*Best wishes for your future
from Fenland Compact*

*Perfect freedom is reserved for the man
who lives by his own work and in that
work does what he wants to do.*

*R.G.Collingwood*

# The Little Oxford Dictionary

**OWLS**

OXFORD ENGLISH
DICTIONARY
WORD AND
LANGUAGE
SERVICE

Do you have a query about
words, their origin, meaning,
use, spelling, or pronunciation,
or any other aspect of the
English language? Then write to
OWLS at Oxford University Press,
Walton Street, Oxford OX2 6DP

# The Little Oxford Dictionary

## of Current English

First edited by George Ostler

**Seventh Edition**

Edited by Maurice Waite

Clarendon Press · Oxford

1994

*Oxford University Press, Walton Street, Oxford OX2 6DP*

*Oxford New York*
*Athens Auckland Bangkok Bombay*
*Calcutta Cape Town Dar es Salaam Delhi*
*Florence Hong Kong Istanbul Karachi*
*Kuala Lumpur Madras Madrid Melbourne*
*Mexico City Nairobi Paris Singapore*
*Taipei Tokyo Toronto*
*and associated companies in*
*Berlin Ibadan*

*Oxford is a trade mark of Oxford University Press*

*Published in the United States*
*by Oxford University Press Inc., New York*

© *Oxford University Press 1969, 1980, 1986, 1994*

*First Edition 1930*
*Second Edition 1937*
*Third Edition 1941*
*Fourth Edition 1969*
*Fifth Edition 1980*
*Sixth Edition 1986*
*Seventh Edition 1994*

*British Library Cataloguing in Publication Data*
*Data available*

*Library of Congress Cataloging in Publication Data*
*Data available*

*ISBN 0–19–861298–2*

10 9 8 7 6 5 4 3 2 1

*Typeset by Latimer Trend Ltd., Plymouth*

*Printed in Great Britain*
*by Clay PLC, Bungay, Suffolk*

# Contents

# Editorial staff

**Editor**                         Maurice Waite

**Assistant Editor**               Andrew Hodgson

**Contributing Editors**           Anna Howes
                                   Louise Jones
                                   Bernadette Paton
                                   Anne St John-Hall

**Keyboarders**                    Anne Whear

                                   Pam Marjara
                                   Kay Pepler

**Schools English Consultant**     Elaine Ashmore-Short

# Features of the dictionary

**Headwords** (words given their own entries) are in bold type:

**abandon** /əˈbænd(ə)n/ ● *verb* desert ...

or in bold italic type if they are borrowed from another language and are usually printed in italics:

***autobahn***

Variant spellings are shown:

**almanac** ... (also **almanack**)

Words that are different but are spelt the same way (homographs) are printed with raised numbers:

**abode¹**
**abode²**

Variant American spellings are labelled *US*:

**anaemia** ... (*US* **anemia**)

**Pronunciations** are given in the International Phonetic Alphabet. See p. xi for an explanation.

**Parts of speech** are shown in italic:

**abhor** ... *verb*
**abhorrence** ... *noun*

If a word is used as more than one part of speech, each comes after a ●:

**abandon** ... ● *noun* ... ● *verb* ...

For explanations of parts of speech, see the panels at the dictionary entries for *noun, verb,* etc.

**Inflections** Irregular and difficult forms are given for:

*nouns*:

**ability** ... (*plural* **-ies**)
**sheep** ... (*plural* same)
**tomato** ... (*plural* **-es**)

(Irregular plurals are not given for compounds such as *footman* and *schoolchild*.)

| *verbs*: | **abate** ... (-ting) |
| | **abut** ... (-tt-) [indicating **abutted**, **abutting**] |
| | **ring** ... (*past tense* **rang**; *past participle* **rung**) |

| *adjectives*: | **good** ... (**better, best**) |
| | **narrow** ... (-er, -est) |
| | **able** ... (-r, -st) |

| *adverbs*: | **well** ... (**better, best**) |

**Definitions** Round brackets are used for

**a**  optional words, e.g. at

**back** ... *verb* (cause to) go backwards

(because *back* can mean either 'go backwards' or 'cause to go backwards')

**b**  typical objects of verbs:

**bank** ... *verb* deposit (money) at bank

**c**  typical subjects of verbs:

**break** ... *verb* (of waves) curl over and foam

**d**  typical nouns qualified by an adjective:

**catchy** ... (of tune) easily remembered

**Subject labels** are sometimes used to help define a word:

**sharp** ... *Music* above true pitch

**Register labels** are used if a word is slang, colloquial, or formal:

**ace** ... *adjective slang* excellent

*Coarse slang* means that a word, although widely used, is still unacceptable to many people.

*Offensive* means that a word is offensive to members of a particular ethnic, religious, or other group.

**Phrases** are entered under their main word:

**company** ... **in company with**

A comma in a phrase indicates alternatives:

**in, to excess**

means that *in excess* and *to excess* are both phrases.

**Compounds** are entered under their main word or element (usually the first):

**air** ... **air speed** ... **airstrip**

unless they need entries of their own:

**broad**
**broadcast**
**broadside**

A comma in a compound indicates alternatives:

**block capitals, letters**

means that *block capitals* and *block letters* are both compounds.

**Derivatives** are put at the end of the entry for the word they are derived from:

**rob** ... **robber** *noun*

unless they need defining:

**drive** ...
**driver** *noun* person who drives; golf club
  for driving from tee.

**Cross-references** are printed in small capitals:

**anatto** = ANNATTO.
**arose** *past* of ARISE.

Definitions will be found at the entries referred to.

# Note on proprietary terms

This dictionary includes some words which are, or are asserted to be, proprietary names or trade marks. Their inclusion does not imply that they have acquired for legal purposes a non-proprietary or general significance, nor is any other judgement implied concerning their legal status. In cases where the editor has some evidence that a word is used as a proprietary name or trade mark this is indicated by the label *proprietary term*, but no judgement concerning the legal status of such words is made or implied thereby.

# Pronunciation symbols

**Consonants**

| | | | | | |
|---|---|---|---|---|---|
| b | *but* | n | *no* | ʃ | *she* |
| d | *dog* | p | *pen* | ʒ | vi*s*ion |
| f | *few* | r | *red* | θ | *th*in |
| g | *get* | s | *sit* | ð | *th*is |
| h | *he* | t | *top* | ŋ | ri*ng* |
| j | *yes* | v | *voice* | x | lo*ch* |
| k | *cat* | w | *we* | tʃ | *ch*ip |
| l | *leg* | z | *zoo* | dʒ | *j*ar |
| m | *man* | | | | |

**Vowels**

| | | | | | |
|---|---|---|---|---|---|
| æ | *cat* | ʌ | *run* | əʊ | *no* |
| ɑː | *arm* | ʊ | *put* | eə | *hair* |
| e | *bed* | uː | *too* | ɪə | *near* |
| ɜː | *her* | ə | *ago* | ɔɪ | *boy* |
| ɪ | *sit* | aɪ | *my* | ʊə | *poor* |
| iː | *see* | aʊ | *how* | aɪə | *fire* |
| ɒ | *hot* | eɪ | *day* | aʊə | *sour* |
| ɔː | *saw* | | | | |

(ə) signifies the indeterminate sound in gar*d*en, carn*a*l, and rhyth*m*.

The mark ˜ indicates a nasalized sound, as in the following vowels that are not natural in English:

> æ̃ (*ing*énue)
> ɑ̃ (él*an*)
> ɔ̃ (b*on* voyage)

The main or primary stress of a word is shown by ' before the relevant syllable.

# Aa

**A** *abbreviation* ampere(s). □ **A-bomb** atomic bomb; **A level** advanced level in GCE exam.

**a** /ə, eɪ/ *adjective* (called the indefinite article) (also **an** /æn, ən/ before vowel sound) one, some, any; per.

**AA** *abbreviation* Automobile Association; Alcoholics Anonymous; anti-aircraft.

**aardvark** /'ɑːdvɑːk/ *noun* mammal with tubular snout and long tongue.

**aback** /ə'bæk/ *adverb* □ **taken aback** disconcerted, surprised.

**abacus** /'æbəkəs/ *noun* (*plural* **-es**) frame with wires along which beads are slid for calculating.

**abaft** /ə'bɑːft/ *Nautical* ● *adverb* in or towards stern of ship. ● *preposition* nearer stern than.

**abandon** /ə'bænd(ə)n/ ● *verb* desert; give up (hope etc.). ● *noun* freedom from inhibitions. □ **abandonment** *noun*.

**abandoned** *adjective* deserted; unrestrained.

**abase** /ə'beɪs/ *verb* (**-sing**) humiliate; degrade. □ **abasement** *noun*.

**abashed** /ə'bæʃt/ *adjective* embarrassed; disconcerted.

**abate** /ə'beɪt/ *verb* (**-ting**) make or become less strong etc. □ **abatement** *noun*.

**abattoir** /'æbətwɑː/ *noun* slaughterhouse.

**abbess** /'æbɪs/ *noun* female head of abbey of nuns.

**abbey** /'æbɪ/ *noun* (*plural* **-s**) (building occupied by) community of monks or nuns.

**abbot** /'æbət/ *noun* head of community of monks.

**abbreviate** /ə'briːvɪeɪt/ *verb* shorten. □ **abbreviation** *noun*.

**ABC** /eɪbiː'siː/ *noun* alphabet; rudiments of subject; alphabetical guide.

**abdicate** /'æbdɪkeɪt/ *verb* renounce or resign from (throne etc.). □ **abdication** *noun*.

**abdomen** /'æbdəmən/ *noun* belly; rear part of insect etc. □ **abdominal** /æb-'dɒmɪn(ə)l/ *adjective*.

**abduct** /əb'dʌkt/ *verb* carry off illegally, kidnap. □ **abduction** *noun*; **abductor** *noun*.

**aberrant** /æ'berənt/ *adjective* showing aberration.

**aberration** /æbə'reɪʃ(ə)n/ *noun* deviation from normal type or accepted standard; distortion.

**abet** /ə'bet/ *verb* encourage (offender), assist (offence). □ **abetter**, *Law* **abettor** *noun*.

**abeyance** /ə'beɪəns/ *noun* (usually after *in*, *into*) temporary disuse; suspension.

**abhor** /əb'hɔː/ *verb* (**-rr-**) detest; regard with disgust.

**abhorrence** /əb'hɒrəns/ *noun* disgust, detestation.

**abhorrent** *adjective* (often + *to*) disgusting.

**abide** /ə'baɪd/ *verb* (**-ding**, *past & past participle* **abode** /ə'bəʊd/ or **abided**) tolerate; (+ *by*) act in accordance with (rule); keep (promise).

**abiding** /ə'baɪdɪŋ/ *adjective* enduring, permanent.

**ability** /ə'bɪlɪtɪ/ *noun* (*plural* **-ies**) (often + *to do*) capacity, power; cleverness, talent.

**abject** /'æbdʒekt/ *adjective* miserable; degraded; despicable. □ **abjection** /-'dʒek-/ *noun*.

**abjure** /əb'dʒʊə/ *verb* renounce on oath. □ **abjuration** /-dʒʊ'reɪ-/ *noun*.

**ablaze** /ə'bleɪz/ *adjective & adverb* on fire; glittering; excited.

**able** /'eɪb(ə)l/ *adjective* (**-r**, **-st**) (+ *to do*) having power; talented. □ **able-bodied** healthy, fit. □ **ably** *adverb*.

**ablution** /ə'bluːʃ(ə)n/ *noun* (usually in *plural*) ceremonial washing of hands etc.; *colloquial* washing onself.

**abnegate** /'æbnɪgeɪt/ *verb* (**-ting**) give up, renounce. □ **abnegation** *noun*.

**abnormal** /æb'nɔːm(ə)l/ *adjective* exceptional; deviating from the norm. □ **abnormality** /-'mæl-/ *noun*; **abnormally** *adverb*.

**aboard** /ə'bɔːd/ *adverb & preposition* on or into (ship, aircraft, etc.).

**abode**[1] /ə'bəʊd/ *noun* dwelling place.

**abode**[2] *past & past participle of* ABIDE.

**abolish** /ə'bɒlɪʃ/ *verb* end existence of. □ **abolition** /æbə'lɪʃ(ə)n/ *noun*; **abolitionist** /æbə'lɪʃənɪst/ *noun*.

**abominable** /ə'bɒmɪnəb(ə)l/ *adjective* detestable, loathsome; *colloquial* very unpleasant. □ **Abominable Snowman** yeti. □ **abominably** *adverb*.

**abominate** /ə'bɒmɪneɪt/ *verb* (**-ting**) detest, loathe. □ **abomination** *noun*.

**aboriginal** /æbə'rɪdʒɪn(ə)l/ ● *adjective* indigenous; (usually **Aboriginal**) of the Australian Aborigines. ● *noun* aboriginal inhabitant, esp. (usually **Aboriginal**) of Australia.

**aborigines** /æbə'rɪdʒɪniːz/ *plural noun* aboriginal inhabitants, esp. (usually **Aborigines**) of Australia.

■ **Usage** It is best to refer to one *Aboriginal* but several *Aborigines*, although *Aboriginals* is also acceptable.

**abort** /ə'bɔːt/ *verb* miscarry; effect abortion of; (cause to) end before completion.

**abortion** /ə'bɔːʃ(ə)n/ *noun* natural or (esp.) induced expulsion of foetus before it can survive; stunted or misshapen creature. □ **abortionist** *noun*.

**abortive** /ə'bɔːtɪv/ *adjective* fruitless, unsuccessful.

**abound** /ə'baʊnd/ *verb* be plentiful; (+ *in, with*) be rich in, teem with.

**about** /ə'baʊt/ ● *preposition* on subject of; relating to, in relation to; at a time near to; around (in); surrounding; here and there in. ● *adverb* approximately; nearby; in every direction; on the move, in action; all around. □ **about-face, -turn** turn made so as to face opposite direction, change of policy etc.; **be about to do** be on the point of doing.

**above** /ə'bʌv/ ● *preposition* over, on top of, higher than; more than; higher in rank, importance, etc. than; too great or good for; beyond reach of. ● *adverb* at or to higher point, overhead; earlier on page or in book. □ **above all** more than anything else; **above-board** without concealment.

**abracadabra** /æbrəkə'dæbrə/ *interjection* supposedly magic word.

**abrade** /ə'breɪd/ *verb* (**-ding**) scrape or wear away by rubbing.

**abrasion** /ə'breɪʒ(ə)n/ *noun* rubbing or scraping away; resulting damaged area.

**abrasive** /ə'breɪsɪv/ ● *adjective* capable of rubbing or grinding down; harsh or hurtful in manner. ● *noun* abrasive substance.

**abreast** /ə'brest/ *adverb* side by side and facing same way; (+ *of*) up to date with.

**abridge** /ə'brɪdʒ/ *verb* (**-ging**) shorten (a book etc.). □ **abridgement** *noun*.

**abroad** /ə'brɔːd/ *adverb* in or to foreign country; widely; in circulation.

**abrogate** /'æbrəgeɪt/ *verb* (**-ting**) repeal, abolish (law etc.). □ **abrogation** *noun*.

**abrupt** /ə'brʌpt/ *adjective* sudden, hasty; curt; steep. □ **abruptly** *adverb*; **abruptness** *noun*.

**abscess** /'æbsɪs/ *noun* (*plural* **-es**) swelling containing pus.

**abscond** /əb'skɒnd/ *verb* flee, esp. to avoid arrest; escape.

**abseil** /'æbseɪl/ ● *verb* descend (building etc.) by using doubled rope fixed at higher point. ● *noun* such a descent.

**absence** /'æbsəns/ *noun* being away; duration of this; (+ *of*) lack. □ **absence of mind** inattentiveness.

**absent** ● *adjective* /'æbsənt/ not present or existing; lacking; inattentive. ● *verb* /əb'sent/ (**absent oneself**) go or stay away. □ **absently** *adverb*.

**absentee** /æbsən'tiː/ *noun* person not present.

**absenteeism** /æbsən'tiːɪz(ə)m/ *noun* absenting oneself from work, school, etc.

**absent-minded** *adjective* forgetful, inattentive. □ **absent-mindedly** *adverb*; **absent-mindedness** *noun*.

**absinthe** /'æbsɪnθ/ *noun* wormwood-based, aniseed-flavoured liqueur.

**absolute** /'æbsəluːt/ *adjective* complete, utter; unconditional; despotic; not relative; (of adjective or transitive verb) without expressed noun or object; (of decree etc.) final. □ **absolute majority** one over all rivals combined; **absolute temperature** one measured from absolute zero; **absolute zero** lowest possible temperature (−273.15°C or 0°K).

**absolutely** *adverb* completely; in an absolute sense; *colloquial* quite so, yes.

**absolution** /æbsə'lu:ʃ(ə)n/ *noun* formal forgiveness of sins.

**absolutism** /'æbsəlu:tɪz(ə)m/ *noun* absolute government. □ **absolutist** *noun*.

**absolve** /əb'zɒlv/ *verb* (**-ving**) (often + *from, of*) free from blame or obligation.

**absorb** /əb'sɔ:b/ *verb* incorporate; assimilate; take in (heat etc.); deal with easily, reduce intensity of; (often as **absorbing** *adjective*) engross attention of; consume (resources).

**absorbent** /əb'sɔ:bənt/ ● *adjective* tending to absorb. ● *noun* absorbent substance.

**absorption** /əb'sɔ:pʃ(ə)n/ *noun* absorbing, being absorbed. □ **absorptive** *adjective*.

**abstain** /əb'steɪn/ *verb* (usually + *from*) refrain (from indulging); decline to vote.

**abstemious** /əb'sti:mɪəs/ *adjective* moderate or ascetic, esp. in eating and drinking. □ **abstemiously** *adverb*.

**abstention** /əb'stenʃ(ə)n/ *noun* abstaining, esp. from voting.

**abstinence** /'æbstɪnəns/ *noun* abstaining, esp. from food or alcohol. □ **abstinent** *adjective*.

**abstract** ● *adjective* /'æbstrækt/ of or existing in theory rather than practice, not concrete; (of art etc.) not representational. ● *verb* /əb'strækt/ (often + *from*) remove; summarize. ● *noun* /'æbstrækt/ summary; abstract idea, work of art, etc.

**abstracted** *adjective* inattentive. □ **abstractedly** *adverb*.

**abstraction** /əb'strækʃ(ə)n/ *noun* abstracting; abstract idea; abstract qualities in art; absent-mindedness.

**abstruse** /əb'stru:s/ *adjective* hard to understand; profound.

**absurd** /əb'sɜ:d/ *adjective* wildly inappropriate; ridiculous. □ **absurdity** *noun* (*plural* **-ies**); **absurdly** *adverb*.

**ABTA** /'æbtə/ *abbreviation* Association of British Travel Agents.

**abundance** /ə'bʌnd(ə)ns/ *noun* plenty; more than enough; wealth.

**abundant** *adjective* plentiful; (+ *in*) rich. □ **abundantly** *adverb*.

**abuse** ● *verb* /ə'bju:z/ (**-sing**) use improperly; misuse; maltreat; insult verbally. ● *noun* /ə'bju:s/ misuse; insulting language; corrupt practice. □ **abuser** /ə'bju:zə/ *noun*.

**abusive** /ə'bju:sɪv/ *adjective* insulting, offensive. □ **abusively** *adverb*.

**abut** /ə'bʌt/ *verb* (**-tt-**) (+ *on*) border on; (+ *on, against*) touch or lean on.

**abysmal** /ə'bɪzm(ə)l/ *adjective* very bad; dire. □ **abysmally** *adverb*.

**abyss** /ə'bɪs/ *noun* deep chasm.

**AC** *abbreviation* alternating current.

**a/c** *abbreviation* account.

**acacia** /ə'keɪʃə/ *noun* tree with yellow or white flowers.

**academia** /ækə'di:mɪə/ *noun* the world of scholars.

**academic** /ækə'demɪk/ ● *adjective* scholarly; of learning; of no practical relevance. ● *noun* teacher or scholar in university etc. □ **academically** *adverb*.

**academician** /əkædə'mɪʃ(ə)n/ *noun* member of Academy.

**academy** /ə'kædəmɪ/ *noun* (*plural* **-ies**) place of specialized training; (**Academy**) society of distinguished scholars, artists, scientists, etc.; *Scottish* secondary school.

**acanthus** /ə'kænθəs/ *noun* (*plural* **-es**) spring herbaceous plant with spiny leaves.

**ACAS** /'eɪkæs/ *abbreviation* Advisory, Conciliation, and Arbitration Service.

**accede** /æk'si:d/ *verb* (**-ding**) (+ *to*) take office, esp. as monarch; assent to.

**accelerate** /ək'seləreɪt/ *verb* (**-ting**) increase speed (of); (cause to) happen earlier. □ **acceleration** *noun*.

**accelerator** *noun* device for increasing speed, esp. pedal in vehicle; *Physics* apparatus for imparting high speeds to charged particles.

**accent** ● *noun* /'æksənt/ style of pronunciation of region or social group (see panel); emphasis; prominence given to syllable by stress or pitch; mark on letter indicating pronunciation (see panel). • *verb* /æk'sent/ emphasize; write or print accents on.

**accentuate** /ək'sentʃʊeɪt/ *verb* (**-ting**) emphasize, make prominent. □ **accentuation** *noun*.

**accept** /ək'sept/ *verb* willingly receive; answer (invitation etc.) affirmatively; regard favourably; receive as valid or suitable. □ **acceptance** *noun*.

**acceptable** *adjective* worth accepting; tolerable. □ **acceptability** *noun*; **acceptably** *adverb*.

**access** /'ækses/ • *noun* way of approach or entry; right or opportunity to reach, use, or visit. • *verb* gain access to (data) in computer.

**accessible** /ək'sesɪb(ə)l/ *adjective* reachable or obtainable; easy to understand. □ **accessibility** *noun*.

**accession** /ək'seʃ(ə)n/ *noun* taking office, esp. as monarch; thing added.

**accessory** /ək'sesərɪ/ *noun* (*plural* **-ies**) additional or extra thing; (usually in *plural*) small attachment or item of dress; (often + *to*) person who abets in or is privy to illegal act.

**accident** /'æksɪd(ə)nt/ *noun* unintentional unfortunate esp. harmful event; event without apparent cause; unexpected event. □ **accident-prone** clumsy; **by accident** unintentionally.

**accidental** /æksɪ'dent(ə)l/ • *adjective* happening or done by chance or accident. • *noun Music* sharp, flat, or natural indicating momentary departure of note from key signature. □ **accidentally** *adverb*.

**acclaim** /ə'kleɪm/ • *verb* welcome or applaud enthusiastically. • *noun* applause; welcome; public praise. □ **acclamation** /æklə-/ *noun*.

**acclimatize** /ə'klaɪmətaɪz/ *verb* (also **-ise**) (**-zing** or **-sing**) adapt to new climate or conditions. □ **acclimatization** *noun*.

**accolade** /'ækəleɪd/ *noun* praise given; touch made with sword at conferring of knighthood.

**accommodate** /ə'kɒmədeɪt/ *verb* (**-ting**) provide lodging or room for; adapt, harmonize, reconcile; do favour to; (+ *with*) supply.

■ **Usage** *Accommodate, accommodation,* etc. are spelt with two *m*s, not one.

**accommodating** *adjective* obliging.

**accommodation** *noun* lodgings; adjustment, adaptation; convenient arrangement. □ **accommodation address** postal address used instead of permanent one.

## Accent

**1** A person's accent is the way he or she pronounces words, and people from different regions and different groups in society have different accents. For instance, most people in northern England say *path* with a 'short' *a*, while most people in southern England say it with a 'long' *a*, and in America and Canada the *r* in *far* and *port* is generally pronounced, while in south-eastern England, for example, it is not. Everyone speaks with an accent, although some accents may be regarded as having more prestige, such as 'Received Pronunciation' (RP) in the UK.

**2** An accent on a letter is a mark added to it to alter the sound it stands for. In French, for example, there are

´ (acute), as in *état*
` (grave), as in *mère*
^ (circumflex), as in *guêpe*

" (diaeresis), as in *Noël*
, (cedilla), as in *français*

and German has

" (umlaut), as in *München*.

There are no accents on native English words, but many words borrowed from other languages still have them, such as *blasé* and *façade*.

**accompaniment** /əˈkʌmpənɪmənt/ *noun* instrumental or orchestral support for solo instrument, voice, or group; accompanying thing.

**accompany** /əˈkʌmpənɪ/ *verb* (**-ies, -ied**) go with, attend; (usually in *passive*; + *by*) be done or found with; *Music* play accompaniment for. □ **accompanist** *noun* Music.

**accomplice** /əˈkʌmplɪs/ *noun* partner in crime.

**accomplish** /əˈkʌmplɪʃ/ *verb* succeed in doing; achieve, complete.

**accomplished** *adjective* clever, skilled.

**accomplishment** *noun* completion (of task etc.); acquired esp. social skill; thing achieved.

**accord** /əˈkɔːd/ ● *verb* (often + *with*) be consistent or in harmony; grant, give. ● *noun* agreement; consent. □ **of one's own accord** on one's own initiative.

**accordance** *noun* □ **in accordance with** in conformity to.

**according** *adverb* ( + *to*) as stated by; ( + *to, as*) in proportion to or as.

**accordingly** *adverb* as circumstances suggest or require; consequently.

**accordion** /əˈkɔːdɪən/ *noun* musical reed instrument with concertina-like bellows, keys, and buttons.

**accost** /əˈkɒst/ *verb* approach and speak boldly to.

**account** /əˈkaʊnt/ ● *noun* narration, description; arrangement at bank etc. for depositing and withdrawing money etc.; statement of financial transactions with balance; importance; behalf. ● *verb* consider as. □ **account for** explain, answer for; kill, destroy; **on account** to be paid for later, in part payment; **on account of** because of; **on no account** under no circumstances; **take account of, take into account** consider.

**accountable** *adjective* responsible, required to account for one's conduct; explicable. □ **accountability** *noun*.

**accountant** *noun* professional keeper or verifier of financial accounts. □ **accountancy** *noun*; **accounting** *noun*.

**accoutrements** /əˈkuːtrəmənts/ *plural noun* equipment, trappings.

**accredit** /əˈkredɪt/ *verb* (**-t-**) ( + *to*) attribute; ( + *with*) credit; (usually + *to, at*)

send (ambassador etc.) with credentials.

**accredited** *adjective* officially recognized; generally accepted.

**accretion** /əˈkriːʃ(ə)n/ *noun* growth by accumulation or organic enlargement; the resulting whole; matter so added.

**accrue** /əˈkruː/ *verb* (**-ues, -ued, -uing**) (often + *to*) come as natural increase or advantage, esp. financial.

**accumulate** /əˈkjuːmjʊleɪt/ *verb* (**-ting**) acquire increasing number or quantity of; amass, collect; grow numerous; increase. □ **accumulation** *noun*; **accumulative** /-lətɪv/ *adjective*.

**accumulator** *noun* rechargeable electric cell; bet placed on sequence of events, with winnings and stake from each placed on next.

**accurate** /ˈækjʊrət/ *adjective* precise; conforming exactly with truth etc. □ **accuracy** *noun*; **accurately** *adverb*.

**accursed** /əˈkɜːsɪd/ *adjective* under a curse; *colloquial* detestable, annoying.

**accusative** /əˈkjuːzətɪv/ *Grammar* ● *noun* case expressing object of action. ● *adjective* of or in an accusative.

**accuse** /əˈkjuːz/ *verb* (**-sing**) (often + *of*) charge with fault or crime; blame. □ **accusation** /æk-/ *noun*; **accusatory** *adjective*.

**accustom** /əˈkʌstəm/ *verb* ( + *to*) make used to.

**accustomed** *adjective* (usually + *to*) used (to a thing); customary.

**ace** ● *noun* playing card with single spot; person who excels in some activity; *Tennis* unreturnable service. ● *adjective* *slang* excellent. □ **within an ace of** on the verge of.

**acerbic** /əˈsɜːbɪk/ *adjective* harsh and sharp, esp. in speech or manner. □ **acerbity** *noun* (*plural* **-ies**).

**acetate** /ˈæsɪteɪt/ *noun* compound of acetic acid, esp. the cellulose ester; fabric made from this.

**acetic** /əˈsiːtɪk/ *adjective* of or like vinegar. □ **acetic acid** clear liquid acid in vinegar.

**acetone** /ˈæsɪtəʊn/ *noun* colourless volatile solvent of organic compounds.

**acetylene** /əˈsetɪliːn/ *noun* inflammable hydrocarbon gas, used esp. in welding.

**ache** /eɪk/ ● noun continuous dull pain; mental distress. ● verb (**-aching**) suffer from or be the source of an ache.

**achieve** /əˈtʃiːv/ verb (**-ving**) reach or attain by effort; accomplish (task etc.); be successful. □ **achiever** noun; **achievement** noun.

**Achilles** /əˈkɪliːz/ noun □ **Achilles heel** vulnerable point; **Achilles tendon** tendon attaching calf muscles to heel.

**achromatic** /ˌækrəʊˈmætɪk/ adjective transmitting light without separating it into colours; free from colour. □ **achromatically** adverb.

**achy** /ˈeɪkɪ/ adjective (**-ier, -iest**) suffering from aches.

**acid** /ˈæsɪd/ ● noun Chemistry substance that neutralizes alkalis, turns litmus red, and usually contains hydrogen and is sour; slang drug LSD. ● adjective having properties of acid; sour; biting, sharp. □ **acid drop** sharp-tasting boiled sweet; **acid house** synthesized music with simple beat, associated with hallucinogenic drugs; **acid rain** rain containing acid formed from industrial waste in atmosphere; **acid test** severe or conclusive test. □ **acidic** /əˈsɪd-/ adjective; **acidify** /əˈsɪd-/ verb (**-ies, -ied**); **acidity** /-ˈsɪd-/ noun.

**acidulous** /əˈsɪdjʊləs/ adjective somewhat acid.

**acknowledge** /əkˈnɒlɪdʒ/ verb (**-ging**) recognize, accept truth of; confirm receipt of (letter etc.); show that one has noticed; express gratitude for.

**acknowledgement** noun (also **acknowledgment**) acknowledging; thing given or done in gratitude; letter etc. confirming receipt; (usually in plural) author's thanks, prefacing book.

**acme** /ˈækmɪ/ noun highest point.

**acne** /ˈæknɪ/ noun skin condition with red pimples.

**acolyte** /ˈækəlaɪt/ noun assistant, esp. of priest.

**aconite** /ˈækənaɪt/ noun any of various poisonous plants, esp. monkshood; drug made from these.

**acorn** /ˈeɪkɔːn/ noun fruit of oak.

**acoustic** /əˈkuːstɪk/ adjective of sound or sense of hearing; (of musical instrument etc.) without electrical amplification. □ **acoustically** adverb.

**acoustics** plural noun properties (of a room etc.) in transmitting sound; (treated as singular) science of sound.

**acquaint** /əˈkweɪnt/ verb (+ with) make aware of or familiar with. □ **be acquainted with** know.

**acquaintance** noun being acquainted; person one knows slightly. □ **acquaintanceship** noun.

**acquiesce** /ˌækwɪˈes/ verb (**-cing**) agree, esp. tacitly. □ **acquiescence** noun; **acquiescent** adjective.

**acquire** /əˈkwaɪə/ verb (**-ring**) gain possession of. □ **acquired immune deficiency syndrome** = AIDS; **acquired taste** liking developed by experience.

**acquirement** noun thing acquired or attained.

**acquisition** /ˌækwɪˈzɪʃ(ə)n/ noun (esp. useful) thing acquired; acquiring, being acquired.

**acquisitive** /əˈkwɪzɪtɪv/ adjective keen to acquire things.

**acquit** /əˈkwɪt/ verb (**-tt-**) (often + of) declare not guilty; (**acquit oneself**) behave, perform, (+ of) discharge (duty etc.). □ **acquittal** noun.

**acre** /ˈeɪkə/ noun measure of land, 4840 sq. yards, 0.405 ha.

**acreage** /ˈeɪkərɪdʒ/ noun number of acres.

**acrid** /ˈækrɪd/ adjective bitterly pungent. □ **acridity** /-ˈkrɪd-/ noun.

**acrimonious** /ˌækrɪˈməʊnɪəs/ adjective bitter in manner or temper. □ **acrimony** /ˈækrɪmənɪ/ noun.

**acrobat** /ˈækrəbæt/ noun performer of acrobatics. □ **acrobatic** /-ˈbæt-/ adjective.

**acrobatics** /ˌækrəˈbætɪks/ plural noun gymnastic feats.

**acronym** /ˈækrənɪm/ noun word formed from initial letters of other words (e.g. laser, NATO).

**acropolis** /əˈkrɒpəlɪs/ noun citadel of ancient Greek city.

**across** /əˈkrɒs/ ● preposition to or on other side of; from one side to another side of. ● adverb to or on other side; from one side to another. □ **across the board** applying to all.

**acrostic** /əˈkrɒstɪk/ noun poem etc. in which first (or first and last) letters of lines form word(s).

**acrylic** /ə'krılık/ ●adjective made from acrylic acid. ●noun acrylic fibre, fabric, or paint.

**acrylic acid** noun a pungent liquid organic acid.

**act** ●noun thing done, deed; process of doing; item of entertainment; pretence; main division of play; decree of legislative body. ●verb behave; perform actions or functions; (often + on) have effect; perform in play etc.; pretend; play part of. □ **act for** be (legal) representative of; **act up** colloquial misbehave, give trouble.

**acting** adjective serving temporarily as.

**actinism** /'æktınız(ə)m/ noun property of short-wave radiation that produces chemical changes, as in photography.

**action** /'ækʃ(ə)n/ noun process of doing or acting; forcefulness, energy; exertion of energy or influence; deed, act; (**the action**) series of events in story, play, etc., slang exciting activity; battle; mechanism of instrument; style of movement; lawsuit. □ **action-packed** full of action or excitement; **action replay** playback of part of television broadcast; **out of action** not functioning.

**actionable** adjective providing grounds for legal action.

**activate** /'æktıveıt/ verb (-ting) make active or radioactive. □ **activation** noun.

**active** /'æktıv/ ●adjective marked by action; energetic, diligent; working, operative; Grammar (of verb) of which subject performs action (e.g. saw in he saw a film). ●noun Grammar active form or voice. □ **active service** military service in wartime. □ **actively** adverb.

**activism** noun policy of vigorous action, esp. for a political cause. □ **activist** noun.

**activity** /æk'tıvıtı/ noun (plural -ies) being active; busy or energetic action; (often in plural) occupation, pursuit.

**actor** /'æktə/ noun person who acts in play, film, etc.

**actress** /'æktrıs/ noun female actor.

**actual** /'æktʃʊəl/ adjective existing, real; current. □ **actuality** /-'æl-/ noun (plural -ies).

**actually** adverb in fact, really.

**actuary** /'æktʃʊərı/ noun (plural -ies) statistician, esp. one calculating insurance risks and premiums. □ **actuarial** /-'eər-/ adjective.

**actuate** /'æktʃʊeıt/ verb (-ting) cause to move, function, act.

**acuity** /ə'kju:ıtı/ noun acuteness.

**acumen** /'ækjʊmen/ noun keen insight or discernment.

**acupuncture** /'ækjʊ:pʌŋktʃə/ noun medical treatment using needles in parts of the body. □ **acupuncturist** noun.

**acute** /ə'kju:t/ adjective (-r, -st) keen, penetrating; shrewd; (of disease) coming quickly to crisis; (of angle) less than 90°. □ **acute** (**accent**) mark (´) over letter indicating pronunciation. □ **acutely** adverb.

**AD** abbreviation of the Christian era (Anno Domini).

**ad** noun colloquial advertisement.

**adage** /'ædıdʒ/ noun proverb, maxim.

**adagio** /ə'dɑ:ʒıəʊ/ Music ●adverb & adjective in slow time. ●noun (plural -s) adagio passage.

**adamant** /'ædəmənt/ adjective stubbornly resolute. □ **adamantly** adverb.

**Adam's apple** /'ædəmz/ noun cartilaginous projection at front of neck.

**adapt** /ə'dæpt/ verb (+ to) fit, adjust; (+ to, for) make suitable, modify; (usually + to) adjust to new conditions. □ **adaptable** adjective; **adaptation** /æd-/ noun.

**adaptor** noun device for making equipment compatible; Electricity device for connecting several electrical plugs to one socket.

**add** verb join as increase or supplement; unite (numbers) to get their total; say further. □ **add up** find total of; (+ to) amount to.

**addendum** /ə'dendəm/ noun (plural -da) thing to be added; material added at end of book.

**adder** /'ædə/ noun small venomous snake.

**addict** /'ædıkt/ noun person addicted, esp. to drug; colloquial devotee.

**addicted** /ə'dıktıd/ adjective (usually + to) dependent on a drug as a habit;

devoted to an interest. □ **addiction** noun.

**addictive** /ə'dɪktɪv/ adjective causing addiction.

**addition** /ə'dɪʃ(ə)n/ noun adding; person or thing added. □ **in addition** (often + to) also, as well.

**additional** adjective added, extra. □ **additionally** adverb.

**additive** /'ædɪtɪv/ noun substance added, esp. to colour, flavour, or preserve food.

**addle** /'æd(ə)l/ verb (**-ling**) muddle, confuse; (usually as **addled** adjective) (of egg) become rotten.

**address** /ə'dres/ ● noun place where person lives or organization is situated; particulars of this, esp. for postal purposes; speech delivered to an audience. ● verb write postal directions on; direct (remarks etc.); speak or write to; direct one's attention to.

**addressee** /ædre'si:/ noun person to whom letter etc. is addressed.

**adduce** /ə'dju:s/ verb (**-cing**) cite as proof or instance. □ **adducible** adjective.

**adenoids** /'ædɪnɔɪdz/ plural noun enlarged lymphatic tissue between nose and throat, often hindering breathing. □ **adenoidal** /-'nɔɪ-/ adjective.

**adept** ● adjective /ə'dept, 'ædept/ (+ at, in) skilful. ● noun /'ædept/ adept person.

**adequate** /'ædɪkwət/ adjective sufficient, satisfactory. □ **adequacy** noun, **adequately** adverb.

**adhere** /əd'hɪə/ verb (**-ring**) (usually + to) stick fast; behave according to (rule etc.); give allegiance.

**adherent** ● noun supporter. ● adjective adhering. □ **adherence** noun.

**adhesion** /əd'hi:ʒ(ə)n/ noun adhering.

**adhesive** /əd'hi:sɪv/ ● adjective sticky, causing adhesion. ● noun adhesive substance.

**ad hoc** /æd 'hɒk/ adverb & adjective for one particular occasion or use.

**adieu** /ə'dju:/ interjection goodbye.

**ad infinitum** /æd ɪnfɪ'naɪtəm/ adverb without limit; for ever.

**adipose** /'ædɪpəʊz/ adjective of fat, fatty. □ **adiposity** /-'pɒs-/ noun.

**adjacent** /ə'dʒeɪs(ə)nt/ adjective lying near; adjoining. □ **adjacency** noun.

**adjective** /'ædʒɪktɪv/ noun word indicating quality of noun or pronoun (see panel). □ **adjectival** /-'taɪv-/ adjective.

**adjoin** /ə'dʒɔɪn/ verb be next to and joined with.

**adjourn** /ə'dʒɜ:n/ verb postpone, break off; (+ to) transfer to (another place). □ **adjournment** noun.

---

## Adjective

An adjective is a word that describes a noun or pronoun, e.g.

*red, clever, German, depressed, battered, sticky, shining*

Most can be used either before a noun, e.g.

*the red house*                    *a clever woman*

or after a verb like *be, seem,* or *call,* e.g.

*The house is red.*                *I wouldn't call him lazy.*
*She seems very clever.*

Some can be used only before a noun, e.g.

*the chief reason* (one cannot say \*the reason is chief)

Some can be used only after a verb, e.g.

*The ship is still afloat.* (one cannot say \*an afloat ship)

A few can be used only immediately after a noun, e.g.

*the president elect* (one cannot say either \*an elect president or
\*The president is elect)

---

**adjudge** /ə'dʒʌdʒ/ verb (-ging) pronounce judgement on; pronounce or award judicially. □ **adjudg(e)ment** noun.

**adjudicate** /ə'dʒuːdɪkeɪt/ verb (-ting) act as judge; adjudge. □ **adjudication** noun; **adjudicator** noun.

**adjunct** /'ædʒʌŋkt/ noun (+ to, of) subordinate or incidental thing.

**adjure** /ə'dʒʊə/ verb (-ring) (usually + to do) beg or command. □ **adjuration** noun.

**adjust** /ə'dʒʌst/ verb order, position; regulate; arrange; (usually + to) adapt; harmonize. □ **adjustable** adjective; **adjustment** noun.

**adjutant** /'ædʒʊt(ə)nt/ noun army officer assisting superior in administrative duties.

**ad lib** /æd 'lɪb/ • verb (-bb-) improvise. • adjective improvised. • adverb to any desired extent.

**Adm.** abbreviation Admiral.

**administer** /əd'mɪnɪstə/ verb manage (affairs); formally deliver, dispense.

**administration** /ədmɪnɪ'streɪʃ(ə)n/ noun administering, esp. public affairs; government in power.

**administrative** /əd'mɪnɪstrətɪv/ adjective of the management of affairs.

**administrator** /əd'mɪnɪstreɪtə/ noun manager of business, public affairs, or person's estate.

**admirable** /'ædmərəb(ə)l/ adjective deserving admiration; excellent. □ **admirably** adverb.

**admiral** /'ædmər(ə)l/ noun commander-in-chief of navy; high-ranking naval officer, commander.

**Admiralty** noun (plural -ies) (in full **Admiralty Board**) historical committee superintending Royal Navy.

**admire** /əd'maɪə/ verb regard with approval, respect, or satisfaction; express admiration of. □ **admiration** /ædmə'reɪ-/ noun; **admirer** noun; **admiring** adjective; **admiringly** adverb.

**admissible** /əd'mɪsɪb(ə)l/ adjective worth accepting or considering; allowable. □ **admissibility** noun.

**admission** /əd'mɪʃ(ə)n/ noun acknowledgement (of error etc.); (right of) entering; entrance charge.

**admit** /əd'mɪt/ verb (-tt-) (often + to be, that) acknowledge, recognize as true; (+ to) confess to; let in; accommodate; take (patient) into hospital; (+ of) allow as possible.

**admittance** noun admitting or being admitted, usually to a place.

**admittedly** adverb as must be admitted.

**admixture** /æd'mɪkstʃə/ noun thing added, esp. minor ingredient; adding of this.

**admonish** /əd'mɒnɪʃ/ verb reprove; urge; (+ of) warn. □ **admonishment** noun; **admonition** /ædmə'nɪ-/ noun; **admonitory** adjective.

**ad nauseam** /æd 'nɔːzɪæm/ adverb to a sickening extent.

**ado** /ə'duː/ noun fuss; trouble.

**adobe** /ə'dəʊbɪ/ noun sun-dried brick.

**adolescent** /ædə'lesənt/ • adjective between childhood and adulthood. • noun adolescent person. □ **adolescence** noun.

**adopt** /ə'dɒpt/ verb legally take (child) as one's own; take over (another's idea etc.); choose; accept responsibility for; approve (report etc.). □ **adoption** noun.

**adoptive** adjective because of adoption.

**adorable** /ə'dɔːrəb(ə)l/ adjective deserving adoration; colloquial delightful, charming.

**adore** /ə'dɔː/ verb (-ring) love intensely; worship; colloquial like very much. □ **adoration** /ædə'reɪ-/ noun; **adorer** noun.

**adorn** /ə'dɔːn/ verb add beauty to, decorate. □ **adornment** noun.

**adrenal** /ə'driːn(ə)l/ • adjective of adrenal glands. • noun (in full **adrenal gland**) either of two ductless glands above the kidneys.

**adrenalin** /ə'drenəlɪn/ noun stimulative hormone secreted by adrenal glands.

**adrift** /ə'drɪft/ adverb & adjective drifting; colloquial unfastened, out of order.

**adroit** /ə'drɔɪt/ adjective dexterous, skilful.

**adsorb** /æd'sɔːb/ verb attract and hold thin layer of (gas or liquid) on its surface. □ **adsorbent** adjective & noun; **adsorption** noun.

**adulation** /ˌædjʊˈleɪʃ(ə)n/ *noun* obsequious flattery.

**adult** /ˈædʌlt/ ● *adjective* grown-up, mature; of or for adults. ● *noun* adult person. □ **adulthood** *noun*.

**adulterate** /əˈdʌltəreɪt/ *verb* (**-ting**) debase (esp. food) by adding other substances. □ **adulteration** *noun*.

**adultery** /əˈdʌltərɪ/ *noun* voluntary sexual intercourse of married person other than with spouse. □ **adulterer**, **adulteress** *noun*; **adulterous** *adjective*.

**adumbrate** /ˈædʌmbreɪt/ *verb* (**-ting**) indicate faintly or in outline; foreshadow. □ **adumbration** *noun*.

**advance** /ədˈvɑːns/ ● *verb* (**-cing**) move or put forward; progress; pay or lend beforehand; promote; present (idea etc.). ● *noun* going forward; progress; prepayment, loan; payment beforehand; (in *plural*) amorous approaches; rise in price. ● *adjective* done etc. beforehand. □ **advance on** approach threateningly; **in advance** ahead, beforehand.

**advanced** *adjective* well ahead; socially progressive. □ **advanced level** high level GCE exam.

**advancement** *noun* promotion of person, cause, etc.

**advantage** /ədˈvɑːntɪdʒ/ ● *noun* beneficial feature; benefit, profit; (often + *over*) superiority; *Tennis* next point after deuce. ● *verb* (**-ging**) benefit, favour. □ **take advantage of** make good use of; exploit. □ **advantageous** /ædvənˈteɪdʒəs/ *adjective*.

**Advent** /ˈædvent/ *noun* season before Christmas; coming of Christ; (**advent**) arrival.

**Adventist** *noun* member of sect believing in imminent second coming of Christ.

**adventure** /ədˈventʃə/ ● *noun* unusual and exciting experience; enterprise. ● *verb* (**-ring**) dare, venture. □ **adventure playground** one with climbing frames etc.

**adventurer** *noun* (*feminine* **adventuress**) person who seeks adventure esp. for personal gain or pleasure; financial speculator.

**adventurous** *adjective* venturesome, enterprising.

**adverb** /ˈædvɜːb/ *noun* word indicating manner, degree, circumstance, etc. used to modify verb, adjective, or other adverb (see panel). □ **adverbial** /ədˈvɜː-/ *adjective*.

**adversary** /ˈædvəsərɪ/ *noun* (*plural* **-ies**) enemy; opponent. □ **adversarial** /-ˈseə-/ *adjective*.

**adverse** /ˈædvɜːs/ *adjective* unfavourable; harmful. □ **adversely** *adverb*.

**adversity** /ədˈvɜːsɪtɪ/ *noun* misfortune.

**advert** /ˈædvɜːt/ *noun colloquial* advertisement.

**advertise** /ˈædvətaɪz/ *verb* (**-sing**) promote publicly to increase sales; make generally known; seek to sell, (fill (vacancy), or (+ *for*) buy or employ by notice in newspaper etc.

**advertisement** /ədˈvɜːtɪsmənt/ *noun* public announcement advertising something; advertising.

**advice** /ədˈvaɪs/ *noun* recommendation on how to act; information; notice of transaction.

**advisable** /ədˈvaɪzəb(ə)l/ *adjective* to be recommended; expedient. □ **advisability** *noun*.

**advise** /ədˈvaɪz/ *verb* (**-sing**) give advice (to); recommend; (usually + *of, that*) inform.

**advisedly** /ədˈvaɪzɪdlɪ/ *adverb* deliberately.

**adviser** *noun* person who advises, esp. officially.

**advisory** /ədˈvaɪzərɪ/ *adjective* giving advice.

**advocaat** /ˈædvəkɑːt/ *noun* liqueur of eggs, sugar, and brandy.

**advocacy** /ˈædvəkəsɪ/ *noun* support or argument for cause etc.

**advocate** ● *noun* /ˈædvəkət/ (+ *of*) person who speaks in favour; person who pleads for another, esp. in law court. ● *verb* /ˈædvəkeɪt/ (**-ting**) recommend by argument.

**adze** /ædz/ *noun* (*US* **adz**) axe with arched blade at right angles to handle.

**aegis** /ˈiːdʒɪs/ *noun* protection; support.

**aeolian harp** /iːˈəʊlɪən/ *noun* (*US* **eolian harp**) stringed instrument sounding when wind passes through it.

**aeon** /ˈiːɒn/ *noun* (also **eon**) long or indefinite period; an age.

**aerate** /'eəreɪt/ *verb* (**-ting**) charge with carbon dioxide; expose to air. □ **aeration** *noun*.

**aerial** /'eərɪəl/ ● *noun* device for transmitting or receiving radio signals. ● *adjective* from the air; existing in the air; like air.

**aero-** *combining form* air; aircraft.

**aerobatics** /eərə'bætɪks/ *plural noun* feats of spectacular flying of aircraft; (treated as *singular*) performance of these.

**aerobics** /eə'rəʊbɪks/ *plural noun* vigorous exercises designed to increase oxygen intake. □ **aerobic** *adjective*.

**aerodrome** /'eərədrəʊm/ *noun* small airport or airfield.

**aerodynamics** /eərəʊdaɪ'næmɪks/ *plural noun* (usually treated as *singular*) dynamics of solid bodies moving through air. □ **aerodynamic** *adjective*.

**aerofoil** /'eərəfɔɪl/ *noun* structure with curved surfaces (e.g. aircraft wing), designed to give lift in flight.

**aeronautics** /eərəʊ'nɔːtɪks/ *plural noun* (usually treated as *singular*) science or practice of motion in the air. □ **aeronautical** *adjective*.

**aeroplane** /'eərəpleɪn/ *noun* powered heavier-than-air aircraft with wings.

**aerosol** /'eərəsɒl/ *noun* pressurized container releasing substance as fine spray.

**aerospace** /'eərəʊspeɪs/ *noun* earth's atmosphere and outer space; aviation in this.

**aesthete** /'iːsθiːt/ *noun* person who appreciates beauty.

**aesthetic** /iːs'θetɪk/ *adjective* of or sensitive to beauty; tasteful. □ **aesthetically** *adverb*; **aestheticism** /-sɪz(ə)m/ *noun*.

**aetiology** /iːtɪ'ɒlədʒɪ/ *noun* (*US* **etiology**) study of causation or of causes of disease. □ **aetiological** /-ə'lɒdʒ-/ *adjective*.

**afar** /ə'fɑː/ *adverb* at or to a distance.

**affable** /'æfəb(ə)l/ *adjective* friendly; courteous. □ **affability** *noun*; **affably** *adverb*.

........................................................................................

## Adverb

An adverb is used:

**1** with a verb, to say:
   **a** how something happens, e.g. *He walks* quickly.
   **b** where something happens, e.g. *I live* here.
   **c** when something happens, e.g. *They visited us* yesterday.
   **d** how often something happens, e.g. *We usually have coffee.*

**2** to strengthen or weaken the meaning of:
   **a** a verb, e.g. *He really meant it. I almost fell asleep.*
   **b** an adjective, e.g. *She is very clever. This is a slightly better result.*
   **c** another adverb, e.g. *It comes off terribly easily. The boys nearly always get home late.*

**3** to add to the meaning of a whole sentence, e.g.
   *He is probably our best player. Luckily, no one was hurt.*

In writing or in formal speech, it is **incorrect** to use an adjective instead of an adverb. For example, use
   *Do it properly.*   and not   **Do it proper.*
but note that many words are both an adjective and an adverb, e.g.

| adjective | adverb |
|---|---|
| a fast *horse* | He ran fast. |
| a long *time* | Have you been here long? |

........................................................................................

**affair** /ə'feə/ *noun* matter, concern; love affair; *colloquial* thing, event; (in *plural*) business.

**affect** /ə'fekt/ *verb* produce effect on; (of disease etc.) attack; move emotionally; use for effect; pretend to feel; (+ *to do*) pretend.

■ **Usage** *Affect* is often confused with *effect*, which means 'to bring about'.

**affectation** /æfek'teɪʃ(ə)n/ *noun* artificial manner; pretentious display.

**affected** *adjective* pretended; full of affectation.

**affection** /ə'fekʃ(ə)n/ *noun* goodwill, fond feeling; disease.

**affectionate** /ə'fekʃənət/ *adjective* loving. □ **affectionately** *adverb*.

**affidavit** /æfɪ'deɪvɪt/ *noun* written statement on oath.

**affiliate** /ə'fɪlɪeɪt/ *verb* (**-ting**) (+ *to, with*) attach to, connect to, or adopt as member or branch.

**affiliation** *noun* affiliating, being affiliated. □ **affiliation order** legal order compelling supposed father to support illegitimate child.

**affinity** /ə'fɪnɪtɪ/ *noun* (*plural* **-ies**) attraction; relationship; resemblance; *Chemistry* tendency of substances to combine with others.

**affirm** /ə'fɜ:m/ *verb* state as fact; make solemn declaration in place of oath. □ **affirmation** /æfə'meɪʃ(ə)n/ *noun*.

**affirmative** /ə'fɜ:mətɪv/ ● *adjective* affirming, expressing approval. ● *noun* affirmative statement.

**affix** ● *verb* /ə'fɪks/ attach, fasten; add in writing. ● *noun* /'æfɪks/ addition; prefix, suffix.

**afflict** /ə'flɪkt/ *verb* distress physically or mentally.

**affliction** *noun* distress, suffering; cause of this.

**affluent** /'æflʊənt/ *adjective* rich. □ **affluence** *noun*.

**afford** /ə'fɔ:d/ *verb* (after *can, be able to*) have enough money, time, etc., for; be able to spare (time etc.); (+ *to do*) be in a position; provide.

**afforest** /ə'fɒrɪst/ *verb* convert into forest; plant with trees. □ **afforestation** *noun*.

**affray** /ə'freɪ/ *noun* breach of peace by fighting or rioting in public.

**affront** /ə'frʌnt/ ● *noun* open insult. ● *verb* insult openly; embarrass.

**Afghan** /'æfgæn/ ● *noun* native, national, or language of Afghanistan. ● *adjective* of Afghanistan. □ **Afghan hound** tall dog with long silky hair.

**afield** /ə'fi:ld/ *adverb* to or at a distance.

**aflame** /ə'fleɪm/ *adverb* & *adjective* in flames; very excited.

**afloat** /ə'fləʊt/ *adverb* & *adjective* floating; at sea; out of debt.

**afoot** /ə'fʊt/ *adverb* & *adjective* in operation; progressing.

**afore** /ə'fɔ:/ *preposition* & *adverb* archaic before.

**afore-** *combining form* previously.

**aforethought** *adjective* (after *noun*) premeditated.

**a fortiori** /eɪ fɔ:tɪ'ɔ:raɪ/ *adverb* & *adjective* with stronger reason. [Latin]

**afraid** /ə'freɪd/ *adjective* alarmed, frightened. □ **be afraid** *colloquial* politely regret.

**afresh** /ə'freʃ/ *adverb* anew; with fresh start.

**African** /'æfrɪkən/ ● *noun* native of Africa; person of African descent. ● *adjective* of Africa.

**Afrikaans** /æfrɪ'kɑ:ns/ *noun* language derived from Dutch, used in S. Africa.

**Afrikaner** /æfrɪ'kɑ:nə/ *noun* Afrikaans-speaking white person in S. Africa.

**Afro** /'æfrəʊ/ ● *adjective* (of hair) tightly-curled and bushy. ● *noun* (*plural* **-s**) Afro hairstyle.

**Afro-** *combining form* African.

**aft** /ɑ:ft/ *adverb* at or towards stern or tail.

**after** /'ɑ:ftə/ ● *preposition* following in time; in view of; despite; behind; in pursuit or quest of; about, concerning; in allusion to or imitation of. ● *conjunction* later than. ● *adverb* later; behind. ● *adjective* later. □ **after all** in spite of everything; **afterbirth** placenta etc. discharged after childbirth; **aftercare** attention after leaving hospital etc.; **after-effect** delayed effect of accident etc.; **afterlife** life after death; **afters** *colloquial* sweet dessert; **aftershave** lotion applied to face after shaving; **afterthought** thing thought of or added later.

**aftermath** /ˈɑːftəmæθ/ noun consequences.

**afternoon** /ɑːftəˈnuːn/ noun time between midday and evening.

**afterwards** /ˈɑːftəwədz/ adverb later, subsequently.

**again** /əˈgen/ adverb another time; as previously; in addition; on the other hand. □ **again and again** repeatedly.

**against** /əˈgenst/ preposition in opposition to; into collision or in contact with; to the disadvantage of; in contrast to; in anticipation of; as compensating factor to; in return for.

**agape** /əˈgeɪp/ adjective gaping.

**agate** /ˈægət/ noun usually hard streaked chalcedony.

**agave** /əˈgeɪvɪ/ noun spiny-leaved plant.

**age** ● noun length of past life or existence; colloquial (often in plural) a long time; historical period; old age. ● verb (**ageing**) (cause to) show signs of age; grow old; mature. □ **come of age** reach legal adult status; **under age** not old enough.

**aged** adjective /eɪdʒd/ of the age of; /ˈeɪdʒɪd/ old.

**ageism** /ˈeɪdʒɪz(ə)m/ noun prejudice or discrimination on grounds of age.

**ageless** /ˈeɪdʒlɪs/ adjective never growing or appearing old.

**agency** /ˈeɪdʒənsɪ/ noun (plural **-ies**) business or premises of agent; action; intervention.

**agenda** /əˈdʒendə/ noun (plural **-s**) list of items to be considered at meeting; things to be done.

**agent** /ˈeɪdʒ(ə)nt/ noun person acting for another in business etc.; person or thing producing effect.

**agent provocateur** /ɑːʒɑ̃ prəvɒkəˈtɜː/ noun (plural **agents provocateurs** same pronunciation) person tempting suspected offenders to self-incriminating action. [French]

**agglomerate** /əˈglɒməreɪt/ verb (**-ting**) collect into mass. □ **agglomeration** noun.

**agglutinate** /əˈgluːtɪneɪt/ verb (**-ting**) stick as with glue. □ **agglutination** noun; **agglutinative** /-nətɪv/ adjective.

**aggrandize** /əˈgrændaɪz/ verb (also **-ise**) (**-zing** or **-sing**) increase power, rank, or wealth of; make seem greater. □ **aggrandizement** /-dɪz-/ noun.

**aggravate** /ˈægrəveɪt/ verb (**-ting**) increase seriousness of; colloquial annoy. ■ **aggravation** noun.

■ **Usage** The use of aggravate to mean 'annoy' is considered incorrect by some people, but it is common in informal use.

**aggregate** ● noun /ˈægrɪgət/ sum total; crushed stone etc. used in making concrete. ● adjective /ˈægrɪgət/ collective, total. ● verb /ˈægrɪgeɪt/ collect together, unite; colloquial amount to. □ **aggregation** noun.

**aggression** /əˈgreʃ(ə)n/ noun unprovoked attack; hostile act or feeling. □ **aggressor** noun.

**aggressive** /əˈgresɪv/ adjective given to aggression; forceful, self-assertive. ■ **aggressively** adverb.

**aggrieved** /əˈgriːvd/ adjective having grievance.

**aggro** /ˈægrəʊ/ noun slang aggression; difficulty.

**aghast** /əˈgɑːst/ adjective amazed and horrified.

**agile** /ˈædʒaɪl/ adjective quick-moving; nimble. □ **agility** /əˈdʒɪlɪtɪ/ noun.

**agitate** /ˈædʒɪteɪt/ verb (**-ting**) disturb, excite; (often + for, against) campaign, esp. politically; shake briskly. ■ **agitation** noun; **agitator** noun.

**AGM** abbreviation annual general meeting.

**agnail** /ˈægneɪl/ noun torn skin at root of fingernail; resulting soreness.

**agnostic** /ægˈnɒstɪk/ ● noun person who believes that existence of God is not provable. ● adjective of agnosticism. □ **agnosticism** /-sɪz(ə)m/ noun.

**ago** /əˈgəʊ/ adverb in the past.

**agog** /əˈgɒg/ adjective eager, expectant.

**agonize** /ˈægənaɪz/ verb (also **-ise**) (**-zing** or **-sing**) undergo mental anguish; (cause to) suffer agony; (as **agonized** adjective) expressing agony.

**agony** /ˈægənɪ/ noun (plural **-ies**) extreme physical or mental suffering; severe struggle. □ **agony aunt** colloquial writer answering letters in **agony column** colloquial, section of magazine etc. offering personal advice.

**agoraphobia** /ˌægərəˈfəʊbɪə/ noun extreme fear of open spaces. □ **agoraphobic** adjective.

**agrarian** /əˈɡreərɪən/ ● adjective of land or its cultivation. ● noun advocate of redistribution of land.

**agree** /əˈɡriː/ verb (**-ees, -eed**) (often + with) hold similar opinion, be or become in harmony, suit, be compatible; (+ to do) consent; reach agreement about.

**agreeable** adjective pleasing; willing to agree. □ **agreeably** adverb.

**agreement** noun act or state of agreeing; arrangement, contract.

**agriculture** /ˈæɡrɪkʌltʃə/ noun cultivation of the soil and rearing of animals. □ **agricultural** /-ˈkʌl-/ adjective; **agriculturalist** /-ˈkʌl-/ noun.

**agronomy** /əˈɡrɒnəmɪ/ noun science of soil management and crop production. □ **agronomist** noun.

**aground** /əˈɡraʊnd/ adjective & adverb on(to) bottom of shallow water.

**ague** /ˈeɪɡjuː/ noun shivering fit; historical malarial fever.

**ah** /ɑː/ interjection expressing surprise, pleasure, or realization.

**aha** /ɑːˈhɑː/ interjection expressing surprise, triumph, mockery, etc.

**ahead** /əˈhed/ adverb in advance, in front; (often + on) in the lead (on points etc.).

**ahoy** /əˈhɔɪ/ interjection Nautical call used in hailing.

**AI** abbreviation artificial insemination; artificial intelligence.

**aid** ● noun help; person or thing that helps. ● verb help; promote (recovery etc.). □ **in aid of** in support of, colloquial for purpose of.

**aide** /eɪd/ noun aide-de-camp; assistant.

**aide-de-camp** /eɪd də ˈkɑ̃/ noun (plural **aides-** same pronunciation) officer assisting senior officer.

**Aids** noun (also **AIDS**) acquired immune deficiency syndrome.

**ail** verb be ill or in poor condition.

**aileron** /ˈeɪlərɒn/ noun hinged flap on aircraft wing.

**ailment** noun illness, esp. minor one.

**aim** ● verb intend, try; (usually + at) direct, point; take aim. ● noun purpose,

object; directing of weapon etc. at object. □ **take aim** direct weapon etc. at object.

**aimless** adjective purposeless. □ **aimlessly** adverb.

**ain't** /eɪnt/ colloquial am not, is not, are not; has not, have not.

■ **Usage** The use of *ain't* is incorrect in standard English.

**air** ● noun mixture chiefly of oxygen and nitrogen surrounding earth; open space; earth's atmosphere, often as place where aircraft operate; appearance, manner; (in plural) affected manner; tune. ● verb expose (room, clothes, etc.) to air, ventilate; express and discuss publicly. □ **airbase** base for military aircraft; **air-bed** inflatable mattress; **airborne** transported by air, (of aircraft) in the air; **airbrick** brick perforated for ventilation; **Air Commodore** RAF officer next above Group Captain; **air-conditioned** adjective equipped with **air-conditioning**, regulation of humidity and temperature in building, apparatus for this; **airfield** area with runway(s) for aircraft; **air force** branch of armed forces fighting in the air; **airgun** gun using compressed air to fire pellets; **air hostess** stewardess in aircraft; **air letter** sheet of paper forming airmail letter; **airlift** noun emergency transport of supplies etc. by air, verb transport thus; **airline** public air transport company; **airliner** large passenger aircraft; **airlock** stoppage of flow by airbubble in pipe etc., compartment giving access to pressurized chamber; **airmail** system of transporting mail by air, mail carried thus; **airman** pilot or member of aircraft crew; **Air (Chief, Vice-) Marshal** high ranks in RAF; **airplane** US aeroplane; **airport** airfield with facilities for passengers and cargo; **air raid** attack by aircraft; **air rifle** rifle using compressed air to fire pellets; **airs and graces** affected manner; **airship** powered aircraft lighter than air; **airsick** nauseous from air travel; **airspace** air above a country; **air speed** aircraft's speed relative to air; **airstrip** strip of ground for take-off and landing of aircraft; **air terminal** building with transport to and from airport; **air traffic**

**controller** official who controls air traffic by radio; **airway** recognized route of aircraft, passage for air into lungs; **airwoman** woman pilot or member of aircraft crew; **by air** by or in aircraft; **on the air** being broadcast.

**aircraft** *noun* (*plural* same) aeroplane, helicopter. □ **aircraft carrier** warship that carries and acts as base for aircraft; **aircraftman**, **aircraftwoman** lowest rank in RAF.

**Airedale** /'eədeɪl/ *noun* terrier of large rough-coated breed.

**airless** *adjective* stuffy; still, calm.

**airtight** *adjective* impermeable to air.

**airworthy** *adjective* (of aircraft) fit to fly. □ **airworthiness** *noun*.

**airy** *adjective* (**-ier**, **-iest**) well-ventilated; flippant; light as air. □ **airy-fairy** *colloquial* unrealistic, impractical.

**aisle** /aɪl/ *noun* side part of church divided by pillars from nave; passage between rows of pews, seats, etc.

**aitchbone** /'eɪtʃbəʊn/ *noun* rump bone of animal; cut of beef over this.

**ajar** /ə'dʒɑː/ *adverb & adjective* (of door etc.) slightly open.

**Akela** /ɑː'keɪlə/ *noun* adult leader of Cub Scouts.

**akimbo** /ə'kɪmbəʊ/ *adverb* (of arms) with hands on hips and elbows out.

**akin** /ə'kɪn/ *adjective* related; similar.

**alabaster** /'æləbɑːstə/ ● *noun* translucent usually white form of gypsum. ● *adjective* of alabaster; white, smooth.

**à la carte** /æ lɑː 'kɑːt/ *adverb & adjective* with individually priced dishes.

**alacrity** /ə'lækrɪtɪ/ *noun* briskness; readiness.

**à la mode** /æ lɑː 'məʊd/ *adverb & adjective* in fashion; fashionable.

**alarm** /ə'lɑːm/ ● *noun* warning of danger etc.; warning sound or device; alarm clock; apprehension. ● *verb* frighten, disturb; warn. □ **alarm clock** clock that rings at set time. □ **alarming** *adjective*.

**alarmist** /ə'lɑːmɪst/ *noun* person spreading unnecessary alarm.

**alas** /ə'læs/ *interjection expressing grief or regret.*

**alb** *noun* long white vestment worn by Christian priests.

**albatross** /'ælbətrɒs/ *noun* long-winged seabird related to petrel; *Golf* score of 3 strokes under par for hole.

**albeit** /ɔːl'biːɪt/ *conjunction* although.

**albino** /æl'biːnəʊ/ *noun* (*plural* -**s**) person or animal lacking pigment in skin, hair, and eyes. □ **albinism** /'ælbɪnɪz(ə)m/ *noun*.

**album** /'ælbəm/ *noun* book for displaying photographs etc.; long-playing gramophone record; set of these.

**albumen** /'ælbjʊmɪn/ *noun* egg white.

**albumin** /'ælbjʊmɪn/ *noun* water-soluble protein found in egg white, milk, blood, etc.

**alchemy** /'ælkəmɪ/ *noun* medieval chemistry, esp. seeking to turn base metals into gold. □ **alchemist** *noun*.

**alcohol** /'ælkəhɒl/ *noun* colourless volatile liquid, esp. as intoxicant present in wine, beer, spirits, etc. and as a solvent, fuel, etc.; liquor containing this; other compound of this type.

**alcoholic** /ælkə'hɒlɪk/ ● *adjective* of, like, containing, or caused by alcohol. ● *noun* person suffering from alcoholism.

**alcoholism** /'ælkəhɒlɪz(ə)m/ *noun* condition resulting from addiction to alcohol.

**alcove** /'ælkəʊv/ *noun* recess in wall of room, garden, etc.

**alder** /'ɔːldə/ *noun* tree related to birch.

**alderman** /'ɔːldəmən/ *noun esp. historical* civic dignitary next in rank to mayor.

**ale** *noun* beer.

**alert** /ə'lɜːt/ ● *adjective* watchful. ● *noun* alarm; state or period of special vigilance. ● *verb* (often + *to*) warn.

**alfalfa** /æl'fælfə/ *noun* clover-like plant used for fodder.

**alfresco** /æl'freskəʊ/ *adjective & adverb* in the open air.

**alga** /'ælgə/ *noun* (*plural* -**gae** /-dʒiː/) (usually in *plural*) non-flowering stemless water plant.

**algebra** /'ældʒɪbrə/ *noun* branch of mathematics using letters to represent numbers. □ **algebraic** /-'breɪk/ *adjective*.

**Algol** /'ælgɒl/ *noun* high-level computer-programming language.

**algorithm** /'ælgərɪð(ə)m/ *noun* process or rules for (esp. computer) calculation etc.

**alias** /'eɪlɪəs/ ● *adverb* also known as. ● *noun* assumed name.

**alibi** /'ælɪbaɪ/ *noun* (*plural* **-s**) proof that one was elsewhere; excuse.

■ **Usage** The use of *alibi* to mean 'an excuse' is considered incorrect by some people.

**alien** /'eɪlɪən/ ● *adjective* (often + *to*) unfamiliar, repugnant; foreign; of beings from another world. ● *noun* non-naturalized foreigner; a being from another world.

**alienate** /'eɪlɪəneɪt/ *verb* (**-ting**) estrange; transfer ownership of. □ **alienation** *noun*.

**alight**[1] /ə'laɪt/ *adjective* on fire; lit up.

**alight**[2] /ə'laɪt/ *verb* (often + *from*) get down or off; come to earth, settle.

**align** /ə'laɪn/ *verb* place in or bring into line; (usually + *with*) ally (oneself etc.). □ **alignment** *noun*.

**alike** /ə'laɪk/ ● *adjective* similar, like. ● *adverb* in similar way.

**alimentary** /ælɪ'mentərɪ/ *adjective* concerning nutrition; nourishing. □ **alimentary canal** channel through which food passes during digestion.

**alimony** /'ælɪmənɪ/ *noun* money payable to a divorced or separated spouse.

**alive** /ə'laɪv/ *adjective* living; lively; active; (usually + *to*) alert to; (usually + *with*) swarming with.

**alkali** /'ælkəlaɪ/ *noun* (*plural* **-s**) substance that neutralizes acids, turns litmus blue, and forms caustic solutions in water. □ **alkaline** *adjective*; **alkalinity** /-'lɪn-/ *noun*.

**alkaloid** /'ælkəlɔɪd/ *noun* plant-based compound often used as drug, e.g. morphine, quinine.

**all** /ɔːl/ ● *adjective* whole amount, number, or extent of. ● *noun* all people or things concerned; (+ *of*) the whole of. ● *adverb* entirely, quite. □ **all along** from the beginning; **all but** very nearly; **all for** *colloquial* strongly in favour of; **all-clear** signal that danger or difficulty is over; **all fours** hands and knees; **all in** exhausted; **all-in** inclusive of all; **all in all** everything considered; **all out** (**all-out** before noun) involving all one's strength etc.; **all over** completely finished, in or on all parts of one's body;

**all-purpose** having many uses; **all right** satisfactory, safe and sound, in good condition, satisfactorily, I consent; **all-right** (before noun) *colloquial* acceptable; **all round** in all respects, for each person; **all-round** (of person) versatile; **all-rounder** versatile person; **All Saints' Day** 1 Nov.; **all the same** nevertheless; **all there** *colloquial* mentally alert or normal; **all together** all at once, all in one place; **at all** (with negative or in questions) in any way, to any extent; **in all** in total, altogether.

■ **Usage** See note at ALTOGETHER.

**Allah** /'ælə/ *noun*: Muslim name of God.

**allay** /ə'leɪ/ *verb* lessen; alleviate.

**allege** /ə'ledʒ/ *verb* declare, esp. without proof. □ **allegation** /ælɪ'geɪʃ(ə)n/ *noun*; **allegedly** /ə'ledʒɪdlɪ/ *adverb*.

**allegiance** /ə'liːdʒ(ə)ns/ *noun* loyalty; duty of subject.

**allegory** /'ælɪgərɪ/ *noun* (*plural* **-ies**) story with moral represented symbolically. □ **allegorical** /-'gɒr-/ *adjective*; **allegorize** *verb* (also **-ise**) (**-zing** or **-sing**).

**allegretto** /ælɪ'gretəʊ/ *Music* ● *adverb* & *adjective* in fairly brisk tempo. ● *noun* (*plural* **-s**) allegretto movement or passage.

**allegro** /ə'legrəʊ/ *Music* ● *adverb* & *adjective* in lively tempo. ● *noun* (*plural* **-s**) allegro movement or passage.

**alleluia** /ælɪ'luːjə/ (also **hallelujah** /hæl-/) ● *interjection* God be praised. ● *noun* (*plural* **-s**) song of praise to God.

**allergic** /ə'lɜːdʒɪk/ *adjective* (+ *to*) having allergy to; *colloquial* having strong dislike for; caused by allergy.

**allergy** /'ælədʒɪ/ *noun* (*plural* **-ies**) reaction to certain substances.

**alleviate** /ə'liːvɪeɪt/ *verb* make (pain etc.) less severe. □ **alleviation** *noun*.

**alley** /'ælɪ/ *noun* narrow street or passage; enclosure for skittles, bowling, etc.

**alliance** /ə'laɪəns/ *noun* formal union or association of states, political parties, etc. or of families by marriage.

**allied** /'ælaɪd/ *adjective* connected or related; (also **Allied**) associated in an alliance.

**alligator** /'ælɪgeɪtə/ *noun* large reptile of crocodile family.

**alliteration** /əlɪtəˈreɪʃ(ə)n/ *noun* recurrence of same initial letter or sound in adjacent or nearby words, as in *The fair breeze blew, the white foam flew, the furrow followed free.* ▫ **alliterate** /-ˈlɪt-/ *verb*; **alliterative** /əˈlɪtərətɪv/ *adjective*.

**allocate** /ˈæləkeɪt/ *verb* (**-ting**) (usually + *to*) assign. ▫ **allocation** *noun*.

**allot** /əˈlɒt/ *verb* (**-tt-**) apportion or distribute to (person).

**allotment** /əˈlɒtmənt/ *noun* small plot of land rented for cultivation; share; allotting.

**allow** /əˈlaʊ/ *verb* (often + *to do*) permit; assign fixed sum to; (usually + *for*) provide or set aside for a purpose. ▫ **allow for** take into consideration.

**allowance** *noun* amount or sum allowed, esp. regularly; deduction, discount. ▫ **make allowances** (often + *for*) judge leniently.

**alloy** ●*noun* /ˈælɔɪ/ mixture of metals; inferior metal mixed esp. with gold or silver. ●*verb* mix (metals); /əˈlɔɪ/ debase by admixture; spoil (pleasure).

**allspice** /ˈɔːlspaɪs/ *noun* spice made from berry of pimento plant; this berry.

**allude** /əˈluːd/ *verb* (**-ding**) (+ *to*) make allusion to.

**allure** /əˈljʊə/ ●*verb* (**-ring**) attract, charm, entice. ●*noun* attractiveness, charm. ▫ **allurement** *noun*.

**allusion** /əˈluːʒ(ə)n/ *noun* (often + *to*) passing or indirect reference. ▫ **allusive** /-sɪv/ *adjective*.

**alluvium** /əˈluːvɪəm/ *noun* (*plural* **-via**) deposit left by flood, esp. in river valley. ▫ **alluvial** *adjective*.

**ally** ●*noun* /ˈælaɪ/ (*plural* **-ies**) state or person formally cooperating or united with another, esp. in war. ●*verb* (also /əˈlaɪ/) (**-ies, -ied**) (often **ally oneself with**) combine in alliance (with).

**Alma Mater** /ælmə ˈmɑːtə/ *noun* one's university, school, or college.

**almanac** /ˈɔːlmənæk/ *noun* (also **almanack**) calendar, usually with astronomical data.

**almighty** /ɔːlˈmaɪtɪ/ ●*adjective* infinitely powerful; very great. ●*noun* (**the Almighty**) God.

**almond** /ˈɑːmənd/ *noun* kernel of nutlike fruit related to plum; tree bearing this.

**almoner** /ˈɑːmənə/ *noun* social worker attached to hospital.

**almost** /ˈɔːlməʊst/ *adverb* all but, very nearly.

**alms** /ɑːmz/ *plural noun historical* donation of money or food to the poor. ▫ **almshouse** charitable institution for the poor.

**aloe** /ˈæləʊ/ *noun* plant with toothed fleshy leaves; (in *plural*) strong laxative from aloe juice. ▫ **aloe vera** /ˈvɪərə/ variety used to make laxative and in cosmetics.

**aloft** /əˈlɒft/ *adjective & adverb* high up, overhead.

**alone** /əˈləʊn/ ●*adjective* without company or help; lonely. ●*adverb* only, exclusively.

**along** /əˈlɒŋ/ ●*preposition* beside or through (part of) the length of. ●*adverb* onward, into more advanced state; with oneself or others; beside or through (part of) thing's length. ▫ **alongside** at or close to side (of); **along with** in addition to.

**aloof** /əˈluːf/ ●*adjective* unconcerned, unsympathetic. ●*adverb* away, apart.

**aloud** /əˈlaʊd/ *adverb* audibly.

**alp** *noun* high mountain, esp. (**the Alps**) those in Switzerland and adjacent countries.

**alpaca** /ælˈpækə/ *noun* S. American llama-like animal; its long wool; fabric made from this.

**alpha** /ˈælfə/ *noun* first letter of Greek alphabet (A, α). ▫ **alpha and omega** beginning and end; **alpha particle** helium nucleus emitted by radioactive substance.

**alphabet** /ˈælfəbet/ *noun* set of letters or signs used in a language. ▫ **alphabetical** /-ˈbet-/ *adjective*.

**alphanumeric** /ælfənjuːˈmerɪk/ *adjective* containing both letters and numbers.

**alpine** /ˈælpaɪn/ ●*adjective* of high mountains or (**Alpine**) the Alps. ●*noun* plant suited to mountain regions; = rock plant.

**already** /ɔːlˈredɪ/ *adverb* before the time in question; as early as this.

**alright** *adverb* = ALL RIGHT.

■ **Usage** Although *alright* is widely used, it is not correct in standard English.

**Alsatian** /æl'seɪʃ(ə)n/ *noun* large dog of a breed of wolfhound.

**also** /'ɔːlsəʊ/ *adverb* in addition, besides. □ **also-ran** loser in race, undistinguished person.

**altar** /'ɔːltə/ *noun* flat table or block for offerings to deity; Communion table.

**alter** /'ɔːltə/ *verb* change in character, shape, etc. □ **alteration** *noun*.

**altercation** /ɔːltə'keɪʃ(ə)n/ *noun* dispute, wrangle.

**alternate** ● *adjective* /ɔːl'tɜːnət/ (with noun in *plural*) every other; (of things of two kinds) alternating. ● *verb* /'ɔːltəneɪt/ (-ting) (often + *with*) arrange or occur by turns; (+ *between*) go repeatedly from one to another. □ **alternating current** electric current regularly reversing direction. □ **alternately** *adverb*; **alternation** *noun*.

■ **Usage** See note at ALTERNATIVE.

**alternative** /ɔːl'tɜːnətɪv/ ● *adjective* available as another choice; unconventional. ● *noun* any of two or more possibilities; choice. □ **alternatively** *adverb*.

■ **Usage** The adjective *alternative* is often confused with *alternate*, which is correctly used in 'there will be a dance on alternate Saturdays'.

**alternator** /'ɔːltəneɪtə/ *noun* dynamo generating alternating current.

**although** /ɔːl'ðəʊ/ *conjunction* though.

**altimeter** /'æltɪmiːtə/ *noun* instrument measuring altitude.

**altitude** /'æltɪtjuːd/ *noun* height, esp. of object above sea level or horizon.

**alto** /'æltəʊ/ ● *noun* (*plural* **-s**) = CONTRALTO; highest adult male singing voice; singer with this. ● *adjective* having range of alto.

**altogether** /ɔːltə'geðə/ *adverb* totally; on the whole; in total.

■ **Usage** Note that *altogether* means 'in total', as in *six rooms altogether*, whereas *all together* means 'all at once' or 'all in one place' as in *six rooms all together*.

**altruism** /'æltruːɪz(ə)m/ *noun* unselfishness as principle of action. □ **altruist** *noun*; **altruistic** /-'ɪs-/ *adjective*.

**alumina** /ə'luːmɪnə/ *noun* aluminium oxide; emery.

**aluminium** /ælju'mɪnɪəm/ *noun* (*US* **aluminum** /ə'luːmɪnəm/) a light silvery metallic element.

**alumnus** /ə'lʌmnəs/ *noun* (*plural* **-ni** /-naɪ/) former pupil or student.

**always** /'ɔːlweɪz/ *adverb* at all times; whatever the circumstances; repeatedly.

**Alzheimer's disease** /'æltshaɪməz/ *noun* brain disorder causing senility.

**AM** *abbreviation* amplitude modulation.

**am** *1st singular present of* BE.

**a.m.** *abbreviation* before noon (*ante meridiem*).

**amalgam** /ə'mælgəm/ *noun* mixture, blend; alloy of any metal with mercury.

**amalgamate** /ə'mælgəmeɪt/ *verb* (**-ting**) mix; unite. □ **amalgamation** *noun*.

**amanuensis** /əmænjuː'ensɪs/ *noun* (*plural* **-enses** /-siːz/) assistant, esp. writing from dictation.

**amaranth** /'æmərænθ/ *noun* plant with green, red, or purple flowers; imaginary unfading flower. □ **amaranthine** /-'rænθaɪn/ *adjective*.

**amaryllis** /æmə'rɪlɪs/ *noun* plant with lily-like flowers.

**amass** /ə'mæs/ *verb* heap together, accumulate.

**amateur** /'æmətə/ *noun* person engaging in pursuit as pastime not profession; person with limited skill. □ **amateurish** *adjective*; **amateurism** *noun*.

**amatory** /'æmətərɪ/ *adjective* of sexual love.

**amaze** /ə'meɪz/ *verb* (**-zing**) fill with surprise or wonder. □ **amazement** *noun*; **amazing** *adjective*.

**Amazon** /'æməzən/ *noun* one of a mythical race of female warriors; (**amazon**) strong or athletic woman. □ **Amazonian** /-'zəʊ-/ *adjective*.

**ambassador** /æm'bæsədə/ *noun* diplomat living abroad as representative of his or her country; promoter. □ **ambassadorial** /-'dɔː-/ *adjective*.

**amber** /'æmbə/ ● *noun* yellow translucent fossil resin; colour of this. ● *adjective* of or like amber.

**ambergris** /'æmbəgrɪs/ *noun* waxlike substance from sperm whale, used in perfumes.

**ambidextrous** /ˌæmbɪˈdekstrəs/ *adjective* able to use either hand equally well.

**ambience** /ˈæmbɪəns/ *noun* surroundings, atmosphere.

**ambient** /ˈæmbɪənt/ *adjective* surrounding.

**ambiguous** /æmˈbɪɡjʊəs/ *adjective* having a double meaning; difficult to classify. □ **ambiguity** /-ˈɡjuː-/ *noun* (*plural* **-ies**).

**ambit** /ˈæmbɪt/ *noun* scope, bounds.

**ambition** /æmˈbɪʃ(ə)n/ *noun* determination to succeed; object of this.

**ambitious** *adjective* full of ambition.

**ambivalent** /æmˈbɪvələnt/ *adjective* having mixed feelings towards person or thing. □ **ambivalence** *noun*.

**amble** /ˈæmb(ə)l/ ● *verb* (**-ling**) walk at leisurely pace. ● *noun* leisurely pace.

**ambrosia** /æmˈbrəʊzɪə/ *noun* food of the gods in classical mythology; delicious food etc.

**ambulance** /ˈæmbjʊləns/ *noun* vehicle for taking patients to hospital; mobile army hospital.

**ambulatory** /ˈæmbjʊlətərɪ/ *adjective* of or for walking.

**ambuscade** /æmbəsˈkeɪd/ *noun & verb* (**-ding**) ambush.

**ambush** /ˈæmbʊʃ/ ● *noun* surprise attack by people hiding; hiding place for this. ● *verb* attack from ambush; waylay.

**ameliorate** /əˈmiːlɪəreɪt/ *verb* (**-ting**) make or become better. □ **amelioration** *noun*; **ameliorative** /-rətɪv/ *adjective*.

**amen** /ɑːˈmen/ *interjection* (esp. at end of prayer) so be it.

**amenable** /əˈmiːnəb(ə)l/ *adjective* responsive, docile; (often + *to*) answerable (to law etc.).

**amend** /əˈmend/ *verb* correct error in; make minor alterations in.

**amendment** *noun* minor alteration or addition in document etc.

**amends** *noun* □ **make amends** (often + *for*) give compensation.

**amenity** /əˈmiːnɪtɪ/ *noun* (*plural* **-ies**) pleasant or useful feature or facility; pleasantness (of a place etc.).

**American** /əˈmerɪkən/ ● *adjective* of America, esp. the US. ● *noun* native, citizen, or inhabitant of America, esp. the US; English as spoken in the US.

□ **Americanize** *verb* (also **-ise**) (**-zing** or **-sing**).

**Americanism** *noun* word etc. of US origin or usage.

**amethyst** /ˈæməθɪst/ *noun* purple or violet semiprecious stone.

**amiable** /ˈeɪmɪəb(ə)l/ *adjective* friendly and pleasant, likeable. □ **amiability** *noun*; **amiably** *adverb*.

**amicable** /ˈæmɪkəb(ə)l/ *adjective* friendly. □ **amicably** *adverb*.

**amid** /əˈmɪd/ *preposition* in the middle of.

**amidships** /əˈmɪdʃɪps/ *adverb* in(to) the middle of a ship.

**amidst** /əˈmɪdst/ = AMID.

**amino acid** /əˈmiːnəʊ/ *noun* organic acid found in proteins.

**amir** = EMIR.

**amiss** /əˈmɪs/ ● *adjective* out of order, wrong. ● *adverb* wrong(ly), inappropriately. □ **take amiss** be offended by.

**amity** /ˈæmɪtɪ/ *noun* friendship.

**ammeter** /ˈæmɪtə/ *noun* instrument for measuring electric current.

**ammo** /ˈæməʊ/ *noun slang* ammunition.

**ammonia** /əˈməʊnɪə/ *noun* pungent strongly alkaline gas; solution of this in water.

**ammonite** /ˈæmənaɪt/ *noun* coil-shaped fossil shell.

**ammunition** /æmjʊˈnɪʃ(ə)n/ *noun* bullets, shells, grenades, etc.; information usable in argument.

**amnesia** /æmˈniːzɪə/ *noun* loss of memory. □ **amnesiac** *adjective & noun*.

**amnesty** /ˈæmnɪstɪ/ *noun* (*plural* **-ies**) general pardon, esp. for political offences.

**amniocentesis** /æmnɪəʊsenˈtiːsɪs/ *noun* (*plural* **-teses** /-siːz/) sampling of amniotic fluid to detect foetal abnormality.

**amniotic fluid** /æmnɪˈɒtɪk/ *noun* fluid surrounding embryo.

**amoeba** /əˈmiːbə/ *noun* (*plural* **-s**) microscopic single-celled organism living in water.

**amok** /əˈmɒk/ *adverb* □ **run amok**, **amuck** /əˈmʌk/ run wild.

**among** /əˈmʌŋ/ *preposition* (also **amongst**) surrounded by; included in or in the category of; from the joint resources of; between.

**amoral** /eɪˈmɒr(ə)l/ *adjective* beyond morality; without moral principles.

**amorous** /ˈæmərəs/ *adjective* showing or feeling sexual love.

**amorphous** /əˈmɔːfəs/ *adjective* of no definite shape; vague; non-crystalline.

**amount** /əˈmaʊnt/ ●*noun* total number, size, value, extent, etc. ●*verb* (+ *to*) be equivalent in number, size, etc. to.

**amour** /əˈmʊə/ *noun* (esp. secret) love affair.

**amp** *noun* ampere; *colloquial* amplifier.

**ampere** /ˈæmpeə/ *noun* SI unit of electric current.

**ampersand** /ˈæmpəsænd/ *noun* the sign '&' (= *and*).

**amphetamine** /æmˈfetəmiːn/ *noun* synthetic stimulant drug.

**amphibian** /æmˈfɪbɪən/ *noun* amphibious animal or vehicle.

**amphibious** /æmˈfɪbɪəs/ *adjective* living or operating on land and in water; involving military forces landed from the sea.

**amphitheatre** /ˈæmfɪθɪətə/ *noun* round open building with tiers of seats surrounding central space.

**amphora** /ˈæmfərə/ *noun* (*plural* **-rae** /-riː/) Greek or Roman two-handled jar.

**ample** /ˈæmp(ə)l/ *adjective* (**-r, -st**) plentiful, extensive; more than enough. □ **amply** *adverb*.

**amplifier** /ˈæmplɪfaɪə/ *noun* device for amplifying sounds or electrical signals.

**amplify** /ˈæmplɪfaɪ/ *verb* (**-ies, -ied**) increase strength of (sound or electrical signal); add details to (story etc.). □ **amplification** *noun*.

**amplitude** /ˈæmplɪtjuːd/ *noun* spaciousness; maximum departure from average of oscillation, alternating current, etc. □ **amplitude modulation** modulation of a wave by variation of its amplitude.

**ampoule** /ˈæmpuːl/ *noun* small sealed capsule holding solution for injection.

**amputate** /ˈæmpjʊteɪt/ *verb* (**-ting**) cut off surgically (limb etc.). □ **amputation** *noun*, **amputee** /-ˈtiː/ *noun*.

**amuck** = AMOK.

**amulet** /ˈæmjʊlɪt/ *noun* charm worn against evil.

**amuse** /əˈmjuːz/ *verb* (**-sing**) cause to laugh or smile; interest, occupy. □ **amusing** *adjective*.

**amusement** *noun* being amused; thing that amuses, esp. device for entertainment at fairground etc. □ **amusement arcade** indoor area with slot machines etc.

**an** see A.

**anabolic steroid** /ænəˈbɒlɪk/ *noun* synthetic steroid hormone used to build muscle.

**anachronism** /əˈnækrənɪz(ə)m/ *noun* attribution of custom, event, etc. to wrong period; thing thus attributed; out-of-date person or thing. □ **anachronistic** /-ˈnɪs-/ *adjective*.

**anaconda** /ænəˈkɒndə/ *noun* large S. American constrictor.

**anaemia** /əˈniːmɪə/ *noun* (US **anemia**) deficiency of red blood cells or their haemoglobin, causing pallor and listlessness. □ **anaemic** *adjective*.

**anaesthesia** /ænɪsˈθiːzɪə/ *noun* (US **anes-**) artificially induced insensibility to pain.

**anaesthetic** /ænɪsˈθetɪk/ (US **anes-**) ●*noun* drug, gas, etc., producing anaesthesia. ●*adjective* producing anaesthesia.

**anaesthetist** /əˈniːsθətɪst/ *noun* (US **anes-**) person who administers anaesthetics.

**anaesthetize** /əˈniːsθətaɪz/ *verb* (also **-ise**; US also **anes-**) (**-zing** or **-sing**) administer anaesthetic to.

**anagram** /ˈænəgræm/ *noun* word or phrase formed by transposing letters of another.

**anal** /ˈeɪn(ə)l/ *adjective* of the anus.

**analgesia** /ænælˈdʒiːzɪə/ *noun* absence or relief of pain.

**analgesic** /ænælˈdʒiːsɪk/ ●*noun* pain-killing drug. ●*adjective* pain-killing.

**analogous** /əˈnæləgəs/ *adjective* (usually + *to*) partially similar or parallel.

**analogue** /ˈænəlɒg/ (US **analog**) ●*noun* analogous thing. ●*adjective* (of computer (usually **analog**), watch, etc.) using physical variables (e.g. voltage, position of hands) to represent numbers.

**analogy** /əˈnælədʒɪ/ *noun* (*plural* **-ies**) correspondence, similarity; reasoning from parallel cases.

**analyse** /ˈænəlaɪz/ verb (-sing) (US ana-lyze; -zing) perform analysis on.

**analysis** /əˈnælɪsɪs/ noun (plural -lyses /-siːz/) detailed examination; Chemistry determination of constituent parts; psychoanalysis.

**analyst** /ˈænəlɪst/ noun person who analyses.

**analytical** /ænəˈlɪtɪkəl/ adjective (also **analytic**) of or using analysis.

**analyze** US = ANALYSE.

**anarchism** /ˈænəkɪz(ə)m/ noun belief that government and law should be abolished. □ **anarchist** noun; **anarchistic** /-ˈkɪstɪk/ adjective.

**anarchy** /ˈænəkɪ/ noun disorder, esp. political. □ **anarchic** /əˈnɑːkɪk/ adjective.

**anathema** /əˈnæθəmə/ noun (plural -s) detested thing; Church's curse.

**anatomy** /əˈnætəmɪ/ noun (plural -ies) (science of) animal or plant structure. □ **anatomical** /ænəˈtɒmɪk(ə)l/ adjective; **anatomist** noun.

**anatto** = ANNATTO.

**ANC** abbreviation African National Congress.

**ancestor** /ˈænsestə/ noun person, animal, or plant from which another has descended or evolved; prototype.

**ancestral** /ænˈsestr(ə)l/ adjective inherited from ancestors.

**ancestry** /ˈænsestrɪ/ noun (plural -ies) lineage; ancestors collectively.

**anchor** /ˈæŋkə/ ● noun metal device used to moor ship to sea-bottom. ● verb secure with anchor; fix firmly; cast anchor. □ **anchorman** coordinator, esp. compère in broadcast.

**anchorage** /ˈæŋkərɪdʒ/ noun place for anchoring; lying at anchor.

**anchorite** /ˈæŋkəraɪt/ noun hermit, recluse.

**anchovy** /ˈæntʃəvɪ/ noun (plural -ies) small strong-flavoured fish of herring family.

**ancien régime** /ɑ̃sjæ̃ reˈʒiːm/ noun superseded regime, esp. that of pre-Revolutionary France. [French]

**ancient** /ˈeɪnʃ(ə)nt/ adjective of times long past; very old.

**ancillary** /ænˈsɪlərɪ/ ● adjective subsidiary, auxiliary; (esp. of health workers) providing essential support.

● noun (plural -ies) auxiliary; ancillary worker.

**and** conjunction connecting words, clauses, or sentences.

**andante** /ænˈdæntɪ/ Music ● adverb & adjective in moderately slow time. ● noun andante movement or passage.

**androgynous** /ænˈdrɒdʒɪnəs/ adjective hermaphrodite.

**android** /ˈændrɔɪd/ noun robot with human appearance.

**anecdote** /ˈænɪkdəʊt/ noun short, esp. true, story. □ **anecdotal** /-ˈdəʊt(ə)l/ adjective.

**anemia** US = ANAEMIA.

**anemic** US = ANAEMIC.

**anemometer** /ænɪˈmɒmɪtə/ noun instrument for measuring wind force.

**anemone** /əˈnemənɪ/ noun plant related to buttercup.

**aneroid barometer** /ˈænərɔɪd/ noun barometer that measures air pressure by registering its action on lid of box containing vacuum.

**anesthesia** etc. US = ANAESTHESIA etc.

**aneurysm** /ˈænjʊrɪz(ə)m/ noun (also **aneurism**) excessive enlargement of artery.

**anew** /əˈnjuː/ adverb again; in different way.

**angel** /ˈeɪndʒ(ə)l/ noun attendant or messenger of God usually represented as human with wings; kind or virtuous person. □ **angel cake** light sponge cake; **angelfish** small fish with winglike fins. □ **angelic** /ænˈdʒelɪk/ adjective; **angelically** adverb.

**angelica** /ænˈdʒelɪkə/ noun aromatic plant; its candied stalks.

**angelus** /ˈændʒɪləs/ noun RC prayers said at morning, noon, and sunset; bell rung for this.

**anger** /ˈæŋgə/ ● noun extreme displeasure. ● verb make angry.

**angina** /ænˈdʒaɪnə/ noun (in full **angina pectoris**) chest pain brought on by exertion, owing to poor blood supply to heart.

**angle**[1] /ˈæŋg(ə)l/ ● noun space between two meeting lines or surfaces, esp. as measured in degrees; corner; point of view. ● verb (-ling) move or place obliquely; present (information) in biased way.

**angle**[2] /'æŋg(ə)l/ *verb* (**-ling**) fish with line and hook; (+ *for*) seek objective indirectly. □ **angler** *noun*.

**Anglican** /'æŋglıkən/ ● *adjective* of Church of England. ● *noun* member of Anglican Church. □ **Anglicanism** *noun*.

**Anglicism** /'æŋglısız(ə)m/ *noun* English expression or custom.

**Anglicize** /'æŋglısaız/ *verb* (also **-ise**) (**-zing** or **-sing**) make English in character etc.

**Anglo-** *combining form* English or British (and).

**Anglo-Catholic** /æŋgləʊ'kæθəlık/ ● *adjective* of High Church Anglican group emphasizing its Catholic tradition. ● *noun* member of this group.

**Anglo-Indian** /æŋgləʊ'ındıən/ ● *adjective* of England and India; of British descent but Indian residence. ● *noun* Anglo-Indian person.

**Anglophile** /'æŋgləʊfaıl/ *noun* admirer of England or the English.

**Anglo-Saxon** /æŋgləʊ'sæks(ə)n/ ● *adjective* of English Saxons before Norman Conquest; of English descent. ● *noun* Anglo-Saxon person or language; *colloquial* plain (esp. crude) English.

**angora** /æŋ'gɔːrə/ *noun* fabric made from hair of angora goat or rabbit. □ **angora cat**, **goat**, **rabbit** long-haired varieties.

**angostura** /æŋgə'stjʊərə/ *noun* aromatic bitter bark of S. American tree.

**angry** /'æŋgrı/ *adjective* (**-ier**, **-iest**) feeling or showing anger; (of wound etc.) inflamed, painful. □ **angrily** *adverb*.

**angst** /æŋst/ *noun* anxiety, neurotic fear; guilt.

**angstrom** /'æŋstrəm/ *noun* unit of wavelength measurement.

**anguish** /'æŋgwıʃ/ *noun* severe mental or physical pain. □ **anguished** *adjective*.

**angular** /'æŋgjʊlə/ *adjective* having sharp corners or (of person) features; (of distance) measured by angle. □ **angularity** /-'lær-/ *noun*.

**aniline** /'ænıliːn/ *noun* colourless oily liquid used in dyes, drugs, and plastics.

**animadvert** /ænımæd'vɜːt/ *verb* (+ *on*) *literary* criticize, censure. □ **animadversion** *noun*.

**animal** /'ænım(ə)l/ ● *noun* living organism, esp. other than man, having sensation and usually ability to move; brutish person. ● *adjective* of or like animal; carnal.

**animality** /ænı'mælıtı/ *noun* the animal world; animal behaviour.

**animate** ● *adjective* /'ænımət/ having life; lively. ● *verb* /'ænımeıt/ (**-ting**) enliven; give life to.

**animated** /'ænımeıtıd/ *adjective* lively; living; (of film) using animation.

**animation** /ænı'meıʃ(ə)n/ *noun* liveliness; being alive; technique of film-making by photographing sequence of drawings or positions of puppets etc. to create illusion of movement.

**animator** /'ænımeıtə/ *noun* artist who prepares animated films.

**animism** /'ænımız(ə)m/ *noun* belief that inanimate objects and natural phenomena have souls. □ **animist** *noun*; **animistic** /-'mıs-/ *adjective*.

**animosity** /ænı'mɒsıtı/ *noun* (*plural* **-ies**) hostility.

**animus** /'ænıməs/ *noun* hostility, ill feeling.

**anion** /'ænaıən/ *noun* negatively charged ion.

**anise** /'ænıs/ *noun* plant with aromatic seeds.

**aniseed** /'ænısiːd/ *noun* seed of anise.

**ankle** /'æŋk(ə)l/ *noun* joint connecting foot with leg.

**anklet** /'æŋklıt/ *noun* ornament worn round ankle.

**ankylosis** /æŋkı'ləʊsıs/ *noun* stiffening of joint by fusing of bones.

**annals** /'æn(ə)lz/ *plural noun* narrative of events year by year; historical records. □ **annalist** *noun*.

**annatto** /ə'nætəʊ/ *noun* (also **anatto**) orange-red food colouring made from tropical fruit.

**anneal** /ə'niːl/ *verb* heat (metal, glass) and cool slowly, esp. to toughen.

**annelid** /'ænəlıd/ *noun* segmented worm, e.g. earthworm.

**annex** /æ'neks/ *verb* (often + *to*) add as subordinate part; take possession of. □ **annexation** *noun*.

**annexe** /'æneks/ *noun* supplementary building.

**annihilate** /ə'naɪəleɪt/ verb (-ting) destroy utterly. □ **annihilation** noun.

**anniversary** /ænɪ'vɜːsərɪ/ noun (plural -ies) yearly return of date of event; celebration of this.

**Anno Domini** /ænəʊ 'dɒmɪnaɪ/ see AD.

**annotate** /'ænəteɪt/ verb (-ting) add explanatory notes to. □ **annotation** noun.

**announce** /ə'naʊns/ verb (-cing) make publicly known; make known the approach of. □ **announcement** noun.

**announcer** noun person who announces, esp. in broadcasting.

**annoy** /ə'nɔɪ/ verb (often in passive + at, with) anger or distress slightly; harass. □ **annoyance** noun.

**annual** /'ænjʊəl/ • adjective reckoned by the year; recurring yearly. • noun book etc. published yearly; plant living only one year. □ **annually** adverb.

**annuity** /ə'njuːɪtɪ/ noun (plural -ies) yearly grant or allowance; investment yielding fixed annual sum for stated period.

**annul** /ə'nʌl/ verb (-ll-) declare invalid; cancel, abolish. □ **annulment** noun.

**annular** /'ænjʊlə/ adjective ring-shaped.

**annulate** /'ænjʊlət/ adjective marked with or formed of rings.

**annunciation** /ənʌnsɪ'eɪʃ(ə)n/ noun announcement, esp. (**Annunciation**) that made by the angel Gabriel to Mary.

**anode** /'ænəʊd/ noun positive electrode.

**anodize** /'ænədaɪz/ verb (also -ise) (-zing or -sing) coat (metal) with protective layer by electrolysis.

**anodyne** /'ænədaɪn/ • adjective pain-relieving; soothing. • noun anodyne drug etc.

**anoint** /ə'nɔɪnt/ verb apply oil or ointment to, esp. ritually.

**anomalous** /ə'nɒmələs/ adjective irregular, abnormal.

**anomaly** /ə'nɒməlɪ/ noun (plural -ies) anomalous thing.

**anon** /ə'nɒn/ adverb archaic soon.

**anon.** abbreviation anonymous.

**anonymous** /ə'nɒnɪməs/ adjective of unknown name or authorship; featureless. □ **anonymity** /ænə'nɪm-/ noun.

**anorak** /'ænəræk/ noun waterproof usually hooded jacket.

**anorexia** /ænə'reksɪə/ noun lack of appetite, esp. (in full **anorexia nervosa** /nɜː'vəʊsə/) obsessive desire to lose weight by refusing to eat. □ **anorexic** adjective & noun.

**another** /ə'nʌðə/ • adjective an additional or different. • pronoun an additional or different person or thing.

**answer** /'ɑːnsə/ • noun something said or done in reaction to a question, statement, or circumstance; solution to problem. • verb make an answer or response (to); suit; (+ to, for) be responsible to or for; (+ to) correspond to (esp. description). □ **answer back** answer insolently; **answering machine**, **answerphone** tape recorder which answers telephone calls and takes messages.

**answerable** adjective (usually + to, for) responsible; that can be answered.

**ant** noun small usually wingless insect living in complex social group. □ **anteater** mammal feeding on ants; **anthill** moundlike ants' nest.

**antacid** /æn'tæsɪd/ noun & adjective preventive or corrective of acidity.

**antagonism** /æn'tægənɪz(ə)m/ noun active hostility.

**antagonist** /æn'tægənɪst/ noun opponent. □ **antagonistic** /-'nɪs-/ adjective.

**antagonize** /æn'tægənaɪz/ verb (also -ise) (-zing or -sing) provoke.

**Antarctic** /æn'tɑːktɪk/ • adjective of south polar region. • noun this region.

**ante** /'æntɪ/ noun stake put up by poker player before receiving cards; amount payable in advance.

**ante-** /'æntɪ/ prefix before.

**antecedent** /æntɪ'siːd(ə)nt/ • noun preceding thing or circumstance; Grammar word, phrase, etc., to which another word refers; (in plural) person's ancestors. • adjective previous.

**antechamber** /'æntɪtʃeɪmbə/ noun ante-room.

**antedate** /æntɪ'deɪt/ verb (-ting) precede in time; give earlier than true date to.

**antediluvian** /æntɪdɪ'luːvɪən/ adjective before the Flood; colloquial very old.

**antelope** /'æntɪləʊp/ noun (plural same or -s) swift deerlike animal.

**antenatal** /æntɪ'neɪtəl/ adjective before birth; of pregnancy.

**antenna** /æn'tenə/ *noun* (*plural* **-tennae** /-niː/) each of pair of feelers on head of insect or crustacean; (*plural* **-s**) aerial.

**anterior** /æn'tɪərɪə/ *adjective* nearer the front; (often + *to*) prior.

**ante-room** /'æntɪruːm/ *noun* small room leading to main one.

**anthem** /'ænθəm/ *noun* choral composition for church use; song of praise, esp. for nation.

**anther** /'ænθə/ *noun* part of stamen containing pollen.

**anthology** /æn'θɒlədʒɪ/ *noun* (*plural* **-ies**) collection of poems, essays, stories, etc.

**anthracite** /'ænθrəsaɪt/ *noun* hard kind of coal.

**anthrax** /'ænθræks/ *noun* disease of sheep and cattle transmissible to humans.

**anthropocentric** /ænθrəpəʊ'sentrɪk/ *adjective* regarding humankind as centre of existence.

**anthropoid** /'ænθrəpɔɪd/ ● *adjective* human in form. ● *noun* anthropoid ape.

**anthropology** /ænθrə'pɒlədʒɪ/ *noun* study of humankind, esp. societies and customs. □ **anthropological** /-pə'lɒdʒɪ-/ *adjective*; **anthropologist** *noun*.

**anthropomorphism** /ænθrəpə'mɔːfɪz(ə)m/ *noun* attributing of human characteristics to god, animal, or thing. □ **anthropomorphic** *adjective*; **anthropomorphize** *verb* (also **-ise**) (**-zing** or **-sing**).

**anthropomorphous** /ænθrəpə'mɔːfəs/ *adjective* human in form.

**anti-** /'æntɪ/ *prefix* opposed to; preventing; opposite of; unconventional.

**anti-abortion** /-ə'bɔːʃ(ə)n/ *adjective* opposing abortion. □ **anti-abortionist** *noun*.

**anti-aircraft** /-'eəkrɑːft/ *adjective* for defence against enemy aircraft.

**antibiotic** /-baɪ'ɒtɪk/ ● *noun* substance that can inhibit or destroy bacteria etc. ● *adjective* functioning as antibiotic.

**antibody** /'æntɪbɒdɪ/ *noun* (*plural* **-ies**) blood protein produced in reaction to antigens.

**antic** /'æntɪk/ *noun* (usually in *plural*) foolish behaviour.

**anticipate** /æn'tɪsɪpeɪt/ *verb* (**-ting**) deal with or use before proper time; expect;

forestall. □ **anticipation** *noun*; **anticipatory** *adjective*.

**anticlimax** /-'klaɪmæks/ *noun* disappointing conclusion to something significant.

**anticlockwise** /-'klɒkwaɪz/ ● *adverb* in opposite direction to hands of clock. ● *adjective* moving anticlockwise.

**anticyclone** /-'saɪkləʊn/ *noun* system of winds rotating outwards from area of high pressure, producing fine weather.

**antidepressant** /-dɪ'pres(ə)nt/ ● *noun* drug etc. alleviating depression. ● *adjective* alleviating depression.

**antidote** /'æntɪdəʊt/ *noun* medicine etc. to counteract poison.

**antifreeze** /'æntɪfriːz/ *noun* substance added to water (esp. in vehicle's radiator) to lower its freezing point.

**antigen** /'æntɪdʒ(ə)n/ *noun* foreign substance causing body to produce antibodies.

**anti-hero** /'æntɪhɪərəʊ/ *noun* (*plural* **-es**) central character in story, lacking conventional heroic qualities.

**antihistamine** /-'hɪstəmiːn/ *noun* drug that counteracts effect of histamine, used esp. to treat allergies.

**anti-lock** /'æntɪlɒk/ *adjective* (of brakes) not locking when applied suddenly.

**antimony** /'æntɪmənɪ/ *noun* brittle silvery metallic element.

**anti-nuclear** /-'njuːklɪə/ *adjective* opposed to development of nuclear weapons or power.

**antipathy** /æn'tɪpəθɪ/ *noun* (*plural* **-ies**) (often + *to*, *for*, *between*) strong aversion or dislike. □ **antipathetic** /-'θet-/ *adjective*.

**antiperspirant** /-'pɜːspərənt/ *noun* substance inhibiting perspiration.

**antiphon** /'æntɪf(ə)n/ *noun* hymn sung alternately by two groups. □ **antiphonal** /-'tɪf-/ *adjective*.

**antipodes** /æn'tɪpədiːz/ *plural noun* places diametrically opposite each other on the earth, esp. (also **Antipodes**) Australasia in relation to Europe. □ **antipodean** /-'diːən/ *adjective* & *noun*.

**antiquarian** /æntɪ'kweərɪən/ ● *adjective* of or dealing in rare books. ● *noun* antiquary.

**antiquary** /ˈæntɪkwərɪ/ noun (plural -ies) student or collector of antiques etc.

**antiquated** /ˈæntɪkweɪtɪd/ adjective old-fashioned.

**antique** /ænˈtiːk/ ● noun old valuable object, esp. piece of furniture etc. ● adjective of or existing since old times; old-fashioned.

**antiquity** /ænˈtɪkwətɪ/ noun (plural -ies) ancient times, esp. before Middle Ages; (in plural) great age; remains from ancient times.

**antirrhinum** /æntɪˈraɪnəm/ noun snapdragon.

**anti-Semitic** /-sɪˈmɪtɪk/ adjective prejudiced against Jews. □ **anti-Semite** /-ˈsiːmaɪt/ noun; **anti-Semitism** /-ˈsemɪ-/ noun.

**antiseptic** /-ˈseptɪk/ ● adjective counteracting sepsis by destroying germs. ● noun antiseptic substance.

**antisocial** /-ˈsəʊʃ(ə)l/ adjective not sociable; opposed or harmful to society.

■ **Usage** It is a mistake to use antisocial instead of unsocial in the phrase unsocial hours.

**antistatic** /-ˈstætɪk/ adjective counteracting effect of static electricity.

**antithesis** /ænˈtɪθəsɪs/ noun (plural -theses /-siːz/) (often + of, to) direct opposite; contrast; rhetorical use of strongly contrasted words. □ **antithetical** /-ˈθet-/ adjective.

**antitoxin** /-ˈtɒksɪn/ noun antibody counteracting toxin. □ **antitoxic** adjective.

**antitrades** /-ˈtreɪdz/ plural noun winds blowing above and in opposite direction to trade winds.

**antiviral** /-ˈvaɪər(ə)l/ adjective effective against viruses.

**antler** /ˈæntlə/ noun branched horn of deer.

**antonym** /ˈæntənɪm/ noun word opposite in meaning to another, e.g. wet is an antonym of dry.

**anus** /ˈeɪnəs/ noun (plural -es) excretory opening at end of alimentary canal.

**anvil** /ˈænvɪl/ noun iron block on which metals are worked.

**anxiety** /æŋˈzaɪətɪ/ noun (plural -ies) troubled state of mind; worry; eagerness.

**anxious** /ˈæŋkʃəs/ adjective mentally troubled; marked by anxiety; (+ to do) uneasily wanting. □ **anxiously** adverb.

**any** /ˈenɪ/ ● adjective one or some, no matter which. ● pronoun any one; any number or amount. ● adverb at all. □ **anybody** pronoun any person, noun an important person; **anyhow** anyway, at random; **anyone** anybody; **anything** any thing, a thing of any kind; **anyway** in any way, in any case; **anywhere** (in or to) any place.

**AOB** abbreviation any other business.

**aorta** /eɪˈɔːtə/ noun (plural -s) main artery carrying blood from heart.

**apace** /əˈpeɪs/ adverb literary swiftly.

**apart** /əˈpɑːt/ adverb separately; into pieces; at or to a distance.

**apartheid** /əˈpɑːteɪt/ noun racial segregation, esp. in S. Africa.

**apartment** /əˈpɑːtmənt/ noun (US or esp. for holidays) flat; (usually in plural) room.

**apathy** /ˈæpəθɪ/ noun lack of interest, indifference. □ **apathetic** /-ˈθet-/ adjective.

**apatosaurus** /əpætəˈsɔːrəs/ noun (plural -ruses) large long-necked plant-eating dinosaur.

**ape** ● noun tailless monkey; imitator. ● verb (-ping) imitate.

**aperient** /əˈpɪərɪənt/ adjective & noun laxative.

**aperitif** /əperɪˈtiːf/ noun alcoholic drink before meal.

**aperture** /ˈæpətʃə/ noun opening or gap, esp. variable one letting light into camera.

**apex** /ˈeɪpeks/ noun (plural -es) highest point; tip.

**aphasia** /əˈfeɪzɪə/ noun loss of verbal understanding or expression.

**aphelion** /əˈfiːlɪən/ noun (plural -lia) point of orbit farthest from sun.

**aphid** /ˈeɪfɪd/ noun insect infesting plants.

**aphis** /ˈeɪfɪs/ noun (plural **aphides** /-diːz/) aphid.

**aphorism** /ˈæfərɪz(ə)m/ noun short wise saying. □ **aphoristic** /-ˈrɪs-/ adjective.

**aphrodisiac** /æfrəˈdɪzɪæk/ ● adjective arousing sexual desire. ● noun aphrodisiac substance.

**apiary** /ˈeɪpɪərɪ/ noun (plural -ies) place where bees are kept. □ **apiarist** noun.

**apiculture** /ˈeɪpɪkʌltʃə/ noun bee-keeping.

**apiece** /əˈpiːs/ adverb for each one.

**aplomb** /əˈplɒm/ noun self-assurance.

**apocalypse** /əˈpɒkəlɪps/ noun destructive event; revelation, esp. about the end of the world. □ **apocalyptic** /-ˈlɪp-/ adjective.

**Apocrypha** /əˈpɒkrɪfə/ plural noun Old Testament books not in Hebrew Bible; (**apocrypha**) writings etc. not considered genuine. □ **apocryphal** adjective.

**apogee** /ˈæpədʒiː/ noun highest point; point farthest from earth in orbit of moon etc.

**apolitical** /eɪpəˈlɪtɪk(ə)l/ adjective not interested or involved in politics.

**apologetic** /əpɒləˈdʒetɪk/ adjective expressing regret. □ **apologetically** adverb.

**apologia** /æpəˈləʊdʒə/ noun formal defence of conduct or opinions.

**apologist** /əˈpɒlədʒɪst/ noun person who defends by argument.

**apologize** /əˈpɒlədʒaɪz/ verb (also **-ise**) (**-zing** or **-sing**) make apology.

**apology** /əˈpɒlədʒɪ/ noun (plural **-ies**) regretful acknowledgement of offence or failure; explanation.

**apophthegm** /ˈæpəθem/ noun short wise saying.

**apoplexy** /ˈæpəpleksɪ/ noun sudden paralysis caused by blockage or rupture of brain artery. □ **apoplectic** /-ˈplek-/ adjective.

**apostasy** /əˈpɒstəsɪ/ noun (plural **-ies**) abandonment of belief, faith, etc.

**apostate** /əˈpɒsteɪt/ noun person who renounces belief. □ **apostatize** /-tət-/ verb (also **-ise**) (**-zing** or **-sing**).

**a posteriori** /eɪ pɒsterɪˈɔːraɪ/ adjective & adverb from effects to causes.

**Apostle** /əˈpɒs(ə)l/ noun any of twelve men sent by Christ to preach gospel; (**apostle**) leader of reform.

**apostolic** /æpɒsˈtɒlɪk/ adjective of Apostles; of the Pope.

**apostrophe** /əˈpɒstrəfɪ/ noun punctuation mark (') indicating possession or marking omission of letter(s) or number(s) (see panel).

**apostrophize** verb (also **-ise**) (**-zing** or **-sing**) address (esp. absent person or thing).

**apothecary** /əˈpɒθəkərɪ/ noun (plural **-ies**) archaic pharmacist.

**apotheosis** /əpɒθɪˈəʊsɪs/ noun (plural **-oses** /-siːz/) deification; glorification or sublime example (of thing).

**appal** /əˈpɔːl/ verb (**-ll-**) dismay; horrify.

**apparatus** /æpəˈreɪtəs/ noun equipment for scientific or other work.

**apparel** /əˈpær(ə)l/ noun formal clothing. □ **apparelled** adjective.

**apparent** /əˈpærənt/ adjective obvious; seeming. □ **apparently** adverb.

**apparition** /æpəˈrɪʃ(ə)n/ noun thing that appears, esp. of startling kind; ghost.

**appeal** /əˈpiːl/ ● verb make earnest or formal request; (usually + to) be attractive; (+ to) resort to for support; (often + to) apply to higher court for revision of judicial decision; Cricket ask umpire to declare batsman out. ● noun appealing; request for aid; attractiveness.

**appear** /əˈpɪə/ verb become or be visible; seem; present oneself; be published.

**appearance** noun appearing; outward form; (in plural) outward show of prosperity, virtue, etc.

**appease** /əˈpiːz/ verb (**-sing**) make calm or quiet, esp. conciliate (aggressor) with concessions; satisfy (appetite etc.). □ **appeasement** noun.

**appellant** /əˈpelənt/ noun person who appeals to higher court.

**appellation** /æpəˈleɪʃ(ə)n/ noun formal name, title.

**append** /əˈpend/ verb (usually + to) attach, affix; add.

**appendage** /əˈpendɪdʒ/ noun thing attached; addition.

**appendectomy** /æpenˈdektəmɪ/ noun (also **appendicectomy** /əpendɪˈsektəmɪ/) (plural **-ies**) surgical removal of appendix.

**appendicitis** /əpendɪˈsaɪtɪs/ noun inflammation of appendix.

**appendix** /əˈpendɪks/ noun (plural **-dices** /-siːz/) tubular sac attached to large intestine; addition to book etc.

**appertain** /æpəˈteɪn/ verb (+ to) belong, relate to.

**appetite** /ˈæpɪtaɪt/ noun (usually + for) desire (esp. for food); inclination, desire.

**appetizer** /ˈæpɪtaɪzə/ noun (also **-iser**) thing eaten or drunk to stimulate appetite.

**appetizing** /ˈæpɪtaɪzɪŋ/ adjective (also **-ising**) (esp. of food) stimulating appetite.

**applaud** /əˈplɔːd/ verb express approval (of), esp. by clapping; commend.

**applause** /əˈplɔːz/ noun warm approval, esp. clapping.

**apple** /ˈæp(ə)l/ noun roundish firm fruit. □ **apple of one's eye** cherished person or thing; **apple-pie bed** bed with sheets folded so that one cannot stretch out one's legs; **apple-pie order** extreme neatness.

**appliance** /əˈplaɪəns/ noun device etc. for specific task.

**applicable** /ˈæplɪkəb(ə)l/ adjective (often + to) that may be applied. □ **applicability** noun.

**applicant** /ˈæplɪkənt/ noun person who applies for job etc.

**application** /æplɪˈkeɪʃ(ə)n/ noun formal request; applying; thing applied; diligence; relevance; use.

**applicator** /ˈæplɪkeɪtə/ noun device for applying ointment etc.

**appliqué** /æˈpliːkeɪ/ ● noun work in which cut-out fabric is fixed on to other fabric. ● verb (**-qués**, **-quéd**, **-quéing**) decorate with appliqué.

---

## Apostrophe '

This is used:

**1** to indicate possession:

with a singular noun:

*a boy's book; a week's work; the boss's salary.*

with a plural already ending with *s*:

*a girls' school; two weeks' newspapers; the bosses' salaries.*

with a plural not already ending with *s*:

*the children's books; women's liberation.*

with a singular name:

*Bill's book; John's coat; Barnabas' (or Barnabas's) book; Nicholas' (or Nicholas's) coat.*

with a name ending in *-es* that is pronounced /-ɪz/:

*Bridges' poems; Moses' mother*

and before the word *sake*:

*for God's sake; for goodness' sake; for Nicholas' sake*

but it is often omitted in a business name:

*Barclays Bank.*

**2** to mark an omission of one or more letters or numbers:

*he's (he is or he has)*　　　*haven't (have not)*
*can't (cannot)*　　　　　*we'll (we shall)*
*won't (will not)*　　　　 *o'clock (of the clock)*
*the summer of '68 (1968)*

**3** when letters or numbers are referred to in plural form:

*mind your p's and q's; find all the number 7's.*

but it is unnecessary in, e.g.

*MPs; the 1940s.*

**apply** /əˈplaɪ/ *verb* (**-ies, -ied**) (often + *for, to, to do*) make formal request; (often + *to*) be relevant; make use of; (often + *to*) put or spread (on); (**apply oneself**; often + *to*) devote oneself.

**appoint** /əˈpɔɪnt/ *verb* assign job or office to; (often + *for*) fix (time etc.); (as **appointed** *adjective*) equipped, furnished.

**appointment** *noun* appointing, being appointed; arrangement for meeting; job available; (in *plural*) equipment, fittings.

**apportion** /əˈpɔːʃ(ə)n/ *verb* (often + *to*) share out. □ **apportionment** *noun*.

**apposite** /ˈæpəzɪt/ *adjective* (often + *to*) well expressed, appropriate.

**apposition** /æpəˈzɪʃ(ə)n/ *noun* juxtaposition, esp. of syntactically parallel words etc. (e.g. *my friend Sue*).

**appraise** /əˈpreɪz/ *verb* (**-sing**) estimate value or quality of. □ **appraisal** *noun*.

**appreciable** /əˈpriːʃəb(ə)l/ *adjective* significant; considerable.

**appreciate** /əˈpriːʃɪeɪt/ *verb* (**-ting**) (highly) value; be grateful for; understand, recognize; rise in value. □ **appreciation** *noun*; **appreciative** /-ʃətɪv/ *adjective*.

**apprehend** /æprɪˈhend/ *verb* arrest; understand.

**apprehension** /æprɪˈhenʃ(ə)n/ *noun* fearful anticipation; arrest; understanding.

**apprehensive** /æprɪˈhensɪv/ *adjective* uneasy, fearful. □ **apprehensively** *adverb*.

**apprentice** /əˈprentɪs/ ● *noun* person learning trade by working for agreed period. ● *verb* (usually + *to*) engage as apprentice. □ **apprenticeship** *noun*.

**apprise** /əˈpraɪz/ *verb* (**-sing**) (usually + *of*) inform.

**approach** /əˈprəʊtʃ/ ● *verb* come nearer (to) in space or time; be similar to; approximate to; set about; make tentative proposal to. ● *noun* act or means of approaching; approximation; technique; part of aircraft's flight before landing.

**approachable** /əˈprəʊtʃəb(ə)l/ *adjective* friendly; able to be approached.

**approbation** /æprəˈbeɪʃ(ə)n/ *noun* approval, consent.

**appropriate** ● *adjective* /əˈprəʊprɪət/ suitable, proper. ● *verb* (**-ting**) /əˈprəʊprɪeɪt/ take possession of; devote (money etc.) to special purpose. □ **appropriately** *adverb*; **appropriation** *noun*.

**approval** /əˈpruːv(ə)l/ *noun* approving; consent. □ **on approval** returnable if not satisfactory.

**approve** /əˈpruːv/ *verb* (**-ving**) sanction; (often + *of*) regard with favour.

**approx.** *abbreviation* approximate(ly).

**approximate** ● *adjective* /əˈprɒksɪmət/ fairly correct; near to the actual. ● *verb* /əˈprɒksɪmeɪt/ (**-ting**) (often + *to*) be or make near. □ **approximately** *adverb*; **approximation** *noun*.

**appurtenances** /əˈpɜːtɪnənsɪz/ *plural noun* accessories; belongings.

**APR** *abbreviation* annual(ized) percentage rate.

**Apr.** *abbreviation* April.

**après-ski** /æprɛˈskiː/ ● *noun* activities after a day's skiing. ● *adjective* suitable for these. [French]

**apricot** /ˈeɪprɪkɒt/ ● *noun* small orange-yellow peachlike fruit; its colour. ● *adjective* orange-yellow.

**April** /ˈeɪpr(ə)l/ *noun* fourth month of year. □ **April Fool** victim of hoax on 1 Apr.

**a priori** /eɪ praɪˈɔːraɪ/ ● *adjective* from cause to effect; not derived from experience; assumed without investigation. ● *adverb* deductively; as far as one knows.

**apron** /ˈeɪprən/ *noun* garment protecting front of clothes; area on airfield for manoeuvring or loading; part of stage in front of curtain.

**apropos** /æprəˈpəʊ/ ● *adjective* appropriate; *colloquial* (often + *of*) in respect of. ● *adverb* appropriately; incidentally.

**apse** /æps/ *noun* arched or domed recess esp. at end of church.

**apsis** /ˈæpsɪs/ *noun* (*plural* **apsides** /-diːz/) aphelion or perihelion of planet, apogee or perigee of moon.

**apt** *adjective* suitable, appropriate; (+ *to do*) having a tendency; quick to learn.

**aptitude** /ˈæptɪtjuːd/ *noun* talent; ability, esp. specified.

**aqualung** /ˈækwəlʌŋ/ *noun* portable underwater breathing-apparatus.

**aquamarine** /ˌækwəməˈriːn/ ● *noun* bluish-green beryl; its colour. ● *adjective* bluish-green.

**aquaplane** /ˈækwəpleɪn/ ● *noun* board for riding on water, pulled by speedboat. ● *verb* (**-ning**) ride on this; (of vehicle) glide uncontrollably on wet surface.

**aquarelle** /ˌækwəˈrel/ *noun* painting in transparent water-colours.

**aquarium** /əˈkweərɪəm/ *noun* (*plural* **-s**) tank for keeping fish etc.

**Aquarius** /əˈkweərɪəs/ *noun* eleventh sign of zodiac.

**aquatic** /əˈkwætɪk/ *adjective* growing or living in water; done in or on water.

**aquatint** /ˈækwətɪnt/ *noun* etched print like water colour.

**aqueduct** /ˈækwɪdʌkt/ *noun* water channel, esp. raised structure across valley.

**aqueous** /ˈeɪkwɪəs/ *adjective* of or like water.

**aquiline** /ˈækwɪlaɪn/ *adjective* of or like an eagle; (of nose) curved.

**Arab** /ˈærəb/ ● *noun* member of Semitic people inhabiting originally Saudi Arabia, now Middle East generally; horse of breed originally native to Arabia. ● *adjective* of Arabia or Arabs.

**arabesque** /ˌærəˈbesk/ *noun* decoration with intertwined leaves, scrollwork, etc.; ballet posture with one leg extended horizontally backwards.

**Arabian** /əˈreɪbɪən/ ● *adjective* of Arabia. ● *noun* Arab.

**Arabic** /ˈærəbɪk/ ● *noun* language of Arabs. ● *adjective* of Arabs or their language. □ **arabic numerals** 1, 2, 3, etc.

**arable** /ˈærəb(ə)l/ *adjective* fit for growing crops.

**arachnid** /əˈræknɪd/ *noun* creature of class comprising spiders, scorpions, etc.

**Aramaic** /ˌærəˈmeɪɪk/ ● *noun* language of Syria at time of Christ. ● *adjective* of or in Aramaic.

**arbiter** /ˈɑːbɪtə/ *noun* arbitrator; person influential in specific field.

**arbitrary** /ˈɑːbɪtrərɪ/ *adjective* random; capricious; despotic. □ **arbitrarily** *adverb*.

**arbitrate** /ˈɑːbɪtreɪt/ *verb* (**-ting**) settle dispute between others. □ **arbitration** *noun*; **arbitrator** *noun*.

**arboreal** /ɑːˈbɔːrɪəl/ *adjective* of or living in trees.

**arboretum** /ˌɑːbəˈriːtəm/ *noun* (*plural* **-ta**) tree-garden.

**arboriculture** /ˈɑːbərɪkʌltʃə/ *noun* cultivation of trees and shrubs.

**arbour** /ˈɑːbə/ *noun* (*US* **arbor**) shady garden alcove enclosed by trees etc.

**arc** *noun* part of circumference of circle or other curve; luminous discharge between two electrodes. □ **arc lamp** one using electric arc; **arc welding** using electric arc to melt metals to be welded.

**arcade** /ɑːˈkeɪd/ *noun* covered walk, esp. lined with shops; series of arches supporting or along wall.

**Arcadian** /ɑːˈkeɪdɪən/ *adjective* ideally rustic.

**arcane** /ɑːˈkeɪn/ *adjective* mysterious, secret.

**arch¹** ● *noun* curved structure supporting bridge, floor, etc. as opening or ornament. ● *verb* form arch; provide with or form into arch.

**arch²** *adjective* self-consciously or affectedly playful.

**archaeology** /ˌɑːkɪˈɒlədʒɪ/ *noun* (*US* **archeology**) study of ancient cultures, esp. by excavation of physical remains. □ **archaeological** /-əˈlɒdʒ-/ *adjective*; **archaeologist** *noun*.

**archaic** /ɑːˈkeɪɪk/ *adjective* antiquated; (of word) no longer in ordinary use; of early period in culture.

**archaism** /ˈɑːkeɪɪz(ə)m/ *noun* archaic word etc.; use of the archaic. □ **archaistic** /-ˈɪst-/ *adjective*.

**archangel** /ˈɑːkeɪndʒ(ə)l/ *noun* angel of highest rank.

**archbishop** /ɑːtʃˈbɪʃəp/ *noun* chief bishop.

**archbishopric** *noun* office or diocese of archbishop.

**archdeacon** /ɑːtʃˈdiːkən/ *noun* church dignitary next below bishop. □ **archdeaconry** *noun* (*plural* **-ies**).

**archdiocese** /ɑːtʃˈdaɪəsɪs/ *noun* archbishop's diocese. □ **archdiocesan** /-daɪˈɒsɪs(ə)n/ *adjective*.

**arch-enemy** /ɑːtʃˈenəmɪ/ *noun* (*plural* **-ies**) chief enemy.

**archeology** *US* = ARCHAEOLOGY.

**archer** /'ɑːtʃə/ noun person who shoots with bow and arrows.

**archery** /'ɑːtʃərɪ/ noun shooting with bow and arrows.

**archetype** /'ɑːkɪtaɪp/ noun original model, typical specimen. □ **archetypal** /-'taɪp-/ adjective.

**archipelago** /ɑːkɪ'peləgəʊ/ noun (plural **-s**) group of islands; sea with many islands.

**architect** /'ɑːkɪtekt/ noun designer of buildings etc.; (+ of) person who brings about specified thing.

**architectonic** /ɑːkɪtek'tɒnɪk/ adjective of architecture.

**architecture** /'ɑːkɪtektʃə/ noun design and construction of buildings; style of building. □ **architectural** /-'tek-/ adjective.

**architrave** /'ɑːkɪtreɪv/ noun moulded frame round doorway or window; main beam laid across tops of classical columns.

**archive** /'ɑːkaɪv/ noun (usually in plural) collection of documents or records; place where these are kept.

**archivist** /'ɑːkɪvɪst/ noun keeper of archives.

**archway** /'ɑːtʃweɪ/ noun arched entrance or passage.

**Arctic** /'ɑːktɪk/ ● adjective of north polar region; (**arctic**) very cold. ● noun Arctic region.

**ardent** /'ɑːd(ə)nt/ adjective eager, fervent, passionate; burning. □ **ardently** adverb.

**ardour** /'ɑːdə/ noun zeal, enthusiasm.

**arduous** /'ɑːdjʊəs/ adjective hard to accomplish; strenuous.

**are** see BE.

**area** /'eərɪə/ noun extent or measure of surface; region; space set aside for a purpose; scope, range; space in front of house basement.

**arena** /ə'riːnə/ noun centre of amphitheatre; scene of conflict; sphere of action.

**aren't** /ɑːnt/ are not; (in questions) am not.

**arête** /æ'reɪt/ noun sharp mountain ridge.

**argon** /'ɑːgɒn/ noun inert gaseous element.

**argot** /'ɑːgəʊ/ noun jargon of group or class.

**argue** /'ɑːgjuː/ verb (**-ues**, **-ued**, **-uing**) exchange views, esp. heatedly; (often + that) maintain by reasoning; (+ for, against) reason. □ **arguable** adjective, **arguably** adverb.

**argument** /'ɑːgjʊmənt/ noun (esp. heated) exchange of views; reason given; reasoning; summary of book etc. □ **argumentation** /-men-/ noun.

**argumentative** /ɑːgjʊ'mentətɪv/ adjective fond of arguing.

**argy-bargy** /ɑːdʒɪ'bɑːdʒɪ/ noun jocular dispute, wrangle.

**aria** /'ɑːrɪə/ noun song for one voice in opera, oratorio, etc.

**arid** /'ærɪd/ noun dry, parched. □ **aridity** /ə'rɪd-/ noun.

**Aries** /'eəriːz/ noun first sign of zodiac.

**aright** /ə'raɪt/ adverb rightly.

**arise** /ə'raɪz/ verb (**-sing**; past **arose** /ə'rəʊz/; past participle **arisen** /ə'rɪz(ə)n/) originate; (usually + from, out of) result; emerge; rise.

**aristocracy** /ærɪs'tɒkrəsɪ/ noun (plural **-ies**) ruling class, nobility.

**aristocrat** /'ærɪstəkræt/ noun member of aristocracy.

**aristocratic** /ærɪstə'krætɪk/ adjective of the aristocracy; grand, distinguished.

**arithmetic** ● noun /ə'rɪθmətɪk/ science of numbers; computation, use of numbers. ● adjective /ærɪθ'metɪk/ (also **arithmetical**) of arithmetic.

**ark** noun ship in which Noah escaped the Flood. □ **Ark of the Covenant** wooden chest containing tables of Jewish law.

**arm**[1] noun upper limb of human body; sleeve; raised side part of chair; branch; armlike thing. □ **armchair** chair with arms, theoretical rather than active; **arm in arm** with arms linked; **armpit** hollow under arm at shoulder; **at arm's length** at a distance; **with open arms** cordially. □ **armful** noun.

**arm**[2] ● noun (usually in plural) weapon; branch of military forces; (in plural) heraldic devices. ● verb equip with arms; equip oneself with arms; make (bomb) ready. □ **up in arms** (usually + against, about) actively resisting.

**armada** /ɑːˈmɑːdə/ *noun* fleet of warships.

**armadillo** /ɑːməˈdɪləʊ/ *noun* (*plural* **-s**) S. American burrowing mammal with plated body.

**Armageddon** /ɑːməˈɡed(ə)n/ *noun* huge battle at end of world.

**armament** /ˈɑːməmənt/ *noun* military weapon etc.; equipping for war.

**armature** /ˈɑːmətʃə/ *noun* rotating coil or coils of dynamo or electric motor; iron bar placed across poles of magnet; framework on which sculpture is moulded.

**armistice** /ˈɑːmɪstɪs/ *noun* truce.

**armlet** /ˈɑːmlɪt/ *noun* band worn round arm.

**armorial** /ɑːˈmɔːrɪəl/ *adjective* of heraldic arms.

**armour** /ˈɑːmə/ *noun* protective covering formerly worn in fighting; metal plates etc. protecting ship, car, tank, etc.; armoured vehicles. □ **armoured** *adjective*.

**armourer** *noun* maker of arms or armour; official in charge of arms.

**armoury** /ˈɑːmərɪ/ *noun* (*plural* **-ies**) arsenal.

**army** /ˈɑːmɪ/ *noun* (*plural* **-ies**) organized armed land force; vast number; organized body.

**arnica** /ˈɑːnɪkə/ *noun* plant with yellow flowers; medicine made from it.

**aroma** /əˈrəʊmə/ *noun* pleasing smell; subtle quality. □ **aromatic** /ærəˈmætɪk/ *adjective*.

**aromatherapy** *noun* use of plant extracts and oils in massage. □ **aromatherapist** *noun*.

**arose** *past* of ARISE.

**around** /əˈraʊnd/ ● *adverb* on every side; all round; *colloquial* in existence, near at hand. ● *preposition* on or along the circuit of; on every side of; here and there in or near; about.

**arouse** /əˈraʊz/ *verb* (**-sing**) induce (esp. emotion); awake from sleep; stir into activity; stimulate sexually. □ **arousal** *noun*.

**arpeggio** /ɑːˈpedʒɪəʊ/ *noun* (*plural* **-s**) notes of chord played in rapid succession.

**arrack** /ˈærək/ *noun* alcoholic spirit made esp. from rice.

**arraign** /əˈreɪn/ *verb* indict, accuse; find fault with. □ **arraignment** *noun*.

**arrange** /əˈreɪndʒ/ *verb* (**-ging**) put in order; plan or provide for; (+ *to do, for*) take measures; (+ *with* person) agree about procedure for; *Music* adapt (piece). □ **arrangement** *noun*.

**arrant** /ˈærənt/ *adjective* downright, utter.

**arras** /ˈærəs/ *noun* tapestry wallhanging.

**array** /əˈreɪ/ ● *noun* imposing series; ordered arrangement, esp. of troops. ● *verb* deck, adorn; set in order; marshal (forces).

**arrears** /əˈrɪəz/ *plural noun* outstanding debt; what remains undone. □ **in arrears** behindhand, esp. in payment.

**arrest** /əˈrest/ ● *verb* lawfully seize; stop; catch attention of. ● *noun* arresting, being arrested; stoppage.

**arrival** /əˈraɪv(ə)l/ *noun* arriving; person or thing arriving.

**arrive** /əˈraɪv/ *verb* (**-ving**) come to destination; (+ *at*) reach (conclusion); *colloquial* become successful; be born.

**arrogant** /ˈærəɡənt/ *adjective* aggressively assertive or presumptuous. □ **arrogance** *noun*, **arrogantly** *adverb*.

**arrogate** /ˈærəɡeɪt/ *verb* (**-ting**) claim without right. □ **arrogation** *noun*.

**arrow** /ˈærəʊ/ *noun* pointed missile shot from bow; representation of this, esp. to show direction. □ **arrowhead** pointed tip of arrow.

**arrowroot** /ˈærəʊruːt/ *noun* nutritious starch.

**arsenal** /ˈɑːsən(ə)l/ *noun* place where weapons and ammunition are made or stored.

**arsenic** /ˈɑːsnɪk/ *noun* brittle semimetallic element; its highly poisonous trioxide.

**arson** /ˈɑːsən/ *noun* crime of deliberately setting property on fire. □ **arsonist** *noun*.

**art** *noun* human creative skill, its application; branch of creative activity concerned with imitative and imaginative designs, sounds, or ideas, e.g. painting, music, writing; creative activity resulting in visual representation; thing in which skill can be exercised; (in *plural*) certain branches of learning (esp. languages, literature, history, etc.) as distinct from sciences; knack; cunning. □ **art nouveau** /ɑ: nu:'vəʊ/ art style of late 19th c., with flowing lines.

**artefact** /'ɑ:tɪfækt/ *noun* (also **artifact**) man-made object.

**arterial** /ɑ:'tɪərɪəl/ *adjective* of or like artery. □ **arterial road** important main road.

**arteriosclerosis** /ɑ:tɪərɪəʊsklɪə'rəʊsɪs/ *noun* hardening and thickening of artery walls.

**artery** /'ɑ:tərɪ/ *noun* ( *plural* **-ies**) blood vessel carrying blood from heart; main road or railway line.

**artesian well** /ɑ:'ti:zɪən/ well in which water rises by natural pressure through vertically drilled hole.

**artful** /'ɑ:tfʊl/ *adjective* sly, crafty. □ **artfully** *adverb*.

**arthritis** /ɑ:'θraɪtɪs/ *noun* inflammation of joint. □ **arthritic** /-'θrɪt-/ *adjective & noun*.

**arthropod** /'ɑ:θrəpɒd/ *noun* animal with segmented body and jointed limbs, e.g. insect, spider, crustacean.

**artichoke** /'ɑ:tɪtʃəʊk/ *noun* plant allied to thistle; its partly edible flower; Jerusalem artichoke.

**article** /'ɑ:tɪk(ə)l/ ● *noun* item or thing; short piece of non-fiction in newspaper etc.; clause of agreement etc.; = DEFINITE ARTICLE, INDEFINITE ARTICLE. ● *verb* employ under contract as trainee.

**articular** /ɑ:'tɪkjʊlə/ *adjective* of joints.

**articulate** ● *adjective* /ɑ:'tɪkjʊlət/ fluent and clear in speech; (of speech) in which separate sounds and words are clear; having joints. ● *verb* /ɑ:'tɪkjʊlert/ (**-ting**) speak distinctly; express clearly; connect with joints. □ **articulated lorry** one with sections connected by flexible joint. □ **articulately** *adverb*; **articulation** *noun*.

**artifact** = ARTEFACT.

**artifice** /'ɑ:tɪfɪs/ *noun* trick; cunning; skill.

**artificer** /ɑ:'tɪfɪsə/ *noun* craftsman.

**artificial** /ɑ:tɪ'fɪʃ(ə)l/ *adjective* not natural; imitating nature; insincere. □ **artificial insemination** non-sexual

injection of semen into uterus; **artificial intelligence** (use of) computers replacing human intelligence; **artificial respiration** manual or mechanical stimulation of breathing. □ **artificiality** /-ʃɪ'æl-/ *noun*; **artificially** *adverb*.

**artillery** /ɑ:'tɪlərɪ/ *noun* large guns used in fighting on land; branch of army using these. □ **artilleryman** *noun*.

**artisan** /ɑ:tɪ'zæn/ *noun* skilled worker or craftsman.

**artist** /'ɑ:tɪst/ *noun* person who practises any art, esp. painting; artiste. □ **artistic** *adjective*; **artistically** *adverb*; **artistry** *noun*.

**artiste** /ɑ:'ti:st/ *noun* professional singer, dancer, etc.

**artless** *adjective* guileless, ingenuous; natural; clumsy. □ **artlessly** *adverb*.

**arty** *adjective* (**-ier, -iest**) pretentiously or affectedly artistic.

**arum** /'eərəm/ *noun* plant with arrow-shaped leaves.

**Aryan** /'eərɪən/ ● *noun* speaker of any Indo-European language. ● *adjective* of Aryans.

**as** /æz, əz/ ● *adverb* to the same extent. ● *conjunction* in the same way that; while, when; since, seeing that; although. ● *preposition* in the capacity or form of. □ **as ... as ...** to the same extent that ... is, does, etc.

**asafoetida** /æsə'fetɪdə/ *noun* (*US* **asafetida**) resinous pungent gum.

**asbestos** /æs'bestɒs/ *noun* fibrous silicate mineral; heat-resistant or insulating substance made from this.

**ascend** /ə'send/ *verb* slope upwards; go or come up, climb.

**ascendancy** *noun* (often + *over*) dominant control.

**ascendant** *adjective* rising. □ **in the ascendant** gaining or having power or authority.

**ascension** /ə'senʃ(ə)n/ *noun* ascent, esp. (**Ascension**) of Christ into heaven.

**ascent** /ə'sent/ *noun* ascending, rising; upward path or slope.

**ascertain** /æsə'teɪn/ *verb* find out for certain. □ **ascertainment** *noun*.

**ascetic** /ə'setɪk/ ● *adjective* severely abstinent; self-denying. ● *noun* ascetic person. □ **asceticism** /-tɪs-/ *noun*.

**ascorbic acid** /əˈskɔːbɪk/ *noun* vitamin C.

**ascribe** /əˈskraɪb/ *verb* (**-bing**) (usually + *to*) attribute; regard as belonging. □ **ascription** /-ˈskrɪp-/ *noun*.

**asepsis** /eɪˈsepsɪs/ *noun* absence of sepsis or harmful bacteria; aseptic method in surgery. □ **aseptic** *adjective*.

**asexual** /eɪˈseksjʊəl/ *adjective* without sex or sexuality; (of reproduction) not involving fusion of gametes. □ **asexually** *adverb*.

**ash**[1] *noun* (often in *plural*) powdery residue left after burning; (in *plural*) human remains after cremation; (**the Ashes**) trophy in cricket between England and Australia. □ **ashcan** *US* dustbin; **ashtray** receptacle for tobacco ash; **Ash Wednesday** first day of Lent.

**ash**[2] *noun* tree with silver-grey bark; its wood.

**ashamed** /əˈʃeɪmd/ *adjective* embarrassed by shame; (+ *to do*) reluctant owing to shame.

**ashen** /ˈæʃ(ə)n/ *adjective* grey, pale.

**ashore** /əˈʃɔː/ *adverb* to or on shore.

**ashram** /ˈæʃræm/ *noun* religious retreat for Hindus.

**Asian** /ˈeɪʃ(ə)n/ ● *adjective* of Asia. ● *noun* native of Asia; person of Asian descent.

**aside** /əˈsaɪd/ ● *adverb* to or on one side; away, apart. ● *noun* words spoken aside, esp. by actor to audience.

**asinine** /ˈæsɪnaɪn/ *adjective* asslike; stupid.

**ask** /ɑːsk/ *verb* call for answer to or about; seek to obtain from another person; invite; (+ *for*) seek to obtain or meet. □ **ask after** inquire about (esp. person).

**askance** /əˈskæns/ *adverb* sideways. □ **look askance at** regard suspiciously.

**askew** /əˈskjuː/ ● *adverb* crookedly. ● *adjective* oblique; awry.

**aslant** /əˈslɑːnt/ ● *adverb* at a slant. ● *preposition* obliquely across.

**asleep** /əˈsliːp/ ● *adjective* sleeping; *colloquial* inattentive; (of limb) numb. ● *adverb* into state of sleep.

**asp** /æsp/ *noun* small venomous snake.

**asparagus** /əˈspærəgəs/ *noun* plant of lily family; its edible shoots.

**aspect** /ˈæspekt/ *noun* feature, viewpoint, etc. to be considered; appearance, look; side facing specified direction.

**aspen** /ˈæspən/ *noun* poplar with fluttering leaves.

**asperity** /æsˈperɪtɪ/ *noun* sharpness of temper or tone; roughness.

**aspersion** /əsˈpɜːʃ(ə)n/ *noun* □ **cast aspersions on** defame.

**asphalt** /ˈæsfælt/ ● *noun* bituminous pitch; mixture of this with gravel etc. for surfacing roads etc. ● *verb* surface with asphalt.

**asphodel** /ˈæsfədel/ *noun* kind of lily.

**asphyxia** /æsˈfɪksɪə/ *noun* lack of oxygen in blood; suffocation.

**asphyxiate** /əsˈfɪksɪeɪt/ *verb* (**-ting**) suffocate. □ **asphyxiation** *noun*.

**aspic** /ˈæspɪk/ *noun* clear savoury jelly.

**aspidistra** /æspɪˈdɪstrə/ *noun* house plant with broad tapering leaves.

**aspirant** /ˈæspɪrənt/ ● *adjective* aspiring. ● *noun* person who aspires.

**aspirate** ● *noun* /ˈæspərət/ sound of *h*; consonant blended with this. ● *verb* /ˈæspəreɪt/ (**-ting**) pronounce with *h*; draw (fluid) by suction from cavity.

**aspiration** /æspəˈreɪʃ(ə)n/ *noun* ambition, desire; aspirating.

**aspire** /əˈspaɪə/ *verb* (**-ring**) (usually + *to, after, to do*) have ambition or strong desire.

**aspirin** /ˈæsprɪn/ *noun* (*plural* same or **-s**) white powder used to reduce pain and fever; tablet of this.

**ass** *noun* 4-legged animal with long ears, related to horse; donkey; stupid person.

**assail** /əˈseɪl/ *verb* attack physically or verbally. □ **assailant** *noun*.

**assassin** /əˈsæsɪn/ *noun* killer, esp. of political or religious leader.

**assassinate** /əˈsæsɪneɪt/ *verb* (**-ting**) kill for political or religious motives. □ **assassination** *noun*.

**assault** /əˈsɔːlt/ ● *noun* violent physical or verbal attack; *Law* threat or display of violence against person. ● *verb* make assault on. □ **assault and battery** *Law* threatening act resulting in physical harm to person.

**assay** /ə'seɪ/ ● *noun* test of metal or ore for ingredients and quality. ● *verb* make assay of.

**assegai** /'æsɪgaɪ/ *noun* light iron-tipped S. African spear.

**assemblage** /ə'semblɪdʒ/ *noun* assembled group.

**assemble** /ə'semb(ə)l/ *verb* (**-ling**) fit together parts of; fit (parts) together; bring or come together.

**assembly** /ə'semblɪ/ *noun* (*plural* **-ies**) assembling; assembled group, esp. as parliament etc.; fitting together of parts. □ **assembly line** machinery arranged so that product can be progressively assembled.

**assent** /ə'sent/ ● *noun* consent, approval. ● *verb* (usually + *to*) agree, consent.

**assert** /ə'sɜːt/ *verb* declare; enforce claim to; (**assert oneself**) insist on one's rights.

**assertion** /ə'sɜːʃ(ə)n/ *noun* declaration; forthright statement.

**assertive** *adjective* asserting oneself; forthright, positive. □ **assertively** *adverb*; **assertiveness** *noun*.

**assess** /ə'ses/ *verb* estimate size or quality of; estimate value of (property etc.) for taxation. □ **assessment** *noun*.

**assessor** *noun* person who assesses taxes etc.; judge's technical adviser in court.

**asset** /'æset/ *noun* useful or valuable person or thing; (usually in *plural*) property and possessions.

**assiduous** /ə'sɪdjʊəs/ *adjective* persevering, hard-working. □ **assiduity** /æsɪ-'djuːɪtɪ/ *noun*; **assiduously** *adverb*.

**assign** /ə'saɪn/ *verb* allot; appoint; fix (time, place, etc.); (+ *to*) ascribe to, *Law* transfer formally to.

**assignation** /æsɪg'neɪʃ(ə)n/ *noun* appointment, esp. made by lovers; assigning, being assigned.

**assignee** /əsaɪ'niː/ *noun Law* person to whom property or right is assigned.

**assignment** /ə'saɪnmənt/ *noun* task or mission; assigning, being assigned.

**assimilate** /ə'sɪmɪleɪt/ *verb* (**-ting**) absorb or be absorbed into system; (usually + *to*) make like. □ **assimilable** *adjective*; **assimilation** *noun*; **assimilative** /-lətɪv/ *adjective*.

**assist** /ə'sɪst/ *verb* (often + *in*) help. □ **assistance** *noun*.

**assistant** *noun* helper; subordinate worker; = SHOP ASSISTANT.

**assizes** /ə'saɪzɪz/ *plural noun historical* court periodically administering civil and criminal law.

**Assoc.** *abbreviation* Association.

**associate** ● *verb* /ə'səʊʃɪeɪt/ (**-ting**) connect mentally; join, combine; (usually + *with*) have frequent dealings. ● *noun* /ə'səʊʃɪət/ partner, colleague; friend, companion. ● *adjective* /ə'səʊʃɪət/ joined, allied.

**association** /əsəʊsɪ'eɪʃ(ə)n/ *noun* group organized for joint purpose; associating, being associated; connection of ideas. □ **association football** kind played with round ball which may be handled only by goalkeeper.

**assonance** /'æsənəns/ *noun* partial resemblance of sound between syllables, as in *run-up*, or *wary* and *barely*. □ **assonant** *adjective*.

**assorted** /ə'sɔːtɪd/ *adjective* of various sorts, mixed.

**assortment** /ə'sɔːtmənt/ *noun* diverse group or mixture.

**assuage** /ə'sweɪdʒ/ *verb* (**-ging**) soothe; appease.

**assume** /ə'sjuːm/ *verb* (**-ming**) take to be true; undertake; simulate; take on (aspect, attribute, etc.).

**assumption** /ə'sʌmpʃ(ə)n/ *noun* assuming; thing assumed; (**Assumption**) reception of Virgin Mary bodily into heaven.

**assurance** /ə'ʃʊərəns/ *noun* declaration; insurance, esp. of life; certainty; self-confidence.

**assure** /ə'ʃʊə/ *verb* (**-ring**) (often + *of*) convince; tell (person) confidently; ensure, guarantee (result etc.); insure (esp. life).

**assuredly** /ə'ʃʊərɪdlɪ/ *adverb* certainly.

**aster** /'æstə/ *noun* plant with bright daisy-like flowers.

**asterisk** /'æstərɪsk/ *noun* symbol (*) used to indicate omission etc.

**astern** /ə'stɜːn/ *adverb* in or to rear of ship or aircraft; backwards.

**asteroid** /'æstərɔɪd/ *noun* any of numerous small planets between orbits of Mars and Jupiter.

**asthma** /'æsmə/ *noun* condition marked by difficulty in breathing. □ **asthmatic** /-'mæt-/ *adjective & noun.*

**astigmatism** /ə'stɪgmətɪz(ə)m/ *noun* eye or lens defect resulting in distorted images. □ **astigmatic** /æstɪg'mætɪk/ *adjective.*

**astir** /ə'stɜː/ *adverb & adjective* in motion; out of bed.

**astonish** /ə'stɒnɪʃ/ *verb* amaze, surprise. □ **astonishment** *noun.*

**astound** /ə'staʊnd/ *verb* astonish greatly.

**astrakhan** /æstrə'kæn/ *noun* dark curly fleece of Astrakhan lamb; cloth imitating this.

**astral** /'æstr(ə)l/ *adjective* of stars; starry.

**astray** /ə'streɪ/ *adverb & adjective* away from right way. □ **go astray** be lost.

**astride** /ə'straɪd/ ● *adverb* (often + *of*) with one leg on each side. ● *preposition* astride of.

**astringent** /ə'strɪndʒənt/ ● *adjective* contracting body tissue, esp. to check bleeding; austere, severe. ● *noun* astringent substance. □ **astringency** *noun.*

**astrolabe** /'æstrəleɪb/ *noun* instrument for measuring altitude of stars etc.

**astrology** /ə'strɒlədʒɪ/ *noun* study of supposed planetary influence on human affairs. □ **astrologer** *noun*; **astrological** /æstrə'lɒdʒ-/ *adjective.*

**astronaut** /'æstrənɔːt/ *noun* space traveller.

**astronautics** /æstrə'nɔːtɪks/ *plural noun* (treated as *singular*) science of space travel. □ **astronautical** *adjective.*

**astronomical** /æstrə'nɒmɪk(ə)l/ *adjective* (also **astronomic**) of astronomy; vast. □ **astronomically** *adverb.*

**astronomy** /ə'strɒnəmɪ/ *noun* science of celestial bodies. □ **astronomer** *noun.*

**astrophysics** /æstrəʊ'fɪzɪks/ *plural noun* (treated as *singular*) study of physics and chemistry of celestial bodies. □ **astrophysical** *adjective*; **astrophysicist** *noun.*

**astute** /ə'stjuːt/ *adjective* shrewd. □ **astutely** *adverb*; **astuteness** *noun.*

**asunder** /ə'sʌndə/ *adverb literary* apart.

**asylum** /ə'saɪləm/ *noun* sanctuary; = POLITICAL ASYLUM; *historical* mental institution.

**asymmetry** /eɪ'sɪmətrɪ/ *noun* lack of symmetry. □ **asymmetric(al)** /-'met-/ *adjective.*

**at** /æt, ət/ *preposition expressing position, point in time or on scale, engagement in activity, value or rate, or motion or aim towards.*

**atavism** /'ætəvɪz(ə)m/ *noun* resemblance to remote ancestors; reversion to earlier type. □ **atavistic** /-'vɪs-/ *adjective.*

**ate** *past of* EAT.

**atelier** /ə'telɪeɪ/ *noun* workshop; artist's studio.

**atheism** /'eɪθɪɪz(ə)m/ *noun* belief that no God exists. □ **atheist** *noun*; **atheistic** /-'ɪst-/ *adjective.*

**atherosclerosis** /æθərəʊsklə'rəʊsɪs/ *noun* formation of fatty deposits in the arteries.

**athlete** /'æθliːt/ *noun* person who engages in athletics, exercises, etc. □ **athlete's foot** fungal foot disease.

**athletic** /æθ'letɪk/ *adjective* of athletes or athletics; physically strong or agile. □ **athletically** *adverb*; **athleticism** *noun.*

**athletics** *plural noun* (usually treated as *singular*) physical exercises, esp. track and field events.

**atlas** /'ætləs/ *noun* book of maps.

**atmosphere** /'ætməsfɪə/ *noun* gases enveloping earth, other planet, etc.; tone, mood, etc., of place, book, etc.; unit of pressure. □ **atmospheric** /-'fer-/ *adjective.*

**atmospherics** /ætməs'ferɪks/ *plural noun* electrical disturbance in atmosphere; interference with telecommunications caused by this.

**atoll** /'ætɒl/ *noun* ring-shaped coral reef enclosing lagoon.

**atom** /'ætəm/ *noun* smallest particle of chemical element that can take part in chemical reaction; this as source of nuclear energy; minute portion or thing. □ **atom bomb** bomb in which energy is released by nuclear fission.

**atomic** /ə'tɒmɪk/ *adjective* of atoms; of or using atomic energy or atom bombs. □ **atomic bomb** atom bomb; **atomic energy** nuclear energy; **atomic number** number of protons in nucleus of atom; **atomic weight** ratio of mass of one atom of element to 1/12 mass of atom of carbon-12.

**atomize** /ˈætəmaɪz/ verb (also **-ise**) (**-zing** or **-sing**) reduce to atoms or fine spray. □ **atomizer** noun.

**atomizer** noun (also **-iser**) aerosol.

**atonal** /eɪˈtəʊn(ə)l/ adjective Music not written in any key. □ **atonality** /-ˈnæl-/ noun.

**atone** /əˈtəʊn/ verb (**-ning**) (usually + for) make amends. □ **atonement** noun.

**atrium** /ˈeɪtrɪəm/ noun (plural **-s** or **atria**) either of upper cavities of heart.

**atrocious** /əˈtrəʊʃəs/ adjective very bad; wicked. □ **atrociously** adverb.

**atrocity** /əˈtrɒsɪtɪ/ noun (plural **-ies**) wicked or cruel act.

**atrophy** /ˈætrəfɪ/ ● noun wasting away, esp. through disuse. ● verb (**-ies**, **-ied**) suffer atrophy; cause atrophy in.

**atropine** /ˈætrəpiːn/ noun poisonous alkaloid in deadly nightshade.

**attach** /əˈtætʃ/ verb fasten, affix, join; (in passive; + to) be very fond of; (+ to) attribute or be attributable to.

**attaché** /əˈtæʃeɪ/ noun specialist member of ambassador's staff. □ **attaché case** small rectangular document case.

**attachment** noun thing attached, esp. for particular purpose; affection, devotion; attaching, being attached.

**attack** /əˈtæk/ ● verb try to hurt or deflect using force; criticize adversely; act harmfully on; Sport try to score against; vigorously apply oneself to. ● noun act of attacking; sudden onset of illness. □ **attacker** noun.

**attain** /əˈteɪn/ verb gain, accomplish; reach; (+ to) arrive at (goal etc.).

**attainment** noun attaining; (often in plural) skill, achievement.

**attar** /ˈætɑː/ noun perfume made from rose-petals.

**attempt** /əˈtempt/ ● verb try; try to accomplish or conquer. ● noun (often + at, on) attempting; endeavour.

**attend** /əˈtend/ verb be present at; go regularly to; (often + to) apply mind or oneself; (+ to) deal with; accompany, wait on. □ **attender** noun.

**attendance** noun attending; number of people present.

**attendant** ● noun person attending, esp. to provide service. ● adjective accompanying; (often + on) waiting.

**attention** /əˈtenʃ(ə)n/ noun act or faculty of applying one's mind, notice; consideration, care; Military erect attitude of readiness; (in plural) courtesies.

**attentive** /əˈtentɪv/ adjective (+ to) paying attention. □ **attentively** adverb.

**attenuate** /əˈtenjʊeɪt/ verb (**-ting**) make thin; reduce in force or value. □ **attenuation** noun.

**attest** /əˈtest/ verb certify validity of; (+ to) bear witness to. □ **attestation** /æt-/ noun.

**attic** /ˈætɪk/ noun room or space immediately under roof of house.

**attire** /əˈtaɪə/ noun clothes, esp. formal.

**attired** adjective dressed, esp. formally.

**attitude** /ˈætɪtjuːd/ noun opinion, way of thinking; (often + to) behaviour reflecting this; bodily posture.

**attitudinize** /ætɪˈtjuːdɪnaɪz/ verb (also **-ise**) (**-zing** or **-sing**) adopt attitudes.

**attorney** /əˈtɜːnɪ/ noun person, esp. lawyer, appointed to act for another in business or legal matters; US qualified lawyer. □ **Attorney-General** chief legal officer of government.

**attract** /əˈtrækt/ verb (of magnet etc.) draw to itself or oneself; arouse interest or admiration in.

**attraction** /əˈtrækʃ(ə)n/ noun attracting, being attracted; attractive quality; person or thing that attracts.

**attractive** /əˈtræktɪv/ adjective attracting esp. interest or admiration; pleasing. □ **attractively** noun.

**attribute** ● verb /əˈtrɪbjuːt/ (**-ting**) (usually + to) regard as belonging to or as written, said, or caused by, etc. ● noun /ˈætrɪbjuːt/ quality ascribed to person or thing; characteristic quality; object frequently associated with person, office, or status. □ **attributable** /əˈtrɪbjʊtəb(ə)l/ adjective, **attribution** /ætrɪˈbjuːʃ(ə)n/ noun.

**attributive** /əˈtrɪbjʊtɪv/ adjective expressing an attribute; (of adjective or noun) preceding word it describes.

**attrition** /əˈtrɪʃ(ə)n/ noun gradual wearing down; friction, abrasion.

**attune** /əˈtjuːn/ verb (**-ning**) (usually + to) adjust; Music tune.

**atypical** /eɪˈtɪpɪk(ə)l/ adjective not typical. □ **atypically** adverb.

**aubergine** /ˈəʊbəʒiːn/ noun (plant with) oval usually purple fruit used as vegetable.

**aubrietia** /ɔːˈbriːʃə/ noun (also **aubretia**) dwarf perennial rock plant.

**auburn** /ˈɔːbən/ adjective (usually of hair) reddish-brown.

**auction** /ˈɔːkʃ(ə)n/ ● noun sale in which each article is sold to highest bidder. ● verb sell by auction.

**auctioneer** /ɔːkʃəˈnɪə/ noun person who conducts auctions.

**audacious** /ɔːˈdeɪʃəs/ adjective daring, bold; impudent. □ **audacity** /-ˈdæs-/ noun.

**audible** /ˈɔːdɪb(ə)l/ adjective that can be heard. □ **audibility** noun; **audibly** adverb.

**audience** /ˈɔːdɪəns/ noun group of listeners or spectators; group of people reached by any spoken or written message; formal interview.

**audio** /ˈɔːdɪəʊ/ noun (reproduction of) sound. □ **audiotape** magnetic tape for recording sound; **audio typist** person who types from tape recording; **audio-visual** using both sight and sound.

**audit** /ˈɔːdɪt/ ● noun official scrutiny of accounts. ● verb (-t-) conduct audit of. □ **auditor** noun.

**audition** /ɔːˈdɪʃ(ə)n/ ● noun test of performer's ability. ● verb assess or be assessed at audition.

**auditorium** /ɔːdɪˈtɔːrɪəm/ noun (plural -s) part of theatre etc. for audience.

**auditory** /ˈɔːdɪtərɪ/ adjective of hearing.

**au fait** /əʊ ˈfeɪ/ adjective (usually + with) conversant.

**Aug.** abbreviation August.

**auger** /ˈɔːgə/ noun tool with screw point for boring holes in wood.

**aught** /ɔːt/ noun archaic anything.

**augment** /ɔːgˈment/ verb make greater, increase. □ **augmentation** noun.

**augur** /ˈɔːgə/ verb portend; serve as omen.

**augury** /ˈɔːgjʊrɪ/ noun (plural -ies) omen; interpretation of omens.

**August** /ˈɔːgəst/ noun eighth month of year.

**august** /ɔːˈgʌst/ adjective venerable, imposing.

**auk** /ɔːk/ noun black and white seabird with small wings.

**aunt** /ɑːnt/ noun parent's sister; uncle's wife. □ **Aunt Sally** game in which sticks or balls are thrown at dummy, target of general abuse.

**aunty** /ˈɑːntɪ/ noun (also **auntie**) (plural -ies) colloquial aunt.

**au pair** /əʊ ˈpeə/ noun young foreign woman who helps with housework in return for room and board.

**aura** /ˈɔːrə/ noun distinctive atmosphere; subtle emanation.

**aural** /ˈɔːr(ə)l/ adjective of ear or hearing. □ **aurally** adverb.

**aureole** /ˈɔːrɪəʊl/ noun (also **aureola** /ɔːˈriːələ/) halo.

**au revoir** /əʊ rəˈvwɑː/ interjection & noun goodbye (until we meet again). [French]

**auricle** /ˈɔːrɪk(ə)l/ noun external ear of animal; atrium of heart.

**auriferous** /ɔːˈrɪfərəs/ adjective yielding gold.

**aurora** /ɔːˈrɔːrə/ noun (plural -s or -rae /-riː/) streamers of light above northern (**aurora borealis** /bɒrɪˈeɪlɪs/) or southern (**aurora australis** /ɔːˈstreɪlɪs/) polar region.

**auscultation** /ɔːskəlˈteɪʃ(ə)n/ noun listening to sound of heart etc. to help diagnosis.

**auspice** /ˈɔːspɪs/ noun omen; (in plural) patronage.

**auspicious** /ɔːˈspɪʃəs/ adjective promising; favourable.

**Aussie** /ˈɒzɪ/ noun & adjective slang Australian.

**austere** /ɔːˈstɪə/ adjective (-r, -st) severely simple; stern; morally strict. □ **austerity** /-ˈter-/ noun.

**austral** /ˈɔːstr(ə)l/ adjective southern.

**Australasian** /ɒstrəˈleɪʒ(ə)n/ adjective of Australia and SW Pacific islands.

**Australian** /ɒˈstreɪlɪən/ ● adjective of Australia. ● noun native or national of Australia.

**autarchy** /ˈɔːtɑːkɪ/ noun absolute rule.

**autarky** /ˈɔːtɑːkɪ/ noun self-sufficiency.

**authentic** /ɔːˈθentɪk/ adjective of undisputed origin, genuine; trustworthy. □ **authentically** adverb; **authenticity** /-ˈtɪs-/ noun.

**authenticate** /ɔː'θentɪkeɪt/ *verb* (**-ting**) establish as true, genuine, or valid. □ **authentication** *noun*.

**author** /'ɔːθə/ *noun* (*feminine* **authoress** /'ɔːθrɪs/) writer of book etc.; originator. □ **authorship** *noun*.

**authoritarian** /ɔːθɒrɪ'teərɪən/ ● *adjective* favouring strict obedience to authority. ● *noun* authoritarian person.

**authoritative** /ɔː'θɒrɪtətɪv/ *adjective* reliable, esp. having authority.

**authority** /ɔː'θɒrɪtɪ/ *noun* (*plural* **-ies**) power or right to enforce obedience; (esp. in *plural*) body having this; delegated power; influence based on recognized knowledge or expertise; expert.

**authorize** /'ɔːθəraɪz/ *verb* (*also* **-ise**) (**-zing** *or* **-sing**) (+ *to do*) give authority to (person); sanction officially. □ **Authorized Version** English translation (1611) of Bible. □ **authorization** *noun*.

**autism** /'ɔːtɪz(ə)m/ *noun* condition characterized by self-absorption and withdrawal. □ **autistic** /-'tɪs-/ *adjective*.

**auto-** *combining form* self; one's own; of or by oneself or itself.

**autobahn** /'ɔːtəʊbɑːn/ *noun* German, Austrian, or Swiss motorway. [German]

**autobiography** /ɔːtəʊbaɪ'ɒgrəfɪ/ *noun* (*plural* **-ies**) story of one's own life. □ **autobiographer** *noun*; **autobiographical** /-ə'græf-/ *adjective*.

**autocracy** /ɔː'tɒkrəsɪ/ *noun* (*plural* **-ies**) absolute rule by one person.

**autocrat** /'ɔːtəkræt/ *noun* absolute ruler. □ **autocratic** /-'kræt-/ *adjective*; **autocratically** /-'kræt-/ *adverb*.

**autocross** /'ɔːtəʊkrɒs/ *noun* motor racing across country or on unmade roads.

**autograph** /'ɔːtəgrɑːf/ ● *noun* signature, esp. of celebrity. ● *verb* write on or sign in one's own handwriting.

**automate** /'ɔːtəmeɪt/ *verb* (**-ting**) convert to or operate by automation.

**automatic** /ɔːtə'mætɪk/ ● *adjective* working by itself, without direct human involvement; done spontaneously; following inevitably; (of firearm) that can be loaded and fired continuously; (of vehicle or its transmission) using gears

that change automatically. ● *noun* automatic firearm, vehicle, etc. □ **automatically** *adverb*.

**automation** *noun* use of automatic equipment in place of manual labour.

**automaton** /ɔː'tɒmət(ə)n/ *noun* (*plural* **-mata** *or* **-s**) machine controlled automatically.

**automobile** /'ɔːtəməbiːl/ *noun* US motor car.

**automotive** /ɔːtə'məʊtɪv/ *adjective* of motor vehicles.

**autonomous** /ɔː'tɒnəməs/ *adjective* self-governing; free to act independently. □ **autonomy** *noun*.

**autopsy** /'ɔːtɒpsɪ/ *noun* (*plural* **-ies**) post-mortem.

**auto-suggestion** /ɔːtəʊsə'dʒestʃ(ə)n/ *noun* hypnotic or subconscious suggestion made to oneself.

**autumn** /'ɔːtəm/ *noun* season between summer and winter. □ **autumnal** /ɔː'tʌmn(ə)l/ *adjective*.

**auxiliary** /ɔːg'zɪljərɪ/ ● *adjective* giving help; additional, subsidiary. ● *noun* (*plural* **-ies**) auxiliary person or thing; (in *plural*) foreign or allied troops in service of nation at war; auxiliary verb. □ **auxiliary verb** one used with another verb to form tenses etc. (see panel).

**avail** /ə'veɪl/ ● *verb* (often + *to*) be of use; help; (**avail oneself of**) use, profit by. ● *noun* use, profit.

**available** *adjective* at one's disposal; (of person) free, able to be contacted. □ **availability** *noun*.

**avalanche** /'ævəlɑːntʃ/ *noun* mass of snow and ice rapidly sliding down mountain; sudden abundance.

**avant-garde** /ævɑ̃'gɑːd/ ● *noun* innovators, esp. in the arts. ● *adjective* new, pioneering.

**avarice** /'ævərɪs/ *noun* greed for wealth. □ **avaricious** /-'rɪʃ-/ *adjective*.

**avatar** /'ævətɑː/ *noun* *Hindu Mythology* descent of god to earth in bodily form.

**avenge** /ə'vendʒ/ *verb* (**-ging**) inflict retribution on behalf of; exact retribution for.

**avenue** /'ævənjuː/ *noun* road or path, usually tree-lined; way of approach.

**aver** /ə'vɜː/ *verb* (**-rr-**) *formal* assert, affirm.

**average** /ˈævərɪdʒ/ ● *noun* usual amount, extent, or rate; number obtained by dividing sum of given numbers by how many there are. ● *adjective* usual, ordinary; mediocre; constituting average. ● *verb* (**-ging**) amount on average to; do on average; estimate average of. □ **average out (at)** result in average (of); **on average** as an average rate etc.

**averse** /əˈvɜːs/ *adjective* (usually + *to*) opposed, disinclined.

**aversion** /əˈvɜːʃ(ə)n/ *noun* (usually + *to*, *for*) dislike, unwillingness; object of this.

**avert** /əˈvɜːt/ *verb* prevent; (often + *from*) turn away.

**aviary** /ˈeɪvɪərɪ/ *noun* (*plural* **-ies**) large cage or building for keeping birds.

**aviation** /eɪvɪˈeɪʃ(ə)n/ *noun* the flying of aircraft.

**aviator** /ˈeɪvɪeɪtə/ *noun* person who flies aircraft.

**avid** /ˈævɪd/ *adjective* eager; greedy. □ **avidity** /-ˈvɪd-/ *noun*; **avidly** *adverb*.

**avocado** /ævəˈkɑːdəʊ/ *noun* (*plural* **-s**) (in full *avocado pear*) dark green pear-shaped fruit with creamy flesh.

**avocet** /ˈævəset/ *noun* wading bird with long upturned bill.

**avoid** /əˈvɔɪd/ *verb* keep away or refrain from; escape; evade. □ **avoidable** *adjective*; **avoidance** *noun*.

**avoirdupois** /ævədəˈpɔɪz/ *noun* system of weights based on pound of 16 ounces.

**avow** /əˈvaʊ/ *verb formal* declare; confess. □ **avowal** *noun*; **avowedly** /əˈvaʊɪdlɪ/ *adverb*.

**avuncular** /əˈvʌŋkjʊlə/ *adjective* of or like an uncle.

**await** /əˈweɪt/ *verb* wait for; be in store for.

**awake** /əˈweɪk/ ● *verb* (**-king**; *past* **awoke**; *past participle* **awoken**) (also *awaken*) rouse from sleep; cease to sleep; (often + *to*) become alert, aware, or active. ● *adjective* not asleep; alert.

**award** /əˈwɔːd/ ● *verb* give or order to be given as payment, penalty, or prize. ● *noun* thing awarded; judicial decision.

**aware** /əˈweə/ *adjective* (often + *of*, *that*) conscious, having knowledge. □ **awareness** *noun*.

**awash** /əˈwɒʃ/ *adjective* at surface of and just covered by water; (+ *with*) abounding.

**away** ● *adverb* to or at distance; into non-existence; constantly, persistently. ● *adjective* (of match etc.) played on opponent's ground.

**awe** /ɔː/ ● *noun* reverential fear or wonder. ● *verb* (**awing**) inspire with awe. □ **awe-inspiring** awesome, magnificent.

**aweigh** /əˈweɪ/ *adjective* (of anchor) just lifted from sea bottom.

**awesome** *adjective* inspiring awe.

---

## Auxiliary verb

An auxiliary verb is used in front of another verb to alter its meaning. Mainly, it expresses:

**1**  when something happens, by forming a tense of the main verb, e.g. *I shall go. He was going.*

**2**  permission, obligation, or ability to do something, e.g. *They may go. You must go. I can't go.*

**3**  the likelihood of something happening, e.g. *I might go. She would go if she could.*

The principal auxiliary verbs are:

| | | | |
|---|---|---|---|
| *be* | *have* | *must* | *will* |
| *can* | *let* | *ought* | *would* |
| *could* | *may* | *shall* | |
| *do* | *might* | *should* | |

---

**awful** /'ɔːfʊl/ *adjective colloquial* very bad; very great; *poetical* inspiring awe.

**awfully** *adverb colloquial* badly; very.

**awhile** /ə'waɪl/ *adverb* for a short time.

**awkward** /'ɔːkwəd/ *adjective* difficult to use; clumsy; embarrassing, embarrassed; hard to deal with.

**awl** /ɔːl/ *noun* small tool for pricking holes, esp. in leather.

**awning** /'ɔːnɪŋ/ *noun* fabric roof, shelter.

**awoke** *past of* AWAKE.

**awoken** *past participle of* AWAKE.

**AWOL** /'eɪwɒl/ *abbreviation colloquial* absent without leave.

**awry** /ə'raɪ/ ● *adverb* crookedly; amiss. ● *adjective* crooked; unsound.

**axe** /æks/ ● *noun* (*US* **ax**) chopping-tool with heavy blade; (**the axe**) dismissal (of employees); abandonment of project etc. ● *verb* (**axing**) cut (staff, services, etc.); abandon (project).

**axial** /'æksɪəl/ *adjective* of, forming, or placed round axis.

**axiom** /'æksɪəm/ *noun* established principle; self-evident truth. □ **axiomatic** /-'mæt-/ *adjective*.

**axis** /'æksɪs/ *noun* (*plural* **axes** /-siːz/) imaginary line about which object rotates; line dividing regular figure symmetrically; reference line for measurement of coordinates etc.

**axle** /'æks(ə)l/ *noun* spindle on which wheel turns or is fixed.

**ayatollah** /aɪə'tɒlə/ *noun* religious leader in Iran.

**aye** /aɪ/ ● *adverb archaic or dialect* yes. ● *noun* affirmative answer or vote.

**azalea** /ə'zeɪlɪə/ *noun* kind of rhododendron.

**azimuth** /'æzɪməθ/ *noun* angular distance between point below star etc. and north or south. □ **azimuthal** *adjective*.

**azure** /'æʒə/ *adjective & noun* sky-blue.

# Bb

**B** *abbreviation* black (pencil-lead).

**b.** *abbreviation* born.

**BA** *abbreviation* Bachelor of Arts.

**baa** /bɑː/ *noun & verb* (**baas**, **baaed** or **baa'd**) bleat.

**babble** /'bæb(ə)l/ ● *verb* (**-ling**) talk, chatter, or say incoherently or excessively; (of stream) murmur; repeat foolishly. ● *noun* babbling; murmur of water etc.

**babe** *noun* baby.

**babel** /'beɪb(ə)l/ *noun* confused noise, esp. of voices.

**baboon** /bə'buːn/ *noun* large kind of monkey.

**baby** /'beɪbɪ/ *noun* (*plural* **-ies**) very young child; childish person; youngest member of family etc.; very young animal; small specimen. □ **baby boom** *colloquial* temporary increase in birth rate; **baby grand** small grand piano.

**babysit** *verb* (**-tt-**; *past & past participle* **-sat**) look after child while parents are out. □ **babysitter** *noun*.

**baccarat** /'bækərɑː/ *noun* gambling card games.

**bachelor** /'bætʃələ/ *noun* unmarried man; person with a university first degree.

**bacillus** /bə'sɪləs/ *noun* (*plural* **bacilli** /-laɪ/) rod-shaped bacterium. □ **bacillary** *adjective*.

**back** ● *noun* rear surface of human body from shoulders to hips; upper surface of animal's body; spine; reverse or more distant part; part of garment covering back; defensive player in football etc. ● *adverb* to rear; away from front; in(to) the past or an earlier or normal position or condition; in return; at a distance. ● *verb* help with money or moral support; (often + *up*) (cause to) go backwards; bet on; provide with or serve as back, support, or backing to; *Music* accompany. ● *adjective* situated to rear; past, not current; reversed. □ **backache** ache in back; **backbencher** MP without senior office; **backbiting** malicious talk; **back boiler** one behind domestic fire etc.; **backbone** spine, main support, firmness of character; **backchat** *colloquial* verbal insolence; **backcloth** painted cloth at back of stage; **backdate** make retrospectively valid, put earlier date to; **back door** secret or ingenious means; **back down** withdraw from confrontation; **backdrop** backcloth; **backfire** (of engine or vehicle) undergo premature explosion in cylinder or exhaust pipe, (of plan etc.) have opposite of intended effect; **backhand** *Tennis etc.* (stroke) made with hand across body; **backhanded** indirect, ambiguous; **backhander** *slang* bribe; **backlash** violent, usually hostile, reaction; **backlog** arrears (of work etc.); **back number** old issue of magazine etc.; **back out** (often + *of*) withdraw; **backpack** rucksack; **back-pedal** reverse previous action or opinion; **back room** place where (esp. secret) work goes on; **back seat** less prominent or important position; **backside** *colloquial* buttocks; **backslide** return to bad ways; **backstage** behind the scenes; **backstreet** *noun* side-street, alley, *adjective* illicit, illegal; **backstroke** stroke made by swimmer lying on back; **back to front** with back and front reversed; **backtrack** retrace one's steps, reverse one's policy or opinion; **back up** give (esp. moral) support to, *Computing* make backup of; **backup** support, *Computing* (making of) spare copy of data; **backwash** receding waves, repercussions; **backwater** peaceful, secluded, or dull place, stagnant water fed from stream; **backwoods** remote uncleared forest land.

**backgammon** /ˈbækgæmən/ *noun* board game with pieces moved according to throw of dice.

**background** /ˈbækgraʊnd/ *noun* back part of scene etc.; inconspicuous position; person's education, social circumstances, etc.; explanatory information etc.

**backing** *noun* help or support; material used for thing's back or support; musical accompaniment.

**backward** *adjective* directed backwards; slow in learning; shy.

**backwards** *adverb* away from one's front; back foremost; in reverse of usual way; into worse state; into past; back towards starting point □ **bend over backwards** *colloquial* make every effort.

**bacon** /ˈbeɪkən/ *noun* cured meat from back and sides of pig.

**bacteriology** /bæktɪərɪˈɒlədʒɪ/ *noun* study of bacteria.

**bacterium** /bækˈtɪərɪəm/ *noun* (*plural* **-ria**) single-celled micro-organism. □ **bacterial** *adjective*.

■ **Usage** It is a mistake to use the plural form *bacteria* when only one bacterium is meant.

**bad** *adjective* (**worse, worst**) inadequate, defective; unpleasant; harmful; decayed; ill, injured; regretful, guilty; serious, severe; wicked; naughty; incorrect, not valid. □ **bad debt** debt that is not recoverable; **bad-tempered** irritable.

**bade** *archaic past of* BID.

**badge** *noun* small flat emblem worn as sign of office, membership, etc. or bearing slogan etc.

**badger** /ˈbædʒə/ ● *noun* nocturnal burrowing mammal with black and white striped head. ● *verb* pester.

**badinage** /ˈbædɪnɑːʒ/ *noun* banter. [French]

**badly** *adverb* (**worse, worst**) in bad manner; severely; very much.

**badminton** /ˈbædmɪnt(ə)n/ *noun* game played with rackets and shuttlecock.

**baffle** /ˈbæf(ə)l/ ● *verb* perplex; frustrate. ● *noun* device that hinders flow of fluid or sound. □ **bafflement** *noun*.

**bag** ● *noun* soft open-topped receptacle; piece of luggage; (in *plural*, usually + *of*) *colloquial* large amount; animal's sac; amount of game shot by one person. ● *verb* secure, take possession of; bulge, hang loosely; put in bag; shoot (game).

**bagatelle** /bægəˈtel/ *noun* game in which small balls are struck into holes on inclined board; mere trifle.

**bagel** /ˈbeɪg(ə)l/ *noun* ring-shaped bread roll.

**baggage** /ˈbægɪdʒ/ *noun* luggage; portable equipment of army.

**baggy** *adjective* (**-ier**, **-iest**) hanging loosely.

**bagpipes** /'bægpaɪps/ *plural noun* musical instrument with windbag for pumping air through reeded pipes.

**baguette** /bæ'get/ *noun* long thin French loaf.

**bail**[1] ● *noun* security given for released prisoner's return for trial; person(s) pledging this. ● *verb* (usually + *out*) give bail for and secure release of (prisoner).

**bail**[2] *noun* Cricket either of two crosspieces resting on stumps.

**bail**[3] *verb* (also **bale**) (usually + *out*) scoop (water) out of (boat etc.). □ **bail out** = BALE OUT.

**bailey** /'beɪlɪ/ *noun* (*plural* **-s**) outer wall of castle; court enclosed by this.

**bailiff** /'beɪlɪf/ *noun* sheriff's officer who executes writs, performs distraints, etc.; landlord's agent or steward.

**bailiwick** /'beɪlɪwɪk/ *noun* district of bailiff.

**bairn** /beən/ *noun Scottish & Northern English* child.

**bait** ● *noun* food to entice prey; allurement. ● *verb* torment (chained animal); harrass (person); put bait on or in (fishhook, trap, etc.).

**baize** /beɪz/ *noun* usually green felted woollen fabric used for coverings etc.

**bake** *verb* (**-king**) cook or become cooked by dry heat esp. in oven; *colloquial* be very hot; harden by heat. □ **baking powder** mixture used as raising agent.

**Bakelite** /'beɪkəlaɪt/ *noun proprietary term* kind of plastic.

**baker** /'beɪkə/ *noun* professional breadmaker. □ **baker's dozen** thirteen.

**bakery** /'beɪkərɪ/ *noun* (*plural* **-ies**) place where bread is made or sold.

**baksheesh** /'bækʃiːʃ/ *noun* gratuity, tip.

**Balaclava** /bælə'klɑːvə/ *noun* (in full **Balaclava helmet**) woollen covering for head and neck.

**balalaika** /bælə'laɪkə/ *noun* Russian triangular-bodied guitar-like musical instrument.

**balance** /'bæləns/ ● *noun* even distribution of weight or amount; stability of body or mind; weighing apparatus; counteracting weight or force; regulating device in clock etc.; decisive weight or amount; difference between credits and debits; remainder. ● *verb* (**-cing**) bring or come into or keep in equilibrium; offset, compare; equal, neutralize; (usually as **balanced** *adjective*) make well-proportioned and harmonious; equalize debits and credits of account, have debits and credits equal. □ **balance of payments** difference between payments into and out of a country; **balance of power** position in which no country etc. predominates, power held by small group when larger groups are of (almost) equal strength; **balance of trade** difference between exports and imports; **balance sheet** statement giving balance of account; **on balance** all things considered.

**balcony** /'bælkənɪ/ *noun* (*plural* **-ies**) outside balustraded or railed platform with access from upper floor; upper tier of seats in theatre etc.

**bald** /bɔːld/ *adjective* lacking some or all hair on scalp; without fur, feathers, etc.; with surface worn away; direct. □ **baldly** *adverb*; **baldness** *noun*.

**balderdash** /'bɔːldədæʃ/ *noun* nonsense.

**balding** /'bɔːldɪŋ/ *adjective* becoming bald.

**bale**[1] ● *noun* bundle of merchandise or hay. ● *verb* (**-ling**) make up into bales. □ **bale out** (also **bail out**) make emergency parachute jump from aircraft.

**bale**[2] = BAIL[3].

**baleful** /'beɪlfʊl/ *adjective* menacing; destructive; malignant.

**balk** = BAULK.

**ball**[1] /bɔːl/ *noun* spherical object or mass; usually spherical object used in game; rounded part of foot or hand at base of big toe or thumb; cannon ball; delivery or pass of ball in game. □ **ball-bearing** bearing using ring of small balls between its two parts, one such ball; **ballcock** valve operated by floating ball that controls level of water in cistern; **ball game** *US* baseball game, *colloquial* affair or matter; **ballpoint** (**pen**) pen with tiny ball as writing point.

**ball**[2] /bɔːl/ *noun* formal social gathering for dancing; *slang* enjoyable time.

**ballad** /'bæləd/ *noun* poem or song narrating popular story; slow sentimental song. □ **balladry** *noun*.

**ballast** /'bæləst/ *noun* heavy material stabilizing ship, controlling height of balloon, etc.; coarse stone etc. as bed of road or railway. ● *verb* provide with ballast.

**ballerina** /bælə'ri:nə/ *noun* female ballet dancer.

**ballet** /'bæleɪ/ *noun* dramatic or representational style of dancing to music; piece or performance of ballet. □ **ballet dancer** dancer of ballet. □ **balletic** /bə'letɪk/ *adjective*.

**ballistic** /bə'lɪstɪk/ *adjective* of projectiles. □ **ballistic missile** one that is powered and guided but falls by gravity.

**ballistics** *plural noun* (usually treated as *singular*) science of projectiles and firearms.

**balloon** /bə'lu:n/ ● *noun* small inflatable rubber toy or decoration; large inflatable flying bag, esp. one with basket below for passengers; outline containing words or thoughts in strip cartoon. ● *verb* (cause to) swell out like balloon. □ **balloonist** *noun*.

**ballot** /'bælət/ ● *noun* voting in writing and usually secret; votes recorded in ballot. ● *verb* (**-t-**) hold ballot; vote by ballot; take ballot of (voters). □ **ballot box** container for **ballot papers**, slips for marking votes.

**ballroom** /'bɔ:lrʊm/ *noun* large room for dancing. □ **ballroom dancing** formal social dancing for couples.

**bally** /'bælɪ/ *adjective & adverb slang* mild form of BLOODY.

**ballyhoo** /bælɪ'hu:/ *noun* loud noise, fuss; noisy publicity.

**balm** /bɑ:m/ *noun* aromatic ointment; fragrant oil or resin exuded from some trees; thing that heals or soothes; aromatic herb.

**balmy** /'bɑ:mɪ/ *adjective* (**-ier**, **-iest**) fragrant, mild, soothing; *slang* crazy.

**balsa** /'bɔ:lsə/ *noun* lightweight tropical American wood used for making models.

**balsam** /'bɔ:lsəm/ *noun* balm from trees; ointment; tree yielding balsam; any of several flowering plants.

**baluster** /'bæləstə/ *noun* short pillar supporting rail.

**balustrade** /bælə'streɪd/ *noun* railing supported by balusters, esp. on balcony.

**bamboo** /bæm'bu:/ *noun* tropical giant woody grass; its hollow stem.

**bamboozle** /bæm'bu:z(ə)l/ *verb* (**-ling**) *colloquial* cheat; mystify.

**ban** ● *verb* (**-nn-**) prohibit, esp. formally. ● *noun* formal prohibition.

**banal** /bə'nɑ:l/ *adjective* commonplace, trite. □ **banality** /-'næl-/ *noun* (*plural* **-ies**).

**banana** /bə'nɑ:nə/ *noun* long curved yellow tropical fruit; treelike plant bearing it.

**band** ● *noun* flat strip or loop of thin material; stripe; group of musicians; organized group of criminals etc.; range of values, esp. frequencies or wavelengths. ● *verb* (usually + *together*) unite; put band on; mark with stripes. □ **bandbox** hatbox; **bandmaster** conductor of band; **bandsman** player in band; **bandstand** outdoor platform for musicians.

**bandage** /'bændɪdʒ/ ● *noun* strip of material for binding wound etc. ● *verb* (**-ging**) bind with bandage.

**bandanna** /bæn'dænə/ *noun* large patterned handkerchief.

**bandeau** /'bændəʊ/ *noun* (*plural* **-x** /-z/) narrow headband.

**bandit** /'bændɪt/ *noun* robber, esp. of travellers. □ **banditry** *noun*.

**bandolier** /bændə'lɪə/ *noun* (also **bandoleer**) shoulder belt with loops or pockets for cartridges.

**bandwagon** *noun*. □ **climb, jump on the bandwagon** join popular or successful cause.

**bandy**[1] /'bændɪ/ *adjective* (**-ier**, **-iest**) (of legs) curved wide apart at knees. □ **bandy-legged** *adjective*.

**bandy**[2] /'bændɪ/ *verb* (**-ies**, **-ied**) (often + *about*) pass (story etc.) to and fro; discuss disparagingly; (often + *with*) exchange (blows, insults, etc.).

**bane** *noun* cause of ruin or trouble.

**bang** ● *noun* loud short sound; sharp blow. ● *verb* strike or shut noisily; (cause to) make bang. ● *adverb* with bang; *colloquial* exactly. □ **bang on** *colloquial* exactly right.

**banger** *noun* firework making bang; *slang* sausage, noisy old car.

**bangle** /'bæŋg(ə)l/ *noun* rigid bracelet or anklet.

**banian** = BANYAN.

**banish** /'bænɪʃ/ *verb* condemn to exile; dismiss from one's mind. □ **banishment** *noun*.

**banister** /'bænɪstə/ *noun* (also **bannister**) (usually in *plural*) uprights and handrail beside staircase.

**banjo** /'bændʒəʊ/ *noun* (*plural* **-s** or **-es**) round-bodied guitar-like musical instrument. □ **banjoist** *noun*.

**bank¹** ●*noun* sloping ground on each side of river; raised shelf of ground, esp. in sea; mass of cloud etc. ●*verb* (often + *up*) heap or rise into banks; pack (fire) tightly for slow burning; (cause to) travel round curve with one side higher than the other.

**bank²** ●*noun* establishment, usually a public company, where money is deposited, withdrawn, and borrowed; pool of money in gambling game; storage place. ●*verb* deposit (money) at bank; (often + *at, with*) keep money (at bank). □ **bank card** cheque card; **bank holiday** public holiday when banks are closed; **banknote** piece of paper money; **bank on** *colloquial* rely on.

**bank³** *noun* row (of lights, switches, organ keys, etc.).

**banker** *noun* owner or manager of bank; keeper of bank in gambling game. □ **banker's card** cheque card.

**bankrupt** /'bæŋkrʌpt/ ●*adjective* insolvent; (often + *of*) drained (of emotion etc.). ●*noun* insolvent person. ●*verb* make bankrupt. □ **bankruptcy** *noun* (*plural* **-ies**).

**banner** /'bænə/ *noun* large portable cloth sign bearing slogan or design; flag.

**bannister** = BANISTER.

**bannock** /'bænək/ *noun* *Scottish & Northern English* round flat loaf, usually unleavened.

**banns** *plural noun* announcement of intended marriage read in church.

**banquet** /'bæŋkwɪt/ ●*noun* sumptuous esp. formal dinner. ●*verb* (**-t-**) give banquet for; attend banquet.

**banquette** /bæŋ'ket/ *noun* upholstered bench along wall.

**banshee** /bæn'ʃiː/ *noun* female spirit whose wail warns of death in a house.

**bantam** /'bæntəm/ *noun* kind of small domestic fowl; small but aggressive person. □ **bantamweight** boxing weight (51–54 kg).

**banter** /'bæntə/ ●*noun* good-humoured teasing. ●*verb* tease; exchange banter.

**banyan** /'bænjən/ *noun* (also **banian**) Indian fig tree with self-rooting branches.

**baobab** /'beɪəʊbæb/ *noun* African tree with massive trunk and edible fruit.

**bap** *noun* soft flattish bread roll.

**baptism** /'bæptɪz(ə)m/ *noun* symbolic admission to Christian Church, with immersing in or sprinkling with water and usually name-giving. □ **baptismal** /-'tɪz-/ *adjective*.

**Baptist** /'bæptɪst/ *noun* member of Church practising adult baptism by immersion.

**baptize** /bæp'taɪz/ *verb* (also **-ise**) (**-zing** or **-sing**) administer baptism to; give name to.

**bar¹** ●*noun* long piece of rigid material, esp. used to confine or obstruct; (often + *of*) oblong piece (of chocolate, soap, etc.); band of colour or light; counter for serving alcoholic drinks etc., room or building containing it; counter for particular service; barrier; prisoner's enclosure in law court; section of music between vertical lines; heating element of electric fire; strip below clasp of medal as extra distinction; (**the Bar**) barristers, their profession. ●*verb* (**-rr-**) fasten with bar; (usually + *in, out*) keep in or out; obstruct, prevent; (usually + *from*) exclude. ●*preposition* except. □ **bar code** machine-readable striped code on packaging etc.; **barmaid**, **barman**, **bartender** woman, man, person serving in pub etc.

**bar²** *noun* unit of atmospheric pressure.

**barathea** /bærə'θiːə/ *noun* fine wool cloth.

**barb** ●*noun* backward-facing point on arrow, fish-hook, etc.; hurtful remark. ●*verb* fit with barb. □ **barbed wire** wire with spikes, used for fences.

**barbarian** /bɑːˈbeərɪən/ • *noun* uncultured or primitive person. • *adjective* uncultured; primitive.

**barbaric** /bɑːˈbærɪk/ *adjective* uncultured; cruel; primitive.

**barbarism** /ˈbɑːbərɪz(ə)m/ *noun* barbaric state or act; non-standard word or expression.

**barbarity** /bɑːˈbærɪtɪ/ *noun* (*plural* -ies) savage cruelty; barbaric act.

**barbarous** /ˈbɑːbərəs/ *adjective* uncultured; cruel.

**barbecue** /ˈbɑːbɪkjuː/ • *noun* meal cooked over charcoal etc. out of doors; party for this; grill etc. used for this. • *verb* (-cues, -cued, -cuing) cook on barbecue.

**barber** /ˈbɑːbə/ *noun* person who cuts men's hair.

**barbican** /ˈbɑːbɪkən/ *noun* outer defence, esp. double tower over gate or bridge.

**barbiturate** /bɑːˈbɪtjʊərət/ *noun* sedative derived from **barbituric acid** /bɑːˈtjʊərɪk/, an organic acid.

**bard** *noun* poet; *historical* Celtic minstrel; prizewinner at Eisteddfod. □ **bardic** *adjective*.

**bare** /beə/ • *adjective* unclothed, uncovered; leafless; unadorned, plain; scanty, just sufficient. • *verb* (-ring) uncover, reveal. □ **bareback** without saddle; **barefaced** shameless, impudent; **barefoot** with bare feet; **bareheaded** without hat.

**barely** *adverb* scarcely; scantily.

**bargain** /ˈbɑːgɪn/ • *noun* agreement on terms of sale etc.; cheap thing. • *verb* discuss terms of sale etc. □ **bargain for** be prepared for; **into the bargain** moreover.

**barge** /bɑːdʒ/ • *noun* large flat-bottomed cargo boat on canal or river; long ornamental pleasure boat. • *verb* (-ging) (+ *into*) collide with. □ **barge in** interrupt.

**bargee** /bɑːˈdʒiː/ *noun* person in charge of barge.

**baritone** /ˈbærɪtəʊn/ *noun* adult male singing voice between tenor and bass; singer with this.

**barium** /ˈbeərɪəm/ *noun* white metallic element. □ **barium meal** mixture swallowed to reveal digestive tract on X-ray.

**bark**[1] • *noun* sharp explosive cry of dog etc. • *verb* give a bark; speak or utter sharply or brusquely.

**bark**[2] • *noun* tough outer layer of tree. • *verb* graze (shin etc.); strip bark from.

**barker** *noun* tout at auction or sideshow.

**barley** /ˈbɑːlɪ/ *noun* cereal used as food and in spirits; (also **barleycorn**) its grain. □ **barley sugar** hard sweet made from sugar; **barley water** drink made from boiled barley.

**barm** *noun* froth on fermenting malt liquor.

**bar mitzvah** /bɑː ˈmɪtsvə/ *noun* religious initiation of Jewish boy at 13.

**barmy** /ˈbɑːmɪ/ *adjective* (-ier, -iest) *slang* crazy.

**barn** *noun* building for storing grain etc. □ **barn dance** social gathering for country dancing; **barn owl** kind of owl frequenting barns.

**barnacle** /ˈbɑːnək(ə)l/ *noun* small shellfish clinging to rocks, ships' bottoms, etc. □ **barnacle goose** kind of Arctic goose.

**barney** /ˈbɑːnɪ/ *noun* (*plural* -s) *colloquial* noisy quarrel.

**barometer** /bəˈrɒmɪtə/ *noun* instrument measuring atmospheric pressure. □ **barometric** /bærəˈmetrɪk/ *adjective*.

**baron** /ˈbærən/ *noun* member of lowest order of British or foreign nobility; powerful businessman etc. □ **baronial** /bəˈrəʊnɪəl/ *adjective*.

**baroness** /ˈbærənɪs/ *noun* woman holding rank of baron; baron's wife or widow.

**baronet** /ˈbærənɪt/ *noun* member of lowest British hereditary titled order. □ **baronetcy** *noun* (*plural* -ies).

**barony** /ˈbærənɪ/ *noun* (*plural* -ies) rank or domain of baron.

**baroque** /bəˈrɒk/ • *adjective* (esp. of 17th- & 18th-c. European architecture and music) ornate and extravagant in style. • *noun* baroque style.

**barque** /bɑːk/ *noun* kind of sailing ship.

**barrack**[1] /ˈbærək/ *noun* (usually in *plural*, often treated as *singular*) housing for soldiers; large bleak building.

**barrack**[2] /ˈbærək/ *verb* shout or jeer (at).

**barracuda** /ˌbærəˈkuːdə/ *noun* (*plural* same or **-s**) large voracious tropical sea fish.

**barrage** /ˈbærɑːʒ/ *noun* concentrated artillery bombardment; rapid succession of questions etc.; artificial barrier in river etc.

**barrel** /ˈbær(ə)l/ *noun* cylindrical usually convex container; contents or capacity of this; tube forming part of thing, esp. gun or pen. ● *verb* (**-ll-**; *US* **-l-**) put in barrels. □ **barrel organ** musical instrument with rotating pin-studded cylinder.

**barren** /ˈbærən/ *adjective* (**-er**, **-est**) unable to bear young; unable to produce fruit or vegetation; unprofitable; dull. □ **barrenness** *noun*.

**barricade** /ˌbærɪˈkeɪd/ ● *noun* barrier, esp. improvised. ● *verb* (**-ding**) block or defend with this.

**barrier** /ˈbærɪə/ *noun* fence etc. barring advance or access; obstacle to communication etc. □ **barrier cream** protective skin cream; **barrier reef** coral reef separated from land by channel.

**barrister** /ˈbærɪstə/ *noun* advocate practising in higher courts.

**barrow**[1] /ˈbærəʊ/ *noun* two-wheeled handcart; wheelbarrow.

**barrow**[2] /ˈbærəʊ/ *noun* ancient grave mound.

**Bart.** *abbreviation* Baronet.

**barter** /ˈbɑːtə/ ● *verb* exchange goods, rights, etc., without using money. ● *noun* trade by bartering.

**basal** /ˈbeɪs(ə)l/ *adjective* of, at, or forming base.

**basalt** /ˈbæsɔːlt/ *noun* dark volcanic rock. □ **basaltic** /bəˈsɔːltɪk/ *adjective*.

**base**[1] ● *noun* what a thing rests or depends on; foundation; principle; starting point; headquarters; main ingredient; number in terms of which other numbers are expressed; substance combining with acid to form salt. ● *verb* (**-sing**) (usually + *on*, *upon*) found, establish; station. □ **base rate** interest rate set by Bank of England and used as basis for other banks' rates.

**base**[2] *adjective* cowardly; despicable; menial; (of coin) alloyed; (of metal) low in value.

**baseball** *noun* game played esp. in US with bat and ball and circuit of 4 bases.

**baseless** *adjective* unfounded, groundless.

**basement** /ˈbeɪsmənt/ *noun* floor below ground level.

**bases** *plural* of BASE[1], BASIS.

**bash** ● *verb* strike bluntly or heavily; (often + *up*) *colloquial* attack violently. ● *noun* heavy blow; *slang* attempt, party.

**bashful** /ˈbæʃfʊl/ *adjective* shy; diffident.

**BASIC** /ˈbeɪsɪk/ *noun* computer programming language using familiar English words.

**basic** /ˈbeɪsɪk/ ● *adjective* serving as base; fundamental; simplest, lowest in level. ● *noun* (usually in *plural*) fundamental fact or principle. □ **basically** *adverb*.

**basil** /ˈbæz(ə)l/ *noun* aromatic herb.

**basilica** /bəˈzɪlɪkə/ *noun* ancient Roman hall with apse and colonnades; similar church.

**basilisk** /ˈbæzɪlɪsk/ *noun* mythical reptile with lethal breath and look; American crested lizard.

**basin** /ˈbeɪs(ə)n/ *noun* round vessel for liquids or preparing food in; washbasin; hollow depression; sheltered mooring area; round valley; area drained by river.

**basis** /ˈbeɪsɪs/ *noun* (*plural* **bases** /-siːz/) foundation; main ingredient or principle; starting point for discussion etc.

**bask** /bɑːsk/ *verb* relax in warmth and light; (+ *in*) revel in.

**basket** /ˈbɑːskɪt/ *noun* container made of woven canes, wire, etc.; amount held by this. □ **basketball** team game in which goals are scored by putting ball through high nets; **basketry**, **basketwork** art of weaving cane etc., work so produced.

**bas-relief** /ˈbæsrɪliːf/ *noun* carving or sculpture projecting slightly from background.

**bass**[1] /beɪs/ ● *noun* lowest adult male voice; singer with this; *colloquial* double bass, bass guitar; low-frequency sound of radio, record player, etc. ● *adjective* lowest in pitch; deep-sounding. □ **bass guitar** electric guitar playing low notes. □ **bassist** *noun*.

**bass**[2] /bæs/ *noun* (*plural* same or **-es**) common perch; other fish of perch family.

**basset** /ˈbæsɪt/ noun (in full **basset-hound**) short-legged hunting dog.

**bassoon** /bəˈsuːn/ noun bass instrument of oboe family. □ **bassoonist** noun.

**bast** /bæst/ noun fibre from inner bark of tree, esp. lime.

**bastard** /ˈbɑːstəd/ often offensive ● noun person born of parents not married to each other; slang person regarded with dislike or pity, difficult or awkward thing. ● adjective illegitimate by birth; hybrid. □ **bastardy** noun.

**bastardize** /ˈbɑːstədaɪz/ verb (also -ise) (-zing or -sing) corrupt, debase; declare illegitimate.

**baste**[1] /beɪst/ verb (-ting) moisten (roasting meat etc.) with fat etc.; beat, thrash.

**baste**[2] /beɪst/ verb (-ting) sew with long loose stitches, tack.

**bastinado** /bæstɪˈneɪdəʊ/ ● noun caning on soles of feet. ● verb (-es, -ed) punish with this.

**bastion** /ˈbæstɪən/ noun projecting part of fortification; thing regarded as protection.

**bat**[1] ● noun implement with handle for hitting ball in games; turn at using this; batsman. ● verb (-tt-) use bat; hit (as) with bat; take one's turn at batting. □ **batsman** person who bats, esp. at cricket.

**bat**[2] noun mouselike nocturnal flying mammal. □ **bats** slang crazy.

**bat**[3] verb (-tt-) □ **not bat an eyelid** colloquial show no reaction.

**batch** ● noun group, collection, set; loaves baked at one time. ● verb arrange in batches.

**bated** /ˈbeɪtɪd/ adjective □ **with bated breath** anxiously.

**Bath** /bɑːθ/ noun □ **Bath bun** round spiced bun with currants; **Bath chair** invalid's wheelchair.

**bath** /bɑːθ/ ● noun (plural -s /bɑːðz/) container for sitting in and washing the body; its contents; act of washing in it; (usually in plural) building for swimming or bathing. ● verb wash in bath. □ **bath cube** cube of **bath salts**, substance for scenting and softening bath water; **bathroom** room with bath, US room with lavatory.

**bathe** /beɪð/ ● verb (-thing) immerse oneself in water etc., esp. to swim or wash; immerse in or treat with liquid; (of sunlight etc.) envelop. ● noun swim. □ **bathing costume** garment worn for swimming.

**bathos** /ˈbeɪθɒs/ noun lapse from sublime to trivial; anticlimax. □ **bathetic** /bəˈθetɪk/ adjective.

**bathyscaphe** /ˈbæθɪskæf/, **bathysphere** /-sfɪə/ nouns vessel for deep-sea diving.

**batik** /bəˈtiːk/ noun method of dyeing textiles by waxing parts to be left uncoloured.

**batiste** /bæˈtiːst/ noun fine cotton or linen fabric.

**batman** /ˈbætmən/ noun army officer's servant.

**baton** /ˈbæt(ə)n/ noun thin stick for conducting orchestra etc.; short stick carried in relay race; stick carried by drum major; staff of office.

**batrachian** /bəˈtreɪkɪən/ ● noun amphibian that discards gills and tail, esp. frog or toad. ● adjective of batrachians.

**battalion** /bəˈtæljən/ noun army unit usually of 300–1000 men.

**batten**[1] /ˈbæt(ə)n/ ● noun long narrow piece of squared timber; strip for securing tarpaulin over ship's hatchway. ● verb strengthen or (often + down) fasten with battens.

**batten**[2] /ˈbæt(ə)n/ verb (often + on) thrive at the expense of.

**batter** /ˈbætə/ ● verb strike hard and repeatedly; (esp. as **battered** adjective) subject to long-term violence. ● noun mixture of flour and eggs beaten up with liquid for cooking. □ **battering ram** historical swinging beam for breaching walls.

**battery** /ˈbætərɪ/ noun (plural -ies) portable container of cell or cells for supplying electricity; series of cages etc. for poultry or cattle; set of connected or similar instruments etc.; emplacement for heavy guns; Law physical violence inflicted on person.

**battle** /ˈbæt(ə)l/ ● noun prolonged fight, esp. between armed forces; contest. ● verb (-ling) (often + with, for) struggle. □ **battleaxe** medieval weapon, colloquial domineering middle-aged woman;

**battle-cruiser** *historical* heavy-gunned ship of higher speed and lighter armour than battleship; **battledress** soldier's everyday uniform; **battlefield** scene of battle; **battleship** most heavily armed and armoured warship.

**battlement** /'bæt(ə)lmənt/ *noun* (usually in *plural*) parapet with gaps at intervals at top of wall.

**batty** /'bætɪ/ *adjective* (**-ier**, **-iest**) *slang* crazy.

**batwing** *adjective* (esp. of sleeve) shaped like a bat's wing.

**bauble** /'bɔːb(ə)l/ *noun* showy trinket.

**baulk** /bɔːlk/ (also **balk**) • *verb* (often + *at*) jib, hesitate; thwart, hinder, disappoint. • *noun* hindrance; stumbling block.

**bauxite** /'bɔːksaɪt/ *noun* claylike mineral, chief source of aluminium.

**bawdy** /'bɔːdɪ/ • *adjective* (**-ier**, **-iest**) humorously indecent. • *noun* bawdy talk or writing. □ **bawdy house** brothel.

**bawl** *verb* shout or weep noisily. □ **bawl out** *colloquial* reprimand severely.

**bay**[1] *noun* broad curving inlet of sea.

**bay**[2] *noun* laurel with deep green leaves; (in *plural*) victor's or poet's bay wreath, fame. □ **bay leaf** leaf of bay tree, used for flavouring.

**bay**[3] *noun* recess; alcove in wall; compartment; allotted area. □ **bay window** window projecting from line of wall.

**bay**[4] • *adjective* reddish-brown (esp. of horse). • *noun* bay horse.

**bay**[5] • *verb* bark loudly. • *noun* bark of large dog, esp. chorus of pursuing hounds. □ **at bay** unable to escape; **keep at bay** ward off.

**bayonet** /'beɪənɪt/ • *noun* stabbing-blade attachable to rifle. • *verb* (**-t-**) stab with bayonet. □ **bayonet fitting** connecting-part engaged by pushing and twisting.

**bazaar** /bə'zɑː/ *noun* oriental market; sale of goods, esp. for charity.

**bazooka** /bə'zuːkə/ *noun* anti-tank rocket launcher.

**BBC** *abbreviation* British Broadcasting Corporation.

**BC** *abbreviation* before Christ; British Columbia.

**BCG** *abbreviation* Bacillus Calmette-Guérin, an anti-tuberculosis vaccine.

**be** /biː/ • *verb* (*present singular 1st* **am**, *2nd* **are** /ɑː/, *3rd* **is** /ɪz/, *plural* **are** /ɑː/; *past singular 1st* **was** /wɒz/, *2nd* **were** /wɜː/, *3rd* **was** /wɒz/, *plural* **were** /wɜː/; *present participle* **being**; *past participle* **been**) exist, live; occur; remain, continue; have specified identity, state, or quality. • *auxiliary verb* with past participle to form passive, with present participle to form continuous tenses, with infinitive to express duty, intention, possibility, etc. □ **be-all and end-all** *colloquial* whole being, essence.

**beach** • *noun* sandy or pebbly shore of sea, lake, etc. • *verb* run or haul (boat etc.) on shore. □ **beachcomber** person who searches beaches for articles of value; **beachhead** fortified position set up on beach by landing forces.

**beacon** /'biːkən/ *noun* signal-fire on hill or pole; signal; signal-station; Belisha beacon.

**bead** • *noun* small ball of glass, stone, etc. pierced for threading with others; drop of liquid; small knob in front sight of gun. • *verb* adorn with bead(s) or beading.

**beading** *noun* moulding like series of beads.

**beadle** /'biːd(ə)l/ *noun* ceremonial officer of church, college, etc.

**beady** *adjective* (**-ier**, **-iest**) (of eyes) small and bright. □ **beady-eyed** with beady eyes, observant.

**beagle** /'biːg(ə)l/ *noun* small hound used for hunting hares.

**beak** *noun* bird's horny projecting jaws; *slang* hooked nose; *historical* prow of warship; spout.

**beaker** /'biːkə/ *noun* tall cup for drinking; lipped glass vessel for scientific experiments.

**beam** • *noun* long piece of squared timber or metal used in house-building etc.; ray of light or radiation; bright smile; series of radio or radar signals as guide to ship or aircraft; crossbar of balance; (in *plural*) horizontal cross-timbers of ship. • *verb* emit (light, radio waves, etc.); shine; smile radiantly. □ **off beam** *colloquial* mistaken.

**bean** *noun* climbing plant with kidney-shaped seeds in long pods; seed of this or of coffee or other plant. □ **beanbag** small bag filled with dried beans and used as ball, large bag filled with polystyrene pieces and used as seat; **bean sprout** sprout of bean seed as food; **full of beans** *colloquial* lively, exuberant; **not a bean** *slang* no money.

**beano** /'biːnəʊ/ *noun* ( *plural* **-s** ) *slang* party, celebration.

**bear¹** /beə/ *verb* ( *past* **bore**; *past participle* **borne** or **born**) carry; show; produce, yield (fruit); give birth to; sustain; endure, tolerate.

**bear²** /beə/ *noun* heavy thick-furred mammal; rough surly person; person who sells shares for future delivery in hope of buying them more cheaply before then. □ **beargarden** noisy or rowdy scene; **bear-hug** powerful embrace; **bearskin** guardsman's tall furry cap.

**bearable** *adjective* endurable.

**beard** /bɪəd/ ● *noun* facial hair on chin etc.; part on animal (esp. goat) resembling beard. ● *verb* oppose, defy. □ **bearded** *adjective*.

**bearer** *noun* carrier of message, cheque, etc.; carrier of coffin, equipment, etc.

**bearing** *noun* outward behaviour, posture; (usually + *on*, *upon*) relation, relevance; part of machine supporting rotating part; direction relative to fixed point; (in *plural*) relative position; heraldic device or design.

**beast** *noun* animal, esp. wild mammal; brutal person; *colloquial* disliked person or thing.

**beastly** *adjective* (**-ier**, **-iest**) like a beast; *colloquial* unpleasant.

**beat** ● *verb* ( *past* **beat**; *past participle* **beaten**) strike repeatedly or persistently; inflict blows on; overcome, surpass, exhaust, perplex; (often + *up*) whisk (eggs etc.) vigorously; (often + *out*) shape (metal etc.) by blows; pulsate; mark (time of music) with baton, foot, etc.; move or cause (wings) to move up and down. ● *noun* main accent in music or verse; strongly marked rhythm of popular music etc.; stroke on drum; movement of conductor's baton; throbbing; police officer's appointed course; one's habitual round.

● *adjective slang* exhausted, tired out. □ **beat about the bush** not come to the point; **beat down** cause (seller) to lower price by bargaining; (of sun, rain, etc.) shine or fall relentlessly; **beat it** *slang* go away; **beat up** beat with punches and kicks; **beat-up** *colloquial* dilapidated.

**beater** *noun* whisk; implement for beating carpet; person who rouses game at a shoot.

**beatific** /biːə'tɪfɪk/ *adjective* making blessed; *colloquial* blissful.

**beatify** /biː'ætɪfaɪ/ *verb* (**-ies**, **-ied**) *RC Church* declare to be blessed as first step to canonization; make happy. □ **beatification** *noun*.

**beatitude** /biː'ætɪtjuːd/ *noun* blessedness; (in *plural*) blessings in Matthew 5: 3–11.

**beau** /bəʊ/ *noun* ( *plural* **-x** /-z/) boyfriend; dandy.

**Beaufort scale** /'bəʊfət/ *noun* scale of wind speeds.

**Beaujolais** /'bəʊʒəleɪ/ *noun* red or white wine from Beaujolais district of France.

**beauteous** /'bjuːtɪəs/ *adjective poetical* beautiful.

**beautician** /bjuː'tɪʃ(ə)n/ *noun* specialist in beauty treatment.

**beautiful** /'bjuːtɪful/ *adjective* having beauty; *colloquial* excellent. □ **beautifully** *adverb*.

**beautify** /'bjuːtɪfaɪ/ *verb* (**-ies**, **-ied**) make beautiful, adorn. □ **beautification** *noun*.

**beauty** /'bjuːtɪ/ *noun* ( *plural* **-ies**) combination of qualities that delights the sight or other senses or the mind; person or thing having this. □ **beauty queen** woman judged most beautiful in contest; **beauty parlour**, **salon** establishment for cosmetic treatment; **beauty spot** beautiful locality.

**beaver** ● *noun* large amphibious broad-tailed rodent; its fur; hat of this; (**Beaver**) member of most junior branch of Scout Association. ● *verb colloquial* (usually + *away*) work hard.

**becalm** /bɪ'kɑːm/ *verb* deprive (ship etc.) of wind.

**became** *past* of BECOME.

**because** /bɪˈkɒz/ *conjunction* for the reason that. □ **because of** by reason of.

**beck¹** *noun* brook, mountain stream.

**beck²** *noun* □ **at (person's) beck and call** subject to his or her constant orders.

**beckon** /ˈbekən/ *verb* (often + *to*) summon by gesture; entice.

**become** /bɪˈkʌm/ *verb* (**-ming**; *past* **became**; *past participle* **become**) come to be, begin to be; suit, look well on. □ **become of** happen to.

**becquerel** /ˈbekərel/ *noun* SI unit of radioactivity.

**bed** ● *noun* place to sleep or rest, esp. piece of furniture for sleeping on; garden plot for plants; bottom of sea, river, etc.; flat base on which thing rests; stratum. ● *verb* (**-dd-**) (usually + *down*) put or go to bed; plant in bed; fix firmly; *colloquial* have sexual intercourse with. □ **bedclothes** sheets, blankets, etc.; **bedpan** pan for use as toilet by invalid in bed; **bedridden** confined to bed by infirmity; **bedrock** solid rock under alluvial deposits etc., basic principles; **bedroom** room for sleeping in; **bedsitting room**, **bedsitter** combined bedroom and sitting-room; **bedsore** sore developed by lying in bed; **bedspread** coverlet; **bedstead** framework of bed; **bedtime** hour for going to bed.

**bedaub** /bɪˈdɔːb/ *verb* smear with paint etc.

**bedding** *noun* mattress and bedclothes; litter for cattle etc. □ **bedding plant** annual flowering plant put in garden bed.

**bedeck** /bɪˈdek/ *verb* adorn, decorate.

**bedevil** /bɪˈdev(ə)l/ *verb* (**-ll-**; *US* **-l-**) torment, confuse, trouble. □ **bedevilment** *noun*.

**bedlam** /ˈbedləm/ *noun* scene of confusion or uproar.

**Bedouin** /ˈbeduɪn/ *noun* (*plural* same) nomadic Arab of the desert.

**bedraggled** /bɪˈdræg(ə)ld/ *adjective* dishevelled, untidy.

**bee** *noun* 4-winged stinging insect, collecting nectar and pollen and producing wax and honey; busy worker; meeting for combined work or amusement. □ **beehive** hive; **beeline** straight line

between two places; **beeswax** wax secreted by bees for honeycomb.

**Beeb** *noun* (**the Beeb**) *colloquial* the BBC.

**beech** *noun* smooth-barked glossy-leaved tree; its wood. □ **beechmast** fruit of beech.

**beef** ● *noun* meat of ox, bull, or cow; (*plural* **beeves** or *US* **-s**) beef animal; (*plural* **-s**) *slang* protest. ● *verb slang* complain. □ **beefburger** hamburger; **beefeater** warder in Tower of London; **beefsteak** thick slice of beef for grilling or frying; **beef tea** stewed beef extract for invalids; **beef tomato** large tomato.

**beefy** *adjective* (**-ier**, **-iest**) like beef; solid, muscular.

**been** *past participle* of BE.

**beep** ● *noun* short high-pitched sound. ● *verb* emit beep.

**beer** /bɪə/ *noun* alcoholic liquor made from fermented malt etc. flavoured esp. with hops. □ **beer garden** garden where beer is sold and drunk; **beer mat** small mat for beer glass.

**beery** *adjective* (**-ier**, **-iest**) showing influence of beer; like beer.

**beeswing** /ˈbiːzwɪŋ/ *noun* filmy crust on old port wine etc.

**beet** *noun* plant with succulent root used for salads etc. and sugar-making (see BEETROOT, SUGAR BEET).

**beetle¹** /ˈbiːt(ə)l/ ● *noun* insect with hard protective outer wings. ● *verb* (**-ling**) *colloquial* (+ *about*, *off*, etc.) hurry, scurry.

**beetle²** /ˈbiːt(ə)l/ ● *adjective* projecting, shaggy, scowling. ● *verb* (usually as **beetling** *adjective*) overhang.

**beetle³** /ˈbiːt(ə)l/ *noun* heavy-headed tool for ramming, crushing, etc.

**beetroot** *noun* beet with dark red root used as vegetable.

**befall** /bɪˈfɔːl/ *verb* (*past* **befell**; *past participle* **befallen**) *poetical* happen; happen to.

**befit** /bɪˈfɪt/ *verb* (**-tt-**) be appropriate for.

**befog** /bɪˈfɒg/ *verb* (**-gg-**) obscure; envelop in fog.

**before** /bɪˈfɔː/ ● *conjunction* sooner than; rather than. ● *preposition* earlier than; in front of, ahead of; in presence of. ● *adverb* ahead, in front; previously, already; in the past.

**beforehand** *adverb* in anticipation, in readiness, before time.

**befriend** /bɪˈfrend/ *verb* act as friend to; help.

**befuddle** /bɪˈfʌd(ə)l/ *verb* (**-ling**) make drunk; confuse.

**beg** *verb* (**-gg-**) ask for as gift; ask earnestly, entreat; live by begging; ask formally. □ **beg the question** assume truth of thing to be proved; **go begging** be unwanted.

■ **Usage** The expression *beg the question* is often used incorrectly to mean 'to invite the obvious question (that ... )'.

**began** *past of* BEGIN.

**begat** *archaic past of* BEGET.

**beget** /bɪˈɡet/ *verb* (**-tt-**; *past* **begot**, *archaic* **begat**; *past participle* **begotten**) *literary* be the father of; give rise to.

**beggar** /ˈbeɡə/ ● *noun* person who begs or lives by begging; *colloquial* person. ● *verb* make poor; be too extraordinary for (belief, description, etc.).

**beggarly** *adjective* mean; poor, needy.

**begin** /bɪˈɡɪn/ *verb* (**-nn-**; *past* **began**; *past participle* **begun**) perform first part of; come into being; (often + *to do*) start, take first step, (usually in negative) *colloquial* show any likelihood, be sufficient.

**beginner** *noun* learner.

**beginning** *noun* time at which thing begins; source, origin; first part.

**begone** /bɪˈɡɒn/ *interjection poetical* go away at once!

**begonia** /bɪˈɡəʊnɪə/ *noun* plant with ornamental foliage and bright flowers.

**begot** *past of* BEGET.

**begotten** *past participle of* BEGET.

**begrudge** /bɪˈɡrʌdʒ/ *verb* (**-ging**) grudge; feel or show resentment at or envy of; be dissatisfied at.

**beguile** /bɪˈɡaɪl/ *verb* (**-ling**) charm, divert; delude, cheat. □ **beguilement** *noun*.

**beguine** /bɪˈɡiːn/ *noun* W. Indian dance.

**begum** /ˈbeɪɡəm/ *noun* (in India, Pakistan, and Bangladesh) Muslim woman of high rank; (**Begum**) *title of married Muslim woman*.

**begun** *past participle of* BEGIN.

**behalf** /bɪˈhɑːf/ *noun* □ **on behalf of, on (person's) behalf** in the interests of, as representative of.

**behave** /bɪˈheɪv/ *verb* (**-ving**) react or act in specified way; (often **behave oneself**) conduct oneself properly; work well (or in specified way).

**behaviour** /bɪˈheɪvjə/ *noun* (*US* **behavior**) manners, conduct, way of behaving. □ **behavioural** *adjective*.

**behaviourism** *noun* (*US* **behaviorism**) study of human actions by analysis of stimulus and response. □ **behaviourist** *noun*.

**behead** /bɪˈhed/ *verb* cut head from (person); execute thus.

**beheld** *past & past participle of* BEHOLD.

**behest** /bɪˈhest/ *noun literary* command, request.

**behind** /bɪˈhaɪnd/ ● *preposition* in or to rear of; hidden by, on farther side of; in past in relation to; inferior to; in support of. ● *adverb* in or to rear; on far side; remaining after others' departure; (usually + *with*) in arrears. ● *noun colloquial* buttocks. □ **behindhand** in arrears, behind time, too late; **behind time** unpunctual; **behind the times** old-fashioned, antiquated.

**behold** /bɪˈhəʊld/ *verb* (*past & past participle* **beheld**) *literary* look at; take notice, observe.

**beholden** /bɪˈhəʊld(ə)n/ *adjective* (usually + *to*) under obligation.

**behove** /bɪˈhəʊv/ *verb* (**-ving**) *formal* be incumbent on; befit.

**beige** /beɪʒ/ ● *noun* pale sandy fawn colour. ● *adjective* of this colour.

**being** /ˈbiːɪŋ/ *noun* existence; constitution, nature; existing person etc.

**belabour** /bɪˈleɪbə/ *verb* (*US* **belabor**) attack physically or verbally.

**belated** /bɪˈleɪtɪd/ *adjective* coming (too) late. □ **belatedly** *adverb*.

**bel canto** /bel ˈkæntəʊ/ *noun* singing marked by full rich tone.

**belch** ● *verb* emit wind from stomach through mouth; (of volcano, gun, etc.) emit (fire, smoke, etc.). ● *noun* act of belching.

**beleaguer** /bɪˈliːɡə/ *verb* besiege; vex; harass.

**belfry** /ˈbelfrɪ/ *noun* (*plural* **-ies**) bell tower; space for bells in church tower.

**belie** /bɪˈlaɪ/ *verb* (**belying**) give false impression of; fail to confirm, fulfil, or justify.

**belief** /bɪˈliːf/ *noun* act of believing; what one believes; trust, confidence; acceptance as true.

**believe** /bɪˈliːv/ *verb* (**-ving**) accept as true; think; (+ *in*) have faith or confidence in; trust word of; have religious faith. □ **believable** *adjective*; **believer** *noun*.

**Belisha beacon** /bəˈliːʃə/ *noun* flashing orange ball on striped post, marking pedestrian crossing.

**belittle** /bɪˈlɪt(ə)l/ *verb* (**-ling**) disparage. □ **belittlement** *noun*.

**bell** *noun* hollow esp. cup-shaped metal body emitting musical sound when struck; sound of bell; bell-shaped thing. □ **bell-bottomed** (of trousers) widening below knee; **bell pull** cord pulled to sound bell; **bell push** button pressed to ring electric bell; **give (person) a bell** *colloquial* telephone him or her.

**belladonna** /beləˈdɒnə/ *noun* deadly nightshade; drug obtained from this.

**belle** /bel/ *noun* handsome woman; reigning beauty.

**belles-lettres** /bel ˈletr/ *plural noun* (also treated as *singular*) writings or studies of purely literary kind.

**bellicose** /ˈbelɪkəʊs/ *adjective* eager to fight.

**belligerent** /bɪˈlɪdʒərənt/ ● *adjective* engaged in war; given to constant fighting; pugnacious. ● *noun* belligerent person or nation. □ **belligerence** *noun*.

**bellow** /ˈbeləʊ/ ● *verb* emit deep loud roar. ● *noun* bellowing sound.

**bellows** /ˈbeləʊz/ *plural noun* (also treated as *singular*) device for driving air into fire, organ, etc.; expandable part of camera etc.

**belly** /ˈbelɪ/ ● *noun* (*plural* **-ies**) cavity of body containing stomach, bowels, etc.; stomach; front of body from waist to groin; underside of animal; cavity or bulging part of anything. ● *verb* (**-ies**, **-ied**) swell out. □ **bellyache** *noun* *colloquial* stomach pain, *verb* *slang* complain noisily or persistently; **belly button** *colloquial* navel; **belly dance** dance by woman (**belly dancer**) with voluptuous movements of belly; **belly laugh** loud unrestrained laugh.

**bellyful** *noun* enough to eat; *colloquial* more than one can tolerate.

**belong** /bɪˈlɒŋ/ *verb* (+ *to*) be property of, assigned to, or member of; fit socially; be rightly placed or classified.

**belongings** *plural noun* possessions, luggage.

**beloved** /bɪˈlʌvɪd/ ● *adjective* loved. ● *noun* beloved person.

**below** /bɪˈləʊ/ ● *preposition* under; lower than; less than; of lower rank or importance etc. than; unworthy of. ● *adverb* at or to lower point or level; further on in book etc.

**belt** ● *noun* strip of leather etc. worn round waist or across chest; continuous band in machinery; distinct strip of colour etc.; zone, district. ● *verb* put belt round; *slang* thrash; *slang* move rapidly. □ **below the belt** unfair(ly); **belt out** *slang* sing or play (music) loudly; **belt up** *slang* be quiet, *colloquial* put on seat belt; **tighten one's belt** economize; **under one's belt** securely acquired.

**bemoan** /bɪˈməʊn/ *verb* lament, complain about.

**bemuse** /bɪˈmjuːz/ *verb* (**-sing**) make (person) confused.

**bench** *noun* long seat of wood or stone; carpenter's or laboratory table; magistrate's or judge's seat; lawcourt. □ **benchmark** surveyor's mark at point in line of levels; standard, point of reference.

**bend** ● *verb* (*past & past participle* **bent** except in *bended knee*) force into curve or angle; be altered in this way; incline from vertical; bow, stoop; interpret or modify (rule) to suit oneself; (force to) submit. ● *noun* bending, curve; bent part of thing; (**the bends**) *colloquial* symptoms due to too rapid decompression under water. □ **round the bend** *colloquial* crazy, insane.

**bender** *noun* *slang* wild drinking spree.

**beneath** /bɪˈniːθ/ ● *preposition* below, under; unworthy of. ● *adverb* below, underneath.

**Benedictine** /benɪˈdɪktɪn/ ● *noun* monk or nun of Order of St Benedict; /-tiːn/ *proprietary term* kind of liqueur. ● *adjective* of St Benedict or his order.

**benediction** /benɪˈdɪkʃ(ə)n/ *noun* utterance of blessing. □ **benedictory** *adjective*.

**benefaction** /benɪˈfækʃ(ə)n/   *noun* charitable gift; doing good.

**benefactor** /ˈbenɪfæktə/ *noun* (*feminine* **benefactress**) person who has given financial or other help.

**benefice** /ˈbenɪfɪs/ *noun* living from a church office.

**beneficent** /bɪˈnefɪsənt/ *adjective* doing good; actively kind. □ **beneficence** *noun*.

**beneficial** /benɪˈfɪʃ(ə)l/ *adjective* advantageous. □ **beneficially** *adverb*.

**beneficiary** /benɪˈfɪʃərɪ/ *noun* (*plural* **-ies**) receiver of benefits; holder of church living.

**benefit** /ˈbenɪfɪt/ ● *noun* advantage, profit; payment made under insurance or social security; performance or game etc. of which proceeds go to particular player or charity. ● *verb* (**-t-**; *US* **-tt-**) do good to; receive benefit. □ **benefit of the doubt** assumption of innocence rather than guilt.

**benevolent** /bɪˈnevələnt/ *adjective* wishing to do good; charitable; kind and helpful. □ **benevolence** *noun*.

**Bengali** /beŋˈɡɔːlɪ/ ● *noun* (*plural* **-s**) native or language of Bengal. ● *adjective* of Bengal.

**benighted** /bɪˈnaɪtɪd/ *adjective* intellectually or morally ignorant.

**benign** /bɪˈnaɪn/ *adjective* kindly, gentle; favourable; salutary; *Medicine* mild, not malignant. □ **benignity** /bɪˈnɪɡnɪtɪ/ *noun*.

**benignant** /bɪˈnɪɡnənt/ *adjective* kindly; beneficial. □ **benignancy** *noun*.

**bent** ● *past & past participle of* BEND. ● *adjective* curved or having angle; *slang* dishonest, illicit; (+ *on*) set on doing or having. ● *noun* inclination, bias; (+ *for*) talent for.

**benumb** /bɪˈnʌm/ *verb* make numb; deaden; paralyse.

**benzene** /ˈbenziːn/ *noun* chemical got from coal tar and used as solvent.

**benzine** /ˈbenziːn/ *noun* spirit obtained from petroleum and used as cleaning agent.

**benzoin** /ˈbenzəʊɪn/ *noun* fragrant resin of E. Asian tree. □ **benzoic** /-ˈzəʊɪk/ *adjective*.

**bequeath** /bɪˈkwiːð/ *verb* leave by will; transmit to posterity.

**bequest** /bɪˈkwest/ *noun* bequeathing; thing bequeathed.

**berate** /bɪˈreɪt/ *verb* (**-ting**) scold.

**bereave** /bɪˈriːv/ *verb* (**-ving**) (esp. as **bereaved** *adjective*) (often + *of*) deprive of relative, friend, etc., esp. by death. □ **bereavement** *noun*.

**bereft** /bɪˈreft/ *adjective* (+ *of*) deprived of.

**beret** /ˈbereɪ/ *noun* round flat brimless cap of felt etc.

**berg** *noun* iceberg.

**bergamot** /ˈbɜːɡəmɒt/ *noun* perfume from fruit of a dwarf orange tree; an aromatic herb.

**beriberi** /berɪˈberɪ/ *noun* nervous disease caused by deficiency of vitamin $B_1$.

**Bermuda shorts** /bəˈmjuːdə/ *plural noun* close-fitting knee-length shorts.

**berry** /ˈberɪ/ *noun* (*plural* **-ies**) any small round juicy stoneless fruit.

**berserk** /bəˈzɜːk/ *adjective* (esp. after *go*) wild, frenzied.

**berth** ● *noun* sleeping place; ship's place at wharf; sea-room; *colloquial* situation, appointment. ● *verb* moor (ship) in berth; provide sleeping berth for.

**beryl** /ˈberɪl/ *noun* transparent (esp. green) precious stone; mineral species including this and emerald.

**beryllium** /bəˈrɪlɪəm/ *noun* hard white metallic element.

**beseech** /bɪˈsiːtʃ/ *verb* (*past & past participle* **besought** /-ˈsɔːt/ *or* **beseeched**) entreat; ask earnestly for.

**beset** /bɪˈset/ *verb* (**-tt-**; *past & past participle* **beset**) attack or harass persistently.

**beside** /bɪˈsaɪd/ *preposition* at side of, close to; compared with; irrelevant to. □ **beside oneself** frantic with anger or worry etc.

**besides** ● *preposition* in addition to; apart from. ● *adverb* also, as well.

**besiege** /bɪˈsiːdʒ/ *verb* (**-ging**) lay siege to; crowd round eagerly; assail with requests.

**besmirch** /bɪˈsmɜːtʃ/ *verb* soil, dishonour.

**besom** /ˈbiːz(ə)m/ *noun* broom made of twigs.

**besotted** /bɪˈsɒtɪd/ *adjective* infatuated; stupefied.

**besought** *past & past participle of* BESEECH.

**bespatter** /bɪ'spætə/ *verb* spatter all over; defame.

**bespeak** /bɪ'spiːk/ *verb* (*past* **bespoke**; *past participle* **bespoken**) engage beforehand; order (goods); be evidence of.

**bespectacled** /bɪ'spektək(ə)ld/ *adjective* wearing spectacles.

**bespoke** /bɪ'spəʊk/ *adjective* made to order.

**best** ● *adjective* (*superlative* of GOOD) most excellent. ● *adverb* (*superlative* of WELL[1]) in the best way; to greatest degree. ● *noun* that which is best. ● *verb colloquial* defeat, outwit. □ **best man** bridegroom's chief attendant at wedding; **best-seller** book with large sale, author of such book; **do one's best** do all one can.

**bestial** /'bestɪəl/ *adjective* brutish; of or like beasts. □ **bestiality** /-'æl-/ *noun*.

**bestiary** /'bestɪərɪ/ *noun* (*plural* **-ies**) medieval treatise on beasts.

**bestir** /bɪ'stɜː/ *verb* (**-rr-**) (**bestir oneself**) exert or rouse oneself.

**bestow** /bɪ'stəʊ/ *verb* (+ *on*, *upon*) confer as gift. □ **bestowal** *noun*.

**bestrew** /bɪ'struː/ *verb* (*past participle* **bestrewed** or **bestrewn**) strew; lie scattered over.

**bestride** /bɪ'straɪd/ *verb* (**-ding**; *past* **bestrode**; *past participle* **bestridden**) sit astride on; stand astride over.

**bet** ● *verb* (**-tt-**; *past & past participle* **bet** or **betted**) risk one's money etc. against another's on result of event. ● *noun* such arrangement; sum of money bet.

**beta** /'biːtə/ *noun* second letter of Greek alphabet (Β, β). □ **beta-blocker** drug used to prevent unwanted stimulation of the heart in angina etc.; **beta particle** fast-moving electron emitted by radioactive substance.

**betake** /bɪ'teɪk/ *verb* (**-king**; *past* **betook**; *past participle* **betaken**) (**betake oneself**) go.

**betatron** /'biːtətrɒn/ *noun* apparatus for accelerating electrons.

**betel** /'biːt(ə)l/ *noun* leaf chewed with betel-nut. □ **betel-nut** seed of tropical palm.

**bête noire** /beɪt 'nwɑː/ *noun* (*plural* **bêtes noires** same pronunciation) particularly disliked person or thing. [French]

**bethink** /bɪ'θɪŋk/ *verb* (*past & past participle* **bethought** /-'θɔːt/) (**bethink oneself**)

*formal* reflect, stop to think; be reminded.

**betide** /bɪ'taɪd/ *verb* □ **woe betide (person)** misfortune will befall him or her.

**betimes** /bɪ'taɪmz/ *adverb literary* in good time, early.

**betoken** /bɪ'təʊkən/ *verb* be sign of.

**betook** *past* of BETAKE.

**betray** /bɪ'treɪ/ *verb* be disloyal to (a person, one's country, etc.); give up or reveal treacherously; reveal involuntarily; be evidence of. □ **betrayal** *noun*.

**betroth** /bɪ'trəʊð/ *verb* (usually as **betrothed** *adjective*) bind with promise to marry. □ **betrothal** *noun*.

**better** /'betə/ ● *adjective* (*comparative* of GOOD) more excellent; partly or fully recovered from illness. ● *adverb* (*comparative* of WELL[1]) in better manner; to greater degree. ● *noun* better thing or person. ● *verb* improve (upon); surpass. □ **better off** in better (esp. financial) situation; **get the better of** defeat, outwit.

**betterment** *noun* improvement.

**between** /bɪ'twiːn/ ● *preposition* in or into space or interval; separating; shared by; to and from; taking one or other of. ● *adverb* (also **in between**) between two or more points, between two extremes.

**bevel** /'bev(ə)l/ ● *noun* slope from horizontal or vertical in carpentry etc.; sloping edge or surface; tool for marking angles. ● *verb* (**-ll-**; *US* **-l-**) impart bevel to, slant.

**beverage** /'bevərɪdʒ/ *noun formal* drink.

**bevvy** /'bevɪ/ *slang* ● *noun* (*plural* **-ies**) ● *verb* (**-ies**, **-ied**) drink.

**bevy** /'bevɪ/ *noun* (*plural* **-ies**) company, flock.

**bewail** /bɪ'weɪl/ *verb* wail over; mourn for.

**beware** /bɪ'weə/ *verb* (only in *imperative* or *infinitive*) take heed; (+ *of*) be cautious of.

**bewilder** /bɪ'wɪldə/ *verb* perplex, confuse. □ **bewilderment** *noun*.

**bewitch** /bɪ'wɪtʃ/ *verb* enchant, greatly delight; cast spell on.

**beyond** /bɪ'jɒnd/ ● *preposition* at or to further side of; outside the range or understanding of; more than. ● *adverb* at or to further side, further on. ● *noun*

**(the beyond)** life after death. □ **back of beyond** very remote place.

**bezel** /ˈbez(ə)l/ noun sloped edge of chisel etc.; oblique face of cut gem; groove holding watch-glass or gem.

**bezique** /brˈziːk/ noun card game for two.

**biannual** /barˈænjʊəl/ adjective occurring etc. twice a year.

**bias** /ˈbaɪəs/ ● noun predisposition, prejudice; distortion of statistical results; edge cut obliquely across weave of fabric; Sport bowl's curved course due to its lopsided form. ● verb (-s- or -ss-) give bias to; prejudice; (as **biased** adjective) influenced (usually unfairly). □ **bias binding** strip of fabric cut obliquely and used to bind edges.

**biathlon** /barˈæθlən/ noun athletic contest in skiing and shooting. □ **biathlete** noun.

**bib** noun cloth put under child's chin while eating; upper part of apron etc.

**Bible** /ˈbaɪb(ə)l/ noun Christian scriptures; (**bible**) copy of these; (**bible**) colloquial any authoritative book. □ **biblical** /ˈbɪb-/ adjective.

**bibliography** /bɪblɪˈɒɡrəfɪ/ noun (plural -ies) list of books of any author, subject, etc.; history of books, their editions, etc. □ **bibliographer** noun; **bibliographical** /-əˈɡræf-/ adjective.

**bibliophile** /ˈbɪblɪəfaɪl/ noun collector of books, book-lover.

**bibulous** /ˈbɪbjʊləs/ adjective fond of or addicted to alcoholic drink.

**bicameral** /barˈkæmər(ə)l/ adjective having two legislative chambers.

**bicarb** /ˈbaɪkɑːb/ noun colloquial bicarbonate of soda.

**bicarbonate** /barˈkɑːbənɪt/ noun any acid salt of carbonic acid; (in full **bicarbonate of soda**) compound used in cooking and as antacid.

**bicentenary** /baɪsenˈtiːnərɪ/ noun (plural -ies) 200th anniversary.

**bicentennial** /baɪsenˈtenɪəl/ ● noun bicentenary. ● adjective recurring every 200 years.

**biceps** /ˈbaɪseps/ noun (plural same) muscle with double head or attachment, esp. that at front of upper arm.

**bicker** /ˈbɪkə/ verb quarrel, wrangle pettily.

**bicuspid** /barˈkʌspɪd/ ● adjective having two cusps. ● noun bicuspid premolar tooth.

**bicycle** /ˈbaɪsɪk(ə)l/ ● noun two-wheeled pedal-driven vehicle. ● verb (-ling) ride bicycle.

**bid** ● verb (-dd-; past **bid**, archaic **bade** /bæd, beɪd/; past participle **bid**, archaic **bidden**) make offer; make bid; command, invite; literary utter (greeting, farewell) to; Cards state before play number of tricks intended. ● noun act of bidding; amount bid; colloquial attempt, effort.

**biddable** adjective obedient, docile.

**bidding** noun command, invitation.

**bide** verb (-ding) archaic or dialect stay, remain. □ **bide one's time** wait for good opportunity.

**bidet** /ˈbiːdeɪ/ noun low basin that one can sit astride to wash crotch area.

**biennial** /barˈenɪəl/ ● adjective lasting 2 years; recurring every 2 years. ● noun plant that flowers, fruits, and dies in second year.

**bier** /bɪə/ noun movable stand on which coffin or corpse rests.

**biff** slang ● noun smart blow. ● verb strike.

**bifid** /ˈbaɪfɪd/ adjective divided by cleft into two parts.

**bifocal** /barˈfəʊk(ə)l/ ● adjective (of spectacle lenses) with two parts of different focal lengths. ● noun (in plural) bifocal spectacles.

**bifurcate** /ˈbaɪfəkeɪt/ verb (-ting) divide into two branches; fork. □ **bifurcation** noun.

**big** ● adjective (-gg-) large; important; grown-up; boastful; colloquial ambitious, generous; (usually + with) advanced in pregnancy. ● adverb colloquial in big manner; with great effect, impressively. □ **Big Apple** US slang New York City; **Big Brother** seemingly benevolent dictator; **big business** large-scale commerce; **big end** end of connecting rod in engine, encircling crank-pin; **big-head** colloquial conceited person; **big-headed** conceited; **big-hearted** generous; **big shot** colloquial important person; **big time** slang highest rank among entertainers; **big top** main tent at circus; **bigwig** colloquial important person; **in a big way** colloquial with great enthusiasm. □ **biggish** adjective.

**bigamy** /ˈbɪgəmɪ/ *noun* (*plural* **-ies**) crime of making second marriage while first is still valid. □ **bigamist** *noun*; **bigamous** *adjective*.

**bight** /baɪt/ *noun* recess of coast, bay; loop of rope.

**bigot** /ˈbɪgət/ *noun* obstinate and intolerant adherent of creed or view. □ **bigoted** *adjective*; **bigotry** *noun*.

**bijou** /ˈbiːʒuː/ ● *noun* (*plural* **-x** same pronunciation) jewel, trinket. ● *adjective* (**bijou**) small and elegant. [French]

**bike** *colloquial* ● *noun* bicycle, motorcycle. ● *verb* (**-king**) ride a bike. □ **biker** *noun*.

**bikini** /bɪˈkiːnɪ/ *noun* (*plural* **-s**) woman's brief two-piece bathing suit.

**bilateral** /baɪˈlætər(ə)l/ *adjective* of, on, or with two sides; between two parties. □ **bilaterally** *adverb*.

**bilberry** /ˈbɪlbərɪ/ *noun* (*plural* **-ies**) N. European heathland shrub; its small dark blue edible berry.

**bile** *noun* bitter fluid secreted by liver to aid digestion; bad temper, peevishness.

**bilge** /bɪldʒ/ *noun* nearly flat part of ship's bottom; (in full **bilge-water**) foul water in bilge; *slang* nonsense, rubbish.

**bilharzia** /bɪlˈhɑːtsɪə/ *noun* disease caused by tropical parasitic flatworm.

**biliary** /ˈbɪlɪərɪ/ *adjective* of bile.

**bilingual** /baɪˈlɪŋgw(ə)l/ *adjective* of, in, or speaking two languages.

**bilious** /ˈbɪlɪəs/ *adjective* affected by disorder of the bile; bad-tempered.

**bilk** *verb slang* evade payment of, cheat.

**bill**[1] ● *noun* statement of charges for goods, work done, etc.; draft of proposed law; poster; programme of entertainment; *US* banknote. ● *verb* send statement of charges to; announce, put in programme; (+ *as*) advertise as. □ **bill of exchange** written order to pay sum on given date; **bill of fare** menu; **billposter**, **billsticker** person who pastes up advertisements on hoardings etc.

**bill**[2] ● *noun* beak (of bird); narrow promontory. ● *verb* (of doves etc.) stroke bill with bill. □ **bill and coo** exchange caresses.

**bill**[3] *noun historical* weapon with hook-shaped blade.

**billabong** /ˈbɪləbɒŋ/ *noun* Australian branch of river forming backwater.

**billboard** *noun* large outdoor board for advertisements.

**billet**[1] ● *noun* place where soldier etc. is lodged; *colloquial* appointment, job. ● *verb* (**-t-**) quarter (soldiers etc.).

**billet**[2] *noun* thick piece of firewood; small metal bar.

**billet-doux** /bɪlɪˈduː/ *noun* (*plural* **billets-doux** /-ˈduːz/) love letter.

**billhook** *noun* concave-edged pruning-instrument.

**billiards** /ˈbɪljədz/ *noun* game played with cues and 3 balls on cloth-covered table. □ **billiard ball**, **room**, **table**, etc., ones used for billiards.

**billion** /ˈbɪljən/ *noun* (*plural* same) thousand million; million million; (**billions**) *colloquial* very large number. □ **billionth** *adjective & noun*.

**billow** /ˈbɪləʊ/ ● *noun* wave; any large mass. ● *verb* rise or move in billows. □ **billowy** *adjective*.

**billy**[1] /ˈbɪlɪ/ *noun* (*plural* **-ies**) (in full **billycan**) *Australian* tin or enamel outdoor cooking pot.

**billy**[2] /ˈbɪlɪ/ *noun* (*plural* **-ies**) (in full **billy goat**) male goat.

**bin** *noun* large receptacle for rubbish or storage. □ **bin-liner** bag for lining rubbish bin; **binman** *colloquial* dustman.

**binary** /ˈbaɪnərɪ/ *adjective* of two parts, dual; of system using digits 0 and 1 to code information.

**bind** /baɪnd/ ● *verb* (*past & past participle* **bound** /baʊnd/) tie or fasten tightly; restrain; (cause to) cohere; compel, impose duty on; edge with braid etc.; fasten (pages of book) into cover. ● *noun colloquial* nuisance; restriction.

**binder** *noun* cover for loose papers; substance that binds things together; *historical* sheaf-binding machine; book-binder.

**bindery** *noun* (*plural* **-ies**) bookbinder's workshop.

**binding** ● *noun* book cover; braid etc. for edging. ● *adjective* obligatory.

**bindweed** *noun* convolvulus.

**binge** /bɪndʒ/ *slang* ● *noun* bout of excessive eating, drinking, etc.; spree. ● *verb* (**-ging**) indulge in binge.

**bingo** /ˈbɪŋɡəʊ/ *noun* gambling game in which each player marks off numbers on card as they are called.

**binnacle** /ˈbɪnək(ə)l/ *noun* case for ship's compass.

**binocular** /baɪˈnɒkjʊlə/ *adjective* for both eyes.

**binoculars** /bɪˈnɒkjʊləz/ *plural noun* instrument with lens for each eye, for viewing distant objects.

**binomial** /baɪˈnəʊmɪəl/ ● *noun* algebraic expression of sum or difference of two terms. ● *adjective* consisting of two terms.

**bio-** *combining form* biological; life.

**biochemistry** /baɪəʊˈkemɪstrɪ/ *noun* chemistry of living organisms. □ **biochemical** *adjective*; **biochemist** *noun*.

**biodegradable** /baɪəʊdɪˈɡreɪdəb(ə)l/ *adjective* able to be decomposed by bacteria or other living organisms.

**biography** /baɪˈɒɡrəfɪ/ *noun* (*plural* **-ies**) written life of person. □ **biographer** *noun*; **biographical** /-əˈɡræf-/ *adjective*.

**biological** /baɪəˈlɒdʒɪk(ə)l/ *adjective* of biology; of living organisms. □ **biological warfare** use of bacteria etc. to spread disease among enemy. □ **biologically** *adverb*.

**biology** /baɪˈɒlədʒɪ/ *noun* study of living organisms. □ **biologist** *noun*.

**bionic** /baɪˈɒnɪk/ *adjective* having electronically operated body parts.

**biorhythm** /ˈbaɪəʊrɪð(ə)m/ *noun* biological cycle thought to affect person's physical or mental state.

**biosphere** /ˈbaɪəʊsfɪə/ *noun* earth's crust and atmosphere containing life.

**bipartite** /baɪˈpɑːtaɪt/ *adjective* of two parts; involving two parties.

**biped** /ˈbaɪped/ ● *noun* two-footed animal. ● *adjective* two-footed.

**biplane** /ˈbaɪpleɪn/ *noun* aeroplane with two pairs of wings, one above the other.

**birch** ● *noun* tree with thin peeling bark; bundle of birch twigs used for flogging. ● *verb* flog with birch.

**bird** *noun* feathered vertebrate with two wings and two feet; *slang* young woman. □ **a bird in the hand** something secured or certain; **birdlime** sticky stuff spread to catch birds; **bird of passage** migratory bird, person who travels habitually; **bird of prey** one hunting animals for food; **birdseed** seeds as food for caged birds; **bird's-eye view** general view from above; **birds of a feather** similar people; **bird table** platform on which food for wild birds is placed.

**birdie** /ˈbɜːdɪ/ *noun colloquial* little bird; *Golf* hole played in one under par.

**biretta** /bɪˈretə/ *noun* square cap of RC priest.

**Biro** /ˈbaɪərəʊ/ *noun* (*plural* **-s**) *proprietary term* kind of ballpoint pen.

**birth** *noun* emergence of young from mother's body; origin, beginning; ancestry; inherited position. □ **birth control** prevention of undesired pregnancy; **birthday** anniversary of birth; **birthmark** unusual mark on body from birth; **birth rate** number of live births per thousand of population per year; **birthright** rights belonging to one by birth; **give birth to** produce (young).

**biscuit** /ˈbɪskɪt/ *noun* thin unleavened cake, usually crisp and sweet; fired unglazed pottery; light brown colour.

**bisect** /baɪˈsekt/ *verb* divide into two (usually equal) parts. □ **bisection** *noun*; **bisector** *noun*.

**bisexual** /baɪˈsekʃʊəl/ ● *adjective* feeling or involving sexual attraction to members of both sexes; hermaphrodite. ● *noun* bisexual person. □ **bisexuality** /-ˈæl-/ *noun*.

**bishop** /ˈbɪʃəp/ *noun* senior clergyman usually in charge of diocese; mitre-shaped chess piece.

**bishopric** /ˈbɪʃəprɪk/ *noun* office or diocese of bishop.

**bismuth** /ˈbɪzməθ/ *noun* reddish-white metallic element; compound of it used medicinally.

**bison** /ˈbaɪs(ə)n/ *noun* (*plural* same) wild ox.

**bisque**[1] /biːsk/ *noun* rich soup.

**bisque**[2] /bɪsk/ *noun* advantage of one free point or stroke in certain games.

**bisque**[3] /bɪsk/ *noun* fired unglazed pottery.

**bistre** /ˈbɪstə/ *noun* brown pigment made from soot.

**bistro** /ˈbiːstrəʊ/ *noun* (*plural* **-s**) small informal restaurant.

**bit**[1] *noun* small piece or amount; short time or distance; mouthpiece of bridle; cutting part of tool etc. □ **bit by bit** gradually.

**bit**[2] *past of* BITE.

**bit**[3] *noun Computing* unit of information expressed as choice between two possibilities.

**bitch** /bɪtʃ/ ● *noun* female dog, fox, or wolf; *offensive slang* spiteful woman. ● *verb colloquial* speak spitefully; grumble.

**bitchy** *adjective slang* spiteful. □ **bitchily** *adverb*; **bitchiness** *noun*.

**bite** ● *verb* (**-ting**; *past* **bit**; *past participle* **bitten**) nip or cut into or off with teeth; sting; penetrate, grip; accept bait; be harsh in effect, esp. intentionally. ● *noun* act of biting; wound so made; small amount to eat; pungency; incisiveness.

**bitter** /ˈbɪtə/ ● *adjective* having sharp pungent taste, not sweet; showing or feeling resentment; harsh, virulent; piercingly cold. ● *noun* bitter beer, strongly flavoured with hops; (in *plural*) liquor with bitter flavour, esp. of wormwood. □ **bitterly** *adverb*; **bitterness** *noun*.

**bittern** /ˈbɪt(ə)n/ *noun* wading bird of heron family.

**bitty** *adjective* (**-ier**, **-iest**) made up of bits.

**bitumen** /ˈbɪtjʊmɪn/ *noun* tarlike mixture of hydrocarbons derived from petroleum. □ **bituminous** /bɪˈtjuːmɪnəs/ *adjective*.

**bivalve** /ˈbaɪvælv/ ● *noun* aquatic mollusc with hinged double shell. ● *adjective* with such a shell.

**bivouac** /ˈbɪvʊæk/ ● *noun* temporary encampment without tents. ● *verb* (**-ck-**) make, or camp in, bivouac.

**bizarre** /bɪˈzɑː/ *adjective* strange in appearance or effect; grotesque.

**blab** *verb* (**-bb-**) talk or tell foolishly or indiscreetly.

**black** ● *adjective* colourless from absence or complete absorption of light; very dark-coloured; of human group with dark skin, esp. African; heavily overcast; angry, gloomy; sinister, wicked; declared untouchable by workers in dispute. ● *noun* black colour, paint, clothes, etc.; (player using) darker pieces in chess etc.; (of tea or coffee) without milk; member of dark-skinned race, esp. African. ● *verb* make black; declare (goods etc.) 'black'. □ **black and blue** badly bruised; **black and white** not in colour, comprising only opposite extremes, (after *in*) in print; **black art** black magic; **blackball** exclude from club, society, etc.; **black beetle** common cockroach; **black belt** (holder of) highest grade of proficiency in judo, karate, etc.; **black box** flight recorder; **black comedy** comedy presenting tragedy in comic terms; **black eye** bruised skin round eye; **blackfly** kind of aphid; **Black Forest gateau** chocolate sponge with cherries and whipped cream; **blackhead** black-topped pimple; **black hole** region of space from which matter and radiation cannot escape; **black ice** thin hard transparent ice; **blacklead** graphite; **blackleg** *derogatory* person refusing to join strike etc.; **black magic** magic supposed to invoke evil spirits; **Black Maria** *slang* police van; **black market** illicit traffic in rationed, prohibited, or scarce commodities; **Black Mass** travesty of Mass in worship of Satan; **black out** effect blackout on, undergo blackout; **blackout** temporary loss of consciousness or memory; loss of electric power, radio reception, etc.; compulsory darkness as precaution against air raids; **black pudding** sausage of blood, suet, etc.; **Black Rod** chief usher of House of Lords; **black sheep** disreputable member; **blackshirt** *historical* Fascist; **black spot** place of danger or trouble; **blackthorn** thorny shrub bearing white flowers and sloes; **black tie** man's formal evening dress; **black velvet** mixture of stout and champagne; **black widow** venomous spider of which female devours male; **in the black** in credit or surplus.

**blackberry** *noun* (*plural* **-ies**) dark edible fruit of bramble.

**blackbird** *noun* European songbird.

**blackboard** *noun* board for chalking on in classroom etc.

**blackcurrant** *noun* small black fruit; shrub on which it grows.

**blacken** *verb* make or become black; slander.

**blackguard** /'blægɑːd/ *noun* villain, scoundrel. □ **blackguardly** *adjective*.

**blacking** *noun* black polish for boots and shoes.

**blacklist** ● *noun* list of people etc. in disfavour. ● *verb* put on blacklist.

**blackmail** ● *noun* extortion of payment in return for silence; use of threats or pressure. ● *verb* extort money from thus. □ **blackmailer** *noun*.

**blacksmith** *noun* smith working in iron.

**bladder** /'blædə/ *noun* sac in humans and other animals, esp. that holding urine.

**blade** *noun* cutting part of knife etc.; flat part of oar, spade, propeller, etc.; flat narrow leaf of grass and cereals; flat bone in shoulder.

**blame** ● *verb* (**-ming**) assign fault or responsibility to; (+ *on*) assign responsibility for (error etc.) to. ● *noun* responsibility for bad result; blaming, attributing of responsibility. □ **blameworthy** deserving blame. □ **blameless** *adjective*.

**blanch** /blɑːntʃ/ *verb* make or grow pale; peel (almonds etc.) by scalding; immerse briefly in boiling water; whiten (plant) by depriving it of light.

**blancmange** /blə'mɒndʒ/ *noun* sweet opaque jelly of flavoured cornflour and milk.

**bland** *adjective* mild; insipid, tasteless; gentle, suave. □ **blandly** *adverb*.

**blandishment** /'blændɪʃmənt/ *noun* (usually in *plural*) flattering attention; cajolery.

**blank** ● *adjective* not written or printed on; (of form etc.) not filled in; (of space) empty; without interest, result, or expression. ● *noun* space to be filled up in form etc.; blank cartridge; empty surface; dash written in place of word. □ **blank cartridge** one without bullet; **blank cheque** one with amount left for payee to fill in; **blank verse** unrhymed verse, esp. iambic pentameters. □ **blankly** *adverb*.

**blanket** /'blæŋkɪt/ ● *noun* large esp. woollen sheet as bed-covering etc.; thick covering layer. ● *adjective* general, covering all cases or classes. ● *verb* (**-t-**) cover (as) with blanket. □ **blanket stitch** stitch used to finish edges of blanket etc.

**blare** ● *verb* (**-ring**) sound or utter loudly; make sound of trumpet. ● *noun* blaring sound.

**blarney** /'blɑːnɪ/ ● *noun* cajoling talk, flattery. ● *verb* (**-eys**, **-eyed**) flatter, use blarney.

**blasé** /'blɑːzeɪ/ *adjective* bored or indifferent, esp. through familiarity.

**blaspheme** /blæs'fiːm/ *verb* (**-ming**) treat religious name or subject irreverently; talk irreverently about.

**blasphemy** /'blæsfəmɪ/ *noun* (*plural* **-ies**) (instance of) blaspheming. □ **blasphemous** *adjective*.

**blast** /blɑːst/ ● *noun* strong gust; explosion; destructive wave of air from this; loud note from wind instrument, car horn, whistle, etc.; *colloquial* severe reprimand. ● *verb* blow up with explosive; blight; (cause to) make explosive sound. ● *interjection* damn. □ **blast furnace** one for smelting with compressed hot air driven in; **blast off** (of rocket) take off from launching site; **blast-off** *noun*.

**blasted** *colloquial* ● *adjective* annoying. ● *adverb* extremely.

**blatant** /'bleɪt(ə)nt/ *adjective* flagrant, unashamed. □ **blatantly** *adverb*.

**blather** /'blæðə/ ● *noun* (also **blether** /'bleðə/) foolish talk. ● *verb* talk foolishly.

**blaze**[1] ● *noun* bright flame or fire; violent outburst of passion; bright display or light. ● *verb* (**-zing**) burn or shine brightly or fiercely; burn with excitement etc. □ **blaze away** shoot continuously.

**blaze**[2] ● *noun* white mark on face of horse or chipped in bark of tree. ● *verb* (**-zing**) mark (tree, path) with blaze(s).

**blazer** *noun* jacket without matching trousers, esp. lightweight and part of uniform.

**blazon** /'bleɪz(ə)n/ *verb* proclaim; describe or paint (coat of arms). □ **blazonry** *noun*.

**bleach** ● *verb* whiten in sunlight or by chemical process. ● *noun* bleaching substance or process.

**bleak** *adjective* exposed, windswept; dreary, grim.

**bleary** /'blɪərɪ/ *adjective* (**-ier**, **-iest**) dim-sighted, blurred. □ **bleary-eyed** having dim sight.

**bleat** ● *verb* utter cry of sheep, goat, etc.; speak plaintively. ● *noun* bleating cry.

**bleed** *verb* (*past & past participle* **bled**) emit blood; draw blood from; *colloquial* extort money from.

**bleep** ● *noun* intermittent high-pitched sound. ● *verb* make bleep; summon by bleep.

**bleeper** *noun* small electronic device alerting person to message by bleeping.

**blemish** /'blemɪʃ/ ● *noun* flaw, defect, stain. ● *verb* spoil, mark, stain.

**blench** *verb* flinch, quail.

**blend** ● *verb* mix (various sorts) into required sort; become one; mingle intimately. ● *noun* mixture.

**blender** *noun* machine for liquidizing or chopping food.

**blenny** /'blenɪ/ *noun* (*plural* **-ies**) spiny-finned sea fish.

**bless** *verb* ask God to look favourably on; consecrate; glorify (God); thank; make happy.

**blessed** /'blesɪd/ *adjective* holy; *euphemistic* cursed; *RC Church* beatified.

**blessing** *noun* invocation of divine favour; grace said at meals; benefit, advantage.

**blether** = BLATHER.

**blew** *past* of BLOW[1].

**blight** /blaɪt/ ● *noun* disease of plants caused esp. by insects; such insect; harmful or destructive force. ● *verb* affect with blight; destroy; spoil.

**blighter** *noun colloquial* annoying person.

**blimey** /'blaɪmɪ/ *interjection slang*: expressing surprise.

**blimp** *noun* small non-rigid airship; (also (**Colonel**) **Blimp**) reactionary person.

**blind** /blaɪnd/ ● *adjective* without sight; without adequate foresight, discernment, or information; (often + *to*) unwilling or unable to appreciate (a factor); not governed by purpose; reckless; concealed; closed at one end. ● *verb* deprive of sight or judgement; deceive. ● *noun* screen for window; thing used to hide truth; obstruction to sight or light. ● *adverb* blindly. □ **blind date** *colloquial* date between two people who have not met before; **blind man's buff** game in which blindfold player tries to catch others; **blind spot** spot on retina insensitive to light, area where vision or judgement fails; **blindworm** slow-worm. □ **blindly** *adverb*; **blindness** *noun*.

**blindfold** ● *verb* cover eyes of (person) with tied cloth etc. ● *noun* cloth etc. so used. ● *adjective & adverb* with eyes covered; without due care.

**blink** ● *verb* shut and open eyes quickly; (often + *back*) prevent (tears) by blinking; shine unsteadily, flicker. ● *noun* act of blinking; momentary gleam. □ **blink at** ignore, shirk; **on the blink** *slang* (of machine etc.) out of order.

**blinker** ● *noun* (usually in *plural*) either of screens on bridle preventing horse from seeing sideways. ● *verb* obscure with blinkers; (as **blinkered** *adjective*) prejudiced, narrow-minded.

**blinking** *adjective & adverb slang*: expressing mild annoyance.

**blip** *noun* minor deviation or error; quick popping sound; small image on radar screen.

**bliss** *noun* perfect joy; being in heaven. □ **blissful** *adjective*; **blissfully** *adverb*.

**blister** /'blɪstə/ ● *noun* small bubble on skin filled with watery fluid; any swelling resembling this. ● *verb* become covered with blisters; raise blister on.

**blithe** /blaɪð/ *adjective* cheerful, happy; carefree, casual. □ **blithely** *adverb*.

**blithering** /'blɪðərɪŋ/ *adjective colloquial* utter, hopeless; contemptible.

**blitz** /blɪts/ *colloquial* ● *noun* intensive (esp. aerial) attack. ● *verb* inflict blitz on.

**blizzard** /'blɪzəd/ *noun* severe snow-storm.

**bloat** *verb* inflate, swell.

**bloater** *noun* herring cured by salting and smoking.

**blob** *noun* small drop or spot.

**bloc** *noun* group of governments etc. sharing some common purpose.

**block** ● *noun* solid piece of hard material; large building, esp. when subdivided; group of buildings surrounded by streets; obstruction; large quantity as a unit; piece of wood or metal engraved for printing. ● *verb* obstruct; restrict use of; stop (cricket ball) with bat.

☐ **blockbuster** *slang* very successful film, book, etc.; **blockhead** stupid person; **block capitals**, **letters** separate capital letters; **block out** shut out (light, noise, view, etc.); **block up** shut in, fill (window etc.) in; **block vote** vote proportional in size to number of people voter represents; **mental block** mental inability due to subconscious factors.

**blockade** /blɒˈkeɪd/ ● *noun* surrounding or blocking of place by enemy. ● *verb* (**-ding**) subject to blockade.

**blockage** *noun* obstruction.

**bloke** *noun slang* man, fellow.

**blond** (of woman, usually **blonde**) ● *adjective* light-coloured, fair-haired. ● *noun* blond person.

**blood** /blʌd/ ● *noun* fluid, usually red, circulating in arteries and veins of animals; killing, bloodshed; passion, temperament; race, descent; relationship. ● *verb* give first taste of blood to (hound); initiate (person). ☐ **blood bank** store of blood for transfusion; **bloodbath** massacre; **blood count** number of corpuscles in blood; **blood-curdling** horrifying; **blood donor** giver of blood for transfusion; **blood group** any of types of human blood; **bloodhound** large keen-scented dog used for tracking; **bloodletting** surgical removal of blood; **blood orange** red-fleshed orange; **blood poisoning** diseased condition due to bacteria in blood; **blood pressure** pressure of blood in arteries; **blood relation** one related by birth; **bloodshed** killing; **bloodshot** (of eyeball) inflamed; **blood sport** one involving killing of animals; **bloodstream** circulating blood; **bloodsucker** leech, extortioner; **bloodthirsty** eager for bloodshed; **blood vessel** vein, artery, or capillary carrying blood.

**bloodless** *adjective* without blood or bloodshed; unemotional; pale.

**bloody** ● *adjective* (**-ier**, **-iest**) of or like blood; running or stained with blood; involving bloodshed, cruel; *coarse slang* annoying, very great. ● *adverb coarse slang* extremely. ● *verb* (**-ies**, **-ied**) stain with blood. ☐ **bloody-minded** *colloquial* deliberately uncooperative.

**bloom** /bluːm/ ● *noun* flower; flowering state; prime; freshness; fine powder on

fruit etc. ● *verb* bear flowers; be in flower; flourish.

**bloomer**[1] *noun slang* blunder.

**bloomer**[2] *noun* long loaf with diagonal marks.

**bloomers** *plural noun colloquial* woman's long loose knickers.

**blooming** ● *adjective* flourishing, healthy; *slang* annoying, very great. ● *adverb slang* extremely.

**blossom** /ˈblɒsəm/ ● *noun* flower; mass of flowers on tree. ● *verb* open into flower; flourish.

**blot** ● *noun* spot of ink etc.; disgraceful act; blemish. ● *verb* (**-tt-**) make blot on; stain; dry with blotting paper. ☐ **blot out** obliterate, obscure; **blotting paper** absorbent paper for drying wet ink.

**blotch** *noun* inflamed patch on skin; irregular patch of colour. ☐ **blotchy** *adjective* (**-ier**, **-iest**).

**blotter** *noun* device holding blotting paper.

**blouse** /blaʊz/ *noun* woman's shirtlike garment; type of military jacket.

**blow**[1] /bləʊ/ ● *verb* (*past* **blew** /bluː/; *past participle* **blown**) send directed air-current esp. from mouth; drive or be driven by blowing; move as wind does; sound (wind instrument); (*past participle* **blowed**) *slang* curse, confound; clear (nose) by forceful breath; pant; make or shape by blowing; break or burst suddenly; (cause to) break electric circuit; *slang* squander. ● *noun* blowing; short spell in fresh air. ☐ **blow-dry** arrange (hair) while drying it; **blowfly** bluebottle; **blow in** send inwards by explosion, *colloquial* arrive unexpectedly; **blowlamp** device with flame for plumbing, burning off paint, etc.; **blow out** extinguish by blowing, send outwards by explosion; **blow-out** *colloquial* burst tyre, *slang* large meal; **blow over** fade away; **blowpipe** tube for blowing through, esp. one from which dart or arrow is projected; **blowtorch** *US* blowlamp; **blow up** explode, *colloquial* rebuke strongly, inflate, *colloquial* enlarge (photograph); **blow-up** *colloquial* enlargement of photograph.

**blow**[2] /bləʊ/ *noun* hard stroke with hand or weapon; disaster, shock.

**blower** /'bləʊə/ *noun* device for blowing; *colloquial* telephone.

**blowy** /'bləʊɪ/ *adjective* (**-ier, -iest**) windy.

**blowzy** /'blaʊzɪ/ *adjective* (**-ier, -iest**) coarse-looking, red-faced; dishevelled.

**blub** *verb* (**-bb-**) *slang* sob.

**blubber** /'blʌbə/ ● *noun* whale fat. ● *verb* sob noisily. □ **blubbery** *adjective*.

**bludgeon** /'blʌdʒ(ə)n/ ● *noun* heavy club. ● *verb* beat with bludgeon; coerce.

**blue** /bluː/ ● *adjective* (**-r, -st**) coloured like clear sky; sad, depressed; pornographic. ● *noun* blue colour, paint, clothes, etc.; person who represents Oxford or Cambridge University at sport; (in *plural*) type of melancholy music of American black origin, (**the blues**) depression. ● *verb* (**blues, blued, bluing** or **blueing**) *slang* squander. □ **blue baby** one with congenital heart defect; **bluebell** woodland plant with bell-shaped blue flowers; **blueberry** small edible blue or blackish fruit of various plants; **blue blood** noble birth; **bluebottle** large buzzing fly; **blue cheese** cheese with veins of blue mould; **blue-collar** manual, industrial; **blue-eyed boy** *colloquial* favourite; **bluegrass** type of country and western music; **Blue Peter** blue flag with central white square hoisted before sailing; **blueprint** photographic print of building plans etc. in white on blue paper, detailed plan; **bluestocking** *usually derogatory* intellectual woman; **blue tit** small blue and yellow bird; **blue whale** rorqual (largest known living mammal).

**bluff**[1] ● *verb* pretend to have strength, knowledge, etc. ● *noun* bluffing.

**bluff**[2] ● *adjective* blunt, frank, hearty; with steep or vertical broad front. ● *noun* bluff headland.

**blunder** /'blʌndə/ ● *noun* serious or foolish mistake. ● *verb* make blunder; move about clumsily.

**blunderbuss** /'blʌndəbʌs/ *noun historical* short large-bored gun.

**blunt** ● *adjective* without sharp edge or point; plain-spoken. ● *verb* make blunt. □ **bluntly** *adverb*; **bluntness** *noun*.

**blur** ● *verb* (**-rr-**) make or become less distinct; smear. ● *noun* indistinct object, sound, memory, etc.

**blurb** *noun* promotional description, esp. of book.

**blurt** *verb* (usually + *out*) utter abruptly or tactlessly.

**blush** ● *verb* be or become red (as) with shame or embarrassment; be ashamed. ● *noun* blushing; pink tinge.

**blusher** *noun* coloured cosmetic for cheeks.

**bluster** /'blʌstə/ ● *verb* behave pompously; storm boisterously. ● *noun* noisy pompous talk, empty threats. □ **blustery** *adjective*.

**BMA** *abbreviation* British Medical Association.

**BMX** *noun* organized bicycle racing on dirt track; bicycle used for this.

**BO** *abbreviation colloquial* body odour.

**boa** /'bəʊə/ *noun* large snake that kills its prey by crushing it; long stole of fur or feathers. □ **boa constrictor** species of boa.

**boar** *noun* male wild pig; uncastrated male pig.

**board** ● *noun* thin piece of sawn timber; material resembling this; slab of wood etc., e.g. ironing board, notice board; thick stiff card; provision of meals; directors of company; committee; (**the boards**) stage. ● *verb* go on board (ship etc.); receive, or provide with, meals and usually lodging; (usually + *up*) cover with boards. □ **board game** game played on a board; **boarding house** unlicensed house providing board and lodging; **boarding school** one in which pupils live in term-time; **boardroom** room where board of directors meets; **on board** on or into ship, train, aircraft, etc.

**boarder** *noun* person who boards, esp. at boarding school.

**boast** ● *verb* declare one's achievements etc. with excessive pride; have (desirable thing). ● *noun* boasting; thing one is proud of. □ **boastful** *adjective*.

**boat** ● *noun* small vessel propelled by oars, sails, or engine; ship; long jug for sauce etc. ● *verb* go in boat, esp. for pleasure. □ **boat-hook** long pole with hook for moving boats; **boathouse** shed at water's edge for boats; **boatman** person who hires out or provides transport by boats; **boat people**

**boater | boloney**

refugees travelling by sea; **boat-train** train scheduled to connect with ship.

**boater** noun flat straw hat with straight brim.

**boatswain** /'bəʊs(ə)n/ noun (also **bo-sun**) ship's officer in charge of equipment and crew.

**bob**[1] ● verb (**-bb-**) move up and down; rebound; cut (hair) in bob; curtsy. ● noun bobbing movement; curtsy; hairstyle with hair hanging evenly above shoulders; weight on pendulum etc. □ **bobtail** docked tail, horse or dog with this.

**bob**[2] noun (plural same) historical slang shilling (= 5p).

**bobbin** /'bɒbɪn/ noun spool or reel for thread etc.

**bobble** /'bɒb(ə)l/ noun small woolly ball on hat etc.

**bobby** /'bɒbɪ/ noun (plural **-ies**) colloquial police officer.

**bobsled** noun US bobsleigh.

**bobsleigh** noun racing sledge steered and braked mechanically.

**bod** noun colloquial person.

**bode** verb (**-ding**) □ **bode well, ill** be good or bad sign.

**bodge** /bɒdʒ/ = BOTCH.

**bodice** /'bɒdɪs/ noun part of woman's dress above waist.

**bodily** /'bɒdɪlɪ/ ● adjective of the body. ● adverb as a whole (body); in person.

**bodkin** /'bɒdkɪn/ noun blunt thick needle for drawing tape etc. through hem.

**body** /'bɒdɪ/ noun (plural **-ies**) physical structure of person or animal, alive or dead; person's or animal's trunk; main part; group of people regarded as unit; quantity, mass; piece of matter; colloquial person; full or substantial quality of flavour etc.; body stocking. □ **body-building** exercises to enlarge and strengthen muscles; **bodyguard** escort or personal guard; **body politic** state, nation; **body shop** workshop where bodywork is repaired; **body stocking** woman's undergarment covering trunk; **bodywork** outer shell of vehicle.

**Boer** /'bɔː/ noun S. African of Dutch descent.

**boffin** /'bɒfɪn/ noun colloquial research scientist.

**bog** noun (area of) wet spongy ground; slang lavatory. □ **bogged down** unable to move or make progress. □ **boggy** adjective (**-ier, -iest**).

**bogey**[1] /'bəʊgɪ/ noun (plural **-s**) Golf score of one more than par for hole; (formerly) par.

**bogey**[2] /'bəʊgɪ/ noun (also **bogy**) (plural **-eys** or **-ies**) evil or mischievous spirit; awkward thing.

**boggle** /'bɒg(ə)l/ verb (**-ling**) colloquial be startled or baffled.

**bogie** /'bəʊgɪ/ noun wheeled undercarriage below locomotive etc.

**bogus** /'bəʊgəs/ adjective sham, spurious.

**bogy** = BOGEY[2].

**Bohemian** /bəʊ'hiːmɪən/ ● noun native of Bohemia; (also **bohemian**) unconventional person, esp. artist or writer. ● adjective of Bohemia; (also **bohemian**) socially unconventional. □ **bohemianism** noun.

**boil**[1] ● verb (of liquid or its vessel) bubble up with heat, reach temperature at which liquid turns to vapour; bring to boiling point; subject to heat of boiling water, cook thus; be agitated like boiling water. ● noun boiling; boiling point. □ **boiling (hot)** colloquial very hot; **boiling point** temperature at which a liquid boils; **boil over** spill over in boiling.

**boil**[2] noun inflamed pus-filled swelling under skin.

**boiler** noun apparatus for heating hot-water supply; tank for heating water or turning it into steam; vessel for boiling things in. □ **boiler suit** protective garment combining trousers and shirt.

**boisterous** /'bɔɪstərəs/ adjective noisily cheerful; violent, rough.

**bold** /bəʊld/ adjective confident; adventurous; courageous; impudent; distinct, vivid. □ **boldly** adverb; **boldness** noun.

**bole** noun trunk of tree.

**bolero** noun (plural **-s**) /bə'leərəʊ/ Spanish dance; /'bɒlərəʊ/ woman's short jacket without fastenings.

**boll** /bəʊl/ noun round seed vessel of cotton, flax, etc.

**bollard** /'bɒlɑːd/ noun short thick post in street etc.; post on ship or quay for securing ropes to.

**boloney** /bə'ləʊnɪ/ noun slang nonsense.

**bolshie** /'bɒlʃɪ/ adjective (**-r, -st**) (also **Bolshie**) slang rebellious, uncooperative.

**bolster** /'bəʊlstə/ ● noun long cylindrical pillow. ● verb (usually + up) encourage, support, prop up.

**bolt**[1] /bəʊlt/ ● noun door-fastening of metal bar and socket; headed metal pin secured with rivet or nut; discharge of lightning; bolting. ● verb fasten with bolt; (+ in, out) keep in or out by bolting door; dart off, run away; (of horse) escape from control; gulp down unchewed; run to seed. □ **bolt-hole** means of escape; **bolt upright** erect.

**bolt**[2] /bəʊlt/ verb (also **boult**) sift.

**bomb** /bɒm/ ● noun container filled with explosive, incendiary material, etc., designed to explode and cause damage; (**the bomb**) the atomic bomb; slang large amount of money. ● verb attack with bombs; drop bombs on; colloquial travel fast. □ **bombshell** great surprise or disappointment.

**bombard** /bɒm'bɑːd/ verb attack with heavy guns etc.; question or abuse persistently; subject to stream of high-speed particles. □ **bombardment** noun.

**bombardier** /bɒmbə'dɪə/ noun artillery NCO below sergeant; US airman who releases bombs from aircraft.

**bombast** /'bɒmbæst/ noun pompous or extravagant language. □ **bombastic** /-'bæs-/ adjective.

**Bombay duck** /'bɒmbeɪ/ noun dried fish eaten as relish, esp. with curry.

**bomber** noun aircraft equipped for bombing; person who throws or plants bomb. □ **bomber jacket** one gathered at waist and cuffs.

**bona fide** /bəʊnə 'faɪdɪ/ adjective & adverb in good faith, genuine(ly).

**bonanza** /bə'nænzə/ noun source of great wealth; large output, esp. from mine.

**bon-bon** noun sweet.

**bond** ● noun thing or force that unites or (usually in plural) restrains; binding agreement; certificate issued by government or company promising to repay money at fixed rate of interest; adhesiveness; document binding person to pay or repay money; linkage of atoms in molecule. ● verb bind or connect together; put in bond. □ **bond**

**paper** high-quality writing paper; **in bond** stored by Customs until duty is paid.

**bondage** /'bɒndɪdʒ/ noun slavery; subjection to constraint.

**bondsman** /'bɒndzmən/ noun serf, slave.

**bone** ● noun any of separate parts of vertebrate skeleton; (in plural) skeleton, esp. as remains; substance of which bones consist. ● verb (**-ning**) remove bones from. □ **bone china** fine semi-translucent earthenware; **bone dry** completely dry; **bone idle** completely idle; **bone marrow** fatty substance in cavity of bones; **bonemeal** crushed bone as fertilizer; **boneshaker** jolting vehicle.

**bonfire** noun open-air fire.

**bongo** /'bɒŋgəʊ/ noun (plural **-s** or **-es**) either of pair of small drums played with fingers.

**bonhomie** /bɒnɒ'miː/ noun geniality.

**bonkers** /'bɒŋkəz/ adjective slang crazy.

**bonnet** /'bɒnɪt/ noun woman's or child's hat tied under chin; Scotsman's floppy beret; hinged cover over engine of vehicle.

**bonny** /'bɒnɪ/ adjective (**-ier, -iest**) esp. Scottish & Northern English healthy-looking, attractive.

**bonsai** /'bɒnsaɪ/ noun (plural same) dwarfed tree or shrub; art of growing these.

**bonus** /'bəʊnəs/ noun extra benefit or payment.

**bon voyage** /bɔ̃ vwaː'jɑːʒ/ interjection have a good trip. [French]

**bony** /'bəʊnɪ/ adjective (**-ier, -iest**) thin with prominent bones; having many bones; of or like bone.

**boo** ● interjection expressing disapproval or contempt; sound intended to surprise. ● noun utterance of 'boo'. ● verb (**boos, booed**) utter boos (at).

**boob** ● noun colloquial silly mistake; slang woman's breast. ● verb colloquial make mistake.

**booby** /'buːbɪ/ noun (plural **-ies**) silly or awkward person. □ **booby prize** prize for coming last; **booby trap** practical joke in form of trap, disguised bomb etc. triggered by unknowing victim.

**book** /bʊk/ ● *noun* written or printed work with pages bound along one side; work intended for publication; bound set of tickets, stamps, matches, cheques, etc.; (in *plural*) set of records or accounts; main division of literary work or Bible; telephone directory; *colloquial* magazine; libretto; record of bets made. ● *verb* reserve (seat etc.) in advance; engage (entertainer etc.); take personal details of (offender); enter in book or list. □ **bookcase** cabinet of shelves for books; **bookend** prop to keep books upright; **bookkeeper** person who keeps accounts; **bookmaker** professional taker of bets; **bookmark** thing for marking place in book; **bookplate** decorative personalized label in book; **book token** voucher exchangeable for books; **bookworm** *colloquial* devoted reader, larva that eats through books.

**bookie** /ˈbʊkɪ/ *noun colloquial* bookmaker.

**bookish** *adjective* fond of reading; getting knowledge mainly from books.

**booklet** /ˈbʊklɪt/ *noun* small usually paper-covered book.

**boom**[1] /buːm/ ● *noun* deep resonant sound. ● *verb* make or speak with boom.

**boom**[2] /buːm/ ● *noun* period of economic prosperity or activity. ● *verb* be suddenly prosperous.

**boom**[3] /buːm/ *noun* pivoted spar to which sail is attached; long pole carrying camera, microphone, etc.; barrier across harbour etc.

**boomerang** /ˈbuːməræŋ/ ● *noun* flat V-shaped Australian hardwood missile returning to thrower. ● *verb* (of plan) backfire.

**boon**[1] /buːn/ *noun* advantage; blessing.

**boon**[2] /buːn/ *adjective* intimate, favourite.

**boor** /bʊə/ *noun* ill-mannered person. □ **boorish** *adjective*.

**boost** /buːst/ *colloquial* ● *verb* promote, encourage; increase, assist; push from below. ● *noun* boosting.

**booster** *noun* device for increasing power or voltage; auxiliary engine or rocket for initial speed; dose renewing effect of earlier one.

**boot** /buːt/ ● *noun* outer foot-covering reaching above ankle; luggage compartment of car; *colloquial* firm kick,

dismissal. ● *verb* kick; (often + *out*) eject forcefully; (usually + *up*) make (computer) ready.

**bootee** /buːˈtiː/ *noun* baby's soft shoe.

**booth** /buːð/ *noun* temporary structure used esp. as market stall; enclosure for telephoning, voting, etc.

**bootleg** /ˈbuːtleg/ ● *adjective* smuggled, illicit. ● *verb* (**-gg-**) illicitly make or deal in. □ **bootlegger** *noun*.

**bootstrap** /ˈbuːtstræp/ *noun* □ **pull oneself up by one's bootstraps** better oneself by one's unaided effort.

**booty** /ˈbuːtɪ/ *noun* loot, spoils; *colloquial* prize.

**booze** *colloquial* ● *noun* alcoholic drink. ● *verb* (**-zing**) drink alcohol, esp. excessively. □ **boozy** *adjective* (**-ier, -iest**).

**boozer** *noun colloquial* habitual drinker; public house.

**bop** *colloquial* ● *noun* spell of dancing, esp. to pop music; *colloquial* hit, blow. ● *verb* (**-pp-**) dance, esp. to pop music; *colloquial* hit.

**boracic** /bəˈræsɪk/ *adjective* of borax. □ **boracic acid** boric acid.

**borage** /ˈbɒrɪdʒ/ *noun* plant with leaves used as flavouring.

**borax** /ˈbɔːræks/ *noun* salt of boric acid used as antiseptic.

**border** /ˈbɔːdə/ ● *noun* edge, boundary, or part near it; line or region separating countries; distinct edging, esp. ornamental strip; long narrow flower-bed. ● *verb* put or be border to; adjoin. □ **borderline** *noun* line marking boundary or dividing two conditions, *adjective* on borderline.

**bore**[1] ● *verb* (**-ring**) make (hole), esp. with revolving tool; make hole in. ● *noun* hollow of firearm barrel or cylinder; diameter of this; deep hole made to find water etc.

**bore**[2] ● *noun* tiresome or dull person or thing. ● *verb* (**-ring**) weary by tedious talk or dullness. □ **bored** *adjective*; **boring** *adjective*.

**bore**[3] *noun* very high tidal wave rushing up estuary.

**bore**[4] *past of* BEAR[1].

**boredom** *noun* being bored (BORE[2]).

**boric acid** /ˈbɔːrɪk/ *noun* acid used as antiseptic.

**born** *adjective* existing as a result of birth; being (specified thing) by nature; (usually + *to do*) destined.

**borne** *past participle of* BEAR[1].

**boron** /ˈbɔːrɒn/ *noun* non-metallic element.

**borough** /ˈbʌrə/ *noun* administrative area, esp. of Greater London; *historical* town with municipal corporation.

**borrow** /ˈbɒrəʊ/ *verb* get temporary use of (something to be returned); use another's (invention, idea, etc.). □ **borrower** *noun.*

**Borstal** /ˈbɔːst(ə)l/ *noun historical* residential institution for youth custody.

**bosom** /ˈbʊz(ə)m/ *noun* person's breasts; *colloquial* each of woman's breasts; enclosure formed by breast and arms; emotional centre. □ **bosom friend** intimate friend.

**boss**[1] *colloquial* ● *noun* employer, manager, or supervisor. ● *verb* (usually + *about, around*) give orders to.

**boss**[2] *noun* round knob or stud.

**boss-eyed** *adjective colloquial* cross-eyed; crooked.

**bossy** *adjective* (**-ier, -iest**) *colloquial* domineering. □ **bossiness** *noun.*

**bosun** = BOATSWAIN.

**botany** /ˈbɒtənɪ/ *noun* study of plants. □ **botanic(al)** /bəˈtæn-/ *adjective;* **botanist** *noun.*

**botch** ● *verb* bungle; patch clumsily. ● *noun* bungled or spoilt work.

**both** /bəʊθ/ ● *adjective & pronoun* the two (not only one). ● *adverb* with equal truth in two cases.

**bother** /ˈbɒðə/ ● *verb* trouble, worry; take trouble. ● *noun* person or thing that bothers; nuisance; trouble, worry. ● *interjection of irritation.* □ **bothersome** /-səm/ *adjective.*

**bottle** /ˈbɒt(ə)l/ ● *noun* container, esp. glass or plastic, for storing liquid; liquid in bottle; *slang* courage. ● *verb* (**-ling**) put into bottles; preserve (fruit etc.) in jars; (+ *up*) restrain (feelings etc.). □ **bottle bank** place for depositing bottles for recycling; **bottle green** dark green; **bottleneck** narrow congested area esp. on road etc., thing that impedes; **bottle party** one to which guests bring bottles of drink.

**bottom** /ˈbɒtəm/ ● *noun* lowest point or part; buttocks; less honourable end of table, class, etc.; ground under water; basis; essential character. ● *adjective* lowest, last. ● *verb* (usually + *out*) reach its lowest level; find extent of; touch bottom (of). □ **bottom line** *colloquial* underlying truth, ultimate criterion.

**bottomless** *adjective* without bottom; inexhaustible.

**botulism** /ˈbɒtjʊlɪz(ə)m/ *noun* poisoning caused by bacillus in badly preserved food.

**boudoir** /ˈbuːdwɑː/ *noun* woman's private room.

**bougainvillaea** /buːgənˈvɪlɪə/ *noun* tropical plant with large coloured bracts.

**bough** /baʊ/ *noun* branch of tree.

**bought** *past & past participle of* BUY.

**bouillon** /ˈbuːjɒn/ *noun* clear broth.

**boulder** /ˈbəʊldə/ *noun* large smooth rock.

**boulevard** /ˈbuːləvɑːd/ *noun* broad tree-lined street.

**boult** = BOLT[2].

**bounce** /baʊns/ ● *verb* (**-cing**) (cause to) rebound; *slang* (of cheque) be returned to payee by bank when there are no funds to meet it; rush boisterously. ● *noun* rebound; *colloquial* swagger, self-confidence; *colloquial* liveliness. □ **bouncy** *adjective* (**-ier, -iest**).

**bouncer** *noun slang* doorman ejecting troublemakers from nightclub etc.

**bouncing** *adjective* big and healthy.

**bound**[1] /baʊnd/ ● *verb* spring, leap; (of ball etc.) bounce. ● *noun* springy leap; bounce.

**bound**[2] /baʊnd/ ● *noun* (usually in *plural*) limitation, restriction; border, boundary. ● *verb* limit; be boundary of. □ **out of bounds** outside permitted area.

**bound**[3] /baʊnd/ *adjective* (usually + *for*) starting or having started.

**bound**[4] /baʊnd/ *past & past participle of* BIND. □ **bound to** certain to; **bound up with** closely associated with.

**boundary** /ˈbaʊndərɪ/ *noun* (*plural* **-ies**) line marking limits; *Cricket* hit crossing limit of field, runs scored for this.

**boundless** *adjective* unlimited.

**bounteous** /ˈbaʊntɪəs/ *adjective poetical* bountiful.

**bountiful** /ˈbaʊntɪfʊl/ *adjective* generous; ample.

**bounty** /ˈbʊntɪ/ *noun* (*plural* **-ies**) generosity; official reward; gift.

**bouquet** /buːˈkeɪ/ *noun* bunch of flowers; scent of wine; compliment. □ **bouquet garni** (/ˈgɑːnɪ/) bunch or bag of herbs for flavouring.

**bourbon** /ˈbɜːbən/ *noun US* whisky from maize and rye.

**bourgeois** /ˈbʊəʒwɑː/ *often derogatory* ● *adjective* conventionally middle-class; materialist; capitalist. ● *noun* (*plural* same) bourgeois person.

**bourgeoisie** /ˌbʊəʒwɑːˈziː/ *noun* bourgeois class.

**bourn** /bɔːn/ *noun* stream.

**bourse** /bʊəs/ *noun* money market, esp. (**Bourse**) Stock Exchange in Paris.

**bout** *noun* spell of work etc.; fit of illness; wrestling or boxing match.

**boutique** /buːˈtiːk/ *noun* small shop selling fashionable clothes etc.

**bouzouki** /buːˈzuːkɪ/ *noun* (*plural* **-s**) form of Greek mandolin.

**bovine** /ˈbəʊvaɪn/ *adjective* of cattle; dull, stupid.

**bow¹** /bəʊ/ ● *noun* weapon for shooting arrows; rod with horsehair stretched from end to end for playing violin etc.; knot with two loops, ribbon etc. so tied; shallow curve or bend. ● *verb* use bow on (violin etc.). □ **bow-legged** having bandy legs; **bow tie** necktie in form of bow; **bow window** curved bay window.

**bow²** /baʊ/ ● *verb* incline head or body, esp. in greeting or acknowledgement; submit; incline (head etc.). ● *noun* bowing.

**bow³** /baʊ/ *noun* (often in *plural*) front end of boat or ship; rower nearest bow.

**bowdlerize** /ˈbaʊdləraɪz/ *verb* (also **-ise**) (**-zing** or **-sing**) expurgate. □ **bowdlerization** *noun*.

**bowel** /ˈbaʊəl/ *noun* (often in *plural*) intestine; (in *plural*) innermost parts.

**bower** /ˈbaʊə/ *noun* arbour; summer house. □ **bowerbird** Australasian bird, the male of which constructs elaborate runs.

**bowie knife** /ˈbəʊɪ/ *noun* long hunting knife.

**bowl¹** /bəʊl/ *noun* dish, esp. for food or liquid; hollow part of tobacco pipe, spoon, etc.

**bowl²** /bəʊl/ ● *noun* hard heavy ball made with bias to run in curve; (in *plural*, usually treated as *singular*) game with these on grass. ● *verb* roll (ball etc.); play bowls; *Cricket* deliver ball, (often + *out*) put (batsman) out by knocking off bails with bowled ball; (often + *along*) go along rapidly. □ **bowling alley** long enclosure for skittles or tenpin bowling; **bowling green** lawn for playing bowls.

**bowler¹** /ˈbəʊlə/ *noun Cricket etc.* player who bowls.

**bowler²** /ˈbəʊlə/ *noun* hard round felt hat.

**bowsprit** /ˈbəʊsprɪt/ *noun* spar running forward from ship's bow.

**box¹** ● *noun* container, usually flat-sided and firm; amount contained in this; compartment in theatre, law court, etc.; telephone box; facility at newspaper office for replies to advertisement; (**the box**) *colloquial* television; enclosed area or space. ● *verb* put in or provide with box. □ **box girder** hollow girder with square cross-section; **box junction** yellow-striped road area which vehicle may enter only if exit is clear; **box office** ticket office at theatre etc.; **box pleat** two parallel pleats forming raised band.

**box²** ● *verb* fight with fists as sport; slap (person's ears). ● *noun* slap on ear.

**box³** *noun* evergreen shrub with small dark green leaves; its wood.

**boxer** *noun* person who boxes; short-haired dog with puglike face. □ **boxer shorts** man's loose underpants.

**boxing** *noun* fighting with fists, esp. as sport. □ **boxing glove** padded glove worn in this.

**Boxing Day** *noun* first weekday after Christmas Day.

**boy** ● *noun* male child, young man; son; male servant. ● *interjection* expressing pleasure, surprise, etc. □ **boyfriend** person's regular male companion; **boy scout** Scout. □ **boyhood** *noun*; **boyish** *adjective*.

**boycott** /ˈbɔɪkɒt/ ● *verb* refuse social or commercial relations with; refuse to handle (goods). ● *noun* such refusal.

**bra** /brɑː/ *noun* woman's undergarment supporting breasts.

**brace** ● *noun* device that clamps or fastens tightly; timber etc. strengthening framework; (in *plural*) straps supporting trousers from shoulders; wire device for straightening teeth; (*plural* same) pair. ● *verb* (**-cing**) make steady by supporting; fasten tightly; (esp. as **bracing** *adjective*) invigorate; (often **brace oneself**) prepare for difficulty, shock, etc.

**bracelet** /'breɪslɪt/ *noun* ornamental band or chain worn on wrist or arm; *slang* handcuff.

**brachiosaurus** /brækɪə'sɔːrəs/ *noun* (*plural* **-ruses**) huge long-necked plant-eating dinosaur.

**bracken** /'brækən/ *noun* large coarse fern; mass of these.

**bracket** /'brækɪt/ ● *noun* support projecting from vertical surface; shelf fixed to wall with this; punctuation mark used in pairs—( ), [ ]—enclosing words or figures (see panel); group classified as similar or falling between limits. ● *verb* (**-t-**) enclose in brackets; group in same category.

**brackish** /'brækɪʃ/ *adjective* (of water) slightly salty.

**bract** *noun* leaflike part of plant growing before flower.

**brad** *noun* thin flat nail.

**bradawl** /'brædɔːl/ *noun* small boring-tool.

**brae** /breɪ/ *noun Scottish* hillside.

**brag** ● *verb* (**-gg-**) talk boastfully. ● *noun* card game like poker; boastful statement or talk.

**braggart** /'brægət/ *noun* boastful person.

**Brahma** /'brɑːmə/ *noun* Hindu Creator; supreme Hindu reality.

**Brahman** /'brɑːmən/ *noun* (*plural* **-s**) (also **Brahmin**) member of Hindu priestly caste.

**braid** ● *noun* woven band as edging or trimming; *US* plait of hair. ● *verb US* plait; trim with braid.

**Braille** /breɪl/ *noun* system of writing and printing for the blind, with patterns of raised dots.

**brain** ● *noun* organ of soft nervous tissue in vertebrate's skull; centre of sensation or thought; (often in *plural*) intelligence, *colloquial* intelligent person. ● *verb* dash out brains of. □ **brainchild** *colloquial* person's clever idea or invention; **brain drain** *colloquial* emigration of

---

## Brackets ( ) [ ]

Round brackets, also called parentheses, are used mainly to enclose:

**1** explanations and extra information or comment, e.g.

> *Zimbabwe (formerly Rhodesia)*
> *He is (as he always was) a rebel.*
> *This is done using integrated circuits (see page 38).*

**2** in this dictionary, optional words or parts of words, e.g.

> **crossword (puzzle)**          **king-size(d)**

and the type of word which can be used with the word being defined, e.g.

> **low** ... (of opinion) unfavourable
> **can** ... preserve (food etc.) in can

Square brackets are used mainly to enclose:

**1** words added by someone other than the original writer or speaker, e.g.

> *Then the man said, 'He [the police officer] can't prove I did it.'*

**2** various special types of information, such as stage directions, e.g.

> HEDLEY: Goodbye! [Exit].

skilled people; **brainstorm** mental disturbance; **brainstorming** pooling of spontaneous ideas about problem etc.; **brains trust** group of experts answering questions, usually impromptu; **brainwash** implant ideas or esp. ideology into (person) by repetition etc.; **brainwave** colloquial bright idea.

**brainy** adjective (**-ier, -iest**) intellectually clever.

**braise** /breɪz/ verb (**-sing**) stew slowly in closed container with little liquid.

**brake** ● noun device for stopping or slowing wheel or vehicle; thing that impedes. ● verb (**-king**) apply brake; slow or stop with brake.

**bramble** /ˈbræmb(ə)l/ noun wild thorny shrub, esp. blackberry.

**bran** noun husks separated from flour.

**branch** /brɑːntʃ/ ● noun limb or bough of tree; lateral extension or subdivision of river, railway, family, etc.; local office of business. ● verb (often + off) divide, diverge. □ **branch out** extend one's field of interest.

**brand** ● noun particular make of goods; trade mark, label, etc.; (usually + of) characteristic kind; identifying mark made with hot iron, iron stamp for this; piece of burning or charred wood; stigma; poetical torch. ● verb mark with hot iron; stigmatize; assign trade mark etc. to; impress unforgettably. □ **brand new** completely new.

**brandish** /ˈbrændɪʃ/ verb wave or flourish.

**brandy** /ˈbrændɪ/ noun (plural **-ies**) strong spirit distilled from wine or fermented fruit juice. □ **brandy snap** crisp rolled gingerbread wafer.

**brash** adjective vulgarly assertive; impudent. □ **brashly** adverb; **brashness** noun.

**brass** /brɑːs/ ● noun yellow alloy of copper and zinc; brass objects; brass wind instruments; slang money; brass memorial tablet; colloquial effrontery. ● adjective made of brass. □ **brass band** band of brass instruments; **brass rubbing** reproducing of design from engraved brass on paper by rubbing with heelball, impression obtained thus; **brass tacks** slang essential details.

**brasserie** /ˈbræsərɪ/ noun restaurant, originally one serving beer with food.

**brassica** /ˈbræsɪkə/ noun plant of cabbage family.

**brassière** /ˈbræzɪə/ noun bra.

**brassy** /ˈbrɑːsɪ/ adjective (**-ier, -iest**) of or like brass; impudent; vulgarly showy; loud and blaring.

**brat** noun usually derogatory child.

**bravado** /brəˈvɑːdəʊ/ noun show of boldness.

**brave** ● adjective (**-r, -st**) able to face and endure danger or pain; formal splendid, spectacular. ● verb (**-ving**) face bravely or defiantly. ● noun N. American Indian warrior. □ **bravely** adverb; **bravery** noun.

**bravo** /brɑːˈvəʊ/ interjection & noun (plural **-s**) cry of approval.

**bravura** /brəˈvjʊərə/ noun brilliance of execution; music requiring brilliant technique.

**brawl** ● noun noisy quarrel or fight. ● verb engage in brawl; (of stream) flow noisily.

**brawn** noun muscular strength; muscle, lean flesh; jellied meat made esp. from pig's head. □ **brawny** adjective (**-ier, -iest**).

**bray** ● noun cry of donkey; harsh sound. ● verb make a bray; utter harshly.

**braze** verb (**-zing**) solder with alloy of brass.

**brazen** /ˈbreɪz(ə)n/ ● adjective shameless; of or like brass. ● verb (+ out) face or undergo defiantly. □ **brazenly** adverb.

**brazier** /ˈbreɪzɪə/ noun pan or stand for holding burning coals.

**Brazil nut** /brəˈzɪl/ noun large 3-sided S. American nut.

**breach** /briːtʃ/ ● noun breaking or neglect of rule, duty, promise, etc.; breaking off of relations, quarrel; gap. ● verb break through; make gap in; break (law etc.).

**bread** /bred/ noun baked dough of flour usually leavened with yeast; necessary food; slang money. □ **breadcrumb** small fragment of bread, esp. (in plural) for use in cooking; **breadline** subsistence level; **breadwinner** person whose work supports a family.

**breadth** /bredθ/ noun broadness, distance from side to side; freedom from mental limitations or prejudices.

**break** /breɪk/ ● *verb* (*past* **broke**; *past participle* **broken** /ˈbrəʊk(ə)n/) separate into pieces under blow or strain; shatter; make or become inoperative; break bone in (limb etc.); interrupt, pause; fail to observe or keep; make or become weak, destroy; weaken effect of (fall, blow, etc.); tame, subdue; surpass (record); reveal or be revealed; come, produce, change, etc., with suddenness or violence; (of waves) curl over and foam; (of voice) change in quality at manhood or with emotion; escape, emerge from. ● *noun* breaking; point where thing is broken; gap; pause in work etc.; sudden dash; a chance; *Cricket* deflection of ball on bouncing; points scored in one sequence at billiards etc. □ **break away** make or become free or separate; **break down** fail or collapse, demolish, analyse; **breakdown** mechanical failure, loss of (esp. mental) health, collapse, analysis; **break even** make neither profit nor loss; **break in** intrude forcibly esp. as thief, interrupt, accustom to habit; **breakneck** (of speed) dangerously fast; **break off** detach by breaking, bring to an end, cease talking etc.; **break open** open forcibly; **break out** escape by force, begin suddenly, (+ *in*) become covered in (rash etc.); **breakthrough** major advance in knowledge etc.; **break up** break into pieces, disband, part; **breakup** disintegration, collapse; **breakwater** barrier breaking force of waves; **break wind** release gas from anus.

**breakable** *adjective* easily broken.

**breakage** *noun* broken thing; breaking.

**breaker** *noun* heavy breaking wave.

**breakfast** /ˈbrekfəst/ ● *noun* first meal of day. ● *verb* have breakfast.

**bream** *noun* (*plural* same) yellowish freshwater fish; similar sea fish.

**breast** /brest/ ● *noun* either of two milk-secreting organs on woman's chest; chest; part of garment covering this; seat of emotions. ● *verb* contend with; reach top of (hill). □ **breastbone** bone connecting ribs in front; **breastfeed** feed (baby) from breast; **breastplate** armour covering chest; **breaststroke** stroke made while swimming on breast by extending arms forward and sweeping them back.

**breath** /breθ/ *noun* air drawn into or expelled from lungs; one respiration; breath as perceived by senses; slight movement of air. □ **breathtaking** astounding, awe-inspiring; **breath test** test with Breathalyser.

**breathalyse** *verb* give breath test to.

**Breathalyser** /ˈbreθəlaɪzə/ *noun* *proprietary term* instrument for measuring alcohol in breath.

**breathe** /briːð/ *verb* (**-thing**) take air into lungs and send it out again; live; utter or sound, esp. quietly; pause; send out or take in (as) with breathed air. □ **breathing-space** time to recover, pause.

**breather** /ˈbriːðə/ *noun* short rest period.

**breathless** /ˈbreθlɪs/ *adjective* panting, out of breath; still, windless. □ **breathlessly** *adverb*.

**bred** *past & past participle* of BREED.

**breech** /briːtʃ/ *noun* back part of gun or gun barrel; (in *plural*) short trousers fastened below knee. □ **breech birth** birth in which buttocks emerge first.

**breed** ● *verb* (*past & past participle* **bred**) produce offspring; propagate; raise (animals); yield, result in; arise, spread; train, bring up; create (fissile material) by nuclear reaction. ● *noun* stock of animals within species; race, lineage; sort, kind. □ **breeder reactor** nuclear reactor creating surplus fissile material. □ **breeder** *noun*.

**breeding** *noun* raising of offspring; social behaviour; ancestry.

**breeze**[1] ● *noun* gentle wind. ● *verb* (**-zing**) (+ *in*, *out*, *along*, etc.) *colloquial* saunter casually.

**breeze**[2] *noun* small cinders. □ **breeze-block** lightweight building block made from breeze.

**breezy** *adjective* (**-ier**, **-iest**) slightly windy.

**Bren** *noun* lightweight quick-firing machine-gun.

**brent** *noun* small migratory goose.

**brethren** see BROTHER.

**Breton** /ˈbret(ə)n/ ● *noun* native or language of Brittany. ● *adjective* of Brittany.

**breve** /briːv/ *noun* *Music* note equal to two semibreves; mark (˘) indicating short or unstressed vowel.

**breviary** /'briːvɪərɪ/ *noun* (*plural* **-ies**) book containing RC daily office.

**brevity** /'brevɪtɪ/ *noun* conciseness, shortness.

**brew** ● *verb* make (beer etc.) by infusion, boiling, and fermenting; make (tea etc.) by infusion; undergo these processes; be forming. ● *noun* amount brewed; liquor brewed. □ **brewer** *noun*.

**brewery** /'bruːərɪ/ *noun* (*plural* **-ies**) factory for brewing beer etc.

**briar**[1,2] = BRIER[1,2].

**bribe** ● *verb* (**-bing**) persuade to act improperly by gift of money etc. ● *noun* money or services offered in bribing. □ **bribery** *noun*.

**bric-a-brac** /'brɪkəbræk/ *noun* cheap ornaments, trinkets, etc.

**brick** ● *noun* small rectangular block of baked clay, used in building; toy building block; brick-shaped thing; *slang* generous or loyal person. ● *verb* (+ *in*, *up*) close or block with brickwork. ● *adjective* made of bricks. □ **brickbat** piece of brick, esp. as missile, insult; **bricklayer** person who builds with bricks; **brickwork** building or work in brick.

**bridal** /'braɪd(ə)l/ *adjective* of bride or wedding.

**bride** *noun* woman on her wedding day and shortly before and after it. □ **bridegroom** man on his wedding day and shortly before and after it; **bridesmaid** woman or girl attending bride at wedding.

**bridge**[1] ● *noun* structure providing way over road, railway, river, etc.; thing joining or connecting; superstructure from which ship is directed; upper bony part of nose; prop under strings of violin etc.; bridgework. ● *verb* (**-ging**) be or make bridge over. □ **bridgehead** position held on enemy's side of river etc.; **bridgework** dental structure covering gap and joined to teeth on either side; **bridging loan** loan to cover interval between buying one house and selling another.

**bridge**[2] *noun* card games derived from whist.

**bridle** /'braɪd(ə)l/ ● *noun* headgear for controlling horse etc.; restraining thing. ● *verb* (**-ling**) put bridle on, control, curb; express resentment, esp. by throwing up head and drawing in chin. □ **bridle path** rough path for riders or walkers.

**Brie** /briː/ *noun* flat round soft creamy French cheese.

**brief** /briːf/ ● *adjective* of short duration; concise; scanty. ● *noun* (in *plural*) short pants; summary of case for guidance of barrister; instructions for a task. ● *verb* instruct (barrister) by brief; inform or instruct in advance. □ **in brief** to sum up. □ **briefly** *adverb*.

**briefcase** /'briːfkeɪs/ *noun* flat document case.

**brier**[1] /braɪə/ *noun* (also **briar**) wild-rose bush.

**brier**[2] /braɪə/ *noun* (also **briar**) white heath of S. Europe; tobacco pipe made from its root.

**brig**[1] *noun* two-masted square-rigged ship.

**brig**[2] *noun* *Scottish & Northern English* bridge.

**brigade** /brɪ'geɪd/ *noun* military unit forming part of division; organized band of workers etc.

**brigadier** /brɪgə'dɪə/ *noun* army officer next below major-general.

**brigand** /'brɪgənd/ *noun* member of robber gang.

**bright** /braɪt/ *adjective* emitting or reflecting much light, shining; vivid; clever; cheerful. □ **brighten** *verb*; **brightly** *adverb*; **brightness** *noun*.

**brill**[1] *noun* (*plural* same) flatfish resembling turbot.

**brill**[2] *adjective* *colloquial* excellent.

**brilliant** /'brɪlɪənt/ ● *adjective* bright, sparkling; highly talented; showy; *colloquial* excellent. ● *noun* diamond of finest quality. □ **brilliance** *noun*; **brilliantly** *adverb*.

**brilliantine** /'brɪljəntiːn/ *noun* cosmetic for making hair glossy.

**brim** ● *noun* edge of vessel; projecting edge of hat. ● *verb* (**-mm-**) fill or be full to brim.

**brimstone** /'brɪmstəʊn/ *noun* *archaic* sulphur.

**brindled** /'brɪnd(ə)ld/ *adjective* brown with streaks of other colour.

**brine** *noun* salt water; sea water.

**bring** *verb* (*past & past participle* **brought** /brɔːt/) come with, carry, convey;

cause, result in; be sold for; submit (criminal charge); initiate (legal action). □ **bring about** cause to happen; **bring down** cause to fall; **bring forward** move to earlier time, transfer from previous page or account, draw attention to; **bring in** introduce, produce as profit; **bring off** succeed in; **bring on** cause to happen, appear or progress; **bring out** emphasize, publish; **bring round** restore to consciousness, win over; **bring up** raise and educate, vomit, draw attention to.

**brink** *noun* edge of precipice etc.; furthest point before danger, discovery, etc. □ **brinkmanship** policy of pursuing dangerous course to brink of catastrophe.

**briny** /'braɪnɪ/ ●*adjective* (-ier, -iest) of brine or sea, salt. ●*noun* (**the briny**) *slang* the sea.

**briquette** /brɪ'ket/ *noun* block of compressed coal dust as fuel.

**brisk** *adjective* active, lively, quick. □ **briskly** *adverb*.

**brisket** /'brɪskɪt/ *noun* animal's breast, esp. as joint of meat.

**brisling** /'brɪzlɪŋ/ *noun* (*plural* same or **-s**) small herring or sprat.

**bristle** /'brɪs(ə)l/ ●*noun* short stiff hair, esp. one used in brushes etc. ●*verb* (-ling) (of hair etc.) stand up; cause to bristle; show irritation; (usually + *with*) be covered (with) or abundant (in). □ **bristly** *adjective*.

**British** /'brɪtɪʃ/ ●*adjective* of Britain. ●*plural noun* (**the British**) the British people. □ **British Summer Time** = SUMMER TIME.

**Briton** /'brɪt(ə)n/ *noun* inhabitant of S. Britain before Roman conquest; native of Great Britain.

**brittle** /'brɪt(ə)l/ *adjective* apt to break, fragile.

**broach** /brəʊtʃ/ *verb* raise for discussion; pierce (cask) to draw liquor; open and start using.

**broad** /brɔːd/ ●*adjective* large across, extensive; of specified breadth; full, clear; explicit; general; tolerant; coarse; (of accent) marked, strong. ●*noun* broad part; *US slang* woman; (**the Broads**) large areas of water in E. Anglia. □ **broad bean** bean with large flat seeds, one such seed; **broadloom** (carpet) woven in broad width; **broad-minded** tolerant, liberal; **broadsheet** large-sized newspaper. □ **broaden** *verb*; **broadly** *adverb*.

**broadcast** ●*verb* (*past & past participle* -cast) transmit by radio or television; take part in such transmission; scatter (seed) etc.; disseminate widely. ●*noun* radio or television programme or transmission. □ **broadcaster** *noun*; **broadcasting** *noun*.

**broadside** *noun* vigorous verbal attack; firing of all guns on one side of ship. □ **broadside on** sideways on.

**brocade** /brə'keɪd/ *noun* fabric woven with raised pattern.

**broccoli** /'brɒkəlɪ/ *noun* brassica with greenish flower heads.

**brochure** /'brəʊʃə/ *noun* booklet, pamphlet, esp. containing descriptive information.

**broderie anglaise** /brəʊdərɪ ɑ̃'gleɪz/ *noun* open embroidery on usually white cotton or linen.

**brogue** /brəʊg/ *noun* strong shoe with ornamental perforations; rough shoe of untanned leather; marked local, esp. Irish, accent.

**broil** *verb* grill (meat); make or be very hot.

**broiler** *noun* young chicken for broiling.

**broke** ●*past* of BREAK. ●*adjective colloquial* having no money, bankrupt.

**broken** /'brəʊkən/ ●*past participle* of BREAK. ●*adjective* that has been broken; reduced to despair; (of language) spoken imperfectly; interrupted. □ **broken-hearted** crushed by grief; **broken home** family disrupted by divorce or separation.

**broker** *noun* middleman, agent; stockbroker. □ **broking** *noun*.

**brokerage** *noun* broker's fee or commission.

**brolly** /'brɒlɪ/ *noun* (*plural* **-ies**) *colloquial* umbrella.

**bromide** /'brəʊmaɪd/ *noun* binary compound of bromine, esp. one used as sedative; trite remark.

**bromine** /'brəʊmiːn/ *noun* poisonous liquid non-metallic element with choking smell.

**bronchial** /ˈbrɒŋkɪəl/ *adjective* of two main divisions of windpipe or smaller tubes into which they divide.

**bronchitis** /brɒŋˈkaɪtɪs/ *noun* inflammation of bronchial mucous membrane.

**bronco** /ˈbrɒŋkəʊ/ *noun* ( *plural* **-s**) wild or half-tamed horse of western US.

**brontosaurus** /ˌbrɒntəˈsɔːrəs/ *noun* ( *plural* **-ruses**) = APATOSAURUS.

**bronze** /brɒnz/ ● *noun* brown alloy of copper and tin; its colour; work of art or medal in it. ● *adjective* made of or coloured like bronze. ● *verb* (**-zing**) make or grow brown; tan. □ **Bronze Age** period when tools were of bronze; **bronze medal** medal given usually as third prize.

**brooch** /brəʊtʃ/ *noun* ornamental hinged pin.

**brood** /bruːd/ ● *noun* bird's or other animal's young produced at one hatch or birth; *colloquial* children of a family. ● *verb* worry or ponder, esp. resentfully; (of hen) sit on eggs.

**broody** *adjective* (**-ier, -iest**) (of hen) wanting to brood; sullenly thoughtful; *colloquial* (of woman) wanting pregnancy.

**brook**[1] /brʊk/ *noun* small stream.

**brook**[2] /brʊk/ *verb* tolerate; allow.

**broom** /bruːm/ *noun* long-handled brush for sweeping; yellow-flowered shrub. □ **broomstick** broom-handle.

**Bros.** *abbreviation* Brothers.

**broth** /brɒθ/ *noun* thin meat or fish soup.

**brothel** /ˈbrɒθ(ə)l/ *noun* premises for prostitution.

**brother** /ˈbrʌðə/ *noun* man or boy in relation to his siblings; close man friend; ( *plural* also **brethren** /ˈbreðrɪn/) member of male religious order; ( *plural* also **brethren**) fellow Christian etc.; fellow human being. □ **brother-in-law** ( *plural* **brothers-in-law**) wife's or husband's brother, sister's husband. □ **brotherly** *adjective*.

**brotherhood** *noun* relationship (as) between brothers; (members of) association for mutual help etc.

**brought** *past & past participle* of BRING.

**brow** /braʊ/ *noun* forehead; (usually in *plural*) eyebrow; summit of hill; edge of cliff etc.

**browbeat** *verb* (*past* **-beat**, *past participle* **-beaten**) intimidate, bully.

**brown** /braʊn/ ● *adjective* of colour of dark wood or rich soil; dark-skinned; tanned. ● *noun* brown colour, paint, clothes, etc. ● *verb* make or become brown. □ **brown bread** bread made of wholemeal or wheatmeal flour; **browned off** *colloquial* bored, fed up; **Brown Owl** adult leader of Brownies; **brown rice** unpolished rice; **brown sugar** partially refined sugar. □ **brownish** *adjective*.

**Brownie** /ˈbraʊnɪ/ *noun* junior Guide; (**brownie**) small square of chocolate cake with nuts; (**brownie**) benevolent elf.

**browse** /braʊz/ ● *verb* (**-sing**) read or look around desultorily; feed on leaves and young shoots. ● *noun* browsing; twigs, shoots, etc. as fodder.

**bruise** /bruːz/ ● *noun* discoloration of skin caused by blow or pressure; similar damage on fruit etc. ● *verb* (**-sing**) inflict bruise on; be susceptible to bruises.

**bruiser** *noun* *colloquial* tough brutal person.

**bruit** /bruːt/ *verb* (often + *abroad*, *about*) spread (report or rumour).

**brunch** *noun* combination of breakfast and lunch.

**brunette** /bruːˈnet/ *noun* woman with dark hair.

**brunt** *noun* chief impact of attack etc.

**brush** ● *noun* cleaning or hairdressing or painting implement of bristles etc. set in holder; application of brush; short esp. unpleasant encounter; fox's tail; carbon or metal piece serving as electrical contact. ● *verb* use brush on; touch lightly, graze in passing. □ **brush off** dismiss abruptly; **brush-off** dismissal, rebuff; **brush up** clean up or smarten, revise (subject, skill); **brushwood** undergrowth, thicket, cut or broken twigs etc.; **brushwork** painter's way of using brush.

**brusque** /brʊsk/ *adjective* abrupt, offhand. □ **brusquely** *adverb*; **brusqueness** *noun*.

**Brussels sprout** /ˈbrʌs(ə)lz/ *noun* brassica with small cabbage-like buds on stem; such bud.

**brutal** /'bru:t(ə)l/ *adjective* savagely cruel; mercilessly frank. □ **brutality** /-'tæl-/ *noun* (*plural* **-ies**); **brutalize** *verb* (also **-ise**) (**-zing, -sing**).

**brute** /bru:t/ ● *noun* cruel person; *colloquial* unpleasant person; animal other than man. ● *adjective* unthinking, cruel, stupid. □ **brutish** *adjective*.

**bryony** /'braɪənɪ/ *noun* (*plural* **-ies**) climbing hedge plant.

**B.Sc.** *abbreviation* Bachelor of Science.

**BST** *abbreviation* British Summer Time.

**Bt.** *abbreviation* Baronet.

**bubble** /'bʌb(ə)l/ ● *noun* thin sphere of liquid enclosing air or gas; air-filled cavity in glass etc.; transparent domed cavity. ● *verb* (**-ling**) send up or rise in bubbles; make sound of boiling. □ **bubble and squeak** cooked potatoes and cabbage fried together; **bubble bath** additive to make bathwater bubbly; **bubblegum** chewing gum that can be blown into bubbles.

**bubbly** ● *adjective* (**-ier, -iest**) full of bubbles; exuberant. ● *noun* *colloquial* champagne.

**bubonic** /bju:'bɒnɪk/ *adjective* (of plague) marked by swellings esp. in groin and armpits.

**buccaneer** /bʌkə'nɪə/ *noun* pirate; adventurer. □ **buccaneering** *adjective* & *noun*.

**buck**[1] ● *noun* male deer, hare, or rabbit. ● *verb* (of horse) jump vertically with back arched, throw (rider) thus; (usually + *up*) *colloquial* cheer up, hurry up. □ **buckshot** coarse shot for gun; **buck-tooth** projecting upper tooth.

**buck**[2] *noun* *US & Australian slang* dollar.

**buck**[3] *noun* *slang* small object placed before dealer at poker. □ **pass the buck** *colloquial* shift responsibility.

**bucket** /'bʌkɪt/ ● *noun* usually round open container with handle, for carrying or holding water etc.; amount contained in this; (in *plural*) *colloquial* large quantities; compartment or scoop in waterwheel, dredger, or grain elevator. ● *verb* (**-t-**) *colloquial* (often + *down*) (esp. of rain) pour heavily; (often + *along*) move jerkily or bumpily. □ **bucket seat** one with rounded back, to fit one person; **bucket shop** agency dealing in cheap airline tickets, unregistered broking agency.

**buckle** /'bʌk(ə)l/ ● *noun* clasp with usually hinged pin for securing strap or belt etc. ● *verb* (**-ling**) fasten with buckle; (cause to) crumple under pressure. □ **buckle down** make determined effort.

**buckram** /'bʌkrəm/ *noun* coarse linen etc. stiffened with paste etc.

**buckshee** /bʌk'ʃi:/ *adjective & adverb* *slang* free of charge.

**buckwheat** *noun* seed of plant related to rhubarb.

**bucolic** /bju:'kɒlɪk/ *adjective* of shepherds, rustic, pastoral.

**bud** ● *noun* projection from which branch, leaf, or flower develops; flower or leaf not fully open; asexual growth separating from organism as new animal. ● *verb* (**-dd-**) form buds; begin to grow or develop; graft bud of (plant) on another plant.

**Buddhism** /'bʊdɪz(ə)m/ *noun* Asian religion founded by Gautama Buddha. □ **Buddhist** *adjective* & *noun*.

**buddleia** /'bʌdlɪə/ *noun* shrub with flowers attractive to butterflies.

**buddy** /'bʌdɪ/ *noun* (*plural* **-ies**) *colloquial* friend; mate.

**budge** *verb* (**-ging**) move in slightest degree; (+ *up*) move to make room for another person.

**budgerigar** /bʌdʒərɪ'gɑ:/ *noun* small parrot often kept as pet.

**budget** /'bʌdʒɪt/ ● *noun* amount of money needed or available; (**the Budget**) annual estimate of country's revenue and expenditure; similar estimate for person or group. ● *verb* (**-t-**) (often + *for*) allow or arrange for in budget. □ **budgetary** *adjective*.

**budgie** /'bʌdʒɪ/ *noun* *colloquial* budgerigar.

**buff** ● *adjective* of yellowish beige colour. ● *noun* this colour; *colloquial* enthusiast; velvety dull yellow leather. ● *verb* polish; make (leather) velvety. □ **in the buff** *colloquial* naked.

**buffalo** /'bʌfələʊ/ *noun* (*plural* same or **-es**) any of various kinds of ox; American bison.

**buffer**[1] *noun* apparatus for deadening impact esp. of railway vehicles. □ **buffer state** minor one between two larger ones, regarded as reducing friction.

**buffer**[2] *noun slang* old or incompetent fellow.

**buffet**[1] /'bʊfeɪ/ *noun* room or counter where refreshments are sold; self-service meal of several dishes set out at once; (also /'bʌfɪt/) sideboard. □ **buffet car** railway coach in which refreshments are served.

**buffet**[2] /'bʌfɪt/ ● *verb* (**-t-**) strike repeatedly. ● *noun* blow with hand; shock.

**buffoon** /bə'fuːn/ *noun* silly or ludicrous person; jester. ● **buffoonery** *noun*.

**bug** ● *noun* small insect; concealed microphone; *colloquial* error in computer program etc.; *slang* virus, infection; *slang* enthusiasm, obsession. ● *verb* (**-gg-**) conceal microphone in; *slang* annoy.

**bugbear** *noun* cause of annoyance; object of baseless fear.

**buggy** /'bʌgɪ/ *noun* (*plural* **-ies**) small sturdy motor vehicle; lightweight pushchair; light horse-drawn vehicle for one or two people.

**bugle** /'bjuːg(ə)l/ ● *noun* brass instrument like small trumpet. ● *verb* (**-ling**) sound bugle. □ **bugler** *noun*.

**build** /bɪld/ ● *verb* (*past & past participle* **built** /bɪlt/) construct or cause to be constructed; develop or establish. ● *noun* physical proportions; style of construction. □ **build in** incorporate; **build up** increase in size or strength, praise, gradually establish or be established; **build-up** favourable description in advance, gradual approach to climax, accumulation.

**builder** *noun* contractor who builds houses etc.

**building** *noun* house or other structure with roof and walls. □ **building society** financial organization (not public company) that pays interest on savings accounts, lends money esp. for mortgages, etc.

**built** /bɪlt/ *past & past participle* of BUILD. □ **built-in** integral; **built-up** covered with buildings.

**bulb** *noun* rounded base of stem of some plants; light bulb; bulb-shaped thing or part.

**bulbous** /'bʌlbəs/ *adjective* bulb-shaped; bulging.

**bulge** ● *noun* irregular swelling; *colloquial* temporary increase. ● *verb* (**-ging**) swell outwards. □ **bulgy** *adjective*.

**bulimia** /bjʊ'lɪmɪə/ *noun* (in full **bulimia nervosa** /nɜː'vəʊsə/) disorder in which overeating alternates with self-induced vomiting, fasting, etc.

**bulk** ● *noun* size, magnitude, esp. when great; (**the bulk**) the greater part; large quantity. ● *verb* seem (in size or importance); make thicker. □ **bulk buying** buying in quantity at discount; **bulkhead** upright partition in ship, aircraft, etc.

**bulky** /'bʌlkɪ/ *adjective* (**-ier**, **-iest**) large, unwieldy.

**bull**[1] /bʊl/ *noun* uncastrated male ox; male whale or elephant etc.; bull's-eye of target; person who buys shares in hope of selling at higher price later. □ **bulldog** short-haired heavy-jowled sturdy dog, tenacious and courageous person; **Bulldog clip** strong sprung clip for papers etc.; **bulldoze** clear with bulldozer, *colloquial* intimidate, *colloquial* make (one's way) forcibly; **bulldozer** powerful tractor with broad upright blade for clearing ground; **bullfight** public baiting, and usually killing, of bulls; **bullfinch** pink and black finch; **bullfrog** large American frog with booming croak; **bullring** arena for bullfight; **bull's-eye** centre of target, hard minty sweet; **bull terrier** cross between bulldog and terrier. □ **bullish** *adjective*.

**bull**[2] /bʊl/ *noun* papal edict.

**bull**[3] /bʊl/ *noun slang* nonsense; *slang* unnecessary routine tasks; absurdly illogical statement.

**bullet** /'bʊlɪt/ *noun* small pointed missile fired from revolver etc. □ **bulletproof** resistant to bullets.

**bulletin** /'bʊlɪtɪn/ *noun* short official statement; short broadcast news report.

**bullion** /'bʊlɪən/ *noun* gold or silver in lump or valued by weight.

**bullock** /'bʊlək/ *noun* castrated bull.

**bully**[1] /'bʊlɪ/ ● *noun* (*plural* **-ies**) person coercing others by fear. ● *verb* (**-ies**, **-ied**) persecute or oppress by force or threats. ● *interjection* (+ *for*) very good.

**bully**[2] /'bʊlɪ/ (in full **bully off**) ● *noun* (*plural* **-ies**) putting ball into play in hockey. ●verb (**-ies**, **-ied**) start play thus.

**bully**[3] /'bʊlɪ/ noun (in full **bully beef** ) corned beef.

**bulrush** /'bʊlrʌʃ/ noun tall rush; Biblical papyrus.

**bulwark** /'bʊlwək/ noun defensive wall, esp. of earth; person or principle that protects; (usually in plural) ship's side above deck.

**bum**[1] noun slang buttocks. □ **bumbag** small pouch worn round waist.

**bum**[2] US slang ●noun loafer, dissolute person. ●verb (**-mm-**) (often + around) loaf, wander around; cadge. ●adjective of poor quality.

**bumble** /'bʌmb(ə)l/ verb (**-ling**) (+ on) speak ramblingly; be inept; blunder. □ **bumble-bee** large bee with loud hum.

**bump** ●noun dull-sounding blow or collision; swelling caused by it; uneven patch on road etc.; prominence on skull, thought to indicate mental faculty. ●verb come or strike with bump against; hurt thus; (usually + along) move along with jolts. □ **bump into** colloquial meet by chance; **bump off** slang murder; **bump up** colloquial increase. □ **bumpy** adjective (**-ier**, **-iest**).

**bumper** ●noun horizontal bar on motor vehicle to reduce damage in collisions; Cricket ball rising high after pitching; brim-full glass. ●adjective unusually large or abundant.

**bumpkin** /'bʌmpkɪn/ noun rustic or awkward person.

**bumptious** /'bʌmpʃəs/ adjective self-assertive, conceited.

**bun** noun small sweet cake or bread roll often with dried fruit; small coil of hair at back of head.

**bunch** ●noun cluster of things growing or fastened together; lot; colloquial gang, group. ●verb arrange in bunch(es); gather in folds; come, cling, or crowd together.

**bundle** /'bʌnd(ə)l/ ●noun collection of things tied or fastened together; set of nerve fibres etc.; slang large amount of money. ●verb (**-ling**) (usually + up) tie in bundle; (usually + into) throw or move carelessly; (usually + out, off, away, etc.) send away hurriedly.

**bung** ●noun stopper, esp. for cask. ●verb stop with bung; slang throw. □ **bunged up** blocked up.

**bungalow** /'bʌŋgələʊ/ noun one-storeyed house.

**bungee** /'bʌndʒɪ/ noun elasticated cord. □ **bungee jumping** sport of jumping from great height while secured by bungee.

**bungle** /'bʌŋg(ə)l/ ●verb (**-ling**) mismanage, fail to accomplish; work awkwardly. ●noun bungled work or attempt.

**bunion** /'bʌnjən/ noun swelling on foot, esp. on side of big toe.

**bunk**[1] noun shelflike bed against wall. □ **bunk bed** each of two or more bunks one above the other.

**bunk**[2] slang □ **do a bunk** run away.

**bunk**[3] noun slang nonsense, humbug.

**bunker** noun container for fuel; reinforced underground shelter; sandy hollow in golf course.

**bunkum** /'bʌŋkəm/ noun nonsense, humbug.

**bunny** /'bʌnɪ/ noun (plural **-ies**) childish name for rabbit.

**Bunsen burner** /'bʌns(ə)n/ noun small adjustable gas burner used in laboratory.

**bunting**[1] /'bʌntɪŋ/ noun small bird related to finches.

**bunting**[2] /'bʌntɪŋ/ noun flags and other decorations; loosely woven fabric for these.

**buoy** /bɔɪ/ ●noun anchored float as navigational mark etc.; lifebuoy. ●verb (usually + up) keep afloat, encourage; (often + out) mark with buoy(s).

**buoyant** /'bɔɪənt/ adjective apt to float; resilient; exuberant. □ **buoyancy** noun.

**bur** noun (also **burr**) clinging seed vessel or flower head, plant producing burs; clinging person.

**burble** /'bɜːb(ə)l/ verb (**-ling**) talk rambling; make bubbling sound.

**burden** /'bɜːd(ə)n/ ●noun thing carried, load; oppressive duty, expense, emotion, etc.; refrain of song; theme. ●verb load, encumber, oppress. □ **burden of proof** obligation to prove one's case. □ **burdensome** adjective.

**burdock** /'bɜːdɒk/ *noun* plant with prickly flowers and docklike leaves.

**bureau** /'bjʊərəʊ/ *noun* ( *plural* **-s** or **-x** /-z/) writing desk with drawers; *US* chest of drawers; office or department for specific business; government department.

**bureaucracy** /bjʊə'rɒkrəsɪ/ *noun* ( *plural* **-ies**) government by central administration; government officials esp. regarded as oppressive and inflexible; conduct typical of these.

**bureaucrat** /'bjʊərəkræt/ *noun* official in bureaucracy. □ **bureaucratic** /-'krætɪk/ *adjective*.

**burgeon** /'bɜːdʒ(ə)n/ *verb* grow rapidly, flourish.

**burger** /'bɜːgə/ *noun colloquial* hamburger.

**burgher** /'bɜːgə/ *noun* citizen, esp. of foreign town.

**burglar** /'bɜːglə/ *noun* person who commits burglary.

**burglary** *noun* ( *plural* **-ies**) illegal entry into building to commit theft or other crime.

**burgle** /'bɜːg(ə)l/ *verb* (**-ling**) commit burglary (on).

**burgundy** /'bɜːgəndɪ/ *noun* ( *plural* **-ies**) red or white wine produced in Burgundy; dark red colour.

**burial** /'berɪəl/ *noun* burying, esp. of corpse; funeral.

**burlesque** /bɜː'lesk/ ● *noun* comic imitation, parody; *US* variety show, esp. with striptease. ● *adjective* of or using burlesque. ● *verb* (**-ques**, **-qued**, **-quing**) parody.

**burly** /'bɜːlɪ/ *adjective* (**-ier**, **-iest**) large and sturdy.

**burn**[1] ● *verb* ( *past & past participle* **burnt** or **burned**) (cause to) be consumed by fire; blaze or glow with fire; (cause to) be injured or damaged by fire, sun, or great heat; use or be used as fuel; produce (hole etc.) by fire or heat; char in working; brand; give or feel sensation or pain (as) of heat. ● *noun* sore or mark made by burning. □ **burn out** be reduced to nothing by burning, (cause to) fail by burning, (usually **burn oneself out**) suffer exhaustion; **burnt offering** sacrifice offered by burning.

**burn**[2] *noun Scottish* brook.

**burner** *noun* part of lamp or cooker etc. that emits flame.

**burnish** /'bɜːnɪʃ/ *verb* polish by rubbing.

**burnt** *past & past participle* of BURN[1].

**burp** *verb & noun colloquial* belch.

**burr**[1] *noun* whirring sound; rough sounding of *r*; rough edge on metal etc.

**burr**[2] = BUR.

**burrow** /'bʌrəʊ/ ● *noun* hole dug by animal as dwelling. ● *verb* make burrow; make by digging; (+ *into*) investigate or search.

**bursar** /'bɜːsə/ *noun* treasurer of college etc.; holder of bursary.

**bursary** /'bɜːsərɪ/ *noun* ( *plural* **-ies**) grant, esp. scholarship.

**burst** ● *verb* ( *past & past participle* **burst**) fly violently apart or give way suddenly, explode; rush, move, speak, be spoken, etc. suddenly or violently. ● *noun* bursting, explosion, outbreak; spurt.

**burton** /'bɜːt(ə)n/ *noun* □ **go for a burton** *slang* be lost, destroyed, or killed.

**bury** /'berɪ/ *verb* (**-ies**, **-ied**) place (corpse) in ground, tomb, or sea; put underground, hide in earth; consign to obscurity; (**bury oneself** or in *passive*) involve (oneself) deeply. □ **bury the hatchet** cease to quarrel.

**bus** ● *noun* ( *plural* **buses**, *US* **busses**) large public passenger vehicle usually plying on fixed route. ● *verb* (**buses** or **busses**, **bussed**, **bussing**) go by bus; *US* transport by bus (esp. to aid racial integration). □ **busman's holiday** leisure spent in same occupation as working hours; **bus shelter** shelter for people waiting for bus; **bus station** centre where buses depart and arrive; **bus stop** regular stopping place of bus.

**busby** /'bʌzbɪ/ *noun* ( *plural* **-ies**) tall fur cap worn by hussars etc.

**bush**[1] *noun* shrub, clump of shrubs; clump of hair or fur; *Australian etc.* uncultivated land, woodland. □ **bush-baby** small African lemur; **Bushman** member or language of a S. African aboriginal people; **bushman** dweller or traveller in Australian bush; **bush telegraph** rapid informal spreading of information etc.

**bush**[2] /bʊʃ/ *noun* metal lining of axlehole etc.; electrically insulating sleeve.

**bushel** /'bʊʃ(ə)l/ noun measure of capacity for corn, fruit, etc. (8 gallons, 36.4 litres).

**bushy** adjective (**-ier, -iest**) growing thickly or like bush; having many bushes.

**business** /'bɪznɪs/ noun one's occupation or profession; one's own concern, task, duty; serious work; (difficult or unpleasant) matter or affair; thing(s) needing dealing with; buying and selling, trade; commercial firm. □ **businesslike** practical, systematic; **businessman, businesswoman** person engaged in trade or commerce.

**busk** verb perform esp. music in street etc. for tips. □ **busker** noun.

**bust** [1] noun human chest, esp. of woman; sculpture of head, shoulders, and chest.

**bust** [2] colloquial ● verb (past & past participle **bust** or **busted**) burst, break; raid, search; arrest. ● adjective burst, broken; bankrupt. □ **bust-up** quarrel, violent split or separation.

**bustard** /'bʌstəd/ noun large swift-running bird.

**bustle** [1] /'bʌs(ə)l/ ● verb (**-ling**) (often + about) move busily and energetically; make (person) hurry; (as **bustling** adjective) active, lively. ● noun excited activity.

**bustle** [2] /'bʌs(ə)l/ noun historical padding worn under skirt to puff it out behind.

**busy** /'bɪzɪ/ ● adjective (**-ier, -iest**) occupied or engaged in work etc.; full of activity; fussy. ● verb (**-ies, -ied**) occupy, keep busy. □ **busybody** meddlesome person; **busy Lizzie** house plant with usually red, pink, or white flowers. □ **busily** adverb.

**but** ● conjunction however; on the other hand; otherwise than. ● preposition except, apart from. ● adverb only. □ **but for** without the help or hindrance etc. of; **but then** however.

**butane** /'bjuːteɪn/ noun hydrocarbon used in liquefied form as fuel.

**butch** /bʊtʃ/ adjective slang masculine, tough-looking.

**butcher** /'bʊtʃə/ ● noun person who sells meat; slaughterer of animals for food; brutal murderer. ● verb slaughter or cut up (animal); kill wantonly or cruelly;

colloquial ruin through incompetence. □ **butchery** noun (plural **-ies**).

**butler** /'bʌtlə/ noun chief manservant of household.

**butt** [1] ● verb push with head; (cause to) meet end to end. ● noun push or blow with head or horns. □ **butt in** interrupt, meddle.

**butt** [2] noun (often + of) object of ridicule etc.; mound behind target; (in plural) shooting range.

**butt** [3] noun thicker end, esp. of tool or weapon; stub of cigarette etc.

**butt** [4] noun cask.

**butter** /'bʌtə/ ● noun yellow fatty substance made from cream, used as spread and in cooking; substance of similar texture. ● verb spread, cook, etc., with butter. □ **butter-bean** dried large flat white kind; **buttercup** plant with yellow flowers; **butter-fingers** colloquial person likely to drop things; **buttermilk** liquid left after butter-making; **butter muslin** thin loosely woven cloth; **butterscotch** sweet made of butter and sugar; **butter up** colloquial flatter.

**butterfly** /'bʌtəflaɪ/ noun (plural **-ies**) insect with 4 often showy wings; (in plural) nervous sensation in stomach. □ **butterfly nut** kind of wing-nut; **butterfly stroke** method of swimming with both arms lifted at same time.

**buttery** [1] adjective like or containing butter.

**buttery** [2] noun (plural **-ies**) food store or snack-bar, esp. in college.

**buttock** /'bʌtək/ noun either protuberance on lower rear part of human trunk; corresponding part of animal.

**button** /'bʌt(ə)n/ ● noun disc or knob sewn to garment etc. as fastening or for ornament; knob etc. pressed to operate electronic equipment. ● verb (often + up) fasten with buttons. □ **button mushroom** small unopened mushroom.

**buttonhole** ● noun slit in cloth for button; flower(s) worn in lapel buttonhole. ● verb (**-ling**) colloquial accost and detain (reluctant listener).

**buttress** /'bʌtrɪs/ ● noun support built against wall etc. ● verb support or strengthen.

**buxom** /ˈbʌksəm/ *adjective* plump and rosy, large and shapely.

**buy** /baɪ/ ● *verb* (**buys, buying**; *past & past participle* **bought** /bɔːt/) obtain in exchange for money etc.; procure by bribery, bribe; get by sacrifice etc.; *slang* accept, believe. ● *noun colloquial* purchase. □ **buy out** pay (a person) for ownership, an interest, etc.; **buyout** purchase of controlling share in company; **buy up** buy as much as possible of.

**buyer** *noun* person who buys, esp. stock for large shop. □ **buyer's market** time when goods are plentiful and cheap.

**buzz** ● *noun* hum of bee etc.; sound of buzzer; low murmur; hurried activity; *slang* telephone call; *slang* thrill. ● *verb* hum; summon with buzzer; (often + *about*) move busily; be filled with activity or excitement. □ **buzzword** *colloquial* fashionable technical word, catchword.

**buzzard** /ˈbʌzəd/ *noun* large bird of hawk family.

**buzzer** *noun* electrical buzzing device as signal.

**by** /baɪ/ ● *preposition* near, beside, along; through action, agency, or means of; not later than; past; via; during; to extent of; according to. ● *adverb* near, aside, in reserve; past. □ **by and by** before long; **by-election** parliamentary election between general elections;

**by-product** substance etc. produced incidentally in making of something else; **byroad** minor road; **by the by, by the way** incidentally; **byway** byroad or secluded path; **byword** person or thing as notable example, proverb.

**bye**[1] /baɪ/ *noun Cricket* run made from ball that passes batsman without being hit; (in tournament) position of competitor left without opponent in round.

**bye**[2] /baɪ/ *interjection* (also **bye-bye**) *colloquial* goodbye.

**bygone** *adjective* past, departed. □ **let bygones be bygones** forgive and forget past quarrels.

**by-law** *noun* regulation made by local authority etc.

**byline** *noun* line in newspaper etc. naming writer of article etc.

**bypass** ● *noun* main road round town or its centre. ● *verb* avoid.

**byre** /baɪə/ *noun* cowshed.

**bystander** *noun* person present but not taking part.

**byte** /baɪt/ *noun Computing* group of 8 binary digits, often representing one character.

**Byzantine** /bɪˈzæntaɪn/ *adjective* of Byzantium or E. Roman Empire; of architectural etc. style developed in Eastern Empire; complicated, underhand.

# Cc

**C**[1] *noun* (also **c**) (Roman numeral) 100.

**C**[2] *abbreviation* Celsius; centigrade.

**c.**[1] *abbreviation* century; cent(s).

**c.**[2] *abbreviation* circa.

**ca.** *abbreviation* circa.

**CAA** *abbreviation* Civil Aviation Authority.

**cab** *noun* taxi; driver's compartment in lorry, train, crane, etc.

**cabal** /kə'bæl/ *noun* secret intrigue; political clique.

**cabaret** /'kæbəreɪ/ *noun* entertainment in restaurant etc.

**cabbage** /'kæbɪdʒ/ *noun* vegetable with green or purple leaves forming a round head; *colloquial* dull or inactive person. □ **cabbage white** kind of white butterfly.

**cabby** /'kæbɪ/ *noun* (*plural* **-ies**) *colloquial* taxi driver.

**caber** /'keɪbə/ *noun* tree trunk tossed as sport in Scotland.

**cabin** /'kæbɪn/ *noun* small shelter or house, esp. of wood; room or compartment in aircraft, ship, etc. □ **cabin boy** boy steward on ship; **cabin cruiser** large motor boat with accommodation.

**cabinet** /'kæbɪnɪt/ *noun* cupboard or case for storing or displaying things; casing of radio, television, etc.; (**Cabinet**) group of senior ministers in government. □ **cabinetmaker** skilled joiner.

**cable** /'keɪb(ə)l/ ● *noun* encased group of insulated wires for transmitting electricity etc.; thick rope of wire or hemp; cablegram. ● *verb* (**-ling**) send (message) or inform (person) by cable. □ **cable car** small cabin on loop of cable for carrying passengers up and down mountain etc.; **cablegram** message sent by undersea cable etc.; **cable stitch** knitting stitch resembling twisted rope; **cable television** transmission of television programmes by cable to subscribers.

**caboodle** /kə'buːd(ə)l/ *noun.* □ **the whole caboodle** *slang* the whole lot.

**caboose** /kə'buːs/ *noun* kitchen on ship's deck; *US* guard's van on train.

**cabriolet** /kæbrɪəʊ'leɪ/ *noun* car with folding top.

**cacao** /kə'kaʊ/ *noun* (*plural* **-s**) seed from which cocoa and chocolate are made; tree bearing it.

**cache** /kæʃ/ ● *noun* hiding place for treasure, supplies, etc.; things so hidden. ● *verb* (**-ching**) place in cache.

**cachet** /'kæʃeɪ/ *noun* prestige; distinguishing mark or seal; flat capsule for medicine.

**cack-handed** /kæk'hændɪd/ *adjective colloquial* clumsy, left-handed.

**cackle** /'kæk(ə)l/ ● *noun* clucking of hen; raucous laugh; noisy chatter. ● *verb* (**-ling**) emit cackle; chatter noisily.

**cacophony** /kə'kɒfənɪ/ *noun* (*plural* **-ies**) harsh discordant sound. □ **cacophonous** *adjective*.

**cactus** /'kæktəs/ *noun* (*plural* **-ti** /-taɪ/ or **-tuses**) plant with thick fleshy stem and usually spines but no leaves.

**CAD** *abbreviation* computer-aided design.

**cad** *noun* man who behaves dishonourably. □ **caddish** *adjective*.

**cadaver** /kə'dævə/ *noun* corpse. □ **cadaverous** *adjective*.

**caddie** /'kædɪ/ (also **caddy**) ● *noun* (*plural* **-ies**) golfer's attendant carrying clubs etc. ● *verb* (**caddying**) act as caddie.

**caddis** /'kædɪs/ *noun* □ **caddis-fly** small nocturnal insect living near water; **caddis-worm** larva of caddis-fly.

**caddy**[1] /'kædɪ/ *noun* (*plural* **-ies**) small container for tea.

**caddy**[2] = CADDIE.

**cadence** /'keɪd(ə)ns/ *noun* rhythm; fall in pitch of voice; tonal inflection; close of musical phrase.

**cadenza** /kə'denzə/ *noun* Music virtuoso passage for soloist during concerto.

**cadet** /kə'det/ *noun* young trainee in armed services or police force.

**cadge** *verb* (**-ging**) *colloquial* get or seek by begging.

**cadi** /'kɑːdɪ/ noun (plural **-s**) judge in Muslim country.

**cadmium** /'kædmɪəm/ noun soft bluish-white metallic element.

**cadre** /'kɑːdə/ noun basic unit, esp. of servicemen; group of esp. Communist activists.

**caecum** /'siːkəm/ noun (US **cecum**) (plural **-ca**) pouch between small and large intestines.

**Caerphilly** /keə'fɪlɪ/ noun kind of mild pale cheese.

**Caesarean** /sɪ'zeərɪən/ (US **Cesarean**, **Cesarian**) ● adjective (of birth) effected by Caesarean section. ● noun (in full **Caesarean section**) delivery of child by cutting into mother's abdomen.

**caesura** /sɪ'zjʊərə/ noun (plural **-s**) pause in line of verse.

**café** /'kæfeɪ/ noun coffee house, restaurant.

**cafeteria** /kæfɪ'tɪərɪə/ noun self-service restaurant.

**cafetière** /kæfə'tjeə/ noun coffee pot with plunger for pressing grounds to bottom.

**caffeine** /'kæfiːn/ noun alkaloid stimulant in tea leaves and coffee beans.

**caftan** /'kæftæn/ noun (also **kaftan**) long tunic worn by men in Near East; long loose dress.

**cage** ● noun structure of bars or wires, esp. for confining animals; open framework, esp. lift in mine etc. ● verb (**-ging**) confine in cage.

**cagey** /'keɪdʒɪ/ adjective (**-ier**, **-iest**) colloquial cautious and non-committal. □ **cagily** adverb.

**cagoule** /kə'guːl/ noun light hooded windproof jacket.

**cahoots** /kə'huːts/ plural noun □ **in cahoots** slang in collusion.

**caiman** = CAYMAN.

**cairn** /keən/ noun mound of stones. □ **cairn terrier** small shaggy short-legged terrier.

**cairngorm** /'keəngɔːm/ noun yellow or wine-coloured semiprecious stone.

**caisson** /'keɪs(ə)n/ noun watertight chamber for underwater construction work.

**cajole** /kə'dʒəʊl/ verb (**-ling**) persuade by flattery, deceit, etc. □ **cajolery** noun.

**cake** ● noun mixture of flour, butter, eggs, sugar, etc. baked in oven; flattish compact mass. ● verb (**-king**) form into compact mass; (usually + with) cover (with sticky mass).

**calabash** /'kæləbæʃ/ noun tropical American tree bearing gourds; bowl or pipe made from gourd.

**calabrese** /'kæləbriːs, kælə'breɪsɪ/ noun variety of broccoli.

**calamine** /'kæləmaɪn/ noun powdered zinc carbonate and ferric oxide used in skin lotion.

**calamity** /kə'læmɪtɪ/ noun (plural **-ies**) disaster. □ **calamitous** adjective.

**calcareous** /kæl'keərɪəs/ adjective of or containing calcium carbonate.

**calceolaria** /kælsɪə'leərɪə/ noun plant with slipper-shaped flowers.

**calcify** /'kælsɪfaɪ/ verb (**-ies**, **-ied**) harden by deposit of calcium salts. □ **calcification** noun.

**calcine** /'kælsaɪn/ verb (**-ning**) decompose or be decomposed by roasting or burning. □ **calcination** /-sɪn-/ noun.

**calcium** /'kælsɪəm/ noun soft grey metallic element.

**calculate** /'kælkjʊleɪt/ verb (**-ting**) ascertain or forecast by exact reckoning; plan deliberately. □ **calculable** adjective; **calculation** noun.

**calculated** adjective done with awareness of likely consequences; (+ to do) designed.

**calculating** adjective scheming, mercenary.

**calculator** noun device (esp. small electronic one) used for making calculations.

**calculus** /'kælkjʊləs/ noun (plural **-luses** or **-li** /-laɪ/) Mathematics particular method of calculation; stone in body.

**Caledonian** /kælɪ'dəʊnɪən/ literary ● adjective of Scotland. ● noun Scot.

**calendar** /'kælɪndə/ noun system fixing year's beginning, length, and subdivision; chart etc. showing such subdivisions; list of special dates or events. □ **calendar year** period from 1 Jan. to 31 Dec. inclusive.

**calends** /'kælendz/ plural noun (also **kalends**) first of month in ancient Roman calendar.

**calf**[1] /kɑːf/ noun (plural **calves** /kɑːvz/) young cow, bull, elephant, whale, etc.; calf leather. □ **calf-love** romantic adolescent love.

**calf**[2] /kɑːf/ noun (plural **calves** /kɑːvz/) fleshy hind part of human leg below knee.

**calibrate** /'kælɪbreɪt/ verb (**-ting**) mark (gauge) with scale of readings; correlate readings of (instrument) with standard; find calibre of (gun). □ **calibration** noun.

**calibre** /'kælɪbə/ noun (US **caliber**) internal diameter of gun or tube; diameter of bullet or shell; strength or quality of character; ability; importance.

**calico** /'kælɪkəʊ/ ● noun (plural **-es** or US **-s**) cotton cloth, esp. white or unbleached; US printed cotton cloth. ● adjective of calico; US multicoloured.

**caliper** = CALLIPER.

**caliph** /'keɪlɪf/ noun historical chief Muslim civil and religious ruler.

**calk** US = CAULK.

**call** /kɔːl/ ● verb (often + out) cry, shout, speak loudly; emit characteristic sound; communicate with by radio or telephone; summon; make brief visit; order to take place; name, describe, or regard as; rouse from sleep; (+ for) demand. ● noun shout; bird's cry; brief visit; telephone conversation; summons; need, demand. □ **call box** telephone box; **call-girl** prostitute accepting appointments by telephone; **call in** withdraw from circulation, seek advice or services of; **call off** cancel, order (pursuer) to desist; **call the shots, tune** colloquial be in control; **call up** verb telephone, recall, summon (esp. to do military service); **call-up** noun summons to do military service. □ **caller** noun.

**calligraphy** /kə'lɪɡrəfɪ/ noun beautiful handwriting; art of this. □ **calligrapher** noun; **calligraphic** /kælɪ'ɡræfɪk/ adjective.

**calling** noun profession, occupation; vocation.

**calliper** /'kælɪpə/ noun (also **caliper**) metal splint to support leg; (in plural) compasses for measuring diameters.

**callisthenics** /kælɪs'θenɪks/ plural noun exercises for fitness and grace. □ **callisthenic** adjective.

**callosity** /kə'lɒsɪtɪ/ noun (plural **-ies**) callus.

**callous** /'kæləs/ adjective unfeeling, unsympathetic; (also **calloused**) (of skin) hardened. □ **callously** adverb; **callousness** noun.

**callow** /'kæləʊ/ adjective inexperienced, immature.

**callus** /'kæləs/ noun (plural **calluses**) area of hard thick skin.

**calm** /kɑːm/ ● adjective tranquil, windless; not agitated. ● noun calm condition or period. ● verb (often + down) make or become calm. □ **calmly** adverb; **calmness** noun.

**calomel** /'kæləmel/ noun compound of mercury used as laxative.

**Calor gas** /'kælə/ noun proprietary term liquefied butane under pressure in containers for domestic use.

**calorie** /'kælərɪ/ noun unit of heat, amount required to raise temperature of one gram (**small calorie**) or one kilogram (**large calorie**) of water by 1°C.

**calorific** /kælə'rɪfɪk/ adjective producing heat.

**calumny** /'kæləmnɪ/ noun (plural **-ies**) slander; malicious misrepresentation. □ **calumnious** /kə'lʌm-/ adjective.

**calvados** /'kælvədɒs/ noun apple brandy.

**calve** /kɑːv/ verb (**-ving**) give birth to (calf).

**calves** plural of CALF[1,2].

**Calvinism** /'kælvɪnɪz(ə)m/ noun Calvin's theology, stressing predestination. □ **Calvinist** noun & adjective; **Calvinistic** /-'nɪs-/ adjective.

**calx** noun (plural **calces** /'kælsiːz/) powdery residue left after heating of ore or mineral.

**calypso** /kə'lɪpsəʊ/ noun (plural **-s**) W. Indian song with improvised usually topical words.

**calyx** /'keɪlɪks/ noun (plural **calyces** /-lɪsiːz/ or **-es**) leaves forming protective case of flower in bud.

**cam** noun projection on wheel etc., shaped to convert circular into reciprocal or variable motion.

**camaraderie** /kæmə'rɑːdəri/ noun friendly comradeship.

**camber** /'kæmbə/ ● noun convex surface of road, deck, etc. ● verb construct with camber.

**cambric** /'kæmbrɪk/ noun fine linen or cotton cloth.

**camcorder** /'kæmkɔːdə/ noun combined portable video camera and recorder.

**came** past of COME.

**camel** /'kæm(ə)l/ noun long-legged ruminant with one hump (**Arabian camel**) or two humps (**Bactrian camel**); fawn colour.

**camellia** /kə'miːlɪə/ noun evergreen flowering shrub.

**Camembert** /'kæməmbeə/ noun kind of soft creamy cheese.

**cameo** /'kæmɪəʊ/ noun (plural **-s**) small piece of hard stone carved in relief; short literary sketch or acted scene; small part in play or film.

**camera** /'kæmrə/ noun apparatus for taking photographs or for making motion film or television pictures. □ **cameraman** operator of film or television camera; **in camera** in private.

**camiknickers** /'kæmɪnɪkəz/ plural noun woman's knickers and vest combined.

**camisole** /'kæmɪsəʊl/ noun woman's under-bodice.

**camomile** /'kæməmaɪl/ noun (also **chamomile**) aromatic herb with flowers used to make tea.

**camouflage** /'kæməflɑːʒ/ ● noun disguising of soldiers, tanks, etc., so that they blend into background; such disguise; animal's natural blending colouring. ● verb (**-ging**) hide by camouflage.

**camp**[1] ● noun place where troops are lodged or trained; temporary accommodation of tents, huts, etc., for detainees, holiday-makers, etc.; fortified site; party supporters regarded collectively. ● verb set up or live in camp. □ **camp bed** portable folding bed; **camp follower** civilian worker in military camp, disciple; **campsite** place for camping.

**camp**[2] colloquial ● adjective affected, theatrically exaggerated; effeminate; homosexual. ● noun camp manner. ● verb behave or do in camp way.

**campaign** /kæm'peɪn/ ● noun organized course of action, esp. to gain publicity; series of military operations. ● verb take part in campaign. □ **campaigner** noun.

**campanile** /kæmpə'niːlɪ/ noun bell tower, usually free-standing.

**campanology** /kæmpə'nɒlədʒɪ/ noun study of bells; bell-ringing. □ **campanologist** noun.

**campanula** /kæm'pænjʊlə/ noun plant with bell-shaped flowers.

**camper** noun person who camps; motor vehicle with beds.

**camphor** /'kæmfə/ noun pungent crystalline substance used in medicine and formerly mothballs.

**camphorate** verb (**-ting**) impregnate with camphor.

**campion** /'kæmpɪən/ noun wild plant with usually pink or white notched flowers.

**campus** /'kæmpəs/ noun (plural **-es**) grounds of university or college.

**camshaft** noun shaft carrying cam(s).

**can**[1] auxiliary verb (3rd singular present **can**; past **could** /kʊd/) be able to; have the potential to; be permitted to.

**can**[2] ● noun metal vessel for liquid; sealed tin container for preservation of food or drink; (in plural) slang headphones; (**the can**) slang prison, US lavatory. ● verb (**-nn-**) preserve (food etc.) in can. □ **canned music** pre-recorded music; **carry the can** bear responsibility; **in the can** colloquial completed.

**canal** /kə'næl/ noun artificial inland waterway; tubular duct in plant or animal.

**canalize** /'kænəlaɪz/ verb (also **-ise**) (**-zing** or **-sing**) convert (river) into canal; provide (area) with canal(s); channel. □ **canalization** noun.

**canapé** /'kænəpeɪ/ noun small piece of bread or pastry with savoury topping.

**canard** /'kænɑːd/ noun unfounded rumour.

**canary** /kə'neərɪ/ noun (plural **-ies**) small songbird with yellow feathers.

**canasta** /kə'næstə/ noun card games resembling rummy.

**cancan** /'kænkæn/ noun high-kicking dance.

**cancel** /'kæns(ə)l/ *verb* (**-ll-**; *US* **-l-**) revoke, discontinue (arrangement); delete; mark (ticket, stamp, etc.) to invalidate it; annul; (often + *out*) neutralize, counterbalance; *Mathematics* strike out (equal factor) on each side of equation etc. □ **cancellation** *noun*.

**cancer** /'kænsə/ *noun* malignant tumour, disease caused by this; corruption; (**Cancer**) fourth sign of zodiac. □ **cancerous** *adjective*.

**candela** /kæn'di:lə/ *noun* SI unit of luminous intensity.

**candelabrum** /kændr'lɑ:brəm/ *noun* (also **-bra**) (*plural* **-bra**, *US* **-brums**, **-bras**) large branched candlestick or lamp-holder.

**candid** /'kændɪd/ *adjective* frank; (of photograph) taken informally, usually without subject's knowledge. □ **candidly** *adverb*.

**candidate** /'kændɪdət/ *noun* person nominated for, seeking, or likely to gain, office, position, award, etc.; person entered for exam. □ **candidacy** *noun*; **candidature** *noun*.

**candle** /'kænd(ə)l/ *noun* (usually cylindrical) block of wax or tallow enclosing wick which gives light when burning. □ **candlelight** light from candle(s); **candlelit** lit by candle(s); **candlestick** holder for candle(s); **candlewick** thick soft yarn, tufted material made from this.

**candour** /'kændə/ *noun* (*US* **candor**) frankness.

**candy** /'kændɪ/ *noun* (*plural* **-ies**) (in full **sugar-candy**) sugar crystallized by repeated boiling and evaporation; *US* sweets, a sweet. • *verb* (**-ies**, **-ied**) (usually as **candied** *adjective*) preserve (fruit etc.) in candy. □ **candyfloss** fluffy mass of spun sugar; **candy stripe** alternate white and esp. pink stripes.

**candytuft** /'kændɪtʌft/ *noun* plant with white, pink, or purple flowers in tufts.

**cane** • *noun* hollow jointed stem of giant reed or grass, or solid stem of slender palm, used for wickerwork or as walking stick, plant support, instrument of punishment, etc.; sugar cane. • *verb* (**-ning**) beat with cane; weave cane into (chair etc.).

**canine** /'keɪnaɪn/ • *adjective* of a dog or dogs. • *noun* dog; (in full **canine tooth**) tooth between incisors and molars.

**canister** /'kænɪstə/ *noun* small usually metal box for tea etc.; cylinder of shot, tear gas, etc.

**canker** /'kæŋkə/ • *noun* disease of trees and plants; ulcerous ear disease of animals; corrupting influence. • *verb* infect with canker; corrupt. □ **cankerous** *adjective*.

**cannabis** /'kænəbɪs/ *noun* hemp plant; parts of it used as narcotic.

**cannelloni** /kænə'ləʊnɪ/ *plural noun* tubes of pasta stuffed with savoury mixture.

**cannibal** /'kænɪb(ə)l/ *noun* person or animal that eats its own species. □ **cannibalism** *noun*; **cannibalistic** /-'lɪs-/ *adjective*.

**cannibalize** /'kænɪbəlaɪz/ *verb* (also **-ise**) (**-zing** or **-sing**) use (machine etc.) as source of spare parts.

**cannon** /'kænən/ • *noun* automatic aircraft gun firing shells; *historical* (*plural* usually same) large gun; hitting of two balls successively by player's ball in billiards. • *verb* (usually + *against*, *into*) collide. □ **cannon ball** *historical* large ball fired by cannon.

**cannot** /'kænɒt/ can not.

**canny** /'kænɪ/ *adjective* (**-ier**, **-iest**) shrewd; thrifty.

**canoe** /kə'nu:/ • *noun* light narrow boat, usually paddled. • *verb* (**-noes**, **-noed**, **-noeing**) travel in canoe. □ **canoeist** *noun*.

**canon** /'kænən/ *noun* general law, rule, principle, or criterion; church decree; member of cathedral chapter; set of (esp. sacred) writings accepted as genuine; part of RC Mass containing words of consecration; *Music* piece with different parts taking up same theme successively. □ **canon law** ecclesiastical law.

**canonical** /kə'nɒnɪk(ə)l/ • *adjective* according to canon law; included in canon of Scripture; authoritative, accepted; of (member of) cathedral chapter. • *noun* (in *plural*) canonical dress of clergy.

**canonize** /'kænənaɪz/ *verb* (also **-ise**) (**-zing** or **-sing**) declare officially to be saint. □ **canonization** *noun*.

**canopy** /ˈkænəpɪ/ ● noun (plural **-ies**) suspended covering over throne, bed, etc.; sky; overhanging shelter; roofline projection. ● verb (**-ies, -ied**) supply or be canopy to.

**cant**[1] ● noun insincere pious or moral talk; language peculiar to class, profession, etc.; jargon. ● verb use cant.

**cant**[2] ● noun slanting surface, bevel; oblique push or jerk; tilted position. ● verb push or pitch out of level.

**can't** /kɑːnt/ can not.

**cantabile** /kænˈtɑːbɪleɪ/ Music ● adverb & adjective in smooth flowing style. ● noun cantabile passage or movement.

**cantaloupe** /ˈkæntəluːp/ noun (also **cantaloup**) small round ribbed melon.

**cantankerous** /kænˈtæŋkərəs/ adjective bad-tempered, quarrelsome. □ **cantankerously** adverb; **cantankerousness** noun.

**cantata** /kænˈtɑːtə/ noun composition for vocal soloists and usually chorus and orchestra.

**canteen** /kænˈtiːn/ noun restaurant for employees in office, factory, etc.; shop for provisions in barracks or camp; case of cutlery; soldier's or camper's water-flask.

**canter** /ˈkæntə/ ● noun horse's pace between trot and gallop. ● verb (cause to) go at a canter.

**canticle** /ˈkæntɪk(ə)l/ noun song or chant with biblical text.

**cantilever** /ˈkæntɪliːvə/ noun bracket, beam, etc. projecting from wall to support balcony etc.; beam or girder fixed at one end only. □ **cantilever bridge** bridge made of cantilevers projecting from piers and connected by girders. □ **cantilevered** adjective.

**canto** /ˈkæntəʊ/ noun (plural **-s**) division of long poem.

**canton** ● noun /ˈkæntɒn/ subdivision of country, esp. Switzerland. ● verb /kænˈtuːn/ put (troops) into quarters.

**cantonment** /kænˈtuːnmənt/ noun lodgings of troops.

**cantor** /ˈkæntɔː/ noun church choir leader; precentor in synagogue.

**canvas** /ˈkænvəs/ noun strong coarse cloth used for sails and tents etc. and for oil painting; a painting on canvas.

**canvass** /ˈkænvəs/ ● verb solicit votes (from), ascertain opinions of; seek custom from; propose (idea etc.). ● noun canvassing. □ **canvasser** noun.

**canyon** /ˈkænjən/ noun deep gorge.

**CAP** abbreviation Common Agricultural Policy (of EC).

**cap** ● noun soft brimless hat, often with peak; head-covering of nurse etc.; cap as sign of membership of sports team; academic mortarboard; cover resembling cap, or designed to close, seal, or protect something; contraceptive diaphragm; percussion cap; dental crown. ● verb (**-pp-**) put cap on; cover top or end of; limit; award sports cap to; form top of; surpass.

**capable** /ˈkeɪpəb(ə)l/ adjective competent, able; (+ of) having ability, fitness, etc. for. □ **capability** noun (plural **-ies**); **capably** adverb.

**capacious** /kəˈpeɪʃəs/ adjective roomy. □ **capaciousness** noun.

**capacitance** /kəˈpæsɪt(ə)ns/ noun ability to store electric charge.

**capacitor** /kəˈpæsɪtə/ noun type of device for storing electric charge.

**capacity** /kəˈpæsɪtɪ/ ● noun (plural **-ies**) power to contain, receive, experience, or produce; maximum amount that can be contained etc.; mental power; position or function. ● adjective fully occupying available space etc.

**caparison** /kəˈpærɪs(ə)n/ literary ● noun horse's trappings; finery. ● verb adorn.

**cape**[1] noun short cloak.

**cape**[2] noun headland, promontory; (**the Cape**) Cape of Good Hope.

**caper**[1] /ˈkeɪpə/ ● verb jump playfully. ● noun playful leap; prank; slang illicit activity.

**caper**[2] /ˈkeɪpə/ noun bramble-like shrub; (in plural) its pickled buds.

**capercaillie** /kæpəˈkeɪlɪ/ noun (also **capercailzie** /-ˈkeɪlzɪ/) large European grouse.

**capillarity** /kæprˈlærɪtɪ/ noun rise or depression of liquid in narrow tube.

**capillary** /kəˈpɪlərɪ/ ● adjective of hair; of narrow diameter. ● noun (plural **-ies**) capillary tube or blood vessel. □ **capillary action** capillarity.

**capital** /ˈkæpɪt(ə)l/ ● noun chief town or city of a country or region; money etc.

with which company starts in business; accumulated wealth; capital letter; head of column or pillar. ● *adjective* involving punishment by death; most important; *colloquial* excellent. □ **capital gain** profit from sale of investments or property; **capital goods** machinery, plant, etc.; **capital letter** large kind, used to begin sentence or name; **capital transfer tax** *historical* tax levied on transfer of capital by gift or bequest etc.

**capitalism** *noun* economic and political system dependent on private capital and profit-making.

**capitalist** ● *noun* person using or possessing capital; advocate of capitalism. ● *adjective* of or favouring capitalism. □ **capitalistic** /-'lɪs-/ *adjective*.

**capitalize** *verb* (also **-ise**) (**-zing** or **-sing**) convert into or provide with capital; write (letter of alphabet) as capital, begin (word) with capital letter; (+ *on*) use to one's advantage. □ **capitalization** *noun*.

**capitulate** /kə'pɪtjʊleɪt/ *verb* (**-ting**) surrender. □ **capitulation** *noun*.

**capon** /'keɪpən/ *noun* castrated cock.

**cappuccino** /kæpʊ'tʃiːnəʊ/ *noun* (*plural* **-s**) frothy milky coffee.

**caprice** /kə'priːs/ *noun* whim; lively or fanciful work of music etc.

**capricious** /kə'prɪʃəs/ *adjective* subject to whims, unpredictable. □ **capriciously** *adverb*; **capriciousness** *noun*.

**Capricorn** /'kæprɪkɔːn/ *noun* tenth sign of zodiac.

**capsicum** /'kæpsɪkəm/ *noun* plant with edible fruits; red, green, or yellow fruit of this.

**capsize** /kæp'saɪz/ *verb* (**-zing**) (of boat) be overturned; overturn (boat).

**capstan** /'kæpst(ə)n/ *noun* thick revolving cylinder for winding cable etc.; revolving spindle controlling speed of tape on tape recorder. □ **capstan lathe** lathe with revolving tool holder.

**capsule** /'kæpsjuːl/ *noun* small soluble case enclosing medicine; detachable compartment of spacecraft or nosecone of rocket; enclosing membrane; dry fruit releasing seeds when ripe.

**Capt.** *abbreviation* Captain.

**captain** /'kæptɪn/ ● *noun* chief, leader; leader of team; commander of ship; pilot of civil aircraft; army officer next above lieutenant. ● *verb* be captain of. □ **captaincy** *noun* (*plural* **-ies**).

**caption** /'kæpʃ(ə)n/ ● *noun* wording appended to illustration or cartoon; wording on cinema or television screen; heading of chapter, article etc. ● *verb* provide with caption.

**captious** /'kæpʃəs/ *adjective* faultfinding.

**captivate** /'kæptɪveɪt/ *verb* (**-ting**) fascinate, charm. □ **captivation** *noun*.

**captive** /'kæptɪv/ ● *noun* confined or imprisoned person or animal. ● *adjective* taken prisoner; confined; unable to escape. □ **captivity** /-'tɪv-/ *noun*.

**captor** /'kæptə/ *noun* person who captures.

**capture** /'kæptʃə/ ● *verb* (**-ring**) take prisoner; seize; portray in permanent form; record on film or for use in computer. ● *noun* act of capturing; thing or person captured.

**Capuchin** /'kæpjʊtʃɪn/ *noun* friar of branch of Franciscans; (**capuchin**) monkey with hair like black hood.

**car** *noun* motor vehicle for driver and small number of passengers; railway carriage of specified type; *US* any railway carriage or van. □ **car bomb** terrorist bomb placed in or under parked car; **car boot sale** sale of goods from (tables stocked from) boots of cars; **car park** area for parking cars; **car phone** radio-telephone for use in car etc.; **carport** roofed open-sided shelter for car; **carsick** nauseous through car travel.

**caracul** = KARAKUL.

**carafe** /kə'ræf/ *noun* glass container for water or wine.

**caramel** /'kærəmel/ *noun* burnt sugar or syrup; kind of soft toffee. □ **caramelize** *verb*.

**carapace** /'kærəpeɪs/ *noun* upper shell of tortoise or crustacean.

**carat** /'kærət/ *noun* unit of weight for precious stones; measure of purity of gold.

**caravan** /'kærəvæn/ *noun* vehicle equipped for living in and usually towed by car; people travelling together, esp. across desert. □ **caravanner** noun.

**caravanserai** /kærə'vænsəraɪ/ noun Eastern inn with central courtyard.

**caravel** /'kærəvel/ noun historical small light fast ship.

**caraway** /'kærəweɪ/ noun plant with small aromatic fruit (**caraway seed**) used in cakes etc.

**carbide** /'kɑːbaɪd/ noun binary compound of carbon.

**carbine** /'kɑːbaɪn/ noun kind of short rifle.

**carbohydrate** /kɑːbə'haɪdreɪt/ noun energy-producing compound of carbon, hydrogen, and oxygen.

**carbolic** /kɑː'bɒlɪk/ noun (in full **carbolic acid**) kind of disinfectant and antiseptic. □ **carbolic soap** soap containing this.

**carbon** /'kɑːbən/ noun non-metallic element occurring as diamond, graphite, and charcoal, and in all organic compounds; carbon copy, carbon paper. □ **carbon copy** copy made with carbon paper; **carbon dating** determination of age of object from decay of carbon-14; **carbon dioxide** gas found in atmosphere and formed by respiration; **carbon fibre** thin filament of carbon used as strengthening material; **carbon-14** radioactive carbon isotope of mass 14; **carbon monoxide** poisonous gas formed by burning carbon incompletely; **carbon paper** thin carbon-coated paper for making copies; **carbon tax** on fuels producing greenhouse gases; **carbon-12** stable isotope of carbon used as a standard.

**carbonate** /'kɑːbəneɪt/ ● noun salt of carbonic acid. ● verb (**-ting**) fill with carbon dioxide.

**carbonic** /kɑː'bɒnɪk/ adjective containing carbon. □ **carbonic acid** weak acid formed from carbon dioxide in water.

**carboniferous** /kɑːbə'nɪfərəs/ adjective producing coal.

**carbonize** /'kɑːbənaɪz/ verb (also **-ise**) (**-zing** or **-sing**) reduce to charcoal or coke; convert to carbon; coat with carbon. □ **carbonization** noun.

**carborundum** /kɑːbə'rʌndəm/ noun compound of carbon and silicon used esp. as abrasive.

**carboy** /'kɑːbɔɪ/ noun large globular glass bottle.

**carbuncle** /'kɑːbʌŋk(ə)l/ noun severe skin abscess; bright red jewel.

**carburettor** /kɑːbə'retə/ noun apparatus mixing air with petrol vapour in internal-combustion engine.

**carcass** /'kɑːkəs/ noun (also **carcase**) dead body of animal or bird or (colloquial) person; framework; worthless remains.

**carcinogen** /kɑː'sɪnədʒ(ə)n/ noun substance producing cancer. □ **carcinogenic** /-'dʒen-/ adjective.

**card**[1] noun thick stiff paper or thin pasteboard; piece of this for writing or printing on, esp. to send greetings, to identify person, or to record information; small rectangular piece of plastic used to obtain credit etc.; playing card; (in plural) card-playing; (in plural) colloquial employee's tax etc. documents; programme of events at race meeting etc.; colloquial eccentric person. □ **card-carrying** registered as member (esp. of political party); **card index** index with separate card for each item; **cardphone** public telephone operated by card instead of money; **card-sharp** swindler at card games; **card vote** block vote.

**card**[2] ● noun wire brush etc. for raising nap on cloth etc. ● verb brush with card.

**cardamom** /'kɑːdəməm/ noun seeds of SE Asian aromatic plant used as spice.

**cardboard** noun pasteboard or stiff paper.

**cardiac** /'kɑːdɪæk/ adjective of the heart.

**cardigan** /'kɑːdɪgən/ noun knitted jacket.

**cardinal** /'kɑːdɪn(ə)l/ ● adjective chief, fundamental; deep scarlet. ● noun one of leading RC dignitaries who elect Pope. □ **cardinal number** number representing quantity (1, 2, 3, etc.); compare ORDINAL.

**cardiogram** /'kɑːdɪəʊgræm/ noun record of heart movements.

**cardiograph** /'kɑːdɪəʊgrɑːf/ noun instrument recording heart movements. □ **cardiographer** /-'ɒgrəfə/ noun; **cardiography** /-'ɒgrəfɪ/ noun.

**cardiology** /kɑːdɪ'ɒlədʒɪ/ noun branch of medicine concerned with heart. □ **cardiologist** noun.

**cardiovascular** /ˌkɑːdɪəʊˈvæskjʊlə/ *adjective* of heart and blood vessels.

**care** /keə/ ● *noun* (cause of) anxiety or concern; serious attention; caution; protection, charge; task. ● *verb* (**-ring**) (usually + *about, for, whether*) feel concern or interest or affection. □ **in care** (of child) under local authority supervision; **take care** be careful, (+ *to do*) not fail or neglect; **take care of** look after, deal with, dispose of.

**careen** /kəˈriːn/ *verb* turn (ship) on side for repair; move or swerve wildly.

**career** /kəˈrɪə/ ● *noun* professional etc. course through life; profession or occupation; swift course. ● *adjective* pursuing or wishing to pursue a career; working permanently in specified profession. ● *verb* move or swerve wildly.

**careerist** *noun* person predominantly concerned with professional advancement.

**carefree** *adjective* light-hearted, joyous.

**careful** *adjective* painstaking; cautious; taking care, not neglecting. □ **carefully** *adverb*; **carefulness** *noun*.

**careless** *adjective* lacking care or attention; unthinking, insensitive; light-hearted. □ **carelessly** *adverb*; **carelessness** *noun*.

**carer** *noun* person who cares for sick or elderly person, esp. at home.

**caress** /kəˈres/ ● *verb* touch lovingly. ● *noun* loving touch.

**caret** /ˈkærət/ *noun* mark indicating insertion in text.

**caretaker** ● *noun* person in charge of maintenance of building. ● *adjective* taking temporary control.

**careworn** *adjective* showing effects of prolonged anxiety.

**cargo** /ˈkɑːgəʊ/ *noun* (*plural* **-es** or **-s**) goods carried by ship or aircraft.

**Caribbean** /kærəˈbiːən/ *adjective* of the West Indies.

**caribou** /ˈkærɪbuː/ *noun* (*plural* same) N. American reindeer.

**caricature** /ˈkærɪkətʊə/ ● *noun* grotesque usually comically exaggerated representation. ● *verb* (**-ring**) make or give caricature of. □ **caricaturist** *noun*.

**caries** /ˈkeərɪːz/ *noun* (*plural* same) decay of tooth or bone.

**carillon** /kəˈrɪljən/ *noun* set of bells sounded from keyboard or mechanically; tune played on this.

**Carmelite** /ˈkɑːməlaɪt/ ● *noun* friar of Order of Our Lady of Mount Carmel; nun of similar order. ● *adjective* of Carmelites.

**carminative** /ˈkɑːmɪnətɪv/ ● *adjective* relieving flatulence. ● *noun* carminative drug.

**carmine** /ˈkɑːmaɪn/ ● *adjective* of vivid crimson colour. ● *noun* this colour; pigment from cochineal.

**carnage** /ˈkɑːnɪdʒ/ *noun* great slaughter.

**carnal** /ˈkɑːn(ə)l/ *adjective* worldly; sensual; sexual. □ **carnality** *noun*.

**carnation** /kɑːˈneɪʃ(ə)n/ ● *noun* clove-scented pink; rosy-pink colour. ● *adjective* rosy-pink.

**carnelian** = CORNELIAN.

**carnival** /ˈkɑːnɪv(ə)l/ *noun* festivities or festival, esp. preceding Lent; merry-making.

**carnivore** /ˈkɑːnɪvɔː/ *noun* animal or plant that feeds on flesh. □ **carnivorous** /-ˈnɪvərəs-/ *adjective*.

**carob** /ˈkærəb/ *noun* seed pod of Mediterranean tree used as chocolate substitute.

**carol** /ˈkær(ə)l/ ● *noun* joyous song, esp. Christmas hymn. ● *verb* (**-ll-**; *US* **-l-**) sing carols; sing joyfully.

**carotene** /ˈkærətiːn/ *noun* orange-coloured pigment in carrots etc.

**carotid** /kəˈrɒtɪd/ ● *noun* each of two main arteries carrying blood to head. ● *adjective* of these arteries.

**carouse** /kəˈraʊz/ ● *verb* (**-sing**) have lively drinking party. ● *noun* such party. □ **carousal** *noun*; **carouser** *noun*.

**carp**[1] *noun* (*plural* same) freshwater fish often bred for food.

**carp**[2] *verb* find fault, complain. □ **carper** *noun*.

**carpal** /ˈkɑːp(ə)l/ ● *adjective* of the wristbones. ● *noun* wrist-bone.

**carpel** /ˈkɑːp(ə)l/ *noun* female reproductive organ of flower.

**carpenter** /ˈkɑːpɪntə/ ● *noun* person skilled in woodwork. ● *verb* do woodwork; make by woodwork. □ **carpentry** *noun*.

**carpet** /ˈkɑːpɪt/ • noun thick fabric for covering floors etc.; piece of this; thing resembling this. • verb (-t-) cover (as) with carpet; colloquial rebuke. □ **carpet-bag** travelling bag originally made of carpet-like material; **carpet-bagger** colloquial political candidate etc. without local connections; **carpet slipper** soft slipper; **carpet sweeper** implement for sweeping carpets.

**carpeting** noun material for carpets; carpets collectively.

**carpus** /ˈkɑːpəs/ noun (plural **-pi** /-paɪ/) group of small bones forming wrist.

**carrageen** /ˈkærəgiːn/ noun edible red seaweed.

**carriage** /ˈkærɪdʒ/ noun railway passenger vehicle; wheeled horse-drawn passenger vehicle; conveying of goods; cost of this; bearing, deportment; part of machine that carries other parts; gun carriage. □ **carriage clock** portable clock with handle; **carriageway** part of road used by vehicles.

**carrier** /ˈkærɪə/ noun person or thing that carries; transport or freight company; carrier bag; framework on bicycle for carrying luggage or passenger; person or animal that may transmit disease without suffering from it; aircraft carrier. □ **carrier bag** plastic or paper bag with handles; **carrier pigeon** pigeon trained to carry messages; **carrier wave** high-frequency electromagnetic wave used to convey signal.

**carrion** /ˈkærɪən/ noun dead flesh; filth. □ **carrion crow** crow feeding on carrion.

**carrot** /ˈkærət/ noun plant with edible tapering orange root; this root; incentive. □ **carroty** adjective.

**carry** /ˈkærɪ/ verb (**-ies, -ied**) support or hold up, esp. while moving; have with one; convey; (often + to) take (process etc.) to specified point; involve; transfer (figure) to column of higher value; hold in specified way; (of newspaper etc.) publish; (of radio or television station) broadcast; keep (goods) in stock; (of sound) be audible at a distance; win victory or acceptance for; win acceptance from; capture. □ **carry away** remove, inspire, deprive of self-control; **carrycot** portable cot for baby; **carry forward** transfer (figure) to new page or account; **carry it off** do well under difficulties; **carry off** remove (esp. by force), win, (esp. of disease) kill; **carry on** continue, colloquial behave excitedly, (often + with) colloquial flirt; **carry-on** colloquial fuss; **carry out** put into practice; **carry-out** takeaway; **carry over** carry forward, postpone; **carry through** complete, bring safely out of difficulties.

**cart** • noun open usually horse-drawn vehicle for carrying loads; light vehicle for pulling by hand. • verb carry in cart; slang carry with difficulty. □ **cart horse** horse of heavy build; **cartwheel** wheel of cart, sideways somersault with arms and legs extended.

**carte blanche** /kɑːt ˈblɑːʃ/ noun full discretionary power.

**cartel** /kɑːˈtel/ noun union of suppliers etc. set up to control prices.

**Cartesian coordinates** /kɑːˈtiːzɪən/ plural noun system of locating point by its distance from two perpendicular axes.

**Carthusian** /kɑːˈθjuːzɪən/ • noun monk of contemplative order founded by St Bruno. • adjective of this order.

**cartilage** /ˈkɑːtɪlɪdʒ/ noun firm flexible connective tissue in vertebrates. □ **cartilaginous** /-ˈlædʒ-/ adjective.

**cartography** /kɑːˈtɒgrəfɪ/ noun map-drawing. □ **cartographer** noun, **cartographic** /-təˈgræf-/ adjective.

**carton** /ˈkɑːt(ə)n/ noun light esp. cardboard container.

**cartoon** /kɑːˈtuːn/ noun humorous esp. topical drawing in newspaper etc.; sequence of drawings telling story; such sequence animated on film; full-size preliminary design for work of art. □ **cartoonist** noun.

**cartouche** /kɑːˈtuːʃ/ noun scroll-like ornament; oval enclosing name and title of pharaoh.

**cartridge** /ˈkɑːtrɪdʒ/ noun case containing explosive charge or bullet; sealed container of film etc.; component carrying stylus on record player; ink-container for insertion in pen. □ **cartridge-belt** belt with pockets or loops for cartridges; **cartridge paper** thick paper for drawing etc.

**carve** verb (**-ving**) make or shape by cutting; cut pattern etc. in; (+ into) form pattern etc. from; cut (meat) into slices. □ **carve out** take from larger whole; **carve up** subdivide, drive aggressively into path of (another vehicle). □ **carver** *noun*.

**carvery** *noun* (*plural* **-ies**) restaurant etc. with joints displayed for carving.

**carving** *noun* carved object, esp. as work of art. □ **carving knife** knife for carving meat.

**cascade** /kæsˈkeɪd/ ● *noun* waterfall, esp. one in series. ● *verb* (**-ding**) fall in or like cascade.

**case¹** /keɪs/ *noun* instance of something occurring; hypothetical or actual situation; person's illness, circumstances, etc. as regarded by doctor, social worker, etc.; such a person; crime etc. investigated by detective or police; suit at law; sum of arguments on one side; (valid) set of arguments; *Grammar* relation of word to others in sentence, form of word expressing this. □ **case law** law as established by decided cases; **casework** social work concerned with individual's background; **in any case** whatever the truth or possible outcome is; **in case** in the event that, lest, in provision against a possibility; **in case of** in the event of; **is (not) the case** is (not) so.

**case²** /keɪs/ ● *noun* container or cover enclosing something. ● *verb* (**-sing**) enclose in case; (+ *with*) surround with; *slang* inspect closely, esp. for criminal purpose. □ **case-harden** harden surface of (esp. steel), make callous.

**casein** /ˈkeɪsɪn/ *noun* main protein in milk and cheese.

**casement** /ˈkeɪsmənt/ *noun* (part of) window hinged to open like door.

**cash** ● *noun* money in coins or notes; full payment at time of purchase. ● *verb* give or obtain cash for. □ **cash and carry** (esp. wholesaling) system of cash payment for goods removed by buyer, store where this operates; **cashcard** plastic card for use in cash dispenser; **cash crop** crop produced for sale; **cash desk** counter etc. where goods are paid for; **cash dispenser** automatic machine for withdrawal of cash; **cash flow** movement of money into and out of a business; **cash in** obtain cash for, (usually + *on*) *colloquial* profit

(from); **cash register** till recording sales, totalling receipts, etc.; **cash up** count day's takings.

**cashew** /ˈkæʃuː/ *noun* evergreen tree bearing kidney-shaped edible nut; this nut.

**cashier¹** /kæˈʃɪə/ *noun* person dealing with cash transactions in bank etc.

**cashier²** /kæˈʃɪə/ *verb* dismiss from service.

**cashmere** /kæʃˈmɪə/ *noun* fine soft (material of) wool, esp. of Kashmir goat.

**casing** *noun* enclosing material or cover.

**casino** /kəˈsiːnəʊ/ *noun* (*plural* **-s**) public room etc. for gambling.

**cask** /kɑːsk/ *noun* barrel, esp. for alcoholic liquor.

**casket** /ˈkɑːskɪt/ *noun* small box for holding valuables; *US* coffin.

**cassava** /kəˈsɑːvə/ *noun* plant with starchy roots; starch or flour from these.

**casserole** /ˈkæsərəʊl/ ● *noun* covered dish for cooking food in oven; food cooked in this. ● *verb* (**-ling**) cook in casserole.

**cassette** /kəˈset/ *noun* sealed case containing magnetic tape, film, etc., ready for insertion in tape recorder, camera, etc.

**cassia** /ˈkæsɪə/ *noun* tree whose leaves and pod yield senna.

**cassis** /kæˈsiːs/ *noun* blackcurrant flavouring for drinks etc.

**cassock** /ˈkæsək/ *noun* long usually black or red clerical garment.

**cassowary** /ˈkæsəweərɪ/ *noun* (*plural* **-ies**) large flightless Australian bird.

**cast** /kɑːst/ ● *verb* (*past & past participle* **cast**) throw; direct, cause to fall; express (doubts etc.); let down (anchor etc.); shed or lose; register (vote); shape (molten metal etc.) in mould; make (product) thus; (usually + *as*) assign (actor) to role; allocate roles in (play, film, etc.); (+ *in, into*) arrange (facts etc.) in specified form. ● *noun* throwing of missile, dice, fishing line, etc.; thing made in mould; moulded mass of solidified material; actors in play etc.; form, type, or quality; tinge of colour; slight squint; worm-cast. □ **cast about, around** search; **cast aside** abandon; **casting vote** deciding vote when votes on two sides are equal; **cast iron** hard but brittle iron alloy; **cast-iron** of cast iron, very strong, unchallengeable; **cast off** abandon, finish piece of knitting; **cast-off** abandoned or discarded (thing, esp. garment); **cast on** make first row of piece of knitting.

**castanet** /kæstə'net/ *noun* (usually in *plural*) each of pair of hand-held wooden or ivory shells clicked together in time with esp. Spanish dancing.

**castaway** /'kɑːstəweɪ/ ●*noun* shipwrecked person. ●*adjective* shipwrecked.

**caste** /kɑːst/ *noun* any of Hindu hereditary classes whose members have no social contact with other classes; exclusive social class.

**castellated** /'kæstəleɪtɪd/ *adjective* built with battlements. □ **castellation** *noun.*

**caster** = CASTOR.

**castigate** /'kæstɪgeɪt/ *verb* (**-ting**) rebuke; punish. □ **castigation** *noun.*

**castle** /'kɑːs(ə)l/ ●*noun* large fortified residential building; *Chess* rook. ●*verb* (**-ling**) *Chess* make combined move of king and rook.

**castor** /'kɑːstə/ *noun* (also **caster**) small swivelled wheel enabling heavy furniture to be moved; container perforated for sprinkling sugar etc. □ **castor sugar** finely granulated white sugar.

**castor oil** *noun* vegetable oil used as laxative and lubricant.

**castrate** /kæs'treɪt/ *verb* (**-ting**) remove testicles of. □ **castration** *noun.*

**casual** /'kæʒʊəl/ ●*adjective* chance; not regular or permanent; unconcerned, careless; (of clothes etc.) informal. ●*noun* casual worker; (usually in *plural*) casual clothes or shoes. □ **casually** *adverb.*

**casualty** /'kæʒʊəltɪ/ *noun* (*plural* **-ies**) person killed or injured in war or accident; thing lost or destroyed; casualty department; accident. □ **casualty department** part of hospital for treatment of casualties.

**casuist** /'kæʒʊɪst/ *noun* person who resolves cases of conscience etc., esp. cleverly but falsely; sophist, quibbler.

□ **casuistic** *adjective;* **casuistry** /-'ɪs-/ *noun.*

**cat** *noun* small furry domestic quadruped; wild animal of same family; *colloquial* malicious or spiteful woman; cat-o'-nine-tails. □ **cat burglar** burglar who enters by climbing to upper storey; **catcall** (make) shrill whistle of disapproval; **catfish** fish with whisker-like filaments round mouth; **cat flap** small flap allowing cat passage through outer door; **catnap** (have) short sleep; **cat-o'-nine-tails** *historical* whip with nine knotted cords; **cat's cradle** child's game with string; **cat's-eye** *proprietary term* reflector stud set into road; **cat's-paw** person used as tool by another; **catsuit** close-fitting garment with trouser legs, covering whole body; **catwalk** narrow walkway; **rain cats and dogs** rain hard.

**catachresis** /kætə'kriːsɪs/ *noun* (*plural* **-chreses** /-siːz/) incorrect use of words. □ **catachrestic** /-'kres-/ *adjective.*

**cataclysm** /'kætəklɪz(ə)m/ *noun* violent upheaval. □ **cataclysmic** /-'klɪz-/ *adjective.*

**catacomb** /'kætəkuːm/ *noun* (often in *plural*) underground cemetery.

**catafalque** /'kætəfælk/ *noun* decorated bier, esp. for state funeral etc.

**Catalan** /'kætəlæn/ ●*noun* native or language of Catalonia in Spain. ●*adjective* of Catalonia.

**catalepsy** /'kætəlepsɪ/ *noun* trance or seizure with rigidity of body. □ **cataleptic** /-'lep-/ *adjective & noun.*

**catalogue** /'kætəlɒg/ (*US* **catalog**) ●*noun* complete or extensive list, usually in alphabetical or other systematic order. ●*verb* (**-logues, -logued, -loguing;** *US* **-logs, -loged, -loging**) make catalogue of; enter in catalogue.

**catalysis** /kə'tælɪsɪs/ *noun* (*plural* **-lyses** /-siːz/) acceleration of chemical reaction by catalyst. □ **catalyse** *verb* (**-sing**) (*US* **-lyze; -zing**).

**catalyst** /'kætəlɪst/ *noun* substance speeding chemical reaction without itself permanently changing; person or thing that precipitates change.

**catalytic** /kætə'lɪtɪk/ *adjective* involving or causing catalysis. □ **catalytic converter** device in vehicle for converting pollutant gases into less harmful ones.

**catamaran** /kætəˈmæn/ *noun* boat or raft with two parallel hulls.

**catapult** /ˈkætəpʌlt/ ● *noun* forked stick with elastic for shooting stones; *historical* military machine for hurling stones etc.; device for launching glider etc. ● *verb* launch with catapult; fling forcibly; leap or be hurled forcibly.

**cataract** /ˈkætərækt/ *noun* waterfall, downpour; progressive opacity of eye lens.

**catarrh** /kəˈtɑː/ *noun* inflammation of mucous membrane, air-passages, etc; mucous in nose caused by this. □ **catarrhal** *adjective*.

**catastrophe** /kəˈtæstrəfɪ/ *noun* great usually sudden disaster; denouement of drama. □ **catastrophic** /kætəˈstrɒf-/ *adjective*; **catastrophically** /kætəˈstrɒf-/ *adverb*.

**catch** /kætʃ/ ● *verb* (*past & past participle* **caught** /kɔːt/) capture in trap, hands, etc.; detect or surprise; intercept and hold (moving thing) in hand etc.; *Cricket* dismiss (batsman) by catching ball before it hits ground; contract (disease) by infection etc.; reach in time and board (train etc.); apprehend; check or be checked; become entangled; (of artist etc.) reproduce faithfully; reach or overtake. ● *noun* act of catching; *Cricket* chance or act of catching ball; amount of thing caught; thing or person caught or worth catching; question etc. intended to deceive etc.; unexpected difficulty or disadvantage; device for fastening door etc.; musical round. □ **catch fire** begin to burn; **catch on** *colloquial* become popular, understand what is meant; **catch out** detect in mistake etc., *Cricket* catch; **catchpenny** intended merely to sell quickly; **catchphrase** phrase in frequent use; **catch up** (often + *with*) reach (person etc. ahead), make up arrears, involve, fasten; **catchword** phrase or word in frequent use, word so placed as to draw attention.

**catching** *adjective* infectious.

**catchment area** *noun* area served by school, hospital, etc.; area from which rainfall flows into river etc.

**catchy** *adjective* (**-ier**, **-iest**) (of tune) easily remembered, attractive.

**catechism** /ˈkætɪkɪz(ə)m/ *noun* (book containing) principles of a religion in form of questions and answers; series of questions.

**catechize** /ˈkætɪkaɪz/ *verb* (also **-ise**) (**-zing** or **-sing**) instruct by question and answer. □ **catechist** *noun*.

**catechumen** /kætɪˈkjuːmən/ *noun* person being instructed before baptism.

**categorical** /kætɪˈgɒrɪk(ə)l/ *adjective* unconditional, absolute, explicit. □ **categorically** *adverb*.

**categorize** /ˈkætɪgəraɪz/ *verb* (also **-ise**) (**-zing** or **-sing**) place in category. □ **categorization** *noun*.

**category** /ˈkætɪgərɪ/ *noun* (*plural* **-ies**) class or division of things, ideas, etc.

**cater** /ˈkeɪtə/ *verb* supply food; (+ *for*) provide what is required for. □ **caterer** *noun*.

**caterpillar** /ˈkætəpɪlə/ *noun* larva of butterfly or moth; (**Caterpillar**) (in full **Caterpillar track**) *proprietary term* articulated steel band passing round wheels of vehicle for travel on rough ground.

**caterwaul** /ˈkætəwɔːl/ *verb* howl like cat.

**catgut** *noun* thread made from intestines of sheep etc. used for strings of musical instruments etc.

**catharsis** /kəˈθɑːsɪs/ *noun* (*plural* **catharses** /-siːz/) emotional release; emptying of bowels.

**cathartic** /kəˈθɑːtɪk/ ● *adjective* effecting catharsis. ● *noun* laxative.

**cathedral** /kəˈθiːdr(ə)l/ *noun* principal church of diocese.

**Catherine wheel** /ˈkæθrɪn/ *noun* rotating firework.

**catheter** /ˈkæθɪtə/ *noun* tube inserted into body cavity to introduce or drain fluid.

**cathode** /ˈkæθəʊd/ *noun* negative electrode of cell; positive terminal of battery. □ **cathode ray** beam of electrons from cathode of vacuum tube; **cathode ray tube** vacuum tube in which cathode rays produce luminous image on fluorescent screen.

**catholic** /ˈkæθlɪk/ ● *adjective* universal; broad-minded; all-embracing; (**Catholic**) Roman Catholic; (**Catholic**) including all Christians or all of Western Church. ● *noun* (**Catholic**) Roman Catholic. □ **Catholicism** /kəˈθɒlɪs-/ *noun*; **catholicity** /-əˈlɪs-/ *noun*.

**cation** /'kætaɪən/ *noun* positively charged ion. □ **cationic** /-'ɒnɪk/ *adjective*.

**catkin** /'kætkɪn/ *noun* spike of usually hanging flowers of willow, hazel, etc.

**catmint** *noun* pungent plant attractive to cats.

**catnip** *noun* catmint.

**cattery** *noun* (*plural* **-ies**) place where cats are boarded.

**cattle** /'kæt(ə)l/ *plural noun* large ruminants, bred esp. for milk or meat. □ **cattle grid** grid over ditch, allowing vehicles to pass over but not livestock.

**catty** *adjective* (**-ier**, **-iest**) spiteful. □ **cattily** *adverb*; **cattiness** *noun*.

**Caucasian** /kɔː'keɪʒ(ə)n/ ● *adjective* of the white or light-skinned race. ● *noun* Caucasian person.

**caucus** /'kɔːkəs/ *noun* (*plural* **-es**) US meeting of party members to decide policy; *often derogatory* (meeting of) group within larger organization.

**caudal** /'kɔːd(ə)l/ *adjective* of, like, or at tail.

**caudate** /'kɔːdeɪt/ *adjective* tailed.

**caught** *past & past participle* of CATCH.

**caul** /kɔːl/ *noun* membrane enclosing foetus; part of this sometimes found on child's head at birth.

**cauldron** /'kɔːldrən/ *noun* large vessel for boiling things in.

**cauliflower** /'kɒlɪflaʊə/ *noun* cabbage with large white flower head.

**caulk** /kɔːk/ *verb* (*US* **calk**) stop up (ship's seams); make watertight.

**causal** /'kɔːz(ə)l/ *adjective* relating to cause (and effect). □ **causality** /-'zæl-/ *noun*.

**causation** /kɔː'zeɪʃ(ə)n/ *noun* causing, causality.

**cause** /kɔːz/ ● *noun* thing producing effect; reason or motive; justification; principle, belief, or purpose; matter to be settled, or case offered, at law. ● *verb* (**-sing**) be cause of; produce; (+ *to do*) make.

**cause célèbre** /kɔːz se'lebr/ *noun* (*plural* **causes célèbres** same pronunciation) lawsuit that excites much interest. [French]

**causeway** /'kɔːzweɪ/ *noun* raised road across low ground or water; raised path by road.

**caustic** /'kɔːstɪk/ ● *adjective* corrosive, burning; sarcastic, biting. ● *noun* caustic substance. □ **caustic soda** sodium hydroxide. □ **causticity** /-'tɪs-/ *noun*.

**cauterize** /'kɔːtəraɪz/ *verb* (also **-ise**) (**-zing** or **-sing**) burn (tissue), esp. to stop bleeding.

**caution** /'kɔːʃ(ə)n/ ● *noun* attention to safety; warning; *colloquial* amusing or surprising person or thing. ● *verb* warn, admonish.

**cautionary** *adjective* warning.

**cautious** /'kɔːʃəs/ *adjective* having or showing caution. □ **cautiously** *adverb*; **cautiousness** *noun*.

**cavalcade** /kævəl'keɪd/ *noun* procession of riders, cars, etc.

**cavalier** /kævə'lɪə/ ● *noun* courtly gentleman; *archaic* horseman; (**Cavalier**) *historical* supporter of Charles I in English Civil War. ● *adjective* offhand, supercilious, curt.

**cavalry** /'kævəlrɪ/ *noun* (*plural* **-ies**) (usually treated as *plural*) soldiers on horseback or in armoured vehicles.

**cave** ● *noun* large hollow in side of cliff, hill, etc., or underground. ● *verb* (**-ving**) explore caves. □ **cave in** (cause to) subside or collapse, yield, submit.

**caveat** /'kævɪæt/ *noun* warning, proviso.

**cavern** /'kæv(ə)n/ *noun* cave, esp. large or dark one.

**cavernous** *adjective* full of caverns; huge or deep as cavern.

**caviar** /'kævɪɑː/ *noun* (also **caviare**) pickled sturgeon-roe.

**cavil** /'kævɪl/ ● *verb* (**-ll-**; *US* **-l-**) (usually + *at, about*) make petty objections. ● *noun* petty objection.

**cavity** /'kævɪtɪ/ *noun* (*plural* **-ies**) hollow within solid body; decayed part of tooth. □ **cavity wall** two walls separated by narrow space.

**cavort** /kə'vɔːt/ *verb* caper.

**caw** ● *noun* cry of rook etc. ● *verb* utter this cry.

**cayenne** /keɪ'en/ *noun* (in full **cayenne pepper**) powdered red pepper.

**cayman** /'keɪmən/ *noun* (also **caiman**) (*plural* **-s**) S. American alligator-like reptile.

**CB** *abbreviation* citizens' band; Commander of the Order of the Bath.

**CBE** *abbreviation* Commander of the Order of the British Empire.

**CBI** *abbreviation* Confederation of British Industry.

**cc** *abbreviation* cubic centimetre(s).

**CD** *abbreviation* compact disc; *Corps Diplomatique*.

**cease** /siːs/ *formal verb* (**-sing**) stop; bring or come to an end. □ **cease-fire** (order for) truce; **without cease** unending.

**ceaseless** *adjective* without end. □ **ceaselessly** *adverb*.

**cedar** /ˈsiːdə/ *noun* evergreen conifer; its durable fragrant wood.

**cede** /siːd/ *verb* (**-ding**) *formal* give up one's rights to or possession of.

**cedilla** /sɪˈdɪlə/ *noun* mark ( ˌ ) under *c* (in French, to show it is pronounced /s/, not /k/).

**ceilidh** /ˈkeɪlɪ/ *noun* informal gathering for music, dancing, etc.

**ceiling** /ˈsiːlɪŋ/ *noun* upper interior surface of room or other compartment; upper limit; maximum altitude of aircraft.

**celandine** /ˈselǝndaɪn/ *noun* yellow-flowered plant.

**celebrant** /ˈselɪbrǝnt/ *noun* person performing rite, esp. priest at Eucharist.

**celebrate** /ˈselɪbreɪt/ *verb* (**-ting**) mark with or engage in festivities; perform (rite or ceremony); praise publicly. □ **celebration** *noun*, **celebratory** /-ˈbreɪt-/ *adjective*.

**celebrity** /sɪˈlebrɪtɪ/ *noun* (*plural* **-ies**) well-known person; fame.

**celeriac** /sɪˈlerɪæk/ *noun* variety of celery.

**celerity** /sɪˈlerɪtɪ/ *noun archaic* swiftness.

**celery** /ˈselǝrɪ/ *noun* plant of which stalks are used as vegetable.

**celesta** /sɪˈlestǝ/ *noun* keyboard instrument with steel plates struck with hammers.

**celestial** /sɪˈlestɪǝl/ *adjective* of sky or heavenly bodies; heavenly, divinely good.

**celibate** /ˈselɪbǝt/ ● *adjective* unmarried, or abstaining from sexual relations, often for religious reasons. ● *noun* celibate person. □ **celibacy** *noun*.

**cell** /sel/ *noun* small room, esp. in prison or monastery; small compartment, e.g. in honeycomb; small active political group; unit of structure of organic matter; enclosed cavity in organism etc.; vessel containing electrodes for current-generation or electrolysis. □ **cellphone** portable radio-telephone.

**cellar** /ˈselǝ/ *noun* underground storage room; stock of wine in cellar.

**cello** /ˈtʃelǝʊ/ *noun* (*plural* **-s**) bass instrument of violin family, held between legs of seated player. □ **cellist** *noun*.

**Cellophane** /ˈselǝfeɪn/ *noun proprietary term* thin transparent wrapping material.

**cellular** /ˈseljʊlǝ/ *adjective* consisting of cells; of open texture, porous. □ **cellularity** /-ˈlær-/ *noun*.

**cellulite** /ˈseljʊlaɪt/ *noun* lumpy fat, esp. on women's hips and thighs.

**celluloid** /ˈseljʊlɔɪd/ *noun* plastic made from camphor and cellulose nitrate; cinema film.

**cellulose** /ˈseljʊlǝʊs/ *noun* carbohydrate forming plant-cell walls; paint or lacquer consisting of cellulose acetate or nitrate in solution.

**Celsius** /ˈselsɪǝs/ *adjective* of scale of temperature on which water freezes at 0° and boils at 100°.

**Celt** /kelt/ *noun* (also **Kelt**) member of an ethnic group including inhabitants of Ireland, Wales, Scotland, Cornwall, and Brittany.

**Celtic** /ˈkeltɪk/ ● *adjective* of the Celts. ● *noun* group of Celtic languages.

**cement** /sɪˈment/ ● *noun* substance made from lime and clay, mixed with water, sand, etc. to form mortar or concrete; adhesive. ● *verb* unite firmly, strengthen; apply cement to.

**cemetery** /ˈsemɪtrɪ/ *noun* (*plural* **-ies**) burial ground, esp. one not in churchyard.

**cenotaph** /ˈsenǝtɑːf/ *noun* tomblike monument to person(s) whose remains are elsewhere.

**Cenozoic** /siːnǝˈzǝʊɪk/ ● *adjective* of most recent geological era, marked by evolution of mammals etc. ● *noun* this era.

**censer** /ˈsensǝ/ *noun* incense-burning vessel.

**censor** /ˈsensə/ ● noun official with power to suppress or expurgate books, films, news, etc., on grounds of obscenity, threat to security, etc. ● verb act as censor of; make deletions or changes in. □ **censorial** /-ˈsɔːr-/ adjective; **censorship** noun.

■ **Usage** As a verb, *censor* is often confused with *censure*, which means 'to criticize harshly'.

**censorious** /senˈsɔːrɪəs/ adjective severely critical.

**censure** /ˈsenʃə/ ● verb (-ring) criticize harshly; reprove. ● noun hostile criticism; disapproval.

**census** /ˈsensəs/ noun (plural **-suses**) official count of population etc.

**cent** /sent/ noun one-hundredth of dollar or other decimal unit of currency.

**cent.** abbreviation century.

**centaur** /ˈsentɔː/ noun creature in Greek mythology with head, arms, and trunk of man joined to body and legs of horse.

**centenarian** /sentɪˈneərɪən/ ● noun person 100 or more years old. ● adjective 100 or more years old.

**centenary** /senˈtiːnərɪ/ ● noun (plural **-ies**) (celebration of) 100th anniversary. ● adjective of a centenary; recurring every 100 years.

**centennial** /senˈtenɪəl/ ● adjective lasting 100 years; recurring every 100 years. ● noun US centenary.

**centi-** combining form one-hundredth.

**centigrade** /ˈsentɪɡreɪd/ adjective Celsius.

■ **Usage** *Celsius* is the better term to use in technical contexts.

**centilitre** /ˈsentɪliːtə/ noun (US **centiliter**) one-hundredth of litre (0.018 pint).

**centime** /ˈsɑ̃tiːm/ noun one-hundredth of franc.

**centimetre** /ˈsentɪmiːtə/ noun (US **centimeter**) one-hundredth of metre (0.394 in.).

**centipede** /ˈsentɪpiːd/ noun arthropod with wormlike body and many legs.

**central** /ˈsentr(ə)l/ adjective of, forming, at, or from centre; essential, principal. □ **central bank** national bank issuing currency etc.; **central heating** heating of building from central source; **central processor**, **central processing unit** computer's main operating part. □ **centrality** noun; **centrally** adverb.

**centralize** verb (also **-ise**) (**-zing** or **-sing**) concentrate (administration etc.) at single centre; subject (state etc.) to this system. □ **centralization** noun.

**centre** /ˈsentə/ (US **center**) ● noun middle point; pivot; place or buildings forming a central point or main area for an activity; point of concentration or dispersion; political party holding moderate opinions; filling in chocolate etc. ● verb (**-ring**) (+ *in*, *on*, *round*) have as main centre; place in centre. □ **centrefold** centre spread that folds out, esp. with nude photographs; **centre forward, back** Football etc. middle player in forward or half-back line; **centre of gravity** point at which the mass of an object effectively acts; **centrepiece** ornament for middle of table, main item; **centre spread** two facing middle pages of magazine etc.

**centrifugal** /sentrɪˈfjuːɡ(ə)l/ adjective moving or tending to move from centre. □ **centrifugal force** apparent force acting outwards on body revolving round centre. □ **centrifugally** adverb.

**centrifuge** /ˈsentrɪfjuːdʒ/ noun rapidly rotating machine for separating e.g. cream from milk.

**centripetal** /senˈtrɪpɪt(ə)l/ adjective moving or tending to move towards centre. □ **centripetally** adverb.

**centrist** /ˈsentrɪst/ noun often derogatory person holding moderate views. □ **centrism** noun.

**cents.** abbreviation centuries.

**centurion** /senˈtjʊərɪən/ noun commander of century in ancient Roman army.

**century** /ˈsentʃərɪ/ noun (plural **-ies**) 100 years; Cricket score of 100 runs by one batsman; company in ancient Roman army.

■ **Usage** Strictly speaking, because the 1st century ran from the year 1 to the year 100, the first year of a century ends in 1. However, a century is commonly regarded as starting with a year ending in 00, the 20th century thus running from 1900 to 1999.

**cephalic** /sə'fælɪk/ *adjective* of or in head.

**cephalopod** /'sefələpɒd/ *noun* mollusc with tentacles on head, e.g. octopus.

**ceramic** /sɪ'ræmɪk/ ● *adjective* made of esp. baked clay; of ceramics. ● *noun* ceramic article.

**ceramics** *plural noun* ceramic products collectively; (usually treated as *singular*) ceramic art.

**cereal** /'sɪərɪəl/ ● *noun* edible grain; breakfast food made from cereal. ● *adjective* of edible grain.

**cerebellum** /serɪ'beləm/ *noun* ( *plural* **-s** or **-bella**) part of brain at back of skull.

**cerebral** /'serɪbr(ə)l/ *adjective* of brain; intellectual. □ **cerebral palsy** paralysis resulting from brain damage before or at birth.

**cerebration** /serɪ'breɪʃ(ə)n/ *noun* working of brain.

**cerebrospinal** /serɪbrəʊ'spaɪn(ə)l/ *adjective* of brain and spine.

**cerebrum** /'serɪbrəm/ *noun* ( *plural* **-bra**) principal part of brain, at front of skull.

**ceremonial** /serɪ'məʊnɪəl/ ● *adjective* of or with ceremony, formal. ● *noun* system of rites or ceremonies.

**ceremonious** /serɪ'məʊnɪəs/ *adjective* fond of or characterized by ceremony, formal. □ **ceremoniously** *adverb*.

**ceremony** /'serɪmənɪ/ *noun* ( *plural* **-ies**) formal procedure; formalities, esp. ritualistic; excessively polite behaviour. □ **stand on ceremony** insist on formality.

**cerise** /sə'riːz/ *noun & adjective* light clear red.

**cert** /sɜːt/ *noun* (esp. **dead cert**) *slang* a certainty.

**certain** /'sɜːt(ə)n/ *adjective* convinced; indisputable; (often + *to do*) sure, destined; reliable; particular but not specified; some.

**certainly** *adverb* undoubtedly; (in answer) yes.

**certainty** *noun* ( *plural* **-ies**) undoubted fact; absolute conviction; reliable thing or person.

**certificate** ● *noun* /sə'tɪfɪkət/ document formally attesting fact. ● *verb* /sə'tɪfɪkeɪt/ (**-ting**) (esp. as **certificated** *adjective*) provide with certificate; license or attest by certificate. □ **certification** /sɜː-/ *noun*.

**certify** /'sɜːtɪfaɪ/ *verb* (**-ies**, **-ied**) attest (to); declare by certificate; officially declare insane. □ **certifiable** *adjective*.

**certitude** /'sɜːtɪtjuːd/ *noun* feeling certain.

**cerulean** /sə'ruːlɪən/ *adjective* sky-blue.

**cervical** /sə'vaɪk(ə)l/ *adjective* of cervix or neck. □ **cervical smear** specimen from neck of womb for examination.

**cervix** /'sɜːvɪks/ *noun* ( *plural* **cervices** /-siːz/) necklike structure, esp. neck of womb; neck.

**Cesarean** (also **Cesarian**) *US* = CAESAREAN.

**cessation** /se'seɪʃ(ə)n/ *noun* ceasing.

**cession** /'seʃ(ə)n/ *noun* ceding; territory ceded.

**cesspit** /'sespɪt/ *noun* pit for liquid waste or sewage.

**cesspool** /'sespuːl/ *noun* cesspit.

**cetacean** /sɪ'teɪʃ(ə)n/ ● *noun* member of order of marine mammals including whales. ● *adjective* of cetaceans.

**cf.** *abbreviation* compare (Latin *confer*).

**CFC** *abbreviation* chlorofluorocarbon (compound used as refrigerant, aerosol propellant, etc.).

**cg** *abbreviation* centigram(s).

**CH** *abbreviation* Companion of Honour.

**Chablis** /'ʃæbliː/ *noun* ( *plural* same /-liːz/) dry white wine from Chablis in France.

**chaconne** /ʃə'kɒn/ *noun* musical variations over ground bass; dance to this.

**chafe** /tʃeɪf/ ● *verb* (**-fing**) make or become sore or damaged by rubbing; irritate; show irritation, fret; rub (esp. skin) to warm. ● *noun* sore caused by rubbing.

**chaff** /tʃɑːf/ ● *noun* separated grain-husks; chopped hay or straw; good-humoured teasing; worthless stuff. ● *verb* tease, banter.

**chaffinch** /'tʃæfɪntʃ/ *noun* a common European finch.

**chafing dish** /'ʃeɪfɪŋ/ noun vessel in which food is cooked or kept warm at table.

**chagrin** /'ʃægrɪn/ • noun acute vexation or disappointment. • verb affect with this.

**chain** • noun connected series of links, thing resembling this; (in plural) fetters, restraining force; sequence, series, or set; unit of length (66 ft). • verb (often + up) secure with chain. □ **chain gang** historical convicts chained together at work etc.; **chain mail** armour made from interlaced rings; **chain reaction** reaction forming products which themselves cause further reactions, series of events each due to previous one; **chainsaw** motor-driven saw with teeth on loop of chain; **chain-smoke** smoke continuously, esp. by lighting next cigarette etc. from previous one; **chain store** one of series of shops owned by one firm.

**chair** • noun seat usually with back for one person; (office of) chairperson; professorship; US electric chair. • verb be chairperson of (meeting); carry aloft in triumph. □ **chairlift** series of chairs on loop of cable for carrying passengers up and down mountain etc.; **chairman**, **chairperson**, **chairwoman** person who presides over meeting, board, or committee.

**chaise** /ʃeɪz/ noun horse-drawn usually open carriage for one or two people.

**chaise longue** /ʃeɪz 'lɒŋ/ noun (plural **chaise longues** or **chaises longues** /'lɒŋ(z)/) sofa with one arm rest.

**chalcedony** /kæl'sedənɪ/ noun (plural **-ies**) type of quartz.

**chalet** /'ʃæleɪ/ noun Swiss hut or cottage; similar house; small cabin in holiday camp etc.

**chalice** /'tʃælɪs/ noun goblet; Eucharistic cup.

**chalk** /tʃɔːk/ • noun white soft limestone; (piece of) similar, sometimes coloured, substance for writing or drawing. • verb rub, mark, draw, or write with chalk. □ **chalky** adjective (**-ier**, **-iest**).

**challenge** /'tʃælɪndʒ/ • noun call to take part in contest etc. or to prove or justify something; demanding or difficult task; call to respond. • verb (**-ging**) issue challenge to; dispute; (as **challenging** adjective) stimulatingly difficult. □ **challenger** noun.

**chamber** /'tʃeɪmbə/ noun hall used by legislative or judicial body; body that meets in it, esp. a house of a parliament; (in plural) set of rooms for barrister(s), esp. in Inns of Court; (in plural) judge's room for hearing cases not needing to be taken in court; archaic room, esp. bedroom; cavity or compartment in body, machinery, etc. (esp. part of gun that contains charge). □ **chambermaid** woman who cleans hotel bedrooms; **chamber music** music for small group of instruments; **Chamber of Commerce** association to promote local commercial interests; **chamber pot** vessel for urine etc., used in bedroom.

**chamberlain** /'tʃeɪmbəlɪn/ noun officer managing royal or noble household; treasurer of corporation etc.

**chameleon** /kə'miːlɪən/ noun lizard able to change colour for camouflage.

**chamfer** /'tʃæmfə/ • verb bevel symmetrically. • noun bevelled surface.

**chamois** noun (plural same /-wɑːz/) small mountain antelope; /'ʃæmɪ/ (piece of) soft leather from sheep, goats, etc.

**chamomile** = CAMOMILE.

**champ¹** • verb munch or bite noisily. • noun chewing noise. □ **champ at the bit** show impatience.

**champ²** noun slang champion.

**champagne** /ʃæm'peɪn/ noun white sparkling wine from Champagne in France.

**champion** /'tʃæmpɪən/ • noun person or thing that has defeated all rivals; person who fights for cause or another person. • verb support cause of, defend. • adjective colloquial splendid.

**championship** noun (often in plural) contest to decide champion in sport etc.; position of champion.

**chance** /tʃɑːns/ • noun possibility; (often in plural) probability; unplanned occurrence; fate. • adjective fortuitous. • verb (**-cing**) colloquial risk; happen. □ **chance on** happen to find.

**chancel** /'tʃɑːns(ə)l/ noun part of church near altar.

**chancellery** /'tʃɑːnsələrɪ/ *noun* (*plural* **-ies**) chancellor's department, staff, or residence; *US* office attached to embassy.

**chancellor** /'tʃɑːnsələ/ *noun* state or legal official; head of government in some European countries; non-resident honorary head of university; (in full **Lord Chancellor**) highest officer of the Crown, presiding in House of Lords; (in full **Chancellor of the Exchequer**) UK finance minister.

**Chancery** /'tʃɑːnsərɪ/ *noun* Lord Chancellor's division of High Court of Justice.

**chancy** /'tʃɑːnsɪ/ *adjective* (**-ier**, **-iest**) uncertain; risky.

**chandelier** /ʃændə'lɪə/ *noun* branched hanging support for lights.

**chandler** /'tʃɑːndlə/ *noun* dealer in oil, candles, soap, paint, etc.

**change** /tʃeɪndʒ/ ● *noun* making or becoming different; low-value money in small coins; money returned as balance of that given in payment; new experience; substitution of one thing or person for another; one of different orders in which bells can be rung. ● *verb* (**-ging**) undergo, show, or subject to change; take or use another instead of; interchange; give or get money in exchange for; put fresh clothes or coverings on; (often + *with*) exchange. □ **change hands** be passed to different owner. □ **changeful** *adjective*; **change-less** *adjective*.

**changeable** *adjective* inconstant; able to change or be changed.

**changeling** *noun* child believed to be substitute for another.

**channel** /'tʃæn(ə)l/ ● *noun* piece of water connecting two seas; (**the Channel**) the English Channel; medium of communication, agency; band of frequencies used for radio and television transmission; course in which thing moves; hollow bed of water; navigable part of waterway; passage for liquid; lengthwise strip on recording tape etc. ● *verb* (**-ll-**; *US* **-l-**) guide, direct; form channel(s) in.

**chant** /tʃɑːnt/ ● *noun* spoken singsong phrase; melody for reciting unmetrical texts; song. ● *verb* talk or repeat monotonously; sing or intone (psalm etc.).

**chanter** *noun* melody-pipe of bagpipes.

**chantry** /'tʃɑːntrɪ/ *noun* (*plural* **-ies**) endowment for singing of masses; priests, chapel, etc., so endowed.

**chaos** /'keɪɒs/ *noun* utter confusion; formless matter supposed to have existed before universe's creation. □ **chaotic** /keɪ'ɒtɪk/ *adjective*.

**chap**[1] *noun colloquial* man, boy.

**chap**[2] ● *verb* (**-pp-**) (esp. of skin) develop cracks or soreness; (of wind etc.) cause this. ● *noun* (usually in *plural*) crack in skin etc.

**chaparral** /ʃæpə'ræl/ *noun US* dense tangled brushwood.

**chapatti** /tʃə'pɑːtɪ/ *noun* (also **chupatty**) (*plural* **chapattis** or **chupatties**) flat thin cake of unleavened bread.

**chapel** /'tʃæp(ə)l/ *noun* place for private worship in cathedral or church, with its own altar; place of worship attached to private house, institution, etc.; place or service of worship for Nonconformists; branch of printers' or journalists' trade union at a workplace.

**chaperon** /'ʃæpərəʊn/ ● *noun* person, esp. older woman, in charge of young unmarried woman on certain social occasions. ● *verb* act as chaperon to.

**chaplain** /'tʃæplɪn/ *noun* member of clergy attached to private chapel, institution, ship, regiment, etc. □ **chaplaincy** *noun* (*plural* **-ies**).

**chaplet** /'tʃæplɪt/ *noun* wreath or circlet for head; string of beads, short rosary.

**chapter** /'tʃæptə/ *noun* division of book; period of time; canons of cathedral etc.; meeting of these.

**char**[1] *verb* (**-rr-**) blacken with fire, scorch; burn to charcoal.

**char**[2] *colloquial* ● *noun* charwoman. ● *verb* (**-rr-**) work as charwoman. □ **charlady**, **charwoman** one employed to do housework.

**char**[3] *noun slang* tea.

**char**[4] *noun* (*plural* same) a kind of trout.

**charabanc** /'ʃærəbæŋ/ *noun* early form of motor coach.

**character** /'kærɪktə/ *noun* distinguishing qualities or characteristics; moral strength; reputation; person in novel, play, etc.; *colloquial* (esp. eccentric) person; letter, symbol; testimonial.

**characteristic** /kærɪktəˈrɪstɪk/ ● *adjective* typical, distinctive. ● *noun* characteristic feature or quality. □ **characteristically** *adverb*.

**characterize** *verb* (also **-ise**) (**-zing** or **-sing**) describe character of; (+ *as*) describe as; be characteristic of. □ **characterization** *noun*.

**charade** /ʃəˈrɑːd/ *noun* (usually in *plural*, treated as *singular*) game of guessing word(s) from acted clues; absurd pretence.

**charcoal** *noun* black residue of partly burnt wood etc.

**charge** ● *verb* (**-ging**) ask (amount) as price; ask (person) for amount as price; (+ *to*, *up to*) debit cost of to; (often + *with*) accuse (of offence); (+ *to do*) instruct or urge to do; (+ *with*) entrust with; make rushing attack (on); (often + *up*) give electric charge to, store energy in; (often + *with*) load, fill. ● *noun* price, financial liability; accusation; task; custody; person or thing entrusted; (signal for) impetuous attack, esp. in battle; appropriate amount of material to be put in mechanism at one time, esp. explosive in gun; cause of electrical phenomena in matter. □ **charge card** credit card, esp. used at particular shop; **in charge** having command. □ **chargeable** *adjective*.

**chargé d'affaires** /ʃɑːʒeɪ dæˈfeə/ *noun* (*plural* **chargés d'affaires** same pronunciation) ambassador's deputy; envoy to minor country.

**charger** *noun* cavalry horse; apparatus for charging battery.

**chariot** /ˈtʃærɪət/ *noun historical* two-wheeled horse-drawn vehicle used in ancient warfare and racing.

**charioteer** /tʃærɪəˈtɪə/ *noun* chariot driver.

**charisma** /kəˈrɪzmə/ *noun* power to inspire or attract others; divinely conferred power or talent. □ **charismatic** /kʌrɪzˈmætɪk/ *adjective*.

**charitable** /ˈtʃærɪtəb(ə)l/ *adjective* generous to those in need; of or connected with a charity; lenient in judging others. □ **charitably** *adverb*.

**charity** /ˈtʃærɪtɪ/ *noun* (*plural* **-ies**) giving voluntarily to those in need; organization for helping those in need; love of fellow men; lenience in judging others.

**charlatan** /ˈʃɑːlət(ə)n/ *noun* person falsely claiming knowledge or skill. □ **charlatanism** *noun*.

**charlotte** /ˈʃɑːlɒt/ *noun* pudding of stewed fruit under bread etc.

**charm** ● *noun* power of delighting, attracting, or influencing; trinket on bracelet etc.; object, act, or word(s) supposedly having magic power. ● *verb* delight, captivate; influence or protect (as) by magic; obtain or gain by charm. □ **charmer** *noun*.

**charming** *adjective* delightful. □ **charmingly** *adverb*.

**charnel house** /ˈtʃɑːn(ə)l/ *noun* place containing corpses or bones.

**chart** ● *noun* map esp. for sea or air navigation or showing weather conditions etc.; sheet of information in form of tables or diagrams; (usually in *plural*) *colloquial* list of currently best-selling pop records. ● *verb* make chart of.

**charter** ● *noun* written grant of rights, esp. by sovereign or legislature; written description of organization's functions etc. ● *verb* grant charter to; hire (aircraft etc.). □ **charter flight** flight by chartered aircraft.

**chartered** *adjective* qualified as member of professional body that has royal charter.

**Chartism** *noun* working-class reform movement of 1837–48. □ **Chartist** *noun*.

**chartreuse** /ʃɑːˈtrɜːz/ *noun* green or yellow brandy liqueur.

**chary** /ˈtʃeərɪ/ *adjective* (**-ier**, **-iest**) cautious; sparing.

**chase¹** /tʃeɪs/ ● *verb* (**-sing**) pursue; (+ *from*, *out of*, *to*, etc.) drive; hurry; (usually + *up*) *colloquial* pursue (thing overdue); *colloquial* try to attain; court persistently. ● *noun* pursuit; unenclosed hunting-land.

**chase²** /tʃeɪs/ *verb* (**-sing**) emboss or engrave (metal).

**chaser** *noun* horse for steeplechasing; *colloquial* drink taken after another of different kind.

**chasm** /'kæz(ə)m/ noun deep cleft in earth, rock, etc.; wide difference in opinion etc.

**chassis** /'ʃæsɪ/ noun (plural same /-sɪz/) base frame of vehicle; frame for (radio etc.) components.

**chaste** /tʃeɪst/ adjective abstaining from extramarital or from all sexual intercourse; pure, virtuous; unadorned. □ **chastely** adverb; **chasteness** noun.

**chasten** /'tʃeɪs(ə)n/ verb (esp. as **chastening, chastened** adjectives) restrain; punish.

**chastise** /tʃæs'taɪz/ verb (-sing) rebuke severely; punish, beat. □ **chastisement** noun.

**chastity** /'tʃæstɪtɪ/ noun being chaste.

**chasuble** /'tʃæzjʊb(ə)l/ noun sleeveless outer vestment worn by celebrant of Eucharist.

**chat** • verb (-tt-) talk in light familiar way. • noun informal talk. □ **chatline** telephone service setting up conversations between groups of people on separate lines; **chat show** television or radio broadcast with informal celebrity interviews; **chat up** colloquial chat to, esp. flirtatiously.

**chateau** /'ʃætəʊ/ noun (plural -x /-z/) large French country house.

**chatelaine** /'ʃætəleɪn/ noun mistress of large house; historical appendage to woman's belt for carrying keys etc.

**chattel** /'tʃæt(ə)l/ noun (usually in plural) movable possession.

**chatter** /'tʃætə/ • verb talk fast, incessantly, or foolishly. • noun such talk.

**chatty** adjective (-ier, -iest) fond of or resembling chat.

**chauffeur** /'ʃəʊfə/ noun person employed to drive car. • verb drive (car or person).

**chauvinism** /'ʃəʊvɪnɪz(ə)m/ noun exaggerated or aggressive patriotism; excessive or prejudiced support or loyalty for something. □ **chauvinist** noun; **chauvinistic** /-'nɪs-/ adjective.

**cheap** adjective low in price; charging low prices; of low quality or worth; easily got. □ **cheaply** adverb; **cheapness** noun.

**cheapen** verb make or become cheap; degrade.

**cheapskate** noun esp. US colloquial stingy person.

**cheat** • verb (often + into, out of) deceive; (+ of) deprive of; gain unfair advantage. • noun person who cheats; deception. □ **cheat on** colloquial be sexually unfaithful to.

**check** • verb test, examine, verify; stop or slow motion of; colloquial rebuke; threaten opponent's king at chess; US agree on comparison; US deposit (luggage etc.). • noun test for accuracy, quality, etc.; stopping or slowing of motion; rebuff; restraint; pattern of small squares; fabric so patterned; (also as interjection) exposure of chess king to attack; US restaurant bill; US cheque; US token of identification for left luggage etc.; US counter used in card games. □ **check in** register at hotel, airport, etc.; **check-in** act or place of checking in; **check out** leave hotel etc. with due formalities; **checkout** act of checking out, pay-desk in supermarket etc.; **check-up** thorough (esp. medical) examination.

**checked** adjective having a check pattern.

**checker** = CHEQUER.

**checkmate** • noun (also as interjection) check at chess from which king cannot escape. • verb (-ting) put into checkmate; frustrate.

**Cheddar** /'tʃedə/ noun kind of firm smooth cheese.

**cheek** • noun side of face below eye; impertinence, impertinent speech; slang buttock. • verb be impertinent to.

**cheeky** adjective (-ier, -iest) impertinent. □ **cheekily** adverb; **cheekiness** noun.

**cheep** • noun shrill feeble note of young bird. • verb make such cry.

**cheer** • noun shout of encouragement or applause; mood, disposition; (as **cheers** interjection) colloquial: expressing good wishes or thanks. • verb applaud; (usually + on) urge with shouts; shout for joy; gladden, comfort. □ **cheer up** make or become less sad.

**cheerful** adjective in good spirits; bright, pleasant. □ **cheerfully** adverb; **cheerfulness** noun.

**cheerless** adjective gloomy, dreary.

**cheery** *adjective* (**-ier**, **-iest**) cheerful. □ **cheerily** *adverb*.

**cheese** /tʃiːz/ *noun* food made from milk curds; cake of this with rind; thick conserve of fruit. □ **cheeseburger** hamburger with cheese in or on it; **cheesecake** tart filled with sweetened curds, *slang* sexually stimulating display of women; **cheesecloth** thin loosely woven cloth; **cheesed** *slang* (often + *off*) bored, fed up; **cheese-paring** stingy; **cheese plant** climbing plant with holey leaves. □ **cheesy** *adjective*.

**cheetah** /ˈtʃiːtə/ *noun* swift-running spotted feline resembling leopard.

**chef** /ʃef/ *noun* (esp. chief) cook in restaurant etc.

**Chelsea** /ˈtʃelsɪ/ *noun* □ **Chelsea bun** kind of spiral-shaped currant bun; **Chelsea pensioner** inmate of Chelsea Royal Hospital for old or disabled soldiers.

**chemical** /ˈkemɪk(ə)l/ ● *adjective* of, made by, or employing chemistry. ● *noun* substance obtained or used in chemistry. □ **chemical warfare** warfare using poison gas and other chemicals. □ **chemically** *adverb*.

**chemise** /ʃəˈmiːz/ *noun historical* woman's loose-fitting undergarment or dress.

**chemist** /ˈkemɪst/ *noun* dealer in medicinal drugs etc.; expert in chemistry.

**chemistry** /ˈkemɪstrɪ/ *noun* (*plural* **-ies**) science of elements and their laws of combination and change; *colloquial* sexual attraction.

**chenille** /ʃəˈniːl/ *noun* tufted velvety yarn; fabric made of this.

**cheque** /tʃek/ *noun* written order to bank to pay sum of money; printed form for this. □ **chequebook** book of forms for writing cheques; **cheque card** card issued by bank to guarantee honouring of cheques up to stated amount.

**chequer** /ˈtʃekə/ (also **checker**) ● *noun* (often in *plural*) pattern of squares often alternately coloured; (in *plural*, usually **checkers**) *US* game of draughts. ● *verb* mark with chequers; variegate, break uniformity of; (as **chequered** *adjective*) with varied fortunes.

**cherish** /ˈtʃerɪʃ/ *verb* tend lovingly; hold dear; cling to.

**cheroot** /ʃəˈruːt/ *noun* cigar with both ends open.

**cherry** /ˈtʃerɪ/ ● *noun* (*plural* **-ies**) small stone fruit, tree bearing it; wood of this; light red. ● *adjective* of light red colour.

**cherub** /ˈtʃerəb/ *noun* representation of winged child; beautiful child; (*plural* **-im**) angelic being. □ **cherubic** /tʃɪˈruːbɪk/ *adjective*.

**chervil** /ˈtʃɜːvɪl/ *noun* herb with aniseed flavour.

**chess** *noun* game for two players with 16 **chessmen** each, on chequered **chessboard** of 64 squares.

**chest** *noun* large strong box; part of body enclosed by ribs, front surface of body from neck to bottom of ribs; small cabinet for medicines etc. □ **chest of drawers** piece of furniture with set of drawers in frame.

**chesterfield** /ˈtʃestəfiːld/ *noun* sofa with arms and back of same height.

**chestnut** /ˈtʃesnʌt/ *noun* glossy hard brown edible nut; tree bearing it; horse chestnut; reddish-brown horse; *colloquial* stale joke etc.; reddish-brown. ● *adjective* reddish-brown.

**chesty** *adjective* (**-ier**, **-iest**) *colloquial* inclined to or symptomatic of chest disease. □ **chestily** *adverb*; **chestiness** *noun*.

**cheval glass** /ʃəˈvæl/ *noun* tall mirror pivoting in upright frame.

**chevalier** /ʃevəˈlɪə/ *noun* member of certain orders of knighthood etc.

**chevron** /ˈʃevrən/ *noun* V-shaped line or stripe.

**chew** ● *verb* work (food etc.) between teeth. ● *noun* act of chewing; chewy sweet. □ **chewing gum** flavoured gum for chewing; **chew on** work continuously between teeth, think about; **chew over** discuss, think about.

**chewy** *adjective* (**-ier**, **-iest**) requiring or suitable for chewing.

**chez** /ʃeɪ/ *preposition* at the home of. [French]

**Chianti** /kɪˈæntɪ/ *noun* (*plural* **-s**) red wine from Chianti in Italy.

**chiaroscuro** /kɪɑːrəˈskʊərəʊ/ *noun* treatment of light and shade in painting; use of contrast in literature etc.

**chic** /ʃiːk/ ● *adjective* (**chic-er**, **chic-est**) stylish, elegant. ● *noun* stylishness, elegance.

**chicane** /ʃɪ'keɪn/ ● noun artificial barrier or obstacle on motor-racing course; chicanery. ● verb (**-ning**) archaic use chicanery; (usually + into, out of, etc.) cheat (person).

**chicanery** /ʃɪ'keɪnərɪ/ noun (plural **-ies**) clever but misleading talk; trickery, deception.

**chick** noun young bird; slang young woman.

**chicken** /'tʃɪkɪn/ ● noun domestic fowl; its flesh as food; young domestic fowl; youthful person. ● adjective colloquial cowardly. ● verb (+ out) colloquial withdraw through cowardice. □ **chicken feed** food for poultry, colloquial insignificant amount esp. of money; **chickenpox** infectious disease with rash of small blisters; **chicken wire** light wire netting.

**chickpea** noun pealike seed used as vegetable.

**chickweed** noun a small weed.

**chicle** /'tʃɪk(ə)l/ noun juice of tropical tree, used in chewing gum.

**chicory** /'tʃɪkərɪ/ noun (plural **-ies**) salad plant; its root, roasted and ground and used with or instead of coffee; endive.

**chide** verb (**-ding**; past **chided** or **chid**; past participle **chided** or **chidden**) archaic scold, rebuke.

**chief** /tʃiːf/ ● noun leader, ruler; head of tribe, clan, etc.; head of department etc. ● adjective first in position, importance, or influence; prominent, leading.

**chiefly** adverb above all; mainly but not exclusively.

**chieftain** /'tʃiːft(ə)n/ noun leader of tribe, clan, etc. □ **chieftaincy** noun (plural **-ies**).

**chiffchaff** /'tʃɪftʃæf/ noun small European warbler.

**chiffon** /'ʃɪfɒn/ noun diaphanous silky fabric.

**chignon** /'ʃiːnjɔ̃/ noun coil of hair at back of head.

**chihuahua** /tʃɪ'wɑːwə/ noun tiny smooth-coated dog.

**chilblain** /'tʃɪlbleɪn/ noun itching swelling on hand, foot, etc., caused by exposure to cold.

**child** /tʃaɪld/ noun (plural **children** /'tʃɪldrən/) young human being; one's son or daughter; (+ of) descendant, follower, or product of. □ **child benefit** regular state payment to parents of child up to certain age; **childbirth** giving birth to child; **child's play** easy task. □ **childless** adjective.

**childhood** noun state or period of being a child.

**childish** adjective of or like child; immature, silly. □ **childishly** adverb; **childishness** noun.

**childlike** adjective innocent, frank, etc., like child.

**chili** = CHILLI.

**chill** ● noun cold sensation; feverish cold; unpleasant coldness (of air etc.); depressing influence. ● verb make or become cold; depress, horrify; preserve (food or drink) by cooling. ● adjective literary chilly.

**chilli** /'tʃɪlɪ/ noun (also **chili**) (plural **-es**) hot-tasting dried red capsicum pod. □ **chilli con carne** /kɒn 'kɑːnɪ/ chilli-flavoured mince and beans.

**chilly** adjective (**-ier**, **-iest**) rather cold; sensitive to cold; unfriendly, unemotional.

**chime** ● noun set of attuned bells; sounds made by this. ● verb (**-ming**) (of bells) ring; show (time) by chiming; (usually + together, with) be in agreement. □ **chime in** interject remark, join in harmoniously.

**chimera** /kaɪ'mɪərə/ noun monster in Greek mythology with lion's head, goat's body, and serpent's tail; bogey; wild impossible scheme or fancy. □ **chimerical** /-'merɪk(ə)l/ adjective.

**chimney** /'tʃɪmnɪ/ noun (plural **-s**) channel conducting smoke etc. away from fire etc.; part of this above roof; glass tube protecting lamp-flame. □ **chimney breast** projecting wall round chimney; **chimney pot** pipe at top of chimney; **chimney sweep** person who clears chimneys of soot.

**chimp** noun colloquial chimpanzee.

**chimpanzee** /tʃɪmpən'ziː/ noun manlike African ape.

**chin** noun front of lower jaw. □ **chinless wonder** ineffectual person; **chinwag** noun & verb slang chat.

**china** /'tʃaɪnə/ ● noun fine white or translucent ceramic ware; things made of this. ● *adjective* made of china. □ **china clay** kaolin.

**chinchilla** /tʃɪnˈtʃɪlə/ *noun* S. American rodent; its soft grey fur; breed of cat or rabbit.

**chine** ● *noun* backbone; joint of meat containing this; ridge. ● *verb* (**-ning**) cut (meat) through backbone.

**Chinese** /tʃaɪˈniːz/ ● *adjective* of China. ● *noun* Chinese language; (*plural* same) native or national of China, person of Chinese descent. □ **Chinese lantern** collapsible paper lantern, plant with inflated orange-red calyx; **Chinese leaf** lettuce-like cabbage.

**chink**¹ *noun* narrow opening.

**chink**² ● *verb* (cause to) make sound of glasses or coins striking together. ● *noun* this sound.

**chintz** *noun* printed multicoloured usually glazed cotton cloth.

**chip** ● *noun* small piece cut or broken off; place where piece has been broken off; strip of potato usually fried; *US* potato crisp; counter used as money in some games; microchip. ● *verb* (**-pp-**) (often + *off*) cut or break (piece) from hard material; (often + *at*, *away at*) cut pieces off (hard material); be apt to break at edge; (usually as **chipped** *adjective*) make (potato) into chips. □ **chipboard** board made of compressed wood chips.

**chipmunk** /ˈtʃɪpmʌŋk/ *noun* N. American striped ground squirrel.

**chipolata** /tʃɪpəˈlɑːtə/ *noun* small thin sausage.

**Chippendale** /ˈtʃɪpəndeɪl/ *adjective* of an 18th-c. elegant style of furniture.

**chiropody** /kɪˈrɒpədɪ/ *noun* treatment of feet and their ailments. □ **chiropodist** *noun*.

**chiropractic** /kaɪərəʊˈpræktɪk/ *noun* treatment of disease by manipulation of spinal column. □ **chiropractor** /ˈkaɪə-/ *noun*.

**chirp** ● *verb* (of small bird etc.) utter short thin sharp note; speak merrily. ● *noun* chirping sound.

**chirpy** *adjective* (**-ier**, **-iest**) *colloquial* cheerful. □ **chirpily** *adverb*.

**chirrup** /ˈtʃɪrəp/ ● *verb* (**-p-**) chirp, esp. repeatedly. ● *noun* chirruping sound.

**chisel** /ˈtʃɪz(ə)l/ ● *noun* tool with bevelled blade for shaping wood, stone, or metal. ● *verb* (**-ll-**; *US* **-l-**) cut or shape with chisel; (as **chiselled** *adjective*) (of features) clear-cut; *slang* defraud.

**chit**¹ *noun* *derogatory or jocular* young small woman; young child.

**chit**² *noun* written note.

**chit-chat** *noun* *colloquial* light conversation, gossip.

**chivalry** /ˈʃɪvəlrɪ/ *noun* medieval knightly system; honour and courtesy, esp. to the weak. □ **chivalrous** *adjective*; **chivalrously** *adverb*.

**chive** *noun* herb related to onion.

**chivvy** /ˈtʃɪvɪ/ *verb* (**-ies**, **-ied**) urge persistently, nag.

**chloral** /ˈklɔːr(ə)l/ *noun* compound used in making DDT, sedatives, etc.

**chloride** /ˈklɔːraɪd/ *noun* compound of chlorine and another element or group.

**chlorinate** /ˈklɔːrɪneɪt/ *verb* (**-ting**) impregnate or treat with chlorine. □ **chlorination** *noun*.

**chlorine** /ˈklɔːriːn/ *noun* poisonous gas used for bleaching and disinfecting.

**chlorofluorocarbon** see CFC.

**chloroform** /ˈklɒrəfɔːm/ ● *noun* colourless volatile liquid formerly used as general anaesthetic. ● *verb* render unconscious with this.

**chlorophyll** /ˈklɒrəfɪl/ *noun* green pigment in most plants.

**choc** *noun* *colloquial* chocolate. □ **choc ice** bar of ice cream covered with chocolate.

**chock** ● *noun* block of wood, wedge. ● *verb* make fast with chock(s). □ **chock-a-block** (often + *with*) crammed together, full; **chock-full** (often + *of*) crammed full.

**chocolate** /ˈtʃɒklət/ ● *noun* food made as paste, powder, or solid block from ground cacao seeds; sweet made of or covered with this; drink containing chocolate; dark brown. ● *adjective* made from chocolate; dark brown.

**choice** ● *noun* act of choosing; thing or person chosen; range to choose from; power to choose. ● *adjective* of superior quality.

**choir** /kwaɪə/ *noun* regular group of singers; chancel in large church.

**choirboy, choirgirl** boy or girl singer in church choir.

**choke** • *verb* (**-king**) stop breathing of (person or animal); suffer such stoppage; block up; (as **choked** *adjective*) speechless from emotion, disgusted, disappointed. • *noun* valve in carburettor controlling inflow of air; device for smoothing variations of alternating electric current.

**choker** *noun* close-fitting necklace.

**choler** /ˈkɒlə/ *noun historical* bile; *archaic* anger, irascibility.

**cholera** /ˈkɒlərə/ *noun* infectious often fatal bacterial disease of small intestine.

**choleric** /ˈkɒlərɪk/ *adjective* easily angered.

**cholesterol** /kəˈlestərɒl/ *noun* sterol present in human tissues including the blood.

**choose** /tʃuːz/ *verb* (**-sing**; *past* **chose** /tʃəʊz/; *past participle* **chosen**) select out of greater number; (usually + *between*, *from*) take one or another; (usually + *to do*) decide.

**choosy** /ˈtʃuːzɪ/ *adjective* (**-ier**, **-iest**) *colloquial* fussy; hard to please.

**chop**[1] • *verb* (**-pp-**) (usually + *off*, *down*, etc.) cut with axe etc.; (often + *up*) cut into small pieces; strike (ball) with heavy edgewise blow. • *noun* cutting blow; thick slice of meat usually including rib; (**the chop**) *slang* dismissal from job, killing, being killed.

**chop**[2] *noun* (usually in *plural*) jaw.

**chop**[3] *verb* (**-pp-**) □ **chop and change** vacillate.

**chopper** *noun* large-bladed short axe; cleaver; *colloquial* helicopter.

**choppy** *adjective* (**-ier**, **-iest**) (of sea etc.) fairly rough.

**chopstick** /ˈtʃɒpstɪk/ *noun* each of pair of sticks held in one hand as eating utensils by Chinese, Japanese, etc.

**chop suey** /tʃɒpˈsuːɪ/ *noun* (*plural* **-s**) Chinese-style dish of meat fried with vegetables.

**choral** /ˈkɔːr(ə)l/ *adjective* of, for, or sung by choir or chorus.

**chorale** /kəˈrɑːl/ *noun* simple stately hymn tune; choir.

**chord**[1] /kɔːd/ *noun* combination of notes sounded together.

**chord**[2] /kɔːd/ *noun* straight line joining ends of arc; string of harp etc.

**chore** *noun* tedious or routine task, esp. domestic.

**choreography** /kɒrɪˈɒɡrəfɪ/ *noun* design or arrangement of ballet etc. □ **choreograph** /ˈkɒrɪəɡrɑːf/ *verb*; **choreographer** *noun*; **choreographic** /-ə-ˈɡræf-/ *adjective*.

**chorister** /ˈkɒrɪstə/ *noun* member of choir, esp. choirboy.

**chortle** /ˈtʃɔːt(ə)l/ • *noun* gleeful chuckle. • *verb* (**-ling**) chuckle gleefully.

**chorus** /ˈkɔːrəs/ *noun* (*plural* **-es**) group of singers, choir; music for choir; refrain of song; simultaneous utterance; group of singers and dancers performing together; group of performers commenting on action in ancient Greek play, any of its utterances. • *verb* (**-s-**) utter simultaneously.

**chose** *past* of CHOOSE.

**chosen** *past participle* of CHOOSE.

**chough** /tʃʌf/ *noun* red-legged crow.

**choux pastry** /ʃuː/ *noun* very light pastry made with eggs.

**chow** *noun slang* food; Chinese breed of dog.

**chow mein** /tʃaʊ ˈmeɪn/ *noun* Chinese-style dish of fried noodles usually with shredded meat and vegetables.

**christen** /ˈkrɪs(ə)n/ *verb* baptize; name. □ **christening** *noun*.

**Christendom** /ˈkrɪsəndəm/ *noun* Christians worldwide.

**Christian** /ˈkrɪstʃ(ə)n/ • *adjective* of Christ's teaching; believing in or following Christian religion; charitable, kind. • *noun* adherent of Christianity. □ **Christian era** era counted from Christ's birth; **Christian name** forename, esp. given at christening; **Christian Science** system of belief including power of healing by prayer alone; **Christian Scientist** adherent of this.

**Christianity** /krɪstɪˈænɪtɪ/ *noun* Christian religion, quality, or character.

**Christmas** /ˈkrɪsməs/ *noun* (period around) festival of Christ's birth celebrated on 25 Dec. □ **Christmas box** present or tip given at Christmas; **Christmas Day** 25 Dec.; **Christmas**

Eve 24 Dec.; **Christmas pudding** rich boiled pudding with dried fruit; **Christmas rose** white-flowered hellebore flowering in winter; **Christmas tree** evergreen tree decorated at Christmas. □ **Christmassy** adjective.

**chromatic** /krə'mætɪk/ adjective of colour, in colours; Music of or having notes not belonging to prevailing key. □ **chromatic scale** scale that proceeds by semitones. □ **chromatically** adverb.

**chrome** /krəʊm/ noun chromium; yellow pigment got from a compound of chromium.

**chromium** /'krəʊmɪəm/ noun metallic element used as shiny decorative or protective coating.

**chromosome** /'krəʊməsəʊm/ noun Biology threadlike structure occurring in pairs in cell nucleus, carrying genes.

**chronic** /'krɒnɪk/ adjective (of disease) long-lasting; (of patient) having chronic illness; colloquial bad, intense, severe. □ **chronically** adverb.

**chronicle** /'krɒnɪk(ə)l/ ● noun record of events in order of occurrence. ● verb (-ling) record (events) thus.

**chronological** /krɒnə'lɒdʒɪk(ə)l/ adjective according to order of occurrence. □ **chronologically** adverb.

**chronology** /krə'nɒlədʒɪ/ noun ( plural -ies) science of computing dates; (document displaying) arrangement of events etc. according to date.

**chronometer** /krə'nɒmɪtə/ noun time-measuring instrument, esp. one used in navigation.

**chrysalis** /'krɪsəlɪs/ noun ( plural -lises) pupa of butterfly or moth; case enclosing it.

**chrysanthemum** /krɪ'sænθəməm/ noun garden plant flowering in autumn.

**chub** noun ( plural same) thick-bodied river fish.

**chubby** adjective (-ier, -iest) plump, round.

**chuck**[1] ● verb colloquial fling or throw carelessly; (often + in, up) give up; touch playfully, esp. under chin. ● noun act of chucking; (**the chuck**) slang dismissal. □ **chuck out** colloquial expel, discard.

**chuck**[2] ● noun cut of beef from neck to ribs; device for holding workpiece or bit. ● verb fix in chuck.

**chuckle** /'tʃʌk(ə)l/ ● verb (-ling) laugh quietly or inwardly. ● noun quiet or suppressed laugh.

**chuff** verb (of engine etc.) work with regular sharp puffing sound.

**chuffed** adjective slang delighted.

**chug** verb (-gg-) make intermittent explosive sound; move with this.

**chukker** /'tʃʌkə/ noun period of play in polo.

**chum** noun colloquial close friend. □ **chum up** (-mm-) (often + with) become close friend (of). □ **chummy** adjective (-ier, -iest).

**chump** noun colloquial foolish person; thick end of loin of lamb or mutton; lump of wood.

**chunk** noun lump cut or broken off.

**chunky** adjective (-ier, -iest) consisting of or resembling chunks; small and sturdy.

**chunter** /'tʃʌntə/ verb colloquial mutter, grumble.

**chupatty** = CHAPATTI.

**church** noun building for public Christian worship; public worship; (**Church**) Christians collectively, clerical profession, organized Christian society. □ **churchgoer** person attending church regularly; **churchman** member of clergy or Church; **churchwarden** elected lay representative of Anglican parish; **churchyard** enclosed ground round church, esp. used for burials.

**churl** noun bad-mannered, surly, or stingy person. □ **churlish** adjective.

**churn** ● noun large milk can; butter-making machine. ● verb agitate (milk etc.) in churn; make (butter) in churn; (usually + up) upset, agitate. □ **churn out** produce in large quantities.

**chute**[1] /ʃuːt/ noun slide for taking things to lower level.

**chute**[2] /ʃuːt/ noun colloquial parachute.

**chutney** /'tʃʌtnɪ/ noun ( plural -s) relish made of fruits, vinegar, spices, etc.

**chyle** /kaɪl/ noun milky fluid into which chyme is converted.

**chyme** /kaɪm/ noun pulp formed from partly-digested food.

**CIA** abbreviation (in US) Central Intelligence Agency.

**ciabatta** /tʃəˈbɑːtə/ *noun* Italian bread made with olive oil.

**ciao** /tʃaʊ/ *interjection colloquial* goodbye; hello.

**cicada** /sɪˈkɑːdə/ *noun* winged chirping insect.

**cicatrice** /ˈsɪkətrɪs/ *noun* scar of healed wound.

**cicely** /ˈsɪsəlɪ/ *noun* (*plural* **-ies**) flowering plant related to parsley and chervil.

**CID** *abbreviation* Criminal Investigation Department.

**cider** /ˈsaɪdə/ *noun* drink of fermented apple juice.

**cigar** /sɪˈɡɑː/ *noun* roll of tobacco leaves for smoking.

**cigarette** /sɪɡəˈret/ *noun* finely-cut tobacco rolled in paper for smoking.

**cilium** /ˈsɪlɪəm/ *noun* (*plural* **cilia**) hairlike structure on animal cells; eyelash. □ **ciliary** *adjective*.

**cinch** /sɪntʃ/ *noun colloquial* certainty; easy task.

**cinchona** /sɪŋˈkəʊnə/ *noun* S. American evergreen tree; (drug from) its bark which contains quinine.

**cincture** /ˈsɪŋktʃə/ *noun literary* girdle, belt, or border.

**cinder** /ˈsɪndə/ *noun* residue of coal etc. after burning.

**Cinderella** /sɪndəˈrelə/ *noun* person or thing of unrecognized merit.

**cine** /ˈsɪnɪ/ *adjective* cinematographic.

**cinema** /ˈsɪnɪmɑː/ *noun* theatre where films are shown; films collectively; art or industry of producing films. □ **cinematic** /-ˈmæt-/ *adjective*.

**cinematography** /sɪnɪməˈtɒɡrəfɪ/ *noun* art of making films. □ **cinematographer** *noun*, **cinematographic** /-mætəˈɡræfɪk/ *adjective*.

**cineraria** /sɪnəˈreərɪə/ *noun* plant with bright flowers and downy leaves.

**cinnabar** /ˈsɪnəbɑː/ *noun* red mercuric sulphide; vermilion.

**cinnamon** /ˈsɪnəmən/ *noun* aromatic spice from bark of SE Asian tree; this tree; yellowish-brown.

**cinquefoil** /ˈsɪŋkfɔɪl/ *noun* plant with compound leaf of 5 leaflets.

**Cinque Port** /sɪŋk/ *noun* any of (originally 5) ports in SE England with ancient privileges.

**cipher** /ˈsaɪfə/ (also **cypher**) ● *noun* secret or disguised writing, key to this; arithmetical symbol 0; person or thing of no importance. ● *verb* write in cipher.

**circa** /ˈsɜːkə/ *preposition* (usually before date) about. [Latin]

**circle** /ˈsɜːk(ə)l/ ● *noun* perfectly round plane figure; roundish enclosure or structure; curved upper tier of seats in theatre etc.; circular route; set or restricted group; people grouped round centre of interest. ● *verb* (**-ling**) (often + *round*, *about*) move in or form circle.

**circlet** /ˈsɜːklɪt/ *noun* small circle; circular band, esp. as ornament.

**circuit** /ˈsɜːkɪt/ *noun* line, course, or distance enclosing an area; path of electric current, apparatus through which current passes; judge's itinerary through district, such a district; chain of theatres, cinemas, etc. under single management; motor-racing track; sphere of operation; sequence of sporting events.

**circuitous** /sɜːˈkjuːɪtəs/ *adjective* indirect, roundabout.

**circuitry** /ˈsɜːkɪtrɪ/ *noun* (*plural* **-ies**) system of electric circuits.

**circular** /ˈsɜːkjʊlə/ ● *adjective* having form of or moving in circle; (of reasoning) using point to be proved as argument for its own truth; (of letter etc.) distributed to several people. ● *noun* circular letter etc. □ **circular saw** power saw with rotating toothed disc. □ **circularity** /-ˈlærɪtɪ/ *noun*.

**circularize** *verb* (also **-ise**) (**-zing** or **-sing**) send circular to.

**circulate** /ˈsɜːkjʊleɪt/ *verb* (**-ting**) be or put in circulation; send circulars to; mingle among guests etc.

**circulation** *noun* movement from and back to starting point, esp. that of blood from and to heart; transmission, distribution; number of copies sold. □ **circulatory** *adjective*.

**circumcise** /ˈsɜːkəmsaɪz/ *verb* (**-sing**) cut off foreskin or clitoris of. □ **circumcision** /-ˈsɪʒ(ə)n/ *noun*.

**circumference** /səˈkʌmfərəns/ *noun* line enclosing circle; distance round.

**circumflex** /ˈsɜːkəmfleks/ *noun* (in full **circumflex accent**) mark (ˆ) over vowel indicating pronunciation.

**circumlocution** /sɜːkəmləˈkjuːʃ(ə)n/ *noun* roundabout expression; evasive speech; verbosity. □ **circumlocutory** /-ˈlɒkjʊt-/ *adjective*.

**circumnavigate** /sɜːkəmˈnævɪgeɪt/ *verb* (-ting) sail round. □ **circumnavigation** *noun*.

**circumscribe** /ˈsɜːkəmskraɪb/ *verb* (-bing) enclose or outline; lay down limits of; confine, restrict. □ **circumscription** /-ˈskrɪpʃ(ə)n/ *noun*.

**circumspect** /ˈsɜːkəmspekt/ *adjective* cautious, taking everything into account. □ **circumspection** /-ˈspekʃ(ə)n/ *noun*; **circumspectly** *adverb*.

**circumstance** /ˈsɜːkəmst(ə)ns/ *noun* fact, occurrence, or condition, esp. (in *plural*) connected with or affecting an event etc.; (in *plural*) financial condition; ceremony, fuss.

**circumstantial** /sɜːkəmˈstænʃ(ə)l/ *adjective* (of account, story) detailed; (of evidence) tending to establish a conclusion by reasonable inference.

**circumvent** /sɜːkəmˈvent/ *verb* evade, outwit.

**circus** /ˈsɜːkəs/ *noun* (*plural* **-es**) travelling show of performing acrobats, clowns, animals, etc.; *colloquial* scene of lively action, group of people in common activity; open space in town, where several streets converge; *historical* arena for sports and games.

**cirrhosis** /sɪˈrəʊsɪs/ *noun* chronic liver disease.

**cirrus** /ˈsɪrəs/ *noun* (*plural* **cirri** /-raɪ/) white wispy cloud.

**cissy** = SISSY.

**Cistercian** /sɪsˈtɜːʃ(ə)n/ ● *noun* monk or nun of strict Benedictine order. ● *adjective* of the Cistercians.

**cistern** /ˈsɪst(ə)n/ *noun* tank for storing water; underground reservoir.

**citadel** /ˈsɪtəd(ə)l/ *noun* fortress protecting or dominating city.

**citation** /saɪˈteɪʃ(ə)n/ *noun* citing or passage cited; description of reasons for award.

**cite** *verb* (-ting) mention as example; quote (book etc.) in support; mention in military dispatches; summon to law court.

**citizen** /ˈsɪtɪz(ə)n/ *noun* native or national of state; inhabitant of a city.

□ **citizen's band** system of local inter-communication by radio. □ **citizenship** *noun*.

**citrate** /ˈsɪtreɪt/ *noun* salt of citric acid.

**citric** /ˈsɪtrɪk/ *adjective* □ **citric acid** sharp-tasting acid in citrus fruits.

**citron** /ˈsɪtrən/ *noun* tree bearing large lemon-like fruits; this fruit.

**citronella** /sɪtrəˈnelə/ *noun* a fragrant oil; grass from S. Asia yielding it.

**citrus** /ˈsɪtrəs/ *noun* (*plural* **-es**) tree of group including orange, lemon, and grapefruit; (in full **citrus fruit**) fruit of such tree.

**city** /ˈsɪtɪ/ *noun* (*plural* **-ies**) large town; town created city by charter and containing cathedral; (**the City**) part of London governed by Lord Mayor and Corporation, business quarter of this, commercial circles.

**civet** /ˈsɪvɪt/ *noun* (in full **civet cat**) catlike animal of Central Africa; strong musky perfume got from this.

**civic** /ˈsɪvɪk/ *adjective* of city or citizenship.

**civics** *plural noun* (usually treated as *singular*) study of civic rights and duties.

**civil** /ˈsɪv(ə)l/ *adjective* of or belonging to citizens; non-military; polite, obliging; *Law* concerning private rights and not criminal offences. □ **civil defence** organization for protecting civilians in wartime; **civil engineer** person who designs or maintains roads, bridges, etc.; **civil list** annual allowance by Parliament for royal family's household expenses; **civil marriage** one solemnized without religious ceremony; **civil servant** member of civil service; **civil service** all non-military and non-judicial branches of state administration; **civil war** one between citizens of same country.

**civilian** /sɪˈvɪlɪən/ ● *noun* person not in armed forces. ● *adjective* of or for civilians.

**civility** /sɪˈvɪlɪtɪ/ *noun* (*plural* **-ies**) politeness; act of politeness.

**civilization** *noun* (also **-sation**) advanced stage of social development; peoples regarded as having achieved, or been instrumental in evolving, this.

**civilize** /ˈsɪvɪlaɪz/ verb (also **-ise**) (**-zing** or **-sing**) bring out of barbarism; enlighten, refine.

**cl** abbreviation centilitre(s).

**clack** ● verb make sharp sound as of boards struck together. ● noun such sound.

**clad** adjective clothed; provided with cladding.

**cladding** noun protective covering or coating.

**claim** ● verb assert; demand as one's due; represent oneself as having; (+ to do) profess. ● noun demand; (+ to, on) right or title; assertion; thing claimed.

**claimant** noun person making claim, esp. in lawsuit or for state benefit.

**clairvoyance** /kleəˈvɔɪəns/ noun supposed faculty of perceiving the future or the unseen. □ **clairvoyant** noun & adjective.

**clam** ● noun edible bivalve mollusc. ● verb (**-mm-**) (+ up) colloquial refuse to talk.

**clamber** /ˈklæmbə/ verb climb using hands or with difficulty.

**clammy** /ˈklæmɪ/ adjective (**-ier**, **-iest**) damp and sticky.

**clamour** /ˈklæmə/ (US **clamor**) ● noun shouting, confused noise; protest, demand. ● verb make clamour, shout. □ **clamorous** adjective.

**clamp**[1] ● noun device, esp. brace or band of iron etc., for strengthening or holding things together; device for immobilizing illegally parked vehicles. ● verb strengthen or fasten with clamp; immobilize with clamp. □ **clamp down** (usually + on) become stricter (about).

**clamp**[2] noun heap of earth and straw over harvested potatoes etc.

**clan** noun group of families with common ancestor, esp. in Scotland; family holding together; group with common interest. □ **clannish** adjective; **clansman**, **clanswoman** noun.

**clandestine** /klænˈdestɪn/ adjective surreptitious, secret.

**clang** ● noun loud resonant metallic sound. ● verb (cause to) make clang.

**clangour** /ˈklæŋgə/ noun (US **clangor**) continued clanging. □ **clangorous** adjective.

**clank** ● noun sound as of metal on metal. ● verb (cause to) make clank.

**clap** ● verb (**-pp-**) strike palms of hands together, esp. as applause; put or place quickly or with determination; (+ on) give friendly slap on. ● noun act of clapping; explosive noise, esp. of thunder; slap. □ **clap eyes on** colloquial see.

**clapper** noun tongue or striker of bell. □ **clapperboard** device in film-making for making sharp noise to synchronize picture and sound.

**claptrap** noun insincere or pretentious talk; nonsense.

**claque** /klæk/ noun people hired to applaud.

**claret** /ˈklærət/ noun red Bordeaux wine.

**clarify** /ˈklærɪfaɪ/ verb (**-ies**, **-ied**) make or become clear; free from impurities; make transparent. □ **clarification** noun.

**clarinet** /klærɪˈnet/ noun woodwind instrument with single reed. □ **clarinettist** noun.

**clarion** /ˈklærɪən/ noun rousing sound; historical war-trumpet.

**clarity** /ˈklærɪtɪ/ noun clearness.

**clash** ● noun loud jarring sound as of metal objects struck together; collision; conflict; discord of colours etc. ● verb (cause to) make clash; coincide awkwardly; (often + with) be at variance or discordant.

**clasp** /klɑːsp/ ● noun device with interlocking parts for fastening; embrace, handshake; bar on medal-ribbon. ● verb fasten (as) with clasp; grasp, embrace. □ **clasp-knife** large folding knife.

**class** /klɑːs/ ● noun any set of people or things grouped together or differentiated from others; division or order of society; colloquial high quality; set of students taught together; their time of meeting; their course of instruction. ● verb place in a class. □ **classmate** person in same class at school; **classroom** room where class of students is taught. □ **classless** adjective.

**classic** /ˈklæsɪk/ ● adjective first-class; of lasting importance; typical; of ancient Greek or Latin culture etc.; (of style) simple and harmonious; famous because long-established. ● noun classic writer, artist, work, or example; (in plural) study of ancient Greek and Latin.

**classical** *adjective* of ancient Greek or Latin literature etc.; (of language) having form used by standard authors; (of music) serious or conventional.

**classicism** /ˈklæsɪsɪz(ə)m/ *noun* following of classic style; classical scholarship. □ **classicist** *noun*.

**classify** /ˈklæsɪfaɪ/ *verb* (**-ies, -ied**) arrange in classes; class; designate as officially secret. □ **classification** *noun*.

**classy** /ˈklɑːsɪ/ *adjective* (**-ier, -iest**) *colloquial* superior. □ **classiness** *noun*.

**clatter** /ˈklætə/ ●*noun* sound as of hard objects struck together. ●*verb* (cause to) make clatter.

**clause** /klɔːz/ *noun* group of words including finite verb (see panel); single statement in treaty, law, contract, etc.

**claustrophobia** /klɔːstrəˈfəʊbɪə/ *noun* abnormal fear of confined places. □ **claustrophobic** *adjective*.

**clavichord** /ˈklævɪkɔːd/ *noun* small keyboard instrument with very soft tone.

**clavicle** /ˈklævɪk(ə)l/ *noun* collar-bone.

**claw** ●*noun* pointed nail on animal's foot; foot armed with claws; pincers of shellfish; device for grappling, holding, etc. ●*verb* scratch, maul, or pull with claws or fingernails.

**clay** *noun* stiff sticky earth, used for bricks, pottery. etc. □ **clay pigeon** breakable disc thrown into air as target for shooting. □ **clayey** *adjective*.

**claymore** /ˈkleɪmɔː/ *noun* *historical* Scottish two-edged broad-bladed sword.

**clean** ●*adjective* free from dirt; clear; pristine; not obscene or indecent; attentive to cleanliness; clear-cut; without record of crime etc.; fair. ●*adverb* completely; simply; in a clean way.

●*verb* make or become clean. ●*noun* process of cleaning. □ **clean-cut** sharply outlined, (of person) clean and tidy; **clean out** clean thoroughly, *slang* empty or deprive (esp. of money); **clean-shaven** without beard or moustache; **clean up** make tidy or clean, *slang* acquire as or make profit. □ **cleaner** *noun*; **cleanness** *noun*.

**cleanly**[1] *adverb* in a clean way.

**cleanly**[2] /ˈklɛnlɪ/ *adjective* (**-ier, -iest**) habitually clean; attentive to cleanliness and hygiene. □ **cleanliness** *noun*.

**cleanse** /klɛnz/ *verb* (**-sing**) make clean or pure. □ **cleanser** *noun*.

**clear** ●*adjective* free from dirt or contamination; not clouded; transparent; readily perceived or understood; able to discern readily; convinced; (of conscience) guiltless; unobstructed; net; complete; (often + *of*) free, unhampered. ●*adverb* clearly; completely; apart. ●*verb* make or become clear; (often + *of*) free from obstruction etc.; (often + *of*) show (person) to be innocent; approve (person etc.) for special duty, access, etc.; pass through (customs); pass over or by without touching; make (sum) as net gain; pass (cheque) through clearing house. □ **clear-cut** sharply defined; **clear off** *colloquial* go away; **clear out** empty, remove, *colloquial* go away; **clear-out** tidying by emptying and sorting; **clear up** tidy, solve; **clearway** road where vehicles may not stop. □ **clearly** *adverb*; **clearness** *noun*.

**clearance** *noun* removal of obstructions etc.; space allowed for passing of two objects; special authorization; clearing for special duty, of cheque, etc.; clearing out.

---

## Clause

A clause is a group of words that includes a finite verb. If it makes complete sense by itself, it is known as a main clause, e.g.

*The sun came out.*

Otherwise, although it makes some sense, it must be attached to a main clause; this is known as a subordinate clause, e.g.

*when the sun came out*
(as in *When the sun came out, we went outside.*)

**clearing** *noun* treeless area in forest. □ **clearing bank** member of clearing house; **clearing house** bankers' institution where cheques etc. are exchanged, agency for collecting and distributing information etc.

**cleat** *noun* device for fastening ropes to projection on gangway, sole, etc. to provide grip.

**cleavage** *noun* hollow between woman's breasts; division; line along which rocks etc. split.

**cleave**[1] *verb* (**-ving**; *past* **clove** /kləʊv/, **cleft**, or **cleaved**; *past participle* **cloven**, **cleft**, or **cleaved**) *literary* break or come apart; make one's way through.

**cleave**[2] *verb* (**-ving**) (+ *to*) *literary* adhere.

**cleaver** *noun* butcher's heavy chopping tool.

**clef** *noun* *Music* symbol at start of staff showing pitch of notes on it.

**cleft**[1] *adjective* split, partly divided. □ **cleft palate** congenital split in roof of mouth.

**cleft**[2] *noun* split, fissure.

**clematis** /ˈklemətɪs/ *noun* climbing flowering plant.

**clement** /ˈklemənt/ *adjective* mild; merciful. □ **clemency** *noun*.

**clementine** /ˈklemənti:n/ *noun* small tangerine-like fruit.

**clench** ● *verb* close tightly; grasp firmly. ● *noun* clenching action; clenched state.

**clergy** /ˈklɜ:dʒɪ/ *noun* (*plural* **-ies**) (usually treated as *plural*) those ordained for religious duties.

**clergyman** /ˈklɜ:dʒɪmən/ *noun* member of clergy.

**cleric** /ˈklerɪk/ *noun* member of clergy.

**clerical** *adjective* of clergy or clergymen; of or done by clerks.

**clerihew** /ˈklerɪhju:/ *noun* witty or comic 4-line biographical verse.

**clerk** /klɑ:k/ ● *noun* person employed to keep records, accounts, etc.; secretary or agent of local council, court, etc.; lay officer of church. ● *verb* work as clerk.

**clever** /ˈklevə/ *adjective* (**-er**, **-est**) skilful, talented, quick to understand and learn; adroit; ingenious. □ **cleverly** *adverb*; **cleverness** *noun*.

**cliché** /ˈkli:ʃeɪ/ *noun* hackneyed phrase or opinion.

**clichéd** *adjective* hackneyed, full of clichés.

**click** ● *noun* slight sharp sound. ● *verb* (cause to) make click; *colloquial* become clear, understood, or popular; (+ *with*) become friendly with.

**client** /ˈklaɪənt/ *noun* person using services of lawyer or other professional person; customer.

**clientele** /kli:ɒnˈtel/ *noun* clients collectively; customers.

**cliff** *noun* steep rock face, esp. on coast. □ **cliff-hanger** story etc. with strong element of suspense.

**climacteric** /klaɪˈmæktərɪk/ *noun* period of life when fertility and sexual activity are in decline.

**climate** /ˈklaɪmɪt/ *noun* prevailing weather conditions of an area; region with particular weather conditions; prevailing trend of opinion etc. □ **climatic** /-ˈmæt-/ *adjective*; **climatically** /-ˈmæt-/ *adverb*.

**climax** /ˈklaɪmæks/ ● *noun* event or point of greatest intensity or interest, culmination. ● *verb* *colloquial* reach or bring to a climax. □ **climactic** *adjective*.

**climb** /klaɪm/ ● *verb* (often + *up*) ascend, mount, go up; (of plant) grow up wall etc. by clinging etc.; rise, esp. in social rank. ● *noun* action of climbing; hill etc. (to be) climbed. □ **climber** *noun*.

**clime** *noun* *literary* region; climate.

**clinch** ● *verb* confirm or settle conclusively; (of boxers) become too closely engaged; secure (nail or rivet) by driving point sideways when through. ● *noun* clinching, resulting state; *colloquial* embrace.

**cling** *verb* (*past & past participle* **clung**) (often + *to*) adhere; (+ *to*) be emotionally dependent on or unwilling to give up; (often + *to*) maintain grasp. □ **cling film** thin transparent plastic covering for food. □ **clingy** *adjective* (**-ier**, **-iest**).

**clinic** /ˈklɪnɪk/ *noun* private or specialized hospital; place or occasion for giving medical treatment or specialist advice; teaching of medicine at hospital bedside.

**clinical** *adjective* of or for the treatment of patients; objective, coldly detached;

(of room etc.) bare, functional. □ **clinically** adverb.

**clink**[1] ● noun sharp ringing sound. ● verb (cause to) make clink.

**clink**[2] noun slang prison.

**clinker** /'klɪŋkə/ noun mass of slag or lava; stony residue from burnt coal.

**clinker-built** adjective (of boat) with external planks overlapping downwards.

**clip**[1] ● noun device for holding things together; piece of jewellery fastened by clip; set of attached cartridges for firearm. ● verb (**-pp-**) fix with clip. □ **clipboard** board with spring clip for holding papers etc.

**clip**[2] ● verb (**-pp-**) cut with shears or scissors; cut hair or wool of; colloquial hit sharply; omit (letter) from word; omit parts of (words uttered); punch hole in (ticket) to show it has been used; cut from newspaper etc. ● noun clipping; colloquial sharp blow; extract from motion picture; yield of wool.

**clipper** noun (usually in plural) instrument for clipping; historical fast sailing ship.

**clipping** noun piece clipped, esp. from newspaper.

**clique** /kli:k/ noun exclusive group of people. □ **cliquey** adjective (**cliquier, cliquiest**); **cliquish** adjective.

**clitoris** /'klɪtərɪs/ noun small erectile part of female genitals.

**Cllr.** abbreviation Councillor.

**cloak** ● noun loose usually sleeveless outdoor garment; covering. ● verb cover with cloak; conceal, disguise. □ **cloakroom** room for outdoor clothes or luggage, euphemistic lavatory.

**clobber**[1] /'klɒbə/ verb slang hit (repeatedly); defeat; criticize severely.

**clobber**[2] /'klɒbə/ noun slang clothing, belongings.

**cloche** /klɒʃ/ noun small translucent cover for outdoor plants; woman's close-fitting bell-shaped hat.

**clock**[1] ● noun instrument measuring and showing time; measuring device resembling this; colloquial speedometer, taximeter, or stopwatch; seed-head of dandelion. ● verb colloquial (often + up) attain or register (distance etc.); time (race etc.) by stopwatch. □ **clock in** (or

on), or **out** (or **off**) register time of arrival, or departure, by automatic clock; **clockwise** (moving) in same direction as hands of clock; **clockwork** mechanism with coiled springs etc. on clock principle; **like clockwork** with mechanical precision.

**clock**[2] noun ornamental pattern on side of stocking or sock.

**clod** noun lump of earth or clay.

**clog** ● noun wooden-soled shoe. ● verb (**-gg-**) (often + up) (cause to) become obstructed, impede; choke; impede.

**cloister** /'klɔɪstə/ noun covered walk esp. in college or ecclesiastical building; monastic life; seclusion. ● verb seclude.

**clone** ● noun group of organisms produced asexually from one ancestor; one such organism; colloquial person or thing regarded as identical to another. ● verb (**-ning**) propagate as clone.

**close**[1] /kləʊs/ ● adjective (often + to) at short distance or interval; having strong or immediate relation; (almost) in contact; dense, compact; nearly equal; rigorous; concentrated; stifling; shut; secret; niggardly. ● adverb at short distance or interval. ● noun street closed at one end; precinct of cathedral. □ **close harmony** singing of parts within an octave; **close-knit** tightly interlocked, closely united; **close season** season when killing of game etc. is illegal; **close shave** colloquial narrow escape; **close-up** photograph etc. taken at short range. □ **closely** adverb; **closeness** noun.

**close**[2] /kləʊz/ ● verb (**-sing**) shut; block up; bring or come to an end; end day's business; bring or come closer or into contact; make (electric circuit) continuous. ● noun conclusion, end. □ **closed-circuit** (of television) transmitted by wires to restricted number of receivers; **closed shop** business etc. where employees must belong to specified trade union.

**closet** /'klɒzɪt/ ● noun small room; cupboard; water-closet. ● adjective secret. ● verb (**-t-**) shut away, esp. in private consultation etc.

**closure** /'kləʊʒə/ noun closing, closed state; procedure for ending debate.

**clot** • *noun* thick lump formed from liquid, esp. blood; *colloquial* foolish person. • *verb* (**-tt-**) form into clots.

**cloth** /klɒθ/ *noun* woven or felted material; piece of this; (**the cloth**) the clergy.

**clothe** /kləʊð/ *verb* (**-thing**; *past & past participle* **clothed** or **clad**) put clothes on; provide with clothes; cover as with clothes.

**clothes** /kləʊðz/ *plural noun* things worn to cover body and limbs; bedclothes. □ **clothes-horse** frame for airing washed clothes.

**clothier** /ˈkləʊðɪə/ *noun* dealer in men's clothes.

**clothing** /ˈkləʊðɪŋ/ *noun* clothes.

**cloud** /klaʊd/ • *noun* visible mass of condensed watery vapour floating in air; mass of smoke or dust; (+ *of*) great number of (birds, insects, etc.) moving together; state of gloom, trouble, or suspicion. • *verb* cover or darken with cloud(s); (often + *over*, *up*) become overcast or gloomy; make unclear. □ **cloudburst** sudden violent rainstorm. □ **cloudless** *adjective*.

**cloudy** *adjective* (**-ier**, **-iest**) covered with clouds; not transparent, unclear. □ **cloudiness** *noun*.

**clout** /klaʊt/ • *noun* heavy blow; *colloquial* influence, power of effective action; piece of cloth or clothing. • *verb* hit hard.

**clove**[1] /kləʊv/ *noun* dried bud of tropical tree, used as spice.

**clove**[2] /kləʊv/ *noun* segment of compound bulb, esp. of garlic.

**clove**[3] *past of* CLEAVE[1].

**clove hitch** *noun* knot for fastening rope round pole etc.

**cloven** /ˈkləʊv(ə)n/ *adjective* split. □ **cloven hoof, foot** divided hoof, as of oxen, sheep, etc., or the Devil.

**clover** /ˈkləʊvə/ *noun* kind of trefoil used as fodder. □ **in clover** in ease and luxury.

**clown** /klaʊn/ • *noun* comic entertainer, esp. in circus; foolish or playful person. • *verb* (often + *about*, *around*) behave like clown.

**cloy** *verb* satiate or sicken by sweetness, richness, etc.

**club** • *noun* heavy stick used as weapon; stick with head, used in golf; association of people for social, sporting, etc.

purposes; premises of this; playing card of suit marked with black trefoils; (in *plural*) this suit. • *verb* (**-bb-**) strike (as) with club; (+ *together*) combine, esp. to make up sum of money. □ **club foot** congenitally deformed foot; **clubhouse** premises of club; **clubland** area with many nightclubs; **clubroot** disease of cabbages etc.; **club sandwich** sandwich with 2 layers of filling and 3 slices of bread or toast.

**cluck** • *noun* chattering cry of hen. • *verb* emit cluck(s).

**clue** • *noun* guiding or suggestive fact; piece of evidence used in detection of crime; word(s) used to indicate word(s) for insertion in crossword. • *verb* (**clues**, **clued**, **cluing** or **clueing**) provide clue to. □ **clue in**, **up** *slang* inform.

**clump** • *noun* (+ *of*) cluster, esp. of trees. • *verb* form clump; heap or plant together; tread heavily.

**clumsy** /ˈklʌmzɪ/ *adjective* (**-ier**, **-iest**) awkward in movement or shape; difficult to handle or use; tactless. □ **clumsily** *adverb*; **clumsiness** *noun*.

**clung** *past & past participle of* CLING.

**cluster** /ˈklʌstə/ • *noun* close group or bunch of similar people or things. • *verb* be in or form into cluster(s); (+ *round*, *around*) gather round.

**clutch**[1] • *verb* seize eagerly; grasp tightly; (+ *at*) snatch at. • *noun* tight or (in *plural*) cruel grasp; (in vehicle) device for connecting engine to transmission, pedal operating this. □ **clutch bag** handbag without handles.

**clutch**[2] *noun* set of eggs; brood of chickens.

**clutter** /ˈklʌtə/ • *noun* crowded untidy collection of things. • *verb* (often + *up*, *with*) crowd untidily, fill with clutter.

**cm** *abbreviation* centimetre(s).

**Cmdr.** *abbreviation* Commander.

**CND** *abbreviation* Campaign for Nuclear Disarmament.

**CO** *abbreviation* Commanding Officer.

**Co.** *abbreviation* company; county.

**c/o** *abbreviation* care of.

**coach** • *noun* single-decker bus usually for longer journeys; railway carriage; closed horse-drawn carriage; sports trainer or private tutor. • *verb* train or teach. □ **coachload** group of tourists etc. travelling by coach; **coachman** driver of horse-drawn carriage; **coachwork** bodywork of road or rail vehicle.

**coagulate** /kəʊˈægjʊleɪt/ verb (**-ting**) change from liquid to semi-solid; clot, curdle. □ **coagulant** noun; **coagulation** noun.

**coal** noun hard black mineral used as fuel etc.; piece of this. □ **coalface** exposed surface of coal in mine; **coalfield** area yielding coal; **coal gas** mixed gases formerly extracted from coal and used for heating, cooking, etc.; **coal mine** place where coal is dug; **coal miner** worker in coal mine; **coal scuttle** container for coal for domestic fire; **coal tar** tar extracted from coal; **coal tit** small bird with greyish plumage.

**coalesce** /kəʊəˈles/ verb (**-cing**) come together and form a whole. □ **coalescence** noun; **coalescent** adjective.

**coalition** /kəʊəˈlɪʃ(ə)n/ noun temporary alliance, esp. of political parties; fusion into one whole.

**coaming** /ˈkəʊmɪŋ/ noun raised border round ship's hatches etc.

**coarse** /kɔːs/ adjective rough or loose in texture; of large particles; lacking refinement; crude, obscene. □ **coarse fish** freshwater fish other than salmon and trout. □ **coarsely** adverb; **coarsen** verb; **coarseness** noun.

**coast** • noun border of land near sea; seashore. • verb ride or move (usually downhill) without use of power; make progress without exertion; sail along coast. □ **coastguard** (member of) group of people employed to keep watch on coasts, prevent smuggling, etc.; **coastline** line of seashore, esp. with regard to its shape. □ **coastal** adjective.

**coaster** noun ship that sails along coast; tray or mat for bottle or glass.

**coat** • noun sleeved outer garment, overcoat, jacket; animal's fur or hair; layer of paint etc. • verb (usually + with, in) cover with coat or layer; form covering on. □ **coat of arms** heraldic bearings on shield; **coat-hanger** shaped piece of wood etc. for hanging clothes on.

**coating** noun layer of paint etc.; cloth for coats.

**coax** verb persuade gradually or by flattery; (+ out of) obtain (thing) from (person) thus; manipulate gently.

**coaxial** /kəʊˈæksɪəl/ adjective having common axis; (of electric cable etc.) transmitting by means of two concentric conductors separated by insulator.

**cob** noun roundish lump; domed loaf; corn cob; large hazelnut; sturdy short-legged riding-horse; male swan.

**cobalt** /ˈkəʊbɔːlt/ noun silvery-white metallic element; (colour of) deep blue pigment made from it.

**cobber** /ˈkɒbə/ noun Australian & NZ colloquial companion, friend.

**cobble**[1] /ˈkɒb(ə)l/ • noun (in full **cobblestone**) rounded stone used for paving. • verb (**-ling**) pave with cobbles.

**cobble**[2] /ˈkɒb(ə)l/ verb (**-ling**) mend or patch (esp. shoes); (often + together) assemble roughly.

**cobbler** noun mender of shoes; (in plural) slang nonsense.

**COBOL** /ˈkəʊbɒl/ noun computer language for use in business operations.

**cobra** /ˈkəʊbrə/ noun venomous hooded snake.

**cobweb** /ˈkɒbweb/ noun spider's network or thread. □ **cobwebby** adjective.

**coca** /ˈkəʊkə/ noun S. American shrub; its leaves chewed as stimulant.

**cocaine** /kəʊˈkeɪn/ noun drug from coca, used as local anaesthetic and as stimulant.

**coccyx** /ˈkɒksɪks/ noun (plural **coccyges** /-dʒiːz/) bone at base of spinal column.

**cochineal** /kɒtʃɪˈniːl/ noun scarlet dye; insects whose dried bodies yield this.

**cock**[1] • noun male bird, esp. domestic fowl; slang (as form of address) friend, fellow; slang nonsense; firing lever in gun released by trigger; tap or valve controlling flow. • verb raise or make upright; turn or move (eye or ear) attentively or knowingly; set (hat etc.) aslant; raise cock of (gun). □ **cock-a-hoop** exultant; **cock-a-leekie** Scottish soup of boiled fowl with leeks; **cockcrow** dawn; **cock-eyed** colloquial crooked, askew, absurd.

**cock**[2] noun conical heap of hay or straw.

**cockade** /kɒˈkeɪd/ noun rosette etc. worn in hat.

**cockatoo** /kɒkə'tu:/ noun crested parrot.

**cockchafer** /'kɒktʃeɪfə/ noun large pale brown beetle.

**cocker** /'kɒkə/ noun (in full **cocker spaniel**) small spaniel.

**cockerel** /'kɒkər(ə)l/ noun young cock.

**cockle** /'kɒk(ə)l/ noun edible bivalve shellfish; its shell; (in full **cockleshell**) small shallow boat; pucker or wrinkle. □ **cockles of the heart** innermost feelings.

**cockney** /'kɒknɪ/ ● noun (plural **-s**) native of London, esp. East End; cockney dialect. ● adjective of cockneys.

**cockpit** noun place for pilot etc. in aircraft or spacecraft or for driver in racing car; arena of war etc.

**cockroach** /'kɒkrəʊtʃ/ noun dark brown insect infesting esp. kitchens.

**cockscomb** /'kɒkskəʊm/ noun cock's crest.

**cocksure** /kɒk'ʃɔː/ adjective arrogantly confident.

**cocktail** /'kɒkteɪl/ noun drink of spirits, fruit juices, etc.; appetizer containing shellfish etc.; any hybrid mixture. □ **cocktail stick** small pointed stick.

**cocky** adjective (**-ier**, **-iest**) colloquial conceited, arrogant. □ **cockiness** noun.

**coco** /'kəʊkəʊ/ noun (plural **-s**) coconut palm.

**cocoa** /'kəʊkəʊ/ noun powder of crushed cacao seeds; drink made from this.

**coconut** /'kəʊkənʌt/ noun large brown seed of coco, with edible white lining enclosing milky juice. □ **coconut matting** matting made from fibre of coconut husks; **coconut shy** fairground sideshow where balls are thrown to dislodge coconuts.

**cocoon** /kə'ku:n/ ● noun silky case spun by larva to protect it as pupa; protective covering. ● verb wrap (as) in cocoon.

**cocotte** /kə'kɒt/ noun small fireproof dish for cooking and serving food.

**COD** abbreviation cash (US collect) on delivery.

**cod**[1] noun (also **codfish**) (plural same) large sea fish. □ **cod liver oil** medicinal oil rich in vitamins.

**cod**[2] noun & verb (**-dd-**) slang hoax, parody.

**coda** /'kəʊdə/ noun final passage of piece of music.

**coddle** /'kɒd(ə)l/ verb (**-ling**) treat as an invalid, pamper; cook in water just below boiling point. □ **coddler** noun.

**code** ● noun system of signals or of symbols etc. used for secrecy, brevity, or computer processing of information; systematic set of laws etc.; standard of moral behaviour. ● verb (**-ding**) put into code.

**codeine** /'kəʊdi:n/ noun alkaloid derived from morphine, used as pain-killer.

**codex** /'kəʊdeks/ noun (plural **codices** /'kəʊdɪsi:z/) manuscript volume esp. of ancient texts.

**codger** /'kɒdʒə/ noun (usually in **old codger**) colloquial (strange) person.

**codicil** /'kəʊdɪsɪl/ noun addition to will.

**codify** /'kəʊdɪfaɪ/ verb (**-ies**, **-ied**) arrange (laws etc.) into code. □ **codification** noun.

**codling**[1] /'kɒdlɪŋ/ noun (also **codlin**) variety of apple; moth whose larva feeds on apples.

**codling**[2] noun (plural same) small cod.

**co-education** /kəʊedjuː'keɪʃ(ə)n/ noun education of both sexes together. □ **co-educational** adjective.

**coefficient** /kəʊɪ'fɪʃ(ə)nt/ noun Mathematics quantity or expression placed before and multiplying another; Physics multiplier or factor by which a property is measured.

**coeliac disease** /'si:lɪæk/ noun intestinal disease whose symptoms include adverse reaction to gluten.

**coequal** /kəʊ'i:kw(ə)l/ adjective & noun equal.

**coerce** /kəʊ'ɜːs/ verb (**-cing**) persuade or restrain by force. □ **coercion** /-'ɜːʃ(ə)n/ noun; **coercive** adjective.

**coeval** /kəʊ'i:v(ə)l/ formal ● adjective of the same age; contemporary. ● noun coeval person or thing.

**coexist** /kəʊɪg'zɪst/ verb (often + with) exist together, esp. in mutual tolerance. □ **coexistence** noun; **coexistent** adjective.

**coextensive** /kəʊɪk'stensɪv/ adjective extending over same space or time.

**C. of E.** abbreviation Church of England.

**coffee** /'kɒfɪ/ *noun* drink made from roasted and ground seeds of tropical shrub; cup of this; the shrub; the seeds; pale brown. □ **coffee bar** café selling coffee and light refreshments from bar; **coffee bean** seed of coffee; **coffee mill** small machine for grinding coffee beans; **coffee morning** morning gathering, esp. for charity, at which coffee is served; **coffee shop** small restaurant, esp. in hotel or store; **coffee table** small low table; **coffee-table book** large illustrated book.

**coffer** /'kɒfə/ *noun* large box for valuables; (in *plural*) funds, treasury; sunken panel in ceiling etc.

**coffin** /'kɒfɪn/ *noun* box in which corpse is buried or cremated.

**cog** *noun* each of series of projections on wheel etc. transferring motion by engaging with another series.

**cogent** /'kəʊdʒ(ə)nt/ *adjective* (of argument etc.) convincing, compelling. □ **cogency** *noun*; **cogently** *adverb*.

**cogitate** /'kɒdʒɪteɪt/ *verb* (**-ting**) ponder, meditate. □ **cogitation** *noun*.

**cognac** /'kɒnjæk/ *noun* French brandy.

**cognate** /'kɒgneɪt/ ● *adjective* descended from same ancestor or root. ● *noun* cognate person or word.

**cognition** /kɒg'nɪʃ(ə)n/ *noun* knowing, perceiving, or conceiving, as distinct from emotion and volition. □ **cognitive** /'kɒg-/ *adjective*.

**cognizance** /'kɒgnɪz(ə)ns/ *noun formal* knowledge or awareness.

**cognizant** /'kɒgnɪz(ə)nt/ *adjective formal* (+ *of*) having knowledge or being aware of.

**cognomen** /kɒg'nəʊmen/ *noun* nickname; *Roman History* surname.

**cohabit** /kəʊ'hæbɪt/ *verb* (**-t-**) live together as husband and wife. □ **cohabitation** *noun*.

**cohere** /kəʊ'hɪə/ *verb* (**-ring**) stick together; (of reasoning) be logical or consistent.

**coherent** *adjective* intelligible; consistent, easily understood. □ **coherence** *noun*; **coherently** *adverb*.

**cohesion** /kəʊ'hiːʒ(ə)n/ *noun* sticking together; tendency to cohere. □ **cohesive** /-sɪv/ *adjective*.

**cohort** /'kəʊhɔːt/ *noun* one-tenth of Roman legion; people banded together.

**coif** /kɔɪf/ *noun historical* close-fitting cap.

**coiffeur** /kwa:'fɜː/ *noun* (*feminine* **coiffeuse** /-'fɜːz/) hairdresser.

**coiffure** /kwa:'fjʊə/ *noun* hairstyle.

**coil** ● *verb* arrange or be arranged in concentric rings; move sinuously. ● *noun* coiled arrangement (of rope, electrical conductor, etc.); single turn of something coiled; flexible contraceptive device in womb.

**coin** ● *noun* stamped disc of metal as official money; metal money. ● *verb* make (coins) by stamping; invent (word, phrase). □ **coin box** telephone operated by coins.

**coinage** *noun* coining; system of coins in use; invention of word, invented word.

**coincide** /kəʊɪn'saɪd/ *verb* (**-ding**) occur at same time; (often + *with*) agree or be identical.

**coincidence** /kəʊ'ɪnsɪd(ə)ns/ *noun* remarkable concurrence of events etc., apparently by chance. □ **coincident** *adjective*.

**coincidental** /kəʊɪnsɪ'dent(ə)l/ *adjective* in the nature of or resulting from coincidence. □ **coincidentally** *adverb*.

**coir** /'kɔɪə/ *noun* coconut fibre used for ropes, matting, etc.

**coition** /kəʊ'ɪʃ(ə)n/ *noun* coitus.

**coitus** /'kəʊɪtəs/ *noun* sexual intercourse. □ **coital** *adjective*.

**coke**[1] ● *noun* solid left after gases have been extracted from coal. ● *verb* (**-king**) convert (coal) into coke.

**coke**[2] *noun slang* cocaine.

**Col.** *abbreviation* Colonel.

**col** *noun* depression in summit-line of mountain chain.

**cola** /'kəʊlə/ *noun* W. African tree with seeds containing caffeine; carbonated drink flavoured with these.

**colander** /'kʌləndə/ *noun* perforated vessel used as strainer in cookery.

**cold** /kəʊld/ ● *adjective* of or at low temperature; not heated; having lost heat; feeling cold; (of colour) suggesting cold; *colloquial* unconscious; lacking ardour or friendliness; dispiriting; (of hunting-scent) grown faint. ● noun prevalence of low temperature; cold weather; infection of nose or throat. ● adverb unrehearsed. □ **cold-blooded** having body temperature varying with that of environment, callous; **cold call** marketing call on person not previously interested in product; **cold cream** cleansing ointment; **cold feet** fear, reluctance; **cold fusion** nuclear fusion at room temperature; **cold shoulder** unfriendly treatment; **cold turkey** *slang* abrupt withdrawal from addictive drugs; **cold war** hostility between nations without actual fighting; **in cold blood** without emotion; **throw cold water on** discourage. □ **coldly** *adverb*; **coldness** *noun*.

**coleslaw** /ˈkəʊlslɔː/ *noun* salad of sliced raw cabbage etc.

**coley** /ˈkəʊlɪ/ *noun* (*plural* **-s**) any of several edible fish, esp. rock-salmon.

**colic** /ˈkɒlɪk/ *noun* spasmodic abdominal pain. □ **colicky** *adjective*.

**colitis** /kəˈlaɪtɪs/ *noun* inflammation of colon.

**collaborate** /kəˈlæbəreɪt/ *verb* (**-ting**) (often + *with*) work jointly. □ **collaboration** *noun*; **collaborative** /-rətɪv/ *adjective*; **collaborator** *noun*.

**collage** /ˈkɒlɑːʒ/ *noun* picture made by gluing pieces of paper etc. on to backing.

**collapse** /kəˈlæps/ ● *noun* falling down of structure; sudden failure of plan etc.; physical or mental breakdown. ● *verb* (**-sing**) (cause to) undergo collapse; *colloquial* relax completely after effort. □ **collapsible** *adjective*.

**collar** /ˈkɒlə/ ● *noun* neckband, upright or turned over, of coat, shirt, dress, etc.; leather band round animal's neck; band, ring, or pipe in machinery. ● *verb* capture, seize, appropriate; *colloquial* accost. □ **collar-bone** bone joining breastbone and shoulder blade.

**collate** /kəˈleɪt/ *verb* (**-ting**) collect and put in order. □ **collator** *noun*.

**collateral** /kəˈlætər(ə)l/ ● *noun* security pledged as guarantee for repayment of loan. ● *adjective* side by side; additional but subordinate; descended from same ancestor but by different line. □ **collaterally** *adverb*.

**collation** *noun* collating; light meal.

**colleague** /ˈkɒliːg/ *noun* fellow worker, esp. in profession or business.

**collect**[1] /kəˈlekt/ ● *verb* bring or come together; assemble, accumulate; seek and acquire (books, stamps, etc.); obtain (contributions, taxes, etc.) from people; call for, fetch; concentrate (one's thoughts etc.); (as **collected** *adjective*) not perturbed or distracted. ● *adjective & adverb US* (of telephone call, parcel, etc.) to be paid for by recipient.

**collect**[2] /ˈkɒlekt/ *noun* short prayer of Anglican or RC Church.

**collectable** /kəˈlektəb(ə)l/ *adjective* worth collecting.

**collection** /kəˈlekʃ(ə)n/ *noun* collecting, being collected; things collected; money collected, esp. at church service etc.

**collective** /kəˈlektɪv/ ● *adjective* of or relating to group or society as a whole; joint; shared. ● *noun* cooperative enterprise; its members. □ **collective bargaining** negotiation of wages etc. by organized group of employees; **collective noun** singular noun denoting group of individuals. □ **collectively** *adverb*; **collectivize** *verb* (also **-ise**) (**-zing** or **-sing**).

**collectivism** *noun* theory or practice of collective ownership of land and means of production. □ **collectivist** *noun & adjective*.

**collector** *noun* person collecting things of interest; person collecting taxes, rents, etc.

**colleen** /ˈkɒliːn/ *noun* *Irish* girl.

**college** /ˈkɒlɪdʒ/ *noun* establishment for further, higher, or professional education; teachers and students in a college; school; organized group of people with shared functions and privileges.

**collegiate** /kəˈliːdʒɪət/ *adjective* of or constituted as college, corporate; (of university) consisting of different colleges.

**collide** /kəˈlaɪd/ *verb* (**-ding**) (often + *with*) come into collision or conflict.

**collie** /ˈkɒlɪ/ *noun* sheepdog originally of Scottish breed.

**collier** /ˈkɒlɪə/ *noun* coal miner; coal ship, member of its crew.

**colliery** /ˈkɒlɪərɪ/ *noun* (*plural* **-ies**) coal mine and its buildings.

**collision** /kəˈlɪʒ(ə)n/ *noun* violent impact of moving body against another or fixed object; clashing of interests etc.

**collocate** /ˈkɒləkeɪt/ *verb* (**-ting**) place (word etc.) next to another. □ **collocation** *noun.*

**colloid** /ˈkɒlɔɪd/ *noun* substance consisting of minute particles; mixture, esp. viscous solution, of this and another substance. □ **colloidal** *adjective.*

**colloquial** /kəˈləʊkwɪəl/ *adjective* of ordinary or familiar conversation, informal. □ **colloquially** *adverb.*

**colloquialism** /kəˈləʊkwɪəlɪz(ə)m/ *noun* colloquial word or phrase.

**colloquy** /ˈkɒləkwɪ/ *noun* (*plural* **-quies**) *literary* talk, dialogue.

**collude** /kəˈluːd/ *verb* (**-ding**) conspire. □ **collusion** /-ʒ(ə)n/ *noun;* **collusive** /-sɪv/ *adjective.*

**collywobbles** /ˈkɒlɪwɒb(ə)lz/ *plural noun colloquial* ache or rumbling in stomach; apprehensive feeling.

**cologne** /kəˈləʊn/ *noun* eau-de-Cologne or similar toilet water.

**colon**[1] /ˈkəʊlən/ *noun* punctuation mark (:) used between main clauses or before list or quotation (see panel).

**colon**[2] /ˈkəʊlən/ *noun* lower and greater part of large intestine.

**colonel** /ˈkɜːn(ə)l/ *noun* army officer commanding regiment, next in rank below brigadier. □ **colonelcy** *noun* (*plural* **-ies**).

**colonial** /kəˈləʊnɪəl/ ● *adjective* of a colony or colonies; of colonialism. ● *noun* inhabitant of colony.

**colonialism** *noun* policy of having colonies.

**colonist** /ˈkɒlənɪst/ *noun* settler in or inhabitant of colony.

**colonize** /ˈkɒlənaɪz/ *verb* (also **-ise**) (**-zing** or **-sing**) establish colony in; join colony. □ **colonization** *noun.*

**colonnade** /kɒləˈneɪd/ *noun* row of columns, esp. supporting roof. □ **colonnaded** *adjective.*

**colony** /ˈkɒlənɪ/ *noun* (*plural* **-ies**) settlement or settlers in new territory remaining subject to mother country; people of one nationality, occupation, etc. forming community in town etc.; group of animals that live close together.

**colophon** /ˈkɒləf(ə)n/ *noun* tailpiece in book.

**color** etc. *US* = **colour** etc.

**Colorado beetle** /kɒləˈrɑːdəʊ/ *noun* small beetle destructive to potato.

**coloration** /kʌləˈreɪʃ(ə)n/ *noun* (also **colouration**) colouring, arrangement of colours.

**coloratura** /kɒlərəˈtʊərə/ *noun* elaborate passages in vocal music; singer of these, esp. soprano.

**colossal** /kəˈlɒs(ə)l/ *adjective* huge; *colloquial* splendid. □ **colossally** *adverb.*

**colossus** /kəˈlɒsəs/ *noun* (*plural* **-ssi** /-saɪ/ or **-ssuses**) statue much bigger than life size; gigantic or remarkable person etc.

**colour** /ˈkʌlə/ (*US* **color**) ● *noun* one, or any mixture, of the constituents into

---

## Colon :

This is used:

**1** between two main clauses of which the second explains, enlarges on, or follows from the first, e.g.

*It was not easy: to begin with I had to find the right house.*

**2** to introduce a list of items (a dash should not be added), and after expressions such as *namely, for example, to resume, to sum up,* and *the following,* e.g.

*You will need: a tent, a sleeping bag, cooking equipment, and a rucksack.*

**3** before a quotation, e.g.

*The poem begins: 'Earth has not anything to show more fair'.*

which light is separated in rainbow etc.; use of all colours as in photography; colouring substance, esp. paint; skin pigmentation, esp. when dark; ruddiness of face; appearance or aspect; (in *plural*) flag of regiment or ship etc.; coloured ribbon, rosette, etc. worn as symbol of school, club, political party, etc. ● *verb* give colour to; paint, stain, dye; blush; influence. □ **colour-blind** unable to distinguish certain colours; **colour-blindness** *noun*; **colour scheme** arrangement of colours; **colour supplement** magazine with colour printing, sold with newspaper.

**coloured** (*US* **colored**) ● *adjective* having colour; wholly or partly of non-white descent; *South African* of mixed white and non-white descent. ● *noun* coloured person.

**colourful** *adjective* (*US* **colorful**) full of colour or interest. □ **colourfully** *adverb*.

**colouring** *noun* (*US* **coloring**) appearance as regards colour, esp. facial complexion; application of colour; substance giving colour.

**colourless** *adjective* (*US* **colorless**) without colour, lacking interest.

**colt** /kəʊlt/ *noun* young male horse; *Sport* inexperienced player.

**colter** *US* = COULTER.

**coltsfoot** *noun* (*plural* **-s**) yellow wild flower with large leaves.

**columbine** /ˈkɒləmbaɪn/ *noun* garden plant with purple-blue flowers.

**column** /ˈkɒləm/ *noun* pillar, usually round, with base and capital; column-shaped thing; series of numbers, one under the other; vertical division of printed page; part of newspaper regularly devoted to particular subject or written by one writer; long, narrow arrangement of advancing troops, vehicles, etc.

**columnist** /ˈkɒləmnɪst/ *noun* journalist contributing regularly to newspaper etc.

**coma** /ˈkəʊmə/ *noun* (*plural* **-s**) prolonged deep unconsciousness.

**comatose** /ˈkəʊmətəʊs/ *adjective* in coma; sleepy.

**comb** /kəʊm/ ● *noun* toothed strip of rigid material for arranging hair; thing like comb, esp. for dressing wool etc.; red fleshy crest of fowl, esp. cock etc.; honeycomb. ● *verb* draw comb through (hair), dress (wool etc.) with comb; *colloquial* search (place) thoroughly.

**combat** /ˈkɒmbæt/ ● *noun* struggle, fight. ● *verb* (**-t-**) do battle (with); strive against, oppose.

**combatant** /ˈkɒmbət(ə)nt/ ● *noun* fighter. ● *adjective* fighting.

**combative** /ˈkɒmbətɪv/ *adjective* pugnacious.

**combe** = COOMB.

**combination** /kɒmbɪˈneɪʃ(ə)n/ *noun* combining, being combined; combined state; combined set of things or people; motorcycle with side-car; sequence of numbers etc. used to open **combination lock**.

**combine** ● *verb* /kəmˈbaɪn/ (**-ning**) join together; unite; form into chemical compound. ● *noun* /ˈkɒmbaɪn/ combination of esp. businesses. □ **combine harvester** /ˈkɒmbaɪn/ combined reaping and threshing machine.

**combustible** /kəmˈbʌstɪb(ə)l/ ● *adjective* capable of or used for burning. ● *noun* combustible substance. □ **combustibility** *noun*.

**combustion** /kəmˈbʌstʃ(ə)n/ *noun* burning; development of light and heat from combination of substance with oxygen.

**come** /kʌm/ *verb* (**-ming**; *past* **came**; *past participle* **come**) move or be brought towards or reach a place, time, situation, or result; be available; occur; become; traverse; *colloquial* behave like. □ **come about** happen; **come across** meet or find by chance, give specified impression, *colloquial* be effective or understood; **come again** *colloquial* what did you say?; **come along** make progress, hurry up; **come apart** disintegrate; **come at** attack; **comeback** return to success, *slang* retort or retaliation; **come back to** recur to memory (of); **come by** obtain; **come clean** *colloquial* confess; **comedown** loss of status; **come down** lose position, be handed down, be reduced; **come forward** offer oneself for task etc.; **come in** become fashionable or seasonable, prove to be; **come in for** receive; **come into** inherit; **come off** succeed, occur, fare; **come off it** *colloquial* expression of *disbelief*; **come on** make progress; **come out** emerge, become known, be published, go on strike, (of photograph or its subject) be (re)produced clearly, (of stain) be removed; **come out with** declare, disclose; **come over** come some distance to visit, (of feeling) affect, appear or sound in specifed way; **come round** pay informal visit, recover consciousness, be converted to another's opinion; **come through** survive; **come to** recover consciousness, amount to; **come up** arise, be mentioned or discussed, attain position; **come up with** produce (idea etc.); **come up against** be faced with; **come upon** meet or find by chance.

**comedian** /kəˈmiːdɪən/ *noun* humorous performer; actor in comedy; *slang* buffoon.

**comedienne** /kəmiːdɪˈen/ *noun* female comedian.

**comedy** /ˈkɒmədɪ/ *noun* (*plural* **-ies**) play or film of amusing character; humorous kind of drama etc.; humour; amusing aspects. □ **comedic** /kəˈmiːdɪk/ *adjective*.

**comely** /ˈkʌmlɪ/ *adjective* (**-ier**, **-iest**) *literary* handsome, good-looking. □ **comeliness** *noun*.

**comestibles** /kəˈmestɪb(ə)lz/ *plural noun formal* things to eat.

**comet** /ˈkɒmɪt/ *noun* hazy object with 'tail' moving in path round sun.

**comeuppance** /kʌmˈʌpəns/ *noun colloquial* deserved punishment.

**comfort** /ˈkʌmf(ə)t/ *noun* physical or mental well-being; consolation; person or thing bringing consolation; (usually in *plural*) things that make life comfortable. ● *verb* console. □ **comfortless** *adjective*.

**comfortable** /ˈkʌmfətəb(ə)l/ *adjective* giving ease; at ease; having adequate standard of living; appreciable. □ **comfortably** *adverb*.

**comforter** /ˈkʌmfətə/ *noun* person who comforts; baby's dummy; *archaic* woollen scarf.

**comfrey** /ˈkʌmfrɪ/ *noun* tall plant with bell-like flowers.

**comfy** /ˈkʌmfɪ/ *adjective* (**-ier**, **-iest**) *colloquial* comfortable.

**comic** /ˈkɒmɪk/ ● *adjective* of or like comedy; funny. ● *noun* comedian; periodical

in form of comic strips. □ **comic strip** sequence of drawings telling comic story. □ **comical** *adjective*; **comically** *adverb*.

**comma** /ˈkɒmə/ *noun* punctuation mark (,) indicating pause or break between parts of sentence (see panel).

**command** /kəˈmɑːnd/ ● *verb* give formal order to; have authority or control over; have at one's disposal; deserve and get; look down over, dominate. ● *noun* order, instruction; holding of authority, esp. in armed forces; mastery; troops or district under commander. □ **command module** control compartment in spacecraft; **command performance** one given at royal request.

**commandant** /ˈkɒməndænt/ *noun* commanding officer, esp. of military academy.

**commandeer** /kɒmənˈdɪə/ *verb* seize (esp. goods) for military use; take possession of without permission.

**commander** *noun* person who commands, esp. naval officer next below captain. □ **commander-in-chief** (*plural* **commanders-in-chief**) supreme commander, esp. of nation's forces.

**commanding** *adjective* impressive; giving wide view; substantial.

**commandment** *noun* divine command.

**commando** /kəˈmɑːndəʊ/ *noun* (*plural* **-s**) unit of shock troops; member of this.

**commemorate** /kəˈmeməreɪt/ *verb* (**-ting**) preserve in memory by celebration or ceremony; be memorial of. □ **commemoration** *noun*; **commemorative** /-rətɪv/ *adjective*.

**commence** /kəˈmens/ *verb* (**-cing**) *formal* begin. □ **commencement** *noun*.

**commend** /kəˈmend/ *verb* praise; recommend; entrust. □ **commendation** /kɒm-/ *noun*.

**commendable** *adjective* praiseworthy. □ **commendably** *adverb*.

**commensurable** /kəˈmenʃərəb(ə)l/ *adjective* (often + *with*, *to*) measurable by same standard; (+ *to*) proportionate to. □ **commensurability** *noun*.

**commensurate** /kəˈmenʃərət/ *adjective* (usually + *with*) extending over same space or time; (often + *to*, *with*) proportionate.

## Comma ,

The comma marks a slight break between words, phrases, etc. In particular, it is used:

**1** to separate items in a list, e.g.

*red, white, and blue* or *red, white and blue*
*We bought some shoes, socks, gloves, and handkerchiefs.*
*potatoes, peas, or carrots* or *potatoes, peas or carrots*

**2** to separate adjectives that describe something in the same way, e.g.

*It is a hot, dry, dusty place.*

but not if they describe it in different ways, e.g.

*a distinguished foreign author*

or if one adjective adds to or alters the meaning of another, e.g.

*a bright red tie.*

**3** to separate main clauses, e.g.

*Cars will park here, and coaches will turn left.*

**4** to separate a name or word used to address someone, e.g.

*David, I'm here.*
*Well, Mr Jones, we meet again.*
*Have you seen this, my friend?*

**5** to separate a phrase, e.g.

*Having had lunch, we went back to work.*

especially in order to clarify meaning, e.g.

*In the valley below, the village looked very small.*

**6** after words that introduce direct speech, or after direct speech where there is no question mark or exclamation mark, e.g.

*They answered, 'Here we are.'*
*'Here we are,' they answered.*

**7** after *Dear Sir, Dear Sarah*, etc., and *Yours faithfully, Yours sincerely*, etc. in letters.

**8** to separate a word, phrase, or clause that is secondary or adds information or a comment, e.g.

*I am sure, however, that it will not happen.*
*Fred, who is bald, complained of the cold.*

but not with a relative clause (one usually beginning with *who, which*, or *that*) that restricts the meaning of the noun it follows, e.g.

*Men who are bald should wear hats.*

No comma is needed between a month and a year in dates, e.g.

*in December 1993*

or between a number and a road in addresses, e.g.

*17 Devonshire Avenue*

**comment** /'kɒment/ ● *noun* brief critical or explanatory note or remark; opinion; commenting. ● *verb* (often + *on*, *that*) make comment(s). □ **no comment** *colloquial* I decline to answer your question.

**commentary** /'kɒməntərɪ/ *noun* (*plural* **-ies**) broadcast description of event happening; series of comments on book or performance etc.

**commentate** /'kɒmənteɪt/ *verb* (**-ting**) act as commentator.

**commentator** *noun* writer or speaker of commentary.

**commerce** /'kɒmɜːs/ *noun* buying and selling; trading.

**commercial** /kə'mɜːʃ(ə)l/ ● *adjective* of, in, or for commerce; done or run primarily for financial profit; (of broadcasting) financed by advertising. ● *noun* television or radio advertisement. □ **commercial broadcasting** broadcasting financed by advertising; **commercial traveller** firm's representative visiting shops etc. to get orders. □ **commercially** *adverb*.

**commercialize** *verb* (also **-ise**) (**-zing** or **-sing**) exploit or spoil for profit; make commercial. □ **commercialization** *noun*.

**Commie** /'kɒmɪ/ *noun slang derogatory* Communist.

**commingle** /kə'mɪŋg(ə)l/ *verb* (**-ling**) *literary* mix, unite.

**commiserate** /kə'mɪzəreɪt/ *verb* (**-ting**) (usually + *with*) have or express sympathy. □ **commiseration** *noun*.

**commissar** /'kɒmɪsɑː/ *noun historical* head of government department in USSR.

**commissariat** /kɒmɪ'seərɪət/ *noun* department responsible for supply of food etc. for army; food supplied.

**commissary** /'kɒmɪsərɪ/ *noun* (*plural* **-ies**) deputy, delegate.

**commission** /kə'mɪʃ(ə)n/ ● *noun* authority to perform task; person(s) given such authority; order for specially produced thing; warrant conferring officer rank in armed forces; rank so conferred; pay or percentage received by agent; committing. ● *verb* empower, give authority to; give (artist etc.) order for work; order (work) to be written etc.; give (officer) command of ship; prepare (ship) for active service; bring (machine etc.) into operation. □ **in** or **out of commission** ready or not ready for active service.

**commissionaire** /kəmɪʃə'neə/ *noun* uniformed door attendant.

**commissioner** *noun* person commissioned to perform specific task; member of government commission; representative of government in district etc.

**commit** /kə'mɪt/ *verb* (**-tt-**) do or make (crime, blunder, etc.); (usually + *to*) entrust, consign; send (person) to prison; pledge or bind (esp. oneself) to policy or course of action; (as **committed** *adjective*) (often + *to*) dedicated, obliged.

**commitment** *noun* engagement, obligation; committing, being committed; dedication, committing oneself.

**committal** *noun* act of committing esp. to prison, grave, etc.

**committee** /kə'mɪtɪ/ *noun* group of people appointed for special function by (and usually out of) larger body.

**commode** /kə'məʊd/ *noun* chamber pot in chair or box with cover; chest of drawers.

**commodious** /kə'məʊdɪəs/ *adjective* roomy.

**commodity** /kə'mɒdɪtɪ/ *noun* (*plural* **-ies**) article of trade.

**commodore** /'kɒmədɔː/ *noun* naval officer next above captain; commander of squadron or other division of fleet; president of yacht club.

**common** /'kɒmən/ ● *adjective* (**-er**, **-est**) occurring often; ordinary, of the most familiar kind; shared by all; belonging to the whole community; *derogatory* inferior, vulgar; *Grammar* (of gender) referring to individuals of either sex. ● *noun* piece of open public land. □ **common ground** point or argument accepted by both sides; **common law** unwritten law based on custom and precedent; **common-law husband, wife** partner recognized by common law without formal marriage; **Common Market** European Community; **common or garden** *colloquial* ordinary; **common room** room for social use of students or teachers at college etc.; **common sense** good practical sense; **common time** *Music* 4 crotchets in a bar; **in common** shared, in joint use.

**commonalty** /ˈkɒmənəltɪ/ *noun* (*plural* -ies) general community, common people.

**commoner** *noun* person below rank of peer.

**commonly** *adverb* usually, frequently.

**commonplace** /ˈkɒmənpleɪs/ ● *adjective* lacking originality; ordinary. ● *noun* event, topic, etc. that is ordinary or usual; trite remark.

**commons** /ˈkɒmənz/ *plural noun* the common people; (**the Commons**) House of Commons.

**commonwealth** /ˈkɒmənwelθ/ *noun* independent state or community; (**the Commonwealth**) association of UK with states previously part of British Empire; republican government of Britain 1649–60.

**commotion** /kəˈməʊʃ(ə)n/ *noun* noisy disturbance.

**communal** /ˈkɒmjʊn(ə)l/ *adjective* shared between members of group or community; (of conflict etc.) between communities. □ **communally** *adverb*.

**commune**[1] /ˈkɒmjuːn/ *noun* group of people sharing accommodation and goods; small administrative district in France etc.

**commune**[2] /kəˈmjuːn/ *verb* (-ning) (usually + *with*) speak intimately; feel in close touch.

**communicant** /kəˈmjuːnɪkənt/ *noun* receiver of Holy Communion.

**communicate** /kəˈmjuːnɪkeɪt/ *verb* (-ting) impart, transmit (news, feelings, disease, ideas, etc.); (often + *with*) have social dealings. □ **communicator** *noun*.

**communication** *noun* communicating, being communicated; letter, message, etc.; connection or means of access; social dealings; (in *plural*) science and practice of transmitting information. □ **communication cord** cord or chain pulled to stop train in emergency; **communication(s) satellite** artificial satellite used to relay telephone calls, TV, radio, etc.

**communicative** /kəˈmjuːnɪkətɪv/ *adjective* ready to talk and impart information.

**communion** /kəˈmjuːnɪən/ *noun* sharing, esp. of thoughts, interests, etc.; fellowship; group of Christians of same denomination; (**Holy Communion**) Eucharist.

**communiqué** /kəˈmjuːnɪkeɪ/ *noun* official communication, esp. news report.

**communism** /ˈkɒmjʊnɪz(ə)m/ *noun* social system based on public ownership of most property; political theory advocating this; (usually **Communism**) form of socialist society in Cuba, China, etc. □ **communist**, **Communist** *noun & adjective*; **communistic** /-ˈnɪstɪk/ *adjective*.

**community** /kəˈmjuːnɪtɪ/ (*plural* -ies) *noun* group of people living in one place or having same religion, ethnic origin, profession, etc.; commune; joint ownership. □ **community centre** place providing social facilities for neighbourhood; **community charge** *historical* tax levied locally on every adult; **community home** institution housing young offenders; **community singing** singing by large group; **community spirit** feeling of belonging to community.

**commute** /kəˈmjuːt/ *verb* (-ting) travel some distance to and from work; (usually + *to*) change (punishment) to one less severe.

**commuter** *noun* person who commutes to and from work.

**compact**[1] ● *adjective* /kəmˈpækt/ closely packed together; economically designed; concise; (of person) small but well-proportioned. ● *verb* /kəmˈpækt/ make compact. ● *noun* /ˈkɒmpækt/ small flat case for face powder etc. □ **compact disc** disc from which digital information or sound is reproduced by reflection of laser light. □ **compactly** *adverb*; **compactness** *noun*.

**compact**[2] /ˈkɒmpækt/ *noun* agreement, contract.

**companion** /kəmˈpænjən/ *noun* person who accompanies or associates with another; person paid to live with another; handbook, reference book; thing that matches another; (**Companion**) member of some orders of knighthood. □ **companionway** staircase from ship's deck to cabins etc.

**companionable** *adjective* sociable, friendly. □ **companionably** *adverb*.

**companionship** *noun* friendship; being together.

**company** /'kʌmpənɪ/ *noun* (*plural* **-ies**) number of people assembled; guest(s); commercial business; actors etc. working together; subdivision of infantry battalion. □ **in company with** together with; **part company** (often + *with*) separate; **ship's company** entire crew.

**comparable** /'kɒmpərəb(ə)l/ *adjective* (often + *with*, *to*) able to be compared. □ **comparability** *noun*; **comparably** *adverb*.

■ **Usage** *Comparable* is often pronounced /kəm'pærəb(ə)l/ (with the stress on the *-par-*), but this is considered incorrect by some people.

**comparative** /kəm'pærətɪv/ ● *adjective* perceptible or estimated by comparison; relative; of or involving comparison; *Grammar* (of adjective or adverb) expressing higher degree of a quality. ● *noun Grammar* comparative expression or word. □ **comparatively** *adverb*.

**compare** /kəm'peə/ *verb* (**-ring**) (usually + *to*) express similarities in; (often + *to*, *with*) estimate similarity of; (often + *with*) bear comparison. ● *noun* comparison. □ **compare notes** exchange ideas or opinions.

**comparison** /kəm'pærɪs(ə)n/ *noun* comparing; example of similarity; (in full **degrees of comparison**) *Grammar* positive, comparative, and superlative forms of adjectives and adverbs. □ **bear comparison** (often + *with*) able to be compared favourably.

**compartment** /kəm'pɑːtmənt/ *noun* space partitioned off within larger space.

**compass** /'kʌmpəs/ *noun* instrument showing direction of magnetic north and bearings from it; (usually in *plural*) V-shaped hinged instrument for drawing circles and taking measurements; scope, range.

**compassion** /kəm'pæʃ(ə)n/ *noun* pity.

**compassionate** /kəm'pæʃənət/ *adjective* showing compassion; sympathetic.

□ **compassionate leave** leave granted on grounds of bereavement etc. □ **compassionately** *adverb*.

**compatible** /kəm'pætɪb(ə)l/ *adjective* (often + *with*) able to coexist; (of equipment) able to be used in combination. □ **compatibility** *noun*.

**compatriot** /kəm'pætrɪət/ *noun* person from one's own country.

**compel** /kəm'pel/ *verb* (**-ll-**) force, constrain; arouse irresistibly; (as **compelling** *adjective*) arousing strong interest.

**compendious** /kəm'pendɪəs/ *adjective* comprehensive but brief.

**compendium** /kəm'pendɪəm/ *noun* (*plural* **-s** or **-dia**) abridgement, summary; collection of table games etc.

**compensate** /'kɒmpenseɪt/ *verb* (**-ting**) recompense, make amends; counterbalance.

**compensation** *noun* compensating, being compensated; money etc. given as recompense. □ **compensatory** /-'seɪt-/ *adjective*.

**compère** /'kɒmpeə/ ● *noun* person introducing variety show. ● *verb* (**-ring**) act as compère (to).

**compete** /kəm'piːt/ *verb* (**-ting**) take part in contest etc.; (often + *with* or *against* person, *for* thing) strive.

**competence** /'kɒmpɪt(ə)ns/ *noun* being competent; ability.

**competent** *adjective* adequately qualified or capable; effective. □ **competently** *adverb*.

**competition** /kɒmpə'tɪʃ(ə)n/ *noun* (often + *for*) competing; event in which people compete; other people competing; opposition.

**competitive** /kəm'petɪtɪv/ *adjective* of or involving competition; (of prices etc.) comparing well with those of rivals; having strong urge to win. □ **competitiveness** *noun*.

**competitor** /kəm'petɪtə/ *noun* person who competes; rival, esp. in business.

**compile** /kəm'paɪl/ *verb* (**-ling**) collect and arrange (material) into list, book, etc. □ **compilation** /kɒmpɪ'leɪʃ(ə)n/ *noun*.

**complacent** /kəm'pleɪs(ə)nt/ *adjective* smugly self-satisfied or contented. □ **complacency** *noun*.

**complain** /kəm'pleɪn/ verb express dissatisfaction; (+ of) say that one is suffering from (an ailment), state grievance concerning. □ **complainant** noun.

**complaint** noun complaining; grievance, cause of dissatisfaction; formal protest; ailment.

**complaisant** /kəm'pleɪz(ə)nt/ adjective formal deferential; willing to please; acquiescent. □ **complaisance** noun.

**complement** ● noun /'kɒmplɪmənt/ thing that completes; full number; word(s) added to verb to complete predicate of sentence; amount by which angle is less than 90°. ● verb /-ment/ complete; form complement of. □ **complementary** /-'men-/ adjective.

**complete** /kəm'pliːt/ ● adjective having all its parts; finished, total. ● verb (**-ting**) finish; make complete; fill in (form etc.). □ **completely** adverb; **completeness** noun; **completion** noun.

**complex** /'kɒmpleks/ ● noun buildings, rooms, etc. made up of related parts; group of usually repressed feelings or thoughts causing abnormal behaviour or mental state. ● adjective complicated; consisting of related parts. □ **complexity** /kəm'pleks-/ noun (plural **-ies**).

**complexion** /kəm'plekʃ(ə)n/ noun natural colour, texture, and appearance of skin, esp. of face; aspect.

**compliance** /kəm'plaɪəns/ noun obedience to request, command, etc.; capacity to yield.

**compliant** adjective obedient; yielding. □ **compliantly** adverb.

**complicate** /'kɒmplɪkeɪt/ verb (**-ting**) make difficult or complex; (as **complicated** adjective) complex, intricate.

**complication** noun involved or confused condition; complicating circumstance; difficulty; (often in plural) disease or condition arising out of another.

**complicity** /kəm'plɪsɪtɪ/ noun partnership in wrongdoing.

**compliment** ● noun /'kɒmplɪmənt/ polite expression of praise; (in plural) formal greetings accompanying gift etc. ● verb /-ment/ (often + on) congratulate; praise.

**complimentary** /kɒmplɪ'mentərɪ/ adjective expressing compliment; given free of charge.

**comply** /kəm'plaɪ/ verb (**-ies, -ied**) (often + with) act in accordance (with request or command).

**component** /kəm'pəʊnənt/ ● adjective being part of larger whole. ● noun component part.

**comport** /kəm'pɔːt/ verb (**comport oneself**) literary conduct oneself; behave. □ **comportment** noun.

**compose** /kəm'pəʊz/ verb (**-sing**) create in music or writing; make up, constitute; arrange artistically; set up (type); arrange in type; (as **composed** adjective) calm, self-possessed.

**composer** noun person who composes esp. music.

**composite** /'kɒmpəzɪt/ ● adjective made up of parts; (of plant) having head of many flowers forming one bloom. ● noun composite thing or plant.

**composition** /kɒmpə'zɪʃ(ə)n/ noun act of putting together; thing composed; school essay; arrangement of parts of picture etc.; constitution of substance; compound artificial substance.

**compositor** /kəm'pɒzɪtə/ noun person who sets up type for printing.

**compost** /'kɒmpɒst/ noun mixture of decayed organic matter used as fertilizer.

**composure** /kəm'pəʊʒə/ noun calm manner.

**compote** /'kɒmpəʊt/ noun fruit in syrup.

**compound¹** /'kɒmpaʊnd/ ● noun mixture of two or more things; word made up of two or more existing words; substance formed from two or more elements chemically united. ● adjective made up of two or more ingredients or parts; combined, collective. ● verb /kəm'paʊnd/ mix or combine; increase (difficulties etc.); make up (whole); settle (matter) by mutual agreement. □ **compound fracture** one complicated by wound; **compound interest** interest paid on capital and accumulated interest.

**compound²** /'kɒmpaʊnd/ noun enclosure, fenced-in space.

**comprehend** /kɒmprɪ'hend/ verb understand; include.

**comprehensible** *adjective* that can be understood.

**comprehension** *noun* understanding; text set as test of understanding; inclusion.

**comprehensive** ● *adjective* including all or nearly all; (of motor insurance) providing protection against most risks. ● *noun* (in full **comprehensive school**) secondary school for children of all abilities. □ **comprehensively** *adverb*.

**compress** ● *verb* /kəm'pres/ squeeze together, bring into smaller space or shorter time. ● *noun* /'kɒmpres/ pad pressed on part of body to relieve inflammation, stop bleeding, etc. □ **compressible** *adjective*.

**compression** /kəm'preʃ(ə)n/ *noun* compressing; reduction in volume of fuel mixture in internal-combustion engine before ignition.

**compressor** *noun* machine for compressing air or other gas.

**comprise** /kəm'praɪz/ *verb* (-**sing**) include; consist of.

■ **Usage** It is a mistake to use *comprise* to mean 'to compose or make up'.

**compromise** /'kɒmprəmaɪz/ ● *noun* agreement reached by mutual concession; (often + *between*) intermediate state between conflicting opinions etc. ● *verb* (-**sing**) settle dispute by compromise; modify one's opinions, demands, etc.; bring into disrepute or danger by indiscretion.

**comptroller** /kən'trəʊlə/ *noun* controller.

**compulsion** /kəm'pʌlʃ(ə)n/ *noun* compelling, being compelled; irresistible urge.

**compulsive** *adjective* compelling; resulting or acting (as if) from compulsion; irresistible. □ **compulsively** *adverb*.

**compulsory** *adjective* required by law or rule. □ **compulsorily** *adverb*.

**compunction** /kəm'pʌŋkʃ(ə)n/ *noun* guilty feeling; slight regret.

**compute** /kəm'pjuːt/ *verb* (-**ting**) calculate; use computer. □ **computation** /kɒm-/ *noun*.

**computer** *noun* electronic device for storing and processing data, making calculations, or controlling machinery. □ **computer-literate** able to use computers; **computer science** study of computers; **computer virus** code maliciously introduced into program to destroy data etc.

**computerize** /kəm'pjuːtəraɪz/ *verb* (also **-ise**) (-**zing** or **-sing**) equip with or store, perform, or produce by computer. □ **computerization** *noun*.

**comrade** /'kɒmreɪd/ *noun* companion in some activity; fellow socialist or Communist. □ **comradeship** *noun*.

**con**[1] *slang* ● *noun* confidence trick. ● *verb* (-**nn**-) swindle, deceive.

**con**[2] *noun* (usually in *plural*) reason against.

**con**[3] *verb* (US **conn**) (-**nn**-) direct steering of (ship).

**concatenation** /kɒnkætɪ'neɪʃ(ə)n/ *noun* series of linked things or events.

**concave** /kɒn'keɪv/ *adjective* curved like interior of circle or sphere. □ **concavity** /-'kæv-/ *noun*.

**conceal** /kən'siːl/ *verb* hide; keep secret. □ **concealment** *noun*.

**concede** /kən'siːd/ *verb* (-**ding**) admit to be true; admit defeat in; grant.

**conceit** /kən'siːt/ *noun* personal vanity; *literary* far-fetched comparison.

**conceited** *adjective* vain. □ **conceitedly** *adverb*.

**conceive** /kən'siːv/ *verb* (-**ving**) become pregnant (with); (often + *of*) imagine; (usually in *passive*) formulate (plan etc.). □ **conceivable** *adjective*; **conceivably** *adverb*.

**concentrate** /'kɒnsəntreɪt/ ● *verb* (-**ting**) (often + *on*) focus one's attention; bring together to one point; increase strength of (liquid etc.) by removing water etc.; (as **concentrated** *adjective*) strong. ● *noun* concentrated solution.

**concentration** *noun* concentrating, being concentrated; weight of substance in given amount of mixture; mental attention. □ **concentration camp** place for detention of political prisoners etc.

**concentric** /kən'sentrɪk/ *adjective* having common centre. □ **concentrically** *adverb*.

**concept** /'kɒnsept/ *noun* general notion; abstract idea.

**conception** /kən'sepʃ(ə)n/ *noun* conceiving, being conceived; idea; understanding.

**conceptual** /kən'septjʊəl/ *adjective* of mental concepts. □ **conceptually** *adverb*.

**conceptualize** *verb* (also **-ise**) (**-zing** or **-sing**) form concept or idea of. □ **conceptualization** *noun*.

**concern** /kən'sɜːn/ ● *verb* be relevant or important to; relate to; be about; worry, affect; (**concern oneself**; often + *with, about, in*) interest or involve oneself. ● *noun* anxiety, worry; matter of interest or importance to one; firm, business.

**concerned** *adjective* involved, interested; anxious, troubled.

**concerning** *preposition* about, regarding.

**concert** /'kɒnsət/ *noun* musical performance; agreement.

**concerted** /kən'sɜːtɪd/ *adjective* jointly planned.

**concertina** /kɒnsə'tiːnə/ ● *noun* portable musical instrument like accordion but smaller. ● *verb* (**-nas, -naed** /-nəd/ or **-na'd, -naing**) compress or collapse in folds like those of concertina.

**concerto** /kən'tʃeətəʊ/ *noun* ( *plural* **-tos** or **-ti** /-tɪ/) composition for solo instrument(s) and orchestra.

**concession** /kən'seʃ(ə)n/ *noun* conceding, thing conceded; reduction in price for certain category of people; right to use land, sell goods, etc. □ **concessionary** *adjective*.

**conch** /kɒntʃ/ *noun* large spiral shell of various marine gastropod molluscs; such gastropod.

**conchology** /kɒŋ'kɒlədʒɪ/ *noun* study of shells.

**conciliate** /kən'sɪlɪeɪt/ *verb* (**-ting**) make calm; pacify; reconcile. □ **conciliation** *noun*, **conciliator** *noun*; **conciliatory** *adjective*.

**concise** /kən'saɪs/ *adjective* brief but comprehensive. □ **concisely** *adverb*; **conciseness** *noun*; **concision** *noun*.

**conclave** /'kɒnkleɪv/ *noun* private meeting; assembly or meeting-place of cardinals for election of pope.

**conclude** /kən'kluːd/ *verb* (**-ding**) bring or come to end; (often + *from, that*) infer; settle (treaty etc.).

**conclusion** /kən'kluːʒ(ə)n/ *noun* ending; judgement reached by reasoning; summing-up; settling of peace etc. □ **in conclusion** lastly.

**conclusive** /kən'kluːsɪv/ *adjective* decisive, convincing. □ **conclusively** *adverb*.

**concoct** /kən'kɒkt/ *verb* make by mixing ingredients; invent (story, lie, etc.). □ **concoction** *noun*.

**concomitant** /kən'kɒmɪt(ə)nt/ ● *adjective* (often + *with*) accompanying. ● *noun* accompanying thing. □ **concomitance** *noun*.

**concord** /'kɒnkɔːd/ *noun* agreement, harmony. □ **concordant** /kən'kɔː-d(ə)nt/ *adjective*.

**concordance** /kən'kɔːd(ə)ns/ *noun* agreement; index of words used in book or by author.

**concordat** /kən'kɔːdæt/ *noun* agreement, esp. between Church and state.

**concourse** /'kɒŋkɔːs/ *noun* crowd; large open area in railway station etc.

**concrete** /'kɒŋkriːt/ ● *adjective* existing in material form, real; definite. ● *noun* mixture of gravel, sand, cement, and water used for building. ● *verb* (**-ting**) cover with or embed in concrete.

**concretion** /kən'kriːʃ(ə)n/ *noun* hard solid mass; forming of this by coalescence.

**concubine** /'kɒŋkjʊbaɪn/ *noun literary* mistress; (among polygamous peoples) secondary wife.

**concupiscence** /kən'kjuːpɪs(ə)ns/ *noun formal* lust. □ **concupiscent** *adjective*.

**concur** /kən'kɜː/ *verb* (**-rr-**) (often + *with*) agree; coincide.

**concurrent** /kən'kʌrənt/ *adjective* (often + *with*) existing or in operation at the same time. □ **concurrence** *noun*; **concurrently** *adverb*.

**concuss** /kən'kʌs/ *verb* subject to concussion.

**concussion** /kən'kʌʃ(ə)n/ *noun* temporary unconsciousness or incapacity due to head injury; violent shaking.

**condemn** /kən'dem/ *verb* express strong disapproval of; (usually + *to*) sentence

**condensation | confessedly**

(to punishment), doom (to something unpleasant); pronounce unfit for use. □ **condemnation** /kɒndem'neɪʃ(ə)n/ noun.

**condensation** /kɒnden'seɪʃ(ə)n/ noun condensing, being condensed; condensed liquid; abridgement.

**condense** /kən'dens/ verb (**-sing**) make denser or more concise; reduce or be reduced from gas to liquid.

**condescend** /kɒndɪ'send/ verb (+ to do) graciously consent to do a thing while showing one's superiority; (+ to) pretend to be on equal terms with (inferior); (as **condescending** adjective) patronizing. □ **condescendingly** adverb; **condescension** noun.

**condiment** /'kɒndɪmənt/ noun seasoning or relish for food.

**condition** /kən'dɪʃ(ə)n/ ● noun stipulation; thing on fulfilment of which something else depends; state of being or fitness of person or thing; ailment; (in plural) circumstances. ● verb bring into desired state; accustom; determine; be essential to.

**conditional** adjective (often + on) dependent, not absolute; Grammar (of clause, mood, etc.) expressing condition. □ **conditionally** adverb.

**condole** /kən'dəʊl/ verb (**-ling**) (+ with) express sympathy with (person) over loss etc.

■ **Usage** Condole is commonly confused with console, which means 'to comfort'.

**condolence** noun (often in plural) expression of sympathy.

**condom** /'kɒndɒm/ noun contraceptive sheath.

**condominium** /kɒndə'mɪnɪəm/ noun joint rule or sovereignty; US building containing individually owned flats.

**condone** /kən'dəʊn/ verb (**-ning**) forgive, overlook.

**condor** /'kɒndɔː/ noun large S. American vulture.

**conducive** /kən'djuːsɪv/ adjective (often + to) contributing or helping (towards someting).

**conduct** ● noun /'kɒndʌkt/ behaviour; manner of conducting business, war,

etc. ● verb /kən'dʌkt/ lead, guide; control, manage; be conductor of (orchestra etc.); transmit by conduction; (**conduct oneself**) behave.

**conduction** /kən'dʌkʃ(ə)n/ noun transmission of heat, electricity, etc.

**conductive** /kən'dʌktɪv/ adjective transmitting heat, electricity, etc. □ **conductivity** /kɒndʌk'tɪv-/ noun.

**conductor** noun director of orchestra etc.; (feminine **conductress**) person who collects fares on bus etc.; conductive thing.

**conduit** /'kɒndɪt/ noun channel or pipe for conveying liquid or protecting insulated cable.

**cone** noun solid figure with usually circular base and tapering to a point; cone-shaped object; dry fruit of pine or fir; ice cream cornet.

**coney** = CONY.

**confab** /'kɒnfæb/ noun colloquial confabulation.

**confabulate** /kən'fæbjʊleɪt/ verb (**-ting**) talk together. □ **confabulation** noun.

**confection** /kən'fekʃ(ə)n/ noun sweet dish or delicacy.

**confectioner** noun dealer in sweets or pastries etc. □ **confectionery** noun.

**confederacy** /kən'fedərəsɪ/ noun (plural **-ies**) alliance or league, esp. of confederate states.

**confederate** /kən'fedərət/ ● adjective esp. Politics allied. ● noun ally; accomplice. ● verb /-reɪt/ (**-ting**) (often + with) bring or come into alliance. □ **Confederate States** those which seceded from US in 1860–1.

**confederation** /kənfedə'reɪʃ(ə)n/ noun union or alliance, esp. of states.

**confer** /kən'fɜː/ verb (**-rr-**) (often + on, upon) grant, bestow; (often + with) meet for discussion.

**conference** /'kɒnfər(ə)ns/ noun consultation; meeting for discussion.

**conferment** /kən'fɜːmənt/ noun conferring (of honour etc.).

**confess** /kən'fes/ verb acknowledge, admit; declare one's sins, esp. to priest; (of priest) hear confession of.

**confessedly** /kən'fesɪdlɪ/ adverb by one's own or general admission.

**confession** /kənˈfeʃ(ə)n/ noun act of confessing; thing confessed; statement of principles etc.

**confessional** • noun enclosed place where priest hears confession. • adjective of confession.

**confessor** noun priest who hears confession.

**confetti** /kənˈfeti/ noun small bits of coloured paper thrown by wedding guests at bride and groom.

**confidant** /ˈkɒnfidænt/ noun (feminine **confidante** same pronunciation) person trusted with knowledge of one's private affairs.

**confide** /kənˈfaɪd/ verb (**-ding**) (usually + to) tell (secret) or entrust (task). □ **confide in** talk confidentially to.

**confidence** /ˈkɒnfɪd(ə)ns/ noun firm trust; feeling of certainty; self-reliance; boldness; something told as a secret. □ **confidence trick** swindle in which victim is persuaded to trust swindler; **confidence trickster** person using confidence tricks; **in confidence** as a secret; **in (person's) confidence** trusted with his or her secrets.

**confident** adjective feeling or showing confidence. □ **confidently** adverb.

**confidential** /kɒnfɪˈdenʃ(ə)l/ adjective spoken or written in confidence; entrusted with secrets; confiding. □ **confidentiality** /-ʃɪˈæl-/ noun; **confidentially** adjective.

**configuration** /kənfɪgjʊˈreɪʃ(ə)n/ noun manner of arrangement; shape; outline. □ **configure** /-ˈfɪgə/ verb.

**confine** • verb /kənˈfaɪn/ (**-ning**) keep or restrict within certain limits; imprison. • noun /ˈkɒnfaɪn/ (usually in plural) boundary. □ **be confined** be in childbirth.

**confinement** /kənˈfaɪnmənt/ noun confining, being confined; childbirth.

**confirm** /kənˈfɜːm/ verb provide support for truth or correctness of; establish more firmly; formally make definite; administer confirmation to.

**confirmation** /kɒnfəˈmeɪʃ(ə)n/ noun confirming circumstance or statement; rite confirming baptized person as member of Christian Church.

**confirmed** adjective firmly settled in habit or condition.

**confiscate** /ˈkɒnfɪskeɪt/ verb (**-ting**) take or seize by authority. □ **confiscation** noun.

**conflagration** /kɒnfləˈgreɪʃ(ə)n/ noun large destructive fire.

**conflate** /kənˈfleɪt/ verb (**-ting**) fuse together, blend. □ **conflation** noun.

**conflict** • noun /ˈkɒnflɪkt/ struggle, fight; opposition; (often + of) clashing of opposed interests etc. • verb /kənˈflɪkt/ clash, be incompatible.

**confluent** /ˈkɒnfluənt/ • adjective merging into one. • noun stream joining another. □ **confluence** noun.

**conform** /kənˈfɔːm/ verb comply with rules or general custom; (+ to, with) be in accordance with.

**conformable** adjective (often + to) similar; (often + with) consistent.

**conformation** /kɒnfɔːˈmeɪʃ(ə)n/ noun thing's structure or shape.

**conformist** • noun person who conforms to established practice. • adjective conventional. □ **conformism** noun.

**conformity** noun conforming with established practice; suitability.

**confound** /kənˈfaʊnd/ • verb baffle; confuse; archaic defeat. □ **confound (person, thing)!** interjection expressing annoyance.

**confounded** adjective colloquial damned.

**confront** /kənˈfrʌnt/ verb meet or stand facing, esp. in hostility or defiance; (of problem etc.) present itself to; (+ with) bring face to face with. □ **confrontation** /kɒn-/ noun; **confrontational** /kɒn-/ adjective.

**confuse** /kənˈfjuːz/ verb (**-sing**) bewilder; mix up; make obscure; (often as **confused** adjective) throw into disorder. □ **confusing** adjective; **confusion** noun.

**confute** /kənˈfjuːt/ verb (**-ting**) prove to be false or wrong. □ **confutation** /kɒn-/ noun.

**conga** /ˈkɒŋgə/ noun Latin American dance, usually performed in single file; tall narrow drum beaten with hands.

**congeal** /kənˈdʒiːl/ verb make or become semi-solid by cooling; (of blood) coagulate.

**congenial** /kənˈdʒiːnɪəl/ adjective having sympathetic nature, similar interests, etc.; (often + to) suited or agreeable.

□ **congeniality** /-'æl-/ *noun*; **congenially** *adverb*.

**congenital** /kən'dʒenɪt(ə)l/ *adjective* existing or as such from birth. □ **congenitally** *adverb*.

**conger** /'kɒŋgə/ *noun* large sea eel.

**congest** /kən'dʒest/ *verb* (esp. as **congested** *adjective*) affect with congestion.

**congestion** *noun* abnormal accumulation or obstruction, esp. of traffic etc. or of mucus in nose etc.

**conglomerate** /kən'glɒmərət/ ● *adjective* gathered into rounded mass. ● *noun* heterogeneous mass; business etc. corporation of merged firms. ● *verb* /-reɪt/ (**-ting**) collect into coherent mass. □ **conglomeration** *noun*.

**congratulate** /kən'grætʃʊleɪt/ *verb* (**-ting**) (often + *on*) express pleasure at happiness, excellence, or good fortune of (person). □ **congratulatory** /-lətərɪ/ *adjective*.

**congratulation** *noun* congratulating, (usually in *plural*) expression of this.

**congregate** /'kɒŋgrɪgeɪt/ *verb* (**-ting**) collect or gather in crowd.

**congregation** *noun* assembly of people, esp. for religious worship; group of people regularly attending particular church etc.

**congregational** *adjective* of a congregation; (**Congregational**) of or adhering to Congregationalism.

**Congregationalism** *noun* system in which individual churches are self-governing. □ **Congregationalist** *noun*.

**congress** /'kɒŋgres/ *noun* formal meeting of delegates for discussion; (**Congress**) national legislative body of US etc. □ **congressman**, **congresswoman** member of US Congress. □ **congressional** /kən'greʃ-/ *adjective*.

**congruent** /'kɒŋgrʊənt/ *adjective* (often + *with*) suitable, agreeing; *Geometry* (of figures) coinciding exactly when superimposed. □ **congruence** *noun*.

**conic** /'kɒnɪk/ *adjective* of a cone.

**conical** *adjective* cone-shaped.

**conifer** /'kɒnɪfə/ *noun* cone-bearing tree. □ **coniferous** /kə'nɪfərəs/ *adjective*.

**conjectural** /kən'dʒektʃər(ə)l/ *adjective* involving conjecture.

**conjecture** /kən'dʒektʃə/ ● *noun* formation of opinion on incomplete information, guess. ● *verb* (**-ring**) guess.

**conjoin** /kən'dʒɔɪn/ *verb formal* join, combine.

**conjoint** /kən'dʒɔɪnt/ *adjective formal* associated, conjoined.

**conjugal** /'kɒndʒʊg(ə)l/ *adjective* of marriage; between husband and wife.

**conjugate** ● *verb* /'kɒndʒʊgeɪt/ (**-ting**) give the different forms of (verb); unite, become fused. ● *adjective* /-gət/ joined together.

**conjugation** *noun Grammar* system of verbal inflection.

**conjunct** /kən'dʒʌŋkt/ *adjective* joined; combined; associated.

**conjunction** *noun* joining, connection; word used to connect sentences, clauses, or words (see panel); combination of events or circumstances. □ **conjunctive** *adjective*.

**conjunctiva** /kɒndʒʌŋk'taɪvə/ *noun* (*plural* **-s**) mucous membrane covering front of eye and inside of eyelid.

**conjunctivitis** /kəndʒʌŋktɪ'vaɪtɪs/ *noun* inflammation of conjunctiva.

**conjure** /'kʌndʒə/ *verb* (**-ring**) perform seemingly magical tricks, esp. by movement of hands. □ **conjure up** produce as if by magic, evoke.

**conjuror** *noun* (also **conjurer**) performer of conjuring tricks.

**conk**[1] *verb colloquial* (usually + *out*) break down; become exhausted; faint; fall asleep.

**conk**[2] *slang* ● *noun* (punch on) nose or head. ● *verb* hit on nose or head.

**conker** /'kɒŋkə/ *noun* horse chestnut fruit; (in *plural*) children's game played with conkers on strings.

**con man** *noun* confidence trickster.

**connect** /kə'nekt/ *verb* (often + *to, with*) join, be joined; associate mentally or practically; (+ *with*) (of train etc.) arrive in time for passengers to transfer to another; put into communication by telephone; (usually in *passive*; + *with*) unite or associate with (others) in relationship etc. □ **connecting rod** rod between piston and crankpin etc. in engine. □ **connector** *noun*.

**connection** *noun* (also **connexion**) connecting, being connected; point at which things are connected; association of ideas; link, esp. by telephone;

(often in *plural*) (esp. influential) relative or associate; connecting train etc.

**connective** *adjective* connecting. □ **connective tissue** body tissue forming tendons and ligaments, supporting organs, etc.

**conning tower** /'kɒnɪŋ/ *noun* raised structure of submarine containing periscope; wheelhouse of warship.

**connive** /kə'naɪv/ *verb* (**-ving**) (+ *at*) tacitly consent to (wrongdoing); conspire. □ **connivance** *noun*.

**connoisseur** /kɒnə'sɜː/ *noun* (often + *of*, *in*) person with good taste and judgement.

**connote** /kə'nəʊt/ *verb* (**-ting**) imply in addition to literal meaning; mean. □ **connotation** /kɒnə-/ *noun*; **connotative** /'kɒnəteɪtɪv/ *adjective*.

**connubial** /kə'njuːbɪəl/ *adjective* conjugal.

**conquer** /'kɒŋkə/ *verb* overcome, defeat; be victorious; subjugate. □ **conqueror** *noun*.

**conquest** /'kɒŋkwest/ *noun* conquering; something won; person whose affections have been won.

**consanguineous** /kɒnsæŋ'gwɪnɪəs/ *adjective* descended from same ancestor; akin. □ **consanguinity** *noun*.

**conscience** /'kɒnʃ(ə)ns/ *noun* moral sense of right and wrong, esp. as affecting behaviour. □ **conscience money** money paid to relieve conscience,

esp. in respect of evaded payment etc.; **conscience-stricken** made uneasy by bad conscience.

**conscientious** /kɒnʃɪ'enʃəs/ *adjective* diligent and scrupulous. □ **conscientious objector** person who refuses to do military service on grounds of conscience. □ **conscientiously** *adverb*; **conscientiousness** *noun*.

**conscious** /'kɒnʃəs/ *adjective* awake and aware of one's surroundings etc.; (usually + *of*, *that*) aware, knowing; intentional. □ **consciously** *adverb*; **consciousness** *noun*.

**conscript** ● *verb* /kən'skrɪpt/ summon for compulsory state (esp. military) service. ● *noun* /'kɒnskrɪpt/ conscripted person. □ **conscription** *noun*.

**consecrate** /'kɒnsɪkreɪt/ *verb* (**-ting**) make or declare sacred; dedicate formally to religious purpose; (+ *to*) devote to (a purpose). □ **consecration** *noun*.

**consecutive** /kən'sekjʊtɪv/ *adjective* following continuously; in unbroken or logical order. □ **consecutively** *adverb*.

**consensus** /kən'sensəs/ *noun* (often + *of*) general agreement or opinion.

**consent** /kən'sent/ ● *verb* (often + *to*) express willingness, give permission; agree. ● *noun* agreement; permission.

**consequence** /'kɒnsɪkwəns/ *noun* result of what has gone before; importance.

---

## Conjunction

A conjunction is used to join parts of sentences which usually, but not always, contain their own verbs, e.g.

*He found it difficult but I helped him.*
*They made lunch for Alice and Mary.*
*I waited until you came.*

The most common conjunctions are:

| | | | |
|---|---|---|---|
| after | for | since | unless |
| although | if | so | until |
| and | in order that | so that | when |
| as | like | than | where |
| because | now | that | whether |
| before | once | though | while |
| but | or | till | |

**consequent** /'kɒnsɪkwənt/ *adjective* that results; (often + *on, upon*) following as consequence. □ **consequently** *adverb.*

**consequential** /kɒnsɪ'kwenʃ(ə)l/ *adjective* resulting, esp. indirectly; important.

**conservancy** /kən'sɜːvənsɪ/ *noun* (*plural* **-ies**) body controlling river, port, etc. or concerned with conservation; official environmental conservation.

**conservation** /kɒnsə'veɪʃ(ə)n/ *noun* preservation, esp. of natural environment. □ **conservationist** *noun.*

**conservative** /kən'sɜːvətɪv/ ● *adjective* averse to rapid change; (of estimate) purposely low; (usually **Conservative**) of Conservative Party. ● *noun* conservative person; (usually **Conservative**) member or supporter of Conservative Party. □ **Conservative Party** political party promoting free enterprise. □ **conservatism** *noun.*

**conservatoire** /kən'sɜːvətwɑː/ *noun* (usually European) school of music or other arts.

**conservatory** /kən'sɜːvətərɪ/ *noun* (*plural* **-ies**) greenhouse for tender plants; esp. *US* conservatoire.

**conserve** ● *verb* /kən'sɜːv/ (**-ving**) preserve, keep from harm or damage. ● *noun* /'kɒnsɜːv/ fruit etc. preserved in sugar; fresh fruit jam.

**consider** /kən'sɪdə/ *verb* contemplate; deliberate thoughtfully; make allowance for, take into account; (+ *that*) have the opinion that; show consideration for; regard as; (as **considered** *adjective*) (esp. of an opinion) formed after careful thought.

**considerable** *adjective* a lot of; notable, important. □ **considerably** *adverb.*

**considerate** /kən'sɪdərət/ *adjective* giving thought to feelings or rights of others. □ **considerately** *adverb.*

**consideration** /kənsɪdə'reɪʃ(ə)n/ *noun* careful thought; being considerate; fact or thing taken into account; compensation, payment. □ **take into consideration** make allowance for.

**considering** *preposition* in view of.

**consign** /kən'saɪn/ *verb* (often + *to*) commit, deliver; send (goods etc.). □ **consignee** /kɒnsaɪ'niː/ *noun*; **consignor** *noun.*

**consignment** *noun* consigning; goods consigned.

**consist** /kən'sɪst/ *verb* (+ *of*) be composed of; (+ *in, of*) have its essential features in.

**consistency** *noun* (*plural* **-ies**) degree of density or firmness, esp. of thick liquids; being consistent.

**consistent** *adjective* constant to same principles; (usually + *with*) compatible. □ **consistently** *adverb.*

**consistory** *noun* (*plural* **-ies**) *RC Church* council of cardinals.

**consolation** /kɒnsə'leɪʃ(ə)n/ *noun* alleviation of grief or disappointment; consoling person or thing. □ **consolation prize** one given to competitor just failing to win main prize. □ **consolatory** /kən'sɒl-/ *adjective.*

**console**¹ /kən'səʊl/ *verb* (**-ling**) bring consolation to.

■ **Usage** *Console* is often confused with *condole*. To condole with someone is to express sympathy with them.

**console**² /'kɒnsəʊl/ *noun* panel for switches, controls, etc.; cabinet for television etc.; cabinet with keys and stops of organ; bracket supporting shelf etc.

**consolidate** /kən'sɒlɪdeɪt/ *verb* (**-ting**) make or become strong or secure; combine (territories, companies, debts, etc.) into one whole. □ **consolidation** *noun.*

**consommé** /kən'sɒmeɪ/ *noun* clear meat soup.

**consonance** /'kɒnsənəns/ *noun* agreement, harmony.

**consonant** ● *noun* speech sound that forms syllable only in combination with vowel; letter(s) representing this. ● *adjective* (+ *with, to*) consistent with; in agreement or harmony. □ **consonantal** /-'næn-/ *adjective.*

**consort**¹ ● *noun* /'kɒnsɔːt/ wife or husband, esp. of royalty. ● *verb* /kən'sɔːt/ (usually + *with, together*) keep company; harmonize.

**consort**² /'kɒnsɔːt/ *noun* *Music* group of players or instruments.

**consortium** /kən'sɔːtɪəm/ *noun* (*plural* **-tia** or **-s**) association, esp. of several business companies.

**conspicuous** /kən'spɪkjʊəs/ *adjective* clearly visible; attracting attention. □ **conspicuously** *adverb.*

**conspiracy** /kən'spɪrəsɪ/ noun (plural **-ies**) act of conspiring; plot.

**conspirator** /kən'spɪrətə/ noun person who takes part in conspiracy. □ **conspiratorial** /-'tɔː-/ adjective.

**conspire** /kən'spaɪə/ verb (**-ring**) combine secretly for unlawful or harmful purpose; (of events) seemingly work together.

**constable** /'kʌnstəb(ə)l/ noun (also **police constable**) police officer of lowest rank; governor of royal castle. □ **Chief Constable** head of police force of county etc.

**constabulary** /kən'stæbjʊlərɪ/ noun (plural **-ies**) police force.

**constancy** /'kɒnstənsɪ/ noun dependability; faithfulness.

**constant** ● adjective continuous; frequently occurring; having constancy. ● noun Mathematics & Physics unvarying quantity. □ **constantly** adverb.

**constellation** /kɒnstə'leɪʃ(ə)n/ noun group of fixed stars.

**consternation** /kɒnstə'neɪʃ(ə)n/ noun amazement, dismay.

**constipate** /'kɒnstɪpeɪt/ verb (**-ting**) (esp. as **constipated** adjective) affect with constipation.

**constipation** noun difficulty in emptying bowels.

**constituency** /kən'stɪtjʊənsɪ/ noun (plural **-ies**) body electing representative; area represented.

**constituent** /kən'stɪtjʊənt/ ● adjective making part of whole; appointing, electing. ● noun member of constituency; component part.

**constitute** /'kɒnstɪtjuːt/ verb be essence or components of; amount to; establish.

**constitution** /kɒnstɪ'tjuːʃ(ə)n/ noun composition; set of principles by which state etc. is governed; person's inherent state of health, strength, etc.

**constitutional** ● adjective of or in line with the constitution; inherent. ● noun walk taken as exercise. □ **constitutionally** adverb.

**constitutive** /'kɒnstɪtjuːtɪv/ adjective able to form or appoint; constituent.

**constrain** /kən'streɪn/ verb compel; confine; (as **constrained** adjective) forced, embarrassed.

**constraint** noun compulsion; restriction; self-control.

**constrict** /kən'strɪkt/ verb make narrow or tight; compress. □ **constriction** noun; **constrictive** adjective.

**constrictor** noun snake that kills by compressing; muscle that contracts a part.

**construct** ● verb /kən'strʌkt/ fit together, build; Geometry draw. ● noun /'kɒnstrʌkt/ thing constructed, esp. by the mind. □ **constructor** /kən'strʌktə/ noun.

**construction** /kən'strʌkʃ(ə)n/ noun structing; thing constructed; syntactical arrangement; interpretation. □ **constructional** adjective.

**constructive** /kən'strʌktɪv/ adjective positive, helpful. □ **constructively** adverb.

**construe** /kən'struː/ verb (**-strues**, **-strued**, **struing**) interpret; (often + with) combine (words) grammatically; translate literally.

**consubstantiation** /kɒnsəbstænʃɪ'eɪʃ(ə)n/ noun presence of Christ's body and blood together with bread and wine in Eucharist.

**consul** /'kɒns(ə)l/ noun official appointed by state to protect its interests and citizens in foreign city; historical either of two annually-elected magistrates in ancient Rome. □ **consular** /-sjʊlə/ adjective.

**consulate** /'kɒnsjʊlət/ noun offices or position of consul.

**consult** /kən'sʌlt/ verb seek information or advice from; (often + with) refer to; take into consideration.

**consultant** /kən'sʌlt(ə)nt/ noun person who gives professional advice; senior medical specialist. □ **consultancy** noun.

**consultation** /kɒnsəl'teɪʃ(ə)n/ noun (meeting for) consulting.

**consultative** /kən'sʌltətɪv/ adjective of or for consultation.

**consume** /kən'sjuːm/ verb (**-ming**) eat or drink; use up; destroy. □ **consumable** adjective.

**consumer** noun user of product or service. □ **consumer goods** goods for consumers, not for producing other goods.

**consumerism** *noun* protection or promotion of consumers' interests; *often derogatory* continual increase in consumption. □ **consumerist** *adjective.*

**consummate** ● *verb* /'kɒnsəmeɪt/ (**-ting**) complete (esp. marriage by sexual intercourse). ● *adjective* /kən'sʌmɪt/ complete, perfect; fully skilled. □ **consummation** /kɒnsə-/ *noun.*

**consumption** /kən'sʌmpʃ(ə)n/ *noun* consuming, being consumed; purchase and use of goods etc.; *archaic* tuberculosis of lungs.

**consumptive** /kən'sʌmptɪv/ *archaic* ● *adjective* suffering or tending to suffer from tuberculosis. ● *noun* consumptive person.

**cont.** *abbreviation* continued.

**contact** /'kɒntækt/ ● *noun* condition or state of touching, meeting, or communicating; person who is, or may be, contacted for information etc.; person likely to carry contagious disease through being near infected person; connection for passage of electric current. ● *verb* get in touch with. □ **contact lens** small lens placed on eyeball to correct vision.

**contagion** /kən'teɪdʒ(ə)n/ *noun* spreading of disease by contact; moral corruption. □ **contagious** *adjective.*

**contain** /kən'teɪn/ *verb* hold or be capable of holding within itself; include; comprise; prevent from moving or extending; control, restrain.

**container** *noun* box etc. for holding things; large metal box for transporting goods.

**containment** /kən'teɪnmənt/ *noun* action or policy of preventing expansion of hostile country or influence.

**contaminate** /kən'tæmɪneɪt/ *verb* (**-ting**) pollute; infect. □ **contaminant** *noun*; **contamination** *noun.*

**contemplate** /'kɒntəmpleɪt/ *verb* (**-ting**) survey with eyes or mind; regard as possible; intend. □ **contemplation** *noun.*

**contemplative** /kən'templətɪv/ *adjective* of or given to (esp. religious) contemplation.

**contemporaneous** /kəntempə'reɪnɪəs/ *adjective* (usually + *with*) existing or occurring at same time.

**contemporary** /kən'tempərərɪ/ ● *adjective* belonging to same time; of same age; modern in style or design. ● *noun* (*plural* **-ies**) contemporary person or thing.

**contempt** /kən'tempt/ *noun* feeling that person or thing deserves scorn or reproach; condition of being held in contempt; (in full **contempt of court**) disobedience to or disrespect for court of law. □ **contemptible** *adjective.*

**contemptuous** *adjective* feeling or showing contempt. □ **contemptuously** *adverb.*

**contend** /kən'tend/ *verb* compete; (usually + *with*) argue; (+ *that*) maintain that. □ **contender** *noun.*

**content**[1] /kən'tent/ ● *adjective* satisfied; (+ *to do*) willing. ● *verb* make content; satisfy. ● *noun* contented state; satisfaction. □ **contented** *adjective*; **contentment** *noun.*

**content**[2] /'kɒntent/ *noun* (usually in *plural*) what is contained, esp. in vessel, house, or book; amount contained; substance of book etc. as opposed to form; capacity, volume.

**contention** /kən'tenʃ(ə)n/ *noun* dispute, rivalry; point contended for in argument.

**contentious** /kən'tenʃəs/ *adjective* quarrelsome; likely to cause argument.

**contest** ● *noun* /'kɒntest/ contending; a competition. ● *verb* /kən'test/ dispute; contend or compete for; compete in.

**contestant** /kən'test(ə)nt/ *noun* person taking part in contest.

**context** /'kɒntekst/ *noun* what precedes and follows word or passage; relevant circumstances. □ **contextual** /kən'tekstjʊəl/ *adjective.*

**contiguous** /kən'tɪgjʊəs/ *adjective* (usually + *with*, *to*) touching; in contact.

**continent**[1] /'kɒntɪnənt/ *noun* any of the earth's main continuous bodies of land; (**the Continent**) the mainland of Europe.

**continent**[2] /'kɒntɪnənt/ *adjective* able to control bowels and bladder; exercising esp. sexual self-restraint. □ **continence** *noun.*

**continental** /kɒntɪ'nent(ə)l/ *adjective* of or characteristic of a continent or (**Continental**) the Continent. □ **continental breakfast** light breakfast of coffee, rolls, etc.; **continental quilt** duvet; **continental shelf** shallow sea-bed bordering continent.

**contingency** /kən'tɪndʒənsɪ/ noun (plural **-ies**) event that may or may not occur; something dependent on another uncertain event.

**contingent** ● adjective (usually + on, upon) conditional, dependent; that may or may not occur; fortuitous. ● noun group (of troops, ships, etc.) forming part of larger group; people sharing interest, origin, etc.

**continual** /kən'tɪnjʊəl/ adjective frequently recurring; always happening. □ **continually** adverb.

**continuance** /kən'tɪnjʊəns/ noun continuing in existence or operation; duration.

**continuation** /kəntɪnjʊ'eɪʃ(ə)n/ noun continuing, being continued; thing that continues something else.

**continue** /kən'tɪnjuː/ verb (**-ues, -ued, -uing**) maintain; resume; prolong; remain.

**continuity** /kɒntɪ'njuːɪtɪ/ noun (plural **-ies**) being continuous; logical sequence; detailed scenario of film; linkage of broadcast items.

**continuo** /kən'tɪnjʊəʊ/ noun (plural **-s**) Music bass accompaniment played usually on keyboard instrument.

**continuous** /kən'tɪnjʊəs/ adjective connected without break; uninterrupted. □ **continuously** adverb.

**continuum** /kən'tɪnjʊəm/ noun (plural **-nua**) thing with continuous structure.

**contort** /kən'tɔːt/ verb twist or force out of normal shape. □ **contortion** noun.

**contortionist** noun entertainer who adopts contorted postures.

**contour** /'kɒntʊə/ noun outline; (in full **contour line**) line on map joining points at same altitude.

**contraband** /'kɒntrəbænd/ ● noun smuggled goods. ● adjective forbidden to be imported or exported.

**contraception** /kɒntrə'sepʃ(ə)n/ noun use of contraceptives.

**contraceptive** /kɒntrə'septɪv/ ● adjective preventing pregnancy. ● noun contraceptive device or drug.

**contract** ● noun /'kɒntrækt/ written or spoken agreement, esp. one enforceable by law; document recording it.

● verb /kən'trækt/ make or become smaller; (usually + with) make contract; (often + out) arrange (work) to be done by contract; become affected by (a disease); incur (debt); draw together; shorten. □ **contract bridge** type of bridge in which only tricks bid and won count towards game; **contract in** (or **out**) elect (not) to enter scheme etc.

**contraction** /kən'trækʃ(ə)n/ noun contracting; shortening of uterine muscles during childbirth; shrinking; diminution; shortened word.

**contractor** /kən'træktə/ noun person who undertakes contract, esp. in building, engineering, etc.

**contractual** /kən'træktjʊəl/ adjective of or in the nature of a contract.

**contradict** /kɒntrə'dɪkt/ verb deny; oppose verbally; be at variance with. □ **contradiction** noun; **contradictory** adjective.

**contradistinction** /kɒntrədɪs'tɪŋkʃ(ə)n/ noun distinction made by contrasting.

**contraflow** /'kɒntrəfləʊ/ noun transfer of traffic from usual half of road to lane(s) of other half.

**contralto** /kən'træltəʊ/ noun (plural **-s**) lowest female singing voice; singer with this voice.

**contraption** /kən'træpʃ(ə)n/ noun machine or device, esp. strange one.

**contrapuntal** /kɒntrə'pʌnt(ə)l/ adjective Music of or in counterpoint.

**contrariwise** /kən'treərɪwaɪz/ adverb on the other hand; in the opposite way.

**contrary** /'kɒntrərɪ/ ● adjective (usually + to) opposed in nature, tendency, or direction; /kən'treərɪ/ perverse, self-willed. ● noun (**the contrary**) the opposite. ● adverb (+ to) in opposition. □ **on the contrary** the opposite is true.

**contrast** ● noun /'kɒntrɑːst/ comparison showing differences; difference so revealed; (often + to) thing or person having different qualities; degree of difference between tones in photograph or television picture. ● verb /kən'trɑːst/ (often + with) compare to reveal contrast; show contrast.

**contravene** /kɒntrə'viːn/ verb (**-ning**) infringe; conflict with. □ **contravention** /-'ven-/ noun.

**contretemps** /'kɒntrətɑ̃/ noun (plural same /-tɑ̃z/) unlucky accident; unfortunate occurrence.

**contribute** /kən'trɪbjuːt/ verb (**-ting**) (often + to) give jointly with others to common purpose; supply (article etc.) for publication with others; (+ to) help to bring about. □ **contribution** /kɒntrɪ'bjuːʃ(ə)n/ noun; **contributor** noun; **contributory** adjective.

■ **Usage** Contribute is often pronounced /'kɒntrɪbjuːt/ (with the stress on the con-), but this is considered incorrect by some people.

**contrite** /kən'traɪt/ adjective penitent, feeling guilt. □ **contrition** /-'trɪʃ-/ noun.

**contrivance** noun something contrived, esp. device or plan; act of contriving.

**contrive** /kən'traɪv/ verb (**-ving**) devise, plan; (often + to do) manage.

**contrived** adjective artificial, forced.

**control** /kən'trəʊl/ ● noun power of directing or restraining; self-restraint; means of restraining or regulating; (usually in plural) device to operate machine, vehicle, etc.; place where something is controlled or verified; standard of comparison for checking results of experiment. ● verb (**-ll-**) have control of; regulate; hold in check; verify. □ **in control** (often + of) in charge; **out of control** no longer manageable.

**controller** noun person or thing that controls; person controlling expenditure.

**controversial** /kɒntrə'vɜːʃ(ə)l/ adjective causing or subject to controversy.

**controversy** /'kɒntrəvɜːsɪ/ noun (plural **-ies**) dispute, argument.

■ **Usage** Controversy is often pronounced /kən'trɒvəsɪ/ (with the stress on the -trov-), but this is considered incorrect by some people.

**controvert** /kɒntrə'vɜːt/ verb dispute, deny.

**contuse** /kən'tjuːz/ verb (**-sing**) bruise. □ **contusion** noun.

**conundrum** /kə'nʌndrəm/ noun riddle; hard question.

**conurbation** /kɒnɜː'beɪʃ(ə)n/ noun group of towns united by expansion.

**convalesce** /kɒnvə'les/ verb (**-cing**) recover health after illness.

**convalescent** /kɒnvə'les(ə)nt/ ● adjective recovering from illness. ● noun convalescent person. □ **convalescence** noun.

**convection** /kən'vekʃ(ə)n/ noun heat transfer by upward movement of heated medium.

**convector** /kən'vektə/ noun heating appliance that circulates warm air by convection.

**convene** /kən'viːn/ verb (**-ning**) summon; assemble. □ **convener**, **convenor** noun.

**convenience** /kən'viːnɪəns/ noun state of being convenient; suitability; advantage; useful thing; public lavatory. □ **convenience food** food needing little preparation.

**convenient** adjective serving one's comfort or interests; suitable; available or occurring at suitable time or place; well situated. □ **conveniently** adverb.

**convent** /'kɒnv(ə)nt/ noun religious community, esp. of nuns; its house.

**convention** /kən'venʃ(ə)n/ noun general agreement on social behaviour etc. by implicit consent of majority; customary practice; assembly, conference; agreement, treaty.

**conventional** adjective depending on or according with convention; bound by social conventions; not spontaneous or sincere; (of weapons etc.) non-nuclear. □ **conventionally** adverb.

**converge** /kən'vɜːdʒ/ verb (**-ging**) come together or towards same point; (+ on, upon) approach from different directions. □ **convergence** noun, **convergent** adjective.

**conversant** /kən'vɜːs(ə)nt/ adjective (+ with) well acquainted with.

**conversation** /kɒnvə'seɪʃ(ə)n/ noun informal spoken communication; instance of this.

**conversational** adjective of or in conversation; colloquial. □ **conversationally** adverb.

**conversationalist** noun person fond of or good at conversation.

**converse¹** /kən'vɜːs/ verb (**-sing**) (often + with) talk.

**converse²** /'kɒnvɜːs/ ● *adjective* opposite, contrary, reversed. ● *noun* converse statement or proposition. □ **conversely** *adverb*.

**conversion** /kən'vɜːʃ(ə)n/ *noun* converting, being converted; converted (part of) building.

**convert** ● *verb* /kən'vɜːt/ (usually + *into*) change; cause (person) to change belief etc.; change (money etc.) into different form or currency etc.; alter (building) for new purpose; *Rugby* kick goal after (try). ● *noun* /'kɒnvɜːt/ person converted, esp. to religious faith.

**convertible** /kən'vɜːtɪb(ə)l/ ● *adjective* able to be converted. ● *noun* car with folding or detachable roof.

**convex** /'kɒnveks/ *adjective* curved like outside of sphere or circle.

**convey** /kən'veɪ/ *verb* transport, carry; communicate (meaning etc.); transfer by legal process; transmit (sound etc.).

**conveyance** *noun* conveying, being conveyed; vehicle; legal transfer of property, document effecting this.

**conveyancing** *noun* branch of law dealing with transfer of property. □ **conveyancer** *noun*.

**conveyor** *noun* person or thing that conveys. □ **conveyor belt** endless moving belt conveying articles in factory etc.

**convict** ● *verb* /kən'vɪkt/ (often + *of*) prove or declare guilty. ● *noun* /'kɒnvɪkt/ *esp. historical* sentenced criminal.

**conviction** /kən'vɪkʃ(ə)n/ *noun* convicting, being convicted; being convinced; firm belief.

**convince** /kən'vɪns/ *verb* (**-cing**) firmly persuade. □ **convincing** *adjective*; **convincingly** *adverb*.

**convivial** /kən'vɪvɪəl/ *adjective* fond of company; sociable, lively. □ **conviviality** /-'æl-/ *noun*.

**convocation** /kɒnvə'keɪʃ(ə)n/ *noun* convoking; large formal gathering.

**convoke** /kən'vəʊk/ *verb* (**-king**) call together; summon to assemble.

**convoluted** /kɒnvə'luːtɪd/ *adjective* coiled, twisted; complex.

**convolution** /kɒnvə'luːʃ(ə)n/ *noun* coiling; coil, twist; complexity.

**convolvulus** /kən'vɒlvjʊləs/ *noun* (*plural* **-es**) twining plant, esp. bindweed.

**convoy** /'kɒnvɔɪ/ *noun* group of ships, vehicles, etc. travelling together. □ **in convoy** as a group.

**convulse** /kən'vʌls/ *verb* (**-sing**) affect with convulsions.

**convulsion** *noun* (usually in *plural*) violent irregular motion of limbs or body caused by involuntary contraction of muscles; violent disturbance; (in *plural*) uncontrollable laughter. □ **convulsive** *adjective*; **convulsively** *adverb*.

**cony** /'kəʊnɪ/ *noun* (*plural* **-ies**) (also **coney**) rabbit; its fur.

**coo** ● *noun* soft murmuring sound as of doves. ● *verb* (**coos**, **cooed**) emit coo.

**cooee** /'kuːiː/ *interjection* used to attract attention.

**cook** /kʊk/ ● *verb* prepare (food) by heating; undergo cooking; *colloquial* falsify (accounts etc.). ● *noun* person who cooks. □ **cookbook** *US* cookery book; **cooking apple** one suitable for eating cooked.

**cooker** *noun* appliance or vessel for cooking food; fruit (esp. apple) suitable for cooking.

**cookery** *noun* art of cooking. □ **cookery book** book containing recipes.

**cookie** /'kʊkɪ/ *noun US* sweet biscuit.

**cool** /kuːl/ ● *adjective* of or at fairly low temperature; suggesting or achieving coolness; calm; lacking enthusiasm; unfriendly; *slang esp. US* marvellous. ● *noun* coolness; cool place; *slang* composure. ● *verb* (often + *down*, *off*) make or become cool. □ **coolly** /'kuːllɪ/ *adverb*; **coolness** *noun*.

**coolant** *noun* cooling agent, esp. fluid.

**cooler** *noun* vessel in which thing is cooled; *slang* prison cell.

**coomb** /kuːm/ *noun* (also **combe**) valley on side of hill; short valley running up from coast.

**coon** /kuːn/ *noun US* racoon.

**coop** /kuːp/ ● *noun* cage for keeping poultry. ● *verb* (often + *up*, *in*) confine.

**co-op** /'kəʊɒp/ *noun colloquial* cooperative society or shop.

**cooper** *noun* maker or repairer of casks and barrels.

**cooperate** /kəʊ'ɒpəreɪt/ *verb* (also **co-operate**) (**-ting**) (often + *with*) work or act together. □ **cooperation** noun.

**cooperative** /kəʊˈɒpərətɪv/ (also **co-operative**) ● adjective willing to cooperate; (of business etc.) jointly owned and run by members, with profits shared. ● noun cooperative society or enterprise.

**co-opt** /kəʊˈɒpt/ verb appoint to committee etc. by invitation of existing members. □ **co-option** noun; **co-optive** adjective.

**coordinate** (also **co-ordinate**) ● verb /kəʊˈɔːdɪneɪt/ (-ting) cause to work together efficiently; work or act together effectively. ● adjective /-nət/ equal in status. ● noun /-nət/ Mathematics each of set of quantities used to fix position of point, line, or plane; (in plural) matching items of clothing. □ **coordination** noun; **coordinator** noun.

**coot** /kuːt/ noun black waterfowl with white horny plate on head; colloquial stupid person.

**cop** slang ● noun police officer; capture. ● verb (-pp-) catch. □ **cop-out** cowardly evasion; **not much cop** of little value or use.

**copal** /ˈkəʊp(ə)l/ noun kind of resin used for varnish.

**copartner** /kəʊˈpɑːtnə/ noun partner, associate. □ **copartnership** noun.

**cope**[1] verb (-ping) deal effectively or contend; (often + with) manage.

**cope**[2] noun priest's long cloaklike vestment.

**copeck** /ˈkəʊpek/ noun (also **kopek, kopeck**) hundredth of rouble.

**copier** /ˈkɒpɪə/ noun machine that copies (esp. documents).

**copilot** /ˈkəʊpaɪlət/ noun second pilot in aircraft.

**coping** /ˈkəʊpɪŋ/ noun top (usually sloping) course of masonry in wall. □ **coping stone** stone used in coping.

**copious** /ˈkəʊpɪəs/ adjective abundant; producing much. □ **copiously** adverb.

**copper**[1] /ˈkɒpə/ ● noun red-brown metal; bronze coin; large metal vessel for boiling laundry. ● adjective made of or coloured like copper. □ **copperplate** copper plate for engraving or etching, print taken from it, ornate sloping handwriting.

**copper**[2] /ˈkɒpə/ noun slang police officer.

**coppice** /ˈkɒpɪs/ noun area of undergrowth and small trees.

**copulate** /ˈkɒpjuleɪt/ verb (-ting) (often + with) (esp. of animals) have sexual intercourse. □ **copulation** noun.

**copy** /ˈkɒpɪ/ ● noun (plural -ies) thing made to look like another; specimen of book etc.; material to be printed, esp. regarded as good etc. reading matter. ● verb (-ies, -ied) make copy of; imitate. □ **copy-typist** typist working from document or recording; **copywriter** writer of copy, esp. for advertisements.

**copyist** /ˈkɒpɪɪst/ noun person who makes copies.

**copyright** ● noun exclusive right to print, publish, perform, etc., material. ● adjective protected by copyright. ● verb secure copyright for (material).

**coquette** /kəˈket/ noun woman who flirts. □ **coquettish** adjective; **coquetry** /ˈkɒkɪtrɪ/ noun (plural -ies).

**coracle** /ˈkɒrək(ə)l/ noun small boat of wickerwork covered with waterproof material.

**coral** /ˈkɒr(ə)l/ ● noun hard substance built up by marine polyps. ● adjective (of red or pink colour) of coral. □ **coral island, reef** one formed by growth of coral.

**cor anglais** /kɔːr ˈɒŋgleɪ/ noun (plural **cors anglais** /kɔːz/) woodwind instrument like oboe but lower in pitch.

**corbel** /ˈkɔːb(ə)l/ noun stone or timber projection from wall, acting as supporting bracket.

**cord** ● noun thick string; piece of this; similar structure in body; ribbed cloth, esp. corduroy; (in plural) corduroy trousers; electric flex. ● verb secure with cords.

**cordial** /ˈkɔːdɪəl/ ● adjective heartfelt; friendly. ● noun fruit-flavoured drink. □ **cordiality** /-ˈæl-/ noun; **cordially** adverb.

**cordite** /ˈkɔːdaɪt/ noun smokeless explosive.

**cordless** adjective (of handheld electric device) battery-powered.

**cordon** /ˈkɔːd(ə)n/ ● noun line or circle of police etc.; ornamental cord or braid; fruit tree trained to grow as single stem. ● verb (often + off) enclose or separate with cordon of police etc.

**cordon bleu** /ˌkɔːdɒn ˈblɜː/ adjective (of cooking) first-class.

**corduroy** /ˈkɔːdərɔɪ/ noun fabric with velvety ribs.

**core** ● noun horny central part of certain fruits, containing seeds; centre or most important part; part of nuclear reactor containing fissile material; inner strand of electric cable; piece of soft iron forming centre of magnet etc. ● verb (**-ring**) remove core from.

**co-respondent** /ˌkəʊrɪˈspɒnd(ə)nt/ noun person cited in divorce case as having committed adultery with respondent.

**corgi** /ˈkɔːgɪ/ noun (plural **-s**) short-legged breed of dog.

**coriander** /ˌkɒrɪˈændə/ noun aromatic plant; its seed, used as flavouring.

**cork** ● noun thick light bark of S. European oak; bottle-stopper made of cork etc. ● verb (often + up) stop, confine; restrain (feelings etc.).

**corkage** noun charge made by restaurant etc. for serving customer's own wine etc.

**corked** adjective (of wine) spoilt by defective cork.

**corkscrew** ● noun spiral steel device for extracting corks from bottles. ● verb move spirally.

**corm** noun swollen underground stem in certain plants, e.g. crocus.

**cormorant** /ˈkɔːmərənt/ noun diving seabird with black plumage.

**corn**[1] noun cereal before or after harvesting, esp. chief crop of a region; grain or seed of cereal plant; colloquial something corny. □ **corn cob** cylindrical centre of maize ear; **corncrake** ground-nesting bird with harsh cry; **corn dolly** plaited straw figure; **cornflakes** breakfast cereal of toasted maize flakes; **cornflour** fine-ground maize flour; **cornflower** blue-flowered plant originally growing in cornfields; **corn on the cob** maize eaten from the corn cob.

**corn**[2] noun small tender hard area of skin, esp. on toe.

**cornea** /ˈkɔːnɪə/ noun transparent circular part of front of eyeball.

**corned** adjective preserved in salt or brine.

**cornelian** /kɔːˈniːlɪən/ noun (also **carnelian** /kɑː-/) dull red variety of chalcedony.

**corner** /ˈkɔːnə/ ● noun place where converging sides, edges, streets, etc. meet; recess formed by meeting of two internal sides of room, box, etc.; difficult or inescapable position; remote or secluded place; action or result of buying whole available stock of a commodity; Football & Hockey free kick or hit from corner of pitch. ● verb force into difficult or inescapable position; buy whole available stock of (commodity); dominate (market) in this way; go round corner. □ **cornerstone** stone in projecting angle of wall, indispensable part or basis.

**cornet** /ˈkɔːnɪt/ noun brass instrument resembling trumpet; conical wafer for holding ice cream.

**cornice** /ˈkɔːnɪs/ noun ornamental moulding, esp. along top of internal wall.

**Cornish** /ˈkɔːnɪʃ/ ● adjective of Cornwall. ● noun Celtic language of Cornwall. □ **Cornish pasty** pastry envelope containing meat and vegetables.

**cornucopia** /ˌkɔːnjʊˈkəʊpɪə/ noun horn overflowing with flowers, fruit, etc., as symbol of plenty.

**corny** adjective (**-ier**, **-iest**) colloquial banal; feebly humorous; sentimental.

**corolla** /kəˈrɒlə/ noun whorl of petals forming inner envelope of flower.

**corollary** /kəˈrɒlərɪ/ noun (plural **-ies**) proposition that follows from one proved; (often + of) natural consequence.

**corona** /kəˈrəʊnə/ noun (plural **-nae** /-niː/) halo round sun or moon, esp. that seen in total eclipse of sun.

**coronary** /ˈkɒrənərɪ/ noun (plural **-ies**) coronary thrombosis. □ **coronary artery** artery supplying blood to heart; **coronary thrombosis** blockage of coronary artery by blood clot.

**coronation** /ˌkɒrəˈneɪʃ(ə)n/ noun ceremony of crowning sovereign.

**coroner** /ˈkɒrənə/ noun official holding inquest on deaths thought to be violent or accidental.

**coronet** /ˈkɒrənɪt/ noun small crown.

**corpora** plural of CORPUS.

**corporal**[1] /'kɔːpr(ə)l/ *noun* army or air-force NCO next below sergeant.

**corporal**[2] /'kɔːpər(ə)l/ *adjective* of human body. □ **corporal punishment** physical punishment.

**corporate** /'kɔːpərət/ *adjective* of, being, or belonging to a corporation or group.

**corporation** /kɔːpə'reɪʃ(ə)n/ *noun* group of people authorized to act as individual, esp. in business; civic authorities.

**corporative** /'kɔːpərətɪv/ *adjective* of corporation; governed by or organized in corporations.

**corporeal** /kɔː'pɔːrɪəl/ *adjective* bodily, physical, material.

**corps** /kɔː/ *noun* (*plural* same /kɔːz/) military unit with particular function; organized group of people.

**corpse** /kɔːps/ *noun* dead body.

**corpulent** /'kɔːpjʊlənt/ *adjective* fleshy, bulky. □ **corpulence** *noun*.

**corpus** /'kɔːpəs/ *noun* (*plural* **-pora** /-pərə/) body or collection of writings, texts, etc.

**corpuscle** /'kɔːpʌs(ə)l/ *noun* minute body or cell in organism, esp. (in *plural*) red or white cells in blood of vertebrates. □ **corpuscular** /-'pʌskjʊlə/ *adjective*.

**corral** /kə'rɑːl/ ● *noun* US pen for horses, cattle, etc.; enclosure for capturing wild animals. ● *verb* (**-ll-**) put or keep in corral.

**correct** /kə'rekt/ ● *adjective* true, accurate; proper, in accordance with taste, standards, etc. ● *verb* set right; mark errors in; admonish; counteract. □ **correctly** *adverb*; **correctness** *noun*.

**correction** *noun* correcting, being corrected; thing substituted for what is wrong.

**correctitude** /kə'rektɪtjuːd/ *noun* consciously correct behaviour.

**corrective** ● *adjective* serving to correct or counteract. ● *noun* corrective measure or thing.

**correlate** /'kɒrəleɪt/ ● *verb* (**-ting**) (usually + *with*, *to*) have or bring into mutual relation. ● *noun* either of two related or complementary things. □ **correlation** *noun*.

**correlative** /kə'relətɪv/ ● *adjective* (often + *with*, *to*) having a mutual relation; (of words) corresponding and regularly used together. ● *noun* correlative thing or word.

**correspond** /kɒrɪ'spɒnd/ *verb* (usually + *to*) be similar or equivalent; (usually + *to*, *with*) agree; (usually + *with*) exchange letters.

**correspondence** *noun* agreement or similarity; (exchange of) letters. □ **correspondence course** course of study conducted by post.

**correspondent** *noun* person who writes letter(s); person employed to write or report for newspaper or broadcasting.

**corridor** /'kɒrɪdɔː/ *noun* passage giving access into rooms; passage in train giving access into compartments; strip of territory of one state running through that of another; route for aircraft over foreign country.

**corrigendum** /kɒrɪ'dʒendəm/ *noun* (*plural* **-da**) error to be corrected.

**corrigible** /'kɒrɪdʒɪb(ə)l/ *adjective* able to be corrected.

**corroborate** /kə'rɒbəreɪt/ *verb* (**-ting**) give support to, confirm. □ **corroboration** *noun*; **corroborative** /-rət-/ *adjective*; **corroboratory** /-rət(ə)rɪ/ *adjective*.

**corrode** /kə'rəʊd/ *verb* (**-ding**) wear away, esp. by chemical action; destroy gradually; decay.

**corrosion** /kə'rəʊʒ(ə)n/ *noun* corroding, being corroded; corroded area. □ **corrosive** /-sɪv/ *adjective* & *noun*.

**corrugate** /'kɒrəgeɪt/ *verb* (**-ting**) (esp. as **corrugated** *adjective*) bend into wavy ridges. □ **corrugation** *noun*.

**corrupt** /kə'rʌpt/ ● *adjective* influenced by or using bribery; immoral, wicked. ● *verb* make or become corrupt. □ **corruptible** *adjective*; **corruption** *noun*; **corruptly** *adverb*.

**corsage** /kɔː'sɑːʒ/ *noun* small bouquet worn by woman.

**corsair** /'kɔː'seə/ *noun* pirate ship; pirate.

**corset** /'kɔːsɪt/ *noun* tight-fitting supporting undergarment worn esp. by women. □ **corsetry** *noun*.

**cortège** /kɔː'teɪʒ/ *noun* procession, esp. for funeral.

**cortex** /'kɔːteks/ *noun* (*plural* **-tices** /-tɪsiːz/) outer part of organ, esp. brain. □ **cortical** *adjective*.

**cortisone** /'kɔːtɪzəʊn/ *noun* hormone used in treating inflammation and allergy.

**corvette** /kɔːˈvet/ *noun* small naval escort-vessel.

**cos**[1] /kɒs/ *noun* crisp long-leaved lettuce.

**cos**[2] /kɒz/ *abbreviation* cosine.

**cosh** *colloquial* ● *noun* heavy blunt weapon. ● *verb* hit with cosh.

**cosine** /'kəʊsaɪn/ *noun* ratio of side adjacent to acute angle (in right-angled triangle) to hypotenuse.

**cosmetic** /kɒzˈmetɪk/ ● *adjective* beautifying, enhancing; superficially improving; (of surgery etc.) restoring or enhancing normal appearance. ● *noun* cosmetic preparation. □ **cosmetically** *adverb*.

**cosmic** /'kɒzmɪk/ *adjective* of the cosmos; of or for space travel. □ **cosmic rays** high-energy radiations from outer space.

**cosmogony** /kɒzˈmɒɡənɪ/ *noun* (*plural* **-ies**) (theory about) origin of universe.

**cosmology** /kɒzˈmɒlədʒɪ/ *noun* science or theory of universe. □ **cosmological** /-məˈlɒdʒ-/ *adjective*; **cosmologist** *noun*.

**cosmonaut** /'kɒzmənɔːt/ *noun* Russian astronaut.

**cosmopolitan** /kɒzməˈpɒlɪt(ə)n/ ● *adjective* of or knowing all parts of world; free from national limitations. ● *noun* cosmopolitan person. □ **cosmopolitanism** *noun*.

**cosmos** /'kɒzmɒs/ *noun* universe as a well-ordered whole.

**Cossack** /'kɒsæk/ *noun* member of S. Russian people famous as horsemen.

**cosset** /'kɒsɪt/ *verb* (**-t-**) pamper.

**cost** ● *verb* (*past & past participle* **cost**) have as price; involve as loss or sacrifice; (*past & past participle* **costed**) fix or estimate cost of. ● *noun* price; loss, sacrifice; (in *plural*) legal expenses. □ **cost-effective** effective in relation to cost; **cost of living** cost of basic necessities of life; **cost price** price paid for thing by person who later sells it.

**costal** /'kɒst(ə)l/ *adjective* of ribs.

**costermonger** /'kɒstəmʌŋɡə/ *noun* person who sells fruit etc. from barrow.

**costive** /'kɒstɪv/ *adjective* constipated.

**costly** *adjective* (**-ier, -iest**) costing much, expensive. □ **costliness** *noun*.

**costume** /'kɒstjuːm/ ● *noun* style of dress, esp. of particular place or period; set of clothes; clothing for particular activity; actor's clothes for part. ● *verb* provide with costume. □ **costume jewellery** artificial jewellery.

**costumier** /kɒsˈtjuːmɪə/ *noun* person who deals in or makes costumes.

**cosy** /'kəʊzɪ/ (*US* **cozy**) ● *adjective* (**-ier, -iest**) snug, comfortable. ● *noun* (*plural* **-ies**) cover to keep teapot etc. hot. □ **cosily** *adverb*; **cosiness** *noun*.

**cot** *noun* small high-sided bed for child etc.; small light bed. □ **cot death** unexplained death of sleeping baby.

**cote** *noun* shelter for birds or animals.

**coterie** /'kəʊtərɪ/ *noun* exclusive group of people sharing interests.

**cotoneaster** /kətəʊnɪˈæstə/ *noun* shrub bearing red or orange berries.

**cottage** /'kɒtɪdʒ/ *noun* small house, esp. in the country. □ **cottage cheese** soft white lumpy cheese; **cottage industry** small business carried on at home; **cottage pie** shepherd's pie.

**cottager** *noun* person who lives in cottage.

**cotter** /'kɒtə/ *noun* (also **cotter pin**) wedge or pin for securing machine part such as bicycle pedal crank.

**cotton** /'kɒt(ə)n/ *noun* soft white fibrous substance covering seeds of certain plants; such a plant; thread or cloth from this. □ **cotton on** (often + *to*) *colloquial* begin to understand; **cotton wool** wadding originally made from raw cotton.

**cotyledon** /kɒtɪˈliːd(ə)n/ *noun* first leaf produced by plant embryo.

**couch**[1] /kaʊtʃ/ ● *noun* upholstered piece of furniture for several people; sofa. ● *verb* (+ *in*) express in (language of specified kind). □ **couch potato** *US slang* person who likes lazing at home.

**couch**[2] /kuːtʃ/ *noun* (in full **couch grass**) kind of grass with long creeping roots.

**couchette** /kuːˈʃet/ *noun* railway carriage with seats convertible into sleeping berths; berth in this.

**cougar** /'kuːɡə/ *noun* *US* puma.

**cough** /kɒf/ ● *verb* expel air from lungs with sudden sharp sound. ● *noun* (sound of) coughing; condition of respiratory organs causing coughing. □ **cough mixture** medicine to relieve cough; **cough up** eject with coughs, *slang* give (money, information, etc.) reluctantly.

**could** *past of* CAN¹.

**couldn't** /ˈkʊd(ə)nt/ could not.

**coulomb** /ˈkuːlɒm/ *noun* SI unit of electrical charge.

**coulter** /ˈkəʊltə/ *noun* (*US* **colter**) vertical blade in front of ploughshare.

**council** /ˈkaʊns(ə)l/ *noun* (meeting of) advisory, deliberative, or administrative body; local administrative body of county, city, town, etc. □ **council flat, house** one owned and let by local council; **council tax** local tax based on value of property and number of residents.

**councillor** *noun* member of (esp. local) council.

**counsel** /ˈkaʊns(ə)l/ ● *noun* advice, esp. formal; consultation; (*plural* same) legal adviser, esp. barrister; group of these. ● *verb* (-**ll**-; *US* -**l**-) advise, esp. on personal problems. □ **counsellor** (*US* **counselor**) *noun*.

**count¹** ● *verb* find number of, esp. by assigning successive numerals; repeat numbers in order; (+ *in*) include or be included in reckoning; consider to be. ● *noun* counting, reckoning; total; *Law* each charge in an indictment. □ **countdown** counting numbers backwards to zero, esp. before launching rocket etc.; **count on** rely on; **count out** exclude, disregard.

**count²** *noun* foreign noble corresponding to earl.

**countenance** /ˈkaʊntɪnəns/ ● *noun* face or its expression; composure; moral support. ● *verb* (-**cing**) support, approve.

**counter¹** *noun* flat-topped fitment in shop etc. across which business is conducted; small disc used for playing or scoring in board games, cards, etc.; device for counting things.

**counter²** ● *verb* oppose, contradict; meet by countermove. ● *adverb* in opposite direction. ● *adjective* opposite. ● *noun* parry, countermove.

**counteract** /kaʊntəˈrækt/ *verb* neutralize or hinder by contrary action. □ **counteraction** *noun*.

**counter-attack** *verb* & *noun* attack in reply to enemy's attack.

**counterbalance** ● *noun* weight or influence balancing another. ● *verb* (-**cing**) act as counterbalance to.

**counter-clockwise** *adverb* & *adjective US* anticlockwise.

**counter-espionage** *noun* action taken against enemy spying.

**counterfeit** /ˈkaʊntəfɪt/ ● *adjective* imitation; forged; not genuine. ● *noun* forgery, imitation. ● *verb* imitate fraudulently; forge.

**counterfoil** *noun* part of cheque, receipt, etc. retained as record.

**counter-intelligence** *noun* counterespionage.

**countermand** /kaʊntəˈmɑːnd/ *verb* revoke, recall by contrary order.

**countermeasure** *noun* action taken to counteract danger, threat, etc.

**countermove** *noun* move or action in opposition to another.

**counterpane** *noun* bedspread.

**counterpart** *noun* person or thing equivalent or complementary to another; duplicate.

**counterpoint** *noun* harmonious combination of melodies in music; melody combined with another; contrasting argument, plot, literary theme, etc.

**counterpoise** ● *noun* counterbalance; state of equilibrium. ● *verb* (-**sing**) counterbalance.

**counter-productive** *adjective* having opposite of desired effect.

**counter-revolution** *noun* revolution opposing former one or reversing its results.

**countersign** ● *verb* add confirming signature to. ● *noun* password spoken to person on guard.

**countersink** *verb* (*past* & *past participle* -**sunk**) shape (screw-hole) so that screw-head lies level with surface; provide (screw) with countersunk hole.

**counter-tenor** *noun* male alto singing voice; singer with this.

**countervailing** /ˈkaʊntəveɪlɪŋ/ *adjective* (of influence etc.) counterbalancing.

**counterweight** *noun* counterbalancing weight.

**countess** /'kauntɪs/ *noun* earl's or count's wife or widow; woman with rank of earl or count.

**countless** *adjective* too many to count.

**countrified** /'kʌntrɪfaɪd/ *adjective* rustic.

**country** /'kʌntrɪ/ *noun* (*plural* **-ies**) nation's territory, state; land of person's birth or citizenship; rural districts, as opposed to towns; region with regard to its aspect, associations, etc.; national population, esp. as voters. □ **country and western** type of folk music originated by southern US whites; **country dance** traditional dance; **countryman, countrywoman** person of one's own country or district; person living in rural area; **countryside** rural areas.

**county** /'kaʊntɪ/ *noun* (*plural* **-ies**) territorial division of country, forming chief unit of local administration; *US* political and administrative division of State; people, esp. gentry, of county. □ **county council** elected governing body of county; **county court** law court for civil cases; **county town** administrative capital of county.

**coup** /kuː/ *noun* (*plural* **-s** /kuːz/) successful stroke or move; *coup d'état*.

**coup de grâce** /kuː də ˈgrɑːs/ *noun* finishing stroke. [French]

**coup d'état** /kuː deɪˈtɑː/ *noun* (*plural* **coups d'état** same pronunciation) sudden overthrow of government, esp. by force. [French]

**coupé** /'kuːpeɪ/ *noun* (*US* **coupe** /kuːp/) two-door car with hard roof and sloping back.

**couple** /'kʌp(ə)l/ ● *noun* (about) two; two people who are married or in a sexual relationship; pair of partners in a dance etc. ● *verb* (**-ling**) link, fasten, or associate together; copulate.

**couplet** /'kʌplɪt/ *noun* two successive lines of rhyming verse.

**coupling** /'kʌplɪŋ/ *noun* link connecting railway carriages or parts of machinery.

**coupon** /'kuːpɒn/ *noun* ticket or form entitling holder to something.

**courage** /'kʌrɪdʒ/ *noun* ability to disregard fear; bravery. □ **courageous** /kəˈreɪdʒəs/ *adjective*; **courageously** *adverb*.

**courgette** /kʊəˈʒet/ *noun* small vegetable marrow.

**courier** /'kʊrɪə/ *noun* person employed to guide and assist group of tourists; special messenger.

**course** /kɔːs/ ● *noun* onward movement or progression; direction taken; line of conduct; series of lectures, lessons, etc.; each successive part of meal; golf course, race-course, etc.; sequence of medical treatment etc.; continuous line of masonry or bricks at one level of building; channel in which water flows. ● *verb* (**-sing**) use hounds to hunt (esp. hares); move or flow freely. □ **in the course of** during; **of course** naturally, as expected, admittedly.

**court** /kɔːt/ ● *noun* number of houses enclosing a yard; courtyard; rectangular area for a game; (in full **court of law**) judicial body hearing legal cases; courtroom; sovereign's establishment and retinue. ● *verb* pay amorous attention to, seek to win favour of; try to win (fame etc.); unwisely invite. □ **court card** playing card that is king, queen, or jack; **court house** building in which judicial court is held, *US* county administrative offices; **court martial** (*plural* **courts martial**) judicial court of military officers; **court-martial** (**-ll-**; *US* **-l-**) try by court martial; **courtroom** room in which court of law sits; **court shoe** woman's light shoe with low-cut upper; **courtyard** space enclosed by walls or buildings.

**courteous** /'kɜːtɪəs/ *adjective* polite, considerate. □ **courteously** *adverb*; **courteousness** *noun*.

**courtesan** /kɔːtɪˈzæn/ *noun* prostitute, esp. one with wealthy or upper-class clients.

**courtesy** /'kɜːtəsɪ/ *noun* (*plural* **-ies**) courteous behaviour or act. □ **by courtesy of** with formal permission of; **courtesy light** light in car switched on when door is opened.

**courtier** /'kɔːtɪə/ *noun* person who attends sovereign's court.

**courtly** *adjective* (**-ier**, **-iest**) dignified; refined in manners. □ **courtliness** *noun*.

**courtship** *noun* courting, wooing.

**couscous** /'ku:sku:s/ *noun* N. African dish of cracked wheat steamed over broth.

**cousin** /'kʌz(ə)n/ *noun* (also **first cousin**) child of one's uncle or aunt.

**couture** /ku:'tjʊə/ *noun* design and making of fashionable garments.

**couturier** /ku:'tjʊərɪeɪ/ *noun* fashion designer.

**cove** /kəʊv/ *noun* small bay or inlet; sheltered recess.

**coven** /'kʌv(ə)n/ *noun* assembly of witches.

**covenant** /'kʌvənənt/ ● *noun* agreement; *Law* sealed contract. ● *verb* agree, esp. by legal covenant.

**Coventry** /'kɒvəntrɪ/ *noun* □ **send to Coventry** refuse to associate with or speak to.

**cover** /'kʌvə/ ● *verb* (often + *with*) protect or conceal with cloth, lid, etc.; extend over; protect, clothe; include; (of sum) be large enough to meet (expense); protect by insurance; report on for newspaper, television, etc.; travel (specified distance); aim gun etc. at; protect by aiming gun. ● *noun* thing that covers, esp. lid, wrapper, etc.; shelter, protection; funds to meet liability or contingent loss; place-setting at table. □ **cover charge** service charge per person in restaurant; **cover note** temporary certificate of insurance; **cover up** *verb* cover completely, conceal; **cover-up** *noun* concealing of facts; **take cover** find shelter.

**coverage** *noun* area or amount covered; reporting of events in newspaper etc.

**covering letter** *noun* explanatory letter with other documents.

**coverlet** /'kʌvəlɪt/ *noun* bedspread.

**covert** /'kʌvət/ ● *adjective* secret, disguised. ● *noun* shelter, esp. thicket hiding game. □ **covertly** *adverb*.

**covet** /'kʌvɪt/ *verb* (**-t-**) desire greatly (esp. thing belonging to another person). □ **covetous** *adjective*.

**covey** /'kʌvɪ/ *noun* (*plural* **-s**) brood of partridges; family, set.

**coving** /'kəʊvɪŋ/ *noun* curved surface at junction of wall and ceiling.

**cow**[1] /kaʊ/ *noun* fully-grown female of esp. domestic bovine animal; female of

elephant, rhinoceros, whale, seal, etc. □ **cowboy**, **cowgirl** person who tends cattle, esp. in western US, *colloquial* unscrupulous or incompetent business person; **cowherd** person who tends cattle; **cowhide** (leather made from) cow's hide; **cow-pat** tropical flat piece of cow-dung; **cowpox** disease of cows, source of smallpox vaccine.

**cow**[2] /kaʊ/ *verb* intimidate.

**coward** /'kaʊəd/ *noun* person easily frightened. □ **cowardly** *adjective*.

**cowardice** /'kaʊədɪs/ *noun* lack of bravery.

**cower** /'kaʊə/ *verb* crouch or shrink back in fear.

**cowl** /kaʊl/ *noun* (hood of) monk's cloak; (also **cowling**) hood-shaped covering of chimney or shaft. □ **cowl neck** wide loose roll neck on garment.

**cowrie** /'kaʊrɪ/ *noun* tropical mollusc with bright shell; its shell as money in parts of Asia etc.

**cowslip** /'kaʊslɪp/ *noun* yellow-flowered primula growing in pastures etc.

**cox** ● *noun* coxswain. ● *verb* act as cox (of).

**coxcomb** /'kɒkskəʊm/ *noun* conceited showy person.

**coxswain** /'kɒks(ə)n/ *noun* person who steers esp. rowing boat.

**coy** *adjective* affectedly shy; irritatingly reticent. □ **coyly** *adverb*.

**coyote** /kɔɪ'əʊtɪ/ *noun* (*plural* same or **-s**) N. American wild dog.

**coypu** /'kɔɪpu:/ *noun* (*plural* **-s**) amphibious rodent like small beaver, originally from S. America.

**cozen** /'kʌz(ə)n/ *verb* *literary* cheat, defraud; beguile.

**cozy** *US* = COSY.

**crab** ● *noun* shellfish with 10 legs; this as food; (in full **crab-louse**) (often in *plural*) parasite infesting human body. ● *verb* (**-bb-**) *colloquial* criticize, grumble; spoil. □ **catch a crab** (in rowing) get oar jammed under water, miss water; **crab-apple** wild apple tree, its sour fruit.

**crabbed** /kræbɪd/ *adjective* crabby; (of handwriting) ill-formed, illegible.

**crabby** *adjective* (**-ier**, **-iest**) morose, irritable. □ **crabbily** *adverb*.

**crack** ● *noun* sudden sharp noise; sharp blow; narrow opening; break or split; *colloquial* joke, malicious remark; sudden change in vocal pitch; *slang* crystalline cocaine. ● *verb* (cause to) make crack; suffer crack or partial break; (of voice) change pitch sharply; tell (joke); open (bottle of wine etc.); break into (safe); find solution to (problem); give way, yield; hit sharply; (as **cracked** *adjective*) crazy, (of wheat) coarsely broken. □ **crack-brained** *adjective* crazy; **crack-down** *colloquial* severe measures (esp. against law-breakers); **crack down on** *colloquial* take severe measures against; **crack of dawn** daybreak; **crackpot** *colloquial* eccentric or impractical person; **crack up** *colloquial* collapse under strain.

**cracker** *noun* small paper cylinder containing paper hat, joke, etc., exploding with crack when ends are pulled; explosive firework; thin crisp savoury biscuit.

**crackers** *adjective slang* crazy.

**crackle** /'kræk(ə)l/ ● *verb* (**-ling**) make repeated light crackling sound. ● *noun* such a sound. □ **crackly** *adjective*.

**crackling** *noun* crisp skin of roast pork.

**cracknel** /'krækn(ə)l/ *noun* light crisp biscuit.

**cradle** /'kreɪd(ə)l/ ● *noun* baby's bed, esp. on rockers; place regarded as origin of something; supporting framework or structure. ● *verb* (**-ling**) contain or shelter as in cradle.

**craft** /krɑːft/ *noun* special skill or technique; occupation needing this; (*plural* same) boat, vessel, aircraft, or spacecraft; cunning.

**craftsman** /'krɑːftsmən/ *noun* (*feminine* **-woman**) person who practises a craft. □ **craftsmanship** *noun*.

**crafty** *adjective* (**-ier**, **-iest**) cunning, artful. □ **craftily** *adverb*.

**crag** *noun* steep rugged rock.

**craggy** *adjective* (**-ier**, **-iest**) rugged; rough-textured.

**cram** *verb* (**-mm-**) fill to bursting; (often + *in*, *into*) force; study or teach intensively for exam.

**crammer** *noun* institution that crams pupils for exam.

**cramp** ● *noun* painful involuntary contraction of muscles. ● *verb* affect with cramp; restrict, confine.

**cramped** *adjective* (of space) small; (of handwriting) small and with the letters close together.

**crampon** /'kræmpɒn/ *noun* spiked iron plate fixed to boot for climbing on ice.

**cranberry** /'krænbərɪ/ *noun* (*plural* **-ies**) (shrub bearing) small red acid berry.

**crane** ● *noun* machine with projecting arm for moving heavy weights; large long-legged wading bird. ● *verb* (**-ning**) stretch (one's neck) in order to see something. □ **crane-fly** two-winged long-legged fly; **cranesbill** kind of wild geranium.

**cranium** /'kreɪnɪəm/ *noun* (*plural* **-s** or **-nia**) bones enclosing brain, skull. □ **cranial** *adjective*.

**crank** ● *noun* part of axle or shaft bent at right angles for converting rotary into reciprocal motion or vice versa; eccentric person. ● *verb* turn with crank. □ **crankpin** pin attaching connecting rod to crank; **crankshaft** shaft driven by crank; **crank up** start (engine) by turning crank.

**cranky** *adjective* (**-ier**, **-iest**) eccentric; shaky; *esp. US* crotchety.

**cranny** /'krænɪ/ *noun* (*plural* **-ies**) chink, crevice.

**crape** *noun* crêpe, usually of black silk, formerly used for mourning.

**craps** *plural noun* (also **crap game**) *US* gambling game played with dice.

**crapulent** /'kræpjʊlənt/ *adjective* suffering the effects of drunkenness. □ **crapulence** *noun*; **crapulous** *adjective*.

**crash** ● *verb* (cause to) make loud smashing noise; (often + *into*) (cause to) collide or fall violently; fail, esp. financially; *colloquial* gatecrash; (of computer, system, etc.) fail suddenly; (often + *out*) *slang* fall asleep, sleep. ● *noun* sudden violent noise; violent fall or impact, esp. of vehicle; ruin, esp. financial; sudden collapse, esp. of computer, system, etc. ● *adjective* done rapidly or urgently. □ **crash barrier** barrier to prevent car leaving road; **crash-dive** *verb* (of submarine) dive hastily and steeply, (of aircraft) dive and crash, *noun* such a dive; **crash-helmet** helmet worn to protect head; **crash-land** land or cause (aircraft etc.) to land with crash; **crash landing** instance of crash-landing.

**crass** adjective grossly stupid; insensitive. □ **crassly** adverb; **crassness** noun.

**crate** ●noun slatted wooden case; slang old aircraft, car, etc. ●verb (**-ting**) pack in crate.

**crater** /'kreɪtə/ noun mouth of volcano; bowl-shaped cavity, esp. hollow on surface of moon etc.

**cravat** /krə'væt/ noun man's scarf worn inside open-necked shirt.

**crave** verb (**-ving**) (often + for) long or beg for.

**craven** /'kreɪv(ə)n/ adjective cowardly, abject.

**craving** noun strong desire, longing.

**craw** noun crop of bird or insect.

**crawfish** noun (plural same) large spiny sea-lobster.

**crawl** ●verb move slowly, esp. on hands and knees or with body close to ground; colloquial behave obsequiously; (often + with) be filled with moving people or things; (esp. of skin) creep. ●noun crawling motion; slow rate of motion; fast swimming stroke.

**crayfish** /'kreɪfɪʃ/ noun (plural same) lobster-like freshwater crustacean; crawfish.

**crayon** /'kreɪən/ ●noun stick or pencil of coloured wax, chalk, etc. ●verb draw or colour with crayons.

**craze** ●verb (**-zing**) (usually as **crazed** adjective) make insane; produce fine surface cracks on, develop such cracks. ●noun usually temporary enthusiasm; object of this.

**crazy** adjective (**-ier**, **-iest**) insane, mad; foolish; (usually + about) colloquial extremely enthusiastic. □ **crazy paving** paving made of irregular pieces. □ **crazily** adverb.

**creak** ●noun harsh scraping or squeaking sound. ●verb emit creak; move stiffly. □ **creaky** adjective (**-ier**, **-iest**).

**cream** ●noun fatty part of milk; its yellowish-white colour; food or drink like or made with cream; creamlike cosmetic etc.; (usually + the) best part or pick of something. ●verb take cream from; make creamy; form cream or scum. ●adjective yellowish-white. □ **cream cheese** soft rich cheese made of cream and unskimmed milk; **cream cracker** crisp unsweetened biscuit; **cream off** remove best part of; **cream of tartar** purified tartar, used in medicine, baking powder, etc.; **cream tea** afternoon tea with scones, jam, and cream. □ **creamy** adjective (**-ier**, **-iest**).

**creamer** noun cream substitute for coffee; jug for cream.

**creamery** noun (plural **-ies**) factory producing dairy products; dairy.

**crease** /kriːs/ ●noun line made by folding or crushing; Cricket line defining position of bowler or batsman. ●verb (**-sing**) make creases in, develop creases.

**create** /kriː'eɪt/ verb (**-ting**) bring into existence; originate; invest with rank; slang make fuss.

**creation** /kriː'eɪʃ(ə)n/ noun creating, being created; (usually **the Creation**) God's creating of the universe; (usually **Creation**) all created things; product of imaginative work.

**creative** /kriː'eɪtɪv/ adjective inventive, imaginative. □ **creatively** adverb; **creativity** /-'tɪv-/ noun.

**creator** /kriː'eɪtə/ noun person who creates; (**the Creator**) God.

**creature** /'kriːtʃə/ noun living being, esp. animal; person, esp. one in subservient position; anything created.

**crèche** /kreʃ/ noun day nursery.

**credence** /'kriːd(ə)ns/ noun belief.

**credentials** /krɪ'denʃ(ə)lz/ plural noun documents attesting to person's education, character, etc.

**credible** /'kredɪb(ə)l/ adjective believable; worthy of belief. □ **credibility** noun.

■ **Usage** Credible is sometimes confused with credulous, which means 'gullible'.

**credit** /'kredɪt/ ●noun belief, trust; good reputation; person's financial standing; power to obtain goods before payment; acknowledgement of payment by entry in account, sum entered; acknowledgement of merit or (usually in plural) of contributor's services to film, book, etc.; grade above pass in exam; educational course counting towards degree. ● *verb* (**-t-**) believe; (usually + *to*, *with*) enter on credit side of account. □ **credit card** card authorizing purchase of goods on credit; **credit (person) with** ascribe to him or her; **credit rating** estimate of person's suitability for commercial credit; **creditworthy** suitable to receive credit; **on credit** with arrangement to pay later; **to one's credit** in one's favour.

**creditable** *adjective* praiseworthy. □ **creditably** *adverb.*

**creditor** *noun* person to whom debt is owing.

**credo** /'kri:dəʊ/ *noun* (*plural* **-s**) creed.

**credulous** /'kredjʊləs/ *adjective* too ready to believe; gullible. □ **credulity** /krɪ'dju:-/ *noun.*

■ **Usage** *Credulous* is sometimes confused with *credible*, which means 'believable'.

**creed** *noun* set of beliefs; system of beliefs; (often **the Creed**) formal summary of Christian doctrine.

**creek** *noun* inlet on sea-coast; arm of river; stream.

**creel** *noun* fisherman's wicker basket.

**creep** ● *verb* (*past & past participle* **crept**) crawl; move stealthily, timidly, or slowly; (of plant) grow along ground or up wall etc.; advance or develop gradually; (of flesh) shudder with horror etc. ● *noun* act of creeping; (**the creeps**) *colloquial* feeling of revulsion or fear; *slang* unpleasant person; gradual change in shape of metal under stress.

**creeper** *noun* creeping or climbing plant.

**creepy** *adjective* (**-ier**, **-iest**) *colloquial* feeling or causing horror or fear. □ **creepy-crawly** (*plural* **-crawlies**) small crawling insect etc. □ **creepily** *adverb.*

**cremate** /krɪ'meɪt/ *verb* (**-ting**) burn (corpse) to ashes. □ **cremation** *noun.*

**crematorium** /kremə'tɔ:rɪəm/ *noun* (*plural* **-ria** or **-s**) place where corpses are cremated.

**crenellated** /'krenəleɪtɪd/ *adjective* having battlements. □ **crenellation** *noun.*

**Creole** /'kri:əʊl/ ● *noun* descendant of European settlers in W. Indies or Central or S. America, or of French settlers in southern US; person of mixed European and black descent; language formed from a European and African language. ● *adjective* of Creoles; (usually **creole**) of Creole origin etc.

**creosote** /'kri:əsəʊt/ ● *noun* oily wood-preservative distilled from coal tar. ● *verb* (**-ting**) treat with creosote.

**crêpe** /kreɪp/ *noun* fine crinkled fabric; thin pancake with savoury or sweet filling; wrinkled sheet rubber used for shoe-soles etc. □ **crêpe de Chine** /də 'ʃi:n/ fine silk crêpe; **crêpe paper** thin crinkled paper.

**crept** *past & past participle* of CREEP.

**crepuscular** /krɪ'pʌskjʊlə/ *adjective* of twilight; (of animal) active etc. at twilight.

**crescendo** /krɪ'ʃendəʊ/ *Music* ● *noun* (*plural* **-s**) gradual increase in loudness. ● *adjective & adverb* increasing in loudness.

■ **Usage** *Crescendo* is sometimes wrongly used to mean a climax rather than the progress towards it.

**crescent** /'kres(ə)nt/ ● *noun* sickle shape, as of waxing or waning moon; thing with this shape, esp. curved street. ● *adjective* crescent-shaped.

**cress** *noun* plant with pungent edible leaves.

**crest** ● *noun* comb or tuft on animal's head; plume of helmet; top of mountain, wave, etc.; *Heraldry* device above shield or on writing paper etc. ● *verb* reach crest of; crown; serve as crest to; form crest. □ **crestfallen** dejected. □ **crested** *adjective.*

**cretaceous** /krɪ'teɪʃəs/ *adjective* chalky.

**cretin** /'kretɪn/ *noun* person with deformity and mental retardation caused by thyroid deficiency; *colloquial* stupid person. □ **cretinism** *noun*; **cretinous** *adjective.*

**cretonne** /kre'tɒn/ *noun* heavy cotton usually floral upholstery fabric.

**crevasse** /krə'væs/ *noun* deep open crack in glacier.

**crevice** /'krevɪs/ *noun* narrow opening or fissure, esp. in rock.

**crew**[1] /kru:/ • *noun* group of people working together, esp. manning ship, aircraft, spacecraft, etc.; these, other than the officers. • *verb* supply or act as crew (member) for; act as crew. □ **crew cut** close-cropped hairstyle; **crew neck** round close-fitting neckline.

**crew**[2] *archaic* past of CROW.

**crewel** /ˈkruːəl/ *noun* thin worsted yarn for embroidery.

**crib** • *noun* baby's small bed or cot; model of Nativity with manger; *colloquial* plagiarism; translation; *colloquial* cribbage. • *verb* (**-bb-**) copy unfairly; confine in small space.

**cribbage** /ˈkrɪbɪdʒ/ *noun* a card game.

**crick** • *noun* sudden painful stiffness, esp. in neck. • *verb* cause crick in.

**cricket**[1] /ˈkrɪkɪt/ *noun* team game, played on grass pitch, in which ball is bowled at wicket defended with bat by player of other team. □ **not cricket** *colloquial* unfair behaviour. □ **cricketer** *noun*.

**cricket**[2] /ˈkrɪkɪt/ *noun* jumping chirping insect.

**cried** past & past participle of CRY.

**crier** /ˈkraɪə/ *noun* (also **cryer**) making public announcements in law court or street.

**crikey** /ˈkraɪkɪ/ *interjection slang*: expressing astonishment.

**crime** *noun* act punishable by law; such acts collectively; evil act; *colloquial* shameful act.

**criminal** /ˈkrɪmɪn(ə)l/ • *noun* person guilty of crime. • *adjective* of, involving, or concerning crime; *colloquial* deplorable. □ **criminality** /-ˈnæl-/ *noun*; **criminally** *adverb*.

**criminology** /krɪmɪˈnɒlədʒɪ/ *noun* study of crime. □ **criminologist** *noun*.

**crimp** *verb* press into small folds or waves; corrugate.

**Crimplene** /ˈkrɪmpliːn/ *noun* proprietary term synthetic crease-resistant fabric.

**crimson** /ˈkrɪmz(ə)n/ *adjective & noun* rich deep red.

**cringe** *verb* (**-ging**) cower; (often + *to*) behave obsequiously.

**crinkle** /ˈkrɪŋk(ə)l/ • *noun* wrinkle, crease. • *verb* (**-ling**) form crinkles (in). □ **crinkly** *adjective*.

**crinoline** /ˈkrɪnəlɪn/ *noun* hooped petticoat.

**cripple** /ˈkrɪp(ə)l/ • *noun* lame person. • *verb* (**-ling**) lame, disable; damage seriously.

**crisis** /ˈkraɪsɪs/ *noun* (*plural* **crises** /-siːz/) time of acute danger or difficulty; decisive moment.

**crisp** • *adjective* hard but brittle; bracing; brisk, decisive; clear-cut; crackling; curly. • *noun* (in full **potato crisp**) very thin fried slice of potato. • *verb* make or become crisp. □ **crispbread** thin crisp biscuit. □ **crisply** *adverb*; **crispness** *noun*.

**crispy** *adjective* (**-ier**, **-iest**) crisp.

**criss-cross** • *noun* pattern of crossing lines. • *adjective* crossing; in crossing lines. • *adverb* crosswise. • *verb* intersect repeatedly; mark with criss-cross lines.

**criterion** /kraɪˈtɪərɪən/ *noun* (*plural* **-ria**) principle or standard of judgement.

■ **Usage** It is a mistake to use the plural form *criteria* when only one criterion is meant.

**critic** /ˈkrɪtɪk/ *noun* person who criticizes; reviewer of literary, artistic, etc. works.

**critical** *adjective* fault-finding; expressing criticism; providing textual criticism; of the nature of a crisis, decisive; marking transition from one state to another. □ **critically** *adverb*.

**criticism** /ˈkrɪtɪsɪz(ə)m/ *noun* finding fault, censure; work of critic; critical article, remark, etc.

**criticize** /ˈkrɪtɪsaɪz/ *verb* (also **-ise**) (**-zing** or **-sing**) find fault with; discuss critically.

**critique** /krɪˈtiːk/ *noun* critical analysis.

**croak** • *noun* deep hoarse sound, esp. of frog. • *verb* utter or speak with croak; *slang* die. □ **croaky** *adjective* (**-ier**, **-iest**); **croakily** *adverb*.

**Croat** /ˈkrəʊæt/ (also **Croatian** /krəʊˈeɪʃ(ə)n/) • *noun* native of Croatia; person of Croatian descent; Slavonic dialect of Croats. • *adjective* of Croats or their dialect.

**crochet** /ˈkrəʊʃeɪ/ • *noun* needlework of hooked yarn producing lacy patterned fabric. • *verb* (**crocheted** /-ʃeɪd/; **crocheting** /-ʃeɪɪŋ/) make by crochet.

**crock¹** *noun colloquial* old or worn-out person or vehicle.

**crock²** *noun* earthenware jar; broken piece of this.

**crockery** *noun* earthenware or china dishes, plates, etc.

**crocodile** /'krɒkədaɪl/ *noun* large amphibious reptile; *colloquial* line of school children etc. walking in pairs. □ **crocodile tears** insincere grief.

**crocus** /'krəʊkəs/ *noun (plural* **-es**) small plant with corm and yellow, purple, or white flowers.

**croft** ● *noun* small piece of arable land; small rented farm in Scotland or N. England. ● *verb* farm croft.

**crofter** *noun* person who farms croft.

**Crohn's disease** /krəʊnz/ *noun* inflammatory disease of alimentary tract.

**croissant** /'krwʌsɑ̃/ *noun* rich crescent-shaped roll.

**cromlech** /'krɒmlek/ *noun* dolmen; prehistoric stone circle.

**crone** *noun* withered old woman.

**crony** /'krəʊnɪ/ *noun (plural* **-ies**) friend; companion.

**crook** /krʊk/ ● *noun* hooked staff of shepherd or bishop; bend, curve; *colloquial* swindler, criminal. ● *verb* bend, curve.

**crooked** /'krʊkɪd/ *adjective* (**-er**, **-est**) not straight, bent; *colloquial* dishonest. □ **crookedly** *adverb*; **crookedness** *noun*.

**croon** /kru:n/ ● *verb* hum or sing in low voice. ● *noun* such singing. □ **crooner** *noun*.

**crop** ● *noun* produce of any cultivated plant or of land; group or amount produced at one time; handle of whip; very short haircut; pouch in bird's gullet where food is prepared for digestion. ● *verb* (**-pp-**) cut off; bite off, eat down; cut (hair) short; raise crop on (land); bear crop. □ **crop circle** circle of crops inexplicably flattened; **crop up** occur unexpectedly.

**cropper** *noun slang* □ **come a cropper** fall heavily, fail badly.

**croquet** /'krəʊkeɪ/ ● *noun* lawn game with hoops, wooden balls, and mallets; croqueting. ● *verb* (**croqueted** /-keɪd/; **croqueting** /-keɪɪŋ/) drive away (opponent's ball) by striking one's own ball placed in contact with it.

**croquette** /krə'ket/ *noun* fried breaded ball of meat, potato, etc.

**crosier** /'krəʊzɪə/ *noun* (also **crozier**) bishop's ceremonial hooked staff.

**cross** ● *noun* upright stake with transverse bar, used in antiquity for crucifixion; representation of this as emblem of Christianity; cross-shaped thing or mark, esp. two short intersecting lines (+ or ×); cross-shaped military etc. decoration; intermixture of breeds, hybrid; (+ *between*) mixture of two things; trial, affliction. ● *verb* (often + *over*) go across; place crosswise; draw line(s) across; make sign of cross on or over; meet and pass; thwart; (cause to) interbreed; cross-fertilize (plants). ● *adjective* (often + *with*) peevish, angry; transverse; reaching from side to side; intersecting; reciprocal. □ **at cross purposes** misunderstanding each other; **crossbar** horizontal bar, esp. between uprights; **cross-bench** bench in House of Lords for non-party members; **crossbones** see SKULL AND CROSSBONES; **crossbow** bow fixed across wooden stock with mechanism working string; **cross-breed** (produce) hybrid animal or plant; **cross-check** check by alternative method; **cross-country** across fields etc., not following roads, *noun* such a race; **cross-examine** question (esp. opposing witness in law court); **cross-examination** such questioning; **cross-eyed** having one or both eyes turned inwards; **cross-fertilize** fertilize (animal or plant) from another of same species; **crossfire** firing of guns in two crossing directions; **cross-grained** (of wood) with grain running irregularly, (of person) perverse or intractable; **cross-hatch** shade with crossing parallel lines; **cross-legged** (sitting) with legs folded across each other; **cross off**, **out** cancel, expunge; **crossover** point or process of crossing; **crosspatch** *colloquial* bad-tempered person; **cross-ply** (of tyre) having crosswise layers of cords; **cross-question** cross-examine, quiz; **cross-reference** reference to another passage in same book; **crossroad** (usually in *plural*) intersection of roads; **cross-section** drawing etc. of thing as if cut through, representative sample; **cross stitch** cross-shaped stitch; **crosswise** intersecting, diagonally; **crossword (puzzle)** puzzle in which words crossing each other vertically and horizontally have to be filled in from clues; **on the cross** diagonally. □ **crossly** *adverb*; **crossness** *noun*.

**crossing** *noun* place where things (esp. roads) meet; place for crossing street; journey across water.

**crotch** *noun* fork, esp. between legs (of person, trousers, etc.).

**crotchet** /ˈkrɒtʃɪt/ *noun* Music black-headed note with stem, equal to quarter of semibreve and usually one beat.

**crotchety** *adjective* peevish.

**crouch** ● *verb* stand, squat, etc. with legs bent close to body. ● *noun* this position.

**croup**[1] /kru:p/ *noun* laryngitis in children, with sharp cough.

**croup**[2] /kru:p/ *noun* rump, esp. of horse.

**croupier** /ˈkru:pɪə/ *noun* person in charge of gaming table.

**croûton** /ˈkru:tɒn/ *noun* small piece of fried or toasted bread served esp. with soup.

**crow** /krəʊ/ ● *noun* any of various kinds of large black-plumaged bird; cry of cock or baby. ● *verb* (past **crowed** or *archaic* **crew** /kru:/) (of cock) utter loud cry; (of baby) utter happy sounds; exult. □ **crow's-foot** wrinkle at outer corner of eye; **crow's-nest** shelter for look-out man at ship's masthead.

**crowbar** *noun* iron bar used as lever.

**crowd** /kraʊd/ ● *noun* large gathering of people; *colloquial* particular set of people. ● *verb* (cause to) collect in crowd; (+ *with*) cram with; (+ *into, through*, etc.) force way into, through, etc.; *colloquial* come aggressively close to. □ **crowd out** exclude by crowding.

**crown** /kraʊn/ ● *noun* monarch's jewelled headdress; (**the Crown**) monarch as head of state, his or her authority; wreath for head as emblem of victory; top part of head, hat, etc.; visible part of tooth, artificial replacement for this; coin worth 5 shillings or 25 pence. ● *verb* put crown on; make king or queen; (often as **crowning** *adjective*) be consummation, reward, or finishing touch to;

*slang* hit on head. □ **Crown colony** British colony controlled by the Crown; **Crown Court** court of criminal jurisdiction in England and Wales; **Crown jewels** sovereign's regalia; **crown prince** male heir to throne; **crown princess** wife of crown prince, female heir to throne.

**crozier** = CROSIER.

**CRT** *abbreviation* cathode ray tube.

**cruces** *plural* of CRUX.

**crucial** /ˈkru:ʃ(ə)l/ *adjective* decisive, critical; very important; *slang* excellent. □ **crucially** *adverb*.

**crucible** /ˈkru:sɪb(ə)l/ *noun* melting pot for metals.

**cruciferous** /kru:ˈsɪfərəs/ *adjective* with 4 equal petals arranged crosswise.

**crucifix** /ˈkru:sɪfɪks/ *noun* image of Christ on Cross.

**crucifixion** /kru:sɪˈfɪkʃ(ə)n/ *noun* crucifying, esp. of Christ.

**cruciform** /ˈkru:sɪfɔ:m/ *adjective* cross-shaped.

**crucify** /ˈkru:sɪfaɪ/ *verb* (-**ies**, -**ied**) put to death by fastening to cross; persecute, torment.

**crude** ● *adjective* in natural or raw state; lacking finish, unpolished; rude, blunt; indecent. ● *noun* natural mineral oil. □ **crudely** *adverb*; **crudeness** *noun*; **crudity** *noun*.

**crudités** /kru:dɪˈteɪ/ *plural noun* hors d'oeuvre of mixed raw vegetables. [French]

**cruel** /ˈkru:əl/ *adjective* (-**ll**- or -**l**-) causing pain or suffering, esp. deliberately; harsh, severe. □ **cruelly** *adverb*; **cruelty** *noun* (*plural* -**ies**).

**cruet** /ˈkru:ɪt/ *noun* set of small salt, pepper, etc. containers for use at table.

**cruise** /kru:z/ ● *verb* (-**sing**) sailabout, esp. travel by sea for pleasure, calling at ports; travel at relaxed or economical speed; achieve objective with ease. ● *noun* cruising voyage. □ **cruise missile** one able to fly low and guide itself.

**cruiser** *noun* high-speed warship; cabin cruiser. □ **cruiserweight** light heavyweight.

**crumb** /krʌm/ ● *noun* small fragment esp. of bread; soft inner part of loaf;

(**crumbs** interjection) slang: expressing dismay. • verb coat with breadcrumbs; crumble (bread). □ **crumby** adjective.

**crumble** /ˈkrʌmb(ə)l/ • verb (-ling) break or fall into fragments, disintegrate. • noun dish of cooked fruit with crumbly topping. □ **crumbly** adjective (-ier, -iest).

**crumhorn** = KRUMMHORN.

**crummy** /ˈkrʌmɪ/ adjective (-ier, -iest) slang squalid, inferior.

**crumpet** /ˈkrʌmpɪt/ noun flat soft yeasty cake eaten toasted.

**crumple** /ˈkrʌmp(ə)l/ verb (-ling) (often + up) crush or become crushed into creases; give way, collapse.

**crunch** • verb crush noisily with teeth; make or emit crunch. • noun crunching sound; colloquial decisive event. □ **crunchy** adjective (-ier, -iest).

**crupper** /ˈkrʌpə/ noun strap looped under horse's tail to hold harness back.

**crusade** /kruːˈseɪd/ • noun historical medieval Christian military expedition to recover Holy Land from Muslims; vigorous campaign for cause. • verb (-ding) take part in crusade. □ **crusader** noun.

**cruse** /kruːz/ noun archaic earthenware jar.

**crush** • verb compress violently so as to break, bruise, etc.; crease, crumple; defeat or subdue completely. • noun act of crushing; crowded mass of people; drink made from juice of crushed fruit; (usually + on) colloquial infatuation.

**crust** • noun hard outer part of bread etc.; pastry covering pie; rocky outer part of the earth; deposit, esp. on sides of wine bottle. • verb cover with, form into, or become covered with crust.

**crustacean** /krʌˈsteɪʃ(ə)n/ • noun hard-shelled usually aquatic animals, e.g. crab or lobster. • adjective of crustaceans.

**crusty** adjective (-ier, -iest) having a crisp crust; irritable, curt.

**crutch** noun support for lame person, usually with cross-piece fitting under armpit; support; crotch.

**crux** noun (plural -es or **cruces** /ˈkruːsiːz/) decisive point at issue.

**cry** /kraɪ/ • verb (**cries**, **cried**) (often + out) make loud or shrill sound, esp. to express pain, grief, joy, etc.; weep; (often + out) utter loudly, exclaim; (+ for) appeal for. • noun (plural **cries**) loud shout of grief, fear, joy, etc.; loud excited utterance; urgent appeal; fit of weeping; call of animal. □ **cry-baby** person who weeps frequently; **cry down** disparage; **cry off** withdraw from undertaking; **cry out for** need badly; **cry wolf** see WOLF; **a far cry** a long way.

**cryer** = CRIER.

**crying** adjective (of injustice etc.) flagrant, demanding redress.

**cryogenics** /kraɪəʊˈdʒenɪks/ noun branch of physics dealing with very low temperatures. □ **cryogenic** adjective.

**crypt** /krɪpt/ noun vault, esp. below church, usually used as burial place.

**cryptic** adjective obscure in meaning; secret, mysterious. □ **cryptically** adverb.

**cryptogam** /ˈkrɪptəɡæm/ noun plant with no true flowers or seeds, e.g. fern or fungus. □ **cryptogamic** /-ˈɡæm-/ adjective.

**cryptogram** /ˈkrɪptəɡræm/ noun text written in cipher.

**crystal** /ˈkrɪst(ə)l/ • noun (piece of) transparent colourless mineral; (articles of) highly transparent glass; substance solidified in definite geometrical form. • adjective of or as clear as crystal. □ **crystal ball** glass globe supposedly used in foretelling the future.

**crystalline** /ˈkrɪstəlaɪn/ adjective of or as clear as crystal.

**crystallize** /ˈkrɪstəlaɪz/ verb (also **-ise**) (-zing or -sing) form into crystals; make or become definite; preserve or be preserved in sugar. □ **crystallization** noun.

**CS gas** noun tear gas used to control riots.

**cu.** abbreviation cubic.

**cub** • noun young of fox, bear, lion, etc.; **Cub (Scout)** junior Scout; colloquial young newspaper reporter. • verb give birth to (cubs).

**cubby-hole** /ˈkʌbɪhəʊl/ noun very small room; snug space.

**cube** /kjuːb/ • noun solid contained by 6 equal squares; cube-shaped block; product of a number multiplied by its square. ● verb (**-bing**) find cube of; cut into small cubes. □ **cube root** number which produces given number when cubed.

**cubic** /'kju:bɪk/ adjective of 3 dimensions; involving cube of a quantity. □ **cubic metre** etc., volume of cube whose edge is one metre etc. □ **cubical** adjective.

**cubicle** /'kju:bɪk(ə)l/ noun small screened space, esp. sleeping compartment.

**cubism** /'kju:bɪz(ə)m/ noun art style in which objects are represented geometrically. □ **cubist** adjective & noun.

**cubit** /'kju:bɪt/ noun ancient measure of length, approximately length of forearm.

**cuboid** /'kju:bɔɪd/ ● adjective like a cube; cube-shaped. ● noun solid with 6 rectangular faces.

**cuckold** /'kʌkəʊld/ ● noun husband of adulteress. ● verb make cuckold of.

**cuckoo** /'kʊku:/ ● noun bird with characteristic cry and laying eggs in nests of small birds. ● adjective slang crazy. □ **cuckoo clock** clock with figure of cuckoo emerging to make call on the hour; **cuckoo-pint** wild arum; **cuckoo-spit** froth exuded by larvae of certain insects.

**cucumber** /'kju:kʌmbə/ noun long green fleshy fruit used in salads.

**cud** noun half-digested food chewed by ruminant.

**cuddle** /'kʌd(ə)l/ ● verb (**-ling**) hug; lie close and snug; nestle. ● noun prolonged hug.

**cuddly** adjective (**-ier**, **-iest**) soft and yielding.

**cudgel** /'kʌdʒ(ə)l/ ● noun thick stick used as weapon. ● verb (**-ll-**; US **-l-**) beat with cudgel.

**cue**[1] /kju:/ ● noun last words of actor's speech as signal for another to begin; signal, hint. ● verb (**cues, cued, cueing** or **cuing**) give cue to. □ **cue in** insert cue for; **on cue** at correct moment.

**cue**[2] /kju:/ ● noun long rod for striking ball in billiards etc. ● verb (**cues, cued, cueing** or **cuing**) strike with cue. □ **cue ball** ball to be struck with cue.

**cuff**[1] noun end part of sleeve; trouser turn-up; (in plural) colloquial handcuffs.

□ **cuff link** either of pair of fasteners for shirt cuffs; **off the cuff** extempore, without preparation.

**cuff**[2] ● verb strike with open hand. ● noun such a blow.

**cuisine** /kwɪ'zi:n/ noun style of cooking.

**cul-de-sac** /'kʌldəsæk/ noun (plural **culs-de-sac** same pronunciation, or **cul-de-sacs** /-sæks/) road etc. closed at one end.

**culinary** /'kʌlɪnərɪ/ adjective of or for cooking.

**cull** ● verb select, gather; pick (flowers); select and kill (surplus animals). ● noun culling; animal(s) culled.

**culminate** /'kʌlmɪneɪt/ verb (**-ting**) (usually + in) reach highest or final point. □ **culmination** noun.

**culottes** /kju:'lɒts/ plural noun woman's trousers cut like skirt.

**culpable** /'kʌlpəb(ə)l/ adjective deserving blame. □ **culpability** noun.

**culprit** /'kʌlprɪt/ noun guilty person.

**cult** noun religious system, sect, etc.; devotion or homage to person or thing.

**cultivar** /'kʌltɪvɑː/ noun plant variety produced by cultivation.

**cultivate** /'kʌltɪveɪt/ verb (**-ting**) prepare and use (soil) for crops; raise (plant etc.); (often as **cultivated** adjective) improve (manners etc.); nurture (friendship etc.). □ **cultivation** noun.

**cultivator** noun agricultural implement for breaking up ground etc.

**culture** /'kʌltʃə/ ● noun intellectual and artistic achievement or expression; refined appreciation of arts etc.; customs and civilization of a particular time or people; improvement by mental or physical training; cultivation of plants, rearing of bees etc.; quantity of bacteria grown for study. ● verb (**-ring**) grow (bacteria) for study. □ **culture shock** disorientation felt by person subjected to unfamiliar way of life. □ **cultural** adjective.

**cultured** adjective having refined tastes etc. □ **cultured pearl** one formed by oyster after insertion of foreign body into its shell.

**culvert** /'kʌlvət/ noun underground channel carrying water under road etc.

**cumbersome** /'kʌmbəsəm/ adjective (also **cumbrous** /'kʌmbrəs/) inconveniently bulky, unwieldy.

**cumin** /'kʌmɪn/ noun (also **cummin**) plant with aromatic seeds; these as flavouring.

**cummerbund** /'kʌməbʌnd/ noun waist sash.

**cumulative** /'kju:mjʊlətɪv/ adjective increasing in force etc. by successive additions. □ **cumulatively** adverb.

**cumulus** /'kju:mjʊləs/ noun (plural **-li** /-laɪ/) cloud formation of heaped-up rounded masses.

**cuneiform** /'kju:nɪfɔ:m/ ● noun writing made up of wedge shapes. ● adjective of or using cuneiform.

**cunning** /'kʌnɪŋ/ ● adjective (**-er**, **-est**) deceitful, crafty; ingenious. ● noun ingenuity; craft. □ **cunningly** adverb.

**cup** ● noun small bowl-shaped drinking vessel; cupful; cup-shaped thing; flavoured usually chilled wine, cider, etc.; cup-shaped trophy as prize. ● verb (**-pp-**) make cup-shaped; hold as in cup. □ **Cup Final** final match in (esp. football) competition; **cup-tie** match in such competition; **cupful** noun.

■ **Usage** A *cupful* is a measure, and so *three cupfuls* is a quantity of something; *three cups full* means the actual cups and their contents, as in *He brought us three cups full of water.*

**cupboard** /'kʌbəd/ noun recess or piece of furniture with door and usually shelves.

**Cupid** /'kju:pɪd/ noun Roman god of love, pictured as winged boy with bow.

**cupidity** /kju:'pɪdɪtɪ/ noun greed, avarice.

**cupola** /'kju:pələ/ noun small dome; revolving gun-turret on ship or in fort.

**cuppa** /'kʌpə/ noun colloquial cup of (tea).

**cur** noun mangy bad-tempered dog; contemptible person.

**curable** /'kjʊərəb(ə)l/ adjective able to be cured.

**curaçao** /'kjʊərəsəʊ/ noun (plural **-s**) orange-flavoured liqueur.

**curacy** /'kjʊərəsɪ/ noun (plural **-ies**) curate's office or position.

**curare** /kjʊ'rɑ:rɪ/ noun vegetable poison used on arrows by American Indians.

**curate** /'kjʊərət/ noun assistant to parish priest. □ **curate's egg** thing good in parts.

**curative** /'kjʊərətɪv/ ● adjective tending to cure. ● noun curative agent.

**curator** /kjʊə'reɪtə/ noun custodian of museum etc.

**curb** ● noun check, restraint; (bit with) chain etc. passing under horse's lower jaw; kerb. ● verb restrain; put curb on.

**curd** noun (often in plural) coagulated acidic milk product, made into cheese or eaten as food.

**curdle** /'kɜ:d(ə)l/ verb (**-ling**) coagulate. □ **make one's blood curdle** horrify one.

**cure** /kjʊə/ ● verb (often + of) restore to health, relieve; eliminate (evil etc.); preserve (meat etc.) by salting etc. ● noun restoration to health; thing that cures; course of treatment.

**curé** /'kjʊəreɪ/ noun parish priest in France etc. [French]

**curette** /kjʊə'ret/ ● noun surgeon's scraping-instrument. ● verb (**-tting**) scrape with this. □ **curettage** noun.

**curfew** /'kɜ:fju:/ noun signal or time after which people must remain indoors.

**curie** /'kjʊərɪ/ noun unit of radioactivity.

**curio** /'kjʊərɪəʊ/ noun (plural **-s**) rare or unusual object.

**curiosity** /kjʊərɪ'ɒsɪtɪ/ noun (plural **-ies**) desire to know; inquisitiveness; rare or strange thing.

**curious** /'kjʊərɪəs/ adjective eager to learn; inquisitive; strange, surprising. □ **curiously** adverb.

**curl** ● verb (often + up) bend or coil into spiral; move in curve; (of upper lip) be raised in contempt; play curling. ● noun curled lock of hair; anything spiral or curved inwards. □ **curly** adjective (**-ier**, **-iest**).

**curler** noun pin, roller, etc. for curling hair.

**curlew** /'kɜ:lju:/ noun long-billed wading bird with musical cry.

**curling** noun game like bowls played on ice with round flat stones.

**curmudgeon** /kə'mʌdʒ(ə)n/ noun bad-tempered or miserly person. □ **curmudgeonly** adjective.

**currant** /'kʌrənt/ noun small seedless dried grape; (fruit of) any of various shrubs producing red, black, or white berries.

**currency** /'kʌrənsɪ/ noun (plural **-ies**) money in use in a country; being current; prevalence (of ideas etc.).

**current** ● adjective belonging to present time; happening now; in general circulation or use. ● noun body of moving water, air, etc., passing through still water etc.; movement of electrically charged particles; general tendency or course. □ **current account** bank account that may be drawn on by cheque without notice. □ **currently** adverb.

**curriculum** /kə'rɪkjʊləm/ noun (plural **-la** /'vi:taɪ/ brief account of one's education, career, etc.

**curry**[1] /'kʌrɪ/ ● noun (plural **-ies**) meat, vegetables, etc. cooked in spicy sauce, usually served with rice. ● verb (**-ies, -ied**) make into or flavour like curry. □ **curry powder** mixture of spices for making curry.

**curry**[2] /'kʌrɪ/ verb (**-ies, -ied**) groom (horse etc.) with curry-comb; dress (leather). □ **curry-comb** metal device for grooming horses etc.; **curry favour** ingratiate oneself.

**curse** /kɜːs/ ● noun invocation of destruction or punishment; violent or profane exclamation; thing causing evil. ● verb (**-sing**) utter curse against; (usually in passive; + with) afflict with; swear. □ **cursed** /'kɜːsɪd/ adjective.

**cursive** /'kɜːsɪv/ ● adjective (of writing) having joined characters. ● noun cursive writing.

**cursor** /'kɜːsə/ noun indicator on VDU screen showing particular position in displayed matter.

**cursory** /'kɜːsərɪ/ adjective hasty, hurried. □ **cursorily** adverb.

**curt** adjective noticeably or rudely brief. □ **curtly** adverb; **curtness** noun.

**curtail** /kɜː'teɪl/ verb cut short, reduce. □ **curtailment** noun.

**curtain** /'kɜːt(ə)n/ ● noun piece of cloth etc. hung up as screen, esp. at window; rise or fall of stage curtain; curtain-call; (in plural) slang the end. ● verb provide or (+ off) shut off with curtains. □ **curtain-call** audience's applause

summoning actors to take bow; **curtain-raiser** short opening play etc., preliminary event.

**curtsy** /'kɜːtsɪ/ (also **curtsey**) ● noun (plural **-ies** or **-eys**) woman's or girl's acknowledgement or greeting made by bending knees. ● verb (**-ies, -ied** or **-eys, -eyed**) make curtsy.

**curvaceous** /kɜː'veɪʃəs/ adjective colloquial (esp. of woman) shapely.

**curvature** /'kɜːvətʃə/ noun curving; curved form; deviation of curve from plane.

**curve** ● noun line or surface of which no part is straight; curved line on graph. ● verb (**-ving**) bend or shape so as to form curve. □ **curvy** adjective (**-ier, -iest**).

**curvet** /kɜː'vet/ ● noun horse's frisky leap. ● verb (**-tt-** or **-t-**) perform curvet.

**curvilinear** /kɜːvɪ'lɪnɪə/ adjective contained by or consisting of curved lines.

**cushion** /'kʊʃ(ə)n/ ● noun bag stuffed with soft material for sitting on etc.; protection against shock; padded rim of billiard table; air supporting hovercraft. ● verb provide or protect with cushions; mitigate effects of.

**cushy** /'kʊʃɪ/ adjective (**-ier, -iest**) colloquial (of job etc.) easy, pleasant.

**cusp** noun point at which two curves meet, e.g. horn of crescent moon.

**cuss** colloquial ● noun curse; awkward person. ● verb curse.

**cussed** /'kʌsɪd/ adjective colloquial awkward, stubborn.

**custard** /'kʌstəd/ noun pudding or sweet sauce of eggs or flavoured cornflour and milk.

**custodian** /kʌs'təʊdɪən/ noun guardian, keeper.

**custody** /'kʌstədɪ/ noun guardianship; imprisonment. □ **custodial** /-'stəʊ-/ adjective.

**custom** /'kʌstəm/ noun usual behaviour; established usage; business dealings, customers; (in plural, also treated as singular) duty on imports, government department or (part of) building at port etc. dealing with this. □ **custom house** customs office at frontier etc.; **custom-built, -made** made to customer's order.

**customary** /'kʌstəmərɪ/ adjective in accordance with custom; usual. □ **customarily** adverb.

**customer** noun person who buys goods or services; colloquial person of specified (esp. awkward) kind.

**customize** verb (also **-ise**) (**-zing** or **-sing**) make or modify to order; personalize.

**cut** ● verb (**-tt-**; past & past participle **cut**) divide, wound, or penetrate with edged instrument; detach, trim, etc. by cutting; (+ loose, open, etc.) loosen by cutting; (esp. as **cutting** adjective) cause pain to; reduce (prices, wages, services, etc.); make by cutting or removing material; cross, intersect; divide (pack of cards); edit (film), stop cameras; end acquaintance or ignore presence of; US deliberately miss (class etc.); chop (ball); switch off (engine etc.); (+ across, through, etc.) pass through as shorter route. ● noun act of cutting; division or wound made by cutting; stroke with knife, sword, whip, etc.; reduction (in price, wages, services, etc.); cessation (of power supply etc.); removal of part of play, film, etc.; slang commission, share of profits, etc.; style in which hair, clothing, etc. is cut; particular piece of meat; cutting of ball; deliberate ignoring of person. □ **a cut above** noticeably superior to; **cut and dried** completely decided, inflexible; **cut back** reduce (expenditure), prune; **cut-back** reduction in expenditure; **cut both ways** serve both sides; **cut corners** do task perfunctorily; **cut glass** glass with patterns cut on it; **cut in** interrupt, pull in too closely in front of another vehicle; **cut one's losses** abandon an unprofitable scheme; **cut no ice** slang have no influence; **cut off** verb remove by cutting, bring to abrupt end, interrupt, disconnect, adjective isolated; **cut out** shape by cutting, (cause to) cease functioning, stop doing or using; **cut-out** device for automatic disconnection; **cutthroat** noun murderer, adjective murderous, (of competition) intense and merciless; **cutthroat razor** one with long unguarded blade set in handle; **cut a tooth** have it appear through gum; **cut up** cut in pieces, (usually in passive) greatly distress; **cut up rough** show resentment.

**cutaneous** /kjuːˈteɪnɪəs/ adjective of the skin.

**cute** /kjuːt/ adjective colloquial esp. US attractive, sweet; clever, ingenious. □ **cutely** adverb; **cuteness** noun.

**cuticle** /ˈkjuːtɪk(ə)l/ noun skin at base of fingernail or toenail.

**cutlass** /ˈkʌtləs/ noun historical short broad-bladed curved sword.

**cutlery** /ˈkʌtləri/ noun knives, forks, and spoons for use at table.

**cutlet** /ˈkʌtlɪt/ noun neck-chop of mutton or lamb; small piece of veal etc. for frying; flat cake of minced meat etc.

**cutter** noun person or thing that cuts; (in plural) cutting tool; small fast sailing ship; small boat carried by large ship.

**cutting** ● noun piece cut from newspaper etc.; piece cut from plant for replanting; excavated channel in hillside etc. for railway or road. ● adjective that cuts; hurtful. □ **cuttingly** adverb.

**cuttlefish** /ˈkʌt(ə)lfɪʃ/ noun (plural same or **-es**) 10-armed sea mollusc ejecting black fluid when pursued.

**cutwater** noun forward edge of ship's prow; wedge-shaped projection from pier of bridge.

**C.V.** abbreviation (also **CV**) curriculum vitae.

**cwm** /kuːm/ noun (in Wales) coomb.

**cwt** abbreviation hundredweight.

**cyanide** /ˈsaɪənaɪd/ noun highly poisonous substance used in extraction of gold and silver.

**cyanosis** /saɪəˈnəʊsɪs/ noun bluish skin due to oxygen-deficient blood.

**cybernetics** /saɪbəˈnetɪks/ plural noun (usually treated as singular) science of control systems and communications in animals and machines. □ **cybernetic** adjective.

**cyclamen** /ˈsɪkləmən/ noun plant with pink, red, or white flowers with backward-turned petals.

**cycle** /ˈsaɪk(ə)l/ ● noun recurrent round or period (of events, phenomena, etc.); series of related poems etc.; bicycle, tricycle, etc. ● verb (**-ling**) ride bicycle etc.; move in cycles. □ **cycle lane** part of road reserved for bicycles; **cycle track, cycleway** path for bicycles.

**cyclic** /ˈsaɪklɪk/ adjective (also **cyclical** /ˈsɪklɪk(ə)l/) recurring in cycles; belonging to chronological cycle. □ **cyclically** adverb.

**cyclist** /ˈsaɪklɪst/ noun rider of bicycle.

**cyclone** /'saɪkləʊn/ noun winds rotating around low-pressure region; violent destructive form of this. □ **cyclonic** /-'klɒn-/ adjective.

**cyclotron** /'saɪklətrɒn/ noun apparatus for acceleration of charged atomic particles revolving in magnetic field.

**cygnet** /'sɪgnɪt/ noun young swan.

**cylinder** /'sɪlɪndə/ noun solid or hollow roller-shaped body; container for liquefied gas etc.; piston-chamber in engine. □ **cylindrical** /-'lɪn-/ adjective.

**cymbal** /'sɪmb(ə)l/ noun concave disc struck usually with another to make ringing sound.

**cynic** /'sɪnɪk/ noun person with pessimistic view of human nature. □ **cynical** adjective; **cynically** adverb; **cynicism** /-sɪz(ə)m/ noun.

**cynosure** /'saɪnəzjʊə/ noun centre of attention or admiration.

**cypher** = CIPHER.

**cypress** /'saɪprəs/ noun conifer with dark foliage.

**Cypriot** /'sɪprɪət/ (also **Cypriote** /-əʊt/) ● noun native or national of Cyprus. ● adjective of Cyprus.

**Cyrillic** /sɪ'rɪlɪk/ ● adjective of alphabet used esp. for Russian and Bulgarian. ● noun this alphabet.

**cyst** /sɪst/ noun sac formed in body, containing liquid matter.

**cystic** adjective of the bladder; like a cyst. □ **cystic fibrosis** hereditary disease usually with respiratory infections.

**cystitis** /sɪ'staɪtɪs/ noun inflammation of the bladder.

**czar** = TSAR.

**czarina** = TSARINA.

**Czech** /tʃek/ ● noun native or national of Czech Republic, or historical Czechoslovakia; language of Czech people. ● adjective of Czechs or their language; of Czech Republic.

**Czechoslovak** /tʃekə'sləʊvæk/ (also **Czechoslovakian** /-slə'vækɪən/) historical ● noun native or national of Czechoslovakia. ● adjective of Czechoslovaks or Czechoslovakia.

......................................................

# Dd

......................................................

**D** noun (also **d**) (Roman numeral) 500. □ **D-Day** day of Allied invasion of France (6 June 1944), important or decisive day.

**d.** abbreviation died; (pre-decimal) penny.

**dab**[1] ● verb (**-bb-**) (often + at) press briefly and repeatedly with cloth etc.; (+ on) apply by dabbing; (often + at) aim feeble blow; strike lightly. ● noun dabbing; small amount (of paint etc.) dabbed on; light blow.

**dab**[2] noun (plural same) kind of marine flatfish.

**dabble** /'dæb(ə)l/ verb (**-ling**) (usually + in, at) engage (in an activity etc.) superficially; move about in shallow water etc. □ **dabbler** noun.

**dabchick** noun little grebe.

**dab hand** noun (usually + at) expert.

**da capo** /dɑː'kɑːpəʊ/ adverb Music repeat from beginning.

**dace** noun (plural same) small freshwater fish.

**dacha** /'dætʃə/ noun Russian country cottage.

**dachshund** /'dækshʊnd/ noun short-legged long-bodied dog.

**dactyl** /'dæktɪl/ noun metrical foot of one long followed by two short syllables. □ **dactylic** /-'tɪl-/ adjective.

**dad** noun colloquial father.

**daddy** /'dædɪ/ noun (plural **-ies**) colloquial father. □ **daddy-long-legs** crane-fly.

**dado** /'deɪdəʊ/ noun (plural **-s**) lower, differently decorated, part of interior wall.

**daffodil** /'dæfədɪl/ noun spring bulb with trumpet-shaped yellow flowers.

**daft** /dɑːft/ *adjective* (**-er, -est**) foolish, silly, crazy.

**dagger** /'dægə/ *noun* short knifelike weapon; obelus.

**daguerreotype** /də'gerəʊtaɪp/ *noun* early photograph using silvered plate.

**dahlia** /'deɪlɪə/ *noun* garden plant with large showy flowers.

**Dáil (Eireann)** /dɔɪl 'eɪrən/ *noun* lower house of Parliament in Republic of Ireland.

**daily** /'deɪlɪ/ • *adjective* done, produced, or occurring every (week)day. • *adverb* every day; constantly. • *noun* (*plural* **-ies**) *colloquial* daily newspaper; cleaning woman.

**dainty** /'deɪntɪ/ • *adjective* (**-ier, -iest**) delicately pretty or small; choice; fastidious. • *noun* (*plural* **-ies**) delicacy. □ **daintily** *adverb*; **daintiness** *noun*.

**daiquiri** /'dækərɪ/ *noun* (*plural* **-s**) cocktail of rum, lime juice, etc.

**dairy** /'deərɪ/ • *noun* (*plural* **-ies**) place for processing, distributing, or selling milk and milk products. • *adjective* of, containing, or used for milk and milk products. □ **dairymaid** woman employed in dairy; **dairyman** man looking after cows.

**dais** /'deɪɪs/ *noun* low platform, esp. at upper end of hall.

**daisy** /'deɪzɪ/ *noun* (*plural* **-ies**) flowering plant with white radiating petals. □ **daisy chain** string of field daisies threaded together; **daisy wheel** spoked disc bearing printing characters, used in word processors and typewriters.

**dale** *noun* valley.

**dally** /'dælɪ/ *verb* (**-ies, -ied**) delay; waste time; (often + *with*) flirt. □ **dalliance** *noun*.

**Dalmatian** /dæl'meɪʃ(ə)n/ *noun* large white dog with dark spots.

**dam¹** • *noun* barrier across river etc., usually forming reservoir or preventing flooding. • *verb* (**-mm-**) provide or confine with dam; (often + *up*) block up, obstruct.

**dam²** *noun* mother (of animal).

**damage** /'dæmɪdʒ/ • *noun* harm; injury; (in *plural*) financial compensation for loss or injury; (**the damage**) *slang* cost. • *verb* (**-ging**) inflict damage on.

**damask** /'dæməsk/ • *noun* fabric with woven design made visible by reflection of light. • *adjective* made of damask; velvety pink. □ **damask rose** old sweet-scented rose.

**dame** *noun* (**Dame**) (title of) woman who has been knighted; comic female pantomime character played by man; *US slang* woman.

**damn** /dæm/ • *verb* (often as *interjection*) curse; censure; condemn to hell; (often as **damning** *adjective*) show or prove to be guilty. • *noun* uttered curse. • *adjective & adverb* damned. □ **damn all** *slang* nothing.

**damnable** /'dæmnəb(ə)l/ *adjective* hateful; annoying.

**damnation** /dæm'neɪʃ(ə)n/ • *noun* eternal punishment in hell. • *interjection* expressing anger.

**damned** /dæmd/ • *adjective* damnable. • *adverb* extremely.

**damp** • *adjective* slightly wet. • *noun* slight diffused or condensed moisture. • *verb* make damp; (often + *down*) discourage, make burn less strongly; *Music* stop vibration of (string etc.). □ **damp course** layer of damp-proof material in wall to keep damp from rising. □ **dampness** *noun*.

**dampen** *verb* make or become damp; discourage.

**damper** *noun* device that reduces shock, vibration, or noise; discouraging person or thing; metal plate in flue to control draught.

**damsel** /'dæmz(ə)l/ *noun archaic* young unmarried woman.

**damson** /'dæmz(ə)n/ *noun* small dark purple plum.

**dance** /dɑːns/ • *verb* (**-cing**) move rhythmically, usually to music; perform (dance role etc.); jump or bob about. • *noun* dancing as art; style or form of this; social gathering for dancing; lively motion. □ **dance attendance (on)** serve obsequiously. □ **dancer** *noun*.

**dandelion** /'dændɪlaɪən/ *noun* yellow-flowered wild plant.

**dander** *noun* □ **get one's dander up** *colloquial* become angry.

**dandle** /'dænd(ə)l/ *verb* (**-ling**) bounce (child) on one's knees etc.

**dandruff** /'dændrʌf/ noun flakes of dead skin in hair.

**dandy** /'dændɪ/ • noun (plural **-ies**) man excessively devoted to style and fashion. • adjective (**-ier**, **-iest**) colloquial splendid. □ **dandy-brush** stiff brush for grooming horses.

**Dane** noun native or national of Denmark; historical Viking invader of England.

**danger** /'deɪndʒə/ noun liability or exposure to harm; thing causing harm. □ **danger list** list of those dangerously ill; **danger money** extra payment for dangerous work.

**dangerous** adjective involving or causing danger. □ **dangerously** adverb.

**dangle** /'dæŋg(ə)l/ verb (**-ling**) hang loosely; hold or carry swaying loosely; hold out (temptation etc.).

**Danish** /'deɪnɪʃ/ • adjective of Denmark. • noun Danish language; (**the Danish**) the Danish people. □ **Danish blue** white blue-veined cheese; **Danish pastry** yeast cake with icing, nuts, fruit, etc.

**dank** adjective damp and cold.

**daphne** /'dæfnɪ/ noun a flowering shrub.

**dapper** adjective neat and precise, esp. in dress; sprightly.

**dapple** /'dæp(ə)l/ verb (**-ling**) mark with spots of colour or shade; mottle. □ **dapple-grey** (of horse) grey with darker spots; **dapple grey** such a horse.

**Darby and Joan** noun devoted old married couple. □ **Darby and Joan club** social club for pensioners.

**dare** /deə/ • verb (**-ring**; 3rd singular present often **dare**) (+ (to) do) have the courage or impudence (to); (usually + to do) defy, challenge. • noun challenge. □ **daredevil** reckless (person); **I dare say** very likely, I grant that.

**daring** • noun adventurous courage. • adjective bold, prepared to take risks. □ **daringly** adverb.

**dariole** /'dærɪəʊl/ noun dish cooked and served in a small mould.

**dark** • adjective with little or no light; of deep or sombre colour; (of a person) with dark colouring; gloomy; sinister; angry; secret, mysterious. • noun absence of light or darkness; unlit place. □ **after dark** after nightfall; **Dark Ages** 5th–10th-c., unenlightened period; **dark horse** little-known person who is unexpectedly successful; **darkroom** darkened room for photographic work; **in the dark** without information or light. □ **darken** verb; **darkly** adverb; **darkness** noun.

**darling** /'dɑ:lɪŋ/ • noun beloved or endearing person or animal. • adjective beloved, lovable; colloquial charming.

**darn**[1] • verb mend by interweaving wool etc. across hole. • noun darned area.

**darn**[2] verb, interjection, adjective, & adverb colloquial mild form of DAMN.

**darnel** /'dɑ:n(ə)l/ noun grass growing in cereal crops.

**dart** • noun small pointed missile; (in plural treated as singular) indoor game of throwing darts at a dartboard; sudden rapid movement; tapering tuck in garment. • verb (often + out, in, past, etc.) move, send, or go suddenly or rapidly. □ **dartboard** circular target in game of darts.

**Darwinian** /dɑ:'wɪnɪən/ • adjective of Darwin's theory of evolution. • noun adherent of this. □ **Darwinism** /'dɑ:-/ noun; **Darwinist** /'dɑ:-/ noun.

**dash** • verb rush; strike or fling forcefully so as to shatter; frustrate, dispirit; colloquial (as interjection) damn. • noun rush, onset; punctuation mark (—) used to indicate break in sense (see panel); longer signal of two in Morse code; slight admixture; (capacity for) impetuous vigour. □ **dashboard** instrument panel of vehicle or aircraft; **dash off** hurriedly.

**dashing** adjective spirited; showy.

**dastardly** /'dæstədlɪ/ adjective cowardly, despicable.

**data** /'deɪtə/ plural noun (also treated as singular) known facts used for inference or reckoning; quantities or characters operated on by computer. □ **data bank** store or source of data; **database** structured set of data held in computer; **data processing** series of operations on data by computer.

■ **Usage** In scientific, philosophical, and general use, *data* is usually considered to mean a number of items and is treated as plural, with *datum* as its singular. In computing and allied subjects (and sometimes in general use), it is treated as singular, as in *Much useful data has been collected.* However, *data* is not singular, and it is wrong to say *a data* or *every data* or to make the plural form *datas*.

**date¹** ● *noun* day of month; historical day or year; day, month, and year of writing etc. at head of document etc.; period to which work of art etc. belongs; time when an event takes place; *colloquial* social appointment, esp. with person of opposite sex; *US colloquial* person to be met at this. ● *verb* (**-ting**) mark with date; assign date to; (+ *to*) assign to a particular time, period, etc.; (often + *from*, *back to*, etc.) have origin at a particular time; expose as or appear old-fashioned; *US colloquial* make date with, go out together as sexual partners. □ **date line** line partly along meridian 180° from Greenwich, to the east of which date is a day earlier than to the west; date and place of writing at head of newspaper article etc.; **out of date** (**out-of-date** before noun) old-fashioned, obsolete; **to date** until now; **up to date** (**up-to-date** before noun) fashionable, current.

**date²** *noun* oval stone fruit; (in full **date-palm**) tree bearing this.

**dative** /'deɪtɪv/ *Grammar* ● *noun* case expressing indirect object or recipient. ● *adjective* of or in the dative.

**datum** /'deɪtəm/ *singular of* DATA.

**daub** /dɔːb/ ● *verb* paint or spread (paint etc.) crudely or unskilfully; smear (surface) with paint etc. ● *noun* paint etc. daubed on a surface; crude painting; clay etc. coating wattles to form wall.

**daughter** /'dɔːtə/ *noun* female child in relation to her parents; female descendant or member of family etc. □ **daughter-in-law** (*plural* **daughters-in-law**) son's wife.

**daunt** /dɔːnt/ *verb* discourage, intimidate. □ **daunting** *adjective*.

**dauntless** *adjective* intrepid, persevering.

**dauphin** /'dɔːfɪn/ *noun historical* eldest son of King of France.

**Davenport** /'dævənpɔːt/ *noun* kind of writing desk; *US* large sofa.

**davit** /'dævɪt/ *noun* small crane on ship for holding lifeboat.

**daw** *noun* jackdaw.

**dawdle** /'dɔːd(ə)l/ *verb* (**-ling**) walk slowly and idly; waste time, procrastinate.

**dawn** ● *noun* daybreak; beginning. ● *verb* (of day) begin, grow light; (often + *on*, *upon*) become evident (to). □ **dawn chorus** birdsong at daybreak.

**day** *noun* time between sunrise and sunset; 24 hours as a unit of time; daylight; time during which work is normally

......................................................................

## Dash —

This is used:

1  to mark the beginning and end of an interruption in the structure of a sentence:
   *My son—where has he gone?—would like to meet you.*

2  to show faltering speech in conversation:
   *Yes—well—I would—only you see—it's not easy.*

3  to show other kinds of break in a sentence, where a comma, semicolon, or colon would traditionally be used, e.g.
   *Come tomorrow—if you can.*
   *The most important thing is this—don't rush the work.*

   A dash is not used in this way in formal writing.

......................................................................

done; (also *plural*) historical period; (**the day**) present time; period of prosperity. □ **daybreak** first light in morning; **day centre** place for care of elderly or handicapped during day; **daydream** (indulge in) fantasy etc. while awake; **day off** day's holiday; **day release** part-time education for employees; **day return** reduced fare or ticket for a return journey in one day; **day school** school for pupils living at home; **daytime** part of day when there is natural light; **day-to-day** mundane, routine; **day-trip** trip completed in one day.

**daylight** *noun* light of day; dawn; visible gap between things; (usually in *plural*) *slang* life. □ **daylight robbery** blatantly excessive charge; **daylight saving** longer summer evening daylight, achieved by putting clocks forward.

**daze** ● *verb* (**-zing**) stupefy, bewilder. ● *noun* dazed state.

**dazzle** /ˈdæz(ə)l/ ● *verb* (**-ling**) blind or confuse temporarily with sudden bright light; impress or overpower with knowledge, ability, etc. ● *noun* bright confusing light. □ **dazzling** *adjective*.

**dB** *abbreviation* decibel(s).

**DC** *abbreviation* direct current; District of Columbia; da capo.

**DDT** *abbreviation* colourless chlorinated hydrocarbon used as insecticide.

**deacon** /ˈdiːkən/ *noun* (in episcopal churches) minister below priest; (*feminine* **deaconess** /-ˈnes/) (in Nonconformist churches) lay officer.

**deactivate** /diːˈæktɪveɪt/ *verb* (**-ting**) make inactive or less reactive.

**dead** /ded/ ● *adjective* no longer alive; numb; *colloquial* extremely tired or unwell; (+ *to*) insensitive to; not effective; extinct; extinguished; inanimate; lacking vigour; not resonant; quiet; not transmitting sounds; out of play; abrupt; complete. ● *adverb* absolutely, completely; *colloquial* very. ● *noun* time of silence or inactivity. □ **dead beat** utterly exhausted; **dead-beat** tramp; **dead duck** useless person or thing; **dead end** closed end of road etc.; **dead-end** having no prospects; **dead heat** race in which competitors tie; **dead letter** law etc. no longer observed; **deadline** time limit; **deadlock**

*noun* state of unresolved conflict, *verb* bring or come to a standstill; **dead loss** useless person or thing; **dead man's handle** handle on electric train etc. disconnecting power supply if released; **dead march** funeral march; **dead on** exactly right; **deadpan** lacking expression or emotion; **dead reckoning** estimation of ship's position from log, compass, etc., when visibility is bad; **dead shot** unerring marksman; **dead weight** inert mass, heavy burden; **dead wood** *colloquial* useless person(s) or thing(s).

**deaden** *verb* deprive of or lose vitality, force, etc.; (+ *to*) make insensitive.

**deadly** ● *adjective* (**-ier**, **-iest**) causing fatal injury or serious damage; intense; accurate; deathlike; dreary. ● *adverb* as if dead; extremely. □ **deadly nightshade** plant with poisonous black berries.

**deaf** /def/ *adjective* wholly or partly unable to hear; (+ *to*) refusing to listen or comply. □ **deaf-aid** hearing aid; **deaf-and-dumb alphabet**, **language** sign language; **deaf mute** deaf and dumb person. □ **deafness** *noun*.

**deafen** *verb* (often as **deafening** *adjective*) overpower or make deaf with noise, esp. temporarily. □ **deafeningly** *adverb*.

**deal**[1] ● *verb* (*past & past participle* **dealt** /delt/) (+ *with*) take measures to resolve, placate, etc., do business or associate with, treat (subject); (often + *by*, *with*) behave in specified way; (+ *in*) sell; (often + *out*, *round*) distribute; administer. ● *noun* (usually **a good** or **great deal**) large amount, considerably; business arrangement etc.; specified treatment; dealing of cards, player's turn to deal.

**deal**[2] *noun* fir or pine timber, esp. as boards.

**dealer** *noun* trader; player dealing at cards.

**dealings** *plural noun* conduct or transactions.

**dean** *noun* head of ecclesiastical chapter; (usually **rural dean**) clergyman supervising parochial clergy; college or university official with disciplinary functions; head of university faculty.

**deanery** *noun* (*plural* **-ies**) dean's house or position; parishes presided over by rural dean.

**dear** • *adjective* beloved; *used before person's name, esp. at beginning of letter*; (+ *to*) precious; expensive. • *noun* dear person. • *adverb* at great cost. • *interjection* (usually **oh dear!** or **dear me!**) *expressing surprise, dismay, etc.* □ **dearly** *adverb*.

**dearth** /dɜːθ/ *noun* scarcity, lack.

**death** /deθ/ *noun* dying, end of life; being dead; cause of death; destruction. □ **deathblow** blow etc. causing death, or action, event, etc. ending something; **death-mask** cast of dead person's face; **death penalty** capital punishment; **death rate** yearly deaths per 1000 of population; **death-rattle** gurgling in throat at death; **death row** part of prison for those sentenced to death; **death squad** paramilitary group; **death-trap** unsafe place, vehicle, etc.; **death-warrant** order of execution; **death-watch beetle** beetle that bores into wood and makes ticking sound. □ **deathlike** *adjective*.

**deathly** • *adjective* (**-ier**, **-iest**) like death. • *adverb* in deathly manner.

**deb** *noun colloquial* débutante.

**débâcle** /deɪˈbɑːk(ə)l/ *noun* utter collapse; confused rush.

**debar** /dɪˈbɑː/ *verb* (**-rr-**) (+ *from*) exclude. □ **debarment** *noun*.

**debase** /dɪˈbeɪs/ *verb* (**-sing**) lower in character, quality, or value; depreciate (coin) by alloying etc. □ **debasement** *noun*.

**debatable** /dɪˈbeɪtəb(ə)l/ *adjective* questionable.

**debate** /dɪˈbeɪt/ • *verb* (**-ting**) discuss or dispute, argue formally; consider, ponder. • *noun* discussion, esp. formal.

**debauch** /dɪˈbɔːtʃ/ • *verb* corrupt, deprave, debase; (as **debauched** *adjective*) dissolute. • *noun* bout of debauchery.

**debauchee** /dɪbɔːˈtʃiː/ *noun* debauched person.

**debauchery** *noun* excessive sensual indulgence.

**debenture** /dɪˈbentʃə/ *noun* company bond providing for payment of interest.

**debilitate** /dɪˈbɪlɪteɪt/ *verb* (**-ting**) enfeeble. □ **debilitation** *noun*.

**debility** *noun* feebleness, esp. of health.

**debit** /ˈdebɪt/ • *noun* entry in account recording sum owed. • *verb* (**-t-**) (+ *against, to*) enter on debit side of account.

**debonair** /debəˈneə/ *adjective* self-assured; pleasant.

**debouch** /dɪˈbaʊtʃ/ *verb* come out into open ground; (often + *into*) (of river etc.) merge. □ **debouchment** *noun*.

**debrief** /diːˈbriːf/ *verb* question (diplomat etc.) about completed mission. □ **debriefing** *noun*.

**debris** /ˈdebriː/ *noun* scattered fragments; wreckage.

**debt** /det/ *noun* money etc. owing; obligation; state of owing.

**debtor** *noun* person owing money etc.

**debug** /diːˈbʌg/ *verb* (**-gg-**) remove hidden microphones from; remove defects from.

**debunk** /diːˈbʌŋk/ *verb colloquial* expose as spurious or false.

**début** /ˈdeɪbjuː/ *noun* first public appearance.

**débutante** /ˈdebjuːtɑːnt/ *noun* young woman making her social début.

**Dec.** *abbreviation* December.

**deca-** *combining form* ten.

**decade** /ˈdekeɪd/ *noun* 10 years; set or series of 10.

**decadence** /ˈdekəd(ə)ns/ *noun* moral or cultural decline; immoral behaviour. □ **decadent** *adjective*.

**decaffeinated** /diːˈkæfɪneɪtɪd/ *adjective* with caffeine removed.

**decagon** /ˈdekəgən/ *noun* plane figure with 10 sides and angles. □ **decagonal** /-ˈkæg-/ *adjective*.

**decahedron** /dekəˈhiːdrən/ *noun* solid figure with 10 faces. □ **decahedral** *adjective*.

**decamp** /dɪˈkæmp/ *verb* depart suddenly; break up or leave camp.

**decant** /dɪˈkænt/ *verb* pour off (wine etc.) leaving sediment behind.

**decanter** *noun* stoppered glass container for decanted wine or spirit.

**decapitate** /dɪˈkæpɪteɪt/ *verb* (**-ting**) behead. □ **decapitation** *noun*.

**decarbonize** /diːˈkɑːbənaɪz/ *verb* (also **-ise**) (**-zing** or **-sing**) remove carbon etc. from (engine of car etc.). □ **decarbonization** *noun*.

**decathlon** /dɪˈkæθlən/ *noun* athletic contest of 10 events. □ **decathlete** *noun*.

**decay** /dɪˈkeɪ/ • *verb* (cause to) rot or decompose; decline in quality, power, etc. • *noun* rotten state; decline.

**decease** /dɪˈsiːs/ *noun formal esp. Law* death.

**deceased** *formal* • *adjective* dead. • *noun* (**the deceased**) person who has died.

**deceit** /dɪˈsiːt/ *noun* deception; trick. □ **deceitful** *adjective*.

**deceive** /dɪˈsiːv/ *verb* (**-ving**) make (person) believe what is false; (**deceive oneself**) persist in mistaken belief; mislead; be unfaithful to.

**decelerate** /diːˈseləreɪt/ *verb* (**-ting**) (cause to) reduce speed. □ **deceleration** *noun*.

**December** /dɪˈsembə/ *noun* twelfth month of year.

**decency** /ˈdiːsənsɪ/ *noun* ( *plural* **-ies**) correct, honourable, or modest behaviour; (in *plural*) proprieties, manners.

**decennial** /dɪˈsenɪəl/ *adjective* lasting 10 years; recurring every 10 years.

**decent** /ˈdiːs(ə)nt/ *adjective* conforming with standards of decency; not obscene; respectable; acceptable; kind. □ **decently** *adverb*.

**decentralize** /diːˈsentrəlaɪz/ *verb* (also **-ise**) (**-zing** or **-sing**) transfer (power etc.) from central to local authority. □ **decentralization** *noun*.

**deception** /dɪˈsepʃ(ə)n/ *noun* deceiving; being deceived; thing that deceives.

**deceptive** /dɪˈseptɪv/ *adjective* likely to mislead.

**deci-** *combining form* one-tenth.

**decibel** /ˈdesɪbel/ *noun* unit used in comparison of sound etc. levels.

**decide** /dɪˈsaɪd/ *verb* (**-ding**) (usually + *to do, that, on, about*) resolve after consideration; settle (issue etc.); (usually + *between, for, against, in favour of, that*) give judgement.

**decided** *adjective* definite, unquestionable; positive, resolute. □ **decidedly** *adverb*.

**deciduous** /dɪˈsɪdjʊəs/ *adjective* (of tree) shedding leaves annually; (of leaves etc.) shed periodically.

**decimal** /ˈdesɪm(ə)l/ • *adjective* (of system of numbers, weights, measures, etc.) based on 10; of tenths or 10; proceeding by tens. • *noun* decimal fraction. □ **decimal fraction** fraction expressed in tenths, hundredths, etc., esp. by units to right of decimal point; **decimal point** dot placed before fraction in decimal fraction.

**decimalize** *verb* (also **-ise**) (**-zing** or **-sing**) express as decimal; convert to decimal system. □ **decimalization** *noun*.

**decimate** /ˈdesɪmeɪt/ *verb* (**-ting**) destroy large proportion of. □ **decimation** *noun*.

■ **Usage** *Decimate* should not be used to mean 'defeat utterly'.

**decipher** /dɪˈsaɪfə/ *verb* convert (coded information) into intelligible language; determine the meaning of. □ **decipherable** *adjective*.

**decision** /dɪˈsɪʒ(ə)n/ *noun* deciding; resolution after consideration; settlement; resoluteness.

**decisive** /dɪˈsaɪsɪv/ *adjective* conclusive, settling an issue; quick to decide. □ **decisively** *adverb*; **decisiveness** *noun*.

**deck** • *noun* platform in a ship serving as a floor; floor of bus etc.; section for playing discs or tapes etc. in sound system; *US* pack of cards. • *verb* ( often + *out*) decorate. □ **deck-chair** outdoor folding chair.

**declaim** /dɪˈkleɪm/ *verb* speak, recite, etc. as if addressing audience. □ **declamation** *noun*; **declamatory** /-ˈklæm-/ *adjective*.

**declaration** /dekləˈreɪʃ(ə)n/ *noun* declaring; emphatic, deliberate, or formal statement.

**declare** /dɪˈkleə/ *verb* (**-ring**) announce openly or formally; pronounce; (usually + *that*) assert emphatically; acknowledge possession of (dutiable goods, income, etc.); *Cricket* close (innings) voluntarily before team is out; *Cards* name trump suit. □ **declaratory** /-ˈklær-/ *adjective*.

**declassify** /diːˈklæsɪfaɪ/ *verb* (**-ies**, **-ied**) declare (information etc.) to be no longer secret. □ **declassification** *noun*.

**declension** /dɪˈklenʃ(ə)n/ *noun Grammar* variation of form of noun etc., to show grammatical case; class of nouns with same inflections; deterioration.

**declination** /deklr'neɪʃ(ə)n/ *noun* downward bend; angular distance north or south of celestial equator; deviation of compass needle from true north.

**decline** /dɪ'klaɪn/ ● *verb* (**-ning**) deteriorate, lose strength or vigour; decrease; refuse; slope or bend downwards; *Grammar* state case forms of (noun etc.). ● *noun* deterioration.

**declivity** /dɪ'klɪvɪti/ *noun* (*plural* **-ies**) downward slope.

**declutch** /di:'klʌtʃ/ *verb* disengage clutch of motor vehicle.

**decode** /di:'kəʊd/ *verb* (**-ding**) decipher. □ **decoder** *noun*.

**decoke** /di:'kəʊk/ *verb* (**-king**) *colloquial* decarbonize.

**décolletage** /deɪkɒl'tɑ:ʒ/ *noun* low neckline of woman's dress. [French]

**décolleté** /deɪˈkɒlteɪ/ *adjective* (also **décolletée**) having low neckline. [French]

**decompose** /di:kəm'pəʊz/ *verb* (**-sing**) rot; separate into elements. □ **decomposition** /di:kɒmpə'zɪʃ(ə)n/ *noun*.

**decompress** /di:kəm'pres/ *verb* subject to decompression.

**decompression** /di:kəm'preʃ(ə)n/ *noun* release from compression; reduction of pressure on deep-sea diver etc. □ **decompression chamber** enclosed space for decompression.

**decongestant** /di:kən'dʒest(ə)nt/ *noun* medicine etc. that relieves nasal congestion.

**decontaminate** /di:kən'tæmɪneɪt/ *verb* (**-ting**) remove contamination from. □ **decontamination** *noun*.

**décor** /'deɪkɔ:/ *noun* furnishings and decoration of room, stage, etc.

**decorate** /'dekəreɪt/ *verb* (**-ting**) adorn; paint, wallpaper, etc. (room etc.); give medal or award to.

**decoration** *noun* decorating; thing that decorates; medal etc.; (in *plural*) flags etc. put up on festive occasion.

**decorative** /'dekərətɪv/ *adjective* pleasing in appearance. □ **decoratively** *adverb*.

**decorator** *noun* person who decorates for a living.

**decorous** /'dekərəs/ *adjective* having or showing decorum. □ **decorously** *adverb*.

**decorum** /dɪ'kɔ:rəm/ *noun* polite dignified behaviour.

**decoy** ● *noun* /'di:kɔɪ/ thing or person used as lure; bait, enticement. ● *verb* /dɪ'kɔɪ/ lure by decoy.

**decrease** ● *verb* /dɪ'kri:s/ (**-sing**) make or become smaller or fewer. ● *noun* /'di:kri:s/ decreasing; amount of this.

**decree** /dɪ'kri:/ ● *noun* official legal order; legal decision. ● *verb* (**-ees**, **-eed**) ordain by decree. □ **decree absolute** final order for completion of divorce; **decree nisi** /'naɪsaɪ/ provisional order for divorce.

**decrepit** /dɪ'krepɪt/ *adjective* weakened by age or infirmity; dilapidated. □ **decrepitude** *noun*.

**decry** /dɪ'kraɪ/ *verb* (**-ies**, **-ied**) disparage.

**dedicate** /'dedɪkeɪt/ *verb* (**-ting**) (often + *to*) devote (oneself) to a purpose etc.; address (book etc.) to friend or patron etc.; devote (building etc.) to saint etc.; (as **dedicated** *adjective*) having single-minded loyalty. □ **dedicatory** *adjective*.

**dedication** *noun* dedicating; words with which book is dedicated.

**deduce** /dɪ'dju:s/ *verb* (**-cing**) (often + *from*) infer logically. □ **deducible** *adjective*.

**deduct** /dɪ'dʌkt/ *verb* (often + *from*) subtract; take away; withhold.

**deductible** *adjective* that may be deducted esp. from tax or taxable income.

**deduction** /dɪ'dʌkʃ(ə)n/ *noun* deducting; amount deducted; inference from general to particular.

**deductive** *adjective* of or reasoning by deduction.

**deed** *noun* thing done; action; legal document. □ **deed of covenant** agreement to pay regular sum, esp. to charity; **deed poll** deed made by one party only, esp. to change one's name.

**deem** *verb* *formal* consider, judge.

**deep** ● *adjective* extending far down or in; to or at specified depth; low-pitched; intense; profound; (+ *in*) fully absorbed, overwhelmed. ● *adverb* deeply; far down or in. ● *noun* deep state; (**the deep**) *poetical* the sea. □ **deep-freeze** *noun* freezer, verb freeze or store in freezer; **deep-fry** fry with fat covering food. □ **deepen** *verb*; **deeply** *adverb*.

**deer** *noun* (*plural* same) 4-hoofed grazing animal, male usually with antlers. □ **deerstalker** cloth peaked cap with ear-flaps.

**deface** /dɪˈfeɪs/ *verb* (**-cing**) disfigure. □ **defacement** *noun*.

**de facto** /deɪ ˈfæktəʊ/ ● *adjective* existing in fact, whether by right or not. ● *adverb* in fact.

**defame** /dɪˈfeɪm/ *verb* (**-ming**) attack good name of. □ **defamation** /defəˈmeɪʃ(ə)n/ *noun*; **defamatory** /-ˈfæm-/ *adjective*.

**default** /dɪˈfɔːlt/ ● *noun* failure to act, appear, or pay; option selected by computer program etc. unless given alternative instruction. ● *verb* fail to fulfil obligations. □ **by default** because of lack of an alternative etc. □ **defaulter** *noun*.

**defeat** /dɪˈfiːt/ ● *verb* overcome in battle, contest, etc.; frustrate, baffle. ● *noun* defeating, being defeated.

**defeatism** *noun* readiness to accept defeat. □ **defeatist** *noun & adjective*.

**defecate** /ˈdiːfɪkeɪt/ *verb* (**-ting**) evacuate the bowels. □ **defecation** *noun*.

**defect** ● *noun* /ˈdiːfekt/ shortcoming; fault. ● *verb* /dɪˈfekt/ desert one's country, cause, etc., for another. □ **defection** *noun*; **defector** *noun*.

**defective** /dɪˈfektɪv/ *adjective* faulty; imperfect. □ **defectiveness** *noun*.

**defence** /dɪˈfens/ *noun* (US **defense**) (means of) defending; justification; defendant's case or counsel; players in defending position; (in *plural*) fortifications. □ **defenceless** *adjective*.

**defend** /dɪˈfend/ *verb* (often + *against*, *from*) resist attack made on; protect; uphold by argument; *Law* conduct defence of; compete to retain (title). □ **defender** *noun*.

**defendant** *noun* person accused or sued in court of law.

**defense** *US* = DEFENCE.

**defensible** /dɪˈfensɪb(ə)l/ *adjective* able to be defended or justified.

**defensive** /dɪˈfensɪv/ *adjective* done or intended for defence; over-reacting to criticism. □ **on the defensive** expecting criticism, ready to defend. □ **defensively** *adverb*; **defensiveness** *noun*.

**defer**[1] /dɪˈfɜː/ *verb* (**-rr-**) postpone. □ **deferment** *noun*.

**defer**[2] /dɪˈfɜː/ *verb* (**-rr-**) (+ *to*) yield or make concessions.

**deference** /ˈdefərəns/ *noun* respectful conduct; compliance with another's wishes. □ **in deference to** out of respect for.

**deferential** /defəˈrenʃ(ə)l/ *adjective* respectful. □ **deferentially** *adverb*.

**defiance** /dɪˈfaɪəns/ *noun* open disobedience; bold resistance. □ **defiant** *adjective*; **defiantly** *adverb*.

**deficiency** /dɪˈfɪʃənsɪ/ *noun* (*plural* **-ies**) being deficient; (usually + *of*) lack or shortage; thing lacking; deficit. □ **deficiency disease** disease caused by lack of essential element in diet.

**deficient** /dɪˈfɪʃ(ə)nt/ *adjective* (often + *in*) incomplete or insufficient.

**deficit** /ˈdefɪsɪt/ *noun* amount by which total falls short; excess of liabilities over assets.

**defile**[1] /dɪˈfaɪl/ *verb* (**-ling**) make dirty; pollute; profane. □ **defilement** *noun*.

**defile**[2] /dɪˈfaɪl/ ● *noun* narrow gorge or pass. ● *verb* (**-ling**) march in file.

**define** /dɪˈfaɪn/ *verb* (**-ning**) give meaning to; describe scope of; outline; mark out the boundary of. □ **definable** *adjective*.

**definite** /ˈdefɪnɪt/ *adjective* certain; clearly defined; precise. □ **definite article** the word (*the* in English) placed before a noun and implying a specific object, person, or idea. □ **definitely** *adverb*.

**definition** /defɪˈnɪʃ(ə)n/ *noun* defining; statement of meaning of word etc.; distinctness in outline.

**definitive** /dɪˈfɪnɪtɪv/ *adjective* decisive, unconditional, final; most authoritative.

**deflate** /dɪˈfleɪt/ *verb* (**-ting**) let air out of (tyre etc.); (cause to) lose confidence; subject (economy) to deflation.

**deflation** *noun* deflating; reduction of money in circulation to combat inflation. □ **deflationary** *adjective*.

**deflect** /dɪˈflekt/ *verb* bend or turn aside from purpose or course; (often + *from*) (cause to) deviate. □ **deflection** *noun*.

**deflower** /diːˈflaʊə/ *verb* deprive of virginity; ravage.

**defoliate** /di:ˈfəʊlɪeɪt/ verb (**-ting**) destroy leaves of. □ **defoliant** noun; **defoliation** noun.

**deforest** /di:ˈfɒrɪst/ verb clear of forests. □ **deforestation** noun.

**deform** /dɪˈfɔ:m/ verb (often as **deformed** adjective) make ugly or misshapen, disfigure. □ **deformation** /di:-/ noun.

**deformity** /dɪˈfɔ:mɪtɪ/ noun (plural **-ies**) being deformed; malformation.

**defraud** /dɪˈfrɔ:d/ verb (often + of) cheat by fraud.

**defray** /dɪˈfreɪ/ verb provide money for (cost). □ **defrayal** noun.

**defrock** /di:ˈfrɒk/ verb deprive (esp. priest) of office.

**defrost** /di:ˈfrɒst/ verb remove frost or ice from; unfreeze; become unfrozen.

**deft** adjective dexterous, skilful. □ **deftly** adverb; **deftness** noun.

**defunct** /dɪˈfʌŋkt/ adjective no longer existing or in use; dead.

**defuse** /di:ˈfju:z/ verb (**-sing**) remove fuse from (bomb etc.); reduce tension in (crisis etc.).

**defy** /dɪˈfaɪ/ verb (**-ies**, **-ied**) resist openly; present insuperable obstacles to; (+ to do) challenge to do or prove something.

**degenerate** /dɪˈdʒenərət/ ● adjective having lost usual or good qualities; immoral. ● noun degenerate person etc. ● verb /-reɪt/ (**-ting**) become degenerate; get worse. □ **degeneracy** noun; **degeneration** noun.

**degrade** /dɪˈgreɪd/ verb (**-ding**) (often as **degrading** adjective) humiliate; dishonour; reduce to lower rank. □ **degradation** /degrəˈdeɪʃ(ə)n/ noun.

**degree** /dɪˈgri:/ noun stage in scale, series, or process; unit of measurement of angle or temperature; extent of burns; academic rank conferred by university etc.

**dehumanize** /di:ˈhju:mənaɪz/ verb (also **-ise**) (**-zing** or **-sing**) remove human qualities from; make impersonal. □ **dehumanization** noun.

**dehydrate** /di:haɪˈdreɪt/ verb (**-ting**) remove water from; make dry; (often as **dehydrated** adjective) deprive of fluids, make very thirsty. □ **dehydration** noun.

**de-ice** /di:ˈaɪs/ verb (**-cing**) remove ice from; prevent formation of ice on. □ **de-icer** noun.

**deify** /ˈdi:ɪfaɪ/ verb (**-ies**, **-ied**) make god or idol of. □ **deification** noun.

**deign** /deɪn/ verb (+ to do) condescend.

**deism** /ˈdi:ɪz(ə)m/ noun reasoned belief in existence of a god. □ **deist** noun; **deistic** /-ˈɪstɪk/ adjective.

**deity** /ˈdeɪtɪ/ noun (plural **-ies**) god or goddess; divine status or nature.

**déjà vu** /deɪʒa: ˈvu:/ noun illusion of having already experienced present situation. [French]

**dejected** /dɪˈdʒektɪd/ adjective sad, depressed. □ **dejectedly** adverb; **dejection** noun.

**delay** /dɪˈleɪ/ ● verb postpone; make or be late. ● noun delaying, being delayed; time lost by this.

**delectable** /dɪˈlektəb(ə)l/ adjective delightful.

**delectation** /di:lekˈteɪʃ(ə)n/ noun enjoyment.

**delegate** ● noun /ˈdelɪgət/ elected representative sent to conference; member of delegation etc. ● verb /ˈdelɪgeɪt/ (**-ting**) (often + to) commit (power etc.) to deputy etc.; entrust (task) to another; send or authorize as representative.

**delegation** /delɪˈgeɪʃ(ə)n/ noun group representing others; delegating, being delegated.

**delete** /dɪˈli:t/ verb (**-ting**) strike out (word etc.). □ **deletion** noun.

**deleterious** /delɪˈtɪərɪəs/ adjective harmful.

**delft** noun (also **delftware**) type of glazed earthenware.

**deli** /ˈdelɪ/ noun (plural **-s**) colloquial delicatessen.

**deliberate** ● adjective /dɪˈlɪbərət/ intentional, considered; unhurried. ● verb /dɪˈlɪbəreɪt/ (**-ting**) think carefully; discuss. □ **deliberately** adverb.

**deliberation** /dɪlɪbəˈreɪʃ(ə)n/ noun careful consideration or slowness.

**deliberative** /dɪˈlɪbərətɪv/ adjective (esp. of assembly etc.) of or for deliberation.

**delicacy** /ˈdelɪkəsɪ/ noun (plural **-ies**) being delicate; choice food.

**delicate** /ˈdelɪkət/ adjective fine in texture, quality, etc.; subtle, hard to discern; susceptible, tender; requiring tact. □ **delicately** adverb.

**delicatessen** /delɪkə'tes(ə)n/ *noun* shop selling esp. exotic cooked meats, cheeses, etc.

**delicious** /dɪ'lɪʃəs/ *adjective* highly enjoyable esp. to taste or smell. □ **deliciously** *adverb*.

**delight** /dɪ'laɪt/ ● *verb* please greatly; (+ *in*) take great pleasure in. ● *noun* great pleasure; thing that delights. □ **delighted** *adjective*; **delightful** *adjective*; **delightfully** *adverb*.

**delimit** /dɪ'lɪmɪt/ *verb* (-**t**-) fix limits or boundary of. □ **delimitation** *noun*.

**delineate** /dɪ'lɪnɪeɪt/ *verb* (-**ting**) portray by drawing or in words. □ **delineation** *noun*.

**delinquent** /dɪ'lɪŋkwənt/ ● *noun* offender. ● *adjective* guilty of misdeed; failing in a duty. □ **delinquency** *noun*.

**deliquesce** /delɪ'kwes/ *verb* (-**cing**) become liquid; dissolve in moisture from the air. □ **deliquescence** *noun*, **deliquescent** *adjective*.

**delirious** /dɪ'lɪrɪəs/ *adjective* affected with delirium; wildly excited. □ **deliriously** *adverb*.

**delirium** /dɪ'lɪrɪəm/ *noun* disordered state of mind, with incoherent speech etc.; wildly excited mood. □ **delirium tremens** /'tri:menz/ psychosis of chronic alcoholism with tremors and hallucinations.

**deliver** /dɪ'lɪvə/ *verb* convey (letters, goods) to destination; (often + *to*) hand over; (often + *from*) save, rescue, set free; assist in giving birth or at birth of; utter (speech); launch or aim (blow etc.); (in full **deliver the goods**) *colloquial* provide or carry out what is required.

**deliverance** *noun* rescuing.

**delivery** /dɪ'lɪvərɪ/ *noun* (*plural* -**ies**) delivering; distribution of letters etc.; thing delivered; childbirth; manner of delivering.

**dell** *noun* small wooded valley.

**delouse** /di:'laʊs/ *verb* (-**sing**) rid of lice.

**delphinium** /del'fɪnɪəm/ *noun* (*plural* -**s**) garden plant with spikes of usually blue flowers.

**delta** /'deltə/ *noun* triangular alluvial tract at mouth of river; fourth letter of Greek alphabet (Δ, δ); fourth-class mark for work etc. □ **delta wing** triangular swept-back wing of aircraft.

**delude** /dɪ'lu:d/ *verb* (-**ding**) deceive, mislead.

**deluge** /'delju:dʒ/ ● *noun* flood; downpour of rain; overwhelming rush. ● *verb* (-**ging**) flood, inundate.

**delusion** /dɪ'lu:ʒ(ə)n/ *noun* false belief or hope. □ **delusive** *adjective*; **delusory** *adjective*.

**de luxe** /də 'lʌks/ *adjective* luxurious; superior; sumptuous.

**delve** *verb* (-**ving**) (often + *in*, *into*) research, search deeply; *poetical* dig.

**demagogue** /'deməgɒg/ *noun* political agitator appealing to emotion. ● **demagogic** /-'gɒgɪk/ *adjective*; **demagogy** /-gɒgɪ/ *noun*.

**demand** /dɪ'mɑ:nd/ ● *noun* insistent and peremptory request; desire for commodity; urgent claim. ● *verb* (often + *of*, *from*, *to do*, *that*) ask for insistently; require; (as **demanding** *adjective*) requiring effort, attention, etc. □ **demand feeding** feeding baby whenever it cries.

**demarcation** /di:mɑ:'keɪʃ(ə)n/ *noun* marking of boundary or limits; trade union practice of restricting job to one union. □ **demarcate** /'di:-/ *verb* (-**ting**).

**demean** /dɪ'mi:n/ *verb* (usually **demean oneself**) lower dignity of.

**demeanour** /dɪ'mi:nə/ *noun* (*US* **demeanor**) bearing; outward behaviour.

**demented** /dɪ'mentɪd/ *adjective* mad.

**dementia** /dɪ'menʃə/ *noun* chronic insanity. □ **dementia praecox** /'pri:-kɒks/ schizophrenia.

**demerara** /demə'reərə/ *noun* light brown cane sugar.

**demerit** /di:'merɪt/ *noun* fault, defect.

**demesne** /dɪ'mi:n/ *noun* landed property, estate; possession (of land) as one's own.

**demigod** /'demɪgɒd/ *noun* partly divine being; *colloquial* godlike person.

**demijohn** /'demɪdʒɒn/ *noun* large wicker-cased bottle.

**demilitarize** /di:'mɪlɪtəraɪz/ *verb* (also -**ise**) (-**zing** or -**sing**) remove army etc. from (zone etc.).

*demi-monde* /'demɪmɒnd/ *noun* class of women of doubtful morality; semi-respectable group. [French]

**demise** /dɪˈmaɪz/ *noun* death; termination.

**demisemiquaver** /ˌdemɪˈsemɪkweɪvə/ *noun Music* note equal to half semiquaver.

**demist** /diːˈmɪst/ *verb* clear mist from (windscreen etc.). □ **demister** *noun*.

**demo** /ˈdeməʊ/ *noun* (*plural* **-s**) *colloquial* demonstration, esp. political.

**demobilize** /diːˈməʊbɪlaɪz/ *verb* (also **-ise**) (**-zing** or **-sing**) disband (troops etc.). □ **demobilization** *noun*.

**democracy** /dɪˈmɒkrəsɪ/ *noun* (*plural* **-ies**) government by the whole population, usually through elected representatives; state so governed.

**democrat** /ˈdeməkræt/ *noun* advocate of democracy; (**Democrat**) member of US Democratic Party.

**democratic** /deməˈkrætɪk/ *adjective* of, like, or practising democracy; favouring social equality. □ **democratically** *adverb*; **democratize** /dɪˈmɒkrətaɪz/ *verb* (also **-ise**) (**-zing** or **-sing**); **democratization** *noun*.

**demography** /dɪˈmɒgrəfɪ/ *noun* study of statistics of birth, deaths, disease, etc. □ **demographic** /deməˈgræfɪk/ *adjective*.

**demolish** /dɪˈmɒlɪʃ/ *verb* pull down (building); destroy; refute; eat up voraciously. □ **demolition** /deməˈlɪʃ(ə)n/ *noun*.

**demon** /ˈdiːmən/ *noun* devil; evil spirit; forceful or skilful performer. □ **demonic** /dɪˈmɒnɪk/ *adjective*.

**demoniac** /dɪˈməʊnɪæk/ ● *adjective* frenzied; supposedly possessed by evil spirit; or of like demons. ● *noun* demoniac person. □ **demoniacal** /diːməˈnaɪək(ə)l/ *adjective*.

**demonology** /diːməˈnɒlədʒɪ/ *noun* study of demons.

**demonstrable** /ˈdemənstrəb(ə)l/ *adjective* able to be shown or proved. □ **demonstrably** *adverb*.

**demonstrate** /ˈdemənstreɪt/ *verb* (**-ting**) show (feelings etc.); describe and explain by experiment etc.; prove truth or existence of; take part in public demonstration.

**demonstration** *noun* demonstrating; (+ *of*) show of feeling etc.; political public march, meeting, etc.; proof by logic, argument, etc.

**demonstrative** /dɪˈmɒnstrətɪv/ *adjective* showing feelings readily; affectionate; *Grammar* indicating person or thing referred to. □ **demonstratively** *adverb*; **demonstrativeness** *noun*.

**demonstrator** /ˈdemənstreɪtə/ *noun* person making or taking part in demonstration.

**demoralize** /diːˈmɒrəlaɪz/ *verb* (also **-ise**) (**-zing** or **-sing**) destroy morale of. □ **demoralization** *noun*.

**demote** /diːˈməʊt/ *verb* (**-ting**) reduce to lower rank or class. □ **demotion** /-ˈməʊʃ(ə)n/ *noun*.

**demotic** /dɪˈmɒtɪk/ ● *noun* colloquial form of a language. ● *adjective* colloquial, vulgar.

**demotivate** /diːˈməʊtɪveɪt/ *verb* (**-ting**) cause to lose motivation. □ **demotivation** *noun*.

**demur** /dɪˈmɜː/ ● *verb* (**-rr-**) (often + *to*, *at*) raise objections. ● *noun* (usually in negative) objection, objecting.

**demure** /dɪˈmjʊə/ *adjective* (**-r**, **-st**) quiet, modest; coy. □ **demurely** *adverb*.

**demystify** /diːˈmɪstɪfaɪ/ *verb* (**-ies**, **-ied**) remove mystery from.

**den** *noun* wild animal's lair; place of crime or vice; small private room.

**denarius** /dɪˈneərɪəs/ *noun* (*plural* **-rii** /-rɪaɪ/) ancient Roman silver coin.

**denationalize** /diːˈnæʃənəlaɪz/ *verb* (also **-ise**) (**-zing** or **-sing**) transfer (industry etc.) from national to private ownership. □ **denationalization** *noun*.

**denature** /diːˈneɪtʃə/ *verb* (**-ring**) change properties of; make (alcohol) unfit for drinking.

**dendrology** /denˈdrɒlədʒɪ/ *noun* study of trees. □ **dendrologist** *noun*.

**denial** /dɪˈnaɪəl/ *noun* denying or refusing.

**denier** /ˈdenjə/ *noun* unit of weight measuring fineness of silk, nylon, etc.

**denigrate** /ˈdenɪgreɪt/ *verb* (**-ting**) sully reputation of. □ **denigration** *noun*; **denigratory** /-ˈgreɪt-/ *adjective*.

**denim** /ˈdenɪm/ *noun* twilled cotton fabric; (in *plural*) jeans etc. made of this.

**denizen** /ˈdenɪz(ə)n/ *noun* (usually + *of*) inhabitant or occupant.

**denominate** /dɪˈnɒmɪneɪt/ *verb* (**-ting**) give name to, describe as, call.

**denomination** *noun* Church or religious sect; class of measurement or money; name, esp. for classification. □ **denominational** *adjective*.

**denominator** *noun* number below line in vulgar fraction; divisor.

**denote** /dɪˈnəʊt/ *verb* (**-ting**) (often + *that*) be sign of; indicate; be name for, signify. □ **denotation** /diːnəˈteɪʃ(ə)n/ *noun*.

**denouement** /deɪˈnuːmɑ̃/ *noun* final resolution in play, novel, etc.

**denounce** /dɪˈnaʊns/ *verb* (**-cing**) accuse publicly; inform against.

**dense** /dens/ *adjective* closely compacted; crowded together; stupid. □ **densely** *adverb*; **denseness** *noun*.

**density** /ˈdensɪtɪ/ *noun* (*plural* **-ies**) denseness; quantity of mass per unit volume; opacity of photographic image.

**dent** ● *noun* depression in surface; noticeable adverse effect. ● *verb* make dent in.

**dental** /ˈdent(ə)l/ *adjective* of teeth or dentistry; (of sound) made with tongue-tip against front teeth. □ **dental floss** thread used to clean between teeth; **dental surgeon** dentist.

**dentate** /ˈdenteɪt/ *adjective* toothed, notched.

**dentifrice** /ˈdentɪfrɪs/ *noun* tooth powder or toothpaste.

**dentine** /ˈdentiːn/ *noun* hard dense tissue forming most of tooth.

**dentist** /ˈdentɪst/ *noun* person qualified to treat, extract, etc., teeth. □ **dentistry** *noun*.

**denture** /ˈdentʃə/ *noun* (usually in *plural*) removable artificial teeth.

**denude** /dɪˈnjuːd/ *verb* (**-ding**) make naked or bare; (+ *of*) strip of (covering etc.). □ **denudation** /diː-/ *noun*.

**denunciation** /dɪnʌnsɪˈeɪʃ(ə)n/ *noun* denouncing.

**deny** /dɪˈnaɪ/ *verb* (**-ies**, **-ied**) declare untrue or non-existent; repudiate; (often + *to*) withhold from; (**deny oneself**) be abstinent.

**deodorant** /diːˈəʊdərənt/ *noun* substance applied to body or sprayed into air to conceal smells.

**deodorize** /diːˈəʊdəraɪz/ *verb* (also **-ise**) (**-zing** or **-sing**) remove smell of. □ **deodorization** *noun*.

**deoxyribonucleic acid** /diːˌɒksɪraɪbəʊnjuːˈkleɪɪk/ see DNA.

**dep.** *abbreviation* departs; deputy.

**depart** /dɪˈpɑːt/ *verb* (often + *from*) go away, leave; (usually + *for*) set out; (usually + *from*) deviate. □ **depart this life** *formal* die.

**departed** ● *adjective* bygone. ● *noun* (**the departed**) *euphemistic* dead person or people.

**department** *noun* separate part of complex whole, esp. branch of administration; division of school etc.; section of large store; area of expertise; French administrative district. □ **department store** shop with many departments. □ **departmental** /diːpɑːtˈment(ə)l/ *adjective*.

**departure** /dɪˈpɑːtʃə/ *noun* departing; new course of action etc.

**depend** /dɪˈpend/ *verb* (often + *on*, *upon*) be controlled or determined by; (+ *on*, *upon*) need, rely on.

**dependable** *adjective* reliable. □ **dependability** *noun*.

**dependant** *noun* person supported, esp. financially, by another.

**dependence** *noun* depending, being dependent; reliance.

**dependency** *noun* (*plural* **-ies**) country etc. controlled by another; dependence (on drugs etc.).

**dependent** *adjective* (usually + *on*) depending; unable to do without (esp. drug); maintained at another's cost; (of clause etc.) subordinate to word etc.

**depict** /dɪˈpɪkt/ *verb* represent in painting etc.; describe. □ **depiction** *noun*.

**depilate** /ˈdepɪleɪt/ *verb* (**-ting**) remove hair from. □ **depilation** *noun*; **depilator** *noun*.

**depilatory** /dɪˈpɪlətərɪ/ ● *adjective* that removes unwanted hair. ● *noun* (*plural* **-ies**) depilatory substance.

**deplete** /dɪˈpliːt/ *verb* (**-ting**) (esp. as **depleted** *adjective*) reduce in numbers, quantity, etc.; exhaust. □ **depletion** *noun*.

**deplorable** /dɪˈplɔːrəb(ə)l/ *adjective* exceedingly bad. □ **deplorably** *adverb*.

**deplore** /dɪˈplɔː/ *verb* (**-ring**) find deplorable; regret.

**deploy** /dɪˈplɔɪ/ *verb* spread out (troops) into line for action; use (arguments etc.) effectively. □ **deployment** *noun*.

**deponent** /dɪ'pəʊnənt/ *noun* person making deposition under oath.

**depopulate** /diː'pɒpjʊleɪt/ *verb* (**-ting**) reduce population of. □ **depopulation** *noun*.

**deport** /dɪ'pɔːt/ *verb* remove forcibly or exile to another country; (**deport oneself**) behave (well, badly, etc.). □ **deportation** /diː-/ *noun*.

**deportee** /diːpɔː'tiː/ *noun* deported person.

**deportment** *noun* bearing, demeanour.

**depose** /dɪ'pəʊz/ *verb* (**-sing**) remove from office; dethrone; (usually + *to*, *that*) testify on oath.

**deposit** /dɪ'pɒzɪt/ ● *noun* money in bank account; thing stored for safe keeping; payment as pledge or first instalment; returnable sum paid on hire of item; layer of accumulated matter. ● *verb* (**-t-**) entrust for keeping; pay or leave as deposit; put or lay down. □ **deposit account** bank account that pays interest but is not usually immediately accessible.

**depositary** /dɪ'pɒzɪtərɪ/ *noun* (*plural* **-ies**) person to whom thing is entrusted.

**deposition** /depə'zɪʃ(ə)n/ *noun* deposing; sworn evidence; giving of this; depositing.

**depositor** *noun* person who deposits money, property, etc.

**depository** /dɪ'pɒzɪtərɪ/ *noun* (*plural* **-ies**) storehouse; store (of wisdom etc.); repository.

**depot** /'depəʊ/ *noun* military storehouse or headquarters; place where vehicles, e.g. buses, are kept; goods yard.

**deprave** /dɪ'preɪv/ *verb* (**-ving**) corrupt morally.

**depravity** /dɪ'prævɪtɪ/ *noun* (*plural* **-ies**) moral corruption; wickedness.

**deprecate** /'deprɪkeɪt/ *verb* (**-ting**) express disapproval of. □ **deprecation** *noun*; **deprecatory** /-'keɪtərɪ/ *adjective*.

■ **Usage** *Deprecate* is often confused with *depreciate*.

**depreciate** /dɪ'priːʃɪeɪt/ *verb* (**-ting**) diminish in value; belittle. □ **depreciatory** /-ʃətərɪ/ *adjective*.

■ **Usage** *Depreciate* is often confused with *deprecate*.

**depreciation** *noun* depreciating; decline in value.

**depredation** /deprɪ'deɪʃ(ə)n/ *noun* (usually in *plural*) despoiling, ravaging.

**depress** /dɪ'pres/ *verb* make dispirited; lower; push down; reduce activity of (esp. trade); (as **depressed** *adjective*) suffering from depression. □ **depressing** *adjective*; **depressingly** *adverb*.

**depressant** ● *adjective* reducing activity, esp. of body function. ● *noun* depressant substance.

**depression** /dɪ'preʃ(ə)n/ *noun* extreme dejection; long slump; lowering of atmospheric pressure; hollow on a surface.

**depressive** /dɪ'presɪv/ ● *adjective* tending towards depression; tending to depress. ● *noun* chronically depressed person.

**deprivation** /deprɪ'veɪʃ(ə)n/ *noun* depriving, being deprived.

**deprive** /dɪ'praɪv/ *verb* (**-ving**) (usually + *of*) prevent from having or enjoying; (as **deprived** *adjective*) lacking what is needed, underprivileged.

**Dept.** *abbreviation* Department.

**depth** *noun* deepness; measure of this; wisdom; intensity; (usually in *plural*) deep, lowest, or inmost part, middle (of winter etc.), abyss, depressed state. □ **depth-charge** bomb exploding under water; **in depth** thoroughly.

**deputation** /depjʊ'teɪʃ(ə)n/ *noun* delegation.

**depute** /dɪ'pjuːt/ *verb* (**-ting**) (often + *to*) delegate (task, authority); authorize as representative.

**deputize** /'depjʊtaɪz/ *verb* (also **-ise**) (**-zing** or **-sing**) (usually + *for*) act as deputy.

**deputy** /'depjʊtɪ/ *noun* (*plural* **-ies**) person appointed to act for another; parliamentary representative in some countries.

**derail** /diː'reɪl/ *verb* cause (train etc.) to leave rails. □ **derailment** *noun*.

**derange** /dɪ'reɪndʒ/ *verb* (**-ging**) (usually as **deranged** *adjective*) make insane. □ **derangement** *noun*.

**Derby** /'dɑːbɪ/ *noun* (*plural* **-ies**) annual horse race at Epsom; similar race or sporting event.

**derelict** /'derɪlɪkt/ ● *adjective* dilapidated; abandoned. ● *noun* vagrant; abandoned property.

**dereliction** /derɪ'lɪkʃ(ə)n/ *noun* (usually + *of*) neglect (of duty etc.).

**deride** /dɪ'raɪd/ *verb* (-**ding**) mock. □ **derision** /-'rɪʒ-/ *noun*.

**de rigueur** /də rɪ'gɜː/ *adjective* required by fashion or etiquette.

**derisive** /dɪ'raɪsɪv/ *adjective* scoffing, ironical. □ **derisively** *adverb*.

**derisory** /dɪ'raɪsərɪ/ *adjective* (of sum offered etc.) ridiculously small; derisive.

**derivation** /derɪ'veɪʃ(ə)n/ *noun* deriving, being derived; origin or formation of word; tracing of this.

**derivative** /dɪ'rɪvətɪv/ ● *adjective* derived, not original. ● *noun* derived word or thing.

**derive** /dɪ'raɪv/ *verb* (-**ving**) (usually + *from*) get or trace from a source; (+ *from*) arise from; (usually + *from*) assert origin and formation of (word etc.).

**dermatitis** /dɜːmə'taɪtɪs/ *noun* inflammation of skin.

**dermatology** /dɜːmə'tɒlədʒɪ/ *noun* study of skin diseases. □ **dermatological** /-tə'lɒdʒ-/ *adjective*; **dermatologist** *noun*.

**derogatory** /dɪ'rɒgətərɪ/ *adjective* disparaging; insulting.

**derrick** /'derɪk/ *noun* crane; framework over oil well etc. for drilling machinery.

**derris** /'derɪs/ *noun* insecticide made from powdered root of tropical plant.

**derv** *noun* diesel fuel for road vehicles.

**dervish** /'dɜːvɪʃ/ *noun* member of Muslim fraternity vowed to poverty and austerity.

**DES** *abbreviation historical* Department of Education and Science.

**descale** /diː'skeɪl/ *verb* (-**ling**) remove scale from.

**descant** /'deskænt/ *noun* harmonizing treble melody above basic hymn tune etc.

**descend** /dɪ'send/ *verb* come, go, or slope down; sink; (usually + *on*) make sudden attack or visit; (+ *to*) stoop (to unworthy act); be passed on by inheritance. □ **be descended from** have as an ancestor.

**descendant** /dɪ'send(ə)nt/ *noun* person etc. descended from another.

**descent** /dɪ'sent/ *noun* act or way of descending; downward slope; lineage; decline, fall; sudden attack.

**describe** /dɪ'skraɪb/ *verb* (-**bing**) state appearance, characteristics, etc. of; (+ *as*) assert to be; draw or move in (curve etc.).

**description** /dɪ'skrɪpʃ(ə)n/ *noun* describing, being described; sort, kind.

**descriptive** /dɪ'skrɪptɪv/ *adjective* describing, esp. vividly.

**descry** /dɪ'skraɪ/ *verb* (-**ies**, -**ied**) catch sight of; discern.

**desecrate** /'desɪkreɪt/ *verb* (-**ting**) violate sanctity of. □ **desecration** *noun*; **desecrator** *noun*.

**desegregate** /diː'segrɪgeɪt/ *verb* (-**ting**) abolish racial segregation in. □ **desegregation** *noun*.

**deselect** /diːsɪ'lekt/ *verb* reject (esp. sitting MP) in favour of another. □ **deselection** *noun*.

**desensitize** /diː'sensɪtaɪz/ *verb* (also -**ise**) (-**zing** or -**sing**) reduce or destroy sensitivity of. □ **desensitization** *noun*.

**desert**[1] /dɪ'zɜːt/ *verb* leave without intending to return; (esp. as **deserted** *adjective*) forsake, abandon; run away from military service. □ **deserter** *noun Military*; **desertion** *noun*.

**desert**[2] /'dezət/ *noun* dry barren, esp. sandy, tract. □ **desert island** (usually tropical) uninhabited island.

**desertification** /dɪzɜːtɪfɪ'keɪʃ(ə)n/ *noun* making or becoming a desert.

**deserts** /dɪ'zɜːts/ *plural noun* deserved reward or punishment.

**deserve** /dɪ'zɜːv/ *verb* (-**ving**) (often + *to do*) be worthy of (reward, punishment); (as **deserving** *adjective*) (often + *of*) worthy (esp. of help, praise, etc.). □ **deservedly** /-vɪdlɪ/ *adverb*.

**desiccate** /'desɪkeɪt/ *verb* (-**ting**) remove moisture from, dry out. □ **desiccation** *noun*.

**desideratum** /dɪzɪdə'rɑːtəm/ *noun* ( *plural* -**ta**) something lacking but desirable.

**design** /dɪ'zaɪn/ ● *noun* (art of producing) sketch or plan for product; lines or shapes as decoration; layout; established form of product; mental plan;

purpose. ● *verb* produce design for; be designer; intend; (as **designing** *adjective*) crafty, scheming. □ **have designs on** plan to take, seduce, etc.

**designate** ● *verb* /'dezɪgneɪt/ (**-ting**) (often + *as*) appoint to office or function; specify; (often + *as*) describe as. ● *adjective* /'dezɪgnət/ (after noun) appointed but not yet installed.

**designation** /dezɪg'neɪʃ(ə)n/ *noun* name or title; designating.

**designedly** /dɪ'zaɪnɪdlɪ/ *adverb* intentionally.

**designer** ● *noun* person who designs e.g. clothing, machines, theatre sets; draughtsman. ● *adjective* bearing label of famous fashion designer; prestigious. □ **designer drug** synthetic equivalent of illegal drug.

**desirable** /dɪ'zaɪərəb(ə)l/ *adjective* worth having or doing; sexually attractive. □ **desirability** *noun*.

**desire** /dɪ'zaɪə/ ● *noun* unsatisfied longing; expression of this; request; thing desired; sexual appetite. ● *verb* (**-ring**) (often + *to do, that*) long for; request.

**desirous** *adjective* (usually + *of*) desiring, wanting; hoping.

**desist** /dɪ'zɪst/ *verb* (often + *from*) cease.

**desk** *noun* piece of furniture with writing surface, and often drawers; counter in hotel, bank, etc.; section of newspaper office.

**desktop** *noun* working surface of desk; computer for use on ordinary desk. □ **desktop publishing** printing with desktop computer and high-quality printer.

**desolate** ● *adjective* /'desələt/ left alone; uninhabited; dreary, forlorn. ● *verb* /'desəleɪt/ (**-ting**) depopulate; devastate; (esp. as **desolated** *adjective*) make wretched. □ **desolately** /-lətlɪ/ *adverb*; **desolation** *noun*.

**despair** /dɪ'speə/ ● *noun* loss or absence of hope; cause of this. ● *verb* (often + *of*) lose all hope.

**despatch** = DISPATCH.

**desperado** /despə'rɑːdəʊ/ *noun* (*plural* **-es** or *US* **-s**) desperate or reckless criminal etc.

**desperate** /'despərət/ *adjective* reckless from despair; violent and lawless; extremely dangerous or serious; (usually

+ *for*) needing or desiring very much. □ **desperately** *adverb*; **desperation** *noun*.

**despicable** /'despɪkəb(ə)l, dɪ'spɪk-/ *adjective* contemptible. □ **despicably** *adverb*.

**despise** /dɪ'spaɪz/ *verb* (**-sing**) regard as inferior or contemptible.

**despite** /dɪ'spaɪt/ *preposition* in spite of.

**despoil** /dɪ'spɔɪl/ *verb* (often + *of*) plunder, rob. □ **despoliation** /-spəʊlɪ-/ *noun*.

**despondent** /dɪ'spɒnd(ə)nt/ *adjective* in low spirits, dejected. □ **despondence** *noun*; **despondency** *noun*; **despondently** *adverb*.

**despot** /'despɒt/ *noun* absolute ruler; tyrant. □ **despotic** /-'spɒt-/ *adjective*.

**despotism** /'despətɪz(ə)m/ *noun* rule by despot.

**dessert** /dɪ'zɜːt/ *noun* sweet course of a meal. □ **dessertspoon** medium-sized spoon for dessert, (also **dessertspoonful**) amount held by this.

**destabilize** /diː'steɪbɪlaɪz/ *verb* (also **-ise**) (**-zing** or **-sing**) make unstable; subvert (esp. foreign government). □ **destabilization** *noun*.

**destination** /destɪ'neɪʃ(ə)n/ *noun* place to which person or thing is going.

**destine** /'destɪn/ *verb* (**-ning**) (often + *to, for, to do*) appoint; preordain; intend. □ **be destined to** be fated to.

**destiny** /'destɪnɪ/ *noun* (*plural* **-ies**) fate; this as power.

**destitute** /'destɪtjuːt/ *adjective* without food or shelter etc.; (usually + *of*) lacking. □ **destitution** /-'tjuː-/ *noun*.

**destroy** /dɪ'strɔɪ/ *verb* pull or break down; kill; make useless; ruin financially; defeat.

**destroyer** /dɪ'strɔɪə/ *noun* fast medium-sized warship; person or thing that destroys.

**destruct** /dɪ'strʌkt/ *verb* destroy or be destroyed deliberately. □ **destructible** *adjective*.

**destruction** *noun* destroying, being destroyed.

**destructive** *adjective* destroying or tending to destroy; negatively critical.

**desuetude** /dɪ'sjuːɪtjuːd/ *noun* formal state of disuse.

**desultory** /ˈdezəltərɪ/ adjective constantly turning from one subject to another; unmethodical.

**detach** /dɪˈtætʃ/ verb (often + from) unfasten and remove; send (troops) on separate mission; (as **detached** adjective) impartial, unemotional, (of house) standing separate. □ **detachable** adjective.

**detachment** noun indifference; impartiality; detaching, being detached; troops etc. detached for special duty.

**detail** /ˈdiːteɪl/ ● noun small separate item or particular; these collectively; minor or intricate decoration; small part of picture etc. shown alone; small military detachment. ● verb give particulars of, relate in detail; (as **detailed** adjective) containing many details, itemized; assign for special duty. □ **in detail** item by item, minutely.

**detain** /dɪˈteɪn/ verb keep waiting, delay; keep in custody. □ **detainment** noun.

**detainee** /diːteɪˈniː/ noun person kept in custody, esp. for political reasons.

**detect** /dɪˈtekt/ verb discover; perceive. □ **detectable** adjective; **detection** noun; **detector** noun.

**detective** /dɪˈtektɪv/ noun person, usually police officer, investigating crime etc.

**détente** /deɪˈtɑːt/ noun relaxing of strained international relations. [French]

**detention** /dɪˈtenʃ(ə)n/ noun detaining, being detained. □ **detention centre** short-term prison for young offenders.

**deter** /dɪˈtɜː/ verb (**-rr-**) (often + from) discourage or prevent, esp. through fear.

**detergent** /dɪˈtɜːdʒ(ə)nt/ ● noun synthetic cleansing agent used with water. ● adjective cleansing.

**deteriorate** /dɪˈtɪərɪəreɪt/ verb (**-ting**) become worse. □ **deterioration** noun.

**determinant** /dɪˈtɜːmɪnənt/ noun decisive factor.

**determinate** /dɪˈtɜːmɪnət/ adjective limited; of definite scope or nature.

**determination** /dɪtɜːmɪˈneɪʃ(ə)n/ noun resolute purpose; deciding, determining.

**determine** /dɪˈtɜːmɪn/ verb (**-ning**) find out precisely; settle, decide; (+ to do) resolve; be decisive factor in.

**determined** adjective resolute. □ **be determined** (usually + to do) be resolved. □ **determinedly** adverb.

**determinism** /dɪˈtɜːmɪnɪz(ə)m/ noun theory that action is determined by forces independent of will. □ **determinist** noun & adjective; **deterministic** /-ˈnɪs-/ adjective.

**deterrent** /dɪˈterənt/ ● adjective deterring. ● noun thing that deters (esp. nuclear weapon).

**detest** /dɪˈtest/ verb hate, loathe. □ **detestation** /diːtesˈteɪʃ(ə)n/ noun.

**detestable** /dɪˈtestəb(ə)l/ adjective hated, loathed.

**dethrone** /diːˈθrəʊn/ verb (**-ning**) remove from throne or high regard. □ **dethronement** noun.

**detonate** /ˈdetəneɪt/ verb (**-ting**) set off (explosive charge); be set off. □ **detonation** noun.

**detonator** noun device for detonating.

**detour** /ˈdiːtʊə/ noun divergence from usual route; roundabout course.

**detoxify** /diːˈtɒksɪfaɪ/ verb (**-ies, -ied**) remove poison or harmful substances from. □ **detoxification** noun.

**detract** /dɪˈtrækt/ verb (+ from) diminish. □ **detraction** noun.

**detractor** noun person who criticizes unfairly.

**detriment** /ˈdetrɪmənt/ noun damage, harm; cause of this. □ **detrimental** /-ˈmen-/ adjective.

**detritus** /dɪˈtraɪtəs/ noun gravel, rock, etc. produced by erosion; debris.

**de trop** /də ˈtrəʊ/ adjective superfluous; in the way. [French]

**deuce**[1] /djuːs/ noun two on dice or cards; Tennis score of 40 all.

**deuce**[2] /djuːs/ noun (**the deuce**) (in exclamations) the Devil.

**deuterium** /djuːˈtɪərɪəm/ noun stable isotope of hydrogen with mass about twice that of the usual isotope.

**Deutschmark** /ˈdɔɪtʃmɑːk/ noun chief monetary unit of Germany.

**devalue** /diːˈvæljuː/ verb (**-ues, -ued, -uing**) reduce value of, esp. currency relative to others or to gold. □ **devaluation** noun.

**devastate** /ˈdevəsteɪt/ verb (**-ting**) lay waste; cause great destruction to; (often as **devastated** adjective) overwhelm with shock or grief. □ **devastation** noun.

**devastating** adjective crushingly effective; overwhelming; colloquial stunningly beautiful. □ **devastatingly** adverb.

**develop** /dɪˈveləp/ verb (**-p-**) make or become fuller, bigger, or more elaborate, etc.; bring or come to active, visible, or mature state; begin to exhibit or suffer from; build on (land); convert (land) to new use; treat (photographic film) to make image visible. □ **developing country** poor or primitive country. □ **developer** noun.

**development** noun developing, being developed; stage of growth or advancement; newly developed thing, event, etc.; area of developed land, esp. with buildings. □ **developmental** /-ˈment(ə)l/ adjective.

**deviant** /ˈdiːvɪənt/ ● adjective deviating from normal, esp. sexual, behaviour. ● noun deviant person or thing. □ **deviance** noun; **deviancy** noun (plural **-ies**).

**deviate** /ˈdiːvɪeɪt/ verb (**-ting**) (often + from) turn aside; diverge. □ **deviation** noun.

**device** /dɪˈvaɪs/ noun thing made or adapted for particular purpose; scheme; trick; heraldic design. □ **leave (person) to his or her own devices** leave (person) to do as he or she wishes.

**devil** /ˈdev(ə)l/ ● noun (usually **the Devil**) Satan; supreme spirit of evil; personified evil; mischievously clever person. ● verb (**-ll-**; US **-l-**) (usually as **devilled** adjective) cook with hot spices. □ **devil-may-care** cheerful and reckless; **devil's advocate** person who tests proposition by arguing against it.

**devilish** ● adjective of or like a devil; mischievous. ● adverb colloquial very. □ **devilishly** adverb.

**devilment** noun mischief; wild spirits.

**devilry** /ˈdevəlrɪ/ noun (plural **-ies**) wickedness; reckless mischief; black magic.

**devious** /ˈdiːvɪəs/ adjective not straightforward, underhand; winding, circuitous. □ **deviously** adverb; **deviousness** noun.

**devise** /dɪˈvaɪz/ verb (**-sing**) plan or invent; Law leave (real estate) by will.

**devoid** /dɪˈvɔɪd/ adjective (+ of) lacking, free from.

**devolution** /diːvəˈluːʃ(ə)n/ noun delegation of power esp. to local or regional administration. □ **devolutionist** noun & adjective.

**devolve** /dɪˈvɒlv/ verb (**-ving**) (+ on, upon, etc.) (of duties etc.) pass or be passed to another; (+ on, to, upon) (of property) descend to.

**devote** /dɪˈvəʊt/ verb (**-ting**) (+ to) apply or give over to (particular activity etc.).

**devoted** adjective loving, loyal. □ **devotedly** adverb.

**devotee** /devəˈtiː/ noun (usually + of) enthusiast, supporter; pious person.

**devotion** /dɪˈvəʊʃ(ə)n/ noun (usually + to) great love or loyalty; worship; (in plural) prayers. □ **devotional** adjective.

**devour** /dɪˈvaʊə/ verb eat voraciously; (of fire etc.) engulf, destroy; take in greedily (with eyes or ears).

**devout** /dɪˈvaʊt/ adjective earnestly religious or sincere. □ **devoutly** adverb; **devoutness** noun.

**dew** noun condensed water vapour forming on cool surfaces at night; similar glistening moisture. □ **dewberry** fruit like blackberry; **dew-claw** rudimentary inner toe on some dogs; **dewdrop** drop of dew; **dew point** temperature at which dew forms. □ **dewy** adjective (**-ier**, **-iest**).

**Dewey Decimal system** /ˈdjuːɪ/ noun system of library classification.

**dewlap** noun fold of loose skin hanging from throat esp. in cattle.

**dexter** /ˈdekstə/ adjective on or of the right-hand side (observer's left) of a heraldic shield etc.

**dexterous** /ˈdekstrəs/ adjective (also **dextrous**) skilful at handling. □ **dexterity** /-ˈter-/ noun; **dexterously** adverb.

**dhal** /dɑːl/ noun (also **dal**) kind of split pulse from India; dish made with this.

**dharma** /ˈdɑːmə/ noun right behaviour; Buddhist truth; Hindu moral law.

**dhoti** /ˈdəʊtɪ/ noun (plural **-s**) loincloth worn by male Hindus.

**dia.** abbreviation diameter.

**diabetes** /daɪəˈbiːtiːz/ noun disease in which sugar and starch are not properly absorbed by the body.

**diabetic** /daɪəˈbetɪk/ ● adjective of or having diabetes; for diabetics. ● noun diabetic person.

**diabolical** /daɪəˈbɒlɪk(ə)l/ adjective (also **diabolic**) of the Devil; inhumanly cruel or wicked; extremely bad. □ **diabolically** adverb.

**diabolism** /daɪˈæbəlɪz(ə)m/ noun worship of the Devil; sorcery.

**diaconate** /daɪˈækənət/ noun office of deacon; deacons collectively.

**diacritic** /daɪəˈkrɪtɪk/ noun sign (e.g. accent) indicating sound or value of letter.

**diacritical** adjective distinguishing.

**diadem** /ˈdaɪədem/ noun crown.

**diaeresis** /daɪˈɪərəsɪs/ noun (plural **-reses** /-siːz/) (US **dieresis**) mark (¨) over vowel to show it is sounded separately.

**diagnose** /daɪəgˈnəʊz/ verb (**-sing**) make diagnosis of.

**diagnosis** /daɪəgˈnəʊsɪs/ noun (plural **-noses** /-siːz/) identification of disease or fault from symptoms etc.

**diagnostic** /daɪəgˈnɒstɪk/ ● adjective of or assisting diagnosis. ● noun symptom.

**diagnostics** noun (treated as plural) programs etc. used to identify faults in computing; (treated as singular) science of diagnosing disease.

**diagonal** /daɪˈægən(ə)l/ ● adjective crossing a straight-sided figure from corner to corner, oblique. ● noun straight line joining two opposite corners. □ **diagonally** adverb.

**diagram** /ˈdaɪəgræm/ noun outline drawing, plan, etc. of thing or process. □ **diagrammatic** /-grəˈmætɪk/ adjective.

**dial** /ˈdaɪəl/ ● noun plate with scale and pointer for measuring; numbered disc on telephone for making connection; face of clock or watch; disc on television etc. for selecting channel etc. ● verb (**-ll-**; US **-l-**) select (telephone number) with dial. □ **dialling tone** sound indicating that telephone caller may dial.

**dialect** /ˈdaɪəlekt/ noun regional form of language (see panel).

**dialectic** /daɪəˈlektɪk/ noun process or situation involving contradictions or conflict of opposites and their resolution; = DIALECTICS.

**dialectical** adjective of dialectic. □ **dialectical materialism** Marxist theory that historical events arise from conflicting economic (and therefore social) conditions. □ **dialectically** adverb.

**dialectics** noun (treated as singular or plural) art of investigating truth by discussion and logic.

**dialogue** /ˈdaɪəlɒg/ noun (US **dialog**) conversation, esp. in a play, novel, etc.; discussion between people of different opinions.

**dialysis** /daɪˈæləsɪs/ noun (plural **-lyses** /-siːz/) separation of particles in liquid by differences in their ability to pass through membrane; purification of blood by this technique.

**diamanté** /dɪəˈmæteɪ/ adjective decorated with synthetic diamonds etc.

**diameter** /daɪˈæmɪtə/ noun straight line passing through centre of circle or sphere to its edges; transverse measurement.

**diametrical** /daɪəˈmetrɪk(ə)l/ adjective (also **diametric**) of or along diameter; (of opposites) absolute. □ **diametrically** adverb.

**diamond** /ˈdaɪəmənd/ noun transparent very hard precious stone; rhombus;

---

## Dialect

Everyone speaks a particular dialect: that is, a particular type of English distinguished by its vocabulary and its grammar. Different parts of the world and different groups of people speak different dialects: for example, Australians may say *arvo* while others say *afternoon*, and a London Cockney may say *I done it* while most other people say *I did it*. A dialect is not the same thing as an accent, which is the way a person pronounces words.

See also the panel at STANDARD ENGLISH.

playing card of suit marked with red rhombuses. □ **diamond jubilee, wedding** 60th (or 75th) anniversary of reign or wedding.

**diapason** /daɪə'peɪz(ə)n/ *noun* compass of musical instrument or voice; either of two main organ stops.

**diaper** /'daɪəpə/ *noun US* baby's nappy.

**diaphanous** /daɪ'æfənəs/ *adjective* (of fabric etc.) light and almost transparent.

**diaphragm** /'daɪəfræm/ *noun* muscular partititon between thorax and abdomen in mammals; = DUTCH CAP; vibrating disc in microphone, telephone, loudspeaker, etc.; device for varying aperture of camera lens.

**diapositive** /daɪə'pɒsɪtɪv/ *noun* positive photographic transparency.

**diarist** /'daɪərɪst/ *noun* person famous for keeping diary.

**diarrhoea** /daɪə'riːə/ *noun* (*US* **diarrhea**) condition of excessively loose and frequent bowel movements.

**diary** /'daɪərɪ/ *noun* (*plural* **-ies**) daily record of events etc.; book for this or for noting future engagements.

**Diaspora** /daɪ'æspərə/ *noun* dispersion of the Jews; the dispersed Jews.

**diatonic** /daɪə'tɒnɪk/ *adjective Music* (of scale etc.) involving only notes of prevailing key.

**diatribe** /'daɪətraɪb/ *noun* forceful verbal criticism.

**diazepam** /daɪ'æzɪpæm/ *noun* tranquillizing drug.

**dibble** /'dɪb(ə)l/ ● *noun* (also **dibber** /'dɪbə/) tool for making small holes for planting. ● *verb* (**-ling**) plant with dibble.

**dice** ● *noun* (*plural* same) small cube marked on each face with 1–6 spots, used in games or gambling; game played with dice. ● *verb* (**-cing**) gamble, take risks; cut into small cubes.

**dicey** /'daɪsɪ/ *adjective* (**dicier, diciest**) *slang* risky, unreliable.

**dichotomy** /daɪ'kɒtəmɪ/ *noun* (*plural* **-ies**) division into two.

**dichromatic** /daɪkrəʊ'mætɪk/ *adjective* of two colours.

**dick**[1] *noun colloquial* (esp. in **clever dick**) person.

**dick**[2] *noun slang* detective.

**dickens** /'dɪkɪnz/ *noun* (**the dickens**) (usually after *how, what, why,* etc.) *colloquial* the Devil.

**dicky** /'dɪkɪ/ ● *noun* (*plural* **-ies**) *colloquial* false shirt-front. ● *adjective* (**-ier, -iest**) *slang* unsound. □ **dicky bow** *colloquial* bow tie.

**dicotyledon** /daɪkɒtɪ'liːd(ə)n/ *noun* flowering plant with two cotyledons. □ **dicotyledonous** *adjective.*

**Dictaphone** /'dɪktəfəʊn/ *noun proprietary term* machine for recording and playing back dictation for typing.

**dictate** ● *verb* /dɪk'teɪt/ (**-ting**) say or read aloud (material to be recorded etc.); state authoritatively; order peremptorily. ● *noun* /'dɪkt-/ (usually in *plural*) authoritative requirement of conscience etc. □ **dictation** *noun.*

**dictator** *noun* usually unelected absolute ruler; omnipotent or domineering person. □ **dictatorship** *noun.*

**dictatorial** /dɪktə'tɔːrɪəl/ *adjective* of or like a dictator; overbearing. □ **dictatorially** *adverb.*

**diction** /'dɪkʃ(ə)n/ *noun* manner of enunciation.

**dictionary** /'dɪkʃənərɪ/ *noun* (*plural* **-ies**) book listing (usually alphabetically) and explaining words of a language, or giving corresponding words in another language; similar book of terms for reference.

**dictum** /'dɪktəm/ *noun* (*plural* **dicta** or **-s**) formal expression of opinion; a saying.

**did** *past of* DO[1].

**didactic** /dɪ'dæktɪk/ *adjective* meant to instruct; (of person) tediously pedantic. □ **didactically** *adverb;* **didacticism** /-sɪz(ə)m/ *noun.*

**diddle** /'dɪd(ə)l/ *verb* (**-ling**) *colloquial* swindle.

**didgeridoo** /dɪdʒərɪ'duː/ *noun* long tubular Australian Aboriginal instrument.

**didn't** /'dɪd(ə)nt/ did not.

**die**[1] /daɪ/ *verb* (**dying** /'daɪɪŋ/) cease to live or exist; fade away; (of fire) go out; (+ *on*) cease to live or function while in the presence or charge of (person); (+ *of, from, with*) be exhausted or tormented. □ **be dying for, to** desire greatly; **die down** become less loud or strong; **die hard** (of habits etc.) die reluctantly; **die-hard** conservative or

**die | digit**

stubborn person; **die off** die one after another; **die out** become extinct, cease to exist.

**die²** /daɪ/ *noun* engraved device for stamping coins etc.; ( *plural* **dice**) a dice. □ **die-casting** process or product of casting from metal moulds.

**dielectric** /daɪˈlektrɪk/ ● *adjective* not conducting electricity. ● *noun* dielectric substance.

**dierisis** *US* = DIAERESIS.

**diesel** /ˈdiːz(ə)l/ *noun* (in full **diesel engine**) internal-combustion engine in which heat produced by compression of air in the cylinder ignites the fuel; vehicle driven by or fuel for diesel engine. □ **diesel-electric** driven by electric current from diesel-engined generator; **diesel oil** petroleum fraction used in diesel engines.

**diet¹** /ˈdaɪət/ ● *noun* habitual food; prescribed food. ● *verb* (**-t-**) keep to special diet, esp. to slim. □ **dietary** *adjective;* **dieter** *noun.*

**diet²** /ˈdaɪət/ *noun* legislative assembly; *historical* congress.

**dietetic** /daɪəˈtetɪk/ *adjective* of diet and nutrition.

**dietetics** *plural noun* (usually treated as *singular*) study of diet and nutrition.

**dietitian** /daɪəˈtɪʃ(ə)n/ *noun* (also **dietician**) expert in dietetics.

**differ** /ˈdɪfə/ *verb* (often + *from*) be unlike or distinguishable; (often + *with*) disagree.

**difference** /ˈdɪfrəns/ *noun* being different or unlike; degree of this; way in which things differ; remainder after subtraction; disagreement. □ **make a** (or **all the, no,** etc.) **difference** have significant (or very significant, no, etc.) effect; **with a difference** having new or unusual feature.

**different** /ˈdɪfrənt/ *adjective* (often + *from, to*) unlike, of another nature; separate, unusual. □ **differently** *adverb.*

■ **Usage** It is safer to use *different from,* but *different to* is common in informal use.

**differential** /dɪfəˈrenʃ(ə)l/ ● *adjective* constituting or relating to specific difference; of, exhibiting, or depending on a difference; *Mathematics* relating to infinitesimal differences. ● *noun* difference, esp. between rates of interest or wage-rates. □ **differential calculus** method of calculating rates of change, maximum or minimum values, etc.; **differential gear** gear enabling wheels to revolve at different speeds on corners.

**differentiate** /dɪfəˈrenʃɪeɪt/ *verb* (**-ting**) constitute difference between or in; distinguish; become different. □ **differentiation** *noun.*

**difficult** /ˈdɪfɪk(ə)lt/ *adjective* hard to do, deal with, or understand; troublesome.

**difficulty** /ˈdɪfɪkəltɪ/ *noun* (*plural* **-ies**) being difficult; difficult thing; hindrance; (often in *plural*) distress, esp. financial.

**diffident** /ˈdɪfɪd(ə)nt/ *adjective* lacking self-confidence. □ **diffidence** *noun;* **diffidently** *adverb.*

**diffract** /dɪˈfrækt/ *verb* break up (beam of light) into series of dark and light bands or coloured spectra. □ **diffraction** *noun;* **diffractive** *adjective.*

**diffuse** ● *verb* /dɪˈfjuːz/ (**-sing**) spread widely or thinly; intermingle. ● *adjective* /dɪˈfjuːs/ spread out; not concentrated; not concise. □ **diffusible** *adjective;* **diffusive** *adjective;* **diffusion** *noun.*

**dig** ● *verb* (**-gg-**; *past & past participle* **dug**) (often + *up*) break up and turn over (ground etc.); make (hole etc.) by digging; (+ *up, out*) obtain by digging, find, discover; excavate; *slang* like, understand; (+ *in, into*) thrust, prod. ● *noun* piece of digging; thrust, poke; *colloquial* pointed remark; archaeological excavation; (in *plural*) lodgings. □ **dig in** *colloquial* begin eating; **dig oneself in** prepare defensive position.

**digest** ● *verb* /daɪˈdʒest/ assimilate (food, information, etc.). ● *noun* /ˈdaɪdʒest/ periodical synopsis of current news etc.; summary, esp. of laws. □ **digestible** *adjective.*

**digestion** *noun* digesting; capacity to digest food.

**digestive** ● *adjective* of or aiding digestion. ● *noun* (in full **digestive biscuit**) wholemeal biscuit.

**digger** /ˈdɪgə/ *noun* person or machine that digs; *colloquial* Australian, New Zealander.

**digit** /ˈdɪdʒɪt/ *noun* any numeral from 0 to 9; finger or toe.

**digital** /'dɪdʒɪt(ə)l/ *adjective* of digits; (of clock, etc.) giving a reading by displayed digits; (of computer) operating on data represented by digits; (of recording) sound-information represented by digits for more reliable transmission. □ **digitally** *adverb*.

**digitalis** /dɪdʒɪ'teɪlɪs/ *noun* heart stimulant made from foxgloves.

**digitize** *verb* (also **ise**) (**-zing** or **-sing**) convert (computer data etc.) into digital form.

**dignified** /'dɪɡnɪfaɪd/ *adjective* having or showing dignity.

**dignify** /'dɪɡnɪfaɪ/ *verb* (**ies**, **-ied**) give dignity to.

**dignitary** /'dɪɡnɪtərɪ/ *noun* (*plural* **-ies**) person of high rank or office.

**dignity** /'dɪɡnɪtɪ/ *noun* (*plural* **-ies**) composed and serious manner; being worthy of respect; high rank or position.

**digraph** /'daɪɡrɑːf/ *noun* two letters representing one sound, e.g. *sh* in *show*, or *ey* in *key*.

■ *Usage Digraph* is sometimes confused with *ligature*, which means 'two or more letters joined'.

**digress** /daɪ'ɡres/ *verb* depart from main subject. □ **digression** *noun*.

**dike** = DYKE.

**dilapidated** /dɪ'læpɪdeɪtɪd/ *adjective* in disrepair. □ **dilapidation** *noun*.

**dilate** /daɪ'leɪt/ *verb* (**-ting**) widen or expand; speak or write at length. □ **dilatation** *noun*; **dilation** *noun*.

**dilatory** /'dɪlətərɪ/ *adjective* given to or causing delay.

**dilemma** /daɪ'lemə/ *noun* situation in which difficult choice has to be made.

■ *Usage Dilemma* is sometimes also used to mean 'a difficult situation or predicament', but this is considered incorrect by some people.

**dilettante** /dɪlɪ'tæntɪ/ *noun* (*plural* **dilettanti** /-tɪ/ or **-s**) dabbler in a subject. □ **dilettantism** *noun*.

**diligent** /'dɪlɪdʒ(ə)nt/ *adjective* hardworking; showing care and effort. □ **diligence** *noun*; **diligently** *adverb*.

**dill** *noun* herb with aromatic leaves and seeds.

**dilly-dally** /dɪlɪ'dælɪ/ *verb* (**-ies**, **-ied**) *colloquial* dawdle, vacillate.

**dilute** /daɪ'ljuːt/ ● *verb* (**-ting**) reduce strength (of fluid) by adding water etc.; weaken in effect. ● *adjective* diluted. □ **dilution** *noun*.

**diluvial** /daɪ'luːvɪəl/ *adjective* of flood, esp. Flood in Genesis.

**dim** ● *adjective* (**-mm-**) not bright; faintly luminous or visible; indistinctly perceived or remembered; (of eyes) not seeing clearly; *colloquial* stupid. ● *verb* (**-mm-**) make or become dim. □ **dimly** *adverb*; **dimness** *noun*.

**dime** *noun US* 10-cent coin.

**dimension** /daɪ'menʃ(ə)n/ *noun* any measurable extent; (in *plural*) size; aspect. □ **dimensional** *adjective*.

**diminish** /dɪ'mɪnɪʃ/ *verb* make or become smaller or less; (often as **diminished** *adjective*) lessen reputation of (person), humiliate.

**diminuendo** /dɪmɪnjʊ'endəʊ/ *Music* ● *noun* (*plural* **-s**) gradual decrease in loudness. ● *adverb & adjective* decreasing in loudness.

**diminution** /dɪmɪ'njuːʃ(ə)n/ *noun* diminishing.

**diminutive** /dɪ'mɪnjʊtɪv/ ● *adjective* tiny; (of word or suffix) implying smallness or affection. ● *noun* diminutive word or suffix.

**dimmer** *noun* (in full **dimmer switch**) device for varying brightness of electric light.

**dimple** /'dɪmp(ə)l/ ● *noun* small hollow, esp. in cheek or chin. ● *verb* (**-ling**) produce dimples (in).

**din** ● *noun* prolonged loud confused noise. ● *verb* (**-nn-**) (+ *into*) force (information) into person by repetition; make din.

**dinar** /'diːnɑː/ *noun* chief monetary unit of (former) Yugoslavia and several Middle Eastern and N. African countries.

**dine** *verb* (**-ning**) eat dinner; (+ *on*, *upon*) eat for dinner; (esp. in **wine and dine**) entertain with food. □ **dining-car** restaurant on train; **dining-room** room in which meals are eaten.

**diner** *noun* person who dines; small dining-room; dining-car; *US* restaurant.

**ding-dong** /ˈdɪŋdɒŋ/ *noun* sound of chimes; *colloquial* heated argument.

**dinghy** /ˈdɪŋgɪ/ *noun* (*plural* **-ies**) small, often inflatable, boat.

**dingle** /ˈdɪŋg(ə)l/ *noun* deep wooded valley.

**dingo** /ˈdɪŋgəʊ/ *noun* (*plural* **-es**) wild Australian dog.

**dingy** /ˈdɪndʒɪ/ *adjective* (**-ier**, **-iest**) drab; dirty-looking. □ **dinginess** *noun*.

**dinkum** /ˈdɪŋkəm/ *adjective & adverb* (in full **fair dinkum**) *Australian & NZ colloquial* genuine(ly), honest(ly).

**dinky** /ˈdɪŋkɪ/ *adjective* (**-ier**, **-iest**) *colloquial* pretty, small and neat.

**dinner** /ˈdɪnə/ *noun* main meal, at midday or in the evening. □ **dinner-dance** formal dinner followed by dancing; **dinner jacket** man's formal evening jacket; **dinner lady** woman who supervises school dinners; **dinner service** set of matching crockery for dinner.

**dinosaur** /ˈdaɪnəsɔː/ *noun* extinct usually large reptile.

**dint** ● *noun* dent. ● *verb* mark with dints. □ **by dint of** by force or means of.

**diocese** /ˈdaɪəsɪs/ *noun* district under bishop's pastoral care. □ **diocesan** /daɪˈɒsɪs(ə)n/ *adjective*.

**diode** /ˈdaɪəʊd/ *noun* semiconductor allowing current in one direction and having two terminals; thermionic valve with two electrodes.

**dioxide** /daɪˈɒksaɪd/ *noun* oxide with two atoms of oxygen.

**Dip.** *abbreviation* Diploma.

**dip** ● *verb* (**-pp-**) put or lower briefly into liquid etc.; immerse; go below a surface or level; decline slightly or briefly; slope or extend downwards; go briefly under water; (+ *into*) look cursorily into (book, subject, etc.); (+ *into*) put (hand etc.) into (container) to take something out, use part of (resources); lower or be lowered, esp. in salute; lower beam of (headlights). ● *noun* dipping, being dipped; liquid for dipping; brief bathe in sea etc.; downward slope or hollow; sauce into which food is dipped. □ **dip-switch** switch for dipping vehicle's headlights.

**diphtheria** /dɪfˈθɪərɪə/ *noun* infectious disease with inflammation of mucous membrane esp. of throat.

**diphthong** /ˈdɪfθɒŋ/ *noun* union of two vowels in one syllable.

**diplodocus** /dɪˈplɒdəkəs/ *noun* (*plural* **-cuses**) huge long-necked plant-eating dinosaur.

**diploma** /dɪˈpləʊmə/ *noun* certificate of educational qualification; document conferring honour, privilege, etc.

**diplomacy** /dɪˈpləʊməsɪ/ *noun* management of international relations; tact.

**diplomat** /ˈdɪpləmæt/ *noun* member of diplomatic service; tactful person.

**diplomatic** /dɪpləˈmætɪk/ *adjective* of or involved in diplomacy; tactful. □ **diplomatic bag** container for dispatching embassy mail; **diplomatic immunity** exemption of foreign diplomatic staff from arrest, taxation, etc.; **diplomatic service** branch of civil service concerned with representing a country abroad. □ **diplomatically** *adverb*.

**diplomatist** /dɪˈpləʊmətɪst/ *noun* diplomat.

**dipper** /ˈdɪpə/ *noun* diving bird; ladle.

**dippy** /ˈdɪpɪ/ *adjective* (**-ier**, **-iest**) *slang* crazy, silly.

**dipsomania** /dɪpsəˈmeɪnɪə/ *noun* alcoholism. □ **dipsomaniac** *noun*.

**dipstick** *noun* rod for measuring depth, esp. of oil in vehicle's engine.

**dipterous** /ˈdɪptərəs/ *adjective* two-winged.

**diptych** /ˈdɪptɪk/ *noun* painted altarpiece on two hinged panels.

**dire** *adjective* dreadful; ominous; *colloquial* very bad; urgent.

**direct** /daɪˈrekt/ ● *adjective* extending or moving in straight line or by shortest route, not crooked or circuitous; straightforward, frank; without intermediaries; complete, greatest possible. ● *adverb* in a direct way; by direct route. ● *verb* control; guide; (+ *to do*, *that*) order; (+ *to*) tell way to (place); address (letter etc.); (+ *at*, *to*, *towards*) point, aim, or turn; supervise acting etc. of (film, play, etc.). □ **direct current** electric current flowing in one direction only; **direct debit** regular debiting of bank account at request of payee; **direct-grant school** school funded by government, not local authority; **direct object** primary object of verbal action (see panel at OBJECT); **direct**

**speech** words actually spoken, not reported (see panel); **direct tax** tax on income, paid directly to government. □ **directness** noun.

**direction** /daɪˈrekʃ(ə)n/ noun directing; (usually in plural) orders, instructions; point to, from, or along which person or thing moves or looks.

**directional** adjective of or indicating direction; sending or receiving radio or sound waves in one direction only.

**directive** /daɪˈrektɪv/ noun order from an authority.

**directly** • adverb at once, without delay; presently; shortly; exactly; in a direct way. • conjunction colloquial as soon as.

**director** noun person who directs, esp. for stage etc. or as member of board of company. □ **director-general** chief executive. □ **directorial** /-ˈtɔː-/ adjective; **directorship** noun.

**directorate** /daɪˈrektərət/ noun board of directors; office of director.

**directory** /daɪˈrektəri/ noun (plural **-ies**) book with list of telephone subscribers, inhabitants of town etc., members of profession, etc. □ **directory enquiries** telephone service providing subscriber's number on request.

**dirge** noun lament for the dead; dreary piece of music.

**dirham** /ˈdɪrəm/ noun monetary unit of Morocco and United Arab Emirates.

**dirigible** /ˈdɪrɪdʒɪb(ə)l/ • adjective that can be steered. • noun dirigible balloon or airship.

**dirk** noun short dagger.

**dirndl** /ˈdɜːnd(ə)l/ noun dress with close-fitting bodice and full skirt; gathered full skirt with tight waistband.

**dirt** noun unclean matter that soils; earth; foul or malicious talk; excrement. □ **dirt cheap** colloquial extremely cheap; **dirt track** racing track with surface of earth or cinders etc.

**dirty** /ˈdɜːtɪ/ • adjective (**-ier, -iest**) soiled, unclean, sordid, obscene; unfair; (of weather) rough; muddy-looking. • adverb very; in a dirty or obscene way. • verb (**-ies, -ied**) make or become dirty. □ **dirty look** colloquial look of disapproval or disgust. □ **dirtiness** noun.

**disability** /dɪsəˈbɪlɪtɪ/ noun (plural **-ies**) permanent physical or mental incapacity; lack of some capacity, preventing action.

**disable** /dɪˈseɪb(ə)l/ verb (**-ling**) deprive of an ability; (often as **disabled** adjective) physically incapacitate. □ **disablement** noun.

---

## Direct Speech

Direct speech is the actual words of a speaker quoted in writing.

**1** In a novel etc., speech punctuation is used for direct speech:
  **a** The words spoken are usually put in quotation marks.
  **b** Each new piece of speech begins with a capital letter.
  **c** Each paragraph within one person's piece of speech begins with quotation marks, but only the last paragraph ends with them.

**2** In a script (the written words of a play, a film, or a radio or television programme):
  **a** The names of speakers are written in the margin in capital letters.
  **b** Each name is followed by a colon.
  **c** Quotation marks are not needed.
  **d** Any instructions about the way the words are spoken or about the scenery or the actions of the speakers (stage directions) are written in the present tense in brackets or italics.

For example:

CHRISTOPHER: [Looks into box.] There's nothing in here.

**disabuse** /dɪsəˈbjuːz/ verb (-sing) (usually + of) free from mistaken idea; disillusion.

**disadvantage** /dɪsədˈvɑːntɪdʒ/ • noun unfavourable condition or circumstance; loss; damage. • verb (-ging) cause disadvantage to. □ **at a disadvantage** in an unfavourable position. □ **disadvantageous** /dɪsædvənˈteɪdʒəs/ adjective.

**disadvantaged** adjective lacking normal opportunities through poverty, disability, etc.

**disaffected** /dɪsəˈfektɪd/ adjective discontented, alienated (esp. politically). □ **disaffection** noun.

**disagree** /dɪsəˈɡriː/ verb (-ees, -eed) (often + with) hold different opinion; not correspond; upset. □ **disagreement** noun.

**disagreeable** adjective unpleasant; bad-tempered. □ **disagreeably** adverb.

**disallow** /dɪsəˈlaʊ/ verb refuse to allow or accept; prohibit.

**disappear** /dɪsəˈpɪə/ verb cease to be visible or in existence or circulation etc.; go missing. □ **disappearance** noun.

**disappoint** /dɪsəˈpɔɪnt/ verb fail to fulfil desire or expectation of; frustrate. □ **disappointing** adjective; **disappointment** noun.

**disapprobation** /dɪsæprəˈbeɪʃ(ə)n/ noun disapproval.

**disapprove** /dɪsəˈpruːv/ verb (-ving) (usually + of) have or express unfavourable opinion. □ **disapproval** noun.

**disarm** /dɪsˈɑːm/ verb deprive of weapons; abandon or reduce one's own weapons; (often as **disarming** adjective) make less hostile, charm, win over. □ **disarmament** noun; **disarmingly** adverb.

**disarrange** /dɪsəˈreɪndʒ/ verb (-ging) put into disorder.

**disarray** /dɪsəˈreɪ/ noun disorder.

**disassociate** /dɪsəˈsəʊʃɪeɪt/ verb (-ting) dissociate. □ **disassociation** noun.

**disaster** /dɪˈzɑːstə/ noun sudden or great misfortune; colloquial complete failure. □ **disastrous** adjective; **disastrously** adverb.

**disavow** /dɪsəˈvaʊ/ verb disclaim knowledge or approval or responsibility for. □ **disavowal** noun.

**disband** /dɪsˈbænd/ verb break up, disperse.

**disbar** /dɪsˈbɑː/ verb (-rr-) deprive of status of barrister. □ **disbarment** noun.

**disbelieve** /dɪsbɪˈliːv/ verb (-ving) refuse to believe; not believe; be sceptical. □ **disbelief** noun; **disbelievingly** adverb.

**disburse** /dɪsˈbɜːs/ verb (-sing) pay out (money). □ **disbursement** noun.

**disc** noun flat thinnish circular object; round flat or apparently flat surface or mark; layer of cartilage between vertebrae; gramophone record; Computing = DISK. □ **disc brake** one using friction of pads against a disc; **disc jockey** presenter of recorded popular music.

**discard** /dɪsˈkɑːd/ verb reject as unwanted; remove or put aside.

**discern** /dɪˈsɜːn/ verb perceive clearly with mind or senses; make out. □ **discernible** adjective.

**discerning** adjective having good judgement or insight. □ **discernment** noun.

**discharge** • verb /dɪsˈtʃɑːdʒ/ (-ging) release, let go; dismiss from office or employment; fire (gun etc.); throw; eject; emit, pour out; pay or perform (debt, duty); relieve (bankrupt) of residual liability; release an electrical charge from; relieve of cargo; unload. • noun /ˈdɪstʃɑːdʒ/ discharging, being discharged; matter or thing discharged; release of electric charge, esp. with spark.

**disciple** /dɪˈsaɪp(ə)l/ noun follower of a teacher or leader, esp. of Christ.

**disciplinarian** /dɪsɪplɪˈneərɪən/ noun enforcer of or believer in strict discipline.

**disciplinary** /dɪsɪˈplɪnərɪ/ adjective of or enforcing discipline.

**discipline** /ˈdɪsɪplɪn/ • noun control or order exercised over people or animals; system of rules for this; training or way of life aimed at self-control or conformity; branch of learning; punishment. • verb (-ning) punish; control by training in obedience.

**disclaim** /dɪsˈkleɪm/ verb disown, deny; renounce legal claim to.

**disclaimer** noun statement disclaiming something.

**disclose** /dɪsˈkləʊz/ verb (-sing) expose, make known, reveal. □ **disclosure** noun.

**disco** /'dɪskəʊ/ noun (plural **-s**) colloquial discothèque.

**discolour** /dɪs'kʌlə/ verb (US **discolor**) cause to change from its usual colour; stain or become stained. □ **discoloration** noun.

**discomfit** /dɪs'kʌmfɪt/ verb (**-t-**) disconcert; baffle; frustrate. □ **discomfiture** noun.

■ Usage *Discomfit* is sometimes confused with *discomfort*.

**discomfort** /dɪs'kʌmfət/ noun lack of comfort; uneasiness of body or mind.

■ Usage As a verb, *discomfort* is sometimes confused with *discomfit*.

**discompose** /dɪskəm'pəʊz/ verb (**-sing**) disturb composure of. □ **discomposure** noun.

**disconcert** /dɪskən'sɜːt/ verb disturb composure of; fluster.

**disconnect** /dɪskə'nekt/ verb break connection of or between; put (apparatus) out of action by disconnecting parts. □ **disconnection** noun.

**disconnected** adjective incoherent and illogical.

**disconsolate** /dɪs'kɒnsələt/ adjective forlorn, unhappy; disappointed. □ **disconsolately** adverb.

**discontent** /dɪskən'tent/ noun dissatisfaction; lack of contentment. ● verb (esp. as **discontented** adjective) make dissatisfied.

**discontinue** /dɪskən'tɪnjuː/ verb (**-ues, -ued, -uing**) (cause to) cease; not go on with (activity).

**discontinuous** /dɪskən'tɪnjʊəs/ adjective lacking continuity; intermittent. □ **discontinuity** /-kɒntɪ'njuːɪtɪ/ noun.

**discord** /'dɪskɔːd/ noun disagreement; strife; harsh noise, clashing sounds; lack of harmony. □ **discordant** /-'kɔːdənt/ adjective.

**discothèque** /'dɪskətek/ noun nightclub etc. where pop records are played for dancing.

**discount** ● noun /'dɪskaʊnt/ amount deducted from normal price. ● verb /dɪs'kaʊnt/ disregard as unreliable or unimportant; deduct amount from (price etc.); give or get present value of (investment certificate which has yet to mature). □ **at a discount** below nominal or usual price.

**discountenance** /dɪs'kaʊntɪnəns/ verb (**-cing**) disconcert; refuse to approve of.

**discourage** /dɪs'kʌrɪdʒ/ verb (**-ging**) reduce confidence or spirits of; dissuade, deter; show disapproval of. □ **discouragement** noun.

**discourse** ● noun /'dɪskɔːs/ conversation; lengthy treatment of theme; lecture, speech. ● verb /dɪs'kɔːs/ (**-sing**) converse; speak or write at length.

**discourteous** /dɪs'kɜːtɪəs/ adjective rude, uncivil. □ **discourteously** adverb; **discourtesy** noun (plural **-ies**).

**discover** /dɪ'skʌvə/ verb find or find out, by effort or chance; be first to find or find out in particular case; find and promote (little-known performer).

**discovery** noun (plural **-ies**) discovering, being discovered; person or thing discovered.

**discredit** /dɪs'kredɪt/ ● verb (**-t-**) cause to be disbelieved; harm good reputation of; refuse to believe. ● noun harm to reputation; cause of this; lack of credibility.

**discreditable** adjective bringing discredit, shameful.

**discreet** /dɪ'skriːt/ adjective (**-er, -est**) tactful, prudent; cautious in speech or action; unobtrusive. □ **discreetly** adverb; **discreetness** noun.

**discrepancy** /dɪ'skrepənsɪ/ noun (plural **-ies**) difference; inconsistency.

**discrete** /dɪ'skriːt/ adjective separate; distinct.

**discretion** /dɪ'skreʃ(ə)n/ noun being discreet; prudence, judgement; freedom or authority to act as one thinks fit. □ **discretionary** adjective.

**discriminate** /dɪ'skrɪmɪneɪt/ verb (**-ting**) (often + between) make or see a distinction; (usually + against, in favour of) treat badly or well, esp. on the basis of race, gender, etc. □ **discriminating** adjective; **discrimination** noun; **discriminatory** /-nətərɪ/ adjective.

**discursive** /dɪs'kɜːsɪv/ adjective rambling, tending to digress.

**discus** /'dɪskəs/ noun (plural **-cuses**) heavy disc thrown in athletic events.

**discuss** /dɪs'kʌs/ verb talk or write about (subject) in detail. □ **discussion** noun.

**disdain** /dɪsˈdeɪn/ ● noun scorn, contempt. ● verb regard with disdain; refrain or refuse out of disdain. □ **disdainful** adjective.

**disease** /dɪˈziːz/ noun unhealthy condition of organism or part of organism; (specific) disorder or illness. □ **diseased** adjective.

**disembark** /dɪsɪmˈbɑːk/ verb put or go ashore; get off aircraft, bus, etc. □ **disembarkation** /-embə-/ noun.

**disembarrass** /dɪsɪmˈbærəs/ verb (usually + of) rid or relieve (of a load etc.); free from embarrassment. □ **disembarrassment** noun.

**disembodied** /dɪsɪmˈbɒdɪd/ adjective (of soul etc.) separated from body or concrete form; without a body.

**disembowel** /dɪsɪmˈbaʊəl/ verb (**-ll-**; US **-l-**) remove entrails of. □ **disembowelment** noun.

**disenchant** /dɪsɪnˈtʃɑːnt/ verb disillusion. □ **disenchantment** noun.

**disencumber** /dɪsɪnˈkʌmbə/ verb free from encumbrance.

**disenfranchise** /dɪsɪnˈfræntʃaɪz/ verb (**-sing**) deprive of right to vote, of citizen's rights, or of franchise held. □ **disenfranchisement** noun.

**disengage** /dɪsɪnˈɡeɪdʒ/ verb (**-ging**) detach; loosen; release; remove (troops) from battle etc.; become detached. □ **disengaged** adjective) at leisure, uncommitted. □ **disengagement** noun.

**disentangle** /dɪsɪnˈtæŋɡ(ə)l/ verb (**-ling**) free or become free of tangles or complications. □ **disentanglement** noun.

**disestablish** /dɪsɪˈstæblɪʃ/ verb deprive (Church) of state support; end the establishment of. □ **disestablishment** noun.

**disfavour** /dɪsˈfeɪvə/ noun (US **disfavor**) dislike; disapproval; being disliked.

**disfigure** /dɪsˈfɪɡə/ verb (**-ring**) spoil appearance of. □ **disfigurement** noun.

**disgorge** /dɪsˈɡɔːdʒ/ verb (**-ging**) eject from throat; pour forth (food, fluid, etc.).

**disgrace** /dɪsˈɡreɪs/ ● noun shame, ignominy; shameful or very bad person or thing. ● verb (**-cing**) bring shame or discredit on; dismiss from position of honour or favour.

**disgraceful** adjective causing disgrace; shameful. □ **disgracefully** adverb.

**disgruntled** /dɪsˈɡrʌnt(ə)ld/ adjective discontented; sulky.

**disguise** /dɪsˈɡaɪz/ ● verb (**-sing**) conceal identity of, make unrecognizable; conceal. ● noun costume, make-up, etc. used to disguise; action, manner, etc. used to deceive; disguised condition.

**disgust** /dɪsˈɡʌst/ ● noun strong aversion; repugnance. ● verb cause disgust in. □ **disgusting** adjective; **disgustingly** adverb.

**dish** ● noun shallow flat-bottomed container for food; food served in dish; particular kind of food; (in plural) crockery etc. to be washed etc. after a meal; dish-shaped object or cavity; colloquial sexually attractive person. ● verb make dish-shaped; colloquial outmanoeuvre, frustrate. □ **dish out** colloquial distribute, allocate; **dish up** (prepare to) serve meal.

**disharmony** /dɪsˈhɑːmənɪ/ noun lack of harmony, discord.

**dishearten** /dɪsˈhɑːt(ə)n/ verb cause to lose courage or confidence.

**dishevelled** /dɪˈʃev(ə)ld/ adjective (US **disheveled**) ruffled, untidy.

**dishonest** /dɪsˈɒnɪst/ adjective fraudulent; insincere. □ **dishonestly** adverb; **dishonesty** noun.

**dishonour** /dɪsˈɒnə/ (US **dishonor**) ● noun loss of honour, disgrace; cause of this. ● verb disgrace (person, family, etc.); refuse to pay (cheque etc.).

**dishonourable** adjective (US **dishonorable**) causing disgrace; ignominious; unprincipled. □ **dishonourably** adverb.

**dishy** adjective (**-ier**, **-iest**) colloquial sexually attractive.

**disillusion** /dɪsɪˈluːʒ(ə)n/ ● verb free from illusion or mistaken belief, esp. disappointingly. ● noun disillusioned state. □ **disillusionment** noun.

**disincentive** /dɪsɪnˈsentɪv/ noun thing that discourages, esp. from a particular line of action.

**disincline** /dɪsɪnˈklaɪn/ verb (**-ning**) (usually as **disinclined** adjective) make unwilling. □ **disinclination** /-klɪˈneɪ-/ noun.

**disinfect** /dɪsɪnˈfekt/ verb cleanse of infection. □ **disinfection** noun.

**disinfectant** ● *noun* substance that destroys germs etc. ● *adjective* disinfecting.

**disinformation** /dɪsɪnfə'meɪʃ(ə)n/ *noun* false information, propaganda.

**disingenuous** /dɪsɪn'dʒenjʊəs/ *adjective* insincere; not candid. □ **disingenuously** *adverb*; **disingenuousness** *noun*.

**disinherit** /dɪsɪn'herɪt/ *verb* (-t-) deprive of right to inherit; reject as one's heir. □ **disinheritance** *noun*.

**disintegrate** /dɪ'sɪntɪɡreɪt/ *verb* (-ting) separate into component parts; break up; *colloquial* break down, esp. mentally. □ **disintegration** *noun*.

**disinter** /dɪsɪn'tɜː/ *verb* (-rr-) dig up (esp. corpse). □ **disinterment** *noun*.

**disinterested** /dɪ'sɪntrɪstɪd/ *adjective* impartial; uninterested. □ **disinterest** *noun*; **disinterestedly** *adverb*.

■ **Usage** The use of *disinterested* to mean 'uninterested' is common in informal use but is widely considered incorrect. The use of the noun *disinterest* to mean 'lack of interest' is also objected to, but it is rarely used in any other sense and the alternative *uninterest* is rare.

**disjointed** /dɪs'dʒɔɪntɪd/ *adjective* disconnected, incoherent.

**disjunction** /dɪs'dʒʌŋkʃ(ə)n/ *noun* separation.

**disjunctive** /dɪs'dʒʌŋktɪv/ *adjective* involving separation; (of a conjunction) expressing alternative.

**disk** *noun* flat circular computer storage device. □ **disk drive** mechanism for rotating disk and reading or writing data from or to it.

**dislike** /dɪs'laɪk/ ● *verb* (-king) have aversion to, not like. ● *noun* feeling of repugnance or not liking; object of this.

**dislocate** /'dɪsləkeɪt/ *verb* (-ting) disturb normal connection of (esp. a joint in the body); disrupt. □ **dislocation** *noun*.

**dislodge** /dɪs'lɒdʒ/ *verb* (-ging) disturb or move. □ **dislodgement** *noun*.

**disloyal** /dɪs'lɔɪəl/ *adjective* unfaithful; lacking loyalty. □ **disloyalty** *noun*.

**dismal** /'dɪzm(ə)l/ *adjective* gloomy; miserable; dreary; *colloquial* feeble, inept. □ **dismally** *adverb*.

**dismantle** /dɪs'mænt(ə)l/ *verb* (-ling) pull down, take to pieces; deprive of defences, equipment, etc.

**dismay** /dɪs'meɪ/ ● *noun* feeling of intense disappointment and discouragement. ● *verb* affect with dismay.

**dismember** /dɪs'membə/ *verb* remove limbs from; partition (country etc.). □ **dismemberment** *noun*.

**dismiss** /dɪs'mɪs/ *verb* send away; disband; allow to go; terminate employment of, esp. dishonourably; put out of one's thoughts; *Law* refuse further hearing to; *Cricket* put (batsman, side) out. □ **dismissal** *noun*.

**dismissive** *adjective* dismissing rudely or casually; disdainful. □ **dismissively** *adverb*.

**dismount** /dɪs'maʊnt/ *verb* get off or down from cycle or horseback etc.; remove (thing) from mounting.

**disobedient** /dɪsə'biːdɪənt/ *adjective* disobeying; rebellious. □ **disobedience** *noun*; **disobediently** *adverb*.

**disobey** /dɪsə'beɪ/ *verb* fail or refuse to obey.

**disoblige** /dɪsə'blaɪdʒ/ *verb* (-ging) refuse to help or cooperate with (person).

**disorder** /dɪs'ɔːdə/ *noun* confusion; tumult, riot; bodily or mental ailment. □ **disordered** *adjective*.

**disorderly** *adjective* untidy; confused; riotous.

**disorganize** /dɪs'ɔːɡənaɪz/ *verb* (also **-ise**) (-zing or -sing) throw into confusion or disorder; (as **disorganized** *adjective*) badly organized, untidy. □ **disorganization** *noun*.

**disorientate** /dɪs'ɔːrɪənteɪt/ *verb* (also **disorient**) (-ting) confuse (person) as to his or her bearings. □ **disorientation** *noun*.

**disown** /dɪs'əʊn/ *verb* deny or give up any connection with; repudiate.

**disparage** /dɪ'spærɪdʒ/ *verb* (-ging) criticize; belittle. □ **disparagement** *noun*.

**disparate** /'dɪspərət/ *adjective* essentially different, unrelated.

**disparity** /dɪ'spærɪtɪ/ *noun* (plural -ies) inequality, difference; incongruity.

**dispassionate** /dɪ'spæʃənət/ *adjective* free from emotion; impartial. □ **dispassionately** *adverb*.

**dispatch** /dɪ'spætʃ/ (also **despatch**) ● *verb* send off; perform (task etc.) promptly; kill; *colloquial* eat (food) quickly. ● *noun* dispatching, being dispatched; official written message, esp. military or political; promptness, efficiency. □ **dispatch box** case for esp. parliamentary documents; **dispatch rider** motorcyclist etc. carrying messages.

**dispel** /dɪˈspel/ *verb* (**-ll-**) drive away (esp. unwanted ideas or feelings); scatter.

**dispensable** /dɪˈspensəb(ə)l/ *adjective* that can be dispensed with.

**dispensary** /dɪˈspensərɪ/ *noun* (*plural* **-ies**) place where medicines etc. are dispensed.

**dispensation** /ˌdɪspenˈseɪʃ(ə)n/ *noun* distributing, dispensing; exemption from penalty, rule, etc.; ordering or management, esp. of world by Providence.

**dispense** /dɪˈspens/ *verb* (**-sing**) distribute; administer; make up and give out (medicine); (+ *with*) do without, make unnecessary.

**dispenser** *noun* person who dispenses something; device that dispenses selected amount at a time.

**disperse** /dɪˈspɜːs/ *verb* (**-sing**) go or send widely or in different directions, scatter; station at different points; disseminate; separate (light) into coloured constituents. □ **dispersal** *noun*, **dispersion** *noun*.

**dispirit** /dɪˈspɪrɪt/ *verb* (esp. as **dispiriting, dispirited** *adjectives*) make despondent.

**displace** /dɪsˈpleɪs/ *verb* (**-cing**) move from its place; remove from office; oust, take the place of. □ **displaced person** refugee in war etc. or from persecution.

**displacement** *noun* displacing, being displaced; amount of fluid displaced by object floating or immersed in it.

**display** /dɪˈspleɪ/ ● *verb* show; exhibit. ● *noun* displaying; exhibition; ostentation; image shown on a visual display unit etc.

**displease** /dɪsˈpliːz/ *verb* (**-sing**) offend; make angry or upset. □ **displeasure** /-ˈpleʒə/ *noun*.

**disport** /dɪˈspɔːt/ *verb* (also **disport oneself**) frolic, enjoy oneself.

**disposable** *adjective* that can be disposed of; designed to be discarded after one use.

**disposal** *noun* disposing of. □ **at one's disposal** available.

**dispose** /dɪˈspəʊz/ *verb* (**-sing**) (usually + *to, to do*) (usually in *passive*) incline, make willing; (in *passive*) tend; arrange suitably; (as **disposed** *adjective*) having a specified inclination; determine events. □ **dispose of** get rid of, deal with, finish.

**disposition** /ˌdɪspəˈzɪʃ(ə)n/ *noun* natural tendency; temperament; arrangement (of parts etc.).

**dispossess** /ˌdɪspəˈzes/ *verb* (usually + *of*) (esp. as **dispossessed** *adjective*) deprive; oust, dislodge. □ **dispossession** *noun*.

**disproof** /dɪsˈpruːf/ *noun* refutation.

**disproportion** /ˌdɪsprəˈpɔːʃ(ə)n/ *noun* lack of proportion.

**disproportionate** *adjective* out of proportion; relatively too large or too small. □ **disproportionately** *adverb*.

**disprove** /dɪsˈpruːv/ *verb* (**-ving**) prove (theory etc.) false.

**disputable** *adjective* open to question.

**disputant** *noun* person in dispute.

**disputation** /ˌdɪspjuːˈteɪʃ(ə)n/ *noun* debate, esp. formal; argument, controversy.

**disputatious** /ˌdɪspjuːˈteɪʃəs/ *adjective* argumentative.

**dispute** /dɪˈspjuːt/ ● *verb* (**-ting**) hold debate; quarrel; question truth or validity of; contend for; resist. ● *noun* controversy, debate; quarrel; disagreement leading to industrial action.

**disqualify** /dɪsˈkwɒlɪfaɪ/ *verb* (**-ies, -ied**) make or pronounce (competitor, applicant, etc.) unfit or ineligible. □ **disqualification** *noun*.

**disquiet** /dɪsˈkwaɪət/ ● *verb* make anxious. ● *noun* uneasiness, anxiety. □ **disquietude** *noun*.

**disquisition** /ˌdɪskwɪˈzɪʃ(ə)n/ *noun* discursive treatise or discourse.

**disregard** /ˌdɪsrɪˈɡɑːd/ ● *verb* ignore, treat as unimportant. ● *noun* indifference, neglect.

**disrepair** /ˌdɪsrɪˈpeə/ *noun* bad condition due to lack of repairs.

**disreputable** /dɪsˈrepjʊtəb(ə)l/ *adjective* having a bad reputation; not respectable. □ **disreputably** *adverb*.

**disrepute** /ˌdɪsrɪˈpjuːt/ noun lack of good reputation; discredit.

**disrespect** /ˌdɪsrɪˈspekt/ noun lack of respect. □ **disrespectful** adjective.

**disrobe** /dɪsˈrəʊb/ verb (**-bing**) literary undress.

**disrupt** /dɪsˈrʌpt/ verb interrupt continuity of; bring disorder to; break (thing) apart. □ **disruption** noun; **disruptive** adjective.

**dissatisfy** /dɪsˈsætɪsfaɪ/ verb (**-ies, -ied**) (usually as **dissatisfied** adjective; often + with) fail to satisfy; make discontented. □ **dissatisfaction** /-ˈfæk-/ noun.

**dissect** /dɪˈsekt/ verb cut in pieces, esp. for examination or post-mortem; analyse or criticize in detail. □ **dissection** noun.

■ **Usage** Dissect is often wrongly pronounced /daɪˈsekt/ (and sometimes written with only one s) because of confusion with bisect.

**dissemble** /dɪˈsemb(ə)l/ verb (**-ling**) be hypocritical or insincere; conceal or disguise (a feeling, intention, etc.).

**disseminate** /dɪˈsemɪneɪt/ verb (**-ting**) scatter about, spread (esp. ideas) widely. □ **dissemination** noun.

**dissension** /dɪˈsenʃ(ə)n/ noun angry disagreement.

**dissent** /dɪˈsent/ ● verb (often + from) disagree, esp. openly; differ, esp. from established or official opinion. ● noun such difference; expression of this.

**dissenter** noun person who dissents; (**Dissenter**) Protestant dissenting from Church of England.

**dissentient** /dɪˈsenʃ(ə)nt/ ● adjective disagreeing with the established or official view. ● noun person who dissents.

**dissertation** /ˌdɪsəˈteɪʃ(ə)n/ noun detailed discourse, esp. as submitted for academic degree.

**disservice** /dɪsˈsɜːvɪs/ noun harmful action.

**dissident** /ˈdɪsɪd(ə)nt/ ● adjective disagreeing, esp. with established government. ● noun dissident person.

**dissimilar** /dɪˈsɪmɪlə/ adjective not similar. □ **dissimilarity** /-ˈlærɪtɪ/ noun (plural **-ies**).

**dissimulate** /dɪˈsɪmjʊleɪt/ verb (**-ting**) dissemble. □ **dissimulation** noun.

**dissipate** /ˈdɪsɪpeɪt/ verb (**-ting**) dispel, disperse; squander; (as **dissipated** adjective) dissolute.

**dissipation** noun dissolute way of life; dissipating, being dissipated.

**dissociate** /dɪˈsəʊʃɪeɪt/ verb (**-ting**) disconnect or separate; become disconnected; (**dissociate oneself from**) declare oneself unconnected with. □ **dissociation** noun.

**dissolute** /ˈdɪsəluːt/ adjective lax in morals, licentious.

**dissolution** /ˌdɪsəˈluːʃ(ə)n/ noun dissolving, being dissolved; dismissal or dispersal of assembly, esp. parliament; breaking up, abolition (of institution); death.

**dissolve** /dɪˈzɒlv/ verb (**-ving**) make or become liquid, esp. by immersion or dispersion in liquid; (cause to) disappear gradually; dismiss (assembly); put an end to, annul; (often + in, into) be overcome (by tears, laughter, etc.).

**dissonant** /ˈdɪsənənt/ adjective discordant, harsh-toned; incongruous. □ **dissonance** noun.

**dissuade** /dɪˈsweɪd/ verb (**-ding**) (often + from) discourage, persuade against. □ **dissuasion** /-ˈsweɪʒ(ə)n/ noun.

**distaff** /ˈdɪstɑːf/ noun cleft stick holding wool etc. for spinning by hand. □ **distaff side** female branch of family.

**distance** /ˈdɪst(ə)ns/ ● noun being far off; remoteness; space between two points; distant point; aloofness, reserve; remoter field of vision. ● verb (**-cing**) place or cause to seem far off; leave behind in race etc. □ **at a distance** far off; **keep one's distance** remain aloof.

**distant** adjective at specified distance; remote in space, time, relationship, etc.; aloof; abstracted; faint. □ **distantly** adverb.

**distaste** /dɪsˈteɪst/ noun (usually + for) dislike; aversion. □ **distasteful** adjective.

**distemper**[1] /dɪsˈtempə/ ● noun paint for walls, using glue etc. as base. ● verb paint with distemper.

**distemper**[2] /dɪsˈtempə/ noun catarrhal disease of dogs etc.

**distend** /dɪˈstend/ verb swell out by pressure from within. □ **distension** /-ˈsten-/ noun.

**distich** /ˈdɪstɪk/ noun verse couplet.

**distil** /dɪˈstɪl/ *verb* (*US* **distill**) (**-ll-**) purify or extract essence from (substance) by vaporizing and condensing it and collecting remaining liquid; extract gist of (idea etc.); make (whisky, essence, etc.) by distilling. □ **distillation** *noun.*

**distiller** *noun* person who distils, esp. alcoholic liquor.

**distillery** *noun* (*plural* **-ies**) factory etc. for distilling alcoholic liquor.

**distinct** /dɪˈstɪŋkt/ *adjective* (often + *from*) separate, different in quality or kind; clearly perceptible; definite, decided. □ **distinctly** *adverb.*

**distinction** /dɪˈstɪŋkʃ(ə)n/ *noun* discriminating, distinguishing; difference between things; thing that differentiates; special consideration or honour; excellence; mark of honour.

**distinctive** *adjective* distinguishing, characteristic. □ **distinctively** *adverb.* **distinctiveness** *noun.*

**distingué** /dɪˈstæŋɡeɪ/ *adjective* having distinguished air, manners, etc. [French]

**distinguish** /dɪˈstɪŋɡwɪʃ/ *verb* (often + *from, between*) see or draw distinctions; characterize; make out by listening or looking etc.; (usually **distinguish oneself**; often + *by*) make prominent. □ **distinguishable** *adjective.*

**distinguished** *adjective* eminent, famous; dignified.

**distort** /dɪˈstɔːt/ *verb* pull or twist out of shape; misrepresent (facts etc.); transmit (sound) inaccurately. □ **distortion** *noun.*

**distract** /dɪˈstrækt/ *verb* (often + *from*) draw away attention of; bewilder; (as **distracted** *adjective*) confused, mad, or angry; amuse, esp. to divert from pain etc.

**distraction** /dɪˈstrækʃ(ə)n/ *noun* distracting, being distracted; thing which distracts; amusement, relaxation; mental confusion; frenzy, madness.

**distrain** /dɪˈstreɪn/ *verb* (usually + *upon*) impose distraint (on person, goods, etc.).

**distraint** /dɪˈstreɪnt/ *noun* seizure of goods to enforce payment.

**distrait** /dɪˈstreɪ/ *adjective* inattentive; distraught. [French]

**distraught** /dɪˈstrɔːt/ *adjective* distracted with worry, fear, etc.; very agitated.

**distress** /dɪˈstres/ ● *noun* suffering caused by pain, grief, anxiety, etc.; poverty; *Law* distraint. ● *verb* cause distress to; make unhappy. □ **distressed** *adjective;* **distressing** *adjective.*

**distribute** /dɪˈstrɪbjuːt/ *verb* (**-ting**) give shares of; deal out; spread about; put at different points; arrange, classify. □ **distribution** /-ˈbjuː-/ *noun;* **distributive** *adjective.*

■ Usage  *Distribute* is often pronounced /ˈdɪstrɪbjuːt/ (with the stress on the *dis-*), but this is considered incorrect by some people.

**distributor** *noun* agent who supplies goods; device in internal-combustion engine for passing current to each spark plug in turn.

**district** /ˈdɪstrɪkt/ *noun* region; administrative division. □ **district attorney** (in the US) public prosecutor of district; **district nurse** nurse who makes home visits in an area.

**distrust** /dɪsˈtrʌst/ ● *noun* lack of trust; suspicion. ● *verb* have no confidence in. □ **distrustful** *adjective.*

**disturb** /dɪˈstɜːb/ *verb* break rest or quiet of; worry; disorganize; (as **disturbed** *adjective*) emotionally or mentally unstable.

**disturbance** *noun* disturbing, being disturbed; tumult, disorder, agitation.

**disunion** /dɪsˈjuːnɪən/ *noun* separation; lack of union.

**disunite** /dɪsjuːˈnaɪt/ *verb* (**-ting**) separate; divide. □ **disunity** /-ˈjuː-/ *noun.*

**disuse** /dɪsˈjuːs/ *noun* state of no longer being used.

**disused** /dɪsˈjuːzd/ *adjective* no longer in use.

**disyllable** /daɪˈsɪləb(ə)l/ *noun* word or metrical foot of two syllables. □ **disyllabic** /-ˈlæb-/ *adjective.*

**ditch** ● *noun* long narrow excavation esp. for drainage or as boundary. ● *verb* make or repair ditches; *slang* abandon, discard.

**dither** /ˈdɪðə/ ● *verb* hesitate; be indecisive; tremble, quiver. ● *noun* *colloquial* state of agitation or hesitation. □ **ditherer** *noun;* **dithery** *adjective.*

**dithyramb** /ˈdɪθɪræm/ noun ancient Greek wild choral hymn; passionate or inflated poem etc. □ **dithyrambic** /-ˈræmbɪk/ adjective.

**ditto** /ˈdɪtəʊ/ noun (plural -s) the aforesaid, the same (in accounts, lists, etc., or colloquial in speech).

**ditty** /ˈdɪtɪ/ noun (plural -ies) short simple song.

**diuretic** /daɪjʊˈretɪk/ • adjective causing increased output of urine. • noun diuretic drug.

**diurnal** /daɪˈɜːn(ə)l/ adjective in or of day; daily; occupying one day.

**diva** /ˈdiːvə/ noun (plural -s) great woman opera singer.

**divan** /dɪˈvæn/ noun low couch or bed without back or ends.

**dive** • verb (-ving) plunge head foremost into water; (of aircraft) descend fast and steeply; (of submarine or diver) submerge; go deeper; (+ into) colloquial put one's hand into. • noun act of diving; plunge; colloquial disreputable nightclub, bar, etc. □ **dive-bomb** bomb (target) from diving aircraft; **diving board** elevated board for diving from.

**diver** noun person who dives, esp. one who works under water; diving bird.

**diverge** /daɪˈvɜːdʒ/ verb (-ging) (often + from) depart from set course; (of opinions etc.) differ; take different courses; spread outward from central point. □ **divergence** noun; **divergent** adjective.

**divers** /ˈdaɪvəːz/ adjective archaic various, several.

**diverse** /daɪˈvɜːs/ adjective varied.

**diversify** /daɪˈvɜːsɪfaɪ/ verb (-ies, -ied) make diverse; vary; spread (investment) over several enterprises; (often + into) expand range of products. □ **diversification** noun.

**diversion** /daɪˈvɜːʃ(ə)n/ noun diverting, being diverted; recreation, pastime; alternative route when road is temporarily closed; stratagem for diverting attention. □ **diversionary** adjective.

**diversity** /daɪˈvɜːsɪtɪ/ noun variety.

**divert** /daɪˈvɜːt/ verb turn aside; deflect; distract (attention); (often as **diverting** adjective) entertain, amuse.

**divest** /daɪˈvest/ verb (usually + of) unclothe, strip; deprive, rid.

**divide** /dɪˈvaɪd/ • verb (-ding) (often + in, into) separate into parts; split or break up; (often + out) distribute, deal, share; separate (one thing) from another; classify into parts or groups; cause to disagree; (+ by) find how many times number contains another; (+ into) be contained exact number of times; (of parliament) vote (by members entering either of two lobbies). • noun dividing line; watershed.

**dividend** /ˈdɪvɪdend/ noun share of profits paid to shareholders, football pools winners, etc.; number to be divided.

**divider** noun screen etc. dividing room; (in plural) measuring compasses.

**divination** /dɪvɪˈneɪʃ(ə)n/ noun supposed foreseeing of the future, using special technique.

**divine** /dɪˈvaɪn/ • adjective (-r, -st) of, from, or like God or a god; sacred; colloquial excellent. • verb (-ning) discover by intuition or guessing; foresee; practise divination. • noun theologian. □ **divining-rod** dowser's forked twig. □ **divinely** adverb.

**diviner** noun practitioner of divination; dowser.

**divinity** /dɪˈvɪnɪtɪ/ noun (plural -ies) being divine; god; theology.

**divisible** /dɪˈvɪzɪb(ə)l/ adjective capable of being divided. □ **divisibility** noun.

**division** /dɪˈvɪʒ(ə)n/ noun dividing, being divided; dividing one number by another; disagreement; one of parts into which thing is divided; administrative unit, esp. group of army units or of teams in sporting league. □ **divisional** adjective.

**divisive** /dɪˈvaɪsɪv/ adjective causing disagreement. □ **divisively** adverb; **divisiveness** noun.

**divisor** /dɪˈvaɪzə/ noun number by which another is to be divided.

**divorce** /dɪˈvɔːs/ • noun legal dissolution of marriage; separation. • verb (-cing) (usually as **divorced** adjective) (often + from) legally dissolve marriage of; separate by divorce; end marriage with by divorce; separate.

**divorcee** /dɪvɔːˈsiː/ noun divorced person.

**divot** /ˈdɪvət/ noun piece of turf dislodged by head of golf club.

**divulge** /dɑɪ'vʌldʒ/ *verb* (**-ging**) disclose (secret).

**divvy** /'dɪvɪ/ *colloquial* ● *noun* (*plural* **-ies**) dividend. ● *verb* (**-ies, -ied**) (often + *up*) share out.

**Dixie** /'dɪksɪ/ *noun* Southern States of US. □ **Dixieland** Dixie, kind of jazz.

**dixie** /'dɪksɪ/ *noun* large iron cooking pot.

**DIY** *abbreviation* do-it-yourself.

**dizzy** /'dɪzɪ/ *adjective* (**-ier, -iest**) giddy; dazed; causing dizziness. ● *verb* (**-ies, -ied**) make dizzy; bewilder. □ **dizzily** *adverb*; **dizziness** *noun*.

**DJ** *abbreviation* disc jockey; dinner jacket.

**dl** *abbreviation* decilitre(s).

**D.Litt.** *abbreviation* Doctor of Letters.

**DM** *abbreviation* Deutschmark.

**dm** *abbreviation* decimetre(s).

**DNA** *abbreviation* deoxyribonucleic acid (substance carrying genetic information in chromosomes).

**do**¹ /duː/ ● *verb* (*3rd singular present* **does** /dʌz/; *past* **did**; *past participle* **done** /dʌn/; *present participle* **doing**) perform, carry out; produce, make; impart; act, proceed; work at; be suitable, satisfy; attend to, deal with; fare; solve; *colloquial* finish; (as **done** *adjective*) finished, completely cooked; *colloquial* exhaust, defeat, kill; *colloquial* cater for; *slang* rob, swindle, prosecute, convict. ● *auxiliary verb used in questions and negative or emphatic statements and commands; as verbal substitute to avoid repetition.* ● *noun* (*plural* **dos** or **do's**) *colloquial* elaborate party or other undertaking. □ **do away with** *colloquial* abolish, kill; **do down** *colloquial* swindle, overcome; **do for** be sufficient for, *colloquial* (esp. as **done for** *adjective*) destroy or ruin or kill, *colloquial* do housework for; **do in** *slang* kill, *colloquial* exhaust; **do-it-yourself** (to be) done or made by householder etc.; **do up** fasten, *colloquial* restore, repair, dress up; **do with** (after *could*) would appreciate, would profit by; **do without** forgo, manage without.

**do**² = DOH.

**do.** *abbreviation* ditto.

**docile** /'dəʊsaɪl/ *adjective* submissive, easily managed. □ **docility** /-'sɪl-/ *noun*.

**dock**¹ ● *noun* enclosed harbour for loading, unloading, and repair of ships; (usually in *plural*) range of docks with wharves, warehouses, etc. ● *verb* bring or come into dock; join (spacecraft) together in space, be thus joined. □ **dockyard** area with docks and equipment for building and repairing ships.

**dock**² *noun* enclosure in criminal court for accused.

**dock**³ *noun* weed with broad leaves.

**dock**⁴ *verb* cut short (tail); reduce or deduct (money etc.).

**docker** *noun* person employed to load and unload ships.

**docket** /'dɒkɪt/ ● *noun* document listing goods delivered, jobs done, contents of package, etc. ● *verb* (**-t-**) label with or enter on docket.

**doctor** /'dɒktə/ ● *noun* qualified medical practitioner; holder of doctorate. ● *verb* *colloquial* tamper with, adulterate; castrate, spay.

**doctoral** *adjective* of the degree of doctor.

**doctorate** /'dɒktərət/ *noun* highest university degree in any faculty.

**doctrinaire** /dɒktrɪ'neə/ *adjective* applying theory or doctrine dogmatically.

**doctrine** /'dɒktrɪn/ *noun* what is taught; principle or set of principles of religious or political etc. belief. □ **doctrinal** /-'traɪn(ə)l/ *adjective*.

**document** ● *noun* /'dɒkjʊmənt/ something written etc. that provides record or evidence of events, circumstances, etc. ● *verb* /'dɒkjʊment/ prove by or support with documents. □ **documentation** *noun*.

**documentary** /dɒkjʊ'mentərɪ/ ● *adjective* consisting of documents; factual, based on real events. ● *noun* (*plural* **-ies**) documentary film etc.

**dodder** /'dɒdə/ *verb* tremble, totter, be feeble. □ **dodderer** *noun*; **doddery** *adjective*.

**doddle** /'dɒd(ə)l/ *noun colloquial* easy task.

**dodecagon** /dəʊ'dekəgən/ *noun* plane figure with 12 sides.

**dodecahedron** /dəʊdekə'hiːdrən/ *noun* solid figure with 12 faces.

**dodge** ● *verb* (**-ging**) move quickly to elude pursuer, blow, etc.; evade by cunning or trickery. ● *noun* quick evasive movement; trick, clever expedient.

**dodgem** /ˈdɒdʒəm/ *noun* small electrically powered car at funfair, bumped into others in enclosure.

**dodgy** *adjective* (**-ier, -iest**) *colloquial* unreliable, risky.

**dodo** /ˈdəʊdəʊ/ *noun* (*plural* **-s**) large extinct flightless bird.

**DoE** *abbreviation* Department of the Environment.

**doe** *noun* (*plural* same or **-s**) female fallow deer, reindeer, hare, or rabbit.

**does** *3rd singular present of* DO[1].

**doesn't** /ˈdʌz(ə)nt/ does not.

**doff** *verb* take off (hat etc.).

**dog** ● *noun* 4-legged flesh-eating animal of many breeds akin to wolf etc.; male of this or of fox or wolf; *colloquial* despicable person; (**the dogs**) *colloquial* greyhound racing; mechanical device for gripping. ● *verb* (**-gg-**) follow closely; pursue, track. □ **dogcart** two-wheeled driving-cart with cross seats back to back; **dog-collar** *colloquial* clergyman's stiff collar; **dog days** hottest period of year; **dog-eared** (of book-page etc.) with worn corners; **dog-end** *slang* cigarette-end; **dogfight** fight between aircraft, rough fight; **dogfish** small shark; **doghouse** *US & Australian* kennel (**in the doghouse** *slang* in disgrace); **dog rose** wild hedge-rose; **dogsbody** *colloquial* drudge; **dog-star** Sirius; **dog-tired** tired out.

**doge** /dəʊdʒ/ *noun historical* chief magistrate of Venice or Genoa.

**dogged** /ˈdɒgɪd/ *adjective* tenacious. □ **doggedly** *adverb*.

**doggerel** /ˈdɒgər(ə)l/ *noun* poor or trivial verse.

**doggo** /ˈdɒgəʊ/ *adverb slang* □ **lie doggo** wait motionless or hidden.

**doggy** *adjective* of or like dogs; devoted to dogs. □ **doggy bag** bag for restaurant customer to take home leftovers; **doggy-paddle** elementary swimming stroke.

**dogma** /ˈdɒgmə/ *noun* principle, tenet; doctrinal system.

**dogmatic** /dɒgˈmætɪk/ *adjective* imposing personal opinions; authoritative, arrogant. □ **dogmatically** *adverb*; **dogmatism** /ˈdɒgmətɪz(ə)m/ *noun*.

**doh** /dəʊ/ *noun* (also **do**) *Music* first note of scale in tonic sol-fa.

**doily** /ˈdɔɪlɪ/ *noun* (*plural* **-ies**) small lacy paper mat placed on plate for cakes etc.

**doings** /ˈduːɪŋz/ *plural noun* actions, exploits; *slang* thing(s) needed.

**Dolby** /ˈdɒlbɪ/ *noun proprietary term* system used esp. in tape-recording to reduce hiss.

**doldrums** /ˈdɒldrəmz/ *plural noun* (usually **the doldrums**) low spirits; period of inactivity; equatorial ocean region of calms.

**dole** ● *noun* unemployment benefit; charitable (esp. niggardly) gift or distribution. ● *verb* (**-ling**) (usually + *out*) distribute sparingly. □ **on the dole** *colloquial* receiving unemployment benefit.

**doleful** /ˈdəʊlfʊl/ *adjective* mournful; dreary, dismal. □ **dolefully** *adverb*.

**doll** ● *noun* model of esp. infant human figure as child's toy; *colloquial* attractive young woman; ventriloquist's dummy. ● *verb* (+ *up*) *colloquial* dress smartly.

**dollar** /ˈdɒlə/ *noun* chief monetary unit in US, Australia, etc.

**dollop** /ˈdɒləp/ *noun* shapeless lump of food etc.

**dolly** *noun* (*plural* **-ies**) *child's word for* doll; movable platform for cine-camera etc.

**dolman sleeve** /ˈdɒlmən/ *noun* loose sleeve cut in one piece with bodice.

**dolmen** /ˈdɒlmən/ *noun* megalithic tomb with large flat stone laid on upright ones.

**dolomite** /ˈdɒləmaɪt/ *noun* mineral or rock of calcium magnesium carbonate.

**dolphin** /ˈdɒlfɪn/ *noun* large porpoiselike sea mammal.

**dolt** /dəʊlt/ *noun* stupid person. □ **doltish** *adjective*.

**Dom** *noun*: *title prefixed to names of some RC dignitaries and Carthusian and Benedictine monks.*

**domain** /dəˈmeɪn/ *noun* area ruled over; realm; estate etc. under one's control; sphere of authority.

**dome** ● *noun* rounded vault as roof; dome-shaped thing. ● *verb* (**-ming**) (usually as **domed** *adjective*) cover with or shape as dome.

**domestic** /dəˈmestɪk/ ● *adjective* of home, household, or family affairs; of one's own country; (of animal) tamed; fond of home life. ● *noun* household servant.

**domesticate** /də'mestɪkeɪt/ *verb* (**-ting**) tame (animal) to live with humans; accustom to housework etc. □ **domestication** *noun*.

**domesticity** /dɒmə'stɪsɪtɪ/ *noun* being domestic; home life.

**domicile** /'dɒmɪsaɪl/ ● *noun* dwelling place; place of permanent residence. ● *verb* (**-ling**) (usually as **domiciled** *adjective*) (usually + *at, in*) settle in a place.

**domiciliary** /dɒmɪ'sɪlɪərɪ/ *adjective formal* (esp. of doctor's etc. visit) to or at person's home.

**dominant** /'dɒmɪnənt/ ● *adjective* dominating, prevailing. ● *noun Music* 5th note of diatonic scale. □ **dominance** *noun*.

**dominate** /'dɒmɪneɪt/ *verb* (**-ting**) command, control; be most influential or obvious; (of place) overlook. □ **domination** *noun*.

**domineer** /dɒmɪ'nɪə/ *verb* (often as **domineering** *adjective*) behave overbearingly.

**Dominican** /də'mɪnɪkən/ ● *noun* friar or nun of order founded by St Dominic. ● *adjective* of this order.

**dominion** /də'mɪnjən/ *noun* sovereignty; realm; domain; *historical* self-governing territory of British Commonwealth.

**domino** /'dɒmɪnəʊ/ *noun* (*plural* **-es**) any of 28 small oblong pieces marked with 0–6 pips in each half; (in *plural*) game played with these; loose cloak worn with half-mask.

**don**[1] *noun* university teacher, esp. senior member of college at Oxford or Cambridge; (**Don**) *Spanish title prefixed to man's name.*

**don**[2] *verb* (**-nn-**) put on (garment).

**donate** /dəʊ'neɪt/ *verb* (**-ting**) give (money etc.), esp. to charity.

**donation** *noun* donating, being donated; thing (esp. money) donated.

**done** /dʌn/ ● *past participle* of DO[1]. ● *adjective* completed; cooked; *colloquial* socially acceptable; (often + *in*) *colloquial* tired out; (esp. as *interjection* in response to offer etc.) accepted. □ **be done with** have or be finished with; **done for** *colloquial* in serious trouble.

**doner kebab** /'dɒnə kɪ'bæb/ *noun* spiced lamb cooked on spit and served in slices, often with pitta bread.

**donkey** /'dɒŋkɪ/ *noun* (*plural* **-s**) domestic ass; *colloquial* stupid person. □ **donkey jacket** thick weatherproof jacket; **donkey's years** *colloquial* very long time; **donkey-work** drudgery.

**Donna** /'dɒnə/ *noun: title of Italian, Spanish, or Portuguese lady.*

**donnish** *adjective* like a college don; pedantic.

**donor** /'dəʊnə/ *noun* person who donates; person who provides blood for transfusion, organ for transplantation, etc.

**don't** /dəʊnt/ ● *verb* do not. ● *noun* prohibition.

**doodle** /'du:d(ə)l/ ● *verb* (**-ling**) scribble or draw absent-mindedly. ● *noun* such scribble or drawing.

**doom** /du:m/ ● *noun* terrible fate or destiny; ruin, death. ● *verb* (usually + *to*) condemn or destine; (esp. as **doomed** *adjective*) consign to ruin, destruction, etc. □ **doomsday** day of Last Judgement.

**door** /dɔː/ *noun* hinged or sliding barrier closing entrance to building, room, cupboard, etc.; doorway. □ **doormat** mat for wiping shoes on, *colloquial* subservient person; **doorstep** step or area immediately outside esp. outer door, *slang* thick slice of bread; **doorstop** device for keeping door open or to keep it from striking wall; **door-to-door** (of selling etc.) done at each house in turn; **doorway** opening filled by door; **out of doors** in(to) open air.

**dope** ● *noun slang* drug, esp. narcotic; thick liquid used as lubricant etc.; varnish; *slang* stupid person; *slang* information. ● *verb* (**-ping**) give or add drug to; apply dope to.

**dopey** *adjective* (also **dopy**) (**dopier**, **dopiest**) *colloquial* half asleep, stupefied; stupid.

**doppelganger** /'dɒp(ə)lgæŋə/ *noun* (also **doppelgänger** /-geŋə/) apparition or double of living person.

**Doppler effect** /'dɒplə/ *noun* change in frequency of esp. sound waves when source and observer are moving closer or apart.

**dormant** /'dɔ:mənt/ *adjective* lying inactive; sleeping; inactive. □ **dormancy** *noun*.

**dormer** /'dɔ:mə/ *noun* (in full **dormer window**) upright window in sloping roof.

**dormitory** /'dɔ:mɪtərɪ/ *noun* (*plural* **-ies**) sleeping-room with several beds; (in full **dormitory town** etc.) commuter town or suburb.

**dormouse** /'dɔ:maʊs/ *noun* (*plural* **-mice**) small mouselike hibernating rodent.

**dorsal** /'dɔ:s(ə)l/ *adjective* of or on back.

**dory** /'dɔ:rɪ/ *noun* (*plural* same or **-ies**) edible sea fish.

**dosage** *noun* size of dose; giving of dose.

**dose** /dəʊs/ ● *noun* single portion of medicine; amount of radiation received. ● *verb* (**-sing**) give medicine to; (+ *with*) treat with.

**doss** *verb* (often + *down*) *slang* sleep on makeshift bed or in doss-house. □ **doss-house** cheap lodging house. □ **dosser** *noun*.

**dossier** /'dɒsɪeɪ/ *noun* file containing information about person, event, etc.

**dot** *noun* small spot, esp. as decimal point, part of *i* or *j* etc.; shorter signal of the two in Morse code. ● *verb* (**-tt-**) mark or scatter with dot(s); (often + *about*) scatter like dots; place dot over (letter); partly cover as with dots; *slang* hit. □ **dotted line** line of dots for signature etc. on document; **on the dot** exactly on time.

**dotage** /'dəʊtɪdʒ/ *noun* feeble-minded senility.

**dote** *verb* (**-ting**) (usually + *on* or as **doting** *adjective*) be excessively fond of.

**dotterel** /'dɒtər(ə)l/ *noun* small plover.

**dotty** *adjective* (**-ier**, **-iest**) *colloquial* eccentric, silly, crazy; (+ *about*) infatuated with.

**double** /'dʌb(ə)l/ ● *adjective* consisting of two things; multiplied by two; twice as much or many or large etc.; having twice the usual size, quantity, strength, etc.; having some part double; (of flower) with two or more circles of petals; ambiguous; deceitful. ● *adverb* at or to twice the amount; two together. ● *noun* double quantity (of spirits etc.) or thing; twice the amount or quantity; person or thing looking exactly like

another; (in *plural*) game between two pairs of players; pair of victories; bet in which winnings and stake from first bet are transferred to second. ● *verb* (**-ling**) make or become double; increase twofold; amount to twice as much as; fold over upon itself; become folded; play (two parts) in same play etc.; (usually + *as*) play twofold role; turn sharply; *Nautical* get round (headland). □ **at the double** running; **double agent** spy working for two rival countries etc.; **double-barrelled** (of gun) having two barrels, (of surname) hyphenated; **double-bass** largest instrument of violin family; **double-book** mistakenly reserve (seat, room, etc.) for two people at once; **double-breasted** (of garment) overlapping across body; **double chin** chin with fold of flesh below it; **double cream** thick cream with high fat-content; **double-cross** deceive or betray; **double-dealing** (practising) deceit, esp. in business; **double-decker** bus etc. with two decks, *colloquial* sandwich with two layers of filling; **double Dutch** *colloquial* gibberish; **double eagle** figure of eagle with two heads; **double-edged** presenting both a danger and an advantage; **double figures** numbers from 10 to 99; **double glazing** two layers of glass in window; **double negative** *Grammar* negative statement (incorrectly) containing two negative elements (see note below); **double pneumonia** pneumonia of both lungs; **double standard** rule or principle not impartially applied; **double take** delayed reaction to unexpected element of situation; **double-talk** (usually deliberately) ambiguous or misleading speech.

■ **Usage** Double negatives like *He didn't do nothing* and *I'm never going nowhere like that* are mistakes in standard English because one negative element is redundant. However, two negatives are perfectly acceptable in, for instance, *a not ungenerous sum* (meaning 'quite a generous sum').

***double entendre*** /du:b(ə) ɑ:n'tɑ:ndrə/ *noun* phrase capable of two meanings, one usually indecent. [French]

**doublet** /ˈdʌblɪt/ *noun historical* man's close-fitting jacket; one of pair of similar things.

**doubloon** /dʌˈbluːn/ *noun historical* Spanish gold coin.

**doubt** /daʊt/ ● *noun* uncertainty; undecided state of mind; cynicism; uncertain state. ● *verb* feel uncertain or undecided about; hesitate to believe; call in question. □ **in doubt** open to question; **no doubt** certainly, admittedly.

**doubtful** *adjective* feeling or causing doubt; unreliable. □ **doubtfully** *adverb*.

**doubtless** *adverb* certainly; probably.

**douche** /duːʃ/ ● *noun* jet of liquid applied to part of body for cleansing or medicinal purposes; device for producing this. ● *verb* (**-ching**) treat with douche; use douche.

**dough** /dəʊ/ *noun* thick paste of flour mixed with liquid for baking; *slang* money. □ **doughnut** (*US* **donut**) small fried cake of sweetened dough. □ **doughy** *adjective* (**-ier, -iest**).

**doughty** /ˈdaʊtɪ/ *adjective* (**-ier, -iest**) *archaic* valiant. □ **doughtily** *adverb*.

**dour** /dʊə/ *adjective* stern, grim, obstinate.

**douse** /daʊs/ *verb* (also **dowse**) (**-sing**) throw water over; plunge into water; extinguish (light).

**dove** /dʌv/ *noun* bird with short legs and full breast; advocate of peaceful policies; gentle or innocent person. □ **dovecot(e)** pigeon house.

**dovetail** ● *noun* mortise-and-tenon joint shaped like dove's spread tail. ● *verb* fit together, combine neatly; join with dovetails.

**dowager** /ˈdaʊədʒə/ *noun* woman with title or property from her late husband.

**dowdy** /ˈdaʊdɪ/ *adjective* (**-ier, -iest**) (of clothes) unattractively dull; dressed dowdily. □ **dowdily** *adverb*; **dowdiness** *noun*.

**dowel** /ˈdaʊəl/ *noun* cylindrical peg for holding parts of structure together.

**dowelling** *noun* rods for cutting into dowels.

**dower** /ˈdaʊə/ *noun* widow's share for life of husband's estate.

**down¹** /daʊn/ ● *adverb* towards or into lower place, esp. to ground; in lower place or position; to or in place regarded as lower, esp. southwards or away from major city or university; in or into low or weaker position or condition; losing by; (of a computer system) out of action; from earlier to later time; in written or recorded form. ● *preposition* downwards along, through, or into; from top to bottom of; along; at lower part of. ● *adjective* directed downwards. ● *verb colloquial* knock or bring etc. down; swallow. ● *noun* reverse of fortune; *colloquial* period of depression. □ **be down to** be the responsibility of, have nothing left but; **down and out** destitute; **down-and-out** destitute person; **downcast** dejected, (of eyes) looking down; **downfall** fall from prosperity or power, cause of this; **downgrade** reduce in rank etc.; **downhearted** despondent; **downhill** *adverb* in descending direction, on a decline, *adjective* sloping down, declining; **down in the mouth** looking unhappy; **down-market** of or to cheaper sector of market; **downpour** heavy fall of rain; **downside** negative aspect, drawback; **downstairs** *adverb* down the stairs, to or on lower floor, *adjective* situated downstairs; **downstream** in direction of flow of stream etc.; **down-to-earth** practical, realistic; **downtown** *US* (of) lower or central part of town or city; **downtrodden** oppressed; **downturn** decline, esp. in economic activity; **down under** *colloquial* in Australia or NZ; **downwind** in direction in which wind is blowing; **down with** *expressing rejection of person or thing*; **have a down on** *colloquial* be hostile to. □ **downward** *adjective & adverb*; **downwards** *adverb*.

**down²** /daʊn/ *noun* baby birds' fluffy covering; bird's under-plumage; fine soft feathers or hairs.

**down³** /daʊn/ *noun* open rolling land; (in *plural*) chalk uplands of S. England etc.

**downright** ● *adjective* plain, straightforward; utter. ● *adverb* thoroughly.

**Down's syndrome** *noun* congenital disorder with mental retardation and physical abnormalities.

**downy** *adjective* (**-ier, -iest**) of, like, or covered with down.

**dowry** /ˈdaʊərɪ/ *noun* (*plural* **-ies**) property brought by bride to her husband.

**dowse**[1] /daʊz/ verb (-sing) search for underground water or minerals by holding stick or rod which dips abruptly when over right spot. □ **dowser** noun.

**dowse**[2] = DOUSE.

**doxology** /dɒkˈsɒlədʒɪ/ noun (plural -ies) liturgical hymn etc. of praise to God.

**doyen** /ˈdɔɪən/ noun (feminine **doyenne** /dɔɪˈen/) senior member of group.

**doz.** abbreviation dozen.

**doze** ● verb (-zing) sleep lightly, be half asleep. ● noun short light sleep. □ **doze off** fall lightly asleep.

**dozen** /ˈdʌz(ə)n/ noun (plural same (after numeral) or -s) set of twelve; (**dozens**, usually + of) colloquial very many.

**D.Phil.** abbreviation Doctor of Philosophy.

**Dr** abbreviation Doctor.

**drab** adjective (-bb-) dull, uninteresting; of dull brownish colour. □ **drabness** noun.

**drachm** /dræm/ noun weight formerly used by apothecaries, = $^1/_8$ ounce.

**drachma** /ˈdrækmə/ noun (plural -s) chief monetary unit of Greece.

**Draconian** /drəˈkəʊnɪən/ adjective (of laws) harsh, cruel.

**draft** /drɑːft/ ● noun preliminary written outline of scheme or version of speech, document, etc.; written order for payment of money by bank; drawing of money on this; detachment from larger group; selection of this; US conscription; US draught. ● verb prepare draft of; select for special duty or purpose; US conscript.

**draftsman** /ˈdrɑːftsmən/ noun person who drafts documents; person who makes drawings.

**drafty** US = DRAUGHTY.

**drag** ● verb (-gg-) pull along with effort; (allow to) trail; (of time etc.) pass tediously or slowly; search bottom of (river etc.) with grapnels, nets, etc. ● noun obstruction to progress, retarding force; colloquial boring or tiresome task, person, etc.; lure before hounds as substitute for fox; apparatus for dredging; colloquial pull at cigarette; slang women's clothes worn by men. □ **drag out** protract.

**draggle** /ˈdræg(ə)l/ verb (-ling) make dirty and wet by trailing; hang trailing.

**dragon** /ˈdrægən/ noun mythical monster like reptile, usually with wings and able to breathe fire; fierce woman.

**dragonfly** noun (plural -ies) large long-bodied gauzy-winged insect.

**dragoon** /drəˈguːn/ ● noun cavalryman; fierce fellow. ● verb (+ into) coerce or bully into.

**drain** ● verb draw off liquid from; draw off (liquid); flow or trickle away; dry or become dry; exhaust; drink to the dregs; empty (glass etc.) by drinking. ● noun channel or pipe carrying off liquid, sewage, etc.; constant outflow or expenditure. □ **draining board** sloping grooved surface beside sink for draining dishes; **drainpipe** pipe for carrying off water etc.

**drainage** noun draining; system of drains; what is drained off.

**drake** noun male duck.

**dram** noun small drink of spirits etc.; drachm.

**drama** /ˈdrɑːmə/ noun play for stage or broadcasting; art of writing, acting, or presenting plays; dramatic event or quality.

**dramatic** /drəˈmætɪk/ adjective of drama; unexpected and exciting; striking; theatrical. □ **dramatically** adverb.

**dramatics** plural noun (often treated as singular) performance of plays; exaggerated behaviour.

**dramatis personae** /ˈdræmətɪs pɜːˈsəʊnaɪ/ plural noun characters in a play.

**dramatist** /ˈdræmətɪst/ noun writer of plays.

**dramatize** /ˈdræmətaɪz/ verb (also -ise) (-zing or -sing) convert into play; make dramatic; behave dramatically. □ **dramatization** noun.

**drank** past of DRINK.

**drape** ● verb (-ping) cover or hang or adorn with cloth etc.; arrange in graceful folds. ● noun (in plural) US curtains.

**draper** noun retailer of textile fabrics.

**drapery** noun (plural -ies) clothing or hangings arranged in folds; draper's trade or fabrics.

**drastic** /ˈdræstɪk/ adjective far-reaching in effect; severe. □ **drastically** adverb.

**drat** colloquial ● verb (-tt-) (usually as interjection) curse. ● interjection expressing annoyance.

**draught** /drɑːft/ *noun* (*US* **draft**) current of air indoors; traction; depth of water needed to float ship; drawing of liquor from cask etc.; single act of drinking or inhaling; amount so drunk; (in *plural*) game for two with 12 pieces each, on **draughtboard** (like chessboard). □ **draught beer** beer drawn from cask, not bottled.

**draughtsman** /'drɑːftsmən/ *noun* person who makes drawings; piece in game of draughts.

**draughty** *adjective* (*US* **drafty**) (**-ier**, **-iest**) (of a room etc.) letting in sharp currents of air.

**draw** ● *verb* (*past* **drew** /druː/; *past participle* **drawn**) pull or cause to move towards or after one; pull (thing) up, over, or across; attract; pull (curtains) open or shut; take in; (+ *at*, *on*) inhale from; extract; take from or out; make (line, mark, or outline); make (picture) in this way; represent (thing) in this way; finish (game etc.) with equal scores; proceed to specified position; infer; elicit, evoke; induce; haul up (water) from well; bring out (liquid from tap, wound, etc.); draw lots; obtain by lot; (of tea) infuse; (of chimney, pipe, etc.) promote or allow draught; write out (bill, cheque); search (cover) for game etc.; (as **drawn** *adjective*) looking strained and tense. ● *noun* act of drawing; person or thing that draws custom or attention; drawing of lots; raffle; drawn game etc. □ **draw back** withdraw; **drawback** disadvantage; **drawbridge** hinged retractable bridge; **draw in** (of days etc.) become shorter, (of train etc.) arrive at station; **draw out** prolong, induce to talk, (of days etc.) become longer; **drawstring** string or cord threaded through waistband, bag opening, etc.; **draw up** draft (document etc.), bring into order, come to a halt, (**draw oneself up**) make oneself erect.

**drawer** /'drɔːə/ *noun* person who draws; (also /drɔː/) receptacle sliding in and out of frame (**chest of drawers**) or of table etc.; (in *plural*) knickers, underpants.

**drawing** *noun* art of representing by line with pencil etc.; picture etc. made thus. □ **drawing-board** board on which paper is fixed for drawing on;

**drawing-pin** flat-headed pin for fastening paper to a surface.

**drawing-room** *noun* room in private house for sitting or entertaining in.

**drawl** ● *verb* speak with drawn-out vowel sounds. ● *noun* drawling utterance or way of speaking.

**dray** *noun* low cart without sides for heavy loads, esp. beer barrels.

**dread** /dred/ ● *verb* fear greatly, esp. in advance. ● *noun* great fear or apprehension. ● *adjective* dreaded; *archaic* awe-inspiring.

**dreadful** *adjective* terrible; *colloquial* very annoying, very bad. □ **dreadfully** *adverb*.

**dream** ● *noun* series of scenes in mind of sleeping person; daydream or fantasy; ideal; aspiration. ● *verb* (*past & past participle* **dreamt** /dremt/ or **dreamed**) experience dream; imagine as in dream; (esp. in negative; + *of*, *that*) consider possible or acceptable; be inactive or unrealistic. □ **dreamer** *noun*.

**dreamy** *adjective* (**-ier**, **-iest**) given to daydreaming; dreamlike; vague; *colloquial* delightful. □ **dreamily** *adverb*.

**dreary** /'drɪərɪ/ *adjective* (**-ier**, **-iest**) dismal, gloomy, dull. □ **drearily** *adverb*; **dreariness** *noun*.

**dredge**[1] ● *noun* apparatus used to collect oysters etc., or to clear mud etc., from bottom of sea etc. ● *verb* (**-ging**) bring up or clear (mud etc.) with dredge; (+ *up*) bring up (something forgotten); clean with or use dredge.

**dredge**[2] *verb* (**-ging**) sprinkle with flour etc.

**dredger**[1] *noun* boat with dredge; dredge.

**dredger**[2] *noun* container with perforated lid for sprinkling flour etc.

**dregs** *plural noun* sediment, grounds; worst part.

**drench** ● *verb* wet thoroughly; force (animal) to take medicine. ● *noun* dose of medicine for animal.

**dress** ● *verb* put clothes on; have and wear clothes; put on evening dress; arrange or adorn; put dressing on (wound etc.); prepare (poultry, crab, etc.) for cooking or eating; apply manure to. ● *noun* woman's one-piece garment of bodice and skirt; clothing, esp.

whole outfit. □ **dress circle** first gallery in theatre; **dressmaker** person who makes women's clothes, esp. for a living; **dress rehearsal** (esp. final) rehearsal in costume; **dress up** put on special clothes, make (person, thing) more attractive or interesting.

**dressage** /'dresɑːʒ/ noun training of horse in obedience and deportment.

**dresser**[1] /'dresə/ noun tall kitchen sideboard with shelves.

**dresser**[2] noun person who helps actors or actresses to dress for stage.

**dressing** noun putting one's clothes on; sauce, esp. of oil, vinegar, etc., for salads; bandage, ointment, etc. for wound; compost etc. spread over land. □ **dressing down** colloquial scolding; **dressing gown** loose robe worn while one is not fully dressed; **dressing table** table with mirror etc. for use while dressing, applying make-up, etc.

**dressy** adjective (**-ier, -iest**) colloquial (of clothes or person) smart, elegant.

**drew** past of DRAW.

**drey** /dreɪ/ noun squirrel's nest.

**dribble** /'drɪb(ə)l/ ● verb (**-ling**) allow saliva to flow from the mouth; flow or allow to flow in drops; Football etc. move (ball) forward with slight touches of feet etc. ● noun act of dribbling; dribbling flow.

**driblet** /'drɪblɪt/ noun small quantity (of liquid etc.).

**dribs and drabs** plural noun colloquial small scattered amounts.

**dried** past & past participle of DRY.

**drier**[1] comparative of DRY.

**drier**[2] /'draɪə/ noun (also **dryer**) machine for drying hair, laundry, etc.

**driest** superlative of DRY.

**drift** ● noun slow movement or variation; this caused by current; intention, meaning, etc. of what is said etc.; mass of snow etc. heaped up by wind; state of inaction; deviation of craft etc. due to current, wind, etc. ● verb be carried by or as if by current of air or water; progress casually or aimlessly; (of current) carry; heap or be heaped into drifts. □ **drift-net** net for sea fishing, which is allowed to drift; **driftwood** wood floating on moving water or washed ashore.

**drifter** noun aimless person; fishing boat with drift-net.

**drill**[1] ● noun tool or machine for boring holes; instruction in military exercises; routine procedure in emergency; thorough training, esp. by repetition; colloquial recognized procedure. ● verb make hole in or through with drill; make (hole) with drill; train or be trained by drill.

**drill**[2] ● noun machine for making furrows, sowing, and covering seed; small furrow for sowing seed in; row of seeds sown by drill. ● verb plant in drills.

**drill**[3] noun coarse twilled cotton or linen fabric.

**drill**[4] noun W. African baboon related to mandrill.

**drily** adverb (also **dryly**) in a dry way.

**drink** ● verb (past **drank**; past participle **drunk**) swallow (liquid); take alcohol, esp. to excess; (of plant etc.) absorb (moisture). ● noun liquid for drinking; draught or specified amount of this; alcoholic liquor; glass, portion, etc., of this; (**the drink**) colloquial the sea. □ **drink-driver** colloquial person driving with excess alcohol in the blood; **drink in** listen eagerly to; **drink to** toast, wish success to; **drink up** drink all or remainder of. □ **drinker** noun.

**drip** ● verb (**-pp-**) fall or let fall in drops; (often + with) be so wet as to shed drops. ● noun liquid falling in drops; drop of liquid; sound of dripping; colloquial dull or ineffectual person.

**drip-dry** ● verb dry or leave to dry crease-free when hung up. ● adjective able to be drip-dried.

**drip-feed** ● verb feed intravenously in drops. ● noun feeding thus; apparatus for doing this.

**dripping** noun fat melted from roasting meat.

**drive** ● verb (**-ving**; past **drove** /drəʊv/; past participle **driven** /'drɪv(ə)n/) urge forward, esp. forcibly; compel; force into specified state; operate and direct (vehicle etc.); carry or be carried in vehicle; strike golf ball from tee; (of wind etc.) carry along, propel. ● noun excursion in vehicle; driveway; street, road; motivation and energy; inner urge; forcible stroke of bat etc.; organized group effort; transmission of power to machinery or wheels of motor vehicle etc.; organized whist, bingo, etc. competition. □ **drive at** seek, intend, mean; **drive-in** (bank, cinema, etc.) used while one sits in one's car; **driveway** private road from garden to house; **driving licence** licence permitting person to drive vehicle; **driving test** official test of competence to drive; **driving wheel** wheel transmitting power of vehicle to ground.

**drivel** /ˈdrɪv(ə)l/ ● *noun* silly nonsense. ● *verb* (**-ll-**; *US* **-l-**) talk drivel; run at mouth or nose.

**driver** *noun* person who drives; golf club for driving from tee.

**drizzle** /ˈdrɪz(ə)l/ ● *noun* very fine rain. ● *verb* (**-ling**) fall in very fine drops.

**droll** /drəʊl/ *adjective* quaintly amusing, strange, odd. □ **drollery** *noun* (*plural* **-ies**).

**dromedary** /ˈdrɒmɪdərɪ/ *noun* (*plural* **-ies**) one-humped (esp. Arabian) camel bred for riding.

**drone** ● *noun* non-working male of honey-bee; idler; deep humming sound; monotonous speaking tone; bass-pipe of bagpipes or its continuous note. ● *verb* (**-ning**) make deep humming sound; speak or utter monotonously.

**drool** *verb* slobber, dribble; (often + *over*) admire extravagantly.

**droop** /druːp/ ● *verb* bend or hang down, esp. from fatigue or lack of food, drink, etc.; flag. ● *noun* drooping position; loss of spirit. □ **droopy** *adjective*.

**drop** ● *noun* globule of liquid that falls, hangs, or adheres to surface; very small amount of liquid; abrupt fall or slope; amount of this; act of dropping; fall in prices, temperature, etc.; drop-shaped thing, esp. pendant or sweet; (in *plural*) liquid medicine swallowed in drops. ● *verb* (**-pp-**) fall, allow to fall; let go; fall, let fall, or shed in drops; sink down from exhaustion or injury; cease, lapse; abandon; *colloquial* cease to associate with or discuss; set down (passenger etc.); utter or be uttered casually; fall or let fall in direction, amount, degree, pitch, etc.; (of person) jump down lightly; let oneself fall; omit; give birth to (lamb); deliver from the air by parachute etc.; *Football* send (ball) or score (goal) by

drop-kick. □ **drop back**, **behind** fall back, get left behind; **drop in**, **by** *colloquial* visit casually; **drop-kick** kick at football made by dropping ball and kicking it as it touches ground; **drop off** fall asleep, drop (passenger); **drop out** (often + *of*) *colloquial* cease to participate (in); **drop-out** *colloquial* person who has dropped out of esp. course of study or conventional society; **drop scone** scone made by dropping spoonful of mixture into pan etc.; **drop-shot** tennis shot dropping abruptly after clearing net. □ **droplet** *noun*.

**dropper** *noun* device for releasing liquid in drops.

**droppings** *plural noun* dung; thing that falls or has fallen in drops.

**dropsy** /ˈdrɒpsɪ/ *noun* oedema. □ **dropsical** *adjective*.

**dross** *noun* rubbish; scum of molten metal; impurities.

**drought** /draʊt/ *noun* prolonged absence of rain.

**drove¹** *past of* DRIVE.

**drove²** /drəʊv/ *noun* moving crowd; (in *plural*) *colloquial* great number; herd or flock moving together.

**drover** *noun* herder of cattle.

**drown** /draʊn/ *verb* kill or die by submersion; submerge; flood; drench; deaden (grief etc.) by drinking; (often + *out*) overpower (sound) with louder sound.

**drowse** /draʊz/ *verb* (**-sing**) be lightly asleep.

**drowsy** /ˈdraʊzɪ/ *adjective* (**-ier**, **-iest**) very sleepy, almost asleep. □ **drowsily** *adverb*; **drowsiness** *noun*.

**drub** *verb* (**-bb-**) thrash, beat; defeat thoroughly. □ **drubbing** *noun*.

**drudge** ● *noun* person who does dull, laborious, or menial work. ● *verb* (**-ging**) work hard or laboriously. □ **drudgery** *noun*.

**drug** ● *noun* medicinal substance; (esp. addictive) hallucinogen, stimulant, narcotic, etc. ● *verb* (**-gg-**) add drug to (drink, food, etc.); administer drug to; stupefy. □ **drugstore** *US* combined chemist's shop and café.

**drugget** /ˈdrʌgɪt/ *noun* coarse woven fabric used for floor coverings etc.

**druggist** *noun* pharmacist.

**Druid** /'druːɪd/ *noun* ancient Celtic priest; member of a modern Druidic order, esp. the Gorsedd. □ **Druidic** /-'ɪdɪk/ *adjective*; **Druidism** *noun*.

**drum** ● *noun* hollow esp. cylindrical percussion instrument 'covered at one or both ends with plastic, skin, etc.; sound of this; cylindrical structure or object; cylinder used for storage etc.; eardrum. ● *verb* (**-mm-**) play drum; beat or tap continuously with fingers etc.; (of bird etc.) make loud noise with wings. □ **drumbeat** stroke or sound of stroke on drum; **drum brake** kind in which shoes on vehicle press against drum on wheel; **drum into** drive (facts etc.) into (person) by persistence; **drum machine** electronic device that simulates percussion; **drum major** leader of marching band; **drum majorette** female baton-twirling member of parading group; **drum out** dismiss with ignominy; **drumstick** stick for beating drum, lower leg of fowl for eating; **drum up** summon or get by vigorous effort.

**drummer** *noun* player of drum.

**drunk** /drʌŋk/ ● *past participle* of DRINK. ● *adjective* lacking control from drinking alcohol; (often + *with*) overcome with joy, success, power, etc. ● *noun* person who is drunk, esp. habitually.

**drunkard** /'drʌŋkəd/ *noun* person habitually drunk.

**drunken** /'drʌŋkən/ *adjective* drunk; caused by or involving drunkenness; often drunk. □ **drunkenly** *adverb*; **drunkenness** *noun*.

**drupe** /druːp/ *noun* fleshy stone fruit.

**dry** ● *adjective* (**drier, driest**) free from moisture, esp. with moisture having evaporated, drained away, etc; (of eyes) free from tears; (of climate) not rainy; (of river, well, etc.) dried up; (of wine etc.) not sweet; plain, unelaborated; uninteresting; (of sense of humour) ironic, understated; prohibiting sale of alcohol; (of bread) without butter etc.; (of provisions etc.) solid, not liquid; *colloquial* thirsty. ● *verb* (**dries, dried**) make or become dry; (usually as **dried** *adjective*) preserve (food) by removing moisture. □ **dry-clean** clean (clothes etc.) with solvents without water; **dry-fly** (of fishing) with floating artificial fly; **dry ice** solid carbon dioxide;

**dry out** make or become fully dry, treat or be treated for alcoholism; **dry rot** decay in wood not exposed to air, fungi causing this; **dry run** *colloquial* rehearsal; **dry-shod** without wetting one's shoes; **dry up** make or become completely dry, dry dishes. □ **dryness** *noun*.

**dryad** /'draɪæd/ *noun* wood nymph.

**dryer** = DRIER[2].

**dryly** = DRILY.

**D.Sc.** *abbreviation* Doctor of Science.

**DSC, DSM, DSO** *abbreviations* Distinguished Service Cross, Medal, Order.

**DSS** *abbreviation* Department of Social Security (formerly DHSS).

**DT** *abbreviation* (also **DT's** /diː'tiːz/) delirium tremens.

**DTI** *abbreviation* Department of Trade and Industry.

**dual** /'djuːəl/ ● *adjective* in two parts; twofold; double. ● *noun* *Grammar* dual number or form. □ **dual carriageway** road with dividing strip between traffic flowing in opposite directions; **dual control** two linked sets of controls, esp. of vehicle used for teaching driving etc., enabling operation by either of two people. □ **duality** /-'æl-/ *noun*.

**dub**[1] *verb* (**-bb-**) make (person) into knight; give name or nickname to.

**dub**[2] *verb* (**-bb-**) provide (film etc.) with alternative, esp. translated, soundtrack; add (sound effects, music) to film or broadcast.

**dubbin** /'dʌbɪn/ *noun* (also **dubbing**) grease for softening and waterproofing leather.

**dubiety** /dju:'baɪətɪ/ *noun literary* doubt.

**dubious** /'djuːbɪəs/ *adjective* doubtful; questionable; unreliable. □ **dubiously** *adverb*; **dubiousness** *noun*.

**ducal** /'djuːk(ə)l/ *adjective* of or like duke.

**ducat** /'dʌkət/ *noun* gold coin formerly current in most European countries.

**duchess** /'dʌtʃɪs/ *noun* duke's wife or widow; woman holding rank of duke.

**duchy** /'dʌtʃɪ/ *noun* (*plural* **-ies**) duke's or duchess's territory.

**duck** ● *noun* (*plural* same or **-s**) swimming bird, esp. domesticated form of mallard or wild duck; female of this; its flesh as food; *Cricket* batsman's score of 0; (also **ducks**) *colloquial* (esp. as form of address) darling. ● *verb* bob down, esp. to avoid being seen or hit; dip head briefly under water; plunge (person) briefly in water. □ **duckweed** any of various plants that grow on surface of still water.

**duckling** *noun* young duck.

**duct** *noun* channel, tube; tube in body carrying secretions etc.

**ductile** /'dʌktaɪl/ *adjective* (of metal) capable of being drawn into wire; pliable; easily moulded; docile. □ **ductility** /-'tɪl-/ *noun*.

**ductless** *adjective* (of gland) secreting directly into bloodstream.

**dud** *slang* ● *noun* useless or broken thing; counterfeit article; (in *plural*) clothes, rags. ● *adjective* defective, useless.

**dude** /du:d/ *noun slang* fellow; *US* dandy; *US* city man staying on ranch.

**dudgeon** /'dʌdʒ(ə)n/ *noun* resentment; indignation.

**due** ● *adjective* owing, payable; merited, appropriate; (often + *to do*) expected or under obligation to do something or arrive at certain time. ● *noun* what one owes or is owed; (usually in *plural*) fee or amount payable. ● *adverb* (of compass point) exactly, directly. □ **due to** because of, caused by.

■ **Usage** Many people believe that *due to*, meaning 'because of', should only be used after the verb *to be*, as in *The mistake was due to ignorance*, and not as in *All trains may be delayed due to a signal failure*. Instead, *owing to a signal failure* could be used.

**duel** /'dju:əl/ ● *noun* armed contest between two people, usually to the death; two-sided contest. ● *verb* (**-ll-**; *US* **-l-**) fight duel. □ **duellist** *noun*.

**duenna** /dju:'enə/ *noun* older woman acting as chaperon to girls, esp. in Spain.

**duet** /dju:'et/ *noun* musical composition for two performers.

**duff** ● *noun* boiled pudding. ● *adjective slang* worthless, useless, counterfeit.

**duffer** /'dʌfə/ *noun colloquial* inefficient or stupid person.

**duffle** /'dʌf(ə)l/ *noun* (also **duffel**) coarse woollen cloth. □ **duffle bag** cylindrical canvas bag closed by drawstring; **duffle-coat** hooded overcoat of duffle with toggle fastenings.

**dug**[1] *past & past participle* of DIG.

**dug**[2] *noun* udder, teat.

**dugong** /'du:gɒŋ/ *noun* (*plural* same or **-s**) Asian sea mammal.

**dugout** *noun* roofed shelter, esp. for troops in trenches; underground shelter; canoe made from tree trunk.

**duke** /dju:k/ *noun* person holding highest hereditary title of the nobility; sovereign prince ruling duchy or small state. □ **dukedom** *noun*.

**dulcet** /'dʌlsɪt/ *adjective* sweet-sounding.

**dulcimer** /'dʌlsɪmə/ *noun* metal-stringed instrument struck with two hand-held hammers.

**dull** ● *adjective* tedious; not interesting; (of weather) overcast; (of colour, light, sound, etc.) not bright, vivid, or clear; slow-witted; stupid; (of knife-edge etc.) blunt; listless, depressed. ● *verb* make or become dull. □ **dullard** *noun*, **dullness** *noun*, **dully** /'dʌlɪ/ *adverb*.

**duly** /'dju:lɪ/ *adverb* in due time or manner; rightly, properly.

**dumb** /dʌm/ *adjective* unable to speak; silent, taciturn; *colloquial* stupid, ignorant. □ **dumb-bell** short bar with weight at each end, for muscle-building etc.; **dumbstruck** speechless with surprise.

**dumbfound** /dʌm'faʊnd/ *verb* nonplus; make speechless with surprise.

**dumdum** /'dʌmdʌm/ *noun* (in full **dumdum bullet**) soft-nosed bullet that expands on impact.

**dummy** /'dʌmɪ/ *noun* (*plural* **-ies**) model of human figure, esp. as used to display clothes or by ventriloquist or as target; imitation object used to replace real or normal one; baby's rubber teat; *colloquial* stupid person; imaginary player in bridge etc., whose cards are exposed and played by partner. ● *adjective* sham, imitation. ● *verb* (**-ies**, **-ied**) make pretended pass etc. in football. □ **dummy run** trial attempt.

**dump** ● *noun* place for depositing rubbish; *colloquial* unpleasant or dreary place; temporary store of ammunition etc. ● *verb* put down firmly or clumsily; deposit as rubbish; *colloquial* abandon; sell (surplus goods) to foreign market at low price; copy (contents of computer memory etc.) as diagnostic aid or for security.

**dumpling** /'dʌmplɪŋ/ *noun* ball of dough boiled in stew or containing apple etc.

**dumps** *plural noun* (usually in **down in the dumps**) *colloquial* low spirits.

**dumpy** /'dʌmpɪ/ *adjective* (**-ier**, **-iest**) short and stout.

**dun** ● *adjective* greyish-brown. ● *noun* dun colour; dun horse.

**dunce** *noun* person slow at learning.

**dunderhead** /'dʌndəhed/ *noun* stupid person.

**dune** /djuːn/ *noun* drift of sand etc. formed by wind.

**dung** ● *noun* excrement of animals; manure. ● *verb* apply dung to (land). □ **dunghill** heap of dung or refuse.

**dungarees** /dʌŋgə'riːz/ *plural noun* trousers with bib attached.

**dungeon** /'dʌndʒ(ə)n/ *noun* underground prison cell.

**dunk** *verb* dip food into liquid before eating it.

**dunlin** /'dʌnlɪn/ *noun* red-backed sandpiper.

**dunnock** /'dʌnək/ *noun* hedge sparrow.

**duo** /'djuːəʊ/ *noun* (*plural* **-s**) pair of performers; duet.

**duodecimal** /djuːəʊ'desɪm(ə)l/ *adjective* of twelfths or 12; proceeding by twelves.

**duodenum** /djuːəʊ'diːnəm/ *noun* (*plural* **-s**) part of small intestine next to stomach. □ **duodenal** *adjective*.

**duologue** /'djuːəlɒg/ *noun* dialogue between two people.

**dupe** /djuːp/ ● *noun* victim of deception. ● *verb* (**-ping**) deceive, trick.

**duple** /'djuːp(ə)l/ *adjective* of two parts. □ **duple time** *Music* rhythm with two beats to bar.

**duplex** /'djuːpleks/ ● *noun* *US* flat on two floors, house subdivided for two families. ● *adjective* having two elements; twofold.

**duplicate** ● *adjective* /'djuːplɪkət/ identical; doubled. ● *noun* /-kət/ identical thing, esp. copy. ● *verb* /-keɪt/ (**-ting**) double; make or be exact copy of; repeat (an action etc.), esp. unnecessarily. □ **in duplicate** in two exact copies. □ **duplication** *noun*.

**duplicator** *noun* machine for producing multiple copies of texts.

**duplicity** /djuː'plɪsɪtɪ/ *noun* double-dealing; deceitfulness. □ **duplicitous** *adjective*.

**durable** /'djuərəb(ə)l/ *adjective* lasting; hard-wearing. □ **durability** *noun*.

**duration** /djuə'reɪʃ(ə)n/ *noun* time taken by event. □ **for the duration** until end of event, for very long time.

**duress** /djuə'res/ *noun* compulsion, esp. illegal use of force or threats.

**Durex** /'djuəreks/ *noun proprietary term* condom.

**during** /'djuərɪŋ/ *preposition* throughout; at some point in.

**dusk** *noun* darker stage of twilight.

**dusky** *adjective* (**-ier**, **-iest**) shadowy, dim; dark-coloured.

**dust** ● *noun* finely powdered earth or other material etc.; dead person's remains. ● *verb* wipe the dust from (furniture etc.); sprinkle with powder, sugar, etc. □ **dustbin** container for household refuse; **dust bowl** desert made by drought or erosion; **dustcover** dust-sheet, dust-jacket; **dust-jacket** paper cover on hardback book; **dustman** man employed to collect household refuse; **dustpan** pan into which dust is brushed from floor etc.; **dust-sheet** protective cloth over furniture; **dust-up** *colloquial* fight, disturbance.

**duster** *noun* cloth etc. for dusting furniture etc.

**dusty** *adjective* (**-ier**, **-iest**) covered with or full of or like dust.

**Dutch** ● *adjective* of the Netherlands or its people or language. ● *noun* Dutch language; (**the Dutch**) (treated as *plural*) the people of the Netherlands. □ **Dutch auction** one in which price is progressively reduced; **Dutch barn** roof on poles over hay etc.; **Dutch cap** dome-shaped contraceptive device fitting over cervix; **Dutch courage** courage induced by alcohol; **Dutchman**, **Dutchwoman** native or national of the Netherlands; **Dutch treat** party, outing, etc. at which people pay for themselves; **go Dutch** share expenses on outing.

**dutiable** /'djuːtɪəb(ə)l/ *adjective* requiring payment of duty.

**dutiful** /'djuːtɪfʊl/ *adjective* doing one's duty; obedient. □ **dutifully** *adverb*.

**duty** /'djuːtɪ/ *noun* (*plural* **-ies**) moral or legal obligation; responsibility; tax on certain goods, imports, etc.; job or function arising from a business or office. □ **duty-free** (of goods) on which duty is not payable; **on**, **off duty** working or not working).

**duvet** /'duːveɪ/ *noun* thick soft quilt used instead of sheets and blankets.

**dwarf** /dwɔːf/ ● *noun* (*plural* **-s** or **dwarves** /dwɔːvz/) person, animal, or plant much below normal size, esp. with normal-sized head and body but short limbs; small mythological being with magical powers. ● *verb* stunt in growth; make look small by contrast.

**dwell** *verb* (*past & past participle* **dwelt** or **dwelled**) reside, live. □ **dwell on** think, write, or speak at length on. □ **dweller** *noun*.

**dwelling** *noun* house, residence.

**dwindle** /'dwɪnd(ə)l/ *verb* (**-ling**) become gradually less or smaller; lose importance.

**dye** /daɪ/ ● *noun* substance used to change colour of fabric, wood, hair, etc.; colour produced by this. ● *verb* (**dyeing**, **dyed**) colour with dye; dye a specified colour. □ **dyer** *noun*.

**dying** /'daɪɪŋ/ ● *present participle* of DIE[1]. ● *adjective* of, or at the time of, death.

**dyke** /daɪk/ (also **dike**) ● *noun* embankment built to prevent flooding; low wall. ● *verb* (**-king**) provide or protect with dyke(s).

**dynamic** /daɪ'næmɪk/ *adjective* energetic, active; of motive force; of force in operation; of dynamics. □ **dynamically** *adverb*.

**dynamics** *plural noun* (usually treated as *singular*) mathematical study of motion and forces causing it.

**dynamism** /'daɪnəmɪz(ə)m/ *noun* energy; dynamic power.

**dynamite** /'daɪnəmaɪt/ ● *noun* highly explosive mixture containing nitroglycerine. ● *verb* (**-ting**) charge or blow up with this.

**dynamo** /'daɪnəməʊ/ *noun* (*plural* **-s**) machine converting mechanical into electrical energy; *colloquial* energetic person.

**dynast** /'dɪnəst/ *noun* ruler; member of dynasty.

**dynasty** /'dɪnəstɪ/ *noun* (*plural* **-ies**) line of hereditary rulers. □ **dynastic** /-'næs-/ *adjective*.

**dyne** *noun* *Physics* force required to give a mass of one gram an acceleration of one centimetre per second per second.

**dysentery** /'dɪsəntrɪ/ *noun* inflammation of bowels, causing severe diarrhoea.

**dysfunction** /dɪs'fʌŋkʃ(ə)n/ *noun* abnormality or impairment of functioning.

**dyslexia** /dɪs'leksɪə/ *noun* abnormal difficulty in reading and spelling. □ **dyslectic** /-'lektɪk/ *adjective & noun*; **dyslexic** *adjective & noun*.

**dyspepsia** /dɪs'pepsɪə/ *noun* indigestion. □ **dyspeptic** *adjective & noun*.

**dystrophy** /'dɪstrəfɪ/ *noun* defective nutrition.

# Ee

**E** *abbreviation* (also **E.**) east(ern). □ **E-number** number prefixed by letter E identifying food additive.

**each** ● *adjective* every one of two or more, regarded separately. ● *pronoun* each person or thing. □ **each way** (of bet) backing horse etc. to win or come second or third.

**eager** /ˈiːgə/ *adjective* keen, enthusiastic. □ **eagerly** *adverb*; **eagerness** *noun*.

**eagle** /ˈiːg(ə)l/ *noun* large bird of prey; *Golf* score of two under par for hole. □ **eagle eye** keen sight, watchfulness; **eagle-eyed** *adjective*.

**eaglet** /ˈiːglɪt/ *noun* young eagle.

**ear¹** /ɪə/ *noun* organ of hearing, esp. external part; faculty of discriminating sound; attention. □ **all ears** listening attentively; **earache** pain in inner ear; **eardrum** membrane of middle ear; **earphone** (usually in *plural*) device worn on ear to listen to recording, radio, etc.; **earplug** device worn in ear as protection from water, noise, etc.; **earring** jewellery worn on ear; **earshot** hearing-range; **ear-trumpet** trumpet-shaped tube formerly used as hearing aid.

**ear²** /ɪə/ *noun* seed-bearing head of cereal plant.

**earl** /ɜːl/ *noun* British nobleman ranking between marquess and viscount. □ **earldom** *noun*.

**early** /ˈɜːlɪ/ *adjective & adverb* (**-ier, -iest**) before due, usual, or expected time; not far on in day or night or in development etc. □ **early bird** *colloquial* person who arrives, gets up, etc. early; **early days** too soon to expect results etc.

**earmark** *verb* set aside for special purpose.

**earn** /ɜːn/ *verb* obtain as reward for work or merit; bring as income or interest. □ **earner** *noun*.

**earnest** /ˈɜːnɪst/ *adjective* intensely serious. □ **in earnest** serious(ly). □ **earnestly** *adverb*; **earnestness** *noun*.

**earnings** /ˈɜːnɪŋz/ *plural noun* money earned.

**earth** /ɜːθ/ ● *noun* planet we live on (also **Earth**); land and sea as opposed to sky; ground; soil, mould; this world as opposed to heaven or hell; *Electricity* connection to earth as completion of circuit; hole of fox etc. ● *verb Electricity* connect to earth; cover (roots) with earth. □ **earthwork** bank of earth in fortification; **earthworm** worm living in earth; **run to earth** find after long search.

**earthen** *adjective* made of earth or baked clay. □ **earthenware** pottery made of fired clay.

**earthly** *adjective* of earth, terrestrial; *colloquial* (usually with negative) remotely possible. □ **not an earthly** *colloquial* no chance or idea whatever.

**earthquake** *noun* violent shaking of earth's surface.

**earthy** *adjective* (**-ier, -iest**) of or like earth or soil; coarse, crude.

**earwig** *noun* insect with pincers at rear end.

**ease** /iːz/ ● *noun* facility, effortlessness; freedom from pain, trouble, or constraint. ● *verb* (**-sing**) relieve from pain etc.; (often + *off, up*) become less burdensome or severe; relax, slacken; move or be moved by gentle force.

**easel** /ˈiːz(ə)l/ *noun* stand for painting, blackboard, etc.

**easement** *noun Law* right of way over another's property.

**easily** /ˈiːzɪlɪ/ *adverb* without difficulty; by far; very probably.

**east** ● *noun* point of horizon where sun rises at equinoxes; corresponding compass point; (usually **the East**) eastern part of world, country, town, etc. ● *adjective* towards, at, near, or facing east; (of wind) from east. ● *adverb* towards, at, or near east; (+ *of*) further east than. □ **eastbound** travelling or leading east; **East End** part of London east of City; **east-north-east**, **east-south-east** point midway between east and north-east or south-east. □ **eastward** *adjective, adverb, & noun*; **eastwards** *adverb*.

**Easter** /ˈiːstə/ noun festival of Christ's resurrection. □ **Easter egg** artificial usually chocolate egg given at Easter; **Easter Saturday** day before Easter, (properly) Saturday after Easter.

**easterly** /ˈiːstəlɪ/ adjective & adverb in eastern position or direction; (of wind) from east.

**eastern** /ˈiːst(ə)n/ adjective of or in east. □ **Eastern Church** Orthodox Church. □ **easternmost** adjective.

**easterner** noun native or inhabitant of east.

**easy** /ˈiːzɪ/ ● adjective (**-ier, -iest**) not difficult; free from pain, trouble, or anxiety; relaxed and pleasant; compliant. ● adverb with ease, in an effortless or relaxed way. □ **easy chair** large comfortable armchair; **easygoing** placid and tolerant; **go easy** (usually + on, with) be sparing or cautious; **take it easy** proceed gently, relax.

**eat** verb (past **ate** /et, eɪt/; past participle **eaten**) chew and swallow (food); consume food, have meal; destroy, consume. □ **eating apple** one suitable for eating raw; **eat out** have meal away from home, esp. in restaurant; **eat up** eat completely.

**eatable** ● adjective fit to be eaten. ● noun (usually in plural) food.

**eater** noun person who eats; eating apple.

**eau-de-Cologne** /əʊdəkəˈləʊn/ noun toilet water originally from Cologne.

**eaves** /iːvz/ plural noun underside of projecting roof.

**eavesdrop** verb (**-pp-**) listen to private conversation. □ **eavesdropper** noun.

**ebb** ● noun outflow of tide. ● verb flow back; decline.

**ebony** /ˈebənɪ/ ● noun hard heavy black tropical wood. ● adjective made of or black as ebony.

**ebullient** /ɪˈbʌlɪənt/ adjective exuberant. □ **ebullience** noun; **ebulliently** adverb.

**EC** abbreviation European Community; East Central.

**eccentric** /ɪkˈsentrɪk/ ● adjective odd or capricious in behaviour or appearance; not placed centrally, not having axis etc. placed centrally; not concentric; not circular. ● noun eccentric person. □ **eccentrically** adverb; **eccentricity** /eksenˈtrɪs-/ noun (plural **-ies**).

**ecclesiastic** /ɪkliːzɪˈæstɪk/ noun clergyman.

**ecclesiastical** adjective of the Church or clergy.

**ECG** abbreviation electrocardiogram.

**echelon** /ˈeʃəlɒn/ noun level in organization, society, etc.; wedge-shaped formation of troops, aircraft, etc.

**echidna** /ɪˈkɪdnə/ noun Australian egg-laying spiny mammal.

**echo** /ˈekəʊ/ ● noun (plural **-es**) repetition of sound by reflection of sound waves; reflected radio or radar beam; close imitation; circumstance or event reminiscent of earlier one. ● verb (**-es, -ed**) resound with echo; repeat, imitate; be repeated.

**éclair** /eɪˈkleə/ noun finger-shaped iced cake of choux pastry filled with cream.

**éclat** /eɪˈklɑː/ noun brilliant display; conspicuous success; prestige.

**eclectic** /ɪˈklektɪk/ ● adjective selecting ideas, style, etc. from various sources. ● noun eclectic person. □ **eclecticism** /-tɪs-/ noun.

**eclipse** /ɪˈklɪps/ ● noun obscuring of light of sun by moon (**solar eclipse**) or of moon by earth (**lunar eclipse**); loss of light or importance. ● verb (**-sing**) cause eclipse of; intercept (light); outshine, surpass.

**eclogue** /ˈeklɒg/ noun short pastoral poem.

**ecology** /ɪˈkɒlədʒɪ/ noun study of relations of organisms to one another and their surroundings. □ **ecological** /iːkəˈlɒdʒ-/ adjective; **ecologically** /iːkəˈlɒdʒ-/ adverb; **ecologist** noun.

**economic** /iːkəˈnɒmɪk/ adjective of economics; profitable; connected with trade and industry. □ **economically** adverb.

**economical** /iːkəˈnɒmɪk(ə)l/ adjective sparing; avoiding waste. □ **economically** adverb.

**economics** /iːkəˈnɒmɪks/ plural noun (treated as singular) science of production and distribution of wealth; application of this to particular subject. □ **economist** /ɪˈkɒnəmɪst/ noun.

**economize** /ɪˈkɒnəmaɪz/ verb (also **-ise**) (**-zing** or **-sing**) make economies; reduce expenditure.

**economy** /ɪˈkɒnəmɪ/ *noun* (*plural* **-ies**) community's system of wealth creation; frugality, instance of this; sparing use.

**ecosystem** /ˈiːkəʊsɪstəm/ *noun* biological community of interacting organisms and their physical environment.

**ecru** /ˈeɪkruː/ *noun* light fawn colour.

**ecstasy** /ˈekstəsɪ/ *noun* (*plural* **-ies**) overwhelming joy or rapture; *slang* type of hallucinogenic drug. □ **ecstatic** /ɪkˈstætɪk/ *adjective*.

**ECT** *abbreviation* electroconvulsive therapy.

**ectoplasm** /ˈektəʊplæz(ə)m/ *noun* supposed viscous substance exuding from body of spiritualistic medium during trance.

**ecu** /ˈekjuː/ *noun* (also **Ecu**) (*plural* **-s**) European Currency Unit.

**ecumenical** /iːkjuːˈmenɪk(ə)l/ *adjective* of or representing whole Christian world; seeking worldwide Christian unity. □ **ecumenism** /iːˈkjuːmən-/ *noun*.

**eczema** /ˈeksɪmə/ *noun* kind of inflammation of skin.

**ed.** *abbreviation* edited by; edition; editor.

**Edam** /ˈiːdæm/ *noun* round Dutch cheese with red rind.

**eddy** /ˈedɪ/ ● *noun* (*plural* **-ies**) circular movement of water, smoke, etc. ● *verb* (**-ies, -ied**) move in eddies.

**edelweiss** /ˈeɪd(ə)lvaɪs/ *noun* Alpine plant with woolly white bracts.

**Eden** /ˈiːd(ə)n/ *noun* (in full **Garden of Eden**) home of Adam and Eve; delightful place or state.

**edge** ● *noun* boundary-line or margin of area or surface; narrow surface of thin object; meeting-line of surfaces; sharpness; sharpened side of blade; brink of precipice; crest of ridge; effectiveness. ● *verb* (**-ging**) advance gradually or furtively; give or form border to; sharpen. □ **edgeways**, **edgewise** with edge foremost or uppermost; **have the edge on**, **over** have slight advantage over; **on edge** excited or irritable; **set** (**person's**) **teeth on edge** cause unpleasant nervous sensation in.

**edging** *noun* thing forming edge or border.

**edgy** *adjective* (**-ier, -iest**) irritable; anxious.

**edible** /ˈedɪb(ə)l/ *adjective* fit to be eaten.

**edict** /ˈiːdɪkt/ *noun* order proclaimed by authority.

**edifice** /ˈedɪfɪs/ *noun* building, esp. imposing one.

**edify** /ˈedɪfaɪ/ *verb* (**-ies, -ied**) improve morally. □ **edification** *noun*.

**edit** /ˈedɪt/ *verb* (**-t-**) prepare for publication or broadcast; be editor of; cut and collate (films etc.) to make unified sequence; reword, modify; (+ *out*) remove (part) from text, recording, etc.

**edition** /ɪˈdɪʃ(ə)n/ *noun* edited or published form of book etc.; copies of book or newspaper etc. issued at one time; instance of regular broadcast.

**editor** /ˈedɪtə/ *noun* person who edits; person who directs writing of newspaper or news programme or section of one; person who selects material for publication. □ **editorship** *noun*.

**editorial** /edɪˈtɔːrɪəl/ ● *adjective* of editing or an editor. ● *noun* article giving newspaper's views on current topic.

**educate** /ˈedjʊkeɪt/ *verb* (**-ting**) train or instruct mentally and morally; provide systematic instruction for. □ **educable** *adjective*; **education** *noun*; **educational** *adjective*; **educator** *noun*.

**educationist** *noun* (also **educationalist**) expert in educational methods.

**Edwardian** /edˈwɔːdɪən/ ● *adjective* of or characteristic of reign (1901–10) of Edward VII. ● *noun* person of this period.

**EEC** *abbreviation* European Economic Community.

**EEG** *abbreviation* electroencephalogram.

**eel** *noun* snakelike fish.

**eerie** /ˈɪərɪ/ *adjective* (**-r, -st**) strange; weird. □ **eerily** *adverb*.

**efface** /ɪˈfeɪs/ *verb* (**-cing**) rub or wipe out; surpass, eclipse; (**efface oneself**) treat oneself as unimportant. □ **effacement** *noun*.

**effect** /ɪˈfekt/ ● *noun* result, consequence; efficacy; impression; (in *plural*) possessions; (in *plural*) lighting, sound, etc. giving realism to play etc.; physical phenomenon. ● *verb* bring about.

■ **Usage** As a verb, *effect* should not be confused with *affect*. *He effected an entrance* means 'He got in (somehow)', but *This won't affect me* means 'My life won't be changed by this'.

**effective** *adjective* operative; impressive; actual; producing intended result. □ **effectively** *adverb*; **effectiveness** *noun*.

**effectual** /ɪˈfektʃʊəl/ *adjective* producing required effect; valid.

**effeminate** /ɪˈfemɪnət/ *adjective* (of a man) unmanly, womanish. □ **effeminacy** *noun*.

**effervesce** /efəˈves/ *verb* (**-cing**) give off bubbles of gas. □ **effervescence** *noun*; **effervescent** *adjective*.

**effete** /ɪˈfiːt/ *adjective* feeble; effeminate.

**efficacious** /efɪˈkeɪʃəs/ *adjective* producing desired effect. □ **efficacy** /ˈefɪkəsɪ/ *noun*.

**efficient** /ɪˈfɪʃ(ə)nt/ *adjective* productive with minimum waste of effort; competent, capable. □ **efficiency** *noun*; **efficiently** *adverb*.

**effigy** /ˈefɪdʒɪ/ *noun* (*plural* **-ies**) sculpture or model of person.

**effloresce** /eflɔːˈres/ *verb* (**-cing**) burst into flower. □ **efflorescence** *noun*.

**effluence** /ˈefluəns/ *noun* flowing out (of light, electricity, etc.); what flows out.

**effluent** /ˈefluənt/ ● *adjective* flowing out. ● *noun* sewage or industrial waste discharged into river etc.; stream flowing from lake etc.

**effluvium** /ɪˈfluːvɪəm/ *noun* (*plural* **-via**) unpleasant or harmful outflow.

**effort** /ˈefət/ *noun* exertion; determined attempt; force exerted; *colloquial* something accomplished. □ **effortless** *adjective*; **effortlessly** *adverb*.

**effrontery** /ɪˈfrʌntərɪ/ *noun* impudence.

**effuse** /ɪˈfjuːz/ *verb* (**-sing**) pour forth.

**effusion** /ɪˈfjuːʒ(ə)n/ *noun* outpouring.

**effusive** /ɪˈfjuːsɪv/ *adjective* demonstrative; gushing. □ **effusively** *adverb*; **effusiveness** *noun*.

**EFL** *abbreviation* English as a foreign language.

**Efta** /ˈeftə/ *noun* (also **EFTA**) European Free Trade Association.

**e.g.** *abbreviation* for example.

**egalitarian** /ɪgælɪˈteərɪən/ ● *adjective* of or advocating equal rights for all. ● *noun* egalitarian person. □ **egalitarianism** *noun*.

**egg**[1] *noun* body produced by female of birds, insects, etc., capable of developing into new individual; edible egg of domestic hen; ovum. □ **eggcup** cup for holding boiled egg; **egghead** *colloquial* intellectual; **eggplant** aubergine; **egg white** white or clear part round yolk of egg.

**egg**[2] *verb* (+ *on*) urge.

**eglantine** /ˈegləntaɪn/ *noun* sweet-brier.

**ego** /ˈiːgəʊ/ *noun* (*plural* **-s**) the self; part of mind that has sense of individuality; self-esteem.

**egocentric** /iːgəʊˈsentrɪk/ *adjective* self-centred.

**egoism** /ˈiːgəʊɪz(ə)m/ *noun* self-interest as moral basis of behaviour; systematic selfishness; egotism. □ **egoist** *noun*; **egoistic** /-ˈɪs-/ *adjective*.

**egotism** /ˈiːgətɪz(ə)m/ *noun* self-conceit; selfishness. □ **egotist** *noun*; **egotistic(al)** /-ˈtɪs-/ *adjective*.

**egregious** /ɪˈgriːdʒəs/ *adjective* extremely bad; *archaic* remarkable.

**egress** /ˈiːgres/ *noun* going out; way out.

**egret** /ˈiːgrɪt/ *noun* kind of white heron.

**Egyptian** /ɪˈdʒɪpʃ(ə)n/ ● *adjective* of Egypt. ● *noun* native or national of Egypt; language of ancient Egyptians.

**Egyptology** /iːdʒɪpˈtɒlədʒɪ/ *noun* study of ancient Egypt. □ **Egyptologist** *noun*.

**eh** /eɪ/ *interjection colloquial*: expressing inquiry, surprise, etc.

**eider** /ˈaɪdə/ *noun* northern species of duck. □ **eiderdown** quilt stuffed with soft material, esp. down.

**eight** /eɪt/ *adjective & noun* one more than seven; 8-oared boat, its crew. □ **eightsome reel** lively Scottish dance for 8 people. □ **eighth** /eɪtθ/ *adjective & noun*.

**eighteen** /eɪˈtiːn/ *adjective & noun* one more than seventeen. □ **eighteenth** *adjective & noun*.

**eighty** /ˈeɪtɪ/ *adjective & noun* (*plural* **-ies**) eight times ten. □ **eightieth** *adjective & noun*.

**eisteddfod** /aɪˈstedfəd/ *noun* congress of Welsh poets and musicians gathering for musical and literary competition.

**either** /ˈaɪðə, ˈiːðə/ ● *adjective & pronoun* one or other of two; each of two. ● *adverb* (with negative) any more than the other. □ **either ... or ...** as one possibility ... and as the other ...

**ejaculate** /ɪˈdʒækjʊleɪt/ *verb* (**-ting**) emit (semen) in orgasm; exclaim. □ **ejaculation** *noun*.

**eject** /ɪˈdʒekt/ *verb* throw out, expel; (of pilot etc.) cause oneself to be propelled from aircraft in emergency; emit. □ **ejection** *noun*.

**ejector seat** *noun* device in aircraft for emergency ejection of pilot etc.

**eke** *verb* (**eking**) □ **eke out** supplement (income etc.), make (living) or support (existence) with difficulty.

**elaborate** ● *adjective* /ɪˈlæbərət/ minutely worked out; complicated. ● *verb* /ɪˈlæbəreɪt/ (**-ting**) work out or explain in detail. □ **elaborately** *adverb*; **elaboration** *noun*.

**élan** /eɪˈlɑ̃/ *noun* vivacity, dash. [French]

**eland** /ˈiːlənd/ *noun* (*plural* same or **-s**) large African antelope.

**elapse** /ɪˈlæps/ *verb* (**-sing**) (of time) pass by.

**elastic** /ɪˈlæstɪk/ ● *adjective* able to resume normal bulk or shape after being stretched or squeezed; springy; flexible. ● *noun* elastic cord or fabric, usually woven with strips of rubber. □ **elastic band** rubber band. □ **elasticity** /iːlæˈstɪs-/ *noun*.

**elasticated** /ɪˈlæstɪkeɪtɪd/ *adjective* (of fabric) made elastic by weaving with rubber thread.

**elate** /ɪˈleɪt/ *verb* (**-ting**) (esp. as **elated** *adjective*) make delighted or proud. □ **elation** *noun*.

**elbow** /ˈelbəʊ/ ● *noun* joint between forearm and upper arm; part of sleeve covering elbow; elbow-shaped thing. ● *verb* thrust or jostle (person); make (one's way) thus. □ **elbow-grease** *jocular* vigorous polishing, hard work; **elbow-room** sufficient space to move or work in.

**elder**[1] /ˈeldə/ ● *adjective* older; senior. ● *noun* older person; official in early Christian and some modern Churches.

**elder**[2] /ˈeldə/ *noun* tree with white flowers and black **elderberries**.

**elderly** /ˈeldəlɪ/ *adjective* rather old.

**eldest** /ˈeldɪst/ *adjective* first-born; oldest surviving.

**eldorado** /eldəˈrɑːdəʊ/ *noun* (*plural* **-s**) imaginary land of great wealth.

**elect** /ɪˈlekt/ ● *verb* choose by voting; choose, decide. ● *adjective* chosen; select, choice; (after noun) chosen but not yet in office.

**election** /ɪˈlekʃ(ə)n/ *noun* electing, being elected; occasion for this.

**electioneer** /ɪlekʃəˈnɪə/ *verb* take part in election campaign.

**elective** /ɪˈlektɪv/ *adjective* chosen by or derived from election; entitled to elect; optional.

**elector** /ɪˈlektə/ *noun* person entitled to vote in election. □ **electoral** *adjective*.

**electorate** /ɪˈlektərət/ *noun* group of electors.

**electric** /ɪˈlektrɪk/ *adjective* of, worked by, or charged with electricity; causing or charged with excitement. □ **electric blanket** one heated by internal wires; **electric chair** chair used for electrocution of criminals; **electric eel** eel-like fish able to give electric shock; **electric fire** portable electric heater; **electric shock** effect of sudden discharge of electricity through body of person etc. □ **electrically** *adverb*.

**electrical** *adjective* of or worked by electricity. □ **electrically** *adverb*.

**electrician** /ɪlekˈtrɪʃ(ə)n/ *noun* person who installs or maintains electrical equipment.

**electricity** /ɪlekˈtrɪsɪtɪ/ *noun* form of energy present in protons and electrons; science of electricity; supply of electricity.

**electrify** /ɪˈlektrɪfaɪ/ *verb* (**-ies**, **-ied**) charge with electricity; convert to electric working; startle, excite. □ **electrification** *noun*.

**electro-** *combining form* of or caused by electricity.

**electrocardiogram** /ɪlektrəʊˈkɑːdɪəgræm/ *noun* record of electric currents generated by heartbeat. □ **electrocardiograph** instrument for recording such currents.

**electroconvulsive** /ɪlektrəʊkənˈvʌlsɪv/ *adjective* (of therapy) using convulsive response to electric shocks.

**electrocute** /ɪˈlektrəkjuːt/ *verb* (**-ting**) kill by electric shock. □ **electrocution** /-ˈkjuːʃ(ə)n/ *noun*.

**electrode** /ɪ'lektrəʊd/ *noun* conductor through which electricity enters or leaves electrolyte, gas, vacuum, etc.

**electroencephalogram** /ɪlektrəʊm-'sefələgræm/ *noun* record of electrical activity of brain. □ **electroencephalograph** instrument for recording such activity.

**electrolysis** /ɪlek'trɒlɪsɪs/ *noun* chemical decomposition by electric action; breaking up of tumours, hair-roots, etc. thus.

**electrolyte** /ɪ'lektrəlaɪt/ *noun* solution that can conduct electricity; substance that can dissolve to produce this. □ **electrolytic** /-trəʊ'lɪt-/ *adjective*.

**electromagnet** /ɪlektrəʊ'mægnɪt/ *noun* soft metal core made into magnet by electric current through coil surrounding it.

**electromagnetism** /ɪlektrəʊ'mægnɪt-ɪz(ə)m/ *noun* magnetic forces produced by electricity; study of these.

**electron** /ɪ'lektrɒn/ *noun* stable elementary particle with charge of negative electricity, found in all atoms and acting as primary carrier of electricity in solids. □ **electron microscope** one with high magnification, using electron beam instead of light.

**electronic** /ɪlek'trɒnɪk/ *adjective* of electrons or electronics; (of music) produced electronically. □ **electronic mail** messages distributed by a computer system. □ **electronically** *adverb*.

**electronics** *plural noun* (treated as *singular*) science of movement of electrons in vacuum, gas, semiconductor, etc.

**electroplate** /ɪ'lektrəʊpleɪt/ ● *verb* (**-ting**) coat with chromium, silver, etc. by electrolysis. ● *noun* electroplated articles.

**elegant** /'elɪgənt/ *adjective* graceful, tasteful, refined; ingeniously simple. □ **elegance** *noun*; **elegantly** *adverb*.

**elegy** /'elɪdʒɪ/ *noun* (*plural* **-ies**) sorrowful song or poem, esp. for the dead. □ **elegiac** /-'dʒaɪək/ *adjective*.

**element** /'elɪmənt/ *noun* component part; substance which cannot be resolved by chemical means into simpler substances; any of **the four elements** (earth, water, air, fire) formerly supposed to make up all matter; wire that

gives out heat in electric heater, cooker, etc.; (in *plural*) atmospheric agencies; (in *plural*) rudiments, first principles; (in *plural*) bread and wine of Eucharist. □ **in one's element** in one's preferred situation.

**elemental** /elɪ'ment(ə)l/ *adjective* of or like the elements or the forces of nature; basic, essential.

**elementary** /elɪ'mentərɪ/ *adjective* dealing with simplest facts of subject; unanalysable. □ **elementary particle** *Physics* subatomic particle, esp. one not known to consist of simpler ones.

**elephant** /'elɪf(ə)nt/ *noun* (*plural* same or **-s**) largest living land animal, with trunk and ivory tusks.

**elephantiasis** /elɪfən'taɪəsɪs/ *noun* skin disease causing gross enlargement of limbs etc.

**elephantine** /elɪ'fæntaɪn/ *adjective* of elephants; huge; clumsy.

**elevate** /'elɪveɪt/ *verb* (**-ting**) lift up, raise; exalt in rank etc.; (usually as **elevated** *adjective*) raise morally or intellectually.

**elevation** *noun* elevating, being elevated; angle above horizontal; height above given level; drawing showing one side of building.

**elevator** *noun* US lift; movable part of tailplane for changing aircraft's altitude; hoisting machine.

**eleven** /ɪ'lev(ə)n/ *adjective & noun* one more than ten; team of 11 people in cricket etc. □ **eleventh hour** last possible moment. □ **eleventh** *adjective & noun*.

**elevenses** /ɪ'levənzɪz/ *noun colloquial* light mid-morning refreshment.

**elf** *noun* (*plural* **elves** /elvz/) mythological being, esp. small and mischievous one. □ **elfish** *adjective*.

**elfin** /'elfɪn/ *adjective* of elves; elflike.

**elicit** /ɪ'lɪsɪt/ *verb* (**-t-**) draw out (facts, response, etc.).

**elide** /ɪ'laɪd/ *verb* (**-ding**) omit in pronunciation.

**eligible** /'elɪdʒɪb(ə)l/ *adjective* (often + *for*) fit or entitled to be chosen; desirable or suitable, esp. for marriage. □ **eligibility** *noun*.

**eliminate** /ɪ'lɪmɪneɪt/ *verb* (**-ting**) remove, get rid of; exclude. □ **elimination** *noun*; **eliminator** *noun*.

**elision** /ɪ'lɪʒ(ə)n/ noun omission of vowel or syllable in pronunciation.

**élite** /ɪ'liːt/ noun select group or class; (**the élite**) the best (of a group).

**élitism** noun advocacy of or reliance on dominance by select group. □ **élitist** noun & adjective.

**elixir** /ɪ'lɪksɪə/ noun alchemist's preparation supposedly able to change metal into gold or prolong life indefinitely; aromatic medicine.

**Elizabethan** /ɪlɪzə'biːθ(ə)n/ ● adjective of time of Elizabeth I or II. ● noun person of this time.

**elk** noun (plural same or **-s**) large type of deer.

**ellipse** /ɪ'lɪps/ noun regular oval.

**ellipsis** /ɪ'lɪpsɪs/ noun (plural **ellipses** /-siːz/) omission of words needed to complete construction or sense.

**elliptical** /ɪ'lɪptɪk(ə)l/ adjective of or like an ellipse; (of language) confusingly concise.

**elm** noun tree with rough serrated leaves; its wood.

**elocution** /elə'kjuːʃ(ə)n/ noun art of clear and expressive speaking.

**elongate** /'iːlɒŋgeɪt/ verb (**-ting**) extend, lengthen. □ **elongation** noun.

**elope** /ɪ'ləʊp/ verb (**-ping**) run away to marry secretly. □ **elopement** noun.

**eloquence** /'eləkwəns/ noun fluent and effective use of language. □ **eloquent** adjective; **eloquently** adverb.

**else** /els/ adverb besides; instead; otherwise, if not. □ **elsewhere** in or to some other place.

**elucidate** /ɪ'luːsɪdeɪt/ verb (**-ting**) throw light on, explain. □ **elucidation** noun.

**elude** /ɪ'luːd/ verb (**-ding**) escape adroitly from; avoid; baffle.

**elusive** /ɪ'luːsɪv/ adjective difficult to find, catch, or remember; avoiding the point raised. □ **elusiveness** noun.

**elver** /'elvə/ noun young eel.

**elves** plural of ELF.

**Elysium** /ɪ'lɪzɪəm/ noun Greek Mythology home of the blessed after death; place of ideal happiness. □ **Elysian** adjective.

**em** noun Printing unit of measurement approximately equal to width of M.

**emaciate** /ɪ'meɪsɪeɪt/ verb (**-ting**) (esp. as **emaciated** adjective) make thin or feeble. □ **emaciation** noun.

**emanate** /'eməneɪt/ verb (**-ting**) (usually + from) issue or originate (from source). □ **emanation** noun.

**emancipate** /ɪ'mænsɪpeɪt/ verb (**-ting**) free from social, political, or moral restraint. □ **emancipation** noun.

**emasculate** ● verb /ɪ'mæskjʊleɪt/ (**-ting**) enfeeble; castrate. ● adjective /ɪ'mæskjʊlət/ enfeebled; castrated; effeminate. □ **emasculation** noun.

**embalm** /ɪm'bɑːm/ verb preserve (corpse) from decay; preserve from oblivion; make fragrant.

**embankment** /ɪm'bæŋkmənt/ noun bank constructed to confine water or carry road or railway.

**embargo** /ɪm'bɑːgəʊ/ ● noun (plural **-es**) order forbidding ships to enter or leave port; suspension of commerce or other activity. ● verb (**-es**, **-ed**) place under embargo.

**embark** /ɪm'bɑːk/ verb put or go on board ship; (+ on, in) begin (enterprise).

**embarkation** /embɑː'keɪʃ(ə)n/ noun embarking on ship.

**embarrass** /ɪm'bærəs/ verb make (person) feel awkward or ashamed; encumber; (as **embarrassed** adjective) encumbered with debts. □ **embarrassment** noun.

**embassy** /'embəsɪ/ noun (plural **-ies**) ambassador's residence or offices; deputation to foreign government.

**embattled** /ɪm'bæt(ə)ld/ adjective prepared or arrayed for battle; fortified with battlements; under heavy attack, in trying circumstances.

**embed** /ɪm'bed/ verb (also **imbed**) (**-dd-**) (esp. as **embedded** adjective) fix in surrounding mass.

**embellish** /ɪm'belɪʃ/ verb beautify, adorn; make fictitious additions to. □ **embellishment** noun.

**ember** /'embə/ noun (usually in plural) small piece of glowing coal etc. in dying fire. □ **ember days** days of fasting and prayer in Christian Church, associated with ordinations.

**embezzle** /ɪm'bez(ə)l/ verb (**-ling**) divert (money) fraudulently to own use. □ **embezzlement** noun; **embezzler** noun.

**embitter** /ɪm'bɪtə/ verb arouse bitter feelings in. □ **embitterment** noun.

**emblazon** /ɪmˈbleɪz(ə)n/ *verb* portray or adorn conspicuously.

**emblem** /ˈembləm/ *noun* symbol; (+ *of*) type, embodiment; distinctive badge. □ **emblematic** /-ˈmæt-/ *adjective*.

**embody** /ɪmˈbɒdɪ/ *verb* (**-ies, -ied**) give concrete form to; be expression of; include, comprise. □ **embodiment** *noun*.

**embolden** /ɪmˈbəʊld(ə)n/ *verb* encourage.

**embolism** /ˈembəlɪz(ə)m/ *noun* obstruction of artery by blood clot etc.

**emboss** /ɪmˈbɒs/ *verb* carve or decorate with design in relief.

**embrace** /ɪmˈbreɪs/ ● *verb* (**-cing**) hold closely in arms; enclose; accept, adopt; include. ● *noun* act of embracing, clasp.

**embrasure** /ɪmˈbreɪʒə/ *noun* bevelling of wall at sides of window etc.; opening in parapet for gun.

**embrocation** /embrəˈkeɪʃ(ə)n/ *noun* liquid for rubbing on body to relieve muscular pain.

**embroider** /ɪmˈbrɔɪdə/ *verb* decorate with needlework; embellish. □ **embroidery** *noun*.

**embroil** /ɪmˈbrɔɪl/ *verb* (often + *in*) involve (in conflict or difficulties).

**embryo** /ˈembrɪəʊ/ *noun* (*plural* **-s**) unborn or unhatched offspring; thing in rudimentary stage. □ **embryonic** /-ˈɒn-/ *adjective*.

**emend** /ɪˈmend/ *verb* correct, remove errors from (text etc.). □ **emendation** /iː-/ *noun*.

**emerald** /ˈemər(ə)ld/ ● *noun* bright green gem; colour of this. ● *adjective* bright green.

**emerge** /ɪˈmɜːdʒ/ *verb* (**-ging**) come up or out into view or notice. □ **emergence** *noun*; **emergent** *adjective*.

**emergency** /ɪˈmɜːdʒənsɪ/ *noun* (*plural* **-ies**) sudden state of danger etc., requiring immediate action.

**emeritus** /ɪˈmerɪtəs/ *adjective* retired and holding honorary title.

**emery** /ˈemərɪ/ *noun* coarse corundum for polishing metal etc. □ **emery board** emery-coated nail-file.

**emetic** /ɪˈmetɪk/ ● *adjective* that causes vomiting. ● *noun* emetic medicine.

**emigrate** /ˈemɪɡreɪt/ *verb* (**-ting**) leave own country to settle in another. □ **emigrant** *noun & adjective*; **emigration** *noun*.

**émigré** /ˈemɪɡreɪ/ *noun* emigrant, esp. political exile.

**eminence** /ˈemɪnəns/ *noun* recognized superiority; rising ground; (**His, Your Eminence**) title used of or to cardinal.

**eminent** /ˈemɪnənt/ *adjective* distinguished, notable. □ **eminently** *adverb*.

**emir** /eˈmɪə/ *noun* (also **amir** /əˈmɪə/) *title of various Muslim rulers*.

**emirate** /ˈemɪrət/ *noun* position, reign, or domain of emir.

**emissary** /ˈemɪsərɪ/ *noun* (*plural* **-ies**) person sent on diplomatic mission.

**emit** /ɪˈmɪt/ *verb* (**-tt-**) give or send out; discharge. □ **emission** /ɪˈmɪʃ(ə)n/ *noun*.

**emollient** /ɪˈmɒlɪənt/ ● *adjective* softening; soothing. ● *noun* emollient substance.

**emolument** /ɪˈmɒljʊmənt/ *adjective* fee from employment, salary.

**emotion** /ɪˈməʊʃ(ə)n/ *noun* strong instinctive feeling such as love or fear; emotional intensity or sensibility.

**emotional** *adjective* of or expressing emotion(s); especially liable to emotion; arousing emotion. □ **emotionalism** *noun*; **emotionally** *adverb*.

■ **Usage** See note at EMOTIVE.

**emotive** /ɪˈməʊtɪv/ *adjective* of or arousing emotion.

■ **Usage** Although the senses of *emotive* and *emotional* overlap, *emotive* is more common in the sense 'arousing emotion', as in *an emotive issue*, and only *emotional* can mean 'especially liable to emotion', as in *a highly emotional person*.

**empanel** /ɪmˈpæn(ə)l/ *verb* (also **impanel**) (**-ll-**; *US* **-l-**) enter (jury) on panel.

**empathize** /ˈempəθaɪz/ *verb* (also **-ise**) (**-zing** or **-sing**) (usually + *with*) exercise empathy.

**empathy** /ˈempəθɪ/ *noun* ability to identify with person or object.

**emperor** /ˈempərə/ *noun* ruler of empire.

**emphasis** /ˈemfəsɪs/ *noun* (*plural* **emphases** /-siːz/) importance attached to something; significant stress on word(s); vigour of expression etc.

**emphasize** /'emfəsaɪz/ *verb* (also **-ise**) (**-zing** or **-sing**) lay stress on.

**emphatic** /ɪm'fætɪk/ *adjective* forcibly expressive; (of word) bearing emphasis (e.g. *myself* in *I did it myself*). □ **emphatically** *adverb*.

**emphysema** /emfɪ'siːmə/ *noun* disease of lungs causing breathlessness.

**empire** /'empaɪə/ *noun* large group of states under single authority; supreme dominion; large commercial organization etc. owned or directed by one person.

**empirical** /ɪm'pɪrɪk(ə)l/ *adjective* based on observation or experiment, not on theory. □ **empiricism** /-rɪs-/ *noun*; **empiricist** /-rɪs-/ *noun*.

**emplacement** /ɪm'pleɪsmənt/ *noun* platform for gun(s); putting in position.

**employ** /ɪm'plɔɪ/ *verb* use services of (person) in return for payment; use (thing, time, energy, etc.); keep (person) occupied. □ **in the employ of** employed by. □ **employer** *noun*.

**employee** /emplɔɪ'iː/ *noun* person employed for wages.

**employment** *noun* employing, being employed; person's trade or profession. □ **employment office** government office finding work for the unemployed.

**emporium** /em'pɔːrɪəm/ *noun* large shop; centre of commerce.

**empower** /ɪm'paʊə/ *verb* give power to.

**empress** /'emprɪs/ *noun* wife or widow of emperor; woman emperor.

**empty** /'emptɪ/ ● *adjective* (**-ier, -iest**) containing nothing; vacant, unoccupied; hollow, insincere; without purpose; *colloquial* hungry; vacuous, foolish. ● *verb* (**-ies, -ied**) remove contents of; transfer (contents); become empty; (of river) discharge itself. ● *noun* (*plural* **-ies**) *colloquial* emptied bottle etc. □ **empty-handed** bringing or taking nothing. □ **emptiness** *noun*.

**EMS** *abbreviation* European Monetary System.

**emu** /'iːmjuː/ *noun* (*plural* **-s**) large flightless Australian bird.

**emulate** /'emjʊleɪt/ *verb* (**-ting**) try to equal or excel; imitate. □ **emulation** *noun*; **emulator** *noun*.

**emulsify** /ɪ'mʌlsɪfaɪ/ *verb* (**-ies, -ied**) make emulsion of. □ **emulsifier** *noun*.

**emulsion** /ɪ'mʌlʃ(ə)n/ *noun* fine dispersion of one liquid in another, esp. as paint, medicine, etc.

**en** *noun* Printing unit of measurement equal to half em.

**enable** /ɪ'neɪb(ə)l/ *verb* (**-ling**) (+ *to do*) supply with means or authority; make possible.

**enact** /ɪ'nækt/ *verb* ordain, decree; make (bill etc.) law; play (part). □ **enactment** *noun*.

**enamel** /ɪ'næm(ə)l/ ● *noun* glasslike opaque coating on metal; any hard smooth coating; kind of hard gloss paint; hard coating of teeth. ● *verb* (**-ll-**, *US* **-l-**) coat with enamel.

**enamour** /ɪ'næmə/ *verb* (*US* **enamor**) (usually in *passive*; + *of*) inspire with love or delight.

**en bloc** /ɑ̃ 'blɒk/ *adverb* in a block, all at same time. [French]

**encamp** /ɪn'kæmp/ *verb* settle in (esp. military) camp. □ **encampment** *noun*.

**encapsulate** /ɪn'kæpsjʊleɪt/ *verb* (**-ting**) enclose (as) in capsule; summarize.

**encase** /ɪn'keɪs/ *verb* (**-sing**) confine (as) in a case.

**encash** /ɪn'kæʃ/ *verb* convert into cash. □ **encashment** *noun*.

**encephalitis** /ensefə'laɪtɪs/ *noun* inflammation of brain.

**enchant** /ɪn'tʃɑːnt/ *verb* delight; bewitch. □ **enchanting** *adjective*; **enchantment** *noun*.

**enchanter** *noun* (*feminine* **enchantress**) person who enchants, esp. by magic.

**encircle** /ɪn'sɜːk(ə)l/ *verb* (**-ling**) surround. □ **encirclement** *noun*.

**enclave** /'enkleɪv/ *noun* part of territory of one state surrounded by that of another; group of people distinct from those surrounding them, esp. ethnically.

**enclose** /ɪn'kləʊz/ *verb* (**-sing**) surround with wall, fence, etc.; shut in; put in receptacle (esp. in envelope besides letter); (as **enclosed** *adjective*) (of religious community) secluded from outside world.

**enclosure** /ɪn'kləʊʒə/ *noun* enclosing; enclosed space or area; thing enclosed.

**encode** /ɪn'kəʊd/ *verb* (**-ding**) put into code.

**encomium** /ɪn'kəʊmɪəm/ *noun* (*plural* **-s**) formal praise.

**encompass** /ɪn'kʌmpəs/ *verb* contain, include; surround.

**encore** /'ɒŋkɔː/ ● *noun* audience's call for repetition of item, or for further item; such item. ● *verb* (**-ring**) call for repetition of or by. ● *interjection* again.

**encounter** /ɪn'kaʊntə/ ● *verb* meet by chance; meet as adversary. ● *noun* meeting by chance or in conflict.

**encourage** /ɪn'kʌrɪdʒ/ *verb* (**-ging**) give courage to; urge; promote. ☐ **encouragement** *noun*.

**encroach** /ɪn'krəʊtʃ/ *verb* (usually + *on*, *upon*) intrude on other's territory etc. ☐ **encroachment** *noun*.

**encrust** /ɪn'krʌst/ *verb* cover with or form crust; coat with hard casing or deposit.

**encumber** /ɪn'kʌmbə/ *verb* be burden to; hamper.

**encumbrance** /ɪn'kʌmbrəns/ *noun* burden; impediment.

**encyclical** /ɪn'sɪklɪk(ə)l/ *noun* papal letter to all RC bishops.

**encyclopedia** /ɪnsaɪklə'piːdɪə/ *noun* (also **-paedia**) book of information on many subjects or on many aspects of one subject.

**encyclopedic** *adjective* (also **-paedic**) (of knowledge or information) comprehensive.

**end** ● *noun* limit; farthest point; extreme point or part; conclusion; latter part; destruction; death; result; goal; object; remnant. ● *verb* bring or come to end. ☐ **endpaper** blank leaf of paper at beginning or end of book; **end-product** final product of manufacture etc.; **end up** be or become eventually, arrive; **in the end** finally; **make ends meet** live within one's income; **no end** *colloquial* to a great extent.

**endanger** /ɪn'deɪndʒə/ *verb* place in danger. ☐ **endangered species** one in danger of extinction.

**endear** /ɪn'dɪə/ *verb* (usually + *to*) make dear. ☐ **endearing** *adjective*.

**endearment** *noun* expression of affection.

**endeavour** /ɪn'devə/ (US **endeavor**) ● *verb* try, strive. ● *noun* attempt, effort.

**endemic** /en'demɪk/ *adjective* (often + *to*) regularly found among particular people or in particular area. ☐ **endemically** *adverb*.

**ending** *noun* end of word or story.

**endive** /'endaɪv/ *noun* curly-leaved plant used in salads.

**endless** *adjective* infinite; continual. ☐ **endlessly** *adverb*.

**endocrine** /'endəʊkraɪn/ *adjective* (of gland) secreting directly into blood.

**endogenous** /en'dɒdʒɪnəs/ *adjective* growing or originating from within.

**endorse** /ɪn'dɔːs/ *verb* (**-sing**) approve; write on (document), esp. sign (cheque); enter details of offence on (driving licence). ☐ **endorsement** *noun*.

**endoskeleton** /'endəʊskelɪtən/ *noun* internal skeleton.

**endow** /ɪn'daʊ/ *verb* give permanent income to; (esp. as **endowed** *adjective*) provide with talent or ability.

**endowment** *noun* endowing; money with which person or thing is endowed. ☐ **endowment mortgage** one in which borrower pays only premiums until policy repays mortgage capital; **endowment policy** life insurance policy paying out on set date or earlier death.

**endue** /ɪn'djuː/ *verb* (**-dues**, **-dued**, **-duing**) (+ *with*) provide (person) with (quality etc.).

**endurance** *noun* power of enduring.

**endure** /ɪn'djʊə/ *verb* (**-ring**) undergo; bear; last.

**endways** *adverb* with an end facing forwards.

**ENE** *abbreviation* east-north-east.

**enema** /'enɪmə/ *noun* injection of liquid etc. into rectum, esp. to expel its contents; liquid used for this.

**enemy** /'enəmɪ/ ● *noun* (*plural* **-ies**) person actively hostile to another; hostile army or nation; member of this; adversary, opponent. ● *adjective* of or belonging to enemy.

**energetic** /enə'dʒetɪk/ *adjective* full of energy. ☐ **energetically** *adverb*.

**energize** /'enədʒaɪz/ *verb* (also **-ise**) (**-zing** or **-sing**) give energy to.

**energy** /'enədʒɪ/ noun (plural **-ies**) force, vigour, activity; ability of matter or radiation to do work.

**enervate** /'enəveɪt/ verb (**-ting**) deprive of vigour. □ **enervation** noun.

**en famille** /ā fæ'mi:/ adverb in or with one's family. [French]

**enfant terrible** /āfā te'ri:bl/ noun (plural **enfants terribles** same pronunciation) indiscreet or unruly person. [French]

**enfeeble** /ɪn'fi:b(ə)l/ verb (**-ling**) make feeble. □ **enfeeblement** noun.

**enfilade** /enfɪ'leɪd/ ● noun gunfire directed down length of enemy position. ● verb (**-ding**) direct enfilade at.

**enfold** /ɪn'fəʊld/ verb wrap; embrace.

**enforce** /ɪn'fɔ:s/ verb (**-cing**) compel observance of; impose. □ **enforceable** adjective; **enforcement** noun.

**enfranchise** /ɪn'fræntʃaɪz/ verb (**-sing**) give (person) right to vote. □ **enfranchisement** /-tʃɪz-/ noun.

**engage** /ɪn'geɪdʒ/ verb (**-ging**) employ, hire; (as **engaged** adjective) occupied, busy, having promised to marry; hold (person's attention); cause parts of (gear) to interlock; fit, interlock; bring into battle; come into battle with (enemy); (usually + in) take part; (+ that, to do) undertake. □ **engagement** noun.

**engender** /ɪn'dʒendə/ verb give rise to.

**engine** /'endʒɪn/ noun mechanical contrivance of parts working together, esp. as source of power; railway locomotive.

**engineer** /endʒɪ'nɪə/ ● noun person skilled in a branch of engineering; person who makes or is in charge of engines etc.; person who designs and constructs military works; mechanic, technician. ● verb contrive, bring about; act as engineer; construct or manage as engineer.

**engineering** noun application of science to design, building, and use of machines etc.

**English** /'ɪŋglɪʃ/ ● adjective of England. ● noun language of England, now used in UK, US, and most Commonwealth countries; (**the English**) (treated as plural) the people of England. □ **Englishman**, **Englishwoman** native of England.

**engraft** /ɪn'grɑ:ft/ verb (usually + into, on) graft, implant, incorporate.

**engrave** /ɪn'greɪv/ verb (**-ving**) inscribe or cut (design) on hard surface; inscribe (surface) thus; (often + on) impress deeply (on memory etc.). □ **engraver** noun.

**engraving** noun print made from engraved plate.

**engross** /ɪn'grəʊs/ verb (usually as **engrossed** adjective + in) fully occupy.

**engulf** /ɪn'gʌlf/ verb flow over and swamp, overwhelm.

**enhance** /ɪn'hɑ:ns/ verb (**-cing**) intensify; improve. □ **enhancement** noun.

**enigma** /ɪ'nɪgmə/ noun puzzling person or thing; riddle. □ **enigmatic** /enɪg'mætɪk/ adjective.

**enjoin** /ɪn'dʒɔɪn/ verb command, order.

**enjoy** /ɪn'dʒɔɪ/ verb find pleasure in; (**enjoy oneself**) find pleasure; have use or benefit of; experience. □ **enjoyable** adjective; **enjoyably** adverb; **enjoyment** noun.

**enlarge** /ɪn'lɑ:dʒ/ verb (**-ging**) make or become larger; (often + on, upon) describe in greater detail; reproduce on larger scale. □ **enlargement** noun.

**enlarger** noun apparatus for enlarging photographs.

**enlighten** /ɪn'laɪt(ə)n/ verb inform; (as **enlightened** adjective) progressive. □ **enlightenment** noun.

**enlist** /ɪn'lɪst/ verb enrol in armed services; secure as means of help or support. □ **enlistment** noun.

**enliven** /ɪn'laɪv(ə)n/ verb make lively or cheerful. □ **enlivenment** noun.

**en masse** /ā 'mæs/ adverb all together. [French]

**enmesh** /ɪn'meʃ/ verb entangle (as) in net.

**enmity** /'enmɪtɪ/ noun (plural **-ies**) hostility; state of being an enemy.

**ennoble** /ɪ'nəʊb(ə)l/ verb (**-ling**) make noble. □ **ennoblement** noun.

**ennui** /ɒ'nwi:/ noun boredom.

**enormity** /ɪ'nɔ:mɪtɪ/ noun (plural **-ies**) great wickedness; monstrous crime; great size.

■ **Usage** Many people believe it is wrong to use *enormity* to mean 'great size'.

**enormous** /ɪˈnɔːməs/ adjective huge. □ **enormously** adverb.

**enough** /ɪˈnʌf/ ● adjective as much or as many as required. ● adverb to required degree; fairly; very, quite. ● noun sufficient amount or quantity.

**enquire** /ɪnˈkwaɪə/ verb (-ring) seek information; ask question; inquire.

**enquiry** noun (plural -ies) asking; inquiry.

**enrage** /ɪnˈreɪdʒ/ verb (-ging) make furious.

**enrapture** /ɪnˈræptʃə/ verb (-ring) delight intensely.

**enrich** /ɪnˈrɪtʃ/ verb make rich(er). □ **enrichment** noun.

**enrol** /ɪnˈrəʊl/ verb (US **enroll**) (-ll-) enlist; write name of (person) on list; incorporate as member; enrol oneself. □ **enrolment** noun.

**en route** /ɑ̃ ˈruːt/ adverb on the way. [French]

**ensconce** /ɪnˈskɒns/ verb (-cing) (usually **ensconce oneself** or in passive) settle comfortably.

**ensemble** /ɒnˈsɒmb(ə)l/ noun thing viewed as whole; set of clothes worn together; group of performers working together; Music passage for ensemble.

**enshrine** /ɪnˈʃraɪn/ verb (-ning) enclose in shrine; protect, make inviolable.

**ensign** /ˈensaɪn/ noun banner, flag, esp. military or naval flag of nation; standard-bearer; historical lowest commissioned infantry officer; US lowest commissioned naval officer.

**enslave** /ɪnˈsleɪv/ verb (-ving) make slave of. □ **enslavement** noun.

**ensnare** /ɪnˈsneə/ verb (-ring) entrap.

**ensue** /ɪnˈsjuː/ verb (-sues, -sued, -suing) happen later or as a result.

**en suite** /ɑ̃ ˈswiːt/ ● adverb forming single unit. ● adjective (of bathroom) attached to bedroom; (of bedroom) with bathroom attached.

**ensure** /ɪnˈʃʊə/ verb (-ring) make certain or safe.

**ENT** abbreviation ear, nose, and throat.

**entail** /ɪnˈteɪl/ ● verb necessitate or involve unavoidably; Law bequeath (estate) to specified line of beneficiaries. ● noun entailed estate.

**entangle** /ɪnˈtæŋɡ(ə)l/ verb (-ling) catch or hold fast in snare etc.; involve in difficulties; complicate. □ **entanglement** noun.

**entente** /ɒnˈtɒnt/ noun friendly understanding between states. □ **entente cordiale** /ˈentənt/ entente, esp. between Britain and France since 1904.

**enter** /ˈentə/ verb go or come in or into; come on stage; penetrate; put (name, fact, etc.) into list or record etc.; (usually + for) name, or name oneself, as competitor; become member of. □ **enter into** engage in, bind oneself by, form part of, sympathize with; **enter (up)on** begin, begin to deal with, assume possession of.

**enteric** /enˈterɪk/ adjective of intestines.

**enteritis** /entəˈraɪtɪs/ noun inflammation of intestines.

**enterprise** /ˈentəpraɪz/ noun bold undertaking; readiness to engage in this; business firm or venture.

**enterprising** adjective showing enterprise.

**entertain** /entəˈteɪn/ verb amuse; receive as guest; harbour (feelings); consider (idea). □ **entertainer** noun; **entertaining** adjective.

**entertainment** noun entertaining; thing that entertains, performance.

**enthral** /ɪnˈθrɔːl/ verb (US **enthrall**) (-ll-) captivate; please greatly. □ **enthralment** noun.

**enthrone** /ɪnˈθrəʊn/ verb (-ning) place on throne. □ **enthronement** noun.

**enthuse** /ɪnˈθjuːz/ verb (-sing) colloquial be or make enthusiastic.

**enthusiasm** /ɪnˈθjuːzɪæz(ə)m/ noun great eagerness or admiration; object of this. □ **enthusiast** noun; **enthusiastic** /-ˈæst-/ adjective; **enthusiastically** adverb.

**entice** /ɪnˈtaɪs/ verb (-cing) attract by offer of pleasure or reward. □ **enticement** noun; **enticing** adjective; **enticingly** adverb.

**entire** /ɪnˈtaɪə/ adjective complete; unbroken; absolute; in one piece.

**entirely** adverb wholly.

**entirety** /ɪnˈtaɪərəti/ noun (plural -ies) completeness; sum total. □ **in its entirety** in its complete form.

**entitle** /ɪn'taɪt(ə)l/ *verb* (**-ling**) (usually + *to*) give (person) right or claim; give title to. □ **entitlement** *noun*.

**entity** /'entɪtɪ/ *noun* (*plural* **-ies**) thing with distinct existence; thing's existence.

**entomb** /ɪn'tuːm/ *verb* place in tomb; serve as tomb for. □ **entombment** *noun*.

**entomology** /entə'mɒlədʒɪ/ *noun* study of insects. □ **entomological** /-mə'lɒdʒ-/ *adjective*; **entomologist** *noun*.

**entourage** /'ɒntʊrɑːʒ/ *noun* people attending important person.

**entr'acte** /'ɒntrækt/ *noun* (music or dance performed in) interval in play.

**entrails** /'entreɪlz/ *plural noun* intestines; inner parts.

**entrance**[1] /'entrəns/ *noun* place for entering; coming or going in; right of admission.

**entrance**[2] /ɪn'trɑːns/ *verb* (**-cing**) enchant, delight; put into trance.

**entrant** /'entrənt/ *noun* person who enters exam, profession, etc.

**entrap** /ɪn'træp/ *verb* (**-pp-**) catch (as) in trap.

**entreat** /ɪn'triːt/ *verb* ask earnestly, beg.

**entreaty** *noun* (*plural* **-ies**) earnest request.

**entrecôte** /'ɒntrəkəʊt/ *noun* boned steak cut off sirloin.

**entrée** /'ɒntreɪ/ *noun* main dish of meal; dish served between fish and meat courses; right of admission.

**entrench** /ɪn'trentʃ/ *verb* establish firmly; (as **entrenched** *adjective*) (of attitude etc.) not easily modified; surround or fortify with trench. □ **entrenchment** *noun*.

**entrepreneur** /ɒntrəprə'nɜː/ *noun* person who undertakes commercial venture. □ **entrepreneurial** *adjective*.

**entropy** /'entrəpɪ/ *noun* measure of disorganization of universe; measure of unavailability of system's thermal energy for conversion into mechanical work.

**entrust** /ɪn'trʌst/ *verb* (+ *to*) give (person, thing) into care of; (+ *with*) assign responsibility for (person, thing) to.

**entry** /'entrɪ/ *noun* (*plural* **-ies**) coming or going in; entering; item entered; place of entrance; alley.

**entwine** /ɪn'twaɪn/ *verb* (**-ning**) twine round, interweave.

**enumerate** /ɪ'njuːməreɪt/ *verb* (**-ting**) specify (items); count. □ **enumeration** *noun*.

**enunciate** /ɪ'nʌnsɪeɪt/ *verb* (**-ting**) pronounce (words) clearly; state definitely. □ **enunciation** *noun*.

**envelop** /ɪn'veləp/ *verb* (**-p-**) wrap up, cover; surround. □ **envelopment** *noun*.

**envelope** /'envələʊp/ *noun* folded paper cover for letter etc.; wrapper, covering.

**enviable** /'envɪəb(ə)l/ *adjective* likely to excite envy. □ **enviably** *adverb*.

**envious** /'envɪəs/ *adjective* feeling or showing envy.

**environment** /ɪn'vaɪərənmənt/ *noun* surroundings; circumstances affecting person's life. □ **environmental** /-'men-/ *adjective*; **environmentally** /-'men-/ *adverb*.

**environmentalist** /ɪnvaɪərən'mentəlɪst/ *noun* person concerned with protection of natural environment.

**environs** /ɪn'vaɪərəns/ *plural noun* district round town etc.

**envisage** /ɪn'vɪzɪdʒ/ *verb* (**-ging**) visualize, imagine, contemplate.

**envoy** /'envɔɪ/ *noun* messenger, representative; diplomat ranking below ambassador.

**envy** /'envɪ/ ● *noun* (*plural* **-ies**) discontent aroused by another's better fortune etc.; object or cause of this. ● *verb* (**-ies**, **-ied**) feel envy of.

**enzyme** /'enzaɪm/ *noun* protein catalyst of specific biochemical reaction.

**eolian harp** *US* = AEOLIAN HARP.

**eon** = AEON.

**EP** *abbreviation* extended-play (record).

**epaulette** /'epəlet/ *noun* (*US* **epaulet**) ornamental shoulder-piece, esp. on uniform.

**ephedrine** /'efədrɪn/ *noun* alkaloid drug used to relieve asthma etc.

**ephemera** /ɪ'femərə/ *plural noun* things of only short-lived relevance.

**ephemeral** *adjective* short-lived, transitory.

**epic** /'epɪk/ ● *noun* long poem narrating adventures of heroic figure etc.; book or film based on this. ● *adjective* like an epic; grand, heroic.

**epicene** /ˈepisiːn/ *adjective* of or for both sexes; having characteristics of both sexes or of neither sex.

**epicentre** /ˈepisentə/ *noun* (*US* **epicenter**) point at which earthquake reaches earth's surface.

**epicure** /ˈepikjʊə/ *noun* person with refined taste in food and drink. □ **epicurism** *noun.*

**epicurean** /epikjʊəˈriːən/ • *noun* person fond of pleasure and luxury. • *adjective* characteristics of an epicurean. □ **epicureanism** *noun.*

**epidemic** /epiˈdemik/ • *noun* widespread occurrence of particular disease in community at particular time. • *adjective* in the nature of an epidemic.

**epidemiology** /epidiːmɪˈɒlədʒɪ/ *noun* study of epidemics and their control.

**epidermis** /epiˈdɜːmɪs/ *noun* outer layer of skin.

**epidiascope** /epiˈdaɪəskəʊp/ *noun* optical projector giving images of both opaque and transparent objects.

**epidural** /epiˈdjʊərəl/ • *adjective* (of anaesthetic) injected close to spinal cord. • *noun* epidural injection.

**epiglottis** /epiˈɡlɒtɪs/ *noun* flap of cartilage at root of tongue that covers windpipe during swallowing. □ **epiglottal** *adjective.*

**epigram** /ˈepiɡræm/ *noun* short poem with witty ending; pointed saying. □ **epigrammatic** /-ɡrəˈmæt-/ *adjective.*

**epigraph** /ˈepiɡrɑːf/ *noun* inscription.

**epilepsy** /ˈepilepsɪ/ *noun* nervous disorder with convulsions and often loss of consciousness. □ **epileptic** /-ˈlep-/ *adjective & noun.*

**epilogue** /ˈepilɒɡ/ *noun* short piece ending literary work; short speech at end of play etc.

**Epiphany** /ɪˈpɪfənɪ/ *noun* (festival on 6 Jan. commemorating) visit of Magi to Christ.

**episcopacy** /ɪˈpɪskəpəsɪ/ *noun* (*plural* **-ies**) government by bishops; bishops collectively.

**episcopal** /ɪˈpɪskəp(ə)l/ *adjective* of bishop or bishops; (of church) governed by bishops. □ **Episcopal Church** Anglican Church in Scotland and US.

**Episcopalian** /ɪpɪskəˈpeɪlɪən/ • *adjective* of the Episcopal Church or (**episcopalian**) an episcopal church. • *noun* member of the Episcopal Church.

**episcopate** /ɪˈpɪskəpət/ *noun* office or tenure of bishop; bishops collectively.

**episode** /ˈepisəʊd/ *noun* event as part of sequence; part of serial story; incident in narrative. □ **episodic** /-ˈsɒd-/ *adjective.*

**epistemology** /ɪpɪstɪˈmɒlədʒɪ/ *noun* philosophy of knowledge. □ **epistemological** /-əˈlɒdʒ-/ *adjective.*

**epistle** /ɪˈpɪs(ə)l/ *noun* letter; poem etc. in form of letter.

**epistolary** /ɪˈpɪstələrɪ/ *adjective* of or in form of letters.

**epitaph** /ˈepitɑːf/ *noun* words in memory of dead person, esp. on tomb.

**epithelium** /epiˈθiːlɪəm/ *noun* ( *plural* **-s** or **-lia**) *Biology* tissue forming outer layer of body and lining many hollow structures. □ **epithelial** *adjective.*

**epithet** /ˈepiθet/ *noun* adjective etc. expressing quality or attribute.

**epitome** /ɪˈpɪtəmɪ/ *noun* person or thing embodying a quality etc.

**epitomize** *verb* (also **-ise**) (**-zing** or **-sing**) make or be perfect example of (a quality etc.).

**EPNS** *abbreviation* electroplated nickel silver.

**epoch** /ˈiːpɒk/ *noun* period marked by special events; beginning of era. □ **epoch-making** notable, significant.

**eponym** /ˈepənɪm/ *noun* word derived from person's name; person whose name is used in this way. □ **eponymous** /ɪˈpɒnɪməs/ *adjective.*

**epoxy resin** /ɪˈpɒksɪ/ *noun* synthetic thermosetting resin, used esp. as glue.

**Epsom salts** /ˈepsəm/ *noun* magnesium sulphate used as purgative.

**equable** /ˈekwəb(ə)l/ *adjective* not varying; moderate; not easily disturbed. □ **equably** *adverb.*

**equal** /ˈiːkw(ə)l/ • *adjective* same in number, size, merit, etc.; evenly matched; having same rights or status. • *noun* person etc. equal to another. • *verb* (**-ll-**; *US* **-l-**) be equal to; achieve something equal to. □ **equal opportunity** (often in *plural*) opportunity to compete equally for jobs regardless of race, sex, etc. □ **equally** *adverb.*

■ **Usage** It is a mistake to say *equally as*, as in *She was equally as guilty.* The correct version is *She was equally guilty* or possibly, for example, *She was as guilty as he was.*

**equality** /ɪˈkwɒlɪtɪ/ *noun* being equal.

**equalize** *verb* (also **-ise**) (**-zing** or **-sing**) make or become equal; (in games) reach opponent's score. □ **equalization** *noun.*

**equalizer** *noun* (also **-iser**) equalizing goal etc.

**equanimity** /ekwəˈnɪmɪtɪ/ *noun* composure, calm.

**equate** /ɪˈkweɪt/ *verb* (**-ting**) (usually + *to, with*) regard as equal or equivalent; (+ *with*) be equal or equivalent to.

**equation** /ɪˈkweɪʒ(ə)n/ *noun* making or being equal; *Mathematics* statement that two expressions are equal; *Chemistry* symbolic representation of reaction.

**equator** /ɪˈkweɪtə/ *noun* imaginary line round the earth or other body, equidistant from poles.

**equatorial** /ekwəˈtɔːrɪəl/ *adjective* of or near equator.

**equerry** /ˈekwərɪ/ *noun* (*plural* **-ies**) officer attending British royal family.

**equestrian** /ɪˈkwestrɪən/ *adjective* of horse-riding; on horseback. □ **equestrianism** *noun.*

**equiangular** /iːkwɪˈæŋgjʊlə/ *adjective* having equal angles.

**equidistant** /iːkwɪˈdɪst(ə)nt/ *adjective* at equal distances.

**equilateral** /iːkwɪˈlætər(ə)l/ *adjective* having all sides equal.

**equilibrium** /iːkwɪˈlɪbrɪəm/ *noun* state of balance; composure.

**equine** /ˈekwaɪn/ *adjective* of or like horse.

**equinox** /ˈiːkwɪnɒks/ *noun* time or date at which sun crosses equator and day and night are of equal length.

**equip** /ɪˈkwɪp/ *verb* (**-pp-**) supply with what is needed.

**equipment** *noun* necessary tools, clothing, etc.; equipping, being equipped.

**equipoise** /ˈekwɪpɔɪz/ *noun* equilibrium; counterbalancing thing.

**equitable** /ˈekwɪtəb(ə)l/ *adjective* fair, just; *Law* valid in equity. □ **equitably** *adverb.*

**equitation** /ekwɪˈteɪʃ(ə)n/ *noun* horsemanship; horse-riding.

**equity** /ˈekwɪtɪ/ *noun* (*plural* **-ies**) fairness; principles of justice supplementing law; value of shares issued by company; (in *plural*) stocks and shares not bearing fixed interest.

**equivalent** /ɪˈkwɪvələnt/ ● *adjective* (often + *to*) equal in value, meaning, etc.; corresponding. ● *noun* equivalent amount etc. □ **equivalence** *noun.*

**equivocal** /ɪˈkwɪvək(ə)l/ *adjective* of double or doubtful meaning; of uncertain nature; (of person etc.) questionable. □ **equivocally** *adverb.*

**equivocate** /ɪˈkwɪvəkeɪt/ *verb* (**-ting**) use words ambiguously to conceal truth. □ **equivocation** *noun.*

**ER** *abbreviation* Queen Elizabeth (*Elizabetha Regina*).

**era** /ˈɪərə/ *noun* system of chronology starting from particular point; historical or other period.

**eradicate** /ɪˈrædɪkeɪt/ *verb* (**-ting**) root out, destroy. □ **eradication** *noun.*

**erase** /ɪˈreɪz/ *verb* (**-sing**) rub out; obliterate; remove recording from (magnetic tape etc.).

**eraser** *noun* piece of rubber etc. for removing esp. pencil marks.

**erasure** /ɪˈreɪʒə/ *noun* erasing; erased word etc.

**ere** /eə/ *preposition* & *conjunction* poetical or archaic before.

**erect** /ɪˈrekt/ ● *adjective* upright, vertical; (of part of body) enlarged and rigid, esp. from sexual excitement. ● *verb* raise, set upright; build; establish. □ **erection** *noun.*

**erectile** /ɪˈrektaɪl/ *adjective* that can become erect.

**erg** *noun* unit of work or energy.

**ergo** /ˈɜːgəʊ/ *adverb* therefore. [Latin]

**ergonomics** /ɜːgəˈnɒmɪks/ *plural noun* (treated as *singular*) study of relationship between people and their working environment. □ **ergonomic** *adjective.*

**ergot** /ˈɜːgət/ *noun* disease of rye etc. caused by fungus.

**ERM** *abbreviation* Exchange Rate Mechanism.

**ermine** /'ɜ:mɪn/ *noun* (*plural* same or **-s**) stoat, esp. in its white winter fur; this fur.

**Ernie** /'ɜ:nɪ/ *noun* device for drawing prize-winning numbers of Premium Bonds.

**erode** /ɪ'rəʊd/ *verb* (**-ding**) wear away, gradually destroy. □ **erosion** *noun*; **erosive** *adjective*.

**erogenous** /ɪ'rɒdʒɪnəs/ *adjective* (of part of body) sexually sensitive.

**erotic** /ɪ'rɒtɪk/ *adjective* arousing sexual desire or excitement. □ **erotically** *adverb*; **eroticism** /-sɪz-/ *noun*.

**erotica** *plural noun* erotic literature or art.

**err** /ɜ:/ *verb* be mistaken or incorrect; sin.

**errand** /'erənd/ *noun* short journey, esp. on another's behalf, to take message etc.; object of journey.

**errant** /'erənt/ *adjective* erring; *literary* travelling in search of adventure.

**erratic** /ɪ'rætɪk/ *adjective* inconsistent or uncertain in movement or conduct etc. □ **erratically** *adverb*.

**erratum** /ɪ'rɑ:təm/ *noun* (*plural* **-ta**) error in printing etc.

**erroneous** /ɪ'rəʊnɪəs/ *adjective* incorrect. □ **erroneously** *adverb*.

**error** /'erə/ *noun* mistake; condition of being morally wrong; degree of inaccuracy in calculation or measurement.

**ersatz** /'eəzæts/ *adjective* & *noun* substitute; imitation.

**erstwhile** /'ɜ:stwaɪl/ *adjective* former.

**eructation** /i:rʌk'teɪʃ(ə)n/ *noun formal* belching.

**erudite** /'eru:daɪt/ *adjective* learned. □ **erudition** /-'dɪʃ-/ *noun*.

**erupt** /ɪ'rʌpt/ *verb* break out; (of volcano) shoot out lava etc.; (of rash) appear on skin. □ **eruption** *noun*.

**erysipelas** /erɪ'sɪpɪləs/ *noun* disease causing deep red inflammation of skin.

**escalate** /'eskəleɪt/ *verb* (**-ting**) increase or develop by stages. □ **escalation** *noun*.

**escalator** *noun* moving staircase.

**escalope** /'eskəlɒp/ *noun* thin slice of meat, esp. veal.

**escapade** /'eskəpeɪd/ *noun* piece of reckless behaviour.

**escape** /ɪs'keɪp/ ● *verb* (**-ping**) get free; leak; avoid punishment etc.; get free of; elude, avoid. ● *noun* escaping; means of escaping; leakage. □ **escape clause** clause releasing contracting party from obligation in specified circumstances.

**escapee** /ɪskeɪ'pi:/ *noun* person who has escaped.

**escapism** *noun* pursuit of distraction and relief from reality. □ **escapist** *adjective* & *noun*.

**escapology** /eskə'pɒlədʒɪ/ *noun* techniques of escaping from confinement, esp. as entertainment. □ **escapologist** *noun*.

**escarpment** /ɪs'kɑ:pmənt/ *noun* long steep slope at edge of plateau etc.

**eschatology** /eskə'tɒlədʒɪ/ *noun* doctrine of death and final destiny. □ **eschatological** /-tə'lɒdʒ-/ *adjective*.

**escheat** /ɪs'tʃi:t/ ● *noun* lapse of property to the state etc.; property so lapsing. ● *verb* hand over as escheat, confiscate; revert by escheat.

**eschew** /ɪs'tʃu:/ *verb formal* abstain from.

**escort** ● *noun* /'eskɔ:t/ person(s) etc. accompanying another for protection or as courtesy; person accompanying another of opposite sex socially. ● *verb* /ɪ'skɔ:t/ act as escort to.

**escritoire** /eskrɪ'twɑ:/ *noun* writing desk with drawers etc.

**escutcheon** /ɪ'skʌtʃ(ə)n/ *noun* shield bearing coat of arms.

**ESE** *abbreviation* east-south-east.

**Eskimo** /'eskɪməʊ/ ● *noun* (*plural* same or **-s**) member of people inhabiting N. Canada, Alaska, Greenland, and E. Siberia; their language. ● *adjective* of Eskimos or their language.

■ **Usage** The Eskimos of N. America prefer the name *Inuit*.

**ESN** *abbreviation* educationally subnormal.

**esophagus** *US* = OESOPHAGUS.

**esoteric** /esə'terɪk, i:sə'terɪk/ *adjective* intelligible only to those with special knowledge.

**ESP** *abbreviation* extrasensory perception.

**esp.** *abbreviation* especially.

**espadrille** /espəˈdril/ *noun* light canvas shoe with plaited fibre sole.

**espalier** /ɪˈspælɪə/ *noun* framework for training tree etc.; tree trained on espalier.

**esparto** /eˈspɑːtəʊ/ *noun* kind of grass used to make paper.

**especial** /ɪˈspeʃ(ə)l/ *adjective* special, notable.

**especially** *adverb* in particular; more than in other cases; particularly.

**Esperanto** /espəˈræntəʊ/ *noun* artificial universal language.

**espionage** /ˈespɪɑːnɑːʒ/ *noun* spying or using spies.

**esplanade** /espləˈneɪd/ *noun* level space, esp. used as public promenade.

**espousal** /ɪˈspaʊz(ə)l/ *noun* espousing; *archaic* marriage, betrothal.

**espouse** /ɪˈspaʊz/ *verb* (**-sing**) support (cause); *archaic* marry.

**espresso** /eˈspresəʊ/ *noun* (*plural* **-s**) coffee made under steam pressure.

**esprit de corps** /espriː də ˈkɔː/ *noun* devotion to and pride in one's group. [French]

**espy** /ɪˈspaɪ/ *verb* (**-ies**, **-ied**) catch sight of.

**Esq.** *abbreviation* Esquire.

**esquire** /ɪˈskwaɪə/ *noun: title placed after man's name in writing.*

**essay** ●*noun* /ˈeseɪ/ short piece of writing, esp. on given subject; *formal* attempt. ● *verb* /eˈseɪ/ attempt.

**essayist** *noun* writer of essays.

**essence** /ˈes(ə)ns/ *noun* fundamental nature, inherent characteristics; extract obtained by distillation etc.; perfume. □ **in essence** fundamentally.

**essential** /ɪˈsenʃ(ə)l/ ● *adjective* necessary, indispensable; of or constituting a thing's essence. ● *noun* (esp. in *plural*) indispensable element or thing. □ **essential oil** volatile oil with characteristic odour. □ **essentially** *adverb*.

**establish** /ɪˈstæblɪʃ/ *verb* set up; settle; (esp. as **established** *adjective*) achieve permanent acceptance for; place beyond dispute. □ **Established Church** Church recognized by state.

**establishment** *noun* establishing, being established; public institution; place of business; staff, household, etc.;

Church system established by law; (**the Establishment**) social group with authority or influence and resisting change.

**estate** /ɪˈsteɪt/ *noun* landed property; area of homes or businesses planned as a whole; dead person's collective assets and liabilities. □ **estate agent** person whose business is sale and lease of buildings and land on behalf of others; **estate car** car with continuous area for rear passengers and luggage.

**esteem** /ɪˈstiːm/ ● *verb* (usually in *passive*) think highly of; *formal* consider. ● *noun* high regard.

**ester** /estə/ *noun* compound formed by replacing the hydrogen of an acid by an organic radical.

**estimable** /ˈestɪməb(ə)l/ *adjective* worthy of esteem.

**estimate** ● *noun* /ˈestɪmət/ approximate judgement of cost, value, etc.; approximate price stated in advance for work. ● *verb* /ˈestɪmeɪt/ (**-ting**) form estimate of; (+ *that*) make rough calculation; (+ *at*) put (sum etc.) at by estimating.

**estimation** /estɪˈmeɪʃ(ə)n/ *noun* estimating; judgement of worth.

**estrange** /ɪˈstreɪndʒ/ *verb* (**-ging**) (usually in *passive*; often + *from*) alienate, make hostile or indifferent; (as **estranged** *adjective*) no longer living with spouse. □ **estrangement** *noun*.

**estuary** /ˈestjʊərɪ/ *noun* (*plural* **-ies**) tidal mouth of river.

**ETA** *abbreviation* estimated time of arrival.

**et al.** *abbreviation* and others (*et alii*).

**etc.** *abbreviation* et cetera.

**et cetera** /et ˈsetrə/ *adverb* (also **etcetera**) and the rest; and so on. □ **etceteras** *plural noun* the usual extras.

**etch** *verb* reproduce (picture etc.) by engraving metal plate with acid, esp. to print copies; engrave (plate) thus; practise this craft; (usually + *on, upon*) impress deeply.

**etching** *noun* print made from etched plate.

**eternal** /ɪˈtɜːn(ə)l/ *adjective* existing always; without end or beginning; unchanging; *colloquial* constant, too frequent. □ **eternally** *adverb*.

**eternity** /ɪˈtɜːnɪtɪ/ noun infinite time; endless life after death; (**an eternity**) colloquial a very long time.

**ethane** /ˈiːθeɪn/ noun hydrocarbon gas present in petroleum and natural gas.

**ethanol** /ˈeθənɒl/ noun alcohol.

**ether** /ˈiːθə/ noun volatile liquid used as anaesthetic or solvent; clear sky, upper air.

**ethereal** /ɪˈθɪərɪəl/ adjective light, airy; delicate, esp. in appearance; heavenly.

**ethic** /ˈeθɪk/ noun set of moral principles.

**ethical** adjective relating to morals or ethics; morally correct; (of drug etc.) available only on prescription. □ **ethically** adverb.

**ethics** plural noun (also treated as singular) moral philosophy; (set of) moral principles.

**Ethiopian** /iːθɪˈəʊpɪən/ ● noun native or national of Ethiopia. ● adjective of Ethiopia.

**ethnic** /ˈeθnɪk/ adjective (of social) group having common national or cultural tradition; (of clothes etc.) resembling those of an exotic people; (of person) having specified origin by birth or descent rather than nationality. □ **ethnic cleansing** euphemistic expulsion or murder of people of ethnic or religious group in certain area. □ **ethnically** adverb.

**ethnology** /eθˈnɒlədʒɪ/ noun comparative study of peoples. □ **ethnological** /-nəˈlɒdʒ-/ adjective.

**ethos** /ˈiːθɒs/ noun characteristic spirit of community, people, or system.

**ethylene** /ˈeθɪliːn/ noun flammable hydrocarbon gas.

**etiolate** /ˈiːtɪəleɪt/ verb (**-ting**) make pale by excluding light; give sickly colour to. □ **etiolation** noun.

**etiology** US = AETIOLOGY.

**etiquette** /ˈetɪket/ noun conventional rules of social behaviour or professional conduct.

**étude** /eɪˈtjuːd/ noun musical composition designed to develop player's skill.

**etymology** /etɪˈmɒlədʒɪ/ noun (plural **-ies**) origin and sense-development of word; account of these. □ **etymological** /-məˈlɒdʒ-/ adjective.

**eucalyptus** /juːkəˈlɪptəs/ noun (plural **-tuses** or **-ti** /-taɪ/) tall evergreen tree; its oil, used as antiseptic etc.

**Eucharist** /ˈjuːkərɪst/ noun Christian sacrament in which bread and wine are consecrated and consumed; consecrated elements, esp. bread. □ **Eucharistic** /-ˈrɪs-/ adjective.

**eugenics** /juːˈdʒenɪks/ plural noun (also treated as singular) improvement of qualities of race by control of inherited characteristics. □ **eugenic** adjective; **eugenically** adverb.

**eulogize** /ˈjuːlədʒaɪz/ verb (also **-ise**) (**-zing** or **-sing**) extol; praise.

**eulogy** /ˈjuːlədʒɪ/ noun (plural **-ies**) speech or writing in praise or commendation. □ **eulogistic** /-ˈdʒɪs-/ adjective.

**eunuch** /ˈjuːnək/ noun castrated man.

**euphemism** /ˈjuːfɪmɪz(ə)m/ noun mild expression substituted for blunt one. □ **euphemistic** /-ˈmɪs-/ adjective; **euphemistically** /-ˈmɪs-/ adverb.

**euphonium** /juːˈfəʊnɪəm/ noun brass instrument of tuba family.

**euphony** /ˈjuːfənɪ/ noun pleasantness of sound, esp. in words. □ **euphonious** /-ˈfəʊ-/ adjective.

**euphoria** /juːˈfɔːrɪə/ noun intense sense of well-being and excitement. □ **euphoric** /-ˈfɒr-/ adjective.

**Eurasian** /jʊəˈreɪʒ(ə)n/ ● adjective of mixed European and Asian parentage; of Europe and Asia. ● noun Eurasian person.

**eureka** /jʊəˈriːkə/ interjection I have found it!

**Eurodollar** /ˈjʊərəʊdɒlə/ noun dollar held in bank in Europe etc.

**European** /jʊərəˈpɪən/ ● adjective of, in, or extending over Europe. ● noun native or inhabitant of Europe; descendant of one.

**Eustachian tube** /juːˈsteɪʃ(ə)n/ noun passage between middle ear and back of throat.

**euthanasia** /juːθəˈneɪzɪə/ noun killing person painlessly, esp. one who has incurable painful disease.

**evacuate** /ɪˈvækjʊeɪt/ verb (**-ting**) remove (people) from place of danger; make empty, clear; withdraw from (place); empty (bowels). □ **evacuation** noun.

**evacuee** /ɪvækjuːˈiː/ noun person evacuated.

**evade** /ɪ'veɪd/ verb (**-ding**) escape from, avoid; avoid doing or answering directly; avoid paying (tax) illegally.

**evaluate** /ɪ'væljʊeɪt/ verb (**-ting**) assess, appraise; find or state number or amount of. □ **evaluation** noun.

**evanesce** /evə'nes/ verb (**-cing**) literary fade from sight. □ **evanescence** noun; **evanescent** adjective.

**evangelical** /i:væn'dʒelɪk(ə)l/ ● adjective of or according to gospel teaching; of Protestant groups maintaining doctrine of salvation by faith. ● noun member of evangelical group. □ **evangelicalism** noun.

**evangelist** /ɪ'vændʒəlɪst/ noun writer of one of the 4 Gospels; preacher of gospel. □ **evangelism** noun, **evangelistic** /-'lɪs-/ adjective.

**evangelize** verb (also **-ise**) (**-zing** or **-sing**) preach gospel to. □ **evangelization** noun.

**evaporate** /ɪ'væpəreɪt/ verb (**-ting**) turn into vapour; (cause to) lose moisture as vapour; (cause to) disappear. □ **evaporation** noun.

**evasion** /ɪ'veɪʒ(ə)n/ noun evading; evasive answer.

**evasive** /ɪ'veɪsɪv/ adjective seeking to evade.

**eve** noun evening or day before festival etc.; time just before event; archaic evening.

**even** /'i:v(ə)n/ ● adjective (**-er**, **-est**) level, smooth; uniform; equal; equable, calm; divisible by two. ● adverb still, yet; (with negative) so much as. ● verb (often + up) make or become even. □ **even if** in spite of the fact that, no matter whether; **even out** become level or regular, spread (thing) over period or among group. □ **evenly** adverb.

**evening** /'i:vnɪŋ/ noun end part of day, esp. from about 6 p.m. to bedtime. □ **evening class** adult education class held in evening; **evening dress** formal clothes for evening wear; **evening star** planet, esp. Venus, conspicious in west after sunset.

**evensong** noun evening service in Church of England.

**event** /ɪ'vent/ noun thing that happens; fact of thing occurring; item in (esp. sports) programme. □ **in any event, at**

**all events** whatever happens; **in the event** as it turned or turned out; **in the event of** if (thing) happens.

**eventful** adjective marked by noteworthy events.

**eventual** /ɪ'ventʃʊəl/ adjective occurring in due course. □ **eventually** adverb.

**eventuality** /ɪventʃʊ'ælɪtɪ/ noun (plural **-ies**) possible event.

**ever** /'evə/ adverb at all times; always; at any time. □ **ever since** throughout period since (then); **ever so** colloquial very; **ever such a(n)** colloquial a very.

**evergreen** ● adjective retaining green leaves throughout year. ● noun evergreen plant.

**everlasting** adjective lasting for ever or a long time; (of flower) retaining shape and colour when dried.

**evermore** adverb for ever; always.

**every** /'evrɪ/ adjective each; all. □ **everybody** every person; **everyday** occurring every day, ordinary; **Everyman** ordinary or typical human being; **every now and again** or **then** occasionally; **everyone** everybody; **every other** each alternate; **everything** all things, the most important thing; **everywhere** in every place.

**evict** /ɪ'vɪkt/ verb expel (tenant) by legal process. □ **eviction** noun.

**evidence** /'evɪd(ə)ns/ ● noun (often + for, of) indication, sign; information given to establish fact etc.; statement etc. admissible in court of law. ● verb (**-cing**) be evidence of.

**evident** adjective obvious, manifest.

**evidential** /evɪ'denʃ(ə)l/ adjective of or providing evidence.

**evidently** adverb seemingly; as shown by evidence.

**evil** /'i:v(ə)l/ ● adjective wicked; harmful. ● noun evil thing; wickedness. □ **evil eye** gaze believed to cause harm. □ **evilly** adverb.

**evince** /ɪ'vɪns/ verb (**-cing**) show, indicate.

**eviscerate** /ɪ'vɪsəreɪt/ verb (**-ting**) disembowel. □ **evisceration** noun.

**evocative** /ɪ'vɒkətɪv/ adjective evoking (feelings etc.).

**evoke** /ɪ'vəʊk/ verb (**-king**) call up (feeling etc.). □ **evocation** /evə-/ noun.

**evolution** /iːvəˈluːʃ(ə)n/ *noun* evolving; development of species from earlier forms; unfolding of events etc.; change in disposition of troops or ships. □ **evolutionary** *adjective*.

**evolutionist** *noun* person who regards evolution as explaining origin of species.

**evolve** /ɪˈvɒlv/ *verb* (**-ving**) develop gradually and naturally; devise; unfold, open out.

**ewe** /juː/ *noun* female sheep.

**ewer** /ˈjuːə/ *noun* water-jug with wide mouth.

**ex**[1] *preposition* (of goods) sold from (warehouse etc.).

**ex**[2] *noun colloquial* former husband or wife.

**ex-** *prefix* formerly.

**exacerbate** /ekˈsæsəbeɪt/ *verb* (**-ting**) make worse; irritate. □ **exacerbation** *noun*.

**exact** /ɪɡˈzækt/ ● *adjective* accurate; correct in all details. ● *verb* demand and enforce payment of (fees etc.); demand, insist on. □ **exactness** *noun*.

**exaction** *noun* exacting, being exacted; illegal or exorbitant demand.

**exactitude** *noun* exactness.

**exactly** *adverb* precisely; I agree.

**exaggerate** /ɪɡˈzædʒəreɪt/ *verb* (**-ting**) make seem larger or greater than it really is; increase beyond normal or due proportions. □ **exaggeration** *noun*.

**exalt** /ɪɡˈzɔːlt/ *verb* raise in rank, power, etc.; praise, extol; (usually as **exalted** *adjective*) make lofty or noble. □ **exaltation** /eg-/ *noun*.

**exam** /ɪɡˈzæm/ *noun* examination, test.

**examination** /ɪɡzæmɪˈneɪʃ(ə)n/ *noun* examining, being examined; detailed inspection; testing of knowledge or ability by questions; formal questioning of witness etc. in court.

**examine** /ɪɡˈzæmɪn/ *verb* (**-ning**) inquire into; look closely at; test knowledge or ability of; check health of; question formally. □ **examinee** /-ˈniː/ *noun*, **examiner** *noun*.

**example** /ɪɡˈzɑːmp(ə)l/ *noun* thing illustrating general rule; model, pattern; specimen; precedent; warning to

others. □ **for example** by way of illustration.

**exasperate** /ɪɡˈzɑːspəreɪt/ *verb* (**-ting**) irritate intensely. □ **exasperation** *noun*.

**ex cathedra** /eks kəˈθiːdrə/ *adjective* & *adverb* with full authority (esp. of papal pronouncement). [Latin]

**excavate** /ˈekskəveɪt/ *verb* (**-ting**) make (hole etc.) by digging; dig out material from (ground); reveal or extract by digging; dig systematically to explore (archaeological site). □ **excavation** *noun*, **excavator** *noun*.

**exceed** /ɪkˈsiːd/ *verb* be more or greater than; go beyond, do more than is warranted by; surpass.

**exceedingly** *adverb* very.

**excel** /ɪkˈsel/ *verb* (**-ll-**) surpass; be pre-eminent.

**excellence** /ˈeksələns/ *noun* great merit.

**Excellency** *noun* (*plural* **-ies**) (**His, Her, Your Excellency**) *title used of or to ambassador, governor, etc.*

**excellent** *adjective* ● extremely good.

**except** /ɪkˈsept/ ● *verb* exclude from general statement etc. ● *preposition* (often + *for*) not including, other than.

**excepting** *preposition* except.

**exception** /ɪkˈsepʃ(ə)n/ *noun* excepting; thing or case excepted. □ **take exception** (often + *to*) object.

**exceptionable** *adjective* open to objection.

■ *Usage* *Exceptionable* is sometimes confused with *exceptional*.

**exceptional** *adjective* forming exception; unusual. □ **exceptionally** *adverb*.

■ *Usage* *Exceptional* is sometimes confused with *exceptionable*.

**excerpt** ● *noun* /ˈeksɜːpt/ short extract from book, film, etc. ● *verb* /ɪkˈsɜːpt/ take excerpts from. □ **excerption** /ɪkˈsɜːpʃ(ə)n/ *noun*.

**excess** ● *noun* /ɪkˈses/ exceeding; amount by which thing exceeds; intemperance in eating or drinking. ● *adjective* /ˈekses/ that exceeds limit or given amount. □ **in, to excess** exceeding proper amount or degree; **in excess of** more than.

**excessive** /ɪk'sesɪv/ *adjective* too much; too great. □ **excessively** *adverb*.

**exchange** /ɪks'tʃeɪndʒ/ ●*noun* giving one thing and receiving another in its place; exchanging of money for equivalent, esp. in other currency; centre where telephone connections are made; place where merchants, stockbrokers, etc. transact business; employment office; short conversation. ●*verb* (**-ging**) give or receive in exchange; interchange. □ **exchange rate** price of one currency expressed in another. □ **exchangeable** *adjective*.

**exchequer** /ɪks'tʃekə/ *noun* former government department in charge of national revenue; royal or national treasury.

**excise**[1] /'eksaɪz/ *noun* tax levied on goods produced or sold within the country; tax on certain licences.

**excise**[2] /ɪk'saɪz/ *verb* (**-sing**) cut out or away. □ **excision** /-'sɪʒ-/ *noun*.

**excitable** *adjective* easily excited. □ **excitability** *noun*.

**excite** /ɪk'saɪt/ *verb* (**-ting**) move to strong emotion; arouse (feelings etc.); provoke (action etc.); stimulate to activity. □ **excitement** *noun*; **exciting** *adjective*.

**exclaim** /ɪk'skleɪm/ *verb* cry out suddenly; utter or say thus.

**exclamation** /eksklə'meɪʃ(ə)n/ *noun* exclaiming; word(s) etc. exclaimed. □ **exclamation mark** punctuation mark (!) indicating exclamation (see panel). □ **exclamatory** /ɪk'sklæmətərɪ/ *adjective*.

**exclude** /ɪk'sklu:d/ *verb* (**-ding**) shut out, leave out; make impossible, preclude. □ **exclusion** *noun*.

**exclusive** /ɪk'sklu:sɪv/ ●*adjective* excluding other things; (+ *of*) not including;

(of society etc.) tending to exclude outsiders; high-class; not obtainable or published elsewhere. ●*noun* exclusive item of news, film, etc. □ **exclusively** *adverb*; **exclusiveness** *noun*; **exclusivity** /eksklu:'sɪvɪtɪ/ *noun*.

**excommunicate** /ekskə'mju:nɪkeɪt/ *verb* (**-ting**) deprive (person) of membership and sacraments of Church. □ **excommunication** *noun*.

**excoriate** /eks'kɔ:rɪeɪt/ *verb* (**-ting**) remove part of skin of by abrasion; remove (skin); censure severely. □ **excoriation** *noun*.

**excrement** /'ekskrɪmənt/ *noun* faeces.

**excrescence** /ɪk'skres(ə)ns/ *noun* abnormal or morbid outgrowth. □ **excrescent** *adjective*.

**excreta** /ɪk'skri:tə/ *plural noun* faeces and urine.

**excrete** /ɪk'skri:t/ *verb* (**-ting**) (of animal or plant) expel (waste). □ **excretion** *noun*; **excretory** *adjective*.

**excruciating** /ɪk'skru:ʃɪeɪtɪŋ/ *adjective* acutely painful. □ **excruciatingly** *adverb*.

**exculpate** /'ekskʌlpeɪt/ *verb* (**-ting**) *formal* free from blame. □ **exculpation** *noun*.

**excursion** /ɪk'skɜ:ʃ(ə)n/ *noun* journey to place and back, made for pleasure.

**excursive** /ɪk'skɜ:sɪv/ *adjective literary* digressive.

**excuse** ●*verb* /ɪk'skju:z/ (**-sing**) try to lessen blame attaching to; serve as reason to judge (person, act) less severely; (often + *from*) grant exemption to; forgive. ●*noun* /ɪk'skju:s/ reason put forward to mitigate or justify offence; apology. □ **be excused** be allowed not to do something or to leave or be absent; **excuse me** *polite request to*

---

## Exclamation mark !

This is used instead of a full stop at the end of a sentence to show that the speaker or writer is very angry, enthusiastic, insistent, disappointed, hurt, surprised, etc., e.g.

*I am not pleased at all!*　　　　*I wish I could have gone!*
*I just love sweets!*　　　　　　*Ow!*
*Go away!*　　　　　　　　　　*He didn't even say goodbye!*

*be allowed to pass, polite apology for interrupting or disagreeing.* □ **excusable** /-'skuːz-/ *adjective.*

**ex-directory** *adjective* not listed in telephone directory, at subscriber's wish.

**execrable** /'eksɪkrəb(ə)l/ *adjective* abominable.

**execrate** /'eksɪkreɪt/ *verb* (**-ting**) express or feel abhorrence for; curse. □ **execration** *noun.*

**execute** /'eksɪkjuːt/ *verb* (**-ting**) carry out, perform; put to death.

**execution** /eksɪ'kjuːʃ(ə)n/ *noun* carrying out, performance; capital punishment.

**executioner** *noun* person carrying out death sentence.

**executive** /ɪg'zekjʊtɪv/ *noun* person or body with managerial or administrative responsibility; branch of government etc. concerned with executing laws, agreements, etc. ● *adjective* concerned with executing laws, agreements, etc. or with administration etc.

**executor** /ɪg'zekjʊtə/ *noun* (feminine **executrix** /-trɪks/) person appointed to carry out terms of will. □ **executorial** /-'tɔːrɪəl/ *adjective.*

**exegesis** /eksɪ'dʒiːsɪs/ *noun* explanation, esp. of Scripture. □ **exegetic** /-'dʒetɪk/ *adjective.*

**exemplar** /ɪg'zemplə/ *noun* model; typical instance.

**exemplary** *adjective* outstandingly good; serving as example or warning.

**exemplify** /ɪg'zemplɪfaɪ/ *verb* (**-ies, -ied**) give or be example of. □ **exemplification** *noun.*

**exempt** /ɪg'zempt/ ● *adjective* (often + *from*) free from obligation or liability imposed on others. ● *verb* (+ *from*) make exempt from. □ **exemption** *noun.*

**exercise** /'eksəsaɪz/ ● *noun* use of muscles etc., esp. for health; task set for physical or other training; use or application of faculties etc.; practice; (often in *plural*) military drill or manoeuvres. ● *verb* (**-sing**) use; perform (function); take exercise; give exercise to; tax powers of; perplex, worry.

**exert** /ɪg'zɜːt/ *verb* use; bring to bear; (**exert oneself**) make effort. □ **exertion** *noun.*

**exfoliate** /eks'fəʊlɪeɪt/ *verb* (**-ting**) come off in scales or layers. □ **exfoliation** *noun.*

**ex gratia** /eks 'greɪʃə/ ● *adverb* as favour and not under (esp. legal) compulsion. ● *adjective* granted on this basis. [Latin]

**exhale** /eks'heɪl/ *verb* (**-ling**) breathe out; give off or be given off in vapour. □ **exhalation** /-hə-/ *noun.*

**exhaust** /ɪg'zɔːst/ ● *verb* (often as **exhausted** *adjective* or **exhausting** *adjective*) consume, use up; tire out; study or expound completely; empty of contents. ● *noun* waste gases etc. expelled from engine after combustion; pipe or system through which they are expelled. □ **exhaustible** *adjective*; **exhaustion** *noun.*

**exhaustive** *adjective* complete, comprehensive. □ **exhaustively** *adverb.*

**exhibit** /ɪg'zɪbɪt/ ● *verb* (**-t-**) show, esp. publicly; display. ● *noun* thing exhibited. □ **exhibitor** *noun.*

**exhibition** /eksɪ'bɪʃ(ə)n/ *noun* display, public show; exhibiting, being exhibited; scholarship, esp. from funds of college etc.

**exhibitioner** *noun* student receiving exhibition.

**exhibitionism** *noun* tendency towards attention-seeking behaviour; compulsion to expose genitals in public. □ **exhibitionist** *noun.*

**exhilarate** /ɪg'zɪləreɪt/ *verb* (**-ting**) (often as **exhilarating** *adjective* or **exhilarated** *adjective*) enliven, gladden. □ **exhilaration** *noun.*

**exhort** /ɪg'zɔːt/ *verb* (often + *to do*) urge strongly or earnestly. □ **exhortation** /eg-/ *noun*; **exhortative** *adjective*; **exhortatory** *adjective.*

**exhume** /eks'hjuːm/ *verb* (**-ming**) dig up. □ **exhumation** *noun.*

**exigency** /'eksɪdʒənsɪ/ *noun* (*plural* **-ies**) (also **exigence**) urgent need; emergency. □ **exigent** *adjective.*

**exiguous** /eg'zɪgjʊəs/ *adjective* scanty, small. □ **exiguity** /-'gjuːɪtɪ/ *noun.*

**exile** /'eksaɪl/ ● *noun* expulsion or long absence from one's country etc.; person in exile. ● *verb* (**-ling**) send into or condemn to exile.

**exist** /ɪg'zɪst/ *verb* be, have being; occur, be found; live with no pleasure; live.

**existence** *noun* fact or manner of existing; all that exists. □ **existent** *adjective*.

**existential** /ɛgzɪˈstenʃ(ə)l/ *adjective* of or relating to existence.

**existentialism** *noun* philosophical theory emphasizing existence of individual as free and self-determining agent. □ **existentialist** *adjective & noun*.

**exit** /ˈeksɪt/ *noun* way out; going out; place where vehicles leave motorway etc.; departure. ● *verb* (-t-) make one's exit.

**exodus** /ˈeksədəs/ *noun* mass departure; **(Exodus)** that of Israelites from Egypt.

**ex officio** /eks əˈfɪʃɪəʊ/ *adverb & adjective* by virtue of one's office.

**exonerate** /ɪgˈzɒnəreɪt/ *verb* (-ting) free or declare free from blame. □ **exoneration** *noun*.

**exorbitant** /ɪgˈzɔːbɪt(ə)nt/ *adjective* grossly excessive.

**exorcize** /ˈeksɔːsaɪz/ *verb* (also **-ise**) (-zing or -sing) drive out (evil spirit) by prayers etc.; free (person, place) thus. □ **exorcism** *noun*, **exorcist** *noun*.

**exoskeleton** /ˈeksəʊskelɪtən/ *noun* external skeleton.

**exotic** /ɪgˈzɒtɪk/ ● *adjective* introduced from abroad; strange, unusual. ● *noun* exotic plant etc. □ **exotically** *adverb*.

**expand** /ɪkˈspænd/ *verb* increase in size or importance; (often + *on*) give fuller account; become more genial; write out in full; spread out flat. □ **expandable** *adjective*; **expansion** *noun*.

**expanse** /ɪkˈspæns/ *noun* wide area or extent of land, space, etc.

**expansionism** *noun* advocacy of expansion, esp. of state's territory. □ **expansionist** *noun & adjective*.

**expansive** *adjective* able or tending to expand; extensive; genial.

**expatiate** /ɪkˈspeɪʃɪeɪt/ *verb* (-ting) (usually + *on*, *upon*) speak or write at length. □ **expatiation** *noun*.

**expatriate** ● *adjective* /eksˈpætrɪət/ living abroad; exiled. ● *noun* /eksˈpætrɪət/ expatriate person. ● *verb* /eksˈpætrɪeɪt/ (-ting) expel from native country.

**expect** /ɪkˈspekt/ *verb* regard as likely; look for as one's due; *colloquial* suppose. □ **be expecting** *colloquial* be pregnant.

**expectant** *adjective* expecting; expecting to become; pregnant. □ **expectancy** *noun*, **expectantly** *adverb*.

**expectation** /ekspekˈteɪʃ(ə)n/ *noun* expecting, anticipation; what one expects; probability; (in *plural*) prospects of inheritance.

**expectorant** /ekˈspektərənt/ ● *adjective* causing expectoration. ● *noun* expectorant medicine.

**expectorate** /ekˈspektəreɪt/ *verb* (-ting) cough or spit out from chest or lungs; spit. □ **expectoration** *noun*.

**expedient** /ɪkˈspiːdɪənt/ ● *adjective* advantageous; advisable on practical rather than moral grounds. ● *noun* means of achieving an end; resource. □ **expediency** *noun*.

**expedite** /ˈekspɪdaɪt/ *verb* (-ting) assist progress of; accomplish quickly.

**expedition** /ekspɪˈdɪʃ(ə)n/ *noun* journey or voyage for particular purpose; people etc. undertaking this; speed.

**expeditionary** *adjective* of or used on expedition.

**expeditious** /ekspɪˈdɪʃəs/ *adjective* acting or done with speed and efficiency.

**expel** /ɪkˈspel/ *verb* (-ll-) deprive of membership; force out; eject.

**expend** /ɪkˈspend/ *verb* spend (money, time, etc.); use up.

**expendable** *adjective* that may be sacrificed or dispensed with.

**expenditure** /ɪkˈspendɪtʃə/ *noun* expending; amount expended.

**expense** /ɪkˈspens/ *noun* cost, charge; (in *plural*) costs incurred in doing job etc., reimbursement of this.

**expensive** *adjective* costing or charging much. □ **expensively** *adverb*.

**experience** /ɪkˈspɪərɪəns/ ● *noun* personal observation or contact; knowledge or skill based on this; event that affects one. ● *verb* (-cing) have experience of; undergo; feel. □ **experiential** /-ˈen-/ *adjective*.

**experienced** *adjective* having had much experience; skilful through experience.

**experiment** /ɪkˈsperɪmənt/ ● *noun* procedure adopted to test hypothesis or demonstrate known fact. ● *verb* (also /-ment/) make experiment(s). □ **experimentation** /-men-/ *noun*, **experimenter** *noun*.

**experimental** /ɪkˈsperɪˈment(ə)l/ *adjective* based on or done by way of experiment. □ **experimentally** *adverb*.

**expert** /'eksp3:t/ (often + *at, in*) ● *adjective* well informed or skilful in a subject. ● *noun* expert person. □ **expertly** *adverb*.

**expertise** /eksp3:'ti:z/ *noun* special skill or knowledge.

**expiate** /'ekspieit/ *verb* (**-ting**) pay penalty or make amends for (wrong). □ **expiation** *noun*.

**expire** /ik'spaiə/ *verb* (**-ring**) come to an end; cease to be valid; die; breathe out. □ **expiration** /ekspi-/ *noun*.

**expiry** *noun* end of validity or duration.

**explain** /iks'plein/ *verb* make intelligible; make known; say by way of explanation; account for. □ **explanation** /eksplə-/ *noun*.

**explanatory** /ik'splænətəri/ *adjective* serving to explain.

**expletive** /ik'spli:tiv/ *noun* swear-word or exclamation.

**explicable** /ik'splikəb(ə)l/ *adjective* explainable.

**explicit** /ik'splisit/ *adjective* expressly stated; stated in detail; definite; outspoken. □ **explicitly** *adverb*; **explicitness** *noun*.

**explode** /ik'spləud/ (**-ding**) *verb* expand violently with loud noise; cause (bomb etc.) to do this; give vent suddenly to emotion, esp. anger; (of population etc.) increase suddenly; discredit.

**exploit** ● *noun* /'eksplɔit/ daring feat. ● *verb* /ik'splɔit/ use or develop for one's own ends; take advantage of (esp. person). □ **exploitation** /eksplɔi-/ *noun*; **exploitative** /ik'splɔit-/ *adjective*.

**explore** /ik'splɔ:/ *verb* (**-ring**) travel through (country etc.) to learn about it; inquire into; examine (part of body), probe (wound). □ **exploration** /eksplə-/ *noun*; **exploratory** /-'splɒr-/ *adjective*; **explorer** *noun*.

**explosion** /ik'spləuʒ(ə)n/ *noun* exploding; loud noise caused by this; outbreak; sudden increase.

**explosive** /ik'spləusiv/ ● *adjective* tending to explode; likely to cause violent outburst etc. ● *noun* explosive substance.

**exponent** /ik'spəunənt/ *noun* person promoting idea etc.; practitioner of activity, profession, etc.; person who explains or interprets; type, representative; *Mathematics* raised number or symbol showing how many of a number are

to be multiplied together, e.g. $3$ in $2^3 = 2 \times 2 \times 2$.

**exponential** /ekspə'nenʃ(ə)l/ *adjective* (of increase) more and more rapid. □ **exponentially** *adverb*.

**export** /ik'spɔ:t/ ● *verb* sell or send (goods or services) to another country. ● *noun* /'ekspɔ:t/ exporting; exported article or service; (in *plural*) amount exported. □ **exportation** *noun*; **exporter** /ik'spɔ:tə/ *noun*.

**expose** /ik'spəuz/ *verb* (**-sing**) leave unprotected, esp. from weather; (+ *to*) put at risk of, subject to (influence etc.); *Photography* subject (film etc.) to light; reveal, disclose; exhibit, display; (**expose oneself**) display one's genitals indecently in public.

**exposé** /ek'spəuzei/ *noun* orderly statement of facts; disclosure of discreditable thing.

**exposition** /ekspə'ziʃ(ə)n/ *noun* expounding, explanation; *Music* part of movement in which principal themes are presented; exhibition.

**ex post facto** /eks pəust 'fæktəu/ *adjective & adverb* retrospective(ly). [Latin]

**expostulate** /ik'spɒstjuleit/ *verb* (**-ting**) make protest, remonstrate. □ **expostulation** *noun*.

**exposure** /ik'spəuʒə/ *noun* exposing, being exposed; physical condition resulting from being exposed to elements; *Photography* length of time film etc. is exposed, section of film etc. exposed at one time.

**expound** /ik'spaund/ *verb* set out in detail; explain, interpret.

**express** /ik'spres/ ● *verb* represent by symbols etc. or in language; put into words; squeeze out (juice, milk, etc.); (**express oneself**) communicate what one thinks, feels, or means. ● *adjective* operating at high speed; definitely stated; delivered by specially fast service. ● *adverb* with speed; by express messenger or train. ● *noun* express train etc. □ **expressible** *adjective*.

**expression** /ik'spreʃ(ə)n/ *noun* expressing, being expressed; wording, word, phrase; conveying or depiction of feeling; appearance (of face), intonation (of voice); *Mathematics* collection of symbols expressing quantity. □ **expressionless** *adjective*.

**expressionism** *noun* style of painting etc. seeking to express emotion rather than depict external world. □ **expressionist** *noun & adjective.*

**expressive** *adjective* full of expression; (+ *of*) serving to express. □ **expressiveness** *noun.*

**expressly** *adverb* explicitly.

**expropriate** /ɪksˈprəʊprɪeɪt/ *verb* (-ting) take away (property); dispossess. □ **expropriation** *noun;* **expropriator** *noun.*

**expulsion** /ɪkˈspʌlʃ(ə)n/ *noun* expelling, being expelled.

**expunge** /ɪkˈspʌndʒ/ *verb* (-ging) erase, remove.

**expurgate** /ˈekspəɡeɪt/ *verb* (-ting) remove matter considered objectionable from (book etc.); clear away (such matter). □ **expurgation** *noun;* **expurgator** *noun.*

**exquisite** /ˈekskwɪzɪt, ekˈskwɪzɪt/ *adjective* extremely beautiful or delicate; acute, keen. □ **exquisitely** *adverb.*

**ex-serviceman** /eksˈsɜːvɪsmən/ *noun* man formerly member of armed forces.

**extant** /ekˈstænt/ *adjective* still existing.

**extempore** /ɪkˈstempərɪ/ *adverb & adjective* without preparation.

**extemporize** /ɪkˈstempəraɪz/ *verb* (also -ise) (-zing or -sing) improvise. □ **extemporization** *noun.*

**extend** /ɪkˈstend/ *verb* lengthen in space or time; lay out at full length; reach or be or make continuous over certain area; (+ *to*) have certain scope; offer or accord (feeling, invitation, etc.); tax powers of. □ **extendible** *adjective;* **extensible** *adjective.*

**extension** /ɪkˈstenʃ(ə)n/ *noun* extending; enlargement, additional part; subsidiary telephone on same line as main one; additional period of time.

**extensive** /ɪkˈstensɪv/ *adjective* large, far-reaching. □ **extensively** *adverb.*

**extent** /ɪkˈstent/ *noun* space covered; width of application, scope.

**extenuate** /ɪkˈstenjʊeɪt/ *verb* (-ting) (often as **extenuating** *adjective*) make (guilt etc.) seem less serious by partial excuse. □ **extenuation** *noun.*

**exterior** /ɪkˈstɪərɪə/ ● *adjective* outer; coming from outside. ● *noun* exterior aspect or surface; outward demeanour.

**exterminate** /ɪkˈstɜːmɪneɪt/ *verb* destroy utterly. □ **extermination** *noun;* **exterminator** *noun.*

**external** /ɪkˈstɜːn(ə)l/ ● *adjective* of or on the outside; coming from outside; relating to a country's foreign affairs; (of medicine) for use on outside of body. ● *noun* (in *plural*) external features or circumstances. □ **externality** /ekstɜːˈnælɪtɪ/ *noun;* **externally** *adverb.*

**externalize** *verb* (also **-ise**) (-zing or -sing) give or attribute external existence to.

**extinct** /ɪkˈstɪŋkt/ *adjective* no longer existing; no longer burning; (of volcano) that no longer erupts; obsolete.

**extinction** *noun* making or becoming extinct; extinguishing, being extinguished.

**extinguish** /ɪkˈstɪŋgwɪʃ/ *verb* put out (flame, light, etc.); terminate, destroy; wipe out (debt).

**extinguisher** *noun* = FIRE EXTINGUISHER.

**extirpate** /ˈekstəpeɪt/ *verb* (-ting) destroy; root out. □ **extirpation** *noun.*

**extol** /ɪkˈstəʊl/ *verb* (-ll-) praise enthusiastically.

**extort** /ɪkˈstɔːt/ *verb* get by coercion.

**extortion** *noun* extorting, esp. of money; illegal exaction.

**extortionate** /ɪkˈstɔːʃənət/ *adjective* exorbitant.

**extra** /ˈekstrə/ ● *adjective* additional; more than usual or necessary. ● *adverb* more than usually; additionally. ● *noun* extra thing; thing for which one is charged extra; person playing one of crowd etc. in film; special edition of newspaper; *Cricket* run not scored from hit with bat.

**extra-** *combining form* outside, beyond scope of.

**extract** ● *verb* /ɪkˈstrækt/ take out; obtain against person's will; obtain from earth; copy out, quote; obtain (juice etc.) by pressure, distillation, etc.; derive (pleasure etc.); *Mathematics* find (root of number). ● *noun* /ˈekstrækt/ passage from book etc.; preparation containing concentrated constituent of substance.

**extraction** /ɪkˈstrækʃ(ə)n/ *noun* extracting; removal of tooth; lineage.

**extractor** /ɪkˈstræktə/ *noun* machine that extracts. □ **extractor fan** one that extracts bad air etc.

**extracurricular** /ekstrəkəˈrɪkjʊlə/ *adjective* outside normal curriculum.

**extraditable** *adjective* liable to extradition; (of crime) warranting extradition.

**extradite** /ˈekstrədaɪt/ *verb* (**-ting**) hand over (person accused of crime) to state where crime was committed. □ **extradition** /-ˈdɪʃ-/ *noun*.

**extramarital** /ekstrəˈmærɪt(ə)l/ *adjective* (of sexual relationship) outside marriage.

**extramural** /ekstrəˈmjʊər(ə)l/ *adjective* additional to ordinary teaching or studies.

**extraneous** /ɪkˈstreɪnɪəs/ *adjective* of external origin; (often + *to*) separate, irrelevant, unrelated.

**extraordinary** /ɪkˈstrɔːdɪnərɪ/ *adjective* unusual, remarkable; unusually great; (of meeting etc.) additional. □ **extraordinarily** *adverb*.

**extrapolate** /ɪkˈstræpəleɪt/ *verb* (**-ting**) estimate (unknown facts or values) from known data. □ **extrapolation** *noun*.

**extrasensory** /ekstrəˈsensərɪ/ *adjective* derived by means other than known senses.

**extraterrestrial** /ekstrətɪˈrestrɪəl/ ● *adjective* outside the earth or its atmosphere. ● *noun* fictional being from outer space.

**extravagant** /ɪkˈstrævəgənt/ *adjective* spending (esp. money) excessively; excessive; absurd; costing much. □ **extravagance** *noun*; **extravagantly** *adverb*.

**extravaganza** /ɪkstrævəˈgænzə/ *noun* spectacular theatrical or television production; fanciful composition.

**extreme** /ɪkˈstriːm/ ● *adjective* reaching high or highest degree; severe, not moderate; outermost; utmost. ● *noun* either of two things as remote or different as possible; thing at either end; highest degree. □ **extreme unction** anointing by priest of dying person. □ **extremely** *adverb*.

**extremis** see IN EXTREMIS.

**extremism** *noun* advocacy of extreme measures. □ **extremist** *adjective & noun*.

**extremity** /ɪkˈstremɪtɪ/ *noun* (*plural* **-ies**) extreme point, end; (in *plural*) hands and feet; condition of extreme adversity.

**extricate** /ˈekstrɪkeɪt/ *verb* (**-ting**) disentangle, release. □ **extrication** *noun*.

**extrinsic** /ekˈstrɪnsɪk/ *adjective* not inherent or intrinsic; (often + *to*) extraneous. □ **extrinsically** *adverb*.

**extrovert** /ˈekstrəvɜːt/ ● *noun* sociable or unreserved person; person mainly concerned with external things. ● *adjective* typical or having nature of extrovert. □ **extroversion** /-ˈvɜː-/ *noun*.

**extrude** /ɪkˈstruːd/ *verb* (**-ding**) thrust or squeeze out; shape by forcing through nozzle. □ **extrusion** *noun*.

**exuberant** /ɪgˈzjuːbərənt/ *adjective* highspirited, lively; luxuriant, prolific; (of feelings etc.) abounding. □ **exuberance** *noun*.

**exude** /ɪgˈzjuːd/ *verb* (**-ding**) ooze out; give off; display (emotion) freely. □ **exudation** *noun*.

**exult** /ɪgˈzʌlt/ *verb* rejoice. □ **exultant** *adjective*; **exultation** /eg-/ *noun*.

**eye** /aɪ/ ● *noun* organ or faculty of sight; iris of eye; region round eye; gaze; perception; eyelike thing; leaf bud of potato; centre of hurricane; spot, hole, loop. ● *verb* (**eyes, eyed, eyeing** or **eying**) (often + *up*) observe, watch suspiciously or closely. □ **all eyes** watching intently; **eyeball** ball of eye within lids and socket; **eyebath** vessel for applying lotion to eye; **eye-brow** hair growing on ridge over eye; **eye-catching** *colloquial* striking; **eyeglass** lens for defective eye; **eyehole** hole to look through; **eyelash** any of hairs on edge of eyelid; **eyelid** fold of skin that can cover eye; **eyeliner** cosmetic applied as line round eye; **eye-opener** *colloquial* enlightening experience, unexpected revelation; **eyepiece** lens(es) to which eye is applied at end of optical instrument; **eye-shade** device to protect eyes from strong light; **eye-shadow** cosmetic for eyelids; **eyesight** faculty or power of sight; **eyesore** ugly thing; **eye-tooth** canine tooth in upper jaw; **eyewash** lotion for eyes, *slang* nonsense; **eyewitness** person who saw thing happen and can tell of it; **have one's eye on** wish or plan to obtain; **keep an eye on** watch, look after; **see eye to eye** (often + *with*) agree; **set eyes on** see.

**eyeful** *noun* (*plural* **-s**) *colloquial* good look, visually striking person or thing.

**eyelet** /ˈaɪlɪt/ *noun* small hole for passing cord etc. through.

**eyrie** /ˈɪərɪ/ *noun* nest of bird of prey, esp. eagle, built high up.

# Ff

**F** *abbreviation* Fahrenheit.

**f** *abbreviation* (also **f.**) female; feminine; *Music* forte.

**FA** *abbreviation* Football Association.

**fa** = FAH.

**fable** /ˈfeɪb(ə)l/ *noun* fictional tale, esp. legendary, or moral tale, often with animal characters.

**fabled** *adjective* celebrated; legendary.

**fabric** /ˈfæbrɪk/ *noun* woven material; walls, floor, and roof of building; structure.

**fabricate** /ˈfæbrɪkeɪt/ *verb* (**-ting**) construct, esp. from components; invent (fact), forge (document). □ **fabrication** *noun*.

**fabulous** /ˈfæbjʊləs/ *adjective colloquial* marvellous; legendary. □ **fabulously** *adverb*.

**façade** /fəˈsɑːd/ *noun* face or front of building; outward, esp. deceptive, appearance.

**face** ● *noun* front of head; facial expression; surface; façade of building; side of mountain; dial of clock etc.; functional side of tool, bat, etc.; effrontery; aspect, feature. ● *verb* (**-cing**) look or be positioned towards; be opposite; meet resolutely, confront; put facing on (garment, wall, etc.). □ **face-lift** cosmetic surgery to remove wrinkles etc., improvement in appearance; **face up to** accept bravely; **face value** nominal value, superficial appearance; **lose face** be humiliated; **on the face of it** apparently; **pull a face** distort features; **save face** avoid humiliation.

**faceless** *adjective* without identity; not identifiable.

**facet** /ˈfæsɪt/ *noun* aspect; side of cut gem etc.

**facetious** /fəˈsiːʃəs/ *adjective* intended to be amusing, esp. inappropriately. □ **facetiously** *adverb*; **facetiousness** *noun*.

**facia** = FASCIA.

**facial** /ˈfeɪʃ(ə)l/ ● *adjective* of or for the face. ● *noun* beauty treatment for the face. □ **facially** *adverb*.

**facile** /ˈfæsaɪl/ *adjective* easily achieved but of little value; glib.

**facilitate** /fəˈsɪlɪteɪt/ *verb* (**-ting**) ease (process etc.). □ **facilitation** *noun*.

**facility** /fəˈsɪlɪtɪ/ *noun* (*plural* **-ies**) ease, absence of difficulty; dexterity; (esp. in *plural*) opportunity or equipment for doing something.

**facing** *noun* material over part of garment etc. for contrast or strength; outer covering on wall etc.

**facsimile** /fækˈsɪmɪlɪ/ *noun* exact copy of writing, picture, etc.

**fact** *noun* thing known to exist or be true; reality. □ **factsheet** information leaflet; **in fact** in reality, in short; **the facts of life** information on sexual functions etc.

**faction** /ˈfækʃ(ə)n/ *noun* small dissenting group within larger one, esp. in politics; such dissension. □ **factional** *adjective*.

**factious** /ˈfækʃəs/ *adjective* of or inclined to faction.

**factitious** /fækˈtɪʃəs/ *adjective* specially contrived; artificial.

**factor** /ˈfæktə/ *noun* thing contributing to result; whole number etc. that when multiplied produces given number (e.g. 2, 3, 4, and 6 are the factors of 12).

**factorial** /fæk'tɔːrɪəl/ *noun* the product of a number and all whole numbers below it.

**factory** /'fæktərɪ/ *noun* (*plural* **-ies**) building(s) for manufacture of goods. □ **factory farming** using intensive or industrial methods of rearing livestock.

**factotum** /fæk'təʊtəm/ *noun* (*plural* **-s**) employee doing all kinds of work.

**factual** /'fæktjʊəl/ *adjective* based on or concerned with fact. □ **factually** *adverb*.

**faculty** /'fækəltɪ/ *noun* (*plural* **-ies**) aptitude for particular activity; physical or mental power; group of related university departments; *US* teaching staff of university etc.

**fad** *noun* craze; peculiar notion.

**faddy** *adjective* (**-ier**, **-iest**) having petty likes and dislikes.

**fade** ● *verb* (**-ding**) (cause to) lose colour, light, or sound; slowly diminish; lose freshness or strength. ● *noun* action of fading. □ **fade away** die away, disappear, *colloquial* languish, grow thin.

**faeces** /'fiːsiːz/ *plural noun* (*US* **feces**) waste matter from bowels. □ **faecal** /-k(ə)l/ *adjective*.

**fag** ● *noun colloquial* tedious task; *slang* cigarette; (at public schools) junior boy who runs errands for a senior. ● *verb* (**-gg-**) (often + *out*) *colloquial* exhaust; act as fag. □ **fag-end** *slang* cigarette-end.

**faggot** /'fægət/ *noun* (*US* **fagot**) baked or fried ball of seasoned chopped liver etc.; bundle of sticks etc.

**fah** /fɑː/ *noun* (also **fa**) *Music* fourth note of scale in tonic sol-fa.

**Fahrenheit** /'færənhaɪt/ *adjective* of scale of temperature on which water freezes at 32° and boils at 212°.

**faience** /'faɪɑ̃s/ *noun* decorated and glazed earthenware and porcelain.

**fail** ● *verb* not succeed; be or judge to be unsuccessful in (exam etc.); (+ *to do*) be unable, neglect; disappoint; be absent or insufficient; become weaker; cease functioning. ● *noun* failure in exam. □ **fail-safe** reverting to safe condition when faulty; **without fail** for certain, whatever happens.

**failed** *adjective* unsuccessful; bankrupt.

**failing** ● *noun* fault; weakness. ● *preposition* in default of.

**failure** /'feɪljə/ *noun* lack of success; unsuccessful person or thing; nonperformance; breaking down, ceasing to function; running short of supply etc.

**fain** *archaic* ● *adjective* (+ *to do*) willing, obliged. ● *adverb* gladly.

**faint** ● *adjective* dim, pale; weak, giddy; slight; timid. ● *verb* lose consciousness; become faint. ● *noun* act or state of fainting. □ **faint-hearted** cowardly, timid. □ **faintly** *adverb*; **faintness** *noun*.

**fair**[1] ● *adjective* just, equitable; blond, not dark; moderate in quality or amount; (of weather) fine; (of wind) favourable; *archaic* beautiful. ● *adverb* in a fair or just manner; exactly, completely. □ **fair and square** exactly, straightforwardly; **fair copy** transcript free from corrections; **fair game** legitimate target or object; **fair play** just treatment or behaviour; **fair-weather friend** friend or ally who deserts in crisis. □ **fairness** *noun*.

**fair**[2] *noun* stalls, amusements, etc. for public entertainment; periodic market, often with entertainments; trade exhibition. □ **fairground** outside site for fair.

**Fair Isle** *noun* multicoloured knitwear design characteristic of Fair Isle in the Shetlands.

**fairly** *adverb* in a fair way; moderately; to a noticeable degree.

**fairway** *noun* navigable channel; mown grass between golf tee and green.

**fairy** /'feərɪ/ *noun* (*plural* **-ies**) small winged legendary being. □ **fairy cake** small iced sponge cake; **fairy godmother** benefactress; **fairyland** home of fairies, enchanted region; **fairy lights** small coloured lights for decoration; **fairy ring** ring of darker grass caused by fungi; **fairy story, tale** tale about fairies, unbelievable story, lie.

**fait accompli** /feɪt ə'kɒmpliː/ *noun* thing done and past arguing about. [French]

**faith** /feɪθ/ *noun* trust; religious belief; creed; loyalty, trustworthiness. □ **faith-healer** person who practises **faith-healing**, healing dependent on faith rather than treatment.

**faithful** *adjective* showing faith; (often + *to*) loyal, trustworthy; accurate.

**faithfully** *adverb* in a faithful way. □ **Yours faithfully** *written before signature at end of business letter*.

**faithless** *adjective* disloyal; without religious faith.

**fake** ● *noun* thing or person that is not genuine. ● *adjective* counterfeit, not genuine. ● *verb* (**-king**) make fake or imitation of; feign.

**fakir** /'feɪkɪə/ *noun* Muslim or Hindu religious beggar or ascetic.

**falcon** /'fɔ:lkən/ *noun* small hawk trained to hunt.

**falconry** *noun* breeding and training of hawks.

**fall** /fɔ:l/ ● *verb* (*past* **fell**; *past participle* **fallen**) go or come down freely; descend; (often + *over*) lose balance and come suddenly to ground; slope or hang down; sink lower, decline in power, status, etc.; subside; occur; become; (of face) show dismay etc.; be defeated; die. ● *noun* falling; amount or thing that falls; overthrow; (esp. in *plural*) waterfall; *US* autumn. □ **fall back on** have recourse to; **fall behind** be outstripped, be in arrears; **fall down (on)** *colloquial* fail (in); **fall for** be captivated or deceived by; **fall foul of** come into conflict with; **fall guy** *slang* easy victim, scapegoat; **fall in** *Military* take place in parade; **fall in with** meet by chance, agree or coincide with; **falling star** meteor; **fall off** decrease, deteriorate; **fall out** *verb* quarrel; (of hair, teeth, etc.) become detached, result, occur, *Military* come out of formation; **fallout** *noun* radioactive nuclear debris; **fall short of** fail to reach or obtain; **fall through** fail; **fall to** start eating, working, etc.

**fallacy** /'fæləsɪ/ *noun* (*plural* **-ies**) mistaken belief; faulty reasoning; misleading argument. □ **fallacious** /fə'leɪʃəs/ *adjective*.

**fallible** /'fælɪb(ə)l/ *adjective* capable of making mistakes. □ **fallibility** *noun*.

**Fallopian tube** /fə'ləʊpɪən/ *noun* either of two tubes along which ova travel from ovaries to womb.

**fallow** /'fæləʊ/ ● *adjective* (of land) ploughed but left unsown; uncultivated. ● *noun* fallow land.

**fallow deer** *noun* small deer with white-spotted reddish-brown summer coat.

**false** /fɔ:ls/ *adjective* wrong, incorrect; sham, artificial; (+ *to*) deceitful, treacherous, unfaithful; deceptive. □ **false alarm** alarm given needlessly; **false pretences** misrepresentations meant to deceive. □ **falsely** *adverb*; **falsity** *noun*; **falseness** *noun*.

**falsehood** *noun* untrue thing; lying, lie.

**falsetto** /fɔ:l'setəʊ/ *noun* male voice above normal range.

**falsify** /'fɔ:lsɪfaɪ/ *verb* (**-ies**, **-ied**) fraudulently alter; misrepresent. □ **falsification** *noun*.

**falter** /'fɔ:ltə/ *verb* stumble; go unsteadily; lose courage; speak hesitatingly.

**fame** *noun* renown, being famous; *archaic* reputation.

**famed** *adjective* (+ *for*) much spoken of or famous because of.

**familial** /fə'mɪlɪəl/ *adjective* of a family or its members.

**familiar** /fə'mɪlɪə/ ● *adjective* (often + *to*) well known, often encountered; (+ *with*) knowing (a thing) well; (excessively) informal. ● *noun* intimate friend; supposed attendant of witch etc. □ **familiarity** /-'ær-/ *noun* (*plural* **-ies**); **familiarly** *adverb*.

**familiarize** /fə'mɪlɪəraɪz/ *verb* (also **-ise**) (**-zing** or **-sing**) (usually + *with*) make (person etc.) conversant. □ **familiarization** *noun*.

**family** /'fæmɪlɪ/ *noun* (*plural* **-ies**) set of relations, esp. parents and children; person's children; household; all the descendants of common ancestor; group of similar things, people, etc.; group of related genera of animals or plants. □ **family credit** regular state payment to low-income family; **family planning** birth control; **family tree** genealogical chart.

**famine** /'fæmɪn/ *noun* extreme scarcity, esp. of food.

**famish** /'fæmɪʃ/ *verb* (usually as **famished** *adjective colloquial*) make or become extremely hungry.

**famous** /'feɪməs/ *adjective* (often + *for*) well-known; celebrated; *colloquial* excellent. □ **famously** *adverb*.

**fan**[1] ● *noun* apparatus, usually with rotating blades, for ventilation etc.; device, semicircular and folding, waved to cool oneself; fan-shaped thing. ● *verb*

(**-nn-**) blow air on, (as) with fan; (usually + *out*) spread out like fan. □ **fan belt** belt driving fan to cool radiator in vehicle; **fanlight** small, originally semicircular, window over door etc.; **fantail** pigeon with broad tail.

**fan**[2] *noun* devotee. □ **fan club** (club of) devotees; **fan mail** letters from fans.

**fanatic** /fə'nætɪk/ *noun* person obsessively devoted to a belief, activity, etc. ● *adjective* excessively enthusiastic. □ **fanatical** *adjective*; **fanatically** *adverb*; **fanaticism** /-tɪsɪz(ə)m/ *noun*.

**fancier** /'fænsɪə/ *noun* connoisseur, enthusiast; breeder, esp. of pigeons.

**fanciful** /'fænsɪfʊl/ *adjective* imaginary; indulging in fancies. □ **fancifully** *adverb*.

**fancy** /'fænsɪ/ ● *noun* (*plural* **-ies**) inclination, whim; supposition; imagination. ● *adjective* (**-ier**, **-iest**) extravagant; ornamental. ● *verb* (**-ies**, **-ied**) (+ *that*) imagine; suppose; *colloquial* find attractive, desire; have unduly high opinion of. □ **fancy dress** costume for masquerading; **fancy-free** without (emotional) commitments; **fancy man, woman** woman's or man's lover. □ **fancily** *adverb*.

**fandango** /fæn'dæŋɡəʊ/ *noun* (*plural* **-es** or **-s**) lively Spanish dance.

**fanfare** /'fænfeə/ *noun* short showy sounding of trumpets etc.

**fang** *noun* canine tooth, esp. of dog or wolf; tooth of venomous snake; (prong of) root of tooth.

**fantasia** /fæn'teɪzɪə/ *noun* free or improvisatory musical etc. composition.

**fantasize** /'fæntəsaɪz/ *verb* (also **-ise**) (**-zing** or **-sing**) daydream; imagine; create fantasy about.

**fantastic** /fæn'tæstɪk/ *adjective* extravagantly fanciful; grotesque, quaint; *colloquial* excellent, extraordinary. □ **fantastically** *adverb*.

**fantasy** /'fæntəsɪ/ *noun* (*plural* **-ies**) imagination, esp. when unrelated to reality; mental image, daydream; fantastic invention or composition.

**fanzine** /'fænziːn/ *noun* magazine for fans of science fiction, a football team, etc.

**far** (**further**, **furthest** or **farther**, **farthest**) ● *adverb* at, to, or by a great distance in space or time; by much. ● *adjective* distant; remote; extreme. □ **far and wide** over large area; **far-away** remote, dreamy, distant; **the Far East** countries of E. Asia; **far-fetched** unconvincing, exaggerated, fanciful; **far-flung** widely scattered, remote; **far from** almost the opposite of; **far gone** very ill, drunk, etc.; **far-off** remote; **far-out** *slang* unconventional, excellent; **far-reaching** widely influential or applicable; **far-seeing** showing foresight; **far-sighted** having foresight, *esp. US* long-sighted.

**farad** /'færəd/ *noun* SI unit of electrical capacitance.

**farce** /fɑːs/ *noun* comedy with ludicrously improbable plot; absurdly futile proceedings; pretence. □ **farcical** *adjective*.

**fare** ● *noun* price of journey on public transport; passenger; food. ● *verb* (**-ring**) progress; get on. □ **fare-stage** section of bus route for which fixed fare is charged; stop marking this.

**farewell** /feə'wel/ ● *interjection* goodbye. ● *noun* leave-taking.

**farina** /fə'riːnə/ *noun* flour of corn, nuts, or starchy roots. □ **farinaceous** /færɪ'neɪʃəs/ *adjective*.

**farm** ● *noun* land and its buildings used for growing crops, rearing animals, etc.; farmhouse. ● *verb* use (land) thus; be farmer; breed (fish etc.) commercially; (+ *out*) delegate or subcontract (work). □ **farm-hand** worker on farm; **farmhouse** house attached to farm; **farmyard** yard adjacent to farmhouse. □ **farming** *noun*.

**farmer** *noun* owner or manager of farm.

**faro** /'feərəʊ/ *noun* gambling card-game.

**farrago** /fə'rɑːɡəʊ/ *noun* (*plural* **-s** or *US* **-es**) medley, hotchpotch.

**farrier** /'færɪə/ *noun* smith who shoes horses.

**farrow** /'færəʊ/ ● *verb* give birth to (piglets). ● *noun* litter of pigs.

**Farsi** /'fɑːsɪ/ *noun* modern Persian language.

**farther** = FURTHER.

**farthest** = FURTHEST.

**farthing** /'fɑːðɪŋ/ *noun* *historical* coin worth quarter of old penny.

**farthingale** /'fɑːðɪŋɡeɪl/ *noun* *historical* hooped petticoat.

**fascia** /ˈfeɪʃə/ *noun* (also **facia**) (*plural* **-s**) instrument panel of vehicle; similar panel etc. for operating machinery; long flat surface of wood or stone.

**fascicle** /ˈfæsɪk(ə)l/ *noun* instalment of book.

**fascinate** /ˈfæsɪneɪt/ *verb* (**-ting**) (often as **fascinating** *adjective*) capture interest of; attract. □ **fascination** *noun*.

**Fascism** /ˈfæʃɪz(ə)m/ *noun* extreme right-wing totalitarian nationalist movement in Italy (1922–43); (also **fascism**) any similar movement. □ **Fascist, fascist** *noun & adjective*; **Fascistic, fascistic** /-ˈʃɪs-/ *adjective*.

**fashion** /ˈfæʃ(ə)n/ ● *noun* current popular custom or style, esp. in dress; manner of doing something. ● *verb* (often + *into*) form, make. □ **in fashion** fashionable; **out of fashion** not fashionable.

**fashionable** *adjective* of or conforming to current fashion; of or favoured by high society. □ **fashionably** *adverb*.

**fast**[1] /fɑːst/ ● *adjective* rapid; capable of or intended for high speed; (of clock) ahead of correct time; firm, fixed, (of colour) not fading; pleasure-seeking. ● *adverb* quickly; firmly; soundly, completely. □ **fastback** with sloping rear; **fast breeder (reactor)** reactor using neutrons with high kinetic energy; **fast food** restaurant food that is produced quickly; **pull a fast one** *colloquial* try to deceive someone.

**fast**[2] /fɑːst/ ● *verb* abstain from food. ● *noun* act or period of fasting.

**fasten** /ˈfɑːs(ə)n/ *verb* make or become fixed or secure; (+ *in, up*) shut in, lock securely; (+ *on*) direct (attention) towards; (+ *off*) fix with knot or stitches.

**fastener** *noun* (also **fastening**) device that fastens.

**fastidious** /fæˈstɪdɪəs/ *adjective* fussy; easily disgusted, squeamish.

**fastness** /ˈfɑːstnɪs/ *noun* stronghold.

**fat** ● *noun* oily substance, esp. in animal bodies; part of meat etc. containing this. ● *adjective* (**-tt-**) plump; containing much fat; thick, substantial. ● *verb* (**-tt-**) (esp. as **fatted** *adjective*) make or become fat. □ **fat-head** *colloquial* stupid person; **fat-headed** stupid; **a fat lot** *colloquial* very little. □ **fatless** *adjective*, **fatten** *verb*.

**fatal** /ˈfeɪt(ə)l/ *adjective* causing or ending in death or ruin. □ **fatally** *adverb*.

**fatalism** *noun* belief in predetermination; submissive acceptance. □ **fatalist** *noun*; **fatalistic** /-ˈlɪs-/ *adjective*.

**fatality** /fəˈtælɪtɪ/ *noun* (*plural* **-ies**) death by accident, in war, etc.

**fate** ● *noun* supposed power predetermining events; destiny; death, destruction. ● *verb* (**-ting**) preordain; (as **fated** *adjective*) doomed, (+ *to do*) preordained.

**fateful** *adjective* decisive; important; controlled by fate.

**father** /ˈfɑːðə/ ● *noun* male parent; (usually in *plural* forebear); originator; early leader; (also **Father**) priest; (**the Father**) God; (in *plural*) elders. ● *verb* be father of; originate. □ **father-in-law** (*plural* **fathers-in-law**) wife's or husband's father; **fatherland** native country. □ **fatherhood** *noun*; **fatherless** *adjective*.

**fatherly** *adjective* of or like a father.

**fathom** /ˈfæð(ə)m/ ● *noun* measure of 6ft, esp. in soundings. ● *verb* comprehend; measure depth of (water). □ **fathomable** *adjective*.

**fathomless** *adjective* too deep to fathom.

**fatigue** /fəˈtiːg/ ● *noun* extreme tiredness; weakness in metals etc. from repeated stress; non-military army duty, (in *plural*) clothing for this. ● *verb* (**-gues, -gued, -guing**) cause fatigue in.

**fatty** ● *adjective* (**-ier, -iest**) like or containing fat. ● *noun* (*plural* **-ies**) *colloquial* fat person. □ **fatty acid** type of organic compound.

**fatuous** /ˈfætjʊəs/ *adjective* vacantly silly; purposeless. □ **fatuity** /fəˈtjuːɪtɪ/ *noun* (*plural* **-ies**); **fatuously** *adverb*; **fatuousness** *noun*.

**fatwa** /ˈfætwɑː/ *noun* legal ruling by Islamic religious leader.

**faucet** /ˈfɔːsɪt/ *noun esp. US* tap.

**fault** /fɔːlt/ ● *noun* defect, imperfection; responsibility for wrongdoing, error, etc.; break in electric circuit; *Tennis etc.* incorrect service; break in rock strata. ● *verb* find fault with. □ **find fault** (often + *with*) criticize or complain (about); **to a fault** excessively. □ **faultless** *adjective*; **faultlessly** *adverb*.

**faulty** *adjective* (**-ier, -iest**) having faults. □ **faultily** *adverb*.

**faun** /fɔːn/ *noun* Latin rural deity with goat's horns, legs, and tail.

**fauna** /ˈfɔːnə/ *noun* (*plural* **-s**) animal life of a region or period.

**faux pas** /fəʊ ˈpɑː/ *noun* (*plural* same /ˈpɑːz/) tactless mistake. [French]

**favour** /ˈfeɪvə/ (*US* **favor**) *noun* kind act; approval, goodwill; partiality; badge, ribbon, etc. as emblem of support. ● *verb* regard or treat with favour; support, facilitate; tend to confirm (idea etc.); (+ *with*) oblige; (as **favoured** *adjective*) having special advantages. □ **in favour** approved of, (+ *of*) in support of or to the advantage of; **out of favour** disapproved of.

**favourable** *adjective* (*US* **favorable**) well-disposed; approving; promising; helpful, suitable. □ **favourably** *adverb*.

**favourite** /ˈfeɪvərɪt/ (*US* **favorite**) ● *adjective* preferred to all others. ● *noun* favourite person or thing; competitor thought most likely to win.

**favouritism** *noun* (*US* **favoritism**) unfair favouring of one person etc.

**fawn**[1] ● *noun* deer in first year; light yellowish brown. ● *adjective* fawn-coloured. ● *verb* give birth to fawn.

**fawn**[2] *verb* (often + *on*, *upon*) behave servilely; (of dog) show extreme affection.

**fax** ● *noun* electronic transmission of exact copy of document etc.; such copy; (in full **fax machine**) apparatus used for this. ● *verb* transmit in this way.

**faze** *verb* (**-zing**) (often as **fazed** *adjective*) *colloquial* disconcert.

**FBI** *abbreviation* Federal Bureau of Investigation.

**FC** *abbreviation* Football Club.

**FCO** *abbreviation* Foreign and Commonwealth Office.

**FE** *abbreviation* further education.

**fealty** /ˈfiːəltɪ/ *noun* (*plural* **-ies**) fidelity to feudal lord; allegiance.

**fear** ● *noun* panic etc. caused by impending danger, pain, etc.; cause of this; alarm, dread. ● *verb* be afraid of; (+ *for*) feel anxiety about; dread; shrink from; revere (God).

**fearful** *adjective* afraid; terrible, awful; extremely unpleasant. □ **fearfully** *adverb*; **fearfulness** *noun*.

**fearless** *adjective* not afraid; brave. □ **fearlessly** *adverb*; **fearlessness** *noun*.

**fearsome** *adjective* frightening. □ **fearsomely** *adverb*.

**feasible** /ˈfiːzɪb(ə)l/ *adjective* practicable, possible. □ **feasibility** *noun*; **feasibly** *adverb*.

■ Usage *Feasible* should not be used to mean 'likely'. *Possible* or *probable* should be used instead.

**feast** ● *noun* sumptuous meal; religious festival; sensual or mental pleasure. ● *verb* (often + *on*) have feast; eat and drink sumptuously; regale.

**feat** *noun* remarkable act or achievement.

**feather** /ˈfeðə/ ● *noun* one of structures forming bird's plumage, with fringed horny shaft; these as material. ● *verb* cover or line with feathers; turn (oar) through air edgeways. □ **feather bed** *noun* bed with feather-stuffed mattress; **feather-bed** *verb* cushion, esp. financially; **feather-brained**, **-headed** silly; **featherweight** amateur boxing weight (54–57 kg). □ **feathery** *adjective*.

**feature** /ˈfiːtʃə/ ● *noun* characteristic or distinctive part; (usually in *plural*) part of face; specialized article in newspaper etc.; (in full **feature film**) main film in cinema programme. ● *verb* (**-ring**) make or be special feature of; emphasize; take part in. □ **featureless** *adjective*.

**Feb.** *abbreviation* February.

**febrile** /ˈfiːbraɪl/ *adjective* of fever.

**February** /ˈfebrʊərɪ/ *noun* (*plural* **-ies**) second month of year.

**fecal** *US* = FAECAL.

**feces** *US* = FAECES.

**feckless** /ˈfeklɪs/ *adjective* feeble, ineffectual; irresponsible.

**fecund** /ˈfekənd/ *adjective* fertile. □ **fecundity** /fɪˈkʌndɪtɪ/ *noun*.

**fecundate** /ˈfekəndeɪt/ *verb* (**-ting**) make fruitful; fertilize. □ **fecundation** *noun*.

**fed** *past & past participle* of FEED. □ **fed up** (often + *with*) discontented, bored.

**federal** /ˈfedər(ə)l/ *adjective* of system of government in which self-governing states unite for certain functions; of such a federation; (**Federal**) US of Northern States in Civil War. □ **federalism** *noun*; **federalist** *noun*; **federalize** *verb* (also **-ise**) (**-zing** or **-sing**); **federalization** *noun*; **federally** *adverb*.

**federate** ● *verb* /'fedəreɪt/ (**-ting**) unite on federal basis. ● *adjective* /'fedərət/ federally organized. □ **federative** /-rətɪv/ *adjective*.

**federation** /fedə'reɪʃ(ə)n/ *noun* federal group; act of federating.

**fee** *noun* payment for professional advice or services; (often in *plural*) payment for admission, membership, licence, education, exam, etc.; money paid for transfer of footballer etc. □ **fee-paying** paying fee(s), (of school) charging fees.

**feeble** /'fiːb(ə)l/ *adjective* (**-r, -st**) weak; lacking energy, strength, or effectiveness. □ **feebly** *adverb*.

**feed** ● *verb* (*past & past participle* **fed**) supply with food; put food in mouth of; eat; graze; keep supplied with; (+ *into*) supply (material) to machine etc.; (often + *on*) nourish; be nourished by. ● *noun* food, esp. for animals or infants; feeding; *colloquial* meal. □ **feedback** information about result of experiment, response, *Electronics* return of part of output signal to input.

**feeder** *noun* person or thing that feeds in specified way; baby's feeding bottle; bib; tributary; branch road or railway line; electricity main supplying distribution point; feeding apparatus in machine.

**feel** ● *verb* (*past & past participle* **felt**) examine, search, or perceive by touch; experience; be affected by; (+ *that*) have impression; consider, think; seem; be consciously; (+ *for, with*) have sympathy or pity for. ● *noun* feeling; sense of touch; sensation characterizing something. □ **feel like** have wish or inclination for; **feel up to** be ready to face or deal with.

**feeler** *noun* organ in certain animals for touching, foraging, etc. □ **put out feelers** make tentative proposal.

**feeling** ● *noun* capacity to feel; sense of touch; physical sensation; emotion; (in *plural*) susceptibilities; sensitivity; notion, opinion. ● *adjective* sensitive; sympathetic. □ **feelingly** *adverb*.

**feet** *plural of* FOOT.

**feign** /feɪn/ *verb* simulate; pretend.

**feint** /feɪnt/ ● *noun* sham attack or diversionary blow; pretence. ● *verb* make a feint. ● *adjective* (of paper etc.) having faintly ruled lines.

**feldspar** /'feldspɑː/ *noun* (also **felspar** /'felspɑː/) common aluminium silicate.

**felicitation** /fəlɪsɪ'teɪʃ(ə)n/ *noun* (usually in *plural*) congratulation.

**felicitous** /fə'lɪsɪtəs/ *adjective* apt; well-chosen.

**felicity** /fə'lɪsɪtɪ/ *noun* (*plural* **-ies**) *formal* great happiness; capacity for apt expression.

**feline** /'fiːlaɪn/ ● *adjective* of cat family; catlike. ● *noun* animal of cat family.

**fell**[1] *past of* FALL.

**fell**[2] *verb* cut down (tree); strike down.

**fell**[3] *noun* hill or stretch of hills in N. England.

**fell**[4] *adjective* □ **at, in one fell swoop** in a single (originally deadly) action.

**fell**[5] *noun* animal's hide or skin with hair.

**fellow** /'feləʊ/ ● *noun* comrade, associate; counterpart, equal; *colloquial* man, boy; incorporated senior member of college; member of learned society. ● *adjective* of same group etc. □ **fellow-feeling** sympathy; **fellow-traveller** person who travels with another, sympathizer with Communist party.

**fellowship** /'feləʊʃɪp/ *noun* friendly association, companionship; group of associates; position or income of college fellow.

**felon** /'felən/ *noun* person who has committed felony.

**felony** /'felənɪ/ *noun* (*plural* **-ies**) serious usually violent crime. □ **felonious** /fɪ'ləʊ-/ *adjective*.

**felspar** = FELDSPAR.

**felt**[1] ● *noun* fabric of matted and pressed fibres of wool etc. ● *verb* make into or cover with felt; become matted. □ **felt tip** or **pen**, **felt-tip(ped) pen** pen with fibre point.

**felt**[2] *past & past participle of* FEEL.

**female** /'fiːmeɪl/ ● *adjective* of the sex that can give birth or produce eggs; (of plants) fruit-bearing; (of female people, animals, or plants; (of screw, socket, etc.) hollow to receive inserted part. ● *noun* female person, animal, or plant.

**feminine** /'femɪnɪn/ *adjective* of women; womanly; *Grammar* (of noun) belonging to gender including words for most female people and animals. □ **femininity** /-'nɪn-/ *noun*.

**feminism** /'femɪnɪz(ə)m/ *noun* advocacy of women's rights and sexual equality. □ **feminist** *noun & adjective*.

**femme fatale** /fæm fæˈtɑːl/ *noun* (*plural* **femmes fatales** same pronunciation) dangerously seductive woman. [French]

**femur** /'fiːmə/ *noun* (*plural* **-s** or **femora** /'femərə/) thigh-bone. □ **femoral** /'femər(ə)l/ *adjective*.

**fen** *noun* low marshy land.

**fence** ● *noun* barrier or railing enclosing field, garden, etc.; jump for horses; *slang* receiver of stolen goods. ● *verb* (**-cing**) surround (as) with fence; practise sword play; be evasive; deal in (stolen goods). □ **fencer** *noun*.

**fencing** *noun* fences, material for fences; sword-fighting, esp. as sport.

**fend** *verb* (+ *off*) ward off; (+ *for*) look after (esp. oneself).

**fender** *noun* low frame round fireplace; matting etc. to protect side of ship; *US* bumper of vehicle.

**fennel** /'fen(ə)l/ *noun* fragrant plant with edible leaf-stalks and seeds.

**fenugreek** /'fenjuːgriːk/ *noun* leguminous plant with aromatic seeds used for flavouring.

**feral** /'fer(ə)l/ *adjective* wild; (of animal) escaped and living wild.

**ferial** /'fɪərɪəl/ *adjective* (of day) not a church festival or fast.

**ferment** ● *noun* /'fɜːment/ excitement; fermentation; fermenting agent. ● *verb* /fəˈment/ undergo or subject to fermentation; excite.

**fermentation** /fɜːmenˈteɪʃ(ə)n/ *noun* breakdown of substance by yeasts, bacteria, etc.; excitement.

**fern** *noun* flowerless plant usually with feathery fronds.

**ferocious** /fəˈrəʊʃəs/ *adjective* fierce. □ **ferociously** *adverb*; **ferocity** /-'rɒs-/ *noun*.

**ferret** /'ferɪt/ ● *noun* small polecat used in catching rabbits, rats, etc. ● *verb* (**-t-**) hunt with ferrets; (often + *out*, *about*, etc.) rummage; (+ *out*) search out.

**ferric** /'ferɪk/ *adjective* of iron; containing iron in trivalent form.

**Ferris wheel** /'ferɪs/ *noun* tall revolving vertical wheel with passenger cars in fairgrounds etc.

**ferroconcrete** /ferəʊˈkɒŋkriːt/ *noun* reinforced concrete.

**ferrous** /'ferəs/ *adjective* containing iron, esp. in divalent form.

**ferrule** /'feruːl/ *noun* ring or cap on end of stick etc.

**ferry** ● *noun* (*plural* **-ies**) boat etc. for esp. regular transport across water; ferrying place or service. ● *verb* (**-ies**, **-ied**) take or go in ferry; transport from place to place, esp. regularly. □ **ferryman** *noun*.

**fertile** /'fɜːtaɪl/ *adjective* (of soil) abundantly productive; fruitful; (of seed, egg, etc.) capable of growth; inventive; (of animal or plant) able to reproduce. □ **fertility** /-'tɪl-/ *noun*.

**fertilize** /'fɜːtɪlaɪz/ *verb* (also **-ise**) (**-zing** or **-sing**) make fertile; cause (egg, female animal, etc.) to develop new individual. □ **fertilization** *noun*.

**fertilizer** *noun* (also **-iser**) substance added to soil to make it more fertile.

**fervent** /'fɜːv(ə)nt/ *adjective* ardent, intense. □ **fervency** *noun*; **fervently** *adverb*.

**fervid** /'fɜːvɪd/ *adjective* fervent. □ **fervidly** *adverb*.

**fervour** /'fɜːvə/ *noun* (*US* **fervor**) passion, zeal.

**fescue** /'feskjuː/ *noun* pasture and fodder grass.

**fester** /'festə/ *verb* make or become septic; cause continuing bitterness; rot; stagnate.

**festival** /'festɪv(ə)l/ *noun* day or period of celebration; series of cultural events in town etc.

**festive** /'festɪv/ *adjective* of or characteristic of festival; joyous.

**festivity** /fe'stɪvɪtɪ/ *noun* (*plural* **-ies**) gaiety, (in *plural*) celebration; party.

**festoon** /fe'stu:n/ ● *noun* curved hanging chain of flowers, ribbons, etc. ● *verb* (often + *with*) adorn with or form into festoons.

**feta** /'fetə/ *noun* salty white Greek cheese made from ewe's or goat's milk.

**fetal** *US* = FOETAL.

**fetch** *verb* go for and bring back; be sold for; draw forth; deal (blow). □ **fetch up** *colloquial* arrive, come to rest.

**fetching** *adjective* attractive. □ **fetchingly** *adverb*.

**fête** /feɪt/ ● *noun* outdoor fund-raising event. ● *verb* (**-ting**) honour or entertain lavishly.

**fetid** /'fetɪd/ *adjective* (also **foetid**) stinking.

**fetish** /'fetɪʃ/ *noun* abnormal object of sexual desire; object worshipped by primitive peoples; object of obsessive concern. □ **fetishism** *noun*; **fetishist** *noun*; **fetishistic** /-'ʃɪs-/ *adjective*.

**fetlock** /'fetlɒk/ *noun* back of horse's leg where tuft of hair grows above hoof.

**fetter** /'fetə/ ● *noun* shackle for ankles; (in *plural*) captivity; restraint. ● *verb* put into fetters, restrict.

**fettle** /'fet(ə)l/ *noun* condition, trim.

**fetus** *US* = FOETUS.

**feud** /fju:d/ ● *noun* prolonged hostility, esp. between families, tribes, etc. ● *verb* conduct feud.

**feudal** /'fju:d(ə)l/ *adjective* of, like, or according to feudal system; reactionary. □ **feudal system** medieval system in which vassal held land in exchange for allegiance and service to landowner. □ **feudalism** *noun*; **feudalistic** /-'lɪs-/ *adjective*.

**fever** /'fi:və/ ● *noun* abnormally high body temperature; disease characterized by this; nervous agitation. ● *verb* (esp. as **fevered** *adjective*) affect with fever or excitement. □ **fever pitch** state of extreme excitement.

**feverfew** /'fi:vəfju:/ *noun* aromatic plant, used formerly to reduce fever, now to treat migraine.

**feverish** *adjective* having symptoms of fever; excited; restless. □ **feverishly** *adverb*.

**few** ● *adjective* not many. ● *noun* (treated as *plural*) not many; (**a few**) some but not many. □ **a good few** a considerable number (of); **quite a few** *colloquial* a fairly large number (of); **very few** a very small number (of).

**fey** /feɪ/ *adjective* strange, other-worldly; whimsical.

**fez** *noun* (*plural* **fezzes**) man's flat-topped conical red cap, worn by some Muslims.

**ff** *abbreviation Music* fortissimo.

**ff.** *abbreviation* following pages etc.

**fiancé** /fɪ'ɒnseɪ/ *noun* (*feminine* **-cée** same pronunciation) person one is engaged to.

**fiasco** /fɪ'æskəʊ/ *noun* (*plural* **-s**) ludicrous or humiliating failure.

**fiat** /'faɪæt/ *noun* authorization; decree.

**fib** ● *noun* trivial lie. ● *verb* (**-bb-**) tell fib. □ **fibber** *noun*.

**fibre** /'faɪbə/ *noun* (*US* **fiber**) thread or filament forming tissue or textile; piece of threadlike glass; substance formed of fibres; moral character; roughage. □ **fibreboard** board made of compressed wood etc. fibres; **fibreglass** fabric made from woven glass fibres, plastic reinforced with glass fibres; **fibre optics** optics using glass fibres, usually to carry signals. □ **fibrous** *adjective*.

**fibril** /'faɪbrɪl/ *noun* small fibre.

**fibroid** /'faɪbrɔɪd/ ● *adjective* of, like, or containing fibrous tissue or fibres. ● *noun* benign fibrous tumour, esp. in womb.

**fibrosis** /faɪ'brəʊsɪs/ *noun* thickening and scarring of connective tissue.

**fibrositis** /faɪbrə'saɪtɪs/ *noun* rheumatic inflammation of fibrous tissue.

**fibula** /'fɪbjʊlə/ *noun* (*plural* **-lae** /-li:/ or **-s**) bone on outer side of lower leg.

**fiche** /fi:ʃ/ *noun* microfiche.

**fickle** /'fɪk(ə)l/ *adjective* inconstant, changeable. □ **fickleness** *noun*.

**fiction** /'fɪkʃ(ə)n/ *noun* non-factual literature, esp. novels; invented idea, thing, etc.; generally accepted falsehood. □ **fictional** *adjective*.

**fictitious** /fɪk'tɪʃəs/ *adjective* imaginary, unreal; not genuine.

**fiddle** /'fɪd(ə)l/ ● *noun* *colloquial* violin; *colloquial* cheat, fraud; fiddly task. ● *verb* (**-ling**) (often + *with, at*) play restlessly;

(often + *about*) move aimlessly; (usually + *with*) tamper, tinker; *slang* falsify, swindle, get by cheating; play fiddle. □ **fiddler** *noun*.

**fiddling** *adjective* petty, trivial; *colloquial* fiddly.

**fiddly** *adjective* (**-ier, -iest**) *colloquial* awkward to do or use.

**fidelity** /fɪˈdelɪtɪ/ *noun* faithfulness, loyalty; accuracy; precision in sound reproduction.

**fidget** /ˈfɪdʒɪt/ ● *verb* (**-t-**) move restlessly; be or make uneasy. ● *noun* person who fidgets; (**the fidgets**) restless state or mood. □ **fidgety** *adjective*.

**fiduciary** /fɪˈdjuːʃərɪ/ ● *adjective* of a trust, trustee, etc.; held or given in trust; (of currency) dependent on public confidence. ● *noun* (*plural* **-ies**) trustee.

**fief** /fiːf/ *noun* land held under feudal system.

**field** /fiːld/ ● *noun* area of esp. cultivated enclosed land; area rich in some natural product; competitors; expanse of sea, snow, etc.; battlefield; area of activity or study; *Computing* part of record, representing item of data. ● *verb Cricket etc.* act as fielder(s), stop and return (ball); select (player, candidate, etc.); deal with (questions etc.). □ **field-day** exciting or successful time, military exercise or review; **field events** athletic events other than races; **fieldglasses** outdoor binoculars; **Field Marshal** army officer of highest rank; **fieldmouse** small long-tailed rodent; **fieldsman** = FIELDER; **field sports** outdoor sports, esp. hunting, shooting, and fishing; **fieldwork** practical surveying, science, sociology, etc. conducted in natural environment; **fieldworker** person doing fieldwork.

**fielder** *noun Cricket etc.* member (other than bowler) of fielding side.

**fieldfare** *noun* grey thrush.

**fiend** /fiːnd/ *noun* evil spirit; wicked or cruel person; mischievous or annoying person; *slang* devotee; difficult or unpleasant thing. □ **fiendish** *adjective*; **fiendishly** *adverb*.

**fierce** *adjective* (**-r, -st**) violently aggressive or frightening; eager; intense. □ **fiercely** *adverb*; **fierceness** *noun*.

**fiery** /ˈfaɪərɪ/ *adjective* (**-ier, -iest**) consisting of or flaming with fire; bright red; burning hot; spirited.

**fiesta** /fɪˈestə/ *noun* festival, holiday.

**FIFA** /ˈfiːfə/ *abbreviation* International Football Federation (*Fédération Internationale de Football Association*).

**fife** /faɪf/ *noun* small shrill flute.

**fifteen** /fɪfˈtiːn/ *adjective & noun* one more than fourteen; *Rugby* team of fifteen players. □ **fifteenth** *adjective & noun*.

**fifth** ● *adjective & noun* next after fourth; any of 5 equal parts of thing. □ **fifth column** group working for enemy within country at war.

**fifty** /ˈfɪftɪ/ *adjective & noun* (*plural* **-ies**) five times ten. □ **fifty-fifty** half and half, equal(ly). □ **fiftieth** *adjective & noun*.

**fig** *noun* soft fruit with many seeds; tree bearing it. □ **fig leaf** device concealing genitals.

**fig.** *abbreviation* figure.

**fight** /faɪt/ ● *verb* (*past & past participle* **fought** /fɔːt/) (often + *against, with*) contend in war, combat, etc.; engage in (battle etc.); (+ *for*) strive to secure or on behalf of; contest (election); strive to overcome; (as **fighting** *adjective*) able and eager or trained to fight. ● *noun* combat; boxing match; battle; struggle; power or inclination to fight. □ **fight back** counter-attack, suppress (tears etc.); **fighting chance** chance of success if effort is made; **fighting fit** extremely fit; **fight off** repel with effort; **fight shy of** avoid; **put up a fight** offer resistance.

**fighter** *noun* person who fights; aircraft designed for attacking other aircraft.

**figment** /ˈfɪgmənt/ *noun* imaginary thing.

**figurative** /ˈfɪgərətɪv/ *adjective* metaphorical; (of art) not abstract, representational. □ **figuratively** *adverb*.

**figure** /ˈfɪgə/ ● *noun* external form, bodily shape; person of specified kind; representation of human form; image; numerical symbol or number, esp. 0–9; value, amount; (in *plural*) arithmetical calculations; diagram, illustration; dance etc. movement or sequence; (in full **figure of speech**) metaphor, hyperbole, etc. ● *verb* (**-ring**) appear, be mentioned; (usually as **figured** *adjective*) embellish with pattern; calculate; *esp. US colloquial* understand, consider, make sense. □ **figurehead** nominal leader, carved image etc. over ship's prow; **figure on** *esp. US colloquial* count on, expect; **figure out** work out by arithmetic or logic; **figure-skating** skating in prescribed patterns.

**figurine** /ˈfɪɡəˈriːn/ *noun* statuette.

**filament** /ˈfɪləmənt/ *noun* threadlike strand or fibre; conducting wire or thread in electric bulb.

**filbert** /ˈfɪlbət/ *noun* (nut of) cultivated hazel.

**filch** *verb* steal, pilfer.

**file**[1] ● *noun* folder, box, etc. for holding loose papers; paper kept in this; collection of related computer data; row of people or things one behind another. ● *verb* (-**ling**) place in file or among records; submit (petition for divorce etc.); walk in line. □ **filing cabinet** cabinet with drawers for storing files.

**file**[2] ● *noun* tool with rough surface for smoothing wood, fingernails, etc. ● *verb* (-**ling**) smooth or shape with file.

**filial** /ˈfɪlɪəl/ *adjective* of or due from son or daughter.

**filibuster** /ˈfɪlɪbʌstə/ ● *noun* obstruction of progress in legislative assembly; *esp. US* person who engages in this. ● *verb* act as filibuster.

**filigree** /ˈfɪlɪɡriː/ *noun* fine ornamental work in gold etc. wire; similar delicate work.

**filings** *plural noun* particles rubbed off by file.

**Filipino** /fɪlɪˈpiːnəʊ/ ● *noun* (*plural* -**s**) native or national of Philippines. ● *adjective* of Philippines or Filipinos.

**fill** ● *verb* (often + *with*) make or become full; occupy completely; spread over or through; block up (hole, tooth, etc.); appoint to or hold (office etc.); (as **filling** *adjective*) (of food) satisfying. ● *noun* enough to satisfy or fill. □ **fill in** complete (form etc.), fill completely, (often + *for*) act as substitute, *colloquial* inform more fully; **fill out** enlarge or become enlarged, esp. to proper size, fill in (form etc.); **fill up** fill completely, fill petrol tank (of).

**filler** *noun* material used to fill cavity or increase bulk.

**fillet** /ˈfɪlɪt/ ● *noun* boneless piece of fish or meat; (in full **fillet steak**) undercut of sirloin; ribbon etc. binding hair; narrow flat band between mouldings. ● *verb* (-**t**-) remove bones from (fish etc.) or divide into fillets; bind or provide with fillet(s).

**filling** *noun* material used to fill tooth, sandwich, pie, etc. □ **filling-station** garage selling petrol etc.

**fillip** /ˈfɪlɪp/ *noun* stimulus, incentive.

**filly** /ˈfɪlɪ/ *noun* (*plural* -**ies**) young female horse.

**film** ● *noun* thin coating or layer; strip or sheet of plastic etc. coated with light-sensitive emulsion for exposure in camera; story etc. on film; (in *plural*) cinema industry; slight veil, haze, etc. ● *verb* make photographic film of; (often + *over*) cover or become covered (as) with film. □ **film star** well-known film actor or actress. □ **filmy** *adjective* (-**ier**, -**iest**).

**filmsetting** *noun* typesetting by projecting characters on to photographic film. □ **filmset** *verb*; **filmsetter** *noun*.

**Filofax** /ˈfaɪləʊfæks/ *noun* proprietary term personal organizer.

**filo pastry** /ˈfiːləʊ/ *noun* pastry in very thin sheets.

**filter** /ˈfɪltə/ ● *noun* porous esp. paper device for removing impurities from liquid or gas or making coffee; screen for absorbing or modifying light; device for suppressing unwanted electrical or sound waves; arrangement for filtering traffic. ● *verb* pass through filter; (usually as **filtered** *adjective*) make (coffee) by dripping hot water through ground beans; (+ *through, into*, etc.) make way gradually through, into, etc.; (of traffic) be allowed to turn left or right at junction when other traffic is held up. □ **filter tip** (cigarette with) filter for removing some impurities.

**filth** *noun* disgusting dirt; obscenity.

**filthy** ● *adjective* (-**ier**, -**iest**) disgustingly dirty; obscene; (of weather) very unpleasant. ● *adverb colloquial* extremely. □ **filthy lucre** dishonourable gain; money.

**filtrate** /ˈfɪltreɪt/ ● *verb* (-**ting**) filter. ● *noun* filtered liquid. □ **filtration** *noun*.

**fin** noun organ, esp. of fish, for propelling and steering; similar projection for stabilizing aircraft etc.

**finagle** /fɪˈneɪg(ə)l/ verb (**-ling**) colloquial act or obtain dishonestly.

**final** /ˈfaɪn(ə)l/ adjective at the end, coming last; conclusive, decisive. ● noun last or deciding heat or game; last edition of day's newspaper; (usually in plural) exams at end of degree course. □ **finality** /-ˈnæl-/ noun; **finally** adverb.

**finale** /fɪˈnɑːlɪ/ noun last movement or section of drama, piece of music, etc.

**finalist** noun competitor in final.

**finalize** verb (also **-ise**) (**-zing** or **-sing**) put in final form; complete. □ **finalization** noun.

**finance** /ˈfaɪnæns/ ● noun management of money; monetary support for enterprise; (in plural) money resources. ● verb (**-cing**) provide capital for. □ **financial** /-ˈnæn-/ adjective; **financially** /-ˈnæn-/ adverb.

**financier** /faɪˈnænsɪə/ noun capitalist; entrepreneur.

**finch** noun small seed-eating bird.

**find** /faɪnd/ ● verb (past & past participle **found**) discover, get by chance or after search; become aware of; obtain, provide; summon up; perceive, experience; consider to be; (often in passive) discover to be present; reach; Law judge and declare. ● noun discovery of treasure etc.; valued thing or person newly discovered. □ **all found** (of wages) with board and lodging provided free; **find out** (often + about) discover, detect. □ **finder** noun.

**finding** noun (often in plural) conclusion reached by inquiry.

**fine¹** ● adjective of high quality; excellent; good, satisfactory; pure, refined; imposing; bright and clear; small or thin, in small particles; smart, showy; flattering. ● adverb finely; very well. □ **fine arts** poetry, music, painting, sculpture, painting, etc.; **fine-spun** delicate, too subtle; **fine-tune** make small adjustments to. □ **finely** adverb.

**fine²** ● noun money paid as penalty. ● verb (**-ning**) punish by fine.

**finery** /ˈfaɪnərɪ/ noun showy dress or decoration.

**finesse** /fɪˈnes/ ● noun refinement; subtlety; artfulness; Cards attempt to win trick with card that is not the highest held. ● verb (**-ssing**) use or manage by finesse; Cards make finesse.

**finger** /ˈfɪŋgə/ ● noun any of terminal projections of hand (usually excluding thumb); part of glove for finger; finger-like object. ● verb touch, turn about, or play with fingers. □ **finger-bowl** bowl for rinsing fingers during meal; **finger-dry** dry and style hair by running fingers through it; **fingernail** nail on each finger; **fingerprint** impression made on surface by fingers, used in detecting crime; **finger-stall** protective cover for injured finger; **fingertip** tip of finger.

**fingering** noun manner of using fingers in music; indication of this in score.

**finial** /ˈfɪnɪəl/ noun ornamental top to gable, canopy, etc.

**finicky** /ˈfɪnɪkɪ/ adjective (also **finical**, **finicking**) over-particular; fastidious; detailed; fiddly.

**finis** /ˈfɪnɪs/ noun end, esp. of book.

**finish** /ˈfɪnɪʃ/ ● verb (often + off) bring or come to end or end of; complete; (often + off, up) complete consuming; treat surface of. ● noun last stage, completion; end of race etc.; method etc. of surface treatment.

**finite** /ˈfaɪnaɪt/ adjective limited, not infinite; (of verb) having specific number and person.

**Finn** noun native or national of Finland.

**finnan** /ˈfɪnən/ noun (in full **finnan haddock**) smoke-cured haddock.

**Finnish** ● adjective of Finland. ● noun language of Finland.

**fiord** /fjɔːd/ noun (also **fjord**) narrow inlet of sea as in Norway.

**fir** noun evergreen conifer with needles growing singly on the stems; its wood. □ **fir-cone** its fruit.

**fire** ● noun state of combustion of substance with oxygen, giving out light and heat; flame, glow; destructive burning; burning fuel in grate etc.; electric or gas heater; firing of guns; fervour, spirit; burning heat. ● verb (**-ring**) shoot (gun etc. or missile from it); shoot gun or missile; produce (salute etc.) by shooting; (of gun) be discharged; deliver or utter rapidly; detonate; dismiss (employee); set fire to;

supply with fuel; stimulate, enthuse; undergo ignition; bake or dry (pottery, bricks, etc.). □ **fire-alarm** bell etc. warning of fire; **firearm** gun, esp. pistol or rifle; **fire-ball** large meteor, ball of flame; **fire-bomb** incendiary bomb; **firebrand** piece of burning wood, trouble-maker; **fire-break** obstacle preventing spread of fire in forest etc.; **fire-brick** fireproof brick in grate; **fire brigade** group of firefighters; **firedog** support for logs in hearth; **fire door** fire-resistant door; **fire-drill** rehearsal of procedure in case of fire; **fire-engine** vehicle carrying hoses, firefighters, etc.; **fire-escape** emergency staircase etc. for use in fire; **fire extinguisher** apparatus discharging water, foam, etc. to extinguish fire; **firefighter** person who extinguishes fires; **firefly** insect emitting phosphorescent light, e.g. glow-worm; **fire-irons** tongs, poker, and shovel for domestic fire; **fireman** male firefighter, person who tends steam engine or steamship furnace; **fire-place** place in wall for domestic fire; **fire-power** destructive capacity of guns etc.; **fire-practice** fire-drill; **fire-raiser** arsonist; **fireside** area round fireplace; **fire-screen** ornamental screen for fireplace, screen against direct heat of fire; **fire station** headquarters of local fire brigade; **fire-trap** building without fire-escapes etc.; **firework** device producing flashes, bangs, etc. from burning chemicals, (in *plural*) outburst of anger etc.; **on fire** burning, excited; **under fire** being shot at or criticized.

**firing** *noun* discharge of guns. □ **firing line** front line in battle, centre of criticism etc.; **firing squad** soldiers ordered to shoot condemned person.

**firm**[1] ●*adjective* solid; fixed, steady; resolute; steadfast; (of offer etc.) definite. ●*verb* (often + *up*) make or become firm or secure. □ **firmly** *adverb*; **firmness** *noun*.

**firm**[2] *noun* business concern, its members.

**firmament** /ˈfɜːməmənt/ *noun* sky regarded as vault.

**first** ●*adjective* foremost in time, order, or importance. ●*noun* (**the first**) first person or thing; beginning; first occurrence of something notable; first-class

degree; first gear; first place in race. ●*adverb* before all or something else; for the first time. □ **at first hand** directly from original source; **first aid** emergency medical treatment; **first class** *noun* best category or accommodation, mail given priority, highest division in exam; **first-class** *adjective & adverb* of or by first class, excellent(ly); **first floor** (*US* **second floor**) floor above ground floor; **first-footing** first crossing of threshold in New Year; **firsthand** direct, original; **first mate** (on merchant ship) second in command; **first name** personal or Christian name; **first night** first public performance of play etc.; **first-rate** excellent; **first thing** before anything else, very early. □ **firstly** *adverb*.

**firth** /fɜːθ/ *noun* inlet, estuary.

**fiscal** /ˈfɪsk(ə)l/ ●*adjective* of public revenue. ●*noun* Scottish procurator fiscal. □ **fiscal year** financial year.

**fish**[1] ●*noun* (*plural* same or **-es**) vertebrate cold-blooded animal living in water; its flesh as food; person of specified kind. ●*verb* try to catch fish (in); (+ *for*) search for; seek indirectly; (+ *up*, *out*) retrieve with effort. □ **fish cake** fried cake of fish and mashed potato; **fish-eye lens** wide-angled lens; **fish farm** place where fish are bred for food; **fish finger** small oblong piece of fish in breadcrumbs; **fish-hook** barbed hook for catching fish; **fish-kettle** oval pan for boiling fish; **fish-knife** knife for eating or serving fish; **fish-meal** ground dried fish as fertilizer etc.; **fishmonger** dealer in fish; **fishnet** open-meshed fabric; **fish-slice** slotted cooking utensil; **fishwife** coarse or noisy woman, woman selling fish.

**fish**[2] *noun* piece of wood or iron for strengthening mast etc. □ **fish-plate** flat plate of iron etc. holding rails together.

**fisherman** /ˈfɪʃəmən/ *noun* man who catches fish as occupation or sport.

**fishery** *noun* (*plural* **-ies**) place where fish are caught or reared; industry of fishing or breeding fish.

**fishing** *noun* occupation or sport of trying to catch fish. □ **fishing-rod** tapering rod for fishing.

**fishy** *adjective* (**-ier**, **-iest**) of or like fish; *slang* dubious, suspect.

**fissile** /ˈfɪsaɪl/ adjective capable of undergoing nuclear fission; tending to split.

**fission** /ˈfɪʃ(ə)n/ ● noun splitting of atomic nucleus; division of cell as mode of reproduction. ● verb (cause to) undergo fission.

**fissure** /ˈfɪʃə/ ● noun narrow crack or split. ● verb (-ring) split.

**fist** noun clenched hand. □ **fisticuffs** fighting with the fists. □ **fistful** noun (plural -s).

**fistula** /ˈfɪstjʊlə/ noun (plural -s or fistulae /-liː/) abnormal or artificial passage in body. □ **fistular** adjective; **fistulous** adjective.

**fit**[1] ● adjective (-tt-) well suited; qualified, competent; in good health or condition; (+ for) good enough, right; ready. ● verb (-tt-) be of right size and shape; find room for; (often + in, into) be correctly positioned; (+ on, together) fix in place; (+ with) supply; befit. ● noun way thing fits. □ **fit in** (often + with) be compatible, accommodate, make room or time for; **fit out, up** equip. □ **fitness** noun.

**fit**[2] noun sudden esp. epileptic seizure; sudden brief bout or burst.

**fitful** adjective spasmodic, intermittent. □ **fitfully** adverb.

**fitment** noun (usually in plural) fixed item of furniture.

**fitted** adjective made to fit closely; with built-in fittings; built-in.

**fitter** noun mechanic who fits together and adjusts machinery etc.; supervisor of cutting, fitting, etc. of garments.

**fitting** ● noun action of fitting on a garment; (usually in plural) fixture, fitment. ● adjective proper, befitting. □ **fittingly** adverb.

**five** adjective & noun one more than four. □ **five o'clock shadow** beard growth visible in latter part of day; **five-star** of highest class; **fivestones** jacks played with five pieces of metal etc. and usually no ball.

**fiver** noun colloquial five-pound note.

**fives** noun game in which ball is struck with gloved hand or bat against walls of court.

**fix** ● verb make firm, stable, or permanent; fasten, secure; settle, specify; mend, repair; (+ on, upon) direct (eyes etc.) steadily on; attract and hold (attention etc.); identify, locate; US colloquial prepare (food, drink); colloquial kill, deal with (person); arrange result fraudulently. ● noun dilemma, predicament; position determined by bearings etc.; slang dose of addictive drug; colloquial fraudulently arranged result. □ **fix up** arrange, organize; (often + with) provide (person). □ **fixer** noun.

**fixate** /fɪkˈseɪt/ verb (-ting) Psychology (usually in passive, often + on, upon) cause to become abnormally attached to person or thing.

**fixation** /fɪkˈseɪʃ(ə)n/ noun fixating, being fixated; obsession.

**fixative** /ˈfɪksətɪv/ ● adjective tending to fix (colours etc.). ● noun fixative substance.

**fixedly** /ˈfɪksɪdlɪ/ adverb intently.

**fixity** noun fixed state; stability, permanence.

**fixture** /ˈfɪkstʃə/ noun thing fixed in position; (date fixed for) sporting event; (in plural) articles belonging to land or house.

**fizz** ● verb make hissing or spluttering sound; effervesce. ● noun fizzing sound; effervescence; colloquial effervescent drink. □ **fizzy** adjective (-ier, -iest).

**fizzle** /ˈfɪz(ə)l/ ● verb (-ling) hiss or splutter feebly. ● noun fizzling sound. □ **fizzle out** end feebly.

**fjord** = FIORD.

**fl.** abbreviation fluid; floruit.

**flab** noun colloquial fat, flabbiness.

**flabbergast** /ˈflæbəɡɑːst/ verb (esp. as **flabbergasted** adjective) colloquial astonish; dumbfound.

**flabby** /ˈflæbɪ/ adjective (-ier, -iest) (of flesh) limp, not firm; feeble. □ **flabbiness** noun.

**flaccid** /ˈflæksɪd/ adjective flabby. □ **flaccidity** /-ˈsɪd-/ noun.

**flag**[1] ● noun piece of cloth attached by one edge to pole or rope as country's emblem, standard, or signal. ● verb (-gg-) grow tired; lag; droop; mark out with flags. □ **flag-day** day when charity collects money and gives stickers to contributors; **flag down** signal to stop; **flag-officer** admiral or vice or rear admiral; **flag-pole** flag-staff; **flagship** ship with admiral on board, leading example of thing; **flagstaff** pole on which flag is hung; **flag-waving** noun populist agitation, chauvinism, adjective chauvinistic.

**flag²** • noun (also **flagstone**) flat paving stone. • verb (**-gg-**) pave with flags.

**flag³** noun plant with bladed leaf, esp. iris.

**flagellant** /ˈflædʒələnt/ • noun person who flagellates himself, herself, or others. • adjective of flagellation.

**flagellate** /ˈflædʒəleɪt/ verb (**-ting**) whip or flog, esp. as religious discipline or sexual stimulus. □ **flagellation** noun.

**flageolet** /flædʒəˈlet/ noun small flute blown at end.

**flagon** /ˈflæɡən/ noun quart bottle or other vessel for wine etc.

**flagrant** /ˈfleɪɡrənt/ adjective blatant; scandalous. □ **flagrancy** noun; **flagrantly** adverb.

**flagrante** see IN FLAGRANTE DELICTO.

**flail** • verb (often + about) wave or swing wildly; beat (as) with flail. • noun staff with heavy stick swinging from it, used for threshing.

**flair** noun natural talent; style, finesse.

**flak** noun anti-aircraft fire; criticism; abuse.

**flake** • noun thin light piece of snow etc.; thin broad piece peeled or split off. • verb (**-king**) (often + away, off) take or come away in flakes; fall in or sprinkle with flakes. □ **flake out** fall asleep or drop from exhaustion, faint.

**flaky** adjective (**-ier**, **-iest**) of, like, or in flakes. □ **flaky pastry** lighter version of puff pastry.

**flambé** /ˈflɒmbeɪ/ adjective (of food) covered with alcohol and set alight briefly.

**flamboyant** /flæmˈbɔɪənt/ adjective ostentatious, showy; florid. □ **flamboyance** noun; **flamboyantly** adverb.

**flame** • noun ignited gas; portion of this; bright light; brilliant orange colour; passion, esp. love; colloquial sweetheart. • verb (**-ming**) (often + out, up) burn; blaze; (of passion) break out; become angry; shine or glow like flame.

**flamenco** /fləˈmeŋkəʊ/ noun (plural **-s**) Spanish Gypsy guitar music with singing and dancing.

**flaming** adjective emitting flames; very hot; passionate; brightly coloured; colloquial expressing annoyance.

**flamingo** /fləˈmɪŋɡəʊ/ noun (plural **-s** or **-es**) tall long-necked wading bird with usually pink plumage.

**flammable** /ˈflæməb(ə)l/ adjective inflammable.

■ Usage Flammable is often used because inflammable could be taken to mean 'not flammable'. The negative of flammable is non-flammable.

**flan** noun pastry case with savoury or sweet filling; sponge base with sweet topping.

**flange** /flændʒ/ noun projecting flat rim, for strengthening etc.

**flank** • noun side of body between ribs and hip; side of mountain, army, etc. • verb (often as **flanked** adjective) be at or move along side of.

**flannel** /ˈflæn(ə)l/ • noun woven woollen usually napless fabric; (in plural) flannel trousers; face-cloth; slang nonsense, flattery. • verb (**-ll-**; US **-l-**) slang flatter; wash with flannel.

**flannelette** /flænəˈlet/ noun napped cotton fabric like flannel.

**flap** • verb (**-pp-**) move or be moved loosely up and down; beat; flutter; colloquial be agitated or panicky; colloquial (of ears) listen intently. • noun piece of cloth, wood, etc. attached by one side, esp. to cover gap; flapping; colloquial agitation; aileron. □ **flapjack** sweet oatcake, esp. US small pancake.

**flapper** noun person apt to panic; slang (in 1920s) young unconventional woman.

**flare** • verb (**-ring**) blaze with bright unsteady flame; (usually as **flared** adjective) widen gradually; burst out, esp. angrily. • noun bright unsteady flame, outburst of this; flame or bright light as signal etc.; gradual widening; (in plural) wide-bottomed trousers. □ **flare-path** line of lights on runway to guide aircraft; **flare up** verb burst into blaze, anger, activity, etc.; **flare-up** noun outburst.

**flash** • verb (cause) to emit brief or sudden light; gleam; send or reflect like sudden flame; burst suddenly into view etc.; move swiftly; send (news etc.) by radio etc.; signal (to) with vehicle lights; show ostentatiously; *slang* indecently expose oneself. ● *noun* sudden bright light or flame; an instant; sudden brief feeling or display; *Photography* flashlight. ● *adjective colloquial* gaudy, showy; vulgar. □ **flashback** scene set in earlier time than main action; **flash bulb** *Photography* bulb for flashlight; **flash-gun** device operating camera flashlight; **flash in the pan** promising start followed by failure; **flash-lamp** portable flashing electric lamp; **flashlight** *Photography* light giving intense flash, *US* electric torch; **flashpoint** temperature at which vapour from oil etc. will ignite in air, point at which anger is expressed.

**flasher** *noun slang* man who indecently exposes himself; automatic device for switching lights rapidly on and off.

**flashing** *noun* (usually metal) strip to prevent water penetration at roof joint etc.

**flashy** *adjective* (**-ier, -iest**) showy; cheaply attractive. □ **flashily** *adverb*.

**flask** /flɑːsk/ *noun* narrow-necked bulbous bottle; hip-flask; vacuum flask.

**flat**[1] ● *adjective* (**-tt-**) horizontally level; smooth, even; level and shallow; downright; dull; dejected; having lost its effervescence; (of battery) having exhausted its charge; (of tyre etc.) deflated; *Music* below correct or normal pitch, having flats in key signature. ● *adverb* spread out; completely, exactly; flatly. ● *noun* flat part; level esp. marshy ground; *Music* note lowered by semitone, sign (♭) indicating this; flat theatre scenery on frame; punctured tyre; (**the flat**) flat racing, its season. □ **flatfish** fish with flattened body, e.g. sole, plaice; **flat foot** foot with flattened arch; **flat-footed** having flat feet, *colloquial* uninspired; **flat out** at top speed, using all one's strength etc.; **flat race** horse race over level ground without jumps; **flat rate** unvarying rate or charge; **flat spin** aircraft's nearly horizontal spin, *colloquial* state of panic; **flatworm** worm with flattened body, e.g. fluke. □ **flatly** *adverb*; **flatness** *noun*; **flattish** *adjective*.

**flat**[2] *noun* set of rooms, usually on one floor, as residence. □ **flatmate** person sharing flat. □ **flatlet** *noun*.

**flatten** *verb* make or become flat; *colloquial* humiliate; knock down.

**flatter** /ˈflætə/ *verb* compliment unduly; enhance appearance of; (usually **flatter oneself**; usually + *that*) congratulate or delude (oneself etc.). □ **flatterer** *noun*; **flattering** *adjective*; **flatteringly** *adverb*; **flattery** *noun*.

**flatulent** /ˈflætjʊlənt/ *adjective* causing, caused by, or troubled with, intestinal wind; inflated, pretentious. □ **flatulence** *noun*.

**flaunt** /flɔːnt/ *verb* display proudly; show off, parade.

■ Usage *Flaunt* is often confused with *flout*, which means 'to disobey contemptuously'.

**flautist** /ˈflɔːtɪst/ *noun* flute-player.

**flavour** /ˈfleɪvə/ (*US* **flavor**) ● *noun* mixed sensation of smell and taste; distinctive taste, characteristic quality. ● *verb* give flavour to, season. □ **flavour of the month** temporary trend or fashion. □ **flavourless** *adjective*; **flavoursome** *adjective*.

**flavouring** *noun* (*US* **flavoring**) substance used to flavour food or drink.

**flaw** ● *noun* imperfection; blemish; crack; invalidating defect. ● *verb* damage; spoil; (as **flawed** *adjective*) morally etc. defective. □ **flawless** *adjective*.

**flax** *noun* blue-flowered plant grown for its oily seeds (linseed) and for making into linen.

**flaxen** *adjective* of flax; (of hair) pale yellow.

**flay** *verb* strip skin or hide off; criticize severely; peel off.

**flea** *noun* small wingless jumping parasitic insect. □ **flea market** street market selling second-hand goods etc.

**fleck** ● *noun* small patch of colour or light; speck. ● *verb* mark with flecks.

**flection** *US* = FLEXION.

**fled** past & past participle of FLEE.

**fledgling** /ˈfledʒlɪŋ/ (also **fledgeling**) ● *noun* young bird. ● *adjective* new, inexperienced.

**flee** *verb* (**flees**; past & past participle **fled**) run away (from); leave hurriedly.

**fleece** • *noun* woolly coat of sheep etc.; this shorn from sheep; fleecy lining etc. • *verb* (**-cing**) (often + *of*) strip of money etc., swindle; shear; (as **fleeced** *adjective*) cover as with fleece. □ **fleecy** *adjective* (**-ier, -iest**).

**fleet** • *noun* warships under one commander-in-chief; (**the fleet**) navy; vehicles in one company etc. • *adjective* swift, nimble.

**fleeting** *adjective* transitory; brief. □ **fleetingly** *adverb*.

**Fleming** /'flemɪŋ/ *noun* native of medieval Flanders; member of Flemish-speaking people of N. and W. Belgium.

**Flemish** /'flemɪʃ/ • *adjective* of Flanders. • *noun* language of the Flemings.

**flesh** *noun* soft substance between skin and bones; plumpness, fat; body, esp. as sinful; pulpy substance of fruit etc.; (also **flesh-colour**) yellowish pink colour. □ **flesh and blood** human body, human nature, esp. as fallible, humankind, near relations; **flesh out** make or become substantial; **fleshpots** luxurious living; **flesh-wound** superficial wound; **in the flesh** in person. □ **fleshy** *adjective* (**-ier, -iest**).

**fleshly** /'fleʃlɪ/ *adjective* worldly; carnal.

**fleur-de-lis** /flɜːdəˈliː/ *noun* (also **fleur-de-lys**) (*plural* **fleurs-** same pronunciation) iris flower; *Heraldry* lily of 3 petals; former royal arms of France.

**flew** *past* of FLY[1].

**flews** *plural noun* hanging lips of bloodhound etc.

**flex**[1] *verb* bend (joint, limb); move (muscle) to bend joint.

**flex**[2] *noun* flexible insulated cable.

**flexible** /'fleksɪb(ə)l/ *adjective* able to bend without breaking; pliable; adaptable. □ **flexibility** *noun*; **flexibly** *adverb*.

**flexion** /'flekʃ(ə)n/ *noun* (*US* **flection**) bending; bent part.

**flexitime** /'fleksɪtaɪm/ *noun* system of flexible working hours.

**flibbertigibbet** /ˈflɪbətɪˈdʒɪbɪt/ *noun* gossiping, frivolous, or restless person.

**flick** • *noun* light sharp blow; sudden release of bent finger etc. to propel thing; jerk; *colloquial* cinema film, (**the flicks**) the cinema. • *verb* (often + *away, off*) strike or move with flick.

□ **flick-knife** knife with blade that springs out; **flick through** glance at or through by turning over (pages etc.) rapidly.

**flicker** /'flɪkə/ • *verb* shine or burn unsteadily; flutter; waver. • *noun* flickering light or motion; brief feeling (of hope etc.); slightest reaction or degree. □ **flicker out** die away.

**flier** = FLYER.

**flight**[1] /flaɪt/ *noun* act or manner of flying; movement, passage, or journey through air or space; timetabled airline journey; flock of birds etc.; (usually + *of*) series of stairs etc.; imaginative excursion; volley; tail of dart. □ **flight bag** small zipped shoulder bag for air travel; **flight-deck** cockpit of large aircraft, deck of aircraft carrier; **flight lieutenant** RAF officer next below squadron leader; **flight path** planned course of aircraft etc.; **flight recorder** device in aircraft recording technical details of flight; **flight sergeant** RAF rank next above sergeant.

**flight**[2] /flaɪt/ *noun* fleeing; hasty retreat.

**flightless** *adjective* (of bird etc.) unable to fly.

**flighty** *adjective* (**-ier, -iest**) frivolous, fickle.

**flimsy** /'flɪmzɪ/ *adjective* (**-ier, -iest**) insubstantial, rickety; unconvincing; (of clothing) thin. □ **flimsily** *adverb*.

**flinch** *verb* draw back in fear etc.; shrink; wince.

**fling** • *verb* (*past & past participle* **flung**) throw, hurl; rush, esp. angrily; discard rashly. • *noun* flinging; throw; bout of wild behaviour; whirling Scottish dance.

**flint** *noun* hard grey stone; piece of this, esp. as tool or weapon; piece of hard alloy used to produce spark. □ **flintlock** old type of gun fired by spark from flint. □ **flinty** *adjective* (**-ier, -iest**).

**flip** • *verb* (**-pp-**) toss (coin etc.) so that it spins in air; turn or flick (small object) over; *slang* flip one's lid. • *noun* act of flipping. • *adjective* glib; flippant. □ **flip chart** large pad of paper on stand; **flip-flop** sandal with thong between toes; **flip one's lid** *slang* lose self-control, go mad; **flip side** reverse side of gramophone record etc.; **flip through** flick through.

**flippant** /ˈflɪpənt/ *adjective* frivolous; disrespectful. □ **flippancy** *noun*; **flippantly** *adverb*.

**flipper** *noun* limb of turtle, penguin, etc., used in swimming; rubber attachment to foot for underwater swimming.

**flirt** ● *verb* try to attract sexually but without serious intent; (usually + *with*) superficially engage in, trifle. ● *noun* person who flirts. □ **flirtation** *noun*; **flirtatious** *adjective*; **flirtatiously** *adverb*; **flirtatiousness** *noun*.

**flit** ● *verb* (**-tt-**) pass lightly or rapidly; make short flights; disappear secretly, esp. to escape creditors. ● *noun* act of flitting.

**flitch** *noun* side of bacon.

**flitter** *verb* flit about.

**float** ● *verb* (cause to) rest or drift on surface of liquid; move or be suspended freely in liquid or gas; launch (company, scheme); offer (stocks, shares, etc.) on stock market; (cause or allow to) have fluctuating exchange rate; circulate or cause (rumour, idea) to circulate. ● *noun* device or structure that floats; electrically powered vehicle or cart; decorated platform or tableau on lorry in procession etc.; supply of loose change, petty cash.

**floating** *adjective* not settled; variable; not committed. □ **floating rib** lower rib not attached to breastbone.

**floaty** *adjective* (**-ier, -iest**) (of fabric) light and airy.

**flocculent** /ˈflɒkjʊlənt/ *adjective* like tufts of wool.

**flock**[1] ● *noun* animals, esp. birds or sheep, as group or unit; large crowd of people; people in care of priest, teacher, etc. ● *verb* (often + *to, in, out, together*) congregate; mass; troop.

**flock**[2] *noun* shredded wool, cotton, etc. used as stuffing; powdered wool used to make pattern on wallpaper.

**floe** *noun* sheet of floating ice.

**flog** *verb* (**-gg-**) beat with whip, stick, etc.; (often + *off*) *slang* sell.

**flood** /flʌd/ ● *noun* overflowing or influx of water, esp. over land; outburst, outpouring; inflow of tide; (**the Flood**) the

flood described in Genesis. ● *verb* overflow; cover or be covered with flood; irrigate; deluge; come in great quantities; overfill (carburettor) with petrol. □ **floodgate** gate for admitting or excluding water, (usually in *plural*) last restraint against tear, anger, etc.; **floodlight** (illuminate with) large powerful light; **floodlit** lit thus.

**floor** /flɔː/ ● *noun* lower surface of room; bottom of sea, cave, etc.; storey; part of legislative chamber where members sit and speak; right to speak in debate; minimum of prices, wages, etc. ● *verb* provide with floor; knock down; baffle; overcome. □ **floor manager** stage manager of television production; **floor plan** diagram of rooms etc. on one storey; **floor show** cabaret.

**flop** ● *verb* (**-pp-**) sway about heavily or loosely; (often + *down, on, into*) move, fall, sit, etc. awkwardly or suddenly; *slang* collapse, fail; make dull soft thud or splash. ● *noun* flopping motion or sound; *slang* failure. ● *adverb* with a flop.

**floppy** ● *adjective* (**-ier, -iest**) tending to flop; flaccid. ● *noun* (*plural* **-ies**) (in full **floppy disk**) flexible disc for storage of computer data.

**flora** /ˈflɔːrə/ *noun* (*plural* **-s** or **-rae** /-riː/) plant life of region or period.

**floral** *adjective* of or decorated with flowers.

**floret** /ˈflɒrɪt/ *noun* each of small flowers of composite flower head; each stem of head of cauliflower, broccoli, etc.

**florid** /ˈflɒrɪd/ *adjective* ruddy; ornate; showy.

**florin** /ˈflɒrɪn/ *noun historical* gold or silver coin, esp. British two-shilling coin.

**florist** /ˈflɒrɪst/ *noun* person who deals in or grows flowers.

**floruit** /ˈflɒrʊɪt/ *verb* (of painter, writer, etc.) lived and worked.

**floss** ● *noun* rough silk of silkworm's cocoon; dental floss. ● *verb* clean (teeth) with dental floss. □ **flossy** *adjective* (**-ier, -iest**).

**flotation** /fləʊˈteɪʃ(ə)n/ *noun* launching of commercial enterprise etc.

**flotilla** /fləˈtɪlə/ *noun* small fleet; fleet of small ships.

**flotsam** /ˈflɒtsəm/ *noun* floating wreckage. □ **flotsam and jetsam** odds and ends, vagrants.

**flounce¹** /flaʊns/ • verb (-cing) (often + off, out, etc.) go or move angrily or impatiently. • noun flouncing movement.

**flounce²** /flaʊns/ • noun frill on dress, skirt, etc. • verb (-cing) (usually as **flounced** adjective) trim with flounces.

**flounder¹** /ˈflaʊndə/ verb struggle helplessly; do task clumsily.

**flounder²** /ˈflaʊndə/ noun (plural same) small flatfish.

**flour** /flaʊə/ • noun meal or powder from ground wheat etc. • verb sprinkle with flour. □ **floury** adjective (-ier, -iest).

**flourish** /ˈflʌrɪʃ/ • verb grow vigorously; thrive, prosper; wave, brandish. • noun showy gesture; ornamental curve in writing; Music ornate passage; fanfare.

**flout** verb disobey (law etc.) contemptuously.

■ **Usage** Flout is often confused with flaunt, which means 'to display proudly or show off'.

**flow** /fləʊ/ • verb glide along, move smoothly; gush out; circulate; be plentiful or in flood; (often + from) result. • noun flowing movement or liquid; stream; rise of tide. □ **flow chart, diagram, sheet** diagram of movement or action in complex activity.

**flower** /ˈflaʊə/ • noun part of plant from which seed or fruit develops; plant bearing blossom. • verb bloom; reach peak. □ **flower-bed** garden bed for flowers; **the flower of** the best of; **flowerpot** pot for growing plant in; **in flower** blooming. □ **flowered** adjective.

**flowery** adjective florally decorated; (of speech etc.) high-flown; full of flowers.

**flowing** adjective fluent; smoothly continuous; (of hair etc.) unconfined.

**flown** past participle of FLY¹.

**flu** noun colloquial influenza.

**fluctuate** /ˈflʌktʃʊeɪt/ verb (-ting) vary, rise and fall. □ **fluctuation** noun.

**flue** noun smoke duct in chimney; channel for conveying heat.

**fluent** /ˈfluːənt/ adjective expressing oneself easily and naturally, esp. in foreign language. □ **fluency** noun; **fluently** adverb.

**fluff** • noun soft fur, feathers, fabric particles, etc.; slang mistake in performance etc. • verb (often + up) shake into or become soft mass; slang make mistake in performance etc. □ **fluffy** adjective (-ier, -iest).

**flugelhorn** /ˈfluːg(ə)lhɔːn/ noun brass instrument like cornet.

**fluid** /ˈfluːɪd/ • noun substance, esp. gas or liquid, capable of flowing freely; liquid secretion. • adjective able to flow freely; constantly changing. □ **fluid ounce** twentieth or US sixteenth of pint. □ **fluidity** /-ˈɪdɪtɪ/ noun.

**fluke¹** /fluːk/ noun lucky accident. □ **fluky** adjective (-ier, -iest).

**fluke²** /fluːk/ noun parasitic flatworm.

**flummery** /ˈflʌmərɪ/ noun (plural -ies) nonsense; flattery; sweet milk dish.

**flummox** /ˈflʌməks/ verb colloquial bewilder.

**flung** past & past participle of FLING.

**flunk** verb US colloquial fail (esp. exam).

**flunkey** /ˈflʌŋkɪ/ noun (also **flunky**) (plural -eys or -ies) usually derogatory footman.

**fluorescence** /flʊəˈres(ə)ns/ noun light radiation from certain substances; property of absorbing invisible light and emitting visible light. □ **fluoresce** verb (-scing); **fluorescent** adjective.

**fluoridate** /ˈflʊərɪdeɪt/ verb (-ting) add fluoride to (water). □ **fluoridation** noun.

**fluoride** /ˈflʊəraɪd/ noun compound of fluorine with metal, esp. used to prevent tooth decay.

**fluorinate** /ˈflʊərɪneɪt/ verb (-ting) fluoridate; introduce fluorine into (compound). □ **fluorination** noun.

**fluorine** /ˈflʊəriːn/ noun poisonous pale yellow gaseous element.

**flurry** /ˈflʌrɪ/ • noun (plural -ies) gust, squall; burst of activity, excitement, etc. • verb (-ies, -ied) agitate, confuse.

**flush¹** • verb (often as **flushed** adjective + with) (cause to) glow or blush (with pride etc.); cleanse (drain, lavatory, etc.) by flow of water; (often + away, down) dispose of thus. • noun glow, blush; rush of water; cleansing (of lavatory etc.) thus; rush of esp. elation or triumph; freshness, vigour; (also **hot flush**) sudden hot feeling during menopause; feverish redness or temperature etc. • adjective level, in same plane; colloquial having plenty of money.

**flush²** noun hand of cards all of one suit.

**flush**³ verb (cause to) fly up suddenly. □ **flush out** reveal, drive out.

**fluster** /ˈflʌstə/ ● verb confuse, make nervous. ● noun confused or agitated state.

**flute** /fluːt/ ● noun high-pitched woodwind instrument held sideways; vertical groove in pillar etc. ● verb (-ting) (often as **fluted** adjective) make grooves in; play on flute. □ **fluting** noun.

**flutter** /ˈflʌtə/ ● verb flap (wings) in flying or trying to fly; fall quiveringly; wave or flap quickly; move about restlessly; (of pulse etc.) beat feebly or irregularly. ● noun fluttering; tremulous excitement; slang small bet on horse etc.; abnormally rapid heartbeat; rapid variation of pitch, esp. of recorded sound.

**fluvial** /ˈfluːvɪəl/ adjective of or found in rivers.

**flux** noun flowing, flowing out; discharge; continuous change; substance mixed with metal etc. to assist fusion.

**fly**¹ /flaɪ/ ● verb (**flies**; past **flew** /fluː/; past participle **flown** /fləʊn/) move or travel through air with wings or in aircraft; control flight of (aircraft); cause to fly or remain aloft; wave; move swiftly; be driven forcefully; flee (from); (+ at, upon) attack or criticize fiercely. ● noun (plural **-ies**) (usually in plural) flap to cover front fastening on trousers, this fastening; flap at entrance of tent; (in plural) space over stage, for scenery and lighting; act of flying. □ **fly-by-night** unreliable; **fly-half** Rugby stand-off half; **flyleaf** blank leaf at beginning or end of book; **flyover** bridge carrying road etc. over another; **fly-past** ceremonial flight of aircraft; **fly-post** fix (posters etc.) illegally; **flysheet** canvas cover over tent for extra protection, short tract or circular; **fly-tip** illegally dump (waste); **flywheel** heavy wheel regulating machinery or accumulating power.

**fly**² /flaɪ/ (plural **flies**) noun two-winged insect; disease caused by flies; (esp. artificial) fly used as bait in fishing. □ **fly-blown** tainted by flies; **flycatcher** bird that catches flies in flight; **fly-fish** verb fish with fly; **fly in the ointment** minor irritation or setback; **fly on the wall** unnoticed observer; **fly-paper** sticky treated paper for catching flies; **fly-trap** plant that

catches flies; **flyweight** amateur boxing weight (48–51 kg).

**fly**³ /flaɪ/ adjective slang knowing, clever.

**flyer** noun (also **flier**) airman, airwoman; thing or person that flies in specified way; small handbill.

**flying** ● adjective that flies; hasty. ● noun flight. □ **flying boat** boatlike seaplane; **flying buttress** (usually arched) buttress running from upper part of wall to outer support; **flying doctor** doctor who uses aircraft to visit patients; **flying fish** fish gliding through air with winglike fins; **flying fox** fruit-eating bat; **flying officer** RAF officer next below flight lieutenant; **flying saucer** supposed alien spaceship; **flying squad** rapidly mobile police detachment, midwifery unit, etc.; **flying start** start (of race) at full speed, vigorous start.

**FM** abbreviation Field Marshal; frequency modulation.

**FO** abbreviation Flying Officer.

**foal** ● noun young of horse or related animal. ● verb give birth to (foal).

**foam** ● noun froth formed in liquid; froth of saliva or sweat; spongy rubber or plastic. ● verb emit foam; froth. □ **foam at the mouth** be very angry. □ **foamy** adjective (**-ier**, **-iest**).

**fob**¹ noun (attachment to) watch-chain; small pocket for watch etc.

**fob**² verb (**-bb-**) □ **fob off** (often + with) deceive into accepting something inferior, (often + on, on to) offload (unwanted thing on person).

**focal** /ˈfəʊk(ə)l/ adjective of or at a focus. □ **focal distance**, **length** distance between centre of lens etc. and its focus; **focal point** focus, centre of interest or activity.

**fo'c's'le** = FORECASTLE.

**focus** /ˈfəʊkəs/ ● noun (plural **focuses** or **foci** /ˈfəʊsaɪ/) point at which rays etc. meet after reflection or refraction or from which they seem to come; point at which object must be situated to give clearly defined image; adjustment of eye or lens to produce clear image; state of clear definition; centre of interest or activity. ● verb (**-s-** or **-ss-**) bring into focus; adjust focus of (lens, eye); concentrate or be concentrated on; (cause to) converge to focus.

**fodder** /'fɒdə/ noun hay, straw, etc. as animal food.

**foe** noun enemy.

**foetid** = FETID.

**foetus** /'fiːtəs/ noun (US **fetus**) (plural **-tuses**) unborn mammalian offspring, esp. human embryo of 8 weeks or more. □ **foetal** adjective.

**fog** ● noun thick cloud of water droplets or smoke suspended at or near earth's surface; thick mist; cloudiness on photographic negative; confused state. ● verb (**-gg-**) envelop (as) in fog; perplex. □ **fog-bank** mass of fog at sea; **foghorn** horn warning ships in fog, colloquial penetrating voice.

**fogey** /'fəʊgɪ/ noun (also **fogy**) (plural **-ies** or **-eys**) (esp. **old fogey**) dull old-fashioned person.

**foggy** adjective (**-ier**, **-iest**) full of fog; of or like fog; vague. □ **not the foggiest** colloquial no idea.

**foible** /'fɔɪb(ə)l/ noun minor weakness or idiosyncrasy.

**foil**[1] verb frustrate, defeat.

**foil**[2] noun thin sheet of metal; person or thing setting off another to advantage.

**foil**[3] noun blunt fencing sword.

**foist** verb (+ on) force (thing, oneself) on to (unwilling person).

**fold**[1] /fəʊld/ ● verb double (flexible thing) over on itself; bend portion of; become or be able to be folded; (+ away, up) make compact by folding; (often + up) colloquial collapse, cease to function; enfold; clasp; (+ in) mix in gently. ● noun folding; line made by folding; hollow among hills.

**fold**[2] /fəʊld/ noun sheepfold; religious group or congregation.

**folder** noun folding cover or holder for loose papers.

**foliaceous** /fəʊlɪ'eɪʃəs/ adjective of or like leaves; laminated.

**foliage** /'fəʊlɪɪdʒ/ noun leaves, leafage.

**foliar** /'fəʊlɪə/ adjective of leaves. □ **foliar feed** fertilizer supplied to leaves.

**foliate** ● adjective /'fəʊlɪət/ leaflike; having leaves. ● verb /'fəʊlɪeɪt/ (**-ting**) split into thin layers. □ **foliation** noun.

**folio** /'fəʊlɪəʊ/ ● noun (plural **-s**) leaf of paper etc. numbered only on front; sheet of paper folded once; book of such sheets. ● adjective (of book) made of folios.

**folk** /fəʊk/ ● noun (plural same or **-s**) (treated as plural) people in general or of specified class; (in plural, usually **folks**) one's relatives; (treated as singular) a people or nation; (in full **folk-music**) (treated as singular) traditional, esp. working-class, music, or music in style of this. ● adjective of popular origin. □ **folklore** traditional beliefs etc., study of these; **folkweave** rough loosely woven fabric.

**folksy** /'fəʊksɪ/ adjective (**-ier**, **-iest**) of or like folk art; in deliberately popular style.

**follicle** /'fɒlɪk(ə)l/ noun small sac or vesicle, esp. for hair-root. □ **follicular** /fɒ'lɪkjʊlə/ adjective.

**follow** /'fɒləʊ/ verb go or come after; go along; come next in order or time; practise; understand; take as guide; take interest in; (+ with) provide with (sequel etc.); (+ from) result from; be necessary inference. □ **follow on** verb continue, (of cricket team) bat twice in succession; **follow-on** noun instance of this; **follow suit** play card of suit led, conform to another's actions; **follow through** verb continue to conclusion, continue movement of stroke after hitting the ball; **follow-through** noun instance of this; **follow up** verb act or investigate further; **follow-up** noun subsequent action.

**follower** noun supporter, devotee; person who follows.

**following** ● preposition after in time; as sequel to. ● noun group of supporters. ● adjective that follows. □ **the following** what follows, now to be mentioned.

**folly** /'fɒlɪ/ noun (plural **-ies**) foolishness; foolish act, idea, etc.; building for display only.

**foment** /fə'ment/ verb instigate, stir up (trouble etc.). □ **fomentation** /fəʊmen'teɪʃ(ə)n/ noun.

**fond** adjective (+ of) liking; affectionate; doting; foolishly optimistic. □ **fondly** adverb; **fondness** noun.

**fondant** /'fɒnd(ə)nt/ noun soft sugary sweet.

**fondle** /'fɒnd(ə)l/ verb (**-ling**) caress.

**fondue** /'fɒndjuː/ noun dish of melted cheese.

**font**[1] *noun* receptacle for baptismal water.

**font**[2] = FOUNT[2].

**fontanelle** /fontə'nel/ *noun* (*US* **fontanel**) space in infant's skull, which later closes up.

**food** /fuːd/ *noun* substance taken in to maintain life and growth; solid food; mental stimulus. □ **food-chain** series of organisms each dependent on next for food; **food poisoning** illness due to bacteria etc. in food; **food processor** machine for chopping and mixing food; **foodstuff** substance used as food.

**foodie** /'fuːdɪ/ *noun colloquial* person who makes a cult of food.

**fool**[1] ● *noun* unwise or stupid person; *historical* jester, clown. ● *verb* deceive; trick; cheat; joke; tease; (+ *around*, *about*) play, trifle. □ **act, play the fool** behave in silly way; **foolproof** incapable of misuse or mistake; **fool's paradise** illusory happiness; **make a fool of** make (person) look foolish, trick.

**fool**[2] *noun* dessert of fruit purée with cream or custard.

**foolery** *noun* foolish behaviour.

**foolhardy** *adjective* (**-ier, -iest**) foolishly bold; reckless. □ **foolhardily** *adverb*; **foolhardiness** *noun*.

**foolish** *adjective* lacking good sense or judgement. □ **foolishly** *adverb*; **foolishness** *noun*.

**foolscap** /'fuːlskæp/ *noun* large size of paper, about 330 mm x 200 (or 400) mm.

**foot** /fut/ ● *noun* (*plural* **feet**) part of leg below ankle; lower part or end; (*plural* same or **feet**) linear measure of 12 in. (30.48 cm); metrical unit of verse forming part of line; *historical* infantry. ● *verb* pay (bill); (usually as **foot it**) go on foot. □ **foot-and-mouth (disease)** contagious viral disease of cattle etc.; **footfall** sound of footstep; **foot-fault** (in tennis) serving with foot over baseline; **foothill** low hill lying at base of mountain or range; **foothold** secure place for feet in climbing, secure initial position; **footlights** row of floor-level lights along front of stage; **footloose** free to act as one pleases; **footman** liveried servant; **footmark** footprint; **footnote** note at foot of page; **footpath**

path for pedestrians only; **footplate** platform for crew in locomotive; **footprint** impression left by foot or shoe; **footsore** having sore feet, esp. from walking; **footstep** (sound of) step taken in walking; **footstool** stool for resting feet on when sitting; **on foot** walking. □ **footless** *adjective*.

**footage** *noun* a length of TV or cinema film etc.; length in feet.

**football** *noun* large inflated usually leather ball; team game played with this. □ **football pool(s)** organized gambling on results of football matches. □ **footballer** *noun*.

**footing** *noun* foothold; secure position; operational basis; relative position or status; (often in *plural*) foundations of wall.

**footling** /'fuːtlɪŋ/ *adjective colloquial* trivial, silly.

**Footsie** /'futsɪ/ *noun* FT-SE.

**footsie** /'futsɪ/ *noun colloquial* amorous play with feet.

**fop** *noun* dandy. □ **foppery** *noun*; **foppish** *adjective*.

**for** /fə, fɔː/ ● *preposition* in interest, defence, or favour of; appropriate to; regarding; representing; at the price of; as consequence or on account of; in order to get or reach; so as to start promptly at; notwithstanding. ● *conjunction* because, since. □ **be for it** liable or about to be punished.

**forage** /'forɪdʒ/ ● *noun* food for horses and cattle; searching for food. ● *verb* (**-ging**) (often + *for*) search for food; rummage; collect food from. □ **forage cap** infantry undress cap.

**foray** /'foreɪ/ ● *noun* sudden attack, raid. ● *verb* make foray.

**forbade** (also **forbad**) *past* of FORBID.

**forbear**[1] /fɔː'beə/ *verb* (*past* **forbore**; *past participle* **forborne**) *formal* abstain or refrain from.

**forbear**[2] = FOREBEAR.

**forbearance** *noun* patient self-control; tolerance.

**forbid** /fə'bɪd/ *verb* (**forbidding**; *past* **forbade** /-'bæd/ or **forbad**; *past participle* **forbidden**) (+ *to do*) order not; not allow; refuse entry to. □ **forbidden fruit** thing desired esp. because not allowed.

**forbidding** *adjective* stern, threatening. □ **forbiddingly** *adverb*.

**forbore** *past of* FORBEAR[1].

**forborne** *past participle of* FORBEAR[1].

**force** ●*noun* strength, power, intense effort; group of soldiers, police, etc.; coercion, compulsion; influence (person etc.) with moral power. ●*verb* (-cing) compel, coerce; make way, break into or open by force; drive, propel; (+ *on, upon*) impose or press on (person); cause or produce by effort; strain; artificially hasten maturity of; accelerate. □ **forced landing** emergency landing of aircraft; **forced march** lengthy and vigorous march, esp. by troops; **force-feed** feed (prisoner etc.) against his or her will; **force (person's) hand** make him or her act prematurely or unwillingly.

**forceful** *adjective* powerful; impressive. □ **forcefully** *adverb*; **forcefulness** *noun*.

**force majeure** /fɔːs mæˈʒɜː/ *noun* irresistible force; unforeseeable circumstances. [French]

**forcemeat** /ˈfɔːsmiːt/ *noun* minced seasoned meat for stuffing etc.

**forceps** /ˈfɔːseps/ *noun* (*plural* same) surgical pincers.

**forcible** /ˈfɔːsɪb(ə)l/ *adjective* done by or involving force; forceful. □ **forcibly** *adverb*.

**ford** ●*noun* shallow place where river etc. may be crossed. ●*verb* cross (water) at ford. □ **fordable** *adjective*.

**fore** ●*adjective* situated in front. ●*noun* front part; bow of ship. ●*interjection* (*in golf*) warning to person in path of ball. □ **fore-and-aft** (of sails or rigging) lengthwise, at bow and stern; **to the fore** conspicuous.

**forearm**[1] /ˈfɔːrɑːm/ *noun* arm from elbow to wrist or fingertips.

**forearm**[2] /fɔːrˈɑːm/ *verb* arm beforehand, prepare.

**forebear** /ˈfɔːbeə/ *noun* (also **forbear**) (usually in *plural*) ancestor.

**forebode** /fɔːˈbəʊd/ *verb* (-ding) be advance sign of; portend.

**foreboding** *noun* expectation of trouble.

**forecast** ●*verb* (*past & past participle* -cast or -casted) predict; estimate beforehand. ●*noun* prediction, esp. of weather. □ **forecaster** *noun*.

**forecastle** /ˈfəʊks(ə)l/ *noun* (also **fo'c's'le**) forward part of ship, formerly living quarters.

**foreclose** /fɔːˈkləʊz/ *verb* (-sing) stop (mortgage) from being redeemable; repossess mortgaged property of (person) when loan is not duly repaid; exclude, prevent. □ **foreclosure** *noun*.

**forecourt** *noun* part of filling-station with petrol pumps; enclosed space in front of building.

**forefather** *noun* (usually in *plural*) ancestor.

**forefinger** *noun* finger next to thumb.

**forefoot** *noun* front foot of animal.

**forefront** *noun* leading position; foremost part.

**forego** = FORGO.

**foregoing** /fɔːˈgəʊɪŋ/ *adjective* preceding; previously mentioned.

**foregone conclusion** /ˈfɔːgɒn/ *noun* easily foreseeable result.

**foreground** *noun* part of view nearest observer.

**forehand** *Tennis etc.* ●*adjective* (of stroke) played with palm of hand facing forward. ●*noun* forehand stroke.

**forehead** /ˈfɒrɪd, ˈfɔːhed/ *noun* part of face above eyebrows.

**foreign** /ˈfɒrən/ *adjective* of, from, in, or characteristic of country or language other than one's own; dealing with other countries; of another district, society, etc.; (often + *to*) unfamiliar, alien; coming from outside. □ **foreign legion** group of foreign volunteers in (esp. French) army. □ **foreignness** *noun*.

**foreigner** *noun* person born in or coming from another country.

**foreknowledge** /fɔːˈnɒlɪdʒ/ *noun* knowledge in advance of (an event etc.).

**foreleg** *noun* animal's front leg.

**forelock** *noun* lock of hair just above forehead. □ **touch one's forelock** defer to person of higher social rank.

**foreman** /ˈfɔːmən/ *noun* (*feminine* **forewoman**) worker supervising others; spokesman of jury.

**foremast** *noun* mast nearest bow of ship.

**foremost** ●*adjective* most notable, best; first, front. ●*adverb* most importantly.

**forename** *noun* first or Christian name.

**forensic** /fə'rensɪk/ *adjective* of or used in courts of law; of or involving application of science to legal problems.

**foreplay** *noun* stimulation preceding sexual intercourse.

**forerunner** *noun* predecessor.

**foresail** *noun* principal sail on foremast.

**foresee** /fɔː'siː/ *verb* (*past* **-saw**; *past participle* **-seen**) see or be aware of beforehand. □ **foreseeable** *adjective*.

**foreshadow** /fɔː'ʃædəu/ *verb* be warning or indication of (future event).

**foreshore** *noun* shore between high and low water marks.

**foreshorten** /fɔː'ʃɔːt(ə)n/ *verb* portray (object) with apparent shortening due to perspective.

**foresight** *noun* care or provision for future; foreseeing.

**foreskin** *noun* fold of skin covering end of penis.

**forest** /'fɒrɪst/ • *noun* large area of trees; large number, dense mass. • *verb* plant with trees; convert into forest.

**forestall** /fɔː'stɔːl/ *verb* prevent by advance action; deal with beforehand.

**forester** *noun* manager of forest; expert in forestry; dweller in forest.

**forestry** *noun* science or management of forests.

**foretaste** *noun* small preliminary experience of something.

**foretell** /fɔː'tel/ *verb* (*past & past participle* **-told**) predict, prophesy; indicate approach of.

**forethought** *noun* care or provision for future; deliberate intention.

**forever** /fə'revə/ *adverb* always, constantly.

**forewarn** /fɔː'wɔːn/ *verb* warn beforehand.

**foreword** *noun* introductory remarks in book, often not by author.

**forfeit** /'fɔːfɪt/ • *noun* (thing surrendered as) penalty. • *adjective* lost or surrendered as penalty. • *verb* (**-t-**) lose right to, surrender as penalty. □ **forfeiture** *noun*.

**forgather** /fɔː'gæðə/ *verb* assemble; associate.

**forgave** *past* of FORGIVE.

**forge**[1] • *verb* (**-ging**) make or write in fraudulent imitation; shape by heating and hammering. • *noun* furnace etc. for melting or refining metal; blacksmith's workshop. □ **forger** *noun*.

**forge**[2] *verb* (**-ging**) advance gradually. □ **forge ahead** take lead, progress rapidly.

**forgery** /'fɔːdʒərɪ/ *noun* (*plural* **-ies**) (making of) forged document etc.

**forget** /fə'get/ *verb* (**forgetting**; *past* **forgot**; *past participle* **forgotten** or *US* **forgot**) lose remembrance of; neglect, overlook; cease to think of; (**forget oneself**) act without dignity. □ **forget-me-not** plant with small blue flowers. □ **forgettable** *adjective*.

**forgetful** *adjective* apt to forget; (often + *of*) neglectful. □ **forgetfully** *adverb*; **forgetfulness** *noun*.

**forgive** /fə'gɪv/ *verb* (**-ving**; *past* **forgave**; *past participle* **forgiven**) cease to resent; pardon; remit (debt). □ **forgivable** *adjective*; **forgiveness** *noun*; **forgiving** *adjective*.

**forgo** /fɔː'gəu/ *verb* (also **forego**) (**-goes**; *past* **-went**; *past participle* **-gone**) go without, relinquish.

**forgot** *past* of FORGET.

**forgotten** *past participle* of FORGET.

**fork** • *noun* pronged item of cutlery; similar large tool for digging etc.; forked part, esp. of bicycle frame; (place of) divergence of road etc. • *verb* form fork or branch; take one road at fork; dig with fork. □ **fork-lift truck** vehicle with fork for lifting and carrying; **fork out** *slang* pay, esp. reluctantly.

**forlorn** /fə'lɔːn/ *adjective* sad and abandoned; pitiful. □ **forlorn hope** faint remaining hope or chance. □ **forlornly** *adverb*.

**form** • *noun* shape, arrangement of parts, visible aspect; person or animal as visible or tangible; mode in which thing exists or manifests itself; kind, variety; document with blanks to be filled in; class in school; (often as **the form**) customary or correct behaviour or method; set order of words; (of athlete, horse, etc.) condition of health and training; disposition; bench. • *verb* make, be made; constitute; develop or establish as concept, practice, etc.; (+

*into*) organize; (of troops etc.) bring or move into formation; mould, fashion.

**formal** /ˈfɔːm(ə)l/ *adjective* in accordance with rules, convention, or ceremony; (of garden etc.) symmetrical; prim, stiff; perfunctory; drawn up correctly; concerned with outward form. □ **formally** *adverb*.

**formaldehyde** /fɔːˈmældɪhaɪd/ *noun* colourless gas used as preservative and disinfectant.

**formalin** /ˈfɔːməlɪn/ *noun* solution of formaldehyde in water.

**formalism** *noun* strict adherence to external form, esp. in art. □ **formalist** *noun*.

**formality** /fɔːˈmælɪtɪ/ *noun* (*plural* **-ies**) formal, esp. meaningless, regulation or act; rigid observance of rules or convention.

**formalize** *verb* (also **-ise**) (**-zing** or **-sing**) give definite (esp. legal) form to; make formal. □ **formalization** *noun*.

**format** /ˈfɔːmæt/ ● *noun* shape and size (of book etc.); style or manner of procedure etc.; arrangement of computer data etc. ● *verb* (**-tt-**) arrange in format; prepare (storage medium) to receive computer data.

**formation** /fɔːˈmeɪʃ(ə)n/ *noun* forming; thing formed; particular arrangement (e.g. of troops); rocks or strata with common characteristic.

**formative** /ˈfɔːmətɪv/ *adjective* serving to form; of formation.

**former** /ˈfɔːmə/ *adjective* of the past, earlier, previous; (**the former**) the first or first-named of two.

**formerly** *adverb* in former times; previously.

**Formica** /fɔːˈmaɪkə/ *noun* proprietary term hard plastic laminate for surfaces.

**formic acid** /ˈfɔːmɪk/ *noun* colourless irritant volatile acid contained in fluid emitted by ants.

**formidable** /ˈfɔːmɪdəb(ə)l/ *adjective* inspiring awe, respect, or dread; difficult to deal with. □ **formidably** *adverb*.

■ **Usage** *Formidable* is also pronounced /fəˈmɪdəb(ə)l/ (with the stress on the *-mid-*), but this is considered incorrect by some people.

**formless** *adjective* without definite or regular form. □ **formlessness** *noun*.

**formula** /ˈfɔːmjʊlə/ *noun* (*plural* **-s** or **-lae** /-liː/) chemical symbols showing constituents of substance; mathematical rule expressed in symbols; fixed form of words; list of ingredients; classification of racing car, esp. by engine capacity. □ **formulaic** /-ˈleɪk/ *adjective*.

**formulate** /ˈfɔːmjʊleɪt/ *verb* express in formula; express clearly and precisely. □ **formulation** *noun*.

**fornicate** /ˈfɔːnɪkeɪt/ *verb* (**-ting**) *usually jocular* have extramarital sexual intercourse. □ **fornication** *noun*; **fornicator** *noun*.

**forsake** /fəˈseɪk/ *verb* (**-king**; *past* **forsook** /-ˈsʊk/; *past participle* **forsaken**) *literary* give up, renounce; desert, abandon.

**forswear** /fɔːˈsweə/ *verb* (*past* **forswore**; *past participle* **forsworn**) abjure, renounce; (**forswear oneself**) perjure oneself; (as **forsworn** *adjective*) perjured.

**forsythia** /fɔːˈsaɪθɪə/ *noun* shrub with bright yellow flowers.

**fort** *noun* fortified building or position. □ **hold the fort** act as temporary substitute.

**forte**[1] /ˈfɔːteɪ/ *noun* thing in which one excels or specializes.

**forte**[2] /ˈfɔːteɪ/ *Music* ● *adjective* loud. ● *adverb* loudly. ● *noun* loud playing, singing, or passage.

**forth** /fɔːθ/ *adverb* forward(s); out; onwards in time. □ **forthcoming** /fɔːθˈkʌmɪŋ/ coming or available soon, produced when wanted, informative, responsive.

**forthright** *adjective* straightforward, outspoken, decisive.

**forthwith** /fɔːθˈwɪθ/ *adverb* immediately, without delay.

**fortification** /fɔːtɪfɪˈkeɪʃ(ə)n/ *noun* fortifying; (usually in *plural*) defensive works.

**fortify** /ˈfɔːtɪfaɪ/ *verb* (**-ies**, **-ied**) provide with fortifications; strengthen; (usually as **fortified** *adjective*) strengthen (wine etc.) with alcohol, increase nutritive value of (food, esp. with vitamins).

**fortissimo** /fɔːˈtɪsɪməʊ/ *Music* ● *adjective* very loud. ● *adverb* very loudly. ● *noun* (*plural* **-mos** or **-mi** /-miː/) very loud playing, singing, or passage.

**fortitude** /ˈfɔːtɪtjuːd/ *noun* courage in pain or adversity.

**fortnight** /ˈfɔːtnaɪt/ *noun* two weeks.

**fortnightly** ● *adjective* done, produced, or occurring once a fortnight. ● *adverb* every fortnight. ● *noun* (*plural* **-ies**) fortnightly magazine etc.

**Fortran** /ˈfɔːtræn/ *noun* (also **FORTRAN**) computer language used esp. for scientific calculations.

**fortress** /ˈfɔːtrɪs/ *noun* fortified building or town.

**fortuitous** /fɔːˈtjuːɪtəs/ *adjective* happening by chance. □ **fortuitously** *adverb*; **fortuitousness** *noun*; **fortuity** *noun* (*plural* **-ies**).

**fortunate** /ˈfɔːtʃənət/ *adjective* lucky, auspicious. □ **fortunately** *adverb*.

**fortune** /ˈfɔːtʃ(ə)n/ *noun* chance or luck in human affairs; person's destiny; prosperity, wealth; *colloquial* large sum of money. □ **fortune-teller** person claiming to foretell one's destiny.

**forty** /ˈfɔːtɪ/ *adjective* & *noun* (*plural* **-ies**) four times ten. □ **forty winks** *colloquial* short sleep. □ **fortieth** *adjective* & *noun*.

**forum** /ˈfɔːrəm/ *noun* place of or meeting for public discussion; court, tribunal.

**forward** /ˈfɔːwəd/ ● *adjective* onward, towards front; bold, precocious, presumptuous; relating to the future; well-advanced. ● *noun* attacking player in football etc. ● *adverb* to front; into prominence; so as to make progress; towards future; forwards. ● *verb* send (letter etc.) on; dispatch; help to advance, promote.

**forwards** *adverb* in direction one is facing.

**forwent** *past* of FORGO.

**fossil** /ˈfɒs(ə)l/ ● *noun* remains or impression of (usually prehistoric) plant or animal hardened in rock; *colloquial* antiquated or unchanging person or thing. ● *adjective* of or like fossil. □ **fossil fuel** natural fuel extracted from ground. □ **fossilize** *verb* (also **-ise**) (**-zing** or **-sing**); **fossilization** *noun*.

**foster** /ˈfɒstə/ ● *verb* promote growth of; encourage or harbour (feeling); bring up (another's child); assign as foster-child. ● *adjective* related by or concerned with fostering.

**fought** *past* & *past participle* of FIGHT.

**foul** /faʊl/ ● *adjective* offensive, loathsome, stinking; dirty, soiled; *colloquial* awful; noxious; obscene; unfair, against rules; (of weather) rough; entangled. ● *noun* foul blow or play; entanglement. ● *adverb* unfairly. ● *verb* make or become foul; commit foul on (player); (often + *up*) (cause to) become entangled or blocked. □ **foul-mouthed** using obscene or offensive language; **foul play** unfair play, treacherous or violent act, esp. murder. □ **foully** /ˈfaʊllɪ/ *adverb*; **foulness** *noun*.

**found**[1] *past* & *past participle* of FIND.

**found**[2] /faʊnd/ *verb* establish, originate; lay base of; base. □ **founder** *noun*.

**found**[3] /faʊnd/ *verb* melt and mould (metal), fuse (materials for glass); make thus. □ **founder** *noun*.

**foundation** /faʊnˈdeɪʃ(ə)n/ *noun* solid ground or base under building; (usually in *plural*) lowest part of building, usually below ground; basis; underlying principle; establishing (esp. endowed institution); base for cosmetics; (in full **foundation garment**) woman's supporting undergarment. □ **foundation-stone** one laid ceremonially at founding of building, basis.

**founder** /ˈfaʊndə/ *verb* (of ship) fill with water and sink; (of plan) fail; (of horse) stumble, fall lame.

**foundling** /ˈfaʊndlɪŋ/ *noun* abandoned infant of unknown parentage.

**foundry** /ˈfaʊndrɪ/ *noun* (*plural* **-ies**) workshop for casting metal.

**fount**[1] /faʊnt/ *noun* *poetical* source, spring, fountain.

**fount**[2] /fɒnt/ *noun* (also **font**) set of printing type of same size and face.

**fountain** /ˈfaʊntɪn/ *noun* jet(s) of water as ornament or for drinking; spring; (often + *of*) source. □ **fountain-head** source; **fountain pen** pen with reservoir or cartridge for ink.

**four** /fɔː/ *adjective* & *noun* one more than three; 4-oared boat, its crew. □ **four-letter word** short obscene word; **four-poster** bed with 4 posts supporting canopy; **four-square** *adjective* solidly based, steady, *adverb* resolutely; **four-stroke** (of internal-combustion engine) having power cycle completed in two up-and-down movements of piston; **four-wheel drive** drive acting on all 4 wheels of vehicle.

**fourfold** *adjective & adverb* four times as much or many.

**foursome** *noun* group of 4 people; golf match between two pairs.

**fourteen** /fɔːˈtiːn/ *adjective & noun* one more than thirteen. □ **fourteenth** *adjective & noun.*

**fourth** /fɔːθ/ *adjective & noun* next after third; any of four equal parts of thing. □ **fourthly** *adverb.*

**fowl** /faʊl/ *noun* (*plural* same or **-s**) chicken kept for eggs and meat; poultry as food.

**fox** ●*noun* wild canine animal with red or grey fur and bushy tail; its fur; crafty person. ●*verb* deceive; puzzle. □ **foxglove** tall plant with purple or white flowers; **foxhole** hole in ground as shelter etc. in battle; **foxhound** hound bred to hunt foxes; **fox-hunting** hunting foxes with hounds; **fox-terrier** small short-haired terrier; **foxtrot** ballroom dance with slow and quick steps. □ **foxlike** *adjective.*

**foxy** *adjective* (**-ier, -iest**) foxlike; sly, cunning; reddish-brown. □ **foxily** *adverb.*

**foyer** /ˈfɔɪeɪ/ *noun* entrance hall in hotel, theatre, etc.

**FPA** *abbreviation* Family Planning Association.

**Fr.** *abbreviation* Father; French.

**fr.** *abbreviation* franc(s).

**fracas** /ˈfrækɑː/ *noun* (*plural* same /-kɑːz/) noisy quarrel.

**fraction** /ˈfrækʃ(ə)n/ *noun* part of whole number; small part, amount, etc.; portion of mixture obtainable by distillation etc. □ **fractional** *adjective*; **fractionally** *adverb.*

**fractious** /ˈfrækʃəs/ *adjective* irritable, peevish.

**fracture** /ˈfræktʃə/ ●*noun* breakage, esp. of bone. ●*verb* (**-ring**) cause fracture in, suffer fracture.

**fragile** /ˈfrædʒaɪl/ *adjective* easily broken; delicate. □ **fragility** /frəˈdʒɪl-/ *noun.*

**fragment** ●*noun* /ˈfrægmənt/ part broken off; remains or unfinished portion of book etc. ●*verb* /frægˈment/ break into fragments. □ **fragmental** /-ˈmen-/

*adjective*; **fragmentary** *adjective*; **fragmentation** *noun.*

**fragrance** /ˈfreɪgrəns/ *noun* sweetness of smell; sweet scent.

**fragrant** *adjective* sweet-smelling.

**frail** *adjective* fragile, delicate; morally weak. □ **frailly** /ˈfreɪllɪ/ *adverb*; **frailness** *noun.*

**frailty** *noun* (*plural* **-ies**) frail quality; weakness, foible.

**frame** ●*noun* case or border enclosing picture etc.; supporting structure; (in *plural*) structure of spectacles holding lenses; build of person or animal; framework; construction; (in full **frame of mind**) temporary state; single picture on photographic film; (in snooker etc.) triangular structure for positioning balls, round of play; glazed structure to protect plants. ●*verb* (**-ming**) set in frame; serve as frame for; construct, devise; (+ *to, into*) adapt, fit; *slang* concoct false charge etc. against; articulate (words). □ **frame-up** *slang* conspiracy to convict innocent person; **framework** essential supporting structure, basic system.

**franc** *noun* French, Belgian, Swiss, etc. unit of currency.

**franchise** /ˈfræntʃaɪz/ ●*noun* right to vote; citizenship; authorization to sell company's goods etc. in particular area; right granted to person or corporation. ●*verb* (**-sing**) grant franchise to.

**Franciscan** /frænˈsɪskən/ ●*adjective* of (order of) St Francis. ●*noun* Franciscan friar or nun.

**franglais** /ˈfrɑ̃gleɪ/ *noun* French with many English words and idioms. [French]

**Frank** *noun* member of Germanic people that conquered Gaul in 6th c. □ **Frankish** *adjective.*

**frank** ●*adjective* candid, outspoken; undisguised; open. ●*verb* mark (letter etc.) to record payment of postage. ●*noun* franking signature or mark. □ **frankly** *adverb*; **frankness** *noun.*

**frankfurter** /ˈfræŋkfɜːtə/ *noun* seasoned smoked sausage.

**frankincense** /ˈfræŋkɪnsens/ *noun* aromatic gum resin burnt as incense.

**frantic** /ˈfræntɪk/ *adjective* wildly excited; frenzied; hurried, anxious; desperate, violent; *colloquial* extreme. □ **frantically** *adverb*.

**fraternal** /frə'tɜːn(ə)l/ *adjective* of brothers, brotherly; comradely. □ **fraternally** *adverb*.

**fraternity** /frə'tɜːnɪtɪ/ *noun* (*plural* **-ies**) religious brotherhood; group with common interests or of same professional class; *US* male students' society; brotherliness.

**fraternize** /'frætənaɪz/ *verb* (also **-ise**) (**-zing** or **-sing**) (often + *with*) associate, make friends, esp. with enemy etc. □ **fraternization** *noun*.

**fratricide** /'frætrɪsaɪd/ *noun* killing of one's brother or sister; person who does this. □ **fratricidal** /-'saɪd(ə)l/ *adjective*.

**Frau** /frau/ *noun* (*plural* **Frauen** /'frauən/) title used of or to married or widowed German-speaking woman.

**fraud** /frɔːd/ *noun* criminal deception; dishonest trick; impostor.

**fraudulent** /'frɔːdjʊlənt/ *adjective* of, involving, or guilty of fraud. □ **fraudulence** *noun*; **fraudulently** *adverb*.

**fraught** /frɔːt/ *adjective* (+ *with*) filled or attended with (danger etc.); *colloquial* distressing; tense.

**Fräulein** /'frɔɪlaɪn/ *noun*: title used of or to unmarried German-speaking woman.

**fray**[1] *verb* wear or become worn; unravel at edge; (esp. as **frayed** *adjective*) (of nerves) become strained.

**fray**[2] *noun* fight, conflict; brawl.

**frazzle** /'fræz(ə)l/ *colloquial* ● *noun* worn, exhausted, or shrivelled state. ● *verb* (**-ling**) (usually as **frazzled** *adjective*) wear out; exhaust.

**freak** ● *noun* monstrosity; abnormal person or thing; *colloquial* unconventional person, fanatic of specified kind. ● *verb* (often + *out*) *colloquial* make or become very angry; (cause to) undergo esp. drug-induced etc. hallucinations or strong emotional experience. □ **freakish** *adjective*; **freaky** *adjective* (**-ier**, **-iest**).

**freckle** /'frek(ə)l/ ● *noun* light brown spot on skin. ● *verb* (**-ling**) (usually as **freckled** *adjective*) spot or be spotted with freckles. □ **freckly** *adjective* (**-ier**, **-iest**).

**free** ● *adjective* (**freer** /'friːə/, **freest** /'friːɪst/) not a slave; having individual rights and social and political liberty; autonomous; democratic; unrestricted, not confined; (+ *of*, *from* or in combination) exempt from, not containing or subject to; (+ *to do*) permitted, at liberty; costing nothing; available; spontaneous; lavish, unreserved; (of translation) not literal. ● *adverb* freely; without cost. ● *verb* (**frees**, **freed**) make free, liberate; disentangle. □ **for free** *colloquial* gratis; **freebooter** pirate; **freeboard** part of ship's side between waterline and deck; **Free Church** Nonconformist Church; **free enterprise** freedom of private business from state control; **free fall** movement under force of gravity only; **free hand** *noun* liberty to act at one's own discretion; **freehand** *adjective* (of drawing) done without ruler, compasses, etc., *adverb* in a freehand way; **free house** pub not controlled by brewery; **freeloader** *slang* sponger; **freeman** holder of freedom of city etc.; **free port** port without customs duties, or open to all traders; **free-range** (of hens etc.) roaming freely, (of eggs) produced by such hens; **free spirit** independent or uninhibited person; **free-standing** not supported by another structure; **freestyle** swimming race in which any stroke may be used, wrestling allowing almost any hold; **freethinker** /-'θɪŋkə/ person who rejects dogma, esp. in religious belief; **free trade** trade without import restrictions etc.; **freeway** *US* motorway; **freewheel** ride bicycle with pedals at rest, act without constraint; **free will** power of acting independently of fate or without coercion.

**freebie** /'friːbɪ/ *noun colloquial* thing given free of charge.

**freedom** *noun* being free; personal or civil liberty; liberty of action; (+ *from*) exemption from; (+ *of*) honorary membership or citizenship of, unrestricted use of (house etc.).

**freehold** *noun* complete ownership of property for unlimited period; such property. □ **freeholder** *noun*.

**freelance** ● *noun* person working for no fixed employer. ● *verb* work as freelance. ● *adverb* as freelance.

**Freemason** /'fri:meɪs(ə)n/ *noun* member of fraternity for mutual help with secret rituals. □ **Freemasonry** *noun*.

**freesia** /'fri:zjə/ *noun* fragrant flowering African bulb.

**freeze** ● *verb* (**-zing**; *past* **froze**; *past participle* **frozen** /'frəʊz(ə)n/) turn into ice or other solid by cold; make or become rigid from cold; be or feel very cold; cover or be covered with ice; refrigerate below freezing point; make or become motionless; (as **frozen** *adjective*) devoid of emotion; make (assets etc.) unrealizable; fix (prices etc.) at certain level; stop (movement in film). ● *noun* period or state of frost; price-fixing etc.; (in full **freeze-frame**) still film-shot. □ **freeze-dry** preserve (food) by freezing and then drying in vacuum; **freeze up** *verb* obstruct or be obstructed by ice; **freeze-up** *noun* period of extreme cold; **freezing point** temperature at which liquid freezes.

**freezer** *noun* refrigerated cabinet for preserving food in frozen state.

**freight** /freɪt/ *noun* transport of goods; goods transported; charge for transport of goods.

**freighter** *noun* ship or aircraft for carrying freight.

**French** ● *adjective* of France or its people or language. ● *noun* French language; (**the French**) (*plural*) the French people. □ **French bean** kidney or haricot bean as unripe pods or as ripe seeds; **French bread** long crisp loaf; **French dressing** salad dressing of oil and vinegar; **French fried potatoes, French fries** chips; **French horn** coiled brass wind instrument; **French letter** *colloquial* condom; **Frenchman, Frenchwoman** native or national of France; **French polish** *noun* shellac polish for wood; **French-polish** *verb*; **French window** glazed door in outside wall.

**frenetic** /frə'netɪk/ *adjective* frantic, frenzied. □ **frenetically** *adverb*.

**frenzy** /'frenzɪ/ ● *noun* (*plural* **-ies**) wild excitement or fury. ● *verb* (**-ies, -ied**) (usually as **frenzied** *adjective*) drive to frenzy. □ **frenziedly** *adverb*.

**frequency** /'fri:kwənsɪ/ *noun* (*plural* **-ies**) commonness of occurrence; frequent occurrence; rate of recurrence (of vibration etc.). □ **frequency modulation**

*Electronics* modulation by varying carrier-wave frequency.

**frequent** ● *adjective* /'fri:kwənt/ occurring often or in close succession; habitual. ● *verb* /frɪ'kwent/ go to habitually. □ **frequently** /'fri:kwəntlɪ/ *adverb*.

**fresco** /'freskəʊ/ *noun* (*plural* **-s**) painting in water-colour on fresh plaster.

**fresh** ● *adjective* newly made or obtained; other, different; new; additional; (+ *from*) lately arrived from; not stale or faded; (of food) not preserved; (of water) not salty; pure; refreshing; (of wind) brisk; *colloquial* cheeky, amorously impudent; inexperienced. ● *adverb* newly, recently. □ **freshwater** (of fish etc.) not of the sea. □ **freshly** *adverb*; **freshness** *noun*.

**freshen** *verb* make or become fresh; (+ *up*) wash, tidy oneself, etc.; revive.

**fresher** *noun colloquial* first-year student at university or (*US*) high school.

**freshet** /'freʃɪt/ *noun* rush of fresh water into sea; river flood.

**freshman** /'freʃmən/ *noun* fresher.

**fret**[1] ● *verb* (**-tt-**) be worried or distressed. ● *noun* worry, vexation. □ **fretful** *adjective*; **fretfully** *adverb*.

**fret**[2] ● *noun* ornamental pattern of straight lines joined usually at right angles. ● *verb* (**-tt-**) adorn with fret etc. □ **fretsaw** narrow saw on frame for cutting thin wood in patterns; **fretwork** work done with fretsaw.

**fret**[3] *noun* bar or ridge on finger-board of guitar etc.

**Freudian** /'frɔɪdɪən/ ● *adjective* of Freud's theories or method of psychoanalysis. ● *noun* follower of Freud. □ **Freudian slip** unintentional verbal error revealing subconscious feelings.

**Fri.** *abbreviation* Friday.

**friable** /'fraɪəb(ə)l/ *adjective* easily crumbled. □ **friability** *noun*.

**friar** /'fraɪə/ *noun* member of male non-enclosed religious order. □ **friar's balsam** type of inhalant.

**friary** /'fraɪərɪ/ *noun* (*plural* **-ies**) monastery for friars.

**fricassee** /'frɪkəseɪ/ ● *noun* pieces of meat in thick sauce. ● *verb* (**fricassees, fricasseed**) make fricassee of.

**fricative** /'frɪkətɪv/ ● *adjective* sounded by friction of breath in narrow opening. ● *noun* such consonant (e.g. *f, th*).

**friction** /'frɪkʃ(ə)n/ *noun* rubbing of one object against another; resistance so encountered; clash of wills, opinions, etc. □ **frictional** *adjective*.

**Friday** /'fraɪdeɪ/ *noun* day of week following Thursday.

**fridge** *noun colloquial* refrigerator. □ **fridge-freezer** combined refrigerator and freezer.

**friend** /frend/ *noun* supportive and respected associate, esp. one for whom affection is felt; ally; kind person; person already mentioned; (**Friend**) Quaker.

**friendly** ● *adjective* (**-ier, -iest**) outgoing, kindly; (often + *with*) on amicable terms; not hostile; user-friendly. ● *noun* (*plural* **-ies**) friendly match. □ **-friendly** not harming, helping; **friendly match** match played for enjoyment rather than competition; **Friendly Society** society for insurance against sickness etc. □ **friendliness** *noun*.

**friendship** *noun* friendly relationship or feeling.

**frier** = FRYER.

**Friesian** /'friːzɪən/ ● *noun* one of breed of black and white dairy cattle. ● *adjective* of Friesians.

**frieze** /friːz/ *noun* part of entablature, often filled with sculpture, between architrave and cornice; band of decoration, esp. at top of wall.

**frigate** /'frɪgɪt/ *noun* naval escort-vessel.

**fright** /fraɪt/ *noun* (instance of) sudden or extreme fear; grotesque-looking person or thing. □ **take fright** become frightened.

**frighten** *verb* fill with fright; (+ *away, off, out of, into*) drive by fright. □ **frightening** *adjective*; **frighteningly** *adverb*.

**frightful** *adjective* dreadful, shocking; ugly; *colloquial* extremely bad; *colloquial* extreme. □ **frightfully** *adverb*.

**frigid** /'frɪdʒɪd/ *adjective* unfriendly, cold; (of woman) sexually unresponsive; cold. □ **frigidity** /-'dʒɪd-/ *noun*.

**frill** ● *noun* ornamental edging of gathered or pleated material; (in *plural*) unnecessary embellishments. ● *verb* (usually as **frilled** *adjective*) decorate with frill. □ **frilly** *adjective* (**-ier, -iest**).

**fringe** ● *noun* border of tassels or loose threads; front hair cut to hang over forehead; outer limit; unimportant area or part. ● *verb* (**-ging**) adorn with fringe; serve as fringe to. □ **fringe benefit** employee's benefit additional to salary.

**frippery** /'frɪpəri/ *noun* (*plural* **-ies**) showy finery; empty display; (usually in *plural*) knick-knacks.

**frisk** ● *verb* leap or skip playfully; *slang* search (person). ● *noun* playful leap or skip.

**frisky** *adjective* (**-ier, -iest**) lively, playful.

**frisson** /'friːsɒn/ *noun* emotional thrill. [French]

**fritillary** /frɪ'tɪləri/ *noun* (*plural* **-ies**) plant with bell-like flowers; butterfly with red and black chequered wings.

**fritter**[1] /'frɪtə/ *verb* (usually + *away*) waste triflingly.

**fritter**[2] /'frɪtə/ *noun* fruit, meat, etc. coated in batter and fried.

**frivolous** /'frɪvələs/ *adjective* not serious, shallow, silly; trifling. □ **frivolity** /-'vɒl-/ *noun* (*plural* **-ies**).

**frizz** ● *verb* form (hair) into tight curls. ● *noun* frizzed hair or state. □ **frizzy** *adjective* (**-ier, -iest**).

**frizzle**[1] /'frɪz(ə)l/ *verb* (**-ling**) fry or cook with sizzling noise; (often + *up*) burn, shrivel.

**frizzle**[2] /'frɪz(ə)l/ *verb* (**-ling**) & *noun* frizz.

**frock** *noun* woman's or girl's dress; monk's or priest's gown. □ **frock-coat** man's long-skirted coat.

**frog** *noun* tailless leaping amphibian. □ **frog in one's throat** *colloquial* phlegm in throat that hinders speech; **frogman** underwater swimmer equipped with rubber suit and flippers; **frogmarch** hustle forward with arms pinned behind; **frog-spawn** frog's eggs.

**frolic** /'frɒlɪk/ ● *verb* (**-ck-**) play about merrily. ● *noun* merrymaking. □ **frolicsome** *adjective* playful.

**from** /frəm/ *preposition* expressing separation or origin.

**fromage frais** /frɒmɑːʒ 'freɪ/ *noun* type of soft cheese.

**frond** *noun* leaflike part of fern or palm.

**front** /frʌnt/ ●*noun* side or part most prominent or important, or nearer spectator or direction of motion; line of battle; scene of actual fighting; organized political group; demeanour; pretext, bluff; person etc. as cover for subversive or illegal activities; land along edge of sea or lake, esp. in town; forward edge of advancing cold or warm air; auditorium; breast of garment. ●*adjective* of or at front. ●*verb* (+ *on, to, towards,* etc.) have front facing or directed towards; (+ *for*) *slang* act as front for; (usually as **fronted** *adjective* + *with*) provide with or have front; lead (band, organization, etc.). □ **front bench** seats in Parliament for leading members of government and opposition; **front line** foremost part of army or group under attack; **front runner** favourite in race etc.

**frontage** *noun* front of building; land next to street, water, etc.; extent of front.

**frontal** *adjective* of or on front; of forehead.

**frontier** /'frʌntɪə/ *noun* border between countries, district on each side of this; limits of attainment or knowledge in subject; *esp. US historical* border between settled and unsettled country. □ **frontiersman** *noun*.

**frontispiece** /'frʌntɪspiːs/ *noun* illustration facing title-page of book.

**frost** ●*noun* frozen dew or vapour; temperature below freezing point. ●*verb* (usually + *over, up*) become covered with frost; cover (as) with frost; (usually as **frosted** *adjective*) roughen surface of (glass) to make opaque. □ **frostbite** injury to body tissue due to freezing; **frostbitten** *adjective*.

**frosting** *noun* icing for cakes.

**frosty** *adjective* (**-ier, -iest**) cold or covered with frost; unfriendly.

**froth** ●*noun* foam; idle talk. ●*verb* emit or gather froth. □ **frothy** *adjective* (**-ier, -iest**).

**frown** ●*verb* wrinkle brows, esp. in displeasure or concentration; (+ *at, on*) disapprove of. ●*noun* act of frowning, frowning look.

**frowsty** /'fraʊstɪ/ *adjective* (**-ier, -iest**) fusty; stuffy.

**frowzy** /'fraʊzɪ/ *adjective* (also **frowsy**) (**-ier, -iest**) fusty; slatternly, dingy.

**froze** *past* of FREEZE.

**frozen** *past participle* of FREEZE.

**FRS** *abbreviation* Fellow of the Royal Society.

**fructify** /'frʌktɪfaɪ/ *verb* (**-ies, -ied**) bear fruit; make fruitful.

**fructose** /'frʌktəʊz/ *noun* sugar in fruits, honey, etc.

**frugal** /'fruːg(ə)l/ *adjective* sparing; meagre. □ **frugality** /-'gæl-/ *noun*; **frugally** *adverb*.

**fruit** /fruːt/ ●*noun* seed-bearing part of plant or tree; this as food; (usually in *plural*) products, profits, rewards. ●*verb* bear fruit. □ **fruit cake** containing dried fruit; **fruit cocktail** diced fruit salad; **fruit machine** gambling machine operated by coins; **fruit salad** dessert of mixed fruit; **fruit sugar** fructose.

**fruiterer** /'fruːtərə/ *noun* dealer in fruit.

**fruitful** *adjective* productive; successful. □ **fruitfully** *adverb*.

**fruition** /fruː'ɪʃ(ə)n/ *noun* realization of aims or hopes.

**fruitless** *adjective* not bearing fruit; useless, unsuccessful. □ **fruitlessly** *adverb*.

**fruity** *adjective* (**-ier, -iest**) of or resembling fruit; (of voice) deep and rich; *colloquial* slightly indecent.

**frump** *noun* dowdy woman. □ **frumpish** *adjective*; **frumpy** *adjective* (**-ier, -iest**).

**frustrate** /frʌs'treɪt/ *verb* (**-ting**) make (efforts) ineffective; prevent from achieving purpose; (as **frustrated** *adjective*) discontented, unfulfilled. □ **frustrating** *adjective*; **frustratingly** *adverb*; **frustration** *noun*.

**fry**[1] ●*verb* (**fries, fried**) cook in hot fat. ●*noun* fried food, esp. (usually **fries**) chips. □ **frying-pan** shallow long-handled pan for frying; **fry-up** *colloquial* fried bacon, eggs, etc.

**fry**[2] *plural noun* young or freshly hatched fishes.

**fryer** *noun* (also **frier**) person who fries; vessel for frying esp. fish.

**ft** *abbreviation* foot, feet.

**FT-SE** *abbreviation* Financial Times Stock Exchange (100 share index).

**fuchsia** /ˈfjuːʃə/ *noun* shrub with drooping flowers.

**fuddle** /ˈfʌd(ə)l/ ● *verb* (**-ling**) confuse, esp. with alcohol. ● *noun* confusion; intoxication.

**fuddy-duddy** /ˈfʌdɪdʌdɪ/ *slang* ● *adjective* fussy, old-fashioned. ● *noun* (*plural* **-ies**) such person.

**fudge** ● *noun* soft toffee-like sweet; faking. ● *verb* (**-ging**) make or do clumsily or dishonestly; fake.

**fuel** /ˈfjuːəl/ ● *noun* material for burning or as source of heat, power, or nuclear energy; thing that sustains or inflames passion etc. ● *verb* (**-ll-**; *US* **-l-**) supply with fuel; inflame (feeling).

**fug** *noun colloquial* stuffy atmosphere. □ **fuggy** *adjective* (**-ier**, **-iest**).

**fugitive** /ˈfjuːdʒɪtɪv/ ● *noun* (often + *from*) person who flees. ● *adjective* fleeing; transient, fleeting.

**fugue** /fjuːɡ/ *noun* piece of music in which short melody or phrase is introduced by one part and developed by others. □ **fugal** *adjective*.

**fulcrum** /ˈfʌlkrəm/ *noun* (*plural* **-s** or **-cra**) point on which lever is supported.

**fulfil** /fʊlˈfɪl/ *verb* (*US* **fulfill**) (**-ll-**) carry out; satisfy; (as **fulfilled** *adjective*) completely happy; (**fulfil oneself**) realize one's potential. □ **fulfilment** *noun*.

**full** /fʊl/ ● *adjective* holding all it can; replete; abundant; satisfying; (+ *of*) having abundance of, engrossed in; complete, perfect; resonant; plump; ample. ● *adverb* quite, exactly. □ **full back** defensive player near goal in football etc.; **full-blooded** vigorous, sensual, not hybrid; **full-blown** fully developed; **full board** provision of bed and all meals; **full-bodied** rich in quality, tone, etc.; **full frontal** (of nude) fully exposed at front, explicit; **full house** maximum attendance at theatre etc., hand in poker with 3 of a kind and a pair; **full-length** of normal length, not shortened, (of portrait) showing whole figure; **full moon** moon with whole disc illuminated; **full stop** punctuation mark (.) at end of sentence etc. (see panel), complete cessation; **full term**

· · · · · · · · · · · · · · · · · · · · · · · · · · · · · · · · · · · · · · · · · · · · · · · · · · · · · · · · · · · · · · · · · · · · · · · · · ·

## Full stop .

This is used:

**1** at the end of a sentence, e.g.

> *I am going to the cinema tonight.*
> *The film begins at seven.*

The full stop is replaced by a question mark at the end of a question, and by an exclamation mark at the end of an exclamation.

**2** after an abbreviation, e.g.

> *H. G. Wells*      *p. 19* (= *page 19*)      *Sun.* (= *Sunday*)
> *Ex. 6* (= *Exercise 6*).

Full stops are **not** used with:

  **a** numerical abbreviations, e.g. *1st, 2nd, 15th, 23rd*
  **b** acronyms, e.g. *FIFA, NATO*
  **c** abbreviations that are used as ordinary words, e.g. *con, demo, recap*
  **d** chemical symbols, e.g. Fe, K, $H_2O$

Full stops are not essential for:

  **a** abbreviations consisting entirely of capitals, e.g. *BBC, AD, BC, PLC*
  **b** *C* (= *Celsius*), *F* (= *Fahrenheit*)
  **c** measures of length, weight, time, etc., except for *in.* (= *inch*), *st.* (= *stone*)
  **d** *Dr, Revd* (but note *Rev.*), *Mr, Mrs, Ms, Mme, Mlle, St* (= *Saint*), *Hants, Northants, p* (= *penny* or *pence*).

· · · · · · · · · · · · · · · · · · · · · · · · · · · · · · · · · · · · · · · · · · · · · · · · · · · · · · · · · · · · · · · · · · · · · · · · · ·

completion of normal pregnancy; **full-time** adjective for or during whole of working week, adverb on full-time basis. □ **fullness** noun.

**fully** adverb completely; at least.

**fulmar** /'fʊlmə/ noun kind of petrel.

**fulminate** /'fʊlmɪneɪt/ verb (-ting) criticize loudly and forcibly; explode, flash. □ **fulmination** noun.

**fulsome** /'fʊlsəm/ adjective excessive, cloying; insincere. ● **fulsomely** adverb.

∎ **Usage** Fulsome is sometimes wrongly used to mean 'generous', as in fulsome praise or 'generous with praise', as in a fulsome tribute.

**fumble** /'fʌmb(ə)l/ ● verb (-ling) grope about; handle clumsily or nervously. ● noun act of fumbling.

**fume** ● noun (usually in plural) exuded smoke, gas, or vapour. ● verb (-ming) emit fumes; be very angry; subject (oak etc.) to fumes to darken.

**fumigate** /'fju:mɪgeɪt/ verb (-ting) disinfect or purify with fumes. □ **fumigation** noun; **fumigator** noun.

**fun** noun playful amusement; source of this; mockery. □ **funfair** fair consisting of amusements and sideshows; **fun run** colloquial sponsored run for charity; **make fun of, poke fun at** ridicule.

**function** /'fʌŋkʃ(ə)n/ ● noun proper role etc.; official duty; public or social occasion; Mathematics quantity whose value depends on varying values of others. ● verb fulfil function; operate.

**functional** adjective of or serving a function; practical rather than attractive. □ **functionally** adverb.

**functionalism** noun belief that function should determine design. □ **functionalist** noun & adjective.

**functionary** noun (plural **-ies**) official.

**fund** ● noun permanently available stock; money set apart for purpose; (in plural) money resources. ● verb provide with money; make (debt) permanent at fixed interest. □ **fund-raising** raising money for charity etc.; **fund-raiser** noun.

**fundamental** /fʌndə'ment(ə)l/ ● adjective of or serving as base or foundation; essential, primary. ● noun fundamental principle. □ **fundamentally** adverb.

**fundamentalism** noun strict adherence to traditional religious beliefs. □ **fundamentalist** noun & adjective.

**funeral** /'fju:nər(ə)l/ ● noun ceremonial burial or cremation of dead. ● adjective of or used at funerals. □ **funeral director** undertaker; **funeral parlour** establishment where corpses are prepared for funerals.

**funerary** /'fju:nərərɪ/ adjective of or used at funerals.

**funereal** /fju:'nɪərɪəl/ adjective of or appropriate to funeral; dismal, dark.

**fungicide** /'fʌndʒɪsaɪd/ noun substance that kills fungus. □ **fungicidal** /-'saɪd(ə)l/ adjective.

**fungus** /'fʌŋgəs/ noun (plural **-gi** /-gaɪ/ or **-guses**) mushroom, toadstool, or allied plant; spongy morbid growth. □ **fungal** adjective; **fungoid** adjective; **fungous** adjective.

**funicular** /fju:'nɪkjʊlə/ noun (in full **funicular railway**) cable railway with ascending and descending cars counterbalanced.

**funk** slang ● noun fear, panic. ● verb evade through fear.

**funky** adjective (**-ier, -iest**) slang (esp. of jazz etc.) with heavy rhythm.

**funnel** /'fʌn(ə)l/ ● noun tube widening at top, for pouring liquid etc. into small opening; chimney of steam engine or ship. ● verb (**-ll-**; US **-l-**) (cause to) move (as) through funnel.

**funny** /'fʌnɪ/ adjective (**-ier, -iest**) amusing, comical; strange. □ **funny bone** part of elbow over which very sensitive nerve passes. □ **funnily** adverb.

**fur** ● noun short fine animal hair; hide with fur on it; garment of or lined with this; coating inside kettle etc. ● verb (**-rr-**) (esp. as **furred** adjective) line or trim with fur; (often + up) (of kettle etc.) become coated with fur.

**furbelow** /'fɜ:bɪləʊ/ noun (in plural) showy ornaments.

**furbish** /'fɜ:bɪʃ/ verb (often + up) refurbish.

**furcate** /'fɜ:keɪt/ ● adjective forked, branched. ● verb (**-ting**) fork, divide. □ **furcation** noun.

**furious** /'fjʊərɪəs/ adjective very angry, raging, frantic. □ **furiously** adverb.

**furl** verb roll up (sail, umbrella); become furled.

**furlong** /'fɜːlɒŋ/ noun eighth of mile.

**furlough** /'fɜːləʊ/ noun leave of absence.

**furnace** /'fɜːnɪs/ noun chamber for intense heating by fire; very hot place.

**furnish** /'fɜːnɪʃ/ verb provide with furniture; (often + with) supply; (as **furnished** adjective) let with furniture. □ **furnishings** plural noun.

**furniture** /'fɜːnɪtʃə/ noun movable contents of building or room; ship's equipment; accessories, e.g. handles and locks.

**furore** /fjʊə'rɔːrɪ/ noun (US **furor** /'fjʊərɔː/) uproar; enthusiasm.

**furrier** /'fʌrɪə/ noun dealer in or dresser of furs.

**furrow** /'fʌrəʊ/ ● noun narrow trench made by plough; rut; wrinkle. ● verb plough; make furrows in.

**furry** /'fɜːrɪ/ adjective (-ier, -iest) like or covered with fur.

**further** /'fɜːðə/ ● adverb (also **farther** /'fɑːðə/) more distant in space or time; more, to greater extent; in addition. ● adjective (also **farther** /'fɑːðə/) more distant or advanced; more, additional. ● verb promote, favour. □ **further education** education for people above school age; **furthermore** in addition, besides.

**furtherance** noun furthering of scheme etc.

**furthest** /'fɜːðɪst/ (also **farthest** /'fɑːðɪst/) ● adjective most distant. ● adverb to or at the greatest distance.

**furtive** /'fɜːtɪv/ adjective sly, stealthy. □ **furtively** adverb.

**fury** /'fjʊərɪ/ noun (plural **-ies**) wild and passionate anger; violence (of storm etc.); (**Fury**) (usually in plural) avenging goddess; angry woman.

**furze** noun gorse. □ **furzy** adjective (-ier, -iest).

**fuse**[1] /fjuːz/ ● verb (-sing) melt with intense heat; blend by melting; supply with fuse; fail due to melting of fuse; cause fuse(s) of to melt. ● noun easily melted wire in circuit, designed to melt when circuit is overloaded.

**fuse**[2] /fjuːz/ noun combustible device for igniting bomb etc. ● verb (-sing) fit fuse to.

**fuselage** /'fjuːzəlɑːʒ/ noun body of aircraft.

**fusible** /'fjuːzɪb(ə)l/ adjective that can be melted. □ **fusibility** noun.

**fusilier** /fjuːzɪ'lɪə/ noun soldier of any of several regiments formerly armed with light muskets.

**fusillade** /fjuːzɪ'leɪd/ noun continuous discharge of firearms or outburst of criticism etc.

**fusion** /'fjuːʒ(ə)n/ noun fusing; blending, coalition; nuclear fusion.

**fuss** ● noun excited commotion; bustle; excessive concern about trivial thing; sustained protest. ● verb behave with nervous concern; agitate, worry. □ **fusspot** colloquial person given to fussing; **make a fuss** complain vigorously; **make a fuss of, over** treat affectionately.

**fussy** adjective (-ier, -iest) inclined to fuss; over-elaborate; fastidious.

**fustian** /'fʌstɪən/ noun thick usually dark twilled cotton cloth; bombast.

**fusty** /'fʌstɪ/ adjective (-ier, -iest) musty, stuffy; antiquated.

**futile** /'fjuːtaɪl/ adjective useless, ineffectual. □ **futility** /-'tɪl-/ noun.

**futon** /'fuːtɒn/ noun Japanese mattress used as bed; this with frame, convertible into couch.

**future** /'fjuːtʃə/ ● adjective about to happen, be, or become; of time to come; Grammar (of tense) describing event yet to happen. ● noun time to come; future condition or events etc.; prospect of success etc.; Grammar future tense; (in plural) (on stock exchange) goods etc. sold for future delivery. □ **future perfect** Grammar tense giving sense 'will have done'.

**futurism** noun 20th-c. artistic movement celebrating technology etc. □ **futurist** adjective & noun.

**futuristic** /fjuːtʃə'rɪstɪk/ adjective suitable for the future; ultra-modern; of futurism.

**futurity** /fjuː'tjʊərɪtɪ/ noun (plural **-ies**) literary future time, events, etc.

**fuzz** noun fluff; fluffy or frizzy hair; (**the fuzz**) slang police (officer).

**fuzzy** /'fʌzɪ/ adjective (-ier, -iest) fluffy; blurred, indistinct.

# Gg

**G** □ **G-man** *US colloquial* FBI special agent; **G-string** narrow strip of cloth etc. attached to string round waist for covering genitals.

**g** *abbreviation* (also **g.**) gram(s).

**gab** *noun colloquial* talk, chatter.

**gabardine** /ˈɡæbədiːn/ *noun* a strong twilled cloth.

**gabble** /ˈɡæb(ə)l/ ● *verb* (**-ling**) talk or utter unintelligibly or too fast. ● *noun* rapid talk.

**gaberdine** = GABARDINE.

**gable** /ˈɡeɪb(ə)l/ *noun* triangular part of wall at end of ridged roof. □ **gabled** *adjective*.

**gad** *verb* (**-dd-**) (+ *about*) go about idly or in search of pleasure. □ **gadabout** person who gads about.

**gadfly** /ˈɡædflaɪ/ *noun* (*plural* **-ies**) fly that bites cattle.

**gadget** /ˈɡædʒɪt/ *noun* small mechanical device or tool. □ **gadgetry** *noun*.

**Gael** /ɡeɪl/ *noun* Scottish or Gaelic-speaking Celt.

**Gaelic** /ˈɡeɪlɪk/ ● *noun* Celtic language of Scots (also /ˈɡælɪk/) or Irish. ● *adjective* of Gaelic or Gaelic-speaking people.

**gaff**[1] ● *noun* stick with hook for landing fish; barbed fishing-spear. ● *verb* seize (fish) with gaff.

**gaff**[2] *noun slang* □ **blow the gaff** let out secret.

**gaffe** /ɡæf/ *noun* blunder, tactless mistake.

**gaffer** /ˈɡæfə/ *noun* old man; *colloquial* foreman, boss; chief electrician in film unit.

**gag** ● *noun* thing thrust into or tied across mouth to prevent speech etc.; joke or comic scene. ● *verb* (**-gg-**) apply gag to; silence; choke, retch; make jokes.

**gaga** /ˈɡɑːɡɑː/ *adjective slang* senile; crazy.

**gage**[1] *noun* pledge, security; challenge.

**gage**[2] *US* = GAUGE.

**gaggle** /ˈɡæɡ(ə)l/ *noun* flock (of geese); *colloquial* disorganized group.

**gaiety** /ˈɡeɪətɪ/ *noun* (*US* **gayety**) being gay, mirth; merrymaking; bright appearance.

**gaily** /ˈɡeɪlɪ/ *adverb* in a gay way.

**gain** ● *verb* obtain, win; acquire, earn; (often + *in*) increase, improve; benefit; (of clock etc.) become fast (by); reach; (often + *on, upon*) get closer to (person or thing one is following). ● *noun* increase (of wealth), profit; (in *plural*) money made in trade etc.

**gainful** /ˈɡeɪnfʊl/ *adjective* paid, lucrative. □ **gainfully** *adverb*.

**gainsay** /ɡeɪnˈseɪ/ *verb* deny, contradict.

**gait** *noun* manner of walking or proceeding.

**gaiter** /ˈɡeɪtə/ *noun* covering of leather etc. for lower leg.

**gal.** *abbreviation* gallon(s).

**gala** /ˈɡɑːlə/ *noun* festive occasion or gathering.

**galactic** /ɡəˈlæktɪk/ *adjective* of galaxy.

**galantine** /ˈɡæləntiːn/ *noun* cold dish of meat boned, spiced, and covered in jelly.

**galaxy** /ˈɡæləksɪ/ *noun* (*plural* **-ies**) independent system of stars etc. in space; (**the Galaxy**) Milky Way; (+ *of*) gathering of beautiful or famous people.

**gale** *noun* strong wind; outburst, esp. of laughter.

**gall**[1] /ɡɔːl/ *noun colloquial* impudence; rancour; bile. □ **gall bladder** bodily organ containing bile; **gallstone** small hard mass that forms in gall bladder.

**gall**[2] /ɡɔːl/ ● *noun* sore made by chafing; (cause of) vexation; place rubbed bare. ● *verb* rub sore; vex, humiliate.

**gall**[3] /ɡɔːl/ *noun* growth produced on tree etc. by insect etc.

**gallant** /ˈɡælənt/ ● *adjective* brave; fine, stately; (/ɡəˈlænt/) attentive to women. ● *noun* (/ɡəˈlænt/) ladies' man. □ **gallantly** *adverb*.

**gallantry** /ˈɡæləntrɪ/ *noun* (*plural* **-ies**) bravery; courteousness to women; polite act or speech.

**galleon** /ˈgælɪən/ *noun historical* (usually Spanish) warship.

**galleria** /gæləˈriːə/ *noun* group of small shops, cafés, etc. under one roof.

**gallery** /ˈgælərɪ/ *noun* (*plural* **-ies**) room etc. for showing works of art; balcony, esp. in church, hall, etc.; highest balcony in theatre; covered walk, colonnade; passage, corridor.

**galley** /ˈgælɪ/ *noun* (*plural* **-s**) *historical* long flat one-decked vessel usually rowed by slaves or criminals; ship's or aircraft's kitchen; (in full **galley proof**) printer's proof before division into pages.

**Gallic** /ˈgælɪk/ *adjective* (typically) French; of Gaul or Gauls.

**Gallicism** /ˈgælɪsɪz(ə)m/ *noun* French idiom.

**gallimimus** /gælɪˈmaɪməs/ *noun* (*plural* **-muses**) medium-sized dinosaur that ran fast on two legs.

**gallinaceous** /gælɪˈneɪʃəs/ *adjective* of order of birds including domestic poultry.

**gallivant** /ˈgælɪvænt/ *verb colloquial* gad about.

**gallon** /ˈgælən/ *noun* measure of capacity (4.546 litres).

**gallop** /ˈgæləp/ ● *noun* horse's fastest pace; ride at this pace. ● *verb* (**-p-**) (cause to) go at gallop; talk etc. fast; progress rapidly.

**gallows** /ˈgæləʊz/ *plural noun* (usually treated as *singular*) structure for hanging criminals.

**Gallup poll** /ˈgæləp/ *noun* kind of opinion poll.

**galore** /gəˈlɔː/ *adverb* in plenty.

**galosh** /gəˈlɒʃ/ *noun* waterproof overshoe.

**galumph** /gəˈlʌmf/ *verb colloquial* (esp. as **galumphing** *adjective*) move noisily or clumsily.

**galvanic** /gælˈvænɪk/ *adjective* producing an electric current by chemical action; (of electric current) produced thus; stimulating, full of energy.

**galvanize** /ˈgælvənaɪz/ *verb* (also **-ise**) (**-zing** or **-sing**) (often + *into*) rouse by shock; stimulate (as) by electricity; coat (iron, steel) with zinc to protect from rust.

**galvanometer** /gælvəˈnɒmɪtə/ *noun* instrument for measuring electric currents.

**gambit** /ˈgæmbɪt/ *noun Chess* opening with sacrifice of pawn etc.; trick, device.

**gamble** /ˈgæmb(ə)l/ ● *verb* (**-ling**) play games of chance for money; bet (sum of money); (often + *away*) lose by gambling. ● *noun* risky undertaking; spell of gambling. □ **gambler** *noun*.

**gambol** /ˈgæmb(ə)l/ ● *verb* (**-ll-**; *US* **-l-**) jump about playfully. ● *noun* caper.

**game¹** ● *noun* form or period of play or sport, esp. competitive one organized with rules; portion of play forming scoring unit; (in *plural*) athletic contests; piece of fun, (in *plural*) tricks; *colloquial* scheme, activity; wild animals or birds etc. hunted for sport or food; their flesh as food. ● *adjective* spirited, eager. ● *verb* (**-ming**) gamble for money. □ **gamekeeper** person employed to breed and protect game; **gamesmanship** art of winning games by psychological means. □ **gamely** *adverb*.

**game²** *adjective colloquial* (of leg etc.) crippled.

**gamete** /ˈgæmiːt/ *noun* mature germ cell uniting with another in sexual reproduction.

**gamin** /ˈgæmɪn/ *noun* street urchin; impudent child.

**gamine** /gæˈmiːn/ *noun* girl gamin; attractively mischievous or boyish girl.

**gamma** /ˈgæmə/ *noun* third letter of Greek alphabet (Γ, γ). □ **gamma rays** very short X-rays emitted by radioactive substances.

**gammon** /ˈgæmən/ *noun* back end of side of bacon, including leg.

**gammy** /ˈgæmɪ/ *adjective* (**-ier**, **-iest**) *slang* (of leg etc.) crippled.

**gamut** /ˈgæmət/ *noun* entire range or scope. □ **run the gamut of** experience or perform complete range of.

**gamy** /ˈgeɪmɪ/ *adjective* (**-ier**, **-iest**) smelling or tasting like high game.

**gander** /ˈgændə/ *noun* male goose.

**gang** ● *noun* set of associates, esp. for criminal purposes; set of workers, slaves, or prisoners. ● *verb colloquial* (+ *up with*) act together with; (+ *up on*) combine against.

**ganger** /'gæŋə/ noun foreman of gang of workers.

**gangling** /'gæŋglɪŋ/ adjective (of person) tall and thin, lanky.

**ganglion** /'gæŋglɪən/ noun (plural **ganglia** or **-s**) knot on nerve containing assemblage of nerve cells.

**gangly** adjective (**-ier, -iest**) gangling.

**gangplank** /'gæŋplæŋk/ noun plank for walking on to or off boat etc.

**gangrene** /'gæŋgriːn/ noun death of body tissue, usually caused by obstruction of circulation. □ **gangrenous** adjective.

**gangster** /'gæŋstə/ noun member of gang of violent criminals.

**gangue** /gæŋ/ noun valueless part of ore deposit.

**gangway** noun passage, esp. between rows of seats; opening in ship's bulwarks; bridge.

**gannet** /'gænɪt/ noun large seabird; slang greedy person.

**gantry** /'gæntrɪ/ noun (plural **-ies**) structure supporting travelling crane, railway or road signals, rocket-launching equipment, etc.

**gaol** etc. = JAIL etc.

**gap** noun empty space, interval; deficiency; breach in hedge, wall, etc.; wide divergence.

**gape** ● verb (**-ping**) open mouth wide; be or become wide open; (+ at) stare at. ● noun open-mouthed stare; opening.

**garage** /'gæraːdʒ/ ● noun building for keeping vehicle(s) in; establishment selling petrol etc. or repairing and selling vehicles. ● verb (**-ging**) put or keep in garage.

**garb** ● noun clothing, esp. of distinctive kind. ● verb dress.

**garbage** /'gɑːbɪdʒ/ noun US refuse; colloquial nonsense.

**garble** /'gɑːb(ə)l/ verb (**-ling**) (esp. as **garbled** adjective) distort or confuse (facts, statements, etc.).

**garden** /'gɑːd(ə)n/ ● noun piece of ground for growing flowers, fruit, or vegetables, or for recreation; (esp. in plural) public pleasure-grounds. ● verb cultivate or tend garden. □ **garden centre** place selling plants and garden equipment. □ **gardener** noun; **gardening** noun.

**gardenia** /gɑːˈdiːnɪə/ noun tree or shrub with fragrant flowers.

**gargantuan** /gɑːˈgæntjʊən/ adjective gigantic.

**gargle** /'gɑːg(ə)l/ ● verb (**-ling**) rinse (throat) with liquid kept in motion by breath. ● noun liquid so used.

**gargoyle** /'gɑːgɔɪl/ noun grotesque carved spout projecting from gutter of building.

**garish** /'geərɪʃ/ adjective obtrusively bright, gaudy. □ **garishly** adverb; **garishness** noun.

**garland** /'gɑːlənd/ ● noun wreath of flowers etc. as decoration. ● verb adorn or crown with garland(s).

**garlic** /'gɑːlɪk/ noun plant with pungent bulb used in cookery. □ **garlicky** adjective colloquial.

**garment** /'gɑːmənt/ noun article of dress.

**garner** /'gɑːnə/ ● verb collect, store. ● noun storehouse for corn etc.

**garnet** /'gɑːnɪt/ noun glassy mineral, esp. red kind used as gem.

**garnish** /'gɑːnɪʃ/ ● verb decorate (esp. food). ● noun decoration, esp. to food.

**garret** /'gærɪt/ noun room, esp. small, cold, etc. immediately under roof.

**garrison** /'gærɪs(ə)n/ ● noun troops stationed in town. ● verb (**-n-**) provide with or occupy as garrison.

**garrotte** /gəˈrɒt/ (also **garotte**, US **garrote**) ● verb (**garrotting**, US **garroting**) execute by strangulation, esp. with wire collar. ● noun device for this.

**garrulous** /'gærələs/ adjective talkative. □ **garrulity** /gəˈruːlɪtɪ/ noun; **garrulousness** noun.

**garter** /'gɑːtə/ noun band to keep sock or stocking up; (**the Garter**) (badge of) highest order of English knighthood. □ **garter stitch** plain knitting stitch.

**gas** /gæs/ ● noun (plural **-es**) any airlike substance (i.e. not liquid or solid); such substance (esp. coal gas or natural gas) used as fuel; gas used as anaesthetic; poisonous gas used in war; US colloquial petrol; slang empty talk, boasting; slang amusing thing or person. ● verb (**gases, gassed, gassing**) expose to gas, esp. to kill; colloquial talk emptily or boastfully. □ **gasbag** slang empty talker; **gas**

**chamber** room filled with poisonous gas to kill people or animals; **gasholder** gasometer; **gas mask** respirator for protection against harmful gases; **gas ring** ring pierced with gas jet(s) for cooking etc.; **gasworks** place where gas is manufactured.

**gaseous** /'gæsɪəs/ *adjective* of or as gas.

**gash** ●*noun* long deep cut or wound. ●*verb* make gash in.

**gasify** /'gæsɪfaɪ/ *verb* (**-ies**, **-ied**) convert into gas. □ **gasification** *noun*.

**gasket** /'gæskɪt/ *noun* sheet or ring of rubber etc. to seal joint between metal surfaces.

**gasoline** /'gæsəliːn/ *noun* (also **gasolene**) *US* petrol.

**gasometer** /gæ'sɒmɪtə/ *noun* large tank from which gas is distributed.

**gasp** /gɑːsp/ ●*verb* catch breath with open mouth; utter with gasps. ●*noun* convulsive catching of breath.

**gassy** /'gæsɪ/ *adjective* (**-ier**, **-iest**) of, like, or full of gas; *colloquial* verbose.

**gastric** /'gæstrɪk/ *adjective* of stomach. □ **gastric flu** *colloquial* intestinal disorder of unknown cause; **gastric juice** digestive fluid secreted by stomach glands.

**gastritis** /gæ'straɪtɪs/ *noun* inflammation of stomach.

**gastroenteritis** /ˌgæstrəʊentə'raɪtɪs/ *noun* inflammation of stomach and intestines.

**gastronome** /'gæstrənəʊm/ *noun* gourmet. □ **gastronomic** /-'nɒm-/ *adjective*; **gastronomical** /-'nɒm-/ *adjective*; **gastronomically** /-'nɒm-/ *adverb*; **gastronomy** /-'strɒn-/ *noun*.

**gastropod** /'gæstrəpɒd/ *noun* mollusc that moves using underside of abdomen, e.g. snail.

**gate** *noun* barrier, usually hinged, used to close opening in wall, fence, etc.; such opening; means of entrance or exit; numbered place of access to aircraft at airport; device regulating passage of water in lock etc.; number of people paying to enter stadium etc., money thus taken. □ **gateleg (table)** table with legs in gateleg frame for supporting folding flaps; **gatepost** post at either side of gate; **gateway**

opening closed by gate, means of access.

**gateau** /'gætəʊ/ *noun* (*plural* **-s** or **-x** /-z/) large rich elaborate cake.

**gatecrash** *verb* attend (party etc.) uninvited. □ **gatecrasher** *noun*.

**gather** /'gæðə/ ●*verb* bring or come together; collect (harvest, dust, etc.); infer, deduce; increase (speed); summon up (energy etc.); draw together in folds or wrinkles; (of boil etc.) come to a head. ●*noun* fold or pleat.

**gathering** *noun* assembly; pus-filled swelling.

**GATT** /gæt/ *abbreviation* General Agreement on Tariffs and Trade.

**gauche** /gəʊʃ/ *adjective* socially awkward, tactless. □ **gauchely** *adverb*; **gaucheness** *noun*.

**gaucho** /'gaʊtʃəʊ/ *noun* (*plural* **-s**) cowboy in S. American pampas.

**gaudy** /'gɔːdɪ/ *adjective* (**-ier**, **-iest**) tastelessly showy. □ **gaudily** *adverb*; **gaudiness** *noun*.

**gauge** /geɪdʒ/ (*US* **gage**) ●*noun* standard measure; instrument for measuring; distance between rails or opposite wheels; capacity, extent; criterion, test. ●*verb* (**-ging**) measure exactly; measure contents of; estimate.

**Gaul** /gɔːl/ *noun* inhabitant of ancient Gaul. □ **Gaulish** *adjective & noun*.

**gaunt** /gɔːnt/ *adjective* lean, haggard, grim. □ **gauntness** *noun*.

**gauntlet**[1] /'gɔːntlɪt/ *noun* glove with long loose wrist; *historical* armoured glove.

**gauntlet**[2] /'gɔːntlɪt/ *noun* □ **run the gauntlet** undergo criticism, pass between two rows of people wielding sticks etc., as punishment.

**gauze** /gɔːz/ *noun* thin transparent fabric; fine mesh of wire etc. □ **gauzy** *adjective* (**-ier**, **-iest**).

**gave** *past of* GIVE.

**gavel** /'gæv(ə)l/ *noun* auctioneer's, chairman's, or judge's hammer.

**gavotte** /gə'vɒt/ *noun* 18th-c. French dance; music for this.

**gawk** ●*verb colloquial* gawp. ●*noun* awkward or bashful person. □ **gawky** *adjective* (**-ier**, **-iest**).

**gawp** *verb colloquial* stare stupidly.

**gay** ● *adjective* light-hearted, cheerful; showy; homosexual; *colloquial* carefree. ● *noun* (esp. male) homosexual.

**gayety** *US* = GAIETY.

**gaze** ● *verb* (**-zing**) (+ *at*, *into*, *on*, etc.) look fixedly. ● *noun* intent look.

**gazebo** /gə'zi:bəʊ/ *noun* (*plural* **-s**) summerhouse etc. giving view.

**gazelle** /gə'zel/ *noun* (*plural* same or **-s**) small graceful antelope.

**gazette** /gə'zet/ ● *noun* newspaper; official publication. ● *verb* (**-tting**) publish in official gazette.

**gazetteer** /gæzɪ'tɪə/ *noun* geographical index.

**gazump** /gə'zʌmp/ *verb colloquial* raise price after accepting offer from (buyer); swindle.

**gazunder** /gə'zʌndə/ *verb colloquial* lower an offer made to (seller) just before exchange of contracts.

**GB** *abbreviation* Great Britain.

**GBH** *abbreviation* grievous bodily harm.

**GC** *abbreviation* George Cross.

**GCE** *abbreviation* General Certificate of Education.

**GCSE** *abbreviation* General Certificate of Secondary Education.

**GDR** *abbreviation historical* German Democratic Republic.

**gear** /gɪə/ ● *noun* (often in *plural*) set of toothed wheels working together, esp. those connecting engine to road wheels; particular setting of these; equipment; *colloquial* clothing. ● *verb* (+ *to*) adjust or adapt to; (often + *up*) equip with gears; (+ *up*) make ready. □ **gearbox** (case enclosing) gears of machine or vehicle; **gear lever** lever moved to engage or change gear; **in gear** with gear engaged.

**gecko** /'gekəʊ/ *noun* (*plural* **-s**) tropical house-lizard.

**gee** /dʒi:/ *interjection expressing surprise* etc.

**geese** *plural* of GOOSE.

**geezer** /'gi:zə/ *noun slang* man, esp. old one.

**Geiger counter** /'gaɪgə/ *noun* instrument for measuring radioactivity.

**geisha** /'geɪʃə/ *noun* (*plural* same or **-s**) Japanese professional hostess and entertainer.

**gel** /dʒel/ ● *noun* semi-solid jelly-like colloid; jelly-like substance for hair. ● *verb* (**-ll-**) form gel; jell.

**gelatin** /'dʒelətɪn/ *noun* (also **gelatine** /-ti:n/) transparent tasteless substance used in cookery, photography, etc. □ **gelatinous** /dʒɪ'læt-/ *adjective*.

**geld** /geld/ *verb* castrate.

**gelding** /'geldɪŋ/ *noun* castrated horse etc.

**gelignite** /'dʒelɪgnaɪt/ *noun* nitroglycerine explosive.

**gem** /dʒem/ ● *noun* precious stone; thing or person of great beauty or worth. ● *verb* (**-mm-**) adorn (as) with gems.

**Gemini** /'dʒemɪnaɪ/ *noun* third sign of zodiac.

**Gen.** *abbreviation* General.

**gen** /dʒen/ *slang* ● *noun* information. ● *verb* (**-nn-**) (+ *up*) gain or give information.

**gendarme** /'ʒɒndɑːm/ *noun* police officer in France etc.

**gender** /'dʒendə/ *noun* (grammatical) classification roughly corresponding to the two sexes and sexlessness; one of these classes; person's sex.

**gene** /dʒi:n/ *noun* unit in chromosome, controlling particular inherited characteristic.

**genealogy** /dʒi:nɪ'ælədʒɪ/ *noun* (*plural* **-ies**) descent traced continuously from ancestor, pedigree; study of pedigrees. □ **genealogical** /-ə'lɒdʒ-/ *adjective*; **genealogically** /-ə'lɒdʒ-/ *adverb*; **genealogist** *noun*.

**genera** *plural* of GENUS.

**general** /'dʒenər(ə)l/ ● *adjective* including, affecting, or applicable to (nearly) all; prevalent, usual; vague; not partial or particular; lacking detail; chief, head. ● *noun* army officer next below Field Marshal; commander of army. □ **general anaesthetic** one affecting whole body; **general election** national election of representatives to parliament; **general practice** work of general practitioner, doctor treating cases of all kinds; **general strike** simultaneous strike of workers in all or most trades; **in general** as a rule, usually.

**generalissimo** /dʒenərə'lɪsɪməʊ/ *noun* (*plural* **-s**) commander of combined forces.

**generality** /dʒenəˈrælɪtɪ/ noun (plural **-ies**) general statement; general applicability; indefiniteness; (+ *of*) majority of.

**generalize** /ˈdʒenərəlaɪz/ verb (also **-ise**) (**-zing** or **-sing**) speak in general or indefinite terms, form general notion(s); reduce to general statement; infer (rule etc.) from particular cases; bring into general use. □ **generalization** noun.

**generally** /ˈdʒenərəlɪ/ adverb usually; in most respects; in general sense; in most cases.

**generate** /ˈdʒenəreɪt/ verb (**-ting**) bring into existence, produce.

**generation** noun all people born about same time; stage in family history or in (esp. technological) development; period of about 30 years; production, esp. of electricity; procreation.

**generative** /ˈdʒenərətɪv/ adjective of procreation; productive.

**generator** noun dynamo; apparatus for producing gas, steam, etc.

**generic** /dʒɪˈnerɪk/ adjective characteristic of or relating to class or genus; not specific or special; (of esp. drug) with no brand name. □ **generically** adverb.

**generous** /ˈdʒenərəs/ adjective giving or given freely; magnanimous; abundant. □ **generosity** /-ˈrɒs-/ noun; **generously** adverb.

**genesis** /ˈdʒenɪsɪs/ noun origin, mode of formation; (**Genesis**) first book of Old Testament.

**genetic** /dʒɪˈnetɪk/ adjective of genetics; of or in origin. □ **genetic engineering** manipulation of DNA to modify hereditary features; **genetic fingerprinting** identification of individuals by DNA patterns. □ **genetically** adverb.

**genetics** plural noun (treated as *singular*) study of heredity and variation among animals and plants. □ **geneticist** /-sɪst/ noun.

**genial** /ˈdʒiːnɪəl/ adjective sociable, kindly; mild, warm; cheering. □ **geniality** /-ˈæl-/ noun; **genially** adverb.

**genie** /ˈdʒiːnɪ/ noun (plural **genii** /-nɪaɪ/) sprite or goblin of Arabian tales.

**genital** /ˈdʒenɪt(ə)l/ ● adjective of animal reproduction or reproductive organs.

● noun (in *plural*, also **genitalia**) external reproductive organs.

**genitive** /ˈdʒenɪtɪv/ Grammar ● noun case expressing possession, origin, etc., corresponding to *of*, *from*, etc. ● adjective of or in this case.

**genius** /ˈdʒiːnɪəs/ noun (plural **-es**) exceptional natural ability; person having this; guardian spirit.

**genocide** /ˈdʒenəsaɪd/ noun mass murder, esp. among particular race or nation.

**genre** /ˈʒɑːrə/ noun kind or style of art etc.; portrayal of scenes from ordinary life.

**gent** /dʒent/ noun colloquial gentleman; (**the Gents**) colloquial men's public lavatory.

**genteel** /dʒenˈtiːl/ adjective affectedly refined; upper-class.

**gentian** /ˈdʒenʃ(ə)n/ noun mountain plant with usually blue flowers. □ **gentian violet** violet dye used as antiseptic.

**Gentile** /ˈdʒentaɪl/ ● adjective not Jewish; heathen. ● noun non-Jewish person.

**gentility** /dʒenˈtɪlɪtɪ/ noun social superiority; genteel habits.

**gentle** /ˈdʒent(ə)l/ adjective (**-r**, **-st**) not rough or severe; mild, kind; well-born; quiet. □ **gentleness** noun; **gently** adverb.

**gentlefolk** /ˈdʒent(ə)lfəʊk/ noun people of good family.

**gentleman** /ˈdʒentəlmən/ noun man; chivalrous well-bred man; man of good social position. □ **gentlemanly** adjective.

**gentlewoman** noun archaic woman of good birth or breeding.

**gentrification** /dʒentrɪfɪˈkeɪʃ(ə)n/ noun upgrading of working-class urban area by arrival of affluent residents. □ **gentrify** verb (**-ies**, **-ied**).

**gentry** /ˈdʒentrɪ/ plural noun people next below nobility; derogatory people.

**genuflect** /ˈdʒenjuːflekt/ verb bend knee, esp. in worship. □ **genuflection**, **genuflexion** /-ˈflekʃ(ə)n/ noun.

**genuine** /ˈdʒenjuːɪn/ adjective really coming from its reputed source; properly so called; not sham. □ **genuinely** adverb; **genuineness** noun.

**genus** · /ˈdʒiːnəs/ noun (plural **genera** /ˈdʒenərə/) group of animals or plants with common structural character-istics, usually containing several species; kind, class.

**geocentric** /dʒiːə'sentrɪk/ *adjective* considered as viewed from earth's centre; having earth as centre.

**geode** /'dʒiːəʊd/ *noun* cavity lined with crystals; rock containing this.

**geodesic** /dʒiːəʊ'diːzɪk/ *adjective* (also **geodetic** /-'det-/) of geodesy. □ **geodesic line** shortest possible line on surface between two points.

**geodesy** /dʒiː'ɒdɪsɪ/ *noun* study of shape and area of the earth.

**geography** /dʒɪ'ɒɡrəfɪ/ *noun* science of earth's physical features, resources, etc.; features of place. □ **geographer** *noun*, **geographic(al)** /-ə'ɡræf-/ *adjective*; **geographically** /-ə'ɡræf-/ *adverb*.

**geology** /dʒɪ'ɒlədʒɪ/ *noun* science of earth's crust, strata, etc. □ **geological** /-ə'lɒdʒ-/ *adjective*; **geologist** *noun*.

**geometry** /dʒɪ'ɒmɪtrɪ/ *noun* science of properties and relations of lines, surfaces, and solids. □ **geometric(al)** /-ə'met-/ *adjective*; **geometrician** /-'trɪ-ʃ(ə)n/ *noun*.

**Geordie** /'dʒɔːdɪ/ *noun* native of Tyneside.

**georgette** /dʒɔː'dʒet/ *noun* kind of fine dress material.

**Georgian** /'dʒɔːdʒ(ə)n/ *adjective* of time of George I–IV or George V and VI.

**geranium** /dʒə'reɪnɪəm/ *noun* (*plural* **-s**) cultivated pelargonium; herb or shrub with fruit shaped like crane's bill.

**gerbil** /'dʒɜːbɪl/ *noun* mouselike desert rodent with long hind legs.

**geriatric** /dʒerɪ'ætrɪk/ ● *adjective* of geriatrics or old people; *derogatory* old. ● *noun* often *derogatory* old person.

**geriatrics** /dʒerɪ'ætrɪks/ *plural noun* (usually treated as *singular*) branch of medicine dealing with health and care of old people. □ **geriatrician** /-ə'trɪʃ(ə)n/ *noun*.

**germ** /dʒɜːm/ *noun* microbe; portion of organism capable of developing into new one; thing that may develop; rudiment, elementary principle.

**German** /'dʒɜːmən/ ● *noun* (*plural* **-s**) native, national, or language of Germany. ● *adjective* of Germany. □ **German measles** disease like mild measles; **German shepherd (dog)** Alsatian.

**german** /'dʒɜːmən/ *adjective* (placed after *brother*, *sister*, or *cousin*) having same two parents or grandparents.

**germander** /dʒɜː'mændə/ *noun* plant of mint family.

**germane** /dʒɜː'meɪn/ *adjective* (usually + *to*) relevant.

**Germanic** /dʒɜː'mænɪk/ ● *adjective* having German characteristics. ● *noun* group of languages including English, German, Dutch, and Scandinavian languages.

**germicide** /'dʒɜːmɪsaɪd/ *noun* substance that destroys germs. □ **germicidal** /-'saɪd(ə)l/ *adjective*.

**germinal** /'dʒɜːmɪn(ə)l/ *adjective* of germs; in earliest stage of development.

**germinate** /'dʒɜːmɪneɪt/ *verb* (**-ting**) (cause to) sprout or bud. □ **germination** *noun*.

**gerontology** /dʒerɒn'tɒlədʒɪ/ *noun* study of old age and ageing.

**gerrymander** /'dʒerɪmændə/ *verb* manipulate boundaries of (constituency etc.) to gain unfair electoral advantage.

**gerund** /'dʒerənd/ *noun* verbal noun, in English ending in *-ing*.

**Gestapo** /ge'stɑːpəʊ/ *noun historical* Nazi secret police.

**gestation** /dʒe'steɪʃ(ə)n/ *noun* carrying or being carried in womb between conception and birth; this period; development of plan etc. □ **gestate** *verb* (**-ting**).

**gesticulate** /dʒe'stɪkjʊleɪt/ *verb* (**-ting**) use gestures instead of or with speech. □ **gesticulation** *noun*.

**gesture** /'dʒestʃə/ ● *noun* meaningful movement of limb or body; action performed as courtesy or to indicate intention. ● *verb* (**-ring**) gesticulate.

**get** /get/ *verb* (**getting**; *past* **got**; *past participle* **got** or *US* **gotten**) obtain, earn; fetch, procure; go to reach or catch; prepare (meal); (cause to) reach some state or become; obtain from calculation; contract (disease); contact; have (punishment) inflicted on one; succeed in bringing, placing, etc.; (cause to) succeed in coming or going; *colloquial* understand, annoy, harm, attract; *archaic* beget. □ **get about** go from place to place; **get across** communicate; **get along** (often + *with*) live harmoniously; **get around** = GET ABOUT; **get at** reach, get hold of, *colloquial* imply, *colloquial* nag; **get away** escape; **getaway** *noun*; **get by** *colloquial* cope; **get in** obtain place at college etc., win election; **get off** alight (from), *colloquial* escape with little or no punishment, start, depart, (+ *with*) *colloquial* start sexual relationship with; **get on** make progress, manage, advance, enter (bus etc.), (often + *with*) live harmoniously, (usually as **be getting on**) age; **get out of** avoid, escape; **get over** recover from, surmount; **get round** coax or cajole (person), evade (law etc.), (+ *to*) deal with (task) in due course; **get through** pass (exam etc.), use up (resources), make contact by telephone, (+ *to*) succeed in making (person) understand; **get-together** *colloquial* social assembly; **get up** rise esp. from bed, (of wind etc.) strengthen, organize, stimulate, arrange appearance of; **get-up** *colloquial* style of dress etc.; **have got** possess, (+ *to do*) must.

**geyser** /ˈɡiːzə/ *noun* hot spring; apparatus for heating water.

**ghastly** /ˈɡɑːstlɪ/ *adjective* (**-ier, -iest**) horrible, frightful; deathlike, pallid.

**ghee** /ɡiː/ *noun* Indian clarified butter.

**gherkin** /ˈɡɜːkɪn/ *noun* small cucumber for pickling.

**ghetto** /ˈɡetəʊ/ *noun* (*plural* **-s**) part of city occupied by minority group; *historical* Jews' quarter in city; segregated group or area. □ **ghetto-blaster** large portable radio or cassette player.

**ghost** /ɡəʊst/ ● *noun* apparition of dead person etc., disembodied spirit; (+ *of*) semblance; secondary image in defective telescope or television picture. ● *verb* (often + *for*) act as ghost-writer of (book etc.). □ **ghost-writer** writer doing work for which another takes credit. □ **ghostly** *adjective* (**-ier, -iest**).

**ghoul** /ɡuːl/ *noun* person morbidly interested in death etc.; evil spirit; (in Arabic mythology) spirit preying on corpses. □ **ghoulish** *adjective*.

**GHQ** *abbreviation* General Headquarters.

**ghyll** *noun* = GILL³.

**GI** /dʒiːˈaɪ/ *noun* soldier in US army.

**giant** /ˈdʒaɪənt/ ● *noun* mythical being of human form but superhuman size; person, animal, or thing of extraordinary size, ability, etc. ● *adjective* gigantic.

**gibber** /ˈdʒɪbə/ *verb* chatter inarticulately.

**gibberish** /ˈdʒɪbərɪʃ/ *noun* unintelligible or meaningless speech or sounds.

**gibbet** /ˈdʒɪbɪt/ *noun historical* gallows; post with arm from which executed criminal was hung after execution.

**gibbon** /ˈɡɪbən/ *noun* long-armed ape.

**gibbous** /ˈɡɪbəs/ *adjective* convex; (of moon etc.) with bright part greater than semicircle.

**gibe** /dʒaɪb/ (also **jibe**) ● *verb* (**-bing**) (often + *at*) jeer, mock. ● *noun* jeering remark, taunt.

**giblets** /ˈdʒɪblɪts/ *plural noun* liver, gizzard, etc. of bird removed and usually cooked separately.

**giddy** /ˈɡɪdɪ/ *adjective* (**-ier, -iest**) dizzy, tending to fall or stagger; mentally intoxicated; excitable, flighty; making dizzy. □ **giddiness** *noun*.

**gift** /ɡɪft/ *noun* thing given, present; talent; *colloquial* easy task.

**gifted** *adjective* talented.

**gig**¹ /ɡɪɡ/ *noun* light two-wheeled one-horse carriage; light boat on ship; rowing boat, esp. for racing.

**gig**² /ɡɪɡ/ *colloquial* ● *noun* engagement to play music, usually on one occasion. ● *verb* (**-gg-**) perform gig.

**giga-** /ˈɡɪɡə/ *combining form* one thousand million.

**gigantic** /dʒaɪˈɡæntɪk/ *adjective* huge, giant-like.

**giggle** /ˈɡɪɡ(ə)l/ ● *verb* (**-ling**) laugh in half-suppressed spasms. ● *noun* such laugh; *colloquial* amusing person or thing. □ **giggly** *adjective* (**-ier, -iest**).

**gigolo** /ˈdʒɪɡələʊ/ *noun* (*plural* **-s**) young man paid by older woman to be escort or lover.

**gild**¹ /ɡɪld/ *verb* (*past participle* **gilded** or as *adjective* **gilt**) cover thinly with gold; tinge with golden colour.

**gild**² /ɡɪld/ = GUILD.

**gill**¹ /ɡɪl/ *noun* (usually in *plural*) respiratory organ of fish etc.; vertical radial plate on underside of mushroom etc.; flesh below person's jaws and ears.

**gill**² /dʒɪl/ *noun* quarter-pint measure.

**gill**³ /ɡɪl/ *noun* (also **ghyll**) deep wooded ravine; narrow mountain torrent.

**gillie** /ˈgɪlɪ/ *noun Scottish* man or boy attending hunter or angler.

**gillyflower** /ˈdʒɪlɪflaʊə/ *noun* clove-scented flower, e.g. wallflower.

**gilt¹** /gɪlt/ ● *adjective* overlaid (as) with gold. ● *noun* gilding. □ **gilt-edged** (of securities etc.) having high degree of reliability.

**gilt²** /gɪlt/ *noun* young sow.

**gimbals** /ˈdʒɪmb(ə)lz/ *plural noun* contrivance of rings etc. for keeping things horizontal in ship, aircraft, etc.

**gimcrack** /ˈdʒɪmkræk/ ● *adjective* flimsy, tawdry. ● *noun* showy ornament etc.

**gimlet** /ˈgɪmlɪt/ *noun* small boring-tool.

**gimmick** /ˈgɪmɪk/ *noun* trick or device, esp. to attract attention. □ **gimmickry** *noun*; **gimmicky** *adjective*.

**gimp** /gɪmp/ *noun* twist of silk etc. with cord or wire running through.

**gin¹** /dʒɪn/ *noun* spirit distilled from grain or malt and flavoured with juniper berries.

**gin²** /dʒɪn/ ● *noun* snare, trap; machine separating cotton from seeds; kind of crane or windlass. ● *verb* (**-nn-**) treat (cotton) in gin; trap.

**ginger** /ˈdʒɪndʒə/ ● *noun* hot spicy root used in cooking; plant having this root; light reddish-yellow. ● *adjective* of ginger colour. ● *verb* flavour with ginger; (+ *up*) enliven. □ **ginger ale, beer** ginger-flavoured fizzy drinks; **gingerbread** ginger-flavoured treacle cake; **ginger group** group urging party or movement to stronger action; **ginger-nut** kind of ginger-flavoured biscuit. □ **gingery** *adjective*.

**gingerly** /ˈdʒɪndʒəlɪ/ ● *adverb* in a careful or cautious way. ● *adjective* showing extreme care or caution.

**gingham** /ˈgɪŋəm/ *noun* plain-woven usually checked cotton cloth.

**gingivitis** /dʒɪndʒɪˈvaɪtɪs/ *noun* inflammation of the gums.

**ginkgo** /ˈgɪŋkəʊ/ *noun* (*plural* **-s**) tree with fan-shaped leaves and yellow flowers.

**ginseng** /ˈdʒɪnseŋ/ *noun* plant found in E. Asia and N. America; medicinal root of this.

**Gipsy** = GYPSY.

**giraffe** /dʒɪˈrɑːf/ *noun* (*plural* same or **-s**) tall 4-legged African animal with long neck.

**gird** /gɜːd/ (*past & past participle* **girded** or **girt**) encircle or fasten (on) with waistbelt etc. □ **gird (up) one's loins** prepare for action.

**girder** /ˈgɜːdə/ *noun* iron or steel beam or compound structure used for bridges etc.

**girdle¹** /ˈgɜːd(ə)l/ ● *noun* belt or cord worn round waist; corset; thing that surrounds; bony support for limbs. ● *verb* (**-ling**) surround with girdle.

**girdle²** /ˈgɜːd(ə)l/ *noun Scottish & Northern English* = GRIDDLE.

**girl** /gɜːl/ *noun* female child; *colloquial* young woman; *colloquial* girlfriend; female servant. □ **girlfriend** person's regular female companion; **girl guide** Guide; **girl scout** female Scout. □ **girlhood** *noun*; **girlish** *adjective*; **girly** *adjective*.

**giro** /ˈdʒaɪrəʊ/ ● *noun* (*plural* **-s**) system of credit transfer between banks, Post Offices, etc.; cheque or payment by giro. ● *verb* (**-es, -ed**) pay by giro.

**girt** *past & past participle* of GIRD.

**girth** /gɜːθ/ *noun* distance round a thing; band round body of horse securing saddle.

**gist** /dʒɪst/ *noun* substance or essence of a matter.

**gîte** /ʒiːt/ *noun* furnished holiday house in French countryside. [French]

**give** /gɪv/ ● *verb* (**-ving**; *past* **gave**; *past participle* **given**) transfer possession of freely; provide with; administer; deliver; (often + *for*) make over in exchange or payment; confer; accord; pledge; perform (action etc.); utter, declare; yield to pressure; collapse; yield as product; consign; devote; present, offer (one's hand, arm, etc.); impart; be source of; concede; assume, grant, specify. ● *noun* capacity to comply; elasticity. □ **give and take** exchange of talk or ideas, ability to compromise; **give away** transfer as gift, hand over (bride) to bridegroom, betray or expose; **give-away** *colloquial* unintentional disclosure, free or inexpensive thing; **give in** yield, hand in; **give off** emit; **give out** announce, emit, distribute, be exhausted, run short; **give over** *colloquial* desist, hand over, devote; **give up** resign, surrender, part with, renounce hope (of), cease (activity). □ **giver** *noun*.

**given** ● *past participle* of GIVE. ● *adjective* (+ *to*) disposed or prone to; assumed as basis of reasoning etc.; fixed, specified.

**gizmo** /'gɪzməʊ/ *noun* (*plural* **-s**) gadget.

**gizzard** /'gɪzəd/ *noun* bird's second stomach, for grinding food.

**glacé** /'glæseɪ/ *adjective* (of fruit) preserved in sugar; (of cloth etc.) smooth, polished.

**glacial** /'gleɪʃ(ə)l/ *adjective* of ice or glaciers.

**glaciated** /'gleɪsɪeɪtɪd/ *adjective* marked or polished by moving ice; covered with glaciers. □ **glaciation** *noun*.

**glacier** /'glæsɪə/ *noun* slowly moving mass of ice on land.

**glad** *adjective* (**-dd-**) pleased; joyful, cheerful. □ **glad rags** *colloquial* best clothes. □ **gladden** *verb*; **gladly** *adverb*; **gladness** *noun*.

**glade** *noun* clear space in forest.

**gladiator** /'glædɪeɪtə/ *noun historical* trained fighter in ancient Roman shows. □ **gladiatorial** /-ɪə'tɔːrɪəl/ *adjective*.

**gladiolus** /glædɪ'əʊləs/ *noun* (*plural* **-li** /-laɪ/) plant of lily family with bright flower-spikes.

**gladsome** *adjective poetical* cheerful, joyful.

**Gladstone bag** /'glædstən/ *noun* kind of light portmanteau.

**glair** *noun* white of egg; similar or derivative viscous substance.

**glamour** /'glæmə/ *noun* (*US* **glamor**) physical, esp. cosmetic, attractiveness; alluring or exciting beauty or charm. □ **glamorize** *verb* (also **-ise**) (**-zing** or **-sing**); **glamorous** *adjective*; **glamorously** *adverb*.

**glance** /glɑːns/ ● *verb* (**-cing**) (often + *down*, *up*, *over*, etc.) look or refer briefly; (often + *off*) hit at fine angle and bounce off. ● *noun* brief look; flash, gleam; swift oblique stroke in cricket. □ **at a glance** immediately on looking.

**gland** *noun* organ etc. secreting substances for use in body; similar organ in plant.

**glanders** /'glændəz/ *plural noun* contagious horse disease.

**glandular** /'glændjʊlə/ *adjective* of gland(s). □ **glandular fever** infectious disease with swelling of lymph glands.

**glare** /gleə/ ● *verb* (**-ring**) look fiercely; shine oppressively; (esp. as **glaring** *adjective*) be very evident. ● *noun* oppressive light or public attention; fierce look; tawdry brilliance. □ **glaringly** *adverb*.

**glasnost** /'glæznɒst/ *noun* (in former USSR) policy of more open government.

**glass** /glɑːs/ ● *noun* hard, brittle, usually transparent substance made by fusing sand with soda and lime etc.; glass objects collectively; glass drinking vessel, its contents; glazed frame for plants; barometer; covering of watchface; lens; (in *plural*) spectacles, binoculars; mirror. ● *verb* (usually as **glassed** *adjective*) fit with glass. □ **glassblowing** blowing of semi-molten glass to make glass objects; **glass fibre** glass filaments made into fabric or reinforcing plastic; **glasshouse** greenhouse, *slang* military prison; **glass-paper** paper covered with powdered glass, for smoothing etc.; **glass wool** fine glass fibres for packing and insulation. □ **glassful** *noun* (*plural* **-s**).

**glassy** /'glɑːsɪ/ *adjective* (**-ier, -iest**) like glass; (of eye etc.) dull, fixed.

**glaucoma** /glɔː'kəʊmə/ *noun* eye disease with pressure in eyeball and gradual loss of sight.

**glaze** ● *verb* (**-zing**) fit with glass or windows; cover (pottery etc.) with vitreous substance or (surface) with smooth shiny coating; (often + *over*) (of eyes) become glassy. ● *noun* substance used for or surface produced by glazing.

**glazier** /'gleɪzɪə/ *noun* person who glazes windows etc.

**gleam** ● *noun* faint or brief light or show. ● *verb* emit gleam(s).

**glean** *verb* gather (facts etc.); gather (corn left by reapers). □ **gleanings** *plural noun*.

**glebe** *noun* piece of land yielding revenue to benefice.

**glee** *noun* mirth, delight; musical composition for several voices. □ **gleeful** *adjective*; **gleefully** *adverb*.

**glen** *noun* narrow valley.

**glengarry** /glen'gærɪ/ *noun* (*plural* **-ies**) kind of Highland cap.

**glib** *adjective* (**-bb-**) speaking or spoken fluently but insincerely. □ **glibly** *adverb*; **glibness** *noun*.

**glide** ● *verb* (**-ding**) move smoothly or continuously; (of aircraft) fly without engine-power; go stealthily. ● *noun* gliding motion.

**glider** /'glaɪdə/ *noun* light aircraft without engine.

**glimmer** /'glɪmə/ ● *verb* shine faintly or intermittently. ● *noun* faint or wavering light; (also **glimmering**) (usually + *of*) small sign.

**glimpse** /glɪmps/ ● *noun* (often + *of*, *at*) brief view; faint transient appearance. ● *verb* (**-sing**) have brief view of.

**glint** *verb & noun* flash, glitter.

**glissade** /glɪ'sɑːd/ ● *noun* controlled slide down snow slope; gliding. ● *verb* (**-ding**) perform glissade.

**glissando** /glɪ'sændəʊ/ *noun* (*plural* **-di** /-dɪ/ or **-s**) *Music* continuous slide of adjacent notes.

**glisten** /'glɪs(ə)n/ ● *verb* shine like wet or polished surface. ● *noun* glitter.

**glitch** *noun colloquial* irregularity, malfunction.

**glitter** /'glɪtə/ ● *verb* shine with brilliant reflected light, sparkle; (often + *with*) be showy. ● *noun* sparkle; showiness; tiny pieces of glittering material.

**glitz** *noun slang* showy glamour. □ **glitzy** *adjective* (**-ier**, **-iest**).

**gloaming** /'gləʊmɪŋ/ *noun* twilight.

**gloat** *verb* (often + *over* etc.) look or ponder with greedy or malicious pleasure.

**global** /'gləʊb(ə)l/ *adjective* worldwide; all-embracing. □ **global warming** increase in temperature of earth's atmosphere. □ **globally** *adverb*.

**globe** *noun* spherical object; spherical map of earth; (**the globe**) the earth. □ **globe artichoke** partly edible head of artichoke plant; **globe-trotter** person travelling widely.

**globular** /'glɒbjʊlə/ *adjective* globe-shaped; composed of globules.

**globule** /'glɒbjuːl/ *noun* small globe, round particle, or drop.

**glockenspiel** /'glɒkənspiːl/ *noun* musical instrument of bells or metal bars played with hammers.

**gloom** /gluːm/ *noun* darkness; melancholy, depression.

**gloomy** /'gluːmɪ/ *adjective* (**-ier**, **-iest**) dark; depressed, depressing.

**glorify** /'glɔːrɪfaɪ/ *verb* (**-ies**, **-ied**) make glorious; make seem more splendid than is the case; (as **glorified** *adjective*) treated as more important etc. than it is; extol. □ **glorification** *noun*.

**glorious** /'glɔːrɪəs/ *adjective* possessing or conferring glory; *colloquial* splendid, excellent. □ **gloriously** *adverb*.

**glory** /'glɔːrɪ/ ● *noun* (*plural* **-ies**) (thing bringing) renown, honourable fame, etc.; adoring praise; resplendent majesty, beauty, etc.; halo of saint. ● *verb* (**-ies**, **-ied**) (often + *in*) take pride.

**gloss**[1] ● *noun* surface lustre; deceptively attractive appearance; (in full *gloss paint*) paint giving glossy finish. ● *verb* make glossy. □ **gloss over** seek to conceal.

**gloss**[2] ● *noun* explanatory comment added to text; interpretation. ● *verb* add gloss to.

**glossary** /'glɒsərɪ/ *noun* (*plural* **-ies**) dictionary of technical or special words, esp. as appendix.

**glossy** ● *adjective* (**-ier**, **-iest**) smooth and shiny; printed on such paper. ● *noun* (*plural* **-ies**) *colloquial* glossy magazine or photograph.

**glottal** /'glɒt(ə)l/ *adjective* of the glottis. □ **glottal stop** sound produced by sudden opening or shutting of glottis.

**glottis** /'glɒtɪs/ *noun* opening at upper end of windpipe between vocal cords.

**glove** /glʌv/ ● *noun* hand-covering for protection, warmth, etc.; boxing glove. ● *verb* (**-ving**) cover or provide with gloves. □ **glove compartment** recess for small articles in car dashboard; **glove puppet** small puppet fitted on hand.

**glow** /gləʊ/ ● *verb* emit flameless light and heat; (often + *with*) feel bodily heat or strong emotion; show warm colour; (as **glowing** *adjective*) expressing pride or satisfaction. ● *noun* glowing state, appearance, or feeling. □ **glow-worm** beetle that emits green light.

**glower** /'glaʊə/ *verb* (often + *at*) scowl.

**glucose** /'gluːkəʊs/ *noun* kind of sugar found in blood, fruits, etc.

**glue** ● *noun* substance used as adhesive. ● *verb* (**glues**, **glued**, **gluing** or **glueing**) attach (as) with glue; hold closely. □ **glue ear** blocking of (esp. child's) Eustachian tube; **glue-sniffing** inhalation of fumes from adhesives as intoxicant. □ **gluey** adjective (**gluier**, **gluiest**).

**glum** adjective (**-mm-**) dejected, sullen. □ **glumly** adverb; **glumness** noun.

**glut** ● verb (**-tt-**) feed or indulge to the full, satiate; overstock. ● noun excessive supply; surfeit.

**gluten** /ˈgluːt(ə)n/ noun sticky part of wheat flour.

**glutinous** /ˈgluːtɪnəs/ adjective sticky, gluelike.

**glutton** /ˈglʌt(ə)n/ noun excessive eater; (often + for) colloquial insatiably eager person; voracious animal of weasel family. □ **gluttonous** adjective; **gluttonously** adverb; **gluttony** noun.

**glycerine** /ˈglɪsəriːn/ noun (also **glycerol**, US **glycerin**) colourless sweet viscous liquid used in medicines, explosives, etc.

**gm** abbreviation gram(s).

**GMT** abbreviation Greenwich Mean Time.

**gnarled** /nɑːld/ adjective knobbly, twisted, rugged.

**gnash** /næʃ/ verb grind (one's teeth); (of teeth) strike together.

**gnat** /næt/ noun small biting fly.

**gnaw** /nɔː/ verb (usually + away etc.) wear away by biting; (often + at, into) bite persistently; corrode; torment.

**gneiss** /naɪs/ noun coarse-grained rock of feldspar, quartz, and mica.

**gnome** /nəʊm/ noun dwarf, goblin; (esp. in plural) colloquial person with sinister influence, esp. financial.

**gnomic** /ˈnəʊmɪk/ adjective of aphorisms; sententious.

**gnomon** /ˈnəʊmɒn/ noun rod etc. on sundial, showing time by its shadow.

**gnostic** /ˈnɒstɪk/ ● adjective of knowledge; having special mystic knowledge. ● noun (**Gnostic**) early Christian heretic claiming mystical knowledge. □ **Gnosticism** /-sɪz(ə)m/ noun.

**GNP** abbreviation gross national product.

**gnu** /nuː/ noun (plural same or **-s**) oxlike antelope.

**go¹** ● verb (3rd singular present **goes** /gəʊz/; past **went**; past participle **gone** /gɒn/) walk, travel, proceed; participate in (doing

something); extend in a certain direction; depart; move, function; make specified movement or sound, colloquial say; be, become; elapse, be traversed; (of song etc.) have specified wording etc.; match; be regularly kept, fit; be successful; be sold, (of money) be spent; be relinquished, fail, decline, collapse; be acceptable or accepted; (often + by, with, on, upon) be guided by; attend regularly; (+ to, towards) contribute to; (+ for) apply to. ● noun (plural **goes**) animation; vigorous activity; success; turn, attempt. □ **go-ahead** adjective enterprising, noun permission to proceed; **go-between** intermediary; **go down** descend, become less, decrease (in price), subside, sink, (of sun) set, deteriorate, cease to function, be recorded, be swallowed, (+ with) find acceptance with, colloquial leave university, colloquial be sent to prison, (+ with) become ill with; **go for** go to fetch, prefer, choose, pass or be accounted as, colloquial attack, colloquial strive to attain; **go-getter** colloquial pushily enterprising person; **go in for** compete or engage in; **go-kart, -cart** miniature racing car with skeleton body; **go off** explode, deteriorate, fall asleep, begin to dislike; **go off well, badly** succeed, fail; **go on** continue, proceed, colloquial talk at great length, (+ at) colloquial nag, use as evidence; **go out** leave room or house, be extinguished, be broadcast, cease to be fashionable, (often + with) have romantic or sexual relationship, (usually + to) sympathize; **go over** inspect details of, rehearse; **go round** spin, revolve, suffice for all; **go slow** work slowly as industrial protest; **go under** sink, succumb, fail; **go up** rise, increase (in price), be consumed (in flames etc.), explode, colloquial enter university; **go without** manage without or forgo (something); **have a go at** attack, attempt; **on the go** colloquial active.

**go²** noun Japanese board game.

**goad** ● verb urge with goad; (usually + on, into) irritate, stimulate. ● noun spiked stick for urging cattle; thing that torments or incites.

**goal** noun object of effort; destination; structure into or through which ball is to be driven in certain games; point(s) so won; point where race ends.

□ **goalkeeper** player protecting goal; **goalpost** either post supporting crossbar of goal.

**goalie** noun colloquial goalkeeper.

**goat** noun small domesticated mammal with horns and (in male) beard; licentious man; colloquial fool. □ **get (person's) goat** colloquial irritate him or her.

**goatee** /gəʊˈtiː/ noun small pointed beard.

**gob**[1] noun slang mouth. □ **gobsmacked** slang flabbergasted; **gob-stopper** large hard sweet.

**gob**[2] slang ● noun clot of slimy matter. ● verb (-bb-) spit.

**gobbet** /ˈgɒbɪt/ noun lump of flesh, food, etc.; extract from text set for translation or comment.

**gobble**[1] /ˈgɒb(ə)l/ verb (-ling) eat hurriedly and noisily.

**gobble**[2] /ˈgɒb(ə)l/ verb (-ling) (of turkeycock) make guttural sound; speak thus.

**gobbledegook** /ˈgɒbəldɪguːk/ noun (also **gobbledeygook**) colloquial pompous or unintelligible jargon.

**goblet** /ˈgɒblɪt/ noun drinking vessel with foot and stem.

**goblin** /ˈgɒblɪn/ noun mischievous demon.

**goby** /ˈgəʊbɪ/ noun (plural -ies) small fish with sucker on underside.

**god** noun superhuman being worshipped as possessing power over nature, human fortunes, etc.; (**God**) creator and ruler of universe; idol; adored person; (**the gods**) (occupants of) gallery in theatre. □ **godchild** person in relation to godparent; **god-daughter** female godchild; **godfather** male godparent; **God-fearing** religious; **God-forsaken** dismal; **godmother** female godparent; **godparent** person who responds on behalf of candidate at baptism; **godsend** unexpected welcome event or acquisition; **godson** male godchild. □ **godlike** adjective.

**goddess** /ˈgɒdɪs/ noun female deity; adored woman.

**godhead** noun divine nature; deity.

**godless** adjective impious, wicked; not believing in God. □ **godlessness** noun.

**godly** /ˈgɒdlɪ/ adjective (-ier, -iest) pious, devout. □ **godliness** noun.

**goer** /ˈgəʊə/ noun person or thing that goes; colloquial lively or sexually promiscuous person. □ **-goer** regular attender.

**goggle** /ˈgɒg(ə)l/ ● verb (-ling) (often + at) look with wide-open eyes; (of eyes) be rolled, project; roll (eyes). ● adjective (of eyes) protuberant, rolling. ● noun (in plural) spectacles for protecting eyes. □ **goggle-box** colloquial television set.

**going** /ˈgəʊɪŋ/ ● noun condition of ground as affecting riding etc. ● adjective in action; existing, available; current, prevalent. □ **going concern** thriving business; **going-over** (plural **goings-over**) colloquial inspection or overhaul, slang thrashing; **goings-on** strange conduct.

**goitre** /ˈgɔɪtə/ noun (US **goiter**) abnormal enlargement of thyroid gland.

**gold** /gəʊld/ ● noun precious yellow metal; colour of this; coins or articles of gold. ● adjective of or coloured like gold. □ **gold-digger** slang woman who goes after men for their money; **gold field** area with naturally occurring gold; **goldfinch** brightly coloured songbird; **goldfish** small golden-red Chinese carp; **gold leaf** gold beaten into thin sheet; **gold medal** medal given usually as first prize; **gold plate** vessels of gold, material plated with gold; **gold-plate** plate with gold; **gold-rush** rush to newly discovered gold field; **goldsmith** worker in gold; **gold standard** financial system in which value of money is based on gold.

**golden** /ˈgəʊld(ə)n/ adjective of gold; coloured or shining like gold; precious, excellent. □ **golden handshake** colloquial gratuity as compensation for redundancy or compulsory retirement; **golden jubilee** 50th anniversary of reign; **golden mean** principle of moderation; **golden retriever** retriever with gold-coloured coat; **golden wedding** 50th anniversary of wedding.

**golf** ● noun game in which small hard ball is struck with clubs over ground into series of small holes. ● verb play golf. □ **golf ball** ball used in golf, spherical unit carrying type in some electric typewriters; **golf course** area of land on which golf is played; **golf club** club used in golf, (premises of) association for playing golf. □ **golfer** noun.

**golliwog** /ˈgɒlɪwɒg/ noun black-faced soft doll with fuzzy hair.

**gonad** /ˈgəʊnæd/ noun animal organ producing gametes, e.g. testis or ovary.

**gondola** /ˈgɒndələ/ noun light Venetian canal-boat; car suspended from airship.

**gondolier** /gɒndəˈlɪə/ noun oarsman of gondola.

**gone** /gɒn/ ● past participle of GO¹. ● adjective (of time) past; lost, hopeless, dead; colloquial pregnant for specified time.

**goner** /ˈgɒnə/ noun slang person or thing that is doomed or irrevocably lost.

**gong** noun metal disc giving resonant note when struck; saucer-shaped bell; slang medal.

**gonorrhoea** /gɒnəˈriːə/ noun (US **gonorrhea**) a venereal disease.

**goo** noun colloquial sticky or slimy substance; sickly sentiment. □ **gooey** adjective (**gooier, gooiest**).

**good** /gʊd/ ● adjective (**better, best**) having right qualities, adequate; competent, effective; kind, morally excellent, virtuous; well-behaved; agreeable; considerable; not less than; beneficial; valid. ● noun (only in singular) good quality or circumstance; (in plural) movable property, merchandise. □ **good-for-nothing** worthless (person); **good humour** genial mood; **good-looking** handsome; **good nature** kindly disposition; **goodwill** kindly feeling, established value-enhancing reputation of a business.

**goodbye** /gʊdˈbaɪ/ (US **goodby**) ● interjection expressing good wishes at parting. ● noun (plural **-byes** or US **-bys**) parting, farewell.

**goodly** /ˈgʊdlɪ/ adjective (**-ier, -iest**) handsome; of imposing size or number.

**goodness** /ˈgʊdnɪs/ noun virtue; excellence; kindness; nutriment.

**goody** /ˈgʊdɪ/ ● noun (plural **-ies**) colloquial good person; (usually in plural) something good or attractive, esp. to eat. ● interjection expressing childish delight. □ **goody-goody** colloquial (person who is) smugly or obtrusively virtuous.

**goof** /guːf/ slang ● noun foolish or stupid person or mistake. ● verb bungle, blunder. □ **goofy** adjective (**-ier, -iest**).

**googly** /ˈguːglɪ/ noun (plural **-ies**) Cricket ball bowled so as to bounce in unexpected direction.

**goon** /guːn/ noun slang stupid person; esp. US hired ruffian.

**goose** /guːs/ noun (plural **geese** /giːs/) large web-footed bird; female of this; colloquial simpleton. □ **goose-flesh**, **-pimples** (US **-bumps**) bristling state of skin due to cold or fright; **goose-step** stiff-legged marching step.

**gooseberry** /ˈgʊzbərɪ/ noun (plural **-ies**) small green usually sour berry; thorny shrub bearing this.

**gopher** /ˈgəʊfə/ noun American burrowing rodent.

**gore¹** noun clotted blood.

**gore²** verb (**-ring**) pierce with horn, tusk, etc.

**gore³** ● noun wedge-shaped piece in garment; triangular or tapering piece in umbrella etc. ● verb (**-ring**) shape with gore.

**gorge** ● noun narrow opening between hills; surfeit; contents of stomach. ● verb (**-ging**) feed greedily; satiate.

**gorgeous** /ˈgɔːdʒəs/ adjective richly coloured; colloquial splendid; colloquial strikingly beautiful. □ **gorgeously** adverb.

**gorgon** /ˈgɔːgən/ noun (in Greek mythology) any of 3 snake-haired sisters able to turn people to stone; frightening or repulsive woman.

**Gorgonzola** /gɔːgənˈzəʊlə/ noun rich blue-veined Italian cheese.

**gorilla** /gəˈrɪlə/ noun largest anthropoid ape.

**gormless** /ˈgɔːmlɪs/ adjective colloquial foolish, lacking sense. □ **gormlessly** adverb.

**gorse** /gɔːs/ noun prickly shrub with yellow flowers.

**Gorsedd** /ˈgɔːseð/ noun Druidic order meeting before eisteddfod.

**gory** /ˈgɔːrɪ/ adjective (**-ier, -iest**) involving bloodshed; bloodstained.

**gosh** interjection expressing surprise.

**goshawk** /ˈgɒshɔːk/ noun large short-winged hawk.

**gosling** /ˈgɒzlɪŋ/ noun young goose.

**gospel** /ˈgɒsp(ə)l/ noun teaching or revelation of Christ; (**Gospel**) (each of 4 books giving) account of Christ's life in

New Testament; portion of this read at church service; thing regarded as absolutely true. □ **gospel music** black American religious singing.

**gossamer** /'gɒsəmə/ ● *noun* filmy substance of small spiders' webs; delicate filmy material. ● *adjective* light and flimsy as gossamer.

**gossip** /'gɒsɪp/ ● *noun* unconstrained talk or writing, esp. about people; idle talk; person indulging in gossip. ● *verb* (**-p-**) talk or write gossip. □ **gossip column** regular newspaper column of gossip. □ **gossipy** *adjective*.

**got** *past & past participle* of GET.

**Goth** *noun* member of Germanic tribe that invaded Roman Empire in 3rd–5th c.

**Gothic** *adjective* of Goths; *Architecture* in the pointed-arch style prevalent in W. Europe in 12th–16th c.; (of novel etc.) in a style popular in 18th & 19th c., with supernatural or horrifying events.

**gotten** *US past participle* of GET.

**gouache** /guːˈɑːʃ/ *noun* painting with opaque water-colour; pigments used for this.

**Gouda** /'gaʊdə/ *noun* flat round Dutch cheese.

**gouge** /gaʊdʒ/ ● *noun* concave-bladed chisel. ● *verb* (**-ging**) cut or (+ *out*) force out (as) with gouge.

**goulash** /'guːlæʃ/ *noun* stew of meat and vegetables seasoned with paprika.

**gourd** /gʊəd/ *noun* fleshy fruit of trailing or climbing cucumber-like plant; this plant; dried rind of this fruit used as bottle etc.

**gourmand** /'gʊəmənd/ *noun* glutton; gourmet.

■ **Usage** The use of *gourmand* to mean a 'gourmet' is considered incorrect by some people.

**gourmet** /'gʊəmeɪ/ *noun* connoisseur of good food.

**gout** /gaʊt/ *noun* disease with inflammation of small joints. □ **gouty** *adjective*.

**govern** /'gʌv(ə)n/ *verb* rule with authority; conduct policy and affairs of; influence or determine; curb, control.

**governance** *noun* act, manner, or function of governing.

**governess** /'gʌvənɪs/ *noun* woman employed to teach children in private household.

**government** *noun* manner or system of governing; group of people governing state. □ **governmental** /-'men-/ *adjective*.

**governor** *noun* ruler; official governing a province, town, etc.; executive head of each State of US; member of governing body of institution; *slang* one's employer or father; automatic regulator controlling speed of engine etc. □ **Governor-General** representative of Crown in Commonwealth country regarding Queen as head of state. □ **governorship** *noun*.

**gown** /gaʊn/ *noun* woman's, esp. formal or elegant, long dress; official robe of alderman, judge, cleric, academic, etc.; surgeon's overall.

**goy** *noun* (*plural* **-im** or **-s**) *Jewish name for* non-Jew.

**GP** *abbreviation* general practitioner.

**GPO** *abbreviation* General Post Office.

**gr** *abbreviation* (also **gr.**) gram(s); grain(s); gross.

**grab** ● *verb* (**-bb-**) seize suddenly; take greedily; *slang* impress; (+ *at*) snatch at. ● *noun* sudden clutch or attempt to seize; device for clutching.

**grace** ● *noun* elegance of proportions, manner, or movement; courteous good will; attractive feature; unmerited favour of God; goodwill; delay granted; thanksgiving at meals; (**His, Her, Your Grace**) *title used of or to* duke, duchess, *or* archbishop. ● *verb* (**-cing**) (often + *with*) add grace to; bestow honour on. □ **grace note** *Music* note embellishing melody.

**graceful** *adjective* full of grace or elegance. □ **gracefully** *adverb*.

**graceless** *adjective* lacking grace or charm.

**gracious** /'greɪʃəs/ *adjective* kindly, esp. to inferiors; merciful. □ **gracious living** elegant way of life. □ **graciously** *adverb*; **graciousness** *noun*.

**gradate** /grə'deɪt/ *verb* (**-ting**) (cause to) pass gradually from one shade to another; arrange in steps or grades.

**gradation** *noun* (usually in *plural*) stage of transition or advance; degree in rank, intensity, etc.; arrangement in grades. □ **gradational** adjective.

**grade** ● noun degree in rank, merit, etc.; mark indicating quality of student's work; slope; US class in school. ● verb (-ding) arrange in grades; (+ up, down, off, into, etc.) pass between grades; give grade to; reduce to easy gradients. □ **make the grade** succeed.

**gradient** /'greɪdɪənt/ noun sloping road etc.; amount of such slope.

**gradual** /'grædʒʊəl/ adjective happening by degrees; not steep or abrupt. □ **gradually** adverb.

**graduate** ● noun /'grædʒʊət/ holder of academic degree. ● verb /-eɪt/ (-ting) obtain academic degree; (+ to) move up to; mark in degrees or portions; arrange in gradations; apportion (tax etc.) according to scale. □ **graduation** noun.

**graffiti** /grə'fiːtɪ/ plural noun (singular **graffito**) writing or drawing on wall etc.

■ **Usage** Graffiti should be used with plural verbs, as in Graffiti have appeared everywhere.

**graft**[1] /grɑːft/ ● noun shoot or scion planted in slit in another stock; piece of transplanted living tissue; slang hard work. ● verb (often + in, on, together, etc.) insert (graft); transplant (living tissue); (+ in, on) insert or fix (thing) permanently to another; slang work hard.

**graft**[2] /grɑːft/ colloquial ● noun practices for securing illicit gains in politics or business; such gains. ● verb seek or make graft.

**Grail** noun (in full **Holy Grail**) legendary cup or platter used by Christ at Last Supper.

**grain** ● noun fruit or seed of cereal; wheat or allied food-grass; corn; particle of sand, salt, etc.; unit of weight (0.065 g); least possible amount; texture in skin, wood, stone, etc.; arrangement of lines of fibre in wood. ● verb paint in imitation of grain of wood; form into grains.

**gram** noun (also **gramme**) metric unit of weight.

**grammar** /'græmə/ noun study or rules of relations between words in (a) language; application of such rules; book

on grammar. □ **grammar school** esp. historical secondary school with academic curriculum.

**grammarian** /grə'meərɪən/ noun expert in grammar.

**grammatical** /grə'mætɪk(ə)l/ adjective of or according to grammar.

**gramophone** /'græməfəʊn/ noun record player.

**grampus** /'græmpəs/ noun (plural **-es**) sea mammal of dolphin family.

**gran** noun colloquial grandmother.

**granary** /'grænərɪ/ noun (plural **-ies**) storehouse for grain; region producing much corn.

**grand** ● adjective splendid, imposing; chief, of chief importance; (**Grand**) of highest rank; colloquial excellent. ● noun grand piano; (plural same) (usually in plural) slang 1,000 dollars or pounds. □ **grand jury** jury to examine validity of accusation before trial; **grand piano** piano with horizontal strings; **grand slam** winning of all of group of matches; **grand total** sum of other totals. □ **grandly** adverb; **grandness** noun.

**grandad** noun (also **grand-dad**) colloquial grandfather.

**grandchild** noun child of one's son or daughter.

**granddaughter** noun one's child's daughter.

**grandee** /græn'diː/ noun Spanish or Portuguese noble of highest rank; great personage.

**grandeur** /'grændʒə/ noun majesty, splendour, dignity; high rank, eminence.

**grandfather** noun one's parent's father. □ **grandfather clock** clock in tall wooden case.

**grandiloquent** /græn'dɪləkwənt/ adjective pompous or inflated in language. □ **grandiloquence** noun.

**grandiose** /'grændɪəʊs/ adjective imposing; planned on large scale. □ **grandiosity** /-'ɒsɪtɪ/ noun.

**grandma** noun colloquial grandmother.

**grandmother** noun one's parent's mother.

**grandparent** noun one's parent's parent.

**Grand Prix** /grã 'pri:/ *noun* any of several international motor-racing events.

**grandson** *noun* one's child's son.

**grandstand** *noun* main stand for spectators at racecourse etc.

**grange** /greɪndʒ/ *noun* country house with farm buildings.

**granite** /'grænɪt/ *noun* granular crystalline rock of quartz, mica, etc.

**granny** /'grænɪ/ *noun* (also **grannie**) (*plural* **-ies**) *colloquial* grandmother; (in full **granny knot**) reef-knot crossed wrong way.

**grant** /grɑ:nt/ ● *verb* consent to fulfil; allow to have; give formally, transfer legally; (often + *that*) admit, concede. ● *noun* granting; thing, esp. money, granted. □ **take for granted** assume to be true, cease to appreciate through familiarity. □ **grantor** /grɑ:n'tɔ:/ *noun*.

**granular** /'grænjʊlə/ *adjective* of or like grains or granules.

**granulate** /'grænjʊleɪt/ *verb* (**-ting**) form into grains; roughen surface of. □ **granulation** *noun*.

**granule** /'grænju:l/ *noun* small grain.

**grape** *noun* usually green or purple berry growing in clusters on vine. □ **grapeshot** *historical* small balls as scattering charge for cannon etc.; **grapevine** vine, means of transmission of rumour.

**grapefruit** /'greɪpfru:t/ *noun* (*plural* same) large round usually yellow citrus fruit.

**graph** /grɑ:f/ ● *noun* symbolic diagram representing relation between two or more variables. ● *verb* plot on graph.

**graphic** /'græfɪk/ *adjective* of writing, drawing, etc.; vividly descriptive. □ **graphic arts** visual and technical arts involving design or lettering. □ **graphically** *adverb*.

**graphics** *plural noun* (usually treated as *singular*) products of graphic arts; use of diagrams in calculation and design.

**graphite** /'græfaɪt/ *noun* crystalline form of carbon used as lubricant, in pencils, etc.

**graphology** /grə'fɒlədʒɪ/ *noun* study of handwriting. □ **graphologist** *noun*.

**grapnel** /'græpn(ə)l/ *noun* iron-clawed instrument for dragging or grasping; small many-fluked anchor.

**grapple** /'græp(ə)l/ ● *verb* (**-ling**) (often + *with*) fight at close quarters; (+ *with*) try to manage (problem etc.); grip with hands, come to close quarters with; seize. ● *noun* hold (as) of wrestler; contest at close quarters; clutching-instrument. □ **grappling-iron, -hook** grapnel.

**grasp** /grɑ:sp/ ● *verb* clutch at, seize greedily; hold firmly; understand, realize. ● *noun* firm hold, grip; (+ *of*) mastery, mental hold.

**grasping** *adjective* avaricious.

**grass** /grɑ:s/ ● *noun* (any of several) plants with bladelike leaves eaten by ruminants; pasture land; grass-covered ground; grazing; *slang* marijuana; *slang* informer. ● *verb* cover with turf; *US* pasture; *slang* betray, inform police. □ **grass roots** fundamental level or source, rank and file; **grass snake** small non-poisonous snake; **grass widow, widower** person whose husband (or wife) is temporarily absent. □ **grassy** *adjective* (**-ier, -iest**).

**grasshopper** /'grɑ:shɒpə/ *noun* jumping and chirping insect.

**grate**[1] *verb* (**-ting**) reduce to small particles by rubbing on rough surface; (often + *against, on*) rub with, utter with, or make harsh sound, have irritating effect; grind, creak. □ **grater** *noun*.

**grate**[2] *noun* (metal) frame holding fuel in fireplace etc.

**grateful** /'greɪtfʊl/ *adjective* thankful; feeling or showing gratitude. □ **gratefully** *adverb*.

**gratify** /'grætɪfaɪ/ *verb* (**-ies, -ied**) please, delight; indulge. □ **gratification** *noun*.

**grating** /'greɪtɪŋ/ *noun* framework of parallel or crossed metal bars.

**gratis** /'grɑ:tɪs/ *adverb* & *adjective* free, without charge.

**gratitude** /'grætɪtju:d/ *noun* being thankful.

**gratuitous** /grə'tju:ɪtəs/ *adjective* given or done gratis; uncalled-for, motiveless. □ **gratuitously** *adverb*; **gratuitousness** *noun*.

**gratuity** /grə'tju:ɪtɪ/ *noun* (*plural* **-ies**) money given for good service.

**grave**[1] /greɪv/ *noun* hole dug for burial of corpse; mound or monument over this; (**the grave**) death. □ **gravestone**

(usually inscribed) stone over grave; **graveyard** burial ground.

**grave**[2] /greɪv/ *adjective* weighty, serious; dignified, solemn; threatening. □ **gravely** *adverb*.

**grave**[3] /greɪv/ *verb* (**-ving**; *past participle* **graven** or **graved**) (+ *in, on*) fix indelibly on (memory etc.); *archaic* engrave, carve. □ **graven image** idol.

**grave**[4] /grɑːv/ *noun* (in full **grave accent**) mark (ˋ) over letter indicating pronunciation.

**gravel** /ˈgræv(ə)l/ ● *noun* coarse sand and small stones; formation of crystals in bladder. ● *verb* (**-ll-**; *US* **-l-**) lay with gravel.

**gravelly** /ˈgrævəlɪ/ *adjective* of or like gravel; (of voice) deep and rough-sounding.

**gravid** /ˈgrævɪd/ *adjective* pregnant.

**gravitate** /ˈgrævɪteɪt/ *verb* (**-ting**) (+ *to, towards*) move, be attracted, or tend by force of gravity to(wards); sink (as) by gravity.

**gravitation** *noun* attraction between each particle of matter and every other; effect of this, esp. falling of bodies to earth. □ **gravitational** *adjective*.

**gravity** /ˈgrævɪtɪ/ *noun* force that attracts body to centre of earth etc.; intensity of this; weight; importance, seriousness; solemnity.

**gravy** /ˈgreɪvɪ/ *noun* (*plural* **-ies**) (sauce made from) juices exuding from meat in and after cooking. □ **gravy-boat** long shallow jug for gravy; **gravy train** *slang* source of easy financial benefit.

**gray** *US* = GREY.

**grayling** *noun* (*plural* same) silver-grey freshwater fish.

**graze**[1] *verb* (**-zing**) feed on growing grass; pasture cattle.

**graze**[2] ● *verb* (**-zing**) rub or scrape (part of body); (+ *against, along,* etc.) touch lightly in passing, move with such contact. ● *noun* abrasion.

**grazier** /ˈgreɪzɪə/ *noun* person who feeds cattle for market.

**grazing** *noun* grassland suitable for pasturage.

**grease** /griːs/ ● *noun* oily or fatty matter, esp. as lubricant; melted fat of dead animal. ● *verb* (**-sing**) smear or lubricate with grease. □ **greasepaint** actor's make-up; **greaseproof** impervious to grease.

**greasy** /ˈgriːsɪ/ *adjective* (**-ier, -iest**) of, like, smeared with, or having too much grease; (of person, manner) unctuous. □ **greasiness** *noun*.

**great** /greɪt/ ● *adjective* above average in bulk, number, extent, or intensity; important, pre-eminent; imposing, distinguished; of remarkable ability etc.; (+ *at, on*) competent, well-informed; *colloquial* very satisfactory. ● *noun* great person or thing. □ **greatcoat** heavy overcoat; **Great Dane** dog of large short-haired breed. □ **greatness** *noun*.

**great-** /greɪt/ *combining form* (of family relationships) one degree more remote (*great-grandfather, great-niece,* etc.).

**greatly** *adverb* much.

**grebe** *noun* a diving bird.

**Grecian** /ˈgriːʃ(ə)n/ *adjective* Greek.

**greed** *noun* excessive desire, esp. for food or wealth.

**greedy** /ˈgriːdɪ/ *adjective* (**-ier, -iest**) showing greed; (+ *for, to do*) eager. □ **greedily** *adverb*.

**Greek** ● *noun* native, national, or language of Greece. ● *adjective* of Greece.

**green** ● *adjective* coloured like grass; unripe, unseasoned; not dried, smoked, or tanned; inexperienced; jealous; (also **Green**) concerned with protection of environment, not harmful to environment. ● *noun* green colour, paint, clothes, etc.; piece of grassy public land; grassy area for special purpose; (in *plural*) green vegetables; (also **Green**) supporter of protection of environment. □ **green belt** area of open land for preservation round city; **green card** motorist's international insurance document; **greenfinch** bird with greenish plumage; **green fingers** *colloquial* skill in gardening; **greenfly** green aphid; **greengage** round green plum; **greenhorn** novice; **green light** signal or permission to proceed; **green pound** the agreed value of the pound for payments to agricultural producers in EC; **green-room** room in theatre for actors when off stage; **greensward** grassy turf.

**greenery** *noun* green foliage.

**greengrocer** /ˈgriːnˌgrəʊsə/ noun retailer of fruit and vegetables. □ **greengrocery** noun (plural **-ies**).

**greenhouse** noun structure with sides and roof mainly of glass, for rearing plants. □ **greenhouse effect** trapping of sun's warmth in earth's lower atmosphere; **greenhouse gas** gas contributing to greenhouse effect, esp. carbon dioxide.

**greet** verb address on meeting or arrival; receive or acknowledge in specified way; become apparent to (eye, ear, etc.).

**greeting** noun act or words used to greet. □ **greetings card** decorative card carrying goodwill message etc.

**gregarious** /grɪˈgeərɪəs/ adjective fond of company; living in flocks etc. □ **gregariousness** noun.

**Gregorian calendar** /grɪˈgɔːrɪən/ noun calendar introduced in 1582 by Pope Gregory XIII.

**Gregorian chant** /grɪˈgɔːrɪən/ noun form of plainsong named after Pope Gregory I.

**gremlin** /ˈgremlɪn/ noun colloquial mischievous sprite said to cause mechanical faults etc.

**grenade** /grɪˈneɪd/ noun small bomb thrown by hand or shot from rifle.

**grenadier** /grenəˈdɪə/ noun (**Grenadier**) member of first regiment of royal household infantry; historical soldier armed with grenades.

**grew** past of GROW.

**grey** /greɪ/ (US **gray**) ● adjective of colour between black and white; clouded, dull; (of hair) turning white, (of person) having grey hair; anonymous, unidentifiable; undistinguished, boring. ● noun grey colour, paint, clothes, etc.; grey horse. ● verb make or become grey. □ **grey area** indefinite situation or topic; **Grey Friar** Franciscan friar; **grey matter** darker tissues of brain, colloquial intelligence.

**greyhound** noun slender swift dog used in racing.

**greylag** noun European wild goose.

**grid** noun grating; system of numbered squares for map references; network of lines, electric power connections, etc.;

pattern of lines marking starting-place on motor-racing track.

**griddle** /ˈgrɪd(ə)l/ noun iron plate placed over heat for baking etc.

**gridiron** /ˈgrɪdaɪən/ noun barred metal frame for broiling or grilling; American football field.

**grief** /griːf/ noun (cause of) intense sorrow. □ **come to grief** meet with disaster.

**grievance** noun real or imagined cause for complaint.

**grieve** /griːv/ verb (**-ving**) (cause to) feel grief.

**grievous** /ˈgriːvəs/ adjective severe; causing grief; injurious; flagrant, heinous. □ **grievously** adverb.

**griffin** /ˈgrɪfɪn/ noun (also **gryphon** /-f(ə)n/) mythical creature with eagle's head and wings and lion's body.

**griffon** /ˈgrɪf(ə)n/ noun small coarse-haired terrier-like dog; large vulture; griffin.

**grill** ● noun device on cooker for radiating heat downwards; gridiron; grilled food; (in full **grill room**) restaurant specializing in grills. ● verb cook under grill or on gridiron; subject to or experience extreme heat; subject to severe questioning.

**grille** /grɪl/ noun (also **grill**) grating, latticed screen; metal grid protecting vehicle radiator.

**grilse** /grɪls/ noun (plural same or **-s**) young salmon that has been to the sea only once.

**grim** adjective (**-mm-**) of stern appearance; harsh, merciless, ghastly, joyless; unpleasant. □ **grimly** adverb; **grimness** noun.

**grimace** /ˈgrɪməs/ ● noun distortion of face made in disgust etc. or to amuse. ● verb (**-cing**) make grimace.

**grime** ● noun deeply ingrained dirt. ● verb (**-ming**) blacken, befoul. □ **grimy** adjective (**-ier, -iest**).

**grin** ● verb (**-nn-**) smile broadly. ● noun broad smile.

**grind** /graɪnd/ ● verb (past & past participle **ground** /graʊnd/) crush to small particles; sharpen; rub gratingly; (often + down) oppress; (often + away) work or study hard. ● noun grinding; colloquial hard dull work. □ **grindstone** thick revolving abrasive disc for grinding, sharpening, etc. □ **grinder** noun.

**grip** ● verb (**-pp-**) grasp tightly; take firm hold; compel attention of. ● noun firm hold, grasp; way of holding; power of holding attention; intellectual mastery; control of one's behaviour; part of machine that grips; part of weapon etc. that is gripped; hairgrip; travelling bag.

**gripe** ● verb (**-ping**) colloquial complain; affect with colic. ● noun (usually in plural) colic; colloquial complaint. □ **Gripe Water** proprietary term medicine to relieve colic in babies.

**grisly** /ˈgrɪzlɪ/ adjective (**-ier, -iest**) causing horror, disgust, or fear.

**grist** noun corn for grinding. □ **grist to the mill** source of profit or advantage.

**gristle** /ˈgrɪs(ə)l/ noun tough flexible tissue; cartilage. □ **gristly** adjective.

**grit** ● noun small particles of sand etc.; coarse sandstone; colloquial pluck, endurance. ● verb (**-tt-**) spread grit on (icy roads etc.); clench (teeth); make grating sound. □ **gritty** adjective (**-ier, -iest**).

**grits** plural noun coarse oatmeal; unground husked oats.

**grizzle** /ˈgrɪz(ə)l/ verb (**-ling**) colloquial cry fretfully. □ **grizzly** adjective (**-ier, -iest**).

**grizzled** adjective grey-haired.

**grizzly** /ˈgrɪzlɪ/ ● adjective (**-ier, -iest**) grey-haired. ● noun (plural **-ies**) (in full **grizzly bear**) large fierce N. American bear.

**groan** ● verb make deep sound expressing pain, grief, or disapproval; (usually + under, beneath, with) be loaded or oppressed. ● noun sound made in groaning.

**groat** noun historical silver coin worth 4 old pence.

**groats** plural noun hulled or crushed grain, esp. oats.

**grocer** /ˈgrəʊsə/ noun dealer in food and household provisions.

**grocery** /ˈgrəʊsərɪ/ noun (plural **-ies**) grocer's trade, shop, or (in plural) goods.

**grog** noun drink of spirit (originally rum) and water.

**groggy** /ˈgrɒgɪ/ adjective (**-ier, -iest**) incapable, unsteady. □ **groggily** adverb.

**groin**[1] ● noun depression between belly and thigh; edge formed by intersecting vaults. ● verb build with groins.

**groin**[2] US = GROYNE.

**grommet** /ˈgrɒmɪt/ noun eyelet placed in hole to protect or insulate rope or cable passed through it; tube passed through eardrum to middle ear.

**groom** /gruːm/ ● noun person employed to tend horses; bridegroom. ● verb tend (horse); give neat or attractive appearance to; prepare (person) for office or occasion etc.

**groove** ● noun channel, elongated hollow; spiral cut in gramophone record for needle. ● verb (**-ving**) make groove(s) in.

**groovy** /ˈgruːvɪ/ adjective (**-ier, -iest**) slang excellent; of or like a groove.

**grope** ● verb (**-ping**) (usually + for) feel about or search blindly; (+ for, after) search mentally; fondle clumsily for sexual pleasure; feel (one's way). ● noun act of groping.

**grosgrain** /ˈgrəʊgreɪn/ noun corded fabric of silk etc.

**gross** /grəʊs/ ● adjective overfed, bloated; coarse, indecent; flagrant; total, not net. ● verb produce as gross profit. ● noun (plural same) 12 dozen. □ **grossly** adverb.

**grotesque** /grəʊˈtesk/ ● adjective comically or repulsively distorted; incongruous, absurd. ● noun decoration interweaving human and animal features; comically distorted figure or design. □ **grotesquely** adverb.

**grotto** /ˈgrɒtəʊ/ noun (plural **-es** or **-s**) picturesque cave; structure imitating cave.

**grotty** /ˈgrɒtɪ/ adjective (**-ier, -iest**) slang unpleasant, dirty, ugly.

**grouch** /graʊtʃ/ colloquial ● verb grumble. ● noun grumbler; complaint; sulky grumbling mood. □ **grouchy** adjective (**-ier, -iest**).

**ground**[1] /graʊnd/ ● noun surface of earth; extent of subject; (often in plural) foundation, motive; area of special kind; (in plural) enclosed land attached to house etc.; area or basis for agreement etc.; surface worked on in painting; (in plural) dregs; bottom of sea; floor of room etc. ● verb prevent from taking off or flying; run aground, strand; (+

*in*) instruct thoroughly; (often as **grounded** *adjective*) (+ *on*) base cause or principle on. □ **ground control** personnel directing landing etc. of aircraft etc.; **ground cover** low-growing plants; **ground floor** storey at ground level; **ground frost** frost on surface of ground; **groundnut** peanut; **ground-rent** rent for land leased for building; **groundsman** person who maintains sports ground; **ground speed** aircraft's speed relative to ground; **ground swell** heavy sea due to distant or past storm etc.; **groundwork** preliminary or basic work.

**ground**[2] *past & past participle* of GRIND.

**grounding** *noun* basic instruction.

**groundless** *adjective* without motive or foundation.

**groundsel** /'graʊnds(ə)l/ *noun* yellow-flowered weed.

**group** /gruːp/ • *noun* number of people or things near, classed, or working together; number of companies under common ownership; pop group; division of air force. • *verb* form into group; place in group(s). □ **group captain** RAF officer next below air commodore.

**groupie** *noun slang* ardent follower of touring pop group(s).

**grouse**[1] /graʊs/ *noun* (*plural* same) game bird with feathered feet.

**grouse**[2] /graʊs/ *verb* (**-sing**) & *noun colloquial* grumble.

**grout** /graʊt/ • *noun* thin fluid mortar. • *verb* apply grout to.

**grove** /grəʊv/ *noun* small wood; group of trees.

**grovel** /'grɒv(ə)l/ *verb* (**-ll-**; *US* **-l-**) behave obsequiously; lie prone.

**grow** /grəʊ/ *verb* (*past* **grew**; *past participle* **grown**) increase in size, height, amount, etc.; develop or exist as living plant or natural product; produce by cultivation; become gradually; (+ *on*) become more favoured by; (in *passive*; + *over*) be covered with growth. □ **grown-up** adult; **grow up** mature. □ **grower** *noun*.

**growl** /graʊl/ • *verb* (often + *at*) make low guttural sound, usually of anger; rumble. • *noun* growling sound; angry murmur.

**grown** *past participle* of GROW.

**growth** /grəʊθ/ *noun* process of growing; increase; what has grown or is growing; tumour. □ **growth industry** one that is developing rapidly.

**groyne** /grɔɪn/ *noun* (*US* **groin**) wall built out into sea to stop beach erosion.

**grub** • *noun* larva of insect; *colloquial* food. • *verb* (**-bb-**) dig superficially; (+ *up*, *out*) extract by digging.

**grubby** /'grʌbɪ/ *adjective* (**-ier**, **-iest**) dirty.

**grudge** • *noun* persistent resentment or ill will. • *verb* (**-ging**) be unwilling to give or allow, feel resentful about (doing something).

**gruel** /'gruːəl/ *noun* liquid food of oatmeal etc. boiled in milk or water.

**gruelling** (*US* **grueling**) *adjective* exhausting; punishing.

**gruesome** /'gruːsəm/ *adjective* grisly, disgusting.

**gruff** *adjective* rough-voiced; surly. □ **gruffly** *adverb*.

**grumble** /'grʌmb(ə)l/ • *verb* (**-ling**) complain peevishly; rumble. • *noun* complaint; rumble. □ **grumbler** *noun*.

**grumpy** /'grʌmpɪ/ *adjective* (**-ier**, **-iest**) ill-tempered.

**grunt** • *noun* low guttural sound characteristic of pig. • *verb* utter (with) grunt.

**Gruyère** /'gruːjeə/ *noun* kind of Swiss cheese with holes in.

**gryphon** = GRIFFIN.

**guano** /'gwɑːnəʊ/ *noun* (*plural* **-s**) excrement of seabirds, used as manure.

**guarantee** /gærən'tiː/ • *noun* formal promise or assurance; guaranty; giver of guaranty or security. • *verb* (**-tees**, **-teed**) give or serve as guarantee for; promise; secure. □ **guarantor** *noun*.

**guaranty** /'gærəntɪ/ *noun* (*plural* **-ies**) written or other undertaking to answer for performance of obligation; thing serving as security.

**guard** /gɑːd/ • *verb* (often + *from*, *against*) defend, protect; keep watch, prevent from escaping; keep in check; (+ *against*) take precautions against. • *noun* vigilant state; protector; soldiers etc. protecting place or person; official in charge of train; (in *plural*) (usually **Guards**) household troops of monarch; device to prevent injury or accident;

defensive posture. □ **guardhouse, guardroom** building or room for accommodating military guard or for detaining prisoners; **guardsman** soldier in guards or Guards.

**guarded** *adjective* (of remark etc.) cautious. □ **guardedly** *adverb*.

**guardian** /ˈgɑːdɪən/ *noun* protector, keeper; person having custody of another, esp. minor. □ **guardianship** *noun*.

**guava** /ˈgwɑːvə/ *noun* edible orange acid fruit; tropical tree bearing this.

**gubernatorial** /gjuːbənəˈtɔːrɪəl/ *adjective* US of governor.

**gudgeon**[1] /ˈgʌdʒ(ə)n/ *noun* small freshwater fish.

**gudgeon**[2] /ˈgʌdʒ(ə)n/ *noun* kind of pivot or pin; tubular part of hinge; socket for rudder.

**guelder rose** /ˈgeldə/ *noun* shrub with round bunches of white flowers.

**Guernsey** /ˈgɜːnzɪ/ *noun* (*plural* **-s**) one of breed of cattle from Guernsey; (**guernsey**) type of thick knitted woollen jersey.

**guerrilla** /gəˈrɪlə/ *noun* (also **guerilla**) member of one of several independent groups fighting against regular forces.

**guess** /ges/ ● *verb* estimate without calculation or measurement; conjecture, think likely; conjecture rightly. ● *noun* estimate, conjecture. □ **guesswork** guessing.

**guest** /gest/ *noun* person invited to visit another's house or have meal etc. at another's expense, or lodging at hotel etc. □ **guest house** superior boarding house.

**guestimate** /ˈgestɪmət/ *noun* (also **guesstimate**) estimate based on guesswork and calculation.

**guffaw** /gʌˈfɔː/ ● *noun* boisterous laugh. ● *verb* utter guffaw.

**guidance** /ˈgaɪd(ə)ns/ *noun* advice; guiding.

**guide** /gaɪd/ ● *noun* person who shows the way; conductor of tours; adviser; directing principle; guidebook; (**Guide**) member of girls' organization similar to Scouts. ● *verb* (**-ding**) act as guide to; lead, direct. □ **guidebook** book of information about place etc.; **guided missile** missile under remote

control or directed by equipment within itself; **guide-dog** dog trained to lead blind person; **guideline** principle directing action.

**Guider** /ˈgaɪdə/ *noun* adult leader of Guides.

**guild** /gɪld/ *noun* (also **gild**) society for mutual aid or with common object; medieval association of craftsmen. □ **guildhall** meeting-place of medieval guild, town hall.

**guilder** /ˈgɪldə/ *noun* monetary unit of Netherlands.

**guile** /gaɪl/ *noun* sly behaviour; treachery, deceit. □ **guileless** *adjective*.

**guillemot** /ˈgɪlɪmɒt/ *noun* kind of auk.

**guillotine** /ˈgɪlətiːn/ ● *noun* beheading machine; machine for cutting paper; method of shortening debate in parliament by fixing time of vote. ● *verb* (**-ning**) use guillotine on.

**guilt** /gɪlt/ *noun* fact of having committed offence; (feeling of) culpability.

**guiltless** *adjective* (often + *of*) innocent.

**guilty** *adjective* (**-ier, -iest**) having, feeling, or causing feeling of guilt. □ **guiltily** *adverb*.

**guinea** /ˈgɪnɪ/ *noun* (*historical* coin worth) £1.05. □ **guinea fowl** domestic fowl with white-spotted grey plumage; **guinea pig** domesticated S. American rodent, person used in experiment.

**guipure** /ˈgiːpjʊə/ *noun* heavy lace of patterned pieces joined by stitches.

**guise** /gaɪz/ *noun* external, esp. assumed, appearance; pretence.

**guitar** /gɪˈtɑː/ *noun* usually 6-stringed musical instrument played with fingers or plectrum. □ **guitarist** *noun*.

**gulch** *noun* US ravine, gully.

**gulf** *noun* large area of sea with narrow-mouthed inlet; deep hollow, chasm; wide difference of opinion etc. □ **Gulf Stream** warm current from Gulf of Mexico to Europe.

**gull**[1] *noun* long-winged web-footed seabird.

**gull**[2] *verb* dupe, fool.

**gullet** /ˈgʌlɪt/ *noun* food-passage from mouth to stomach.

**gullible** /ˈgʌlɪb(ə)l/ *adjective* easily persuaded or deceived. □ **gullibility** *noun*.

**gully** /ˈgʌlɪ/ *noun* (*plural* **-ies**) water-worn ravine; gutter, drain; *Cricket* fielding position between point and slips.

**gulp** • verb (often + down) swallow hastily or with effort; choke; (+ down, back) suppress. • noun act of gulping; large mouthful.

**gum**¹ • noun sticky secretion of some trees and shrubs, used as glue etc.; chewing gum; (also **gumdrop**) hard jelly sweet. • verb (**-mm-**) (usually + down, together, etc.) fasten with gum; apply gum to. □ **gum arabic** gum exuded by some kinds of acacia; **gumboot** rubber boot; **gum tree** tree exuding gum, esp. eucalyptus; **gum up** colloquial interfere with, spoil.

**gum**² noun (usually in plural) firm flesh around roots of teeth. □ **gumboil** small abscess on gum.

**gummy**¹ /'gʌmɪ/ adjective (**-ier, -iest**) sticky; exuding gum.

**gummy**² /'gʌmɪ/ adjective (**-ier, -iest**) toothless.

**gumption** /'gʌmpʃ(ə)n/ noun colloquial resourcefulness, enterprise; common sense.

**gun** • noun metal tube for throwing missiles with explosive propellant; starting pistol; device for discharging grease, electrons, etc., in desired direction; member of shooting party. • verb (**-nn-**) (usually + down) shoot with gun; (+ for) seek out determinedly to attack or rebuke. □ **gunboat** small warship with heavy guns; **gun carriage** wheeled support for gun; **gun cotton** cotton steeped in acids, used as explosive; **gun dog** dog trained to retrieve game; **gunfire** firing of guns; **gunman** armed lawbreaker; **gun metal** bluish-grey colour, alloy of copper, tin, and usually zinc; **gunpowder** explosive of saltpetre, sulphur, and charcoal; **gunrunner** person selling or bringing guns into country illegally; **gunshot** shot from gun, the range of a gun; **gunslinger** esp. US gunman; **gunsmith** maker and repairer of small firearms.

**gunge** /gʌndʒ/ colloquial • noun sticky substance. • verb (**-ging**) (usually + up) clog with gunge. □ **gungy** adjective.

**gung-ho** /gʌŋ'həʊ/ adjective (arrogantly) eager.

**gunner** /'gʌnə/ noun artillery soldier; Nautical warrant officer in charge of battery, magazine, etc.; airman who operates gun.

**gunnery** /'gʌnərɪ/ noun construction and management, or firing, of large guns.

**gunny** /'gʌnɪ/ noun (plural **-ies**) coarse sacking usually of jute fibre; sack made of this.

**gunwale** /'gʌn(ə)l/ noun upper edge of ship's or boat's side.

**guppy** /'gʌpɪ/ noun (plural **-ies**) very small brightly coloured tropical freshwater fish.

**gurgle** /'gɜːg(ə)l/ • verb (**-ling**) make bubbling sound as of water; utter with such sound. • noun bubbling sound.

**gurnard** /'gɜːnəd/ noun (plural same or **-s**) sea fish with large spiny head.

**guru** /'gʊruː/ noun (plural **-s**) Hindu spiritual teacher; influential or revered teacher.

**gush** • verb flow in sudden or copious stream; speak or behave effusively. • noun sudden or copious stream; effusiveness.

**gusher** /'gʌʃə/ noun oil well emitting unpumped oil; effusive person.

**gusset** /'gʌsɪt/ noun piece let into garment etc. to strengthen or enlarge it.

**gust** • noun sudden violent rush of wind; burst of rain, smoke, anger, etc. • verb blow in gusts. □ **gusty** adjective (**-ier, -iest**).

**gusto** /'gʌstəʊ/ noun zest, enjoyment.

**gut** • noun intestine; (in plural) bowels, entrails; (in plural) colloquial courage and determination; slang stomach; (in plural) contents, essence; material for violin etc. strings or for fishing line; instinctive, fundamental. • verb (**-tt-**) remove or destroy internal fittings of (buildings); remove guts of. □ **gutless** adjective.

**gutsy** /'gʌtsɪ/ adjective (**-ier, iest**) colloquial courageous; greedy.

**gutta-percha** /gʌtə'pɜːtʃə/ noun tough plastic substance made from latex.

**gutted** adjective slang bitterly disappointed.

**gutter** /'gʌtə/ • noun shallow trough below eaves, or channel at side of street, for carrying off rainwater; (**the gutter**) poor or degraded environment; channel, groove. • verb (of candle) burn unsteadily and melt away.

**guttering** noun (material for) gutters.

**guttersnipe** noun street urchin.

**guttural** /ˈɡʌtər(ə)l/ ● *adjective* throaty, harsh-sounding; (of sound) produced in throat. ● *noun* guttural consonant.

**guy¹** /ɡaɪ/ ● *noun colloquial* man; effigy of Guy Fawkes burnt on 5 Nov. ● *verb* ridicule.

**guy²** /ɡaɪ/ ● *noun* rope or chain to secure tent or steady crane-load etc. ● *verb* secure with guy(s).

**guzzle** /ˈɡʌz(ə)l/ *verb* (**-ling**) eat or drink greedily.

**gybe** /dʒaɪb/ *verb* (*US* **jibe**) (**-bing**) (of fore-and-aft sail or boom) swing across boat, momentarily pointing into wind; cause (sail) to do this; (of boat etc.) change course thus.

**gym** /dʒɪm/ *noun colloquial* gymnasium; gymnastics. □ **gymslip, gym tunic** schoolgirl's sleeveless dress.

**gymkhana** /dʒɪmˈkɑːnə/ *noun* horse-riding competition.

**gymnasium** /dʒɪmˈneɪzɪəm/ *noun* (*plural* **-siums** or **-sia**) room etc. equipped for gymnastics.

**gymnast** /ˈdʒɪmnæst/ *noun* expert in gymnastics.

**gymnastic** /dʒɪmˈnæstɪk/ *adjective* of gymnastics. □ **gymnastically** *adverb*.

**gymnastics** *plural noun* (also treated as *singular*) exercises to develop or demonstrate physical (or mental) agility.

**gynaecology** /ɡaɪnɪˈkɒlədʒɪ/ *noun* (*US* **gynecology**) science of physiological functions and diseases of women. □ **gynaecological** /-kəˈlɒdʒ-/ *adjective*; **gynaecologist** *noun*.

**gypsum** /ˈdʒɪpsəm/ *noun* mineral used esp. to make plaster of Paris.

**Gypsy** /ˈdʒɪpsɪ/ *noun* (also **Gipsy**) (*plural* **-ies**) member of nomadic dark-skinned people of Europe.

**gyrate** /dʒaɪəˈreɪt/ *verb* (**-ting**) move in circle or spiral. □ **gyration** *noun*; **gyratory** *adjective*.

**gyro** /ˈdʒaɪərəʊ/ *noun* (*plural* **-s**) *colloquial* gyroscope.

**gyroscope** /ˈdʒaɪərəskəʊp/ *noun* rotating wheel whose axis is free to turn but maintains fixed direction unless perturbed, esp. used for stabilization.

# Hh

**H** *abbreviation* hard (pencil lead); (water) hydrant; *slang* heroin. □ **H-bomb** hydrogen bomb.

**h.** *abbreviation* (also **h**) hour(s); (also **h**) height; hot. □ **h. & c.** hot and cold (water).

**ha¹** /hɑː/ (also **hah**) *interjection expressing* surprise, triumph, *etc.*

**ha²** *abbreviation* hectare(s).

**habeas corpus** /heɪbɪəs ˈkɔːpəs/ *noun* writ requiring person to be brought before judge etc., esp. to investigate lawfulness of his or her detention.

**haberdasher** /ˈhæbədæʃə/ *noun* dealer in dress accessories and sewing goods. □ **haberdashery** *noun* (*plural* **-ies**).

**habit** /ˈhæbɪt/ *noun* settled tendency or practice; practice that is hard to give up; mental constitution or attitude; clothes, esp. of religious order.

**habitable** /ˈhæbɪtəb(ə)l/ *adjective* suitable for living in. □ **habitability** *noun*.

**habitat** /ˈhæbɪtæt/ *noun* natural home of plant or animal.

**habitation** /hæbɪˈteɪʃ(ə)n/ *noun* inhabiting; house, home.

**habitual** /həˈbɪtʃʊəl/ *adjective* done as a habit; usual; given to a habit. □ **habitually** *adverb*.

**habituate** /həˈbɪtʃʊeɪt/ *verb* (**-ting**) (often + *to*) accustom. □ **habituation** *noun*.

**habitué** /həˈbɪtʃʊeɪ/ *noun* (often + *of*) frequent visitor or resident. [French]

**háček** /ˈhætʃek/ *noun* mark used (ˇ) over letter to modify its sound in some languages. [Czech]

**hacienda** /hæsɪˈendə/ *noun* (in Spanish-speaking countries) plantation etc. with dwelling house.

**hack¹** ● verb cut or chop roughly; kick shin of; (often + at) deal cutting blows; cut (one's way) through; colloquial gain unauthorized access to (computer data); slang manage, tolerate. ● noun kick with toe of boot, wound from this. □ **hacksaw** saw for cutting metal.

**hack²** ● noun horse for ordinary riding; hired horse; person hired to do dull routine work, esp. as writer. ● adjective used as hack; commonplace. ● verb ride on horseback on road at ordinary pace.

**hacker** noun colloquial computer enthusiast; person who gains unauthorized access to computer network.

**hacking** adjective (of cough) short, dry, and frequent.

**hackle** /'hæk(ə)l/ noun (in plural) hairs on animal's neck which rise when it is angry or alarmed; long feather(s) on neck of domestic cock etc.; steel flax-comb. □ **make person's hackles rise** arouse anger or indignation.

**hackney** /'hækni/ noun (plural **-s**) horse for ordinary riding. □ **hackney carriage** taxi.

**hackneyed** /'hæknid/ adjective overused, trite.

**had** past & past participle of HAVE.

**haddock** /'hædək/ noun (plural same) common edible sea fish.

**Hades** /'heidi:z/ noun (in Greek mythology) the underworld.

**hadj** = HAJJ.

**hadji** = HAJJI.

**hadn't** /'hæd(ə)nt/ had not.

**haematite** /'hi:mətait/ noun (US **hem-**) red or brown iron ore.

**haematology** /hi:mə'tɒlədʒi/ noun (US **hem-**) study of the blood. □ **haematologist** noun.

**haemoglobin** /hi:mə'gləʊbɪn/ noun (US **hem-**) oxygen-carrying substance in red blood cells.

**haemophilia** /hi:mə'fɪlɪə/ noun (US **hem-**) hereditary tendency to severe bleeding from even a slight injury through failure of blood to clot. □ **haemophiliac** noun.

**haemorrhage** /'hemərɪdʒ/ (US **hem-**) ● noun profuse bleeding. ● verb (**-ging**) suffer haemorrhage.

**haemorrhoids** /'hemərɔɪdz/ plural noun (US **hem-**) swollen veins near anus, piles.

**haft** /hɑːft/ noun handle of knife etc.

**hag** noun ugly old woman; witch. □ **hagridden** afflicted by nightmares or fears.

**haggard** /'hægəd/ adjective looking exhausted and distraught.

**haggis** /'hægɪs/ noun Scottish dish of offal boiled in bag with oatmeal etc.

**haggle** /'hæg(ə)l/ ● verb (**-ling**) (often + over, about) bargain persistently. ● noun haggling.

**hagiography** /hægi'ɒgrəfi/ noun writing about saints' lives. □ **hagiographer** noun.

**hah** = HA¹.

**ha ha** /hɑːˈhɑː/ interjection representing laughter.

**ha-ha** /'hɑːhɑː/ noun ditch with wall in it bounding park or garden.

**haiku** /'haiku:/ noun (plural same) Japanese 3-line poem of usually 17 syllables.

**hail¹** ● noun pellets of frozen rain; (+ of) barrage, onslaught. ● verb (after it) hail falls; pour down as or like hail. □ **hailstone** pellet of hail; **hailstorm** period of heavy hail.

**hail²** ● verb signal (taxi etc.) to stop; greet enthusiastically; (+ from) originate. ● interjection archaic or jocular: expressing greeting. ● noun act of hailing.

**hair** noun any or all of fine filaments growing from skin of mammals, esp. of human head; hairlike thing. □ **haircut** (style of) cutting hair; **hairdo** style of or act of styling hair; **hairdresser** person who cuts and styles hair; **hairdressing** noun; **hair-drier, -dryer** device for drying hair with warm air; **hairgrip** flat hairpin with ends close together; **hairline** edge of person's hair on forehead, very narrow crack or line; **hairnet** piece of netting for confining hair; **hair of the dog** further alcoholic drink taken to cure effects of previous drinking; **hairpiece** false hair augmenting person's natural hair; **hairpin** U-shaped pin for fastening the hair; **hairpin bend** U-shaped bend in road; **hair-raising** terrifying; **hair's breadth** minute distance; **hair shirt** ascetic's or penitent's shirt made of hair; **hair-**

**slide** clip for keeping hair in position; **hair-splitting** quibbling; **hairspray** liquid sprayed on hair to keep it in place; **hairspring** fine spring regulating balance-wheel of watch; **hairstyle** particular way of arranging hair; **hairstylist** *noun*; **hair-trigger** trigger acting on very slight pressure. □ **hairless** *adjective*; **hairy** *adjective* (**-ier, -iest**).

**hajj** /hædʒ/ *noun* (also **hadj**) Islamic pilgrimage to Mecca.

**hajji** /ˈhædʒɪ/ *noun* (also **hadji**) (*plural* **-s**) Muslim who has made pilgrimage to Mecca.

**haka** /ˈhaːkə/ *noun NZ* Maori ceremonial war dance; similar dance by sports team before match.

**hake** *noun* (*plural* same) codlike sea fish.

**halal** /ˈhaːˈlaːl/ *noun* (also **hallal**) meat from animal killed according to Muslim law.

**halberd** /ˈhælbəd/ *noun historical* combined spear and battleaxe.

**halcyon** /ˈhælsɪən/ *adjective* calm, peaceful, happy.

**hale** *adjective* strong and healthy (esp. in **hale and hearty**).

**half** /haːf/ ● *noun* (*plural* **halves** /haːvz/) either of two (esp. equal) parts into which a thing is divided; *colloquial* half pint, esp. of beer; *Sport* either of two equal periods of play, half-back; half-price (esp. child's) ticket. ● *adjective* forming a half. ● *adverb* partly. □ **half and half** being half one thing and half another; **half-back** player between forwards and full back(s) in football etc.; **half-baked** not thoroughly thought out; **half board** provision of bed, breakfast, and one main meal; **half-brother, -sister** one having only one parent in common; **half-crown** *historical* coin worth 2 shillings and 6 pence (= 12½p); **half-dozen** (about) six; **half-hearted** lacking courage or zeal; **half-heartedly** *adverb*; **half holiday** half day as holiday; **half-hour, half an hour** 30 minutes, point of time 30 minutes after any hour o'clock; **half-hourly** *adjective & adverb*; **half-life** time after which radioactivity etc. is half its original value; **half-mast** position of flag halfway down mast as symbol of mourning; **half measures** unsatisfactory compromise etc.; **half-moon** (shape of) moon with disc half illuminated; **half nelson** see NELSON; **half-term** short holiday halfway through school term; **half-timbered** having walls with timber frame and brick or plaster filling; **half-time** (short break at) mid-point of game or contest; **halftone** photograph representing tones by large or small dots; **half-truth** statement that conveys only part of truth; **half-volley** playing of ball as soon as it bounces off ground; **halfwit** stupid person; **halfwitted** *adjective*.

**halfpenny** /ˈheɪpnɪ/ *noun* (*plural* **-pennies** or **-pence** /ˈheɪpəns/) *historical* coin worth half penny (withdrawn in 1984).

**halfway** ● *adverb* at a point midway between two others; to some extent. ● *adjective* situated halfway. □ **halfway house** compromise, halfway point, rehabilitation centre, inn etc. between two towns.

**halibut** /ˈhælɪbət/ *noun* (*plural* same) large flatfish.

**halitosis** /hælɪˈtəʊsɪs/ *noun* bad breath.

**hall** /hɔːl/ *noun* entrance area of house; large room or building for meetings, concerts, etc.; large country house or estate; (in full **hall of residence**) residence for students; college dining-room; large public room; *esp. US* corridor. □ **hallmark** mark used to show standard of gold, silver, and platinum, distinctive feature; **hallway** entrance hall or corridor.

**hallal** = HALAL.

**hallelujah** = ALLELUIA.

**hallo** = HELLO.

**hallow** /ˈhæləʊ/ *verb* (usually as **hallowed** *adjective*) make or honour as holy.

**Hallowe'en** /hæləʊˈiːn/ *noun* eve of All Saints' Day, 31 Oct.

**hallucinate** /həˈluːsɪneɪt/ *verb* (**-ting**) experience hallucinations.

**hallucination** *noun* illusion of seeing or hearing something not actually present. □ **hallucinatory** /həˈluːsɪnətərɪ/ *adjective*.

**hallucinogen** /həˈluːsɪnədʒ(ə)n/ *noun* drug causing hallucinations. □ **hallucinogenic** /-ˈdʒen-/ *adjective*.

**halm** = HAULM.

**halo** /'heɪləʊ/ ● *noun* (*plural* **-es**) disc of light shown round head of sacred person; glory associated with idealized person; circle of light round sun or moon etc. ● *verb* (**-es**, **-ed**) surround with halo.

**halogen** /'hælədʒ(ə)n/ *noun* any of the non-metallic elements (fluorine, chlorine, etc.) which form a salt when combined with a metal.

**halon** /'heɪlɒn/ *noun* gaseous halogen compound used to extinguish fires.

**halt**[1] /hɔːlt/ ● *noun* stop (usually temporary); minor stopping place on local railway line. ● *verb* (cause to) make a halt.

**halt**[2] /hɔːlt/ ● *verb* (esp. as **halting** *adjective*) proceed hesitantly. □ **haltingly** *adverb*.

**halter** /'hɔːltə/ *noun* rope with headstall for leading or tying up horses etc.; strap passing round back of neck holding dress etc. up, (also **halterneck**) dress etc. held by this.

**halva** /'hælvə/ *noun* confection of sesame flour, honey, etc.

**halve** /hɑːv/ *verb* (**-ving**) divide into halves; reduce to half.

**halves** *plural* of HALF.

**halyard** /'hæljəd/ *noun* rope or tackle for raising and lowering sail etc.

**ham** ● *noun* upper part of pig's leg cured for food; back of thigh; thigh and buttock; *colloquial* inexpert or unsubtle performer or actor; *colloquial* operator of amateur radio station. ● *verb* (**-mm-**) (usually in **ham it up**) *colloquial* overact. □ **ham-fisted, -handed** *colloquial* clumsy.

**hamburger** /'hæmbɜːgə/ *noun* cake of minced beef, usually eaten in soft bread roll.

**hamlet** /'hæmlɪt/ *noun* small village, esp. without church.

**hammer** /'hæmə/ ● *noun* tool with heavy metal head at right angles to handle, used for driving nails etc.; similar device, as for exploding charge in gun, striking strings of piano, etc.; auctioneer's mallet; metal ball attached to a wire for throwing as athletic contest. ● *verb* strike or drive (as) with hammer; *colloquial* defeat utterly. □ **hammer and tongs** *colloquial* with great energy;

**hammerhead** shark with flattened hammer-shaped head; **hammerlock** wrestling hold in which twisted arm is bent behind back; **hammer-toe** toe bent permanently downwards. □ **hammering** *noun*.

**hammock** /'hæmək/ *noun* bed of canvas or netting suspended by cords at ends.

**hamper**[1] /'hæmpə/ *noun* large basket, usually with hinged lid and containing food.

**hamper**[2] /'hæmpə/ *verb* obstruct movement of; hinder.

**hamster** /'hæmstə/ *noun* short-tailed mouselike rodent often kept as pet.

**hamstring** ● *noun* any of 5 tendons at back of human knee; (in quadruped) tendon at back of hock. ● *verb* (*past & past participle* **-strung** or **-stringed**) cripple by cutting hamstrings; impair efficiency of.

**hand** ● *noun* end part of human arm beyond wrist; similar member of monkey; (often in *plural*) control, disposal, agency; share in action, active support; handlike thing, esp. pointer of clock etc.; right or left side, direction, etc.; skill or style, esp. of writing; person who does or makes something; person etc. as source; manual worker in factory etc.; pledge of marriage; playing cards dealt to player, round or game of cards; *colloquial* round of applause; measure of horse's height, = 4 in. (10.16 cm). ● *verb* (+ *in, to, over, round*, etc.) deliver or transfer (as) with hand. □ **at hand** close by; **by hand** by person not machine, not by post; **handbag** small bag carried esp. by woman; **handball** game with ball thrown by hand, *Football* foul touching of ball; **handbell** small bell for ringing by hand; **handbook** short manual or guidebook; **handbrake** brake operated by hand; **handcuff** secure (prisoner) with **handcuffs**, pair of lockable metal rings joined by short chain; **handgun** small firearm held in one hand; **handhold** something for hand to grip; **hand in glove** in collusion; **handmade** made by hand (rather than machine); **hand-me-down** article passed on from another person; **handout** from hand to needy person, information etc. distributed to press etc., notes given out in class; **handover** act of handing over; **hand-over-fist** *colloquial* with rapid progress; **hand-picked** carefully chosen; **handrail** rail along edge of stairs etc.; **hands down** without effort; **handset** part of telephone held in hand; **handshake** clasping of person's hand, esp. as greeting etc.; **hands-on** practical rather than theoretical; **handstand** act of supporting oneself vertically on one's hands; **hand-to-hand** (of fighting) at close quarters; **handwriting** (style of) writing by hand; **take in hand** start doing or dealing with, undertake control or reform of; **to hand** within reach.

**handful** *noun* (*plural* **-s**) enough to fill the hand; small number or quantity; *colloquial* troublesome person or task.

**handicap** /'hændɪkæp/ ● *noun* physical or mental disability; thing that makes progress difficult; disadvantage imposed on superior competitor to equalize chances; race etc. in which this is imposed. ● *verb* (**-pp-**) impose handicap on; place at disadvantage.

**handicapped** *adjective* suffering from physical or mental disability.

**handicraft** /'hændɪkrɑːft/ *noun* work requiring manual and artistic skill.

**handiwork** /'hændɪwɜːk/ *noun* work done or thing made by hand, or by particular person.

**handkerchief** /'hæŋkətʃɪf/ *noun* (*plural* **-s** or **-chieves** /-tʃiːvz/) square of cloth used to wipe nose etc.

**handle** /'hænd(ə)l/ ● *noun* part by which thing is held. ● *verb* (**-ling**) touch, feel, operate, etc. with hands; manage, deal with; deal in (goods etc.). □ **handlebar** (usually in *plural*) steering-bar of bicycle etc.

**handler** *noun* person in charge of trained dog etc.

**handsome** /'hænsəm/ *adjective* (**-r, -st**) good-looking; imposing; generous; considerable. □ **handsomely** *adverb*.

**handy** *adjective* (**-ier, -iest**) convenient to handle; ready to hand; clever with hands. □ **handyman** person able to do odd jobs.

**hang** ● *verb* (*past & past participle* **hung** except as below) (cause to) be supported from above, attach by suspending from top; set up on hinges etc.;

place (picture) on wall or in exhibition; attach (wallpaper); (*past & past participle* **hanged**) suspend or be suspended by neck, esp. as capital punishment; let droop; remain or be hung. ● *noun* way thing hangs. □ **get the hang of** *colloquial* get knack of, understand; **hang about, around** loiter, not move away; **hangdog** shamefaced; **hang fire** delay acting; **hang-glider** fabric wing on light frame from which pilot is suspended; **hang-gliding** *noun*; **hangman** executioner by hanging; **hangnail** agnail; **hang on** (often + *to*) continue to hold, retain, wait for short time, not ring off during pause in telephoning; **hangover** after-effects of excess of alcohol; **hang up** *verb* hang from hook etc., end telephone conversation; **hang-up** *noun* *slang* emotional inhibition.

**hangar** /'hæŋə/ *noun* building for housing aircraft etc.

**hanger** *noun* person or thing that hangs; (in full **coat-hanger**) shaped piece of wood etc. for hanging clothes on. □ **hanger-on** (*plural* **hangers-on**) follower, dependant.

**hanging** *noun* execution by suspending by neck; (usually in *plural*) drapery for walls etc.

**hank** *noun* coil of yarn etc.

**hanker** /'hæŋkə/ *verb* (+ *for, after, to do*) crave, long for. □ **hankering** *noun*.

**hanky** /'hæŋkɪ/ *noun* (also **hankie**) (*plural* **-ies**) *colloquial* handkerchief.

**hanky-panky** /hæŋkɪ'pæŋkɪ/ *noun* *slang* misbehaviour; trickery.

**Hansard** /'hænsɑːd/ *noun* verbatim record of parliamentary debates.

**hansom** /'hænsəm/ *noun* (in full **hansom cab**) *historical* two-wheeled horse-drawn cab.

**haphazard** /hæp'hæzəd/ *adjective* casual, random. □ **haphazardly** *adverb*.

**hapless** /'hæplɪs/ *adjective* unlucky.

**happen** /'hæpən/ *verb* occur; (+ *to do*) have the (good or bad) fortune; (+ *to*) be fate or experience of; (+ *on*) come by chance on. □ **happening** *noun*.

**happy** /'hæpɪ/ *adjective* (**-ier, -iest**) feeling or showing pleasure or contentment; fortunate; apt, pleasing. □ **happy-go-lucky** taking things cheerfully as they happen; **happy hour** time of day when drinks are sold at reduced prices; **happy medium** compromise. □ **happily** adverb; **happiness** noun.

**hara-kiri** /ˈhærəˈkɪrɪ/ noun historical Japanese suicide by ritual disembowelling.

**harangue** /həˈræŋ/ ● noun lengthy and earnest speech. ● verb (**-guing**) make harangue to.

**harass** /ˈhærəs/ verb trouble, annoy; attack repeatedly. □ **harassment** noun.

■ **Usage** Harass is often pronounced /həˈræs/ (with the stress on the -rass), but this is considered incorrect by some people.

**harbinger** /ˈhɑːbɪndʒə/ noun person or thing announcing another's approach, forerunner.

**harbour** /ˈhɑːbə/ (US **harbor**) ● noun place of shelter for ships; shelter. ● verb give shelter to; entertain (thoughts etc.).

**hard** ● adjective firm, solid; difficult to bear, do, or understand; unfeeling, harsh, severe; strenuous, enthusiastic; Politics extreme, radical; (of drinks) strongly alcoholic; (of drug) potent and addictive; (of water) difficult to lather; (of currency etc.) not likely to fall in value; not disputable. ● adverb strenuously, severely, intensely. □ **hard and fast** (of rule etc.) strict; **hardback** (book) bound in stiff covers; **hardbitten** colloquial tough, cynical; **hardboard** stiff board of compressed wood pulp; **hard-boiled** (of eggs) boiled until yolk and white are solid, (of person) tough, shrewd; **hard cash** coins and banknotes, not cheques etc.; **hard copy** printed material produced by computer; **hardcore** stones, rubble, etc. as foundation; **hard core** central or most enduring part; **hard disk** Computing rigid storage disk, esp. fixed in computer; **hard-done-by** unfairly treated; **hardheaded** practical, not sentimental; **hard-hearted** unfeeling; **hard line** firm adherence to policy; **hardliner** noun; **hard-nosed** colloquial realistic, uncompromising; **hard of hearing** somewhat deaf; **hard-pressed** closely pursued, burdened with urgent business; **hard sell** aggressive salesmanship; **hard shoulder** strip at side of motorway for emergency stops; **hard up** short of money; **hardware** tools,

weapons, machinery, etc., mechanical and electronic components of computer; **hardwood** wood of deciduous tree. □ **hardness** noun.

**harden** verb make or become hard or unyielding.

**hardihood** /ˈhɑːdɪhʊd/ noun boldness.

**hardly** adverb scarcely; with difficulty.

**hardship** noun severe suffering or privation.

**hardy** /ˈhɑːdɪ/ adjective (**-ier**, **-iest**) robust; capable of endurance; (of plant) able to grow in the open all year. □ **hardiness** noun.

**hare** /heə/ ● noun mammal like large rabbit, with long ears, short tail, and long hind legs. ● verb(**-ring**) run rapidly. □ **hare-brained** rash, wild.

**harebell** noun plant with pale blue bell-shaped flowers.

**harem** /ˈhɑːriːm/ noun women of Muslim household; their quarters.

**haricot** /ˈhærɪkəʊ/ noun (in full **haricot bean**) French bean with small white seeds; these as vegetable.

**hark** verb (usually in imperative) archaic listen. □ **hark back** revert to earlier topic.

**Harlequin** /ˈhɑːlɪkwɪn/ ● noun masked pantomime character in diamond-patterned costume. ● adjective (**harlequin**) in varied colours.

**harlot** /ˈhɑːlət/ noun archaic prostitute.

**harm** noun & verb damage, hurt.

**harmful** adjective causing or likely to cause harm. □ **harmfully** adverb.

**harmless** adjective not able or likely to harm. □ **harmlessly** adverb.

**harmonic** /hɑːˈmɒnɪk/ ● adjective of or relating to harmony; harmonious. ● noun Music overtone accompanying (and forming a note with) a fundamental at a fixed interval.

**harmonica** /hɑːˈmɒnɪkə/ noun small rectangular instrument played by blowing and sucking air through it.

**harmonious** /hɑːˈməʊnɪəs/ adjective sweet-sounding, tuneful; forming a pleasant or consistent whole; free from dissent. □ **harmoniously** adverb.

**harmonium** /hɑːˈməʊnɪəm/ noun keyboard instrument with bellows and metal reeds.

**harmonize** /ˈhɑːmənaɪz/ verb (also **-ise**) (**-zing** or **-sing**) add notes to (melody) to produce harmony; bring into or be in harmony. □ **harmonization** noun.

**harmony** /ˈhɑːmənɪ/ noun (plural **-ies**) combination of notes to form chords; melodious sound; agreement, concord.

**harness** /ˈhɑːnɪs/ ● noun straps etc. by which horse is fastened to cart etc. and controlled; similar arrangement for fastening thing to person. ● verb put harness on; utilize (natural forces), esp. to produce energy.

**harp** ● noun large upright stringed instrument plucked with fingers. ● verb (+ on, on about) dwell on tediously. □ **harpist** noun.

**harpoon** /hɑːˈpuːn/ ● noun spearlike missile for shooting whales etc. ● verb spear with harpoon.

**harpsichord** /ˈhɑːpsɪkɔːd/ noun keyboard instrument with strings plucked mechanically. □ **harpsichordist** noun.

**harpy** /ˈhɑːpɪ/ noun (plural **-ies**) mythological monster with woman's face and bird's wings and claws; grasping unscrupulous person.

**harridan** /ˈhærɪd(ə)n/ noun bad-tempered old woman.

**harrier** /ˈhærɪə/ noun hound used in hunting hares; kind of falcon.

**harrow** /ˈhærəʊ/ ● noun frame with metal teeth or discs for breaking clods of earth. ● verb draw harrow over; (usually as **harrowing** adjective) distress greatly.

**harry** /ˈhærɪ/ verb (**-ies**, **-ied**) ravage, despoil; harass.

**harsh** adjective rough to hear, taste, etc.; severe, cruel. □ **harshly** adverb; **harshness** noun.

**hart** noun (plural same or **-s**) male of (esp. red) deer.

**hartebeest** /ˈhɑːtɪbiːst/ noun large African antelope with curved horns.

**harum-scarum** /heərəmˈskeərəm/ adjective colloquial reckless, wild.

**harvest** /ˈhɑːvɪst/ ● noun gathering in of crops etc.; season for this; season's yield; product of any action. ● verb reap and gather in.

**harvester** noun reaper, reaping machine.

**has** 3rd singular present of HAVE.

**hash**[1] ● noun dish of reheated pieces of cooked meat; mixture, jumble; recycled material. ● verb (often + up) recycle (old material). □ **make a hash of** colloquial make a mess of, bungle.

**hash**[2] noun colloquial hashish.

**hashish** /ˈhæʃɪʃ/ noun narcotic drug got from hemp.

**hasn't** /ˈhæz(ə)nt/ has not.

**hasp** /hɑːsp/ noun hinged metal clasp passing over staple and secured by padlock.

**hassle** /ˈhæs(ə)l/ colloquial ● noun trouble, problem; argument. ● verb (**-ling**) harass.

**hassock** /ˈhæsək/ noun kneeling-cushion.

**haste** /heɪst/ noun urgency of movement; hurry. □ **make haste** be quick.

**hasten** /ˈheɪs(ə)n/ verb (cause to) proceed or go quickly.

**hasty** /ˈheɪstɪ/ adjective (**-ier**, **-iest**) hurried; said, made, or done too quickly. □ **hastily** adverb; **hastiness** noun.

**hat** noun (esp. outdoor) head-covering. □ **hat trick** Cricket taking 3 wickets with successive balls, Football scoring of 3 goals in one match by same player, 3 consecutive successes.

**hatch**[1] noun opening in wall between kitchen and dining-room for serving food; opening or door in aircraft etc.; (cover for) hatchway. □ **hatchback** car with rear door hinged at top; **hatchway** opening in ship's deck for lowering cargo.

**hatch**[2] ● verb (often + out) emerge from egg; (of egg) produce young animal; incubate; (also + up) devise (plot). ● noun hatching; brood hatched.

**hatch**[3] verb mark with parallel lines. □ **hatching** noun.

**hatchet** /ˈhætʃɪt/ noun light short axe.

**hate** ● verb (**-ting**) dislike intensely. ● noun hatred.

**hateful** adjective arousing hatred.

**hatred** /ˈheɪtrɪd/ noun intense dislike; ill will.

**hatter** noun maker or seller of hats.

**haughty** /ˈhɔːtɪ/ adjective (**-ier**, **-iest**) proud, arrogant. □ **haughtily** adverb; **haughtiness** noun.

**haul** /hɔːl/ ● *verb* pull or drag forcibly; transport by lorry, cart, etc. ● *noun* hauling; amount gained or acquired; distance to be traversed.

**haulage** *noun* (charge for) commercial transport of goods.

**haulier** /ˈhɔːlɪə/ *noun* person or firm engaged in transport of goods.

**haulm** /hɔːm/ *noun* (also **halm**) stalk or stem; stalks of beans, peas, potatoes, etc. collectively.

**haunch** /hɔːntʃ/ *noun* fleshy part of buttock and thigh; leg and loin of deer etc. as food.

**haunt** /hɔːnt/ ● *verb* (of ghost etc.) visit regularly; frequent (place); linger in mind of (person). ● *noun* place frequented by person.

**haunting** *adjective* (of memory, melody, etc.) lingering; poignant, evocative.

**haute couture** /əʊt kuːˈtjʊə/ *noun* (world of) high fashion.

**hauteur** /əʊˈtɜː/ *noun* haughtiness.

**have** /hæv/ ● *verb* (**having**; *3rd singular present* **has** /hæz/; *past & past participle* **had**) *used as auxiliary verb with past participle to form past tenses*; hold in possession or relationship, be provided with; contain as part or quality; experience; (come to) be subjected to a specified state; engage in; tolerate, permit; give birth to; receive; obtain or know (qualification, language, etc.); *colloquial* get the better of, (usually in *passive*) cheat. ● *noun* (usually in *plural*) *colloquial* wealthy person; *slang* swindle. □ **have on** wear (clothes), have (engagement), *colloquial* hoax; **have-not** (usually in *plural*) person lacking wealth; **have to** be obliged to, must.

**haven** /ˈheɪv(ə)n/ *noun* refuge; harbour.

**haven't** /ˈhæv(ə)nt/ have not.

**haver** /ˈheɪvə/ *verb* hesitate; talk foolishly.

**haversack** /ˈhævəsæk/ *noun* canvas bag carried on back or over shoulder.

**havoc** /ˈhævək/ *noun* devastation, confusion.

**haw** *noun* hawthorn berry.

**hawk**[1] ● *noun* bird of prey with rounded wings; *Politics* person who advocates aggressive policy. ● *verb* hunt with hawk.

**hawk**[2] *verb* carry (goods) about for sale.

**hawk**[3] *verb* clear throat noisily; (+ *up*) bring (phlegm etc.) up thus.

**hawker** *noun* person who hawks goods.

**hawser** /ˈhɔːzə/ *noun* thick rope or cable for mooring ship.

**hawthorn** *noun* thorny shrub with red berries.

**hay** *noun* grass mown and dried for fodder. □ **haycock** conical heap of hay; **hay fever** allergic irritation of nose, throat, etc. caused by pollen, dust, etc.; **haymaking** mowing grass and spreading it to dry; **hayrick, haystack** packed pile of hay; **haywire** *colloquial* badly disorganized, out of control.

**hazard** /ˈhæzəd/ ● *noun* danger, risk; obstacle on golf course. ● *verb* venture on (guess etc.); risk.

**hazardous** *adjective* risky.

**haze** *noun* slight mist; mental obscurity, confusion.

**hazel** /ˈheɪz(ə)l/ *noun* nut-bearing hedgerow shrub; greenish-brown. □ **hazelnut** nut of hazel.

**hazy** *adjective* (**-ier, -iest**) misty; vague; confused. □ **hazily** *adverb*; **haziness** *noun*.

**HB** *abbreviation* hard black (pencil lead).

**HE** *abbreviation* His or Her Excellency; high explosive.

**he** /hiː/ *pronoun* (as subject of verb) the male person or animal in question; person of unspecified sex. □ **he-man** masterful or virile man.

**head** /hed/ ● *noun* uppermost part of human body, or foremost part of body of animal, containing brain, sense organs, etc.; seat of intellect; thing like head in form or position; top, front, or upper end; person in charge, esp. of school; position of command; individual as unit; side of coin bearing image of head, (in *plural*) this as call when tossing coin; signal-converting device on tape recorder etc.; foam on top of beer etc.; confined body of water or steam, pressure exerted by this; (usually in **come to a head**) climax, crisis. ● *verb* be at front or in charge of; (often + *for*) move or send in specified direction; provide with heading; *Football* strike (ball) with head. □ **headache** continuous pain in head, *colloquial* troublesome problem; **headachy** adjective; **headband** band worn round head as decoration or to confine hair; **headboard** upright panel at head of bed; **headcount** (counting of) total number of people; **headdress** (esp. ornamental) covering for head; **head-hunting** collecting of enemies' heads as trophies, seeking of staff by approaching people employed elsewhere; **headlamp, headlight** (main) light at front of vehicle; **headland** promontory; **headline** heading at top of page, newspaper article, etc., (in plural) summary of broadcast news; **headlock** wrestling hold round opponent's head; **headlong** with head foremost, in a rush; **headman** tribal chief; **headmaster, headmistress** head teacher; **head-on** (of collision etc.) with front foremost; **headphones** pair of earphones fitting over head; **headquarters** (treated as *singular* or *plural*) organization's administrative centre; **headroom** overhead space; **headset** headphones, often with microphone; **headshrinker** *slang* psychiatrist; **headstall** part of bridle or halter fitting round horse's head; **head start** advantage granted or gained at early stage; **headstone** stone set up at head of grave; **headstrong** self-willed; **head teacher** teacher in charge of school; **headway** progress; **head wind** one blowing from directly in front.

**header** noun Football act of heading ball; colloquial headlong dive or plunge.

**heading** noun title at head of page etc.

**heady** adjective (-**ier, -iest**) (of liquor etc.) potent; exciting; intoxicating; impetuous; headachy.

**heal** verb (often + up) become healthy again; cure; put right (differences). □ **healer** noun.

**health** /helθ/ noun state of being well in body or mind; mental or physical condition. □ **health centre** building containing local medical services; **health food** natural food, thought to promote good health; **health service** public medical service; **health visitor** nurse who visits mothers and babies, the elderly, etc. at home.

**healthy** adjective (-**ier, -iest**) having, conducive to, or indicative of, good health. □ **healthily** adverb; **healthiness** noun.

**heap** ● noun disorderly pile; (esp. in plural) colloquial large number or amount; slang dilapidated vehicle. ● verb (+ up, together, etc.) pile or collect in heap; (+ with) load copiously with; (+ on, upon) offer copiously.

**hear** verb (past & past participle **heard** /hɜːd/) perceive with ear; listen to; listen judicially to; be informed; (+ from) receive message etc. from. □ **hearsay** rumour, gossip. □ **hearer** noun.

**hearing** noun faculty of perceiving sounds; range within which sounds may be heard; opportunity to state one's case; trial of case before court. □ **hearing-aid** small sound-amplifier worn by deaf person.

**hearse** /hɜːs/ noun vehicle for carrying coffin.

**heart** /hɑːt/ noun organ in body keeping up circulation of blood by contraction and dilation; region of heart, breast; seat of thought, feeling, or emotion (esp. love); courage; mood; central or innermost part, essence; tender inner part of vegetable etc.; (conventionally) heart-shaped thing; playing card of suit marked with red hearts. □ **at heart** in inmost feelings; **by heart** from memory; **have the heart** (usually in negative, + to do) be hard-hearted enough; **heartache** mental anguish; **heart attack** sudden heart failure; **heartbeat** pulsation of heart; **heartbreak** overwhelming distress; **heartbreaking** adjective; **heartbroken** adjective; **heartburn** burning sensation in chest from indigestion; **heartfelt** sincere; **heart-rending** very distressing; **heartsick** despondent; **heartstrings** deepest affections or pity; **heartthrob** colloquial object of (esp. immature) romantic feelings; **heart-to-heart** frank (talk); **heart-warming** emotionally moving and encouraging; **take to heart** be much affected by.

**hearten** verb make or become more cheerful. □ **heartening** adjective.

**hearth** /hɑːθ/ noun floor of fireplace. □ **hearthrug** rug laid before fireplace.

**heartless** adjective unfeeling, pitiless. □ **heartlessly** adverb.

**hearty** adjective (-**ier, -iest**) strong, vigorous; (of meal or appetite) large; warm, friendly. □ **heartily** adverb; **heartiness** noun.

**heat** • *noun* condition or sensation of being hot; energy arising from motion of molecules; hot weather; warmth of feeling; anger; most intense part or period of activity; preliminary contest, winner(s) of which compete in final. • *verb* make or become hot; inflame. □ **heatproof** able to resist great heat; **heatwave** period of very hot weather; **on heat** (of female animals) sexually receptive.

**heated** *adjective* angry, impassioned. □ **heatedly** *adverb*.

**heater** *noun* device for heating room, water, etc.

**heath** /hiːθ/ *noun* flattish tract of uncultivated land with low shrubs; plant growing on heath, esp. heather.

**heathen** /ˈhiːð(ə)n/ • *noun* person not belonging to predominant religion. • *adjective* of heathens; having no religion.

**heather** /ˈheðə/ *noun* purple-flowered plant of moors and heaths.

**heating** *noun* equipment used to heat building.

**heave** • *verb* (**-ving**) *past & past participle* **heaved** or *esp. Nautical* **hove** /həʊv/ lift, haul, or utter with effort; *colloquial* throw; rise and fall periodically; *Nautical* haul by rope; retch. • *noun* heaving. □ **heave in sight** come into view; **heave to** bring vessel to standstill.

**heaven** /ˈhev(ə)n/ *noun* home of God and of blessed after death; place or state of bliss, delightful thing; (**the heavens**) sky as seen from earth. □ **heavenly** *adjective*.

**heavy** /ˈhevɪ/ • *adjective* (**-ier**, **-iest**) of great weight, difficult to lift; of great density; abundant; severe, extensive; striking or falling with force; (of machinery etc.) very large of its kind; needing much physical effort; hard to digest; hard to read or understand; (of ground) difficult to travel over; dull, tedious, oppressive; coarse, ungraceful. • *noun* (*plural* **-ies**) *colloquial* thug (often hired); villain. □ **heavy-duty** designed to withstand hard use; **heavy-handed** clumsy, oppressive; **heavy hydrogen** deuterium; **heavy industry** that concerned with production of metal and machines etc.; **heavy metal** *colloquial* loud rock music with pounding rhythm; **heavy water** water composed of deuterium and oxygen; **heavyweight** amateur boxing weight (over 81 kg). □ **heavily** *adverb*; **heaviness** *noun*.

**Hebraic** /hiːˈbreɪk/ *adjective* of Hebrew or the Hebrews.

**Hebrew** /ˈhiːbruː/ • *noun* member of a Semitic people in ancient Palestine; their language; modern form of this, used esp. in Israel. • *adjective* of or in Hebrew; of the Jews.

**heckle** /ˈhek(ə)l/ • *verb* (**-ling**) interrupt or harass (speaker). • *noun* act of heckling. □ **heckler** *noun*.

**hectare** /ˈhekteə/ *noun* metric unit of square measure (2.471 acres).

**hectic** /ˈhektɪk/ *adjective* busy and confused; excited; feverish. □ **hectically** *adverb*.

**hecto-** /ˈhektəʊ/ *combining form* one hundred.

**hector** /ˈhektə/ *verb* bluster, bully. □ **hectoring** *adjective*.

**he'd** /hiːd/ he had; he would.

**hedge** • *noun* fence of bushes or low trees; protection against possible loss. • *verb* (**-ging**) surround with hedge; (+ *in*) enclose; secure oneself against loss on (bet etc.); avoid committing oneself. □ **hedgehog** small spiny insect-eating mammal; **hedge-hop** fly at low altitude; **hedgerow** row of bushes forming hedge; **hedge sparrow** common brown-backed bird.

**hedonism** /ˈhiːdənɪz(ə)m/ *noun* (behaviour based on) belief in pleasure as humankind's proper aim. □ **hedonist** *noun*; **hedonistic** /-ˈnɪs-/ *adjective*.

**heed** • *verb* attend to; take notice of. • *noun* care, attention. □ **heedless** *adjective*; **heedlessly** *adverb*.

**hee-haw** /ˈhiːhɔː/ *noun & verb* bray.

**heel¹** • *noun* back of foot below ankle; part of sock etc. covering this, or of shoe etc. supporting it; crust end of loaf; *colloquial* scoundrel; (as *interjection*) command to dog to walk near owner's heel. • *verb* fit or renew heel on (shoe); touch ground with heel; (+ *out*) *Rugby* pass ball with heel. □ **cool, kick one's heels** be kept waiting; **heelball** shoemaker's polishing mixture of wax etc., esp. used in brass rubbing.

**heel**[2] ● *verb* (often + *over*) (of ship etc.) lean over; cause (ship) to do this. ● *noun* heeling.

**hefty** /ˈheftɪ/ *adjective* (**-ier**, **-iest**) (of person) big, strong; (of thing) heavy, powerful.

**hegemony** /hɪˈɡemənɪ/ *noun* leadership.

**heifer** /ˈhefə/ *noun* young cow, esp. one that has not had more than one calf.

**height** /haɪt/ *noun* measurement from base to top; elevation above ground or other level; high point; top; extreme example.

**heighten** *verb* make or become higher or more intense.

**heinous** /ˈheɪnəs/ *adjective* atrocious.

**heir** /eə/ *noun* (*feminine* **heiress**) person entitled to property or rank as legal successor of former holder. □ **heir apparent** one whose claim cannot be superseded by birth of nearer heir; **heirloom** piece of property that has been in family for generations; **heir presumptive** one whose claim may be superseded by birth of nearer heir.

**held** past & past participle of HOLD[1].

**helical** /ˈhelɪk(ə)l/ *adjective* spiral.

**helices** *plural* of HELIX.

**helicopter** /ˈhelɪkɒptə/ *noun* wingless aircraft lifted and propelled by overhead blades revolving horizontally.

**heliograph** /ˈhiːlɪəɡrɑːf/ ● *noun* signalling apparatus reflecting flashes of sunlight. ● *verb* send (message) thus.

**heliotrope** /ˈhiːlɪətrəʊp/ *noun* plant with fragrant purple flowers.

**heliport** /ˈhelɪpɔːt/ *noun* place where helicopters take off and land.

**helium** /ˈhiːlɪəm/ *noun* light nonflammable gaseous element.

**helix** /ˈhiːlɪks/ *noun* (*plural* **helices** /ˈhiːlɪsiːz/) spiral or coiled curve.

**hell** *noun* home of the damned after death; place or state of misery. □ **hellish** *adjective*; **hellishly** *adverb*.

**he'll** /hiːl/ he will; he shall.

**hellebore** /ˈhelɪbɔː/ *noun* evergreen plant of kind including Christmas rose.

**Hellene** /ˈheliːn/ *noun* Greek. □ **Hellenic** /-ˈlen-/ *adjective*; **Hellenism** /-lɪn-/ *noun*; **Hellenist** /-lɪn-/ *noun*.

**Hellenistic** /helɪˈnɪstɪk/ *adjective* of Greek history, language, and culture of late 4th to late 1st c. BC.

**hello** /həˈləʊ/ (also **hallo**, **hullo**) ● *interjection* expressing informal greeting or surprise, or calling attention. ● *noun* (*plural* **-s**) cry of 'hello'.

**helm** *noun* tiller or wheel for managing rudder. □ **at the helm** in control; **helmsman** person who steers ship.

**helmet** /ˈhelmɪt/ *noun* protective headcover of policeman, motorcyclist, etc.

**help** ● *verb* provide with means to what is needed or sought; be useful to; (usually in negative) prevent, refrain from. ● *noun* act of helping; person or thing that helps; *colloquial* domestic assistant or assistance; remedy etc.; (**help oneself**) (often + *to*) serve oneself, take without permission. □ **helpline** telephone service providing help with problems. □ **helper** *noun*.

**helpful** *adjective* giving help, useful. □ **helpfully** *adverb*; **helpfulness** *noun*.

**helping** *noun* portion of food.

**helpless** *adjective* lacking help, defenceless; unable to act without help. □ **helplessly** *adverb*; **helplessness** *noun*.

**helter-skelter** /heltəˈskeltə/ ● *adverb* & *adjective* in disorderly haste. ● *noun* spiral slide at funfair.

**hem**[1] ● *noun* border of cloth where edge is turned under and sewn down. ● *verb* (**-mm-**) sew edge thus. □ **hem in** confine, restrict; **hemline** lower edge of skirt etc.; **hemstitch** (make hem with) ornamental stitch.

**hem**[2] *interjection* expressing hesitation or calling attention by slight cough.

**hemisphere** /ˈhemɪsfɪə/ *noun* half sphere; half earth, esp. as divided by equator or by line passing through poles; each half of brain. □ **hemispherical** /-ˈsfer-/ *adjective*.

**hemlock** /ˈhemlɒk/ *noun* poisonous plant with small white flowers; poison made from it.

**hemp** *noun* (in full **Indian hemp**) Asian herbaceous plant; its fibre used for rope etc.; narcotic drug made from it.

**hempen** *adjective* made of hemp.

**hen** *noun* female bird, esp. of domestic fowl. □ **henbane** poisonous hairy plant; **hen-party** *colloquial* party of women only; **henpecked** (of husband) domineered over by his wife.

**hence** *adverb* from now; for this reason. □ **henceforth, henceforward** from this time onwards.

**henchman** /'hentʃmən/ *noun usually derogatory* trusted supporter.

**henge** *noun* prehistoric circle of wood or stone uprights, as at *Stonehenge*.

**henna** /'henə/ ●*noun* tropical shrub; reddish dye made from it and used esp. to colour hair. ●*verb* (**hennaed, hennaing**) dye with henna.

**henry** /'henrɪ/ *noun* (*plural* **-s, -ies**) SI unit of inductance.

**hep** = HIP⁴.

**hepatitis** /hepə'taɪtɪs/ *noun* inflammation of the liver.

**hepta-** *combining form* seven.

**heptagon** /'heptəgən/ *noun* plane figure with 7 sides and angles. □ **heptagonal** /-'tæg-/ *adjective*.

**her** ●*pronoun* (as object of verb) the female person or thing in question; *colloquial* she. ●*adjective* of or belonging to her.

**herald** /'her(ə)ld/ ●*noun* messenger; forerunner; official. ●*verb* proclaim approach of; usher in. □ **heraldic** /-'ræld-/ *adjective*.

**heraldry** /'herəldrɪ/ *noun* (science or art of) armorial bearings.

**herb** *noun* non-woody seed-bearing plant; plant with leaves, seeds, or flowers used for flavouring, medicine, etc.

**herbaceous** /hɜː'beɪʃəs/ *adjective* of or like herbs. □ **herbaceous border** border in garden etc. containing flowering plants.

**herbage** *noun* vegetation collectively, esp. pasturage.

**herbal** ●*adjective* of herbs. ●*noun* book about herbs.

**herbalist** *noun* dealer in medicinal herbs; writer on herbs.

**herbarium** /hɜː'beərɪəm/ *noun* (*plural* **-ria**) collection of dried plants.

**herbicide** /'hɜːbɪsaɪd/ *noun* poison used to destroy unwanted vegetation.

**herbivore** /'hɜːbɪvɔː/ *noun* plant-eating animal. □ **herbivorous** /-'bɪvərəs/ *adjective*.

**Herculean** /hɜːkjʊ'liːən/ *adjective* having or requiring great strength or effort.

**herd** ●*noun* number of cattle etc. feeding or travelling together; (**the herd**) *derogatory* large number of people. ●*verb* (cause to) go in herd; tend. □ **herdsman** keeper of herds.

**here** ●*adverb* in or to this place; *indicating a person or thing*; at this point. ●*noun* this place. □ **hereabout(s)** somewhere near here; **hereafter** (in) future, (in) next world; **hereby** by this means; **herein** *formal* in this place, book, etc.; **hereinafter** *formal* from this point on, below (in document); **hereof** *formal* of this; **hereto** *formal* to this; **heretofore** *formal* formerly; **hereupon** after or in consequence of this; **herewith** with this.

**hereditary** /hɪ'redɪtərɪ/ *adjective* transmitted genetically from one generation to another; descending by inheritance; holding position by inheritance.

**heredity** /hɪ'redɪtɪ/ *noun* genetic transmission of physical or mental characteristics; these characteristics; genetic constitution.

**heresy** /'herəsɪ/ *noun* (*plural* **-ies**) *esp. RC Church* religious belief contrary to orthodox doctrine; opinion contrary to what is normally accepted.

**heretic** /'heretɪk/ *noun* believer in heresy. □ **heretical** /hɪ'ret-/ *adjective*.

**heritable** /'herɪtəb(ə)l/ *adjective* that can be inherited.

**heritage** /'herɪtɪdʒ/ *noun* what is or may be inherited; inherited circumstances, benefits, etc.; nation's historic buildings, countryside, etc.

**hermaphrodite** /hɜː'mæfrədaɪt/ ●*noun* person, animal, or plant with organs of both sexes. ●*adjective* combining both sexes. □ **hermaphroditic** /-'dɪt-/ *adjective*.

**hermetic** /hɜː'metɪk/ *adjective* with an airtight seal. □ **hermetically** *adverb*.

**hermit** /'hɜːmɪt/ *noun* person living in solitude. □ **hermit-crab** crab which lives in mollusc's cast-off shell.

**hermitage** *noun* hermit's dwelling; secluded residence.

**hernia** /'hɜːnɪə/ *noun* protrusion of part of organ through wall of cavity containing it.

**hero** /'hɪərəʊ/ *noun* (*plural* **-es**) person admired for courage, outstanding achievements, etc.; chief male character in play, story, etc. □ **hero-worship** idealization of admired person.

**heroic** /hɪˈrəʊɪk/ ● *adjective* fit for, or like, a hero; very brave. ● *noun* (in *plural*) overdramatic talk or behaviour. □ **heroically** *adverb*.

**heroin** /ˈherəʊɪn/ *noun* sedative addictive drug prepared from morphine.

**heroine** /ˈherəʊɪn/ *noun* female hero; chief female character in play, story, etc.

**heroism** /ˈherəʊɪz(ə)m/ *noun* heroic conduct.

**heron** /ˈherən/ *noun* long-necked long-legged wading bird.

**herpes** /ˈhɜːpiːz/ *noun* virus disease causing blisters.

**Herr** /heə/ *noun* (*plural* **Herren** /ˈherən/) title of German man.

**herring** /ˈherɪŋ/ *noun* (*plural* same or **-s**) N. Atlantic edible fish. □ **herring-bone** stitch or weave of small 'V' shapes making zigzag pattern.

**hers** /hɜːz/ *pronoun* the one(s) belonging to her.

**herself** /həˈself/ *pronoun:* emphatic *form of* SHE *or* HER; reflexive *form of* HER.

**hertz** /hɜːts/ *noun* (*plural* same) SI unit of frequency (one cycle per second).

**he's** /hiːz/ he is; he has.

**hesitant** /ˈhezɪt(ə)nt/ *adjective* hesitating. □ **hesitance** *noun;* **hesitancy** *noun;* **hesitantly** *adverb.*

**hesitate** /ˈhezɪteɪt/ *verb* (**-ting**) feel or show indecision; pause; (often + *to do*) be reluctant. □ **hesitation** *noun.*

**hessian** /ˈhesɪən/ *noun* strong coarse hemp or jute sacking.

**heterodox** /ˈhetərəʊdɒks/ *adjective* not orthodox. □ **heterodoxy** *noun.*

**heterogeneous** /ˌhetərəʊˈdʒiːnɪəs/ *adjective* diverse; varied in content. □ **heterogeneity** /-dʒɪˈniːɪtɪ/ *noun.*

**heteromorphic** /ˌhetərəʊˈmɔːfɪk/ *adjective* (also **heteromorphous** /-ˈmɔːfəs/) *Biology* of dissimilar forms.

**heterosexual** /ˌhetərəʊˈsekʃʊəl/ ● *adjective* feeling or involving sexual attraction to opposite sex. ● *noun* heterosexual person. □ **heterosexuality** /-ˈælɪ-/ *noun.*

**het up** *adjective colloquial* overwrought.

**heuristic** /hjʊəˈrɪstɪk/ *adjective* serving to discover; using trial and error.

**hew** *verb* (*past participle* **hewn** /hjuːn/ or **hewed**) chop or cut with axe, sword, etc.; cut into shape.

**hex** ● *verb* practise witchcraft; bewitch. ● *noun* magic spell.

**hexa-** *combining form* six.

**hexagon** /ˈheksəɡən/ *noun* plane figure with 6 sides and angles. □ **hexagonal** /-ˈsæɡ-/ *adjective.*

**hexagram** /ˈheksəɡræm/ *noun* 6-pointed star formed by two intersecting equilateral triangles.

**hexameter** /hekˈsæmɪtə/ *noun* verse line of 6 metrical feet.

**hey** /heɪ/ *interjection* calling attention or expressing surprise, inquiry, etc. □ **hey presto!** *conjuror's phrase on completing trick.*

**heyday** /ˈheɪdeɪ/ *noun* time of greatest success, prime.

**HF** *abbreviation* high frequency.

**HGV** *abbreviation* heavy goods vehicle.

**HH** *abbreviation* Her or His Highness; His Holiness; double-hard (pencil lead).

**hi** /haɪ/ *interjection* calling attention or as greeting.

**hiatus** /haɪˈeɪtəs/ *noun* (*plural* **-tuses**) gap in series etc.; break between two vowels coming together but not in same syllable.

**hibernate** /ˈhaɪbəneɪt/ *verb* (**-ting**) (of animal) spend winter in dormant state. □ **hibernation** *noun.*

**Hibernian** /haɪˈbɜːnɪən/ *archaic poetical* ● *adjective* of Ireland. ● *noun* native of Ireland.

**hibiscus** /hɪˈbɪskəs/ *noun* (*plural* **-cuses**) cultivated shrub with large brightly coloured flowers.

**hiccup** /ˈhɪkʌp/ (also **hiccough**) ● *noun* involuntary audible spasm of respiratory organs; temporary or minor stoppage or difficulty. ● *verb* (**-p-**) make hiccup.

**hick** *noun esp. US colloquial* yokel.

**hickory** /ˈhɪkərɪ/ *noun* (*plural* **-ies**) N. American tree related to walnut; its wood.

**hid** *past of* HIDE[1].

**hidden** *past participle of* HIDE[1]. □ **hidden agenda** secret motivation behind policy etc., ulterior motive.

**hide**[1] • *verb* (**-ding**; *past* **hid**; *past participle* **hidden**) /'hɪd(ə)n/) put or keep out of sight; conceal oneself; (usually + *from*) conceal (fact). • *noun* camouflaged shelter for observing wildlife. □ **hide-and-seek** game in which players hide and another searches for them; **hideaway** hiding place, retreat; **hide-out** *colloquial* hiding place.

**hide**[2] *noun* animal's skin, esp. tanned; *colloquial* human skin. □ **hidebound** rigidly conventional.

**hideous** /'hɪdɪəs/ *adjective* repulsive, revolting. □ **hideously** *adverb*.

**hiding** *noun colloquial* thrashing.

**hierarchy** /'haɪərɑːkɪ/ *noun* (*plural* **-ies**) system of grades of authority ranked one above another. □ **hierarchical** /-'rɑːk-/ *adjective*.

**hieroglyph** /'haɪərəglɪf/ *noun* picture representing word or syllable, esp. in ancient Egyptian. □ **hieroglyphic** /-'glɪf/ *adjective*; **hieroglyphics** /-'glɪf/ *plural noun*.

**hi-fi** /'haɪfaɪ/ *colloquial* • *adjective* of high fidelity. • *noun* (*plural* **-s**) equipment for such sound reproduction.

**higgledy-piggledy** /hɪgəldɪ'pɪgəldɪ/ *adverb & adjective* in disorder.

**high** /haɪ/ • *adjective* of great or specified upward extent; far above ground or sea level; coming above normal level; of exalted rank or position, of superior quality; extreme, intense; (often + *on*) *colloquial* intoxicated by alcohol or drugs; (of sound) shrill; (of period etc.) at its peak; (of meat etc.) beginning to go bad. • *noun* high or highest level or number; area of high barometric pressure; *slang* euphoric state, esp. drug-induced. • *adverb* far up, aloft; in or to high degree; at high price; (of sound) at high pitch. □ **high altar** chief altar in church; **highball** *US* drink of spirits and soda etc.; **highbrow** *colloquial* (person) of superior intellect or culture; **high chair** child's chair with long legs and meal-tray; **High Church** section of Church of England emphasizing ritual, priestly authority, and sacraments; **high command** army commander-in-chief and associated staff; **High Commission** embassy from one Commonwealth country to another; **High Court** supreme court of justice for civil cases;

**highfalutin(g)** *colloquial* pompous, pretentious; **high fidelity** high-quality sound reproduction; **high-flown** extravagant, bombastic; **high-flyer, -flier** person of great potential or ambition; **high frequency** *Radio* 3–30 megahertz; **high-handed** overbearing; **high-handedly** *adverb*; **high-handedness** *noun*; **high heels** woman's shoes with high heels; **high jump** athletic event consisting of jumping over high bar, *colloquial* drastic punishment; **high-level** conducted by people of high rank, (of computer language) close to ordinary language; **high-minded** of firm moral principles; **high-mindedness** *noun*; **high pressure** high degree of activity, atmospheric condition with pressure above average; **high priest** chief priest, head of cult; **high-rise** (of building) having many storeys; **high road** main road; **high school** secondary school; **high sea(s)** seas outside territorial waters; **high-spirited** cheerful; **high street** principal shopping street of town; **high tea** early evening meal of tea and cooked food; **high-tech** employing, requiring, or involved in high technology, imitating its style; **high technology** advanced (esp. electronic) technology; **high tension, voltage** electrical potential large enough to injure or damage; **high tide, water time** or level of tide at its peak; **high water mark** level reached at high water.

**highland** /'haɪlənd/ • *noun* (usually in *plural*) mountainous country, esp. (**the Highlands**) of N. Scotland. • *adjective* of highland or Highlands. □ **highlander**, **Highlander** *noun*.

**highlight** • *noun* moment or detail of vivid interest; bright part of picture; bleached streak in hair. • *verb* bring into prominence; mark with highlighter.

**highlighter** *noun* coloured marker pen for emphasizing printed word.

**highly** *adverb* in high degree, favourably. □ **highly-strung** sensitive, nervous.

**highness** *noun* state of being high; (**His, Her, Your Highness**) *title of prince, princess, etc.*

**highway** *noun* public road, main route. □ **Highway Code** official handbook for road-users; **highwayman** *historical* (usually mounted) robber of stagecoaches.

**hijack** /ˈhaɪdʒæk/ ● *verb* seize control of (vehicle, aircraft, etc.), esp. to force it to different destination; steal (goods) in transit. ● *noun* hijacking. □ **hijacker** *noun*.

**hike** ● *noun* long walk, esp. in country for pleasure; rise in prices etc. ● *verb* (**-king**) go on hike. □ **hiker** *noun*.

**hilarious** /hɪˈleərɪəs/ *adjective* extremely funny; boisterously merry. □ **hilariously** *adverb*; **hilarity** /-ˈlær-/ *noun*.

**hill** *noun* natural elevation of ground, lower than mountain; heap, mound. □ **hill-billy** *US colloquial often derogatory* person from remote rural area. □ **hilly** *adjective* (**-ier, -iest**).

**hillock** /ˈhɪlək/ *noun* small hill, mound.

**hilt** *noun* handle of sword, dagger, etc.

**him** *pronoun* (as object of verb) the male person or animal in question, person of unspecified sex; *colloquial* he.

**himself** /hɪmˈself/ *pronoun: emphatic form* of HE *or* HIM; *reflexive form* of HIM.

**hind**[1] /haɪnd/ *adjective* at back. □ **hindquarters** rump and hind legs of quadruped; **hindsight** wisdom after event. □ **hindmost** *adjective*.

**hind**[2] /haɪnd/ *noun* female (esp. red) deer.

**hinder**[1] /ˈhɪndə/ *verb* impede; delay.

**hinder**[2] /ˈhaɪndə/ *adjective* rear, hind.

**Hindi** /ˈhɪndiː/ *noun* group of spoken languages in N. India; one of official languages of India, literary form of Hindustani.

**Hindu** /ˈhɪnduː/ ● *noun* (*plural* **-s**) follower of Hinduism. ● *adjective* of Hindus or Hinduism.

**Hinduism** /ˈhɪnduːɪz(ə)m/ *noun* main religious and social system of India, including belief in reincarnation and worship of several gods.

**Hindustani** /hɪnduˈstɑːnɪ/ *noun* language based on Hindi, used in much of India.

**hinge** ● *noun* movable joint on which door, lid, etc. swings; principle on which all depends. ● *verb* (**-ging**) (+ *on*) depend on (event etc.); attach or be attached with hinge.

**hinny** /ˈhɪnɪ/ *noun* (*plural* **-ies**) offspring of female donkey and male horse.

**hint** ● *noun* indirect suggestion; slight indication; small piece of practical information; faint trace. ● *verb* suggest indirectly. □ **hint at** refer indirectly to.

**hinterland** /ˈhɪntəlænd/ *noun* district behind that lying along coast etc.

**hip**[1] *noun* projection of pelvis and upper part of thigh-bone. □ **hip-flask** small flask for spirits.

**hip**[2] *noun* fruit of rose.

**hip**[3] *interjection* used to introduce cheer.

**hip**[4] *adjective* (also **hep**) (**-pp-**) *slang* trendy, stylish. □ **hip hop, hip-hop** subculture combining rap music, graffiti art, and break-dancing.

**hippie** /ˈhɪpɪ/ *noun* (also **hippy**) (*plural* **-ies**) *colloquial* person (esp. in 1960s) rejecting convention, typically with long hair, jeans, etc.

**hippo** /ˈhɪpəʊ/ *noun* (*plural* **-s**) *colloquial* hippopotamus.

**Hippocratic oath** /hɪpəˈkrætɪk/ *noun* statement of ethics of medical profession.

**hippodrome** /ˈhɪpədrəʊm/ *noun* musichall, dance hall, etc.; *historical* course for chariot races etc.

**hippopotamus** /hɪpəˈpɒtəməs/ *noun* (*plural* **-muses** or **-mi** /-maɪ/) large African mammal with short legs and thick skin, living by rivers etc.

**hippy** = HIPPIE.

**hipster**[1] /ˈhɪpstə/ ● *adjective* (of garment) hanging from hips rather than waist. ● *noun* (in *plural*) such trousers.

**hipster**[2] /ˈhɪpstə/ *noun* *slang* hip person.

**hire** ● *verb* (**-ring**) obtain use of (thing) or services of (person) for payment. ● *noun* hiring, being hired; payment for this. □ **hire out** grant temporary use of (thing) for payment; **hire purchase** system of purchase by paying in instalments. □ **hirer** *noun*.

**hireling** /ˈhaɪəlɪŋ/ *noun* *usually derogatory* person who works for hire.

**hirsute** /ˈhɜːsjuːt/ *adjective* hairy.

**his** /hɪz/ ● *adjective* of or belonging to him. ● *pronoun* the one(s) belonging to him.

**Hispanic** /hɪˈspænɪk/ ● *adjective* of Spain or Spain and Portugal; of Spain and other Spanish-speaking countries.

• *noun* Spanish-speaking person living in US.

**hiss** /hɪs/ • *verb* make sharp sibilant sound, as of letter *s*; express disapproval of thus; whisper urgently or angrily. • *noun* sharp sibilant sound.

**histamine** /'hɪstəmiːn/ *noun* chemical compound in body tissues associated with allergic reactions.

**histology** /hɪ'stɒlədʒɪ/ *noun* study of tissue structure.

**historian** /hɪ'stɔːrɪən/ *noun* writer of history; person learned in history.

**historic** /hɪ'stɒrɪk/ *adjective* famous in history or potentially so; *Grammar* (of tense) used to narrate past events.

**historical** *adjective* of history; belonging to or dealing with the past; not legendary; studying development over period of time. □ **historically** *adverb*.

**historicity** /hɪstə'rɪsɪtɪ/ *noun* historical genuineness or accuracy.

**historiography** /hɪstɔːrɪ'ɒɡrəfɪ/ *noun* writing of history; study of this. □ **historiographer** *noun*.

**history** /'hɪstərɪ/ *noun* (*plural* **-ies**) continuous record of (esp. public) events; study of past events; total accumulation of these; (esp. eventful) past or record.

**histrionic** /hɪstrɪ'ɒnɪk/ • *adjective* (of behaviour) theatrical, dramatic. • *noun* (in *plural*) insincere and dramatic behaviour designed to impress.

**hit** • *verb* (**-tt-**; *past & past participle* **hit**) strike with blow or missile; (of moving body) strike with force; affect adversely; (often + *at*) aim blow; propel (ball etc.) with bat etc.; achieve, reach; *colloquial* encounter, arrive at. • *noun* blow; shot that hits target; *colloquial* popular success. □ **hit it off** (often + *with*, *together*) get on well; **hit-and-run** (of person) causing damage or injury and leaving immediately, (of accident etc.) caused by such person(s); **hit-or-miss** random.

**hitch** • *verb* fasten with loop etc.; move (thing) with jerk; *colloquial* hitchhike; obtain (lift). • *noun* temporary difficulty, snag; jerk; kind of noose or knot; *colloquial* free ride in vehicle. □ **hitchhike** travel by means of free lifts in passing vehicles; **hitchhiker** *noun*.

**hi-tech** /'haɪtek/ *adjective* high-tech.

**hither** /'hɪðə/ *adverb formal* to this place. □ **hitherto** up to now.

**HIV** *abbreviation* human immunodeficiency virus, either of two viruses causing Aids.

**hive** *noun* beehive. □ **hive off** (**-ving**) separate from larger group.

**hives** /haɪvz/ *plural noun* skin eruption, esp. nettle-rash.

**HM** *abbreviation* Her or His Majesty('s).

**HMG** *abbreviation* Her or His Majesty's Government.

**HMI** *abbreviation* Her or His Majesty's Inspector (of Schools).

**HMS** *abbreviation* Her or His Majesty's Ship.

**HMSO** *abbreviation* Her or His Majesty's Stationery Office.

**HNC, HND** *abbreviations* Higher National Certificate, Diploma.

**ho** /həʊ/ *interjection expressing triumph, derision, etc., or calling attention etc.*

**hoard** /hɔːd/ • *noun* store (esp. of money or food). • *verb* amass and store. □ **hoarder** *noun*.

**hoarding** /'hɔːdɪŋ/ *noun* structure erected to carry advertisements; temporary fence round building site etc.

**hoar-frost** /'hɔːfrɒst/ *noun* frozen water vapour on lawns.

**hoarse** /hɔːs/ *adjective* (of voice) rough, husky; having hoarse voice. □ **hoarsely** *adverb*; **hoarseness** *noun*.

**hoary** /'hɔːrɪ/ *adjective* (**-ier, -iest**) white or grey with age; aged; old and trite.

**hoax** • *noun* humorous or malicious deception. • *verb* deceive with hoax.

**hob** *noun* hotplates etc. on cooker or as separate unit; flat metal shelf at side of fire for heating pans etc. □ **hobnail** heavy-headed nail for boot-sole.

**hobble** /'hɒb(ə)l/ • *verb* (**-ling**) walk lamely, limp; tie together legs of horse etc.) to keep it from straying. • *noun* limping gait; rope etc. used to hobble horse.

**hobby** /'hɒbɪ/ *noun* (*plural* **-ies**) leisure-time activity pursued for pleasure. □ **hobby-horse** stick with horse's head, used as toy, favourite subject or idea.

**hobgoblin** /'hɒbgɒblɪn/ noun mischievous imp; bogy.

**hobnob** /'hɒbnɒb/ verb (-bb-) (usually + with) mix socially or informally.

**hobo** /'həʊbəʊ/ noun (plural **-es** or **-s**) US wandering worker; tramp.

**hock¹** noun joint of quadruped's hind leg between knee and fetlock.

**hock²** noun German white wine.

**hock³** verb esp. US colloquial pawn. □ **in hock** in pawn, in debt, in prison.

**hockey** /'hɒkɪ/ noun team game played with ball and hooked sticks.

**hocus-pocus** /həʊkəs'pəʊkəs/ noun trickery.

**hod** noun trough on pole for carrying bricks etc.; portable container for coal.

**hodgepodge** = HOTCHPOTCH.

**hoe** ● noun long-handled tool for weeding etc. ● verb (**hoes, hoed, hoeing**) weed (crops), loosen (soil), or dig up etc. with hoe.

**hog** ● noun castrated male pig; colloquial greedy person. ● verb (**-gg-**) colloquial take greedily; monopolize. □ **go the whole hog** colloquial do thing thoroughly; **hogwash** colloquial nonsense.

**hogmanay** /'hɒgməneɪ/ noun Scottish New Year's Eve.

**hogshead** /'hɒgzhed/ noun large cask; liquid or dry measure (about 50 gals.).

**ho-ho** /həʊ'həʊ/ interjection representing deep jolly laugh or expressing surprise, triumph, or derision.

**hoick** verb colloquial (often + out) lift or jerk.

**hoi polloi** /hɔɪ pəˈlɔɪ/ noun the masses; ordinary people. [Greek]

**hoist** ● verb raise or haul up; raise with ropes and pulleys etc. ● noun act of hoisting; apparatus for hoisting. □ **hoist with one's own petard** caught by one's own trick etc.

**hoity-toity** /hɔɪtɪ'tɔɪtɪ/ adjective haughty.

**hokum** /'həʊkəm/ noun esp. US slang sentimental or unreal material in film etc.; bunkum, rubbish.

**hold¹** /həʊld/ ● verb (past & past participle **held**) keep fast; grasp; keep in particular position; contain, have capacity for; possess, have (property, qualifications, job, etc.); conduct, celebrate; detain; think, believe; not give way; reserve. ● noun (+ on, over) power over; grasp; manner or means of holding. □ **holdall** large soft travelling bag; **hold back** impede, keep for oneself, (often + from) refrain; **hold down** repress, colloquial be competent enough to keep (job); **hold forth** speak at length or tediously; **hold on** maintain grasp, wait, not ring off; **hold one's tongue** colloquial remain silent; **hold out** stretch forth (hand etc.), offer (inducement etc.), maintain resistance, (+ for) continue to demand; **hold over** postpone; **hold up** verb sustain, display, obstruct, stop and rob by force; **hold-up** noun stoppage, delay, robbery by force; **hold with** (usually in negative) colloquial approve of.

**hold²** /həʊld/ noun cavity in lower part of ship or aircraft for cargo.

**holder** noun device for holding something; possessor of title, shares, etc.; occupant of office etc.

**holding** noun tenure of land; stocks, property, etc. held. □ **holding company** one formed to hold shares of other companies.

**hole** noun empty space in solid body; opening in or through something; burrow; colloquial small or gloomy place; colloquial awkward situation; (in games) cavity or receptacle for ball, Golf section of course from tee to hole. □ **hole up** (**-ling**) US colloquial hide oneself. □ **holey** adjective.

**holiday** /'hɒlɪdeɪ/ ● noun (often in plural) extended period of recreation, esp. spent away from home; break from work or school. ● verb spend holiday.

**holiness** /'həʊlɪnɪs/ noun being holy or sacred; (**His, Your Holiness**) title of Pope.

**holism** /'həʊlɪz(ə)m/ noun (also **wholism**) theory that certain wholes are greater than sum of their parts; Medicine treating of whole person rather than symptoms of disease. □ **holistic** /-'lɪst-/ adjective.

**hollandaise sauce** /hɒlən'deɪz/ noun creamy sauce of butter, egg yolks, vinegar, etc.

**holler** /'hɒlə/ verb & noun US colloquial shout.

**hollow** /'hɒləʊ/ ● adjective having cavity; not solid; sunken; echoing; empty;

hungry; meaningless; insincere. ● *noun* hollow place; hole; valley. ● *verb* (often + *out*) make hollow, excavate. ● *adverb colloquial* completely.

**holly** /'hɒlɪ/ *noun* (*plural* **-ies**) evergreen prickly-leaved shrub with red berries.

**hollyhock** /'hɒlɪhɒk/ *noun* tall plant with showy flowers.

**holm** /həʊm/ *noun* (in full **holm-oak**) evergreen oak.

**holocaust** /'hɒləkɔ:st/ *noun* wholesale destruction; (**the Holocaust**) mass murder of Jews by Nazis 1939–45.

**hologram** /'hɒləgræm/ *noun* photographic pattern having 3-dimensional effect.

**holograph** /'hɒləgrɑ:f/ ● *adjective* wholly in handwriting of person named as author. ● *noun* such document.

**holography** /hə'lɒgrəfɪ/ *noun* study or production of holograms.

**holster** /'həʊlstə/ *noun* leather case for pistol or revolver on belt etc.

**holy** /'həʊlɪ/ *adjective* (**-ier, -iest**) morally and spiritually excellent; belonging or devoted to God. □ **Holy Ghost** Holy Spirit; **Holy Land** area between River Jordan and Mediterranean; **holy of holies** inner chamber of Jewish temple, thing regarded as most sacred; **holy orders** those of bishop, priest, and deacon; **Holy Saturday** day before Easter; **Holy See** papacy, papal court; **Holy Spirit** Third Person of Trinity; **Holy Week** week before Easter; **Holy Writ** Bible.

**homage** /'hɒmɪdʒ/ *noun* tribute, expression of reverence.

**Homburg** /'hɒmbɜ:g/ *noun* man's felt hat with narrow curled brim and lengthwise dent in crown.

**home** ● *noun* place where one lives; residence; (esp. good or bad) family circumstances; native land; institution caring for people or animals; place where thing originates, is kept, is most common, etc.; (in games) finishing line in race, goal, home match or win etc. ● *adjective* of or connected with home; carried on or done at home; not foreign; played etc. on team's own ground. ● *adverb* to or at home; to point aimed at. ● *verb* (**-ming**) (of pigeon) return home; (often + *on, in on*) (of missile etc.) be

guided to destination. □ **at home** *adjective* in one's house or native land, at ease, well-informed, available to callers; **at-home** *noun* social reception in person's home; **home-brew** beer etc. brewed at home; **Home Counties** those lying round London; **home economics** study of household management; **homeland** native land, any of several areas reserved for black South Africans; **Home Office** British government department concerned with immigration, law and order, etc.; **home rule** self-government; **Home Secretary** minister in charge of Home Office; **homesick** depressed by absence from home; **homesickness** such depression; **homestead** house with outbuildings, farm; **homework** lessons to be done by schoolchild at home. □ **homeless** *adjective*; **homeward** *adjective & adverb*; **homewards** *adverb*.

**homely** *adjective* (**-ier, -iest**) plain; unpretentious; *US* unattractive; cosy. □ **homeliness** *noun*.

**homeopathy** etc. *US* = HOMOEOPATHY etc.

**Homeric** /həʊ'merɪk/ *adjective* of or in style of the ancient Greek poet Homer; of Bronze Age Greece.

**homey** *adjective* (**-mier, -miest**) suggesting home; cosy.

**homicide** /'hɒmɪsaɪd/ *noun* killing of person by another; person who kills another. □ **homicidal** /-'saɪd-/ *adjective*.

**homily** /'hɒmɪlɪ/ *noun* (*plural* **-ies**) short sermon; moralizing lecture. □ **homiletic** /-'let-/ *adjective*.

**homing** *adjective* (of pigeon) trained to fly home; (of device) for guiding to target etc.

**hominid** /'hɒmɪnɪd/ ● *adjective* of mammal family of existing and fossil man. ● *noun* member of this.

**hominoid** /'hɒmɪnɔɪd/ ● *adjective* like a human. ● *noun* animal resembling human.

**homoeopathy** /həʊmɪ'ɒpəθɪ/ *noun* (*US* **homeopathy**) treatment of disease by drugs that in healthy person would produce symptoms of the disease. □ **homoeopath** /'həʊmɪəʊpæθ/ *noun*; **homoeopathic** /-'pæθ-/ *adjective*.

**homogeneous** /hɒmə'dʒi:nɪəs/ *adjective* (having parts) of same kind or nature;

uniform. □ **homogeneity** /-dʒɪˈniːɪtɪ/ *noun*; **homogeneously** *adverb*.

■ **Usage** *Homogeneous* is often confused with *homogenous* (and pronounced /həˈmɒdʒənəs/, with the stress on the *-mog-*), but that is a term in biology meaning 'similar owing to common descent'.

**homogenize** /həˈmɒdʒɪnaɪz/ *verb* (also **-ise**) (**-zing** or **-sing**) make homogeneous; treat (milk) so that cream does not separate.

**homologous** /həˈmɒləgəs/ *adjective* having same relation, relative position, etc.; corresponding.

**homology** /həˈmɒlədʒɪ/ *noun* homologous relation, correspondence.

**homonym** /ˈhɒmənɪm/ *noun* word spelt or pronounced like another but of different meaning.

**homophobia** /hɒməˈfəʊbɪə/ *noun* hatred or fear of homosexuals. □ **homophobe** /ˈhɒm-/ *noun*; **homophobic** *adjective*.

**homophone** /ˈhɒməfəʊn/ *noun* word pronounced like another but having different meaning, e.g. *beach*, *beech*.

**Homo sapiens** /ˌhəʊməʊ ˈsæpɪenz/ *noun* modern humans regarded as a species. [Latin]

**homosexual** /hɒməˈsekʃʊəl/ ● *adjective* feeling or involving sexual attraction to people of same sex. ● *noun* homosexual person. □ **homosexuality** /-ˈæl-/ *noun*.

**Hon.** *abbreviation* Honorary; Honourable.

**hone** ● *noun* whetstone, esp. for razors. ● *verb* (**-ning**) sharpen (as) on hone.

**honest** /ˈɒnɪst/ ● *adjective* not lying, cheating, or stealing; sincere; fairly earned. ● *adverb colloquial* genuinely, really. □ **honestly** *adverb*.

**honesty** /ˈɒnɪstɪ/ *noun* being honest, truthfulness; plant with purple or white flowers and flat round pods.

**honey** /ˈhʌnɪ/ *noun* (*plural* **-s**) sweet sticky yellowish fluid made by bees from nectar; colour of this; sweetness; darling.

**honeycomb** ● *noun* beeswax structure of hexagonal cells for honey and eggs; pattern arranged hexagonally. ● *verb* fill with cavities; mark with honeycomb pattern.

**honeydew** *noun* sweet substance excreted by aphids; variety of melon.

**honeyed** *adjective* sweet, sweetsounding.

**honeymoon** ● *noun* holiday of newly married couple; initial period of enthusiasm or goodwill. ● *verb* spend honeymoon.

**honeysuckle** *noun* climbing shrub with fragrant flowers.

**honk** ● *noun* sound of car horn; cry of wild goose. ● *verb* (cause to) make honk.

**honky-tonk** /ˈhɒŋkɪtɒŋk/ *noun colloquial* ragtime piano music.

**honor** *US* = HONOUR.

**honorable** *US* = HONOURABLE.

**honorarium** /ɒnəˈreərɪəm/ *noun* (*plural* **-s** or **-ria**) voluntary payment for professional services.

**honorary** /ˈɒnərərɪ/ *adjective* conferred as honour; unpaid.

**honorific** /ɒnəˈrɪfɪk/ *adjective* conferring honour; implying respect.

**honour** /ˈɒnə/ (*US* **honor**) ● *noun* high respect, public regard; adherence to what is right; nobleness of mind; thing conferred as distinction (esp. official award for bravery or achievement); privilege; (**Her, His, Your Honour**) *title of judge etc.*; person or thing that brings honour; chastity, reputation for this; (in *plural*) specialized degree course or special distinction in exam; (in *plural*) (in card games) 4 or 5 highest-ranking cards; *Golf* right of driving off first. ● *verb* respect highly; confer honour on; accept or pay (bill, cheque) when due. □ **do the honours** perform duties of host etc.

**honourable** *adjective* (*US* **honorable**) deserving, bringing, or showing honour; (**Honourable**) courtesy title of MPs, certain officials, and children of certain ranks of the nobility. □ **honourably** *adverb*.

**hooch** /huːtʃ/ *noun US colloquial* alcoholic spirits, esp. inferior or illicit.

**hood**[1] /hʊd/ ● *noun* covering for head and neck, esp. as part of garment; separate hoodlike garment; folding top of car etc.; *US* bonnet of car etc.; protective cover. ● *verb* cover with hood. □ **hooded** *adjective*.

**hood**[2] /hʊd/ *noun US slang* gangster, gunman.

**hoodlum** /'huːdləm/ *noun* hooligan; gangster.

**hoodoo** /'huːduː/ *noun US* bad luck; thing or person that brings this.

**hoodwink** *verb* deceive, delude.

**hoof** /huːf/ *noun* (*plural* **-s** or **hooves** /huːvz/) horny part of foot of horse etc. □ **hoof it** *slang* go on foot.

**hook** /hʊk/ *noun* bent piece of metal etc. for catching hold of or hanging things on; curved cutting instrument; hook-shaped thing; hooking stroke; *Boxing* short swinging blow. *● verb* grasp, secure, fasten, or catch with hook; (in sports) send (ball) in curving or deviating path; *Rugby* secure (ball) in scrum with foot. □ **hook and eye** small hook and loop as fastener; **hook, line, and sinker** completely; **hook-up** connection, esp. of broadcasting equipment; **hookworm** worm infesting intestines of humans and animals.

**hookah** /'hʊkə/ *noun* tobacco pipe with long tube passing through water to cool smoke.

**hooked** *adjective* hook-shaped; (often + *on*) *slang* addicted or captivated.

**hooker** *noun Rugby* player in front row of scrum who tries to hook ball; *slang* prostitute.

**hooligan** /'huːlɪgən/ *noun* young ruffian. □ **hooliganism** *noun*.

**hoop** /huːp/ *● noun* circular band of metal, wood, etc., esp. as part of framework; wooden etc. circle bowled by child or used by circus performer etc.; arch through which balls are hit in croquet. *● verb* bind with hoop(s). □ **hoop-la** game with rings thrown to encircle prizes.

**hoopoe** /'huːpuː/ *noun* bird with variegated plumage and fanlike crest.

**hooray** = HURRAH.

**hoot** /huːt/ *● noun* owl's cry; sound of car's horn etc.; shout of derision etc.; *colloquial* (cause of) laughter; (also **two hoots**) *slang* anything, in the slightest. *● verb* utter hoot(s); greet or drive away with hoots; sound (horn).

**hooter** *noun* thing that hoots, esp. car's horn or siren; *slang* nose.

**Hoover** /'huːvə/ *● noun* proprietary term vacuum cleaner. *● verb* (**hoover**) clean or (+ *up*) suck up with vacuum cleaner.

**hooves** *plural* of HOOF.

**hop**[1] *● verb* (**-pp-**) (of bird, frog, etc.) spring with all feet at once; (of person) jump on one foot; move or go quickly, leap. *● noun* hopping movement; *colloquial* dance; short journey, esp. flight. □ **hop in**, **out** *colloquial* get into or out of car etc.; **hopscotch** child's game of hopping over squares marked on ground.

**hop**[2] *noun* climbing plant with bitter cones used to flavour beer etc.; (in *plural*) these cones.

**hope** *● noun* expectation and desire; person or thing giving cause for hope; what is hoped for. *● verb* (**-ping**) feel hope; expect and desire.

**hopeful** *adjective* feeling or inspiring hope, promising.

**hopefully** *adverb* in a hopeful way; it is to be hoped.

■ **Usage** The use of *hopefully* to mean 'it is to be hoped' is common, but it is considered incorrect by some people.

**hopeless** *adjective* feeling or admitting no hope; inadequate, incompetent. □ **hopelessly** *adverb*; **hopelessness** *noun*.

**hopper** *noun* funnel-like device for feeding grain into mill etc.; hopping insect.

**horde** *noun usually derogatory* large group, gang.

**horehound** /'hɔːhaʊnd/ *noun* herb with aromatic bitter juice.

**horizon** /hə'raɪz(ə)n/ *noun* line at which earth and sky appear to meet; limit of mental perception, interest, etc.

**horizontal** /hɒrɪ'zɒnt(ə)l/ *● adjective* parallel to plane of horizon; level, flat. *● noun* horizontal line, plane, etc. □ **horizontally** *adverb*.

**hormone** /'hɔːməʊn/ *noun* substance produced by body and transported in tissue fluids to stimulate cells or tissues to growth etc.; similar synthetic substance. □ **hormone replacement therapy** treatment with hormones to relieve menopausal symptoms. □ **hormonal** /-'məʊn-/ *adjective*.

**horn** *noun* hard outgrowth, often curved and pointed, on head of animal; horn-like projection; substance of horns;

brass wind instrument; instrument giving warning. □ **hornbeam** tough-wooded hedgerow tree; **hornbill** bird with hornlike excrescence on bill; **horn of plenty** cornucopia; **horn-rimmed** (of spectacles) having rims of horn or similar substance. □ **horned** adjective.

**hornblende** /'hɔːnblend/ noun dark brown etc. mineral constituent of granite etc.

**hornet** /'hɔːnɪt/ noun large species of wasp.

**hornpipe** noun (music for) lively dance associated esp. with sailors.

**horny** adjective (-ier, -iest) of or like horn; hard; slang sexually excited. □ **horniness** noun.

**horology** /hə'rɒlədʒɪ/ noun clock-making. □ **horological** /hɒrə'lɒdʒ-/ adjective.

**horoscope** /'hɒrəskəʊp/ noun predic-tion of person's future based on relat-ive position of stars at his or her birth.

**horrendous** /hə'rendəs/ adjective horri-fying. □ **horrendously** adverb.

**horrible** /'hɒrɪb(ə)l/ adjective causing horror; colloquial unpleasant. □ **horribly** adverb.

**horrid** /'hɒrɪd/ adjective horrible; colloquial unpleasant.

**horrific** /hə'rɪfɪk/ adjective horrifying. □ **horrifically** adverb.

**horrify** /'hɒrɪfaɪ/ verb (-ies, -ied) arouse horror in; shock. □ **horrifying** adjective.

**horror** /'hɒrə/ • noun intense loathing or fear; (often + of) deep dislike; colloquial intense dismay; horrifying thing. • ad-jective (of films etc.) designed to arouse feelings of horror.

**hors d'oeuvre** /ɔː 'dɜːvr/ noun appetizer served at start of meal.

**horse** • noun large 4-legged hoofed mam-mal with mane, used for riding etc.; adult male horse; vaulting-block; sup-porting frame. • verb (-sing) (+ around) fool about. □ **horsebox** closed vehicle for transporting horse(s); **horse brass** brass ornament originally for horse's harness; **horse chestnut** tree with conical clusters of flowers, its dark brown fruit; **horse-drawn** pulled by horse(s); **horsefly** biting insect troublesome to horses; **Horse Guards** cavalry brigade of British household

troops; **horsehair** (padding etc. of) hair from mane or tail of horse; **horseman** (skilled) rider on horseback; **horsemanship** skill in riding; **horseplay** boisterous play; **horsepower** (plural same) unit of rate of doing work; **horse race** race between horses with riders; **horse racing** sport of rac-ing horses; **horseradish** plant with pungent root used to make sauce; **horse sense** colloquial plain common sense; **horseshoe** U-shaped iron shoe for horse, thing of this shape; **horsetail** (plant resembling) horse's tail; **horsewhip** noun whip for horse, verb beat (person) with this; **horsewoman** (skilled) woman rider on horseback.

**horsy** adjective (-ier, -iest) of or like horse; concerned with horses.

**horticulture** /'hɔːtɪkʌltʃə/ noun art of gardening. □ **horticultural** /-'kʌlt-/ ad-jective; **horticulturist** /-'kʌlt-/ noun.

**hosanna** /həʊ'zænə/ noun & interjection cry of adoration.

**hose** /həʊz/ • noun (also **hose-pipe**) flex-ible tube for conveying liquids; (treated as plural) stockings and socks collect-ively; historical breeches. • verb (-sing) (often + down) water, spray, or drench with hose.

**hosier** /'həʊzɪə/ noun dealer in stockings and socks. □ **hosiery** noun.

**hospice** /'hɒspɪs/ noun home for (esp. terminally) ill or destitute people; trav-ellers' lodging kept by religious order etc.

**hospitable** /hɒs'pɪtəb(ə)l/ adjective giv-ing hospitality. □ **hospitably** adverb.

**hospital** /'hɒspɪt(ə)l/ noun institution providing medical and surgical treat-ment and nursing for ill and injured people; historical hospice.

**hospitality** /hɒspɪ'tælɪtɪ/ noun friendly and generous reception of guests or strangers.

**hospitalize** /'hɒspɪtəlaɪz/ verb (also **-ise**) (-zing or -sing) send or admit to hos-pital. □ **hospitalization** noun.

**host**[1] /həʊst/ noun (usually + of) large number of people or things.

**host**[2] /həʊst/ • noun person who enter-tains another as guest; compère; animal or plant having parasite; re-cipient of transplanted organ; landlord of inn. ● *verb* be host to (person) or of (event).

**host**[3] /həʊst/ *noun* (usually **the Host**) bread consecrated in Eucharist.

**hostage** /ˈhɒstɪdʒ/ *noun* person seized or held as security for fulfilment of a condition.

**hostel** /ˈhɒst(ə)l/ *noun* house of residence for students etc.; youth hostel.

**hostelling** *noun* (*US* **hosteling**) practice of staying in youth hostels. □ **hosteller** *noun*.

**hostelry** *noun* (*plural* **-ies**) *archaic* inn.

**hostess** /ˈhəʊstɪs/ *noun* woman who entertains guests, or customers at nightclub.

**hostile** /ˈhɒstaɪl/ *adjective* of enemy; (often + *to*) unfriendly, opposed.

**hostility** /hɒˈstɪlɪtɪ/ *noun* (*plural* **-ies**) being hostile; enmity; warfare; (in *plural*) acts of war.

**hot** ● *adjective* (**-tt-**) having high temperature, very warm; causing sensation of or feeling heat; pungent; excited; (often + *on, for*) eager; (of news) fresh; skilful, formidable; (+ *on*) knowledgeable about; *slang* (of stolen goods) difficult to dispose of. ● *verb* (**-tt-**) (usually + *up*) *colloquial* make or become hot; become more active, exciting, or dangerous. □ **hot air** *slang* empty or boastful talk; **hot-air balloon** balloon containing air heated by burners, causing it to rise; **hotbed** (+ *of*) environment conducive to (vice etc.), bed of earth heated by fermenting manure; **hot cross bun** bun marked with cross, eaten on Good Friday; **hot dog** *colloquial* hot sausage in bread roll; **hotfoot** in eager haste; **hothead** impetuous person; **hotheaded** impetuous; **hothouse** heated (mainly glass) building for growing plants, environment conducive to rapid growth; **hotline** direct telephone line; **hotplate** heated metal plate for cooking food or keeping it hot; **hotpot** dish of stewed meat and vegetables; **hot rod** vehicle modified for extra power and speed; **hot seat** *slang* awkward or responsible position, electric chair; **hot water** *colloquial* difficulty, trouble; **hot-water bottle** container filled with hot water to warm bed etc. □ **hotly** *adverb*.

**hotchpotch** /ˈhɒtʃpɒtʃ/ *noun* (also **hodgepodge** /ˈhɒdʒpɒdʒ/) confused mixture, jumble, esp. of ideas.

**hotel** /həʊˈtel/ *noun* (usually licensed) place providing meals and accommodation for payment.

**hotelier** /həʊˈtelɪə/ *noun* hotel-keeper.

**houmous** = HUMMUS.

**hound** /haʊnd/ ● *noun* dog used in hunting; *colloquial* despicable man. ● *verb* harass or pursue.

**hour** /aʊə/ *noun* twenty-fourth part of day and night, 60 minutes; time of day, point in time; (in *plural* after numerals in form 18.00, 20.30, etc.) this number of hours and minutes past midnight on the 24-hour clock; period set aside for some purpose; (in *plural*) working or open period; short time; time for action etc.; (**the hour**) each time o'clock of a whole number of hours. □ **hourglass** two connected glass bulbs containing sand that takes an hour to pass from upper to lower bulb. □ **hourly** *adjective & adverb*.

**houri** /ˈhʊərɪ/ *noun* (*plural* **-s**) beautiful young woman in Muslim paradise.

**house** ● *noun* /haʊs/ (*plural* /ˈhaʊzɪz/) building for human habitation; building for special purpose or for keeping animals or goods; (buildings of) religious community; section of boarding school etc.; division of school for games etc.; royal family, dynasty; (premises of) firm or institution; (building for) legislative etc. assembly; audience or performance in theatre etc. ● *verb* /haʊz/ (**-sing**) provide house for; store; enclose or encase (part etc.); fix in socket etc. □ **house arrest** detention in one's own house; **houseboat** boat equipped for living in; **housebound** confined to one's house through illness etc.; **housebreaker** burglar; **housebreaking** burglary; **housefly** common fly; **house-husband** man who does wife's traditional duties; **housekeeper** woman managing affairs of house; **housekeeping** management of house, money for this, record-keeping etc.; **houseman** resident junior doctor of hospital; **house-martin** bird which builds nests on house walls etc.; **housemaster**, **housemistress** teacher in charge of house in boarding school; **house music** pop music with synthesized drums and bass and fast beat; **House of Commons** elected chamber of Parliament; **House of Lords** chamber of Parliament that is mainly hereditary; **house plant** one grown indoors; **house-proud** attentive to care etc. of home; **house-trained** (of domestic animal) trained to be clean in house; **house-warming** party celebrating move to new house; **housewife** woman whose chief occupation is managing household; **housewifely** *adjective*; **housework** regular cleaning and cooking etc. in home.

**household** *noun* occupants of house; house and its affairs. □ **household name** well-known name; **household troops** those nominally guarding sovereign; **household word** well-known saying or name.

**householder** *noun* person who owns or rents house; head of household.

**housing** /ˈhaʊzɪŋ/ *noun* (provision of) houses; protective casing. □ **housing estate** residential area planned as a unit.

**hove** *past* of HEAVE.

**hovel** /ˈhɒv(ə)l/ *noun* small miserable dwelling.

**hover** /ˈhɒvə/ *verb* remain in one place in air; (often + *about*, *round*) linger.

**hovercraft** *noun* (*plural* same) vehicle moving on air-cushion provided by downward blast.

**hoverport** *noun* terminal for hovercraft.

**how** /haʊ/ *interrogative & relative adverb* by what means, in what way; in what condition; to what extent. □ **however** nevertheless, in whatever way, to whatever extent.

**howdah** /ˈhaʊdə/ *noun* (usually canopied) seat for riding elephant or camel.

**howitzer** /ˈhaʊɪtsə/ *noun* short gun firing shells at high elevation.

**howl** /haʊl/ ● *noun* long doleful cry of dog etc.; prolonged wailing noise; loud cry of pain, rage, derision, or laughter. ● *verb* make howl; weep loudly; utter with howl.

**howler** *noun colloquial* glaring mistake.

**hoy** *interjection* used to call attention.

**hoyden** /ˈhɔɪd(ə)n/ *noun* boisterous girl.

**HP** *abbreviation* hire purchase; (also **hp**) horsepower.

**HQ** *abbreviation* headquarters.

**hr.** *abbreviation* hour.

**HRH** *abbreviation* Her or His Royal Highness.

**HRT** *abbreviation* hormone replacement therapy.

**HT** *abbreviation* high tension.

**hub** *noun* central part of wheel, rotating on or with axle; centre of interest, activity, etc.

**hubble-bubble** /ˈhʌb(ə)lbʌb(ə)l/ *noun* simple hookah; confused sound or talk.

**hubbub** /ˈhʌbʌb/ *noun* confused noise of talking; disturbance.

**hubby** /ˈhʌbɪ/ *noun* (*plural* **-ies**) *colloquial* husband.

**hubris** /ˈhjuːbrɪs/ *noun* arrogant pride, presumption.

**huckleberry** /ˈhʌkəlbərɪ/ *noun* (*plural* **-ies**) low N. American shrub; its fruit.

**huckster** /ˈhʌkstə/ ● *noun* hawker; aggressive salesman. ● *verb* haggle; hawk (goods).

**huddle** /ˈhʌd(ə)l/ ● *verb* (**-ling**) (often + *up*) crowd together; nestle closely; (often + *up*) curl one's body up. ● *noun* confused mass; *colloquial* secret conference.

**hue** *noun* colour, tint.

**hue and cry** *noun* loud outcry.

**huff** ● *noun colloquial* fit of petulance. ● *verb* blow air, steam, etc.; (esp. **huff and puff**) bluster; remove (opponent's man) as forfeit in draughts. □ **huffy** *adjective* (**-ier**, **-iest**).

**hug** ● *verb* (**-gg-**) squeeze tightly in one's arms, esp. with affection; keep close to, fit tightly around. ● *noun* close clasp.

**huge** /hjuːdʒ/ *adjective* very large or great.

**hugely** *adverb* extremely, very much.

**hugger-mugger** /ˈhʌgəmʌgə/ *adjective & adverb* in secret; in confusion.

**Huguenot** /ˈhjuːgənəʊ/ *noun historical* French Protestant.

**hula** /ˈhuːlə/ *noun* (also **hula-hula**) Polynesian women's dance. □ **hula hoop** large hoop spun round the body.

**hulk** *noun* body of dismantled ship; *colloquial* large clumsy-looking person or thing.

**hulking** *adjective colloquial* bulky, clumsy.

**hull**[1] *noun* body of ship etc.

**hull²** ● *noun* outer covering of fruit. ● *verb* remove hulls of.

**hullabaloo** /ˌhʌləbə'luː/ *noun* uproar.

**hullo** = HELLO.

**hum** ● *verb* (**-mm-**) make low continuous sound like bee; sing with closed lips; make slight inarticulate sound; *colloquial* be active; *colloquial* smell unpleasantly. ● *noun* humming sound. □ **hummingbird** small tropical bird whose wings hum.

**human** /'hjuːmən/ ● *adjective* of or belonging to species *Homo sapiens*; consisting of human beings; having characteristics of humankind, as being weak, fallible, sympathetic, etc. ● *noun* (*plural* **-s**) human being. □ **human being** man, woman, or child; **human chain** line of people for passing things along etc.; **humankind** human beings collectively; **human rights** those held to belong to all people; **human shield** person(s) placed in line of fire to discourage attack.

**humane** /hjuː'meɪn/ *adjective* benevolent, compassionate; inflicting minimum pain; (of studies) tending to civilize. □ **humanely** *adverb*.

**humanism** /'hjuːmənɪz(ə)m/ *noun* non-religious philosophy based on liberal human values; (often **Humanism**) literary culture, esp. in Renaissance. □ **humanist** *noun*; **humanistic** /-'nɪst-/ *adjective*.

**humanitarian** /hjuːmænɪ'teərɪən/ ● *noun* person who seeks to promote human welfare. ● *adjective* of humanitarians. □ **humanitarianism** *noun*.

**humanity** /hjuː'mænɪtɪ/ *noun* (*plural* **-ies**) human race; human nature; humaneness, benevolence; (usually in *plural*) subjects concerned with human culture.

**humanize** *verb* (also **-ise**) (**-zing** or **-sing**) make human or humane. □ **humanization** *noun*.

**humanly** *adverb* within human capabilities; in a human way.

**humble** /'hʌmb(ə)l/ ● *adjective* (**-r**, **-st**) having or showing low self-esteem; lowly, modest. ● *verb* (**-ling**) make humble; lower rank of. □ **eat humble pie** apologize humbly, accept humiliation. □ **humbly** *adverb*.

**humbug** /'hʌmbʌg/ ● *noun* deception, hypocrisy; impostor; striped peppermint-flavoured boiled sweet. ● *verb* (**-gg-**) be impostor; hoax.

**humdinger** /'hʌmdɪŋə/ *noun slang* remarkable person or thing.

**humdrum** /'hʌmdrʌm/ *adjective* dull, commonplace.

**humerus** /'hjuːmərəs/ *noun* (*plural* **-ri** /-raɪ/) bone of upper arm.

**humid** /'hjuːmɪd/ *adjective* warm and damp.

**humidifier** /hjuː'mɪdɪfaɪə/ *noun* device for keeping atmosphere moist.

**humidify** /hjuː'mɪdɪfaɪ/ *verb* (**-ies**, **-ied**) make (air etc.) humid.

**humidity** /hjuː'mɪdɪtɪ/ *noun* (*plural* **-ies**) dampness; degree of moisture, esp. in atmosphere.

**humiliate** /hjuː'mɪlɪeɪt/ *verb* (**-ting**) injure dignity or self-respect of. □ **humiliating** *adjective*; **humiliation** *noun*.

**humility** /hjuː'mɪlɪtɪ/ *noun* humbleness; meekness.

**hummock** /'hʌmək/ *noun* hillock, hump.

**hummus** /'hʊmʊs/ *noun* (also **houmous**) dip of chickpeas, sesame paste, lemon juice, and garlic.

**humor** *US* = HUMOUR.

**humorist** /'hjuːmərɪst/ *noun* humorous writer, talker, or actor.

**humorous** /'hjuːmərəs/ *adjective* showing humour, comic. □ **humorously** *adverb*.

**humour** /'hjuːmə/ (*US* **humor**) ● *noun* quality of being amusing; expression of humour in literature etc.; (in full **sense of humour**) ability to perceive or express humour; state of mind, mood; each of 4 fluids formerly held to determine physical and mental qualities. ● *verb* gratify or indulge (person, taste, etc.). □ **humourless** *adjective*.

**hump** ● *noun* rounded lump, esp. on back; rounded raised mass of earth etc.; (**the hump**) *slang* fit of depression or annoyance. ● *verb* (often + *about*) *colloquial* lift or carry with difficulty; make hump-shaped. □ **humpback** (**whale**) whale with dorsal fin; **humpback bridge** one with steep approach to top; **over the hump** past the most difficult stage.

**humph** /hʌmf/ *interjection & noun* inarticulate sound of dissatisfaction etc.

**humus** /'hju:məs/ *noun* organic constituent of soil formed by decomposition of plants.

**hunch** ● *verb* bend or arch into a hump. ● *noun* intuitive feeling; hump.

**hundred** /'hʌndrəd/ *adjective & noun* (*plural* same in first sense) ten times ten; *historical* subdivision of county; (**hundreds**) *colloquial* large number. □ **hundreds and thousands** tiny coloured sweets; **hundredweight** (*plural* same or **-s**) 112 lb (50.80 kg), *US* 100 lb. (45.4 kg) □ **hundredth** *adjective & noun*.

**hundredfold** *adjective & adverb* a hundred times as much or many.

**hung** *past & past participle of* HANG. □ **hung-over** suffering from hangover; **hung parliament** parliament in which no party has clear majority.

**Hungarian** /hʌŋ'geəriən/ ● *noun* native, national, or language of Hungary. ● *adjective* of Hungary or its people or language.

**hunger** /'hʌŋgə/ ● *noun* lack of food; discomfort or exhaustion caused by this; (often + *for, after*) strong desire. ● *verb* (often + *for, after*) crave; desire; feel hunger. □ **hunger strike** refusal of food as protest.

**hungry** /'hʌŋgrɪ/ *adjective* (**-ier, -iest**) feeling, showing, or inducing hunger; craving. □ **hungrily** *adverb*.

**hunk** *noun* large piece cut off; *colloquial* sexually attractive man.

**hunt** ● *verb* pursue wild animals for food or sport; (of animal) pursue prey; (+ *after, for*) search; (as **hunted** *adjective*) (of look) frightened. ● *noun* hunting; hunting area or society. □ **huntsman** hunter, person in charge of hounds. □ **hunting** *noun*.

**hunter** *noun* (*feminine* **huntress**) person who hunts; horse ridden for hunting.

**hurdle** /'hɜ:d(ə)l/ ● *noun* frame to be jumped over by athlete in race; (in *plural*) hurdle race; obstacle; portable rectangular frame used as temporary fence. ● *verb* (**-ling**) run in hurdle race. □ **hurdler** *noun*.

**hurdy-gurdy** /hɜ:dɪ'gɜ:dɪ/ *noun* (*plural* **-ies**) droning musical instrument played by turning handle; *colloquial* barrel organ.

**hurl** ● *verb* throw violently. ● *noun* violent throw.

**hurley** /'hɜ:lɪ/ *noun* (also **hurling**) (stick used in) Irish game resembling hockey.

**hurly-burly** /hɜ:lɪ'bɜ:lɪ/ *noun* boisterous activity; commotion.

**hurrah** /hʊ'rɑ:/ (also **hurray** /hʊ'reɪ/) ● *interjection expressing joy or approval*. ● *noun* utterance of 'hurrah'.

**hurricane** /'hʌrɪkən/ *noun* storm with violent wind, esp. W. Indian cyclone. □ **hurricane lamp** lamp with flame protected from wind.

**hurry** /'hʌrɪ/ ● *noun* great haste; eagerness; (with negative or in questions) need for haste. ● *verb* (**-ies, -ied**) (cause to) move or act hastily; (as **hurried** *adjective*) hasty, done rapidly. □ **hurriedly** *adverb*.

**hurt** ● *verb* (*past & past participle* **hurt**) cause pain, injury, or distress to; suffer pain. ● *noun* injury; harm. □ **hurtful** *adjective*; **hurtfully** *adverb*.

**hurtle** /'hɜ:t(ə)l/ *verb* (**-ling**) move or hurl rapidly or noisily; come with crash.

**husband** /'hʌzbənd/ ● *noun* married man in relation to his wife. ● *verb* use (resources) economically.

**husbandry** *noun* farming; management of resources.

**hush** ● *verb* make, become, or be silent. ● *interjection calling for silence*. ● *noun* silence. □ **hush-hush** *colloquial* highly secret; **hush money** *slang* sum paid to ensure discretion; **hush up** suppress (fact).

**husk** ● *noun* dry outer covering of fruit or seed. ● *verb* remove husk from.

**husky**[1] /'hʌskɪ/ *adjective* (**-ier, -iest**) dry in the throat, hoarse; strong, hefty. □ **huskily** *adverb*.

**husky**[2] /'hʌskɪ/ *noun* (*plural* **-ies**) powerful dog used for pulling sledges.

**hussar** /hʊ'zɑ:/ *noun* light-cavalry soldier.

**hussy** /'hʌsɪ/ *noun* (*plural* **-ies**) pert girl; promiscuous woman.

**hustings** /'hʌstɪŋz/ *noun* election proceedings.

**hustle** /'hʌs(ə)l/ ● *verb* (**-ling**) jostle; (+ *into, out of,* etc.) force, hurry; *slang* solicit business. ● *noun* act or instance of hustling. □ **hustler** *noun*.

**hut** *noun* small simple or crude house or shelter.

**hutch** *noun* box or cage for rabbits etc.

**hyacinth** /'haɪəsɪnθ/ *noun* bulbous plant with bell-shaped flowers.

**hybrid** /'haɪbrɪd/ ● *noun* offspring of two animals or plants of different species etc.; thing of mixed origins. ● *adjective* bred as hybrid; heterogeneous. □ **hybridism** *noun*; **hybridization** *noun*; **hybridize** *verb* (also **-ise**) (**-zing** or **-sing**).

**hydra** /'haɪdrə/ *noun* freshwater polyp; something hard to destroy.

**hydrangea** /haɪ'dreɪndʒə/ *noun* shrub with globular clusters of white, blue, or pink flowers.

**hydrant** /'haɪdrənt/ *noun* outlet for drawing water from main.

**hydrate** /'haɪdreɪt/ ● *noun* chemical compound of water with another compound etc. ● *verb* (**-ting**) (cause to) combine with water. □ **hydration** *noun*.

**hydraulic** /haɪ'drɔːlɪk/ *adjective* (of water etc.) conveyed through pipes etc.; operated by movement of liquid. □ **hydraulically** *adverb*.

**hydraulics** *plural noun* (usually treated as *singular*) science of conveyance of liquids through pipes etc., esp. as motive power.

**hydro** /'haɪdrəʊ/ *noun* (*plural* **-s**) *colloquial* hotel etc. originally providing hydropathic treatment; hydroelectric powerplant.

**hydro-** *combining form* water; combined with hydrogen.

**hydrocarbon** /haɪdrəʊ'kɑːbən/ *noun* compound of hydrogen and carbon.

**hydrocephalus** /haɪdrə'sefələs/ *noun* accumulated fluid in brain, esp. in young children. □ **hydrocephalic** /-sɪ'fælɪk/ *adjective*.

**hydrochloric acid** /haɪdrə'klɒrɪk/ *noun* solution of hydrogen chloride in water.

**hydrodynamics** /haɪdrəʊdaɪ'næmɪks/ *plural noun* (usually treated as *singular*) science of forces acting on or exerted by liquids.

**hydroelectric** /haɪdrəʊɪ'lektrɪk/ *adjective* generating electricity by waterpower; (of electricity) so generated. □ **hydroelectricity** /-'trɪs-/ *noun*.

**hydrofoil** /'haɪdrəfɔɪl/ *noun* boat fitted with planes for raising hull out of water at speed; such a plane.

**hydrogen** /'haɪdrədʒ(ə)n/ *noun* light colourless odourless gas combining with oxygen to form water. □ **hydrogen bomb** immensely powerful bomb utilizing explosive fusion of hydrogen nuclei; **hydrogen peroxide** see PEROXIDE.

**hydrogenate** /haɪ'drɒdʒɪneɪt/ *verb* (**-ting**) charge with or cause to combine with hydrogen. □ **hydrogenation** *noun*.

**hydrography** /haɪ'drɒɡrəfɪ/ *noun* science of surveying and charting seas, lakes, rivers, etc. □ **hydrographer** *noun*; **hydrographic** /-drə'ɡræf-/ *adjective*.

**hydrology** /haɪ'drɒlədʒɪ/ *noun* science of relationship between water and land.

**hydrolyse** /'haɪdrəlaɪz/ *verb* (**-lyse**; **-zing**) decompose by hydrolysis.

**hydrolysis** /haɪ'drɒlɪsɪs/ *noun* decomposition by chemical reaction with water.

**hydrometer** /haɪ'drɒmɪtə/ *noun* instrument for measuring density of liquids.

**hydropathy** /haɪ'drɒpəθɪ/ *noun* (medically unorthodox) treatment of disease by water. □ **hydropathic** /-drə'pæθ-/ *adjective*.

**hydrophobia** /haɪdrə'fəʊbɪə/ *noun* aversion to water, esp. as symptom of rabies in humans; rabies. □ **hydrophobic** *adjective*.

**hydroplane** /'haɪdrəpleɪn/ *noun* light fast motor boat; finlike device enabling submarine to rise or fall.

**hydroponics** /haɪdrə'pɒnɪks/ *noun* growing plants without soil, in sand, water, etc. with added nutrients.

**hydrostatic** /haɪdrə'stætɪk/ *adjective* of the equilibrium of liquids and the pressure exerted by liquids at rest.

**hydrostatics** *plural noun* (usually treated as *singular*) study of hydrostatic properties of liquids.

**hydrotherapy** /haɪdrə'θerəpɪ/ *noun* use of water, esp. swimming, in treatment of disease.

**hydrous** /'haɪdrəs/ *adjective* containing water.

**hyena** /haɪˈiːnə/ noun doglike flesh-eating mammal.

**hygiene** /ˈhaɪdʒiːn/ noun conditions or practices conducive to maintaining health; cleanliness; sanitary science. □ **hygienic** /-ˈdʒiːn-/ adjective; **hygienically** /-ˈdʒiːn-/ adverb; **hygienist** noun.

**hygrometer** /haɪˈɡrɒmɪtə/ noun instrument for measuring humidity of air etc.

**hygroscopic** /haɪɡrəˈskɒpɪk/ adjective tending to absorb moisture from air.

**hymen** /ˈhaɪmən/ noun membrane at opening of vagina, usually broken at first sexual intercourse.

**hymenopterous** /haɪməˈnɒptərəs/ adjective of order of insects with 4 membranous wings, including bees and wasps.

**hymn** /hɪm/ ● noun song of esp. Christian praise. ● verb praise or celebrate in hymns.

**hymnal** /ˈhɪmn(ə)l/ noun book of hymns.

**hymnology** /hɪmˈnɒlədʒɪ/ noun composition or study of hymns. □ **hymnologist** noun.

**hyoscine** /ˈhaɪəsiːn/ noun alkaloid used to prevent motion sickness etc.

**hype** /haɪp/ slang ● noun intensive promotion of product etc. ● verb (**-ping**) promote with hype. □ **hyped up** excited.

**hyper** /ˈhaɪpə/ adjective slang hyperactive.

**hyper-** /ˈhaɪpə/ prefix over, above; too.

**hyperbola** /haɪˈpɜːbələ/ noun (plural **-s** or **-lae** /-liː/) curve produced when cone is cut by plane making larger angle with base than side of cone makes. □ **hyperbolic** /-pəˈbɒl-/ adjective.

**hyperbole** /haɪˈpɜːbəlɪ/ noun exaggeration, esp. for effect. □ **hyperbolical** /-ˈbɒl-/ adjective.

**hyperglycaemia** /haɪpəɡlaɪˈsiːmɪə/ noun (US **hyperglycemia**) excess of glucose in bloodstream.

**hypermarket** /ˈhaɪpəmɑːkɪt/ noun very large supermarket.

**hypermedia** /ˈhaɪpəmiːdɪə/ noun provision of several media (audio, video, etc.) on one computer system.

**hypersensitive** /haɪpəˈsensɪtɪv/ adjective excessively sensitive. □ **hypersensitivity** /-ˈtɪv-/ noun.

**hypersonic** /haɪpəˈsɒnɪk/ adjective of speeds more than 5 times that of sound.

**hypertension** /haɪpəˈtenʃ(ə)n/ noun abnormally high blood pressure; extreme tension.

**hypertext** /ˈhaɪpətekst/ noun provision of several texts on one computer system.

**hyperthermia** /haɪpəˈθɜːmɪə/ noun abnormally high body-temperature.

**hyperthyroidism** /haɪpəˈθaɪrɔɪdɪz(ə)m/ noun overactivity of thyroid gland.

**hyperventilation** /haɪpəˌventɪˈleɪʃ(ə)n/ noun abnormally rapid breathing. □ **hyperventilate** verb (**-ting**).

**hyphen** /ˈhaɪf(ə)n/ ● noun punctuation mark (-) used to join or divide words (see panel). ● verb hyphenate.

**hyphenate** /ˈhaɪfəneɪt/ verb (**-ting**) join or divide with hyphen. □ **hyphenation** noun.

**hypnosis** /hɪpˈnəʊsɪs/ noun state like sleep in which subject acts only on external suggestion; artificially induced sleep.

**hypnotherapy** /hɪpnəʊˈθerəpɪ/ noun treatment of mental disorders by hypnosis.

**hypnotic** /hɪpˈnɒtɪk/ ● adjective of or causing hypnosis; sleep-inducing. ● noun hypnotic drug or influence. □ **hypnotically** adverb.

**hypnotism** /ˈhɪpnətɪz(ə)m/ noun study or practice of hypnosis. □ **hypnotist** noun.

**hypnotize** /ˈhɪpnətaɪz/ verb (also **-ise**) (**-zing** or **-sing**) produce hypnosis in; fascinate.

**hypo** /ˈhaɪpəʊ/ noun sodium thiosulphate, used as photographic fixer.

**hypo-** /ˈhaɪpəʊ/ prefix under; below normal; slightly.

**hypochondria** /haɪpəˈkɒndrɪə/ noun abnormal anxiety about one's health.

**hypochondriac** /haɪpəˈkɒndrɪæk/ ● noun person given to hypochondria. ● adjective of hypochondria.

**hypocrisy** /hɪˈpɒkrɪsɪ/ noun (plural **-ies**) simulation of virtue; insincerity.

**hypocrite** /ˈhɪpəkrɪt/ noun person guilty of hypocrisy. □ **hypocritical** /-ˈkrɪt-/ adjective; **hypocritically** /-ˈkrɪt-/ adverb.

**hypodermic** /haɪpəˈdɜːmɪk/ ● adjective (of drug, syringe, etc.) introduced under the skin. ● *noun* hypodermic injection or syringe.

**hypotension** /haɪpəʊˈtenʃ(ə)n/ *noun* abnormally low blood pressure.

**hypotenuse** /haɪˈpɒtənjuːz/ *noun* side opposite right angle of right-angled triangle.

**hypothalamus** /haɪpəˈθæləməs/ *noun* (*plural* **-mi** /-maɪ/) region of brain controlling body temperature, thirst, hunger, etc.

**hypothermia** /haɪpəʊˈθɜːmɪə/ *noun* abnormally low body-temperature.

**hypothesis** /haɪˈpɒθɪsɪs/ *noun* (*plural* **-theses** /-siːz/) supposition made as basis for reasoning etc. □ **hypothesize** *verb* (also **-ise**) (**-zing** or **-sing**).

**hypothetical** /haɪpəˈθetɪk(ə)l/ *adjective* of or resting on hypothesis. □ **hypothetically** *adverb*.

**hypothyroidism** /haɪpəʊˈθaɪrɔɪdɪz(ə)m/ *noun* subnormal activity of the thyroid gland.

**hypoventilation** /haɪpəʊventɪˈleɪʃ(ə)n/ *noun* abnormally slow breathing.

**hyssop** /ˈhɪsəp/ *noun* small bushy aromatic herb.

**hysterectomy** /hɪstəˈrektəmɪ/ *noun* (*plural* **-ies**) surgical removal of womb.

---

## Hyphen -

This is used:

**1** to join two or more words so as to form a compound or single expression, e.g.

   *mother-in-law, non-stick, dressing-table*

This use is growing less common; often you can do without such hyphens:

   *nonstick, treelike, dressing table*

**2** to join words in an attributive compound (one put before a noun, like an adjective), e.g.

   *a well-known man* (but *the man is well known*)
   *an out-of-date list* (but *the list is out of date*)

**3** to join a prefix etc. to a proper name, e.g.

   *anti-Darwinian; half-Italian; non-British*

**4** to make a meaning clear by linking words, e.g.

   *twenty-odd people*/*twenty odd people*

or by separating a prefix, e.g.

   *re-cover*/*recover; re-present*/*represent; re-sign*/*resign*

**5** to separate two identical letters in adjacent parts of a word, e.g.

   *pre-exist, Ross-shire*

**6** to represent a common second element in the items of a list, e.g.

   *two-, three-, or fourfold.*

**7** to divide a word if there is no room to complete it at the end of the line, e.g.

   *... diction-*
   *ary ...*

The hyphen comes at the end of the line, not at the beginning of the next line. In general, words should be divided at the end of a syllable: *dicti-onary* would be quite wrong. In handwriting, typing, and word-processing, it is safest (and often neatest) not to divide words at all.

**hysteria** /hɪˈstɪərɪə/ *noun* uncontrollable emotion or excitement; functional disturbance of nervous system.

**hysteric** /hɪˈsterɪk/ *noun* (in *plural*) fit of hysteria, *colloquial* overwhelming laughter; hysterical person. ☐ **hysterical** *adjective*; **hysterically** *adverb*.

**Hz** *abbreviation* hertz.

∙∙∙∙∙∙∙∙∙∙∙∙∙∙∙∙∙∙∙∙∙∙∙∙∙∙∙∙∙∙∙∙∙∙∙∙∙∙∙∙∙∙∙∙∙∙∙∙∙∙∙∙∙∙∙∙∙∙∙∙∙∙∙∙∙

# Ii

∙∙∙∙∙∙∙∙∙∙∙∙∙∙∙∙∙∙∙∙∙∙∙∙∙∙∙∙∙∙∙∙∙∙∙∙∙∙∙∙∙∙∙∙∙∙∙∙∙∙∙∙∙∙∙∙∙∙∙∙∙∙∙∙∙

**I**[1] *noun* (also **i**) (Roman numeral) 1.

**I**[2] /aɪ/ *pronoun used by speaker or writer to refer to himself or herself as subject of verb*.

**I**[3] *abbreviation* (also **I.**) Island(s); Isle(s).

**iambic** /aɪˈæmbɪk/ ● *adjective* of or using iambuses. ● *noun* (usually in *plural*) iambic verse.

**iambus** /aɪˈæmbəs/ *noun* (*plural* **-buses** or **-bi** /-baɪ/) metrical foot of one short followed by one long syllable.

**IBA** *abbreviation* Independent Broadcasting Authority.

**ibex** /ˈaɪbeks/ *noun* (*plural* **-es**) wild mountain goat with large backward-curving ridged horns.

**ibid.** /ˈɪbɪd/ *abbreviation* in same book or passage etc. (*ibidem*).

**ibis** /ˈaɪbɪs/ *noun* (*plural* **-es**) storklike bird with long curved bill.

**ice** ● *noun* frozen water; portion of ice cream etc. ● *verb* (**icing**) mix with or cool in ice; (often + *over*, *up*) cover or become covered (as) with ice; freeze; cover (a cake etc.) with icing. ☐ **ice age** glacial period; **icebox** compartment in refrigerator for making or storing ice, *US* refrigerator; **ice-breaker** boat designed to break through ice; **icecap** mass of thick ice permanently covering polar region etc.; **ice cream** sweet creamy frozen food; **ice field** extensive sheet of floating ice; **ice hockey** form of hockey played on ice with flat disc instead of ball; **ice lolly** flavoured ice on stick; **ice rink** area of ice for skating etc.; **ice-skate** *noun* boot with blade attached for gliding over ice, *verb* move on ice-skates; **on ice** performed by ice-skaters, *colloquial* in reserve.

**iceberg** /ˈaɪsbɜːɡ/ *noun* mass of floating ice at sea. ☐ **tip of the iceberg** small

perceptible part of something very large or complex.

**Icelander** /ˈaɪsləndə/ *noun* native of Iceland.

**Icelandic** /aɪsˈlændɪk/ ● *adjective* of Iceland. ● *noun* language of Iceland.

**ichneumon** /ɪkˈnjuːmən/ *noun* (in full **ichneumon fly**) wasplike insect parasitic on other insects; mongoose of N. Africa etc.

**ichthyology** /ɪkθɪˈɒlədʒɪ/ *noun* study of fishes. ☐ **ichthyological** /-əˈlɒdʒɪk(ə)l/ *adjective*; **ichthyologist** *noun*.

**ichthyosaur** /ˈɪkθɪəsɔː/ *noun* large extinct reptile like dolphin.

**icicle** /ˈaɪsɪk(ə)l/ *noun* tapering hanging spike of ice, formed from dripping water.

**icing** *noun* sugar etc. coating for cake etc.; formation of ice on ship or aircraft. ☐ **icing sugar** finely powdered sugar.

**icon** /ˈaɪkɒn/ *noun* (also **ikon**) sacred painting, mosaic, etc.; image, statue. ☐ **iconic** /-ˈkɒn-/ *adjective*.

**iconoclast** /aɪˈkɒnəklæst/ *noun* person who attacks cherished beliefs; *historical* breaker of religious images. ☐ **iconoclasm** *noun*; **iconoclastic** /-ˈklæstɪk/ *adjective*.

**iconography** /aɪkəˈnɒɡrəfɪ/ *noun* illustration of subject by drawings etc.; study of portraits, esp. of one person, or of artistic images or symbols.

**icy** /ˈaɪsɪ/ *adjective* (**-ier**, **-iest**) very cold; covered with or abounding in ice; (of manner) unfriendly.

**ID** *abbreviation* identification, identity.

**I'd** /aɪd/ I had; I should; I would.

**id** *noun* *Psychology* part of mind comprising instinctive impulses of individual etc.

**idea** /aɪˈdɪə/ noun plan etc. formed by mental effort; mental impression or concept; vague belief or fancy; purpose, intention. □ **have no idea** colloquial not know at all, be completely incompetent.

**ideal** /aɪˈdiːəl/ ● adjective perfect; existing only in idea; visionary. ● noun perfect type, thing, principle, etc. as standard for imitation.

**idealism** noun forming or pursuing ideals; representation of things in ideal form; philosophy in which objects are held to be dependent on mind. □ **idealist** noun; **idealistic** /-ˈlɪst-/ adjective.

**idealize** verb (also **-ise**) (**-zing** or **-sing**) regard or represent as ideal. □ **idealization** noun.

**identical** /aɪˈdentɪk(ə)l/ adjective (often + with) absolutely alike; same; (of twins) developed from single ovum and very similar in appearance. □ **identically** adverb.

**identify** /aɪˈdentɪfaɪ/ verb (**-ies**, **-ied**) establish identity of; select, discover; (+ with) closely associate with; (+ with) regard oneself as sharing basic characteristics with; (often + with) treat as identical. □ **identification** noun.

**identity** /aɪˈdentɪtɪ/ noun (plural **-ies**) being specified person or thing; individuality; identification or the result of it; absolute sameness.

**ideogram** /ˈɪdɪəgræm/ noun (also **ideograph** /-grɑːf/) symbol representing thing or idea without indicating sounds in its name (e.g. Chinese character, or ' = ' for 'equals').

**ideology** /aɪdɪˈɒlədʒɪ/ noun (plural **-ies**) scheme of ideas at basis of political etc. theory or system; characteristic thinking of class etc. □ **ideological** /-ə'lɒdʒ-/ adjective.

**idiocy** /ˈɪdɪəsɪ/ noun (plural **-ies**) utter foolishness; foolish act; mental condition of idiot.

**idiom** /ˈɪdɪəm/ noun phrase etc. established by usage and not immediately comprehensible from the words used; form of expression peculiar to a language; language; characteristic mode of expression. □ **idiomatic** /-ˈmæt-/ adjective.

**idiosyncrasy** /ɪdɪəʊˈsɪŋkrəsɪ/ noun (plural **-ies**) attitude or form of behaviour peculiar to person. □ **idiosyncratic** /-ˈkræt-/ adjective.

**idiot** /ˈɪdɪət/ noun stupid person; person too deficient in mind to be capable of rational conduct. □ **idiotic** /-ˈɒt-/ adjective.

**idle** /ˈaɪd(ə)l/ ● adjective (**-r**, **-st**) lazy, indolent; not in use; unoccupied; useless, purposeless. ● verb (**-ling**) be idle; (of engine) run slowly without doing any work; pass (time) in idleness. □ **idleness** noun; **idler** noun; **idly** adverb.

**idol** /ˈaɪd(ə)l/ noun image as object of worship; object of devotion.

**idolater** /aɪˈdɒlətə/ noun worshipper of idols; devout admirer. □ **idolatrous** adjective; **idolatry** noun.

**idolize** verb (also **-ise**) (**-zing** or **-sing**) venerate or love to excess; treat as idol. □ **idolization** noun.

**idyll** /ˈɪdɪl/ noun account of picturesque scene or incident etc.; such scene etc. □ **idyllic** /ɪˈdɪlɪk/ adjective.

**i.e.** abbreviation that is to say (id est).

**if** conjunction on condition or supposition that; (with past tense) implying that the condition is not fulfilled; even though; whenever; whether; expressing wish, request, or (with negative) surprise. □ **if only** even if for no other reason than, I wish that.

**igloo** /ˈɪgluː/ noun dome-shaped snow house.

**igneous** /ˈɪgnɪəs/ adjective of fire; (esp. of rocks) produced by volcanic action.

**ignite** /ɪgˈnaɪt/ verb (**-ting**) set fire to; catch fire; provoke or excite (feelings etc.).

**ignition** /ɪgˈnɪʃ(ə)n/ noun mechanism for starting combustion in cylinder of motor engine; igniting.

**ignoble** /ɪgˈnəʊb(ə)l/ adjective (**-r**, **-st**) dishonourable; of low birth or position.

**ignominious** /ɪgnəˈmɪnɪəs/ adjective humiliating. □ **ignominiously** adverb.

**ignominy** /ˈɪgnəmɪnɪ/ noun dishonour, infamy.

**ignoramus** /ɪgnəˈreɪməs/ noun (plural **-muses**) ignorant person.

**ignorant** /ˈɪgnərənt/ adjective lacking knowledge; (+ of) uninformed; colloquial uncouth. □ **ignorance** noun.

**ignore** /ɪgˈnɔː/ *verb* (**-ring**) refuse to take notice of.

**iguana** /ɪgˈwɑːnə/ *noun* large Central and S. American tree lizard.

**iguanodon** /ɪgˈwɑːnədɒn/ *noun* large plant-eating dinosaur.

**ikebana** /ɪkɪˈbɑːnə/ *noun* Japanese art of flower arrangement.

**ikon** = ICON.

**ilex** /ˈaɪleks/ *noun* (*plural* **-es**) plant of genus including holly; holm-oak.

**iliac** /ˈɪlɪæk/ *adjective* of flank or hip-bone.

**ilk** *noun colloquial* sort, kind. □ **of that ilk** *Scottish* of ancestral estate of same name as family.

**I'll** /aɪl/ I shall; I will.

**ill** ● *adjective* in bad health, sick; harmful, unfavourable; hostile, unkind; faulty, deficient. ● *adverb* badly, unfavourably; scarcely. ● *noun* harm; evil. □ **ill-advised** unwise; **ill-bred** rude; **ill-favoured** unattractive; **ill-gotten** gained unlawfully or wickedly; **ill health** poor physical condition; **ill-mannered** rude; **ill-natured** churlish; **ill-tempered** morose, irritable; **ill-timed** done or occurring at unsuitable time; **ill-treat, -use** treat badly.

**illegal** /ɪˈliːg(ə)l/ *adjective* contrary to law. □ **illegality** /-ˈgæl-/ *noun* (*plural* **-ies**); **illegally** *adverb*.

**illegible** /ɪˈledʒɪb(ə)l/ *adjective* not legible, unreadable. □ **illegibility** *noun*; **illegibly** *adverb*.

**illegitimate** /ɪlɪˈdʒɪtɪmət/ *adjective* born of parents not married to each other; unlawful; improper; wrongly inferred. □ **illegitimacy** *noun*.

**illiberal** /ɪˈlɪbər(ə)l/ *adjective* narrow-minded; stingy. □ **illiberality** /-ˈræl-/ *noun*.

**illicit** /ɪˈlɪsɪt/ *adjective* unlawful; forbidden. □ **illicitly** *adverb*.

**illiterate** /ɪˈlɪtərət/ ● *adjective* unable to read; uneducated. ● *noun* illiterate person. □ **illiteracy** *noun*.

**illness** *noun* disease; ill health.

**illogical** /ɪˈlɒdʒɪk(ə)l/ *adjective* devoid of or contrary to logic. □ **illogicality** /-ˈkæl-/ *noun* (*plural* **-ies**); **illogically** *adverb*.

**illuminate** /ɪˈluːmɪneɪt/ *verb* (**-ting**) light up; decorate with lights; decorate (manuscript etc.) with gold, colour, etc.; help to explain (subject etc.); enlighten spiritually or intellectually. □ **illuminating** *adjective*; **illumination** *noun*.

**illumine** /ɪˈljuːmɪn/ *verb* (**-ning**) *literary* light up; enlighten.

**illusion** /ɪˈluːʒ(ə)n/ *noun* false belief; deceptive appearance. □ **be under the illusion** (+ *that*) believe mistakenly. □ **illusive** *adjective*; **illusory** *adjective*.

**illusionist** *noun* conjuror.

**illustrate** /ˈɪləstreɪt/ *verb* (**-ting**) provide with pictures; make clear, esp. by examples or drawings; serve as example of. □ **illustrator** *noun*.

**illustration** *noun* drawing etc. in book; explanatory example; illustrating.

**illustrative** /ˈɪləstrətɪv/ *adjective* (often + *of*) explanatory.

**illustrious** /ɪˈlʌstrɪəs/ *adjective* distinguished, renowned.

**I'm** /aɪm/ I am.

**image** /ˈɪmɪdʒ/ ● *noun* representation of object, esp. figure of saint or divinity; reputation or persona of person, company, etc.; appearance as seen in mirror or through lens; idea, conception; simile, metaphor. ● *verb* (**-ging**) make image of; mirror; picture.

**imagery** /ˈɪmɪdʒərɪ/ *noun* figurative illustration; use of images in literature etc.; images, statuary; mental images collectively.

**imaginary** /ɪˈmædʒɪnərɪ/ *adjective* existing only in imagination.

**imagination** /ɪmædʒɪˈneɪʃ(ə)n/ *noun* mental faculty of forming images of objects not present to senses; creative faculty of mind.

**imaginative** /ɪˈmædʒɪnətɪv/ *adjective* having or showing high degree of imagination. □ **imaginatively** *adverb*.

**imagine** /ɪˈmædʒɪn/ *verb* (**-ning**) form mental image of, conceive; suppose, think.

**imago** /ɪˈmeɪgəʊ/ *noun* (*plural* **-s** or **imagines** /ɪˈmædʒɪniːz/) fully developed stage of insect.

**imam** /ɪˈmɑːm/ *noun* prayer-leader of mosque; *title of some Muslim leaders*.

**imbalance** /ɪmˈbæləns/ *noun* lack of balance; disproportion.

**imbecile** /ˈɪmbɪsiːl/ ●*noun colloquial* stupid person; adult with mental age of about 5. ●*adjective* mentally weak, stupid. □ **imbecilic** /-ˈsɪlɪk/ *adjective*; **imbecility** /-ˈsɪlɪtɪ/ *noun* (*plural* **-ies**).

**imbed** = EMBED.

**imbibe** /ɪmˈbaɪb/ *verb* (**-bing**) drink; drink in; absorb; inhale.

**imbroglio** /ɪmˈbrəʊlɪəʊ/ *noun* (*plural* **-s**) confused or complicated situation.

**imbue** /ɪmˈbjuː/ *verb* (**-bues**, **-bued**, **-buing**) (often + *with*) inspire; saturate, dye.

**imitate** /ˈɪmɪteɪt/ *verb* (**-ting**) follow example of; mimic; make copy of; be like. □ **imitable** *adjective*; **imitative** /-tətɪv/ *adjective*; **imitator** *noun*.

**imitation** *noun* imitating, being imitated; copy; counterfeit.

**immaculate** /ɪˈmækjʊlət/ *adjective* perfectly clean, spotless; faultless; innocent, sinless. □ **immaculately** *adverb*; **immaculateness** *noun*.

**immanent** /ˈɪmənənt/ *adjective* inherent; (of God) omnipresent. □ **immanence** *noun*.

**immaterial** /ɪməˈtɪərɪəl/ *adjective* unimportant; irrelevant; not material. □ **immateriality** /-ˈæl-/ *noun*.

**immature** /ɪməˈtjʊə/ *adjective* not mature; undeveloped, esp. emotionally. □ **immaturity** *noun*.

**immeasurable** /ɪˈmeʒərəb(ə)l/ *adjective* not measurable, immense. □ **immeasurably** *adverb*.

**immediate** /ɪˈmiːdɪət/ *adjective* occurring at once; direct; nearest; having priority. □ **immediacy** *noun*; **immediately** *adverb*.

**immemorial** /ɪmɪˈmɔːrɪəl/ *adjective* ancient beyond memory.

**immense** /ɪˈmens/ *adjective* vast, huge. □ **immensity** *noun*.

**immensely** *adverb colloquial* vastly, very much.

**immerse** /ɪˈmɜːs/ *verb* (**-sing**) (often + *in*) dip, plunge; put under water; (often **immerse oneself** or in *passive*; often + *in*) involve deeply, embed.

**immersion** /ɪˈmɜːʃ(ə)n/ *noun* immersing, being immersed. □ **immersion heater** electric heater designed to be immersed in liquid to be heated.

**immigrant** /ˈɪmɪgrənt/ ●*noun* person who immigrates. ●*adjective* immigrating; of immigrants.

**immigrate** /ˈɪmɪgreɪt/ *verb* (**-ting**) enter a country to settle permanently. □ **immigration** *noun*.

**imminent** /ˈɪmɪnənt/ *adjective* soon to happen. □ **imminence** *noun*; **imminently** *adverb*.

**immobile** /ɪˈməʊbaɪl/ *adjective* motionless; immovable. □ **immobility** *noun*.

**immobilize** /ɪˈməʊbɪlaɪz/ *verb* (also **-ise**) (**-zing** or **-sing**) prevent from being moved. □ **immobilization** *noun*.

**immoderate** /ɪˈmɒdərət/ *adjective* excessive. □ **immoderately** *adverb*.

**immodest** /ɪˈmɒdɪst/ *adjective* conceited; indecent. □ **immodesty** *noun*.

**immolate** /ˈɪməleɪt/ *verb* (**-ting**) kill as sacrifice. □ **immolation** *noun*.

**immoral** /ɪˈmɒr(ə)l/ *adjective* opposed to, or not conforming to, (esp. sexual) morality; dissolute. □ **immorality** /ɪməˈrælɪtɪ/ *noun*.

**immortal** /ɪˈmɔːt(ə)l/ ●*adjective* living for ever; unfading; divine; famous for all time. ●*noun* immortal being, esp. (in *plural*) gods of antiquity. □ **immortality** /-ˈtæl-/ *noun*; **immortalize** *verb* (also **-ise**) (**-zing** or **-sing**).

**immovable** /ɪˈmuːvəb(ə)l/ *adjective* not movable; unyielding. □ **immovability** *noun*.

**immune** /ɪˈmjuːn/ *adjective* having immunity; relating to immunity; exempt.

**immunity** *noun* (*plural* **-ies**) living organism's power of resisting and overcoming infection; (often + *from*) freedom, exemption.

**immunize** /ˈɪmjuːnaɪz/ *verb* (also **-ise**) (**-zing** or **-sing**) make immune. □ **immunization** *noun*.

**immure** /ɪˈmjʊə/ *verb* (**-ring**) imprison.

**immutable** /ɪˈmjuːtəb(ə)l/ *adjective* unchangeable. □ **immutability** *noun*.

**imp** *noun* mischievous child; little devil.

**impact** ●*noun* /ˈɪmpækt/ collision, striking; (immediate) effect or influence. ●*verb* /ɪmˈpækt/ drive or wedge together; (as **impacted** *adjective*) (of tooth) wedged between another tooth and jaw. □ **impaction** /ɪmˈpækʃ(ə)n/ *noun*.

**impair** /ɪmˈpeə/ *verb* damage, weaken. □ **impairment** *noun*.

**impala** /ɪmˈpɑːlə/ noun (plural same or -s) small African antelope.

**impale** /ɪmˈpeɪl/ verb (-ling) transfix on stake. □ **impalement** noun.

**impalpable** /ɪmˈpælpəb(ə)l/ adjective not easily grasped; imperceptible to touch.

**impart** /ɪmˈpɑːt/ verb communicate (news etc.); give share of.

**impartial** /ɪmˈpɑːʃ(ə)l/ adjective fair, not partial. □ **impartiality** /-ʃɪˈæl-/ noun; **impartially** adverb.

**impassable** /ɪmˈpɑːsəb(ə)l/ adjective that cannot be traversed. □ **impassability** noun.

**impasse** /ˈæmpæs/ noun deadlock.

**impassioned** /ɪmˈpæʃ(ə)nd/ adjective filled with passion, ardent.

**impassive** /ɪmˈpæsɪv/ adjective not feeling or showing emotion. □ **impassively** adverb; **impassivity** /-ˈsɪv-/ noun.

**impasto** /ɪmˈpæstəʊ/ noun technique of laying on paint thickly.

**impatiens** /ɪmˈpeɪʃɪenz/ noun any of several plants including busy Lizzie.

**impatient** /ɪmˈpeɪʃ(ə)nt/ adjective not patient; intolerant; restlessly eager. □ **impatience** noun; **impatiently** adverb.

**impeach** /ɪmˈpiːtʃ/ verb accuse, esp. of treason etc.; call in question; disparage. □ **impeachment** noun.

**impeccable** /ɪmˈpekəb(ə)l/ adjective faultless; exemplary. □ **impeccability** noun; **impeccably** adverb.

**impecunious** /ɪmpɪˈkjuːnɪəs/ adjective having little or no money.

**impedance** /ɪmˈpiːd(ə)ns/ noun total effective resistance of electric circuit etc. to alternating current.

**impede** /ɪmˈpiːd/ verb (-ding) obstruct; hinder.

**impediment** /ɪmˈpedɪmənt/ noun hindrance; defect in speech, esp. lisp or stammer.

**impedimenta** /ɪmpedɪˈmentə/ plural noun encumbrances; baggage, esp. of army.

**impel** /ɪmˈpel/ verb (-ll-) drive, force; propel.

**impend** /ɪmˈpend/ verb be imminent; hang. □ **impending** adjective.

**impenetrable** /ɪmˈpenɪtrəb(ə)l/ adjective not penetrable; inscrutable; inaccessible to influences etc. □ **impenetrability** noun.

**impenitent** /ɪmˈpenɪt(ə)nt/ adjective not penitent. □ **impenitence** noun.

**imperative** /ɪmˈperətɪv/ ● adjective urgent, obligatory; peremptory; Grammar (of mood) expressing command. ● noun Grammar imperative mood; command; essential or urgent thing.

**imperceptible** /ɪmpəˈseptɪb(ə)l/ adjective not perceptible; very slight or gradual. □ **imperceptibility** noun; **imperceptibly** adverb.

**imperfect** /ɪmˈpɜːfɪkt/ ● adjective not perfect; incomplete; faulty; Grammar (of past tense) implying action going on but not completed. ● noun imperfect tense. □ **imperfectly** adverb.

**imperfection** /ɪmpəˈfekʃ(ə)n/ noun imperfectness; fault, blemish.

**imperial** /ɪmˈpɪərɪəl/ adjective of empire or sovereign state ranking with this; of emperor; majestic; (of non-metric weights and measures) used by statute in UK.

**imperialism** noun imperial system of government etc.; usually derogatory policy of dominating other nations by acquisition of dependencies or through trade etc. □ **imperialist** noun & adjective.

**imperil** /ɪmˈperɪl/ verb (-ll-; US -l-) endanger.

**imperious** /ɪmˈpɪərɪəs/ adjective overbearing, domineering. □ **imperiously** adverb.

**imperishable** /ɪmˈperɪʃəb(ə)l/ adjective that cannot perish.

**impermanent** /ɪmˈpɜːmənənt/ adjective not permanent. **impermanence** noun.

**impermeable** /ɪmˈpɜːmɪəb(ə)l/ adjective not permeable. □ **impermeability** noun.

**impersonal** /ɪmˈpɜːsən(ə)l/ adjective having no personality or personal feeling or reference; impartial; unfeeling; Grammar (of verb) used esp. with it as subject. □ **impersonality** /-ˈnæl-/ noun.

**impersonate** /ɪmˈpɜːsəneɪt/ verb (-ting) pretend to be, play part of. □ **impersonation** noun; **impersonator** noun.

**impertinent** /ɪmˈpɜːtɪnənt/ adjective insolent, saucy; irrelevant. □ **impertinence** noun; **impertinently** adverb.

**imperturbable** /ɪmpəˈtɜːbəb(ə)l/ adjective not excitable; calm. □ **imperturbability** noun; **imperturbably** adverb.

**impervious** /ɪmˈpɜːvɪəs/ *adjective* (usually + *to*) impermeable; not responsive.

**impetigo** /ɪmpɪˈtaɪɡəʊ/ *noun* contagious skin disease.

**impetuous** /ɪmˈpetjʊəs/ *adjective* acting or moving rashly or suddenly; moving violently or fast. □ **impetuosity** /-ˈɒs-/ *noun*; **impetuously** *adverb*.

**impetus** /ˈɪmpɪtəs/ *noun* moving force; momentum; impulse.

**impiety** /ɪmˈpaɪətɪ/ *noun* (*plural* **-ies**) lack of piety; act showing this.

**impinge** /ɪmˈpɪndʒ/ *verb* (**-ging**) (usually + *on*) make impact; (usually + *upon*) encroach.

**impious** /ˈɪmpɪəs/ *adjective* not pious; wicked.

**impish** *adjective* of or like imp, mischievous. □ **impishly** *adverb*.

**implacable** /ɪmˈplækəb(ə)l/ *adjective* not appeasable. □ **implacability** *noun*; **implacably** *adverb*.

**implant** ● *verb* /ɪmˈplɑːnt/ insert, fix; instil; plant; (in *passive*) (of fertilized ovum) become attached to wall of womb. ● *noun* /ˈɪmplɑːnt/ thing implanted. □ **implantation** *noun*.

**implausible** /ɪmˈplɔːzɪb(ə)l/ *adjective* not plausible. □ **implausibly** *adverb*.

**implement** ● *noun* /ˈɪmplɪmənt/ tool, utensil. ● *verb* /ˈɪmplɪment/ carry into effect. □ **implementation** *noun*.

**implicate** /ˈɪmplɪkeɪt/ *verb* (**-ting**) (often + *in*) show (person) to be involved (in crime etc.); imply.

**implication** *noun* thing implied; implying; implicating.

**implicit** /ɪmˈplɪsɪt/ *adjective* implied though not expressed; unquestioning. □ **implicitly** *adverb*.

**implode** /ɪmˈpləʊd/ *verb* (**-ding**) (cause to) burst inwards. □ **implosion** /ɪmˈpləʊʒ(ə)n/ *noun*.

**implore** /ɪmˈplɔː/ *verb* (**-ring**) beg earnestly.

**imply** /ɪmˈplaɪ/ *verb* (**-ies**, **-ied**) (often + *that*) insinuate, hint; mean.

**impolite** /ɪmpəˈlaɪt/ *adjective* uncivil, rude. □ **impolitely** *adverb*; **impoliteness** *noun*.

**impolitic** /ɪmˈpɒlɪtɪk/ *adjective* inexpedient, not advisable. □ **impoliticly** *adverb*.

**imponderable** /ɪmˈpɒndərəb(ə)l/ ● *adjective* that cannot be estimated; very light. ● *noun* (usually in *plural*) imponderable thing. □ **imponderability** *noun*; **imponderably** *adverb*.

**import** ● *verb* /ɪmˈpɔːt/ bring in (esp. foreign goods) from abroad; imply, mean. ● *noun* /ˈɪmpɔːt/ article or (in *plural*) amount imported; importing; meaning, implication; importance. □ **importation** *noun*; **importer** /-ˈpɔːtə/ *noun*.

**important** /ɪmˈpɔːt(ə)nt/ *adjective* (often + *to*) of great consequence; momentous; (of person) having position of authority or rank; pompous. □ **importance** *noun*; **importantly** *adverb*.

**importunate** /ɪmˈpɔːtjʊnət/ *adjective* making persistent or pressing requests. □ **importunity** /-ˈtjuː-/ *noun*.

**importune** /ɪmpəˈtjuːn/ *verb* (**-ning**) pester (person) with requests; solicit as prostitute.

**impose** /ɪmˈpəʊz/ *verb* (**-sing**) enforce compliance with; (often + *on*) inflict, lay (tax etc.); (+ *on*, *upon*) take advantage of.

**imposing** *adjective* impressive, esp. in appearance.

**imposition** /ɪmpəˈzɪʃ(ə)n/ *noun* imposing, being imposed; unfair demand or burden; tax, duty.

**impossible** /ɪmˈpɒsɪb(ə)l/ *adjective* not possible; not easy or convenient; *colloquial* outrageous, intolerable. □ **impossibility** *noun*; **impossibly** *adverb*.

**impost** /ˈɪmpəʊst/ *noun* tax, duty.

**impostor** /ɪmˈpɒstə/ *noun* (also **imposter**) person who assumes false character; swindler.

**imposture** /ɪmˈpɒstʃə/ *noun* fraudulent deception.

**impotent** /ˈɪmpət(ə)nt/ *adjective* powerless; (of male) unable to achieve erection of penis or have sexual intercourse. □ **impotence** *noun*.

**impound** /ɪmˈpaʊnd/ *verb* confiscate; shut up in pound.

**impoverish** /ɪmˈpɒvərɪʃ/ *verb* make poor. □ **impoverishment** *noun*.

**impracticable** /ɪmˈpræktɪkəb(ə)l/ *adjective* impossible in practice. □ **practicability** *noun*; **impracticably** *adverb*.

**impractical** /ɪmˈpræktɪk(ə)l/ adjective not practical; *esp.* US not practicable. □ **impracticality** /-ˈkæl-/ noun.

**imprecation** /ɪmprɪˈkeɪʃ(ə)n/ noun formal curse.

**imprecise** /ɪmprɪˈsaɪs/ adjective not precise.

**impregnable** /ɪmˈpregnəb(ə)l/ adjective safe against attack. □ **impregnability** noun.

**impregnate** /ˈɪmpregneɪt/ verb (-ting) fill, saturate; make pregnant. □ **impregnation** noun.

**impresario** /ɪmprɪˈsɑːrɪəʊ/ noun (plural -s) organizer of public entertainments.

**impress** ● verb /ɪmˈpres/ affect or influence deeply; arouse admiration or respect in; (often + on) emphasize; imprint, stamp. ● noun /ˈɪmpres/ mark impressed; characteristic quality.

**impression** /ɪmˈpreʃ(ə)n/ noun effect produced on mind; belief; imitation of person or sound, esp. done to entertain; impressing, mark impressed; unaltered reprint of book etc.; issue of book or newspaper etc.; print from type or engraving.

**impressionable** adjective easily influenced.

**impressionism** noun school of painting concerned with conveying effect of natural light on objects; style of music or writing seeking to convey esp. fleeting feelings or experience. □ **impressionist** noun; **impressionistic** /-ˈnɪs-/ adjective.

**impressive** /ɪmˈpresɪv/ adjective arousing respect, approval, or admiration. □ **impressively** adverb.

**imprimatur** /ɪmprɪˈmɑːtə/ noun licence to print; official approval.

**imprint** ● verb /ɪmˈprɪnt/ (often + on) impress firmly, esp. on mind; make impression of (figure etc.) on thing; make impression on with stamp etc. ● noun /ˈɪmprɪnt/ impression; printer's or publisher's name in book etc.

**imprison** /ɪmˈprɪz(ə)n/ verb (-n-) put into prison; confine. □ **imprisonment** noun.

**improbable** /ɪmˈprɒbəb(ə)l/ adjective not likely, difficult to believe. □ **improbability** noun; **improbably** adverb.

**improbity** /ɪmˈprəʊbɪtɪ/ noun (plural -ies) wickedness; dishonesty; wicked or dishonest act.

**impromptu** /ɪmˈprɒmptjuː/ ● adverb & adjective unrehearsed. ● noun (plural -s) impromptu performance or speech; short, usually solo, musical piece, often improvisatory in style.

**improper** /ɪmˈprɒpə/ adjective unseemly, indecent; inaccurate, wrong. □ **improperly** adverb.

**impropriety** /ɪmprəˈpraɪətɪ/ noun (plural -ies) indecency; instance of this; incorrectness, unfitness.

**improve** /ɪmˈpruːv/ verb (-ving) make or become better; (+ on) produce something better than; (as **improving** adjective) giving moral benefit. □ **improvement** noun.

**improvident** /ɪmˈprɒvɪd(ə)nt/ adjective lacking foresight; wasteful. □ **improvidence** noun; **improvidently** adverb.

**improvise** /ˈɪmprəvaɪz/ verb (-sing) compose extempore; provide or construct from materials etc. not intended for the purpose. □ **improvisation** noun; **improvisational** adjective; **improvisatory** /-ˈzeɪtərɪ/ adjective.

**imprudent** /ɪmˈpruːd(ə)nt/ adjective rash, indiscreet. □ **imprudence** noun; **imprudently** adverb.

**impudent** /ˈɪmpjʊd(ə)nt/ adjective impertinent. □ **impudence** noun; **impudently** adverb.

**impugn** /ɪmˈpjuːn/ verb challenge; call in question.

**impulse** /ˈɪmpʌls/ noun sudden urge; tendency to follow such urges; impelling; impetus.

**impulsive** /ɪmˈpʌlsɪv/ adjective apt to act on impulse; done on impulse; tending to impel. □ **impulsively** adverb; **impulsiveness** noun.

**impunity** /ɪmˈpjuːnɪtɪ/ noun exemption from punishment or injurious consequences. □ **with impunity** without punishment etc.

**impure** /ɪmˈpjʊə/ adjective adulterated; dirty; unchaste.

**impurity** noun (plural -ies) being impure; impure thing or part.

**impute** /ɪmˈpjuːt/ verb (-ting) (+ to) ascribe (fault etc.) to. □ **imputation** noun.

**in** ● preposition expressing inclusion or position within limits of space, time, circumstance, etc.; after (specified period of time); with respect to; as proportionate part of; with form or arrangement of; as member of; involved with; within ability of; having the condition of; affected by; having as aim; by means of; meaning; into (with verb of motion or change). ● *adverb expressing position bounded by certain limits, or movement to point enclosed by them*; into room etc.; at home etc.; so as to be enclosed; as part of a publication; in fashion, season, or office; (of player etc.) having turn or right to play; (of transport) at platform etc.; (of season, harvest, ordered goods, etc.) having arrived or been received; (of fire etc.) burning; (of tide) at highest point. ● *adjective* internal, living etc. inside; fashionable; (of joke etc.) confined to small group. □ **in-between** *colloquial* intermediate; **in-house** within an institution, company, etc.; **ins and outs** (often + *of*) details; **in so far as** to the extent that; **in that** because, in so far as; **in-tray** tray for incoming documents etc.; **in with** on good terms with.

**in.** *abbreviation* inch(es).

**inability** /ɪnəˈbɪlɪtɪ/ *noun* being unable.

**inaccessible** /ɪnəkˈsesɪb(ə)l/ *adjective* not accessible; unapproachable. □ **inaccessibility** *noun*.

**inaccurate** /ɪnˈækjʊrət/ *adjective* not accurate. □ **inaccuracy** *noun* ( *plural* **-ies**); **inaccurately** *adverb*.

**inaction** /ɪnˈækʃ(ə)n/ *noun* absence of action.

**inactive** /ɪnˈæktɪv/ *adjective* not active; not operating. □ **inactivity** /-ˈtɪv-/ *noun*.

**inadequate** /ɪnˈædɪkwət/ *adjective* insufficient; incompetent. □ **inadequacy** *noun* ( *plural* **-ies**); **inadequately** *adverb*.

**inadmissible** /ɪnədˈmɪsɪb(ə)l/ *adjective* not allowable. □ **inadmissibility** *noun*; **inadmissibly** *adverb*.

**inadvertent** /ɪnədˈvɜːt(ə)nt/ *adjective* unintentional; inattentive. □ **inadvertence** *noun*; **inadvertently** *adverb*.

**inadvisable** /ɪnədˈvaɪzəb(ə)l/ *adjective* not advisable. □ **inadvisability** *noun*.

**inalienable** /ɪnˈeɪlɪənəb(ə)l/ *adjective* that cannot be transferred to another or taken away.

**inane** /ɪˈneɪn/ *adjective* silly, senseless; empty. □ **inanity** /-ˈnæn-/ *noun* ( *plural* **-ies**).

**inanimate** /ɪnˈænɪmət/ *adjective* not endowed with animal life; spiritless, dull.

**inapplicable** /məˈplɪkəb(ə)l/ *adjective* not applicable; irrelevant. □ **inapplicability** *noun*.

**inapposite** /ɪnˈæpəzɪt/ *adjective* not apposite.

**inappropriate** /ɪnəˈprəʊprɪət/ *adjective* not appropriate. □ **inappropriately** *adverb*; **inappropriateness** *noun*.

**inapt** /ɪnˈæpt/ *adjective* not suitable; unskilful. □ **inaptitude** *noun*.

**inarticulate** /ɪnɑːˈtɪkjʊlət/ *adjective* unable to express oneself clearly; not articulate, indistinct; dumb; not jointed. □ **inarticulately** *adverb*.

**inasmuch** /ɪnəzˈmʌtʃ/ *adverb* (+ *as*) since, because; to the extent that.

**inattentive** /ɪnəˈtentɪv/ *adjective* not paying attention; neglecting to show courtesy. □ **inattention** *noun*; **inattentively** *adverb*.

**inaudible** /ɪnˈɔːdɪb(ə)l/ *adjective* that cannot be heard. □ **inaudibly** *adverb*.

**inaugural** /ɪnˈɔːgjʊr(ə)l/ ● *adjective* of inauguration. ● *noun* inaugural speech or lecture.

**inaugurate** /ɪnˈɔːgjʊreɪt/ *verb* (**-ting**) admit (person) to office; initiate use of or begin with ceremony; begin, introduce. □ **inauguration** *noun*.

**inauspicious** /ɪnɔːˈspɪʃəs/ *adjective* not of good omen; unlucky.

**inborn** /ˈɪnbɔːn/ *adjective* existing from birth; innate.

**inbred** /ɪnˈbred/ *adjective* inborn; produced by inbreeding.

**inbreeding** /ɪnˈbriːdɪŋ/ *noun* breeding from closely related animals or people.

**Inc.** *abbreviation US* Incorporated.

**incalculable** /ɪnˈkælkjʊləb(ə)l/ *adjective* too great for calculation; not calculable beforehand; uncertain. □ **incalculability** *noun*; **incalculably** *adverb*.

**incandesce** /ɪnkænˈdes/ *verb* (**-cing**) (cause to) glow with heat.

**incandescent** /ɪnkænˈdes(ə)nt/ *adjective* glowing with heat, shining; (of artificial light) produced by glowing filament etc. □ **incandescence** *noun*.

**incantation** /ɪnkænˈteɪʃ(ə)n/ *noun* spell, charm. □ **incantational** *adjective*.

**incapable** /ɪnˈkeɪpəb(ə)l/ *adjective* not capable; too honest, kind, etc. to do something; not capable of rational conduct. □ **incapability** *noun.*

**incapacitate** /ɪnkəˈpæsɪteɪt/ *verb* (**-ting**) make incapable or unfit.

**incapacity** /ɪnkəˈpæsɪtɪ/ *noun* inability; legal disqualification.

**incarcerate** /ɪnˈkɑːsəreɪt/ *verb* (**-ting**) imprison. □ **incarceration** *noun.*

**incarnate** /ɪnˈkɑːnət/ *adjective* in esp. human form.

**incarnation** /ɪnkɑːˈneɪʃ(ə)n/ *noun* embodiment in flesh; (**the Incarnation**) embodiment of God in Christ; (often + *of*) living type (of a quality etc.).

**incautious** /ɪnˈkɔːʃəs/ *adjective* rash. □ **incautiously** *adverb.*

**incendiary** /ɪnˈsendɪərɪ/ ● *adjective* (of bomb) filled with material for causing fires; of arson; guilty of arson; inflammatory. ● *noun* (*plural* **-ies**) incendiary person or bomb.

**incense**[1] /ˈɪnsens/ *noun* gum or spice giving sweet smell when burned; smoke of this, esp. in religious ceremonial.

**incense**[2] /ɪnˈsens/ *verb* (**-sing**) make angry.

**incentive** /ɪnˈsentɪv/ ● *noun* motive, incitement; payment etc. encouraging effort in work. ● *adjective* serving to motivate or incite.

**inception** /ɪnˈsepʃ(ə)n/ *noun* beginning.

**incessant** /ɪnˈses(ə)nt/ *adjective* unceasing, continual; repeated. □ **incessantly** *adverb.*

**incest** /ˈɪnsest/ *noun* crime of sexual intercourse between people prohibited from marrying because of closeness of their blood relationship.

**incestuous** /ɪnˈsestjʊəs/ *adjective* of or guilty of incest; having relationships restricted to a particular group etc.

**inch** ● *noun* twelfth of (linear) foot (2.54 cm); this as unit of map-scale (e.g. 1 inch to 1 mile) or as unit of rainfall (= 1 inch depth of water). ● *verb* move gradually. □ **every inch** entirely; **within an inch of one's life** almost to death.

**inchoate** /ɪnˈkəʊeɪt/ *adjective* just begun; undeveloped. □ **inchoation** *noun.*

**incidence** /ˈɪnsɪd(ə)ns/ *noun* range, scope, extent, manner, or rate of occurrence; falling of line, ray, particles, etc.

on surface; coming into contact with thing.

**incident** /ˈɪnsɪd(ə)nt/ ● *noun* event, occurrence; violent episode, civil or military; episode in play, film, etc. ● *adjective* (often + *to*) apt to occur, naturally attaching; (often + *on*, *upon*) (of light etc.) falling.

**incidental** /ɪnsɪˈdent(ə)l/ *adjective* (often + *to*) minor, supplementary; not essential. □ **incidental music** music played during or between scenes of play, film, etc.

**incidentally** *adverb* by the way; in an incidental way.

**incinerate** /ɪnˈsɪnəreɪt/ *verb* (**-ting**) burn to ashes. □ **incineration** *noun.*

**incinerator** *noun* furnace or device for incineration.

**incipient** /ɪnˈsɪpɪənt/ *adjective* beginning, in early stage.

**incise** /ɪnˈsaɪz/ *verb* (**-sing**) make cut in; engrave.

**incision** /ɪnˈsɪʒ(ə)n/ *noun* cutting, esp. by surgeon; cut.

**incisive** /ɪnˈsaɪsɪv/ *adjective* sharp; clear and effective.

**incisor** /ɪnˈsaɪzə/ *noun* cutting-tooth, esp. at front of mouth.

**incite** /ɪnˈsaɪt/ *verb* (**-ting**) (often + *to*) urge on, stir up. □ **incitement** *noun.*

**incivility** /ɪnsɪˈvɪlɪtɪ/ *noun* (*plural* **-ies**) rudeness; impolite act.

**inclement** /ɪnˈklemənt/ *adjective* (of weather) severe, stormy. □ **inclemency** *noun.*

**inclination** /ɪnklɪˈneɪʃ(ə)n/ *noun* propensity; liking, affection; slope, slant.

**incline** ● *verb* /ɪnˈklaɪn/ (**-ning**) (usually in *passive*) dispose, influence; have specified tendency; be disposed, tend; (cause to) lean or bend. ● *noun* /ˈɪnklaɪn/ slope.

**include** /ɪnˈkluːd/ *verb* (**-ding**) comprise, regard or treat as part of whole. □ **inclusion** /-ʒ(ə)n/ *noun.*

**inclusive** /ɪnˈkluːsɪv/ *adjective* (often + *of*) including; including the limits stated; comprehensive; including all accessory payments. □ **inclusively** *adverb;* **inclusiveness** *noun.*

**incognito** /ɪnkɒɡˈniːtəʊ/ ● *adjective & adverb* with one's name or identity concealed. ● *noun* (*plural* **-s**) person who is incognito; pretended identity.

**incoherent** /ˌɪnkəʊˈhɪərənt/ adjective unintelligible; lacking logic or consistency; not clear. □ **incoherence** noun; **incoherently** adverb.

**incombustible** /ˌɪnkəmˈbʌstɪb(ə)l/ adjective that cannot be burnt.

**income** /ˈɪnkʌm/ noun money received, esp. periodically, from work, investments, etc. □ **income tax** tax levied on income.

**incoming** adjective coming in; succeeding another.

**incommensurable** /ˌɪnkəˈmenʃərəb(ə)l/ adjective (often + with) not comparable in size, value, etc.; having no common factor. □ **incommensurability** noun.

**incommensurate** /ˌɪnkəˈmenʃərət/ adjective (often + with, to) out of proportion; inadequate; incommensurable.

**incommode** /ˌɪnkəˈməʊd/ verb (**-ding**) formal inconvenience; trouble, annoy.

**incommodious** /ˌɪnkəˈməʊdɪəs/ adjective formal too small for comfort; inconvenient.

**incommunicable** /ˌɪnkəˈmjuːnɪkəb(ə)l/ adjective that cannot be shared or communicated.

**incommunicado** /ˌɪnkəmjuːnɪˈkɑːdəʊ/ adjective without means of communication, in solitary confinement in prison etc.

**incomparable** /ɪnˈkɒmpərəb(ə)l/ adjective without an equal; matchless. □ **incomparability** noun; **incomparably** adverb.

**incompatible** /ˌɪnkəmˈpætɪb(ə)l/ adjective not compatible. □ **incompatibility** noun.

**incompetent** /ɪnˈkɒmpɪt(ə)nt/ adjective inept; (often + to) lacking the necessary skill, not legally qualified. □ **incompetence** noun.

**incomplete** /ˌɪnkəmˈpliːt/ adjective not complete.

**incomprehensible** /ɪnˌkɒmprɪˈhensɪb(ə)l/ adjective that cannot be understood.

**incomprehension** /ɪnˌkɒmprɪˈhenʃ(ə)n/ noun failure to understand.

**inconceivable** /ˌɪnkənˈsiːvəb(ə)l/ adjective that cannot be imagined. □ **inconceivably** adverb.

**inconclusive** /ˌɪnkənˈkluːsɪv/ adjective (of argument etc.) not convincing or decisive.

**incongruous** /ɪnˈkɒŋɡrʊəs/ adjective out of place; absurd; (often + with) out of keeping. □ **incongruity** /-ˈɡruːɪtɪ/ noun (plural **-ies**); **incongruously** adverb.

**inconsequent** /ɪnˈkɒnsɪkwənt/ adjective irrelevant; not following logically; disconnected. □ **inconsequence** noun.

**inconsequential** /ˌɪnkɒnsɪˈkwenʃ(ə)l/ adjective unimportant; inconsequent. □ **inconsequentially** adverb.

**inconsiderable** /ˌɪnkənˈsɪdərəb(ə)l/ adjective of small size, value, etc.; not worth considering. □ **inconsiderably** adverb.

**inconsiderate** /ˌɪnkənˈsɪdərət/ adjective not considerate of others; thoughtless. □ **inconsiderately** adverb; **inconsiderateness** noun.

**inconsistent** /ˌɪnkənˈsɪst(ə)nt/ adjective not consistent. □ **inconsistency** noun (plural **-ies**); **inconsistently** adverb.

**inconsolable** /ˌɪnkənˈsəʊləb(ə)l/ adjective that cannot be consoled. □ **inconsolably** adverb.

**inconspicuous** /ˌɪnkənˈspɪkjʊəs/ adjective not conspicuous; not easily noticed. □ **inconspicuously** adverb; **inconspicuousness** noun.

**inconstant** /ɪnˈkɒnst(ə)nt/ adjective fickle; variable. □ **inconstancy** noun (plural **-ies**).

**incontestable** /ˌɪnkənˈtestəb(ə)l/ adjective that cannot be disputed. □ **incontestably** adverb.

**incontinent** /ɪnˈkɒntɪnənt/ adjective unable to control bowels or bladder; lacking self-restraint. □ **incontinence** noun.

**incontrovertible** /ˌɪnkɒntrəˈvɜːtɪb(ə)l/ adjective indisputable. □ **incontrovertibly** adverb.

**inconvenience** /ˌɪnkənˈviːnɪəns/ ● noun lack of ease or comfort; trouble; cause or instance of this. ● verb (**-cing**) cause inconvenience to.

**inconvenient** adjective causing trouble, difficulty, or discomfort; awkward. □ **inconveniently** adverb.

**incorporate** ● verb /ɪnˈkɔːpəreɪt/ (**-ting**) include as part or ingredient; (often + in, with) unite (in one body); admit as member of company etc.; (esp. as **incorporated** adjective) constitute as legal corporation. ● *adjective* /ɪnˈkɔːpərət/ incorporated. □ **incorporation** *noun.*

**incorporeal** /ɪnkɔːˈpɔːrɪəl/ *adjective* without substance or material existence. □ **incorporeally** *adverb.*

**incorrect** /ɪnkəˈrekt/ *adjective* untrue, inaccurate; improper, unsuitable. □ **incorrectly** *adverb.*

**incorrigible** /ɪnˈkɒrɪdʒɪb(ə)l/ *adjective* that cannot be corrected or improved. □ **incorrigibility** *noun*, **incorrigibly** *adverb.*

**incorruptible** /ɪnkəˈrʌptɪb(ə)l/ *adjective* that cannot decay or be corrupted. □ **incorruptibility** *noun*, **incorruptibly** *adverb.*

**increase** ● *verb* /ɪnˈkriːs/ (**-sing**) become or make greater or more numerous. ● *noun* /ˈɪnkriːs/ growth, enlargement; (of people, animals, or plants) multiplication; increased amount. □ **on the increase** increasing.

**increasingly** /ɪnˈkriːsɪŋli/ *adverb* more and more.

**incredible** /ɪnˈkredɪb(ə)l/ *adjective* that cannot be believed; *colloquial* surprising, extremely good. □ **incredibility** *noun*, **incredibly** *adverb.*

**incredulous** /ɪnˈkredjʊləs/ *adjective* unwilling to believe; showing disbelief. □ **incredulity** /ɪnkrɪˈdjuːlɪti/ *noun*, **incredulously** *adverb.*

**increment** /ˈɪŋkrɪmənt/ *noun* amount of increase; added amount. □ **incremental** /-ˈment(ə)l/ *adjective.*

**incriminate** /ɪnˈkrɪmɪneɪt/ *verb* (**-ting**) indicate as guilty; charge with crime. □ **incrimination** *noun*, **incriminatory** *adjective.*

**incrustation** /ɪnkrʌsˈteɪʃ(ə)n/ *noun* encrusting, being encrusted; crust, hard coating; deposit on surface.

**incubate** /ˈɪŋkjʊbeɪt/ *verb* (**-ting**) hatch (eggs) by sitting on them or by artificial heat; cause (bacteria etc.) to develop; develop slowly.

**incubation** *noun* incubating, being incubated; period between infection and appearance of first symptoms.

**incubator** *noun* apparatus providing warmth for hatching eggs, rearing premature babies, or developing bacteria.

**incubus** /ˈɪŋkjʊbəs/ *noun* (*plural* **-buses** or **-bi** /-baɪ/) demon or male spirit formerly believed to have sexual intercourse with sleeping women; nightmare; oppressive person or thing.

**inculcate** /ˈɪnkʌlkeɪt/ *verb* (**-ting**) (often + *upon, in*) urge, impress persistently. □ **inculcation** *noun.*

**incumbency** /ɪnˈkʌmbənsi/ *noun* (*plural* **-ies**) office or tenure of incumbent.

**incumbent** /ɪnˈkʌmbənt/ ● *adjective* lying, pressing; currently holding office. ● *noun* holder of office, esp. benefice. □ **it is incumbent on a person** (+ *to do*) it is a person's duty.

**incur** /ɪnˈkɜː/ *verb* (**-rr-**) bring on oneself.

**incurable** /ɪnˈkjʊərəb(ə)l/ ● *adjective* that cannot be cured. ● *noun* incurable person. □ **incurability** *noun*, **incurably** *adverb.*

**incurious** /ɪnˈkjʊərɪəs/ *adjective* lacking curiosity.

**incursion** /ɪnˈkɜːʃ(ə)n/ *noun* invasion; sudden attack. □ **incursive** *adjective.*

**indebted** /ɪnˈdetɪd/ *adjective* (usually + *to*) owing money or gratitude. □ **indebtedness** *noun.*

**indecent** /ɪnˈdiːs(ə)nt/ *adjective* offending against decency; unbecoming; unsuitable. □ **indecent assault** sexual attack not involving rape. □ **indecency** *noun*, **indecently** *adverb.*

**indecipherable** /ɪndɪˈsaɪfərəb(ə)l/ *adjective* that cannot be deciphered.

**indecision** /ɪndɪˈsɪʒ(ə)n/ *noun* inability to decide; hesitation.

**indecisive** /ɪndɪˈsaɪsɪv/ *adjective* not decisive; irresolute; not conclusive. □ **indecisively** *adverb*, **indecisiveness** *noun.*

**indecorous** /ɪnˈdekərəs/ *adjective* improper, undignified; in bad taste. □ **indecorously** *adverb.*

**indeed** /ɪnˈdiːd/ ● *adverb* in truth; really; admittedly. ● *interjection expressing irony, incredulity, etc.*

**indefatigable** /ɪndɪˈfætɪgəb(ə)l/ *adjective* unwearying, unremitting. □ **indefatigably** *adverb.*

**indefeasible** /ɪndɪˈfiːzɪb(ə)l/ *adjective literary* (esp. of claim, rights, etc.) that cannot be forfeited or annulled.

**indefensible** /ɪndɪˈfensɪb(ə)l/ *adjective* that cannot be defended. □ **indefensibility** *noun*, **indefensibly** *adverb.*

**indefinable** /ɪndɪˈfaɪnəb(ə)l/ *adjective* that cannot be defined; mysterious. □ **indefinably** *adverb*.

**indefinite** /ɪnˈdefɪnɪt/ *adjective* vague, undefined; unlimited; (of adjectives, adverbs, and pronouns) not determining the person etc. referred to. □ **indefinite article** word (*a*, *an* in English) placed before noun and meaning 'one, some, any'.

**indefinitely** *adverb* for an unlimited time; in an indefinite manner.

**indelible** /ɪnˈdelɪb(ə)l/ *adjective* that cannot be rubbed out; permanent. □ **indelibly** *adverb*.

**indelicate** /ɪnˈdelɪkət/ *adjective* coarse, unrefined; tactless. □ **indelicacy** *noun* (*plural* -ies); **indelicately** *adverb*.

**indemnify** /ɪnˈdemnɪfaɪ/ *verb* (-ies, -ied) (often + *against*, *from*) secure against loss or legal responsibility; (often + *for*) exempt from penalty; compensate. □ **indemnification** *noun*.

**indemnity** /ɪnˈdemnɪtɪ/ *noun* (*plural* -ies) compensation for damage; sum exacted by victor in war; security against damage or loss; exemption from penalties.

**indent** • *verb* /ɪnˈdent/ make or impress notches, dents, or recesses in; set back (beginning of line) inwards from margin; draw up (legal document) in duplicate; (often + *for*) make requisition. • *noun* /ˈɪndent/ order (esp. from abroad) for goods; official requisition for stores; indented line; indentation; indenture.

**indentation** /ɪndenˈteɪʃ(ə)n/ *noun* denting, being indented; notch.

**indenture** /ɪnˈdentʃə/ • *noun* (usually in *plural*) sealed agreement; formal list, certificate, etc. • *verb* (-ring) *historical* bind by indentures, esp. as apprentice.

**independent** /ɪndɪˈpend(ə)nt/ • *adjective* (often + *of*) not depending on authority; self-governing; not depending on another person for one's livelihood or opinions; (of income) making it unnecessary to earn one's livelihood; unwilling to be under obligation to others; not depending on something else for validity etc.; (of institution) not supported by public funds. • *noun* politician etc. independent of any political party. □ **independence** *noun*, **independently** *adverb*.

**indescribable** /ɪndɪˈskraɪbəb(ə)l/ *adjective* beyond description; that cannot be described. □ **indescribably** *adverb*.

**indestructible** /ɪndɪˈstrʌktɪb(ə)l/ *adjective* that cannot be destroyed. □ **indestructibility** *noun*; **indestructibly** *adverb*.

**indeterminable** /ɪndɪˈtɜːmɪnəb(ə)l/ *adjective* that cannot be ascertained or settled.

**indeterminate** /ɪndɪˈtɜːmɪnət/ *adjective* not fixed in extent, character, etc.; vague. □ **indeterminacy** *noun*.

**index** /ˈɪndeks/ • *noun* (*plural* -es or **indices** /ˈɪndɪsiːz/) alphabetical list of subjects etc. with references, usually at end of book; card index; measure of prices or wages compared with a previous month, year, etc.; *Mathematics* exponent. • *verb* furnish (book) with index, enter in index; relate (wages, investment income, etc.) to a price index. □ **index finger** finger next to thumb; **index-linked** related to value of price index.

**Indian** /ˈɪndɪən/ • *noun* native or national of India; person of Indian descent; (in full **American Indian**) original inhabitant of America. • *adjective* of India; of the subcontinent comprising India, Pakistan, and Bangladesh; of the original inhabitants of America. □ **Indian corn** maize; **Indian file** single file; **Indian ink** black pigment, ink made from this; **Indian summer** period of calm dry warm weather in late autumn, happy tranquil period late in life.

**indiarubber** *noun* rubber, esp. for rubbing out pencil marks etc.

**indicate** /ˈɪndɪkeɪt/ *verb* (-ting) point out, make known; show; be sign of; require, call for; state briefly; give as reading or measurement; point by hand; use a vehicle's indicator. □ **indication** *noun*.

**indicative** /ɪnˈdɪkətɪv/ • *adjective* (+ *of*) suggestive, giving indications; *Grammar* (of mood) stating thing as fact. • *noun* *Grammar* indicative mood; verb in this mood.

**indicator** *noun* flashing light on vehicle showing direction in which it is about to turn; person or thing that indicates; device indicating condition of machine etc.; recording instrument; board giving current information.

**indices** plural of INDEX.

**indict** /ɪnˈdaɪt/ verb accuse formally by legal process.

**indictable** adjective (of an offence) rendering person liable to be indicted; so liable.

**indictment** noun indicting, accusation; document containing this; thing that serves to condemn or censure.

**indifference** /ɪnˈdɪfrəns/ noun lack of interest or attention; unimportance.

**indifferent** adjective (+ to) showing indifference; neither good nor bad; of poor quality or ability. □ **indifferently** adverb.

**indigenous** /ɪnˈdɪdʒɪnəs/ adjective (often + to) native or belonging naturally to a place.

**indigent** /ˈɪndɪdʒ(ə)nt/ adjective formal needy, poor. □ **indigence** noun.

**indigestible** /ɪndɪˈdʒestɪb(ə)l/ adjective difficult or impossible to digest.

**indigestion** /ɪndɪˈdʒestʃ(ə)n/ noun difficulty in digesting food; pain caused by this.

**indignant** /ɪnˈdɪgnənt/ adjective feeling or showing indignation. □ **indignantly** adverb.

**indignation** /ɪndɪgˈneɪʃ(ə)n/ noun anger at supposed injustice etc.

**indignity** /ɪnˈdɪgnɪti/ noun (plural -ies) humiliating treatment; insult.

**indigo** /ˈɪndɪgəʊ/ noun (plural -s) deep violet-blue; dye of this colour.

**indirect** /ɪndaɪˈrekt/ adjective not going straight to the point; (of route etc.) not straight. □ **indirect object** word or phrase representing person or thing affected by action of verb but not acted on (see panel at OBJECT); **indirect speech** reported speech; **indirect tax** tax on goods and services, not income. □ **indirectly** adverb.

**indiscernible** /ɪndɪˈsɜːnɪb(ə)l/ adjective that cannot be discerned.

**indiscipline** /ɪnˈdɪsɪplɪn/ noun lack of discipline.

**indiscreet** /ɪndɪˈskriːt/ adjective not discreet; injudicious, unwary. □ **indiscreetly** adverb.

**indiscretion** /ɪndɪˈskreʃ(ə)n/ noun indiscreet conduct or action.

**indiscriminate** /ɪndɪˈskrɪmɪnət/ adjective making no distinctions; done or acting at random. □ **indiscriminately** adverb.

**indispensable** /ɪndɪˈspensəb(ə)l/ adjective that cannot be dispensed with; necessary. □ **indispensably** adverb.

**indisposed** /ɪndɪˈspəʊzd/ adjective slightly unwell; averse, unwilling. □ **indisposition** /-spəˈzɪʃ(ə)n/ noun.

**indisputable** /ɪndɪˈspjuːtəb(ə)l/ adjective that cannot be disputed. □ **indisputably** adverb.

**indissoluble** /ɪndɪˈsɒljʊb(ə)l/ adjective that cannot be dissolved; lasting, stable. □ **indissolubly** adverb.

**indistinct** /ɪndɪˈstɪŋkt/ adjective not distinct; confused, obscure. □ **indistinctly** adverb.

**indistinguishable** /ɪndɪˈstɪŋgwɪʃəb(ə)l/ adjective (often + from) not distinguishable.

**indite** /ɪnˈdaɪt/ verb (-ting) formal or jocular put into words; write (letter etc.).

**individual** /ɪndɪˈvɪdʒʊəl/ ● adjective of, for, or characteristic of single person or thing; having distinct character; designed for use by one person; single; particular. ● noun single member of class, group, etc.; single human being; colloquial person; distinctive person.

**individualism** noun social theory favouring free action by individuals; being independent or different. □ **individualist** noun; **individualistic** /-ˈlɪs-/ adjective.

**individuality** /ɪndɪvɪdʒʊˈælɪti/ noun individual character, esp. when strongly marked; separate existence.

**individualize** verb (also **-ise**) (-zing or -sing) give individual character to; (esp. as **individualized** adjective) personalize.

**individually** adverb one by one; personally; distinctively.

**indivisible** /ɪndɪˈvɪzɪb(ə)l/ adjective not divisible.

**indoctrinate** /ɪnˈdɒktrɪneɪt/ verb (-ting) teach to accept a particular belief uncritically. □ **indoctrination** noun.

**Indo-European** /ɪndəʊjʊərəˈpɪən/ ● adjective of family of languages spoken over most of Europe and Asia as far as N. India; of hypothetical parent language of this family. ● *noun* Indo-European family of languages; hypothetical parent language of these.

**indolent** /'ɪndələnt/ *adjective* lazy; averse to exertion. □ **indolence** *noun*, **indolently** *adverb*.

**indomitable** /ɪn'dɒmɪtəb(ə)l/ *adjective* unconquerable; unyielding. □ **indomitably** *adverb*.

**indoor** /'ɪndɔː/ *adjective* done etc. in building or under cover.

**indoors** /ɪn'dɔːz/ *adverb* in(to) a building.

**indubitable** /ɪn'djuːbɪtəb(ə)l/ *adjective* that cannot be doubted. □ **indubitably** *adverb*.

**induce** /ɪn'djuːs/ *verb* (**-cing**) prevail on, persuade; bring about; bring on (labour) artificially; bring on labour in (mother); speed up birth of (baby); produce by induction; infer. □ **inducible** *adjective*.

**inducement** *noun* attractive offer; incentive; bribe.

**induct** /ɪn'dʌkt/ *verb* install into office etc.

**inductance** *noun* property of electric circuit in which variation in current produces electromotive force.

**induction** /ɪn'dʌkʃ(ə)n/ *noun* inducting, inducing; act of bringing on (esp. labour) artificially; general inference from particular instances; formal introduction to new job etc.; production of electric or magnetic state by proximity to electric circuit or magnetic field.

**inductive** /ɪn'dʌktɪv/ *adjective* (of reasoning etc.) based on induction; of electric or magnetic induction.

**indulge** /ɪn'dʌldʒ/ *verb* (**-ging**) (often + *in*) take one's pleasure freely; yield freely to (desire etc.); gratify by compliance with wishes.

**indulgence** *noun* indulging; thing indulged in; *RC Church* remission of punishment still due after absolution; privilege granted.

**indulgent** *adjective* lenient; willing to overlook faults; indulging. □ **indulgently** *adverb*.

**industrial** /ɪn'dʌstrɪəl/ *adjective* of, engaged in, for use in, or serving the needs of, industry; having highly developed industries. □ **industrial action** strike or disruptive action by workers as protest; **industrial estate** area of land zoned for factories etc. □ **industrially** *adverb*.

**industrialism** *noun* system in which manufacturing industries predominate.

**industrialist** *noun* owner or manager in industry.

**industrialize** *verb* (also **-ise**) (**-zing** or **-sing**) make (nation etc.) industrial. □ **industrialization** *noun*.

**industrious** /ɪn'dʌstrɪəs/ *adjective* hardworking. □ **industriously** *adverb*.

**industry** /'ɪndəstrɪ/ *noun* (*plural* **-ies**) branch of trade or manufacture; commercial enterprise; trade or manufacture collectively; concerted activity; diligence.

**inebriate** ● *verb* /ɪn'iːbrɪeɪt/ (**-ting**) make drunk; excite. ● *adjective* /ɪn'iːbrɪət/ drunken. ● *noun* /ɪn'iːbrɪət/ drunkard. □ **inebriation** *noun*.

**inedible** /ɪn'edɪb(ə)l/ *adjective* not suitable for eating.

**ineducable** /ɪn'edjʊkəb(ə)l/ *adjective* incapable of being educated.

**ineffable** /ɪn'efəb(ə)l/ *adjective* too great for description in words; that must not be uttered. □ **ineffability** *noun*, **ineffably** *adverb*.

**ineffective** /ɪnɪ'fektɪv/ *adjective* not achieving desired effect or results. □ **ineffectively** *adverb*, **ineffectiveness** *noun*.

**ineffectual** /ɪnɪ'fektʃʊəl/ *adjective* ineffective, feeble. □ **ineffectually** *adverb*.

**inefficient** /ɪnɪ'fɪʃ(ə)nt/ *adjective* not efficient or fully capable; (of machine etc.) wasteful. □ **inefficiency** *noun*, **inefficiently** *adverb*.

**inelegant** /ɪn'elɪɡənt/ *adjective* ungraceful, unrefined. □ **inelegance** *noun*, **inelegantly** *adverb*.

**ineligible** /ɪn'elɪdʒɪb(ə)l/ *adjective* not eligible or qualified. □ **ineligibility** *noun*.

**ineluctable** /ɪnɪ'lʌktəb(ə)l/ *adjective* inescapable, unavoidable.

**inept** /ɪ'nept/ *adjective* unskilful; absurd, silly; out of place. □ **ineptitude** *noun*, **ineptly** *adverb*.

**inequality** /ɪnɪˈkwɒlɪtɪ/ noun (plural -ies) lack of equality; variability; unevenness.

**inequitable** /ɪnˈekwɪtəb(ə)l/ adjective unfair, unjust.

**inequity** /ɪnˈekwɪtɪ/ noun (plural -ies) unfairness, injustice.

**ineradicable** /ɪnɪˈrædɪkəb(ə)l/ adjective that cannot be rooted out.

**inert** /ɪˈnɜːt/ adjective without inherent power of action etc.; chemically inactive; sluggish, slow; lifeless.

**inertia** /ɪˈnɜːʃə/ noun property by which matter continues in existing state of rest or motion unless acted on by external force; inertness; tendency to remain unchanged. □ **inertia reel** reel allowing seat belt to unwind freely but locking on impact; **inertia selling** sending of unsolicited goods in hope of making a sale.

**inescapable** /ɪnɪˈskeɪpəb(ə)l/ adjective that cannot be escaped or avoided. □ **inescapably** adverb.

**inessential** /ɪnɪˈsenʃ(ə)l/ ● adjective not necessary; dispensable. ● noun inessential thing.

**inestimable** /ɪnˈestɪməb(ə)l/ adjective too great etc. to be estimated. □ **inestimably** adverb.

**inevitable** /ɪnˈevɪtəb(ə)l/ adjective unavoidable; bound to happen or appear; colloquial tiresomely familiar. □ **inevitability** noun; **inevitably** adverb.

**inexact** /ɪnɪɡˈzækt/ adjective not exact. □ **inexactitude** noun.

**inexcusable** /ɪnɪkˈskjuːzəb(ə)l/ adjective that cannot be justified. □ **inexcusably** adverb.

**inexhaustible** /ɪnɪɡˈzɔːstɪb(ə)l/ adjective that cannot be used up.

**inexorable** /ɪnˈeksərəb(ə)l/ adjective relentless. □ **inexorably** adverb.

**inexpedient** /ɪnɪkˈspiːdɪənt/ adjective not expedient.

**inexpensive** /ɪnɪkˈspensɪv/ adjective not expensive.

**inexperience** /ɪnɪkˈspɪərɪəns/ noun lack of experience. □ **inexperienced** adjective.

**inexpert** /ɪnˈekspɜːt/ adjective unskilful.

**inexpiable** /ɪnˈekspɪəb(ə)l/ adjective that cannot be expiated.

**inexplicable** /ɪnɪkˈsplɪkəb(ə)l/ adjective that cannot be explained. □ **inexplicably** adverb.

**inexpressible** /ɪnɪkˈspresɪb(ə)l/ adjective that cannot be expressed. □ **inexpressibly** adverb.

**in extremis** /ɪn ɪkˈstriːmɪs/ adjective at point of death; in great difficulties. [Latin]

**inextricable** /ɪnɪkˈstrɪkəb(ə)l/ adjective that cannot be separated, loosened, or resolved; inescapable. □ **inextricably** adverb.

**infallible** /ɪnˈfælɪb(ə)l/ adjective incapable of error; unfailing, sure. □ **infallibility** noun; **infallibly** adverb.

**infamous** /ˈɪnfəməs/ adjective notoriously vile, evil; abominable. □ **infamously** adverb; **infamy** noun (plural -ies).

**infant** /ˈɪnf(ə)nt/ noun child during earliest period of life; thing in early stage of development; Law person under 18. □ **infancy** noun.

**infanta** /ɪnˈfæntə/ noun historical daughter of Spanish or Portuguese king.

**infanticide** /ɪnˈfæntɪsaɪd/ noun killing of infant, esp. soon after birth; person guilty of this.

**infantile** /ˈɪnfəntaɪl/ adjective of or like infants. □ **infantile paralysis** poliomyelitis.

**infantry** /ˈɪnfəntrɪ/ noun (plural -ies) (group of) foot-soldiers. □ **infantryman** soldier of infantry regiment.

**infatuate** /ɪnˈfætjʊeɪt/ verb (-ting) (usually as **infatuated** adjective) inspire with intense fondness. □ **infatuation** noun.

**infect** /ɪnˈfekt/ verb affect or contaminate with germ, virus, or disease; imbue, taint.

**infection** /ɪnˈfekʃ(ə)n/ noun infecting, being infected; disease; communication of disease.

**infectious** /ɪnˈfekʃəs/ adjective infecting; transmissible by infection; apt to spread. □ **infectiously** adverb.

**infelicity** /ɪnfɪˈlɪsɪtɪ/ noun (plural -ies) inapt expression; unhappiness. □ **infelicitous** adjective.

**infer** /ɪnˈfɜː/ verb (-rr-) deduce, conclude.

■ **Usage** It is a mistake to use *infer* to mean 'imply', as in *Are you inferring that I'm a liar?*

**inference** /'ɪnfərəns/ *noun* act of inferring; thing inferred. □ **inferential** /-'ren(ə)l/ *adjective*.

**inferior** /ɪn'fɪərɪə/ ● *adjective* lower in rank etc.; of poor quality; situated below. ● *noun* inferior person.

**inferiority** /ɪnfɪərɪ'ɒrɪtɪ/ *noun* being inferior. □ **inferiority complex** feeling of inadequacy, sometimes marked by compensating aggressive behaviour.

**infernal** /ɪn'fɜːn(ə)l/ *adjective* of hell; hellish; *colloquial* detestable, tiresome. □ **infernally** *adverb*.

**inferno** /ɪn'fɜːnəʊ/ *noun* (*plural* **-s**) raging fire; scene of horror or distress; hell.

**infertile** /ɪn'fɜːtaɪl/ *adjective* not fertile. □ **infertility** /-fə'tɪl-/ *noun*.

**infest** /ɪn'fest/ *verb* overrun in large numbers. □ **infestation** *noun*.

**infidel** /'ɪnfɪd(ə)l/ ● *noun* disbeliever in esp. the supposed true religion. ● *adjective* of infidels; unbelieving.

**infidelity** /ɪnfɪ'delɪtɪ/ *noun* (*plural* **-ies**) being unfaithful.

**infighting** *noun* conflict or competitiveness in organization; boxing within arm's length.

**infiltrate** /'ɪnfɪltreɪt/ *verb* (**-ting**) enter (territory, political party, etc.) gradually and imperceptibly; cause to do this; permeate by filtration; (often + *into*, *through*) introduce (fluid) by filtration. □ **infiltration** *noun*; **infiltrator** *noun*.

**infinite** /'ɪnfɪnɪt/ *adjective* boundless; endless; very great or many. □ **infinitely** *adverb*.

**infinitesimal** /ɪnfɪnɪ'tesɪm(ə)l/ *adjective* infinitely or very small. □ **infinitesimally** *adverb*.

**infinitive** /ɪn'fɪnɪtɪv/ ● *noun* verb-form expressing verbal notion without particular subject, tense, etc. ● *adjective* having this form.

**infinitude** /ɪn'fɪnɪtjuːd/ *noun literary* infinite number etc.; being infinite.

**infinity** /ɪn'fɪnɪtɪ/ *noun* (*plural* **-ies**) infinite number or extent; being infinite; boundlessness; infinite distance; *Mathematics* infinite quantity.

**infirm** /ɪn'fɜːm/ *adjective* weak.

**infirmary** /ɪn'fɜːmərɪ/ *noun* (*plural* **-ies**) hospital; sickbay in school etc.

**infirmity** *noun* (*plural* **-ies**) being infirm; particular physical weakness.

**in flagrante delicto** /ɪn flə'græntɪ dɪ'lɪktəʊ/ *adverb* in act of committing offence. [Latin]

**inflame** /ɪn'fleɪm/ *verb* (**-ming**) provoke to strong feeling; cause inflammation in; aggravate; make hot; (cause to) catch fire.

**inflammable** /ɪn'flæməb(ə)l/ *adjective* easily set on fire or excited. □ **inflammability** *noun*.

■ **Usage** Because *inflammable* could be thought to mean 'not easily set on fire', *flammable* is often used instead. The negative of *inflammable* is *non-inflammable*.

**inflammation** /ɪnflə'meɪʃ(ə)n/ *noun* inflaming; disordered bodily condition marked by heat, swelling, redness, and usually pain.

**inflammatory** /ɪn'flæmətərɪ/ *adjective* tending to inflame; of inflammation.

**inflatable** ● *adjective* that can be inflated. ● *noun* inflatable object.

**inflate** /ɪn'fleɪt/ *verb* (**-ting**) distend with air or gas; (usually + *with*; usually in *passive*) puff up (with pride etc.); resort to inflation (of currency); raise (prices) artificially; (as **inflated** *adjective*) (esp. of language, opinions, etc.) bombastic, exaggerated.

**inflation** *noun* inflating, being inflated; general rise in prices, increase in supply of money regarded as cause of such rise. □ **inflationary** *adjective*.

**inflect** /ɪn'flekt/ *verb* change or vary pitch of (voice); modify (word) to express grammatical relation; undergo such modification.

**inflection** /ɪn'flekʃ(ə)n/ *noun* (also **inflexion**) inflecting, being inflected; inflected form; inflecting suffix etc.; modulation of voice. □ **inflectional** *adjective*.

**inflexible** /ɪn'fleksɪb(ə)l/ *adjective* unbendable; unbending; unyielding. □ **inflexibility** *noun*, **inflexibly** *adverb*.

**inflexion** = INFLECTION.

**inflict** /ɪn'flɪkt/ *verb* deal (blow etc.); impose. □ **infliction** *noun*.

**inflight** *adjective* occurring or provided during a flight.

**inflorescence** /ɪnfləˈres(ə)ns/ noun collective flower head of plant; arrangement of flowers on plant; flowering.

**inflow** noun flowing in; that which flows in.

**influence** /ˈɪnfluəns/ ● noun (usually + on) effect a person or thing has on another; (usually + over, with) ascendancy, moral power; thing or person exercising this. ● verb (**-cing**) exert influence on; affect. □ **under the influence** colloquial drunk.

**influential** /ɪnfluˈenʃ(ə)l/ adjective having great influence.

**influenza** /ɪnfluˈenzə/ noun infectious viral disease with fever, severe aching, and catarrh.

**influx** /ˈɪnflʌks/ noun flowing in.

**inform** /ɪnˈfɔːm/ verb tell; (usually + against, on) give incriminating information about person to authorities.

**informal** /ɪnˈfɔːm(ə)l/ adjective without formality; not formal. □ **informality** /-ˈmæl-/ noun (plural **-ies**); **informally** adverb.

**informant** noun giver of information.

**information** /ɪnfəˈmeɪʃ(ə)n/ noun what is told; knowledge; news; formal charge or accusation. □ **information retrieval** tracing of information stored in books, computers, etc.; **information technology** study or use of processes (esp. computers etc.) for storing, retrieving, and sending information.

**informative** /ɪnˈfɔːmətɪv/ adjective giving information, instructive.

**informed** adjective knowing the facts; having some knowledge.

**informer** noun person who informs, esp. against others.

**infraction** /ɪnˈfrækʃ(ə)n/ noun infringement.

**infra dig** /ɪnfrə ˈdɪg/ adjective colloquial beneath one's dignity.

**infrared** /ɪnfrəˈred/ adjective of or using radiation just beyond red end of spectrum.

**infrastructure** /ˈɪnfrəstrʌktʃə/ noun structural foundations of a society or enterprise; roads, bridges, sewers, etc., regarded as country's economic foundation; permanent installations as basis for military etc. operations.

**infrequent** /ɪnˈfriːkwənt/ adjective not frequent. □ **infrequently** adverb.

**infringe** /ɪnˈfrɪndʒ/ verb (**-ging**) break or violate (law, another's rights, etc.); (usually + on) encroach, trespass. □ **infringement** noun.

**infuriate** /ɪnˈfjʊərɪeɪt/ verb (**-ting**) enrage; irritate greatly. □ **infuriating** adjective.

**infuse** /ɪnˈfjuːz/ verb (**-sing**) (usually + with) fill (with a quality); steep or be steeped in liquid to extract properties; (usually + into) instil (life etc.).

**infusible** /ɪnˈfjuːzɪb(ə)l/ adjective that cannot be melted. □ **infusibility** noun.

**infusion** /ɪnˈfjuːʒ(ə)n/ noun infusing; liquid extract so obtained; infused element.

**ingenious** /ɪnˈdʒiːnɪəs/ adjective clever at contriving; cleverly contrived. □ **ingeniously** adverb.

■ Usage *Ingenious* is sometimes confused with *ingenuous*.

**ingénue** /æʒeɪˈnjuː/ noun artless young woman, esp. as stage type. [French]

**ingenuity** /ɪndʒɪˈnjuːɪtɪ/ noun inventiveness, cleverness.

**ingenuous** /ɪnˈdʒenjʊəs/ adjective artless, frank. □ **ingenuously** adverb.

■ Usage *Ingenuous* is sometimes confused with *ingenious*.

**ingest** /ɪnˈdʒest/ verb take in (food etc.); absorb (knowledge etc.). □ **ingestion** noun.

**inglenook** /ˈɪŋg(ə)lnʊk/ noun space within opening either side of old-fashioned wide fireplace.

**inglorious** /ɪnˈglɔːrɪəs/ adjective shameful; not famous.

**ingoing** adjective going in.

**ingot** /ˈɪŋgət/ noun (usually oblong) mass of cast metal, esp. gold, silver, or steel.

**ingrained** /ɪnˈgreɪnd/ adjective deeply rooted, inveterate; (of dirt etc.) deeply embedded.

**ingratiate** /ɪnˈgreɪʃɪeɪt/ verb (**-ting**) (**ingratiate oneself**; usually + with) bring oneself into favour. □ **ingratiating** adjective.

**ingratitude** /ɪnˈgrætɪtjuːd/ noun lack of due gratitude.

**ingredient** /ɪnˈgriːdɪənt/ noun component part in mixture.

**ingress** /ˈɪngres/ noun going in; right to go in.

**ingrowing** adjective (of nail) growing into the flesh.

**inhabit** /ɪnˈhæbɪt/ verb (-t-) dwell in, occupy. □ **inhabitable** adjective; **inhabitant** noun.

**inhalant** /ɪnˈheɪlənt/ noun medicinal substance to be inhaled.

**inhale** /ɪnˈheɪl/ verb (-ling) breathe in. □ **inhalation** /-həˈleɪʃ(ə)n/ noun.

**inhaler** noun device for administering inhalant, esp. to relieve asthma.

**inhere** /ɪnˈhɪə/ verb (-ring) be inherent.

**inherent** /ɪnˈhɜːrənt/ adjective (often + in) existing in something as essential or permanent attribute. □ **inherently** adverb.

**inherit** /ɪnˈherɪt/ verb (-t-) receive as heir; derive (characteristic) from ancestors; derive or take over (situation) from predecessor. □ **inheritor** noun.

**inheritance** noun what is inherited; inheriting.

**inhibit** /ɪnˈhɪbɪt/ verb (-t-) hinder, restrain, prevent; (as **inhibited** adjective) suffering from inhibition; (usually + from) prohibit.

**inhibition** /ɪnhɪˈbɪʃ(ə)n/ noun restraint of direct expression of instinct; colloquial emotional resistance to thought or action; inhibiting, being inhibited.

**inhospitable** /ɪnhɒsˈpɪtəb(ə)l/ adjective not hospitable; affording no shelter.

**inhuman** /ɪnˈhjuːmən/ adjective brutal, unfeeling, barbarous. □ **inhumanity** /-ˈmæn-/ noun (plural **-ies**); **inhumanly** adverb.

**inhumane** /ɪnhjuːˈmeɪn/ adjective not humane, callous.

**inimical** /ɪˈnɪmɪk(ə)l/ adjective hostile; harmful.

**inimitable** /ɪˈnɪmɪtəb(ə)l/ adjective that cannot be imitated. □ **inimitably** adverb.

**iniquity** /ɪˈnɪkwɪtɪ/ noun (plural **-ies**) wickedness; gross injustice. □ **iniquitous** adjective.

**initial** /ɪˈnɪʃ(ə)l/ ● adjective of or at beginning. ● noun first letter, esp. of person's name. ● verb (-ll-; US -l-) mark or sign with one's initials. □ **initially** adverb.

**initiate** ● verb /ɪˈnɪʃɪeɪt/ (-ting) originate, set going; admit into society, office, etc., esp. with ritual; (+ into) instruct in subject. ● noun /ɪˈnɪʃɪət/ initiated person. □ **initiation** noun; **initiatory** /ɪˈnɪʃɪətərɪ/ adjective.

**initiative** /ɪˈnɪʃətɪv/ noun ability to initiate, enterprise; first step; (**the initiative**) power or right to begin.

**inject** /ɪnˈdʒekt/ verb (usually + into) force (medicine etc.) (as) by syringe; administer medicine etc. to (person) by injection; place (quality etc.) where needed in something. □ **injection** noun.

**injudicious** /ɪndʒuːˈdɪʃəs/ adjective unwise, ill-judged.

**injunction** /ɪnˈdʒʌŋkʃ(ə)n/ noun authoritative order; judicial order restraining from specified act or compelling restitution etc.

**injure** /ˈɪndʒə/ verb (-ring) hurt, harm, impair; do wrong to.

**injurious** /ɪnˈdʒʊərɪəs/ adjective hurtful; defamatory; wrongful.

**injury** /ˈɪndʒərɪ/ noun (plural **-ies**) physical damage, harm; offence to feelings etc.; esp. Law wrongful treatment. □ **injury time** extra time at football match etc. to compensate for that lost in dealing with injuries.

**injustice** /ɪnˈdʒʌstɪs/ noun unfairness; unjust act.

**ink** ● noun coloured fluid or paste for writing or printing; black liquid ejected by cuttlefish etc. ● verb mark, cover, or smear with ink. □ **ink-jet printer** printing machine firing tiny jets of ink at paper; **inkwell** pot for ink, esp. in hole in desk. □ **inky** adjective (-**ier**, -**iest**).

**inkling** /ˈɪŋklɪŋ/ noun (often + of) hint, slight knowledge or suspicion.

**inland** ● adjective /ˈɪnlənd/ remote from sea or border within a country; carried on within country. ● adverb /ɪnˈlænd/ in or towards interior of country. □ **Inland Revenue** government department assessing and collecting taxes.

**in-laws** /ˈɪnlɔːz/ plural noun relatives by marriage.

**inlay** ● verb /ɪnˈleɪ/ (past & past participle **inlaid** /ɪnˈleɪd/) embed (thing in another); decorate (thing) thus. ● noun

/'ɪnleɪ/ inlaid material or work; filling shaped to fit tooth-cavity.

**inlet** /'ɪnlət/ noun small arm of sea etc.; piece inserted; way of admission.

**inmate** /'ɪnmeɪt/ noun occupant of house, hospital, prison, etc.

**in memoriam** /ɪn mɪ'mɔːrɪæm/ preposition in memory of.

**inmost** /'ɪnməʊst/ adjective most inward.

**inn** noun pub, sometimes with accommodation; historical house providing lodging etc. for payment, esp. for travellers. □ **innkeeper** keeper of inn; **Inns of Court** 4 legal societies admitting people to English bar.

**innards** /'ɪnədz/ plural noun colloquial entrails.

**innate** /ɪ'neɪt/ adjective inborn; natural. □ **innately** adverb.

**inner** /'ɪnə/ ● adjective interior, internal. ● noun circle nearest bull's-eye of target. □ **inner city** central area of city, esp. regarded as having social problems; **inner tube** separate inflatable tube in pneumatic tyre. □ **innermost** adjective.

**innings** /'ɪnɪŋz/ noun (plural same) esp. Cricket batsman's or side's turn at batting; term of office etc. when person, party, etc. can achieve something.

**innocent** /'ɪnəs(ə)nt/ ● adjective free from moral wrong; not guilty; guileless; harmless. ● noun innocent person, esp. young child. □ **innocence** noun; **innocently** adverb.

**innocuous** /ɪ'nɒkjʊəs/ adjective harmless.

**innovate** /'ɪnəveɪt/ verb (-ting) bring in new ideas etc.; make changes. □ **innovation** noun; **innovative** /-vətɪv/ adjective; **innovator** noun.

**innuendo** /ɪnju:'endəʊ/ noun (plural -es or -s) allusive (usually depreciatory or sexually suggestive) remark.

**innumerable** /ɪ'nju:mərəb(ə)l/ adjective countless.

**innumerate** /ɪ'nju:mərət/ adjective not knowing basic mathematics. □ **innumeracy** noun.

**inoculate** /ɪ'nɒkjʊleɪt/ verb (-ting) treat with vaccine or serum to promote immunity against a disease. □ **inoculation** noun.

**inoffensive** /ɪnə'fensɪv/ adjective not objectionable; harmless.

**inoperable** /ɪ'nɒpərəb(ə)l/ adjective that cannot be cured by surgical operation.

**inoperative** /ɪ'nɒpərətɪv/ adjective not working or taking effect.

**inopportune** /ɪ'nɒpətju:n/ adjective not appropriate, esp. as regards time.

**inordinate** /ɪ'nɔːdɪnət/ adjective excessive. □ **inordinately** adverb.

**inorganic** /ɪnɔː'gænɪk/ adjective Chemistry not organic; without organized physical structure; extraneous.

**input** /'ɪnpʊt/ ● noun what is put in; place of entry of energy, information, etc.; action of putting in or feeding in; contribution of information etc. ● verb (**inputting**; past & past participle **input** or **inputted**) put in; supply (data, programs, etc.) to computer.

**inquest** /'ɪŋkwest/ noun inquiry held by coroner into cause of death.

**inquietude** /ɪn'kwaɪɪtju:d/ noun uneasiness.

**inquire** /ɪn'kwaɪə/ verb (-ring) seek information formally; make inquiry; ask question.

**inquiry** /ɪn'kwaɪərɪ/ noun (plural -ies) investigation, esp. official; asking; question.

**inquisition** /ɪnkwɪ'zɪʃ(ə)n/ noun investigation; official inquiry; (**the Inquisition**) RC Church History ecclesiastical tribunal for suppression of heresy. □ **inquisitional** adjective.

**inquisitive** /ɪn'kwɪzɪtɪv/ adjective curious, prying; seeking knowledge. □ **inquisitively** adverb; **inquisitiveness** noun.

**inquisitor** /ɪn'kwɪzɪtə/ noun investigator; historical officer of Inquisition.

**inquisitorial** /ɪnkwɪzɪ'tɔːrɪəl/ adjective inquisitor-like; prying.

**inroad** noun (often in plural) encroachment; using up of resources etc.; hostile incursion.

**inrush** noun rapid influx.

**insalubrious** /ɪnsə'lu:brɪəs/ adjective (of climate or place) unhealthy.

**insane** /ɪn'seɪn/ adjective mad; colloquial extremely foolish. □ **insanely** adverb; **insanity** /ɪn'sænɪtɪ/ noun (plural -ies).

**insanitary** /ɪn'sænɪtərɪ/ adjective not sanitary.

**insatiable** /ɪnˈseɪʃəb(ə)l/ *adjective* that cannot be satisfied; extremely greedy. □ **insatiability** *noun*; **insatiably** *adverb*.

**insatiate** /ɪnˈseɪʃɪət/ *adjective* never satisfied.

**inscribe** /ɪnˈskraɪb/ *verb* (**-bing**) (usually + *in, on*) write or carve (words etc.) on surface; mark (surface) with characters; (usually + *to*) write informal dedication in or on (book etc.); enter on list; *Geometry* draw (figure) within another so that some points of their boundaries coincide.

**inscription** /ɪnˈskrɪpʃ(ə)n/ *noun* words inscribed; inscribing.

**inscrutable** /ɪnˈskruːtəb(ə)l/ *adjective* mysterious, impenetrable. □ **inscrutability** *noun*; **inscrutably** *adverb*.

**insect** /ˈɪnsekt/ *noun* small invertebrate animal with segmented body, 6 legs, and usually wings.

**insecticide** /ɪnˈsektɪsaɪd/ *noun* preparation used for killing insects.

**insectivore** /ɪnˈsektɪvɔː/ *noun* animal or plant that feeds on insects. □ **insectivorous** /-ˈtɪvərəs/ *adjective*.

**insecure** /ɪnsɪˈkjʊə/ *adjective* not secure or safe; not feeling safe. □ **insecurity** /-ˈkjʊr-/ *noun*.

**inseminate** /ɪnˈsemɪneɪt/ *verb* (**-ting**) introduce semen into; sow (seed etc.). □ **insemination** *noun*.

**insensate** /ɪnˈsenseɪt/ *adjective* without esp. physical sensibility; stupid.

**insensible** /ɪnˈsensɪb(ə)l/ *adjective* unconscious; unaware; callous; imperceptible. □ **insensibility** *noun*; **insensibly** *adverb*.

**insensitive** /ɪnˈsensɪtɪv/ *adjective* not sensitive. □ **insensitively** *adverb*; **insensitiveness** *noun*; **insensitivity** /-ˈtɪv-/ *noun*.

**insentient** /ɪnˈsenʃ(ə)nt/ *adjective* inanimate.

**inseparable** /ɪnˈsepərəb(ə)l/ *adjective* that cannot be separated. □ **inseparability** *noun*; **inseparably** *adverb*.

**insert** • *verb* /ɪnˈsɜːt/ place or put (thing into another). • *noun* /ˈɪnsɜːt/ thing inserted.

**insertion** /ɪnˈsɜːʃ(ə)n/ *noun* inserting; thing inserted.

**inset** • *noun* /ˈɪnset/ extra piece inserted in book, garment, etc.; small map etc.

within border of larger. • *verb* /ɪnˈset/ (**insetting**; *past & past participle* **inset** or **insetted**) put in as inset; decorate with inset.

**inshore** /ɪnˈʃɔː/ *adverb & adjective* at sea but close to shore.

**inside** *noun* /ɪnˈsaɪd/ inner side or part; interior; side of path away from road; (usually in *plural*) *colloquial* stomach and bowels. • *adjective* /ˈɪnsaɪd/ of, on, or in the inside; nearer to centre of games field. • *adverb* /ɪnˈsaɪd/ on, in, or to the inside; *slang* in prison. • *preposition* /ɪnˈsaɪd/ within, on the inside of; in less than. □ **inside out** with inner side turned outwards; **know inside out** know thoroughly.

**insider** /ɪnˈsaɪdə/ *noun* person within organization etc.; person privy to secret.

**insidious** /ɪnˈsɪdɪəs/ *adjective* proceeding inconspicuously but harmfully. □ **insidiously** *adverb*.

**insight** *noun* capacity for understanding hidden truths etc.; instance of this.

**insignia** /ɪnˈsɪɡnɪə/ *plural noun* badges or marks of office etc.

**insignificant** /ɪnsɪɡˈnɪfɪkənt/ *adjective* unimportant; trivial. □ **insignificance** *noun*.

**insincere** /ɪnsɪnˈsɪə/ *adjective* not sincere. □ **insincerely** *adverb*; **insincerity** /-ˈser-/ *noun*.

**insinuate** /ɪnˈsɪnjʊeɪt/ *verb* (**-ting**) hint obliquely; (usually + *into*) introduce subtly or deviously. □ **insinuation** *noun*.

**insipid** /ɪnˈsɪpɪd/ *adjective* dull, lifeless; flavourless. □ **insipidity** /-ˈpɪd-/ *noun*; **insipidly** *adverb*.

**insist** /ɪnˈsɪst/ *verb* demand or maintain emphatically. □ **insistence** *noun*; **insistent** *adjective*; **insistently** *adverb*.

**in situ** /ɪn ˈsɪtjuː/ *adverb* in its original place. [Latin]

**insobriety** /ɪnsəˈbraɪətɪ/ *noun* intemperance, esp. in drinking.

**insole** *noun* removable inner sole for use in shoe.

**insolent** /ˈɪnsələnt/ *adjective* impertinently insulting. □ **insolence** *noun*; **insolently** *adverb*.

**insoluble** /ɪnˈsɒljʊb(ə)l/ *adjective* that cannot be solved or dissolved. □ **insolubility** *noun*; **insolubly** *adverb*.

**insolvent** /ɪnˈsɒlv(ə)nt/ • *adjective* unable to pay debts. • *noun* insolvent debtor. □ **insolvency** *noun*.

**insomnia** /ɪnˈsɒmnɪə/ *noun* sleeplessness.

**insomniac** /ɪnˈsɒmnɪæk/ *noun* person suffering from insomnia.

**insouciant** /ɪnˈsuːsɪənt/ *adjective* carefree, unconcerned. □ **insouciance** *noun*.

**inspect** /ɪnˈspekt/ *verb* look closely at; examine officially. □ **inspection** *noun*.

**inspector** *noun* official employed to inspect or supervise; police officer next above sergeant in rank. □ **inspectorate** *noun*.

**inspiration** /ɪnspəˈreɪʃ(ə)n/ *noun* creative force or influence; person etc. stimulating creativity etc.; sudden brilliant idea; divine influence, esp. on writing of Scripture.

**inspire** /ɪnˈspaɪə/ *verb* (**-ring**) stimulate (person) to esp. creative activity; animate; instil thought or feeling into; prompt, give rise to; (as **inspired** *adjective*) characterized by inspiration. □ **inspiring** *adjective*.

**inspirit** /ɪnˈspɪrɪt/ *verb* (**-t-**) put life into, animate; encourage.

**inst.** *abbreviation* instant, of current month.

**instability** /ɪnstəˈbɪlɪtɪ/ *noun* lack of stability.

**install** /ɪnˈstɔːl/ *verb* place (equipment etc.) in position ready for use; place (person) in office with ceremony. □ **installation** /-stəˈleɪ-/ *noun*.

**instalment** *noun* (*US* **installment**) any of several usually equal payments for something; any of several parts, esp. of broadcast or published story.

**instance** /ˈɪnst(ə)ns/ • *noun* example; particular case. • *verb* (**-cing**) cite as instance.

**instant** /ˈɪnst(ə)nt/ • *adjective* occurring immediately; (of food etc.) processed for quick preparation; urgent, pressing; of current month. • *noun* precise moment; short space of time.

**instantaneous** /ɪnstənˈteɪnɪəs/ *adjective* occurring or done in an instant. □ **instantaneously** *adverb*.

**instantly** *adverb* immediately.

**instead** /ɪnˈsted/ *adverb* (+ *of*) in place of; as substitute or alternative.

**instep** /ˈɪnstep/ *noun* inner arch of foot between toes and ankle; part of shoe etc. fitting this.

**instigate** /ˈɪnstɪɡeɪt/ *verb* (**-ting**) bring about by persuasion; incite. □ **instigation** *noun*; **instigator** *noun*.

**instil** /ɪnˈstɪl/ *verb* (*US* **instill**) (**-ll-**) (often + *into*) put (ideas etc. into mind etc.) gradually; put in by drops. □ **instillation** *noun*; **instilment** *noun*.

**instinct** /ˈɪnstɪŋkt/ *noun* inborn pattern of behaviour; innate impulse; intuition. □ **instinctive** /-ˈstɪŋktɪv/ *adjective*; **instinctively** /-ˈstɪŋktɪvlɪ/ *adverb*; **instinctual** /-ˈstɪŋktjʊəl/ *adjective*.

**institute** /ˈɪnstɪtjuːt/ • *noun* organized body for promotion of science, education, etc. • *verb* (**-ting**) establish; initiate (inquiry etc.); (usually + *to*, *into*) appoint (person) as cleric in church etc.

**institution** /ɪnstɪˈtjuːʃ(ə)n/ *noun* (esp. charitable) organization or society; established law or custom; *colloquial* well-known person; instituting, being instituted.

**institutional** *adjective* of or like an institution; typical of institutions.

**institutionalize** *verb* (also **-ise**) (**-zing** or **-sing**) (as **institutionalized** *adjective*) made dependent by long period in institution; place or keep in institution; make institutional.

**instruct** /ɪnˈstrʌkt/ *verb* teach; (usually + *to do*) direct, command; employ (lawyer); inform. □ **instructor** *noun*.

**instruction** /ɪnˈstrʌkʃ(ə)n/ *noun* (often in *plural*) order, direction (as to how thing works etc.); teaching. □ **instructional** *adjective*.

**instructive** /ɪnˈstrʌktɪv/ *adjective* tending to instruct; enlightening.

**instrument** /ˈɪnstrəmənt/ *noun* tool, implement; (in full **musical instrument**) contrivance for producing musical sounds; thing used in performing action; person made use of; measuring device, esp. in aircraft; *formal* (esp. legal) document.

**instrumental** /ɪnstrəˈment(ə)l/ *adjective* serving as instrument or means; (of music) performed on instruments.

**instrumentalist** *noun* performer on musical instrument.

**instrumentality** /ˌɪnstrəmen'tælɪtɪ/ *noun* agency, means.

**instrumentation** /ˌɪnstrəmen'teɪʃ(ə)n/ *noun* provision or use of instruments; arrangement of music for instruments; particular instruments used in piece.

**insubordinate** /ˌɪnsə'bɔːdɪnət/ *adjective* disobedient; unruly. □ **insubordination** *noun*.

**insubstantial** /ˌɪnsəb'stænʃ(ə)l/ *adjective* lacking solidity or substance; not real.

**insufferable** /ɪn'sʌfərəb(ə)l/ *adjective* unbearable; unbearably conceited etc. □ **insufferably** *adverb*.

**insufficient** /ˌɪnsə'fɪʃ(ə)nt/ *adjective* not enough, inadequate. □ **insufficiency** *noun*; **insufficiently** *adverb*.

**insular** /'ɪnsjʊlə/ *adjective* of or like an island; separated, remote; narrow-minded. □ **insularity** /-'lær-/ *noun*.

**insulate** /'ɪnsjʊleɪt/ *verb* (**-ting**) isolate, esp. by non-conductor of electricity, heat, sound, etc. □ **insulation** *noun*; **insulator** *noun*.

**insulin** /'ɪnsjʊlɪn/ *noun* hormone regulating the amount of glucose in the blood, the lack of which causes diabetes.

**insult** ● *verb* /ɪn'sʌlt/ abuse scornfully; offend self-respect etc. of. ● *noun* /'ɪnsʌlt/ insulting remark or action. □ **insulting** *adjective*; **insultingly** *adverb*.

**insuperable** /ɪn'suːpərəb(ə)l/ *adjective* impossible to surmount; impossible to overcome. □ **insuperability** *noun*; **insuperably** *adverb*.

**insupportable** /ˌɪnsə'pɔːtəb(ə)l/ *adjective* unbearable; unjustifiable.

**insurance** /ɪn'ʃʊərəns/ *noun* procedure or contract securing compensation for loss, damage, injury, or death on payment of premium; sum paid to effect insurance.

**insure** /ɪn'ʃʊə/ *verb* (**-ring**) (often + *against*) effect insurance with respect to.

**insurgent** /ɪn'sɜːdʒ(ə)nt/ ● *adjective* in revolt; rebellious. ● *noun* rebel. □ **insurgence** *noun*.

**insurmountable** /ˌɪnsə'maʊntəb(ə)l/ *adjective* insuperable.

**insurrection** /ˌɪnsə'rekʃ(ə)n/ *noun* rising in resistance to authority; incipient rebellion. □ **insurrectionist** *noun*.

**intact** /ɪn'tækt/ *adjective* unimpaired; entire; untouched.

**intaglio** /ɪn'tɑːlɪəʊ/ *noun* (*plural* **-s**) gem with incised design; engraved design.

**intake** *noun* action of taking in; people, things, or quantity taken in; place where water is taken into pipe, or fuel or air into engine.

**intangible** /ɪn'tændʒɪb(ə)l/ *adjective* that cannot be touched or mentally grasped. □ **intangibility** *noun*; **intangibly** *adverb*.

**integer** /'ɪntɪdʒə/ *noun* whole number.

**integral** /'ɪntɪgr(ə)l/ *adjective* of or essential to a whole; complete; of or denoted by an integer.

■ **Usage** *Integral* is often pronounced /ɪn'tegr(ə)l/ (with the stress on the -*teg*-), but this is considered incorrect by some people.

**integrate** /'ɪntɪgreɪt/ *verb* (**-ting**) combine (parts) into whole; complete by adding parts; bring or come into equal membership of society; desegregate (school etc.), esp. racially. □ **integrated circuit** small piece of material replacing electrical circuit of many components. □ **integration** *noun*.

**integrity** /ɪn'tegrɪtɪ/ *noun* honesty; wholeness; soundness.

**integument** /ɪn'tegjʊmənt/ *noun* skin, husk, or other (natural) covering.

**intellect** /'ɪntəlekt/ *noun* faculty of knowing and reasoning; understanding.

**intellectual** /ˌɪntə'lektʃʊəl/ ● *adjective* of, requiring, or using intellect; having highly developed intellect. ● *noun* intellectual person. □ **intellectualize** *verb* (also **-ise**) (**-zing** or **-sing**); **intellectually** *adverb*.

**intelligence** /ɪn'telɪdʒ(ə)ns/ *noun* intellect; quickness of understanding; collecting of information, esp. secretly for military or political purposes; information so collected; people employed in this. □ **intelligence quotient** number denoting ratio of person's intelligence to the average.

**intelligent** *adjective* having or showing good intelligence, clever. □ **intelligently** *adverb*.

**intelligentsia** /ɪnˌtelɪ'dʒentsɪə/ *noun* class of intellectuals regarded as cultured and politically enterprising.

**intelligible** /ɪn'telɪdʒɪb(ə)l/ *adjective* that can be understood. □ **intelligibility** *noun*; **intelligibly** *adverb*.

**intemperate** /ɪn'tempərət/ *adjective* immoderate; excessive in consumption of alcohol, or in general indulgence of appetite. □ **intemperance** *noun*.

**intend** /ɪn'tend/ *verb* have as one's purpose; (usually + *for, as, to do*) design, destine.

**intended** ● *adjective* done on purpose. ● *noun colloquial* fiancé(e).

**intense** /ɪn'tens/ *adjective* (**-r, -st**) existing in high degree; vehement; violent, forceful; extreme; very emotional. □ **intensity** *noun* (*plural* **-ies**); **intensely** *adverb*.

■ **Usage** *Intense* is sometimes confused with *intensive*, and wrongly used to describe a course of study etc.

**intensify** *verb* (**-ies, -ied**) make or become (more) intense. □ **intensification** *noun*.

**intensive** /ɪn'tensɪv/ *adjective* thorough, vigorous; concentrated; of or relating to intensity; increasing production relative to cost. □ **-intensive** making much use of; **intensive care** medical treatment with constant supervision of dangerously ill patient. □ **intensively** *adverb*.

**intent** /ɪn'tent/ ● *noun* intention; purpose. ● *adjective* (usually + *on*) resolved, bent; attentively occupied; eager. □ **to all intents and purposes** practically. □ **intently** *adverb*.

**intention** /ɪn'tenʃ(ə)n/ *noun* purpose, aim; intending.

**intentional** *adjective* done on purpose. □ **intentionally** *adverb*.

**inter** /ɪn'tɜː/ *verb* (**-rr-**) bury (corpse etc.).

**inter-** *combining form* among, between; mutually, reciprocally.

**interact** /ɪntər'ækt/ *verb* act on each other. □ **interaction** *noun*.

**interactive** *adjective* reciprocally active; (of computer etc.) allowing two-way flow of information between itself and user. □ **interactively** *adverb*.

**interbreed** /ɪntə'briːd/ *verb* (*past & past participle* **-bred**) (cause to) produce hybrid individual.

**intercalary** /ɪn'tɜːkələrɪ/ *adjective* inserted to harmonize calendar with solar year; having such addition; interpolated.

**intercede** /ɪntə'siːd/ *verb* (**-ding**) intervene on behalf of another; plead.

**intercept** /ɪntə'sept/ *verb* seize, catch, stop, etc. in transit; cut off. □ **interception** *noun*; **interceptor** *noun*.

**intercession** /ɪntə'seʃ(ə)n/ *noun* interceding. □ **intercessor** *noun*.

**interchange** ● *verb* /ɪntə'tʃeɪndʒ/ (**-ging**) (of two people) exchange (things) with each other; make exchange of (two things); alternate. ● *noun* /'ɪntətʃeɪndʒ/ reciprocal exchange; alternation; road junction where traffic streams do not cross. □ **interchangeable** *adjective*.

**inter-city** /ɪntə'sɪtɪ/ *adjective* existing or travelling between cities.

**intercom** /'ɪntəkɒm/ *noun colloquial* system of intercommunication by telephone or radio.

**intercommunicate** /ɪntəkə'mjuːnɪkeɪt/ *verb* (**-ting**) have communication with each other; (of rooms etc.) open into each other. □ **intercommunication** *noun*.

**intercommunion** /ɪntəkə'mjuːnɪən/ *noun* mutual communion, esp. between religious bodies.

**interconnect** /ɪntəkə'nekt/ *verb* connect with each other. □ **interconnection** *noun*.

**intercontinental** /ɪntəkɒntɪ'nent(ə)l/ *adjective* connecting or travelling between continents.

**intercourse** /'ɪntəkɔːs/ *noun* social, international, etc. communication or dealings; sexual intercourse.

**interdenominational** /ɪntədɪnɒmɪ'neɪʃən(ə)l/ *adjective* of or involving more than one Christian denomination.

**interdependent** /ɪntədɪ'pend(ə)nt/ *adjective* mutually dependent. □ **interdependence** *noun*.

**interdict** ● *noun* /'ɪntədɪkt/ *formal* prohibition; *RC Church* sentence debarring person, or esp. place, from ecclesiastical functions and privileges. ● *verb* /ɪntə'dɪkt/ prohibit (action); forbid use of; (usually + *from*) restrain (person).

□ **interdiction** /-'dɪk-/ *noun*; **interdictory** /-'dɪk-/ *adjective*.

**interdisciplinary** /ɪntədɪsɪ'plɪnərɪ/ *adjective* of or involving different branches of learning.

**interest** /'ɪntrəst/ ● *noun* concern, curiosity; quality causing this; subject, hobby, etc., towards which one feels it; advantage; money paid for use of money borrowed etc.; thing in which one has stake or concern; financial stake; legal concern, title, or right. ● *verb* arouse interest of; (usually + *in*) cause to take interest; (as **interested** *adjective*) having private interest, not impartial.

**interesting** *adjective* causing curiosity; holding the attention. □ **interestingly** *adverb*.

**interface** /'ɪntəfeɪs/ ● *noun* surface forming common boundary of two regions; place where interaction occurs between two systems etc.; apparatus for connecting two pieces of esp. computing equipment so they can be operated jointly. ● *verb* (**-cing**) connect by means of interface; interact.

**interfere** /ɪntə'fɪə/ *verb* (**-ring**) (often + *with*) meddle; be an obstacle; intervene; (+ *with*) molest sexually.

**interference** *noun* interfering; fading of received radio signals.

**interferon** /ɪntə'fɪərɒn/ *noun* protein inhibiting development of virus in cell.

**interfuse** /ɪntə'fju:z/ *verb* (**-sing**) mix, blend. □ **interfusion** *noun*.

**interim** /'ɪntərɪm/ ● *noun* intervening time. ● *adjective* provisional, temporary.

**interior** /ɪn'tɪərɪə/ ● *adjective* inner; inland; internal, domestic. ● *noun* inner part; inside; inland region; home affairs of country; representation of inside of room etc.

**interject** /ɪntə'dʒekt/ *verb* make (remark etc.) abruptly or parenthetically; interrupt.

**interjection** /ɪntə'dʒekʃ(ə)n/ *noun* exclamation.

**interlace** /ɪntə'leɪs/ *verb* (**-cing**) bind intricately together; interweave.

**interlard** /ɪntə'lɑ:d/ *verb* mix (speech etc.) with unusual words or phrases.

**interleave** /ɪntə'li:v/ *verb* (**-ving**) insert (usually blank) leaves between leaves of (book).

**interline** /ɪntə'laɪn/ *verb* (**-ning**) put extra layer of material between fabric of (garment) and its lining.

**interlink** /ɪntə'lɪŋk/ *verb* link together.

**interlock** /ɪntə'lɒk/ ● *verb* engage with each other by overlapping etc.; lock together. ● *noun* machine-knitted fabric with fine stitches.

**interlocutor** /ɪntə'lɒkjutə/ *noun formal* person who takes part in conversation. □ **interlocutory** *adjective*.

**interloper** /'ɪntələupə/ *noun* intruder; person who thrusts himself or herself into others' affairs.

**interlude** /'ɪntəlu:d/ *noun* interval between parts of play etc., performance filling this; contrasting time, event, etc. in middle of something.

**intermarry** /ɪntə'mærɪ/ *verb* (**-ies, -ied**) (+ *with*) (of races, castes, families, etc.) become connected by marriage. □ **intermarriage** /-rɪdʒ/ *noun*.

**intermediary** /ɪntə'mi:dɪərɪ/ ● *noun* (*plural* **-ies**) mediator. ● *adjective* acting as mediator; intermediate.

**intermediate** /ɪntə'mi:dɪət/ ● *adjective* coming between in time, place, order, etc. ● *noun* intermediate thing.

**interment** /ɪn'tɜ:mənt/ *noun* burial.

**intermezzo** /ɪntə'metsəu/ *noun* (*plural* **-mezzi** /-sɪ/ or **-s**) *Music* short connecting movement or composition.

**interminable** /ɪn'tɜ:mɪnəb(ə)l/ *adjective* endless; tediously long. □ **interminably** *adverb*.

**intermingle** /ɪntə'mɪŋg(ə)l/ *verb* (**-ling**) mix together, mingle.

**intermission** /ɪntə'mɪʃ(ə)n/ *noun* pause, cessation; interval in cinema etc.

**intermittent** /ɪntə'mɪt(ə)nt/ *adjective* occurring at intervals, not continuous or steady. □ **intermittently** *adverb*.

**intermix** /ɪntə'mɪks/ *verb* mix together.

**intern** ● *noun* /'ɪntɜ:n/ *US* resident junior doctor in hospital. ● *verb* /ɪn'tɜ:n/ confine within prescribed limits. □ **internee** /-'ni:/ *noun*; **internment** *noun*.

**internal** /ɪn'tɜ:n(ə)l/ *adjective* of or in the inside of thing; relating to inside of the body; of domestic affairs of country; (of students) attending a university as well as taking its exams; used or applying within an organization; intrinsic; of mind or soul. □ **internal-combustion engine** engine in which motive power comes from explosion of gas or vapour with air in cylinder. □ **internally** *adverb*.

**international** /ɪntəˈnæʃən(ə)l/ ● *adjective* existing or carried on between nations; agreed on by many nations. ● *noun* contest (usually in sports) between representatives of different nations; such representative; (**International**) any of 4 successive associations for socialist or Communist action. □ **internationality** /-ˈnæl-/ *noun*; **internationally** *adverb*.

**internationalism** *noun* advocacy of community of interests among nations. □ **internationalist** *noun*.

**internationalize** *verb* (also **-ise**) (**-zing** or **-sing**) make international; bring under joint protection etc. of different nations.

**internecine** /ɪntəˈniːsaɪn/ *adjective* mutually destructive.

**interpenetrate** /ɪntəˈpenɪtreɪt/ *verb* (**-ting**) penetrate each other; pervade. □ **interpenetration** *noun*.

**interpersonal** /ɪntəˈpɜːsən(ə)l/ *adjective* between people.

**interplanetary** /ɪntəˈplænɪtəri/ *adjective* between planets.

**interplay** /ˈɪntəpleɪ/ *noun* reciprocal action.

**Interpol** /ˈɪntəpɒl/ *noun* International Criminal Police Organization.

**interpolate** /ɪnˈtɜːpəleɪt/ *verb* (**-ting**) insert or introduce between other things; make (esp. misleading) insertions in. □ **interpolation** *noun*.

**interpose** /ɪntəˈpəʊz/ *verb* (**-sing**) insert (thing between others); introduce, use, say, etc. as interruption or interference; interrupt; advance (objection etc.) so as to interfere; intervene. □ **interposition** /-pəˈzɪʃ(ə)n/ *noun*.

**interpret** /ɪnˈtɜːprɪt/ *verb* (**-t-**) explain the meaning of (esp. words); render, represent; act as interpreter. □ **interpretation** *noun*.

**interpreter** *noun* person who translates orally.

**interracial** /ɪntəˈreɪʃ(ə)l/ *adjective* between or affecting different races.

**interregnum** /ɪntəˈregnəm/ *noun* (*plural* **-s**) interval with suspension of normal

government between successive reigns or regimes; interval, pause.

**interrelated** /ɪntərɪˈleɪtɪd/ *adjective* related to each other. □ **interrelation** *noun*; **interrelationship** *noun*.

**interrogate** /ɪnˈterəgeɪt/ *verb* (**-ting**) question closely or formally. □ **interrogation** *noun*; **interrogator** *noun*.

**interrogative** /ɪntəˈrɒgətɪv/ ● *adjective* of, like, or used in questions. ● *noun* interrogative word.

**interrogatory** /ɪntəˈrɒgətəri/ ● *adjective* questioning. ● *noun* (*plural* **-ies**) set of questions.

**interrupt** /ɪntəˈrʌpt/ *verb* break continuity of (action, speech, etc.); obstruct (view etc.). □ **interruption** *noun*.

**intersect** /ɪntəˈsekt/ *verb* divide by passing or lying across; cross or cut each other.

**intersection** /ɪntəˈsekʃ(ə)n/ *noun* intersecting; place where two roads intersect; point or line common to lines or planes that intersect.

**intersperse** /ɪntəˈspɜːs/ *verb* (**-sing**) (usually + *between, among*) scatter; (+ *with*) vary (thing) by scattering others among it.

**interstate** /ˈɪntəsteɪt/ *adjective* existing etc. between states, esp. of US.

**interstellar** /ɪntəˈstelə/ *adjective* between stars.

**interstice** /ɪnˈtɜːstɪs/ *noun* gap, chink, crevice.

**interstitial** /ɪntəˈstɪʃ(ə)l/ *adjective* forming or in interstices.

**intertwine** /ɪntəˈtwaɪn/ *verb* (**-ning**) (often + *with*) twine closely together.

**interval** /ˈɪntəv(ə)l/ *noun* intervening time or space; pause; break; *Music* difference of pitch between two sounds. □ **at intervals** here and there, now and then.

**intervene** /ɪntəˈviːn/ *verb* (**-ning**) occur in meantime; interfere; prevent or modify events; come between people or things; mediate.

**intervention** /ɪntəˈvenʃ(ə)n/ *noun* intervening; interference; mediation.

**interview** /ˈɪntəvjuː/ ● *noun* oral examination of applicant; conversation with reporter, for broadcast or publication; meeting of people, esp. for discussion.

●*verb* hold interview with. □ **interviewee** /-vjuː'iː/ *noun;* **interviewer** *noun.*

**interweave** /ɪntə'wiːv/ *verb* (-ving; *past* -wove; *past participle* -woven) weave together; blend intimately.

**intestate** /ɪn'testeɪt/ ●*adjective* not having made a will before death. ●*noun* person who has died intestate. □ **intestacy** /-təsɪ/ *noun.*

**intestine** /ɪn'testɪn/ *noun* (in *singular* or *plural*) lower part of alimentary canal. □ **intestinal** *adjective.*

**intimate**[1] ●*adjective* /'ɪntɪmət/ closely acquainted; familiar; closely personal; (usually + *with*) having sexual relations; (of knowledge) thorough; close. ●*noun* intimate friend. □ **intimacy** /-məsɪ/ *noun;* **intimately** *adverb.*

**intimate**[2] /'ɪntɪmeɪt/ *verb* (-ting) state or make known; imply. □ **intimation** *noun.*

**intimidate** /ɪn'tɪmɪdeɪt/ *verb* (-ting) frighten, esp. in order to influence conduct. □ **intimidation** *noun.*

**into** /'ɪntʊ, 'ɪntə/ *preposition* expressing motion or direction to point within, direction of attention, or change of state; after the beginning of; *colloquial* interested in.

**intolerable** /ɪn'tɒlərəb(ə)l/ *adjective* that cannot be endured. □ **intolerably** *adverb.*

**intolerant** /ɪn'tɒlərənt/ *adjective* not tolerant. □ **intolerance** *noun.*

**intonation** /ɪntə'neɪʃ(ə)n/ *noun* modulation of voice, accent; intoning.

**intone** /ɪn'təʊn/ *verb* (-ning) recite with prolonged sounds, esp. in monotone.

**in toto** /ɪn 'təʊtəʊ/ *adverb* entirely. [Latin]

**intoxicant** /ɪn'tɒksɪkənt/ ●*adjective* intoxicating. ●*noun* intoxicating substance.

**intoxicate** /ɪn'tɒksɪkeɪt/ *verb* (-ting) make drunk; excite or elate beyond self-control. □ **intoxication** *noun.*

**intractable** /ɪn'træktəb(ə)l/ *adjective* not easily dealt with; stubborn. □ **intractability** *noun.*

**intramural** /ɪntrə'mjʊər(ə)l/ *adjective* situated or done within walls of institution etc.

**intransigent** /ɪn'trænsɪdʒ(ə)nt/ ●*adjective* uncompromising. ●*noun* such person. □ **intransigence** *noun.*

**intransitive** /ɪn'trænsɪtɪv/ *adjective* (of verb) not taking direct object.

**intrauterine** /ɪntrə'juːtəraɪn/ *adjective* within the womb.

**intravenous** /ɪntrə'viːnəs/ *adjective* in(to) vein(s). □ **intravenously** *adverb.*

**intrepid** /ɪn'trepɪd/ *adjective* fearless; brave.

**intricate** /'ɪntrɪkət/ *adjective* complicated; perplexingly detailed. □ **intricacy** /-kəsɪ/ *noun* ( *plural* -ies); **intricately** *adverb.*

**intrigue** ●*verb* /ɪn'triːg/ (-gues, -gued, -guing) carry on underhand plot; use secret influence; rouse curiosity of. ●*noun* /'ɪntriːg/ underhand plotting or plot; secret arrangement, esp. with romantic associations. □ **intriguing** *adjective;* **intriguingly** *adverb.*

**intrinsic** /ɪn'trɪnzɪk/ *adjective* inherent; essential. □ **intrinsically** *adverb.*

**intro** /'ɪntrəʊ/ *noun* ( *plural* -s) *colloquial* introduction.

**introduce** /ɪntrə'djuːs/ *verb* (-cing) make (person) known by name to another; announce or present to audience; bring (custom etc.) into use; bring (bill etc.) before Parliament; (+ *to*) initiate (person) in subject; insert; bring in; usher in, bring forward. □ **introducible** *adjective.*

**introduction** /ɪntrə'dʌkʃ(ə)n/ *noun* introducing, being introduced; formal presentation; preliminary matter in book; introductory treatise. □ **introductory** *adjective.*

**introspection** /ɪntrə'spekʃ(ə)n/ *noun* examination of one's own thoughts. □ **introspective** *adjective.*

**introvert** ●*noun* person chiefly concerned with his or her own thoughts; shy thoughtful person. ●*adjective* (also **introverted**) characteristic of an introvert. □ **introversion** /-'vɜːʃ(ə)n/ *noun.*

**intrude** /ɪn'truːd/ *verb* (-ding) (+ *on, upon, into*) come uninvited or unwanted; force on a person. □ **intruder** *noun;* **intrusion** /-ʒ(ə)n/ *noun;* **intrusive** /-sɪv/ *adjective.*

**intuition** /ɪntjuː'ɪʃ(ə)n/ *noun* immediate apprehension by mind without reasoning; immediate insight. □ **intuit** /ɪn'tjuːɪt/ *verb;* **intuitional** *adjective.*

**intuitive** /ɪn'tjuːɪtɪv/ *adjective* of, having, or perceived by intuition. □ **intuitively** *adverb*; **intuitiveness** *noun*.

**Inuit** /'ɪnjuːɪt/ ● *noun* (*plural* same or **-s**) N. American Eskimo; language of Inuit. ● *adjective* of Inuit or their language.

**inundate** /'ɪnʌndeɪt/ *verb* (**-ting**) (often + *with*) flood, overwhelm. □ **inundation** *noun*.

**inure** /ɪ'njʊə/ *verb* (**-ring**) habituate, accustom. □ **inurement** *noun*.

**invade** /ɪn'veɪd/ *verb* (**-ding**) enter (country etc.) with arms to control or subdue it; swarm into; (of disease etc.) attack; encroach on. □ **invader** *noun*.

**invalid¹** /'ɪnvəlɪd, -liːd/ ● *noun* person enfeebled or disabled by illness or injury. ● *adjective* of or for invalids; sick, disabled. ● *verb* (**-d-**) (often + *out* etc.) remove from active service; disable (person) by illness. □ **invalidism** *noun*; **invalidity** /-'lɪd-/ *noun*.

**invalid²** /ɪn'vælɪd/ *adjective* not valid. □ **invalidity** /-və'lɪd-/ *noun*.

**invalidate** /ɪn'vælɪdeɪt/ *verb* (**-ting**) make invalid. □ **invalidation** *noun*.

**invaluable** /ɪn'væljʊəb(ə)l/ *adjective* beyond price, very valuable.

**invariable** /ɪn'veərɪəb(ə)l/ *adjective* unchangeable; always the same. □ **invariably** *adverb*.

**invasion** /ɪn'veɪʒ(ə)n/ *noun* invading, being invaded. □ **invasive** /-sɪv/ *adjective*.

**invective** /ɪn'vektɪv/ *noun* violent attack in words.

**inveigh** /ɪn'veɪ/ *verb* (+ *against*) speak or write with strong hostility against.

**inveigle** /ɪn'veɪg(ə)l/ *verb* (**-ling**) (+ *into*, *to do*) entice, persuade by guile. □ **inveiglement** *noun*.

**invent** /ɪn'vent/ *verb* create by thought; originate; fabricate. □ **inventor** *noun*.

**invention** /ɪn'venʃ(ə)n/ *noun* inventing, being invented; thing invented; inventiveness.

**inventive** *adjective* able to invent; imaginative. □ **inventively** *adverb*; **inventiveness** *noun*.

**inventory** /'ɪnvəntərɪ/ ● *noun* (*plural* **-ies**) list of goods etc. ● *verb* (**-ies**, **-ied**) make inventory of; enter in inventory.

**inverse** /ɪn'vɜːs/ ● *adjective* inverted in position, order, or relation. ● *noun* inverted state; (often + *of*) direct opposite. □ **inverse proportion, ratio** relation between two quantities such that one increases in proportion as the other decreases.

**inversion** /ɪn'vɜːʃ(ə)n/ *noun* inverting, esp. reversal of normal order of words.

**invert** /ɪn'vɜːt/ *verb* turn upside down; reverse position, order, or relation of. □ **inverted commas** quotation marks.

**invertebrate** /ɪn'vɜːtɪbrət/ ● *adjective* without backbone. ● *noun* invertebrate animal.

**invest** /ɪn'vest/ *verb* (often + *in*) apply or use (money) for profit; devote (time etc.) to an enterprise; (+ *in*) buy (something useful or otherwise rewarding); (+ *with*) endue with qualities etc.; (often + *with*, *in*) clothe with insignia of office. □ **investor** *noun*.

**investigate** /ɪn'vestɪgeɪt/ *verb* (**-ting**) inquire into, examine. □ **investigation** *noun*; **investigative** /-gətɪv/ *adjective*; **investigator** *noun*.

**investiture** /ɪn'vestɪtʃə/ *noun* formal investing of person with honours etc.

**investment** *noun* investing; money invested; property etc. in which money is invested.

**inveterate** /ɪn'vetərət/ *adjective* (of person) confirmed in (usually undesirable) habit etc.; (of habit etc.) longestablished. □ **inveteracy** *noun*.

**invidious** /ɪn'vɪdɪəs/ *adjective* likely to excite ill-will against performer, possessor, etc.

**invigilate** /ɪn'vɪdʒɪleɪt/ *verb* (**-ting**) supervise examinees. □ **invigilation** *noun*; **invigilator** *noun*.

**invigorate** /ɪn'vɪgəreɪt/ *verb* (**-ting**) give vigour to. □ **invigorating** *adjective*.

**invincible** /ɪn'vɪnsɪb(ə)l/ *adjective* unconquerable. □ **invincibility** *noun*; **invincibly** *adverb*.

**inviolable** /ɪn'vaɪələb(ə)l/ *adjective* not to be violated. □ **inviolability** *noun*.

**inviolate** /ɪn'vaɪələt/ *adjective* not violated; safe (from harm). □ **inviolacy** *noun*.

**invisible** /ɪn'vɪzɪb(ə)l/ *adjective* that cannot be seen. □ **invisible exports, imports** items for which payment is made by or to another country but which are not goods. □ **invisibility** *noun*; **invisibly** *adverb*.

**invite** ● *verb* /ɪnˈvaɪt/ (**-ting**) request courteously to come, to do, etc.; solicit courteously; tend to evoke unintentionally; attract. ● *noun* /ˈɪnvaɪt/ *colloquial* invitation. □ **invitation** /ɪnvɪˈteɪʃ(ə)n/ *noun*.

**inviting** *adjective* attractive. □ **invitingly** *adverb*.

*in vitro* /ɪn ˈviːtrəʊ/ *adverb* (of biological processes) taking place in test-tube or other laboratory environment. [Latin]

**invocation** /ɪnvəˈkeɪʃ(ə)n/ *noun* invoking; calling on, esp. in prayer or for inspiration etc. □ **invocatory** /ɪnˈvɒkətərɪ/ *adjective*.

**invoice** /ˈɪnvɔɪs/ ● *noun* bill for usually itemized goods etc. ● *verb* (**-cing**) send invoice to; make invoice of.

**invoke** /ɪnˈvəʊk/ *verb* (**-king**) call on in prayer or as witness; appeal to (law, authority, etc.); summon (spirit) by charms; ask earnestly for (vengeance, justice, etc.).

**involuntary** /ɪnˈvɒləntərɪ/ *adjective* done etc. without exercise of will; not controlled by will. □ **involuntarily** *adverb*.

**involute** /ˈɪnvəluːt/ *adjective* intricate; curled spirally.

**involution** /ɪnvəˈluːʃ(ə)n/ *noun* involving; intricacy; curling inwards, part so curled.

**involve** /ɪnˈvɒlv/ *verb* (**-ving**) (often + *in*) cause (person, thing) to share experience or effect; imply, make necessary; (often + *in*) implicate (person) in charge, crime, etc.; include or affect in its operation; (as **involved** *adjective*) complicated. □ **involvement** *noun*.

**invulnerable** /ɪnˈvʌlnərəb(ə)l/ *adjective* that cannot be wounded. □ **invulnerability** *noun*.

**inward** /ˈɪnwəd/ ● *adjective* directed towards inside; going in; situated within; mental, spiritual. ● *adverb* (also **inwards**) towards inside; in mind or soul.

**inwardly** *adverb* on the inside; in mind or spirit; not aloud.

**inwrought** /ɪnˈrɔːt/ *adjective* (often + *with*) decorated (with pattern); (often + *in, on*) (of pattern) wrought (in or on fabric).

**iodine** /ˈaɪədiːn/ *noun* black solid halogen element forming violet vapour; solution of this used as antiseptic.

**IOM** *abbreviation* Isle of Man.

**ion** /ˈaɪən/ *noun* atom or group of atoms that has lost or gained one or more electrons.

**ionic** /aɪˈɒnɪk/ *adjective* of or using ions.

**ionize** *verb* (also **-ise**) (**-zing** or **-sing**) convert or be converted into ion(s). □ **ionization** *noun*.

**ionosphere** /aɪˈɒnəsfɪə/ *noun* ionized region in upper atmosphere. □ **ionospheric** /-ˈsfer-/ *adjective*.

**iota** /aɪˈəʊtə/ *noun* ninth letter of Greek alphabet (I, ι); (usually with negative) a jot.

**IOU** /aɪəʊˈjuː/ *noun* (*plural* **-s**) signed document acknowledging debt.

**IOW** *abbreviation* Isle of Wight.

**IPA** *abbreviation* International Phonetic Alphabet.

**ipecacuanha** /ɪpɪkækjʊˈɑːnə/ *noun* root of S. American plant used as emetic etc.

*ipso facto* /ɪpsəʊ ˈfæktəʊ/ *adverb* by that very fact. [Latin]

**IQ** *abbreviation* intelligence quotient.

**IRA** *abbreviation* Irish Republican Army.

**Iranian** /ɪˈreɪnɪən/ ● *adjective* of Iran (formerly Persia); of group of languages including Persian. ● *noun* native or national of Iran.

**Iraqi** /ɪˈrɑːkɪ/ ● *adjective* of Iraq. ● *noun* (*plural* **-s**) native or national of Iraq.

**irascible** /ɪˈræsɪb(ə)l/ *adjective* irritable; hot-tempered. □ **irascibility** *noun*.

**irate** /aɪˈreɪt/ *adjective* angry, enraged.

**ire** /ˈaɪə/ *noun literary* anger.

**iridescent** /ɪrɪˈdes(ə)nt/ *adjective* showing rainbow-like glowing colours; changing colour with position. □ **iridescence** *noun*.

**iris** /ˈaɪərɪs/ *noun* circular coloured membrane surrounding pupil of eye; bulbous or tuberous plant with sword-shaped leaves and showy flowers.

**Irish** /ˈaɪərɪʃ/ ● *adjective* of Ireland. ● *noun* Celtic language of Ireland; (**the Irish**; treated as *plural*) the Irish people. □ **Irish coffee** coffee with dash of whiskey and a little sugar, topped with cream; **Irishman**, **Irishwoman** native of Ireland; **Irish stew** dish of stewed mutton, onions, and potatoes.

**irk** verb irritate, annoy.

**irksome** adjective annoying, tiresome.

**iron** /'aɪən/ ● noun common strong grey metallic element; this as symbol of strength or firmness; tool etc. of iron; implement heated to smooth clothes etc.; golf club with iron or steel head; (in plural) fetters; (in plural) stirrups; (often in plural) leg-support to rectify malformations. ● adjective of iron; robust; unyielding. ● verb smooth (clothes etc.) with heated iron. □ **Iron Age** era characterized by use of iron weapons etc.; **Iron Curtain** historical notional barrier to passage of people and information between Soviet bloc and West; **ironing board** narrow folding table etc. for ironing clothes on; **iron lung** rigid case over patient's body for administering prolonged artificial respiration; **ironmonger** dealer in **ironmongery**, household and building hardware; **iron rations** small emergency supply of food; **ironstone** hard iron ore, kind of hard white pottery.

**ironic** /aɪ'rɒnɪk/ adjective (also **ironical**) using or displaying irony. □ **ironically** adverb.

**irony** /'aɪrənɪ/ noun (plural -**ies**) expression of meaning, usually humorous or sarcastic, by use of words normally conveying opposite meaning; apparent perversity of fate or circumstances.

**irradiate** /ɪ'reɪdɪeɪt/ verb (-**ting**) subject to radiation; shine on; throw light on; light up. □ **irradiation** noun.

**irrational** /ɪ'ræʃ(ə)n(ə)l/ adjective unreasonable, illogical; not endowed with reason; Mathematics not expressible as an ordinary fraction. □ **irrationality** /-'næl-/ noun; **irrationally** adverb.

**irreconcilable** /ɪ'rekənsaɪləb(ə)l/ adjective implacably hostile; (of ideas etc.) incompatible. □ **irreconcilably** adverb.

**irrecoverable** /ɪrɪ'kʌvərəb(ə)l/ adjective that cannot be recovered or remedied.

**irredeemable** /ɪrɪ'diːməb(ə)l/ adjective that cannot be redeemed, hopeless. □ **irredeemably** adverb.

**irreducible** /ɪrɪ'djuːsɪb(ə)l/ adjective not able to be reduced or simplified.

**irrefutable** /ɪrɪ'fjuːtəb(ə)l/ adjective that cannot be refuted. □ **irrefutably** adverb.

**irregular** /ɪ'regjʊlə/ ● adjective not regular; unsymmetrical, uneven; varying in form; not occurring at regular intervals; contrary to rule; (of troops) not in regular army; (of verb, noun, etc.) not inflected according to usual rules. ● noun (in plural) irregular troops. □ **irregularity** /-'lær-/ noun (plural -**ies**); **irregularly** adverb.

**irrelevant** /ɪ'relɪv(ə)nt/ adjective not relevant. □ **irrelevance** noun; **irrelevancy** noun (plural -**ies**).

**irreligious** /ɪrɪ'lɪdʒəs/ adjective lacking or hostile to religion; irreverent.

**irremediable** /ɪrɪ'miːdɪəb(ə)l/ adjective that cannot be remedied. □ **irremediably** adverb.

**irremovable** /ɪrɪ'muːvəb(ə)l/ adjective not removable. □ **irremovably** adverb.

**irreparable** /ɪ'repərəb(ə)l/ adjective that cannot be rectified or made good. □ **irreparably** adverb.

**irreplaceable** /ɪrɪ'pleɪsəb(ə)l/ adjective that cannot be replaced.

**irrepressible** /ɪrɪ'presɪb(ə)l/ adjective that cannot be repressed. □ **irrepressibly** adverb.

**irreproachable** /ɪrɪ'prəʊtʃəb(ə)l/ adjective faultless, blameless. □ **irreproachably** adverb.

**irresistible** /ɪrɪ'zɪstɪb(ə)l/ adjective too strong, convincing, charming, etc. to be resisted. □ **irresistibly** adverb.

**irresolute** /ɪ'rezəluːt/ adjective hesitating; lacking in resolution. □ **irresoluteness** noun; **irresolution** /-'luːʃ(ə)n/ noun.

**irrespective** /ɪrɪ'spektɪv/ adjective (+ of) not taking into account, regardless of.

**irresponsible** /ɪrɪ'spɒnsɪb(ə)l/ adjective acting or done without due sense of responsibility; not responsible. □ **irresponsibility** noun; **irresponsibly** adverb.

**irretrievable** /ɪrɪ'triːvəb(ə)l/ adjective that cannot be retrieved or restored. □ **irretrievably** adverb.

**irreverent** /ɪ'revərənt/ adjective lacking in reverence. □ **irreverence** noun; **irreverently** adverb.

**irreversible** /ɪrɪ'vɜːsɪb(ə)l/ adjective that cannot be reversed or altered. □ **irreversibly** adverb.

**irrevocable** /ɪˈrevəkəb(ə)l/ adjective unalterable; gone beyond recall. □ **irrevocably** adverb.

**irrigate** /ˈɪrɪgeɪt/ verb (**-ting**) water (land) by system of artificial channels; (of stream etc.) supply (land) with water; Medicine moisten (wound etc.) with constant flow of liquid. □ **irrigable** adjective; **irrigation** noun; **irrigator** noun.

**irritable** /ˈɪrɪtəb(ə)l/ adjective easily annoyed; very sensitive to contact. □ **irritability** noun; **irritably** adverb.

**irritant** /ˈɪrɪt(ə)nt/ ● adjective causing irritation. ● noun irritant substance or agent.

**irritate** /ˈɪrɪteɪt/ verb (**-ting**) excite to anger, annoy; stimulate discomfort in (part of body). □ **irritating** adjective; **irritation** noun.

**is.** abbreviation Island(s); Isle(s).

**is** 3rd singular present of BE.

**isinglass** /ˈaɪzɪŋglɑːs/ noun kind of gelatin obtained from sturgeon etc.

**Islam** /ˈɪzlɑːm/ noun religion of Muslims, proclaimed by Prophet Muhammad; the Muslim world. □ **Islamic** /-ˈlæm-/ adjective.

**island** /ˈaɪlənd/ noun piece of land surrounded by water; traffic island; detached or isolated thing.

**islander** noun native or inhabitant of island.

**isle** /aɪl/ noun literary (usually small) island.

**islet** /ˈaɪlɪt/ noun small island.

**isn't** /ˈɪz(ə)nt/ is not.

**isobar** /ˈaɪsəbɑː/ noun line on map connecting places with same atmospheric pressure. □ **isobaric** /-ˈbær-/ adjective.

**isolate** /ˈaɪsəleɪt/ verb (**-ting**) place apart or alone; separate (esp. infectious patient from others); insulate (electrical apparatus), esp. by gap; disconnect. □ **isolation** noun.

**isolationism** noun policy of holding aloof from affairs of other countries or groups. □ **isolationist** noun.

**isomer** /ˈaɪsəmə/ noun one of two or more compounds with same molecular formula but different arrangement of atoms. □ **isomeric** /-ˈmer-/ adjective; **isomerism** /aɪˈsɒmərɪz(ə)m/ noun.

**isosceles** /aɪˈsɒsɪliːz/ adjective (of triangle) having two sides equal.

**isotherm** /ˈaɪsəθɜːm/ noun line on map connecting places with same temperature. □ **isothermal** /-ˈθɜːm(ə)l/ adjective.

**isotope** /ˈaɪsətəʊp/ noun any of two or more forms of chemical element with different relative atomic mass and different nuclear but not chemical properties. □ **isotopic** /-ˈtɒp-/ adjective.

**Israeli** /ɪzˈreɪlɪ/ ● adjective of modern state of Israel. ● noun (plural **-s**) native or national of Israel.

**issue** /ˈɪʃuː/ ● noun giving out or circulation of shares, notes, stamps, etc.; copies of journal etc. circulated at one time; each of regular series of magazine etc.; outgoing, outflow; point in question; essential subject of dispute; result, outcome; offspring. ● verb (**issues**, **issued**, **issuing**) go or come out; give or send out; publish, circulate; supply, (+ with) supply with equipment etc.; (+ from) be derived; result; (+ from) emerge.

**isthmus** /ˈɪsməs/ noun (plural **-es**) neck of land connecting two larger land masses.

**IT** abbreviation information technology.

**it** pronoun the thing in question; indefinite, undefined, or impersonal subject, action, condition, object, etc.; substitute for deferred subject or object; exactly what is needed; perfection; slang sexual intercourse; sex appeal. □ **that's it** colloquial that is what is required, that is the difficulty, that is the end, enough.

**Italian** /ɪˈtæljən/ ● noun native, national, or language of Italy. ● adjective of Italy.

**italic** /ɪˈtælɪk/ ● adjective (of type etc.) of sloping kind; (of handwriting) neat and pointed; (**Italic**) of ancient Italy. ● noun (usually in plural) italic type.

**italicize** /ɪˈtælɪsaɪz/ verb (also **-ise**) (**-zing** or **-sing**) print in italics.

**itch** ● noun irritation in skin; restless desire; disease with itch. ● verb feel irritation or restless desire.

**itchy** adjective (**-ier**, **-iest**) having or causing itch. □ **have itchy feet** colloquial be restless, have urge to travel.

**it'd** /ɪtəd/ it had; it would.

**item** /ˈaɪtəm/ noun any one of enumerated things; separate or distinct piece of news etc.

**itemize** verb (also **-ise**) (**-zing** or **-sing**) state by items. □ **itemization** noun.

**iterate** /ˈɪtəreɪt/ verb (**-ting**) repeat; state repeatedly. □ **iteration** noun; **iterative** /-rətɪv/ adjective.

**itinerant** /aɪˈtɪnərənt/ ● adjective travelling from place to place. ● noun itinerant person.

**itinerary** /aɪˈtɪnərərɪ/ noun (plural **-ies**) route; record of travel; guidebook.

**it'll** /ˈɪt(ə)l/ it will; it shall.

**its** adjective of or belonging to it.

**it's** /ɪts/ it is; it has.

■ **Usage** Because it has an apostrophe, *it's* is easily confused with *its*. Both are correctly used in *Where's the dog?—It's in its kennel, and it's eaten its food* (= *It is in its kennel, and it has eaten its food.*)

**itself** /ɪtˈself/ pronoun: emphatic & reflexive form of IT.

**ITV** abbreviation Independent Television.

**IUD** abbreviation intrauterine (contraceptive) device.

**I've** /aɪv/ I have.

**ivory** /ˈaɪvərɪ/ noun (plural **-ies**) white substance of tusks of elephant etc.; colour of this; (in plural) slang things made of or resembling ivory, esp. dice, piano keys, or teeth. □ **ivory tower** seclusion from harsh realities of life.

**ivy** /ˈaɪvɪ/ noun (plural **-ies**) climbing evergreen with shiny 5-angled leaves.

# Jj

**jab** ● verb (**-bb-**) poke roughly; stab; (+ into) thrust (thing) abruptly or abruptly. ● noun abrupt blow or thrust; colloquial hypodermic injection.

**jabber** ● verb chatter volubly; utter fast and indistinctly. ● noun chatter, gabble.

**jabot** /ˈʒæbəʊ/ noun frill on front of shirt or blouse.

**jacaranda** /dʒækəˈrændə/ noun tropical American tree with blue flowers or one with hard scented wood.

**jacinth** /ˈdʒæsɪnθ/ noun reddish-orange zircon used as gem.

**jack** ● noun device for lifting heavy objects, esp. vehicles; lowest-ranking court card; ship's flag, esp. showing nationality; device using single-pronged plug to connect electrical equipment; small white target ball in bowls; (in plural) game played with jackstones. ● verb (usually + up) raise (as) with jack. □ **jackboot** boot reaching above knee; **jack in** slang abandon (attempt etc.); **jack-in-the-box** toy figure that springs out of box; **jack of all trades** person with many skills; **jack plug** electrical plug with single prong; **jackstone** metal etc. piece used in tossing games.

**jackal** /ˈdʒæk(ə)l/ noun African or Asian wild animal of dog family.

**jackass** noun male ass; stupid person.

**jackdaw** noun grey-headed bird of crow family.

**jacket** /ˈdʒækɪt/ noun short coat with sleeves; covering round boiler etc.; outside wrapper of book; skin of potato. □ **jacket potato** one baked in its skin.

**jackknife** ● noun large clasp-knife. ● verb (**-fing**) (of articulated vehicle) fold against itself in accident.

**jackpot** noun large prize, esp. accumulated in game, lottery, etc.

**Jacobean** /dʒækəˈbiːən/ adjective of reign of James I.

**Jacobite** /ˈdʒækəbaɪt/ noun historical supporter of James II in exile, or of Stuarts.

**Jacuzzi** /dʒəˈkuːzɪ/ noun (plural **-s**) proprietary term large bath with massaging
underwater jets.

**jade**[1] noun hard usually green stone for
ornaments; green colour of jade.

**jade**[2] noun inferior or worn-out horse.

**jaded** adjective tired out, surfeited.

**jag** ● noun sharp projection of rock etc.
● verb (**-gg-**) cut or tear unevenly; make
indentations in.

**jagged** /ˈdʒægɪd/ adjective unevenly cut
or torn. □ **jaggedly** adverb; **jaggedness**
noun.

**jaguar** /ˈdʒægjʊə/ noun large American
spotted animal of cat family.

**jail** /dʒeɪl/ (also **gaol**) ● noun place for
detention of prisoners; confinement in
jail. ● verb put in jail. □ **jailbird**
prisoner, habitual criminal. □ **jailer**
noun.

**jalap** /ˈdʒæləp/ noun purgative drug.

**jalopy** /dʒəˈlɒpɪ/ noun (plural **-ies**) colloquial
dilapidated old motor vehicle.

**jalousie** /ˈʒæluːziː/ noun slatted blind or
shutter.

**jam**[1] ● verb (**-mm-**) (usually + into, together, etc.) squeeze or cram into space;
become wedged; cause (machinery) to
become wedged and so unworkable,
become wedged in this way; block (exit,
road, etc.) by crowding; (usually + on)
apply (brakes) suddenly; make (radio
transmission) unintelligible with interference. ● noun squeeze; stoppage;
crowded mass, esp. of traffic; colloquial
predicament. □ **jam session** (in jazz
etc.) improvised ensemble playing.

**jam**[2] noun conserve of boiled fruit and
sugar; colloquial easy or pleasant thing.

**jamb** /dʒæm/ noun side post or side face
of doorway or window frame.

**jamboree** /dʒæmbəˈriː/ noun celebration; large rally of Scouts.

**jammy** adjective (**-ier, -iest**) covered with
jam; colloquial lucky, profitable.

**Jan.** abbreviation January.

**jangle** /ˈdʒæŋɡ(ə)l/ ● verb (**-ling**) (cause
to) make harsh metallic sound. ● noun
such sound.

**janitor** /ˈdʒænɪtə/ noun doorkeeper;
caretaker.

**January** /ˈdʒænjʊərɪ/ noun (plural **-ies**)
first month of year.

**japan** /dʒəˈpæn/ ● noun hard usually
black varnish. ● verb (**-nn-**) make black
and glossy (as) with japan.

**Japanese** /dʒæpəˈniːz/ ● noun (plural
same) native, national, or language of
Japan. ● adjective of Japan or its people
or language.

**jape** noun practical joke.

**japonica** /dʒəˈpɒnɪkə/ noun flowering
shrub with red flowers and edible
fruits.

**jar**[1] noun container, usually of glass and
cylindrical.

**jar**[2] ● verb (**-rr-**) (often + on) (of sound,
manner, etc.) strike discordantly,
grate; (often + against, on) (cause to)
strike (esp. part of body) with vibration
or shock; (often + with) be at variance.
● noun jarring sound, shock, or
vibration.

**jardinière** /ʒɑːdɪˈnjeə/ noun ornamental
pot or stand for plants.

**jargon** /ˈdʒɑːɡən/ noun words used by
particular group or profession; de-
based or pretentious language.

**jasmine** /ˈdʒæzmɪn/ noun shrub with
white or yellow flowers.

**jasper** /ˈdʒæspə/ noun red, yellow, or
brown opaque quartz.

**jaundice** /ˈdʒɔːndɪs/ ● noun yellowing of
skin caused by liver disease, bile disorder, etc. ● verb (as **jaundiced** adjective)
affected with jaundice; envious, resentful.

**jaunt** /dʒɔːnt/ ● noun pleasure trip. ● verb
take a jaunt.

**jaunty** adjective (**-ier, -iest**) cheerful and
self-confident; sprightly. □ **jauntily** adverb; **jauntiness** noun.

**javelin** /ˈdʒævlɪn/ noun light spear
thrown in sport or, formerly, as
weapon.

**jaw** ● noun bony structure containing
teeth; (in plural) mouth, gripping parts
of tool etc.; colloquial tedious talk.
● verb slang speak at tedious length.
□ **jawbone** lower jaw in most
mammals.

**jay** noun noisy European bird of crow
family with vivid plumage. □ **jaywalk**
walk across road carelessly or dangerously; **jaywalker** person who does this.

**jazz** noun rhythmic syncopated esp. improvised music of American black origin. □ **and all that jazz** colloquial and
other related things; **jazz up** enliven.

**jazzy** *adjective* (**-ier, -iest**) of or like jazz; vivid.

**jealous** /ˈdʒeləs/ *adjective* resentful of rivalry in love; (often + *of*) envious (of person etc.), protective (of rights etc.). □ **jealously** *adverb*; **jealousy** *noun* (*plural* **-ies**).

**jeans** /dʒiːnz/ *plural noun* casual esp. denim trousers.

**Jeep** *noun proprietary term* small sturdy esp. military vehicle with 4-wheel drive.

**jeer** ● *verb* (often + *at*) scoff, deride. ● *noun* taunt.

**Jehovah** /dʒəˈhəʊvə/ *noun* (in Old Testament) God. □ **Jehovah's Witness** member of unorthodox Christian sect.

**jejune** /dʒɪˈdʒuːn/ *adjective* (of ideas, writing, etc.) shallow, naïve, or dry and uninteresting.

**jell** *verb colloquial* set as jelly; (of ideas etc.) take definite form; cohere.

**jellied** /ˈdʒelɪd/ *adjective* (of food etc.) set as or in jelly.

**jelly** /ˈdʒelɪ/ *noun* (*plural* **-ies**) (usually fruit-flavoured) semi-transparent dessert set with gelatin; similar preparation as jam or condiment; *slang* gelignite. □ **jelly baby** jelly-like baby-shaped sweet; **jellyfish** (*plural* same or **-es**) marine animal with jelly-like body and stinging tentacles.

**jemmy** /ˈdʒemɪ/ *noun* (*plural* **-ies**) burglar's crowbar.

**jeopardize** *verb* (also **-ise**) (**-zing** or **-sing**) endanger.

**jeopardy** /ˈdʒepədɪ/ *noun* danger, esp. severe.

**jerboa** /dʒɜːˈbəʊə/ *noun* small jumping desert rodent.

**Jeremiah** /dʒerɪˈmaɪə/ *noun* dismal prophet.

**jerk**[1] ● *noun* sharp sudden pull, twist, etc.; spasmodic muscular twitch; *slang* fool. ● *verb* move, pull, throw, etc. with jerk. □ **jerky** *adjective* (**-ier, -iest**); **jerkily** *adverb*; **jerkiness** *noun*.

**jerk**[2] *verb* cure (beef) by cutting in long slices and drying in the sun.

**jerkin** /ˈdʒɜːkɪn/ *noun* sleeveless jacket.

**jeroboam** /dʒerəˈbəʊəm/ *noun* wine bottle of 4–12 times ordinary size.

**jerry-building** *noun* building of shoddy houses with bad materials. □ **jerry-builder** *noun*; **jerry-built** *adjective*.

**jerrycan** *noun* kind of petrol- or water-can.

**jersey** /ˈdʒɜːzɪ/ *noun* (*plural* **-s**) knitted usually woollen pullover; knitted fabric; (**Jersey**) dairy cow from Jersey.

**Jerusalem artichoke** /dʒəˈruːsələm/ *noun* kind of sunflower with edible tubers; this tuber as vegetable.

**jest** ● *noun* joke; fun; banter; object of derision. ● *verb* joke; fool about. □ **in jest** in fun.

**jester** *noun historical* professional clown at medieval court etc.

**Jesuit** /ˈdʒezjʊɪt/ *noun* member of RC Society of Jesus. □ **Jesuitical** /-ˈɪt-/ *adjective*.

**jet**[1] ● *noun* stream of water, steam, gas, flame, etc. shot esp. from small opening; spout or nozzle for this; jet engine or plane. ● *verb* (**-tt-**) spurt out in jet(s); *colloquial* send or travel by jet plane. □ **jet engine** one using jet propulsion; **jet lag** exhaustion felt after long flight across time zones; **jet plane** one with jet engine; **jet-propelled** having jet propulsion, very fast; **jet propulsion** propulsion by backward ejection of high-speed jet of gas etc.; **jet set** wealthy people who travel widely, esp. for pleasure; **jet-setter** such a person.

**jet**[2] *noun* hard black lignite, often carved and highly polished. □ **jet black** deep glossy black.

**jetsam** /ˈdʒetsəm/ *noun* objects washed ashore, esp. jettisoned from ship.

**jettison** /ˈdʒetɪs(ə)n/ *verb* throw (cargo, fuel, etc.) from ship or aircraft to lighten it; abandon; get rid of.

**jetty** /ˈdʒetɪ/ *noun* (*plural* **-ies**) pier or breakwater protecting or defending harbour etc.; landing-pier.

**Jew** /dʒuː/ *noun* person of Hebrew descent or whose religion is Judaism.

**jewel** /ˈdʒuːəl/ ● *noun* precious stone; this used in watchmaking; jewelled personal ornament; precious person or thing. ● *verb* (**-ll-**; *US* **-l-**) (esp. as **jewelled** *adjective*) adorn or set with jewels.

**jeweller** *noun* (*US* **jeweler**) maker of or dealer in jewels or jewellery.

**jewellery** /ˈdʒuːəlrɪ/ noun (also **jewelry**) rings, brooches, necklaces, etc. collectively.

**Jewish** adjective of Jews or Judaism. □ **Jewishness** noun.

**Jewry** /ˈdʒʊərɪ/ noun Jews collectively.

**Jezebel** /ˈdʒezəbəl/ noun shameless or immoral woman.

**jib** ● noun projecting arm of crane; triangular staysail. ● verb (**-bb-**) (esp. of horse) stop and refuse to go on; (+ at) show aversion to.

**jibe¹** = GIBE.

**jibe²** US = GYBE.

**jiffy** /ˈdʒɪfɪ/ noun (plural **-ies**) (also **jiff**) colloquial short time, moment. □ **Jiffy bag** proprietary term padded envelope.

**jig** ● noun lively dance; music for this; device that holds piece of work and guides tools operating on it. ● verb (**-gg-**) dance jig; (often + about) move quickly up and down; fidget.

**jigger** /ˈdʒɪgə/ noun small glass for measure of spirits.

**jiggery-pokery** /dʒɪgərɪˈpəʊkərɪ/ noun colloquial trickery; swindling.

**jiggle** /ˈdʒɪg(ə)l/ ● verb (**-ling**) (often + about) rock or jerk lightly; fidget. ● noun light shake.

**jigsaw** noun (in full **jigsaw puzzle**) picture on board etc. cut into irregular interlocking pieces to be reassembled as pastime; mechanical fine-bladed fret saw.

**jihad** /dʒɪˈhæd/ noun Muslim holy war against unbelievers.

**jilt** verb abruptly reject or abandon (esp. lover).

**jingle** /ˈdʒɪŋg(ə)l/ ● noun mixed ringing or clinking noise; repetition of sounds in phrase; short catchy verse in advertising etc. ● verb (**-ling**) (cause to) make jingling sound.

**jingo** /ˈdʒɪŋgəʊ/ noun (plural **-es**) blustering patriot. □ **jingoism** noun; **jingoist** noun; **jingoistic** /-ˈɪs-/ adjective.

**jink** ● verb move elusively; elude by dodging. ● noun jinking. □ **high jinks** boisterous fun.

**jinnee** /ˈdʒɪniː/ noun (also **jinn**, **djinn** /dʒɪn/) (plural **jinn** or **djinn**) (in Muslim mythology) spirit of supernatural power in human or animal form.

**jinx** colloquial ● noun person or thing that seems to bring bad luck. ● verb (esp. as **jinxed** adjective) subject to bad luck.

**jitter** /ˈdʒɪtə/ colloquial ● noun (**the jitters**) extreme nervousness. ● verb be nervous; act nervously. □ **jittery** adjective.

**jive** ● noun lively dance of 1950s; music for this. ● verb (**-ving**) dance to or play jive music. □ **jiver** noun.

**Jnr.** abbreviation Junior.

**job** ● noun piece of work (to be) done; paid employment; colloquial difficult task; slang a crime, esp. a robbery. ● verb (**-bb-**) do jobs; do piece-work; buy and sell (stocks etc.); deal corruptly with (matter). □ **jobcentre** local government office advertising available jobs; **job-hunt** colloquial seek employment; **job lot** mixed lot bought at auction etc.

**jobber** /ˈdʒɒbə/ noun person who jobs; historical principal or wholesaler on Stock Exchange.

**jobbery** noun corrupt dealing.

**jobless** adjective unemployed. □ **joblessness** noun.

**job-sharing** noun sharing of full-time job by two or more people. □ **job-share** noun & verb.

**jockey** /ˈdʒɒkɪ/ ● noun rider in horse races. ● verb (**-eys**, **-eyed**) cheat, trick. □ **jockey for position** manoeuvre for advantage.

**jockstrap** /ˈdʒɒkstræp/ noun support or protection for male genitals worn esp. in sport.

**jocose** /dʒəˈkəʊs/ adjective playful; jocular. □ **jocosely** adverb; **jocosity** /-ˈkɒs-/ noun (plural **-ies**).

**jocular** /ˈdʒɒkjʊlə/ adjective fond of joking; humorous. □ **jocularity** /-ˈlær-/ noun (plural **-ies**); **jocularly** adverb.

**jocund** /ˈdʒɒkənd/ adjective literary merry, cheerful. □ **jocundity** /dʒəˈkʌn-/ noun (plural **-ies**); **jocundly** adverb.

**jodhpurs** /ˈdʒɒdpəz/ plural noun riding breeches tight below knee.

**jog** ● verb (**-gg-**) run slowly, esp. as exercise; push, jerk; nudge, esp. to alert; stimulate (person's memory). ● noun spell of jogging; slow walk or trot; push, jerk; nudge. □ **jogtrot** slow regular trot. □ **jogger** noun.

**joggle** /ˈdʒɒg(ə)l/ ● verb (**-ling**) move in jerks. ● noun slight shake.

**joie de vivre** /ʒwɑː də 'viːvrə/ *noun* exuberance; high spirits. [French]

**join** ● *verb* (often + *to*, *together*) put together, fasten, unite; connect (points) by line etc.; become member of (club etc.); take one's place with (person, group, etc.); (+ *in*, *for*, etc.) take part with (others) in activity etc.; (often + *with*, *to*) come together, be united; (of river etc.) become connected or continuous with. ● *noun* point, line, or surface of junction. □ **join in** take part in (activity); **join up** enlist for military service.

**joiner** *noun* maker of furniture and light woodwork. □ **joinery** *noun*.

**joint** ● *noun* place at which two or more things are joined; device for doing this; point at which two bones fit together; division of animal carcass as meat; *slang* restaurant, bar, etc.; *slang* marijuana cigarette. ● *adjective* held by, done by, or belonging to two or more people etc.; sharing with another. ● *verb* connect by joint(s); divide at joint or into joints. □ **joint stock** capital held jointly.

**jointure** /'dʒɔɪntʃə/ *noun* estate settled on wife by husband for use after his death.

**joist** *noun* supporting beam in floor, ceiling, etc.

**jojoba** /həʊ'həʊbə/ *noun* plant with seeds yielding oil used in cosmetics etc.

**joke** ● *noun* thing said or done to cause laughter; witticism; ridiculous person or thing. ● *verb* (**-king**) make jokes. □ **jokily** *adverb*; **jokiness** *noun*; **jokingly** *adverb*; **jokey**, **joky** *adjective*.

**joker** *noun* person who jokes; playing card used in some games.

**jollification** /dʒɒlɪfɪ'keɪʃ(ə)n/ *noun* merry-making.

**jolly** /'dʒɒlɪ/ ● *adjective* (**-ier**, **-iest**) cheerful; festive, jovial; *colloquial* pleasant, delightful. ● *adverb colloquial* very. ● *verb* (**-ies**, **-ied**) (usually + *along*) *colloquial* coax, humour. □ **jollity** *noun* (*plural* **-ies**).

**jolt** /dʒəʊlt/ ● *verb* shake (esp. in vehicle) with jerk; shock, perturb; move along jerkily. ● *noun* jerk; surprise, shock.

**jonquil** /'dʒɒŋkwɪl/ *noun* narcissus with white or yellow fragrant flowers.

**josh** *slang* ● *verb* tease, make fun of. ● *noun* good-natured joke.

**joss** *noun* Chinese idol. □ **joss-stick** incense stick for burning.

**jostle** /'dʒɒs(ə)l/ ● *verb* (**-ling**) (often + *against*) knock; elbow; (+ *with*) struggle. ● *noun* jostling.

**jot** ● *verb* (**-tt-**) (usually + *down*) write briefly or hastily. ● *noun* very small amount.

**jotter** *noun* small pad or notebook.

**joule** /dʒuːl/ *noun* SI unit of work and energy.

**journal** /'dʒɜː(ə)l/ *noun* newspaper, periodical; daily record of events; diary; account book; part of shaft or axle resting on bearings.

**journalese** /dʒɜːnə'liːz/ *noun* hackneyed style of writing characteristic of newspapers.

**journalism** /'dʒɜːnəlɪz(ə)m/ *noun* work of journalist.

**journalist** /'dʒɜːnəlɪst/ *noun* person writing for or editing newspapers etc. □ **journalistic** /-'lɪs-/ *adjective*.

**journey** /'dʒɜːnɪ/ ● *noun* (*plural* **-s**) act of going from one place to another; distance travelled, time taken. ● *verb* (**-s**, **-ed**) make journey, travel. □ **journeyman** qualified mechanic or artisan working for another.

**joust** /dʒaʊst/ *historical* ● *noun* combat with lances between two mounted knights. ● *verb* engage in joust. □ **jouster** *noun*.

**jovial** /'dʒəʊvɪəl/ *adjective* merry, convivial, hearty. □ **joviality** /-'æl-/ *noun*; **jovially** *adverb*.

**jowl** /dʒaʊl/ *noun* jaw, jawbone; cheek; loose skin on throat.

**joy** *noun* gladness, pleasure; thing causing joy; *colloquial* satisfaction. □ **joyride** *colloquial* (go for) pleasure ride in esp. stolen car; **joystick** control column of aircraft, lever for moving image on VDU screen. □ **joyful** *adjective*; **joyfully** *adverb*; **joyfulness** *noun*; **joyless** *adjective*; **joyous** *adjective*; **joyously** *adverb*.

**JP** *abbreviation* Justice of the Peace.

**Jr.** *abbreviation* Junior.

**jubilant** /'dʒuːbɪlənt/ *adjective* exultant, rejoicing. □ **jubilantly** *adverb*; **jubilation** *noun*.

**jubilee** /'dʒuːbɪliː/ *noun* anniversary (esp. 25th or 50th); time of rejoicing.

**Judaic** /dʒu:'deɪɪk/ *adjective* of or characteristic of Jews.

**Judaism** /'dʒu:deɪɪz(ə)m/ *noun* religion of Jews.

**Judas** /'dʒu:dəs/ *noun* traitor.

**judder** /'dʒʌdə/ ● *verb* shake noisily or violently. ● *noun* juddering.

**judge** /dʒʌdʒ/ ● *noun* public official appointed to hear and try legal cases; person appointed to decide dispute or contest; person who decides question; person having judgement of specified type. ● *verb* (**-ging**) form opinion (about); estimate; act as judge (of); try legal case; (often + *to do, that*) conclude, consider.

**judgement** *noun* (also **judgment**) critical faculty, discernment, good sense; opinion; sentence of court of justice; *often jocular* deserved misfortune. □ **Judgement Day** day on which God will judge humankind. □ **judgemental** /-'men-/ *adjective*.

**judicature** /'dʒu:dɪkətʃə/ *noun* administration of justice; judge's position; judges collectively.

**judicial** /dʒu:'dɪʃ(ə)l/ *adjective* of, done by, or proper to court of law; of or proper to a judge; having function of judge; impartial. □ **judicially** *adverb*.

**judiciary** /dʒu:'dɪʃərɪ/ *noun* (*plural* **-ies**) judges collectively.

**judicious** /dʒu:'dɪʃəs/ *adjective* sensible, prudent. □ **judiciously** *adverb*.

**judo** /'dʒu:dəʊ/ *noun* sport derived from ju-jitsu.

**jug** ● *noun* deep vessel for liquids, with handle and lip; contents of this; *slang* prison. ● *verb* (**-gg-**) (usually as **jugged** *adjective*) stew (hare) in casserole. □ **jugful** *noun* (*plural* **-s**).

**juggernaut** /'dʒʌgənɔːt/ *noun* large heavy lorry; overwhelming force or object.

**juggle** /'dʒʌg(ə)l/ ● *verb* (**-ling**) (often + *with*) keep several objects in the air at once by throwing and catching; manipulate or rearrange (facts). ● *noun* juggling; fraud. □ **juggler** *noun*.

**jugular** /'dʒʌgjʊlə/ ● *adjective* of neck or throat. ● *noun* jugular vein. □ **jugular vein** any of large veins in neck carrying blood from head.

**juice** /dʒu:s/ *noun* liquid part of vegetable, fruit, or meat; animal fluid, esp. secretion; *colloquial* petrol, electricity.

**juicy** /'dʒu:sɪ/ *adjective* (**-ier, -iest**) full of juice; *colloquial* interesting, scandalous; *colloquial* profitable. □ **juicily** *adverb*.

**ju-jitsu** /dʒu:'dʒɪtsu:/ *noun* Japanese system of unarmed combat.

**ju-ju** /'dʒu:dʒu:/ *noun* (*plural* **-s**) charm or fetish of some W. African peoples; supernatural power attributed to this.

**jujube** /'dʒu:dʒu:b/ *noun* flavoured jelly-like lozenge.

**jukebox** /'dʒu:kbɒks/ *noun* coin-operated machine playing records or compact discs.

**Jul.** *abbreviation* July.

**julep** /'dʒu:lep/ *noun* sweet drink, esp. medicated; *US* spirits and water iced and flavoured.

**julienne** /dʒu:lɪ'en/ ● *noun* vegetables cut into thin strips. ● *adjective* cut into thin strips.

**Juliet cap** /'dʒu:lɪət/ *noun* small close-fitting cap worn by brides etc.

**July** /dʒu:'laɪ/ *noun* (*plural* **Julys**) seventh month of year.

**jumble** /'dʒʌmb(ə)l/ ● *verb* (**-ling**) (often + *up*) mix; confuse; muddle. ● *noun* confused heap etc.; muddle; articles in jumble sale. □ **jumble sale** sale of second-hand articles, esp. for charity.

**jumbo** /'dʒʌmbəʊ/ *noun* (*plural* **-s**) big animal (esp. elephant), person, or thing. □ **jumbo jet** large airliner for several hundred passengers, esp. Boeing 747.

**jump** ● *verb* spring from ground etc.; (often + *up, from, in, out,* etc.) rise or move suddenly; jerk from shock or excitement; pass over (obstacle) by jumping; (+ *to, at*) reach (conclusion) hastily; (of train etc.) leave (rails); pass (red traffic light); get on or off (train etc.) quickly, esp. illegally; attack (person) unexpectedly. ● *noun* act of jumping; sudden movement caused by shock etc.; abrupt rise in price, status, etc.; obstacle to be jumped, esp. by horse; gap in series etc. □ **jump at** accept eagerly; **jumped-up** *adjective* *colloquial* upstart; **jump the gun** start prematurely; **jump-jet** vertical take-off jet plane; **jump-lead** cable for carrying current from one battery to another; **jump-off** deciding round in show-jumping; **jump the queue** take unfair precedence; **jump ship** (of seaman) desert; **jump suit** one-piece garment for whole body; **jump to it** colloquial act promptly and energetically.

**jumper** /'dʒʌmpə/ noun knitted pullover; loose outer jacket worn by sailors; US pinafore dress.

**jumpy** adjective (**-ier, -iest**) nervous, easily startled. □ **jumpiness** noun.

**Jun.** abbreviation June; Junior.

**junction** /'dʒʌŋkʃ(ə)n/ noun joining-point; place where railway lines or roads meet. □ **junction box** box containing junction of electric cables etc.

**juncture** /'dʒʌŋktʃə/ noun point in time, esp. critical one; joining-point.

**June** noun sixth month of year.

**jungle** /'dʒʌŋg(ə)l/ noun land overgrown with tangled vegetation, esp. in tropics; tangled mass; place of bewildering complexity or struggle.

**junior** /'dʒuːnɪə/ ● adjective (often + to) lower in age, standing, or position; the younger (esp. after name); (of school) for younger pupils. ● noun junior person.

**juniper** /'dʒuːnɪpə/ noun prickly evergreen shrub or tree with purple berry-like cones.

**junk**¹ ● noun discarded articles, rubbish; anything regarded as of little value; slang narcotic drug, esp. heroin. ● verb discard as junk. □ **junk food** food which is not nutritious; **junk mail** unsolicited advertising sent by post.

**junk**² noun flat-bottomed sailing vessel in China seas.

**junket** /'dʒʌŋkɪt/ ● noun pleasure outing; official's tour at public expense; sweetened and flavoured milk curds; feast. ● verb (**-t-**) feast, picnic.

**junkie** /'dʒʌŋkɪ/ noun slang drug addict.

**junta** /'dʒʌntə/ noun (usually military) clique taking power after coup d'état.

**juridical** /dʒʊə'rɪdɪk(ə)l/ adjective of judicial proceedings, relating to the law.

**jurisdiction** /dʒʊərɪs'dɪkʃ(ə)n/ noun (often + over) administration of justice; legal or other authority; extent of this.

**jurisprudence** /dʒʊərɪs'pruːd(ə)ns/ noun science or philosophy of law.

**jurist** /'dʒʊərɪst/ noun expert in law. □ **juristic** /-'rɪs-/ adjective.

**juror** /'dʒʊərə/ noun member of jury.

**jury** /'dʒʊərɪ/ noun (plural **-ies**) group of people giving verdict in court of justice; judges of competition. □ **jury-box** enclosure in court for jury.

**just** ● adjective morally right, fair; deserved; well-grounded; justified. ● adverb exactly; very recently; barely; quite; colloquial simply, merely, positively. □ **just now** at this moment, a little time ago. □ **justly** adverb.

**justice** /'dʒʌstɪs/ noun fairness; authority exercised in maintenance of right; judicial proceedings; magistrate, judge. □ **do justice to** treat fairly, appreciate properly; **Justice of the Peace** lay magistrate.

**justify** /'dʒʌstɪfaɪ/ verb (**-ies, -ied**) show justice or truth of; (esp. in passive) be adequate grounds for, vindicate; Printing adjust (line of type) to fill space evenly; (as **justified** adjective) just, right. □ **justifiable** adjective; **justification** noun.

**jut** ● verb (**-tt-**) (often + out) protrude. ● noun projection.

**jute** /dʒuːt/ noun fibre from bark of E. Indian plant, used for sacking, mats, etc.; plant yielding this.

**juvenile** /'dʒuːvənaɪl/ ● adjective youthful; of or for young people; often derogatory immature. ● noun young person; actor playing juvenile part. □ **juvenile delinquency** offences committed by people below age of legal responsibility; **juvenile delinquent** such offender.

**juvenilia** /dʒuː'vəˈnɪlɪə/ plural noun youthful works of author or artist.

**juxtapose** /dʒʌkstə'pəʊz/ verb (**-sing**) put side by side; (+ with) put (thing) beside another. □ **juxtaposition** /-pə-'zɪʃ(ə)n/ noun.

# Kk

**K** *abbreviation* (also **K.**) kelvin(s); Köchel (list of Mozart's works); (also **k**) 1,000.

**k** *abbreviation* kilo-; knot(s).

**kaftan** = CAFTAN.

**kaiser** /ˈkaɪzə/ *noun historical* emperor, esp. of Germany or Austria.

**kale** *noun* variety of cabbage, esp. with wrinkled leaves.

**kaleidoscope** /kəˈlaɪdəskəʊp/ *noun* tube containing angled mirrors and pieces of coloured glass producing reflected patterns when shaken; constantly changing scene, group, etc. □ **kaleidoscopic** /-ˈskɒp-/ *adjective*.

**kalends** = CALENDS.

**kamikaze** /kæmɪˈkɑːzɪ/ ● *noun historical* explosive-laden Japanese aircraft deliberately crashed on to target in 1939–45 war; pilot of this. ● *adjective* reckless, esp. suicidal.

**kangaroo** /kæŋgəˈruː/ *noun* ( *plural* **-s**) Australian marsupial with strong hind legs for jumping. □ **kangaroo court** illegal court held by strikers, mutineers, etc.

**kaolin** /ˈkeɪəlɪn/ *noun* fine white clay used esp. for porcelain and in medicines.

**kapok** /ˈkeɪpɒk/ *noun* fine cotton-like material from tropical tree, used to stuff cushions etc.

**kaput** /kəˈpʊt/ *adjective slang* broken, ruined.

**karabiner** /kærəˈbiːnə/ *noun* coupling link used by mountaineers.

**karakul** /ˈkærəkʊl/ *noun* (also **caracul**) Asian sheep whose lambs have dark curled fleece; fur of this.

**karaoke** /kærɪˈəʊkɪ/ *noun* entertainment in nightclubs etc. with customers singing to backing music.

**karate** /kəˈrɑːtɪ/ *noun* Japanese system of unarmed combat.

**karma** /ˈkɑːmə/ *noun Buddhism & Hinduism* person's actions in one life, believed to decide fate in next; destiny.

**kauri** /kaʊˈrɪ/ *noun* ( *plural* **-s**) coniferous NZ timber tree.

**kayak** /ˈkaɪæk/ *noun* Eskimo one-man canoe.

**kazoo** /kəˈzuː/ *noun* toy musical instrument into which player sings wordlessly.

**KBE** *abbreviation* Knight Commander of the Order of the British Empire.

**kea** /ˈkiːə/ *noun* green and red NZ parrot.

**kebab** /kɪˈbæb/ *noun* pieces of meat and sometimes vegetables grilled on skewer.

**kedge** ● *verb* (**-ging**) move (ship) with hawser attached to small anchor. ● *noun* (in full **kedge-anchor**) small anchor for this purpose.

**kedgeree** /kedʒəˈriː/ *noun* dish of fish, rice, hard-boiled eggs, etc.

**keel** ● *noun* main lengthwise member of base of ship etc. ● *verb* (often + *over*) (cause to) fall down or over; turn keel upwards. □ **keelhaul** drag (person) under keel as punishment; **on an even keel** steady, balanced.

**keen**¹ *adjective* enthusiastic, eager; (often + *on*) enthusiastic about, fond of; intellectually acute; (of knife) sharp; (of price) competitive. □ **keenly** *adverb*. **keenness** *noun*.

**keen**² ● *noun* Irish wailing funeral song. ● *verb* (often + *over*, *for*) wail mournfully, esp. at funeral.

**keep** ● *verb* (*past & past participle* **kept**) have charge of; retain possession of; (+ *for*) retain or reserve (for future); maintain or remain in good or specified condition; restrain; detain; observe or respect (law, secret, etc.); own and look after (animal); clothe, feed, etc. (person); carry on (a business); maintain, guard, protect. ● *noun* maintenance, food; *historical* tower, stronghold. □ **for keeps** *colloquial* permanently; **keep at** (cause to) persist with; **keep away** (often + *from*) avoid, prevent from being near; **keep-fit** regular physical exercises; **keep off** (cause to) stay away from, abstain from, avoid; **keep**

**on** continue, (+ *at*) nag; **keep out** (cause to) stay outside; **keep up** maintain, prevent from going to bed, (often + *with*) not fall behind; **keep up with the Joneses** compete socially with neighbours.

**keeper** *noun* person who looks after or is in charge of an animal, person, or thing; custodian of museum, forest, etc.; wicket-keeper, goalkeeper; ring holding another on finger.

**keeping** *noun* custody, charge; (esp. in **in** or **out of keeping with**) agreement, harmony.

**keepsake** *noun* souvenir, esp. of person.

**keg** *noun* small barrel. □ **keg beer** beer kept in pressurized metal keg.

**kelp** *noun* large seaweed suitable for manure.

**kelpie** /ˈkelpɪ/ *noun Scottish* malevolent water-spirit; Australian sheepdog.

**Kelt** = CELT.

**kelter** = KILTER.

**kelvin** /ˈkelvɪn/ *noun* SI unit of temperature.

**ken** ● *noun* range of knowledge or sight. ● *verb* (**-nn-**; *past & past participle* **kenned** or **kent**) *Scottish & Northern English* recognize, know.

**kendo** /ˈkendəʊ/ *noun* Japanese fencing with bamboo swords.

**kennel** /ˈken(ə)l/ ● *noun* small shelter for dog; (in *plural*) breeding or boarding place for dogs. ● *verb* (**-ll-**; *US* **-l-**) put or keep in kennel.

**Kenyan** /ˈkenjən/ ● *adjective* of Kenya. ● *noun* native or national of Kenya.

**kept** *past & past participle* of KEEP.

**keratin** /ˈkerətɪn/ *noun* fibrous protein in hair, hooves, claws, etc.

**kerb** *noun* stone etc. edging to pavement etc. □ **kerb-crawling** *colloquial* driving slowly to pick up prostitute; **kerb drill** rules taught to children about crossing roads.

**kerfuffle** /kəˈfʌf(ə)l/ *noun colloquial* fuss, commotion.

**kermes** /ˈkɜːmɪz/ *noun* female of insect with berry-like appearance that feeds on **kermes oak**, evergreen oak; red dye made from these insects.

**kernel** /ˈkɜːn(ə)l/ *noun* (usually soft) edible centre within hard shell of nut, fruit stone, seed, etc.; central or essential part.

**kerosene** /ˈkerəsiːn/ *noun esp. US* fuel oil distilled from petroleum etc.; paraffin oil.

**kestrel** /ˈkestr(ə)l/ *noun* small hovering falcon.

**ketch** *noun* kind of two-masted sailing boat.

**ketchup** /ˈketʃəp/ *noun* (*US* **catsup** /ˈkætsəp/) spicy sauce made esp. from tomatoes.

**kettle** /ˈket(ə)l/ *noun* vessel for boiling water in. □ **kettledrum** large bowl-shaped drum.

**key** /kiː/ ● *noun* (*plural* **-s**) instrument for moving bolt of lock, operating switch, etc.; instrument for winding clock etc. or grasping screw, nut, etc.; finger-operated button or lever on typewriter, piano, computer terminal, etc.; explanation, word, or system for understanding list of symbols, code, etc.; *Music* system of related notes based on particular note; roughness of surface helping adhesion of plaster etc. ● *verb* fasten with pin, wedge, bolt, etc.; (often + *in*) enter (data) by means of (computer) keyboard; roughen (surface) to help adhesion of plaster etc. □ **keyed up** tense, excited; **keyhole** hole by which key is put into lock; **keynote** prevailing tone or idea, *Music* note on which key is based; **keypad** miniature keyboard etc. for telephone, portable computer, etc.; **keyring** ring for keeping keys on; **keystone** central principle of policy, system, etc., central stone of arch.

**keyboard** ● *noun* set of keys on typewriter, computer, piano, etc. ● *verb* enter (data) by means of keyboard. □ **keyboarder** *noun Computing*.

**KG** *abbreviation* Knight of the Order of the Garter.

**kg** *abbreviation* kilogram(s).

**KGB** *noun historical* secret police of USSR.

**khaki** /ˈkɑːkɪ/ ● *adjective* dull brownish-yellow. ● *noun* (*plural* **-s**) khaki colour, cloth, or uniform.

**khan** /kɑːn/ *noun: title of ruler or official in Central Asia.* □ **khanate** *noun.*

**kHz** *abbreviation* kilohertz.

**kibbutz** /kɪˈbʊts/ noun (plural **-im** /-iːm/) communal esp. farming settlement in Israel.

**kibosh** /ˈkaɪbɒʃ/ noun slang nonsense. □ **put the kibosh on** put an end to.

**kick** ● verb strike, strike out, or propel forcibly with foot or hoof; (often + at, against) protest, rebel; slang give up (habit); (often + out) expel, dismiss; (**kick oneself, could kick oneself**) be annoyed with oneself; score (goal) by kicking. ● noun kicking action or blow; recoil of gun; colloquial temporary enthusiasm, sharp stimulant effect; (often in plural) thrill. □ **kick about** drift idly, discuss informally; **kickback** recoil, payment esp. for illegal help; **kick the bucket** slang die; **kick off** verb begin football game, remove (shoes etc.) by kicking, colloquial start; **kick-off** noun start, esp. of football game; **kick-start(er)** (pedal on) device to start engine of motorcycle etc.; **kick up a fuss** colloquial create disturbance, object; **kick upstairs** get rid of by promotion.

**kid**[1] ● noun young goat; leather from this; colloquial child. ● verb (**-dd-**) (of goat) give birth to kid.

**kid**[2] verb (**-dd-**) colloquial deceive, tease. □ **no kidding** slang that is the truth.

**kidnap** /ˈkɪdnæp/ verb (**-pp-**; US **-p-**) carry off (person) illegally, esp. to obtain ransom. □ **kidnapper** noun.

**kidney** /ˈkɪdnɪ/ noun (plural **-s**) either of two organs serving to excrete urine; animal's kidney as food. □ **kidney bean** red-skinned kidney-shaped bean; **kidney machine** apparatus able to perform function of damaged kidney; **kidney-shaped** having one side concave and the other convex.

**kill** ● verb deprive of life or vitality; end; (**kill oneself**) colloquial overexert oneself, laugh heartily; colloquial overwhelm with amusement; switch off; pass (time) while waiting; Computing delete; Sport stop (ball) dead. ● noun (esp. in hunting) act of killing, animal(s) killed. □ **killjoy** depressing person; **kill off** destroy completely, bring about death of (fictional character).

**killer** noun person or thing that kills; murderer. □ **killer whale** dolphin with prominent dorsal fin.

**killing** ● noun causing death; colloquial great financial success. ● adjective colloquial very funny; exhausting.

**kiln** noun oven for burning, baking, or drying esp. pottery.

**kilo** /ˈkiːləʊ/ noun (plural **-s**) kilogram.

**kilo-** combining form one thousand.

**kilobyte** /ˈkɪləbaɪt/ noun Computing 1,024 bytes as measure of memory size etc.

**kilocalorie** /ˈkɪləkælərɪ/ noun large calorie (see CALORIE).

**kilocycle** /ˈkɪləsaɪk(ə)l/ noun historical kilohertz.

**kilogram** /ˈkɪləgræm/ noun SI unit of mass (2.205 lb).

**kilohertz** /ˈkɪləhɜːts/ noun 1,000 hertz.

**kilolitre** /ˈkɪlɪliːtə/ noun (US **-liter**) 1,000 litres.

**kilometre** /ˈkɪlɪmiːtə/ noun (US **-meter**) 1,000 metres (0.6214 mile).

■ Usage *Kilometre* is often pronounced /kɪˈlɒmɪtə/ (with the stress on the *-lom-*), but this is considered incorrect by some people.

**kiloton** /ˈkɪlətʌn/ noun (also **kilotonne**) unit of explosive power equal to that of 1,000 tons of TNT.

**kilovolt** /ˈkɪləvəʊlt/ noun 1,000 volts.

**kilowatt** /ˈkɪləwɒt/ noun 1,000 watts. □ **kilowatt-hour** electrical energy equal to 1 kilowatt used for 1 hour.

**kilt** ● noun pleated skirt usually of tartan, traditionally worn by Highland man. ● verb tuck up (skirts) round body; (esp. as **kilted** adjective) gather in vertical pleats.

**kilter** /ˈkɪltə/ noun (also **kelter** /ˈkeltə/) good working order.

**kimono** /kɪˈməʊnəʊ/ noun (plural **-s**) wide-sleeved Japanese robe; similar dressing gown.

**kin** ● noun one's relatives or family. ● adjective related.

**kind** /kaɪnd/ ● noun species, natural group of animals, plants, etc.; class, type, variety. ● adjective (often + to) friendly, benevolent. □ **in kind** in same form, (of payment) in goods etc. instead of money.

**kindergarten** /ˈkɪndəgɑːt(ə)n/ noun class or school for young children.

**kind-hearted** *adjective* of kind disposition. □ **kind-heartedly** *adverb*; **kind-heartedness** *noun*.

**kindle** /'kɪnd(ə)l/ *verb* (**-ling**) set on fire, light; inspire; become aroused or animated.

**kindling** /'kɪndlɪŋ/ *noun* small sticks etc. for lighting fires.

**kindly** /'kaɪndlɪ/ ● *adverb* in a kind way; please. ● *adjective* (**-ier, -iest**) kind; (of climate etc.) pleasant, mild.

**kindred** /'kɪndrɪd/ ● *adjective* related, allied, similar. ● *noun* blood relationship; one's relations.

**kinetic** /kɪ'netɪk/ *adjective* of or due to motion. □ **kinetic energy** energy of motion. □ **kinetically** *adverb*.

**king** *noun* (as title usually **King**) male sovereign, esp. hereditary; outstanding man or thing in specified field; largest kind of a thing; chess piece which must be checkmated for a win; crowned piece in draughts; court card depicting king; (**the King**) national anthem when sovereign is male. □ **King Charles spaniel** small black and tan kind; **kingcup** marsh marigold; **kingpin** main or large bolt, essential person or thing; **king-size(d)** large. □ **kingly** *adjective*; **kingship** *noun*.

**kingdom** *noun* state or territory ruled by king or queen; spiritual reign of God; domain; division of natural world. □ **kingdom come** *colloquial* the next world.

**kingfisher** *noun* small river bird with brilliant blue plumage, which dives for fish.

**kink** ● *noun* twist or bend in wire etc.; tight wave in hair; mental peculiarity. ● *verb* (cause to) form kink.

**kinky** *adjective* (**-ier, -iest**) *colloquial* sexually perverted or unconventional; (of clothing) bizarre and sexually provocative. □ **kinkily** *adverb*.

**kinship** *noun* blood relationship; similarity.

**kinsman** /'kɪnzmən/ *noun* (*feminine* **kinswoman**) blood relation.

**kiosk** /'kiːɒsk/ *noun* open-fronted booth selling newspapers, food, etc.; telephone box.

**kip** *slang* ● *noun* sleep, bed. ● *verb* (**-pp-**) (often + *down*) sleep.

**kipper** /'kɪpə/ ● *noun* fish, esp. herring, split, salted, dried, and usually smoked. ● *verb* treat (herring etc.) this way.

**kir** /kɪə/ *noun* dry white wine with blackcurrant liqueur.

**kirk** *noun* *Scottish & Northern English* church. □ **Kirk-session** lowest court in Church of Scotland.

**kirsch** /kɪəʃ/ *noun* spirit distilled from cherries.

**kismet** /'kɪzmet/ *noun* destiny.

**kiss** ● *verb* touch with lips, esp. as sign of love, reverence, etc.; touch lightly. ● *noun* touch of lips; light touch. □ **kiss-curl** small curl of hair on forehead or nape of neck; **kiss of life** mouth-to-mouth resuscitation.

**kisser** *noun* *slang* mouth; face.

**kissogram** *noun* novelty greeting delivered with kiss.

**kit** ● *noun* equipment, clothing, etc. for particular purpose; specialized, esp. sports, clothing or uniform; set of parts needed to assemble furniture, model, etc. ● *verb* (**-tt-**) supply; (often + *out*) equip with kit. □ **kitbag** usually cylindrical canvas etc. bag for carrying soldier's etc. kit.

**kitchen** /'kɪtʃɪn/ *noun* place where food is cooked; kitchen fitments. □ **kitchen garden** garden for growing fruit and vegetables.

**kitchenette** /kɪtʃɪ'net/ *noun* small kitchen or cooking area.

**kite** *noun* light framework with thin covering flown on long string in wind; soaring bird of prey.

**kith** /kɪθ/ *noun* □ **kith and kin** friends and relations.

**kitsch** /kɪtʃ/ *noun* vulgar, pretentious, or worthless art. ●

**kitten** /'kɪt(ə)n/ ● *noun* young cat, ferret, etc. ● *verb* give birth to (kittens).

**kittenish** *adjective* playful; flirtatious.

**kittiwake** /'kɪtɪweɪk/ *noun* kind of small seagull.

**kitty** [1] /'kɪtɪ/ *noun* (*plural* **-ies**) joint fund; pool in some card games.

**kitty** [2] /'kɪtɪ/ *noun* (*plural* **-ies**) *childish name for* kitten or cat.

**kiwi** /'kiːwiː/ *noun* flightless NZ bird; (**Kiwi**) *colloquial* New Zealander. □ **kiwi fruit** green-fleshed fruit.

**Klaxon** /'klæks(ə)n/ *noun proprietary term* horn, warning hooter.

**Kleenex** /'kli:neks/ *noun (plural same or -es) proprietary term* disposable paper handkerchief.

**kleptomania** /kleptə'meɪnɪə/ *noun* irresistible urge to steal. □ **kleptomaniac** /-nɪæk/ *adjective & noun.*

**km** *abbreviation* kilometre(s).

**knack** /næk/ *noun* acquired faculty of doing something skilfully; habit of action, speech, etc.

**knacker** /'nækə/ ● *noun* buyer of useless horses for slaughter. ● *verb slang* (esp. as **knackered** *adjective*) exhaust, wear out.

**knapsack** /'næpsæk/ *noun* soldier's or hiker's bag carried on back.

**knapweed** /'næpwi:d/ *noun* plant with thistle-like flower.

**knave** /neɪv/ *noun* rogue, scoundrel; jack (in playing cards). □ **knavery** *noun,* **knavish** *adjective.*

**knead** /ni:d/ *verb* work into dough, paste, etc., esp. by hand; make (bread, pottery) thus; massage.

**knee** /ni:/ ● *noun* joint between thigh and lower leg; lap of sitting person; part of garment covering knee. ● *verb* (**knees, kneed, kneeing**) touch or strike with knee. □ **kneecap** convex bone in front of knee; **knees-up** *colloquial* lively party or gathering.

**kneel** /ni:l/ *verb* (*past & past participle* **knelt**) rest or lower oneself on knee(s).

**kneeler** *noun* cushion for kneeling on.

**knell** /nel/ *noun* sound of bell, esp. for death or funeral; event etc. seen as bad omen.

**knelt** *past & past participle of* KNEEL.

**knew** *past of* KNOW.

**knickerbockers** /'nɪkəbɒkəz/ *plural noun* loose-fitting breeches gathered in at knee. □ **Knickerbocker Glory** ice cream and fruit in tall glass.

**knickers** /'nɪkəz/ *plural noun* woman's or girl's undergarment for lower torso.

**knick-knack** /'nɪknæk/ *noun* (also **nick-nack**) trinket, small ornament.

**knife** /naɪf/ ● *noun* (*plural* **knives**) cutting blade or weapon with long sharpened edge fixed in handle; cutting-blade in machine; (**the knife**) *colloquial* surgery. ● *verb* (**-fing**) cut or stab with knife. □ **knife-edge** edge of knife, position of extreme uncertainty; **knife-pleat** overlapping narrow flat pleat.

**knight** /naɪt/ ● *noun* man awarded non-hereditary title (*Sir*) by sovereign; *historical* man raised to honourable military rank; *historical* lady's champion in tournament etc.; chess piece usually in shape of horse's head. ● *verb* confer knighthood on. □ **knighthood** *noun,* **knightly** *adjective.*

**knit** /nɪt/ *verb* (**-tt-**; *past & past participle* **knitted** or **knit**) make (garment etc.) by interlocking loops of esp. wool with knitting-needles or knitting machine; make (plain stitch) in knitting; wrinkle (brow); (often + *together*) make or become close, (of broken bone) become joined. □ **knitwear** knitted garments.

**knitting** *noun* work being knitted. □ **knitting-needle** thin pointed rod used usually in pairs for knitting.

**knob** /nɒb/ *noun* rounded protuberance, e.g. door handle, radio control, etc.; small lump (of butter, coal, etc.). □ **knobby** *adjective.*

**knobbly** /'nɒblɪ/ *adjective* (**-ier, -iest**) hard and lumpy.

**knock** /nɒk/ ● *verb* strike with audible sharp blow; (often + *at*) strike (door etc.) for admittance; (usually + *in, off,* etc.) drive by striking; make (hole) by knocking; (of engine) make thumping etc. noise; *slang* criticize. ● *noun* audible sharp blow; rap, esp. at door. □ **knock about, around** treat roughly, wander about aimlessly, (usually + *with*) associate socially; **knock back** *slang* eat or drink, esp. quickly; **knock down** *verb* strike (esp. person) to ground, demolish, (usually + *to*) (at auction) sell to bidder, *colloquial* lower price of; **knock-down** *adjective* (of price) very low; **knock knees** legs curved inward at the knee; **knock-kneed** with knock knees; **knock off** strike off with blow, *colloquial* finish work, do or make rapidly, (often + *from*) deduct (amount) from price, *slang* steal, kill; **knock on the head** put end to (scheme etc.);

**knock on wood** *US* touch wood; **knock out** *verb* make unconscious by blow to head, defeat (boxer) by knocking down for count of 10, defeat in knockout competition, *colloquial* tire out; **knock-out** *noun* blow that knocks boxer out, competition in which loser of each match is eliminated, *slang* outstanding person or thing; **knock together** construct hurriedly; **knock up** *verb* make hastily, arouse by knock at door, practise tennis etc. before formal game begins, *US slang* make pregnant; **knock-up** *noun* practice at tennis etc.

**knocker** *noun* hinged metal device on door for knocking with.

**knoll** /nəʊl/ *noun* small hill, mound.

**knot** /nɒt/ ● *noun* intertwining of rope, string, etc. so as to fasten; set method of this; tangle in hair, knitting, etc.; unit of ship's or aircraft's speed equal to one nautical mile per hour; hard mass formed in tree trunk where branch grows out; round cross-grained piece in board caused by this; (usually + *of*) cluster. ● *verb* (**-tt-**) tie in knot; entangle. □ **knotgrass** wild plant with creeping stems and pink flowers; **knot-hole** hole in timber where knot has fallen out.

**knotty** *adjective* (**-ier, -iest**) full of knots; puzzling.

**know** /nəʊ/ *verb* (*past* **knew** /njuː/; *past participle* **known**) (often + *that, how, what*, etc.) have in the mind, have learnt; be acquainted with; recognize, identify; (often + *from*) be able to distinguish; (as **known** *adjective*) publicly acknowledged. □ **in the know** having inside information; **know-how** practical knowledge or skill.

**knowing** *adjective* cunning; showing knowledge, shrewd.

**knowingly** *adverb* in a knowing way; consciously, intentionally.

**knowledge** /ˈnɒlɪdʒ/ *noun* (usually + *of*) awareness, familiarity, person's range of information, understanding (of subject); sum of what is known.

**knowledgeable** *adjective* (also **knowledgable**) well-informed, intelligent. □ **knowledgeably** *adverb*.

**known** *past participle* of KNOW.

**knuckle** /ˈnʌk(ə)l/ ● *noun* bone at finger-joint; knee- or ankle-joint of quadruped; this as joint of meat. ● *verb* (**-ling**) strike, rub, etc. with knuckles. □ **knuckle down** (often + *to*) apply oneself earnestly; **knuckleduster** metal guard worn over knuckles in fighting, esp. to inflict greater damage; **knuckle under** give in, submit.

**KO** *abbreviation* knockout.

**koala** /kəʊˈɑːlə/ *noun* (in full **koala bear**) small Australian bearlike marsupial with thick grey fur.

**kohl** /kəʊl/ *noun* black powder used as eye make-up, esp. in Eastern countries.

**kohlrabi** /kəʊlˈrɑːbɪ/ *noun* (*plural* **-bies**) cabbage with edible turnip-like stem.

**kookaburra** /ˈkʊkəbʌrə/ *noun* Australian kingfisher with strange laughing cry.

**Koran** /kɔːˈrɑːn/ *noun* Islamic sacred book.

**Korean** /kəˈriːən/ ● *noun* native or national of N. or S. Korea; language of Korea. ● *adjective* of Korea or its people or language.

**kosher** /ˈkəʊʃə/ ● *adjective* (of food or food-shop) fulfilling requirements of Jewish law; *colloquial* correct, genuine. ● *noun* kosher food or shop.

**kowtow** /kaʊˈtaʊ/ ● *noun historical* Chinese custom of touching ground with forehead, esp. in submission. ● *verb* (usually + *to*) act obsequiously; perform kowtow.

**k.p.h.** *abbreviation* kilometres per hour.

**kraal** /krɑːl/ *noun South African* village of huts enclosed by fence; enclosure for cattle etc.

**kremlin** /ˈkremlɪn/ *noun* citadel within Russian town; (**the Kremlin**) that in Moscow, Russian government.

**krill** *noun* tiny plankton crustaceans eaten by whales etc.

**krugerrand** /ˈkruːɡərænd/ *noun* S. African gold coin.

**krummhorn** /ˈkrʌmhɔːn/ *noun* (also **crumhorn**) medieval wind instrument.

**krypton** /ˈkrɪptɒn/ *noun* gaseous element used in lamps etc.

**Kt.** *abbreviation* Knight.

**kts.** *abbreviation* knots.

**kudos** /'kju:dɒs/ *noun colloquial* glory, renown.

**kumquat** /'kʌmkwɒt/ *noun* (also **cumquat**) small orange-like fruit.

**kung fu** /kʌŋ 'fu:/ *noun* Chinese form of karate.

**kV** *abbreviation* kilovolt(s).

**kW** *abbreviation* kilowatt(s).

**kWh** *abbreviation* kilowatt-hour(s).

# Ll

**L¹** *noun* (also **l**) (Roman numeral) 50.

**L²** *abbreviation* Lake. □ **L-plate** sign bearing letter L, attached to vehicle to show that driver is learner.

**l** *abbreviation* left; line; litre(s).

**LA** *abbreviation* Los Angeles.

**la** = LAH.

**Lab.** *abbreviation* Labour.

**lab** *noun colloquial* laboratory.

**label** /'leɪb(ə)l/ ● *noun* piece of paper attached to object to give information about it; classifying phrase etc.; logo, title, or trademark of company. ● *verb* (-**ll**-; *US* -**l**-) attach label to; (usually + *as*) assign to category.

**labial** /'leɪbɪəl/ ● *adjective* of lips; *Phonetics* pronounced with (closed) lips. ● *noun Phonetics* labial sound.

**labium** /'leɪbɪəm/ *noun* (*plural* **labia**) each fold of skin of pairs enclosing vulva.

**labor** etc. *US & Australian* = LABOUR etc.

**laboratory** /lə'bɒrətərɪ/ *noun* (*plural* -**ies**) place used for scientific experiments and research.

**laborious** /lə'bɔːrɪəs/ *adjective* needing hard work; (esp. of literary style) showing signs of effort. □ **laboriously** *adverb*.

**labour** /'leɪbə/ (*US & Australian* **labor**) ● *noun* physical or mental work, exertion; workers, esp. as political force; (**Labour**) the Labour Party; process of giving birth; task. ● *verb* work hard, exert oneself; elaborate needlessly; proceed with difficulty; (as **laboured** *adjective*) done with great effort; (+ *under*) suffer because of. □ **labour**

**camp** prison camp enforcing hard labour; **Labour Exchange** *colloquial or historical* jobcentre; **Labour Party** political party formed to represent workers' interests; **labour-saving** designed to reduce or eliminate work.

**labourer** *noun* (*US* **laborer**) person doing unskilled paid manual work.

**Labrador** /'læbrədɔː/ *noun* dog of retriever breed with black or golden coat.

**laburnum** /lə'bɜːnəm/ *noun* tree with drooping golden flowers and poisonous seeds.

**labyrinth** /'læbərɪnθ/ *noun* complicated network of passages; intricate or tangled arrangement. □ **labyrinthine** /-'rɪnθaɪn/ *adjective*.

**lac** *noun* resinous substance from SE Asian insect, used to make varnish and shellac.

**lace** ● *noun* open patterned fabric or trimming made by twisting, knotting, or looping threads; cord etc. passed through eyelets or hooks for fastening shoes etc. ● *verb* (-**cing**) (usually + *up*) fasten or tighten with lace(s); add spirits to (drink); (+ *through*) pass (shoelace etc.) through. □ **lace-up** shoe fastened with lace.

**lacerate** /'læsəreɪt/ *verb* (-**ting**) tear (esp. flesh etc.) roughly; wound (feelings etc.). □ **laceration** *noun*.

**lachrymal** /'lækrɪm(ə)l/ *adjective* (also **lacrimal**) of tears.

**lachrymose** /'lækrɪməʊs/ *adjective formal* often weeping; tearful.

**lack** ● *noun* (usually + *of*) deficiency, want. ● *verb* be without or deficient in.

□ **lacklustre** (*US* **lackluster**) dull, lacking in vitality etc.

**lackadaisical** /ˌlækəˈdeɪzɪk(ə)l/ *adjective* languid; unenthusiastic.

**lackey** /ˈlækɪ/ *noun* (*plural* **-s**) servile follower; footman, manservant.

**lacking** *adjective* undesirably absent; ( + *in*) deficient in.

**laconic** /ləˈkɒnɪk/ *adjective* using few words. □ **laconically** *adverb*.

**lacquer** /ˈlækə/ ● *noun* hard shiny shellac or synthetic varnish; substance sprayed on hair to keep it in place. ● *verb* coat with lacquer.

**lacrimal** = LACHRYMAL.

**lacrosse** /ləˈkrɒs/ *noun* hockey-like game played with ball carried in net at end of stick.

**lactate** /lækˈteɪt/ *verb* (**-ting**) (of mammals) secrete milk. □ **lactation** *noun*.

**lactic** /ˈlæktɪk/ *adjective* of milk.

**lactose** /ˈlæktəʊs/ *noun* sugar present in milk.

**lacuna** /ləˈkjuːnə/ *noun* (*plural* **-s** or **-nae** /-niː/) missing part, esp. in manuscript; gap.

**lacy** /ˈleɪsɪ/ *adjective* (**-ier**, **-iest**) like lace fabric.

**lad** *noun* boy, youth; *colloquial* man.

**ladder** /ˈlædə/ ● *noun* set of horizontal bars fixed at intervals between two uprights for climbing up and down; unravelled stitching in stocking etc.; means of advancement in career etc. ● *verb* cause or develop ladder in (stocking etc.).

**lade** *verb* (**-ding**; *past participle* **laden**) load (ship); ship (goods); (as **laden** *adjective*) (usually + *with*) loaded, burdened.

**la-di-da** /ˌlɑːdɪˈdɑː/ *adjective colloquial* pretentious or affected, esp. in manner or speech.

**ladle** /ˈleɪd(ə)l/ ● *noun* deep long-handled spoon for serving liquids. ● *verb* (**-ling**) (often + *out*) transfer with ladle.

**lady** /ˈleɪdɪ/ *noun* (*plural* **-ies**) woman regarded as having superior status or refined manners; *polite form of address for woman*; *colloquial* wife, girlfriend; (**Lady**) title used before name of peeresses, peers' female relatives, etc.; (**Ladies**) women's public lavatory. □ **ladybird**

small beetle, usually red with black spots; **Lady chapel** chapel dedicated to Virgin Mary; **Lady Day** Feast of the Annunciation, 25 Mar.; **ladylike** like or appropriate to lady.

**Ladyship** *noun* □ **Her** or **Your Ladyship** *title used of or to Lady*.

**lag**[1] ● *verb* (**-gg-**) fall behind; not keep pace. ● *noun* delay.

**lag**[2] *verb* (**-gg-**) enclose (boiler etc.) with heat-insulating material.

**lag**[3] *noun slang* habitual convict.

**lager** /ˈlɑːgə/ *noun* kind of light beer. □ **lager lout** *colloquial* youth behaving violently through drinking too much.

**laggard** /ˈlægəd/ *noun* person lagging behind.

**lagging** *noun* insulating material for boiler etc.

**lagoon** /ləˈguːn/ *noun* salt-water lake separated from sea by sandbank, reef, etc.

**lah** *noun* (also **la**) *Music* sixth note of scale in tonic sol-fa.

**laid** *past & past participle* of LAY[1]. □ **laid-back** relaxed, easy-going.

**lain** *past participle* of LIE[1].

**lair** *noun* wild animal's home; person's hiding place.

**laird** /leəd/ *noun Scottish* landed proprietor.

**laissez-faire** /ˌleɪseɪˈfeə/ *noun* (also **laisser-faire**) policy of not interfering. [French]

**laity** /ˈleɪɪtɪ/ *noun* lay people, as distinct from clergy.

**lake**[1] *noun* large body of water surrounded by land. □ **Lake District** region of lakes in Cumbria.

**lake**[2] *noun* reddish pigment originally made from lac.

**lam** *verb* (**-mm-**) *slang* hit hard, thrash.

**lama** /ˈlɑːmə/ *noun* Tibetan or Mongolian Buddhist monk.

**lamasery** /ˈlɑːməsərɪ/ *noun* (*plural* **-ies**) lama monastery.

**lamb** /læm/ ● *noun* young sheep; its flesh as food; gentle, innocent, or weak person. ● *verb* (of sheep) give birth.

**lambaste** /læmˈbeɪst/ *verb* (**-ting**) (also **lambast** /-ˈbæst/) *colloquial* thrash, beat.

**lambent** /ˈlæmbənt/ *adjective* (of flame etc.) playing on a surface; (of eyes, wit, etc.) gently brilliant. □ **lambency** *noun*.

**lambswool** *noun* soft fine wool from young sheep.

**lame** ● *adjective* disabled in foot or leg; (of excuse etc.) unconvincing; (of verse etc.) halting. ● *verb* (**-ming**) make lame, disable. □ **lame duck** helpless person or firm. □ **lamely** *adverb*; **lameness** *noun*.

**lamé** /ˈlɑːmeɪ/ *noun* fabric with gold or silver thread woven in.

**lament** /ləˈment/ ● *noun* passionate expression of grief; song etc. of mourning. ● *verb* express or feel grief for or about; utter lament; (as **lamented** *adjective*) recently dead. □ **lamentation** /læmən-/ *noun*.

**lamentable** /ˈlæməntəb(ə)l/ *adjective* deplorable, regrettable. □ **lamentably** *adverb*.

**lamina** /ˈlæmɪnə/ *noun* ( *plural* **-nae** /-niː/) thin plate or layer. □ **laminar** *adjective*.

**laminate** ● *verb* /ˈlæmɪneɪt/ (**-ting**) beat or roll into thin plates; overlay with plastic layer etc.; split into layers. ● *noun* /ˈlæmɪnət/ laminated structure, esp. of layers fixed together. □ **lamination** *noun*.

**lamp** *noun* device for giving light from electricity, gas, oil, etc.; apparatus producing esp. ultraviolet or infrared radiation. □ **lamppost** post supporting street light; **lampshade** usually partial cover for lamp.

**lampoon** /læmˈpuːn/ ● *noun* satirical attack on person etc. ● *verb* satirize. □ **lampoonist** *noun*.

**lamprey** /ˈlæmprɪ/ *noun* ( *plural* **-s**) eel-like fish with sucker mouth.

**Lancastrian** /læŋˈkæstrɪən/ ● *noun* native of Lancashire or Lancaster. ● *adjective* of Lancashire or Lancaster; of House of Lancaster in Wars of Roses.

**lance** /lɑːns/ ● *noun* long spear, esp. one used by horseman. ● *verb* (**-cing**) prick or open with lancet. □ **lance-corporal** army NCO below corporal.

**lanceolate** /ˈlɑːnsɪələt/ *adjective* shaped like spearhead, tapering to each end.

**lancer** /ˈlɑːnsə/ *noun historical* soldier of cavalry regiment originally armed with lances; (in *plural*) quadrille.

**lancet** /ˈlɑːnsɪt/ *noun* small broad two-edged surgical knife with sharp point.

**land** ● *noun* solid part of earth's surface; ground, soil, expanse of country; region, state; landed property; (in *plural*) estates. ● *verb* set or go ashore; bring (aircraft) down; alight on ground etc.; bring (fish) to land; often + *up* bring to or arrive at certain situation or place; *colloquial* deal (person etc. a blow etc.); (+ *with*); present (person) with (problem etc.); *colloquial* win (prize, appointment, etc.). □ **landfall** approach to land after sea or air journey; **landfill** waste material used to landscape or reclaim land, disposing of waste in this way; **landlady** woman owning rented property or keeping pub, guest-house, etc.; **landlocked** (almost) enclosed by land; **landlord** man owning rented property or keeping pub, guest-house, etc.; **landlubber** person unfamiliar with sea and ships; **landmark** conspicuous object, notable event; **land-mine** explosive mine laid in or on ground; **landslide** sliding down of mass of land from cliff or mountain, overwhelming majority in election.

**landau** /ˈlændɔː/ *noun* ( *plural* **-s**) 4-wheeled enclosed carriage with divided top.

**landed** *adjective* owning or consisting of land.

**landing** /ˈlændɪŋ/ *noun* platform or passage at top of or part way up stairs. □ **landing-craft** craft used for putting troops and equipment ashore; **landing-gear** undercarriage of aircraft; **landing-stage** platform for disembarking passengers and goods.

**landscape** /ˈlændskeɪp/ ● *noun* scenery in area of land; picture of this. ● *verb* (**-ping**) improve (piece of land) by **landscape gardening**, laying out of grounds to resemble natural scenery.

**lane** *noun* narrow road; division of road for one line of traffic; strip of track or water for competitor in race; regular course followed by ship or aircraft.

**language** /ˈlæŋgwɪdʒ/ *noun* use of words in agreed way as means of human communication; system of words of particular community, country, etc.; faculty of speech; style of expression;

system of symbols and rules for computer programs. □ **language laboratory** room with tape recorders etc. for learning foreign language.

**languid** /ˈlæŋgwɪd/ *adjective* lacking vigour; idle. □ **languidly** *adverb*.

**languish** /ˈlæŋgwɪʃ/ *verb* lose or lack vitality. □ **languish for** long for; **languish under** live under (depression etc.).

**languor** /ˈlæŋgə/ *noun* lack of energy; idleness; soft or tender mood or effect. □ **languorous** *adjective*.

**lank** *adjective* (of grass, hair, etc.) long and limp; thin and tall.

**lanky** *adjective* (**-ier**, **-iest**) ungracefully thin and long or tall.

**lanolin** /ˈlænəlɪn/ *noun* fat from sheep's wool used in cosmetics, ointments, etc.

**lantern** /ˈlænt(ə)n/ *noun* lamp with transparent case protecting flame etc.; glazed structure on top of dome or room; light-chamber of lighthouse. □ **lantern jaws** long thin jaws.

**lanyard** /ˈlænjəd/ *noun* cord round neck or shoulder for holding knife etc.; *Nautical* short rope.

**lap**[1] *noun* front of sitting person's body from waist to knees; clothing covering this. □ **lap-dog** small pet dog; **laptop** (microcomputer) suitable for use while travelling.

**lap**[2] ● *noun* one circuit of racetrack etc.; section of journey etc.; amount of overlap. ● *verb* (**-pp-**) overtake (competitor in race who is a lap behind); (often + *about*, *around*) fold or wrap (garment etc.).

**lap**[3] ● *verb* (**-pp-**) (esp. of animal) drink by scooping with tongue; (usually + *up*, *down*) drink greedily; (usually + *up*) receive (gossip, praise, etc.) eagerly; (of waves etc.) ripple; make lapping sound against (shore). ● *noun* act or sound of lapping.

**lapel** /ləˈpel/ *noun* part of coat-front folded back.

**lapidary** /ˈlæpɪdərɪ/ ● *adjective* concerned with stones; engraved on stone; concise, well-expressed. ● *noun* (*plural* **-ies**) cutter, polisher, or engraver of gems.

**lapis lazuli** /ˌlæpɪs ˈlæzjʊlɪ/ *noun* bright blue gem; its colour.

**lapse** /læps/ ● *noun* slight error; slip of memory etc.; weak or careless decline into inferior state. ● *verb* (**-sing**) fail to maintain position or standard; (+ *into*) fall back into (inferior or previous state); (of right etc.) become invalid.

**lapwing** /ˈlæpwɪŋ/ *noun* plover with shrill cry.

**larceny** /ˈlɑːsənɪ/ *noun* (*plural* **-ies**) theft of personal property. □ **larcenous** *adjective*.

**larch** *noun* deciduous coniferous tree with bright foliage; its wood.

**lard** ● *noun* pig fat used in cooking etc. ● *verb* insert strips of bacon in (meat etc.) before cooking; (+ *with*) embellish (talk etc.) with (strange terms etc.).

**larder** *noun* room or cupboard for storing food.

**lardy-cake** *noun* cake made with lard, currants, etc.

**large** *adjective* of relatively great size or extent; of larger kind; comprehensive. □ **at large** at liberty, as a body or whole; **large as life** in person, esp. prominently. □ **largeness** *noun*; **largish** *adjective*.

**largely** *adverb* to a great extent.

**largesse** /lɑːˈʒes/ *noun* (also **largess**) money or gifts freely given.

**largo** /ˈlɑːgəʊ/ *Music* ● *adverb* & *adjective* in slow time and dignified style. ● *noun* (*plural* **-s**) largo movement or passage.

**lariat** /ˈlærɪət/ *noun* lasso; rope for tethering animal.

**lark**[1] *noun* small bird with tuneful song, esp. skylark.

**lark**[2] *colloquial* ● *noun* frolic; amusing incident; type of activity. ● *verb* (+ *about*) play tricks.

**larkspur** *noun* plant with spur-shaped calyx.

**larva** /ˈlɑːvə/ *noun* (*plural* **-vae** /-viː/) insect in stage between egg and pupa. □ **larval** *adjective*.

**laryngeal** /ləˈrɪndʒɪəl/ *adjective* of the larynx.

**laryngitis** /ˌlærɪnˈdʒaɪtɪs/ *noun* inflammation of larynx.

**larynx** /ˈlærɪŋks/ *noun* (*plural* **larynges** /ləˈrɪndʒiːz/ or **-xes**) cavity in throat holding vocal cords.

**lasagne** /ləˈsænjə/ *noun* pasta sheets.

**lascivious** /ləˈsɪvɪəs/ adjective lustful.
□ **lasciviously** adverb.

**laser** /ˈleɪzə/ noun device producing intense beam of special kind of light.
□ **laser printer** printing machine using laser to produce image.

**lash** ● verb make sudden whiplike movement; beat with whip; (often + against, down) (of rain etc.) beat, strike; criticize harshly; rouse, incite; (often + together, down) fasten with rope etc. ● noun sharp blow with whip etc.; flexible part of whip; eyelash.
□ **lash out** speak or hit out angrily, colloquial spend money extravagantly.

**lashings** plural noun colloquial (often + of) plenty.

**lass** noun esp. Scottish & Northern English or poetical girl.

**lassitude** /ˈlæsɪtjuːd/ noun languor; disinclination to exert oneself.

**lasso** /læˈsuː/ ● noun (plural -s or -es) rope with running noose used esp. for catching cattle. ● verb (-es, -ed) catch with lasso.

**last**[1] /lɑːst/ ● adjective after all others; coming at end; most recent; only remaining. ● adverb after all others; on most recent occasion. ● noun last, last-mentioned, or most recent person or thing; last mention, sight, etc.; end; death. □ **at (long) last** in the end, after much delay; **the last straw** slight addition to task etc. making it unbearable.

**last**[2] /lɑːst/ verb remain unexhausted, adequate, or alive for specified or long time. □ **last out** be sufficient for whole of given period.

**last**[3] /lɑːst/ noun shoemaker's model for shaping shoe etc. □ **stick to one's last** keep to what one understands.

**lasting** adjective permanent, durable.

**lastly** adverb finally.

**lat.** abbreviation latitude.

**latch** ● noun bar with catch as fastening of gate etc.; spring-lock as fastening of outer door. ● verb fasten with latch.
□ **latchkey** key of outer door; **latch on to** colloquial attach oneself to, understand.

**late** ● adjective after due or usual time; far on in day, night, period, etc.; flowering, ripening, etc. towards end of season; no longer alive or having specified status; of recent date. ● adverb after due or usual time; far on in time; at or till late hour; at late stage of development; formerly but not now. □ **late in the day** at late stage of proceedings etc.
□ **lateness** noun.

**lateen sail** /ləˈtiːn/ noun triangular sail on long yard at angle of 45° to mast.

**lately** adverb not long ago; recently.

**latent** /ˈleɪt(ə)nt/ adjective existing but not developed or manifest; concealed, dormant. □ **latency** noun.

**lateral** /ˈlætər(ə)l/ ● adjective of, at, towards, or from side(s). ● noun lateral shoot or branch. □ **lateral thinking** method of solving problems by indirect or illogical methods. □ **laterally** adverb.

**latex** /ˈleɪteks/ noun milky fluid of esp. rubber tree; synthetic substance like this.

**lath** /lɑːθ/ noun thin flat strip of wood.

**lathe** /leɪð/ noun machine for shaping wood, metal, etc. by rotating article against cutting tools.

**lather** /ˈlɑːðə/ ● noun froth made by agitating soap etc. and water; frothy sweat; state of agitation. ● verb (of soap) form lather; cover with lather; colloquial thrash.

**Latin** /ˈlætɪn/ ● noun language of ancient Rome. ● adjective of or in Latin; of countries or peoples speaking languages developed from Latin; of RC Church.
□ **Latin America** parts of Central and S. America where Spanish or Portuguese is main language.

**Latinate** /ˈlætɪneɪt/ adjective having character of Latin.

**latitude** /ˈlætɪtjuːd/ noun angular distance N. or S. of equator; (usually in plural) regions, climes; freedom from restriction in action or opinion.

**latrine** /ləˈtriːn/ noun communal lavatory, esp. in camp.

**latter** /ˈlætə/ ● adjective second-mentioned of two; nearer the end. ● noun (the latter) the latter thing or person.
□ **latter-day** modern, contemporary.

**latterly** adverb recently; in latter part of life or period.

**lattice** /ˈlætɪs/ noun structure of crossed laths or bars with spaces between, used as fence, screen, etc.; arrangement resembling this. □ **lattice window** one with small panes set in lead. □ **latticed** adjective.

**Latvian** /'lætvɪən/ ● noun native, national, or language of Latvia. ● adjective of Latvia.

**laud** /lɔːd/ verb praise, extol.

**laudable** adjective praiseworthy. □ **laudably** adverb.

**laudanum** /'lɔːdənəm/ noun solution prepared from opium.

**laudatory** /'lɔːdətərɪ/ adjective praising.

**laugh** /lɑːf/ ● verb make sounds etc. usual in expressing amusement, scorn, etc.; express by laughing; (+ at) make fun of, ridicule. ● noun sound or act of laughing; colloquial comical person or thing. □ **laugh off** shrug off (embarrassment etc.) by joking.

**laughable** adjective amusing; ridiculous. □ **laughably** adverb.

**laughing** noun laughter. □ **laughing gas** nitrous oxide as anaesthetic; **laughing jackass** kookaburra; **laughing stock** object of general derision. □ **laughingly** adverb.

**laughter** /'lɑːftə/ noun act or sound of laughing.

**launch**[1] /lɔːntʃ/ ● verb set (vessel) afloat; hurl or send forth (rocket etc.); start or set in motion (enterprise, person, etc.); formally introduce (new product) with publicity; (+ into) make start on; (+ out) make start on new enterprise. ● noun launching. □ **launch pad** platform with structure for launching rockets from.

**launch**[2] /lɔːntʃ/ noun large motor boat.

**launder** /'lɔːndə/ verb wash and iron etc. (clothes etc.); colloquial transfer (money) to conceal its origin.

**launderette** /lɔːn'dret/ noun (also **laundrette**) establishment with coin-operated washing machines and driers for public use.

**laundress** /'lɔːndrɪs/ noun woman who launders.

**laundry** /'lɔːndrɪ/ noun (plural **-ies**) place where clothes etc. are laundered; clothes etc. that need to be or have been laundered.

**laurel** /'lɒr(ə)l/ noun any of various kinds of shrub with dark green glossy leaves; (in singular or plural) wreath of bay-leaves

as emblem of victory or poetic merit. □ **look to one's laurels** beware of losing one's pre-eminence; **rest on one's laurels** stop seeking further success.

**lava** /'lɑːvə/ noun matter flowing from volcano and solidifying as it cools.

**lavatorial** /lævə'tɔːrɪəl/ adjective of or like lavatories; (esp. of humour) relating to excretion.

**lavatory** /'lævətərɪ/ noun (plural **-ies**) receptacle for urine and faeces, usually with means of disposal; room etc. containing this.

**lave** verb (**-ving**) literary wash, bathe; wash against; flow along.

**lavender** /'lævɪndə/ noun evergreen fragrant-flowered shrub; its dried flowers used to scent linen; pale purplish colour. □ **lavender-water** light perfume.

**laver** /'leɪvə/ noun kind of edible seaweed.

**lavish** /'lævɪʃ/ ● adjective profuse; abundant; generous. ● verb (often + on) bestow or spend (money, praise, etc.) abundantly. □ **lavishly** adverb.

**law** noun rule or set of rules established in a community, demanding or prohibiting certain actions; such rules as social system or branch of study; binding force; (**the law**) legal profession, colloquial police; law courts, legal remedy; science or philosophy of law; statement of regularity of natural occurrences. □ **law-abiding** obedient to the laws; **law court** court of law; **Law Lord** member of House of Lords qualified to perform its legal work; **lawsuit** bringing of claim etc. before law court; **lay down the law** give dogmatic opinions; **take the law into one's own hands** get one's rights without help of the law.

**lawful** adjective permitted, appointed, or recognized by law; not illegal. □ **lawfully** adverb; **lawfulness** noun.

**lawless** adjective having no laws; disregarding laws. □ **lawlessness** noun.

**lawn**[1] noun piece of close-mown grass in garden etc. □ **lawnmower** machine for cutting lawns; **lawn tennis** tennis played with soft ball on grass or hard court.

**lawn**[2] noun kind of fine linen or cotton.

**lawyer** /'lɔɪə/ noun person practising law, esp. solicitor.

**lax** *adjective* lacking care or precision; not strict. □ **laxity** *noun*; **laxly** *adverb*; **laxness** *noun*.

**laxative** /ˈlæksətɪv/ ● *adjective* helping evacuation of bowels. ● *noun* laxative medicine.

**lay**[1] ● *verb* (*past & past participle* **laid**) place on surface, esp. horizontally; put or bring into required position or state; make by laying; (of bird) produce (egg); cause to subside or lie flat; (usually + *on*) attribute (blame etc.); make ready (trap, plan); prepare (table) for meal; put fuel ready to light (fire); put down as bet. ● *noun* way, position, or direction in which something lies. □ **lay bare** expose, reveal; **lay-by** extra strip beside road where vehicles may park; **lay claim to** claim as one's own; **lay down** relinquish, make (rule), store (wine) in cellar, sacrifice (one's life); **lay in** provide oneself with stock of; **lay into** *colloquial* attack violently with blows or verbally; **lay it on thick** or **with a trowel** *colloquial* flatter, exaggerate grossly; **lay off** discharge (workers) temporarily, *colloquial* desist; **lay on** provide, spread on; **lay out** spread, expose to view, prepare (body) for burial, *colloquial* knock unconscious, expend (money); **layout** way in which land, building, printed matter, etc., is arranged or set out; **lay up** store, save (money), (as **laid up** *adjective*) confined to bed or the house; **lay waste** ravage, destroy.

■ **Usage** It is incorrect in standard English to use *lay* to mean 'lie', as in *She was laying on the floor.*

**lay**[2] *adjective* not ordained into the clergy; not professionally qualified; of or done by such people. □ **layman**, **laywoman** person not in holy orders, one without professional or special knowledge; **lay reader** lay person licensed to conduct some religious services.

**lay**[3] *noun* short poem meant to be sung; song.

**lay**[4] *past* of LIE[1].

**layer** ● *noun* thickness of matter, esp. one of several, covering surface; hen that lays eggs. ● *verb* arrange in layers; propagate (plant) by fastening shoot down to take root.

**layette** /leɪˈet/ *noun* clothes etc. prepared for newborn child.

**lay figure** *noun* artist's jointed wooden model of human figure; unrealistic character in novel etc.

**laze** ● *verb* (**-zing**) spend time idly. ● *noun* spell of lazing.

**lazy** *adjective* (**-ier**, **-iest**) disinclined to work, doing little work; of or inducing idleness. □ **lazybones** *colloquial* lazy person. □ **lazily** *adverb*; **laziness** *noun*.

**lb** *abbreviation* pound(s) weight.

■ **Usage** It is a common mistake to write *lbs* as an abbreviation for *pounds*. *28 lb* is correct.

**l.b.w.** *abbreviation* leg before wicket.

**l.c.** *abbreviation* loc. cit.; lower case.

**LCD** *abbreviation* liquid crystal display.

**L/Cpl** *abbreviation* Lance-Corporal.

**LEA** *abbreviation* Local Education Authority.

**lea** *noun poetical* meadow, field.

**leach** *verb* make (liquid) percolate through some material; subject (bark, ore, ash, soil) to this; (usually + *away*, *out*) remove (soluble matter) or be removed in this way.

**lead**[1] /liːd/ ● *verb* (*past & past participle* **led**) conduct, esp. by going in front; direct actions or opinions of; (often + *to*) guide by persuasion; provide access to; pass or spend (life etc.) in; have first place in; go or be first; play (card) as first player in trick; (+ *to*) result in; (+ *with*) (of newspapers or broadcast) have as main story. ● *noun* guidance, example; leader's place; amount by which competitor is ahead of others; clue; strap etc. for leading dog etc.; *Electricity* conductor carrying current to place of use; chief part in play etc.; *Cards* act or right of playing first. □ **lead by the nose** make (someone) do all one wishes them to; **lead-in** introduction, opening; **lead on** entice dishonestly; **lead up the garden path** *colloquial* mislead; **lead up to** form preparation for, direct conversation towards.

**lead**[2] /led/ ● *noun* heavy soft grey metal; graphite used in pencils; lump of lead used in sounding; blank space between lines of print. ● *verb* cover, frame, or space with lead(s). □ **lead-free** (of petrol) without added lead compounds.

**leaded** /'ledɪd/ *adjective* (of petrol) with added lead compounds; (of window pane) framed with lead.

**leaden** /'led(ə)n/ *adjective* of or like lead; heavy, slow; lead-coloured.

**leader**/'liːdə/ *noun* person or thing that leads; leading performer in orchestra, quartet, etc.; leading article. □ **leadership** *noun*.

**leading**/'liːdɪŋ/ *adjective* chief, most important. □ **leading aircraftman** one ranking just below NCO in RAF; **leading article** newspaper article giving editorial opinion; **leading light** prominent influential person; **leading note** *Music* seventh note of ascending scale; **leading question** one prompting the answer wanted.

■ Usage *Leading question* does not mean a 'principal' or 'loaded' or 'searching' question.

**leaf** ● *noun* (*plural* **leaves**) flat usually green part of plant growing usually on stem; foliage; single thickness of paper, esp. in book; very thin sheet of metal etc.; hinged part, extra section, or flap of table etc. ● *verb* (of plants etc.) begin to grow leaves; (+ *through*) turn over pages of (book etc.). □ **leaf-mould** soil composed chiefly of decaying leaves. □ **leafage** *noun*; **leafy** *adjective* (**-ier, -iest**).

**leaflet** /'liːflɪt/ *noun* sheet of paper, pamphlet, etc., giving information; young leaf.

**league**[1] /liːg/ ● *noun* people, countries, etc., joining together for particular purpose; group of sports clubs who contend for championship; class of contestants. ● *verb* (**-gues, -gued, -guing**) (often + *together*) join in league. □ **in league** allied, conspiring; **league table** list in order of success.

**league**[2] /liːg/ *noun* archaic measure of travelling distance, usually about 3 miles.

**leak** ● *noun* hole through which liquid etc. passes accidentally in or out; liquid etc. thus passing through; similar escape of electric charge; disclosure of secret information. ● *verb* (let) pass out or in through leak; disclose (secret); (often + *out*) become known. □ **leaky** *adjective* (**-ier, -iest**).

**leakage** *noun* action or result of leaking.

**lean**[1] ● *verb* (*past & past participle* **leaned** or **leant** /lent/) (often + *across, back, over*, etc.) be or place in sloping position; (usually + *against, on*) rest for support against; (usually + *on, upon*) rely, depend; (usually + *to, towards*) be inclined or partial. ● *noun* inclination, slope. □ **lean on** *colloquial* put pressure on (person) to act in certain way; **lean-to** building with roof resting against larger building or wall.

**lean**[2] ● *adjective* (of person etc.) having no superfluous fat; (of meat) containing little fat; meagre. ● *noun* lean part of meat. □ **lean years** time of scarcity. □ **leanness** *noun*.

**leaning** *noun* tendency or inclination.

**leap** ● *verb* (*past & past participle* **leaped** or **leapt** /lept/) jump, spring forcefully. ● *noun* forceful jump. □ **by leaps and bounds** with very rapid progress; **leap-frog** game in which player vaults with parted legs over another bending down; **leap year** year with 29 Feb. as extra day.

**learn** /lɜːn/ *verb* (*past & past participle* **learned** /lɜːnt, lɜːnd/ or **learnt**) get knowledge of or skill in by study, experience, or being taught; commit to memory; (usually + *of, about*) be told about, find out.

**learned** /'lɜːnɪd/ *adjective* having much knowledge from studying; showing or requiring learning.

**learner** *noun* person learning, beginner; (in full **learner driver**) person who is learning to drive but has not yet passed driving test.

**learning** *noun* knowledge got by study.

**lease** /liːs/ ● *noun* contract by which owner of land or building allows another to use it for specified time, usually for rent. ● *verb* (**-sing**) grant or take on lease. □ **leasehold** holding of property by lease; **leaseholder** *noun*; **new lease of** (*US* **on**) **life** improved prospect of living, or of use after repair.

**leash** ● *noun* strap for holding dog(s). ● *verb* put leash on; restrain. □ **straining at the leash** eager to begin.

**least** ● *adjective* smallest, slightest. ● *noun* least amount. ● *adverb* in the least degree. □ **at least** at any rate; **to say the least** putting the case moderately.

**leather** /'leðə/ ● *noun* material made from skin of animal by tanning etc.; piece of leather for cleaning esp. windows; *slang* cricket ball, football. ● *verb* beat, thrash; cover or polish with leather. □ **leather-jacket** larva of crane-fly.

**leatherette** /leðə'ret/ *noun* imitation leather.

**leathery** *adjective* like leather; tough.

**leave**[1] *verb* (**-ving**; *past & past participle* **left**) go away (from); cause or allow to remain; depart without taking; cease to reside at, belong to, work for, etc.; abandon; (usually + *to*) commit to another person; bequeath; deposit or entrust (object, message, etc.) to be dealt with in one's absence; not consume or deal with. □ **leave off** come to or make an end, stop; **leave out** omit.

**leave**[2] *noun* permission; (in full **leave of absence**) permission to be absent from duty; period for which this lasts. □ **on leave** absent thus; **take one's leave of** say goodbye to.

**leaven** /'lev(ə)n/ ● *noun* substance used to make dough ferment and rise; transforming influence. ● *verb* ferment (dough) with leaven; permeate, transform.

**leavings** *plural noun* what is left.

**Lebanese** /lebə'ni:z/ ● *adjective* of Lebanon. ● *noun* (*plural* same) native or national of Lebanon.

**lecher** /'letʃə/ *noun* lecherous man.

**lecherous** *adjective* lustful. □ **lecherously** *adverb*; **lechery** *noun*.

**lectern** /'lekt(ə)n/ *noun* stand for holding Bible etc. in church; similar stand for lecturer etc.

**lecture** /'lektʃə/ ● *noun* talk giving information to class etc.; admonition, reprimand. ● *verb* (**-ring**) (often + *on*) deliver lecture(s); admonish, reprimand.

**lecturer** *noun* person who lectures, esp. as teacher in higher education.

**lectureship** *noun* university post as lecturer.

**led** *past & past participle* of LEAD[1].

**ledge** *noun* narrow shelf or projection from vertical surface.

**ledger** /'ledʒə/ *noun* book in which firm's accounts are kept.

**lee** *noun* shelter given by neighbouring object; side of thing away from the wind. □ **leeway** allowable deviation, drift of ship to leeward.

**leech** *noun* bloodsucking worm formerly used medicinally for bleeding; person who sponges on others.

**leek** *noun* vegetable of onion family with long cylindrical white bulb.

**leer** ● *verb* look slyly, lasciviously, or maliciously. ● *noun* leering look.

**leery** *adjective* (**-ier, -iest**) *slang* knowing, sly; (usually + *of*) wary.

**lees** /li:z/ *plural noun* sediment of wine etc.; dregs.

**leeward** /'li:wəd, *Nautical* 'lu:əd/ ● *adjective & adverb* on or towards sheltered side. ● *noun* this direction.

**left**[1] ● *adjective* on or towards west side of person or thing facing north; (also **Left**) *Politics* of the Left. ● *adverb* on or to left side. ● *noun* left part, region, or direction; *Boxing* left hand, blow with this; (often **Left**) *Politics* group favouring socialism, radicals collectively. □ **left-hand** on left side; **left-handed** naturally using left hand for writing etc.; made by or for left hand, turning to left, (of screw) turned anti-clockwise to tighten, awkward, clumsy, (of compliment etc.) ambiguous; **left-handedness** *noun*; **left-hander** left-handed person or blow; **left wing** more radical section of political party, left side of army, football team, etc.; **left-wing** socialist, radical; **left-winger** member of left wing. □ **leftward** *adjective & adverb*; **leftwards** *adverb*.

**left**[2] *past & past participle* of LEAVE[1].

**leg** *noun* each of limbs on which person or animal walks and stands; leg of animal as food; part of garment covering leg; support of chair, table, etc.; section of journey, race, competition, etc.; *Cricket* half of field behind batsman's back. □ **leg before wicket** *Cricket* (of batsman) declared out for illegal obstruction of ball that would have hit wicket; **leg it** (**-gg-**) *colloquial* walk or run hard; **leg warmer** either of pair of tubular knitted garments covering leg from ankle to thigh; **pull (person's) leg** deceive playfully. □ **legged** adjective.

**legacy** /'legəsɪ/ noun (plural **-ies**) gift left by will; anything handed down by predecessor.

**legal** /'li:g(ə)l/ adjective of, based on, or concerned with law; appointed, required, or permitted by law. □ **legal aid** state help with cost of legal advice; **legal tender** currency that cannot legally be refused in payment of debt. □ **legality** /lɪ'gælɪtɪ/ noun; **legally** adverb.

**legalize** /'li:gəlaɪz/ verb (also **-ise**) (**-zing** or **-sing**) make lawful; bring into harmony with law. □ **legalization** noun.

**legate** /'legət/ noun papal ambassador.

**legatee** /legə'ti:/ noun recipient of legacy.

**legation** /lɪ'geɪʃ(ə)n/ noun diplomatic minister and his or her staff; this minister's official residence.

**legato** /lɪ'gɑːtəʊ/ Music ● adverb & adjective in smooth flowing manner. ● noun (plural **-s**) legato passage.

**legend** /'ledʒ(ə)nd/ noun traditional story, myth; colloquial famous or remarkable person or event; inscription; explanation on map etc. of symbols used.

**legendary** adjective existing in legend; colloquial remarkable, famous.

**legerdemain** /ledʒədə'meɪn/ noun sleight of hand; trickery, sophistry.

**leger line** /'ledʒə/ noun Music short line added for notes above or below range of staff.

**legging** noun (usually in plural) close-fitting trousers for women or children; outer covering of leather etc. for lower leg.

**leggy** adjective (**-ier**, **-iest**) long-legged; long-stemmed and weak.

**legible** /'ledʒɪb(ə)l/ adjective easily read. □ **legibility** noun; **legibly** adverb.

**legion** /'li:dʒ(ə)n/ ● noun division of 3,000–6,000 men in ancient Roman army; other large organized body. ● adjective great in number.

**legionary** ● adjective of legions. ● noun (plural **-ies**) member of legion.

**legionnaire** /li:dʒə'neə/ noun member of foreign legion. □ **legionnaires' disease** form of bacterial pneumonia.

**legislate** /'ledʒɪsleɪt/ verb (**-ting**) make laws. □ **legislator** noun.

**legislation** noun making laws; laws made.

**legislative** /'ledʒɪslətɪv/ adjective of or empowered to make legislation.

**legislature** /'ledʒɪsleɪtʃə/ noun legislative body of a state.

**legitimate** /lɪ'dʒɪtɪmət/ adjective (of child) born of parents married to one another; lawful, proper, regular; logically admissible. □ **legitimacy** noun; **legitimately** adverb.

**legitimize** /lɪ'dʒɪtɪmaɪz/ verb (also **-ise**) (**-zing** or **-sing**) make legitimate; serve as justification for. □ **legitimization** noun.

**legume** /'legju:m/ noun leguminous plant; edible part of this.

**leguminous** /lɪ'gju:mɪnəs/ adjective of the family of plants with seeds in pods, e.g. peas and beans.

**lei** /'leɪ/ noun Polynesian garland of flowers.

**leisure** /'leʒə/ noun free time, time at one's own disposal. □ **at leisure** not occupied, in an unhurried way; **at one's leisure** when one has time; **leisure centre** public building with sports facilities etc.; **leisurewear** informal clothes, esp. sportswear.

**leisured** adjective having ample leisure.

**leisurely** ● adjective relaxed, unhurried. ● adverb without hurry.

**leitmotif** /'laɪtməʊti:f/ noun (also **leitmotiv**) recurring theme in musical etc. composition representing particular person, idea, etc.

**lemming** /'lemɪŋ/ noun Arctic rodent reputed to rush, during migration, in large numbers into sea and drown.

**lemon** /'lemən/ noun acid yellow citrus fruit; tree bearing it; pale yellow colour. □ **lemon cheese**, **curd** thick creamy lemon spread. □ **lemony** adjective.

**lemonade** /lemə'neɪd/ noun drink made from lemons; synthetic substitute for this, often fizzy.

**lemon sole** /'lemən/ noun (plural same or **-s**) fish of plaice family.

**lemur** /'li:mə/ noun tree-dwelling primate of Madagascar.

**lend** *verb* (*past & past participle* **lent**) grant temporary use of (thing); allow use of (money) in return for interest; bestow, contribute; (**lend itself to**) be suitable for. □ **lend an ear** listen. □ **lender** *noun*.

**length** *noun* measurement from end to end; extent in or of time; length of horse, boat, etc. as measure of lead in race; long stretch or extent; degree of thoroughness in action. □ **at length** in detail, after a long time. □ **lengthways** *adverb*; **lengthwise** *adverb & adjective*.

**lengthen** *verb* make or become longer.

**lengthy** *adjective* (**-ier, -iest**) of unusual length, prolix, tedious.

**lenient** /'liːnɪənt/ *adjective* merciful, not severe, mild. □ **lenience** *noun*; **leniency** *noun*; **leniently** *adverb*.

**lens** /lenz/ *noun* piece of transparent substance with one or both sides curved, used in spectacles, telescopes, cameras, etc.; combination of lenses used in photography.

**Lent** *noun* religious period of fasting and penitence from Ash Wednesday to Easter Eve. □ **Lenten** *adjective*.

**lent** *past & past participle of* LEND.

**lentil** /'lentɪl/ *noun* edible seed of leguminous plant; this plant.

**lento** /'lentəʊ/ *Music* ● *adjective* slow. ● *adverb* slowly. ● *noun* lento movement or passage.

**Leo** /'liːəʊ/ *noun* fifth sign of zodiac.

**leonine** /'liːənaɪn/ *adjective* lionlike; of lions.

**leopard** /'lepəd/ *noun* large animal of cat family with dark-spotted fawn or all black coat, panther.

**leotard** /'liːətɑːd/ *noun* close-fitting one-piece garment worn by dancers etc.

**leper** /'lepə/ *noun* person with leprosy.

**leprechaun** /'leprəkɔːn/ *noun* small mischievous sprite in Irish folklore.

**leprosy** /'leprəsɪ/ *noun* contagious disease of skin and nerves. □ **leprous** *adjective*.

**lesbian** /'lezbɪən/ ● *noun* homosexual woman. ● *adjective* of homosexuality in women. □ **lesbianism** *noun*.

**lesion** /'liːʒ(ə)n/ *noun* damage; injury; change in part of body due to injury or disease.

**less** ● *adjective* smaller; of smaller quantity; not so much. ● *adverb* to smaller extent, in lower degree. ● *noun* smaller amount, quantity, or number. ● *preposition* minus, deducting.

■ **Usage** The use of *less* to mean 'fewer', as in *There are less people than yesterday*, is incorrect in standard English.

**lessee** /le'siː/ *noun* (often + *of*) person holding property by lease.

**lessen** /'les(ə)n/ *verb* diminish.

**lesser** *adjective* not so great as the other(s).

**lesson** /'les(ə)n/ *noun* period of teaching; (in *plural*, usually + *in*) systematic instruction; thing learnt by pupil; experience that serves to warn or encourage; passage from Bible read aloud during church service.

**lessor** /le'sɔː/ *noun* person who lets property by lease.

**lest** *conjunction* in order that not, for fear that.

**let**¹ ● *verb* (**-tt-**; *past & past participle* **let**) allow, enable, or cause to; grant use of (rooms, land, etc.) for rent or hire. ● *auxiliary verb* in exhortations, commands, assumptions, etc. ● *noun* act of letting. □ **let alone** not to mention; **let be** not interfere with; **let down** *verb* lower, fail to support or satisfy, disappoint; **let-down** *noun* disappointment; **let go** release, lose hold of; **let in** allow to enter, (usually + *for*) involve (person, often oneself) in loss, problem, etc., (usually + *on*) allow (person) to share secret etc.; **let off** fire (gun), cause (steam etc.) to escape, not punish or compel; **let on** *colloquial* reveal secret; **let out** *verb* reléase, reveal (secret etc.), slacken, put out to rent; **let-out** *noun* *colloquial* opportunity to escape; **let up** *verb* *colloquial* become less severe, diminish; **let-up** *noun* *colloquial* relaxation of effort, diminution.

**let**² *noun* obstruction of ball or player in tennis etc. after which ball must be served again. □ **without let or hindrance** unimpeded.

**lethal** /'liːθ(ə)l/ *adjective* causing or sufficient to cause death. □ **lethally** *adverb*.

**lethargy** /'leθədʒɪ/ noun lack of energy; unnatural sleepiness. □ **lethargic** /lɪ-'θɑːdʒɪk/ adjective; **lethargically** /lɪ'θɑːdʒ-ɪkəlɪ/ adverb.

**letter** /'letə/ ● noun character representing one or more of sounds used in speech; written or printed communication, usually sent in envelope by post; precise terms of statement; (in plural) literature. ● verb inscribe letters on; classify with letters. □ **letter bomb** terrorist explosive device sent by post; **letter box** box for delivery or posting of letters, slit in door for delivery of letters; **letterhead** printed heading on stationery; **letterpress** printed words in illustrated book, printing from raised type; **to the letter** keeping to every detail.

**lettuce** /'letɪs/ noun plant with crisp leaves used in salad.

**leucocyte** /'luːkəsaɪt/ noun white blood cell.

**leukaemia** /luː'kiːmɪə/ noun (US **leukemia**) malignant progressive disease in which too many white blood cells are produced.

**Levant** /lɪ'vænt/ noun (**the Levant**) archaic East-Mediterranean region.

**Levantine** /'levəntaɪn/ ● adjective of or trading to the Levant. ● noun native or inhabitant of the Levant.

**levee** /'levɪ/ noun US embankment against river floods.

**level** /'lev(ə)l/ ● noun horizontal line or plane; height or value reached; position on real or imaginary scale; social, moral, or intellectual standard; plane of rank or authority; instrument giving line parallel to plane of horizon; level surface, flat country. ● adjective flat, not bumpy; horizontal; (often + with) on same horizontal plane as something else, having equality with something else; even, uniform, well-balanced. ● verb (**-ll-**; US **-l-**) make level; raze, completely destroy; (usually + at) aim (gun etc.); (usually + at, against) direct (accusation etc.). □ **do one's level best** colloquial do one's utmost; **find one's level** reach right social, intellectual, etc., position; **level crossing** crossing of road and railway etc. at same level; **level-headed** mentally well-balanced, cool; **level pegging**

equality of scores etc.; **on the level** colloquial truthfully, honestly.

**lever** /'liːvə/ ● noun bar pivoted about fulcrum to transfer force; bar used on pivot to prise or lift; projecting handle used to operate mechanism; means of exerting moral pressure. ● verb use lever; lift, move, etc. (as) with lever.

**leverage** noun action or power of lever; means of accomplishing a purpose.

**leveret** /'levərɪt/ noun young hare.

**leviathan** /lɪ'vaɪəθ(ə)n/ noun Biblical sea monster; very large or powerful thing.

**Levis** /'liːvaɪz/ plural noun proprietary term type of (originally blue) denim jeans.

**levitate** /'levɪteɪt/ verb (**-ting**) (cause to) rise and float in air. □ **levitation** noun.

**levity** /'levɪtɪ/ noun lack of serious thought; frivolity.

**levy** /'levɪ/ ● verb (**-ies, -ied**) impose or collect (payment etc.) compulsorily; enrol (troops etc.). ● noun (plural **-ies**) levying; payment etc. or (in plural) troops levied.

**lewd** /ljuːd/ adjective lascivious, indecent.

**lexical** /'leksɪk(ə)l/ adjective of the words of a language; (as) of a lexicon.

**lexicography** /leksɪ'kɒgrəfɪ/ noun compiling of dictionaries. □ **lexicographer** noun.

**lexicon** /'leksɪkən/ noun dictionary.

**Leyden jar** /'laɪd(ə)n/ noun early kind of capacitor.

**LF** abbreviation low frequency.

**liability** /laɪə'bɪlɪtɪ/ noun (plural **-ies**) being liable; troublesome person or thing; handicap; (in plural) debts for which one is liable.

**liable** /'laɪəb(ə)l/ adjective legally bound; (+ to) subject to; (+ to do) under an obligation; (+ to) exposed or open to (something undesirable); (+ for) answerable for.

■ **Usage** Liable is often used to mean 'likely', as in It is liable to rain, but this is considered incorrect by some people.

**liaise** /lɪ'eɪz/ verb (**-sing**) (usually + with, between) colloquial establish cooperation; act as link.

**liaison** /lɪ'eɪzɒn/ noun communication, cooperation; illicit sexual relationship.

**liana** /lɪ'ɑːnə/ noun climbing plant in tropical forests.

**liar** /'laɪə/ noun person who tells lies.

**Lib.** abbreviation Liberal.

**lib** noun colloquial liberation.

**libation** /laɪ'beɪʃ(ə)n/ noun (pouring out of) drink-offering to a god.

**libel** /'laɪb(ə)l/ ● noun Law published false statement damaging to person's reputation, publishing of this; false defamatory statement. ● verb (**-ll-**; US **-l-**) Law publish libel against. □ **libellous** adjective.

**liberal** /'lɪbər(ə)l/ ● adjective abundant; giving freely; generous; open-minded; not rigorous; (of studies) for general broadening of mind; Politics favouring moderate reforms. ● noun person of liberal views, esp. (**Liberal**) member of a Liberal Party. □ **Liberal Democrat** member of **Liberal Democrats**, UK political party. □ **liberalism** noun; **liberality** /-'ræl-/ noun; **liberally** adverb.

**liberalize** verb (also **-ise**) (**-zing** or **-sing**) make or become more liberal or less strict. □ **liberalization** noun.

**liberate** /'lɪbəreɪt/ verb (**-ting**) (often + from) set free; free (country etc.) from aggressor; (as **liberated** adjective) (of person etc.) freed from oppressive social conventions. □ **liberation** noun; **liberator** noun.

**libertine** /'lɪbətiːn/ noun licentious person.

**liberty** /'lɪbətɪ/ noun (plural **-ies**) being free, freedom; right or power to do as one pleases; (in plural) privileges granted by authority. □ **at liberty** free, (+ to do) permitted; **take liberties** (often + with) behave in unacceptably familiar way.

**libidinous** /lɪ'bɪdɪnəs/ adjective lustful.

**libido** /lɪ'biːdəʊ/ noun (plural **-s**) psychic impulse or drive, esp. that associated with sex instinct. □ **libidinal** /lɪ'bɪdɪn(ə)l/ adjective.

**Libra** /'liːbrə/ noun seventh sign of zodiac.

**librarian** /laɪ'breərɪən/ noun person in charge of or assistant in library. □ **librarianship** noun.

**library** /'laɪbrərɪ/ noun (plural **-ies**) a collection of books, films, records, etc.; room or building etc. where these are kept; series of books issued in similar bindings.

**libretto** /lɪ'bretəʊ/ noun (plural **-ti** /-tɪ/ or **-s**) text of opera etc. □ **librettist** noun.

**lice** plural of LOUSE.

**licence** /'laɪs(ə)ns/ noun (US **license**) official permit to own, use, or do, something, or carry on trade; permission; excessive liberty of action; writer's etc. deliberate deviation from fact.

**license** /'laɪs(ə)ns/ ● verb (**-sing**) grant licence to; authorize use of (premises) for certain purpose. ● noun US = LICENCE.

**licensee** /laɪsən'siː/ noun holder of licence, esp. to sell alcoholic liquor.

**licentiate** /laɪ'senʃɪət/ noun holder of certificate of professional competence.

**licentious** /laɪ'senʃəs/ adjective sexually promiscuous.

**lichee** = LYCHEE.

**lichen** /'laɪkən/ noun plant composed of fungus and alga in association, growing on rocks, trees, etc.

**lich-gate** /'lɪtʃgeɪt/ noun (also **lychgate**) roofed gateway of churchyard.

**licit** /'lɪsɪt/ adjective formal lawful, permitted.

**lick** ● verb pass tongue over; bring into specified condition by licking; (of flame etc.) play lightly over; colloquial thrash, defeat. ● noun act of licking with tongue; colloquial pace, speed; smart blow. □ **lick one's lips**, **chops** look forward with great pleasure.

**licorice** = LIQUORICE.

**lid** noun hinged or removable cover, esp. at top of container; eyelid. □ **put the lid on** colloquial be the culmination of, put stop to. □ **lidded** adjective.

**lido** /'liːdəʊ/ noun (plural **-s**) public open-air swimming pool or bathing beach.

**lie**[1] /laɪ/ ● verb (**lying**; past **lay**; past participle **lain**) be in or assume horizontal position on supporting surface; (of thing) rest on flat surface; remain undisturbed or undiscussed; be kept, remain, or be in specified place etc.; (of abstract things) be in certain relation; be situated or spread out to view etc. ● noun way, position, or direction in which something lies. □ **lie in** stay in bed late in morning; **lie-in** *noun*; **lie low** keep quiet or unseen; **lie of the land** state of affairs.

■ **Usage** It is incorrect in standard English to use *lie* to mean 'lay', as in *lie her on the bed*.

**lie**[2] /laɪ/ ● *noun* intentional false statement; something that deceives. ● *verb* (**lies, lied, lying**) tell lie(s); (of thing) be deceptive. □ **give the lie to** show the falsity of.

**lied** /liːd/ *noun* (*plural* **lieder**) German song of Romantic period for voice and piano.

**liege** /liːdʒ/ *historical* ● *adjective* entitled to receive, or bound to give, feudal service or allegiance. ● *noun* (in full **liege lord**) feudal superior; (usually in *plural*) vassal, subject.

**lien** /ˈliːən/ *noun* Law right to hold another's property till debt on it is paid.

**lieu** /ljuː/ *noun* □ **in lieu** instead; (+ *of*) in place of.

**Lieut.** *abbreviation* Lieutenant.

**lieutenant** /lefˈtenənt/ *noun* army officer next below captain; naval officer next below lieutenant commander; deputy. □ **lieutenant colonel, commander, general** officers ranking next below colonel etc. □ **lieutenancy** *noun* (*plural* **-ies**).

**life** *noun* (*plural* **lives**) capacity for growth, functional activity, and continual change until death; living things and their activity; period during which life lasts; period from birth to present time or from present time to death; duration of thing's existence or ability to function; person's state of existence; living person; business and pleasures of the world; energy, liveliness; biography; *colloquial* imprisonment for life. □ **life assurance** life insurance; **lifebelt** buoyant ring to keep person afloat; **lifeblood** blood as necessary to life, vital factor or influence; **lifeboat** boat for rescues at sea, ship's boat for emergency use; **lifebuoy** buoyant support to keep person afloat; **life cycle** series of changes in life of organism; **lifeguard** expert swimmer employed to rescue bathers from drowning; **Life Guards** regiment of royal household cavalry; **life insurance**

insurance which makes payment on death of insured person; **life-jacket** buoyant jacket to keep person afloat; **lifeline** rope etc. used for life-saving, sole means of communication or transport; **life peer** peer whose title lapses on death; **life sentence** imprisonment for life; **life-size(d)** of same size as person or thing represented; **lifestyle** way of life; **life-support machine** respirator; **lifetime** duration of person's life.

**lifeless** *adjective* dead; unconscious; lacking movement or vitality. □ **lifelessly** *adverb*.

**lifelike** *adjective* closely resembling life or person or thing represented.

**lifer** *noun* *slang* person serving life sentence.

**lift** ● *verb* (often + *up, of,* etc.) raise to higher position, go up, be raised; yield to upward force; give upward direction to (eyes etc.); add interest to; (of fog etc.) rise, disperse; remove (barrier etc.); transport supplies, troops, etc. by air; *colloquial* steal, plagiarize. ● *noun* lifting; ride in another person's vehicle; apparatus for raising and lowering people or things to different floors of building, or for carrying people up or down mountain etc.; transport by air; upward pressure on aerofoil; supporting or elevating influence; elated feeling. □ **lift-off** vertical take-off of spacecraft or rocket.

**ligament** /ˈlɪgəmənt/ *noun* band of tough fibrous tissue linking bones.

**ligature** /ˈlɪgətʃə/ *noun* tie, bandage; *Music* slur, tie; *Printing* two or more letters joined, e.g. æ.

■ **Usage** *Ligature*, in the *Printing* sense, is sometimes confused with *digraph*, which means 'two letters representing one sound'.

**light**[1] /laɪt/ ● *noun* electromagnetic radiation that stimulates sight and makes things visible; appearance of brightness; source of light; (often in *plural*) traffic light; flame, spark, or device for igniting; aspect in which thing is regarded; mental or spiritual illumination; vivacity, esp. in person's eyes. ● *verb* (*past* **lit**; *past participle* **lit** or **lighted**) set burning, begin to burn; (often +

up) give light to; make prominent by light; show (person) way etc. with light; (usually + up) (of face or eyes) brighten with pleasure etc. ● *adjective* well-provided with light, not dark; (of colour) pale. □ **bring** or **come to light** reveal or be revealed; **in the light of** taking account of; **light bulb** glass bulb containing metal filament giving light when current is passed through it; **lighthouse** tower with beacon light to warn or guide ships at sea; **lightship** anchored ship with beacon light; **light year** distance light travels in one year.

**light²** /laɪt/ ● *adjective* not heavy; relatively low in weight, amount, density, or intensity; (of railway) suitable for small loads; carrying only light arms; (of food) easy to digest; (of music etc.) intended only as entertainment; not profound; (of sleep or sleeper) easily disturbed; easily done; nimble; cheerful. ● *adverb* lightly; with light load. ● *verb* (*past & past participle* **lit** or **lighted**) (+ *on*, *upon*) come upon or find by chance. □ **light-fingered** given to stealing; **light flyweight** amateur boxing weight (up to 48 kg); **light-headed** giddy, delirious; **light-hearted** cheerful; **light heavyweight** amateur boxing weight (75–81 kg); **light industry** manufacture of small or light articles; **light middleweight** amateur boxing weight (67–71 kg); **lightweight** *adjective* below average weight, of little importance, *noun* lightweight person or thing, amateur boxing weight (57–60kg); **light welterweight** amateur boxing weight (60–63.5 kg). □ **lightly** *adverb*; **lightness** *noun*.

**lighten¹** *verb* make or become lighter in weight; reduce weight or load of.

**lighten²** *verb* shed light on, make or grow bright.

**lighter¹** *noun* device for lighting cigarettes etc.

**lighter²** *noun* boat for transporting goods between ship and wharf etc.

**lightning** /'laɪtnɪŋ/ *noun* flash of light produced by electric discharge between clouds or between clouds and ground. □ **lightning-conductor** metal rod or wire fixed to building or mast to divert lightning to earth or sea.

**lights** *plural noun* lungs of sheep, pigs, etc. as food, esp. for pets.

**ligneous** /'lɪgnɪəs/ *adjective* of the nature of wood.

**lignite** /'lɪgnaɪt/ *noun* brown coal of woody texture.

**lignum vitae** /lɪgnəm 'vaɪtɪ/ *noun* a hard-wooded tree.

**like¹** ● *adjective* (**more like, most like**) similar to another, each other, or original; resembling; such as; characteristic of; in suitable state or mood for. ● *preposition* in manner of, to same degree as. ● *adverb slang* so to speak; *colloquial* probably. ● *conjunction colloquial* as, as if (see note below). ● *noun* counterpart, equal; similar person or thing.

■ **Usage** It is incorrect in standard English to use *like* as a conjunction, as in *Tell it like it is* or *He's spending money like it was going out of fashion.*

**like²** ● *verb* (**-king**) find agreeable or enjoyable; feel attracted by, choose to have, prefer. ● *noun* (in *plural*) things one likes or prefers.

**likeable** *adjective* (also **likable**) pleasant, easy to like. □ **likeably** *adverb*.

**likelihood** /'laɪklɪhʊd/ *noun* probability.

**likely** /'laɪklɪ/ ● *adjective* (**-ier, -iest**) probable; such as may well happen or be true; to be expected; promising, apparently suitable. ● *adverb* probably. □ **not likely!** *colloquial* certainly not.

**liken** *verb* (+ *to*) point out resemblance between (person, thing) and (another).

**likeness** *noun* (usually + *between, to*) resemblance; (+ *of*) semblance, guise; portrait, representation.

**likewise** *adverb* also, moreover; similarly.

**liking** *noun* what one likes; one's taste; (+ *for*) fondness, taste, fancy.

**lilac** /'laɪlək/ ● *noun* shrub with fragrant pinkish-violet or white flowers; pale pinkish-violet colour. ● *adjective* of this colour.

**liliaceous** /lɪlɪ'eɪʃəs/ *adjective* of the lily family.

**lilliputian** /lɪlɪ'pjuːʃ(ə)n/ ● *noun* diminutive person or thing. ● *adjective* diminutive.

**lilt** ● *noun* light springing rhythm; tune with this. ● *verb* (esp. as **lilting** *adjective*) speak etc. with lilt.

**lily** /'lɪlɪ/ *noun* (*plural* **-ies**) tall bulbous plant with large trumpet-shaped flowers; heraldic fleur-de-lis. □ **lily of the valley** plant with fragrant white bell-shaped flowers.

**limb**[1] /lɪm/ *noun* leg, arm, wing; large branch of tree; branch of cross. □ **out on a limb** isolated.

**limb**[2] /lɪm/ *noun* specified edge of sun, moon, etc.

**limber**[1] /'lɪmbə/ ● *adjective* lithe, flexible; agile. ● *verb* (usually + *up*) make oneself supple; warm up for athletic etc. activity.

**limber**[2] /'lɪmbə/ ● *noun* detachable front of gun-carriage. ● *verb* attach limber to.

**limbo**[1] /'lɪmbəʊ/ *noun* (*plural* **-s**) supposed abode of souls of unbaptized infants, and of the just who died before Christ; intermediate state or condition of awaiting decision.

**limbo**[2] /'lɪmbəʊ/ *noun* (*plural* **-s**) W. Indian dance in which dancer bends backwards to pass under progressively lowered horizontal bar.

**lime**[1] ● *noun* white caustic substance got by heating limestone. ● *verb* (**-ming**) treat with lime. □ **limekiln** kiln for heating limestone. □ **limy** *adjective* (**-ier**, **-iest**).

**lime**[2] *noun* round green acid fruit; tree producing this fruit. □ **lime-green** yellowish-green colour.

**lime**[3] *noun* (in full **lime tree**) tree with heart-shaped leaves and fragrant creamy blossom.

**limelight** *noun* intense white light used formerly in theatres; glare of publicity.

**limerick** /'lɪmərɪk/ *noun* humorous 5-line verse.

**limestone** *noun* rock composed mainly of calcium carbonate.

**limit** /'lɪmɪt/ ● *noun* point, line, or level beyond which something does not or may not extend or pass; greatest or smallest amount permitted. ● *verb* (**-t-**) set or serve as limit to; (+ *to*) restrict to. □ **limitless** *adjective*.

**limitation** /lɪmɪ'teɪʃ(ə)n/ *noun* limiting, being limited; limit of ability; limiting circumstance.

**limn** /lɪm/ *verb* *archaic* paint.

**limousine** /lɪmʊ'ziːn/ *noun* large luxurious car.

**limp**[1] ● *verb* walk or proceed lamely or awkwardly. ● *noun* lame walk.

**limp**[2] *adjective* not stiff or firm; without will or energy. □ **limply** *adverb*; **limpness** *noun*.

**limpet** /'lɪmpɪt/ *noun* mollusc with conical shell sticking tightly to rocks.

**limpid** /'lɪmpɪd/ *adjective* clear, transparent. □ **limpidity** /-'pɪd-/ *noun*.

**linage** /'laɪnɪdʒ/ *noun* number of lines in printed or written page etc.; payment by the line.

**linchpin** /'lɪntʃpɪn/ *noun* pin passed through axle-end to keep wheel on; person or thing vital to organization etc.

**linctus** /'lɪŋktəs/ *noun* syrupy medicine, esp. soothing cough mixture.

**linden** /'lɪnd(ə)n/ *noun* = LIME TREE.

**line**[1] ● *noun* continuous mark made on surface; furrow, wrinkle; use of lines in art; straight or curved track of moving point; outline; limit, boundary; row of persons or things; *US* queue; mark defining area of play or start or finish of race; row of printed or written words; portion of verse written in line; (in *plural*) piece of poetry, words of actor's part; length of cord, rope, etc. serving specified purpose; wire or cable for telephone or telegraph; connection by means of this; single track or branch of railway; regular succession of buses, ships, aircraft, etc., plying between certain places, company conducting this; several generations of family; stock; manner of procedure, conduct, thought, etc.; channel; department of activity, branch of business; type of product; connected series of military field works, arrangement of soldiers or ships side by side; each of very narrow horizontal sections forming television picture. ● *verb* (**-ning**) mark with lines; position or stand at intervals along. □ **line printer** machine that prints computer output a line at a time; **linesman** umpire's or referee's assistant who decides whether ball has fallen within playing area or not; **line up** *verb* arrange or be arranged in lines, have ready; **line-up** *noun* line of people for inspection, arrangement of team, band, etc.

**line**[2] *verb* (**-ning**) apply layer of usually different material to cover inside of (garment, box, etc.); serve as lining for; *colloquial* fill (purse etc.).

**lineage** /'lɪnɪɪdʒ/ *noun* lineal descent, ancestry.

**lineal** /'lɪnɪəl/ *adjective* in direct line of descent or ancestry; linear. □ **lineally** *adverb.*

**lineament** /'lɪnɪəmənt/ *noun* (usually in *plural*) distinctive feature or characteristic, esp. of face.

**linear** /'lɪnɪə/ *adjective* of or in lines; long and narrow and of uniform breadth.

**linen** /'lɪnɪn/ *noun* cloth woven from flax; articles made or originally made of linen, as sheets, shirts, underwear, etc. ● *adjective* made of linen.

**liner**[1] *noun* ship or aircraft carrying passengers on regular line.

**liner**[2] *noun* removable lining.

**ling**[1] *noun* (*plural* same) long slender marine fish.

**ling**[2] *noun* kind of heather.

**linger** /'lɪŋɡə/ *verb* stay about; (+ *over, on,* etc.) dally; be protracted; (often + *on*) die slowly.

**lingerie** /'læʒərɪ/ *noun* women's underwear and nightclothes.

**lingo** /'lɪŋɡəʊ/ *noun* (*plural* **-s** or **-es**) *colloquial* foreign language.

**lingual** /'lɪŋɡw(ə)l/ *adjective* of tongue; of speech or languages.

**linguist** /'lɪŋɡwɪst/ *noun* person skilled in languages or linguistics.

**linguistic** /lɪŋ'ɡwɪstɪk/ *adjective* of language or the study of languages. □ **linguistically** *adverb.*

**linguistics** *noun* study of language and its structure.

**liniment** /'lɪnɪmənt/ *noun* embrocation.

**lining** *noun* material to line surface.

**link** ● *noun* one loop or ring of chain etc.; one in series; means of connection. ● *verb* (+ *together, to, with*) connect, join; clasp or intertwine (hands etc.).

**linkage** *noun* linking or being linked.

**links** *noun* (treated as *singular* or *plural*) golf course.

**Linnaean** /lɪ'niːən/ *adjective* of Linnaeus or his system of classifying plants and animals.

**linnet** /'lɪnɪt/ *noun* brown-grey finch.

**lino** /'laɪnəʊ/ *noun* (*plural* **-s**) linoleum. □ **linocut** design carved in relief on block of linoleum, print made from this.

**linoleum** /lɪ'nəʊlɪəm/ *noun* canvas-backed material coated with linseed oil, cork, etc.

**linseed** /'lɪnsiːd/ *noun* seed of flax.

**lint** *noun* linen or cotton with one side made fluffy, used for dressing wounds; fluff.

**lintel** /'lɪnt(ə)l/ *noun* horizontal timber, stone, etc. over door or window.

**lion** /'laɪən/ *noun* (*feminine* **lioness**) large tawny flesh-eating wild cat of Africa and S. Asia; brave or celebrated person.

**lionize** *verb* (also **-ise**) (**-zing** or **-sing**) treat as celebrity.

**lip** *noun* either edge of opening of mouth; edge of cup, vessel, cavity, etc., esp. part shaped for pouring from; *colloquial* impudent talk. □ **lip-read** understand (speech) by observing speaker's lip-movements; **lip-service** insincere expression of support; **lipstick** stick of cosmetic for colouring lips.

**liquefy** /'lɪkwɪfaɪ/ *verb* (**-ies, -ied**) make or become liquid. □ **liquefaction** /-'fækʃ(ə)n/ *noun.*

**liqueur** /lɪ'kjʊə/ *noun* any of several strong sweet alcoholic spirits.

**liquid** /'lɪkwɪd/ ● *adjective* having consistency like that of water or oil, flowing freely but of constant volume; having appearance of water; (of sounds) clear, pure; (of assets) easily convertible into cash. ● *noun* liquid substance; *Phonetics* sound of *l* or *r*. □ **liquid crystal** liquid in state approaching that of crystalline solid; **liquid crystal display** visual display in some electronic devices.

**liquidate** /'lɪkwɪdeɪt/ *verb* (**-ting**) wind up affairs of (firm etc.); pay off (debt); wipe out; kill. □ **liquidator** *noun.*

**liquidation** /lɪkwɪ'deɪʃ(ə)n/ *noun* liquidating, esp. of firm. □ **go into liquidation** be wound up and have assets apportioned.

**liquidity** /lɪ'kwɪdɪtɪ/ *noun* (*plural* **-ies**) state of being liquid; having liquid assets.

**liquidize** *verb* (also **-ise**) (**-zing** or **-sing**) reduce to liquid state.

**liquidizer** *noun* (also **-iser**) machine for liquidizing foods.

**liquor** /'lɪkə/ *noun* alcoholic (esp. distilled) drink; other liquid, esp. that produced in cooking.

**liquorice** /'lɪkərɪs/ *noun* (also **licorice**) black root extract used as sweet and in medicine; plant from which it is obtained.

**lira** /'lɪərə/ *noun* chief monetary unit of Italy ( *plural* **lire** /-rɪ/ ) and Turkey ( *plural* **-s**).

**lisle** /laɪl/ *noun* fine cotton thread for stockings etc.

**lisp** • *noun* speech defect in which *s* is pronounced like *th* in *thick* and *z* like *th* in *this*. • *verb* speak or utter with lisp.

**lissom** /'lɪsəm/ *adjective* lithe, agile.

**list**[1] • *noun* number of items, names, etc. written or printed together as record; (in *plural*) palisades enclosing tournament area. • *verb* arrange as or enter in list; (as **listed** *adjective*) approved for Stock Exchange dealings, (of a building) of historical importance and officially protected. □ **enter the lists** issue or accept challenge.

**list**[2] • *verb* (of ship etc.) lean over to one side. • *noun* listing position, tilt.

**listen** /'lɪs(ə)n/ *verb* make effort to hear something, attentively hear person speaking; (+ *to*) give attention with ear to, take notice of. □ **listen in** tap telephonic communication, use radio receiving set. □ **listener** *noun*.

**listless** /'lɪstlɪs/ *adjective* lacking energy or enthusiasm. □ **listlessly** *adverb*; **listlessness** *noun*.

**lit** *past & past participle* of LIGHT[1,2].

**litany** /'lɪtənɪ/ *noun* ( *plural* **-ies**) series of supplications to God used in church services; (**the Litany**) that in Book of Common Prayer.

**litchi** /'laɪ'tʃiː/ = LYCHEE.

**liter** *US* = LITRE.

**literacy** /'lɪtərəsɪ/ *noun* ability to read and write.

**literal** /'lɪtər(ə)l/ *adjective* taking words in their basic sense without metaphor etc.; corresponding exactly to original words; prosaic; matter-of-fact. □ **literalism** *noun*; **literally** *adverb*.

**literary** /'lɪtərərɪ/ *adjective* of or concerned with or interested in literature.

**literate** /'lɪtərət/ • *adjective* able to read and write. • *noun* literate person.

**literati** /lɪtə'rɑːtɪ/ *plural noun* the class of learned people.

**literature** /'lɪtərətʃə/ *noun* written works, esp. those valued for form and style; writings of country or period or on particular subject; *colloquial* printed matter, leaflets, etc.

**lithe** /laɪð/ *adjective* flexible, supple.

**litho** /'laɪðəʊ/ *colloquial* • *noun* lithography. • *verb* (**-oes, -oed**) lithograph.

**lithograph** /'lɪθəgrɑːf/ • *noun* lithographic print. • *verb* print by lithography.

**lithography** /lɪ'θɒgrəfɪ/ *noun* process of printing from plate so treated that ink sticks only to design to be printed. □ **lithographer** *noun*; **lithographic** /lɪθə'græfɪk/ *adjective*.

**Lithuanian** /lɪθjuːˈeɪnɪən/ • *noun* native, national, or language of Lithuania. • *adjective* of Lithuania.

**litigant** /'lɪtɪgənt/ • *noun* party to lawsuit. • *adjective* engaged in lawsuit.

**litigate** /'lɪtɪgeɪt/ *verb* (**-ting**) go to law; contest (point) at law. □ **litigation** *noun*; **litigator** *noun*.

**litigious** /lɪ'tɪdʒəs/ *adjective* fond of litigation; contentious.

**litmus** /'lɪtməs/ *noun* dye turned red by acid and blue by alkali.

**litre** /'liːtə/ *noun* (*US* **liter**) metric unit of capacity (1.76 pints).

**litter** /'lɪtə/ • *noun* refuse, esp. paper, discarded in public place, odds and ends lying about; young animals brought forth at one birth; vehicle containing couch and carried on men's shoulders or by animals; kind of stretcher for sick and wounded; straw etc. as bedding for animals; material for animal's, esp. cat's, indoor toilet. • *verb* make (place) untidy; give birth to (puppies etc.); provide (horse etc.) with bedding.

**little** /'lɪt(ə)l/ • *adjective* (**-r, -st**; **less** or **lesser**, **least**) small in size, amount, degree, etc.; short in stature; of short distance or duration; (**a little**) certain but small amount of; trivial; only small amount; operating on small scale; humble, ordinary; young, younger. • *noun* not much, only small amount;

short time or distance. ● adverb (**less**, **least**) to small extent only; not at all. □ **little by little** by degrees, gradually; **the little people** fairies.

**littoral** /'lɪtər(ə)l/ ● adjective of or on the shore. ● noun region lying along shore.

**liturgy** /'lɪtədʒɪ/ noun (plural **-ies**) fixed form of public worship; (**the Liturgy**) the Book of Common Prayer. □ **liturgical** /-'tɜːdʒ-/ adjective.

**live**[1] /lɪv/ verb (**-ving**) have life; be or remain alive; have one's home; (+ on, off) subsist or feed on; keep one's position; pass, spend; conduct oneself in specified way; enjoy life to the full. □ **live down** cause (scandal etc.) to be forgotten through blameless behaviour thereafter; **live it up** colloquial live exuberantly and extravagantly.

**live**[2] /laɪv/ ● adjective that is alive, living; (of broadcast, performance, etc.) heard or seen while happening or with audience present; of current interest; glowing, burning; (of match, bomb, etc.) not yet kindled or exploded; charged with electricity. ● adverb as live performance. □ **livestock** (usually treated as plural) animals kept on farm for use or profit; **live wire** spirited person.

**liveable** /'lɪvəb(ə)l/ adjective (also **livable**) colloquial (usually **liveable-in**) (of house etc.) fit to live in; (of life) worth living; colloquial (usually **liveable-with**) (of person) easy to live with.

**livelihood** /'laɪvlɪhʊd/ noun means of living; job, income.

**livelong** /'lɪvlɒŋ/ adjective in its entire length.

**lively** /'laɪvlɪ/ adjective (**-ier**, **-iest**) full of life, energetic; (of imagination) vivid; cheerful; jocular exciting, dangerous. □ **liveliness** noun.

**liven** /'laɪv(ə)n/ verb (often + up) make or become lively, cheer up.

**liver**[1] /'lɪvə/ noun large glandular organ in abdomen of vertebrates; liver of some animals as food.

**liver**[2] /'lɪvə/ noun person who lives in specified way.

**liverish** /'lɪvərɪʃ/ adjective suffering from liver disorder; peevish, glum.

**liverwort** noun mosslike plant sometimes lobed like liver.

**livery** /'lɪvərɪ/ noun (plural **-ies**) distinctive uniform of member of City Company or servant; distinctive guise or marking; distinctive colour scheme for company's vehicles etc. □ **at livery** (of horse) kept for owner at fixed charge; **livery stable** stable where horses are kept at livery or let out for hire.

**lives** plural of **life**.

**livid** /'lɪvɪd/ adjective colloquial furious; of bluish leaden colour.

**living** /'lɪvɪŋ/ ● noun being alive; livelihood; position held by clergyman, providing income. ● adjective contemporary; now alive; (of likeness) exact; (of language) still in vernacular use. □ **living-room** room for general day use; **living wage** wage on which one can live without privation; **within living memory** within memory of living people.

**lizard** /'lɪzəd/ noun reptile with usually long body and tail, 4 legs, and scaly hide.

**llama** /'lɑːmə/ noun S. American ruminant kept as beast of burden and for woolly fleece.

**Lloyd's** /lɔɪdz/ noun incorporated society of underwriters in London. □ **Lloyd's Register** annual classified list of all ships.

**lo** interjection archaic look.

**loach** noun (plural same or **-es**) small freshwater fish.

**load** ● noun what is (to be) carried; amount usually or actually carried; burden of work, responsibility, care, etc.; (in plural, often + of) plenty; (**a load of**) a quantity of; amount of power carried by electrical circuit or supplied by generating station. ● verb put load on or aboard; place (load) aboard ship or on vehicle etc.; (often + up) (of vehicle or person) take load aboard; (often + with) burden, strain, overwhelm; put ammunition in (gun), film in (camera), cassette in (tape recorder), program in (computer), etc. □ **load line** Plimsoll line.

**loaded** adjective slang rich, drunk, US drugged; (of dice etc.) weighted; (of question or statement) carrying hidden implication.

**loadstone** = LODESTONE.

**loaf**[1] *noun* (*plural* **loaves**) unit of baked bread, usually of standard size or shape; other cooked food in loaf shape; *slang* head.

**loaf**[2] *verb* (often + *about*) spend time idly, hang about.

**loam** *noun* rich soil of clay, sand, and humus. □ **loamy** *adjective*.

**loan** ● *noun* thing lent, esp. money; lending, being lent. ● *verb* lend (money, works of art, etc.). □ **on loan** being lent.

**loath** *adjective* (also **loth**) disinclined, reluctant.

**loathe** /ləʊð/ *verb* (**-thing**) detest, hate. □ **loathing** *noun*.

**loathsome** /ˈləʊðsəm/ *adjective* arousing hatred or disgust; repulsive.

**loaves** *plural* of LOAF[1].

**lob** ● *verb* (**-bb-**) hit or throw (ball etc.) slowly or in high arc. ● *noun* such ball.

**lobar** /ˈləʊbə/ *adjective* of a lobe, esp. of lung.

**lobate** /ˈləʊbeɪt/ *adjective* having lobe(s).

**lobby** /ˈlɒbɪ/ ● *noun* (*plural* **-ies**) porch, ante-room, entrance hall, corridor; (in House of Commons) large hall used esp. for interviews between MPs and the public; (also **division lobby**) each of two corridors to which MPs retire to vote; group of lobbyists. ● *verb* (**-ies**, **-ied**) solicit support of (influential person); inform (legislators etc.) in order to influence them. □ **lobby correspondent** journalist who receives unattributable briefings from government.

**lobbyist** *noun* person who lobbies MP etc.

**lobe** *noun* lower soft pendulous part of outer ear; similar part of other organs. □ **lobed** *adjective*.

**lobelia** /ləˈbiːlɪə/ *noun* plant with bright, esp. blue, flowers.

**lobotomy** /ləˈbɒtəmɪ/ *noun* (*plural* **-ies**) incision into frontal lobe of brain to relieve mental disorder.

**lobster** /ˈlɒbstə/ *noun* marine crustacean with two pincer-like claws; its flesh as food. □ **lobster pot** basket for trapping lobsters.

**lobworm** *noun* large earthworm used as fishing bait.

**local** /ˈləʊk(ə)l/ ● *adjective* belonging to, existing in, or peculiar to particular place; of the neighbourhood; of or affecting a part and not the whole; (of telephone call) to nearby place and at lower charge. ● *noun* inhabitant of particular place; (often **the local**) *colloquial* local public house. □ **local authority** administrative body in local government; **local colour** touches of detail in story etc. designed to provide realistic background; **local government** system of administration of county, district, parish, etc. by elected representatives of those who live there. □ **locally** *adverb*.

**locale** /ləʊˈkɑːl/ *noun* scene or locality of event or occurrence.

**locality** /ləʊˈkælɪtɪ/ *noun* (*plural* **-ies**) district; thing's site or scene; thing's position.

**localize** /ˈləʊkəlaɪz/ *verb* (also **-ise**) (**-zing** or **-sing**) restrict or assign to particular place; invest with characteristics of place; decentralize.

**locate** /ləʊˈkeɪt/ *verb* (**-ting**) discover exact place of; establish in a place, situate; state locality of.

■ **Usage** In standard English, it is incorrect to use *locate* to mean merely 'find' as in *I can't locate my key*.

**location** *noun* particular place; locating; natural, not studio, setting for film etc.

**loc. cit.** *abbreviation* in the passage cited (*loco citato*).

**loch** /lɒx, lɒk/ *noun* Scottish lake or narrow inlet of the sea.

**lock**[1] ● *noun* mechanism for fastening door etc. with bolt requiring key of particular shape; section of canal or river confined within sluice-gates for moving boats from one level to another; turning of vehicle's front wheels; interlocked or jammed state; wrestling hold. ● *verb* fasten with lock; (+ *up*) shut (house etc.) thus; (of door etc.) be lockable; (+ *up*, *in*, *into*) enclose (person, thing) by locking; (often + *up*, *away*) store inaccessibly; make or become rigidly fixed; (cause to) jam or catch. □ **lockjaw** form of tetanus in which jaws become rigidly closed; **lock-keeper** keeper of river or canal lock; **lock on to** (of missile etc.) automatically find and then track (target);

**lock out** *verb* keep out by locking door, (of employer) subject (employees) to lockout; **lockout** *noun* employer's exclusion of employees from workplace until certain terms are accepted; **locksmith** maker and mender of locks; **lock-up** house or room for temporary detention of prisoners, premises that can be locked up. □ **lockable** *adjective*.

**lock²** *noun* portion of hair that hangs together; (in *plural*) the hair.

**locker** *noun* (usually lockable) cupboard, esp. for public use.

**locket** /'lɒkɪt/ *noun* small ornamental case for portrait etc., usually on chain round neck.

**locomotion** /ləʊkə'məʊʃ(ə)n/ *noun* motion or power of motion from place to place.

**locomotive** /ləʊkə'məʊtɪv/ ● *noun* engine for pulling trains. ● *adjective* of, having, or bringing about locomotion.

**locum tenens** /ləʊkəm 'ti:nenz/ *noun* (*plural* **locum tenentes** /tɪ'nenti:z/) (also *colloquial* **locum**) deputy acting esp. for doctor or member of clergy.

**locus** /'ləʊkəs/ *noun* (*plural* **loci** /-saɪ/) position, place; line or curve etc. made by all points satisfying certain conditions or by defined motion of point, line, or surface.

**locust** /'ləʊkəst/ *noun* African or Asian grasshopper migrating in swarms and consuming all vegetation.

**locution** /lə'kju:ʃ(ə)n/ *noun* phrase, word, or idiom; style of speech.

**lode** *noun* vein of metal ore. □ **lodestar** star used as guide in navigation, esp. pole star; **lodestone, loadstone** magnetic oxide of iron, piece of this as magnet.

**lodge** ● *noun* small house, esp. one for gatekeeper at entrance to park or grounds of large house; porter's room etc.; members or meeting-place of branch of society such as Freemasons; beaver's or otter's lair. ● *verb* (-**ging**) reside, esp. as lodger; provide with sleeping quarters; submit (complaint etc.); become fixed or caught; deposit for security; settle, place.

**lodger** *noun* person paying for accommodation in another's house.

**lodging** *noun* temporary accommodation; (in *plural*) room(s) rented for lodging in.

**loft** ● *noun* attic; room over stable; gallery in church or hall; pigeon house. ● *verb* send (ball etc.) high up.

**lofty** *adjective* (-**ier**, -**iest**) of imposing height; haughty, aloof; exalted, noble. □ **loftily** *adverb*; **loftiness** *noun*.

**log¹** ● *noun* unhewn piece of felled tree; any large rough piece of wood; *historical* floating device for ascertaining ship's speed; record of ship's or aircraft's voyage; any systematic record of experiences etc. ● *verb* (-**gg**-) enter (ship's speed or other transport details) in logbook; enter (data etc.) in regular record; cut into logs. □ **logbook** book containing record or log, vehicle registration document; **log on** or **off, log in** or **out** begin or end operations at terminal of esp. multi-access computer.

**log²** *noun* logarithm.

**logan** /'ləʊgən/ *noun* (in full **logan-stone**) poised heavy stone rocking at a touch.

**loganberry** /'ləʊgənbərɪ/ *noun* (*plural* -**ies**) dark red fruit, hybrid of blackberry and raspberry.

**logarithm** /'lɒgərɪð(ə)m/ *noun* an arithmetic exponent used in computation. □ **logarithmic** /-'rɪðmɪk/ *adjective*.

**loggerhead** /'lɒgəhed/ *noun* □ **at loggerheads** (often + *with*) disagreeing or disputing.

**loggia** /'ləʊdʒə/ *noun* open-sided gallery or arcade.

**logging** *noun* work of cutting and preparing forest timber.

**logic** /'lɒdʒɪk/ *noun* science of reasoning; chain of reasoning; use of or ability in argument; inexorable force; principles used in designing computer etc.; circuits based on these. □ **logician** /lə'dʒɪʃ(ə)n/ *noun*.

**logical** *adjective* of or according to logic; correctly reasoned, consistent; capable of correct reasoning. □ **logicality** /-'kæl-/ *noun*; **logically** *adverb*.

**logistics** /lə'dʒɪstɪks/ *plural noun* organization of (originally military) services and supplies. □ **logistic** *adjective*; **logistical** *adjective*; **logistically** *adverb*.

**logo** /'ləʊgəʊ/ *noun* (*plural* -**s**) organization's emblem used in display material.

**loin** *noun* (in *plural*) side and back of body between ribs and hip-bones; joint of meat from this part of animal. □ **loincloth** cloth worn round hips, esp. as sole garment.

**loiter** /'lɔɪtə/ *verb* stand about idly; linger. □ **loiter with intent** linger to commit felony.

**loll** *verb* stand, sit, or recline in lazy attitude; hang loosely.

**lollipop** /'lɒlɪpɒp/ *noun* hard sweet on stick. □ **lollipop man**, **lady** *colloquial* warden using circular sign on pole to stop traffic for children to cross road.

**lollop** /'lɒləp/ *verb* (-p-) *colloquial* flop about; move in ungainly bounds.

**lolly** /'lɒlɪ/ *noun* (*plural* **-ies**) *colloquial* lollipop; ice lolly; *slang* money.

**lone** *adjective* solitary; without companions; isolated; unmarried. □ **lone hand** hand played or player playing against the rest at cards, person or action without allies; **lone wolf** loner.

**lonely** /'ləʊnlɪ/ *adjective* (-**ier**, -**iest**) without companions; sad because of this; isolated; uninhabited. □ **loneliness** *noun*.

**loner** *noun* person or animal preferring to be alone.

**lonesome** *adjective esp. US* lonely; causing loneliness.

**long**[1] ● *adjective* (**longer** /'lɒŋgə/, **longest** /'lɒŋgɪst/) measuring much from end to end in space or time; (following measurement) in length or duration; consisting of many items; tedious; of elongated shape; reaching far back or forward in time; involving great interval or difference. ● *noun* long interval or period. ● *adverb* (**longer** /'lɒŋgə/, **longest** /'lɒŋgɪst/) by or for a long time; (following nouns of duration) throughout specified time; (in *comparative*) after implied point of time. □ **as, so long as** provided that; **before long** soon; **in the long run** eventually; **longboat** sailing ship's largest boat; **longbow** one drawn by hand and shooting long arrow; **long-distance** travelling or operating between distant places; **long face** dismal expression; **longhand** ordinary handwriting; **long johns** *colloquial* long underpants; **long jump** athletic contest of jumping along ground in one leap;

**long-life** (of milk etc.) treated to prolong shelf-life; **long odds** chances with low probability; **long-playing** (of gramophone record) playing for about 20–30 minutes on each side; **long-range** having a long range, relating to period of time far into future; **longshore** existing on or frequenting the shore; **long shot** wild guess or venture; **long sight** ability to see clearly only what is comparatively distant; **long-sighted** having long sight, far-sighted; **long-suffering** bearing provocation patiently; **long-term** of or for long period of time; **long-winded** (of speech or writing) tediously lengthy.

**long**[2] *verb* (+ *for*, *to do*) have strong wish or desire for. □ **longing** *noun* & *adjective*; **longingly** *adverb*.

**long.** *abbreviation* longitude.

**longevity** /lɒn'dʒevɪtɪ/ *noun formal* long life.

**longitude** /'lɒŋgɪtjuːd/ *noun* angular distance E. or W. of (esp. Greenwich) meridian.

**longitudinal** /lɒŋgɪ'tjuːdɪn(ə)l/ *adjective* of or in length; running lengthwise; of longitude. □ **longitudinally** *adverb*.

**longways** *adverb* (also **longwise**) in direction parallel with thing's length.

**loo** *noun colloquial* lavatory.

**loofah** /'luːfə/ *noun* rough bath-sponge made from dried pod of type of gourd.

**look** /lʊk/ ● *verb* (often + *at*, *down*, *up*, etc.) use or direct one's eyes; examine; make visual or mental search; (+ *at*) consider; (+ *for*) seek; have specified appearance, seem; (+ *into*) investigate; (of thing) face some direction; indicate (emotion) by looks; (+ *to do*) expect. ● *noun* act of looking; gaze, glance; appearance of face, expression; (in *plural*) personal appearance. □ **look after** attend to; **look back** (+ *on*, *to*) turn one's thoughts to (something past); **look down (up)on** regard with contempt; **look forward to** await (expected event) eagerly or with specified feelings; **look in** *verb* make short visit; **look-in** *noun colloquial* chance of participation or success; **looking-glass** mirror; **look on** be spectator; **look out** *verb* (often + *for*) be vigilant or prepared; **lookout** *noun* watch, observation-post, person etc. stationed to keep watch, prospect, *colloquial* person's own concern; **look up** search for (esp. information in book), *colloquial* visit (person), improve in prospect; **look up to** respect.

**loom**[1] /luːm/ *noun* apparatus for weaving.

**loom**[2] /luːm/ *verb* appear dimly, esp. as vague often threatening shape.

**loon** /luːn/ *noun* kind of diving bird; *colloquial* crazy person.

**loony** /ˈluːnɪ/ *slang* ● *noun* ( *plural* **-ies**) lunatic. ● *adjective* (**-ier**, **-iest**) crazy.

**loop** /luːp/ ● *noun* figure produced by curve or doubled thread etc. crossing itself; thing, path, etc. forming this figure; similarly shaped attachment used as fastening; contraceptive coil; endless band of tape or film allowing continuous repetition; repeated sequence of computer operations. ● *verb* form or bend into loop; fasten with loop(s); form loop. □ **loop line** railway or telegraph line that diverges from main line and joins it again.

**loophole** *noun* means of evading rule etc. without infringing it; narrow vertical slit in wall of fort etc.

**loopy** *adjective* (**-ier**, **-iest**) *slang* crazy.

**loose** /luːs/ ● *adjective* not tightly held; free from bonds or restraint; not held together; not compact or dense; inexact; morally lax. ● *verb* (**-sing**) free; untie, detach; release; relax (hold etc.). □ **at a loose end** unoccupied; **let loose** release; **loose cover** removable cover for armchair etc.; **loose-leaf** (of notebook etc.) with pages that can be removed and replaced; **on the loose** escaped from captivity, enjoying oneself freely. □ **loosely** *adverb*.

**loosen** *verb* make or become loose or looser. □ **loosen up** relax.

**loot** /luːt/ ● *noun* spoil, booty; *slang* money. ● *verb* rob or steal, esp. after rioting etc.; plunder.

**lop** *verb* (**-pp-**) (often + *off*) cut or remove (part or parts) from whole, esp. branches from tree; prune (tree).

**lope** ● *verb* (**-ping**) run with long bounding stride. ● *noun* such stride.

**lop-eared** *adjective* having drooping ears.

**lopsided** *adjective* unevenly balanced.

**loquacious** /ləˈkweɪʃəs/ *adjective* talkative. □ **loquacity** /-ˈkwæsɪtɪ/ *noun*.

**lord** ● *noun* master, ruler; *historical* feudal superior, esp. of manor; peer of realm, person with title Lord; (**Lord**) (often **the Lord**) God, Christ; (**Lord**) *title used before name of certain male peers and officials*; (**the Lords**) House of Lords. ● *interjection expressing surprise, dismay, etc.* □ **lord it over** domineer; **Lord Mayor** title of mayor in some large cities; **Lord's Day** Sunday; **Lord's Prayer** the Our Father; **Lord's Supper** Eucharist.

**lordly** *adjective* (**-ier**, **-iest**) haughty, imperious; suitable for a lord.

**Lordship** *noun* □ **His**, **Your Lordship** title used of or to man with rank of Lord.

**lore** *noun* body of tradition and information on a subject or held by particular group.

**lorgnette** /lɔːˈnjet/ *noun* pair of eyeglasses or opera-glasses on long handle.

**lorn** *adjective archaic* desolate, forlorn.

**lorry** /ˈlɒrɪ/ *noun* ( *plural* **-ies**) large vehicle for transporting goods etc.

**lose** /luːz/ *verb* (**-sing**; *past & past participle* **lost**) be deprived of; cease to have, esp. by negligence; be deprived of (person) by death; become unable to find, follow, or understand; let pass from one's control; be defeated in; get rid of; forfeit (right to something); suffer loss or detriment; cause (person) the loss of; (of clock etc.) become slow; (in *passive*) disappear, perish. □ **be lost without** be dependent on.

**loser** *noun* person or thing that loses esp. contest; *colloquial* person who regularly fails.

**loss** *noun* losing, being lost; what is lost; detriment resulting from losing. □ **at a loss** (sold etc.) for less than was paid for it; **be at a loss** be puzzled or uncertain; **loss-leader** item sold at a loss to attract customers.

**lost** *past & past participle of* LOSE.

**lot** *noun colloquial* (**a lot**, or **lots**) large number or amount; each of set of objects used to make chance selection; this method of deciding, share or responsibility resulting from it; destiny, fortune, condition; *esp. US* plot, allotment; article or set of articles for sale at auction etc.; group of associated people or things. □ **draw**, **cast lots** decide by lots; **the (whole) lot** total number or quantity.

■ **Usage** A lot of, as in a lot of people, is fairly informal, though acceptable in serious writing, but lots of people is not acceptable.

**loth** = LOATH.

**lotion** /ˈləʊʃ(ə)n/ noun medical or cosmetic liquid preparation applied externally.

**lottery** /ˈlɒtərɪ/ noun (plural **-ies**) means of raising money by selling numbered tickets and giving prizes to holders of numbers drawn at random.

**lotto** /ˈlɒtəʊ/ noun game of chance like bingo.

**lotus** /ˈləʊtəs/ noun legendary plant inducing luxurious langour when eaten; kind of water lily. □ **lotus position** cross-legged position of meditation.

**loud** ● adjective strongly audible; noisy; (of colours etc.) gaudy, obtrusive. ● adverb loudly. □ **loudspeaker** apparatus that converts electrical signals into sounds. □ **loudly** adverb; **loudness** noun.

**lough** /lɒk, lɒx/ noun Irish lake, sea inlet.

**lounge** ● verb (**-ging**) recline comfortably; loll; stand or move idly. ● noun place for lounging, esp. sitting-room in house; public room (in hotel etc.); place in airport etc. with seats for waiting passengers; spell of lounging. □ **lounge suit** man's suit for ordinary day wear.

**lour** /laʊə/ verb (also **lower** /laʊə/) frown, look sullen; (of sky etc.) look dark and threatening.

**louse** /laʊs/ ● noun (plural **lice**) parasitic insect; (plural **louses**) slang contemptible person. ● verb (**-sing**) delouse.

**lousy** /ˈlaʊzɪ/ adjective (**-ier**, **-iest**) colloquial very bad, disgusting, ill; (often + with) colloquial well supplied; infested with lice.

**lout** noun rough-mannered person. □ **loutish** adjective.

**louvre** /ˈluːvə/ noun (also **louver**) each of set of overlapping slats designed to admit air and some light and exclude rain; domed structure on roof with side openings for ventilation etc.

**lovable** /ˈlʌvəb(ə)l/ adjective (also **loveable**) inspiring affection.

**lovage** /ˈlʌvɪdʒ/ noun herb used for flavouring etc.

**love** /lʌv/ ● noun deep affection or fondness; sexual passion; sexual relations; beloved one; sweetheart; colloquial form of address regardless of affection; colloquial person of whom one is fond; affectionate greetings; (in games) no score, nil. ● verb (**-ving**) feel love for; delight in, admire; colloquial like very much. □ **fall in love** (often + with) suddenly begin to love; **in love** (often + with) enamoured (of); **love affair** romantic or sexual relationship between two people; **love-bird** kind of parakeet; **love-in-a-mist** blue-flowered cultivated plant; **lovelorn** pining from unrequited love; **lovesick** languishing with love; **make love** (often + to) have sexual intercourse (with), pay amorous attention (to).

**loveable** = LOVABLE.

**loveless** adjective unloving or unloved or both.

**lovely** adjective (**-ier**, **-iest**) colloquial pleasing, delightful; beautiful. □ **loveliness** noun.

**lover** noun person in love with another, or having sexual relations with another; (in plural) unmarried couple in love or having sexual relations; person who enjoys specified thing.

**loving** ● adjective feeling or showing love, affectionate. ● noun affection. □ **loving cup** two-handled drinking cup passed round at banquets. □ **lovingly** adverb.

**low¹** /ləʊ/ ● adjective not high or tall; not elevated in position; (of sun) near horizon; of humble rank; of small or less than normal amount, extent, or intensity; dejected; lacking vigour; (of sound) not shrill or loud; commonplace; (of opinion) unfavourable; mean, vulgar. ● noun low or lowest level or number; area of low pressure. ● adverb in or to low position; in low tone, at low pitch. □ **lowbrow** colloquial not intellectual or cultured; **Low Church** section of Church of England attaching little importance to ritual, priestly authority, and sacraments; **Low Countries** Netherlands, Belgium, and Luxembourg; **low-down** adjective mean, dishonourable, noun colloquial (**the low-down**) usually + on) relevant information; **lower case** small letters, not capitals; **low frequency** *Radio* 30–300 kilohertz; **low pressure** low degree of activity, atmospheric condition with pressure below average; **Low Sunday** Sunday after Easter; **low tide, water** time or level of tide at its ebb; **low water mark** level reached at low water.

**low²** /ləʊ/ ● *noun* sound made by cattle; moo. ● *verb* make this sound.

**lower¹** *verb* let or haul down; make or become lower; degrade.

**lower²** = LOUR.

**lowland** /ˈləʊlənd/ ● *noun* (usually in *plural*) low-lying country. ● *adjective* of or in lowland. □ **lowlander** *noun*.

**lowly** *adjective* (**-ier, -iest**) humble; unpretentious. □ **lowliness** *noun*.

**loyal** /ˈlɔɪəl/ *adjective* (often + *to*) faithful; steadfast in allegiance etc. □ **loyally** *adverb*; **loyalty** *noun* ( *plural* **-ies**).

**loyalist** *noun* person remaining loyal to legitimate sovereign etc.; (**Loyalist**) supporter of union between Great Britain and Northern Ireland. □ **loyalism** *noun*.

**lozenge** /ˈlɒzɪndʒ/ *noun* rhombus; small sweet or medicinal tablet to be dissolved in mouth; lozenge-shaped object.

**LP** *abbreviation* long-playing (record).

**LSD** *abbreviation* lysergic acid diethylamide, a powerful hallucinogenic drug.

**Lt.** *abbreviation* Lieutenant; light.

**Ltd.** *abbreviation* Limited.

**lubber** /ˈlʌbə/ *noun* clumsy fellow, lout.

**lubricant** /ˈluːbrɪkənt/ *noun* substance used to reduce friction.

**lubricate** /ˈluːbrɪkeɪt/ *verb* (**-ting**) apply oil, grease, etc. to; make slippery. □ **lubrication** *noun*.

**lubricious** /luːˈbrɪʃəs/ *adjective* slippery, evasive; lewd. □ **lubricity** *noun*.

**lucerne** /luːˈsɜːn/ *noun* alfalfa.

**lucid** /ˈluːsɪd/ *adjective* expressing or expressed clearly; sane. □ **lucidity** /-ˈsɪd-/ *noun*; **lucidly** *adverb*.

**luck** *noun* good or bad fortune; circumstances brought by this; success due to chance.

**luckless** *adjective* unlucky; ending in failure.

**lucky** *adjective* (**-ier, -iest**) having or resulting from good luck; bringing good luck. □ **lucky dip** tub containing articles from which one chooses at random. □ **luckily** *adverb*.

**lucrative** /ˈluːkrətɪv/ *adjective* profitable. □ **lucratively** *adverb*.

**lucre** /ˈluːkə/ *noun derogatory* financial gain.

**ludicrous** /ˈluːdɪkrəs/ *adjective* absurd, ridiculous, laughable. □ **ludicrously** *adverb*; **ludicrousness** *noun*.

**ludo** /ˈluːdəʊ/ *noun* board game played with dice and counters.

**lug** ● *verb* (**-gg-**) drag or carry with effort; pull hard. ● *noun* hard or rough pull; *colloquial* ear; projection on object by which it may be carried, fixed in place, etc.

**luggage** /ˈlʌgɪdʒ/ *noun* suitcases, bags, etc., for traveller's belongings.

**lugger** /ˈlʌgə/ *noun* small ship with 4-cornered sails (**lugsails**).

**lugubrious** /luˈguːbrɪəs/ *adjective* doleful. □ **lugubriously** *adverb*; **lugubriousness** *noun*.

**lukewarm** /luːkˈwɔːm/ *adjective* moderately warm, tepid; unenthusiastic.

**lull** ● *verb* soothe, send to sleep; (usually + *into*) deceive (person) into undue confidence; allay (suspicions etc.); (of noise, storm, etc.) lessen, fall quiet. ● *noun* temporary quiet period.

**lullaby** /ˈlʌləbaɪ/ *noun* ( *plural* **-ies**) soothing song to send child to sleep.

**lumbago** /lʌmˈbeɪgəʊ/ *noun* rheumatic pain in muscles of lower back.

**lumbar** /ˈlʌmbə/ *adjective* of lower back. □ **lumbar puncture** withdrawal of spinal fluid from lower back for diagnosis.

**lumber** /ˈlʌmbə/ ● *noun* disused and cumbersome articles; partly prepared timber. ● *verb* (usually + *with*) encumber (person); move in slow clumsy way; cut and prepare forest timber for transporting. □ **lumberjack** person who fells and transports lumber; **lumber-room** room where things in disuse are kept.

**lumen** /ˈluːmen/ *noun* SI unit of luminous flux.

**luminary** /ˈluːmɪnərɪ/ *noun* ( *plural* **-ies**) *literary* natural light-giving body; wise person; celebrated member of group.

**luminescence** /luːmɪˈnes(ə)ns/ noun emission of light without heat. □ **luminescent** adjective.

**luminous** /ˈluːmɪnəs/ adjective shedding light; phosphorescent, visible in darkness. □ **luminosity** /-ˈnɒs-/ noun.

**lump**[1] ● noun compact shapeless mass; tumour; swelling, bruise; heavy ungainly person etc. ● verb (usually + together etc.) class, mass. □ **lump sugar** sugar in small lumps or cubes; **lump sum** sum including number of items or paid down all at once.

**lump**[2] verb colloquial (in contrast with like) put up with ungraciously.

**lumpish** adjective heavy, clumsy; stupid.

**lumpy** adjective (**-ier, -iest**) full of or covered with lumps. □ **lumpily** adverb; **lumpiness** noun.

**lunacy** /ˈluːnəsɪ/ noun (plural **-ies**) insanity; great folly.

**lunar** /ˈluːnə/ adjective of, like, concerned with, or determined by the moon. □ **lunar module** craft for travelling between moon and orbiting spacecraft; **lunar month** period of moon's revolution, (in general use) 4 weeks.

**lunate** /ˈluːneɪt/ adjective crescent-shaped.

**lunatic** /ˈluːnətɪk/ ● noun insane person; wildly foolish person. ● adjective insane; very reckless or foolish.

**lunation** /luːˈneɪʃ(ə)n/ noun interval between new moons, about 29½ days.

**lunch** ● noun midday meal. ● verb take lunch; provide lunch for.

**luncheon** /ˈlʌntʃ(ə)n/ noun formal lunch. □ **luncheon voucher** voucher issued to employees and exchangeable for food at restaurant etc.

**lung** noun either of pair of respiratory organs in humans and many other vertebrates.

**lunge** ● noun sudden movement forward; attacking move in fencing. ● verb (**-ging**) (usually + at) deliver or make lunge.

**lupin** /ˈluːpɪn/ noun cultivated plant with long tapering spikes of flowers.

**lupine** /ˈluːpaɪn/ adjective of or like wolves.

**lupus** /ˈluːpəs/ noun inflammatory skin disease.

**lurch**[1] ● noun stagger; sudden unsteady movement or tilt. ● verb stagger, move unsteadily.

**lurch**[2] noun □ **leave in the lurch** desert (friend etc.) in difficulties.

**lurcher** /ˈlɜːtʃə/ noun crossbred dog, usually working dog crossed with greyhound.

**lure** ● verb (**-ring**) (usually + away, into) entice; recall with lure. ● noun thing used to entice, enticing quality (of chase etc.); falconer's apparatus for recalling hawk.

**lurid** /ˈljʊərɪd/ adjective bright and glaring in colour; sensational, shocking; ghastly, wan. □ **luridly** adverb.

**lurk** verb linger furtively; lie in ambush; (usually + in, about, etc.) hide, esp. for sinister purpose; (as **lurking** adjective) latent.

**luscious** /ˈlʌʃəs/ adjective richly sweet in taste or smell; voluptuously attractive.

**lush**[1] adjective luxuriant and succulent.

**lush**[2] noun slang alcoholic, drunkard.

**lust** ● noun strong sexual desire; (usually + for, of) passionate desire for or enjoyment of; sensuous appetite seen as sinful. ● verb (usually + after, for) have strong or excessive (esp. sexual) desire. □ **lustful** adjective; **lustfully** adverb.

**lustre** /ˈlʌstə/ noun (US **luster**) gloss, shining surface; brilliance, splendour; iridescent glaze on pottery and porcelain. □ **lustrous** adjective.

**lusty** adjective (**-ier, -iest**) healthy and strong; vigorous, lively. □ **lustily** adverb.

**lute**[1] /luːt/ noun guitar-like instrument with long neck and pear-shaped body.

**lute**[2] /luːt/ ● noun clay or cement for making joints airtight. ● verb (**-ting**) apply lute to.

**lutenist** /ˈluːtənɪst/ noun lute-player.

**Lutheran** /ˈluːθərən/ ● noun follower of Martin Luther; member of Lutheran Church. ● adjective of Luther, the doctrines associated with him, or the Protestant Reformation. □ **Lutheranism** noun.

**lux** /lʌks/ noun (plural same) SI unit of illumination.

**luxuriant** /lʌɡˈzjʊərɪənt/ adjective growing profusely; exuberant, florid. □ **luxuriance** noun; **luxuriantly** adverb.

■ **Usage** *Luxuriant* is sometimes confused with *luxurious*.

**luxuriate** /lʌgˈzjʊərɪeɪt/ *verb* (**-ting**) (+ *in*) take self-indulgent delight in, enjoy as luxury.

**luxurious** /lʌgˈzjʊərɪəs/ *adjective* supplied with luxuries; very comfortable; fond of luxury. □ **luxuriously** *adverb*.

■ **Usage** *Luxurious* is sometimes confused with *luxuriant*.

**luxury** /ˈlʌkʃərɪ/ ● *noun* (*plural* **-ies**) choice or costly surroundings, possessions, etc.; thing giving comfort or enjoyment but inessential. ● *adjective* comfortable, expensive, etc.

**LV** *abbreviation* luncheon voucher.

**lychee** /ˈlaɪtʃɪ/ *noun* (also **litchi**, **lichee**) sweet white juicy brown-skinned fruit; tree bearing this.

**lych-gate** = LICH-GATE.

**Lycra** /ˈlaɪkrə/ *noun proprietary term* elastic polyurethane fabric.

**lye** /laɪ/ *noun* water made alkaline with wood ashes; any alkaline solution for washing.

**lying** *present participle of* LIE[1,2].

**lymph** /lɪmf/ *noun* colourless fluid from tissues of body, containing white blood cells; this fluid as vaccine.

**lymphatic** /lɪmˈfætɪk/ *adjective* of, secreting, or carrying lymph; (of person) pale, flabby. □ **lymphatic system** vessels carrying lymph.

**lynch** /lɪntʃ/ *verb* put (person) to death by mob action without legal trial. □ **lynching** *noun*.

**lynx** /lɪŋks/ *noun* (*plural* same or **-es**) wild cat with short tail, spotted fur, and proverbially keen sight.

**lyre** /laɪə/ *noun* ancient U-shaped stringed instrument.

**lyric** /ˈlɪrɪk/ ● *adjective* (of poetry) expressing writer's emotion, usually briefly; (of poet) writing in this way; meant or fit to be sung; songlike. ● *noun* lyric poem; (in *plural*) words of song.

**lyrical** *adjective* lyric; resembling, or using language appropriate to, lyric poetry; *colloquial* highly enthusiastic. □ **lyrically** *adverb*.

**lyricism** /ˈlɪrɪsɪz(ə)m/ *noun* quality of being lyrical.

**lyricist** /ˈlɪrɪsɪst/ *noun* writer of lyrics.

# Mm

**M[1]** *noun* (also **m**) (Roman numeral) 1,000.

**M[2]** *abbreviation* (also **M.**) Master; *Monsieur*; motorway; mega-.

**m** *abbreviation* (also **m.**) male; masculine; married; mile(s); metre(s); million(s); minute(s); milli-.

**MA** *abbreviation* Master of Arts.

**ma** /mɑː/ *noun colloquial* mother.

**ma'am** /mæm/ *noun* madam (esp. used in addressing royal lady).

**mac** *noun* (also **mack**) *colloquial* mackintosh.

**macabre** /məˈkɑːbr/ *adjective* gruesome, grim.

**macadam** /məˈkædəm/ *noun* broken stone as material for road-making; tarmacadam. □ **macadamize** *verb* (also **-ise**) (**-zing** or **-sing**).

**macaroni** /mækəˈrəʊnɪ/ *noun* pasta tubes.

**macaroon** /mækəˈruːn/ *noun* biscuit made of ground almonds etc.

**macaw** /məˈkɔː/ *noun* kind of parrot.

**mace[1]** *noun* staff of office, esp. symbol of Speaker's authority in House of Commons.

**mace[2]** *noun* dried outer covering of nutmeg as spice.

**macédoine** /ˈmæsɪdwɑːn/ *noun* mixture of fruits or vegetables, esp. cut up small.

**macerate** /ˈmæsəreɪt/ *verb* (**-ting**) soften by soaking. □ **maceration** *noun*.

**machete** /məˈʃetɪ/ *noun* broad heavy knife used in Central America and W. Indies.

**machiavellian** /mækɪəˈveliən/ *adjective* unscrupulous, cunning.

**machination** /mækɪˈneɪʃ(ə)n/ *noun* (usually in *plural*) intrigue, plot.

**machine** /məˈʃiːn/ ● *noun* apparatus for applying mechanical power, having several interrelated parts; bicycle, motorcycle, etc.; aircraft; computer; controlling system of an organization. ● *verb* (**-ning**) make or operate on with machine. □ **machine-gun** automatic gun that gives continuous fire; **machine-readable** in form that computer can process; **machine tool** mechanically operated tool.

**machinery** *noun* (*plural* **-ies**) machines; mechanism; organized system; means arranged.

**machinist** *noun* person who works machine.

**machismo** /məˈkɪzməʊ/ *noun* being macho; masculine pride.

**macho** /ˈmætʃəʊ/ *adjective* aggressively masculine.

**macintosh** = MACKINTOSH.

**mack** = MAC.

**mackerel** /ˈmækr(ə)l/ *noun* (*plural* same or **-s**) edible sea fish. □ **mackerel sky** sky dappled with rows of small fleecy white clouds.

**mackintosh** /ˈmækɪntɒʃ/ *noun* (also **macintosh**) waterproof coat or cloak; cloth waterproofed with rubber.

**macramé** /məˈkrɑːmɪ/ *noun* art of knotting cord or string in patterns; work so made.

**macrobiotic** /mækrəʊbaɪˈɒtɪk/ *adjective* of diet intended to prolong life, esp. consisting of wholefoods.

**macrocosm** /ˈmækrəʊkɒz(ə)m/ *noun* universe; whole of a complex structure.

**mad** *adjective* (**-dd-**) insane; frenzied; wildly foolish; infatuated; *colloquial* annoyed. □ **madcap** *adjective* wildly impulsive, *noun* reckless person; **madhouse** *colloquial* confused uproar, *archaic* mental home or hospital; **madman**, **madwoman** mad person; **madly** *adverb*; **madness** *noun*.

**madam** /ˈmædəm/ *noun* polite formal address to woman; *colloquial* conceited or precocious girl or young woman; woman brothel-keeper.

**Madame** /məˈdɑːm/ *noun* (*plural* **Mesdames** /merˈdɑːm/) title used of or to French-speaking woman.

**madden** *verb* make mad; irritate. □ **maddening** *adjective*.

**madder** /ˈmædə/ *noun* herbaceous climbing plant; red dye from its root; synthetic substitute for this dye.

**made** *past & past participle* of MAKE.

**Madeira** /məˈdɪərə/ *noun* fortified wine from Madeira; (in full **Madeira cake**) kind of sponge cake.

**Mademoiselle** /mædəmwəˈzel/ *noun* (*plural* **Mesdemoiselles** /meɪdm-/) title used of or to unmarried French-speaking woman.

**Madonna** /məˈdɒnə/ *noun* (**the Madonna**) the Virgin Mary; (**madonna**) picture or statue of her.

**madrigal** /ˈmædrɪg(ə)l/ *noun* part-song for several voices, usually unaccompanied.

**maelstrom** /ˈmeɪlstrəm/ *noun* great whirlpool.

**maestro** /ˈmaɪstrəʊ/ *noun* (*plural* **maestri** /-strɪ/ or **-s**) eminent musician, esp. teacher or conductor.

**Mafia** /ˈmæfɪə/ *noun* organized international group of criminals.

**Mafioso** /mæfɪˈəʊsəʊ/ *noun* (*plural* **Mafiosi** /-sɪ/) member of the Mafia.

**mag** *noun* *colloquial* magazine.

**magazine** /mægəˈziːn/ *noun* periodical publication containing contributions by various writers; chamber containing cartridges fed automatically to breech of gun; similar device in slide projector etc.; store for explosives, arms, or military provisions.

**magenta** /məˈdʒentə/ *noun* shade of crimson; aniline dye of this colour.

**maggot** /ˈmægət/ *noun* larva, esp. of bluebottle. □ **maggoty** *adjective*.

**Magi** /ˈmeɪdʒaɪ/ *plural noun* (**the Magi**) 'wise men from the East' in the Gospel.

**magic** /ˈmædʒɪk/ ● *noun* art of influencing events supernaturally; conjuring tricks; inexplicable influence. ● *adjective* of magic. □ **magic lantern** simple form of slide projector.

**magical** *adjective* of magic; resembling, or produced as if by, magic; wonderful, enchanting. □ **magically** *adverb*.

**magician** /mə'dʒɪʃ(ə)n/ *noun* person skilled in magic; conjuror.

**magisterial** /mædʒɪ'stɪərɪəl/ *adjective* imperious; authoritative; of a magistrate.

**magistracy** /'mædʒɪstrəsɪ/ *noun* ( *plural* -ies) magisterial office; magistrates.

**magistrate** /'mædʒɪstreɪt/ *noun* civil officer administering law, esp. one trying minor offences etc.

**magnanimous** /mæg'nænɪməs/ *adjective* nobly generous, not petty in feelings or conduct. □ **magnanimity** /-nə'nɪm-/ *noun*.

**magnate** /'mægneɪt/ *noun* person of wealth, authority, etc.

**magnesia** /mæg'ni:ʃə/ *noun* magnesium oxide; hydrated magnesium carbonate, used as antacid and laxative.

**magnesium** /mæg'ni:zɪəm/ *noun* silvery metallic element.

**magnet** /'mægnɪt/ *noun* piece of iron, steel, etc., having properties of attracting iron and of pointing approximately north when suspended; lodestone; person or thing that attracts.

**magnetic** /mæg'netɪk/ *adjective* having properties of magnet; produced or acting by magnetism; capable of being attracted by or acquiring properties of magnet; very attractive. □ **magnetic field** area of influence of magnet; **magnetic north** point indicated by north end of compass needle; **magnetic storm** disturbance of earth's magnetic field; **magnetic tape** coated plastic strip for recording sound or pictures.

**magnetism** /'mægnɪtɪz(ə)m/ *noun* magnetic phenomena; science of these; personal charm.

**magnetize** /'mægnɪtaɪz/ *verb* (also -ise) (-zing or -sing) make into magnet; attract like magnet. □ **magnetization** *noun*.

**magneto** /mæg'ni:təʊ/ *noun* ( *plural* -s) electric generator using permanent magnets (esp. for ignition in internal-combustion engine).

**magnificent** /mæg'nɪfɪs(ə)nt/ *adjective* splendid; imposing; *colloquial* excellent. □ **magnificence** *noun*; **magnificently** *adverb*.

**magnify** /'mægnɪfaɪ/ *verb* (-ies, -ied) make (thing) appear larger than it is, as

with lens (**magnifying glass**) etc.; exaggerate; intensify; *archaic* extol. □ **magnification** *noun*.

**magnitude** /'mægnɪtjuːd/ *noun* largeness, size; importance.

**magnolia** /mæg'nəʊlɪə/ *noun* kind of flowering tree; very pale pinkish colour of its flowers.

**magnum** /'mægnəm/ *noun* ( *plural* -s) wine bottle twice normal size.

**magpie** /'mægpaɪ/ *noun* crow with long tail and black and white plumage; chatterer; indiscriminate collector.

**Magyar** /'mægjɑː/ ● *noun* member of the chief ethnic group in Hungary; their language. ● *adjective* of this people.

**maharaja** /mɑːhə'rɑːdʒə/ *noun* (also **maharajah**) *historical* title of some *Indian* princes.

**maharanee** /mɑːhə'rɑːnɪ/ *noun* (also **maharani**) ( *plural* -s) *historical* maharaja's wife or widow.

**maharishi** /mɑːhə'rɪʃɪ/ *noun* ( *plural* -s) great Hindu sage.

**mahatma** /mə'hætmə/ *noun* (in India etc.) revered person.

**mah-jong** /mɑː'dʒɒŋ/ *noun* (also **-jongg**) originally Chinese game played with 136 or 144 pieces.

**mahogany** /mə'hɒgənɪ/ *noun* ( *plural* -ies) reddish-brown wood used for furniture etc.; colour of this.

**mahout** /mə'haʊt/ *noun* elephant driver.

**maid** *noun* female servant; *archaic* girl, young woman. □ **maidservant** female servant.

**maiden** /'meɪd(ə)n/ ● *noun* *archaic* girl, young unmarried woman; *Cricket* maiden over. ● *adjective* unmarried; (of voyage, speech by MP, etc.) first. □ **maidenhair** delicate kind of fern; **maiden name** woman's surname before marriage; **maiden over** *Cricket* over in which no runs are scored. □ **maidenly** *adjective*.

**mail**[1] ● *noun* letters etc. conveyed by post; the post. ● *verb* send by mail. □ **mail order** purchase of goods by post.

**mail**[2] *noun* armour of metal rings or plates.

**maim** *verb* cripple, mutilate.

**main** ● *adjective* chief, principal. ● *noun* principal channel for water, gas, etc., or (usually in *plural*) electricity; (in *plural*) domestic electricity supply as distinct from batteries; *archaic* high seas. □ **in the main** mostly, on the whole; **mainframe** central processing unit of large computer, large computer system; **mainland** continuous extent of land excluding nearby islands etc.; **mainmast** principal mast; **mainsail** lowest sail or sail set on after part of mainmast; **mainspring** principal spring of watch or clock, chief motive power etc.; **mainstay** chief support; **mainstream** prevailing trend of opinion, fashion, etc.

**mainly** *adverb* mostly; chiefly.

**maintain** /meɪn'teɪn/ *verb* keep up; keep going; support; assert as true; keep in repair.

**maintenance** /'meɪntənəns/ *noun* maintaining, being maintained; provision of enough to support life; alimony.

**maiolica** /mə'jɒlɪkə/ *noun* (also **majolica**) kind of decorated Italian earthenware.

**maisonette** /meɪzə'net/ *noun* flat on more than one floor; small house.

**maize** *noun* N. American cereal plant; cobs or grain of this.

**Maj.** *abbreviation* Major.

**majestic** /mə'dʒestɪk/ *adjective* stately and dignified; imposing. □ **majestically** *adverb*.

**majesty** /'mædʒɪstɪ/ *noun* (*plural* **-ies**) stateliness of aspect, language, etc.; sovereign power; (**His, Her, Your Majesty**) title used of or to sovereign or sovereign's wife or widow.

**majolica** = MAIOLICA.

**major** /'meɪdʒə/ ● *adjective* greater or relatively great in size etc.; unusually serious or significant; *Music* of or based on scale having semitone next above third and seventh notes; of full legal age. ● *noun* army officer next below lieutenant colonel; person of full legal age; *US* student's main subject or course, student of this. ● *verb* (+ *in*) *US* study or qualify in as a major. □ **major-domo** /-'dəʊməʊ/ (*plural* **-s**) house-steward; **major-general** army officer next below lieutenant general.

**majority** /mə'dʒɒrɪtɪ/ *noun* (*plural* **-ies**) (usually + *of*) greater number or part;

number by which winning vote exceeds next; full legal age.

■ **Usage** *Majority* should strictly be used of a number of people or things, as in *the majority of people*, and not of a quantity of something, as in *the majority of the work*.

**make** ● *verb* (**-king**; *past & past participle* **made**) construct, frame, create, esp. from parts or other substance; compel; bring about, give rise to; cause to become or seem; write, compose; constitute, amount to; undertake; perform; gain, acquire, obtain as result; prepare for consumption or use; proceed; *colloquial* arrive at or in time for, manage to attend; *colloquial* achieve place in; establish, enact; consider to be, estimate as; secure success or advancement of; accomplish; become; represent as; form in the mind. ● *noun* origin of manufactured goods, brand; way thing is made. □ **make believe** *verb* pretend; **make-believe** *noun* pretence, *adjective* pretended; **make do** (often + *with*) manage (with substitute etc.); **make for** tend to result in, proceed towards; **make good** compensate for, repair, succeed in an undertaking; **make off** depart hastily; **make out** discern, understand, assert, pretend, *colloquial* progress, write out, fill in; **makeshift** (serving as) temporary substitute or device; **make up** *verb* act to overcome (deficiency), complete, (+ *for*) compensate for, be reconciled, put together, prepare, invent (story), apply cosmetics (to); **make-up** *noun* cosmetics, similar preparation used as disguise by actor, person's temperament etc., composition; **makeweight** small quantity added to make full weight; **on the make** *colloquial* intent on gain.

**maker** *noun* person who makes, esp. (**Maker**) God.

**making** *noun* (in *plural*) earnings, profit; essential qualities for becoming. □ **be the making of** ensure success of; **in the making** in the course of being made.

**malachite** /'mæləkaɪt/ *noun* green mineral used for ornament.

**maladjusted** /mælə'dʒʌstɪd/ *adjective* (of person) unable to cope with demands of social environment. □ **maladjust-ment** noun.

**maladminister** /mælǝd'mɪnɪstǝ/ verb manage badly or improperly. □ **mal-administration** noun.

**maladroit** /mælǝ'drɔɪt/ adjective bungling, clumsy.

**malady** /'mælǝdɪ/ noun (plural **-ies**) ailment, disease.

**malaise** /mǝ'leɪz/ noun feeling of illness or uneasiness.

**malapropism** /'mælǝprɒpɪz(ǝ)m/ noun comical confusion between words.

**malaria** /mǝ'leǝrɪǝ/ noun fever transmitted by mosquitoes. □ **malarial** adjective.

**Malay** /mǝ'leɪ/ ● noun member of a people predominating in Malaysia and Indonesia; their language. ● adjective of this people or language.

**malcontent** /'mælkǝntent/ ● noun discontented person. ● adjective discontented.

**male** ● adjective of the sex that can beget offspring by fertilizing; (of plants or flowers) containing stamens but no pistil; (of parts of machinery) designed to enter or fill corresponding hollow part. ● noun male person or animal.

**malediction** /mælɪ'dɪkʃ(ǝ)n/ noun curse. □ **maledictory** adjective.

**malefactor** /'mælɪfæktǝ/ noun criminal; evil-doer. □ **malefaction** /-'fækʃ(ǝ)n/ noun.

**malevolent** /mǝ'levǝlǝnt/ adjective wishing evil to others. □ **malevolence** noun.

**malformation** /mælfɔː'meɪʃ(ǝ)n/ noun faulty formation. □ **malformed** /-'fɔːmd/ adjective.

**malfunction** /mæl'fʌŋkʃ(ǝ)n/ ● noun failure to function normally. ● verb function faultily.

**malice** /'mælɪs/ noun ill-will; desire to do harm.

**malicious** /mǝ'lɪʃǝs/ adjective given to or arising from malice. □ **maliciously** adverb.

**malign** /mǝ'laɪn/ ● adjective injurious; malignant; malevolent. ● verb speak ill of; slander. □ **malignity** /mǝ'lɪgnɪtɪ/ noun.

**malignant** /mǝ'lɪgnǝnt/ adjective (of disease) very virulent; (of tumour) spreading, recurring, cancerous; feeling or

showing intense ill-will. □ **malignancy** noun.

**malinger** /mǝ'lɪŋgǝ/ verb pretend to be ill, esp. to escape duty.

**mall** /mæl, mɔːl/ noun sheltered walk; shopping precinct.

**mallard** /'mælɑːd/ noun (plural same) kind of wild duck.

**malleable** /'mælɪǝb(ǝ)l/ adjective that can be shaped by hammering; pliable. □ **malleability** noun.

**mallet** /'mælɪt/ noun hammer, usually of wood; implement for striking croquet or polo ball.

**mallow** /'mæləʊ/ noun flowering plant with hairy stems and leaves.

**malmsey** /'mɑːmzɪ/ noun a strong sweet wine.

**malnutrition** /mælnjuː'trɪʃ(ǝ)n/ noun lack of foods necessary for health.

**malodorous** /mæl'ǝʊdǝrǝs/ adjective evil-smelling.

**malpractice** /mæl'præktɪs/ noun improper, negligent, or criminal professional conduct.

**malt** /mɔːlt/ ● noun barley or other grain prepared for brewing etc.; colloquial malt whisky. ● verb convert (grain) into malt. □ **malted milk** drink made from dried milk and extract of malt; **malt whisky** whisky made from malted barley.

**Maltese** /mɔːl'tiːz/ ● noun native, national, or language of Malta. ● adjective of Malta. □ **Maltese cross** one with equal arms broadened at ends.

**maltreat** /mæl'triːt/ verb ill-treat. □ **maltreatment** noun.

**mama** /mǝ'mɑː/ noun (also **mamma**) archaic mother.

**mamba** /'mæmbǝ/ noun venomous African snake.

**mamma** = MAMA.

**mammal** /'mæm(ǝ)l/ noun animal of class secreting milk to feed young. □ **mammalian** /-'meɪlɪǝn/ adjective.

**mammary** /'mæmǝrɪ/ adjective of breasts.

**Mammon** /'mæmǝn/ noun wealth regarded as god or evil influence.

**mammoth** /'mæmǝθ/ ● noun large extinct elephant. ● adjective huge.

**man** ● noun (plural **men**) adult human male; human being, person; the human race; employee, workman; (usually in *plural*) soldier, sailor, etc.; suitable or appropriate person; husband; *colloquial* boyfriend; human being of specified type; piece in chess, draughts, etc. ● *verb* (**-nn-**) supply with person(s) for work or defence. □ **manhole** opening giving person access to sewer, conduit, etc.; **man-hour** work done by one person in one hour; **man in the street** ordinary person; **man-of-war** warship; **manpower** people available for work or military service; **manservant** (*plural* **menservants**) male servant; **mantrap** trap set to catch esp. trespassers.

**manacle** /ˈmænək(ə)l/ ● *noun* (usually in *plural*) handcuff. ● *verb* (**-ling**) put manacles on.

**manage** /ˈmænɪdʒ/ *verb* (**-ging**) organize, regulate; succeed in achieving, contrive; succeed with limited resources, cope; succeed in controlling; cope with. □ **managing director** director with executive control or authority. □ **manageable** *adjective*.

**management** *noun* managing, being managed; administration; people managing a business.

**manager** *noun* person controlling or administering business etc.; person controlling activities of person, team, etc.; person who manages money etc. in specified way. □ **managerial** /-ˈdʒɪərɪəl/ *adjective*.

**manageress** /mænɪdʒəˈres/ *noun* woman manager, esp. of shop, hotel, etc.

**mañana** /mænˈjɑːnə/ *adverb & noun* some time in the future. [Spanish]

**manatee** /mænəˈtiː/ *noun* large aquatic plant-eating mammal.

**Mancunian** /mænˈkjuːnɪən/ ● *noun* native of Manchester. ● *adjective* of Manchester.

**mandarin** /ˈmændərɪn/ *noun* (**Mandarin**) official language of China; *historical* Chinese official; influential person, esp. bureaucrat; (in full **mandarin orange**) tangerine.

**mandate** /ˈmændeɪt/ ● *noun* official command; authority given by electors to government etc.; authority to act for another. ● *verb* (**-ting**) instruct (delegate) how to act or vote.

**mandatory** /ˈmændətərɪ/ *adjective* compulsory; of or conveying a command.

**mandible** /ˈmændɪb(ə)l/ *noun* jaw, esp. lower one; either part of bird's beak; either half of crushing organ in mouth-parts of insect etc.

**mandolin** /mændəˈlɪn/ *noun* kind of lute with paired metal strings plucked with a plectrum.

**mandrake** /ˈmændreɪk/ *noun* narcotic plant with forked root.

**mandrill** /ˈmændrɪl/ *noun* large W. African baboon.

**mane** *noun* long hair on horse's or lion's neck; *colloquial* person's long hair.

**manège** /mæˈneɪʒ/ *noun* riding-school; movements of trained horse; horsemanship.

**maneuver** *US* = MANOEUVRE.

**manful** *adjective* brave, resolute. □ **manfully** *adverb*.

**manganese** /ˈmæŋgəniːz/ *noun* grey brittle metallic element; black oxide of this.

**mange** /meɪndʒ/ *noun* skin disease of dogs etc.

**mangel-wurzel** /ˈmæŋg(ə)l wɜːz(ə)l/ *noun* large beet used as cattle food.

**manger** /ˈmeɪndʒə/ *noun* eating-trough in stable.

**mangle**[1] /ˈmæŋg(ə)l/ *verb* (**-ling**) hack, cut about; mutilate, spoil.

**mangle**[2] /ˈmæŋg(ə)l/ ● *noun* machine with rollers for pressing water out of washed clothes. ● *verb* (**-ling**) put through mangle.

**mango** /ˈmæŋgəʊ/ *noun* (*plural* **-es** or **-s**) tropical fruit with yellowish flesh; tree bearing it.

**mangold** /ˈmæŋg(ə)ld/ *noun* mangel-wurzel.

**mangrove** /ˈmæŋgrəʊv/ *noun* tropical seashore tree with many tangled roots above ground.

**mangy** /ˈmeɪndʒɪ/ *adjective* (**-ier**, **-iest**) having mange; squalid, shabby.

**manhandle** *verb* (**-ling**) *colloquial* handle roughly; move by human effort.

**manhood** *noun* state of being a man; manliness; a man's sexual potency; men of a country.

**mania** /ˈmeɪnɪə/ *noun* mental illness marked by excitement and violence;

(often + *for*) excessive enthusiasm, obsession.

**maniac** /'meɪnɪæk/ ● *noun colloquial* person behaving wildly; *colloquial* obsessive enthusiast; person suffering from mania. ● *adjective* of or behaving like maniac. □ **maniacal** /məˈnaɪək(ə)l/ *adjective*.

**manic** /'mænɪk/ *adjective* of or affected by mania. □ **manic-depressive** *adjective* relating to mental disorder with alternating periods of elation and depression, *noun* person having such disorder.

**manicure** /'mænɪkjʊə/ ● *noun* cosmetic treatment of the hands. ● *verb* (**-ring**) give manicure to. □ **manicurist** *noun*.

**manifest** /'mænɪfest/ ● *adjective* clear to sight or mind; indubitable. ● *verb* make manifest; (**manifest itself**) reveal itself. ● *noun* cargo or passenger list. □ **manifestation** *noun*; **manifestly** *adverb*.

**manifesto** /mænɪˈfestəʊ/ *noun* (*plural* **-s**) declaration of policies.

**manifold** /'mænɪfəʊld/ ● *adjective* many and various; having various forms, applications, parts, etc. ● *noun* manifold thing; pipe etc. with several outlets.

**manikin** /'mænɪkɪn/ *noun* little man, dwarf.

**Manila** /məˈnɪlə/ *noun* strong fibre of Philippine tree; (also **manila**) strong brown paper made of this.

**manipulate** /məˈnɪpjʊleɪt/ *verb* (**-ting**) handle, esp. with skill; manage to one's own advantage, esp. unfairly. □ **manipulation** *noun*; **manipulator** *noun*.

**manipulative** /məˈnɪpjʊlətɪv/ *adjective* tending to exploit a situation, person, etc., for one's own ends.

**mankind** *noun* human species.

**manly** *adjective* (**-ier**, **-iest**) having qualities associated with or befitting a man. □ **manliness** *noun*.

**manna** /'mænə/ *noun* food miraculously supplied to Israelites in wilderness.

**mannequin** /'mænɪkɪn/ *noun* fashion model; dummy for display of clothes.

**manner** /'mænə/ *noun* way thing is done or happens; (in *plural*) social behaviour; style; (in *plural*) polite behaviour; outward bearing, way of speaking, etc.; kind, sort.

**mannered** *adjective* behaving in specified way; showing mannerisms.

**mannerism** *noun* distinctive gesture or feature of style; excessive use of these in art etc.

**mannerly** *adjective* well-behaved, polite.

**mannish** *adjective* (of woman) masculine in appearance or manner; characteristic of man as opposed to woman.

**manoeuvre** /məˈnuːvə/ (*US* **maneuver**) ● *noun* planned movement of vehicle or troops; (in *plural*) large-scale exercise of troops etc.; agile or skilful movement; artful plan. ● *verb* (**-ring**) move (thing, esp. vehicle) carefully; perform or cause to perform manoeuvres; manipulate by scheming or adroitness; use artifice. □ **manoeuvrable** *adjective*.

**manor** /'mænə/ *noun* large country house with lands; *historical* feudal lordship over lands. □ **manorial** /məˈnɔːrɪəl/ *adjective*.

**mansard** /'mænsɑːd/ *noun* roof with 4 sloping sides, each of which becomes steeper halfway down.

**manse** /mæns/ *noun* (esp. Scottish Presbyterian) minister's house.

**mansion** /'mænʃ(ə)n/ *noun* large grand house; (in *plural*) block of flats.

**manslaughter** *noun* unintentional but not accidental unlawful killing of human being.

**mantel** /'mænt(ə)l/ *noun* mantelpiece, mantelshelf. □ **mantelpiece** structure above and around fireplace, mantelshelf; **mantelshelf** shelf above fireplace.

**mantilla** /mænˈtɪlə/ *noun* Spanish woman's lace scarf worn over head and shoulders.

**mantis** /'mæntɪs/ *noun* (*plural* same or **mantises**) kind of predatory insect.

**mantle** /'mænt(ə)l/ ● *noun* loose sleeveless cloak; covering; fragile tube round gas jet to give incandescent light. ● *verb* (**-ling**) clothe; conceal, envelop.

**manual** /'mænjʊəl/ ● *adjective* of or done with hands. ● *noun* reference book; organ keyboard played with hands, not feet. □ **manually** *adverb*.

**manufacture** /mænjʊˈfæktʃə/ ● *noun* making of articles, esp. in factory etc.; branch of industry. ● *verb* (**-ring**) make, esp. on industrial scale; invent, fabricate. □ **manufacturer** *noun.*

**manure** /mə'njʊə/ ● *noun* fertilizer, esp. dung. ● *verb* (**-ring**) treat with manure.

**manuscript** /'mænjʊskrɪpt/ ● *noun* book or document written by hand or typed, not printed. ● *adjective* written by hand.

**Manx** ● *adjective* of Isle of Man. ● *noun* Celtic language of Isle of Man. □ **Manx cat** tailless variety.

**many** /'menɪ/ ● *adjective* (**more, most**) numerous, great in number. ● *noun* (treated as *plural*) many people or things; (**the many**) the majority of people.

**Maori** /'maʊrɪ/ ● *noun* (*plural* same or **-s**) member of aboriginal NZ race; their language. ● *adjective* of this people.

**map** ● *noun* flat representation of (part of) earth's surface, or of sky; diagram. ● *verb* (**-pp-**) represent on map. □ **map out** plan in detail.

**maple** /'meɪp(ə)l/ *noun* kind of tree. □ **maple leaf** emblem of Canada; **maple sugar** sugar got by evaporating sap of some kinds of maple; **maple syrup** syrup got from maple sap or maple sugar.

**maquette** /mə'ket/ *noun* preliminary model or sketch.

**Mar.** *abbreviation* March.

**mar** *verb* (**-rr-**) spoil; disfigure.

**marabou** /'mærəbuː/ *noun* (*plural* **-s**) large W. African stork; its down as trimming etc.

**maraca** /mə'rækə/ *noun* clublike bean-filled gourd etc., shaken as percussion instrument.

**maraschino** /mærə'skiːnəʊ/ *noun* (*plural* **-s**) liqueur made from cherries. □ **maraschino cherry** one preserved in maraschino.

**marathon** /'mærəθ(ə)n/ *noun* long-distance foot race; long-lasting, esp. difficult, undertaking.

**maraud** /mə'rɔːd/ *verb* make raid; pillage. □ **marauder** *noun.*

**marble** /'maːb(ə)l/ ● *noun* kind of limestone used in sculpture and architecture; anything of or like marble; small ball of glass etc. as toy; (in *plural*; treated as *singular*) game played with these; (in *plural*) *slang* one's mental faculties; (in

*plural*) collection of sculptures. ● *verb* (**-ling**) (esp. as **marbled** *adjective*) give veined or mottled appearance to (esp. paper).

**marcasite** /'maːkəsaɪt/ *noun* crystalline iron sulphide; crystals of this used in jewellery.

**March** *noun* third month of year. □ **March hare** hare in breeding season.

**march** [1] ● *verb* walk in military manner or with regular paces; proceed steadily; cause to march or walk. ● *noun* act of marching; uniform military step; long difficult walk; procession as demonstration; progress; piece of music suitable for marching to. □ **march past** ceremonial march of troops past saluting point. □ **marcher** *noun.*

**march** [2] *noun* *historical* boundary (often in *plural*); tract of (often disputed) land between countries etc.

**marchioness** /maːʃə'nes/ *noun* marquess's wife or widow; woman holding rank of marquess.

**mare** /meə/ *noun* female equine animal, esp. horse. □ **mare's nest** illusory discovery.

**margarine** /maːdʒə'riːn/ *noun* butter substitute made from edible oils etc.

**marge** /maːdʒ/ *noun* *colloquial* margarine.

**margin** /'maːdʒɪn/ *noun* edge or border of surface; plain space round printed page etc.; amount by which thing exceeds, falls short, etc. □ **margin of error** allowance for miscalculation or mischance.

**marginal** *adjective* written in margin; of or at edge; (of constituency) having elected MP with small majority; close to limit, esp. of profitability; insignificant; barely adequate. □ **marginally** *adverb.*

**marginalize** *verb* (also **-ise**) (**-zing** or **-sing**) make or treat as insignificant. □ **marginalization** *noun.*

**marguerite** /maːgə'riːt/ *noun* ox-eye daisy.

**marigold** /'mærɪgəʊld/ *noun* plant with golden or bright yellow flowers.

**marijuana** /mærɪ'hwaːnə/ *noun* dried leaves etc. of hemp smoked as drug.

**marimba** /mə'rɪmbə/ *noun* African and Central American xylophone; orchestral instrument developed from this.

**marina** /məˈriːnə/ noun harbour for pleasure boats.

**marinade** /mærɪˈneɪd/ ● noun mixture of wine, vinegar, oil, spices, etc., for soaking fish or meat. ● verb (-ding) soak in marinade.

**marinate** /ˈmærɪneɪt/ verb (-ting) marinade.

**marine** /məˈriːn/ ● adjective of, found in, or produced by, the sea; of shipping; for use at sea. ● noun member of corps trained to fight on land or sea; country's shipping, fleet, or navy.

**mariner** /ˈmærɪnə/ noun seaman.

**marionette** /mærɪəˈnet/ noun puppet worked with strings.

**marital** /ˈmærɪt(ə)l/ adjective of or between husband and wife; of marriage.

**maritime** /ˈmærɪtaɪm/ adjective connected with the sea or seafaring; living or found near the sea.

**marjoram** /ˈmɑːdʒərəm/ noun aromatic herb used in cookery.

**mark**[1] ● noun visible sign left by person or thing; stain, scar, etc; written or printed symbol; number or letter denoting conduct or proficiency; (often + of) sign, indication; lasting effect; target, thing aimed at; line etc. serving to indicate position; (followed by numeral) particular design of piece of equipment. ● verb make mark on; distinguish with mark; correct and assess (student's work etc.); attach price to; notice, observe; characterize; acknowledge, celebrate; indicate on map etc.; keep close to (opposing player) in games; (in passive) have natural marks. □ **mark down** reduce price of; **mark off** separate by boundary; **mark out** plan (course), destine, trace out (boundaries etc.); **mark time** march on spot without moving forward, await opportunity to advance; **mark up** verb increase price of; **mark-up** noun amount added to price by retailer for profit.

**mark**[2] noun Deutschmark.

**marked** /mɑːkt/ adjective having a visible mark; clearly noticeable. □ **markedly** /-kɪdlɪ/ adverb.

**marker** noun thing that marks a position; person or thing that marks; pen with broad felt tip; scorer, esp. at billiards.

**market** /ˈmɑːkɪt/ ● noun gathering for sale of commodities, livestock, etc.; space for this; (often + for) demand for commodity etc.; place or group providing such demand; conditions for buying and selling; stock market. ● verb (-t-) offer for sale; archaic buy or sell goods in market. □ **market garden** place where vegetables are grown for market; **market-place** open space for market, commercial world; **market research** surveying of consumers' needs and preferences; **market town** town where market is held; **market value** value as saleable thing; **on the market** offered for sale. □ **marketing** noun.

**marketable** adjective able or fit to be sold.

**marking** noun (usually in plural) identification mark; colouring of fur, feathers, etc.

**marksman** /ˈmɑːksmən/ noun skilled shot, esp. with rifle. □ **marksmanship** noun.

**marl** noun soil composed of clay and lime, used as fertilizer.

**marlinspike** /ˈmɑːlɪnspaɪk/ noun pointed tool used to separate strands of rope or wire.

**marmalade** /ˈmɑːməleɪd/ noun preserve of oranges or other citrus fruit.

**Marmite** /ˈmɑːmaɪt/ noun proprietary term thick brown spread made from yeast and vegetable extract.

**marmoreal** /mɑːˈmɔːrɪəl/ adjective of or like marble.

**marmoset** /ˈmɑːməzet/ noun small bushy-tailed monkey.

**marmot** /ˈmɑːmət/ noun burrowing rodent with short bushy tail.

**marocain** /ˈmærəkeɪn/ noun fabric of ribbed crêpe.

**maroon**[1] /məˈruːn/ adjective & noun brownish-crimson.

**maroon**[2] /məˈruːn/ verb put and leave ashore on desolate island or coast; leave stranded.

**marquee** /mɑːˈkiː/ noun large tent.

**marquess** /ˈmɑːkwəs/ noun British nobleman ranking between duke and earl.

**marquetry** /ˈmɑːkɪtrɪ/ noun inlaid work in wood etc.

**marquis** /ˈmɑːkwɪs/ noun (plural **-quises**) foreign nobleman ranking between duke and count.

**marquise** /mɑːˈkiːz/ noun marquise's wife or widow; woman holding rank of marquis.

**marriage** /ˈmærɪdʒ/ noun legal union of man and woman for the purpose of living together; act or ceremony establishing this; particular matrimonial union. □ **marriage certificate, lines** certificate stating that marriage has taken place; **marriage guidance** counselling of people with marital problems.

**marriageable** adjective free, ready, or fit for marriage.

**marrow** /ˈmærəʊ/ noun large fleshy gourd, cooked as vegetable; bone marrow. □ **marrowbone** bone containing edible marrow; **marrowfat** kind of large pea.

**marry** /ˈmærɪ/ verb (**-ies, -ied**) take, join, or give in marriage; enter into marriage; (+ into) become member of (family) by marriage; unite intimately.

**Marsala** /mɑːˈsɑːlə/ noun dark sweet fortified wine.

**Marseillaise** /mɑːseɪˈjeɪz/ noun French national anthem.

**marsh** noun low watery ground. □ **marsh gas** methane; **marsh mallow** shrubby herb; **marshmallow** soft sweet made from sugar, albumen, gelatin, etc. □ **marshy** adjective (**-ier, -iest**).

**marshal** /ˈmɑːʃ(ə)l/ ● noun (**Marshal**) high-ranking officer of state or in armed forces; officer arranging ceremonies, controlling procedure at races, etc. ● verb (**-ll-**) arrange in due order; conduct (person) ceremoniously. □ **marshalling yard** yard in which goods trains etc. are assembled.

**marsupial** /mɑːˈsuːpɪəl/ ● noun mammal giving birth to underdeveloped young subsequently carried in pouch. ● adjective of or like a marsupial.

**mart** noun trade centre; auction-room; market.

**Martello tower** /mɑːˈteləʊ/ noun small circular coastal fort.

**marten** /ˈmɑːtɪn/ noun weasel-like flesh-eating mammal with valuable fur; its fur.

**martial** /ˈmɑːʃ(ə)l/ adjective of warfare; warlike. □ **martial arts** fighting sports such as judo or karate; **martial law** military government with ordinary law suspended.

**Martian** /ˈmɑːʃ(ə)n/ ● adjective of planet Mars. ● noun hypothetical inhabitant of Mars.

**martin** /ˈmɑːtɪn/ noun bird of swallow family.

**martinet** /mɑːtɪˈnet/ noun strict disciplinarian.

**Martini** /mɑːˈtiːnɪ/ noun (plural **-s**) proprietary term type of vermouth; cocktail of gin and vermouth.

**martyr** /ˈmɑːtə/ ● noun person who undergoes death or suffering for great cause; (+ to) colloquial constant sufferer from. ● verb put to death as martyr; torment. □ **martyrdom** noun.

**marvel** /ˈmɑːv(ə)l/ ● noun wonderful thing; (+ of) wonderful example of. ● verb (**-ll-**; US **-l-**) (+ at, that) feel surprise or wonder.

**marvellous** /ˈmɑːvələs/ adjective (US **marvelous**) astonishing; excellent. □ **marvellously** adverb.

**Marxism** /ˈmɑːksɪz(ə)m/ noun doctrines of Marx, predicting common ownership of means of production. □ **Marxist** noun & adjective.

**marzipan** /ˈmɑːzɪpæn/ noun paste of ground almonds, sugar, etc.

**mascara** /mæsˈkɑːrə/ noun cosmetic for darkening eyelashes.

**mascot** /ˈmæskɒt/ noun person, animal, or thing supposed to bring luck.

**masculine** /ˈmæskjʊlɪn/ adjective of men; manly; Grammar belonging to gender including words for most male people and animals. □ **masculinity** /-ˈlɪn-/ noun.

**maser** /ˈmeɪzə/ noun device for amplifying or generating microwaves.

**mash** ● noun soft or confused mixture; mixture of boiled bran etc. fed to horses; colloquial mashed potatoes. ● verb crush (potatoes etc.) to pulp.

**mask** /mɑːsk/ ● noun covering for all or part of face, worn as disguise or for protection, or by surgeon etc. to prevent infection of patient; respirator; likeness of person's face, esp. one made by taking mould from face; disguise.

● *verb* cover with mask; conceal; protect.

**masochism** /ˈmæsəkɪz(ə)m/ *noun* pleasure in suffering physical or mental pain, esp. as form of sexual perversion. □ **masochist** *noun*; **masochistic** /-ˈkɪs-/ *adjective*.

**mason** /ˈmeɪs(ə)n/ *noun* person who builds with stone; **(Mason)** Freemason.

**Masonic** /məˈsɒnɪk/ *adjective* of Freemasons.

**masonry** /ˈmeɪsənrɪ/ *noun* stonework; mason's work; **(Masonry)** Freemasonry.

**masque** /mɑːsk/ *noun* musical drama with mime, esp. in 16th & 17th c.

**masquerade** /mæskəˈreɪd/ ● *noun* false show, pretence; masked ball. ● *verb* **(-ding)** appear in disguise; assume false appearance.

**mass**[1] ● *noun* cohesive body of matter; dense aggregation; (in *singular* or *plural*, usually + *of*) large number or amount; (usually + *of*) unbroken expanse (of colour etc.); **(the mass)** the majority; **(the masses)** ordinary people; *Physics* quantity of matter body contains. ● *verb* gather into mass; assemble into one body. ● *adjective* of or relating to large numbers of people or things. □ **mass media** means of communication to large numbers of people; **mass production** mechanical production of large quantities of standardized article.

**mass**[2] *noun* (often **Mass**) Eucharist, esp. in RC Church; (musical setting of) liturgy used in this.

**massacre** /ˈmæsəkə/ ● *noun* general slaughter. ● *verb* **(-ring)** make massacre of.

**massage** /ˈmæsɑːʒ/ ● *noun* kneading and rubbing of muscles etc., usually with hands. ● *verb* **(-ging)** treat thus.

**masseur** /mæˈsɜː/ *noun* (*feminine* **masseuse** /mæˈsɜːz/) person who gives massage.

**massif** /ˈmæsiːf/ *noun* mountain heights forming compact group.

**massive** /ˈmæsɪv/ *adjective* large and heavy or solid; unusually large or severe; substantial. □ **massively** *adverb*.

**mast**[1] /mɑːst/ *noun* upright to which ship's yards and sails are attached; tall

metal structure supporting radio or television aerial; flag-pole.

**mast**[2] /mɑːst/ *noun* fruit of beech, oak, etc., esp. as food for pigs.

**mastectomy** /mæˈstektəmɪ/ *noun* (*plural* **-ies**) surgical removal of a breast.

**master** /ˈmɑːstə/ ● *noun* person having control or ownership; ship's captain; male teacher; prevailing person; skilled workman; skilled practitioner; holder of university degree above bachelor's; revered teacher; great artist; *Chess etc.* player at international level; thing from which series of copies is made; **(Master)** *title prefixed to name of boy.* ● *adjective* commanding; main, principal; controlling others. ● *verb* overcome, conquer; acquire complete knowledge of. □ **master-key** one opening several different locks; **mastermind** *noun* person with outstanding intellect, *verb* plan and direct (enterprise); **Master of Ceremonies** person introducing speakers at banquet or entertainers at variety show; **masterpiece** outstanding piece of artistry, one's best work; **master-switch** switch controlling electricity etc. supply to entire system.

**masterful** *adjective* imperious, domineering; very skilful. □ **masterfully** *adverb*.

■ **Usage** *Masterful* is normally used of a person, whereas *masterly* is used of achievements, abilities, etc.

**masterly** *adjective* very skilful.

■ **Usage** See note at MASTERFUL.

**mastery** *noun* control, dominance; (often + *of*) comprehensive skill or knowledge.

**mastic** /ˈmæstɪk/ *noun* gum or resin from certain trees; such tree; waterproof filler and sealant.

**masticate** /ˈmæstɪkeɪt/ *verb* **(-ting)** chew. □ **mastication** *noun*.

**mastiff** /ˈmæstɪf/ *noun* large strong kind of dog.

**mastodon** /ˈmæstədɒn/ *noun* (*plural* same or **-s**) extinct animal resembling elephant.

**mastoid** /ˈmæstɔɪd/ ● *adjective* shaped like woman's breast. ● *noun* (in full **mastoid process**) conical prominence on temporal bone; (usually in *plural*) *colloquial* inflammation of mastoid.

**masturbate** /'mæstəbeɪt/ *verb* (-ting) produce sexual arousal (of) by manual stimulation of genitals. □ **masturbation** *noun*.

**mat**[1] ● *noun* piece of coarse fabric on floor, esp. for wiping shoes on; piece of material laid on table etc. to protect surface. ● *verb* (-tt-) (esp. as **matted** *adjective*) bring or come into thickly tangled state. □ **on the mat** *slang* being reprimanded.

**mat**[2] = MATT.

**matador** /'mætədɔ:/ *noun* bullfighter whose task is to kill bull.

**match**[1] ● *noun* contest, game; person or thing equal to, exactly resembling, or corresponding to another; marriage; person viewed as marriage prospect. ● *verb* be equal, correspond; be or find match for; (+ *against, with*) place in conflict or competition with. □ **matchboard** tongued and grooved board fitting into others; **matchmaker** person who arranges marriages or schemes to bring couples together; **match point** state of game when one side needs only one point to win match; **match up** (often + *with*) fit to form whole, tally; **match up to** be equal to.

**match**[2] *noun* short thin piece of wood etc., tipped with substance that ignites when rubbed on rough or specially prepared surface. □ **matchbox** box for holding matches; **matchstick** stem of match; **matchwood** wood suitable for matches, minute splinters.

**matchless** *adjective* incomparable.

**mate**[1] ● *noun* companion, fellow worker; *colloquial form of address, esp. to another man*; each of a breeding pair, esp. of birds; *colloquial* partner in marriage; subordinate officer on merchant ship; assistant to worker. ● *verb* (-ting) come or bring together for breeding.

**mate**[2] *noun & verb* (-ting) checkmate.

**material** /mə'tɪərɪəl/ ● *noun* that from which thing is made; cloth, fabric; (in *plural*) things needed for activity; person or thing of specified kind or suitable for purpose; (in *singular* or *plural*) information etc. for book etc.; (in *singular* or *plural*) elements. ● *adjective* of matter; not

spiritual; of bodily comfort etc.; important, relevant.

**materialism** *noun* greater interest in material possessions and comfort than in spiritual values; theory that nothing exists but matter. □ **materialist** *noun*; **materialistic** /-'lɪs-/ *adjective*.

**materialize** *verb* (also **-ise**) (-zing or -sing) become fact, happen; *colloquial* appear, be present; represent in or assume bodily form. □ **materialization** *noun*.

**maternal** /mə'tɜ:n(ə)l/ *adjective* of or like a mother; motherly; related on mother's side.

**maternity** /mə'tɜ:nɪtɪ/ ● *noun* motherhood; motherliness. ● *adjective* for women in pregnancy or childbirth.

**matey** *adjective* (also **maty**) (-tier, -tiest) familiar and friendly. □ **matily** *adverb*.

**math** *noun US colloquial* mathematics.

**mathematics** /mæθə'mætɪks/ *plural noun* (also treated as *singular*) science of space, number, and quantity. □ **mathematical** *adjective*; **mathematician** /-mə'tɪʃ(ə)n/ *noun*.

**maths** *noun colloquial* mathematics.

**matinée** /'mætɪneɪ/ *noun* (*US* **matinee**) theatrical etc. performance in afternoon. □ **matinée coat** baby's short coat.

**matins** /'mætɪnz/ *noun* (also **mattins**) morning prayer.

**matriarch** /'meɪtrɪɑ:k/ *noun* female head of family or tribe. □ **matriarchal** /-'ɑ:k(ə)l/ *adjective*.

**matriarchy** /'meɪtrɪɑ:kɪ/ *noun* (*plural* **-ies**) female-dominated system of society.

**matrices** *plural of* MATRIX.

**matricide** /'meɪtrɪsaɪd/ *noun* killing of one's mother; person who does this.

**matriculate** /mə'trɪkjʊleɪt/ *verb* (-ting) admit (student) to university; be thus admitted. □ **matriculation** *noun*.

**matrimony** /'mætrɪmənɪ/ *noun* marriage. □ **matrimonial** /-'məʊnɪəl/ *adjective*.

**matrix** /'meɪtrɪks/ *noun* (*plural* **matrices** /-si:z/ or **-es**) mould in which thing is cast or shaped; place etc. in which thing is developed; rock in which gems etc. are embedded; *Mathematics* rectangular array of quantities treated as single quantity.

**matron** /'meɪtrən/ *noun* woman in charge of nursing in hospital; married, esp. staid, woman; woman nurse and housekeeper at school etc.

**matronly** *adjective* like a matron, esp. portly or staid.

**matt** *adjective* (also **mat**) dull, not shiny or glossy.

**matter** /'mætə/ ●*noun* physical substance; thing(s), material; (**the matter**; often + *with*) thing that is amiss; content as opposed to form, substance; affair, concern; purulent discharge. ●*verb* (often + *to*) be of importance. □ **a matter of** approximately, amounting to; **matter of course** natural or expected thing; **matter-of-fact** prosaic, unimaginative, unemotional; **no matter** (+ *when, how,* etc.) regardless of.

**matting** *noun* fabric for mats.

**mattins** = MATINS.

**mattock** /'mætək/ *noun* tool like pickaxe with adze and chisel edge as ends of head.

**mattress** /'mætrɪs/ *noun* fabric case filled with soft or firm material or springs, used on or as bed.

**mature** /mə'tʃʊə/ ●*adjective* (**-r, -st**) fully developed, ripe; adult; careful, considered; (of bill etc.) due for payment. ●*verb* (**-ring**) bring to or reach mature state. □ **maturity** *noun*.

**matutinal** /mætjuː'taɪn(ə)l/ *adjective* of or in morning.

**maty** = MATEY.

**maudlin** /'mɔːdlɪn/ *adjective* weakly sentimental.

**maul** /mɔːl/ ●*verb* injure by clawing etc.; handle roughly; damage. ●*noun* Rugby loose scrum; brawl; heavy hammer.

**maulstick** /'mɔːlstɪk/ *noun* stick held to support hand in painting.

**maunder** /'mɔːndə/ *verb* talk ramblingly.

**Maundy** /'mɔːndɪ/ *noun* distribution of **Maundy money**, silver coins minted for English sovereign to give to the poor on **Maundy Thursday**, Thursday before Easter.

**mausoleum** /mɔːsə'liːəm/ *noun* magnificent tomb.

**mauve** /məʊv/ *adjective & noun* pale purple.

**maverick** /'mævərɪk/ *noun* unorthodox or independent-minded person; *US* unbranded calf etc.

**maw** *noun* stomach of animal.

**mawkish** /'mɔːkɪʃ/ *adjective* feebly sentimental.

**maxillary** /mæk'sɪlərɪ/ *adjective* of the jaw.

**maxim** /'mæksɪm/ *noun* general truth or rule of conduct briefly expressed.

**maxima** *plural* of MAXIMUM.

**maximal** /'mæksɪm(ə)l/ *adjective* greatest possible in size, duration, etc.

**maximize** /'mæksɪmaɪz/ *verb* (also **-ise**) (**-zing** or **-sing**) make as large or great as possible. □ **maximization** *noun*.

■ **Usage** *Maximize* should not be used in standard English to mean 'to make as good as possible' or 'to make the most of'.

**maximum** /'mæksɪməm/ ●*noun* (*plural* **maxima**) highest possible amount, size, etc. ●*adjective* greatest in amount, size, etc.

**May** *noun* fifth month of year; (**may**) hawthorn, esp. in blossom. □ **May Day** 1 May as Spring festival or as international holiday in honour of workers; **mayfly** insect living briefly in spring as adult; **maypole** decorated pole danced round on May Day; **May queen** girl chosen to preside over May Day festivities.

**may** *auxiliary verb* (*3rd singular present* **may**; *past* **might** /maɪt/) *expressing possibility, permission, request, wish,* etc. □ **be that as it may** although that is possible.

■ **Usage** Both *can* and *may* are used for asking permission, as in *Can I move?* and *May I move?*, but *may* is better in formal English because *Can I move?* also means 'Am I physically able to move?'

**maybe** /'meɪbiː/ *adverb* perhaps.

**mayday** /'meɪdeɪ/ *noun* international radio distress signal.

**mayhem** /'meɪhem/ *noun* destruction, havoc.

**mayonnaise** /meɪə'neɪz/ *noun* creamy dressing of oil, egg yolk, vinegar, etc.; dish dressed with this.

**mayor** /meə/ *noun* head of corporation of city or borough; head of district council with status of borough. □ **mayoral** *adjective*.

**mayoralty** /ˈmeərəltɪ/ *noun* (*plural* **-ies**) office of mayor; period of this.

**mayoress** /ˈmeərɪs/ *noun* woman mayor; wife or consort of mayor.

**maze** *noun* network of paths and hedges designed as puzzle; labyrinth; confused network, mass, etc.

**mazurka** /məˈzɜːkə/ *noun* lively Polish dance in triple time; music for this.

**MB** *abbreviation* Bachelor of Medicine.

**MBE** *abbreviation* Member of the Order of the British Empire.

**MC** *abbreviation* Master of Ceremonies; Military Cross.

**MCC** *abbreviation* Marylebone Cricket Club.

**MD** *abbreviation* Doctor of Medicine; Managing Director.

**me**[1] /miː/ *pronoun used by speaker or writer to refer to himself or herself as object of verb*; *colloquial* I.

■ **Usage** Some people consider it correct to use only *It is I*, but this is very formal or old-fashioned in most situations, and *It is me* is normally quite acceptable. On the other hand, it is not standard English to say *Me and him went* rather than *He and I went*.

**me**[2] /miː/ *noun* (also **mi**) *Music* third note of scale in tonic sol-fa.

**mead** *noun* alcoholic drink of fermented honey and water.

**meadow** /ˈmedəʊ/ *noun* piece of grassland, esp. used for hay; low ground, esp. near river. □ **meadowsweet** a fragrant flowering plant.

**meagre** /ˈmiːɡə/ *adjective* (*US* **meager**) scanty in amount or quality.

**meal**[1] *noun* occasion when food is eaten; the food eaten on one occasion. □ **meal-ticket** *colloquial* source of income.

**meal**[2] *noun* grain or pulse ground to powder.

**mealy** *adjective* (**-ier**, **-iest**) of, like, or containing meal. □ **mealy-mouthed** afraid to speak plainly.

**mean**[1] *verb* (*past & past participle* **meant** /ment/) have as one's purpose, design; intend to convey or indicate; involve, portend; (of word) have as equivalent in same or another language; (+ *to*) be of specified significance to.

**mean**[2] *adjective* niggardly; not generous; ignoble; of low degree or poor quality; malicious; *US* vicious, aggressive. □ **meanness** *noun*.

**mean**[3] ● *noun* condition, quality, or course of action equally far from two extremes; term midway between first and last terms of progression; quotient of the sum of several quantities and their number. ● *adjective* (of quantity) equally far from two extremes; calculated as mean.

**meander** /mɪˈændə/ ● *verb* wander at random; wind about. ● *noun* (in *plural*) sinuous windings; circuitous journey.

**meaning** ● *noun* what is meant; significance. ● *adjective* expressive; significant. □ **meaningful** *adjective*; **meaningfully** *adverb*; **meaningless** *adjective*; **meaninglessness** *noun*.

**means** *plural noun* (often treated as *singular*) action, agent, device, or method producing result; money resources. □ **means test** inquiry into financial resources of applicant for assistance etc.

**meantime** ● *adverb* meanwhile. ● *noun* intervening period.

**meanwhile** *adverb* in the intervening time; at the same time.

**measles** /ˈmiːz(ə)lz/ *plural noun* (also treated as *singular*) infectious viral disease with red rash.

**measly** /ˈmiːzlɪ/ *adjective* (**-ier**, **-iest**) *colloquial* meagre, contemptible.

**measure** /ˈmeʒə/ ● *noun* size or quantity found by measuring; system or unit of measuring; vessel, rod, tape, etc., for measuring; degree, extent; factor determining evaluation etc.; (usually in *plural*) suitable action; legislative enactment; prescribed extent or amount; poetic metre. ● *verb* (**-ring**) find size, quantity, proportions, etc. of by comparison with known standard; be of specified size; estimate by some criterion; (often + *off*) mark (line etc. of given length); (+ *out*) distribute in measured quantities; (+ *with*, *against*) bring into competition with. □ **measurable** *adjective*; **measurement** *noun*.

**measured** *adjective* rhythmical; (of language) carefully considered.

**measureless** *adjective* not measurable; infinite.

**meat** *noun* animal flesh as food; (often + *of*) chief part.

**meaty** *adjective* (**-ier, -iest**) full of meat; fleshy; of or like meat; substantial, satisfying.

**Mecca** /'mekə/ *noun* place one aspires to visit.

**mechanic** /mɪ'kænɪk/ *noun* person skilled in using or repairing machinery.

**mechanical** *adjective* of, working, or produced by, machines or mechanism; automatic; lacking originality; of mechanics as a science. □ **mechanically** *adverb*.

**mechanics** /mɪ'kænɪks/ *plural noun* (usually treated as *singular*) branch of applied mathematics dealing with motion; science of machinery; routine technical aspects of thing.

**mechanism** /'mekənɪz(ə)m/ *noun* structure or parts of machine; system of parts working together; process, method.

**mechanize** /'mekənaɪz/ *verb* (also **-ise**) (**-zing** or **-sing**) introduce machines in; make mechanical; equip with tanks, armoured cars, etc. □ **mechanization** *noun*.

**medal** /'med(ə)l/ *noun* commemorative metal disc etc., esp. awarded for military or sporting prowess.

**medallion** /mɪ'dæljən/ *noun* large medal; thing so shaped, e.g. portrait.

**medallist** /'medəlɪst/ *noun* (*US* **medalist**) winner of (specified) medal.

**meddle** /'med(ə)l/ *verb* (**-ling**) (often + *with, in*) interfere in others' concerns.

**meddlesome** *adjective* interfering.

**media** *plural* of MEDIUM.

■ **Usage** It is a mistake to use *media* with a singular verb, as in *The media is biased*.

**mediaeval** = MEDIEVAL.

**median** /'mi:dɪən/ ● *adjective* situated in the middle. ● *noun* straight line from angle of triangle to middle of opposite side; middle value of series.

**mediate** /'mi:dɪeɪt/ *verb* (**-ting**) act as go-between or peacemaker. □ **mediation** *noun*; **mediator** *noun*.

**medical** /'medɪk(ə)l/ ● *adjective* of medicine in general or as distinct from surgery. ● *noun* colloquial medical examination. □ **medical certificate** certificate of fitness or unfitness to work etc.; **medical examination** examination to determine person's physical fitness. □ **medically** *adverb*.

**medicament** /mɪ'dɪkəmənt/ *noun* substance used in curative treatment.

**medicate** /'medɪkeɪt/ *verb* (**-ting**) treat medically; impregnate with medicinal substance.

**medication** /medɪ'keɪʃ(ə)n/ *noun* medicinal drug; treatment using drugs.

**medicinal** /mə'dɪsɪn(ə)l/ *adjective* (of substance) healing.

**medicine** /'meds(ə)n/ *noun* science or practice of diagnosis, treatment, and prevention of disease, esp. as distinct from surgery; substance, esp. one taken by mouth, used in this. □ **medicine man** witch-doctor.

**medieval** /medɪ'i:v(ə)l/ *adjective* (also **mediaeval**) of Middle Ages.

**mediocre** /mi:dɪ'əʊkə/ *adjective* indifferent in quality; second-rate.

**mediocrity** /mi:dɪ'ɒkrɪtɪ/ *noun* (*plural* **-ies**) being mediocre; mediocre person.

**meditate** /'medɪteɪt/ *verb* (**-ting**) engage in (esp. religious) contemplation; plan mentally. □ **meditation** *noun*; **meditative** /-tətɪv/ *adjective*.

**Mediterranean** /medɪtə'reɪnɪən/ *adjective* of the sea between Europe and N. Africa, or the countries bordering on it.

**medium** /'mi:dɪəm/ ● *noun* (*plural* **media** or **-s**) middle quality, degree, etc. between extremes; environment; means of communication; physical material or form used by artist, composer, etc.; (*plural* **-s**) person claiming to communicate with the dead. ● *adjective* between two qualities etc.; average. □ **medium-range** (of aircraft, missile, etc.) able to travel medium distance.

**medlar** /'medlə/ *noun* tree bearing fruit like apple, eaten when decayed; such fruit.

**medley** /'medlɪ/ *noun* (*plural* **-s**) varied mixture.

**medulla** /mɪˈdʌlə/ *noun* inner part of certain bodily organs; soft internal tissue of plants. □ **medulla oblongata** /ˌɒblɒŋˈɡɑːtə/ lowest part of brainstem. □ **medullary** *adjective*.

**meek** *adjective* humble and submissive or gentle. □ **meekly** *adverb*; **meekness** *noun*.

**meerschaum** /ˈmɪəʃəm/ *noun* soft white clay-like substance; tobacco pipe with bowl made from this.

**meet¹** ● *verb* (*past & past participle* **met**) encounter or (of two or more people) come together; be present at arrival of (person, train, etc.); come into contact (with); make acquaintance of; deal with (demand etc.); (often + *with*) experience, receive. ● *noun* assembly for a hunt; assembly for athletics.

**meet²** *adjective archaic* fitting, proper.

**meeting** *noun* coming together; assembly of esp. a society, committee, etc.; race meeting.

**mega-** *combining form* large; one million; *slang* extremely, very big.

**megabyte** /ˈmeɡəbaɪt/ *noun* $2^{20}$ bytes (approx. 1,000,000) as unit of computer storage.

**megalith** /ˈmeɡəlɪθ/ *noun* large stone, esp. prehistoric monument. □ **megalithic** /-ˈlɪθ-/ *adjective*.

**megalomania** /ˌmeɡələˈmeɪnɪə/ *noun* mental disorder producing delusions of grandeur; passion for grandiose schemes. □ **megalomaniac** *adjective & noun*.

**megaphone** /ˈmeɡəfəʊn/ *noun* large funnel-shaped device for amplifying voice.

**megaton** /ˈmeɡətʌn/ *noun* unit of explosive power equal to that of 1,000,000 tons of TNT.

**meiosis** /maɪˈəʊsɪs/ *noun* (*plural* **meioses** /-siːz/) cell division resulting in gametes with half normal chromosome number; ironical understatement.

**melamine** /ˈmeləmiːn/ *noun* crystalline compound producing resins; plastic made from this.

**melancholia** /ˌmelənˈkəʊlɪə/ *noun* depression and anxiety.

**melancholy** /ˈmelənkəlɪ/ ● *noun* pensive sadness; depression; tendency to this.

● *adjective* sad; depressing. □ **melancholic** /-ˈkɒl-/ *adjective*.

**mêlée** /ˈmeleɪ/ *noun* (*US* **melee**) confused fight or scuffle; muddle.

**mellifluous** /mɪˈlɪfluəs/ *adjective* (of voice etc.) pleasing, musical.

**mellow** /ˈmeləʊ/ ● *adjective* (of sound, colour, light, or flavour) soft and rich, free from harshness; (of character) gentle; mature; genial. ● *verb* make or become mellow.

**melodic** /mɪˈlɒdɪk/ *adjective* of melody; melodious.

**melodious** /mɪˈləʊdɪəs/ *adjective* of, producing, or having melody; sweet-sounding. □ **melodiously** *adverb*.

**melodrama** /ˈmelədrɑːmə/ *noun* sensational play etc. appealing blatantly to emotions; this type of drama. □ **melodramatic** /-drəˈmæt-/ *adjective*.

**melody** /ˈmelədɪ/ *noun* (*plural* **-ies**) arrangement of notes to make distinctive pattern; tune; principal part in harmonized music; tunefulness.

**melon** /ˈmelən/ *noun* sweet fleshy fruit of various climbers of gourd family.

**melt** *verb* become liquid or change from solid to liquid by action of heat; dissolve; (as **molten** *adjective*) (esp. of metals etc.) liquefied by heat; soften; be softened; (usually + *into*) merge; (often + *away*) leave unobtrusively. □ **melt down** melt (esp. metal) for reuse, become liquid and lose structure; **melting point** temperature at which solid melts; **melting pot** place for mixing races, theories, etc.

**member** /ˈmembə/ *noun* person etc. belonging to society, team, group, etc.; (**Member**) person elected to certain assemblies; part of larger structure; part or organ of body, esp. limb.

**membership** *noun* being a member; number or group of members.

**membrane** /ˈmembreɪn/ *noun* pliable tissue connecting or lining organs in plants and animals; pliable sheet or skin. □ **membranous** /-brən-/ *adjective*.

**memento** /mɪˈmentəʊ/ *noun* (*plural* **-es** or **-s**) souvenir of person or event.

**memo** /ˈmeməʊ/ *noun* (*plural* **-s**) *colloquial* memorandum.

**memoir** /'memwɑː/ noun historical account etc. written from personal knowledge or special sources; (in plural) autobiography.

**memorable** /'memərəb(ə)l/ adjective worth remembering; easily remembered. □ **memorably** adverb.

**memorandum** /memə'rændəm/ noun (plural **-da** or **-s**) note or record for future use; informal written message, esp. in business etc.

**memorial** /mɪ'mɔːrɪəl/ • noun object etc. established in memory of person or event. • adjective commemorative.

**memoriam** see IN MEMORIAM.

**memorize** /'meməraɪz/ verb (also **-ise**) (**-zing** or **-sing**) commit to memory.

**memory** /'memərɪ/ noun (plural **-ies**) faculty by which things are recalled to or kept in mind; store of things remembered; remembrance, esp. of person etc.; storage capacity of computer etc.; posthumous reputation.

**memsahib** /'memsɑːb/ noun historical European married woman in India.

**men** plural of MAN.

**menace** /'menɪs/ • noun threat; dangerous thing or person; jocular nuisance. • verb (**-cing**) threaten. □ **menacingly** adverb.

**ménage** /meɪ'nɑːʒ/ noun household.

**menagerie** /mɪ'nædʒərɪ/ noun small zoo.

**mend** • verb restore to good condition; repair; regain health; improve. • noun darn or repair in material etc. □ **on the mend** recovering, esp. in health.

**mendacious** /men'deɪʃəs/ adjective lying, untruthful. □ **mendacity** /-'dæs-/ noun (plural **-ies**).

**mendicant** /'mendɪkənt/ • adjective begging; (of friar) living solely on alms. • noun beggar; mendicant friar.

**menfolk** plural noun men, esp. men of family.

**menhir** /'menhɪə/ noun usually prehistoric monument of tall upright stone.

**menial** /'miːnɪəl/ • adjective (of work) degrading, servile. • noun domestic servant.

**meningitis** /menɪn'dʒaɪtɪs/ noun (esp. viral) infection and inflammation of membranes enclosing brain and spinal cord.

**meniscus** /mɪ'nɪskəs/ noun (plural **menisci** /-saɪ/) curved upper surface of liquid in tube; lens convex on one side and concave on the other.

**menopause** /'menəpɔːz/ noun ceasing of menstruation; period in woman's life when this occurs. □ **menopausal** /-'pɔːz(ə)l/ adjective.

**menses** /'mensiːz/ plural noun flow of menstrual blood etc.

**menstrual** /'menstrʊəl/ adjective of menstruation.

**menstruate** /'menstrʊeɪt/ verb (**-ting**) undergo menstruation.

**menstruation** noun discharge of blood etc. from uterus, usually at monthly intervals.

**mensuration** /mensjʊə'reɪʃ(ə)n/ noun measuring; measuring of lengths, areas, and volumes.

**mental** /'ment(ə)l/ adjective of, in, or done by mind; caring for mental patients; colloquial insane. □ **mental age** degree of mental development in terms of average age at which such development is attained; **mental deficiency** abnormally low intelligence; **mental patient** sufferer from mental illness. □ **mentally** adverb.

**mentality** /men'tælɪtɪ/ noun (plural **-ies**) mental character or disposition.

**menthol** /'menθɒl/ noun mint-tasting organic alcohol found in oil of peppermint etc., used as flavouring and to relieve local pain.

**mention** /'menʃ(ə)n/ • verb refer to briefly or by name; disclose. • noun reference, esp. by name.

**mentor** /'mentɔː/ noun experienced and trusted adviser.

**menu** /'menjuː/ noun (plural **-s**) list of dishes available in restaurant etc., or to be served at meal; Computing list of options displayed on VDU.

**MEP** abbreviation Member of European Parliament.

**mercantile** /'mɜːkəntaɪl/ adjective of trade, trading; commercial. □ **mercantile marine** merchant shipping.

**mercenary** /'mɜːsɪnərɪ/ • adjective primarily concerned with or working for money etc. • noun (plural **-ies**) hired soldier in foreign service.

**mercer** /'mɜːsə/ noun dealer in textile fabrics.

**mercerize** /'mɜːsəraɪz/ verb (also **-ise**) (**-zing** or **-sing**) treat (cotton) with caustic alkali to strengthen and make lustrous.

**merchandise** /'mɜːtʃəndaɪz/ ● noun goods for sale. ● verb (**-sing**) trade (in); promote (goods, ideas, etc.).

**merchant** /'mɜːtʃ(ə)nt/ noun wholesale trader, esp. with foreign countries; esp. US & Scottish retail trader. □ **merchant bank** bank dealing in commercial loans and finance; **merchantman** merchant ship; **merchant navy** nation's commercial shipping; **merchant ship** ship carrying merchandise.

**merchantable** adjective saleable.

**merciful** /'mɜːsɪfʊl/ adjective showing mercy. □ **mercifulness** noun.

**mercifully** adverb in a merciful way; fortunately.

**merciless** /'mɜːsɪləs/ adjective showing no mercy. □ **mercilessly** adverb.

**mercurial** /mɜːˈkjʊərɪəl/ adjective (of person) volatile; of or containing mercury.

**mercury** /'mɜːkjʊrɪ/ noun silvery heavy liquid metal used in barometers, thermometers, etc.; (**Mercury**) planet nearest to the sun. □ **mercuric** /-ˈkjʊər-/ adjective; **mercurous** adjective.

**mercy** /'mɜːsɪ/ noun (plural **-ies**) compassion towards defeated enemies or offenders or as quality; act of mercy; thing to be thankful for. □ **at the mercy of** in the power of; **mercy killing** killing done out of pity.

**mere**[1] /mɪə/ adjective (**-st**) being only what is specified. □ **merely** adverb.

**mere**[2] /mɪə/ noun dialect or poetical lake.

**meretricious** /merəˈtrɪʃəs/ adjective showily but falsely attractive.

**merganser** /mɜːˈgænsə/ noun (plural same or **-s**) a diving duck.

**merge** verb (**-ging**) (often + with) combine, join or blend gradually; (+ in) (cause to) lose character and identity in (something else).

**merger** noun combining, esp. of two commercial companies etc. into one.

**meridian** /məˈrɪdɪən/ noun circle of constant longitude passing through given place and N. & S. Poles; corresponding line on map etc.

**meridional** /məˈrɪdɪən(ə)l/ adjective of or in the south (esp. of Europe); of a meridian.

**meringue** /məˈræŋ/ noun sugar, whipped egg whites, etc. baked crisp; cake of this.

**merino** /məˈriːnəʊ/ noun (plural **-s**) variety of sheep with long fine wool; soft material, originally of merino wool; fine woollen yarn.

**merit** /'merɪt/ ● noun quality of deserving well; excellence; worth; (usually in plural) thing that entitles to reward or gratitude. ● verb (**-t-**) deserve.

**meritocracy** /merɪˈtɒkrəsɪ/ noun (plural **-ies**) government by those selected for merit; group selected in this way.

**meritorious** /merɪˈtɔːrɪəs/ adjective praiseworthy.

**merlin** /'mɜːlɪn/ noun kind of small falcon.

**mermaid** /'mɜːmeɪd/ noun legendary creature with woman's head and trunk and fish's tail.

**merry** /'merɪ/ adjective (**-ier, -iest**) joyous; full of laughter or gaiety; colloquial slightly drunk. □ **merry-go-round** fairground ride with revolving model horses, cars, etc.; **merrymaking** festivity. □ **merrily** adverb; **merriment** noun.

**mésalliance** /merˈzælɪɑ̃s/ noun marriage with social inferior. [French]

**mescal** /'meskæl/ noun peyote cactus. □ **mescal buttons** disc-shaped dried tops from mescal, esp. as intoxicant.

**mescaline** /'meskəlɪn/ noun (also **mescalin**) hallucinogenic alkaloid present in mescal buttons.

**Mesdames, Mesdemoiselles** plural of MADAME, MADEMOISELLE.

**mesh** ● noun network structure; each of open spaces in net, sieve, etc.; (in plural) network, snare. ● verb (often + with) (of teeth of wheel) be engaged; be harmonious; catch in net.

**mesmerize** /'mezməraɪz/ verb (also **-ise**) (**-zing** or **-sing**) hypnotize; fascinate. □ **mesmerism** noun.

**meso-** combining form middle, intermediate.

**mesolithic** /mezəʊˈlɪθɪk/ adjective of Stone Age between palaeolithic and neolithic periods.

**meson** /'miːzɒn/ • *noun* elementary particle with mass between that of electron and proton.

**Mesozoic** /mesəʊ'zəʊɪk/ • *adjective* of geological era marked by development of dinosaurs. • *noun* this era.

**mess** • *noun* dirty or untidy state; state of confusion or trouble; something spilt etc.; disagreeable concoction; soldiers etc. dining together; army dininghall; meal taken there; domestic animal's excreta; *archaic* portion of liquid or pulpy food. • *verb* (often + *up*) make mess of, dirty, muddle; *US* (+ *with*) interfere with; take one's meals; *colloquial* defecate. □ **make a mess of** bungle; **mess about, around** potter.

**message** /'mesɪdʒ/ *noun* communication sent by one person to another; exalted or spiritual communication.

**messenger** /'mesɪndʒə/ *noun* person who carries message(s).

**Messiah** /mɪ'saɪə/ *noun* promised deliverer of Jews; Jesus regarded as this. □ **Messianic** /mesɪ'ænɪk/ *adjective*.

**Messieurs** *plural of* MONSIEUR.

**Messrs** /'mesəz/ *plural of* MR.

**messy** *adjective* (**-ier, -iest**) untidy, dirty; causing or accompanied by a mess; difficult to deal with; awkward. □ **messily** *adverb*.

**met** *past & past participle of* MEET[1].

**metabolism** /mɪ'tæbəlɪz(ə)m/ *noun* all chemical processes in living organism producing energy and growth. □ **metabolic** /metə'bɒlɪk/ *adjective*.

**metacarpus** /metə'kɑːpəs/ *noun* (*plural* **-carpi** /-paɪ/) set of bones forming part of hand between wrist and fingers. □ **metacarpal** *adjective*.

**metal** /'met(ə)l/ • *noun* any of class of mainly workable elements such as gold, silver, iron, or tin; alloy of any of these; (in *plural*) rails of railway; roadmetal. • *adjective* made of metal. • *verb* (**-ll-**; *US* **-l-**) make or mend (road) with road-metal; cover or fit with metal.

**metallic** /mɪ'tælɪk/ *adjective* of or like metal(s); sounding like struck metal.

**metallurgy** /mɪ'tælədʒɪ/ *noun* science of metals and their application; extraction and purification of metals. □ **metallurgic** /metə'lɜːdʒɪk/ *adjective*; **metallurgical** /metə'lɜːdʒɪk(ə)l/ *adjective*; **metallurgist** *noun*.

**metamorphic** /metə'mɔːfɪk/ *adjective* of metamorphosis; (of rock) transformed naturally. □ **metamorphism** *noun*.

**metamorphose** /metə'mɔːfəʊz/ *verb* (**-sing**) (often + *to, into*) change in form or nature.

**metamorphosis** /metə'mɔːfəsɪs/ *noun* (*plural* **-phoses** /-siːz/) change of form, esp. from pupa to insect; change of character, conditions, etc.

**metaphor** /'metəfə/ *noun* application of name or description to something to which it is not literally applicable (see panel). □ **metaphoric** /-'fɒr-/ *adjective*; **metaphorical** /-'fɒr-/ *adjective*; **metaphorically** /-'fɒr-/ *adverb*.

**metaphysics** /metə'fɪzɪks/ *plural noun* (usually treated as *singular*) philosophy dealing with nature of existence, truth, and knowledge. □ **metaphysical** *adjective*.

**metatarsus** /metə'tɑːsəs/ *noun* (*plural* **-tarsi** /-saɪ/) set of bones forming part of foot between ankle and toes. □ **metatarsal** *adjective*.

---

## Metaphor

A metaphor is a figure of speech that goes further than a simile, either by saying that something is something else that it could not normally be called, e.g.

*The moon was a ghostly galleon tossed upon cloudy seas.*
*Stockholm, the Venice of the North*

or by suggesting that something appears, sounds, or behaves like something else, e.g.

*burning ambition*　　　　　　　　*blindingly obvious*
*the long arm of the law*

**mete** verb (**-ting**) (usually + *out*) *literary* apportion, allot.

**meteor** /'miːtɪə/ noun small solid body from outer space becoming incandescent when entering earth's atmosphere.

**meteoric** /miːtɪ'ɒrɪk/ adjective rapid; dazzling; of meteors.

**meteorite** /'miːtɪəraɪt/ noun fallen meteor; fragment of rock or metal from outer space.

**meteorology** /miːtɪə'rɒlədʒɪ/ noun study of atmospheric phenomena, esp. for forecasting weather. □ **meteorological** /-rə'lɒdʒ-/ adjective; **meteorologist** noun.

**meter**[1] /'miːtə/ ● noun instrument that measures or records, esp. gas, electricity, etc. used, distance travelled, etc.; parking meter. ● verb measure or record by meter.

**meter**[2] US = METRE.

**methane** /'miːθeɪn/ noun colourless odourless inflammable gaseous hydrocarbon, the main constituent of natural gas.

**methanol** /'meθənɒl/ noun colourless inflammable organic liquid, used as solvent.

**methinks** /mɪ'θɪŋks/ verb (past **methought** /mɪ'θɔːt/) *archaic* it seems to me.

**method** /'meθəd/ noun way of doing something; procedure; orderliness.

**methodical** /mɪ'θɒdɪk(ə)l/ adjective characterized by method or order. □ **methodically** adverb.

**Methodist** /'meθədɪst/ ● noun member of Protestant denomination originating in 18th-c. Wesleyan evangelistic movement. ● adjective of Methodists or Methodism. □ **Methodism** noun.

**methought** past of METHINKS.

**meths** noun *colloquial* methylated spirit.

**methyl** /'meθɪl/ noun hydrocarbon radical $CH_3$. □ **methyl alcohol** methanol.

**methylate** /'meθɪleɪt/ verb (**-ting**) mix or impregnate with methanol; introduce methyl group into (molecule).

**meticulous** /mə'tɪkjʊləs/ adjective giving great attention to detail; very careful and precise. □ **meticulously** adverb.

**métier** /'metɪeɪ/ noun one's trade, profession, or field of activity; one's forte. [French]

**metonymy** /mɪ'tɒnɪmɪ/ noun substitution of name of attribute for that of thing meant.

**metre** /'miːtə/ noun (*US* **meter**) SI unit of length (about 39.4 in.); any form of poetic rhythm; basic rhythm of music.

**metric** /'metrɪk/ adjective of or based on the metre. □ **metric system** decimal measuring system with metre, litre, and gram or kilogram as units of length, volume, and mass; **metric ton** 1,000 kg.

**metrical** adjective of or composed in metre; of or involving measurement. □ **metrically** adverb.

**metronome** /'metrənəʊm/ noun device ticking at selected rate to mark musical time.

**metropolis** /mɪ'trɒpəlɪs/ noun chief city, capital.

**metropolitan** /metrə'pɒlɪt(ə)n/ ● adjective of metropolis; of mother country as distinct from colonies. ● noun bishop with authority over bishops of province.

**mettle** /'met(ə)l/ noun quality or strength of character; spirit, courage. □ **mettlesome** adjective.

**mew**[1] ● noun cat's cry. ● verb utter this sound.

**mew**[2] noun gull, esp. common gull.

**mews** /mjuːz/ noun (treated as *singular*) stabling round yard etc., now used esp. for housing.

**mezzanine** /'metsəniːn/ noun storey between two others (usually ground and first floors).

**mezzo** /'metsəʊ/ *Music* ● adverb moderately. ● noun (in full **mezzo-soprano**) (plural **-s**) female singing voice between soprano and contralto, singer with this voice. □ **mezzo forte** fairly loud(ly); **mezzo piano** fairly soft(ly).

**mezzotint** /'metsəʊtɪnt/ noun method of copper or steel engraving; print so produced.

**mf** abbreviation mezzo forte.

**mg** abbreviation milligram(s).

**Mgr.** abbreviation Manager; *Monseigneur*; Monsignor.

**MHz** abbreviation megahertz.

**mi** = ME[2].

**miaow** /mɪˈaʊ/ ●*noun* characteristic cry of cat. ●*verb* make this cry.

**miasma** /mɪˈæzmə/ *noun* (*plural* **-mata** or **-s**) *archaic* infectious or noxious vapour.

**mica** /ˈmaɪkə/ *noun* silicate mineral found as glittering scales in granite etc. or crystals separable into thin plates.

**mice** *plural* of MOUSE.

**Michaelmas** /ˈmɪkəlməs/ *noun* feast of St Michael, 29 Sept. □ **Michaelmas daisy** autumn-flowering aster.

**mickey** /ˈmɪkɪ/ *noun* (also **micky**) □ **take the mickey** (often + *out of*) *slang* tease, mock.

**micro** /ˈmaɪkrəʊ/ *noun* (*plural* **-s**) *colloquial* microcomputer; microprocessor.

**micro-** *combining form* small; one-millionth.

**microbe** /ˈmaɪkrəʊb/ *noun* micro-organism (esp. bacterium) causing disease or fermentation. □ **microbial** /-ˈkrəʊb-/ *adjective*.

**microbiology** /maɪkrəʊbaɪˈɒlədʒɪ/ *noun* study of micro-organisms. □ **microbiologist** *noun*.

**microchip** /ˈmaɪkrəʊtʃɪp/ *noun* small piece of semiconductor used to carry integrated circuits.

**microcomputer** /ˈmaɪkrəʊkəmpjuːtə/ *noun* small computer with microprocessor as central processor.

**microcosm** /ˈmaɪkrəkɒz(ə)m/ *noun* (often + *of*) miniature representation, e.g. humankind seen as small-scale model of universe; epitome. □ **microcosmic** /-ˈkɒz-/ *adjective*.

**microdot** /ˈmaɪkrəʊdɒt/ *noun* microphotograph of document etc. reduced to size of dot.

**microfiche** /ˈmaɪkrəʊfiːʃ/ *noun* small flat square of film bearing microphotographs of documents etc.

**microfilm** /ˈmaɪkrəʊfɪlm/ ●*noun* length of film bearing microphotographs of documents etc. ●*verb* photograph on microfilm.

**microlight** /ˈmaɪkrəʊlaɪt/ *noun* kind of motorized hang-glider.

**micrometer** /maɪˈkrɒmɪtə/ *noun* gauge for accurate small-scale measurement.

**micron** /ˈmaɪkrɒn/ *noun* millionth of a metre.

**micro-organism** /maɪkrəʊˈɔːɡənɪz(ə)m/ *noun* microscopic organism.

**microphone** /ˈmaɪkrəfəʊn/ *noun* instrument for converting sound waves into electrical energy for reconversion into sound.

**microphotograph** /maɪkrəʊˈfəʊtəɡrɑːf/ *noun* photograph reduced to very small size.

**microprocessor** /maɪkrəʊˈprəʊsesə/ *noun* data processor using integrated circuits contained on microchip(s).

**microscope** /ˈmaɪkrəskəʊp/ *noun* instrument with lenses for magnifying objects or details invisible to naked eye.

**microscopic** /maɪkrəˈskɒpɪk/ *adjective* visible only with microscope; extremely small; of the microscope. □ **microscopically** *adverb*.

**microscopy** /maɪˈkrɒskəpɪ/ *noun* use of microscopes.

**microsurgery** /ˈmaɪkrəʊsɜːdʒərɪ/ *noun* intricate surgery using microscopes.

**microwave** /ˈmaɪkrəʊweɪv/ ●*noun* electromagnetic wave of length between 1 mm and 30 cm; (in full **microwave oven**) oven using microwaves to cook or heat food quickly. ●*verb* (**-ving**) cook in microwave oven.

**micturition** /mɪktjʊəˈrɪʃ(ə)n/ *noun formal* urination.

**mid-** *combining form* middle of. □ **midday** middle of day, noon; **mid-life** middle age; **mid-off**, **-on** *Cricket* position of fielder near bowler on off or on side.

**midden** /ˈmɪd(ə)n/ *noun* dunghill; refuse heap.

**middle** /ˈmɪd(ə)l/ ●*adjective* at equal distance, time, or number from extremities; central; intermediate in rank, quality, etc.; average. ●*noun* (often + *of*) middle point, position, or part; waist. □ **in the middle of** in the process of; **middle age** period between youth and old age; **the Middle Ages** period of European history from *c.* 1000 to 1453; **middle class** *noun* social class between upper and lower, including professional and business workers; **middle-class** *adjective*; **the Middle East** countries from Egypt to Iran inclusive;

**middleman** trader who handles commodity between producer and consumer; **middleweight** amateur boxing weight (71–75 kg).

**middling** ●adjective moderately good. ●adverb fairly, moderately.

**midge** noun gnatlike insect.

**midget** /'mɪdʒɪt/ noun extremely small person or thing.

**midland** /'mɪdlənd/ ●noun (**the Midlands**) inland counties of central England; middle part of country. ●adjective of or in midland or Midlands.

**midnight** noun middle of night; 12 o'clock at night. □ **midnight sun** sun visible at midnight during summer in polar regions.

**midriff** /'mɪdrɪf/ noun front of body just above waist.

**midshipman** /'mɪdʃɪpmən/ noun naval officer ranking next above cadet.

**midst** noun middle. □ **in the midst of** among.

**midsummer** noun period of or near summer solstice, about 21 June. □ **Midsummer Day, Midsummer's Day** 24 June.

**midwife** /'mɪdwaɪf/ noun (plural **-wives**) person trained to assist at childbirth. □ **midwifery** /-wɪfrɪ/ noun.

**midwinter** noun period of or near winter solstice, about 22 Dec.

**mien** /miːn/ noun literary person's look or bearing.

**might**[1] past of MAY.

**might**[2] /maɪt/ noun strength, power.

**mightn't** /'maɪt(ə)nt/ might not.

**mighty** ●adjective (**-ier, -iest**) powerful, strong; massive. ●adverb colloquial very. □ **mightily** adverb.

**mignonette** /mɪɡjə'net/ noun plant with fragrant grey-green flowers.

**migraine** /'miːɡreɪn/ noun recurrent throbbing headache often with nausea and visual disturbance.

**migrant** /'maɪɡrənt/ ●adjective migrating. ●noun migrant person or animal, esp. bird.

**migrate** /maɪ'ɡreɪt/ verb (**-ting**) move from one place, esp. one country, to settle in another; (of bird etc.) change habitation seasonally. □ **migration** noun, **migratory** /'maɪɡrətərɪ/ adjective.

**mikado** /mɪ'kɑːdəʊ/ noun (plural **-s**) historical emperor of Japan.

**mike** noun colloquial microphone.

**milch** adjective (of cow etc.) giving milk.

**mild** /maɪld/ adjective (esp. of person) gentle; not severe or harsh; (of weather) moderately warm; (of flavour) not sharp or strong. □ **mild steel** tough low-carbon steel. □ **mildly** adverb; **mildness** noun.

**mildew** /'mɪldjuː/ ●noun destructive growth of minute fungi on plants, damp paper, leather, etc. ●verb taint or be tainted with mildew.

**mile** noun unit of linear measure (1,760 yds, approx. 1.6 km); (in plural) colloquial great distance or amount; race extending over one mile. □ **milestone** stone beside road to mark distance in miles, significant point (in life, history, etc.).

**mileage** noun (also **milage**) number of miles travelled; colloquial profit, advantage.

**miler** noun colloquial person or horse specializing in races of one mile.

**milfoil** /'mɪlfɔɪl/ noun common yarrow.

**milieu** /mɪ'ljɜː/ noun (plural **-x** or **-s** /-z/) person's environment or social surroundings.

**militant** /'mɪlɪt(ə)nt/ ●adjective combative; aggressively active in support of cause; engaged in warfare. ●noun militant person. □ **militancy** noun, **militantly** adverb.

**militarism** /'mɪlɪtərɪz(ə)m/ noun aggressively military policy etc.; military spirit. □ **militarist** noun; **militaristic** /-'rɪst-/ adjective.

**military** /'mɪlɪtərɪ/ ●adjective of or characteristic of soldiers or armed forces. ●noun (treated as singular or plural; **the military**) the army.

**militate** /'mɪlɪteɪt/ verb (**-ting**) (usually + against) have force or effect.

■ **Usage** Militate is often confused with mitigate, which means 'to make less intense or severe'.

**militia** /mɪ'lɪʃə/ noun military force, esp. one conscripted in emergency. □ **militiaman** noun.

**milk** ●noun opaque white fluid secreted by female mammals for nourishing young; milk of cows, goats, etc. as food;

milklike liquid of coconut etc. ● *verb* draw milk from (cow etc.); exploit (person, situation). □ **milk chocolate** chocolate made with milk; **milk float** small usually electric vehicle used in delivering milk; **milkmaid** woman who milks cows or works in dairy; **milkman** person who sells or delivers milk; **milk run** routine expedition etc.; **milk shake** drink of whisked milk, flavouring, etc.; **milksop** weak or timid man or youth; **milk tooth** temporary tooth in young mammals.

**milky** *adjective* (**-ier**, **-iest**) of, like, or mixed with milk; (of gem or liquid) cloudy. □ **Milky Way** luminous band of stars, the Earth's galaxy.

**mill** ● *noun* building fitted with mechanical device for grinding corn; such device; device for grinding any solid to powder; building fitted with machinery for manufacturing processes etc.; such machinery. ● *verb* grind or treat in mill; (esp. as **milled** *adjective*) produce ribbed edge on (coin); (often + *about*, *round*) move aimlessly. □ **millpond** pond retained by dam for operating mill-wheel; **mill-race** current of water driving mill-wheel; **millstone** each of two circular stones for grinding corn, heavy burden, great responsibility; **mill-wheel** wheel used to drive water-mill.

**millennium** /mɪˈlenɪəm/ *noun* (*plural* **-s** or **millennia**) thousand-year period; (esp. future) period of happiness on earth. □ **millennial** *adjective*.

**miller** /ˈmɪlə/ *noun* person who owns or works mill, esp. corn-mill; person operating milling machine.

**millesimal** /mɪˈlesɪm(ə)l/ ● *adjective* thousandth; of, belonging to, or dealing with, thousandth or thousandths. ● *noun* thousandth part.

**millet** /ˈmɪlɪt/ *noun* cereal plant bearing small nutritious seeds; seed of this.

**milli-** *combining form* one-thousandth.

**millibar** /ˈmɪlɪbɑː/ *noun* unit of atmospheric pressure equivalent to 100 pascals.

**milligram** /ˈmɪlɪɡræm/ *noun* (also **-gramme**) one-thousandth of a gram.

**millilitre** /ˈmɪlɪliːtə/ *noun* (*US* **-liter**) one-thousandth of a litre (0.002 pint).

**millimetre** /ˈmɪlɪmiːtə/ *noun* (*US* **-meter**) one-thousandth of a metre.

**milliner** /ˈmɪlɪnə/ *noun* maker or seller of women's hats. □ **millinery** *noun*.

**million** /ˈmɪljən/ *noun* (*plural* same) one thousand thousand; (**millions**) *colloquial* very large number. □ **millionth** *adjective & noun*.

**millionaire** /mɪljəˈneə/ *noun* (*feminine* **millionairess**) person possessing over a million pounds, dollars, etc.

**millipede** /ˈmɪlɪpiːd/ *noun* (also **millepede**) small crawling invertebrate with many legs.

**millisecond** /ˈmɪlɪsekənd/ *noun* one-thousandth of a second.

**milometer** /maɪˈlɒmɪtə/ *noun* instrument for measuring number of miles travelled by vehicle.

**milt** *noun* spleen in mammals; reproductive gland or sperm of male fish.

**mime** ● *noun* acting without words, using only gestures; performance using mime. ● *verb* (**-ming**) express or represent by mime.

**mimeograph** /ˈmɪmɪəɡrɑːf/ ● *noun* machine which duplicates from stencil; copy so produced. ● *verb* reproduce in this way.

**mimetic** /mɪˈmetɪk/ *adjective* of or practising imitation or mimicry.

**mimic** /ˈmɪmɪk/ ● *verb* (**-ck-**) imitate (person, gesture, etc.), esp. to entertain or ridicule; copy minutely or servilely; resemble closely. ● *noun* person who mimics. □ **mimicry** *noun*.

**mimosa** /mɪˈməʊzə/ *noun* shrub with globular usually yellow flowers; acacia plant.

**Min.** *abbreviation* Minister; Ministry.

**min.** *abbreviation* minute(s); minimum; minim (fluid measure).

**minaret** /mɪnəˈret/ *noun* tall slender turret next to mosque, used by muezzin.

**minatory** /ˈmɪnətərɪ/ *adjective* formal threatening.

**mince** ● *verb* (**-cing**) cut or grind (meat etc.) finely; (usually as **mincing** *adjective*) walk or speak in affected way. ● *noun* minced meat. □ **mincemeat** mixture of currants, sugar, spices, suet, etc.; **mince pie** (usually small) pie containing mincemeat. □ **mincer** *noun*.

**mind** /maɪnd/ ● *noun* seat of consciousness, thought, volition, and feeling; attention; concentration; intellect; memory; opinion; sanity. ● *verb* object to; be upset; (often + *out*) heed, take care; look after; concern oneself with. □ **be in two minds** be undecided.

**minded** *adjective* (usually + *to do*) disposed, inclined. □ **-minded** inclined to think in specified way, or with specified interest.

**minder** *noun* person employed to look after person or thing; *slang* bodyguard.

**mindful** *adjective* (often + *of*) taking heed or care.

**mindless** *adjective* lacking intelligence; brutish; not requiring thought or skill. □ **mindlessly** *adverb;* **mindlessness** *noun.*

**mine**¹ *pronoun* the one(s) belonging to me.

**mine**² ● *noun* hole dug to extract metal, coal, salt, etc.; abundant source (of information etc.); *military* explosive device placed in ground or water. ● *verb* (**-ning**) obtain (minerals) from mine; (often + *for*) dig in (earth etc.) for ore etc. or to tunnel; lay explosive mines under or in. □ **minefield** area planted with explosive mines; **minesweeper** ship for clearing explosive mines from sea. □ **mining** *noun.*

**miner** *noun* worker in mine.

**mineral** /ˈmɪnər(ə)l/ *noun* inorganic substance; substance obtained by mining; (often in *plural*) artificial mineral water or other carbonated drink. □ **mineral water** water naturally or artificially impregnated with dissolved salts.

**mineralogy** /mɪnəˈrælədʒɪ/ *noun* study of minerals. □ **mineralogical** /-rəˈlɒdʒ-/ *adjective;* **mineralogist** *noun.*

**minestrone** /mɪnɪˈstrəʊnɪ/ *noun* soup containing vegetables and pasta, beans, or rice.

**mingle** /ˈmɪŋɡ(ə)l/ *verb* (**-ling**) mix, blend.

**mingy** /ˈmɪndʒɪ/ *adjective* (**-ier, -iest**) *colloquial* stingy.

**mini** /ˈmɪnɪ/ *noun* (*plural* **-s**) *colloquial* miniskirt; (**Mini**) *proprietary term* make of small car.

**mini-** *combining form* miniature; small of its kind.

**miniature** /ˈmɪnɪtʃə/ ● *adjective* much smaller than normal; represented on small scale. ● *noun* miniature object; detailed small-scale portrait. □ **in miniature** on small scale.

**miniaturist** *noun* painter of miniatures.

**miniaturize** *verb* (also **-ise**) (**-zing** or **-sing**) produce in smaller version; make small. □ **miniaturization** *noun.*

**minibus** /ˈmɪnɪbʌs/ *noun* small bus for about 12 passengers.

**minicab** /ˈmɪnɪkæb/ *noun* car used as taxi, hireable only by telephone.

**minim** /ˈmɪnɪm/ *noun Music* note equal to two crotchets or half a semibreve; one-sixtieth of fluid drachm.

**minimal** /ˈmɪnɪm(ə)l/ *adjective* very minute or slight; being a minimum. □ **minimally** *adverb.*

**minimize** /ˈmɪnɪmaɪz/ *verb* (also **-ise**) (**-zing** or **-sing**) reduce to or estimate at minimum; estimate or represent at less than true value etc.

**minimum** /ˈmɪnɪməm/ ● *noun* (*plural* **minima**) least possible or attainable amount. ● *adjective* that is a minimum. □ **minimum wage** lowest wage permitted by law or agreement.

**minion** /ˈmɪnjən/ *noun derogatory* servile subordinate.

**miniskirt** /ˈmɪnɪskɜːt/ *noun* very short skirt.

**minister** /ˈmɪnɪstə/ ● *noun* head of government department; member of clergy, esp. in Presbyterian and Nonconformist Churches; diplomat, usually ranking below ambassador. ● *verb* (usually + *to*) help, serve, look after. □ **ministerial** /-ˈstɪər-/ *adjective.*

**ministration** /mɪnɪˈstreɪʃ(ə)n/ *noun* (usually in *plural*) help, service; ministering, esp. in religious matters.

**ministry** /ˈmɪnɪstrɪ/ *noun* (*plural* **-ies**) government department headed by minister; building for this; (**the ministry**) profession of religious minister, ministers of government or religion.

**mink** *noun* (*plural* same or **-s**) small semi-aquatic stoatlike animal; its fur; coat of this.

**minke** /ˈmɪŋkɪ/ *noun* small whale.

**minnow** /ˈmɪnəʊ/ *noun* (*plural* same or **-s**) small freshwater carp.

**Minoan** /mɪˈnəʊən/ ● *adjective* of Cretan Bronze Age civilization. ● *noun* person of this civilization.

**minor** /ˈmaɪnə/ ● *adjective* lesser or comparatively small in size or importance; *Music* (of scale) having semitone above second, fifth, and seventh notes; (of key) based on minor scale. ● *noun* person under full legal age; *US* student's subsidiary subject or course. ● *verb US* (+ *in*) study (subject) as subsidiary.

**minority** /maɪˈnɒrɪtɪ/ *noun* (*plural* **-ies**) (often + *of*) smaller number or part, esp. in politics; smaller group of people differing from larger in race, religion, language, etc.; being under full legal age; period of this.

**minster** /ˈmɪnstə/ *noun* large or important church; church of monastery.

**minstrel** /ˈmɪnstr(ə)l/ *noun* medieval singer or musician; musical entertainer with blacked face.

**mint**¹ *noun* aromatic herb used in cooking; peppermint; peppermint sweet. □ **minty** *adjective* (**-ier, -iest**).

**mint**² ● *noun* (esp. state) establishment where money is coined; *colloquial* vast sum. ● *verb* make (coin); invent (word, phrase, etc.).

**minuet** /mɪnjʊˈet/ *noun* slow stately dance in triple time; music for this.

**minus** /ˈmaɪnəs/ ● *preposition* with subtraction of; less than zero; *colloquial* lacking. ● *adjective Mathematics* negative. ● *noun* minus sign; negative quantity; *colloquial* disadvantage. □ **minus sign** symbol (−) indicating subtraction or negative value.

**minuscule** /ˈmɪnəskjuːl/ *adjective colloquial* extremely small or unimportant.

**minute**¹ /ˈmɪnɪt/ ● *noun* sixtieth part of hour; distance covered in minute; moment; sixtieth part of angular degree; (in *plural*) summary of proceedings of meeting; official memorandum. ● *verb* (**-ting**) record in minutes; send minutes to. □ **up to the minute** up to date.

**minute**² /maɪˈnjuːt/ *adjective* (**-est**) very small; accurate, detailed. □ **minutely** *adverb*.

**minutiae** /maɪˈnjuːʃɪɪ/ *plural noun* very small, precise, or minor details.

**minx** /mɪŋks/ *noun* pert, sly, or playful girl.

**miracle** /ˈmɪrək(ə)l/ *noun* extraordinary, supposedly supernatural, event; remarkable happening. □ **miracle play** medieval play on biblical themes.

**miraculous** /mɪˈrækjʊləs/ *adjective* being a miracle; supernatural; surprising. □ **miraculously** *adverb*.

**mirage** /ˈmɪrɑːʒ/ *noun* optical illusion caused by atmospheric conditions, esp. appearance of water in desert; illusory thing.

**mire** ● *noun* area of swampy ground; mud. ● *verb* (**-ring**) sink in mire; bespatter with mud. □ **miry** *adjective*.

**mirror** /ˈmɪrə/ ● *noun* polished surface, usually of coated glass, reflecting image; anything reflecting state of affairs etc. ● *verb* reflect in or as in mirror. □ **mirror image** identical image or reflection with left and right reversed.

**mirth** *noun* merriment, laughter. □ **mirthful** *adjective*.

**misadventure** /mɪsədˈventʃə/ *noun Law* accident without crime or negligence; bad luck.

**misalliance** /mɪsəˈlaɪəns/ *noun* unsuitable alliance, esp. marriage.

**misanthrope** /ˈmɪsənθrəʊp/ *noun* (also **misanthropist** /mɪˈsænθrəpɪst/) person who hates humankind. □ **misanthropic** /-ˈθrɒp-/ *adjective*.

**misanthropy** /mɪˈsænθrəpɪ/ *noun* condition or habits of misanthrope.

**misapply** /mɪsəˈplaɪ/ *verb* (**-ies, -ied**) apply (esp. funds) wrongly. □ **misapplication** /-æplɪˈkeɪ-/ *noun*.

**misapprehend** /mɪsæprɪˈhend/ *verb* misunderstand (words, person). □ **misapprehension** *noun*.

**misappropriate** /mɪsəˈprəʊprɪeɪt/ *verb* (**-ting**) take (another's money etc.) for one's own use; embezzle. □ **misappropriation** *noun*.

**misbegotten** /mɪsbɪˈɡɒt(ə)n/ *adjective* illegitimate, bastard; contemptible.

**misbehave** /mɪsbɪˈheɪv/ *verb* (**-ving**) behave badly. □ **misbehaviour** *noun*.

**miscalculate** /mɪsˈkælkjʊleɪt/ *verb* (**-ting**) calculate wrongly. □ **miscalculation** *noun*.

**miscarriage** /ˈmɪskærɪdʒ/ *noun* spontaneous abortion. □ **miscarriage of justice** failure of judicial system.

**miscarry** /mɪsˈkærɪ/ *verb* (**-ies**, **-ied**) (of woman) have miscarriage; (of plan etc.) fail.

**miscast** /mɪsˈkɑːst/ *verb* (*past & past participle* **-cast**) allot unsuitable part to (actor) or unsuitable actors to (play etc.).

**miscegenation** /mɪsɪdʒɪˈneɪʃ(ə)n/ *noun* interbreeding of races.

**miscellaneous** /mɪsəˈleɪnɪəs/ *adjective* of mixed composition or character; (+ plural noun) of various kinds. □ **miscellaneously** *adverb*.

**miscellany** /mɪˈselənɪ/ *noun* (*plural* **-ies**) mixture, medley.

**mischance** /mɪsˈtʃɑːns/ *noun* bad luck; instance of this.

**mischief** /ˈmɪstʃɪf/ *noun* troublesome, but not malicious, conduct, esp. of children; playfulness; malice; harm, injury. □ **mischievous** /ˈmɪstʃɪvəs/ *adjective*, **mischievously** /ˈmɪstʃɪvəslɪ/ *adverb*.

**misconceive** /mɪskənˈsiːv/ *verb* (**-ving**) (often + *of*) have wrong idea or conception; (as **misconceived** *adjective*) badly organized etc. □ **misconception** /-ˈsep-/ *noun*.

**misconduct** /mɪsˈkɒndʌkt/ *noun* improper or unprofessional conduct.

**misconstrue** /mɪskənˈstruː/ *verb* (**-strues**, **-strued**, **-struing**) interpret wrongly. □ **misconstruction** /-ˈstrʌk-/ *noun*.

**miscount** /mɪsˈkaʊnt/ ● *verb* count inaccurately. ● *noun* inaccurate count.

**miscreant** /ˈmɪskrɪənt/ *noun* vile wretch, villain.

**misdeed** /mɪsˈdiːd/ *noun* evil deed, wrongdoing.

**misdemeanour** /mɪsdɪˈmiːnə/ *noun* (*US* **misdemeanor**) misdeed; *historical* indictable offence less serious than felony.

**misdirect** /mɪsdaɪˈrekt/ *verb* direct wrongly. □ **misdirection** *noun*.

**miser** /ˈmaɪzə/ *noun* person who hoards wealth and lives miserably. □ **miserly** *adjective*.

**miserable** /ˈmɪzərəb(ə)l/ *adjective* wretchedly unhappy or uncomfortable; contemptible, mean; causing discomfort. □ **miserably** *adverb*.

**misericord** /mɪˈzerɪkɔːd/ *noun* projection under hinged choir stall seat to support person standing.

**misery** /ˈmɪzərɪ/ *noun* (*plural* **-ies**) condition or feeling of wretchedness; cause of this; *colloquial* constantly grumbling person.

**misfire** /mɪsˈfaɪə/ ● *verb* (**-ring**) (of gun, motor engine, etc.) fail to go off, start, or function smoothly; (of plan etc.) fail to be effective. ● *noun* such failure.

**misfit** /ˈmɪsfɪt/ *noun* person unsuited to surroundings, occupation, etc.; garment etc. that does not fit.

**misfortune** /mɪsˈfɔːtʃ(ə)n/ *noun* bad luck; instance of this.

**misgiving** *noun* (usually in *plural*) feeling of mistrust or apprehension.

**misgovern** /mɪsˈgʌv(ə)n/ *verb* govern badly. □ **misgovernment** *noun*.

**misguided** /mɪsˈgaɪdɪd/ *adjective* mistaken in thought or action. □ **misguidedly** *adverb*.

**mishandle** /mɪsˈhænd(ə)l/ *verb* (**-ling**) deal with incorrectly or inefficiently; handle roughly.

**mishap** /ˈmɪshæp/ *noun* unlucky accident.

**mishear** /mɪsˈhɪə/ *verb* (*past & past participle* **-heard** /-ˈhɜːd/) hear incorrectly or imperfectly.

**mishmash** /ˈmɪʃmæʃ/ *noun* confused mixture.

**misinform** /mɪsɪnˈfɔːm/ *verb* give wrong information to, mislead. □ **misinformation** /-fəˈm-/ *noun*.

**misinterpret** /mɪsɪnˈtɜːprɪt/ *verb* (**-t-**) interpret wrongly. □ **misinterpretation** *noun*.

**misjudge** /mɪsˈdʒʌdʒ/ *verb* (**-ging**) judge wrongly. □ **misjudgement** *noun*.

**mislay** /mɪsˈleɪ/ *verb* (*past & past participle* **-laid**) accidentally put (thing) where it cannot readily be found.

**mislead** /mɪsˈliːd/ *verb* (*past & past participle* **-led**) cause to infer what is not true; deceive. □ **misleading** *adjective*.

**mismanage** /mɪsˈmænɪdʒ/ *verb* (**-ging**) manage badly or wrongly. □ **mismanagement** *noun*.

**misnomer** /mɪsˈnəʊmə/ *noun* wrongly used name or term.

**misogyny** /mɪˈsɒdʒɪnɪ/ *noun* hatred of women. □ **misogynist** *noun*.

**misplace** /mɪsˈpleɪs/ *verb* (**-cing**) put in wrong place; bestow (affections, confidence, etc.) on inappropriate object. □ **misplacement** *noun*.

**misprint** ● noun /'mɪsprɪnt/ printing error. ● verb /mɪs'prɪnt/ print wrongly.

**mispronounce** /mɪsprə'naʊns/ verb (-cing) pronounce (word etc.) wrongly. □ **mispronunciation** /-nʌnsɪ'eɪ-/ noun.

**misquote** /mɪs'kwəʊt/ verb (-ting) quote inaccurately. □ **misquotation** noun.

**misread** /mɪs'riːd/ verb (past & past participle **-read** /-'red/) read or interpret wrongly.

**misrepresent** /mɪsreprɪ'zent/ verb represent wrongly; give false account of. □ **misrepresentation** noun.

**misrule** /mɪs'ruːl/ ● noun bad government. ● verb (-ling) govern badly.

**Miss** noun title of girl or unmarried woman.

**miss** ● verb fail to hit, reach, meet, find, catch, or perceive; fail to seize (opportunity etc.); regret absence of; avoid; (of engine etc.) misfire. ● noun failure. □ **give (thing) a miss** colloquial avoid; **miss out** omit.

**missal** /'mɪs(ə)l/ noun RC Church book of texts for Mass; book of prayers.

**misshapen** /mɪs'ʃeɪpən/ adjective deformed, distorted.

**missile** /'mɪsaɪl/ noun object, esp. weapon, suitable for throwing at target or discharging from machine; weapon directed by remote control or automatically.

**missing** adjective not in its place; lost; (of person) not traced but not known to be dead.

**mission** /'mɪʃ(ə)n/ noun task or goal assigned to person or group; journey undertaken as part of this; military or scientific expedition; group of people sent to conduct negotiations or to evangelize; missionary post.

**missionary** /'mɪʃənərɪ/ ● adjective of or concerned with religious missions, esp. abroad. ● noun (plural **-ies**) person doing missionary work.

**missis** = MISSUS.

**missive** /'mɪsɪv/ noun jocular letter; official letter.

**misspell** /mɪs'spel/ verb (past & past participle **-spelt** or **-spelled**) spell wrongly.

**misspend** /mɪs'spend/ verb (past & past participle **-spent**) (esp. as **misspent** adjective) spend wrongly or wastefully.

**misstate** /mɪs'steɪt/ verb (-ting) state wrongly or inaccurately. □ **misstatement** noun.

**missus** /'mɪsɪz/ noun (also **missis**) colloquial or jocular form of address to woman; **(the missis)** colloquial my or your wife.

**mist** ● noun water vapour in minute drops limiting visibility; condensed vapour obscuring glass etc.; dimness or blurring of sight caused by tears etc. ● verb cover or be covered (as) with mist.

**mistake** /mɪ'steɪk/ ● noun incorrect idea or opinion; thing incorrectly done, thought, or judged. ● verb (-king; past **mistook** /-'stʊk/; past participle **mistaken**) misunderstand meaning of; (+ for) wrongly take (person, thing) for another.

**mistaken** /mɪ'steɪkən/ adjective wrong in opinion or judgement; based on or resulting from error. □ **mistakenly** adverb.

**mister** /'mɪstə/ noun colloquial or jocular form of address to man.

**mistime** /mɪs'taɪm/ verb (-ming) say or do at wrong time.

**mistle thrush** /'mɪs(ə)l/ noun large thrush that eats mistletoe berries.

**mistletoe** /'mɪs(ə)ltəʊ/ noun parasitic white-berried plant.

**mistook** past of MISTAKE.

**mistral** /'mɪstr(ə)l/ noun cold N or NW wind in S. France.

**mistreat** /mɪs'triːt/ verb treat badly. □ **mistreatment** noun.

**mistress** /'mɪstrɪs/ noun female head of household; woman in authority; female owner of pet; female teacher; woman having illicit sexual relationship with (usually married) man.

**mistrial** /mɪs'traɪəl/ noun trial made invalid by error.

**mistrust** /mɪs'trʌst/ ● verb be suspicious of; feel no confidence in. ● noun suspicion; lack of confidence. □ **mistrustful** adjective; **mistrustfully** adverb.

**misty** adjective (-ier, -iest) of or covered with mist; dim in outline; obscure. □ **mistily** adverb.

**misunderstand** /mɪsʌndə'stænd/ verb (past & past participle **-stood** /-'stʊd/) understand incorrectly; misinterpret words or actions of (person). □ **misunderstanding** noun.

**misuse** ● verb /mɪsˈjuːz/ (**-sing**) use wrongly; ill-treat. ● noun /mɪsˈjuːs/ wrong or improper use.

**mite**¹ noun small arachnid, esp. of kind found in cheese etc.

**mite**² noun small monetary unit; small object or child; modest contribution.

**miter** US = MITRE.

**mitigate** /ˈmɪtɪɡeɪt/ verb (**-ting**) make less intense or severe. □ **mitigation** noun.

■ **Usage** Mitigate is often confused with militate, which means 'to have force or effect'.

**mitre** (US **miter**) ● noun bishop's or abbot's tall deeply cleft headdress; joint of two pieces of wood at angle of 90°, such that line of junction bisects this angle. ● verb (**-ring**) bestow mitre on; join with mitre.

**mitt** noun (also **mitten**) glove with only one compartment for the 4 fingers and another for thumb; glove leaving fingers and thumb-tip bare; slang hand; baseball glove.

**mix** ● verb combine or put together (two or more substances or things) so that constituents of each are diffused among those of the other(s); prepare (compound, cocktail, etc.) by combining ingredients; combine (activities etc.); join, be mixed, combine; be compatible; be sociable; (+ with) be harmonious with; combine (two or more sound signals) into one. ● noun mixing, mixture; proportion of materials in mixture; ingredients prepared commercially for making cake, concrete, etc.

**mixed** /mɪkst/ adjective of diverse qualities or elements; containing people from various backgrounds, of both sexes, etc. □ **mixed marriage** marriage between people of different race or religion; **mixed-up** colloquial mentally or emotionally confused, socially ill-adjusted.

**mixer** noun machine for mixing foods etc.; person who manages socially in specified way; (usually soft) drink to be mixed with spirit; device combining separate signals from microphones etc.

**mixture** /ˈmɪkstʃə/ noun process or result of mixing; combination of ingredients, qualities, etc.

**mizen-mast** /ˈmɪz(ə)n/ noun mast next aft of mainmast.

**ml** abbreviation millilitre(s); mile(s).

**Mlle** abbreviation (plural **-s**) Mademoiselle.

**MM** abbreviation Messieurs; Military Medal.

**mm** abbreviation millimetre(s).

**Mme** abbreviation (plural **-s**) Madame.

**mnemonic** /nɪˈmɒnɪk/ ● adjective of or designed to aid memory. ● noun mnemonic word, verse, etc. □ **mnemonically** adverb.

**MO** abbreviation Medical Officer; money order.

**mo** /məʊ/ noun (plural **-s**) colloquial moment.

**moan** ● noun low murmur expressing physical or mental suffering or pleasure; colloquial complaint. ● verb make moan or moans; colloquial complain, grumble. □ **moaner** noun.

**moat** noun defensive ditch round castle etc., usually filled with water.

**mob** ● noun disorderly crowd; rabble; (**the mob**) usually derogatory the populace; colloquial gang, group. ● verb (**-bb-**) crowd round to attack or admire.

**mob-cap** noun historical woman's indoor cap covering all the hair.

**mobile** /ˈməʊbaɪl/ ● adjective movable; able to move easily; (of face etc.) readily changing expression; (of shop etc.) accommodated in vehicle to serve various places; (of person) able to change social status. ● noun decoration that may be hung so as to turn freely. □ **mobility** /məˈbɪl-/ noun.

**mobilize** /ˈməʊbɪlaɪz/ verb (also **-ise**) (**-zing** or **-sing**) make or become ready for (esp. military) service or action. □ **mobilization** noun.

**mobster** /ˈmɒbstə/ noun slang gangster.

**moccasin** /ˈmɒkəsɪn/ noun soft flat-soled shoe originally worn by N. American Indians.

**mock** ● verb (often + at) ridicule, scoff (at); treat with scorn or contempt; mimic contemptuously. ● adjective sham; imitation; as a trial run. □ **mock turtle soup** soup made from calf's head etc.; **mock-up** experimental model of proposed structure etc. □ **mockingly** *adverb*.

**mockery** *noun* (*plural* **-ies**) derision; counterfeit or absurdly inadequate representation; travesty.

**mode** *noun* way in which thing is done; prevailing fashion; *Music* any of several types of scale.

**model** /'mɒd(ə)l/ ● *noun* representation in 3 dimensions of existing person or thing or of proposed structure, esp. on smaller scale; simplified description of system etc.; clay, wax, etc. figure for reproduction in another material; particular design or style, esp. of car; exemplary person or thing; person employed to pose for artist or photographer, or to wear clothes etc. for display; (copy of) garment etc. by well-known designer. ● *adjective* exemplary; ideally perfect. ● *verb* (**-ll-**; *US* **-l-**) fashion or shape (figure) in clay, wax, etc.; (+ *after, on*, etc.) form (thing) in imitation of; act or pose as model; (of person acting as model) display (garment).

**modem** /'məʊdem/ *noun* device for sending and receiving computer data by means of telephone line.

**moderate** /'mɒdərət/ ● *adjective* avoiding extremes; temperate in conduct or expression; fairly large or good; (of wind) of medium strength; (of prices) fairly low. ● *noun* person of moderate views. ● *verb* /-reɪt/ (**-ting**) make or become less violent, intense, rigorous, etc.; act as moderator of or to. □ **moderately** /-rətlɪ/ *adverb*; **moderation** *noun*.

**moderator** *noun* arbitrator, mediator; presiding officer; Presbyterian minister presiding over ecclesiastical body.

**modern** /'mɒd(ə)n/ ● *adjective* of present and recent times; in current fashion, not antiquated. ● *noun* person living in modern times. □ **modernity** /mə'dɜːnɪtɪ/ *noun*.

**modernism** *noun* modern ideas or methods, esp. in art. □ **modernist** *noun & adjective*.

**modernize** *verb* (also **-ise**) (**-zing** or **-sing**) make modern; adapt to modern needs or habits. □ **modernization** *noun*.

**modest** /'mɒdɪst/ *adjective* having humble or moderate estimate of one's own merits; bashful; decorous; not excessive; unpretentious, not extravagant. □ **modestly** *adverb*; **modesty** *noun*.

**modicum** /'mɒdɪkəm/ *noun* (+ *of*) small quantity.

**modify** /'mɒdɪfaɪ/ *verb* (**-ies, -ied**) make less severe; make partial changes in. □ **modification** *noun*.

**modish** /'məʊdɪʃ/ *adjective* fashionable. □ **modishly** *adverb*.

**modulate** /'mɒdjʊleɪt/ *verb* (**-ting**) regulate, adjust; moderate; adjust or vary tone or pitch of (speaking voice); alter amplitude or frequency of (wave) by using wave of lower frequency to convey signal; *Music* pass from one key to another. □ **modulation** *noun*.

**module** /'mɒdjuːl/ *noun* standardized part or independent unit in construction, esp. of furniture, building, spacecraft, or electronic system; unit or period of training or education. □ **modular** *adjective*.

**modus operandi** /məʊdəs ɒpə'rændɪ/ *noun* (*plural* **modi operandi** /məʊdiː/) method of working. [Latin]

**modus vivendi** /məʊdəs vɪ'vendɪ/ *noun* (*plural* **modi vivendi** /məʊdiː/) way of living or coping; compromise between people agreeing to differ. [Latin]

**mog** *noun* (also **moggie**) *slang* cat.

**mogul** /'məʊɡ(ə)l/ *noun colloquial* important or influential person.

**mohair** /'məʊheə/ *noun* hair of angora goat; yarn or fabric from this.

**Mohammedan** = Muhammadan.

**moiety** /'mɔɪətɪ/ *noun* (*plural* **-ies**) half; each of two parts of thing.

**moiré** /'mwɑːreɪ/ *adjective* (of silk) watered; (of metal) having clouded appearance.

**moist** *adjective* slightly wet; damp. □ **moisten** *verb*.

**moisture** /'mɔɪstʃə/ *noun* water or other liquid diffused as vapour or within solid, or condensed on surface.

**moisturize** *verb* (also **-ise**) (**-zing** or **-sing**) make less dry (esp. skin by use of cosmetic). □ **moisturizer** *noun*.

**molar** /'məʊlə/ ● *adjective* (usually of mammal's back teeth) serving to grind. ● *noun* molar tooth.

**molasses** /məˈlæsɪz/ *plural noun* (treated as *singular*) uncrystallized syrup extracted from raw sugar; *US* treacle.

**mold** *US* = MOULD[1,2,3].

**molder** *US* = MOULDER.

**molding** *US* = MOULDING.

**moldy** *US* = MOULDY.

**mole**[1] *noun* small burrowing animal with dark velvety fur and very small eyes; *slang* spy established in position of trust in organization. □ **molehill** small mound thrown up by mole in burrowing.

**mole**[2] *noun* small permanent dark spot on skin.

**mole**[3] *noun* massive structure as pier, breakwater, or causeway; artificial harbour.

**mole**[4] *noun* SI unit of amount of substance.

**molecule** /ˈmɒlɪkjuːl/ *noun* group of atoms forming smallest fundamental unit of chemical compound. □ **molecular** /məˈlekjʊlə/ *adjective*.

**molest** /məˈlest/ *verb* annoy or pester (person); attack or interfere with (person), esp. sexually. □ **molestation** *noun*; **molester** *noun*.

**moll** *noun slang* gangster's female companion; prostitute.

**mollify** /ˈmɒlɪfaɪ/ *verb* (**-ies, -ied**) soften, appease. □ **mollification** *noun*.

**mollusc** /ˈmɒləsk/ *noun* (*US* **mollusk**) invertebrate with soft body and usually hard shell, e.g. snail or oyster.

**mollycoddle** /ˈmɒlɪkɒd(ə)l/ *verb* (**-ling**) coddle, pamper.

**molt** *US* = MOULT.

**molten** /ˈməʊlt(ə)n/ *adjective* melted, esp. made liquid by heat.

**molto** /ˈmɒltəʊ/ *adverb* Music very.

**molybdenum** /məˈlɪbdɪnəm/ *noun* silver-white metallic element added to steel to give strength and resistance to corrosion.

**moment** /ˈməʊmənt/ *noun* very brief portion of time; exact point of time; importance; product of force and distance from its line of action to a point.

**momentary** *adjective* lasting only a moment; transitory. □ **momentarily** *adverb*.

**momentous** /məˈmentəs/ *adjective* very important.

**momentum** /məˈmentəm/ *noun* (*plural* **-ta**) quantity of motion of moving body, the product of its mass and velocity; impetus gained by movement or initial effort.

**Mon.** *abbreviation* Monday.

**monarch** /ˈmɒnək/ *noun* sovereign with title of king, queen, emperor, empress, or equivalent. □ **monarchic** /məˈnɑːk-/ *adjective*; **monarchical** /məˈnɑːk-/ *adjective*.

**monarchist** *noun* advocate of monarchy.

**monarchy** *noun* (*plural* **-ies**) government headed by monarch; state with this.

**monastery** /ˈmɒnəstrɪ/ *noun* (*plural* **-ies**) residence of community of monks.

**monastic** /məˈnæstɪk/ *adjective* of or like monasteries or monks, nuns, etc. □ **monastically** *adverb*; **monasticism** /-sɪz(ə)m/ *noun*.

**Monday** /ˈmʌndeɪ/ *noun* day of week following Sunday.

**monetarism** /ˈmʌnɪtərɪz(ə)m/ *noun* control of supply of money as chief method of stabilizing economy. □ **monetarist** *adjective & noun*.

**monetary** /ˈmʌnɪtərɪ/ *adjective* of the currency in use; of or consisting of money.

**money** /ˈmʌnɪ/ *noun* (*plural* **-s** or **monies**) coins and banknotes as medium of exchange; (in *plural*) sums of money; wealth. □ **moneylender** person lending money at interest; **money market** trade in short-term stocks, loans, etc.; **money order** order for payment of specified sum, issued by bank or Post Office; **money-spinner** thing that brings in a profit.

**moneyed** /ˈmʌnɪd/ *adjective* rich.

**Mongol** /ˈmɒŋɡ(ə)l/ ● *adjective* of Asian people now inhabiting Mongolia; resembling this people. ● *noun* Mongolian.

**Mongolian** /mɒŋˈɡəʊlɪən/ ● *noun* native, national, or language of Mongolia. ● *adjective* of or relating to Mongolia or its people or language.

**Mongoloid** /ˈmɒŋɡəlɔɪd/ ● *adjective* characteristic of Mongolians, esp. in having broad flat yellowish face. ● *noun* Mongoloid person.

**mongoose** /ˈmɒŋguːs/ *noun* (*plural* **-s**) small flesh-eating civet-like mammal.

**mongrel** /ˈmʌŋɡr(ə)l/ ● *noun* dog of no definable type or breed; any animal or plant resulting from crossing of different breeds or types. ● *adjective* of mixed origin or character.

**monies** *plural* of **money**.

**monitor** /ˈmɒnɪtə/ ● *noun* person or device for checking; school pupil with disciplinary etc. duties; television set used to select or verify picture being broadcast or to display computer data; person who listens to and reports on foreign broadcasts etc.; detector of radioactive contamination. ● *verb* act as monitor of; maintain regular surveillance over.

**monk** /mʌŋk/ *noun* member of religious community of men living under vows. □ **monkish** *adjective*.

**monkey** /ˈmʌŋkɪ/ ● *noun* (*plural* **-eys**) any of various primates, e.g. baboons, marmosets; mischievous person, esp. child. ● *verb* (**-eys**, **-eyed**) (often + *with*) play mischievous tricks. □ **monkey-nut** peanut; **monkey-puzzle** tree with hanging prickly branches; **monkey wrench** wrench with adjustable jaw.

**monkshood** /ˈmʌŋkshʊd/ *noun* poisonous plant with hood-shaped flowers.

**mono** /ˈmɒnəʊ/ *colloquial* ● *adjective* monophonic. ● *noun* monophonic reproduction.

**mono-** *combining form* (usually **mon-** before vowel) one, alone, single.

**monochromatic** /mɒnəkrəˈmætɪk/ *adjective* (of light or other radiation) of single colour or wavelength; containing only one colour.

**monochrome** /ˈmɒnəkrəʊm/ ● *noun* photograph or picture in one colour, or in black and white only. ● *adjective* having or using one colour or black and white only.

**monocle** /ˈmɒnək(ə)l/ *noun* single eyeglass.

**monocular** /məˈnɒkjʊlə/ *adjective* with or for one eye.

**monody** /ˈmɒnədɪ/ *noun* (*plural* **-ies**) ode sung by one actor in Greek tragedy; poem lamenting person's death.

**monogamy** /məˈnɒɡəmɪ/ *noun* practice or state of being married to one person at a time. □ **monogamous** *adjective*.

**monogram** /ˈmɒnəɡræm/ *noun* two or more letters, esp. initials, interwoven.

**monograph** /ˈmɒnəɡrɑːf/ *noun* treatise on single subject.

**monolith** /ˈmɒnəlɪθ/ *noun* single block of stone, esp. shaped into pillar etc.; person or thing like monolith in being massive, immovable, or solidly uniform. □ **monolithic** /-ˈlɪθ-/ *adjective*.

**monologue** /ˈmɒnəlɒɡ/ *noun* scene in drama in which person speaks alone; dramatic composition for one performer; long speech by one person in conversation etc.

**monomania** /mɒnəˈmeɪnɪə/ *noun* obsession by single idea or interest. □ **monomaniac** *noun & adjective*.

**monophonic** /mɒnəˈfɒnɪk/ *adjective* (of sound-reproduction) using only one channel of transmission.

**monoplane** /ˈmɒnəpleɪn/ *noun* aeroplane with one set of wings.

**monopolist** /məˈnɒpəlɪst/ *noun* person who has or advocates monopoly. □ **monopolistic** /-ˈlɪs-/ *adjective*.

**monopolize** /məˈnɒpəlaɪz/ *verb* (also **-ise**) (**-zing** or **-sing**) obtain exclusive possession or control of (trade etc.); dominate (conversation) etc. □ **monopolization** *noun*; **monopolizer** *noun*.

**monopoly** /məˈnɒpəlɪ/ *noun* (*plural* **-ies**) exclusive possession or control of trade in commodity or service; (+ *of*, US *on*) sole possession or control.

**monorail** /ˈmɒnəʊreɪl/ *noun* railway with single-rail track.

**monosodium glutamate** /mɒnəʊˈsəʊdɪəm ˈɡluːtəmeɪt/ *noun* sodium salt of glutamic acid used to enhance flavour of food.

**monosyllable** /ˈmɒnəsɪləb(ə)l/ *noun* word of one syllable. □ **monosyllabic** /-ˈlæb-/ *adjective*.

**monotheism** /ˈmɒnəθiːɪz(ə)m/ *noun* doctrine that there is only one God. □ **monotheist** *noun*; **monotheistic** /-ˈɪst-/ *adjective*.

**monotone** /ˈmɒnətəʊn/ *noun* sound continuing or repeated on one note or without change of pitch.

**monotonous** /məˈnɒtənəs/ *adjective* lacking in variety, tedious through sameness. □ **monotonously** *adverb*; **monotony** *noun*.

**monoxide** /məˈnɒksaɪd/ *noun* oxide containing one oxygen atom.

**Monseigneur** /mɒnsenˈjɜː/ *noun* (*plural* **Messeigneurs** /mesenˈjɜː/) *title given to eminent French person, esp. prince, cardinal, etc.* [French]

**Monsieur** /məˈsjɜː/ *noun* (*plural* **Messieurs** /mesˈjɜː/) *title used of or to French-speaking man.*

**Monsignor** /mɒnˈsiːnjə/ *noun* (*plural* **-nori** /-ˈnjɔːrɪ/) *title of various RC priests and officials.*

**monsoon** /mɒnˈsuːn/ *noun* wind in S. Asia, esp. in Indian Ocean; rainy season accompanying summer monsoon.

**monster** /ˈmɒnstə/ ●*noun* imaginary creature, usually large and frightening; inhumanly wicked person; misshapen animal or plant; large, usually ugly, animal or thing. ●*adjective* huge.

**monstrance** /ˈmɒnstrəns/ *noun* RC Church vessel in which host is exposed for veneration.

**monstrosity** /mɒnˈstrɒsɪtɪ/ *noun* (*plural* **-ies**) huge or outrageous thing.

**monstrous** /ˈmɒnstrəs/ *adjective* like a monster; abnormally formed; huge; outrageously wrong; atrocious. □ **monstrously** *adverb*.

**montage** /mɒnˈtɑːʒ/ *noun* selection, cutting, and arrangement as consecutive whole, of separate sections of cinema or television film; composite whole made from juxtaposed photographs etc.

**month** /mʌnθ/ *noun* (in full **calendar month**) each of 12 divisions of year; period of time between same dates in successive calendar months; period of 28 days.

**monthly** ●*adjective* done, produced, or occurring once every month. ●*adverb* every month. ●*noun* (*plural* **-ies**) monthly periodical.

**monument** /ˈmɒnjʊmənt/ *noun* anything enduring that serves to commemorate, esp. structure, building, or memorial stone.

**monumental** /mɒnjʊˈment(ə)l/ *adjective* extremely great; stupendous; massive and permanent; of or serving as monument.

**moo** ●*noun* (*plural* **-s**) characteristic sound of cattle. ●*verb* (**moos, mooed**) make this sound.

**mooch** *verb colloquial* (usually + *about, around*) wander aimlessly; *esp. US* cadge.

**mood**[1] *noun* state of mind or feeling; fit of bad temper or depression.

**mood**[2] *noun* Grammar form(s) of verb indicating whether it expresses fact, command, wish, etc.

**moody** *adjective* (**-ier, -iest**) given to changes of mood; gloomy, sullen.

**moon** ●*noun* natural satellite of the earth, orbiting it monthly, illuminated by and reflecting sun; satellite of any planet. ●*verb* (often + *about, around*) wander aimlessly or listlessly. □ **moonbeam** ray of moonlight; **moonlight** *noun* light of moon, *verb colloquial* have other paid occupation, esp. one by night as well as one by day; **moonlit** lit by the moon; **moonshine** foolish or visionary talk, illicit alcohol; **moonshot** launching of spacecraft to moon; **moonstone** feldspar of pearly appearance; **moonstruck** slightly mad.

**moony** *adjective* (**-ier, -iest**) listless; stupidly dreamy.

**Moor** /mʊə/ *noun* member of a Muslim people of NW Africa. □ **Moorish** *adjective*.

**moor**[1] /mʊə/ *noun* open uncultivated upland, esp. when covered with heather. □ **moorhen** small waterfowl; **moorland** large area of moor.

**moor**[2] /mʊə/ *verb* attach (boat etc.) to fixed object. □ **moorage** *noun*.

**mooring** *noun* (often in *plural*) place where boat etc. is moored; (in *plural*) set of permanent anchors and chains.

**moose** *noun* (*plural* same) N. American deer; elk.

**moot** ●*adjective* debatable, undecided. ●*verb* raise (question) for discussion. ●*noun historical* assembly.

**mop** ●*noun* bundle of yarn or cloth or a sponge on end of stick for cleaning floors etc.; thick mass of hair. ●*verb* (**-pp-**) wipe or clean (as) with mop. □ **mop up** wipe with mop, *colloquial* absorb, dispose of, complete occupation of (area etc.) by capturing or killing enemy troops left there.

**mope** ●*verb* (**-ping**) be depressed or listless. ●*noun* person who mopes. □ **mopy** *adjective* (**-ier, -iest**).

**moped** /ˈməʊped/ *noun* low-powered motorized bicycle.

**moquette** /mɒˈket/ *noun* thick pile or looped material used for upholstery etc.

**moraine** /məˈreɪn/ *noun* area of debris carried down and deposited by glacier.

**moral** /ˈmɒr(ə)l/ ● *adjective* concerned with goodness or badness of character or behaviour, or with difference between right and wrong; virtuous in conduct. ● *noun* moral lesson of story etc.; (in *plural*) moral principles or behaviour. □ **moral support** psychological rather than physical help. □ **morally** *adverb*.

**morale** /məˈrɑːl/ *noun* confidence, determination, etc. of person or group.

**moralist** /ˈmɒrəlɪst/ *noun* person who practises or teaches morality. □ **moralistic** /-ˈlɪs-/ *adjective*.

**morality** /məˈrælɪtɪ/ *noun* (*plural* **-ies**) degree of conformity to moral principles; moral conduct; science of morals.

**moralize** /ˈmɒrəlaɪz/ *verb* (also **-ise**) (**-zing** or **-sing**) (often + *on*) indulge in moral reflection or talk. □ **moralization** *noun*.

**morass** /məˈræs/ *noun* entanglement; *literary* bog.

**moratorium** /mɒrəˈtɔːrɪəm/ *noun* (*plural* **-s** or **-ria**) (often + *on*) temporary prohibition or suspension (of activity); legal authorization to debtors to postpone payment.

**morbid** /ˈmɔːbɪd/ *adjective* (of mind, ideas, etc.) unwholesome; *colloquial* melancholy; of or indicative of disease. □ **morbidity** /-ˈbɪd-/ *noun*; **morbidly** *adverb*.

**mordant** /ˈmɔːd(ə)nt/ ● *adjective* (of sarcasm etc.) caustic, biting; smarting; corrosive, cleansing. ● *noun* mordant substance.

**more** /mɔː/ ● *adjective* greater in quantity or degree; additional. ● *noun* greater quantity, number, or amount. ● *adverb* to greater degree or extent; *forming comparative of adjectives and adverbs*.

**morello** /məˈreləʊ/ *noun* (*plural* **-s**) sour kind of dark cherry.

**moreover** /mɔːˈrəʊvə/ *adverb* besides, in addition.

**mores** /ˈmɔːreɪz/ *plural noun* customs or conventions of community.

**morganatic** /mɔːgəˈnætɪk/ *adjective* (of marriage) between person of high rank and one of lower rank, the latter and the latter's children having no claim to possessions of former.

**morgue** /mɔːg/ *noun* mortuary; room or file of miscellaneous information kept by newspaper office.

**moribund** /ˈmɒrɪbʌnd/ *adjective* at point of death; lacking vitality.

**Mormon** /ˈmɔːmən/ *noun* member of Church of Jesus Christ of Latter-Day Saints. □ **Mormonism** *noun*.

**morn** *noun poetical* morning.

**morning** /ˈmɔːnɪŋ/ *noun* early part of day till noon or lunchtime. □ **morning coat** tailcoat with front cut away; **morning dress** man's morning coat and striped trousers; **morning glory** climbing plant with trumpet-shaped flowers; **morning sickness** nausea felt in morning in pregnancy; **morning star** planet, usually Venus, seen in east before sunrise.

**morocco** /məˈrɒkəʊ/ *noun* (*plural* **-s**) fine flexible leather of goatskin tanned with sumac.

**moron** /ˈmɔːrɒn/ *noun colloquial* very stupid person; adult with mental age of 8–12. □ **moronic** /məˈr-/ *adjective*.

**morose** /məˈrəʊs/ *adjective* sullen, gloomy. □ **morosely** *adverb*; **moroseness** *noun*.

**morphia** /ˈmɔːfɪə/ *noun* morphine.

**morphine** /ˈmɔːfiːn/ *noun* narcotic drug from opium.

**morphology** /mɔːˈfɒlədʒɪ/ *noun* study of forms of things, esp. of animals and plants and of words and their structure. □ **morphological** /-fəˈlɒdʒ-/ *adjective*.

**morris dance** /ˈmɒrɪs/ *noun* traditional English dance in fancy costume. □ **morris dancer** *noun*; **morris dancing** *noun*.

**morrow** /ˈmɒrəʊ/ *noun* (usually **the morrow**) *literary* following day.

**Morse** /mɔːs/ *noun* (in full **Morse code**) code in which letters, numbers, etc. are represented by combinations of long and short light or sound signals.

**morsel** /'mɔːs(ə)l/ ● *noun* mouthful; small piece (esp. of food).

**mortal** /'mɔːt(ə)l/ ● *adjective* subject to or causing death; (of combat) fought to the death; (of enemy) implacable. ● *noun* human being. □ **mortal sin** sin depriving soul of salvation. □ **mortally** *adverb*.

**mortality** /mɔː'tælɪtɪ/ *noun* (*plural* **-ies**) being subject to death; loss of life on large scale; (in full **mortality rate**) death rate.

**mortar** /'mɔːtə/ *noun* mixture of lime or cement, sand, and water, for bonding bricks or stones; short cannon for firing shells at high angles; vessel in which ingredients are pounded with pestle. □ **mortarboard** stiff flat square-topped academic cap, flat board for holding mortar.

**mortgage** /'mɔːgɪdʒ/ ● *noun* conveyance of property to creditor as security for debt (usually one incurred by purchase of property); sum of money lent by this. ● *verb* (**-ging**) convey (property) by mortgage.

**mortgagee** /mɔːgɪ'dʒiː/ *noun* creditor in mortgage.

**mortgager** /'mɔːgɪdʒə/ *noun* (also **mortgagor** /-'dʒɔː/) debtor in mortgage.

**mortician** = MORTISE.

**mortician** /mɔː'tɪʃ(ə)n/ *noun US* undertaker.

**mortify** /'mɔːtɪfaɪ/ *verb* (**-ies**, **-ied**) humiliate, wound (person's feelings); bring (body etc.) into subjection by self-denial; (of flesh) be affected by gangrene. □ **mortification** *noun*; **mortifying** *adjective*.

**mortise** /'mɔːtɪs/ (also **mortice**) ● *noun* hole in framework to receive end of another part, esp. tenon. ● *verb* (**-sing**) join, esp. by mortise and tenon; cut mortise in. □ **mortise lock** lock recessed in frame of door etc.

**mortuary** /'mɔːtjʊərɪ/ ● *noun* (*plural* **-ies**) room or building in which dead bodies are kept until burial or cremation. ● *adjective* of death or burial.

**Mosaic** /məʊ'zeɪɪk/ *adjective* of Moses.

**mosaic** /məʊ'zeɪɪk/ *noun* picture or pattern made with small variously coloured pieces of glass, stone, etc.; diversified thing.

**moselle** /məʊ'zel/ *noun* dry German white wine.

**Moslem** = MUSLIM.

**mosque** /mɒsk/ *noun* Muslim place of worship.

**mosquito** /mɒs'kiːtəʊ/ *noun* (*plural* **-es**) biting insect, esp. with long proboscis to suck blood. □ **mosquito-net** net to keep off mosquitoes.

**moss** *noun* small flowerless plant growing in dense clusters in bogs and on trees, stones, etc.; *Scottish & N English* peatbog. □ **mossy** *adjective* (**-ier**, **-iest**).

**most** /məʊst/ ● *adjective* greatest in quantity or degree; the majority of. ● *noun* greatest quantity or number; the majority. ● *adverb* in highest degree; *forming superlative of adjectives and adverbs.*

**mostly** *adverb* mainly; usually.

**MOT** *abbreviation* (in full **MOT test**) compulsory annual test, instituted by Ministry of Transport, of vehicles over specified age.

**mot** /məʊ/ *noun* (*plural* **mots** same pronunciation) (usually **bon mot** /bɔ̃/) witty saying. □ **mot juste** /'ʒuːst/ most appropriate expression. [French]

**mote** *noun* speck of dust.

**motel** /məʊ'tel/ *noun* roadside hotel for motorists.

**moth** /mɒθ/ ● *noun* nocturnal insect like butterfly; insect of this type breeding in cloth etc., on which its larva feeds. □ **mothball** ball of naphthalene etc. kept with stored clothes to deter moths; **moth-eaten** damaged by moths, time-worn.

**mother** /'mʌðə/ ● *noun* female parent; woman or condition etc. giving rise to something else; (in full **Mother Superior**) head of female religious community. ● *verb* treat as mother does. □ **mother country** country in relation to its colonies; **mother-in-law** (*plural* **mothers-in-law**) husband's or wife's mother; **motherland** native country; **mother-of-pearl** iridescent substance forming lining of oyster and other shells; **mother tongue** native language. □ **motherhood** *noun*; **motherly** *adjective*.

**motif** /məʊ'tiːf/ *noun* theme repeated and developed in artistic work; decorative design; ornament sewn separately on garment.

**motion** /'məʊʃ(ə)n/ ● *noun* moving; changing position; gesture; formal proposal put to committee etc.; application to court for order; evacuation of bowels. ● *verb* (often + *to do*) direct (person) by gesture. □ **motion picture** *esp. US* cinema film. □ **motionless** *adjective*.

**motivate** /'məʊtɪveɪt/ *verb* (**-ting**) supply motive to, be motive of; cause (person) to act in particular way; stimulate interest of (person in activity). □ **motivation** *noun*.

**motive** /'məʊtɪv/ ● *noun* what induces person to act; motif. ● *adjective* tending to initiate movement.

**motley** /'mɒtlɪ/ ● *adjective* (**-ier, -iest**) diversified in colour; of varied character. ● *noun historical* jester's particoloured costume.

**motor** /'məʊtə/ ● *noun* thing that imparts motion; machine (esp. using electricity or internal combustion) supplying motive power for vehicle or other machine; car. ● *adjective* giving, imparting, or producing motion; driven by motor; of or for motor vehicles. ● *verb* go or convey by motor vehicle. □ **motor bike** *colloquial*, **motorcycle** two-wheeled motor vehicle without pedal propulsion; **motor car** car; **motorway** fast road with separate carriageways limited to motor vehicles.

**motorcade** /'məʊtəkeɪd/ *noun* procession of motor vehicles.

**motorist** *noun* driver of car.

**motorize** *verb* (also **-ise**) (**-zing** or **-sing**) equip with motor transport; provide with motor.

**mottle** /'mɒt(ə)l/ *verb* (**-ling**) (esp. as **mottled** *adjective*) mark with spots or smears of colour.

**motto** /'mɒtəʊ/ *noun* (*plural* **-es**) maxim adopted as rule of conduct; words accompanying coat of arms; appropriate inscription; joke, maxim, etc. in paper cracker.

**mould**[1] /məʊld/ (*US* **mold**) ● *noun* hollow container into which substance is poured or pressed to harden into required shape; pudding etc. shaped in mould; form, shape; character, type. ● *verb* shape (as) in mould; give shape to; influence development of.

**mould**[2] /məʊld/ *noun* (*US* **mold**) furry growth of fungi, esp. in moist warm conditions.

**mould**[3] /məʊld/ *noun* (*US* **mold**) loose earth; upper soil of cultivated land, esp. when rich in organic matter.

**moulder** /'məʊldə/ *verb* (*US* **molder**) decay to dust; (+ *away*) rot, crumble.

**moulding** *noun* (*US* **molding**) ornamental strip of plaster etc. applied as architectural feature, esp. in cornice; similar feature in woodwork etc.

**mouldy** *adjective* (*US* **moldy**) (**-ier, -iest**) covered with mould; stale; out of date; *colloquial* dull, miserable.

**moult** /məʊlt/ (*US* **molt**) ● *verb* shed (feathers, hair, shell, etc.) in renewing plumage, coat, etc. ● *noun* moulting.

**mound** /maʊnd/ *noun* raised mass of earth, stones, etc.; heap, pile; hillock.

**mount**[1] *verb* ascend; climb on to; get up on (horse etc.); set on horseback; (as **mounted** *adjective*) serving on horseback; (often + *up*) accumulate, increase; set in frame etc., esp. for viewing; organize, arrange (exhibition, attack, etc.). ● *noun* backing etc. on which picture etc. is set for display; horse for riding; setting for gem etc.

**mount**[2] *noun* (*poetical* except before name) mountain, hill.

**mountain** /'maʊntɪn/ *noun* large abrupt elevation of ground; large heap or pile; huge quantity; large surplus stock. □ **mountain ash** tree with scarlet berries; **mountain bike** sturdy bicycle with straight handlebars and many gears.

**mountaineer** /maʊntɪ'nɪə/ ● *noun* person practising mountain climbing. ● *verb* climb mountains as sport. □ **mountaineering** *noun*.

**mountainous** *adjective* having many mountains; huge.

**mountebank** /'maʊntɪbæŋk/ *noun* swindler, charlatan.

**Mountie** /'maʊntɪ/ *noun colloquial* member of Royal Canadian Mounted Police.

**mourn** /mɔːn/ *verb* (often + *for, over*) feel or show sorrow or regret; grieve for loss of (dead person etc.).

**mourner** *noun* person who mourns, esp. at funeral.

**mournful** *adjective* doleful, sad. □ **mournfully** *adverb*.

**mourning** *noun* expression of sorrow for dead, esp. by wearing black clothes; such clothes.

**mouse** /maʊs/ ● *noun* (*plural* **mice**) small rodent; timid or feeble person; *Computing* small device controlling cursor on VDU screen. ● *verb* (*also* /maʊz/) (**-sing**) (of cat etc.) hunt mice. □ **mouser** *noun*; **mousy** *adjective*.

**mousse** /muːs/ *noun* dish of whipped cream, eggs, etc., flavoured with fruit, chocolate, etc., or with meat or fish purée.

**moustache** /məˈstɑːʃ/ *noun* (*US* **mustache**) hair left to grow on upper lip.

**mouth** *noun* /maʊθ/ (*plural* **mouths** /maʊðz/) external opening in head, for taking in food and emitting sound; cavity behind it containing teeth and vocal organs; opening of container, cave, trumpet, volcano, etc.; place where river enters sea. ● *verb* /maʊð/ (**-thing**) say or speak by moving lips silently; utter insincerely or without understanding. □ **mouth-organ** harmonica; **mouthpiece** part of musical instrument, telephone, etc., placed next to lips; **mouthwash** liquid antiseptic etc. for rinsing mouth.

**mouthful** *noun* (*plural* **-s**) quantity of food etc. that fills the mouth; *colloquial* something difficult to say.

**move** /muːv/ ● *verb* (**-ving**) (cause to) change position, posture, home, or place of work; put or keep in motion; rouse, stir; (*often* + *about, away, off*, etc.) go, proceed; take action; (+ *in*) be socially active in; affect with emotion; (cause to) change attitude; propose as resolution. ● *noun* act or process of moving; change of house, premises, etc.; step taken to secure object; moving of piece in board game. □ **move in with** start to share accommodation with; **move out** leave one's home. □ **movable** *adjective*.

**movement** *noun* moving, being moved; moving parts of mechanism; group of people with common object; (*in plural*) person's activities and whereabouts; chief division of longer musical work; bowel motion; rise or fall of stockmarket prices.

**movie** /ˈmuːvɪ/ *noun esp. US colloquial* cinema film.

**moving** *adjective* emotionally affecting.

**mow** /maʊ/ *verb* (*past participle* **mowed** *or* **mown**) cut (grass, hay, etc.) with scythe or machine. □ **mower** *noun*.

**MP** *abbreviation* Member of Parliament.

**mp** *abbreviation* mezzo piano.

**m.p.g.** *abbreviation* miles per gallon.

**m.p.h.** *abbreviation* miles per hour.

**Mr** /ˈmɪstə/ *noun* (*plural* **Messrs**) *title prefixed to name of man or to designation of office etc.*

**Mrs** /ˈmɪsɪz/ *noun* (*plural* same) *title of married woman.*

**MS** *abbreviation* (*plural* **MSS** /emˈesɪz/) manuscript; multiple sclerosis.

**Ms** /mɪz/ *noun title of married or unmarried woman.*

**M.Sc.** *abbreviation* Master of Science.

**Mt.** *abbreviation* Mount.

**much** ● *adjective* existing or occurring in great quantity. ● *noun* great quantity; (usually in negative) noteworthy example. ● *adverb* in great degree; for large part of one's time; often. □ **a bit much** *colloquial* excessive; **much of a muchness** very nearly the same.

**mucilage** /ˈmjuːsɪlɪdʒ/ *noun* viscous substance obtained from plants; adhesive gum.

**muck** ● *noun colloquial* dirt, filth; anything disgusting; manure. ● *verb* (usually + *up*) *colloquial* bungle; make dirty; (+ *out*) remove manure from. □ **muck about, around** *colloquial* potter or fool about; **muck in** (*often* + *with*) *colloquial* share tasks etc.; **muckraking** seeking out and revealing of scandals etc. □ **mucky** *adjective* (**-ier, -iest**).

**mucous** /ˈmjuːkəs/ *adjective* of or covered with mucus. □ **mucous membrane** mucus-secreting tissue lining body cavities etc.

**mucus** /ˈmjuːkəs/ *noun* slimy substance secreted by mucous membrane.

**mud** *noun* soft wet earth. □ **mudguard** curved strip over wheel to protect against mud; **mud-slinging** abuse, slander.

**muddle** /ˈmʌd(ə)l/ ● *verb* (**-ling**) (*often* + *up*) bring into disorder; bewilder; confuse. ● *noun* disorder; confusion.

□ **muddle along** progress in haphazard way.

**muddy** ● adjective (**-ier, -iest**) like mud; covered in or full of mud; (of liquid, colour, or sound) not clear; confused. ● verb (**-ies, -ied**) make muddy.

**muesli** /ˈmjuːzlɪ/ noun breakfast food of crushed cereals, dried fruit, nuts, etc.

**muezzin** /muːˈezɪn/ noun Muslim crier who proclaims hours of prayer.

**muff** [1] noun covering, esp. of fur, for keeping hands or ears warm.

**muff** [2] verb colloquial bungle; miss (catch etc.).

**muffin** /ˈmʌfɪn/ noun light flat round spongy cake, eaten toasted and buttered; US similar cake made from batter or dough.

**muffle** /ˈmʌf(ə)l/ verb (**-ling**) (often + up) wrap for warmth or to deaden sound.

**muffler** noun wrap or scarf worn for warmth; thing used to deaden sound.

**mufti** /ˈmʌftɪ/ noun civilian clothes.

**mug** [1] ● noun drinking vessel, usually cylindrical with handle and no saucer; its contents; gullible person; slang face, mouth. ● verb (**-gg-**) attack and rob, esp. in public place. □ **mugger** noun; **mugging** noun.

**mug** [2] verb (**-gg-**) (usually + up) slang learn (subject) by concentrated study.

**muggins** /ˈmʌgɪnz/ noun (plural same or **mugginses**) colloquial gullible person (often meaning oneself).

**muggy** /ˈmʌgɪ/ adjective (**-ier, -iest**) (of weather etc.) oppressively humid.

**Muhammadan** /məˈhæməd(ə)n/ noun & adjective (also **Mohammedan**) Muslim.

■ **Usage** The term Muhammadan is not used by Muslims and is often regarded as offensive.

**mulatto** /mjuːˈlætəʊ/ noun (plural **-s** or **-es**) person of mixed white and black parentage.

**mulberry** /ˈmʌlbərɪ/ noun (plural **-ies**) tree bearing edible purple or white berries; its fruit; dark red, purple.

**mulch** noun layer of wet straw, leaves, plastic, etc., put round plant's roots to enrich or insulate soil. ● verb treat with mulch.

**mule** [1] /mjuːl/ noun offspring of male donkey and female horse or (in general use) vice versa; obstinate person; kind of spinning machine.

**mule** [2] /mjuːl/ noun backless slipper.

**muleteer** /mjuːləˈtɪə/ noun mule driver.

**mulish** adjective stubborn.

**mull** [1] verb (often + over) ponder.

**mull** [2] verb heat and spice (wine, beer).

**mullah** /ˈmʌlə/ noun Muslim learned in theology and sacred law.

**mullet** /ˈmʌlɪt/ noun (plural same) edible sea fish.

**mulligatawny** /mʌlɪgəˈtɔːnɪ/ noun highly seasoned soup originally from India.

**mullion** /ˈmʌljən/ noun vertical bar between panes in window. □ **mullioned** adjective.

**multi-** combining form many.

**multicoloured** /ˈmʌltɪkʌləd/ adjective of many colours.

**multifarious** /mʌltɪˈfeərɪəs/ adjective many and various; of great variety.

**multiform** /ˈmʌltɪfɔːm/ adjective having many forms; of many kinds.

**multilateral** /mʌltɪˈlætər(ə)l/ adjective (of agreement etc.) in which 3 or more parties participate; having many sides. □ **multilaterally** adverb.

**multilingual** /mʌltɪˈlɪŋgw(ə)l/ adjective in, speaking, or using many languages.

**multinational** /mʌltɪˈnæʃən(ə)l/ ● adjective operating in several countries; of several nationalities. ● noun multinational company.

**multiple** /ˈmʌltɪp(ə)l/ ● adjective having several parts, elements, or components; many and various. ● noun quantity exactly divisible by another. □ **multiple sclerosis** see SCLEROSIS.

**multiplicand** /mʌltɪplɪˈkænd/ noun quantity to be multiplied.

**multiplication** /mʌltɪplɪˈkeɪʃ(ə)n/ noun multiplying.

**multiplicity** /mʌltɪˈplɪsɪtɪ/ noun (plural **-ies**) manifold variety; (+ of) great number.

**multiplier** /ˈmʌltɪplaɪə/ noun quantity by which given number is multiplied.

**multiply** /ˈmʌltɪplaɪ/ verb (**-ies, -ied**) obtain from (number) another a specified number of times its value; increase in number, esp. by procreation.

**multi-purpose** /mʌltɪ'pɜ:pəs/ adjective having several purposes.

**multiracial** /mʌltɪ'reɪʃ(ə)l/ adjective of several races.

**multitude** /'mʌltɪtjuːd/ noun (often + of) great number; large gathering of people; (**the multitude**) the common people. □ **multitudinous** /-'tjuːdɪnəs/ adjective.

**mum¹** noun colloquial mother.

**mum²** adjective colloquial silent. □ **mum's the word** say nothing.

**mumble** /'mʌmb(ə)l/ • verb (-ling) speak or utter indistinctly. • noun indistinct utterance.

**mumbo-jumbo** /mʌmbəʊ'dʒʌmbəʊ/ noun (plural -s) meaningless ritual; meaningless or unnecessarily complicated language; nonsense.

**mummer** /'mʌmə/ noun actor in traditional play or mime.

**mummery** /'mʌmərɪ/ noun (plural -ies) ridiculous (esp. religious) ceremonial; performance by mummers.

**mummify** /'mʌmɪfaɪ/ verb (-ies, -ied) preserve (body) as mummy. □ **mummification** noun.

**mummy¹** /'mʌmɪ/ noun (plural -ies) colloquial mother.

**mummy²** /'mʌmɪ/ noun (plural -ies) dead body preserved by embalming, esp. in ancient Egypt.

**mumps** plural noun (treated as singular) infectious disease with swelling of neck and face.

**munch** verb chew steadily.

**mundane** /mʌn'deɪn/ adjective dull, routine; of this world. □ **mundanely** adverb.

**municipal** /mjuː'nɪsɪp(ə)l/ adjective of municipality or its self-government.

**municipality** /mjuːnɪsɪ'pælɪtɪ/ noun (plural -ies) town or district with local self-government; its governing body.

**munificent** /mjuː'nɪfɪs(ə)nt/ adjective (of giver or gift) splendidly generous. □ **munificence** noun.

**muniment** /'mjuːnɪmənt/ noun (usually in plural) document kept as evidence of rights or privileges.

**munition** /mjuː'nɪʃ(ə)n/ noun (usually in plural) military weapons, ammunition, etc.

**mural** /'mjʊər(ə)l/ • noun painting executed directly on wall. • adjective of, on, or like wall.

**murder** /'mɜːdə/ • noun intentional unlawful killing of human being by another; colloquial unpleasant or dangerous state of affairs. • verb kill (human being) intentionally and unlawfully; colloquial utterly defeat; spoil by bad performance, mispronunciation, etc. □ **murderer**, **murderess** noun; **murderous** adjective.

**murky** /'mɜːkɪ/ (-ier, -iest) adjective dark, gloomy; (of liquid etc.) dirty.

**murmur** /'mɜːmə/ • noun subdued continuous sound; softly spoken utterance; subdued expression of discontent. • verb make murmur; utter in low voice.

**murrain** /'mʌrɪn/ noun infectious disease of cattle.

**Muscadet** /'mʌskədeɪ/ noun dry white wine of France from Loire region; variety of grape used for this.

**muscat** /'mʌskət/ noun sweet usually fortified white wine made from musk-flavoured grapes; this grape.

**muscatel** /mʌskə'tel/ noun muscat wine or grape; raisin made from muscat grape.

**muscle** /'mʌs(ə)l/ • noun fibrous tissue producing movement in or maintaining position of animal body; part of body composed of muscles; strength, power. • verb (-ling) (+ in, in on) colloquial force oneself on others. □ **muscle-bound** with muscles stiff and inelastic through excessive exercise; **muscle-man** man with highly developed muscles.

**Muscovite** /'mʌskəvaɪt/ • noun native or citizen of Moscow. • adjective of Moscow.

**muscular** /'mʌskjʊlə/ adjective of or affecting muscles; having well-developed muscles. □ **muscular dystrophy** hereditary progressive wasting of muscles. □ **muscularity** /-'lær-/ noun.

**muse¹** /mjuːz/ verb (-sing) (usually + on, upon) ponder, reflect.

**muse²** /mjuːz/ noun Greek & Roman Mythology any of 9 goddesses inspiring poetry, music, etc.; (usually **the muse**) poet's inspiration.

**museum** /mjuː'ziːəm/ noun building for storing and exhibiting objects of historical, scientific, or cultural interest. □ **museum piece** object fit for museum, *derogatory* old-fashioned person etc.

**mush** noun soft pulp; feeble sentimentality; *US* maize porridge. □ **mushy** adjective (**-ier, -iest**).

**mushroom** /'mʌʃrʊm/ ● noun edible fungus with stem and domed cap; pinkish-brown colour. ● verb appear or develop rapidly. □ **mushroom cloud** mushroom-shaped cloud from nuclear explosion.

**music** /'mjuːzɪk/ noun art of combining vocal or instrumental sounds in harmonious or expressive way; sounds so produced; musical composition; written or printed score of this; pleasant sound. □ **music centre** equipment combining radio, record player, tape recorder, etc.; **music-hall** variety entertainment, theatre for this.

**musical** ● adjective of music; (of sounds) melodious, harmonious; fond of or skilled in music; set to or accompanied by music. ● noun musical film or play. □ **musicality** /-'kæl-/ noun; **musically** adverb.

**musician** /mjuː'zɪʃ(ə)n/ noun person skilled in practice of music, esp. professional instrumentalist. □ **musicianship** noun.

**musicology** /mjuːzɪ'kɒlədʒɪ/ noun study of history and forms of music. □ **musicological** /-kə'lɒdʒ-/ adjective; **musicologist** noun.

**musk** noun substance secreted by male musk deer and used in perfumes; plant which originally had smell of musk. □ **musk deer** small hornless Asian deer; **muskrat** large N. American aquatic rodent with smell like musk, its fur; **musk-rose** rambling rose smelling of musk. □ **musky** adjective (**-ier, -iest**).

**musket** /'mʌskɪt/ noun historical infantryman's (esp. smooth-bored) light gun.

**musketeer** /mʌskə'tɪə/ noun historical soldier armed with musket.

**musketry** /'mʌskɪtrɪ/ noun muskets; soldiers armed with muskets; knowledge of handling small arms.

**Muslim** /'mʊzlɪm/ (also **Moslem** /'mɒzləm/) ● noun follower of Islamic religion. ● adjective of Muslims or their religion.

**muslin** /'mʌzlɪn/ noun fine delicately woven cotton fabric.

**musquash** /'mʌskwɒʃ/ noun muskrat; its fur.

**mussel** /'mʌs(ə)l/ noun edible bivalve mollusc.

**must**¹ ● auxiliary verb (3rd singular present **must**; past **had to**) be obliged to; be certain to; ought to. ● noun colloquial thing that should not be missed.

■ **Usage** The negative *I must not go* means 'I am not allowed to go'. To express a lack of obligation, use *I am not obliged to go, I need not go*, or *I haven't got to go*.

**must**² noun grape juice before fermentation is complete.

**mustache** *US* = MOUSTACHE.

**mustang** /'mʌstæŋ/ noun small wild horse of Mexico and California.

**mustard** /'mʌstəd/ noun plant with yellow flowers; seeds of this crushed into paste and used as spicy condiment. □ **mustard gas** colourless oily liquid whose vapour is powerful irritant.

**muster** /'mʌstə/ ● verb collect (originally soldiers); come together; summon (courage etc.). ● noun assembly of people for inspection. □ **pass muster** be accepted as adequate.

**mustn't** /'mʌs(ə)nt/ must not.

**musty** /'mʌstɪ/ adjective (**-ier, -iest**) mouldy, stale; dull, antiquated. □ **mustiness** noun.

**mutable** /'mjuːtəb(ə)l/ adjective literary liable to change. □ **mutability** noun.

**mutant** /'mjuːt(ə)nt/ ● adjective resulting from mutation. ● noun mutant organism or gene.

**mutate** /mjuː'teɪt/ (cause to) undergo mutation.

**mutation** noun change; genetic change which when transmitted to offspring gives rise to heritable variations.

**mute** /mjuːt/ ● adjective silent; refraining from or temporarily bereft of speech; dumb; soundless. ● noun dumb person; device for damping sound of musical instrument. ● verb (**-ting**) muffle or deaden sound of; (as **muted** *adjective*) (of colours etc.) subdued. □ **mute swan** common white swan. □ **mutely** *adverb*.

**mutilate** /'mjuːtɪleɪt/ *verb* (**-ting**) deprive (person, animal) of limb etc.; destroy usefulness of (limb etc.); excise or damage part of (book etc.). □ **mutilation** *noun*.

**mutineer** /mjuːtɪ'nɪə/ *noun* person who mutinies.

**mutinous** /'mjuːtɪnəs/ *adjective* rebellious.

**mutiny** /'mjuːtɪnɪ/ ● *noun* (*plural* **-ies**) open revolt, esp. by soldiers or sailors against officers. ● *verb* (**-ies**, **-ied**) engage in mutiny.

**mutt** *noun* *slang* stupid person.

**mutter** /'mʌtə/ ● *verb* speak in barely audible manner; (often + *against*, *at*) grumble. ● *noun* muttered words etc.; muttering.

**mutton** /'mʌt(ə)n/ *noun* flesh of sheep as food.

**mutual** /'mjuːtʃʊəl/ *adjective* (of feelings, actions, etc.) experienced or done by each of two or more parties to the other(s); *colloquial* common to two or more people; having same (specified) relationship to each other. □ **mutuality** /-'æl-/ *noun*; **mutually** *adverb*.

■ **Usage** The use of *mutual* to mean 'common to two or more people' is considered incorrect by some people, who use *common* instead.

**muzzle** /'mʌz(ə)l/ ● *noun* projecting part of animal's face, including nose and mouth; guard put over animal's nose and mouth; open end of firearm. ● *verb* (**-ling**) put muzzle on; impose silence on.

**muzzy** /'mʌzɪ/ *adjective* (**-ier**, **-iest**) confused, dazed; blurred, indistinct. □ **muzzily** *adverb*.

**MW** *abbreviation* megawatt(s); medium wave.

**my** /maɪ/ *adjective* of or belonging to me.

**mycology** /maɪ'kɒlədʒɪ/ *noun* study of fungi; fungi of particular region.

**mynah** /'maɪnə/ *noun* (also **myna**) talking bird of starling family.

**myopia** /maɪ'əʊpɪə/ *noun* short-sightedness; lack of imagination. □ **myopic** /-'ɒp-/ *adjective*.

**myriad** /'mɪrɪəd/ *literary* ● *noun* indefinitely great number. ● *adjective* innumerable.

**myrrh** /mɜː/ *noun* gum resin used in perfume, medicine, incense, etc.

**myrtle** /'mɜːt(ə)l/ *noun* evergreen shrub with shiny leaves and white scented flowers.

**myself** /maɪ'self/ *pronoun*: emphatic form of I[2] or ME[1]; reflexive form of ME[1].

**mysterious** /mɪs'tɪərɪəs/ *adjective* full of or wrapped in mystery. □ **mysteriously** *adverb*.

**mystery** /'mɪstərɪ/ *noun* (*plural* **-ies**) hidden or inexplicable matter; secrecy; obscurity; fictional work dealing with puzzling event, esp. murder; religious truth divinely revealed; (in *plural*) secret ancient religious rites. □ **mystery play** miracle play; **mystery tour** pleasure trip to unspecified destination.

**mystic** /'mɪstɪk/ ● *noun* person who seeks unity with deity through contemplation etc., or believes in spiritual apprehension of truths beyond understanding. □ **mysticism** /-sɪz(ə)m/ *noun*.

**mystical** *adjective* of mystics or mysticism; of hidden meaning; spiritually symbolic.

**mystify** /'mɪstɪfaɪ/ *verb* (**-ies**, **-ied**) bewilder, confuse. □ **mystification** *noun*.

**mystique** /mɪs'tiːk/ *noun* atmosphere of mystery and veneration attending some activity, person, profession, etc.

**myth** /mɪθ/ *noun* traditional story usually involving supernatural or imaginary people and embodying popular ideas on natural or social phenomena; widely held but false idea; fictitious person, thing, or idea. □ **mythical** *adjective*.

**mythology** /mɪ'θɒlədʒɪ/ *noun* (*plural* **-ies**) body or study of myths. □ **mythological** /-θə'lɒdʒ-/ *adjective*; **mythologize** *verb* (also **-ise**) (**-zing** or **-sing**).

**myxomatosis** /mɪksəmə'təʊsɪs/ *noun* viral disease of rabbits.

**N** abbreviation (also **N.**) north(ern).

**n** [1] noun indefinite number.

**n.** abbreviation (also **n**) noun; neuter.

**NAAFI** /ˈnæfɪ/ abbreviation Navy, Army, and Air Force Institutes (canteen for servicemen).

**nab** verb (**-bb-**) slang arrest; catch in wrongdoing; grab.

**nacre** /ˈneɪkə/ noun mother-of-pearl from any shelled mollusc. □ **nacreous** /ˈneɪkrɪəs/ adjective.

**nadir** /ˈneɪdɪə/ noun point on celestial sphere directly below observer; lowest point; time of despair.

**naff** adjective slang unfashionable; rubbishy.

**nag** [1] verb (**-gg-**) persistently criticize or scold; (often + at) find fault or urge, esp. continually; (of pain) be persistent.

**nag** [2] noun colloquial horse.

**naiad** /ˈnaɪæd/ noun water nymph.

**nail** ● noun small metal spike hammered in to fasten things; horny covering on upper surface of tip of human finger or toe. ● verb fasten with nail(s); fix or hold tight; secure, catch (person, thing).

**naïve** /naɪˈiːv/ adjective (also **naive**) innocent, unaffected; foolishly credulous. □ **naïvely** adverb; **naïvety** noun.

**naked** /ˈneɪkɪd/ adjective unclothed, nude; without usual covering; undisguised; (of light, flame, sword, etc.) unprotected. □ **nakedly** adverb; **nakedness** noun.

**namby-pamby** /næmbɪˈpæmbɪ/ ● adjective insipidly pretty or sentimental; weak. ● noun (plural **-ies**) namby-pamby person.

**name** ● noun word by which individual person, animal, place, or thing is spoken of etc.; (usually abusive) term used of person; word denoting object or class of objects; reputation, esp. good. ● verb (**-ming**) give name to; state name of; mention; specify; cite. □ **name-day** feast-day of saint after whom person is named; **namesake**

person or thing having same name as another.

**nameless** adjective having, or showing, no name; left unnamed.

**namely** adverb that is to say; in other words.

**nanny** /ˈnænɪ/ noun (plural **-ies**) child's nurse; colloquial grandmother; (in full **nanny goat**) female goat.

**nano-** /ˈnænəʊ/ combining form one thousand millionth.

**nap** [1] ● noun short sleep, esp. by day. ● verb (**-pp-**) have nap.

**nap** [2] noun raised pile on cloth, esp. velvet.

**nap** [3] ● noun card game; racing tip claimed to be almost a certainty. ● verb (**-pp-**) name (horse) as probable winner. □ **go nap** try to take all 5 tricks in nap, risk everything.

**napalm** /ˈneɪpɑːm/ noun thick jellied hydrocarbon mixture used in bombs.

**nape** noun back of neck.

**naphtha** /ˈnæfθə/ noun inflammable hydrocarbon distilled from coal etc.

**naphthalene** /ˈnæfθəliːn/ noun white crystalline substance produced by distilling tar.

**napkin** /ˈnæpkɪn/ noun piece of linen etc. for wiping lips, fingers, etc. at table; baby's nappy.

**nappy** /ˈnæpɪ/ noun (plural **-ies**) piece of towelling etc. wrapped round baby to absorb urine and faeces.

**narcissism** /ˈnɑːsɪsɪz(ə)m/ noun excessive or erotic interest in oneself. □ **narcissistic** /-ˈsɪstɪk/ adjective.

**narcissus** /nɑːˈsɪsəs/ noun (plural **-cissi** /-saɪ/) any of several flowering bulbs, including daffodil.

**narcosis** /nɑːˈkəʊsɪs/ noun unconsciousness; induction of this.

**narcotic** /nɑːˈkɒtɪk/ ● adjective (of substance) inducing drowsiness etc.; (of drug) affecting the mind. ● noun narcotic substance or drug.

**nark** slang ● noun police informer. ● verb annoy.

**narrate** /nəˈreɪt/ verb (**-ting**) give continuous story or account of; provide spoken accompaniment for (film etc.). □ **narration** noun; **narrator** noun.

**narrative** /ˈnærətɪv/ ● noun ordered account of connected events. ● adjective of or by narration.

**narrow** /ˈnærəʊ/ ● adjective (**-er**, **-est**) of small width; restricted; of limited scope; with little margin; precise, exact; narrow-minded. ● noun (usually in plural) narrow part of strait, river, pass, etc. ● verb become or make narrower; contract; lessen. □ **narrow boat** canal boat; **narrow-minded** rigid or restricted in one's views, intolerant. □ **narrowly** adverb; **narrowness** noun.

**narwhal** /ˈnɑːw(ə)l/ noun Arctic white whale, male of which has long tusk.

**nasal** /ˈneɪz(ə)l/ ● adjective of nose; (of letter or sound) pronounced with breath passing through nose, e.g. m, n, ng; (of voice etc.) having many nasal sounds. ● noun nasal letter or sound. □ **nasally** adverb.

**nascent** /ˈnæs(ə)nt/ adjective in act of being born; just beginning to be. □ **nascency** /-ənsɪ/ noun.

**nasturtium** /nəˈstɜːʃəm/ noun trailing garden plant with edible leaves and bright orange, red, or yellow flowers.

**nasty** /ˈnɑːstɪ/ ● adjective (**-ier**, **-iest**) unpleasant; difficult to negotiate; (of person or animal) ill-natured, spiteful. ● noun ( plural **-ies**) colloquial violent horror film, esp. on video. □ **nastily** adverb; **nastiness** noun.

**Nat.** abbreviation National(ist); Natural.

**natal** /ˈneɪt(ə)l/ adjective of or from birth.

**nation** /ˈneɪʃ(ə)n/ noun community of people having mainly common descent, history, language, etc., forming state or inhabiting territory. □ **nationwide** extending over whole nation.

**national** /ˈnæʃən(ə)l/ ● adjective of nation; characteristic of particular nation. ● noun citizen of specified country. □ **national anthem** song adopted by nation, intended to inspire patriotism; **national grid** network of high-voltage electric power lines between major power stations; **National Insurance** system of compulsory payments from employee and employer to provide state assistance in sickness, retirement, etc.; **national service** historical conscripted peacetime military service. □ **nationally** adverb.

**nationalism** noun patriotic feeling, principles, etc.; policy of national independence. □ **nationalist** noun; **nationalistic** /-ˈlɪs-/ adjective.

**nationality** /næʃəˈnælɪtɪ/ noun ( plural **-ies**) membership of nation; being national; ethnic group within one or more political nations.

**nationalize** /ˈnæʃənəlaɪz/ verb (also **-ise**) (**-zing** or **-sing**) take (industry etc.) into state ownership; make national. □ **nationalization** noun.

**native** /ˈneɪtɪv/ ● noun (usually + of) person born in specified place; local inhabitant; indigenous animal or plant. ● adjective inherent; innate; of one's birth; (usually + to) belonging to specified place; born in a place.

**nativity** /nəˈtɪvɪtɪ/ noun ( plural **-ies**) (esp. **the Nativity**) Christ's birth; birth.

**NATO** /ˈneɪtəʊ/ abbreviation (also **Nato**) North Atlantic Treaty Organization.

**natter** /ˈnætə/ colloquial ● verb chatter idly. ● noun aimless chatter.

**natty** /ˈnætɪ/ adjective (**-ier**, **-iest**) trim; smart.

**natural** /ˈnætʃər(ə)l/ ● adjective existing in or caused by nature; not surprising; to be expected; unaffected; innate; physically existing; Music not flat or sharp. ● noun colloquial (usually + for) person or thing naturally suitable, adept, etc.; Music sign (♮) showing return to natural pitch, natural note. □ **natural gas** gas found in earth's crust; **natural history** study of animals and plants; **natural number** whole number greater than 0; **natural selection** process favouring survival of organisms best adapted to environment.

**naturalism** noun realistic representation in art and literature; philosophy based on nature alone. □ **naturalistic** /-ˈlɪs-/ adjective.

**naturalist** noun student of natural history.

**naturalize** verb (also **-ise**) (**-zing** or **-sing**) admit (foreigner) to citizenship;

introduce (plant etc.) into another region; adopt (foreign word, custom, etc.). □ **naturalization** noun.

**naturally** adverb in a natural way; as might be expected, of course.

**nature** /ˈneɪtʃə/ noun thing's or person's essential qualities or character; physical power causing material phenomena; these phenomena; kind, class.

**naturism** noun nudism. □ **naturist** noun.

**naught** /nɔːt/ archaic ● noun nothing. ● adjective worthless.

**naughty** /ˈnɔːtɪ/ adjective (**-ier, -iest**) (esp. of children) disobedient; badly behaved; colloquial jocular indecent. □ **naughtily** adverb; **naughtiness** noun.

**nausea** /ˈnɔːsɪə/ noun inclination to vomit; revulsion.

**nauseate** /ˈnɔːsɪeɪt/ verb (**-ting**) affect with nausea. □ **nauseating** adjective.

**nauseous** /ˈnɔːsɪəs/ adjective causing or inclined to vomit; disgusting.

**nautical** /ˈnɔːtɪk(ə)l/ adjective of sailors or navigation. □ **nautical mile** unit of approx. 2,025 yards (1,852 metres).

**nautilus** /ˈnɔːtɪləs/ noun (plural **nautiluses** or **nautili** /-laɪ/) kind of mollusc with spiral shell.

**naval** /ˈneɪv(ə)l/ adjective of navy; of ships.

**nave**[1] noun central part of church excluding chancel and side aisles.

**nave**[2] noun hub of wheel.

**navel** /ˈneɪv(ə)l/ noun depression in belly marking site of attachment of umbilical cord. □ **navel orange** one with navel-like formation at top.

**navigable** /ˈnævɪɡəb(ə)l/ adjective (of river etc.) suitable for ships; seaworthy; steerable. □ **navigability** noun.

**navigate** /ˈnævɪɡeɪt/ verb (**-ting**) manage or direct course of (ship, aircraft); sail on (sea, river, etc.); fly through (air); help car-driver etc. by map-reading etc. □ **navigator** noun.

**navigation** noun act or process of navigating; art or science of navigating.

**navvy** /ˈnævɪ/ noun (plural **-ies**) labourer employed in building roads, canals, etc.

**navy** /ˈneɪvɪ/ noun (plural **-ies**) state's warships with their crews, maintenance systems, etc.; (in full **navy blue**) dark blue colour.

**nay** ● adverb or rather; and even; archaic no. ● noun 'no' vote.

**Nazi** /ˈnɑːtsɪ/ ● noun (plural **-s**) historical member of German National Socialist party. ● adjective of Nazis or Nazism. □ **Nazism** noun.

**NB** abbreviation note well (nota bene).

**NCB** abbreviation historical National Coal Board.

**NCO** abbreviation non-commissioned officer.

**NE** abbreviation north-east(ern).

**Neanderthal** /nɪˈændətɑːl/ adjective of type of human found in palaeolithic Europe.

**neap** noun (in full **neap tide**) tide with smallest rise and fall.

**Neapolitan** /nɪəˈpɒlɪt(ə)n/ ● noun native of Naples. ● adjective of Naples.

**near** /nɪə/ ● adverb (often + to) to or at short distance in space or time; closely. ● preposition to or at a short distance from in space, time, condition, or resemblance. ● adjective close (to); not far in place or time; closely related; (of part of vehicle, animal, or road) on left side; colloquial stingy; with little margin. ● verb approach, draw near to. □ **the Near East** countries of eastern Mediterranean; **near-sighted** short-sighted.

**nearby** ● adjective near in position. ● adverb close.

**nearly** adverb almost; closely. □ **not nearly** nothing like, far from.

**neat** adjective tidy, methodical; elegantly simple; brief and clear; cleverly done; dexterous; (of alcoholic liquor) undiluted. □ **neaten** verb; **neatly** adverb; **neatness** noun.

**neath** preposition poetical beneath.

**nebula** /ˈnebjʊlə/ noun (plural **nebulae** /-liː/) cloud of gas and dust seen in night sky, appearing luminous or as dark silhouette. □ **nebular** adjective.

**nebulous** /ˈnebjʊləs/ adjective cloudlike; indistinct, vague.

**necessary** /ˈnesəsərɪ/ ● adjective requiring to be done; essential; inevitable. ● noun (plural **-ies**) (usually in plural) any of basic requirements of life. □ **necessarily** adverb.

**necessitate** /nɪˈsesɪteɪt/ verb (**-ting**) make necessary (esp. as result).

**necessitous** /nɪˈsesɪtəs/ *adjective* poor, needy.

**necessity** /nɪˈsesɪtɪ/ *noun* (*plural* **-ies**) indispensable thing; pressure of circumstances; imperative need; poverty; constraint or compulsion seen as natural law governing human action.

**neck** ● *noun* part of body connecting head to shoulders; part of garment round neck; narrow part of anything. ● *verb colloquial* kiss and caress amorously. □ **neckline** outline of garment-opening at neck; **necktie** strip of material worn round shirt-collar, knotted at front.

**necklace** /ˈnekləs/ *noun* string of beads, precious stones, etc. worn round neck; *South African* petrol-soaked tyre placed round victim's neck and lighted.

**necromancy** /ˈnekrəʊmænsɪ/ *noun* divination by supposed communication with the dead; magic. □ **necromancer** *noun*.

**necrophilia** /nekrəˈfɪlɪə/ *noun* morbid esp. sexual attraction to corpses.

**necropolis** /neˈkrɒpəlɪs/ *noun* ancient cemetery.

**necrosis** /neˈkrəʊsɪs/ *noun* death of tissue. □ **necrotic** /-ˈkrɒt-/ *adjective*.

**nectar** /ˈnektə/ *noun* sugary substance produced by plants and made into honey by bees; *Mythology* drink of gods.

**nectarine** /ˈnektərɪn/ *noun* smooth-skinned variety of peach.

**NEDC** *abbreviation* National Economic Development Council.

**née** /neɪ/ *adjective* (*US* **nee**) (before married woman's maiden name) born.

**need** ● *verb* stand in want of; require; (usually + *to do*) be under necessity or obligation. ● *noun* requirement; circumstances requiring action; destitution; poverty; emergency.

**needful** *adjective* requisite.

**needle** /ˈniːd(ə)l/ ● *noun* very thin pointed rod with slit ('eye') for thread, used in sewing; knitting-needle; pointer on dial; any small thin pointed instrument, esp. end of hypodermic syringe; obelisk; pointed rock or peak; leaf of fir or pine. ● *verb* (**-ling**) *colloquial* annoy, provoke. □ **needlecord** fine-ribbed corduroy fabric; **needlework** sewing or embroidery.

**needless** *adjective* unnecessary. □ **needlessly** *adverb*.

**needy** *adjective* (**-ier**, **-iest**) poor, destitute.

**ne'er** /neə/ *adverb poetical* never. □ **ne'er-do-well** good-for-nothing person.

**nefarious** /nɪˈfeərɪəs/ *adjective* wicked.

**negate** /nɪˈgeɪt/ *verb* (**-ting**) nullify; deny existence of.

**negation** *noun* absence or opposite of something positive; act of denying; negative statement; negative or unreal thing.

**negative** /ˈnegətɪv/ ● *adjective* expressing or implying denial, prohibition, or refusal; lacking positive attributes; opposite to positive; (of quantity) less than zero, to be subtracted; *Electricity* of, containing, or producing, kind of charge carried by electrons. ● *noun* negative statement or word; *Photography* image with black and white reversed or colours replaced by complementary ones. ● *verb* (**-ving**) refuse to accept; veto; disprove; contradict; neutralize. □ **negatively** *adverb*.

**neglect** /nɪˈglekt/ ● *verb* fail to care for or do; (+ *to do*) fail; pay no attention to; disregard. ● *noun* negligence; neglecting, being neglected. □ **neglectful** *adjective*; **neglectfully** *adverb*.

**negligée** /ˈneglɪʒeɪ/ *noun* (also **négligé**) woman's flimsy dressing gown.

**negligence** /ˈneglɪdʒ(ə)ns/ *noun* lack of proper care or attention; culpable carelessness. □ **negligent** *adjective*; **negligently** *adverb*.

**negligible** /ˈneglɪdʒɪb(ə)l/ *adjective* not worth considering; insignificant.

**negotiate** /nɪˈgəʊʃɪeɪt/ *verb* (**-ting**) confer in order to reach agreement; obtain (result) by negotiating; deal successfully with (obstacle etc.); convert (cheque etc.) into money. □ **negotiable** /-ʃəb-/ *adjective*; **negotiation** *noun*; **negotiator** *noun*.

**Negress** /ˈniːgrɪs/ *noun* female Negro.

■ **Usage** The term *Negress* is often considered offensive; *black* is usually preferred.

**Negro** /ˈniːgrəʊ/ ● *noun* (*plural* **-es**) member of dark-skinned (originally) African race; black. ● *adjective* of this race; black.

■ **Usage** The term *Negro* is often considered offensive; *black* is usually preferred.

**Negroid** /'ni:grɔɪd/ ● *adjective* (of physical features etc.) characteristic of black people. ● *noun* black person.

**neigh** /neɪ/ ● *noun* cry of horse. ● *verb* make a neigh.

**neighbour** /'neɪbə/ (*US* **neighbor**) *noun* person living next door or nearby; fellow human being. ● *verb* border on, adjoin.

**neighbourhood** *noun* (*US* **neighborhood**) district; vicinity; people of a district.

**neighbourly** *adjective* (*US* **neighborly**) like good neighbour, friendly, helpful. □ **neighbourliness** *noun*.

**neither** /'naɪðə/ *adjective, pronoun & adverb* not either.

**nelson** /'nels(ə)n/ *noun* wrestling hold in which arm is passed under opponent's arm from behind and hand applied to neck (**half nelson**), or both arms and hands are applied (**full nelson**).

**nem. con.** *abbreviation* with no one dissenting (*nemine contradicente*). [Latin]

**nemesis** /'neməsɪs/ *noun* justice bringing deserved punishment.

**neo-** *combining form* new; new form of.

**neolithic** /ni:ə'lɪθɪk/ *adjective* of later Stone Age.

**neologism** /ni:'ɒlədʒɪz(ə)m/ *noun* new word; coining of new words.

**neon** /'ni:ɒn/ *noun* inert gas giving orange glow when electricity is passed through it.

**neophyte** /'ni:əfaɪt/ *noun* new convert; novice of religious order; beginner.

**nephew** /'nefju:/ *noun* son of one's brother or sister or of one's spouse's brother or sister.

**nephritic** /nɪ'frɪtɪk/ *adjective* of or in kidneys.

**nephritis** /nɪ'fraɪtɪs/ *noun* inflammation of kidneys.

**nepotism** /'nepətɪz(ə)m/ *noun* favouritism to relatives in conferring offices.

**nereid** /'nɪərɪd/ *noun* sea nymph.

**nerve** ● *noun* fibre or bundle of fibres conveying impulses of sensation or motion between brain and other parts of body; coolness in danger; *colloquial* impudence; (in *plural*) nervousness, mental or physical stress. ● *verb* (**-ving**) (usually **nerve oneself**) brace or prepare (oneself). □ **nerve-cell** cell transmitting impulses in nerve tissue.

**nerveless** *adjective* lacking vigour.

**nervous** *adjective* easily upset, timid, highly strung; anxious; affecting the nerves; (+ *of*) afraid of. □ **nervous breakdown** period of mental illness, usually after stress; **nervous system** body's network of nerves. □ **nervously** *adverb*; **nervousness** *noun*.

**nervy** *adjective* (**-ier, -iest**) *colloquial* nervous; easily excited.

**nest** ● *noun* structure or place where bird lays eggs and shelters young; breeding-place, lair; snug retreat, shelter; brood, swarm; group or set of similar objects. ● *verb* use or build nest; (of objects) fit one inside another. □ **nest egg** money saved up as reserve.

**nestle** /'nes(ə)l/ *verb* (**-ling**) settle oneself comfortably; press oneself against another in affection etc.; (+ *in, into*, etc.) push (head, shoulders, etc.) affectionately or snugly; lie half hidden or embedded.

**nestling** /'nestlɪŋ/ *noun* bird too young to leave nest.

**net**[1] ● *noun* open-meshed fabric of cord, rope, etc.; piece of net used esp. to contain, restrain, or delimit, or to catch fish; structure with net used in various games. ● *verb* (**-tt-**) cover, confine, or catch with net; hit (ball) into net, esp. of goal. □ **netball** game similar to basketball.

**net**[2] (also **nett**) ● *adjective* remaining after necessary deductions; (of price) not reducible; (of weight) excluding packaging etc. ● *verb* (**-tt-**) gain or yield (sum) as net profit.

**nether** /'neðə/ *adjective archaic* lower.

**nett** = NET[2].

**netting** *noun* meshed fabric of cord or wire.

**nettle** /'net(ə)l/ ● *noun* plant covered with stinging hairs; plant resembling this. ● *verb* (**-ling**) irritate, provoke. □ **nettle-rash** skin eruption like nettle stings.

**network** ● *noun* arrangement of intersecting horizontal and vertical lines;

complex system of railways etc.; people connected by exchange of information etc.; group of broadcasting stations connected for simultaneous broadcast of a programme; system of interconnected computers. ● *verb* broadcast on network.

**neural** /'njʊər(ə)l/ *adjective* of nerve or central nervous system.

**neuralgia** /njʊə'rældʒə/ *noun* intense pain along a nerve, esp. in face or head. □ **neuralgic** *adjective*.

**neuritis** /njʊə'raɪtɪs/ *noun* inflammation of nerve(s).

**neuro-** /'njʊərəʊ/ *combining form* nerve(s).

**neurology** /njʊə'rɒlədʒɪ/ *noun* study of nerve systems. □ **neurological** /-rə-'lɒdʒ-/ *adjective*; **neurologist** *noun*.

**neuron** /'njʊərɒn/ *noun* (also **neurone** /-rəʊn/) nerve cell.

**neurosis** /njʊə'rəʊsɪs/ *noun* (*plural* **-roses** /-siːz/) disturbed behaviour pattern associated with nervous distress.

**neurotic** /njʊə'rɒtɪk/ ● *adjective* caused by or relating to neurosis; suffering from neurosis; *colloquial* abnormally sensitive or obsessive. ● *noun* neurotic person.

**neuter** /'njuːtə/ ● *adjective* neither masculine nor feminine. ● *verb* castrate, spay.

**neutral** /'njuːtr(ə)l/ ● *adjective* supporting neither of two opposing sides, impartial; vague, indeterminate; (of a gear) in which engine is disconnected from driven parts; (of colours) not strong or positive; *Chemistry* neither acid nor alkaline; *Electricity* neither positive nor negative. ● *noun* neutral state or person. □ **neutrality** /-'træl-/ *noun*.

**neutralize** *verb* (also **-ise**) (**-zing** or **-sing**) make neutral; make ineffective by opposite force. □ **neutralization** *noun*.

**neutrino** /njuː'triːnəʊ/ *noun* (*plural* **-s**) elementary particle with zero electric charge and probably zero mass.

**neutron** /'njuːtrɒn/ *noun* elementary particle of about same mass as proton but without electric charge.

**never** /'nevə/ *adverb* at no time, on no occasion; not ever; not at all; *colloquial* surely not. □ **the never-never** *colloquial* hire purchase.

**nevermore** *adverb* at no future time.

**nevertheless** /nevəðə'les/ *adverb* in spite of that; notwithstanding.

**new** *adjective* of recent origin or arrival; made, discovered, acquired, or experienced for first time; not worn; renewed; reinvigorated; different; unfamiliar. □ **New Age** set of alternative beliefs replacing traditional Western culture; **newborn** recently born; **newcomer** person recently arrived; **newfangled** different from what one is used to; **new moon** moon when first seen as crescent; **New Testament** part of Bible concerned with Christ and his followers; **New World** N. & S. America; **New Year's Day, Eve** 1 Jan., 31 Dec.

**newel** /'njuːəl/ *noun* supporting central post of winding stairs; top or bottom post of stair-rail.

**newly** *adverb* recently; afresh.

**news** /njuːz/ *plural noun* (usually treated as *singular*) information about important or interesting recent events, esp. when published or broadcast; (**the news**) broadcast report of news. □ **newsagent** seller of newspapers etc.; **newscast** radio or television broadcast of news reports; **newsletter** informal printed bulletin of club etc.; **newspaper** /'njuːs-/ printed publication of loose folded sheets with news etc.; **newsprint** low-quality paper for printing newspapers; **newsreader** person who reads out broadcast news bulletins; **newsreel** short cinema film of recent events; **news room** room where news is prepared for publication or broadcasting; **newsworthy** topical, worth reporting as news.

**newsy** *adjective* (**-ier, -iest**) *colloquial* full of news.

**newt** /njuːt/ *noun* small tailed amphibian.

**newton** /'njuːt(ə)n/ *noun* SI unit of force.

**next** ● *adjective* (often + *to*) being, placed, or living nearest; nearest in time. ● *adverb* (often + *to*) nearest in place or degree, on first or soonest occasion. ● *noun* next person or thing. ● *preposition colloquial* next to. □ **next door** in next house or room; **next of kin** closest living relative(s).

**nexus** /'neksəs/ *noun* (*plural* same) connected group or series.

**NHS** *abbreviation* National Health Service.

**NI** *abbreviation* Northern Ireland; National Insurance.

**niacin** /'naɪəsɪn/ *noun* nicotinic acid.

**nib** *noun* pen-point; (in *plural*) crushed coffee or cocoa beans.

**nibble** /'nɪb(ə)l/ ● *verb* (**-ling**) (+ *at*) take small bites at; eat in small amounts; bite gently or playfully. ● *noun* act of nibbling; very small amount of food.

**nice** *adjective* pleasant, satisfactory; kind, good-natured; fine, (of distinctions) subtle; fastidious. □ **nicely** *adverb*; **niceness** *noun*.

**nicety** /'naɪsɪtɪ/ *noun* (*plural* **-ies**) subtle distinction or detail; precision. □ **to a nicety** exactly.

**niche** /niːʃ/ *noun* shallow recess, esp. in wall; comfortable or apt position in life or employment.

**nick** ● *noun* small cut or notch; *slang* prison, police station; *colloquial* state, condition. ● *verb* make nick(s) in; *slang* steal, arrest, catch. □ **in the nick of time** only just in time.

**nickel** /'nɪk(ə)l/ *noun* silver-white metallic element used esp. in magnetic alloys; *colloquial* US 5-cent coin.

**nickname** /'nɪkneɪm/ ● *noun* familiar or humorous name added to or substituted for real name of person or thing. ● *verb* (**-ming**) give nickname to.

**nicotine** /'nɪkətiːn/ *noun* poisonous alkaloid present in tobacco.

**nicotinic acid** /nɪkə'tɪnɪk/ *noun* vitamin of B group.

**nictitate** /'nɪktɪteɪt/ *verb* (**-ting**) blink, wink. □ **nictitation** *noun*.

**niece** /niːs/ *noun* daughter of one's brother or sister or of one's spouse's brother or sister.

**nifty** /'nɪftɪ/ *adjective* (**-ier, -iest**) *colloquial* clever, adroit; smart, stylish.

**niggard** /'nɪgəd/ *noun* stingy person.

**niggardly** *adjective* stingy. □ **niggardliness** *noun*.

**niggle** /'nɪg(ə)l/ *verb* (**-ling**) fuss over details, find fault in petty way; *colloquial* nag. □ **niggling** *adjective*.

**nigh** /naɪ/ *adverb* & *preposition archaic* near.

**night** /naɪt/ *noun* period of darkness from one day to next; time from sunset to sunrise; nightfall; darkness of night; evening. □ **nightcap** *historical* cap worn in bed, drink before going to bed; **nightclub** club providing entertainment etc. late at night; **nightdress** woman's or child's loose garment worn in bed; **nightfall** end of daylight; **nightjar** nocturnal bird with harsh cry; **night-life** entertainment available at night; **nightmare** terrifying dream or *colloquial* experience; **night safe** safe with access from outer wall of bank for deposit of money when bank is closed; **nightshade** any of various plants with poisonous berries; **nightshirt** long shirt worn in bed.

**nightingale** /'naɪtɪŋgeɪl/ *noun* small reddish-brown bird, of which the male sings tunefully, esp. at night.

**nightly** ● *adjective* happening, done, or existing in the night; recurring every night. ● *adverb* every night.

**nihilism** /'naɪlɪz(ə)m/ *noun* rejection of all religious and moral principles. □ **nihilist** *noun*; **nihilistic** /-'lɪs-/ *adjective*.

**nil** *noun* nothing.

**nimble** /'nɪmb(ə)l/ *adjective* (**-r, -st**) quick and light in movement or function; agile. □ **nimbly** *adverb*.

**nimbus** /'nɪmbəs/ *noun* (*plural* **nimbi** /-baɪ/ or **nimbuses**) halo; rain-cloud.

**nincompoop** /'nɪŋkəmpuːp/ *noun* foolish person.

**nine** *adjective* & *noun* one more than eight. □ **ninepins** (usually treated as *singular*) kind of skittles. □ **ninth** /naɪnθ/ *adjective* & *noun*.

**nineteen** /naɪn'tiːn/ *adjective* & *noun* one more than eighteen. □ **nineteenth** *adjective* & *noun*.

**ninety** /'naɪntɪ/ *adjective* & *noun* (*plural* **-ies**) nine times ten. □ **ninetieth** *adjective* & *noun*.

**ninny** /'nɪnɪ/ *noun* (*plural* **-ies**) foolish person.

**nip**¹ ● *verb* (**-pp-**) pinch, squeeze sharply, bite; (often + *off*) remove by pinching etc.; *colloquial* go nimbly. ● *noun* pinch, sharp squeeze, bite; biting cold. □ **nip in the bud** suppress or destroy at very beginning.

**nip**² *noun* small quantity of spirits.

**nipper** *noun* person or thing that nips; claw of crab etc.; *colloquial* young child; (in *plural*) tool with jaws for gripping or cutting.

**nipple** /'nɪp(ə)l/ *noun* small projection in mammals from which in females milk for young is secreted; teat of feeding-bottle; device like nipple in function; nipple-like protuberance.

**nippy** *adjective* (**-ier, -iest**) *colloquial* quick, nimble; chilly.

**nirvana** /nɪə'vɑːnə/ *noun* (in Buddhism) perfect bliss attained by extinction of individuality.

**nit** *noun* egg or young of louse or other parasitic insect; *slang* stupid person. □ **nit-picking** *colloquial* fault-finding in a petty way.

**niter** *US* = NITRE.

**nitrate** /'naɪtreɪt/ *noun* salt of nitric acid; potassium or sodium nitrate as fertilizer.

**nitre** /'naɪtə/ *noun* (*US* **niter**) saltpetre.

**nitric acid** /'naɪtrɪk/ *noun* colourless corrosive poisonous liquid.

**nitrogen** /'naɪtrədʒ(ə)n/ *noun* gaseous element forming four-fifths of atmosphere. □ **nitrogenous** /-'trɒdʒɪnəs/ *adjective*.

**nitroglycerine** /naɪtrəʊ'glɪsərɪn/ *noun* (*US* **nitroglycerin**) explosive yellow liquid.

**nitrous oxide** /'naɪtrəs/ *noun* colourless gas used as anaesthetic.

**nitty-gritty** /nɪtɪ'grɪtɪ/ *noun slang* realities or practical details of a matter.

**nitwit** *noun colloquial* stupid person.

**NNE** *abbreviation* north-north-east.

**NNW** *abbreviation* north-north-west.

**No** = NOH.

**No.** *abbreviation* number.

**no** /nəʊ/ ● *adjective* not any; not a; hardly any; *used to forbid thing specified*. ● *adverb* by no amount, not at all. ● *interjection* expressing negative reply to question, request, etc. ● *noun* (*plural* **noes**) utterance of word *no*, denial or refusal; 'no' vote. □ **no-ball** unlawfully delivered ball in cricket etc.; **no longer** not now as formerly; **no one** nobody; **no way** *colloquial* it is impossible.

**nob**[1] *noun slang* person of wealth or high social position.

**nob**[2] *noun slang* head.

**nobble** /'nɒb(ə)l/ *verb* (**-ling**) *slang* try to influence (e.g. judge); tamper with (racehorse etc.); steal; seize; catch.

**nobility** /nəʊ'bɪlɪtɪ/ *noun* (*plural* **-ies**) nobleness of character, birth, or rank; class of nobles.

**noble** /'nəʊb(ə)l/ ● *adjective* (**-r, -st**) belonging to the aristocracy; of excellent character; magnanimous; of imposing appearance. ● *noun* nobleman; noblewoman. □ **nobleman** peer; **noblewoman** peeress. □ **nobly** *adverb*.

**noblesse oblige** /nəʊbles ɒ'bliːʒ/ *noun* privilege entails responsibility. [French]

**nobody** /'nəʊbədɪ/ ● *pronoun* no person. ● *noun* (*plural* **-ies**) person of no importance.

**nocturnal** /nɒk'tɜːn(ə)l/ *adjective* of or in the night; done or active by night.

**nocturne** /'nɒktɜːn/ *noun Music* short romantic composition, usually for piano; picture of night scene.

**nod** ● *verb* (**-dd-**) incline head slightly and briefly; let head droop in drowsiness; be drowsy; show (assent etc.) by nod; (of flowers etc.) bend and sway; make momentary slip or mistake. ● *noun* nodding of head. □ **nod off** *colloquial* fall asleep.

**noddle** /'nɒd(ə)l/ *noun colloquial* head.

**node** *noun* part of plant stem from which leaves emerge; knob on root or branch; natural swelling; intersecting point, esp. of planet's orbit with plane of celestial equator; point or line of least disturbance in vibrating system; point at which curve crosses itself; component in computer network. □ **nodal** *adjective*.

**nodule** /'nɒdjuːl/ *noun* small rounded lump of anything; small tumour, ganglion, swelling on legume root. □ **nodular** *adjective*.

**noggin** /'nɒgɪn/ *noun* small mug; small measure of spirits.

**Noh** /nəʊ/ *noun* (also **No**) traditional Japanese drama.

**noise** /nɔɪz/ ● *noun* sound, esp. loud or unpleasant one; confusion of loud sounds. ● *verb* (**-sing**) (usually in *passive*) make public, spread abroad.

**noisome** /'nɔɪsəm/ *adjective literary* harmful, noxious; evil-smelling.

**noisy** *adjective* (**-ier, -iest**) making much noise; full of noise. □ **noisily** *adverb*.

**nomad** /'nəʊmæd/ *noun* member of tribe roaming from place to place for pasture; wanderer. □ **nomadic** /-'mæd-/ *adjective*.

**nom de plume** /nɒm də 'pluːm/ *noun* (*plural* **noms de plume** same pronunciation) writer's assumed name. [French]

**nomenclature** /nəʊ'menklətʃə/ *noun* system of names for things; terminology of a science etc.

**nominal** /'nɒmɪn(ə)l/ *adjective* existing in name only; not real or actual; (of sum of money etc.) very small; of, as, or like noun. □ **nominally** *adverb*.

**nominate** /'nɒmɪneɪt/ *verb* (**-ting**) propose (candidate) for election; appoint to office; appoint (date or place). □ **nomination** *noun*; **nominator** *noun*.

**nominative** /'nɒmɪnətɪv/ *Grammar* ● *noun* case expressing subject of verb. ● *adjective* of or in this case.

**nominee** /nɒmɪ'niː/ *noun* person who is nominated.

**non-** *prefix* not. For words starting with *non-* that are not found below, the rootwords should be consulted.

**nonagenarian** /nəʊnædʒɪ'neərɪən/ *noun* person from 90 to 99 years old.

**non-belligerent** /nɒnbə'lɪdʒərənt/ ● *adjective* not engaged in hostilities. ● *noun* non-belligerent state etc.

**nonce** /nɒns/ *noun* □ **for the nonce** for the time being, for the present; **nonce-word** word coined for one occasion.

**nonchalant** /'nɒnʃələnt/ *adjective* calm and casual. □ **nonchalance** *noun*; **nonchalantly** *adverb*.

**non-combatant** /nɒn'kɒmbət(ə)nt/ *noun* person not fighting in a war, esp. civilian, army chaplain, etc.

**non-commissioned** /nɒnkə'mɪʃ(ə)nd/ *adjective* (of officer) not holding commission.

**noncommittal** /nɒnkə'mɪt(ə)l/ *adjective* avoiding commitment to definite opinion or course of action.

**non-conductor** /nɒnkən'dʌktə/ *noun* substance that does not conduct heat or electricity.

**nonconformist** /nɒnkən'fɔːmɪst/ *noun* person who does not conform to doctrine of established Church, esp. (**Nonconformist**) member of Protestant sect dissenting from Anglican Church; person not conforming to prevailing principle.

**nonconformity** /nɒnkənfɔː'mɪtɪ/ *noun* nonconformists as body; (+ *to*) failure to conform.

**non-contributory** /nɒnkən'trɪbjʊtərɪ/ *adjective* not involving contributions.

**nondescript** /'nɒndɪskrɪpt/ ● *adjective* lacking distinctive characteristics, not easily classified. ● *noun* such person or thing.

**none** /nʌn/ *pronoun* (often + *of*) not any; no person(s). □ **none the** (+ *comparative*), **none too** not in the least.

■ **Usage** The verb following *none* can be singular or plural when it means 'not any of several', e.g. *None of us knows* or *None of us know*.

**nonentity** /nɒ'nentɪtɪ/ *noun* (*plural* **-ies**) person or thing of no importance; nonexistence; non-existent thing.

**nonet** /nəʊ'net/ *noun* musical composition for 9 performers; the performers; any group of 9.

**nonetheless** /nʌnðə'les/ *adverb* nevertheless.

**non-event** /nɒnɪ'vent/ *noun* insignificant event, esp. contrary to hopes or expectations.

**non-existent** /nɒnɪg'zɪst(ə)nt/ *adjective* not existing. □ **non-existence** *noun*.

**non-fiction** /nɒn'fɪkʃ(ə)n/ *noun* literary work other than fiction.

**non-interference** /nɒnɪntə'fɪərəns/ *noun* non-intervention.

**non-intervention** /nɒnɪntə'venʃ(ə)n/ *noun* policy of not interfering in others' affairs.

**nonpareil** /nɒnpə'reɪl/ ● *adjective* unrivalled, unique. ● *noun* such person or thing.

**non-party** /nɒn'pɑːtɪ/ *adjective* independent of political parties.

**nonplus** /nɒn'plʌs/ *verb* (**-ss-**) completely perplex.

**nonsense** /'nɒns(ə)ns/ *noun* (often as *interjection*) absurd or meaningless words or ideas; foolish conduct. □ **nonsensical** /-'sen-/ *adjective*.

**non sequitur** /nɒn 'sekwɪtə/ *noun* conclusion that does not logically follow from the premises. [Latin]

**non-slip** /nɒnˈslɪp/ *adjective* that does not slip; that prevents slipping.

**non-smoker** /nɒnˈsməʊkə/ *noun* person who does not smoke; train compartment etc. where smoking is forbidden. □ **non-smoking** *adjective*.

**non-starter** /nɒnˈstɑːtə/ *noun colloquial* person or scheme not worth considering.

**non-stick** /nɒnˈstɪk/ *adjective* that does not allow things to stick to it.

**non-stop** /nɒnˈstɒp/ ● *adjective* (of train etc.) not stopping at intermediate stations; done without stopping. ● *adverb* without stopping.

**noodle**[1] /ˈnuːd(ə)l/ *noun* strip or ring of pasta.

**noodle**[2] /ˈnuːd(ə)l/ *noun* simpleton.

**nook** /nʊk/ *noun* corner or recess; secluded place.

**noon** *noun* 12 o'clock in day, midday. □ **noonday** midday.

**noose** ● *noun* loop with running knot; snare. ● *verb* (**-sing**) catch with or enclose in noose.

**nor** *conjunction* and not.

**Nordic** /ˈnɔːdɪk/ *adjective* of tall blond Germanic people of Scandinavia.

**norm** *noun* standard, type; standard amount of work etc.; customary behaviour.

**normal** /ˈnɔːm(ə)l/ ● *adjective* conforming to standard; regular, usual, typical; *Geometry* (of line) at right angles. ● *noun* normal value of a temperature etc.; usual state, level, etc. □ **normalcy** *noun esp. US*; **normality** /-ˈmæl-/ *noun*; **normalize** *verb* (also **-ise**) (**-zing** or **-sing**); **normally** *adverb*.

**Norman** /ˈnɔːmən/ ● *noun* (*plural* **-s**) native of medieval Normandy; descendant of people established there in 10th c. ● *adjective* of Normans; of style of medieval architecture found in Britain under Normans.

**Norse** ● *noun* Norwegian language; Scandinavian language group. ● *adjective* of ancient Scandinavia, esp. Norway. □ **Norseman** *noun*.

**north** ● *noun* point of horizon 90° anticlockwise from east; corresponding compass point; (usually **the North**) northern part of world, country, town, etc. ● *adjective* towards, at, near, or facing north; (of wind) from north. ● *adverb* towards, at, or near north; (+ *of*) further north than. □ **northbound** travelling or leading north; **north-east, -west** point midway between north and east or west; **north-north-east, north-north-west** point midway between north and north-east or north-west; **North Star** pole star. □ **northward** *adjective, adverb, & noun*; **northwards** *adverb*.

**northerly** /ˈnɔːðəlɪ/ *adjective & adverb* in northern position or direction; (of wind) from north.

**northern** /ˈnɔːð(ə)n/ *adjective* of or in the north. □ **northern lights** aurora borealis. □ **northernmost** *adjective*.

**northerner** *noun* native or inhabitant of north.

**Norwegian** /nɔːˈwiːdʒ(ə)n/ ● *noun* native, national, or language of Norway. ● *adjective* of or relating to Norway.

**nose** /nəʊz/ ● *noun* organ above mouth, used for smelling and breathing; sense of smell; odour or perfume of wine etc.; projecting part or front end of car, aircraft, etc. ● *verb* (**-sing**) (usually + *about* etc.) search; (often + *out*) perceive smell of, discover by smell; thrust nose against or into; make one's way cautiously forward. □ **nosebag** fodder-bag hung on horse's head; **nosebleed** bleeding from nose; **nosedive** (make) steep downward plunge.

**nosegay** *noun* small bunch of flowers.

**nosh** *slang* ● *verb* eat. ● *noun* food or drink. □ **nosh-up** large meal.

**nostalgia** /nɒsˈtældʒə/ *noun* (often + *for*) yearning for past period; homesickness. □ **nostalgic** *adjective*.

**nostril** /ˈnɒstr(ə)l/ *noun* either of two openings in nose.

**nostrum** /ˈnɒstrəm/ *noun* quack remedy, patent medicine; pet scheme.

**nosy** *adjective* (**-ier, -iest**) *colloquial* inquisitive, prying.

**not** *adverb* expressing negation, *refusal, or denial*. □ **not half** *slang* very much, very, not nearly, *colloquial* not at all; **not quite** almost.

**notable** /'nəʊtəb(ə)l/ ● adjective worthy of note; remarkable; eminent. ● noun eminent person. □ **notability** noun; **notably** adverb.

**notary** /'nəʊtəri/ noun (plural **-ies**) solicitor etc. who certifies deeds etc. □ **notarial** /-'teər-/ adjective.

**notation** /nəʊ'teɪʃ(ə)n/ noun representation of numbers, quantities, musical notes, etc. by symbols; set of such symbols.

**notch** ● noun V-shaped indentation on edge or surface. ● verb make notches in; (usually + up) score, win, achieve (esp. amount or quantity).

**note** ● noun brief written record as memory aid; short letter; formal diplomatic message; additional explanation in book; banknote; notice, attention; eminence; single musical tone of definite pitch; written sign representing its pitch and duration; quality or tone of speaking. ● verb (**-ting**) observe, notice; (often + down) record as thing to be remembered; (in passive; often + for) be well known. □ **notebook** book for making notes in; **notecase** wallet for banknotes; **notelet** small folded card for informal letter; **notepaper** paper for writing letters; **noteworthy** worthy of attention, remarkable.

**nothing** /'nʌθɪŋ/ ● noun no thing, not anything; person or thing of no importance; non-existence; no amount; nought. ● adverb not at all; in no way.

**nothingness** noun non-existence; worthlessness.

**notice** /'nəʊtɪs/ ● noun attention; displayed sheet etc. with announcement; intimation, warning; formal declaration of intention to end agreement or employment at specified time; short published review of new play, book, etc. ● verb (**-cing**) (often + that, how, etc.) perceive, observe. □ **noticeable** adjective; **noticeably** adverb.

**notifiable** /'nəʊtɪfaɪəb(ə)l/ adjective (esp. of disease) that must be notified to authorities.

**notify** /'nəʊtɪfaɪ/ verb (**-ies**, **-ied**) (often + of, that) inform, give notice to (person); make known. □ **notification** noun.

**notion** /'nəʊʃ(ə)n/ noun concept, idea; opinion; vague understanding; intention.

**notional** adjective hypothetical, imaginary. □ **notionally** adverb.

**notorious** /nəʊ'tɔːrɪəs/ adjective well known, esp. unfavourably. □ **notoriety** /-tə'raɪətɪ/ noun; **notoriously** adverb.

**notwithstanding** /nɒtwɪð'stændɪŋ/ ● preposition in spite of. ● adverb nevertheless.

**nougat** /'nuːgɑː/ noun sweet made from nuts, egg white, and sugar or honey.

**nought** /nɔːt/ noun digit 0; cipher; poetical or archaic nothing.

**noun** /naʊn/ noun word used to name person or thing (see panel).

**nourish** /'nʌrɪʃ/ verb sustain with food; foster, cherish (feeling etc.). □ **nourishing** adjective.

**nourishment** noun sustenance, food.

**nous** /naʊs/ noun colloquial common sense.

**Nov.** abbreviation November.

**nova** /'nəʊvə/ noun (plural **novae** /-viː/ or **-s**) star showing sudden burst of brightness and then subsiding.

**novel** /'nɒv(ə)l/ ● noun fictitious prose story of book length. ● adjective of new kind or nature.

**novelette** /nɒvə'let/ noun short (esp. romantic) novel.

**novelist** /'nɒvəlɪst/ noun writer of novels.

**novella** /nə'velə/ noun (plural **-s**) short novel or narrative story.

**novelty** /'nɒvəltɪ/ noun (plural **-ies**) newness; new thing or occurrence; small toy etc.

**November** /nəʊ'vembə/ noun eleventh month of year.

**novena** /nə'viːnə/ noun RC Church special prayers or services on 9 successive days.

**novice** /'nɒvɪs/ noun probationary member of religious order; beginner.

**noviciate** /nə'vɪʃɪət/ noun (also **noviatiate**) period of being a novice; religious novice; novices' quarters.

**now** ● adverb at present or mentioned time; immediately; by this time: in the immediate past. ● conjunction (often + that) because. ● noun this time; the present. □ **now and again** or **then** occasionally.

**nowadays | nude**

**nowadays** /'naʊədeɪz/ ● *adverb* at present time or age. ● *noun* the present time.

**nowhere** /'nəʊweə/ ● *adverb* in or to no place. ● *pronoun* no place.

**nowt** *noun colloquial or dialect* nothing.

**noxious** /'nɒkʃəs/ *adjective* harmful, unwholesome.

**nozzle** /'nɒz(ə)l/ *noun* spout on hose etc.

**nr.** *abbreviation* near.

**NSPCC** *abbreviation* National Society for Prevention of Cruelty to Children.

**NSW** *abbreviation* New South Wales.

**NT** *abbreviation* New Testament; Northern Territory (of Australia); National Trust.

**nuance** /'njuːɑ̃s/ *noun* subtle shade of meaning, feeling, colour, etc.

**nub** *noun* point or gist (of matter or story).

**nubile** /'njuːbaɪl/ *adjective* (of woman) marriageable, sexually attractive. □ **nubility** *noun*.

**nuclear** /'njuːklɪə/ *adjective* of, relating to, or constituting a nucleus; using nuclear energy. □ **nuclear energy** energy obtained by nuclear fission or fusion; **nuclear family** couple and their child(ren); **nuclear fission** nuclear reaction in which heavy nucleus splits with release of energy; **nuclear fuel** source of nuclear energy; **nuclear fusion** nuclear reaction in which nuclei of low atomic number fuse with release of energy; **nuclear physics** physics of atomic nuclei; **nuclear power** power derived from nuclear energy, country that has nuclear weapons.

**nucleic acid** /njuː'kliːɪk/ *noun* either of two complex organic molecules (DNA and RNA) present in all living cells.

**nucleon** /'njuːklɒn/ *noun* proton or neutron.

**nucleus** /'njuːklɪəs/ *noun* (*plural* **nuclei** /-lɪaɪ/) central part or thing round which others collect; kernel; initial part; central core of atom; part of cell containing genetic material.

**nude** /njuːd/ ● *adjective* naked, unclothed. ● *noun* painting etc. of nude human figure; nude person. □ **in the nude** naked. □ **nudity** *noun*.

---

## Noun

A noun is the name of a person or thing. There are four kinds:

**1** common nouns (the words for articles and creatures), e.g.

| | | |
|---|---|---|
| shoe | in | *The red shoe was left on the shelf.* |
| box | in | *The large box stood in the corner.* |
| plant | in | *The plant grew to two metres.* |
| horse | in | *A horse and rider galloped by.* |

**2** proper nouns (the names of people, places, ships, institutions, and animals, which always begin with a capital letter), e.g.

| | | |
|---|---|---|
| Jane | USS Enterprise | Bambi |
| London | Grand Hotel | |

**3** abstract nouns (the words for qualities, things we cannot see or touch, and things which have no physical reality), e.g.

| | |
|---|---|
| truth | absence |
| explanation | warmth |

**4** collective nouns (the words for groups of things), e.g.

| | | |
|---|---|---|
| committee | squad | the Cabinet |
| herd | swarm | the clergy |
| majority | team | the public |

---

**nudge** • *verb* (**-ging**) prod gently with elbow to draw attention; push gradually. • *noun* gentle push.

**nudist** /'nju:dɪst/ *noun* person who advocates or practises going unclothed. □ **nudism** *noun*.

**nugatory** /'nju:gətərɪ/ *adjective* futile, trifling; inoperative, not valid.

**nugget** /'nʌgɪt/ *noun* lump of gold etc., as found in earth; lump of anything.

**nuisance** /'nju:s(ə)ns/ *noun* person, thing, or circumstance causing annoyance.

**null** *adjective* (esp. **null and void**) invalid; non-existent; expressionless. □ **nullity** *noun*.

**nullify** /'nʌlɪfaɪ/ *verb* (**-ies, -ied**) neutralize; invalidate. □ **nullification** *noun*.

**numb** /nʌm/ • *adjective* deprived of feeling; paralysed. • *verb* make numb; stupefy, paralyse. □ **numbness** *noun*.

**number** /'nʌmbə/ • *noun* arithmetical value representing a quantity; word, symbol, or figure representing this; total count or aggregate; numerical reckoning; quantity, amount; person or thing having place in a series, esp. single issue of magazine, item in programme, etc. • *verb* include; assign number(s) to; amount to specified number. □ **number one** *colloquial* oneself; **number plate** plate bearing number esp. of motor vehicle.

■ **Usage** The phrase *a number of* is normally used with a plural verb, as in *a number of problems remain.*

**numberless** *adjective* innumerable.

**numeral** /'nju:mər(ə)l/ • *noun* symbol or group of symbols denoting a number. • *adjective* of or denoting a number.

**numerate** /'nju:mərət/ *adjective* familiar with basic principles of mathematics. □ **numeracy** *noun*.

**numeration** /nju:mə'reɪʃ(ə)n/ *noun* process of numbering; calculation.

**numerator** /'nju:məreɪtə/ *noun* number above line in vulgar fraction.

**numerical** /nju:'merɪk(ə)l/ *adjective* of or relating to number(s). □ **numerically** *adverb*.

**numerology** /nju:mə'rɒlədʒɪ/ *noun* study of supposed occult significance of numbers.

**numerous** /'nju:mərəs/ *adjective* many; consisting of many.

**numinous** /'nju:mɪnəs/ *adjective* indicating presence of a god; awe-inspiring.

**numismatic** /nju:mɪz'mætɪk/ *adjective* of or relating to coins or medals.

**numismatics** *plural noun* (usually treated as *singular*) study of coins and medals. □ **numismatist** /-'mɪzmətɪst/ *noun*.

**nun** *noun* member of community of women living under religious vows.

**nuncio** /'nʌnsɪəʊ/ *noun* (*plural* **-s**) papal ambassador.

**nunnery** *noun* (*plural* **-ies**) religious house of nuns.

**nuptial** /'nʌpʃ(ə)l/ • *adjective* of marriage or weddings. • *noun* (usually in *plural*) wedding.

**nurse** /nɜ:s/ • *noun* person trained to care for sick and help doctors or dentists; nursemaid. • *verb* (**-sing**) work as nurse; attend to (sick person); feed or be fed at breast; hold or treat carefully; foster; harbour. □ **nursing home** private hospital or home.

**nursemaid** *noun* woman in charge of child(ren).

**nursery** /'nɜ:sərɪ/ *noun* (*plural* **-ies**) room or place equipped for young children; place where plants are reared for sale. □ **nurseryman** grower of plants for sale; **nursery rhyme** traditional song or rhyme for young children; **nursery school** school for children between ages of 3 and 5.

**nurture** /'nɜ:tʃə/ • *noun* bringing up, fostering care; nourishment. • *verb* (**-ring**) bring up, rear.

**nut** *noun* fruit consisting of hard shell or pod around edible kernel or seeds; this kernel; small usually hexagonal flat piece of metal with threaded hole through it for screwing on end of bolt to secure it; *slang* head; *slang* crazy person; small lump (of coal etc.). □ **nutcase** *slang* crazy person; **nutcracker** (usually in *plural*) device for cracking nuts; **nuthatch** small bird climbing up and down tree trunks; **nuts** *slang* crazy.

**nutmeg** /'nʌtmeg/ *noun* hard aromatic seed used as spice etc.; E. Indian tree bearing this.

**nutria** /'nju:trɪə/ *noun* coypu fur.

**nutrient** /'njuːtrɪənt/ ● *noun* substance providing essential nourishment. ● *adjective* serving as or providing nourishment.

**nutriment** /'njuːtrɪmənt/ *noun* nourishing food.

**nutrition** /njuːˈtrɪʃ(ə)n/ *noun* food, nourishment. □ **nutritional** *adjective*; **nutritionist** *noun*.

**nutritious** /njuːˈtrɪʃəs/ *adjective* efficient as food.

**nutritive** /'njuːtrɪtɪv/ *adjective* of nutrition; nutritious.

**nutshell** *noun* hard covering of nut. □ **in a nutshell** in few words.

**nutter** *noun slang* crazy person.

**nutty** *adjective* (**-ier, -iest**) full of nuts; tasting like nuts; *slang* crazy.

**nux vomica** /nʌks ˈvɒmɪkə/ *noun* E. Indian tree; its seeds, containing strychnine.

**nuzzle** /'nʌz(ə)l/ *verb* (**-ling**) prod or rub gently with nose; nestle, lie snug.

**NW** *abbreviation* north-west(ern).

**NY** *abbreviation US* New York.

**nylon** /'naɪlɒn/ *noun* strong light synthetic fibre; nylon fabric; (in *plural*) stockings of nylon.

**nymph** /nɪmf/ *noun* mythological semi-divine female spirit associated with rivers, woods, etc.; immature form of some insects.

**nymphomania** /nɪmfəˈmeɪnɪə/ *noun* excessive sexual desire in a woman. □ **nymphomaniac** *noun & adjective*.

**NZ** *abbreviation* New Zealand.

# Oo

**O**[1] □ **O level** *historical* ordinary level in GCE exam.

**O**[2] /əʊ/ *interjection* = OH; *used before name in exclamation*.

**oaf** *noun* (*plural* **-s**) awkward lout. □ **oafish** *adjective*; **oafishly** *adverb*; **oafishness** *noun*.

**oak** *noun* acorn-bearing hardwood tree with lobed leaves; its wood. □ **oak-apple, -gall** abnormal growth produced on oak trees by insects.

**oakum** /'əʊkəm/ *noun* loose fibre got by picking old rope to pieces.

**OAP** *abbreviation* old-age pensioner.

**oar** /ɔː/ *noun* pole with blade used to propel boat by leverage against water; rower.

**oarsman** /'ɔːzmən/ *noun* (*feminine* **-woman**) rower. □ **oarsmanship** *noun*.

**oasis** /əʊˈeɪsɪs/ *noun* (*plural* **oases** /-siːz/) fertile spot in desert.

**oast** *noun* hop-drying kiln. □ **oast house** building containing this.

**oat** *noun* cereal plant grown as food; (in *plural*) grain of this; tall grass resembling this. □ **oatcake** thin oatmeal biscuit; **oatmeal** meal ground from oats,

greyish-fawn colour; **sow one's wild oats** indulge in youthful follies before becoming steady. □ **oaten** *adjective*.

**oath** /əʊθ/ *noun* (*plural* **-s**) solemn declaration naming God etc. as witness; curse. □ **on, under oath** having sworn solemn oath.

**ob.** *abbreviation* died (*obiit*).

**obbligato** /ɒblɪˈgɑːtəʊ/ *noun* (*plural* **-s**) *Music* accompaniment forming integral part of a composition.

**obdurate** /'ɒbdjʊrət/ *adjective* stubborn; hardened. □ **obduracy** *noun*.

**OBE** *abbreviation* Officer of the Order of the British Empire.

**obedient** /əʊˈbiːdɪənt/ *adjective* obeying or ready to obey; submissive to another's will. □ **obedience** *noun*; **obediently** *adverb*.

**obeisance** /əʊˈbeɪs(ə)ns/ *noun* gesture expressing submission, respect, etc.; homage. □ **obeisant** *adjective*.

**obelisk** /'ɒbəlɪsk/ *noun* tapering usually 4-sided stone pillar.

**obelus** /'ɒbələs/ *noun* (*plural* **obeli** /-laɪ/) dagger-shaped mark of reference (†).

**obese** /əʊˈbiːs/ *adjective* very fat. □ **obesity** *noun*.

**obey** /əʊˈbeɪ/ verb carry out command of; do what one is told to do.

**obfuscate** /ˈɒbfʌskeɪt/ verb (-ting) obscure, confuse; bewilder. □ **obfuscation** noun.

**obituary** /əˈbɪtjʊərɪ/ • noun (plural -ies) notice of death(s); brief biography of deceased person. • adjective of or serving as obituary.

**object** • noun /ˈɒbdʒɪkt/ material thing; person or thing to which action or feeling is directed; thing sought or aimed at; word or phrase representing person or thing affected by action of verb (see panel). • verb /əbˈdʒekt/ (often + to, against) express opposition, disapproval, or reluctance; protest. □ **no object** not an important factor. □ **objector** noun.

**objectify** /əbˈdʒektɪfaɪ/ verb (-ies, -ied) present as an object, embody.

**objection** /əbˈdʒekʃ(ə)n/ noun expression of disapproval or opposition; objecting; adverse reason or statement.

**objectionable** adjective unpleasant, offensive; open to objection. □ **objectionably** adverb.

**objective** /əbˈdʒektɪv/ • adjective external to the mind; actually existing; dealing with outward things uncoloured by opinions or feelings; Grammar (of case or word) in form appropriate to object. • noun object or purpose; Grammar objective case. □ **objectively** adverb; **objectivity** /ɒbdʒekˈtɪvɪtɪ/ noun.

**objet d'art** /ɒbʒeɪ ˈdɑː/ noun (plural **objets d'art** same pronunciation) small decorative object. [French]

**oblate** /ˈɒbleɪt/ adjective (of spheroid) flattened at poles.

**oblation** /əʊˈbleɪʃ(ə)n/ noun thing offered to a divine being.

**obligate** /ˈɒblɪgeɪt/ verb (-ting) bind (person) legally or morally.

**obligation** /ɒblɪˈgeɪʃ(ə)n/ noun compelling power of law, duty, etc.; duty; binding agreement; indebtedness for service or benefit.

**obligatory** /əˈblɪgətərɪ/ adjective binding, compulsory. □ **obligatorily** adverb.

**oblige** /əˈblaɪdʒ/ verb (-ging) compel, require; be binding on; do (person) small favour; (as **obliged** adjective) grateful.

**obliging** adjective helpful, accommodating. □ **obligingly** adverb.

**oblique** /əˈbliːk/ • adjective slanting; at an angle; not going straight to the point, indirect; Grammar (of case) other than nominative or vocative. • noun oblique stroke. □ **obliquely** adverb; **obliqueness** noun; **obliquity** /əˈblɪkwɪtɪ/ noun.

---

## Object

There are two types of object:

**1** A direct object is a person or thing directly affected by the verb and can usually be found by asking the question 'whom or what?' after the verb, e.g.

> The electors chose Mr Smith.
> Charles wrote a letter.

**2** An indirect object is usually a person or thing receiving something from the subject of the verb, e.g.

> He gave me the pen.
> (me is the indirect object, and the pen is the direct object.)

> I sent my bank a letter.
> (my bank is the indirect object, and a letter is the direct object.)

Sentences containing an indirect object usually contain a direct object as well, but not always, e.g.

> Pay me.

'Object' on its own usually means a direct object.

**obliterate** /əˈblɪtəreɪt/ verb (-ting) blot out, leave no clear trace of. □ **obliteration** noun.

**oblivion** /əˈblɪvɪən/ noun state of having or being forgotten.

**oblivious** /əˈblɪvɪəs/ adjective unaware or unconscious. □ **obliviously** adverb; **obliviousness** noun.

**oblong** /ˈɒblɒŋ/ ● adjective rectangular with adjacent sides unequal. ● noun oblong figure or object.

**obloquy** /ˈɒbləkwɪ/ noun abuse, being ill spoken of.

**obnoxious** /əbˈnɒkʃəs/ adjective offensive, objectionable. □ **obnoxiously** adverb; **obnoxiousness** noun.

**oboe** /ˈəʊbəʊ/ noun double-reeded wood-wind instrument. □ **oboist** noun.

**obscene** /əbˈsiːn/ adjective offensively indecent; colloquial highly offensive; Law (of publication) tending to deprave and corrupt. □ **obscenely** adverb; **obscenity** /-ˈsen-/ noun (plural **-ies**).

**obscure** /əbˈskjʊə/ ● adjective not clearly expressed or easily understood; unexplained; dark, indistinct; hidden, undistinguished. ● verb (-ring) make obscure or invisible. □ **obscurity** noun.

**obsequies** /ˈɒbsɪkwɪz/ plural noun funeral.

**obsequious** /əbˈsiːkwɪəs/ adjective fawning, servile. □ **obsequiously** adverb; **obsequiousness** noun.

**observance** /əbˈzɜːv(ə)ns/ noun keeping or performance of law, duty, etc.; rite, ceremonial act.

**observant** adjective good at observing. □ **observantly** adverb.

**observation** /ɒbzəˈveɪʃ(ə)n/ noun observing, being observed; comment, remark; power of perception. □ **observational** adjective.

**observatory** /əbˈzɜːvətərɪ/ noun (plural **-ies**) building for astronomical or other observation.

**observe** /əbˈzɜːv/ verb (-ving) perceive, become aware of; watch; keep (rules etc.); celebrate (rite etc.); remark; take note of scientifically. □ **observable** adjective.

**observer** noun person who observes; interested spectator; person attending meeting to note proceedings but without participating.

**obsess** /əbˈses/ verb fill mind of (person) all the time; preoccupy. □ **obsession** noun; **obsessional** adjective; **obsessive** adjective; **obsessively** adverb; **obsessiveness** noun.

**obsidian** /əbˈsɪdɪən/ noun dark glassy rock formed from lava.

**obsolescent** /ɒbsəˈles(ə)nt/ adjective becoming obsolete. □ **obsolescence** noun.

**obsolete** /ˈɒbsəliːt/ adjective no longer used, antiquated.

**obstacle** /ˈɒbstək(ə)l/ noun thing obstructing progress.

**obstetrics** /əbˈstetrɪks/ plural noun (usually treated as singular) branch of medicine or surgery dealing with childbirth. □ **obstetric** adjective; **obstetrician** /ɒbstəˈtrɪʃ(ə)n/ noun.

**obstinate** /ˈɒbstɪnət/ adjective stubborn, intractable. □ **obstinacy** noun; **obstinately** adverb.

**obstreperous** /əbˈstrepərəs/ adjective noisy, unruly. □ **obstreperously** adverb; **obstreperousness** noun.

**obstruct** /əbˈstrʌkt/ verb block up; make hard or impossible to pass along or through; retard or prevent progress of.

**obstruction** /əbˈstrʌkʃ(ə)n/ noun obstructing, being obstructed; thing that obstructs; Sport unlawfully obstructing another player.

**obstructive** adjective causing or meant to cause obstruction.

**obtain** /əbˈteɪn/ verb acquire; get; have granted to one; be prevalent or established. □ **obtainable** adjective.

**obtrude** /əbˈtruːd/ verb (-ding) (often + on, upon) thrust (oneself etc.) importunately forward. □ **obtrusion** noun.

**obtrusive** /əbˈtruːsɪv/ adjective unpleasantly noticeable; obtruding oneself. □ **obtrusively** adverb; **obtrusiveness** noun.

**obtuse** /əbˈtjuːs/ adjective dull-witted; (of angle) between 90° and 180°; blunt, not sharp or pointed. □ **obtuseness** noun.

**obverse** /ˈɒbvɜːs/ noun counterpart, opposite; side of coin or medal that bears head or principal design; front or top side.

**obviate** /ˈɒbvɪeɪt/ verb (-ting) get round or do away with (need, inconvenience, etc.).

**obvious** /'ɒbvɪəs/ *adjective* easily seen, recognized, or understood. □ **obviously** *adverb*; **obviousness** *noun*.

**OC** *abbreviation* Officer Commanding.

**ocarina** /ɒkə'riːnə/ *noun* egg-shaped musical wind instrument.

**occasion** /ə'keɪʒ(ə)n/ ●*noun* special event or happening; time of this; reason, need; suitable juncture, opportunity. ●*verb* cause, esp. incidentally.

**occasional** *adjective* happening irregularly and infrequently; made or meant for, acting on, etc. special occasion(s). □ **occasional table** small table for use as required. □ **occasionally** *adverb*.

**Occident** /'ɒksɪd(ə)nt/ *noun* (**the Occident**) West, esp. Europe and America as distinct from the Orient. □ **occidental** /-'den-/ *adjective*.

**occiput** /'ɒksɪpʌt/ *noun* back of head. □ **occipital** /-'sɪpɪt-/ *adjective*.

**occlude** /ə'kluːd/ *verb* (**-ding**) stop up; obstruct; *Chemistry* absorb (gases); (as **occluded** *adjective*) *Meteorology* (of frontal system) formed when cold front overtakes warm front, raising warm air. □ **occlusion** *noun*.

**occult** /ɒ'kʌlt, 'ɒkʌlt/ *adjective* involving the supernatural, mystical; esoteric. □ **the occult** occult phenomena generally.

**occupant** /'ɒkjʊpənt/ *noun* person occupying dwelling, office, or position. □ **occupancy** *noun* (*plural* **-ies**).

**occupation** /ɒkjʊ'peɪʃ(ə)n/ *noun* profession or employment; pastime; occupying or being occupied, esp. by armed forces of another country.

**occupational** *adjective* of or connected with one's occupation. □ **occupational disease, hazard** one to which a particular occupation renders someone especially liable; **occupational therapy** programme of mental or physical activity to assist recovery from disease or injury.

**occupier** /'ɒkjʊpaɪə/ *noun* person living in house etc. as owner or tenant.

**occupy** /'ɒkjʊpaɪ/ *verb* (**-ies, -ied**) live in; be tenant of; take up, fill (space, time, or place); take military possession of; place oneself in (building etc.) without authority as protest etc.; hold (office); keep busy.

**occur** /ə'kɜː/ *verb* (**-rr-**) take place, happen; be met with or found in some place or conditions; (+ *to*) come into one's mind.

**occurrence** /ə'kʌrəns/ *noun* happening; incident.

**ocean** /'əʊʃ(ə)n/ *noun* large expanse of sea, esp. one of the 5 named divisions of this, e.g. Atlantic Ocean; (often in *plural*) *colloquial* immense expanse or quantity. □ **oceanic** /əʊʃɪ'ænɪk/ *adjective*.

**oceanography** /əʊʃə'nɒgrəfɪ/ *noun* study of the oceans. □ **oceanographer** *noun*.

**ocelot** /'ɒsɪlɒt/ *noun* S. American leopard-like cat.

**ochre** /'əʊkə/ *noun* (*US* **ocher**) earth used as pigment; pale brownish-yellow colour. □ **ochreous** /'əʊkrɪəs/ *adjective*.

**o'clock** /ə'klɒk/ *adverb* of the clock (used to specify hour).

**Oct.** *abbreviation* October.

**octa-** *combining form* (also **oct-** before vowel) eight.

**octagon** /'ɒktəgən/ *noun* plane figure with 8 sides and angles. □ **octagonal** /-'tæg-/ *adjective*.

**octahedron** /ɒktə'hiːdrən/ *noun* (*plural* **-s**) solid figure contained by 8 (esp. triangular) plane faces. □ **octahedral** *adjective*.

**octane** /'ɒkteɪn/ *noun* colourless inflammable hydrocarbon occurring in petrol. □ **high-octane** (of fuel used in internal-combustion engines) not detonating rapidly during power stroke; **octane number, rating** figure indicating antiknock properties of fuel.

**octave** /'ɒktɪv/ *noun* *Music* interval of 8 diatonic degrees between two notes, 8 notes occupying this interval, each of two notes at this interval's extremes; 8-line stanza.

**octavo** /ɒk'teɪvəʊ/ *noun* (*plural* **-s**) size of book or page when sheets folded into 8 leaves.

**octet** /ɒk'tet/ *noun* musical composition for 8 performers; the performers; any group of 8.

**octo-** *combining form* (also **oct-** before vowel) eight.

**October** /ɒk'təʊbə/ *noun* tenth month of year.

**octogenarian** /ɒktəʊdʒɪˈneərɪən/ *noun* person from 80 to 89 years old.

**octopus** /ˈɒktəpəs/ *noun* (*plural* **-puses**) mollusc with 8 suckered tentacles.

**ocular** /ˈɒkjʊlə/ *adjective* of, for, or by the eyes; visual.

**oculist** /ˈɒkjʊlɪst/ *noun* specialist in treatment of eyes.

**OD** /əʊˈdiː/ *slang* ●*noun* drug overdose. ●*verb* (**OD's**, **OD'd**, **OD'ing**) take overdose.

**odd** *adjective* extraordinary, strange; (of job etc.) occasional, casual; not normally considered, unconnected; (of numbers) not divisible by 2; left over, detached from set etc.; (added to weight, sum, etc.) rather more than. □ **oddball** *colloquial* eccentric person. □ **oddly** *adverb*; **oddness** *noun*.

**oddity** /ˈɒdɪtɪ/ *noun* (*plural* **-ies**) strange person, thing, or occurrence; peculiar trait; strangeness.

**oddment** *noun* odd article; something left over.

**odds** *plural noun* ratio between amounts staked by parties to a bet; chances in favour of or against result; balance of advantage; difference giving an advantage. □ **at odds** (often + *with*) in conflict; **odds and ends** remnants, stray articles; **odds-on** state when success is more likely than failure; **over the odds** above general price etc.

**ode** *noun* lyric poem of exalted style and tone.

**odious** /ˈəʊdɪəs/ *adjective* hateful, repulsive. □ **odiously** *adverb*; **odiousness** *noun*.

**odium** /ˈəʊdɪəm/ *noun* general dislike or disapproval.

**odor** *US* = ODOUR.

**odoriferous** /əʊdəˈrɪfərəs/ *adjective* diffusing (usually pleasant) odours.

**odour** /ˈəʊdə/ *noun* (*US* **odor**) smell or fragrance; favour or repute. □ **odorous** *adjective*; **odourless** *adjective*.

**odyssey** /ˈɒdɪsɪ/ *noun* (*plural* **-s**) long adventurous journey.

**OED** *abbreviation* Oxford English Dictionary.

**Oedipus complex** /ˈiːdɪpəs/ *noun* attraction of child to parent of opposite sex (esp. son to mother). □ **Oedipal** *adjective*.

**oesophagus** /iːˈsɒfəgəs/ *noun* (*US* **esophagus**) (*plural* **-gi** /-dʒaɪ/ or **-guses**) passage from mouth to stomach, gullet.

**oestrogen** /ˈiːstrədʒ(ə)n/ *noun* (*US* **estrogen**) sex hormone developing and maintaining female physical characteristics; this produced artificially for medical use.

**oeuvre** /ˈɜːvr/ *noun* works of creative artist considered collectively. [French]

**of** /ɒv/ *preposition* belonging to, from; concerning; out of; among; relating to; *US* (of time in relation to following hour) to. □ **be of** possess, give rise to; **of late** recently; **of old** formerly.

**off** ●*adverb* away, at or to distance; out of position; loose, separate, gone; so as to be rid of; discontinued, stopped; not available on menu. ●*preposition* from; not on. ●*adjective* further; far; right-hand; *colloquial* annoying; not acceptable; *Cricket* of, in, or into half of field which batsman faces. ●*noun* start of race; *Cricket* the off side. □ **off and on** now and then; **offbeat** unconventional, *Music* not coinciding with beat; **off chance** remote possibility; **off colour** unwell, *US* rather indecent; **offhand** without preparation, casual, curt; **off-licence** shop selling alcoholic drink for consumption away from premises; **offline** *Computing* *adjective* not online, *adverb* with delay between data production and its processing; **off-peak** (of electricity, traffic, etc.) used or for use at times of lesser demand; **offprint** reprint of part of publication; **offshoot** side-shoot or branch, derivative; **offside** (of player in field game) in position where he or she may not play the ball; **off the wall** *slang* crazy, absurd; **off white** white with grey or yellowish tinge.

**offal** /ˈɒf(ə)l/ *noun* edible organs of animal, esp. heart, liver, etc.; refuse, scraps.

**offence** /əˈfens/ *noun* (*US* **offense**) illegal act; transgression; upsetting of person's feelings, insult; aggressive action.

**offend** /əˈfend/ *verb* cause offence to, upset; displease, anger; (often + *against*) do wrong. □ **offender** *noun*; **offending** *adjective*.

**offense** *US* = OFFENCE.

**offensive** /ə'fensɪv/ ● *adjective* causing offence; insulting; disgusting; aggressive; (of weapon) for attacking. ● *noun* aggressive attitude, action, or campaign. □ **offensively** *adverb*; **offensiveness** *noun*.

**offer** /'ɒfə/ ● *verb* present for acceptance, refusal, or consideration; (+ *to do*) express readiness, show intention; attempt; present by way of sacrifice. ● *noun* expression of readiness to do or give if desired, or buy or sell; amount offered; proposal, esp. of marriage; bid. □ **on offer** for sale at certain (esp. reduced) price.

**offering** *noun* contribution, gift; thing offered.

**offertory** /'ɒfətərɪ/ *noun* (*plural* -**ies**) offering of bread and wine at Eucharist; collection of money at religious service.

**office** /'ɒfɪs/ *noun* room or building where administrative or clerical work is done; place for transacting business; department or local branch, esp. for specified purpose; position with duties attached to it; tenure of official position; duty, task, function; (usually in *plural*) piece of kindness, service; authorized form of worship.

**officer** /'ɒfɪsə/ *noun* person holding position of authority or trust, esp. one with commission in armed forces; policeman or policewoman; president, treasurer, etc. of society etc.

**official** /ə'fɪʃ(ə)l/ ● *adjective* of office or its tenure; characteristic of people in office; properly authorized. ● *noun* person holding office or engaged in official duties. □ **official secrets** confidential information involving national security. □ **officialdom** *noun*; **officially** *adverb*.

**officialese** /əfɪʃə'liːz/ *noun derogatory* officials' jargon.

**officiate** /ə'fɪʃɪeɪt/ *verb* (-**ting**) act in official capacity; conduct religious service.

**officious** /ə'fɪʃəs/ *adjective* domineering; intrusive in correcting etc. □ **officiously** *adverb*; **officiousness** *noun*.

**offing** /'ɒfɪŋ/ *noun* □ **in the offing** at hand, ready or likely to happen etc.

**offset** ● *noun* side-shoot of plant used for propagation; compensation; sloping ledge. ● *verb* (-**setting**; *past & past participle* -**set**) counterbalance, compensate.

**offspring** *noun* (*plural* same) person's child, children, or descendants; animal's young or descendants.

**oft** *adverb archaic* often.

**often** /'ɒf(ə)n/ *adverb* (**oftener, oftenest**) frequently; many times; at short intervals; in many instances.

**ogee** /'əʊdʒiː/ *noun* S-shaped curve or moulding.

**ogive** /'əʊdʒaɪv/ *noun* pointed arch; diagonal rib of vault.

**ogle** /'əʊg(ə)l/ ● *verb* (-**ling**) look lecherously or flirtatiously (at). ● *noun* flirtatious glance.

**ogre** /'əʊgə/ *noun* (*feminine* **ogress** /-grɪs/) man-eating giant. □ **ogreish, ogrish** /'əʊgərɪʃ/ *adjective*.

**oh** /əʊ/ *interjection* (also **O**) *expressing surprise, pain, etc.*

**ohm** /əʊm/ *noun* SI unit of electrical resistance.

**OHMS** *abbreviation* On Her or His Majesty's Service.

**oho** /əʊ'həʊ/ *interjection expressing surprise or exultation.*

**OHP** *abbreviation* overhead projector.

**oil** ● *noun* viscous usually inflammable liquid insoluble in water; petroleum. ● *verb* apply oil to, lubricate; treat with oil. □ **oilcake** compressed linseed etc. as cattle food or manure; **oilfield** district yielding mineral oil; **oil paint** paint made by mixing pigment with oil; **oil painting** use of picture in oil paints; **oil rig** equipment for drilling an oil well; **oilskin** cloth waterproofed with oil, garment or (in *plural*) suit of it; **oil slick** patch of oil, esp. on sea; **oil well** well from which mineral oil is drawn.

**oily** *adjective* (-**ier**, -**iest**) of, like, covered or soaked with, oil; (of manner) fawning.

**ointment** /'ɔɪntmənt/ *noun* smooth greasy healing or cosmetic preparation for skin.

**OK** /əʊ'keɪ/ (also **okay**) *colloquial* ● *adjective & adverb* all right. ● *noun* (*plural* **OKs**) approval, sanction. ● *verb* (**OK's, OK'd, OK'ing**) approve, sanction.

**okapi** /əʊˈkɑːpɪ/ noun (plural same or **-s**) African partially striped ruminant mammal.

**okay** = OK.

**okra** /ˈəʊkrə/ noun tall originally African plant with edible seed pods.

**old** /əʊld/ adjective (**-er, -est**) advanced in age; not young or near its beginning; worn, dilapidated, or shabby from age; practised, inveterate; dating from far back; long established; former; colloquial used to indicate affection. □ **old age** later part of normal lifetime; **old-age pension** state retirement pension; **old-age pensioner** person receiving this; **Old Bill** slang the police; **old boy** former male pupil of school, colloquial elderly man; **old-fashioned** in or according to fashion no longer current, antiquated; **old girl** former female pupil of school, colloquial elderly woman; **Old Glory** US Stars and Stripes; **old guard** original, past, or conservative members of group; **old hand** experienced or practised person; **old hat** colloquial hackneyed; **old maid** derogatory elderly unmarried woman, prim and fussy person; **old man** colloquial one's father, husband, or employer etc.; **old man's beard** wild clematis; **old master** great painter of former times, painting by such painter; **Old Testament** part of Bible dealing with pre-Christian times; **old wives' tale** unscientific belief; **old woman** colloquial one's wife or mother, fussy or timid man; **Old World** Europe, Asia, and Africa. □ **oldish** adjective; **oldness** noun.

**olden** adjective archaic old, of old.

**oldie** noun colloquial old person or thing.

**oleaginous** /əʊlɪˈædʒɪnəs/ adjective like or producing oil; oily.

**oleander** /əʊlɪˈændə/ noun evergreen flowering Mediterranean shrub.

**olfactory** /ɒlˈfæktərɪ/ adjective of the sense of smell.

**oligarch** /ˈɒlɪɡɑːk/ noun member of oligarchy.

**oligarchy** /ˈɒlɪɡɑːkɪ/ noun (plural **-ies**) government by small group of people; members of such government; state so governed. □ **oligarchic(al)** /-ˈɡɑːk-/ adjective.

**olive** /ˈɒlɪv/ ● noun oval hard-stoned fruit yielding oil; tree bearing this; dull yellowish green. ● adjective olive-green; (of complexion) yellowish-brown. □ **olive branch** gesture of peace or reconciliation.

**Olympiad** /əˈlɪmpɪæd/ noun period of 4 years between Olympic Games; celebration of modern Olympic Games.

**Olympian** /əˈlɪmpɪən/ adjective of Olympus; magnificent, condescending; aloof.

**Olympic** /əˈlɪmpɪk/ ● adjective of the Olympic Games. ● plural noun (**the Olympics**) Olympic Games. □ **Olympic Games** ancient Greek athletic festival held every 4 years, or modern international revival of this.

**OM** abbreviation Order of Merit.

**ombudsman** /ˈɒmbʊdzmən/ noun official appointed to investigate complaints against public authorities.

**omega** /ˈəʊmɪɡə/ noun last letter of Greek alphabet (Ω, ω); last of series.

**omelette** /ˈɒmlɪt/ noun beaten eggs fried and often folded over filling.

**omen** /ˈəʊmən/ noun event supposedly warning of good or evil; prophetic significance.

**ominous** /ˈɒmɪnəs/ adjective threatening; inauspicious. □ **ominously** adverb.

**omit** /əˈmɪt/ verb (**-tt-**) leave out; not include; leave undone; (+ to do) neglect. □ **omission** /əʊˈmɪʃ(ə)n/ noun.

**omni-** combining form all.

**omnibus** /ˈɒmnɪbəs/ ● noun formal bus; volume containing several novels etc. previously published separately. ● adjective serving several purposes at once; comprising several items.

**omnipotent** /ɒmˈnɪpət(ə)nt/ adjective all-powerful. □ **omnipotence** noun.

**omnipresent** /ɒmnɪˈprez(ə)nt/ adjective present everywhere. □ **omnipresence** noun.

**omniscient** /ɒmˈnɪsɪənt/ adjective knowing everything. □ **omniscience** noun.

**omnivorous** /ɒmˈnɪvərəs/ adjective feeding on both plant and animal material; jocular reading everything that comes one's way. □ **omnivore** /ˈɒmnɪvɔː/ noun; **omnivorousness** noun.

**on** ● preposition (so as to be) supported by, covering, attached to, etc.; (of time) exactly at; during; close to, in direction of; at, near, concerning, about; added to. ● *adverb* (so as to be) on something; in some direction, forward; in advance; with movement; in operation or activity; *colloquial* willing to participate, approve, bet, etc.; *colloquial* practicable, acceptable; being shown or performed. ● *adjective Cricket* of, in, or into half of field behind batsman's back. ● *noun Cricket* the on side. □ **be on about** *colloquial* discuss, esp. tiresomely; **online** directly controlled by or connected to computer; **onscreen** when being filmed; **on to** to a position on.

■ **Usage** See note at ONTO.

**ONC** *abbreviation* Ordinary National Certificate.

**once** /wʌns/ ● *adverb* on one occasion only; at some time in past; ever or at all. ● *conjunction* as soon as. ● *noun* one time or occasion. □ **at once** immediately, simultaneously; **once-over** *colloquial* rapid inspection.

**oncology** /ɒŋ'kɒlədʒɪ/ *noun* study of tumours.

**oncoming** *adjective* approaching from the front.

**OND** *abbreviation* Ordinary National Diploma.

**one** /wʌn/ ● *adjective* single and integral in number; only such; without others; identical; forming a unity. ● *noun* lowest cardinal numeral; thing numbered with it; unit, unity; single thing, person, or example; *colloquial* drink. ● *pronoun* any person. □ **one-armed bandit** *colloquial* fruit machine with long handle; **one-horse** *colloquial* small, poorly equipped; **one-man** involving or operated by one person only; **one-off** made as the only one, not repeated; **one-sided** unfair, partial; **one-way** allowing movement etc. in one direction only.

**oneness** *noun* singleness; uniqueness; agreement, sameness.

**onerous** /'əʊnərəs/ *adjective* burdensome. □ **onerousness** *noun*.

**oneself** *pronoun* emphatic & reflexive form of ONE. □ **be oneself** act in one's natural manner.

**ongoing** *adjective* continuing, in progress.

**onion** /'ʌnjən/ *noun* vegetable with edible bulb of pungent smell and flavour.

**onlooker** *noun* spectator. □ **onlooking** *adjective*.

**only** /'əʊnlɪ/ ● *adverb* solely, merely, exclusively. ● *adjective* existing alone of its or their kind. ● *conjunction colloquial* except that; but then. □ **if only** even if for no other reason than, I wish that.

**o.n.o.** *abbreviation* or near offer.

**onomatopoeia** /ɒnəmætə'piːə/ *noun* formation of word from sound associated with thing named, e.g. *whizz*, *cuckoo*. □ **onomatopoeic** *adjective*.

**onset** *noun* attack; impetuous beginning.

**onslaught** /'ɒnslɔːt/ *noun* fierce attack.

**onto** *preposition* = ON TO.

■ **Usage** *Onto* is much used but is still not as widely accepted as *into*. It is, however, useful in distinguishing between, e.g., *We drove on to the beach* (i.e. towards it) and *we drove onto the beach* (i.e. into contact with it).

**ontology** /ɒn'tɒlədʒɪ/ *noun* branch of metaphysics concerned with the nature of being. □ **ontological** /-tə'lɒdʒ-/ *adjective*; **ontologically** /-tə'lɒdʒ-/ *adverb*; **ontologist** *noun*.

**onus** /'əʊnəs/ *noun* (*plural* **onuses**) burden, duty, responsibility.

**onward** /'ɒnwəd/ ● *adverb* (also **onwards**) advancing; into the future. ● *adjective* forward, advancing.

**onyx** /'ɒnɪks/ *noun* semiprecious variety of agate with coloured layers.

**oodles** /'uːd(ə)lz/ *plural noun colloquial* very great amount.

**ooh** /uː/ *interjection expressing surprised pleasure, pain, excitement, etc.*

**oolite** /'əʊəlaɪt/ *noun* granular limestone. □ **oolitic** /-'lɪt-/ *adjective*.

**oomph** /ʊmf/ *noun slang* energy, enthusiasm; attractiveness, esp. sex appeal.

**ooze**[1] ● *verb* (**-zing**) trickle or leak slowly out; (of substance) exude fluid; (often + *with*) give off (a feeling) freely. ● *noun* sluggish flow. □ **oozy** *adjective*.

**ooze**[2] *noun* wet mud. □ **oozy** *adjective*.

**op** *noun colloquial* operation.

**op.** *abbreviation* opus.

**opacity** /əʊ'pæsɪtɪ/ *noun* opaqueness.

**opal** /ˈəʊp(ə)l/ *noun* semiprecious milk-white or bluish stone with iridescent reflections.

**opalescent** /əʊpəˈles(ə)nt/ *adjective* iridescent. □ **opalescence** *noun*.

**opaline** /ˈəʊpəlaɪn/ *adjective* opal-like; opalescent.

**opaque** /əʊˈpeɪk/ *adjective* (**-r, -st**) not transmitting light; impenetrable to sight; unintelligible; stupid. □ **opaquely** *adverb*; **opaqueness** *noun*.

**op. cit.** *abbreviation* in the work already quoted (*opere citato*).

**OPEC** /ˈəʊpek/ *abbreviation* Organization of Petroleum Exporting Countries.

**open** /ˈəʊpən/ ● *adjective* not closed, locked, or blocked up; not covered or confined; exposed; (of goal etc.) undefended; undisguised, public; unfolded; spread out; (of fabric) with gaps; frank; open-minded; accessible to visitors or customers; (of meeting, competition, etc.) not restricted; (+ *to*) willing to receive, vulnerable to. ● *verb* make or become open or more open; (+ *into* etc.) give access; establish, set going; start; ceremonially declare open. ● *noun* (**the open**) open air; open competition etc. □ **open air** *noun* outdoors; **open-air** *adjective* outdoor; **open day** day when public may visit place normally closed to them; **open-ended** with no limit or restriction; **open-handed** generous; **open-heart surgery** surgery with heart exposed and blood made to bypass it; **open house** hospitality for all visitors; **open letter** one addressed to individual and printed in newspaper etc.; **open-minded** accessible to new ideas, unprejudiced; **open-plan** (of house, office, etc.) having large undivided rooms; **open prison** one with few physical restraints on prisoners; **open question** matter on which different views are legitimate; **open sandwich** one without bread on top; **open sea** expanse of sea away from land. □ **openness** *noun*.

**opener** *noun* device for opening tins or bottles etc.

**opening** ● *noun* gap, aperture; opportunity; beginning, initial part. ● *adjective* initial, first.

**openly** *adverb* publicly, frankly.

**opera**[1] /ˈɒpərə/ *noun* musical drama with sung or spoken dialogue. □ **opera-glasses** small binoculars for use in theatres etc.; **opera house** theatre for operas.

**opera**[2] *plural of* OPUS.

**operable** /ˈɒpərəb(ə)l/ *adjective* that can be operated; suitable for treatment by surgical operation.

**operate** /ˈɒpəreɪt/ *verb* (**-ting**) work, control (machine etc.); be in action; perform surgical operation(s); direct military etc. action. □ **operating theatre** room for surgical operations.

**operatic** /ɒpəˈrætɪk/ *adjective* of or like opera.

**operation** *noun* action, working; performance of surgery on a patient; military manoeuvre; financial transaction. □ **operational** *adjective*; **operationally** *adverb*.

**operative** /ˈɒpərətɪv/ ● *adjective* in operation; having principal relevance; of or by surgery. ● *noun* worker, artisan.

**operator** *noun* person operating machine, esp. connecting lines in telephone exchange; person engaging in business.

**operetta** /ɒpəˈretə/ *noun* light opera.

**ophidian** /əʊˈfɪdɪən/ ● *noun* member of suborder of reptiles including snakes. ● *adjective* of this order.

**ophthalmia** /ɒfˈθælmɪə/ *noun* inflammation of eye.

**ophthalmic** /ɒfˈθælmɪk/ *adjective* of or relating to the eye and its diseases. □ **ophthalmic optician** one qualified to prescribe as well as dispense spectacles.

**ophthalmology** /ɒfθælˈmɒlədʒɪ/ *noun* study of the eye. □ **ophthalmologist** *noun*.

**ophthalmoscope** /ɒfˈθælməskəʊp/ *noun* instrument for examining the eye.

**opiate** /ˈəʊpɪət/ ● *adjective* containing opium; soporific. ● *noun* drug containing opium, usually to ease pain or induce sleep; soothing influence.

**opine** /əʊˈpaɪn/ *verb* (**-ning**) (often + *that*) express or hold as opinion.

**opinion** /əˈpɪnjən/ *noun* unproven belief; view held as probable; professional advice; estimation. □ **opinion poll** assessment of public opinion by questioning representative sample.

**opinionated** /əˈpɪnjəneɪtɪd/ *adjective* unduly confident in one's opinions.

**opium** /ˈəʊpɪəm/ *noun* drug made from juice of certain poppy, used as narcotic or sedative.

**opossum** /əˈpɒsəm/ *noun* tree-living American marsupial; *Australian & NZ* marsupial resembling this.

**opponent** /əˈpəʊnənt/ *noun* person who opposes.

**opportune** /ˈɒpətjuːn/ *adjective* well-chosen, specially favourable; (of action, event, etc.) well-timed.

**opportunism** /ɒpəˈtjuːnɪz(ə)m/ *noun* adaptation of policy to circumstances, esp. regardless of principle. □ **opportunist** *noun*; **opportunistic** /-ˈnɪs-/ *adjective*; **opportunistically** /-ˈnɪs-/ *adverb*.

**opportunity** /ɒpəˈtjuːnɪtɪ/ *noun* (*plural* -**ies**) favourable chance or opening offered by circumstances.

**oppose** /əˈpəʊz/ *verb* (-**sing**) set oneself against; resist; argue against; (+ *to*) place in opposition or contrast. □ **as opposed to** in contrast with. □ **opposer** *noun*.

**opposite** /ˈɒpəzɪt/ ● *adjective* facing, on other side; (often + *to, from*) contrary; diametrically different. ● *noun* opposite thing, person, or term. ● *adverb* in opposite position. ● *preposition* opposite to. □ **opposite number** person in corresponding position in another group etc.; **the opposite sex** either sex in relation to the other.

**opposition** /ɒpəˈzɪʃ(ə)n/ *noun* antagonism, resistance; being in conflict or disagreement; contrast; group or party of opponents; chief parliamentary party, or group of parties, opposed to party in office; act of placing opposite.

**oppress** /əˈpres/ *verb* govern tyrannically; treat with gross harshness or injustice; weigh down. □ **oppression** *noun*; **oppressor** *noun*.

**oppressive** *adjective* that oppresses; (of weather) sultry, close. □ **oppressively** *adverb*; **oppressiveness** *noun*.

**opprobrious** /əˈprəʊbrɪəs/ *adjective* (of language) severely scornful; abusive.

**opprobrium** /əˈprəʊbrɪəm/ *noun* disgrace; cause of this.

**opt** *verb* (usually + *for*) make choice; decide. □ **opt out** (**of**) choose not to take part etc. (in).

**optic** /ˈɒptɪk/ *adjective* of eye or sight.

**optical** *adjective* visual; of or according to optics; aiding sight. □ **optical fibre** thin glass fibre used to carry light signals; **optical illusion** image which deceives the eye, mental misapprehension caused by this.

**optician** /ɒpˈtɪʃ(ə)n/ *noun* maker, seller, or prescriber of spectacles, contact lenses, etc.

**optics** *plural noun* (treated as *singular*) science of light and vision.

**optimal** /ˈɒptɪm(ə)l/ *adjective* best, most favourable.

**optimism** /ˈɒptɪmɪz(ə)m/ *noun* inclination to hopefulness and confidence. □ **optimist** *noun*; **optimistic** /-ˈmɪs-/ *adjective*; **optimistically** /-ˈmɪs-/ *adverb*.

**optimize** /ˈɒptɪmaɪz/ *verb* (also -**ise**) (-**zing** or -**sing**) make best or most effective use of. □ **optimization** *noun*.

**optimum** /ˈɒptɪməm/ ● *noun* (*plural* -**ma**) most favourable conditions; best practical solution. ● *adjective* optimal.

**option** /ˈɒpʃ(ə)n/ *noun* choice, choosing; right to choose; right to buy, sell, etc., on specified conditions at specified time. □ **keep, leave one's options open** not commit oneself.

**optional** *adjective* not obligatory. □ **optionally** *adverb*.

**opulent** /ˈɒpjʊlənt/ *adjective* wealthy; luxurious; abundant. □ **opulence** *noun*.

**opus** /ˈəʊpəs/ *noun* (*plural* **opuses** or **opera** /ˈɒpərə/) musical composition numbered as one of composer's works; any artistic work.

**or** *conjunction* introducing *alternatives*. □ **or else** otherwise, *colloquial* expressing *threat*.

**oracle** /ˈɒrək(ə)l/ *noun* place at which ancient Greeks etc. consulted gods for advice or prophecy; response received there; person or thing regarded as source of wisdom etc. □ **oracular** /ɒˈrækjʊlə/ *adjective*.

**oral** /ˈɔːr(ə)l/ ● *adjective* spoken, verbal; by word of mouth; done or taken by mouth. ● *noun colloquial* spoken exam. □ **orally** *adverb*.

**orange** /ˈɒrɪndʒ/ ●noun roundish reddish-yellow citrus fruit; its colour; tree bearing it. ●adjective orange-coloured.

**orangeade** /ɒrɪndʒˈeɪd/ noun drink made from or flavoured like oranges, usually fizzy.

**orang-utan** /ɔːræŋuːˈtæn/ noun (also **orang-outang** /-uːˈtæŋ/) large anthropoid ape.

**oration** /ɔːˈreɪʃ(ə)n/ noun formal or ceremonial speech.

**orator** /ˈɒrətə/ noun maker of a formal speech; eloquent public speaker.

**oratorio** /ɒrəˈtɔːrɪəʊ/ noun (plural -s) semi-dramatic musical composition usually on sacred theme.

**oratory** /ˈɒrətərɪ/ noun (plural -ies) art of or skill in public speaking; small private chapel. □ **oratorical** /-ˈtɒr-/ adjective.

**orb** noun globe surmounted by cross as part of coronation regalia; sphere, globe; poetical celestial body; poetical eye.

**orbicular** /ɔːˈbɪkjʊlə/ adjective formal spherical, circular.

**orbit** /ˈɔːbɪt/ ●noun curved course of planet, comet, satellite, etc.; one complete passage round another body; range or sphere of action. ●verb (-t-) go round in orbit; put into orbit. □ **orbiter** noun.

**orbital** adjective of orbits; (of road) passing round outside of city.

**Orcadian** /ɔːˈkeɪdɪən/ ●adjective of Orkney. ●noun native of Orkney.

**orchard** /ˈɔːtʃəd/ noun enclosed piece of land with fruit trees.

**orchestra** /ˈɔːkɪstrə/ noun large group of instrumental performers. □ **orchestra pit** part of theatre where orchestra plays. □ **orchestral** /ɔːˈkestr(ə)l/ adjective.

**orchestrate** /ˈɔːkɪstreɪt/ verb (-ting) compose or arrange for orchestral performance; arrange (elements) for desired effect.

**orchid** /ˈɔːkɪd/ noun any of various plants, often with brilliantly coloured or grotesquely shaped flowers.

**ordain** /ɔːˈdeɪn/ verb confer holy orders on; decree, order.

**ordeal** /ɔːˈdiːl/ noun severe trial; painful or horrific experience.

**order** /ˈɔːdə/ ●noun condition in which every part, unit, etc. is in its right place; tidiness; specified sequence; authoritative direction or instruction; state of obedience to law, authority, etc.; direction to supply something, thing(s) (to be) supplied; social class or rank; kind, sort; constitution or nature of the world, society, etc.; Biology grouping of animals or plants below class and above family; religious fraternity; grade of Christian ministry; any of 5 classical styles of architecture; company of people distinguished by particular honour, etc., insignia worn by its members; stated form of divine service; system of rules etc. (at meetings etc.). ●verb command, prescribe; command or direct (person) to specified destination; direct manufacturer, tradesman, etc. to supply; direct waiter to serve; (often as **ordered** adjective) put in order; (of God, fate, etc.) ordain. □ **in** or **out of order** in correct or incorrect sequence; **of** or **in the order of** approximately.

**orderly** ●adjective methodically arranged; tidy; not unruly. ●noun (plural -ies) soldier in attendance on officer; hospital attendant. □ **orderly room** room in barracks for company's business.

**ordinal** /ˈɔːdɪn(ə)l/ noun (in full **ordinal number**) number defining position in a series; compare CARDINAL NUMBER.

**ordinance** /ˈɔːdɪnəns/ noun decree; religious rite.

**ordinand** /ˈɔːdɪnænd/ noun candidate for ordination.

**ordinary** /ˈɔːdɪnərɪ/ adjective normal; not exceptional; commonplace. □ **ordinary level** historical lowest in GCE exam; **ordinary seaman** sailor of lowest rank. □ **ordinarily** adverb; **ordinariness** noun.

**ordination** /ɔːdɪˈneɪʃ(ə)n/ noun conferring of holy orders; ordaining.

**ordnance** /ˈɔːdnəns/ noun artillery and military supplies; government service dealing with these. □ **Ordnance Survey** government survey of UK producing detailed maps.

**ordure** /ˈɔːdjʊə/ noun dung.

**ore** noun naturally occurring mineral yielding metal or other valuable minerals.

**oregano** /ɒrɪ'gɑːnəʊ/ noun dried wild marjoram as seasoning.

**organ** /'ɔːgən/ noun musical instrument consisting of pipes that sound when air is forced through them, operated by keys and pedals; similar instrument producing sound electronically; part of body serving some special function; medium of opinion, esp. newspaper. □ **organ-grinder** player of barrel organ.

**organdie** /'ɔːgəndɪ/ noun fine translucent muslin, usually stiffened.

**organic** /ɔː'gænɪk/ adjective of or affecting bodily organ(s); (of animals and plants) having organs or organized physical structure; (of food) produced without artificial fertilizers or pesticides; (of chemical compound etc.) containing carbon; organized; inherent, structural. □ **organic chemistry** that of carbon compounds. □ **organically** adverb.

**organism** /'ɔːgənɪz(ə)m/ noun individual animal or plant; living being with interdependent parts; system made up of interdependent parts.

**organist** noun player of organ.

**organization** /ɔːgənaɪ'zeɪʃ(ə)n/ noun (also **-isation**) organized body, system, or society; organizing, being organized.

**organize** /'ɔːgənaɪz/ verb (also **-ise**) (**-zing** or **-sing**) give orderly structure to; make arrangements for (person, oneself); initiate, arrange for; (as **organized** adjective) make organic or into living tissue. □ **organizer** noun.

**orgasm** /'ɔːgæz(ə)m/ ● noun climax of sexual excitement. ● verb have sexual orgasm. □ **orgasmic** /-'gæz-/ adjective.

**orgy** /'ɔːdʒɪ/ noun (plural **-ies**) wild party with indiscriminate sexual activity; excessive indulgence in an activity. □ **orgiastic** /-'æs-/ adjective.

**oriel** /'ɔːrɪəl/ noun window projecting from wall at upper level.

**orient** /'ɔːrɪənt/ ● noun (**the Orient**) the East, countries east of Mediterranean, esp. E. Asia. ● verb place or determine position of with aid of compass; find bearings of; (often + towards) direct; place (building etc.) to face east; turn eastward or in specified direction.

**oriental** /ɔːrɪ'ent(ə)l/ (often **Oriental**) ● adjective of the East, esp. E. Asia; of the Orient. ● noun native of Orient.

**orientate** /'ɔːrɪənteɪt/ verb (**-ting**) orient.

**orientation** noun orienting, being oriented; relative position; person's adjustment in relation to circumstances; briefing.

**orienteering** /ɔːrɪən'tɪərɪŋ/ noun competitive sport of running across rough country with map and compass.

**orifice** /'ɒrɪfɪs/ noun aperture; mouth of cavity.

**origami** /ɒrɪ'gɑːmɪ/ noun Japanese art of folding paper into decorative shapes.

**origan** /'ɒrɪgən/ noun (also **origanum** /ə'rɪgənəm/) wild marjoram.

**origin** /'ɒrɪdʒɪn/ noun source; starting point; (often in plural) parentage.

**original** /ə'rɪdʒɪn(ə)l/ ● adjective existing from the beginning; earliest; innate; not imitative or derived; creative not copied; by artist etc. himself or herself. ● noun original pattern, picture, etc. from which another is copied or translated. □ **original sin** innate sinfulness held to be common to all human beings after the Fall. □ **originality** /-'næl-/ noun; **originally** adverb.

**originate** /ə'rɪdʒɪneɪt/ verb (**-ting**) begin; initiate or give origin to, be origin of. □ **origination** noun; **originator** noun.

**oriole** /'ɔːrɪəʊl/ noun kind of bird, esp. **golden oriole** with black and yellow plumage in male.

**ormolu** /'ɔːməluː/ noun gilded bronze; gold-coloured alloy; articles made of or decorated with these.

**ornament** ● noun /'ɔːnəmənt/ thing used to adorn or decorate; decoration; quality or person bringing honour or distinction. ● verb /-ment/ adorn, beautify. □ **ornamental** /-'men-/ adjective; **ornamentation** /-men-/ noun.

**ornate** /ɔː'neɪt/ adjective elaborately adorned; (of literary style) flowery. □ **ornately** adverb.

**ornithology** /ɔːnɪ'θɒlədʒɪ/ noun study of birds. □ **ornithological** /-θə'lɒdʒ-/ adjective; **ornithologist** noun.

**orotund** /'ɒrətʌnd/ adjective (of voice) full, round; imposing; (of writing, style, etc.) pompous; pretentious.

**orphan** /'ɔːf(ə)n/ ● *noun* child whose parents are dead. ● *verb* bereave of parents.

**orphanage** *noun* home for orphans.

**orrery** /'ɒrərɪ/ *noun* (*plural* **-ies**) clockwork model of solar system.

**orris root** /'ɒrɪs/ *noun* fragrant iris root used in perfumery.

**ortho-** *combining form* straight, correct.

**orthodontics** /ɔːθə'dɒntɪks/ *plural noun* (usually treated as *singular*) correction of irregularities in teeth and jaws.

**orthodox** /'ɔːθədɒks/ *adjective* holding usual or accepted views, esp. on religion, morals, etc.; conventional. □ **Orthodox Church** Eastern Church headed by Patriarch of Constantinople, including Churches of Russia, Romania, Greece, etc. □ **orthodoxy** *noun*.

**orthography** /ɔː'θɒgrəfɪ/ *noun* (*plural* **-ies**) spelling, esp. with reference to its correctness. □ **orthographic** /-'græf-/ *adjective*.

**orthopaedics** /ɔːθə'piːdɪks/ *plural noun* (treated as *singular*) (*US* **-pedics**) branch of medicine dealing with correction of diseased or injured bones or muscles. □ **orthopaedic** *adjective*; **orthopaedist** *noun*.

**OS** *abbreviation* old style; Ordinary Seaman; Ordnance Survey; outsize.

**Oscar** /'ɒskə/ *noun* statuette awarded annually in US for excellence in film acting, directing, etc.

**oscillate** /'ɒsɪleɪt/ *verb* (**-ting**) (cause to) swing to and fro; vacillate; *Electricity* (of current) undergo high-frequency alternations. □ **oscillation** *noun*; **oscillator** *noun*.

**oscilloscope** /ə'sɪləskəʊp/ *noun* device for viewing oscillations usually on screen of cathode ray tube.

**osier** /'əʊzɪə/ *noun* willow used in basketwork; shoot of this.

**osmosis** /ɒz'məʊsɪs/ *noun* passage of solvent through semipermeable partition into another solution; process by which something is acquired by absorption. □ **osmotic** /-'mɒt-/ *adjective*.

**osprey** /'ɒspreɪ/ *noun* (*plural* **-s**) large bird preying on fish.

**osseous** /'ɒsɪəs/ *adjective* of bone; bony; having bones.

**ossify** /'ɒsɪfaɪ/ *verb* (**-ies**, **-ied**) turn into bone; harden; make or become rigid or unprogressive. □ **ossification** *noun*.

**ostensible** /ɒ'stensɪb(ə)l/ *adjective* professed; used to conceal real purpose or nature. □ **ostensibly** *adverb*.

**ostentation** /ɒsten'teɪʃ(ə)n/ *noun* pretentious display of wealth; showing off. □ **ostentatious** *adjective*.

**osteoarthritis** /ɒstɪəʊɑː'θraɪtɪs/ *noun* degenerative disease of the joints. □ **osteoarthritic** /-'θrɪt-/ *adjective*.

**osteopath** /'ɒstɪəpæθ/ *noun* person who treats disease by manipulation of bones. □ **osteopathy** /-'ɒp-/ *noun*.

**osteoporosis** /ɒstɪəʊpə'rəʊsɪs/ *noun* brittle bones caused by hormonal change or deficiency of calcium or vitamin D.

**ostler** /'ɒslə/ *noun historical* stableman at inn.

**ostracize** /'ɒstrəsaɪz/ *verb* (also **-ise**) (**-zing** or **-sing**) exclude from society, refuse to associate with. □ **ostracism** /-sɪz(ə)m/ *noun*.

**ostrich** /'ɒstrɪtʃ/ *noun* large flightless swift-running African bird; person refusing to acknowledge awkward truth.

**OT** *abbreviation* Old Testament.

**other** /'ʌðə/ ● *adjective* further, additional; different; (**the other**) the only remaining. ● *noun* other person or thing. □ **the other day**, **week**, etc. a few days etc. ago; **other half** *colloquial* one's wife or husband; **other than** apart from.

**otherwise** /'ʌðəwaɪz/ ● *adverb* or else; in different circumstances; in other respects; in a different way; as an alternative. ● *adjective* different.

**otiose** /'əʊtɪəʊs/ *adjective* not required, serving no practical purpose.

**OTT** *abbreviation colloquial* over-the-top.

**otter** /'ɒtə/ *noun* furred aquatic fish-eating mammal.

**Ottoman** /'ɒtəmən/ ● *adjective historical* of Turkish Empire. ● *noun* (*plural* **-s**) Turk of Ottoman period; (**ottoman**) cushioned seat without back or arms, storage-box with padded top.

**OU** *abbreviation* Open University; Oxford University.

**oubliette** /uːblɪ'et/ *noun* secret dungeon with trapdoor entrance.

**ouch** /aʊtʃ/ *interjection expressing sharp or sudden pain*.

**ought** /ɔːt/ *auxiliary verb expressing duty, rightness, probability, etc.*

**oughtn't** /ˈɔːt(ə)nt/ ought not.

**Ouija** /ˈwiːdʒə/ *noun* (in full **Ouija board**) *proprietary term* board marked with letters or signs used with movable pointer to try to obtain messages in seances.

**ounce** /aʊns/ *noun* unit of weight (1/16 lb, 28.35 g); very small quantity.

**our** /aʊə/ *adjective* of or belonging to us.

**ours** /aʊəz/ *pronoun* the one(s) belonging to us.

**ourselves** /aʊəˈselvz/ *pronoun: emphatic form of* WE *or* US; *reflexive form of* US.

**ousel** = OUZEL.

**oust** /aʊst/ *verb* drive out of office or power, esp. by seizing place of.

**out** /aʊt/ ● *adverb* away from or not in place, not at home, office, etc.; into open, not sight, notice, etc.; to or at an end; not burning; in error; *colloquial* unconscious; (+ *to do*) determined; (of limb etc.) dislocated. ● *preposition* out of. ● *noun* way of escape. □ **out for** intent on, determined to get; **out of** from inside, not inside, from among, lacking, having no more of, because of. ● *verb* emerge.

■ **Usage** The use of *out* as a preposition, as in *He walked out the room*, is not standard English. *Out of* should be used instead.

**out-** *prefix* so as to surpass; external; out of.

**outback** *noun Australian* remote inland areas.

**outbalance** /aʊtˈbæləns/ *verb* (**-cing**) outweigh.

**outbid** /aʊtˈbɪd/ *verb* (**-dd-**; *past & past participle* **-bid**) bid higher than.

**outboard motor** *noun* portable engine attached to outside of boat.

**outbreak** /ˈaʊtbreɪk/ *noun* sudden eruption of emotion, war, disease, fire, etc.

**outbuilding** *noun* shed, barn, etc. detached from main building.

**outburst** *noun* bursting out, esp. of emotion in vehement words.

**outcast** ● *noun* person cast out from home and friends. ● *adjective* homeless; rejected.

**outclass** /aʊtˈklɑːs/ *verb* surpass in quality.

**outcome** *noun* result.

**outcrop** *noun* rock etc. emerging at surface; noticeable manifestation.

**outcry** *noun* (*plural* **-ies**) loud public protest.

**outdated** /aʊtˈdeɪtɪd/ *adjective* out of date, obsolete.

**outdistance** /aʊtˈdɪst(ə)ns/ *verb* (**-cing**) leave (competitor) behind completely.

**outdo** /aʊtˈduː/ *verb* (**-doing**; *3rd singular present* **-does**; *past* **-did**; *past participle* **-done**) surpass, excel.

**outdoor** *adjective* done, existing, or used out of doors; fond of the open air.

**outdoors** /aʊtˈdɔːz/ ● *adverb* in(to) the open air. ● *noun* the open air.

**outer** *adjective* outside, external; farther from centre or inside. □ **outer space** universe beyond earth's atmosphere. □ **outermost** *adjective*.

**outface** /aʊtˈfeɪs/ *verb* (**-cing**) disconcert by staring or by confident manner.

**outfall** *noun* outlet of river, drain, etc.

**outfield** *noun* outer part of cricket or baseball pitch. □ **outfielder** *noun*.

**outfit** *noun* set of equipment or clothes; *colloquial* (organized) group or company.

**outfitter** *noun* supplier of clothing.

**outflank** /aʊtˈflæŋk/ *verb* get round the flank of (enemy); outmanoeuvre.

**outflow** *noun* outward flow; what flows out.

**outgoing** ● *adjective* friendly; retiring from office; going out. ● *noun* (in *plural*) expenditure.

**outgrow** /aʊtˈɡrəʊ/ *verb* (*past* **-grew**; *past participle* **-grown**) get too big for (clothes etc.); leave behind (childish habit etc.); grow faster or taller than.

**outgrowth** *noun* offshoot.

**outhouse** *noun* shed etc., esp. adjoining main house.

**outing** *noun* pleasure trip.

**outlandish** /aʊtˈlændɪʃ/ *adjective* bizarre, strange. □ **outlandishly** *adverb*; **outlandishness** *noun*.

**outlast** /aʊtˈlɑːst/ *verb* last longer than.

**outlaw** ● *noun* fugitive from law; *historical* person deprived of protection of law. ● *verb* declare (person) an outlaw; make illegal; proscribe.

**outlay** *noun* expenditure.

**outlet** noun means of exit; means of expressing feelings; market for goods.

**outline** ● noun rough draft; summary; line(s) enclosing visible object; contour; external boundary; (in plural) main features. ● verb (**-ning**) draw or describe in outline; mark outline of.

**outlive** /aʊtˈlɪv/ verb (**-ving**) live longer than, beyond, or through.

**outlook** noun view, prospect; mental attitude.

**outlying** adjective far from centre; remote.

**outmanoeuvre** /aʊtməˈnuːvə/ verb (**-ring**) (US **-maneuver**) outdo by skilful manoeuvring.

**outmatch** /aʊtˈmætʃ/ verb be more than a match for.

**outmoded** /aʊtˈməʊdɪd/ adjective outdated; out of fashion.

**outnumber** /aʊtˈnʌmbə/ verb exceed in number.

**outpace** /aʊtˈpeɪs/ verb (**-cing**) go faster than; outdo in contest.

**outpatient** noun non-resident hospital patient.

**outplacement** noun help in finding new job after redundancy.

**outpost** noun detachment on guard at some distance from army; outlying settlement etc.

**outpouring** noun (usually in plural) copious expression of emotion.

**output** ● noun amount produced (by machine, worker, etc.); electrical power etc. supplied by apparatus; printout, results, etc. from computer; place where energy, information, etc., leaves a system. ● verb (**-tt-**; past & past participle **-put** or **-putted**) (of computer) supply (results etc.).

**outrage** ● noun forcible violation of others' rights, sentiments, etc.; gross offence or indignity; fierce resentment. ● verb (**-ging**) subject to outrage; insult; shock and anger.

**outrageous** /aʊtˈreɪdʒəs/ adjective immoderate; shocking; immoral, offensive. □ **outrageously** adverb.

**outrank** /aʊtˈræŋk/ verb be superior in rank to.

**outré** /ˈuːtreɪ/ adjective eccentric, violating decorum. [French]

**outrider** noun motorcyclist or mounted guard riding ahead of car(s) etc.

**outrigger** noun spar or framework projecting from or over side of ship, canoe, etc. to give stability; boat with this.

**outright** ● adverb altogether, entirely; not gradually; without reservation. ● adjective downright, complete; undisputed.

**outrun** /aʊtˈrʌn/ verb (**-nn-**; past **-ran**; past participle **-run**) run faster or farther than; go beyond.

**outsell** /aʊtˈsel/ verb (past & past participle **-sold**) sell more than; be sold in greater quantities than.

**outset** noun □ **at, from the outset** at or from the beginning.

**outshine** /aʊtˈʃaɪn/ verb (**-ning**; past & past participle **-shone**) be more brilliant than.

**outside** ● noun /aʊtˈsaɪd, ˈaʊtsaɪd/ external surface, outer part(s); external appearance; position on outer side. ● adjective /ˈaʊtsaɪd/ of, on, or nearer outside; not belonging to particular circle or institution; (of chance etc.) remote; greatest existent or possible. ● adverb /aʊtˈsaɪd/ on or to outside; out of doors; not within or enclosed. ● preposition /aʊtˈsaɪd/ not in; to or at the outside of; external to; beyond limits of. □ **at the outside** (of estimate etc.) at the most; **outside interest** hobby etc. unconnected with one's work.

**outsider** /aʊtˈsaɪdə/ noun non-member of circle, party, profession, etc.; competitor thought to have little chance.

**outsize** adjective unusually large.

**outskirts** plural noun outer area of town etc.

**outsmart** /aʊtˈsmɑːt/ verb outwit; be too clever for.

**outspoken** /aʊtˈspəʊkən/ adjective saying openly what one thinks; frank. □ **outspokenly** adverb; **outspokenness** noun.

**outspread** /aʊtˈspred/ adjective spread out.

**outstanding** /aʊtˈstændɪŋ/ adjective conspicuous, esp. from excellence; still to be dealt with; (of debt) not yet settled. □ **outstandingly** adverb.

**outstation** noun remote branch or outpost.

**outstay** /aʊt'steɪ/ verb stay longer than (one's welcome etc.).

**outstretched** /aʊt'stretʃt/ adjective stretched out.

**outstrip** /aʊt'strɪp/ verb (**-pp-**) go faster than; surpass in progress, competition, etc.

**out-take** noun film or tape sequence cut out in editing.

**out-tray** noun tray for outgoing documents.

**outvote** /aʊt'vəʊt/ verb (**-ting**) defeat by majority of votes.

**outward** /'aʊtwəd/ ● adjective directed towards outside; going out; physical; external, apparent. ● adverb (also **outwards**) in outward direction, towards outside. □ **outwardly** adverb.

**outweigh** /aʊt'weɪ/ verb exceed in weight, value, influence, etc.

**outwit** /aʊt'wɪt/ verb (**-tt-**) be too clever for; overcome by greater ingenuity.

**outwith** /aʊt'wɪθ/ preposition Scottish outside.

**outwork** noun advanced or detached part of fortress etc.; work done off premises of shop, factory, etc. supplying it.

**outworn** /aʊt'wɔːn/ adjective worn out; obsolete.

**ouzel** /'uːz(ə)l/ noun (also **ousel**) small bird of thrush family.

**ouzo** /'uːzəʊ/ noun (plural **-s**) Greek aniseed-flavoured alcoholic spirit.

**ova** plural of OVUM.

**oval** /'əʊv(ə)l/ ● adjective shaped like egg, elliptical. ● noun elliptical closed curve; thing with oval outline.

**ovary** /'əʊvərɪ/ noun (plural **-ies**) either of two ovum-producing organs in female; seed vessel in plant. □ **ovarian** /əʊ'veər-/ adjective.

**ovation** /əʊ'veɪʃ(ə)n/ noun enthusiastic applause or reception.

**oven** /'ʌv(ə)n/ noun enclosed chamber for cooking food in. □ **ovenproof** heat-resistant; **oven-ready** (of food) prepared before sale for immediate cooking; **ovenware** dishes for cooking food in oven.

**over** /'əʊvə/ ● adverb outward and downward from brink or from erect position; so as to cover whole surface; so as to produce fold or reverse position; above in place or position; from one side, end, etc. to other; from beginning to end with repetition; in excess; settled, finished. ● preposition above; out and down from; so as to cover; across; on or to other side, end, etc. of; concerning. ● noun Cricket sequence of 6 balls bowled from one end before change is made to other; play during this time. □ **over the way** (in street etc.) facing or across from.

**over-** prefix excessively; upper, outer; over; completely.

**overact** /əʊvə'rækt/ verb act (a role) with exaggeration.

**over-active** /əʊvə'ræktɪv/ adjective too active.

**overall** ● adjective /'əʊvərɔːl/ taking everything into account, inclusive, total. ● adverb /əʊvər'ɔːl/ including everything; on the whole. ● noun /'əʊvərɔːl/ protective outer garment; (in plural) protective trousers or suit.

**overarm** adjective & adverb with arm raised above shoulder.

**overawe** /əʊvə'rɔː/ verb (**-wing**) awe into submission.

**overbalance** /əʊvə'bæləns/ verb (**-cing**) lose balance and fall; cause to do this.

**overbearing** /əʊvə'beərɪŋ/ adjective domineering; oppressive.

**overblown** /əʊvə'bləʊn/ adjective inflated, pretentious; (of flower etc.) past its prime.

**overboard** adverb from ship into water. □ **go overboard** colloquial show extreme enthusiasm, behave immoderately.

**overbook** /əʊvə'bʊk/ verb make too many bookings for (aircraft, hotel, etc.).

**overcame** past of OVERCOME.

**overcast** adjective (of sky) covered with cloud; (in sewing) edged with stitching.

**overcharge** /əʊvə'tʃɑːdʒ/ verb (**-ging**) charge too high a price to; put too much charge into (battery, gun, etc.).

**overcoat** noun warm outdoor coat.

**overcome** /əʊvə'kʌm/ verb (**-coming**; past **-came**; past participle **-come**) prevail over, master; be victorious; (usually as **overcome** adjective) make faint; (often + with) make weak or helpless.

**overcrowd** /əʊvəˈkraʊd/ *verb* (usually as **overcrowded** *adjective*) cause too many people or things to be in (a place). □ **overcrowding** *noun.*

**overdevelop** /əʊvədɪˈveləp/ *verb* (**-p-**) develop too much.

**overdo** /əʊvəˈduː/ *verb* (**-doing**; *3rd singular present* **-does**; *past* **-did**; *past participle* **-done**) carry to excess; (as **overdone** *adjective*) overcooked. □ **overdo it, things** *colloquial* exhaust oneself.

**overdose** ● *noun* excessive dose of drug etc. ● *verb* (**-sing**) take overdose.

**overdraft** *noun* overdrawing of bank account; amount by which account is overdrawn.

**overdraw** /əʊvəˈdrɔː/ *verb* (*past* **-drew**; *past participle* **-drawn**) draw more from (bank account) than amount in credit; (as **overdrawn** *adjective*) having overdrawn one's account.

**overdress** /əʊvəˈdres/ *verb* dress ostentatiously or with too much formality.

**overdrive** *noun* mechanism in vehicle providing gear above top gear for economy at high speeds; state of high activity.

**overdue** /əʊvəˈdjuː/ *adjective* past the time when due or ready; late, in arrears.

**overestimate** ● *verb* /əʊvərˈestɪmeɪt/ (**-ting**) form too high an estimate of. ● *noun* /əʊvərˈestɪmət/ too high an estimate. □ **overestimation** *noun.*

**overexpose** /əʊvərɪkˈspəʊz/ *verb* (**-sing**) expose too much to public; expose (film) for too long.

**overfish** /əʊvəˈfɪʃ/ *verb* deplete (stream etc.) by too much fishing.

**overflow** ● *verb* /əʊvəˈfləʊ/ flow over; be so full that contents overflow; (of crowd etc.) extend beyond limits or capacity of; flood; (of kindness, harvest, etc.) be very abundant. ● *noun* /ˈəʊvəfləʊ/ what overflows or is superfluous; outlet for excess liquid.

**overgrown** /əʊvəˈɡrəʊn/ *adjective* grown too big; covered with weeds etc. □ **overgrowth** *noun.*

**overhang** ● *verb* /əʊvəˈhæŋ/ (*past & past participle* **-hung**) project or hang over. ● *noun* /ˈəʊvəhæŋ/ fact or amount of overhanging.

**overhaul** *verb* /əʊvəˈhɔːl/ check over thoroughly and make repairs to if necessary; overtake. ● *noun* /ˈəʊvəhɔːl/ thorough examination, with repairs if necessary.

**overhead** ● *adverb* /əʊvəˈhed/ above one's head; in sky. ● *adjective* /ˈəʊvəhed/ placed overhead. ● *noun* /ˈəʊvəhed/ (in *plural*) routine administrative and maintenance expenses of a business. □ **overhead projector** projector for producing enlarged image of transparency above and behind user.

**overhear** /əʊvəˈhɪə/ *verb* (*past & past participle* **-heard**) hear as hidden or unintentional listener.

**overindulge** /əʊvərɪnˈdʌldʒ/ *noun* (**-ging**) indulge to excess.

**overjoyed** /əʊvəˈdʒɔɪd/ *adjective* filled with great joy.

**overkill** *noun* excess of capacity to kill or destroy; excess.

**overland** *adjective & adverb* by land and not sea.

**overlap** ● *verb* /əʊvəˈlæp/ (**-pp-**) partly cover; cover and extend beyond; partly coincide. ● *noun* /ˈəʊvəlæp/ overlapping; overlapping part or amount.

**overlay** ● *verb* /əʊvəˈleɪ/ (*past & past participle* **-laid**) lay over; (+ *with*) cover (thing) with (coating etc.). ● *noun* /ˈəʊvəleɪ/ thing laid over another.

**overleaf** /əʊvəˈliːf/ *adverb* on other side of page of book.

**overlie** /əʊvəˈlaɪ/ *verb* (**-lying**; *past* **-lay**; *past participle* **-lain**) lie on top of.

**overload** ● *verb* /əʊvəˈləʊd/ load too heavily (with baggage, work, etc.); put too great a demand on (electrical circuit etc.). ● *noun* /ˈəʊvələʊd/ excessive quantity or demand.

**overlook** /əʊvəˈlʊk/ *verb* fail to observe; tolerate; have view of from above.

**overlord** *noun* supreme lord.

**overly** *adverb* excessively.

**overman** /əʊvəˈmæn/ *verb* (**-nn-**) provide with too large a crew, staff, etc.

**overmuch** /əʊvəˈmʌtʃ/ *adverb & adjective* too much.

**overnight** /əʊvəˈnaɪt/ ● *adverb* for or during night; on preceding evening; suddenly. ● *adjective* done or for use etc. overnight; instant.

**over-particular** /ˌəʊvəpəˈtɪkjʊlə/ *adjective* fussy or excessively particular.

**overpass** *noun esp. US* bridge by which road or railway line crosses another.

**overplay** /ˌəʊvəˈpleɪ/ *verb* give undue importance or emphasis to. □ **overplay one's hand** act on unduly optimistic estimate of one's chances.

**overpower** /ˌəʊvəˈpaʊə/ *verb* subdue, reduce to submission; (esp. as **overpowering** *adjective*) be too intense or overwhelming for.

**over-produce** /ˌəʊvəprəˈdjuːs/ *verb* (**-cing**) produce in excess of demand or of defined amount. □ **overproduction** *noun*.

**overrate** /ˌəʊvəˈreɪt/ *verb* (**-ting**) assess or value too highly; (as **overrated** *adjective*) not as good as it is said to be.

**overreach** /ˌəʊvəˈriːtʃ/ *verb* (**overreach oneself**) fail by attempting too much.

**overreact** /ˌəʊvərɪˈækt/ *verb* respond more violently etc. than is justified. □ **overreaction** *noun*.

**override** ● *verb* /ˌəʊvəˈraɪd/ (**-ding**; *past* **-rode**; *past participle* **-ridden**) have priority over; intervene and make ineffective; interrupt action of (automatic device). ● *noun* /ˈəʊvəraɪd/ suspension of automatic function.

**overrider** *noun* each of pair of projecting pieces on bumper of car.

**overrule** /ˌəʊvəˈruːl/ *verb* (**-ling**) set aside (decision etc.) by superior authority; reject proposal of (person) in this way.

**overrun** /ˌəʊvəˈrʌn/ *verb* (**-nn-**; *past* **-ran**; *past participle* **-run**) spread over; conquer (territory) by force; exceed time etc. allowed.

**overseas** ● *adverb* /ˌəʊvəˈsiːz/ across or beyond sea. ● *adjective* /ˈəʊvəsiːz/ of places across sea; foreign.

**oversee** /ˌəʊvəˈsiː/ *verb* (**-sees**; *past* **-saw**; *past participle* **-seen**) superintend (workers etc.). □ **overseer** *noun*.

**over-sensitive** /ˌəʊvəˈsensɪtɪv/ *adjective* excessively sensitive; easily hurt; quick to react. □ **over-sensitiveness** *noun*; **over-sensitivity** /-ˈtɪv-/ *noun*.

**oversew** *verb* (*past participle* **-sewn** or **-sewed**) sew (two edges) with stitches lying over them.

**oversexed** /ˌəʊvəˈsekst/ *adjective* having unusually strong sexual desires.

**overshadow** /ˌəʊvəˈʃædəʊ/ *verb* appear much more prominent or important than; cast into shade.

**overshoe** *noun* shoe worn over another for protection in wet weather etc.

**overshoot** /ˌəʊvəˈʃuːt/ *verb* (*past & past participle* **-shot**) pass or send beyond (target or limit); go beyond runway when landing or taking off. □ **overshoot the mark** go beyond what is intended or proper.

**oversight** *noun* failure to notice; inadvertent omission or mistake; supervision.

**oversimplify** /ˌəʊvəˈsɪmplɪfaɪ/ *verb* (**-ies**, **-ied**) distort (problem etc.) by putting it in too simple terms. □ **oversimplification** *noun*.

**oversleep** /ˌəʊvəˈsliːp/ *verb* (*past & past participle* **-slept**) sleep beyond intended time of waking.

**overspend** /ˌəʊvəˈspend/ *verb* (*past & past participle* **-spent**) spend beyond one's means.

**overspill** *noun* what is spilt over or overflows; surplus population leaving one area for another.

**overspread** /ˌəʊvəˈspred/ *verb* (*past & past participle* **-spread**) cover surface of; (as **overspread** *adjective*) (usually + *with*) covered.

**overstate** /ˌəʊvəˈsteɪt/ *verb* (**-ting**) state too strongly; exaggerate. □ **overstatement** *noun*.

**overstep** /ˌəʊvəˈstep/ *verb* (**-pp-**) pass beyond. □ **overstep the mark** go beyond conventional behaviour.

**overstrain** /ˌəʊvəˈstreɪn/ *verb* damage by exertion; stretch too far.

**overstrung** *adjective* /əʊvəˈstrʌŋ/ (of person, nerves, etc.) too highly strung; /ˈəʊvəstrʌŋ/ (of piano) with strings crossing each other obliquely.

**oversubscribe** /ˌəʊvəsəbˈskraɪb/ *verb* (**-bing**) (usually as **oversubscribed** *adjective*) subscribe for more than available amount or number of (offer, shares, places, etc.).

**overt** /əʊˈvɜːt/ *adjective* openly done, unconcealed. □ **overtly** *adverb*.

**overtake** /ˌəʊvəˈteɪk/ *verb* (**-king**; *past* **-took**; *past participle* **-taken**) catch up and pass; (of bad luck etc.) come suddenly upon.

**overtax** /əʊvə'tæks/ verb make excessive demands on; tax too highly.

**over-the-top** adjective colloquial excessive.

**overthrow** • verb /əʊvə'θrəʊ/ (past **-threw**; past participle **-thrown**) remove forcibly from power; conquer. • noun /'əʊvəθrəʊ/ defeat; downfall.

**overtime** • noun time worked in addition to regular hours; payment for this. • adverb in addition to regular hours.

**overtone** noun Music any of tones above lowest in harmonic series; subtle extra quality or implication.

**overture** /'əʊvətjʊə/ noun orchestral prelude; (usually in plural) opening of negotiations; formal proposal or offer.

**overturn** /əʊvə't3:n/ verb (cause to) fall down or over; upset, overthrow.

**overview** noun general survey.

**overweening** /əʊvə'wi:nɪŋ/ adjective arrogant.

**overweight** • adjective /əʊvə'weɪt/ above the weight allowed or desirable. • noun /'əʊvəweɪt/ excess weight.

**overwhelm** /əʊvə'welm/ verb overpower with emotion; overcome by force of numbers; bury, submerge utterly.

**overwhelming** adjective too great to resist or overcome; by a great number. □ **overwhelmingly** adverb.

**overwork** /əʊvə'wɜ:k/ • verb (cause to) work too hard; weary or exhaust with work; (esp. as **overworked** adjective) make excessive use of. • noun excessive work.

**overwrought** /əʊvə'rɔːt/ adjective overexcited, nervous, distraught; too elaborate.

**oviduct** /'əʊvɪdʌkt/ noun tube through which ova pass from ovary.

**oviform** /'əʊvɪfɔːm/ adjective egg-shaped.

**ovine** /'əʊvaɪn/ adjective of or like sheep.

**oviparous** /əʊ'vɪpərəs/ adjective egg-laying.

**ovoid** /'əʊvɔɪd/ adjective (of solid) egg-shaped.

**ovulate** /'ɒvjʊleɪt/ verb (**-ting**) produce ova or ovules, or discharge them from ovary. □ **ovulation** noun.

**ovule** /'ɒvju:l/ noun structure containing germ cell in female plant.

**ovum** /'əʊvəm/ noun (plural **ova** /'əʊvə/) female egg cell from which develop after fertilization with male sperm.

**ow** /aʊ/ interjection expressing sudden pain.

**owe** /əʊ/ verb (**owing**) be under obligation to (re)pay or render; (usually + for) be in debt; (usually + to) be indebted to person, thing, etc. for.

**owing** /'əʊɪŋ/ adjective owed, yet to be paid; (+ to) caused by, because of.

**owl** /aʊl/ noun night bird of prey; solemn or wise-looking person. □ **owlish** adjective.

**owlet** /'aʊlɪt/ noun small or young owl.

**own** /əʊn/ • adjective (after my, your, etc.) belonging to myself, yourself, etc.; not another's. • verb have as property, possess; acknowledge as true or belonging to one. □ **come into one's own** achieve recognition, receive one's due; **hold one's own** maintain one's position, not be defeated; **on one's own** alone, independently, unaided; **own goal** goal scored by mistake against scorer's own side, action etc. having unintended effect of harming person's own interests; **own up** confess.

**owner** noun possessor. □ **owner-occupier** person who owns and occupies house. □ **ownership** noun.

**ox** noun (plural **oxen**) large usually horned ruminant; castrated male of domestic species of cattle. □ **ox-eye daisy** daisy with large white petals and yellow centre; **oxtail** tail of ox, often used in making soup.

**oxalic acid** /ɒk'sælɪk/ noun intensely sour poisonous acid found in wood sorrel and rhubarb leaves.

**oxidation** /ɒksɪ'deɪʃ(ə)n/ noun oxidizing, being oxidized.

**oxide** /'ɒksaɪd/ noun compound of oxygen with another element.

**oxidize** /'ɒksɪdaɪz/ verb (also **-ise**) (**-zing** or **-sing**) combine with oxygen; rust; cover with coating of oxide. □ **oxidization** noun.

**oxyacetylene** /ɒksɪə'setɪli:n/ adjective of or using mixture of oxygen and acetylene, esp. in cutting or welding metals.

**oxygen** /'ɒksɪdʒ(ə)n/ noun colourless odourless tasteless gaseous element essential to life and to combustion.

□ **oxygen tent** enclosure to allow patient to breathe air with increased oxygen content.

**oxygenate** /ˈɒksɪdʒəneɪt/ *verb* (**-ting**) supply, treat, or mix with oxygen; oxidize.

**oyez** /əʊˈjes/ *interjection* (also **oyes**) *uttered by public crier or court officer to call for attention.*

**oyster** /ˈɔɪstə/ ● *noun* bivalve mollusc living on seabed, esp. edible kind. ● *adjective* (in full **oyster-white**) greyish white.

**oz** *abbreviation* ounce(s).

**ozone** /ˈəʊzəʊn/ *noun* form of oxygen with pungent odour; *colloquial* invigorating seaside air. □ **ozone-friendly** not containing chemicals destructive to ozone layer; **ozone layer** layer of ozone in stratosphere that absorbs most of sun's ultraviolet radiation.

# Pp

**p** *abbreviation* (also **p.**) penny, pence; page; piano (softly). □ **p. & p.** postage and packing.

**PA** *abbreviation* personal assistant; public address.

**pa** /pɑː/ *noun colloquial* father.

**p.a.** *abbreviation* per annum.

**pace**[1] ● *noun* single step in walking or running; distance covered in this; speed, rate of progression; gait. ● *verb* (**-cing**) walk (over, about), esp. with slow or regular step; set pace for; (+ *out*) measure (distance) by pacing. □ **pacemaker** person who sets pace, natural or electrical device for stimulating heart muscle.

**pace**[2] /ˈpɑːtʃeɪ/ *preposition* with all due deference to. [Latin]

**pachyderm** /ˈpækɪdɜːm/ *noun* large thick-skinned mammal, esp. elephant or rhinoceros. □ **pachydermatous** /-ˈdɜːmətəs/ *adjective*.

**pacific** /pəˈsɪfɪk/ ● *adjective* tending to peace, peaceful; (**Pacific**) of or adjoining the Pacific. ● *noun* (**the Pacific**) ocean between America to the east and Asia to the west.

**pacifist** /ˈpæsɪfɪst/ *noun* person opposed to war. □ **pacifism** *noun*.

**pacify** /ˈpæsɪfaɪ/ *verb* (**-ies**, **-ied**) appease (person, anger, etc.); bring (country etc.) to state of peace. □ **pacification** *noun*.

**pack** ● *noun* collection of things tied or wrapped together for carrying; backpack; set of packaged items; set of playing cards; *usually derogatory* lot, set; group of wild animals or hounds; organized group of Cub Scouts or Brownies; forwards of Rugby team; area of large crowded pieces of floating ice in sea. ● *verb* put together into bundle, box, etc., fill with clothes etc. for transport or storing; cram, crowd together, form into pack; (esp. in *passive*; often + *with*) fill; wrap tightly. □ **packed out** full, crowded; **packhorse** horse for carrying loads; **pack in** *colloquial* stop, give up; **pack it in, up** *colloquial* end or stop it; **pack up** *colloquial* stop working, break down, retire from contest, activity, etc.; **send packing** *colloquial* dismiss summarily.

**package** ● *noun* parcel; box etc. in which goods are packed; (in full **package deal**) set of proposals or items offered or agreed to as a whole. ● *verb* (**-ging**) make up into or enclose in package. □ **package holiday, tour**, etc., one with fixed inclusive price. □ **packaging** *noun*.

**packet** /ˈpækɪt/ *noun* small package; *colloquial* large sum of money; *historical* mail-boat.

**pact** *noun* agreement, treaty.

**pad**[1] ● *noun* piece of soft stuff used to diminish jarring, raise surface, absorb fluid, etc.; sheets of blank writing paper fastened together at one edge; fleshy cushion forming sole of foot of some animals; leg-guard in games; flat surface for helicopter take-off or rocket-launching; *slang* lodging. ● *verb* (**-dd-**) provide with pad or padding, stuff; (+ *out*) fill out (book etc.) with superfluous matter.

**pad²** ● *verb* (**-dd-**) walk softly; tramp (along) on foot; travel on foot. ● *noun* sound of soft steady steps.

**padding** *noun* material used to pad.

**paddle¹** /'pæd(ə)l/ ● *noun* short oar with broad blade at one or each end; paddle-shaped instrument; fin, flipper; board on paddle-wheel or mill-wheel; action or spell of paddling. ● *verb* (**-ling**) move on water or propel (boat etc.) with paddle(s); row gently. □ **paddle-wheel** wheel for propelling ship, with boards round circumference.

**paddle²** /'pæd(ə)l/ ● *verb* (**-ling**) wade about in shallow water. ● *noun* action or spell of paddling.

**paddock** /'pædək/ *noun* small field, esp. for keeping horses in; enclosure where horses or cars are assembled before race.

**paddy¹** /'pædɪ/ *noun* (*plural* **-ies**) (in full **paddy field**) field where rice is grown; rice before threshing or in the husk.

**paddy²** /'pædɪ/ *noun* (*plural* **-ies**) *colloquial* rage, temper.

**padlock** /'pædlɒk/ ● *noun* detachable lock hanging by pivoted hook. ● *verb* secure with padlock.

**padre** /'pɑːdrɪ/ *noun* chaplain in army etc.

**paean** /'piːən/ *noun* (*US* **pean**) song of praise or triumph.

**paediatrics** /piːdɪˈætrɪks/ *plural noun* (treated as *singular*) (*US* **pediatrics**) branch of medicine dealing with children's diseases. □ **paediatric** *adjective*; **paediatrician** /-əˈtrɪʃ(ə)n/ *noun*.

**paedophile** /'piːdəfaɪl/ *noun* (*US* **pedophile**) person feeling sexual attraction towards children.

**paella** /paɪˈelə/ *noun* Spanish dish of rice, saffron, chicken, seafood, etc.

**paeony** = PEONY.

**pagan** /'peɪgən/ ● *noun* heathen, pantheist, etc. ● *adjective* of pagans; heathen; pantheistic. □ **paganism** *noun*.

**page¹** ● *noun* leaf of book etc.; each side of this. ● *verb* (**-ging**) number pages of.

**page²** ● *noun* boy or man employed as liveried servant or personal attendant. ● *verb* (**-ging**) call name of (person sought) in public rooms of hotel etc. □ **page-boy** boy attending bride etc., woman's short hairstyle.

**pageant** /'pædʒ(ə)nt/ *noun* spectacular performance, usually illustrative of historical events; any brilliant show.

**pageantry** *noun* spectacular show or display.

**pager** *noun* bleeping device calling bearer to telephone etc.

**paginate** /'pædʒɪneɪt/ *verb* (**-ting**) number pages of (book etc.). □ **pagination** *noun*.

**pagoda** /pəˈgəʊdə/ *noun* temple or sacred tower in China etc.; ornamental imitation of this.

**pah** *interjection expressing disgust*.

**paid** *past & past participle of* PAY.

**pail** *noun* bucket.

**pain** ● *noun* bodily suffering caused by injury, pressure, illness, etc.; mental suffering; *colloquial* troublesome person or thing. ● *verb* cause pain to. □ **be at** or **take pains** take great care; **in pain** suffering pain; **painkiller** pain-relieving drug.

**painful** *adjective* causing or (esp. of part of the body) suffering pain; causing trouble or difficulty. □ **painfully** *adverb*.

**painless** *adjective* not causing pain. □ **painlessly** *adverb*.

**painstaking** /'peɪnzteɪkɪŋ/ *adjective* careful, industrious, thorough. □ **painstakingly** *adverb*.

**paint** ● *noun* colouring matter, esp. in liquid form, for applying to surface. ● *verb* cover surface of with paint; portray or make pictures in colours; describe vividly; apply liquid or cosmetic to. □ **paintbox** box holding dry paints for painting pictures; **painted lady** butterfly with spotted orange-red wings; **paintwork** painted, esp. wooden, surface or area in building etc.

**painter¹** *noun* person who paints, esp. as artist or decorator.

**painter²** *noun* rope at bow of boat for tying it up.

**painting** *noun* process or art of using paint; painted picture.

**pair** • *noun* set of two people or things; thing with two joined or corresponding parts; engaged or married or mated couple; two playing cards of same denomination; (either of) two MPs etc. on opposite sides agreeing not to vote on certain occasions. • *verb* (often + *off*) arrange or unite as pair, in pairs, or in marriage; mate.

**Paisley** /ˈpeɪzlɪ/ *noun* (*plural* **-s**) pattern of curved feather-shaped figures.

**pajamas** *US* = PYJAMAS.

**Pakistani** /pɑːkɪsˈtɑːnɪ/ • *noun* (*plural* **-s**) native or national of Pakistan; person of Pakistani descent. • *adjective* of Pakistan.

**pal** *colloquial* • *noun* friend. • *verb* (**-ll-**) (+ *up*) make friends.

**palace** /ˈpælɪs/ *noun* official residence of sovereign, president, archbishop, or bishop; stately or spacious building.

**palaeo-** *combining form* (*US* **paleo-**) ancient; prehistoric.

**palaeography** /pælɪˈɒɡrəfɪ/ *noun* (*US* **paleography**) study of ancient writing and documents.

**palaeolithic** /pælɪəʊˈlɪθɪk/ *adjective* (*US* **paleolithic**) of earlier Stone Age.

**palaeontology** /pælɪɒnˈtɒlədʒɪ/ *noun* (*US* **paleontology**) study of life in geological past. □ **palaeontologist** *noun*.

**Palaeozoic** /pælɪəʊˈzəʊɪk/ (*US* **Paleozoic**) • *adjective* of geological era marked by appearance of plants and animals, esp. invertebrates. • *noun* this era.

**palais** /ˈpæleɪ/ *noun colloquial* public dance hall.

**palanquin** /pælənˈkiːn/ *noun* (also **palankeen**) Eastern covered litter for one.

**palatable** /ˈpælətəb(ə)l/ *adjective* pleasant to taste; (of idea etc.) acceptable, satisfactory.

**palatal** /ˈpælət(ə)l/ • *adjective* of the palate; (of sound) made with tongue against palate. • *noun* palatal sound.

**palate** /ˈpælət/ *noun* roof of mouth in vertebrates; sense of taste; liking.

**palatial** /pəˈleɪʃ(ə)l/ *adjective* like palace, splendid.

**palaver** /pəˈlɑːvə/ *noun colloquial* tedious fuss and bother.

**pale**[1] • *adjective* (of complexion etc.) whitish; faintly coloured; (of colour) faint, (of light) dim. • *verb* (**-ling**) grow or make pale; (often + *before, beside*) seem feeble in comparison (with). □ **palely** *adverb*.

**pale**[2] *noun* pointed piece of wood for fencing etc.; stake; boundary. □ **beyond the pale** outside bounds of acceptable behaviour.

**paleo-** *US* = PALEO-.

**Palestinian** /pælɪˈstɪnɪən/ • *adjective* of Palestine. • *noun* native or inhabitant of Palestine.

**palette** /ˈpælɪt/ *noun* artist's flat tablet for mixing colours on; range of colours used by artist. □ **palette-knife** knife with long round-ended flexible blade, esp. for mixing colours or applying or removing paint.

**palimony** /ˈpælɪmənɪ/ *noun esp. US colloquial* allowance paid by either of a separated unmarried couple to the other.

**palimpsest** /ˈpælɪmpsest/ *noun* writing material used for second time after original writing has been erased.

**palindrome** /ˈpælɪndrəʊm/ *noun* word or phrase that reads same backwards as forwards. □ **palindromic** /-ˈdrɒm-/ *adjective*.

**paling** *noun* (in *singular* or *plural*) fence of pales; pale.

**palisade** /pælɪˈseɪd/ • *noun* fence of pointed stakes. • *verb* (**-ding**) enclose or provide with palisade.

**pall**[1] /pɔːl/ *noun* cloth spread over coffin etc.; ecclesiastical vestment; dark covering. □ **pallbearer** person helping to carry or escort coffin at funeral.

**pall**[2] /pɔːl/ *verb* become uninteresting.

**pallet**[1] /ˈpælɪt/ *noun* straw mattress; makeshift bed.

**pallet**[2] /ˈpælɪt/ *noun* portable platform for transporting and storing loads.

**palliasse** /ˈpælɪæs/ *noun* straw mattress.

**palliate** /ˈpælɪeɪt/ *verb* (**-ting**) alleviate without curing; excuse, extenuate. □ **palliative** /-ətɪv/ *adjective & noun*.

**pallid** /ˈpælɪd/ *adjective* pale, sickly-looking.

**pallor** /ˈpælə/ *noun* paleness.

**pally** *adjective* (**-ier**, **-iest**) *colloquial* friendly.

**palm¹** /pɑːm/ noun (also **palm tree**) (usually tropical) treelike plant with unbranched stem and crown of large esp. sickle- or fan-shaped leaves; leaf of this as symbol of victory. □ **Palm Sunday** Sunday before Easter.

**palm²** /pɑːm/ ● noun inner surface of hand between wrist and fingers. ● verb conceal in hand. □ **palm off** (often + on) impose fraudulently (on person).

**palmate** /'pælmeɪt/ adjective shaped like open hand.

**palmetto** /pæl'metəʊ/ noun (plural -s) small palm tree.

**palmist** /'pɑːmɪst/ noun teller of character or fortune from lines etc. in palm of hand. □ **palmistry** noun.

**palmy** /'pɑːmɪ/ adjective (-ier, -iest) of, like, or abounding in palms; flourishing.

**palomino** /pælə'miːnəʊ/ noun (plural -s) golden or cream-coloured horse with light-coloured mane and tail.

**palpable** /'pælpəb(ə)l/ adjective that can be touched or felt; readily perceived. □ **palpably** adverb.

**palpate** /'pælpeɪt/ verb (-ting) examine (esp. medically) by touch. □ **palpation** noun.

**palpitate** /'pælpɪteɪt/ verb (-ting) pulsate, throb; tremble. □ **palpitation** noun.

**palsy** /'pɔːlzɪ/ ● noun (plural -ies) paralysis, esp. with involuntary tremors. ● verb (-ies, -ied) affect with palsy.

**paltry** /'pɔːltrɪ/ adjective (-ier, -iest) worthless, contemptible, trifling.

**pampas** /'pæmpəs/ plural noun large treeless S. American plains. □ **pampas grass** large ornamental grass.

**pamper** /'pæmpə/ verb overindulge.

**pamphlet** /'pæmflɪt/ noun small unbound booklet, esp. controversial treatise.

**pamphleteer** /pæmflɪ'tɪə/ noun writer of (esp. political) pamphlets.

**pan¹** ● noun flat-bottomed usually metal vessel used in cooking etc.; shallow receptacle or tray; bowl of scales or of lavatory. ● verb (-nn-) colloquial criticize harshly; (+ off, out) wash (gold-bearing gravel) in pan; search for gold in this way. □ **pan out** turn out, work out well or in specified way.

**pan²** ● verb (-nn-) swing (film-camera) horizontally to give panoramic effect or follow moving object; (of camera) be moved thus. ● noun panning movement.

**pan-** combining form all; the whole of (esp. referring to a continent, racial group, religion, etc.).

**panacea** /pænə'siːə/ noun universal remedy.

**panache** /pə'næʃ/ noun assertively flamboyant or confident style.

**panama** /pænə'mɑː/ noun hat of strawlike material with brim and indented crown.

**panatella** /pænə'telə/ noun long thin cigar.

**pancake** noun thin flat cake of fried batter, usually folded or rolled up with filling. □ **Pancake Day** Shrove Tuesday (when pancakes are traditionally eaten); **pancake landing** colloquial emergency aircraft landing with undercarriage still retracted.

**panchromatic** /pænkrəʊ'mætɪk/ adjective (of film etc.) sensitive to all visible colours of spectrum.

**pancreas** /'pæŋkrɪəs/ noun gland near stomach supplying digestive fluid and insulin. □ **pancreatic** /-'æt-/ adjective.

**panda** /'pændə/ noun (also **giant panda**) large rare bearlike black and white mammal native to China and Tibet; (also **red panda**) racoon-like Himalayan mammal. □ **panda car** police patrol car.

**pandemic** /pæn'demɪk/ adjective (of disease) widespread; universal.

**pandemonium** /pændɪ'məʊnɪəm/ noun uproar; utter confusion; scene of this.

**pander** /'pændə/ ● verb (+ to) indulge (person or weakness). ● noun procurer, pimp.

**pandit** = PUNDIT.

**pane** noun single sheet of glass in window or door.

**panegyric** /pænɪ'dʒɪrɪk/ noun eulogy; speech or essay of praise.

**panel** /'pæn(ə)l/ ● noun distinct, usually rectangular, section of surface, esp. of wall, door, or vehicle; group or team of people assembled for discussion, consultation, etc.; strip of material in garment; list of available jurors; jury.

● *verb* (**-ll-**; *US* **-l-**) fit with panels. □ **panel game** broadcast quiz etc. played by panel. □ **panelling** *noun*.

**panellist** *noun* (*US* **panelist**) member of panel.

**pang** *noun* sudden sharp pain or distressing emotion.

**pangolin** /pæŋˈgəʊlɪn/ *noun* scaly anteater.

**panic** /ˈpænɪk/ ● *noun* sudden alarm; infectious fright. ● *verb* (**-ck-**) (often + *into*) affect or be affected with panic. □ **panic-stricken**, **-struck** affected with panic. □ **panicky** *adjective*.

**panicle** /ˈpænɪk(ə)l/ *noun* loose branching cluster of flowers.

**panjandrum** /pænˈdʒændrəm/ *noun*: *mock title of great personage*.

**pannier** /ˈpænɪə/ *noun* one of pair of baskets or bags etc. carried by beast of burden or on bicycle or motorcycle.

**panoply** /ˈpænəplɪ/ *noun* (*plural* **-ies**) complete or splendid array; full armour.

**panorama** /pænəˈrɑːmə/ *noun* unbroken view of surrounding region; picture or photograph containing wide view. □ **panoramic** /-ˈræm-/ *adjective*.

**pansy** /ˈpænzɪ/ *noun* (*plural* **-ies**) garden plant of violet family with richly coloured flowers.

**pant** ● *verb* breathe with quick breaths; yearn. ● *noun* panting breath.

**pantaloons** /pæntəˈluːnz/ *plural noun* baggy trousers gathered at ankles.

**pantechnicon** /pænˈteknɪkən/ *noun* large furniture van.

**pantheism** /ˈpænθɪɪz(ə)m/ *noun* doctrine that God is everything and everything is God. □ **pantheist** *noun*, **pantheistic** /-ˈɪs-/ *adjective*.

**pantheon** /ˈpænθɪən/ *noun* building with memorials of illustrious dead; deities of a people collectively; temple of all gods.

**panther** /ˈpænθə/ *noun* leopard, esp. black; *US* puma.

**panties** /ˈpæntɪz/ *plural noun colloquial* short-legged or legless knickers.

**pantile** /ˈpæntaɪl/ *noun* curved roof-tile.

**pantograph** /ˈpæntəɡrɑːf/ *noun* instrument for copying plan etc. on any scale.

**pantomime** /ˈpæntəmaɪm/ *noun* dramatic usually Christmas entertainment based on fairy tale; *colloquial* absurd or outrageous behaviour; gestures and facial expressions conveying meaning.

**pantry** /ˈpæntrɪ/ *noun* (*plural* **-ies**) room in which provisions, crockery, cutlery, etc. are kept.

**pants** *plural noun* underpants; knickers; *US* trousers.

**pap**[1] *noun* soft or semi-liquid food; trivial reading matter.

**pap**[2] *noun archaic* nipple.

**papa** /pəˈpɑː/ *noun archaic: child's name for* father.

**papacy** /ˈpeɪpəsɪ/ *noun* (*plural* **-ies**) Pope's office or tenure; papal system.

**papal** /ˈpeɪp(ə)l/ *adjective* of the Pope or his office.

**paparazzo** /pæpəˈrætsəʊ/ *noun* (*plural* **-zzi** /-tsɪ/) freelance photographer who pursues celebrities to photograph them.

**papaya** = PAWPAW.

**paper** /ˈpeɪpə/ ● *noun* substance made in very thin sheets from pulp of wood etc., used for writing, printing, wrapping, etc.; newspaper; (in *plural*) documents; set of exam questions or answers; wallpaper; essay. ● *adjective* not actual, theoretical. ● *verb* decorate (wall etc.) with paper. □ **paper-boy**, **-girl** one who delivers or sells newspapers; **paper-clip** clip of bent wire or plastic for holding sheets of paper together; **paper-knife** blunt knife for opening envelopes etc.; **paper money** banknotes etc.; **paper round** job of regularly delivering newspapers, route for doing this; **paperweight** small heavy object to hold papers down; **paperwork** office record-keeping and administration.

**paperback** ● *adjective* bound in stiff paper, not boards. ● *noun* paperback book.

**papier mâché** /pæpɪeɪ ˈmæʃeɪ/ *noun* moulded paper pulp used for making models etc.

**papilla** /pəˈpɪlə/ *noun* (*plural* **papillae** /-liː/) small nipple-like protuberance. □ **papillary** *adjective*.

**papoose** /pəˈpuːs/ *noun* young N. American Indian child.

**paprika** /ˈpæprɪkə/ *noun* ripe red pepper; condiment made from this.

**papyrus** /pəˈpaɪərəs/ *noun* ( *plural* **papyri** /-raɪ/) aquatic plant of N. Africa; ancient writing material made from stem of this; manuscript written on this.

**par** *noun* average or normal value, degree, condition, etc.; equality, equal footing; *Golf* number of strokes needed by first-class player for hole or course; face value. □ **par for the course** *colloquial* what is normal or to be expected.

**para** /ˈpærə/ *noun* colloquial paratrooper.

**para-** *prefix* beside, beyond.

**parable** /ˈpærəb(ə)l/ *noun* story used to illustrate moral or spiritual truth.

**parabola** /pəˈræbələ/ *noun* plane curve formed by intersection of cone with plane parallel to its side. □ **parabolic** /pærəˈbɒlɪk/ *adjective*.

**paracetamol** /pærəˈsiːtəmɒl/ *noun* compound used to relieve pain and reduce fever; tablet of this.

**parachute** /ˈpærəʃuːt/ ● *noun* usually umbrella-shaped apparatus allowing person or heavy object to descend safely from a height, esp. from aircraft. ● *verb* (**-ting**) convey or descend by parachute. □ **parachutist** *noun*.

**parade** /pəˈreɪd/ ● *noun* public procession; muster of troops etc. for inspection; parade ground; display, ostentation; public square, row of shops. ● *verb* (**-ding**) march ceremonially; assemble for parade; display ostentatiously. □ **parade ground** place for muster of troops.

**paradigm** /ˈpærədaɪm/ *noun* example or pattern, esp. of inflection of word.

**paradise** /ˈpærədaɪs/ *noun* heaven; place or state of complete bliss; garden of Eden.

**paradox** /ˈpærədɒks/ *noun* seemingly absurd or self-contradictory though often true statement etc. □ **paradoxical** /-ˈdɒks-/ *adjective*; **paradoxically** /-ˈdɒks-/ *adverb*.

**paraffin** /ˈpærəfɪn/ *noun* inflammable waxy or oily substance got by distillation from petroleum etc., used in liquid form esp. as fuel. □ **paraffin wax** solid paraffin.

**paragon** /ˈpærəgən/ *noun* (often + *of*) model of excellence.

**paragraph** /ˈpærəɡrɑːf/ *noun* distinct passage in book etc. usually marked by indentation of first line; mark of reference (¶); short separate item in newspaper etc.

**parakeet** /ˈpærəkiːt/ *noun* small usually long-tailed parrot.

**parallax** /ˈpærəlæks/ *noun* apparent difference in position or direction of object caused by change of observer's position; angular amount of this.

**parallel** /ˈpærəlel/ ● *adjective* (of lines) continuously equidistant; precisely similar, analogous, or corresponding; (of processes etc.) occurring or performed simultaneously. ● *noun* person or thing analogous to another; comparison; imaginary line on earth's surface or line on map marking degree of latitude. ● *verb* (**-l-**) be parallel or correspond to; represent as similar; compare. □ **parallelism** *noun*.

**parallelepiped** /pærəleləˈpaɪped/ *noun* solid bounded by parallelograms.

**parallelogram** /pærəˈleləɡræm/ *noun* 4-sided rectilinear figure whose opposite sides are parallel.

**paralyse** /ˈpærəlaɪz/ *verb* (**-sing**) (*US* **-lyze**; **-zing**) affect with paralysis; render powerless, cripple.

**paralysis** /pəˈrælɪsɪs/ *noun* impairment or loss of esp. motor function of nerves, causing immobility; powerlessness.

**paralytic** /pærəˈlɪtɪk/ ● *adjective* affected with paralysis; *slang* very drunk. ● *noun* person affected with paralysis.

**paramedic** /pærəˈmedɪk/ *noun* paramedical worker.

**paramedical** /pærəˈmedɪk(ə)l/ *adjective* supplementing and supporting medical work.

**parameter** /pəˈræmɪtə/ *noun Mathematics* quantity constant in case considered, but varying in different cases; (esp. measurable or quantifiable) characteristic or feature; (loosely) boundary, esp. of subject for discussion.

**paramilitary** /pærəˈmɪlɪtəri/ ● *adjective* similarly organized to military forces. ● *noun* ( *plural* **-ies**) member of unofficial paramilitary organization.

**paramount** /ˈpærəmaʊnt/ *adjective* supreme; most important or powerful.

**paramour** /ˈpærəmʊə/ *noun archaic* illicit lover of married person.

**paranoia** /pærə'nɔɪə/ noun mental derangement with delusions of grandeur, persecution, etc.; abnormal tendency to suspect and mistrust others. □ **paranoiac** adjective & noun; **paranoid** /'pærənɔɪd/ adjective & noun.

**paranormal** /pærə'nɔːm(ə)l/ adjective beyond the scope of normal scientific investigations etc.

**parapet** /'pærəpɪt/ noun low wall at edge of roof, balcony, bridge, etc.; mound along front of trench etc.

**paraphernalia** /pærəfə'neɪlɪə/ plural noun (also treated as singular) personal belongings, miscellaneous accessories, etc.

**paraphrase** /'pærəfreɪz/ ● noun restatement of sense of passage etc. in other words. ● verb (singular) express meaning of in other words.

**paraplegia** /pærə'pliːdʒə/ noun paralysis below waist. □ **paraplegic** adjective & noun.

**parapsychology** /pærəsaɪ'kɒlədʒɪ/ noun study of mental phenomena outside sphere of ordinary psychology.

**paraquat** /'pærəkwɒt/ noun quick-acting highly toxic herbicide.

**parasite** /'pærəsaɪt/ noun animal or plant living in or on another and feeding on it; person exploiting another or others. □ **parasitic** /-'sɪt-/ adjective; **parasitism** noun.

**parasol** /'pærəsɒl/ noun light umbrella giving shade from the sun.

**paratroops** /'pærətruːps/ plural noun airborne troops landing by parachute. □ **paratrooper** noun.

**paratyphoid** /pærə'taɪfɔɪd/ noun fever resembling typhoid.

**parboil** /'pɑːbɔɪl/ verb partly cook by boiling.

**parcel** /'pɑːs(ə)l/ ● noun goods etc. packed up in single wrapping; piece of land. ● verb (-ll-; US -l-) (+ up) wrap into parcel; (+ out) divide into portions.

**parch** verb make or become hot and dry; slightly roast.

**parchment** /'pɑːtʃmənt/ noun skin, esp. of sheep or goat, prepared for writing etc.; manuscript written on this.

**pardon** /'pɑːd(ə)n/ ● noun forgiveness; remission of punishment. ● verb forgive; excuse; release from legal consequences of offence etc. ● interjection

(also **pardon me** or **I beg your pardon**) formula of apology or disagreement; request to repeat something said. □ **pardonable** adjective.

**pare** /peə/ verb (-ring) trim or reduce by cutting away edge or surface of; (often + away, down) whittle away.

**parent** /'peərənt/ noun person who has had or adopted a child; father, mother; source, origin. □ **parent company** company of which others are subsidiaries; **parent-teacher association** social and fund-raising organization of school's teachers and parents. □ **parental** /pə'rent(ə)l/ adjective; **parenthood** noun.

**parentage** noun lineage, descent from or through parents.

**parenthesis** /pə'renθəsɪs/ noun (plural **-theses** /-siːz/) word, clause, or sentence inserted as explanation etc. into passage independently of grammatical sequence; (in plural) round brackets used to mark this; interlude. □ **parenthetic** /pærən'θetɪk/ adjective.

**par excellence** /pɑːr eksə'lɑ̃s/ adverb superior to all others so called. [French]

**parfait** /'pɑːfeɪ/ noun rich iced pudding of whipped cream, eggs, etc.; layers of ice cream, meringue, etc., served in tall glass.

**pariah** /pə'raɪə/ noun social outcast; historical member of low or no caste.

**parietal** /pə'raɪət(ə)l/ adjective of wall of body or any of its cavities. □ **parietal bone** either of pair forming part of skull.

**paring** noun strip pared off.

**parish** /'pærɪʃ/ noun division of diocese having its own church and clergyman; local government district; inhabitants of parish.

**parishioner** /pə'rɪʃənə/ noun inhabitant of parish.

**parity** /'pærɪtɪ/ noun (plural **-ies**) equality; equal status etc.; equivalence; being at par.

**park** ● noun large public garden in town; large enclosed piece of ground attached to country house or laid out or preserved for public use; place where vehicles may be parked; area for specified purpose. ● verb place and leave (esp.

vehicle) temporarily. □ **parking-lot** *US* outdoor car park; **parking meter** coin-operated meter allocating period of time for which a vehicle may be parked in street; **parking ticket** notice of fine etc. imposed for parking vehicle illegally.

**parka** /'pɑːkə/ *noun* jacket with hood, as worn by Eskimos, mountaineers, etc.

**parkin** /'pɑːkɪn/ *noun* oatmeal ginger-bread.

**parky** /'pɑːkɪ/ *adjective* (**-ier, -iest**) *colloquial or dialect* chilly.

**parlance** /'pɑːləns/ *noun* way of speaking.

**parley** /'pɑːlɪ/ ● *noun* (*plural* **-s**) meeting between representatives of opposed forces to discuss terms. ● *verb* (**-leys, -leyed**) (often + *with*) hold parley.

**parliament** /'pɑːləmənt/ *noun* body consisting of House of Commons and House of Lords and forming (with Sovereign) legislature of UK; similar legislature in other states.

**parliamentarian** /pɑːləmen'teərɪən/ *noun* member of parliament.

**parliamentary** /pɑːlə'mentərɪ/ *adjective* of, in, concerned with, or enacted by parliament.

**parlour** /'pɑːlə/ *noun* (*US* **parlor**) *archaic* sitting-room in private house; *esp. US* shop providing specified goods or services. □ **parlour game** indoor game, esp. word game.

**parlous** /'pɑːləs/ *adjective archaic* perilous; hard to deal with.

**Parmesan** /pɑːmɪ'zæn/ *noun* hard Italian cheese usually used grated as flavouring.

**parochial** /pə'rəʊkɪəl/ *adjective* of a parish; of narrow range, merely local. □ **parochialism** *noun*.

**parody** /'pærədɪ/ ● *noun* (*plural* **-ies**) humorous exaggerated imitation of author, style, etc.; travesty. ● *verb* (**-ies, -ied**) write parody of; mimic humorously. □ **parodist** *noun*.

**parole** /pə'rəʊl/ ● *noun* temporary or permanent release of prisoner before end of sentence, on promise of good behaviour; such promise. ● *verb* (**-ling**) put (prisoner) on parole.

**parotid** /pə'rɒtɪd/ ● *adjective* situated near ear. ● *noun* (in full **parotid gland**) salivary gland in front of ear.

**paroxysm** /'pærəksɪz(ə)m/ *noun* (often + *of*) fit (of pain, rage, coughing, etc.).

**parquet** /'pɑːkeɪ/ ● *noun* flooring of wooden blocks arranged in a pattern. ● *verb* (**-eted** /-eɪd/, **-eting** /-eɪŋ/) floor (room) thus.

**parricide** /'pærɪsaɪd/ *noun* person who kills his or her parent; such a killing. □ **parricidal** /-'saɪd(ə)l/ *adjective*.

**parrot** /'pærət/ ● *noun* mainly tropical bird with short hooked bill, of which some species can be taught to repeat words; unintelligent imitator or chatterer. ● *verb* (**-t-**) repeat mechanically. □ **parrot-fashion** (learning or repeating) mechanically, by rote.

**parry** /'pærɪ/ ● *verb* (**-ies, -ied**) ward off, avert. ● *noun* (*plural* **-ies**) act of parrying.

**parse** /pɑːz/ *verb* (**-sing**) describe (word) or analyse (sentence) in terms of grammar.

**parsec** /'pɑːsek/ *noun* unit of stellar distance, about 3.25 light years.

**parsimony** /'pɑːsɪmənɪ/ *noun* carefulness in use of money etc.; meanness. □ **parsimonious** /-'məʊn-/ *adjective*.

**parsley** /'pɑːslɪ/ *noun* herb used for seasoning and garnishing.

**parsnip** /'pɑːsnɪp/ *noun* plant with pale yellow tapering root used as vegetable; this root.

**parson** /'pɑːs(ə)n/ *noun* parish clergyman; *colloquial* any clergyman. □ **parson's nose** fatty flesh at rump of cooked fowl.

**parsonage** *noun* parson's house.

**part** ● *noun* some but not all; component, division, portion; share, allotted portion; person's share in an action etc.; assigned character or role; *Music* one of melodies making up harmony of concerted music; side in agreement or dispute; (usually in *plural*) region, direction, way; (in *plural*) abilities. ● *verb* divide into parts; separate; (+ *with*) give up, hand over; make parting in (hair). ● *adverb* partly, in part. □ **on the part of** made or done by; **part and parcel** (usually + *of*) essential part; **part-exchange** *noun* transaction in which article is given as part of payment for more expensive one, *verb* give (article) thus; **part of speech** grammatical class of words (noun, pronoun, adjective, adverb, verb, etc.); **part-song** song for 3 or more voice parts; **part-time** employed for or occupying less than normal working week etc.; **part-timer** part-time worker.

**partake** /pɑːˈteɪk/ verb (-**king**; past **partook**; past participle **partaken**) (+ of, in) take share of; (+ of) eat or drink some of.

**parterre** /pɑːˈteə/ noun level garden space filled with flower-beds etc.; US pit of theatre.

**partial** /ˈpɑːʃ(ə)l/ adjective not total or complete; biased, unfair; (+ to) having a liking for. □ **partiality** /-ʃɪˈæl-/ noun; **partially** adverb.

**participate** /pɑːˈtɪsɪpeɪt/ verb (-**ting**) (often + in) have share or take part. □ **participant** noun; **participation** noun.

**participle** /pɑːˈtɪsɪp(ə)l/ noun word (either **present participle**, e.g. writing, or **past participle**, e.g. written) formed from verb and used in complex verb-forms or as adjective. □ **participial** /-ˈsɪp-/ adjective.

**particle** /ˈpɑːtɪk(ə)l/ noun minute portion of matter; smallest possible amount; minor esp. undeclinable part of speech.

**particoloured** /ˈpɑːtɪkʌləd/ adjective (US **-colored**) of more than one colour.

**particular** /pəˈtɪkjʊlə/ ● adjective relating to or considered as one as distinct from others; special; scrupulously exact; fastidious. ● noun detail, item; (in plural) detailed account. □ **in particular** specifically. □ **particularity** /-ˈlær-/ noun.

**particularize** /pəˈtɪkjʊləraɪz/ verb (also **-ise**) (-**zing** or **-sing**) name specially or one by one; specify (items). □ **particularization** noun.

**particularly** adverb very; specifically; in a fastidious way.

**parting** noun leave-taking; dividing line of combed hair.

**partisan** /pɑːtɪˈzæn/ ● noun strong supporter of party, side, or cause; guerrilla. ● adjective of partisans; biased. □ **partisanship** noun.

**partition** /pɑːˈtɪʃ(ə)n/ ● noun structure dividing a space, esp. light interior wall; division into parts. ● verb divide into parts; (+ off) separate with partition.

**partitive** /ˈpɑːtɪtɪv/ ● adjective (of word) denoting part of collective whole. ● noun partitive word.

**partly** adverb with respect to a part; to some extent.

**partner** /ˈpɑːtnə/ ● noun sharer; person associated with others in business; either of pair in marriage etc. or dancing or game. ● verb be partner of. □ **partnership** noun.

**partridge** /ˈpɑːtrɪdʒ/ noun (plural same or **-s**) kind of game bird.

**parturition** /pɑːtjʊˈrɪʃ(ə)n/ noun formal childbirth.

**party** /ˈpɑːtɪ/ noun (plural **-ies**) social gathering; group of people travelling or working together; political group putting forward candidates in elections and usually organized on national basis; each side in agreement or dispute. □ **party line** set policy of political party etc., shared telephone line; **party wall** wall common to adjoining rooms, buildings, etc.

**parvenu** /ˈpɑːvənjuː/ noun (plural **-s**; feminine **parvenue**, plural **-s**) newly rich social climber; upstart.

**pascal** /ˈpæsk(ə)l/ noun SI unit of pressure; (**Pascal** /pæsˈkɑːl/) computer language designed for training.

**paschal** /ˈpæsk(ə)l/ adjective of Passover; of Easter.

**pasha** /ˈpɑːʃə/ noun historical Turkish officer of high rank.

**pasque-flower** /ˈpæskflaʊə/ noun kind of anemone.

**pass**[1] /pɑːs/ ● verb move onward, proceed; go past; leave on one side or behind; (cause to) be transferred from one person or place to another; surpass; go unremarked or uncensured; move; cause to go; be successful in (exam); allow (bill in Parliament) to proceed; be approved; elapse; happen; spend (time etc.); Football etc. kick, hand, or hit (ball etc.) to player of one's own side; (+ into, from) change; come to an end; be accepted as adequate; discharge from body as or with excreta; utter (judgement etc.). ● noun passing, esp. of exam; status of degree without honours; written permission, ticket, or order; Football etc. passing of ball; critical position. □ **make a pass at** colloquial make sexual advances to; **pass away** die; **passbook** book recording customer's transactions with bank etc.; **passer-by** (*plural* **passers-by**) person who goes past, esp. by chance; **pass for** be accepted as; **passkey** private key to gate etc., master-key; **pass off** fade away, be carried through (in specified way), lightly dismiss, (+ *as*) misrepresent as something false; **pass on** proceed, die, transmit to next person in a series; **pass out** become unconscious, complete military training; **pass over** omit, overlook, make no remark on, die; **pass round** distribute, give to one person after another; **pass up** *colloquial* refuse or neglect (opportunity etc.); **password** prearranged word or phrase to secure recognition, admission, etc.

**pass²** /pɑːs/ *noun* narrow way through mountains.

**passable** *adjective* adequate, fairly good.

**passage** /ˈpæsɪdʒ/ *noun* process or means of passing, transit; passageway; right to pass through; journey by sea or air; transition from one state to another; short part of book or piece of music etc.; duct etc. in body.

**passageway** *noun* narrow way for passing along; corridor.

**passé** /ˈpæseɪ/ *adjective* (*feminine* **passée**) outmoded; past its prime.

**passenger** /ˈpæsɪndʒə/ *noun* traveller in or on vehicle (other than driver, pilot, crew, etc.); *colloquial* idle member of team etc.

**passerine** /ˈpæsəriːn/ • *noun* bird able to grip branch etc. with claws. • *adjective* of passerines.

**passim** /ˈpæsɪm/ *adverb* throughout. [Latin]

**passion** /ˈpæʃ(ə)n/ *noun* strong emotion; outburst of anger; intense sexual love; strong enthusiasm; object arousing this; (**the Passion**) sufferings of Christ during his last days, Gospel narrative of this or musical setting of it. □ **passion-flower** plant with flower supposed to suggest instruments of Crucifixion; **passion-fruit** edible fruit of some species of passion-flower. □ **passionless** *adjective*.

**passionate** /ˈpæʃənət/ *adjective* dominated by, easily moved to, or showing passion. □ **passionately** *adverb*.

**passive** /ˈpæsɪv/ *adjective* acted upon, not acting; submissive; inert; *Grammar* (of verb) of which subject undergoes action (e.g. *was written* in *it was written by me*). □ **passive smoking** involuntary inhalation of others' cigarette smoke. □ **passively** *adverb*; **passivity** /-ˈsɪv-/ *noun*.

**Passover** /ˈpɑːsəʊvə/ *noun* Jewish spring festival commemorating Exodus from Egypt.

**passport** /ˈpɑːspɔːt/ *noun* official document showing holder's identity and nationality etc. and authorizing travel abroad.

**past** /pɑːst/ • *adjective* gone by; just over; of former time; *Grammar* expressing past action or state. • *noun* past time or events; person's past life or career; past tense. • *preposition* beyond. • *adverb* so as to pass by. □ **past it** *colloquial* old and useless; **past master** expert.

**pasta** /ˈpæstə/ *noun* dried flour paste in various shapes.

**paste** /peɪst/ • *noun* any moist fairly stiff mixture; dough of flour with fat, water, etc.; flour and water or other mixture as adhesive; meat or fish spread; hard glasslike material used for imitation gems. • *verb* (**-ting**) fasten or coat with paste; *slang* beat, thrash. □ **pasteboard** stiff substance made by pasting together sheets of paper. □ **pasting** *noun*.

**pastel** /ˈpæst(ə)l/ • *noun* pale shade of colour; crayon made of dry pigment-paste; drawing in pastel. • *adjective* of pale shade of colour.

**pastern** /ˈpæst(ə)n/ *noun* part of horse's foot between fetlock and hoof.

**pasteurize** /ˈpɑːstʃəraɪz/ *verb* (also **-ise**) (**-zing** or **-sing**) partially sterilize (milk etc.) by heating. □ **pasteurization** *noun*.

**pastiche** /pæˈstiːʃ/ *noun* picture or musical composition made up from various sources; literary or other work imitating style of author or period etc.

**pastille** /ˈpæstɪl/ *noun* small sweet or lozenge.

**pastime** /ˈpɑːstaɪm/ *noun* recreation; hobby.

**pastor** /ˈpɑːstə/ *noun* minister, esp. of Nonconformist church.

**pastoral** /ˈpɑːstər(ə)l/ • *adjective* of shepherds; of (esp. romanticized) rural life; of pastor. ● *noun* pastoral poem, play, picture, etc; letter from bishop or other pastor to clergy or people.

**pastrami** /pæˈstrɑːmɪ/ *noun* seasoned smoked beef.

**pastry** /ˈpeɪstrɪ/ *noun* (*plural* **-ies**) dough of flour, fat, and water; (item of) food made wholly or partly of this.

**pasturage** *noun* pasture land; pasturing.

**pasture** /ˈpɑːstʃə/ ● *noun* land covered with grass etc. for grazing animals; herbage for animals. ● *verb* (**-ring**) put (animals) to pasture; graze.

**pasty**[1] /ˈpæstɪ/ *noun* (*plural* **-ies**) pie of meat etc. wrapped in pastry and baked without dish.

**pasty**[2] /ˈpeɪstɪ/ *adjective* (**-ier**, **-iest**) pallid.

**pat**[1] ● *verb* (**-tt-**) strike gently with flat palm or other flat surface, esp. in affection etc. ● *noun* light stroke or tap, esp. with hand in affection etc.; patting sound; small mass, esp. of butter, made (as) by patting.

**pat**[2] ● *adjective* known thoroughly; apposite, opportune, esp. glibly so. ● *adverb* in a pat way. □ **have off pat** have memorized perfectly.

**patch** ● *noun* piece put on in mending or as reinforcement; cover protecting injured eye; large or irregular spot on surface; distinct area or period; small plot of ground. ● *verb* mend with patch(es); (often + *up*) piece together; (+ *up*) settle (quarrel etc.), esp. hastily. □ **not a patch on** *colloquial* very much inferior to; **patchwork** stitching together of small pieces of differently coloured cloth to form pattern.

**patchy** *adjective* (**-ier**, **-iest**) uneven in quality; having patches. □ **patchily** *adverb*.

**pate** *noun colloquial* head.

**pâté** /ˈpæteɪ/ *noun* smooth paste of meat etc. □ **pâté de foie gras** /də fwɑː ˈgrɑː/ pâté made from livers of fatted geese.

**patella** /pəˈtelə/ *noun* (*plural* **patellae** /-liː/) kneecap.

**paten** /ˈpæt(ə)n/ *noun* plate for bread at Eucharist.

**patent** /ˈpeɪt(ə)nt, ˈpæt-/ ● *noun* official document conferring right, title, etc., esp. sole right to make, use, or sell some invention; invention or process so protected. ● *adjective* /ˈpeɪt/ plain, obvious; conferred or protected by patent; (of food, medicine, etc.) proprietary. ● *verb* obtain patent for (invention). □ **patent leather** glossy varnished leather. □ **patently** *adverb*.

**patentee** /peɪtənˈtiː/ *noun* holder of patent.

**paterfamilias** /peɪtəfəˈmɪlɪæs/ *noun* male head of family etc.

**paternal** /pəˈtɜːn(ə)l/ *adjective* of father, fatherly; related through father.

**paternalism** *noun* policy of restricting freedom and responsibility by well-meant regulations. □ **paternalistic** /-ˈlɪs-/ *adjective*.

**paternity** /pəˈtɜːnɪtɪ/ *noun* fatherhood; one's paternal origin.

**paternoster** /pætəˈnɒstə/ *noun* Lord's Prayer, esp. in Latin.

**path** /pɑːθ/ *noun* (*plural* **paths** /pɑːðz/) footway, track; line along which person or thing moves. □ **pathway** path, its course.

**pathetic** /pəˈθetɪk/ *adjective* exciting pity, sadness, or contempt. □ **pathetically** *adverb*.

**pathogen** /ˈpæθədʒ(ə)n/ *noun* agent causing disease. □ **pathogenic** /-ˈdʒen-/ *adjective*.

**pathological** /pæθəˈlɒdʒɪk(ə)l/ *adjective* of pathology; or of caused by mental or physical disorder. □ **pathologically** *adverb*.

**pathology** /pəˈθɒlədʒɪ/ *noun* study of disease. □ **pathologist** *noun*.

**pathos** /ˈpeɪθɒs/ *noun* quality that excites pity or sadness.

**patience** /ˈpeɪʃ(ə)ns/ *noun* ability to endure delay, hardship, provocation, pain, etc.; perseverance; solo card game.

**patient** ● *adjective* having or showing patience. ● *noun* person under medical etc. treatment. □ **patiently** *adverb*.

**patina** /ˈpætɪnə/ *noun* (*plural* **-s**) film, usually green, on surface of old bronze etc.; gloss produced by age on woodwork etc.

**patio** /ˈpætɪəʊ/ *noun* (*plural* **-s**) paved usually roofless area adjoining house; roofless inner courtyard.

**patisserie** /pəˈtiːsərɪ/ *noun* shop where pastries are made and sold; pastries collectively.

**patois** /ˈpætwɑː/ *noun (plural same* /-wɑːz/) regional dialect differing from literary language.

**patriarch** /ˈpeɪtrɪɑːk/ *noun* male head of family or tribe; chief bishop in Orthodox and RC Churches; venerable old man. □ **patriarchal** /-ˈɑːk-/ *adjective*.

**patriarchate** /ˈpeɪtrɪəkət/ *noun* office, see, or residence of patriarch; rank of tribal patriarch.

**patriarchy** /ˈpeɪtrɪɑːkɪ/ *noun (plural* **-ies**) male-dominated social system, with descent reckoned through male line.

**patrician** /pəˈtrɪʃ(ə)n/ ● *noun* person of noble birth, esp. in ancient Rome. ● *adjective* of nobility; aristocratic.

**patricide** /ˈpætrɪsaɪd/ *noun* parricide. □ **patricidal** /-ˈsaɪd(ə)l/ *adjective*.

**patrimony** /ˈpætrɪmənɪ/ *noun (plural* **-ies**) property inherited from father or ancestors; heritage.

**patriot** /ˈpeɪtrɪət/ *noun* person devoted to and ready to defend his or her country. □ **patriotic** /-ˈɒt-/ *adjective*; **patriotism** *noun*.

**patrol** /pəˈtrəʊl/ ● *noun* act of walking or travelling round area etc. to protect or supervise it; person(s) or vehicle(s) sent out on patrol; unit of usually 6 in Scout troop or Guide company. ● *verb* (**-ll-**) carry out patrol of; act as patrol. □ **patrol car** car used by police etc. for patrol.

**patron** /ˈpeɪtrən/ *noun (feminine* **patroness**) person who gives financial or other support; customer of shop etc. □ **patron saint** saint regarded as protecting person, place, activity, etc.

**patronage** /ˈpætrənɪdʒ/ *noun* patron's or customer's support; right of bestowing or recommending for appointments; condescending manner.

**patronize** /ˈpætrənaɪz/ *verb* (also **-ise**) (**-zing** or **-sing**) treat condescendingly; act as patron to; be customer of. □ **patronizing** *adjective*.

**patronymic** /pætrəˈnɪmɪk/ *noun* name derived from that of father or ancestor.

**patten** /ˈpæt(ə)n/ *noun historical* wooden sole mounted on iron ring for raising wearer's shoe above mud etc.

**patter¹** /ˈpætə/ ● *noun* sound of quick light taps or steps. ● *verb* (of rain etc.) make this sound.

**patter²** /ˈpætə/ ● *noun* rapid often glib or deceptive talk. ● *verb* say or talk glibly.

**pattern** /ˈpæt(ə)n/ ● *noun* decorative design on surface; regular or logical form, order, etc.; model, design, or instructions from which thing is to be made; excellent example. ● *verb* decorate with pattern; model (thing) on design etc.

**patty** /ˈpætɪ/ *noun (plural* **-ies**) small pie or pasty.

**paucity** /ˈpɔːsɪtɪ/ *noun* smallness of number or quantity.

**paunch** /pɔːntʃ/ *noun* belly, stomach. □ **paunchy** *adjective*.

**pauper** /ˈpɔːpə/ *noun* very poor person. □ **pauperism** *noun*.

**pause** /pɔːz/ ● *noun* temporary stop or silence; *Music* mark denoting lengthening of note or rest. ● *verb* (**-sing**) make a pause; wait.

**pavane** /pəˈvɑːn/ *noun* (also **pavan** /ˈpæv(ə)n/) *historical* stately dance; music for this.

**pave** *verb* (**-ving**) cover (street, floor, etc.) with durable surface. □ **pave the way** (usually + *for*) make preparations. □ **paving** *noun*.

**pavement** *noun* paved footway at side of road. □ **pavement artist** artist who draws in chalk on pavement for tips.

**pavilion** /pəˈvɪljən/ *noun* building on sports ground for spectators or players; summerhouse etc. in park; large tent; building or stand at exhibition.

**pavlova** /pævˈləʊvə/ *noun* meringue dessert with cream and fruit filling.

**paw** ● *noun* foot of animal with claws; *colloquial* person's hand. ● *verb* touch with paw; *colloquial* fondle awkwardly or indecently.

**pawn¹** *noun* chessman of smallest size and value; person subservient to others' plans.

**pawn²** *verb* deposit (thing) as security for money borrowed; pledge. □ **in pawn** held as security; **pawnbroker** person who lends money at interest on security of personal property;

**pawnshop** pawnbroker's place of business.

**pawpaw** /ˈpɔːpɔː/ *noun* (also **papaya** /pəˈpaɪə/) pear-shaped mango-like fruit with pulpy orange flesh; tropical tree bearing this.

**pay** ● *verb* (*past & past participle* **paid**) discharge debt to; give as due; render, bestow (attention etc.); yield adequate return; let out (rope) by slackening it; reward or punish. ● *noun* wages. □ **in the pay of** employed by; **pay-as-you-earn** collection of income tax by deduction at source from wages etc.; **pay-claim** demand for increase in pay; **payday** day on which wages are paid; **pay for** hand over money for, bear cost of, suffer or be punished for; **paying guest** lodger; **payload** part of (esp. aircraft's) load from which revenue is derived; **paymaster** official who pays troops, workmen, etc.; **Paymaster General** Treasury minister responsible for payments; **pay off** pay in full and discharge, *colloquial* yield good results; **pay-off** *slang* payment, climax, end result; **pay phone** coin box telephone; **payroll** list of employees receiving regular pay. □ **payee** /peɪˈiː/ *noun*.

**payable** *adjective* that must or may be paid.

**PAYE** *abbreviation* pay-as-you-earn.

**payment** *noun* paying, amount paid; recompense.

**payola** /peɪˈəʊlə/ *noun* esp. US *slang* bribe offered for unofficial media promotion of product etc.

**PC** *abbreviation* Police Constable; personal computer; politically correct; political correctness; Privy Councillor.

**p.c.** *abbreviation* per cent; postcard.

**pd.** *abbreviation* paid.

**PE** *abbreviation* physical education.

**pea** *noun* climbing plant bearing round edible seeds in pods; one of its seeds; similar plant. □ **pea-souper** *colloquial* thick yellowish fog.

**peace** *noun* quiet, calm; freedom from or cessation of war; civil order. □ **peacemaker** person who brings about peace; **peacetime** time when country is not at war.

**peaceable** *adjective* disposed or tending to peace, peaceful.

**peaceful** *adjective* characterized by or not infringing peace. □ **peacefully** *adverb*; **peacefulness** *noun*.

**peach**[1] *noun* roundish juicy fruit with downy yellow or rosy skin; tree bearing it; yellowish-pink colour; *colloquial* person or thing of superlative merit. □ **peach Melba** dish of ice cream and peaches. **peachy** *adjective* (**-ier, -iest**).

**peach**[2] *verb* *colloquial* turn informer; inform.

**peacock** /ˈpiːkɒk/ *noun* (*plural* same or **-s**) male peafowl, bird with brilliant plumage and erectile fanlike tail. □ **peacock blue** bright lustrous greenish blue of peacock's neck; **peacock butterfly** butterfly with eyelike markings resembling those on peacock's tail.

**peafowl** /ˈpiːfaʊl/ *noun* kind of pheasant, peacock or peahen.

**peahen** /ˈpiːhen/ *noun* female peafowl.

**peak**[1] ● *noun* pointed top, esp. of mountain; stiff projecting brim at front of cap; highest point of achievement, intensity, etc. ● *verb* reach highest value, quality, etc.

**peak**[2] *verb* waste away; (as **peaked** *adjective*) pinched-looking.

**peaky** *adjective* (**-ier, -iest**) sickly, puny.

**peal** ● *noun* loud ringing of bell(s); set of bells; loud repeated sound. ● *verb* (cause to) sound in peal; utter sonorously.

**peanut** *noun* plant bearing underground pods containing seeds used as food and yielding oil; its seed; (in *plural*) *colloquial* trivial amount, esp. of money. □ **peanut butter** paste of ground roasted peanuts.

**pear** /peə/ *noun* fleshy fruit tapering towards stalk; tree bearing it.

**pearl** /pɜːl/ ● *noun* rounded lustrous usually white solid formed in shell of certain oysters and prized as gem; imitation of this; precious thing, finest example. ● *verb* *poetical* (of moisture) form drops, form drops on; fish for pearls. □ **pearl barley** barley rubbed into small rounded grains; **pearl button** button of (real or imitation) mother-of-pearl.

**pearly** ● *adjective* (**-ier, -iest**) resembling a pearl; adorned with pearls. ● *noun* (*plural* **-ies**) pearly king or queen; (in *plural)* pearly king's or queen's clothes. □ **Pearly Gates** *colloquial* gates of Heaven; **pearly king, queen** London costermonger, or his wife, wearing clothes covered with pearl buttons.

**peasant** /'pez(ə)nt/ *noun* (in some countries) worker on land, farm labourer; small farmer; *derogatory* lout, boor. □ **peasantry** *noun* (*plural* **-ies**).

**pease-pudding** /piːz/ *noun* dried peas boiled in cloth.

**peat** *noun* vegetable matter decomposed by water and partly carbonized; piece of this as fuel. □ **peatbog** bog composed of peat. □ **peaty** *adjective*.

**pebble** /'peb(ə)l/ *noun* small stone made smooth by action of water. □ **pebble-dash** mortar with pebbles in it as wall-coating. □ **pebbly** *adjective*.

**pecan** /'piːkən/ *noun* pinkish-brown smooth nut; kind of hickory producing it.

**peccadillo** /pekə'dɪləʊ/ *noun* (*plural* **-es** or **-s**) trivial offence.

**peck**[1] • *verb* strike, pick up, pluck out, or make (hole) with beak; kiss hastily or perfunctorily; *colloquial* (+ *at*) eat (meal) listlessly or fastidiously. • *noun* stroke with beak; hasty or perfunctory kiss. □ **pecking order** social hierarchy.

**peck**[2] *noun* measure of capacity for dry goods (2 gallons, 9.092 litres).

**pecker** *noun* □ **keep your pecker up** *colloquial* stay cheerful.

**peckish** *adjective colloquial* hungry.

**pectin** /'pektɪn/ *noun* soluble gelatinous substance in ripe fruits, causing jam etc. to set.

**pectoral** /'pektər(ə)l/ • *adjective* of or for breast or chest. • *noun* pectoral fin or muscle.

**peculiar** /prˈkjuːlɪə/ *adjective* odd; (usually + *to*) belonging exclusively; belonging to the individual; particular, special.

**peculiarity** /pɪkjuːlɪˈærɪtɪ/ *noun* (*plural* **-ies**) oddity; characteristic; being peculiar.

**peculiarly** *adverb* more than usually, especially; oddly.

**pecuniary** /prˈkjuːnɪərɪ/ *adjective* of or in money.

**pedagogue** /'pedəgɒg/ *noun archaic* or *derogatory* schoolmaster.

**pedagogy** /'pedəgɒdʒɪ/ *noun* science of teaching. □ **pedagogic(al)** /-'gɒg-/ *adjective*.

**pedal** /'ped(ə)l/ • *noun* lever or key operated by foot, esp. in bicycle, motor vehicle, or some musical instruments. • *verb* (**-ll-;** *US* **-l-**) work pedals (of); ride bicycle. • *adjective* /'piːd(ə)l/ of foot or feet.

**pedant** /'ped(ə)nt/ *noun derogatory* person who insists on strict adherence to literal meaning or formal rules. □ **pedantic** /prˈdæntɪk/ *adjective*; **pedantry** *noun*.

**peddle** /'ped(ə)l/ *verb* (**-ling**) sell as pedlar; advocate; sell (drugs) illegally; engage in selling, esp. as pedlar.

**peddler** *noun* person who sells drugs illegally; *US* = PEDLAR.

**pedestal** /'pedɪst(ə)l/ *noun* base of column; block on which something stands.

**pedestrian** /prˈdestrɪən/ • *noun* walker, esp. in town. • *adjective* prosaic, dull. □ **pedestrian crossing** part of road where crossing pedestrians have right of way.

**pedicure** /'pedɪkjʊə/ *noun* care or treatment of feet, esp. of toenails.

**pedigree** /'pedɪgriː/ *noun* recorded (esp. distinguished) line of descent of person or animal; genealogical table; *colloquial* thing's history.

**pediment** /'pedɪmənt/ *noun* triangular part crowning front of building, esp. over portico.

**pedlar** /'pedlə/ *noun* (*US* **peddler**) travelling seller of small wares.

**pedometer** /prˈdɒmɪtə/ *noun* instrument for estimating distance travelled on foot.

**pedophile** *US* = PAEDOPHILE.

**peduncle** /prˈdʌŋk(ə)l/ *noun* stalk of flower, fruit, or cluster, esp. main stalk bearing solitary flower.

**pee** *colloquial* • *verb* (**pees, peed**) urinate. • *noun* urination; urine.

**peek** *noun* & *verb* peep, glance.

**peel** • *verb* strip rind etc. from; (usually + *off*) take off (skin etc.); become bare of bark, skin, etc.; (often + *off*) flake off. ● *noun* rind or outer coating of fruit, potato, etc.

**peeling** *noun* (usually in *plural*) piece peeled off.

**peep**[1] ● *verb* look furtively or through narrow aperture; come cautiously or partly into view; emerge. ● *noun* furtive or peering glance; (usually + *of*) first light of dawn. □ **peep-hole** small hole to peep through; **Peeping Tom** furtive voyeur; **peep-show** exhibition of pictures etc. viewed through lens or peep-hole.

**peep**[2] ● *verb* cheep, squeak. ● *noun* cheep, squeak; slight sound, utterance, or complaint.

**peer**[1] *verb* look closely or with difficulty.

**peer**[2] *noun* (*feminine* **peeress**) duke, marquis, earl, viscount, or baron; equal (esp. in civil standing or rank). □ **peer group** person's associates of same status.

**peerage** *noun* peers as a class; rank of peer or peeress.

**peerless** *adjective* unequalled.

**peeve** *colloquial* ● *verb* (**-ving**) (usually as **peeved** *adjective*) irritate. ● *noun* cause or state of annoyance.

**peevish** *adjective* querulous, irritable. □ **peevishly** *adverb*.

**peewit** /'piːwɪt/ *noun* lapwing.

**peg** ● *noun* wooden, metal, etc. bolt or pin for holding things together, hanging things on, etc.; each of pins used to tighten or loosen strings of violin etc.; forked wooden peg etc. for hanging washing on line; drink, esp. of spirits. ● *verb* (**-gg-**) (usually + *down*, *in*, etc.) fix, mark, or hang out (as with peg(s); keep (prices etc.) stable. □ **off the peg** (of clothes) ready-made; **peg away** (often + *at*) work persistently; **pegboard** board with holes for pegs; **peg out** *slang* die, mark out boundaries of.

**pejorative** /prɪˈdʒɒrətɪv/ ● *adjective* derogatory. ● *noun* derogatory word.

**peke** *noun colloquial* Pekingese.

**Pekingese** /piːkɪˈniːz/ *noun* (also **Pekinese**) (*plural* same) dog of small short-legged snub-nosed breed with long silky hair.

**pelargonium** /peləˈɡəʊnɪəm/ *noun* plant with showy flowers; geranium.

**pelf** *noun* money, wealth.

**pelican** /'pelɪkən/ *noun* large waterfowl with pouch below bill for storing fish. □ **pelican crossing** road crossing-place with traffic lights operated by pedestrians.

**pellagra** /pəˈlæɡrə/ *noun* deficiency disease with cracking of skin.

**pellet** /'pelɪt/ *noun* small compressed ball of a substance; pill; small shot.

**pellicle** /'pelɪk(ə)l/ *noun* thin skin; membrane; film.

**pell-mell** /pel'mel/ *adverb* headlong; in disorder.

**pellucid** /prɪˈluːsɪd/ *adjective* transparent, clear.

**pelmet** /'pelmɪt/ *noun* hanging border concealing curtain-rods etc.

**pelt**[1] ● *verb* assail with missiles, abuse, etc.; (of rain) come down hard; run at full speed. ● *noun* pelting.

**pelt**[2] *noun* skin of animal, esp. with hair or fur still on it.

**pelvis** /'pelvɪs/ *noun* lower abdominal cavity in most vertebrates, formed by haunch bones etc. □ **pelvic** *adjective*.

**pen**[1] ● *noun* implement for writing with ink. ● *verb* (**-nn-**) write. □ **penfriend** friend with whom one communicates by letter only; **penknife** small folding knife; **pen-name** literary pseudonym; **pen-pal** *colloquial* penfriend.

**pen**[2] ● *noun* small enclosure for cows, sheep, poultry, etc. ● *verb* (**-nn-**) enclose; put or keep in confined space.

**pen**[3] *noun* female swan.

**penal** /'piːn(ə)l/ *adjective* of or involving punishment; punishable.

**penalize** /'piːnəlaɪz/ *verb* (also **-ise**) (**-zing** or **-sing**) subject to penalty or disadvantage; make punishable.

**penalty** /'penəltɪ/ *noun* (*plural* **-ies**) fine or other punishment; disadvantage, loss, etc., esp. as result of one's own actions; disadvantage imposed in sports for breach of rules etc. □ **penalty area** *Football* area in front of goal within which breach of rules involves award of penalty kick for opposing team; **penalty kick** free kick at goal from close range.

**penance** /'penəns/ *noun* act of self-punishment, esp. imposed by priest, performed as expression of penitence.

**pence** *plural* of PENNY.

**penchant** /'pãʃã/ noun (+ for) inclination or liking for.

**pencil** /'pens(ə)l/ ● noun instrument for drawing or writing, esp. of graphite enclosed in wooden cylinder or metal case with tapering end; something used or shaped like this. ● verb (-ll-; US -l-) write, draw, or mark with pencil.

**pendant** /'pend(ə)nt/ noun ornament hung from necklace etc.

**pendent** /'pend(ə)nt/ adjective formal hanging; overhanging; pending.

**pending** /'pendɪŋ/ ● adjective awaiting decision or settlement. ● preposition until; during.

**pendulous** /'pendjʊləs/ adjective hanging down; swinging.

**pendulum** /'pendjʊləm/ noun (plural -s) body suspended so as to be free to swing, esp. regulating movement of clock's works.

**penetrate** /'penɪtreɪt/ verb (-ting) make way into or through; pierce; permeate; see into or through; be absorbed by the mind; (as **penetrating** adjective) having or suggesting insight, (of voice) easily heard above other sounds, piercing. □ **penetrable** /-trəb(ə)l/ adjective; **penetration** noun.

**penguin** /'peŋgwɪn/ noun flightless seabird of southern hemisphere.

**penicillin** /penɪ'sɪlɪn/ noun antibiotic obtained from mould.

**peninsula** /pɪ'nɪnsjʊlə/ noun piece of land almost surrounded by water or projecting far into sea etc. □ **peninsular** adjective.

**penis** /'piːnɪs/ noun sexual and (in mammals) urinary organ of male animal.

**penitent** /'penɪt(ə)nt/ ● adjective repentant. ● noun penitent person; person doing penance. □ **penitence** noun; **penitently** adverb.

**penitential** /penɪ'tenʃ(ə)l/ adjective of penitence or penance.

**penitentiary** /penɪ'tenʃərɪ/ ● noun (plural -ies) US prison. ● adjective of penance or reformatory treatment.

**pennant** /'penənt/ noun tapering flag, esp. that at masthead of ship in commission.

**penniless** /'penɪlɪs/ adjective destitute.

**pennon** /'penən/ noun long narrow triangular or swallow-tailed flag; long pointed streamer on ship.

**penny** /'penɪ/ noun (plural **pence** or, for separate coins only, **pennies**) British coin worth 1/100 of pound, or formerly 1/240 of pound. □ **penny-farthing** early kind of bicycle with large front wheel and small rear one; **penny-pinching** noun meanness, adjective mean; **a pretty penny** a large sum of money.

**pennyroyal** /penɪ'rɔɪəl/ noun creeping kind of mint.

**penology** /piː'nɒlədʒɪ/ noun study of punishment and prison management.

**pension¹** /'penʃ(ə)n/ ● noun periodic payment made by government, exemployer, private fund, etc. to person above specified age or to retired, widowed, disabled, etc. person. ● verb grant pension to. □ **pension off** dismiss with pension.

**pension²** /'pãˈsjõ/ noun European, esp. French, boarding house. [French]

**pensionable** adjective entitled or entitling person to pension.

**pensioner** noun recipient of (esp. retirement) pension.

**pensive** /'pensɪv/ adjective deep in thought. □ **pensively** adverb.

**pent** adjective (often + in, up) closely confined; shut in.

**penta-** combining form five.

**pentacle** /'pentək(ə)l/ noun figure used as symbol, esp. in magic, e.g. pentagram.

**pentagon** /'pentəgən/ noun plane figure with 5 sides and angles; (**the Pentagon**) (pentagonal headquarters of) leaders of US defence forces. □ **pentagonal** /-'tæg-/ adjective.

**pentagram** /'pentəgræm/ noun 5-pointed star.

**pentameter** /pen'tæmɪtə/ noun line of verse with 5 metrical feet.

**Pentateuch** /'pentətjuːk/ noun first 5 books of Old Testament.

**pentathlon** /pen'tæθlən/ noun athletic contest of 5 events. □ **pentathlete** noun.

**Pentecost** /'pentɪkɒst/ noun Whit Sunday; Jewish harvest festival 50 days after second day of Passover.

**pentecostal** /pentɪ'kɒst(ə)l/ adjective (of religious group) emphasizing divine gifts, esp. healing, and often fundamentalist.

**penthouse** /'pɛnthaʊs/ *noun* flat on roof or top floor of tall building.

**penultimate** /pɪ'nʌltɪmət/ *adjective & noun* last but one.

**penumbra** /pɪ'nʌmbrə/ *noun* (*plural* **-s** or **-brae** /-briː/) partly shaded region round shadow of opaque body; partial shadow. □ **penumbral** *adjective*.

**penurious** /pɪ'njʊərɪəs/ *adjective* poor; stingy.

**penury** /'pɛnjʊrɪ/ *noun* (*plural* **-ies**) destitution, poverty.

**peon** /'piːən/ *noun* Spanish-American day-labourer.

**peony** /'piːənɪ/ *noun* (also **paeony**) (*plural* **-ies**) plant with large globular red, pink, or white flowers.

**people** /'piːp(ə)l/ ● *plural noun* persons in general; (*singular*) race or nation; (**the people**) ordinary people, esp. as electorate; parents or other relatives; subjects. ● *verb* (**-ling**) (usually + *with*) fill with people; populate; (esp. as **peopled** *adjective*) inhabit.

**PEP** /pɛp/ *abbreviation* Personal Equity Plan.

**pep** *colloquial* ● *noun* vigour, spirit. ● *verb* (**-pp-**) (usually + *up*) fill with vigour. □ **pep pill** one containing stimulant drug; **pep talk** exhortation to greater effort or courage.

**pepper** /'pɛpə/ ● *noun* hot aromatic condiment from dried berries of some plants; capsicum plant, its fruit. ● *verb* sprinkle or flavour with pepper; pelt with missiles. □ **pepper-and-salt** of closely mingled dark and light colour; **peppercorn** dried pepper berry, (in full **peppercorn rent**) nominal rent; **pepper-mill** mill for grinding peppercorns by hand.

**peppermint** *noun* species of mint grown for its strong-flavoured oil; sweet flavoured with this oil; the oil.

**pepperoni** /pepə'rəʊnɪ/ *noun* sausage seasoned with pepper.

**peppery** *adjective* of, like, or abounding in pepper; hot-tempered.

**pepsin** /'pɛpsɪn/ *noun* enzyme contained in gastric juice.

**peptic** /'pɛptɪk/ *adjective* digestive. □ **peptic ulcer** one in stomach or duodenum.

**per** *preposition* for each; by, by means of, through.

**peradventure** /pərəd'vɛntʃə/ *adverb* archaic perhaps.

**perambulate** /pə'ræmbjʊleɪt/ *verb* (**-ting**) walk through, over, or about. □ **perambulation** *noun*.

**perambulator** *noun* formal pram.

**per annum** /pər 'ænəm/ *adverb* for each year.

**per capita** /pə 'kæpɪtə/ *adverb & adjective* for each person.

**perceive** /pə'siːv/ *verb* (**-ving**) become aware of by one of senses; apprehend; understand. □ **perceivable** *adjective*.

**per cent** /pə 'sɛnt/ (*US* **percent**) ● *adverb* in every hundred. ● *noun* percentage; one part in every hundred.

**percentage** *noun* rate or proportion per cent; proportion.

**percentile** /pə'sɛntaɪl/ *noun* each of 99 points at which a range of data is divided to make 100 groups of equal size; each of these groups.

**perceptible** /pə'sɛptɪb(ə)l/ *adjective* that can be perceived. □ **perceptibility** *noun*; **perceptibly** *adverb*.

**perception** /pə'sɛpʃ(ə)n/ *noun* act or faculty of perceiving. □ **perceptual** /-'sɛptʃʊəl/ *adjective*.

**perceptive** /pə'sɛptɪv/ *adjective* sensitive; discerning; capable of perceiving. □ **perceptively** *adverb*; **perceptiveness** *noun*.

**perch**[1] ● *noun* bird's resting-place above ground; high place for person or thing to rest on; *historical* measure of length (5½ yds). ● *verb* rest or place on perch.

**perch**[2] *noun* (*plural* same or **-s**) edible spiny-finned freshwater fish.

**perchance** /pə'tʃɑːns/ *adverb* archaic maybe.

**percipient** /pə'sɪpɪənt/ *adjective* perceiving; conscious.

**percolate** /'pɜːkəleɪt/ *verb* (**-ting**) (often + *through*) filter gradually; (of idea etc.) permeate gradually; prepare (coffee) in percolator. □ **percolation** *noun*.

**percolator** *noun* apparatus for making coffee by circulating boiling water through ground beans.

**percussion** /pə'kʌʃ(ə)n/ *noun* playing of music by striking instruments with sticks etc.; such instruments collectively; gentle tapping of body in medical diagnosis; forcible striking of body against another. □ **percussionist** noun; **percussive** adjective.

**perdition** /pə'dɪʃ(ə)n/ noun damnation.

**peregrine** /'perɪɡrɪn/ noun (in full **peregrine falcon**) kind of falcon.

**peremptory** /pə'remptərɪ/ adjective admitting no denial or refusal; imperious. □ **peremptorily** adverb.

**perennial** /pə'renɪəl/ ● adjective lasting through the year; (of plant) living several years; lasting long or for ever. ● noun perennial plant. □ **perennially** adverb.

**perestroika** /pere'strɔɪkə/ noun (in former USSR) reform of economic and political system.

**perfect** ● adjective /'pɜːfɪkt/ complete; faultless; not deficient; very enjoyable; exact, precise; entire, unqualified; Grammar (of tense) expressing completed action. ● verb /pə'fekt/ make perfect; complete. ● noun /'pɜːfɪkt/ perfect tense. □ **perfect pitch** Music ability to recognize pitch of note.

**perfection** /pə'fekʃ(ə)n/ noun being or making perfect; perfect state; perfect person, specimen, etc.

**perfectionism** noun uncompromising pursuit of perfection. □ **perfectionist** noun.

**perfectly** adverb quite, completely; in a perfect way.

**perfidy** /'pɜːfɪdɪ/ noun breach of faith, treachery. □ **perfidious** /-'fɪd-/ adjective.

**perforate** /'pɜːfəreɪt/ verb (-ting) pierce, make hole(s) through; make row of small holes in (paper etc.). □ **perforation** noun.

**perforce** /pə'fɔːs/ adverb archaic unavoidably, necessarily.

**perform** /pə'fɔːm/ verb carry into effect; go through, execute; act, sing, etc., esp. in public; (of animals) do tricks etc. □ **performing arts** drama, music, dance, etc. □ **performer** noun.

**performance** noun act, process, or manner of doing or functioning; execution (of duty etc.); performing of or in play etc.; colloquial fuss, emotional scene.

**perfume** /'pɜːfjuːm/ ● noun sweet smell; fragrant liquid, esp. for application to

the body, scent. ● verb (**-ming**) impart perfume to.

**perfumer** /pə'fjuːmə/ noun maker or seller of perfumes. □ **perfumery** noun (plural **-ies**).

**perfunctory** /pə'fʌŋktərɪ/ adjective done merely out of duty; superficial. □ **perfunctorily** adverb; **perfunctoriness** noun.

**pergola** /'pɜːɡələ/ noun arbour or covered walk arched with climbing plants.

**perhaps** /pə'hæps/ adverb it may be, possibly.

**perianth** /'perɪænθ/ noun outer part of flower.

**perigee** /'perɪdʒiː/ noun point nearest to earth in orbit of moon etc.

**perihelion** /perɪ'hiːlɪən/ noun (plural **-lia**) point nearest to sun in orbit of planet, comet, etc. round it.

**peril** /'perɪl/ noun serious and immediate danger. □ **perilous** adjective; **perilously** adverb.

**perimeter** /pə'rɪmɪtə/ noun circumference or outline of closed figure; length of this; outer boundary.

**period** /'pɪərɪəd/ ● noun amount of time during which something runs its course; distinct portion of history, life, etc.; occurrence of menstruation, time of this; complete sentence; esp. US full stop. ● adjective characteristic of past period.

**periodic** /pɪərɪ'ɒdɪk/ adjective appearing or recurring at intervals. □ **periodic table** arrangement of chemical elements by atomic number and chemical properties. □ **periodicity** /-rɪə'dɪsɪtɪ/ noun.

**periodical** ● noun magazine etc. published at regular intervals. ● adjective periodic. □ **periodically** adverb.

**peripatetic** /perɪpə'tetɪk/ adjective (of teacher) working in more than one establishment; going from place to place; itinerant.

**peripheral** /pə'rɪfər(ə)l/ ● adjective of minor importance; of periphery. ● noun input, output, or storage device connected to computer.

**periphery** /pə'rɪfərɪ/ noun (plural **-ies**) bounding line, esp. of round surface; outer or surrounding area.

**periphrasis** /pə'rɪfrəsɪs/ noun (plural **-phrases** /-siːz/) circumlocution, roundabout speech or phrase. □ **periphrastic** /perɪ'fræstɪk/ adjective.

**periscope** /'perɪskəʊp/ *noun* apparatus with tube and mirrors or prisms for viewing objects otherwise out of sight.

**perish** /'perɪʃ/ *verb* suffer destruction, die; lose natural qualities; (cause to) rot or deteriorate; (in *passive*) suffer from cold.

**perishable** ● *adjective* subject to speedy decay; liable to perish. ● *noun* perishable thing (esp. food).

**perisher** *noun slang* annoying person.

**perishing** *colloquial* ● *adjective* confounded; intensely cold. ● *adverb* confoundedly.

**peritoneum** /perɪtə'niːəm/ *noun* ( *plural* -s or -na) membrane lining abdominal cavity. □ **peritoneal** *adjective*.

**peritonitis** /perɪtə'naɪtɪs/ *noun* inflammation of peritoneum.

**periwig** /'perɪwɪg/ *noun historical* wig.

**periwinkle**[1] /'perɪwɪŋk(ə)l/ *noun* evergreen trailing plant with blue or white flower.

**periwinkle**[2] /'perɪwɪŋk(ə)l/ *noun* winkle.

**perjure** /'pɜːdʒə/ *verb* (-ring) (**perjure oneself**) commit perjury; (as **perjured** *adjective*) guilty of perjury. □ **perjurer** *noun*.

**perjury** /'pɜːdʒərɪ/ *noun* ( *plural* -ies) wilful lying while on oath.

**perk**[1] *verb* □ **perk up** (cause to) recover courage, smarten up, raise (head etc.) briskly.

**perk**[2] *noun colloquial* perquisite.

**perky** *adjective* (-ier, -iest) lively and cheerful.

**perm**[1] ● *noun* permanent wave. ● *verb* give permanent wave to.

**perm**[2] *colloquial* ● *noun* permutation. ● *verb* make permutation of.

**permafrost** /'pɜːməfrɒst/ *noun* permanently frozen subsoil, as in polar regions.

**permanent** /'pɜːmənənt/ *adjective* lasting or intended to last indefinitely. □ **permanent wave** long-lasting artificial wave in hair. □ **permanence** *noun*; **permanently** *adverb*.

**permeable** /'pɜːmɪəb(ə)l/ *adjective* capable of being permeated. □ **permeability** *noun*.

**permeate** /'pɜːmɪeɪt/ *verb* (-ting) penetrate, saturate, pervade; be diffused. □ **permeation** *noun*.

**permissible** /pə'mɪsɪb(ə)l/ *adjective* allowable. □ **permissibility** *noun*.

**permission** /pə'mɪʃ(ə)n/ *noun* consent, authorization.

**permissive** /pə'mɪsɪv/ *adjective* tolerant, liberal; giving permission. □ **permissiveness** *noun*.

**permit** ● *verb* /pə'mɪt/ (-tt-) give consent to; authorize; allow; give opportunity; ( + *of*) allow as possible. ● *noun* /'pɜːmɪt/ written order giving permission or allowing entry.

**permutation** /pɜːmjʊ'teɪʃ(ə)n/ *noun* one of possible ordered arrangements of set of things; combination or selection of specified number of items from larger group.

**pernicious** /pə'nɪʃəs/ *adjective* destructive, injurious. □ **pernicious anaemia** defective formation of red blood cells through lack of vitamin B.

**pernickety** /pə'nɪkɪtɪ/ *adjective colloquial* fastidious, over-precise.

**peroration** /perə'reɪʃ(ə)n/ *noun* concluding part of speech.

**peroxide** /pə'rɒksaɪd/ ● *noun* (in full **hydrogen peroxide**) colourless liquid used in water solution, esp. to bleach hair; oxide containing maximum proportion of oxygen. ● *verb* (-ding) bleach (hair) with peroxide.

**perpendicular** /pɜːpən'dɪkjʊlə/ ● *adjective* (usually + *to*) at right angles; upright; very steep; (**Perpendicular**) of or in style of English Gothic architecture of 15th & 16th c. ● *noun* perpendicular line etc. □ **perpendicularity** /-'lærɪtɪ/ *noun*.

**perpetrate** /'pɜːpɪtreɪt/ *verb* (-ting) commit. □ **perpetration** *noun*; **perpetrator** *noun*.

**perpetual** /pə'petʃʊəl/ *adjective* lasting for ever or indefinitely; continuous; *colloquial* frequent. □ **perpetually** *adverb*.

**perpetuate** /pə'petʃʊeɪt/ *verb* (-ting) make perpetual; cause to be always remembered. □ **perpetuation** *noun*.

**perpetuity** /pɜːpɪ'tjuːɪtɪ/ *noun* ( *plural* -ies) perpetual continuance or possession. □ **in perpetuity** for ever.

**perplex** /pə'pleks/ *verb* bewilder, puzzle; complicate, tangle. □ **perplexing** *adjective*; **perplexity** *noun*.

**per pro.** /pɜː 'prəʊ/ *abbreviation* through the agency of (used in signatures) (*per procurantionem*). [Latin].

■ **Usage** The abbreviation *per pro.* (or *p.p.*) is frequently written before the wrong name: "T. Jones, *p.p.* P. Smith" means that P. Smith is signing on behalf of T. Jones.

**perquisite** /'pɜːkwɪzɪt/ *noun* extra profit additional to main income etc.; customary extra right or privilege.

■ **Usage** *Perquisite* is sometimes confused with *prerequisite*, which means 'a thing required as a precondition'.

**perry** /'perɪ/ *noun* (*plural* **-ies**) drink made from fermented pear juice.

**per se** /pɜː 'seɪ/ *adverb* by or in itself, intrinsically. [Latin]

**persecute** /'pɜːsɪkjuːt/ *verb* (**-ting**) subject to constant hostility and ill-treatment; harass, worry. □ **persecution** /-'kjuːʃ(ə)n/ *noun*, **persecutor** *noun*.

**persevere** /pɜːsɪ'vɪə/ *verb* (**-ring**) continue steadfastly, persist. □ **perseverance** *noun*.

**Persian** /'pɜːʃ(ə)n/ ● *noun* native, national, or language of Persia (now Iran); (in full **Persian cat**) cat with long silky hair. ● *adjective* of Persia (Iran). □ **Persian lamb** silky curled fur of young karakul.

**persiflage** /'pɜːsɪflɑːʒ/ *noun* banter; light raillery.

**persimmon** /pɜː'sɪmən/ *noun* tropical tree; its edible orange tomato-like fruit.

**persist** /pə'sɪst/ *verb* (often + *in*) continue to exist or do something in spite of obstacles. □ **persistence** *noun*, **persistent** *adjective*; **persistently** *adverb*.

**person** /'pɜːs(ə)n/ *noun* individual human being; living body of human being; *Grammar* one of 3 classes of pronouns, verb-forms, etc., denoting person etc. speaking, spoken to, or spoken of. □ **in person** physically present.

**persona** /pə'səʊnə/ *noun* (*plural* **-nae** /-niː/) aspect of personality as perceived by others. ● **persona grata** /'grɑːtə/ (*plural* **personae gratae** /-niː, -tiː/) person acceptable to certain others; **persona non grata** /nɒn/ (*plural* **personae non gratae**) person not acceptable.

**personable** *adjective* pleasing in appearance or demeanour.

**personage** *noun* person, esp. important one.

**personal** /'pɜːsən(ə)l/ *adjective* one's own; individual, private; done etc. in person; directed to or concerning individual; referring (esp. in hostile way) to individual's private life; *Grammar* of or denoting one of the 3 persons. □ **personal column** part of newspaper devoted to private advertisements and messages; **personal computer** computer designed for use by single individual; **personal equity plan** scheme for tax-free personal investments; **personal organizer** means of keeping track of personal affairs, esp. loose-leaf notebook divided into sections; **personal pronoun** pronoun replacing subject, object, etc., of clause etc.; **personal property** all property except land.

**personality** /pɜːsə'nælɪtɪ/ *noun* (*plural* **-ies**) distinctive personal character; well-known person; (in *plural*) personal remarks.

**personalize** *verb* (also **-ise**) (**-zing** or **-sing**) identify as belonging to particular person.

**personally** *adverb* in person; for one's own part; in a personal way.

**personification** /pəsɒnɪfɪ'keɪʃ(ə)n/ *noun* type of metaphor in which human qualities are attributed to object, plant, animal, nature, etc., e.g. *Life can play some nasty tricks.*

**personify** /pə'sɒnɪfaɪ/ *verb* (**-ies**, **-ied**) attribute human characteristics to; symbolize by human figure; (usually as **personified** *adjective*) embody, exemplify typically. □ **personification** *noun*.

**personnel** /pɜːsə'nel/ *noun* staff of an organization; people engaged in particular service, profession, etc. □ **personnel department** department of firm etc. dealing with appointment, training, and welfare of employees.

**perspective** /pə'spektɪv/ ● *noun* art of drawing so as to give effect of solidity and relative position and size; relation as to position and distance, or proportion between visible objects, parts of subject, etc.; mental view of relative importance of things; view, prospect. ● *adjective* of or in perspective. □ **in** or **out of perspective** according or not according to rules of perspective, in or not in proportion.

**Perspex** /'pɜːspeks/ *noun* proprietary term tough light transparent plastic.

**perspicacious** /pɜːspɪ'keɪʃəs/ adjective having mental penetration or discernment. □ **perspicacity** /-'kæs-/ noun.

**perspicuous** /pə'spɪkjʊəs/ adjective lucid; clearly expressed. □ **perspicuity** /-'kjuː-/ noun.

**perspire** /pə'spaɪə/ verb (**-ring**) sweat. □ **perspiration** /pɜːspɪ'reɪʃ(ə)n/ noun.

**persuade** /pə'sweɪd/ verb (**-ding**) cause (person) by argument etc. to believe or do something; convince.

**persuasion** /pə'sweɪʒ(ə)n/ noun persuading; conviction; religious belief or sect.

**persuasive** /pə'sweɪsɪv/ adjective able or tending to persuade. □ **persuasively** adverb; **persuasiveness** noun.

**pert** adjective saucy, impudent; jaunty. □ **pertly** adverb; **pertness** noun.

**pertain** /pə'teɪn/ verb belong, relate.

**pertinacious** /pɜːtɪ'neɪʃəs/ adjective persistent, obstinate. □ **pertinacity** /-'næs-/ noun.

**pertinent** /'pɜːtɪnənt/ adjective relevant. □ **pertinence** noun; **pertinency** noun.

**perturb** /pə'tɜːb/ verb throw into agitation; disquiet. □ **perturbation** noun.

**peruke** /pə'ruːk/ noun historical wig.

**peruse** /pə'ruːz/ verb (**-sing**) read; scan. □ **perusal** noun.

**pervade** /pə'veɪd/ verb (**-ding**) spread through, permeate; be rife among. □ **pervasion** noun; **pervasive** adjective.

**perverse** /pə'vɜːs/ adjective obstinately or wilfully in the wrong; wayward. □ **perversely** adverb; **perversity** noun.

**perversion** /pə'vɜːʃ(ə)n/ noun perverting, being perverted; preference for abnormal form of sexual activity.

**pervert** ● verb /pə'vɜːt/ turn (thing) aside from proper or normal use; lead astray from right behaviour or belief etc.; (as **perverted** adjective) showing perversion. ● noun /'pɜːvɜːt/ person who is perverted, esp. sexually.

**pervious** /'pɜːvɪəs/ adjective permeable; allowing passage or access.

**peseta** /pə'seɪtə/ noun Spanish monetary unit.

**peso** /'peɪsəʊ/ noun (plural **-s**) monetary unit in several Latin American countries.

**pessary** /'pesərɪ/ noun (plural **-ies**) device worn in vagina; vaginal suppository.

**pessimism** /'pesɪmɪz(ə)m/ noun tendency to take worst view or expect worst outcome. □ **pessimist** noun; **pessimistic** /-'mɪst-/ adjective.

**pest** noun troublesome or destructive person, animal, or thing.

**pester** /'pestə/ verb trouble or annoy, esp. with persistent requests.

**pesticide** /'pestɪsaɪd/ noun substance for destroying harmful insects etc.

**pestilence** /'pestɪləns/ noun fatal epidemic disease, esp. bubonic plague.

**pestilent** /'pestɪlənt/ adjective deadly; harmful or morally destructive.

**pestilential** /pestɪ'lenʃ(ə)l/ adjective of pestilence; pestilent.

**pestle** /'pes(ə)l/ noun instrument for pounding substances in a mortar.

**pet**[1] ● noun domestic animal kept for pleasure or companionship; favourite. ● adjective as, of, or for a pet; favourite; expressing fondness. ● verb (**-tt-**) fondle, esp. erotically; treat as pet.

**pet**[2] noun fit of ill humour.

**petal** /'pet(ə)l/ noun each division of flower corolla.

**peter** /'piːtə/ verb □ **peter out** diminish, come to an end.

**petersham** /'piːtəʃəm/ noun thick ribbed silk ribbon.

**petiole** /'petɪəʊl/ noun leaf-stalk.

**petite** /pə'tiːt/ adjective (of woman) of small dainty build. [French]

**petit four** /petɪ'fɔː/ noun (plural **petits fours** /'fɔːz/) very small fancy cake.

**petition** /pə'tɪʃ(ə)n/ ● noun request, supplication; formal written request, esp. one signed by many people, to authorities etc. ● verb make petition to; ask humbly.

**petit point** /petɪ 'pwæ̃/ noun embroidery on canvas using small stitches.

**petrel** /'petr(ə)l/ noun seabird, usually flying far from land.

**petrify** /'petrɪfaɪ/ verb (**-ies**, **-ied**) paralyse with terror or astonishment etc.; turn or be turned into stone. □ **petrifaction** /-'fækʃ(ə)n/ noun.

**petrochemical** /petrəʊ'kemɪk(ə)l/ noun substance obtained from petroleum or natural gas.

**petrodollar** /'petrəʊdɒlə/ noun notional unit of currency earned by petroleum-exporting country.

**petrol** /'petr(ə)l/ *noun* refined petroleum used as fuel in motor vehicles, aircraft, etc.

**petroleum** /pɪ'trəʊlɪəm/ *noun* hydrocarbon oil found in upper strata of earth, refined for use as fuel etc. □ **petroleum jelly** translucent solid mixture of hydrocarbons got from petroleum and used as lubricant etc.

**petticoat** /'petɪkəʊt/ *noun* woman's or girl's undergarment hanging from waist or shoulders.

**pettifogging** /'petɪfɒgɪŋ/ *adjective* quibbling; petty; dishonest.

**pettish** *adjective* fretful, peevish.

**petty** /'petɪ/ *adjective* (**-ier**, **-iest**) unimportant, trivial; small-minded; minor, inferior. □ **petty cash** money kept for small items of expenditure; **petty officer** naval NCO. □ **pettiness** *noun*.

**petulant** /'petjʊlənt/ *adjective* peevishly impatient or irritable. □ **petulance** *noun*; **petulantly** *adverb*.

**petunia** /pɪ'tjuːnɪə/ *noun* cultivated plant with vivid funnel-shaped flowers.

**pew** *noun* (in church) enclosed compartment or fixed bench with back; *colloquial* seat.

**pewter** /'pjuːtə/ *noun* grey alloy of tin, antimony, and copper; articles made of this.

**peyote** /per'əʊtɪ/ *noun* a Mexican cactus; hallucinogenic drug prepared from it.

**pfennig** /'fenɪg/ *noun* one-hundredth of Deutschmark.

**PG** *abbreviation* (of film) classified as suitable for children subject to parental guidance.

**pH** /piː'eɪtʃ/ *noun* measure of acidity or alkalinity of a solution.

**phagocyte** /'fægəsaɪt/ *noun* blood corpuscle etc. capable of absorbing foreign matter.

**phalanx** /'fælæŋks/ *noun* (*plural* **phalanxes** or **phalanges** /fə'lændʒiːz/) group of infantry in close formation; united or organized party or company.

**phallus** /'fæləs/ *noun* (*plural* **phalli** /-laɪ/ or **phalluses**) (esp. erect) penis; image of this. □ **phallic** *adjective*.

**phantasm** /'fæntæz(ə)m/ *noun* illusion; phantom. □ **phantasmal** /-'tæzm(ə)l/ *adjective*.

**phantasmagoria** /ˌfæntæzmə'gɔːrɪə/ *noun* shifting scene of real or imaginary figures. □ **phantasmagoric** /-'gɒrɪk/ *adjective*.

**phantom** /'fæntəm/ ● *noun* spectre, apparition; mental illusion. ● *adjective* illusory.

**Pharaoh** /'feərəʊ/ *noun* ruler of ancient Egypt.

**Pharisee** /'færɪsiː/ *noun* member of ancient Jewish sect distinguished by strict observance of traditional and written law; self-righteous person; hypocrite. □ **Pharisaic** /-'seɪɪk/ *adjective*.

**pharmaceutical** /ˌfɑːmə'sjuːtɪk(ə)l/ *adjective* of pharmacy; of use or sale of medicinal drugs. □ **pharmaceutics** *noun*.

**pharmacist** /'fɑːməsɪst/ *noun* person qualified to practise pharmacy.

**pharmacology** /ˌfɑːmə'kɒlədʒɪ/ *noun* study of action of drugs on the body. □ **pharmacological** /-kə'lɒdʒ-/ *adjective*; **pharmacologist** *noun*.

**pharmacopoeia** /ˌfɑːməkə'piːə/ *noun* book with list of drugs and directions for use; stock of drugs.

**pharmacy** /'fɑːməsɪ/ *noun* (*plural* **-ies**) preparation and dispensing of drugs; pharmacist's shop; dispensary.

**pharynx** /'færɪŋks/ *noun* (*plural* **pharynges** /-rɪndʒiːz/ or **-xes**) cavity behind mouth and nose. □ **pharyngeal** /ˌfærɪn'dʒiːəl/ *adjective*.

**phase** /feɪz/ ● *noun* stage of development, process, or recurring sequence; aspect of moon or planet. ● *verb* (**-sing**) carry out by phases. □ **phase in**, **out** bring gradually into or out of use.

**Ph.D.** *abbreviation* Doctor of Philosophy.

**pheasant** /'fez(ə)nt/ *noun* long-tailed game bird.

**phenomenal** /fɪ'nɒmɪn(ə)l/ *adjective* extraordinary, remarkable; of or concerned with phenomena. □ **phenomenally** *adverb*.

**phenomenon** /fɪ'nɒmɪnən/ *noun* (*plural* **-mena**) observed or apparent object, fact, or occurrence; remarkable person or thing.

■ **Usage** It is a mistake to use the plural form *phenomena* when only one phenomenon is meant.

**phew** /fju:/ *interjection expressing disgust, relief, etc.*

**phial** /'faɪəl/ *noun* small glass bottle.

**philander** /fɪ'lændə/ *verb* flirt or have casual affairs with women. □ **philanderer** *noun*.

**philanthropy** /fɪ'lænθrəpɪ/ *noun* love of all humankind; practical benevolence. □ **philanthropic** /-'θrɒp-/ *adjective*; **philanthropist** *noun*.

**philately** /fɪ'lætəlɪ/ *noun* stamp-collecting. □ **philatelist** *noun*.

**philharmonic** /fɪlhɑː'mɒnɪk/ *adjective* devoted to music.

**philippic** /fɪ'lɪpɪk/ *noun* bitter verbal attack.

**philistine** /'fɪlɪstaɪn/ ●*noun* person who is hostile or indifferent to culture. ●*adjective* hostile or indifferent to culture. □ **philistinism** /-stɪn-/ *noun*.

**Phillips** /'fɪlɪps/ *noun proprietary term* □ **Phillips screw, screwdriver** screw with cross-shaped slot, corresponding screwdriver.

**philology** /fɪ'lɒlədʒɪ/ *noun* study of language. □ **philological** /-lə'lɒdʒ-/ *adjective*; **philologist** *noun*.

**philosopher** /fɪ'lɒsəfə/ *noun* expert in or student of philosophy; person who acts philosophically.

**philosophical** /fɪlə'sɒfɪk(ə)l/ *adjective* (also **philosophic**) of or according to philosophy; calm under adverse circumstances. □ **philosophically** *adverb*.

**philosophize** /fɪ'lɒsəfaɪz/ *verb* (also **-ise**) (**-zing** or **-sing**) reason like philosopher; theorize.

**philosophy** /fɪ'lɒsəfɪ/ *noun* (*plural* **-ies**) use of reason and argument in seeking truth and knowledge, esp. of ultimate reality or of general causes and principles; philosophical system; system for conduct of life.

**philtre** /'fɪltə/ *noun* (*US* **philter**) love potion.

**phlebitis** /flɪ'baɪtɪs/ *noun* inflammation of vein. □ **phlebitic** /-'bɪt-/ *adjective*.

**phlegm** /flem/ *noun* bronchial mucus ejected by coughing; calmness; sluggishness.

**phlegmatic** /fleg'mætɪk/ *adjective* calm; sluggish.

**phlox** /flɒks/ *noun* (*plural* same or **-es**) plant with clusters of white or coloured flowers.

**phobia** /'fəʊbɪə/ *noun* abnormal fear or aversion. □ **phobic** *adjective & noun*.

**phoenix** /'fi:nɪks/ *noun* bird, the only one of its kind, fabled to burn itself and rise from its ashes.

**phone** *noun & verb* (**-ning**) *colloquial* telephone. □ **phone book** telephone directory; **phonecard** card holding prepaid units for use with cardphone; **phone-in** broadcast programme in which listeners or viewers participate by telephone.

**phonetic** /fə'netɪk/ *adjective* of or representing vocal sounds; (of spelling) corresponding to pronunciation. □ **phonetically** *adverb*.

**phonetics** *plural noun* (usually treated as *singular*) study or representation of vocal sounds. □ **phonetician** /fəʊnɪ'tɪʃ(ə)n/ *noun*.

**phoney** /'fəʊnɪ/ (also **phony**) *colloquial* ●*adjective* (**-ier, -iest**) false, sham, counterfeit. ●*noun* (*plural* **-eys** or **-ies**) phoney person or thing. □ **phoniness** *noun*.

**phonic** /'fɒnɪk/ *adjective* of (vocal) sound.

**phonograph** /'fəʊnəɡrɑːf/ *noun* early form of gramophone.

**phonology** /fə'nɒlədʒɪ/ *noun* study of sounds in language. □ **phonological** /fəʊnə'lɒdʒɪk(ə)l/ *adjective*.

**phony** = PHONEY.

**phosphate** /'fɒsfeɪt/ *noun* salt of phosphoric acid, esp. used as fertilizer.

**phosphorescence** /fɒsfə'res(ə)ns/ *noun* emission of light without combustion or perceptible heat. □ **phosphoresce** *verb* (**-cing**); **phosphorescent** *adjective*.

**phosphorus** /'fɒsfərəs/ *noun* non-metallic element occurring esp. as waxlike substance appearing luminous in dark. □ **phosphoric** /-'fɒrɪk/ *adjective*; **phosphorous** *adjective*.

**photo** /'fəʊtəʊ/ *noun* (*plural* **-s**) photograph. □ **photo finish** close finish of race in which winner is distinguishable only on photograph; **photofit** picture of suspect constructed from composite photographs.

**photo-** *combining form* light; photography.

**photocopier** /'fəʊtəʊkɒpɪə/ *noun* machine for photocopying documents.

**photocopy** /ˈfəʊtəʊkɒpɪ/ ● *noun* (*plural* **-ies**) photographic copy of document. ● *verb* (**-ies, -ied**) make photocopy of.

**photoelectric** /fəʊtəʊrˈlektrɪk/ *adjective* with or using emission of electrons from substances exposed to light. □ **photoelectric cell** device using this effect to generate current. □ **photoelectricity** /-ˈtrɪsɪtɪ/ *noun*.

**photogenic** /fəʊtəʊˈdʒenɪk/ *adjective* looking attractive in photographs; producing or emitting light.

**photograph** /ˈfəʊtəɡrɑːf/ ● *noun* picture formed by chemical action of light on sensitive film. ● *verb* take photograph (of). □ **photographer** /fəˈtɒɡrəfə/ *noun*; **photographic** /-ˈɡræf-/ *adjective*; **photography** /fəˈtɒɡrəfɪ/ *noun*.

**photogravure** /fəʊtəʊɡrəˈvjʊə/ *noun* picture produced from photographic negative transferred to metal plate and etched in; this process.

**photojournalism** /fəʊtəʊˈdʒɜːnəlɪz(ə)m/ *noun* reporting of news by photographs in magazines etc.

**photolithography** /fəʊtəʊlɪˈθɒɡrəfɪ/ *noun* lithography using plates made photographically.

**photometer** /fəʊˈtɒmɪtə/ *noun* instrument for measuring light. □ **photometric** /fəʊtəʊˈmetrɪk/ *adjective*; **photometry** /-ˈtɒmɪtrɪ/ *noun*.

**photon** /ˈfəʊtɒn/ *noun* quantum of electromagnetic radiation energy.

**Photostat** /ˈfəʊtəʊstæt/ ● *noun proprietary term* type of photocopier; copy made by

it. ● *verb* (**photostat**) (**-tt-**) make Photostat of.

**photosynthesis** /fəʊtəʊˈsɪnθəsɪs/ *noun* process in which energy of sunlight is used by green plants to form carbohydrates from carbon dioxide and water. □ **photosynthesize** *verb* (also **-ise**) (**-zing** or **-sing**).

**phrase** /freɪz/ ● *noun* group of words forming conceptual unit but not sentence (see panel); short pithy expression; *Music* short sequence of notes. ● *verb* (**-sing**) express in words; divide (music) into phrases. □ **phrase book** book listing phrases and their foreign equivalents, for use by tourists etc. □ **phrasal** *adjective*.

**phraseology** /freɪzɪˈɒlədʒɪ/ *noun* (*plural* **-ies**) choice or arrangement of words. □ **phraseological** /-zɪəˈlɒdʒ-/ *adjective*.

**phrenology** /frɪˈnɒlədʒɪ/ *noun historical* study of external form of cranium as supposed indication of mental faculties etc. □ **phrenologist** *noun*.

**phut** /fʌt/ *adverb colloquial* □ **go phut** collapse, break down.

**phylactery** /fɪˈlæktərɪ/ *noun* (*plural* **-ies**) small box containing Hebrew texts, worn by Jewish man at prayer.

**phylum** /ˈfaɪləm/ *noun* (*plural* **phyla**) major division of plant or animal kingdom.

**physic** /ˈfɪzɪk/ *noun esp. archaic* medicine; medical art or profession.

**physical** /ˈfɪzɪk(ə)l/ ● *adjective* of the body; of matter; of nature or according

---

### Phrase

A phrase is a group of words that has meaning but does not have a subject, verb, or object (unlike a clause or sentence). It can be:

**1**   a noun phrase, functioning as a noun, e.g.

> I went to see *my friend Tom*.
> *The only ones they have* are too small.

**2**   an adjective phrase, functioning as an adjective, e.g.

> I was *very pleased* indeed.
> *This one* is better than mine.

**3**   an adverb phrase, functioning as an adverb, e.g.

> They drove *off* in their car.
> I was *there* ten days ago.

to its laws; of physics. ● noun US medical examination. □ **physically** adverb.

**physician** /fɪˈzɪʃ(ə)n/ noun doctor, esp. specialist in medical diagnosis and treatment.

**physics** /ˈfɪzɪks/ plural noun (usually treated as singular) science of properties and interaction of matter and energy. □ **physicist** noun.

**physiognomy** /fɪzɪˈɒnəmɪ/ noun (plural -ies) features or type of face; art of judging character from face etc.

**physiology** /fɪzɪˈɒlədʒɪ/ noun science of functioning of living organisms. □ **physiological** /-əˈlɒdʒ-/ adjective; **physiologist** noun.

**physiotherapy** /fɪzɪəʊˈθerəpɪ/ noun treatment of injury or disease by exercise, heat, or other physical agencies. □ **physiotherapist** noun.

**physique** /fɪˈziːk/ noun bodily structure and development.

**pi** /paɪ/ noun sixteenth letter of Greek alphabet (Π, π); (as π) symbol of ratio of circumference of circle to diameter (approx. 3.14).

**pia mater** /paɪə ˈmeɪtə/ noun inner membrane enveloping brain and spinal cord.

**pianissimo** /pɪəˈnɪsɪməʊ/ Music ● adjective very soft. ● adverb very softly. ● noun (plural -s or -mi /-mɪ/) very soft playing, singing, or passage.

**pianist** /ˈpɪənɪst/ noun player of piano.

**piano**¹ /pɪˈænəʊ/ noun (plural -s) keyboard instrument with metal strings struck by hammers. □ **piano-accordion** accordion with small keyboard like that of piano.

**piano**² /ˈpjɑːnəʊ/ Music ● adjective soft. ● adverb softly. ● noun (plural -s or -ni /-nɪ/) soft playing, singing, or passage.

**pianoforte** /pɪænəʊˈfɔːtɪ/ noun formal or archaic = PIANO¹.

**piazza** /pɪˈætsə/ noun public square or market-place.

**pibroch** /ˈpiːbrɒk/ noun martial or funeral bagpipe music.

**picador** /ˈpɪkədɔː/ noun mounted man with lance in bullfight.

**picaresque** /pɪkəˈresk/ adjective (of style of fiction) dealing with episodic adventures of rogues.

**piccalilli** /ˈpɪkəˌlɪlɪ/ noun (plural -s) pickle of chopped vegetables, mustard, and spices.

**piccolo** /ˈpɪkələʊ/ noun (plural -s) small high-pitched flute.

**pick** ● verb select carefully; pluck, gather (flower, fruit, etc.); probe with fingers or instrument to remove unwanted matter; clear (bone etc.) of scraps of meat etc.; eat (food, meal, etc.) in small bits. ● noun picking, selection; (usually + of) best; pickaxe; colloquial plectrum; instrument for picking. □ **pick a lock** open lock with instrument other than proper key, esp. with criminal intent; **pick on** nag at, find fault with, select; **pickpocket** person who steals from pockets; **pick up** take hold of and lift, acquire casually, learn routinely, stop for and take with one, make acquaintance of casually, recover, improve, arrest, detect, manage to receive (broadcast signal etc.), accept responsibility of paying (bill etc.), resume; **pick-up** person met casually, small open truck, part of record player carrying stylus, device on electric guitar etc. that converts string vibrations into electrical signals, act of picking up; **pick-your-own** (of fruit and vegetables) dug or picked by customer at farm etc.

**pickaxe** /ˈpɪkæks/ noun (US **pickax**) tool with sharp-pointed iron cross-bar for breaking up ground etc.

**picket** /ˈpɪkɪt/ ● noun one or more people stationed to dissuade workers from entering workplace during strike etc.; pointed stake driven into ground; small group of troops sent to watch for enemy. ● verb (-t-) place or act as picket outside; post as military picket; secure with stakes. □ **picket line** boundary established by workers on strike, esp. at workplace entrance, which others are asked not to cross.

**pickings** plural noun perquisites, gleanings.

**pickle** /ˈpɪk(ə)l/ ● noun (often in plural) vegetables etc. preserved in vinegar etc.; liquid used for this; colloquial plight. ● verb (-ling) preserve in or treat with pickle; (as **pickled** adjective) slang drunk.

**picky** adjective (-ier, -iest) colloquial highly fastidious.

**picnic** /ˈpɪknɪk/ ● noun outing including outdoor meal; such meal; something pleasantly or easily accomplished. ● verb (**-ck-**) eat meal outdoors.

**pictograph** /ˈpɪktəgrɑːf/ noun (also **pictogram** /-græm/) pictorial symbol used as form of writing.

**pictorial** /pɪkˈtɔːrɪəl/ adjective of, expressed in, illustrated with a picture or pictures. □ **pictorially** adverb.

**picture** /ˈpɪktʃə/ ● noun painting, drawing, photograph, etc., esp. as work of art; portrait; beautiful object; scene; mental image; cinema film; (**the pictures**) cinema (performance). ● verb (**-ring**) imagine; represent in picture; describe graphically. □ **picture postcard** postcard with picture on one side; **picture window** large window of one pane of glass.

**picturesque** /pɪktʃəˈresk/ adjective striking and pleasant to look at; (of language etc.) strikingly graphic.

**piddle** /ˈpɪd(ə)l/ verb (**-ling**) colloquial urinate; (as **piddling** adjective) colloquial trivial; work or act in trifling way.

**pidgin** /ˈpɪdʒɪn/ noun simplified language, esp. used between speakers of different languages.

**pie** noun dish of meat, fruit, etc., encased in or covered with pastry etc. and baked. □ **pie chart** diagram representing relative quantities as sectors of circle; **pie-eyed** slang drunk.

**piebald** /ˈpaɪbɔːld/ ● adjective having irregular patches of two colours, esp. black and white. ● noun piebald animal.

**piece** /piːs/ ● noun distinct portion forming part of or broken off from larger object; coin; picture, literary or musical composition; example; item; chessman, man at draughts, etc. ● verb (**-cing**) (usually + together) form into a whole; join. □ **of a piece** uniform or consistent; **piece-work** work paid for according to amount done.

**pièce de résistance** /pjes də reɪˈziːstɑːs/ noun (plural **pièces de résistance** same pronunciation) most important or remarkable item.

**piecemeal** ● adverb piece by piece, part at a time. ● adjective gradual; unsystematic.

**pied** /paɪd/ adjective of mixed colours.

**pied-à-terre** /pjeɪdɑːˈteə/ noun (plural **pieds-** same pronunciation) (usually small) flat, house, etc. kept for occasional use. [French]

**pier** /pɪə/ noun structure built out into sea etc. used as promenade and landing-stage or breakwater; support of arch or of span of bridge; pillar; solid part of wall between windows etc. □ **pier-glass** large tall mirror.

**pierce** /pɪəs/ verb (**-cing**) go through or into like spear or needle; make hole in; make (hole etc.).

**pierrot** /ˈpɪərəʊ/ noun (feminine **pierrette** /pɪəˈret/) French white-faced pantomime character with clown's costume; itinerant entertainer so dressed.

**pietà** /pɪeˈtɑː/ noun representation of Virgin Mary holding dead body of Christ. [Italian]

**pietism** /ˈpaɪətɪz(ə)m/ noun extreme or affected piety.

**piety** /ˈpaɪətɪ/ noun piousness.

**piffle** /ˈpɪf(ə)l/ colloquial ● noun nonsense. ● verb (**-ling**) talk or act feebly.

**pig** ● noun wild or domesticated animal with broad snout and stout bristly body; colloquial greedy, dirty, obstinate, or annoying person; oblong mass of smelted iron or other metal. ● verb (**-gg-**) colloquial eat (food) greedily. □ **pigheaded** obstinate; **pig-iron** crude iron from smelting-furnace; **pig it** colloquial live in disorderly fashion; **pig out** esp. US slang eat greedily; **pigsty** sty for pigs; **pigtail** plait of hair hanging from back or each side of head.

**pigeon** /ˈpɪdʒ(ə)n/ noun bird of dove family. □ **pigeon-hole** noun each of set of compartments in cabinet etc. for papers etc., verb classify mentally, put in pigeon-hole, put aside for future consideration; **pigeon-toed** having toes turned inwards.

**piggery** noun (plural **-ies**) pig farm; pigsty.

**piggish** adjective greedy; dirty; mean.

**piggy** ● noun (plural **-ies**) colloquial little pig. ● adjective (**-ier**, **-iest**) like a pig; (of features etc.) like those of a pig. □ **piggyback** (a ride) on shoulders and back of another person; **piggy bank** pig-shaped money box.

**piglet** /ˈpɪglɪt/ noun young pig.

**pigment** /'pɪgmənt/ ● noun coloured substance used as paint etc., or occurring naturally in plant or animal tissue. ● verb colour (as) with natural pigment. □ **pigmentation** noun.

**pigmy** = PYGMY.

**pike** noun (plural same or -s) large voracious freshwater fish; spear formerly used by infantry. □ **pikestaff** wooden shaft of pike (**plain as a pikestaff** quite obvious).

**pilaff** = PILAU.

**pilaster** /pɪ'læstə/ noun rectangular column, esp. one fastened into wall.

**pilau** /pɪ'laʊ/ noun (also **pilaff** /pɪ'lɑːf/) Middle Eastern or Indian dish of rice with meat, spices, etc.

**pilchard** /'pɪltʃəd/ noun small sea fish related to herring.

**pile**[1] ● noun heap of things laid on one another; large imposing building; colloquial large amount, esp. of money; series of plates of dissimilar metals laid alternately for producing electric current; nuclear reactor; pyre. ● verb (-ling) heap; (+ with) load with; (+ in, into, on, out of, etc.) crowd. □ **pile up** accumulate, heap up; **pile-up** colloquial collision of several motor vehicles.

**pile**[2] noun heavy beam driven vertically into ground as support for building etc.

**pile**[3] noun soft projecting surface of velvet, carpet, etc.

**piles** plural noun colloquial haemorrhoids.

**pilfer** /'pɪlfə/ verb steal or thieve in petty way.

**pilgrim** /'pɪlgrɪm/ noun person who journeys to sacred place; traveller. □ **Pilgrim Fathers** English Puritans who founded colony in Massachusetts in 1620.

**pilgrimage** noun pilgrim's journey.

**pill** noun ball or flat piece of medicinal substance to be swallowed whole; (usually **the pill**) colloquial contraceptive pill. □ **pillbox** small round shallow box for pills, hat shaped like this, Military small round concrete shelter, mainly underground.

**pillage** /'pɪlɪdʒ/ verb (-ging) & noun plunder.

**pillar** /'pɪlə/ noun slender upright structure used as support or ornament; person regarded as mainstay; upright mass. □ **pillar-box** public postbox shaped like pillar.

**pillion** /'pɪljən/ noun seat for passenger behind motorcyclist etc.

**pillory** /'pɪlərɪ/ ● noun (plural -ies) historical frame with holes for head and hands, allowing an offender to be exposed to public ridicule. ● verb (-ies, -ied) expose to ridicule; historical set in pillory.

**pillow** /'pɪləʊ/ ● noun cushion as support for head, esp. in bed; pillow-shaped support. ● verb rest (as) on pillow. □ **pillowcase**, **pillowslip** washable cover for pillow.

**pilot** /'paɪlət/ ● noun person operating controls of aircraft; person in charge of ships entering or leaving harbour etc.; experimental or preliminary study or undertaking; guide, leader. ● adjective experimental, preliminary. ● verb (-t-) act as pilot to; guide course of. □ **pilot-light** small gas burner kept alight to light another; **pilot officer** lowest commissioned rank in RAF.

**pimento** /pɪ'mentəʊ/ noun (plural -s) allspice; sweet pepper.

**pimiento** /pɪmɪ'entəʊ/ noun (plural -s) sweet pepper.

**pimp** ● noun person who lives off earnings of prostitute or brothel. ● verb act as pimp, esp. procure clients for prostitute.

**pimpernel** /'pɪmpənel/ noun scarlet pimpernel.

**pimple** /'pɪmp(ə)l/ noun small hard inflamed spot on skin. □ **pimply** adjective.

**pin** ● noun small thin pointed piece of metal with head, used as fastening; wooden or metal peg, rivet, etc.; (in plural) colloquial legs. ● verb (-nn-) fasten with pin(s); transfix with pin, lance, etc.; (usually + on) fix (responsibility, blame, etc.); seize and hold fast. □ **pinball** game in which small metal balls are shot across board and strike obstacles; **pincushion** small pad for holding pins; **pin down** (often + to) bind (person etc.) to promise, arrangement, etc., make (person) declare position or intentions; **pin-money** small sum of money, esp. earned by woman; **pinpoint** noun very small or sharp thing, adjective precise, verb locate with precision; **pinprick** petty irritation; **pins and needles** tingling sensation in limb recovering from numbness; **pinstripe** very narrow stripe in cloth; **pin-table** table used in pinball; **pintail** duck or grouse with pointed tail; **pin-tuck** narrow ornamental tuck; **pin-up** picture of attractive or famous person, pinned up on wall etc.; **pinwheel** small Catherine wheel.

**pina colada** /ˈpiːnə kəˈlɑːdə/ noun cocktail of pineapple juice, rum, and coconut.

**pinafore** /ˈpɪnəfɔː/ noun apron, esp. with bib; (in full **pinafore dress**) dress without collar or sleeves, worn over blouse or jumper.

**pince-nez** /ˈpænsneɪ/ noun (plural same) pair of eyeglasses with spring that clips on nose.

**pincers** /ˈpɪnsəz/ plural noun gripping-tool forming pair of jaws; pincer-shaped claw in crustaceans etc. □ **pincer movement** converging movement by two wings of army against enemy position.

**pinch** ● verb grip tightly, esp. between finger and thumb; constrict painfully; (of cold etc.) affect painfully; slang steal, arrest; stint, be niggardly. ● noun pinching; (as **pinched** adjective) (of features) drawn; amount that can be taken up with fingers and thumb; stress of poverty etc. □ **at a pinch** in an emergency.

**pinchbeck** /ˈpɪntʃbek/ ● noun goldlike copper and zinc alloy used in cheap jewellery etc. ● adjective spurious, sham.

**pine**[1] noun evergreen needle-leaved coniferous tree; its wood. □ **pine cone** fruit of pine; **pine nut, kernel** edible seed of some pines.

**pine**[2] verb (**-ning**) (often + away) waste away with grief, disease, etc.; (usually + for) long.

**pineal** /ˈpɪnɪəl/ adjective shaped like pine cone. □ **pineal gland, body** conical gland in brain, secreting hormone-like substance.

**pineapple** /ˈpaɪnæp(ə)l/ noun large juicy tropical fruit with yellow flesh and tough skin.

**ping** ● noun abrupt single ringing sound. ● verb (cause to) emit ping.

**ping-pong** noun colloquial table tennis.

**pinion**[1] /ˈpɪnjən/ ● noun outer part of bird's wing; poetical wing; flight feather. ● verb cut off pinion of (wing or bird) to prevent flight; restrain by binding arms to sides.

**pinion**[2] /ˈpɪnjən/ noun small cogwheel engaging with larger.

**pink**[1] ● noun pale red colour; garden plant with clove-scented flowers; (**the pink**) the most perfect condition. ● adjective pink-coloured; colloquial mildly socialist. □ **in the pink** colloquial in very good health. □ **pinkish** adjective; **pinkness** noun.

**pink**[2] verb pierce slightly; cut scalloped or zigzag edge on. □ **pinking shears** dressmaker's serrated shears for cutting zigzag edge.

**pink**[3] verb (of vehicle engine) emit high-pitched explosive sounds caused by faulty combustion.

**pinnace** /ˈpɪnɪs/ noun ship's small boat.

**pinnacle** /ˈpɪnək(ə)l/ noun culmination, climax; natural peak; small ornamental turret crowning buttress, roof, etc.

**pinnate** /ˈpɪneɪt/ adjective (of compound leaf) with leaflets on each side of leaf-stalk.

**pinny** /ˈpɪnɪ/ noun (plural **-ies**) colloquial pinafore.

**pint** /paɪnt/ noun measure of capacity (1/8 gal., 0.568 litre); colloquial pint of beer. □ **pint-sized** colloquial very small.

**pinta** /ˈpaɪntə/ noun colloquial pint of milk.

**pintle** /ˈpɪnt(ə)l/ noun bolt or pin, esp. one on which some other part turns.

**Pinyin** /pɪnˈjɪn/ noun system of romanized spelling for transliterating Chinese.

**pioneer** /paɪəˈnɪə/ ● noun beginner of enterprise etc.; explorer or settler. ● verb initiate (enterprise etc.) for others to follow; act as pioneer.

**pious** /ˈpaɪəs/ adjective devout, religious; sanctimonious; dutiful. □ **piously** adverb.

**pip**[1] noun seed of apple, pear, orange, etc.

**pip**[2] noun short high-pitched sound.

**pip**[3] verb (**-pp-**) colloquial hit with a shot; (also **pip at** or **to the post**) defeat narrowly.

**pip**⁴ *noun* each spot on dominoes, dice, or playing cards; star on army officer's shoulder.

**pip**⁵ *noun* disease of poultry etc.; (esp. **the pip**) *colloquial* (fit of) depression, boredom, or bad temper.

**pipe** ● *noun* tube of earthenware, metal, etc., esp. for carrying gas, water, etc.; narrow tube with bowl at one end containing tobacco for smoking; quantity of tobacco held by this; wind instrument of single tube; each tube by which sound is produced in organ; (in *plural*) bagpipes; tubular organ etc. in body; high note or song, esp. of bird; boatswain's whistle; measure of capacity for wine (105 gals., 477 litres). ● *verb* (**-ping**) convey (as) through pipes; play on pipe; (esp. as **piped** *adjective*) transmit (recorded music etc.) by wire or cable; utter shrilly; summon, lead, etc. by sound of pipe or whistle; trim with piping; furnish with pipe(s). □ **pipeclay** fine white clay for tobacco pipes or for whitening leather etc.; **pipe-cleaner** piece of flexible tuft-covered wire to clean inside tobacco pipe; **pipe down** *colloquial* be quiet; **pipedream** extravagant fancy, impossible wish, etc.; **pipeline** pipe conveying oil etc. across country, channel of supply or communication; **pipe up** begin to play, sing, etc.

**piper** *noun* person who plays on pipe, esp. bagpipes.

**pipette** /pɪˈpet/ *noun* slender tube for transferring or measuring small quantities of liquid.

**piping** *noun* ornamentation of dress, upholstery, etc. by means of cord enclosed in pipelike fold; ornamental cordlike lines of sugar etc. on cake etc.; length or system of pipes. □ **piping hot** (of food, water, etc.) very or suitably hot.

**pipit** /ˈpɪpɪt/ *noun* small bird resembling lark.

**pippin** /ˈpɪpɪn/ *noun* apple grown from seed; dessert apple.

**piquant** /ˈpiːkənt/ *adjective* agreeably pungent, sharp, appetizing, stimulating. □ **piquancy** *noun.*

**pique** /piːk/ ● *verb* (**piques, piqued, piquing**) wound pride of; stir (curiosity). ● *noun* resentment; hurt pride.

**piquet** /pɪˈket/ *noun* card game for two players.

**piracy** /ˈpaɪrəsɪ/ *noun* (*plural* **-ies**) activity of pirate.

**piranha** /pɪˈrɑːnə/ *noun* voracious S. American freshwater fish.

**pirate** /ˈpaɪərət/ ● *noun* seafaring robber attacking ships; ship used by pirate; person who infringes copyright or regulations or encroaches on rights of others etc. ● *verb* (**-ting**) reproduce (book etc.) or trade (goods) without permission. □ **piratical** /-ˈræt-/ *adjective.*

**pirouette** /pɪrʊˈet/ ● *noun* dancer's spin on one foot or point of toe. ● *verb* (**-tting**) perform pirouette.

**piscatorial** /pɪskəˈtɔːrɪəl/ *adjective* of fishing.

**Pisces** /ˈpaɪsiːz/ *noun* twelfth sign of zodiac.

**piscina** /pɪˈsiːnə/ *noun* (*plural* **-nae** /-niː/ or **-s**) stone basin near altar in church, for draining water after use.

**pistachio** /pɪsˈtɑːʃɪəʊ/ *noun* (*plural* **-s**) kind of nut with green kernel.

**piste** /piːst/ *noun* ski run of compacted snow.

**pistil** /ˈpɪstɪl/ *noun* female organ in flowers. □ **pistillate** *adjective.*

**pistol** /ˈpɪst(ə)l/ *noun* small firearm.

**piston** /ˈpɪst(ə)n/ *noun* sliding cylinder fitting closely in tube and moving up and down in it, used in steam or petrol engine to impart motion; sliding valve in trumpet etc. □ **piston rod** rod connecting piston to other parts of machine.

**pit**¹ ● *noun* large hole in ground; coal mine; covered hole as trap; depression in skin or any surface; orchestra pit; (**the pits**) *slang* worst imaginable place, situation, person, etc.; area to side of track where racing cars are refuelled etc. during race; sunken area in floor of workshop etc. for inspection or repair of underside of vehicle. ● *verb* (**-tt-**) (usually + *against*) set (one's wits, strength, etc.) in competition; (usually as **pitted** *adjective*) make pit(s) in; store in pit. □ **pit bull terrier** small American dog noted for ferocity; **pitfall** unsuspected danger or drawback, covered pit as trap; **pit-head** top of shaft of coal mine, area surrounding this; **pit**

**of the stomach** hollow below base of breastbone.

**pit**² *verb* (**-tt-**) (usually as **pitted** *adjective*) remove stones from (fruit).

**pita** = PITTA.

**pit-a-pat** /ˈpɪtəpæt/ (also **pitter-patter** /ˈpɪtəpætə/) ● *adverb* with sound as of light quick steps; falteringly. ● *noun* such sound.

**pitch**¹ ● *verb* set up (esp. tent, camp, etc.) in chosen position; throw; express in particular style or at particular level; fall heavily; (of ship etc.) plunge in lengthwise direction; set at particular musical pitch. ● *noun* area of play in esp. outdoor game; height, degree, intensity, etc.; gradient, esp. of roof; *Music* degree of highness or lowness of tone; act or process of pitching; *colloquial* salesman's persuasive talk; place, esp. in street or market, where one is stationed; distance between successive points, lines, etc. □ **pitched battle** vigorous argument etc., planned battle between sides in prepared positions; **pitched roof** sloping roof; **pitchfork** *noun* fork with long-handle and two prongs for tossing hay etc., *verb* (+ *into*) thrust forcibly or hastily into office, position, etc.; **pitch in** *colloquial* set to work vigorously; **pitch into** *colloquial* attack vigorously.

**pitch**² ● *noun* dark resinous tarry substance. ● *verb* coat with pitch. □ **pitch-black**, **-dark** intensely dark; **pitch pine** resinous kinds of pine. □ **pitchy** *adjective* (**-ier**, **-iest**).

**pitchblende** /ˈpɪtʃblend/ *noun* uranium oxide yielding radium.

**pitcher**¹ /ˈpɪtʃə/ *noun* large jug, ewer.

**pitcher**² *noun* player who delivers ball in baseball.

**piteous** /ˈpɪtɪəs/ *adjective* deserving or arousing pity. □ **piteously** *adverb*; **piteousness** *noun*.

**pith** *noun* spongy tissue in stems of plants or lining rind of orange etc.; chief part; vigour, energy. □ **pith helmet** sun-helmet made from dried pith of plants.

**pithy** /ˈpɪθɪ/ *adjective* (**-ier**, **-iest**) condensed and forcible, terse. □ **pithily** *adverb*; **pithiness** *noun*.

**pitiable** /ˈpɪtɪəb(ə)l/ *adjective* deserving or arousing pity or contempt. □ **pitiably** *adverb*.

**pitiful** /ˈpɪtɪfʊl/ *adjective* arousing pity; contemptible. □ **pitifully** *adverb*.

**pitiless** /ˈpɪtɪlɪs/ *adjective* showing no pity. □ **pitilessly** *adverb*.

**piton** /ˈpiːtɒn/ *noun* peg driven in to support climber or rope.

**pitta** /ˈpɪtə/ *noun* (also **pita**) originally Turkish unleavened bread which can be split and filled.

**pittance** /ˈpɪt(ə)ns/ *noun* scanty allowance, small amount.

**pitter-patter** = PIT-A-PAT.

**pituitary** /prˈtjuːɪtərɪ/ *noun* (*plural* **-ies**) (in full **pituitary gland**) small ductless gland at base of brain.

**pity** /ˈpɪtɪ/ ● *noun* sorrow for another's suffering; cause for regret. ● *verb* (**-ies**, **-ied**) feel pity for. □ **pitying** *adjective*.

**pivot** /ˈpɪvət/ ● *noun* shaft or pin on which something turns; crucial person or point. ● *verb* (**-t-**) turn (as) on pivot; provide with pivot. □ **pivotal** *adjective*.

**pixie** /ˈpɪksɪ/ *noun* (also **pixy**) (*plural* **-ies**) fairy-like being.

**pizza** /ˈpiːtsə/ *noun* flat piece of dough baked with topping of cheese, tomatoes, etc.

**pizzeria** /piːtsəˈriːə/ *noun* pizza restaurant.

**pizzicato** /pɪtsɪˈkɑːtəʊ/ *Music* ● *adverb* plucking. ● *adjective* performed thus. ● *noun* (*plural* **-s** or **-ti** /-tɪ/) pizzicato note or passage.

**pl.** *abbreviation* plural; place; plate.

**placable** /ˈplækəb(ə)l/ *adjective* easily appeased; mild-tempered. □ **placability** *noun*.

**placard** /ˈplækɑːd/ ● *noun* large notice for public display. ● *verb* post placards on.

**placate** /pləˈkeɪt/ *verb* (**-ting**) conciliate, pacify. □ **placatory** *adjective*.

**place** ● *noun* particular part of space; space or room of or for person etc.; city, town, village, residence, building; rank, station, position; building or spot devoted to specified purpose; office, employment; duties of this. ● *verb* (**-cing**) put or dispose in place; assign rank, order, or class to; give (order for goods etc.) to firm etc.; (in *passive*) be among first 3 (or 4) in race. □ **in place** suitable, in the right position; **in place of** instead of; **out of place** unsuitable, in the wrong position; **place-kick** *Football* kick made with ball placed on ground; **place-mat** small mat on table at person's place; **place setting** set of cutlery etc. for one person to eat with; **take place** happen; **take the place of** be substituted for. □ **placement** noun.

**placebo** /plə'siːbəʊ/ noun ( plural -**s**) medicine with no physiological effect prescribed for psychological reasons; dummy pill etc. used in controlled trial.

**placenta** /plə'sentə/ noun ( plural -**tae** /-tiː/ or -**s**) organ in uterus of pregnant mammal that nourishes foetus. □ **placental** adjective.

**placid** /'plæsɪd/ adjective calm, unruffled; not easily disturbed. □ **placidity** /plə'sɪdɪtɪ/ noun; **placidly** adverb.

**placket** /'plækɪt/ noun opening or slit in garment, for fastenings or access to pocket.

**plagiarize** /'pleɪdʒəraɪz/ verb (also -**ise**) (-**zing** or -**sing**) take and use (another's writings etc.) as one's own. □ **plagiarism** noun; **plagiarist** noun; **plagiarizer** noun.

**plague** /pleɪg/ ●noun deadly contagious disease; (+ *of*) colloquial infestation; great trouble or affliction. ●verb (**pla-guing**) colloquial annoy, bother; afflict, hinder; affect with plague.

**plaice** /pleɪs/ noun ( plural same) marine flatfish.

**plaid** /plæd/ noun chequered or tartan, esp. woollen, cloth; long piece of this as part of Highland costume.

**plain** ●adjective clear, evident; readily understood; simple; not beautiful or distinguished-looking; straightforward in speech; not luxurious; adverb clearly; simply. ●noun level tract of country; ordinary stitch in knitting. □ **plain chocolate** chocolate made without milk; **plain clothes** ordinary clothes as distinct from esp. police uniform; **plain flour** flour with no raising agent; **plain sailing** simple situation or course of action; **plainsong** traditional church music sung in unison in medieval modes and free

rhythm; **plain-spoken** frank. □ **plainly** adverb.

**plaint** noun Law accusation, charge; literary lamentation.

**plaintiff** /'pleɪntɪf/ noun person who brings case against another in law court.

**plaintive** /'pleɪntɪv/ adjective mournful-sounding. □ **plaintively** adverb.

**plait** /plæt/ ●noun length of hair, straw, etc. in 3 or more interlaced strands. ●verb form into plait.

**plan** ●noun method or procedure for doing something; drawing exhibiting relative position and size of parts of building etc.; diagram; map. ●verb (-**nn**-) arrange beforehand; scheme; make plan of; design; (as **planned** adjective) in accordance with plan; make plans. □ **plan on** (often + present participle) colloquial aim at, intend. □ **planning** noun.

**planchette** /plaːn'ʃet/ noun small board on castors, with pencil, said to write messages from spirits when person's fingers rest on it.

**plane**[1] ●noun flat surface (not necessarily horizontal); colloquial aeroplane; level of attainment etc. ●adjective level as or lying in a plane.

**plane**[2] ●noun tool for smoothing surface of wood by paring shavings from it. ●verb (-**ning**) smooth or pare with plane.

**plane**[3] noun tall spreading broad-leaved tree.

**planet** /'plænɪt/ noun heavenly body orbiting star. □ **planetary** adjective.

**planetarium** /plænɪ'teərɪəm/ noun ( plural -**s** or -**ria**) building in which image of night sky as seen at various times and places is projected; device for such projection.

**plangent** /'plændʒ(ə)nt/ adjective literary loudly lamenting; plaintive; reverberating.

**plank** ●noun long flat piece of timber; item of political or other programme. ●verb provide or cover with planks; (usually + *down*) colloquial put down roughly, deposit (esp. money).

**plankton** /'plæŋkt(ə)n/ noun chiefly microscopic organisms drifting in sea or fresh water.

**planner** noun person who plans new town etc.; person who makes plans; list, table, chart, etc. with information helpful in planning.

**plant** /plɑ:nt/ ● noun organism capable of living wholly on inorganic substances and lacking power of locomotion; small plant (other than trees and shrubs); equipment for industrial process; *colloquial* thing deliberately placed for discovery, esp. to incriminate another. ● verb place (seed etc.) in ground to grow; fix firmly, establish; cause (idea etc.) to be established, esp. in another person's mind; deliver (blow etc.); *colloquial* place (something incriminating) for later discovery.

**plantain¹** /'plæntɪn/ noun herb yielding seed used as food for birds.

**plantain²** /'plæntɪn/ noun plant related to banana; banana-like fruit of this.

**plantation** /plɑ:n'teɪʃ(ə)n/ noun estate for cultivation of cotton, tobacco, etc.; number of growing plants, esp. trees, planted together; *historical* colony.

**planter** noun owner or manager of plantation; container for house-plants.

**plaque** /plæk/ noun ornamental tablet of metal, porcelain, etc.; deposit on teeth, where bacteria proliferate.

**plasma** /'plæzmə/ noun (also **plasm** /'plæz(ə)m/) colourless fluid part of blood etc. in which corpuscles etc. float; protoplasm; gas of positive ions and free electrons in about equal numbers. □ **plasmic** adjective.

**plaster** /'plɑ:stə/ noun mixture esp. of lime, sand, and water spread on walls etc.; sticking plaster; plaster of Paris. ● verb cover with or like plaster; apply, stick, etc. like plaster to; (as **plastered** adjective) *slang* drunk. □ **plasterboard** two boards with core of plaster used for walls etc.; **plaster cast** bandage stiffened with plaster of Paris and wrapped round broken limb etc.; **plaster of Paris** fine white gypsum powder for plaster casts etc. □ **plasterer** noun.

**plastic** /'plæstɪk/ ● noun synthetic resinous substance that can be given any shape; (in full **plastic money**) *colloquial* credit card(s). ● adjective made of plastic; capable of being moulded; giving form to clay, wax, etc. □ **plastic arts** those

involving modelling; **plastic explosive** putty-like explosive; **plastic surgery** repair or restoration of lost or damaged etc. tissue. □ **plasticity** /-'tɪs-/ noun; **plasticize** /-saɪz/ verb (also **-ise**) (**-zing** or **-sing**); **plasticky** adjective.

**Plasticine** /'plæstəsi:n/ noun proprietary term pliant substance used for modelling.

**plate** ● noun shallow usually circular vessel from which food is eaten or served; similar vessel used for collection in church etc.; table utensils of gold, silver, or other metal; objects of plated metal; piece of metal with inscription, for fixing to door etc.; illustration on special paper in book; sheet of metal, glass, etc. coated with sensitive film for photography; flat thin sheet of metal etc.; part of denture fitting to mouth and holding teeth; each of several sheets of rock thought to form earth's crust. ● verb (**-ting**) cover (other metal) with thin coating of silver, gold, etc.; cover with plates of metal. □ **plate glass** thick fine-quality glass for mirrors, windows, etc.; **platelayer** workman laying and repairing railway lines. □ **plateful** noun (plural **-s**).

**plateau** /'plætəʊ/ ● noun (plural **-x** or **-s** /-z/) area of level high ground; state of little variation following an increase. ● verb (**plateaus**, **plateaued**, **plateauing**) (often + out) reach level or static state after period of increase.

**platelet** /'pleɪtlɪt/ noun small disc in blood, involved in clotting.

**platen** /'plæt(ə)n/ noun plate in printing press by which paper is pressed against type; corresponding part in typewriter etc.

**platform** /'plætfɔ:m/ noun raised level surface, esp. one from which speaker addresses audience, or one along side of line at railway station; floor area at entrance to bus etc.; thick sole of shoe; declared policy of political party.

**platinum** /'plætɪnəm/ noun white heavy precious metallic element that does not tarnish. □ **platinum blonde** adjective silvery-blond, noun person with such hair.

**platitude** /'plætɪtjuːd/ noun commonplace remark. □ **platitudinous** /-'tjuːd-/ adjective.

**Platonic** /plə'tɒnɪk/ *adjective* of Plato or his philosophy; (**platonic**) (of love or friendship) not sexual.

**platoon** /plə'tu:n/ *noun* subdivision of infantry company.

**platter** /'plætə/ *noun* flat plate or dish.

**platypus** /'plætɪpəs/ *noun* (*plural* **-puses**) Australian aquatic egg-laying mammal with ducklike beak.

**plaudit** /'plɔ:dɪt/ *noun* (usually in *plural*) round of applause; commendation.

**plausible** /'plɔ:zɪb(ə)l/ *adjective* reasonable, probable; (of person) persuasive but deceptive. □ **plausibility** *noun*; **plausibly** *adverb*.

**play** ● *verb* occupy or amuse oneself pleasantly; (+ *with*) act light-heartedly or flippantly with (feelings etc.); perform on (musical instrument), perform (piece of music etc.); cause (record etc.) to produce sounds; perform (drama, role); (+ *on*) perform (trick or joke etc.) on; *colloquial* cooperate, do what is wanted; take part in (game); have as opponent in game; move (piece) in game, put (card) on table, strike (ball), etc.; move about in lively or unrestrained way; (often + *on*) touch gently; pretend to be; allow (fish) to exhaust itself pulling against line. ● *noun* recreation; amusement; playing of game; dramatic piece for stage etc.; freedom of movement; fitful or light movement; gambling. □ **play along** pretend to cooperate; **play back** play (what has been recorded); **play-back** *noun*; **play ball** *colloquial* cooperate; **playbill** poster announcing play etc.; **playboy** pleasure-seeking usually wealthy man; **play by ear** perform (music) without having seen it written down, (also **play it by ear**) *colloquial* proceed gradually according to results; **play one's cards right** *colloquial* make best use of opportunities and advantages; **play down** minimize; **playfellow** playmate; **play the game** behave honourably; **playground** outdoor area for children to play in; **playgroup** group of preschool children who play together under supervision; **playhouse** theatre; **playing card** small usually oblong card used in games, one of set of usually 52 divided into 4 suits; **play it cool** *colloquial* appear relaxed or indifferent; **playmate** child's companion in play; **play-off** extra match played to decide draw or tie; **plaything** toy; **play up** behave mischievously, annoy in this way, cause trouble; **play with fire** take foolish risks; **playwright** dramatist. □ **player** *noun*.

**playful** *adjective* fond of or inclined to play; done in fun. □ **playfully** *adverb*; **playfulness** *noun*.

**plc** *abbreviation* (also **PLC**) Public Limited Company.

**plea** *noun* appeal, entreaty; *Law* formal statement by or on behalf of defendant; excuse.

**pleach** *verb* entwine or interlace (esp. branches to form a hedge).

**plead** *verb* (+ *with*) make earnest appeal to; address court as advocate or party; allege as excuse; (+ *guilty*, *not guilty*) declare oneself to be guilty or not guilty of a charge; make appeal or entreaty.

**pleading** *noun* (usually in *plural*) formal statement of cause of action or defence.

**pleasant** /'plez(ə)nt/ *adjective* (**-er**, **-est**) agreeable; giving pleasure. □ **pleasantly** *adverb*.

**pleasantry** *noun* (*plural* **-ies**) joking remark; polite remark.

**please** /pli:z/ *verb* (**-sing**) be agreeable to; give joy or gratification to; think fit; (in *passive*) be willing, like; *used in polite requests*. □ **pleased** *adjective*; **pleasing** *adjective*.

**pleasurable** /'pleʒərəb(ə)l/ *adjective* causing pleasure. □ **pleasurably** *adverb*.

**pleasure** /'pleʒə/ ● *noun* satisfaction, delight; sensuous enjoyment; source of gratification; will, choice. ● *adjective* done or used for pleasure.

**pleat** ● *noun* flattened fold in cloth etc. ● *verb* make pleat(s) in.

**pleb** *noun* *colloquial* plebeian.

**plebeian** /plɪ'bi:ən/ ● *noun* commoner, esp. in ancient Rome; working-class person (esp. uncultured). ● *adjective* of the common people; uncultured, coarse.

**plebiscite** /'plebɪsaɪt/ *noun* referendum.

**plectrum** /'plektrəm/ *noun* (*plural* **-s** or **-tra**) thin flat piece of plastic etc. for plucking strings of musical instrument.

**pledge** • *noun* solemn promise; thing given as security for payment of debt etc.; thing put in pawn; token; drinking of health. • *verb* (**-ging**) deposit as security, pawn; promise solemnly by pledge; bind by solemn promise; drink to the health of.

**Pleiades** /ˈplaɪədiːz/ *plural noun* cluster of stars in constellation Taurus.

**plenary** /ˈpliːnərɪ/ *adjective* (of assembly) to be attended by all members; entire, unqualified.

**plenipotentiary** /plenɪpəˈtenʃərɪ/ • *noun* (*plural* **-ies**) person (esp. diplomat) having full authority to act. • *adjective* having such power.

**plenitude** /ˈplenɪtjuːd/ *noun literary* fullness; completeness; abundance.

**plenteous** /ˈplentɪəs/ *adjective literary* plentiful.

**plentiful** /ˈplentɪfʊl/ *adjective* existing in ample quantity. □ **plentifully** *adverb*.

**plenty** /ˈplentɪ/ • *noun* abundance; quite enough. • *adjective colloquial* plentiful. • *adverb colloquial* fully.

**plenum** /ˈpliːnəm/ *noun* full assembly of people or a committee etc.

**pleonasm** /ˈpliːənæz(ə)m/ *noun* use of more words than are needed. □ **pleonastic** /-ˈnæstɪk/ *adjective*.

**plesiosaur** /ˈpliːsɪəsɔː/ *noun* large extinct reptile with flippers and long neck.

**plethora** /ˈpleθərə/ *noun* overabundance.

**pleurisy** /ˈplʊərəsɪ/ *noun* inflammation of membrane enclosing lungs. □ **pleuritic** /-ˈrɪt-/ *adjective*.

**plexus** /ˈpleksəs/ *noun* (*plural* same or **plexuses**) network of nerves or blood vessels.

**pliable** /ˈplaɪəb(ə)l/ *adjective* easily bent or influenced; supple; compliant. □ **pliability** *noun*.

**pliant** /ˈplaɪənt/ *adjective* pliable. □ **pliancy** *noun*.

**pliers** /ˈplaɪəz/ *plural noun* pincers with parallel flat surfaces for bending wire etc.

**plight¹** /plaɪt/ *noun* unfortunate condition or state.

**plight²** /plaɪt/ *verb archaic* pledge. □ **plight one's troth** promise to marry.

**plimsoll** /ˈplɪms(ə)l/ *noun* rubber-soled canvas shoe. □ **Plimsoll line**, **mark** marking on ship's side showing limit of legal submersion under various conditions.

**plinth** *noun* base supporting column, vase, statue, etc.

**plod** *verb* (**-dd-**) walk or work laboriously. □ **plodder** *noun*.

**plonk¹** • *verb* set down hurriedly or clumsily; (*usually* + *down*) set down firmly. • *noun* heavy thud.

**plonk²** *noun colloquial* cheap or inferior wine.

**plop** • *noun* sound as of smooth object dropping into water. • *verb* (**-pp-**) (cause to) fall with plop. • *adverb* with a plop.

**plot** • *noun* small piece of land; plan or interrelationship of main events of tale, play, etc.; secret plan, conspiracy. • *verb* (**-tt-**) make chart, diagram, graph, etc. of; hatch secret plans; devise secretly; mark on chart or diagram. □ **plotter** *noun*.

**plough** /plaʊ/ (*US* **plow**) • *noun* implement for furrowing and turning up soil; similar instrument for clearing away snow etc. • *verb* (*often* + *up*, *out*, etc.) turn up or extract with plough; furrow, make (furrow); (+ *through*) advance laboriously or cut or force way through; *colloquial* fail in exam. □ **plough back** reinvest (profits) in business; **ploughman** user of plough; **ploughman's lunch** meal of bread, cheese, pickles, etc.; **ploughshare** blade of plough.

**plover** /ˈplʌvə/ *noun* plump-breasted wading bird.

**plow** *US* = PLOUGH.

**ploy** *noun* manoeuvre to gain advantage.

**pluck** • *verb* pick or pull out or away; strip (bird) of feathers; pull at, twitch; (+ *at*) tug or snatch at; sound (string of musical instrument) with finger or plectrum. • *noun* courage; twitch; animal's heart, liver, and lungs. □ **pluck up** summon up (one's courage etc.).

**plucky** *adjective* (**-ier**, **-iest**) brave, spirited.

**plug** • *noun* something fitting into hole or filling cavity; device of metal pins etc. for making electrical connection; spark plug; *colloquial* piece of free publicity; cake or stick of tobacco. ● *verb* (-gg-) (often + *up*) stop with plug; *slang* shoot; *colloquial* seek to popularize by frequent recommendation. □ **plug away** (often + *at*) *colloquial* work steadily; **plug-hole** hole for plug, esp. in sink or bath; **plug in** *verb* connect electrically by inserting plug into socket; **plug-in** *adjective* designed to be plugged into socket; **pull the plug** *colloquial* flush toilet; (+ *on*) put an end to by withdrawing resources etc.

**plum** *noun* roundish fleshy stone fruit; tree bearing this; reddish-purple colour; raisin; *colloquial* prized thing. □ **plum pudding** Christmas pudding.

**plumage** /ˈpluːmɪdʒ/ *noun* bird's feathers.

**plumb** /plʌm/ ● *noun* lead ball attached to line for testing water's depth or whether wall etc. is vertical. ● *adverb* exactly; vertically; *US slang* quite, utterly. ● *adjective* vertical. ● *verb* provide with plumbing; fit as part of plumbing system; work as plumber; test with plumb; experience (extreme feeling); learn detailed facts about. □ **plumb line** string with plumb attached.

**plumber** *noun* person who fits and repairs apparatus of water supply, heating, etc.

**plumbing** *noun* system or apparatus of water supply etc.; plumber's work.

**plume** /pluːm/ ● *noun* feather, esp. large and showy one; feathery ornament in hat, hair, etc.; feather-like formation, esp. of smoke. ● *verb* (-ming) furnish with plume(s); **(plume oneself on, upon)** pride oneself on.

**plummet** /ˈplʌmɪt/ ● *noun* plumb, plumb line; sounding line. ● *verb* (-t-) fall rapidly.

**plummy** *adjective* (-ier, -iest) *colloquial* (of voice) affectedly rich in tone; *colloquial* good, desirable.

**plump**[1] ● *adjective* having full rounded shape; fleshy. ● *verb* (often + *up*, *out*) make or become plump. □ **plumpness** *noun*.

**plump**[2] ● *verb* (+ *for*) decide on, choose. ● *noun* abrupt or heavy fall. ● *adverb* *colloquial* with plump.

**plunder** /ˈplʌndə/ ● *verb* rob or steal, esp. in war; embezzle. ● *noun* plundering; property plundered.

**plunge** ● *verb* (-ging) (usually + *in, into*) throw forcefully, dive, (cause to) become or enter into impetuously, immerse completely; move suddenly downward; move with a rush; *colloquial* run up gambling debts. ● *noun* plunging, dive; decisive step.

**plunger** *noun* part of mechanism that works with plunging or thrusting motion; rubber cup on handle for removing blockages by plunging action.

**pluperfect** /pluːˈpɜːfɪkt/ *Grammar* ● *adjective* expressing action completed prior to some past point of time. ● *noun* pluperfect tense.

**plural** /ˈplʊər(ə)l/ ● *adjective* more than one in number; denoting more than one. ● *noun* plural word, form, or number.

**pluralism** *noun* form of society in which minority groups retain independent traditions; holding of more than one office at a time. □ **pluralist** *noun*; **pluralistic** /-ˈlɪst-/ *adjective*.

**plurality** /plʊəˈrælɪtɪ/ *noun* (*plural* -ies) state of being plural; pluralism; large number; non-absolute majority (of votes etc.).

**pluralize** *verb* (also -ise) (-zing or -sing) make plural; express as plural.

**plus** ● *preposition* with addition of; (of temperature) above zero; *colloquial* having gained. ● *adjective* (after number) at least, (after grade) better than; *Mathematics* positive; additional, extra. ● *noun* plus sign; advantage. □ **plus sign** symbol (+) indicating addition or positive value.

■ **Usage** The use of *plus* as a conjunction, as in *they arrived late, plus they wanted a meal*, is considered incorrect except in very informal use.

**plush** ● *noun* cloth of silk, cotton, etc., with long soft pile. ● *adjective* made of plush; *colloquial* plushy.

**plushy** *adjective* (-ier, -iest) *colloquial* stylish, luxurious.

**plutocracy** /pluːˈtɒkrəsɪ/ *noun* (*plural* -ies) state in which power belongs to rich; wealthy élite. □ **plutocrat** /'pluːtə-kræt/ *noun*; **plutocratic** /-təˈkræt-/ *adjective*.

**plutonium** /pluːˈtəʊnɪəm/ *noun* radioactive metallic element.

**pluvial** /'pluːvɪəl/ *adjective* of or caused by rain.

**ply**¹ /plaɪ/ *noun* (*plural* **-ies**) thickness, layer; strand.

**ply**² /plaɪ/ *verb* (**-ies, -ied**) wield; work at; (+ *with*) supply continuously or approach repeatedly with; (often + *between*) (of vehicle etc.) go to and fro.

**plywood** *noun* strong thin board made by gluing layers of wood with the direction of the grain alternating.

**PM** *abbreviation* prime minister.

**p.m.** *abbreviation* after noon (*post meridiem*).

**PMS** *abbreviation* premenstrual syndrome.

**PMT** *abbreviation* premenstrual tension.

**pneumatic** /njuːˈmætɪk/ *adjective* filled with air or wind; operated by compressed air.

**pneumonia** /njuːˈməʊnɪə/ *noun* inflammation of lung(s).

**PO** *abbreviation* Post Office; postal order; Petty Officer; Pilot Officer.

**po** *noun* (*plural* **-s**) *colloquial* chamber pot. □ **po-faced** solemn-faced, humourless, smug.

**poach**¹ *verb* cook (egg) without shell in boiling water; cook (fish etc.) by simmering in small amount of liquid. □ **poacher** *noun*.

**poach**² *verb* catch (game or fish) illicitly; (often + *on*) trespass, encroach; appropriate (another's ideas, staff, etc.). □ **poacher** *noun*.

**pock** *noun* (also **pock-mark**) small pus-filled spot, esp. in smallpox. □ **pock-marked** *adjective*.

**pocket** /'pɒkɪt/ ● *noun* small bag sewn into or on garment for carrying small articles; pouchlike compartment in suitcase, car door, etc.; financial resources; isolated group or area; cavity in earth etc. containing ore; pouch at corner or on side of billiard or snooker table into which balls are driven. ● *adjective* small, esp. small enough for carrying in pocket. ● *verb* (**-t-**) put into pocket; appropriate; submit to (affront

etc.); conceal (feelings). □ **in** or **out of pocket** having gained or lost in transaction; **pocketbook** notebook, folding case for papers, paper money, etc.; **pocket knife** small folding knife; **pocket money** money for minor expenses, esp. given to child.

**pod** ● *noun* long seed vessel, esp. of pea or bean. ● *verb* (**-dd-**) form pods; remove (peas etc.) from pods.

**podgy** /'pɒdʒɪ/ *adjective* (**-ier, -iest**) short and fat.

**podium** /'pəʊdɪəm/ *noun* (*plural* **-s** or **-dia**) rostrum.

**poem** /'pəʊɪm/ *noun* metrical composition; elevated composition in verse or prose; something with poetic qualities.

**poesy** /'pəʊəzɪ/ *noun archaic* poetry.

**poet** /'pəʊɪt/ *noun* (*feminine* **poetess**) writer of poems. □ **Poet Laureate** poet appointed to write poems for state occasions.

**poetaster** /pəʊɪˈtæstə/ *noun* inferior poet.

**poetic** /pəʊˈetɪk/ *adjective* (also **poetical**) of or like poetry or poets. □ **poetic justice** well-deserved punishment or reward; **poetic licence** departure from truth etc. for effect. □ **poetically** *adverb*.

**poetry** /'pəʊɪtrɪ/ *noun* poet's art or work; poems; poetic or tenderly pleasing quality.

**pogo** /'pəʊgəʊ/ *noun* (*plural* **-s**) (also **pogo stick**) stiltlike toy with spring, used to jump about on.

**pogrom** /'pɒgrəm/ *noun* organized massacre (originally of Jews in Russia).

**poignant** /'pɔɪnjənt/ *adjective* painfully sharp, deeply moving; arousing sympathy; pleasantly piquant. □ **poignance** *noun*; **poignancy** *noun*; **poignantly** *adverb*.

**poinsettia** /pɔɪnˈsetɪə/ *noun* plant with large scarlet bracts surrounding small yellowish flowers.

**point** ● *noun* sharp end, tip; geometric entity with position but no magnitude; particular place; precise moment; very small mark on surface; decimal point; stage or degree in progress or increase; single item or particular; unit of scoring in games etc., or in evaluation etc.;

significant thing, thing actually intended or under discussion; sense, purpose, advantage; characteristic; each of 32 directions marked on compass; (usually in *plural*) pair of tapering movable rails to direct train from one line to another; power point; *Cricket* (position of) fielder near batsman on off side; promontory. ● *verb* (usually + *to*, *at*) direct (finger, weapon, etc.); direct attention; (+ *at*, *towards*) aim or be directed to; (+ *to*) indicate; give force to (words, action); fill joints of (brickwork) with smoothed mortar or cement; (of dog) indicate presence of game by acting as pointer. □ **at** or **on the point of** on the verge of; **point-blank** at close range, directly, flatly; **point-duty** traffic control by police officer; **point of view** position from which thing is viewed, way of considering a matter; **point out** indicate, draw attention to; **point-to-point** steeplechase for hunting horses; **point up** emphasize.

**pointed** *adjective* having point; (of remark etc.) cutting, emphasized. □ **pointedly** *adverb*.

**pointer** *noun* indicator on gauge etc.; rod for pointing at features on screen etc.; *colloquial* hint; dog of breed trained to stand rigid looking at game.

**pointless** *adjective* purposeless, meaningless; ineffective. □ **pointlessly** *adverb*; **pointlessness** *noun*.

**poise** /pɔɪz/ ● *noun* composure; equilibrium; carriage (of head etc.). ● *verb* (**-sing**) balance, hold suspended or supported; be balanced or suspended.

**poised** *adjective* self-assured; carrying oneself with dignity; (often + *for*) ready.

**poison** /ˈpɔɪz(ə)n/ ● *noun* substance that when absorbed by living organism kills or injures it; *colloquial* harmful influence. ● *verb* administer poison to; kill or injure with poison; treat (weapon) with poison; corrupt, pervert; spoil. □ **poison ivy** N. American climbing plant secreting irritant oil from leaves; **poison-pen letter** malicious anonymous letter. □ **poisoner** *noun*; **poisonous** *adjective*.

**poke** ● *verb* (**-king**) push with (end of) finger, stick, etc.; (+ *out*, *up*, etc.) (be)

thrust forward; (+ *at* etc.) make thrusts; (+ *in*) produce (hole etc.) in by poking; stir (fire). ● *noun* poking; thrust, nudge. □ **poke fun at** ridicule.

**poker**[1] *noun* metal rod for stirring fire.

**poker**[2] /ˈpəʊkə/ *noun* card game in which players bet on value of their hands. □ **poker-face** impassive countenance assumed by poker player.

**poky** /ˈpəʊkɪ/ *adjective* (**-ier**, **-iest**) (of room etc.) small and cramped.

**polar** /ˈpəʊlə/ *adjective* of or near either pole of earth etc.; having magnetic or electric polarity; directly opposite in character. □ **polar bear** large white bear living in Arctic.

**polarity** /pəˈlærɪtɪ/ *noun* (*plural* **-ies**) tendency of magnet etc. to point to earth's magnetic poles or of body to lie with axis in particular direction; possession of two poles having contrary qualities; possession of two opposite tendencies, opinions, etc.; electrical condition of body (positive or negative).

**polarize** /ˈpəʊləraɪz/ *verb* (also **-ise**) (**-zing** or **-sing**) restrict vibrations of (light-waves etc.) to one direction; give polarity to; divide into two opposing groups. □ **polarization** *noun*.

**Polaroid** /ˈpəʊlərɔɪd/ *noun* proprietary term material in thin sheets polarizing light passing through it; camera that produces print immediately after each exposure; (in *plural*) sunglasses with Polaroid lenses.

**Pole** *noun* native or national of Poland.

**pole**[1] *noun* long slender rounded piece of wood, metal, etc., esp. as support etc.; *historical* measure of length (5½ yds). □ **pole-vault** jump over high bar with aid of pole held in hands.

**pole**[2] *noun* each of two points in celestial sphere (in full **north**, **south pole**) about which stars appear to revolve; each end of axis of earth (in full **North**, **South Pole**) or of other body; each of two opposite points on surface of magnet at which magnetic forces are strongest; positive or negative terminal of electric cell, battery, etc.; each of two opposed principles. □ **pole star** star near N. pole of heavens, thing serving as guide.

**poleaxe** /ˈpəʊlæks/ (*US* **-ax**) ● *noun* *historical* battleaxe; butcher's axe. ● *verb*

**(-xing)** hit or kill with poleaxe; (esp. as **poleaxed** *adjective*) *colloquial/*dumbfound, overwhelm.

**polecat** /ˈpəʊlkæt/ *noun* small dark brown mammal of weasel family.

**polemic** /pəˈlemɪk/ *noun* verbal attack; controversy; (in *plural*) art of controversial discussion. ● *adjective* (also **polemical**) involving dispute, controversial. □ **polemicist** /-sɪst/ *noun*.

**police** /pəˈliːs/ ● *noun* (treated as *plural*) civil force responsible for maintaining public order; its members; force with similar functions. ● *verb* **(-cing)** control or provide with police; keep in order, control, administer. □ **police dog** dog used in police work; **police force** body of police of country, district, or town; **policeman**, **policewoman**, **police officer** member of police force; **police state** totalitarian state controlled by political police; **police station** office of local police force.

**policy¹** /ˈpɒlɪsɪ/ *noun* (*plural* **-ies**) course of action adopted by government, business, etc.; prudent conduct.

**policy²** /ˈpɒlɪsɪ/ *noun* (*plural* **-ies**) (document containing) contract of insurance. □ **policyholder** person or body holding insurance policy.

**polio** /ˈpəʊlɪəʊ/ *noun* poliomyelitis.

**poliomyelitis** /ˌpəʊlɪəʊmaɪəˈlaɪtɪs/ *noun* infectious viral disease of grey matter of central nervous system, with temporary or permanent paralysis.

**Polish** /ˈpəʊlɪʃ/ ● *adjective* of Poland. ● *noun* language of Poland.

**polish** /ˈpɒlɪʃ/ ● *verb* (often + *up*) make or become smooth or glossy by rubbing; (esp. as **polished** *adjective*) refine, improve. ● *noun* substance used for polishing; smoothness, glossiness; refinement. □ **polish off** finish quickly.

**polite** /pəˈlaɪt/ *adjective* **(-r, -st)** having good manners, courteous; cultivated, refined. □ **politely** *adverb*; **politeness** *noun*.

**politic** /ˈpɒlɪtɪk/ ● *adjective* judicious, expedient; prudent, sagacious. ● *verb* **(-ck-)** engage in politics.

**political** /pəˈlɪtɪk(ə)l/ *adjective* of state or its government; of public affairs; of, engaged in, or taking a side in politics; relating to pursuit of power, status, etc.

□ **political asylum** state protection for foreign refugee; **political correctness** avoidance of language or action which excludes ethnic or cultural minorities; **political economy** study of economic aspects of government; **political geography** geography dealing with boundaries etc. of states; **political prisoner** person imprisoned for political reasons.

**politically** *adverb* in a political way. □ **politically correct** exhibiting political correctness.

**politician** /pɒlɪˈtɪʃ(ə)n/ *noun* person engaged in politics.

**politicize** /pəˈlɪtɪsaɪz/ *verb* (also **-ise**) **(-zing** or **-sing)** give political character or awareness to.

**politics** /ˈpɒlɪtɪks/ *plural noun* (treated as *singular* or *plural*) art and science of government; political life, affairs, principles, etc.; activities relating to pursuit of power, status, etc.

**polity** /ˈpɒlɪtɪ/ *noun* (*plural* **-ies**) form of civil administration; organized society, state.

**polka** /ˈpɒlkə/ ● *noun* lively dance; music for this. ● *verb* **(-kas, -kaed** /-kəd/ or **-ka'd, -kaing** /-kəŋ/) dance polka. □ **polka dot** round dot as one of many forming regular pattern on textile fabric etc.

**poll** /pəʊl/ ● *noun* (often in *plural*) voting; counting of votes; result of voting, number of votes recorded; questioning of sample of population to estimate trend of public opinion; head. ● *verb* take or receive vote(s) of, vote; record opinion of (person, group); cut off top of (tree etc.) or (esp. as **polled** *adjective*) horns of (cattle). □ **polling booth** cubicle where voter stands to mark ballot paper; **polling station** building used for voting; **poll tax** *historical* tax levied on every adult.

**pollack** /ˈpɒlək/ *noun* (also **pollock**) (*plural* same or **-s**) edible marine fish related to cod.

**pollard** /ˈpɒləd/ ● *noun* hornless animal; tree polled to produce close head of young branches. ● *verb* make pollard of (tree).

**pollen** /ˈpɒlən/ *noun* fertilizing powder discharged from flower's anther.

□ **pollen count** index of amount of pollen in air.

**pollinate** /'pɒlɪneɪt/ verb (**-ting**) sprinkle (stigma of flower) with pollen. □ **pollination** noun.

**pollock** = POLLACK.

**pollster** noun person who organizes opinion poll.

**pollute** /pə'lu:t/ verb (**-ting**) contaminate; make impure. □ **pollutant** noun; **polluter** noun; **pollution** noun.

**polo** /'pəʊləʊ/ noun game like hockey played on horseback. □ **polo-neck** (sweater with) high round turned-over collar.

**polonaise** /pɒlə'neɪz/ noun slow processional dance; music for this.

**poltergeist** /'pɒltəgaɪst/ noun noisy mischievous ghost.

**poltroon** /pɒl'tru:n/ noun coward. □ **poltroonery** noun.

**poly-** combining form many; polymerized.

**polyandry** /'pɒlɪændrɪ/ noun polygamy in which one woman has more than one husband.

**polyanthus** /pɒlɪ'ænθəs/ noun (plural **-thuses**) cultivated primula.

**polychromatic** /pɒlɪkrəʊ'mætɪk/ adjective many-coloured.

**polychrome** /'pɒlɪkrəʊm/ ● adjective in many colours. ● noun polychrome work of art.

**polyester** /pɒlɪ'estə/ noun synthetic fibre or resin.

**polyethylene** /pɒlɪ'eθɪli:n/ noun polythene.

**polygamy** /pə'lɪgəmɪ/ noun practice of having more than one wife or husband at once. □ **polygamist** noun; **polygamous** adjective.

**polyglot** /'pɒlɪglɒt/ ● adjective knowing, using, or written in several languages. ● noun polyglot person.

**polygon** /'pɒlɪgən/ noun figure with many sides and angles. □ **polygonal** /pə'lɪg-/ adjective.

**polyhedron** /pɒlɪ'hi:drən/ noun (plural **-dra**) solid figure with many faces. □ **polyhedral** adjective.

**polymath** /'pɒlɪmæθ/ noun person of great or varied learning.

**polymer** /'pɒlɪmə/ noun compound of molecule(s) formed from repeated units of smaller molecules. □ **polymeric** /-'mer-/ adjective; **polymerization** noun; **polymerize** verb (also **-ise**) (**-zing** or **-sing**).

**polyp** /'pɒlɪp/ noun simple organism with tube-shaped body; small growth on mucous membrane.

**polyphony** /pə'lɪfənɪ/ noun (plural **-ies**) contrapuntal music. □ **polyphonic** /pɒlɪ'fɒnɪk/ adjective.

**polypropylene** /pɒlɪ'prəʊpɪli:n/ noun any of various thermoplastic materials used for films, fibres, or moulding.

**polystyrene** /pɒlɪ'staɪəri:n/ noun kind of hard plastic.

**polysyllabic** /pɒlɪsɪ'læbɪk/ adjective having many syllables; using polysyllables.

**polysyllable** /'pɒlɪsɪləb(ə)l/ noun polysyllabic word.

**polytechnic** /pɒlɪ'teknɪk/ noun college providing courses in esp. vocational subjects up to degree level.

**polytheism** /'pɒlɪθi:ɪz(ə)m/ noun belief in or worship of more than one god. □ **polytheistic** /-'ɪst-/ adjective.

**polythene** /'pɒlɪθi:n/ noun a tough light plastic.

**polyunsaturated** /pɒlɪʌn'sætʃəreɪtɪd/ adjective (of fat) containing several double or triple bonds in each molecule and therefore capable of combining with hydrogen and not associated with accumulation of cholesterol.

**polyurethane** /pɒlɪ'jʊərəθeɪn/ noun synthetic resin or plastic used esp. in paints or foam.

**polyvinyl chloride** /pɒlɪ'vaɪnɪl/ noun see PVC.

**pomade** /pə'mɑ:d/ noun scented ointment for hair.

**pomander** /pə'mændə/ noun ball of mixed aromatic substances; container for this.

**pomegranate** /'pɒmɪgrænɪt/ noun tropical tough-rinded many-seeded fruit; tree bearing this.

**pommel** /'pʌm(ə)l/ noun knob of sword hilt; projecting front of saddle.

**pomp** noun splendid display, splendour; specious glory.

**pom-pom** /'pɒmpɒm/ noun automatic quick-firing gun.

**pompon** /ˈpɒmpɒn/ *noun* (also **pompom**) decorative tuft or ball on hat, shoe, etc.

**pompous** /ˈpɒmpəs/ *adjective* self-important, affectedly grand or solemn. □ **pomposity** /-ˈpɒs-/ *noun* (*plural* **-ies**); **pompously** *adverb*; **pompousness** *noun*.

**ponce** *slang* ● *noun* man who lives off prostitute's earnings. ● *verb* (**-cing**) act as ponce. □ **ponce about** move about effeminately.

**poncho** /ˈpɒntʃəʊ/ *noun* (*plural* **-s**) cloak of rectangular piece of material with slit in middle for head.

**pond** *noun* small body of still water.

**ponder** /ˈpɒndə/ *verb* think over; muse.

**ponderable** /ˈpɒndərəb(ə)l/ *adjective literary* having appreciable weight.

**ponderous** /ˈpɒndərəs/ *adjective* heavy and unwieldy; laborious, dull. □ **ponderously** *adverb*; **ponderousness** *noun*.

**pong** *noun & verb colloquial* stink. □ **pongy** *adjective* (**-ier**, **-iest**).

**poniard** /ˈpɒnjəd/ *noun* dagger.

**pontiff** /ˈpɒntɪf/ *noun* Pope.

**pontifical** /pɒnˈtɪfɪk(ə)l/ *adjective* papal; pompously dogmatic.

**pontificate** ● *verb* /pɒnˈtɪfɪkeɪt/ (**-ting**) be pompously dogmatic. ● *noun* /pɒnˈtɪfɪkət/ office of bishop or Pope; period of this.

**pontoon**[1] /pɒnˈtuːn/ *noun* card game in which players try to acquire cards with face value totalling 21.

**pontoon**[2] /pɒnˈtuːn/ *noun* flat-bottomed boat; boat etc. as one of supports of temporary bridge.

**pony** /ˈpəʊnɪ/ *noun* (*plural* **-ies**) horse of any small breed. □ **pony-tail** hair drawn back, tied, and hanging down behind head; **pony-trekking** travelling across country on ponies for pleasure.

**poodle** /ˈpuːd(ə)l/ *noun* dog of breed with thick curling hair.

**pooh** /puː/ *interjection expressing contempt or disgust.* □ **pooh-pooh** express contempt for, ridicule.

**pool**[1] *noun* small body of still water; small shallow body of any liquid; swimming pool; deep place in river.

**pool**[2] ● *noun* common supply of people, vehicles, etc., for sharing by group; group of people sharing duties etc.; common fund, e.g. of profits or of gamblers' stakes; arrangement between competing parties to fix prices and share business; game like billiards with usually 16 balls; (**the pools**) football pool. ● *verb* put into common fund; share in common.

**poop** *noun* stern of ship; furthest aft and highest deck.

**poor** /pʊə/ *adjective* having little money or means; (+ *in*) deficient in; inadequate; inferior; deserving pity; despicable. □ **poor man's** inferior substitute for.

**poorly** ● *adverb* in poor manner; badly. ● *adjective* unwell.

**pop**[1] ● *noun* abrupt explosive sound; *colloquial* effervescent drink. ● *verb* (**-pp-**) (cause to) make pop; (+ *in, out, up,* etc.) move, come, or put unexpectedly or suddenly; *slang* pawn. ● *adverb* with the sound pop. □ **popcorn** maize kernels burst open when heated; **pop-eyed** *colloquial* with eyes bulging or wide open; **popgun** toy gun shooting pellet etc. by compressed air or spring; **popping crease** *Cricket* line in front of and parallel to wicket; **pop-up** involving parts that pop up automatically.

**pop**[2] *noun colloquial* (in full **pop music**) highly successful commercial music; pop record or song. □ **pop art** art based on modern popular culture and the mass media; **pop culture** commercial culture based on popular taste; **pop group** ensemble playing pop music.

**pop**[3] *noun esp. US colloquial* father.

**popadam** = POPPADAM.

**pope** *noun* (also **Pope**) head of RC Church.

**popinjay** /ˈpɒpɪndʒeɪ/ *noun* fop, conceited person.

**poplar** /ˈpɒplə/ *noun* slender tree with straight trunk and often tremulous leaves.

**poplin** /ˈpɒplɪn/ *noun* closely woven corded fabric.

**poppadam** /ˈpɒpədəm/ *noun* (also **poppadom, popadam**) thin crisp spiced Indian bread.

**popper** *noun colloquial* press-stud; thing that pops.

**poppet** /ˈpɒpɪt/ *noun colloquial* (esp. as term of endearment) small or dainty person.

**poppy** /'pɒpɪ/ *noun* (*plural* **-ies**) plant with bright flowers and milky narcotic juice; artificial poppy worn on Remembrance Sunday. □ **Poppy Day** Remembrance Sunday.

**poppycock** /'pɒpɪkɒk/ *noun slang* nonsense.

**populace** /'pɒpjʊləs/ *noun* the common people.

**popular** /'pɒpjʊlə/ *adjective* generally liked or admired; of, for, or prevalent among the general public. □ **popularity** /-'lærɪtɪ/ *noun*; **popularize** *verb* (also **-ise**) (**-zing** or **-sing**); **popularly** *adverb*.

**populate** /'pɒpjʊleɪt/ *verb* (**-ting**) form population of; supply with inhabitants.

**population** /pɒpjʊ'leɪʃ(ə)n/ *noun* inhabitants of town, country, etc.; total number of these.

**populous** /'pɒpjʊləs/ *adjective* thickly inhabited.

**porcelain** /'pɔːsəlɪn/ *noun* fine translucent ceramic; things made of this.

**porch** *noun* covered entrance to building.

**porcine** /'pɔːsaɪn/ *adjective* of or like pigs.

**porcupine** /'pɔːkjʊpaɪn/ *noun* large rodent with body and tail covered with erectile spines.

**pore**[1] *noun* minute opening in surface through which fluids may pass.

**pore**[2] *verb* (**-ring**) (+ *over*) be absorbed in studying (book etc.).

**pork** *noun* flesh of pig used as food.

**porker** *noun* pig raised for food.

**porn** (also **porno**) *colloquial* ● *noun* pornography. ● *adjective* pornographic.

**pornography** /pɔː'nɒgrəfɪ/ *noun* explicit presentation of sexual activity in literature, films, etc., to stimulate erotic rather than aesthetic feelings. □ **pornographic** /-nə'græf-/ *adjective*.

**porous** /'pɔːrəs/ *adjective* having pores; permeable. □ **porosity** /-'rɒs-/ *noun*.

**porphyry** /'pɔːfɪrɪ/ *noun* (*plural* **-ies**) hard rock with feldspar crystals in fine-grained red mass.

**porpoise** /'pɔːpəs/ *noun* sea mammal of whale family.

**porridge** /'pɒrɪdʒ/ *noun* oatmeal or other cereal boiled in water or milk.

**porringer** /'pɒrɪndʒə/ *noun* small soup-bowl.

**port**[1] *noun* harbour; town possessing harbour.

**port**[2] *noun* strong sweet fortified wine.

**port**[3] ● *noun* left-hand side of ship or aircraft looking forward. ● *verb* turn (helm) to port.

**port**[4] *noun* opening in ship's side for entrance, loading, etc.; porthole. □ **porthole** (esp. glazed) aperture in ship's side to admit light.

**portable** /'pɔːtəb(ə)l/ *adjective* easily movable, convenient for carrying; adaptable in altered circumstances. □ **portability** *noun*.

**portage** /'pɔːtɪdʒ/ *noun* carrying of boats or goods between two navigable waters.

**Portakabin** /'pɔːtəkæbɪn/ *noun proprietary term* prefabricated small building.

**portal** /'pɔːt(ə)l/ *noun* doorway, gate.

**portcullis** /pɔːt'kʌlɪs/ *noun* strong heavy grating lowered in defence of fortress gateway.

**portend** /pɔː'tend/ *verb* foreshadow as an omen; give warning of.

**portent** /'pɔːtent/ *noun* omen, significant sign; marvellous thing.

**portentous** /pɔː'tentəs/ *adjective* like or being portent; pompously solemn.

**porter**[1] /'pɔːtə/ *noun* person employed to carry luggage etc.; dark beer brewed from charred or browned malt. □ **porterhouse steak** choice cut of beef.

**porter**[2] /'pɔːtə/ *noun* gatekeeper or doorkeeper, esp. of large building.

**porterage** *noun* (charge for) hire of porters.

**portfolio** /pɔːt'fəʊlɪəʊ/ *noun* (*plural* **-s**) folder for loose sheets of paper, drawings, etc.; samples of artist's work; list of investments held by investor etc.; office of government minister. □ **Minister without Portfolio** government minister not in charge of department.

**portico** /'pɔːtɪkəʊ/ *noun* (*plural* **-es** or **-s**) colonnade; roof supported by columns, usually serving as porch to building.

**portion** /'pɔːʃ(ə)n/ ● *noun* part, share; helping; destiny or lot. ● *verb* divide into portions; (+ *out*) distribute.

**Portland** /'pɔːtlənd/ *noun* □ **Portland cement** cement manufactured from chalk and clay; **Portland stone** a valuable building limestone.

**portly** /'pɔːtlɪ/ *adjective* (**-ier**, **-iest**) corpulent.

**portmanteau** /pɔːt'mæntəʊ/ *noun* (*plural* **-s** or **-x** /-z/) case for clothes etc., opening into two equal parts. □ **portmanteau word** word combining sounds and meanings of two others.

**portrait** /'pɔːtrɪt/ *noun* drawing, painting, photograph, etc. of person or animal; description.

**portraiture** /'pɔːtrɪtʃə/ *noun* portraying; description; portrait.

**portray** /pɔː'treɪ/ *verb* make likeness of; describe. □ **portrayal** *noun*.

**Portuguese** /pɔːtʃʊ'giːz/ ● *noun* (*plural* same) native, national, or language of Portugal. ● *adjective* of Portugal.

**pose** /pəʊz/ ● *verb* (**-sing**) assume attitude, esp. for artistic purpose; (+ *as*) pretend to be; behave affectedly for effect; propound (question, problem); arrange in required attitude. ● *noun* attitude of body or mind; affectation, pretence.

**poser** *noun* poseur; *colloquial* puzzling question or problem.

**poseur** /pəʊ'zɜː/ *noun* person who behaves affectedly.

**posh** *colloquial* ● *adjective* smart; upperclass. ● *adverb* in an upper-class way. □ **poshly** *adverb*; **poshness** *noun*.

**posit** /'pɒzɪt/ *verb* (**-t-**) assume as fact, postulate.

**position** /pə'zɪʃ(ə)n/ ● *noun* place occupied by person or thing; way thing is placed; proper place; advantage; mental attitude; situation; rank, status; paid employment; strategic location. ● *verb* place in position. □ **in a position to** able to. □ **positional** *adjective*.

**positive** /'pɒzɪtɪv/ ● *adjective* explicit, definite, unquestionable; convinced, confident, cocksure; absolute, not relative; *Grammar* (of adjective or adverb) expressing simple quality without comparison; constructive; marked by presence and not absence of qualities; favourable; dealing only with matters of fact, practical; *Mathematics* (of quantity) greater than zero; *Electricity* (of current, or producing kind of charge produced by rubbing glass with silk;

*Photography* showing lights and shades or colours as seen in original image. ● *noun* positive adjective, photograph, quantity, etc. □ **positive discrimination** making distinctions in favour of groups believed to be underprivileged; **positive vetting** inquiry into background etc. of candidate for post involving national security. □ **positively** *adverb*; **positiveness** *noun*.

**positivism** *noun* philosophical system recognizing only facts and observable phenomena. □ **positivist** *noun* & *adjective*.

**positron** /'pɒzɪtrɒn/ *noun* elementary particle with same mass as but opposite charge to electron.

**posse** /'pɒsɪ/ *noun* strong force or company; group of law-enforcers.

**possess** /pə'zes/ *verb* hold as property, own; have; occupy, dominate mind of. □ **possessor** *noun*.

**possession** /pə'zeʃ(ə)n/ *noun* possessing, being possessed; thing possessed; occupancy; (in *plural*) property; control of ball by player.

**possessive** /pə'zesɪv/ ● *adjective* wanting to retain what one possesses; jealous and domineering; *Grammar* indicating possession. ● *noun Grammar* possessive case or word. □ **possessiveness** *noun*.

**possibility** /pɒsɪ'bɪlɪtɪ/ *noun* (*plural* **-ies**) state or fact of being possible; thing that may exist or happen; (usually in *plural*) capability of being used.

**possible** /'pɒsɪb(ə)l/ ● *adjective* capable of existing, happening, being done, etc.; potential. ● *noun* possible candidate, member of team, etc.; highest possible score.

**possibly** *adverb* perhaps; in accordance with possibility.

**possum** /'pɒsəm/ *noun colloquial* opossum. □ **play possum** *colloquial* pretend to be unconscious or unaware.

**post**[1] /pəʊst/ ● *noun* upright of timber or metal as support in building, to mark boundary, carry notices, etc.; pole etc. marking start or finish of race. ● *verb* (often + *up*) display (notice etc.) in prominent place; advertise by poster or list.

**post**[2] /pəʊst/ ● *noun* official conveying of parcels, letters, etc.; single collection or delivery of these; letters etc. dispatched; place where letters etc. are collected. ● *verb* put (letter etc.) into post; (esp. as **posted** *adjective*) (often + *up*) supply with information; enter in ledger. □ **postbox** public box for posting mail; **postcard** card for posting without envelope; **postcode** group of letters and figures in postal address to assist sorting; **post-haste** with great speed; **postman**, **postwoman** person who collects or delivers post; **postmark** official mark on letters to cancel stamp; **postmaster**, **postmistress** official in charge of post office; **post office** room or building for postal business; **Post Office** public department or corporation providing postal services.

**post**[3] /pəʊst/ ● *noun* appointed place of soldier etc. on duty; occupying force; fort; paid employment; trading post. ● *verb* place (soldier etc.) at post; appoint to post or command.

**post-** *prefix* after, behind.

**postage** *noun* charge for sending letter etc. by post. □ **postage stamp** small adhesive label indicating amount of postage paid.

**postal** *adjective* of or by post. □ **postal order** money order issued by Post Office.

**postdate** /pəʊst'deɪt/ *verb* (**-ting**) give later than actual date to; follow in time.

**poster** *noun* placard in public place; large printed picture. □ **poster paint** gummy opaque paint.

**poste restante** /pəʊst re'stɑːt/ *noun* department in post office where letters are kept till called for.

**posterior** /pɒ'stɪərɪə/ ● *adjective* later in time or order; at the back. ● *noun* (in *singular* or *plural*) buttocks.

**posterity** /pɒ'sterɪtɪ/ *noun* later generations; descendants.

**postern** /'pɒst(ə)n/ *noun archaic* back or side entrance.

**postgraduate** /pəʊst'grædjʊət/ ● *noun* person on course of study after taking first degree. ● *adjective* relating to postgraduates.

**posthumous** /'pɒstjʊməs/ *adjective* occurring after death; published after author's death; born after father's death. □ **posthumously** *adverb*.

**postilion** /pɒ'stɪljən/ *noun* (also **postillion**) rider on near horse of team drawing coach etc. without coachman.

**post-impressionism** /pəʊstɪm'preʃənɪz(ə)m/ *noun* art intending to express individual artist's conception of objects represented. □ **post-impressionist** *noun* & *adjective*.

**post-industrial** /pəʊstɪn'dʌstrɪəl/ *adjective* of society or economy no longer reliant on heavy industry.

**post-mortem** /pəʊst'mɔːtəm/ ● *noun* examination of body made after death; *colloquial* discussion after conclusion (of game etc.). ● *adverb* & *adjective* after death.

**postnatal** /pəʊst'neɪt(ə)l/ *adjective* existing or occurring after birth.

**postpone** /pəʊst'pəʊn/ *verb* (**-ning**) cause to take place at later time. □ **postponement** *noun*.

**postscript** /'pəʊstskrɪpt/ *noun* addition at end of letter etc. after signature.

**postulant** /'pɒstjʊlənt/ *noun* candidate, esp. for admission to religious order.

**postulate** ● *verb* /'pɒstjʊleɪt/ (**-ting**) (often + *that*) assume or require to be true, take for granted; claim. ● *noun* /'pɒstjʊlət/ thing postulated; prerequisite.

**posture** /'pɒstʃə/ ● *noun* relative position of parts, esp. of body; bearing; mental attitude; condition or state (of affairs etc.). ● *verb* (**-ring**) assume posture, esp. for effect; pose (person).

**postwar** /pəʊst'wɔː/ *adjective* occurring or existing after a war.

**posy** /'pəʊzɪ/ *noun* (*plural* **-ies**) small bunch of flowers.

**pot**[1] ● *noun* rounded ceramic, metal, or glass vessel; flowerpot, teapot, etc.; contents of pot; chamber pot; total amount bet in game etc.; (usually in *plural*) *colloquial* large sum; *slang* cup etc. as prize. ● *verb* (**-tt-**) plant in pot; (usually as **potted** *adjective*) preserve (food) in sealed pot; pocket (ball) in billiards etc.; abridge, condense; shoot at, hit, or kill (animal). □ **go to pot** *colloquial* be ruined; **pot-belly** protuberant belly; **pot-boiler** work of literature etc. done merely to earn money; **pot-herb** herb grown in kitchen garden; **pothole** deep hole in rock, hole in road surface; **potluck** whatever is available; **pot**

**plant** plant grown in flowerpot; **pot roast** piece of braised meat; **pot-roast** braise; **potsherd** broken piece of ceramic material; **pot-shot** random shot. □ **potful** noun (plural **-s**).

**pot**[2] noun slang marijuana.

**potable** /'pəʊtəb(ə)l/ adjective drinkable.

**potash** /'pɒtæʃ/ noun any of various compounds of potassium.

**potassium** /pə'tæsɪəm/ noun soft silver-white metallic element.

**potation** /pə'teɪʃ(ə)n/ noun a drink; drinking.

**potato** /pə'teɪtəʊ/ noun (plural **-es**) edible plant tuber; plant bearing this. □ **potato crisp** crisp.

**poteen** /pɒ'tʃiːn/ noun Irish illicit distilled spirit.

**potent** /'pəʊt(ə)nt/ adjective powerful, strong; cogent; (of male) able to achieve erection of penis or have sexual intercourse. □ **potency** noun.

**potentate** /'pəʊtənteɪt/ noun monarch, ruler.

**potential** /pə'tenʃ(ə)l/ ● adjective capable of coming into being; latent. ● noun capability for use or development; usable resources; quantity determining energy of mass in gravitational field or of charge in electric field. □ **potentiality** /-ʃɪ'æl-/ noun; **potentially** adverb.

**pother** /'pɒðə/ noun literary din, fuss.

**potion** /'pəʊʃ(ə)n/ noun liquid dose of medicine, poison, etc.

**pot-pourri** /pəʊ'pʊərɪ/ noun (plural **-s**) scented mixture of dried petals and spices; musical or literary medley.

**pottage** /'pɒtɪdʒ/ noun archaic soup, stew.

**potter**[1] /'pɒtə/ verb (US **putter**) (often + about, around) work etc. in aimless or desultory manner; go slowly.

**potter**[2] /'pɒtə/ noun maker of ceramic vessels.

**pottery** /'pɒtərɪ/ noun (plural **-ies**) vessels etc. made of baked clay; potter's work or workshop.

**potty**[1] /'pɒtɪ/ adjective (**-ier**, **-iest**) slang crazy; insignificant. □ **pottiness** noun.

**potty**[2] noun (plural **-ies**) colloquial chamber pot, esp. for child.

**pouch** ● noun small bag, detachable pocket; baggy area of skin under eyes

etc.; baglike receptacle in which marsupials carry undeveloped young, other baglike natural structure. ● verb put or make into pouch; take possession of.

**pouffe** /puːf/ noun firm cushion as low seat or footstool.

**poulterer** /'pəʊltərə/ noun dealer in poultry and game.

**poultice** /'pəʊltɪs/ ● noun soft usually hot dressing applied to sore or inflamed part of body. ● verb (**-cing**) apply poultice to.

**poultry** /'pəʊltrɪ/ noun domestic fowls.

**pounce** ● verb (**-cing**) spring, swoop; (often + on, upon) make sudden attack, seize eagerly. ● noun act of pouncing.

**pound**[1] noun unit of weight equal to 16 oz (454 g); (in full **pound sterling**) monetary unit of UK etc.

**pound**[2] verb crush or beat with repeated strokes; (+ at, on) deliver heavy blows or gunfire to; (+ along etc.) walk, run, etc. heavily.

**pound**[3] noun enclosure where stray animals or officially removed vehicles are kept until claimed.

**poundage** noun commission or fee of so much per pound sterling or weight.

**-pounder** combining form thing or person weighing specified number of pounds; gun firing shell weighing specified number of pounds.

**pour** /pɔː/ verb (usually + down, out, over, etc.) (cause to) flow in stream or shower; dispense (drink); rain heavily; (usually + in, out, etc.) come or go in profusion or in a rush; discharge copiously.

**pout** ● verb push lips forward, esp. as sign of displeasure; (of lips) be pushed forward. ● noun pouting expression.

**pouter** noun kind of pigeon able to inflate crop.

**poverty** /'pɒvətɪ/ noun being poor, want; (often + of, in) scarcity, lack; inferiority, poorness. □ **poverty-stricken** very poor; **poverty trap** situation in which increase of income incurs greater loss of state benefits.

**POW** abbreviation prisoner of war.

**powder** /'paʊdə/ ● noun mass of fine dry particles; medicine or cosmetic in this form; gunpowder. ● *verb* apply powder to; (esp. as **powdered** *adjective*) reduce to powder. □ **powder blue** pale blue; **powder-puff** soft pad for applying cosmetic powder to skin; **powder-room** *euphemistic* women's lavatory. □ **powdery** *adjective*.

**power** /'pauə/ ● *noun* ability to do or act; mental or bodily faculty; influence, authority; ascendancy; authorization; influential person etc.; state with international influence; vigour, energy; *colloquial* large number or amount; capacity for exerting mechanical force; mechanical or electrical energy; electricity supply; particular source or form of energy; product obtained by multiplying a number by itself a specified number of times; magnifying capacity of lens. ● *verb* supply with mechanical or electrical energy; (+ *up, down*) increase or decrease power supplied to (device), switch on or off. □ **power cut** temporary withdrawal or failure of electric power supply; **powerhouse** power station, person or thing of great energy; **power of attorney** authority to act for another in legal and financial matters; **power point** socket for connection of electrical appliance etc. to mains; **power-sharing** coalition government; **power station** building where electric power is generated for distribution.

**powerful** *adjective* having great power or influence. □ **powerfully** *adverb*; **powerfulness** *noun*.

**powerless** *adjective* without power; wholly unable. □ **powerlessness** *noun*.

**powwow** /'pauwau/ ● *noun* meeting for discussion (originally among N. American Indians). ● *verb* hold powwow.

**pox** *noun* virus disease leaving pocks; *colloquial* syphilis.

**pp** *abbreviation* pianissimo.

**pp.** *abbreviation* pages.

**p.p.** *abbreviation* (also **pp**) *per pro*.

**PPS** *abbreviation* Parliamentary Private Secretary; further postscript (*post-postscriptum*).

**PR** *abbreviation* public relations; proportional representation.

**practicable** /'præktɪkəb(ə)l/ *adjective* that can be done or used. □ **practicability** *noun*.

**practical** /'præktɪk(ə)l/ ● *adjective* of or concerned with practice rather than theory; functional; good at making, organizing, or mending things; realistic; that is such in effect, virtual. ● *noun* practical exam. □ **practical joke** trick played on person. □ **practicality** /-'kæl-/ *noun* (*plural* **-ies**).

**practically** *adverb* virtually, almost; in a practical way.

**practice** /'præktɪs/ *noun* habitual action; repeated exercise to improve skill; action as opposed to theory; doctor's or lawyer's professional business etc.; procedure, esp. of specified kind. □ **in practice** when applied, in reality, skilled from recent practice; **out of practice** lacking former skill.

**practise** /'præktɪs/ *verb* (**-sing**; (*US*-**tice**; -**cing**) carry out in action; do repeatedly to improve skill; exercise oneself in or on; (as **practised** *adjective*) expert; engage in (profession, religion, etc.).

**practitioner** /præk'tɪʃənə/ *noun* professional worker, esp. in medicine.

**praesidium** = PRESIDIUM.

**praetorian guard** /priː'tɔːrɪən/ *noun* bodyguard of ancient Roman emperor etc.

**pragmatic** /præg'mætɪk/ *adjective* dealing with matters from a practical point of view. □ **pragmatically** *adverb*.

**pragmatism** /'prægmətɪz(ə)m/ *noun* pragmatic attitude or procedure; *Philosophy* doctrine that evaluates assertions according to their practical consequences. □ **pragmatist** *noun*.

**prairie** /'preərɪ/ *noun* large treeless tract of grassland, esp. in N. America.

**praise** /preɪz/ ● *verb* (**-sing**) express warm approval or admiration of; glorify. ● *noun* praising; commendation. □ **praiseworthy** worthy of praise.

**praline** /'prɑːliːn/ *noun* sweet made of nuts browned in boiling sugar.

**pram** *noun* carriage for baby, pushed by person on foot.

**prance** /prɑːns/ ● *verb* (**-cing**) (of horse) spring from hind legs; walk or behave in an elated or arrogant way. ● *noun* prancing; prancing movement.

**prank** *noun* practical joke.

**prat** *noun* *slang* fool.

**prate** ● *verb* (**-ting**) talk too much; chatter foolishly. ● *noun* idle talk.

**prattle** /'præt(ə)l/ ● *verb* (**-ling**) talk in childish or inconsequential way. ● *noun* prattling talk.

**prawn** *noun* edible shellfish like large shrimp.

**pray** *verb* (often + *for, to do, that*) say prayers; make devout supplication; entreat.

**prayer** /preə/ *noun* request or thanksgiving to God or object of worship; formula used in praying; entreaty. □ **prayer book** book of set prayers; **prayer-mat** small carpet on which Muslims kneel when praying; **prayer-shawl** one worn by male Jews when praying.

**pre-** *prefix* before (in time, place, order, degree, or importance).

**preach** *verb* deliver (sermon); proclaim (the gospel etc.); give moral advice obtrusively; advocate, inculcate. □ **preacher** *noun*.

**preamble** /pri:'æmb(ə)l/ *noun* preliminary statement; introductory part of statute, deed, etc.

**prearrange** /pri:ə'reɪndʒ/ *verb* (**-ging**) arrange beforehand. □ **prearrangement** *noun*.

**prebend** /'prebənd/ *noun* stipend of canon or member of chapter; portion of land etc. from which this is drawn. □ **prebendal** /prɪ'bend(ə)l/ *adjective*.

**prebendary** /'prebəndərɪ/ *noun* (*plural* **-ies**) holder of prebend; honorary canon.

**Precambrian** /pri:'kæmbrɪən/ ● *adjective* of earliest geological era. ● *noun* this era.

**precarious** /prɪ'keərɪəs/ *adjective* uncertain, dependent on chance; perilous. □ **precariously** *adverb*; **precariousness** *noun*.

**precast** /pri:'kɑ:st/ *adjective* (of concrete) cast in required shape before positioning.

**precaution** /prɪ'kɔ:ʃ(ə)n/ *noun* action taken beforehand to avoid risk or ensure good result. □ **precautionary** *adjective*.

**precede** /prɪ'si:d/ *verb* (**-ding**) come or go before in time, order, importance, etc.; (+ *by*) cause to be preceded by.

**precedence** /'presɪd(ə)ns/ *noun* priority; right of preceding others. □ **take precedence** (often + *over, of*) have priority.

**precedent** ● *noun* /'presɪd(ə)nt/ previous case taken as guide or justification etc. ● *adjective* /prɪ'si:d(ə)nt/ preceding.

**precentor** /prɪ'sentə/ *noun* leader of singing or (in synagogue) prayers of congregation.

**precept** /'pri:sept/ *noun* rule for action or conduct.

**preceptor** /prɪ'septə/ *noun* teacher, instructor. □ **preceptorial** /pri:sep'tɔ:rɪəl/ *adjective*.

**precession** /prɪ'seʃ(ə)n/ *noun* slow movement of axis of spinning body around another axis; such change causing equinoxes to occur earlier in each successive sidereal year.

**precinct** /'pri:sɪŋkt/ *noun* enclosed area, esp. around building; district in town, esp. where traffic is excluded; (in *plural*) environs.

**preciosity** /preʃɪ'ɒsɪtɪ/ *noun* affected refinement in art.

**precious** /'preʃəs/ ● *adjective* of great value; much prized; affectedly refined. ● *adverb colloquial* extremely, very.

**precipice** /'presɪpɪs/ *noun* vertical or steep face of rock, cliff, mountain, etc.

**precipitate** ● *verb* /prɪ'sɪpɪteɪt/ (**-ting**) hasten occurrence of; (+ *into*) cause to go into (war etc.) hurriedly or violently; throw down headlong; *Chemistry* cause (substance) to be deposited in solid form from solution; *Physics* condense (vapour) into drops. ● *adjective* /prɪ'sɪpɪtət/ headlong; hasty, rash. ● *noun* /prɪ'sɪpɪtət/ solid matter precipitated; moisture condensed from vapour.

**precipitation** /prɪsɪpɪ'teɪʃ(ə)n/ *noun* precipitating, being precipitated; rash haste; rain, snow, etc., falling to ground.

**precipitous** /prɪ'sɪpɪtəs/ *adjective* of or like precipice; steep.

**précis** /'preɪsi:/ ● *noun* (*plural* same *-si:z*/) summary, abstract. ● *verb* (**-cises** /-si:z/, **-cised** /-si:d/, **-cising** /-si:ɪŋ/) make précis of.

**precise** /prɪ'saɪs/ *adjective* accurately worded; definite, exact; punctilious.

**precisely** /prɪ'saɪslɪ/ *adverb* in a precise way, exactly; quite so.

**precision** /prɪ'sɪʒ(ə)n/ • *noun* accuracy. • *adjective* designed for or produced by precise work.

**preclude** /prɪ'kluːd/ *verb* (**-ding**) (+ *from*) prevent; make impossible.

**precocious** /prɪ'kəʊʃəs/ *adjective* prematurely developed in some respect. □ **precociously** *adverb*; **precociousness** *noun*; **precocity** /-'kɒsɪ-/ *noun*.

**precognition** /priːkɒg'nɪʃ(ə)n/ *noun* (esp supernatural) foreknowledge.

**preconceive** /priːkən'siːv/ *verb* (**-ving**) form (opinion etc.) beforehand.

**preconception** /priːkən'sepʃ(ə)n/ *noun* preconceived idea; prejudice.

**precondition** /priːkən'dɪʃ(ə)n/ *noun* condition that must be fulfilled beforehand.

**precursor** /priː'kɜːsə/ *noun* forerunner; person who precedes in office etc.; harbinger.

**predate** /priː'deɪt/ *verb* (**-ting**) precede in time.

**predator** /'predətə/ *noun* predatory animal; exploiter of others.

**predatory** /'predətərɪ/ *adjective* (of animal) preying naturally on others; plundering or exploiting others.

**predecease** /priːdɪ'siːs/ *verb* (**-sing**) die before (another).

**predecessor** /'priːdɪsesə/ *noun* previous holder of office or position; ancestor; thing to which another has succeeded.

**predestine** /priː'destɪn/ *verb* (**-ning**) determine beforehand; ordain by divine will or as if by fate. □ **predestination** *noun*.

**predetermine** /priːdɪ'tɜːmɪn/ *verb* (**-ning**) decree beforehand; predestine.

**predicament** /prɪ'dɪkəmənt/ *noun* difficult or unpleasant situation.

**predicate** • *verb* /'predɪkeɪt/ (**-ting**) assert (something) about subject or proposition; (+ *on*) base (statement etc.) on. • *noun* /'predɪkət/ *Grammar & Logic* what is said about subject of sentence or proposition. □ **predicable** *adjective*; **predication** *noun*.

**predicative** /prɪ'dɪkətɪv/ *adjective* *Grammar* (of adjective or noun) forming part or all of predicate; that predicates.

**predict** /prɪ'dɪkt/ *verb* forecast; prophesy. □ **predictable** *adjective*; **predictably** *adverb*; **prediction** *noun*.

**predilection** /priːdɪ'lekʃ(ə)n/ *noun* (often + *for*) preference, special liking.

**predispose** /priːdɪs'pəʊz/ *verb* (**-sing**) influence favourably in advance; (+ *to*, *to do*) render liable or inclined beforehand to. □ **predisposition** /-pə'zɪʃ(ə)n/ *noun*.

**predominate** /prɪ'dɒmɪneɪt/ *verb* (**-ting**) (+ *over*) have control over; prevail; preponderate. □ **predominance** *noun*; **predominant** *adjective*; **predominantly** *adverb*.

**pre-eminent** /priː'emɪnənt/ *adjective* excelling others; outstanding. □ **pre-eminence** *noun*; **pre-eminently** *adverb*.

**pre-empt** /priː'empt/ *verb* forestall; obtain by pre-emption.

■ *Usage* **Pre-empt** is sometimes used to mean *prevent*, but this is considered incorrect in standard English.

**pre-emption** /priː'empʃ(ə)n/ *noun* purchase or taking of thing before it is offered to others.

**pre-emptive** /priː'emptɪv/ *adjective* pre-empting; *Military* intended to prevent attack by disabling enemy.

**preen** *verb* (of bird) tidy (feathers, itself) with beak; (of person) smarten or admire (oneself, one's hair, clothes, etc.); (often + *on*) pride (oneself).

**prefab** /'priːfæb/ *noun colloquial* prefabricated building.

**prefabricate** /priː'fæbrɪkeɪt/ *verb* (**-ting**) manufacture sections of (building etc.) prior to assembly on site.

**preface** /'prefəs/ • *noun* introduction to book stating subject, scope, etc.; preliminary part of speech. • *verb* (**-cing**) (often + *with*) introduce or begin (as) with preface; (of event etc.) lead up to (another). □ **prefatory** *adjective*.

**prefect** /'priːfekt/ *noun* chief administrative officer of district in France etc.; senior pupil in school, authorized to maintain discipline.

**prefecture** /'priːfektʃə/ *noun* district under government of prefect; prefect's office or tenure.

**prefer** /prɪ'fɜː/ *verb* (**-rr-**) (often + *to*, *to do*) like better; submit (information, accusation, etc.); promote (person).

**preferable** /ˈprefərəb(ə)l/ *adjective* to be preferred, more desirable. □ **preferably** *adverb*.

**preference** /ˈprefərəns/ *noun* preferring, being preferred; thing preferred; favouring of one person etc. before others; prior right.

**preferential** /prefəˈrenʃ(ə)l/ *adjective* of, giving, or receiving preference. □ **preferentially** *adverb*.

**preferment** /prɪˈfɜːmənt/ *noun formal* promotion to higher office.

**prefigure** /priːˈfɪgə/ *verb* (**-ring**) represent or imagine beforehand.

**prefix** /ˈpriːfɪks/ *noun* part-word added to beginning of word to alter meaning, e.g. *re-* in *retake*, *ex-* in *ex-president*; title before name. ● *verb* (often + *to*) add as introduction; join (word, element) as prefix.

**pregnant** /ˈpregnənt/ *adjective* having child or young developing in womb; significant, suggestive. □ **pregnancy** *noun* (*plural* **-ies**).

**preheat** /priːˈhiːt/ *verb* heat beforehand.

**prehensile** /prɪˈhensaɪl/ *adjective* (of tail, limb, etc.) capable of grasping.

**prehistoric** /priːhɪsˈtɒrɪk/ *adjective* of period before written records. □ **prehistory** /-ˈhɪstərɪ/ *noun*.

**prejudge** /priːˈdʒʌdʒ/ *verb* (**-ging**) form premature judgement on (person etc.).

**prejudice** /ˈpredʒʊdɪs/ ● *noun* preconceived opinion; (+ *against*, *in favour of*) bias; harm (possibly) resulting from action or judgement. ● *verb* (**-cing**) impair validity of; (esp. as **prejudiced** *adjective*) cause (person) to have prejudice. □ **prejudicial** /-ˈdɪʃ-/ *adjective*.

**prelacy** /ˈpreləsɪ/ *noun* (*plural* **-ies**) church government by prelates; (**the prelacy**) prelates collectively; office or rank of prelate.

**prelate** /ˈprelət/ *noun* high ecclesiastical dignitary, e.g. bishop.

**preliminary** /prɪˈlɪmɪnərɪ/ ● *adjective* introductory, preparatory. ● *noun* (*plural* **-ies**) (usually in *plural*) preliminary action or arrangement; preliminary trial or contest.

**prelude** /ˈpreljuːd/ ● *noun* (often + *to*) action, event, etc. serving as introduction; introductory part of poem etc.; *Music* introductory piece of suite, short

piece of similar type. ● *verb* (**-ding**) serve as prelude to; introduce with prelude.

**premarital** /priːˈmærɪt(ə)l/ *adjective* occurring etc. before marriage.

**premature** /ˈpremətʃə/ *adjective* occurring or done before usual or right time; too hasty; (of baby) born 3 or more weeks before expected time. □ **prematurely** *adverb*.

**premed** /priːˈmed/ *noun colloquial* premedication.

**premedication** /priːmedɪˈkeɪʃ(ə)n/ *noun* medication in preparation for operation.

**premeditate** /priːˈmedɪteɪt/ *verb* (**-ting**) think out or plan beforehand. □ **premeditation** *noun*.

**premenstrual** /priːˈmenstrʊəl/ *adjective* of the time immediately before menstruation.

**premier** /ˈpremɪə/ ● *noun* prime minister. ● *adjective* first in importance, order, or time. □ **premiership** *noun*.

**première** /ˈpremɪeə/ ● *noun* first performance or showing of play or film. ● *verb* (**-ring**) give première of.

**premise** /ˈpremɪs/ *noun* premiss; (in *plural*) house or other building with its grounds etc.; (in *plural*) *Law* previously specified houses, lands, or tenements. □ **on the premises** in the house etc. concerned.

**premiss** /ˈpremɪs/ *noun* previous statement from which another is inferred.

**premium** /ˈpriːmɪəm/ ● *noun* amount to be paid for contract of insurance; sum added to interest, wages, etc.; reward, prize. ● *adjective* of best quality and highest price. □ **at a premium** highly valued, above usual or nominal price; **Premium (Savings) Bond** government security not bearing interest but with periodic prize draw.

**premonition** /premǝˈnɪʃ(ə)n/ *noun* forewarning; presentiment. □ **premonitory** /prɪˈmɒnɪtərɪ/ *adjective*.

**prenatal** /priːˈneɪt(ə)l/ *adjective* existing or occurring before birth.

**preoccupy** /priːˈɒkjʊpaɪ/ *verb* (**-ies**, **-ied**) dominate mind of; (as **preoccupied** *adjective*) otherwise engrossed. □ **preoccupation** *noun*.

**preordain** /priːɔːˈdeɪn/ *verb* ordain or determine beforehand.

**prep** *noun colloquial* homework; time when this is done.

**prepack** /priːˈpæk/ *verb* (also **pre-package** /-ˈpækɪdʒ/) pack (goods) before retail.

**preparation** /prepəˈreɪʃ(ə)n/ *noun* preparing, being prepared; (often in *plural*) thing done to make ready; substance specially prepared.

**preparatory** /prɪˈpærətərɪ/ ● *adjective* (often + *to*) serving to prepare; introductory. ● *adverb* (often + *to*) as a preparation. □ **preparatory school** private primary or (*US*) secondary school.

**prepare** /prɪˈpeə/ *verb* (**-ring**) make or get ready; get oneself ready.

**prepay** /priːˈpeɪ/ *verb* (*past & past participle* **prepaid**) pay (charge) beforehand; pay postage on beforehand. □ **prepayment** *noun*.

**preponderate** /prɪˈpɒndəreɪt/ *verb* (**-ting**) (often + *over*) be superior in influence, quantity, or number; predominate. □ **preponderance** *noun*; **preponderant** *adjective*.

**preposition** /prepəˈzɪʃ(ə)n/ *noun* word used before noun or pronoun to indicate its relationship to another word (see panel). □ **prepositional** *adjective*.

**prepossess** /priːpəˈzes/ *verb* (usually in *passive*) take possession of; prejudice, usually favourably; (as **prepossessing** *adjective*) attractive. □ **prepossession** *noun*.

**preposterous** /prɪˈpɒstərəs/ *adjective* utterly absurd; contrary to nature or reason. □ **preposterously** *adverb*.

**prepuce** /ˈpriːpjuːs/ *noun* foreskin.

**Pre-Raphaelite** /priːˈræfəlaɪt/ ● *noun* member of group of 19th-c. Eng. artists. ● *adjective* of Pre-Raphaelites; (**pre-Raphaelite**) (esp. of woman) of type painted by Pre-Raphaelites.

**pre-record** /priːrɪˈkɔːd/ *verb* record in advance.

**prerequisite** /priːˈrekwɪzɪt/ ● *adjective* required as precondition. ● *noun* prerequisite thing.

■ **Usage** *Prerequisite* is sometimes confused with *perquisite* which means 'an extra profit, right, or privilege'.

**prerogative** /prɪˈrɒgətɪv/ *noun* right or privilege exclusive to individual or class.

**Pres.** *abbreviation* President.

**presage** /ˈpresɪdʒ/ ● *noun* omen; presentiment. ● *verb* (**-ging**) portend; indicate (future event etc.); foretell, foresee.

**presbyopia** /prezbɪˈəʊpɪə/ *noun* longsightedness. □ **presbyopic** *adjective*.

**presbyter** /ˈprezbɪtə/ *noun* priest of Episcopal Church; elder of Presbyterian Church.

**Presbyterian** /prezbɪˈtɪərɪən/ ● *adjective* (of Church, esp. Church of Scotland) governed by elders all of equal rank.

---

## Preposition

A preposition is used in front of a noun or pronoun to form a phrase. It often describes the position of something, e.g. *under the chair*, or the time at which something happens, e.g. *in the evening*.

Prepositions in common use are:

| | | | |
|---|---|---|---|
| about | behind | into | through |
| above | beside | like | till |
| across | between | near | to |
| after | by | of | towards |
| against | down | off | under |
| along | during | on | underneath |
| among | except | outside | until |
| around | for | over | up |
| as | from | past | upon |
| at | in | round | with |
| before | inside | since | without |

● *noun* member of Presbyterian Church.
□ **Presbyterianism** *noun.*

**presbytery** /'prezbɪtərɪ/ *noun* (*plural* **-ies**) eastern part of chancel; body of presbyters; RC priest's house.

**prescient** /'presɪənt/ *adjective* having foreknowledge or foresight. □ **prescience** *noun.*

**prescribe** /prɪ'skraɪb/ *verb* (**-bing**) advise use of (medicine etc.); lay down authoritatively.

■ *Usage* *Prescribe* is sometimes confused with *proscribe*, which means 'forbid'.

**prescript** /'priːskrɪpt/ *noun* ordinance, command.

**prescription** /prɪ'skrɪpʃ(ə)n/ *noun* prescribing; doctor's (usually written) instruction for composition and use of medicine; medicine thus prescribed.

**prescriptive** /prɪ'skrɪptɪv/ *adjective* prescribing, laying down rules; arising from custom.

**presence** /'prez(ə)ns/ *noun* being present; place where person is; personal appearance; person or spirit that is present. □ **presence of mind** calmness and quick-wittedness in sudden difficulty etc.

**present**[1] /'prez(ə)nt/ ● *adjective* being in place in question; now existing, occurring, or being dealt with etc.; *Grammar* expressing present action or state. ● *noun* (**the present**) now; present tense. □ **at present** now; **for the present** just now; **present-day** of this time, modern.

**present**[2] /prɪ'zent/ *verb* introduce; exhibit; offer or give (thing) to; (+ *with*) provide (person) with; put (play, film, etc.) before public; reveal; deliver (cheque etc.) for payment etc. □ **present arms** hold rifle etc. in saluting position.

**present**[3] /'prez(ə)nt/ *noun* gift.

**presentable** /prɪ'zentəb(ə)l/ *adjective* of good appearance; fit to be shown. □ **presentability** *noun*; **presentably** *adverb.*

**presentation** /prezən'teɪʃ(ə)n/ *noun* presenting, being presented; thing presented; manner or quality of presenting; demonstration of materials etc., lecture.

**presenter** *noun* person introducing broadcast programme.

**presentiment** /prɪ'zentɪmənt/ *noun* vague expectation, foreboding.

**presently** *adverb* before long; *US & Scottish* at present.

**preservative** /prɪ'zɜːvətɪv/ ● *noun* substance for preserving food etc. ● *adjective* tending to preserve.

**preserve** /prɪ'zɜːv/ ● *verb* (**-ving**) keep safe or free from decay; maintain, retain; treat (food) to prevent decomposition or fermentation; keep (game etc.) undisturbed for private use. ● *noun* (in *singular* or *plural*) preserved fruit, jam; place where game etc. is preserved; sphere of activity regarded by person as his or hers alone. □ **preservation** /prezə'veɪʃ(ə)n/ *noun.*

**preshrunk** /priː'ʃrʌŋk/ *adjective* (of fabric etc.) treated so as to shrink during manufacture and not in use.

**preside** /prɪ'zaɪd/ *verb* (**-ding**) (often + *at*, *over*) be chairperson or president; exercise control or authority.

**presidency** /'prezɪdənsɪ/ *noun* (*plural* **-ies**) office of president; period of this.

**president** /'prezɪd(ə)nt/ *noun* head of republic; head of society or council etc., of certain colleges, or (*US*) of university, company, etc.; person in charge of meeting. □ **presidential** /-'den-/ *adjective.*

**presidium** /prɪ'sɪdɪəm/ *noun* (also **praesidium**) standing committee, esp. in Communist country.

**press**[1] ● *verb* apply steady force to; flatten, shape, smooth (esp. clothes); (+ *out of, from*, etc.) squeeze (juice etc.); embrace, caress firmly; (+ *on, against*, etc.) exert pressure on; be urgent, urge; (+ *for*) demand insistently; (+ *up, round*, etc.) crowd; (+ *on, forward*, etc.) hasten; (+ *on, upon*) force (offer etc.) on; manufacture (gramophone record, car part, etc.) using pressure. ● *noun* pressing; device for compressing, flattening, extracting juice, etc.; machine for printing; (**the press**) newspapers; publicity in newspapers; printing house; publishing company; crowding, crowd; pressure of affairs; large usually shelved cupboard. □ **press agent** person employed to manage advertising and press publicity; **press**

**conference** meeting with journalists; **press gallery** gallery for reporters, esp. in legislative assembly; **press release** statement issued to newspapers etc.; **press-stud** small device fastened by pressing to engage two parts; **press-up** exercise in which prone body is raised by pressing down on hands to straighten arms.

**press²** verb historical force to serve in army or navy; bring into use as makeshift. □ **press-gang** noun historical group of men employed to press men for navy, verb force into service.

**pressing** ● adjective urgent; insistent. ● noun thing made by pressing, e.g. gramophone record; series of these made at one time; act of pressing. □ **pressingly** adverb.

**pressure** /ˈpreʃə/ ● noun exertion of continuous force, force so exerted, amount of this; urgency; affliction, difficulty; constraining or compelling influence. ● verb (-ring) (often + into) apply pressure to, coerce, persuade. □ **pressure-cooker** pan for cooking quickly under high pressure; **pressure group** group formed to influence public policy.

**pressurize** verb (also **-ise**) (**-zing** or **-sing**) (esp. as **pressurized** adjective) maintain normal atmospheric pressure in (aircraft cabin etc.) at high altitude; raise to high pressure; pressure (person).

**prestidigitator** /prestɪˈdɪdʒɪteɪtə/ noun formal conjuror. □ **prestidigitation** noun.

**prestige** /presˈtiːʒ/ ● noun respect or reputation. ● adjective having or conferring prestige. □ **prestigious** /-ˈstɪdʒəs/ adjective.

**presto** /ˈprestəʊ/ Music ● adverb & adjective in quick tempo. ● noun (plural **-s**) presto movement or passage.

**prestressed** /priːˈstrest/ adjective (of concrete) strengthened by stretched wires in it.

**presumably** /prɪˈzjuːməblɪ/ adverb as may reasonably be presumed.

**presume** /prɪˈzjuːm/ verb (**-ming**) (often + that) suppose to be true, take for granted; (often + to do) venture; be presumptuous; (+ on, upon) make unscrupulous use of.

**presumption** /prɪˈzʌmpʃ(ə)n/ noun arrogance, presumptuous behaviour; taking for granted; thing presumed to be true; ground for presuming.

**presumptive** /prɪˈzʌmptɪv/ adjective giving grounds for presumption.

**presumptuous** /prɪˈzʌmptʃʊəs/ adjective unduly confident, arrogant. □ **presumptuously** adverb; **presumptuousness** noun.

**presuppose** /priːsəˈpəʊz/ verb (**-sing**) assume beforehand; imply. □ **presupposition** /-sʌpəˈzɪʃ(ə)n/ noun.

**pre-tax** /priːˈtæks/ adjective (of income) before deduction of taxes.

**pretence** /prɪˈtens/ noun (US **pretense**) pretending, make-believe; pretext; (+ to) (esp. false) claim; ostentation.

**pretend** /prɪˈtend/ ● verb claim or assert falsely; imagine in play; (as **pretended** adjective) falsely claimed to be; (+ to) profess to have. ● adjective colloquial pretended.

**pretender** noun person who claims throne, title, etc.

**pretense** US = PRETENCE.

**pretension** /prɪˈtenʃ(ə)n/ noun (often + to) assertion of claim; pretentiousness.

**pretentious** /prɪˈtenʃəs/ adjective making excessive claim to merit or importance; ostentatious. □ **pretentiously** adverb; **pretentiousness** noun.

**preternatural** /priːtəˈnætʃər(ə)l/ adjective extraordinary; supernatural.

**pretext** /ˈpriːtekst/ noun ostensible reason; excuse.

**pretty** /ˈprɪtɪ/ ● adjective (**-ier**, **-iest**) attractive in delicate way; fine, good; considerable. ● adverb colloquial fairly, moderately. ● verb (**-ies**, **-ied**) (often + up) make pretty. □ **pretty-pretty** colloquial too pretty. □ **prettify** verb (**-ies**, **-ied**); **prettily** adverb; **prettiness** noun.

**pretzel** /ˈprets(ə)l/ noun crisp knotshaped salted biscuit.

**prevail** /prɪˈveɪl/ verb (often + against, over) be victorious; be the more usual or predominant; exist or occur in general use; (+ on, upon) persuade.

**prevalent** /ˈprevələnt/ adjective generally existing or occurring. □ **prevalence** noun.

**prevaricate** /prɪˈværɪkeɪt/ verb (**-ting**) speak or act evasively or misleadingly.

□ **prevarication** *noun*; **prevaricator** *noun*.

■ **Usage** *Prevaricate* is often confused with *procrastinate*, which means 'to defer action'.

**prevent** /prɪ'vent/ *verb* (often + *from doing*) stop, hinder. □ **preventable** *adjective* (also **preventible**); **prevention** *noun*.

■ **Usage** The use of *prevent* without 'from' as in *She prevented me going* is informal. An acceptable further alternative is *She prevented my going*.

**preventative** /prɪ'ventətɪv/ *adjective & noun* preventive.

**preventive** /prɪ'ventɪv/ ● *adjective* serving to prevent, esp. disease. ● *noun* preventive agent, measure, drug, etc.

**preview** /'pri:vju:/ ● *noun* showing of film, play, etc. before it is seen by general public. ● *verb* view or show in advance.

**previous** /'pri:vɪəs/ ● *adjective* (often + *to*) coming before in time or order; *colloquial* hasty, premature. ● *adverb* (+ *to*) before. □ **previously** *adverb*.

**pre-war** /pri:'wɔ:/ *adjective* existing or occurring before a war.

**prey** /preɪ/ ● *noun* animal hunted or killed by another for food; (often + *to*) victim. ● *verb* (+ *on, upon*) seek or take as prey; exert harmful influence.

**price** ● *noun* amount of money for which thing is bought or sold; what must be given, done, etc. to obtain thing; odds. ● *verb* (**-cing**) fix or find price of; estimate value of. □ **at a price** at high cost; **price tag** label on item showing its price.

**priceless** *adjective* invaluable; *colloquial* very amusing or absurd.

**pricey** *adjective* (**pricier, priciest**) *colloquial* expensive.

**prick** ● *verb* pierce slightly, make small hole in; (+ *off, out*) mark with pricks or dots; trouble mentally; tingle. ● *noun* pricking, mark of it; pain caused as by pricking, mental pain. □ **prick out** plant (seedlings etc.) in small holes pricked in earth; **prick up one's ears** (of dog) erect the ears when alert, (of person) become suddenly attentive.

**prickle** /'prɪk(ə)l/ ● *noun* small thorn; hard-pointed spine; prickling sensation. ● *verb* (**-ling**) cause or feel sensation as of prick(s).

**prickly** *adjective* (**-ier, -iest**) having prickles; irritable; tingling. □ **prickly heat** itchy inflammation of skin near sweat glands; **prickly pear** cactus with pear-shaped edible fruit, its fruit. □ **prickliness** *noun*.

**pride** ● *noun* elation or satisfaction at one's achievements, possessions, etc.; object of this; unduly high opinion of oneself; proper sense of one's own worth, position, etc.; group (of lions etc.). ● *verb* (**-ding**) (**pride oneself on, upon**) be proud of. □ **pride of place** most important position; **take (a) pride in** be proud of.

**prie-dieu** /pri:'djɜ:/ *noun* (*plural* **-x** same pronunciation) kneeling-desk for prayer.

**priest** /pri:st/ *noun* ordained minister of some Christian churches (above deacon and below bishop); (*feminine* **priestess**) official minister of non-Christian religion. □ **priesthood** *noun*; **priestly** *adjective*.

**prig** *noun* self-righteous or moralistic person. □ **priggish** *adjective*; **priggishness** *noun*.

**prim** *adjective* (**-mm-**) stiffly formal and precise; prudish. □ **primly** *adverb*; **primness** *noun*.

**prima** /'pri:mə/ *adjective* □ **prima ballerina** chief female dancer in ballet; **prima donna** chief female singer in opera, temperamental person.

**primacy** /'praɪməsɪ/ *noun* (*plural* **-ies**) pre-eminence; office of primate.

**prima facie** /praɪmə 'feɪʃɪ/ ● *adverb* at first sight. ● *adjective* (of evidence) based on first impression.

**primal** /'praɪm(ə)l/ *adjective* primitive, primeval; fundamental.

**primary** /'praɪmərɪ/ ● *adjective* of first importance; fundamental; original. ● *noun* (*plural* **-ies**) primary colour, feather, school, etc.; *US* primary election. □ **primary colour** one not obtained by mixing others; **primary education** education for children under 11; **primary election** *US* election to select candidate(s) for principal election;

**primary feather** large flight feather of bird's wing; **primary school** school for primary education. □ **primarily** /ˈpraɪmərɪlɪ, praɪˈmeərɪlɪ/ adverb.

**primate** /ˈpraɪmeɪt/ noun member of highest order of mammals, including apes, man, etc.; archbishop.

**prime**[1] ● adjective chief, most important; of highest quality; primary, fundamental; (of number etc.) divisible only by itself and unity. ● noun best or most vigorous stage. □ **prime minister** chief minister of government; **prime time** time when television etc. audience is largest.

**prime**[2] verb (**-ming**) prepare (thing) for use; prepare (gun) for firing or (explosive) for detonation; pour liquid into (pump) to start it working; cover (wood, metal, etc.) with primer; equip (person) with information etc.

**primer**[1] noun substance applied to bare wood, metal, etc. before painting.

**primer**[2] noun elementary school-book; introductory book.

**primeval** /praɪˈmiːv(ə)l/ adjective of first age of world; ancient, primitive.

**primitive** /ˈprɪmɪtɪv/ ● adjective at early stage of civilization; crude, simple. ● noun untutored painter with naïve style; picture by such painter. □ **primitively** adverb; **primitiveness** noun.

**primogeniture** /praɪməʊˈdʒenɪtʃə/ noun being first-born; first-born's right to inheritance.

**primordial** /praɪˈmɔːdɪəl/ adjective existing at or from beginning, primeval.

**primrose** /ˈprɪmrəʊz/ noun plant bearing pale yellow spring flower; this flower; pale yellow. □ **primrose path** pursuit of pleasure.

**primula** /ˈprɪmjʊlə/ noun cultivated plant with flowers of various colours.

**Primus** /ˈpraɪməs/ noun proprietary term portable cooking stove burning vaporized oil.

**prince** noun (as title usually **Prince**) male member of royal family other than king; ruler of small state; nobleman of some countries; (often + of) the greatest. □ **Prince Consort** husband of reigning queen who is himself a prince.

**princely** adjective (**-ier**, **-iest**) of or worthy of a prince; sumptuous, splendid.

**princess** /prɪnˈses/ noun (as title usually **Princess** /ˈprɪnses/) prince's wife; female member of royal family other than queen.

**principal** /ˈprɪnsɪp(ə)l/ ● adjective first in importance, chief; leading. ● noun chief person; head of some institutions; principal actor, singer, etc.; capital sum lent or invested; person for whom another is agent etc. □ **principal boy** (usually actress playing) leading male role in pantomime. □ **principally** adverb.

**principality** /prɪnsɪˈpælɪtɪ/ noun (plural **-ies**) state ruled by prince; (**the Principality**) Wales.

**principle** /ˈprɪnsɪp(ə)l/ noun fundamental truth or law as basis of reasoning or action; personal code of conduct; fundamental source or element. □ **in principle** in theory; **on principle** from moral motive.

**principled** adjective based on or having (esp. praiseworthy) principles of behaviour.

**prink** verb (usually **prink oneself**; often + up) smarten, dress up.

**print** ● verb produce by applying inked type, plates, etc. to paper etc.; express or publish in print; (often + on, with) impress, stamp; write in letters that are not joined; produce (photograph) from negative; (usually + out) produce computer output in printed form; mark (fabric) with design. ● noun mark left on surface by pressure; printed lettering, words, or publication (esp. newspaper); engraving; photograph; printed fabric. □ **in print** (of book etc.) available from publisher, in printed form; **out of print** (of book etc.) no longer available from publisher; **printed circuit** electric circuit with thin conducting strips printed on flat sheet; **printing press** machine for printing from type, plates, etc.; **printout** computer output in printed form.

**printer** noun person who prints books etc.; owner of printing business; device that prints esp. computer output.

**prior** /ˈpraɪə/ ● adjective earlier; (often + to) coming before in time, order, or importance. ● *adverb* ( + *to*) before. ● *noun* ( *feminine* **prioress**) superior of religious house; (in abbey) deputy of abbot.

**priority** /praɪˈɒrɪtɪ/ *noun* ( *plural* **-ies**) thing considered more important than others; precedence in time, rank, etc.; right to do something before other people. □ **prioritize** *verb* (also **-ise**) (**-zing** or **-sing**).

**priory** /ˈpraɪərɪ/ *noun* ( *plural* **-ies**) religious house governed by prior or prioress.

**prise** /praɪz/ *verb* (also **prize**) (**-sing** or **-zing**) force open or out by leverage.

**prism** /ˈprɪz(ə)m/ *noun* solid figure whose two ends are equal parallel rectilinear figures, and whose sides are parallelograms; transparent body of this form with refracting surfaces.

**prismatic** /prɪzˈmætɪk/ *adjective* of, like, or using prism; (of colours) distributed (as if) by transparent prism.

**prison** /ˈprɪz(ə)n/ *noun* place of captivity, esp. building to which people are consigned while awaiting trial or for punishment.

**prisoner** /ˈprɪznə/ *noun* person kept in prison; person or thing confined by illness, another's grasp, etc.; (in full **prisoner of war**) person captured in war.

**prissy** /ˈprɪsɪ/ *adjective* (**-ier**, **-iest**) prim, prudish. □ **prissily** *adverb*; **prissiness** *noun*.

**pristine** /ˈprɪstiːn/ *adjective* in original condition, unspoilt; ancient.

**privacy** /ˈprɪvəsɪ/ *noun* (right to) being private; freedom from intrusion or publicity.

**private** /ˈpraɪvət/ ● *adjective* belonging to an individual, personal; confidential, secret; not public; secluded; not holding public office or official position; not supported, managed, or provided by state. ● *noun* private soldier; (in *plural*) *colloquial* genitals. □ **in private** privately; **private detective** detective outside police force; **private enterprise** business(es) not under state control; **private eye** *colloquial* private detective; **private means** unearned income from investments etc.; **private member** MP not holding government office; **private parts** *euphemistic* genitals; **private sol-**

**dier** ordinary soldier, not officer. □ **privately** *adverb*.

**privateer** /praɪvəˈtɪə/ *noun* (commander of) privately owned and government-commissioned warship.

**privation** /praɪˈveɪʃ(ə)n/ *noun* lack of comforts or necessities.

**privatize** /ˈpraɪvətaɪz/ *verb* (also **-ise**) (**-zing** or **-sing**) transfer from state to private ownership. □ **privatization** *noun*.

**privet** /ˈprɪvɪt/ *noun* bushy evergreen shrub used for hedges.

**privilege** /ˈprɪvɪlɪdʒ/ ● *noun* right, advantage, or immunity belonging to person, class, or office; special benefit or honour. ● *verb* (**-ging**) invest with privilege.

**privy** /ˈprɪvɪ/ ● *adjective* ( + *to*) sharing secret of; *archaic* hidden, secret. ● *noun* ( *plural* **-ies**) lavatory. □ **Privy Council** group of advisers appointed by sovereign; **Privy Councillor, Counsellor** member of this; **privy purse** allowance from public revenue for monarch's private expenses; **privy seal** state seal formerly affixed to minor documents.

**prize**[1] ● *noun* reward in competition, lottery, etc.; reward given as symbol of victory or superiority; thing (to be) striven for. ● *adjective* to which prize is awarded; excellent of its kind. ● *verb* (**-zing**) value highly. □ **prizefight** boxing match for money.

**prize**[2] *noun* ship or property captured in naval warfare.

**prize**[3] = PRISE.

**PRO** *abbreviation* Public Record Office; public relations officer.

**pro**[1] *noun* ( *plural* **-s**) *colloquial* professional.

**pro**[2] ● *adjective* in favour. ● *noun* ( *plural* **-s**) reason in favour. ● *preposition* in favour of. □ **pros and cons** reasons for and against.

**proactive** /prəʊˈæktɪv/ *adjective* (of person, policy, etc.) taking the initiative.

**probability** *noun* ( *plural* **-ies**) being probable; likelihood; (most) probable event; extent to which thing is likely to occur, measured by ratio of favourable cases to all cases possible. □ **in all probability** most probably.

**probable** /ˈprɒbəb(ə)l/ ● *adjective* (often + *that*) that may be expected to happen or prove true; likely. ● *noun* probable candidate, member of team, etc. □ **probably** *adverb*.

**probate** /ˈprəʊbeɪt/ *noun* official proving of will; verified copy of will.

**probation** /prəˈbeɪʃ(ə)n/ *noun* system of supervising behaviour of offenders as alternative to prison; testing of character and abilities of esp. new employee. □ **probation officer** official supervising offenders on probation. □ **probationary** *adjective*.

**probationer** *noun* person on probation.

**probe** ● *noun* investigation; device for measuring, testing, etc.; blunt-ended surgical instrument for exploring wound etc.; unmanned exploratory spacecraft. ● *verb* (**-bing**) examine closely; explore with probe.

**probity** /ˈprəʊbɪtɪ/ *noun* uprightness, honesty.

**problem** /ˈprɒbləm/ ● *noun* doubtful or difficult question; thing hard to understand or deal with. ● *adjective* causing problems.

**problematic** /prɒbləˈmætɪk/ *adjective* (also **problematical**) attended by difficulty; doubtful, questionable.

**proboscis** /prəˈbɒsɪs/ *noun* (*plural* **-sces**) long flexible trunk or snout, e.g. of elephant; elongated mouth-parts of some insects.

**procedure** /prəˈsiːdʒə/ *noun* way of conducting business etc. or performing task; set series of actions. □ **procedural** *adjective*.

**proceed** /prəˈsiːd/ *verb* (often + *to*) go forward or on further, make one's way; (often + *with, to do*) continue or resume; adopt course of action; go on to say; (+ *against*) start lawsuit against; (often + *from*) originate.

**proceeding** *noun* action, piece of conduct; (in *plural*) legal action, published report of discussions or conference.

**proceeds** /ˈprəʊsiːdz/ *plural noun* profits from sale etc.

**process**[1] /ˈprəʊses/ ● *noun* course of action or proceeding, esp. series of stages in manufacture etc.; progress or course; natural or involuntary course of change; action at law; summons; writ; *Biology* natural appendage or outgrowth of organism. ● *verb* subject to particular process; (as **processed** *adjective*) (of food) treated, esp. to prevent decay.

**process**[2] /prəˈses/ *verb* walk in procession.

**procession** /prəˈseʃ(ə)n/ *noun* people etc. advancing in orderly succession, esp. at ceremony, demonstration, or festivity.

**processional** ● *adjective* of processions; used, carried, or sung in processions. ● *noun* processional hymn (book).

**processor** /ˈprəʊsesə/ *noun* machine that processes things; central processor; food processor.

**proclaim** /prəˈkleɪm/ *verb* (often + *that*) announce publicly or officially; declare to be. □ **proclamation** /prɒklə-/ *noun*.

**proclivity** /prəˈklɪvɪtɪ/ *noun* (*plural* **-ies**) natural tendency.

**procrastinate** /prəʊˈkræstɪneɪt/ *verb* (**-ting**) defer action. □ **procrastination** *noun*.

■ **Usage** *Procrastinate* is often confused with *prevaricate*, which means 'to speak or act evasively or misleadingly'.

**procreate** /ˈprəʊkrɪeɪt/ *verb* (**-ting**) produce (offspring) naturally. □ **procreation** *noun*; **procreative** /-krɪˈeɪ-/ *adjective*.

**proctor** /ˈprɒktə/ *noun* university disciplinary official. □ **proctorial** /-ˈtɔːrɪəl/ *adjective*.

**procuration** /prɒkjʊˈreɪʃ(ə)n/ *noun* formal procuring; action of attorney.

**procurator** /ˈprɒkjʊreɪtə/ *noun* agent or proxy, esp. with power of attorney. □ **procurator fiscal** (in Scotland) local coroner and public prosecutor.

**procure** /prəˈkjʊə/ *verb* (**-ring**) succeed in getting; bring about; act as procurer. □ **procurement** *noun*.

**procurer** *noun* (*feminine* **procuress**) person who obtains women for prostitution.

**prod** ● *verb* (**-dd-**) poke with finger, stick, etc.; stimulate to action. ● *noun* poke, thrust; stimulus to action.

**prodigal** /ˈprɒdɪg(ə)l/ ● *adjective* wasteful; (+ *of*) lavish of. ● *noun* spendthrift. □ **prodigal son** repentant wastrel. □ **prodigality** /-ˈgæl-/ *noun*.

**prodigious** /prəˈdɪdʒəs/ *adjective* marvellous; enormous; abnormal.

**prodigy** /ˈprɒdɪdʒɪ/ *noun* (*plural* **-ies**) exceptionally gifted person, esp. precocious child; marvellous thing; (+ *of*) wonderful example of.

**produce** ● *verb* /prəˈdjuːs/ (**-cing**) manufacture or prepare; bring forward for inspection etc.; bear, yield, or bring into existence; cause or bring about; *Geometry* extend or continue (line); bring (play etc.) before public. ● *noun* /ˈprɒdjuːs/ what is produced, esp. agricultural products; amount produced; (often + *of*) result.

**producer** *noun* person who produces goods etc.; person who supervises production of play, film, broadcast, etc.

**product** /ˈprɒdʌkt/ *noun* thing or substance produced, esp. by manufacture; result; *Mathematics* quantity obtained by multiplying.

**production** /prəˈdʌkʃ(ə)n/ *noun* producing, being produced; total yield; thing produced, esp. play etc. □ **production line** systematized sequence of operations to produce commodity.

**productive** /prəˈdʌktɪv/ *adjective* producing, esp. abundantly. □ **productively** *adverb*; **productiveness** *noun*.

**productivity** /prɒdʌkˈtɪvɪtɪ/ *noun* capacity to produce; effectiveness of industry, workforce, etc.

**Prof.** *abbreviation* Professor.

**profane** /prəˈfeɪn/ ● *adjective* irreverent, blasphemous; obscene; not sacred. ● *verb* (**-ning**) treat irreverently; violate, pollute. □ **profanation** /prɒfə-/ *noun*.

**profanity** /prəˈfænɪtɪ/ *noun* (*plural* **-ies**) blasphemy; swear-word.

**profess** /prəˈfes/ *verb* claim openly to have; (often + *to do*) pretend, declare; affirm one's faith in or allegiance to.

**professed** *adjective* self-acknowledged; alleged, ostensible. □ **professedly** /-sɪdlɪ/ *adverb*.

**profession** /prəˈfeʃ(ə)n/ *noun* occupation or calling, esp. learned or scientific; people in a profession; declaration, avowal.

**professional** ● *adjective* of, belonging to, or connected with a profession; competent, worthy of professional; engaged in specified activity as paid occupation, or (*derogatory*) fanatically. ● *noun* professional person. □ **professionally** *adverb*.

**professionalism** *noun* qualities of professionals, esp. competence, skill, etc.

**professor** /prəˈfesə/ *noun* highest-ranking academic in university department, *US* university teacher; person who professes a religion etc. □ **professorial** /prɒfɪˈsɔːrɪəl/ *adjective*; **professorship** *noun*.

**proffer** /ˈprɒfə/ *verb* offer.

**proficient** /prəˈfɪʃ(ə)nt/ *adjective* (often + *in*, *at*) adept, expert. □ **proficiency** *noun*; **proficiently** *adverb*.

**profile** /ˈprəʊfaɪl/ ● *noun* side view or outline, esp. of human face; short biographical sketch. ● *verb* (**-ling**) represent by profile. □ **keep a low profile** remain inconspicuous.

**profit** /ˈprɒfɪt/ ● *noun* advantage, benefit; financial gain, excess of returns over outlay. ● *verb* (**-t-**) be beneficial to; obtain financial gain. □ **at a profit** with financial gain; **profit margin** profit after deduction of costs.

**profitable** *adjective* yielding profit; beneficial. □ **profitability** *noun*; **profitably** *adverb*.

**profiteer** /prɒfɪˈtɪə/ ● *verb* make or seek excessive profits, esp. illegally. ● *noun* person who profiteers.

**profiterole** /prəˈfɪtərəʊl/ *noun* small hollow cake of choux pastry with filling.

**profligate** /ˈprɒflɪɡət/ ● *adjective* recklessly extravagant; licentious, dissolute. ● *noun* profligate person. □ **profligacy** *noun*; **profligately** *adverb*.

**pro forma** /prəʊ ˈfɔːmə/ ● *adverb & adjective* for form's sake. ● *noun* (in full **pro forma invoice**) invoice sent in advance of goods supplied.

**profound** /prəˈfaʊnd/ *adjective* (**-er**, **-est**) having or demanding great knowledge, study, or insight; intense, thorough; deep. □ **profoundly** *adverb*; **profoundness** *noun*; **profundity** /-ˈfʌndɪtɪ/ *noun* (*plural* **-ies**).

**profuse** /prəˈfjuːs/ *adjective* (often + *in*, *of*) lavish, extravagant, copious. □ **profusely** *adverb*; **profusion** *noun*.

**progenitor** /prəʊˈdʒenɪtə/ *noun* ancestor; predecessor; original.

**progeny** /ˈprɒdʒɪnɪ/ *noun* offspring, descendants; outcome, issue.

**progesterone** /prəʊˈdʒestərəʊn/ noun a sex hormone that helps to initiate and maintains pregnancy.

**prognosis** /prɒgˈnəʊsɪs/ noun (plural -noses /-siːz/) forecast, esp. of course of disease.

**prognostic** /prɒgˈnɒstɪk/ • noun (often + of) advance indication; prediction. • adjective (often + of) foretelling, predictive.

**prognosticate** /prɒgˈnɒstɪkeɪt/ verb (-ting) (often + that) foretell; betoken. □ **prognostication** noun.

**programme** /ˈprəʊɡræm/ (US **program**) • noun list of events, performers, etc.; radio or television broadcast; plan of events; course or series of studies, lectures, etc.; (usually **program**) series of instructions for computer. • verb (-mm-; US -m-) make programme of; (usually **program**) express (problem) or instruct (computer) by means of program. □ **programmable** adjective; **programmer** noun.

**progress** • noun /ˈprəʊɡres/ forward movement; advance, development, improvement; historical state journey, esp. by royalty. • verb /prəˈɡres/ move forward or onward; advance, develop, improve. □ **in progress** developing, going on.

**progression** /prəˈɡreʃ(ə)n/ noun progressing; succession, series.

**progressive** /prəˈɡresɪv/ • adjective moving forward; proceeding step by step; cumulative; favouring rapid reform; modern, efficient; (of disease etc.) increasing in severity or extent; (of taxation) increasing with the sum taxed. • noun (also **Progressive**) advocate of progressive policy. □ **progressively** adverb.

**prohibit** /prəˈhɪbɪt/ verb (-t-) (often + from) forbid; prevent.

**prohibition** /prəʊhɪˈbɪʃ(ə)n/ noun forbidding, being forbidden; edict or order that forbids; (usually **Prohibition**) legal ban on manufacture and sale of alcohol. □ **prohibitionist** noun.

**prohibitive** /prəˈhɪbɪtɪv/ adjective prohibiting; (of prices, taxes, etc.) extremely high. □ **prohibitively** adverb.

**project** • noun /ˈprɒdʒekt/ plan, scheme; extensive essay, piece of research, etc.

by student(s). • verb /prəˈdʒekt/ protrude, jut out; throw, impel; forecast; plan; cause (light, image, etc.) to fall on surface; cause (voice etc.) to be heard at distance.

**projectile** /prəˈdʒektaɪl/ • noun object to be fired (esp. by rocket) or hurled. • adjective of or serving as projectile; projecting, impelling.

**projection** /prəˈdʒekʃ(ə)n/ noun projecting, being projected; thing that protrudes; presentation of image(s) etc. on surface; forecast, estimate; mental image viewed as objective reality; transfer of feelings to other people etc.; representation of earth etc. on plane surface.

**projectionist** noun person who operates projector.

**projector** /prəˈdʒektə/ noun apparatus for projecting image or film on screen.

**prolactin** /prəʊˈlæktɪn/ noun hormone that stimulates milk production after childbirth.

**prolapse** • noun /ˈprəʊlæps/ (also **prolapsus** /-ˈlæpsəs/) slipping forward or downward of part or organ; prolapsed womb, rectum, etc. • verb /prəˈlæps/ (-sing) undergo prolapse.

**prolate** /ˈprəʊleɪt/ adjective (of spheroid) lengthened along polar diameter.

**prolegomenon** /prəʊlɪˈɡɒmɪnən/ noun (plural -mena) (usually in plural) preface to book etc., esp. discursive or critical.

**proletarian** /prəʊlɪˈteərɪən/ • adjective of proletariat. • noun member of proletariat.

**proletariat** /prəʊlɪˈteərɪət/ noun working class; esp. derogatory lowest class.

**proliferate** /prəˈlɪfəreɪt/ verb (-ting) reproduce; produce (cells etc.) rapidly; increase rapidly, multiply. □ **proliferation** noun.

**prolific** /prəˈlɪfɪk/ adjective producing many offspring or much output; (often + of) abundantly productive; copious.

**prolix** /ˈprəʊlɪks/ adjective lengthy; tedious. □ **prolixity** /-ˈlɪks-/ noun.

**prologue** /ˈprəʊlɒɡ/ noun introduction to poem, play, etc.; (usually + to) introductory event.

**prolong** /prəˈlɒŋ/ verb extend; (as **prolonged** adjective) (tediously) lengthy. □ **prolongation** /prəʊlɒŋˈɡeɪʃ(ə)n/ noun.

**prom** *noun colloquial* promenade; promenade concert.

**promenade** /prɒmə'nɑːd/ ● *noun* paved public walk, esp. at seaside; leisure walk. ● *verb* (**-ding**) make promenade (through); lead about, esp. for display. □ **promenade concert** one at which (part of) audience is not seated; **promenade deck** upper deck on liner.

**promenader** *noun* person who promenades; regular attender at promenade concerts.

**prominent** /'prɒmɪnənt/ *adjective* jutting out; conspicuous; distinguished. □ **prominence** *noun.*

**promiscuous** /prə'mɪskjʊəs/ *adjective* having frequent casual sexual relationships; mixed and indiscriminate; *colloquial* casual. □ **promiscuously** *adverb;* **promiscuity** /prɒmɪs'kjuːɪtɪ/ *noun.*

**promise** /'prɒmɪs/ ● *noun* explicit undertaking to do or not to do something; favourable indications. ● *verb* (**-sing**) (usually + *to, that*) make promise; (often + *to do*) seem likely; *colloquial* assure.

**promising** *adjective* likely to turn out well; hopeful, full of promise. □ **promisingly** *adverb.*

**promissory** /'prɒmɪsərɪ/ *adjective* expressing or implying promise. □ **promissory note** signed document containing promise to pay stated sum.

**promontory** /'prɒməntərɪ/ *noun* (*plural* **-ies**) point of high land jutting out into sea etc.; headland.

**promote** /prə'məʊt/ *verb* (**-ting**) (often + *to*) advance (person) to higher office or position; help forward, encourage; publicize and sell. □ **promotion** *noun;* **promotional** *adjective.*

**promoter** *noun* person who promotes, esp. sporting event, theatrical production, etc., or formation of joint-stock company.

**prompt** ● *adjective* acting, made, or done immediately; ready. ● *adverb* punctually. ● *verb* (usually + *to, to do*) incite; supply (actor, speaker) with next words or with suggestion; inspire. ● *noun* prompting; thing said to prompt actor etc.; sign on computer screen inviting input. □ **promptitude** *noun;* **promptly** *adverb;* **promptness** *noun.*

**prompter** *noun* person who prompts actors.

**promulgate** /'prɒmʌlgeɪt/ *verb* (**-ting**) make known to the public; proclaim. □ **promulgation** *noun.*

**prone** *adjective* lying face downwards; lying flat, prostrate; (usually + *to, to do*) disposed, liable. □ **-prone** likely to suffer. □ **proneness** *noun.*

**prong** *noun* spike of fork.

**pronominal** /prəʊ'nɒmɪn(ə)l/ *adjective* of, concerning, or being a pronoun.

**pronoun** /'prəʊnaʊn/ *noun* word used as substitute for noun or noun phrase usually already mentioned or known (see panel).

**pronounce** /prə'naʊns/ *verb* (**-cing**) utter or speak, esp. in approved manner; utter formally; state (as) one's opinion; (usually + *on, for, against,* etc.) pass judgement. □ **pronounceable** *adjective;* **pronouncement** *noun.*

**pronounced** *adjective* strongly marked.

---

## Pronoun

A pronoun is used as a substitute for a noun or a noun phrase, e.g.

He *was* upstairs.               *Did you see* that?
Anything *can happen now.*        It's *lovely weather.*

Using a pronoun often avoids repetition, e.g.

I *found Jim*—he *was upstairs.*
(instead of I *found Jim*—Jim *was upstairs.*)

*Where are your keys?*—I've *got them.*
(instead of *Where are your keys?*—I've *got my keys.*)

**pronto** /ˈprɒntəʊ/ *adverb colloquial* promptly, quickly.

**pronunciation** /prənʌnsɪˈeɪʃ(ə)n/ *noun* pronouncing of word, esp. with reference to standard; act of pronouncing; way of pronouncing words.

**proof** /pruːf/ ● *noun* fact, evidence, reasoning, or demonstration that proves something; test, trial; standard of strength of distilled alcohol; trial impression of printed matter for correction. ● *adjective* (often + *against*) impervious to penetration, damage, etc. by a specified thing. ● *verb* make proof, esp. against water or bullets. □ **proofread** read and correct (printed proof); **proofreader** person who does this.

**prop**[1] ● *noun* rigid support; person or thing that supports, comforts, etc. ● *verb* (**-pp-**) (often + *against, up*, etc.) support (as) with prop.

**prop**[2] *noun colloquial* stage property.

**prop**[3] *noun colloquial* propeller.

**propaganda** /prɒpəˈgændə/ *noun* organized propagation of a doctrine etc.; *usually derogatory* ideas etc. so propagated. □ **propagandist** *noun.*

**propagate** /ˈprɒpəgeɪt/ *verb* (**-ting**) breed from parent stock; (often **propagate itself**) (of plant etc.) reproduce itself; disseminate; transmit. □ **propagation** *noun*; **propagator** *noun.*

**propane** /ˈprəʊpeɪn/ *noun* gaseous hydrocarbon used as fuel.

**propel** /prəˈpel/ *verb* (**-ll-**) drive or push forward; urge on. □ **propellant** *noun & adjective.*

**propeller** *noun* revolving shaft with blades, esp. for propelling ship or aircraft.

**propensity** /prəˈpensɪtɪ/ *noun* ( *plural* **-ies**) inclination, tendency.

**proper** /ˈprɒpə/ *adjective* accurate, correct; suitable, appropriate; decent, respectable; (usually + *to*) belonging, relating; strictly so called, genuine; *colloquial* thorough. □ **proper name**, *noun* name of person, place, etc. □ **properly** *adverb.*

**property** /ˈprɒpətɪ/ *noun* ( *plural* **-ies**) thing(s) owned; landed estate; quality, characteristic; movable article used on theatre stage or in film.

**prophecy** /ˈprɒfɪsɪ/ *noun* ( *plural* **-ies**) prophetic utterance; prediction; prophesying.

**prophesy** /ˈprɒfɪsaɪ/ *verb* (**-ies, -ied**) (usually + *that, who*, etc.) foretell; speak as prophet.

**prophet** /ˈprɒfɪt/ *noun* ( *feminine* **prophetess**) teacher or interpreter of divine will; person who predicts; (**the Prophet**) Muhammad.

**prophetic** /prəˈfetɪk/ *adjective* (often + *of* ) containing a prediction, predicting; of prophet.

**prophylactic** /prɒfɪˈlæktɪk/ ● *adjective* tending to prevent disease etc. ● *noun* preventive medicine or action; *esp. US* condom.

**prophylaxis** /prɒfɪˈlæksɪs/ *noun* preventive treatment against disease.

**propinquity** /prəˈpɪŋkwɪtɪ/ *noun* nearness; close kinship; similarity.

**propitiate** /prəˈpɪʃɪeɪt/ *verb* (**-ting**) appease. □ **propitiation** *noun*; **propitiatory** /-ʃətərɪ/ *adjective.*

**propitious** /prəˈpɪʃəs/ *adjective* favourable, auspicious; (often + *for, to*) suitable.

**proponent** /prəˈpəʊnənt/ *noun* person advocating proposal etc.

**proportion** /prəˈpɔːʃ(ə)n/ ● *noun* comparative part, share; comparative ratio; correct relation between things or parts of thing; (in *plural*) dimensions. ● *verb* (usually + *to*) make proportionate.

**proportional** *adjective* in correct proportion; comparable. □ **proportional representation** representation of parties in parliament in proportion to votes they receive. □ **proportionally** *adverb.*

**proportionate** /prəˈpɔːʃənət/ *adjective* proportional. □ **proportionately** *adverb.*

**proposal** /prəˈpəʊz(ə)l/ *noun* proposing; scheme etc. proposed; offer of marriage.

**propose** /prəˈpəʊz/ *verb* (**-sing**) put forward for consideration; (usually + *to do*) purpose; (usually + *to*) offer marriage; nominate as member of society etc. □ **propose a toast** ask people to drink to health or in honour of person or thing. □ **proposer** *noun.*

**proposition** /propə'zɪʃ(ə)n/ ● noun statement, assertion; scheme proposed, proposal; statement subject to proof or disproof; colloquial problem, opponent, prospect, etc.; Mathematics formal statement of theorem or problem; likely commercial enterprise, person, etc.; sexual proposal. ● verb colloquial put (esp. sexual) proposal to.

**propound** /prə'paund/ verb offer for consideration.

**proprietary** /prə'praɪətərɪ/ adjective of or holding property; of proprietor; held in private ownership; manufactured by one particular firm. □ **proprietary name, term** name of product etc. registered as trade mark.

**proprietor** /prə'praɪətə/ noun (feminine **proprietress**) owner. □ **proprietorial** /-'tɔːr-/ adjective.

**propriety** /prə'praɪtɪ/ noun (plural **-ies**) fitness, rightness; correctness of behaviour or morals; (in plural) rules of polite behaviour.

**propulsion** /prə'pʌlʃ(ə)n/ noun driving or pushing forward; force causing this. □ **propulsive** /-'pʌlsɪv/ adjective.

**pro rata** /prəu 'rɑːtə/ ● adjective proportional. ● adverb proportionally. [Latin]

**prorogue** /prə'rəug/ verb (**-gues**, **-gued**, **-guing**) discontinue meetings of (parliament etc.) without dissolving it; be prorogued. □ **prorogation** /prəurə-/ noun.

**prosaic** /prə'zeɪɪk/ adjective like prose; unromantic; commonplace. □ **prosaically** adverb.

**proscenium** /prə'siːnɪəm/ noun (plural **-s** or **-nia**) part of theatre stage in front of curtain and enclosing arch.

**proscribe** /prə'skraɪb/ verb (**-bing**) forbid; denounce; outlaw. □ **proscription** /-'skrɪp-/ noun; **proscriptive** /-'skrɪp-/ adjective.

■ **Usage** Proscribe is sometimes confused with prescribe which means 'to impose'.

**prose** /prəuz/ ● noun ordinary language; not in verse; passage of this, esp. for translation; dullness. ● verb (**-sing**) talk tediously.

**prosecute** /'prɒsɪkjuːt/ verb (**-ting**) institute legal proceedings against; formal carry on (trade etc.). □ **prosecutor** noun.

**prosecution** /prɒsɪ'kjuːʃ(ə)n/ noun prosecuting, being prosecuted; prosecuting party.

**proselyte** /'prɒsəlaɪt/ noun convert, esp. recent; convert to Jewish faith. □ **proselytism** /-lɪtɪz(ə)m/ noun.

**proselytize** /'prɒsəlɪtaɪz/ verb (also **-ise**) (**-zing** or **-sing**) (seek to) convert.

**prosody** /'prɒsədɪ/ noun science of versification. □ **prosodist** noun.

**prospect** ● noun /'prɒspekt/ (often in plural) expectation; extensive view; mental picture; possible or likely customer etc. ● verb /prə'spekt/ (usually + for) explore (for gold etc.). □ **prospector** noun.

**prospective** /prəs'pektɪv/ adjective some day to be, expected; future.

**prospectus** /prəs'pektəs/ noun (plural **-tuses**) pamphlet etc. advertising or describing school, business, etc.

**prosper** /'prɒspə/ verb succeed, thrive.

**prosperity** /prɒ'sperɪtɪ/ noun prosperous state.

**prosperous** /'prɒspərəs/ adjective successful, rich, thriving; auspicious. □ **prosperously** adverb.

**prostate** /'prɒsteɪt/ noun (in full **prostate gland**) gland secreting component of semen. □ **prostatic** /-'stæt-/ adjective.

**prostitute** /'prɒstɪtjuːt/ ● noun person who offers sexual intercourse for payment. ● verb (**-ting**) make prostitute of; misuse, offer for sale unworthily. □ **prostitution** noun.

**prostrate** ● adjective /'prɒstreɪt/ lying face downwards, esp. in submission; lying horizontally; overcome, esp. exhausted. ● verb /prɒs'treɪt/ (**-ting**) lay or throw flat; overcome, make weak. □ **prostration** noun.

**prosy** /'prəuzɪ/ adjective (**-ier**, **-iest**) tedious, commonplace, dull.

**protagonist** /prə'tægənɪst/ noun chief person in drama, story, etc.; supporter of cause.

■ **Usage** The use of protagonist to mean 'a supporter of a cause' is considered incorrect by some people.

**protean** /'prəʊtɪən/ *adjective* variable, versatile.

**protect** /prə'tekt/ *verb* (often + *from*, *against*) keep (person etc.) safe; shield.

**protection** /prə'tekʃ(ə)n/ *noun* protecting, being protected; defence; person etc. that protects; protectionism; *colloquial* immunity from violence etc. by paying gangsters etc.

**protectionism** *noun* theory or practice of protecting home industries. □ **protectionist** *noun & adjective*.

**protective** /prə'tektɪv/ *adjective* protecting; intended for or giving protection. □ **protective custody** detention of person for his or her own protection. □ **protectively** *adverb*; **protectiveness** *noun*.

**protector** *noun* (*feminine* **protectress**) person or thing that protects; *historical* regent ruling during minority or absence of sovereign. □ **protectorship** *noun*.

**protectorate** /prə'tektərət/ *noun* state controlled and protected by another; such protectorship; *historical* office of protector of kingdom or state; period of this.

**protégé** /'prɒtɪʒeɪ/ *noun* (*feminine* **protégée** same pronunciation) person under protection, patronage, etc. of another.

**protein** /'prəʊtiːn/ *noun* any of a class of nitrogenous compounds essential in all living organisms.

**pro tem** /prəʊ 'tem/ *adjective & adverb colloquial* for the time being (*pro tempore*).

**protest** ● *noun* /'prəʊtest/ expression of dissent or disapproval; legal written refusal to pay or accept bill. ● *verb* /prə'test/ (usually + *against, at, about*, etc.) make protest; affirm (innocence etc.); write or get protest relating to (bill); *US* object to. □ **protester, protestor** *noun*.

**Protestant** /'prɒtɪst(ə)nt/ ● *noun* member or adherent of any of Churches separated from RC Church in Reformation. ● *adjective* of Protestant Churches or Protestants. □ **Protestantism** *noun*.

**protestation** /prɒtɪs'teɪʃ(ə)n/ *noun* strong affirmation; protest.

**proto-** *combining form* first.

**protocol** /'prəʊtəkɒl/ ● *noun* official formality and etiquette; draft, esp. of terms of treaty. ● *verb* (**-ll-**) draft or record in protocol.

**proton** /'prəʊtɒn/ *noun* elementary particle with positive electric charge equal to electron's, and occurring in all atomic nuclei.

**protoplasm** /'prəʊtəplæz(ə)m/ *noun* viscous translucent substance comprising living part of cell in organism. □ **protoplasmic** /-'plæzmɪk/ *adjective*.

**prototype** /'prəʊtətaɪp/ *noun* original as pattern for copy, improved form, etc.; trial model of vehicle, machine, etc. □ **prototypic** /-'tɪp-/ *adjective*; **prototypical** /-'tɪp-/ *adjective*.

**protozoan** /prəʊtə'zəʊən/ ● *noun* (*plural* **-s**) (also **protozoon** /-'zəʊɒn/, *plural* **-zoa** /-'zəʊə/) one-celled microscopic organism. ● *adjective* (also **protozoic** /-'zəʊɪk/) of protozoa.

**protract** /prə'trækt/ *verb* (often as **protracted** *adjective*) prolong, lengthen. □ **protraction** *noun*.

**protractor** *noun* instrument for measuring angles, usually in form of graduated semicircle.

**protrude** /prə'truːd/ *verb* (**-ding**) thrust forward; stick out. □ **protrusion** *noun*; **protrusive** *adjective*.

**protuberant** /prə'tjuːbərənt/ *adjective* bulging out; prominent. □ **protuberance** *noun*.

**proud** /praʊd/ *adjective* feeling greatly honoured; haughty, arrogant; (often + *of*) feeling or showing (proper) pride; imposing, splendid; (often + *of*) slightly projecting. □ **do** (**person**) **proud** *colloquial* treat with great generosity or honour. □ **proudly** *adverb*.

**prove** /pruːv/ *verb* (**-ving**; *past participle* **proved** or *esp. US & Scottish* **proven** /'pruːv(ə)n/) (often + *that*) demonstrate to be true by evidence or argument; (**prove oneself**) show one's abilities etc.; (usually + *to be*) be found; test accuracy of; establish validity of (will); (of dough) rise. □ **provable** *adjective*.

■ **Usage** The use of *proven* as the past participle is uncommon except in certain expressions, such as *of proven ability*. It is, however, standard in Scots and American English.

**provenance** /'prɒvɪnəns/ noun (place of) origin; history.

**provender** /'prɒvɪndə/ noun fodder; jocular food.

**proverb** /'prɒvɜːb/ noun short pithy saying in general use.

**proverbial** /prə'vɜːbɪəl/ adjective notorious; of or referred to in proverbs. □ **proverbially** adverb.

**provide** /prə'vaɪd/ verb (-ding) supply; (usually + for, against) make due preparation; (usually + for) take care of person etc. with money, food, etc.; (often + that) stipulate. □ **provided, providing** (often + that) on condition or understanding that.

**providence** /'prɒvɪd(ə)ns/ noun protective care of God or nature; (**Providence**) God; foresight, thrift.

**provident** /'prɒvɪd(ə)nt/ adjective having or showing foresight, thrifty.

**providential** /prɒvɪ'denʃ(ə)l/ adjective of or by divine foresight or intervention; opportune, lucky. □ **providentially** adverb.

**province** /'prɒvɪns/ noun principal administrative division of country etc.; (**the provinces**) whole of country outside capital; sphere of action; branch of learning.

**provincial** /prə'vɪnʃ(ə)l/ ● adjective of province(s); unsophisticated, uncultured. ● noun inhabitant of province(s); unsophisticated or uncultured person. □ **provincialism** noun.

**provision** /prə'vɪʒ(ə)n/ ● noun providing; (in plural) food and drink, esp. for expedition; legal or formal stipulation. ● verb supply with provisions.

**provisional** ● adjective providing for immediate needs only, temporary; (**Provisional**) of the unofficial wing of the IRA. ● noun (**Provisional**) member of unofficial wing of IRA. □ **provisionally** adverb.

**proviso** /prə'vaɪzəʊ/ noun (plural -s) stipulation; limiting clause. □ **provisory** adjective.

**provocation** /prɒvə'keɪʃ(ə)n/ noun provoking, being provoked; cause of annoyance.

**provocative** /prə'vɒkətɪv/ adjective (usually + of) tending or intended to provoke anger, lust, etc. □ **provocatively** adverb.

**provoke** /prə'vəʊk/ verb (-king) (often + to, to do) rouse, incite; call forth, cause; (usually + into) irritate, stimulate; tempt.

**provost** /'prɒvəst/ noun head of some colleges; head of cathedral chapter; /prə'vəʊ/ (in full **provost marshal**) head of military police in camp or on active service.

**prow** /praʊ/ noun bow of ship; pointed or projecting front part.

**prowess** /'praʊɪs/ noun skill, expertise; valour, gallantry.

**prowl** /praʊl/ ● verb (often + about, around) roam, esp. stealthily in search of prey, plunder, etc. ● noun prowling. □ **prowler** noun.

**prox.** abbreviation proximo.

**proximate** /'prɒksɪmət/ adjective nearest, next before or after.

**proximity** /prɒk'sɪmɪtɪ/ noun nearness.

**proximo** /'prɒksɪməʊ/ adjective of next month.

**proxy** /'prɒksɪ/ noun (plural -ies) authorization given to deputy; person authorized to deputize; document authorizing person to vote on another's behalf; vote so given.

**prude** noun excessively squeamish or sexually modest person. □ **prudery** noun; **prudish** adjective; **prudishly** adverb; **prudishness** noun.

**prudent** /'pruːd(ə)nt/ adjective cautious; politic. □ **prudence** noun; **prudently** adverb.

**prudential** /pruː'denʃ(ə)l/ adjective of or showing prudence.

**prune**[1] noun dried plum.

**prune**[2] verb (-ning) (often + down) trim (tree etc.) by cutting away dead or overgrown parts; (usually + off, away) remove (branches etc.) thus; reduce (costs etc.); (often + of) clear superfluities from; remove (superfluities).

**prurient** /'prʊərɪənt/ adjective having or encouraging unhealthy sexual curiosity. □ **prurience** noun.

**Prussian** /'prʌʃ(ə)n/ ● adjective of Prussia. ● noun native of Prussia. □ **Prussian blue** deep blue (pigment).

**prussic acid** /'prʌsɪk/ noun highly poisonous liquid.

**pry** /praɪ/ *verb* (**pries, pried**) (usually + *into* etc.) inquire impertinently, look inquisitively.

**PS** *abbreviation* postscript.

**psalm** /sɑːm/ *noun* (also **Psalm**) sacred song; (**the (Book of) Psalms**) book of these in Old Testament.

**psalmist** /'sɑːmɪst/ *noun* author or composer of psalm(s).

**psalmody** /'sɑːmədɪ/ *noun* practice or art of singing psalms.

**Psalter** /'sɔːltə/ *noun* Book of Psalms; (**psalter**) version or copy of this.

**psaltery** /'sɔːltərɪ/ *noun* (*plural* -**ies**) ancient and medieval plucked stringed instrument.

**psephology** /sɪ'fɒlədʒɪ/ *noun* statistical study of voting etc. □ **psephologist** *noun*.

**pseudo-** *combining form* (also **pseud-** before vowel) false, not genuine; resembling, imitating.

**pseudonym** /'sjuːdənɪm/ *noun* fictitious name, esp. of author.

**psoriasis** /sə'raɪəsɪs/ *noun* skin disease with red scaly patches.

**PSV** *abbreviation* public service vehicle.

**psych** /saɪk/ *verb colloquial* (usually + *up*) prepare mentally; (often + *out*) intimidate; (usually + *out*) analyse (person's motivation etc.).

**psyche** /'saɪkɪ/ *noun* soul, spirit, mind.

**psychedelic** /saɪkə'delɪk/ *adjective* expanding the mind's awareness, hallucinatory; vivid in colour, design, etc.

**psychiatry** /saɪ'kaɪətrɪ/ *noun* study and treatment of mental disease. □ **psychiatric** /-kɪ'ætrɪk/ *adjective*; **psychiatrist** *noun*.

**psychic** /'saɪkɪk/ ● *adjective* (of person) regarded as having paranormal powers, clairvoyant; of the soul or mind. ● *noun* psychic person, medium.

**psychical** *adjective* concerning psychic phenomena or faculties; of the soul or mind.

**psycho-** *combining form* of mind or psychology.

**psychoanalysis** /saɪkəʊə'nælɪsɪs/ *noun* treatment of mental disorders by bringing repressed fears etc. into conscious mind. □ **psychoanalyse** /-'ænəl-/ *verb* (**-sing**); **psychoanalyst** /-'ænəl-/ *noun*; **psychoanalytical** /-ænə'lɪt-/ *adjective*.

**psychokinesis** /saɪkəʊkɪ'niːsɪs/ *noun* movement of objects by telepathy.

**psychological** /saɪkə'lɒdʒɪk(ə)l/ *adjective* of the mind; of psychology; *colloquial* imaginary. □ **psychological block** inhibition caused by emotion; **psychological moment** best time to achieve purpose; **psychological warfare** campaign to reduce enemy's morale. □ **psychologically** *adverb*.

**psychology** /saɪ'kɒlədʒɪ/ *noun* (*plural* -**ies**) study of human mind; treatise on or theory of this; mental characteristics. □ **psychologist** *noun*.

**psychopath** /'saɪkəpæθ/ *noun* mentally deranged person, esp. with abnormal social behaviour; mentally or emotionally unstable person. □ **psychopathic** /-'pæθ-/ *adjective*.

**psychosis** /saɪ'kəʊsɪs/ *noun* (*plural* -**choses** /-siːz/) severe mental derangement involving loss of contact with reality.

**psychosomatic** /saɪkəʊsə'mætɪk/ *adjective* (of disease) mental, not physical, in origin; of both mind and body.

**psychotherapy** /saɪkəʊ'θerəpɪ/ *noun* treatment of mental disorder by psychological means. □ **psychotherapist** *noun*.

**psychotic** /saɪ'kɒtɪk/ ● *adjective* of or suffering from psychosis. ● *noun* psychotic person.

**PT** *abbreviation* physical training.

**pt** *abbreviation* part; pint; point; port.

**PTA** *abbreviation* parent–teacher association.

**ptarmigan** /'tɑːmɪgən/ *noun* bird of grouse family.

**Pte.** *abbreviation* Private (soldier).

**pteridophyte** /'terɪdəfaɪt/ *noun* flowerless plant.

**pterodactyl** /terə'dæktɪl/ *noun* large extinct flying reptile.

**PTO** *abbreviation* please turn over.

**ptomaine** /'təʊmeɪn/ *noun* any of a group of compounds (some toxic) in putrefying matter.

**pub** *noun colloquial* public house.

**puberty** /'pjuːbətɪ/ *noun* period of sexual maturing.

**pubes**[1] /'pjuːbiːz/ *noun* ( *plural* same) lower part of abdomen.

**pubes**[2] *plural of* **pubis**.

**pubescence** /pjuː'bes(ə)ns/ *noun* beginning of puberty; soft down on plant or animal. □ **pubescent** *adjective*.

**pubic** /'pjuːbɪk/ *adjective* of pubes or pubis.

**pubis** /'pjuːbɪs/ *noun* ( *plural* **pubes** -biːz/) front portion of hip bone.

**public** /'pʌblɪk/ ● *adjective* of the people as a whole; open to or shared by all; done or existing openly; of or from government; involved in community affairs. ● *noun* (treated as *singular* or *plural*) (members of) community as a whole; section of community. □ **go public** (of company) start selling shares on open market, reveal one's plans; **in public** publicly, openly; **public address system** equipment of loudspeakers etc.; **public convenience** public lavatory; **public figure** famous person; **public house** place selling alcoholic drink for consumption on premises; **public lending right** right of authors to payment when their books are lent by public libraries; **public relations** professional promotion of company, product, etc.; **public school** independent fee-paying school; *US, Australian, Scottish, etc.* non-fee-paying school; **public-spirited** ready to do things for the community; **public transport** buses, trains, etc. available for public use on fixed routes; **public utility** organization supplying water, gas, etc. to community. □ **publicly** *adverb*.

**publican** /'pʌblɪkən/ *noun* keeper of public house.

**publication** /pʌblɪ'keɪʃ(ə)n/ *noun* publishing; published book, periodical, etc.

**publicist** /'pʌblɪsɪst/ *noun* publicity agent, public relations officer.

**publicity** /pʌb'lɪsɪtɪ/ *noun* (means of attracting) public attention; (material used for) advertising.

**publicize** /'pʌblɪsaɪz/ *verb* (also **-ise**) (**-zing** or **-sing**) advertise, make publicly known.

**publish** /'pʌblɪʃ/ *verb* prepare and issue (book, magazine, etc.) for public sale; make generally known; formally announce.

**publisher** *noun* person or firm that publishes books etc.

**puce** /pjuːs/ *adjective & noun* purplebrown.

**puck**[1] *noun* rubber disc used in ice hockey.

**puck**[2] *noun* mischievous sprite. □ **puckish** *adjective*; **puckishly** *adverb*; **puckishness** *noun*.

**pucker** /'pʌkə/ ● *verb* gather (often + *up*) into wrinkles, folds, or bulges. ● *noun* such wrinkle etc.

**pudding** /'pʊdɪŋ/ *noun* sweet cooked dish; savoury dish containing flour, suet, etc.; sweet course of meal; kind of sausage.

**puddle** /'pʌd(ə)l/ *noun* small (dirty) pool; clay made into watertight coating.

**pudenda** /pjuː'dendə/ *plural noun* genitals, esp. of woman.

**pudgy** /'pʌdʒɪ/ *adjective* (**-ier**, **-iest**) *colloquial* plump, podgy.

**puerile** /'pjʊəraɪl/ *adjective* childish, immature. □ **puerility** /-'rɪl-/ *noun* ( *plural* **-ies**).

**puerperal** /pjuː'ɜːpər(ə)l/ *adjective* of or due to childbirth.

**puff** ● *noun* short quick blast of breath or wind; sound (as) of this; vapour or smoke sent out in one blast; light pastry cake; gathered material in dress etc.; unduly enthusiastic review, advertisement, etc. ● *verb* emit puff(s); smoke or move with puffs; (usually in *passive*, often + *out*) *colloquial* put out of breath; pant; (usually + *up*, *out*) inflate; (usually as **puffed up** *adjective*) elate, make boastful; advertise in exaggerated terms. □ **puff-adder** large venomous African viper; **puffball** ballshaped fungus; **puff pastry** pastry consisting of thin layers.

**puffin** /'pʌfɪn/ *noun* N. Atlantic and N. Pacific auk with short striped bill.

**puffy** *adjective* (**-ier**, **-iest**) swollen, puffed out; *colloquial* short-winded.

**pug** *noun* (in full **pug-dog**) dog of small breed with flat nose. □ **pug-nose** short flat or snub nose.

**pugilist** /'pjuːdʒɪlɪst/ *noun* boxer. □ **pugilism** *noun*; **pugilistic** /-'lɪs-/ *adjective*.

**pugnacious** /pʌg'neɪʃəs/ *adjective* disposed to fight. □ **pugnaciously** *adverb*; **pugnacity** /-'næs-/ *noun*.

**puissance** /'pwiːsɑ̃s/ noun jumping of large obstacles in showjumping.

**puissant** /'pwiːsɒnt/ adjective literary powerful; mighty.

**puke** /pjuːk/ verb & noun (**-king**) slang vomit. □ **pukey** adjective.

**pukka** /'pʌkə/ adjective colloquial genuine; reliable.

**pulchritude** /'pʌlkrɪtjuːd/ noun literary beauty. □ **pulchritudinous** /-'tjuːdməs/ adjective.

**pull** /pʊl/ ● verb exert force on (thing etc.) to move it to oneself or origin of force; exert pulling force; extract by pulling; damage (muscle etc.) by abnormal strain; proceed with effort; (+ on) draw (weapon) against (person); attract; draw (liquor) from barrel etc.; (+ at) pluck at; (often + on, at) inhale or drink deeply, suck. ● noun act of pulling; force thus exerted; influence; advantage; attraction; deep draught of liquor; prolonged effort; handle etc. for applying pull; printer's rough proof; suck at cigarette. □ **pull back** retreat; **pull down** demolish; **pull in** arrive to take passengers, move to side of or off road, colloquial earn, colloquial arrest; **pull-in** roadside café etc.; **pull off** remove, win, manage successfully; **pull oneself together** recover control of oneself; **pull out** take out, depart, withdraw, leave station or stop, move towards off side; **pull-out** removable section of magazine; **pull round**, **through** (cause to) recover from illness; **pull strings** exert (esp. clandestine) influence; **pull together** work in harmony; **pull up** (cause to) stop moving, pull out of ground, reprimand, check oneself.

**pullet** /'pʊlɪt/ noun young hen, esp. less than one year old.

**pulley** /'pʊlɪ/ noun (plural **-s**) grooved wheel(s) for cord etc. to run over, mounted in block and used to lift weight etc.; wheel or drum mounted on shaft and turned by belt, used to increase speed or power.

**Pullman** /'pʊlmən/ noun (plural **-s**) luxurious railway carriage or motor coach; sleeping car.

**pullover** noun knitted garment put on over the head.

**pullulate** /'pʌljʊleɪt/ verb (**-ting**) sprout; swarm; develop; (+ with) abound with. □ **pullulation** noun.

**pulmonary** /'pʌlmənərɪ/ adjective of lungs; having (organs like) lungs; affected with or subject to lung disease.

**pulp** ● noun fleshy part of fruit etc.; soft shapeless mass, esp. of materials for papermaking; cheap fiction. ● verb reduce to or become pulp. □ **pulpy** adjective; **pulpiness** noun.

**pulpit** /'pʊlpɪt/ noun raised enclosed platform for preaching from; (**the pulpit**) preachers collectively; preaching.

**pulsar** /'pʌlsɑː/ noun cosmic source of regular rapid pulses of radiation.

**pulsate** /pʌl'seɪt/ verb (**-ting**) expand and contract rhythmically; throb, vibrate, quiver. □ **pulsation** noun.

**pulse**[1] ● noun rhythmical throbbing of arteries; each beat of arteries or heart; throb or thrill of life or emotion; general feeling; single vibration of sound, electromagnetic radiation, etc.; rhythmical (esp. musical) beat. ● verb (**-sing**) pulsate.

**pulse**[2] noun (treated as singular or plural) (plant producing) edible seeds of peas, beans, lentils, etc.

**pulverize** /'pʌlvəraɪz/ verb (also **-ise**) (**-zing** or **-sing**) reduce or crumble to powder or dust; colloquial demolish, crush. □ **pulverization** noun.

**puma** /'pjuːmə/ noun large tawny American feline.

**pumice** /'pʌmɪs/ noun (in full **pumice stone**) light porous lava used as abrasive; piece of this.

**pummel** /'pʌm(ə)l/ verb (**-ll-**; US **-l-**) strike repeatedly, esp. with fists.

**pump**[1] ● noun machine or device for raising or moving liquids or gases; act of pumping. ● verb (often + in, out, up, etc.) raise, remove, inflate, empty, etc. (as) with pump; work pump; persistently question (person) to elicit information; move vigorously up and down. □ **pump iron** colloquial exercise with weights.

**pump**[2] noun plimsoll; light shoe for dancing etc.

**pumpernickel** /'pʌmpənɪk(ə)l/ noun wholemeal rye bread.

**pumpkin** /'pʌmpkɪn/ noun large yellow or orange fruit used as vegetable; plant bearing it.

**pun** ●*noun* humorous use of word(s) with two or more meanings, play on words. ●*verb* (**-nn-**) (usually + *on*) make pun(s).

**Punch** *noun* grotesque humpbacked puppet in *Punch and Judy* shows.

**punch**[1] ●*verb* strike with fist; make hole in (as) with punch; pierce (hole) thus. ●*noun* blow with fist; *colloquial* vigour, effective force; instrument or machine for piercing holes or impressing design in leather, metal, etc. □ **pull one's punches** avoid using full force; **punchball** stuffed or inflated ball used for practice in punching; **punch-drunk** stupefied (as) with repeated punches; **punchline** words giving point of joke etc.; **punch-up** *colloquial* fist-fight, brawl. □ **puncher** *noun*.

**punch**[2] *noun* hot or cold mixture of wine or spirit with water, fruit, spices, etc. □ **punch-bowl** bowl for punch; deep round hollow in hill.

**punchy** *adjective* (**-ier**, **-iest**) vigorous, forceful.

**punctilio** /pʌŋk'tɪlɪəʊ/ *noun* (*plural* **-s**) delicate point of ceremony or honour; petty formality.

**punctilious** /pʌŋk'tɪlɪəs/ *adjective* attentive to formality or etiquette; precise in behaviour. □ **punctiliously** *adverb*; **punctiliousness** *noun*.

**punctual** /'pʌŋktʃʊəl/ *adjective* observing appointed time; prompt. □ **punctuality** /-'æl-/ *noun*; **punctually** *adverb*.

**punctuate** /'pʌŋktʃʊeɪt/ *verb* (**-ting**) insert punctuation marks in; interrupt at intervals.

**punctuation** *noun* (system of) punctuating. □ **punctuation mark** any of the marks used in writing to separate sentences, phrases, etc.

**puncture** /'pʌŋktʃə/ ●*noun* prick, pricking; hole made by this. ●*verb* (**-ring**) make or suffer puncture (in); deflate.

**pundit** /'pʌndɪt/ *noun* (also **pandit**) learned Hindu; expert.

**pungent** /'pʌndʒ(ə)nt/ *adjective* having sharp or strong taste or smell; biting, caustic. □ **pungency** *noun*.

**punish** /'pʌnɪʃ/ *verb* inflict penalty on (offender) or for (offence); tax, abuse, or treat severely. □ **punishable** *adjective*; **punishment** *noun*.

**punitive** /'pju:nɪtɪv/ *adjective* inflicting or intended to inflict punishment; extremely severe.

**punk** *noun* (in full **punk rock**) deliberately outrageous style of rock music; (in full **punk rocker**) fan of this; *esp. US* hooligan, lout.

**punkah** /'pʌŋkə/ *noun* large swinging fan on frame worked by cord or electrically.

**punnet** /'pʌnɪt/ *noun* small basket for fruit etc.

**punster** /'pʌnstə/ *noun* maker of puns.

**punt**[1] ●*noun* square-ended flat-bottomed boat propelled by long pole. ●*verb* travel or carry in punt.

**punt**[2] ●*verb* kick (football) dropped from hands before it reaches ground. ●*noun* such kick.

**punt**[3] *verb colloquial* bet, speculate in shares etc.; (in some card games) lay stake against bank.

**punt**[4] /pʊnt/ *noun* chief monetary unit of Republic of Ireland.

**punter** *noun colloquial* person who gambles or bets; customer, client.

**puny** /'pju:nɪ/ *adjective* (**-ier**, **-iest**) undersized; feeble.

**pup** ●*noun* young dog, wolf, rat, seal, etc. ●*verb* (**-pp-**) give birth to (pups).

**pupa** /'pju:pə/ *noun* (*plural* **pupae** /-pi:/) insect in stage between larva and imago.

**pupil**[1] /'pju:pɪl/ *noun* person being taught.

**pupil**[2] /'pju:pɪl/ *noun* opening in centre of iris of eye.

**puppet** /'pʌpɪt/ *noun* small figure moved esp. by strings as entertainment; person controlled by another. □ **puppet state** country apparently independent but actually under control of another power. □ **puppetry** *noun*.

**puppy** /'pʌpɪ/ *noun* (*plural* **-ies**) young dog; conceited young man. □ **puppy fat** temporary fatness of child or adolescent; **puppy love** calf love.

**purblind** /'pɜ:blaɪnd/ *adjective* partly blind, dim-sighted; obtuse, dull. □ **purblindness** *noun*.

**purchase** /'pɜ:tʃəs/ ●*verb* (**-sing**) buy. ●*noun* buying; thing bought; firm hold on thing, leverage; equipment for moving heavy objects. □ **purchaser** noun.

**purdah** /'pɜːdə/ noun screening of Muslim or Hindu women from strangers.

**pure** /pjʊə/ adjective unmixed, unadulterated; chaste; not morally corrupt; guiltless; sincere; not discordant; (of science) abstract, not applied. □ **pureness** noun; **purity** noun.

**purée** /'pjʊəreɪ/ ● noun smooth pulp of vegetables or fruit etc. ● verb (**-ées, -éed**) make purée of.

**purely** adverb in a pure way; merely, solely, exclusively.

**purgative** /'pɜːɡətɪv/ ● adjective serving to purify; strongly laxative. ● noun purgative thing.

**purgatory** /'pɜːɡətərɪ/ ● noun ( plural **-ies**) place or state of spiritual cleansing, esp. after death and before entering heaven; place or state of temporary suffering or expiation. ● adjective purifying. □ **purgatorial** /-'tɔːrɪəl/ adjective.

**purge** /pɜːdʒ/ ● verb (**-ging**) (often + of, from) make physically or spiritually clean; remove by cleansing; rid of unacceptable members; empty (bowels); Law atone for (offence). ● noun purging, purgative.

**purify** /'pjʊərɪfaɪ/ verb (**-ies, -ied**) clear of extraneous elements, make pure; (often + of, from) cleanse. □ **purification** noun; **purificatory** /-fɪkeɪtərɪ/ adjective.

**purist** /'pjʊərɪst/ noun stickler for correctness, esp. in language. □ **purism** noun.

**puritan** /'pjʊərɪt(ə)n/ ● noun (**Puritan**) historical member of English Protestant group regarding Reformation as incomplete; purist member of any party; strict observer of religion or morals. ● adjective (**Puritan**) historical of Puritans; scrupulous in religion or morals. □ **puritanical** /-'tæn-/ adjective; **puritanically** /-'tæn-/ adverb; **puritanism** noun.

**purl¹** ● noun knitting stitch with needle moved in opposite to normal direction; chain of minute loops. ● verb knit with purl stitch.

**purl²** verb flow with babbling sound.

**purler** /'pɜːlə/ noun colloquial heavy fall.

**purlieu** /'pɜːljuː/ noun ( plural **-s**) person's limits or usual haunts; historical tract on

border of forest; (in plural) outskirts, outlying region.

**purlin** /'pɜːlɪn/ noun horizontal beam along length of roof.

**purloin** /pə'lɔɪn/ verb formal or jocular steal, pilfer.

**purple** /'pɜːp(ə)l/ ● noun colour between red and blue; purple robe, esp. of emperor etc.; cardinal's scarlet official dress. ● adjective of purple. ● verb (**-ling**) make or become purple. □ **purplish** adjective.

**purport** ● verb /pə'pɔːt/ profess, be intended to seem; (often + that) have as its meaning. ● noun /'pɜːpɔːt/ ostensible meaning; tenor of document or statement. □ **purportedly** adverb.

**purpose** /'pɜːpəs/ ● noun object to be attained, thing intended; intention to act; resolution, determination. ● verb (**-sing**) have as one's purpose, intend. □ **on purpose** intentionally; **to good, little, no,** etc. **purpose** with good, little, no, etc., effect or result; **to the purpose** relevant, useful.

**purposeful** adjective having or indicating purpose; intentional. □ **purposefully** adverb; **purposefulness** noun.

**purposeless** adjective having no aim or plan.

**purposely** adverb on purpose.

**purposive** /'pɜːpəsɪv/ adjective having, serving, or done with a purpose; purposeful.

**purr** /pɜː/ ● verb make low vibratory sound of cat expressing pleasure; (of machinery etc.) run smoothly and quietly. ● noun purring sound.

**purse** /pɜːs/ ● noun small pouch for carrying money in; US handbag; funds; sum given as present or prize. ● verb (**-sing**) (often + up) contract (esp. lips); become wrinkled. □ **hold the purse-strings** have control of expenditure.

**purser** /'pɜːsə/ noun ship's officer who keeps accounts, esp. head steward in passenger vessel.

**pursuance** /pə'sjuːəns/ noun (+ of) carrying out or observance (of plan, rules, etc.).

**pursuant** /pə'sjuːənt/ adverb (+ to) in accordance with.

**pursue** /pə'sjuː/ *verb* (**-sues, -sued, -su-ing**) follow with intent to overtake, capture, or harm; proceed along; engage in (study etc.); carry out (plan etc.); seek after; continue to investigate etc.; persistently importune or assail. □ **pursuer** *noun*.

**pursuit** /pə'sjuːt/ *noun* pursuing; occupation or activity pursued. □ **in pursuit of** pursuing.

**purulent** /'pjʊərʊlənt/ *adjective* of, containing, or discharging pus. □ **purulence** *noun*.

**purvey** /pə'veɪ/ *verb* provide or supply food etc. as one's business. □ **purveyor** *noun*.

**purview** /'pɜːvjuː/ *noun* scope of document etc.; range of physical or mental vision.

**pus** /pʌs/ *noun* thick yellowish liquid produced from infected tissue.

**push** /pʊʃ/ ● *verb* exert force on (thing) to move it away, cause to move thus; exert such force; thrust forward or upward; (cause to) project; make (one's way) forcibly or persistently; exert oneself; (often + *to, into, to do*) urge, impel; (often + *for*) pursue (claim etc.) persistently; promote, advertise; *colloquial* sell (drug) illegally. ● *noun* act of pushing; force thus exerted; vigorous effort; determination; use of influence to advance person. □ **give** or **get the push** *colloquial* dismiss, be dismissed; **push-bike** *colloquial* bicycle; **pushchair** child's folding chair on wheels; **push off** *colloquial* go away; **pushover** *colloquial* opponent or difficulty easily overcome.

**pusher** *noun colloquial* seller of illegal drugs.

**pushing** *adjective* pushy; *colloquial* having nearly reached (specified age).

**pushy** *adjective* (**-ier, -iest**) *colloquial* excessively self-assertive. □ **pushily** *adverb*; **pushiness** *noun*.

**pusillanimous** /pjuːsɪ'lænɪməs/ *adjective* *formal* cowardly, timid. □ **pusillanimity** /-lə'nɪm/ *noun*.

**puss** /pʊs/ *noun colloquial* cat; sly or coquettish girl.

**pussy** /'pʊsɪ/ *noun* (*plural* **-ies**) (also **pussy-cat**) *colloquial* cat. □ **pussyfoot** *colloquial* move stealthily, equivocate; **pussy willow** willow with furry catkins.

**pustulate** /'pʌstjʊleɪt/ *verb* (**-ting**) form into pustules.

**pustule** /'pʌstjuːl/ *noun* pimple containing pus. □ **pustular** *adjective*.

**put** /pʊt/ ● *verb* (**-tt-**; *past & past participle* **put**) move to or cause to be in specified place, position, or state; (often + *on, to*) impose; (+ *for*) substitute (thing) for (another); express in specified way; (+ *at*) estimate; (+ *into*) express or translate in (words etc.); (+ *into*) invest (money) in; (+ *on*) stake (money) on; (+ *to*) submit for attention; hurl (shot etc.) as sport. ● *noun* throw of shot. □ **put about** spread (rumour etc.); **put across** make understood, achieve by deceit; **put away** restore to usual place, lay aside for future, imprison, consume (food or drink); **put back** restore to usual place, change (meeting etc.) to later time, move back hands of (clock or watch); **put by** lay aside for future; **put down** suppress, *colloquial* snub, record in writing, enter on list, (+ *as, for*) account or reckon, (+ *to*) attribute to, kill (old etc. animal), pay as deposit; **put in** submit (claim), (+ *for*) be candidate for (election etc.), spend (time); **put off** postpone, evade (person) with excuse, dissuade, disconcert; **put on** clothe oneself with, cause (light etc.) to operate, make (transport) available, stage (play etc.), advance hands of (clock or watch), feign, increase one's weight by (specified amount); **put out** disconcert, annoy, inconvenience, extinguish; **put over** put across; **put through** complete, connect by telephone; **put together** make from parts, combine (parts) into whole; **put up** *verb* build, raise, lodge (person), engage in (fight etc.), propose, provide (money) as backer, display (notice), offer for sale etc.; **put-up** *adjective* fraudulent; **put upon** (usually in *passive*) *colloquial* unfairly burden or deceive; **put (person) up to** instigate him or her to; **put up with** endure, tolerate.

**putative** /'pjuːtətɪv/ *adjective formal* reputed, supposed.

**putrefy** /'pjuːtrɪfaɪ/ *verb* (**-ies, -ied**) become or make putrid, go bad; fester; become morally corrupt. □ **putrefaction** /-'fæk-/ *noun*; **putrefactive** /-'fæk-/ *adjective*.

**putrescent** /pju:'tres(ə)nt/ *adjective* rotting. □ **putrescence** *noun*.

**putrid** /'pju:trɪd/ *adjective* decomposed, rotten; noxious; corrupt; *slang* contemptible, very unpleasant. □ **putridity** /-'trɪd-/ *noun*.

**putsch** /pʊtʃ/ *noun* attempt at revolution.

**putt** /pʌt/ ● *verb* (-tt-) strike (golf ball) on putting-green. ● *noun* putting stroke. □ **putting green** smooth turf round hole on golf course.

**puttee** /'pʌti/ *noun historical* long strip of cloth wound round leg for protection and support.

**putter¹** *noun* golf club used in putting.

**putter²** *US* = POTTER¹.

**putty** /'pʌti/ ● *noun* paste of chalk, linseed oil, etc. for fixing panes of glass etc. ● *verb* (-ies, -ied) fix, fill, etc. with putty.

**puzzle** /'pʌz(ə)l/ ● *noun* difficult or confusing problem; problem or toy designed to test ingenuity etc. ● *verb* (-ling) perplex, (usually + *over* etc.) be perplexed; (usually as **puzzling** *adjective*) require much mental effort; (+ *out*) solve using ingenuity etc. □ **puzzlement** *noun*.

**PVC** *abbreviation* polyvinyl chloride, a plastic used for pipes, electrical insulation, etc.

**pyaemia** /paɪ'i:mɪə/ *noun* (*US* **pyemia**) severe bacterial infection of blood.

**pygmy** /'pɪgmi/ (also **pigmy**) ● *noun* (*plural* **-ies**) member of dwarf people of esp. equatorial Africa; very small person, animal, or thing. ● *adjective* very small.

**pyjamas** /pə'dʒɑ:məz/ *plural noun* (*US* **pajamas**) suit of trousers and top for sleeping in etc.; loose trousers worn in some Asian countries.

**pylon** /'paɪlən/ *noun* tall structure esp. as support for electric cables.

**pyorrhoea** /paɪə'rɪə/ *noun* (*US* **pyorrhea**) gum disease; discharge of pus.

**pyramid** /'pɪrəmɪd/ *noun* monumental (esp. ancient Egyptian) stone structure with square base and sloping sides meeting at apex; solid of this shape with base of 3 or more sides; pyramid-shaped thing. □ **pyramidal** /-'ræm-/ *adjective*.

**pyre** /'paɪə/ *noun* pile of combustible material, esp. for burning corpse.

**pyrethrum** /paɪ'ri:θrəm/ *noun* aromatic chrysanthemum; insecticide from its dried flowers.

**Pyrex** /'paɪəreks/ *noun proprietary term* a hard heat-resistant glass.

**pyrites** /paɪ'raɪti:z/ *noun* (in full **iron pyrites**) yellow sulphide of iron.

**pyromania** /paɪərəʊ'meɪnɪə/ *noun* obsessive desire to start fires. □ **pyromaniac** *noun & adjective*.

**pyrotechnics** /paɪərəʊ'tekniks/ *plural noun* art of making fireworks; display of fireworks. □ **pyrotechnic** *adjective*.

**pyrrhic** /'pɪrɪk/ *adjective* (of victory) achieved at too great cost.

**python** /'paɪθ(ə)n/ *noun* large snake that crushes its prey.

**pyx** /pɪks/ *noun* vessel for consecrated bread of Eucharist.

# Qq

**Q** *abbreviation* (also **Q.**) question.

**QC** *abbreviation* Queen's Counsel.

**QED** *abbreviation* which was to be proved (*quod erat demonstrandum*).

**QM** *abbreviation* Quartermaster.

**qr.** *abbreviation* quarter(s).

**qt** *abbreviation* quart(s).

**qua** /kwɑː, kweɪ/ *conjunction* in the capacity of.

**quack**¹ ● *noun* harsh sound made by ducks. ● *verb* utter this sound.

**quack**² *noun* unqualified practitioner, esp. of medicine; *slang* any doctor. □ **quackery** *noun*.

**quad** /kwɒd/ *colloquial* ● *noun* quadrangle; quadruplet; quadraphonics. ● *adjective* quadraphonic.

**quadrangle** /'kwɒdræŋg(ə)l/ *noun* 4-sided plane figure, esp. square or rectangle; 4-sided court, esp. in college etc. □ **quadrangular** /-'ræŋgjʊlə/ *adjective*.

**quadrant** /'kwɒdrənt/ *noun* quarter of circle or sphere or of circle's circumference; optical instrument for measuring angle between distant objects.

**quadraphonic** /kwɒdrə'fɒnɪk/ *adjective* (of sound reproduction) using 4 transmission channels. □ **quadraphonically** *adverb*; **quadraphonics** *plural noun*.

**quadrate** ● *adjective* /'kwɒdrət/ square, rectangular. ● *noun* /'kwɒdrət, -dreɪt/ rectangular object. ● *verb* /kwɒ'dreɪt/ (**-ting**) make square.

**quadratic** /kwɒ'drætɪk/ *Mathematics* ● *adjective* involving the square (and no higher power) of unknown quantity or variable. ● *noun* quadratic equation.

**quadriceps** /'kwɒdrɪseps/ *noun* 4-headed muscle at front of thigh.

**quadrilateral** /kwɒdrɪ'lætər(ə)l/ ● *adjective* having 4 sides. ● *noun* 4-sided figure.

**quadrille** /kwɒ'drɪl/ *noun* square dance; music for this.

**quadruped** /'kwɒdrʊped/ *noun* 4-footed animal, esp. mammal.

**quadruple** /'kwɒdrʊp(ə)l/ ● *adjective* fourfold; having 4 parts; (of time in music) having 4 beats in bar. ● *noun* fourfold number or amount. ● *verb* /kwɒ'druːp(ə)l/ multiply by 4.

**quadruplet** /'kwɒdrʊplɪt/ *noun* each of 4 children born at one birth.

**quadruplicate** ● *adjective* /kwɒ'druːplɪkət/ fourfold; of which 4 copies are made. ● *verb* /-keɪt/ (**-ting**) multiply by 4.

**quaff** /kwɒf/ *verb literary* drink deeply; drain (cup etc.) in long draughts.

**quagmire** /'kwɒgmaɪə, 'kwæg-/ *noun* muddy or boggy area; hazardous situation.

**quail**¹ *noun* (*plural* same or **-s**) small game bird related to partridge.

**quail**² *verb* flinch, show fear.

**quaint** *adjective* attractively odd or old-fashioned. □ **quaintly** *adverb*; **quaintness** *noun*.

**quake** ● *verb* (**-king**) shake, tremble. ● *noun colloquial* earthquake.

**Quaker** *noun* member of Society of Friends. □ **Quakerism** *noun*.

**qualification** /kwɒlɪfɪ'keɪʃ(ə)n/ *noun* accomplishment fitting person for position or purpose; thing that modifies or limits; qualifying, being qualified. □ **qualificatory** /'kwɒl-/ *adjective*.

**qualify** /'kwɒlɪfaɪ/ *verb* (**-ies, -ied**) (often as **qualified** *adjective*) make competent or fit for purpose or position; make legally entitled; (usually + *for*) satisfy conditions; modify, limit; *Grammar* (of word) attribute quality to (esp. noun); moderate, mitigate; (+ *as*) be describable as. □ **qualifier** *noun*.

**qualitative** /'kwɒlɪtətɪv/ *adjective* concerned with quality as opposed to quantity. □ **qualitatively** *adverb*.

**quality** /'kwɒlɪtɪ/ ● *noun* (*plural* **-ies**) excellence; degree of excellence; attribute, faculty; relative nature or character; timbre. ● *adjective* of high quality.

**qualm** /kwɑːm/ *noun* misgiving; scruple of conscience; momentary faint or sick feeling.

**quandary** /ˈkwɒndərɪ/ noun (plural **-ies**) perplexed state; practical dilemma.

**quango** /ˈkwæŋɡəʊ/ noun (plural **-s**) semi-public administrative body appointed by government.

**quanta** plural of QUANTUM.

**quantify** /ˈkwɒntɪfaɪ/ verb (**-ies**, **-ied**) determine quantity of; express as quantity. □ **quantifiable** adjective.

**quantitative** /ˈkwɒntɪtətɪv/ adjective concerned with quantity as opposed to quality; measured or measurable by quantity.

**quantity** /ˈkwɒntɪtɪ/ noun (plural **-ies**) property of things that is measurable; size, extent, weight, amount, or number; (in plural) large amounts or numbers; length or shortness of vowel sound or syllable; Mathematics value, component, etc. that may be expressed in numbers. □ **quantity surveyor** person who measures and prices building work.

**quantum** /ˈkwɒntəm/ noun (plural **-ta**) discrete amount of energy proportional to frequency of radiation it represents; required or allowed amount. □ **quantum mechanics**, theory assuming that energy exists in discrete units.

**quarantine** /ˈkwɒrəntiːn/ ● noun isolation imposed on person or animal to prevent infection or contagion; period of this. ● verb (**-ning**) put in quarantine.

**quark**[1] /kwɑːk/ noun Physics component of elementary particles.

**quark**[2] /kwɑːk/ noun kind of low-fat curd cheese.

**quarrel** /ˈkwɒr(ə)l/ ● noun severe or angry dispute; break in friendly relations; cause of complaint. ● verb (**-ll-**; US **-l-**) (often + with) find fault; dispute; break off friendly relations. □ **quarrelsome** adjective.

**quarry**[1] /ˈkwɒrɪ/ ● noun (plural **-ies**) place from which stone etc. is extracted. ● verb (**-ies**, **-ied**) extract (stone etc.) from quarry. □ **quarry tile** unglazed floor-tile.

**quarry**[2] /ˈkwɒrɪ/ noun (plural **-ies**) intended victim or prey; object of pursuit.

**quart** /kwɔːt/ noun liquid measure equal to quarter of gallon; two pints (1.136 litre).

**quarter** /ˈkwɔːtə/ ● noun each of 4 equal parts; period of 3 months; point of time 15 minutes before or after any hour; 25 US or Canadian cents, coin worth this; part of town, esp. as occupied by particular class; point of compass, region at this; direction, district; source of supply; (in plural) lodgings, accommodation of troops etc.; one-fourth of a lunar month; mercy towards enemy etc. on condition of surrender; grain measure equivalent to 8 bushels, colloquial one-fourth of a pound weight. ● verb divide into quarters; put (troops etc.) into quarters; provide with lodgings; Heraldry place (coats of arms) on 4 quarters of shield. □ **quarterback** player in American football who directs attacking play; **quarter day** day on which quarterly payments are due; **quarterdeck** part of ship's upper deck near stern; **quarter-final** Sport match or round preceding semifinal; **quarter-hour** period of 15 minutes; **quartermaster** regimental officer in charge of quartering, rations, etc., naval petty officer in charge of steering, signals, etc.

**quarterly** ● adjective produced or occurring once every quarter of year. ● adverb once every quarter of year. ● noun (plural **-ies**) quarterly journal.

**quartet** /kwɔːˈtet/ noun musical composition for 4 performers; the performers; any group of 4.

**quarto** /ˈkwɔːtəʊ/ noun (plural **-s**) size of book or page made by folding sheet of standard size twice to form 4 leaves.

**quartz** /kwɔːts/ ● noun silica in various mineral forms. ● adjective (of clock or watch) operated by vibrations of electrically driven quartz crystal.

**quasar** /ˈkweɪzɑː/ noun starlike object with large red shift.

**quash** /kwɒʃ/ verb annul; reject as not valid; suppress, crush.

**quasi-** /ˈkweɪzaɪ/ combining form seemingly, not really; almost.

**quaternary** /kwəˈtɜːnərɪ/ adjective having 4 parts.

**quatrain** /ˈkwɒtreɪn/ noun 4-line stanza.

**quatrefoil** /ˈkætrəfɔɪl/ noun leaf consisting of 4 leaflets; design or ornament in this shape.

**quaver** /ˈkweɪvə/ ● verb (esp. of voice or sound) vibrate, shake, tremble; sing or say with quavering voice. ● *noun Music* note half as long as crotchet; trill in singing; tremble in speech. □ **quavery** *adjective*.

**quay** /kiː/ *noun* artificial landing-place for loading and unloading ships. □ **quayside** land forming or near quay.

**queasy** /'kwiːzɪ/ *adjective* (**-ier**, **-iest**) (of person) nauseous; (of stomach) easily upset; (of the conscience etc.) overscrupulous. □ **queasily** *adverb*; **queasiness** *noun*.

**queen** ● *noun* (as title usually **Queen**) female sovereign; (in full **queen consort**) king's wife; woman, country, or thing pre-eminent of its kind; fertile female among bees, ants, etc.; most powerful piece in chess; court card depicting queen; (**the Queen**) national anthem when sovereign is female; *offensive slang* male homosexual. ● *verb* convert (pawn in chess) to queen when it reaches opponent's side of board. □ **queen mother** king's widow who is mother of sovereign; **Queen's Bench** division of High Court of Justice; **Queen's Counsel** counsel to the Crown, taking precedence over other barristers; **the Queen's English** English language correctly written or spoken. □ **queenly** *adjective* (**-ier**, **-iest**).

**Queensberry Rules** /'kwiːnzbərɪ/ *plural noun* standard rules, esp. of boxing.

**queer** ● *adjective* strange, odd, eccentric; suspect, of questionable character; slightly ill, faint; *offensive slang* (esp. of a man) homosexual. ● *noun offensive slang* homosexual. ● *verb slang* spoil, put out of order. □ **in Queer Street** *slang* in difficulty, esp. in debt.

**quell** *verb* suppress, crush.

**quench** *verb* satisfy (thirst) by drinking; extinguish (fire or light); cool, esp. with water; stifle, suppress.

**quern** *noun* hand mill for grinding corn.

**querulous** /'kwerʊləs/ *adjective* complaining; peevish. □ **querulously** *adverb*.

**query** /'kwɪərɪ/ ● *noun* (*plural* **-ies**) question; question mark. ● *verb* (**-ies**, **-ied**) ask, inquire; call in question; dispute accuracy of.

**quest** ● *noun* search, seeking; thing sought, esp. by medieval knight. ● *verb* (often + *about*) go about in search of something.

**question** /'kwestʃ(ə)n/ ● *noun* sentence worded or expressed so as to seek information or answer; doubt or dispute about matter, raising of such doubt etc.; matter to be discussed or decided; problem requiring solution. ● *verb* ask questions of; subject (person) to examination; throw doubt on. □ **be just a question of time** be certain to happen sooner or later; **be a question of** be at issue, be a problem; **call in** or **into question** express doubts about; **in question** being discussed or referred to; **out of the question** not worth questioning, impossible; **question mark** punctuation mark (?) indicating question (see panel); **question-master** person presiding over quiz game etc.; **question time** period in Parliament when MPs may question ministers. □ **questioner** *noun*; **questioning** *adjective & noun*; **questioningly** *adverb*.

**questionable** *adjective* doubtful as regards truth, quality, honesty, wisdom, etc.

---

## Question mark **?**

This is used instead of a full stop at the end of a sentence to show that it is a question, e.g.

    *Have you seen the film yet?*
    *You didn't lose my purse, did you?*

It is **not** used at the end of a reported question, e.g.

    *I asked you whether you'd seen the film yet.*

---

**questionnaire** /kwestʃəˈneə/ *noun* list of questions for obtaining information esp. for statistical analysis.

**queue** /kjuː/ • *noun* line or sequence of people, vehicles, etc. waiting their turn. • *verb* (**-s, -d,** queuing or **queue-ing**) (often + *up*) form or join queue. □ **queue-jump** push forward out of turn in queue.

**quibble** /ˈkwɪb(ə)l/ • *noun* petty objection, trivial point of criticism; evasion. • *verb* (**-ling**) use quibbles.

**quiche** /kiːʃ/ *noun* savoury flan.

**quick** • *adjective* taking only a short time; arriving after only a short time, prompt; with only a short interval; lively, alert, intelligent; (of temper) easily roused. • *adverb* quickly. • *noun* soft sensitive flesh, esp. below nails or skin; seat of emotion. □ **quicklime** unslaked lime; **quicksand** (often in *plural*) area of loose wet sand that sucks in anything placed on it, treacherous situation etc.; **quickset** (of hedge etc.) formed of cuttings, esp. hawthorn; **quicksilver** mercury; **quickstep** fast foxtrot; **quick-tempered** easily angered; **quick-witted** quick to grasp situation, make repartee, etc.; **quickwittedness** *noun.* □ **quickly** *adverb.*

**quicken** *verb* make or become quicker, accelerate; give life or vigour to, rouse; (of woman) reach stage in pregnancy when movements of foetus can be felt; (of foetus) begin to show signs of life.

**quid**[1] *noun* slang (*plural* same) one pound sterling.

**quid**[2] *noun* lump of tobacco for chewing.

**quid pro quo** /kwɪd prəʊ ˈkwəʊ/ *noun* (*plural* **quid pro quos**) gift, favour, etc. exchanged for another.

**quiescent** /kwɪˈes(ə)nt/ *adjective* inert, dormant. □ **quiescence** *noun.*

**quiet** /ˈkwaɪət/ • *adjective* with little or no sound or motion; of gentle or peaceful disposition; unobtrusive, not showy; not overt, disguised; undisturbed, uninterrupted; not busy. • *noun* silence, stillness; undisturbed state, tranquillity. • *verb* (often + *down*) make or become quiet, calm. □ **be quiet** (esp. in *imperative*) cease talking etc.; **keep quiet** (often + *about*) say nothing; **on the quiet** secretly. □ **quietly** *adverb;* **quietness** *noun.*

**quieten** *verb* (often + *down*) make or become quiet or calm.

**quietism** *noun* passive contemplative attitude towards life. □ **quietist** *noun & adjective.*

**quietude** /ˈkwaɪɪtjuːd/ *noun* state of quiet.

**quietus** /kwaɪˈiːtəs/ *noun* release from life; death, final riddance.

**quiff** *noun* man's tuft of hair brushed upwards in front.

**quill** *noun* (in full **quill-feather**) large feather in wing or tail; hollow stem of this; (in full **quill pen**) pen made of quill; (usually in *plural*) porcupine's spine.

**quilt** • *noun* bedspread, esp. of quilted material. • *verb* line bedspread or garment with padding enclosed between layers of fabric by lines of stitching. □ **quilter** *noun;* **quilting** *noun.*

**quin** *noun* colloquial quintuplet.

**quince** *noun* (tree bearing) acid pear-shaped fruit used in jams etc.

**quincentenary** /kwɪnsenˈtiːnərɪ/ • *noun* (*plural* **-ies**) 500th anniversary; celebration of this. • *adjective* of this anniversary.

**quinine** /ˈkwɪniːn/ *noun* bitter drug used as a tonic and to reduce fever.

**Quinquagesima** /kwɪŋkwəˈdʒesɪmə/ *noun* Sunday before Lent.

**quinquennial** /kwɪŋˈkwenɪəl/ *adjective* lasting 5 years; recurring every 5 years. □ **quinquennially** *adverb.*

**quintessence** /kwɪnˈtes(ə)ns/ *noun* (usually + *of*) purest and most perfect form, manifestation, or embodiment of quality etc.; highly refined extract. □ **quintessential** /-tɪˈsen-/ *adjective;* **quintessentially** /-tɪˈsen-/ *adverb.*

**quintet** /kwɪnˈtet/ *noun* musical composition for 5 performers; the performers; any group of 5.

**quintuple** /ˈkwɪntjʊp(ə)l/ • *adjective* fivefold, having 5 parts. • *noun* fivefold number or amount. • *verb* (**-ling**) multiply by 5.

**quintuplet** /ˈkwɪntjʊplɪt/ *noun* each of 5 children born at one birth.

**quip** • *noun* clever saying, epigram. • *verb* (**-pp-**) make quips.

**quire** *noun* 25 sheets of paper.

**quirk** *noun* peculiar feature; trick of fate. □ **quirky** *adjective* (**-ier**, **-iest**).

**quisling** /'kwɪzlɪŋ/ *noun* collaborator with invading enemy.

**quit** • *verb* (**-tting**; *past & past participle* **quitted** or **quit**) give up, let go, abandon; *US* cease, stop; leave or depart from. • *adjective* (+ *of*) rid of.

**quitch** *noun* couch grass.

**quite** *adverb* completely, altogether, absolutely; rather, to some extent; (often + *so*) *said to indicate agreement*. □ **quite a**, **quite some** a remarkable; **quite a few** *colloquial* a fairly large number (of); **quite something** *colloquial* a remarkable thing or person.

**quits** *adjective* on even terms by retaliation or repayment. □ **call it quits** acknowledge that things are now even, agree to stop quarrelling.

**quiver**[1] /'kwɪvə/ • *verb* tremble or vibrate with slight rapid motion. • *noun* quivering motion or sound.

**quiver**[2] /'kwɪvə/ *noun* case for arrows.

**quixotic** /kwɪk'sɒtɪk/ *adjective* extravagantly and romantically chivalrous. □ **quixotically** *adverb*.

**quiz** • *noun* (*plural* **quizzes**) test of knowledge, esp. as entertainment; interrogation, examination. • *verb* examine by questioning.

**quizzical** /'kwɪzɪk(ə)l/ *adjective* mocking, gently amused. □ **quizzically** *adverb*.

**quod** *noun slang* prison.

**quoin** /kɔɪn/ *noun* external angle of building; cornerstone; wedge used in printing or gunnery.

**quoit** /kɔɪt/ *noun* ring thrown to encircle peg; (in *plural*) game using these.

**quondam** /'kwɒndæm/ *adjective* that once was, former.

**quorate** /'kwɔːreɪt/ *adjective* constituting or having quorum.

**Quorn** /kwɔːn/ *noun proprietary term* vegetable protein food made from fungus.

**quorum** /'kwɔːrəm/ *noun* minimum number of members that must be present to constitute valid meeting.

---

## Quotation marks ' ' " "

Also called inverted commas, these are used:

**1** round a direct quotation (closing quotation marks come after any punctuation which is part of the quotation), e.g.

> He said, 'That is nonsense.'
> 'That', he said, 'is nonsense.'
> 'That, however,' he said, 'is nonsense.'
> Did he say, 'That is nonsense'?
> He asked, 'Is that nonsense?'

**2** round a quoted word or phrase, e.g.

> What does 'integrated circuit' mean?

**3** round a word or phrase that is not being used in its central sense, e.g.

> the 'king' of jazz
> He said he had enough 'bread' to buy a car.

**4** round the title of a book, song, poem, magazine article, television programme, etc. (but not a book of the Bible), e.g.

> 'Hard Times' by Charles Dickens

**5** as double quotation marks round a quotation within a quotation, e.g.

> He asked, 'Do you know what "integrated circuit" means?'

In handwriting, double quotation marks are usual.

---

**quota** /'kwəʊtə/ *noun* share to be contributed to or received from total; number of goods, people, etc. stipulated or permitted.

**quotable** *adjective* worth quoting.

**quotation** /kwəʊ'teɪʃ(ə)n/ *noun* passage or remark quoted; quoting, being quoted; contractor's estimate. □ **quotation marks** inverted commas (' ' or " ") used at beginning and end of quotation etc. (see panel).

**quote** ● *verb* (**-ting**) cite or appeal to as example, authority, etc.; repeat or copy out passage from; (+ *from*) cite (author, book, etc.); (+ *as*) cite (author etc.) as proof, evidence, etc.; (as *interjection*) *used in dictation* etc. to indicate opening quotation marks; (often + *at*) state price of; state (price) for job. ● *noun colloquial* passage quoted; (usually in *plural*) quotation marks.

**quoth** /kwəʊθ/ *verb* (only in 1st & 3rd persons) *archaic* said.

**quotidian** /kwɒ'tɪdɪən/ *adjective* occurring or recurring daily; commonplace, trivial.

**quotient** /'kwəʊʃ(ə)nt/ *noun* result of division sum.

**q.v.** *abbreviation* which see (*quod vide*).

# Rr

**R** *abbreviation* (also **R.**) *Regina*; *Rex*; River; (also ®) registered as trademark. □ **R & D** research and development.

**r.** *abbreviation* (also **r**) right; radius.

**RA** *abbreviation* Royal Academy or Academician; Royal Artillery.

**rabbet** /'ræbɪt/ ● *noun* step-shaped channel cut along edge or face of wood etc. to receive edge or tongue of another piece. ● *verb* (**-t-**) join with rabbet; make rabbet in.

**rabbi** /'ræbaɪ/ *noun* (*plural* **-s**) Jewish religious leader; Jewish scholar or teacher, esp. of the law. □ **rabbinical** /rə'bɪn-/ *adjective*.

**rabbit** /'ræbɪt/ ● *noun* burrowing mammal of hare family; its fur. ● *verb* (**-t-**) hunt rabbits; (often + *on*, *away*) *colloquial* talk pointlessly; chatter. □ **rabbit punch** blow with edge of hand on back of neck.

**rabble** /'ræb(ə)l/ *noun* disorderly crowd, mob; contemptible or inferior set of people. □ **rabble-rouser** person who stirs up rabble, esp. to agitate for social change.

**Rabelaisian** /ræbə'leɪzɪən/ *adjective* exuberantly and coarsely humorous.

**rabid** /'ræbɪd/ *adjective* affected with rabies, mad; violent, fanatical. □ **rabidity** /rə'bɪd-/ *noun*.

**rabies** /'reɪbiːz/ *noun* contagious viral disease of esp. dogs; hydrophobia.

**RAC** *abbreviation* Royal Automobile Club.

**raccoon** /rə'kuːn/ *noun* (also **racoon**) (*plural* same or **-s**) N. American mammal with bushy tail; its fur.

**race¹** ● *noun* contest of speed or to be first to achieve something; (in *plural*) series of races for horses etc.; strong current in sea or river; channel. ● *verb* (**-cing**) take part in race; have race with; (+ *with*) compete in speed; cause to race; go at full speed; (usually as **racing** *adjective*) follow or take part in horse racing. □ **racecourse** ground for horse racing; **racehorse** one bred or kept for racing; **race meeting** sequence of horse races at one place; **racetrack** racecourse, track for motor racing; **racing car** one built for racing; **racing driver** driver of racing car.

**race²** *noun* each of the major divisions of humankind, each having distinct physical characteristics; group of people, animals, or plants connected by common descent; any great division of living creatures. □ **race relations** relations between members of different races in same country.

**raceme** /rə'siːm/ *noun* flower cluster with flowers attached by short stalks at equal distances along stem.

**racial** /ˈreɪʃ(ə)l/ *adjective* of or concerning race; on grounds of or connected with difference in race. □ **racially** *adverb*.

**racialism** *noun* = RACISM. □ **racialist** *noun & adjective*.

**racism** *noun* (prejudice based on) belief in superiority of particular race; antagonism towards other races. □ **racist** *noun & adjective*.

**rack**¹ ● *noun* framework, usually with rails, bars, etc., for holding things; cogged or toothed rail or bar engaging with wheel, pinion, etc.; *historical* instrument of torture stretching victim's joints. ● *verb* inflict suffering on; *historical* torture on rack. □ **rack one's brains** make great mental effort; **rack-rent** extortionate rent.

**rack**² *noun* destruction (esp. in **rack and ruin**).

**rack**³ *verb* (often + *off*) draw off (wine etc.) from lees.

**racket**¹ /ˈrækɪt/ *noun* (also **racquet**) bat with round or oval frame strung with catgut, nylon, etc., used in tennis etc.; (in *plural*) game like squash but in larger court.

**racket**² ● *noun* uproar, din; *slang* scheme for obtaining money etc. by dishonest means; dodge; sly game; *colloquial* line of business.

**racketeer** /rækɪˈtɪə/ *noun* person who operates dishonest business. □ **racketeering** *noun*.

**raconteur** /rækɒnˈtɜː/ *noun* teller of anecdotes.

**racoon** = RACCOON.

**racy** *adjective* (**-ier**, **-iest**) lively and vigorous in style; risqué; of distinctive quality. □ **raciness** *noun*.

**rad** *noun* unit of absorbed dose of ionizing radiation.

**RADA** /ˈrɑːdə/ *abbreviation* Royal Academy of Dramatic Art.

**radar** /ˈreɪdɑː/ *noun* radio system for detecting the direction, range, or presence of objects; apparatus for this. □ **radar trap** device using radar to detect speeding vehicles.

**raddled** /ˈræd(ə)ld/ *adjective* worn out.

**radial** /ˈreɪdɪəl/ ● *adjective* of or arranged like rays or radii; having spokes or radiating lines; acting or moving along

such lines; (in full **radial-ply**) (of tyre) having fabric layers arranged radially. ● *noun* radial-ply tyre. □ **radially** *adverb*.

**radian** /ˈreɪdɪən/ *noun* SI unit of plane angle (about 57°).

**radiant** /ˈreɪdɪənt/ ● *adjective* emitting or issuing in rays; beaming with joy etc.; splendid, dazzling. ● *noun* point or object from which heat or light radiates. □ **radiance** *noun*; **radiantly** *adverb*.

**radiate** /ˈreɪdɪeɪt/ *verb* (**-ting**) emit rays of light, heat, etc.; be emitted in rays; emit or spread from a centre; transmit or demonstrate.

**radiation** *noun* radiating; emission of energy as electromagnetic waves; energy thus transmitted, esp. invisibly; (in full **radiation therapy**) treatment of cancer etc. using e.g. X-rays or ultraviolet light. □ **radiation sickness** sickness caused by exposure to radiation such as gamma rays.

**radiator** *noun* device for heating room etc. by circulation of hot water etc.; engine-cooling device in motor vehicle or aircraft.

**radical** /ˈrædɪk(ə)l/ ● *adjective* fundamental; far-reaching, thorough; advocating fundamental reform; forming the basis; primary; of the root of a number or plant. ● *noun* person holding radical views; atom or group of atoms forming base of compound and remaining unchanged during reactions; quantity forming or expressed as root of another. □ **radicalism** *noun*; **radically** *adverb*.

**radicchio** /rəˈdiːkɪəʊ/ *noun* (*plural* **-s**) chicory with purplish leaves.

**radicle** /ˈrædɪk(ə)l/ *noun* part of seed that develops into root.

**radii** *plural of* **radius**.

**radio** /ˈreɪdɪəʊ/ ● *noun* (*plural* **-s**) transmission and reception of messages etc. by electromagnetic waves of radio frequency; apparatus for receiving, broadcasting, or transmitting radio signals; sound broadcasting (station or channel). ● *verb* (**-es**, **-ed**) send (message) by radio; send message to (person) by radio; communicate or broadcast by radio. □ **radio-controlled** controlled from a distance by radio; **radio telephone** one operating by radio; **radio**

**telescope** aerial system for analysing radiation in the radio-frequency range from stars etc.

**radioactive** *adjective* of or exhibiting radioactivity.

**radioactivity** *noun* spontaneous disintegration of atomic nuclei, with emission of usually penetrating radiation or particles.

**radiocarbon** *noun* radioactive isotope of carbon.

**radiogram** /ˈreɪdɪəʊɡræm/ *noun* combined radio and record player; picture obtained by X-rays etc.; telegram sent by radio.

**radiograph** /ˈreɪdɪəʊɡrɑːf/ ● *noun* instrument recording intensity of radiation; picture obtained by X-rays etc. ● *verb* obtain picture of by X-rays, gamma rays, etc. □ **radiographer** /-ˈɒɡrəfə/ *noun*; **radiography** /-ˈɒɡrəfɪ/ *noun*.

**radiology** /reɪdɪˈɒlədʒɪ/ *noun esp. Medicine* study of X-rays and other high-energy radiation. □ **radiologist** *noun*.

**radiophonic** *adjective* of electronically produced sound, esp. music.

**radioscopy** /reɪdɪˈɒskəpɪ/ *noun* examination by X-rays etc. of objects opaque to light.

**radiotherapy** *noun* treatment of disease by X-rays or other forms of radiation.

**radish** /ˈrædɪʃ/ *noun* plant with crisp pungent root; this root, esp. eaten raw.

**radium** /ˈreɪdɪəm/ *noun* radioactive metallic element.

**radius** /ˈreɪdɪəs/ *noun* ( *plural* **radii** /-dɪaɪ/ or **-es**) straight line from centre to circumference of circle or sphere; distance from a centre; bone of forearm on same side as thumb.

**radon** /ˈreɪdɒn/ *noun* gaseous radioactive inert element arising from disintegration of radium.

**RAF** *abbreviation* Royal Air Force.

**raffia** /ˈræfɪə/ *noun* palm tree native to Madagascar; fibre from its leaves.

**raffish** /ˈræfɪʃ/ *adjective* disreputable, rakish; tawdry.

**raffle** /ˈræf(ə)l/ ● *noun* fund-raising lottery with prizes. ● *verb* (**-ling**) (often + *off* ) sell by raffle.

**raft** /rɑːft/ *noun* flat floating structure of wood etc., used for transport.

**rafter** /ˈrɑːftə/ *noun* any of sloping beams forming framework of roof.

**rag** [1] *noun* torn, frayed, or worn piece of woven material; remnant; (in *plural* ) old or worn clothes; *derogatory* newspaper. □ **rag-bag** miscellaneous collection; **rag doll** stuffed cloth doll; **ragtime** form of highly syncopated early jazz; **the rag trade** *colloquial* the clothing business; **ragwort** yellow-flowered ragged-leaved plant.

**rag** [2] ● *noun* fund-raising programme of stunts etc. staged by students; prank; rowdy celebration, disorderly scene. ● *verb* (**-gg-**) tease; play rough jokes on; engage in rough play.

**ragamuffin** /ˈrægəmʌfɪn/ *noun* child in ragged dirty clothes.

**rage** ● *noun* violent anger; fit of this. ● *verb* (**-ging**) be full of anger; (often + *at, against*) speak furiously; be violent, be at its height; (as **raging** *adjective*) extreme, very painful. □ **all the rage** very popular, fashionable.

**ragged** /ˈrægɪd/ *adjective* torn; frayed; in ragged clothes; with a broken or jagged outline or surface; lacking finish, smoothness, or uniformity.

**raglan** /ˈræglən/ *adjective* (of sleeve) running up to neck of garment.

**ragout** /ræˈguː/ *noun* highly seasoned stew of meat and vegetables.

**raid** ● *noun* rapid surprise attack by armed forces or thieves; surprise visit by police etc. to arrest suspects or seize illicit goods. ● *verb* make raid on. □ **raider** *noun*.

**rail** [1] ● *noun* bar used to hang things on or as protection, part of fence, top of banisters, etc.; steel bar(s) making railway track; railway. ● *verb* provide or enclose with rail(s). □ **railcard** pass entitling holder to reduced rail fares.

**rail** [2] *verb* (often + *at, against*) complain or protest strongly; rant.

**rail** [3] *noun* marsh wading bird.

**railing** *noun* (often in *plural*) fence or barrier made of rails.

**raillery** /ˈreɪlərɪ/ *noun* good-humoured ridicule.

**railroad** ● *noun esp. US* railway. ● *verb* (often + *into, through*) coerce, rush.

**railway** /ˈreɪlweɪ/ *noun* track or set of tracks of steel rails on which trains run; organization and people required to work such a system. □ **railwayman** male railway employee.

**raiment** /'reɪmənt/ noun archaic clothing.

**rain** ● noun condensed atmospheric moisture falling in drops; fall of these; falling liquid or objects; (**the rains**) rainy season. ● verb (after it) rain falls, send in large quantities; fall or send down like rain; lavishly bestow. □ **raincoat** waterproof or water-resistant coat; **rainfall** total amount of rain falling within given area in given time; **rainforest** tropical forest with heavy rainfall; **take a rain check on** reserve right to postpone taking up (offer) until convenient.

**rainbow** /'reɪnbəʊ/ ● noun arch of colours formed in sky by reflection, refraction, and dispersion of sun's rays in falling rain etc. ● adjective many-coloured. □ **rainbow trout** large trout originally of N. America.

**rainy** adjective (**-ier, -iest**) (of weather, day, climate, etc.) in or on which rain is falling or much rain usually falls. □ **rainy day** time of need in the future.

**raise** /reɪz/ ● verb (**-sing**) put or take into higher position; (often + up) cause to rise or stand up or be vertical; increase amount, value, or strength of; (often + up) build up; levy; collect; cause to be heard or considered; bring up, educate; breed; remove (barrier); rouse. ● noun Cards increase in stake or bid; US rise in salary. □ **raise Cain, hell, the roof** be very angry, cause an uproar; **raise a laugh** cause others to laugh.

**raisin** /'reɪz(ə)n/ noun dried grape.

**raison d'être** /reɪzõ 'detr/ noun (plural **raisons d'être** same pronunciation) purpose that accounts for, justifies, or originally caused thing's existence. [French]

**raj** /rɑːdʒ/ noun (**the raj**) historical British rule in India.

**raja** /'rɑːdʒə/ noun (also **rajah**) historical Indian king or prince.

**rake**[1] ● noun implement with long handle and toothed crossbar for drawing hay etc. together, smoothing loose soil, etc.; similar implement. ● verb (**-king**) collect or gather (as) with rake; ransack, search thoroughly; direct

gunfire along (line) from end to end. □ **rake in** colloquial amass (profits etc.); **rake-off** colloquial commission or share; **rake up** revive (unwelcome) memory of.

**rake**[2] noun dissolute man of fashion.

**rake**[3] ● verb (**-king**) set or be set at sloping angle. ● noun raking position or build; amount by which things rakes.

**rakish** adjective dashing, jaunty; dissolute. □ **rakishly** adverb.

**rallentando** /rælən'tændəʊ/ Music ● adverb & adjective with gradual decrease of speed. ● noun (plural **-s** or **-di** /-dɪ/) rallentando passage.

**rally** /'rælɪ/ ● verb (**-ies, -ied**) (often + round) bring or come together as support for action; recover after illness etc., revive; (of prices etc.) increase after fall. ● noun (plural **-ies**) rallying, being rallied; mass meeting; competition for motor vehicles over public roads; extended exchange of strokes in tennis etc. □ **rallycross** motor racing across country.

**RAM** abbreviation Royal Academy of Music; random-access memory.

**ram** ● noun uncastrated male sheep; (**the Ram**) zodiacal sign or constellation Aries; falling weight of pile-driving machine; hydraulic water pump. ● verb (**-mm-**) force into place; (usually + down, in, etc.) beat down or drive in by blows; (of ship, vehicle, etc.) strike, crash against. □ **ram-raid** crashing vehicle into shop front in order to steal contents; **ram-raider** noun.

**Ramadan** /'ræmədæn/ noun ninth month of Muslim year, with strict fasting from sunrise to sunset.

**ramble** /'ræmb(ə)l/ ● verb (**-ling**) walk for pleasure; talk or write incoherently. ● noun walk taken for pleasure.

**rambler** noun person who rambles; straggling or spreading rose.

**rambling** adjective wandering; disconnected, incoherent; irregularly arranged; (of plant) straggling, climbing.

**RAMC** abbreviation Royal Army Medical Corps.

**ramekin** /'ræmɪkɪn/ noun small dish for baking and serving individual portion of food.

**ramification** /ˌræmɪfɪˈkeɪʃ(ə)n/ *noun* (usually in *plural*) consequence; subdivision.

**ramify** /ˈræmɪfaɪ/ *verb* (**-ies**, **-ied**) (cause to) form branches or subdivisions; branch out.

**ramp** *noun* slope joining two levels of ground, floor, etc.; stairs for entering or leaving aircraft; transverse ridge in road making vehicles slow down.

**rampage** ● *verb* /ræmˈpeɪdʒ/ (**-ging**) (often + *about*) rush wildly; rage, storm. ● *noun* /ˈræmpeɪdʒ/ wild or violent behaviour. □ **on the rampage** rampaging.

**rampant** /ˈræmpənt/ *adjective* unchecked, flourishing excessively; rank, luxuriant; *Heraldry* (of lion etc.) standing on left hind foot with forepaws in air; fanatical. □ **rampancy** *noun*.

**rampart** /ˈræmpɑːt/ *noun* defensive broad-topped wall; defence, protection.

**ramrod** *noun* rod for ramming down charge of muzzle-loading firearm; thing that is very straight or rigid.

**ramshackle** /ˈræmʃæk(ə)l/ *adjective* rickety, tumbledown.

**ran** *past of* RUN.

**ranch** /rɑːntʃ/ ● *noun* cattle-breeding establishment, esp. in US & Canada; farm where other animals are bred. ● *verb* farm on ranch. □ **rancher** *noun*.

**rancid** /ˈrænsɪd/ *adjective* smelling or tasting like rank stale fat. □ **rancidity** /-ˈsɪd-/ *noun*.

**rancour** /ˈræŋkə/ *noun* (*US* **rancor**) inveterate bitterness; malignant hate. □ **rancorous** *adjective*.

**rand** *noun* monetary unit of South Africa.

**random** /ˈrændəm/ *adjective* made, done, etc. without method or conscious choice. □ **at random** without particular aim; **random-access** (of computer memory) having all parts directly accessible. □ **randomly** *adverb*.

**randy** /ˈrændɪ/ *adjective* (**-ier**, **-iest**) eager for sexual satisfaction.

**ranee** /ˈrɑːniː/ *noun* (also **rani**) (*plural* **-s**) *historical* raja's wife or widow.

**rang** *past of* RING².

**range** /reɪndʒ/ ● *noun* region between limits of variation, esp. scope of operation; such limits; area relevant to something; distance attainable by gun or projectile, distance between gun etc. and target; row, series, etc., esp. of mountains; area with targets for shooting; fireplace for cooking; area over which a thing is distributed; distance that can be covered by vehicle without refuelling; stretch of open land for grazing or hunting. ● *verb* (**-ging**) reach; extend; vary between limits; (usually in *passive*) line up, arrange; rove, wonder; traverse in all directions. □ **range-finder** instrument for determining distance of object.

**ranger** *noun* keeper of royal or national park, or of forest; (**Ranger**) senior Guide.

**rangy** /ˈreɪndʒɪ/ *adjective* (**-ier**, **-iest**) tall and slim.

**rani** = RANEE.

**rank**¹ ● *noun* position in hierarchy; grade of advancement; distinct social class, grade of dignity or achievement; high social position; place in scale; row or line; single line of soldiers drawn up abreast; place where taxis wait for customers. ● *verb* have rank or place; classify, give a certain grade to; arrange in rank. □ **rank and file** (usually treated as *plural*) ordinary members of organization; **the ranks** common soldiers.

**rank**² *adjective* luxuriant; coarse; choked with weeds etc.; foul-smelling; loathsome; flagrant; gross, complete.

**rankle** /ˈræŋk(ə)l/ *verb* (**-ling**) cause persistent annoyance or resentment.

**ransack** /ˈrænsæk/ *verb* pillage, plunder; thoroughly search.

**ransom** /ˈrænsəm/ ● *noun* sum demanded or paid for release of prisoner. ● *verb* buy freedom or restoration of; hold (prisoner) to ransom; release for a ransom. □ **hold to ransom** keep (prisoner) and demand ransom, demand concessions from by threats.

**rant** ● *verb* speak loudly, bombastically, or violently. ● *noun* piece of ranting. □ **rant and rave** express anger noisily and forcefully.

**ranunculus** /rəˈnʌŋkjʊləs/ *noun* (*plural* **-luses** or **-li** /-laɪ/) plant of genus including buttercup.

**RAOC** *abbreviation* Royal Army Ordnance Corps.

**rap¹** • noun smart slight blow; sound of this, tap; slang blame, punishment; rhythmic monologue recited to music; (in full **rap music**) style of rock music with words recited. • verb (**-pp-**) strike smartly; make sharp tapping sound; criticize adversely; Music perform rap. □ **take the rap** suffer the consequences. □ **rapper** noun Music.

**rap²** noun the least bit.

**rapacious** /rəˈpeɪʃəs/ adjective grasping, extortionate, predatory. □ **rapacity** /-ˈpæs-/ noun.

**rape¹** • noun act of forcing woman or girl to have sexual intercourse against her will; (often + of) violent assault or plunder. • verb (**-ping**) commit rape on.

**rape²** noun plant grown as fodder and for oil from its seed.

**rapid** /ˈræpɪd/ • adjective (**-er, -est**) quick, swift. • noun (usually in plural) steep descent in river bed, with swift current. □ **rapid eye movement** jerky movement of eyes during dreaming. □ **rapidity** /rəˈpɪd-/ noun; **rapidly** adverb.

**rapier** /ˈreɪpɪə/ noun light slender sword for thrusting.

**rapine** /ˈræpaɪn/ noun rhetorical plundering.

**rapist** noun person who commits rape.

**rapport** /ræˈpɔː/ noun communication or relationship, esp. when useful and harmonious.

**rapprochement** /ræˈprɒʃmɑ̃/ noun resumption of harmonious relations, esp. between states. [French]

**rapscallion** /ræpˈskæljən/ noun archaic rascal.

**rapt** adjective absorbed; intent; carried away with feeling or thought.

**rapture** /ˈræptʃə/ noun ecstatic delight; (in plural) great pleasure or enthusiasm or expression of it. □ **rapturous** adjective.

**rare¹** adjective (**-r, -st**) seldom done, found, or occurring; uncommon; exceptionally good; of less than usual density. □ **rareness** noun.

**rare²** adjective (**-r, -st**) (of meat) underdone.

**rarebit** noun see WELSH RAREBIT.

**rarefy** /ˈreərɪfaɪ/ verb (**-ies, -ied**) (often as **rarefied** adjective) make or become

less dense or solid; refine, make (idea etc.) subtle. □ **rarefaction** /-ˈfækʃ(ə)n/ noun.

**rarely** adverb seldom, not often.

**raring** /ˈreərɪŋ/ adjective colloquial eager (esp. in **raring to go**).

**rarity** /ˈreərətɪ/ noun (plural **-ies**) rareness; uncommon thing.

**rascal** /ˈrɑːsk(ə)l/ noun dishonest or mischievous person. □ **rascally** adjective.

**rase** = RAZE.

**rash¹** adjective reckless; hasty, impetuous. □ **rashly** adverb; **rashness** noun.

**rash²** noun skin eruption in spots or patches; (usually + of) sudden widespread phenomenon.

**rasher** /ˈræʃə/ noun thin slice of bacon or ham.

**rasp** /rɑːsp/ • noun coarse file; grating noise or utterance. • verb scrape roughly or with rasp; make grating sound; say gratingly; grate on.

**raspberry** /ˈrɑːzbərɪ/ noun (plural **-ies**) red fruit like blackberry; shrub bearing this; colloquial sound made by blowing through lips, expressing derision or disapproval.

**Rastafarian** /ræstəˈfeərɪən/ (also **Rasta** /ˈræstə/) • noun member of Jamaican sect regarding Haile Selassie of Ethiopia (d. 1975) as God. • adjective of this sect.

**rat** • noun large mouselike rodent; colloquial unpleasant or treacherous person. • verb (**-tt-**) hunt or kill rats; (also + on) inform (on), desert, betray. □ **ratbag** slang obnoxious person; **rat race** colloquial fiercely competitive struggle.

**ratable** = RATEABLE.

**ratatouille** /rætəˈtuːɪ/ noun dish of stewed onions, courgettes, tomatoes, aubergines, and peppers.

**ratchet** /ˈrætʃɪt/ noun set of teeth on edge of bar or wheel with catch ensuring motion in one direction only; (in full **ratchet-wheel**) wheel with rim so toothed.

**rate** • noun numerical proportion between two sets of things or as basis of calculating amount or value; charge, cost, or value; measure of this; pace of movement or change; (in plural) tax levied by local authorities according to

value of buildings and land occupied.
● *verb* (**-ting**) estimate worth or value of;
assign value to; consider, regard as; (+
*as*) rank or be considered as; subject to
payment of local rate; deserve. □ **at
any rate** in any case, whatever happens; **at this rate** if this example is
typical; **rate-capping** *historical* imposition of upper limit on local authority
rates; **ratepayer** person liable to pay
rates.

**rateable** /ˈreɪtəb(ə)l/ *adjective* (also
**ratable** /ˈreɪtəb(ə)l/) liable to rates.
□ **rateable value** value at which business etc. is assessed for rates.

**rather** /ˈrɑːðə/ *adverb* by preference;
(usually + *than*) more truly; as a more
likely alternative; more precisely; to
some extent; /rɑːˈðɜː/ most emphatically.

**ratify** /ˈrætɪfaɪ/ *verb* (**-ies, -ied**) confirm
or accept by formal consent, signature,
etc. □ **ratification** *noun*.

**rating** /ˈreɪtɪŋ/ *noun* placing in rank or
class; estimated standing of person as
regards credit etc.; non-commissioned
sailor; (usually in *plural*) popularity of a
broadcast as determined by estimated
size of audience.

**ratio** /ˈreɪʃɪəʊ/ *noun* (*plural* **-s**) quantitative relation between similar magnitudes.

**ratiocinate** /rætɪˈɒsɪneɪt/ *verb* (**-ting**) *literary* reason, esp. using syllogisms.
□ **ratiocination** *noun*.

**ration** /ˈræʃ(ə)n/ ● *noun* official allowance of food, clothing, etc., in time of
shortage; (usually in *plural*) fixed daily
allowance of food. ● *verb* limit (food etc.
or people) to fixed ration; (usually +
*out*) share (out) in fixed quantities.

**rational** /ˈræʃən(ə)l/ *adjective* of or based
on reason; sensible; endowed with reason; rejecting what is unreasonable;
*Mathematics* expressible as ratio of whole
numbers. □ **rationality** /-ˈnæl-/ *noun*;
**rationally** *adverb*.

**rationale** /ræʃəˈnɑːl/ *noun* fundamental
reason, logical basis.

**rationalism** *noun* practice of treating
reason as basis of belief and knowledge. □ **rationalist** *noun & adjective*; **rationalistic** /-ˈlɪs-/ *adjective*.

**rationalize** *verb* (also **-ise**) (**-zing** or
**-sing**) (often + *away*) offer rational but

specious explanation of (behaviour or
attitude); make logical and consistent;
make (industry etc.) more efficient
by reducing waste. □ **rationalization**
*noun*.

**ratline** /ˈrætlɪn/ *noun* (also **ratlin**) (usually in *plural*) any of the small lines
fastened across ship's shrouds like ladder rungs.

**rattan** /rəˈtæn/ *noun* palm with long thin
many-jointed stems; cane of this.

**rattle** /ˈræt(ə)l/ ● *verb* (**-ling**) (cause to)
give out rapid succession of short
sharp sounds; cause such sounds by
shaking something; move or travel
with rattling noise; (usually + *off*) say
or recite rapidly; (usually + *on*) talk in
lively thoughtless way; *colloquial* disconcert, alarm. ● *noun* rattling sound; device or plaything made to rattle.
□ **rattlesnake** poisonous American
snake with rattling rings on tail. □ **rattly** *adjective*.

**rattling** ● *adjective* that rattles; brisk,
vigorous. ● *adverb colloquial* remarkably
(good etc.).

**raucous** /ˈrɔːkəs/ *adjective* harsh-sounding; hoarse. □ **raucously** *adverb*; **raucousness** *noun*.

**raunchy** /ˈrɔːntʃɪ/ *adjective* (**-ier, -iest**)
*colloquial* sexually boisterous.

**ravage** /ˈrævɪdʒ/ ● *verb* (**-ging**) devastate, plunder. ● *noun* (usually in *plural*; +
*of*) destructive effect.

**rave** ● *verb* (**-ving**) talk wildly or deliriously; (usually + *about, over*) speak
with rapturous admiration; *colloquial* enjoy oneself freely. ● *noun colloquial* highly
enthusiastic review; (also **rave-up**)
lively party.

**ravel** /ˈræv(ə)l/ *verb* (**-ll-**; *US* **-l-**) entangle,
become entangled; fray out.

**raven** /ˈreɪv(ə)n/ ● *noun* large glossy
black crow with hoarse cry. ● *adjective*
glossy black.

**ravening** /ˈrævənɪŋ/ *adjective* hungrily
seeking prey; voracious.

**ravenous** /ˈrævənəs/ *adjective* very
hungry; voracious; rapacious. □ **ravenously** *adverb*.

**raver** *noun colloquial* uninhibited
pleasure-loving person.

**ravine** /rəˈviːn/ *noun* deep narrow gorge.

**raving** ● *noun* (usually in *plural*) wild or delirious talk. ● *adjective colloquial* utter, absolute. ● *adverb colloquial* utterly, absolutely.

**ravioli** /rævɪˈəʊlɪ/ *noun* small square pasta envelopes containing meat, spinach, etc.

**ravish** /ˈrævɪʃ/ *verb archaic* rape (woman); enrapture.

**ravishing** *adjective* lovely, beautiful. □ **ravishingly** *adverb*.

**raw** *adjective* uncooked; in natural state, not processed or manufactured; inexperienced, untrained; stripped of skin; unhealed; sensitive to touch; (of weather) cold and damp; crude. □ **in the raw** in its natural state, naked; **raw-boned** gaunt; **raw deal** unfair treatment; **rawhide** untanned hide, rope or whip of this; **raw material** material from which manufactured goods are made.

**Rawlplug** /ˈrɔːlplʌg/ *noun proprietary term* cylindrical plug for holding screw in masonry.

**ray**[1] *noun* single line or narrow beam of light; straight line in which radiation travels; (in *plural*) radiation; trace or beginning of enlightening influence; any of set of radiating lines, parts, or things; marginal part of daisy etc.

**ray**[2] *noun* large edible marine fish with flat body.

**ray**[3] *noun* (also **re**) *Music* second note of scale in tonic sol-fa.

**rayon** /ˈreɪɒn/ *noun* textile fibre or fabric made from cellulose.

**raze** *verb* (also **rase**) (**-zing** or **-sing**) completely destroy, tear down.

**razor** /ˈreɪzə/ *noun* instrument for shaving. □ **razorbill** auk with sharp-edged bill; **razor-blade** flat piece of metal with sharp edge, used in safety razor; **razor-edge**, **razor's edge** keen edge, sharp mountain ridge, critical situation, sharp line of division.

**razzle** /ˈræz(ə)l/ *noun colloquial* spree. □ **razzle-dazzle** excitement, bustle, extravagant publicity.

**razzmatazz** /ˌræzməˈtæz/ *noun* (also **razzamatazz** /ˌræzə-/) *colloquial* glamorous excitement; insincere activity.

**RC** *abbreviation* Roman Catholic.

**Rd.** *abbreviation* Road.

**RE** *abbreviation* Religious Education; Royal Engineers.

**re**[1] /riː/ *preposition* in the matter of; about, concerning.

**re**[2] = RAY[3].

**re-** *prefix attachable to almost any verb or its derivative, meaning*: once more, anew, afresh; back. For words starting with *re-* that are not found below, the root-words should be consulted.

**reach** ● *verb* (often + *out*) stretch out, extend; (often + *for*) stretch hand etc.; get as far as, get to or attain; make contact with; pass, hand; take with outstretched hand; *Nautical* sail with wind abeam. ● *noun* extent to which hand etc. can be reached out, influence exerted, etc.; act of reaching out; continuous extent, esp. of river or canal. □ **reach-me-down** *colloquial* ready-made garment. □ **reachable** *adjective*.

**react** /rɪˈækt/ *verb* (often + *to*) respond to stimulus; change or behave differently due to some influence; (often + *with*) undergo chemical reaction (with other substance); (often + *against*) respond with repulsion to; tend in reverse or contrary direction.

**reaction** /rɪˈækʃ(ə)n/ *noun* reacting; response; bad physical response to drug etc.; occurrence of condition after its opposite; tendency to oppose change or reform; interaction of substances undergoing chemical change.

**reactionary** ● *adjective* tending to oppose (esp. political) change or reform. ● *noun* (*plural* **-ies**) reactionary person.

**reactivate** /rɪˈæktɪveɪt/ *verb* (**-ting**) restore to state of activity. □ **reactivation** *noun*.

**reactive** /rɪˈæktɪv/ *adjective* showing reaction; reacting rather than taking initiative; susceptible to chemical reaction.

**reactor** *noun* (in full **nuclear reactor**) device in which nuclear chain reaction is used to produce energy.

**read** ● *verb* (*past & past participle* **read** /red/) reproduce (written or printed words) mentally or (often + *aloud, out, off,* etc.) vocally; (be able to) convert (written or printed words or other symbols) into intended words or meaning; interpret; (of meter) show (figure); interpret state of (meter); study (subject) at university; (as **read** /red/ *adjective*) versed in subject (esp. literature) by reading; (of computer) copy or transfer (data); hear and understand (over radio); substitute (word etc.) for incorrect one. • *noun* spell of reading; *colloquial* book etc. as regards readability. □ **take as read** treat (thing) as if it has been agreed.

**readable** *adjective* able to be read; interesting to read. □ **readability** *noun*.

**reader** *noun* person who reads; book intended for reading pratice; device for producing image that can be read from microfilm etc.; (also **Reader**) university lecturer of highest grade below professor; publisher's employee who reports on submitted manuscripts; printer's proof-corrector.

**readership** *noun* readers of a newspaper etc.; (also **Readership**) position of Reader.

**readily** *adverb* without reluctance; willingly; easily.

**readiness** *noun* prepared state; willingness; facility; promptness in argument or action.

**reading** *noun* act of reading; matter to be read; literary knowledge; entertainment at which something is read; figure etc. shown by recording instrument; interpretation or view taken; interpretation made (of music etc.); presentation of bill to legislature.

**ready** /'redɪ/ • *adjective* (**-ier**, **-iest**) with preparations complete; in fit state; willing; (of income etc.) easily secured; fit for immediate use; prompt, enthusiastic; (+ *to do*) about to; provided beforehand. • *adverb* usually in combination beforehand; in readiness. • *noun slang* (**the ready**) ready money; (**readies**) bank notes. • *verb* (**-ies**, **-ied**) prepare. □ **at the ready** ready for action; **ready-made**, **ready-to-wear** (esp. of clothes) made in standard size, not to measure; **ready money** cash, actual coin; **ready reckoner** book or table listing standard numerical calculations.

**reagent** /riːˈeɪdʒ(ə)nt/ *noun* substance used to produce chemical reaction.

**real** • *adjective* actually existing or occurring; genuine; appraised by purchasing power. • *adverb Scottish & US colloquial* really, very. □ **real ale** beer regarded as brewed in traditional way; **real estate** property such as land and houses; **real tennis** original form of tennis played on indoor court.

**realism** *noun* practice of regarding things in their true nature and dealing with them as they are; fidelity to nature in representation. □ **realist** *noun*.

**realistic** /rɪəˈlɪstɪk/ *adjective* regarding things as they are; based on facts rather than ideals. □ **realistically** *adverb*.

**reality** /rɪˈælɪtɪ/ *noun* (*plural* **-ies**) what is real or existent or underlies appearances; (+ *of*) real nature of; real existence; being real; likeness to original. □ **in reality** in fact.

**realize** *verb* (also **-ise**) (**-zing** or **-sing**) (often + *that*) be or become fully aware of; understand clearly; convert into actuality; convert into money; acquire (profit); be sold for. □ **realizable** *adjective*, **realization** *noun*.

**really** /'rɪəlɪ/ *adverb* in fact; very; I assure you; *expression of mild protest or surprise*.

**realm** /relm/ *noun formal* kingdom; domain.

**realty** /'riːəltɪ/ *noun* real estate.

**ream** *noun* 500 sheets of paper; (in *plural*) large quantity of writing.

**reap** *verb* cut (grain etc.) as harvest; receive as consequences of actions. □ **reaper** *noun*.

**rear¹** • *noun* back part of anything; space or position at back. • *adjective* at the back. □ **bring up the rear** come last; **rear admiral** naval officer below vice admiral. □ **rearmost** *adjective*.

**rear²** *verb* bring up and educate; breed and care for; cultivate; (of horse etc.) raise itself on hind legs; raise, build.

**rearguard** *noun* troops detached to protect rear, esp. in retreat. □ **rearguard action** engagement undertaken by rearguard, defensive stand or struggle, esp. when losing.

**rearm** /riːˈɑːm/ *verb* arm again, esp. with improved weapons. □ **rearmament** *noun*.

**rearward** /'rɪəwəd/ • *noun* rear. • *adjective* to the rear. • *adverb* (also **rearwards**) towards the rear.

**reason** /'ri:z(ə)n/ ● noun motive, cause, or justification; fact adduced or serving as this; intellectual faculty by which conclusions are drawn; sanity; sense, sensible conduct; moderation. ● verb form or try to reach conclusions by connected thought; (+ with) use argument with person by way of persuasion; (+ that) conclude or assert in argument; (+ out) think out.

**reasonable** adjective having sound judgement; moderate; ready to listen to reason; sensible; inexpensive; tolerable. □ **reasonableness** noun; **reasonably** adverb.

**reassure** /ri:ə'ʃʊə/ verb (-ring) restore confidence to; confirm in opinion etc. □ **reassurance** noun; **reassuring** adjective.

**rebate**[1] /'ri:beɪt/ noun partial refund; deduction from sum to be paid, discount.

**rebate**[2] /'ri:beɪt/ noun & verb (-ting) rabbet.

**rebel** ● noun /'reb(ə)l/ person who fights against, resists, or refuses allegiance to, established government; person etc. who resists authority or control. ● verb /rɪ'bel/ (-ll-; US -l-) (usually + against) act as rebel; feel or show repugnance.

**rebellion** /rɪ'beljən/ noun open resistance to authority, esp. organized armed resistance to established government.

**rebellious** /rɪ'beljəs/ adjective disposed to rebel; in rebellion; unmanageable. □ **rebelliously** adverb; **rebelliousness** noun.

**rebound** ● verb /rɪ'baʊnd/ spring back after impact; (+ upon) have adverse effect on (doer). ● noun /'ri:baʊnd/ rebounding, recoil; reaction. □ **on the rebound** while still recovering from emotional shock, esp. rejection by lover.

**rebuff** /rɪ'bʌf/ ● noun rejection of person who makes advances, offers help, etc.; snub. ● verb give rebuff to.

**rebuke** /rɪ'bju:k/ ● verb (-king) express sharp disapproval to (person) for fault; censure. ● noun rebuking, being rebuked.

**rebus** /'ri:bəs/ noun (plural **rebuses**) representation of word (esp. name) by pictures etc. suggesting its parts.

**rebut** /rɪ'bʌt/ verb (-tt-) refute, disprove; force back. □ **rebuttal** noun.

**recalcitrant** /rɪ'kælsɪtrənt/ adjective obstinately disobedient; objecting to restraint. □ **recalcitrance** noun.

**recall** /rɪ'kɔ:l/ ● verb summon to return; recollect, remember; bring back to memory; revoke, annul; revive, resuscitate. ● noun (also /'ri:kɔ:l/) summons to come back; act of remembering; ability to remember; possibility of recalling.

**recant** /rɪ'kænt/ verb withdraw and renounce (belief or statement) as erroneous or heretical. □ **recantation** /ri:kæn'teɪʃ(ə)n/ noun.

**recap** /'ri:kæp/ colloquial ● verb (-pp-) recapitulate. ● noun recapitulation.

**recapitulate** /ri:kə'pɪtjʊleɪt/ verb (-ling) summarize, restate briefly. □ **recapitulation** noun.

**recast** /ri:'kɑ:st/ ● verb (past & past participle **recast**) cast again; put into new form; improve arrangement of. ● noun recasting; recast form.

**recce** /'rekɪ/ colloquial ● noun reconnaissance. ● verb (**recced, recceing**) reconnoitre.

**recede** /rɪ'si:d/ verb (-ding) go or shrink back; be left at an increasing distance; slope backwards; decline in force or value.

**receipt** /rɪ'si:t/ ● noun receiving, being received; written or printed acknowledgement of payment received; (usually in plural) amount of money received. ● verb place written or printed receipt on (bill). □ **in receipt of** having received.

**receive** /rɪ'si:v/ verb (-ving) take or accept (thing offered, sent, or given); acquire; have conferred etc. on one; react to (news etc.) in particular way; stand degree or weight of; consent to hear or consider; admit, entertain as guest, greet, welcome; be able to hold; convert (broadcast signals) into sound or pictures (as **received** adjective) accepted as authoritative or true. □ **Received Pronunciation** standard pronunciation of English in Britain (see panel at ACCENT).

**receiver** *noun* part of telephone containing earpiece; (in full **official receiver**) person appointed to administer property of bankrupt person etc. or property under litigation; radio or television receiving apparatus; person who receives stolen goods.

**receivership** *noun* □ **in receivership** being dealt with by receiver.

**recent** /'riːs(ə)nt/ *adjective* not long past, that happened or existed lately; not long established, modern. □ **recently** *adverb*.

**receptacle** /rɪ'septək(ə)l/ *noun* object or space used to contain something.

**reception** /rɪ'sepʃ(ə)n/ *noun* receiving, being received; way in which person or thing is received; social occasion for receiving guests, esp. after wedding; place where visitors register on arriving at hotel, office, etc.; (quality of) receiving of broadcast signals. □ **reception room** room for receiving guests, clients, etc.

**receptionist** *noun* person employed to receive guests, clients, etc.

**receptive** /rɪ'septɪv/ *adjective* able or quick to receive ideas etc. □ **receptively** *adverb*; **receptiveness** *noun*; **receptivity** /riːsep'tɪv-/ *noun*.

**recess** /rɪ'ses/ ● *noun* space set back in wall; (often in *plural*) remote or secret place; temporary cessation from work, esp. of Parliament. ● *verb* make recess in; place in recess; *US* take recess, adjourn.

**recession** /rɪ'seʃ(ə)n/ *noun* temporary decline in economic activity or prosperity; receding, withdrawal.

**recessive** /rɪ'sesɪv/ *adjective* tending to recede; (of inherited characteristic) appearing in offspring only when not masked by inherited dominant characteristic.

**recherché** /rə'ʃeəʃeɪ/ *adjective* carefully sought out; far-fetched.

**recidivist** /rɪ'sɪdɪvɪst/ *noun* person who relapses into crime. □ **recidivism** *noun*.

**recipe** /'resɪpɪ/ *noun* statement of ingredients and procedure for preparing dish etc.; (+ *for*) certain means to.

**recipient** /rɪ'sɪpɪənt/ *noun* person who receives something.

**reciprocal** /rɪ'sɪprək(ə)l/ ● *adjective* in return; mutual; *Grammar* expressing mutual relation. ● *noun Mathematics* function or expression so related to another that their product is unity. □ **reciprocally** *adverb*.

**reciprocate** /rɪ'sɪprəkeɪt/ *verb* (-**ting**) requite, return; (+ *with*) give in return; interchange; (of machine part) move backwards and forwards. □ **reciprocation** *noun*.

**reciprocity** /resɪ'prɒsɪtɪ/ *noun* condition of being reciprocal; mutual action; give and take.

**recital** /rɪ'saɪt(ə)l/ *noun* reciting, being recited; concert of classical music by soloist or small group; (+ *of*) detailed account of (facts etc.); narrative.

**recitation** /resɪ'teɪʃ(ə)n/ *noun* reciting; piece recited.

**recitative** /resɪtə'tiːv/ *noun* passage of singing in speech rhythm, esp. in narrative or dialogue section of opera or oratorio.

**recite** /rɪ'saɪt/ *verb* (-**ting**) repeat aloud or declaim from memory; enumerate.

**reckless** /'reklɪs/ *adjective* disregarding consequences or danger etc. □ **recklessly** *adverb*; **recklessness** *noun*.

**reckon** /'rekən/ *verb* (often + *that*) think, consider; count or compute by calculation; (+ *on*) rely or base plans on; (+ *with*, *without*) take (or fail to take) into account.

**reckoning** *noun* calculating; opinion; settlement of account.

**reclaim** /rɪ'kleɪm/ *verb* seek return of (one's property etc.); bring (land) under cultivation from sea etc.; win back from vice, error, or waste condition. □ **reclaimable** *adjective*; **reclamation** /reklə-/ *noun*.

**recline** /rɪ'klaɪn/ *verb* (-**ning**) assume or be in horizontal or leaning position.

**recluse** /rɪ'kluːs/ *noun* person given to or living in seclusion. □ **reclusive** *adjective*.

**recognition** /rekəg'nɪʃ(ə)n/ *noun* recognizing, being recognized.

**recognizance** /rɪ'kɒgnɪz(ə)ns/ *noun Law* bond by which person undertakes to observe some condition; sum pledged as surety for this.

**recognize** /ˈrekəgnaɪz/ *verb* (also **-ise**) (**-zing** or **-sing**) identify as already known; realize or discover nature of; (+ *that*) realize or admit; acknowledge existence, validity, character, or claims of; show appreciation of; reward. □ **recognizable** *adjective*.

**recoil** ● *verb* /rɪˈkɔɪl/ jerk or spring back in horror, disgust, or fear; shrink mentally in this way; rebound; (of gun) be driven backwards by discharge. ● *noun* /ˈriːkɔɪl/ act or sensation of recoiling.

**recollect** /rekəˈlekt/ *verb* remember; call to mind.

**recollection** /rekəˈlekʃ(ə)n/ *noun* act or power of recollecting; thing recollected; person's memory, time over which it extends.

**recommend** /rekəˈmend/ *verb* suggest as fit for purpose or use; advise (course of action etc.); (of qualities etc.) make acceptable or desirable; (+ *to*) commend or entrust. □ **recommendation** *noun*.

**recompense** /ˈrekəmpens/ ● *verb* (**-sing**) make amends to; compensate; reward or punish. ● *noun* reward; compensation; retribution.

**reconcile** /ˈrekənsaɪl/ *verb* (**-ling**) make friendly again after estrangement; (usually **reconcile oneself** or in *passive*; + *to*) make resigned to; settle (quarrel etc.); harmonize; make compatible; show compatibility of. □ **reconcilable** /-ˈsaɪl-/ *adjective*; **reconciliation** /-sɪli-/ *noun*.

**recondite** /ˈrekəndaɪt/ *adjective* abstruse; obscure.

**recondition** /riːkənˈdɪʃ(ə)n/ *verb* overhaul, renovate, make usable again.

**reconnaissance** /rɪˈkɒnɪs(ə)ns/ *noun* survey of region to locate enemy or ascertain strategic features; preliminary survey.

**reconnoitre** /rekəˈnɔɪtə/ *verb* (*US* **reconnoiter**) (**-ring**) make reconnaissance (of).

**reconsider** /riːkənˈsɪdə/ *verb* consider again, esp. for possible change of decision.

**reconstitute** /riːˈkɒnstɪtjuːt/ *verb* (**-ting**) reconstruct; reorganize; rehydrate (dried food etc.). □ **reconstitution** /-ˈtjuːʃ(ə)n/ *noun*.

**reconstruct** /riːkənˈstrʌkt/ *verb* build again; form impression of (past events) by assembling evidence; re-enact (crime); reorganize. □ **reconstruction** *noun*.

**record** ● *noun* /ˈrekɔːd/ evidence etc. constituting account of occurrence, statement, etc.; document etc. preserving this; (in full **gramophone record**) disc carrying recorded sound in grooves, for reproduction by record player; facts known about person's past, esp. criminal convictions; best performance or most remarkable event of its kind. ● *verb* /rɪˈkɔːd/ put in writing or other permanent form for later reference; convert (sound etc.) into permanent form for later reproduction. □ **have a record** have criminal conviction; **off the record** unofficially, confidentially; **on record** officially recorded, publicly known; **recorded delivery** Post Office service in which dispatch and receipt are recorded; **record player** apparatus for reproducing sounds from gramophone records.

**recorder** /rɪˈkɔːdə/ *noun* apparatus for recording; woodwind instrument; (also **Recorder**) barrister or solicitor serving as part-time judge.

**recording** /rɪˈkɔːdɪŋ/ *noun* process of recording sound etc. for later reproduction; material or programme recorded.

**recordist** /rɪˈkɔːdɪst/ *noun* person who records sound.

**recount** /rɪˈkaʊnt/ *verb* narrate; tell in detail.

**re-count** ● *verb* /riːˈkaʊnt/ count again. ● *noun* /ˈriːkaʊnt/ re-counting, esp. of votes.

**recoup** /rɪˈkuːp/ *verb* recover or regain (loss); compensate or reimburse for loss.

**recourse** /rɪˈkɔːs/ *noun* resort to possible source of help; person or thing resorted to.

**recover** /rɪˈkʌvə/ *verb* regain possession, use, or control of; return to health, consciousness, or normal state or position; secure by legal process; make up for; retrieve. □ **recoverable** *adjective*.

**re-cover** /riːˈkʌvə/ *verb* cover again; provide (chairs etc.) with new cover.

**recovery** noun (plural **-ies**) recovering, being recovered.

**recreant** /ˈrekrɪənt/ literary ● adjective cowardly. ● noun coward.

**re-create** /riːkrɪˈeɪt/ verb (**-ting**) create anew; reproduce. □ **re-creation** noun.

**recreation** /rekrɪˈeɪʃ(ə)n/ noun (means of) entertaining oneself; pleasurable activity. □ **recreation ground** public land for sports etc. □ **recreational** adjective.

**recriminate** /rɪˈkrɪmɪneɪt/ verb (**-ting**) make mutual or counter accusations. □ **recrimination** noun; **recriminatory** adjective.

**recrudesce** /riːkruːˈdes/ verb (**-cing**) formal (of disease, problem, etc.) break out again. □ **recrudescence** noun; **recrudescent** adjective.

**recruit** /rɪˈkruːt/ ● noun newly enlisted serviceman or servicewoman; new member of a society etc. ● verb enlist (person) as recruit; form (army etc.) by enlisting recruits; replenish, reinvigorate. □ **recruitment** noun.

**rectal** /ˈrekt(ə)l/ adjective of or by means of rectum.

**rectangle** /ˈrektæŋg(ə)l/ noun plane figure with 4 straight sides and 4 right angles. □ **rectangular** /-ˈtæŋɡjʊlə/ adjective.

**rectify** /ˈrektɪfaɪ/ verb (**-ies, -ied**) adjust or make right; purify, esp. by repeated distillation; convert (alternating current) to direct current. □ **rectifiable** adjective; **rectification** noun.

**rectilinear** /rektɪˈlɪnɪə/ adjective bounded or characterized by straight lines; in or forming straight line.

**rectitude** /ˈrektɪtjuːd/ noun moral uprightness.

**recto** /ˈrektəʊ/ noun (plural **-s**) right-hand page of open book; front of printed leaf.

**rector** /ˈrektə/ noun incumbent of C. of E. parish where in former times all tithes passed to incumbent; head priest of church or religious institution; head of university or college. □ **rectorship** noun.

**rectory** noun (plural **-ies**) rector's house.

**rectum** /ˈrektəm/ noun (plural **-s**) final section of large intestine.

**recumbent** /rɪˈkʌmbənt/ adjective lying down, reclining.

**recuperate** /rɪˈkuːpəreɪt/ verb (**-ting**) recover from illness, exhaustion, loss, etc.; regain (health, loss, etc.). □ **recuperation** noun; **recuperative** /-rətɪv/ adjective.

**recur** /rɪˈkɜː/ verb (**-rr-**) occur again or repeatedly; (+ to) go back to in thought or speech; (as **recurring** adjective) (of decimal fraction) with same figure(s) repeated indefinitely.

**recurrent** /rɪˈkʌrənt/ adjective recurring. □ **recurrence** noun.

**recusant** /ˈrekjʊz(ə)nt/ noun person refusing submission or compliance, esp. (historical) one who refused to attend services of the Church of England. □ **recusancy** noun.

**recycle** /riːˈsaɪk(ə)l/ verb (**-ling**) convert (waste) to reusable material. □ **recyclable** adjective.

**red** ● adjective (**-dd-**) of colour from that of blood to deep pink or orange; flushed; bloodshot; (of hair) reddish-brown; having to do with bloodshed, burning, violence, or revolution; colloquial Communist. ● noun red colour, paint, clothes, etc.; colloquial Communist. □ **in the red** in debt or deficit; **red admiral** butterfly with red bands; **red-blooded** virile, vigorous; **redbrick** (of university) founded in the 19th or early 20th c.; **red card** Football card shown by referee to player being sent off; **red carpet** privileged treatment of eminent visitor; **redcoat** historical British soldier; **Red Crescent** equivalent of Red Cross in Muslim countries; **Red Cross** international relief organization; **redcurrant** small red edible berry, shrub bearing it; **red flag** symbol of revolution, danger signal; **red-handed** in act of crime; **redhead** person with red hair; **red herring** irrelevant diversion; **red-hot** heated until red, colloquial highly exciting or excited, colloquial (of news) completely new; **red lead** red oxide of lead as pigment; **red-letter day** joyfully noteworthy or memorable day; **red light** stop signal, warning; **red meat** meat that is red when raw (e.g. beef); **red neck** conservative working-class white in southern US; **red pepper** cayenne pepper, red fruit of capsicum; **red rag** thing that excites rage; **redshank** sandpiper with bright red legs; **red shift** displacement of spectrum to longer wavelengths in light from receding galaxies; **redstart** red-tailed songbird; **red tape** excessive bureaucracy or formality; **redwing** thrush with red underwings; **redwood** tree with red wood. □ **reddish** *adjective*; **redness** *noun*.

**redden** *verb* make or become red; blush.

**redeem** /rɪˈdiːm/ *verb* recover by expenditure of effort; make single payment to cancel (regular charge etc.); convert (tokens or bonds) into goods or cash; deliver from sin and damnation; (often as **redeeming** *adjective*) make amends or compensate for; save, rescue, reclaim; fulfil (promise). □ **redeemable** *adjective*.

**redeemer** *noun* one who redeems, esp. Christ.

**redemption** /rɪˈdempʃ(ə)n/ *noun* redeeming, being redeemed.

**redeploy** /riːdɪˈplɔɪ/ *verb* send (troops, workers, etc.) to new place or task. □ **redeployment** *noun*.

**rediffusion** /riːdɪˈfjuːʒ(ə)n/ *noun* relaying of broadcast programmes, esp. by cable from central receiver.

**redolent** /ˈredələnt/ *adjective* (+ *of*, *with*) strongly smelling or suggestive of. □ **redolence** *noun*.

**redouble** /riːˈdʌb(ə)l/ *verb* (-**ling**) make or grow greater or more intense or numerous; double again.

**redoubt** /rɪˈdaʊt/ *noun Military* outwork or fieldwork without flanking defences.

**redoubtable** /rɪˈdaʊtəb(ə)l/ *adjective* formidable.

**redound** /rɪˈdaʊnd/ *verb* (+ *to*) make great contribution to (one's advantage etc.); (+ *upon*, *on*) come back or recoil upon.

**redress** /rɪˈdres/ ● *verb* remedy; put right again. ● *noun* reparation; (+ *of*) redressing.

**reduce** /rɪˈdjuːs/ *verb* (-**cing**) make or become smaller or less; (+ *to*) bring by force or necessity; convert to another (esp. simpler) form; bring lower in status, rank, or price; lessen one's weight or size; make (sauce etc.) more concentrated by boiling; weaken; impoverish; subdue. □ **reduced circumstances** poverty after relative prosperity. □ **reducible** *adjective*.

**reduction** /rɪˈdʌkʃ(ə)n/ *noun* reducing, being reduced; amount by which prices etc. are reduced; smaller copy of picture etc. □ **reductive** *adjective*.

**redundant** /rɪˈdʌnd(ə)nt/ *adjective* superfluous; that can be omitted without loss of significance; no longer needed at work and therefore unemployed. □ **redundancy** *noun* (*plural* -**ies**).

**reduplicate** /rɪˈdjuːplɪkeɪt/ *verb* (-**ting**) make double; repeat. □ **reduplication** *noun*.

**re-echo** /riːˈekəʊ/ *verb* (-**es**, -**ed**) echo repeatedly; resound.

**reed** *noun* firm-stemmed water or marsh plant; tall straight stalk of this; vibrating part of some wind instruments. □ **reedy** *adjective* (-**ier**, -**iest**).

**reef¹** *noun* ridge of rock or coral etc. at or near surface of sea; lode of ore, bedrock surrounding this.

**reef²** ● *noun* each of several strips across sail, for taking it in etc. ● *verb* take in reef(s) of (sail). □ **reef-knot** symmetrical double knot.

**reefer** *noun slang* marijuana cigarette; thick double-breasted jacket.

**reek** ● *verb* (often + *of*) smell unpleasantly; have suspicious associations. ● *noun* foul or stale smell; *esp. Scottish* smoke; vapour, exhalation.

**reel** ● *noun* cylindrical device on which thread, paper, film, wire, etc. are wound; device for winding and unwinding line as required, esp. in fishing; lively folk or Scottish dance, music for this. ● *verb* wind on reel; (+ *in*, *up*) draw in or up with reel; stand, walk, etc. unsteadily; be shaken physically or mentally; dance reel. □ **reel off** recite rapidly and without apparent effort.

**re-entrant** /riːˈentrənt/ *adjective* (of angle) pointing inwards.

**re-entry** /riːˈentrɪ/ *noun* (*plural* -**ies**) act of entering again, esp. (of spacecraft etc.) of re-entering earth's atmosphere.

**reeve** *noun historical* chief magistrate of town or district; official supervising landowner's estate.

**ref¹** *noun colloquial* referee.

**ref²** *noun colloquial* reference.

**refectory** /rɪ'fektərɪ/ noun (plural **-ies**) dining-room, esp. in monastery or college. □ **refectory table** long narrow table.

**refer** /rɪ'fɜː/ verb (**-rr-**) (usually + to) have recourse to (some authority or source of information); send on or direct; make allusion or be relevant. □ **referred pain** pain felt in part of body other than actual source. □ **referable** adjective.

**referee** /refə'riː/ • noun umpire, esp. in football or boxing; person referred to for decision in dispute etc.; person willing to testify to character of applicant for employment etc. • verb (**-rees**, **-reed**) act as referee (for).

**reference** /'refərəns/ noun referring to some authority; scope given to such authority; (+ to) relation, respect, or allusion to; direction to page, book, etc. for information; written testimonial, person giving it. □ **reference book** book for occasional consultation. □ **referential** /-'ren-/ adjective.

**referendum** /refə'rendəm/ noun (plural **-s** or **-da**) vote on political question open to entire electorate.

**referral** /rɪ'fɜːr(ə)l/ noun referring of person to medical specialist etc.

**refill** • verb /riː'fɪl/ fill again. • noun /'riːfɪl/ thing that refills; act of refilling. □ **refillable** adjective.

**refine** /rɪ'faɪn/ verb (**-ning**) free from impurities or defects; (esp. as **refined** adjective) make or become more elegant or cultured.

**refinement** noun refining, being refined; fineness of feeling or taste; elegance; added development or improvement; subtle reasoning; fine distinction.

**refiner** noun person or firm refining crude oil, metal, sugar, etc.

**refinery** noun (plural **-ies**) place where oil etc. is refined.

**refit** • verb /riː'fɪt/ (**-tt-**) esp. Nautical make or become serviceable again by repairs etc. • noun /'riːfɪt/ refitting.

**reflate** /riː'fleɪt/ verb (**-ting**) cause reflation of (currency, economy, etc.).

**reflation** noun inflation of financial system to restore previous condition after deflation. □ **reflationary** adjective.

**reflect** /rɪ'flekt/ verb throw back (light, heat, sound, etc.); (of mirror etc.) show image of, reproduce to eye or mind; correspond in appearance or effect to; bring (credit, discredit, etc.); (usually + on, upon) bring discredit; (often + on, upon) meditate; (+ that, how, etc.) consider.

**reflection** /rɪ'flekʃ(ə)n/ noun reflecting, being reflected; reflected light, heat, colour, or image; reconsideration; (often + on) thing bringing discredit; (often + on, upon) comment.

**reflective** adjective (of surface) reflecting; (of mental faculties) concerned in reflection or thought; thoughtful. □ **reflectively** adverb.

**reflector** noun piece of glass or metal for reflecting light in required direction; telescope etc. using mirror to produce images.

**reflex** /'riːfleks/ • adjective (of action) independent of will; (of angle) larger than 180°. • noun reflex action; sign, secondary manifestation; reflected light or image. □ **reflex camera** camera in which image is reflected by mirror to enable correct focusing.

**reflexive** /rɪ'fleksɪv/ Grammar • adjective (of word or form) referring back to subject (e.g. myself in I hurt myself); (of verb) having reflexive pronoun as object. • noun reflexive word or form.

**reflexology** /riːflek'sɒlədʒɪ/ noun massage to areas of soles of feet. □ **reflexologist** noun.

**reform** /rɪ'fɔːm/ • verb make or become better; abolish or cure (abuse etc.). • noun removal of abuses, esp. political; improvement. □ **reformative** adjective.

**reformation** /refə'meɪʃ(ə)n/ noun reforming or being reformed, esp. radical improvement in political, religious, or social affairs; (**the Reformation**) 16th-c. movement for reform of abuses in Roman Church ending in establishment of Reformed or Protestant Churches.

**reformatory** /rɪ'fɔːmətərɪ/ • noun (plural **-ies**) US historical institution for reform of young offenders. • adjective producing reform.

**reformer** noun advocate of reform.

**reformism** *noun* policy of reform rather than abolition or revolution. □ **reformist** *noun & adjective*.

**refract** /rɪˈfrækt/ *verb* deflect (light) at certain angle when it enters obliquely from another medium. □ **refraction** *noun*; **refractive** *adjective*.

**refractor** *noun* refracting medium or lens; telescope using lens to produce image.

**refractory** /rɪˈfræktərɪ/ *adjective* stubborn, unmanageable, rebellious; resistant to treatment; hard to fuse or work.

**refrain**¹ /rɪˈfreɪn/ *verb* (+ *from*) avoid doing (action).

**refrain**² /rɪˈfreɪn/ *noun* recurring phrase or lines, esp. at ends of stanzas.

**refresh** /rɪˈfreʃ/ *verb* give fresh spirit or vigour to; revive (memory). □ **refreshing** *adjective*; **refreshingly** *adverb*.

**refresher** *noun* something that refreshes, esp. drink; extra fee to counsel in prolonged lawsuit. □ **refresher course** course reviewing or updating previous studies.

**refreshment** *noun* refreshing, being refreshed; (usually in *plural*) food or drink.

**refrigerant** /rɪˈfrɪdʒərənt/ ● *noun* substance used for refrigeration. ● *adjective* cooling.

**refrigerate** /rɪˈfrɪdʒəreɪt/ *verb* (**-ting**) cool or freeze (esp. food). □ **refrigeration** *noun*.

**refrigerator** *noun* cabinet or room in which food etc. is refrigerated.

**refuge** /ˈrefjuːdʒ/ *noun* shelter from pursuit, danger, or trouble; person or place offering this.

**refugee** /refjʊˈdʒiː/ *noun* person taking refuge, esp. in foreign country, from war, persecution, etc.

**refulgent** /rɪˈfʌldʒ(ə)nt/ *adjective literary* shining, gloriously bright. □ **refulgence** *noun*.

**refund** ● *verb* /rɪˈfʌnd/ pay back (money etc.); reimburse. ● *noun* /ˈriːfʌnd/ act of refunding; sum refunded. □ **refundable** /rɪˈfʌn-/ *adjective*.

**refurbish** /riːˈfɜːbɪʃ/ *verb* brighten up, redecorate. □ **refurbishment** *noun*.

**refusal** /rɪˈfjuːz(ə)l/ *noun* refusing, being refused; (in full **first refusal**) chance of taking thing before it is offered to others.

**refuse**¹ /rɪˈfjuːz/ *verb* (**-sing**) withhold acceptance of or consent to; (often + *to do*) indicate unwillingness; not grant (request) made by (person); (of horse) be unwilling to jump (fence etc.).

**refuse**² /ˈrefjuːs/ *noun* items rejected as worthless; waste.

**refusenik** /rɪˈfjuːznɪk/ *noun historical* Soviet Jew refused permission to emigrate to Israel.

**refute** /rɪˈfjuːt/ *verb* (**-ting**) prove falsity or error of; rebut by argument; deny or contradict (without argument). □ **refutation** /refjʊˈteɪʃ(ə)n/ *noun*.

■ **Usage** The use of *refute* to mean 'deny, contradict' is considered incorrect by some people. *Repudiate* can be used instead.

**reg** /redʒ/ *noun colloquial* registration mark.

**regain** /rɪˈgeɪn/ *verb* obtain possession or use of after loss.

**regal** /ˈriːg(ə)l/ *adjective* of or by monarch(s); magnificent. □ **regality** /rɪˈgælɪ-/ *noun*; **regally** *adverb*.

**regale** /rɪˈgeɪl/ *verb* (**-ling**) entertain lavishly with feasting; (+ *with*) entertain with (talk etc.).

**regalia** /rɪˈgeɪlɪə/ *plural noun* insignia of royalty or an order, mayor, etc.

**regard** /rɪˈgɑːd/ ● *verb* gaze on; heed, take into account; look upon or think of in specified way. ● *noun* gaze; steady look; attention, care; esteem; (in *plural*) expression of *friendliness in letter etc.* □ **as regards** as regards, in respect of; **in this regard** on this point; **in, with regard to** in respect of.

**regardful** *adjective* (+ *of*) mindful of.

**regarding** *preposition* concerning; in respect of.

**regardless** ● *adjective* (+ *of*) without regard or consideration for. ● *adverb* without paying attention.

**regatta** /rɪˈgætə/ *noun* event consisting of rowing or yacht races.

**regency** /ˈriːdʒənsɪ/ *noun* (*plural* **-ies**) office of regent; commission acting as regent; regent's or regency commission's period of office; (**Regency**) (in UK) 1811–1820.

**regenerate** ● *verb* /rɪˈdʒenəreɪt/ (**-ting**) bring or come into renewed existence;

improve moral condition of; impart new, more vigorous, or spiritually higher life or nature to; regrow or cause (new tissue) to regrow. ● *adjective* /-rət/ spiritually born again, reformed. □ **regeneration** *noun*; **regenerative** /-rətɪv/ *adjective*.

**regent** /'riːdʒ(ə)nt/ ● *noun* person acting as head of state because monarch is absent, ill, or a child. ● *adjective* (after *noun*) acting as regent.

**reggae** /'reɡeɪ/ *noun* W. Indian style of music with strongly accented subsidiary beat.

**regicide** /'redʒɪsaɪd/ *noun* person who kills or helps to kill a king; killing of a king.

**regime** /reɪ'ʒiːm/ *noun* (also **régime**) method of government; prevailing system; regimen.

**regimen** /'redʒɪmən/ *noun* prescribed course of exercise, way of life, and diet.

**regiment** ● *noun* /'redʒɪmənt/ permanent unit of army consisting of several companies, troops, or batteries; (usually + *of*) large or formidable array or number. ● *verb* /-ment/ organize in groups or according to system; form into regiment(s). □ **regimentation** /-men-/ *noun*.

**regimental** /redʒɪ'ment(ə)l/ ● *adjective* of a regiment. ● *noun* (in *plural*) military uniform, esp. of particular regiment.

**Regina** /rɪ'dʒaɪnə/ *noun* (after *name*) reigning queen; *Law* the Crown. [Latin]

**region** /'riːdʒ(ə)n/ *noun* geographical area or division, having definable boundaries or characteristics; administrative area, esp. in Scotland; part of body; sphere, realm. □ **in the region of** approximately. □ **regional** *adjective*; **regionally** *adverb*.

**register** /'redʒɪstə/ ● *noun* official list; book in which items are recorded for reference; device recording speed, force, etc.; compass of voice or instrument; form of language used in particular circumstances; adjustable plate for regulating draught etc. ● *verb* set down formally, record in writing; enter or cause to be entered in register; send (letter) by registered post; record automatically, indicate; make mental note of; show (emotion etc.) in face etc.;

make impression. □ **registered post** postal procedure with special precautions and compensation in case of loss; **register office** state office where civil marriages are conducted and births, marriages, and deaths are recorded.

**registrar** /redʒɪ'strɑː/ *noun* official keeping register; chief administrator in university etc.; hospital doctor training as specialist.

**registration** /redʒɪ'streɪʃ(ə)n/ *noun* registering, being registered. □ **registration mark**, **number** combination of letters and numbers identifying vehicle.

**registry** /'redʒɪstrɪ/ *noun* (*plural* **-ies**) place where registers or records are kept. □ **registry office** register office (the official name).

**Regius professor** /'riːdʒɪəs/ *noun* holder of university chair founded by sovereign or filled by Crown appointment.

**regress** ● *verb* /rɪ'ɡres/ move backwards; return to former stage or state. ● *noun* /'riːɡres/ act of regressing. □ **regression** /rɪ'ɡreʃ(ə)n/ *noun*; **regressive** /rɪ'ɡresɪv/ *adjective*.

**regret** /rɪ'ɡret/ ● *verb* (**-tt-**) feel or express sorrow, repentance, or distress over (action or loss); say with sorrow or remorse. ● *noun* sorrow, repentance, or distress over action or loss. □ **regretful** *adjective*; **regretfully** *adverb*.

**regrettable** *adjective* undesirable, unwelcome; deserving censure. □ **regrettably** *adverb*.

**regular** /'reɡjʊlə/ ● *adjective* acting, done, or recurring uniformly; habitual, orderly; conforming to rule or principle; symmetrical; conforming to correct procedure etc.; *Grammar* (of verb etc.) following normal type of inflection; *colloquial* absolute, thorough; (of soldier etc.) permanent, professional. ● *noun* regular soldier; *colloquial* regular customer, visitor, etc.; one of regular clergy. □ **regularity** /-'lærɪtɪ/ *noun*; **regularize** *verb* (also **-ise**) (**-zing** or **-sing**); **regularly** *adverb*.

**regulate** /'reɡjʊleɪt/ *verb* (**-ting**) control by rule, subject to restrictions; adapt to requirements; adjust (clock, watch, etc.) to work accurately. □ **regulator** *noun*.

**regulation** ● *noun* regulating, being regulated; prescribed rule. ● *adjective* in accordance with regulations, of correct pattern etc.

**regulo** /'regjʊləʊ/ *noun* (usually + numeral) number on scale denoting temperature in gas oven.

**regurgitate** /rɪ'gɜːdʒɪteɪt/ *verb* (**-ting**) bring (swallowed) food up again to mouth; reproduce (information etc.). □ **regurgitation** *noun*.

**rehabilitate** /riːhə'bɪlɪteɪt/ *verb* (**-ting**) restore to normal life by training, etc. esp. after imprisonment or illness; restore to former privileges or reputation or to proper condition. □ **rehabilitation** *noun*.

**rehash** ● *verb* /riː'hæʃ/ put into new form without significant change or improvement. ● *noun* /'riːhæʃ/ material rehashed; rehashing.

**rehearsal** /rɪ'hɜːs(ə)l/ *noun* trial performance or practice; rehearsing.

**rehearse** /rɪ'hɜːs/ *verb* (**-sing**) practise before performing in public; recite or say over; give list of, enumerate.

**Reich** /raɪx/ *noun* former German state, esp. Third Reich (1933–45).

**reign** /reɪn/ ● *verb* be king or queen; prevail; (as **reigning** *adjective*) currently holding title. ● *noun* sovereignty, rule; sovereign's period of rule.

**reimburse** /riːɪm'bɜːs/ *verb* (**-sing**) repay (person); refund. □ **reimbursement** *noun*.

**rein** /reɪn/ ● *noun* (in *singular* or *plural*) long narrow strap used to guide horse; means of control. ● *verb* (+ *back*, *up*, *in*) pull back or up or hold in (as) with reins; govern, control.

**reincarnate** ● *verb* /riːɪn'kɑːneɪt/ (**-ting**) give esp. human form to again. ● *adjective* /-nət/ reincarnated.

**reincarnation** /riːɪnkɑː'neɪʃ(ə)n/ *noun* rebirth of soul in new body.

**reindeer** /'reɪndɪə/ *noun* (*plural* same or **-s**) subarctic deer with large antlers.

**reinforce** /riːɪn'fɔːs/ *verb* (**-cing**) support or strengthen, esp. with additional personnel or material. □ **reinforced concrete** concrete with metal bars etc. embedded in it.

**reinforcement** *noun* reinforcing, being reinforced; (in *plural*) additional personnel, equipment, etc.

**reinstate** /riːɪn'steɪt/ *verb* (**-ting**) replace in former position; restore to former privileges. □ **reinstatement** *noun*.

**reinsure** /riːɪn'ʃʊə/ *verb* (**-ring**) insure again (esp. of insurer transferring risk to another insurer). □ **reinsurance** *noun*.

**reiterate** /riː'ɪtəreɪt/ *verb* (**-ting**) say or do again or repeatedly. □ **reiteration** *noun*.

**reject** ● *verb* /rɪ'dʒekt/ put aside or send back as not to be used, done, or complied with; refuse to accept or believe in; rebuff. ● *noun* /'riːdʒekt/ rejected thing or person. □ **rejection** /rɪ'dʒek-/ *noun*.

**rejoice** /rɪ'dʒɔɪs/ *verb* (**-cing**) feel joy, be glad; (+ *in*, *at*) take delight in.

**rejoin**[1] /riː'dʒɔɪn/ *verb* join again; reunite.

**rejoin**[2] /rɪ'dʒɔɪn/ *verb* say in answer; retort.

**rejoinder** /rɪ'dʒɔɪndə/ *noun* reply, retort.

**rejuvenate** /rɪ'dʒuːvəneɪt/ *verb* (**-ting**) make (as if) young again. □ **rejuvenation** *noun*.

**relapse** /rɪ'læps/ ● *verb* (**-sing**) (usually + *into*) fall back (into worse state after improvement). ● *noun* relapsing, esp. deterioration in patient's condition after partial recovery.

**relate** /rɪ'leɪt/ *verb* (**-ting**) narrate, recount; (usually + *to*, *with*) connect in thought or meaning; have reference to; (+ *to*) feel connected or sympathetic to.

**related** *adjective* connected, esp. by blood or marriage.

**relation** /rɪ'leɪʃ(ə)n/ *noun* connection between people or things; relative; (in *plural*) dealings (with others); narration.

**relationship** *noun* state of being related; connection, association; *colloquial* emotional association between two people.

**relative** /'relətɪv/ ● *adjective* in relation or proportion to something else; implying comparison or relation; (+ *to*) having application or reference to; *Grammar* (of word, clause, etc.) referring to expressed or implied antecedent, attached to antecedent by such word. ● *noun* person connected by blood or marriage; species related to another by common origin; relative word, esp. pronoun. □ **relative density** ratio between density of substance and that of a standard (usually water or air). □ **relatively** adverb.

**relativity** /relə'tɪvɪtɪ/ noun relativeness; Physics theory based on principle that all motion is relative and that light has constant velocity in a vacuum.

**relax** /rɪ'læks/ verb make or become less stiff, rigid, tense, formal, or strict; reduce (attention, efforts); cease work or effort; (as **relaxed** adjective) at ease, unperturbed.

**relaxation** /ri:læk'seɪʃ(ə)n/ noun relaxing; recreation.

**relay** /'ri:leɪ/ ● noun fresh set of people etc. to replace tired ones; supply of material similarly used; relay race; device activating electric circuit; device transmitting broadcast; relayed transmission. ● verb /also rɪ'leɪ/ receive (esp. broadcast message) and transmit to others. □ **relay race** one between teams of which each member in turn covers part of distance.

**release** /rɪ'li:s/ ● verb (-sing) (often + from) set free, liberate, unfasten; allow to move from fixed position; make (information) public; issue (film etc.) generally. ● noun liberation from restriction, duty, or difficulty; handle, catch, etc. that releases part of mechanism; item made available for publication; film, record, etc. that is released; releasing of film etc.

**relegate** /'relɪgeɪt/ verb (-ting) consign or dismiss to inferior position; transfer (team) to lower division of league. □ **relegation** noun.

**relent** /rɪ'lent/ verb relax severity; yield to compassion.

**relentless** adjective unrelenting. □ **relentlessly** adverb.

**relevant** /'relɪv(ə)nt/ adjective (often + to) bearing on or pertinent to matter in hand. □ **relevance** noun.

**reliable** /rɪ'laɪəb(ə)l/ adjective that may be relied on. □ **reliability** noun, **reliably** adverb.

**reliance** /rɪ'laɪəns/ noun (+ in, on) trust or confidence in. □ **reliant** adjective.

**relic** /'relɪk/ noun object interesting because of its age or associations; part of

holy person's body or belongings kept as object of reverence; surviving custom, belief, etc. from past age; (in plural) dead body or remains of person, what has survived.

**relict** /'relɪkt/ noun object surviving in primitive form.

**relief** /rɪ'li:f/ noun (feeling accompanying) alleviation of or deliverance from pain, distress, etc.; feature etc. that diversifies monotony or relaxes tension; assistance given to people in special need; replacing of person(s) on duty by another or others; person(s) thus bringing relief; thing supplementing another in some service; method of carving, moulding, etc., in which design projects from surface; piece of sculpture etc. in relief; effect of being done in relief given by colour or shading etc.; vividness, distinctness. □ **relief map** one showing hills and valleys by shading or colouring etc.

**relieve** /rɪ'li:v/ verb (-ving) bring or give relief to; mitigate tedium of; release (person) from duty by acting as or providing substitute; (+ of) take (burden or duty) away from; (**relieve oneself**) urinate, defecate. □ **relieved** adjective.

**religion** /rɪ'lɪdʒ(ə)n/ noun belief in superhuman controlling power, esp. in personal God or gods entitled to obedience; system of faith and worship.

**religiosity** /rɪlɪdʒɪ'ɒsɪtɪ/ noun state of being religious or too religious.

**religious** /rɪ'lɪdʒəs/ ● adjective devoted to religion, devout; of or concerned with religion; of or belonging to monastic order; scrupulous. ● noun (plural same) person bound by monastic vows. □ **religiously** adverb.

**relinquish** /rɪ'lɪŋkwɪʃ/ verb give up, let go, resign, surrender. □ **relinquishment** noun.

**reliquary** /'relɪkwərɪ/ noun (plural -ies) receptacle for relic(s).

**relish** /'relɪʃ/ ● noun (often + for) liking or enjoyment; appetizing flavour, attractive quality; thing eaten with plainer food to add flavour; (+ of) distinctive flavour or taste. ● verb get pleasure out of, enjoy greatly; anticipate with pleasure.

**reluctant** /rɪˈlʌkt(ə)nt/ *adjective* (often + *to do*) unwilling, disinclined. □ **reluctance** *noun*; **reluctantly** *adverb*.

**rely** /rɪˈlaɪ/ *verb* (**-ies**, **-ied**) (+ *on*, *upon*) depend with confidence on; be dependent on.

**REM** *abbreviation* rapid eye movement.

**remade** *past & past participle of* REMAKE.

**remain** /rɪˈmeɪn/ *verb* be left over; stay in same place or condition; be left behind; continue to be.

**remainder** /rɪˈmeɪndə/ ● *noun* residue; remaining people or things; number left after subtraction or division; (any of) copies of book left unsold. ● *verb* dispose of remainder of (book) at reduced prices.

**remains** /rɪˈmeɪnz/ *plural noun* what remains after other parts have been removed or used; relics of antiquity etc.; dead body.

**remake** ● *verb* /riːˈmeɪk/ (**-king**; *past & past participle* **remade**) make again or differently. ● *noun* /ˈriːmeɪk/ remade thing, esp. cinema film.

**remand** /rɪˈmɑːnd/ ● *verb* return (prisoner) to custody, esp. to allow further inquiry. ● *noun* committal to custody. □ **on remand** in custody pending trial; **remand centre** institution for remand of accused people.

**remark** /rɪˈmɑːk/ ● *verb* (often + *that*) say by way of comment; (usually + *on*, *upon*) make comment; *archaic* take notice of. ● *noun* comment, thing said; noticing.

**remarkable** *adjective* worth notice; exceptional, striking. □ **remarkably** *adverb*.

**REME** /ˈriːmiː/ *abbreviation* Royal Electrical and Mechanical Engineers.

**remedial** /rɪˈmiːdɪəl/ *adjective* affording or intended as a remedy; (of teaching) for slow or disadvantaged pupils.

**remedy** /ˈremɪdɪ/ ● *noun* (*plural* **-ies**) (often + *for*, *against*) medicine or treatment; means of removing anything undesirable; redress. ● *verb* (**-ies**, **-ied**) rectify, make good. □ **remediable** /rɪˈmiːdɪəb(ə)l/ *adjective*.

**remember** /rɪˈmembə/ *verb* (often + *to do*, *that*) keep in the memory; not forget; bring back into one's thoughts; acknowledge in making gift etc.; convey greetings from.

**remembrance** /rɪˈmembrəns/ *noun* remembering, being remembered; recollection; keepsake, souvenir; (in *plural*) greetings conveyed through third person.

**remind** /rɪˈmaɪnd/ *verb* (usually + *of*, *to do*, *that*) cause (person) to remember or think of.

**reminder** *noun* thing that reminds; (often + *of*) memento.

**reminisce** /remɪˈnɪs/ *verb* (**-cing**) indulge in reminiscence.

**reminiscence** /remɪˈnɪs(ə)ns/ *noun* remembering things past; (in *plural*) *literary* account of things remembered.

**reminiscent** *adjective* (+ *of*) reminding or suggestive of; concerned with reminiscence.

**remiss** /rɪˈmɪs/ *adjective* careless of duty; negligent.

**remission** /rɪˈmɪʃ(ə)n/ *noun* reduction of prison sentence for good behaviour; remittance of debt etc.; diminution of force etc.; (often + *of*) forgiveness (of sins etc.).

**remit** ● *verb* /rɪˈmɪt/ (**-tt-**) refrain from exacting or inflicting (debt, punishment, etc.); abate, slacken; send (esp. money); (+ *to*) refer to some authority, send back to lower court; postpone, defer; pardon (sins etc.). ● *noun* /ˈriːmɪt/ terms of reference of committee etc.; item remitted.

**remittance** *noun* money sent; sending of money.

**remittent** *adjective* (of disease etc.) abating at intervals.

**remix** ● *verb* /riːˈmɪks/ mix again. ● *noun* /ˈriːmɪks/ remixed recording.

**remnant** /ˈremnənt/ *noun* small remaining quantity; piece of cloth etc. left when greater part has been used or sold.

**remold** *US* = REMOULD.

**remonstrate** /ˈremənstreɪt/ *verb* (**-ting**) (+ *with*) make protest; argue forcibly. □ **remonstrance** /rɪˈmɒnstrəns/ *noun*; **remonstration** *noun*.

**remorse** /rɪˈmɔːs/ *noun* bitter repentance; compunction; mercy.

**remorseful** *adjective* filled with repentance. □ **remorsefully** *adverb*.

**remorseless** *adjective* without compassion. □ **remorselessly** *adverb*.

**remote** /rɪ'məʊt/ *adjective* (**-r**, **-st**) distant in place or time; secluded; distantly related; slight, faint; aloof, not friendly. □ **remote control** (device for) control of apparatus etc. from a distance. □ **remotely** *adverb*; **remoteness** *noun*.

**remould** ● *verb* /riː'məʊld/ (*US* **remold**) mould again, refashion; reconstruct tread of (tyre). ● *noun* /'riː'məʊld/ remoulded tyre.

**removal** /rɪ'muːv(ə)l/ *noun* removing, being removed; transfer of furniture etc. on moving house.

**remove** /rɪ'muːv/ ● *verb* (**-ving**) take off or away from place occupied; convey to another place; dismiss; cause to be no longer available; (in *passive*; + *from*) be distant in condition; (as **removed** *adjective*) (esp. of cousins) separated by a specified number of generations. ● *noun* distance, degree of remoteness; stage in gradation; form or division in some schools. □ **removable** *adjective*.

**remunerate** /rɪ'mjuːnəreɪt/ *verb* (**-ting**) pay for service rendered. □ **remuneration** *noun*; **remunerative** /-rətɪv/ *adjective*.

**Renaissance** /rɪ'neɪs(ə)ns/ *noun* revival of classical art and literature in 14th–16th c.; period of this; style of art and architecture developed by it; (**renaissance**) any similar revival. □ **Renaissance man** person with many talents.

**renal** /'riːn(ə)l/ *adjective* of kidneys.

**renascent** /rɪ'næs(ə)nt/ *adjective* springing up anew; being reborn. □ **renascence** *noun*.

**rend** *verb* (*past & past participle* **rent**) *archaic* tear or wrench forcibly.

**render** /'rendə/ *verb* cause to be or become; give in return; pay as due; (often + *to*) give (assistance), show (obedience etc.); present, submit; represent, portray; perform; translate; (often + *down*) melt (fat) down; cover (stone or brick) with plaster. □ **rendering** *noun*.

**rendezvous** /'rɒndɪvuː/ ● *noun* (*plural* same /-vuːz/) agreed or regular meeting-place; meeting by arrangement. ● *verb* (**rendezvouses** /-vuːz/; **rendezvoused** /-vuːd/; **rendezvousing** /-vuːɪŋ/) meet at rendezvous.

**rendition** /ren'dɪʃ(ə)n/ *noun* interpretation or rendering of dramatic or musical piece.

**renegade** /'renɪgeɪd/ *noun* deserter of party or principles.

**renege** /rɪ'niːg, rɪ'neɪg/ *verb* (**-ging**) (often + *on*) go back on promise made.

**renew** /rɪ'njuː/ *verb* make new again; restore to original state; replace; repeat; resume after interruption; grant or be granted continuation of (licence etc.). □ **renewable** *adjective*; **renewal** *noun*.

**rennet** /'renɪt/ *noun* curdled milk from calf's stomach, or artificial preparation, used in making cheese etc.

**renounce** /rɪ'naʊns/ *verb* (**-cing**) consent formally to abandon; repudiate; decline further association with.

**renovate** /'renəveɪt/ *verb* (**-ting**) restore to good condition; repair. □ **renovation** *noun*; **renovator** *noun*.

**renown** /rɪ'naʊn/ *noun* fame, high distinction. □ **renowned** *adjective*.

**rent**[1] ● *noun* periodical payment for use of land or premises; payment for hire of machinery etc. ● *verb* (often + *from*) take, occupy, or use for rent; (often + *out*) let or hire for rent; (often + *at*) be let at specified rate.

**rent**[2] *noun* tear in garment etc.; gap, cleft, fissure.

**rent**[3] *past & past participle* of REND.

**rental** /'rent(ə)l/ *noun* amount paid or received as rent; act of renting.

**rentier** /'rɑ̃tɪeɪ/ *noun* person living on income from property or investments. [French]

**renunciation** /rɪnʌnsɪ'eɪʃ(ə)n/ *noun* renouncing, self-denial, giving up of things.

**rep**[1] *noun colloquial* representative, esp. commercial traveller.

**rep**[2] *noun colloquial* repertory; repertory theatre or company.

**repair**[1] /rɪ'peə/ ● *verb* restore to good condition after damage or wear; set right or make amends for. ● *noun* (result of) restoring to sound condition; good or relative condition for working or using. □ **repairable** *adjective*; **repairer** *noun*.

**repair**[2] /rɪ'peə/ *verb* (usually + *to*) resort; go.

**reparable** /ˈrepərəb(ə)l/ *adjective* that can be made good.

**reparation** /repəˈreɪʃ(ə)n/ *noun* making amends; (esp. in *plural*) compensation.

**repartee** /repɑːˈtiː/ *noun* (making of) witty retorts.

**repast** /rɪˈpɑːst/ *noun* formal meal.

**repatriate** /riːˈpætrɪeɪt/ *verb* (**-ting**) return (person) to native land. □ **repatriation** *noun*.

**repay** /rɪˈpeɪ/ *verb* (*past & past participle* **repaid**) pay back (money); make repayment to (person); reward (action etc.). □ **repayable** *adjective*; **repayment** *noun*.

**repeal** /rɪˈpiːl/ ● *verb* annul, revoke. ● *noun* repealing.

**repeat** /rɪˈpiːt/ ● *verb* say or do over again; recite, report; recur. ● *noun* repeating; thing repeated, esp. broadcast; *Music* passage intended to be repeated. □ **repeatable** *adjective*; **repeatedly** *adverb*.

**repeater** *noun* person or thing that repeats; firearm that fires several shots without reloading; watch that strikes last quarter etc. again when required; device for retransmitting electrical message.

**repel** /rɪˈpel/ *verb* drive back; ward off; be repulsive or distasteful to; resist mixing with; push away from itself. □ **repellent** *adjective & noun*.

**repent** /rɪˈpent/ *verb* (often + *of*) feel sorrow about one's actions etc.; wish one had not done, resolve not to continue (wrongdoing etc.). □ **repentance** *noun*; **repentant** *adjective*.

**repercussion** /riːpəˈkʌʃ(ə)n/ *noun* indirect effect or reaction following event etc.; recoil after impact.

**repertoire** /ˈrepətwɑː/ *noun* stock of works that performer etc. knows or is prepared to perform.

**repertory** /ˈrepətərɪ/ *noun* (*plural* **-ies**) performance of various plays for short periods by one company; repertory theatres collectively; store of information etc.; repertoire. □ **repertory company** one performing plays from repertoire; **repertory theatre** one with repertoire of plays.

**repetition** /repəˈtɪʃ(ə)n/ *noun* repeating, being repeated; thing repeated, copy.

□ **repetitious** *adjective*; **repetitive** /rɪˈpetɪtɪv/ *adjective*.

**repine** /rɪˈpaɪn/ *verb* (**-ning**) (often + *at*, *against*) fret, be discontented.

**replace** /rɪˈpleɪs/ *verb* (**-cing**) put back in place; take place of, be or provide substitute for; (often + *with*, *by*) fill up place of.

**replacement** *noun* replacing, being replaced; person or thing that replaces another.

**replay** ● *verb* /riːˈpleɪ/ play (match, recording, etc.) again. ● *noun* /ˈriːpleɪ/ replaying of match, recorded incident in game, etc.

**replenish** /rɪˈplenɪʃ/ *verb* (often + *with*) fill up again. □ **replenishment** *noun*.

**replete** /rɪˈpliːt/ *adjective* (often + *with*) well-fed; filled or well-supplied. □ **repletion** *noun*.

**replica** /ˈreplɪkə/ *noun* exact copy, esp. duplicate made by original artist; model, esp. small-scale.

**replicate** /ˈreplɪkeɪt/ *verb* make replica of. □ **replication** *noun*.

**reply** /rɪˈplaɪ/ ● *verb* (**-ies**, **-ied**) (often + *to*) make an answer, respond; say in answer. ● *noun* (*plural* **-ies**) replying; what is replied.

**report** /rɪˈpɔːt/ ● *verb* bring back or give account of; tell as news; describe, esp. as eyewitness; make official or formal statement; (often + *to*) bring to attention of authorities, present oneself as arrived; take down, write description of, etc. for publication; (+ *to*) be responsible to. ● *noun* account given or opinion formally expressed after investigation; description, reproduction, or summary of speech, law case, scene, etc., esp. for newspaper publication or broadcast; common talk, rumour; repute; periodical statement on (esp. pupil's) work etc.; sound of gunshot. □ **reportedly** *adverb*.

**reporter** *noun* person employed to report news etc. for media.

**repose**[1] /rɪˈpəʊz/ ● *noun* rest; sleep; tranquillity. ● *verb* (**-sing**) rest; lie, esp. when dead.

**repose**[2] /rɪˈpəʊz/ *verb* (**-sing**) (+ *in*) place (trust etc.) in.

**repository** /rɪˈpɒzɪtərɪ/ *noun* (*plural* **-ies**) place where things are stored or may be found; receptacle; (often + *of*) book, person, etc. regarded as store of information, recipient of secrets etc.

**reprehend** /reprɪ'hend/ *verb formal* rebuke, blame.

**reprehensible** /reprɪ'hensɪb(ə)l/ *adjective* blameworthy.

**represent** /reprɪ'zent/ *verb* stand for, correspond to; be specimen of; symbolize; present likeness of to mind or senses; (often + *as, to be*) describe or depict, declare; (+ *that*) allege; show or play part of; be substitute or deputy for; be elected by as member of legislature etc.

**representation** /reprɪzen'teɪʃ(ə)n/ *noun* representing, being represented; thing that represents another.

**representational** *adjective* (of art) seeking to portray objects etc. realistically.

**representative** /reprɪ'zentətɪv/ ● *adjective* typical of class; containing typical specimens of all or many classes; (of government etc.) of elected deputies or based on representation. ● *noun* (+ *of*) sample, specimen, or typical embodiment of; agent; commercial traveller; delegate or deputy, esp. in representative assembly.

**repress** /rɪ'pres/ *verb* keep under; put down; suppress (esp. unwelcome thought). □ **repression** *noun*; **repressive** *adjective*.

**reprieve** /rɪ'priːv/ ● *verb* (**-ving**) remit or postpone execution of; give respite to. ● *noun* reprieving, being reprieved.

**reprimand** /'reprɪmɑːnd/ ● *noun* official rebuke. ● *verb* rebuke officially.

**reprint** ● *verb* /riː'prɪnt/ print again. ● *noun* /'riːprɪnt/ reprinting of book etc.; quantity reprinted.

**reprisal** /rɪ'praɪz(ə)l/ *noun* act of retaliation.

**reprise** /rɪ'priːz/ *noun Music* repeated passage or song etc.

**repro** /'riːprəʊ/ *noun* (*plural* **-s**) *colloquial* reproduction, copy.

**reproach** /rɪ'prəʊtʃ/ ● *verb* express disapproval to (person) for fault etc. ● *noun* rebuke, censure; (often + *to*) thing that brings discredit.

**reproachful** *adjective* full of or expressing reproach. □ **reproachfully** *adverb*.

**reprobate** /'reprəbeɪt/ *noun* unprincipled or immoral person.

**reproduce** /riːprə'djuːs/ *verb* (**-cing**) produce copy or representation of; produce further members of same species by natural means; (**reproduce itself**) produce offspring. □ **reproducible** *adjective*.

**reproduction** /riːprə'dʌkʃ(ə)n/ ● *noun* reproducing, esp. of further members of same species; copy of work of art. ● *adjective* (of furniture etc.) imitating earlier style. □ **reproductive** *adjective*.

**reproof** /rɪ'pruːf/ *noun formal* blame; rebuke.

**reprove** /rɪ'pruːv/ *verb* (**-ving**) *formal* rebuke.

**reptile** /'reptaɪl/ *noun* cold-blooded scaly animal of class including snakes, lizards, etc.; grovelling or repulsive person. □ **reptilian** /-'tɪl-/ *adjective*.

**republic** /rɪ'pʌblɪk/ *noun* state in which supreme power is held by the people or their elected representatives.

**republican** ● *adjective* of or characterizing republic(s); advocating or supporting republican government. ● *noun* supporter or advocate of republican government; (**Republican**) member of political party styled 'Republican'. □ **republicanism** *noun*.

**repudiate** /rɪ'pjuːdɪeɪt/ *verb* (**-ting**) disown, disavow, deny; refuse to recognize or obey (authority) or discharge (obligation or debt). □ **repudiation** *noun*.

**repugnance** /rɪ'pʌgnəns/ *noun* aversion, antipathy; inconsistency or incompatibility of ideas etc.

**repugnant** /rɪ'pʌgn(ə)nt/ *adjective* distasteful; inconsistency or contradictory.

**repulse** /rɪ'pʌls/ ● *verb* (**-sing**) drive back; rebuff, reject. ● *noun* defeat, rebuff.

**repulsion** /rɪ'pʌlʃ(ə)n/ *noun* aversion, disgust; *Physics* tendency of bodies to repel each other.

**repulsive** /rɪ'pʌlsɪv/ *adjective* causing aversion or loathing. □ **repulsively** *adverb*.

**reputable** /'repjʊtəb(ə)l/ *adjective* of good reputation, respectable.

**reputation** /repjʊ'teɪʃ(ə)n/ *noun* what is generally said or believed about character of person or thing; credit, respectability.

**repute** /rɪˈpjuːt/ ● noun reputation. ● verb (as **reputed** adjective) be generally considered. □ **reputedly** adverb.

**request** /rɪˈkwest/ ● noun asking for something, thing asked for. ● verb ask to be given, allowed, etc.; (+ to do) ask (person) to do something; (+ that) ask that.

**Requiem** /ˈrekwɪəm/ noun (also **requiem**) esp. RC Church mass for the dead.

**require** /rɪˈkwaɪə/ verb (-ring) need; depend on for success etc.; lay down as imperative; command, instruct; demand, insist on. □ **requirement** noun.

**requisite** /ˈrekwɪzɪt/ ● adjective required, necessary. ● noun (often + for) thing needed.

**requisition** /rekwɪˈzɪʃ(ə)n/ ● noun official order laying claim to use of property or materials; formal written demand. ● verb demand use or supply of.

**requite** /rɪˈkwaɪt/ verb (-ting) make return for; reward, avenge; (often + for) give in return. □ **requital** noun.

**reredos** /ˈrɪədɒs/ noun ornamental screen covering wall above back of altar.

**rescind** /rɪˈsɪnd/ verb abrogate, revoke, cancel. □ **rescission** /-ˈsɪʒ-/ noun.

**rescue** /ˈreskjuː/ ● verb (-ues, -ued, -uing) (often + from) save or set free from danger or harm. ● noun rescuing, being rescued. □ **rescuer** noun.

**research** /rɪˈsɜːtʃ, ˈriːsɜːtʃ/ ● noun systematic investigation of materials, sources, etc. to establish facts. ● verb do research into or for. □ **researcher** noun.

**resemble** /rɪˈzemb(ə)l/ verb (-ling) be like; have similarity to. □ **resemblance** noun.

**resent** /rɪˈzent/ verb feel indignation at; be aggrieved by. □ **resentful** adjective; **resentfully** adverb; **resentment** noun.

**reservation** /rezəˈveɪʃ(ə)n/ noun reserving, being reserved; thing reserved (e.g. room in hotel); spoken or unspoken limitation or exception; (in full **central reservation**) strip of land between carriageways of road; area reserved for occupation of aboriginal peoples.

**reserve** /rɪˈzɜːv/ ● verb (-ving) put aside or keep back for later occasion or special use; order to be retained or allocated for person at particular time; retain, secure. ● noun thing reserved for future use; limitation or exception attached to something; self-restraint, reticence; company's profit added to capital; (in singular or plural) assets kept readily available, troops withheld from action to reinforce or protect others, forces outside regular ones but available in emergency; extra player chosen as possible substitute in team; land reserved for special use, esp. as habitat.

**reserved** adjective reticent, uncommunicative; set apart for particular use.

**reservist** noun member of reserve forces.

**reservoir** /ˈrezəvwɑː/ noun large natural or artificial lake as source of water supply; receptacle for fluid; supply of facts etc.

**reshuffle** /riːˈʃʌf(ə)l/ ● verb (-ling) shuffle again; change posts of (government ministers etc.). ● noun reshuffling.

**reside** /rɪˈzaɪd/ verb (-ding) have one's home; (+ in) (of right etc.) be vested in, (of quality) be present in.

**residence** /ˈrezɪd(ə)ns/ noun residing; place where one resides; house, esp. large one. □ **in residence** living or working at specified place.

**resident** /ˈrezɪd(ə)nt/ ● noun (often + of) permanent inhabitant; guest staying at hotel. ● adjective residing, in residence; living at one's workplace etc.; (+ in) located in.

**residential** /rezɪˈdenʃ(ə)l/ adjective suitable for or occupied by dwellings; used as residence; connected with residence.

**residual** /rɪˈzɪdjʊəl/ adjective left as residue or residuum.

**residuary** /rɪˈzɪdjʊərɪ/ adjective of the residue of an estate; residual.

**residue** /ˈrezɪdjuː/ noun remainder, what is left over; what remains of estate when liabilities have been discharged.

**residuum** /rɪˈzɪdjʊəm/ noun (plural **-dua**) substance left after combustion or evaporation; residue.

**resign** /rɪˈzaɪn/ *verb* (often + *from*) give up job, position, etc.; relinquish, surrender; **(resign oneself to)** accept (situation etc.) reluctantly.

**resignation** /rezɪgˈneɪʃ(ə)n/ *noun* resigning, esp. from job or office; reluctant acceptance of the inevitable.

**resigned** *adjective* (often + *to*) having resigned oneself; resolved to endure; indicative of this. □ **resignedly** /-nɪdlɪ/ *adverb*.

**resilient** /rɪˈzɪlɪənt/ *adjective* resuming original form after compression etc.; readily recovering from setback. □ **resilience** *noun*.

**resin** /ˈrezɪn/ ● *noun* sticky secretion of trees and plants; (in full **synthetic resin**) organic compound made by polymerization etc. and used in plastics. ● *verb* (**-n-**) rub or treat with resin. □ **resinous** *adjective*.

**resist** /rɪˈzɪst/ *verb* withstand action or effect of; abstain from (pleasure etc.); strive against, oppose; offer opposition. □ **resistible** *adjective*.

**resistance** /rɪˈzɪst(ə)ns/ *noun* resisting; power to resist; ability to withstand disease; impeding effect exerted by one thing on another; *Physics* property of hindering passage of electric current, heat, etc.; resistor; secret organization resisting regime, esp. in occupied country. □ **resistant** *adjective*.

**resistor** *noun* device having resistance to passage of electric current.

**resit** ● *verb* /riːˈsɪt/ (**-tt-**; *past & past participle* **resat**) sit (exam) again after failing. ● *noun* /ˈriːsɪt/ resitting of exam; exam for this.

**resoluble** /rɪˈzɒljʊb(ə)l/ *adjective* resolvable; (+ *into*) analysable into.

**resolute** /ˈrezəluːt/ *adjective* determined, decided; purposeful. □ **resolutely** *adverb*.

**resolution** /rezəˈluːʃ(ə)n/ *noun* resolute temper or character; thing resolved on; formal expression of opinion of meeting; (+ *of*) solving of question etc.; resolving, being resolved.

**resolve** /rɪˈzɒlv/ ● *verb* (**-ving**) make up one's mind, decide firmly; cause to do this; solve, settle; (+ *that*) pass resolution by vote; (often + *into*) (cause to) separate into constituent parts, analyse; *Music* convert or be converted into

concord. ● *noun* firm mental decision; determination. □ **resolved** *adjective*.

**resonant** /ˈrezənənt/ *adjective* echoing, resounding; continuing to sound; causing reinforcement or prolongation of sound, esp. by vibration. □ **resonance** *noun*.

**resonate** /ˈrezəneɪt/ *verb* (**-ting**) produce or show resonance; resound. □ **resonator** *noun*.

**resort** /rɪˈzɔːt/ ● *noun* place frequented, esp. for holidays etc.; thing to which recourse is had, expedient; (+ *to*) recourse to, use of. ● *verb* (+ *to*) turn to as expedient; (+ *to*) go often or in numbers to. □ **in the** or **as a last resort** when all else has failed.

**resound** /rɪˈzaʊnd/ *verb* (often + *with*) ring, echo; produce echoes, go on sounding, fill place with sound; be much talked of, produce sensation.

**resounding** *adjective* ringing, echoing; unmistakable, emphatic.

**resource** /rɪˈzɔːs/ ● *noun* expedient, device; (often in *plural*) means available; stock that can be drawn on; (in *plural*) country's collective wealth, person's inner strength; skill in devising expedients. ● *verb* (**-cing**) provide with resources.

**resourceful** *adjective* good at devising expedients. □ **resourcefully** *adverb*; **resourcefulness** *noun*.

**respect** /rɪˈspekt/ ● *noun* deferential esteem; (+ *of, for*) heed, regard; detail, aspect; reference, relation; (in *plural*) polite greetings. ● *verb* regard with deference or esteem; treat with consideration, spare. □ **respectful** *adjective*, **respectfully** *adverb*.

**respectable** *adjective* of acceptable social standing, decent in appearance or behaviour; reasonably good in condition, appearance, size, etc. □ **respectability** *noun*; **respectably** *adverb*.

**respecting** *preposition* with regard to.

**respective** /rɪˈspektɪv/ *adjective* of or relating to each of several individually.

**respectively** *adverb* for each separately or in turn, and in the order mentioned.

**respiration** /respəˈreɪʃ(ə)n/ *noun* breathing; single breath in or out; plant's absorption of oxygen and emission of carbon dioxide.

**respirator** /'respəreɪtə/ *noun* apparatus worn over mouth and nose to filter inhaled air; apparatus for maintaining artificial respiration.

**respire** /rɪ'spaɪə/ *verb* (**-ring**) breathe; inhale and exhale; (of plant) carry out respiration. □ **respiratory** /-'spɪr-/ *adjective*.

**respite** /'respaɪt/ *noun* interval of rest or relief; delay permitted before discharge of obligation or suffering of penalty.

**resplendent** /rɪ'splend(ə)nt/ *adjective* brilliant, dazzlingly or gloriously bright. □ **resplendence** *noun*.

**respond** /rɪ'spɒnd/ *verb* answer, reply; (often + *to*) act etc. in response.

**respondent** *noun* defendant, esp. in appeal or divorce case. • *adjective* in position of defendant.

**response** /rɪ'spɒns/ *noun* answer, reply; action, feeling, etc. caused by stimulus etc.; (often in *plural*) part of liturgy said or sung in answer to priest.

**responsibility** /rɪspɒnsə'bɪlɪtɪ/ *noun* (*plural* **-ies**) (often + *for*, *of*) being responsible, authority; person or thing for which one is responsible.

**responsible** /rɪ'spɒnsəb(ə)l/ *adjective* (often + *to*, *for*) liable to be called to account; morally accountable for actions; of good credit and repute; trustworthy; (often + *for*) being the cause; involving responsibility. □ **responsibly** *adverb*.

**responsive** /rɪ'spɒnsɪv/ *adjective* (often + *to*) responding readily (to some influence); sympathetic; answering; by way of answer. □ **responsiveness** *noun*.

**rest¹** • *verb* cease from exertion or action; be still, esp. to recover strength; lie in sleep or death; give relief or repose to; be left without further investigation or discussion; (+ *on*, *upon*, *against*) place, lie, lean, or depend on; (as **rested** *adjective*) refreshed by resting. • *noun* repose or sleep; resting; prop or support for steadying something; *Music* (sign denoting) interval of silence. □ **at rest** not moving, not agitated or troubled; **rest-cure** prolonged rest as medical treatment; **rest home** place where elderly or convalescent people are cared for; **rest room** *esp. US* public lavatory; **set at rest** settle, reassure.

**rest²** • *noun* (**the rest**) remainder or remaining parts or individuals. • *verb* remain in specified state; (+ *with*) be left in the charge of. □ **for the rest** as regards anything else.

**restaurant** /'restərɒnt/ *noun* public premises where meals may be bought and eaten.

**restaurateur** /restərə'tɜ:/ *noun* keeper of restaurant.

**restful** *adjective* quiet, soothing.

**restitution** /restɪ'tju:ʃ(ə)n/ *noun* restoring of property etc. to its owner; reparation.

**restive** /'restɪv/ *adjective* fidgety; intractable; resisting control.

**restless** *adjective* without rest; uneasy, agitated, fidgeting. □ **restlessly** *adverb*; **restlessness** *noun*.

**restoration** /restə'reɪʃ(ə)n/ *noun* restoring, being restored; model or drawing representing supposed original form of thing; (**Restoration**) re-establishment of British monarchy in 1660.

**restorative** /rɪ'stɒrətɪv/ • *adjective* tending to restore health or strength. • *noun* restorative food, medicine, etc.

**restore** /rɪ'stɔ:/ *verb* (**-ring**) bring back to original state by rebuilding, repairing, etc.; give back; reinstate; bring back to former place, condition, or use; make restoration of (extinct animal, ruined building, etc.). □ **restorer** *noun*.

**restrain** /rɪ'streɪn/ *verb* (usually + *from*) check or hold in; keep under control; repress; confine.

**restraint** /rɪ'streɪnt/ *noun* restraining, being restrained; restraining agency or influence; self-control, moderation; reserve of manner.

**restrict** /rɪ'strɪkt/ *verb* confine, limit; withhold from general disclosure. □ **restriction** *noun*.

**restrictive** /rɪ'strɪktɪv/ *adjective* restricting. □ **restrictive practice** agreement or practice that limits competition or output in industry.

**result** /rɪ'zʌlt/ • *noun* consequence; issue; satisfactory outcome; answer etc. got by calculation; (in *plural*) list of scores, winners, etc. in sporting events or exams. • *verb* (often + *from*) arise as consequence; (+ *in*) end in.

**resultant** ● *adjective* resulting. ● *noun* force etc. equivalent to two or more acting in different directions at same point.

**resume** /rɪ'zju:m/ *verb* (**-ming**) begin again; recommence; take again or back. □ **resumption** /-'zʌmp-/ *noun*; **resumptive** /-'zʌmp-/ *adjective*.

**résumé** /'rezjʊmeɪ/ *noun* summary.

**resurgent** /rɪ'sɜ:dʒ(ə)nt/ *adjective* rising or arising again. □ **resurgence** *noun*.

**resurrect** /rezə'rekt/ *verb* *colloquial* revive practice or memory of; raise or rise from dead.

**resurrection** /rezə'rekʃ(ə)n/ *noun* rising from the dead; revival from disuse or decay etc.

**resuscitate** /rɪ'sʌsɪteɪt/ *verb* (**-ting**) revive from unconsciousness or apparent death; revive, restore. □ **resuscitation** *noun*.

**retail** /'ri:teɪl/ ● *noun* sale of goods to the public in small quantities. ● *adjective & adverb* by retail; at retail price. ● *verb* sell by retail; (often + *at, of*) (of goods) be sold by retail; (also /rɪ'teɪl/) recount. □ **retailer** *noun*.

**retain** /rɪ'teɪn/ *verb* keep possession of, continue to have, use, etc.; keep in mind; keep in place, hold fixed; secure services of (esp. barrister) by preliminary fee.

**retainer** *noun* fee for securing person's services; faithful servant; reduced rent paid to retain unoccupied accommodation; person or thing that retains.

**retake** ● *verb* /ri:'teɪk/ (**-king**; *past* **retook**; *past participle* **retaken**) take (photograph, exam, etc.) again; recapture. ● *noun* /'ri:teɪk/ filming, recording, etc. again; taking of exam etc. again.

**retaliate** /rɪ'tælɪeɪt/ *verb* (**-ting**) repay in kind; attack in return. □ **retaliation** *noun*; **retaliatory** /-'tælɪət-/ *adjective*.

**retard** /rɪ'tɑ:d/ *verb* make slow or late; delay progress or accomplishment of. □ **retardant** *adjective & noun*; **retardation** /ri:-/ *noun*.

**retarded** *adjective* backward in mental or physical development.

**retch** *verb* make motion of vomiting.

**retention** /rɪ'tenʃ(ə)n/ *noun* retaining, being retained.

**retentive** /rɪ'tentɪv/ *adjective* tending to retain; (of memory) not forgetful.

**rethink** ● *verb* /ri:'θɪŋk/ (*past & past participle* **rethought** /-'θɔ:t/) consider again, esp. with view to making changes. ● *noun* /'ri:θɪŋk/ rethinking, reassessment.

**reticence** /'retɪs(ə)ns/ *noun* avoidance of saying all one knows or feels; taciturnity. □ **reticent** *adjective*.

**reticulate** ● *verb* /rɪ'tɪkjʊleɪt/ (**-ting**) divide or be divided in fact or appearance into network. ● *adjective* /rɪ'tɪkjʊlət/ reticulated. □ **reticulation** *noun*.

**retina** /'retɪnə/ *noun* (*plural* **-s** or **-nae** /-ni:/) light-sensitive layer at back of eyeball. □ **retinal** *adjective*.

**retinue** /'retɪnju:/ *noun* group of people attending important person.

**retire** /rɪ'taɪə/ *verb* (**-ring**) leave office or employment, esp. because of age; cause (employee) to retire; withdraw, retreat, seek seclusion or shelter; go to bed; *Cricket* (of batsman) suspend one's innings. □ **retired** *adjective*.

**retirement** *noun* retiring; period spent as retired person; seclusion. □ **retirement pension** pension paid by state to retired people above certain age.

**retiring** *adjective* shy, fond of seclusion.

**retort**[1] /rɪ'tɔ:t/ ● *noun* incisive, witty, or angry reply. ● *verb* say by way of retort; repay in kind.

**retort**[2] /rɪ'tɔ:t/ *noun* vessel with long downward-bent neck for distilling liquids; vessel for heating coal to generate gas.

**retouch** /ri:'tʌtʃ/ *verb* improve (esp. photograph) by minor alterations.

**retrace** /rɪ'treɪs/ *verb* (**-cing**) go back over (one's steps etc.); trace back to source or beginning.

**retract** /rɪ'trækt/ *verb* withdraw (statement etc.); draw or be drawn back or in. □ **retractable** *adjective*; **retraction** *noun*.

**retractile** /rɪ'træktaɪl/ *adjective* retractable.

**retread** ● *verb* /ri:'tred/ (*past* **retrod**; *past participle* **retrodden**) tread (path etc.) again; (*past & past participle* **retreaded**) put new tread on (tyre). ● *noun* /'ri:tred/ retreaded tyre.

**retreat** /rɪ'triːt/ ● *verb* go back, retire; recede. ● *noun* (signal for) act of retreating; withdrawing into privacy; place of seclusion or shelter; period of seclusion for prayer and meditation.

**retrench** /rɪ'trentʃ/ *verb* cut down expenses; reduce amount of (costs); economize. □ **retrenchment** *noun*.

**retrial** /riː'traɪəl/ *noun* retrying of case.

**retribution** /retrɪ'bjuːʃ(ə)n/ *noun* recompense, usually for evil; vengeance. □ **retributive** /rɪ'trɪb-/ *adjective*.

**retrieve** /rɪ'triːv/ *verb* regain possession of; find again; obtain (information in computer); (of dog) find and bring in game; (+ *from*) rescue from (bad state etc.); restore to good state; repair, set right. □ **retrievable** *adjective*; **retrieval** *noun*.

**retriever** *noun* dog of breed used for retrieving game.

**retro** /'retrəʊ/ *slang* ● *adjective* reviving or harking back to past. ● *noun* (*plural* **retros**) retro fashion or style.

**retro-** *combining form* backwards, back.

**retroactive** /retrəʊ'æktɪv/ *adjective* having retrospective effect.

**retrod** *past* of RETREAD.

**retrodden** *past participle* of RETREAD.

**retrograde** /'retrəgreɪd/ ● *adjective* directed backwards; reverting, esp. to inferior state. ● *verb* move backwards; decline, revert.

**retrogress** /retrə'gres/ *verb* move backwards; deteriorate. □ **retrogression** *noun*; **retrogressive** *adjective*.

**retrorocket** /'retrəʊrɒkɪt/ *noun* auxiliary rocket for slowing down spacecraft etc.

**retrospect** /'retrəspekt/ *noun* □ **in retrospect** when looking back.

**retrospection** /retrə'spekʃ(ə)n/ *noun* looking back into the past.

**retrospective** /retrə'spektɪv/ ● *adjective* looking back on or dealing with the past; (of statute etc.) applying to the past as well as the future. ● *noun* exhibition etc. showing artist's lifetime development. □ **retrospectively** *adverb*.

**retroussé** /rə'truːseɪ/ *adjective* (of nose) turned up at tip.

**retroverted** /'retrəʊvɜːtɪd/ *adjective* (of womb) inclining backwards.

**retry** /riː'traɪ/ *verb* (**-ies**, **-ied**) try (defendant, law case) again.

**retsina** /ret'siːnə/ *noun* resin-flavoured Greek white wine.

**return** /rɪ'tɜːn/ ● *verb* come or go back; bring, put, or send back; give in response; yield (profit); say in reply; send (ball) back in tennis etc.; state in answer to formal demand; elect as MP etc. ● *noun* coming, going, putting, giving, sending, or paying back; what is returned; (in full **return ticket**) ticket for journey to place and back again; (in *singular* or *plural*) proceeds, profit; coming in of these; formal statement or report; (in full **return match**, **game**) second game between same opponents; (announcement of) person's election as MP etc. □ **by return** (**of post**) by the next available post in the return direction; **returning officer** official conducting election in constituency etc. and announcing result.

**returnee** /rɪtɜː'niː/ *noun* person who returns home, esp. after war service.

**reunify** /riː'juːnɪfaɪ/ *verb* (**-ies**, **-ied**) restore to political unity. □ **reunification** *noun*.

**reunion** /riː'juːnjən/ *noun* reuniting, being reunited; social gathering, esp. of former associates.

**reunite** /riːjuː'naɪt/ *verb* (**-ting**) (cause to) come together again.

**reuse** ● *verb* /riː'juːz/ (**-sing**) use again. ● *noun* /riː'juːs/ second or further use. □ **reusable** *adjective*.

**Rev.** *abbreviation* Reverend.

**rev** *colloquial* ● *noun* (in *plural*) revolutions of engine per minute. ● *verb* (**-vv-**) (of engine) revolve; (often + *up*) cause (engine) to run quickly.

**revalue** /riː'væljuː/ *verb* (**-ues**, **-ued**, **-uing**) give different, esp. higher, value to (currency etc.). □ **revaluation** *noun*.

**revamp** /riː'væmp/ *verb* renovate, revise; patch up.

**Revd** *abbreviation* Reverend.

**reveal** /rɪ'viːl/ *verb* display, show, allow to appear; (often as **revealing** *adjective*) disclose, divulge.

**reveille** /rɪ'vælɪ/ *noun* military waking-signal.

**revel** /'rev(ə)l/ ● *verb* (**-ll-**; *US* **-l-**) make merry, be riotously festive; (+ *in*) take keen delight in. ●*noun* (in *singular* or *plural*) revelling. □ **reveller** *noun*; **revelry** *noun* (*plural* **-ies**).

**revelation** /revəˈleɪʃ(ə)n/ *noun* revealing; knowledge supposedly disclosed by divine or supernatural agency; striking disclosure or realization; (**Revelation** or *colloquial* **Revelations**) last book of New Testament.

**revenge** /rɪˈvendʒ/ ●*noun* (act of) retaliation; desire for this. ●*verb* (**-ging**) avenge; (**revenge oneself** or in *passive*, often + *on*, *upon*) inflict retaliation.

**revengeful** *adjective* eager for revenge.

**revenue** /ˈrevənjuː/ *noun* income, esp. annual income of state; department collecting state revenue.

**reverberate** /rɪˈvɜːbəreɪt/ *verb* (**-ting**) (of sound, light, or heat) be returned or reflected repeatedly; return (sound etc.) thus; (of event) produce continuing effect. □ **reverberant** *adjective*; **reverberation** *noun*; **reverberative** /-rətɪv/ *adjective*.

**revere** /rɪˈvɪə/ *verb* (**-ring**) regard with deep and affectionate or religious respect.

**reverence** /ˈrevərəns/ ●*noun* revering, being revered; deep respect. ●*verb* (**-cing**) treat with reverence.

**reverend** /ˈrevərənd/ *adjective* (esp. as title of member of clergy) deserving reverence. □ **Reverend Mother** Mother Superior of convent.

**reverent** /ˈrevərənt/ *adjective* feeling or showing reverence. □ **reverently** *adverb*.

**reverential** /revəˈrenʃ(ə)l/ *adjective* of the nature of, due to, or characterized by reverence. □ **reverentially** *adverb*.

**reverie** /ˈrevərɪ/ *noun* fit of musing; daydream.

**revers** /rɪˈvɪə/ *noun* (*plural* same /-ˈvɪəz/) (material of) turned-back front edge of garment.

**reverse** /rɪˈvɜːs/ ●*verb* (**-sing**) turn the other way round or up, turn inside out; convert to opposite character or effect; (cause to) travel backwards; make (engine) work in contrary direction; revoke, annul. ●*adjective* backward, upside down; opposite or contrary in character or order, inverted. ●*noun* opposite or contrary; contrary of usual

manner; piece of misfortune, disaster; reverse gear or motion; reverse side; side of coin etc. bearing secondary design; verso of printed leaf. □ **reverse the charges** have recipient of telephone call pay for it; **reverse gear** gear used to make vehicle etc. go backwards; **reversing light** light at rear of vehicle showing it is in reverse gear. □ **reversal** *noun*; **reversible** *adjective*.

**reversion** /rɪˈvɜːʃ(ə)n/ *noun* return to previous state or earlier type; legal right (esp. of original owner) to possess or succeed to property on death of present possessor.

**revert** /rɪˈvɜːt/ *verb* (+ *to*) return to (former condition, practice, subject, opinion, etc.); return by reversion. □ **revertible** *adjective*.

**review** /rɪˈvjuː/ ●*noun* general survey or assessment; survey of past; revision, reconsideration; published criticism of book, play, etc.; periodical in which events, books, etc. are reviewed; inspection of troops etc. ●*verb* survey, look back on; reconsider, revise; hold review of (troops etc.); write review of (book etc.). □ **reviewer** *noun*.

**revile** /rɪˈvaɪl/ *verb* (**-ling**) abuse verbally.

**revise** /rɪˈvaɪz/ *verb* (**-sing**) examine and improve or amend; reconsider and alter (opinion etc.); go over (work etc.) again, esp. for examination. □ **revisory** *adjective*.

**revision** /rɪˈvɪʒ(ə)n/ *noun* revising, being revised; revised edition or form.

**revisionism** *noun* often *derogatory* revision or modification of orthodoxy, esp. of Marxism. □ **revisionist** *noun* & *adjective*.

**revitalize** /riːˈvaɪtəlaɪz/ *verb* (also **-ise**) (**-zing** or **-sing**) imbue with new vitality.

**revival** /rɪˈvaɪv(ə)l/ *noun* reviving, being revived; new production of old play etc.; (campaign to promote) reawakening of religious fervour.

**revivalism** *noun* promotion of esp. religious revival. □ **revivalist** *noun* & *adjective*.

**revive** /rɪˈvaɪv/ *verb* (**-ving**) come or bring back to consciousness, life, vigour, use, or notice.

**revivify** /rɪˈvɪvɪfaɪ/ *verb* (**-ies, -ied**) restore to life, strength, or activity. □ **revivification** *noun*.

**revoke** /rɪˈvəʊk/ ● *verb* (**-king**) rescind, withdraw, cancel; *Cards* fail to follow suit though able to. ● *noun Cards* revoking. □ **revocable** /ˈrevəkəb(ə)l/ *adjective*; **revocation** /revəˈkeɪʃ(ə)n/ *noun*.

**revolt** /rɪˈvəʊlt/ ● *verb* rise in rebellion; affect with disgust; (often + *at, against*) feel revulsion. ● *noun* insurrection; sense of disgust; rebellious mood.

**revolting** *adjective* disgusting, horrible. □ **revoltingly** *adverb*.

**revolution** /revəˈluːʃ(ə)n/ *noun* forcible overthrow of government or social order; fundamental change; revolving; single completion of orbit or rotation.

**revolutionary** ● *adjective* involving great change; of political revolution. ● *noun* (*plural* **-ies**) instigator or supporter of political revolution.

**revolutionize** *verb* (also **-ise**) (**-zing** or **-sing**) change fundamentally.

**revolve** /rɪˈvɒlv/ *verb* (**-ving**) turn round; rotate; move in orbit; ponder in the mind; (+ *around*) be centred on.

**revolver** *noun* pistol with revolving chambers enabling user to fire several shots without reloading.

**revue** /rɪˈvjuː/ *noun* theatrical entertainment of usually comic sketches and songs.

**revulsion** /rɪˈvʌlʃ(ə)n/ *noun* abhorrence; sudden violent change of feeling.

**reward** /rɪˈwɔːd/ ● *noun* return or recompense for service or merit; requital for good or evil; sum offered for detection of criminal, recovery of lost property, etc. ● *verb* give or serve as reward to. □ **rewarding** *adjective*.

**rewind** /riːˈwaɪnd/ *verb* (*past & past participle* **rewound** /-ˈwaʊnd/) wind (film, tape, etc.) back.

**rewire** /riːˈwaɪə/ *verb* (**-ring**) provide with new electrical wiring.

**rework** /riːˈwɜːk/ *verb* revise, refashion, remake. □ **reworking** *noun*.

**Rex** *noun* (after name) reigning king; *Law* the Crown. [Latin].

**rhapsodize** /ˈræpsədaɪz/ *verb* (also **-ise**) (**-zing** or **-sing**) speak or write rhapsodies.

**rhapsody** /ˈræpsədɪ/ *noun* (*plural* **-ies**) enthusiastic or extravagant speech or composition; melodic musical piece often based on folk culture. □ **rhapsodic** /-ˈsɒd-/ *adjective*.

**rhea** /ˈriːə/ *noun* large flightless S. American bird.

**rheostat** /ˈriːəstæt/ *noun* instrument used to control electric current by varying resistance.

**rhesus** /ˈriːsəs/ *noun* (in full **rhesus monkey**) small Indian monkey. □ **rhesus factor** antigen occurring on red blood cells of most humans and some other primates; **rhesus-positive, -negative** having or not having rhesus factor.

**rhetoric** /ˈretərɪk/ *noun* art of persuasive speaking or writing; language intended to impress, esp. seen as inflated, exaggerated, or meaningless.

**rhetorical** /rɪˈtɒrɪk(ə)l/ *adjective* expressed artificially or extravagantly; of the nature of rhetoric. □ **rhetorical question** question asked not for information but to produce effect. □ **rhetorically** *adverb*.

**rheumatic** /ruːˈmætɪk/ ● *adjective* of, caused by, or suffering from rheumatism. ● *noun* person suffering from rheumatism; (in *plural*, often treated as *singular*) *colloquial* rheumatism. □ **rheumatic fever** fever with pain in the joints. □ **rheumatically** *adverb*; **rheumaticky** *adjective colloquial*.

**rheumatism** /ˈruːmətɪz(ə)m/ *noun* disease marked by inflammation and pain in joints etc.

**rheumatoid** /ˈruːmətɔɪd/ *adjective* having the character of rheumatism. □ **rheumatoid arthritis** chronic progressive disease causing inflammation and stiffening of joints.

**rhinestone** /ˈraɪnstəʊn/ *noun* imitation diamond.

**rhino** /ˈraɪnəʊ/ *noun* (*plural* same or **-s**) *colloquial* rhinoceros.

**rhinoceros** /raɪˈnɒsərəs/ *noun* (*plural* same or **-roses**) large thick-skinned animal with usually one horn on nose.

**rhizome** /ˈraɪzəʊm/ *noun* underground rootlike stem bearing both roots and shoots.

**rhododendron** /ˌrəʊdə'dendrən/ noun (plural **-s** or **-dra**) evergreen shrub with large flowers.

**rhomboid** /'rɒmbɔɪd/ • adjective (also **rhomboidal** /-'bɔɪd-/) like a rhombus. • noun quadrilateral of which only opposite sides and angles are equal.

**rhombus** /'rɒmbəs/ noun (plural **-buses** or **-bi** /-baɪ/) oblique equilateral parallelogram, e.g. diamond on playing card.

**rhubarb** /'ruːbɑːb/ noun (stalks of) plant with fleshy leaf-stalks cooked and eaten as dessert; colloquial indistinct conversation or noise, from repeated use of word 'rhubarb' by stage crowd.

**rhyme** /raɪm/ • noun identity of sound at ends of words or verse-lines; (in singular or plural) rhymed verse; use of rhyme; word providing rhyme. • verb (**-ming**) (of words or lines) produce rhyme; ( + with) be or use as rhyme; write rhymes; put into rhyme.

**rhythm** /'rɪð(ə)m/ noun periodical accent and duration of notes in music; type of structure formed by this; measured flow of words in verse or prose; Physiology pattern of successive strong and weak movements; regularly occurring sequence of events. □ **rhythm method** contraception by avoiding sexual intercourse near times of ovulation. □ **rhythmic** adjective; **rhythmical** adjective; **rhythmically** adverb.

**rib** • noun each of the curved bones joined to spine and protecting organs of chest; joint of meat from this part of animal; supporting ridge, timber, rod, etc. across surface or through structure; combination of plain and purl stitches producing ribbed design. • verb (**-bb-**) provide or mark (as) with ribs; colloquial tease. □ **ribcage** wall of bones formed by ribs round chest; **rib-tickler** something amusing. □ **ribbed** adjective; **ribbing** noun.

**ribald** /'rɪb(ə)ld/ adjective irreverent, coarsely humorous. □ **ribaldry** noun.

**riband** /'rɪbənd/ noun ribbon.

**ribbon** /'rɪbən/ noun narrow strip or band of fabric; material in this form; ribbon worn to indicate some honour, membership of sports team, etc.; long narrow strip; (in plural) ragged strips. □ **ribbon development** building of houses along main road outwards from town.

**riboflavin** /ˌraɪbəʊ'fleɪvɪn/ noun (also **riboflavine** /-viːn/) vitamin of B complex, found in liver, milk, and eggs.

**ribonucleic acid** /ˌraɪbəʊnjuː'kliːɪk/ noun substance controlling protein synthesis in cells.

**rice** noun (grains from) swamp grass grown esp. in Asia. □ **rice-paper** edible paper made from pith of an oriental tree and used for painting and in cookery.

**rich** adjective having much wealth; splendid, costly; valuable; abundant, ample; (often + in, with) abounding; fertile; (of food) containing much fat, spice, etc.; mellow, strong and full; highly amusing or ludicrous. □ **richness** noun.

**riches** plural noun abundant means; valuable possessions.

**richly** adverb in a rich way; fully, thoroughly.

**Richter scale** /'rɪktə/ noun scale of 0–10 for representing strength of earthquake.

**rick**[1] noun stack of hay etc.

**rick**[2] (also **wrick**) • noun slight sprain or strain. • verb slightly strain or sprain.

**rickets** /'rɪkɪts/ noun (treated as singular or plural) children's deficiency disease with softening of the bones.

**rickety** /'rɪkɪtɪ/ adjective shaky, insecure; suffering from rickets.

**rickshaw** /'rɪkʃɔː/ noun (also **ricksha** /-ʃə/) light two-wheeled hooded vehicle drawn by one or more people.

**ricochet** /'rɪkəʃeɪ/ • noun rebounding of esp. shell or bullet off surface; hit made after this. • verb (**-cheted** /-ʃeɪd/ or **-chetted** /-ʃetɪd/; **-cheting** /-ʃeɪɪŋ/ or **-chetting** /-ʃetɪŋ/) (of projectile) make ricochet.

**ricotta** /rɪ'kɒtə/ noun soft Italian cheese.

**rid** verb (**-dd-**; past & past participle **rid** ) ( + of ) make (person, place) free of.

**riddance** /'rɪd(ə)ns/ noun □ **good riddance** expression of relief at getting rid of something or someone.

**ridden** past participle of RIDE.

**riddle**[1] /'rɪd(ə)l/ • noun verbal puzzle or test, often with trick answer; puzzling fact, thing, or person. ● *verb* **(-ling)** speak in riddles.

**riddle**[2] /'rɪd(ə)l/ ● *verb* **(-ling)** (usually + *with*) make many holes in, esp. with gunshot; (in *passive*) fill, permeate; pass through riddle. ● *noun* coarse sieve.

**ride** ● *verb* **(-ding**; *past* **rode**; *past participle* **ridden** /'rɪd(ə)n/) (often + *on, in*) travel or be carried on or in (bicycle, vehicle, horse, etc.); be carried or supported by; cross, be conveyed over; float buoyantly; (as **ridden** *adjective*) (+ *by, with*) dominated by or infested with. ● *noun* journey or spell of riding in vehicle, on horse, etc.; path (esp. through woods) for riding on; amusement for riding on at fairground. □ **ride up** (of garment) work upwards when worn; **take for a ride** *colloquial* hoax, deceive.

**rider** *noun* person riding; additional remark following statement, verdict, etc.

**ridge** *noun* line of junction of two surfaces sloping upwards towards each other; long narrow hilltop; mountain range; any narrow elevation across surface. □ **ridge-pole** horizontal pole of long tent; **ridgeway** road along ridge.

**ridicule** /'rɪdɪkjuːl/ ● *noun* derision, mockery. ● *verb* **(-ling)** make fun of; mock; laugh at.

**ridiculous** /rɪ'dɪkjʊləs/ *adjective* deserving to be laughed at; unreasonable. □ **ridiculously** *adverb*; **ridiculousness** *noun*.

**riding**[1] /'raɪdɪŋ/ *noun* sport or pastime of travelling on horseback.

**riding**[2] /'raɪdɪŋ/ *noun historical* former division of Yorkshire.

**Riesling** /'riːzlɪŋ/ *noun* (white wine made from) type of grape.

**rife** *adjective* widespread; (+ *with*) abounding in.

**riff** *noun* short repeated phrase in jazz etc.

**riffle** /'rɪf(ə)l/ ● *verb* **(-ling)** (often + *through*) leaf quickly through (pages); shuffle (cards). ● *noun* riffling; *US* patch of ripples in stream etc.

**riff-raff** /'rɪfræf/ *noun* rabble, disreputable people.

**rifle**[1] /'raɪf(ə)l/ ● *noun* gun with long rifled barrel; (in *plural*) troops armed

with these. ● *verb* **(-ling)** make spiral grooves in (gun etc.) to make projectile spin. □ **rifle range** place for rifle practice.

**rifle**[2] /'raɪf(ə)l/ *verb* **(-ling)** (often + *through*) search and rob; carry off as booty.

**rift** *noun* crack, split; cleft; disagreement, dispute. □ **rift-valley** one formed by subsidence of section of earth's crust.

**rig**[1] ● *verb* **(-gg-)** provide (ship) with rigging; (often + *out, up*) fit with clothes or equipment; (+ *up*) set up hastily or as makeshift. ● *noun* arrangement of ship's masts, sails, etc.; equipment for special purpose; oil rig; *colloquial* style of dress, uniform. □ **rig-out** *colloquial* outfit of clothes. □ **rigger** *noun*.

**rig**[2] ● *verb* **(-gg-)** manage or fix fraudulently. ● *noun* trick, swindle.

**rigging** *noun* ship's spars, ropes, etc.

**right** /raɪt/ ● *adjective* just, morally or socially correct; correct, true; preferable, suitable; in good or normal condition; on or towards east side of person or thing facing north; (also **Right**) *Politics* of the Right; (of side of fabric etc.) meant to show; *colloquial* real, complete. ● *noun* what is just; fair treatment; fair claim; legal or moral entitlement; right-hand part, region, or direction; *Boxing* right hand, blow with this; (often **Right**) *Politics* conservatives collectively. ● *verb* (often *reflexive*) restore to proper, straight, or vertical position; correct, avenge; set in order; make reparation for. ● *adverb* straight; *colloquial* immediately; (+ *to, round, through*, etc.) all the way; (+ *off, out*, etc.) completely; quite, very; justly, properly, correctly, truly; on or to right side. ● *interjection colloquial*: expressing agreement or consent. □ **by right(s)** if right were done; **in the right** having justice or truth on one's side; **right angle** angle of 90°; **right-hand** on right side; **right-handed** naturally using right hand for writing etc., made by or for right hand, turning to right, (of screw) turning clockwise to tighten; **right-hander** right-handed person or blow; **right-hand man** essential or chief assistant; **Right Honourable** *title of certain high officials, e.g.* Privy Counsellors; **right-minded, -thinking** having sound views and principles; **right**

**of way** right to pass over another's ground, path subject to such right, precedence granted to one vehicle over another; **Right Reverend** *title of bishop*; **right wing** more conservative section of political party etc., right side of football etc. team; **right-wing** conservative, reactionary; **right-winger** member of right wing. □ **rightward** *adjective & adverb*; **rightwards** *adverb*.

**righteous** /ˈraɪtʃəs/ *adjective* morally right; virtuous, law-abiding. □ **righteously** *adverb*; **righteousness** *noun*.

**rightful** *adjective* legitimately entitled to (position etc.); that one is entitled to. □ **rightfully** *adverb*.

**rightly** *adverb* justly, correctly, properly, justifiably.

**rigid** /ˈrɪdʒɪd/ *adjective* not flexible, unbendable; inflexible, harsh. □ **rigidity** /-ˈdʒɪd-/ *noun*; **rigidly** *adverb*.

**rigmarole** /ˈrɪɡmərəʊl/ *noun* complicated procedure; rambling tale etc.

**rigor** *US* = RIGOUR.

**rigor mortis** /ˌrɪɡə ˈmɔːtɪs/ *noun* stiffening of body after death.

**rigorous** /ˈrɪɡərəs/ *adjective* strict, severe; exact, accurate. □ **rigorously** *adverb*; **rigorousness** *noun*.

**rigour** /ˈrɪɡə/ *noun* (*US* **rigor**) severity, strictness, harshness; (in *plural*) harsh conditions; strict application or observance etc.

**rile** *verb* (**-ling**) *colloquial* anger, irritate.

**rill** *noun* small stream.

**rim** *noun* edge or border, esp. of something circular; outer ring of wheel, holding tyre; part of spectacle frames around lens. □ **rimless** *adjective*; **rimmed** *adjective*.

**rime** ● *noun* frost; hoar-frost. ● *verb* (**-ming**) cover with rime.

**rind** /raɪnd/ *noun* tough outer layer or covering of fruit and vegetables, cheese, bacon, etc.

**ring¹** ● *noun* circular band, usually of metal, worn on finger; circular band of any material; line or band round cylindrical or circular object; mark or part etc. resembling ring; ring in cross-section of tree representing one year's growth; enclosure for circus, boxing, betting at races, etc.; people or things arranged in circle, such arrangement; combination of traders, politicians, spies, etc. acting together; gas ring; disc or halo round planet, moon, etc. ● *verb* (often + *round, about, in*) encircle; put ring on (bird etc.). □ **ring-binder** loose-leaf binder with ring-shaped clasps; **ring-dove** woodpigeon; **ring finger** finger next to little finger, esp. on left hand; **ringleader** instigator in crime or mischief etc.; **ringmaster** director of circus performance; **ring-pull** (of tin) having ring for pulling to break seal; **ring road** bypass encircling town; **ringside** area immediately beside boxing or circus ring etc.; **ringworm** skin infection forming circular inflamed patches.

**ring²** ● *verb* (*past* **rang**; *past participle* **rung**) (often + *out* etc.) give clear resonant sound; make (bell) ring; call by telephone; (usually + *with, to*) (of place) resound, re-echo; (of ears) be filled with sensation of ringing; (+ *in, out*) usher in or out with bell-ringing; give specified impression. ● *noun* ringing sound or tone; act of ringing bell, sound caused by this; *colloquial* telephone call; set of esp. church bells; specified feeling conveyed by words etc.. □ **ring back** make return telephone call to; **ring off** end telephone call; **ring up** make telephone call (to), record (amount) on cash register.

**ringlet** /ˈrɪŋlɪt/ *noun* curly lock of esp. long hair.

**rink** *noun* area of ice for skating, curling, etc.; enclosed area for roller-skating; building containing either of these; strip of bowling green; team in bowls or curling.

**rinse** ● *verb* (**-sing**) (often + *through, out*) wash or treat with clean water etc.; wash lightly; put through clean water after washing; (+ *out, away*) remove by rinsing. ● *noun* rinsing; temporary hair tint.

**riot** /ˈraɪət/ ● *noun* disturbance of peace by crowd; loud revelry; (+ *of*) lavish display of; *colloquial* very amusing thing or person. ● *verb* make or engage in riot. □ **run riot** throw off all restraint, spread uncontrolled. □ **rioter** *noun*, **riotous** *adjective*.

**RIP** *abbreviation* may he, she, or they rest in peace (*requiesca(n)t in pace*).

**rip** ● *verb* (**-pp-**) tear or cut quickly or forcibly away or apart; make (hole etc.) thus; make long tear or cut in; come violently apart, split. ● *noun* long tear or cut; act of ripping. □ **let rip** *colloquial* (allow to) proceed or act without restraint or interference; **rip-cord** cord for releasing parachute from its pack; **rip off** *colloquial* swindle, exploit, steal; **rip-off** *colloquial* □ **ripper** *noun*.

**riparian** /raɪ'peərɪən/ *adjective* of or on riverbank.

**ripe** *adjective* ready to be reaped, picked, or eaten; mature; (often + *for*) fit, ready. □ **ripen** *verb*; **ripeness** *noun*.

**riposte** /rɪ'pɒst/ ● *noun* quick retort; quick return thrust in fencing. ● *verb* (**-ting**) deliver riposte.

**ripple** /'rɪp(ə)l/ ● *noun* ruffling of water's surface; small wave(s); gentle lively sound, e.g. of laughter or applause; slight variation in strength of current etc.; ice cream with veins of syrup. ● *verb* (**-ling**) (cause to) form or flow in ripples; show or sound like ripples.

**rise** /raɪz/ ● *verb* (**-sing**; *past* **rose** /rəʊz/; *past participle* **risen** /'rɪz(ə)n/) come or go up; project or swell upwards; appear above horizon; get up from lying, sitting, or kneeling; get out of bed; (of meeting etc.) adjourn; reach higher level; make social progress; (often + *up*) rebel; come to surface; react to provocation; ascend, soar; have origin, begin to flow. ● *noun* rising; upward slope; increase in amount, extent, pitch, etc.; increase in salary; increase in status or power; height of step, incline, etc.; origin. □ **give rise to** cause, induce; **get, take a rise out of** *colloquial* provoke reaction from; **on the rise** on the increase.

**riser** *noun* person who rises from bed; vertical piece between treads of staircase.

**risible** /'rɪzɪb(ə)l/ *adjective* laughable, ludicrous.

**rising** ● *adjective* advancing; approaching specified age; going up. ● *noun* insurrection. □ **rising damp** moisture absorbed from ground into wall.

**risk** ● *noun* chance of danger, injury, loss, etc.; person or thing causing risk. ● *verb* expose to risk; venture on, take chances of. □ **at risk** exposed to danger; **at one's (own) risk** accepting responsibility for oneself; **at the risk of** with the possibility of (adverse consequences).

**risky** *adjective* (**-ier, -iest**) involving risk; risqué. □ **riskily** *adverb*; **riskiness** *noun*.

**risotto** /rɪ'zɒtəʊ/ *noun* (*plural* **-s**) Italian savoury rice dish cooked in stock.

**risqué** /'rɪskeɪ/ *adjective* (of story etc.) slightly indecent.

**rissole** /'rɪsəʊl/ *noun* fried cake of minced meat coated in breadcrumbs.

**ritardando** /rɪtɑː'dændəʊ/ *adverb, adjective, & noun* (*plural* **-s** or **-di** /-dɪ/) *Music* = RALLENTANDO.

**rite** *noun* religious or solemn ceremony or observance. □ **rite of passage** (often in *plural*) event marking change or stage in life.

**ritual** /'rɪtʃʊəl/ ● *noun* prescribed order esp. of religious ceremony; solemn or colourful pageantry etc.; procedure regularly followed. ● *adjective* of or done as ritual or rite. □ **ritually** *adverb*.

**ritualism** *noun* regular or excessive practice of ritual. □ **ritualist** *noun*; **ritualistic** /-'lɪs-/ *adjective*; **ritualistically** /-'lɪs-/ *adverb*.

**rival** /'raɪv(ə)l/ ● *noun* person or thing that competes with another or equals another in quality. ● *verb* (**-ll-**; *US* **-l-**) be rival of or comparable to.

**rivalry** *noun* (*plural* **-ies**) being rivals; competition.

**riven** /'rɪv(ə)n/ *adjective literary* split, torn.

**river** /'rɪvə/ *noun* large natural stream of water flowing to sea, lake, etc.; copious flow. □ **riverside** ground along riverbank.

**rivet** /'rɪvɪt/ ● *noun* nail or bolt for joining metal plates etc. ● *verb* (**-t-**) join or fasten with rivets; fix, make immovable; (+ *on, upon*) direct intently; (esp. as **riveting** *adjective*) engross.

**riviera** /rɪvɪ'eərə/ *noun* coastal subtropical region, esp. that of SE France and NW Italy.

**rivulet** /'rɪvjʊlɪt/ *noun* small stream.

**RLC** *abbreviation* Royal Logistics Corps.

**RM** *abbreviation* Royal Marines.

**rm.** *abbreviation* room.

**RN** *abbreviation* Royal Navy.

**RNA** *abbreviation* ribonucleic acid.

**RNLI** *abbreviation* Royal National Lifeboat Institution.

**roach** *noun* (*plural* same or **-es**) small freshwater fish.

**road** *noun* way with prepared surface for vehicles, etc.; route; (usually in *plural*) piece of water near shore in which ships can ride at anchor. □ **any road** *dialect* anyway; **in the** or **one's road** *dialect* forming obstruction; **on the road** travelling; **roadbed** foundation of road or railway, *US* part of road for vehicles; **roadblock** barrier on road to detain traffic; **road fund licence** = TAX DISC; **road-hog** *colloquial* reckless or inconsiderate motorist etc.; **roadhouse** inn etc. on main road; **road-metal** broken stone for road-making; **roadshow** touring entertainment etc., esp. radio or television series broadcast from changing venue; **roadstead** sea road for ships; **road tax** payable on vehicles; **road test** test of vehicle's roadworthiness; **roadway** part of road used by vehicles; **roadworks** construction or repair of roads; **roadworthy** (of vehicle) fit to be used on road; **roadworthiness** *noun*.

**roadie** *noun colloquial* assistant of touring band etc., responsible for equipment.

**roadster** *noun* open car without rear seats.

**roam** *verb* ramble, wander; travel unsystematically over, through, or about.

**roan** ● *adjective* (esp. of horse) with coat thickly interspersed with hairs of another colour. ● *noun* roan animal.

**roar** /rɔː/ ● *noun* loud deep hoarse sound as of lion; loud laugh. ● *verb* (often + *out*) utter loudly, or make roar, roaring laugh, etc.; travel in vehicle at high speed. □ **roaring drunk** very drunk and noisy; **roaring forties** stormy ocean tracts between latitudes 40° and 50°S; **roaring success** great success; **roaring twenties** decade of 1920s.

**roast** ● *verb* cook or be cooked by exposure to open heat or in oven; criticize severely. ● *adjective* roasted. ● *noun* (dish of) roast meat; meat for roasting; process of roasting.

**rob** *verb* (**-bb-**) (often + *of*) take unlawfully from, esp. by force; deprive of. □ **robber** *noun*; **robbery** *noun* (*plural* **-ies**).

**robe** ● *noun* long loose garment, esp. (often in *plural*) as indication of rank,

office, etc.; *esp. US* dressing gown. ● *verb* (**-bing**) clothe in robe; dress.

**robin** /ˈrɒbɪn/ *noun* (also **robin redbreast**) small brown red-breasted bird.

**Robin Hood** *noun* person who steals from rich to give to poor.

**robot** /ˈrəʊbɒt/ *noun* automaton resembling or functioning like human; automatic mechanical device; machine-like person. □ **robotic** /-ˈbɒt-/ *adjective*; **robotize** *verb* (also **-ise**) (**-zing** or **-sing**).

**robotics** /rəʊˈbɒtɪks/ *plural noun* (usually treated as *singular*) science or study of robot design and operation.

**robust** /rəʊˈbʌst/ *adjective* (**-er**, **-est**) strong, esp. in health and physique; (of exercise etc.) vigorous; straightforward; (of statement etc.) bold. □ **robustly** *adverb*; **robustness** *noun*.

**roc** *noun* gigantic bird of Eastern legend.

**rock**¹ *noun* solid part of earth's crust; material or projecting mass of this; (**the Rock**) Gibraltar; large detached stone; *US* stone of any size; firm support or protection; hard sweet usually as peppermint-flavoured stick; *slang* precious stone, esp. diamond. □ **on the rocks** *colloquial* short of money, (of marriage) broken down, (of drink) served with ice cubes; **rock-bottom** very lowest (level); **rock-cake** bun with rough surface; **rock crystal** crystallized quartz; **rock face** vertical surface of natural rock; **rock-garden** rockery; **rock plant** plant that grows on or among rocks; **rock-salmon** catfish, dogfish, etc.; **rock salt** common salt as solid mineral.

**rock**² ● *verb* move gently to and fro; set, keep, or be in such motion; (cause to) sway; oscillate; shake, reel. ● *noun* rocking motion; rock and roll, popular music influenced by this. □ **rock and roll**, **rock 'n' roll** popular dance music with heavy beat and blues influence; **rocking-chair** chair on rockers or springs; **rocking-horse** toy horse on rockers or springs.

**rocker** *noun* device for rocking, esp. curved bar etc. on which something rocks; rocking-chair; rock music devotee, esp. leather-clad motorcyclist.

**rockery** *noun* (*plural* **-ies**) pile of rough stones with soil between them for growing rock plants on.

**rocket** /'rɒkɪt/ ● *noun* firework or signal propelled to great height after ignition; engine operating on same principle; rocket-propelled missile, spacecraft, etc. ● *verb* (**-t-**) move rapidly upwards or away; bombard with rockets.

**rocketry** *noun* science or practice of rocket propulsion.

**rocky**[1] *adjective* (**-ier, -iest**) of, like, or full of rocks.

**rocky**[2] *adjective* (**-ier, -iest**) *colloquial* unsteady, tottering.

**rococo** /rə'kəʊkəʊ/ ● *adjective* of ornate style of art, music, and literature in 18th-c. Europe. ● *noun* this style.

**rod** *noun* slender straight round stick or bar; cane for flogging; fishing-rod; *historical* measure of length (5½ yds.).

**rode** *past of* RIDE.

**rodent** /'rəʊd(ə)nt/ *noun* mammal with strong incisors and no canine teeth (e.g. rat, squirrel, beaver).

**rodeo** /'rəʊdɪəʊ/ *noun* (*plural* **-s**) exhibition of cowboys' skills; round-up of cattle for branding etc.

**roe**[1] *noun* (also **hard roe**) mass of eggs in female fish; (also **soft roe**) male fish's milt.

**roe**[2] *noun* (*plural* same or **-s**) (also **roe-deer**) small kind of deer. □ **roebuck** male roe.

**roentgen** /'rʌntjən/ *noun* (also **röntgen**) unit of exposure to ionizing radiation.

**rogation** /rəʊ'geɪʃ(ə)n/ *noun* (usually in *plural*) litany of the saints chanted on the 3 days (**Rogation Days**) before Ascension Day.

**roger** /'rɒdʒə/ *interjection* your message has been received and understood; *slang* I agree.

**rogue** /rəʊg/ *noun* dishonest or unprincipled person; *jocular* mischievous person; wild fierce animal driven or living apart from herd; inferior or defective specimen. □ **roguery** *noun* (*plural* **-ies**) **roguish** *adjective*.

**roister** /'rɔɪstə/ *verb* (esp. as **roistering** *adjective*) revel noisily, be uproarious. □ **roisterer** *noun*.

**role** *noun* (also **rôle**) actor's part; person's or thing's function. □ **role model** person on whom others model themselves; **role-playing, -play** acting of

characters or situations as aid in psychotherapy, teaching, etc.; **role-play** *verb*.

**roll** /rəʊl/ ● *verb* (cause to) move or go in some direction by turning over and over on axis; make cylindrical or spherical by revolving between two surfaces or over on itself; gather into mass; (often + *along, by*, etc.) move or be carried on or as if on wheels; flatten with roller; rotate; sway or rock; proceed unsteadily; undulate, show undulating motion or surface; sound with vibration. ● *noun* rolling motion or gait; undulation; act of rolling; rhythmic rumbling sound; anything forming cylinder by being turned over on itself without folding; small loaf of bread for one person; official list or register. □ **roll-call** calling of list of names to establish presence; **rolled gold** thin coating of gold applied by roller to base metal; **rolled oats** husked and crushed oats; **rolling-mill** machine or factory for rolling metal into shape; **rolling-pin** roller for pastry; **rolling-stock** company's railway or (*US*) road vehicles; **rollmop** rolled pickled herring fillet; **roll-neck** having high loosely turned-over collar; **roll-on** applied by means of rotating ball; **roll-on roll-off** (of ship etc.) in which vehicles are driven directly on and off; **roll-top desk** desk with flexible cover sliding in curved grooves; **roll-up** hand-rolled cigarette; **strike off the rolls** debar from practising as solicitor.

**roller** *noun* revolving cylinder for smoothing, flattening, crushing, spreading, etc.; small cylinder on which hair is rolled for setting; long swelling wave. □ **roller bearing** bearing with cylinders instead of balls; **roller coaster** switchback at fair etc.; **roller-skate** *noun* frame with small wheels, strapped to shoes; boot with small wheels underneath; *verb* move on roller-skates; **roller towel** towel with ends joined.

**rollicking** /'rɒlɪkɪŋ/ *adjective* jovial, exuberant.

**roly-poly** /rəʊlɪ'pəʊlɪ/ ● *noun* (*plural* **-ies**) (also **roly-poly pudding**) pudding of rolled-up suet pastry covered with jam and boiled or baked. ● *adjective* podgy, plump.

**ROM** *noun Computing* read-only memory.

**Roman** /ˈrəʊmən/ ● *adjective* of ancient Rome or its territory or people; of medieval or modern Rome; Roman Catholic; (**roman**) (of type) plain and upright, used in ordinary print; (of the alphabet etc.) based on the ancient Roman system with letters A–Z. ● *noun* (*plural* -**s**) citizen of ancient Roman Republic or Empire, or of modern Rome; Roman Catholic; (**roman**) roman type. □ **Roman candle** firework discharging coloured sparks; **Roman Catholic** *adjective* of part of Christian Church acknowledging Pope as its head, *noun* member of this; **Roman Catholicism** *noun*; **Roman Empire** *historical* that established in 27 BC and divided in AD 395; **Roman law** law code of ancient Rome, forming basis of many modern codes; **Roman nose** one with high bridge; **roman numerals** numerals expressed in letters of Roman alphabet. □ **romanize** *verb* (also -**ise**) (-**zing** or -**sing**); **romanization** *noun*.

**romance** /rəʊˈmæns/ ● *noun* (also /ˈrəʊ-/) idealized, poetic, or unworldly atmosphere or tendency; love affair; (work of) literature concerning romantic love, stirring action, etc.; medieval tale of chivalry; exaggeration, picturesque falsehood. ● *adjective* (**Romance**) (of a language) descended from Latin. ● *verb* (-**cing**) exaggerate, fantasize; woo.

**Romanesque** /rəʊməˈnesk/ ● *noun* style of European architecture *c.* 900–1200, with massive vaulting and round arches. ● *adjective* of this style.

**Romanian** /rəʊˈmeɪnɪən/ (also **Rumanian** /ruː-/) ● *noun* native, national, or language of Romania. ● *adjective* of Romania or its people or language.

**romantic** /rəʊˈmæntɪk/ ● *adjective* of, characterized by, or suggestive of romance; imaginative, visionary; (of literature or music etc.) concerned more with emotion than with form; (also **Romantic**) of the 18th–19th-c. romantic movement or style in European arts. ● *noun* romantic person; romanticist. □ **romantically** *adverb*.

**romanticism** /rəʊˈmæntɪsɪz(ə)m/ *noun* (also **Romanticism**) adherence to romantic style in literature, art, etc. □ **romanticist, Romanticist** *noun*.

**romanticize** /rəʊˈmæntɪsaɪz/ *verb* (also -**ise**) (-**zing** or -**sing**) make romantic; exaggerate; indulge in romance.

**Romany** /ˈrɒmənɪ/ ● *noun* (*plural* -**ies**) Gypsy; language of Gypsies. ● *adjective* of Gypsies or Romany language.

**Romeo** /ˈrəʊmɪəʊ/ *noun* (*plural* -**s**) passionate male lover or seducer.

**romp** ● *verb* play roughly and energetically; (+ *along, past,* etc.) *colloquial* proceed without effort. ● *noun* spell of romping. □ **romp in, home** *colloquial* win easily.

**rompers** *plural noun* (also **romper suit**) young child's one-piece garment.

**rondeau** /ˈrɒndəʊ/ *noun* (*plural* -**x** same pronunciation or /-z/) short poem with two rhymes only, and opening words used as refrains.

**rondel** /ˈrɒnd(ə)l/ *noun* rondeau.

**rondo** /ˈrɒndəʊ/ *noun* (*plural* -**s**) musical form with recurring leading theme.

**röntgen** = ROENTGEN.

**rood** /ruːd/ *noun* crucifix, esp. on roodscreen; quarter-acre. □ **rood-screen** carved screen separating nave and chancel.

**roof** /ruːf/ ● *noun* (*plural* **roofs** /ruːvz/) upper covering of building; top of covered vehicle etc.; top interior surface of oven, cave, mine, etc. ● *verb* (often + *in, over*) cover with roof; be roof of. □ **roof of the mouth** palate; **roof-rack** framework for luggage on top of vehicle; **rooftop** outer surface of roof, (in *plural*) tops of houses etc.

**rook¹** /rʊk/ ● *noun* black bird of crow family nesting in colonies. ● *verb colloquial* charge (customer) extortionately; win money at cards etc., esp. by swindling.

**rook²** /rʊk/ *noun* chess piece with battlement-shaped top.

**rookery** *noun* (*plural* -**ies**) colony of rooks, penguins, or seals.

**rookie** /ˈrʊkɪ/ *noun slang* recruit.

**room** /ruːm/ ● *noun* space for, or occupied by, something; capacity; part of building enclosed by walls; (in *plural*) apartments or lodgings. ● verb US have room(s), lodge. □ **room service** provision of food etc. in hotel bedroom.

**roomy** adjective (-ier, -iest) having much room, spacious. □ **roominess** noun.

**roost** /ruːst/ ● noun bird's perch. ● verb (of bird) settle for rest or sleep.

**rooster** noun domestic cock.

**root**[1] /ruːt/ ● noun part of plant below ground conveying nourishment from soil; (in plural) fibres or branches of this; plant with edible root, such root; (in plural) emotional attachment or family ties in a place; embedded part of hair or tooth etc.; basic cause, source; Mathematics number which multiplied by itself a given number of times yields a given number, esp. square root; core of a word. ● verb (cause to) take root; esp. as **rooted** adjective) fix or establish firmly; pull up by roots. □ **root out** find and get rid of; **rootstock** rhizome, plant into which graft is inserted, source from which offshoots have arisen; **take root** begin to draw nourishment from the soil, become established. □ **rootless** adjective.

**root**[2] /ruːt/ verb (often + up) turn up (ground) with snout etc. in search of food; (+ around, in, etc.) rummage; (+ out, up) extract by rummaging; (+ for) US slang encourage by applause or support.

**rope** ● noun stout cord made by twisting together strands of hemp or wire etc.; (+ of) string of onions, pearls etc.; (**the rope**) halter for) execution by hanging. ● verb (-ping) fasten or catch with rope; (+ off, in) enclose with rope. □ **know, learn,** or **show the ropes** know, learn, show how to do a thing properly; **rope into** persuade to take part (in).

**ropy** adjective (also **ropey**) (-ier, -iest) colloquial poor in quality. □ **ropiness** noun.

**Roquefort** /ˈrɒkfɔː/ noun proprietary term soft blue ewe's-milk cheese.

**rorqual** /ˈrɔːkw(ə)l/ noun whale with dorsal fin.

**rosaceous** /rəʊˈzeɪʃəs/ adjective of plant family including the rose.

**rosary** /ˈrəʊzərɪ/ noun (plural -ies) RC Church repeated sequence of prayers; string of beads for keeping count in this.

**rose**[1] /rəʊz/ ● noun prickly shrub bearing fragrant red, pink, yellow, or white flowers; this flower; pinkish-red colour or (usually in plural) complexion; rose-shaped design; circular fitting on ceiling from which electric light hangs by cable; spray nozzle of watering-can etc.; (in plural) used to express ease, luck, etc. ● adjective rose-coloured. □ **rosebowl** bowl for cut roses, esp. given as prize; **rosebud** bud of rose, pretty girl; **rose-coloured** pinkish-red, cheerful, optimistic; **rose-hip** fruit of rose; **rose-water** perfume made from roses; **rose-window** circular window with roselike tracery; **rosewood** close-grained wood used in making furniture.

**rose**[2] past of RISE.

**rosé** /ˈrəʊzeɪ/ noun light pink wine. [French]

**rosemary** /ˈrəʊzmərɪ/ noun evergreen fragrant shrub used as herb.

**rosette** /rəʊˈzet/ noun rose-shaped ornament made of ribbons etc. or carved in stone etc.

**rosin** /ˈrɒzɪn/ ● noun resin, esp. in solid form. ● verb (-n-) rub with rosin.

**RoSPA** /ˈrɒspə/ abbreviation Royal Society for the Prevention of Accidents.

**roster** /ˈrɒstə/ ● noun list or plan of turns of duty etc. ● verb place on roster.

**rostrum** /ˈrɒstrəm/ noun (plural **rostra** or **-s**) platform for public speaking etc.

**rosy** /ˈrəʊzɪ/ adjective (-ier, -iest) pink, red; optimistic, hopeful.

**rot** ● verb (-tt-) undergo decay by putrefaction; perish, waste away; cause to rot, make rotten. ● noun decay, rottenness; slang nonsense; decline in standards etc. ● interjection expressing incredulity or ridicule. □ **rot-gut** slang cheap harmful alcohol.

**rota** /ˈrəʊtə/ noun list of duties to be done or people to do them in turn.

**rotary** /ˈrəʊtərɪ/ ● adjective acting by rotation. ● noun (plural -ies) rotary machine; (**Rotary**; in full **Rotary International**) worldwide charitable society of businessmen.

**rotate** /rəʊˈteɪt/ verb (-ting) move round axis or centre, revolve; arrange or take in rotation. □ **rotatory** /'rəʊtətəri/ adjective.

**rotation** noun rotating, being rotated; recurrent series or period; regular succession; growing of different crops in regular order. □ **rotational** adjective.

**rote** noun (usually in **by rote**) mechanical repetition (in order to memorize).

**rotisserie** /rəʊ'tɪsəri/ noun restaurant etc. where meat is roasted; revolving spit for roasting food.

**rotor** /'rəʊtə/ noun rotary part of machine; rotating aerofoil on helicopter.

**rotten** /'rɒt(ə)n/ adjective (**-er, -est**) rotting or rotted; fragile from age etc.; morally or politically corrupt; slang disagreeable, worthless. □ **rotten borough** historical (before 1832) English borough electing MP though having very few voters. □ **rottenness** noun.

**rotter** noun slang objectionable person.

**Rottweiler** /'rɒtvaɪlə/ noun black-and-tan dog noted for ferocity.

**rotund** /rəʊ'tʌnd/ adjective plump, podgy. □ **rotundity** noun.

**rotunda** /rəʊ'tʌndə/ noun circular building, esp. domed.

**rouble** /ru:b(ə)l/ noun (also **ruble**) monetary unit of Russia etc.

**roué** /'ru:eɪ/ noun (esp. elderly) debauchee.

**rouge** /ru:ʒ/ ● noun red cosmetic used to colour cheeks. ● verb (**-ging**) colour with or apply rouge; blush.

**rough** /rʌf/ ● adjective having uneven surface, not smooth or level; shaggy; coarse, violent; not mild, quiet, or gentle; (of wine) harsh; insensitive; unpleasant, severe; lacking finish etc.; approximate, rudimentary. ● adverb in a rough way. ● noun (usually **the rough**) hardship; rough ground; hooligan; unfinished or natural state. ● verb make rough; (+ out, in) sketch or plan roughly. □ **rough-and-ready** rough or crude but effective, not over-particular; **rough-and-tumble** adjective irregular, disorderly, noun scuffle; **roughcast** noun plaster of lime and gravel, verb coat with this; **rough diamond** uncut diamond, rough but honest person; **rough house** slang disturbance, rough fight; **rough it** colloquial do without basic comforts; **rough justice** treatment that is

approximately fair, unfair treatment; **roughneck** colloquial worker on oil rig, rough person; **rough up** slang attack violently. □ **roughen** verb; **roughly** adverb; **roughness** noun.

**roughage** noun fibrous material in food, stimulating intestinal action.

**roughshod** /'rʌfʃɒd/ □ **ride roughshod over** treat arrogantly.

**roulade** /ru:'lɑ:d/ noun filled rolled piece of meat, sponge, etc.; quick succession of notes.

**roulette** /ru:'let/ noun gambling game with ball dropped on revolving numbered wheel.

**round** /raʊnd/ ● adjective shaped like circle, sphere, or cylinder; done with circular motion; (of number etc.) without odd units; entire, continuous, complete; candid; (of voice etc.) sonorous. ● noun round object; revolving motion, circular or recurring course, series; route for deliveries, inspection, etc.; drink etc. for each member of group; one bullet, shell, etc.; slice of bread, sandwich made from two slices, joint of beef from haunch; one period of play etc., one stage in competition, playing of all holes in golf course once; song for unaccompanied voices overlapping at intervals; rung of ladder; (+ of) circumference or extent of. ● adverb with circular motion, with return to starting point or change to opposite position; to, at, or affecting circumference, area, group, etc.; in every direction from a centre; measuring (specified distance) in girth. ● preposition so as to encircle or enclose; at or to points on circumference of; with successive visits to; within a radius of; having as central point; so as to pass in curved course, having thus passed. ● verb give or take round shape; pass round (corner etc.); (usually + up, down) express (number) approximately. □ **in the round** with all angles or features shown or considered, with audience all round theatre stage; **Roundhead** historical member of Parliamentary party in English Civil War; **round off** make complete or less angular; **round on** attack unexpectedly; **round out** provide with more details, finish; **round robin** petition with signatures in circle to conceal order of writing, tournament in which each competitor plays every other; **Round Table** international charitable association; **round table** assembly for discussion, esp. at conference; **round trip** trip to one or more places and back; **round up** gather or bring together; **round-up** rounding-up, summary.

**roundabout** ● noun road junction with traffic passing in one direction round central island; revolving device in children's playground; merry-go-round. ● adjective circuitous.

**roundel** /'raʊnd(ə)l/ noun circular mark; small disc, medallion.

**roundelay** /'raʊndɪleɪ/ noun short simple song with refrain.

**rounders** /'raʊndəz/ noun team game in which players hit ball and run through round of bases.

**roundly** adverb bluntly, severely.

**rouse** /raʊz/ verb (-sing) (cause to) wake; (often + up) make or become active or excited; anger; evoke (feelings). □ **rousing** adjective.

**roustabout** /'raʊstəbaʊt/ noun labourer on oil rig; unskilled or casual labourer.

**rout** /raʊt/ ● noun disorderly retreat of defeated troops; overthrow, defeat. ● verb put to flight, defeat.

**route** /ruːt/ ● noun way taken (esp. regularly) from one place to another. ● verb (-teing) send etc. by particular route. □ **route march** training-march for troops.

**routine** /ruːˈtiːn/ ● noun regular course or procedure, unvarying performance of certain acts; set sequence in dance, comedy act, etc.; sequence of instructions to computer. ● adjective performed as routine; of customary or standard kind. □ **routinely** adverb.

**roux** /ruː/ noun (plural same) mixture of fat and flour used in sauces etc.

**rove** /raʊv/ verb (-ving) wander without settling, roam; (of eyes) look about.

**rover** noun wanderer.

**row**¹ /raʊ/ noun line of people or things; line of seats in theatre etc. □ **in a row** forming a row, colloquial in succession.

**row**² /raʊ/ ● verb propel (boat) with oars; convey thus. ● noun spell of rowing; trip in rowing boat. □ **rowing boat** (US

**row-boat**) small boat propelled by oars. □ **rower** noun.

**row**³ /raʊ/ colloquial ● noun loud noise, commotion; quarrel, dispute; severe reprimand. ● verb make or engage in row; reprimand.

**rowan** /'raʊən/ noun (in full **rowan tree**) mountain ash; (in full **rowan-berry**) its scarlet berry.

**rowdy** /'raʊdɪ/ ● adjective (-ier, -iest) noisy and disorderly. ● noun (plural -ies) rowdy person. □ **rowdily** adverb; **rowdiness** noun; **rowdyism** noun.

**rowel** /'raʊəl/ noun spiked revolving disc at end of spur.

**rowlock** /'rɒlək/ noun device for holding oar in place.

**royal** /'rɔɪəl/ ● adjective of, suited to, or worthy of king or queen; in service or under patronage of king or queen; of family of king or queen; splendid, on great scale. ● noun colloquial member of royal family. □ **royal blue** deep vivid blue; **Royal Commission** commission of inquiry appointed by Crown at request of government; **royal flush** straight poker flush headed by ace; **royal jelly** substance secreted by worker bees and fed to future queen bees; **Royal Navy** British navy; **royal 'we'** use of 'we' instead of 'I' by single person. □ **royally** adverb.

**royalist** noun supporter of monarchy, esp. historical of King's side in English Civil War.

**royalty** noun (plural -ies) being royal; royal people; member of royal family; percentage of profit from book, public performance, patent, etc. paid to author etc.; royal right (now esp. over minerals) granted by sovereign; payment made by producer of minerals etc. to owner of site etc.

**RP** abbreviation Received Pronunciation.

**RPI** abbreviation retail price index.

**rpm** abbreviation revolutions per minute.

**RSA** abbreviation Royal Society of Arts; Royal Scottish Academy; Royal Scottish Academician.

**RSC** abbreviation Royal Shakespeare Company.

**RSM** abbreviation Regimental Sergeant-Major.

**RSPB** *abbreviation* Royal Society for the Protection of Birds.

**RSPCA** *abbreviation* Royal Society for the Prevention of Cruelty to Animals.

**RSV** *abbreviation* Revised Standard Version (of Bible).

**RSVP** *abbreviation* please answer (*répondez s'il vous plaît*).

**Rt. Hon.** *abbreviation* Right Honourable.

**Rt Revd** *abbreviation* (also **Rt. Rev.**) Right Reverend.

**rub** ● *verb* (**-bb-**) move hand etc. firmly over surface of; (usually + *against, in, on, over*) apply (hand etc.) thus; polish, clean, abrade, chafe, or make dry, sore, or bare by rubbing; (+ *in, into, through, over*) apply by rubbing; (often + *together, against, on*) move with friction or slide (objects) against each other; get frayed or worn by friction. ● *noun* action or spell of rubbing; impediment or difficulty. □ **rub off** (usually + *on*) be transferred by contact, be transmitted; **rub out** erase with rubber; **rub up the wrong way** irritate.

**rubato** /ruːˈbɑːtəʊ/ *noun* Music (*plural* **-s** or **-ti** /-tɪ/) temporary disregarding of strict tempo.

**rubber¹** /ˈrʌbə/ *noun* elastic substance made from latex of plants or synthetically; piece of this or other substance for erasing pencil marks; (in *plural*) US galoshes. □ **rubber band** loop of rubber to hold papers etc.; **rubberneck** *colloquial* (be) inquisitive sightseer; **rubber plant** tropical plant often grown as house-plant, (also **rubber tree**) tree yielding latex; **rubber stamp** device for inking and imprinting on surface, (person giving) mechanical endorsement of actions etc.; **rubber-stamp** approve automatically. □ **rubberize** *verb* (also **-ise**) (**-zing** or **-sing**); **rubbery** *adjective*.

**rubber²** /ˈrʌbə/ *noun* series of games between same sides or people at whist, bridge, cricket, etc.

**rubbish** /ˈrʌbɪʃ/ ● *noun* waste or worthless matter; litter; trash; (often as *interjection*) nonsense. ● *verb colloquial* criticize contemptuously. □ **rubbishy** *adjective*.

**rubble** /ˈrʌb(ə)l/ *noun* rough fragments of stone, brick, etc.

**rubella** /ruːˈbelə/ *noun formal* German measles.

**Rubicon** /ˈruːbɪkɒn/ *noun* point from which there is no going back.

**rubicund** /ˈruːbɪkʌnd/ *adjective* ruddy, red-faced.

**ruble** = ROUBLE.

**rubric** /ˈruːbrɪk/ *noun* heading or passage in red or special lettering; explanatory words; established custom or rule; direction for conduct of divine service in liturgical book.

**ruby** /ˈruːbɪ/ ● *noun* (*plural* **-ies**) crimson or rose-coloured precious stone; deep red colour. ● *adjective* ruby-coloured. □ **ruby wedding** 40th wedding anniversary.

**RUC** *abbreviation* Royal Ulster Constabulary.

**ruche** /ruːʃ/ *noun* frill or gathering of lace etc. □ **ruched** *adjective*.

**ruck¹** *noun* (**the ruck**) main group of competitors not likely to overtake leaders; undistinguished crowd of people or things; Rugby loose scrum.

**ruck²** ● *verb* (often + *up*) crease, wrinkle. ● *noun* crease, wrinkle.

**rucksack** /ˈrʌksæk/ *noun* bag carried on back, esp. by hikers.

**ruckus** /ˈrʌkəs/ *noun esp. US* row, commotion.

**ruction** /ˈrʌkʃ(ə)n/ *noun colloquial* disturbance, tumult; (in *plural*) row.

**rudder** /ˈrʌdə/ *noun* flat piece hinged to vessel's stern or rear of aeroplane for steering. □ **rudderless** *adjective*.

**ruddy** /ˈrʌdɪ/ *adjective* (**-ier**, **-iest**) freshly or healthily red; reddish; *colloquial* bloody, damnable.

**rude** *adjective* impolite, offensive; roughly made; primitive, uneducated; abrupt, sudden; *colloquial* indecent, lewd; vigorous, hearty. □ **rudely** *adverb*; **rudeness** *noun*.

**rudiment** /ˈruːdɪmənt/ *noun* (in *plural*) elements or first principles of subject, imperfect beginning of something undeveloped; vestigial or undeveloped part or organ. □ **rudimentary** /-ˈmentərɪ/ *adjective*.

**rue¹** *verb* (**rues**, **rued**, **rueing** or **ruing**) repent of; wish undone or non-existent.

**rue²** *noun* evergreen shrub with bitter strong-scented leaves.

**rueful** *adjective* genuinely or humorously sorrowful. □ **ruefully** *adverb*.

**uff**[1] noun projecting starched frill worn round neck; projecting or coloured ring of feathers or hair round bird's or animal's neck; domestic pigeon.

**uff**[2] • verb trump at cards. • noun trumping.

**uffian** /'rʌfɪən/ noun violent lawless person.

**uffle** /'rʌf(ə)l/ • verb (-ling) disturb smoothness or tranquillity of; gather into ruffle; (often + up) (of bird) erect (feathers) in anger, display, etc. • noun frill of lace etc.

**ufous** /'ru:fəs/ adjective reddish-brown.

**ug** noun floor-mat; thick woollen wrap or coverlet.

**Rugby** /'rʌgbɪ/ noun (in full **Rugby football**) team game played with oval ball that may be kicked or carried. □ **Rugby League** partly professional Rugby with teams of 13; **Rugby Union** amateur Rugby with teams of 15.

**ugged** /'rʌgɪd/ adjective (esp. of ground) rough, uneven; (of features) furrowed, irregular; harsh; robust. □ **ruggedly** adverb; **ruggedness** noun.

**ugger** /'rʌgə/ noun colloquial Rugby.

**uin** /'ru:ɪn/ • noun wrecked or spoiled state; downfall; loss of property or position; (in singular or plural) remains of building etc. that has suffered ruin; cause of ruin. • verb bring to ruin; spoil, damage; (esp. as **ruined** adjective) reduce to ruins. □ **ruination** noun.

**uinous** adjective bringing ruin; disastrous; dilapidated.

**ule** • noun compulsory principle governing action; prevailing custom, standard, normal state of things; government, dominion; straight measuring device, ruler; code of discipline of religious order; Printing thin line or dash. • verb (-ling) dominate; keep under control; (often + over) have sovereign control of; (often + that) pronounce authoritatively; make parallel lines across (paper), make (straight line) with ruler etc. □ **as a rule** usually; **rule of thumb** rule based on experience or practice, not theory; **rule out** exclude.

**uler** noun person exercising government or dominion; straight strip of plastic etc. used to draw or measure.

**ruling** noun authoritative pronouncement.

**rum**[1] noun spirit distilled from sugar cane or molasses. □ **rum baba** sponge cake soaked in rum syrup.

**rum**[2] adjective (**-mm-**) colloquial queer, strange.

**Rumanian** = ROMANIAN.

**rumba** /'rʌmbə/ noun ballroom dance of Cuban origin; music for this.

**rumble** /'rʌmb(ə)l/ • verb (**-ling**) make continuous deep sound as of thunder; (+ along, by, past, etc.) (esp. of vehicle) move with such sound; slang see through, detect. • noun rumbling sound.

**rumbustious** /rʌm'bʌstʃəs/ adjective colloquial boisterous, uproarious.

**ruminant** /'ru:mɪnənt/ • noun animal that chews the cud. • adjective of ruminants; meditative.

**ruminate** /'ru:mɪneɪt/ verb (**-ting**) meditate, ponder; chew the cud. □ **rumination** noun; **ruminative** /-nətɪv/ adjective.

**rummage** /'rʌmɪdʒ/ • verb (**-ging**) search, esp. unsystematically; (+ up, out) find among other things. • noun rummaging. □ **rummage sale** esp. US jumble sale.

**rummy** /'rʌmɪ/ noun card game played usually with two packs.

**rumour** /'ru:mə/ (US **rumor**) • noun (often + of, that) general talk, assertion, or hearsay of doubtful accuracy. • verb (usually in passive) report by way of rumour.

**rump** noun hind part of mammal or bird, esp. buttocks; remnant of parliament etc. □ **rump steak** cut of beef from rump.

**rumple** /'rʌmp(ə)l/ verb (**-ling**) crease, ruffle.

**rumpus** /'rʌmpəs/ noun colloquial row, uproar.

**run** • verb (**-nn-**; past **ran**; past participle **run**) go at pace faster than walk; flee; go or travel hurriedly, briefly, etc.; advance smoothly or (as) by rolling or on wheels; (cause to) be in action or operation; (of bus, train, etc.) travel on its route; (of play etc.) be presented; extend, have course or tendency; compete in or enter (horse etc.) in race etc.; (often + for) seek election; (cause to) flow or emit liquid; spread rapidly; perform (errand); publish (article etc.); direct (business etc.); own and use (vehicle); smuggle; (of thought, the eye, etc.) pass quickly; (of tights etc.) ladder. ●*noun* running; short excursion; distance travelled; general tendency; regular route; continuous stretch, spell, or course; (often + *on*) high general demand; quantity produced at one time; general or average type or class; point scored in cricket or baseball; (+ *of*) free use of; animal's regular track; enclosure for fowls etc.; range of pasture; ladder in tights etc.; *Music* rapid scale passage. □ **give (person) the run-around** deceive, evade; **on the run** fleeing; **runabout** light car or aircraft; **run across** happen to meet; **run after** pursue; **run away** *verb* (often + *from*) flee, abscond; **runaway** *noun* person, animal, vehicle, etc. running away or out of control; **run down** *verb* knock down, reduce numbers of (of clock etc.) stop, discover after search, *colloquial* disparage; **run-down** *noun* reduction in numbers, detailed analysis, *adjective* dilapidated, decayed, exhausted; **run dry** cease to flow; **run in** *verb* run (vehicle, engine) carefully when new, *colloquial* arrest; **run-in** *noun colloquial* quarrel; **run into** collide with, encounter, reach as many as; **run low, short** become depleted, have too little; **run off** flee, produce (copies) on machine, decide (race) after tie or heats, write or recite fluently; **run-of-the-mill** ordinary, not special; **run on** continue in operation, speak volubly, continue on same line as preceding matter; **run out** come to an end, (+ *of*) exhaust one's stock of, put down wicket of (running batsman); **run out on** *colloquial* desert; **run over** (of vehicle) knock down or crush, overflow, review quickly; **run through** *verb* examine or rehearse briefly, deal successively with, spend money rapidly, pervade, pierce with blade; **run-through** *noun* rehearsal; **run to** have money or ability for, reach (amount etc.), show tendency to; **run up** *verb* accumulate (debt etc.), build or make hurriedly, raise (flag); **run-up** *noun* (often + *to*) preparatory period; **run up against** meet with

(difficulty etc.); **runway** specially prepared airfield surface for taking off and landing.

**rune** *noun* letter of earliest Germanic alphabet; similar character of mysterious or magic significance. □ **runic** *adjective*.

**rung**[1] *noun* step of ladder; strengthening crosspiece of chair etc.

**rung**[2] *past participle* of RING[2].

**runnel** /ˈrʌn(ə)l/ *noun* brook; gutter.

**runner** *noun* racer; creeping rooting plant-stem; groove, rod, etc. for thing to slide along or on; sliding ring on rod etc.; messenger; long narrow ornamental cloth or rug; (in full **runner bean**) kind of climbing bean. □ **runner-up** (*plural* **runners-up** or **runner-ups**) competitor taking second place.

**running** ●*noun* act or manner of running; race etc. ●*adjective* continuous; consecutive; done with a run. □ **in** or **out of the running** with good or poor chance of success; **running commentary** verbal description of events in progress; **running knot** one that slips along rope etc. to allow tightening; **running mate** *US* vice-presidential candidate, horse setting pace for another; **running repairs** minor or temporary repairs; **running water** flowing water esp. on tap.

**runny** *adjective* (**-ier, -iest**) tending to run or flow; excessively fluid.

**runt** *noun* smallest pig etc. of litter; undersized person.

**rupee** /ruːˈpiː/ *noun* monetary unit of India, Pakistan, etc.

**rupiah** /ruːˈpiːə/ *noun* monetary unit of Indonesia.

**rupture** /ˈrʌptʃə/ ●*noun* breaking; breach; breach in relationship; abdominal hernia. ●*verb* (**-ring**) burst (cell, membrane, etc.); sever (connection); affect or suffer hernia.

**rural** /ˈrʊər(ə)l/ *adjective* in, of, or suggesting country.

**ruse** /ruːz/ *noun* stratagem, trick.

**rush**[1] ●*verb* go, move, flow, or act precipitately or with great speed; move or transport with great haste; perform or deal with hurriedly; force (person) to act hastily; attack or capture by sudden assault. ●*noun* rushing; violent advance or attack; sudden flow; period of great activity; sudden migration of large numbers; (+ *on, for*) strong demand for a commodity; (in *plural*) *colloquial* first uncut prints of film. ● *adjective* done hastily. □ **rush hour** time each day when traffic is heaviest.

**rush**[2] *noun* marsh plant with slender pith-filled stem; its stem esp. used for making basketware etc.

**rusk** *noun* slice of bread rebaked as light biscuit, esp. for infants.

**russet** /'rʌsɪt/ ● *adjective* reddish-brown. ● *noun* russet colour; rough-skinned russet-coloured apple.

**Russian** /'rʌʃ(ə)n/ ● *noun* native or national of Russia or (loosely) former USSR; person of Russian descent; language of Russia. ● *adjective* of Russia or (loosely) former USSR or its people; of or in Russian. □ **Russian roulette** firing of revolver held to one's head after spinning cylinder with one chamber loaded; **Russian salad** mixed diced cooked vegetables with mayonnaise.

**rust** ● *noun* reddish corrosive coating formed on iron etc. by oxidation; plant disease with rust-coloured spots; reddish-brown. ● *verb* affect or be affected with rust; become impaired through disuse. □ **rustproof** not susceptible to corrosion by rust.

**rustic** /'rʌstɪk/ ● *adjective* of or like country people or country life; unsoph-isticated; of rough workmanship; made of untrimmed branches or rough timber; *Architecture* with roughened surface. ● *noun* country person, peasant. □ **rusticity** /-'tɪs-/ *noun*.

**rusticate** /'rʌstɪkeɪt/ *verb* (-**ting**) expel temporarily from university; retire to or live in the country; make rustic. □ **rustication** *noun*.

**rustle** /'rʌs(ə)l/ ● *verb* (-**ling**) (cause to) make sound as of dry blown leaves; steal (cattle or horses). ● *noun* rustling sound. □ **rustle up** *colloquial* produce at short notice. □ **rustler** *noun*.

**rusty** *adjective* (-**ier**, -**iest**) rusted, affected by rust; stiff with age or disuse; (of knowledge etc.) impaired by neglect; rust-coloured; discoloured by age.

**rut**[1] ● *noun* deep track made by passage of wheels; fixed (esp. tedious) practice or routine. ● *verb* (-**tt**-) (esp. as **rutted** *adjective*) mark with ruts.

**rut**[2] ● *noun* periodic sexual excitement of male deer etc. ● *verb* (-**tt**-) be affected with rut.

**ruthless** /'ruːθlɪs/ *adjective* having no pity or compassion. □ **ruthlessly** *adverb*; **ruthlessness** *noun*.

**RV** *abbreviation* Revised Version (of Bible).

**rye** /raɪ/ *noun* cereal plant; grain of this, used for bread, fodder, etc.; (in full **rye whisky**) whisky distilled from rye.

# Ss

**S** *abbreviation* (also **S.**) Saint; south(ern).

**s.** *abbreviation* second(s); *historical* shilling(s); son.

**SA** *abbreviation* Salvation Army; South Africa; South Australia.

**sabbath** /'sæbəθ/ *noun* religious rest-day kept by Christians on Sunday and Jews on Saturday.

**sabbatical** /sə'bætɪk(ə)l/ ● *adjective* (of leave) granted at intervals to university teacher for study or travel. ● *noun* period of sabbatical leave.

**saber** *US* = SABRE.

**sable** /'seɪb(ə)l/ ● *noun* ( *plural* same or **-s**) small dark-furred mammal; its skin or fur. ● *adjective* Heraldry black; *esp. poetical* gloomy.

**sabot** /'sæbəʊ/ *noun* wooden or wooden-soled shoe.

**sabotage** /'sæbətɑːʒ/ ● *noun* deliberate destruction or damage, esp. for political purpose. ● *verb* (**-ging**) commit sabotage on; destroy, spoil.

**saboteur** /sæbə'tɜː/ *noun* person who commits sabotage.

**sabre** /'seɪbə/ *noun* (*US* **saber**) curved cavalry sword; light fencing-sword. □ **sabre-rattling** display or threat of military force.

**sac** *noun* membranous bag in animal or plant.

**saccharin** /'sækərɪn/ *noun* a sugar substitute.

**saccharine** /'sækəriːn/ *adjective* excessively sentimental or sweet.

**sacerdotal** /sækə'dəʊt(ə)l/ *adjective* of priests or priestly office.

**sachet** /'sæʃeɪ/ *noun* small bag or packet containing shampoo, perfumed substances, etc.

**sack¹** ● *noun* large strong bag for coal, food, mail, etc.; amount held by sack; (**the sack**) *colloquial* dismissal, *US slang* bed. ● *verb* put in sack(s); *colloquial* dismiss from employment. □ **sackcloth** coarse fabric of flax or hemp.

**sack²** ● *verb* plunder and destroy (town etc.). ● *noun* such sacking.

**sack³** *noun* *historical* white wine from Spain etc.

**sackbut** /'sækbʌt/ *noun* early form of trombone.

**sacking** *noun* sackcloth.

**sacral** /'seɪkr(ə)l/ *adjective* of sacrum.

**sacrament** /'sækrəmənt/ *noun* symbolic Christian ceremony, esp. Eucharist; sacred thing. □ **sacramental** /-'men-/ *adjective*.

**sacred** /'seɪkrɪd/ *adjective* (often + *to*) dedicated to a god, connected with religion; safeguarded or required, esp. by tradition; inviolable. □ **sacred cow** *colloquial* idea or institution unreasonably held to be above criticism.

**sacrifice** /'sækrɪfaɪs/ ● *noun* voluntary relinquishing of something valued; thing thus relinquished; loss entailed; slaughter of animal or person, or surrender of possession, as offering to deity; animal, person, or thing thus offered. ● *verb* (**-cing**) give up; (+ *to*) devote to; offer or kill (as) sacrifice. □ **sacrificial** /-'fɪʃ-/ *adjective*.

**sacrilege** /'sækrɪlɪdʒ/ *noun* violation of what is sacred. □ **sacrilegious** /-'lɪdʒəs/ *adjective*.

**sacristan** /'sækrɪst(ə)n/ *noun* person in charge of sacristy and church contents.

**sacristy** /'sækrɪstɪ/ *noun* ( *plural* **-ies**) room in church for vestments, vessels, etc.

**sacrosanct** /'sækrəʊsæŋkt/ *adjective* most sacred; inviolable. □ **sacrosanctity** /-'sæŋkt-/ *noun*.

**sacrum** /'seɪkrəm/ *noun* ( *plural* **sacra** or **-s**) triangular bone between hip-bones.

**sad** *adjective* (**-dd-**) sorrowful; causing sorrow; regrettable; deplorable. □ **sadden** *verb*; **sadly** *adverb*; **sadness** *noun*.

**saddle** /'sæd(ə)l/ ● *noun* seat of leather etc. fastened on horse etc.; bicycle etc. seat; joint of meat consisting of the two

loins; ridge rising to a summit at each
end. ● *verb* (**-ling**) put saddle on (horse
etc.); (+ *with*) burden with task etc.
□ **saddle-bag** each of pair of bags laid
across back of horse etc., bag attached
behind bicycle etc. saddle.

**saddler** *noun* maker of or dealer in
saddles etc. □ **saddlery** *noun* (*plural*
**-ies**).

**sadism** /ˈseɪdɪz(ə)m/ *noun colloquial* enjoyment of cruelty to others; sexual perversion characterized by this. □ **sadist**
*noun*, **sadistic** /səˈdɪs-/ *adjective*, **sadistic-
ally** /səˈdɪs-/ *adverb*.

**sadomasochism** /seɪdəʊˈmæsəkɪz
(ə)m/ *noun* sadism and masochism in
one person. □ **sadomasochist** *noun*,
**sadomasochistic** /-ˈkɪs-/ *adjective*.

**s.a.e.** *abbreviation* stamped addressed
envelope.

**safari** /səˈfɑːrɪ/ *noun* (*plural* **-s**) expedition,
esp. in Africa, to observe or hunt
animals. □ **safari park** area where
wild animals are kept in open for viewing.

**safe** ● *adjective* free of danger or injury;
secure, not risky; reliable, sure; prevented from escaping or doing harm;
cautious. ● *noun* strong lockable cupboard for valuables; ventilated cupboard for provisions. □ **safe conduct**
immunity from arrest or harm; **safe
deposit** building containing strong-
rooms and safes for hire. □ **safely**
*adverb*.

**safeguard** ● *noun* protecting proviso,
circumstance, etc. ● *verb* guard or protect (rights etc.).

**safety** /ˈseɪftɪ/ *noun* being safe; freedom
from danger. □ **safety-belt** belt or
strap preventing injury, esp. seat-belt;
**safety-catch** device preventing accidental operation of gun trigger or
machinery; **safety curtain** fireproof
curtain to divide theatre auditorium
from stage; **safety match** match that
ignites only on specially prepared surface; **safety net** net placed to catch
acrobat etc. in case of fall; **safety pin**
pin with guarded point; **safety razor**
razor with guard to prevent user cutting skin; **safety-valve** valve relieving
excessive pressure of steam, means of
harmlessly venting excitement etc.

**saffron** /ˈsæfrən/ ● *noun* deep yellow colouring and flavouring from dried crocus stigmas; colour of this. ● *adjective*
deep yellow.

**sag** ● *verb* (**-gg-**) sink or subside; have
downward bulge or curve in middle.
● *noun* state or amount of sagging.
□ **saggy** *adjective*.

**saga** /ˈsɑːgə/ *noun* long heroic story, esp.
medieval Icelandic or Norwegian; long
family chronicle; long involved story.

**sagacious** /səˈgeɪʃ(ə)s/ *adjective* showing
insight or good judgement. □ **sagacity**
/-ˈgæs-/ *noun*.

**sage** [1] *noun* aromatic herb with dull
greyish-green leaves.

**sage** [2] ● *noun* wise man. ● *adjective* wise,
judicious, experienced. □ **sagely** *adverb*.

**Sagittarius** /sædʒɪˈteərɪəs/ *noun* ninth
sign of zodiac.

**sago** /ˈseɪgəʊ/ *noun* (*plural* **-s**) starch used
in puddings etc.; (in full **sago palm**)
any of several tropical trees yielding
this.

**sahib** /sɑːb/ *noun historical* form of address
to European men in India.

**said** *past & past participle* of SAY.

**sail** ● *noun* piece of material extended on
rigging to catch wind and propel vessel; ship's sails collectively; voyage or
excursion in sailing vessel; wind-catch-
ing apparatus of windmill. ● *verb* travel
on water by use of sails or engine-
power; begin voyage; navigate (ship
etc.); travel on (sea); glide or move
smoothly or with dignity; (often +
*through*) *colloquial* succeed easily.
□ **sailboard** board with mast and sail,
used in windsurfing; **sailcloth** material for sails, kind of coarse linen;
**sailing boat**, **ship**, etc., vessel moved
by sails; **sailplane** kind of glider.

**sailor** *noun* seaman or mariner, esp.
below officer's rank. □ **bad**, **good
sailor** person very liable or not liable
to seasickness.

**sainfoin** /ˈsænfɔɪn/ *noun* pink-flowered
plant used as fodder.

**saint** /seɪnt, before a name usually sənt/
● *noun* holy or canonized person, regarded as deserving special veneration; very virtuous person. ● *verb*
(as **sainted** *adjective*) holy, virtuous.

□ **sainthood** *noun*; **saintlike** *adjective*; **saintliness** *noun*; **saintly** (**-ier**, **-iest**) *adjective*.

**sake**[1] *noun* □ **for the sake of** out of consideration for, in the interest of, in order to please, get, etc.

**sake**[2] /'saːkɪ/ *noun* Japanese rice wine.

**salaam** /sə'lɑːm/ ● *noun* (*chiefly as Muslim greeting*) Peace!; low bow. ● *verb* make salaam.

**salacious** /sə'leɪʃəs/ *adjective* erotic; lecherous. □ **salaciousness** *noun*; **salacity** /-'læs-/ *noun*.

**salad** /'sæləd/ *noun* cold mixture of usually raw vegetables etc. often with dressing. □ **salad cream** creamy salad dressing; **salad days** period of youthful inexperience; **salad dressing** sauce of oil, vinegar, etc. for salads.

**salamander** /'sæləmændə/ *noun* newt-like amphibian formerly supposed to live in fire; similar mythical creature.

**salami** /sə'lɑːmɪ/ *noun* (*plural* **-s**) highly-seasoned sausage, originally Italian.

**sal ammoniac** /sæl ə'məʊnɪæk/ *noun* ammonium chloride.

**salary** /'sælərɪ/ ● *noun* (*plural* **-ies**) fixed regular payment by employer to employee. ● *verb* (**-ies**, **-ied**) (usually as **salaried** *adjective*) pay salary to.

**sale** /seɪl/ *noun* exchange of commodity for money etc.; act or instance of selling; amount sold; temporary offering of goods at reduced prices; event at which goods are sold. □ **on, for sale** offered for purchase; **saleroom** room where auctions are held; **salesman, salesperson, saleswoman** person employed to sell goods etc.

**saleable** *adjective* fit or likely to be sold. □ **saleability** *noun*.

**salesmanship** *noun* skill in selling.

**salient** /'seɪlɪənt/ ● *adjective* prominent, conspicuous; (of angle) pointing outwards. ● *noun* salient angle; outward bulge in military line.

**saline** /'seɪlaɪn/ ● *adjective* containing or tasting of salt(s); of salt(s). ● *noun* salt lake, spring, etc.; saline solution. □ **salinity** /sə'lɪn-/ *noun*.

**saliva** /sə'laɪvə/ *noun* colourless liquid produced by glands in mouth. □ **salivary** *adjective*.

**salivate** /'sælɪveɪt/ *verb* (**-ting**) secrete saliva, esp. in excess.

**sallow**[1] /'sæləʊ/ *adjective* (**-er**, **-est**) (esp. of complexion) yellowish.

**sallow**[2] /'sæləʊ/ *noun* low-growing willow; shoot or wood of this.

**sally** /'sælɪ/ ● *noun* (*plural* **-ies**) witticism; military rush; excursion. ● *verb* (**-ies**, **-ied**) (usually + *out, forth*) set out for walk etc., make sally.

**salmon** /'sæmən/ ● *noun* (*plural* same) large silver-scaled fish with orange-pink flesh. ● *adjective* orange-pink. □ **salmon-pink** orange-pink; **salmon trout** large silver-coloured trout.

**salmonella** /sælmə'nelə/ *noun* (*plural* **-llae** /-liː/) bacterium causing food poisoning; such food poisoning.

**salon** /'sælɒn/ *noun* room or establishment of hairdresser, fashion designer, etc.; *historical* meeting of eminent people at fashionable home; reception room of large house.

**saloon** /sə'luːn/ *noun* large room or hall on ship, in hotel, etc., or for specified purpose; saloon car; *US* drinking bar; saloon bar. □ **saloon bar** more comfortable bar in public house; **saloon car** car with body closed off from luggage area.

**salsa** /'sælsə/ *noun* dance music of Cuban origin; kind of spicy tomato sauce.

**salsify** /'sælsɪfɪ/ *noun* (*plural* **-ies**) plant with long fleshy edible root.

**salt** /sɔːlt/ ● *noun* (also **common salt**) sodium chloride, esp. mined or evaporated from sea water, and used esp. for seasoning or preserving food; *Chemistry* substance formed in reaction of an acid with a base; piquancy, wit; (in *singular* or *plural*) substance resembling salt in taste, form, etc.; (esp. in *plural*) substance used as laxative; (also **old salt**) experienced sailor. ● *adjective* containing, tasting of, or preserved with salt. ● *verb* cure, preserve, or season with salt; sprinkle salt on (road etc.). □ **salt away, down** *slang* put (money etc.) by; **salt-cellar** container for salt at table; **salt-mine** mine yielding rock salt; **salt of the earth** finest or most honest people; **salt-pan** vessel, or hollow near sea, used for getting salt by evaporation; **salt-water** of or living in sea;

**take with a pinch** or **grain of salt** be sceptical about; **worth one's salt** efficient, capable.

**salting** *noun* (esp. in *plural*) marsh overflowed by sea.

**saltire** /'sɔːltaɪə/ *noun* X-shaped cross.

**saltpetre** /sɔːlt'piːtə/ *noun* (*US* **saltpeter**) white crystalline salty substance used in preserving meat and in gunpowder.

**salty** *adjective* (**-ier**, **-iest**) tasting of or containing salt; witty, piquant. □ **saltiness** *noun*.

**salubrious** /sə'luːbrɪəs/ *adjective* healthgiving. □ **salubrity** *noun*.

**saluki** /sə'luːkɪ/ *noun* (*plural* **-s**) dog of tall slender silky-coated breed.

**salutary** /'sæljʊtərɪ/ *adjective* producing good effect.

**salutation** /sælju'teɪʃ(ə)n/ *noun formal* sign or expression of greeting.

**salute** /sə'luːt/ ● *noun* gesture of respect, homage, greeting, etc.; *Military etc.* prescribed gesture or use of weapons or flags as sign of respect etc. ● *verb* (**-ting**) make salute (to); greet; commend.

**salvage** /'sælvɪdʒ/ ● *noun* rescue of property from sea, fire, etc.; saving and utilization of waste materials; property or materials salvaged. ● *verb* (**-ging**) save from wreck etc. □ **salvageable** *adjective*.

**salvation** /sæl'veɪʃ(ə)n/ *noun* saving, being saved; deliverance from sin and damnation; religious conversion; person or thing that saves. □ **Salvation Army** worldwide quasi-military Christian charitable organization.

**Salvationist** *noun* member of Salvation Army.

**salve**[1] ● *noun* healing ointment; (often + *for*) thing that soothes. ● *verb* (**-ving**) soothe.

**salve**[2] *verb* (**-ving**) save from wreck, fire, etc. □ **salvable** *adjective*.

**salver** /'sælvə/ *noun* tray for drinks, letters, etc.

**salvo** /'sælvəʊ/ *noun* (*plural* **-es** or **-s**) simultaneous firing of guns etc.; round of applause.

**sal volatile** /sæl və'lætɪlɪ/ *noun* solution of ammonium carbonate, used as smelling salts.

**SAM** *abbreviation* surface-to-air missile.

**Samaritan** /sə'mærɪt(ə)n/ *noun* (in full **good Samaritan**) charitable or helpful person; member of counselling organization.

**samba** /'sæmbə/ ● *noun* ballroom dance of Brazilian origin; music for this. ● *verb* (**-bas**, **-baed** or **-ba'd** /-bəd/, **-baing** /-baɪŋ/) dance samba.

**same** ● *adjective* identical; unvarying; just mentioned. ● *pronoun* (**the same**) the same person or thing. ● *adverb* (**the same**) in the same manner. □ **all** or **just the same** nevertheless; **at the same time** simultaneously, notwithstanding. □ **sameness** *noun*.

**samosa** /sə'məʊsə/ *noun* Indian fried triangular pastry containing spiced vegetables or meat.

**samovar** /'sæməvɑː/ *noun* Russian tea-urn.

**Samoyed** /'sæməjed/ *noun* member of a northern Siberian people; (also **samoyed**) dog of white Arctic breed.

**sampan** /'sæmpæn/ *noun* small boat used in Far East.

**samphire** /'sæmfaɪə/ *noun* cliff plant used in pickles.

**sample** /'sɑːmp(ə)l/ ● *noun* small representative part or quantity; specimen; typical example. ● *verb* (**-ling**) take samples of; try qualities of; experience briefly.

**sampler** /'sɑːmplə/ *noun* piece of embroidery worked to show proficiency.

**samurai** /'sæmʊraɪ/ *noun* (*plural* same) Japanese army officer; *historical* member of Japanese military caste.

**sanatorium** /sænə'tɔːrɪəm/ *noun* (*plural* **-riums** or **-ria**) residential clinic, esp. for convalescents and the chronically sick; accommodation for sick people in school etc.

**sanctify** /'sæŋktɪfaɪ/ *verb* (**-ies**, **-ied**) consecrate, treat as holy; purify from sin; sanction. □ **sanctification** *noun*.

**sanctimonious** /sæŋktɪ'məʊnɪəs/ *adjective* ostentatiously pious. □ **sanctimoniously** *adverb*; **sanctimony** /'sæŋktɪmənɪ/ *noun*.

**sanction** /'sæŋkʃ(ə)n/ ● *noun* approval by custom or tradition; express permission; confirmation of law etc.; penalty or reward attached to law; moral impetus for obedience to rule; (esp. in *plural*) (esp. economic) action to coerce state to conform to agreement etc. • *verb* authorize, countenance; make (law etc.) binding.

**sanctity** /'sæŋktɪtɪ/ *noun* holiness, sacredness; inviolability.

**sanctuary** /'sæŋktʃʊərɪ/ *noun* (*plural* **-ies**) holy place; place where birds, wild animals, etc. are protected; place of refuge.

**sanctum** /'sæŋktəm/ *noun* (*plural* **-s**) holy place, esp. in temple or church; *colloquial* person's den.

**sand** • *noun* fine grains resulting from erosion of esp. siliceous rocks; (in *plural*) grains of sand, expanse of sand, sandbank. • *verb* smooth or treat with sandpaper or sand. □ **sandbag** *noun* bag filled with sand, esp. for making temporary defences, *verb* defend or hit with sandbag(s); **sandbank** sand forming shallow place in sea or river; **sandblast** *verb* treat with jet of sand driven by compressed air or steam, *noun* this jet; **sandcastle** model castle of sand on beach; **sand-dune**, **-hill** dune; **sand-martin** bird nesting in sandy banks; **sandpaper** *noun* paper with abrasive coating for smoothing or polishing wood etc., *verb* treat with this; **sandpiper** bird inhabiting wet sandy places; **sandpit** hollow or box containing sand for children to play in; **sandstone** sedimentary rock of compressed sand; **sandstorm** storm with clouds of sand raised by wind.

**sandal** /'sænd(ə)l/ *noun* shoe with openwork upper or no upper, fastened with straps.

**sandal-tree** /'sændəltri:/ *noun* tree yielding sandalwood.

**sandalwood** /'sændəlwʊd/ *noun* scented wood of sandal-tree.

**sandwich** /'sænwɪdʒ/ • *noun* two or more slices of bread with filling; layered cake with jam, cream, etc. • *verb* put (thing, statement, etc.) between two of different kind; squeeze in between others. □ **sandwich-board** each of two advertising boards worn front and back; **sandwich course** course with alternate periods of study and work experience.

**sandy** *adjective* (**-ier**, **-iest**) containing or covered with sand; (of hair) reddish; sand-coloured.

**sane** *adjective* of sound mind, not mad; (of opinion etc.) moderate, sensible.

**sang** *past* of SING.

**sang-froid** /sɑ̃'frwɑ:/ *noun* calmness in danger or difficulty.

**sangria** /sæŋ'gri:ə/ *noun* Spanish drink of red wine with fruit etc.

**sanguinary** /'sæŋgwɪnərɪ/ *adjective* bloody; bloodthirsty.

**sanguine** /'sæŋgwɪn/ *adjective* optimistic; (of complexion) florid, ruddy.

**Sanhedrin** /'sænɪdrɪn/ *noun* court of justice and supreme council in ancient Jerusalem.

**sanitarium** /sænɪ'teərɪəm/ *noun* (*plural* **-s** or **-ria**) *US* sanatorium.

**sanitary** /'sænɪtərɪ/ *adjective* (of conditions etc.) affecting health; hygienic. □ **sanitary towel** (*US* **sanitary napkin**) absorbent pad used during menstruation. □ **sanitariness** *noun*.

**sanitation** /sænɪ'teɪʃ(ə)n/ *noun* sanitary conditions; maintenance etc. of these; disposal of sewage, refuse, etc.

**sanitize** /'sænɪtaɪz/ *verb* (also **-ise**) (**-zing** or **-sing**) make sanitary, disinfect; *colloquial* censor.

**sanity** /'sænɪtɪ/ *noun* being sane; moderation.

**sank** *past* of SINK.

**Sanskrit** /'sænskrɪt/ • *noun* ancient and sacred language of Hindus in India. • *adjective* of or in Sanskrit.

**Santa Claus** /'sæntə klɔ:z/ *noun* person said to bring children presents at Christmas.

**sap**[1] • *noun* vital juice of plants; vitality; *slang* foolish person. • *verb* (**-pp-**) drain of sap; weaken. □ **sappy** *adjective* (**-ier**, **-iest**).

**sap**[2] • *noun* tunnel or trench for concealed approach to enemy. • *verb* (**-pp-**) dig saps; undermine.

**sapient** /'seɪpɪənt/ *adjective literary* wise; aping wisdom. □ **sapience** *noun*.

**sapling** /'sæplɪŋ/ *noun* young tree.

**sapper** *noun* digger of saps; private of Royal Engineers.

**sapphire** /'sæfaɪə/ • *noun* transparent blue precious stone; its colour. • *adjective* (also **sapphire blue**) bright blue.

**saprophyte** /'sæprəfaɪt/ *noun* plant or micro-organism living on dead organic matter.

**saraband** /'særəbænd/ *noun* slow Spanish dance; music for this.

**Saracen** /'særəs(ə)n/ *noun* Arab or Muslim of time of Crusades.

**sarcasm** /'sɑːkæz(ə)m/ *noun* ironically scornful remark(s). □ **sarcastic** /sɑː-'kæstɪk/ *adjective*; **sarcastically** /sɑː'kæs-tɪkəlɪ/ *adverb*.

**sarcophagus** /sɑː'kɒfəgəs/ *noun* (*plural* **-gi** /-gaɪ/) stone coffin.

**sardine** /sɑː'diːn/ *noun* (*plural* same or **-s**) young pilchard etc. tinned tightly packed.

**sardonic** /sɑː'dɒnɪk/ *adjective* bitterly mocking; cynical. □ **sardonically** *adverb*.

**sardonyx** /'sɑːdəniks/ *noun* onyx in which white layers alternate with yellow or orange ones.

**sargasso** /sɑː'gæsəʊ/ *noun* (*plural* **-s** or **-es**) seaweed with berry-like air-vessels.

**sarge** *noun slang* sergeant.

**sari** /'sɑːrɪ/ *noun* (*plural* **-s**) length of material draped round body, worn traditionally by Hindu etc. women.

**sarky** /'sɑːkɪ/ *adjective* (**-ier**, **-iest**) *slang* sarcastic.

**sarong** /sə'rɒŋ/ *noun* garment of long strip of cloth tucked round waist or under armpits.

**sarsaparilla** /sɑːsəpə'rɪlə/ *noun* dried roots of esp. smilax used to flavour drinks and medicines and formerly as tonic; plant yielding these.

**sarsen** /'sɑːs(ə)n/ *noun* sandstone boulder carried by ice in glacial period.

**sarsenet** /'sɑːsnɪt/ *noun* soft silk fabric used esp. for linings.

**sartorial** /sɑː'tɔːrɪəl/ *adjective* of men's clothes or tailoring. □ **sartorially** *adverb*.

**SAS** *abbreviation* Special Air Service.

**sash**¹ *noun* strip or loop of cloth worn over one shoulder or round waist.

**sash**² *noun* frame holding glass in window sliding up and down in grooves.

**sass** *US colloquial* ● *noun* impudence. ● *verb* be impudent to. □ **sassy** *adjective* (**-ier**, **-iest**).

**sassafras** /'sæsəfræs/ *noun* small N. American tree; medicinal preparation from its leaves or bark.

**Sassenach** /'sæsənæk/ *noun Scottish usually derogatory* English person.

**Sat.** *abbreviation* Saturday.

**sat** *past & past participle* of SIT.

**Satan** /'seɪt(ə)n/ *noun* the Devil.

**satanic** /sə'tænɪk/ *adjective* of or like Satan; hellish, evil.

**Satanism** *noun* worship of Satan. □ **Satanist** *noun*.

**satchel** /'sætʃ(ə)l/ *noun* small bag, esp. for carrying school-books.

**sate** *verb* (**-ting**) *formal* gratify fully, surfeit.

**sateen** /sæ'tiːn/ *noun* glossy cotton fabric like satin.

**satellite** /'sætəlaɪt/ ● *noun* heavenly or artificial body orbiting earth or other planet; (in full **satellite state**) small country controlled by another. ● *adjective* transmitted by satellite; receiving signal from satellite.

**satiate** /'seɪʃɪeɪt/ *verb* (**-ting**) sate. □ **satiation** *noun*.

**satiety** /sə'taɪɪtɪ/ *noun formal* being sated.

**satin** /'sætɪn/ ● *noun* silk etc. fabric glossy on one side. ● *adjective* smooth as satin. □ **satinwood** kind of yellow glossy timber. □ **satiny** *adjective*.

**satire** /'sætaɪə/ *noun* ridicule, irony, etc. used to expose folly, vice, etc.; literary work using satire. □ **satirical** /sə'tɪr-ɪk(ə)l/ *adjective*; **satirically** /sə'tɪrɪkəlɪ/ *adverb*.

**satirist** /'sætərɪst/ *noun* writer of satires; satirical person.

**satirize** /'sætəraɪz/ *verb* (also **-ise**) (**-zing** or **-sing**) attack or describe with satire.

**satisfaction** /sætɪs'fækʃ(ə)n/ *noun* satisfying, being satisfied; thing that satisfies; atonement; compensation.

**satisfactory** /sætɪs'fæktərɪ/ *adjective* adequate; causing satisfaction. □ **satisfactorily** *adverb*.

**satisfy** /'sætɪsfaɪ/ *verb* (**-ies**, **-ied**) meet expectations or wishes of; be adequate; meet (an appetite or want); rid (person) of an appetite or want; pay; fulfil, comply with; convince.

**satsuma** /sæt'suːmə/ *noun* kind of tangerine.

**saturate** /'sætʃəreɪt/ *verb* (**-ting**) fill with moisture; fill to capacity; cause (substance) to absorb, hold, etc. as much as possible of another substance; supply (market) beyond demand; (as **saturated** *adjective*) (of fat) containing the most possible hydrogen atoms.

**saturation** *noun* saturating, being saturated. □ **saturation point** stage beyond which no more can be absorbed or accepted.

**Saturday** /'sætədeɪ/ *noun* day of week following Friday.

**Saturnalia** /sætə'neɪlɪə/ *noun* (*plural* same or **-s**) ancient Roman festival of Saturn; (**saturnalia**) (treated as *singular* or *plural*) scene of wild revelry.

**saturnine** /'sætənaɪn/ *adjective* of gloomy temperament or appearance.

**satyr** /'sætə/ *noun* Greek & Roman Mythology part-human part-animal woodland deity; lecherous man.

**sauce** /sɔːs/ ● *noun* liquid or viscous accompaniment to food; something that adds piquancy; *colloquial* impudence. ● *verb* (**-cing**) *colloquial* be impudent to. □ **sauce-boat** jug or dish for serving sauce; **saucepan** cooking vessel usually with handle, used on hob.

**saucer** /'sɔːsə/ *noun* shallow circular dish, esp. for standing cup on.

**saucy** *adjective* (**-ier, -iest**) impudent, cheeky. □ **saucily** *adverb*; **sauciness** *noun*.

**sauerkraut** /'saʊəkraʊt/ *noun* German dish of pickled cabbage.

**sauna** /'sɔːnə/ *noun* period spent in room with steam bath; this room.

**saunter** /'sɔːntə/ ● *verb* stroll. ● *noun* leisurely walk.

**saurian** /'sɔːrɪən/ *adjective* of or like a lizard.

**sausage** /'sɒsɪdʒ/ *noun* seasoned minced meat etc. in edible cylindrical case; sausage-shaped object. □ **sausage meat** minced meat for sausages etc.; **sausage roll** sausage meat in pastry cylinder.

**sauté** /'səʊteɪ/ ● *adjective* fried quickly in a little fat. ● *noun* food cooked thus. ● *verb* (*past & past participle* **sautéed** or **sautéed**) cook thus.

**savage** /'sævɪdʒ/ ● *adjective* fierce, cruel; wild, primitive. ● *noun* *derogatory* member of primitive tribe; brutal or barbarous person. ● *verb* (**-ging**) attack and

maul; attack verbally. □ **savagely** *adverb*; **savagery** *noun* (*plural* **-ies**).

**savannah** /sə'vænə/ *noun* (also **savanna**) grassy plain in tropical or subtropical region.

**savant** /'sæv(ə)nt/ *noun* (*feminine* **savante** same pronunciation) learned person.

**save**[1] ● *verb* (**-ving**) (often + *from*) rescue or preserve from danger or harm; (often + *up*) keep for future use; relieve (person) from spending (money, time, etc.); prevent exposure to (annoyance etc.); prevent need for; rescue spiritually; Football etc. avoid losing (match), prevent (goal) from being scored. ● *noun* Football etc. act of saving goal. □ **savable, saveable** *adjective*; **saver** *noun*.

**save**[2] *preposition & conjunction* archaic or poetical except; but.

**saveloy** /'sævəlɔɪ/ *noun* highly seasoned sausage.

**saving** ● *noun* anything saved; an economy; (usually in *plural*) money saved; act of preserving or rescuing. ● *preposition* except; without offence to. □ **-saving** making economical use of specified thing; **saving grace** redeeming feature.

**saviour** /'seɪvjə/ *noun* (US **savior**) person who saves from danger etc.; (**the, our Saviour**) Christ.

**savoir faire** /sævwɑː 'feə/ *noun* ability to behave appropriately; tact. [French]

**savory**[1] /'seɪvərɪ/ *noun* aromatic herb used in cookery.

**savory**[2] US = SAVOURY.

**savour** /'seɪvə/ (US **savor**) ● *noun* characteristic taste, flavour, etc.; tinge or hint. ● *verb* appreciate, enjoy; (+ *of*) imply, suggest.

**savoury** /'seɪvərɪ/ (US **savory**) ● *adjective* with appetizing taste or smell; (of food) salty or piquant, not sweet; pleasant. ● *noun* (*plural* **-ies**) savoury dish.

**savoy** /sə'vɔɪ/ *noun* rough-leaved winter cabbage.

**savvy** /'sævɪ/ *slang* ● *verb* (**-ies, -ied**) know. ● *noun* knowingness, understanding. ● *adjective* (**-ier, -iest**) US knowing, wise.

**saw**[1] ● *noun* implement with toothed blade etc. for cutting wood etc. ● *verb* (*past participle* **sawn** or **sawed**) cut or make with saw; use saw; make to-and-fro sawing motion. □ **sawdust** fine wood fragments produced in sawing; **sawfish** (*plural* same or **-es**) large sea fish with toothed flat snout; **sawmill** factory for sawing wood into planks; **sawtooth(ed)** serrated.

**saw²** *past of* SEE¹.

**saw³** *noun* proverb, maxim.

**sawyer** /'sɔːjə/ *noun* person who saws timber.

**sax** *noun colloquial* saxophone.

**saxe** /sæks/ *noun & adjective* (in full **saxe blue**; as *adjective* often hyphenated) light greyish-blue.

**saxifrage** /'sæksɪfreɪdʒ/ *noun* small-flowered rock-plant.

**Saxon** /'sæks(ə)n/ ● *noun historical* member or language of Germanic people that occupied parts of England in 5th–6th c.; Anglo-Saxon. ● *adjective historical* of the Saxons; Anglo-Saxon.

**saxophone** /'sæksəfəʊn/ *noun* keyed brass reed instrument used esp. in jazz. □ **saxophonist** /'sɒfən-/ *noun.*

**say** ● *verb* (3rd singular present **says** /sez/; *past & past participle* **said** /sed/) utter, remark; express; state; indicate; (in *passive*; usually + *to do*) be asserted; (+ *to do*) *colloquial* direct, order; convey (information); adduce, plead; decide; take as example or as near enough; (**the said**) *Law or jocular* the previously mentioned. ● *noun* opportunity to express view; share in decision. □ **say-so** *colloquial* power of decision, mere assertion.

**saying** *noun* maxim, proverb, etc.

**sc.** *abbreviation* scilicet.

**scab** ● *noun* crust over healing cut, sore, etc.; skin disease; plant disease; *colloquial derogatory* blackleg. ● *verb* (**-bb-**) form scab; *colloquial derogatory* act as blackleg. □ **scabby** *adjective* (**-ier, -iest**).

**scabbard** /'skæbəd/ *noun historical* sheath of sword etc.

**scabies** /'skeɪbɪːz/ *noun* contagious skin disease causing itching.

**scabious** /'skeɪbɪəs/ *noun* plant with pincushion-shaped flowers.

**scabrous** /'skeɪbrəs/ *adjective* rough, scaly; indecent.

**scaffold** /'skæfəʊld/ *noun* scaffolding; *historical* platform for execution of criminal.

**scaffolding** *noun* temporary structure of poles, planks, etc. for building work; materials for this.

**scald** /skɔːld/ ● *verb* burn (skin etc.) with hot liquid or vapour; heat (esp. milk) to near boiling point; (usually + *out*) clean with boiling water. ● *noun* burn etc. caused by scalding.

**scale¹** ● *noun* each of thin horny plates protecting skin of fish and reptiles; thing resembling this; incrustation inside kettle etc.; tartar on teeth. ● *verb* (**-ling**) remove scale(s) from; form or come off in scales. □ **scaly** *adjective* (**-ier, -iest**).

**scale²** *noun* (often in *plural*) weighing machine; (also **scale-pan**) pan of weighing-balance. □ **tip, turn the scales** be decisive factor, (+ *at*) weigh (specified amount).

**scale³** ● *noun* graded classification system; ratio of reduction or enlargement in map, picture, etc.; relative dimensions; *Music* set of notes at fixed intervals, arranged in order of pitch; set of marks on line used in measuring etc., rule determining distances between these, rod on which these are marked. ● *verb* (**-ling**) climb; represent in proportion; reduce to common scale. □ **scale down, up** make or become smaller or larger in proportion; **to scale** uniformly in proportion.

**scalene** /'skeɪliːn/ *adjective* (of triangle) having unequal sides.

**scallion** /'skæljən/ *noun* esp. US shallot; spring onion.

**scallop** /'skæləp/ ● *noun* edible bivalve with fan-shaped ridged shells; (in full **scallop shell**) one shell of this, esp. used for cooking or serving food on; (in *plural*) ornamental edging of semicircular curves. ● *verb* (**-p-**) ornament with scallops.

**scallywag** /'skælɪwæg/ *noun* scamp, rascal.

**scalp** ● *noun* skin and hair on head; *historical* this cut off as trophy by N. American Indian. ● *verb historical* take scalp of.

**scalpel** /'skælp(ə)l/ *noun* small surgical knife.

**scam** *noun* US slang trick, fraud.

**scamp** *noun colloquial* rascal, rogue.

**scamper** /'skæmpə/ ● *verb* run and skip. ● *noun* act of scampering.

**scampi** /'skæmpɪ/ *plural noun* large prawns.

**scan** ● *verb* (**-nn-**) look at intently or quickly; (of verse etc.) be metrically correct; examine (surface etc.) for radioactivity etc.; traverse (region) with radar etc. beam; resolve (picture) into elements of light and shade for esp. television transmission; analyse metre of (line etc.); obtain image of (part of body) using scanner. ● *noun* scanning; image obtained by scanning.

**scandal** /'skænd(ə)l/ *noun* disgraceful event; public outrage; malicious gossip. □ **scandalmonger** /-mʌŋgə/ person who spreads scandal. □ **scandalous** *adjective*; **scandalously** *adverb*.

**scandalize** *verb* (also **-ise**) (**-zing** or **-sing**) offend morally, shock.

**Scandinavian** /skændɪ'neɪvɪən/ ● *noun* native or inhabitant, or family of languages, of Scandinavia. ● *adjective* of Scandinavia.

**scanner** *noun* device for scanning; diagnostic apparatus measuring radiation, ultrasound reflections, etc. from body.

**scansion** /'skænʃ(ə)n/ *noun* metrical scanning of verse.

**scant** *adjective* barely sufficient; deficient.

**scanty** *adjective* (**-ier**, **-iest**) of small extent or amount; barely sufficient. □ **scantily** *adverb*; **scantiness** *noun*.

**scapegoat** /'skeɪpgəʊt/ *noun* person blamed for others' faults.

**scapula** /'skæpjʊlə/ *noun* (*plural* **-lae** /-liː/ or **-s**) shoulder blade.

**scapular** /'skæpjʊlə/ ● *adjective* of scapula. ● *noun* monastic short cloak.

**scar**[1] ● *noun* mark left on skin etc. by wound etc.; emotional damage. ● *verb* (**-rr-**) (esp. as **scarred** *adjective*) mark with or form scar(s).

**scar**[2] *noun* (also **scaur**) steep craggy part of mountainside.

**scarab** /'skærəb/ *noun* kind of beetle; gem cut in form of beetle.

**scarce** /skeəs/ ● *adjective* in short supply; rare. ● *adverb* archaic or literary scarcely. □ **make oneself scarce** *colloquial* keep out of the way, disappear.

**scarcely** /'skeəslɪ/ *adverb* hardly, only just.

**scarcity** *noun* (*plural* **-ies**) lack or shortage.

**scare** /skeə/ ● *verb* (**-ring**) frighten; (as **scared** *adjective*) (usually + *of*) frightened; (usually + *away*, *off*, etc.) drive away by frightening. ● *noun* sudden fright or alarm, esp. caused by rumours. □ **scarecrow** human figure used for frightening birds away from crops, *colloquial* badly-dressed or grotesque person; **scaremonger** /-mʌŋgə/ person who spreads scare(s).

**scarf**[1] *noun* (*plural* **scarves** /skɑːvz/ or **-s**) piece of material worn round neck or over head for warmth or ornament.

**scarf**[2] ● *verb* join ends of (timber etc.) by thinning or notching them and bolting them together. ● *noun* (*plural* **-s**) joint made thus.

**scarify** /'skærɪfaɪ/ *verb* (**-ies**, **-ied**) make slight incisions in; scratch; criticize etc. mercilessly; loosen (soil). □ **scarification** *noun*.

**scarlatina** /skɑːlə'tiːnə/ *noun* scarlet fever.

**scarlet** /'skɑːlət/ ● *adjective* of brilliant red tinged with orange. ● *noun* scarlet colour, pigment, clothes, etc. □ **scarlet fever** infectious fever with scarlet rash; **scarlet pimpernel** wild plant with small esp. scarlet flowers.

**scarp** ● *noun* steep slope, esp. inner side of ditch in fortification. ● *verb* make perpendicular or steep.

**scarper** /'skɑːpə/ *verb* slang run away, escape.

**scarves** *plural* of SCARF[1].

**scary** *adjective* (**-ier**, **-iest**) *colloquial* frightening.

**scat** ● *noun* wordless jazz singing. ● *verb* (**-tt-**) sing scat.

**scathing** /'skeɪðɪŋ/ *adjective* witheringly scornful. □ **scathingly** *adverb*.

**scatology** /skæ'tɒlədʒɪ/ *noun* preoccupation with excrement or obscenity. □ **scatological** /-tə'lɒdʒ-/ *adjective*.

**scatter** /'skætə/ ● *verb* throw about, strew; cover by scattering; (cause) to flee; (cause to) disperse; (as **scattered** *adjective*) wide apart, sporadic; *Physics* deflect or diffuse (light, particles, etc.). ● *noun* act of scattering; small amount scattered; extent of distribution. □ **scatterbrain** person lacking concentration; **scatterbrained** adjective.

**scatty** /'skæti/ adjective (**-ier, -iest**) colloquial lacking concentration. □ **scattily** adverb; **scattiness** noun.

**scavenge** /'skævɪndʒ/ verb (**-ging**) (usually + for) search for and collect (discarded items).

**scavenger** /'skævɪndʒə/ noun person who scavenges; animal etc. feeding on carrion.

**SCE** abbreviation Scottish Certificate of Education.

**scenario** /sɪ'nɑːrɪəʊ/ noun (plural **-s**) synopsis of film, play, etc.; imagined sequence of future events.

■ Usage Scenario should not be used in standard English to mean 'situation', as in It was an unpleasant scenario.

**scene** /siːn/ noun place of actual or fictitious occurrence; incident; public display of emotion, temper, etc.; piece of continuous action in a play, film, book, etc.; piece(s) of scenery for a play; landscape, view; colloquial area of interest or activity. □ **behind the scenes** out of view of audience, secret, secretly; **scene-shifter** person who moves scenery in theatre.

**scenery** /'siːnəri/ noun features (esp. picturesque) of landscape; backcloths, properties, etc. representing scene in a play etc.

**scenic** /'siːnɪk/ adjective picturesque; of scenery. □ **scenically** adverb.

**scent** /sent/ ●noun characteristic, esp. pleasant, smell; liquid perfume; smell left by animal; clues etc. leading to discovery; power of scenting. ●verb discern by smell; sense; (esp. as **scented** adjective) make fragrant.

**scepter** US = SCEPTRE.

**sceptic** /'skeptɪk/ noun (US **skeptic**) sceptical person; person who questions truth of religions, or the possibility of knowledge. □ **scepticism** /-sɪz(ə)m/ noun.

**sceptical** /'skeptɪk(ə)l/ adjective (US **skeptical**) inclined to doubt accepted opinions; critical; incredulous. □ **sceptically** adverb.

**sceptre** /'septə/ noun (US **scepter**) staff borne as symbol of sovereignty.

**schedule** /'ʃedjuːl/ ●noun timetable; list, esp. of rates or prices. ●verb (**-ling**) include in schedule; make schedule of; list (building) for preservation. □ **on schedule** at time appointed; **scheduled flight**, **service**, etc., regular public one.

**schema** /'skiːmə/ noun (plural **schemata** or **-s**) synopsis, outline, diagram.

**schematic** /skɪ'mætɪk/ ●adjective of or as scheme or diagram. ●noun diagram, esp. of electronic circuit.

**schematize** /'skiːmətaɪz/ verb (also **-ise**) (**-zing** or **-sing**) put in schematic form.

**scheme** /skiːm/ ●noun systematic arrangement; artful plot; outline, syllabus, etc. ●verb (**-ming**) plan, esp. secretly or deceitfully. □ **scheming** adjective.

**scherzo** /'skeətsəʊ/ noun (plural **-s**) Music vigorous and lively movement or composition.

**schism** /'skɪz(ə)m/ noun division of esp. religious group into sects etc. □ **schismatic** /-'mæt-/ adjective & noun.

**schist** /ʃɪst/ noun layered crystalline rock.

**schizo** /'skɪtsəʊ/ colloquial ●adjective schizophrenic. ●noun (plural **-s**) schizophrenic person.

**schizoid** /'skɪtsɔɪd/ ●adjective tending to schizophrenia. ●noun schizoid person.

**schizophrenia** /skɪtsə'friːnɪə/ noun mental disorder marked by disconnection between thoughts, feelings, and actions. □ **schizophrenic** /-'fren-/ adjective & noun.

**schmaltz** /ʃmɔːlts/ noun colloquial sickly sentimentality. □ **schmaltzy** adjective (**-ier, -iest**).

**schnapps** /ʃnæps/ noun any of various spirits drunk in N. Europe.

**schnitzel** /'ʃnɪts(ə)l/ noun veal escalope.

**scholar** /'skɒlə/ noun learned person; holder of scholarship; person of specified academic ability. □ **scholarly** adjective.

**scholarship** noun learning, erudition; award of money etc. towards education.

**scholastic** /skə'læstɪk/ adjective of schools, education, etc.; academic.

**school**[1] /skuːl/ ● *noun* educational institution for pupils up to 19 years old or (*US*) at any level; school buildings, pupils, staff, etc; (time given to) teaching; university department or faculty; group of artists, disciples, etc. following or holding similar principles, opinions, etc.; instructive circumstances. ● *verb* send to school; discipline, train, control; (as **schooled** *adjective*) (+ *in*) educated, trained. □ **schoolboy**, **schoolchild**, **schoolgirl** one who attends school; **school-leaver** person who has just left school; **schoolmaster**, **schoolmistress**, **schoolteacher** teacher in school; **schoolroom** room used for lessons, esp. in private house.

**school**[2] /skuːl/ *noun* shoal of fish, whales, etc.

**schooling** *noun* education.

**schooner** /ˈskuːnə/ *noun* two-masted fore-and-aft rigged ship; large glass, esp. for sherry; *US & Australian* tall beer glass.

**schottische** /ʃɒˈtiːʃ/ *noun* kind of slow polka.

**sciatic** /saɪˈætɪk/ *adjective* of hip or sciatic nerve; of or having sciatica. □ **sciatic nerve** large nerve from pelvis to thigh.

**sciatica** /saɪˈætɪkə/ *noun* neuralgia of hip and leg.

**science** /ˈsaɪəns/ *noun* branch of knowledge involving systematized observation, experiment, and induction; knowledge so gained; pursuit or principles of this; skilful technique. □ **science fiction** fiction with scientific theme; **science park** area containing science-based businesses.

**scientific** /saɪənˈtɪfɪk/ *adjective* following systematic methods of science; systematic, accurate; of or concerned with science.

**scientist** /ˈsaɪəntɪst/ *noun* student or expert in science.

**sci-fi** /ˈsaɪfaɪ/ *noun colloquial* science fiction.

**scilicet** /ˈsaɪlɪset/ *adverb* that is to say.

**scimitar** /ˈsɪmɪtə/ *noun* curved oriental sword.

**scintillate** /ˈsɪntɪleɪt/ (**-ting**) (esp. as **scintillating** *adjective*) talk or act cleverly; sparkle, twinkle. □ **scintillation** *noun*.

**scion** /ˈsaɪən/ *noun* shoot cut for grafting; young member of family.

**scissors** /ˈsɪzəz/ *plural noun* (also **pair of scissors** *singular*) cutting instrument with pair of pivoted blades.

**sclerosis** /skləˈrəʊsɪs/ *noun* abnormal hardening of tissue; (in full **multiple sclerosis**) serious progressive disease of nervous system. □ **sclerotic** /-ˈrɒt-/ *adjective*.

**scoff**[1] ● *verb* (usually + *at*) speak derisively, mock. ● *noun* mocking words, taunt.

**scoff**[2] *colloquial* ● *verb* eat (food) greedily. ● *noun* food.

**scold** /skəʊld/ ● *verb* rebuke; find fault noisily. ● *noun archaic* nagging woman.

**sconce** *noun* wall-bracket holding candlestick or light-fitting.

**scone** /skɒn, skəʊn/ *noun* small cake of flour etc. baked quickly.

**scoop** /skuːp/ ● *noun* short-handled deep shovel; long-handled ladle; excavating part of digging machine etc.; device for serving ice cream etc.; quantity taken up by scoop; scooping movement; exclusive news item; large profit made quickly. ● *verb* (usually + *out*) hollow out or (usually + *up*) lift (as) with scoop; forestall (rival newspaper etc.) with scoop; secure (large profit etc.), esp. suddenly.

**scoot** /skuːt/ *verb* (esp. in *imperative*) *colloquial* shoot along; depart, flee.

**scooter** *noun* child's toy with footboard on two wheels and long steering-handle; low-powered motorcycle.

**scope** *noun* range, opportunity; extent of ability, outlook, etc.

**scorch** ● *verb* burn or discolour surface of with dry heat; become so discoloured etc.; (as **scorching** *adjective*) *colloquial* (of weather) very hot, (of criticism etc.) stringent. ● *noun* mark of scorching. □ **scorched earth policy** policy of destroying everything that might be of use to invading enemy.

**scorcher** *noun colloquial* extremely hot day.

**score** *noun* number of points, goals, etc. made by player or side in game etc.; respective scores at end of game; act of gaining esp. goal; (*plural* same or **-s**) (set of) 20; (in *plural*) a great many; reason, motive; *Music* copy of composition with parts arranged one below another; music for film or play; notch, line, etc. made on surface; record of money owing. ● verb **(-ring)** win, gain; make (points etc.) in game; keep score; mark with notches etc.; have an advantage; *Music* (often + *for*) orchestrate or arrange (piece of music); *slang* obtain drugs illegally, make sexual conquest. □ **keep (the) score** register points etc. as they are made; **score (points) off** *colloquial* humiliate, esp. verbally; **scoreboard** large board for displaying score in match etc.

**scoria** /ˈskɔːrɪə/ *noun* (*plural* **scoriae** /-rɪiː/) (fragments of) cellular lava; slag.

**scorn** ● *noun* disdain, contempt, derision. ● *verb* hold in contempt; reject or refuse to do as unworthy.

**scornful** *adjective* (often + *of*) contemptuous. □ **scornfully** *adverb*.

**Scorpio** /ˈskɔːpɪəʊ/ *noun* eighth sign of zodiac.

**scorpion** /ˈskɔːpɪən/ *noun* lobster-like arachnid with jointed stinging tail.

**Scot** *noun* native of Scotland.

**Scotch** ● *adjective* Scottish, Scots. ● *noun* Scottish, Scots; Scotch whisky. □ **Scotch broth** meat soup with pearl barley etc.; **Scotch egg** hard-boiled egg in sausage meat; **Scotch fir** Scots pine; **Scotch mist** thick mist and drizzle; **Scotch terrier** small rough-coated terrier; **Scotch whisky** whisky distilled in Scotland.

■ **Usage** Scots or Scottish is preferred to Scotch in Scotland, except in the compound nouns given above.

**scotch** *verb* decisively put an end to; *archaic* wound without killing.

**scot-free** *adverb* unharmed, unpunished.

**Scots** ● *adjective* Scottish. ● *noun* Scottish; form of English spoken in (esp. Lowlands of) Scotland. □ **Scotsman, Scotswoman** Scot; **Scots pine** kind of pine tree.

**Scottish** ● *adjective* of Scotland or its inhabitants. ● *noun* (**the Scottish**) (treated as *plural*) people of Scotland.

**scoundrel** /ˈskaʊndr(ə)l/ *noun* unscrupulous villain; rogue.

**scour**[1] /skaʊə/ ● *verb* rub clean; (usually + *away*, *off*, etc.) clear by rubbing; clear out (pipe etc.) by flushing through. ● *noun* scouring, being scoured. □ **scourer** *noun*.

**scour**[2] /skaʊə/ *verb* search thoroughly.

**scourge** /skɜːdʒ/ ● *noun* person or thing regarded as causing suffering; whip. ● *verb* **(-ging)** whip; punish, oppress.

**Scouse** /skaʊs/ *colloquial* ● *noun* Liverpool dialect; (also **Scouser**) native of Liverpool. ● *adjective* of Liverpool.

**scout** /skaʊt/ ● *noun* person sent out to get information or reconnoitre; search for this; talent-scout; (also **Scout**) member of (originally boys') association intended to develop character. ● *verb* (often + *for*) seek information etc.; (often + *about*, *around*) make search; (often + *out*) *colloquial* explore. □ **Scoutmaster** person in charge of group of Scouts. □ **scouting** *noun*.

**Scouter** *noun* adult leader of Scouts.

**scowl** /skaʊl/ ● *noun* sullen or bad-tempered look. ● *verb* wear scowl.

**scrabble** /ˈskræb(ə)l/ ● *verb* **(-ling)** scratch or grope busily about. ● *noun* scrabbling; (**Scrabble**) *proprietary term* game in which players build up words from letter-blocks on board.

**scrag** ● *noun* (also **scrag-end**) inferior end of neck of mutton; skinny person or animal. ● *verb* **(-gg-)** *slang* strangle, hang; handle roughly, beat up.

**scraggy** *adjective* (**-ier, -iest**) thin and bony. □ **scragginess** *noun*.

**scram** *verb* **(-mm-)** (esp. in *imperative*) *colloquial* go away.

**scramble** /ˈskræmb(ə)l/ ● *verb* **(-ling)** clamber, crawl, climb, etc.; (+ *for*, *at*) struggle with competitors (for thing or share); mix indiscriminately; cook (eggs) by stirring in heated pan; alter sound frequencies of (broadcast or telephone conversation) so as to make it unintelligible without special receiver; (of fighter aircraft or pilot) take off rapidly. ● *noun* scrambling; difficult climb or walk; (+ *for*) eager struggle or competition; motorcycle race over rough ground; emergency take-off by fighter aircraft.

**scrambler** *noun* device for scrambling telephone conversations; motorcycle used for scrambles.

**scrap**[1] ●*noun* small detached piece, fragment; waste material; discarded metal for reprocessing; (with negative) smallest piece or amount; (in *plural*) odds and ends, bits of uneaten food. ●*verb* (**-pp-**) discard as useless. □ **scrapbook** book in which cuttings etc. are kept; **scrap heap** collection of waste material, state of being discarded as useless; **scrapyard** place where (esp. metal) scrap is collected.

**scrap**[2] *colloquial* ●*noun* fight or rough quarrel. ●*verb* (**-pp-**) have scrap.

**scrape** ●*verb* (**-ping**) move hard edge across (surface), esp. to smoothe or clean; (+ *away*, *off*, etc.) remove by scraping; rub (surface) harshly against another; scratch, damage, or make by scraping; draw or move with sound (as) of scraping; produce such sound from; (often + *along*, *by*, *through*, etc.) move while (almost) touching; narrowly achieve; (often + *by*, *through*) barely manage, pass exam etc. with difficulty; (+ *together*, *up*) provide or amass with difficulty; be economical; make clumsy bow; (+ *back*) draw (hair) tightly back. ●*noun* act or sound of scraping; scraped place, graze; *colloquial* predicament caused by rashness. □ **scraper** *noun*.

**scrapie** /'skreɪpɪ/ *noun* viral disease of sheep.

**scrappy** *adjective* (**-ier**, **-iest**) consisting of scraps; incomplete.

**scratch** ●*verb* score or wound superficially, esp. with sharp object; scrape with the nails to relieve itching; make or form by scratching; (+ *out*, *off*, *through*) erase; withdraw from race or competition; (often + *about*, *around*, etc.) scratch ground etc. in search, search haphazardly. ●*noun* mark, wound, or sound made by scratching; act of scratching oneself; *colloquial* trifling wound; starting line for race etc.; position of those receiving no handicap. ●*adjective* collected by chance; collected or made from whatever is available; with no handicap given. □ **from scratch** from the beginning, without help; **up to scratch** up to required standard.

**scratchy** *adjective* (**-ier**, **-iest**) tending to make scratches or scratching noise;

causing itchiness; (of drawing etc.) careless. □ **scratchily** *adverb*; **scratchiness** *noun*.

**scrawl** ●*verb* write in hurried untidy way. ●*noun* hurried writing; scrawled note. □ **scrawly** *adjective* (**-ier**, **-iest**).

**scrawny** /'skrɔːnɪ/ *adjective* (**-ier**, **-iest**) lean, scraggy.

**scream** ●*noun* piercing cry (as) of terror or pain; *colloquial* hilarious occurrence or person. ●*verb* emit scream; utter in or with scream; move with scream; laugh uncontrollably; be blatantly obvious.

**scree** *noun* (in *singular* or *plural*) small loose stones; mountain slope covered with these.

**screech** ●*noun* harsh scream or squeal. ●*verb* utter with or make screech. □ **screech-owl** barn owl.

**screed** *noun* long usually tiresome letter or harangue; layer of cement etc. applied to level a surface.

**screen** ●*noun* fixed or movable upright partition for separating, concealing, or protecting from heat etc.; thing used to conceal or shelter; concealing stratagem; protection thus given; blank surface on which images are projected; (**the screen**) cinema industry, films collectively; windscreen; large sieve; system for detecting disease, ability, attribute, etc. ●*verb* shelter, hide; protect from detection, censure, etc.; (+ *off*) conceal behind screen; show (film etc.); prevent from causing, or protect from, electrical interference; test (person or group) for disease, reliability, loyalty, etc.; sieve. □ **screenplay** film script; **screen printing** printing process with ink forced through areas of sheet of fine mesh; **screen test** audition for film part; **screenwriter** person who writes for cinema.

**screw** /skruː/ ●*noun* cylinder or cone with spiral ridge running round it outside (**male screw**) or inside (**female screw**); (in full **woodscrew**) metal male screw with slotted head and sharp point; (in full **screw-bolt**) blunt metal male screw on which nut is threaded; straight screw used to exert pressure; (in *singular* or *plural*) instrument of torture acting thus; (in full **screw propeller**) propeller with twisted blades; one turn of screw; (+ *of*) small twisted-up paper (of tobacco etc.); oblique curling motion; *slang* prison keeper. ● *verb* fasten or tighten (as) with screw(s); (of ball etc.) swerve; (+ *out*, *of*) extort from; swindle. □ **screwball** *US slang* crazy or eccentric person; **screwdriver** tool for turning screws by putting tool's tip into screw's slot; **screw up** contract, crumple, or contort, summon up (courage etc.), *slang* bungle, spoil, or upset; **screw-up** *slang* bungle.

**screwy** *adjective* (**-ier**, **-iest**) *slang* mad, eccentric; absurd. □ **screwiness** *noun*.

**scribble** /'skrɪb(ə)l/ ● *verb* (**-ling**) write or draw carelessly or hurriedly; *jocular* be author or writer. ● *noun* scrawl; hasty note etc.

**scribe** ● *noun* ancient or medieval copyist of manuscripts; pointed instrument for marking wood etc.; *colloquial* writer. ● *verb* (**-bing**) mark with scribe. □ **scribal** *adjective*.

**scrim** *noun* open-weave fabric for lining, upholstery, etc.

**scrimmage** /'skrɪmɪdʒ/ ● *noun* tussle, brawl. ● *verb* (**-ging**) engage in scrimmage.

**scrimp** *verb* skimp.

**scrip** *noun* provisional certificate of money subscribed to company etc.; extra share(s) instead of dividend.

**script** ● *noun* text of play, film, or broadcast (see panel at DIRECT SPEECH); handwriting; typeface imitating handwriting; alphabet or other system of writing; examinee's written answer(s). ● *verb* write script for (film etc.). □ **scriptwriter** person who writes scripts for films, etc.

**scripture** /'skrɪptʃə/ *noun* sacred writings; (**Scripture, the Scriptures**) the Bible. □ **scriptural** *adjective*.

**scrivener** /'skrɪvənə/ *noun* historical copyist, drafter of documents; notary.

**scrofula** /'skrɒfjʊlə/ *noun* disease with glandular swellings. □ **scrofulous** *adjective*.

**scroll** /skrəʊl/ ● *noun* roll of parchment or paper; book in ancient roll form; ornamental design imitating roll of parchment. ● *verb* (often + *down*, *up*) move (display on VDU screen) to view later or earlier material.

**scrotum** /'skrəʊtəm/ *noun* (*plural* **scrota** or **-s**) pouch of skin enclosing testicles. □ **scrotal** *adjective*.

**scrounge** /skraʊndʒ/ *verb* (**-ging**) obtain (things) by cadging. □ **on the scrounge** scrounging. □ **scrounger** *noun*.

**scrub**[1] ● *verb* (**-bb-**) clean by hard rubbing, esp. with hard brush; (often + *up*) (of surgeon etc.) clean and disinfect hands etc. before operating; *colloquial* cancel; pass (gas etc.) through scrubber. ● *noun* scrubbing, being scrubbed.

**scrub**[2] *noun* brushwood or stunted trees etc.; land covered with this. □ **scrubby** *adjective* (**-ier**, **-iest**).

**scrubber** *noun slang* promiscuous woman; apparatus for purifying gases etc.

**scruff**[1] *noun* back of neck.

**scruff**[2] *noun colloquial* scruffy person.

**scruffy** /'skrʌfɪ/ *adjective* (**-ier**, **-iest**) *colloquial* shabby, slovenly, untidy. □ **scruffily** *adverb*; **scruffiness** *noun*.

**scrum** *noun* scrummage; *colloquial* scrimmage. □ **scrum-half** *Rugby* half-back who puts ball into scrum.

**scrummage** /'skrʌmɪdʒ/ *noun Rugby* massed forwards on each side pushing to gain possession of ball thrown on ground between them.

**scrumptious** /'skrʌmpʃəs/ *adjective colloquial* delicious.

**scrumpy** /'skrʌmpɪ/ *noun colloquial* rough cider.

**scrunch** ● *verb* (usually + *up*) crumple; crunch. ● *noun* crunch.

**scruple** /'skru:p(ə)l/ ● *noun* (often in *plural*) moral concern; doubt caused by this. ● *verb* (**-ling**) (+ *to do*; usually in negative) hesitate owing to scruples.

**scrupulous** /'skru:pjʊləs/ *adjective* conscientious, thorough; careful to avoid doing wrong; over-attentive to details. □ **scrupulously** *adverb*.

**scrutineer** /skru:tɪ'nɪə/ *noun* person who scrutinizes ballot papers.

**scrutinize** /'skru:tɪnaɪz/ *verb* (also **-ise**) (**-zing** or **-sing**) subject to scrutiny.

**scrutiny** /'skru:tɪnɪ/ *noun* (*plural* **-ies**) critical gaze; close examination; official examination of ballot papers.

**scuba** /'sku:bə/ *noun* (*plural* **-s**) aqualung. □ **scuba-diving** swimming underwater using scuba.

**scud** • verb (**-dd-**) move straight and fast; skim along; *Nautical* run before wind. • noun scudding; vapoury driving clouds or shower.

**scuff** • verb graze or brush against; mark or wear out (shoes etc.) thus; shuffle or drag feet. • noun mark of scuffing.

**scuffle** /'skʌf(ə)l/ • noun confused struggle or fight at close quarters. • verb (**-ling**) engage in scuffle.

**scull** • noun each of pair of small oars; oar used to propel boat from stern; (in *plural*) sculling race. • verb propel with scull(s).

**scullery** /'skʌlərɪ/ noun (*plural* **-ies**) back kitchen; room where dishes are washed etc.

**sculpt** verb sculpture.

**sculptor** /'skʌlptə/ noun (feminine **sculptress**) person who sculptures.

**sculpture** /'skʌlptʃə/ • noun art of making 3-dimensional forms by chiselling, carving, modelling, casting, etc.; work of sculpture. • verb (**-ring**) represent in or adorn with sculpture; practise sculpture. □ **sculptural** adjective.

**scum** • noun layer of dirt etc. at surface of liquid; *derogatory* worst part, person, or group. • verb (**-mm-**) remove scum from; form scum (on). □ **scumbag** slang contemptible person. □ **scummy** adjective (**-ier**, **-iest**).

**scupper**[1] /'skʌpə/ noun hole in ship's side draining water from deck.

**scupper**[2] /'skʌpə/ verb slang sink (ship, crew); defeat or ruin (plan etc.); kill.

**scurf** noun dandruff. □ **scurfy** adjective (**-ier**, **-iest**).

**scurrilous** /'skʌrɪləs/ adjective grossly or obscenely abusive. □ **scurrility** /skə'rɪlɪ-/ noun (*plural* **-ies**); **scurrilously** adverb; **scurrilousness** noun.

**scurry** /'skʌrɪ/ • verb (**-ies**, **-ied**) run hurriedly, scamper. • noun (*plural* **-ies**) scurrying sound or movement; flurry of rain or snow.

**scurvy** /'skɜːvɪ/ • noun disease resulting from deficiency of vitamin C. • adjective (**-ier**, **-iest**) paltry, contemptible. □ **scurvily** adverb.

**scut** noun short tail, esp. of hare, rabbit, or deer.

**scutter** /'skʌtə/ verb & noun colloquial scurry.

**scuttle**[1] /'skʌt(ə)l/ noun coal scuttle; part of car body between windscreen and bonnet.

**scuttle**[2] /'skʌt(ə)l/ • verb (**-ling**) scurry; flee in undignified way. • noun hurried gait; precipitate flight.

**scuttle**[3] /'skʌt(ə)l/ • noun hole with lid in ship's deck or side. • verb (**-ling**) let water into (ship) to sink it.

**scythe** /saɪð/ • noun mowing and reaping implement with long handle and curved blade. • verb (**-thing**) cut with scythe.

**SDLP** abbreviation (in N. Ireland) Social Democratic and Labour Party.

**SDP** abbreviation (in UK) Social Democratic Party.

**SE** abbreviation south-east(ern).

**sea** noun expanse of salt water covering most of earth; area of this; large inland lake; (motion or state of) waves of sea; (+ *of*) vast quantity or expanse. □ **at sea** in ship on the sea, confused; **sea anchor** bag to reduce drifting of ship; **sea anemone** polyp with petal-like tentacles; **seabed** ocean floor; **seaboard** coastline, coastal area; **sea dog** old sailor; **seafarer** traveller by sea; **seafood** edible marine fish or shellfish; **sea front** part of seaside town facing sea; **seagoing** designed for open sea; **seagull** = GULL[1]; **sea horse** small fish with head like horse's; **seakale** plant with young shoots used as vegetable; **sea legs** ability to keep one's balance at sea; **sea level** mean level of sea's surface, used in reckoning heights of hills etc. and as barometric standard; **sea lion** large, eared seal; **seaman** person whose work is at sea, sailor, sailor below rank of officer; **seaplane** aircraft designed to take off from and land on water; **seaport** town with harbour; **sea salt** salt got by evaporating sea water; **seascape** picture or view of sea; **seashell** shell of salt-water mollusc; **seashore** land next to sea; **seasick** nauseous from motion of ship at sea; **seasickness** noun; **seaside** sea-coast, esp. as holiday resort; **sea urchin** small marine animal with spiny shell; **seaweed** plant growing in sea; **seaworthy** fit to put to sea.

**seal**[1] ● *noun* piece of stamped wax etc. attached to document or to receptacle, envelope, etc. to guarantee authenticity or security; metal stamp etc. used in making seal; substance or device used to close gap etc.; anything regarded as confirmation or guarantee; decorative adhesive stamp. ● *verb* close securely or hermetically; stamp, fasten, or fix with seal; certify as correct with seal; (+ *off*) prevent access to or from; (often + *up*) confine securely; settle, decide. □ **sealing wax** mixture softened by heating and used for seals.

**seal**[2] ● *noun* fish-eating amphibious marine mammal with flippers. ● *verb* hunt seals.

**sealant** *noun* material for sealing, esp. to make watertight.

**seam** ● *noun* line where two edges join, esp. of cloth or boards; fissure between parallel edges; wrinkle; stratum of coal etc. ● *verb* join with seam; (esp. as **seamed** *adjective*) mark or score with seam. □ **seamless** *adjective*.

**seamstress** /'siːmstrɪs/ *noun* woman who sews.

**seamy** *adjective* (**-ier, -iest**) disreputable, sordid; showing seams. □ **seaminess** *noun*.

**seance** /'seɪɑ̃s/ *noun* meeting at which spiritualist attempts to contact the dead.

**sear** /sɪə/ *verb* scorch, cauterize; cause anguish to; brown (meat) quickly.

**search** /sɜːtʃ/ ● *verb* examine thoroughly to find something; make investigation; (+ *for*, *out*) look for, seek out; (as **searching** *adjective*) keenly questioning. ● *noun* act of searching; investigation. □ **searchlight** outdoor lamp designed to throw strong beam of light in any direction, light or beam from this; **search party** group of people conducting organized search; **search warrant** official authorization to enter and search building. □ **searcher** *noun*; **searchingly** *adverb*.

**season** /'siːz(ə)n/ ● *noun* each of climatic divisions of year; proper or suitable time; time when something is plentiful, active, etc.; (**the season**) (also **high season**) busiest period at resort etc.; *colloquial* season ticket. ● *verb* flavour with salt, herbs, etc.; enhance with wit

etc.; moderate; (esp. as **seasoned** *adjective*) make or become suitable by exposure to weather or experience. □ **in season** (of food) available plentifully, (of animal) on heat; **season ticket** one entitling holder to unlimited travel, access, etc. in given period.

**seasonable** *adjective* suitable to season; opportune.

■ **Usage** *Seasonable* is sometimes confused with *seasonal*.

**seasonal** *adjective* of, depending on, or varying with seasons.

■ **Usage** *Seasonal* is sometimes confused with *seasonable*.

**seasoning** *noun* salt, herbs, etc. as flavouring for food.

**seat** ● *noun* thing made or used for sitting on; buttocks, part of garment covering them; part of chair etc. on which buttocks rest; place for one person in theatre etc.; position as MP, committee member, etc., or right to occupy it; machine's supporting or guiding part; location; country mansion; posture on horse. ● *verb* cause to sit; provide sitting accommodation for; (as **seated** *adjective*) sitting; establish in position. □ **seat belt** belt securing seated person in vehicle or aircraft.

**seating** *noun* seats collectively; sitting accommodation.

**sebaceous** /sɪ'beɪʃəs/ *adjective* fatty; secreting oily matter.

**Sec.** *abbreviation* (also **sec.**) secretary.

**sec.** *abbreviation* second(s).

**sec**[1] *noun* *colloquial* (in phrases) second, moment.

**sec**[2] *adjective* (of wine) dry.

**secateurs** /sekə'tɜːz/ *plural noun* pruning clippers.

**secede** /sɪ'siːd/ *verb* (**-ding**) withdraw formally from political or religious body.

**secession** /sɪ'seʃ(ə)n/ *noun* seceding. □ **secessionist** *noun & adjective*.

**seclude** /sɪ'kluːd/ *verb* (**-ding**) keep (person, place) apart from others; (esp. as **secluded** *adjective*) screen from view.

**seclusion** /sɪ'kluːʒ(ə)n/ *noun* secluded state or place.

**second¹** /'sekənd/ ● *adjective* next after first; additional; subordinate; inferior; comparable to. ● *noun* runner-up; person or thing coming second; second gear; (in *plural*) inferior goods; *colloquial* second helping or course; assistant to boxer, duellist, etc. ● *verb* formally support (nomination, proposal, etc.). □ **second-best** next after best; **second class** second-best group, category, postal service, or accommodation; **second cousin** child of parent's first cousin; **second fiddle** subordinate position; **second-guess** *colloquial* anticipate by guesswork, criticize with hindsight; **second-hand** (of goods) having had previous owner, (of information etc.) obtained indirectly; **second nature** acquired tendency that has become instinctive; **second-rate** inferior; **second sight** clairvoyance; **second string** alternative course of action etc.; **second thoughts** revised opinion; **second wind** renewed capacity for effort after breathlessness or tiredness. □ **seconder** *noun*.

**second²** /'sekənd/ *noun* SI unit of time (1/60 of minute); 1/60 of minute of angle; *colloquial* very short time.

**second³** /sɪ'kɒnd/ *verb* transfer (person) temporarily to another department etc. □ **secondment** *noun*.

**secondary** /'sekəndərɪ/ ● *adjective* coming after or next below what is primary; derived from or supplementing what is primary; (of education etc.) following primary. ● *noun* (*plural* **-ies**) secondary thing. □ **secondary colour** result of mixing two primary colours.

**secondly** *adverb* furthermore; as a second item.

**secrecy** /'si:krəsɪ/ *noun* being secret; keeping of secrets.

**secret** /'si:krɪt/ ● *adjective* not (to be) made known or seen; working etc. secretly; liking secrecy. ● *noun* thing (to be) kept secret; mystery; effective but not widely known method. □ **in secret** secretly; **secret agent** spy; **secret police** police operating secretly for political ends; **secret service** government department concerned with espionage. □ **secretly** *adverb*.

**secretariat** /sekrɪ'teərɪət/ *noun* administrative office or department; its members or premises.

**secretary** /'sekrɪtərɪ/ *noun* (*plural* **-ies**) employee who deals with correspondence, records, making appointments, etc.; official of society etc. who writes letters, organizes business, etc.; principal assistant of government minister, ambassador, etc. □ **secretary bird** long-legged crested African bird; **Secretary-General** principal administrative officer of organization; **Secretary of State** head of major government department, (in US) foreign minister. □ **secretarial** /-'teərɪəl/ *adjective*.

**secrete** /sɪ'kri:t/ *verb* (**-ting**) (of cell, organ, etc.) produce and discharge (substance); conceal. □ **secretory** *adjective*.

**secretion** /sɪ'kri:ʃ(ə)n/ *noun* process or act of secreting; secreted substance.

**secretive** /'si:krətɪv/ *adjective* inclined to make or keep secrets; uncommunicative. □ **secretively** *adverb*; **secretiveness** *noun*.

**sect** *noun* group sharing (usually unorthodox) religious etc. doctrines; religious denomination.

**sectarian** /sek'teərɪən/ ● *adjective* of sect(s); bigoted in following one's sect. ● *noun* member of a sect. □ **sectarianism** *noun*.

**section** /'sekʃ(ə)n/ ● *noun* each of parts into which something is divisible or divided; part cut off; subdivision; *US* area of land, district of town; surgical separation or cutting; cutting of solid by plane, resulting figure or area of this; thin slice cut off for microscopic examination. ● *verb* arrange in or divide into sections; compulsorily commit to psychiatric hospital.

**sectional** *adjective* of a social group; partisan; made in sections; local rather than general. □ **sectionally** *adverb*.

**sector** /'sektə/ *noun* branch of an enterprise, the economy, etc.; *Military* section of battle area; plane figure enclosed between two radii of circle etc.

**secular** /'sekjʊlə/ *adjective* not concerned with religion, not sacred; (of clerics) not monastic. □ **secularism** *noun*; **secularization** *noun*; **secularize** *verb* (also **-ise**) (**-zing** or **-sing**).

**secure** /sɪ'kjʊə/ ● *adjective* untroubled by danger or fear; safe; reliable, stable, fixed. • verb (**-ring**) make secure or safe; fasten or close securely; obtain. □ **securely** adverb.

**security** noun (plural **-ies**) secure condition or feeling; thing that guards or guarantees; safety against espionage, theft, etc.; organization for ensuring this; thing deposited as guarantee for undertaking or loan; (often in plural) document as evidence of loan, certificate of stock, bonds, etc. □ **security risk** person or thing threatening security.

**sedan** /sɪˈdæn/ noun (in full **sedan chair**) historical enclosed chair for one person, usually carried on poles by two; US saloon car.

**sedate** /sɪˈdeɪt/ • adjective tranquil, serious. • verb (**-ting**) put under sedation. □ **sedately** adverb; **sedateness** noun.

**sedation** noun treatment with sedatives.

**sedative** /ˈsedətɪv/ • noun calming drug or influence. • adjective calming, soothing.

**sedentary** /ˈsedəntərɪ/ adjective sitting; (of work etc.) done while sitting; (of person) disinclined to exercise.

**sedge** noun grasslike waterside or marsh plant. □ **sedgy** adjective.

**sediment** /ˈsedmənt/ noun dregs; matter deposited on land by water or wind. □ **sedimentary** /-ˈmen-/ adjective; **sedimentation** noun.

**sedition** /sɪˈdɪʃ(ə)n/ noun conduct or speech inciting to rebellion. □ **seditious** adjective.

**seduce** /sɪˈdjuːs/ verb (**-cing**) entice into sexual activity or wrongdoing; coax or lead astray. □ **seducer** noun.

**seduction** /sɪˈdʌkʃ(ə)n/ noun seducing, being seduced; tempting or attractive thing.

**seductive** /sɪˈdʌktɪv/ adjective alluring, enticing. □ **seductively** adverb; **seductiveness** noun.

**sedulous** /ˈsedjʊləs/ adjective persevering, diligent, painstaking. □ **sedulity** /sɪˈdjuː-/ noun; **sedulously** adverb.

**see**[1] verb (**sees**; past **saw**; past participle **seen**) perceive with the eyes; have or use this power; discern mentally, understand; watch; experience; ascertain; imagine, foresee; look at; meet; visit, be visited by; meet regularly; reflect, get clarification; (+ in) find attractive in; escort, conduct; witness (event etc.); ensure. □ **see about** attend to, consider; **see off** be present at departure of, colloquial get the better of; **see over** inspect, tour; **see red** colloquial become enraged; **see through** not be deceived by, support (person) during difficult time, complete (project); **see-through** translucent; **see to** attend to, repair; **see to it** (+ that) ensure.

**see**[2] noun area under (arch)bishop's authority; (arch)bishop's office or jurisdiction.

**seed** • noun part of plant capable of developing into another such plant; seeds collectively, esp. for sowing; semen; prime cause, beginning; offspring; Tennis etc. seeded player. • verb place seed(s) in; sprinkle (as) with seed; sow seeds; produce or drop seed; remove seeds from (fruit etc.); place crystal etc. in (cloud) to produce rain; Tennis etc. designate (competitor in knockout tournament) so that strong competitors do not meet each other until later rounds, arrange (order of play) thus. □ **go**, **run to seed** cease flowering as seed develops, become degenerate, unkempt, etc.; **seed-bed** bed prepared for sowing, place of development; **seed-pearl** very small pearl; **seed-potato** potato kept for planting; **seedsman** dealer in seeds.

**seedling** noun young plant raised from seed.

**seedy** adjective (**-ier**, **-iest**) shabby; colloquial unwell; full of seed.

**seeing** conjunction (usually + that) considering that, inasmuch as, because.

**seek** verb (past & past participle **sought** /sɔːt/) (often + for, after) search, inquire; try or want to obtain or reach; request; endeavour. □ **seek out** search for and find. □ **seeker** noun.

**seem** verb (often + to do) appear, give the impression.

**seeming** adjective apparent but doubtful. □ **seemingly** adverb.

**seemly** /ˈsiːmlɪ/ adjective (**-ier**, **-iest**) in good taste, decorous. □ **seemliness** noun.

**seen** past participle of SEE[1].

**seep** verb ooze, percolate.

**seepage** noun act of seeping; quantity that seeps.

**seer** /sɪə/ noun person who sees; prophet, visionary.

**seersucker** /'sɪəsʌkə/ noun thin cotton etc. fabric with puckered surface.

**see-saw** /'siːsɔː/ ● noun long board supported in middle so that children etc. sitting on ends move alternately up and down; this game; up-and-down or to-and-fro motion, contest, etc. ● verb play or move (as) on see-saw; vacillate. ● adjective & adverb with up-and-down or to-and-fro motion.

**seethe** /siːð/ verb (**-thing**) boil, bubble; be very angry, resentful, etc.

**segment** ● noun /'segmənt/ part cut off or separable from other parts; part of circle or sphere cut off by intersecting line or plane. ● verb /seg'ment/ divide into segments. □ **segmental** /-'ment-/ adjective; **segmentation** noun.

**segregate** /'segrɪgeɪt/ verb (**-ting**) put apart, isolate; separate (esp. ethnic group) from the rest of the community. □ **segregation** noun; **segregationist** noun & adjective.

**seigneur** /seɪn'jɜː/ noun feudal lord. □ **seigneurial** adjective.

**seine** /seɪn/ ● noun large vertical fishing net. ● verb (**-ning**) fish with seine.

**seismic** /'saɪzmɪk/ adjective of earth-quake(s).

**seismograph** /'saɪzməgrɑːf/ noun instrument for recording earthquake details. □ **seismographic** /-'græf-/ adjective.

**seismology** /saɪz'mɒlədʒɪ/ noun the study of earthquakes. □ **seismological** /-mə'lɒdʒ-/ adjective; **seismologist** noun.

**seize** /siːz/ verb (**-zing**) (often + on, upon) take hold or possession of, esp. forcibly, suddenly, or by legal power; take advantage of; comprehend quickly or clearly; affect suddenly; (also **seise**) (usually + of) Law put in possession of. □ **seize up** (of mechanism) become jammed, (of part of body etc.) become stiff.

**seizure** /'siːʒə/ noun seizing, being seized; sudden attack of epilepsy, apoplexy, etc.

**seldom** /'seldəm/ adverb rarely, not often.

**select** /sɪ'lekt/ ● verb choose, esp. with care. ● adjective chosen for excellence or suitability; exclusive. □ **select committee** parliamentary committee conducting special inquiry. □ **selector** noun.

**selection** /sɪ'lekʃ(ə)n/ noun selecting, being selected; person or thing selected; things from which choice may be made; = NATURAL SELECTION.

**selective** adjective of or using selection; able to select; selecting what is convenient. □ **selectively** adverb; **selectivity** /-'tɪv-/ noun.

**selenium** /sɪ'liːnɪəm/ noun non-metallic element in some sulphide ores.

**self** noun ( plural **selves** /selvz/) individuality, essence; object of introspection or reflexive action; one's own interests or pleasure, concentration on these.

**self-** combining form expressing reflexive action, automatic or independent action, or sameness. □ **self-addressed** addressed to oneself; **self-adhesive** (of envelope etc.) adhesive, esp. without wetting; **self-aggrandizement** enriching oneself, making oneself powerful; **self-assertive** confident or assertive in promoting oneself, one's claims, etc.; **self-assertion** noun; **self-assured** self-confident; **self-catering** providing cooking facilities but no food; **self-centred** preoccupied with oneself; **self-confessed** openly admitting oneself to be; **self-confident** having confidence in oneself; **self-confidence** noun; **self-conscious** nervous, shy, embarrassed; **self-consciously** adverb; **self-contained** uncommunicative, complete in itself; **self-control** control of oneself, one's behaviour, etc.; **self-critical** critical of oneself, one's abilities, etc.; **self-defence** defence of oneself, one's reputation, etc.; **self-denial** abstinence, esp. as discipline; **self-deprecating** belittling oneself; **self-determination** nation's right to determine own government etc., free will; **self-destruct** (of device etc.) explode or disintegrate automatically, esp. when pre-set to do so; **self-effacing** retiring, modest; **self-employed** working as freelance or for one's own business etc.; **self-employment** noun; **self-esteem** good opinion of oneself; **self-**

**evident** needing no proof or explanation; **self-explanatory** not needing explanation; **self-financing** not needing subsidy; **self-fulfilling** (of prophecy etc.) assured fulfilment by its utterance; **self-governing** governing itself or oneself; **self-government** *noun*; **self-help** use of one's own abilities etc. to achieve success etc.; **self-image** one's conception of oneself; **self-important** conceited, pompous; **self-importance** *noun*; **self-indulgent** indulging one's own pleasures, feelings, etc., (of work of art etc.) lacking control; **self-indulgence** *noun*; **self-interest** one's own interest or advantage; **self-interested** *adjective*; **self-made** successful or rich by one's own efforts; **self-opinionated** obstinate in one's opinion; **self-pity** pity for oneself; **self-portrait** portrait of oneself by oneself; **self-possessed** unperturbed, calm; **self-possession** *noun*; **self-preservation** keeping oneself safe, instinct for this; **self-raising** (of flour) containing a raising agent; **self-reliance** reliance on one's own abilities etc.; **self-reliant** *adjective*; **self-respect** respect for oneself; **self-restraint** self-control; **self-righteous** smugly sure of one's righteousness; **self-righteously** *adverb*; **self-righteousness** *noun*; **self-rule** self-government; **self-sacrifice** selflessness, self-denial; **self-satisfied** complacent; **self-satisfaction** *noun*; **self-seeking** selfish; **self-service** with customers helping themselves and paying cashier afterwards; **self-starter** electric device for starting engine, ambitious person with initiative; **self-styled** called so by oneself; **self-sufficient** capable of supplying one's own needs; **self-sufficiency** *noun*; **self-willed** obstinately pursuing one's own wishes; **self-worth** self-esteem.

**selfish** *adjective* concerned chiefly with one's own interests or pleasure; actuated by or appealing to self-interest. □ **selfishness** *noun*.

**selfless** *adjective* unselfish.

**selfsame** /ˈselfseɪm/ *adjective* (**the selfsame**) the very same, the identical.

**sell** ● *verb* (*past & past participle* **sold** /səʊld/) exchange or be exchanged for money; stock for sale; (+ *at, for*) have specified price; betray or prostitute for money etc.; advertise, publicize; cause to be sold; *colloquial* make (person) enthusiastic about (idea etc.). ● *noun colloquial* manner of selling; deception, disappointment. □ **sell-by date** latest recommended date of sale; **sell off** sell at reduced prices; **sell out** sell (all one's stock or shares etc.), betray, be treacherous; **sell-out** commercial success, betrayal; **sell short** disparage, underestimate; **sell up** sell one's business, house, etc.

**seller** *noun* person who sells; thing that sells well or badly as specified. □ **seller's market** time when goods are scarce and expensive.

**Sellotape** /ˈseləteɪp/ ● *noun proprietary term* adhesive usually transparent cellulose tape. ● *verb* (**sellotape**) (**-ping**) fix with Sellotape.

**selvage** /ˈselvɪdʒ/ *noun* (also **selvedge**) edge of cloth woven to prevent fraying.

**selves** *plural of* SELF.

**semantic** /sɪˈmæntɪk/ *adjective* of meaning in language.

**semantics** *plural noun* (usually treated as *singular*) branch of linguistics concerned with meaning.

**semaphore** /ˈseməfɔː/ ● *noun* system of signalling with arms or two flags; railway signalling apparatus with arm(s). ● *verb* (**-ring**) signal or send by semaphore.

**semblance** /ˈsembləns/ *noun* (+ *of*) appearance, show.

**semen** /ˈsiːmən/ *noun* reproductive fluid of males.

**semester** /sɪˈmestə/ *noun* half-year term in universities.

**semi** /ˈsemi/ *noun colloquial* (*plural* **-s**) semi-detached house.

**semi-** *prefix* half; partly.

**semibreve** /ˈsemibriːv/ *noun Music* note equal to 4 crotchets.

**semicircle** /ˈsemisɜːk(ə)l/ *noun* half of circle or its circumference. □ **semicircular** /-ˈsɜːkjʊlə/ *adjective*.

**semicolon** /semɪˈkəʊlən/ *noun* punctuation mark (;) of intermediate value between comma and full stop (see panel).

**semiconductor** /semɪkənˈdʌktə/ *noun* substance that is a poor electrical conductor when either pure or cold and a good conductor when either impure or hot.

**semi-detached** /semɪdɪ'tætʃt/ ● *adjective* (of house) joined to another on one side only. ● *noun* such house.

**semifinal** /semɪ'faɪn(ə)l/ *noun Sport* match or round preceding final. □ **semifinalist** *noun*.

**seminal** /'semɪn(ə)l/ *adjective* of seed, semen, or reproduction; germinal; (of idea etc.) providing basis for future development.

**seminar** /'semɪnɑː/ *noun* small class for discussion etc.; short intensive course of study; specialists' conference.

**seminary** /'semɪnərɪ/ *noun* ( *plural* **-ies**) training college for priests etc. □ **seminarist** *noun*.

**semipermeable** /semɪ'pɜːmɪəb(ə)l/ *adjective* (of membrane etc.) allowing small molecules to pass through.

**semiprecious** /semɪ'preʃəs/ *adjective* (of gem) less valuable than a precious stone.

**semi-professional** /semɪprə'feʃən(ə)l/ ● *adjective* (of footballer, musician, etc.) paid for activity but not relying on it for living; of semi-professionals. ● *noun* semi-professional person.

**semiquaver** /'semɪkweɪvə/ *noun Music* note equal to half a quaver.

**semi-skimmed** /semɪ'skɪmd/ *adjective* (of milk) with some of cream skimmed off.

**Semite** /'siːmaɪt/ *noun* member of peoples supposedly descended from Shem, including Jews and Arabs.

**Semitic** /sɪ'mɪtɪk/ *adjective* of Semites, esp. Jews; of languages of family including Hebrew and Arabic.

**semitone** /'semɪtəʊn/ *noun* half a tone in musical scale.

**semivowel** /'semɪvaʊəl/ *noun* sound intermediate between vowel and consonant; letter representing this.

**semolina** /semə'liːnə/ *noun* hard round grains of wheat used for puddings etc.; pudding of this.

**Semtex** /'semteks/ *noun proprietary term* odourless plastic explosive.

**SEN** *abbreviation* State Enrolled Nurse.

**Sen.** *abbreviation* Senior; Senator.

**senate** /'senɪt/ *noun* upper house of legislature in some countries; governing body of some universities or (*US*) colleges; ancient Roman state council.

**senator** /'senətə/ *noun* member of senate. □ **senatorial** /-'tɔː-/ *adjective*.

**send** *verb* (*past & past participle* **sent**) order or cause to go or be conveyed; cause to become; send message etc.; grant, bestow, inflict, cause to be. □ **send away for** order (goods) by post; **send down** rusticate or expel from university, send to prison; **send for** summon, order by post; **send off** dispatch, attend departure of; **send-off** party etc. at departure of person; **send off for** send away for; **send on** transmit further or in advance of oneself; **send up** *colloquial* ridicule (by mimicking); **send-up** *noun* □ **sender** *noun*.

**senescent** /sɪ'nes(ə)nt/ *adjective* growing old. □ **senescence** *noun*.

---

## Semicolon ;

This is used:

**1** between clauses that are too short or too closely related to be made into separate sentences; such clauses are not usually connected by a conjunction, e.g.

> *To err is human; to forgive, divine.*
> *You could wait for him here; on the other hand I could wait in your place; this would save you valuable time.*

**2** between items in a list which themselves contain commas, if it is necessary to avoid confusion, e.g.

> *The party consisted of three teachers, who had already climbed with the leader; seven pupils; and two parents.*

---

**seneschal** /ˈsenɪʃ(ə)l/ *noun* steward of medieval great house.

**senile** /ˈsiːnaɪl/ *adjective* of old age; mentally or physically infirm because of old age. □ **senile dementia** illness of old people with loss of memory etc. □ **senility** /sɪˈnɪl-/ *noun*.

**senior** /ˈsiːnɪə/ ● *adjective* higher in age or standing; (placed after person's name) senior to relative of same name. ● *noun* senior person; one's elder or superior. □ **senior citizen** old-age pensioner. □ **seniority** /-ˈɒr-/ *noun*.

**senna** /ˈsenə/ *noun* cassia; laxative from leaves and pods of this.

**señor** /senˈjɔː/ *noun* (*plural* **señores** /-rez/) title used of or to Spanish-speaking man.

**señora** /senˈjɔːrə/ *noun* title used of or to Spanish-speaking *esp. married woman*.

**señorita** /senjəˈriːtə/ *noun* title used of or to young Spanish-speaking *esp. unmarried woman*.

**sensation** /senˈseɪʃ(ə)n/ *noun* feeling in one's body; awareness; impression; intense feeling, esp. in community; cause of this; sense of touch.

**sensational** *adjective* causing or intended to cause public excitement etc.; wonderful. □ **sensationalism** *noun*; **sensationalist** *noun & adjective*; **sensationalize** *verb* (also **-ise**) (**-zing** or **-sing**).

**sense** ● *noun* any of bodily faculties transmitting sensation; sensitiveness of any of these; ability to perceive; (+ *of*) consciousness; appreciation; instinct; practical wisdom; meaning of word etc.; intelligibility, coherence; prevailing opinion; (in *plural*) sanity, ability to think. ● *verb* (**-sing**) perceive by sense(s); be vaguely aware of; (of machine etc.) detect. □ **make sense** be intelligible or practicable; **make sense of** show or find meaning of. □ **sense of humour** SEE HUMOUR.

**senseless** *adjective* pointless, foolish; unconscious. □ **senselessly** *adverb*; **senselessness** *noun*.

**sensibility** *noun* (*plural* **-ies**) capacity to feel; (exceptional) sensitiveness; (in *plural*) tendency to feel offended etc.

■ **Usage** *Sensibility* should not be used in standard English to mean 'possession of good sense'.

**sensible** /ˈsensɪb(ə)l/ *adjective* having or showing good sense; perceptible by senses; (of clothing etc.) practical; (+ *of*) aware of. □ **sensibly** *adverb*.

**sensitive** /ˈsensɪtɪv/ *adjective* (often + *to*) acutely affected by external impressions, having sensibility; easily offended or hurt; (often + *to*) responsive to or recording slight changes of condition; *Photography* responding (esp. rapidly) to light; (of topic etc.) requiring tact or secrecy. □ **sensitively** *noun*; **sensitiveness** *noun*; **sensitivity** /-ˈtɪv-/ *noun* (*plural* **-ies**).

**sensitize** /ˈsensɪtaɪz/ *verb* (also **-ise**) (**-zing** or **-sing**) make sensitive. □ **sensitization** *noun*.

**sensor** /ˈsensə/ *noun* device to detect or measure a physical property.

**sensory** /ˈsensərɪ/ *adjective* of sensation or senses.

**sensual** /ˈsensjʊəl/ *adjective* of physical, esp. sexual, pleasure; enjoying, giving, or showing this. □ **sensuality** /-ˈæl-/ *noun*; **sensually** *adverb*.

■ **Usage** *Sensual* is sometimes confused with *sensuous*.

**sensuous** /ˈsensjʊəs/ *adjective* of or affecting senses, esp. aesthetically. □ **sensuously** *adverb*; **sensuousness** *noun*.

■ **Usage** *Sensuous* is sometimes confused with *sensual*.

**sent** *past & past participle* of SEND.

**sentence** /ˈsent(ə)ns/ ● *noun* grammatically complete series of words with (implied) subject and predicate (see panel); punishment allotted to person convicted in criminal trial; declaration of this. ● *verb* (**-cing**) declare sentence of, condemn.

**sententious** /senˈtenʃəs/ *adjective* pompously moralizing; affectedly formal; using maxims. □ **sententiousness** *noun*.

**sentient** /ˈsenʃ(ə)nt/ *adjective* capable of perception and feeling. □ **sentience** *noun*; **sentiently** *adverb*.

**sentiment** /'sentɪmənt/ noun mental feeling; (often in plural) opinion; emotional or irrational view(s); tendency to be swayed by feeling; mawkish tenderness.

**sentimental** /sentɪ'ment(ə)l/ adjective of or showing sentiment; showing or affected by emotion rather than reason. □ **sentimentalism** noun; **sentimentalist** noun; **sentimentality** /-'tæl-/ noun; **sentimentalize** verb (also **-ise**) (**-zing** or **-sing**); **sentimentally** adverb.

**sentinel** /'sentɪn(ə)l/ noun sentry.

**sentry** /'sentrɪ/ noun (plural **-ies**) soldier etc. stationed to keep guard. □ **sentry-box** cabin to shelter standing sentry.

**sepal** /'sep(ə)l/ noun division or leaf of calyx.

**separable** /'sepərəb(ə)l/ adjective able to be separated. □ **separability** noun.

**separate** ● adjective /'sepərət/ forming unit by itself, existing apart; disconnected, distinct, individual. ● noun /'sepərət/ (in plural) articles of dress not parts of suits. ● verb /'sepəreɪt/ (**-ting**) make separate, sever; prevent union or contact of; go different ways; (esp. as **separated** adjective) cease to live with spouse; secede; divide or sort into parts or sizes; (often + out) extract or remove (ingredient etc.). □ **separately** adverb; **separateness** noun; **separator** noun.

■ **Usage** Separate, separation, etc. are not spelt with an e in the middle.

**separation** /sepə'reɪʃ(ə)n/ noun separating, being separated; arrangement by which couple remain married but live apart.

**separatist** /'sepərətɪst/ noun person who favours separation, esp. political independence. □ **separatism** noun.

**sepia** /'siːpɪə/ noun dark reddish-brown colour or paint; brown tint used in photography.

**sepoy** /'siːpɔɪ/ noun historical Indian soldier under European, esp. British, discipline.

**sepsis** /'sepsɪs/ noun septic condition.

**Sept.** abbreviation September.

**sept** noun clan, esp. in Ireland.

**September** /sep'tembə/ noun ninth month of year.

**septet** /sep'tet/ noun musical composition for 7 performers; the performers; any group of 7.

**septic** /'septɪk/ adjective contaminated with bacteria, putrefying. □ **septic tank** tank in which sewage is disintegrated through bacterial activity.

**septicaemia** /septɪ'siːmɪə/ noun (US **septicemia**) blood poisoning.

**septuagenarian** /septjʊədʒɪ'neərɪən/ noun person between 70 and 79 years old.

**Septuagesima** /septjʊə'dʒesɪmə/ noun third Sunday before Lent.

**Septuagint** /'septjʊədʒɪnt/ noun ancient Greek version of Old Testament.

**septum** /'septəm/ noun (plural **septa**) partition such as that between nostrils.

---

## Sentence

A sentence is the basic unit of language in use and expresses a complete thought. There are three types of sentence, each starting with a capital letter, and each normally ending with a full stop, a question mark, or an exclamation mark:

| Statement: | *You're happy.* |
| Question: | *Is it raining?* |
| Exclamation: | *I wouldn't have believed it!* |

A sentence, especially a statement, often has no punctuation at the end in a public notice, a newspaper headline, or a legal document, e.g.

*Government cuts public spending*

A sentence normally contains a subject and a verb, but may not, e.g.

*What a mess!*      *Where?*      *In the sink.*

**sepulchral** /sɪˈpʌlkr(ə)l/ *adjective* of tomb or burial; funereal, gloomy.

**sepulchre** /ˈsepəlkə/ (*US* **sepulcher**) ● *noun* tomb, burial cave or vault. ● *verb* (**-ring**) lay in sepulchre.

**sequel** /ˈsiːkw(ə)l/ *noun* what follows; novel, film, etc. that continues story of earlier one.

**sequence** /ˈsiːkwəns/ *noun* succession; order of succession; set of things belonging next to one another; unbroken series; episode or incident in film etc.

**sequential** /sɪˈkwenʃ(ə)l/ *adjective* forming sequence or consequence. □ **sequentially** *adverb*.

**sequester** /sɪˈkwestə/ *verb* (esp. as **sequestered** *adjective*) seclude, isolate; sequestrate.

**sequestrate** /ˈsiːkwɪstreɪt/ *verb* (**-ting**) confiscate; take temporary possession of (debtor's estate etc.). □ **sequestration** *noun*.

**sequin** /ˈsiːkwɪn/ *noun* circular spangle on dress etc. □ **sequined, sequinned** *adjective*.

**sequoia** /sɪˈkwɔɪə/ *noun* extremely tall Californian conifer.

**sera** *plural of* SERUM.

**seraglio** /səˈrɑːlɪəʊ/ *noun* (*plural* **-s**) harem; *historical* Turkish palace.

**seraph** /ˈseraf/ *noun* (*plural* **-im** or **-s**) member of highest of 9 orders of angels. □ **seraphic** /səˈræfɪk/ *adjective*.

**Serb** ● *noun* native of Serbia; person of Serbian descent. ● *adjective* Serbian.

**Serbian** /ˈsɜːbɪən/ ● *noun* Slavonic dialect of Serbs; Serb. ● *adjective* of Serbs or their dialect.

**Serbo-Croat** /sɜːbəʊˈkrəʊæt/ (also **Serbo-Croatian** /-krəʊˈeɪʃ(ə)n/) ● *noun* main official language of former Yugoslavia, combining Serbian and Croatian dialects. ● *adjective* of this language.

**serenade** /serəˈneɪd/ ● *noun* piece of music performed at night, esp. under lover's window; orchestral suite for small ensemble. ● *verb* (**-ding**) perform serenade to.

**serendipity** /serənˈdɪpɪtɪ/ *noun* faculty of making happy discoveries by accident. □ **serendipitous** *adjective*.

**serene** /sɪˈriːn/ *adjective* (**-r, -st**) clear and calm; placid, unperturbed. □ **serenely** *adverb*; **serenity** /-ˈren-/ *noun*.

**serf** *noun historical* labourer not allowed to leave the land on which he worked; oppressed person, drudge. □ **serfdom** *noun*.

**serge** *noun* durable woollen fabric.

**sergeant** /ˈsɑːdʒ(ə)nt/ *noun* non-commissioned army or RAF officer next below warrant officer; police officer next below inspector. □ **sergeant major** warrant officer assisting adjutant of regiment or battalion.

**serial** /ˈsɪərɪəl/ ● *noun* story published, broadcast, or shown in instalments. ● *adjective* of, in, or forming series. □ **serial killer** person who murders repeatedly. □ **serially** *adverb*.

**serialize** *verb* (also **-ise**) (**-zing** or **-sing**) publish or produce in instalments. □ **serialization** *noun*.

**series** /ˈsɪərɪːz/ *noun* (*plural* same) number of similar or related things, events, etc.; succession, row, set; *Broadcasting* set of related but individually complete programmes. □ **in series** in ordered succession, (of set of electrical circuits) arranged so that same current passes through each circuit.

**serif** /ˈserɪf/ *noun* fine cross-line at extremities of printed letter.

**serious** /ˈsɪərɪəs/ *adjective* thoughtful, earnest; important, requiring thought; not negligible, dangerous; sincere, in earnest; (of music, literature, etc.) intellectual, not popular. □ **seriously** *adverb*; **seriousness** *noun*.

**serjeant** /ˈsɑːdʒ(ə)nt/ *noun* (in full **serjeant-at-law**, plural **serjeants-at-law**) *historical* barrister of highest rank. □ **serjeant-at-arms** official of court, city, or parliament, with ceremonial duties.

**sermon** /ˈsɜːmən/ *noun* discourse on religion or morals, esp. delivered in church; admonition, reproof.

**sermonize** *verb* (also **-ise**) (**-zing** or **-sing**) (often + *to*) moralize.

**serous** /ˈsɪərəs/ *adjective* of or like serum, watery; (of gland etc.) having serous secretion.

**serpent** /ˈsɜːpənt/ *noun* snake, esp. large; cunning or treacherous person.

**serpentine** /ˈsɜːpəntaɪn/ ● *adjective* of or like serpent; coiling, sinuous; cunning, treacherous. ● *noun* soft usually dark green rock, sometimes mottled.

**SERPS** *abbreviation* State Earnings-Related Pension Scheme.

**serrated** /sə'reɪtɪd/ *adjective* with saw-like edge. □ **serration** *noun*.

**serried** /'serɪd/ *adjective* (of ranks of soldiers etc.) close together.

**serum** /'sɪərəm/ *noun* (*plural* **sera** or **-s**) liquid separating from clot when blood coagulates, esp. used for inoculation; watery fluid in animal bodies.

**servant** /'sɜ:v(ə)nt/ *noun* person employed for domestic work; devoted follower or helper.

**serve** ● *verb* (**-ving**) do service for; be servant to; carry out duty; (+ *in*) be employed in (esp. armed forces); be useful to or serviceable for; meet needs, perform function; go through due period of (apprenticeship, prison sentence, etc.); go through (specified period) of imprisonment etc.; (often + *up*) present (food) to eat; act as waiter; attend to (customer etc.); (+ *with*) supply with (goods); treat (person) in specified way; *Law* (often + *on*) deliver (writ etc.), (+ *with*) deliver writ etc. to; set (ball) in play at tennis etc.; (of male animal) copulate with (female). ● *noun* Tennis etc. service. □ **serve (person) right** be his or her deserved misfortune. □ **server** *noun*.

**service** /'sɜ:vɪs/ ● *noun* (often in *plural*) work done or doing of work for employer or for community etc.; work done by machine etc.; assistance or benefit given; provision of some public need, e.g. transport or (often in *plural*) water, gas, etc.; employment as servant; state or period of employment; Crown or public department or organization; (in *plural*) the armed forces; ceremony of worship; liturgical form for this; (routine) maintenance and repair of machine etc. after sale; assistance given to customers; serving of food etc.; quality of this, nominal charge for this; (in *plural*) motorway service area; set of dishes etc. for serving meal; act of serving in tennis etc., person's turn to serve, game in which one serves. ● *verb* (**-cing**) maintain or repair (car, machine, etc.); provide service for. □ **at (person's) service** ready to serve him or her; **of service** useful; **service area** area near road supplying petrol,

refreshments, etc.; **service charge** additional charge for service in restaurant etc.; **service flat** one in which domestic service etc. is provided; **service industry** one providing services, not goods; **serviceman**, **servicewoman** person in armed services; **service road** one giving access to houses etc. lying back from main road; **service station** establishment selling petrol etc. to motorists.

**serviceable** *adjective* useful, usable; durable but plain. □ **serviceability** *noun*.

**serviette** /sɜ:vɪ'et/ *noun* table napkin.

**servile** /'sɜ:vaɪl/ *adjective* of or like slave(s); fawning, subservient. □ **servility** /-'vɪl-/ *noun*.

**servitude** /'sɜ:vɪtju:d/ *noun* slavery, subjection.

**servo-** /'sɜ:vəʊ/ *combining form* power-assisted.

**sesame** /'sesəmɪ/ *noun* E. Indian plant with oil-yielding seeds; its seeds.

**sesqui-** /'seskwɪ/ *combining form* one and a half.

**sessile** /'sesaɪl/ *adjective* Biology attached directly by base without stalk or peduncle; fixed, immobile.

**session** /'seʃ(ə)n/ *noun* period devoted to an activity; assembly of parliament, court, etc.; single meeting for this; period during which such meetings are regularly held; academic year. □ **in session** assembled for business, not on vacation. □ **sessional** *adjective*.

**set** ● *verb* (**-tt-**; *past & past participle* **set**) put, lay, or stand in certain position etc.; apply; fix or place ready; dispose suitably for use, action, or display; adjust hands or mechanism of (clock, trap, etc.); insert (jewel) in ring etc.; lay (table) for meal; style (hair) while damp; (+ *with*) ornament or provide (surface) with; bring into specified state, cause to be; harden, solidify; (of sun, moon, etc.) move towards or below earth's horizon; show (story etc.) as happening in a certain time or place; (+ *to do*) cause (person) to do specified thing; (+ *present participle*) start (person, thing) doing something; present or impose as work to be done, problem to be solved, etc.; exhibit as model etc.; initiate (fashion etc.); establish (record etc.); determine, decide; appoint, establish; put parts of (broken or dislocated bone, limb, etc.) together for healing; provide (song, words) with music; arrange (type) or type for (book etc.); (of tide, current, etc.) have a certain motion or direction; (of face) assume hard expression; (of eyes etc.) become motionless; have a certain tendency; (of blossom) form into fruit; (of dancer) take position facing partner; (of hunting dog) take rigid attitude indicating presence of game. ● *noun* group of linked or similar things or persons; section of society; collection of objects for specified purpose; radio or television receiver; *Tennis etc.* group of games counting as unit towards winning match; *Mathematics* collection of things sharing a property; direction or position in which something sets or is set; slip, shoot, bulb, etc. for planting; setting, stage furniture, etc. for play, film, etc.; setting of sun, hair, etc.; = SETT. ● *adjective* prescribed or determined in advance; unchanging; fixed; prepared for action; (+ *on, upon*) determined to get, achieve, etc. □ **set about** begin, take steps towards, *colloquial* attack; **set aside** put to one side, keep for future, disregard or reject; **set back** place further back in space or time, impede or reverse progress of, *colloquial* cost (person) specified amount; **set-back** reversal or arrest of progress; **set down** record in writing, allow to alight; **set forth** begin journey, expound; **set in** begin, become established, insert; **set off** begin journey, detonate (bomb etc.), initiate, stimulate, cause (person) to start laughing etc., adorn, enhance, (+ *against*) use as compensating item against; **set on** (cause or urge to) attack; **set out** begin journey, (+ *to do*) intend, exhibit, arrange; **set piece** formal or elaborate arrangement, esp. in art or literature; **set square** right-angled triangular plate for drawing lines at certain angles; **set to** begin doing something vigorously; **set theory** study or use of sets in mathematics; **set-to** (*plural* **-tos**) *colloquial* fight, argument; **set up** place in position or view, start, establish, equip, prepare, *colloquial* cause (person) to look guilty or foolish; **set-up** arrangement

or organization, manner or structure of this, instance of setting person up; **set upon** set on.

**sett** *noun* (also **set**) badger's burrow, paving-block.

**settee** /se'tiː/ *noun* sofa.

**setter** *noun* dog of long-haired breed trained to stand rigid on scenting game.

**setting** *noun* position or manner in which thing is set; surroundings; period, place, etc. of story, film, etc.; frame etc. for jewel; music to which words are set; cutlery etc. for one person at table; operating level of machine.

**settle**[1] /'set(ə)l/ *verb* (**-ling**) (often + *down, in*) establish or become established in abode or lifestyle; (often + *down*) regain calm after disturbance, adopt regular or secure way of life, (+ *to*) apply oneself to; (cause to) sit down or come to rest; make or become composed etc.; determine, decide, agree on; resolve (dispute etc.); agree to terminate (lawsuit); (+ *for*) accept or agree to; pay (bill); (as **settled** *adjective*) established; colonize; subside, sink. □ **settle up** pay money owed etc.

**settle**[2] /'set(ə)l/ *noun* high-backed bench, often with box under seat.

**settlement** *noun* settling, being settled; place occupied by settlers, small village; political etc. agreement; arrangement ending dispute; terms on which property is given to person; deed stating these; amount or property given.

**settler** *noun* person who settles in newly developed region.

**seven** /'sev(ə)n/ *adjective & noun* one more than six. □ **seventh** *adjective & noun*.

**seventeen** /sevən'tiːn/ *adjective & noun* one more than sixteen. □ **seventeenth** *adjective & noun*.

**seventy** /'sevəntɪ/ *adjective & noun* (*plural* **-ies**) seven times ten. □ **seventieth** *adjective & noun*.

**sever** /'sevə/ *verb* divide, break, or make separate, esp. by cutting.

**several** /'sevr(ə)l/ ● *adjective* a few; quite a large number; *formal* separate, respective. ● *pronoun* a few; quite a large number. □ **severally** *adverb*.

**severance** /ˈsevr(ə)ns/ *noun* severing; severed state. □ **severance pay** payment to employee on termination of contract.

**severe** /sɪˈvɪə/ *adjective* rigorous and harsh; not negligible, worrying; forceful; extreme; exacting; unadorned. □ **severely** *adverb*; **severity** /-ˈver-/ *noun.*

**sew** /səʊ/ *verb* (*past participle* **sewn** or **sewed**) fasten, join, etc. with needle and thread or sewing machine. □ **sewing machine** machine for sewing or stitching.

**sewage** /ˈsuːɪdʒ/ *noun* waste matter carried in sewers. □ **sewage farm, works** place where sewage is treated.

**sewer** /ˈsuːə/ *noun* (usually underground) conduit for carrying off drainage water and waste matter.

**sewerage** /ˈsuːərɪdʒ/ *noun* system of or drainage by sewers.

**sewing** /ˈsəʊɪŋ/ *noun* material or work to be sewn.

**sewn** *past participle* of SEW.

**sex** ● *noun* group of males or females collectively; fact of belonging to either group; sexual instincts, desires, activity, etc.; *colloquial* sexual intercourse. ● *adjective* of or relating to sex or sexual differences. ● *verb* determine sex of; (as **sexed** *adjective*) having specified sexual appetite. □ **sex appeal** sexual attractiveness; **sex life** person's sexual activity; **sex symbol** person famed for sex appeal.

**sexagenarian** /seksədʒɪˈneərɪən/ *noun* person between 60 and 69 years old.

**Sexagesima** /seksəˈdʒesɪmə/ *noun* second Sunday before Lent.

**sexism** *noun* prejudice or discrimination against people (esp. women) because of their sex. □ **sexist** *adjective & noun.*

**sexless** *adjective* neither male nor female; lacking sexual desire or attractiveness.

**sextant** /ˈsekst(ə)nt/ *noun* optical instrument for measuring angle between distant objects, esp. sun and horizon in navigation.

**sextet** /seksˈtet/ *noun* musical composition for 6 performers; the performers; any group of 6.

**sexton** /ˈsekst(ə)n/ *noun* person who looks after church and churchyard, often acting as bell-ringer and gravedigger.

**sextuple** /ˈsekstjuːp(ə)l/ *adjective* sixfold.

**sextuplet** /ˈsekstjʊplɪt/ *noun* each of 6 children born at one birth.

**sexual** /ˈsekʃʊəl/ *adjective* of sex, the sexes, or relations between them. □ **sexual intercourse** insertion of man's penis into woman's vagina. □ **sexuality** /-ˈæl-/ *noun*; **sexually** *adverb.*

**sexy** *adjective* (**-ier, -iest**) sexually attractive or provocative; *colloquial* (of project etc.) exciting. □ **sexily** *adverb*; **sexiness** *noun.*

**SF** *abbreviation* science fiction.

**Sgt.** *abbreviation* Sergeant.

**sh** *interjection* hush.

**shabby** /ˈʃæbɪ/ *adjective* (**-ier, -iest**) faded and worn, dingy, dilapidated; poorly dressed; contemptible. □ **shabbily** *adverb*; **shabbiness** *noun.*

**shack** ● *noun* roughly built hut or cabin. ● *verb* (+ *up*) *slang* cohabit.

**shackle** /ˈʃæk(ə)l/ ● *noun* metal loop or link closed by bolt, coupling link; fetter; (usually in *plural*) restraint. ● *verb* (**-ling**) fetter, impede, restrain.

**shad** *noun* (*plural* same or **-s**) large edible marine fish.

**shade** ● *noun* comparative darkness caused by shelter from direct light and heat; area so sheltered; darker part of picture etc.; a colour, esp. as darker or lighter than one similar; comparative obscurity; slight amount; lampshade; screen moderating light; (in *plural*) esp. US *colloquial* sunglasses; *literary* ghost; (in *plural*, + *of*) reminder of. ● *verb* (**-ding**) screen from light; cover or moderate light of; darken, esp. with parallel lines to represent shadow etc.; (often + *away, off, into*) pass or change gradually. □ **shading** *noun.*

**shadow** /ˈʃædəʊ/ ● *noun* shade; patch of shade; dark shape projected by body blocking out light; inseparable attendant or companion; person secretly following another; (with negative) slightest trace; insubstantial remnant; shaded part of picture; gloom, sadness. ● *verb* cast shadow over; secretly follow and watch. □ **shadow-boxing** boxing against imaginary opponent; **Shadow Cabinet, Minister**, etc., members of opposition party holding posts parallel to those of government. □ **shadowy** *adjective*.

**shady** /ˈʃeɪdɪ/ *adjective* (**-ier, -iest**) giving or situated in shade; disreputable, of doubtful honesty.

**shaft** /ʃɑːft/ *noun* narrow usually vertical space for access to mine or (in building) for lift, ventilation, etc.; (+ *of*) ray of (light), stroke of (lightning); handle of tool etc.; long narrow part supporting, connecting, or driving thicker part(s) etc.; *archaic* arrow, spear, its long slender stem; hurtful or provocative remark; each of pair of poles between which horse is harnessed to vehicle; central stem of feather; column, esp. between base and capital.

**shag** ●*noun* coarse tobacco; rough mass of hair; (crested) cormorant. ●*adjective* (of carpet) with long rough pile.

**shaggy** *adjective* (**-ier, -iest**) hairy, rough-haired; tangled. □ **shaggy-dog story** lengthy 'joke' without funny ending. □ **shagginess** *noun*.

**shagreen** /ʃæˈɡriːn/ *noun* kind of untanned granulated leather; sharkskin.

**shah** /ʃɑː/ *noun historical* ruler of Iran.

**shake** ●*verb* (**-king; past shook** /ʃʊk/; *past participle* **shaken**) move violently or quickly up and down or to and fro; (cause to) tremble or vibrate; agitate, shock, disturb; weaken, impair; *colloquial* shake hands. ●*noun* shaking, being shaken; jerk, shock; (**the shakes**) *colloquial* fit of trembling. □ **shake down** settle or cause to fall by shaking, become comfortably settled or established; **shake hands** (often + *with*) clasp hands, esp. at meeting or parting or as sign of bargain; **shake off** get rid of, evade; **shake up** mix (ingredients) or restore to shape by shaking, disturb or make uncomfortable, rouse from lethargy etc.; **shake-up** upheaval, reorganization.

**shaker** *noun* person or thing that shakes; container for shaking together ingredients of cocktails etc.

**Shakespearian** /ʃeɪkˈspɪərɪən/ *adjective* (also **Shakespearean**) of Shakespeare.

**shako** /ˈʃækəʊ/ *noun* (*plural* **-s**) cylindrical plumed military peaked cap.

**shaky** *adjective* (**-ier, -iest**) unsteady, trembling; infirm; unreliable. □ **shakily** *adverb*; **shakiness** *noun*.

**shale** *noun* soft rock that splits easily. □ **shaly** *adjective*.

**shall** *auxiliary verb* (*3rd singular present* **shall**) *used to form future tenses.*

**shallot** /ʃəˈlɒt/ *noun* onion-like plant with cluster of small bulbs.

**shallow** /ˈʃæləʊ/ ●*adjective* having little depth; superficial, trivial. ●*noun* (often in *plural*) shallow place. □ **shallowness** *noun*.

**sham** ●*verb* (**-mm-**) feign; pretend (to be). ●*noun* imposture, pretence; bogus or false person or thing. ●*adjective* pretended, counterfeit.

**shamble** /ˈʃæmb(ə)l/ ●*verb* (**-ling**) walk or run awkwardly, dragging feet. ●*noun* shambling gait.

**shambles** *plural noun* (usually treated as *singular*) *colloquial* mess, muddle; butcher's slaughterhouse; scene of carnage.

**shambolic** /ʃæmˈbɒlɪk/ *adjective colloquial* chaotic, disorganized.

**shame** ●*noun* humiliation caused by consciousness of guilt or folly; capacity for feeling this; state of disgrace or discredit; person or thing that brings disgrace etc.; wrong or regrettable thing. ●*verb* (**-ming**) bring disgrace on, make ashamed; (+ *into, out of*) force by shame into or out of. □ **shamefaced** showing shame, bashful.

**shameful** *adjective* disgraceful, scandalous. □ **shamefully** *adverb*; **shamefulness** *noun*.

**shameless** *adjective* having or showing no shame; impudent. □ **shamelessly** *adverb*.

**shammy** /ˈʃæmɪ/ *noun* (*plural* **-ies**) *colloquial* chamois leather.

**shampoo** /ʃæmˈpuː/ ●*noun* liquid for washing hair; similar substance for washing cars, carpets, etc. ●*verb* (**-poos, -pooed**) wash with shampoo.

**shamrock** /ˈʃæmrɒk/ *noun* trefoil, as national emblem of Ireland.

**shandy** /ˈʃændɪ/ *noun* (*plural* **-ies**) beer with lemonade or ginger beer.

**shanghai** /ʃæŋˈhaɪ/ *verb* (**-hais, -haied, -haiing**) *colloquial* trick or force (person) to do something, esp. be sailor.

**shank** noun leg, lower part of leg; shaft or stem, esp. joining tool's handle to its working end.

**shan't** /ʃɑːnt/ shall not.

**shantung** /ʃænˈtʌŋ/ noun soft undressed Chinese silk.

**shanty**[1] /ˈʃæntɪ/ noun (plural **-ies**) hut, cabin. □ **shanty town** area with makeshift housing.

**shanty**[2] /ˈʃæntɪ/ noun (plural **-ies**) (in full **sea shanty**) sailors' work song.

**shape** ● noun outline; form; specific form or guise; good or specified condition; person or thing seen indistinctly; mould, pattern. ● verb (**-ping**) give a certain form to, fashion, create; influence; (usually + up) show promise; (+ to) make conform to. □ **take shape** assume distinct form, develop.

**shapeless** adjective lacking definite or attractive shape. □ **shapelessness** noun.

**shapely** adjective (**-ier**, **-iest**) of pleasing shape, well-proportioned. □ **shapeliness** noun.

**shard** noun broken fragment of pottery, glass, etc.

**share**[1] /ʃeə/ ● noun portion of whole given to or taken from person; each of equal parts into which company's capital is divided, entitling owner to proportion of profits. ● verb (**-ring**) have or use with another or others; get, have, or give share of; (+ in) participate in; (+ out) divide and distribute. □ **shareholder** owner of shares in a company; **share-out** division and distribution.

**shark** noun large voracious sea fish; colloquial swindler, extortioner. □ **sharkskin** skin of shark, smooth slightly shiny fabric.

**sharp** ● adjective having edge or point able to cut or pierce; tapering to a point or edge; abrupt, steep, angular; well-defined; severe, intense; pungent, acid; shrill, piercing; harsh; acute, sensitive, clever; unscrupulous; vigorous, brisk; Music above true pitch, a semitone higher than note named. ● noun Music sharp note; sign (♯) indicating this; colloquial swindler, cheat. ● adverb punctually; suddenly; at a sharp angle; Music above true pitch. □ **sharp practice** barely honest dealings; **sharpshooter**

skilled marksman; **sharp-witted** keenly perceptive or intelligent. □ **sharpen** verb; **sharpener** noun; **sharply** adverb; **sharpness** noun.

**sharper** noun swindler, esp. at cards.

**shatter** /ˈʃætə/ verb break suddenly in pieces; severely damage, destroy; (esp. in passive) severely upset; (usually as **shattered** adjective) colloquial exhaust.

**shave** ● verb (**-ving**; past participle **shaved** or (as adjective) **shaven**) remove (hair, bristles) with razor; remove hair with razor from (leg, head, etc.) or from face of (person); reduce by small amount; pare (wood etc.) to shape it; miss or pass narrowly. ● noun shaving, being shaved; narrow miss or escape.

**shaver** noun thing that shaves; electric razor; colloquial young lad.

**shaving** noun (esp. in plural) thin paring of wood.

**shawl** noun large usually rectangular piece of fabric worn over shoulders etc. or wrapped round baby.

**she** pronoun (as subject of verb) the female person or animal in question.

**s/he** pronoun: written representation of 'he or she'.

**sheaf** ● noun (plural **sheaves**) bundle of things laid lengthways together and usually tied, esp. reaped corn or collection of papers. ● verb make into sheaves.

**shear** ● verb (past **sheared**; past participle **shorn** or **sheared**) clip wool off (sheep etc.); remove by cutting; cut with scissors, shears, etc.; strip bare, deprive; (often + of) distort, be distorted, or break. ● noun strain produced by pressure in structure of substance; (in plural) (also **pair of shears** singular) scissor-shaped clipping or cutting instrument. □ **shearer** noun.

**sheath** /ʃiːθ/ noun (plural **-s** /ʃiːðz/) close-fitting cover, esp. for blade; condom. □ **sheath knife** dagger-like knife carried in sheath.

**sheathe** /ʃiːð/ verb (**-thing**) put into sheath; encase or protect with sheath.

**sheaves** plural of SHEAF.

**shebeen** /ʃɪˈbiːn/ noun esp. Irish unlicensed drinking place.

**shed**[1] noun one-storeyed building for storage or shelter or as workshop etc.

**shed²** *verb* (**-dd-;** *past & past participle* **shed**) let, or cause to, fall off; take off (clothes); reduce (electrical power load); cause to fall or flow; disperse, diffuse, radiate; get rid of.

**she'd** /ʃiːd/ she had; she would.

**sheen** *noun* lustre, brightness.

**sheep** *noun* (*plural* same) mammal with thick woolly coat, esp. kept for its wool or meat; timid, silly, or easily-led person; (usually in *plural*) member of minister's congregation. □ **sheep-dip** preparation or place for cleansing sheep of vermin etc.; **sheepdog** dog trained to guard and herd sheep, dog of breed suitable for this; **sheepfold** enclosure for sheep; **sheepshank** knot for temporarily shortening rope; **sheepskin** sheep's skin with wool on.

**sheepish** *adjective* embarrassed or shy; ashamed. □ **sheepishly** *adverb.*

**sheer¹** ● *adjective* mere, complete; (of cliff etc.) perpendicular; (of textile) diaphanous. ● *adverb* directly, perpendicularly.

**sheer²** *verb* swerve or change course; (often + *away, off*) turn away, esp. from person that one dislikes or fears.

**sheet¹** ● *noun* rectangular piece of cotton etc. as part of bedclothes; broad thin flat piece of paper, metal, etc.; wide expanse of water, ice, flame, etc. ● *verb* cover (as) with sheet; (of rain etc.) fall in sheets. □ **sheet metal** metal rolled or hammered etc. into thin sheets; **sheet music** music published in separate sheets.

**sheet²** *noun* rope at lower corner of sail to control it. □ **sheet anchor** emergency anchor, person or thing depended on as last hope.

**sheikh** /ʃeɪk/ *noun* chief or head of Arab tribe, family, or village; Muslim leader.

**sheila** /ˈʃiːlə/ *noun* *Australian & NZ offensive slang* girl, young woman.

**shekel** /ˈʃek(ə)l/ *noun* chief monetary unit of Israel; *historical* weight and coin in ancient Israel etc.; (in *plural*) *colloquial* money.

**shelduck** /ˈʃeldʌk/ *noun* (*plural* same or **-s**; *masculine* **sheldrake**, *plural* same or **-s**) brightly coloured wild duck.

**shelf** *noun* (*plural* **shelves**) wooden etc. board projecting from wall or forming part of bookcase or cupboard; ledge on cliff face etc.; reef, sandbank. □ **on the shelf** (of woman) considered past marriageable age, put aside; **shelf-life** time for which stored thing remains usable; **shelf-mark** code on book to show its place in library.

**shell** ● *noun* hard outer case of many molluscs, tortoise, egg, nut-kernel, seed, etc.; explosive artillery projectile; hollow container for fireworks, cartridges, etc.; light racing boat; framework of vehicle etc.; walls of unfinished or gutted building etc. ● *verb* remove shell or pod from; fire shells at. □ **come out of one's shell** become less shy; **shellfish** aquatic mollusc with shell, crustacean; **shell out** *colloquial* pay (money); **shell-shock** nervous breakdown caused by warfare; **shell-shocked** *adjective* □ **shell-like** *adjective.*

**she'll** /ʃiːl/ she will; she shall.

**shellac** /ʃəˈlæk/ ● *noun* resin used for making varnish. ● *verb* (**-ck-**) varnish with shellac.

**shelter** /ˈʃeltə/ ● *noun* protection from danger, bad weather, etc.; place providing this. ● *verb* act or serve as shelter to; shield; take shelter.

**shelve** *verb* (**-ving**) put aside, esp. temporarily; put on shelf; provide with shelves; (of ground) slope.

**shelving** *noun* shelves; material for shelves.

**shepherd** /ˈʃepəd/ *noun* (*feminine* **shepherdess**) person who tends sheep; pastor. ● *verb* tend (sheep); marshal or guide like sheep. □ **shepherd's pie** minced meat baked with covering of (esp. mashed) potato.

**sherbet** /ˈʃɜːbət/ *noun* flavoured effervescent powder or drink.

**sherd** *noun* potsherd.

**sheriff** /ˈʃerɪf/ *noun* (also **High Sheriff**) chief executive officer of Crown in county, administering justice etc.; *US* chief law-enforcing officer of county; (also **sheriff-depute**) *Scottish* chief judge of county or district.

**sherry** /ˈʃerɪ/ *noun* (*plural* **-ies**) fortified wine originally from Spain.

**she's** /ʃiːz/ she is; she has.

**Shetland pony** /ˈʃetlənd/ *noun* pony of small hardy breed.

**shew** *archaic* = SHOW.

**shiatsu** /ʃɪˈætsu:/ *noun* Japanese therapy involving pressure on specific points of body.

**shibboleth** /ˈʃɪbəleθ/ *noun* long-standing formula, doctrine, phrase, etc. espoused by party or sect.

**shied** *past & past participle of* SHY².

**shield** /ʃi:ld/ ● *noun* piece of defensive armour held in front of body when fighting; person or thing giving protection; shield-shaped trophy; protective plate or screen in machinery etc.; representation of shield for displaying person's coat of arms. ● *verb* protect, screen.

**shier** *comparative of* SHY¹.

**shiest** *superlative of* SHY¹.

**shift** ● *verb* (cause to) change or move from one position to another; remove, esp. with effort; *slang* hurry; *US* change (gear). ● *noun* shifting; relay of workers; period for which they work; device, expedient, trick; woman's loose straight dress; displacement of spectral line; key on keyboard for switching between lower and upper case etc.; *US* gear lever in motor vehicle. □ **make shift** manage, get along; **shift for oneself** rely on one's own efforts; **shift one's ground** alter stance in argument etc.

**shiftless** *adjective* lacking resourcefulness; lazy.

**shifty** *adjective* (**-ier, -iest**) *colloquial* evasive, deceitful.

**Shiite** /ˈʃi:aɪt/ ● *noun* member of esp. Iranian branch of Islam opposed to Sunnis. ● *adjective* of this branch.

**shillelagh** /ʃɪˈleɪlɪ/ *noun* Irish cudgel.

**shilling** /ˈʃɪlɪŋ/ *noun historical* former British coin and monetary unit, worth 1/20 of pound; monetary unit in some other countries.

**shilly-shally** /ˈʃɪlɪʃælɪ/ *verb* (**-ies, -ied**) be undecided, vacillate.

**shimmer** /ˈʃɪmə/ ● *verb* shine tremulously or faintly. ● *noun* tremulous or faint light.

**shin** ● *noun* front of leg below knee; cut of beef from this part. ● *verb* (**-nn-**) (usually

+ *up, down*) climb quickly using arms and legs. □ **shin-bone** tibia.

**shindig** /ˈʃɪndɪɡ/ *noun* (also **shindy**) *colloquial* lively noisy party; brawl, disturbance.

**shine** ● *verb* (**-ning**; *past & past participle* **shone** /ʃɒn/ *or* **shined**) emit or reflect light, be bright, glow; (of sun, star, etc.) be visible; cause to shine; be brilliant, excel; (*past & past participle* **shined**) polish. ● *noun* light, brightness; polish, lustre. □ **take a shine to** *colloquial* take a liking to.

**shiner** *noun colloquial* black eye.

**shingle¹** /ˈʃɪŋɡ(ə)l/ *noun* small rounded pebbles on seashore. ● **shingly** *adjective*.

**shingle²** /ˈʃɪŋɡ(ə)l/ ● *noun* rectangular wooden tile used on roofs etc.; *archaic* shingled hair. ● *verb* (**-ling**) roof with shingles; *archaic* cut (woman's hair) short and tapering.

**shingles** /ˈʃɪŋɡ(ə)lz/ *plural noun* (usually treated as *singular*) painful viral infection of nerves with rash, esp. round waist.

**Shinto** /ˈʃɪntəʊ/ *noun* (also **Shintoism**) Japanese religion with worship of ancestors and nature-spirits.

**shinty** /ˈʃɪntɪ/ *noun* (*plural* **-ies**) game resembling hockey; stick or ball for this.

**shiny** *adjective* (**-ier, -iest**) having shine; (of clothing) with nap worn off.

**ship** ● *noun* large seagoing vessel; *US* aircraft; spaceship. ● *verb* (**-pp-**) transport, esp. in ship; take in (water) over ship's side etc.; lay (oars) at bottom of boat; fix (rudder etc.) in place; embark; be hired to work on ship. □ **shipmate** fellow member of ship's crew; **ship off** send away; **shipshape** trim, neat, tidy; **shipwreck** *noun* destruction of ship by storm or collision etc., ship so destroyed, *verb* (usually in *passive*) cause to suffer this; **shipwright** shipbuilder, ship's carpenter; **shipyard** place where ships are built.

**shipment** *noun* goods shipped; act of shipping goods etc.

**shipper** *noun* person or company that ships goods.

**shipping** *noun* transport of goods etc.; ships collectively.

**shire** /ʃaɪə/ *noun* county. □ **shire horse** heavy powerful horse.

**shirk** *verb* avoid (duty, work, etc.). □ **shirker** *noun*.

**shirr** ● *noun* elasticated gathered threads forming smocking. ● *verb* gather (material) with parallel threads. □ **shirring** *noun*.

**shirt** *noun* upper-body garment of cotton etc., usually with sleeves and collar. □ **in shirtsleeves** not wearing jacket; **shirt dress**, **shirtwaister** dress with bodice like shirt.

**shirty** *adjective* (**-ier, -iest**) *colloquial* annoyed. □ **shirtily** *adverb*; **shirtiness** *noun*.

**shish kebab** /ʃɪʃ/ *noun* pieces of meat and vegetables grilled on skewer.

**shiver**[1] /ˈʃɪvə/ ● *verb* tremble with cold, fear, etc. ● *noun* momentary shivering movement; (**the shivers**) attack of shivering. □ **shivery** *adjective*.

**shiver**[2] /ˈʃɪvə/ ● *noun* (esp. in *plural*) small fragment, splinter. ● *verb* break into shivers.

**shoal**[1] ● *noun* multitude, esp. of fish swimming together. ● *verb* form shoal(s).

**shoal**[2] ● *noun* area of shallow water; submerged sandbank. ● *verb* (of water) become shallow.

**shock**[1] ● *noun* violent collision, impact, etc.; sudden and disturbing emotional effect; acute prostration following wound, pain, etc.; electric shock; disturbance in stability of organization etc. ● *verb* horrify, outrage; cause shock; affect with electric or pathological shock. □ **shock absorber** device on vehicle etc. for absorbing shock and vibration; **shockproof** resistant to effects of shock; **shock therapy** electroconvulsive therapy; **shock wave** moving region of high air pressure caused by explosion etc.

**shock**[2] *noun* unkempt or shaggy mass of hair.

**shocker** *noun colloquial* shocking person or thing; sensational novel etc.

**shocking** *adjective* causing shock, scandalous; *colloquial* very bad. □ **shocking pink** vibrant shade of pink. □ **shockingly** *adverb*.

**shod** *past & past participle* of SHOE.

**shoddy** /ˈʃɒdɪ/ *adjective* (**-ier, -iest**) poorly made; counterfeit. □ **shoddily** *adverb*; **shoddiness** *noun*.

**shoe** /ʃuː/ ● *noun* foot-covering of leather etc., esp. one not reaching above ankle; protective metal rim for horse's hoof; thing like shoe in shape or use. ● *verb* (**shoes, shoeing**; *past & past participle* **shod**) fit with shoe(s). □ **-shod** having shoes of specified kind; **shoehorn** curved implement for easing heel into shoe; **shoelace** cord for lacing shoe; **shoestring** shoelace, *colloquial* small esp. inadequate amount of money; **shoe-tree** shaped block for keeping shoe in shape.

**shone** *past & past participle* of SHINE.

**shoo** ● *interjection used to frighten animals etc. away.* ● *verb* (**shoos, shooed**) utter such sound; (usually + *away*) drive away thus.

**shook** *past* of SHAKE.

**shoot** /ʃuːt/ ● *verb* (*past & past participle* **shot**) cause (weapon) to discharge missile; kill or wound with bullet, arrow, etc.; send out or discharge rapidly; come or go swiftly or suddenly; (of plant) put forth buds etc.; (of bud etc.) appear; hunt game etc. with gun; film, photograph; *esp. Football* score or take shot at (goal); (often + *up*) *slang* inject (drug). ● *noun* young branch or sucker; hunting party or expedition; land on which game is shot. □ **shooting gallery** place for shooting at targets with rifles etc.; **shooting star** small rapidly moving meteor; **shooting stick** walking stick with foldable seat.

**shop** ● *noun* place for retail sale of goods or services; act of shopping; place for making or repairing something; *colloquial* place of business etc. ● *verb* (**-pp-**) go to shop(s) to make purchases; *slang* inform against. □ **shop around** look for best bargain; **shop assistant** person serving in shop; **shop-floor** production area in factory etc., workers as distinct from management; **shopkeeper** owner or manager of shop; **shoplift** steal goods while appearing to shop; **shoplifter** *noun*; **shop-soiled** soiled or faded by display in shop; **shop steward** elected representative of workers in factory etc.; **shopwalker** supervisor in large shop; **talk shop** talk about one's occupation. □ **shopper** *noun*.

**shopping** noun purchase of goods; goods bought. □ **shopping centre** area containing many shops.

**shore**[1] noun land adjoining sea, lake, etc.; (usually in plural) country. □ **on shore** ashore; **shoreline** line where shore meets water.

**shore**[2] verb (-ring) (often + up) support (as if) with prop(s) or beam(s).

**shorn** past participle of SHEAR.

**short** ●adjective measuring little from end to end in space or time, or from head to foot; (usually + of, on) deficient, scanty; concise, brief; curt, uncivil; (of memory) unable to remember distant events; (of vowel or syllable) having the less of two recognized durations; (of pastry) easily crumbled; (of a drink of spirits) undiluted. ●adverb before the natural or expected time or place; abruptly; rudely. ●noun short circuit; colloquial short drink; short film. ●verb short-circuit. □ **short back and sides** short simple haircut; **shortbread**, **shortcake** rich crumbly biscuit or cake made of flour, butter, and sugar; **short-change** cheat, esp. by giving insufficient change; **short circuit** electric circuit through small resistance, esp. instead of through normal circuit; **short-circuit** cause short circuit in, have short circuit, shorten or avoid by taking short cut; **shortcoming** deficiency, defect; **short cut** path or course shorter than usual or normal; **shortfall** deficit; **shorthand** method of rapid writing using special symbols, abbreviated or symbolic means of expression; **short-handed**, **-staffed** understaffed; **shorthorn** animal of breed of cattle with short horns; **short list** list of candidates from whom final selection will be made; **short-list** put on short list; **short-lived** ephemeral; **short-range** having short range, relating to immediate future; **short shrift** curt or dismissive treatment; **short sight** inability to focus except at close range; **short-tempered** easily angered; **short-term** of or for a short period of time; **short-winded** easily becoming breathless. □ **shorten** verb.

**shortage** noun (often + of) deficiency; lack.

**shortening** noun fat for pastry.

**shortly** adverb (often + before, after) soon; curtly.

**shorts** plural noun trousers reaching to knees or higher; US underpants.

**short-sighted** adjective having short sight; lacking imagination or foresight. □ **short-sightedly** adverb; **short-sightedness** noun.

**shot**[1] noun firing of gun etc.; attempt to hit by shooting or throwing etc.; single missile for gun etc.; (plural same or -s) small lead pellet of which several are used for single charge; (treated as plural) these collectively; photograph, film sequence; stroke or kick in ball game; colloquial attempt, guess; person of specified skill in shooting; heavy metal ball thrown in shot-put; colloquial drink of spirits; injection of drug etc. □ **shotgun** gun for firing small shot at short range; **shotgun wedding** colloquial wedding enforced because of bride's pregnancy; **shot-put** athletic contest in which shot is thrown; **shot-putter** noun.

**shot**[2] ●past & past participle of SHOOT. ●adjective woven so as to show different colours at different angles.

**should** /ʃʊd/ auxiliary verb (3rd singular present **should**) used in reported speech; expressing obligation, likelihood, or tentative suggestion; used to form conditional clause or (in 1st person) conditional mood.

**shoulder** /ˈʃəʊldə/ ●noun part of body to which arm, foreleg, or wing is attached; either of two projections below neck; animal's upper foreleg as joint of meat; (also in plural) shoulder regarded as supportive, comforting, etc.; strip of land next to road; part of garment covering shoulder. ●verb push with shoulder; make one's way thus; take on (burden, responsibility, etc.). □ **shoulder blade** either flat bone of upper back; **shoulder-length** (of hair etc.) reaching to shoulders; **shoulder pad** pad in garment to bulk out shoulder; **shoulder strap** strap going over shoulder from front to back of garment, strap suspending bag etc. from shoulder.

**shouldn't** /ˈʃʊd(ə)nt/ should not.

**shout** /ʃaʊt/ ●verb speak or cry loudly; say or express loudly. ●noun loud cry calling attention or expressing joy, defiance, approval, etc. □ **shout down** reduce to silence by shouting.

**shove** /ʃʌv/ ● verb (**-ving**) push, esp. vigorously or roughly; colloquial put casually. ● noun act of shoving. □ **shove-halfpenny** form of shovelboard played with coins etc. on table; **shove off** start from shore, mooring, etc. in boat, slang depart.

**shovel** /ʃʌv(ə)l/ ● noun spadelike scoop used to shift earth or coal etc. ● verb (**-ll-**; US **-l-**) move (as) with shovel. □ **shovelboard** game played esp. on ship's deck by pushing discs over marked surface.

**shoveller** /ʃʌvələ/ noun (also **shoveler**) duck with shovel-like beak.

**show** /ʃəʊ/ ● verb (past participle **shown** or **showed**) be, or allow or cause to be, seen; manifest; offer for inspection; express (one's feelings); accord, grant (favour, mercy, etc.); (of feelings etc.) be manifest; instruct by example; demonstrate, make understood; exhibit; (often + in, round, etc.) conduct, lead; colloquial appear, arrive. ● noun showing; spectacle, exhibition, display; public entertainment or performance; outward appearance, impression produced; ostentation, mere display; colloquial undertaking, business. □ **good** (or **bad** or **poor**) **show!** colloquial that was well (or badly) done; **showbiz** colloquial show business; **show business** colloquial the entertainment profession; **showcase** glass case or event etc. for displaying goods or exhibits; **showdown** final test or confrontation; **show house**, **flat** furnished and decorated new house or flat on show to prospective buyers; **showjumping** competitive jumping on horseback; **show off** display to advantage, colloquial act pretentiously; **show-off** colloquial person who shows off; **show-piece** excellent specimen suitable for display; **showroom** room where goods are displayed for sale; **show trial** judicial trial designed to frighten or impress the public; **show up** make or be visible or conspicuous, expose, humiliate, colloquial appear or arrive; **show willing** show willingness to help etc.

**shower** /ʃaʊə/ ● noun brief fall of rain, snow, etc.; brisk flurry of bullets, dust,

etc.; sudden copious arrival of gifts, honours, etc.; (in full **shower-bath**) bath in which water is sprayed from above. ● verb descend, send, or give in shower; take shower-bath; (+ upon, with) bestow lavishly. □ **showery** adjective.

**showing** noun display; quality of performance, achievement, etc.; evidence; putting of case etc.

**shown** past participle of SHOW.

**showy** adjective (**-ier**, **-iest**) gaudy; striking. □ **showily** adverb; **showiness** noun.

**shrank** past of SHRINK.

**shrapnel** /ʃræpn(ə)l/ noun fragments of exploded bomb etc.

**shred** ● noun scrap, fragment; least amount. ● verb (**-dd-**) tear, cut, etc. to shreds. □ **shredder** noun.

**shrew** noun small long-snouted mouse-like animal; bad-tempered or scolding woman. □ **shrewish** adjective.

**shrewd** adjective astute; clever. □ **shrewdly** adverb; **shrewdness** noun.

**shriek** ● noun shrill cry or sound. ● verb make a shriek; say in shrill tones.

**shrike** noun bird with strong hooked beak.

**shrill** ● adjective piercing and high-pitched. ● verb sound or utter shrilly. □ **shrillness** noun; **shrilly** adverb.

**shrimp** noun (plural same or **-s**) small edible crustacean; colloquial very small person.

**shrine** noun sacred or revered place; casket or tomb holding relics.

**shrink** ● verb (past **shrank**; past participle **shrunk** or (esp. as adjective) **shrunken**) become or make smaller, esp. by action of moisture, heat, or cold; (usually + from) recoil, flinch. ● noun slang psychiatrist. □ **shrink-wrap** wrap (article) in material that shrinks tightly round it.

**shrinkage** noun process or degree of shrinking; allowance for loss by theft or wastage.

**shrivel** /ʃrɪv(ə)l/ verb (**-ll-**; US **-l-**) contract into wrinkled or dried-up state.

**shroud** /ʃraʊd/ ● noun wrapping for corpse; something which conceals; rope supporting mast. ● verb clothe (corpse) for burial; cover, disguise.

**Shrove Tuesday** /ʃrəʊv/ noun day before Ash Wednesday.

**shrub** noun woody plant smaller than tree and usually branching from near ground. □ **shrubby** adjective.

**shrubbery** noun ( plural **-ies**) area planted with shrubs.

**shrug** ● verb (**-gg-**) draw up (shoulders) momentarily as gesture of indifference, ignorance, etc. ● noun shrugging movement.

**shrunk** (also **shrunken**) past participle of SHRINK.

**shudder** /'ʃʌdə/ ● verb shiver from fear, cold, etc.; feel strong repugnance, fear, etc.; vibrate. ● noun act of shuddering.

**shuffle** /'ʃʌf(ə)l/ ● verb (**-ling**) drag or slide (feet) in walking; mix up or rearrange (esp. cards); be evasive; keep shifting one's position. ● noun shuffling action or movement; change of relative positions; shuffling dance. □ **shuffle off** remove, get rid of.

**shufti** /'ʃʊftɪ/ noun ( plural **-s**) colloquial look, glimpse.

**shun** verb (**-nn-**) avoid, keep clear of.

**shunt** ● verb move (train etc.) to another track; (of train) be shunted; redirect. ● noun shunting, being shunted; conductor joining two points in electric circuit for diversion of current; slang collision of vehicles.

**shush** /ʃʊʃ/ interjection & verb hush.

**shut** verb (**-tt-**; past & past participle **shut**) move (door, window, lid, etc.) into position to block opening; become or be capable of being shut; shut door etc. of; become or make closed for trade; fold or contract (book, hand, telescope); bar access to (place). □ **shut down** close, cease working; **shut-eye** colloquial sleep; **shut off** stop flow of (water, gas, etc.), separate; **shut out** exclude, screen from view, prevent; **shut up** close all doors and windows of, imprison, put away in box etc., (esp. in imperative) colloquial stop talking.

**shutter** ● noun movable hinged cover for window; device for exposing film in camera. ● verb provide or close with shutter(s).

**shuttle** /'ʃʌt(ə)l/ ● noun part of loom which carries weft-thread between threads of warp; thread-carrier for lower thread in sewing machine; train, bus, aircraft, etc. used in shuttle service; space shuttle. ● verb (**-ling**) (cause to) move to and fro like shuttle. □ **shuttlecock** cork with ring of feathers, or similar plastic device, struck to and fro in badminton; **shuttle diplomacy** negotiations conducted by mediator travelling between disputing parties; **shuttle service** transport system operating to and fro over short distance.

**shy**[1] ● adjective (**-er**, **-est**) timid and nervous in company; self-conscious; easily startled. ● verb (**shies**, **shied**) (usually + at) (esp. of horse) start back or aside in fright. ● noun sudden startled movement. □ **-shy** showing fear or dislike of. □ **shyly** adverb; **shyness** noun.

**shy**[2] ● verb (**shies**, **shied**) throw, fling. ● noun ( plural **shies**) throw, fling.

**shyster** /'ʃaɪstə/ noun colloquial person who acts unscrupulously or unprofessionally.

**SI** abbreviation international system of units of measurement (Système International).

**si** /siː/ noun Music te.

**Siamese** /saɪə'miːz/ ● noun ( plural same) native or language of Siam (now Thailand); (in full **Siamese cat**) cat of cream-coloured dark-faced short-haired breed with blue eyes. ● adjective of Siam. □ **Siamese twins** twins joined together at birth.

**sibilant** /'sɪbɪlənt/ ● adjective hissing, sounded with hiss. ● noun sibilant speech sound or letter. □ **sibilance** noun.

**sibling** /'sɪblɪŋ/ noun each of two or more children having one or both parents in common.

**sibyl** /'sɪbɪl/ noun pagan prophetess.

**sic** adverb used or spelt thus (confirming form of quoted words). [Latin]

**sick** ● adjective vomiting, disposed to vomit; esp. US ill, unwell; (often + of) colloquial disgusted, surfeited; colloquial (of humour) cruel, morbid, perverted, offensive. ● noun colloquial vomit. ● verb (esp. + up) colloquial vomit. □ **sickbay** place for sick people; **sickbed** invalid's bed; **sick leave** leave granted because of illness; **sick pay** pay given during sick leave.

**sicken** verb make or become sick, disgusted, etc.; ( often + for) show symptoms of illness; (as **sickening** adjective) disgusting, *colloquial* very annoying. □ **sickeningly** *adverb*.

**sickle** /'sɪk(ə)l/ *noun* short-handled implement with semicircular blade for reaping, lopping, etc.

**sickly** *adjective* (**-ier, -iest**) liable to be ill, weak; faint, pale; causing sickness; mawkish, weakly sentimental.

**sickness** *noun* being ill; disease; vomiting, nausea.

**side** ● *noun* each of inner or outer surfaces of object, esp. as distinct from top and bottom or front and back or ends; right or left part of person's or animal's body; part of object, place, etc. that faces specified direction or that is on observer's right or left; either surface of thing regarded as having two; aspect of question, character, etc.; each of sets of opponents in war, game, etc.; cause represented by this; part or region near edge; *colloquial* television channel; each of lines bounding triangle, rectangle, etc.; position nearer or farther than, or to right or left of, dividing line; line of descent through father or mother; spinning motion given to ball by striking it on side; *slang* swagger, assumption of superiority. ● *adjective* of, on, from, or to side; oblique, indirect; subordinate, subsidiary, not main. ● *verb* (**-ding**) take side in dispute etc.; (+ *with*) be on or join same side as. □ **on the side** as sideline, illicitly, *US* as side dish; **sideboard** table or flat-topped chest with drawers and cupboards for crockery etc.; **sideboards, sideburns** short side-whiskers; **side by side** standing close together, esp. for mutual encouragement; **sidecar** passenger car attached to side of motorcycle; **side drum** small double-headed drum; **side effect** secondary (usually undesirable) effect; **sidekick** *colloquial* close associate; **sidelight** light from side, small light at side of front of vehicle etc.; **sideline** work etc. done in addition to one's main activity, (usually in *plural*) line bounding side of sports pitch etc., space just outside these for spectators to sit; **side-saddle** *noun* saddle for woman riding with both legs on same side of horse, *adverb* sitting thus on horse; **sideshow** minor show

or stall in exhibition, fair, etc.; **sidesman** assistant churchwarden; **sidestep** *noun* step taken sideways, *verb* avoid, evade; **sidetrack** divert from course, purpose, etc.; **sidewalk** *US* pavement; **side-whiskers** hair left unshaven on cheeks; **take sides** support either of (usually) two opposing sides in argument etc.

**sidelong** ● *adjective* directed to the side. ● *adverb* to the side.

**sidereal** /saɪ'dɪərɪəl/ *adjective* of or measured or determined by stars.

**sideways** *adverb & adjective* to or from a side; with one side facing forward.

**siding** *noun* short track by side of railway line for shunting etc.

**sidle** /'saɪd(ə)l/ *verb* (**-ling**) walk timidly or furtively.

**siege** /siːdʒ/ ● *noun* surrounding and blockading of town, castle, etc. □ **lay siege to** conduct siege of; **raise siege** end it.

**siemens** /'siːmənz/ *noun* (*plural* same) SI unit of electrical conductance.

**sienna** /sɪ'enə/ *noun* kind of earth used as pigment; its colour of reddish- or yellowish-brown.

**sierra** /sɪ'erə/ *noun* long jagged mountain chain, esp. in Spain or Spanish America.

**siesta** /sɪ'estə/ *noun* afternoon nap or rest in hot countries.

**sieve** /sɪv/ ● *noun* utensil with network or perforated bottom through which liquids or fine particles can pass. ● *verb* (**-ving**) sift.

**sift** *verb* separate with or cause to pass through sieve; sprinkle through perforated container; closely examine details of, analyse; (of snow, light, etc.) fall as if from sieve.

**sigh** /saɪ/ ● *verb* emit long deep audible breath in sadness, weariness, relief, etc.; yearn; express with sighs. ● *noun* act of sighing; sound (like that) made in sighing.

**sight** /saɪt/ ● *noun* faculty of seeing; seeing, being seen; thing seen; range of vision; (usually in *plural*) notable features of a place; device assisting aim with gun or observation with telescope etc.; aim or observation so gained;

*colloquial* unsightly person or thing; *colloquial* great deal. ● *verb* get sight of; observe presence of; aim (gun etc.) with sight. □ **at first sight** on first glimpse or impression; **on, at sight** as soon as person or thing is seen; **sight-read** read (music) at sight; **sight-screen** *Cricket* large white screen placed near boundary in line with wicket to help batsman see ball; **sightseer** person visiting sights of place; **sightseeing** *noun.*

**sighted** *adjective* not blind. □ **-sighted** having specified vision.

**sightless** *adjective* blind.

**sign** /saɪn/ ● *noun* indication of quality, state, future event, etc.; mark, symbol, etc.; motion or gesture used to convey information, order, etc.; signboard; each of the 12 divisions of the zodiac. ● *verb* write one's name on (document etc.) as authorization; write (one's name) thus; communicate by gesture. □ **signboard** board bearing name, symbol, etc. displayed outside shop, inn, etc.; **sign in** sign register on arrival, get (person) admitted by signing register; **sign language** series of signs used esp. by deaf or dumb people for communication; **sign off** end contract, work, etc.; **sign on** register to obtain unemployment benefit; **sign out** sign register on departing; **signpost** post etc. showing directions of roads, *verb* provide with signpost(s); **sign up** engage (person), enlist in armed forces; **signwriter** person who paints signboards etc.

**signal**[1] /ˈsɪgn(ə)l/ ● *noun* sign, esp. prearranged one, conveying information or direction; message of such signs; event which causes immediate activity; *Electricity* transmitted impulses or radio waves; sequence of these; device on railway giving instructions or warnings to train drivers etc. ● *verb* (**-ll-**; *US* **-l-**) make signal(s) (to); (often + *to do*) transmit, announce, or direct by signal(s). □ **signal-box** building from which railway signals are controlled; **signalman** railway signal operator.

**signal**[2] /ˈsɪgn(ə)l/ *adjective* remarkable, noteworthy. □ **signally** *adverb.*

**signalize** *verb* (also **-ise**) (**-zing** or **-sing**) make conspicuous or remarkable; indicate.

**signatory** /ˈsɪgnətərɪ/ ● *noun* (*plural* **-ies**) party that has signed an agreement, esp. a treaty. ● *adjective* having signed such an agreement.

**signature** /ˈsɪgnətʃə/ *noun* person's name or initials used in signing; act of signing; *Music* key signature, time signature; section of book made from one sheet folded and cut. □ **signature tune** tune used esp. in broadcasting to announce a particular programme, performer, etc.

**signet** /ˈsɪgnɪt/ *noun* small seal. □ **signet ring** ring with seal set in it.

**significance** /sɪgˈnɪfɪkəns/ *noun* importance; meaning; being significant; extent to which result deviates from hypothesis such that difference is due to more than errors in sampling.

**significant** /sɪgˈnɪfɪkənt/ *adjective* having or conveying meaning; important. □ **significant figure** *Mathematics* digit conveying information about a number containing it. □ **significantly** *adverb.*

**signify** /ˈsɪgnɪfaɪ/ *verb* (**-ies**, **-ied**) be sign or symbol of; represent, mean, denote; make known; be of importance, matter. □ **signification** *noun.*

**signor** /ˈsiːnjɔː/ *noun* (*plural* **-i** /-ˈnjɔːriː/) title used of or to Italian man.

**signora** /siːˈnjɔːrə/ *noun* title used of or to Italian esp. married woman.

**signorina** /siːnjəˈriːnə/ *noun* title used of or to Italian unmarried woman.

**Sikh** /siːk/ *noun* member of Indian monotheistic sect.

**silage** /ˈsaɪlɪdʒ/ *noun* green fodder stored in silo; storage in silo.

**silence** /ˈsaɪləns/ ● *noun* absence of sound; abstinence from speech or noise; neglect or omission to mention, write, etc. ● *verb* (**-cing**) make silent, esp. by force or superior argument.

**silencer** *noun* device for reducing noise made by gun, vehicle's exhaust, etc.

**silent** /ˈsaɪlənt/ *adjective* not speaking; making or accompanied by little or no sound. □ **silently** *adverb.*

**silhouette** /sɪluːˈet/ ● *noun* dark outline or shadow in profile against lighter background; contour, outline, profile; portrait in profile showing outline only, usually cut from paper or in black on white. ● *verb* (**-tting**) represent or show in silhouette.

**silica** /ˈsɪlɪkə/ *noun* silicon dioxide, occurring as quartz and as main constituent of sand etc. □ **siliceous** /sɪˈlɪʃəs/ *adjective*.

**silicate** /ˈsɪlɪkeɪt/ *noun* compound of metal(s), silicon, and oxygen.

**silicon** /ˈsɪlɪkən/ *noun* non-metallic element occurring in silica and silicates. □ **silicon chip** silicon microchip.

**silicone** /ˈsɪlɪkəʊn/ *noun* any organic compound of silicon with high resistance to cold, heat, water, etc.

**silicosis** /sɪlɪˈkəʊsɪs/ *noun* lung disease caused by inhaling dust containing silica.

**silk** *noun* fine strong soft lustrous fibre produced by silkworms; thread or cloth made from this; (in *plural*) cloth or garments of silk; *colloquial* Queen's Counsel. □ **silk-screen printing** screen printing; **silkworm** caterpillar which spins cocoon of silk; **take silk** become Queen's Counsel.

**silken** *adjective* of or resembling silk; soft, smooth, lustrous.

**silky** *adjective* (**-ier**, **-iest**) like silk in smoothness, softness, etc.; suave. □ **silkily** *adverb*.

**sill** *noun* slab of wood, stone, etc. at base of window or doorway.

**silly** /ˈsɪlɪ/ ● *adjective* (**-ier**, **-iest**) foolish, imprudent; weak-minded; *Cricket* (of fielder or position) very close to batsman. ● *noun* (*plural* **-ies**) *colloquial* silly person. □ **silliness** *noun*.

**silo** /ˈsaɪləʊ/ *noun* (*plural* **-s**) pit or airtight structure in which green crops are stored for fodder; tower or pit for storage of grain, cement, etc.; underground storage chamber for guided missile.

**silt** ● *noun* sediment in channel, harbour, etc. ● *verb* (often + *up*) block or be blocked with silt.

**silvan** = SYLVAN.

**silver** /ˈsɪlvə/ ● *noun* greyish-white lustrous precious metal; coins or articles made of or looking like this; colour of silver. ● *adjective* of or coloured like silver. ● *verb* coat or plate with silver; provide (mirror-glass) with backing of tin amalgam etc.; make silvery; turn grey or white. □ **silver birch** common birch with silvery white bark; **silverfish** (*plural* same or **-es**) small silvery wingless insect, silver-coloured fish; **silver jubilee** 25th anniversary of reign; **silver medal** medal awarded as second prize; **silver paper** aluminium foil; **silver plate** articles plated with silver; **silver-plated** plated with silver; **silver sand** fine pure kind used in gardening; **silver screen** (usually **the silver screen**) cinema films collectively; **silverside** upper side of round of beef; **silversmith** worker in silver; **silver wedding** 25th anniversary of wedding.

**silvery** *adjective* like silver in colour or appearance; having clear soft ringing sound.

**simian** /ˈsɪmɪən/ ● *adjective* of anthropoid apes; resembling ape, monkey. ● *noun* ape or monkey.

**similar** /ˈsɪmɪlə/ *adjective* like, alike; (often + *to*) having resemblance. □ **similarity** /-ˈlær-/ *noun* (*plural* **-ies**); **similarly** *adverb*.

**simile** /ˈsɪmɪlɪ/ *noun* esp. poetical comparison of two things using *like* or *as* (see panel).

**similitude** /sɪˈmɪlɪtjuːd/ *noun* guise, appearance; comparison or its expression.

**simmer** /ˈsɪmə/ ● *verb* be or keep just below boiling point; be in state of suppressed anger or laughter. ● *noun* simmering state. □ **simmer down** become less agitated.

**simnel cake** /ˈsɪmn(ə)l/ *noun* rich fruit cake, usually with almond paste.

**simony** /ˈsaɪmənɪ/ *noun* buying or selling of ecclesiastical privileges.

**simoom** /sɪˈmuːm/ *noun* hot dry dust-laden desert wind.

**simper** /ˈsɪmpə/ ● *verb* smile in silly affected way; utter with simper. ● *noun* such smile.

**simple** /ˈsɪmp(ə)l/ *adjective* (**-r**, **-st**) easily understood or done, presenting no difficulty; not complicated or elaborate; plain; not compound or complex; absolute, unqualified, straightforward; foolish, feeble-minded. □ **simple-minded** foolish, feeble-minded. □ **simpleness** *noun*.

**simpleton** /ˈsɪmpəlt(ə)n/ *noun* stupid or gullible person.

**simplicity** /sɪmˈplɪsɪtɪ/ *noun* fact or condition of being simple.

**simplify** /ˈsɪmplɪfaɪ/ *verb* (**-ies, -ied**) make simple or simpler. □ **simplification** *noun*.

**simplistic** /sɪmˈplɪstɪk/ *adjective* excessively or affectedly simple. □ **simplistically** *adverb*.

**simply** *adverb* in a simple way; absolutely; merely.

**simulate** /ˈsɪmjʊleɪt/ *verb* (**-ting**) pretend to be, have, or feel; counterfeit; reproduce conditions of (situation etc.), e.g. for training. □ **simulation** *noun*, **simulator** *noun*.

**simultaneous** /sɪmalˈteɪnɪəs/ *adjective* (often + *with*) occurring or operating at same time. □ **simultaneity** /-tə'neɪɪtɪ/ *noun*, **simultaneously** *adverb*.

**sin** ● *noun* breaking of divine or moral law; offence against good taste etc. ● *verb* (**-nn-**) commit sin; (+ *against*) offend. □ **sinner** *noun*.

**since** ● *preposition* throughout or within period after. ● *conjunction* during or in time after; because. ● *adverb* from that time or event until now.

**sincere** /sɪnˈsɪə/ *adjective* (**-r, -st**) free from pretence, genuine, honest, frank. □ **sincerity** /-ˈser-/ *noun*.

**sincerely** *adverb* in a sincere way. □ **Yours sincerely** *written before signature at end of informal letter*.

**sine** *noun* ratio of side opposite angle (in right-angled triangle) to hypotenuse.

**sinecure** /ˈsaɪnɪkjʊə/ *noun* position that requires little or no work but usually yields profit or honour.

*sine die* /ˈsɪneɪ ˈdiːeɪ/ *adverb formal* indefinitely. [Latin]

*sine qua non* /ˈsɪneɪ kwɑː ˈnəʊn/ *noun* indispensable condition or qualification. [Latin]

**sinew** /ˈsɪnjuː/ *noun* tough fibrous tissue joining muscle to bone; tendon; (in *plural*) muscles, strength; framework of thing. □ **sinewy** *adjective*.

**sinful** *adjective* committing or involving sin. □ **sinfully** *adverb*; **sinfulness** *noun*.

**sing** *verb* (*past* **sang**; *past participle* **sung**) utter musical sounds, esp. words in set tune; utter (song, tune); (of wind, kettle, etc.) hum, buzz, or whistle; *slang* become informer; (+ *of*) *literary* celebrate in verse. □ **sing out** shout; **singsong** *noun* session of informal singing, *adjective* (of voice) monotonously rising and falling. □ **singer** *noun*.

**singe** /sɪndʒ/ ● *verb* (**-geing**) burn superficially; burn off tips or edges of (esp. hair). ● *noun* superficial burn.

**single** /ˈsɪŋɡ(ə)l/ ● *adjective* one only, not double or multiple; united, undivided; of or for one person or thing; solitary; taken separately; unmarried; (with negative or in questions) even one. ● *noun* single thing, esp. room in hotel; (in full **single ticket**) ticket for one-way journey; pop record with one piece of music on each side; *Cricket* hit for one run; (usually in *plural*) game with one player on each side. ● *verb* (**-ling**) (+ *out*) choose for special attention. □ **single-breasted** (of coat etc.) with only one vertical row of buttons, and overlapping little at the front; **single-decker** bus with only one

---

## Simile

A simile is a figure of speech involving the comparison of one thing with another of a different kind, using *as* or *like*, e.g.

> *The water was as clear as glass.*
> *Cherry blossom lay like driven snow upon the lawn.*

Everyday language is rich in similes:

| with *as*: | as like as two peas | as poor as a church mouse |
| | as strong as an ox | as rich as Croesus |
| with *like*: | spread like wildfire | run like the wind |
| | sell like hot cakes | like a bull in a china shop |

deck; **single file** line of people one behind another; **single-handed** without help; **single-handedly** *adverb*; **single-minded** intent on only one aim; **single parent** parent bringing up child or children alone. □ **singly** /'sɪŋglɪ/ *adverb*.

**singlet** /'sɪŋglɪt/ *noun* sleeveless vest.

**singleton** /'sɪŋgəlt(ə)n/ *noun* player's only card of particular suit.

**singular** /'sɪŋgjʊlə/ ● *adjective* unique; outstanding; extraordinary, strange; *Grammar* denoting one person or thing. ● *noun Grammar* singular word or form. □ **singularity** /-'lær-/ *noun* (*plural* **-ies**); **singularly** *adverb*.

**Sinhalese** /sɪnhə'liːz/ ● *noun* (*plural* same) member of a people from N. India now forming majority of population of Sri Lanka; their language. ● *adjective* of this people or language.

**sinister** /'sɪnɪstə/ *adjective* suggestive of evil; wicked, criminal; ominous; *Heraldry* on left side of shield etc. (i.e. to observer's right).

**sink** ● *verb* (*past* **sank** or **sunk**; *past participle* **sunk** or (as *adjective*) **sunken**) fall or come slowly downwards; disappear below horizon; go or penetrate below surface of liquid; go to bottom of sea etc.; settle down; decline in strength and vitality; descend in pitch or volume; cause or allow to sink or penetrate; cause failure of; dig (well), bore (shaft); engrave (die); invest (money); cause (ball) to enter pocket at billiards or hole at golf etc. ● *noun* plumbed-in basin, esp. in kitchen; place where foul liquid collects; place of vice. □ **sinking fund** money set aside for eventual repayment of debt.

**sinker** *noun* weight used to sink fishing or sounding line.

**Sino-** /'saɪnəʊ/ *combining form* Chinese.

**sinology** /saɪ'nɒlədʒɪ/ *noun* study of China and its language, history, etc. □ **sinologist** *noun*.

**sinuous** /'sɪnjʊəs/ *adjective* with many curves, undulating. □ **sinuosity** /-'ɒs-/ *noun*.

**sinus** /'saɪnəs/ *noun* either of cavities in skull communicating with nostrils.

**sinusitis** /saɪnə'saɪtɪs/ *noun* inflammation of sinus.

**sip** ● *verb* (**-pp-**) drink in small mouthfuls. ● *noun* small mouthful of liquid; act of taking this.

**siphon** /'saɪf(ə)n/ ● *noun* tube shaped like inverted V or U with unequal legs, used for transferring liquid from one container to another by atmospheric pressure; bottle from which fizzy water is forced by pressure of gas. ● *verb* (often + *off*) conduct or flow through siphon, divert or set aside (funds etc.).

**sir** /sɜː/ *noun* polite form of address or reference to a man; (**Sir**) title used before forename of knight or baronet.

**sire** ● *noun* male parent of animal, esp. stallion; *archaic* form of address to king; *archaic* father or other male ancestor. ● *verb* (**-ring**) beget.

**siren** /'saɪərən/ *noun* device for making loud prolonged signal or warning sound; *Greek Mythology* woman or winged creature whose singing lured unwary sailors on to rocks; dangerously fascinating woman.

**sirloin** /'sɜːlɔɪn/ *noun* best part of loin of beef.

**sirocco** /sɪ'rɒkəʊ/ *noun* (*plural* **-s**) Saharan simoom; hot moist wind in S. Europe.

**sisal** /'saɪs(ə)l/ *noun* fibre from leaves of agave.

**siskin** /'sɪskɪn/ *noun* small songbird.

**sissy** /'sɪsɪ/ (also **cissy**) *colloquial* ● *noun* (*plural* **-ies**) effeminate or cowardly person. ● *adjective* (**-ier**, **-iest**) effeminate; cowardly.

**sister** /'sɪstə/ *noun* woman or girl in relation to her siblings; female fellow member of trade union, sect, human race, etc.; member of female religious order; senior female nurse. □ **sister-in-law** (*plural* **sisters-in-law**) husband's or wife's sister, brother's wife. □ **sisterly** *adjective*.

**sisterhood** *noun* relationship (as) of sisters; society of women bound by monastic vows or devoting themselves to religious or charitable work; community of feeling among women.

**sit** *verb* (**-tt-**; *past* & *past participle* **sat**) support body by resting buttocks on ground, seat, etc.; cause to sit; place in sitting position; (of bird) perch or remain on nest to hatch eggs; (of animal) rest with hind legs bent and buttocks on ground; (of parliament, court, etc.) be in session; (usually + *for*) pose (for portrait); (+ *for*) be MP for (constituency); (often + *for*) take (exam). □ **be sitting pretty** be comfortably placed; **sit back** relax one's efforts; **sit down** sit after standing, cause to sit, (+ *under*) suffer tamely (humiliation etc.); **sit in** occupy place as protest; **sit-in** *noun*; **sit in on** be present as guest etc. at (meeting); **sit on** be member of (committee etc.), *colloquial* delay action about, *slang* repress or snub; **sit out** take no part in (dance etc.), stay till end of, sit outdoors; **sit tight** *colloquial* remain firmly in one's place, not yield; **sit up** rise from lying to sitting, sit firmly upright, defer going to bed, *colloquial* become interested, aroused, etc.; **sit-up** physical exercise of sitting up from supine position without using arms or hands.

**sitar** /'sɪtɑː/ *noun* long-necked Indian lute.

**sitcom** /'sɪtkɒm/ *noun colloquial* situation comedy.

**site** ●*noun* ground chosen or used for town or building; ground set apart for some purpose. ●*verb* (**-ting**) locate, place.

**sitter** *noun* person who sits for portrait etc.; babysitter.

**sitting** ●*noun* continuous period spent engaged in an activity; time during which assembly is engaged in business; session in which meal is served. ●*adjective* having sat down; (of animal or bird) still; (of MP etc.) current. □ **sitting-room** room in which to sit and relax.

**situ** see IN SITU.

**situate** /'sɪtjʊeɪt/ *verb* (**-ting**) (usually in *passive*) place or put in position, situation, etc.

**situation** *noun* place and its surroundings; circumstances; position; state of affairs; *formal* paid job. □ **situation comedy** broadcast comedy series involving characters dealing with awkward esp. domestic or everyday situations. □ **situational** *adjective*.

**six** *adjective & noun* one more than five; *Cricket* hit scoring six runs. □ **hit, knock for six** *colloquial* utterly surprise or defeat.

**sixpence** /'sɪkspəns/ *noun* sum of 6 (esp. old) pence; *historical* coin worth this.

**sixpenny** /'sɪkspəni/ *adjective* costing or worth 6 (esp. old) pence.

**sixteen** /sɪks'tiːn/ *adjective & noun* one more than fifteen. □ **sixteenth** *adjective & noun*.

**sixth** ●*adjective & noun* next after fifth; any of 6 equal parts of thing. □ **sixth form** form in secondary school for pupils over 16; **sixth-form college** separate college for pupils over 16; **sixth sense** supposed intuitive or extrasensory faculty.

**sixty** /'sɪkstɪ/ *adjective & noun* (*plural* **-ies**) six times ten. □ **sixtieth** *adjective & noun*.

**sizable** = SIZEABLE.

**size**[1] ●*noun* relative bigness or extent of a thing; dimensions, magnitude; each of classes into which things are divided by size. ●*verb* (**-zing**) sort in sizes or by size. □ **size up** *colloquial* form judgement of.

**size**[2] ●*noun* sticky solution used for glazing paper and stiffening textiles etc. ●*verb* (**-zing**) treat with size.

**sizeable** *adjective* (also **sizable**) fairly large.

**sizzle** /'sɪz(ə)l/ ●*verb* (**-ling**) sputter or hiss, esp. in frying. ●*noun* sizzling sound. □ **sizzling** *adjective & adverb*.

**SJ** *abbreviation* Society of Jesus.

**skate**[1] ●*noun* ice-skate; roller-skate. ●*verb* (**-ting**) move, glide, or perform (as) on skates; (+ *over*) refer fleetingly to, disregard. □ **skateboard** *noun* short narrow board on roller-skate wheels for riding on standing up, *verb* ride on skateboard. □ **skater** *noun*.

**skate**[2] *noun* (*plural* same or **-s**) large edible marine flatfish.

**skedaddle** /skɪ'dæd(ə)l/ *verb* (**-ling**) *colloquial* run away, retreat hastily.

**skein** /skeɪn/ *noun* quantity of yarn etc. coiled and usually loosely twisted; flock of wild geese etc. in flight.

**skeleton** /'skelɪt(ə)n/ ●*noun* hard framework of bones etc. of animal; supporting framework or structure of thing; very thin person or animal; useless or dead remnant; outline sketch. ●*adjective* having only essential or minimum number of people, parts, etc.

□ **skeleton key** key fitting many locks.
□ **skeletal** *adjective.*

**skerry** /'skɛrɪ/ *noun* (*plural* **-ies**) *Scottish* reef, rocky islet.

**sketch** ● *noun* rough or unfinished drawing or painting; rough draft, general outline; short usually humorous play. ● *verb* make or give sketch of; make sketches.

**sketchy** *adjective* (**-ier**, **-iest**) giving only a rough outline; *colloquial* insubstantial or imperfect, esp. through haste. □ **sketchily** *adverb.*

**skew** ● *adjective* oblique, slanting, set askew. ● *noun* slant. ● *verb* make skew; distort; move obliquely.

**skewbald** /'skju:bɔ:ld/ ● *adjective* (of animal) with irregular patches of white and another colour. ● *noun* skewbald animal, esp. horse.

**skewer** /'skju:ə/ *noun* long pin for holding meat compactly together while cooking. ● *verb* fasten together or pierce (as) with skewer.

**ski** /ski:/ ● *noun* (*plural* **-s**) each of pair of long narrow pieces of wood etc. fastened under feet for travelling over snow; similar device under vehicle. ● *verb* (**skis**, **ski'd** or **skied** /ski:d/; **skiing**) travel on skis. □ **skier** *noun.*

**skid** ● *verb* (**-dd-**) (of vehicle etc.) slide esp. sideways or obliquely on slippery road etc.; cause (vehicle) to skid. ● *noun* act of skidding; runner used as part of landing-gear of aircraft. □ **skid-pan** slippery surface for drivers to practise control of skidding; **skid row** *US slang* district frequented by vagrants.

**skiff** *noun* light boat, esp. for rowing or sculling.

**skilful** /'skɪlfʊl/ *adjective* (*US* **skillful**) having or showing skill. □ **skilfully** *adverb.*

**skill** *noun* practised ability, expertness, technique; craft, art, etc. requiring skill.

**skilled** *adjective* skilful; (of work or worker) requiring or having skill or special training.

**skillet** /'skɪlɪt/ *noun* long-handled metal cooking pot; *US* frying-pan.

**skim** *verb* (**-mm-**) take scum or cream etc. from surface of (liquid); barely touch (surface) in passing over; (often + *over*) deal with or treat (matter)

superficially; (often + *over*, *along*) glide lightly; read or look over superficially. □ **skim**, **skimmed milk** milk with cream removed.

**skimp** *verb* (often + *on*) economize; supply meagrely, use too little of.

**skimpy** *adjective* (**-ier**, **-iest**) meagre, insufficient.

**skin** ● *noun* flexible covering of body; skin removed from animal, material made from this; complexion; outer layer or covering; film like skin on liquid etc.; container for liquid, made of animal's skin. ● *verb* (**-nn-**) strip skin from; graze (part of body); *slang* swindle. □ **skin-deep** superficial; **skin-diver** person who swims under water without diving suit; **skin-diving** *noun*; **skinflint** miser; **skin-graft** surgical transplanting of skin, skin thus transferred; **skintight** very close-fitting.

**skinful** *noun colloquial* enough alcohol to make one drunk.

**skinny** *adjective* (**-ier**, **-iest**) thin, emaciated.

**skint** *adjective slang* having no money.

**skip**[1] ● *verb* (**-pp-**) move along lightly, esp. by taking two hops with each foot in turn; jump lightly esp. over skipping rope; frisk; gambol; move quickly from one subject etc. to another; omit or make omissions in reading; *colloquial* not attend etc.; *colloquial* leave hurriedly. ● *noun* skipping movement or action. □ **skipping-rope** length of rope turned over head and under feet while jumping it.

**skip**[2] *noun* large container for refuse etc.; container in which men or materials are lowered or raised in mines etc.

**skipjack** *noun* (in full **skipjack tuna**) (*plural* same or **-s**) small Pacific tuna.

**skipper** /'skɪpə/ ● *noun* captain of ship, aircraft, team, etc. ● *verb* be captain of.

**skirl** ● *noun* shrill sound of bagpipes. ● *verb* make skirl.

**skirmish** /'skɜ:mɪʃ/ ● *noun* minor battle; short argument etc. ● *verb* engage in skirmish.

**skirt** ● *noun* woman's garment hanging from waist, or this part of complete dress; part of coat etc. that hangs below waist; hanging part at base of hover-craft; (in *singular* or *plural*) border, outly-ing part; flank of beef etc. ● *verb* go or be along or round edge of. □ **skirting board** narrow board etc. round bottom of room-wall.

**skit** *noun* light piece of satire, burlesque.

**skittish** /'skɪtɪʃ/ *adjective* lively, playful; (of horse etc.) nervous, inclined to shy.

**skittle** /'skɪt(ə)l/ *noun* pin used in game of skittles, in which number of wooden pins are set up to be bowled or knocked down.

**skive** *verb* (**-ving**) (often + *off*) *slang* evade work; play truant.

**skivvy** /'skɪvɪ/ *noun* (*plural* **-ies**) *colloquial derogatory* female domestic servant.

**skua** /'skjuːə/ *noun* large predatory seabird.

**skulduggery** /skʌl'dʌgərɪ/ *noun* trick-ery, unscrupulous behaviour.

**skulk** *verb* lurk or conceal oneself or move stealthily.

**skull** *noun* bony case of brain; bony framework of head; head as site of intelligence. □ **skull and crossbones** representation of skull over two crossed thigh-bones, esp. on pirate flag or as emblem of death; **skullcap** close-fitting peakless cap.

**skunk** *noun* (*plural* same or **-s**) black white-striped bushy-tailed mammal, emitting powerful stench when at-tacked; *colloquial* contemptible person.

**sky** /skaɪ/ *noun* (*plural* **skies**) (in *singular* or *plural*) atmosphere and outer space seen from the earth. □ **sky blue** bright clear blue; **skydiving** sport of performing acrobatic manoeuvres under free fall before opening parachute; **skylark** *noun* lark that sings while soaring, *verb* play tricks and practical jokes; **skylight** window in roof; **skyline** out-line of hills, buildings, etc. against sky; **sky-rocket** *noun* firework shooting into air and exploding, *verb* rise steeply; **skyscraper** very tall building.

**slab** *noun* flat thickish esp. rectangular piece of solid material; mortuary table.

**slack**[1] ● *adjective* (of rope etc.) not taut; inactive; sluggish; negligent, remiss; (of tide etc.) neither ebbing nor flowing. ● *noun* slack part of rope etc.; slack period; (in *plural*) casual trousers. ● *verb*

slacken; *colloquial* take a rest, be lazy. □ **slack off** loosen; **slack up** reduce level of activity or speed. □ **slackness** *noun*.

**slack**[2] *noun* coal dust, coal fragments.

**slacken** *verb* make or become slack. □ **slacken off** slack off.

**slacker** *noun* shirker.

**slag** ● *noun* refuse left after ore has been smelted etc. ● *verb* (**-gg-**) form slag; (often + *off*) *slang* insult, slander. □ **slag-heap** hill of refuse from mine etc.

**slain** *past participle* of SLAY.

**slake** *verb* (**-king**) assuage or satisfy (thirst etc.); cause (lime) to heat and crumble by action of water.

**slalom** /'slɑːləm/ *noun* downhill ski-race on zigzag course between artificial obstacles.

**slam**[1] ● *verb* (**-mm-**) shut, throw, or put down violently or with bang; *slang* criti-cize severely. ● *noun* sound or action of slamming.

**slam**[2] *noun* winning of all tricks at cards.

**slander** /'slɑːndə/ ● *noun* false and dam-aging utterance about person. ● *verb* utter slander about. □ **slanderous** *adjective*.

**slang** ● *noun* very informal words, phrases, or meanings, not regarded as standard and often peculiar to profes-sion, class, etc. ● *verb* use abusive lan-guage (to). □ **slanging match** pro-longed exchange of insults. □ **slangy** *adjective*.

**slant** /slɑːnt/ ● *verb* slope, (cause to) lie or go obliquely; (often as **slanted** *adjective*) present (news etc.) in biased or particu-lar way. ● *noun* slope, oblique position; point of view, esp. biased one. ● *adjective* sloping, oblique.

**slantwise** *adverb* aslant.

**slap** ● *verb* (**-pp-**) strike (as) with palm of hand; lay forcefully; put hastily or carelessly. ● *noun* slapping stroke or sound. ● *adverb* suddenly, fully, dir-ectly. □ **slapdash** hasty, careless; **slap-happy** *colloquial* cheerfully cas-ual; **slapstick** boisterous comedy; **slap-up** *colloquial* lavish.

**slash** ● *verb* cut or gash with knife etc.; (often + *at*) deliver or aim cutting blows; reduce (prices etc.) drastically; criticize harshly. ● *noun* slashing cut; *Printing* oblique stroke; *slang* act of urinating.

**slat** *noun* long narrow strip of wood, plastic, or metal, used in fences, venetian blinds, etc.

**slate** ● *noun* fine-grained bluish-grey rock easily split into thin smooth plates; piece of this used esp. in roofing or *historical* for writing on; colour of slate; list of nominees for office etc. ● *verb* (**-ting**) roof with slates; *colloquial* criticize severely; *US* make arrangements for (event etc.), nominate for office. ● *adjective* (of colour of) slate. □ **slating** *noun*; **slaty** *adjective*.

**slattern** /'slæt(ə)n/ *noun* slovenly woman. □ **slatternly** *adjective*.

**slaughter** /'slɔːtə/ ● *verb* kill (animals) for food etc.; kill (people) ruthlessly or in large numbers; *colloquial* defeat utterly. ● *noun* act of slaughtering. □ **slaughterhouse** place for slaughter of animals for food. □ **slaughterer** *noun*.

**Slav** /slɑːv/ ● *noun* member of group of peoples of central and eastern Europe speaking Slavonic languages. ● *adjective* of the Slavs.

**slave** ● *noun* person who is owned by and has to serve another; drudge, very hard worker; (+ *of*, *to*) obsessive devotee. ● *verb* (**-ving**) work very hard. □ **slave-driver** overseer of slaves, hard taskmaster; **slave trade** dealing in slaves, esp. African blacks.

**slaver**[1] *noun historical* ship or person engaged in slave trade.

**slaver**[2] /'slævə/ ● *verb* dribble; drool. ● *noun* dribbling saliva; flattery; drivel.

**slavery** /'sleɪvərɪ/ *noun* condition of slave; drudgery; practice of having slaves.

**Slavic** /'slɑːvɪk/ *adjective & noun* Slavonic.

**slavish** /'sleɪvɪʃ/ *adjective* like slaves; without originality. □ **slavishly** *adverb*.

**Slavonic** /slə'vɒnɪk/ ● *adjective* of group of languages including Russian, Polish, and Czech. ● *noun* Slavonic group of languages.

**slay** *verb* (*past* **slew** /sluː/; *past participle* **slain**) kill. □ **slayer** *noun*.

**sleaze** *noun colloquial* sleaziness.

**sleazy** /'sliːzɪ/ *adjective* (**-ier, -iest**) squalid, tawdry. □ **sleazily** *adverb*; **sleaziness** *noun*.

**sled** *noun & verb* (**-dd-**) *US* sledge.

**sledge** ● *noun* vehicle on runners for use on snow. ● *verb* (**-ging**) travel or carry on sledge.

**sledgehammer** /'sledʒhæmə/ *noun* large heavy hammer.

**sleek** ● *adjective* (of hair, skin, etc.) smooth and glossy; looking well-fed and comfortable. ● *verb* make sleek. □ **sleekly** *adverb*; **sleekness** *noun*.

**sleep** ● *noun* condition in which eyes are closed, muscles and nerves relaxed, and consciousness suspended; period of this; rest, quiet, death. ● *verb* (*past & past participle* **slept**) be or fall asleep; spend the night; provide sleeping accommodation for; (+ *with, together*) have sexual intercourse; (+ *on*) defer (decision) until next day; (+ *through*) fail to be woken by; be inactive or dead; (+ *off*) cure by sleeping. □ **sleeping bag** padded bag to sleep in when camping etc.; **sleeping car, carriage** railway coach with beds or berths; **sleeping partner** partner not sharing in actual work of a firm; **sleeping pill** pill to induce sleep; **sleeping policeman** ramp etc. in road to slow traffic; **sleepwalk** walk about while asleep; **sleepwalker** *noun* □ **sleepless** *adjective*; **sleeplessness** *noun*.

**sleeper** *noun* sleeping person or animal; beam supporting railway track; sleeping car; ring worn in pierced ear to keep hole open.

**sleepy** *adjective* (**-ier, -iest**) feeling need of sleep; quiet, inactive. □ **sleepily** *adverb*; **sleepiness** *noun*.

**sleet** ● *noun* snow and rain together; hail or snow melting as it falls. ● *verb* (after *it*) sleet falls. □ **sleety** *adjective*.

**sleeve** *noun* part of garment covering arm; cover for gramophone record; tube enclosing rod etc. □ **up one's sleeve** in reserve. □ **sleeved** *adjective*; **sleeveless** *adjective*.

**sleigh** /sleɪ/ ● *noun* sledge, esp. for riding on. ● *verb* travel on sleigh.

**sleight of hand** /slaɪt/ *noun* dexterity, esp. in conjuring.

**slender** /'slendə/ *adjective* (**-er**, **-est**) of small girth or breadth; slim; slight, scanty, meagre.

**slept** *past & past participle* of SLEEP.

**sleuth** /sluːθ/ *colloquial* ● *noun* detective. ● *verb* investigate crime etc.

**slew**[1] /sluː/ ● *verb* (often + *round*) turn or swing to new position. ● *noun* such turn.

**slew**[2] *past* of SLAY.

**slice** ● *noun* thin flat piece or wedge cut from something; share; kitchen utensil with thin broad blade; stroke sending ball obliquely. ● *verb* (**-cing**) (often + *up*) cut into slices; (+ *off*) cut off; (+ *into*, *through*) cut (as) with knife; strike (ball) with slice.

**slick** ● *adjective colloquial* skilful, efficient; superficially dexterous, glib; sleek, smooth. ● *noun* patch of oil etc., esp. on sea. ● *verb colloquial* make smooth or sleek. □ **slickly** *adverb*; **slickness** *noun*.

**slide** ● *verb* (*past & past participle* **slid**) (cause to) move along smooth surface touching it always with same part; move quietly or smoothly; glide over ice without skates; (+ *into*) pass unobtrusively. ● *noun* act of sliding; rapid decline; smooth slope down which people or things slide; track for sliding, esp. on ice; part of machine or instrument that slides; mounted transparency viewed with projector; piece of glass holding object for microscope; hair-slide. □ **let things slide** be negligent, allow deterioration; **slide-rule** ruler with sliding central strip, graduated logarithmically for rapid calculations; **sliding scale** scale of fees, taxes, wages, etc. that varies according to some other factor.

**slight** /slaɪt/ ● *adjective* small, insignificant; inadequate; slender, frail-looking. ● *verb* treat disrespectfully, ignore. ● *noun* act of slighting. □ **slightly** *adverb*; **slightness** *noun*.

**slim** ● *adjective* (**-mm-**) not fat, slender; small, insufficient. ● *verb* (**-mm-**) (often + *down*) become slim, esp. by dieting etc.; make slim. □ **slimline** of slender design, not fattening. □ **slimmer** *noun*; **slimming** *noun*.

**slime** *noun* oozy or sticky substance.

**slimy** *adjective* (**-ier**, **-iest**) like, covered with, or filled with slime; *colloquial* disgustingly obsequious. □ **sliminess** *noun*.

**sling**[1] ● *noun* strap etc. used to support or raise thing; bandage supporting injured arm; strap etc. used to throw small missile. ● *verb* (*past & past participle* **slung**) suspend with sling; *colloquial* throw. □ **sling-back** shoe held in place by strap above heel; **sling one's hook** *slang* go away.

**sling**[2] *noun* sweetened drink of spirits (esp. gin) with water.

**slink** *verb* (*past & past participle* **slunk**) (often + *off*, *away*, *by*) move stealthily or guiltily.

**slinky** *adjective* (**-ier**, **-iest**) (of garment) close-fitting and sinuous.

**slip**[1] ● *verb* (**-pp-**) slide unintentionally or momentarily, lose footing or balance; go with sliding motion; escape or fall because hard to grasp; go unobserved or quietly; make careless or slight mistake; fall below standard; place stealthily or casually; release from restraint or connection; (+ *on*, *off*) pull (garment) easily or hastily on or off; escape from, evade. ● *noun* act of slipping; careless or slight error; pillowcase; petticoat; (in *singular* or *plural*) slipway; *Cricket* fielder behind wicket on off side, (in *singular* or *plural*) this position. □ **give** (**person**) **the slip** escape from, evade; **slip-knot** knot that can be undone by pull, running knot; **slip-on** (of shoes or clothes) easily slipped on or off; **slipped disc** displaced disc between vertebrae; **slip-road** road for entering or leaving motorway etc.; **slipstream** current of air or water driven backwards by propeller etc.; **slip up** *colloquial* make mistake; **slip-up** *noun*; **slipway** ramp for shipbuilding or landing boats.

**slip**[2] *noun* small piece of paper, esp. for making notes; cutting from plant for grafting or planting.

**slippage** *noun* act or instance of slipping.

**slipper** *noun* light loose indoor shoe.

**slippery** /'slɪpərɪ/ *adjective* difficult to grasp, stand on, etc., because smooth or wet; unreliable, unscrupulous. □ **slipperiness** *noun*.

**slippy** *adjective* (**-ier**, **-iest**) *colloquial* slippery.

**slipshod** *adjective* careless, slovenly.

**slit** ● *noun* straight narrow incision or opening. ● *verb* (**-tt-**; *past & past participle* **slit**) make slit in; cut in strips.

**slither** /ˈslɪðə/ ● *verb* slide unsteadily. ● *noun* act of slithering. □ **slithery** *adjective*.

**sliver** /ˈslɪvə/ ● *noun* long thin slice or piece. ● *verb* cut or split into slivers.

**slob** *noun colloquial derogatory* lazy, untidy, or fat person.

**slobber** /ˈslɒbə/ *verb & noun* slaver. □ **slobbery** *adjective*.

**sloe** *noun* blackthorn; its small bluish-black fruit.

**slog** ● *verb* (**-gg-**) hit hard and usually unskilfully; work or walk doggedly. ● *noun* heavy random hit; hard steady work or walk; spell of this.

**slogan** /ˈsləʊgən/ *noun* catchy phrase used in advertising etc.; party cry, watchword.

**sloop** /sluːp/ *noun* small one-masted fore-and-aft rigged vessel.

**slop** ● *verb* (**-pp-**) (often + *over*) spill over edge of vessel; spill or splash liquid on. ● *noun* liquid spilled or splashed; (in *plural*) dirty waste water, wine, etc.; (in *singular* or *plural*) unappetizing liquid food.

**slope** ● *noun* inclined position, direction, or state; piece of rising or falling ground; difference in level between two ends or sides of a thing; place for skiing. ● *verb* (**-ping**) have or take slope, slant; cause to slope. □ **slope off** *slang* go away, esp. to evade work etc.

**sloppy** *adjective* (**-ier**, **-iest**) wet, watery, too liquid; careless, untidy; foolishly sentimental. □ **sloppily** *adverb*; **sloppiness** *noun*.

**slosh** ● *verb* (often + *about*) splash or flounder; *slang* hit, esp. heavily; *colloquial* pour (liquid) clumsily. ● *noun* slush; act or sound of splashing; *slang* heavy blow.

**sloshed** *adjective slang* drunk.

**slot** ● *noun* slit in machine etc. for something (esp. coin) to be inserted; slit, groove, etc. for thing; allotted place in schedule. ● *verb* (**-tt-**) (often + *in*, *into*) place or be placed (as if) into slot;

provide with slot(s). □ **slot machine** machine worked by insertion of coin, esp. delivering small items or providing amusement.

**sloth** /sləʊθ/ *noun* laziness, indolence; slow-moving arboreal S. American mammal.

**slothful** *adjective* lazy. □ **slothfully** *adverb*.

**slouch** /slaʊtʃ/ ● *verb* stand, move, or sit in drooping fashion. ● *noun* slouching posture or movement; *slang* incompetent or slovenly worker etc. □ **slouch hat** hat with wide flexible brim.

**slough**[1] /slaʊ/ *noun* swamp, miry place. □ **Slough of Despond** state of hopeless depression.

**slough**[2] /slʌf/ ● *noun* part that animal (esp. snake) casts or moults. ● *verb* (often + *off*) cast or drop as slough.

**Slovak** /ˈsləʊvæk/ ● *noun* member of Slavonic people inhabiting Slovakia; their language. ● *adjective* of this people or language.

**sloven** /ˈslʌv(ə)n/ *noun* untidy or careless person.

**Slovene** /ˈsləʊviːn/ (also **Slovenian** /-ˈviːnɪən/) ● *noun* member of Slavonic people in Slovenia; their language. ● *adjective* of Slovenia or its people or language.

**slovenly** ● *adjective* careless and untidy, unmethodical. ● *adverb* in a slovenly way. □ **slovenliness** *noun*.

**slow** /sləʊ/ ● *adjective* taking relatively long time to do thing(s); acting, moving, or done without speed; not conducive to speed; (of clock etc.) showing earlier than correct time; dull-witted, stupid; tedious; slack, sluggish; (of fire or oven) not very hot; (of photographic film) needing long exposure; reluctant. ● *adverb* slowly. ● *verb* (usually + *down*, *up*) (cause to) move, act, or work with reduced speed or vigour. □ **slowcoach** *colloquial* slow person; **slow motion** speed of film or videotape in which actions etc. appear much slower than usual, simulation of this in real action; **slow-worm** small European legless lizard. □ **slowly** *adverb*; **slowness** *noun*.

**sludge** *noun* thick greasy mud or sediment; sewage. □ **sludgy** *adjective*.

**slug**[1] ● *noun* slimy shell-less mollusc; bullet, esp. irregularly shaped; missile for airgun; *Printing* metal bar for spacing; mouthful of liquor.

**slug**[2] *US* ● *verb* (**-gg-**) hit hard. ● *noun* hard blow.

**sluggard** /ˈslʌɡəd/ *noun* lazy person.

**sluggish** *adjective* inert, slow-moving. □ **sluggishly** *adverb*; **sluggishness** *noun*.

**sluice** /sluːs/ ● *noun* (also **sluice-gate**, **-valve**) sliding gate or other contrivance for regulating volume or flow of water; water so regulated; (also **sluice-way**) artificial water-channel; place for or act of rinsing. ● *verb* (**-cing**) provide or wash with sluice(s); rinse; (of water) rush out (as if) from sluice.

**slum** ● *noun* house unfit for human habitation; (often in *plural*) overcrowded and squalid district in city. ● *verb* (**-mm-**) visit slums, esp. out of curiosity. □ **slum it** *colloquial* put up with conditions less comfortable than usual. □ **slummy** *adjective*.

**slumber** /ˈslʌmbə/ *verb & noun* poetical sleep.

**slump** ● *noun* sudden severe or prolonged fall in prices and trade. ● *verb* undergo slump; sit or fall heavily or limply.

**slung** *past & past participle of* SLING[1].

**slunk** *past & past participle of* SLINK.

**slur** ● *verb* (**-rr-**) sound (words, musical notes, etc.) so that they run into one another; *archaic or US* put slur on (person, character); (usually + *over*) pass over lightly. ● *noun* imputation of wrongdoing; act of slurring; *Music* curved line joining notes to be slurred.

**slurp** *colloquial* ● *verb* eat or drink noisily. ● *noun* sound of slurping.

**slurry** /ˈslʌrɪ/ *noun* thin semi-liquid cement, mud, manure, etc.

**slush** *noun* thawing snow; silly sentimentality. □ **slush fund** reserve fund, esp. for bribery. □ **slushy** *adjective* (**-ier, -iest**).

**slut** *noun derogatory* slovenly or promiscuous woman. □ **sluttish** *adjective*.

**sly** *adjective* (**-er, -est**) crafty, wily; secretive; knowing, insinuating. □ **on the sly** secretly. □ **slyly** *adverb*; **slyness** *noun*.

**smack**[1] ● *noun* sharp slap or blow; hard hit; loud kiss; loud sharp sound. ● *verb* slap; part (lips) noisily in anticipation of food; move, hit, etc. with smack. ● *adverb colloquial* with a smack; suddenly, violently; exactly.

**smack**[2] (+ *of*) ● *verb* taste of, suggest. ● *noun* flavour or suggestion of.

**smack**[3] *noun* single-masted sailing boat.

**smack**[4] *noun slang* heroin, other hard drug.

**smacker** *noun slang* loud kiss; £1, *US* $1.

**small** /smɔːl/ ● *adjective* not large or big; not great in importance, amount, number, etc.; not much; insignificant; of small particles; on small scale; poor, humble; mean; young. ● *noun* slenderest part, esp. of back; (in *plural*) *colloquial* underwear, esp. as laundry. ● *adverb* into small pieces. □ **small arms** portable firearms; **small change** coins, not notes; **small fry** unimportant people, children; **smallholding** agricultural holding smaller than farm; **small hours** night-time after midnight; **small-minded** petty, narrow in outlook; **smallpox** *historical* acute contagious disease with fever and pustules usually leaving scars; **small print** matter printed small, esp. limitations in contract; **small talk** trivial social conversation; **small-time** *colloquial* unimportant, petty. □ **smallness** *noun*.

**smarmy** /ˈsmɑːmɪ/ *adjective* (**-ier, -iest**) *colloquial* ingratiating. □ **smarmily** *adverb*; **smarminess** *noun*.

**smart** ● *adjective* well-groomed, neat; bright and fresh in appearance; stylish, fashionable; *esp. US* clever, ingenious, quickwitted; quick, brisk; painfully severe, sharp, vigorous. ● *verb* feel or give pain; rankle; (+ *for*) suffer consequences of. ● *noun* sharp bodily or mental pain, stinging sensation. ● *adverb* smartly. □ **smartish** *adjective & adverb*; **smartly** *adverb*; **smartness** *noun*.

**smarten** *verb* (usually + *up*) make or become smart.

**smash** ● *verb* (often + *up*) break to pieces; bring or come to destruction, defeat, or disaster; (+ *into, through*) move forcefully; (+ *in*) break with crushing blow; hit (ball) hard, esp. downwards. ● *noun* act or sound of smashing; (in full **smash hit**) very successful play, song, etc. ● *adverb* with smash. □ **smash-and-grab** robbery with goods snatched from broken shop window etc.

**smashing** *adjective colloquial* excellent, wonderful.

**smattering** /'smætərɪŋ/ *noun* slight knowledge.

**smear** /smɪə/ ● *verb* daub or mark with grease etc.; smudge; defame. ● *noun* action of smearing; material smeared on microscope slide etc. for examination; specimen of this. □ **smear test** cervical smear. □ **smeary** *adjective*.

**smell** ● *noun* sense of odour perception; property perceived by this; unpleasant odour; act of inhaling to ascertain smell. ● *verb* (*past & past participle* **smelt** or **smelled**) perceive or examine by smell; stink; seem by smell to be; (+ *of*) emit smell of, suggest; detect; have or use sense of smell. □ **smelling salts** sharp-smelling substances sniffed to relieve faintness.

**smelly** *adjective* (**-ier**, **-iest**) strong- or evil-smelling.

**smelt**[1] *verb* melt (ore) to extract metal; obtain (metal) thus. □ **smelter** *noun*.

**smelt**[2] *past & past participle* of SMELL.

**smelt**[3] *noun* (*plural* same or **-s**) small edible green and silver fish.

**smilax** /'smaɪlæks/ *noun* any of several climbing plants.

**smile** ● *verb* (**-ling**) have or assume facial expression of amusement or pleasure, with ends of lips turned upward; express by smiling; give (smile); (+ *on*, *upon*) favour. ● *noun* act of smiling; smiling expression or aspect.

**smirch** *verb & noun* stain, smear.

**smirk** ● *noun* conceited or silly smile. ● *verb* give smirk.

**smite** *verb* (**-ting**; *past* **smote**; *past participle* **smitten** /'smɪt(ə)n/) *archaic or literary* hit, chastise, defeat; (in *passive*) affect strongly, seize.

**smith** *noun* blacksmith; worker in metal, craftsman.

**smithereens** /smɪðə'ri:nz/ *plural noun* small fragments.

**smithy** /'smɪðɪ/ *noun* (*plural* **-ies**) blacksmith's workshop, forge.

**smitten** *past participle* of SMITE.

**smock** ● *noun* loose shirtlike garment, often adorned with smocking. ● *verb* adorn with smocking.

**smocking** *noun* ornamentation on cloth made by gathering it tightly with stitches.

**smog** *noun* dense smoky fog. □ **smoggy** *adjective* (**-ier**, **-iest**).

**smoke** ● *noun* visible vapour from burning substance; act of smoking tobacco etc.; *colloquial* cigarette, cigar. ● *verb* (**-king**) inhale and exhale smoke of (cigarette etc.); do this habitually; emit smoke or visible vapour; darken or preserve with smoke. □ **smoke bomb** bomb emitting dense smoke on bursting; **smoke-free** free from smoke, where smoking is not permitted; **smoke out** drive out by means of smoke, drive out of hiding etc.; **smokescreen** cloud of smoke concealing esp. military operations, ruse for disguising activities; **smokestack** funnel of locomotive or steamship, tall chimney.

**smoker** *noun* person who habitually smokes tobacco; compartment on train where smoking is permitted.

**smoky** *adjective* (**-ier**, **-iest**) emitting, filled with, or obscured by, smoke; coloured by or like smoke; having flavour of smoked food.

**smolder** *US* = SMOULDER.

**smooch** /smu:tʃ/ ● *verb* kiss and caress. ● *noun* smooching.

**smooth** /smu:ð/ ● *adjective* having even surface; free from projections and roughness; that can be traversed uninterrupted; (of sea etc.) calm, flat; (of journey etc.) easy; not harsh in sound or taste; conciliatory, slick; not jerky. ● *verb* (often + *out*, *down*) make or become smooth; (often + *out*, *down*, *over*, *away*) get rid of (differences, faults, etc.). ● *noun* smoothing touch or stroke. □ **smooth-tongued** insincerely flattering. □ **smoothly** *adverb*; **smoothness** *noun*.

**smorgasbord** /'smɔ:gəsbɔ:d/ *noun* Swedish hors d'oeuvres; buffet meal with various esp. savoury dishes.

**smote** *past* of SMITE.

**smother** /'smʌðə/ *verb* suffocate, stifle; (+ *in*, *with*) overwhelm or cover with (kisses, gifts, etc.); extinguish (fire) by heaping with ashes etc.; have difficulty breathing; (often + *up*) suppress, conceal.

**smoulder** /ˈsməʊldə/ (*US* **smolder**) ● *verb* burn without flame or internally; (of person) show silent emotion. ● *noun* smouldering.

**smudge** ● *noun* blurred or smeared line, mark, etc. ● *verb* (**-ging**) make smudge on or with; become smeared or blurred. □ **smudgy** *adjective*.

**smug** *adjective* (**-gg-**) self-satisfied. □ **smugly** *adverb*; **smugness** *noun*.

**smuggle** /ˈsmʌg(ə)l/ *verb* (**-ling**) import or export illegally, esp. without paying duties; convey secretly. □ **smuggler** *noun*; **smuggling** *noun*.

**smut** ● *noun* small piece of soot; spot or smudge made by this; obscene talk, pictures, or stories; fungous disease of cereals. ● *verb* (**-tt-**) mark with smut(s). □ **smutty** *adjective* (**-ier**, **-iest**).

**snack** ● *noun* light, casual, or hasty meal. □ **snack bar** place where snacks are sold.

**snaffle** /ˈsnæf(ə)l/ ● *noun* (in full **snaffle-bit**) simple bridle-bit without curb. ● *verb* (**-ling**) *colloquial* steal, seize.

**snag** ● *noun* unexpected obstacle or drawback; jagged projection; tear in material etc. ● *verb* (**-gg-**) catch or tear on snag.

**snail** *noun* slow-moving mollusc with spiral shell.

**snake** ● *noun* long limbless reptile; (also **snake in the grass**) traitor, secret enemy. ● *verb* (**-king**) move or twist like a snake. □ **snakes and ladders** board game with counters moved up 'ladders' and down 'snakes'; **snakeskin** *noun* skin of snake, *adjective* made of snakeskin.

**snaky** *adjective* of or like a snake; sinuous; treacherous.

**snap** ● *verb* (**-pp-**) break sharply; (cause to) emit sudden sharp sound; open or close with snapping sound; speak irritably; (often + *at*) make sudden audible bite; move quickly; photograph. ● *noun* act or sound of snapping; crisp biscuit; snapshot; (in full **cold snap**) sudden brief period of cold weather; card game in which players call 'snap'

when two similar cards are exposed; vigour. ● *adverb* with snapping sound. ● *adjective* done without forethought. □ **snapdragon** plant with two-lipped flowers; **snap-fastener** press-stud; **snap out of** *slang* get out of (mood etc.) by sudden effort; **snapshot** informal or casual photograph; **snap up** accept (offer etc.) hastily or eagerly.

**snapper** *noun* any of several edible marine fish.

**snappish** *adjective* curt, ill-tempered.

**snappy** *adjective* (**-ier**, **-iest**) *colloquial* brisk, lively; neat and elegant; snappish. □ **snappily** *adverb*.

**snare** /sneə/ ● *noun* trap, esp. with noose, for birds or animals; trap, trick, temptation; (in *singular* or *plural*) twisted strings of gut, hide, or wire stretched across lower head of side drum to produce rattle; (in full **snare drum**) side drum with snares. ● *verb* (**-ring**) catch in snare, trap.

**snarl**[1] ● *verb* growl with bared teeth; speak angrily. ● *noun* act or sound of snarling.

**snarl**[2] ● *verb* (often + *up*) twist, entangle, hamper movement of (traffic etc.), become entangled. ● *noun* tangle.

**snatch** ● *verb* (often + *away, from*) seize quickly, eagerly, or unexpectedly; steal by grabbing; *slang* kidnap; (+ *at*) try to seize, take eagerly. ● *noun* act of snatching; fragment of song, talk, etc.; short spell of activity etc.

**snazzy** /ˈsnæzɪ/ *adjective* (**-ier**, **-iest**) *slang* smart, stylish; showy.

**sneak** ● *verb* go or convey furtively; *slang* steal unobserved; *slang* tell tales; (as **sneaking** *adjective*) furtive, persistent and puzzling. ● *noun* mean-spirited, underhand person; *slang* tell-tale. ● *adjective* acting or done without warning, secret. □ **sneak-thief** person who steals without breaking in. □ **sneaky** *adjective* (**-ier**, **-iest**).

**sneaker** *noun* *slang* soft-soled shoe.

**sneer** ● *noun* derisive smile or remark. ● *verb* (often + *at*) make sneer; utter with sneer. □ **sneering** *adjective*; **sneeringly** *adverb*.

**sneeze** ● *noun* sudden involuntary explosive expulsion of air from irritated nostrils. ● *verb* (**-zing**) make sneeze.

□ **not to be sneezed at** *colloquial* worth having or considering.

**snick** ● *verb* make small notch or cut in; *Cricket* deflect (ball) slightly with bat. ● *noun* such notch or deflection.

**snicker** /'snɪkə/ *noun & verb* snigger.

**snide** *adjective* sneering, slyly derogatory.

**sniff** ● *verb* inhale air audibly through nose; (often + *up*) draw in through nose; smell scent of by sniffing. ● *noun* act or sound of sniffing. □ **sniff at** show contempt for; **sniffer-dog** *colloquial* dog trained to find drugs or explosives by scent.

**sniffle** /'snɪf(ə)l/ ● *verb* (**-ling**) sniff repeatedly or slightly. ● *noun* act of sniffling; (in *singular* or *plural*) cold in the head causing sniffling.

**snifter** /'snɪftə/ *noun slang* small alcoholic drink.

**snigger** /'snɪgə/ ● *noun* half-suppressed laugh. ● *verb* utter snigger.

**snip** ● *verb* (**-pp-**) cut with scissors etc., esp. in small quick strokes. ● *noun* act of snipping; piece snipped off; *slang* something easily done, bargain.

**snipe** ● *noun* (*plural* same or **-s**) wading bird with long straight bill. ● *verb* (**-ping**) fire shots from hiding usually at long range; (often + *at*) make sly critical attack. □ **sniper** *noun*.

**snippet** /'snɪpɪt/ *noun* small piece cut off; (usually in *plural*) scrap of information etc., short extract from book etc.

**snitch** ● *verb slang* steal; (often + *on*) inform on person. ● *noun* informer.

**snivel** /'snɪv(ə)l/ ● *verb* (**-ll-**; *US* **-l-**) sniffle; weep with sniffling; show maudlin emotion. ● *noun* act of snivelling.

**snob** *noun* person who despises people with inferior social position, wealth, intellect, tastes, etc. □ **snobbery** *noun*; **snobbish** *adjective*; **snobby** *adjective* (**-ier**, **-iest**).

**snood** /snuːd/ *noun* woman's loose hairnet.

**snook** /snuːk/ *noun slang* contemptuous gesture with thumb to nose and fingers spread. □ **cock a snook** (**at**) make this gesture (at), show contempt (for).

**snooker** /'snuːkə/ ● *noun* game played on oblong cloth-covered table with 1

white, 15 red, and 6 other coloured balls; position in this game where direct shot would lose points. ● *verb* subject (player) to snooker; (esp. as **snookered** *adjective*) *slang* thwart, defeat.

**snoop** /snuːp/ *colloquial* ● *verb* pry into another's affairs; (often + *about*, *around*) investigate (often stealthily) transgressions of rules etc. ● *noun* act of snooping. □ **snooper** *noun*.

**snooty** /'snuːtɪ/ *adjective* (**-ier**, **-iest**) *colloquial* supercilious, snobbish. □ **snootily** *adverb*.

**snooze** /snuːz/ *colloquial* ● *noun* short sleep, nap. ● *verb* (**-zing**) take snooze.

**snore** ● *noun* snorting or grunting sound of breathing during sleep. ● *verb* (**-ring**) make this sound.

**snorkel** /'snɔːk(ə)l/ ● *noun* device for supplying air to underwater swimmer or submerged submarine. ● *verb* (**-ll-**; *US* **-l-**) use snorkel.

**snort** ● *noun* explosive sound made by driving breath violently through nose, esp. by horses, or by humans to show contempt, incredulity, etc.; *colloquial* small drink of liquor; *slang* inhaled dose of powdered cocaine. ● *verb* make snort; *slang* inhale (esp. cocaine); express or utter with snort.

**snot** *noun slang* nasal mucus.

**snotty** *adjective* (**-ier**, **-iest**) *slang* running or covered with nasal mucus; snooty; contemptible. □ **snottily** *adverb*; **snottiness** *noun*.

**snout** /snaʊt/ *noun* projecting nose (and mouth) of animal; *derogatory* person's nose; pointed front of thing.

**snow** /snəʊ/ ● *noun* frozen vapour falling to earth in light white flakes; fall or layer of this; thing resembling snow in whiteness or texture etc.; *slang* cocaine. ● *verb* (after *it*) snow falls; (+ *in*, *over*, *up*, etc.) confine or block with snow. □ **snowball** snow pressed into ball for throwing in play, *verb* throw or pelt with snowballs, increase rapidly; **snow-blind** temporarily blinded by glare from snow; **snowbound** prevented by snow from going out; **snowcap** snow-covered mountain peak; **snowdrift** bank of snow piled up by wind; **snowdrop** spring-flowering plant with white drooping flowers; **snowed under** overwhelmed, esp. with work; **snowflake** each of the flakes in which snow falls; **snow goose** white Arctic goose; **snowline** level above which snow never melts entirely; **snowman** figure made of snow; **snowplough** device for clearing road of snow; **snowshoe** racket-shaped attachment to boot for walking on surface of snow; **snowstorm** heavy fall of snow, esp. with wind; **snow white** pure white. □ **snowy** *adjective* (**-ier, iest**).

**SNP** *abbreviation* Scottish National Party.

**Snr.** *abbreviation* Senior.

**snub** ● *verb* (**-bb-**) rebuff or humiliate in a sharp or cutting way. ● *noun* snubbing, rebuff. ● *adjective* (of nose) short and turned up.

**snuff¹** ● *noun* charred part of candle-wick. ● *verb* trim snuff from (candle). □ **snuff it** *slang* die; **snuff out** extinguish (candle), put an end to (hopes etc.).

**snuff²** ● *noun* powdered tobacco or medicine taken by sniffing. ● *verb* take snuff.

**snuffle** /'snʌf(ə)l/ ● *verb* (**-ling**) make sniffing sounds; speak nasally; breathe noisily, esp. with blocked nose. ● *noun* snuffling sound or speech.

**snug** ● *adjective* (**-gg-**) cosy, comfortable, sheltered; close-fitting. ● *noun* small room in pub. □ **snugly** *adverb*.

**snuggle** /'snʌg(ə)l/ *verb* (**-ling**) settle or move into warm comfortable position.

**so¹** /səʊ/ ● *adverb* to such an extent, in this or that manner or state; also; indeed, actually; very; thus. ● *conjunction* (often + *that*) consequently, in order that; and then; (introducing question) after that. □ **so-and-so** particular but unspecified person or thing, *colloquial* objectionable person; **so as to** in order to; **so-called** commonly called but often incorrectly; **so long** *colloquial* good-bye; **so so** *colloquial* only moderately good or well.

**so²** = SOH.

**soak** ● *verb* make or become thoroughly wet through saturation; (of rain etc.) drench; (+ *in, up*) absorb (liquid, knowledge, etc.); (+ *in, into, through*) penetrate by saturation; *colloquial* extort money from; *colloquial* drink heavily.

● *noun* soaking; *colloquial* hard drinker. □ **soakaway** arrangement for disposal of waste water by percolation through soil.

**soaking** *adjective* (in full **soaking wet**) wet through.

**soap** ● *noun* cleansing substance yielding lather when rubbed in water; *colloquial* soap opera. ● *verb* apply soap to. □ **soapbox** makeshift stand for street orator; **soap opera** domestic broadcast serial; **soap powder** powdered soap usually with additives, for washing clothes etc.; **soapstone** steatite; **soapsuds** suds.

**soapy** *adjective* (**-ier, -iest**) of or like soap; containing or smeared with soap; unctuous, flattering.

**soar** /sɔː/ *verb* fly or rise high; reach high level or standard; fly without flapping wings or using motor power.

**sob** ● *verb* (**-bb-**) inhale convulsively, usually with weeping; utter with sobs. ● *noun* act or sound of sobbing. □ **sob story** *colloquial* story or explanation appealing for sympathy.

**sober** /'səʊbə/ ● *adjective* (**-er, -est**) not drunk; not given to drink; moderate, tranquil, serious; (of colour) dull. ● *verb* (often + *down, up*) make or become sober. □ **soberly** *adverb*.

**sobriety** /sə'braɪɪtɪ/ *noun* being sober.

**sobriquet** /'səʊbrɪkeɪ/ *noun* (also **soubriquet** /'suː-/) nickname.

**Soc.** *abbreviation* Socialist; Society.

**soccer** /'sɒkə/ *noun* Association football.

**sociable** /'səʊʃəb(ə)l/ *adjective* liking company, gregarious, friendly. □ **sociability** *noun*; **sociably** *adverb*.

**social** /'səʊʃ(ə)l/ ● *adjective* of society or its organization, esp. of relations (of classes of) people; living in communities; gregarious. ● *noun* social gathering. □ **social science** study of society and social relationships; **social security** state assistance to the poor and unemployed; **social services** welfare services provided by the State, esp. education, health care, and housing; **social work** professional or voluntary work with disadvantaged groups; **social worker** *noun*. □ **socially** *adverb*.

**socialism** *noun* political and economic theory advocating state ownership and control of means of production, distribution, and exchange; social system based on this. □ **socialist** noun & adjective; **socialistic** /-'lɪs-/ adjective.

**socialite** /'səʊʃəlaɪt/ noun person moving in fashionable society.

**socialize** /'səʊʃəlaɪz/ verb (also **-ise**) (**-zing** or **-sing**) mix socially; make social; organize in a socialistic way.

**society** /sə'saɪətɪ/ noun (plural **-ies**) organized and interdependent community; system and organization of this; (members of) aristocratic part of this; mixing with other people, companionship, company; association, club. □ **societal** adjective.

**sociology** /səʊsɪ'ɒlədʒɪ/ noun study of society and social problems. □ **sociological** /-ə'lɒdʒ-/ adjective; **sociologist** noun.

**sock**[1] noun knitted covering for foot and lower leg; insole.

**sock**[2] colloquial ● verb hit hard. ● noun hard blow. □ **sock it to** attack or address vigorously.

**socket** /'sɒkɪt/ noun hollow for thing to fit into etc., esp. device receiving electric plug, light bulb, etc.

**Socratic** /sə'krætɪk/ adjective of Socrates or his philosophy.

**sod** noun turf, piece of turf; surface of ground.

**soda** /'səʊdə/ noun any of various compounds of sodium in common use; (in full **soda water**) effervescent water used esp. with spirits etc. as drink. □ **soda fountain** device supplying soda water, shop or counter with this.

**sodden** /'sɒd(ə)n/ adjective saturated, soaked through; stupid, dull, etc. with drunkenness.

**sodium** /'səʊdɪəm/ noun soft silver-white metallic element. □ **sodium bicarbonate** white compound used in baking-powder; **sodium chloride** common salt; **sodium lamp** lamp using sodium vapour and giving yellow light; **sodium nitrate** white powdery compound in fertilizers etc.

**sofa** /'səʊfə/ noun long upholstered seat with raised back and ends. □ **sofa bed** sofa that can be converted into bed.

**soffit** /'sɒfɪt/ noun undersurface of arch, lintel, etc.

**soft** ● adjective not hard, easily cut or dented, malleable; (of cloth etc.) smooth, fine, not rough; mild; (of water) low in mineral salts which prevent lathering; not brilliant or glaring; not strident or loud; sibilant; not sharply defined; gentle, conciliatory; compassionate, sympathetic; feeble, half-witted, silly, sentimental; colloquial easy; (of drug) not highly addictive. ● adverb softly. □ **have a soft spot for** be fond of; **softball** form of baseball with softer larger ball; **soft-boiled** (of egg) boiled leaving yolk soft; **soft-centred** having soft centre, soft-hearted; **soft drink** non-alcoholic drink; **soft fruit** small stoneless fruit; **soft furnishings** curtains, rugs, etc.; **soft-hearted** tender, compassionate; **soft option** easier alternative; **soft palate** back part of palate; **soft pedal** noun pedal on piano softening tone; **soft-pedal** verb refrain from emphasizing; **soft sell** restrained salesmanship; **soft soap** colloquial persuasive flattery; **soft-spoken** having gentle voice; **soft target** vulnerable person or thing; **soft touch** colloquial gullible person, esp. over money; **software** computer programs; **softwood** wood of coniferous tree. □ **softly** adverb; **softness** noun.

**soften** /'sɒf(ə)n/ verb make or become soft(er); (often + *up*) reduce strength, resistance, etc. of. □ **softener** noun.

**softie** noun (also **softy**) (plural **-ies**) colloquial weak, silly, or soft-hearted person.

**soggy** /'sɒgɪ/ adjective (**-ier**, **-iest**) sodden, waterlogged.

**soh** noun (also **so**) Music fifth note of scale in tonic sol-fa.

**soil**[1] noun upper layer of earth, in which plants grow; ground, territory.

**soil**[2] ● verb make dirty, smear, stain; defile; discredit. ● noun dirty mark; filth, refuse. □ **soil pipe** discharge-pipe of lavatory.

**soirée** /'swɑːreɪ/ noun evening party.

**sojourn** /'sɒdʒ(ə)n/ ● noun temporary stay. ● verb stay temporarily.

**sola** /'səʊlə/ noun pithy-stemmed E. Indian swamp plant. □ **sola topi** sun-helmet made from pith of this.

**solace** /'sɒləs/ ● noun comfort in distress or disappointment. ● verb (**-cing**) give solace to.

**solan** /ˈsəʊlən/ noun (in full **solan goose**) large gooselike gannet.

**solar** /ˈsəʊlə/ adjective of or reckoned by sun. □ **solar battery, cell** device converting solar radiation into electricity; **solar panel** panel absorbing sun's rays as energy source; **solar plexus** complex of nerves at pit of stomach; **solar system** sun and the planets etc. whose motion is governed by it.

**solarium** /sə'leəriəm/ noun (plural **-ria**) room with sunlamps, glass roof, etc.

**sold** past & past participle of SELL.

**solder** /ˈsəʊldə/ ● noun fusible alloy used for joining metals, wires, etc. ● verb join with solder. □ **soldering iron** tool for melting and applying solder.

**soldier** /ˈsəʊldʒə/ ● noun member of army, esp. (in full **common soldier**) private or NCO; colloquial bread finger, esp. for dipping in egg. ● verb serve as soldier. □ **soldier on** colloquial persevere doggedly. □ **soldierly** adjective.

**soldiery** noun soldiers collectively.

**sole**[1] ● noun undersurface of foot; part of shoe, sock, etc. below foot, esp. part other than heel; lower surface or base of plough, golf-club head, etc. ● verb (-ling) provide with sole.

**sole**[2] noun (plural same or **-s**) type of flatfish.

**sole**[3] adjective one and only single; exclusive. □ **solely** adverb.

**solecism** /ˈsɒlɪsɪz(ə)m/ noun mistake of grammar or idiom; offence against etiquette.

**solemn** /ˈsɒləm/ adjective serious and dignified; formal; awe-inspiring; of cheerless manner; grave. □ **solemnness** noun; **solemnity** /sə'lem-/ (plural **-ies**); **solemnly** adverb.

**solemnize** /ˈsɒləmnaɪz/ verb (also **-ise**) (**-zing** or **-sing**) duly perform (esp. marriage ceremony); make solemn. □ **solemnization** noun.

**solenoid** /ˈsəʊlənɔɪd/ noun cylindrical coil of wire acting as magnet when carrying electric current.

**sol-fa** /ˈsɒlfɑː/ noun system of syllables representing musical notes.

**solicit** /sə'lɪsɪt/ verb (**-t-**) seek repeatedly or earnestly; (of prostitute) accost (man) concerning sexual activity. □ **solicitation** noun.

**solicitor** /sə'lɪsɪtə/ noun lawyer qualified to advise clients and instruct barristers.

**solicitous** /sə'lɪsɪtəs/ adjective showing concern; (+ to do) eager, anxious. □ **solicitously** adverb.

**solicitude** /sə'lɪsɪtjuːd/ noun being solicitous.

**solid** /ˈsɒlɪd/ ● adjective (**-er, -est**) of firm and stable shape, not liquid or fluid; of such material throughout, not hollow; alike all through; sturdily built, not flimsy; 3-dimensional; of solids; sound, reliable; uninterrupted; unanimous. ● noun solid substance or body; (in plural) solid food. ● adverb solidly. □ **solid-state** using electronic properties of solids to replace those of valves. □ **solidity** /sə'lɪd-/ noun; **solidly** adverb; **solidness** noun.

**solidarity** /sɒlɪ'dærɪtɪ/ noun unity, esp. political or in industrial dispute; mutual dependence.

**solidify** /sə'lɪdɪfaɪ/ verb (**-ies, -ied**) make or become solid.

**soliloquy** /sə'lɪləkwɪ/ noun (plural **-quies**) talking without or regardless of hearers; this part of a play. □ **soliloquize** verb (also -ise) (**-zing** or **-sing**).

**solipsism** /ˈsɒlɪpsɪz(ə)m/ noun theory that self is all that exists or can be known.

**solitaire** /ˈsɒlɪteə/ noun jewel set by itself; ring etc. with this; game for one player who removes pegs etc. from board on jumping others over them; US card game for one person.

**solitary** /ˈsɒlɪtərɪ/ ● adjective living or being alone; not gregarious; lonely; secluded; single. ● noun (plural **-ies**) recluse; colloquial solitary confinement. □ **solitary confinement** isolation in separate prison cell.

**solitude** /ˈsɒlɪtjuːd/ noun being solitary; solitary place.

**solo** /ˈsəʊləʊ/ ● noun (plural **-s**) piece of music or dance performed by one person; thing done by one person, esp. unaccompanied flight; (in full **solo whist**) type of whist in which one player may oppose the others. ● verb (**-es, -ed**) perform a solo. ● adjective & adverb unaccompanied, alone.

**soloist** /ˈsəʊləʊɪst/ noun performer of solo.

**solstice** /ˈsɒlstɪs/ *noun* either of two times (**summer**, **winter solstice**) when sun is farthest from equator.

**soluble** /ˈsɒljʊb(ə)l/ *adjective* that can be dissolved or solved. □ **solubility** *noun*.

**solution** /səˈluːʃ(ə)n/ *noun* (means of) solving a problem; conversion of solid or gas into liquid by mixture with liquid; state or substance resulting from this; dissolving, being dissolved.

**solve** *verb* (**-ving**) answer, remove, or deal with (problem). □ **solvable** *adjective*.

**solvency** /ˈsɒlvənsɪ/ *noun* being financially solvent.

**solvent** /ˈsɒlv(ə)nt/ ● *adjective* able to pay one's debts; able to dissolve or form solution. ● *noun* solvent liquid etc.

**somatic** /səˈmætɪk/ *adjective* of the body, not of the mind.

**sombre** /ˈsɒmbə/ *adjective* (also *US* **somber**) dark, gloomy, dismal. □ **sombrely** *adverb*; **sombreness** *noun*.

**sombrero** /sɒmˈbreərəʊ/ *noun* (*plural* **-s**) broad-brimmed hat worn esp. in Latin America.

**some** /sʌm/ ● *adjective* unspecified amount or number of; unknown, unspecified; approximately; considerable; at least a small amount of; such to a certain extent; remarkable. ● *pronoun* some people or things, some number or amount. ● *adverb* colloquial to some extent. □ **somebody** *pronoun* some person, *noun* important person; **someday** at some time in the future; **somehow** for some reason, in some way, by some means; **someone** somebody; **something** unspecified or unknown thing, unexpressed or intangible quantity or quality, *colloquial* notable person or thing; **sometime** at some time, former(ly); **sometimes** occasionally; **somewhat** to some extent; **somewhere** (in or to) some place.

**somersault** /ˈsʌməsɒlt/ ● *noun* leap or roll in which one turns head over heels. ● *verb* perform somersault.

**somnambulism** /sɒmˈnæmbjʊlɪz(ə)n/ *noun* sleepwalking. □ **somnambulant** *adjective*; **somnambulist** *noun*.

**somnolent** /ˈsɒmnələnt/ *adjective* sleepy, drowsy; inducing drowsiness. □ **somnolence** *noun*.

**son** /sʌn/ *noun* male in relation to his parent(s); male descendant; (+ *of*) male member of (family etc.); male inheritor of a quality etc.; *form of address, esp. to boy*. □ **son-in-law** (*plural* **sons-in-law**) daughter's husband.

**sonar** /ˈsəʊnɑː/ *noun* system for detecting objects under water by reflected sound; apparatus for this.

**sonata** /səˈnɑːtə/ *noun* musical composition for one or two instruments in several related movements.

**song** *noun* words set to music or for singing; vocal music; composition suggestive of song; cry of some birds. □ **for a song** *colloquial* very cheaply; **songbird** bird with musical call; **song thrush** common thrush; **songwriter** writer of (music for) songs.

**songster** /ˈsɒŋstə/ *noun* (*feminine* **songstress**) singer; songbird.

**sonic** /ˈsɒnɪk/ *adjective* of or using sound or sound waves. □ **sonic bang, boom** noise made by aircraft flying faster than sound.

**sonnet** /ˈsɒnɪt/ *noun* poem of 14 lines with fixed rhyme scheme.

**sonny** /ˈsʌnɪ/ *noun colloquial familiar form of address to young boy*.

**sonorous** /ˈsɒnərəs/ *adjective* having a loud, full, or deep sound; (of speech etc.) imposing. □ **sonority** /səˈnɒr-/ *noun* (*plural* **-ies**).

**soon** /suːn/ *adverb* in a short time; relatively early; readily, willingly. □ **sooner or later** at some future time. □ **soonish** *adverb*.

**soot** /sʊt/ *noun* black powdery deposit from smoke.

**soothe** /suːð/ *verb* (**-thing**) calm; soften, mitigate.

**soothsayer** /ˈsuːθseɪə/ *noun* seer, prophet.

**sooty** *adjective* (**-ier**, **-iest**) covered with soot; black, brownish black.

**sop** ● *noun* thing given or done to pacify or bribe; piece of bread etc. dipped in gravy etc. ● *verb* (**-pp-**) (+ *up*) soak up.

**sophism** /ˈsɒfɪz(ə)m/ *noun* false argument, esp. one meant to deceive.

**sophist** /ˈsɒfɪst/ *noun* captious or clever but fallacious reasoner. □ **sophistic** /səˈfɪs-/ *adjective*.

**sophisticate** /səˈfɪstɪkət/ *noun* sophisticated person.

**sophisticated** /səˈfɪstɪkeɪtɪd/ *adjective* worldly-wise, cultured, elegant; highly developed and complex. □ **sophistication** *noun*.

**sophistry** /ˈsɒfɪstrɪ/ *noun* (*plural* **-ies**) use of sophisms; a sophism.

**sophomore** /ˈsɒfəmɔ:/ *noun* US second-year university or high-school student.

**soporific** /sɒpəˈrɪfɪk/ ● *adjective* inducing sleep. ● *noun* soporific drug or influence. □ **soporifically** *adverb*.

**sopping** *adjective* drenched.

**soppy** *adjective* (**-ier**, **-iest**) *colloquial* mawkishly sentimental, silly.

**soprano** /səˈprɑ:nəʊ/ ● *noun* (*plural* **-s**) highest singing voice; singer with this. ● *adjective* having range of soprano.

**sorbet** /ˈsɔ:beɪ/ *noun* water-ice; sherbet.

**sorcerer** /ˈsɔ:sərə/ *noun* (*feminine* **sorceress**) magician, wizard. □ **sorcery** *noun* (*plural* **-ies**).

**sordid** /ˈsɔ:dɪd/ *adjective* dirty, squalid; ignoble, mercenary. □ **sordidly** *adverb*; **sordidness** *noun*.

**sore** ● *adjective* painful; suffering pain; aggrieved, vexed; *archaic* grievous, severe. ● *noun* sore place, subject, etc. ● *adverb* *archaic* grievously, severely. □ **soreness** *noun*.

**sorely** *adverb* extremely.

**sorghum** /ˈsɔ:gəm/ *noun* tropical cereal grass.

**sorority** /səˈrɒrɪtɪ/ *noun* (*plural* **-ies**) US female students' society in university or college.

**sorrel**[1] /ˈsɒr(ə)l/ *noun* sour-leaved herb.

**sorrel**[2] /ˈsɒr(ə)l/ ● *adjective* of light reddish-brown colour. ● *noun* this colour; sorrel animal, esp. horse.

**sorrow** /ˈsɒrəʊ/ ● *noun* mental distress caused by loss, disappointment, etc.; cause of sorrow. ● *verb* feel sorrow, mourn. □ **sorrowful** *adjective*.

**sorry** /ˈsɒrɪ/ *adjective* (**-ier**, **-iest**) pained, regretful, penitent; feeling pity; wretched.

**sort** ● *noun* class, kind; *colloquial* person of specified kind. ● *verb* (often + *out*, *over*) arrange systematically. □ **of a sort**, **of sorts** *colloquial* barely deserving the name; **out of sorts** slightly unwell, in

low spirits; **sort out** separate into sorts, select from miscellaneous group, disentangle, put into order, solve, *colloquial* deal with or punish.

**sortie** /ˈsɔ:tɪ/ ● *noun* sally, esp. from besieged garrison; operational military flight. ● *verb* (**sortieing**) make sortie.

**SOS** *noun* (*plural* **SOSs**) international code-signal of extreme distress; urgent appeal for help.

**sot** *noun* habitual drunkard. □ **sottish** *adjective*.

**sotto voce** /sɒtəʊ ˈvəʊtʃɪ/ *adverb* in an undertone. [Italian]

**sou** /su:/ *noun* (*plural* **-s**) *colloquial* very small amount of money; *historical* former French coin of low value.

**soubrette** /su:ˈbret/ *noun* pert maidservant etc. in comedy; actress taking this part.

**soubriquet** = SOBRIQUET.

**soufflé** /ˈsu:fleɪ/ *noun* light spongy dish made with stiffly beaten egg white.

**sough** /saʊ, sʌf/ ● *noun* moaning or rustling sound, e.g. of wind in trees. ● *verb* make this sound.

**sought** /sɔ:t/ *past & past participle* of SEEK. □ **sought-after** much in demand.

**souk** /su:k/ *noun* market-place in Muslim countries.

**soul** /səʊl/ *noun* spiritual or immaterial part of person; moral, emotional, or intellectual nature of person; personification, pattern; an individual; animating or essential part; energy, intensity; soul music. □ **soul-destroying** tedious, monotonous; **soul mate** person ideally suited to another; **soul music** type of black American music; **soul-searching** introspection.

**soulful** *adjective* having, expressing, or evoking deep feeling. □ **soulfully** *adverb*.

**soulless** *adjective* lacking sensitivity or noble qualities; undistinguished, uninteresting.

**sound**[1] /saʊnd/ ● *noun* sensation produced in ear when surrounding air etc. vibrates; vibrations causing this; what is or may be heard; idea or impression give by words. ● *verb* (cause to) emit sound; utter, pronounce; convey specified impression; give audible signal for; test condition of by sound produced.

□ **sound barrier** high resistance of air to objects moving at speeds near that of sound; **sound effect** sound other than speech or music produced artificially for film, broadcast, etc.; **sounding-board** person etc. used to test or disseminate opinion(s), canopy projecting sound towards audience; **sound off** talk loudly, express one's opinions forcefully; **soundproof** *adjective* impervious to sound, *verb* make soundproof; **sound system** equipment for reproducing sound; **soundtrack** sound element of film or videotape, recording of this available separately; **sound wave** wave of compression and rarefaction by which sound is transmitted in air etc.

**sound²** /saʊnd/ ● *adjective* healthy, not diseased or rotten, uninjured; correct, well-founded; financially secure; undisturbed; thorough. ● *adverb* soundly. □ **soundly** *adverb*; **soundness** *noun*.

**sound³** /saʊnd/ ● *verb* test depth or quality of bottom of (sea, river, etc.); (often + *out*) inquire (esp. discreetly) into views etc. of (person).

**sound⁴** /saʊnd/ ● *noun* strait (of water).

**sounding** *noun* measurement of depth of water; (in *plural*) region near enough to shore for sounding; (in *plural*) cautious investigation.

**soup** /suːp/ ● *noun* liquid food made by boiling meat, fish, or vegetables. ● *verb* (usually + *up*) *colloquial* increase power of (engine), enliven. □ **in the soup** *colloquial* in difficulties; **soup-kitchen** place supplying free soup etc. to the poor; **soup-spoon** large round-bowled spoon. □ **soupy** *adjective* (**-ier**, **-iest**).

**soupçon** /ˈsuːpsɔ̃/ *noun* small quantity, trace.

**sour** /saʊə/ ● *adjective* having acid taste or smell (as) from unripeness or fermentation; morose, bitter; unpleasant, distasteful; (of soil) dank. ● *verb* make or become sour. □ **sour grapes** resentful disparagement of something coveted; **sourpuss** *colloquial* bad-tempered person. □ **sourly** *adverb*; **sourness** *noun*.

**source** /sɔːs/ *noun* place from which river or stream issues; place of origination; person, book, etc. providing information. □ **at source** at point of origin or issue.

**souse** /saʊs/ ● *verb* (**-sing**) immerse in pickle or other liquid; (as **soused** *adjective*) *colloquial* drunk; (usually + *in*) soak (thing). ● *noun* pickle made with salt; *US* food in pickle; a plunge or drenching in water.

**soutane** /suːˈtɑːn/ *noun* cassock of RC priest.

**south** /saʊθ/ ● *noun* point of horizon opposite north; corresponding compass point; (usually **the South**) southern part of world, country, town, etc. ● *adjective* towards, at, near, or facing south; (of wind) from south. ● *adverb* towards, at, or near south; (+ *of*) further south than. □ **southbound** travelling or leading south; **south-east, -west** point midway between south and east or west; **southpaw** *colloquial* left-handed person, esp. boxer; **south-south-east, south-south-west** point midway between south and south-east or south-west. □ **southward** *adjective, adverb, & noun*; **southwards** *adverb*.

**southerly** /ˈsʌðəlɪ/ *adjective & adverb* in southern position or direction; (of wind) from south.

**southern** /ˈsʌð(ə)n/ *adjective* of or in south. □ **Southern Cross** constellation with stars forming cross; **southern lights** aurora australis. □ **southernmost** *adjective*.

**southerner** *noun* native or inhabitant of south.

**souvenir** /suːvəˈnɪə/ *noun* memento of place, occasion, etc.

**sou'wester** /saʊˈwestə/ *noun* waterproof hat with broad flap at back; SW wind.

**sovereign** /ˈsɒvrɪn/ ● *noun* supreme ruler, esp. monarch; *historical* British gold coin nominally worth £1. ● *adjective* supreme; self-governing; royal; (of remedy etc.) effective. □ **sovereignty** *noun* (*plural* **-ies**).

**Soviet** /ˈsəʊvɪət/ *historical* ● *adjective* of USSR. ● *noun* citizen of USSR; (**soviet**) elected council in USSR.

**sow¹** /səʊ/ *verb* (*past* **sowed**; *past participle* **sown** or **sowed**) scatter (seed) on or in earth, (often + *with*) plant with seed; initiate.

**sow²** /saʊ/ *noun* adult female pig.

**soy** *noun* (in full **soy sauce**) sauce made from pickled soya beans.

**soya** /'sɔɪə/ *noun* (in full **soya bean**) (seed of) leguminous plant yielding edible oil and flour.

**sozzled** /'sɒz(ə)ld/ *adjective colloquial* very drunk.

**spa** /spɑː/ *noun* curative mineral spring; resort in this.

**space** ● *noun* continuous expanse in which things exist and move; amount of this taken by thing or available; interval between points or objects; empty area; outdoor urban recreation area; outer space; interval of time; expanse of paper used in writing, available for advertising, etc.; blank between printed, typed, or written words etc.; *Printing* piece of metal separating words etc. ● *verb* (**-cing**) set or arrange at intervals; put spaces between. □ **space age** era of space travel; **space-age** very modern; **spacecraft** vehicle for travelling in outer space; **spaceman**, **spacewoman** astronaut; **space out** spread out (more) widely; **spaceship** spacecraft; **space shuttle** spacecraft for repeated use; **space station** artificial satellite as base for operations in outer space; **spacesuit** sealed pressurized suit for astronaut in space; **space-time** fusion of concepts of space and time as 4-dimensional continuum.

**spacious** /'speɪʃəs/ *adjective* having ample space, roomy. □ **spaciously** *adverb*; **spaciousness** *noun*.

**spade**[1] *noun* long-handled digging tool with rectangular metal blade. □ **spadework** hard preparatory work. □ **spadeful** *noun* (*plural* **-s**).

**spade**[2] *noun* playing card of suit denoted by black inverted heart-shaped figures with short stems.

**spaghetti** /spə'geti/ *noun* pasta in long thin strands. □ **spaghetti western** cowboy film made cheaply in Italy.

**span**[1] ● *noun* full extent from end to end; each part of bridge between supports; maximum lateral extent of aeroplane or its wing or of bird's wing etc.; distance between outstretched tips of thumb and little finger; 9 inches. ● *verb* (**-nn-**) extend from side to side or end to end of; bridge (river etc.).

**span**[2] *past of* SPIN.

**spandrel** /'spændrɪl/ *noun* space between curve of arch and surrounding

rectangular moulding, or between curves of adjoining arches and moulding above.

**spangle** /'spæŋg(ə)l/ ● *noun* small piece of glittering material, esp. one of many used to ornament dress etc. ● *verb* (**-ling**) (esp. as **spangled** *adjective*) cover (as) with spangles.

**Spaniard** /'spænjəd/ *noun* native or national of Spain.

**spaniel** /'spænj(ə)l/ *noun* dog of breed with long silky coat and drooping ears.

**Spanish** /'spænɪʃ/ ● *adjective* of Spain. ● *noun* language of Spain.

**spank** *verb & noun* slap, esp. on buttocks.

**spanker** *noun Nautical* fore-and-aft sail on mizen-mast.

**spanking** ● *adjective* brisk; *colloquial* striking, excellent. ● *adverb colloquial* very. ● *noun* slapping on buttocks.

**spanner** /'spænə/ *noun* tool for turning nut on bolt etc. □ **spanner in the works** *colloquial* impediment.

**spar**[1] *noun* stout pole, esp. as ship's mast etc.

**spar**[2] ● *verb* (**-rr-**) make motions of boxing; argue. ● *noun* sparring; boxing match. □ **sparring partner** boxer employed to spar with another as training, person with whom one enjoys arguing.

**spar**[3] *noun* easily split crystalline mineral.

**spare** /speə/ ● *adjective* not required for ordinary or present use, extra; for emergency or occasional use; lean, thin; frugal. ● *noun* spare part. ● *verb* (**-ring**) afford to give, dispense with; refrain from killing, hurting, etc.; not inflict; be frugal or grudging of. □ **go spare** *colloquial* become very angry; **spare (person's) life** not kill; **spare part** duplicate, esp. as replacement; **spare-rib** closely trimmed rib of esp. pork; **spare time** leisure; **spare tyre** *colloquial* roll of fat round waist; **to spare** left over. □ **sparely** *adverb*; **spareness** *noun*.

**sparing** *adjective* frugal, economical; restrained. □ **sparingly** *adverb*.

**spark** ● *noun* fiery particle of burning substance; (often + *of*) small amount; flash of light between electric conductors etc.; this for firing explosive mixture in internal-combustion engine;

flash of wit etc.; (also **bright spark**) lively or clever person. ● *verb* emit spark(s); (often + *off*) stir into activity, initiate. □ **spark plug, sparking plug** device for making spark in internal-combustion engine. □ **sparky** *adjective*.

**sparkle** /'spɑːk(ə)l/ ● *verb* (**-ling**) (seem to) emit sparks; glitter, scintillate; (of wine etc.) effervesce. ● *noun* glitter; lively quality. □ **sparkly** *adjective*.

**sparkler** *noun* sparkling firework; *colloquial* diamond.

**sparrow** /'spærəʊ/ *noun* small brownish-grey bird. □ **sparrowhawk** small hawk.

**sparse** /spɑːs/ *adjective* thinly scattered. □ **sparsely** *adverb*; **sparseness** *noun*; **sparsity** *noun*.

**Spartan** /'spɑːt(ə)n/ ● *adjective* of ancient Sparta; austere, rigorous. ● *noun* native or citizen of Sparta.

**spasm** /'spæz(ə)m/ *noun* sudden involuntary muscular contraction; convulsive movement or emotion etc.; (usually + *of*) *colloquial* brief spell.

**spasmodic** /spæz'mɒdɪk/ *adjective* of or in spasms, intermittent. □ **spasmodically** *adverb*.

**spastic** /'spæstɪk/ ● *adjective* of or having cerebral palsy. ● *noun* spastic person.

**spat**[1] *past & past participle* of SPIT[1].

**spat**[2] (usually in *plural*) *historical* short gaiter covering shoe.

**spate** *noun* river-flood; large amount or number (of similar events etc.).

**spathe** /speɪð/ *noun* large bract(s) enveloping flower-cluster.

**spatial** /'speɪʃ(ə)l/ *adjective* of space. □ **spatially** *adverb*.

**spatter** /'spætə/ ● *verb* splash or scatter in drips. ● *noun* splash; pattering.

**spatula** /'spætjʊlə/ *noun* broad-bladed implement used esp. by artists and in cookery.

**spawn** ● *verb* (of fish, frog, etc.) produce (eggs); be produced as eggs or young; produce or generate in large numbers. ● *noun* eggs of fish, frogs, etc.; white fibrous matter from which fungi grow.

**spay** *verb* sterilize (female animal) by removing ovaries.

**speak** *verb* (*past* **spoke**; *past participle* **spoken** /'spəʊk(ə)n/) utter words in ordinary way; utter (words, the truth, etc.); converse; (+ *of, about*) mention; (+ *for*) act as spokesman for; (+ *to*) speak with reference to or in support of; deliver speech; (be able to) use (specified language) in speaking; convey idea; (usually + *to*) affect. □ **speak for itself** be sufficient evidence; **speaking clock** telephone service announcing correct time; **speak out** give one's opinion courageously; **speak up** speak (more) loudly.

**speaker** *noun* person who speaks, esp. in public; person who speaks specified language; (**Speaker**) presiding officer of legislative assembly; loudspeaker.

**spear** ● *noun* thrusting or hurling weapon with long shaft and sharp point; tip and stem of asparagus, broccoli, etc. ● *verb* pierce or strike (as) with spear. □ **spearhead** *noun* point of spear, person(s) leading attack or challenge, *verb* act as spearhead of (attack etc.); **spearmint** common garden mint.

**spec**[1] *noun colloquial* speculation. □ **on spec** as a gamble.

**spec**[2] *noun colloquial* specification.

**special** /'speʃ(ə)l/ ● *adjective* exceptional; peculiar, specific; for particular purpose; for children with special needs. ● *noun* special constable, train, edition of newspaper, dish on menu, etc. □ **Special Branch** police department dealing with political security; **special constable** person assisting police in routine duties or in emergencies; **special effects** illusions created by props, camera-work, etc.; **special licence** licence allowing immediate marriage without banns; **special pleading** biased reasoning. □ **specially** *adverb*.

**specialist** *noun* person trained in particular branch of profession, esp. medicine; person specially studying subject or area.

**speciality** /speʃɪ'ælɪti/ *noun* (*plural* **-ies**) special subject, product, activity, etc.; special feature or skill.

**specialize** *verb* (also **-ise**) (**-zing** of **-sing**) (often + *in*) become or be specialist; devote oneself to an interest, skill, etc.; (esp. in *passive*) adapt for particular purpose; (as **specialized** *adjective*) of a specialist. □ **specialization** *noun*.

**specialty** /'speʃəltɪ/ noun (plural -ies) esp. US **speciality**.

**specie** /'spiːʃiː/ noun coin as opposed to paper money.

**species** /'spiːʃiːz/ noun (plural same) class of things having common characteristics; group of animals or plants within genus; kind, sort.

**specific** /spə'sɪfɪk/ • adjective clearly defined; relating to particular subject, peculiar; exact, giving full details; archaic (of medicine etc.) for particular disease. • noun archaic specific medicine; specific aspect. □ **specific gravity** relative density. □ **specifically** adverb; **specificity** /-'fɪs-/ noun.

**specification** /spesɪfɪ'keɪʃ(ə)n/ noun specifying; (esp. in plural) detailed description of work (to be) done or of invention, patent, etc.

**specify** /'spesɪfaɪ/ verb (-ies, -ied) name or mention expressly or as condition; include in specifications.

**specimen** /'spesɪmɪn/ noun individual or sample taken as example of class or whole, esp. in experiments etc.; colloquial usually derogatory person of specified sort.

**specious** /'spiːʃəs/ adjective plausible but wrong.

**speck** • noun small spot or stain; particle. • verb (esp. as **specked** adjective) mark with specks.

**speckle** /'spek(ə)l/ • noun speck, esp. one of many markings. • verb (-ling) (esp. as **speckled** adjective) mark with speckles.

**specs** plural noun colloquial spectacles.

**spectacle** /'spektək(ə)l/ noun striking, impressive, or ridiculous sight; public show; object of public attention; (in plural) pair of lenses in frame supported on nose and ears, to correct defective eyesight.

**spectacled** adjective wearing spectacles.

**spectacular** /spek'tækjʊlə/ • adjective striking, impressive, lavish. • noun spectacular performance. □ **spectacularly** adverb.

**spectator** /spek'teɪtə/ noun person who watches a show, game, incident, etc. □ **spectator sport** sport attracting

many spectators. □ **spectate** verb (-ting).

**specter** US = SPECTRE.

**spectra** plural of SPECTRUM.

**spectral** /'spektr(ə)l/ adjective of or like spectres or spectra; ghostly.

**spectre** /'spektə/ noun (US **specter**) ghost; haunting presentiment.

**spectroscope** /'spektrəskəʊp/ noun instrument for recording and examining spectra. □ **spectroscopic** /-'skɒp-/ adjective; **spectroscopy** /-'trɒskəpɪ/ noun.

**spectrum** /'spektrəm/ noun (plural -tra) band of colours as seen in rainbow etc.; entire or wide range of subject, emotion, etc.; arrangement of electromagnetic radiation by wavelength.

**speculate** /'spekjʊleɪt/ verb (-ting) (usually + on, upon, about) theorize, conjecture; deal in commodities etc. in expectation of profiting from fluctuating prices. □ **speculation** noun; **speculative** /-lətɪv/ adjective; **speculator** noun.

**sped** past & past participle of SPEED.

**speech** noun faculty, act, or manner of speaking; formal public address; language, dialect. □ **speech day** annual prize-giving day in school; **speech therapy** treatment for defective speech.

**speechify** /'spiːtʃɪfaɪ/ verb (-ies, -ied) jocular make speeches.

**speechless** adjective temporarily silenced by emotion etc.

**speed** • noun rapidity; rate of progress or motion; gear on bicycle; relative sensitivity of photographic film to light; slang amphetamine. • verb (past & past participle **sped**) go or send quickly; (past & past participle **speeded**) travel at illegal or dangerous speed; archaic be or make prosperous or successful. □ **speedboat** fast motor boat; **speed limit** maximum permitted speed on road etc.; **speedway** (dirt track for) motorcycle racing, US road or track for fast vehicles. □ **speeder** noun.

**speedometer** /spiː'dɒmɪtə/ noun instrument on vehicle indicating its speed.

**speedwell** /'spiːdwel/ noun small blue-flowered herbaceous plant.

**speedy** adjective (-ier, -iest) rapid; prompt. □ **speedily** adverb.

**speleology** /spiːlɪˈɒlədʒɪ/ *noun* the study of caves etc.

**spell**[1] *verb* (*past & past participle* **spelt** or **spelled**) write or name correctly the letters of (word etc.); (of letters) form (word etc.); result in. □ **spell out** make out letter by letter, explain in detail. □ **speller** *noun*.

**spell**[2] *noun* words used as charm; effect of these; fascination. □ **spellbound** held as if by spell, fascinated.

**spell**[3] *noun* (fairly) short period; period of some activity or work.

**spelling** *noun* way word is spelt; ability to spell.

**spelt**[1] *past & past participle* of SPELL[1].

**spelt**[2] *noun* kind of wheat giving very fine flour.

**spend** *verb* (*past & past participle* **spent**) pay out (money); use or consume (time or energy); use up; (as **spent** *adjective*) having lost force or strength. □ **spendthrift** extravagant person. □ **spender** *noun*.

**sperm** *noun* (*plural* same or **-s**) spermatozoon; semen. □ **sperm bank** store of semen for artificial insemination; **sperm whale** large whale hunted for spermaceti.

**spermaceti** /spɜːməˈsɛtɪ/ *noun* white waxy substance used for ointments etc.

**spermatozoon** /spɜːmətəʊˈzəʊən/ *noun* (*plural* **-zoa**) fertilizing cell of male organism.

**spermicide** /ˈspɜːmɪsaɪd/ *noun* substance that kills spermatozoa. □ **spermicidal** /-ˈsaɪd-/ *adjective*.

**spew** *verb* (often + *up*) vomit; (often + *out*) (cause to) gush.

**sphagnum** /ˈsfægnəm/ *noun* (*plural* **-na**) (in full **sphagnum moss**) moss growing in bogs, used as packing etc.

**sphere** /sfɪə/ *noun* solid figure with every point on its surface equidistant from centre; ball, globe; field of action, influence, etc.; place in society; *historical* each of revolving shells in which heavenly bodies were thought to be set.

**spherical** /ˈsfɛrɪk(ə)l/ *adjective* shaped like sphere; of spheres. □ **spherically** *adverb*.

**spheroid** /ˈsfɪərɔɪd/ *noun* spherelike but not perfectly spherical body. □ **spheroidal** /-ˈrɔɪd-/ *adjective*.

**sphincter** /ˈsfɪŋktə/ *noun* ring of muscle closing and opening orifice.

**Sphinx** /sfɪŋks/ *noun* ancient Egyptian stone figure with lion's body and human or animal head; (**sphinx**) inscrutable person.

**spice** ● *noun* aromatic or pungent vegetable substance used as flavouring; spices collectively; piquant quality; slight flavour. ● *verb* (**-cing**) flavour with spice; enhance.

**spick and span** *adjective* trim and clean; smart, new-looking.

**spicy** *adjective* (**-ier, -iest**) of or flavoured with spice; piquant, improper. □ **spiciness** *noun*.

**spider** /ˈspaɪdə/ *noun* 8-legged arthropod, many species of which spin webs esp. to capture insects as food. □ **spider plant** house plant with long narrow leaves.

**spidery** *adjective* elongated and thin.

**spiel** /ʃpiːl/ *noun slang* glib speech or story, sales pitch.

**spigot** /ˈspɪgət/ *noun* small peg or plug; device for controlling flow of liquid in tap.

**spike**[1] ● *noun* sharp point; pointed piece of metal, esp. forming top of iron railing; metal point on sole of running shoe to prevent slipping; (in *plural*) spiked running shoes; large nail. ● *verb* (**-king**) put spikes on or into; fix on spike; *colloquial* add alcohol to (drink), contaminate. □ **spike (person's) guns** defeat his or her plans.

**spike**[2] *noun* cluster of flower heads on long stem.

**spikenard** /ˈspaɪknɑːd/ *noun* tall sweet-smelling plant; *historical* aromatic ointment formerly made from this.

**spiky** *adjective* (**-ier, -iest**) like a spike; having spikes; *colloquial* irritable.

**spill**[1] ● *verb* (*past & past participle* **spilt** or **spilled**) allow (liquid etc.) to fall or run out of container, esp. accidentally; (of liquid etc.) fall or run out thus; throw from vehicle, saddle, etc.; (+ *into*, *out*, etc.) leave quickly; *slang* divulge (information etc.); shed (blood). ● *noun* spilling, being spilt; tumble, esp. from horse or vehicle. □ **spill the beans** *colloquial* divulge secret etc. □ **spillage** *noun*.

**spill**[2] *noun* thin strip of wood, paper, etc. for lighting candle etc.

**spillikin** /'spɪlɪkɪn/ *noun* splinter of wood etc.; (in *plural*) game in which thin rods are removed one at a time from heap without disturbing others.

**spilt** *past & past participle of* SPILL[1].

**spin** ● *verb* (**-nn-**; *past* **spun** or **span**; *past participle* **spun**) (cause to) turn or whirl round rapidly; make (yarn) by drawing out and twisting together fibres of wool etc.; make (web etc.) by extruding fine viscous thread; (of person's head) be in a whirl; tell or compose (story etc.); toss (coin); (as **spun** *adjective*) made into threads. ● *noun* revolving motion, whirl; rotating dive of aircraft; secondary twisting motion e.g. of ball in flight; *colloquial* brief drive, esp. in car. □ **spin bowler** *Cricket* one who imparts spin to ball; **spin-drier, -dryer** machine for drying clothes by spinning them in rotating drum; **spin-dry** *verb*; **spinning wheel** household implement for spinning yarn, with spindle driven by wheel with crank or treadle; **spin-off** incidental result, esp. from technology; **spin out** prolong; **spin a yarn** tell story.

**spina bifida** /spaɪnə 'bɪfɪdə/ *noun* congenital spinal defect, with protruding membranes.

**spinach** /'spɪnɪdʒ/ *noun* green vegetable with edible leaves.

**spinal** /'spaɪn(ə)l/ *adjective* of spine. □ **spinal column** spine; **spinal cord** cylindrical nervous structure within spine.

**spindle** /'spɪnd(ə)l/ *noun* slender rod for twisting and winding thread in spinning; pin or axis on which something revolves; turned piece of wood used as banister etc.

**spindly** *adjective* (**-ier, -iest**) long or tall and thin.

**spindrift** /'spɪndrɪft/ *noun* spray on surface of sea.

**spine** *noun* series of vertebrae extending from skull, backbone; needle-like outgrowth of animal or plant; part of book enclosing page-fastening; ridge, sharp projection. □ **spine-chiller** suspense or horror film, story, etc.

**spineless** *adjective* lacking resoluteness.

**spinet** /spɪ'net/ *noun historical* small harpsichord with oblique strings.

**spinnaker** /'spɪnəkə/ *noun* large triangular sail used at bow of yacht.

**spinner** *noun* spin bowler; person or thing that spins, esp. manufacturer engaged in spinning; spin-drier; revolving bait or lure in fishing.

**spinneret** /'spɪnəret/ *noun* spinning-organ in spider etc.

**spinney** /'spɪnɪ/ *noun* (*plural* **-s**) small wood, thicket.

**spinster** /'spɪnstə/ *noun formal* unmarried woman.

**spiny** *adjective* (**-ier, -iest**) having (many) spines.

**spiraea** /spaɪˈrɪə/ *noun* (*US* **spirea**) garden plant related to meadowsweet.

**spiral** /'spaɪər(ə)l/ ● *adjective* coiled in a plane or as round a cylinder or cone; having this shape. ● *noun* spiral curve; progressive rise or fall. ● *verb* (**-ll-**; *US* **-l-**) move in spiral course; (of prices etc.) rise or fall continuously. □ **spiral staircase** circular staircase round central axis.

**spirant** /'spaɪərənt/ ● *adjective* uttered with continuous expulsion of breath. ● *noun* spirant consonant.

**spire** *noun* tapering structure, esp. on church tower; any tapering thing.

**spirea** *US* = SPIRAEA.

**spirit** /'spɪrɪt/ ● *noun* person's essence or intelligence, soul; rational being without material body; ghost; person's character; attitude; type of person; prevailing tendency; (usually in *plural*) distilled alcoholic liquor; distilled volatile liquid; courage, vivacity; (in *plural*) mood; essential as opposed to formal meaning. ● *verb* (**-t-**) (usually + *away*, *off*, etc.) convey mysteriously. □ **spirit gum** quick-drying gum for attaching false hair; **spirit lamp** lamp burning methylated or other volatile spirit; **spirit level** device used to test horizontality.

**spirited** *adjective* lively, courageous. □ **-spirited** in specified mood. □ **spiritedly** *adverb*.

**spiritual** /'spɪrɪtʃʊəl/ ● *adjective* of spirit; religious, divine, inspired; refined, sensitive. ● *noun* (also **Negro spiritual**) religious song originally of American blacks. □ **spirituality** /-'æl-/ noun; **spiritually** adverb.

**spiritualism** noun belief in, and practice of, communication with the dead, esp. through mediums. □ **spiritualist** noun; **spiritualistic** /-'lɪs-/ adjective.

**spirituous** /'spɪrɪtʃʊəs/ adjective very alcoholic; distilled as well as fermented.

**spit**[1] ● verb (**-tt-**; past & past participle **spat** or **spit**) eject (esp. saliva) from mouth; do this as gesture of contempt; utter vehemently; (of fire etc.) throw out with explosion; (of rain etc.) fall lightly; make spitting noise. ● noun spittle; spitting. ● **spitfire** fiery-tempered person; **spitting distance** colloquial very short distance; **spitting image** colloquial exact counterpart or likeness.

**spit**[2] ● noun rod for skewering meat for roasting over fire etc.; point of land projecting into sea; spade-depth of earth. ● verb (**-tt-**) pierce (as) with spit. □ **spit-roast** roast on spit.

**spite** ● noun ill will, malice. ● verb (**-ting**) hurt, thwart. □ **in spite of** notwithstanding.

**spiteful** adjective malicious. □ **spitefully** adverb.

**spittle** /'spɪt(ə)l/ noun saliva.

**spittoon** /spɪ'tuːn/ noun vessel to spit into.

**spiv** noun colloquial man, esp. flashily-dressed one, living from shady dealings. □ **spivvish** adjective; **spivvy** adjective.

**splash** ● verb (cause to) scatter in drops; wet or stain by splashing; (usually + across, along, about, etc.) move with splashing; jump or fall into water etc. with splash; display (news) conspicuously; decorate with scattered colour; spend (money) ostentatiously. ● noun act or noise of splashing; quantity splashed; mark of splashing; prominent news feature, display, etc.; patch of colour; colloquial small quantity of soda water etc. (in drink). □ **splashback** panel behind sink etc. to protect wall from splashes; **splashdown** alighting of spacecraft on sea; **splash down** verb; **splash out** colloquial spend money freely.

**splat** colloquial ● noun sharp splattering sound. ● adverb with splat. ● verb (**-tt-**) fall or hit with splat.

**splatter** /'splætə/ verb & noun splash, esp. with continuous noisy action, spatter.

**splay** ● verb spread apart; (of opening) have sides diverging; make (opening) with divergent sides. ● noun surface at oblique angle to another. ● adjective splayed.

**spleen** noun abdominal organ regulating quality of blood; moroseness, irritability.

**splendid** /'splendɪd/ adjective magnificent; glorious, dignified; excellent. □ **splendidly** adverb.

**splendiferous** /splen'dɪfərəs/ adjective colloquial splendid.

**splendour** /'splendə/ noun (US **splendor**) dazzling brightness; magnificence.

**splenetic** /splɪ'netɪk/ adjective bad-tempered, peevish.

**splenic** /'splenɪk/ adjective of or in spleen.

**splice** ● verb (**-cing**) join (ropes) by interweaving strands; join (pieces of wood, tape, etc.) by overlapping; (esp. as **spliced** adjective) colloquial join in marriage. ● noun join made by splicing.

**splint** ● noun strip of wood etc. bound to broken limb while it heals. ● verb secure with splint.

**splinter** /'splɪntə/ ● noun small sharp fragment of wood, stone, glass, etc. ● verb split into splinters, shatter. □ **splinter group** breakaway political group. □ **splintery** adjective.

**split** ● verb (**-tt-**; past & past participle **split**) break, esp. lengthwise or with grain; break forcibly; (often + up) divide into parts, esp. equal shares; (often + off, away) remove or be removed by breaking or dividing; (usually + on, over, etc.) divide into disagreeing or hostile parties; cause fission of (atom); slang leave, esp. suddenly; (usually + on) colloquial inform; (as **splitting** adjective) (of headache) severe; (of head) suffer severe headache. ● noun splitting; disagreement, schism; (in plural) feat of leaping or sitting with legs straight and pointing in opposite directions. □ **split hairs** make over-subtle distinctions; **split infinitive** one with adverb etc. inserted between to and verb (see note below); **split-level** with more than one level; **split personality** condition of alternating personalities; **split pin** metal cotter with its two ends splayed out after passing through hole; **split second** very short time; **split-second** very rapid, (of timing) very accurate; **split up** separate, end relationship.

■ **Usage** Split infinitives, as in *I want to quickly sum up* and *Your job is to really get to know everybody*, are common in informal English, but many people consider them incorrect and prefer *I want quickly to sum up* or *I want to sum up quickly*. They should therefore be avoided in formal English, but note that just changing the order of words can alter the meaning, e.g. *Your job is really to get to know everybody*.

**splodge** *colloquial* ● *noun* daub, blot, smear. ● *verb* (**-ging**) make splodge on. □ **splodgy** *adjective*.

**splosh** *colloquial* ● *verb* move with splashing sound. ● *noun* splashing sound; splash of water etc.

**splotch** *noun & verb* splodge. □ **splotchy** *adjective*.

**splurge** *colloquial* ● *noun* sudden extravagance; ostentatious display or effort. ● *verb* (**-ging**) (usually + *on*) make splurge.

**splutter** /'splʌtə/ ● *verb* speak or express in choking manner; emit spitting sounds; speak rapidly or incoherently. ● *noun* spluttering speech or sound.

**spoil** ● *verb* (*past & past participle* **spoilt** or **spoiled**) make or become useless or unsatisfactory; reduce enjoyment etc. of; decay, go bad; ruin character of by over-indulgence. ● *noun* (usually in *plural*) plunder, stolen goods; profit or advantages accruing from success or position. □ **spoilsport** person who spoils others' enjoyment; **spoilt for choice** having excessive number of choices.

**spoiler** *noun* device on aircraft to increase drag; device on vehicle to improve road-holding at speed.

**spoilt** *past & past participle* of **spoil**.

**spoke**[1] *noun* each of rods running from hub to rim of wheel. □ **put a spoke in (person's) wheel** thwart, hinder.

**spoke**[2] *past* of SPEAK.

**spoken** *past participle* of SPEAK.

**spokesman** /'spəʊksmən/ *noun* (*feminine* **spokeswoman**) person who speaks for others, representative.

**spokesperson** /'spəʊkspɜːs(ə)n/ *noun* (*plural* **-s** or **spokespeople**) spokesman or spokeswoman.

**spoliation** /spəʊlɪ'eɪʃ(ə)n/ *noun* plundering, pillage.

**spondee** /'spɒndiː/ *noun* metrical foot of two long syllables. □ **spondaic** /-'deɪɪk/ *adjective*.

**sponge** /spʌndʒ/ ● *noun* sea animal with porous body wall and tough elastic skeleton; this skeleton or piece of porous rubber etc. used in bathing, cleaning, etc.; thing like sponge in consistency, esp. sponge cake; act of sponging. ● *verb* (**-ging**) wipe or clean with sponge; (often + *out*, *away*, etc.) wipe off or rub out (as with sponge); (often + *up*) absorb (as with sponge); (often + *on*, *off*) live as parasite. □ **sponge bag** waterproof bag for toilet articles; **sponge cake**, **pudding** one of light spongelike consistency; **sponge rubber** porous rubber.

**sponger** *noun* parasitic person.

**spongy** *adjective* (**-ier**, **-iest**) like a sponge, porous, elastic, absorbent.

**sponsor** /'spɒnsə/ ● *noun* person who pledges money to charity in return for specified activity by someone; patron of artistic or sporting activity etc.; company etc. financing broadcast in return for advertising; person introducing legislation; godparent at baptism. ● *verb* be sponsor for. □ **sponsorship** *noun*.

**spontaneous** /spɒn'teɪnɪəs/ *adjective* acting, done, or occurring without external cause; instinctive, automatic, natural. □ **spontaneity** /-tə'neɪɪtɪ/ *noun*; **spontaneously** *adverb*.

**spoof** /spuːf/ *noun & verb colloquial* parody, hoax, swindle.

**spook** /spuːk/ ● *noun colloquial* ghost. ● *verb esp. US* frighten, unnerve. □ **spooky** *adjective* (**-ier**, **-iest**).

**spool** /spuːl/ ● *noun* reel on which something is wound; revolving cylinder of angler's reel. ● *verb* wind on spool.

**spoon** /spuːn/ ● *noun* utensil with bowl and handle for putting food in mouth or for stirring etc.; spoonful; spoon-shaped thing, esp. (in full **spoon-bait**) revolving metal fish-lure. ● *verb* (often + *up*, *out*) take (liquid etc.) with spoon; hit (ball) feebly upwards. □ **spoonbill** wading bird with broad flat-tipped bill; **spoonfeed** feed with spoon, give help etc. to (person) without demanding any effort from recipient. □ **spoonful** *noun* (*plural* **-s**).

**spoonerism** /'spuːnərɪz(ə)m/ *noun* (usually accidental) transposition of initial sounds of two or more words.

**spoor** /spʊə/ *noun* animal's track or scent.

**sporadic** /spə'rædɪk/ *adjective* occurring only sparsely or occasionally. □ **sporadically** *adverb*.

**spore** *noun* reproductive cell of ferns, fungi, protozoa, etc.

**sporran** /'spɒrən/ *noun* pouch worn in front of kilt.

**sport** ● *noun* game or competitive activity usually involving physical exertion; these collectively; (in *plural*) meeting for competition in athletics; amusement, fun; *colloquial* sportsman, good fellow; person with specified attitude to games, rules, etc. ● *verb* amuse oneself, play about; wear or exhibit, esp. ostentatiously. □ **sports car** low-built racing car; **sports coat**, **jacket** man's informal jacket; **sports ground** piece of land used for sport; **sportswear** clothes for sports, informal clothes.

**sporting** *adjective* of or interested in sport; generous, fair. □ **sporting chance** some possibility of success. □ **sportingly** *adverb*.

**sportive** *adjective* playful.

**sportsman** /'spɔːtsmən/ *noun* (*feminine* **sportswoman**) person engaging in sport; fair and generous person. □ **sportsmanlike** *adjective*; **sportsmanship** *noun*.

**sporty** *adjective* (**-ier**, **-iest**) *colloquial* fond of sport; *colloquial* rakish, showy.

**spot** ● *noun* small mark differing in colour etc. from surface it is on; pimple, blemish; particular place, locality; particular part of one's body or character; *colloquial* one's (regular) position in organization, programme, etc.; *colloquial* small quantity; spotlight. ● *verb* (**-tt-**) *colloquial* pick out, recognize, catch sight of; watch for and take note of (trains,

talent, etc.); (as **spotted** *adjective*) marked with spots; make spots, rain slightly. □ **in a** (**tight**) **spot** *colloquial* in difficulties; **on the spot** at scene of event, *colloquial* in position demanding response or action, without delay, without moving backwards or forwards; **spot cash** money paid immediately after sale; **spot check** sudden or random check; **spotlight** *noun* beam of light directed on small area, lamp projecting this, full publicity, *verb* direct spotlight on; **spot on** *colloquial* precise(ly); **spotted dick** suet pudding containing currants; **spot-weld** join (metal surfaces) by welding at points. □ **spotter** *noun*.

**spotless** *adjective* absolutely clean, unblemished. □ **spotlessly** *adverb*.

**spotty** *adjective* (**-ier**, **-iest**) marked with spots; patchy, irregular.

**spouse** /spaʊz/ *noun* husband or wife.

**spout** /spaʊt/ ● *noun* projecting tube or lip for pouring from teapot, kettle, jug, fountain, roof-gutter, etc.; jet of liquid. ● *verb* discharge or issue forcibly in jet; utter at length or pompously. □ **up the spout** *slang* useless, ruined, pregnant.

**sprain** ● *verb* wrench (ankle, wrist, etc.) causing pain or swelling. ● *noun* such injury.

**sprang** *past* of SPRING.

**sprat** *noun* small sea fish.

**sprawl** ● *verb* sit, lie, or fall with limbs spread out untidily; spread untidily, straggle. ● *noun* sprawling movement, position, or mass; straggling urban expansion.

**spray**¹ ● *noun* water etc. flying in small drops; liquid intended for spraying; device for spraying. ● *verb* throw as spray; sprinkle (as) with spray; (of tomcat) mark environment with urine to attract females. □ **spray-gun** device for spraying paint etc. □ **sprayer** *noun*.

**spray**² ● *noun* sprig with flowers or leaves, small branch; ornament in similar form.

**spread** /spred/ ● *verb* (*past & past participle* **spread**) (often + *out*) open, extend, unfold, cause to cover larger surface, have wide or increasing extent; (cause to) become widely known; cover; lay (table). ● *noun* act, capability, or extent of spreading; diffusion; breadth; increased girth; difference between two rates, prices, etc.; *colloquial* elaborate meal; paste for spreading on bread etc.; bedspread; printed matter spread over more than one column. □ **spread eagle** figure of eagle with legs and wings extended as emblem; **spread-eagle** place (person) with arms and legs spread out, defeat utterly; **spreadsheet** computer program for handling tabulated figures etc., esp. in accounting.

**spree** *noun colloquial* extravagant outing; bout of drinking etc.

**sprig** ● *noun* small branch or shoot; ornament resembling this, esp. on fabric. ● *verb* (**-gg-**) ornament with sprigs.

**sprightly** /'spraɪtlɪ/ *adjective* (**-ier, -iest**) vivacious, lively.

**spring** ● *verb* (*past* **sprang**; *past participle* **sprung**) rise rapidly or suddenly, leap; move rapidly (as by action of a spring; (usually + *from*) originate; (cause to) act or appear unexpectedly; *slang* contrive escape of (person from prison etc.); (usually as **sprung** *adjective*) provide with springs. ● *noun* jump, leap; recoil; elasticity; elastic device usually of coiled metal used esp. to drive clockwork or for cushioning in furniture or vehicles; season of year between winter and summer; (often + *of*) early stage of life etc.; place where water, oil, etc. wells up from earth, basin or flow so formed; motive for or origin of action, custom, etc. □ **spring balance** device measuring weight by tension of spring; **springboard** flexible board for leaping or diving from, source of impetus; **spring-clean** *noun* thorough cleaning of house, esp. in spring, *verb* clean thus; **spring greens** young cabbage leaves; **spring a leak** develop leak; **spring onion** young onion eaten raw; **spring roll** Chinese fried pancake filled with vegetables etc.; **spring tide** tide with greatest rise and fall; **springtime** season or period of spring.

**springbok** /'sprɪŋbɒk/ *noun* ( *plural* same or **-s**) S. African gazelle.

**springer** *noun* small spaniel.

**springy** *adjective* (**-ier, -iest**) elastic.

**sprinkle** /'sprɪŋk(ə)l/ ● *verb* (**-ling**) scatter in small drops or particles; (often +

*with*) subject to sprinkling; (of liquid etc.) fall thus on. ● *noun* (usually + *of*) light shower, sprinkling.

**sprinkler** *noun* device for sprinkling lawn or extinguishing fires.

**sprinkling** *noun* small sparse number or amount.

**sprint** ● *verb* run short distance at top speed. ● *noun* such run; similar short effort in cycling, swimming, etc. □ **sprinter** *noun*.

**sprit** *noun* small diagonal spar from mast to upper outer corner of sail. □ **spritsail** /'sprɪts(ə)l/ sail extended by sprit.

**sprite** *noun* elf, fairy.

**spritzer** /'sprɪtsə/ *noun* drink of white wine with soda water.

**sprocket** /'sprɒkɪt/ *noun* projection on rim of wheel engaging with links of chain.

**sprout** /spraʊt/ ● *verb* put forth (shoots etc.); begin to grow. ● *noun* plant shoot; Brussels sprout.

**spruce**[1] ● *adjective* of trim appearance, smart. ● *verb* (**-cing**) (usually + *up*) make or become smart. □ **sprucely** *adverb*; **spruceness** *noun*.

**spruce**[2] *noun* conifer with dense conical foliage; its wood.

**sprung** *past participle* of SPRING.

**spry** /spraɪ/ *adjective* (**-er, -est**) lively, nimble. □ **spryly** *adverb*.

**spud** ● *noun colloquial* potato; small narrow spade for weeding. ● *verb* (**-dd-**) (+ *up, out*) remove with spud.

**spumante** /spuːˈmæntɪ/ *noun* Italian sparkling white wine.

**spume** /spjuːm/ *noun & verb* (**-ming**) froth, foam. □ **spumy** *adjective* (**-ier, -iest**).

**spun** *past & past participle* of SPIN. □ **spun silk** cheap material containing waste silk.

**spunk** *noun colloquial* mettle, spirit. □ **spunky** *adjective* (**-ier, -iest**).

**spur** ● *noun* small spike or spiked wheel attached to rider's heel for urging horse forward; stimulus, incentive; spur-shaped thing, esp. projection from mountain (range), branch road or railway, or hard projection on cock's leg. ● *verb* (**-rr-**) prick (horse) with spur;

incite, stimulate. □ **on the spur of the moment** on impulse.

**spurge** *noun* plant with acrid milky juice.

**spurious** /'spjʊərɪəs/ *adjective* not genuine, fake.

**spurn** *verb* reject with disdain or contempt.

**spurt** ● *verb* (cause to) gush out in jet or stream; make sudden effort. ● *noun* sudden gushing out, jet; short burst of speed, growth, etc.

**sputnik** /'spʊtnɪk/ *noun* Russian artificial earth satellite.

**sputter** /'spʌtə/ *verb & noun* splutter.

**sputum** /'spju:təm/ *noun* thick coughed-up mucus.

**spy** ● *noun* (*plural* **spies**) person secretly collecting and reporting information for a government, company, etc.; person watching others secretly. ● *verb* (**spies**, **spied**) discern, see; (often + *on*) act as spy. □ **spyglass** small telescope; **spyhole** peep-hole; **spy out** explore or discover, spy secretly.

**sq.** *abbreviation* square.

**Sqn. Ldr.** *abbreviation* Squadron Leader.

**squab** /skwɒb/ ● *noun* young esp. unfledged pigeon etc.; short fat person; stuffed cushion, esp. as part of car-seat; sofa. ● *adjective* short and fat.

**squabble** /'skwɒb(ə)l/ ● *noun* petty or noisy quarrel. ● *verb* (**-ling**) engage in squabble.

**squad** /skwɒd/ *noun* small group sharing task etc., esp. of soldiers or police officers; team. □ **squad car** police car.

**squaddie** *noun* (also **squaddy**) (*plural* **-ies**) *slang* recruit, private.

**squadron** /'skwɒdrən/ *noun* unit of RAF with 10–18 aircraft; detachment of warships employed on particular service; organized group etc., esp. cavalry division of two troops. □ **squadron leader** RAF officer commanding squadron, next below wing commander.

**squalid** /'skwɒlɪd/ *adjective* filthy, dirty; mean in appearance.

**squall** /skwɔ:l/ ● *noun* sudden or violent gust or storm; discordant cry, scream. ● *verb* utter (with) squall, scream. □ **squally** *adjective*.

**squalor** /'skwɒlə/ *noun* filthy or squalid state.

**squander** /'skwɒndə/ *verb* spend wastefully.

**square** /skweə/ ● *noun* rectangle with 4 equal sides; object of (roughly) this shape; open area enclosed by buildings; product of number multiplied by itself; L- or T-shaped instrument for obtaining or testing right angles; *slang* conventional or old-fashioned person. ● *adjective* square-shaped; having or in form of a right angle; angular, not round; designating unit of measure equal to area of square whose side is one of the unit specified; (usually + *with*) level, parallel; (usually + *to*) perpendicular; sturdy, squat; arranged; (also **all square**) with no money owed, (of scores) equal; fair, honest; direct; *slang* conventional, old-fashioned. ● *adverb* squarely. ● *verb* (**-ring**) make square; multiply (number) by itself; (usually + *to, with*) make or be consistent, reconcile; mark out in squares; settle (bill etc.); place (shoulders etc.) squarely facing forwards; *colloquial* pay, bribe; make scores of (match etc.) equal. □ **square brackets** brackets of the form [ ] (see panel at BRACKET); **square dance** dance with 4 couples facing inwards from 4 sides; **square deal** fair bargain or treatment; **square leg** *Cricket* fielding position on batsman's leg side nearly opposite stumps; **square meal** substantial meal; **square-rigged** having 4-sided sails set across length of ship; **square root** number that multiplied by itself gives specified number. □ **squarely** *adverb*.

**squash¹** /skwɒʃ/ ● *verb* crush or squeeze flat or into pulp; (often + *into*) *colloquial* force into small space, crowd; belittle, bully; suppress. ● *noun* crowd, crowded state; drink made of crushed fruit; (in full **squash rackets**) game played with rackets and small ball in closed court. □ **squashy** *adjective* (**-ier, -iest**).

**squash²** /skwɒʃ/ *noun* (*plural* same or **-es**) trailing annual plant; gourd of this.

**squat** /skwɒt/ ● *verb* (**-tt-**) sit on one's heels, or on ground with knees drawn up; *colloquial* sit down; act as squatter. ● *adjective* (**-tt-**) short and thick, dumpy. ● *noun* squatting posture; place occupied by squatter(s).

**squatter** *noun* person who inhabits unoccupied premises without permission.

**squaw** *noun* N. American Indian woman or wife.

**squawk** ● *noun* harsh cry; complaint. ● *verb* utter squawk.

**squeak** ● *noun* short high-pitched cry or sound; (also **narrow squeak**) narrow escape. ● *verb* emit squeak; utter shrilly; (+ *by, through*) *colloquial* pass narrowly; *slang* turn informer.

**squeaky** *adjective* (**-ier, -iest**) making squeaking sound. □ **squeaky clean** *colloquial* completely clean, above criticism. □ **squeakily** *adverb*; **squeakiness** *noun*.

**squeal** ● *noun* prolonged shrill sound or cry. ● *verb* make, or utter with, squeal; *slang* turn informer; *colloquial* protest vociferously.

**squeamish** /ˈskwiːmɪʃ/ *adjective* easily nauseated; fastidious. □ **squeamishly** *adverb*; **squeamishness** *noun*.

**squeegee** /ˈskwiːdʒiː/ *noun* rubber-edged implement on handle, for cleaning windows etc.

**squeeze** ● *verb* (**-zing**) (often + *out*) exert pressure on, esp. to extract moisture; reduce in size or alter in shape by squeezing; force or push into or through small or narrow space; harass, pressure; (usually + *out of*) get by extortion or entreaty; press (person's hand) in sympathy etc. ● *noun* squeezing, being squeezed; close embrace; crowd, crowded state; small quantity produced by squeezing; restriction on borrowing and investment. □ **squeeze-box** *colloquial* accordion, concertina.

**squelch** ● *verb* make sucking sound as of treading in thick mud; move with squelching sound; disconcert, silence. ● *noun* act or sound of squelching. □ **squelchy** *adjective*.

**squib** *noun* small hissing firework; satirical essay.

**squid** *noun* (*plural* same or **-s**) 10-armed marine cephalopod.

**squidgy** /ˈskwɪdʒɪ/ *adjective* (**-ier, -iest**) *colloquial* squashy, soggy.

**squiffy** /ˈskwɪfɪ/ *adjective* (**-ier, -iest**) *slang* slightly drunk.

**squiggle** /ˈskwɪg(ə)l/ *noun* short curling line, esp. in handwriting. □ **squiggly** *adjective*.

**squint** ● *verb* have eyes turned in different directions; (often + *at*) look sidelong. ● *noun* squinting condition; sidelong glance; *colloquial* glance, look; oblique opening in church wall.

**squire** ● *noun* country gentleman, esp. chief landowner of district; *historical* knight's attendant. ● *verb* (**-ring**) (of man) escort (woman).

**squirearchy** /ˈskwaɪərɑːkɪ/ *noun* (*plural* **-ies**) landowners collectively.

**squirm** ● *verb* wriggle, writhe; show or feel embarrassment. ● *noun* squirming movement.

**squirrel** /ˈskwɪr(ə)l/ ● *noun* bushy-tailed usually tree-living rodent; its fur; hoarder. ● *verb* (**-ll-**; *US* **-l-**) (often + *away*) hoard.

**squirt** ● *verb* eject (liquid etc.) in jet; be ejected thus; splash with squirted substance. ● *noun* jet of water etc.; small quantity squirted; syringe; *colloquial* insignificant person.

**squish** *colloquial* ● *noun* slight squelching sound. ● *verb* move with squish; squash. □ **squishy** *adjective* (**-ier, -iest**).

**Sr.** *abbreviation* Senior.

**SRN** *abbreviation* State Registered Nurse.

**SS** *abbreviation* steamship; Saints; *historical* Nazi special police force (*Schutzstaffel*).

**SSE** *abbreviation* south-south-east.

**SSW** *abbreviation* south-south-west.

**St** *abbreviation* Saint.

**St.** *abbreviation* Street.

**st.** *abbreviation* stone (weight).

**stab** ● *verb* (**-bb-**) pierce or wound with knife etc.; (often + *at*) aim blow with such weapon; cause sharp pain to. ● *noun* act or result of stabbing; *colloquial* attempt. □ **stab in the back** *noun* treacherous attack, *verb* betray.

**stability** /stəˈbɪlɪtɪ/ *noun* being stable.

**stabilize** /ˈsteɪbɪlaɪz/ *verb* (also **-ise**) (**-zing** or **-sing**) make or become stable. □ **stabilization** *noun*.

**stabilizer** *noun* (also **-iser**) device to keep aircraft or (in *plural*) child's bicycle steady; food additive for preserving texture.

**stable** /ˈsteɪb(ə)l/ ● adjective (**-r, -st**) firmly fixed or established, not fluctuating or changing; not easily upset or disturbed. ● noun building for keeping horses; establishment for training racehorses; racehorses of particular stable; people, products, etc. having common origin or affiliation; such origin or affiliation. ● verb (**-ling**) put or keep in stable. □ **stably** adverb.

**stabling** noun accommodation for horses.

**staccato** /stəˈkɑːtəʊ/ esp. Music ● adverb & adjective with each sound sharply distinct. ● noun (plural **-s**) staccato passage or delivery.

**stack** ● noun (esp. orderly) pile or heap; haystack; colloquial large quantity; number of chimneys standing together; smokestack; tall factory chimney; stacked group of aircraft; part of library where books are compactly stored. ● verb pile in stack(s); arrange (cards, circumstances, etc.) secretly for cheating; cause (aircraft) to fly in circles while waiting to land.

**stadium** /ˈsteɪdɪəm/ noun (plural **-s**) athletic or sports ground with tiered seats for spectators.

**staff** /stɑːf/ ● noun stick or pole for walking, as weapon, or as symbol of office; supporting person or thing; people employed in a business etc.; those in authority in a school etc.; group of army officers assisting officer in high command; (plural **-s** or **staves**) Music set of usually 5 parallel lines to indicate pitch of notes by position. ● verb provide (institution etc.) with staff. □ **staff nurse** one ranking just below a sister.

**stag** noun male deer; person who applies for new shares to sell at once for profit. □ **stag beetle** beetle with antler-like mandibles; **stag-party** colloquial party for men only.

**stage** ● noun point or period in process or development; raised platform, esp. for performing plays etc. on; (**the stage**) theatrical profession; scene of action; regular stopping place on route; distance between stopping places; section of space rocket with separate engine. ● verb (**-ging**) put (play etc.) on stage; organize and carry out. □ **stagecoach** historical coach running

on regular route; **stage direction** instruction in a play about actors' movements, sound effects, etc.; **stage door** entrance from street to backstage part of theatre; **stage fright** performer's fear of audience; **stage-manage** arrange and control as or like stage manager; **stage manager** person responsible for lighting and mechanical arrangements on stage; **stage-struck** obsessed with becoming actor; **stage whisper** loud whisper meant to be overheard.

**stagger** /ˈstæɡə/ ● verb (cause to) walk unsteadily; shock, confuse; arrange (events etc.) so that they do not coincide; arrange (objects) so that they are not in line. ● noun staggering movement; (in plural) disease, esp. of horses and cattle, causing staggering.

**staggering** adjective astonishing, bewildering. □ **staggeringly** adverb.

**staging** /ˈsteɪdʒɪŋ/ noun presentation of play etc.; (temporary) platform; shelves for plants in greenhouse. □ **staging post** regular stopping place, esp. on air route.

**stagnant** /ˈstæɡnənt/ adjective (of liquid) motionless, without current; dull, sluggish. □ **stagnancy** noun.

**stagnate** /stæɡˈneɪt/ verb (**-ting**) be or become stagnant. □ **stagnation** noun.

**stagy** /ˈsteɪdʒɪ/ adjective (also **stagey**) (**-ier, -iest**) theatrical, artificial, exaggerated.

**staid** adjective sober, steady, sedate.

**stain** ● verb discolour or be discoloured by action of liquid sinking in; spoil, damage; colour (wood, etc.) with penetrating substance; treat with colouring agent. ● noun discoloration, spot, mark; blot, blemish; dye etc. for staining. □ **stained glass** coloured glass in leaded window etc.

**stainless** adjective without stains; not liable to stain. □ **stainless steel** chrome steel resisting rust and tarnish.

**stair** noun each of a set of fixed indoor steps; (usually in plural) such a set. □ **staircase** flight of stairs and supporting structure; **stair-rod** rod securing carpet between two steps; **stairway** staircase; **stairwell** shaft for staircase.

**stake** • *noun* stout pointed stick driven into ground as support, boundary mark, etc.; *historical* post to which person was tied to be burnt alive; sum of money etc. wagered on event; (often + *in*) interest or concern, esp. financial; (in *plural*) prize-money, esp. in horse race, such race. • *verb* (**-king**) secure or support with stake(s); (+ *off, out*) mark off (area) with stakes; wager; *US colloquial* support, esp. financially. □ **at stake** risked, to be won or lost; **stake out** *colloquial* place under surveillance; **stake-out** *esp. US colloquial* period of surveillance.

**stalactite** /'stæləktaɪt/ *noun* icicle-like deposit of calcium carbonate hanging from roof of cave etc.

**stalagmite** /'stæləgmaɪt/ *noun* icicle-like deposit of calcium carbonate rising from floor of cave etc.

**stale** • *adjective* not fresh; musty, insipid, or otherwise the worse for age or use; trite, unoriginal; (of athlete or performer) impaired by excessive training. • *verb* (**-ling**) make or become stale. □ **staleness** *noun*.

**stalemate** • *noun Chess* position counting as draw in which player cannot move except into check; deadlock. • *verb* (**-ting**) *Chess* bring (player) to stalemate; bring to deadlock.

**Stalinism** /'stɑːlɪnɪz(ə)m/ *noun* centralized authoritarian form of socialism associated with Stalin. □ **Stalinist** *noun & adjective*.

**stalk**¹ /stɔːk/ • *noun* main stem of herbaceous plant; slender attachment or support of leaf, flower, fruit, etc.; similar support for organ etc. in animal.

**stalk**² /stɔːk/ • *verb* pursue (game, enemy) stealthily; stride, walk in a haughty way; *formal or rhetorical* move silently or threateningly through (place). • *noun* stalking of game; haughty gait. □ **stalking-horse** horse concealing hunter, pretext concealing real intentions or actions.

**stall**¹ /stɔːl/ • *noun* trader's booth or table in market etc.; compartment for one animal in stable or cowhouse; fixed, usually partly enclosed, seat in choir or chancel of church; (usually in *plural*) each of seats on ground floor of theatre; stalling of engine or aircraft, condition resulting from this. • *verb* (of vehicle or its engine) stop because of overload on engine or inadequate supply of fuel to it; (of aircraft or its pilot) lose control because speed is too low; cause to stall. □ **stallholder** person in charge of stall in market etc.

**stall**² /stɔːl/ *verb* play for time when being questioned etc.; delay, obstruct.

**stallion** /'stæljən/ *noun* uncastrated adult male horse.

**stalwart** /'stɔːlwət/ • *adjective* strong, sturdy; courageous, resolute, reliable. • *noun* stalwart person, esp. loyal comrade.

**stamen** /'steɪmən/ *noun* organ producing pollen in flower.

**stamina** /'stæmɪnə/ *noun* physical or mental endurance.

**stammer** /'stæmə/ • *verb* speak haltingly, esp. with pauses or rapid repetitions of same syllable; (often + *out*) utter (words) in this way. • *noun* tendency to stammer; instance of stammering.

**stamp** • *verb* bring down (one's foot) heavily, esp. on ground, (often + *on*) crush or flatten in this way, walk heavily; impress (design, mark, etc.) on surface, impress (surface) with pattern etc.; affix postage or other stamp to; assign specific character to, mark out. • *noun* instrument for stamping; mark or design made by this; impression of official mark required to be made on deeds, bills of exchange, etc., as evidence of payment of tax; small adhesive piece of paper as evidence of payment, esp. postage stamp; mark, label, etc. on commodity as evidence of quality etc.; act or sound of stamping foot; characteristic mark, quality. □ **stamp duty** duty imposed on certain kinds of legal document; **stamping ground** *colloquial* favourite haunt; **stamp on** impress (idea etc.) on (memory etc.); **stamp out** produce by cutting out with die etc., put end to.

**stampede** /stæm'piːd/ • *noun* sudden flight or hurried movement of animals or people; response of many people at once to a common impulse. • *verb* (**-ding**) (cause to) take part in stampede.

standpoint, atti-
y, esp. when hit-

nt∫/ verb (also
ain flow of (esp.
v from (esp.

noun upright

participle **stood**
ntain upright
sp on feet or
ecified height);
in upright or
o and remain
specified atti-
...ae, remain valid or unaltered; Nautical
hold specified course; endure, tolerate;
provide at one's own expense; (often +
for) be candidate (for office etc.); act in
specified capacity; undergo (trial).
●noun cessation from progress, stoppage; Military (esp. in **make a stand**)
halt made to repel attack; resistance to
attack or compulsion; position taken
up, attitude adopted; rack, set of
shelves, etc. for storage; open-fronted
stall or structure for trader, exhibitor,
etc.; standing-place for vehicles; raised
structure to sit or stand on; US witness-
box; each halt made for performance
on tour; group of growing plants. □ **as
it stands** in its present condition, in
the present circumstances; **stand by**
stand nearby, look on without interfering, uphold, support (person), adhere
to (promise etc.), be ready for action;
**stand-by** (person or thing) ready if
needed in emergency etc., readiness for
duty etc.; **stand down** withdraw from
position or candidacy; **stand for** represent, signify, imply, colloquial endure,
tolerate; **stand in** (usually + for) deputize for; **stand-in** deputy, substitute;
**stand off** move or keep away, temporarily dismiss (employee); **stand-off**

**half** Rugby half-back forming link between scrum-half and three-quarters;
**standoffish** cold or distant in manner;
**stand on** insist on, observe scrupulously; **stand out** be prominent or outstanding, (usually + against, for),
persist in opposition or support;
**standpipe** vertical pipe rising from
water supply, esp. one connecting temporary tap to mains; **standpoint** point
of view; **standstill** stoppage, inability
to proceed; **stand to** Military stand ready
for attack, abide by, be likely or certain
to; **stand to reason** be obvious; **stand
up** rise to one's feet, come to remain in,
or place in standing position, (of argument etc.) be valid, colloquial fail to keep
appointment with; **stand-up** (of meal)
eaten standing, (of fight) violent, thorough, (of collar) not turned down, (of
comedian) telling jokes to audience;
**stand up for** support, side with; **stand
up to** face (opponent) courageously, be
resistant to (wear, use, etc.).

**standard** /'stændəd/ ●noun object, quality, or measure serving as basis, example, or principle to which others
conform or should conform or by
which others are judged; level of excellence etc. required or specified; ordinary procedure etc.; distinctive flag;
upright support or pipe; shrub standing without support, or grafted on
upright stem and trained in tree form.
● adjective serving or used as standard; of
normal or prescribed quality, type, or
size. □ **standard-bearer** person who
carries distinctive flag, prominent
leader in cause; **standard English**
most widely accepted dialect of English
(see panel); **standard lamp** lamp on
tall upright with base; **standard of
living** degree of material comfort of
person or group; **standard time** uniform time established by law or custom
in country or region.

••••••••••••••••••••••••••••••••••••••••••••

### Standard English

Standard English is the dialect of English used by most educated English speakers
and is spoken with a variety of accents (see panel at ACCENT). While not in itself any
better than any other dialect, standard English is the form of English used in all
formal written contexts.

••••••••••••••••••••••••••••••••••••••••••••

**standardize** verb (also **-ise**) (**-zing** or **-sing**) cause to conform to standard. □ **standardization** noun.

**standing** ● noun esteem, repute, esp. high; duration. ● adjective that stands, upright; established, permanent; (of jump, start, etc.) performed with no run-up. □ **standing order** instruction to banker to make regular payments; **standing orders** rules governing procedure in a parliament, council, etc.; **standing ovation** prolonged applause from audience that has risen to its feet; **standing room** space to stand in.

**stank** past of STINK.

**stanza** /'stænzə/ noun group of lines forming division of poem, etc.

**staphylococcus** /stæfɪlə'kɒkəs/ noun (plural **-cocci** /-kaɪ/) bacterium sometimes forming pus. □ **staphylococcal** adjective.

**staple**¹ /'steɪp(ə)l/ ● noun shaped piece of wire with two points for fastening papers together, fixing netting to post, etc. ● verb (**-ling**) fasten with staple(s). □ **stapler** noun.

**staple**² /'steɪp(ə)l/ ● noun principal or important article of commerce; chief element, main component; fibre of cotton, wool, etc. with regard to its quality. ● adjective main, principal; important as product or export.

**star** ● noun celestial body appearing as luminous point in night sky; large luminous gaseous body such as sun; celestial body regarded as influencing fortunes etc.; conventional image of star with radiating lines or points; famous or brilliant person, leading performer. ● adjective outstanding. ● verb (**-rr-**) appear or present as leading performer(s); mark, set, or adorn with star(s). □ **starfish** (plural same or **-es**) sea creature with 5 or more radiating arms; **star-gazer** colloquial usually derogatory or jocular astronomer or astrologer; **starlight** light of stars; **starlit** lit by stars, with stars visible; **Stars and Stripes** US national flag; **star turn** main item in entertainment etc. □ **stardom** noun.

**starboard** /'stɑːbəd/ ● noun right-hand side of ship or aircraft looking forward. ● verb turn (helm) to starboard.

**starch** ● noun white carbohydrate obtained chiefly from cereals and potatoes; preparation of this for stiffening fabric; stiffness of manner, formality. ● verb stiffen (clothing) with starch. □ **starchy** adjective (**-ier, -iest**).

**stare** /steə/ ● verb (**-ring**) (usually + at) look fixedly, esp. in curiosity, surprise, horror, etc. ● noun staring gaze. □ **stare (person) in the face** be evident or imminent; **stare out** stare at (person) until he or she looks away.

**stark** ● adjective sharply evident; desolate, bare; absolute. ● adverb completely, wholly. □ **starkly** adverb.

**starkers** /'stɑːkəz/ adjective slang stark naked.

**starlet** /'stɑːlɪt/ noun promising young performer, esp. film actress.

**starling** /'stɑːlɪŋ/ noun gregarious bird with blackish speckled lustrous plumage.

**starry** adjective (**-ier, -iest**) full of stars; starlike. □ **starry-eyed** colloquial romantic but impractical, euphoric.

**start** ● verb begin; set in motion or action; set oneself in motion or action; (often + out) begin journey etc.; (often + up) (cause to) begin operating; (often + up) establish; give signal to (competitors) to start in race; (often + up, from, etc.) jump in surprise, pain, etc.; rouse (game etc.). ● noun beginning; starting-place of race etc.; advantage given at beginning of race etc.; advantageous initial position in life, business, etc.; sudden movement of surprise, pain, etc. □ **starting block** shaped block against which runner braces feet at start of race; **starting price** odds ruling at start of horse race.

**starter** noun device for starting vehicle engine etc.; first course of meal; person giving signal to start race; horse or competitor starting in race. □ **for starters** colloquial to start with.

**startle** /'stɑːt(ə)l/ verb (**-ling**) shock, surprise.

**starve** verb (**-ving**) (cause to) die of hunger or suffer from malnourishment; colloquial feel very hungry; suffer from mental or spiritual want; (+ of) deprive of; compel by starvation. □ **starvation** noun.

**stash** colloquial ● verb (often + away) conceal, put in safe place; hoard. ● noun hiding place; thing hidden.

**state** ● noun existing condition or position of person or thing; colloquial excited or agitated mental condition, untidy condition; political community under one government, this as part of federal republic; civil government; pomp; (**the States**) USA. ● adjective of, for, or concerned with state; reserved for or done on ceremonial occasions. ● verb (**-ting**) express in speech or writing; fix, specify. □ **lie in state** be laid in public place of honour before burial; **state of the art** current stage of esp. technological development; **state-of-the-art** absolutely up-to-date; **stateroom** state apartment, large private cabin in passenger ship.

**stateless** adjective having no nationality or citizenship.

**stately** adjective (**-ier, -iest**) dignified, imposing. □ **stately home** large historic house, esp. one open to public. □ **stateliness** noun.

**statement** noun stating, being stated; thing stated; formal account of facts; record of transactions in bank account etc.; notification of amount due to tradesman etc.

**statesman** /'steɪtsmən/ noun (feminine **stateswoman**) distinguished and capable politician or diplomat. □ **statesmanlike** adjective; **statesmanship** noun.

**static** /'stætɪk/ ● adjective stationary, not acting or changing; Physics concerned with bodies at rest or forces in equilibrium. ● noun static electricity; atmospherics. □ **static electricity** electricity not flowing as current.

**statics** plural noun (usually treated as singular) science of bodies at rest or forces in equilibrium.

**station** /'steɪʃ(ə)n/ ● noun regular stopping place on railway line; person or thing's allotted place, building, etc.; centre for particular service or activity; establishment involved in broadcasting; military or naval base, inhabitants of this; position in life, rank, status; Australian & NZ large sheep or cattle farm. ● verb assign station to; put in position. □ **stationmaster** official in charge of railway station; **stations of**

**the cross** RC Church series of images representing events in Christ's Passion; **station wagon** esp. US estate car.

**stationary** adjective not moving; not meant to be moved; unchanging.

**stationer** noun dealer in stationery.

**stationery** noun writing materials, office supplies, etc.

**statistic** /stə'tɪstɪk/ noun statistical fact or item.

**statistical** adjective of statistics. □ **statistically** adverb.

**statistics** plural noun (usually treated as singular) science of collecting and analysing significant numerical data; such data. □ **statistician** /stætɪs'tɪʃ(ə)n/ noun.

**statuary** /'stætʃʊərɪ/ ● adjective of or for statues. ● noun statues collectively; making statues.

**statue** /'stætʃuː/ noun sculptured figure of person or animal, esp. life-size or larger.

**statuesque** /stætʃʊ'esk/ adjective like statue, esp. in beauty or dignity.

**statuette** /stætʃʊ'et/ noun small statue.

**stature** /'stætʃə/ noun height of (esp. human) body; calibre (esp. moral), eminence.

**status** /'steɪtəs/ noun rank, social position, relative importance; superior social etc. position. □ **status quo** /'kwəʊ/ existing conditions; **status symbol** possession etc. intended to indicate owner's superiority.

**statute** /'stætʃuːt/ noun written law passed by legislative body; rule of corporation, founder, etc., intended to be permanent.

**statutory** /'stætʃʊtərɪ/ adjective required or enacted by statute.

**staunch**[1] /stɔːntʃ/ adjective trustworthy, loyal. □ **staunchly** adverb.

**staunch**[2] = STANCH.

**stave** ● noun each of curved slats forming sides of cask; Music staff; stanza, verse. ● verb (**-ving**; past & past participle **stove** /stəʊv/ or **staved**) (usually + in) break hole in, damage, crush by forcing inwards. □ **stave off** (past & past participle **staved**) avert or defer (danger etc.).

**stay**[1] ● verb continue in same place or condition, not depart or change; (often

+ *at*, *in*, *with*) reside temporarily; *archaic or literary* stop, check, (esp. in *imperative*) pause; postpone (judgement etc.); assuage (hunger etc.), esp. for short time. ●*noun* act or period of staying; suspension or postponement of sentence, judgement, etc.; prop, support; (in *plural*) *historical* (esp. boned) corset. □ **stay-at-home** (person) rarely going out; **staying power** endurance; **stay the night** remain overnight; **stay put** *colloquial* remain where it is put or where one is; **stay up** not go to bed (until late).

**stay²** ●*noun* rope supporting mast, flagstaff, etc.; supporting cable on aircraft. □ **staysail** sail extended on stay.

**stayer** *noun* person or animal with great endurance.

**STD** *abbreviation* subscriber trunk dialling.

**stead** /sted/ *noun* □ **in (person's, thing's) stead** as substitute; **stand (person) in good stead** be advantageous or useful to him or her.

**steadfast** /'stedfɑːst/ *adjective* constant, firm, unwavering. □ **steadfastly** *adverb*; **steadfastness** *noun*.

**steady** /'stedɪ/ ●*adjective* (**-ier**, **-iest**) firmly fixed or supported, unwavering; uniform, regular; constant, persistent; (of person) serious and dependable; regular, established. ●*verb* (**-ies**, **-ied**) make or become steady. ●*adverb* steadily. ●*noun* (*plural* **-ies**) *colloquial* regular boyfriend or girlfriend. □ **steady state** unvarying condition, esp. in physical process. □ **steadily** *adverb*; **steadiness** *noun*.

**steak** /steɪk/ *noun* thick slice of meat (esp. beef) or fish, usually grilled or fried. □ **steakhouse** restaurant specializing in beefsteaks.

**steal** ●*verb* (*past* **stole**; *past participle* **stolen** /'stəʊl(ə)n/) take (another's property) illegally or without right or permission, esp. in secret; obtain surreptitiously, insidiously, or artfully; (+ *in*, *out*, *away*, *up*, etc.) move, esp. silently or stealthily. ●*noun US colloquial* act of stealing, theft; *colloquial* easy task, bargain. □ **steal a march on** gain advantage over by surreptitious means; **steal the show** outshine other performers, esp. unexpectedly.

**stealth** /stelθ/ *noun* secrecy, secret behaviour.

**stealthy** *adjective* (**-ier**, **-iest**) done or moving with stealth. □ **stealthily** *adverb*.

**steam** ●*noun* gas into which water is changed by boiling; condensed vapour formed from this; power obtained from steam; *colloquial* power, energy. ●*verb* cook (food) in steam; give off steam; move under steam power; (+ *ahead*, *away*, etc.) *colloquial* proceed or travel fast or with vigour. □ **let off steam** relieve pent-up energy or feelings; **steamboat** steam-driven boat; **steam engine** one worked or propelled by steam; **steam iron** electric iron that emits steam; **steamroller** *noun* heavy slow-moving vehicle with roller, used to flatten new-made roads, crushing power or force, *verb* crush or move forcibly or indiscriminately; **steamship** steam-driven ship; **steam train** train pulled by steam engine; **steam up** cover or become covered with condensed steam, (as **steamed up** *adjective*) *colloquial* angry, excited.

**steamer** *noun* steamboat; vessel for steaming food in.

**steamy** *adjective* (**-ier**, **-iest**) like or full of steam; *colloquial* erotic.

**steatite** /'stɪətaɪt/ *noun* impure form of talc, esp. soapstone.

**steed** *noun archaic or poetical* horse.

**steel** ●*noun* strong malleable low-carbon iron alloy, used esp. for making tools, weapons, etc.; strength, firmness; steel rod for sharpening knives. ●*adjective* of or like steel. ●*verb* harden, make resolute. □ **steel band** band playing chiefly calypso-style music on instruments made from oil drums; **steel wool** fine steel shavings used as abrasive; **steelworks** factory producing steel; **steelyard** balance with graduated arm along which weight is moved.

**steely** *adjective* (**-ier**, **-iest**) of or like steel; severe, resolute.

**steep¹** ●*adjective* sloping sharply; (of rise or fall) rapid; *colloquial* exorbitant, unreasonable, exaggerated, incredible. ●*noun* steep slope, precipice. □ **steepen** *verb*; **steeply** *adverb*; **steepness** *noun*.

**steep²** ●*verb* soak or bathe in liquid. ●*noun* act of steeping; liquid for steeping. □ **steep in** imbue with, make deeply acquainted with (subject etc.).

**steeple** /ˈstiːp(ə)l/ *noun* tall tower, esp. with spire, above roof of church. □ **steeplechase** horse race with ditches, hedges, etc. to jump, cross-country foot race; **steeplejack** repairer of tall chimneys, steeples, etc.

**steer¹** *verb* guide (vehicle, ship, etc.) with wheel, rudder, etc.; direct or guide (one's course, other people, conversation, etc.) in specified direction. □ **steer clear of** avoid; **steering column** column on which steering wheel is mounted; **steering committee** one deciding order of business, course of operations etc.; **steering wheel** wheel by which vehicle etc. is steered; **steersman** person who steers ship.

**steer²** *noun* bullock.

**steerage** *noun* act of steering; *archaic* cheapest part of ship's accommodation.

**steering** *noun* apparatus for steering vehicle etc.

**stegosaurus** /stegəˈsɔːrəs/ *noun* (*plural* **-ruses**) large dinosaur with two rows of vertical plates along back.

**stela** /ˈstiːlə/ *noun* (*plural* **stelae** /-liː/) (also **stele** /ˈstiːl/) ancient upright slab or pillar, usually inscribed and sculptured, esp. as gravestone.

**stellar** /ˈstelə/ *adjective* of star or stars.

**stem¹** ● *noun* main body or stalk of plant; stalk of fruit, flower, or leaf; stem-shaped part, e.g. slender part of wineglass; *Grammar* root or main part of noun, verb, etc. to which inflections are added; main upright timber at bow of ship. ● *verb* (**-mm-**) (+ *from*) spring or originate from.

**stem²** *verb* (**-mm-**) check, stop.

**stench** *noun* foul smell.

**stencil** /ˈstensɪl/ ● *noun* thin sheet in which pattern is cut, placed on surface and printed, inked over, etc.; pattern so produced. ● *verb* (**-ll-**; *US* **-l-**) (often + *on*) produce (pattern) with stencil; mark (surface) in this way.

**Sten gun** *noun* lightweight sub-machine-gun.

**stenographer** /steˈnɒɡrəfə/ *noun esp. US* shorthand typist.

**stentorian** /stenˈtɔːrɪən/ *adjective* loud and powerful.

**step** ● *noun* complete movement of leg in walking or running; distance so covered; unit of movement in dancing; measure taken, esp. one of several in course of action; surface of stair, stepladder, etc. tread; short distance; sound or mark made by foot in walking etc.; degree in scale of promotion, precedence, etc.; stepping in unison or to music; state of conforming. ● *verb* (**-pp-**) lift and set down foot or alternate feet in walking; come or go in specified direction by stepping; make progress in specified way; (+ *off, out*) measure (distance) by stepping; perform (dance). □ **mind, watch one's step** be careful; **step down** resign; **step in** enter, intervene; **stepladder** short folding ladder not leant against wall; **step on it** *colloquial* hurry; **step out** be active socially, take large steps; **stepping-stone** large stone set in stream etc. to walk over, means of progress; **step up** increase, intensify.

**step-** *combining form* related by remarriage of parent. □ **stepchild**, **stepdaughter**, **stepson** one's husband's or wife's child by previous partner; **stepfather**, **stepmother**, **step-parent** mother's or father's spouse who is not one's own parent; **stepbrother**, **stepsister** child of one's step-parent by previous partner.

**stephanotis** /stefəˈnəʊtɪs/ *noun* fragrant tropical climbing plant.

**steppe** /step/ *noun* level grassy treeless plain.

**stereo** /ˈsterɪəʊ/ ● *noun* (*plural* **-s**) stereophonic sound reproduction or equipment; stereoscope. ● *adjective* stereophonic; stereoscopic.

**stereo-** *combining form* solid; 3-dimensional.

**stereophonic** /sterɪəʊˈfɒnɪk/ *adjective* using two or more channels, to give effect of naturally distributed sound.

**stereoscope** /ˈsterɪəskəʊp/ *noun* device for producing 3-dimensional effect by viewing two slightly different photographs together. □ **stereoscopic** /-ˈskɒp-/ *adjective*.

**stereotype** /ˈsterɪəʊtaɪp/ ● *noun* person or thing seeming to conform to widely accepted type; such type, idea, or attitude; printing plate cast from mould of composed type. ● verb (**-ping**) (esp. as **stereotyped** adjective) cause to conform to type, standardize; print from stereotype; make stereotype of.

**sterile** /ˈsteraɪl/ adjective not able to produce crop, fruit, or young, barren; lacking ideas or originality, unproductive; free from micro-organisms etc. □ **sterility** /stəˈrɪl-/ noun.

**sterilize** /ˈsterɪlaɪz/ verb (also **-ise**) (**-zing** or **-sing**) make sterile; deprive of reproductive power. □ **sterilization** noun.

**sterling** /ˈstɜːlɪŋ/ ● adjective of or in British money; (of coin or precious metal) genuine, of standard value or purity; (of person etc.) genuine, reliable. ● noun British money. □ **sterling silver** silver of 92½% purity.

**stern**[1] adjective severe, grim; authoritarian. □ **sternly** adverb; **sternness** noun.

**stern**[2] noun rear part, esp. of ship or boat.

**sternum** /ˈstɜːnəm/ noun (plural **-na** or **-nums**) breastbone.

**steroid** /ˈstɪərɔɪd/ noun any of group of organic compounds including many hormones, alkaloids, and vitamins.

**sterol** /ˈsterɒl/ noun naturally occurring steroid alcohol.

**stertorous** /ˈstɜːtərəs/ adjective (of breathing etc.) laboured and noisy.

**stet** verb (**-tt-**) (usually written on proofsheet etc.) ignore or cancel (alteration), let original stand.

**stethoscope** /ˈsteθəskəʊp/ noun instrument used in listening to heart, lungs, etc.

**stetson** /ˈstets(ə)n/ noun slouch hat with wide brim and high crown.

**stevedore** /ˈstiːvədɔː/ noun person employed in loading and unloading ships.

**stew** ● verb cook by long simmering in closed vessel; colloquial swelter; (of tea etc.) become bitter or strong from infusing too long. ● noun dish of stewed meat etc.; colloquial agitated or angry state.

**steward** /ˈstjuːəd/ ● noun passengers' attendant on ship, aircraft, or train; official managing meeting, show, etc.; person responsible for supplies of food etc. for college, club, etc.; property manager. □ **stewardship** noun.

**stewardess** /stjuːəˈdes/ noun female steward, esp. on ship or aircraft.

**stick**[1] noun short slender length of wood, esp. for use as support or weapon; thin rod of wood etc. for particular purpose; gear lever, joystick; sticklike piece of celery, dynamite, etc.; (often **the stick**) punishment, esp. by beating; colloquial adverse criticism; colloquial person, esp. when dull or unsociable. □ **stick insect** insect with twiglike body.

**stick**[2] verb (past & past participle **stuck**) (+ in, into, through) thrust, insert (thing or its point); stab; (+ in, into, on, etc.) fix or be fixed (as) by pointed end; fix or be fixed (as) by adhesive etc.; lose or be deprived of movement or action through adhesion, jamming, etc.; colloquial put in specified position or place, remain; colloquial endure, tolerate; (+ at) colloquial persevere with. □ **get stuck into** slang start in earnest; **stick around** colloquial linger; **sticking plaster** adhesive plaster for wounds etc.; **stick-in-the-mud** colloquial unprogressive or old-fashioned person; **stick it out** colloquial endure to the end; **stick out** (cause to) protrude; **stick out for** persist in demanding; **stick up** be or make erect or protruding upwards, fasten to upright surface, colloquial rob or threaten with gun; **stick up for** support, defend; **stuck for** at a loss for, needing; **stuck with** colloquial unable to get rid of.

**sticker** noun adhesive label.

**stickleback** /ˈstɪk(ə)lbæk/ noun small spiny-backed fish.

**stickler** /ˈstɪklə/ noun (+ for) person who insists on something.

**sticky** adjective (**-ier**, **-iest**) tending or intended to stick or adhere; glutinous, viscous; (of weather) humid; colloquial difficult, awkward, unpleasant, painful. □ **sticky wicket** colloquial difficult situation. □ **stickiness** noun.

**stiff** ● adjective rigid, inflexible; hard to bend, move, turn, etc.; hard to cope with, needing strength or effort; severe, strong, formal, constrained; (of muscle, person, etc.) aching from exertion, injury, etc.; (of esp. alcoholic drink) strong. ● adverb colloquial utterly, extremely. ● noun slang corpse.

**stiff-necked** obstinate, haughty; **stiff upper lip** appearance of firmness or fortitude. □ **stiffen** verb; **stiffly** adverb; **stiffness** noun.

**stifle** /ˈstaɪf(ə)l/ verb (**-ling**) suppress; feel or make unable to breathe easily; suffocate. □ **stifling** adjective.

**stigma** /ˈstɪɡmə/ noun (plural **-s** or **stigmata** /-mətə or -ˈmɑːtə/) shame, disgrace; part of pistil that receives pollen in pollination; (**stigmata**) marks like those on Christ's body after the Crucifixion, appearing on bodies of certain saints etc.

**stigmatize** /ˈstɪɡmətaɪz/ verb (also **-ise**) (**-zing** or **-sing**) (often + as) brand as unworthy or disgraceful.

**stile** noun set of steps etc. allowing people to climb over fence, wall, etc.

**stiletto** /stɪˈletəʊ/ noun (plural **-s**) short dagger; (in full **stiletto heel**) long tapering heel of shoe; pointed implement for making eyelets etc.

**still**¹ ● adjective with little or no movement or sound; calm, tranquil; (of drink) not effervescing. ● noun deep silence; static photograph, esp. single shot from cinema film. ● adverb without moving; even now, at particular time; nevertheless; (+ comparative) even, yet, increasingly. ● verb make or become still, quieten. □ **stillbirth** birth of dead child; **stillborn** born dead, abortive; **still life** painting or drawing of inanimate objects. □ **stillness** noun.

**still**² noun apparatus for distilling spirits etc.

**stilt** noun either of pair of poles with foot supports for walking at a distance above ground; each of set of piles or posts supporting building etc.

**stilted** adjective (of literary style etc.) stiff and unnatural.

**Stilton** /ˈstɪlt(ə)n/ noun proprietary term strong rich esp. blue-veined cheese.

**stimulant** /ˈstɪmjʊlənt/ ● adjective stimulating esp. bodily or mental activity. ● noun stimulant substance or influence.

**stimulate** /ˈstɪmjʊleɪt/ verb (**-ting**) act as stimulus to; animate, excite, rouse. □ **stimulation** noun; **stimulative** /-lətɪv/ adjective; **stimulator** noun.

**stimulus** /ˈstɪmjʊləs/ noun (plural **-li** /-laɪ/) thing that rouses to activity.

**sting** ● noun sharp wounding organ of insect, nettle, etc.; inflicting of wound with this; wound itself, pain caused by it; painful quality or effect; pungency, vigour. ● verb (past & past participle **stung**) wound with sting; be able to sting; feel or cause tingling physical pain or sharp mental pain; (+ into) incite, esp. painfully; slang swindle, charge heavily. □ **stinging-nettle** nettle with stinging hairs; **stingray** broad flatfish with stinging tail.

**stingy** /ˈstɪndʒɪ/ adjective (**-ier**, **-iest**) niggardly, mean. □ **stingily** adverb; **stinginess** noun.

**stink** ● verb (past **stank** or **stunk**; past participle **stunk**) emit strong offensive smell; (often + out) fill (place) with stink; (+ out etc.) drive (person) out etc. by stink; colloquial be or seem very unpleasant. ● noun strong offensive smell; colloquial loud complaint, fuss. □ **stink bomb** device emitting stink when opened.

**stinker** noun slang particularly annoying or unpleasant person; very difficult problem etc.

**stinking** ● adjective that stinks; slang very objectionable. ● adverb slang extremely and usually objectionably.

**stint** ● verb (often + on) supply (food, aid, etc.) meanly or grudgingly; (often **stint oneself**) supply (person etc.) in this way. ● noun allotted amount or period of work.

**stipend** /ˈstaɪpend/ noun salary, esp. of clergyman.

**stipendiary** /staɪˈpendjərɪ/ ● adjective receiving stipend. ● noun (plural **-ies**) person receiving stipend. □ **stipendiary magistrate** paid professional magistrate.

**stipple** /ˈstɪp(ə)l/ ● verb (**-ling**) draw, paint, engrave, etc. with dots instead of lines; roughen surface of (paint, cement, etc.). ● noun stippling; effect of stippling.

**stipulate** /ˈstɪpjʊleɪt/ verb (**-ting**) demand or specify as part of bargain etc. □ **stipulation** noun.

**stir** ● verb (**-rr-**) move spoon etc. round and round in (liquid etc.), esp. to mix ingredients; cause to move, esp. slightly; be or begin to be in motion;

rise from sleep; arouse, inspire, excite; *colloquial* cause trouble by gossiping etc. ● *noun* act of stirring; commotion, excitement. □ **stir-fry** *verb* fry rapidly while stirring, *noun* stir-fried dish; **stir up** mix thoroughly by stirring, stimulate, incite.

**stirrup** /'stɪrəp/ *noun* support for horse-rider's foot, suspended by strap from saddle. □ **stirrup-cup** cup of wine etc. offered to departing traveller, originally rider; **stirrup-pump** hand-operated water-pump with footrest, used to extinguish small fires.

**stitch** ● *noun* single pass of needle, or result of this, in sewing, knitting, or crochet; particular method of sewing etc.; least bit of clothing; sharp pain in side induced by running etc. ● *verb* sew, make stitches (in). □ **in stitches** *colloquial* laughing uncontrollably; **stitch up** join or mend by sewing.

**stoat** *noun* mammal of weasel family with brown fur turning mainly white in winter.

**stock** ● *noun* store of goods etc. ready for sale or distribution; supply or quantity of things for use; equipment or raw material for manufacture, trade, etc.; farm animals or equipment; capital of business; shares in this; reputation, popularity; money lent to government at fixed interest; line of ancestry; liquid made by stewing bones, vegetables, etc.; fragrant garden plant; plant into which graft is inserted; main trunk of tree etc.; (in *plural* *historical*) timber frame with holes for feet in which offenders were locked as public punishment; base, support, or handle for implement or machine; butt of rifle etc.; (in *plural*) supports for ship during building or repair; band of cloth worn round neck. ● *adjective* kept regularly in stock for sale or use; commonly used, hackneyed. ● *verb* have (goods) in stock; provide (shop, farm, etc.) with goods, livestock, etc. □ **stockbroker** member of Stock Exchange dealing in stocks and shares; **stock-car** specially strengthened car used in racing where deliberate bumping is allowed; **Stock Exchange** place for dealing in stocks and shares, dealers working there; **stock-in-trade** requisite(s) of trade or profession;

**stock market** Stock Exchange, transactions on this; **stockpile** *noun* reserve supply of accumulated stock, *verb* accumulate stockpile; **stockpot** pot for making soup stock; **stock-still** motionless; **stocktaking** making inventory of stock; **stock up** (often + *with*) provide with or get stocks or supplies (of); **stockyard** enclosure for sorting or temporary keeping of cattle; **take stock** make inventory of one's stock, (often + *of*) review (situation etc.).

**stockade** /stɒ'keɪd/ ● *noun* line or enclosure of upright stakes. ● *verb* (**-ding**) fortify with this.

**stockinet** /stɒkɪ'net/ *noun* (also **stockinette**) elastic knitted fabric.

**stocking** /'stɒkɪŋ/ *noun* knitted covering for leg and foot, of nylon, wool, silk, etc. □ **stocking stitch** alternate rows of plain and purl.

**stockist** *noun* dealer in specified types of goods.

**stocky** *adjective* (**-ier**, **-iest**) short and strongly built. □ **stockily** *adverb*.

**stodge** *noun colloquial* heavy fattening food.

**stodgy** *adjective* (**-ier**, **-iest**) (of food) heavy, filling; dull, uninteresting. □ **stodginess** *noun*.

**stoic** /'stəʊɪk/ *noun* person having great self-control in adversity. □ **stoical** *adjective*; **stoicism** /-ɪsɪz(ə)m/ *noun*.

**stoke** *verb* (**-king**) (often + *up*) feed and tend (fire, furnace, etc.); *colloquial* fill oneself with food. □ **stokehold** compartment in steamship containing its boilers and furnace; **stokehole** space for stokers in front of furnace.

**stoker** *noun* person who tends furnace, esp. on steamship.

**stole**[1] *noun* woman's garment like long wide scarf worn over shoulders; strip of silk etc. worn similarly by priest.

**stole**[2] past of STEAL.

**stolen** past participle of STEAL.

**stolid** /'stɒlɪd/ *adjective* not easily excited or moved; impassive, unemotional. □ **stolidity** /-'lɪd-/ *noun*; **stolidly** *adverb*.

**stomach** /'stʌmək/ ● *noun* internal organ in which food is digested; lower front of body; (usually + *for*) appetite, inclination, etc. ● *verb* (usually in negative) endure. □ **stomach-pump** syringe for forcing liquid etc. into or out of stomach.

**stomp** ● *verb* tread or stamp heavily. ● *noun* lively jazz dance with heavy stamping.

**stone** ● *noun* solid non-metallic mineral matter, rock; small piece of this; hard case of kernel in some fruits; hard morbid concretion in body; (*plural* same) unit of weight (14 lb, 6.35 kg); precious stone. ● *verb* (**-ning**) pelt with stones; remove stones from (fruit). □ **Stone Age** prehistoric period when weapons and tools were made of stone; **stone-cold** completely cold; **stone-cold sober** completely sober; **stonecrop** succulent rock plant; **stone-dead** completely dead; **stone-deaf** completely deaf; **stone fruit** fruit with flesh enclosing stone; **stoneground** (of flour) ground with millstones; **stone's throw** short distance; **stonewall** obstruct with evasive answers etc., *Cricket* bat with excessive caution; **stoneware** impermeable and partly vitrified but opaque ceramic ware; **stonewashed** (esp. of denim) washed with abrasives to give worn or faded look; **stonework** masonry.

**stoned** *adjective slang* drunk, drugged.

**stony** *adjective* (**-ier, -iest**) full of stones; hard, rigid; unfeeling, unresponsive. □ **stony-broke** *slang* entirely without money. □ **stonily** *adverb*.

**stood** past & past participle of STAND.

**stooge** *colloquial* ● *noun* person acting as butt or foil, esp. for comedian; assistant or subordinate, esp. for unpleasant work. ● *verb* (**-ging**) (+ *for*) act as stooge for; (+ *about, around*, etc.) move about aimlessly.

**stool** /stuːl/ *noun* single seat without back or arms; footstool; (usually in *plural*) faeces. □ **stool-pigeon** person acting as decoy, police informer.

**stoop** ● *verb* bend down; stand or walk with shoulders habitually bent forward; (+ *to do*) condescend; (+ *to*) descend to (shameful act). ● *noun* stooping posture.

**stop** ● *verb* (**-pp-**) put an end to progress, motion, or operation of; effectively hinder or prevent; discontinue; come

to an end; cease from motion, speaking, or action; defeat; *colloquial* remain; stay for short time; (often + *up*) block or close up (hole, leak, etc.); not permit or supply as usual; instruct bank to withhold payment on (cheque); fill (tooth); press (violin etc. string) to obtain required pitch. ● *noun* stopping, being stopped; place where bus, train, etc. regularly stops; full stop; device for stopping motion at particular point; change of pitch effected by stopping string; (in organ) row of pipes of one character, knob etc. operating these; (in camera etc.) diaphragm, effective diameter of lens, device for reducing this; plosive sound. □ **pull out all the stops** make extreme effort; **stopcock** externally operated valve regulating flow through pipe etc.; **stopgap** temporary substitute; **stop off, over** break one's journey; **stop press** late news inserted in newspaper after printing has begun; **stopwatch** watch that can be instantly started and stopped, used in timing of races etc.

**stoppage** *noun* interruption of work due to strike etc.; (in *plural*) sum deducted from pay, for tax, etc.; condition of being blocked or stopped.

**stopper** *noun* plug for closing bottle etc.

**storage** /'stɔːrɪdʒ/ *noun* storing of goods etc.; method of, space for, or cost of storing. □ **storage battery, cell** one for storing electricity; **storage heater** electric heater releasing heat stored outside peak hours.

**store** ● *noun* quantity of something kept ready for use; (in *plural*) articles gathered for particular purpose, supply of, or place for keeping, these; department store; *esp. US* shop; (often in *plural*) shop selling basic necessities; warehouse for keeping furniture etc. temporarily; device in computer for keeping retrievable data. ● *verb* (**-ring**) (often + *up, away*) accumulate for future use; put (furniture etc.) in a store; stock or provide with something useful; keep (data) for retrieval. □ **in store** in reserve, to come, (+ *for*) awaiting; **storehouse** storage place; **storekeeper** person in charge of stores, *US* shopkeeper; **storeroom** storage room.

**storey** /'stɔːrɪ/ *noun* (*plural* **-s**) rooms etc. on one level of building.

**stork** *noun* long-legged usually white wading bird.

**storm** ●*noun* violent disturbance of atmosphere with high winds and usually thunder, rain, or snow; violent disturbance in human affairs; (+ *of*) shower of missiles or blows, outbreak of applause, hisses, etc.; assault on fortified place. ●*verb* attack or capture by storm; rush violently; rage, be violent; bluster. □ **storm centre** comparatively calm centre of cyclonic storm, centre round which controversy etc. rages; **storm cloud** heavy rain-cloud; **storm troops** shock troops, *historical* Nazi political militia; **take by storm** capture by direct assault, quickly captivate.

**stormy** *adjective* (**-ier, -iest**) of or affected by storms; (of wind etc.) violent; full of angry feeling or outbursts. □ **stormily** *adverb*.

**story** /ˈstɔːrɪ/ *noun* (*plural* **-ies**) account of real or imaginary events; tale, anecdote; history of person, institution, etc.; plot of novel, play, etc.; article in newspaper, material for this; *colloquial* fib. □ **storyteller** person who tells or writes stories, *colloquial* liar.

**stoup** /stuːp/ *noun* basin for holy water; *archaic* flagon, beaker.

**stout** /staʊt/ ●*adjective* rather fat, corpulent; thick; strong; brave, resolute, vigorous. ●*noun* strong dark beer. □ **stout-hearted** courageous. □ **stoutly** *adverb*; **stoutness** *noun*.

**stove**[1] /staʊv/ *noun* closed apparatus burning fuel or using electricity etc. for heating or cooking. □ **stove-pipe** pipe carrying smoke and gases from stove to chimney.

**stove**[2] *past & past participle* of STAVE.

**stow** /staʊ/ *verb* pack (goods, cargo, etc.) tidily and compactly. □ **stow away** place (thing) out of the way, hide oneself on ship etc. to travel free; **stowaway** person who stows away.

**stowage** *noun* stowing; place for this.

**straddle** /ˈstræd(ə)l/ ●*verb* (**-ling**) sit or stand across (thing) with legs wide apart; be situated on both sides of; spread legs wide apart.

**strafe** /strɑːf/ *verb* (**-fing**) bombard; attack with gunfire.

**straggle** /ˈstræg(ə)l/ ●*verb* (**-ling**) lack compactness or tidiness; be dispersed or sporadic; trail behind in race etc. ●*noun* straggling group. □ **straggler** *noun*; **straggly** *adjective*.

**straight** /streɪt/ ●*adjective* not curved, bent, crooked or curly; successive, uninterrupted; ordered, level, tidy; honest, candid; (of thinking etc.) logical; (of theatre, music, etc.) not popular or comic; unmodified, (of a drink) undiluted; *colloquial* (of person etc.) conventional, respectable, heterosexual. ●*noun* straight part, esp. concluding stretch of racetrack; straight condition; *colloquial* conventional person, heterosexual. ●*adverb* in straight line, direct; in right direction; correctly. □ **go straight** (of criminal) become honest; **straight away** immediately; **straight face** intentionally expressionless face; **straight fight** *Politics* contest between two candidates only; **straightforward** honest, frank, (of task etc.) simple; **straight man** comedian's stooge; **straight off** *colloquial* without hesitation. □ **straightness** *noun*.

**straighten** *verb* (often + *out*) make or become straight; (+ *up*) stand erect after bending.

**strain**[1] ●*verb* stretch tightly; make or become taut or tense; injure by overuse or excessive demands; exercise (oneself, one's senses, thing, etc.) intensely, press to extremes; strive intensely; distort from true intention or meaning; clear (liquid) of solid matter by passing it through sieve etc. ●*noun* act of straining, force exerted in this; injury caused by straining muscle etc.; severe mental or physical demand or exertion; snatch of music or poetry; tone or tendency in speech or writing.

**strain**[2] *noun* breed or stock of animals, plants, etc.; characteristic tendency.

**strained** *adjective* constrained, artificial; (of relationship) distrustful, tense.

**strainer** *noun* device for straining liquids.

**strait** *noun* (in *singular* or *plural*) narrow channel connecting two large bodies of water; (usually in *plural*) difficulty, distress. □ **strait-jacket** strong garment with long sleeves for confining violent prisoner etc., restrictive measures; **strait-laced** puritanical.

**straitened** /ˈstreɪt(ə)nd/ *adjective* of or marked by poverty.

**strand**[1] ● *verb* run aground; (as **stranded** *adjective*) in difficulties, esp. without money or transport. ● *noun* foreshore, beach.

**strand**[2] *noun* each of twisted threads or wires making rope, cable, etc.; single thread or strip of fibre; lock of hair; element, component.

**strange** /streɪndʒ/ *adjective* unusual, peculiar, surprising, eccentric; (often + *to*) unfamiliar, foreign; (+ *to*) unaccustomed; not at ease. □ **strangely** *adverb*, **strangeness** *noun*.

**stranger** *noun* person new to particular place or company; (often + *to*) person one does not know.

**strangle** /ˈstræŋg(ə)l/ *verb* (**-ling**) squeeze windpipe or neck of, esp. so as to kill; hamper or suppress (movement, cry, etc.). □ **stranglehold** deadly grip, complete control. □ **strangler** *noun*.

**strangulate** /ˈstræŋɡjʊleɪt/ *verb* (**-ting**) compress (vein, intestine, etc.), preventing circulation.

**strangulation** *noun* strangling, being strangled; strangulating.

**strap** ● *noun* strip of leather etc., often with buckle, for holding things together etc.; narrow strip of fabric forming part of garment; loop for grasping to steady oneself in moving vehicle. ● *verb* (**-pp-**) (often + *down*, *up*, etc.) secure or bind with strap; beat with strap. □ **straphanger** *slang* standing passenger in bus or train; **straphang** *verb* □ **strapless** *adjective*.

**strapping** *adjective* large and sturdy.

**strata** *plural* of STRATUM.

■ **Usage** It is a mistake to use the plural form *strata* when only one stratum is meant.

**stratagem** /ˈstrætədʒəm/ *noun* cunning plan or scheme; trickery.

**strategic** /strəˈtiːdʒɪk/ *adjective* of or promoting strategy; (of materials) essential in war; (of bombing or weapons) done or for use as longer-term military policy. □ **strategically** *adverb*.

**strategy** /ˈstrætɪdʒɪ/ *noun* (*plural* **-ies**) long-term plan or policy; art of war; art of moving troops, ships, aircraft, etc.

into favourable positions. □ **strategist** *noun*.

**stratify** /ˈstrætɪfaɪ/ *verb* (**-ies**, **-ied**) (esp. as **stratified** *adjective*) arrange in strata, grades, etc. □ **stratification** *noun*.

**stratosphere** /ˈstrætəsfɪə/ *noun* layer of atmosphere above troposphere, extending to about 50 km from earth's surface.

**stratum** /ˈstrɑːtəm/ *noun* (*plural* **strata**) layer or set of layers of any deposited substance, esp. of rock; atmospheric layer; social class.

**straw** *noun* dry cut stalks of grain; single stalk of straw; thin tube for sucking drink through; insignificant thing; pale yellow colour. □ **clutch at straws** try any remedy in desperation; **straw vote**, **poll** unofficial ballot as test of opinion.

**strawberry** /ˈstrɔːbərɪ/ *noun* (*plural* **-ies**) pulpy red fruit having surface studded with yellow seeds; plant bearing this. □ **strawberry mark** reddish birthmark.

**stray** ● *verb* wander from the right place, from one's companions, etc., go astray; deviate. ● *noun* strayed animal or person. ● *adjective* strayed, lost; isolated, occasional.

**streak** ● *noun* long thin usually irregular line or band, esp. of colour; strain or trait in person's character. ● *verb* mark with streaks; move very rapidly; *colloquial* run naked in public.

**streaky** *adjective* (**-ier**, **-iest**) marked with streaks; (of bacon) with streaks of fat.

**stream** ● *noun* body of running water, esp. small river; current; flow; group of schoolchildren of similar ability taught together. ● *verb* move as stream; run with liquid; be blown in wind; emit stream of (blood etc.); arrange (schoolchildren) in streams. □ **on stream** in operation or production.

**streamer** *noun* long narrow strip of ribbon or paper; long narrow flag.

**streamline** *verb* (**-ning**) give (vehicle etc.) form which presents least resistance to motion; make simple or more efficient.

**street** *noun* road in city, town, or village; this with buildings on each side.

□ **on the streets** living by prostitution; **streetcar** *US* tram; **street credibility**, **cred** *slang* acceptability within urban subculture; **streetwalker** prostitute seeking customers in street; **streetwise** knowing how to survive modern urban life.

**strength** *noun* being strong; degree or manner of this; person or thing giving strength; number of people present or available. □ **on the strength of** on basis of.

**strengthen** *verb* make or become stronger.

**strenuous** /ˈstrenjʊəs/ *adjective* using or requiring great effort; energetic. □ **strenuously** *adverb*.

**streptococcus** /streptəˈkɒkəs/ *noun* (*plural* **-cocci** /-kaɪ/) bacterium causing serious infections. □ **streptococcal** *adjective*.

**streptomycin** /streptəʊˈmaɪsɪn/ *noun* antibiotic effective against many disease-producing bacteria.

**stress** ● *noun* pressure, tension; quantity measuring this; physical or mental strain; emphasis. ● *verb* emphasize; subject to stress.

**stressful** *adjective* causing stress.

**stretch** ● *verb* draw, be drawn, or be able to be drawn out in length or size; make or become taut; place or lie at full length or spread out; extend limbs and tighten muscles after being relaxed; have specified length or extension, extend; strain or exert extremely; exaggerate. ● *noun* continuous extent, expanse, or period; stretching, being stretched; *colloquial* period of imprisonment etc. □ **at a stretch** in one period; **stretch one's legs** exercise oneself by walking; **stretch out** extend (limb etc.), last, prolong; **stretch a point** agree to something not normally allowed. □ **stretchy** *adjective* (**-ier**, **-iest**).

**stretcher** *noun* two poles with canvas etc. between for carrying person in lying position; brick etc. laid along face of wall.

**strew** /struː/ *verb* (*past participle* **strewn** or **strewed**) scatter over surface; (usually + *with*) spread (surface) with scattered things.

**'strewth** = 'STRUTH.

**striated** /straɪˈeɪtɪd/ *adjective* marked with slight ridges or furrows. □ **striation** *noun*.

**stricken** /ˈstrɪkən/ *archaic past participle* of STRIKE. ● *adjective* affected or overcome (with illness, misfortune, etc.).

**strict** *adjective* precisely limited or defined, without deviation; requiring complete obedience or exact performance. □ **strictly** *adverb*; **strictness** *noun*.

**stricture** /ˈstrɪktʃə/ *noun* (usually in *plural*, often + *on*, *upon*) critical or censorious remark.

**stride** ● *verb* (**-ding**; *past* **strode**; *past participle* **stridden** /ˈstrɪd(ə)n/) walk with long firm steps; cross with one step; bestride. ● *noun* single long step; length of this; gait as determined by length of stride; (usually in *plural*) progress. □ **take in one's stride** manage easily.

**strident** /ˈstraɪd(ə)nt/ *adjective* loud and harsh. □ **stridency** *noun*; **stridently** *adverb*.

**strife** *noun* conflict, struggle.

**strike** ● *verb* (**-king**; *past* **struck**; *past participle* **struck** or *archaic* **stricken**) deliver (blow), inflict blow on; come or bring sharply into contact with; propel or divert with blow; (cause to) penetrate; ignite (match) or produce (sparks etc.) by rubbing; make (coin) by stamping; produce (musical note) by striking; (of clock) indicate (time) with chime etc., (of time) be so indicated; attack suddenly; (of disease) afflict; cause to become suddenly; reach, achieve; agree on (bargain); assume (attitude); find (oil etc.) by drilling; come to attention of or appear to; (of employees) engage in strike; lower or take down (flag, tent, etc.); take specified direction. ● *noun* act of striking; employees' organized refusal to work until grievance is remedied; similar refusal to participate; sudden find or success; attack, esp. from air. □ **on strike** taking part in industrial strike; **strikebreaker** person working or employed in place of strikers; **strike home** deal effective blow; **strike off** remove with stroke, delete; **strike out** hit out, act vigorously, delete; **strike up** start (acquaintance, conversation, etc.), esp. casually, begin playing (tune etc.).

**striker** *noun* employee on strike; *Football* attacking player positioned forward.

**striking** *adjective* impressive, noticeable. □ **strikingly** *adverb*.

**string** ● *noun* twine, narrow cord; length of this or similar material used for tying, holding together, pulling, forming head of racket, etc.; piece of catgut, wire, etc. on musical instrument, producing note by vibration; (in *plural*) stringed instruments in orchestra etc.; (in *plural*) condition or complication attached to offer etc.; set of things strung together; tough side of bean-pod etc. ● *verb* (*past & past participle* **strung**) fit with string(s); thread on string; arrange in or as string; remove strings from (bean-pod etc.). □ **string along** *colloquial* deceive, (often + *with*) keep company (with); **string-course** raised horizontal band of bricks etc. on building; **string up** hang up on strings etc., kill by hanging, (usually as **strung up** *adjective*) make tense.

**stringed** *adjective* (of musical instrument) having strings.

**stringent** /ˈstrɪndʒ(ə)nt/ *adjective* (of rules etc.) strict, precise. □ **stringency** *noun*; **stringently** *adverb*.

**stringer** *noun* longitudinal structural member in framework, esp. of ship or aircraft; *colloquial* freelance newspaper correspondent.

**stringy** *adjective* (**-ier, -iest**) like string, fibrous.

**strip**[1] ● *verb* (**-pp-**) (often + *of*) remove clothes or covering from, undress; deprive (person) of property or titles; leave bare; (often + *down*) remove accessory fittings of or take apart (machine etc.); remove old paint etc. from with solvent; damage thread of (screw) or teeth of (gearwheel). ● *noun* act of stripping, esp. in striptease; *colloquial* distinctive outfit worn by sports team. □ **strip club** club where striptease is performed; **striptease** entertainment in which performer slowly and erotically undresses.

**strip**[2] *noun* long narrow piece. □ **strip cartoon** comic strip; **strip light** tubular fluorescent lamp; **tear (person) off a strip** *colloquial* rebuke.

**stripe** *noun* long narrow band or strip differing in colour or texture from surface on either side of it; *Military* chevron etc. denoting military rank. □ **stripy** *adjective* (**-ier, -iest**).

**striped** *adjective* having stripes.

**stripling** /ˈstrɪplɪŋ/ *noun* youth not yet fully grown.

**stripper** *noun* device or solvent for removing paint etc.; performer of striptease.

**strive** *verb* (**-ving**; *past* **strove** /strəʊv/; *past participle* **striven** /ˈstrɪv(ə)n/) try hard; (often + *with*, *against*) struggle.

**strobe** *noun* *colloquial* stroboscope.

**stroboscope** /ˈstrəʊbəskəʊp/ *noun* lamp producing regular intermittent flashes. □ **stroboscopic** /-ˈskɒp-/ *adjective*.

**strode** *past of* STRIDE.

**stroke** ● *noun* act of striking; sudden disabling attack caused esp. by thrombosis; action or movement, esp. as one of series or in game etc.; slightest action; single complete action of moving wing, oar, etc.; whole motion of piston either way; mode of moving limbs in swimming; single mark made by pen, paint brush, etc.; detail contributing to general effect; sound of striking clock; oarsman nearest stern, who sets time of stroke; act or spell of stroking. ● *verb* (**-king**) pass hand gently along surface of (hair, fur, etc.); act as stroke of (boat, crew). □ **at a stroke** by a single action; **on the stroke of** punctually at; **stroke of (good) luck** unexpected fortunate event.

**stroll** /strəʊl/ ● *verb* walk in leisurely fashion. ● *noun* leisurely walk. □ **strolling players** *historical* actors etc. going from place to place performing.

**strong** ● *adjective* (**stronger** /ˈstrɒŋgə/, **strongest** /-gɪst/) physically, morally, or mentally powerful; vigorous, robust; performed with muscular strength; difficult to capture, escape from, etc.; (of suspicion, belief, etc.) firmly held; powerfully affecting senses or mind etc.; (of drink, solution, etc.) with large proportion of alcohol etc.; powerful in numbers or equipment etc.; (of verb) forming inflections by vowel change in root syllable. ● *adverb* strongly. □ **come on strong** act forcefully; **going strong** *colloquial* thriving; **strong-arm** using force; **strongbox** strongly made box for valuables; **stronghold** fortress, centre of support for a cause etc.; **strong language** swearing; **strong-minded** determined; **strongroom** strongly built room for valuables; **strong suit** thing in which one excels. □ **strongish** adjective; **strongly** adverb.

**strontium** /ˈstrɒntɪəm/ noun soft silver-white metallic element. □ **strontium-90** radioactive isotope of this.

**strop** ● noun device, esp. strip of leather, for sharpening razors; colloquial bad temper. ● verb (**-pp-**) sharpen on or with strop.

**stroppy** /ˈstrɒpɪ/ adjective (**-ier, -iest**) colloquial bad-tempered, awkward to deal with.

**strove** past of STRIVE.

**struck** past & past participle of STRIKE.

**structuralism** noun doctrine that structure rather than function is important. □ **structuralist** noun & adjective.

**structure** /ˈstrʌktʃə/ ● noun constructed unit, esp. building; way in which thing is constructed; framework. ● verb (**-ring**) give structure to, organize. □ **structural** adjective; **structurally** adverb.

**strudel** /ˈstruːd(ə)l/ noun thin leaved pastry filled esp. with apple and baked.

**struggle** /ˈstrʌg(ə)l/ ● verb (**-ling**) violently try to get free; (often + for, to do) make great efforts under difficulties; (+ with, against) fight against; (+ along, up, etc.) make one's way with difficulty; (esp. as **struggling** adjective) have difficulty in getting recognition or a living. ● noun act or period of struggling; hard or confused contest.

**strum** ● verb (**-mm-**) (often + on) play on (stringed or keyboard instrument), esp. carelessly or unskilfully. ● noun strumming sound.

**strumpet** /ˈstrʌmpɪt/ noun archaic prostitute.

**strung** past & past participle of STRING.

**strut** ● noun bar in framework to resist pressure; strutting gait. ● verb (**-tt-**) walk in stiff pompous way; brace with strut(s).

**'struth** /struːθ/ interjection (also **'strewth**) colloquial exclamation of surprise.

**strychnine** /ˈstrɪkniːn/ noun highly poisonous alkaloid.

**stub** ● noun remnant of pencil, cigarette, etc.; counterfoil of cheque, receipt, etc.; stump. ● verb (**-bb-**) strike (one's toe) against something; (usually + out) extinguish (cigarette etc.) by pressing lighted end against something.

**stubble** /ˈstʌb(ə)l/ noun cut stalks of corn etc. left in ground after harvest; short stiff hair or bristles, esp. on unshaven face. □ **stubbly** adjective.

**stubborn** /ˈstʌbən/ adjective obstinate, inflexible. □ **stubbornly** adverb; **stubbornness** noun.

**stubby** adjective (**-ier, -iest**) short and thick.

**stucco** /ˈstʌkəʊ/ ● noun (plural **-es**) plaster or cement for coating walls or moulding into architectural decorations. ● verb (**-es, -ed**) coat with stucco.

**stuck** past & past participle of STICK[2]. □ **stuck-up** colloquial conceited, snobbish.

**stud[1]** ● noun large projecting nail, knob, etc. as surface ornament; double button, esp. for use in shirt-front. ● verb (**-dd-**) set with studs; (as **studded** adjective) (+ with) thickly set or strewn with.

**stud[2]** noun number of horses kept for breeding etc.; place where these are kept; stallion. □ **at stud** (of stallion) hired out for breeding. **stud-book** book giving pedigrees of horses; **stud-farm** place where horses are bred; **stud poker** poker with betting after dealing of cards face up.

**student** /ˈstjuːd(ə)nt/ noun person who is studying, esp. at place of higher or further education. □ **studentship** noun.

**studio** /ˈstjuːdɪəʊ/ noun (plural **-s**) work-room of sculptor, painter, photographer, etc.; place for making films, recordings, or broadcasts. □ **studio couch** couch that can be converted into a bed; **studio flat** one-roomed flat.

**studious** /ˈstjuːdɪəs/ adjective diligent in study or reading; painstaking. □ **studiously** adverb.

**study** /ˈstʌdɪ/ ● noun (plural **-ies**) acquiring knowledge, esp. from books; (in plural) pursuit of academic knowledge; private room for reading, writing, etc.; piece of work, esp. in painting, done as exercise or preliminary experiment; portrayal, esp. in literature, of character, behaviour, etc.; Music composition designed to develop player's skill; thing worth observing; thing that is or deserves to be investigated. ● verb (-ies, -ied) make study of; scrutinize; devote time and thought to understanding subject etc. or achieving desired result; (as **studied** adjective) deliberate, affected.

**stuff** ● noun material; fabric; substance or things not needing to be specified; particular knowledge or activity; woollen fabric; nonsense; (**the stuff**) colloquial supply, esp. of drink or drugs. ● verb pack (receptacle) tightly; (+ in, into) force or cram (thing); fill out skin to restore original shape of (bird, animal, etc.); fill (bird, piece of meat, etc.) with mixture, esp. before cooking; (also **stuff oneself**) eat greedily; push, esp. hastily or clumsily; (usually in passive; + up) block up (nose etc.); slang derogatory dispose of. □ **get stuffed** slang go away, get lost; **stuff and nonsense** something ridiculous or incredible.

**stuffing** noun padding for cushions etc.; mixture used to stuff food, esp. before cooking.

**stuffy** adjective (-ier, -iest) (of room etc.) lacking fresh air; dull, uninteresting; conventional, narrow-minded; (of nose etc.) stuffed up. □ **stuffily** adverb; **stuffiness** noun.

**stultify** /'stʌltɪfaɪ/ verb (-ies, -ied) make ineffective or useless, esp. by routine or from frustration. □ **stultification** noun.

**stumble** /'stʌmb(ə)l/ ● verb (-ling) accidentally lurch forward or have partial fall; (often + along) walk with repeated stumbles; speak clumsily; (+ on, upon, across) find by chance. ● noun act of stumbling. □ **stumbling block** circumstance causing difficulty or hesitation.

**stump** ● noun part of cut or fallen tree still in ground; similar part (of branch, limb, tooth, etc.) cut off or worn down; Cricket each of 3 uprights of wicket. ● verb (of question etc.) be too difficult for, baffle; (as **stumped** adjective) at a loss; Cricket put batsman out by touching stumps with ball while he is out of his crease; walk stiffly or clumsily and noisily; US traverse (district) making political speeches. □ **stump up** colloquial produce or pay over (money required).

**stumpy** adjective (-ier, -iest) short and thick. □ **stumpiness** noun.

**stun** verb (-nn-) knock senseless; stupefy; bewilder, shock.

**stung** past & past participle of STING.

**stunk** past & past participle of STINK.

**stunner** noun colloquial stunning person or thing.

**stunning** adjective colloquial extremely attractive or impressive. □ **stunningly** adverb.

**stunt**[1] verb retard growth or development of.

**stunt**[2] noun something unusual done to attract attention; trick, daring manoeuvre. □ **stunt man** employed to take actor's place in performing dangerous stunts.

**stupefy** /'stjuːpɪfaɪ/ verb (-ies, -ied) make stupid or insensible; astonish. □ **stupefaction** noun.

**stupendous** /stjuː'pendəs/ adjective amazing; of vast size or importance. □ **stupendously** adverb.

**stupid** /'stjuːpɪd/ adjective (-er, -est) unintelligent, slow-witted; typical of stupid person; uninteresting; in state of stupor. □ **stupidity** /-'pɪd-/ noun (plural -ies); **stupidly** adverb.

**stupor** /'stjuːpə/ noun dazed or torpid state; utter amazement.

**sturdy** /'stɜːdɪ/ adjective (-ier, -iest) robust; strongly built; vigorous. □ **sturdily** adverb; **sturdiness** noun.

**sturgeon** /'stɜːdʒ(ə)n/ noun (plural same or -s) large edible fish yielding caviar.

**stutter** /'stʌtə/ verb & noun stammer.

**sty**[1] /staɪ/ noun (plural **sties**) enclosure for pigs; filthy room or dwelling.

**sty**[2] /staɪ/ noun (also **stye**) (plural **sties** or **styes**) inflamed swelling on edge of eyelid.

**Stygian** /'stɪdʒɪən/ adjective literary murky, gloomy.

**style** /staɪl/ ● noun kind or sort, esp. in regard to appearance and form (of person, house, etc.); manner of writing, speaking, etc.; distinctive manner of person, artistic school, or period; correct way of designating person or thing; superior quality; fashion in dress etc.; implement for scratching or engraving; part of flower supporting stigma. ● verb (-ling) design or make etc. in particular style; designate in specified way.

**stylish** adjective fashionable, elegant. □ **stylishly** adverb; **stylishness** noun.

**stylist** /'staɪlɪst/ noun designer of fashionable styles; hairdresser; stylish writer or performer.

**stylistic** /staɪ'lɪstɪk/ adjective of literary or artistic style. □ **stylistically** adverb.

**stylized** /'staɪlaɪzd/ adjective (also **-ised**) painted, drawn, etc. in conventional non-realistic style.

**stylus** /'staɪləs/ noun (plural **-luses**) needle-like point for producing or following groove in gramophone record; ancient pointed writing instrument.

**stymie** /'staɪmɪ/ (also **stimy**) ● noun (plural **-ies**) Golf situation where opponent's ball lies between one's ball and the hole; difficult situation. ● verb (**stymying** or **stymieing**) obstruct, thwart.

**styptic** /'stɪptɪk/ ● adjective serving to check bleeding. ● noun styptic substance.

**styrene** /'staɪəri:n/ noun liquid hydrocarbon used in making plastics etc.

**suave** /swɑ:v/ adjective smooth; polite; sophisticated. □ **suavely** adverb; **suavity** noun.

**sub** colloquial ● noun submarine; subscription; substitute; sub-editor. ● verb (**-bb-**) (usually + for) act as substitute; sub-edit.

**sub-** prefix at, to, or from lower position; secondary or inferior position; nearly; more or less.

**subaltern** /'sʌbəlt(ə)n/ noun Military officer below rank of captain, esp. second lieutenant.

**sub-aqua** /sʌb'ækwə/ adjective (of sport etc.) taking place under water.

**subatomic** /sʌbə'tɒmɪk/ adjective occurring in, or smaller than, an atom.

**subcommittee** noun committee formed from main committee for special purpose.

**subconscious** /sʌb'kɒnʃəs/ ● adjective of part of mind that is not fully conscious but influences actions etc. ● noun this part of the mind. □ **subconsciously** adverb.

**subcontinent** /'sʌbkɒntɪnənt/ noun large land mass, smaller than a continent.

**subcontract** ● verb /sʌbkən'trækt/ employ another contractor to do (work) as part of larger project; make or carry out subcontract. ● noun /sʌb'kɒntrækt/ secondary contract. □ **subcontractor** /-'træktə/ noun.

**subculture** /'sʌbkʌltʃə/ noun social group or its culture within a larger culture.

**subcutaneous** /sʌbkju:'teɪnɪəs/ adjective under the skin.

**subdivide** /sʌbdɪ'vaɪd/ verb (**-ding**) divide again after first division. □ **subdivision** /'sʌbdɪvɪʒ(ə)n/ noun.

**subdue** /səb'dju:/ verb (**-dues**, **-dued**, **-duing**) conquer, suppress; tame; (as **subdued** adjective) softened, lacking in intensity.

**sub-editor** /sʌb'edɪtə/ noun assistant editor; person who prepares material for printing. □ **sub-edit** verb (**-t-**).

**subheading** /'sʌbhedɪŋ/ noun subordinate heading or title.

**subhuman** /sʌb'hju:mən/ adjective (of behaviour, intelligence, etc.) less than human.

**subject** ● noun /'sʌbdʒɪkt/ theme of discussion, description, or representation; (+ for) person, circumstance, etc. giving rise to specified feeling, action, etc.; branch of study; word or phrase representing person or thing carrying out action of verb (see panel); person other than monarch living under government; Philosophy thinking or feeling entity, conscious self; Music theme, leading motif. ● adjective /'sʌbdʒɪkt/ (+ to) conditional on, liable or exposed to; owing obedience to government etc. ● adverb /'sʌbdʒɪkt/ (+ to) conditionally on. ● verb /səb'dʒekt/ (+ to) make liable or expose to; (usually + to) subdue (person, nation, etc.) to superior will. □ **subjection** noun.

**subjective** /səb'dʒektɪv/ adjective (of art, written history, opinion, etc.) not impartial or literal; esp. Philosophy of individual consciousness or perception; imaginary, partial, distorted; Grammar of the subject. □ **subjectively** adverb; **subjectivity** /sʌbdʒek'tɪv-/ noun.

**subjoin** /sʌb'dʒɔɪn/ verb add (illustration, anecdote, etc.) at the end.

**sub judice** /sʌb ˈdʒuːdɪsɪ/ *adjective Law* under judicial consideration and therefore prohibited from public discussion. [Latin]

**subjugate** /ˈsʌbdʒʊɡeɪt/ *verb* (**-ting**) conquer, bring into subjection. □ **subjugation** *noun*; **subjugator** *noun*.

**subjunctive** /səbˈdʒʌŋktɪv/ *Grammar* ● *adjective* (of mood) expressing wish, supposition, or possibility. ● *noun* subjunctive mood or form.

**sublease** ● *noun* /ˈsʌbliːs/ lease granted by tenant to subtenant. ● *verb* /sʌbˈliːs/ (**-sing**) lease to subtenant.

**sublet** /sʌbˈlet/ *verb* (**-tt-**; *past & past participle* **-let**) lease to subtenant.

**sub-lieutenant** /sʌblefˈtenənt/ *noun* officer ranking next below lieutenant.

**sublimate** ● *verb* /ˈsʌblɪmeɪt/ (**-ting**) divert energy of (primitive impulse etc.) into socially more acceptable activity; sublime (substance); refine, purify. ● *noun* /ˈsʌblɪmət/ sublimated substance. □ **sublimation** *noun*.

**sublime** /səˈblaɪm/ ● *adjective* (**-r**, **-st**) of most exalted kind; awe-inspiring; arrogantly undisturbed. ● *verb* (**-ming**) convert (substance) from solid into vapour by heat (and usually allow to solidify again); make sublime; become pure (as if) by sublimation. □ **sublimely** *adverb*; **sublimity** /-ˈlɪm-/ *noun*.

**subliminal** /səbˈlɪmɪn(ə)l/ *adjective Psychology* below threshold of sensation or consciousness; too faint or rapid to be consciously perceived. □ **subliminally** *adverb*.

**sub-machine-gun** /sʌbməˈʃiːnɡʌn/ *noun* hand-held lightweight machine-gun.

**submarine** /ˈsʌbməriːn/ ● *noun* vessel, esp. armed warship, which can be submerged and navigated under water. ● *adjective* existing, occurring, done, or used below surface of sea. □ **submariner** /-ˈmærɪnə/ *noun*.

**submerge** /səbˈmɜːdʒ/ *verb* (**-ging**) place, go, or dive beneath water; overwhelm with work, problems, etc. □ **submergence** *noun*; **submersion** *noun*.

**submersible** /səbˈmɜːsɪb(ə)l/ ● *noun* submarine operating under water for short periods. ● *adjective* capable of submerging.

**submicroscopic** /sʌbmaɪkrəˈskɒpɪk/ *adjective* too small to be seen by ordinary microscope.

**submission** /səbˈmɪʃ(ə)n/ *noun* submitting, being submitted; thing submitted; submissive attitude etc.

**submissive** /səbˈmɪsɪv/ *adjective* humble, obedient. □ **submissively** *adverb*; **submissiveness** *noun*.

**submit** /səbˈmɪt/ *verb* (**-tt-**) (often + *to*) cease resistance, yield; present for consideration; (+ *to*) subject or be subjected to (process, treatment, etc.); *Law* argue, suggest.

**subnormal** /sʌbˈnɔːm(ə)l/ *adjective* below or less than normal, esp. in intelligence.

**subordinate** ● *adjective* /səˈbɔːdɪnət/ (usually + *to*) of inferior importance or rank; secondary, subservient. ● *noun* /səˈbɔːdɪnət/ person working under authority of another. ● *verb* /səˈbɔːdɪneɪt/ (**-ting**) (usually + *to*) make or treat as subordinate. □ **subordinate clause** clause serving as noun, adjective, or

## Subject

The subject of a sentence is the person or thing that carries out the action of the verb and can be found by asking the question 'who or what?' before the verb, e.g.

The goalkeeper *made a stunning save.*
Hundreds of books *are now available on CD-ROM.*

In a passive construction, the subject of the sentence is in fact the person or thing to which the action of the verb is done, e.g.

I *was hit by a ball.*
Has the programme *been broadcast yet?*

adverb within sentence. □ **subordination** noun.

**suborn** /sə'bɔːn/ verb induce esp. by bribery to commit perjury or other crime.

**subpoena** /sə'piːnə/ ● noun writ ordering person's attendance in law court. ● verb (past & past participle **-naed** or **-na'd**) serve subpoena on.

**sub rosa** /sʌb 'rəʊzə/ adjective & adverb in confidence or in secret. [Latin]

**subscribe** /səb'skraɪb/ verb (**-bing**) (usually + to, for) pay (specified sum) esp. regularly for membership of organization or receipt of publication etc.; contribute to fund, for cause, etc.; (usually + to) agree with (opinion etc.). □ **subscribe to** arrange to receive (periodical etc.) regularly.

**subscriber** noun person who subscribes, esp. person paying regular sum for hire of telephone line. □ **subscriber trunk dialling** making of trunk calls by subscriber without assistance of operator.

**subscript** /'sʌbskrɪpt/ ● adjective written or printed below the line. ● noun subscript number etc.

**subscription** /səb'skrɪpʃ(ə)n/ noun act of subscribing; money subscribed; membership fee, esp. paid regularly.

**subsequent** /'sʌbsɪkwənt/ adjective (usually + to) following specified or implied event. □ **subsequently** adverb.

**subservient** /səb'sɜːvɪənt/ adjective servile; (usually + to) instrumental, subordinate. □ **subservience** noun.

**subside** /səb'saɪd/ verb (**-ding**) become tranquil, diminish; (of water etc.) sink; (of ground) cave in. □ **subsidence** /-'saɪd-, 'sʌbsɪd-/ noun.

**subsidiary** /səb'sɪdɪərɪ/ ● adjective supplementary; additional; (of company) controlled by another. ● noun (plural **-ies**) subsidiary company, person, or thing.

**subsidize** /'sʌbsɪdaɪz/ verb (also **-ise**) (**-zing** or **-sing**) pay subsidy to; support by subsidies.

**subsidy** /'sʌbsɪdɪ/ noun (plural **-ies**) money contributed esp. by state to keep prices at desired level; any monetary grant.

**subsist** /səb'sɪst/ verb (often + on) keep oneself alive; be kept alive; remain in being, exist.

**subsistence** noun subsisting; means of supporting life; minimal level of existence, income, etc. □ **subsistence farming** farming in which almost all produce is consumed by farmer's household.

**subsoil** /'sʌbsɔɪl/ noun soil just below surface soil.

**subsonic** /sʌb'sɒnɪk/ adjective of speeds less than that of sound.

**substance** /'sʌbst(ə)ns/ noun particular kind of material; reality, solidity; essence of what is spoken or written; wealth and possessions. □ **in substance** generally, essentially.

**substandard** /sʌb'stændəd/ adjective of lower than desired standard.

**substantial** /səb'stænʃ(ə)l/ adjective of real importance or value; large in size or amount; of solid structure; commercially successful; wealthy; largely true; real; existing. □ **substantially** adverb.

**substantiate** /səb'stænʃɪeɪt/ verb (**-ting**) support or prove truth of (charge, claim, etc.). □ **substantiation** noun.

**substantive** /'sʌbstəntɪv/ ● adjective actual, real, permanent; substantial. ● noun noun. □ **substantively** adverb.

**substitute** /'sʌbstɪtjuːt/ ● noun person or thing acting or serving in place of another; artificial alternative to a food etc. ● verb (**-ting**) (often + for) put in place of another; act as substitute for. ● adjective acting as substitute. □ **substitution** noun.

**substratum** /'sʌbstrɑːtəm/ noun (plural **-ta**) underlying layer.

**subsume** /səb'sjuːm/ verb (**-ming**) (usually + under) include under particular rule, class, etc.

**subtenant** /'sʌbtenənt/ noun person renting room or house etc. from its tenant. □ **subtenancy** noun (plural **-ies**).

**subtend** /sʌb'tend/ verb (of line) be opposite (angle, arc).

**subterfuge** /'sʌbtəfjuːdʒ/ noun attempt to avoid blame etc., esp. by lying or deceit.

**subterranean** /sʌbtə'reɪnɪən/ adjective underground.

**subtext** noun underlying theme.

**subtitle** /'sʌbtaɪt(ə)l/ ● noun subordinate or additional title of book etc.; caption of cinema film, esp. translating dialogue. ● verb (-ling) provide with subtitle(s).

**subtle** /'sʌt(ə)l/ adjective (-r, -st) hard to detect or describe; (of scent, colour, etc.) faint, delicate; ingenious, perceptive. □ **subtlety** noun (plural -ies); **subtly** adverb.

**subtract** /səb'trækt/ verb (often + from) deduct (number etc.) from another. □ **subtraction** noun.

**subtropical** /sʌb'trɒpɪk(ə)l/ adjective bordering on the tropics; characteristic of such regions.

**suburb** /'sʌbɜ:b/ noun outlying district of city.

**suburban** /sə'bɜ:bən/ adjective of or characteristic of suburbs; derogatory provincial in outlook. □ **suburbanite** noun.

**suburbia** /sə'bɜ:bɪə/ noun usually derogatory suburbs and their inhabitants etc.

**subvention** /səb'venʃ(ə)n/ noun subsidy.

**subversive** /səb'vɜ:sɪv/ ● adjective seeking to overthrow (esp. government). ● noun subversive person. □ **subversion** noun; **subversively** adverb; **subversiveness** noun.

**subvert** /səb'vɜ:t/ verb overthrow or weaken (government etc.).

**subway** /'sʌbweɪ/ noun underground passage, esp. for pedestrians; US underground railway.

**subzero** /sʌb'zɪərəʊ/ adjective (esp. of temperature) lower than zero.

**succeed** /sək'si:d/ verb (often + in) have success; prosper; follow in order; (often + to) come into inheritance, office, title, or property.

**success** /sək'ses/ noun accomplishment of aim; favourable outcome; attainment of wealth, fame, etc.; successful person or thing. □ **successful** adjective; **successfully** adverb.

**succession** /sək'seʃ(ə)n/ noun following in order; series of things or people following one another; succeeding to inheritance, office, or esp. throne; right to succeed to one of these, set of people with such right. ■ **in succession** one after another; **in succession to** as successor of.

**successive** /sək'sesɪv/ adjective following in succession, consecutive. □ **successively** adverb.

**successor** /sək'sesə/ noun (often + to) person or thing that succeeds another.

**succinct** /sək'sɪŋkt/ adjective brief, concise. □ **succinctly** adverb; **succinctness** noun.

**succour** /'sʌkə/ (US **succor**) archaic or formal ● noun help, esp. in time of need. ● verb give succour to.

**succulent** /'sʌkjʊlənt/ ● adjective juicy; (of plant) thick and fleshy. ● noun succulent plant. □ **succulence** noun.

**succumb** /sə'kʌm/ verb (usually + to) give way; be overcome; die.

**such** ● adjective (often + as) of kind or degree specified or suggested; so great or extreme; unusually, abnormally. ● pronoun such person(s) or thing(s). ■ **as such** as being what has been specified; **such-and-such** particular but unspecified; **suchlike** colloquial of such kind.

**suck** ● verb draw (liquid) into mouth by suction; draw liquid from in this way; roll tongue round (sweet etc.) in mouth; make sucking action or noise; (usually + down) engulf or drown in sucking movement. ● noun act or period of sucking. ■ **suck in** absorb, involve (person); **suck up** (often + to) colloquial behave in a servile way, absorb.

**sucker** noun person easily duped or cheated; (+ for) person susceptible to; rubber etc. cap adhering by suction; similar part of plant or animal; shoot springing from plant's root below ground.

**suckle** /'sʌk(ə)l/ verb (-ling) feed (young) from breast or udder.

**suckling** /'sʌklɪŋ/ noun unweaned child or animal.

**sucrose** /'su:krəʊz/ noun kind of sugar obtained from cane, beet, etc.

**suction** /'sʌkʃ(ə)n/ noun sucking; production of partial vacuum so that external atmospheric pressure forces fluid into vacant space or causes adhesion of surfaces.

**Sudanese** /su:də'ni:z/ ● adjective of Sudan. ● noun (plural same) native or national of Sudan.

**sudden** /'sʌd(ə)n/ adjective done or occurring unexpectedly or abruptly. ■ **all of a sudden** suddenly. □ **suddenly** adverb; **suddenness** noun.

**sudorific** /suːdəˈrɪfɪk/ ● *adjective* causing sweating. ● *noun* sudorific drug.

**suds** *plural noun* froth of soap and water. □ **sudsy** *adjective*.

**sue** *verb* (**sues**, **sued**, **suing**) begin lawsuit against; (often + *for*) make application to law court for compensation etc.; (often + *to*, *for*) make plea to person for favour.

**suede** /sweɪd/ *noun* leather with flesh side rubbed into nap.

**suet** /ˈsuːɪt/ *noun* hard fat surrounding kidneys of cattle and sheep, used in cooking etc. □ **suety** *adjective*.

**suffer** /ˈsʌfə/ *verb* undergo pain, grief, etc.; undergo or be subjected to (pain, loss, punishment, grief, etc.); tolerate. □ **sufferer** *noun*; **suffering** *noun*.

**sufferance** *noun* tacit permission or toleration. □ **on sufferance** tolerated but not supported.

**suffice** /səˈfaɪs/ *verb* (**-cing**) be enough; meet needs of. □ **suffice it to say** I shall say only this.

**sufficiency** /səˈfɪʃənsɪ/ *noun* (*plural* -**ies**) (often + *of*) sufficient amount.

**sufficient** /səˈfɪʃ(ə)nt/ *adjective* sufficing; adequate. □ **sufficiently** *adverb*.

**suffix** /ˈsʌfɪks/ ● *noun* letter(s) added to end of word to form derivative. ● *verb* add as suffix.

**suffocate** /ˈsʌfəkeɪt/ *verb* (**-ting**) kill, stifle, or choke by stopping breathing, esp. by fumes etc.; be or feel suffocated. □ **suffocating** *adjective*; **suffocation** *noun*.

**suffragan** /ˈsʌfrəgən/ *noun* bishop assisting diocesan bishop.

**suffrage** /ˈsʌfrɪdʒ/ *noun* right of voting in political elections.

**suffragette** /sʌfrəˈdʒet/ *noun* *historical* woman who agitated for women's suffrage.

**suffuse** /səˈfjuːz/ *verb* (**-sing**) (of colour, moisture, etc.) spread throughout or over from within. □ **suffusion** /-ʒ(ə)n/ *noun*.

**sugar** /ˈʃʊgə/ ● *noun* sweet crystalline substance obtained from sugar cane and sugar beet, used in cookery, confectionery, etc.; *Chemistry* soluble usually sweet crystalline carbohydrate, e.g. glucose; *esp. US colloquial* darling (as

term of address). ● *verb* sweeten or coat with sugar. □ **sugar beet** white beet yielding sugar; **sugar cane** tall stout perennial tropical grass yielding sugar; **sugar-daddy** *slang* elderly man who lavishes gifts on young woman; **sugar loaf** conical moulded mass of hard refined sugar.

**sugary** *adjective* containing or resembling sugar; cloying, sentimental. □ **sugariness** *noun*.

**suggest** /səˈdʒest/ *verb* (often + *that*) propose (theory, plan, etc.); hint at; evoke (idea etc.); (**suggest itself**) (of idea etc.) come into person's mind.

**suggestible** *adjective* capable of being influenced by suggestion. □ **suggestibility** *noun*.

**suggestion** /səˈdʒestʃ(ə)n/ *noun* suggesting; thing suggested; slight trace, hint; insinuation of belief or impulse into the mind.

**suggestive** /səˈdʒestɪv/ *adjective* (usually + *of*) conveying a suggestion; (of remark, joke, etc.) suggesting something indecent. □ **suggestively** *adverb*.

**suicidal** /suːɪˈsaɪd(ə)l/ *adjective* (of person) liable to commit suicide; of or tending to suicide; destructive to one's own interests. □ **suicidally** *adverb*.

**suicide** /ˈsuːɪsaɪd/ *noun* intentional self-killing; person who commits suicide; action destructive to one's own interests etc.

**sui generis** /sjuːˈaɪˈdʒenərɪs/ *adjective* of its own kind, unique. [Latin]

**suit** /suːt, sjuːt/ ● *noun* set of usually matching clothes consisting usually of jacket and trousers or skirt; clothing for particular purpose; any of the 4 sets into which pack of cards is divided; lawsuit. ● *verb* go well with (person's appearance); meet requirements of; (**suit oneself**) do as one chooses; be in harmony with; make fitting; be convenient; adapt; (as **suited**) appropriate, well-fitted. □ **suitcase** flat case for carrying clothes, usually with hinged lid.

**suitable** *adjective* (usually + *to*, *for*) well-fitted for purpose; appropriate to occasion. □ **suitability** *noun*; **suitably** *adverb*.

**suite** /swiːt/ *noun* set of rooms, furniture, etc.; *Music* set of instrumental pieces.

**suitor** /ˈsuːtə/ *noun* man who woos woman; plaintiff or petitioner in lawsuit.

**sulfur** etc. *US* = SULPHUR etc.

**sulk** ● *verb* be sulky. ● *noun* (also **the sulks**) fit of sullen silence.

**sulky** /ˈsʌlkɪ/ *adjective* (**-ier**, **-iest**) sullen and unsociable from resentment or ill temper. □ **sulkily** *adverb*.

**sullen** /ˈsʌlən/ *adjective* sulky, morose. □ **sullenly** *adverb*; **sullenness** *noun*.

**sully** /ˈsʌlɪ/ *verb* (**-ies**, **-ied**) spoil purity or splendour of (reputation etc.).

**sulphate** /ˈsʌlfeɪt/ *noun* (*US* **sulfate**) salt or ester of sulphuric acid.

**sulphide** /ˈsʌlfaɪd/ *noun* (*US* **sulfide**) binary compound of sulphur.

**sulphite** /ˈsʌlfaɪt/ *noun* (*US* **sulfite**) salt or ester of sulphurous acid.

**sulphonamide** /sʌlˈfɒnəmaɪd/ *noun* (*US* **sulfonamide**) kind of antibiotic drug containing sulphur.

**sulphur** /ˈsʌlfə/ *noun* (*US* **sulfur**) pale yellow non-metallic element burning with blue flame and stifling smell. □ **sulphur dioxide** colourless pungent gas formed by burning sulphur in air and dissolving it in water.

**sulphuric** /sʌlˈfjʊərɪk/ *adjective* (*US* **sulfuric**) of or containing sulphur with valency of 6. □ **sulphuric acid** dense highly corrosive oily acid.

**sulphurous** /ˈsʌlfərəs/ *adjective* (*US* **sulfurous**) of or like sulphur; containing sulphur with valency of 4. □ **sulphurous acid** unstable weak acid used e.g. as bleaching agent.

**sultan** /ˈsʌlt(ə)n/ *noun* Muslim sovereign.

**sultana** /sʌlˈtɑːnə/ *noun* seedless raisin; sultan's wife, mother, concubine, or daughter.

**sultanate** /ˈsʌltəneɪt/ *noun* position of or territory ruled by sultan.

**sultry** /ˈsʌltrɪ/ *adjective* (**-ier**, **-iest**) (of weather) oppressively hot; (of person) passionate, sensual.

**sum** ● *noun* total resulting from addition; amount of money; arithmetical problem; (esp. in *plural*) *colloquial* arithmetic work, esp. elementary. ● *verb* (**-mm-**) find sum of. □ **in sum** briefly, to sum up; **summing-up** judge's review of evidence given to jury, recapitulation of main points of argument etc.; **sum up** (esp. of judge) give summing-up, form or express opinion of (person, situation, etc.), summarize.

**sumac** /ˈsuːmæk/ *noun* (also **sumach**) shrub with reddish fruits used as spice; dried and ground leaves of this for use in tanning and dyeing.

**summarize** /ˈsʌməraɪz/ *verb* (also **-ise**) (**-zing** or **-sing**) make or be summary of.

**summary** /ˈsʌmərɪ/ ● *noun* (*plural* **-ies**) brief account giving chief points. ● *adjective* brief, without details or formalities. □ **summarily** *adverb*.

**summation** /səˈmeɪʃ(ə)n/ *noun* finding of total or sum; summarizing.

**summer** /ˈsʌmə/ *noun* warmest season of year; (often + *of*) mature stage of life etc. □ **summer house** light building in garden etc. for use in summer; **summer pudding** dessert of soft fruit pressed in bread casing; **summer school** course of lectures etc. held in summer, esp. at university; **summer time** period from March to October when clocks etc. are advanced one hour; **summertime** season or period of summer. □ **summery** *adjective*.

**summit** /ˈsʌmɪt/ *noun* highest point, top; highest level of achievement or status; (in full **summit conference**, **meeting**, etc.) discussion between heads of governments.

**summon** /ˈsʌmən/ *verb* order to come or appear, esp. in lawcourt; (usually + *to do*) call on; call together; (often + *up*) gather (courage, resources, etc.).

**summons** /ˈsʌmənz/ ● *noun* (*plural* **summonses**) authoritative call to attend or do something, esp. to appear in court. ● *verb esp. Law* serve with summons.

**sumo** /ˈsuːməʊ/ *noun* Japanese wrestling in which only soles of feet may touch ground.

**sump** *noun* casing holding oil in internal-combustion engine; pit, well, etc. for collecting superfluous liquid.

**sumptuary** /ˈsʌmptʃʊərɪ/ *adjective Law* regulating (esp. private) expenditure.

**sumptuous** /ˈsʌmptʃʊəs/ *adjective* costly, splendid, magnificent. □ **sumptuously** *adverb;* **sumptuousness** *noun.*

**Sun.** *abbreviation* Sunday.

**sun** ●*noun* the star round which the earth travels and from which it receives light and warmth; this light or warmth; any star. ●*verb* (**-nn-**) (often **sun oneself**) expose to sun. □ **sunbathe** bask in sun, esp. to tan one's body; **sunbeam** ray of sunlight; **sunblock** lotion protecting skin from sun; **sunburn** inflammation of skin from exposure to sun; **sunburnt** affected by sunburn; **sundial** instrument showing time by shadow of pointer in sunlight; **sundown** sunset; **sunflower** tall plant with large golden-rayed flowers; **sunglasses** tinted spectacles to protect eyes from glare; **sunlamp** lamp giving ultraviolet rays for therapy or artificial suntan; **sunlight** light from sun; **sunlit** illuminated by sun; **sun lounge** room with large windows etc. to receive much sunlight; **sunrise** (time of) sun's rising; **sunroof** opening panel in car's roof; **sunset** (time of) sun's setting; **sunshade** parasol, awning; **sunshine** sunlight, area illuminated by it, fine weather, cheerfulness; **sunspot** dark patch on sun's surface; **sunstroke** acute prostration from excessive heat of sun; **suntan** brownish skin colour caused by exposure to sun; **suntrap** sunny place, esp. sheltered from wind; **sun-up** *esp. US* sunrise.

**sundae** /ˈsʌndeɪ/ *noun* ice cream with fruit, nuts, syrup, etc.

**Sunday** /ˈsʌndeɪ/ *noun* day of week following Saturday; Christian day of worship; *colloquial* newspaper published on Sundays. □ **month of Sundays** *colloquial* very long period; **Sunday school** religious class held on Sundays for children.

**sunder** /ˈsʌndə/ *verb literary* sever, keep apart.

**sundry** /ˈsʌndrɪ/ ●*adjective* various, several. ●*noun* (*plural* **-ies**) (in *plural*) oddments, accessories, etc. not mentioned individually. □ **all and sundry** everyone.

**sung** *past participle* of SING.

**sunk** *past & past participle* of SINK.

**sunken** *adjective* that has sunk; lying below general surface; (of eyes, cheeks, etc.) shrunken, hollow.

**Sunni** /ˈsʌnɪ/ *noun* (*plural* same or **-s**) one of two main branches of Islam; adherent of this.

**sunny** *adjective* (**-ier, -iest**) bright with or warmed by sunlight; cheerful. □ **sunnily** *adverb;* **sunniness** *noun.*

**sup**[1] ●*verb* (**-pp-**) drink by sips or spoonfuls; *esp. Northern English colloquial* drink (alcohol). ●*noun* sip of liquid.

**sup**[2] *verb* (**-pp-**) *archaic* take supper.

**super** /ˈsuːpə/ ●*adjective colloquial* excellent, unusually good. ●*noun colloquial* superintendent; supernumerary.

**super-** *combining form* on top, over, beyond; to extreme degree; extra good or large of its kind; of higher kind.

**superannuate** /suːpərˈænjʊeɪt/ *verb* (**-ting**) pension (person) off; dismiss or discard as too old; (as **superannuated** *adjective*) too old for work.

**superannuation** *noun* pension; payment made to obtain pension.

**superb** /suːˈpɜːb/ *adjective colloquial* excellent; magnificent. □ **superbly** *adverb.*

**supercargo** /ˈsuːpəkɑːgəʊ/ *noun* (*plural* **-es**) person in merchant ship managing sales etc. of cargo.

**supercharge** /ˈsuːpətʃɑːdʒ/ *verb* (**-ging**) (usually + *with*) charge (atmosphere etc.) with energy, emotion, etc.; use supercharger on.

**supercharger** *noun* device forcing extra air or fuel into internal-combustion engine.

**supercilious** /suːpəˈsɪlɪəs/ *adjective* haughtily contemptuous. □ **superciliously** *adverb;* **superciliousness** *noun.*

**supererogation** /suːpərerəˈgeɪʃ(ə)n/ *noun* doing of more than duty requires.

**superficial** /suːpəˈfɪʃ(ə)l/ *adjective* of or on the surface; lacking depth; swift, cursory; apparent, not real; (esp. of person) of shallow feelings etc. □ **superficiality** /-ʃɪˈæl-/ *noun;* **superficially** *adverb.*

**superfluity** /suːpəˈfluːɪtɪ/ *noun* (*plural* **-ies**) being superfluous; superfluous amount or thing.

**superfluous** /suːˈpɜːfluːəs/ *adjective* more than is needed or wanted; useless.

**supergrass** /ˈsuːpəɡrɑːs/ *noun colloquial* police informer implicating many people.

**superhuman** /suːpəˈhjuːmən/ *adjective* exceeding normal human capacity or power.

**superimpose** /suːpərɪmˈpəʊz/ *verb* (**-sing**) (usually + *on*) place (thing) on or above something else. □ **superimposition** /-pəˈzɪʃ(ə)n/ *noun.*

**superintend** /suːpərɪnˈtend/ *verb* manage, supervise (work etc.). □ **superintendence** *noun.*

**superintendent** /suːpərɪnˈtend(ə)nt/ *noun* police officer above rank of chief inspector; person who superintends; director of institution etc.

**superior** /suːˈpɪərɪə/ ● *adjective* higher in rank, quality, etc.; high-quality; supercilious; (often + *to*) better or greater in some respect; written or printed above the line. ● *noun* person superior to another, esp. in rank; head of monastery etc. □ **superiority** /-ˈɒr-/ *noun.*

**superlative** /suːˈpɜːlətɪv/ ● *adjective* of highest degree; excellent; *Grammar* (of adjective or adverb) expressing highest or very high degree of quality etc. denoted by simple word. ● *noun Grammar* superlative expression or word; (in *plural*) high praise, exaggerated language.

**superman** *noun colloquial* man of exceptional powers or achievement.

**supermarket** /ˈsuːpəmɑːkɪt/ *noun* large self-service store selling food, household goods, etc.

**supernatural** /suːpəˈnætʃər(ə)l/ ● *adjective* not attributable to, or explicable by, natural or physical laws; magical; mystical. ● *noun* (**the supernatural**) supernatural forces etc. □ **supernaturally** *adverb.*

**supernova** /suːpəˈnəʊvə/ *noun* (*plural* **-vae** /-viː/ or **-vas**) star that suddenly increases very greatly in brightness.

**supernumerary** /suːpəˈnjuːmərərɪ/ ● *adjective* in excess of normal number; engaged for extra work; (of actor) with non-speaking part. ● *noun* (*plural* **-ies**) supernumerary person or thing.

**superphosphate** /suːpəˈfɒsfeɪt/ *noun* fertilizer made from phosphate rock.

**superpower** /ˈsuːpəpaʊə/ *noun* extremely powerful nation.

**superscript** /ˈsuːpəskrɪpt/ ● *adjective* written or printed above. ● *noun* superscript number or symbol.

**supersede** /suːpəˈsiːd/ *verb* (**-ding**) take place of; put or use another in place of. □ **supersession** /-ˈseʃ-/ *noun.*

**supersonic** /suːpəˈsɒnɪk/ *adjective* of or having speed greater than that of sound. □ **supersonically** *adverb.*

**superstar** /ˈsuːpəstɑː/ *noun* extremely famous or renowned actor, musician, etc.

**superstition** /suːpəˈstɪʃ(ə)n/ *noun* belief in the supernatural; irrational fear of the unknown or mysterious; practice, belief, or religion based on this. □ **superstitious** *adjective.*

**superstore** /ˈsuːpəstɔː/ *noun* very large supermarket.

**superstructure** /ˈsuːpəstrʌktʃə/ *noun* structure built on top of another; upper part of building, ship, etc.

**supertanker** /ˈsuːpətæŋkə/ *noun* very large tanker.

**supertax** /ˈsuːpətæks/ *noun* surtax.

**supervene** /suːpəˈviːn/ *verb* (**-ning**) *formal* occur as interruption or change from some state. □ **supervention** *noun.*

**supervise** /ˈsuːpəvaɪz/ *verb* (**-sing**) oversee, superintend. □ **supervision** /-ˈvɪʒ(ə)n/ *noun*; **supervisor** *noun*; **supervisory** *adjective.*

**superwoman** *noun colloquial* woman of exceptional ability or power.

**supine** /ˈsuːpaɪn/ ● *adjective* lying face upwards; inactive, indolent. ● *noun* type of Latin verbal noun.

**supper** /ˈsʌpə/ *noun* meal taken late in day, esp. evening meal less formal and substantial than dinner.

**supplant** /səˈplɑːnt/ *verb* take the place of, esp. by underhand means.

**supple** /ˈsʌp(ə)l/ *adjective* (**-r**, **-st**) easily bent, pliant, flexible. □ **suppleness** *noun.*

**supplement** ● *noun* /ˈsʌplɪmənt/ thing or part added to improve or provide further information; separate section of newspaper etc. ● *verb* /ˈsʌplɪment/ provide supplement for. □ **supplemental** /-ˈment(ə)l/ *adjective*; **supplementary** /-ˈmentərɪ/ *adjective*; **supplementation** *noun.*

**suppliant** /'sʌplɪənt/ ● adjective supplicating. ● noun humble petitioner.

**supplicate** /'sʌplɪkeɪt/ verb (-ting) literary make humble petition to or for. □ **supplicant** noun; **supplication** noun; **supplicatory** /-kətərɪ/ adjective.

**supply** /sə'plaɪ/ ● verb (-ies, -ied) provide (thing needed); (often + with) provide (person etc. with something); make up for (deficiency etc.). ● noun (plural -ies) provision of what is needed; stock, store; (in plural) provisions, equipment, etc. for army, expedition, etc.; person, esp. teacher, acting as temporary substitute. □ **supply and demand** quantities available and required, as factors regulating price. □ **supplier** noun.

**support** /sə'pɔːt/ ● verb carry all or part of weight of; keep from falling, sinking, or failing; provide for; strengthen, encourage; give help or corroboration to; speak in favour of; take secondary part to (actor etc.); perform secondary act to (main act) at pop concert. ● noun supporting, being supported; person or thing that supports. □ **in support of** so as to support. □ **supportive** adjective; **supportively** adverb; **supportiveness** noun.

**supporter** noun person or thing that supports particular cause, team, sport, etc.

**suppose** /sə'pəʊz/ verb (-sing) (often + that) assume, be inclined to think; take as possibility or hypothesis; require as condition; (as **supposed** adjective) presumed. □ **be supposed to** be expected or required to; (in negative) ought not, not be allowed to; **I suppose so** expression of hesitant agreement.

**supposedly** /sə'pəʊzɪdlɪ/ adverb as is generally believed.

**supposition** /sʌpə'zɪʃ(ə)n/ noun what is supposed or assumed.

**suppositious** /sʌpə'zɪʃəs/ adjective hypothetical.

**suppository** /sə'pɒzɪtərɪ/ noun (plural -ies) solid medical preparation put into rectum or vagina to melt.

**suppress** /sə'pres/ verb put an end to; prevent (information, feelings, etc.) from being seen, heard, or known; Electricity partially or wholly eliminate (interference etc.), equip (device) to reduce interference due to it. □ **suppressible** adjective; **suppression** noun; **suppressor** noun.

**suppurate** /'sʌpjʊreɪt/ verb (-ting) form or secrete pus; fester. □ **suppuration** noun.

**supra-** prefix above.

**supranational** /suːprə'næʃən(ə)l/ adjective transcending national limits.

**supremacy** /suː'preməsɪ/ noun (plural -ies) being supreme; highest authority.

**supreme** /suː'priːm/ adjective highest in authority or rank; greatest, most important; (of penalty, sacrifice, etc.) involving death. □ **supremely** adverb.

**supremo** /suː'priːməʊ/ noun (plural -s) supreme leader.

**surcharge** /'sɜːtʃɑːdʒ/ ● noun additional charge or payment. ● verb (-ging) exact surcharge from.

**surd** ● adjective (of number) irrational. ● noun surd number.

**sure** /ʃʊə/ ● adjective (often + of, that) convinced; having or seeming to have adequate reason for belief; (+ of) confident in anticipation or knowledge of; reliable, unfailing; (+ to do) certain; undoubtedly true or truthful. ● adverb colloquial certainly. □ **make sure** make or become certain, ensure; **sure-fire** colloquial certain to succeed; **sure-footed** never stumbling; **to be sure** admittedly, indeed, certainly. □ **sureness** noun.

**surely** adverb with certainty or safety; added to statement to express strong belief in its correctness.

**surety** /'ʃʊərətɪ/ noun (plural -ies) money given as guarantee of performance etc.; person taking responsibility for another's debt, obligation, etc.

**surf** ● noun foam of sea breaking on rock or (esp. shallow) shore. ● verb engage in surfing. □ **surfboard** long narrow board used in surfing. □ **surfer** noun.

**surface** /'sɜːfɪs/ ● noun the outside of a thing; any of the limits of a solid; top of liquid, soil, etc.; outward or superficial aspect; Geometry thing with length and breadth but no thickness. ● verb (-cing) give (special) surface to (road, paper, etc.); rise or bring to surface; become visible or known; colloquial wake up, get up. □ **surface mail** mail not carried by air; **surface tension** tension of surface of liquid, tending to minimize its surface area.

**surfeit** /'sɜ:fɪt/ ● *noun* excess, esp. in eating or drinking; resulting fullness. ● *verb* (**-t-**) overfeed; (+ *with*) (cause to) be wearied through excess.

**surfing** *noun* sport of riding surf on board.

**surge** ● *noun* sudden rush; heavy forward or upward motion; sudden increase (in price etc.); sudden but brief increase in pressure, voltage, etc.; surging motion of sea, waves, etc. ● *verb* (**-ging**) move suddenly and powerfully forwards; (of sea etc.) swell.

**surgeon** /'sɜ:dʒ(ə)n/ *noun* medical practitioner qualified to practise surgery; naval or military medical officer.

**surgery** /'sɜ:dʒərɪ/ *noun* (*plural* **-ies**) manual or instrumental treatment of injuries or disorders of body; place where or time when doctor, dentist, etc. gives advice and treatment to patients, or MP, lawyer, etc. gives advice.

**surgical** /'sɜ:dʒɪk(ə)l/ *adjective* of or by surgery or surgeons; used for surgery; (of appliance) worn to correct deformity etc.; (esp. of military action) swift and precise. □ **surgical spirit** methylated spirits used for cleansing etc. □ **surgically** *adverb*.

**surly** /'sɜ:lɪ/ *adjective* (**-ier**, **-iest**) bad-tempered, unfriendly. □ **surliness** *noun*.

**surmise** /sə'maɪz/ ● *noun* conjecture. ● *verb* (**-sing**) (often + *that*) infer doubtfully; suppose; guess.

**surmount** /sə'maʊnt/ *verb* overcome (difficulty, obstacle); (usually in *passive*) cap, crown. □ **surmountable** *adjective*.

**surname** /'sɜ:neɪm/ *noun* name common to all members of family.

**surpass** /sə'pɑ:s/ *verb* outdo, be better than; (as **surpassing** *adjective*) greatly exceeding, excelling others.

**surplice** /'sɜ:plɪs/ *noun* loose full-sleeved white vestment worn by clergy etc.

**surplus** /'sɜ:pləs/ ● *noun* amount left over when requirements have been met; excess of income over spending. ● *adjective* exceeding what is needed or used.

**surprise** /sə'praɪz/ ● *noun* unexpected or astonishing thing; emotion caused by this; catching or being caught unawares. ● *adjective* made, done, etc. without warning. ● *verb* (**-sing**) affect with surprise; (usually in *passive*; + *at*) shock, scandalize; capture by surprise; come upon (person) unawares; (+ *into*) startle, betray, etc. (person) into doing something. □ **surprising** *adjective*; **surprisingly** *adverb*.

**surreal** /sə'rɪəl/ *adjective* unreal; dream-like; bizarre.

**surrealism** /sə'rɪəlɪz(ə)m/ *noun* 20th-c. movement in art and literature aiming to express subconscious mind by dream imagery etc. □ **surrealist** *noun & adjective*; **surrealistic** /-'lɪs-/ *adjective*; **surrealistically** /-'lɪs-/ *adverb*.

**surrender** /sə'rendə/ ● *verb* hand over, relinquish; submit, esp. to enemy; (often **surrender oneself**; + *to*) yield to habit, emotion, influence, etc.; give up rights under (life-insurance policy) in return for smaller sum received immediately. ● *noun* surrendering.

**surreptitious** /sʌrəp'tɪʃəs/ *adjective* done by stealth; underhand. □ **surreptitiously** *adverb*.

**surrogate** /'sʌrəgət/ *noun* substitute; deputy, esp. of bishop. □ **surrogate mother** woman who conceives and gives birth to child on behalf of woman unable to do so. □ **surrogacy** *noun*.

**surround** /sə'raʊnd/ ● *verb* come or be all round; encircle, enclose. ● *noun* border or edging, esp. area between walls and carpet.

**surroundings** *plural noun* things in neighbourhood of, or conditions affecting, person or thing; environment.

**surtax** /'sɜ:tæks/ *noun* additional tax, esp. on high incomes.

**surtitle** /'sɜ:taɪt(ə)l/ *noun* caption translating words of opera, projected on to screen above stage.

**surveillance** /sə'veɪləns/ *noun* close watch undertaken by police etc., esp. on suspected person.

**survey** ● *verb* /sə'veɪ/ take or present general view of; examine condition of (building etc.); determine boundaries,

**extent**, ownership, etc. of (district etc.). ●noun /'sɜːveɪ/ general view or consideration; surveying of property; result of this; investigation of public opinion etc.; map or plan made by surveying.

**surveyor** /sə'veɪə/ noun person who surveys land and buildings, esp. professionally.

**survival** /sə'vaɪv(ə)l/ noun surviving; relic.

**survive** /sə'vaɪv/ verb (-ving) continue to live or exist; live or exist longer than; come alive through or continue to exist in spite of (danger, accident, etc.). □ **survivor** noun.

**sus** = SUSS.

**susceptibility** noun (plural -ies) being susceptible; (in plural) person's feelings.

**susceptible** /sə'septəb(ə)l/ adjective impressionable, sensitive; easily moved by emotion; (+ to) accessible or sensitive to; (+ of) allowing, admitting of (proof etc.).

**suspect** ●verb /səs'pekt/ be inclined to think; have impression of the existence or presence of; (often + of) mentally accuse; doubt innocence, genuineness, or truth of. ●noun /'sʌspekt/ suspected person. ●adjective /'sʌspekt/ subject to suspicion or distrust.

**suspend** /səs'pend/ verb hang up; keep inoperative or undecided temporarily; debar temporarily from function, office, etc.; (as **suspended** adjective) (of particles or body in fluid) floating between top and bottom. □ **suspended animation** temporary deathlike condition; **suspended sentence** judicial sentence remaining unenforced on condition of good behaviour.

**suspender** noun attachment to hold up stocking or sock by its top; (in plural) US pair of braces. □ **suspender belt** woman's undergarment with suspenders.

**suspense** /səs'pens/ noun state of anxious uncertainty or expectation.

**suspension** /səs'penʃ(ə)n/ noun suspending, being suspended; means by which vehicle is supported on its axles; substance consisting of particles suspended in fluid. □ **suspension b** ̇**dge**

bridge with roadway suspended from cables supported by towers.

**suspicion** /səs'pɪʃ(ə)n/ noun unconfirmed belief; distrust; suspecting, being suspected; (+ of) slight trace of.

**suspicious** /səs'pɪʃəs/ adjective prone to or feeling suspicion; indicating or justifying suspicion. □ **suspiciously** adverb.

**suss** /sʌs/ verb (also **sus**) (-ss-) slang (usually + out) investigate, inspect; understand; work out.

**sustain** /səs'teɪn/ verb bear weight of, support, esp. for long period; encourage, support; endure, stand; (of food) nourish; undergo (defeat, injury, loss, etc.); (of court etc.) decide in favour of, uphold; substantiate, corroborate; keep up (effort etc.). □ **sustainable** adjective.

**sustenance** /'sʌstɪnəns/ noun nourishment, food; means of support.

**suture** /'suːtʃə/ ●noun joining edges of wound or incision by stitching; stitch or thread etc. used for this. ●verb (-ring) stitch (wound, incision).

**suzerain** /'suːzərən/ noun historical feudal overlord; archaic sovereign or state having some control over another state that is internally self-governing. □ **suzerainty** noun.

**svelte** /svelt/ adjective slim, slender, graceful.

**SW** abbreviation south-west(ern).

**swab** /swɒb/ ●noun absorbent pad used in surgery; specimen of secretion etc. taken for examination; mop etc. for cleaning or mopping up. ●verb (-bb-) clean with swab; (+ up) absorb (moisture) with swab; mop clean (ship's deck).

**swaddle** /'swɒd(ə)l/ verb (-ling) wrap tightly in bandages, wrappings, etc. □ **swaddling-clothes** narrow bandages formerly wrapped round newborn child to restrain its movements.

**swag** noun slang thief's booty; Australian & NZ traveller's bundle; festoon of flowers, foliage, drapery, etc.

**swagger** /'swægə/ ●verb walk or behave arrogantly or self-importantly. ●noun swaggering gait or manner.

**swain** noun archaic country youth; poetical young lover or suitor.

**swallow**[1] /'swɒləʊ/ ● *verb* make or let (food etc.) pass down one's throat; accept meekly or gullibly; repress (emotion); engulf; say (words etc.) indistinctly. ● *noun* act of swallowing; amount swallowed.

**swallow**[2] /'swɒləʊ/ *noun* migratory swift-flying bird with forked tail. □ **swallow-dive** dive with arms spread sideways; **swallow-tail** deeply forked tail, butterfly etc. with this.

**swam** *past of* SWIM.

**swamp** /swɒmp/ ● *noun* piece of wet spongy ground. ● *verb* submerge, inundate; cause to fill with water and sink; overwhelm with numbers or quantity. □ **swampy** *adjective* (**-ier, -iest**).

**swan** /swɒn/ ● *noun* large web-footed usually white waterfowl with long flexible neck. ● *verb* (**-nn-**) (usually + *about, off,* etc.) *colloquial* move about casually or with superior manner. □ **swansong** person's last work or performance before death, retirement, etc.

**swank** *colloquial* ● *noun* ostentation, swagger. ● *verb* show off. □ **swanky** *adjective* (**-ier, -iest**).

**swap** /swɒp/ (also **swop**) ● *verb* (**-pp-**) exchange, barter. ● *noun* act of swapping; thing suitable for swapping.

**sward** /swɔːd/ *noun literary* expanse of short grass.

**swarf** /swɔːf/ *noun* fine chips or filings of stone, metal, etc.

**swarm**[1] /swɔːm/ ● *noun* cluster of bees leaving hive etc. with queen bee to establish new colony; large group of insects, birds, or people; (in *plural,* + *of*) great numbers. ● *verb* move in or form swarm; (+ *with*) be overrun or crowded with.

**swarm**[2] /swɔːm/ *verb* (+ *up*) climb (rope, tree, etc.) clasping or clinging with arms and legs.

**swarthy** /'swɔːðɪ/ *adjective* (**-ier, -iest**) dark-complexioned, dark in colour.

**swashbuckler** /'swɒʃbʌklə/ *noun* swaggering adventurer. □ **swashbuckling** *adjective* & *noun.*

**swastika** /'swɒstɪkə/ *noun* ancient symbol formed by equal-armed cross with each arm continued at a right angle; this with clockwise continuations as symbol of Nazi Germany.

**swat** /swɒt/ ● *verb* (**-tt-**) crush (fly etc.) with blow; hit hard and abruptly. ● *noun* act of swatting.

**swatch** /swɒtʃ/ *noun* sample, esp. of cloth; collection of samples.

**swath** /swɔːθ/ *noun* (also **swathe** /sweɪð/) ridge of cut grass, corn, etc.; space left clear by mower, scythe, etc.

**swathe** /sweɪð/ *verb* (**-thing**) bind or wrap in bandages, garments, etc.

**sway** ● *verb* (cause to) move unsteadily from side to side; oscillate irregularly; waver; have influence over. ● *noun* rule, government; swaying motion.

**swear** /sweə/ *verb* (*past* **swore**; *past participle* **sworn**) state or promise on oath; cause to take oath; *colloquial* insist; (often + *at*) use profane or obscene language; (+ *by*) appeal to as witness or guarantee of oath, *colloquial* have great confidence in. □ **swear in** admit to office etc. by administering oath; **swear off** *colloquial* promise to keep off (drink etc.); **swear-word** profane or obscene word.

**sweat** /swet/ ● *noun* moisture exuded through pores, esp. when one is hot or nervous; state or period of sweating; *colloquial* state of anxiety; *colloquial* effort, drudgery, laborious task or undertaking; condensed moisture on surface. ● *verb* (*past* & *past participle* **sweated** or *US* **sweat**) exude sweat; be terrified, suffer, etc. (of wall etc.) show surface moisture; (cause to) toil or drudge; emit like sweat; make (horse, athlete, etc.) sweat by exercise; (as **sweated** *adjective*) (of goods, labour, etc.) produced by or subjected to exploitation. □ **no sweat** *colloquial* no bother, no trouble; **sweat-band** band of absorbent material inside hat or round head, wrist, etc. to soak up sweat; **sweatshirt** sleeved cotton sweater; **sweatshop** workshop where sweated labour is employed. □ **sweaty** *adjective* (**-ier, -iest**).

**sweater** *noun* woollen etc. pullover.

**Swede** *noun* native or national of Sweden; (**swede**) large yellow variety of turnip.

**Swedish** /'swiːdɪʃ/ ● *adjective* of Sweden. ● *noun* language of Sweden.

**sweep** ● *verb* (*past* & *past participle* **swept**) clean or clear (room, area, etc.) (as) with a broom; (often + *up*) collect or remove (dirt etc.) by sweeping; (+ *aside*, *away*, etc.) dismiss abruptly; (+ *along*, *down*, etc.) drive or carry along with force; (+ *off*, *away*, etc.) remove or clear forcefully; traverse swiftly or lightly; impart sweeping motion to; glide swiftly; go majestically; (of landscape etc.) be rolling or spacious. ● *noun* act or motion of sweeping; curve in road etc.; range, scope; chimney sweep; sortie by aircraft; *colloquial* sweepstake. □ **sweep the board** win all the money in gambling game, win all possible prizes etc.; **sweepstake** form of gambling on horse races etc. in which money staked is divided among those who have drawn numbered tickets for winners.

**sweeping** *adjective* wide in range or effect; generalized, arbitrary.

**sweet** ● *adjective* tasting like sugar, honey, etc.; smelling pleasant like perfume, roses, etc., fragrant; melodious; fresh; not sour or bitter; gratifying, attractive; amiable, gentle; *colloquial* pretty; (+ *on*) *colloquial* fond of, in love with. ● *noun* small shaped piece of sugar or chocolate confectionery; sweet dish forming course of meal. □ **sweet-and-sour** cooked in sauce with sugar, vinegar, etc.; **sweetbread** pancreas or thymus of animal, as food; **sweet-brier** single-flowered fragrant-leaved wild rose; **sweetcorn** sweet-flavoured maize kernels; **sweetheart** either of pair of lovers; **sweetmeat** a sweet, a small fancy cake; **sweet pea** climbing garden annual with many-coloured scented flowers; **sweet pepper** fruit of capsicum; **sweet potato** tropical plant with edible tuberous roots; **sweet-talk** flatter in order to persuade; **sweet tooth** liking for sweet-tasting things; **sweet william** garden plant with close clusters of sweet-smelling flowers. □ **sweetish** *adjective*; **sweetly** *adverb*.

**sweeten** *verb* make or become sweet(er); make agreeable or less painful. □ **sweetening** *noun*.

**sweetener** *noun* thing that sweetens; *colloquial* bribe.

**sweetie** *noun* *colloquial* a sweet; sweetheart.

**sweetness** *noun* being sweet; fragrance. □ **sweetness and light** (esp.

uncharacteristic) mildness and reason.

**swell** ● *verb* (*past participle* **swollen** /ˈswəʊlən/ or **-ed**) (cause to) grow bigger, louder, or more intense; rise or raise up; (+ *out*) bulge out; (of heart etc.) feel full of joy, pride, etc.; (+ *with*) be hardly able to restrain (pride etc.). ● *noun* act or state of swelling; heaving of sea etc. with unbreaking rolling waves; crescendo; mechanism in organ etc. for gradually varying volume; *colloquial* fashionable or stylish person. ● *adjective colloquial esp. US* fine, excellent.

**swelling** *noun* abnormally swollen place, esp. on body.

**swelter** /ˈsweltə/ ● *verb* be uncomfortably hot. ● *noun* sweltering condition.

**swept** *past & past participle of* SWEEP.

**swerve** ● *verb* (**-ving**) (cause to) change direction, esp. suddenly. ● *noun* swerving motion.

**swift** ● *adjective* rapid, quick; prompt. ● *noun* swift-flying long-winged migratory bird. □ **swiftly** *adverb*; **swiftness** *noun*.

**swig** ● *verb* (**-gg-**) *colloquial* drink in large draughts. ● *noun* swallow of liquid, esp. of large amount.

**swill** ● *verb* (often + *out*) rinse, pour water over or through; drink greedily. ● *noun* swilling; mainly liquid refuse as pig-food.

**swim** ● *verb* (**-mm-**; *past* **swam**; *past participle* **swum**) propel body through water with limbs, fins, etc.; perform (stroke) or cross (river etc.) by swimming; float on liquid; appear to undulate, reel, or whirl; (of head) feel dizzy; (+ *in*, *with*) be flooded. ● *noun* act or spell of swimming. □ **in the swim** *colloquial* involved in or aware of what is going on; **swimming bath**, **pool** pool constructed for swimming; **swimming costume** bathing costume; **swimsuit** swimming costume, esp. one-piece for women and girls; **swimwear** clothing for swimming in. □ **swimmer** *noun*.

**swimmingly** *adverb colloquial* smoothly, without obstruction.

**swindle** /ˈswɪnd(ə)l/ ● *verb* (**-ling**) (often + *out of*) cheat of money etc.; defraud. ● *noun* act of swindling; fraudulent person or thing. □ **swindler** *noun*.

**swine** noun (plural same) formal or US pig; colloquial (plural same or **-s**) disgusting person, unpleasant or difficult thing. □ **swinish** adjective.

**swing** ● verb (past & past participle **swung**) (cause to) move with to-and-fro or curving motion; sway or hang like pendulum or door etc.; oscillate; move by gripping something and leaping etc.; walk with swinging gait; (+ round) move to face opposite direction; (+ at) attempt to hit; colloquial (of party etc.) be lively; have decisive influence on (voting etc.); colloquial be executed by hanging. ● noun act, motion, or extent of swinging; swinging or smooth gait, rhythm, or action; seat slung by ropes, chains, etc. for swinging on or in, spell of swinging thus; smooth rhythmic jazz or jazzy dance music; amount by which votes etc. change from one side to another. □ **swing-boat** boat-shaped swing at fairs etc.; **swing-bridge** bridge that can be swung aside to let ships etc. pass; **swing-door** door that swings in either direction and closes by itself when released; **swings and roundabouts** situation allowing equal gain and loss; **swing-wing** (aircraft) with wings that can pivot to point sideways or backwards. □ **swinger** noun.

**swingeing** /'swɪndʒɪŋ/ adjective (of blow etc.) forcible; huge, far-reaching.

**swipe** colloquial ● verb (**-ping**) (often + at) hit hard and recklessly; steal. ● noun reckless hard hit or attempt to hit.

**swirl** ● verb move, flow, or carry along with whirling motion. ● noun swirling motion; twist, curl. □ **swirly** adjective.

**swish** ● verb swing (cane, scythe, etc.) audibly through air, grass, etc.; move with or make swishing sound. ● noun swishing action or sound. ● adjective colloquial smart, fashionable.

**Swiss** ● adjective of Switzerland. ● noun (plural same) native or national of Switzerland. □ **Swiss roll** cylindrical cake, made by rolling up thin flat sponge cake spread with jam etc.

**switch** ● noun device for making or breaking connection in electric circuit; transfer, changeover, deviation; flexible shoot cut from tree; light tapering rod; US railway points. ● verb (+ on, off)

turn (electrical device) on or off; change or transfer (position, subject, etc.); exchange; whip or flick with switch. □ **switchback** ride at fair etc. with extremely steep ascents and descents, similar railway or road; **switchboard** apparatus for varying connections between electric circuits, esp. in telephony; **switched-on** colloquial up to date, aware of what is going on; **switch off** colloquial cease to pay attention.

**swivel** /'swɪv(ə)l/ ● noun coupling between two parts etc. so that one can turn freely without the other. ● verb (**-ll-**; US **-l-**) turn (as) on swivel, swing round. □ **swivel chair** chair with revolving seat.

**swizz** noun (also **swiz**) colloquial something disappointing; swindle.

**swizzle** /'swɪz(ə)l/ noun colloquial frothy mixed alcoholic drink, esp. of rum or gin and bitters; slang swizz. □ **swizzle-stick** stick used for frothing or flattening drinks.

**swollen** past participle of SWELL.

**swoon** /swuːn/ verb & noun literary faint.

**swoop** /swuːp/ ● verb (often + down) come down with rush like bird of prey; (often + on) make sudden attack. ● noun act of swooping, sudden pounce.

**swop** = SWAP.

**sword** /sɔːd/ noun weapon with long blade for cutting or thrusting. □ **put to the sword** kill; **sword dance** dance with brandishing of swords, or steps about swords laid on ground; **swordfish** (plural same or **-es**) large sea fish with swordlike upper jaw; **swordplay** fencing, repartee, lively arguing; **swordsman** person of (usually specified) skill with sword; **swordstick** hollow walking stick containing sword blade.

**swore** past of SWEAR.

**sworn** ● past participle of SWEAR. ● adjective bound (as) by oath.

**swot** colloquial ● verb (**-tt-**) study hard; (usually + up, up on) study (subject) hard or hurriedly. ● noun usually derogatory person who swots.

**swum** past participle of SWIM.

**swung** past & past participle of SWING.

**sybarite** /'sɪbəraɪt/ noun self-indulgent or luxury-loving person. □ **sybaritic** /-'rɪt-/ adjective.

**sycamore** /'sɪkəmɔː/ noun large maple tree, its wood; US plane tree, its wood.

**sycophant** /'sɪkəfænt/ noun flatterer, toady. □ **sycophancy** noun; **sycophantic** /-'fæn-/ adjective.

**syllabic** /sɪ'læbɪk/ adjective of or in syllables. □ **syllabically** adverb.

**syllable** /'sɪləb(ə)l/ noun unit of pronunciation forming whole or part of word, usually consisting of vowel sound with consonant(s) before or after (see panel). □ **in words of one syllable** plainly, bluntly.

**syllabub** /'sɪləbʌb/ noun dessert of cream or milk sweetened and whipped with wine etc.

**syllabus** /'sɪləbəs/ noun (plural **-buses** or **-bi** /-baɪ/) programme or outline of course of study, teaching, etc.

**syllogism** /'sɪlədʒɪz(ə)m/ noun form of reasoning in which from two propositions a third is deduced. □ **syllogistic** /-'dʒɪs-/ adjective.

**sylph** /sɪlf/ noun elemental spirit of air; slender graceful woman. □ **sylphlike** adjective.

**sylvan** /'sɪlv(ə)n/ adjective (also **silvan**) of the woods, having woods; rural.

**symbiosis** /sɪmbaɪ'əʊsɪs/ noun (plural **-bioses** /-siːz/) (usually mutually advantageous) association of two different organisms living attached to one another etc.; mutually advantageous connection between people. □ **symbiotic** /-'ɒt-/ adjective.

**symbol** /'sɪmb(ə)l/ noun thing generally regarded as typifying, representing, or recalling something; mark, sign, etc.

representing object, idea, process, etc. □ **symbolic** /-'bɒl-/ adjective; **symbolically** /-'bɒl-/ adverb.

**symbolism** noun use of symbols; symbols; artistic movement or style using symbols to express ideas, emotions, etc. □ **symbolist** noun.

**symbolize** verb (also **-ise**) (**-zing** or **-sing**) be symbol of; represent by symbol(s).

**symmetry** /'sɪmɪtrɪ/ noun (plural **-ies**) correct proportion of parts; beauty resulting from this; structure allowing object to be divided into parts of equal shape and size; possession of such structure; repetition of exactly similar parts facing each other or a centre. □ **symmetrical** /-'met-/ adjective; **symmetrically** /-'met-/ adverb.

**sympathetic** /sɪmpə'θetɪk/ adjective of or expressing sympathy; likeable, pleasant; ( + to) favouring (proposal etc.). □ **sympathetically** adverb.

**sympathize** /'sɪmpəθaɪz/ verb (also **-ise**) (**-zing** or **-sing**) (often + with) feel or express sympathy; agree. □ **sympathizer** noun.

**sympathy** /'sɪmpəθɪ/ noun (plural **-ies**) sharing of another's feelings; (often + with) sharing or tendency to share emotion, sensation, condition, etc. of another person; (in singular or plural) compassion, commiseration, condolences; (often + with) agreement (with person etc.) in opinion or desire. □ **in sympathy** (often + with) having, showing, or resulting from sympathy.

**symphony** /'sɪmfənɪ/ noun (plural **-ies**) musical composition in several movements for full orchestra. □ **symphony orchestra** large orchestra playing

• • • • • • • • • • • • • • • • • • • • • • • • • • • • • • • • • • • • • •

### Syllable

A syllable is the smallest unit of speech that can normally occur alone, such as a *a*, *at*, *ta*, or *tat*. A word can be made up of one or more syllables:

*cat*, *fought*, and *twinge* each have one syllable;
*rating*, *deny*, and *collapse* each have two syllables;
*excitement*, *superman*, and *telephoned* each have three syllables;
*American* and *complicated* each have four syllables;
*examination* and *uncontrollable* each have five syllables.

• • • • • • • • • • • • • • • • • • • • • • • • • • • • • • • • • • • • • •

symphonies etc. □ **symphonic** /-'fɒn-/ adjective.

**symposium** /sɪm'pəʊzɪəm/ noun (plural **-sia**) conference, or collection of essays, on particular subject.

**symptom** /'sɪmptəm/ noun physical or mental sign of disease or injury; sign of existence of something. □ **symptomatic** /-'mæt-/ adjective.

**synagogue** /'sɪnəgɒg/ noun building for Jewish religious instruction and worship.

**sync** /sɪŋk/ (also **synch**) colloquial ● noun synchronization. ● verb synchronize. □ **in** or **out of sync** (often + *with*) according or agreeing well or badly.

**synchromesh** /'sɪŋkrəʊmeʃ/ ● noun system of gear-changing, esp. in vehicles, in which gearwheels revolve at same speed during engagement. ● adjective of this system.

**synchronize** /'sɪŋkrənaɪz/ verb (also **-ise**) (**-zing** or **-sing**) (often + *with*) make or be synchronous (with); make sound and picture (of film etc.) coincide; cause (clocks etc.) to show same time. □ **synchronization** noun.

**synchronous** /'sɪŋkrənəs/ adjective (often + *with*) existing or occurring at same time.

**syncopate** /'sɪŋkəpeɪt/ verb (**-ting**) displace beats or accents in (music); shorten (word) by omitting syllable or letter(s) in middle. □ **syncopation** noun.

**syncope** /'sɪŋkəpɪ/ noun Grammar syncopation; Medicine fainting through fall in blood pressure.

**syncretize** /'sɪŋkrətaɪz/ verb (also **-ise**) (**-zing** or **-sing**) attempt to unify or reconcile differing schools of thought. □ **syncretic** /-'kret-/ adjective; **syncretism** noun.

**syndicalism** /'sɪndɪkəlɪz(ə)m/ noun historical movement for transferring industrial control and ownership to workers' unions. □ **syndicalist** noun.

**syndicate** ● noun /'sɪndɪkət/ combination of people, commercial firms, etc. to promote some common interest; agency supplying material simultaneously to a number of periodicals etc.; group of people who gamble, organize crime, etc. ● verb /'sɪndɪkeɪt/ (**-ting**) form into syndicate; publish (material) through syndicate. □ **syndication** noun.

**syndrome** /'sɪndrəʊm/ noun group of concurrent symptoms of disease; characteristic combination of opinions, emotions, etc.

**synod** /'sɪnəd/ noun Church council of clergy and lay people.

**synonym** /'sɪnənɪm/ noun word or phrase that means the same as another (see panel).

**synonymous** /sɪ'nɒnɪməs/ adjective (often + *with*) having same meaning; suggestive of; associated with.

**synopsis** /sɪ'nɒpsɪs/ noun (plural **synopses** /-siːz/) summary; outline.

**synoptic** /sɪ'nɒptɪk/ adjective of or giving synopsis. □ **Synoptic Gospels** those of Matthew, Mark, and Luke.

........................................................

## Synonym

A synonym is a word that has the same meaning as, or a similar meaning to, another word:

    *cheerful, happy, merry,* and *jolly*

are synonyms that are quite close to each other in meaning, as are

    *lazy, indolent,* and *slothful*

In contrast, the following words all mean 'a person who works with another', but their meanings vary considerably:

| | |
|---|---|
| *colleague* | *conspirator* |
| *collaborator* | *accomplice* |
| *ally* | |

........................................................

**syntax** /'sɪntæks/ noun grammatical arrangement of words; rules or analysis of this. □ **syntactic** /-'tæk-/ adjective.

**synthesis** /'sɪnθəsɪs/ noun ( plural **-theses** /-siːz/) putting together of parts or elements to make up complex whole; *Chemistry* artificial production of (esp. organic) substances from simpler ones.

**synthesize** /'sɪnθəsaɪz/ verb (also **-ise**) (**-zing** or **-sing**) make synthesis of.

**synthesizer** noun (also **-iser**) electronic, usually keyboard, instrument producing great variety of sounds.

**synthetic** /sɪn'θetɪk/ ● adjective produced by synthesis, esp. to imitate natural product; affected, insincere. ● noun synthetic substance. □ **synthetically** adverb.

**syphilis** /'sɪfəlɪs/ noun a contagious venereal disease. □ **syphilitic** /-'lɪt-/ adjective.

**Syrian** /'sɪrɪən/ ● noun native or national of Syria. ● adjective of Syria.

**syringa** /sɪ'rɪŋgə/ noun shrub with white scented flowers.

**syringe** /sɪ'rɪndʒ/ ● noun device for drawing in quantity of liquid and ejecting it in fine stream. ● verb (**-ging**) sluice or spray with syringe.

**syrup** /'sɪrəp/ noun (*US* **sirup**) sweet sauce of sugar dissolved in boiling water, often flavoured or medicated; condensed sugar-cane juice; molasses, treacle; excessive sweetness of manner. □ **syrupy** adjective.

**system** /'sɪstəm/ noun complex whole; set of connected things or parts; organized group of things; set of organs in body with common structure or function; human or animal body as organized whole; method, scheme of action, procedure, or classification; orderliness; (**the system**) prevailing political or social order, esp. seen as oppressive. □ **get (thing) out of one's system** get rid of (anxiety etc.); **systems analysis** analysis of complex process etc. so as to improve its efficiency, esp. by using computer.

**systematic** /sɪstə'mætɪk/ adjective methodical; according to system; deliberate. □ **systematically** adverb.

**systematize** /'sɪstəmətaɪz/ verb (also **-ise**) (**-zing** or **-sing**) make systematic. □ **systematization** noun.

**systemic** /sɪ'stemɪk/ adjective *Physiology* of the whole body; (of insecticide etc.) entering plant tissues via roots and shoots. □ **systemically** adverb.

# Tt

**T** *noun* □ **to a T** exactly, to a nicety; **T-bone** T-shaped bone, esp. in steak from thin end of loin; **T-junction** junction, esp. of two roads, in shape of T; **T-shirt** short-sleeved casual top; **T-square** T-shaped instrument for drawing right angles.

**t.** *abbreviation* (also **t**) ton(s); tonne(s).

**TA** *abbreviation* Territorial Army.

**ta** /tɑː/ *interjection colloquial* thank you.

**tab**¹ *noun* small piece of material attached to thing for grasping, fastening, identifying, etc.; *US colloquial* bill; distinguishing mark on officer's collar. □ **keep tabs on** *colloquial* have under observation or in check.

**tab**² *noun* tabulator.

**tabard** /'tæbəd/ *noun* herald's official coat emblazoned with arms of sovereign; woman's or girl's sleeveless jerkin; *historical* knight's short emblazoned garment worn over armour.

**tabasco** /tə'bæskəʊ/ *noun* pungent pepper; (**Tabasco**) *proprietary term* sauce made from this.

**tabby** /'tæbɪ/ *noun* (*plural* **-ies**) grey or brownish cat with dark stripes.

**tabernacle** /'tæbənæk(ə)l/ *noun historical* tent used as sanctuary by Israelites during Exodus; niche or receptacle, esp. for bread and wine of Eucharist; Nonconformist meeting-house.

**tabla** /'tæblə/ *noun* pair of small Indian drums played with hands.

**table** /'teɪb(ə)l/ ● *noun* flat surface on legs used for eating, working at, etc.; food provided at table; group seated for dinner etc.; set of facts or figures arranged esp. in columns; multiplication table. ● *verb* (**-ling**) bring forward for discussion at meeting etc.; *esp. US* postpone consideration of. □ **at table** taking a meal; **tablecloth** cloth spread over table; **tableland** plateau; **tablespoon** large spoon for serving etc., (also **tablespoonful**) amount held by this; **table tennis** game played with small bats on table divided by net;

**tableware** dishes etc. for meals; **table wine** wine of ordinary quality; **turn the tables** (often + *on*) reverse circumstances to one's advantage.

**tableau** /'tæbləʊ/ *noun* (*plural* **-x** /-z/) picturesque presentation; group of silent motionless people representing stage scene.

**table d'hôte** /tɑːb(ə)l 'dəʊt/ *noun* meal from set menu at fixed price.

**tablet** /'tæblɪt/ *noun* small solid dose of medicine etc.; bar of soap etc.; flat slab of stone etc., esp. inscribed.

**tabloid** /'tæblɔɪd/ *noun* small-sized, often popular or sensational, newspaper.

**taboo** /tə'buː/ ● *noun* (*plural* **-s**) ritual isolation of person or thing as sacred or accursed; prohibition. ● *adjective* avoided or prohibited, esp. by social custom. ● *verb* (**-oos, -ooed**) put under taboo; exclude or prohibit, esp. socially.

**tabor** /'teɪbə/ *noun historical* small drum.

**tabular** /'tæbjʊlə/ *adjective* of or arranged in tables.

**tabulate** /'tæbjʊleɪt/ *verb* (**-ting**) arrange (figures, facts) in tabular form. □ **tabulation** *noun*.

**tabulator** *noun* device on typewriter etc. for advancing to sequence of set positions in tabular work.

**tachograph** /'tækəgrɑːf/ *noun* device in vehicle to record speed and travel time.

**tachometer** /tə'kɒmɪtə/ *noun* instrument measuring velocity or rate of shaft's rotation (esp. in vehicle).

**tacit** /'tæsɪt/ *adjective* implied or understood without being stated. □ **tacitly** *adverb*.

**taciturn** /'tæsɪtɜːn/ *adjective* saying little, uncommunicative. □ **taciturnity** /-'tɜːn-/ *noun*.

**tack**¹ ● *noun* small sharp broad-headed nail; *US* drawing-pin; long stitch for fastening materials lightly or temporarily together; (in sailing) direction, temporary change of direction; course of action or policy. ● verb (often + *down* etc.) fasten with tacks; stitch lightly together; (+ *to, on, on to*) add, append; change ship's course by turning head to wind, make series of such tacks.

**tack²** noun horse's saddle, bridle, etc.

**tack³** noun colloquial cheap or shoddy material; tat, kitsch.

**tackle** /'tæk(ə)l/ ● noun equipment for task or sport; rope(s), pulley(s), etc. used in working sails, hoisting weights, etc.; tackling in football etc. ● verb (-ling) try to deal with (problem etc.); grapple with (opponent); confront (person) in discussion; intercept or stop (player running with ball etc.). □ **tackle-block** pulley over which rope runs. □ **tackler** noun.

**tacky¹** /'tækɪ/ adjective (-ier, -iest) slightly sticky.

**tacky²** /'tækɪ/ adjective (-ier, -iest) colloquial in poor taste; cheap, shoddy.

**taco** /'tækəʊ/ noun (plural **-s**) Mexican dish of meat etc. in crisp folded tortilla.

**tact** noun adroitness in dealing with people or circumstances; intuitive perception of right thing to do or say. □ **tactful** adjective; **tactfully** adverb; **tactless** adjective; **tactlessly** adverb.

**tactic** /'tæktɪk/ noun piece of tactics.

**tactical** adjective of tactics; (of bombing etc.) done in immediate support of military or naval operation; adroitly planning or planned. □ **tactically** adverb.

**tactics** /'tæktɪks/ plural noun (also treated as *singular*) disposition of armed forces, esp. in warfare; procedure calculated to gain some end, skilful device(s). □ **tactician** /-'tɪʃ-/ noun.

**tactile** /'tæktaɪl/ adjective of sense of touch; perceived by touch. □ **tactility** /-'tɪl-/ noun.

**tadpole** /'tædpəʊl/ noun larva of frog, toad, etc. at stage of living in water and having gills and tail.

**taffeta** /'tæfɪtə/ noun fine lustrous silk or silklike fabric.

**taffrail** /'tæfreɪl/ noun rail round ship's stern.

**tag** ● noun label, esp. to show address or price; metal point of shoelace etc.; loop or flap for handling or hanging thing; loose or ragged end; trite quotation, stock phrase. ● verb (**-gg-**) furnish with

tag(s); (often + *on, on to*) join, attach. □ **tag along** (often + *with*) go along, accompany passively.

**tagliatelle** /tæljə'telɪ/ noun ribbon-shaped pasta.

**tail¹** ● noun hindmost part of animal, esp. extending beyond body; thing like tail in form or position, esp. rear part of aeroplane, vehicle, etc.; hanging part of back of shirt or coat, end of procession, luminous trail following comet, etc.; inferior, weak, or last part of anything; (in *plural*) colloquial tailcoat, evening dress with this; (in *plural*) reverse of coin turning up in toss; colloquial person following another. ● verb remove stalks of (fruit etc.); colloquial follow closely. □ **tailback** long queue of traffic caused by obstruction; **tailboard** hinged or removable board of lorry etc.; **tailcoat** man's coat divided at back and cut away in front; **tailgate** tailboard, rear door of estate car; **tail-light, -lamp** US rear light on vehicle etc.; **tail off, away** gradually diminish and cease; **tailpiece** final part of thing, decoration at end of chapter etc.; **tailplane** horizontal aerofoil at tail of aircraft; **tailspin** aircraft's spinning dive, state of panic; **tail wind** one blowing in direction of travel. □ **tailless** adjective.

**tail²** Law ● noun limitation of ownership, esp. of estate limited to person and his heirs. ● adjective so limited.

**tailor** /'teɪlə/ ● noun maker of (esp. men's) outer garments to measure. ● verb make (clothes) as tailor; make or adapt for special purpose; work as tailor. □ **tailor-made** made by tailor, made or suited for particular purpose. □ **tailored** adjective.

**taint** ● noun spot or trace of decay, corruption, etc.; corrupt condition, infection. ● verb affect with taint, become tainted; (+ *with*) affect slightly.

**take** ● verb (**-king**; past **took** /tʊk/; past participle **taken**) lay hold of; acquire, capture, earn, win; regularly buy (newspaper etc.); occupy; make use of; be effective; consume; use up; carry, accompany; remove, steal; catch, be infected with; be affected by (pleasure etc.); ascertain and record; grasp mentally, understand; accept, submit to; deal with or regard in specified way;

teach, be taught or examined in; submit to (exam); make (photograph); have as necessary accompaniment, requirement, or part. ● *noun* amount taken or caught; scene or film sequence photographed continuously. □ **take after** resemble (parent etc.); **take against** begin to dislike; **take apart** dismantle, *colloquial* defeat, criticize severely; **take away** remove or carry elsewhere, subtract; **take-away** (cooked meal) bought at restaurant for eating elsewhere, restaurant selling this; **take back** retract (statement), convey to original position, carry in thought to past time, return or accept back (goods); **take down** write down (spoken words), dismantle (structure), lower (garment); **take-home pay** employee's pay after deduction of tax etc.; **take in** receive as lodger etc., undertake (work) at home, make (garment etc.) smaller, understand, cheat, include; **take off** remove (clothing), deduct, mimic, begin a jump, become airborne, (of scheme etc.) become successful; **take-off** act of mimicking or becoming airborne; **take on** undertake, acquire, engage, agree to oppose at game, *colloquial* show strong emotion; **take out** remove, escort on outing, get (licence etc.); **take over** succeed to management or ownership of, assume control; **takeover** *noun*; **take to** begin, have recourse to, form liking for; **take up** adopt as pursuit, accept (offer etc.), occupy (time or space), absorb, (often + *on*) interrupt or correct (speaker), shorten (garment), pursue (matter). □ **taker** *noun*.

**taking** ● *adjective* attractive, captivating. ● *noun* (in *plural*) money taken in business etc.

**talc** *noun* talcum powder; translucent mineral formed in thin plates.

**talcum** /ˈtælkəm/ *noun* talc; (in full **talcum powder**) usually perfumed powdered talc for toilet use.

**tale** *noun* narrative or story, esp. fictitious; allegation or gossip, often malicious.

**talent** /ˈtælənt/ *noun* special aptitude or gift; high mental ability; people of talent; *colloquial* attractive members of opposite sex; ancient weight and money unit. □ **talent-scout, -spotter**

person seeking new talent, esp. in sport or entertainment. □ **talented** *adjective*.

**talisman** /ˈtælɪzmən/ *noun* (*plural* -s) thing believed to bring good luck or protect from harm.

**talk** /tɔːk/ ● *verb* (often + *to*, *with*) converse or communicate verbally; have power of speech; express, utter, discuss; use (language); gossip. ● *noun* conversation; particular piece of speech; short address or lecture; rumour or gossip, its theme; *colloquial* empty boasting; (often in *plural*) discussions, negotiations. □ **talk down** silence by loud or persistent talking, guide (pilot, aircraft) to landing by radio, (+ *to*) speak patronizingly to; **talk into** persuade by talking; **talk of** discuss, express intention of; **talk over** discuss; **talk round** persuade to change opinion etc.; **talk to** rebuke, scold. □ **talker** *noun*.

**talkative** /ˈtɔːkətɪv/ *adjective* fond of talking.

**talkie** *noun* *colloquial* early film with soundtrack.

**talking** ● *adjective* that talks or can talk; expressive. ● *noun* action or process of talking. □ **talking of** while we are discussing; **talking point** topic for discussion; **talking-to** *colloquial* scolding.

**tall** /tɔːl/ ● *adjective* of more than average height; of specified height; higher than surroundings. ● *adverb* as if tall; proudly. □ **tallboy** tall chest of drawers; **tall order** unreasonable demand; **tall ship** high-masted sailing ship; **tall story** *colloquial* extravagant tale.

**tallow** /ˈtæləʊ/ *noun* hard (esp. animal) fat melted down to make candles, soap, etc.

**tally** /ˈtælɪ/ ● *noun* (*plural* -ies) reckoning of debt or score; mark registering number of objects delivered or received; *historical* piece of notched wood for keeping account; identification ticket or label; counterpart, duplicate. ● *verb* (-ies, -ied) (often + *with*) agree, correspond.

**tally-ho** /tælɪˈhəʊ/ *interjection* huntsman's cry as signal on seeing fox.

**Talmud** /ˈtælmʊd/ *noun* body of Jewish civil and ceremonial law. □ **Talmudic** /-ˈmʊd-/ *adjective*; **Talmudist** *noun*.

**talon** /ˈtælən/ *noun* claw, esp. of bird of prey.

**talus** /ˈteɪləs/ noun (plural **tali** /-laɪ/) ankle-bone supporting tibia.

**tamarind** /ˈtæmərɪnd/ noun tropical evergreen tree; its fruit pulp used as food and in drinks.

**tamarisk** /ˈtæmərɪsk/ noun seaside shrub usually with small pink or white flowers.

**tambour** /ˈtæmbʊə/ noun drum; circular frame for stretching embroidery-work on.

**tambourine** /tæmbəˈriːn/ noun small shallow drum with jingling discs in rim, shaken or banged as accompaniment.

**tame** ● adjective (of animal) domesticated, not wild or shy; uninteresting, insipid. ● verb (-ming) make tame, domesticate; subdue. □ **tamely** adverb; **tameness** noun; **tamer** noun.

**Tamil** /ˈtæmɪl/ ● noun member of a people inhabiting South India and Sri Lanka; their language. ● adjective of this people or language.

**tam-o'-shanter** /tæməˈʃæntə/ noun floppy woollen beret of Scottish origin.

**tamp** verb ram down tightly.

**tamper** /ˈtæmpə/ verb (+ with) meddle or interfere with.

**tampon** /ˈtæmpɒn/ noun plug of cotton wool etc. used esp. to absorb menstrual blood.

**tan**[1] ● noun suntan; yellowish-brown colour; bark of oak etc. used for tanning. ● adjective yellowish-brown. ● verb (-nn-) make or become brown by exposure to sun; convert (raw hide) into leather; slang thrash.

**tan**[2] abbreviation tangent.

**tandem** /ˈtændəm/ ● noun bicycle with two or more seats one behind another; vehicle driven tandem. ● adverb with two or more horses harnessed one behind another. □ **in tandem** one behind the other, alongside each other, together.

**tandoor** /ˈtændʊə/ noun clay oven.

**tandoori** /tænˈdʊəri/ noun spiced food cooked in tandoor.

**tang** noun strong taste or smell; characteristic quality; part of tool by which blade is held firm in handle. □ **tangy** adjective (-ier, -iest).

**tangent** /ˈtændʒ(ə)nt/ noun straight line, curve, or surface touching but not intersecting curve; ratio of sides opposite and adjacent to acute angle in right-angled triangle. □ **at a tangent** diverging from previous course or from what is relevant. □ **tangential** /-ˈdʒenʃ(ə)l/ adjective.

**tangerine** /tændʒəˈriːn/ noun small sweet-scented fruit like orange, mandarin; deep orange-yellow colour.

**tangible** /ˈtændʒɪb(ə)l/ adjective perceptible by touch; definite, clearly intelligible, not elusive. □ **tangibility** noun; **tangibly** adverb.

**tangle** /ˈtæŋg(ə)l/ ● verb (-ling) intertwine or become twisted or involved in confused mass; entangle; complicate. ● noun tangled mass or state. □ **tangly** adjective.

**tango** /ˈtæŋgəʊ/ ● noun (plural **-s**) (music for) slow South American ballroom dance. ● verb (-goes, -goed) dance tango.

**tank** noun large receptacle for liquid, gas, etc.; heavy armoured fighting vehicle moving on continuous tracks. □ **tank engine** steam engine with integral fuel and water containers. □ **tankful** noun (plural **-s**).

**tankard** /ˈtæŋkəd/ noun (contents of) tall beer mug with handle.

**tanker** noun ship, aircraft, or road vehicle for carrying liquids, esp. oil, in bulk.

**tanner** noun person who tans hides.

**tannery** noun (plural **-ies**) place where hides are tanned.

**tannic** /ˈtænɪk/ adjective of tan. □ **tannic acid** yellowish organic compound used in cleaning, dyeing, etc.

**tannin** /ˈtænɪn/ noun any of several substances extracted from tree-barks etc. and used in tanning etc.

**Tannoy** /ˈtænɔɪ/ noun proprietary term type of public address system.

**tansy** /ˈtænzi/ noun (plural **-ies**) aromatic herb with yellow flowers.

**tantalize** /ˈtæntəlaɪz/ verb (also **-ise**) (-zing or **-sing**) torment with sight of the unobtainable, raise and then dash the hopes of. □ **tantalization** noun.

**tantamount** /ˈtæntəmaʊnt/ adjective (+ to) equivalent to.

**tantra** /'tæntrə/ *noun* any of a class of Hindu or Buddhist mystical or magical writings.

**tantrum** /'tæntrəm/ *noun* (esp. child's) outburst of bad temper or petulance.

**Taoiseach** /'ti:ʃəx/ *noun* prime minister of Irish Republic.

**tap**[1] ● *noun* device by which flow of liquid or gas from pipe or vessel can be controlled; act of tapping telephone; taproom. ● *verb* (**-pp-**) provide (cask) with tap, let out (liquid) thus; draw sap from (tree) by cutting into it; draw supplies or information from; discover and exploit; fasten listening device to (telephone etc.). □ **on tap** ready to be drawn off, *colloquial* freely available; **taproom** room in pub serving drinks on tap; **tap root** tapering root growing vertically downwards.

**tap**[2] ● *verb* (**-pp-**) (+ *at, on, against,* etc.) strike or cause to strike lightly; (often + *out*) make by taps; tap-dance. ● *noun* light blow or rap; tap-dancing; metal attachment on dancer's shoe. □ **tap-dance** *noun* rhythmic dance performed in shoes with metal taps, *verb* perform this; **tap-dancer** *noun;* **tap-dancing** *noun.*

**tapas** /'tæpæs/ *plural noun* small savoury esp. Spanish dishes.

**tape** ● *noun* narrow woven strip of cotton etc. for fastening etc.; this across finishing line of race; (in full **adhesive tape**) strip of adhesive plastic etc. for fastening, masking, insulating, etc.; magnetic tape; tape recording; tape-measure. ● *verb* (**-ping**) tie up or join with tape; apply tape to; (+ *off*) seal off with tape; record on magnetic tape; measure with tape. □ **have (person, thing) taped** *colloquial* understand fully; **tape deck** machine for using audiotape (separate from speakers etc.); **tape machine** device for recording telegraph messages, tape recorder; **tape-measure** strip of tape or thin flexible metal marked for measuring; **tape recorder** apparatus for recording and replaying sounds on magnetic tape; **tape-record** *verb;* **tape recording** *noun;* **tapeworm** tapelike worm parasitic in alimentary canal.

**taper** /'teɪpə/ ● *noun* wick coated with wax etc. for conveying flame; slender candle. ● *verb* (often + *off*) (cause to) diminish in thickness towards one end, make or become gradually less.

**tapestry** /'tæpɪstrɪ/ *noun* (*plural* **-ies**) thick fabric in which coloured weft threads are woven to form pictures or designs; (usually wool) embroidery imitating this; piece of this.

**tapioca** /tæpɪ'əʊkə/ *noun* starchy granular foodstuff prepared from cassava.

**tapir** /'teɪpə/ *noun* small piglike mammal with short flexible snout.

**tappet** /'tæpɪt/ *noun* lever etc. in machinery giving intermittent motion.

**tar**[1] ● *noun* dark thick inflammable liquid distilled from wood, coal, etc.; similar substance formed in combustion of tobacco. ● *verb* (**-rr-**) cover with tar.

**tar**[2] *noun colloquial* sailor.

**taramasalata** /tærəməsə'lɑːtə/ *noun* (also **taramosalata**) dip made from roe, olive oil, etc.

**tarantella** /tærən'telə/ *noun* (music for) whirling Southern Italian dance.

**tarantula** /tə'ræntjʊlə/ *noun* large hairy tropical spider; large black spider of Southern Europe.

**tarboosh** /tɑː'buːʃ/ *noun* cap like fez.

**tardy** /'tɑːdɪ/ *adjective* (**-ier, -iest**) slow to act, come, or happen; delaying, delayed. □ **tardily** *adverb;* **tardiness** *noun.*

**tare**[1] *noun* vetch, esp. as cornfield weed or fodder; (in *plural*) *Biblical* injurious cornfield weed.

**tare**[2] /teə/ *noun* allowance made for weight of packing around goods; weight of vehicle without fuel or load.

**target** /'tɑːgɪt/ ● *noun* mark fired at, esp. round object marked with concentric circles; person, objective, or result aimed at; butt for criticism etc. ● *verb* (**-t-**) single out as target; aim, direct.

**tariff** /'tærɪf/ *noun* table of fixed charges; duty on particular class of goods; list of duties or customs due.

**tarlatan** /'tɑːlət(ə)n/ *noun* thin stiff muslin.

**Tarmac** /'tɑːmæk/ ● *noun proprietary term* tarmacadam; area surfaced with this. ● *verb* (**tarmac**) (**-ck-**) apply tarmacadam to.

**tarmacadam** /tɑːmə'kædəm/ *noun* bitumen-bound stones etc. used as paving.

**tarn** *noun* small mountain lake.

**tarnish** /ˈtɑːnɪʃ/ ●verb (cause to) lose lustre; impair (reputation etc.). ●noun tarnished state; stain, blemish.

**taro** /ˈtɑːrəʊ/ noun (plural -s) tropical plant with edible tuberous roots.

**tarot** /ˈtærəʊ/ noun (in singular or plural) pack of 78 cards used in fortune-telling.

**tarpaulin** /tɑːˈpɔːlɪn/ noun waterproof cloth, esp. of tarred canvas; sheet or covering of this.

**tarragon** /ˈtærəgən/ noun aromatic herb.

**tarry**[1] /ˈtɑːrɪ/ adjective (-ier, -iest) of or smeared with tar.

**tarry**[2] /ˈtærɪ/ verb (-ies, -ied) archaic linger; wait, stay.

**tarsal** /ˈtɑːs(ə)l/ ●adjective of the ankle-bones. ●noun tarsal bone.

**tarsus** /ˈtɑːsəs/ noun (plural tarsi /-saɪ/) bones of ankle and upper foot.

**tart**[1] noun pastry case containing fruit, jam, etc. □ **tartlet** noun.

**tart**[2] ●noun slang prostitute, promiscuous woman. ●verb (+ up) colloquial smarten or dress up, esp. gaudily. □ **tarty** adjective (-ier, -iest).

**tart**[3] adjective sharp-tasting, acid; (of remark etc.) cutting, biting. □ **tartly** adverb; **tartness** noun.

**tartan** /ˈtɑːt(ə)n/ noun (woollen cloth woven in) pattern of coloured stripes crossing at right angles, esp. denoting a Scottish Highland clan.

**Tartar** /ˈtɑːtə/ noun member of group of Central Asian people including Mongols and Turks; their Turkic language; (**tartar**) harsh or formidable person. □ **tartar sauce** mayonnaise with chopped gherkins etc.

**tartar** /ˈtɑːtə/ noun hard deposit that forms on teeth; deposit forming hard crust in wine casks.

**tartaric** /tɑːˈtærɪk/ adjective of tartar. □ **tartaric acid** organic acid found esp. in unripe grapes.

**tartrazine** /ˈtɑːtrəziːn/ noun brilliant yellow dye from tartaric acid, used to colour food etc.

**task** /tɑːsk/ ●noun piece of work to be done. ●verb make great demands on. □ **take to task** rebuke, scold; **task force** specially organized unit for task; **taskmaster**, **taskmistress** person who makes others work hard.

**Tass** noun official Russian news agency.

**tassel** /ˈtæs(ə)l/ noun tuft of hanging threads etc. as ornament; tassel-like flowerhead of plant. □ **tasselled** adjective (US **tasseled**).

**taste** /teɪst/ ●noun (faculty of perceiving) sensation caused in mouth by contact with substance; flavour; small sample of food etc.; slight experience; (often + for) liking, predilection; aesthetic discernment in art, clothes, conduct, etc. ●verb (-ting) perceive or sample flavour of; eat small portion of; experience; (often + of) have specified flavour. □ **taste bud** organ of taste on surface of tongue.

**tasteful** adjective done in or having good taste. □ **tastefully** adverb; **tastefulness** noun.

**tasteless** adjective flavourless; having or done in bad taste. □ **tastelessly** adverb; **tastelessness** noun.

**taster** noun person employed to test food or drink by tasting; small sample.

**tasting** noun gathering at which food or drink is tasted and evaluated.

**tasty** adjective (-ier, -iest) of pleasing flavour, appetizing; colloquial attractive. □ **tastiness** noun.

**tat**[1] noun colloquial tatty things; junk.

**tat**[2] verb (-tt-) do, or make by, tatting.

**ta-ta** /tæˈtɑː/ interjection colloquial goodbye.

**tatter** /ˈtætə/ noun (usually in plural) rag, irregularly torn cloth, paper, etc. □ **in tatters** colloquial torn in many places, ruined.

**tattered** adjective in tatters.

**tatting** /ˈtætɪŋ/ noun (process of making) kind of handmade knotted lace.

**tattle** /ˈtæt(ə)l/ ●verb (-ling) prattle, chatter, gossip. ●noun gossip, idle talk.

**tattoo**[1] /təˈtuː/ ●verb (-oos, -ooed) mark (skin) by puncturing and inserting pigment; make (design) thus. ●noun such design. □ **tattooer** noun; **tattooist** noun.

**tattoo**[2] /təˈtuː/ noun evening signal recalling soldiers to quarters; elaboration of this with music and marching etc. as entertainment; drumming, rapping; drumbeat.

**tatty** /ˈtætɪ/ adjective (-ier, -iest) colloquial tattered; shabby, inferior, tawdry. □ **tattily** adverb; **tattiness** noun.

**taught** past & past participle of TEACH.

**taunt** ● *noun* insult; provocation. ● *verb* insult; provoke contemptuously.

**taupe** /təʊp/ *noun* grey tinged with esp. brown.

**Taurus** /'tɔːrəs/ *noun* second sign of zodiac.

**taut** *adjective* (of rope etc.) tight; (of nerves etc.) tense; (of ship etc.) in good condition. □ **tauten** *verb*; **tautly** *adverb*; **tautness** *noun*.

**tautology** /tɔː'tɒlədʒɪ/ *noun* (*plural* **-ies**) repetition of same thing in different words. □ **tautological** /-tə'lɒdʒ-/ *adjective*; **tautologous** /-lagəs/ *adjective*.

**tavern** /'tæv(ə)n/ *noun* archaic or literary inn, pub.

**taverna** /tə'vɜːnə/ *noun* Greek restaurant.

**tawdry** /'tɔːdrɪ/ *adjective* (**-ier**, **-iest**) showy but worthless; gaudy.

**tawny** /'tɔːnɪ/ *adjective* (**-ier**, **-iest**) of orange-brown colour. □ **tawny owl** reddish-brown European owl.

**tax** ● *noun* money compulsorily levied by state on person, property, business, etc.; (+ *on*, *upon*) strain, heavy demand. ● *verb* impose tax on; deduct tax from; make demands on; (often + *with*) charge, call to account. □ **tax avoidance** minimizing tax payment by financial manoeuvring; **tax-deductible** (of expenses) legally deductible from income before tax assessment; **tax disc** licence on vehicle certifying payment of road tax; **tax evasion** illegal non-payment of taxes; **tax-free** exempt from tax; **taxman** *colloquial* inspector or collector of taxes; **taxpayer** person who pays taxes; **tax return** declaration of income etc. for taxation purposes.

**taxation** /tæk'seɪʃ(ə)n/ *noun* imposition or payment of tax.

**taxi** /'tæksɪ/ ● *noun* (*plural* **-s**) (in full **taxi-cab**) car plying for hire and usually fitted with taximeter. ● *verb* (**taxis**, **taxied**, **taxiing** or **taxying**) (of aircraft) go along ground before or after flying; go or carry in taxi. □ **taxi rank** (*US* **taxi stand**) place where taxis wait to be hired.

**taxidermy** /'tæksɪdɜːmɪ/ *noun* art of preparing, stuffing, and mounting skins of animals. □ **taxidermist** *noun*.

**taximeter** /'tæksɪmiːtə/ *noun* automatic fare-indicator in taxi.

**taxon** /'tæks(ə)n/ *noun* (*plural* **taxa**) any taxonomic group.

**taxonomy** /tæk'sɒnəmɪ/ *noun* classification of living and extinct organisms. □ **taxonomic** /-sə'nɒm-/ *adjective*; **taxonomical** /-sə'nɒm-/ *adjective*; **taxonomist** *noun*.

**tayberry** /'teɪbərɪ/ *noun* (*plural* **-ies**) hybrid fruit between blackberry and raspberry.

**TB** *abbreviation* tubercle bacillus; tuberculosis.

**tbsp.** *abbreviation* tablespoonful.

**te** /tiː/ *noun* (also **ti**) seventh note of scale in tonic sol-fa.

**tea** *noun* (in full **tea plant**) Asian evergreen shrub or small tree; its dried leaves; infusion of these leaves as drink; infusion made from other leaves etc.; light meal in afternoon or evening. □ **tea bag** small permeable bag of tea for infusion; **tea break** pause in work for drinking tea; **tea caddy** container for tea; **teacake** light usually toasted sweet bun; **tea chest** light metal-lined wooden box for transporting tea; **tea cloth** tea towel; **tea cosy** cover to keep teapot warm; **teacup** cup from which tea is drunk, amount it holds; **tea leaf** leaf of tea, esp. (in *plural*) after infusion; **teapot** pot with handle and spout, in which tea is made; **tearoom** small unlicensed café; **tea rose** rose with scent like tea; **teaset** set of crockery for serving tea; **teashop** tearoom; **teaspoon** small spoon for stirring tea etc., (also **teaspoonful**) amount held by this; **tea towel** cloth for drying washed crockery etc.; **tea trolley** (*US* **tea wagon**) small trolley from which tea is served.

**teach** *verb* (*past & past participle* **taught** /tɔːt/) give systematic information, instruction, or training to (person) or about (subject, skill); practise this as a profession; advocate as moral etc. principle; (+ *to do*) instruct to, *colloquial* discourage from. □ **teachable** *adjective*.

**teacher** *noun* person who teaches, esp. in school.

**teaching** *noun* teacher's profession; (often in *plural*) what is taught; doctrine.

**teak** *noun* a hard durable wood.

**teal** *noun* (*plural* same) small freshwater duck.

**team** ●*noun* set of players etc. in game or sport; set of people working together; set of draught animals. ●*verb* (usually + *up*) join in team or in common action; (+ *with*) coordinate, match. □ **team-mate** fellow member of team; **team spirit** willingness to act for communal good; **teamwork** combined effort, cooperation.

**teamster** /'tiːmstə/ *noun US* lorry driver; driver of team.

**tear**[1] /teə/ ●*verb* (*past* **tore**; *past participle* **torn**) (often + *up*) pull (apart) with some force; make (hole, rent) thus; undergo this; (+ *away*, *off*, *at*, etc.) pull violently; violently disrupt; *colloquial* go hurriedly. ●*noun* hole etc. caused by tearing; torn part of cloth etc. □ **tear apart** search exhaustively, criticize forcefully, divide utterly, distress greatly; **tearaway** *colloquial* unruly young person; **tearing hurry** *colloquial* great hurry; **tear into** *colloquial* severely reprimand, start (activity) vigorously; **tear to shreds** *colloquial* criticize thoroughly.

**tear**[2] /tɪə/ *noun* drop of clear salty liquid secreted from eye and shed esp. in grief. □ **in tears** weeping; **teardrop** single tear; **tear duct** drain carrying tears to or from eye; **tear gas** gas causing severe irritation to the eyes.

**tearful** *adjective* in, given to, or accompanied with tears. □ **tearfully** *adverb*.

**tease** /tiːz/ ●*verb* (**-sing**) make fun of; irritate; entice sexually while refusing to satisfy desire; pick (wool etc.) into separate fibres; raise nap on (cloth) with teasels etc.; (+ *out*) extract or obtain by careful effort. ●*noun colloquial* person fond of teasing; act of teasing.

**teasel** /'tiːz(ə)l/ *noun* (also **teazel**, **teazle**) plant with prickly flower heads, used dried for raising nap on cloth; other device used for this.

**teaser** *noun colloquial* hard question or problem.

**teat** *noun* nipple on breast or udder; rubber etc. nipple for sucking milk from bottle.

**teazel** (also **teazle**) = TEASEL.

**TEC** /tek/ *abbreviation* Training and Enterprise Council.

**tec** *noun colloquial* detective.

**tech** /tek/ *noun* (also **tec**) *colloquial* technical college.

**technic** /'teknɪk/ *noun* (usually in *plural*) technology; technical terms, methods, etc.; technique.

**technical** *adjective* of the mechanical arts and applied sciences; of a particular subject, craft, etc.; using technical language; specialized; due to mechanical failure; in strict legal sense. □ **technical knockout** referee's ruling that boxer has lost because he is unfit to continue. □ **technically** *adverb*.

**technicality** /teknɪ'kælɪtɪ/ *noun* (*plural* **-ies**) being technical; technical expression; technical point or detail.

**technician** /tek'nɪʃ(ə)n/ *noun* person doing practical or maintenance work in laboratory; person skilled in artistic etc. technique; expert in practical science.

**Technicolor** /'teknɪkʌlə/ *noun proprietary term* process of colour cinematography; (usually **technicolour**) *colloquial* vivid or artificial colour.

**technique** /tek'niːk/ *noun* mechanical skill in art; method of achieving purpose, esp. by manipulation; manner of execution in music, painting, etc.

**technocracy** /tek'nɒkrəsɪ/ *noun* (*plural* **-ies**) (instance of) rule or control by technical experts.

**technocrat** /'teknəkræt/ *noun* exponent or advocate of technocracy. □ **technocratic** /-'kræt-/ *adjective*.

**technology** /tek'nɒlədʒɪ/ *noun* (*plural* **-ies**) knowledge or use of mechanical arts and applied sciences; these subjects collectively. □ **technological** /-nə'lɒdʒ-/ *adjective*; **technologically** /-nə'lɒdʒ-/ *adverb*; **technologist** *noun*.

**tectonic** /tek'tɒnɪk/ *adjective* of building or construction; of changes in the earth's crust.

**tectonics** *plural noun* (usually treated as *singular*) study of earth's large-scale structural features.

**teddy** /'tedɪ/ *noun* (also **Teddy**) (*plural* **-ies**) (in full **teddy bear**) soft toy bear.

**Teddy boy** /'tedɪ/ *noun colloquial* 1950s youth with Edwardian-style clothing, hair, etc.

**tedious** /'tiːdɪəs/ *adjective* tiresomely long, wearisome. □ **tediously** *adverb*; **tediousness** *noun*.

**tedium** /'tiːdɪəm/ *noun* tediousness.

**tee¹** *noun* letter T.

**tee²** ● *noun* cleared space from which golf ball is struck at start of play for each hole; small wood or plastic support for golf ball used then; mark aimed at in bowls, quoits, curling, etc. ● *verb* (**tees, teed**) (often + *up*) place (ball) on tee. □ **tee off** make first stroke in golf, *colloquial* start, begin.

**teem¹** *verb* be abundant; (+ *with*) be full of, swarm with.

**teem²** *verb* (often + *down*) pour (esp. of rain).

**teen** *adjective* teenage.

**teenage** /'tiːneɪdʒ/ *adjective* of or characteristic of teenagers. □ **teenaged** *adjective*.

**teenager** /'tiːneɪdʒə/ *noun* person in teens.

**teens** /tiːnz/ *plural noun* years of one's age from 13 to 19.

**teensy** /'tiːnzɪ/ *adjective* (**-ier, -iest**) *colloquial* teeny.

**teeny** /'tiːnɪ/ *adjective* (**-ier, -iest**) *colloquial* tiny.

**teepee** = TEPEE.

**teeter** /'tiːtə/ *verb* totter, stand or move unsteadily.

**teeth** *plural of* TOOTH.

**teethe** /tiːð/ *verb* (**-thing**) grow or cut teeth, esp. milk teeth. □ **teething ring** ring for infant to bite on while teething; **teething troubles** initial troubles in an enterprise etc.

**teetotal** /tiː'təʊt(ə)l/ *adjective* advocating or practising total abstinence from alcohol. □ **teetotalism** *noun*; **teetotaller** *noun*.

**TEFL** /'tef(ə)l/ *abbreviation* teaching of English as a foreign language.

**Teflon** /'teflɒn/ *noun proprietary term* non-stick coating for kitchen utensils.

**Tel.** *abbreviation* (also **tel.**) telephone.

**tele-** *combining form* at or to a distance; television; by telephone.

**telecast** /'telɪkɑːst/ ● *noun* television broadcast. ● *verb* transmit by television. □ **telecaster** *noun*.

**telecommunication** /telɪkəmjuːnɪ'keɪʃ(ə)n/ *noun* communication over distances by cable, fibre optics, satellites, radio, etc.; (in *plural*) technology of this.

**telefax** /'telɪfæks/ *noun* fax.

**telegram** /'telɪgræm/ *noun* message sent by telegraph.

**telegraph** /'telɪgrɑːf/ ● *noun* (device or system for) transmitting messages to a distance by making and breaking electrical connection. ● *verb* (often + *to*) send message or communicate by telegraph. □ **telegraphist** /tɪ'legrə-/ *noun*.

**telegraphic** /telɪ'græfɪk/ *adjective* of or by telegraphs or telegrams; economically worded. □ **telegraphically** *adverb*.

**telegraphy** /tɪ'legrəfɪ/ *noun* communication by telegraph.

**telekinesis** /telɪkaɪ'niːsɪs/ *noun* supposed paranormal force moving objects at a distance. □ **telekinetic** /-'net-/ *adjective*.

**telemessage** /'telɪmesɪdʒ/ *noun* message sent by telephone or telex and delivered in printed form.

**telemetry** /tɪ'lemətrɪ/ *noun* process of recording readings of instrument and transmitting them by radio. □ **telemeter** /tɪ'lemɪtə/ *noun*.

**teleology** /tiːlɪ'ɒlədʒɪ/ *noun* (*plural* **-ies**) *Philosophy* explanation of phenomena by purpose they serve. □ **teleological** /-ə'lɒdʒ-/ *adjective*.

**telepathy** /tɪ'lepəθɪ/ *noun* supposed paranormal communication of thoughts. □ **telepathic** /telɪ'pæθɪk/ *adjective*; **telepathically** /telɪ'pæθ-/ *adverb*.

**telephone** /'telɪfəʊn/ ● *noun* apparatus for transmitting sound (esp. speech) to a distance; instrument used in this; system of communication by network of telephones. ● *verb* (**-ning**) send (message) or speak to by telephone; make telephone call. □ **on the telephone** having or using a telephone; **telephone book, directory** book listing telephone subscribers and numbers; **telephone booth, box, kiosk** booth etc. with telephone for public use; **telephone number** number used to call a particular telephone. □ **telephonic** /-'fɒn-/ *adjective*; **telephonically** /-'fɒn-/ *adverb*.

**telephonist** /tɪˈlefənɪst/ noun operator in telephone exchange or at switchboard.

**telephony** /tɪˈlefənɪ/ noun transmission of sound by telephone.

**telephoto** /telɪˈfəʊtəʊ/ noun (plural **-s**) (in full **telephoto lens**) lens used in telephotography.

**telephotography** /telɪfəˈtɒgrəfɪ/ noun photographing of distant object with combined lenses giving large image. □ **telephotographic** /-fəʊtəˈgræf-/ adjective.

**teleprinter** /ˈtelɪprɪntə/ noun device for sending, receiving, and printing telegraph messages.

**teleprompter** /ˈtelɪprɒmptə/ noun device beside esp. television camera that slowly unrolls script out of sight of audience.

**telesales** /ˈtelɪseɪlz/ plural noun selling by telephone.

**telescope** /ˈtelɪskəʊp/ ● noun optical instrument using lenses or mirrors to magnify distant objects; radio telescope. ● verb (**-ping**) press or drive (sections of tube etc.) one into another; close or be capable of closing thus; compress.

**telescopic** /telɪˈskɒpɪk/ adjective of or made with telescope; (esp. of lens) able to magnify distant objects; consisting of sections that telescope. □ **telescopic sight** telescope on rifle etc. used for sighting. □ **telescopically** adverb.

**teletext** /ˈtelɪtekst/ noun computerized information service transmitted to subscribers' televisions.

**telethon** /ˈtelɪθɒn/ noun long television programme to raise money for charity.

**televise** /ˈtelɪvaɪz/ verb (**-sing**) transmit by television.

**television** /ˈtelɪvɪʒ(ə)n/ noun system for reproducing on a screen visual images transmitted (with sound) by radio signals or cable; (in full **television set**) device with screen for receiving these signals; television broadcasting. □ **televisual** /-ˈvɪʒʊəl/ adjective.

**telex** /ˈteleks/ (also **Telex**) ● noun international system of telegraphy using teleprinters and public telecommunication network. ● verb send, or communicate with, by telex.

**tell** verb (past & past participle **told** /təʊld/) relate in speech or writing; make known, express in words; (often + of, about) divulge information, reveal secret etc.; (+ to do) direct, order; decide about, distinguish; (often + on) produce marked effect or influence. □ **tell apart** distinguish between; **tell off** colloquial scold; **tell-tale** noun person who tells tales, automatic registering device, adjective serving to reveal or betray something; **tell tales** make known person's faults etc.

**teller** noun person employed to receive and pay out money in bank etc.; person who counts votes; person who tells stories.

**telling** adjective having marked effect, striking. □ **tellingly** adverb.

**telly** /ˈtelɪ/ noun (plural **-ies**) colloquial television.

**temerity** /tɪˈmerɪtɪ/ noun rashness, audacity.

**temp** colloquial ● noun temporary employee, esp. secretary. ● verb work as temp.

**temper** /ˈtempə/ ● noun mental disposition, mood; irritation, anger; tendency to become angry; composure, calmness; metal's hardness or elasticity. ● verb bring (clay, metal) to proper consistency or hardness; (+ with) moderate, mitigate.

**tempera** /ˈtempərə/ noun method of painting using emulsion e.g. of pigment with egg.

**temperament** /ˈtemprəmənt/ noun person's or animal's nature and character.

**temperamental** /temprəˈment(ə)l/ adjective regarding temperament; unreliable, moody; colloquial unpredictable. □ **temperamentally** adverb.

**temperance** /ˈtempərəns/ noun moderation, esp. in eating and drinking; abstinence, esp. total, from alcohol.

**temperate** /ˈtempərət/ adjective avoiding excess, moderate; (of region or climate) mild.

**temperature** /ˈtemprɪtʃə/ noun measured or perceived degree of heat or cold of thing, region, etc.; colloquial body temperature above normal.

**tempest** /ˈtempɪst/ noun violent storm.

**tempestuous** /tem'pestʃʊəs/ adjective stormy, turbulent. □ **tempestuously** adverb.

**tempi** plural of TEMPO.

**template** /'templɪt/ noun thin board or plate used as guide in drawing, cutting, drilling, etc.

**temple**[1] /'temp(ə)l/ noun building for worship, or treated as dwelling place, of god(s).

**temple**[2] /'temp(ə)l/ noun flat part of side of head between forehead and ear.

**tempo** /'tempəʊ/ noun (plural **-pos** or **-pi** /-piː/) speed at which music is (to be) played; speed, pace.

**temporal** /'tempər(ə)l/ adjective worldly as opposed to spiritual, secular; of time; of the temples of the head.

**temporary** /'tempərərɪ/ ● adjective lasting or meant to last only for limited time. ● noun (plural **-ies**) person employed temporarily. □ **temporarily** adverb.

**temporize** /'tempəraɪz/ verb (also **-ise**) (**-zing** or **-sing**) avoid committing oneself, so as to gain time; procrastinate; comply temporarily.

**tempt** verb entice, incite to what is forbidden; allure, attract; risk provoking. □ **tempter** noun; **tempting** adjective; **temptingly** adverb; **temptress** noun.

**temptation** /temp'teɪʃ(ə)n/ noun tempting, being tempted; incitement, esp. to wrongdoing; attractive thing or course of action.

**ten** adjective & noun one more than nine. □ **the Ten Commandments** rules of conduct given by God to Moses. □ **tenth** adjective & noun.

**tenable** /'tenəb(ə)l/ adjective maintainable against attack or objection; (+ for, by) (of office etc.) that can be held for period or by (person etc.). □ **tenability** noun.

**tenacious** /tɪ'neɪʃəs/ adjective (often + of) keeping firm hold; persistent, resolute; (of memory) retentive. □ **tenaciously** adverb; **tenacity** /-'næs-/ noun.

**tenancy** /'tenənsɪ/ noun (plural **-ies**) (duration of) tenant's status or possession.

**tenant** /'tenənt/ noun person who rents land or property from landlord; (often + of) occupant of place.

**tenantry** noun tenants of estate etc.

**tench** noun (plural same) freshwater fish of carp family.

**tend**[1] verb (often + to) be apt or inclined; be moving; hold a course.

**tend**[2] verb take care of, look after.

**tendency** /'tendənsɪ/ noun (plural **-ies**) (often + to, towards) leaning, inclination.

**tendentious** /ten'denʃəs/ adjective derogatory designed to advance a particular cause; biased; controversial. □ **tendentiously** adverb; **tendentiousness** noun.

**tender**[1] /'tendə/ adjective (**tenderer**, **tenderest**) not tough or hard; susceptible to pain or grief; compassionate; delicate, fragile; loving, affectionate; requiring tact; immature. □ **tenderfoot** (plural **-s** or **-feet**) novice, newcomer; **tender-hearted** easily moved; **tenderloin** middle part of loin of pork; **tender mercies** harsh treatment. □ **tenderly** adverb; **tenderness** noun.

**tender**[2] /'tendə/ ● verb offer, present (services, resignation, payment, etc.); (often + for) make tender. ● noun offer to execute work or supply goods at fixed price.

**tender**[3] /'tendə/ noun person who looks after people or things; supply vessel attending larger one; truck attached to steam locomotive and carrying fuel etc.

**tenderize** verb (also **-ise**) (**-zing** or **-sing**) render (meat) tender by beating etc.

**tendon** /'tend(ə)n/ noun tough fibrous tissue connecting muscle to bone etc.

**tendril** /'tendrɪl/ noun slender leafless shoot by which some climbing plants cling.

**tenebrous** /'tenɪbrəs/ adjective literary dark, gloomy.

**tenement** /'tenɪmənt/ noun room or flat within house or block of flats; (also **tenement house, block**) house or block so divided.

**tenet** /'tenɪt/ noun doctrine, principle.

**tenfold** adjective & adverb ten times as much or many.

**tenner** /'tenə/ noun colloquial £10 or $10 note.

**tennis** /'tenɪs/ noun ball game played with rackets on court divided by net.

□ **tennis elbow** sprain caused by over-use of forearm muscles.

**tenon** /'tenən/ *noun* wooden projection shaped to fit into mortise of another piece.

**tenor** /'tenə/ ● *noun* male singing voice between alto and baritone; singer with this; (usually + *of*) general purport, prevailing course of one's life or habits. ● *adjective* having range of tenor.

**tenosynovitis** /ˌtenəʊsaɪnə'vaɪtɪs/ *noun* repetitive strain injury, esp. of wrist.

**tenpin bowling** *noun* game in which ten pins or skittles are bowled at in alley.

**tense**[1] ● *adjective* stretched tight; strained; causing tenseness. ● *verb* (**-sing**) make or become tense. □ **tense up** become tense. □ **tensely** *adverb*; **tenseness** *noun*.

**tense**[2] *noun* form of verb indicating time of action etc.; set of such forms for various persons and numbers.

**tensile** /'tensaɪl/ *adjective* of tension; capable of being stretched. □ **tensile strength** resistance to breaking under tension.

**tension** /'tenʃ(ə)n/ *noun* stretching, being stretched; mental strain or excitement; strained state; stress produced by forces pulling apart; degree of tightness of stitches in knitting and machine sewing; voltage.

**tent** *noun* portable shelter or dwelling of canvas etc.

**tentacle** /'tentək(ə)l/ *noun* slender flexible appendage of animal, used for feeling, grasping, or moving.

**tentative** /'tentətɪv/ *adjective* experimental; hesitant, not definite. □ **tentatively** *adverb*.

**tenterhooks** /'tentəhʊks/ *plural noun* □ **on tenterhooks** in suspense, distracted by uncertainty.

**tenuous** /'tenjʊəs/ *adjective* slight, insubstantial; oversubtle; thin, slender. □ **tenuity** /-'juːɪtɪ/ *noun*; **tenuously** *adverb*.

**tenure** /'tenjə/ *noun* (often + *of*) holding of property or office; conditions or period of this; guaranteed permanent employment, esp. as lecturer. □ **tenured** *adjective*.

**tepee** /'tiːpiː/ *noun* (also **teepee**) N. American Indian's conical tent.

**tepid** /'tepɪd/ *adjective* lukewarm; unenthusiastic.

**tequila** /tɪ'kiːlə/ *noun* Mexican liquor made from agave.

**tercel** /'tɜːs(ə)l/ *noun* (also **tiercel** /'tɪəs(ə)l/) male hawk.

**tercentenary** /tɜːsen'tiːnərɪ/ *noun* (*plural* **-ies**) 300th anniversary; celebration of this.

**tergiversate** /'tɜːdʒɪvəseɪt/ *verb* (**-ting**) change one's party or principles; make conflicting or evasive statements. □ **tergiversation** *noun*; **tergiversator** *noun*.

**term** ● *noun* word for definite concept, esp. specialized; (in *plural*) language used, mode of expression; (in *plural*) relation, footing; (in *plural*) stipulations, charge, price; limited period; period of weeks during which instruction is given or during which law court holds sessions; *Logic* word(s) which may be subject or predicate of proposition; *Mathematics* each quantity in ratio or series, part of algebraic expression; completion of normal length of pregnancy. ● *verb* call, name. □ **come to terms with** reconcile oneself to; **in terms of** with reference to; **terms of reference** scope of inquiry etc., definition of this. □ **termly** *adjective*.

**termagant** /'tɜːməgənt/ *noun* overbearing woman, virago.

**terminable** /'tɜːmɪnəb(ə)l/ *adjective* able to be terminated.

**terminal** /'tɜːmɪn(ə)l/ ● *adjective* (of condition or disease) fatal; (of patient) dying; of or forming limit or terminus. ● *noun* terminating thing, extremity; bus or train terminus; air terminal; point of connection for closing electric circuit; apparatus for transmission of messages to and from computer, communications system, etc. □ **terminally** *adverb*.

**terminate** /'tɜːmɪneɪt/ *verb* (**-ting**) bring or come to an end; (+ *in*) end in.

**termination** *noun* terminating, being terminated; ending, result; induced abortion.

**terminology** /tɜːmɪ'nɒlədʒɪ/ *noun* (*plural* **-ies**) system of specialized terms. □ **terminological** /-nə'lɒdʒ-/ *adjective*.

**terminus** /'tɜ:mɪnəs/ *noun* (*plural* **-ni** /-naɪ/ or **-nuses**) point at end of railway or bus route or of pipeline etc.

**termite** /'tɜ:maɪt/ *noun* antlike insect destructive to timber.

**tern** *noun* seabird with long pointed wings and forked tail.

**ternary** /'tɜ:nərɪ/ *adjective* composed of 3 parts.

**terrace** /'terəs/ ● *noun* flat area on slope for cultivation; level paved area next to house; row of houses built in one block of uniform style; terrace house; tiered standing accommodation for spectators at sports ground. ● *verb* (**-cing**) form into or provide with terrace(s). □ **terrace(d) house** house in terrace.

**terracotta** /terə'kɒtə/ *noun* unglazed usually brownish-red earthenware; its colour.

**terra firma** /terə 'fɜ:mə/ *noun* dry land, firm ground.

**terrain** /tə'reɪn/ *noun* tract of land, esp. in military or geographical contexts.

**terra incognita** /terə ɪŋ'kɒgnɪtə/ *noun* unexplored region. [Latin]

**terrapin** /'terəpɪn/ *noun* N. American edible freshwater turtle.

**terrarium** /tə'reərɪəm/ *noun* (*plural* **-s** or **-ria**) place for keeping small land animals; transparent globe containing growing plants.

**terrestrial** /tə'restrɪəl/ *adjective* of or on the earth; earthly; of or on dry land.

**terrible** /'terɪb(ə)l/ *adjective colloquial* very great, bad, or incompetent; causing or likely to cause terror; dreadful.

**terribly** *adverb colloquial* very, extremely; in terrible manner.

**terrier** /'terɪə/ *noun* small active hardy dog.

**terrific** /tə'rɪfɪk/ *adjective colloquial* huge, intense, excellent; causing terror. □ **terrifically** *adverb*.

**terrify** /'terɪfaɪ/ *verb* (**-ies, -ied**) fill with terror. □ **terrifying** *adjective*; **terrifyingly** *adverb*.

**terrine** /tə'ri:n/ *noun* (earthenware vessel for) pâté or similar food.

**territorial** /terɪ'tɔ:rɪəl/ ● *adjective* of territory or district. ● *noun* (**Territorial**) member of Territorial Army.

□ **Territorial Army** local volunteer reserve force; **territorial waters** waters under state's jurisdiction, esp. part of sea within stated distance of shore. □ **territorially** *adverb*.

**territory** /'terɪtərɪ/ *noun* (*plural* **-ies**) extent of land under jurisdiction of ruler, state, etc.; (**Territory**) organized division of a country, esp. if not yet admitted to full rights of a state; sphere of action etc., province; commercial traveller's sales area; area defended by animal or human, or by team etc. in game.

**terror** /'terə/ *noun* extreme fear; terrifying person or thing; *colloquial* troublesome or tiresome person, esp. child; terrorism.

**terrorist** *noun* person using esp. organized violence to secure political ends. □ **terrorism** *noun*.

**terrorize** *verb* (also **-ise**) (**-zing** or **-sing**) fill with terror; use terrorism against.

**terry** /'terɪ/ *noun* looped pile fabric used for nappies, towels, etc.

**terse** /tɜ:s/ *adjective* (**-r, -st**) concise, brief; curt. □ **tersely** *adverb*.

**tertiary** /'tɜ:ʃərɪ/ *adjective* of third order, rank, etc.

**Terylene** /'terɪli:n/ *noun proprietary term* synthetic polyester textile fibre.

**TESL** /'tes(ə)l/ *abbreviation* teaching of English as a second language.

**tesla** /'tezlə/ *noun* SI unit of magnetic flux density.

**tessellated** /'tesəleɪtɪd/ *adjective* of or resembling mosaic; finely chequered.

**tessellation** /tesə'leɪʃ(ə)n/ *noun* close arrangement of polygons, esp. in repeated pattern.

**test** ● *noun* critical exam or trial of person's or thing's qualities; means, procedure, or standard for so doing; minor exam; *colloquial* test match. ● *verb* put to test; try severely, tax. □ **test card** still television picture outside normal programme hours; **test case** *Law* case setting precedent for other similar cases; **test drive** *noun* drive taken to judge vehicle's performance; **test-drive** *verb* take test drive in; **test match** international cricket or Rugby match, usually in series; **test-tube** thin glass tube closed at one end, used for chemical tests etc.; **test-tube baby** *colloquial* baby conceived elsewhere than in a mother's body. □ **tester** *noun*.

**testaceous** /tes'teɪʃəs/ *adjective* having hard continuous shell.

**testament** /'testəmənt/ *noun* a will; (usually + *to*) evidence, proof; *Biblical* covenant; (**Testament**) division of Bible. □ **testamentary** /-'ment-/ *adjective*.

**testate** /'testeɪt/ ● *adjective* having left valid will at death. ● *noun* testate person. □ **testacy** /-təsi/ *noun* (*plural* **-ies**).

**testator** /tes'teɪtə/ *noun* (*feminine* **testatrix** /-trɪks/) (esp. deceased) person who has made a will.

**testes** *plural* of TESTIS.

**testicle** /'testɪk(ə)l/ *noun* male organ that secretes spermatozoa, esp. one of pair in scrotum of man and most mammals.

**testify** /'testɪfaɪ/ *verb* (**-ies**, **-ied**) (often + *to*) bear witness; give evidence; affirm, declare.

**testimonial** /testɪ'məʊnɪəl/ *noun* certificate of character, conduct, or qualifications; gift presented as mark of esteem.

**testimony** /'testɪmənɪ/ *noun* (*plural* **-ies**) witness's statement under oath etc.; declaration, statement of fact; evidence.

**testis** /'testɪs/ *noun* (*plural* **testes** /-tiːz/) testicle.

**testosterone** /te'stɒstərəʊn/ *noun* male sex hormone.

**testy** /'testɪ/ *adjective* (**-ier**, **-iest**) irascible, short-tempered. □ **testily** *adverb*; **testiness** *noun*.

**tetanus** /'tetənəs/ *noun* bacterial disease causing painful spasm of voluntary muscles.

**tetchy** /'tetʃɪ/ *adjective* (**-ier**, **-iest**) peevish, irritable. □ **tetchily** *adverb*; **tetchiness** *noun*.

**tête-à-tête** /teɪtɑː'teɪt/ ● *noun* private conversation between two people. ● *adverb* privately without third person.

**tether** /'teðə/ ● *noun* rope etc. confining grazing animal. ● *verb* fasten with tether. □ **at the end of one's tether** at the limit of one's patience, resources, etc.

**tetra-** *combining form* four.

**tetragon** /'tetrəgɒn/ *noun* plane figure with 4 sides and angles. □ **tetragonal** /tɪ'trægən-/ *adjective*.

**tetrahedron** /tetrə'hiːdrən/ *noun* (*plural* **-dra** or **-s**) 4-sided triangular pyramid. □ **tetrahedral** *adjective*.

**Teutonic** /tjuː'tɒnɪk/ *adjective* of Germanic peoples or languages; German.

**text** *noun* main part of book; original document, esp. as distinct from paraphrase etc.; passage of Scripture, esp. as subject of sermon; subject, theme; (in *plural*) books prescribed for study; data in textual form, esp. in word processor. □ **textbook** book used in studying, esp. standard book in any subject; **text editor** computing program allowing user to edit text.

**textile** /'tekstaɪl/ ● *noun* (often in *plural*) fabric, esp. woven. ● *adjective* of weaving or cloth; woven.

**textual** /'tekstʃʊəl/ *adjective* of, in, or concerning a text.

**texture** /'tekstʃə/ ● *noun* feel or appearance of surface or substance; arrangement of threads in textile fabric. ● *verb* (**-ring**) (usually as **textured** *adjective*) provide with texture; provide (vegetable protein) with texture like meat. □ **textural** *adjective*.

**Thai** /taɪ/ ● *noun* (*plural* same or **-s**) native, national, or language of Thailand. ● *adjective* of Thailand.

**thalidomide** /θə'lɪdəmaɪd/ *noun* sedative drug found in 1961 to cause foetal malformation when taken early in pregnancy.

**than** /ðən/ *conjunction* introducing comparison.

**thane** /θeɪn/ *noun historical* holder of land from English king by military service, or from Scottish king and ranking below earl; clan-chief.

**thank** /θæŋk/ ● *verb* express gratitude to; hold responsible. ● *noun* (in *plural*) *colloquial* gratitude; (as *interjection*) *expression of gratitude*. □ **thanksgiving** expression of gratitude, esp. to God; **Thanksgiving (Day)** US national holiday on fourth Thurs. in Nov.; **thanks to** as result of; **thank you** *polite formula* expressing gratitude.

**thankful** *adjective* grateful, pleased, expressive of thanks.

**thankfully** *adverb* in a thankful way; let us be thankful that.

■ **Usage** The use of *thankfully* to mean 'let us be thankful that' is common, but it is considered incorrect by some people.

**thankless** *adjective* not feeling or expressing gratitude; (of task etc.) unprofitable, unappreciated.

**that** /ðæt/ ● *adjective* (*plural* **those** /ðəʊz/) used to describe the person or thing nearby, indicated, just mentioned, or understood; used to specify the further or less immediate of two. ● *pronoun* (*plural* **those** /ðəʊz/) that one; the one, the person, etc.; /ðət/ (*plural* **that**) who, whom, which (*used to introduce a defining relative clause*). ● *adverb* (+ *adjective or adverb*) to that degree, so, (with *negative*) *colloquial* very. ● *conjunction* /ðət/ used to introduce a subordinate clause expressing esp. a statement, purpose, or result. □ **at that** moreover, then; **that is** (**to say**) in other words, more correctly or intelligibly.

**thatch** /θætʃ/ ● *noun* roofing of straw, reeds, etc. ● *verb* cover with thatch. □ **thatcher** *noun*.

**thaw** /θɔː/ ● *verb* (often + *out*) pass from frozen into liquid or unfrozen state; (of weather) become warm enough to melt ice etc.; warm into life, animation, cordiality, etc. ● *noun* thawing; warmth of weather that thaws.

**the** /ðɪ, ðə, ðiː/ ● *adjective* (called the definite article) denoting person(s) or thing(s) already mentioned or known about; describing as unique; (+ *adjective*) which is, who are, etc.; (with the *stressed*) best known; used with noun which represents or symbolizes a group, activity, etc. ● *adverb* (before comparatives in expressions of proportional variation) in or by that degree, on that account.

**theatre** /ˈθɪətə/ *noun* (*US* **theater**) building or outdoor area for dramatic performances; writing, production, acting, etc. of plays; room or hall for lectures etc. with seats in tiers; operating theatre; scene or field of action.

**theatrical** /θɪˈætrɪk(ə)l/ ● *adjective* of or for theatre or acting; calculated for effect, showy. ● *noun* (in *plural*) dramatic

performances. □ **theatricality** /-ˈkæl-/ *noun*; **theatrically** *adverb*.

**thee** /ðiː/ *pronoun archaic* (as object of verb) you (singular).

**theft** /θeft/ *noun* act of stealing.

**their** /ðeə/ *adjective* of or belonging to them.

**theirs** /ðeəz/ *pronoun* the one(s) belonging to them.

**theism** /ˈθiːɪz(ə)m/ *noun* belief in gods or a god. □ **theist** *noun*; **theistic** /-ˈɪstɪk/ *adjective*.

**them** /ðem, ð(ə)m/ ● *pronoun* (as object of verb) the people or things in question; people in general; people in authority; *colloquial* they. ● *adjective slang or dialect* those.

**theme** /θiːm/ *noun* subject or topic of talk etc.; *Music* leading melody in a composition; *US* school exercise on given subject. □ **theme park** amusement park based on unifying idea; **theme song, tune** signature tune. □ **thematic** /θɪˈmætɪk/ *adjective*; **thematically** /θɪˈmæt-/ *adverb*.

**themselves** /ðəmˈselvz/ *pronoun*: emphatic & reflexive form of THEY; reflexive form of THEM.

**then** /ðen/ ● *adverb* at that time; after that, next; in that case, accordingly. ● *adjective* such at that time. ● *noun* that time. □ **then and there** immediately and on the spot.

**thence** /ðens/ *adverb* (also **from thence**) *archaic or literary* from that place, for that reason. □ **thenceforth, thenceforward** from that time on.

**theo-** *combining form* God or god(s).

**theocracy** /θɪˈɒkrəsɪ/ *noun* (*plural* **-ies**) form of government by God or a god directly or through a priestly order etc. □ **theocratic** /θɪəˈkrætɪk/ *adjective*.

**theodolite** /θɪˈɒdəlaɪt/ *noun* surveying instrument for measuring angles.

**theology** /θɪˈɒlədʒɪ/ *noun* (*plural* **-ies**) study or system of (esp. Christian) religion. □ **theologian** /θɪəˈləʊdʒ-/ *noun*; **theological** /θɪəˈlɒdʒ-/ *adjective*.

**theorem** /ˈθɪərəm/ *noun esp. Mathematics* general proposition not self-evident but demonstrable by argument; algebraic rule.

**theoretical** /θɪəˈretɪk(ə)l/ *adjective* concerned with knowledge but not with its practical application; based on theory rather than experience. □ **theoretically** adverb.

**theoretician** /θɪərə'tɪʃ(ə)n/ noun person concerned with theoretical part of a subject.

**theorist** /'θɪərɪst/ noun holder or inventor of a theory.

**theorize** /'θɪəraɪz/ verb (also **-ise**) (**-zing** or **-sing**) evolve or indulge in theories.

**theory** /'θɪərɪ/ noun (plural **-ies**) supposition or system of ideas explaining something, esp. one based on general principles; speculative view; abstract knowledge or speculative thought; exposition of principles of a science etc.; collection of propositions to illustrate principles of a mathematical subject.

**theosophy** /θɪ'ɒsəfɪ/ noun (plural **-ies**) philosophy professing to achieve knowledge of God by direct intuition, spiritual ecstasy, etc. □ **theosophical** /θɪə'sɒf-/ adjective; **theosophist** noun.

**therapeutic** /θerə'pjuːtɪk/ adjective of, for, or contributing to the cure of diseases; soothing, conducive to wellbeing. □ **therapeutically** adverb.

**therapeutics** plural noun (usually treated as singular) branch of medicine concerned with cures and remedies.

**therapy** /'θerəpɪ/ noun (plural **-ies**) nonsurgical treatment of disease etc. □ **therapist** noun.

**there** /ðeə/ • adverb in, at, or to that place or position; at that point; in that respect; used for emphasis in calling attention; used to indicate the fact or existence of something. • noun that place. • interjection expressing confirmation, triumph, etc.; used to soothe a child etc. □ **thereabout(s)** near that place, amount, or time; **thereafter** formal after that; **thereby** by that means or agency; **therefore** for that reason, accordingly, consequently; **therein** formal in that place or respect; **thereof** formal of that or it; **thereto** formal to that or it, in addition; **thereupon** in consequence of that, directly after that.

**therm** /θɜːm/ noun unit of heat, former UK unit of gas supplied.

**thermal** /'θɜːm(ə)l/ • adjective of, for, producing, or retaining heat. • noun rising current of warm air. □ **thermal unit** unit for measuring heat. □ **thermally** adverb.

**thermionic valve** /θɜːmɪ'ɒnɪk/ noun device giving flow of electrons in one direction from heated substance, used esp. in rectification of current and in radio reception.

**thermo-** combining form heat.

**thermodynamics** /θɜːməʊdaɪ'næmɪks/ plural noun (usually treated as singular) science of relationship between heat and other forms of energy. □ **thermodynamic** adjective.

**thermoelectric** /θɜːməʊɪ'lektrɪk/ adjective producing electricity by difference of temperatures.

**thermometer** /θə'mɒmɪtə/ noun instrument for measuring temperature, esp. graduated glass tube containing mercury or alcohol.

**thermonuclear** /θɜːməʊ'njuːklɪə/ adjective relating to nuclear reactions that occur only at very high temperatures; (of bomb etc.) using such reactions.

**thermoplastic** /θɜːməʊ'plæstɪk/ • adjective becoming plastic on heating and hardening on cooling. • noun thermoplastic substance.

**Thermos** /'θɜːməs/ noun (in full **Thermos flask**) proprietary term vacuum flask.

**thermosetting** /'θɜːməʊsetɪŋ/ adjective (of plastics) setting permanently when heated.

**thermosphere** /'θɜːməsfɪə/ noun region of atmosphere beyond mesosphere.

**thermostat** /'θɜːməstæt/ noun device for automatic regulation of temperature. □ **thermostatic** /-'stæt-/ adjective; **thermostatically** /-'stæt-/ adverb.

**thesaurus** /θɪ'sɔːrəs/ noun (plural **-ri** /-raɪ/ or **-ruses**) dictionary of synonyms etc.

**these** plural of THIS.

**thesis** /'θiːsɪs/ noun (plural **theses** /-siːz/) proposition to be maintained or proved; dissertation, esp. by candidate for higher degree.

**Thespian** /'θespɪən/ • adjective of drama. • noun actor or actress.

**they** /ðeɪ/ pronoun (as subject of verb) the people or things in question; people in general; people in authority.

**they'd** /ðeɪd/ they had; they would.

**they'll** /ðeɪəl/ they will; they shall.

**they're** /ðeə/ they are.

**they've** /ðeɪv/ they have.

**thiamine** /ˈθaɪəmɪn/ *noun* (also **thiamin**) B vitamin found in unrefined cereals, beans, and liver.

**thick** /θɪk/ ● *adjective* of great or specified extent between opposite surfaces; (of line etc.) broad, not fine; closely set; crowded; (usually + *with*) densely filled or covered; firm in consistency; made of thick material; muddy, impenetrable; *colloquial* stupid; (of voice) indistinct; (of accent) marked; *colloquial* intimate. ● *noun* thick part of anything. ● *adverb* thickly. □ **a bit thick** *colloquial* unreasonable, intolerable; **in the thick of** in the busiest part of; **thickhead** *colloquial* stupid person; **thickheaded** *adjective*; **thickset** heavily or solidly built, set or growing close together; **thick-skinned** not sensitive to criticism; **through thick and thin** under all conditions, in spite of all difficulties. □ **thickly** *adverb*; **thickness** *noun*.

**thicken** *verb* make or become thick(er); become more complicated.

**thickener** *noun* substance used to thicken liquid.

**thickening** *noun* thickened part; = THICKENER.

**thicket** /ˈθɪkɪt/ *noun* tangle of shrubs or trees.

**thief** /θiːf/ *noun* (*plural* **thieves** /θiːvz/) person who steals, esp. secretly.

**thieve** /θiːv/ *verb* (**-ving**) be a thief; steal. □ **thievery** *noun*.

**thievish** *adjective* given to stealing.

**thigh** /θaɪ/ *noun* part of leg between hip and knee. □ **thigh-bone** *noun*.

**thimble** /ˈθɪmb(ə)l/ *noun* metal or plastic cap worn to protect finger and push needle in sewing.

**thimbleful** *noun* (*plural* **-s**) small quantity, esp. of drink.

**thin** /θɪn/ ● *adjective* (**-nn-**) having opposite surfaces close together, of small thickness or diameter; (of line etc.) narrow, fine; made of thin material; lean, not plump; not dense or copious; of slight consistency; weak, lacking an important ingredient; (of excuse etc.) transparent, flimsy. ● *adverb* thinly. ● *verb* (**-nn-**) make or become thin(ner); (often + *out*) make or become less dense, crowded, or numerous. □ **thin on the ground** few; **thin on top** balding; **thin-skinned** sensitive to criticism. □ **thinly** *adverb*; **thinness** *noun*.

**thine** /ðaɪn/ *archaic* ● *pronoun* yours (singular). ● *adjective* your (singular).

**thing** /θɪŋ/ *noun* any possible object of thought or perception including people, material objects, events, qualities, ideas, utterances, and acts; *colloquial* one's special interest; (**the thing**) *colloquial* what is proper, fashionable, needed, important, etc.; (in *plural*) personal belongings, clothing, or equipment; (in *plural*) affairs, circumstances. □ **have a thing about** *colloquial* be obsessed by or prejudiced about.

**thingummy** /ˈθɪŋəmɪ/ *noun* (*plural* **-ies**) (also **thingumabob** /-məbɒb/, **thingumajig** /-mədʒɪɡ/) *colloquial* person or thing whose name one forgets or does not know.

**think** /θɪŋk/ ● *verb* (*past & past participle* **thought** /θɔːt/) be of opinion; (+ *of, about*) consider; exercise mind; form ideas, imagine; have half-formed intention. ● *noun colloquial* act of thinking. □ **think of** change one's mind about (intention) after reconsideration; **think out** consider carefully, devise; **think over** reflect on; **think-tank** *colloquial* group of experts providing advice and ideas on national or commercial problems; **think twice** avoid hasty action etc.; **think up** *colloquial* devise.

**thinker** *noun* person who thinks in specified way; person with skilled or powerful mind.

**thinking** ● *adjective* intelligent, rational. ● *noun* opinion, judgement.

**thinner** *noun* solvent for diluting paint etc.

**third** /θɜːd/ *adjective & noun* next after second; any of 3 equal parts of thing. □ **third degree** severe and protracted interrogation by police etc.; **third man** *Cricket* fielder near boundary behind slips; **third party** another party besides the two principals; **third-party insurance** insurance against damage or injury suffered by person other than the insured; **third-rate** inferior, very poor; **Third World** developing countries of Africa, Asia, and Latin America. □ **thirdly** *adverb*.

**thirst** /θɜːst/ ● noun (discomfort caused by) need to drink; desire, craving. ● verb feel thirst.

**thirsty** /'θɜːstɪ/ adjective (-ier, -iest) feeling thirst; (of land, season, etc.) dry, parched; (often + for, after) eager; colloquial causing thirst. □ **thirstily** adverb; **thirstiness** noun.

**thirteen** /θɜː'tiːn/ adjective & noun one more than twelve. □ **thirteenth** adjective & noun.

**thirty** /'θɜːtɪ/ adjective & noun (plural -ies) three times ten. □ **thirtieth** adjective & noun.

**this** /ðɪs/ ● adjective (plural these /ðiːz/) used to describe the person or thing nearby, indicated, just mentioned, or understood; used to specify the nearer or more immediate of two; the present (morning, week, etc.). ● pronoun (plural these /ðiːz/) this one. ● adverb (+ adjective or adverb) to this degree or extent.

**thistle** /'θɪs(ə)l/ noun prickly plant, usually with globular heads of purple flowers; this as Scottish national emblem. □ **thistledown** down containing thistle-seeds. □ **thistly** adjective.

**thither** /'ðɪðə/ adverb archaic or formal to that place.

**tho'** = THOUGH.

**thole** /θəʊl/ noun (in full **thole-pin**) pin in gunwale of boat as fulcrum for oar; each of two such pins forming rowlock.

**thong** /θɒŋ/ noun narrow strip of hide or leather.

**thorax** /'θɔːræks/ noun (plural -races /-rəsiːz/ or -raxes) part of the body between neck and abdomen. □ **thoracic** /-'ræs-/ adjective.

**thorn** /θɔːn/ noun sharp-pointed projection on plant; thorn-bearing shrub or tree. □ **thornless** adjective.

**thorny** adjective (-ier, -iest) having many thorns; (of subject) problematic, causing disagreement.

**thorough** /'θʌrə/ adjective complete, unqualified, not superficial; acting or done with great care etc. □ **thoroughbred** adjective of pure breed, high-spirited, noun such animal, esp. horse; **thoroughfare** public way open at both ends, esp. main road; **thoroughgoing** thorough, complete. □ **thoroughly** adverb; **thoroughness** noun.

**those** plural of THAT.

**thou**¹ /ðaʊ/ pronoun archaic (as subject of verb) you (singular).

**thou**² /θaʊ/ noun (plural same or -s) colloquial thousand; one thousandth.

**though** /ðəʊ/ (also **tho'**) ● conjunction in spite of the fact that; even if; and yet. ● adverb colloquial however, all the same.

**thought**¹ /θɔːt/ noun process, power, faculty, etc. of thinking; particular way of thinking; sober reflection, consideration; idea, notion; intention, purpose; (usually in plural) one's opinion.

**thought**² past & past participle of THINK.

**thoughtful** adjective engaged in or given to meditation; giving signs of serious thought; considerate. ● **thoughtfully** adverb; **thoughtfulness** noun.

**thoughtless** adjective careless of consequences or of others' feelings; caused by lack of thought. □ **thoughtlessly** adverb; **thoughtlessness** noun.

**thousand** /'θaʊz(ə)nd/ adjective & noun (plural same) ten hundred; (**thousands**) colloquial large number. □ **thousandth** adjective & noun.

**thrall** /θrɔːl/ noun literary (often + of, to) slave; slavery.

**thrash** /θræʃ/ verb beat or whip severely; defeat thoroughly; move or fling (esp. limbs) violently. □ **thrash out** discuss to conclusion.

**thread** /θred/ ● noun spun-out cotton, silk, glass, etc.; length of this; thin cord of twisted yarns used esp. in sewing and weaving; continuous aspect of thing; spiral ridge of screw. ● verb pass thread through (needle); put (beads) on thread; arrange (material in strip form, e.g. film) in proper position on equipment; pick (one's way) through maze, crowded place, etc. □ **threadbare** (of cloth) so worn that nap is lost and threads showing, (of person) shabby, (of idea etc.) hackneyed; **threadworm** parasitic threadlike worm.

**threat** /θret/ noun declaration of intention to punish or hurt; indication of something undesirable coming; person or thing regarded as dangerous.

**threaten** /'θret(ə)n/ verb use threats towards; be sign or indication of (something undesirable); (+ to do) announce one's intention to do (undesirable thing); give warning of infliction of (harm etc.); (as **threatened** adjective) (of species etc.) likely to become extinct.

**three** /θriː/ adjective & noun one more than two. □ **three-cornered** triangular, (of contest etc.) between 3 people etc.; **three-dimensional** having or appearing to have length, breadth, and depth; **three-legged race** race for pairs with right leg of one tied to other's left leg; **threepence** /ˈθrepəns/ sum of 3 pence; **threepenny** /ˈθrepənɪ/ costing 3 pence; **three-piece** (suit or suite) consisting of 3 items; **three-ply** (wool etc.) having 3 strands, (plywood) having 3 layers; **three-point turn** method of turning vehicle in narrow space by moving forwards, backwards, and forwards again; **three-quarter** Rugby any of 3 or 4 players just behind half-backs; **the three Rs** reading, writing, and arithmetic.

**threefold** adjective & adverb three times as much or many.

**threesome** noun group of 3 people.

**threnody** /ˈθrenədɪ/ noun (plural **-ies**) song of lamentation.

**thresh** verb beat out or separate grain from (corn etc.). □ **thresher** noun.

**threshold** /ˈθreʃəʊld/ noun plank or stone forming bottom of doorway; point of entry; limit below which stimulus causes no reaction.

**threw** past of THROW.

**thrice** adverb archaic or literary 3 times.

**thrift** noun frugality, economical management. □ **thrifty** adjective (**-ier**, **-iest**).

**thrill** ● noun wave or nervous tremor of emotion or sensation; throb, pulsation. ● verb (cause to) feel thrill; quiver or throb (as) with emotion.

**thriller** noun sensational or exciting play, story, etc.

**thrips** noun (plural same) insect harmful to plants.

**thrive** verb (**-ving**; past **throve** or **thrived**; past participle **thriven** /ˈθrɪv(ə)n/ or **thrived**) prosper; grow vigorously.

**thro'** = THROUGH.

**throat** noun gullet, windpipe; front of neck; literary narrow passage or entrance.

**throaty** adjective (**-ier**, **-iest**) (of voice) hoarsely resonant.

**throb** ● verb (**-bb-**) pulsate; vibrate with persistent rhythm or with emotion. ● noun throbbing, violent beat or pulsation.

**throe** noun (usually in plural) violent pang. □ **in the throes of** struggling with the task of.

**thrombosis** /θrɒmˈbəʊsɪs/ noun (plural **-boses** /-siːz/) coagulation of blood in blood vessel or organ.

**throne** ● noun ceremonial chair for sovereign, bishop, etc.; sovereign power. ● verb (**-ning**) enthrone.

**throng** ● noun (often + of) crowd, esp. of people. ● verb come in multitudes; fill (as) with crowd.

**throstle** /ˈθrɒs(ə)l/ noun song thrush.

**throttle** /ˈθrɒt(ə)l/ ● noun (lever etc. operating) valve controlling flow of steam or fuel in engine; throat. ● verb (**-ling**) choke, strangle; control (engine etc.) with throttle. □ **throttle back**, **down** reduce speed of (engine etc.) by throttling.

**through** /θruː/ (also **thro'**, US **thru**) ● preposition from end to end or side to side of; between, among; from beginning to end of; by agency, means, or fault of; by reason of; US up to and including. ● adverb through something; from end to end; to the end. ● adjective (of journey etc.) done without change of line, vehicle, etc.; (of traffic) going through a place to its destination; (of road) open at both ends. □ **be through** colloquial (often + with) have finished, cease to have dealings; **through and through** thoroughly, completely; **throughput** amount of material put through a manufacturing etc. process or a computer.

**throughout** /θruːˈaʊt/ ● preposition right through; from end to end of. ● adverb in every part or respect.

**throve** past of THRIVE.

**throw** /θrəʊ/ ● verb (past **threw** /θruː/; past participle **thrown**) propel through space; force violently into specified position or state; turn or move (part of body) quickly or suddenly; project (rays, light, etc.); cast (shadow); bring to the ground; colloquial disconcert; (+ on, off, etc.) put (clothes etc.) carelessly or hastily on, off, etc.; cause (dice) to fall on table etc., obtain (specified number) thus; cause to pass or extend suddenly to another state or position; move (switch, lever); shape (pottery) on wheel; have (fit, tantrum, etc.); give (a party). ● *noun* throwing, being thrown; distance a thing is or may be thrown; (**a throw**) *slang* each, per item. □ **throw away** discard as unwanted, waste, fail to make use of; **throw-away** to be thrown away after (one) use, deliberately underemphasized; **throw back** (usually in *passive*, + *on*) compel to rely on; **throwback** (instance of) reversion to ancestral character; **throw in** interpose (word, remark), include at no extra cost, throw (football) from edge of pitch where it has gone out of play; **throw-in** throwing in of football from edge of pitch; **throw off** discard, contrive to get rid of, write or utter in offhand way; **throw open** (often + *to*) cause to be suddenly or widely open, make accessible; **throw out** put out forcibly or suddenly, discard, reject; **throw over** desert, abandon; **throw up** abandon, resign from, vomit, erect hastily, bring to notice.

**thrum** ● *verb* (**-mm-**) play (stringed instrument) monotonously or unskilfully; ( often + *on*) drum idly. ● *noun* such playing; resultant sound.

**thrush**¹ *noun* kind of songbird.

**thrush**² *noun* fungus infection of throat, esp. in children, or of vagina.

**thrust** ● *verb* (*past & past participle* **thrust**) push with sudden impulse or with force; (+ *on*) impose (thing) forcibly on; (+ *at, through*) pierce, stab, lunge suddenly; make (one's way) forcibly; (as **thrusting** *adjective*) aggressive, ambitious. ● *noun* sudden or forcible push or lunge; forward force exerted by propeller or jet etc.; strong attempt to penetrate enemy's line or territory; remark aimed at person; stress between parts of arch etc.; (often + *of*) theme, gist.

**thud** /θʌd/ ● *noun* low dull sound as of blow on non-resonant thing. ● *verb* (**-dd-**) make thud; fall with thud.

**thug** /θʌg/ *noun* vicious or brutal ruffian. □ **thuggery** *noun*; **thuggish** *adjective*.

**thumb** /θʌm/ ● *noun* short thick finger on hand, set apart from other 4; part of glove for thumb. ● *verb* soil or wear with thumb; turn over pages (as) with thumb; request or get (lift) by sticking out thumb. □ **thumb index** set of lettered grooves cut down side of book etc. for easy reference; **thumbnail** *noun* nail of thumb, *adjective* concise; **thumbscrew** instrument of torture for squeezing thumbs; **thumbs up, down** indication of approval or rejection; **under (person's) thumb** dominated by him or her.

**thump** /θʌmp/ ● *verb* beat heavily, esp. with fist; throb strongly; (+ *at, on*, etc.) knock loudly. ● *noun* (sound of) heavy blow.

**thumping** *adjective colloquial* huge.

**thunder** /ˈθʌndə/ ● *noun* loud noise accompanying lightning; resounding loud deep noise; strong censure. ● *verb* sound with or like thunder; move with loud noise; utter loudly; (+ *against*) make violent threats. □ **thunderbolt** flash of lightning with crash of thunder, unexpected occurrence or announcement, supposed bolt or shaft as destructive agent; **thunderclap** crash of thunder; **thundercloud** electrically charged cumulus cloud; **thunderstorm** storm with thunder and lightning; **thunderstruck** amazed. □ **thunderous** *adjective*; **thundery** *adjective*.

**thundering** *adjective colloquial* huge.

**Thur.** *abbreviation* (also **Thurs.**) Thursday.

**thurible** /ˈθjʊərɪb(ə)l/ *noun* censer.

**Thursday** /ˈθɜːzdeɪ/ *noun* day of week following Wednesday.

**thus** /ðʌs/ *adverb formal* in this way, like this; accordingly, as a result or inference; to this extent, so.

**thwack** ● *verb* hit with heavy blow. ● *noun* heavy blow.

**thwart** /θwɔːt/ ● *verb* frustrate, foil. ● *noun* rower's seat.

**thy** /ðaɪ/ *adjective* (also **thine**, esp. before vowel) *archaic* your (singular).

**thyme** /taɪm/ *noun* herb with aromatic leaves.

**thymol** /ˈθaɪmɒl/ *noun* antiseptic made from oil of thyme.

**thymus** /ˈθaɪməs/ *noun* (*plural* **thymi** /-maɪ/) ductless gland near base of neck.

**thyroid** /ˈθaɪrɔɪd/ *noun* thyroid gland. □ **thyroid cartilage** large cartilage of larynx forming Adam's apple; **thyroid gland** large ductless gland near larynx secreting hormone which regulates growth and development, extract of this.

**thyself** /ðaɪˈself/ *pronoun archaic: emphatic & reflexive form of* THOU¹; *reflexive form of* THEE.

**ti** = TE.

**tiara** /tɪˈɑːrə/ *noun* jewelled ornamental band worn on front of woman's hair; 3-crowned diadem formerly worn by pope.

**tibia** /ˈtɪbɪə/ *noun* (*plural* **tibiae** /-bɪiː/) inner of two bones extending from knee to ankle.

**tic** *noun* (in full **nervous tic**) spasmodic contraction of muscles, esp. of face.

**tick¹** ● *noun* slight recurring click, esp. of watch or clock; *colloquial* moment; small mark (√) to denote correctness etc. ● *verb* make sound of tick; (often + *off*) mark with tick. □ **tick off** *colloquial* reprimand; **tick over** (of engine) idle, function at basic level; **tick-tack** kind of manual semaphore used by race-course bookmakers; **tick-tock** ticking of large clock etc.

**tick²** *noun* parasitic arachnid or insect on animals.

**tick³** *noun colloquial* financial credit.

**tick⁴** *noun* case of mattress or pillow; ticking.

**ticker** *noun colloquial* heart; watch; *US* tape machine. □ **ticker-tape** paper strip from tape machine, esp. as thrown from windows to greet celebrity.

**ticket** /ˈtɪkɪt/ ● *noun* piece of paper or card entitling holder to enter place, participate in event, travel by public transport, etc.; notification of traffic offence etc.; certificate of discharge from army or of qualification as ship's master, pilot, etc.; price etc. label; *esp. US* list of candidates put forward by group, esp. political party, principles of party; (**the ticket**) *colloquial* what is needed. ● *verb* (**-t-**) attach ticket to.

**ticking** *noun* strong usually striped material to cover mattresses etc.

**tickle** /ˈtɪk(ə)l/ ● *verb* (**-ling**) touch or stroke lightly so as to produce laughter and spasmodic movement; excite agreeably, amuse; catch (trout etc.) by rubbing it so that it moves backwards into hand. ● *noun* act or sensation of tickling.

**ticklish** /ˈtɪklɪʃ/ *adjective* sensitive to tickling; difficult to handle.

**tidal** /ˈtaɪd(ə)l/ *adjective* related to, like, or affected by tides. □ **tidal wave** exceptionally large ocean wave, esp. one caused by underwater earthquake, widespread manifestation of feeling etc.

**tidbit** *US* = TITBIT.

**tiddler** /ˈtɪdlə/ *noun colloquial* small fish, esp. stickleback or minnow; unusually small thing.

**tiddly¹** /ˈtɪdlɪ/ *adjective* (**-ier, -iest**) *colloquial* slightly drunk.

**tiddly²** /ˈtɪdlɪ/ *adjective* (**-ier, -iest**) *colloquial* little.

**tiddly-wink** /ˈtɪdlɪwɪŋk/ *noun* counter flicked with another into cup; (in *plural*) this game.

**tide** ● *noun* regular rise and fall of sea due to attraction of moon and sun; water as moved by this; time, season; trend of opinion, fortune, or events. ● *verb* (**-ding**) (**tide over**) temporarily provide with what is needed. □ **tidemark** mark made by tide at high water, *colloquial* line of dirt round bath, or on person's body between washed and unwashed parts; **tideway** tidal part of river.

**tidings** /ˈtaɪdɪŋz/ *noun archaic or jocular* (treated as *singular* or *plural*) news.

**tidy** /ˈtaɪdɪ/ ● *adjective* (**-ier, -iest**) neat, orderly; (of person) methodical; *colloquial* considerable. ● *noun* (*plural* **-ies**) receptacle for odds and ends. ● *verb* (**-ies, -ied**) (often + *up*) make (oneself, room, etc.) tidy; put in order. □ **tidily** *adverb*; **tidiness** *noun*.

**tie** ● *verb* (**tying**) attach or fasten with cord etc.; form into knot or bow; (often + *down*) restrict, bind; (often + *with*) make same score as another competitor; bind (rafters etc.) by crosspiece etc.; *Music* unite (notes) by tie. ● *noun* cord etc. used for fastening; strip of material worn round collar and tied in knot at front; thing that unites or restricts people; equality of score, draw, or dead heat among competitors; match between any pair of players or teams; rod or beam holding parts of structure together; *Music* curved line above or below two notes of same pitch that are to be joined as one. □ **tie-break, -breaker** means of deciding winner when competitors have tied; **tie-dye** method of producing dyed patterns by tying string etc. to keep dye from parts of fabric; **tie-pin** ornamental pin to hold necktie in place; **tie up** fasten with cord etc., invest (money etc.) so that it is not immediately available for use, fully occupy (person), bring to satisfactory conclusion; **tie-up** connection, association.

**tied** *adjective* (of dwelling house) occupied subject to tenant's working for house's owner; (of public house etc.) bound to supply only particular brewer's liquor.

**tier** /tɪə/ ●*noun* row, rank, or unit of structure, as one of several placed one above another. □ **tiered** *adjective*.

**tiercel** = TERCEL.

**tiff** *noun* slight or petty quarrel.

**tiger** /'taɪgə/ *noun* large Asian animal of cat family, with yellow-brown coat with black stripes; fierce, formidable, or energetic person. □ **tiger-cat** any moderate-sized feline resembling tiger; **tiger lily** tall garden lily with dark-spotted orange flowers.

**tight** /taɪt/ ●*adjective* closely, held, drawn, fastened, fitting, etc.; impermeable, impervious; tense, stretched; *colloquial* drunk; *colloquial* stingy; (of money or materials) not easily obtainable; stringent, demanding; presenting difficulties; produced by or requiring great exertion or pressure. ●*adverb* tightly. □ **tight corner** difficult situation; **tight-fisted** stingy; **tight-lipped** restraining emotion, determinedly reticent; **tightrope** high tightly stretched rope or wire on which acrobats etc. perform. □ **tighten** *verb*; **tightly** *adverb*; **tightness** *noun*.

**tights** *plural noun* thin close-fitting stretch garment covering legs, feet, and lower torso.

**tigress** /'taɪgrɪs/ *noun* female tiger.

**tilde** /'tɪldə/ *noun* mark (˜) placed over letter, e.g. Spanish *n* in *señor*.

**tile** ●*noun* thin slab of concrete, baked clay, etc. for roofing, paving, etc. ●*verb* (-ling) cover with tiles. □ **tiler** *noun*.

**tiling** *noun* process of fixing tiles; area of tiles.

**till**[1] ●*preposition* up to, as late as. ●*conjunction* up to time when; so long that.

■ **Usage** In all senses, *till* can be replaced by *until*, which is more formal in style.

**till**[2] *noun* money-drawer in bank, shop, etc., esp. with device recording amount and details of each purchase.

**till**[3] *verb* cultivate (land).

**tillage** *noun* preparation of land for growing crops; tilled land.

**tiller** /'tɪlə/ *noun* bar by which boat's rudder is turned.

**tilt** ●*verb* (cause to) assume sloping position or heel over; (+ *at*) thrust or run at with weapon; (+ *with*) engage in contest. ●*noun* tilting; sloping position; (of medieval knights etc.) charging with lance against opponent or mark. □ **(at) full tilt** at full speed, with full force.

**tilth** *noun* tillage, cultivation; cultivated soil.

**timber** /'tɪmbə/ *noun* wood for building, carpentry, etc.; piece of wood, beam, esp. as rib of vessel; large standing trees; (as *interjection*) tree is about to fall.

**timbered** *adjective* made (partly) of timber; (of land) wooded.

**timbre** /'tæmbə/ *noun* distinctive character of musical sound or voice apart from its pitch and volume.

**timbrel** /'tɪmbr(ə)l/ *noun* *archaic* tambourine.

**time** ●*noun* indefinite continuous progress of past, present, and future events etc. regarded as a whole; more or less definite portion of this, historical or other period; allotted or available portion of time; definite or fixed point or portion of time; (**a time**) indefinite period; occasion; moment etc. suitable for purpose; (in *plural*) (after numeral etc.) *expressing multiplication*; lifetime; (in *singular* or *plural*) conditions of life or of period; *slang* prison sentence; apprenticeship; date or expected date of childbirth or death; measured amount of time worked; rhythm or measure of musical composition. ● *verb* (**-ming**) choose time for, do at chosen or appropriate time; ascertain time taken by. □ **at the same time** simultaneously, nevertheless; **at times** now and then; **from time to time** occasionally; **in no time** rapidly, in a moment; **in time** not late, early enough, eventually, following time of music etc.; **on time** punctually; **time-and-motion** measuring efficiency of industrial etc. operations; **time bomb** one designed to explode at pre-set time; **time capsule** box etc. containing objects typical of present time, buried for future discovery; **time-honoured** esteemed by tradition or through custom; **timekeeper** person who records time, watch or clock as regards accuracy; **timekeeping** keeping of time, punctuality; **time-lag** interval between cause and effect; **time off** time used for rest or different activity; **timepiece** clock, watch; **time-server** person who adapts his or her opinions to suit prevailing circumstances; **time-share** share in property under time-sharing scheme; **time-sharing** use of holiday home by several joint owners at different times of year, use of computer by several people for different operations at the same time; **time sheet** sheet of paper for recording hours worked; **time-shift** move from one time to another; **time signal** audible indication of exact time of day; **time signature** *Music* indication of rhythm; **time switch** one operating automatically at preset time; **timetable** *noun* table showing times of public transport services, scheme of lessons, etc., *verb* include or arrange in such schedule; **time zone** range of longitudes where a common standard time is used.

**timeless** *adjective* not affected by passage of time. □ **timelessness** *noun*.

**timely** *adjective* (**-ier**, **-iest**) opportune, coming at right time. □ **timeliness** *noun*.

**timer** *noun* person or device that measures time taken.

**timid** /'tɪmɪd/ *adjective* (**-er**, **-est**) easily alarmed; shy. □ **timidity** /-'mɪd-/ *noun*; **timidly** *adverb*.

**timing** *noun* way thing is timed; regulation of opening and closing of valves in internal-combustion engine.

**timorous** /'tɪmərəs/ *adjective* timid, frightened. □ **timorously** *adverb*.

**timpani** /'tɪmpənɪ/ *plural noun* (also **tympani**) kettledrums. □ **timpanist** *noun*.

**tin** ● *noun* silvery-white metal used esp. in alloys and in making tin plate; container of tin or tin plate, esp. for preserving food; tin plate. ● *verb* (**-nn-**) preserve (food) in tin; cover or coat with tin. □ **tin foil** foil of tin, aluminium, or tin alloy, used to wrap food; **tin hat** *colloquial* military steel helmet; **tin-opener** tool for opening tins; **tin-pan alley** world of composers and publishers of popular music; **tin plate** sheet steel coated with tin; **tinpot** cheap, inferior; **tinsnips** clippers for cutting sheet metal; **tin-tack** tack[1] coated with tin.

**tincture** /'tɪŋktʃə/ ● *noun* (often + *of*) slight flavour or tinge; medicinal solution of drug in alcohol. ● *verb* (**-ring**) colour slightly, tinge, flavour; (often + *with*) affect slightly.

**tinder** /'tɪndə/ *noun* dry substance readily taking fire from spark. □ **tinder-box** *historical* box with tinder, flint, and steel for kindling fires.

**tine** *noun* prong, tooth, or point of fork, comb, antler, etc.

**ting** ● *noun* tinkling sound as of bell. ● *verb* (cause to) emit this.

**tinge** /tɪndʒ/ ● *verb* (**-ging**) (often + *with*; often in *passive*) colour slightly. ● *noun* tendency to or trace of some colour; slight admixture of feeling or quality.

**tingle** /'tɪŋg(ə)l/ ● *verb* (**-ling**) feel or cause slight pricking or stinging sensation. ● *noun* tingling sensation.

**tinker** /'tɪŋkə/ ● *noun* itinerant mender of kettles, pans, etc.; *Scottish & Irish* Gypsy; *colloquial* mischievous person or animal. ● *verb* (+ *at*, *with*) work in amateurish or desultory way; work as tinker.

**tinkle** /'tɪŋk(ə)l/ ● *verb* (**-ling**) (cause to) make short light ringing sounds. ● *noun* tinkling sound.

**tinnitus** /'tɪnɪtəs/ *noun Medicine* condition with ringing in ears.

**tinny** *adjective* (**-ier**, **-iest**) like tin; flimsy; (of sound) thin and metallic.

**tinsel** /'tɪns(ə)l/ *noun* glittering decorative metallic strips, threads, etc.; superficial brilliance or splendour. □ **tinselled** *adjective*.

**tint** ● *noun* a variety of a colour; tendency towards or admixture of a different colour; faint colour spread over surface. ● *verb* apply tint to, colour.

**tintinnabulation** /tɪntɪnæbjʊ'leɪʃ(ə)n/ *noun* ringing of bells.

**tiny** /'taɪnɪ/ *adjective* (**-ier**, **-iest**) very small.

**tip**[1] ● *noun* extremity, esp. of small or tapering thing; small piece or part attached to end of thing. ● *verb* (**-pp-**) provide with tip. □ **tiptop** *colloquial* first-rate, of highest excellence.

**tip**[2] ● *verb* (**-pp-**) (often + *over*, *up*) (cause to) lean or slant; (+ *into* etc.) overturn, cause to overbalance, discharge contents of (container etc.) thus. ● *noun* slight push or tilt; place where refuse is tipped.

**tip**[3] ● *verb* (**-pp-**) give small present of money to, esp. for service; name as likely winner of race or contest; strike or touch lightly. ● *noun* small present of money given esp. for service; piece of private or special information, esp. regarding betting or investment; piece of advice. □ **tip-off** a hint, warning, etc.; **tip off** give warning, hint, or inside information to.

**tippet** /'tɪpɪt/ *noun* cape or collar of fur etc.

**tipple** /'tɪp(ə)l/ ● *verb* (**-ling**) drink intoxicating liquor habitually or repeatedly in small quantities. ● *noun colloquial* alcoholic drink. □ **tippler** *noun*.

**tipster** /'tɪpstə/ *noun* person who gives tips about horse racing etc.

**tipsy** /'tɪpsɪ/ *adjective* (**-ier**, **-iest**) slightly drunk; caused by or showing intoxication.

**tiptoe** /'tɪptəʊ/ ● *noun* the tips of the toes. ● *verb* (**-toes**, **-toed**, **-toeing**) walk on tiptoe or stealthily. ● *adverb* (also **on tiptoe**) with heels off the ground.

**TIR** *abbreviation* international road transport (*transport international routier*).

**tirade** /taɪ'reɪd/ *noun* long vehement denunciation or declamation.

**tire**[1] /taɪə/ *verb* (**-ring**) make or grow weary; exhaust patience or interest of; (in *passive*; + *of*) have had enough of.

**tire**[2] *US* = TYRE.

**tired** *adjective* weary, ready for sleep; (of idea) hackneyed. □ **tiredly** *adverb*; **tiredness** *noun*.

**tireless** *adjective* not tiring easily, energetic. □ **tirelessly** *adverb*; **tirelessness** *noun*.

**tiresome** *adjective* tedious; *colloquial* annoying. □ **tiresomely** *adverb*.

**tiro** /'taɪərəʊ/ *noun* (also **tyro**) (*plural* **-s**) beginner, novice.

**tissue** /'tɪʃuː/ *noun* any of the coherent collections of cells of which animals or plants are made; tissue-paper; disposable piece of thin absorbent paper for wiping, drying, etc.; fine woven esp. gauzy fabric; (often + *of*) connected series (of lies etc.). □ **tissue-paper** thin soft paper for wrapping etc.

**tit**[1] *noun* any of various small birds.

**tit**[2] *noun* □ **tit for tat** blow for blow, retaliation.

**Titan** /'taɪt(ə)n/ *noun* (often **titan**) person of superhuman strength, intellect, or importance.

**titanic** /taɪ'tænɪk/ *adjective* gigantic, colossal.

**titanium** /taɪ'teɪnɪəm/ *noun* dark grey metallic element.

**titbit** /'tɪtbɪt/ *noun* (*US* **tidbit**) dainty morsel; piquant item of news etc.

**titchy** /'tɪtʃɪ/ *adjective* (**-ier**, **-iest**) *colloquial* very small.

**tithe** /taɪð/ *historical* ● *noun* one-tenth of annual produce of land or labour taken as tax for Church. ● *verb* (**-thing**) subject to tithes; pay tithes.

**Titian** /'tɪʃ(ə)n/ *adjective* (of hair) bright auburn.

**titillate** /'tɪtɪleɪt/ *verb* (**-ting**) excite, esp. sexually; tickle. □ **titillation** *noun*.

**titivate** /'tɪtɪveɪt/ *verb* (**-ting**) *colloquial* smarten; put finishing touches to. □ **titivation** *noun*.

**title** /'taɪt(ə)l/ *noun* name of book, work of art, etc.; heading of chapter etc.; title-page; caption or credit in film etc.; name denoting person's status; championship in sport; legal right to ownership of property; (+ *to*) just or recognized claim to. □ **title-deed** legal document constituting evidence of a right;

**title-holder** person holding (esp. sporting) title; **title-page** page at beginning of book giving title, author, etc.; **title role** part in play etc. from which its title is taken.

**titled** *adjective* having title of nobility or rank.

**titmouse** /'tɪtmaʊs/ *noun* (*plural* **titmice**) small active tit.

**titrate** /taɪ'treɪt/ *verb* (**-ting**) ascertain quantity of constituent in (solution) by adding measured amounts of reagent. □ **titration** *noun*.

**titter** /'tɪtə/ • *verb* laugh covertly, giggle. • *noun* covert laugh.

**tittle** /'tɪt(ə)l/ *noun* particle, whit.

**tittle-tattle** /'tɪt(ə)ltæt(ə)l/ *noun & verb* (**-ling**) gossip, chatter.

**tittup** /'tɪtəp/ • *verb* (**-p-** or **-pp-**) go friskily or jerkily, bob up and down, canter. • *noun* such gait or movement.

**titular** /'tɪtjʊlə/ *adjective* of or relating to title; existing or being in name only.

**tizzy** /'tɪzɪ/ *noun* (*plural* **-ies**) *colloquial* state of nervous agitation.

**TNT** *abbreviation* trinitrotoluene.

**to** /tə, before vowel tʊ, when stressed tuː/ • *preposition* in direction of; as far as, not short of; according to; compared with; involved in, comprising; *used to introduce indirect object of verb etc.*, *to introduce or as substitute for infinitive*, *or to express purpose, consequence, or cause*. • *adverb* in normal or required position or condition; (of door) nearly closed. □ **to and fro** backwards and forwards, (repeatedly) from place to place; **to-do** fuss, commotion; **toing and froing** constant movement to and fro, great or dispersed activity.

**toad** *noun* froglike amphibian breeding in water but living chiefly on land; repulsive person. □ **toadflax** plant with yellow or purple flowers; **toad-in-the-hole** sausages baked in batter; **toadstool** fungus (usually poisonous) with round top and slender stalk.

**toady** /'təʊdɪ/ • *noun* (*plural* **-ies**) sycophant. • *verb* (**-ies**, **-ied**) (+ *to*) behave servilely to, fawn on. □ **toadyism** *noun*.

**toast** • *noun* sliced bread browned on both sides by radiant heat; person or thing in whose honour company is requested to drink; call to drink or

instance of drinking thus. • *verb* brown by heat, warm at fire etc.; drink to the health or in honour of. □ **toasting-fork** long-handled fork for toasting bread etc.; **toastmaster**, **toastmistress** person announcing toasts at public occasion; **toast rack** rack for holding slices of toast at table.

**toaster** *noun* electrical device for making toast.

**tobacco** /tə'bækəʊ/ *noun* (*plural* **-s**) plant of American origin with leaves used for smoking, chewing, or snuff; its leaves, esp. as prepared for smoking.

**tobacconist** /tə'bækənɪst/ *noun* dealer in tobacco.

**toboggan** /tə'bɒgən/ • *noun* long light narrow sledge for sliding downhill, esp. over snow. • *verb* ride on toboggan.

**toby jug** /'təʊbɪ/ *noun* jug or mug in shape of stout man in 3-cornered hat.

**toccata** /tə'kɑːtə/ *noun Music* composition for keyboard instrument, designed to exhibit performer's touch and technique.

**tocsin** /'tɒksɪn/ *noun* alarm bell or signal.

**today** /tə'deɪ/ • *adverb* on this present day; nowadays. • *noun* this present day; modern times.

**toddle** /'tɒd(ə)l/ • *verb* (**-ling**) walk with young child's short unsteady steps; *colloquial* walk, stroll, (usually + *off*, *along*) depart. • *noun* toddling walk.

**toddler** *noun* child just learning to walk.

**toddy** /'tɒdɪ/ *noun* (*plural* **-ies**) sweetened drink of spirits and hot water.

**toe** • *noun* any of terminal projections of foot or paw; part of footwear that covers toes; lower end or tip of implement etc. • *verb* (**toes**, **toed**, **toeing**) touch with toe(s). □ **on one's toes** alert; **toecap** (reinforced) part of boot or shoe covering toes; **toe-hold** slight foothold, small beginning or advantage; **toe the line** conform, esp. under pressure; **toenail** nail of each toe.

**toff** *noun slang* upper-class person.

**toffee** /'tɒfɪ/ *noun* firm or hard sweet made of boiled butter, sugar, etc.; this substance. □ **toffee-apple** toffee-coated apple; **toffee-nosed** *slang* snobbish, pretentious.

**tofu** /'təʊfuː/ *noun* curd of mashed soya beans.

**tog**[1] *colloquial* ● *noun* (in *plural*) clothes. ● *verb* (**-gg-**) (+ *out*, *up*) dress.

**tog**[2] *noun* unit of thermal resistance of quilts etc.

**toga** /'təʊgə/ *noun historical* ancient Roman citizen's loose flowing outer garment.

**together** /tə'geðə/ ● *adverb* in(to) company or conjunction; simultaneously; one with another; uninterruptedly. ● *adjective colloquial* well-organized, self-assured, emotionally stable. □ **togetherness** *noun*.

**toggle** /'tɒg(ə)l/ *noun* short bar used like button for fastening clothes; *Computing* key or command which alternately switches function on and off.

**toil** ● *verb* work laboriously or incessantly; make slow painful progress. ● *noun* labour; drudgery. □ **toilsome** *adjective*.

**toilet** /'tɔɪlɪt/ *noun* lavatory; process of washing oneself, dressing, etc. □ **toilet paper** paper for cleaning oneself after using lavatory; **toilet roll** roll of toilet paper; **toilet water** dilute perfume used after washing.

**toiletries** /'tɔɪlɪtriːz/ *plural noun* articles or cosmetics used in washing, dressing, etc.

**toilette** /twɑː'let/ *noun* process of washing oneself, dressing, etc.

**toils** /tɔɪlz/ *plural noun* net, snare.

**token** /'təʊkən/ ● *noun* symbol, reminder, mark; voucher; thing equivalent to something else, esp. money. ● *adjective* perfunctory, chosen by tokenism to represent a group. □ **token strike** brief strike to demonstrate strength of feeling.

**tokenism** *noun* granting of minimum concessions.

**told** *past* & *past participle* of TELL.

**tolerable** /'tɒlərəb(ə)l/ *adjective* endurable; fairly good. □ **tolerably** *adverb*.

**tolerance** /'tɒlərəns/ *noun* willingness or ability to tolerate; permitted variation in dimension, weight, etc.

**tolerant** /'tɒlərənt/ *adjective* disposed to tolerate others; (+ *of*) enduring or patient of.

**tolerate** /'tɒləreɪt/ *verb* (**-ting**) allow the existence or occurrence of without authoritative interference; endure; find or treat as endurable; be able to take or undergo without harm. □ **toleration** *noun*.

**toll**[1] /təʊl/ *noun* charge to use bridge, road, etc.; cost or damage caused by disaster etc. □ **toll-gate** barrier preventing passage until toll is paid.

**toll**[2] /təʊl/ ● *verb* (of bell) ring with slow uniform strokes, ring (bell) thus; announce or mark (death etc.) thus; (of bell) strike (the hour). ● *noun* tolling or stroke of bell.

**toluene** /'tɒljuːiːn/ *noun* colourless liquid hydrocarbon used in manufacture of explosives etc.

**tom** *noun* (in full **tom-cat**) male cat.

**tomahawk** /'tɒməhɔːk/ *noun* N. American Indian war-axe.

**tomato** /tə'mɑːtəʊ/ *noun* (*plural* **-es**) glossy red or yellow fleshy edible fruit; plant bearing this.

**tomb** /tuːm/ *noun* burial-vault; grave; sepulchral monument. □ **tombstone** memorial stone over grave.

**tombola** /tɒm'bəʊlə/ *noun* kind of lottery.

**tomboy** /'tɒmbɔɪ/ *noun* girl who enjoys rough noisy recreations. □ **tomboyish** *adjective*.

**tome** *noun* large book or volume.

**tomfool** /tɒm'fuːl/ ● *noun* fool. ● *adjective* foolish. □ **tomfoolery** *noun*.

**Tommy** /'tɒmɪ/ *noun* (*plural* **-ies**) *colloquial* British private soldier.

**tommy-gun** /'tɒmɪgʌn/ *noun* submachine-gun.

**tomorrow** /tə'mɒrəʊ/ ● *adverb* on day after today; in future. ● *noun* the day after today; the near future.

**tomtit** *noun* tit, esp. blue tit.

**tom-tom** /'tɒmtɒm/ *noun* kind of drum usually beaten with hands.

**ton** /tʌn/ *noun* measure of weight equalling 2,240 lb (**long ton**) or 2,000 lb (**short ton**); metric ton; unit of measurement of ship's tonnage; (usually in *plural*) *colloquial* large number or amount; *slang* speed of 100 m.p.h., score of 100.

**tonal** /'təʊn(ə)l/ *adjective* of or relating to tone or tonality.

**tonality** /təˈnælɪtɪ/ *noun* (*plural* **-ies**) relationship between tones of a musical scale; observance of single tonic key as basis of musical composition; colour scheme of picture.

**tone** ● *noun* sound, esp. with reference to pitch, quality, and strength; (often in *plural*) modulation of voice to express emotion etc.; manner of expression in writing or speaking; musical sound, esp. of definite pitch and character; general effect of colour or of light and shade in picture; tint or shade of colour; prevailing character of morals, sentiments, etc.; proper firmness of body, state of (good) health. ● *verb* (**-ning**) give desired tone to; alter tone of; harmonize. □ **tone-deaf** unable to perceive differences in musical pitch; **tone down** make or become softer in tone; **tone up** make or become stronger in tone. □ **toneless** *adjective*; **tonelessly** *adverb*; **toner** *noun*.

**tongs** *plural noun* implement with two arms for grasping coal, sugar, etc.

**tongue** /tʌŋ/ ● *noun* muscular organ in mouth used in tasting, swallowing, speaking, etc.; tongue of ox etc. as food; faculty or manner of speaking; particular language; thing like tongue in shape. ● *verb* (**-guing**) use tongue to articulate (notes) in playing wind instrument. □ **tongue-in-cheek** ironic(ally); **tongue-tied** too shy to speak; **tongue-twister** sequence of words difficult to pronounce quickly and correctly.

**tonic** /ˈtɒnɪk/ ● *noun* invigorating medicine; anything serving to invigorate; tonic water; *Music* keynote. ● *adjective* invigorating. □ **tonic sol-fa** musical notation used esp. in teaching singing; **tonic water** carbonated drink with quinine.

**tonight** /təˈnaɪt/ ● *adverb* on present or approaching evening or night. ● *noun* the evening or night of today.

**tonnage** /ˈtʌnɪdʒ/ *noun* ship's internal cubic capacity or freight-carrying capacity; charge per ton on freight or cargo.

**tonne** /tʌn/ *noun* 1,000 kg.

**tonsil** /ˈtɒns(ə)l/ *noun* either of two small organs on each side of root of tongue.

**tonsillectomy** /tɒnsəˈlektəmɪ/ *noun* (*plural* **-ies**) surgical removal of tonsils.

**tonsillitis** /tɒnsəˈlaɪtɪs/ *noun* inflammation of tonsils.

**tonsorial** /tɒnˈsɔːrɪəl/ *adjective usually jocular* of hairdresser or hairdressing.

**tonsure** /ˈtɒnʃə/ ● *noun* shaving of crown or of whole head as clerical or monastic symbol; bare patch so made. ● *verb* (**-ring**) give tonsure to.

**too** *adverb* to a greater extent than is desirable or permissible; *colloquial* very; in addition; moreover.

**took** *past of* TAKE.

**tool** /tuːl/ ● *noun* implement for working on something by hand or by machine; thing used in activity; person merely used by another. ● *verb* dress (stone) with chisel; impress design on (leather); ( + *along*, *around*, etc.) *slang* drive or ride esp. in a casual or leisurely way.

**toot** /tuːt/ ● *noun* sound (as) of horn etc. ● *verb* sound (horn etc.); give out such sound.

**tooth** /tuːθ/ *noun* (*plural* **teeth**) each of a set of hard structures in jaws of most vertebrates, used for biting and chewing; toothlike part or projection, e.g. cog of gearwheel, point of saw or comb, etc.; (often + *for*) taste, appetite; (in *plural*) force, effectiveness. □ **fight tooth and nail** fight fiercely; **get one's teeth into** devote oneself seriously to; **in the teeth of** in spite of, contrary to, directly against (wind etc.); **toothache** pain in teeth; **toothbrush** brush for cleaning teeth; **toothpaste** paste for cleaning teeth; **toothpick** small sharp stick for removing food lodged between teeth. □ **toothed** *adjective*; **toothless** *adjective*.

**toothsome** *adjective* (of food) delicious.

**toothy** *adjective* (**-ier**, **-iest**) having large, numerous, or prominent teeth.

**tootle** /ˈtuːt(ə)l/ *verb* (**-ling**) toot gently or repeatedly; (usually + *around*, *along*, etc.) *colloquial* move casually.

**top**[1] ● *noun* highest point or part; highest rank or place, person occupying this; upper end, head; upper surface, upper part; cover or cap of container etc.; garment for upper part of body; utmost degree, height; (in *plural*) *colloquial* person or thing of best quality; (esp. in *plural*) leaves etc. of plant grown chiefly for its root; *Nautical* platform round head of lower mast. ●*adjective* highest in position, degree, or importance. ●*verb* (-**pp**-) furnish with top, cap, etc.; be higher or better than, surpass, be at or reach top of; *slang* kill, hit golf ball above centre. □ **on top of** fully in command of, very close to, in addition to; **top brass** *colloquial* high-ranking officers; **topcoat** overcoat, final coat of paint etc.; **top dog** *colloquial* victor, master; **top drawer** *colloquial* high social position or origin; **top dress** apply fertilizer on top of (earth) without ploughing it in; **top-flight** of highest rank of achievement; **top hat** tall silk hat; **top-heavy** overweighted at top; **topknot** knot, tuft, crest, or bow worn or growing on top of head; **topmast** mast on top of lower mast; **top-notch** *colloquial* first-rate; **top secret** of utmost secrecy; **topside** outer side of round of beef, side of ship above waterline; **topsoil** top layer of soil; **top up** complete (amount), fill up (partly empty container); **top-up** addition, amount that completes or quantity that fills something. □ **topmost** *adjective*.

**top**² *noun* toy spinning on point when set in motion.

**topaz** /ˈtəupæz/ *noun* semiprecious transparent stone, usually yellow.

**tope** *verb* ( -**ping**) *archaic* or *literary* drink alcohol to excess, esp. habitually. □ **toper** *noun*.

**topi** /ˈtəupɪ/ *noun* (also **topee**) (*plural* -**s**) hat, esp sun-helmet.

**topiary** /ˈtəupɪərɪ/ ●*adjective* of or formed by clipping shrubs, trees, etc. into ornamental shapes. ●*noun* topiary art.

**topic** /ˈtɒpɪk/ *noun* subject of discourse, conversation, or argument.

**topical** *adjective* dealing with current affairs, etc. □ **topicality** /-ˈkæl-/ *noun*.

**topless** *adjective* without a top; (of garment) leaving breasts bare; (of woman) bare-breasted; (of place) where women go or work bare-breasted.

**topography** /təˈpɒgrəfɪ/ *noun* detailed description, representation, etc. of features of a district; such features. □ **topographer** *noun*; **topographical** /tɒpəˈgræf-/ *adjective*.

**topology** /təˈpɒlədʒɪ/ *noun* study of geometrical properties unaffected by

changes of shape or size. □ **topological** /tɒpəˈlɒdʒ-/ *adjective*.

**topper** *noun colloquial* top hat.

**topping** *noun* thing that tops, esp. sauce on dessert etc.

**topple** /ˈtɒp(ə)l/ *verb* (-**ling**) (often + *over*, *down*) (cause to) fall as if topheavy; overthrow.

**topsy-turvy** /tɒpsɪˈtɜːvɪ/ *adverb* & *adjective* upside down; in utter confusion.

**toque** /təuk/ *noun* woman's close-fitting brimless hat.

**tor** *noun* hill, rocky peak.

**torch** *noun* battery-powered portable lamp; thing lit for illumination; source of heat, light, or enlightment. □ **carry a torch for** have (esp. unreturned) love for.

**tore** *past* of TEAR¹.

**toreador** /ˈtɒrɪədɔː/ *noun* bullfighter, esp. on horseback.

**torment** ●*noun* /ˈtɔːment/ (cause of) severe bodily or mental suffering. ●*verb* /tɔːˈment/ subject to torment, tease or worry excessively. □ **tormentor** /-ˈmen-/ *noun*.

**torn** *past participle* of TEAR¹.

**tornado** /tɔːˈneɪdəu/ *noun* (*plural* -**es**) violent storm over small area, with whirling winds.

**torpedo** /tɔːˈpiːdəu/ ●*noun* (*plural* -**es**) cigar-shaped self-propelled underwater or aerial missile that explodes on hitting ship. ●*verb* (-**es**, -**ed**) destroy or attack with torpedo(es); make ineffective. □ **torpedo boat** small fast warship armed with torpedoes.

**torpid** /ˈtɔːpɪd/ *adjective* sluggish, apathetic; numb; dormant. □ **torpidity** /-ˈpɪd-/ *noun*.

**torpor** /ˈtɔːpə/ *noun* torpid condition.

**torque** /tɔːk/ *noun* twisting or rotary force, esp. in machine; *historical* twisted metal necklace worn by ancient Gauls and Britons.

**torrent** /ˈtɒrənt/ *noun* rushing stream of liquid; downpour of rain; (in *plural*) (usually + *of*) violent flow. □ **torrential** /təˈrenʃ(ə)l/ *adjective*.

**torrid** /ˈtɒrɪd/ *adjective* intensely hot; scorched, parched; passionate, intense.

**torsion** /ˈtɔːʃ(ə)n/ *noun* twisting. □ **torsional** *adjective*.

**torso** /ˈtɔːsəʊ/ noun (plural **-s**) trunk of human body; statue of this.

**tort** noun breach of legal duty (other than under contract) with liability for damages. □ **tortious** /ˈtɔːʃəs/ adjective.

**tortilla** /tɔːˈtiːjə/ noun thin flat originally Mexican maize cake eaten hot.

**tortoise** /ˈtɔːtəs/ noun slow-moving reptile with horny domed shell. □ **tortoiseshell** mottled yellowish-brown turtle-shell, cat or butterfly with markings resembling tortoiseshell.

**tortuous** /ˈtɔːtʃʊəs/ adjective winding; devious, circuitous. □ **tortuously** adverb.

**torture** /ˈtɔːtʃə/ ● noun infliction of severe bodily pain, esp. as punishment or means of persuasion; severe physical or mental pain. ● verb (**-ring**) subject to torture. □ **torturer** noun, **torturous** adjective.

**Tory** /ˈtɔːrɪ/ colloquial ● noun (plural **-ies**) member of Conservative party. ● adjective Conservative. □ **Toryism** noun.

**tosa** /ˈtəʊsə/ noun dog of a mastiff breed.

**tosh** noun colloquial rubbish, nonsense.

**toss** ● verb throw up, esp. with hand; roll about, throw, or be thrown, restlessly or from side to side; throw lightly or carelessly; throw (coin) into air to decide choice etc. by way it falls, (often + for) settle question or dispute with (person) thus; (of bull etc.) fling up with horns; coat (food) with dressing etc. by shaking it. ● noun tossing; fall, esp. from horseback. □ **toss one's head** throw it back, esp. in anger, impatience, etc.; **toss off** drink off at a draught, dispatch (work) rapidly or easily; **toss up** verb toss coin; **toss-up** noun doubtful matter, tossing of coin.

**tot**[1] noun small child; dram of liquor.

**tot**[2] verb (**-tt-**) (usually + up) add, mount. □ **tot up to** amount to.

**total** /ˈtəʊt(ə)l/ ● adjective complete, comprising the whole; absolute, unqualified. ● noun whole sum or amount. ● verb (**-ll-**; US **-l-**) (often + to, up to) amount to; calculate total of. □ **totality** /-ˈtæl-/ noun (plural **-ies**); **totally** adverb.

**totalitarian** /təʊtælɪˈteərɪən/ adjective of one-party government requiring complete subservience to state. □ **totalitarianism** noun.

**totalizator** /ˈtəʊtəlaɪzeɪtə/ noun (also **totalisator**) device showing number and amount of bets staked on race when total will be divided among those betting on winner; this betting system.

**totalize** /ˈtəʊtəlaɪz/ verb (also **-ise**) (**-zing** or **-sing**) combine into a total.

**tote**[1] noun slang totalizator.

**tote**[2] verb (**-ting**) esp. US colloquial carry, convey. ● **tote bag** large and capacious bag.

**totem** /ˈtəʊtəm/ noun natural object (esp. animal) adopted esp. among N. American Indians as emblem of clan or individual; image of this. □ **totem-pole** post with carved and painted or hung totem(s).

**toto** see IN TOTO.

**totter** /ˈtɒtə/ ● verb stand or walk unsteadily or feebly; shake, be about to fall. ● noun unsteady or shaky movement or gait. □ **tottery** adjective.

**toucan** /ˈtuːkən/ noun tropical American bird with large bill.

**touch** /tʌtʃ/ ● verb come into or be in physical contact with; (often + with) bring hand etc. into contact with; cause (two things) to meet thus; rouse tender or painful feelings in; strike lightly; (usually in negative) disturb, harm, affect, have dealings with, consume, use; concern; reach as far as; (usually in negative) approach in excellence; modify; (as **touched** adjective) colloquial slightly mad; (usually + for) slang request and get money etc. from (person). ● noun act of touching; sense of feeling; small amount, trace; (**a touch**) slightly; Music manner of playing keys or strings, instrument's response to this; artistic, literary, etc. style or skill; slang act of requesting and getting money etc. from person; Football part of field outside touchlines. □ **touch-and-go** critical, risky; **touch** at Nautical call at (port etc.); **touch down** (of aircraft) alight; **touchdown** noun; **touchline** side limit of football etc. pitch; **touch off** explode by touching with match etc., initiate (process) suddenly; **touch on, upon** refer to or mention briefly or casually, verge on; **touch-paper** paper impregnated with nitre for igniting fireworks etc.; **touchstone** dark schist or jasper for testing alloys by marking it with them, criterion; **touch-type** type without looking at keys; **touch-typist** noun, **touch up** give finishing touches to, retouch, *slang* molest sexually; **touch wood** touch something wooden to avert ill luck; **touchwood** readily inflammable rotten wood.

**touché** /tuːˈʃeɪ/ *interjection* acknowledging justified accusation or retort, or hit in fencing. [French]

**touching** ● *adjective* moving, pathetic. ● *preposition literary* concerning. □ **touchingly** *adverb*.

**touchy** *adjective* (**-ier, -iest**) apt to take offence, over-sensitive. □ **touchily** *adverb*; **touchiness** *noun*.

**tough** /tʌf/ ● *adjective* hard to break, cut, tear, or chew; able to endure hardship, hardy; stubborn, difficult; *colloquial* acting sternly, (of luck etc.) hard; *colloquial* criminal, violent. ● *noun* tough person, esp. ruffian. □ **toughen** *verb*; **toughness** *noun*.

**toupee** /ˈtuːpeɪ/ *noun* hairpiece to cover bald spot.

**tour** /tʊə/ ● *noun* holiday journey or excursion including stops at various places; walk round, inspection; spell of military or diplomatic duty; series of performances, matches, etc. at different places. ● *verb* (often + *through*) go on a tour; make a tour of (country etc.). □ **on tour** (esp. of sports team, theatre company, etc.) touring; **tour operator** travel agent specializing in package holidays.

**tour de force** /tʊə də ˈfɔːs/ *noun* (*plural* **tours de force** same pronunciation) outstanding feat or performance. [French]

**tourer** *noun* car or caravan for touring in.

**tourism** *noun* commercial organization and operation of holidays.

**tourist** *noun* holiday traveller; member of touring sports team. □ **tourist class** lowest class of passenger accommodation in ship, aeroplane, etc.

**tourmaline** /ˈtʊəməliːn/ *noun* mineral with unusual electric properties and used as gem.

**tournament** /ˈtʊənəmənt/ *noun* large contest of many rounds; display of military exercises; *historical* pageant with jousting.

**tournedos** /ˈtʊənədəʊ/ *noun* (*plural* same /-dəʊz/) small thick piece of fillet of beef.

**tourney** /ˈtʊənɪ/ ● *noun* (*plural* **-s**) tournament. ● *verb* (**-eys, -eyed**) take part in tournament.

**tourniquet** /ˈtʊənɪkeɪ/ *noun* device for stopping flow of blood through artery by compression.

**tousle** /ˈtaʊz(ə)l/ *verb* (**-ling**) make (esp. hair) untidy; handle roughly.

**tout** /taʊt/ ● *verb* (usually + *for*) solicit custom persistently, pester customers; solicit custom of or for; spy on racehorses in training. ● *noun* person who touts.

**tow**[1] /təʊ/ ● *verb* pull along by rope etc. ● *noun* towing, being towed. □ **in tow** being towed, accompanying or in the charge of a person; **on tow** being towed; **towpath** path beside river or canal originally for horse towing boat.

**tow**[2] /təʊ/ *noun* fibres of flax etc. ready for spinning. □ **tow-headed** having very light-coloured or tousled hair.

**towards** /təˈwɔːdz/ *preposition* (also **toward**) in direction of; as regards, in relation to; as a contribution to; for; near.

**towel** /ˈtaʊəl/ ● *noun* absorbent cloth, paper, etc. for drying after washing etc. ● *verb* (**-ll-**; *US* **-l-**) rub or dry with towel.

**towelling** *noun* thick soft absorbent cloth used esp. for towels.

**tower** /ˈtaʊə/ ● *noun* tall structure, often part of castle, church, etc.; fortress etc. with tower; tall structure housing machinery etc. ● *verb* (usually + *above*, *up*) reach high, be superior; (as **towering** *adjective*) high, lofty, violent. □ **tower block** tall building of offices or flats; **tower of strength** person who gives strong emotional support.

**town** /taʊn/ *noun* densely populated area, between city and village in size; London or the chief city or town in area; central business area in neighbourhood. □ **go to town** *colloquial* act or work with energy or enthusiasm; **on the town** *colloquial* enjoying urban night-life; **town clerk** *US & historical* official in charge of records etc. of town; **town gas** manufactured gas for domestic etc. use; **town hall** headquarters of local government, with public meeting rooms etc.; **town house** town residence, esp. one of terrace;

**town planning** planning of construction and growth of towns; **township** *South African* urban area for occupation by black people, *US & Canadian* administrative division of county, or district 6 miles square, *Australian & NZ* small town; **townspeople** inhabitants of town.

**townie** /ˈtaʊnɪ/ *noun* (also **townee** /-ˈniː/) *derogatory* inhabitant of town.

**toxaemia** /tɒkˈsiːmɪə/ *noun* (*US* **toxemia**) blood poisoning; increased blood pressure in pregnancy.

**toxic** /ˈtɒksɪk/ *adjective* poisonous; of poison. □ **toxicity** /-ˈsɪs-/ *noun*.

**toxicology** /tɒksɪˈkɒlədʒɪ/ *noun* study of poisons. □ **toxicological** /-kəˈlɒdʒ-/ *adjective*; **toxicologist** *noun*.

**toxin** /ˈtɒksɪn/ *noun* poison produced by living organism.

**toy** ● *noun* plaything; thing providing amusement; diminutive breed of dog etc. ● *verb* (usually + *with*) amuse oneself, flirt, move thing idly. □ **toy boy** *colloquial* woman's much younger boyfriend; **toyshop** shop selling toys.

**trace**[1] ● *verb* (**-cing**) find signs of by investigation; (often + *along, through, to,* etc.) follow or mark track, position, or path of; (often + *back*) follow to origins; copy (drawing etc.) by marking its lines on superimposed translucent paper; mark out, delineate, or write, esp. laboriously. ● *noun* indication of existence of something, vestige; very small quantity; track, footprint; mark left by instrument's moving pen etc. □ **trace element** chemical element occurring or required, esp. in soil, only in minute amounts. □ **traceable** *adjective*.

**trace**[2] *noun* each of two side-straps, chains, or ropes by which horse draws vehicle. □ **kick over the traces** become insubordinate or reckless.

**tracer** *noun* bullet etc. made visible in flight by flame etc. emitted; artificial radioisotope which can be followed through body by radiation it produces.

**tracery** /ˈtreɪsərɪ/ *noun* (*plural* **-ies**) decorative stone openwork, esp. in head of Gothic window; lacelike pattern.

**trachea** /trəˈkiːə/ *noun* (*plural* **-cheae** /-ˈkiːiː/) windpipe.

**tracing** *noun* traced copy of drawing etc.; act of tracing. □ **tracing-paper** translucent paper for making tracings.

**track** ● *noun* mark(s) left by person, animal, vehicle, etc.; (in *plural*) such marks, esp. footprints; rough path; line of travel; continuous railway line; racecourse, circuit, prepared course for runners; groove on gramophone record; single song etc. on gramophone record, CD, or magnetic tape; band round wheels of tank, tractor, etc. ● *verb* follow track of; trace (course, development, etc.) from vestiges. □ **in one's tracks** *colloquial* where one stands, instantly; **make tracks** *colloquial* depart; **make tracks for** *colloquial* go in pursuit of or towards; **track down** reach or capture by tracking; **tracker dog** police dog tracking by scent; **track events** running-races; **track record** person's past achievements; **track shoe** runner's spiked shoe; **track suit** warm outfit worn for exercising etc. □ **tracker** *noun*.

**tract**[1] *noun* (esp. large) stretch of territory; bodily organ or system.

**tract**[2] *noun* pamphlet, esp. containing propaganda.

**tractable** /ˈtræktəb(ə)l/ *adjective* easily managed, docile. □ **tractability** *noun*.

**traction** /ˈtrækʃ(ə)n/ *noun* hauling, pulling; therapeutic sustained pull on limb etc. □ **traction-engine** steam or diesel engine for drawing heavy load.

**tractor** /ˈtræktə/ *noun* vehicle for hauling farm machinery etc.; traction-engine.

**trad** *colloquial* ● *noun* traditional jazz. ● *adjective* traditional.

**trade** ● *noun* buying and selling; this between nations etc.; business merely for profit (as distinct from profession); business of specified nature or time; skilled handicraft; (**the trade**) people engaged in specific trade; *US* transaction, esp. swap; (usually in *plural*) trade wind. ● *verb* (**-ding**) (often + *in, with*) engage in trade, buy and sell; exchange; *US* swap; (usually + *with, for*) have transaction. □ **trade in** exchange (esp. used article) in part payment for another; **trade mark** device or name legally registered to represent a company or product, distinctive characteristic; **trade name** name by which a thing is known in a trade, or given by manufacturer to a product, or under which a business trades; **trade off** exchange as compromise; **trade-off** balance, compromise; **trade on** take advantage of; **tradesman, tradeswoman** person engaged in trade, esp. shopkeeper; **trade(s) union** organized association of workers in trade, profession, etc. formed to further their common interests; **trade-unionist** member of trade union; **trade wind** constant wind blowing towards equator from NE or SE. □ **trader** noun.

**tradescantia** /trædɪsˈkæntɪə/ noun (usually trailing) plant with large blue, white, or pink flowers.

**trading** noun engaging in trade. □ **trading estate** area designed for industrial and commercial firms; **trading post** store etc. in remote region; **trading-stamp** token given to customer and exchangeable in quantity usually for goods.

**tradition** /trəˈdɪʃ(ə)n/ noun custom, opinion, or belief handed down to posterity; handing down of these.

**traditional** adjective of, based on, or obtained by tradition; (of jazz) in style of early 20th c. □ **traditionally** adverb.

**traditionalism** noun respect or support for tradition. □ **traditionalist** noun & adjective.

**traduce** /trəˈdjuːs/ verb (**-cing**) slander. □ **traducement** noun; **traducer** noun.

**traffic** /ˈtræfɪk/ ●noun vehicles moving on public highway, in air, or at sea; (usually + in) trade, esp. illegal; coming and going of people or goods by road, rail, air, sea, etc.; dealings between people etc.; (volume of) messages transmitted through communications system. ●verb (**-ck-**) (often + in) deal, esp. illegally; barter. □ **traffic island** raised area in road to divide traffic and provide refuge for pedestrians; **traffic jam** traffic at standstill; **traffic light(s)** signal controlling road traffic by coloured lights; **traffic warden** person employed to control movement and parking of road vehicles. □ **trafficker** noun.

**tragedian** /trəˈdʒiːdɪən/ noun author of or actor in tragedies.

**tragedienne** /trədʒiːdɪˈen/ noun actress in tragedies.

**tragedy** /ˈtrædʒɪdɪ/ noun (plural **-ies**) serious accident, sad event; play with tragic unhappy ending.

**tragic** /ˈtrædʒɪk/ adjective disastrous, distressing, very sad; of tragedy. □ **tragically** adverb.

**tragicomedy** /trædʒɪˈkɒmədɪ/ noun (plural **-ies**) drama or event combining comedy and tragedy.

**trail** ●noun track or scent left by moving person, thing, etc.; beaten path, esp. through wild region; long line of people or things following something; part dragging behind thing or person. ●verb draw or be drawn along behind; (often + behind) walk wearily; follow trail of, pursue; be losing in contest; (usually + away, off) peter out; (of plant etc.) grow or hang over wall, along ground, etc.; hang loosely. □ **trailing edge** rear edge of aircraft's wing.

**trailer** noun set of extracts from film etc. shown in advance to advertise it; vehicle pulled by another; US caravan.

**train** ●verb (often + to do) teach (person etc.) specified skill, esp. by practice; undergo this process; bring or come to physical efficiency by exercise, diet, etc.; (often + up, along) guide growth of (plant); (usually as **trained** adjective) make (mind etc.) discerning through practice etc.; (often + on) point, aim. ●noun series of railway carriages or trucks drawn by engine; thing dragged along behind or forming back part of dress etc.; succession or series of people, things, events, etc.; group of followers, retinue. □ **in train** arranged, in preparation; **train-bearer** person holding up train of another's robe etc.; **train-spotter** person who collects numbers of railway locomotives. □ **trainee** /-ˈniː/ noun.

**trainer** noun person who trains horses, athletes, etc.; aircraft or simulator used to train pilots; soft running shoe.

**training** /ˈtreɪnɪŋ/ noun process of teaching or learning a skill etc.

**traipse** colloquial ●verb (**-sing**) tramp or trudge wearily. ●noun tedious journey on foot.

**trait** /treɪ/ noun characteristic.

**traitor** /ˈtreɪtə/ noun (feminine **traitress**) person guilty of betrayal or disloyalty. □ **traitorous** adjective.

**trajectory** /trə'dʒektərɪ/ *noun* ( *plural* **-ies**) path of object moving under given forces.

**tram** *noun* (also **tramcar**) electrically powered passenger road vehicle running on rails. □ **tramlines** rails for tram, *colloquial* either pair of parallel lines at edge of tennis etc. court.

**trammel** /'træm(ə)l/ ● *noun* (usually in *plural*) impediment, restraint; kind of fishing net. ● *verb* (**-ll-**; *US* **-l-**) hamper.

**tramp** ● *verb* walk heavily and firmly; go on walking expedition; walk laboriously across or along; (often + *down*) tread on, stamp on; live as tramp. ● *noun* itinerant vagrant or beggar; sound of person or people walking or marching; long walk; *slang derogatory* promiscuous woman.

**trample** /'træmp(ə)l/ *verb* (**-ling**) tread under foot; crush thus. □ **trample on** tread heavily on, treat roughly or with contempt.

**trampoline** /'træmpəli:n/ ● *noun* canvas sheet connected by springs to horizontal frame, used for acrobatic exercises. ● *verb* (**-ning**) use trampoline.

**trance** /trɑ:ns/ *noun* sleeplike state; hypnotic or cataleptic state; such state as supposedly entered into by medium; rapture, ecstasy.

**tranny** /'trænɪ/ *noun* ( *plural* **-ies**) *colloquial* transistor radio.

**tranquil** /'træŋkwɪl/ *adjective* serene, calm, undisturbed. □ **tranquillity** /-'kwɪl-/ *noun*; **tranquilly** *adverb*.

**tranquillize** *verb* (also **-ise**; *US* also **tranquilize**) (**-zing** or **-sing**) make tranquil, esp. by drug etc.

**tranquillizer** *noun* (also **-iser**; *US* also **tranquilizer**) drug used to diminish anxiety.

**trans-** *prefix* across, beyond; on or to other side of; through.

**transact** /træn'zækt/ *verb* perform or carry through (business etc.).

**transaction** /træn'zækʃ(ə)n/ *noun* piece of commercial or other dealing; transacting of business; (in *plural*) published reports of discussions and lectures at meetings of learned society.

**transatlantic** /trænzət'læntɪk/ *adjective* beyond or crossing the Atlantic; American; *US* European.

**transceiver** /træn'si:və/ *noun* combined radio transmitter and receiver.

**transcend** /træn'send/ *verb* go beyond or exceed limits of; excel, surpass.

**transcendent** *adjective* excelling, surpassing; transcending human experience; (esp. of God) existing apart from, or not subject to limitations of, material universe. □ **transcendence** *noun*; **transcendency** *noun*.

**transcendental** /trænsen'dent(ə)l/ *adjective* a priori, not based on experience, intuitively accepted; abstract, vague. □ **Transcendental Meditation** meditation seeking to induce detachment from problems, anxiety, etc.

**transcontinental** /trænzkɒntɪ'nent(ə)l/ *adjective* extending across a continent.

**transcribe** /træn'skraɪb/ *verb* (**-bing**) copy out; write out (notes etc.) in full; record for different broadcasting; *Music* adapt for different instrument etc. □ **transcriber** *noun*; **transcription** /-'skrɪp-/ *noun*.

**transcript** /'trænskrɪpt/ *noun* written copy.

**transducer** /trænz'dju:sə/ *noun* device for changing a non-electrical signal (e.g. pressure) into an electrical one (e.g. voltage).

**transept** /'trænsept/ *noun* part of cross-shaped church at right angles to nave; either arm of this.

**transfer** ● *verb* /træns'fɜ:/ (**-rr-**) convey, remove, or hand over (thing etc.); make over possession of (thing, right, etc.) to person; move, change, or be moved to another group, club, etc.; change from one station, route, etc. to another to continue journey; convey (design etc.) from one surface to another. ● *noun* /'trænsfɜ:/ transferring, being transferred; design etc. (to be) conveyed from one surface to another; football player etc. who is transferred; document effecting conveyance of property, a right, etc. □ **transferable** /-'fɜ:rəb(ə)l/ *adjective*; **transference** /'trænsfərəns/ *noun*.

**transfigure** /træns'fɪgə/ *verb* (**-ring**) change appearance of, make more elevated or idealized. □ **transfiguration** *noun*.

**transfix** /ˈtrænsˈfɪks/ *verb* paralyse with horror or astonishment; pierce with sharp implement or weapon.

**transform** /trænsˈfɔːm/ *verb* change form, appearance, character, etc. of, esp. considerably; change voltage etc. of (alternating current). □ **transformation** /-fəˈmeɪ-/ *noun*.

**transformer** *noun* apparatus for reducing or increasing voltage of alternating current.

**transfuse** /trænsˈfjuːz/ *verb* (**-sing**) transfer (blood or other liquid) into blood vessel to replace that lost; permeate. □ **transfusion** *noun*.

**transgress** /trænzˈgres/ *verb* infringe (law etc.); overstep (limit laid down); sin. □ **transgression** *noun*; **transgressor** *noun*.

**transient** /ˈtrænzɪənt/ *adjective* of short duration; passing. □ **transience** *noun*.

**transistor** /trænˈzɪstə/ *noun* semiconductor device capable of amplification and rectification; (in full **transistor radio**) portable radio using transistors.

**transistorize** *verb* (also **-ise**) (**-zing** or **-sing**) equip with transistors rather than valves.

**transit** /ˈtrænzɪt/ *noun* going; conveying; being conveyed; passage, route; apparent passage of heavenly body across meridian of place or across sun or planet. □ **in transit** (while) going or being conveyed.

**transition** /trænˈzɪʃ(ə)n/ *noun* passage or change from one place, state, condition, style, etc. to another. □ **transitional** *adjective*; **transitionally** *adverb*.

**transitive** /ˈtrænsɪtɪv/ *adjective* (of verb) requiring direct object expressed or understood.

**transitory** /ˈtrænzɪtərɪ/ *adjective* not lasting; brief, fleeting.

**translate** /trænsˈleɪt/ *verb* (**-ting**) (often + *into*) express sense of in another language or in another form; be translatable; interpret; move or change, esp. from one person, place, or condition to another. □ **translatable** *adjective*; **translation** *noun*; **translator** *noun*.

**transliterate** /trænzˈlɪtəreɪt/ *verb* (**-ting**) represent (word etc.) in closest corresponding characters of another script. □ **transliteration** *noun*.

**translucent** /trænzˈluːs(ə)nt/ *adjective* allowing light to pass through, semi-transparent. □ **translucence** *noun*.

**transmigrate** /trænzmaɪˈgreɪt/ *verb* (**-ting**) (of soul) pass into different body. □ **transmigration** *noun*.

**transmission** /trænzˈmɪʃ(ə)n/ *noun* transmitting, being transmitted; broadcast programme; device transmitting power from engine to axle in vehicle.

**transmit** /trænzˈmɪt/ *verb* (**-tt-**) pass or hand on, transfer; communicate or be medium for (ideas, emotions, etc.); allow (heat, light, sound, etc.) to pass through. □ **transmissible** *adjective*; **transmittable** *adjective*.

**transmitter** *noun* person or thing that transmits; equipment used to transmit radio etc. signals.

**transmogrify** /trænzˈmɒgrɪfaɪ/ *verb* (**-ies**, **-ied**) *jocular* transform, esp. in magical or surprising way. □ **transmogrification** *noun*.

**transmute** /trænzˈmjuːt/ *verb* (**-ting**) change form, nature, or substance of; *historical* change (base metals) into gold. □ **transmutation** *noun*.

**transom** /ˈtrænsəm/ *noun* horizontal bar in window or above door; (in full **transom window**) window above this.

**transparency** /trænsˈpærənsɪ/ *noun* (*plural* **-ies**) being transparent; picture (esp. photograph) to be viewed by light passing through it.

**transparent** /trænsˈpærənt/ *adjective* allowing light to pass through and giving maximum visibility possible; (of disguise, pretext, etc.) easily seen through; (of quality etc.) obvious; easily understood. □ **transparently** *adverb*.

**transpire** /trænsˈpaɪə/ *verb* (**-ring**) (of secret, fact, etc.) come to be known; happen; emit (vapour, moisture) or be emitted through pores of skin etc. □ **transpiration** /-spɪ-/ *noun*.

■ **Usage** The use of *transpire* to mean 'happen' is considered incorrect by some people.

**transplant** ● *verb* /trænsˈplɑːnt/ plant elsewhere; transfer (living tissue or organ) to another part of body or to another body. ● noun /'trænsplɑːnt/ transplanting of organ or tissue; thing transplanted. □ **transplantation** noun.

**transport** ● verb /træns'pɔːt/ take to another place; historical deport (criminal) to penal colony; (as **transported** adjective) (usually with + with) affected with strong emotion. ● noun /'trænspɔːt/ system of transporting, means of conveyance; ship, aircraft, etc. used to carry troops, military stores, etc.; (esp. in plural) vehement emotion. □ **transportable** /-'pɔːt-/ adjective.

**transportation** /trænspɔː'teɪʃ(ə)n/ noun (system of) conveying, being conveyed; US means of transport; historical deporting of criminals.

**transporter** noun vehicle used to transport other vehicles, heavy machinery, etc. □ **transporter bridge** bridge carrying vehicles etc. across water on suspended moving platform.

**transpose** /træns'pəʊz/ verb (**-sing**) cause (two or more things) to change places; change position of (thing) in series or (word(s)) in sentence; Music write or play in different key. □ **transposition** /-pə'zɪʃ(ə)n/ noun.

**transsexual** /træns'sekʃʊəl/ (also **transexual**) ● adjective having physical characteristics of one sex and psychological identification with the other. ● noun transsexual person; person who has had sex change.

**transship** /træns'ʃɪp/ verb (**-pp-**) transfer from one ship or conveyance to another. □ **transshipment** noun.

**transubstantiation** /trænsəbstænʃɪ'eɪʃ(ə)n/ noun conversion of Eucharistic elements wholly into body and blood of Christ.

**transuranic** /trænzjʊ'rænɪk/ adjective Chemistry (of element) having higher atomic number than uranium.

**transverse** /'trænzvɜːs/ adjective situated, arranged, or acting in crosswise direction. □ **transversely** adverb.

**transvestite** /trænz'vestaɪt/ noun man deriving pleasure from dressing in women's clothes. □ **transvestism** noun.

**trap** ● noun device, often baited, for catching animals; arrangement or trick to catch (out) unsuspecting person; device for releasing clay pigeon to

be shot at or greyhound at start of race etc.; curve in drainpipe etc. that fills with liquid and forms seal against return of gas; two-wheeled carriage; trapdoor; slang mouth. ● verb (**-pp-**) catch (as) in trap; catch (out) using trick etc.; furnish with traps. □ **trapdoor** door in floor, ceiling, or roof.

**trapeze** /trə'piːz/ noun crossbar suspended by ropes as swing for acrobatics etc.

**trapezium** /trə'piːzɪəm/ noun (plural **-s** or **-zia**) quadrilateral with only one pair of sides parallel; US trapezoid.

**trapezoid** /'træpɪzɔɪd/ noun quadrilateral with no sides parallel; US trapezium.

**trapper** noun person who traps wild animals, esp. for their fur.

**trappings** /'træpɪŋz/ plural noun ornamental accessories; (esp. ornamental) harness for horse.

**Trappist** /'træpɪst/ ● noun monk of order vowed to silence. ● adjective of this order.

**trash** ● noun esp. US worthless or waste stuff, rubbish; worthless person(s). ● verb slang wreck, vandalize. □ **trash can** US dustbin. □ **trashy** adjective (**-ier**, **-iest**).

**trauma** /'trɔːmə/ noun (plural **traumata** /-mətə/ or **-s**) emotional shock; physical injury, resulting shock. □ **traumatic** /-'mæt-/ adjective; **traumatize** verb (also **-ise**) (**-zing** or **-sing**).

**travail** /'træveɪl/ literary ● noun laborious effort; pangs of childbirth. ● verb make laborious effort, esp. in childbirth.

**travel** /'træv(ə)l/ ● verb (**-ll-**; US **-l-**) go from one place to another; make journey(s), esp. long or abroad; journey along or through, cover (distance); colloquial withstand long journey; act as commercial traveller; move or proceed as specified; colloquial move quickly; pass from point to point; (of machine or part) move or operate in specified way. ● noun travelling, esp. abroad; (often in plural) spell of this; range, rate, or mode of motion of part in machinery. □ **travel agency** agency making arrangements for travellers; **travelling salesman** commercial traveller; **travel-sick** nauseous owing to motion in travelling.

**travelled** adjective (US **traveled**) experienced in travelling.

**traveller** noun (US **traveler**) person who travels or is travelling; commercial traveller. □ **traveller's cheque** cheque for fixed amount, cashed on signature for equivalent in other currencies; **traveller's joy** wild clematis.

**travelogue** /'trævəlɒg/ noun film or illustrated lecture about travel.

**traverse** ● verb /trə'vɜːs/ (**-sing**) travel or lie across; consider or discuss whole extent of. ● noun /'trævəs/ sideways movement; traversing; thing that crosses another. □ **traversal** noun.

**travesty** /'trævɪstɪ/ ● noun (plural **-ies**) grotesque parody, ridiculous imitation. ● verb (**-ies, -ied**) make or be travesty of.

**trawl** ● verb fish with trawl or seine or in trawler; catch by trawling; (often + for, through) search thoroughly. ● noun trawling; (in full **trawl-net**) large widemouthed fishing net dragged by boat along sea bottom.

**trawler** noun boat used for trawling.

**tray** noun flat board with raised rim for carrying dishes etc.; shallow lidless box for papers or small articles, sometimes forming drawer in cabinet etc.

**treacherous** /'tretʃərəs/ adjective guilty of or involving violation of faith or betrayal of trust; not to be relied on, deceptive. □ **treacherously** adverb; **treachery** noun.

**treacle** /'triːk(ə)l/ noun syrup produced in refining sugar; molasses. □ **treacly** adjective.

**tread** /tred/ ● verb (past **trod**; past participle **trodden** or **trod**) (often + on) set one's foot down; walk on; (often + down, in, into) press (down) or crush with feet; perform (steps etc.) by walking. ● noun manner or sound of walking; top surface of step or stair; thick moulded part of vehicle tyre for gripping road; part of wheel or sole of shoe etc. that touches ground. □ **treadmill** device for producing motion by treading on steps on revolving cylinder, similar device used for exercise, monotonous routine work; **tread water** maintain upright position in water by moving feet and hands.

**treadle** /'tred(ə)l/ noun lever moved by foot and imparting motion to machine.

**treason** /'triːz(ə)n/ noun violation of allegiance to sovereign (e.g. plotting assassination) or state (e.g. helping enemy).

**treasonable** adjective involving or guilty of treason.

**treasure** /'treʒə/ ● noun precious metals or gems; hoard of them; accumulated wealth; thing valued for rarity, workmanship, associations, etc.; colloquial beloved or highly valued person. ● verb (**-ring**) value highly; (often + up) store up as valuable. □ **treasure hunt** search for treasure, game in which players seek hidden object; **treasure trove** treasure of unknown ownership found hidden.

**treasurer** noun person in charge of funds of society etc.

**treasury** /'treʒərɪ/ noun (plural **-ies**) place where treasure is kept; funds or revenue of state, institution, or society; (**Treasury**) (offices and officers of) department managing public revenue of a country. □ **Treasury bench** government front bench in parliament; **treasury bill** bill of exchange issued by government to raise money for temporary needs.

**treat** ● verb act, behave towards, or deal with in specified way; apply process or medical care or attention to; present or handle (subject) in literature or art; (often + to) provide with food, drink, or entertainment at one's own expense; (often + with) negotiate terms; (often + of) give exposition. ● noun event or circumstance that gives great pleasure; meal, entertainment, etc. designed to do this; (**a treat**) colloquial extremely good or well. □ **treatable** adjective.

**treatise** /'triːtɪz/ noun literary composition dealing esp. formally with subject.

**treatment** noun process or manner of behaving towards or dealing with person or thing; medical care or attention.

**treaty** /'triːtɪ/ noun (plural **-ies**) formal agreement between states; agreement between people, esp. for purchase of property.

**treble** /'treb(ə)l/ ● adjective threefold, triple; 3 times as much or many; high-pitched. ● noun treble quantity or thing; (voice of) boy soprano; high-pitched instrument; high-frequency sound of radio, record player, etc. ● *verb* (**-ling**) multiply or be multiplied by 3. □ **trebly** *adverb*.

**tree** ● *noun* perennial plant with woody self-supporting main stem and usually unbranched for some distance from ground; shaped piece of wood for various purposes; family tree. ● *verb* (**trees, treed**) cause to take refuge in tree. □ **treecreeper** small creeping bird feeding on insects in tree-bark; **tree-fern** large fern with upright woody stem; **tree surgeon** person who treats decayed trees in order to preserve them.

**trefoil** /ˈtrefɔɪl/ *noun* plant with leaves of 3 leaflets; 3-lobed ornamentation, esp. in tracery windows.

**trek** ● *verb* (**-kk-**) make arduous journey, esp. (*historical*) migrate or journey by oxwagon. ● *noun* such journey; each stage of it. □ **trekker** *noun*.

**trellis** /ˈtrelɪs/ *noun* (in full **trellis-work**) lattice of light wooden or metal bars, esp. support for climbing plants.

**tremble** /ˈtremb(ə)l/ ● *verb* (**-ling**) shake involuntarily with emotion, cold, etc.; be affected with extreme apprehension; quiver. ● *noun* trembling, quiver. □ **trembly** *adjective* (**-ier, -iest**).

**tremendous** /trɪˈmendəs/ *adjective* colloquial remarkable, considerable, excellent; awe-inspiring, overpowering. □ **tremendously** *adverb*.

**tremolo** /ˈtremələʊ/ *noun* (*plural* **-s**) tremulous effect in music.

**tremor** /ˈtremə/ *noun* shaking, quivering; thrill (of fear, exultation, etc.); (in full **earth tremor**) slight earthquake.

**tremulous** /ˈtremjʊləs/ *adjective* trembling. □ **tremulously** *adverb*.

**trench** ● *noun* deep ditch, esp. one dug by troops as shelter from enemy's fire. ● *verb* dig trench(es) in; make series of trenches (in) so as to bring lower soil to surface. □ **trench coat** lined or padded waterproof coat, loose belted raincoat.

**trenchant** /ˈtrentʃ(ə)nt/ *adjective* incisive, terse, vigorous. □ **trenchancy** *noun*; **trenchantly** *adverb*.

**trencher** /ˈtrentʃə/ *noun* historical wooden etc. platter for serving food.

**trencherman** /ˈtrentʃəmən/ *noun* eater.

**trend** ● *noun* general direction and tendency. ● *verb* turn away in specified direction; have general tendency. □ **trend-setter** person who leads the way in fashion etc.

**trendy** colloquial often derogatory ● *adjective* (**-ier, -iest**) fashionable. ● *noun* (*plural* **-ies**) fashionable person. □ **trendily** *adverb*; **trendiness** *noun*.

**trepan** /trɪˈpæn/ historical ● *noun* surgeon's cylindrical saw for making opening in skull. ● *verb* (**-nn-**) perforate (skull) with trepan.

**trepidation** /trepɪˈdeɪʃ(ə)n/ *noun* fear, anxiety.

**trespass** /ˈtrespəs/ ● *verb* (usually + *on, upon*) enter unlawfully (on another's land, property, etc.); encroach. ● *noun* act of trespassing; *archaic* sin, offence. □ **trespasser** *noun*.

**tress** *noun* lock of hair; (in *plural*) hair.

**trestle** /ˈtres(ə)l/ *noun* supporting structure for table etc. consisting of two frames fixed at an angle or hinged or of bar with two divergent pairs of legs; (in full **trestle-table**) table of board(s) laid on trestles; (in full **trestle-work**) open braced framework to support bridge etc.

**trews** *plural noun* close-fitting usually tartan trousers.

**tri-** *combining form* three (times).

**triad** /ˈtraɪæd/ *noun* group of 3 (esp. notes in chord). □ **triadic** /-ˈæd-/ *adjective*.

**trial** /ˈtraɪəl/ *noun* judicial examination and determination of issues between parties by judge with or without jury; test; trying thing or person; match held to select players for team; contest for horses, dogs, motorcycles, etc. □ **on trial** being tried in court of law, being tested; **trial run** preliminary operational test.

**triangle** /ˈtraɪæŋg(ə)l/ *noun* plane figure with 3 sides and angles; any 3 things not in straight line, with imaginary lines joining them; implement etc. of this shape; *Music* instrument of steel rod bent into triangle, struck with small steel rod; situation involving 3 people. □ **triangular** /-ˈæŋgjʊlə/ *adjective*.

**triangulate** /traɪˈæŋgjʊleɪt/ *verb* (**-ting**) divide (area) into triangles for surveying purposes. □ **triangulation** *noun*.

**triathlon** /traɪˈæθlən/ *noun* athletic contest of 3 events. □ **triathlete** *noun*.

**tribe** *noun* (in some societies) group of families under recognized leader with blood etc. ties and usually having common culture and dialect; any similar natural or political division; *usually derogatory* set or number of people, esp. of one profession etc. or family. □ **tribesman**, **tribeswoman** member of tribe. □ **tribal** *adjective*.

**tribulation** /trɪbjʊˈleɪʃ(ə)n/ *noun* great affliction.

**tribunal** /traɪˈbjuːn(ə)l/ *noun* board appointed to adjudicate on particular question; court of justice.

**tribune** /ˈtrɪbjuːn/ *noun* popular leader, demagogue; (in full **tribune of the people**) *Roman History* officer chosen by the people to protect their liberties.

**tributary** /ˈtrɪbjʊtəri/ ● *noun* (*plural* **-ies**) stream etc. that flows into larger stream or lake; *historical* person or state paying or subject to tribute. ● *adjective* that is a tributary.

**tribute** /ˈtrɪbjuːt/ *noun* thing said or done or given as mark of respect or affection etc.; (+ *to*) indication of (some praiseworthy quality); *historical* periodic payment by one state or ruler to another, obligation to pay this.

**trice** *noun* □ **in a trice** in an instant.

**triceps** /ˈtraɪseps/ *noun* muscle (esp. in upper arm) with 3 points of attachment.

**triceratops** /traɪˈserətɒps/ *noun* large dinosaur with 3 horns.

**trichinosis** /trɪkɪˈnəʊsɪs/ *noun* disease caused by hairlike worms.

**trichology** /trɪˈkɒlədʒɪ/ *noun* study of hair. □ **trichologist** *noun*.

**trichromatic** /traɪkrəˈmætɪk/ *adjective* 3-coloured.

**trick** ● *noun* thing done to deceive or outwit; illusion; knack; feat of skill or dexterity; unusual action learned by animal; foolish or discreditable act; hoax, joke; idiosyncrasy; cards played in one round, point gained in this. ● *verb* deceive by trick; swindle; (+ *into*) cause to do something by trickery; take by surprise.

**trickery** *noun* deception, use of tricks.

**trickle** /ˈtrɪk(ə)l/ ● *verb* (**-ling**) (cause to) flow in drops or small stream; come or go slowly or gradually. ● *noun* trickling flow. □ **trickle charger** *Electricity* device for slow continuous charging of battery.

**trickster** /ˈtrɪkstə/ *noun* deceiver, rogue.

**tricky** *adjective* (**-ier**, **-iest**) requiring care and adroitness; crafty, deceitful. □ **trickily** *adverb*; **trickiness** *noun*.

**tricolour** /ˈtrɪkələ/ *noun* (*US* **tricolor**) flag of 3 colours, esp. French national flag.

**tricot** /ˈtrɪkəʊ/ *noun* knitted fabric.

**tricycle** /ˈtraɪsɪk(ə)l/ *noun* 3-wheeled pedal-driven vehicle.

**trident** /ˈtraɪd(ə)nt/ *noun* 3-pronged spear.

**Tridentine** /traɪˈdentaɪn/ *adjective* of traditional RC orthodoxy.

**triennial** /traɪˈenɪəl/ *adjective* lasting 3 years; recurring every 3 years.

**trifle** /ˈtraɪf(ə)l/ ● *noun* thing of slight value or importance; small amount; (**a trifle**) somewhat; dessert of sponge cakes with custard, cream, etc. ● *verb* (**-ling**) talk or act frivolously; (+ *with*) treat frivolously, flirt heartlessly with.

**trifling** *adjective* unimportant; frivolous.

**trigger** /ˈtrɪgə/ ● *noun* movable device for releasing spring or catch and so setting off mechanism, esp. of gun; event etc. that sets off chain reaction. ● *verb* (often + *off*) set (action, process) in motion, precipitate. □ **trigger-happy** apt to shoot on slight provocation.

**trigonometry** /trɪgəˈnɒmətrɪ/ *noun* branch of mathematics dealing with relations of sides and angles of triangles, and with certain functions of angles. □ **trigonometric** /-nəˈmet-/ *adjective*; **trigonometrical** /-nəˈmet-/ *adjective*.

**trike** *noun colloquial* tricycle.

**trilateral** /traɪˈlætər(ə)l/ *adjective* of, on, or with 3 sides; involving 3 parties.

**trilby** /ˈtrɪlbɪ/ *noun* (*plural* **-ies**) soft felt hat with narrow brim and indented crown.

**trilingual** /traɪˈlɪŋgw(ə)l/ *adjective* speaking or in 3 languages.

**trill** ● *noun* quavering sound, esp. quick alternation of notes; bird's warbling; pronunciation of letter *r* with vibrating tongue. ● *verb* produce trill; warble (song); pronounce (*r* etc.) with trill.

**trillion** /ˈtrɪljən/ *noun* (*plural* same) million million; million million million;

**(trillions)** *colloquial* large number. □ **trillionth** *adjective & noun*.

**trilobite** /ˈtraɪləbaɪt/ *noun* kind of fossil crustacean.

**trilogy** /ˈtrɪlədʒi/ *noun* (*plural* **-ies**) set of 3 related novels, plays, operas, etc.

**trim** ● *verb* (**-mm-**) make neat or tidy or of required size or shape, esp. by cutting away irregular or unwanted parts; (+ *off*, *away*) cut off; ornament; adjust balance of (ship, aircraft) by arranging cargo etc.; arrange (sails) to suit wind. ● *noun* state of readiness or fitness; ornament, decorative material; trimming of hair etc. ● *adjective* (**-mm-**) neat; in good order, well arranged or equipped.

**trimaran** /ˈtraɪmərӕn/ *noun* vessel like catamaran, with 3 hulls side by side.

**trimming** *noun* ornamental addition to dress, hat, etc.; (in *plural*) *colloquial* usual accompaniments.

**trinitrotoluene** /tramaɪtrəˈtɒljuːn/ *noun* (also **trinitrotoluol** /-ˈtɒljʊɒl/) a high explosive.

**trinity** /ˈtrɪnɪti/ *noun* (*plural* **-ies**) being 3; group of 3; (**the Trinity**) the 3 persons of the Christian Godhead. □ **Trinity Sunday** Sunday after Whit Sunday.

**trinket** /ˈtrɪŋkɪt/ *noun* trifling ornament, esp. piece of jewellery.

**trio** /ˈtriːəʊ/ *noun* (*plural* **-s**) group of 3; musical composition for 3 performers; the performers.

**trip** ● *verb* (**-pp-**) (often + *up*) (cause to) stumble, esp. by catching foot; (+ *up*) (cause to) commit fault or blunder; run lightly; make excursion to place; operate (mechanism) suddenly by knocking aside catch etc.; *slang* have drug-induced hallucinatory experience. ● *noun* journey or excursion, esp. for pleasure; stumble, blunder, tripping, being tripped up; nimble step; *slang* drug-induced hallucinatory experience; device for tripping mechanism etc. □ **trip-wire** wire stretched close to ground to operate alarm etc. if disturbed.

**tripartite** /traɪˈpɑːtaɪt/ *adjective* consisting of 3 parts; shared by or involving 3 parties.

**tripe** *noun* first or second stomach of ruminant, esp. ox, as food; *colloquial* nonsense, rubbish.

**triple** /ˈtrɪp(ə)l/ ● *adjective* of 3 parts; threefold; involving 3 parties; 3 times as much or as many. ● *noun* threefold number or amount; set of 3. ● *verb* (**-ling**) multiply by 3. □ **triple crown** winning of 3 important sporting events; **triple jump** athletic contest comprising hop, step, and jump. □ **triply** *adverb*.

**triplet** /ˈtrɪplɪt/ *noun* each of 3 children or animals born at one birth; set of 3 things, esp. of notes played in time of two.

**triplex** /ˈtrɪpleks/ *adjective* triple, threefold.

**triplicate** ● *adjective* /ˈtrɪplɪkət/ existing in 3 examples or copies; having 3 corresponding parts; tripled. ● *noun* /ˈtrɪplɪkət/ each of 3 copies or corresponding parts. ● *verb* (**-ting**) /ˈtrɪplɪkeɪt/ make in 3 copies; multiply by 3. □ **triplication** *noun*.

**tripod** /ˈtraɪpɒd/ *noun* 3-legged or 3-footed stand, stool, table, or utensil.

**tripos** /ˈtraɪpɒs/ *noun* honours exam for primary degree at Cambridge University.

**tripper** *noun* person who goes on pleasure trip.

**triptych** /ˈtrɪptɪk/ *noun* picture etc. with 3 panels usually hinged vertically together.

**trireme** /ˈtraɪriːm/ *noun* ancient Greek warship, with 3 files of oarsmen on each side.

**trisect** /traɪˈsekt/ *verb* divide into 3 (usually equal) parts. □ **trisection** *noun*.

**trite** *adjective* hackneyed. □ **tritely** *adverb*; **triteness** *noun*.

**tritium** /ˈtrɪtɪəm/ *noun* radioactive isotope of hydrogen with mass about 3 times that of ordinary hydrogen.

**triumph** /ˈtraɪʌmf/ ● *noun* state of victory or success; great success or achievement; supreme example; joy at success. ● *verb* gain victory, be successful; *Roman History* ride in triumph; (often + *over*) exult.

**triumphal** /traɪˈʌmf(ə)l/ *adjective* of, used in, or celebrating a triumph.

■ **Usage** *Triumphal*, as in *triumphal arch*, should not be confused with *triumphant*.

**triumphant** /traɪˈʌmf(ə)nt/ *adjective* victorious, successful; exultant. □ **triumphantly** *adverb*.

■ **Usage** See note at TRIUMPHAL.

**triumvirate** /traɪˈʌmvərət/ *noun* ruling group of 3 men.

**trivalent** /traɪˈveɪlənt/ *adjective* Chemistry having a valency of 3. □ **trivalency** *noun.*

**trivet** /ˈtrɪvɪt/ *noun* iron tripod or bracket for pot or kettle to stand on.

**trivia** /ˈtrɪvɪə/ *plural noun* trifles, trivialities.

**trivial** /ˈtrɪvɪəl/ *adjective* of small value or importance; concerned only with trivial things. □ **triviality** /-ˈæl-/ *noun* (*plural* **-ies**); **trivially** *adverb.*

**trivialize** *verb* (also **-ise**) (**-zing** or **-sing**) make or treat as trivial, minimize. □ **trivialization** *noun.*

**trochee** /ˈtrəʊkiː/ *noun* metrical foot of one long followed by one short syllable. □ **trochaic** /trəˈkeɪɪk/ *adjective.*

**trod** *past & past participle* of TREAD.

**trodden** *past participle* of TREAD.

**troglodyte** /ˈtrɒɡlədaɪt/ *noun* cave dweller.

**troika** /ˈtrɔɪkə/ *noun* Russian vehicle drawn by 3 horses abreast.

**Trojan** /ˈtrəʊdʒ(ə)n/ ● *adjective* of ancient Troy. ● *noun* native or inhabitant of ancient Troy; person who works, fights, etc. courageously. □ **Trojan Horse** person or device planted to bring about enemy's downfall.

**troll**[1] /trəʊl/ *noun* supernatural cave-dwelling giant or dwarf in Scandinavian mythology.

**troll**[2] /trəʊl/ *verb* fish by drawing bait along in water.

**trolley** /ˈtrɒlɪ/ *noun* (*plural* **-s**) table, stand, or basket on wheels or castors for serving food, carrying luggage etc., gathering purchases in supermarket, etc.; low truck running along rails; (in full **trolley-wheel**) wheel attached to pole etc. for collecting current from overhead electric wire to drive vehicle. □ **trolley bus** electric bus using trolley-wheel.

**trollop** /ˈtrɒləp/ *noun* disreputable girl or woman.

**trombone** /trɒmˈbəʊn/ *noun* brass wind instrument with sliding tube. □ **trombonist** *noun.*

**troop** /truːp/ ● *noun* assembled company, assemblage of people or animals; (in *plural*) soldiers, armed forces; cavalry unit commanded by captain; artillery unit; group of 3 or more Scout patrols. ● *verb* (+ *in, out, off,* etc.) come together or move in a troop. □ **troop the colour** transfer flag ceremonially at public mounting of garrison guards; **troop-ship** ship for transporting troops.

**trooper** *noun* private soldier in cavalry or armoured unit; *Australian & US* mounted or State police officer; cavalry horse; troop-ship.

**trope** *noun* figurative use of word.

**trophy** /ˈtrəʊfɪ/ *noun* (*plural* **-ies**) cup etc. as prize in contest; memento of any success.

**tropic** /ˈtrɒpɪk/ *noun* parallel of latitude 23° 27′ N. (**tropic of Cancer**) or S. (**tropic of Capricorn**) of Equator; (**the Tropics**) region lying between these.

**tropical** *adjective* of or typical of the Tropics.

**troposphere** /ˈtrɒpəsfɪə/ *noun* layer of atmosphere extending about 8 km upwards from earth's surface.

**trot** ● *verb* (**-tt-**) (of person) run at moderate pace; (of horse) proceed at steady pace faster than walk; traverse (distance) thus. ● *noun* action or exercise of trotting; (**the trots**) *slang* diarrhoea. □ **on the trot** *colloquial* in succession, continually busy; **trot out** *colloquial* introduce (opinion etc.) repeatedly or tediously.

**troth** /trəʊθ/ *noun archaic* faith, fidelity; truth.

**trotter** *noun* (usually in *plural*) animal's foot, esp. as food; horse bred or trained for trotting.

**troubadour** /ˈtruːbədʊə/ *noun* singer, poet; French medieval poet singing of love.

**trouble** /ˈtrʌb(ə)l/ ● *noun* difficulty, distress, vexation, affliction; inconvenience, unpleasant exertion; cause of this; perceived failing; malfunction; disturbance; (in *plural*) public disturbances. ● *verb* (**-ling**) cause distress to, disturb; be disturbed; afflict, cause pain etc. to; subject to or be subjected to inconvenience or unpleasant exertion. □ **in trouble** likely to incur censure or punishment, *colloquial* pregnant and unmarried; **troublemaker** person who habitually causes trouble; **troubleshooter** mediator in dispute, person who traces and corrects faults in machinery etc.

**troublesome** *adjective* causing trouble, annoying.

**trough** /trɒf/ *noun* long narrow open receptacle for water, animal feed, etc.; channel or hollow like this; elongated region of low barometric pressure.

**trounce** /traʊns/ *verb* (**-cing**) inflict severe defeat, beating, or punishment on.

**troupe** /truːp/ *noun* company of actors, acrobats, etc.

**trouper** *noun* member of theatrical troupe; staunch colleague.

**trousers** /ˈtraʊzəz/ *plural noun* two-legged outer garment from waist usually to ankles. □ **trouser suit** woman's suit of trousers and jacket.

**trousseau** /ˈtruːsəʊ/ *noun* (*plural* **-s** or **-x** /-z/) bride's collection of clothes etc.

**trout** /traʊt/ *noun* (*plural* same or **-s**) fish related to salmon.

**trove** /trəʊv/ *noun* treasure trove.

**trowel** /ˈtraʊəl/ *noun* flat-bladed tool for spreading mortar etc.; scoop for lifting small plants or earth.

**troy** *noun* (in full **troy weight**) system of weights used for precious metals etc.

**truant** /ˈtruːənt/ ● *noun* child who does not attend school; person who avoids work etc. ● *adjective* idle, wandering. ● *verb* (also **play truant**) be truant. □ **truancy** *noun* (*plural* **-ies**).

**truce** *noun* temporary agreement to cease hostilities.

**truck**¹ *noun* lorry; open railway wagon for freight.

**truck**² *noun* □ **have no truck with** avoid dealing with.

**trucker** *noun* *esp. US* long-distance lorry driver.

**truckle** /ˈtrʌk(ə)l/ ● *noun* (in full **truckle-bed**) low bed on wheels, stored under another. ● *verb* (**-ling**) (+ *to*) submit obsequiously to.

**truculent** /ˈtrʌkjʊlənt/ *adjective* aggressively defiant. □ **truculence** *noun*; **truculently** *adverb*.

**trudge** ● *verb* (**-ging**) walk laboriously; traverse (distance) thus. ● *noun* trudging walk.

**true** ● *adjective* (**-r, -st**) in accordance with fact or reality; genuine; loyal, faithful; (+ *to*) accurately conforming to (type, standard); correctly positioned or balanced, level; exact, accurate. ● *adverb* *archaic* truly; accurately; without variation. □ **out of true** out of alignment.

**truffle** /ˈtrʌf(ə)l/ *noun* rich-flavoured underground fungus; sweet made of soft chocolate mixture.

**trug** *noun* shallow oblong garden-basket.

**truism** /ˈtruːɪz(ə)m/ *noun* self-evident or hackneyed truth.

**truly** /ˈtruːlɪ/ *adverb* sincerely; really; loyally; accurately. □ **Yours truly** *written before signature at end of informal letter; jocular* I, me.

**trump**¹ ● *noun* playing card(s) of suit temporarily ranking above others; (in *plural*) this suit; *colloquial* helpful or excellent person. ● *verb* defeat with trump; *colloquial* outdo. □ **come** or **turn up trumps** *colloquial* turn out well or successfully, be extremely successful or helpful; **trump card** card belonging to, or turned up to determine, trump suit, *colloquial* valuable resource; **trump up** fabricate, invent (accusation, excuse, etc.).

**trump**² *noun* *archaic* trumpet-blast.

**trumpery** /ˈtrʌmpərɪ/ ● *noun* worthless finery; rubbish. ● *adjective* showy but worthless, trashy, shallow.

**trumpet** /ˈtrʌmpɪt/ ● *noun* brass instrument with flared mouth and bright penetrating tone; trumpet-shaped thing; sound (as) of trumpet. ● *verb* (**-t-**) blow trumpet; (of elephant) make trumpet; proclaim loudly. □ **trumpeter** *noun*.

**truncate** /trʌŋˈkeɪt/ *verb* (**-ting**) cut off top or end of; shorten. □ **truncation** *noun*.

**truncheon** /ˈtrʌntʃ(ə)n/ *noun* short club carried by police officer.

**trundle** /ˈtrʌnd(ə)l/ *verb* (**-ling**) roll or move, esp. heavily or noisily.

**trunk** *noun* main stem of tree; body without limbs or head; large luggage-box with hinged lid; *US* boot of car;

elephant's elongated prehensile nose; (in *plural*) men's close-fitting shorts worn for swimming etc. □ **trunk call** long-distance telephone call; **trunk line** main line of railway, telephone system, etc.; **trunk road** important main road.

**truss** ●*noun* framework supporting roof, bridge, etc.; supporting surgical appliance for hernia etc. sufferers; bundle of hay or straw; cluster of flowers or fruit. ●*verb* tie up (fowl) for cooking; (often + *up*) tie (person) with arms to sides; support with truss(es).

**trust** ●*noun* firm belief that a person or thing may be relied on; confident expectation; responsibility; *Law* arrangement involving trustees, property so held, group of trustees; association of companies for reducing competition. ●*verb* place trust in, believe in, rely on; (+ *with*) give (person) charge of; (often + *that*) hope earnestly that a thing will take place; (+ *to*) consign (thing) to (person); (+ *in*) place reliance in; (+ *to*) place (esp. undue) reliance on. □ **in trust** (of property) managed by person(s) on behalf of another; **trustworthy** deserving of trust, reliable. □ **trustful** *adjective*.

**trustee** /trʌsˈtiː/ *noun* person or member of board managing property in trust with legal obligation to administer it solely for purposes specified. □ **trusteeship** *noun*.

**trusting** *adjective* having trust or confidence. □ **trustingly** *adverb*.

**trusty** ●*adjective* (**-ier**, **-iest**) *archaic or jocular* trustworthy. ●*noun* (*plural* **-ies**) prisoner given special privileges for good behaviour.

**truth** /truːθ/ *noun* (*plural* **truths** /truːðz/) quality or state of being true; what is true.

**truthful** *adjective* habitually speaking the truth; (of story etc.) true. □ **truthfully** *adverb*; **truthfulness** *noun*.

**try** ●*verb* (**-ies**, **-ied**) attempt, endeavour; test (quality), test by use or experiment test qualities of; make severe demands on; examine effectiveness of for purpose; ascertain state of fastening of (door etc.); investigate and decide (case, issue) judicially, (often + *for*) subject (person) to trial; (+ *for*) apply or compete for, seek to attain. ●*noun*

(*plural* **-ies**) attempt; *Rugby* touching-down of ball by player behind opposing goal line, scoring points and entitling player's side to a kick at goal. □ **try one's hand** (often + *at*) have attempt; **try it on** *colloquial* test how much unreasonable behaviour etc. will be tolerated; **try on** put (clothes etc.) on to test fit etc.; **try-on** *colloquial* act of trying it on or trying on clothes etc., attempt to deceive; **try out** put to the test, test thoroughly; **try-out** experimental test.

**trying** *adjective* annoying, exasperating; hard to bear.

**tryst** /trɪst/ *noun archaic* meeting, esp. of lovers.

**tsar** /zɑː/ *noun* (also **czar**) (*feminine* **tsarina** /-ˈriːnə/) *historical* emperor of Russia. □ **tsarist** *noun & adjective*.

**tsetse** /ˈtsetsɪ/ *noun* African fly feeding on blood and transmitting disease.

**tsp.** *abbreviation* (*plural* **tsps.**) teaspoonful.

**TT** *abbreviation* teetotal(ler); tuberculin-tested; Tourist Trophy.

**tub** ●*noun* open flat-bottomed usually round vessel; tub-shaped (usually plastic) carton; *colloquial* bath; *colloquial* clumsy slow boat. ●*verb* (**-bb-**) plant, bathe, or wash in tub. □ **tub-thumper** *colloquial* ranting preacher or orator.

**tuba** /ˈtjuːbə/ *noun* (*plural* **-s**) low-pitched brass wind instrument.

**tubby** /ˈtʌbɪ/ *adjective* (**-ier**, **-iest**) short and fat. □ **tubbiness** *noun*.

**tube** ●*noun* long hollow cylinder; soft metal or plastic cylinder sealed at one end; hollow cylindrical bodily organ; *colloquial* London underground; cathode ray tube, esp. in television; (**the tube**) *esp. US colloquial* television; *US* thermionic valve; inner tube. ●*verb* (**-bing**) equip with tubes; enclose in tube.

**tuber** /ˈtjuːbə/ *noun* short thick rounded root or underground stem of plant.

**tubercle** /ˈtjuːbək(ə)l/ *noun* small rounded swelling on part or in organ of body, esp. as characteristic of tuberculosis. □ **tubercle bacillus** bacterium causing tuberculosis. □ **tuberculous** /-ˈbɜːkjʊləs/ *adjective*.

**tubercular** /tjʊˈbɜːkjʊlə/ *adjective* of or affected with tuberculosis.

**tuberculin** /tjʊˈbɜːkjʊlɪn/ *noun* preparation from cultures of tubercle bacillus used in diagnosis and treatment of tuberculosis. □ **tuberculin-tested** (of milk) from cows shown to be free of tuberculosis.

**tuberculosis** /tjʊbɜːkjuːˈləʊsɪs/ noun infectious bacterial disease marked by tubercles, esp. in lungs.

**tuberose** /ˈtjuːbərəʊz/ noun plant with creamy-white fragrant flowers.

**tuberous** /ˈtjuːbərəs/ adjective having tubers; of or like a tuber.

**tubing** noun length of tube; quantity of or material for tubes.

**tubular** /ˈtjuːbjʊlə/ adjective tube-shaped; having or consisting of tubes.

**TUC** abbreviation Trades Union Congress.

**tuck** ● verb (often + in, up) draw, fold, or turn outer or end parts of (cloth, clothes, etc.) close together, push in edges of bedclothes around (person); draw together into small space; stow (thing) away in specified place or way; make stitched fold in (cloth etc.). ● noun flattened fold sewn in garment etc.; colloquial food, esp. cakes and sweets. □ **tuck in** colloquial eat heartily; **tuck shop** shop selling sweets etc. to schoolchildren.

**tucker** /ˈtʌkə/ ● noun Australian & NZ slang food. ● verb (esp. in passive; often + out) US & Australian colloquial tire.

**Tudor** /ˈtjuːdə/ adjective of royal family of England from Henry VII to Elizabeth I; of this period (1485–1603); of the architectural style of this period.

**Tues.** abbreviation (also **Tue.**) Tuesday.

**Tuesday** /ˈtjuːzdeɪ/ noun day of week following Monday.

**tufa** /ˈtjuːfə/ noun porous rock formed round mineral springs; tuff.

**tuff** noun rock formed from volcanic ash.

**tuft** noun bunch of threads, grass, feathers, hair, etc. held or growing together at base. □ **tufted** adjective; **tufty** adjective.

**tug** ● verb (-gg-) (often + at) pull hard or violently; tow (vessel) by tugboat. ● noun hard, violent, or jerky pull; sudden emotion; (also **tugboat**) small powerful boat for towing ships. □ **tug of war** trial of strength between two sides pulling opposite ways on a rope.

**tuition** /tjuːˈɪʃ(ə)n/ noun teaching; fee for this.

**tulip** /ˈtjuːlɪp/ noun bulbous spring-flowering plant with showy cup-shaped flowers; its flower. □ **tulip-tree** tree with tulip-like flowers.

**tulle** /tjuːl/ noun soft fine silk etc. net for veils and dresses.

**tumble** /ˈtʌmb(ə)l/ ● verb (-ling) (cause to) fall suddenly or headlong; fall rapidly in amount etc.; roll, toss; move or rush in headlong or blundering fashion; (often + to) colloquial grasp meaning of; fling or push roughly or carelessly; perform acrobatic feats, esp. somersaults; rumple, disarrange. ● noun fall; somersault or other acrobatic feat. □ **tumbledown** falling or fallen into ruin, dilapidated; **tumble-drier, -dryer** machine for drying washing in heated rotating drum; **tumble-dry** verb.

**tumbler** noun drinking glass without handle or foot; acrobat; part of mechanism of lock.

**tumbrel** /ˈtʌmbr(ə)l/ noun (also **tumbril**) historical open cart in which condemned people were carried to guillotine during French Revolution.

**tumescent** /tjʊˈmes(ə)nt/ adjective swelling. □ **tumescence** noun.

**tumid** /ˈtjuːmɪd/ adjective swollen, inflated; pompous. □ **tumidity** /-ˈmɪd-/ noun.

**tummy** /ˈtʌmɪ/ noun (plural **-ies**) colloquial stomach.

**tumour** /ˈtjuːmə/ noun (US **tumor**) abnormal or morbid swelling in the body.

**tumult** /ˈtjuːmʌlt/ noun uproar, din; angry demonstration by mob, riot; conflict of emotions etc. □ **tumultuous** /tjʊˈmʌltʃʊəs/ adjective.

**tumulus** /ˈtjuːmjʊləs/ noun (plural **-li** /-laɪ/) ancient burial mound.

**tun** noun large cask; brewer's fermenting-vat.

**tuna** /ˈtjuːnə/ noun (plural same or **-s**) large edible marine fish; (in full **tuna-fish**) its flesh as food.

**tundra** /ˈtʌndrə/ noun vast level treeless Arctic region with permafrost.

**tune** ● noun melody; correct pitch or intonation. ● verb (-ning) put (musical instrument) in tune; (often + in) adjust (radio etc.) to desired frequency etc.; adjust (engine etc.) to run smoothly. □ **change one's tune** voice different opinion, become more respectful; **tune up** bring instrument(s) to proper pitch; **tuning-fork** two-pronged steel fork giving particular note when struck.

**tuneful** *adjective* melodious, musical. □ **tunefully** *adverb*.

**tuneless** *adjective* unmelodious, unmusical. □ **tunelessly** *adverb*.

**tuner** *noun* person who tunes pianos etc.; part of radio or television receiver for tuning.

**tungsten** /ˈtʌŋst(ə)n/ *noun* heavy steel-grey metallic element.

**tunic** /ˈtjuːnɪk/ *noun* close-fitting short coat of police or military uniform; loose often sleeveless garment.

**tunnel** /ˈtʌn(ə)l/ ●*noun* underground passage dug through hill, or under river, road, etc.; underground passage dug by animal. ●*verb* (**-ll-**; *US* **-l-**) (+ *through, into*) make tunnel through (hill etc.); make (one's way) so. □ **tunnel vision** restricted vision, *colloquial* inability to grasp wider implications of situation etc.

**tunny** /ˈtʌnɪ/ *noun* (*plural* same or **-ies**) tuna.

**tuppence** = TWOPENCE.

**tuppenny** = TWOPENNY.

**Tupperware** /ˈtʌpəweə/ *noun proprietary term* range of plastic containers for food.

**turban** /ˈtɜːbən/ *noun* man's headdress of fabric wound round cap or head, worn esp. by Muslims and Sikhs; woman's hat resembling this.

**turbid** /ˈtɜːbɪd/ *adjective* muddy, thick, not clear; confused, disordered. □ **turbidity** /-ˈbɪd-/ *noun*.

■ **Usage** *Turbid* is sometimes confused with *turgid*.

**turbine** /ˈtɜːbaɪn/ *noun* rotary motor driven by flow of water, gas, etc.

**turbo-** *combining form* turbine.

**turbocharger** /ˈtɜːbəʊtʃɑːdʒə/ *noun* (also **turbo**) supercharger driven by turbine powered by engine's exhaust gases.

**turbojet** /ˈtɜːbəʊdʒet/ *noun* jet engine in which jet also operates turbine-driven air-compressor; aircraft with this.

**turboprop** /ˈtɜːbəʊprɒp/ *noun* jet engine in which turbine is used as in turbojet

and also to drive propeller; aircraft with this.

**turbot** /ˈtɜːbət/ *noun* (*plural* same or **-s**) large flatfish valued as food.

**turbulent** /ˈtɜːbjʊlənt/ *adjective* disturbed, in commotion; (of flow of air etc.) varying irregularly; riotous, restless. □ **turbulence** *noun*, **turbulently** *adverb*.

**tureen** /tjʊəˈriːn/ *noun* deep covered dish for soup.

**turf** ●*noun* (*plural* **-s** or **turves**) short grass with surface earth bound together by its roots; piece of this cut from ground; slab of peat for fuel; (**the turf**) horse racing, racecourse. ●*verb* (+ *out*) *colloquial* expel, eject. □ **turf accountant** bookmaker. □ **turfy** *adjective*.

**turgid** /ˈtɜːdʒɪd/ *adjective* swollen, inflated; (of language) pompous, bombastic. □ **turgidity** /-ˈdʒɪd-/ *noun*.

■ **Usage** *Turgid* is sometimes confused with *turbid*.

**Turk** *noun* native or national of Turkey.

**turkey** /ˈtɜːkɪ/ *noun* (*plural* **-s**) large originally American bird bred for food; its flesh. □ **turkeycock** male turkey.

**Turkish** ●*adjective* of Turkey. ●*noun* language of Turkey. □ **Turkish bath** hot-air or steam bath followed by massage etc., (in *singular* or *plural*) building for this; **Turkish carpet** thick-piled woollen carpet with bold design; **Turkish delight** kind of gelatinous sweet; **Turkish towel** one made of cotton terry.

**turmeric** /ˈtɜːmərɪk/ *noun* E. Indian plant of ginger family; its rhizome powdered as flavouring or dye.

**turmoil** /ˈtɜːmɔɪl/ *noun* violent confusion; din and bustle.

**turn** ●*verb* move around point or axis, give or receive rotary motion; change from one side to another, invert, reverse; give new direction to, take new direction, aim in certain way; (+ *into*) change in nature, form, or condition to; (+ *to*) set about, have recourse to, consider next; become; (+ *against*) make or become hostile to; (+ *on, upon*) face hostilely; change colour; (of milk) become sour; (of stomach) be nauseated; cause (milk) to become sour or (stomach) to be nauseated; (of head) become giddy; translate; move to other side of, go round; pass age or time of; ( + *on*) depend on; send, put, cause to go; remake (sheet, shirt collar, etc.); make (profit); divert (bullet); shape (object) in lathe; give (esp. elegant) form to. ● *noun* turning, rotary motion; changed or change of direction or tendency; point of turning or change; turning of road; change of direction of tide; change in course of events; tendency, formation; opportunity, obligation, etc. that comes successively to each of several people etc.; short walk or ride; short performance on stage, in circus, etc.; service of specified kind; purpose; *colloquial* momentary nervous shock; *Music* ornament of principal note with those above and below it. □ **in turn** in succession; **take (it in) turns** act alternately; **turncoat** person who changes sides; **turn down** reject, reduce volume or strength of (sound, heat, etc.) by turning knob, fold down; **turn in** hand in, achieve, *colloquial* go to bed, incline inwards; **turnkey** *archaic* jailer; **turn off** stop flow or working of by means of tap, switch, etc., enter side road, *colloquial* cause to lose interest; **turn on** start flow or working of by means of tap, switch, etc., *colloquial* arouse, esp. sexually; **turn out** expel, extinguish (light etc.), dress, equip, produce (goods etc.), empty, clean out, (cause to) assemble, prove to be the case, result, (usually + *to be*) be found; **turnout** number of people who attend meeting etc., equipage; **turn over** reverse position of, cause (engine etc.) to run, (of engine) start running, consider thoroughly, ( + *to*) transfer care or conduct of (person, thing) to (person); **turnover** turning over, gross amount of money taken in business, rate of sale and replacement of goods, rate at which people enter and leave employment etc., small pie with pastry folded over filling; **turnpike** *US & historical* road on which toll is charged; **turnstile** revolving gate with arms; **turntable** circular revolving plate or platform; **turn to** begin work; **turn turtle** capsize; **turn up** increase (volume or strength of) by turning knob etc.,

discover, reveal, be found, happen, arrive, shorten (garment etc.), fold over or upwards; **turn-up** turned-up end of trouser leg, *colloquial* unexpected happening.

**turner** *noun* lathe-worker.

**turnery** *noun* objects made on lathe; work with lathe.

**turning** *noun* road branching off another, place where this occurs; use of lathe; (in *plural*) chips or shavings from this. □ **turning circle** smallest circle in which vehicle can turn; **turning point** point at which decisive change occurs.

**turnip** /'tɜːnɪp/ *noun* plant with globular root; its root as vegetable.

**turpentine** /'tɜːpəntaɪn/ *noun* resin from any of various trees; (in full **oil of turpentine**) volatile inflammable oil distilled from turpentine and used in mixing paints etc.

**turpitude** /'tɜːpɪtjuːd/ *noun formal* depravity, wickedness.

**turps** *noun colloquial* oil of turpentine.

**turquoise** /'tɜːkwɔɪz/ ● *noun* opaque semiprecious stone, usually greenish-blue; this colour. ● *adjective* of this colour.

**turret** /'tʌrɪt/ *noun* small tower, esp. decorating building; usually revolving armoured structure for gun and gunners on ship, fort, etc.; rotating holder for tools in lathe etc. □ **turreted** *adjective*.

**turtle** /'tɜːt(ə)l/ *noun* aquatic reptile with flippers and horny shell. □ **turtle-neck** high close-fitting neck on knitted garment.

**turtle-dove** /'tɜːt(ə)ldʌv/ *noun* wild dove noted for soft cooing and affection for its mate.

**tusk** *noun* long pointed tooth, esp. projecting beyond mouth as in elephant, walrus, or boar. □ **tusked** *adjective*.

**tussle** /'tʌs(ə)l/ *noun & verb* (**-ling**) struggle, scuffle.

**tussock** /'tʌsək/ *noun* clump of grass etc.

**tut** = TUT-TUT.

**tutelage** /'tjuːtɪlɪdʒ/ *noun* guardianship; being under this; tuition.

**tutelary** /'tjuːtɪlərɪ/ *adjective* serving as guardian or protector; of guardian.

**tutor** /'tjuːtə/ ● *noun* private teacher; university teacher supervising studies or welfare of assigned undergraduates. ● *verb* act as tutor (to). □ **tutorship** *noun*.

**tutorial** /tjuː'tɔːrɪəl/ ● *adjective* of tutor or tuition. ● *noun* period of tuition for single student or small group.

**tutti** /'tʊtɪ/ *Music* ● *adjective & adverb* with all instruments or voices together. ● *noun* (*plural* **-s**) tutti passage.

**tut-tut** /tʌt'tʌt/ (also **tut**) ● *interjection expressing rebuke or impatience.* ● *noun* such exclamation. ● *verb* (**-tt-**) exclaim thus.

**tutu** /'tuːtuː/ *noun* (*plural* **-s**) dancer's short skirt of stiffened frills.

**tuxedo** /tʌk'siːdəʊ/ *noun* (*plural* **-s** or **-es**) *US* (suit including) dinner jacket.

**TV** *abbreviation* television.

**twaddle** /'twɒd(ə)l/ *noun* silly writing or talk.

**twain** *adjective & noun archaic* two.

**twang** ● *noun* sound made by plucked string of musical instrument, bow, etc.; nasal quality of voice. ● *verb* (cause) to emit twang. □ **twangy** *adjective*.

**tweak** ● *verb* pinch and twist; jerk; adjust finely. ● *noun* such action.

**twee** *adjective* (**tweer** /'twiːə/, **tweest** /'twiːɪst/) *derogatory* affectedly dainty or quaint.

**tweed** *noun* rough-surfaced woollen cloth usually of mixed colours; (in *plural*) clothes of tweed.

**tweedy** *adjective* (**-ier**, **-iest**) of or dressed in tweed; heartily informal.

**tweet** ● *noun* chirp of small bird. ● *verb* make this noise.

**tweeter** *noun* loudspeaker for high frequencies.

**tweezers** /'twiːzəz/ *plural noun* small pair of pincers for picking up small objects, plucking out hairs, etc.

**twelfth** *adjective & noun* next after eleventh; any of twelve equal parts of thing. □ **Twelfth Night** evening of 5 Jan.

**twelve** /twelv/ *adjective & noun* one more than eleven.

**twenty** /'twentɪ/ *adjective & noun* (*plural* **-ies**) twice ten. □ **twentieth** *adjective & noun*.

**twerp** *noun slang* stupid or objectionable person.

**twice** *adverb* two times; on two occasions; doubly.

**twiddle** /'twɪd(ə)l/ ● *verb* (**-ling**) twist or play idly about. ● *noun* act of twiddling. □ **twiddle one's thumbs** make them rotate round each other, have nothing to do.

**twig**¹ *noun* very small branch of tree or shrub.

**twig**² *verb* (**-gg-**) *colloquial* understand, realize.

**twilight** /'twaɪlaɪt/ *noun* light from sky when sun is below horizon, esp. in evening; period of this; faint light; period of decline. □ **twilight zone** decrepit urban area, undefined or intermediate area.

**twilit** /'twaɪlɪt/ *adjective* dimly illuminated (as) by twilight.

**twill** *noun* fabric woven with surface of parallel diagonal ridges. □ **twilled** *adjective*.

**twin** ● *noun* each of closely related pair, esp. of children or animals born at a birth; counterpart. ● *adjective* forming, or born as one of, twins. ● *verb* (**-nn-**) join closely, (+ *with*) pair; bear twins; link (town) with one abroad for social and cultural exchange. □ **twin bed** each of pair of single beds; **twin set** woman's matching cardigan and jumper; **twin town** town twinned with another.

**twine** ● *noun* strong coarse string of twisted strands of fibre; coil, twist. ● *verb* (**-ning**) coil, twist; form (string etc.) by twisting strands.

**twinge** /twɪndʒ/ *noun* sharp momentary local pain.

**twinkle** /'twɪŋk(ə)l/ ● *verb* (**-ling**) shine with rapidly intermittent light; sparkle; move rapidly. ● *noun* sparkle or gleam of eyes; twinkling light; light rapid movement. □ **twinkly** *adjective*.

**twirl** ● *verb* spin, swing, or twist quickly and lightly round. ● *noun* twirling; flourish made with pen.

**twist** ● *verb* change the form of by rotating one end and not the other or the two ends opposite ways; undergo such change; wrench or distort by twisting; wind (strands etc.) about each other, form (rope etc.) thus; (cause) to take spiral form; (+ *off*) break off by twisting; misrepresent meaning of (words); take winding course; *colloquial* cheat; (as **twisted** *adjective*) perverted; dance the twist. ● *noun* twisting, being twisted; thing made by twisting; point at which thing twists; *usually derogatory* peculiar tendency of mind, character, etc.; unexpected development; (**the twist**) 1960s dance with twisting hips. ▫ **twisty** *adjective* (**-ier**, **-iest**).

**twister** *noun colloquial* swindler.

**twit**¹ *noun slang* foolish person.

**twit**² *verb* (**-tt-**) reproach, taunt, usually good-humouredly.

**twitch** ● *verb* quiver or jerk spasmodically; pull sharply at. ● *noun* twitching; *colloquial* state of nervousness. ▫ **twitchy** *adjective* (**-ier**, **-iest**).

**twitter** /ˈtwɪtə/ ● *verb* (esp. of bird) utter succession of light tremulous sounds; utter or express thus. ● *noun* twittering; *colloquial* tremulously excited state.

**two** /tuː/ *adjective & noun* more than one. ▫ **two-dimensional** having or appearing to have length and breadth but no depth, superficial; **two-edged** having both good and bad effect, ambiguous; **two-faced** insincere; **two-handed** with 2 hands, used with both hands or by 2 people; **twopence** /ˈtʌpəns/ sum of 2 pence, (esp. with negative) *colloquial* thing of little value; **twopenny** /ˈtʌpənɪ/ costing twopence, *colloquial* cheap, worthless; **two-piece** (suit etc.) comprising 2 matching parts; **two-ply** (wool etc.) having 2 strands, (plywood) having 2 layers; **two-step** dance in march or polka time; **two-stroke** (of internal-combustion engine) having power cycle completed in one up-and-down movement of piston; **two-time** *colloquial* be unfaithful to, swindle; **two-tone** having two colours or sounds; **two-way** involving or operating in two directions, (of radio) capable of transmitting and receiving signals.

**twofold** *adjective & adverb* twice as much or many.

**twosome** *noun* two people together.

**tycoon** /taɪˈkuːn/ *noun* business magnate.

**tying** *present participle* of TIE.

**tyke** /taɪk/ *noun* (also **tike**) objectionable or coarse man; small child.

**tympani** = TIMPANI.

**tympanum** /ˈtɪmpənəm/ *noun* (*plural* **-s** or **-na**) middle ear; eardrum; vertical space forming centre of pediment; space between lintel and arch above door etc.

**type** /taɪp/ ● *noun* sort, class, kind; person, thing, or event exemplifying class or group; *colloquial* person, esp. of specified character; object, idea, or work of art serving as model; small block with raised character on upper surface for printing; printing types collectively; typeset or printed text. ● *verb* (**-ping**) write with typewriter; typecast; assign to type, classify. ▫ **-type** made of, resembling, functioning as; **typecast** cast (performer) repeatedly in similar roles; **typeface** inked surface of type, set of characters in one design; **typescript** typewritten document; **typesetter** compositor, composing machine; **typewriter** machine with keys for producing printlike characters; **typewritten** produced thus.

**typhoid** /ˈtaɪfɔɪd/ *noun* (in full **typhoid fever**) infectious bacterial fever attacking intestines.

**typhoon** /taɪˈfuːn/ *noun* violent hurricane in E. Asian seas.

**typhus** /ˈtaɪfəs/ *noun* an acute infectious fever.

**typical** /ˈtɪpɪk(ə)l/ *adjective* serving as characteristic example; (often + *of*) characteristic of particular person or thing. ▫ **typicality** /-ˈkæl-/ *noun*; **typically** *adverb*.

**typify** /ˈtɪpɪfaɪ/ *verb* (**-ies**, **-ied**) be typical of; represent by or as type. ▫ **typification** *noun*.

**typist** /ˈtaɪpɪst/ *noun* (esp. professional) user of typewriter.

**typo** /ˈtaɪpəʊ/ *noun* (*plural* **-s**) *colloquial* typographical error.

**typography** /taɪˈpɒɡrəfɪ/ *noun* printing as an art; style and appearance of printed matter. ▫ **typographer** *noun*; **typographical** /-pəˈɡræf-/ *adjective*; **typographically** /-pəˈɡræf-/ *adverb*.

**tyrannical** /tɪˈrænɪk(ə)l/ *adjective* acting like or characteristic of tyrant.

**tyrannize** /'tɪrənaɪz/ verb (also **-ise**) (**-zing** or **-sing**) (often + over) treat despotically.

**tyrannosaurus** /tɪrænə'sɔːrəs/ noun (plural **-ruses**) very large carnivorous dinosaur with short front legs and powerful tail.

**tyranny** /'tɪrənɪ/ noun (plural **-ies**) cruel and arbitrary use of authority; rule by tyrant; period of this; state thus ruled. □ **tyrannous** adjective.

**tyrant** /'taɪərənt/ noun oppressive or cruel ruler; person exercising power arbitrarily or cruelly.

**tyre** /'taɪə/ noun (US **tire**) rubber covering, usually inflated, placed round vehicle's wheel for cushioning and grip.

**tyro** = TIRO.

**tzatziki** /tsæt'siːkɪ/ noun Greek dish of yoghurt with cucumber and garlic.

# Uu

**U**[1] □ **U-boat** historical German submarine; **U-turn** U-shaped turn of vehicle to face in opposite direction, reversal of policy.

**U**[2] abbreviation (of film classified as suitable for all) universal.

**UB40** abbreviation card for claiming unemployment benefit; colloquial unemployed person.

**ubiquitous** /juː'bɪkwɪtəs/ adjective (seemingly) present everywhere simultaneously; often encountered. □ **ubiquity** noun.

**UCCA** /'ʌkə/ abbreviation Universities Central Council on Admissions.

**UDA** abbreviation Ulster Defence Association.

**udder** /'ʌdə/ noun baglike milk-producing organ of cow etc.

**UDI** abbreviation unilateral declaration of independence.

**UDR** abbreviation Ulster Defence Regiment.

**UEFA** /juː'eɪfə/ abbreviation Union of European Football Associations.

**UFO** /'juːfəʊ/ noun (also **ufo**) (plural **-s**) unidentified flying object.

**ugh** /əx, ʌɡ/ interjection expressing disgust etc.

**Ugli** /'ʌɡlɪ/ noun (plural **-lis** or **-lies**) proprietary term mottled green and yellow citrus fruit.

**ugly** /'ʌɡlɪ/ adjective (**-ier**, **-iest**) unpleasant to eye, ear, mind, etc.; discreditable; threatening, dangerous; morally repulsive. □ **ugly duckling** person

lacking early promise but blossoming later. □ **uglify** verb (**-ies**, **-ied**); **ugliness** noun.

**UHF** abbreviation ultra-high frequency.

**uh-huh** /'ʌhʌ/ interjection colloquial yes.

**UHT** abbreviation ultra heat treated (esp. of milk, for long keeping).

**UK** abbreviation United Kingdom.

**Ukrainian** /juː'kreɪnɪən/ ● noun native, national, or language of Ukraine. ● adjective of Ukraine.

**ukulele** /juːkə'leɪlɪ/ noun small guitar with 4 strings.

**ulcer** /'ʌlsə/ noun (often pus-forming) open sore on or in body; corrupting influence. □ **ulcerous** adjective.

**ulcerate** /'ʌlsəreɪt/ verb (**-ting**) form into or affect with ulcer. □ **ulceration** noun.

**ullage** /'ʌlɪdʒ/ noun amount by which cask etc. falls short of being full; loss by evaporation or leakage.

**ulna** /'ʌlnə/ noun (plural **ulnae** /-niː/) longer bone of forearm, opposite thumb; corresponding bone in animal's foreleg or bird's wing. □ **ulnar** adjective.

**ulster** /'ʌlstə/ noun long loose overcoat of rough cloth.

**Ulsterman** /'ʌlstəmən/ noun (feminine **Ulsterwoman**) native of Ulster.

**ult.** abbreviation ultimo.

**ulterior** /ʌl'tɪərɪə/ adjective not admitted; hidden, secret.

**ultimate** /'ʌltɪmət/ ● adjective last, final; fundamental, basic. ● noun (**the ultimate**) best achievable or imaginable;

final or fundamental fact or principle. □ **ultimately** *adverb*.

**ultimatum** /ˌʌltɪˈmeɪtəm/ *noun* (*plural* **-s**) final statement of terms, rejection of which could cause hostility etc.

**ultimo** /ˈʌltɪməʊ/ *adjective* of last month.

**ultra** /ˈʌltrə/ ● *adjective* extreme, esp. in religion or politics. ● *noun* extremist.

**ultra-** *combining form* extreme(ly), excessive(ly); beyond.

**ultra-high** /ʌltrəˈhaɪ/ *adjective* (of frequency) between 300 and 3000 megahertz.

**ultramarine** /ˌʌltrəməˈriːn/ ● *noun* (colour of) brilliant deep blue pigment. ● *adjective* of this colour.

**ultrasonic** /ʌltrəˈsɒnɪk/ *adjective* of or using sound waves pitched above range of human hearing. □ **ultrasonically** *adverb*.

**ultrasound** /ˈʌltrəsaʊnd/ *noun* ultrasonic waves.

**ultraviolet** /ʌltrəˈvaɪələt/ *adjective* of or using radiation just beyond violet end of spectrum.

**ultra vires** /ʌltrə ˈvaɪəriːz/ *adverb & adjective* beyond one's legal power or authority. [Latin]

**ululate** /ˈjuːɪjʊleɪt/ *verb* (**-ting**) howl, wail. □ **ululation** *noun*.

**um** *interjection representing hesitation or pause in speech*.

**umbel** /ˈʌmb(ə)l/ *noun* flower-cluster with stalks springing from common centre. □ **umbellate** *adjective*.

**umbelliferous** /ʌmbəˈlɪfərəs/ *adjective* (of plant, e.g. parsley or carrot) bearing umbels.

**umber** /ˈʌmbə/ ● *noun* (colour of) dark brown earth used as pigment. ● *adjective* umber-coloured.

**umbilical** /ʌmˈbɪlɪk(ə)l/ *adjective* of navel. □ **umbilical cord** cordlike structure attaching foetus to placenta.

**umbilicus** /ʌmˈbɪlɪkəs/ *noun* (*plural* **-ci** /-saɪ/ or **-cuses**) navel.

**umbra** /ˈʌmbrə/ *noun* (*plural* **-s** or **-brae** /-briː/) shadow cast by moon or earth in eclipse.

**umbrage** /ˈʌmbrɪdʒ/ *noun* offence taken.

**umbrella** /ʌmˈbrelə/ *noun* collapsible cloth canopy on central stick for protection against rain, sun, etc.; protection, patronage; coordinating agency.

**umlaut** /ˈʊmlaʊt/ *noun* mark (¨) over vowel, esp. in German, indicating change in pronunciation; such a change.

**umpire** /ˈʌmpaɪə/ ● *noun* person enforcing rules and settling disputes in game, contest, etc. ● *verb* (**-ring**) (often + *for*, *in*, etc.) act as umpire (in).

**umpteen** /ˈʌmptiːn/ *adjective & noun colloquial* very many. □ **umpteenth** *adjective & noun*.

**UN** *abbreviation* United Nations.

**un-** *prefix added to adjectives, nouns, and adverbs, meaning:* not; non-; reverse of, lack of; *added to verbs, verbal derivatives, etc. to express contrary or reverse action, deprivation of or removal from. For words starting with un- that are not found below, the root-words should be consulted.*

**unaccountable** /ʌnəˈkaʊntəb(ə)l/ *adjective* without explanation, strange; not answerable for one's actions. □ **unaccountably** *adverb*.

**unadopted** /ʌnəˈdɒptɪd/ *adjective* (of road) not maintained by local authority.

**unadulterated** /ʌnəˈdʌltəreɪtɪd/ *adjective* pure; complete, utter.

**unaffected** /ʌnəˈfektɪd/ *adjective* (usually + *by*) not affected; free from affectation. □ **unaffectedly** *adverb*.

**unalloyed** /ʌnəˈlɔɪd/ *adjective* complete, pure.

**un-American** /ʌnəˈmerɪkən/ *adjective* uncharacteristic of Americans; contrary to US interests, treasonable.

**unanimous** /juːˈnænɪməs/ *adjective* all in agreement; (of vote etc.) by all without exception. □ **unanimity** /-nəˈnɪm-/ *noun*; **unanimously** *adverb*.

**unannounced** /ʌnəˈnaʊnst/ *adjective* not announced, without warning.

**unanswerable** /ʌnˈɑːnsərəb(ə)l/ *adjective* that cannot be answered or refuted.

**unapproachable** /ʌnəˈprəʊtʃəb(ə)l/ *adjective* inaccessible; (of person) unfriendly, aloof.

**unassailable** /ʌnəˈseɪləb(ə)l/ *adjective* that cannot be attacked or questioned.

**unassuming** /ʌnəˈsjuːmɪŋ/ *adjective* not pretentious, modest.

**unattached** /ʌnəˈtætʃt/ *adjective* not engaged, married, etc.; (often + *to*) not attached to particular organization etc.

**unaware** /ʌnə'weə/ ● adjective (usually + of, that) not aware; unperceptive. ● adverb unawares.

**unawares** /ʌnə'weəz/ adverb unexpectedly; inadvertently.

**unbalanced** /ʌn'bælənst/ adjective emotionally unstable; biased.

**unbeknown** /ʌnbɪ'nəʊn/ adjective (also **unbeknownst** /-'nəʊnst/) (+ to) without the knowledge of.

**unbend** /ʌn'bend/ verb (past & past participle **unbent**) straighten; relax; become affable.

**unbending** /ʌn'bendɪŋ/ adjective inflexible; firm, austere.

**unblushing** /ʌn'blʌʃɪŋ/ adjective shameless; frank.

**unbosom** /ʌn'bʊz(ə)m/ verb disclose (thoughts etc.); (**unbosom oneself**) disclose one's thoughts etc.

**unbounded** /ʌn'baʊndɪd/ adjective infinite.

**unbridled** /ʌn'braɪd(ə)ld/ adjective unrestrained, uncontrolled.

**uncalled-for** /ʌn'kɔ:ldfɔ:/ adjective (of remark etc.) rude and unnecessary.

**uncanny** /ʌn'kænɪ/ adjective (**-ier, -iest**) seemingly supernatural, mysterious. □ **uncannily** adverb; **uncanniness** noun.

**uncapped** /ʌn'kæpt/ adjective Sport (of player) not yet awarded his or her cap or never having been selected to represent his or her country.

**unceremonious** /ʌnserɪ'məʊnɪəs/ adjective abrupt, discourteous; informal. □ **unceremoniously** adverb.

**uncertain** /ʌn'sɜ:t(ə)n/ adjective not certain; unreliable; changeable. □ **in no uncertain terms** clearly and forcefully. □ **uncertainly** adverb; **uncertainty** noun (plural **-ies**).

**uncharted** /ʌn'tʃɑ:tɪd/ adjective not mapped or surveyed.

**uncle** /'ʌŋk(ə)l/ noun parent's brother or brother-in-law. □ **Uncle Sam** colloquial US government.

**unclean** /ʌn'kli:n/ adjective not clean; unchaste; religiously impure.

**uncomfortable** /ʌn'kʌmftəb(ə)l/ adjective not comfortable; uneasy. □ **uncomfortably** adverb.

**uncommon** /ʌn'kɒmən/ adjective unusual, remarkable. □ **uncommonly** adverb.

**uncompromising** /ʌn'kɒmprəmaɪzɪŋ/ adjective stubborn; unyielding. □ **uncompromisingly** adverb.

**unconcern** /ʌnkən'sɜ:n/ noun calmness; indifference, apathy. □ **unconcerned** adjective.

**unconditional** /ʌnkən'dɪʃ(ə)n(ə)l/ adjective not subject to conditions, complete. □ **unconditionally** adverb.

**unconscionable** /ʌn'kɒnʃənəb(ə)l/ adjective without conscience; excessive.

**unconscious** /ʌn'kɒnʃəs/ ● adjective not conscious. ● noun normally inaccessible part of mind affecting emotions etc. □ **unconsciously** adverb; **unconsciousness** noun.

**unconsidered** /ʌnkən'sɪdəd/ adjective not considered; disregarded; not premeditated.

**unconstitutional** /ʌnkɒnstɪ'tju:ʃən(ə)l/ adjective in breach of political constitution or procedural rules.

**uncooperative** /ʌnkəʊ'ɒpərətɪv/ adjective not cooperative.

**uncork** /ʌn'kɔ:k/ verb draw cork from (bottle); vent (feelings).

**uncouple** /ʌn'kʌp(ə)l/ verb (**-ling**) release from couples or coupling.

**uncouth** /ʌn'ku:θ/ adjective uncultured, rough.

**uncover** /ʌn'kʌvə/ verb remove cover or covering from; disclose.

**uncrowned** /ʌn'kraʊnd/ adjective having status but not name of.

**unction** /'ʌŋkʃ(ə)n/ noun anointing with oil etc. as religious rite or medical treatment; oil etc. so used; soothing words or thought; excessive or insincere flattery; (pretence of) deep emotion.

**unctuous** /'ʌŋktjʊəs/ adjective unpleasantly flattering; greasy. □ **unctuously** adverb.

**uncut** /ʌn'kʌt/ adjective not cut; (of book) with pages sealed or untrimmed; (of film) not censored; (of diamond) not shaped; (of fabric) with looped pile.

**undeniable** /ʌndɪ'naɪəb(ə)l/ adjective indisputable; certain. □ **undeniably** adverb.

**under** /'ʌndə/ ● preposition in or to position lower than, below; beneath; inferior to, less than; undergoing, liable to;

controlled or bound by; classified or subsumed in. ● *adverb* in or to lower condition or position. ● *adjective* lower.

**underachieve** /ˌʌndərəˈtʃiːv/ *verb* (**-ving**) do less well than might be expected, esp. academically. □ **underachiever** *noun*.

**underarm** *adjective & adverb Cricket etc.* with arm below shoulder level.

**underbelly** *noun* (*plural* **-ies**) under surface of animal etc., esp. as vulnerable to attack.

**underbid** /ˌʌndəˈbɪd/ *verb* (**-dd-**; *past & past participle* **-bid**) make lower bid than; *Bridge etc.* bid too little (on).

**undercarriage** *noun* wheeled retractable landing structure beneath aircraft; supporting framework of vehicle etc.

**undercharge** /ˌʌndəˈtʃɑːdʒ/ *verb* (**-ging**) charge too little to.

**underclothes** *plural noun* (also **underclothing**) clothes worn under others, esp. next to skin.

**undercoat** *noun* layer of paint under another; (in animals) under layer of hair etc.

**undercook** /ˌʌndəˈkʊk/ *verb* cook insufficiently.

**undercover** /ˌʌndəˈkʌvə/ *adjective* surreptitious; spying incognito.

**undercroft** *noun* crypt.

**undercurrent** *noun* current below surface; underlying often contrary feeling, force, etc.

**undercut** ● *verb* /ˌʌndəˈkʌt/ (**-tt-**; *past & past participle* **-cut**) sell or work at lower price than; strike (ball) to make it rise high; undermine. ● *noun* /ˈʌndəkʌt/ underside of sirloin.

**underdeveloped** /ˌʌndədɪˈveləpt/ *adjective* immature; (of country etc.) with unexploited potential.

**underdog** *noun* oppressed person; loser in fight etc.

**underdone** /ˌʌndəˈdʌn/ *adjective* undercooked.

**underemployed** /ˌʌndərɪmˈplɔɪd/ *adjective* not fully occupied.

**underestimate** ● *verb* /ˌʌndərˈestɪmeɪt/ (**-ting**) form too low an estimate of. ● *noun* /ˌʌndərˈestɪmət/ estimate that is too low. □ **underestimation** *noun*.

**underexpose** /ˌʌndərɪkˈspəʊz/ *verb* (**-sing**) expose (film) for too short a time. □ **underexposure** *noun*.

**underfed** /ˌʌndəˈfed/ *adjective* malnourished.

**underfelt** *noun* felt laid under carpet.

**underfloor** /ˌʌndəˈflɔː/ *adjective* (esp. of heating) beneath floor.

**underfoot** /ˌʌndəˈfʊt/ *adverb* (also **under foot**) under one's feet; on the ground.

**underfunded** /ˌʌndəˈfʌndɪd/ *adjective* provided with insufficient money.

**undergarment** *noun* piece of underclothing.

**undergo** /ˌʌndəˈgəʊ/ *verb* (*3rd singular present* **-goes**; *past* **-went**; *past participle* **-gone** /-ˈgɒn/) be subjected to, endure.

**undergraduate** /ˌʌndəˈgrædjʊət/ *noun* person studying for first degree.

**underground** ● *adverb* /ˌʌndəˈgraʊnd/ beneath the ground; in(to) secrecy or hiding. ● *adjective* /ˈʌndəgraʊnd/ situated underground; secret, subversive; unconventional. ● *noun* /ˈʌndəgraʊnd/ underground railway; secret subversive group or activity.

**undergrowth** *noun* dense shrubs etc., esp. in wood.

**underhand** *adjective* secret, deceptive; *Cricket etc.* underarm.

**underlay**[1] ● *verb* /ˌʌndəˈleɪ/ (*past & past participle* **-laid**) lay thing under (another) to support or raise. ● *noun* /ˈʌndəleɪ/ thing so laid (esp. under carpet).

**underlay**[2] *past of* UNDERLIE.

**underlie** /ˌʌndəˈlaɪ/ *verb* (**-lying**; *past* **-lay**; *past participle* **-lain**) lie under (stratum etc.); (esp. as **underlying** *adjective*) be basis of, exist beneath superficial aspect of.

**underline** /ˌʌndəˈlaɪn/ *verb* (**-ning**) draw line under (words etc.); emphasize.

**underling** /ˈʌndəlɪŋ/ *noun* usually derogatory subordinate.

**undermanned** /ˌʌndəˈmænd/ *adjective* having insufficient crew or staff.

**undermine** /ˌʌndəˈmaɪn/ *verb* (**-ning**) injure or wear out insidiously or secretly; wear away base of; make excavation under.

**underneath** /ˌʌndəˈniːθ/ ● *preposition* at or to lower place than, below; on inside of. ● *adverb* at or to lower place; inside.

• *noun* lower surface or part. • *adjective* lower.

**undernourished** /ˌʌndəˈnʌrɪʃt/ *adjective* insufficiently nourished. □ **undernourishment** *noun*.

**underpants** *plural noun* undergarment for lower part of torso.

**underpass** *noun* road etc. passing under another; subway.

**underpay** /ˌʌndəˈpeɪ/ *verb* (*past & past participle* **-paid**) pay too little to (person) or for (thing). □ **underpayment** *noun*.

**underpin** /ˌʌndəˈpɪn/ *verb* (**-nn-**) support from below with masonry etc.; support, strengthen.

**underprivileged** /ˌʌndəˈprɪvɪlɪdʒd/ *adjective* less privileged than others; having below average income, rights, etc.

**underrate** /ˌʌndəˈreɪt/ *verb* (**-ting**) have too low an opinion of.

**underscore** /ˌʌndəˈskɔː/ *verb* (**-ring**) underline.

**undersea** *adjective* below sea or its surface.

**underseal** *verb* seal underpart of (esp. vehicle) against rust etc.).

**under-secretary** /ˌʌndəˈsekrətərɪ/ *noun* (*plural* **-ies**) subordinate official, esp. junior minister or senior civil servant.

**undersell** /ˌʌndəˈsel/ *verb* (*past & past participle* **-sold**) sell at lower price than (another seller).

**undershirt** *noun esp. US* vest.

**undershoot** /ˌʌndəˈʃuːt/ *verb* (*past & past participle* **-shot**) land short of (runway etc.).

**undershot** *adjective* (of wheel) turned by water flowing under it; (of lower jaw) projecting beyond upper jaw.

**underside** *noun* lower side or surface.

**undersigned** /ˌʌndəˈsaɪnd/ *adjective* whose signature is appended.

**undersized** /ˈʌndəˈsaɪzd/ *adjective* smaller than average.

**underspend** /ˌʌndəˈspend/ *verb* (*past & past participle* **-spent**) spend less than (expected amount) or too little.

**understaffed** /ˌʌndəˈstɑːft/ *adjective* having too few staff.

**understand** /ˌʌndəˈstænd/ *verb* (*past & past participle* **-stood**) comprehend, perceive meaning, significance, or cause of; know how to deal with; (often +

*that*) infer, take as implied. □ **understandable** *adjective*; **understandably** *adverb*.

**understanding** • *noun* intelligence; ability to understand; individual's perception of situation; agreement, esp. informal. • *adjective* having understanding or insight; sympathetic. □ **understandingly** *adverb*.

**understate** /ˌʌndəˈsteɪt/ *verb* (**-ting**) express in restrained terms; represent as being less than it really is. □ **understatement** *noun*.

**understudy** /ˈʌndəstʌdɪ/ • *noun* (*plural* **-ies**) person ready to take another's role when required, esp. in theatre. • *verb* (**-ies**, **-ied**) study (role etc.) for this purpose; act as understudy to.

**undersubscribed** /ˌʌndəsəbˈskraɪbd/ *adjective* without sufficient subscribers, participants, etc.

**undertake** /ˌʌndəˈteɪk/ *verb* (**-king**; *past* **-took**; *past participle* **-taken**) agree to perform or be responsible for; engage in; (usually + *to do*) promise; guarantee, affirm.

**undertaker** /ˈʌndəteɪkə/ *noun* professional funeral organizer.

**undertaking** /ˌʌndəˈteɪkɪŋ/ *noun* work etc. undertaken; enterprise; promise; /ˈʌn-/ professional funeral management.

**undertone** *noun* subdued tone; underlying quality or feeling.

**undertow** *noun* current below sea surface contrary to surface current.

**underused** /ˌʌndəˈjuːzd/ *adjective* not used to capacity.

**undervalue** /ˌʌndəˈvæljuː/ *verb* (**-ues**, **-ued**, **-uing**) value insufficiently; underestimate.

**underwater** /ˌʌndəˈwɔːtə/ • *adjective* situated or done under water. • *adverb* under water.

**underwear** *noun* underclothes.

**underweight** /ˌʌndəˈweɪt/ *adjective* below normal weight.

**underwent** *past of* UNDERGO.

**underwhelm** /ˌʌndəˈwelm/ *verb* jocular fail to impress.

**underworld** *noun* those who live by organized crime; mythical home of the dead.

**underwrite** /ˈʌndəˈraɪt/ *verb* (**-ting**; *past* **-wrote**; *past participle* **-written**) sign and accept liability under (insurance policy); accept (liability) thus; undertake to finance or support; engage to buy all unsold stock in (company etc.). □ **underwriter** /ˈʌn-/ *noun*.

**undesirable** /ˌʌndɪˈzaɪərəb(ə)l/ ● *adjective* unpleasant, objectionable. ● *noun* undesirable person. □ **undesirability** *noun*.

**undies** /ˈʌndɪz/ *plural noun colloquial* (esp. women's) underclothes.

**undo** /ʌnˈduː/ *verb* (*3rd singular present* **-does**; *past* **-did**; *past participle* **-done**; *present participle* **-doing**) unfasten; annul; ruin prospects, reputation, or morals of.

**undoing** *noun* (cause of) ruin; reversing of action etc.; unfastening.

**undone** /ʌnˈdʌn/ *adjective* not done; not fastened; *archaic* ruined.

**undoubted** /ʌnˈdaʊtɪd/ *adjective* certain, not questioned. □ **undoubtedly** *adverb*.

**undreamed** /ʌnˈdriːmd, ʌnˈdremt/ *adjective* (also **undreamt** /ʌnˈdremt/) (often + *of*) not thought of, never imagined.

**undress** /ʌnˈdres/ ● *verb* take off one's clothes; take clothes off (person). ● *noun* ordinary dress, esp. as opposed to (full-dress) uniform; naked or scantily clad state.

**undressed** /ʌnˈdrest/ *adjective* no longer dressed; (of food) without dressing; (of leather) untreated.

**undue** /ʌnˈdjuː/ *adjective* excessive, disproportionate. □ **unduly** *adverb*.

**undulate** /ˈʌndjʊleɪt/ *verb* (**-ting**) (cause to) have wavy motion or look. □ **undulation** *noun*.

**undying** /ʌnˈdaɪɪŋ/ *adjective* immortal; never-ending.

**unearth** /ʌnˈɜːθ/ *verb* discover by searching, digging, or rummaging.

**unearthly** /ʌnˈɜːθlɪ/ *adjective* supernatural; mysterious; *colloquial* very early.

**unease** /ʌnˈiːz/ *noun* nervousness, anxiety.

**uneasy** /ʌnˈiːzɪ/ *adjective* (**-ier**, **-iest**) disturbed or uncomfortable in body or mind. □ **uneasily** *adverb*; **uneasiness** *noun*.

**unemployable** /ˌʌnɪmˈplɔɪəb(ə)l/ *adjective* unfit for paid employment.

**unemployed** /ˌʌnɪmˈplɔɪd/ *adjective* out of work; not used.

**unemployment** /ˌʌnɪmˈplɔɪmənt/ *noun* lack of employment. □ **unemployment benefit** state payment made to unemployed worker.

**unencumbered** /ˌʌnɪnˈkʌmbəd/ *adjective* (of estate) having no liabilities; free, not burdened.

**unequivocal** /ˌʌnɪˈkwɪvək(ə)l/ *adjective* not ambiguous, plain, unmistakable. □ **unequivocally** *adverb*.

**UNESCO** /juːˈneskəʊ/ *abbreviation* (also **Unesco**) United Nations Educational, Scientific, and Cultural Organization.

**uneven** /ʌnˈiːv(ə)n/ *adjective* not level; of variable quality; (of contest) unequal. □ **unevenly** *adverb*.

**unexceptionable** /ˌʌnɪkˈsepʃənəb(ə)l/ *adjective* entirely satisfactory.

■ *Usage* *Unexceptionable* is sometimes confused with *unexceptional*.

**unexceptional** /ˌʌnɪkˈsepʃən(ə)l/ *adjective* normal, ordinary.

■ *Usage* *Unexceptional* is sometimes confused with *unexceptionable*

**unfailing** /ʌnˈfeɪlɪŋ/ *adjective* not failing, constant, reliable. □ **unfailingly** *adverb*.

**unfaithful** /ʌnˈfeɪθfʊl/ *adjective* not faithful, esp. adulterous. □ **unfaithfulness** *noun*.

**unfeeling** /ʌnˈfiːlɪŋ/ *adjective* unsympathetic, harsh.

**unfit** /ʌnˈfɪt/ *adjective* (often + *for, to do*) not fit, unsuitable; in poor health.

**unflagging** /ʌnˈflægɪŋ/ *adjective* tireless, persistent.

**unflappable** /ʌnˈflæpəb(ə)l/ *adjective colloquial* imperturbable.

**unfledged** /ʌnˈfledʒd/ *adjective* inexperienced; not fledged.

**unfold** /ʌnˈfəʊld/ *verb* open out; reveal; become opened out; develop.

**unforgettable** /ˌʌnfəˈgetəb(ə)l/ *adjective* memorable, wonderful.

**unfortunate** /ʌnˈfɔːtʃənət/ ● *adjective* unlucky; unhappy; regrettable. ● *noun* unfortunate person. □ **unfortunately** *adverb*.

**unfounded** /ʌnˈfaʊndɪd/ *adjective* (of rumour etc.) without foundation.

**unfreeze** /ʌnˈfriːz/ verb (**-zing**; past **unfroze**; past participle **unfrozen**) (cause to) thaw; derestrict (assets etc.).

**unfrock** /ʌnˈfrɒk/ verb defrock.

**unfurl** /ʌnˈfɜːl/ verb unroll, spread out.

**ungainly** /ʌnˈɡeɪnlɪ/ adjective awkward, clumsy.

**unget-at-able** /ʌnɡetˈætəb(ə)l/ colloquial inaccessible.

**ungodly** /ʌnˈɡɒdlɪ/ adjective impious, wicked; colloquial outrageous.

**ungovernable** /ʌnˈɡʌvənəb(ə)l/ adjective uncontrollable, violent.

**ungracious** /ʌnˈɡreɪʃəs/ adjective discourteous, grudging.

**ungrateful** /ʌnˈɡreɪtfʊl/ adjective not feeling or showing gratitude. □ **ungratefully** adverb.

**ungreen** /ʌnˈɡriːn/ adjective harmful to environment; not concerned with protection of environment.

**unguarded** /ʌnˈɡɑːdɪd/ adjective incautious, thoughtless; not guarded.

**unguent** /ˈʌŋɡwənt/ noun ointment, lubricant.

**ungulate** /ˈʌŋɡjʊlət/ ● adjective hoofed. ● noun hoofed mammal.

**unhallowed** /ʌnˈhæləʊd/ adjective unconsecrated; not sacred; wicked.

**unhand** /ʌnˈhænd/ verb rhetorical or jocular take one's hands off, release (person).

**unhappy** /ʌnˈhæpɪ/ adjective (**-ier, -iest**) miserable; unfortunate; disastrous. □ **unhappily** adverb; **unhappiness** noun.

**unhealthy** /ʌnˈhelθɪ/ adjective (**-ier, -iest**) in poor health; harmful to health; unwholesome; slang dangerous. □ **unhealthily** adverb.

**unheard-of** /ʌnˈhɜːdʊv/ adjective unprecedented.

**unhinge** /ʌnˈhɪndʒ/ verb (**-ging**) take (door etc.) off hinges; (esp. as **unhinged** adjective) derange, disorder (mind).

**unholy** /ʌnˈhəʊlɪ/ adjective (**-ier, -iest**) profane, wicked; colloquial dreadful, outrageous.

**unhorse** /ʌnˈhɔːs/ verb (**-sing**) throw (rider) from horse.

**uni** /ˈjuːnɪ/ noun ( plural **-s**) esp. Australian & NZ colloquial university.

**uni-** combining form having or composed of one.

**Uniate** /ˈjuːnɪət/ ● adjective of Church in E. Europe or Near East acknowledging papal supremacy but retaining its own liturgy etc. ● noun member of such Church.

**unicameral** /juːnɪˈkæmər(ə)l/ adjective having one legislative chamber.

**UNICEF** /ˈjuːnɪsef/ abbreviation United Nations Children's Fund.

**unicellular** /juːnɪˈseljʊlə/ adjective consisting of a single cell.

**unicorn** /ˈjuːnɪkɔːn/ noun mythical horse with single straight horn.

**unicycle** /ˈjuːnɪsaɪk(ə)l/ noun one-wheeled cycle used by acrobats etc.

**unification** /juːnɪfɪˈkeɪʃ(ə)n/ noun unifying, being unified. □ **Unification Church** religious organization funded by Sun Myung Moon. □ **unificatory** adjective.

**uniform** /ˈjuːnɪfɔːm/ ● adjective unvarying; conforming to same standard or rule; constant over a period. ● noun distinctive clothing worn by members of same organization etc. □ **uniformed** adjective; **uniformity** /-ˈfɔːm-/ noun; **uniformly** adverb.

**unify** /ˈjuːnɪfaɪ/ verb (**-ies, -ied**) make or become united or uniform.

**unilateral** /juːnɪˈlætər(ə)l/ adjective done by or affecting one side only. □ **unilaterally** adverb.

**unilateralism** noun unilateral disarmament. □ **unilateralist** noun & adjective.

**unimpeachable** /ʌnɪmˈpiːtʃəb(ə)l/ adjective beyond reproach.

**uninviting** /ʌnɪnˈvaɪtɪŋ/ adjective unattractive, repellent.

**union** /ˈjuːnjən/ noun uniting, being united; whole formed from parts or members; trade union; marriage; concord; university social club or debating society. □ **Union flag, Jack** national flag of UK.

**unionist** noun member of trade union, advocate of trade unions; (usually **Unionist**) supporter of continued union between Britain and Northern Ireland. □ **unionism** noun.

**unionize** verb (also **-ise**) (**-zing** or **-sing**) organize in or into trade union. □ **unionization** noun.

**unique** /juːˈniːk/ adjective being the only one of its kind; having no like, equal, or parallel; remarkable. □ **uniquely** adverb.

■ **Usage** The use of *unique* to mean 'remarkable' is considered incorrect by some people.

**unisex** /'juːnɪseks/ adjective (of clothing etc.) designed for both sexes.

**unison** /'juːnɪs(ə)n/ noun concord; coincidence in pitch of sounds or notes.

**unit** /'juːnɪt/ noun individual thing, person, or group, esp. for calculation; smallest component of complex whole; quantity chosen as standard of measurement; smallest share in unit trust; part with specified function in complex mechanism; fitted item of furniture, esp. as part of set; subgroup with special function; group of buildings, wards, etc. in hospital; single-digit number, esp. 'one'. □ **unit cost** cost of producing one item; **unit trust** company investing contributions from many people in various securities.

**Unitarian** /juːnɪˈteərɪən/ noun member of religious body maintaining that God is one person not Trinity. □ **Unitarianism** noun.

**unitary** /'juːnɪtərɪ/ adjective of unit(s); marked by unity or uniformity.

**unite** /juˈnaɪt/ verb (**-ting**) join together, esp. for common purpose; join in marriage; (cause to) form physical or chemical whole. □ **United Kingdom** Great Britain and Northern Ireland; **United Nations** (treated as *singular* or *plural*) international peace-seeking organization; **United States** = United States of America.

**unity** /'juːnɪtɪ/ noun (plural **-ies**) oneness, being one; interconnecting parts making a whole, the whole made; solidarity, harmony between people etc.; the number 'one'.

**universal** /juːnɪˈvɜːs(ə)l/ ● adjective of, belonging to, or done by etc. all; applicable to all cases. ● noun term, characteristic, or concept of general application. □ **universal coupling, joint** one transmitting rotary power by a shaft at any angle; **universal time** Greenwich Mean Time. □ **universality** /-ˈsæl-/ noun; **universally** adverb.

**universe** /'juːnɪvɜːs/ noun all existing things; Creation; all humankind.

**university** /juːnɪˈvɜːsɪtɪ/ noun (plural **-ies**) educational institution of advanced learning and research, conferring degrees; members of this.

**unkempt** /ʌnˈkempt/ adjective dishevelled, untidy.

**unknown** /ʌnˈnəʊn/ ● adjective (often + to) not known, unfamiliar. ● noun unknown thing, person, or quantity. □ **unknown quantity** mysterious or obscure person or thing; **Unknown Soldier, Warrior** unidentified soldier symbolizing nation's dead in war.

**unlawful** /ʌnˈlɔːfʊl/ adjective illegal, not permissible. □ **unlawfully** adverb.

**unleaded** /ʌnˈledɪd/ adjective (of petrol etc.) without added lead.

**unleash** /ʌnˈliːʃ/ verb free from leash or restraint; set free to pursue or attack.

**unleavened** /ʌnˈlev(ə)nd/ adjective made without yeast etc.

**unless** /ʌnˈles/ conjunction if not; except when.

**unlettered** /ʌnˈletəd/ adjective illiterate.

**unlike** /ʌnˈlaɪk/ ● adjective not like, different. ● preposition differently from.

**unlikely** /ʌnˈlaɪklɪ/ adjective (**-ier, -iest**) improbable; (+ to do) not expected; unpromising.

**unlisted** /ʌnˈlɪstɪd/ adjective not included in list, esp. of Stock Exchange prices or telephone numbers.

**unload** /ʌnˈləʊd/ verb remove load from (vehicle etc.); remove (load) from vehicle etc.; remove ammunition from (gun); colloquial get rid of.

**unlock** /ʌnˈlɒk/ verb release lock of; release or disclose by unlocking; release feelings etc. from.

**unlooked-for** /ʌnˈlʊktfɔː/ adjective unexpected.

**unlucky** /ʌnˈlʌkɪ/ adjective (**-ier, -iest**) not fortunate or successful; wretched; bringing bad luck; ill-judged. □ **unluckily** adverb.

**unman** /ʌnˈmæn/ verb (**-nn-**) deprive of courage, self-control, etc.

**unmannerly** /ʌnˈmænəlɪ/ adjective ill-mannered.

**unmask** /ʌnˈmɑːsk/ verb remove mask from; expose true character of; remove one's mask.

**unmentionable** /ʌnˈmenʃənəb(ə)l/ ●*adjective* unsuitable for polite conversation. ●*noun* (in *plural*) *jocular* undergarments.

**unmistakable** /ʌnmɪˈsteɪkəb(ə)l/ *adjective* clear, obvious, plain. □ **unmistakably** *adverb*.

**unmitigated** /ʌnˈmɪtɪɡeɪtɪd/ *adjective* not modified; absolute.

**unmoved** /ʌnˈmuːvd/ *adjective* not moved; constant in purpose; unemotional.

**unnatural** /ʌnˈnætʃər(ə)l/ *adjective* contrary to nature; not normal; lacking natural feelings; artificial, forced. □ **unnaturally** *adverb*.

**unnecessary** /ʌnˈnesəsərɪ/ *adjective* not necessary; superfluous. □ **unnecessarily** *adverb*.

**unnerve** /ʌnˈnɜːv/ *verb* (**-ving**) deprive of confidence etc.

**unobjectionable** /ʌnəbˈdʒekʃənəb(ə)l/ *adjective* acceptable.

**unobtrusive** /ʌnəbˈtruːsɪv/ *adjective* not making oneself or itself noticed. □ **unobtrusively** *adverb*.

**unofficial** /ʌnəˈfɪʃ(ə)l/ *adjective* not officially authorized or confirmed. □ **unofficial strike** strike not ratified by trade union.

**unpack** /ʌnˈpæk/ *verb* open and empty; take (thing) from package etc.

**unpalatable** /ʌnˈpælətəb(ə)l/ *adjective* (of food, suggestion, etc.) disagreeable, distasteful.

**unparalleled** /ʌnˈpærəleld/ *adjective* unequalled.

**unparliamentary** /ʌnpɑːləˈmentərɪ/ *adjective* contrary to proper parliamentary usage. □ **unparliamentary language** oaths, abuse.

**unpick** /ʌnˈpɪk/ *verb* undo sewing of.

**unplaced** /ʌnˈpleɪst/ *adjective* not placed as one of the first 3 in race etc.

**unpleasant** /ʌnˈplez(ə)nt/ *adjective* disagreeable. □ **unpleasantly** *adverb*; **unpleasantness** *noun*.

**unplug** /ʌnˈplʌɡ/ *verb* (**-gg-**) disconnect (electrical device) by removing plug from socket; unstop.

**unplumbed** /ʌnˈplʌmd/ *adjective* not plumbed; not fully explored or understood.

**unpopular** /ʌnˈpɒpjʊlə/ *adjective* not popular, disliked. □ **unpopularity** /-ˈlær-/ *noun*.

**unpractised** /ʌnˈpræktɪst/ *adjective* (*US* **unpracticed**) not experienced or skilled; not put into practice.

**unprecedented** /ʌnˈpresɪdentɪd/ *adjective* having no precedent, unparalleled.

**unprepossessing** /ʌnpriːpəˈzesɪŋ/ *adjective* unattractive.

**unprincipled** /ʌnˈprɪnsɪp(ə)ld/ *adjective* lacking or not based on moral principles.

**unprintable** /ʌnˈprɪntəb(ə)l/ *adjective* too offensive or indecent to be printed.

**unprofessional** /ʌnprəˈfeʃən(ə)l/ *adjective* contrary to professional standards; unskilled; amateurish.

**unprompted** /ʌnˈprɒmptɪd/ *adjective* spontaneous.

**unputdownable** /ʌnpʊtˈdaʊnəb(ə)l/ *adjective colloquial* compulsively readable.

**unqualified** /ʌnˈkwɒlɪfaɪd/ *adjective* not qualified or competent; complete.

**unquestionable** /ʌnˈkwestʃənəb(ə)l/ *adjective* that cannot be disputed or doubted. □ **unquestionably** *adverb*.

**unquote** /ʌnˈkwəʊt/ *interjection* used in dictation etc. to indicate closing quotation marks.

**unravel** /ʌnˈræv(ə)l/ *verb* (**-ll-**; *US* **-l-**) make or become unknitted, unknotted, etc.; solve (mystery etc.); undo (knitted fabric).

**unreal** /ʌnˈrɪəl/ *adjective* not real; imaginary; *slang* incredible.

**unreasonable** /ʌnˈriːzənəb(ə)l/ *adjective* excessive; not heeding reason. □ **unreasonably** *adverb*.

**unregenerate** /ʌnrɪˈdʒenərət/ *adjective* obstinately wrong or bad.

**unrelenting** /ʌnrɪˈlentɪŋ/ *adjective* not abating; merciless.

**unreliable** /ʌnrɪˈlaɪəb(ə)l/ *adjective* erratic.

**unrelieved** /ʌnrɪˈliːvd/ *adjective* monotonously uniform.

**unremarked** /ʌnrɪˈmɑːkt/ *adjective* not mentioned or remarked on.

**unremitting** /ʌnrɪˈmɪtɪŋ/ *adjective* incessant. □ **unremittingly** *adverb*.

**unremunerative** /ʌnrɪˈmjuːnərətɪv/ *adjective* unprofitable.

**unrequited** /ˌʌnrɪˈkwaɪtɪd/ *adjective* (of love etc.) not returned.

**unreserved** /ˌʌnrɪˈzɜːvd/ *adjective* without reservation. □ **unreservedly** /-vɪdlɪ/ *adverb*.

**unrest** /ʌnˈrest/ *noun* disturbance, turmoil, trouble.

**unrivalled** /ʌnˈraɪv(ə)ld/ *adjective* (US **unrivaled**) having no equal.

**unroll** /ʌnˈrəʊl/ *verb* open out from rolled-up state; display, be displayed.

**unruffled** /ʌnˈrʌf(ə)ld/ *adjective* calm.

**unruly** /ʌnˈruːlɪ/ *adjective* (**-ier, -iest**) undisciplined, disorderly. □ **unruliness** *noun*.

**unsatisfactory** /ˌʌnsætɪsˈfæktərɪ/ *adjective* poor, unacceptable.

**unsaturated** /ʌnˈsætʃəreɪtɪd/ *adjective* Chemistry (of fat) containing double or triple molecular bonds and therefore capable of combining with hydrogen.

**unsavoury** /ʌnˈseɪvərɪ/ *adjective* (US **unsavory**) disgusting; (esp. morally) offensive.

**unscathed** /ʌnˈskeɪðd/ *adjective* uninjured, unharmed.

**unschooled** /ʌnˈskuːld/ *adjective* uneducated, untrained.

**unscientific** /ˌʌnsaɪənˈtɪfɪk/ *adjective* not scientific in method etc. □ **unscientifically** *adverb*.

**unscramble** /ʌnˈskræmb(ə)l/ *verb* (**-ling**) decode, interpret (scrambled transmission etc.).

**unscreened** /ʌnˈskriːnd/ *adjective* (esp. of coal) not passed through screen; not checked, esp. for security or medical problems; not having screen; not shown on screen.

**unscrew** /ʌnˈskruː/ *verb* unfasten by removing screw(s), loosen (screw).

**unscripted** /ʌnˈskrɪptɪd/ *adjective* (of speech etc.) delivered impromptu.

**unscrupulous** /ʌnˈskruːpjʊləs/ *adjective* without scruples; unprincipled. □ **unscrupulously** *adverb*; **unscrupulousness** *noun*.

**unseasonal** /ʌnˈsiːzən(ə)l/ *adjective* not typical of the time or season.

**unseat** /ʌnˈsiːt/ *verb* remove from (esp. parliamentary) seat; dislodge from horseback etc.

**unseeing** /ʌnˈsiːɪŋ/ *adjective* unobservant; blind. □ **unseeingly** *adverb*.

**unseemly** /ʌnˈsiːmlɪ/ *adjective* (**-ier, -iest**) indecent; unbecoming.

**unseen** /ʌnˈsiːn/ ● *adjective* not seen; invisible; (of translation) to be done without preparation. ● *noun* unseen translation.

**unselfish** /ʌnˈselfɪʃ/ *adjective* concerned about others; sharing. □ **unselfishly** *adverb*; **unselfishness** *noun*.

**unsettled** /ʌnˈset(ə)ld/ *adjective* restless, disturbed; open to further discussion; liable to change; not paid.

**unsex** /ʌnˈseks/ *verb* deprive of qualities of one's (esp. female) sex.

**unshakeable** /ʌnˈʃeɪkəb(ə)l/ *adjective* firm; obstinate.

**unsightly** /ʌnˈsaɪtlɪ/ *adjective* ugly. □ **unsightliness** *noun*.

**unskilled** /ʌnˈskɪld/ *adjective* lacking or (of work) not needing special skills.

**unsociable** /ʌnˈsəʊʃəb(ə)l/ *adjective* disliking company.

■ **Usage** *Unsociable* is sometimes confused with *unsocial*.

**unsocial** /ʌnˈsəʊʃ(ə)l/ *adjective* not social; not suitable for or seeking society; outside normal working day; antisocial.

■ **Usage** *Unsocial* is sometimes confused with *unsociable*.

**unsolicited** /ˌʌnsəˈlɪsɪtɪd/ *adjective* voluntary.

**unsophisticated** /ˌʌnsəˈfɪstɪkeɪtɪd/ *adjective* artless, simple, natural.

**unsound** /ʌnˈsaʊnd/ *adjective* unhealthy; rotten; weak; unreliable.

**unsparing** /ʌnˈspeərɪŋ/ *adjective* lavish; merciless.

**unspeakable** /ʌnˈspiːkəb(ə)l/ *adjective* that words cannot express; indescribably bad. □ **unspeakably** *adverb*.

**unstable** /ʌnˈsteɪb(ə)l/ *adjective* (**-r, -st**) likely to fall; not stable emotionally; changeable.

**unsteady** /ʌnˈstedɪ/ *adjective* (**-ier, -iest**) not firm; changeable; not regular. □ **unsteadily** *adverb*; **unsteadiness** *noun*.

**unstick** /ʌnˈstɪk/ *verb* (*past & past participle* **unstuck**) separate (thing stuck to another). □ **come unstuck** *colloquial* fail.

**unstinting** /ʌnˈstɪntɪŋ/ *adjective* lavish; limitless. □ **unstintingly** *adverb*.

**unstressed** /ʌnˈstrest/ *adjective* not pronounced with stress.

**unstring** /ʌnˈstrɪŋ/ *verb* (*past & past participle* **unstrung**) remove string(s) of (bow, harp, etc.); take (beads etc.) off string; (esp. as **unstrung** *adjective*) unnerve.

**unstructured** /ʌnˈstrʌktʃəd/ *adjective* without structure; informal.

**unstudied** /ʌnˈstʌdɪd/ *adjective* easy, natural, spontaneous.

**unsung** /ʌnˈsʌŋ/ *adjective* not celebrated, unrecognized.

**unswerving** /ʌnˈswɜːvɪŋ/ *adjective* constant, steady. □ **unswervingly** *adverb*.

**unthinkable** /ʌnˈθɪŋkəb(ə)l/ *adjective* unimaginable, inconceivable; *colloquial* highly unlikely or undesirable.

**unthinking** /ʌnˈθɪŋkɪŋ/ *adjective* thoughtless; unintentional, inadvertent. □ **unthinkingly** *adverb*.

**untidy** /ʌnˈtaɪdɪ/ *adjective* (**-ier, -iest**) not neat or orderly. □ **untidily** *adverb*; **untidiness** *noun*.

**until** /ənˈtɪl/ *preposition & conjunction* = TILL[1].

■ **Usage** Until, as opposed to *till*, is used especially at the beginning of a sentence and in formal style, as in *Until you told me, I had no idea* or *He resided there until his decease.*

**untimely** /ʌnˈtaɪmlɪ/ *adjective* inopportune; premature.

**untiring** /ʌnˈtaɪərɪŋ/ *adjective* tireless.

**unto** /ˈʌntʊ/ *preposition archaic* to.

**untold** /ʌnˈtəʊld/ *adjective* not told; immeasurable.

**untouchable** /ʌnˈtʌtʃəb(ə)l/ ● *adjective* that may not be touched. ● *noun* Hindu of group believed to defile higher castes on contact.

**untoward** /ʌntəˈwɔːd/ *adjective* inconvenient, unlucky; awkward; refractory; unseemly.

**untrammelled** /ʌnˈtræm(ə)ld/ *adjective* not hampered.

**untruth** /ʌnˈtruːθ/ *noun* being untrue; lie.

**unused** *adjective* /ʌnˈjuːzd/ not in use, never used; /ʌnˈjuːst/ (+ *to*) not accustomed.

**unusual** /ʌnˈjuːʒʊəl/ *adjective* not usual; remarkable. □ **unusually** *adverb*.

**unutterable** /ʌnˈʌtərəb(ə)l/ *adjective* inexpressible; beyond description. □ **unutterably** *adverb*.

**unvarnished** /ʌnˈvɑːnɪʃt/ *adjective* not varnished; plain, direct, simple.

**unveil** /ʌnˈveɪl/ *verb* uncover (statue etc.) ceremonially; reveal (secrets etc.).

**unversed** /ʌnˈvɜːst/ *adjective* (usually + *in*) not experienced or skilled.

**unwarrantable** /ʌnˈwɒrəntəb(ə)l/ *adjective* (also **unwarranted**) unjustified.

**unwashed** /ʌnˈwɒʃt/ *adjective* not washed or clean. □ **the great unwashed** *colloquial* the rabble.

**unwell** /ʌnˈwel/ *adjective* ill.

**unwholesome** /ʌnˈhəʊlsəm/ *adjective* detrimental to moral or physical health; unhealthy-looking.

**unwieldy** /ʌnˈwiːldɪ/ *adjective* (**-ier, -iest**) cumbersome or hard to manage owing to size, shape, etc.

**unwilling** /ʌnˈwɪlɪŋ/ *adjective* reluctant. □ **unwillingly** *adverb*; **unwillingness** *noun*.

**unwind** /ʌnˈwaɪnd/ *verb* (*past & past participle* **unwound**) draw out or become drawn out after having been wound; *colloquial* relax.

**unwitting** /ʌnˈwɪtɪŋ/ *adjective* not knowing, unaware; unintentional. □ **unwittingly** *adverb*.

**unwonted** /ʌnˈwəʊntɪd/ *adjective* not customary or usual.

**unworldly** /ʌnˈwɜːldlɪ/ *adjective* spiritual; naïve.

**unworthy** /ʌnˈwɜːðɪ/ *adjective* (**-ier, -iest**) (often + *of*) not worthy or befitting; discreditable, unseemly. □ **unworthiness** *noun*.

**unwritten** /ʌnˈrɪt(ə)n/ *adjective* not written; (of law etc.) based on tradition or judicial decision, not on statute.

**up** ● *adverb* towards or in higher place or place regarded as higher, e.g. the north, a capital; to or in erect or required position; in or into active condition; in stronger position; (+ *to, till,* etc.) to specified place, person, or time;

higher in price; completely; completed; into compact, accumulated, or secure state; having risen; happening, esp. unusually. ● *preposition* upwards and along, through, or into; at higher part of. ● *noun* spell of good fortune. ● *verb* (**-pp-**) *colloquial* start (abruptly or unexpectedly) to speak or act; raise. □ **on the up (and up)** *colloquial* steadily improving; **up against** close to, in(to) contact with, *colloquial* confronted with; **up-and-coming** *colloquial* (of person) promising, progressing; **up for** available for or standing for (sale, office, etc.); **upstate** *US* (in, to, or of) provincial, esp. northern, part of a state; **upstream** *adverb* against flow of stream etc., *adjective* moving upstream; **up to** until, below or equal to, incumbent on, capable of, occupied or busy with; **uptown** *US* (in, into, or of) residential part of town or city; **upwind** in the direction from which the wind is blowing.

**upbeat** ● *noun* *Music* unaccented beat. ● *adjective* *colloquial* optimistic, cheerful.

**upbraid** /ʌpˈbreɪd/ *verb* (often + *with*, *for*) chide, reproach.

**upbringing** *noun* child's rearing.

**up-country** /ʌpˈkʌntrɪ/ *adjective & adverb* inland.

**update** ● *verb* /ʌpˈdeɪt/ (**-ting**) bring up to date. ● *noun* /ˈʌpdeɪt/ updating; updated information etc.

**up-end** /ʌpˈend/ *verb* set or rise up on end.

**upfront** /ʌpˈfrʌnt/ *colloquial* ● *adverb* (usually **up front**) at the front; in front; (of payments) in advance. ● *adjective* honest, frank, direct; (of payments) made in advance.

**upgrade** /ʌpˈgreɪd/ *verb* (**-ding**) raise in rank etc.; improve (equipment etc.).

**upheaval** /ʌpˈhiːv(ə)l/ *noun* sudden esp. violent change or disturbance.

**uphill** ● *adverb* /ʌpˈhɪl/ up a slope. ● *adjective* /ˈʌphɪl/ sloping up; ascending; arduous.

**uphold** /ʌpˈhəʊld/ *verb* (*past & past participle* **upheld**) support; maintain, confirm. □ **upholder** *noun*.

**upholster** /ʌpˈhəʊlstə/ *verb* provide (furniture) with upholstery. □ **upholsterer** *noun*.

**upholstery** *noun* covering, padding, springs, etc. for furniture; upholsterer's work.

**upkeep** *noun* maintenance in good condition; cost or means of this.

**upland** /ˈʌplənd/ ● *noun* (usually in *plural*) higher parts of country. ● *adjective* of these parts.

**uplift** ● *verb* /ʌpˈlɪft/ raise; (esp as **uplifting** *adjective*) elevate morally or emotionally. ● *noun* /ˈʌplɪft/ elevating influence; support for breasts etc.

**up-market** /ʌpˈmɑːkɪt/ *adjective & adverb* of or to more expensive sector of market.

**upon** /əˈpɒn/ *preposition* on.

■ **Usage** *Upon* is usually more formal than *on*, but it is standard in *once upon a time* and *upon my word*.

**upper** /ˈʌpə/ ● *adjective* higher in place; situated above; superior in rank etc. ● *noun* part of shoe or boot above sole. □ **on one's uppers** *colloquial* extremely short of money; **upper case** capital letters; **the upper crust** *colloquial* the aristocracy; **upper-cut** hit upwards with arm bent; **the upper hand** dominance, control; **Upper House** higher legislative assembly, esp. House of Lords.

**uppermost** ● *adjective* highest, predominant. ● *adverb* on or to the top.

**uppity** /ˈʌpɪtɪ/ *adjective* (also **uppish**) *colloquial* self-assertive, arrogant.

**upright** /ˈʌpraɪt/ ● *adjective* erect, vertical; (of piano) with vertical strings; honourable, honest. ● *noun* upright post or rod, esp. as structural support; upright piano.

**uprising** *noun* insurrection.

**uproar** *noun* tumult, violent disturbance.

**uproarious** /ʌpˈrɔːrɪəs/ *adjective* very noisy; provoking loud laughter; very funny. □ **uproariously** *adverb*.

**uproot** /ʌpˈruːt/ *verb* pull (plant etc.) up from ground; displace (person); eradicate.

**upset** ● *verb* /ʌpˈset/ (**-tt-**; *past & past participle* **upset**) overturn; disturb temper, digestion, or composure of; disrupt. ● *noun* /ˈʌpset/ disturbance, surprising result. ● *adjective* /ʌpˈset, ˈʌp-/ disturbed.

**upshot** *noun* outcome, conclusion.

**upside down** /ˌʌpsaɪd 'daʊn/ *adverb & adjective* with upper and lower parts reversed, inverted; in(to) total disorder.

**upstage** /ʌp'steɪdʒ/ ● *adjective & adverb* nearer back of theatre stage. ● *verb* (**-ging**) move upstage to make (another actor) face away from audience; divert attention from (person) to oneself.

**upstairs** ● *adverb* /ʌp'steəz/ to or on an upper floor. ● *adjective* /ˈʌpsteəz/ situated upstairs. ● *noun* /ʌp'steəz/ upper floor.

**upstanding** /ʌp'stændɪŋ/ *adjective* standing up; strong and healthy; honest.

**upstart** ● *noun* newly successful, esp. arrogant, person. ● *adjective* that is an upstart; of upstarts.

**upsurge** *noun* upward surge.

**upswept** *adjective* (of hair) combed to top of head.

**upswing** *noun* upward movement or trend.

**uptake** *noun colloquial* understanding; taking up (of offer etc.).

**uptight** /ʌp'taɪt/ *adjective colloquial* nervously tense, angry; *US* rigidly conventional.

**upturn** ● *noun* /ˈʌptɜːn/ upward trend, improvement. ● *verb* /ʌp'tɜːn/ turn up or upside down.

**upward** /ˈʌpwəd/ ● *adverb* (also **upwards**) towards what is higher, more important, etc. ● *adjective* moving or extending upwards. □ **upwardly** *adverb*.

**uranium** /jʊ'reɪnɪəm/ *noun* radioactive heavy grey metallic element, capable of nuclear fission and used as source of nuclear energy.

**urban** /ˈɜːbən/ *adjective* of, living in, or situated in city or town. □ **urban guerrilla** terrorist operating in urban area.

**urbane** /ɜː'beɪn/ *adjective* suave; elegant. □ **urbanity** /-'bæn-/ *noun*.

**urbanize** /ˈɜːbənaɪz/ *verb* (also **-ise**) (**-zing** or **-sing**) make urban, esp. by destroying rural quality of (district). □ **urbanization** *noun*.

**urchin** /ˈɜːtʃɪn/ *noun* mischievous, esp. ragged, child; sea urchin.

**Urdu** /ˈʊəduː/ *noun* Persian-influenced language related to Hindi, used esp. in Pakistan.

**urea** /jʊə'riːə/ *noun* soluble nitrogenous compound contained esp. in urine.

**ureter** /jʊə'riːtə/ *noun* duct carrying urine from kidney to bladder.

**urethra** /jʊə'riːθrə/ *noun* (*plural* **-s**) duct carrying urine from bladder.

**urge** /ɜːdʒ/ ● *verb* (**-ging**) (often + *on*) drive forcibly, hasten; entreat or exhort earnestly or persistently; (often + *on, upon*) advocate (action, argument, etc.) emphatically. ● *noun* urging impulse or tendency; strong desire.

**urgent** /ˈɜːdʒ(ə)nt/ *adjective* requiring immediate action or attention; importunate. □ **urgency** *noun*; **urgently** *adverb*.

**uric acid** /ˈjʊərɪk/ *noun* constituent of urine.

**urinal** /jʊə'raɪn(ə)l/ *noun* place or receptacle for urinating by men.

**urinary** /ˈjʊərɪnərɪ/ *adjective* of or relating to urine.

**urinate** /ˈjʊərɪneɪt/ *verb* (**-ting**) discharge urine. □ **urination** *noun*.

**urine** /ˈjʊərɪn/ *noun* waste fluid secreted by kidneys and discharged from bladder.

**urn** *noun* vase with foot, used esp. for ashes of the dead; large vessel with tap, in which tea etc. is made or kept hot.

**urology** /jʊə'rɒlədʒɪ/ *noun* study of the urinary system. □ **urological** /-rə'lɒdʒ-/ *adjective*.

**ursine** /ˈɜːsaɪn/ *adjective* of or like a bear.

**US** *abbreviation* United States.

**us** /ʌs, əs/ *pronoun* used by speaker or writer to refer to himself or herself and one or more others as object of verb; used for ME by sovereign in formal contexts or by editorial writer in newspaper; *colloquial* we.

**USA** *abbreviation* United States of America.

**usable** /ˈjuːzəb(ə)l/ *adjective* that can be used.

**USAF** *abbreviation* United States Air Force.

**usage** /ˈjuːsɪdʒ/ *noun* use, treatment; customary practice, established use (esp. of language).

**use** ● *verb* /juːz/ (**using**) cause to act or serve for purpose; bring into service; treat in specified way; exploit for one's own ends; (as **used** *adjective*) secondhand. ● *noun* /juːs/ using, being used;

right or power of using; benefit, advantage; custom, usage. □ **in use** being used; **make use of** use, benefit from; **used to** /juːst/ *adjective* accustomed to; *verb used before other verb to describe habitual action* (e.g. *I used to live here*); **use up** consume, find use for (leftovers etc.).

■ **Usage** The usual negative and question forms of *used to* are, for example, *You didn't use to go there* and *Did you use to go there?* Both are, however, rather informal, so it is better in formal language to use *You used not to go there* and a different expression such as *Were you in the habit of going there?* or *Did you go there when you lived in London?*

**useful** *adjective* that can be used to advantage; helpful, beneficial; *colloquial* creditable, efficient. □ **usefully** *adverb*; **usefulness** *noun*.

**useless** *adjective* serving no purpose, unavailing; *colloquial* feeble, ineffectual. □ **uselessly** *adverb*; **uselessness** *noun*.

**user** *noun* person who uses a thing. □ **user-friendly** (of computer, program, etc.) easy to use.

**usher** /ˈʌʃə/ ● *noun* person who shows people to their seats in cinema, church, etc.; doorkeeper of court etc. ● *verb* act as usher to; (usually + *in*) announce, show in.

**usherette** /ʌʃəˈret/ *noun* female usher, esp. in cinema.

**USSR** *abbreviation historical* Union of Soviet Socialist Republics.

**usual** /ˈjuːʒʊəl/ *adjective* customary; habitual. □ **as usual** as is (or was) usual. □ **usually** *adverb*.

**usurer** /ˈjuːʒərə/ *noun* person who practises usury.

**usurp** /juˈzɜːp/ *verb* seize (throne, power, etc.) wrongfully. □ **usurpation** /juːzəˈp-/ *noun*; **usurper** *noun*.

**usury** /ˈjuːʒərɪ/ *noun* lending of money at interest, esp. at exorbitant or illegal rate; interest at this rate. □ **usurious** /juːˈʒʊərɪəs/ *adjective*.

**utensil** /juːˈtens(ə)l/ *noun* implement or vessel, esp. for kitchen use.

**uterus** /ˈjuːtərəs/ *noun* (*plural* **uteri** /-raɪ/) womb. □ **uterine** /-raɪn/ *adjective*.

**utilitarian** /juːtɪlɪˈteərɪən/ ● *adjective* designed to be useful rather than attractive; of utilitarianism. ● *noun* adherent of utilitarianism.

**utilitarianism** *noun* doctrine that actions are justified if they are useful or benefit majority.

**utility** /juːˈtɪlɪtɪ/ ● *noun* (*plural* **-ies**) usefulness; useful thing, public utility. ● *adjective* basic and standardized. □ **utility room** room for domestic appliances, e.g. washing machine, boiler, etc.; **utility vehicle** vehicle serving various functions.

**utilize** /ˈjuːtɪlaɪz/ *verb* (also **-ise**) (**-zing** or **-sing**) turn to account, use. □ **utilization** *noun*.

**utmost** /ˈʌtməʊst/ ● *adjective* farthest, extreme; greatest. ● *noun* the utmost point, degree, etc. □ **do one's utmost** do all that one can.

**Utopia** /juːˈtəʊpɪə/ *noun* imagined perfect place or state. □ **Utopian**, **utopian** *adjective*.

**utter**[1] /ˈʌtə/ *adjective* complete, absolute. □ **utterly** *adverb*; **uttermost** *adjective*.

**utter**[2] /ˈʌtə/ *verb* emit audibly; express in words; *Law* put (esp. forged money) into circulation.

**utterance** *noun* uttering; thing spoken; power or manner of speaking.

**UV** *abbreviation* ultraviolet.

**uvula** /ˈjuːvjʊlə/ *noun* (*plural* **uvulae** /-liː/) fleshy part of soft palate hanging above throat. □ **uvular** *adjective*.

**uxorious** /ʌkˈsɔːrɪəs/ *adjective* excessively fond of one's wife.

# Vv

**V¹** noun (also **v**) (Roman numeral) 5.

**V²** abbreviation volt(s).

**v.** abbreviation verse; versus; very; verb; vide.

**vac** noun colloquial vacation.

**vacancy** /'veɪkənsɪ/ noun (plural **-ies**) being vacant; unoccupied post, place, etc.

**vacant** adjective not filled or occupied; not mentally active, showing no interest. □ **vacant possession** ownership of unoccupied house etc. □ **vacantly** adverb.

**vacate** /vəˈkeɪt/ verb (**-ting**) leave vacant, cease to occupy.

**vacation** /vəˈkeɪʃ(ə)n/ noun fixed holiday period, esp. in law courts and universities; US holiday; vacating, being vacated.

**vaccinate** /'væksɪneɪt/ verb (**-ting**) inoculate with vaccine to immunize against disease. □ **vaccination** noun.

**vaccine** /'væksiːn/ noun preparation used for inoculation, originally cowpox virus giving immunity to smallpox.

**vacillate** /'væsɪleɪt/ verb (**-ting**) fluctuate in opinion or resolution. □ **vacillation** noun; **vacillator** noun.

**vacuous** /'vækjʊəs/ adjective expressionless; unintelligent. □ **vacuity** /vəˈkjuːɪtɪ/ noun; **vacuously** adverb.

**vacuum** /'vækjʊəm/ ● noun (plural **-s** or **vacua**) space entirely devoid of matter; space or vessel from which air has been completely or partly removed by pump etc.; absence of normal or previous content; (plural **-s**) colloquial vacuum cleaner. ● verb colloquial clean with vacuum cleaner. □ **vacuum brake** brake worked by exhaustion of air; **vacuum cleaner** machine for removing dust etc. by suction; **vacuum flask** vessel with double wall enclosing vacuum so that contents remain hot or cold; **vacuum-packed** sealed after partial removal of air; **vacuum tube** tube containing near-vacuum for free passage of electric current.

**vagabond** /'vægəbɒnd/ ● noun wanderer, esp. idle one. ● adjective wandering, having no settled habitation or home.

**vagary** /'veɪgərɪ/ noun (plural **-ies**) caprice, eccentric act or idea.

**vagina** /vəˈdʒaɪnə/ noun (plural **-s** or **-nae** /-niː/) canal joining womb and vulva of female mammal. □ **vaginal** adjective.

**vagrant** /'veɪgrənt/ ● noun person without settled home or regular work. ● adjective wandering, roving. □ **vagrancy** noun.

**vague** /veɪg/ adjective uncertain, ill-defined; not clear-thinking, inexact. □ **vaguely** adverb; **vagueness** noun.

**vain** adjective conceited; empty, trivial; unavailing, useless. □ **in vain** without result or success, lightly or profanely. □ **vainly** adverb.

**vainglory** /veɪnˈglɔːrɪ/ noun extreme vanity, boastfulness. □ **vainglorious** adjective.

**valance** /'væləns/ noun short curtain round bedstead, above window, etc.

**vale** noun (archaic except in place names) valley.

**valediction** /vælɪˈdɪkʃ(ə)n/ noun formal bidding farewell; words used in this. □ **valedictory** adjective & noun (plural **-ies**).

**valence** /'veɪləns/ noun valency.

**valency** /'veɪlənsɪ/ noun (plural **-ies**) combining-power of an atom measured by number of hydrogen atoms it can displace or combine with.

**valentine** /'væləntaɪn/ noun (usually anonymous) letter or card sent as mark of love on St Valentine's Day (14 Feb.); sweetheart chosen on that day.

**valerian** /vəˈlɪərɪən/ noun any of various kinds of flowering herb.

**valet** /'vælɪt/ ● noun gentleman's personal servant. ● verb (**-t-**) act as valet (to).

**valetudinarian** /vælɪtjuːdɪˈneərɪən/ ● noun person of poor health or unduly anxious about health. ●*adjective* of a valetudinarian.

**valiant** /'væljənt/ *adjective* brave. □ **valiantly** *adverb*.

**valid** /'vælɪd/ *adjective* (of reason, objection, etc.) sound, defensible; legally acceptable, not yet expired. □ **validity** /və'lɪd-/ *noun*.

**validate** /'vælɪdeɪt/ *verb* (**-ting**) make valid, ratify. □ **validation** *noun*.

**valise** /və'liːz/ *noun* US small portmanteau.

**Valium** /'vælɪəm/ *noun* proprietary term the tranquillizing drug diazepam.

**valley** /'vælɪ/ *noun* (*plural* **-s**) low area between hills, usually with stream or river.

**valour** /'vælə/ *noun* (US **valor**) courage, esp. in battle. □ **valorous** *adjective*.

**valuable** /'væljuəb(ə)l/ ●*adjective* of great value, price, or worth. ●*noun* (usually in *plural*) valuable thing.

**valuation** /væljʊ'eɪʃ(ə)n/ *noun* estimation (esp. by professional valuer) of thing's worth; estimated value.

**value** /'væljuː/ ●*noun* worth, desirability, or qualities on which these depend; worth as estimated; amount for which thing can be exchanged in open market; equivalent of thing; (in full **value for money**) something well worth money spent; ability of a thing to serve a purpose or cause an effect; (in *plural*) one's principles, priorities, or standards; *Music* duration of note; *Mathematics* amount denoted by algebraic term. ●*verb* (**-ues**, **-ued**, **-uing**) estimate value of; have high or specified opinion of. □ **value added tax** tax levied on rise in value of services and goods at each stage of production; **value judgement** subjective estimate of worth etc. □ **valueless** *adjective*.

**valuer** *noun* person who estimates or assesses values.

**valve** *noun* device controlling flow through pipe etc., usually allowing movement in one direction only; structure in organ etc. allowing flow of blood etc. in one direction only; thermionic valve; device to vary length of tube in trumpet etc.; half-shell of oyster, mussel, etc.

**valvular** /'vælvjʊlə/ *adjective* having valve(s); having form or function of valve.

**vamoose** /və'muːs/ *verb* US slang depart hurriedly.

**vamp**[1] ●*noun* upper front part of boot or shoe. ●*verb* (often + *up*) repair, furbish, or make by patching or piecing together; improvise musical accompaniment.

**vamp**[2] *colloquial* ●*noun* woman who uses sexual attraction to exploit men. ●*verb* allure or exploit (man).

**vampire** /'væmpaɪə/ *noun* supposed ghost or reanimated corpse sucking blood of sleeping people; person who preys on others; (in full **vampire bat**) bloodsucking bat.

**van**[1] *noun* covered vehicle or closed railway truck for transporting goods etc.

**van**[2] *noun* vanguard, forefront.

**vanadium** /və'neɪdɪəm/ *noun* hard grey metallic element used to strengthen steel.

**vandal** /'vænd(ə)l/ *noun* person who wilfully or maliciously damages property. □ **vandalism** *noun*.

**vandalize** /'vændəlaɪz/ *verb* (also **-ise**) (**-zing** or **-sing**) destroy or damage wilfully or maliciously (esp. public property).

**vane** *noun* weather vane; blade of windmill, ship's propeller, etc.

**vanguard** /'vænɡɑːd/ *noun* foremost part of advancing army etc.; leaders of movement etc.

**vanilla** /və'nɪlə/ *noun* tropical fragrant climbing orchid; extract of its fruit (**vanilla-pod**), or synthetic substitute, used as flavouring.

**vanish** /'vænɪʃ/ *verb* disappear; cease to exist. □ **vanishing point** point at which receding parallel lines appear to meet.

**vanity** /'vænɪtɪ/ *noun* (*plural* **-ies**) conceit about one's attainments or appearance; futility, unreal thing. □ **vanity bag**, **case** woman's make-up bag or case.

**vanquish** /'vænkwɪʃ/ *verb* literary conquer, overcome.

**vantage** /'vɑːntɪdʒ/ *noun* advantage, esp. in tennis; (also **vantage point**) place giving good view.

**vapid** /'væpɪd/ *adjective* insipid, dull, flat. □ **vapidity** /və'pɪd-/ *noun*.

**vapor** *US* = VAPOUR.

**vaporize** /'veɪpəraɪz/ *verb* (also **-ise**) (**-zing** or **-sing**) change into vapour. □ **vaporization** *noun*.

**vaporous** /'veɪpərəs/ *adjective* in the form of or consisting of vapour.

**vapour** /'veɪpə/ *noun* (*US* **vapor**) moisture or other substance diffused or suspended in air, e.g. mist, smoke; gaseous form of substance. □ **vapour trail** trail of condensed water from aircraft etc.

**variable** /'veərɪəb(ə)l/ ● *adjective* changeable, adaptable; apt to vary, not constant; *Mathematics* (of quantity) indeterminate, able to assume different numerical values. ● *noun* variable thing or quantity. □ **variability** *noun*.

**variance** /'veərɪəns/ *noun* (usually after *at*) difference of opinion; dispute; discrepancy.

**variant** ● *adjective* differing in form or details from standard; having different forms. ● *noun* variant form, spelling, type, etc.

**variation** /veərɪ'eɪʃ(ə)n/ *noun* varying; departure from normal kind, standard, type, etc.; extent of this; thing that varies from type; *Music* theme in changed or elaborated form.

**varicose** /'værɪkəʊs/ *adjective* (esp. of vein etc.) permanently and abnormally dilated.

**variegated** /'veərɪɡeɪtɪd/ *adjective* with irregular patches of different colours; having leaves of two or more colours. □ **variegation** *noun*.

**variety** /və'raɪətɪ/ *noun* (*plural* **-ies**) diversity; absence of uniformity; collection of different things; class of things differing from rest in same general class; member of such class; (+ *of*) different form of thing, quality, etc.; *Biology* subdivision of species; series of dances, songs, comedy acts, etc.

**various** /'veərɪəs/ *adjective* different, diverse; several. □ **variously** *adverb*.

■ **Usage** *Various* (unlike *several*) is not a pronoun and therefore cannot be used with *of*, as (wrongly) in *Various of the guests arrived late.*

**varnish** /'vɑːnɪʃ/ ● *noun* resinous solution used to give hard shiny transparent coating. ● *verb* coat with varnish; conceal with deceptively attractive appearance.

**varsity** /'vɑːsɪtɪ/ *noun* (*plural* **-ies**) *colloquial* university.

**vary** /'veərɪ/ *verb* (**-ies**, **-ied**) be or become different; be of different kinds; modify, diversify.

**vascular** /'væskjʊlə/ *adjective* of or containing vessels for conveying blood, sap, etc.

**vas deferens** /væs 'defərenz/ *noun* (*plural* **vasa deferentia** /veɪsə defə'renʃɪə/) sperm duct of testicle.

**vase** /vɑːz/ *noun* vessel used as ornament or container for flowers.

**vasectomy** /və'sektəmɪ/ *noun* (*plural* **-ies**) removal of part of each vas deferens, esp. for sterilization.

**Vaseline** /'væsɪliːn/ *noun* proprietary term type of petroleum jelly used as ointment etc.

**vassal** /'væs(ə)l/ *noun* humble dependant; *historical* holder of land by feudal tenure.

**vast** /vɑːst/ *adjective* immense, huge. □ **vastly** *adverb*; **vastness** *noun*.

**VAT** *abbreviation* value added tax.

**vat** *noun* tank, esp. for holding liquids in brewing, dyeing, and tanning.

**Vatican** /'vætɪkən/ *noun* palace or government of Pope in Rome.

**vaudeville** /'vɔːdəvɪl/ *noun esp. US* variety entertainment.

**vault** /vɔːlt/ ● *noun* arched roof; vaultlike covering; underground room as place of storage; underground burial chamber; act of vaulting. ● *verb* leap or spring, esp. using hands or pole; spring over in this way; (esp. as **vaulted** *adjective*) make in form of vault, provide with vault(s).

**vaunt** /vɔːnt/ *verb & noun literary* boast.

**VC** *abbreviation* Victoria Cross.

**VCR** *abbreviation* video cassette recorder.

**VD** *abbreviation* venereal disease.

**VDU** *abbreviation* visual display unit.

**veal** *noun* calf's flesh as food.

**vector** /'vektə/ *noun Mathematics & Physics* quantity having both magnitude and direction; carrier of disease.

**veer** /vɪə/ *verb* change direction, esp. (of wind) clockwise; change in opinion, course, etc.

**vegan** /'viːgən/ ● *noun* person who does not eat animals or animal products. ● *adjective* using or containing no animal products.

**vegetable** /'vedʒtəb(ə)l/ ● *noun* plant, esp. edible herbaceous plant. ● *adjective* of, derived from, or relating to plant life or vegetables as food.

**vegetarian** /vedʒɪ'teərɪən/ ● *noun* person who does not eat meat or fish. ● *adjective* excluding animal food, esp. meat. □ **vegetarianism** *noun*.

**vegetate** /'vedʒɪteɪt/ *verb* (**-ting**) lead dull monotonous life; grow as plants do.

**vegetation** /vedʒɪ'teɪʃ(ə)n/ *noun* plants collectively; plant life.

**vegetative** /'vedʒɪtətɪv/ *adjective* concerned with growth and development rather than sexual reproduction; of vegetation.

**vehement** /'viːəmənt/ *adjective* showing or caused by strong feeling, ardent. □ **vehemence** *noun*; **vehemently** *adverb*.

**vehicle** /'viːɪk(ə)l/ *noun* conveyance used on land or in space; thing or person as medium for thought, feeling, or action; liquid etc. as medium for suspending pigments, drugs, etc. □ **vehicular** /vɪ'hɪkjʊlə/ *adjective*.

**veil** /veɪl/ ● *noun* piece of usually transparent material attached to woman's hat or otherwise forming part of headdress, esp. to conceal or protect face; piece of linen etc. as part of nun's headdress; thing that hides or disguises. ● *verb* cover with veil; (esp. as **veiled** *adjective*) partly conceal. □ **beyond the veil** in the unknown state of life after death; **draw a veil over** avoid discussing; **take the veil** become nun.

**vein** /veɪn/ *noun* any of tubes carrying blood to heart; (in general use) any blood vessel; rib of leaf or insect's wing; streak of different colour in wood, marble, cheese, etc.; fissure in rock filled with ore; specified character or tendency, mood. □ **veined** *adjective*.

**Velcro** /'velkrəʊ/ *noun proprietary term* fastener consisting of two strips of fabric which cling when pressed together.

**veld** /velt/ *noun* (also **veldt**) *South African* open country.

**veleta** /və'liːtə/ *noun* ballroom dance in triple time.

**vellum** /'veləm/ *noun* fine parchment, originally calfskin; manuscript on this; smooth writing paper imitating vellum.

**velociraptor** /vɪ'lɒsɪræptə/ *noun* small carnivorous dinosaur with short front legs.

**velocity** /vɪ'lɒsɪtɪ/ *noun* (*plural* **-ies**) speed, esp. of inanimate things.

**velour** /və'lʊə/ *noun* (also **velours** same pronunciation) plushlike fabric.

**velvet** /'velvɪt/ *noun* soft fabric with thick short pile on one side; furry skin on growing antler. ● *adjective* of, like, or soft as velvet. □ **on velvet** in advantageous or prosperous position; **velvet glove** outward gentleness cloaking firmness or inflexibility. □ **velvety** *adjective*.

**velveteen** /velvɪ'tiːn/ *noun* cotton fabric with pile like velvet.

**Ven.** *abbreviation* Venerable.

**venal** /'viːn(ə)l/ *adjective* able to be bribed; involving bribery; corrupt. □ **venality** /-'næl-/ *noun*.

■ **Usage** *Venal* is sometimes confused with *venial*.

**vend** *verb* offer (esp. small wares) for sale. □ **vending machine** slot machine selling small items. □ **vendor** *noun*.

**vendetta** /ven'detə/ *noun* blood feud; prolonged bitter quarrel.

**veneer** /vɪ'nɪə/ ● *noun* thin covering of fine wood; (often + *of*) deceptively pleasing appearance. ● *verb* apply veneer to (wood etc.).

**venerable** /'venərəb(ə)l/ *adjective* entitled to deep respect on account of age, character, etc.; *title of archdeacon.*

**venerate** /'venəreɪt/ *verb* (**-ting**) regard with deep respect. □ **veneration** *noun*.

**venereal** /vɪ'nɪərɪəl/ *adjective* of sexual desire or intercourse; of venereal ease. □ **venereal disease** disease contracted by sexual intercourse with infected person.

**Venetian** /vɪˈniːʃ(ə)n/ ● noun native, citizen, or dialect of Venice. ● adjective of Venice. □ **venetian blind** window-blind of adjustable horizontal slats.

**vengeance** /ˈvendʒ(ə)ns/ noun punishment inflicted for wrong to oneself or to one's cause. □ **with a vengeance** to extreme degree, thoroughly, violently.

**vengeful** /ˈvendʒfʊl/ adjective seeking vengeance, vindictive.

**venial** /ˈviːnɪəl/ adjective (of sin or fault) pardonable, not mortal. □ **veniality** /-ˈæl-/ noun.

■ Usage *Venial* is sometimes confused with *venal*.

**venison** /ˈvenɪs(ə)n/ noun deer's flesh as food.

**Venn diagram** noun diagram using overlapping and intersecting circles etc. to show relationships between mathematical sets.

**venom** /ˈvenəm/ noun poisonous fluid of esp. snakes; malignity, virulence of feeling, language, or conduct. □ **venomous** /ˈvenəməs/ adjective; **venomously** adverb.

**venous** /ˈviːnəs/ adjective of, full of, or contained in veins.

**vent**[1] ● noun opening for passage of air etc.; outlet, free expression; anus, esp. of lower animal. ● verb give vent or free expression to.

**vent**[2] noun slit in garment, esp. in back of jacket.

**ventilate** /ˈventɪleɪt/ verb (-ting) cause air to circulate freely in (room etc.); air (question, grievance, etc.). □ **ventilation** noun.

**ventilator** noun appliance or aperture for ventilating room etc.; apparatus for maintaining artifical respiration.

**ventral** /ˈventr(ə)l/ adjective of or on abdomen.

**ventricle** /ˈventrɪk(ə)l/ noun cavity in body; hollow part of organ, esp. brain or heart.

**ventricular** /venˈtrɪkjʊlə/ adjective of or shaped like ventricle.

**ventriloquism** /venˈtrɪləkwɪz(ə)m/ noun skill of speaking without moving the lips. □ **ventriloquist** noun.

**venture** /ˈventʃə/ ● noun risky undertaking; commercial speculation. ● verb (-ring) dare, not be afraid; dare to go, make, or put forward; take risks, expose to risk, stake. □ **Venture Scout** senior Scout.

**venturesome** adjective disposed to take risks.

**venue** /ˈvenjuː/ noun appointed place for match, meeting, concert, etc.

**Venus fly-trap** /ˈviːnəs/ noun insectivorous plant.

**veracious** /vəˈreɪʃəs/ adjective formal truthful, true. □ **veracity** /-ˈræs-/ noun.

**veranda** /vəˈrændə/ noun (sometimes partly covered) platform along side of house.

**verb** noun word used to indicate action, event, state, or change (see panel).

**verbal** adjective of words; oral, not written; of a verb; (of translation) literal. □ **verbally** adverb.

**verbalize** verb (also **-ise**) (**-zing** or **-sing**) put into words.

**verbatim** /vɜːˈbeɪtɪm/ adverb & adjective in exactly the same words.

**verbena** /vɜːˈbiːnə/ noun (plural same) plant of genus of herbs and small shrubs with fragrant flowers.

**verbiage** /ˈvɜːbɪɪdʒ/ noun derogatory unnecessary number of words.

**verbose** /vɜːˈbəʊs/ adjective using more words than are needed. □ **verbosity** /-ˈbɒs-/ noun.

**verdant** /ˈvɜːd(ə)nt/ adjective (of grass, field, etc.) green, lush. □ **verdancy** noun.

**verdict** /ˈvɜːdɪkt/ noun decision of jury; decision, judgement.

**verdigris** /ˈvɜːdɪgriː/ noun greenish-blue substance that forms on copper or brass.

**verdure** /ˈvɜːdjə/ noun literary green vegetation or its colour.

**verge**[1] noun edge, border; brink; grass edging of road etc.

**verge**[2] verb (**-ging**) (+ on) border on; incline downwards or in specified direction.

**verger** /ˈvɜːdʒə/ noun caretaker and attendant in church; officer carrying staff before dignitaries of cathedral etc.

**verify** /ˈverɪfaɪ/ verb (**-ies**, **-ied**) establish truth or correctness of by examination etc.; fulfil, bear out. □ **verification** noun.

**verily** /ˈverɪlɪ/ adverb archaic truly, really.

**verisimilitude** /ˌverɪsɪˈmɪlɪtjuːd/ *noun* appearance of being true or real.

**veritable** /ˈverɪtəb(ə)l/ *adjective* real, rightly so called.

**verity** /ˈverɪtɪ/ *noun* (*plural* **-ies**) true statement; *archaic* truth.

**vermicelli** /vɜːmɪˈtʃelɪ/ *noun* pasta in long slender threads.

**vermicide** /ˈvɜːmɪsaɪd/ *noun* drug used to kill intestinal worms.

**vermiform** /ˈvɜːmɪfɔːm/ *adjective* worm-shaped. □ **vermiform appendix** small blind tube extending from caecum in man and some other mammals.

**vermilion** /vəˈmɪljən/ ● *noun* brilliant scarlet pigment made esp. from cinnabar; colour of this. ● *adjective* of this colour.

**vermin** /ˈvɜːmɪn/ *noun* (usually treated as *plural*) mammals and birds harmful to game, crops, etc.; parasitic worms or insects; vile people.

**verminous** *adjective* of the nature of or infested with vermin.

**vermouth** /ˈvɜːməθ/ *noun* wine flavoured with aromatic herbs.

**vernacular** /vəˈnækjʊlə/ ● *noun* language or dialect of country; language of particular class or group; homely speech. ● *adjective* (of language) of one's own country, not foreign or formal.

**vernal** /ˈvɜːn(ə)l/ *adjective* of or in spring.

**vernier** /ˈvɜːnɪə/ *noun* small movable scale for reading fractional parts of subdivisions on fixed scale of measuring instrument.

**veronica** /vəˈrɒnɪkə/ *noun* speedwell.

**verruca** /vəˈruːkə/ *noun* (*plural* **verrucae** /-siː/ or **-s**) wart or similar growth, esp. on foot.

**versatile** /ˈvɜːsətaɪl/ *adjective* turning easily or readily from one subject or occupation to another, skilled in many subjects or occupations; having many uses. □ **versatility** /-ˈtɪl-/ *noun*.

**verse** *noun* poetry; stanza of poem or song; each of short numbered divisions of Bible.

**versed** /vɜːst/ *adjective* (+ *in*) experienced or skilled in.

**versicle** /ˈvɜːsɪk(ə)l/ *noun* short sentence, esp. each of series in liturgy said or sung by minister or priest, answered by congregation.

---

## Verb

A verb says what a person or thing does, and can describe:

an action, e.g. *run, hit*
an event, e.g. *rain, happen*
a state, e.g. *be, have, seem, appear*
a change, e.g. *become, grow*

Verbs occur in different forms, usually in one or other of their tenses. The most common tenses are:

| | |
|---|---|
| the simple present tense: | *The boy walks down the road.* |
| the continuous present tense: | *The boy is walking down the road.* |
| the simple past tense: | *The boy walked down the road.* |
| the continuous past tense: | *The boy was walking down the road.* |
| the perfect tense: | *The boy has walked down the road.* |
| the future tense: | *The boy will walk down the road.* |

Each of these forms is a finite verb, which means that it is in a particular tense and that it changes according to the number and person of the subject, as in

| | |
|---|---|
| *I am* | *you walk* |
| *we are* | *he walks* |

An infinitive is the form of a verb that usually appears with 'to', e.g.

*to wander, to look, to sleep.*

**versify** /ˈvɜːsɪfaɪ/ *verb* (**-ies**, **-ied**) turn into or express in verse; compose verses. □ **versification** *noun*.

**version** /ˈvɜːʃ(ə)n/ *noun* account of matter from particular point of view; particular edition or translation of book etc.

**verso** /ˈvɜːsəʊ/ *noun* (*plural* **-s**) left-hand page of open book, back of printed leaf.

**versus** /ˈvɜːsəs/ *preposition* against.

**vertebra** /ˈvɜːtɪbrə/ *noun* (*plural* **-brae** /-briː/) each segment of backbone. □ **vertebral** *adjective*.

**vertebrate** /ˈvɜːtɪbrət/ ● *adjective* having backbone. ● *noun* vertebrate animal.

**vertex** /ˈvɜːteks/ *noun* (*plural* **-tices** /-tɪsiːz/ or **-texes**) highest point, top, apex; meeting-point of lines that form angle.

**vertical** /ˈvɜːtɪk(ə)l/ ● *adjective* at right angles to horizontal plane; in direction from top to bottom of picture etc.; of or at vertex. ● *noun* vertical line or plane. □ **vertical take-off** take-off of aircraft directly upwards. □ **vertically** *adverb*.

**vertiginous** /vɜːˈtɪdʒɪnəs/ *adjective* of or causing vertigo.

**vertigo** /ˈvɜːtɪɡəʊ/ *noun* dizziness.

**vervain** /ˈvɜːveɪn/ *noun* any of several verbenas, esp. one with small blue, white, or purple flowers.

**verve** *noun* enthusiasm, energy, vigour.

**very** /ˈverɪ/ ● *adverb* in high degree; (+ *own* or superlative adjective) in fullest sense. ● *adjective* real, properly so called etc. □ **very good**, **well** *formula of consent or approval;* **very high frequency** 30–300 megahertz (in radio); **Very Reverend** *title of dean.*

**vesicle** /ˈvesɪk(ə)l/ *noun* small bladder, blister, or bubble.

**vespers** /ˈvespəz/ *plural noun* evening church service.

**vessel** /ˈves(ə)l/ *noun* hollow receptacle, esp. for liquid; ship or boat, esp. large one; duct or canal holding or conveying blood, sap, etc.

**vest** ● *noun* undergarment worn on upper part of body; *US & Australian* waistcoat. ● *verb* (+ *with*) bestow (powers, authority, etc.) on; (+ *in*) confer (property or power) on (person) with immediate fixed right of future possession. □ **vested interest** personal interest in state of affairs, usually with

expectation of gain, *Law* interest (usually in land or money held in trust) recognized as belonging to person.

**vestal virgin** /ˈvest(ə)l/ *noun* virgin consecrated to Vesta, Roman goddess of hearth and home, and vowed to chastity.

**vestibule** /ˈvestɪbjuːl/ *noun* lobby, entrance hall.

**vestige** /ˈvestɪdʒ/ *noun* trace, evidence; slight amount, particle; *Biology* part or organ now atrophied that was well-developed in ancestors. □ **vestigial** /-ˈtɪdʒɪəl/ *adjective*.

**vestment** /ˈvestmənt/ *noun* ceremonial garment worn by priest etc.

**vestry** /ˈvestrɪ/ *noun* (*plural* **-ies**) room or part of church for keeping vestments etc. in.

**vet** ● *noun colloquial* veterinary surgeon. ● *verb* (**-tt-**) make careful and critical examination of (scheme, work, candidate, etc.).

**vetch** *noun* plant of pea family largely used for fodder.

**veteran** /ˈvetərən/ *noun* old soldier or long-serving member of any group; *US* ex-serviceman or -woman. □ **veteran car** one made before 1905.

**veterinarian** /vetərɪˈneərɪən/ *noun formal* veterinary surgeon.

**veterinary** /ˈvetərɪnərɪ/ *adjective* of or for diseases and injuries of animals. □ **veterinary surgeon** person qualified to treat animals.

**veto** /ˈviːtəʊ/ ● *noun* (*plural* **-es**) right to reject measure etc. unilaterally; rejection, prohibition. ● *verb* (**-oes**, **-oed**) reject (measure etc.); forbid.

**vex** *verb* annoy, irritate; *archaic* grieve, afflict.

**vexation** /vekˈseɪʃ(ə)n/ *noun* vexing, being vexed; annoying or distressing thing.

**vexatious** /vekˈseɪʃ(ə)s/ *adjective* causing vexation; *Law* lacking sufficient grounds for action and seeking only to annoy defendant.

**vexed** *adjective* (of question) much discussed.

**VHF** *abbreviation* very high frequency.

**via** /ˈvaɪə/ *preposition* by way of, through.

**viable | victual**

**viable** /'vaɪəb(ə)l/ *adjective* (of plan etc.) feasible, esp. economically; (esp. of foetus) capable of living and surviving independently. □ **viability** *noun*.

**viaduct** /'vaɪədʌkt/ *noun* long bridge carrying railway or road over valley.

**vial** /'vaɪəl/ *noun* small glass vessel.

**viands** /'vaɪəndz/ *plural noun formal* articles of food.

**viaticum** /vaɪ'ætɪkəm/ *noun* (*plural* **-ca**) Eucharist given to dying person.

**vibes** /vaɪbz/ *plural noun colloquial* vibrations, esp. feelings communicated; vibraphone.

**vibrant** /'vaɪbrənt/ *adjective* vibrating; resonant; (often + *with*) thrilling; (of colour) bright and striking. □ **vibrancy** *noun*.

**vibraphone** /'vaɪbrəfəʊn/ *noun* percussion instrument with motor-driven resonators under metal bars giving vibrato effect.

**vibrate** /vaɪ'breɪt/ *verb* (**-ting**) move rapidly to and fro; (of sound) throb, resonate; (+ *with*) quiver; swing to and fro, oscillate. □ **vibratory** *adjective*.

**vibration** *noun* vibrating; (in *plural*) mental (esp. occult) influence, atmosphere or feeling communicated.

**vibrato** /vɪ'brɑːtəʊ/ *noun* tremulous effect in musical pitch.

**vibrator** *noun* device that vibrates, esp. instrument used in massage or sexual stimulation.

**viburnum** /vaɪ'bɜːnəm/ *noun* shrub with pink or white flowers.

**vicar** /'vɪkə/ *noun* incumbent of C. of E. parish where in former times incumbent received stipend rather than tithes; *colloquial* any member of the clergy.

**vicarage** *noun* vicar's house.

**vicarious** /vɪ'keərɪəs/ *adjective* experienced indirectly; acting or done etc. for another; deputed, delegated. □ **vicariously** *adverb*.

**vice**[1] *noun* immoral conduct; particular form of this; bad habit. □ **vice ring** group of criminals organizing prostitution; **vice squad** police department concerned with prostitution.

**vice**[2] *noun* (*US* **vise**) clamp with two jaws for holding an object being worked on.

**vice-** *combining form* person acting in place of; person next in rank to.

**vice-chancellor** /vaɪs'tʃɑːnsələ/ *noun* deputy chancellor (esp. administrator of university).

**viceregal** /vaɪs'riːg(ə)l/ *adjective* of viceroy.

**vicereine** /'vaɪsreɪn/ *noun* viceroy's wife; woman viceroy.

**viceroy** /'vaɪsrɔɪ/ *noun* ruler on behalf of sovereign in colony, province, etc.

**vice versa** /vaɪs 'vɜːsə/ *adjective* with order of terms changed, other way round.

**Vichy water** /'viːʃiː/ *noun* effervescent mineral water from Vichy in France.

**vicinity** /vɪ'sɪnɪtɪ/ *noun* (*plural* **-ies**) surrounding district; (+ *to*) nearness to. □ **in the vicinity (of)** near (to).

**vicious** /'vɪʃəs/ *adjective* bad-tempered; spiteful; violent; corrupt. □ **vicious circle** self-perpetuating, harmful sequence of cause and effect. □ **viciously** *adverb*; **viciousness** *noun*.

**vicissitude** /vɪ'sɪsɪtjuːd/ *noun literary* change, esp. of fortune.

**victim** /'vɪktɪm/ *noun* person or thing destroyed or injured; prey, dupe; creature sacrificed to a god etc.

**victimize** *verb* (also **-ise**) (**-zing** or **-sing**) single out for punishment or unfair treatment; make (person etc.) a victim. □ **victimization** *noun*.

**victor** /'vɪktə/ *noun* conqueror, winner of contest.

**Victoria Cross** /vɪk'tɔːrɪə/ *noun* highest decoration for conspicuous bravery in armed services.

**Victorian** /vɪk'tɔːrɪən/ ● *adjective* of time of Queen Victoria; prudish, strict. ● *noun* person of this time.

**Victoriana** /vɪktɔːrɪ'ɑːnə/ *plural noun* articles, esp. collectors' items, of Victorian period.

**victorious** /vɪk'tɔːrɪəs/ *adjective* conquering, triumphant; marked by victory. □ **victoriously** *adverb*.

**victory** /'vɪktərɪ/ *noun* (*plural* **-ies**) success in battle, war, or contest.

**victual** /'vɪt(ə)l/ ● *noun* (usually in *plural*) food, provisions. ● *verb* (**-ll-**; *US* **-l-**) supply with victuals; lay in supply of victuals; eat victuals.

**victualler** /'vɪtlə/ noun (US **victualer**) person who supplies victuals; (in full **licensed victualler**) publican licensed to sell alcohol.

**vicuña** /vɪ'kju:nə/ noun S. American mammal with fine silky wool; cloth made from its wool; imitation of this.

**vide** /'vi:deɪ/ verb (in imperative) see, consult. [Latin]

**videlicet** /vɪ'deliset/ adverb that is to say; namely.

**video** /'vɪdɪəʊ/ ● adjective relating to recording or reproduction of moving pictures on magnetic tape; of broadcasting of these. ● noun (plural **-s**) such recording or broadcasting; colloquial video recorder; colloquial film on videotape. ● verb (**-oes**, **-oed**) record on videotape. □ **video cassette** cassette of videotape; **video game** computer game played on television screen; **video nasty** colloquial horrific or pornographic video film; **video (cassette) recorder** apparatus for recording and playing videotapes.

**videotape** ● noun magnetic tape for recording television pictures and sound. ● verb (**-ping**) record on this.

**vie** /vaɪ/ verb (**vying**) (often + with) contend, compete, strive for superiority.

**Vietnamese** /vjetnə'mi:z/ ● adjective of Vietnam. ● noun (plural same) native, national, or language of Vietnam.

**view** /vju:/ ● noun range of vision; what is seen, scene, prospect, picture etc. of this; opinion; inspection by eye or mind. ● verb look at; survey visually or mentally; form mental impression or opinion of; watch television. □ **in view of** considering; **on view** being shown or exhibited; **viewdata** news and information service from computer source, connected to TV screen by telephone link; **viewfinder** part of camera showing field of photograph; **viewpoint** point of view; **with a view to** with hope or intention of.

**viewer** noun television-watcher; device for looking at film transparencies etc.

**vigil** /'vɪdʒɪl/ noun keeping awake during night etc., esp. to keep watch or pray; eve of festival or holy day.

**vigilance** noun watchfulness; caution. □ **vigilant** adjective.

**vigilante** /vɪdʒɪ'læntɪ/ noun member of self-appointed group for keeping order etc.

**vignette** /vi:'njet/ noun short description, character sketch; illustration not in definite border; photograph etc. with background shaded off.

**vigour** /'vɪgə/ noun (US **vigor**) activity and strength of body or mind; healthy growth; animation. □ **vigorous** adjective; **vigorously** adverb.

**Viking** /'vaɪkɪŋ/ noun Scandinavian raider and pirate of 8th–11th c.

**vile** adjective disgusting; depraved; colloquial abominably bad. □ **vilely** adverb; **vileness** noun.

**vilify** /'vɪlɪfaɪ/ verb (**-ies**, **-ied**) speak ill of, defame. □ **vilification** noun.

**villa** /'vɪlə/ noun country house, mansion; rented holiday home, esp. abroad; detached or semi-detached house in residential district.

**village** /'vɪlɪdʒ/ noun group of houses etc. in country district, larger than hamlet and smaller than town.

**villager** noun inhabitant of village.

**villain** /'vɪlən/ noun wicked person; chief wicked character in play, story, etc.; colloquial criminal, rascal.

**villainous** adjective wicked.

**villainy** noun (plural **-ies**) wicked behaviour or act.

**villein** /'vɪlɪn/ noun historical feudal tenant entirely subject to lord or attached to manor. □ **villeinage** noun.

**vim** noun colloquial vigour, energy.

**vinaigrette** /vɪnɪ'gret/ noun salad dressing of oil and wine vinegar.

**vindicate** /'vɪndɪkeɪt/ verb (**-ting**) clear of suspicion; establish merits, existence, or justice of. □ **vindication** noun; **vindicator** noun; **vindicatory** adjective.

**vindictive** /vɪn'dɪktɪv/ adjective tending to seek revenge. □ **vindictively** adverb; **vindictiveness** noun.

**vine** noun trailing or climbing woody-stemmed plant, esp. bearing grapes.

**vinegar** /'vɪnɪgə/ noun sour liquid produced by fermentation of wine, malt, cider, etc. □ **vinegary** adjective.

**vineyard** /'vɪnjɑːd/ noun plantation of grapevines, esp. for wine-making.

*vingt-et-un* /væ̃teɪˈɒ̃/ *noun* = PONTOON[1]. [French]

**vino** /ˈviːnəʊ/ *noun slang* wine, esp. of inferior kind.

**vinous** /ˈvaɪnəs/ *adjective* of, like, or due to wine.

**vintage** /ˈvɪntɪdʒ/ ● *noun* season's produce of grapes, wine from this; grapeharvest, season of this; wine of high quality from particular year and district; year etc. when thing was made, thing made etc. in particular year etc. ● *adjective* of high or peak quality; of a past season. □ **vintage car** car made 1917–1930.

**vintner** /ˈvɪntnə/ *noun* wine merchant.

**vinyl** /ˈvaɪnɪl/ *noun* any of group of plastics made by polymerization.

**viol** /ˈvaɪəl/ *noun* medieval stringed instrument similar in shape to violin.

**viola**[1] /vɪˈəʊlə/ *noun* instrument like violin but larger and of lower pitch.

**viola**[2] /ˈvaɪələ/ *noun* any plant of genus including violet and pansy, esp. cultivated hybrid.

**viola da gamba** /vɪˌəʊlə də ˈgæmbə/ *noun* viol held between player's legs.

**violate** /ˈvaɪəleɪt/ *verb* (**-ting**) disregard, break (oath, law, etc.); treat profanely; break in on, disturb; rape. □ **violation** *noun*, **violator** *noun*.

**violence** /ˈvaɪələns/ *noun* being violent; violent conduct or treatment; unlawful use of force. □ **do violence to** act contrary to, outrage.

**violent** /ˈvaɪələnt/ *adjective* involving great physical force; intense, vehement; (of death) resulting from violence or poison. □ **violently** *adverb*.

**violet** /ˈvaɪələt/ ● *noun* plant with usually purple, blue, or white flowers; bluishpurple colour at opposite end of spectrum from red; paint, clothes, or material of this colour. ● *adjective* of this colour.

**violin** /vaɪəˈlɪn/ *noun* high-pitched instrument with 4 strings played with bow. □ **violinist** *noun*.

**violoncello** /vaɪələnˈtʃeləʊ/ *noun* (*plural* **-s**) *formal* cello.

**VIP** *abbreviation* very important person.

**viper** /ˈvaɪpə/ *noun* small venomous snake; malignant or treacherous person.

**virago** /vɪˈrɑːgəʊ/ *noun* (*plural* **-s**) fierce or abusive woman.

**viral** /ˈvaɪər(ə)l/ *adjective* of or caused by virus.

**virgin** /ˈvɜːdʒɪn/ ● *noun* person who has never had sexual intercourse; (**the Virgin**) Christ's mother Mary. ● *adjective* not yet used etc.; virginal. □ **the Virgin birth** doctrine of Christ's birth from virgin mother. □ **virginity** /vəˈdʒɪn-/ *noun*.

**virginal** ● *adjective* of or befitting a virgin. ● *noun* (usually in *plural*) legless spinet in box.

**Virginia creeper** /vəˈdʒɪnɪə/ *noun* vine cultivated for ornament.

**Virgo** /ˈvɜːgəʊ/ *noun* sixth sign of zodiac.

**virile** /ˈvɪraɪl/ *adjective* having masculine vigour or strength; sexually potent; of man as distinct from woman or child. □ **virility** /-ˈrɪl-/ *noun*.

**virology** /vaɪˈrɒlədʒɪ/ *noun* study of viruses.

**virtual** /ˈvɜːtʃʊəl/ *adjective* being so for practical purposes though not strictly or in name. □ **virtual reality** computer-generated images, sounds, etc. that appear real to the senses. □ **virtually** *adverb*.

**virtue** /ˈvɜːtʃuː/ *noun* moral goodness; particular form of this; chastity, esp. of woman; good quality; efficacy. □ **by** or **in virtue of** on account of, because of.

**virtuoso** /vɜːtʃʊˈəʊsəʊ/ *noun* (*plural* **-si** /-siː/ or **-sos**) highly skilled artist, esp. musician. □ **virtuosity** /-ˈɒs-/ *noun*.

**virtuous** /ˈvɜːtʃʊəs/ *adjective* morally good; *archaic* chaste. □ **virtuously** *adverb*.

**virulent** /ˈvɪrʊlənt/ *adjective* poisonous; (of disease) violent; bitterly hostile. □ **virulence** *noun*, **virulently** *adverb*.

**virus** /ˈvaɪərəs/ *noun* microscopic organism able to cause diseases; computer virus.

**visa** /ˈviːzə/ *noun* endorsement on passport etc., esp. allowing holder to enter or leave country.

**visage** /ˈvɪzɪdʒ/ *noun literary* face.

**vis-à-vis** /viːzɑːˈviː/ ● *preposition* in relation to; in comparison with. ● *adverb* opposite. [French]

**viscera** /ˈvɪsərə/ *plural noun* internal organs of body. □ **visceral** *adjective*.

**viscid** /ˈvɪsɪd/ *adjective* glutinous, sticky.

**viscose** /'vɪskəʊz/ noun viscous form of cellulose used in making rayon etc.; fabric made from this.

**viscount** /'vaɪkaʊnt/ noun British nobleman ranking between earl and baron.

**viscountess** /'vaɪkaʊntɪs/ noun viscount's wife or widow; woman holding rank of viscount.

**viscous** /'vɪskəs/ adjective glutinous, sticky; semifluid; not flowing freely. □ **viscosity** /-kɒs-/ noun (plural **-ies**).

**visibility** /vɪzɪ'bɪlɪtɪ/ noun being visible; range or possibility of vision as determined by light and weather.

**visible** /'vɪzɪb(ə)l/ adjective able to be seen, perceived, or discovered; in sight; apparent, open, obvious. □ **visibly** adverb.

**vision** /'vɪʒ(ə)n/ noun act or faculty of seeing, sight; thing or person seen in dream or trance; thing seen in imagination; imaginative insight; foresight, good judgement in planning; beautiful person etc.; TV or cinema picture, esp. of specified quality.

**visionary** ● adjective given to seeing visions or to fanciful theories; having vision or foresight; not real, imaginary; unpractical. ● noun (plural **-ies**) visionary person.

**visit** /'vɪzɪt/ ● verb (**-t-**) go or come to see (person, place, etc.); stay temporarily with or at; (of disease, calamity, etc.) attack; (often + upon) inflict punishment for (sin). ● noun act of visiting, temporary stay with person or at place; (+ to) occasion of going to doctor etc.; formal or official call.

**visitant** /'vɪzɪt(ə)nt/ noun visitor, esp. ghost etc.

**visitation** /vɪzɪ'teɪʃ(ə)n/ noun official visit of inspection; trouble etc. seen as divine punishment.

**visitor** noun person who visits; migrant bird.

**visor** /'vaɪzə/ noun movable part of helmet covering face; shield for eyes, esp. one at top of vehicle windscreen.

**vista** /'vɪstə/ noun view, esp. through avenue of trees or other long narrow opening; mental view of long succession of events.

**visual** /'vɪzʊəl/ adjective of or used in seeing. □ **visual display unit** device

for displaying data of computer on screen. □ **visually** adverb.

**visualize** verb (also **-ise**) (**-zing** or **-sing**) imagine visually. □ **visualization** noun.

**vital** /'vaɪt(ə)l/ ● adjective of or essential to organic life; essential to existence, success, etc.; full of life or activity; fatal. ● noun (in plural) vital organs, e.g. lungs and heart. □ **vital statistics** those relating to number of births, marriages, deaths, etc., jocular measurements of woman's bust, waist, and hips. □ **vitally** adverb.

**vitality** /vaɪ'tælɪtɪ/ noun animation, liveliness; ability to survive or endure.

**vitalize** verb (also **-ise**) (**-zing** or **-sing**) endow with life; make lively or vigorous. □ **vitalization** noun.

**vitamin** /'vɪtəmɪn/ noun any of various substances present in many foods and essential to health and growth.

**vitaminize** verb (also **-ise**) (**-zing** or **-sing**) introduce vitamins into (food).

**vitiate** /'vɪʃɪeɪt/ verb (**-ting**) impair, debase; make invalid or ineffectual.

**viticulture** /'vɪtɪkʌltʃə/ noun cultivation of grapes.

**vitreous** /'vɪtrɪəs/ adjective of or like glass.

**vitrify** /'vɪtrɪfaɪ/ verb (**-ies**, **-ied**) change into glass or glassy substance, esp. by heat. □ **vitrification** noun.

**vitriol** /'vɪtrɪəl/ noun sulphuric acid or sulphate; caustic speech or criticism. □ **vitriolic** /-'ɒl-/ adjective.

**vitro** see IN VITRO.

**vituperate** /vɪ'tjuːpəreɪt/ verb (**-ting**) criticize abusively. □ **vituperation** noun; **vituperative** /-rətɪv/ adjective.

**viva**[1] /'vaɪvə/ colloquial ● noun (plural **-s**) viva voce. ● verb (**vivas**, **vivaed**, **vivaing**) viva-voce.

**viva**[2] /'viːvə/ ● interjection long live. ● noun cry of this as salute etc. [Italian]

**vivacious** /vɪ'veɪʃəs/ adjective lively, animated. □ **vivacity** /vɪ'væsɪtɪ/ noun.

**vivarium** /vaɪ'veərɪəm/ noun (plural **-ria** or **-s**) glass bowl etc. for keeping animals for scientific study; place for keeping animals in (nearly) their natural conditions.

**viva voce** /vaɪvə 'vəʊtʃɪ/ ● adjective oral. ● adverb orally. ● noun oral exam.

**viva-voce** *verb* (**-voces**, **-voceed**, **-voceing**) examine orally.

**vivid** /ˈvɪvɪd/ *adjective* (of light or colour) bright, strong, intense; (of memory, description, etc.) lively, incisive, graphic. □ **vividly** *adverb*; **vividness** *noun*.

**vivify** /ˈvɪvɪfaɪ/ *verb* (**-ies**, **-ied**) give life to, animate.

**viviparous** /vɪˈvɪpərəs/ *adjective* bringing forth young alive.

**vivisect** /ˈvɪvɪsekt/ *verb* perform vivisection on.

**vivisection** /vɪvɪˈsekʃ(ə)n/ *noun* surgical experimentation on living animals for scientific research. □ **vivisectionist** *noun*.

**vixen** /ˈvɪks(ə)n/ *noun* female fox; spiteful woman.

**viz.** *abbreviation* videlicet.

**vizier** /vɪˈzɪə/ *noun historical* high official in some Muslim countries.

**V-neck** *noun* V-shaped neckline on pullover etc.

**vocabulary** /vəˈkæbjʊlərɪ/ *noun* (*plural* **-ies**) words used by language, book, branch of science, or author; list of these; person's range of language.

**vocal** /ˈvəʊk(ə)l/ *adjective* of or uttered by voice; speaking one's feelings freely. □ **vocal cords** voice-producing part of larynx. □ **vocally** *adverb*.

**vocalist** *noun* singer.

**vocalize** *verb* (also **-ise**) (**-zing** or **-sing**) form (sound) or utter (word) with voice; articulate, express. □ **vocalization** *noun*.

**vocation** /vəʊˈkeɪʃ(ə)n/ *noun* divine call to, or sense of suitability for, career or occupation; employment, trade, profession. □ **vocational** *adjective*.

**vocative** /ˈvɒkətɪv/ ● *noun* case of noun used in addressing person or thing. ● *adjective* of or in this case.

**vociferate** /vəˈsɪfəreɪt/ *verb* (**-ting**) utter noisily; shout, bawl. □ **vociferation** *noun*.

**vociferous** /vəˈsɪfərəs/ *adjective* noisy, clamorous; loud and insistent in speech. □ **vociferously** *adverb*.

**vodka** /ˈvɒdkə/ *noun* alcoholic spirit distilled esp. in Russia from rye etc.

**vogue** /vəʊg/ *noun* (**the vogue**) prevailing fashion; popular use. □ **in vogue** in fashion. □ **voguish** *adjective*.

**voice** ● *noun* sound formed in larynx and uttered by mouth, esp. in speaking, singing, etc.; ability to produce this; use of voice, spoken or written expression, opinion so expressed, right to express opinion; *Grammar* set of verbal forms showing whether verb is active or passive. ● *verb* (**-cing**) express; (esp. as **voiced** *adjective*) utter with vibration of vocal cords. □ **voice-over** commentary in film by unseen speaker.

**void** ● *adjective* empty, vacant; not valid or binding. ● *noun* empty space, sense of loss. ● *verb* invalidate; excrete.

**voile** /vɔɪl/ *noun* thin semi-transparent fabric.

**vol.** *abbreviation* volume.

**volatile** /ˈvɒlətaɪl/ *adjective* changeable in mood, flighty; unstable; evaporating rapidly. □ **volatility** /-ˈtɪl-/ *noun*.

**vol-au-vent** /ˈvɒləʊvɑ̃/ *noun* small round case of puff pastry with savoury filling.

**volcanic** /vɒlˈkænɪk/ *adjective* of, like, or produced by volcano.

**volcano** /vɒlˈkeɪnəʊ/ *noun* (*plural* **-es**) mountain or hill from which lava, steam, etc. escape through earth's crust.

**vole** *noun* small plant-eating rodent.

**volition** /vəˈlɪʃ(ə)n/ *noun* act or power of willing. □ **of one's own volition** voluntarily.

**volley** /ˈvɒlɪ/ ● *noun* (*plural* **-s**) simultaneous firing of a number of weapons; bullets etc. so fired; (usually + *of*) torrent (of abuse etc.); *Tennis, Football, etc.* playing of ball before it touches ground. ● *verb* (**-eys**, **-eyed**) return or send by volley. □ **volleyball** game for two teams of 6 hitting large ball by hand over net.

**volt** /vəʊlt/ *noun* SI unit of electromotive force. □ **voltmeter** instrument measuring electric potential in volts.

**voltage** *noun* electromotive force expressed in volts.

**volte-face** /vɒltˈfɑːs/ *noun* (*plural* **voltes-face** same pronunciation) complete change of position in one's attitude or opinion.

**voluble** /'vɒljʊb(ə)l/ *adjective* speaking or spoken fluently or with continuous flow of words. □ **volubility** *noun;* **volubly** *adverb.*

**volume** /'vɒljuːm/ *noun* single book forming part or all of work; solid content, bulk; space occupied by gas or liquid; (+ *of*) amount or quantity of; quantity or power of sound; (+ *of*) moving mass of (water, smoke, etc.).

**voluminous** /və'luːmɪnəs/ *adjective* (of drapery etc.) loose and ample; written or writing at great length.

**voluntary** /'vɒləntrɪ/ ● *adjective* done, acting, or given willingly; unpaid; (of institution) supported or built by charity; brought about by voluntary action; (of muscle, limb, etc.) controlled by will. ● *noun* (*plural* **-ies**) organ solo played before or after church service. □ **voluntarily** *adverb.*

**volunteer** /vɒlən'tɪə/ ● *noun* person who voluntarily undertakes task or enters military etc. service. ● *verb* (often + *to*) undertake or offer voluntarily; (often + *for*) be volunteer.

**voluptuary** /və'lʌptʃʊərɪ/ *noun* (*plural* **-ies**) person who seeks luxury and sensual pleasure.

**voluptuous** /və'lʌptʃʊəs/ *adjective* of, tending to, occupied with, or derived from, sensuous or sensual pleasure; (of woman) curvaceous and sexually desirable. □ **voluptuously** *adverb.*

**vomit** /'vɒmɪt/ ● *verb* (**-t-**) eject (contents of stomach) through mouth, be sick; (of volcano, chimney, etc.) eject violently, belch forth. ● *noun* matter vomited from stomach.

**voodoo** /'vuːduː/ ● *noun* religious witchcraft as practised esp. in W. Indies. ● *verb* (**-doos, -dooed**) affect by voodoo, bewitch.

**voracious** /və'reɪʃəs/ *adjective* greedy in eating, ravenous; very eager. □ **voraciously** *adverb;* **voracity** /-'ræs-/ *noun.*

**vortex** /'vɔːteks/ *noun* (*plural* **-texes** or **-tices** /-tɪsiːz/) whirlpool, whirlwind; whirling motion or mass; thing viewed as destructive or devouring.

**votary** /'vəʊtərɪ/ *noun* (*plural* **-ies;** *feminine* **votaress**) (usually + *of*) person dedicated to service of god or cult; devotee of a person, occupation etc.

**vote** ● *noun* formal expression of choice or opinion by ballot, show of hands, etc.; (usually **the vote**) right to vote; opinion expressed by vote; votes given by or for particular group. ● *verb* (**-ting**) (often + *for, against*) give vote; enact etc. by majority of votes; *colloquial* pronounce by general consent; (often + *that*) suggest, urge. □ **vote down** defeat (proposal etc.) by voting; **vote in** elect by voting; **vote with one's feet** *colloquial* indicate opinion by one's presence or absence.

**voter** *noun* person voting or entitled to vote.

**votive** /'vəʊtɪv/ *adjective* given or consecrated in fulfilment of vow.

**vouch** /vaʊtʃ/ *verb* (+ *for*) answer or be surety for.

**voucher** *noun* document exchangeable for goods or services; receipt.

**vouchsafe** /vaʊtʃ'seɪf/ *verb* (**-fing**) *formal* condescend to grant; (+ *to do*) condescend.

**vow** /vaʊ/ ● *noun* solemn, esp. religious, promise. ● *verb* promise solemnly; *archaic* declare solemnly.

**vowel** /'vaʊəl/ *noun* speech sound made by vibrations of vocal cords, but without audible friction; letter(s) representing this.

■ **Usage** The (written) vowels of English are customarily said to be *a, e, i, o,* and *u,* but *y* can be either a consonant (as in *yet*) or a vowel (as in *by*), and combinations of these six, such as *ee* in *keep, ie* in *tied, ou* in *pour,* and *ye* in *rye,* are just as much vowels.

**vox pop** *noun colloquial* popular opinion as represented by informal comments.

**vox populi** /vɒks 'pɒpjʊlaɪ/ *noun* public opinion, popular belief. [Latin]

**voyage** /'vɔɪɪdʒ/ ● *noun* journey, esp. long one by sea or in space. ● *verb* (**-ging**) make voyage. □ **voyager** *noun.*

**voyeur** /vwa:'jɜː/ *noun* person who derives sexual pleasure from secretly observing others' sexual activity or organs; (esp. covert) spectator. □ **voyeurism** *noun;* **voyeuristic** /-'rɪs-/ *adjective.*

**vs.** *abbreviation* versus.

**VSO** *abbreviation* Voluntary Service Overseas.

**VTOL** /ˈviːtɒl/ *abbreviation* vertical take-off and landing.

**vulcanite** /ˈvʌlkənaɪt/ *noun* hard black vulcanized rubber.

**vulcanize** /ˈvʌlkənaɪz/ *verb* (also **-ise**) (**-zing** or **-sing**) make (rubber etc.) stronger and more elastic due to treating with sulphur at high temperature. □ **vulcanization** *noun.*

**vulgar** /ˈvʌlgə/ *adjective* coarse; of or characteristic of the common people; in common use, prevalent. □ **vulgar fraction** fraction expressed by numerator and denominator (e.g. ½), not decimally (e.g. 0.5); **the vulgar tongue** native or vernacular language. □ **vulgarity** /-ˈgær-/ *noun* (*plural* **-ies**); **vulgarly** *adverb.*

**vulgarian** /vʌlˈgeərɪən/ *noun* vulgar (esp. rich) person.

**vulgarism** *noun* vulgar word or expression.

**vulgarize** /ˈvʌlgəraɪz/ *verb* (also **-ise**) (**-zing** or **-sing**) make vulgar; spoil by popularizing. □ **vulgarization** *noun.*

**Vulgate** /ˈvʌlgeɪt/ *noun* 4th-c. Latin version of Bible.

**vulnerable** /ˈvʌlnərəb(ə)l/ *adjective* easily wounded or harmed; (+ *to*) open to attack, injury, or criticism. □ **vulnerability** *noun.*

**vulpine** /ˈvʌlpaɪn/ *adjective* of or like fox; crafty, cunning.

**vulture** /ˈvʌltʃə/ *noun* large carrion-eating bird of prey; rapacious person.

**vulva** /ˈvʌlvə/ *noun* (*plural* **-s**) external female genitals.

**vv.** *abbreviation* verses.

**vying** *present participle* of VIE.

---

# Ww

---

**W** *abbreviation* (also **W.**) watt(s); west(ern).

**w.** *abbreviation* wicket(s); wide(s); with.

**wacky** /ˈwækɪ/ *adjective* (**-ier**, **-iest**) *slang* crazy.

**wad** /wɒd/ ● *noun* lump of soft material to keep things apart or in place or to block hole; roll of banknotes. ● *verb* (**-dd-**) stop up or fix with wad; line, stuff, or protect with wadding.

**wadding** *noun* soft fibrous material for stuffing quilts, packing fragile articles in, etc.

**waddle** /ˈwɒd(ə)l/ ● *verb* (**-ling**) walk with short steps and swaying motion. ● *noun* such walk.

**wade** ● *verb* (**-ding**) walk through water, mud, etc., esp. with difficulty; (+ *through*) go through (tedious task, book, etc.); (+ *into*) *colloquial* attack (person, task). ● *noun* spell of wading. □ **wade in** *colloquial* make vigorous attack or intervention.

**wader** *noun* long-legged waterfowl; (in *plural*) high waterproof boots.

**wadi** /ˈwɒdɪ/ *noun* (*plural* **-s**) rocky watercourse in N. Africa etc., dry except in rainy season.

**wafer** /ˈweɪfə/ *noun* very thin light crisp biscuit; disc of unleavened bread used in Eucharist; disc of red paper stuck on legal document instead of seal. □ **wafer-thin** very thin.

**waffle**[1] /ˈwɒf(ə)l/ *colloquial* ● *noun* aimless verbose talk or writing. ● *verb* (**-ling**) indulge in waffle.

**waffle**[2] /ˈwɒf(ə)l/ *noun* small crisp batter cake. □ **waffle-iron** utensil for cooking waffles.

**waft** /wɒft/ ● *verb* convey or be conveyed smoothly (as) through air or over water. ● *noun* whiff.

**wag**[1] ● *verb* (**-gg-**) shake or wave to and fro. ● *noun* single wagging motion. □ **wagtail** small bird with long tail.

**wag**[2] *noun* facetious person.

**wage** ● *noun* (in *singular* or *plural*) employee's regular pay, esp. paid weekly. ● *verb* (**-ging**) carry on (war etc.).

**waged** *adjective* in regular paid employment.

**wager** /ˈweɪdʒə/ *noun & verb* bet.

**waggish** *adjective* playful, facetious □ **waggishly** *adverb.*

**waggle** /'wæg(ə)l/ *verb* (**-ling**) *colloquial* wag.

**wagon** /'wægən/ *noun* (also **waggon**) 4-wheeled vehicle for heavy loads; open railway truck. □ **on the wagon** *slang* abstaining from alcohol; **wagon-load** as much as wagon can carry.

**wagoner** *noun* (also **waggoner**) driver of wagon.

**waif** *noun* homeless and helpless person, esp. abandoned child; ownerless object or animal.

**wail** ● *noun* prolonged plaintive inarticulate cry of pain, grief, etc.; sound resembling this. ● *verb* utter wail; lament or complain persistently.

**wain** *noun archaic* wagon.

**wainscot** /'weɪnskət/ *noun* (also **wainscoting**) boarding or wooden panelling on room-wall.

**waist** *noun* part of human body between ribs and hips; narrowness marking this; circumference of waist; narrow middle part of anything; part of garment encircling waist; *US* bodice, blouse; part of ship between forecastle and quarterdeck. □ **waistband** strip of cloth forming waist of garment; **waistcoat** usually sleeveless and collarless waist-length garment; **waistline** outline or size of waist.

**wait** ● *verb* defer action until expected event occurs; await (turn etc.); (of thing) remain in readiness; (usually as **waiting** *noun*) park briefly; act as waiter or attendant; (+ *on, upon*) await convenience of, be attendant to. ● *noun* act or period of waiting; (usually + *for*) watching for enemy; (in *plural*) *archaic* street singers of Christmas carols. □ **waiting-list** list of people waiting for thing not immediately available; **waiting-room** room for people to wait in, esp. at surgery or railway station.

**waiter** *noun* (*feminine* **waitress**) person who serves at hotel or restaurant tables.

**waive** *verb* (**-ving**) refrain from insisting on or using.

**waiver** *noun Law* (document recording) waiving.

**wake**[1] ● *verb* (**-king**; *past* **woke**; *past participle* **woken** /'wəʊk(ə)n/) (often + *up*) (cause to) cease to sleep or become alert; *archaic* (except as **waking** *adjective* & *noun*) be awake; disturb with noise; evoke. ● *noun* (chiefly in Ireland) vigil beside corpse before burial, attendant lamentations and merrymaking; (usually in *plural*) annual holiday in (industrial) N. England.

**wake**[2] *noun* track left on water's surface by moving ship etc.; turbulent air left by moving aircraft. □ **in the wake of** following, as result of.

**wakeful** *adjective* unable to sleep; sleepless; vigilant. □ **wakefully** *adverb*; **wakefulness** *noun*.

**waken** /'weɪkən/ *verb* make or become awake.

**walk** /wɔːk/ ● *verb* move by lifting and setting down each foot in turn, never having both feet off the ground at once; (of quadruped) go with slowest gait; travel or go on foot, take exercise thus; traverse (distance) in walking; tread floor or surface of; cause to walk with one. ● *noun* act of walking, ordinary human gait; slowest gait of animal; person's manner of walking; distance walkable in specified time; excursion on foot; place or route meant or fit for walking. □ **walkabout** informal stroll by royal person etc., Australian Aboriginal's period of wandering; **walking frame** tubular metal frame to assist elderly or disabled people in walking; **walking stick** stick carried for support when walking; **walk off with** *colloquial* steal, win easily; **walk of life** one's occupation; **walk-on part** short or non-speaking dramatic role; **walk out** depart suddenly or angrily, stop work in protest; **walk-out** *noun*; **walk out on** desert; **walkover** easy victory; **walk the streets** be prostitute; **walkway** passage or path for walking along. □ **walkable** *adjective*.

**walker** *noun* person etc. that walks; framework in which baby can walk unaided; walking frame.

**walkie-talkie** /wɔːkɪ'tɔːkɪ/ *noun* portable two-way radio.

**Walkman** /'wɔːkmən/ *noun* (*plural* **-s**) *proprietary term* type of personal stereo.

**wall** /wɔːl/ ● *noun* continuous narrow upright structure of usually brick or stone, esp. enclosing or dividing a space or supporting a roof; thing like wall in appearance or effect; outermost layer of animal or plant organ, cell, etc. ● *verb* (esp. as **walled** *adjective*) surround with wall; (usually + *up*, *off*) block with wall; (+ *up*) enclose within sealed space. □ **go to the wall** fare badly in competition; **up the wall** *colloquial* crazy, furious; **wallflower** fragrant garden plant, *colloquial* woman not dancing because partnerless; **wall game** Eton form of football; **wallpaper** *noun* paper for covering interior walls of rooms, *verb* decorate with wallpaper; **wall-to-wall** fitted to cover whole floor, *colloquial* ubiquitous.

**wallaby** /ˈwɒləbɪ/ *noun* (*plural* -**ies**) small kangaroo-like marsupial.

**wallah** /ˈwɒlə/ *noun slang* person connected with a specified occupation or thing.

**wallet** /ˈwɒlɪt/ *noun* small flat case for holding banknotes etc.

**wall-eye** *noun* eye with whitish iris or outward squint. □ **wall-eyed** *adjective*.

**wallop** /ˈwɒləp/ *colloquial* ● *verb* (-**p**-) thrash, beat. ● *noun* whack; beer.

**wallow** /ˈwɒləʊ/ ● *verb* roll about in mud etc.; (+ *in*) indulge unrestrainedly in. ● *noun* act of wallowing; place where animals wallow.

**wally** /ˈwɒlɪ/ *noun* (*plural* -**ies**) *slang* foolish or incompetent person.

**walnut** /ˈwɔːlnʌt/ *noun* tree with aromatic leaves and drooping catkins; its nut; its timber.

**walrus** /ˈwɔːlrəs/ *noun* (*plural* same or **walruses**) long-tusked amphibious arctic mammal. □ **walrus moustache** long thick drooping moustache.

**waltz** /wɔːls/ ● *noun* ballroom dance in triple time; music for this. ● *verb* dance waltz; (often + *in*, *out*, *round*, etc.) *colloquial* move easily, casually, etc.

**wampum** /ˈwɒmpəm/ *noun* strings of shell-beads formerly used by N. American Indians for money, ornament, etc.

**wan** /wɒn/ *adjective* (-**nn**-) pale, weary-looking. □ **wanly** *adverb*.

**wand** /wɒnd/ *noun* fairy's or magician's magic stick; staff as sign of office etc.; *colloquial Music* conductor's baton.

**wander** /ˈwɒndə/ *verb* (often + *in*, *off*, etc.) go from place to place aimlessly; meander; diverge from path etc.; talk or think incoherently, be inattentive or delirious. □ **wanderlust** eagerness to travel or wander, restlessness. □ **wanderer** *noun*.

**wane** ● *verb* (-**ning**) (of moon) decrease in apparent size; decrease in power, vigour, importance, size, etc. ● *noun* process of waning. □ **on the wane** declining.

**wangle** /ˈwæŋɡ(ə)l/ *colloquial* ● *verb* (-**ling**) contrive to obtain (favour etc.). ● *noun* act of wangling.

**wannabe** /ˈwɒnəbɪ/ *noun slang* avid fan who apes person admired; anyone wishing to be someone else.

**want** /wɒnt/ ● *verb* (often + *to do*) desire; wish for possession of; need; (+ *to do*) *colloquial* should; (usually + *for*) lack; be without or fall short by; (as **wanted** *adjective*) (of suspected criminal etc.) sought by police. ● *noun* lack, deficiency; poverty, need.

**wanting** *adjective* lacking (in quality or quantity), unequal to requirements; absent.

**wanton** /ˈwɒnt(ə)n/ ● *adjective* licentious, capricious, arbitrary; luxuriant, wild. ● *noun literary* licentious person. □ **wantonly** *adverb*.

**wapiti** /ˈwɒpɪtɪ/ *noun* (*plural* -**s**) large N. American deer.

**war** /wɔː/ ● *noun* armed hostility, esp. between nations; specific period of this; hostility between people; (often + *on*) efforts against crime, poverty, etc. ● *verb* (-**rr**-) (as **warring** *adjective*) rival, fighting; make war. □ **at war** engaged in war; **go to war** begin war; **on the warpath** going to war, *colloquial* seeking confrontation; **war crime** crime violating international laws of war; **war cry** phrase or name shouted to rally troops, party slogan; **war dance** dance performed by primitive peoples before battle or after victory; **warhead** explosive head of missile; **warhorse** *historical* trooper's horse, *colloquial* veteran soldier; **war memorial** monument to those killed in (a) war; **warmonger** /-mʌŋɡə/ person who promotes war; **warpaint** paint put on body esp. by N. American Indians before battle, *colloquial* make-up; **warship** ship used in war.

**warble** /'wɔːb(ə)l/ ● *verb* (**-ling**) sing in a gentle trilling way. ● *noun* warbling sound.

**warbler** *noun* bird that warbles.

**ward** /wɔːd/ *noun* separate division or room of hospital etc.; administrative division, esp. for elections; minor etc. under care of guardian or court; (in *plural*) corresponding notches and projections in key and lock; *archaic* guardianship. □ **ward off** parry (blow), avert (danger etc.); **wardroom** officers' mess in warship.

**warden** /'wɔːd(ə)n/ *noun* supervising official; president or governor of institution; traffic warden.

**warder** /'wɔːdə/ *noun* (*feminine* **wardress**) prison officer.

**wardrobe** /'wɔːdrəub/ *noun* large cupboard for storing clothes; stock of clothes; theatre's costume department. □ **wardrobe master, mistress** person in charge of theatrical wardrobe.

**wardship** *noun* tutelage.

**ware** *noun* things of specified kind made usually for sale; (usually in *plural*) articles for sale.

**warehouse** ● *noun* building in which goods are stored; wholesale or large retail store. ● *verb* (**-sing**) store in warehouse.

**warfare** /'wɔːfeə/ *noun* waging war, campaigning.

**warlike** *adjective* hostile; soldierly; military.

**warlock** /'wɔːlɒk/ *noun archaic* sorcerer.

**warm** /wɔːm/ ● *adjective* of or at fairly high temperature; (of person) with skin at natural or slightly raised temperature; (of clothes) affording warmth; hearty, enthusiastic; sympathetic, friendly, loving; *colloquial* dangerous, hostile; *colloquial* (in game) near object sought, near to guessing; (of colour) reddish or yellowish, suggesting warmth; (of scent in hunting) fresh and strong. ● *verb* make or become warm. ● *noun* act of warming; warmth. □ **warm-blooded** (of animals) having blood temperature well above that of environment; **warm-hearted** kind, friendly; **warming-pan** *historical* flat closed vessel holding hot coals for warming beds; **warm up** make or become warm, prepare for performance

etc. by practising, reach temperature for efficient working, reheat (food); **warm-up** *noun*. □ **warmly** *adverb*; **warmth** *noun*.

**warn** /wɔːn/ *verb* (often + *of, that*) inform of impending danger or misfortune; (+ *to do*) advise (person) to take certain action; (often + *against*) inform (person) about specific danger. □ **warn off** tell (person) to keep away (from).

**warning** *noun* what is said or done or occurs to warn person.

**warp** /wɔːp/ ● *verb* make or become distorted, esp. through heat, damp, etc.; make or become perverted or strange; haul (ship etc.) by rope attached to fixed point. ● *noun* warped state; mental perversion; lengthwise threads in loom; rope used in warping ship.

**warrant** /'wɒrənt/ ● *noun* thing that authorizes an action; written authorization, money voucher, etc.; written authorization allowing police to carry out search or arrest; certificate of service rank held by warrant officer. ● *verb* serve as warrant for, justify; guarantee. □ **warrant officer** officer ranking between commissioned and non-commissioned officers.

**warranty** /'wɒrəntɪ/ *noun* (*plural* **-ies**) undertaking as to ownership or quality of thing sold etc., often accepting responsibility for repairs needed over specified period; authority, justification.

**warren** /'wɒrən/ *noun* network of rabbit burrows; densely populated or labyrinthine building or district.

**warrior** /'wɒrɪə/ *noun* person skilled in or famed for fighting.

**wart** /wɔːt/ *noun* small round dry growth on skin; protuberance on skin of animal, surface of plant, etc. □ **wart-hog** African wild pig. □ **warty** *adjective*.

**wary** /'weərɪ/ *adjective* (**-ier, -iest**) on one's guard, circumspect; cautious. □ **warily** *adverb*; **wariness** *noun*.

**was** *1st & 3rd singular past of* BE.

**wash** /wɒʃ/ ● *verb* cleanse with liquid; (+ *out, off, away*, etc.) remove or be removed from by washing; wash oneself or one's hands (and face); wash clothes, dishes, etc.; (of fabric or dye) bear washing without damage; bear scrutiny, be believed or acceptable; (of river etc.) touch; (of liquid) carry along in specified direction; sweep, move, splash; (+ *over*) occur without affecting (person); sift (ore) by action of water; brush watery colour over; *poetical* moisten. ●*noun* washing, being washed; clothes for washing or just washed; motion of agitated water or air, esp. due to passage of vessel or aircraft; kitchen slops given to pigs; thin, weak, inferior, or animals' liquid food; liquid to spread over surface to cleanse, heal, or colour. □ **washbasin** basin for washing one's hands etc.; **washboard** ribbed board for washing clothes, this as percussion instrument; **wash down** wash completely, (usually + *with*) accompany or follow (food); **washed out** faded, pale, *colloquial* exhausted; **washed up** *esp. US slang* defeated, having failed; **wash one's hands of** decline responsibility for; **wash out** clean inside of by washing, *colloquial* cause to be cancelled because of rain; **wash-out** *colloquial* complete failure; **washroom** *esp. US* public toilet; **washstand** piece of furniture for holding washbasin, soap-dish, etc.; **wash up** wash (dishes etc.) after use, *US* wash one's face and hands, (of sea) carry on to shore. □ **washable** *adjective*.

**washer** *noun* person or thing that washes; flat ring placed between two surfaces or under plunger of tap, nut, etc. to tighten joint or disperse pressure.

**washerwoman** *noun* laundress.

**washing** *noun* clothes etc. for washing or just washed. □ **washing machine** machine for washing clothes; **washing powder** soap powder or detergent for washing clothes; **washing-up** washing of dishes etc., dishes etc. for washing.

**washy** *adjective* (**-ier, -iest**) too watery or weak; lacking vigour.

**wasn't** /'wɒz(ə)nt/ was not.

**Wasp** /wɒsp/ *noun* (also **WASP**) *US usually derogatory* middle-class white American [Anglo-Saxon] Protestant.

**wasp** /wɒsp/ *noun* stinging insect with black and yellow stripes. □ **wasp-waist** very slender waist.

**waspish** *adjective* irritable, snappish.

**wassail** /'wɒseil/ *archaic* ●*noun* festive drinking. ●*verb* make merry.

**wastage** /'weistidʒ/ *noun* amount wasted; loss by use, wear, or leakage; (also **natural wastage**) loss of employees other than by redundancy.

**waste** ●*verb* (**-ting**) use to no purpose or for inadequate result or extravagantly; fail to use; (often + *on*) give (advice etc.) without effect; (in *passive*) fail to be appreciated or used properly; wear away; make or become weak; devastate. ●*adjective* superfluous, no longer needed; uninhabited, not cultivated. ●*noun* act of wasting; waste material; waste region; diminution by wear; waste pipe. □ **go, run to waste** be wasted; **wasteland** land not productive or developed, spiritually or intellectually barren place or time; **waste paper** used or valueless paper; **waste pipe** pipe carrying off waste material; **waste product** useless by-product of manufacture or organism.

**wasteful** *adjective* extravagant; causing or showing waste. □ **wastefully** *adverb*.

**waster** *noun* wasteful person; *colloquial* wastrel.

**wastrel** /'weistr(ə)l/ *noun* good-for-nothing person.

**watch** /wɒtʃ/ ●*verb* keep eyes fixed on; keep under observation, follow observantly; (often + *for*) be in alert state, be vigilant; (+ *over*) look after, take care of. ●*noun* small portable timepiece for wrist or pocket; state of alert or constant attention; *Nautical* usually 4-hour spell of duty; *historical* (member of) body of men patrolling streets at night. □ **on the watch for** waiting for (anticipated event); **watchdog** dog guarding property, person etc. monitoring others' rights etc.; **watching brief** brief of barrister who follows case for client not directly concerned; **watchman** man employed to look after empty building etc. at night; **watch out** (often + *for*) be on one's guard; **watch-tower** tower for observing prisoners, attackers, etc.; **watchword** phrase summarizing guiding principle. □ **watcher** *noun* (also in *combination*).

**watchful** *adjective* accustomed to watching; on the watch. □ **watchfully** *adverb*; **watchfulness** *noun*.

**water** /ˈwɔːtə/ ● *noun* transparent colourless liquid found in seas and rivers etc. and in rain etc.; sheet or body of water; (in *plural*) part of sea or river; (often **the waters**) mineral water at spa etc.; state of tide; solution of specified substance in water; transparency and lustre of gem; (usually in *plural*) amniotic fluid. ● *verb* sprinkle or soak with water; supply (plant or animal) with water; secrete water; (as **watered** *adjective*) (of silk etc.) having irregular wavy finish; take in supply of water. □ **make water** urinate; **water-bed** mattress filled with water; **water biscuit** thin unsweetened biscuit; **water buffalo** common domestic Indian buffalo; **water cannon** device giving powerful water-jet to disperse crowd etc.; **water chestnut** corm from a sedge, used in Chinese cookery; **water-closet** lavatory that can be flushed; **water colour** pigment mixed with water and not oil, picture painted or art of painting with this; **watercourse** stream of water, bed of this; **watercress** pungent cress growing in running water; **water-diviner** dowser; **water down** dilute, make less forceful or horrifying; **waterfall** stream or river falling over precipice or down steep hill; **waterfowl** bird(s) frequenting water; **waterfront** part of town adjoining river etc.; **waterhole** shallow depression in which water collects; **water-ice** flavoured and frozen water and sugar; **watering-can** portable container for watering plants; **watering-place** pool where animals drink, spa or seaside resort; **water jump** jump over water in steeplechase etc.; **water level** surface of water, height of this, water table; **water lily** aquatic plant with floating leaves and flowers; **waterline** line where surface of water touches ship's side; **waterlogged** saturated or filled with water; **water main** main pipe in water supply system; **waterman** boatman plying for hire; **watermark** faint design made in paper by maker; **water-meadow** meadow periodically flooded by stream; **water melon** large dark green melon with red pulp and watery juice; **water-mill** mill worked by waterwheel; **water pistol** toy pistol shooting

jet of water; **water polo** game [played] by swimmers with ball like fo[otball]; **water-power** mechanical force [from] weight or motion of water; **wate[r]proof]** *adjective* impervious to water, *nou[n]* garment or material, *verb* make [waterproof; **water-rat** water vole; [water-] **rate** charge for use of public [water] supply; **watershed** line be[tween] waters flowing to different [river] basins, turning point in e[vents]; **waterside** edge of sea, lake, or [river]; **water-ski** ski (esp. one of pa[ir] on which person is towed across wa[ter by] motor boat; **waterspout** gy[rating] column of water and spray betwe[en sea] and cloud; **water table** plane [below] which ground is saturated with [water]; **watertight** so closely fastened o[r made] that water cannot leak throu[gh, (of] argument etc.) unassailable; **water** **tower** tower with elevated tank [to give] pressure for distributing water; **water** **vole** aquatic vole; **waterway** nav[igable] channel; **waterwheel** [wheel] driven by water to drive machin[ery or] to raise water; **water-wings** in[flated] floats used to support person le[arning] to swim; **waterworks** establis[hment] for managing water supply, c[olloquial] shedding of tears, *colloquial* urina[ry sys]tem.

**watery** *adjective* containing too [much] water; too thin in consistency; [mainly] consisting of water; vapid, unin[terest]ing; (of colour) pale; (of sun, mo[on, or] sky) rainy-looking; (of eyes) moi[st].

**watt** /wɒt/ *noun* SI unit of power.

**wattage** *noun* amount of ele[ctrical] power expressed in watts.

**wattle**[1] /ˈwɒt(ə)l/ *noun* interlace[d rods] and sticks used for fences etc.; A[ustra]lian acacia with fragrant golden [flowers. □ **wattle and daub** netw[ork of] rods and twigs plastered with c[lay or] mud as building material.

**wattle**[2] /ˈwɒt(ə)l/ *noun* fleshy ap[pend]age hanging from head or ne[ck of] turkey etc.

**wave** ● *verb* (**-ving**) move (hand e[tc.]) to and fro in greeting or as signal; [show] sinuous or sweeping motion; giv[e such] motion to; direct (person) or ex[press] (greeting etc.) by waving; give un[dulat]ing form to, have such form.

moving ridge of water between two depressions; long body of water curling into arch and breaking on shore; thing compared to this; gesture of waving; curved shape in hair; temporary occurrence or heightening of condition or influence; disturbance carrying motion, heat, light, sound, etc. through esp. fluid medium; single curve in this. □ **wave aside** dismiss as intrusive or irrelevant; **waveband** radio wavelengths between certain limits; **wave down** wave to (vehicle or driver) to stop; **wavelength** distance between successive crests of wave, this as distinctive feature of radio waves from a transmitter, *colloquial* person's way of thinking.

**wavelet** *noun* small wave.

**waver** /'weɪvə/ *verb* be or become unsteady or irresolute, begin to give way.

**wavy** *adjective* (**-ier, -iest**) having waves or alternate contrary curves. □ **waviness** *noun*.

**wax**[1] ● *noun* sticky pliable yellowish substance secreted by bees as material of honeycomb; this bleached and purified for candles, modelling, etc.; any similar substance. ● *verb* cover or treat with wax; remove hair from (legs etc.) using wax. □ **waxwork** object, esp. lifelike dummy, modelled in wax, (in *plural*) exhibition of wax dummies.

**wax**[2] *verb* (of moon) increase in apparent size; grow larger or stronger; become.

**waxen** *adjective* smooth or pale like wax; *archaic* made of wax.

**way** ● *noun* road, track, path, street; course, route; direction; method, means; style, manner; habitual course of action; normal course of events; distance (to be) travelled; unimpeded opportunity or space to advance; advance, progress; specified condition or state; respect, sense. ● *adverb colloquial* far. □ **by the way** incidentally; **by way of** by means of, as a form of, passing through; **give way** yield under pressure, give precedence; **in the way, in (person's) way** forming obstruction (to); **lead the way** act as guide or leader; **make one's way** go, prosper; **make way for** allow to pass, be superseded by; **out of the way** not forming obstruction, disposed of, unusual, remote; **pay its** or **one's way** cover costs, pay one's expenses as they arise; **under way** in motion or progress; **way back** *colloquial* long ago; **wayfarer** traveller, esp. on foot; **waylay** lie in wait for, stop to accost or rob; **way of life** principles or habits governing one's actions; **way-out** *colloquial* unusual, eccentric; **wayside** (land at) side of road.

**wayward** /'weɪwəd/ *adjective* childishly self-willed; capricious. □ **waywardness** *noun*.

**WC** *abbreviation* water-closet; West Central.

**W/Cdr.** *abbreviation* Wing Commander.

**we** /wiː/ *pronoun used by speaker or writer to refer to himself or herself and one or more others as subject of verb; used for I by sovereign in formal contexts or by editorial writer in newspaper.*

**weak** *adjective* lacking in strength, power, vigour, resolution, or number; unconvincing; (of verb) forming inflections by suffix. □ **weak-kneed** *colloquial* lacking resolution; **weak-minded** mentally deficient, lacking resolution. □ **weaken** *verb*.

**weakling** *noun* feeble person or animal.

**weakly** ● *adverb* in a weak way. ● *adjective* (**-ier, -iest**) sickly, not robust.

**weakness** *noun* being weak; weak point; self-indulgent liking.

**weal**[1] ● *noun* ridge raised on flesh by stroke of rod or whip. ● *verb* raise weals on.

**weal**[2] *noun literary* welfare.

**wealth** /welθ/ *noun* riches; being rich; abundance.

**wealthy** *adjective* (**-ier, -iest**) having abundance, esp. of money.

**wean** *verb* accustom (infant or other young mammal) to food other than mother's milk; (often + *from, away from*) disengage (from habit etc.) by enforced discontinuance.

**weapon** /'wepən/ *noun* thing designed, used, or usable for inflicting bodily harm; means for gaining advantage in a conflict.

**weaponry** *noun* weapons collectively.

**wear** /weə/ ● *verb* (*past* **wore**; *past participle* **worn**) have on one's person as clothing, ornament, etc.; exhibit (expression etc.); *colloquial* (usually in negative) tolerate; (often + *away*, *down*) damage or deteriorate gradually by use or attrition; make (hole etc.) by attrition; (often + *out*) exhaust; (+ *down*) overcome by persistence; (+ *well* etc.) endure continued use or life; (of time) pass, esp. tediously. ● *noun* wearing, being worn; things worn; fashionable or suitable clothing; (in full **wear and tear**) damage from continuous use. □ **wear out** use or be used until useless, tire or be tired out. □ **wearer** *noun*.

**wearisome** /ˈwɪərɪsəm/ *adjective* tedious, monotonous.

**weary** /ˈwɪərɪ/ ● *adjective* (**-ier, -iest**) very tired, intensely fatigued; (+ *of*) tired of; tiring, tedious. ● *verb* (**-ies, -ied**) make or become weary. □ **wearily** *adverb*; **weariness** *noun*.

**weasel** /ˈwiːz(ə)l/ *noun* small ferocious reddish-brown flesh-eating mammal.

**weather** /ˈweðə/ ● *noun* atmospheric conditions at specified place or time as regards heat, cloudiness, humidity, sunshine, wind, and rain etc. ● *verb* expose to or affect by atmospheric changes, season (wood); be discoloured or worn thus; come safely through (storm etc.); get to windward of. □ **make heavy weather of** *colloquial* exaggerate difficulty of; **under the weather** *colloquial* indisposed; **weather-beaten** affected by exposure to weather; **weatherboard** sloping board attached at bottom of door to keep out rain, each of series of overlapping horizontal boards on wall; **weathercock** weather vane in form of cock, inconstant person; **weather forecast** prediction of likely weather; **weather vane** revolving pointer on church spire etc. to show direction of wind.

**weave**[1] ● *verb* (**-ving**; *past* **wove** /wəʊv/; *past participle* **woven**) form (fabric) by interlacing threads, form (threads) into fabric, esp. in loom; (+ *into*) make (facts etc.) into story or connected whole; make (story etc.) thus. ● *noun* style of weaving.

**weave**[2] *verb* (**-ving**) move repeatedly from side to side; take intricate course.

**weaver** *noun* person who weaves fabric; (in full **weaver-bird**) tropical bird building elaborately woven nest.

**web** *noun* woven fabric; amount woven in one piece; complex series; cobweb or similar tissue; membrane connecting toes of aquatic bird or other animal; large roll of paper for printing. □ **web-footed** having toes connected by web. □ **webbed** *adjective*.

**webbing** *noun* strong narrow closely woven fabric for belts etc.

**weber** /ˈveɪbə/ *noun* SI unit of magnetic flux.

**Wed.** *abbreviation* (also **Weds.**) Wednesday.

**wed** *verb* (**-dd-**; *past & past participle* **wedded** or **wed**) *usually formal or literary* marry; unite; (as **wedded** *adjective*) of or in marriage, (+ *to*) obstinately attached to (pursuit etc.).

**we'd** /wiːd/ we had; we should; we would.

**wedding** /ˈwedɪŋ/ *noun* marriage ceremony. □ **wedding breakfast** meal etc. between wedding and departure for honeymoon; **wedding cake** rich decorated cake served at wedding reception; **wedding ring** ring worn by married person.

**wedge** ● *noun* piece of tapering wood, metal, etc., used for forcing things apart or fixing them immovably etc.; wedge-shaped thing. ● *verb* (**-ging**) secure or force open or apart with wedge; (+ *in, into*) pack or force (thing, oneself) in or into. □ **thin end of the wedge** *colloquial* small beginning that may lead to something more serious.

**wedlock** /ˈwedlɒk/ *noun* married state. □ **born in** or **out of wedlock** born of married or unmarried parents.

**Wednesday** /ˈwenzdeɪ/ *noun* day of week following Tuesday.

**wee** *adjective* (**weer** /ˈwiːə/, **weest** /ˈwiːɪst/) *esp.* Scottish little; *colloquial* tiny.

**weed** ● *noun* wild plant growing where it is not wanted; lanky and weakly person or horse; (**the weed**) *slang* marijuana, tobacco. ● *verb* rid of weeds or unwanted parts; (+ *out*) sort out and remove (inferior or unwanted parts etc.), rid of inferior or unwanted parts etc.; remove or destroy weeds.

**weeds** *plural noun* (in full **widow's weeds**) *archaic* deep mourning worn by widow.

**weedy** *adjective* (**-ier, -iest**) weak, feeble; full of weeds.

**week** *noun* 7-day period reckoned usually from Saturday midnight; any 7-day period; the 6 days between Sundays; the 5 days Monday to Friday, period of work then done. □ **weekday** day other than (Saturday or) Sunday; **weekend** Saturday and Sunday.

**weekly** ● *adjective* done, produced, or occurring once a week. ● *adverb* once a week. ● *noun* (*plural* **-ies**) weekly newspaper or periodical.

**weeny** /ˈwiːnɪ/ *adjective* (**-ier, -iest**) *colloquial* tiny.

**weep** ● *verb* (*past & past participle* **wept**) shed tears; (often + *for*) lament over; be covered with or send forth drops, exude liquid; come or send forth in drops; (as **weeping** *adjective*) (as of trees) have drooping branches. ● *noun* spell of weeping.

**weepie** *noun colloquial* sentimental or emotional film, play, etc.

**weepy** *adjective* (**-ier, -iest**) *colloquial* inclined to weep, tearful.

**weevil** /ˈwiːvɪl/ *noun* destructive beetle feeding esp. on grain.

**weft** *noun* threads woven across warp to make fabric.

**weigh** /weɪ/ *verb* find weight of; balance in hand (as if) to guess weight of; (often + *out*) take definite weight of (substance), measure out (specified weight); estimate relative value or importance of; (+ *with, against*) compare with; be of specified weight or importance; have influence; (often + *on*) be heavy or burdensome (to); raise (anchor). □ **weighbridge** weighing machine for vehicles; **weigh down** bring down by weight, oppress; **weigh in** (of boxer before contest, or jockey after race) be weighed; **weigh-in** *noun*; **weigh in with** *colloquial* advance (argument etc.) confidently; **weigh up** *colloquial* form estimate of; **weigh one's words** carefully choose words to express something.

**weight** /weɪt/ ● *noun* force on a body due to earth's gravitation; heaviness of body; quantitative expression of a body's weight, scale of such weights; body of known weight for use in weighing or weight training; heavy body, esp.

used in mechanism etc.; load, burden; influence, importance; preponderance (of evidence etc.). ● *verb* attach a weight to, hold down with a weight; impede, burden. □ **pull one's weight** do fair share of work; **weightlifting** sport of lifting heavy objects; **weight training** physical training using weights. □ **weightless** *adjective*.

**weighting** *noun* extra pay in special cases.

**weighty** *adjective* (**-ier, -iest**) heavy; momentous; deserving attention; influential, authoritative.

**weir** /wɪə/ *noun* dam across river to retain water and regulate its flow.

**weird** /wɪəd/ *adjective* uncanny, supernatural; *colloquial* queer, incomprehensible. □ **weirdly** *adverb*; **weirdness** *noun*.

**welch** = WELSH.

**welcome** /ˈwelkəm/ ● *noun* kind or glad greeting or reception. ● *interjection* expressing such greeting. ● *verb* (**-ming**) receive with welcome. ● *adjective* gladly received; (+ *to*) cordially allowed or invited to. □ **make welcome** receive hospitably.

**weld** ● *verb* join (pieces of metal or plastic) using heat, usually from electric arc; fashion into effectual or homogeneous whole. ● *noun* welded joint. □ **welder** *noun*.

**welfare** /ˈwelfeə/ *noun* well-being, happiness; health and prosperity (of person, community, etc.); (**Welfare**) financial support from state. □ **welfare state** system of social services controlled or financed by government, state operating this; **welfare work** organized effort for welfare of poor, disabled, etc.

**welkin** /ˈwelkɪn/ *noun poetical* sky.

**well**[1] ● *adverb* (**better, best**) in satisfactory way; with distinction; in kind way; thoroughly, carefully; with heartiness or approval; probably, reasonably; to considerable extent; *slang* extremely. ● *adjective* (**better, best**) in good health; in satisfactory state or position, advisable. ● *interjection* expressing astonishment, resignation, etc., or introducing speech. □ **as well** in addition, advisable, desirable, reasonably; **as well as** in addition to; **well-adjusted** mentally and emotionally stable; **well-advised** prudent; **well and truly** decisively, completely; **well-appointed** properly equipped or fitted out; **well away** having made considerable progress, *colloquial* fast asleep or drunk; **well-balanced** sane, sensible; **well-being** happiness, health, prosperity; **well-born** of noble family; **well-bred** having or showing good breeding or manners; **well-built** big, strong, and shapely; **well-connected** related to good families; **well-disposed** (often + *towards*) friendly, sympathetic; **well-earned** fully deserved; **well-founded** based on good evidence; **well-groomed** with carefully tended hair, clothes, etc.; **well-heeled** *colloquial* wealthy; **well-informed** having much knowledge or information; **well-intentioned** having or showing good intentions; **well-judged** opportunely, skilfully, or discreetly done; **well-known** known to many; **well-meaning, -meant** well-intentioned; **well-nigh** almost; **well off** rich, fortunately situated; **well-read** having read (and learnt) much; **well-spoken** articulate or refined in speech; **well-to-do** prosperous; **well-tried** often tested with good result; **well-wisher** person who wishes one well; **well-worn** much used, trite.

**well²** ● *noun* shaft sunk in ground to obtain water, oil, etc.; enclosed space resembling well-shaft, e.g. central space in building for staircase, lift, light, or ventilation; source; (in *plural*) spa; inkwell; railed space in law court. ● *verb* (+ *out, up*) rise or flow as water from well. □ **well-head, -spring** source.

**we'll** /wiːl/ we shall; we will.

**wellington** /ˈwelɪŋt(ə)n/ *noun* (in full **wellington boot**) waterproof rubber boot usually reaching knee.

**welly** /ˈwelɪ/ *noun* (*plural* **-ies**) *colloquial* wellington.

**Welsh** ● *adjective* of Wales. ● *noun* language of Wales; (**the Welsh**) (treated as *plural*) the Welsh people. □ **Welshman, Welshwoman** native of Wales; **Welsh rarebit** dish of melted cheese etc. on toast.

**welsh** *verb* (also **welch** /weltʃ/) (of loser of bet, esp. bookmaker) evade an obligation; (+ *on*) fail to carry out promise to (person), fail to honour (obligation).

**welt** ● *noun* leather rim sewn to shoe-upper for sole to be attached to; weal; ribbed or reinforced border of garment; heavy blow. ● *verb* provide with welt; raise weals on, thrash.

**welter** /ˈweltə/ ● *verb* roll, wallow; (+ *in*) be soaked in. ● *noun* general confusion; disorderly mixture.

**welterweight** /ˈweltəweɪt/ *noun* amateur boxing weight (63.5–67 kg).

**wen** *noun* benign tumour on skin.

**wench** *noun* jocular girl, young woman.

**wend** *verb* □ **wend one's way** go.

**went** *past* of GO¹.

**wept** *past & past participle* of WEEP.

**were** *2nd singular past, plural past,* and *past subjunctive* of BE.

**we're** /wɪə/ we are.

**weren't** /wɜːnt/ were not.

**werewolf** /ˈweəwʊlf/ *noun* (*plural* **-wolves**) *Mythology* human being who changes into wolf.

**Wesleyan** /ˈwezlɪən/ ● *adjective* of Protestant denomination founded by John Wesley. ● *noun* member of this denomination.

**west** ● *noun* point of horizon where sun sets at equinoxes; corresponding compass point; (usually **the West**) European civilization, western part of world, country, town, etc. ● *adjective* towards, at, near, or facing west; (of wind) from west. ● *adverb* towards; at, or near west; (+ *of*) further west than. □ **go west** *slang* be killed or wrecked etc.; **westbound** travelling or leading west; **West End** fashionable part of London; **west-north-west, west-south-west** point midway between west and north-west or south-west. □ **westward** *adjective, adverb, & noun;* **westwards** *adverb.*

**westering** /ˈwestərɪŋ/ *adjective* (of sun) nearing the west.

**westerly** /ˈwestəlɪ/ ● *adjective & adverb* in western position or direction; (of wind) from west. ● *noun* (*plural* **-ies**) wind from west.

**western** /ˈwest(ə)n/ ● *adjective* of or in west. ● *noun* film or novel about cowboys in western N. America. □ **westernize** *verb* (also **-ise**) (**-zing** or **-sing**); **westernmost** *adjective.*

**westerner** *noun* native or inhabitant of west.

**wet** ● *adjective* (**-tt-**) soaked or covered with water or other liquid; (of weather) rainy; (of paint) not yet dried; used with water; *colloquial* feeble. ● *verb* (**-tt-**; *past & past participle* **wet** or **wetted**) make wet; urinate in or on. ● *noun* liquid that wets something; rainy weather; *colloquial* feeble or spiritless person; *colloquial* liberal Conservative; *colloquial* drink. □ **wet blanket** gloomy person discouraging cheerfulness etc.; **wet-nurse** *noun* woman employed to suckle another's child, *verb* act as wet-nurse to, *colloquial* treat as if helpless.

**wether** /ˈweðə/ *noun* castrated ram.

**we've** /wiːv/ we have.

**Wg. Cdr.** *abbreviation* Wing Commander.

**whack** *colloquial* ● *verb* hit forcefully; (as **whacked** *adjective*) tired out. ● *noun* sharp or resounding blow; *slang* share.

**whacking** *colloquial* ● *adjective* large. ● *adverb* very.

**whale** ● *noun* (*plural* same or **-s**) large fishlike marine mammal. ● *verb* (**-ling**) hunt whales. □ **whalebone** elastic horny substance in upper jaw of some whales.

**whaler** *noun* whaling ship or seaman.

**wham** *interjection colloquial: expressing forcible impact.*

**wharf** /wɔːf/ ● *noun* (*plural* **wharves** /wɔːvz/ or **-s**) quayside structure for loading or unloading of moored vessels. ● *verb* moor (ship) at wharf; store (goods) on wharf.

**what** /wɒt/ ● *interrogative adjective* used in asking someone to specify one or more things from an indefinite number. ● *adjective* (usually in exclamation) how great, how remarkable. ● *relative adjective* the or any ... that. ● *interrogative pronoun* what thing(s); what did you say? ● *relative pronoun* the things which; anything that. □ **whatever** anything at all that, no matter what; (with negative or in questions) at all, of any kind; **what for?** *colloquial* for what reason?; **what have you** *colloquial* anything else similar; **whatnot** unspecified thing; **what not** *colloquial* other similar things; **whatsoever** whatever; **know what's what** *colloquial* have common sense,

know what is useful or important; **what with** *colloquial* because of.

**wheat** *noun* cereal plant bearing dense 4-sided seed-spikes; its grain used for flour etc. □ **wheat germ** wheat embryo extracted as source of vitamins; **wheatmeal** flour from wheat with some bran and germ removed.

**wheatear** /ˈwiːtɪə/ *noun* small migratory bird.

**wheaten** *adjective* made of wheat.

**wheedle** /ˈwiːd(ə)l/ *verb* (**-ling**) coax by flattery or endearments; (+ *out*) get (thing) from person or cheat (person) of thing by wheedling.

**wheel** ● *noun* circular frame or disc revolving on axle and used to propel vehicle or other machinery; wheel-like thing; motion of wheel; movement of line of men etc. with one end as pivot; (in *plural*) slang car. ● *verb* turn on axis or pivot; swing round in line with one end as pivot; (often + *about, around*) (cause to) change direction or face another way; push or pull (wheeled thing, or its load or occupant); go in circles or curves. □ **wheel and deal** engage in political or commercial scheming; **wheelbarrow** small cart with one wheel at front and two handles; **wheelbase** distance between axles of vehicle; **wheelchair** disabled person's chair on wheels; **wheel-spin** rotation of vehicle's wheels without traction; **wheels within wheels** intricate machinery, *colloquial* indirect or secret agencies; **wheelwright** maker or repairer of wheels.

**wheelie** *noun* slang manoeuvre on bicycle or motorcycle with front wheel off the ground.

**wheeze** ● *verb* (**-zing**) breathe or utter with audible whistling sound. ● *noun* sound of wheezing; *colloquial* clever scheme. □ **wheezy** *adjective* (**-ier, -iest**).

**whelk** *noun* spiral-shelled marine mollusc.

**whelp** ● *noun* young dog, puppy; *archaic* cub; ill-mannered child or youth. ● *verb* give birth to puppies.

**when** ● *interrogative adverb* at what time. ● *relative adverb* (time etc.) at or on which. ● *conjunction* at the or any time that; as soon as; although; after which, and then, but just then. ●*pronoun* what time; which time. □ **whenever, whensoever** at whatever time, on whatever occasion, every time that.

**whence** *archaic or formal* ●*interrogative adverb* from what place. ●*relative adverb* (place etc.) from which. ●*conjunction* to the place from which.

**where** /weə/ ●*interrogative adverb* in or to what place; in what direction; in what respect. ●*relative adverb* (place etc.) in or to which. ●*conjunction* in or to the or any place, direction, or respect in which; and there. ●*interrogative pronoun* what place. ●*relative pronoun* the place in or to which. □ **whereabouts** *interrogative adverb* approximately where, *noun* person's or thing's location; **whereas** in contrast or comparison with the fact that, taking into consideration the fact that; **whereby** by what or which means; **wherefore** *archaic* for what or which reason; **wherein** *formal* in what or which; **whereof** *formal* of what or which; **whereupon** immediately after which; **wherever** anywhere at all that, no matter where; **wherewithal** /-wɪðɔ:l/ *colloquial* money etc. needed for a purpose.

**wherry** /ˈwerɪ/ *noun* (*plural* **-ies**) light rowing boat, usually for carrying passengers; large light barge.

**whet** *verb* (**-tt-**) sharpen; stimulate (appetite etc.). □ **whetstone** stone for sharpening cutting-tools.

**whether** /ˈweðə/ *conjunction introducing first or both of alternative possibilities.*

**whew** /hwju:/ *interjection expressing astonishment, consternation, or relief.*

**whey** /weɪ/ *noun* watery liquid left when milk forms curds.

**which** ●*interrogative adjective used in asking someone to specify one or more things from a definite set of alternatives.* ●*relative adjective* being the one just referred to, and this or these. ●*interrogative pronoun* which person(s) or thing(s). ●*relative pronoun* which thing(s). □ **whichever** any which, no matter which.

**whiff** *noun* puff of air, smoke, etc.; smell; (+ *of*) trace of; small cigar.

**Whig** *noun historical* member of British political party succeeded by Liberals. □ **Whiggery** *noun*; **Whiggish** *adjective*; **Whiggism** *noun*.

**while** ●*noun* period of time. ●*conjunction* during the time that, for as long as, at the same time as; although, whereas. ●*verb* (**-ling**) (+ *away*) pass (time etc.) in leisurely or interesting way. ●*relative adverb* (time etc.) during which. □ **for a while** for some time; **in a while** soon; **once in a while** occasionally.

**whilst** /waɪlst/ *adverb & conjunction* while.

**whim** *noun* sudden fancy, caprice.

**whimper** /ˈwɪmpə/ ●*verb* make feeble, querulous, or frightened sounds. ●*noun* such sound.

**whimsical** /ˈwɪmzɪk(ə)l/ *adjective* capricious, fantastic. □ **whimsicality** /-ˈkæl-/ *noun*; **whimsically** *adverb*.

**whimsy** /ˈwɪmzɪ/ *noun* (*plural* **-ies**) whim.

**whin** *noun* (in *singular* or *plural*) gorse. □ **whinchat** small songbird.

**whine** ●*noun* long-drawn complaining cry (as) of dog or child; querulous tone or complaint. ●*verb* (**-ning**) emit or utter whine(s); complain.

**whinge** /wɪndʒ/ *verb* (**-geing** or **-ging**) *colloquial* complain peevishly.

**whinny** /ˈwɪnɪ/ ●*noun* (*plural* **-ies**) gentle or joyful neigh. ●*verb* (**-ies, -ied**) emit whinny.

**whip** ●*noun* lash attached to stick, for urging on or for punishing; person appointed by political party to control its discipline and tactics in Parliament; whip's written notice requesting member's attendance; food made with whipped cream etc.; whipper-in. ●*verb* (**-pp-**) beat or urge on with whip; beat (eggs, cream, etc.) into froth; take or move suddenly or quickly; *slang* steal, excel, defeat; bind with spirally wound twine; sew with overcast stitches. □ **whipcord** tightly twisted cord; **(the) whip hand** advantage, control; **whiplash** sudden jerk; **whipper-in** huntsman's assistant who manages hounds; **whipping boy** scapegoat; **whip-round** *colloquial* informal collection of money among group of people; **whipstock** handle of whip.

**whippersnapper** /ˈwɪpəsnæpə/ *noun* small child; insignificant but presumptuous person.

**whippet** /ˈwɪpɪt/ *noun* crossbred dog of greyhound type, used for racing.

**whippoorwill** /ˈwɪpʊəwɪl/ *noun* N. American nightjar.

**whirl** ● *verb* swing round and round, revolve rapidly; (+ *away*) convey or go rapidly in car etc.; send or travel swiftly in orbit or curve; (of brain etc.) seem to spin round. ● *noun* whirling movement; state of intense activity or confusion. □ **give it a whirl** *colloquial* attempt it; **whirlpool** circular eddy in sea, river, etc.; **whirlwind** *noun* whirling mass or column of air, *adjective* very rapid.

**whirligig** /ˈwɜːlɪgɪg/ *noun* spinning or whirling toy; merry-go-round; revolving motion.

**whirr** ● *noun* continuous buzzing or softly clicking sound. ● *verb* (**-rr-**) make this sound.

**whisk** ● *verb* (+ *away*, *off*) brush with sweeping movement, take suddenly; whip (cream, eggs, etc.); convey or go lightly or quickly; wave (object). ● *noun* whisking movement; utensil for whipping eggs, cream, etc.; bunch of twigs, bristles, etc. for brushing or dusting.

**whisker** /ˈwɪskə/ *noun* (usually in *plural*) hair on cheeks or sides of face of man; each of bristles on face of cat etc.; *colloquial* small distance. □ **whiskered** *adjective*; **whiskery** *adjective*.

**whisky** /ˈwɪskɪ/ *noun* (*Irish* & *US* **whiskey**) (*plural* **-ies** or **-eys**) spirit distilled esp. from malted barley.

**whisper** /ˈwɪspə/ ● *verb* speak using breath instead of vocal cords; talk or say in barely audible tone or confidential way; rustle, murmur. ● *noun* whispering speech or sound; thing whispered.

**whist** *noun* card game, usually for two pairs of opponents. □ **whist drive** whist-party with players moving on from table to table.

**whistle** /ˈwɪs(ə)l/ ● *noun* clear shrill sound made by forcing breath through lips contracted to narrow opening; similar sound made by bird, wind, missile, etc.; instrument used to produce such sound. ● *verb* (**-ling**) emit whistle; give signal or express surprise or derision by whistling; (often + *up*) summon or give signal to thus; produce (tune) by whistling; (+ *for*) seek or desire in vain. □ **whistle-stop** *US* small unimportant town on railway; politician's brief pause for electioneering speech on tour.

**Whit** ● *noun* Whitsuntide. ● *adjective* of Whitsuntide. □ **Whit Sunday** 7th Sunday after Easter, commemorating Pentecost.

**whit** *noun* particle, least possible amount.

**white** ● *adjective* of colour produced by reflection or transmission of all light; of colour of snow or milk; pale; of the human racial group having light-coloured skin; albino; (of hair) having lost its colour; (of coffee) with milk or cream. ● *noun* white colour, paint, clothes, etc.; (in *plural*) white garments worn in cricket, tennis, etc.; (player using) lighter-coloured pieces in chess etc.; egg white; whitish part of eyeball round iris; white person. □ **white ant** termite; **whitebait** small silvery-white food-fish; **white cell** leucocyte; **white-collar** (of worker or work) non-manual, clerical, professional; **white corpuscle** leucocyte; **white elephant** useless possession; **white feather** symbol of cowardice; **white flag** symbol of surrender; **white goods** large domestic electrical equipment; **white heat** degree of heat making metal glow white, state of intense anger or passion; **white-hot** *adjective*; **white hope** person expected to achieve much; **white horses** white-crested waves; **white lead** mixture containing lead carbonate used as white pigment; **white lie** harmless or trivial untruth; **white magic** magic used for beneficent purposes; **white meat** poultry, veal, rabbit, and pork; **White Paper** government report giving information; **white pepper** pepper made by grinding husked berry; **white sauce** sauce of flour, melted butter, and milk or cream; **white slave** woman entrapped for prostitution; **white spirit** light petroleum as solvent; **white sugar** purified sugar; **white tie** man's white bow tie as part of full evening dress; **whitewash** *noun* solution of chalk or lime for whitening walls etc., means of glossing over faults, *verb* apply whitewash (to), gloss over, clear of blame; **white wedding** wedding where bride wears formal white dress; **whitewood** light-coloured wood, esp. prepared for staining etc. □ **whiten** *verb*; **whitener** *noun*; **whiteness** *noun*; **whitish** *adjective*.

**whither** /'wɪðə/ *archaic* ● *interrogative adverb* to what place. ● *relative adverb* (place etc.) to which.

**whiting**¹ /'waɪtɪŋ/ *noun* (*plural* same) small edible sea fish.

**whiting**² /'waɪtɪŋ/ *noun* ground chalk used in whitewashing etc.

**whitlow** /'wɪtləʊ/ *noun* inflammation near fingernail or toenail.

**Whitsun** /'wɪts(ə)n/ ● *noun* Whitsuntide. ● *adjective* of Whitsuntide.

**Whitsuntide** *noun* weekend or week including Whit Sunday.

**whittle** /'wɪt(ə)l/ *verb* (**-ling**) (often + *at*) pare (wood etc.) by cutting thin slices or shavings from surface; (often + *away, down*) reduce by repeated subtractions.

**whiz** (also **whizz**) ● *noun* sound made by object moving through air at great speed. ● *verb* (**-zz-**) move with or make a whiz. □ **whiz-kid** *colloquial* brilliant or highly successful young person.

**WHO** *abbreviation* World Health Organization.

**who** /hu:/ ● *interrogative pronoun* what or which person(s), what sort of person(s). ● *relative pronoun* (person or persons) that. □ **whoever, whosoever** the or any person(s) who; no matter who.

**whoa** /wəʊ/ *interjection* used to stop or slow horse etc.

**who'd** /hu:d/ who had; who would.

**whodunit** /hu:'dʌnɪt/ *noun* (also **whodunnit**) *colloquial* detective story, play, or film.

**whole** /həʊl/ ● *adjective* uninjured, unbroken, intact, undiminished; not less than; all, all of. ● *noun* complete thing; all of a thing; (+ *of*) all members etc. of. □ **on the whole** all things considered; **wholefood** food not artificially processed or refined; **wholehearted** completely devoted, done with all possible effort or sincerity; **wholeheartedly** *adverb*; **wholemeal** meal or flour made from whole grains of wheat.

**wholesale** /'həʊlseɪl/ ● *noun* selling in large quantities, esp. for retail by others. ● *adjective & adverb* by wholesale; on a large scale. ● *verb* (**-ling**) sell wholesale. □ **wholesaler** *noun*.

**wholesome** *adjective* promoting physical, mental, or moral health; prudent.

**wholly** /'həʊllɪ/ *adverb* entirely, without limitation; purely.

**whom** /hu:m/ *pronoun* (as object of verb) who. □ **whomever** (as object of verb) whoever; **whomsoever** (as object of verb) whosoever.

**whoop** /hu:p, wu:p/ ● *noun* cry expressing excitement etc.; characteristic drawing-in of breath after cough in whooping cough. ● *verb* utter whoop. □ **whooping cough** /'hu:pɪŋ/ infectious disease, esp. of children, with violent convulsive cough.

**whoopee** /wʊ'pi:/ *interjection expressing wild joy.* □ **make whoopee** /'wʊpɪ/ *colloquial* make merry, make love.

**whoops** /wʊps/ *interjection colloquial apology for obvious mistake.*

**whop** *verb* (**-pp-**) *slang* thrash, defeat.

**whopper** *noun slang* big specimen; great lie.

**whopping** *adjective colloquial* huge.

**whore** /hɔ:/ *noun* prostitute; *derogatory* promiscuous woman. □ **whorehouse** brothel.

**whorl** /wɜ:l/ *noun* ring of leaves etc. round stem; one turn of spiral.

**whortleberry** /'wɜ:t(ə)lberɪ/ *noun* (*plural* **-ies**) bilberry.

**who's** /hu:z/ who is; who has.

■ **Usage** Because it has an apostrophe, *who's* is easily confused with *whose*. They are each correctly used in *Who's there?* (= *Who is there?*), *Who's taken my pen?* (= *Who has taken my pen?*), and *Whose book is this?* (= *Who does this book belong to?*).

**whose** /hu:z/ ● *interrogative, pronoun, & adjective* of whom. ● *relative adjective* of whom or which.

**why** /waɪ/ ● *interrogative adverb* for what reason or purpose. ● *relative adverb* (reason etc.) for which. ● *interjection expressing surprise, impatience, reflection, or protest.* □ **whys and wherefores** reasons, explanation.

**WI** *abbreviation* West Indies; Women's Institute.

**wick** *noun* strip or thread feeding flame with fuel.

**wicked** /ˈwɪkɪd/ *adjective* (**-er, -est**) sinful, immoral; spiteful; playfully malicious; *colloquial* very bad; *slang* excellent. □ **wickedly** *adverb*; **wickedness** *noun*.

**wicker** /ˈwɪkə/ *noun* plaited osiers etc. as material for chairs, baskets, etc. □ **wickerwork** wicker, things made of wicker.

**wicket** /ˈwɪkɪt/ *noun Cricket* 3 upright stumps with bails in position defended by batsman, ground between the two wickets, state of this, batsman's being got out; (in full **wicket-door, -gate**) small door or gate, esp. beside or in larger one. □ **wicket-keeper** fielder close behind batsman's wicket.

**wide** ● *adjective* having sides far apart, broad, not narrow; (following measurement) in width; extending far, not restricted; liberal, not specialized; open to full extent; (+ *of*) not within reasonable distance of, far from. ● *adverb* to full extent; far from target etc. ● *noun* wide ball. □ **-wide** extending over whole of; **wide awake** fully awake, *colloquial* wary or knowing; **wide ball** *Cricket* ball judged by umpire to be beyond batsman's reach; **wide-eyed** surprised, naïve; **widespread** widely distributed. □ **widen** *verb*.

**widely** *adverb* far apart; extensively; by many people; considerably.

**widgeon** /ˈwɪdʒ(ə)n/ *noun* (also **wigeon**) kind of wild duck.

**widow** /ˈwɪdəʊ/ ● *noun* woman who has lost her husband by death and not married again. ● *verb* make into widow or widower; (as **widowed** *adjective*) bereft by death of spouse. □ **widow's peak** V-shaped growth of hair on forehead. □ **widowhood** *noun*.

**widower** /ˈwɪdəʊə/ *noun* man who has lost his wife by death and not married again.

**width** *noun* measurement from side to side; large extent; liberality of views etc.; piece of material of full width. □ **widthways** *adverb*.

**wield** /wiːld/ *verb* hold and use, control, exert.

**wife** *noun* (*plural* **wives**) married woman, esp. in relation to her husband. □ **wifely** *adjective*.

**wig** *noun* artificial head of hair.

**wigeon** = WIDGEON.

**wiggle** /ˈwɪg(ə)l/ *colloquial* ● *verb* (**-ling**) move from side to side etc. ● *noun* wiggling movement; kink in line etc. □ **wiggly** *adjective* (**-ier, -iest**).

**wight** /waɪt/ *noun archaic* person.

**wigwam** /ˈwɪgwæm/ *noun* N. American Indian's hut or tent.

**wilco** /ˈwɪlkəʊ/ *interjection colloquial*: expressing compliance or agreement.

**wild** /waɪld/ ● *adjective* in original natural state; not domesticated, cultivated, or civilized; unrestrained, disorderly; tempestuous; intensely eager, frantic; (+ *about*) *colloquial* enthusiastically devoted to; *colloquial* infuriated; random, ill-aimed, rash. ● *adverb* in a wild way. ● *noun* wild place, desert. □ **like wildfire** with extraordinary speed; **run wild** grow or stray unchecked or undisciplined; **wild card** card having any rank chosen by its player, person or thing usable in different ways; **wildcat** *noun* hot-tempered or violent person, *adjective* (of strike) sudden and unofficial, reckless, financially unsound; **wild-goose chase** foolish or hopeless quest; **wildlife** wild animals collectively; **Wild West** western US in lawless times. □ **wildly** *adverb*; **wildness** *noun*.

**wildebeest** /ˈwɪldəbiːst/ *noun* (*plural* same or **-s**) gnu.

**wilderness** /ˈwɪldənɪs/ *noun* desert, uncultivated area; confused assemblage.

**wile** ● *noun* (usually in *plural*) stratagem, trick. ● *verb* (**-ling**) lure.

**wilful** /ˈwɪlfʊl/ *adjective* (*US* **willful**) intentional, deliberate; obstinate. □ **wilfully** *adverb*.

**will**[1] *auxiliary verb* (*3rd singular present* **will**) used to form future tenses; expressing request as question; be able to; have tendency to; be likely to.

**will**[2] ● *noun* faculty by which person decides what to do; fixed desire or intention; will-power; legal written directions for disposal of one's property etc. after death; disposition towards others. ● *verb* try to cause by will-power; intend, desire; bequeath by will. □ **at will** whenever one wishes; **will-power** control by purpose over impulse; **with a will** vigorously.

**willing** /ˈwɪlɪŋ/ *adjective* ready to consent or undertake; given etc. by willing person. □ **willingly** adverb; **willingness** noun.

**will-o'-the-wisp** /wɪləðə'wɪsp/ noun phosphorescent light seen on marshy ground; elusive person.

**willow** /'wɪləʊ/ noun waterside tree with pliant branches yielding osiers. □ **willowherb** plant with leaves like willow; **willow-pattern** conventional Chinese design of blue on white china etc.

**willowy** adjective lithe and slender; having willows.

**willy-nilly** /wɪlɪ'nɪlɪ/ adverb whether one likes it or not.

**wilt** ● verb wither, droop; lose energy. ● noun plant disease causing wilting.

**wily** /'waɪlɪ/ adjective (**-ier**, **-iest**) crafty, cunning.

**wimp** noun colloquial feeble or ineffectual person. □ **wimpish** adjective.

**wimple** /'wɪmp(ə)l/ noun headdress covering neck and sides of face, worn by some nuns.

**win** ● verb (**-nn-**; past & past participle **won** /wʌn/) secure as result of fight, contest, bet, etc.; be victor, be victorious in. ● noun victory in game etc. □ **win the day** be victorious in battle, argument, etc.; **win over** gain support of; **win through**, **out** overcome obstacles.

**wince** ● noun start or involuntary shrinking movement of pain etc. ● verb (**-cing**) give wince.

**winceyette** /wɪnsɪ'et/ noun lightweight flannelette.

**winch** ● noun crank of wheel or axle; windlass. ● verb lift with winch.

**wind¹** /wɪnd/ ● noun air in natural motion; breath, esp. as needed in exertion or playing wind instrument; power of breathing easily; empty talk; gas generated in bowels etc.; wind instruments of orchestra etc.; scent carried by the wind. ● verb exhaust wind of by exertion or blow; make (baby) bring up wind after feeding; detect presence of by scent. □ **get wind of** begin to suspect; **get**, **have the wind up** colloquial become, be, frightened; **in the wind** colloquial about to happen; **put the wind up** colloquial frighten; **take the wind out of** (**person's**) **sails** frustrate by anticipation; **windbag** colloquial person who talks a lot but says little of value; **wind-break** thing that breaks force of

wind; **windcheater** windproof jacket; **windfall** fruit blown down by wind, unexpected good fortune, esp. legacy; **wind instrument** musical instrument sounded by air-current; **wind-jammer** merchant sailing ship; **windmill** mill worked by action of wind on sails, toy with curved vanes revolving on stick; **windpipe** air-passage between throat and lungs; **windscreen** screen of glass at front of car etc.; **windscreen wiper** rubber etc. blade to clear windscreen of rain etc.; **windshield** US windscreen; **wind-sock** canvas cylinder or cone on mast to show direction of wind; **windswept** exposed to high winds; **wind-tunnel** enclosed chamber for testing (models or parts of) aircraft etc. in winds of known velocities.

**wind²** /waɪnd/ ● verb (past & past participle **wound** /waʊnd/) go in spiral, crooked, or curved course; make (one's way) thus; wrap closely, coil; provide with coiled thread etc.; surround (as) with coil; wind up (clock etc.). ● noun bend or turn in course. □ **wind down** lower by winding, unwind, approach end gradually; **winding-sheet** sheet in which corpse is wrapped for burial; **wind up** verb coil whole of, tighten coiling or coiled spring of, colloquial increase intensity of, colloquial provoke to anger etc., bring to conclusion, arrange affairs of and dissolve (company), cease business and go into liquidation, colloquial arrive finally; **wind-up** noun conclusion, colloquial attempt to provoke.

**windlass** /'wɪndləs/ noun machine with horizontal axle for hauling or hoisting.

**window** /'wɪndəʊ/ noun opening, usually with glass, in wall etc. to admit light etc.; the glass itself; space for display behind window of shop; window-like opening; transparent part in envelope showing address; opportunity for study or action. □ **window-box** box placed outside window for cultivating plants; **window-dressing** art of arranging display in shop window etc., adroit presentation of facts etc. to give falsely favourable impression; **window-pane** glass pane in window; **window-seat** seat below window, seat next to window in aircraft etc.; **window-shop** look at goods in shop windows without buying anything.

**windsurfing** *noun* sport of riding on water on sailboard. □ **windsurf** *verb*; **windsurfer** *noun*.

**windward** /'wɪndwəd/ ● *adjective & adverb* on or towards side from which wind is blowing. ● *noun* this direction.

**windy** *adjective* (**-ier, -iest**) stormy with or exposed to wind; generating or characterized by flatulence; *colloquial* wordy; *colloquial* apprehensive, frightened. □ **windiness** *noun*.

**wine** ● *noun* fermented grape juice as alcoholic drink; fermented drink resembling this made from other fruits etc.; colour of red wine. ● *verb* (**-ning**) drink wine; entertain with wine. □ **wine bar** bar or small restaurant where wine is main drink available; **wine cellar** cellar for storing wine, its contents; **wineglass** glass for wine, usually with stem and foot; **winepress** press in which grape juice is extracted for wine; **wine waiter** waiter responsible for serving wine.

**wing** ● *noun* each of the limbs or organs by which bird etc. flies; winglike part supporting aircraft; projecting part of building; *Football etc.* forward player at either end of line, side part of playing area; (in *plural*) sides of theatre stage; extreme section of political party; flank of battle array; part of vehicle over wheel; air-force unit of several squadrons. ● *verb* travel or traverse on wings; wound in wing or arm; equip with wings; enable to fly, send in flight. □ **on the wing** flying; **take under one's wing** treat as protégé; **take wing** fly away; **wing-case** horny cover of insect's wing; **wing-chair** chair with side-pieces at top of high back; **wing-collar** man's high stiff collar with turned-down corners; **wing commander** RAF officer next below group captain; **wing-nut** nut with projections to turn it by; **wingspan** measurement right across wings. □ **winged** *adjective*.

**winger** *noun Football etc.* wing player.

**wink** ● *verb* (often + *at*) close and open one eye quickly, esp. as signal; close eye(s) momentarily; (of light) twinkle; (of indicator) flash on and off. ● *noun* act of winking; *colloquial* short sleep. □ **wink at** purposely avoid seeing, pretend not to notice.

**winkle** /'wɪŋk(ə)l/ ● *noun* edible sea snail. ● *verb* (**-ling**) (+ *out*) extract with difficulty.

**winning** ● *adjective* having or bringing victory; attractive. ● *noun* (in *plural*) money won. □ **winning post** post marking end of race. □ **winningly** *adverb*.

**winnow** /'wɪnəʊ/ *verb* blow (grain) free of chaff etc.; (+ *out, away, from,* etc.) rid grain of (chaff etc.); sift, examine.

**winsome** /'wɪnsəm/ *adjective* attractive, engaging. □ **winsomely** *adverb*; **winsomeness** *noun*.

**winter** /'wɪntə/ ● *noun* coldest season of year. ● *verb* (usually + *at, in*) spend the winter. □ **winter garden** garden of plants flourishing in winter; **wintergreen** kind of plant remaining green all winter; **winter sports** sports practised on snow or ice; **wintertime** season or period of winter.

**wintry** /'wɪntrɪ/ *adjective* (**-ier, -iest**) characteristic of winter; lacking warmth. □ **wintriness** *noun*.

**winy** *adjective* (**-ier, -iest**) wine-flavoured.

**wipe** ● *verb* (**-ping**) clean or dry surface of by rubbing; rub (cloth) over surface; spread (liquid etc.) over surface by rubbing; (often + *away, off,* etc.) clear or remove by wiping; erase, eliminate. ● *noun* act of wiping; piece of specially treated cloth for wiping. □ **wipe out** utterly destroy or defeat, clean inside of; **wipe up** dry (dishes etc.), take up (liquid etc.) by wiping.

**wiper** *noun* windscreen wiper.

**wire** ● *noun* metal drawn out into thread or slender flexible rod; piece of this; length of this used for fencing or to carry electric current etc.; *colloquial* telegram. ● *verb* (**-ring**) provide, fasten, strengthen, etc. with wire; (often + *up*) install electrical circuits in; *colloquial* telegraph. □ **get one's wires crossed** become confused; **wire-haired** (of dog) having stiff wiry hair; **wire netting** netting made of meshed wire; **wire-tapping** tapping of telephone wires; **wire wool** mass of fine wire for scouring; **wireworm** destructive larva of a kind of beetle.

**wireless** *noun* radio; radio receiving set.

**wiring** *noun* system or installation of electrical circuits.

**wiry** *adjective* (**-ier**, **-iest**) sinewy, untiring; like wire, tough and coarse.

**wisdom** /ˈwɪzdəm/ *noun* experience, knowledge, and the power of applying them; prudence, common sense; wise sayings. □ **wisdom tooth** hindmost molar usually cut at age of about 20.

**wise**[1] /waɪz/ *adjective* having, showing, or dictated by wisdom; prudent, sensible; having knowledge; suggestive of wisdom; *US colloquial* alert, crafty. □ **be, get wise to** *colloquial* be, become, aware of; **wisecrack** *colloquial noun* smart remark, *verb* make wisecrack; **wise guy** *colloquial* know-all; **wise man** wizard, esp. one of the Magi; **wise up** *esp. US colloquial* inform, get wise. □ **wisely** *adverb.*

**wise**[2] /waɪz/ *noun archaic* way, manner, degree.

**-wise** /waɪz/ *combining form* added to nouns to form adjectives and adverbs: in the manner or direction of (e.g. *clockwise, lengthwise*); with reference to (e.g. *weatherwise*).

**wiseacre** /ˈwaɪzeɪkə/ *noun* person who affects to be wise.

**wish** ● *verb* (often + *for*) have or express desire or aspiration; want, demand; express one's hopes for; *colloquial* foist. ● *noun* desire, request, expression of this; thing desired. □ **wishbone** forked bone between neck and breast of fowl; **wish-fulfilment** tendency of unconscious wishes to be satisfied in fantasy; **wishing-well** well at which wishes are made.

**wishful** *adjective* (often + *to do*) desiring. □ **wishful thinking** belief founded on wishes rather than facts.

**wishy-washy** /ˈwɪʃɪwɒʃɪ/ *adjective colloquial* feeble or poor in quality or character; weak, watery.

**wisp** *noun* small bundle or twist of straw etc.; small separate quantity of smoke, hair, etc.; small thin person. □ **wispy** *adjective* (**-ier**, **-iest**).

**wisteria** /wɪˈstɪərɪə/ *noun* (also **wistaria** /-teər-/) climbing plant with purple, blue, or white hanging flowers.

**wistful** /ˈwɪstfʊl/ *adjective* yearning, mournfully expectant or wishful. □ **wistfully** *adverb*; **wistfulness** *noun.*

**wit** *noun* (in *singular* or *plural*) intelli understanding; (in *singular*) imagin and inventive faculty; amusing in ity of speech or ideas; person not this. □ **at one's wit's** or **wits** utterly at a loss or in despair; **ha keep one's wits about one** be **out of one's wits** mad; **to wit** tha say, namely.

**witch** *noun* woman supposed to dealings with Devil or evil spirit hag; fascinating girl or w □ **witchcraft** use of magic, bewit charm; **witch-doctor** tribal mag of primitive people; **witch, wych** N. American shrub, astringent l from its bark; **witch-hunt** cam against people suspected of unpo or unorthodox views.

**witchery** /ˈwɪtʃərɪ/ *noun* witchcra

**with** /wɪð/ *preposition expressing i ment or means used, company, po of company, cause, possession, ci stances, manner, agreement, disc ment, antagonism, understandin gard.* □ **with it** *colloquial* up to date, and comprehending; **with that** t upon.

**withdraw** /wɪðˈdrɔː/ *verb* (*past -* past participle **-drawn**) pull or take or back; discontinue, cancel, re remove, take away; take (money of an account; retire or go a (as **withdrawn** *adjective*) unsoc □ **withdrawal** *noun.*

**withe** = WITHY.

**wither** /ˈwɪðə/ *verb* (often + *up*) ma become dry and shrivelled; (oft *away*) deprive of or lose vigo freshness; (esp. as **withering** *ad* blight with scorn etc. □ **wither** *adverb.*

**withers** /ˈwɪðəz/ *plural noun* ridg tween horse's shoulder-blades.

**withhold** /wɪðˈhəʊld/ *verb* (*past a* participle **-held**) refuse to give, gra allow; hold back, restrain.

**within** /wɪˈðɪn/ ● *adverb* inside; ind in spirit. ● *preposition* inside; not be or out of; not transgressing or ex ing; not further off than.

**without** /wɪˈðaʊt/ ● *preposition* not ing, feeling, or showing; free fro absence of; with neglect or avoid of; *archaic* outside. ● *adverb archaic or literary* outside, out of doors.

**withstand** /wɪð'stænd/ *verb* (*past & past participle* **-stood**) oppose, hold out against.

**withy** /'wɪðɪ/ *noun* (*plural* **-ies**) tough flexible shoot, esp. of willow.

**witless** *adjective* foolish; crazy.

**witness** /'wɪtnɪs/ ● *noun* eyewitness; person giving sworn testimony; person attesting another's signature to document; (+ *to*, *of*) person or thing whose existence etc. attests or proves something. ● *verb* be eyewitness of; be witness to (signature etc.); serve as evidence or indication of; give or be evidence. □ **bear witness to** attest truth of, state one's belief in; **witness-box** (*US* **-stand**) enclosed space in law court from which witness gives evidence.

**witter** /'wɪtə/ *verb* (often + *on*) *colloquial* chatter annoyingly or on trivial matters.

**witticism** /'wɪtɪsɪz(ə)m/ *noun* witty remark.

**wittingly** /'wɪtɪŋlɪ/ *adverb* consciously, intentionally.

**witty** *adjective* (**-ier**, **-iest**) showing verbal wit. □ **wittily** *adverb*; **wittiness** *noun*.

**wives** *plural* of WIFE.

**wizard** /'wɪzəd/ ● *noun* sorcerer, magician; person of extraordinary powers. ● *adjective slang* wonderful. □ **wizardry** *noun*.

**wizened** /'wɪz(ə)nd/ *adjective* shrivelled-looking.

**WNW** *abbreviation* west-north-west.

**WO** *abbreviation* Warrant Officer.

**woad** *noun* plant yielding blue dye; this dye.

**wobble** /'wɒb(ə)l/ ● *verb* (**-ling**) sway from side to side; stand or go unsteadily, stagger; waver, vacillate. ● *noun* wobbling motion. □ **wobbly** *adjective* (**-ier**, **-iest**).

**woe** *noun* affliction, bitter grief; (in *plural*) calamities. □ **woebegone** dismal-looking.

**woeful** *adjective* sorrowful; causing or feeling affliction; very bad. □ **woefully** *adverb*.

**wok** *noun* bowl-shaped frying-pan used in esp. Chinese cookery.

**woke** *past* of WAKE[1].

**woken** *past participle* of WAKE[1].

**wold** /wəʊld/ *noun* high open uncultivated land or moor.

**wolf** /wʊlf/ ● *noun* (*plural* **wolves** /wʊlvz/) wild animal related to dog; *slang* man who seduces women. ● *verb* (often + *down*) devour greedily. □ **cry wolf** raise false alarm; **keep the wolf from the door** avert starvation; **wolfhound** dog of kind used originally to hunt wolves; **wolfsbane** an aconite; **wolf-whistle** man's whistle to attractive woman. □ **wolfish** *adjective*.

**wolfram** /'wʊlfrəm/ *noun* tungsten; tungsten ore.

**wolverine** /'wʊlvəri:n/ *noun* N. American animal of weasel family.

**wolves** *plural* of WOLF.

**woman** /'wʊmən/ *noun* (*plural* **women** /'wɪmɪn/) adult human female; the female sex; *colloquial* wife, girlfriend.

**womanhood** *noun* female maturity; womanliness; womankind.

**womanish** *adjective derogatory* effeminate, unmanly.

**womanize** *verb* (also **-ise**) (**-zing** or **-sing**) (of man) be promiscuous. □ **womanizer** *noun*.

**womankind** *noun* (also **womenkind**) women in general.

**womanly** *adjective* having or showing qualities associated with women. □ **womanliness** *noun*.

**womb** /wu:m/ *noun* organ of conception and gestation in female mammals.

**wombat** /'wɒmbæt/ *noun* burrowing plant-eating Australian marsupial.

**women** /'wɪmɪn/ *plural* of WOMAN. □ **women's libber** *colloquial* supporter of women's liberation; **women's liberation**, **lib** *colloquial* movement for release of women from subservient status; **women's rights** human rights of women giving equality with men.

**womenfolk** *noun* women in general; women in family.

**won** *past & past participle* of WIN.

**wonder** /'wʌndə/ ● *noun* emotion, esp. admiration, excited by what is unexpected, unfamiliar, or inexplicable;

strange or remarkable thing, specimen, event, etc. ● *adjective* having amazing properties etc. ● *verb* be filled with wonder; (+ *that*) be surprised to find that, be curious to know. □ **no** or **small wonder** it is not surprising; **wonderland** fairyland, place of surprises or marvels.

**wonderful** *adjective* very remarkable or admirable. □ **wonderfully** *adverb*.

**wonderment** *noun* surprise, awe.

**wondrous** /'wʌndrəs/ *poetical* ● *adjective* wonderful. ● *adverb* wonderfully.

**wonky** /'wɒŋkɪ/ *adjective* (**-ier, -iest**) *slang* crooked; unsteady; unreliable.

**wont** /wəunt/ ● *adjective archaic or literary* (+ *to do*) accustomed. ● *noun* formal or jocular custom, habit.

**won't** /wəunt/ will not.

**wonted** /'wəuntɪd/ *adjective* habitual, usual.

**woo** *verb* (**woos, wooed**) court, seek love of; try to win; seek support of; coax, importune.

**wood** /wud/ *noun* hard fibrous substance of tree; this for timber or fuel; (in *singular* or *plural*) growing trees occupying piece of ground; wooden cask for wine etc.; wooden-headed golf club; ball in game of bowls. □ **out of the wood(s)** clear of danger or difficulty; **wood anemone** wild spring-flowering anemone; **woodbine** honeysuckle; **woodchuck** N. American marmot; **woodcock** game bird related to snipe; **woodcut** relief cut on wood, print made from this; **woodcutter** person who cuts timber; **woodland** wooded country; **woodlouse** small land crustacean with many legs; **woodman** forester; **woodpecker** bird that taps tree trunks to find insects; **woodpigeon** dove with white patches round neck; **wood pulp** wood fibre prepared for papermaking; **woodwind** wind instrument(s) of orchestra made originally of wood; **woodwork** making of things in wood, things made of wood; **woodworm** beetle larva that bores in wood, resulting condition of wood.

**wooded** *adjective* having woods.

**wooden** /'wud(ə)n/ *adjective* made of wood; like wood; stiff, clumsy, expressionless. □ **woodenly** *adverb*; **woodenness** *noun*.

**woody** *adjective* (**-ier, -iest**) wooded; like or of wood.

**woof**[1] /wuf/ ● *noun* gruff bark of dog. ● *verb* give woof.

**woof**[2] /wu:f/ *noun* weft.

**woofer** /'wu:fə/ *noun* loudspeaker for low frequencies.

**wool** /wul/ *noun* fine soft wavy hair forming fleece of sheep etc.; woollen yarn, cloth, or garments; wool-like substance. □ **wool-gathering** absent-mindedness; **the Woolsack** Lord Chancellor's seat in House of Lords.

**woollen** /'wulən/ (*US* **woolen**) ● *adjective* made (partly) of wool. ● *noun* woollen fabric; (in *plural*) woollen garments.

**woolly** ● *adjective* (**-ier, -iest**) bearing or like wool; woollen; indistinct; confused. ● *noun* (*plural* **-ies**) *colloquial* woollen (esp. knitted) garment.

**woozy** /'wu:zɪ/ *adjective* (**-ier, -iest**) *colloquial* dizzy; slightly drunk.

**word** /wɜːd/ ● *noun* meaningful element of speech, usually shown with space on either side of it when written or printed; speech as distinct from action; one's promise or assurance; (in *singular* or *plural*) thing said, remark, conversation; (in *plural*) text of song or actor's part; (in *plural*) angry talk; news, message; command. ● *verb* put into words, select words to express. □ **word-blindness** dyslexia; **word for word** in exactly the same words, literally; **the Word (of God)** the Bible; **word of mouth** speech (only); **word-perfect** having memorized one's part etc. perfectly; **word processor** computer software or hardware for storing text entered from keyboard, incorporating corrections, and producing printout; **word-process** *verb*; **word processing** *noun*.

**wording** *noun* form of words used.

**wordy** *adjective* (**-ier, -iest**) using or expressed in (too) many words.

**wore** *past of* WEAR.

**work** /wɜːk/ ● *noun* application of effort to a purpose, use of energy; task to be undertaken; thing done or made by work, result of action; employment, occupation, etc., esp. as means of earning money; literary or musical composition; actions or experiences of specified kind; (in *plural*) operative part of clock etc.; (**the works**) *colloquial* all that is available or needed, full treatment; (in *plural*) operations of building or repair; (in *plural*, often treated as *singular*) factory; (usually in *plural* or *in combination*) defensive structure. ● *verb* be engaged in activity; be employed in certain work; make efforts; be craftsman in (material); operate or function, esp. effectively; operate, manage, control; put or keep in operation or at work, cause to toil; cultivate (land); produce as result; *colloquial* arrange; knead, hammer, bring to desired shape or consistency; do, or make by, needlework etc.; (cause to) make way or make (way) slowly or with difficulty; gradually become (loose etc.) by motion; artificially excite; purchase with labour instead of money; obtain money for by labour; (+ *on*, *upon*) influence; be in motion or agitated, ferment. □ **get worked up** become angry, excited, or tense; **workaday** ordinary, everyday, practical; **work-basket** basket for sewing materials; **workbench** bench for manual work, esp. carpentry; **workbox** box for tools, needlework, etc.; **workday** day on which work is usually done; **work experience** temporary experience of employment for young people; **workforce** workers engaged or available, number of these; **workhouse** *historical* public institution for the poor; **work in** find place for; **workload** amount of work to be done; **workman** man employed to do manual labour, person who works in specified manner; **workmanlike** showing practised skill; **workmanship** degree of skill in doing task or of finish in product; **workmate** person working alongside another; **work off** get rid of by work or activity; **work out** *verb* solve (sum) or find (amount) by calculation, understand (problem, person, etc.), be calculated, have result, provide for all details of, engage in physical exercise; **workout** *noun* session of physical exercise; **work over** examine thoroughly, *colloquial* treat with violence; **workshop** room or building in which goods are manufactured, place or meeting for concerted activity; **work-shy** disinclined to work; **workstation** location of stage in manufacturing process, computer terminal; **worktop** flat (esp. kitchen) surface for working on; **work to rule** follow official working rules exactly to reduce efficiency as protest; **work-to-rule** *noun*; **work up** bring gradually to efficient or advanced state, advance gradually, elaborate or excite by degrees, mingle (ingredients), learn (subject) by study.

**workable** *adjective* that can be worked, will work, or is worth working. □ **workability** *noun*.

**worker** *noun* manual or industrial etc. employee; neuter bee or ant; person who works hard.

**working** ● *adjective* engaged in work; while so engaged; functioning, able to function. ● *noun* activity of work; functioning; mine, quarry; (usually in *plural*) mechanism. □ **working capital** capital used in conducting a business; **working class** social class employed for wages, esp. in manual or industrial work; **working-class** *adjective*; **working day** workday, part of day devoted to work; **working knowledge** knowledge adequate to work with; **working lunch** lunch at which business is conducted; **working order** condition in which machine works; **working party** committee appointed to study and advise on some question.

**world** /wɜːld/ ● *noun* the earth, planetary body like it; the universe, all that exists; time, state, or scene of human existence; (**the**, **this world**) mortal life; secular interests and affairs; human affairs, active life; average, respectable, or fashionable people or their customs or opinions; all that concerns or all who belong to specified class or sphere of activity; vast amount. ● *adjective* of or affecting all nations. □ **out of this world** *colloquial* extremely good etc.; **think the world of** have very high regard for; **world-class** of standard considered high throughout world; **world-famous** known throughout the world; **world music** pop music incorporating ethnic elements; **world war** one involving many important nations; **world-weary** bored with human affairs; **worldwide** *adjective* occurring or known in all parts of the world; *adverb* throughout the world.

**worldly** *adjective* (**-ier, -iest**) temporal, earthly; experienced in life, sophisticated, practical. □ **worldly-wise** prudent in one's dealings with world.

**worm** /wɜːm/ ● *noun* any of several types of creeping invertebrate animal with long slender body and no limbs; larva of insect; (in *plural*) internal parasites; insignificant or contemptible person; spiral of screw. ● *verb* crawl, wriggle; (**worm oneself**) insinuate oneself (into favour etc.); (+ *out*) obtain (secret etc.) by cunning persistence; rid (dog etc.) of worms. □ **worm-cast** convoluted mass of earth left on surface by burrowing earthworm; **wormeaten** eaten into by worms, decayed, dilapidated.

**wormwood** /ˈwɜːmwʊd/ *noun* plant with bitter aromatic taste; bitter humiliation, source of this.

**wormy** *adjective* (**-ier, -iest**) full of worms; wormeaten.

**worn** ● *past participle* of WEAR. ● *adjective* damaged by use or wear; looking tired and exhausted.

**worry** /ˈwʌrɪ/ ● *verb* (**-ies, -ied**) be anxious; harass, importune, be trouble or anxiety to; shake or pull about with teeth; (as **worried** *adjective*) uneasy. ● *noun* (*plural* **-ies**) thing that causes anxiety or disturbs tranquillity; disturbed state of mind, anxiety. □ **worry beads** string of beads manipulated with fingers to occupy or calm oneself. □ **worrier** *noun*.

**worse** /wɜːs/ ● *adjective* more bad; in or into worse health or worse condition. ● *adverb* more badly; more ill. ● *noun* worse thing(s); (**the worse**) worse condition. □ **the worse for wear** damaged by use, injured; **worse off** in a worse (esp. financial) position. □ **worsen** *verb*.

**worship** /ˈwɜːʃɪp/ ● *noun* homage or service to deity; acts, rites, or ceremonies of this; adoration, devotion; (**His, Her, Your Worship**) title used of or to mayor, magistrate, etc. ● *verb* (**-pp-**; *US* **-p-**) adore as divine, honour with religious rites; idolize; attend public worship; be full of adoration. □ **worshipper** *noun*.

**worshipful** *adjective* (also **Worshipful**) *archaic* honourable, distinguished (esp. in old titles of companies or officers).

**worst** /wɜːst/ ● *adjective* most bad. ● *adverb* most badly. ● *noun* worst part or possibility. ● *verb* get the better of, defeat. □ **at (the) worst** in the worst possible case; **do your worst** *expression of defiance*; **get the worst of it** be defeated; **if the worst comes to the worst** if the worst happens.

**worsted** /ˈwʊstɪd/ *noun* fine woollen yarn; fabric made from this.

**wort** /wɜːt/ *noun* infusion of malt before it is fermented into beer.

**worth** /wɜːθ/ ● *adjective* of value equivalent to; such as to justify or repay; possessing property equivalent to. ● *noun* value; equivalent of money etc. in commodity etc. □ **worth it** (*colloquial*), **worth (one's) while**, **worthwhile** worth the time or effort spent.

**worthless** *adjective* without value or merit. □ **worthlessness** *noun*.

**worthy** /ˈwɜːðɪ/ ● *adjective* (**-ier, -iest**) deserving respect, estimable; entitled to recognition; (usually + *of*) deserving; (+ *of*) adequate or suitable for the dignity etc. of. ● *noun* (*plural* **-ies**) worthy person; person of some distinction.

**would** *auxiliary verb* (*3rd singular present* **would**) *used in reported speech or to form conditional mood; expressing habitual past action, request as question, or probability.* □ **would-be** desiring or aspiring to be.

**wouldn't** /ˈwʊd(ə)nt/ would not.

**wound**[1] /wuːnd/ ● *noun* injury done by cut or blow to living tissue; pain inflicted on feelings, injury to reputation. ● *verb* inflict wound on.

**wound**[2] *past & past participle* of WIND[2]. □ **wound up** excited, tense, angry.

**wove** *past* of WEAVE[1].

**woven** *past participle* of WEAVE[1].

**wow** /waʊ/ ● *interjection* expressing astonishment or admiration. ● *noun* *slang* sensational success. ● *verb* *slang* impress greatly.

**WP** *abbreviation* word processor.

**WPC** *abbreviation* woman police constable.

**w.p.m.** *abbreviation* words per minute.

**WRAC** *abbreviation* Women's Royal Army Corps.

**wrack** *noun* seaweed cast up or growing on seashore; destruction.

**WRAF** *abbreviation* Women's Royal Air Force.

**wraith** /reɪθ/ *noun* ghost; spectral appearance of living person supposed to portend that person's death.

**wrangle** /'ræŋg(ə)l/ • *noun* noisy argument or dispute. • *verb* (**-ling**) engage in wrangle.

**wrap** • *verb* (**-pp-**) (often + *up*) envelop in folded or soft encircling material; (+ *round, about*) arrange or draw (pliant covering) round (person). • *noun* shawl, scarf, etc.; wrapper; *esp. US* wrapping material. □ **under wraps** in secrecy; **wraparound, wrapround** (esp. of clothing) designed to wrap round, curving round at edges; **wrap-over** *adjective* (of garment) overlapping when worn, *noun* such garment; **wrapped up in** engrossed or absorbed in; **wrap up** *colloquial* finish off (matter), put on warm clothes.

**wrapper** *noun* cover for sweet, book, posted newspaper, etc.; loose enveloping robe or gown.

**wrapping** *noun* (esp. in *plural*) material used to wrap, wraps, wrappers. □ **wrapping paper** strong or decorative paper for wrapping parcels.

**wrasse** /ræs/ *noun* (*plural* same or **-s**) brilliant-coloured edible sea fish.

**wrath** /rɒθ/ *noun literary* extreme anger. □ **wrathful** *adjective*.

**wreak** *verb* (usually + *upon*) give play to (vengeance etc.); cause (damage etc.).

**wreath** /riːθ/ *noun* (*plural* **-s** /riːðz/) flowers or leaves wound together into ring, esp. as ornament for head or door or for laying on grave etc.; curl or ring of smoke, cloud, or soft fabric.

**wreathe** /riːð/ *verb* (**-thing**) encircle (as with or like wreath; (+ *round*) wind (one's arms etc.) round (person etc.); move in wreaths.

**wreck** • *noun* sinking or running aground of ship; ship that has suffered wreck; greatly damaged building, thing, or person. • *verb* seriously damage (vehicle etc.); ruin (hopes etc.); cause wreck of (ship).

**wreckage** *noun* wrecked material; remnants of wreck; act of wrecking.

**wrecker** *noun* person or thing that wrecks or destroys, esp. (*historical*) person who tries from shore to bring about shipwreck for plunder or profit.

**Wren** *noun* member of WRNS.

**wren** *noun* small usually brown short-winged songbird.

**wrench** • *noun* violent twist or oblique pull or tearing off; tool for gripping and turning nuts etc.; painful uprooting or parting etc. • *verb* twist or pull violently round or sideways; (often + *off, away*, etc.) pull with wrench.

**wrest** *verb* wrench away from person's grasp; (+ *from*) obtain by effort or with difficulty.

**wrestle** /'res(ə)l/ • *noun* contest in which two opponents grapple and try to throw each other to ground; hard struggle. • *verb* (**-ling**) have wrestling match; (often + *with*) struggle; (+ *with*) do one's utmost to deal with. □ **wrestler** *noun*.

**wretch** *noun* unfortunate or pitiable person; reprehensible person.

**wretched** /'retʃɪd/ *adjective* (**-er**, **-est**) unhappy, miserable, unwell; of bad quality, contemptible; displeasing. □ **wretchedly** *adverb*; **wretchedness** *noun*.

**wriggle** /'rɪg(ə)l/ • *verb* (**-ling**) twist or turn body with short writhing movements; make wriggling motions; (+ *along, through*, etc.) go thus; be evasive. • *noun* wriggling movement. □ **wriggly** *adjective*.

**wring** • *verb* (*past & past participle* **wrung**) squeeze tightly; (often + *out*) squeeze and twist, esp. to remove liquid; break by twisting; distress, torture; extract by squeezing; (+ *out, from*) obtain by pressure or importunity. • *noun* act of wringing. □ **wringing** (**wet**) so wet that water can be wrung out; **wring one's hands** clasp them as gesture of grief; **wring the neck of** kill (chicken etc.) by twisting neck.

**wringer** *noun* device for wringing water from washed clothes etc.

**wrinkle** /'rɪŋk(ə)l/ • *noun* crease in skin or other flexible surface; *colloquial* useful hint, clever expedient. • *verb* (**-ling**) make wrinkles in; form wrinkles. □ **wrinkly** *adjective* (**-ier**, **-iest**).

**wrist** *noun* joint connecting hand and forearm; part of garment covering wrist. □ **wrist-watch** small watch worn on strap etc. round wrist.

**wristlet** *noun* band or ring to guard, strengthen, or adorn wrist.

**writ** *noun* formal written court order to do or not do specified act.

**write** *verb* (**-ting**; *past* **wrote**; *past participle* **written** /'rɪt(ə)n/) mark paper or other surface with symbols, letters, or words; form or mark (such symbols etc.); form or mark symbols of (word, document, etc.); fill or complete with writing; put (data) into computer store; (esp. in *passive*) indicate (quality or condition) by appearance; compose for reproduction or publication; (usually + *to*) write and send letter; convey (news etc.) by letter; state in book etc.; (+ *into*, *out of*) include or exclude (character, episode) in or from story. □ **write down** record in writing; **write in** send suggestion etc. in writing, esp. to broadcasting station; **write off** *verb* cancel (debt etc.), acknowledge as lost, completely destroy; (+ *for*) order or request by post; **write-off** *noun* thing written off, esp. vehicle etc. so damaged as not to be worth repair; **write up** *verb* write full account of; **write-up** *noun* written or published account, review.

**writer** *noun* person who writes, esp. author. □ **writer's cramp** muscular spasm due to excessive writing.

**writhe** /raɪð/ *verb* (**-thing**) twist or roll oneself about (as) in acute pain; suffer mental torture.

**writing** *noun* written words etc.; handwriting; (usually in *plural*) writer's works. □ **in writing** in written form.

**written** *past participle* of WRITE.

**WRNS** *abbreviation* Women's Royal Naval Service.

**wrong** ● *adjective* mistaken, not true, in error; unsuitable, less or least desirable; contrary to law or morality; amiss, out of order. ● *adverb* in wrong manner or direction, with incorrect result. ● *noun* what is morally wrong; unjust action. ● *verb* treat unjustly; mistakenly attribute bad motives to. □ **go wrong** take wrong path, stop functioning properly, depart from virtuous behaviour; **in the wrong** responsible for quarrel, mistake, or offence; **wrongdoer** person who behaves immorally or illegally; **wrongdoing** *noun*; **wrong-foot** *colloquial* catch off balance or unprepared; **wrong-headed** perverse and obstinate; **wrong side** worse or undesirable or unusable side; **wrong way round** in opposite of normal orientation or sequence. □ **wrongly** *adverb*; **wrongness** *noun*.

**wrongful** *adjective* unwarranted, unjustified. □ **wrongfully** *adverb*.

**wrote** *past* of WRITE.

**wroth** /rəʊθ/ *adjective archaic* angry.

**wrought** /rɔːt/ *archaic past & past participle* of WORK. □ **wrought iron** form of iron suitable for forging or rolling, not cast.

**wrung** *past & past participle* of WRING.

**WRVS** *abbreviation* Women's Royal Voluntary Service.

**wry** /raɪ/ *adjective* (**-er**, **-est**) distorted, turned to one side; contorted in disgust, disappointment, or mockery; (of humour) dry and mocking. □ **wryneck** small woodpecker able to turn head over shoulder. □ **wryly** *adverb*; **wryness** *noun*.

**WSW** *abbreviation* west-south-west.

**wt** *abbreviation* weight.

**wych hazel** /wɪtʃ/ witch hazel.

**WYSIWYG** /'wɪzɪwɪg/ *adjective indicating that text on computer screen and printout correspond exactly* (*what you see is what you get*).

**X¹** *noun* (also **x**) (Roman numeral) 10; first unknown quantity in algebra; unknown or unspecified number, person, etc.; cross-shaped symbol, esp. used to indicate position or incorrectness, to symbolize kiss or vote, or as signature of person who cannot write. □ **X-ray** *noun* electromagnetic radiation of short wavelength able to pass through opaque bodies, photograph made by X-rays, *verb* photograph, examine, or treat with X-rays.

**X²** *adjective* (of film) classified as suitable for adults only.

**xenophobia** /zenəˈfəʊbɪə/ *noun* hatred or fear of foreigners.

**Xerox** /ˈzɪərɒks/ ● *noun proprietary term* type of photocopier; copy made by it. ● *verb* (**xerox**) make Xerox of.

**Xmas** /ˈkrɪsməs, ˈeksməs/ *noun colloquial* Christmas.

**xylophone** /ˈzaɪləfəʊn/ *noun* musical instrument of graduated wooden or metal bars struck with small wooden hammers.

**Y** *noun* (also **y**) second unknown quantity in algebra; Y-shaped thing.

**yacht** /jɒt/ ● *noun* light sailing vessel for racing or cruising; larger usually power-driven vessel for cruising. ● *verb* race or cruise in yacht. □ **yachtsman**, **yachtswoman** person who yachts.

**yah** /jɑː/ *interjection of derision, defiance, etc.*

**yahoo** /jɑːˈhuː/ *noun* bestial person.

**Yahweh** /ˈjɑːweɪ/ *noun* Jehovah.

**yak** *noun* long-haired Tibetan ox.

**yam** *noun* tropical or subtropical climbing plant; edible starchy tuberous root of this; *US* sweet potato.

**yang** *noun* (in Chinese philosophy) active male principle of universe (compare YIN).

**Yank** *noun colloquial often derogatory* American.

**yank** *verb & noun colloquial* pull with jerk.

**Yankee** /ˈjæŋkɪ/ *noun colloquial* Yank; *US* inhabitant of New England or of northern States.

**yap** ● *verb* (**-pp-**) bark shrilly or fussily; *colloquial* talk noisily, foolishly, or complainingly. ● *noun* sound of yapping.

**yard¹** *noun* unit of linear measure (3 ft, 0.9144 m.); this length of material; square or cubic yard; spar slung across mast for sail to hang from; (in *plural*, + *of*) *colloquial* a great length. □ **yard-arm** either end of ship's yard; **yardstick** standard of comparison, rod a yard long usually divided into inches etc.

**yard²** *noun* piece of enclosed ground, esp. attached to building or used for particular purpose; *US & Australian* garden of house.

**yardage** *noun* number of yards of material etc.

**yarmulke** /ˈjɑːməlkə/ *noun* (also **yarmulka**) skullcap worn by Jewish men.

**yarn** ● *noun* spun thread for weaving, knitting, etc.; *colloquial* story, traveller's tale, anecdote. ● *verb colloquial* tell yarns.

**yarrow** /ˈjærəʊ/ *noun* perennial plant, esp. milfoil.

**yashmak** /ˈjæʃmæk/ *noun* veil concealing face except eyes, worn by some Muslim women.

**yaw** ● *verb* (of ship, aircraft, etc.) fail to hold straight course, go unsteadily. ● *noun* yawing of ship etc. from course.

**yawl** *noun* kind of sailing boat; small fishing boat.

**yawn** ● *verb* open mouth wide and inhale, esp. when sleepy or bored; gape, be wide open. ● *noun* act of yawning.

**yaws** /jɔːz/ *plural noun* (usually treated as *singular*) contagious tropical skin disease.

**yd** *abbreviation* ( *plural* **yds**) yard (measure).

**ye** /jiː/ *pronoun archaic* (as subject of verb) you (plural).

**yea** /jeɪ/ *archaic* ● *adverb* yes. ● *noun* 'yes' vote.

**yeah** /jeə/ *adverb colloquial* yes.

**year** /jɪə/ *noun* time occupied by one revolution of earth round sun, approx. 365¼ days; period from 1 Jan. to 31 Dec. inclusive; period of 12 calendar months; (in *plural*) age, time of life; (usually in *plural*) *colloquial* very long time. □ **yearbook** annual publication bringing information on some subject up to date.

**yearling** *noun* animal between one and two years old.

**yearly** ● *adjective* done, produced, or occurring once every year; of or lasting a year. ● *adverb* once every year.

**yearn** /jɜːn/ *verb* be filled with longing, compassion, or tenderness. □ **yearning** *noun & adjective*.

**yeast** *noun* greyish-yellow fungus, got esp. from fermenting malt liquors and used as fermenting agent, to raise bread, etc.

**yeasty** *adjective* (**-ier**, **-iest**) frothy; in ferment; working like yeast.

**yell** ● *noun* sharp loud cry; shout. ● *verb* cry, shout.

**yellow** /ˈjeləʊ/ ● *adjective* of the colour of lemons, buttercups, etc.; having yellow skin or complexion; *colloquial* cowardly. ● *noun* yellow colour, paint, clothes, etc. ● *verb* turn yellow. □ **yellow-belly** *colloquial* coward; **yellow card** card shown by referee to football-player being cautioned; **yellow fever** tropical virus fever with jaundice etc.; **yellowhammer** bunting of which male has yellow head, neck, and breast; **Yellow Pages** *proprietary term* telephone directory on yellow paper, listing and classifying business subscribers; **yellow streak**

*colloquial* trace of cowardice. □ **yellowish** *adjective*; **yellowness** *noun*; **yellowy** *adjective*.

**yelp** ● *noun* sharp shrill bark or cry as of dog in excitement or pain. ● *verb* utter yelp.

**yen**¹ *noun* (*plural* same) chief monetary unit of Japan.

**yen**² *colloquial* ● *noun* intense desire or longing. ● *verb* (**-nn-**) feel longing.

**yeoman** /ˈjəʊmən/ *noun esp. historical* man holding and farming small estate; member of yeomanry force. □ **Yeoman of the Guard** member of bodyguard of English sovereign.

**yeomanry** *noun* (*plural* **-ies**) group of yeomen; *historical* volunteer cavalry force in British army.

**yes** ● *adverb* indicating *affirmative* reply to question, statement, request, command, etc.; (**yes?**) indeed?, is that so?, what do you want? ● *noun* utterance of word yes. □ **yes-man** *colloquial* weakly acquiescent person.

**yesterday** /ˈjestədeɪ/ ● *adverb* on the day before today. ● *noun* the day before today.

**yesteryear** /ˈjestəjɪə/ *noun archaic or rhetorical* last year; the recent past.

**yet** ● *adverb* up to now or then; (with negative or in questions) so soon as, or by, now or then; again, in addition; in the remaining time available; (+ *comparative*) even; nevertheless. ● *conjunction* but nevertheless.

**yeti** /ˈjetɪ/ *noun* supposed manlike or bearlike Himalayan animal.

**yew** *noun* dark-leaved evergreen coniferous tree; its wood.

**YHA** *abbreviation* Youth Hostels Association.

**Yiddish** /ˈjɪdɪʃ/ ● *noun* language used by Jews in or from Europe. ● *adjective* of this language.

**yield** /jiːld/ ● *verb* produce or return as fruit, profit, or result; concede, give up; (often + *to*) surrender, submit, defer; (as **yielding** *adjective*) soft and pliable, submissive; (+ *to*) give right of way to. ● *noun* amount yielded or produced.

**yin** *noun* (in Chinese philosophy) passive female principle of universe (compare YANG).

**yippee** /jɪˈpiː/ interjection expressing delight or excitement.

**YMCA** abbreviation Young Men's Christian Association.

**yob** /jɒb/ noun (also **yobbo**, plural **-s**) slang lout, hooligan. □ **yobbish** adjective.

**yodel** /ˈjəʊd(ə)l/ ● verb (**-ll-**; US **-l-**) sing with melodious inarticulate sounds and frequent changes between falsetto and normal voice, in manner of Swiss mountain-dwellers. ● noun yodelling cry.

**yoga** /ˈjəʊɡə/ noun Hindu system of meditation and asceticism; system of physical exercises and breathing control used in yoga.

**yoghurt** /ˈjɒɡət/ noun (also **yogurt**) rather sour semi-solid food made from milk fermented by added bacteria.

**yogi** /ˈjəʊɡɪ/ noun (plural **-s**) devotee of yoga.

**yoke** ● noun wooden crosspiece fastened over necks of two oxen etc. and attached to plough or wagon to be pulled; (plural same or **-s**) pair (of oxen etc.); object like yoke in form or function, e.g. wooden shoulder-piece for carrying pair of pails, top part of garment from which rest hangs; sway, dominion, servitude; bond of union, esp. of marriage. ● verb (**-king**) put yoke on; couple or unite (pair); link (one thing) to (another); match or work together.

**yokel** /ˈjəʊk(ə)l/ noun country bumpkin.

**yolk** /jəʊk/ noun yellow inner part of egg.

**Yom Kippur** /jɒm ˈkɪpə/ noun most solemn religious fast day of Jewish year, Day of Atonement.

**yon** adjective & adverb literary & dialect yonder.

**yonder** /ˈjɒndə/ ● adverb over there, at some distance in that direction, in place indicated. ● adjective situated yonder.

**yore** noun □ **of yore** a long time ago.

**york** verb Cricket bowl out with yorker.

**yorker** noun Cricket ball that pitches immediately under bat.

**Yorkist** /ˈjɔːkɪst/ noun historical follower of House of York, esp. in Wars of the Roses. ● adjective of House of York.

**Yorkshire pudding** /ˈjɔːkʃə/ noun baked batter usually eaten with roast beef.

**Yorkshire terrier** /ˈjɔːkʃə/ noun small long-haired blue and tan kind of terrier.

**you** /juː/ pronoun the person(s) or thing(s) addressed; one, a person.

**you'd** /juːd/ you had; you would.

**you'll** /juːl/ you will; you shall.

**young** /jʌŋ/ ● adjective (**younger** /ˈjʌŋɡə/, **youngest** /ˈjʌŋɡɪst/) not far advanced in life, development, or existence, not yet old; immature, inexperienced, youthful; of or characteristic of youth. ● noun offspring, esp. of animals. □ **youngish** adjective.

**youngster** noun child, young person.

**your** /jɔː/ adjective of or belonging to you.

**you're** /jɔː/ you are.

**yours** /jɔːz/ pronoun the one(s) belonging to you.

**yourself** /jɔːˈself/ pronoun (plural **yourselves**): emphatic & reflexive form of YOU.

**youth** /juːθ/ noun (plural **-s** /juːðz/) being young; early part of life, esp. adolescence; quality or condition characteristic of the young; young man; (treated as plural) young people collectively. □ **youth club** place for young people's leisure activities; **youth hostel** any of chain of cheap lodgings where (esp. young) holiday-makers can stay for the night.

**youthful** adjective young or still having characteristics of youth. □ **youthfulness** noun.

**you've** /juːv/ you have.

**yowl** /jaʊl/ ● noun loud wailing cry (as) of cat or dog in distress. ● verb utter yowl.

**yo-yo** /ˈjəʊjəʊ/ noun (plural **yo-yos**) toy consisting of pair of discs with deep groove between them in which string is attached and wound, and which can be made to fall and rise.

**yr.** abbreviation year(s); younger; your.

**yrs.** abbreviation years; yours.

**YTS** abbreviation Youth Training Scheme.

**yuan** /juːˈɑːn/ noun (plural same) chief monetary unit of China.

**yucca** /ˈjʌkə/ noun white-flowered plant with swordlike leaves, often grown as house plant.

**yuck** /jʌk/ *interjection* (also **yuk**) *slang* expression of strong distaste.

**yucky** *adjective* (also **yukky**) (**-ier, -iest**) *slang* messy, repellent; sickly, sentimental.

**Yugoslav** /'ju:ɡəslɑːv/ *historical* ● *adjective* of Yugoslavia. ● *noun* native or national of Yugoslavia. □ **Yugoslavian** /-'slɑːv-/ *adjective & noun*.

**yuk** = YUCK.

**yukky** = YUCKY.

**yule** *noun* (in full **yule-tide**) *archaic* festival of Christmas. □ **yule-log** large log burnt at Christmas.

**yummy** /'jʌmɪ/ *adjective* (**-ier, -iest**) *colloquial* tasty, delicious.

**yuppie** /'jʌpɪ/ *noun* (also **yuppy**) (*plural* **-ies**) *colloquial usually derogatory* young ambitious professional person working in city.

**YWCA** *abbreviation* Young Women's Christian Association.

# Zz

**zabaglione** /zæbə'ljəʊnɪ/ *noun* Italian dessert of whipped and heated egg yolks, sugar, and wine.

**zany** /'zeɪnɪ/ *adjective* (**-ier, -iest**) comically idiotic; crazily ridiculous.

**zap** *verb* (**-pp-**) *slang* kill, destroy; attack; hit hard.

**zeal** *noun* fervour, eagerness; hearty persistent endeavour. □ **zealous** /'zeləs/ *adjective*.

**zealot** /'zelət/ *noun* extreme partisan, fanatic.

**zebra** /'zebrə, 'zi:-/ *noun* (*plural* same or **-s**) African black and white striped horse-like animal. □ **zebra crossing** striped street-crossing where pedestrians have precedence.

***Zeitgeist*** /'tsaɪtɡaɪst/ *noun* spirit of times. [German]

**Zen** *noun* form of Buddhism emphasizing meditation and intuition.

**zenith** /'zenɪθ/ *noun* point of heavens directly overhead; highest point (of power, prosperity, etc.).

**zephyr** /'zefə/ *noun literary* mild gentle breeze.

**zero** /'zɪərəʊ/ ● *noun* (*plural* **-s**) figure 0, nought, nil; point on scale of thermometer etc. from which positive or negative quantity is reckoned; (in full **zero-hour**) hour at which planned, esp. military, operation is timed to begin, crucial moment; lowest or earliest point. ● *adjective* no, not any. ● *verb* (**zeroes, zeroed**) adjust (instrument etc.) to zero. □ **zero in on** take aim at, focus attention on; **zero-rated** on which no VAT is charged.

**zest** *noun* piquancy; keen interest or enjoyment, relish, gusto; outer layer of orange or lemon peel.

**zigzag** /'zɪɡzæɡ/ ● *adjective* with abrupt alternate right and left turns. ● *noun* zigzag line, thing having sharp turns. ● *adverb* with zigzag manner or course. ● *verb* (**-gg-**) move in zigzag course.

**zilch** *noun esp. US slang* nothing.

**zillion** /'zɪljən/ *noun* (*plural* same) *colloquial* indefinite large number; (**zillions**) very large number.

**Zimmer frame** /'zɪmə/ *noun proprietary term* kind of walking frame.

**zinc** *noun* greyish-white metallic element.

**zing** *colloquial* ● *noun* vigour, energy. ● *verb* move swiftly, esp. with shrill sound.

**zinnia** /'zɪnɪə/ *noun* garden plant with showy flowers.

**zip** ● *noun* light sharp sound; energy, vigour; (in full **zip-fastener**) fastening device of two flexible strips with interlocking projections, closed or opened by sliding clip along them. ● *verb* (**-pp-**) (often + *up*) fasten with zip-fastener; move with zip or at high speed.

**zipper** *noun esp. US* zip-fastener.

**zircon** /'zɜːkən/ *noun* translucent varieties of zirconium silicate cut into gems.

**zirconium** /zəˈkəʊnɪəm/ noun grey metallic element.

**zit** noun esp. US slang pimple.

**zither** /ˈzɪðə/ noun stringed instrument with flat soundbox, placed horizontally and played by plucking.

**zloty** /ˈzlɒtɪ/ noun (plural same or **-s**) chief monetary unit of Poland.

**zodiac** /ˈzəʊdɪæk/ noun belt of heavens including all apparent positions of sun, moon, and planets as known to ancient astronomers, and divided into 12 equal parts (**signs of the zodiac**).

**zombie** /ˈzɒmbɪ/ noun corpse said to have been revived by witchcraft; colloquial dull or apathetic person.

**zone** ●noun area having particular features, properties, purpose, or use; well-defined region of more or less beltlike form; area between two concentric circles; encircling band of colour etc.; archaic girdle, belt. ● verb (**-ning**) encircle as or with zone; arrange or distribute by zones; assign as or to specific area. □ **zonal** adjective.

**zonked** /zɒŋkt/ adjective slang (often + out) exhausted; intoxicated.

**zoo** noun zoological garden.

**zoological** /zəʊəˈlɒdʒɪk(ə)l, zuːə-/ adjective of zoology. □ **zoological garden(s)** public garden or park with collection of animals for exhibition and study.

■ **Usage** See note at ZOOLOGY.

**zoology** /zəʊˈɒlədʒɪ, zuːˈɒl-/ noun scientific study of animals. □ **zoologist** noun.

■ **Usage** The second pronunciation given for zoology, zoological, and zoologist (with the first syllable pronounced as in zoo), although extremely common, is considered incorrect by some people.

**zoom** ● verb move quickly, esp. with buzzing sound; cause aeroplane to mount at high speed and steep angle; (often + in, in on) (of camera) change rapidly from long shot to close-up (of). ● noun aeroplane's steep climb. □ **zoom lens** lens allowing camera to zoom by varying focal length.

**zoophyte** /ˈzəʊəfaɪt/ noun plantlike animal, esp. coral, sea anemone, or sponge.

**zucchini** /zuːˈkiːnɪ/ noun (plural same or **-s**) esp. US & Australian courgette.

**zygote** /ˈzaɪgəʊt/ noun Biology cell formed by union of two gametes.

# Appendix 1 Countries of the world

(Countries are given for linguistic information on the names in use; some regions and dependent territories are included.)

| country | person (name in general use) | related adjective (in general use) |
| --- | --- | --- |
| Afghanistan | Afghan | Afghan |
| Albania | Albanian | Albanian |
| Algeria | Algerian | Algerian |
| America see United States of America | | |
| Andorra | Andorran | Andorran |
| Angola | Angolan | Angolan |
| Anguilla | Anguillan | Anguillan or Anguilla |
| Antigua and Barbuda | citizen of Antigua and Barbuda | Antiguan or Barbudan, or Antigua and Barbuda |
| Argentina | Argentine or Argentinian | Argentine or Argentinian |
| Armenia | Armenian | Armenian |
| Australia | Australian | Australian |
| Austria | Austrian | Austrian |
| Azerbaijan | Azerbaijani | Azerbaijani |
| Bahamas | Bahamian | Bahamian |
| Bahrain | Bahraini | Bahraini or Bahrain |
| Bangladesh | Bangladeshi | Bangladeshi |
| Barbados | Barbadian | Barbadian |
| Belgium | Belgian | Belgian |
| Belize | Belizean | Belizean |
| Belarus (formerly Belorussia) | Belorussian or Belarussian | Belorussian or Belarussian |
| Benin | Beninese | Beninese |
| Bermuda (dependent territory) | Bermudan | Bermudan |
| Bhutan | Bhutanese | Bhutanese |
| Bolivia | Bolivian | Bolivian |

| country | person (name in general use) | related adjective (in general use) |
|---|---|---|
| Bosnia and Herzegovina | citizen of Bosnia and Herzegovina | Bosnian or Bosnian and Herzegovinian |
| Botswana | Botswanan | Botswanan |
| Brazil | Brazilian | Brazilian |
| Britain see Great Britain | | |
| Brunei | citizen of Brunei | Bruneian or Brunei |
| Bulgaria | Bulgarian | Bulgarian |
| Burkina (official name Burkina Faso) | Burkinan | Burkinan or Burkine |
| Burma | Burmese | Burmese |
| Burundi | citizen of Burundi | Burundi |
| | | |
| Cambodia (formerly Kampuchea) | Cambodian | Cambodian |
| Cameroon | Cameroonian | Cameroonian |
| Canada | Canadian | Canadian |
| Cape Verde Islands | Cape Verdean | Cape Verdean |
| Cayman Islands (dependent territory) | Cayman Islander or Caymanian | Cayman Islands |
| Central African Republic | citizen of the Central African Republic | Central African Republic |
| Chad | Chadian | Chadian |
| Chile | Chilean | Chilean |
| China | Chinese | Chinese |
| Colombia | Colombian | Colombian |
| Comoros | Comorian | Comorian |
| Congo | Congolese | Congolese |
| Costa Rica | Costa Rican | Costa Rican |
| Croatia | Croat | Croatian |
| Cuba | Cuban | Cuban |
| Cyprus | Cypriot | Cypriot or Cyprus |
| Czech Republic | Czech | Czech |
| | | |
| Denmark | Dane | Danish |
| Djibouti | Djiboutian | Djiboutian |
| Dominica | Dominican | Dominican |
| Dominican Republic | citizen of the Dominican Republic | Dominican Republic |
| Ecuador | Ecuadorean | Ecuadorean |
| Egypt | Egyptian | Egyptian |

| country | person (*name in general use*) | related adjective (*in general use*) |
|---|---|---|
| El Salvador | Salvadorean | Salvadorean |
| England | Englishman/ Englishwoman | English |
| Equatorial Guinea | Equatorial Guinean | Equatorial Guinea |
| Estonia | Estonian | Estonian |
| Ethiopia | Ethiopian | Ethiopian |
| Falkland Islands (*dependent territory*) | Falkland Islander | Falkland Islands |
| Fiji | Fijian | Fijian *or* Fiji |
| Finland | Finn | Finnish |
| France | Frenchman/ Frenchwoman | French |
| Gabon | Gabonese | Gabonese |
| Gambia | Gambian | Gambian |
| Georgia | Georgian | Georgian |
| Germany | German | German |
| Ghana | Ghanaian | Ghanaian *or* Ghana |
| Gibraltar (*dependent territory*) | Gibraltarian | Gibraltarian *or* Gibraltar |
| Great Britain | Briton | British |
| Greece | Greek | Greek |
| Grenada | Grenadian | Grenadian |
| Guatemala | Guatemalan | Guatemalan |
| Guinea | Guinean | Guinean |
| Guinea-Bissau | citizen of Guinea-Bissau | Guinea-Bissau |
| Guyana | Guyanese | Guyanese |
| Haiti | Haitian | Haitian |
| Holland *see* Netherlands | | |
| Honduras | Honduran | Honduran |
| Hong Kong (*dependent territory*) | inhabitant of Hong Kong | Hong Kong |
| Hungary | Hungarian | Hungarian |
| Iceland | Icelander | Icelandic |
| India | Indian | Indian |

| country | person (*name in general use*) | related adjective (*in general use*) |
|---|---|---|
| Indonesia | Indonesian | Indonesian |
| Iran | Iranian | Iranian |
| Iraq | Iraqi | Iraqi or Iraq |
| Ireland, Republic of | Irishman/ Irishwoman | Irish |
| Israel | Israeli | Israeli or Israel |
| Italy | Italian | Italian |
| Ivory Coast | citizen of the Ivory Coast | Ivory Coast or Ivorian |
| Jamaica | Jamaican | Jamaican |
| Japan | Japanese | Japanese |
| Jordan | Jordanian | Jordanian |
| Kampuchea *see* Cambodia | | |
| Kazakhstan | Kazakh | Kazakh |
| Kenya | Kenyan | Kenyan |
| Kiribati | citizen of Kiribati | Kiribati |
| Korea, North | North Korean | North Korean |
| Korea, South | South Korean | South Korean |
| Kuwait | Kuwaiti | Kuwaiti or Kuwait |
| Kyrgyzstan | Kyrgyz | Kyrgyz |
| Laos | Laotian | Laotian |
| Latvia | Latvian | Latvian |
| Lebanon | Lebanese | Lebanese |
| Lesotho | Mosotho, *plural* Basotho | Lesotho |
| Liberia | Liberian | Liberian |
| Libya | Libyan | Libyan |
| Liechtenstein | Liechtensteiner | Liechtenstein |
| Lithuania | Lithuanian | Lithuanian |
| Luxemburg | Luxemburger | Luxemburg |
| Macedonia | Macedonian | Macedonian |
| Madagascar | Madagascan | Malagasy or Madagascan |
| Malawi | Malawian | Malawian |
| Malaysia | Malaysian | Malaysian |
| Maldives | Maldivian | Maldivian |

| country | person (name in general use) | related adjective (in general use) |
|---|---|---|
| Mali | Malian | Malian |
| Malta | Maltese | Maltese |
| Marshall Islands | Marshall Islander | Marshall Islands |
| Mauritania | Mauritanian | Mauritanian |
| Mauritius | Mauritian | Mauritian |
| Mexico | Mexican | Mexican |
| Micronesia | Micronesian | Micronesian |
| Moldavia | Moldavian | Moldavian |
| Monaco | Monegasque | Monegasque |
| Mongolia | Mongolian | Mongolian |
| Montenegro | Montenegrin | Montenegrin |
| Montserrat (dependent territory) | Montserratian | Monserrat |
| Morocco | Moroccan | Moroccan |
| Mozambique | Mozambican | Mozambican or Mozambique |
| | | |
| Namibia | Namibian | Namibian |
| Nauru | Nauruan | Nauruan |
| Nepal | Nepalese | Nepalese |
| Netherlands | Dutchman/ Dutchwoman or Netherlander | Dutch or Netherlands |
| New Zealand | New Zealander | New Zealand |
| Nicaragua | Nicaraguan | Nicaraguan |
| Niger | citizen of Niger | Niger |
| Nigeria | Nigerian | Nigerian |
| Northern Ireland | Ulsterman/ Ulsterwoman | Northern Irish or Northern Ireland or Ulster |
| Norway | Norwegian | Norwegian |
| Oman | Omani | Omani or Oman |
| | | |
| Pakistan | Pakistani | Pakistani |
| Panama | Panamian | Panamian |
| Papua New Guinea | Papua New Guinean | Papua New Guinean |
| Paraguay | Paraguayan | Paraguayan |
| Peru | Peruvian | Peruvian |
| Philippines | Filipino/Filipina | Philippine or Filipino/Filipina |

| country | person (*name in general use*) | related adjective (*in general use*) |
|---|---|---|
| Pitcairn Islands (*dependent territory*) | Pitcairn Islander | Pitcairn |
| Poland | Pole | Polish |
| Portugal | Portuguese | Portuguese |
| Puerto Rico | Puerto Rican | Puerto Rican |
| Qatar | Qatari | Qatari *or* Qatar |
| Romania | Romanian | Romanian |
| Russia | Russian | Russian |
| Rwanda | Rwandan | Rwandan |
| St Helena (*dependent territory*) | St Helenian | St Helenian *or* St Helena |
| St Kitts and Nevis | citizen of St Kitts and Nevis | Kittitian *or* Nevisian *or* St Kitts and Nevis |
| St Lucia | St Lucian | St Lucian *or* St Lucia |
| St Vincent | Vincentian | Vincentian *or* St Vincent |
| San Marino | citizen of San Marino | San Marino |
| São Tomé and Príncipe | citizen of São Tomé and Príncipe | São Tomé and Príncipe |
| Saudi Arabia | Saudi Arabian *or* Saudi | Saudi Arabian *or* Saudi |
| Scotland | Scot *or* Scotsman/Scotswoman | Scottish *or* Scots *or* Scotch |
| Senegal | Senegalese | Senegalese |
| Serbia | Serb *or* Serbian | Serb *or* Serbian |
| Seychelles | Seychellois | Seychelles *or* Seychellois |
| Sierra Leone | Sierra Leonean | Sierra Leonean *or* Sierra Leone |
| Singapore | Singaporean | Singaporean |
| Slovakia | Slovak | Slovak |
| Slovenia | Slovene | Slovenian |
| Solomon Islands | Solomon Islander | Solomon Islands |
| Somalia | Somali | Somali |
| South Africa | South African | South African |
| Spain | Spaniard | Spanish |

| country | person (name in general use) | related adjective (in general use) |
|---|---|---|
| Sri Lanka | Sri Lankan | Sri Lankan |
| Sudan | Sudanese | Sudanese |
| Suriname | Surinamer | Surinamese |
| Swaziland | Swazi | Swazi |
| Sweden | Swede | Swedish |
| Switzerland | Swiss | Swiss |
| Syria | Syrian | Syrian |
| Taiwan | Taiwanese | Taiwanese |
| Tajikistan | Tajik | Tajik |
| Tanzania | Tanzanian | Tanzanian |
| Thailand | Thai | Thai |
| Togo | Togolese | Togolese |
| Tonga | Tongan | Tongan |
| Trinidad and Tobago | Trinidadian or Tobagan or Tobagonian or Trinidad and Tobago citizen | Trinidadian or Tobagan or Tobagonian or Trinidad and Tobago |
| Tunisia | Tunisian | Tunisian |
| Turkey | Turk | Turkish |
| Turkmenistan | Turkmen | Turkmen |
| Tuvalu | Tuvaluan | Tuvaluan |
| Uganda | Ugandan | Ugandan |
| Ukraine | Ukrainian | Ukrainian |
| United Arab Emirates | citizen of the United Arab Emirates | United Arab Emirates |
| United Kingdom see also Great Britain | United Kingdom citizen | United Kingdom |
| United States of America | United States citizen or American | United States or American |
| Uruguay | Uruguayan | Uruguayan |
| Uzbekistan | Uzbek | Uzbek |
| Vanuatu | citizen of Vanuatu | Vanuatu |
| Vatican City | Vatican citizen | Vatican |
| Venezuela | Venezuelan | Venezuelan |
| Vietnam | Vietnamese | Vietnamese |

| country | person (*name in general use*) | related adjective (*in general use*) |
|---|---|---|
| Virgin Islands | Virgin Islander | Virgin Islands |
| Wales | Welshman/ Welshwoman | Welsh |
| Western Samoa | Western Samoan | Western Samoan |
| Yemen Arab Republic | Yemeni | Yemeni |
| Yemen, People's Democratic Republic of | South Yemeni | South Yemeni |
| Yugoslavia | Yugoslav | Yugoslav |
| Zaire | Zairean | Zairean |
| Zambia | Zambian | Zambian |
| Zimbabwe | Zimbabwean | Zimbabwean *or* Zimbabwe |

# **Appendix 2** Weights and measures

*Note.* The conversion factors are not exact unless so marked. They are given only to the accuracy likely to be needed in everyday calculations.

## 1  British and American, with metric equivalents

*Linear measure*

| | |
|---|---|
| 1 inch | = 25.4 millimetres exactly |
| 1 foot = 12 inches | = 0.3048 metre exactly |
| 1 yard = 3 feet | = 0.9144 metre exactly |
| 1 (statute) mile = 1,760 yards | = 1.609 kilometres |

*Square measure*

| | |
|---|---|
| 1 square inch | = 6.45 sq. centimetres |
| 1 square foot = 144 sq. in. | = 9.29 sq. decimetres |
| 1 square yard = 9 sq. ft. | = 0.836 sq. metre |
| 1 acre = 4,840 sq. yd. | = 0.405 hectare |
| 1 square mile = 640 acres | = 259 hectares |

*Cubic measure*

| | |
|---|---|
| 1 cubic inch | = 16.4 cu. centimetres |
| 1 cubic foot = 1,728 cu. in. | = 0.0283 cu. metre |
| 1 cubic yard = 27 cu. ft. | = 0.765 cu. metre |

*Capacity measure*

*British*

| | |
|---|---|
| 1 pint = 20 fluid oz. | = 0.568 litre |
| = 34.68 cu. in. | |
| 1 quart = 2 pints | = 1.136 litres |
| 1 gallon = 4 quarts | = 4.546 litres |
| 1 peck = 2 gallons | = 9.092 litres |
| 1 bushel = 4 pecks | = 36.4 litres |
| 1 quarter = 8 bushels | = 2.91 hectolitres |

## Weights and measures

### American dry

| | |
|---|---|
| 1 pint = 33.60 cu. in. | = 0.550 litre |
| 1 quart = 2 pints | = 1.101 litres |
| 1 peck = 8 quarts | = 8.81 litres |
| 1 bushel = 4 pecks | = 35.3 litres |

### American liquid

| | |
|---|---|
| 1 pint = 16 fluid oz. = 28.88 cu. in | = 0.473 litre |
| 1 quart = 2 pints | = 0.946 litre |
| 1 gallon = 4 quarts | = 3.785 litres |

### Avoirdupois weight

| | |
|---|---|
| 1 grain | = 0.065 gram |
| 1 dram | = 1.772 grams |
| 1 ounce = 16 drams | = 28.35 grams |
| 1 pound = 16 ounces = 7,000 grains | = 0.4536 kilogram (0.45359237 exactly) |
| 1 stone = 14 pounds | = 6.35 kilograms |
| 1 quarter = 2 stones | = 12.70 kilograms |
| 1 hundredweight = 4 quarters | = 50.80 kilograms |
| 1 (long) ton = 20 hundredweight | = 1.016 tonnes |
| 1 short ton = 2,000 pounds | = 0.907 tonne |

## 2  Metric, with British equivalents

### Linear measure

| | |
|---|---|
| 1 millimetre | = 0.039 inch |
| 1 centimetre = 10 mm | = 0.394 inch |
| 1 decimetre = 10 cm | = 3.94 inches |
| 1 metre = 10 dm | = 1.094 yards |
| 1 decametre = 10 m | = 10.94 yards |
| 1 hectometre = 100 m | = 109.4 yards |
| 1 kilometre = 1,000 m | = 0.6214 mile |

### Square measure

| | |
|---|---|
| 1 square centimetre | = 0.155 sq. inch |
| 1 square metre = 10,000 sq. cm | = 1.196 sq. yards |
| 1 are = 100 sq. metres | = 119.6 sq. yards |
| 1 hectare = 100 ares | = 2.471 acres |

1 square kilometre     = 0.386 sq. mile
  = 100 hectares

*Cubic measure*

1 cubic centimetre     = 0.061 cu. inch
1 cubic metre     = 1.308 cu. yards
  = 1,000,000 cu. cm

*Capacity measure*

1 millilitre     = 0.002 pint (British)
1 centilitre = 10 ml     = 0.018 pint
1 decilitre = 10 cl     = 0.176 pint
1 litre = 10 dl     = 1.76 pints
1 decalitre = 10 l     = 2.20 gallons
1 hectolitre = 100 l     = 2.75 bushels
1 kilolitre = 1,000 l     = 3.44 quarters

*Weight*

1 milligram     = 0.015 grain
1 centigram = 10 mg     = 0.154 grain
1 decigram = 10 cg     = 1.543 grain
1 gram = 10 dg     = 15.43 grain
1 decagram = 10 g     = 5.64 drams
1 hectogram = 100 g     = 3.527 ounces
1 kilogram = 1,000 g     = 2.205 pounds
1 tonne (metric ton) = 1,000 kg     = 0.984 (long) ton

## 3 Temperature

Fahrenheit: Water boils (under standard conditions) at 212° and
  freezes at 32°.
Celsius or Centigrade: Water boils at 100° and freezes at 0°.
Kelvin: Water boils at 373.15 K and freezes at 273.15 K.

| Celsius | Fahrenheit |
|---|---|
| —17.8° | 0° |
| —10° | 14° |
| 0° | 32° |
| 10° | 50° |
| 20° | 68° |
| 30° | 86° |
| 40° | 104° |
| 50° | 122° |
| 60° | 140° |
| 70° | 158° |
| 80° | 176° |
| 90° | 194° |
| 100° | 212° |

To convert Celsius into Fahrenheit: multiply by 9, divide by 5, and
  add 32.
To convert Fahrenheit into Celsius: subtract 32, multiply by 5,
  and divide by 9.